A TIBETAN - ENGLISH DICTIONARY

A TIBETAN-ENGLISH DICTIONARY

With Special Reference to the Prevailing Dialects

To which is added AN ENGLISH-TIBETAN VOCABULARY

H. Jäschke

MOTILAL BANARSIDASS
INTERNATIONAL
DELHI

Reprint Edition Delhi, 2022
First Edition, London, 1881

ISBN : 978-93-90696-42-0 (Cloth)

Also available at
MOTILAL BANARSIDASS INTERNATIONAL
41 U.A. Bungalow Road, (Back Lane) Jawahar Nagar, Delhi - 110 007
4261 (basement) Lane #3,Ansari Road, Darya Ganj, New Delhi - 110 002
203 Royapettah High Road, Mylapore, Chennai - 600 004
12/1A,Bankim Chatterjee Street, Kolkata - 700 073
Stockist : Motilal Books, Ashok Rajpath, Near Kali Mandir, Patna - 800 004

Printed & Bound by
MOTILAL BANARSIDASS INTERNATIONAL

PREFACE.

This work represents a new and thoroughly revised edition of a Tibetan-German Dictionary, which appeared in a lithographed form between the years 1871 and 1876.

During a residence, which commenced in 1857 and extended over a number of years, on the borders of Tibet and among Tibetan tribes, I and my colleagues gathered the materials for this Dictionary.

We had to take primarily into account the needs of missionaries entering upon new regions, and then of those who might hereafter follow into the same field of enterprize. The chief motive of all our exertions lay always in the desire to facilitate and to hasten the spread of the Christian religion and of Christian civilization, among the millions of Buddhists, who inhabit Central Asia, and who speak and read in Tibetan idioms.

A yet more definite object influenced my own personal linguistic researches, in as much as I had undertaken to make preparations for the translation of the Holy Scriptures into the Tibetan speech. I approached and carried forward this task by way of a careful examination of the full sense and exact range of words in their ordinary and common usage. For it seemed to me that, if Buddhist readers were to be brought into contact with Biblical and Christian ideas, the introduction to so foreign and strange a train of thought, and one making the largest demands upon the character and the imagination, had best be made through the medium of a phraseology and diction as simple, as clear, and as popular as possible. My instrument must be, as in the case of every successful translator of the Bible, so to say, not a technical, but the vulgar tongue.

Thus, in contrast to the business of the European philologist, engaged in the same domain, who quite rightly occupies himself with the analysis and commentary of a literary language, the vocabulary and terminology of which he finds mainly deposited in the speculative writings of the Buddhist philosophers, it became my duty to embrace every opportunity, with which my presence on the spot favoured me, to trace the living powers of words and of expressions through their consecutive historical applications, till I reached their last signification in their modern equivalents, as these are embodied in the provincial dialects of the native tribes of our own time.

These circumstances, it is hoped, will excuse and explain the system of my work.

As an inventory of the whole treasure of the language, as a finished key to its literature, this Dictionary, when judged by the high standard of modern lexicography, may seem inadequate; I have, for instance, been unable to consult, much as I could have wished to have done so, all the original and translated treatises in Tibetan which, down to the present, have appeared in Europe, and the reader of a Tibetan work may thus, here and there, look in vain for the assistance he expects. On the other hand, a consistent attempt is here made for the first time, 1. to give a rational account of the development of the values and meanings of words in this language; 2. to distinguish precisely the various transitions in periods of literature and varieties of dialect; 3. to make sure of each step by the help of accurate and copious illustrations and examples. I have done my utmost to arrive at certainty where, heretofore, much was mere guess-work, and I cherish the hope that, from this point of view, my contribution will be welcomed by the comparative philologist, and will be serviceable to the general cause of learning, as well as a useful volume within that narrower circle, whose requirements I was specially bound not to overlook, of persons whose main purpose is to be taught how to write and speak the modern Tibetan tongue.

There are two chief periods of literary activity to be noticed in studying the origin and growth of Tibetan literature and the landmarks in the history of the language. The first is the Period of Translations which, however, might also be entitled the Classical Period, for the sanctity of the religious message conferred a corresponding reputation and tradition of excellence upon the form, in which it was conveyed. This period begins in the first half of the seventh century, when Thonmi Sambhota, the minister of king Srongtsangampo, was sent to India to learn Sanskrit. His invention of the Tibetan alphabet gave a twofold impulse: for several centuries the wisdom of India and the ingenuity of Tibet laboured in unison and with the greatest industry and enthusiasm at the work of translation. The tribute due to real genius must be awarded to these early pioneers of Tibetan grammar. They had to grapple with the infinite wealth and refinement of Sanskrit, they had to save the independence of their own tongue, while they strove to subject it to the rule of scientific principles, and it is most remarkable, how they managed to produce translations at once literal and faithful to the spirit of the original. The first masters had made for their later disciples a comparatively easy road, for the style and contexts of the writings, with which the translators had to deal, present very uniform features. When once typical patterns had been furnished, it was possible for the literary manufacture to be extended by a sort of mechanical process.

A considerable time elapsed before natives of Tibet began to indulge in compositions of their own. When they did so, the subject matter, chosen by them to operate upon, was either of an historical or a legendary kind. In this Second Period the language shows much resemblance to the modern tongue, approaching most closely the present idiom of Central Tibet. We find a greater freedom in construction, a tendency to use abbreviated forms (thus the mere verbal root is often inflected in the place of a complete infinitive), and a certain number of new grammatical combinations.

The present language of the people has as many dialects, as the country has provinces. Indeed, as in most geographically similar districts, well nigh every separate mountain valley has its own singularities as to modes of utterance and favourite collocations of words. Especially is it interesting to note, in respect to pronunciation, how the old consonants, which would seem to have been generally sounded and spoken twelve centuries ago, when the Tibetan written character came into existence, and which, at any rate, are marked by the primitive system of writing, remain still extant; every one of them can still be disinterred, somewhere or other, from some local peculiarity of language, and thus even the very diversity of modern practice can be made to bear testimony to the standards imposed by what was termed above the Classical Period. (Compare my Essay on the Phonetic System of the Tibetan language in the Monthly Reports of the Royal Academy of Science at Berlin 1867, p. 148 etc.)

I have already adverted to the circumstances which, especially in the case of the student, who has for immediate object to learn how to read and write the Tibetan language, render existing dictionaries almost if not quite useless. They give but scanty information concerning modes of construction, variations and limits of actual application, shades of meaning etc. In my own case, I was forced from the beginning to compile my own German-Tibetan dictionary, and found myself for all practical purposes thrown back upon my own resources. But the cause of truth appears to require a further word or two in regard to the Lexicon by Professor I. J. Schmidt of St. Petersburg, the relation of that work to its predecessors having been left by its author in some obscurity.

The first Tibetan dictionary, intended for European students, was published at Serampore, as long ago as 1826. It contains the collections, amassed in view of a dictionary and grammar, by a Roman Catholic missionary, who was stationed in eastern Tibet or close to the frontier in Bhotan. There was nothing to assist him, except the scanty contributions, given by Georgi, in his Alphabetum Tibetanum. He had to cope with an entirely unworked language. He evidently took the one way possible of making acquaintance with it, sufficient to enable him to understand, to speak, to read and write. Each word or sentence was jotted down, as soon as it was heard, or was committed to writing, at the request of the learner, by some native expert. After a while, the attempt could be made to master a book. In the instance of our missionary, Padma Sambhava's book of legends appears to have been selected, a work which represents rather a low level of literature, yet just on that account, perhaps, as a specimen of popular and current literature, not unsuitable to start from. Then, step by step, as best he could, our missionary had to possess himself of some abstract views, which would serve as a preliminary basis for a grammar. And had it been granted to this first occupant of the field to reduce his materials to an ordered system and to prepare them himself for publication, it is possible, that in Europe the knowledge of the Tibetan language might have reached, some fifty years earlier, the stage at which it has now arrived. The very name of that Roman Catholic missionary, however, has been lost. The papers which he left behind him, unsorted and unsifted, came into the hands of Major Latter, an English officer, and were passed on by him to Mr. Schröter, a missionary in Bengal. English was substituted for the Italian of the manuscript, and the East India Company made a grant which defrayed the cost of the Tibetan types and the further expenses of printing. But there was no Tibetan scholar to correct the proofs. The author himself would doubtless, on reconsideration, have detected and dismissed much erroneous or unnecessary matter. As it was, many additional mistakes crept in during the passage through the press. Thus the work, though it has a richer vocabulary than can be found in the later dictionaries, cannot on any questionable point be accepted as an authority, and has only value for those who are already competent, for themselves, to weigh and decide upon the statements and interpretations it advances. I have not been able to extract from it much that was serviceable to me. Nevertheless, any one who knows by experience what time and toil such a work must have cost, though its design remained unfulfilled and its object unaccomplished, will not easily be able to repress his indignation at the tone, in which this book in the preface to his Grammar (p. VI) is recklessly and absolutely condemned by Professor Schmidt.

High praise, however, is awarded by the Professor to a second work, the Tibetan-English Dictionary by Csoma de Körös, which appeared in 1834. This work deserves all eulogy; but the Professor's manner, which imitates that of a master commending a pupil, is, though on other grounds, as unwarranted and as offensive in this as in the former case. The work of Csoma de Körös is that of an original investigator and the fruit of almost unparalleled determination and patience. The compiler, in order to dedicate himself to the study of Tibetan literature, lived like a monk for years among the inmates of a Tibetan monastery. It is to be regretted that, with the knowledge he certainly must have possessed of the later language and literature, he should have restricted the scope of his labours to the earlier periods of literature, and when in his Grammar conversational phrases are quoted as examples, they are almost without exception in the dialect of the Kangyur, and of little practical value.

This Tibetan-English dictionary by Csoma has been adapted for a German public by Professor I. J. Schmidt of St. Petersburg. The translation from English into German is good; in the general alphabetical arrangement improvements have been introduced, and such as are in conformity with the spirit of the language; moreover, three Mongolian dictionaries have been consulted, and from these a certain number of words have been supplemented. But it cannot be said that even on the work of revision Professor Schmidt has bestowed much pains. For example, Csoma's rough grouping of words under the principal headings is left unaltered, though here especially a reduction to alphabetical order was obviously required. Mistakes and superfluities, very pardonable in the case of a first issue of an original publication, are repeated in this translation, and these cannot be so readily overlooked and condoned, when they are made at second hand, and are sanctioned and subscribed to by one, who has assumed so severe a critical and editorial attitude.

The national dictionaries of Tibet itself, so far as I have met with such, are either little handbooks, meant only to furnish a correct orthography, or they are glossaries of antiquated forms. The absence of an alphabetical order in them makes the business of reference very troublesome. It is by great good luck that one sometimes finds an otherwise unknown word after a prolonged search.

My own dictionary, in the main, pursues the object and accepts the plan of the work, which was published by Mr. Schröter. As I said at the beginning, I have not restricted myself to the Classical Period, but I have endeavoured to deal with the Tibetan language as a whole, though I do not pretend to have performed this task exhaustively. My dictionary derives its matter and its principles, so far as possible, equally from the literature and from the speech of the people. Each word has been made the object of observation in its relation to the context as it occurs in books, and in its value and place among others when it is used in common conversation, and then the attempt has been made to define its range and to fix its meaning.

All the words, cited by Csoma and Schmidt, even such as I myself had never seen or heard, I have embodied in this work, stating, in each case, the source from whence I drew them.

The signification in Sanskrit has been added, whenever this seemed likely to be useful or interesting to the student of Tibetan literature. Of proper names only the most important are given.

The great number of diacritical marks will perhaps prove irksome to the English reader; yet, they were not to be dispensed with, if the pronunciation of Tibetan letters and words was to be represented with any degree of exactness, and the method of Prof. Lepsius seemed the most eligible among all the systems available for my purpose. The student, however, need not be disheartened, as he is not obliged to make himself acquainted with all the minutiae of the system, but need only direct his attention to the peculiarities of that dialect, within the limits of which his inquiries, for the time, are confined. And by-the-by it may be observed, that the multitude of little marks, of manifold description, cannot be startling to the Indian reader, who was ever necessitated to make himself familiar with systems quite as complicated, as e.g. the Urdu alphabet.

One word more of apology. Of publications in general it has been said, that "when human care has done its best, there will be found a certain percentage of error". And the probability is but too great, that this dictionary will exhibit a number of deficiencies and faults, in the English text as well as in the Tibetan transcript. Still, I venture to hope that an indulgent Public will be ready to make every reasonable allowance in consideration of the peculiar difficulties, which attach to the execution of a work like the present, and which, moreover, were not a little increased, in this instance, by the fact that the compositors of the press were altogether unacquainted with English.

I should be guilty of great ingratitude, if I were not to mention my obligations to two friends, without whose kind and efficient aid it would have been impossible for me in my present infirm state, to complete this work, which was commenced in the days of health and vigour, viz. to the Rev. T. Reichelt, formerly a Missionary of the Moravian Church in South Africa, and to Mr. F. W. Petersen, a relative of mine.

Further, I desire to record my obligations for various acts of kindness, encouragement, assistance and advice, during the prosecution of my researches and the completion of my work, to A. C. Burnell Esq. M. R. A. S., in India; Dr. E. Schlagintweit in Bavaria, Dr. Thomson and Dr. Aitchison of Kew, Dr. Kurz of Calcutta, and R. Laing Esq. M.A., Fellow of Corpus Christi College, Oxford.

Not the least debt of gratitude is that which I owe to Dr. R. Rost in London, Secretary of the Royal Asiatic Society, to whose exertions, indeed, the execution of this work is, properly speaking, entirely due, inas much as he kindly interested the Indian Government on behalf of my undertaking.

Herrnhut, January 1881.

H. J.

INTRODUCTION

I. THE TIBETAN ALPHABET.

CONSONANTS.

The names of all the Consonants sound in a, pronounced like the a in the English word 'far'.

ཀ *ka* pronounced like the French c — car
ཁ *ḱa* like the English c or k — cart
ག *ga* harder than the English (hard) g
ང *ṅa* ng — pang
ཅ *ċa* the soft English g — ginger
ཆ *ča* ch — chart
ཇ *ja* j — jar
ཉ *nya* the French gn — campagne
ཏ *ta* the French t — tard
ཐ *t́a* the English t — tart
ད *da* dart
ན *na* nard
པ *pa* the French p — pas
ཕ *ṗa* the English p — part
བ *ba* bard
མ *ma* mart
ཙ *tsa* (ts) parts
ཚ *t́sa* (aspirated)
ཛ *dza* (ds) — guards
ཝ *wa* waft
ཞ *ża* (zh) like the English s in leisure
ཟ *za* like the English z — zeal
འ *a* (basis for vowels)
ཡ *) *ya* yard
ར **) *ra* rasp
ལ *la* last
ཤ *śa* (sh) — sharp
ས *sa* salve
ཧ *ha* half
ཨ *'a* (basis for vowels)

*) ཡ *ya*, when combined, as second consonant, with k- and p-sounds, or with m, is written under the first letter, assuming the shape of ◌ྱ, thus ཀྱ *kya*, པྱ *pya*, མྱ *mya* etc.

**) ར *ra*, when combined as second letter, with k-, t- and p-sounds is written under the first, in the shape of ◌ྲ, thus: ཀྲ, *kra*, ཏྲ *tra*, བྲ *bra* etc. — When combined with another consonant as *first* letter, it is written over the second, thus: རྐ *rka*, རྔ *rṅa*, རྡ *rda* etc., but it is seldom heard in speaking.

The so-called Sanskrit Cerebrals are represented in Tibetan letters by ཊ, ཋ, ཌ, ཎ, ཥ,

and when in this dictionary they are transcribed, they are marked by a dot underneath: ṭ, ṭ', ḍ, ṇ, ṣ.

The figure ◂ (*wa-zur* or small *wa*) attached to the foot of a letter, is often used to distinguish homonyms in writing, e.g. ཚ *tsa* hot and ཚྭ *tsa* (*tswa*) salt.

The dot, which stands at the end of every syllable and of every word, is called Tseg (*tseg*) and is indispensable for a correct writing or reading.

When ག stands as a prefix, it is, when transcribed, represented by *γ*, e.g. གཅིག་ *γčig*, གཏམ་ *γtam* etc.

VOWELS.

The alphabetical order of the vowels is: a, i, u, e, o; they have in Tibetan the same sound as they have in German, Italian, and most other European languages: *a* sounds like the English a in 'far', *i* like ee in 'peer' or i in 'pin', *u* like u in 'rule' or in 'pull', *e* like a in 'fate' or e in 'met', *o* like o in 'note' or in 'not'.

As the vowel a is inherent in every consonant, so that even a single letter may form a word, e.g. བ་ *ba* (cow), ས་ *sa* (earth), there is no special character or letter required for this vowel. The other four vowels are represented by little hooks: ི standing for *i*, ུ for *u*, ེ for *e*, ོ for *o*. The marks for *i*, *e*, *o* are placed over the letter, that for *u* under it. Examples: པད་མ་ *pad-ma*, རི་ *ri*, མེ་ *me*, བུ་མོ་ *bu-mo*.

The letter ཨ is used as a basis for initial vowels, thus: ཨ་མ་ *'a-ma;* the letter འ serves as a basis for initial and final vowels: འོ་མ་ *˛o-ma*, དགའ་ *dga*.

The vowel-sounds of འ, when transcribed, are indicated by the mark ˛: འ *˛a*, འི *˛i*, འུ *˛u*, འེ *˛e*, འོ *˛o*, whilst the ཨ-vowels are denoted by the mark ' placed over the respective letters: ཨ *'a*, ཨི *'i*, ཨུ *'u*, ཨེ *'e*, ཨོ *'o*. — The real nature of the letters འ and ཨ is treated of in the latter part of the Introduction.

Whenever འ is a prefixed letter, the mark ˳, in transcribing, is put under the consonant following the འ e.g. འདུ *˳du*, འགྲོ་བ་ *˳gro-ba*.

Note. For a ready 'finding of words' in the Dictionary, it should be borne in mind, that the articles are arranged in the alphabetical order of the *initial* consonants *and* their *prefixed* and *superscribed* letters. Thus: ཀ—དཀ—བཀ—རྐ—ལྐ—སྐ—; ཁ—མཁ—འཁ— etc. etc.

II. PRONUNCIATION.

With regard to the language, with which I am dealing, it must, on the one hand, be admitted, that distinctions between sounds and, especially, variations in the mode of expressing their values as embodied in a written character, are far more numerous in Tibetan than either in Sanskrit or Hindi, in which two languages there is really little or no opening for mistake or ambiguity in this respect. But on the other hand, Tibetan is scarcely more irregular than French pronunciation, and a few definite rules enjoy universally recognized acceptation.

There is, however, one special difficulty in the case of Tibetan which, at the present stage of that language, renders it practically impossible to set up an equable and authoritative standard of pronunciation, and this is the existence of a great number of independent and well-defined *dialects*. An attempt to deal partially with this difficulty, — to append, let me suppose, to every word from three to five different pronunciations would involve a waste of time and an extension of space quite disproportionate to the value of the result. And yet, if one has to strike a preference in favour of one particular dialect, it is very hard to determine, which is to be selected. At first sight, it might seem the most natural course to fix upon the speech of the best educated classes in the capital city Lhasa. But when this method was followed, or when at least an endeavour was made to act upon it, by Georgi and then by Schröter, only scant approval was bestowed upon it by European critics, and there were and are several reasonable arguments to be urged against its adoption. Of all the dialects this presents to the European ear and tongue the greatest difficulties, and accommodates itself least readily to the written character. Moreover, in my own case, I have to add that I do not consider myself sufficiently master of it to care to risk its application to each individual word. Besides, modern political circumstances make this dialect, for the present, the least available for general use.

Csoma chose a much more manageable and a much more widely circulating mode of pronunciation, though one which presents problems of its own, when it has to be fitted to the written character: the West-Tibetan dialect. Here again, in representing each separate word, one has, in reality, to make choice between two, three or four pronunciations, of which one agrees best with the written character, another conforms closest to the rules of spelling, a third recommends itself as that most frequent in conversational language. In my own smaller Tibetan dictionary I went no farther than to distinguish between two principal groups, which I termed West-Tibetan and Central-Tibetan; but in a more scientific work like the present I may permit myself to call more minute attention to the niceties and refinements of the language before us. I have, accordingly, published a number of specimens from my note-book, in which I kept a collection of typical words, of which I availed myself as often as I had the opportunity of meeting the representatives of remote districts, and of enquiring concerning their manner of speech at home. Whenever in this collection a word had not been entered on sound native authority, or had not been sufficiently discussed, I preferred to mark it with a note of interrogation, and not to allow any conclusion from analogy, or any theory of pronunciation to interfere with the design of my handy-book and its simple and unprejudiced statement of fact. I may therefore, I hope, claim for this list a high degree of trustworthiness, even among collections of the kind, into which words can sometimes have slipped, as they had been heard once, and perhaps were not heard again.

In order to denote the pronunciation, I follow the scheme of Professor Lepsius. Some objections have been urged against this scheme; yet, amongst all systems of the kind, so far as I have become acquainted with them, I have no hesitation in affirming that of Professor Lepsius to be the best, and it is certainly also that most appropriate for my purpose. A thorough study of the 'Standard Alphabet by R. Lepsius, 2nd edition, London, Williams and Norgate. Berlin, Hertz, 1863' may be recommended to all persons, who interest themselves in phonetic investigations. As I can scarcely take it for granted, that the work mentioned will be already in the hands of every one, who may consult my dictionary, I shall endeavour, as briefly as possible, to indicate its essential plan and principles. Its rules may be stated as follows:

In order to mark sound, Lepsius uses the letters of the ordinary Latin alphabet. Where these are insufficient, he calls in the aid of a few Greek letters. Letters are used with the powers they most generally possess in European languages. (Thus z has its usual force, and does not stand for the peculiar sound ts, which belongs to it in the German language alone.) Sounds which lack exact representation are indicated by *diacritical marks*, placed above or below the letters which most nearly correspond. Every simple sound is represented by one and only one simple mark. Explosive and fricative consonants (these terms will be explained below) are denoted by different letters.

The following marks or signs are for *vowels:* the well known sign(˘) for a short, and (¯) for a long vowel; the mark of a modified vowel (¨), German ä, ö, ü, is placed by Lepsius, for practical reasons, below, not above the vowel (*a̤, o̤. ṳ*); a dot under the vowel denotes a close vowel-sound (*ẹ* = a in fate, *ọ* in note); a horizontal line under the vowel denotes a more open vowel-sound (*e̱* in 'there', *o̱* in 'or, cord', which, indeed, supersedes the *a̤* mentioned above); the mark (˜) above the vowel indicates a nasal quality, the breath passing, while uttering the sound, to a considerable extent through the nose (the French '*an, in, on, un*' = *ã, ẽ̱, õ̱, ö̤̃*).

In marking *consonants*, there is first the distinction to be noted, that they are partly *explosives*, formed by a rapid process of closing and re-opening the passage of the air at a certain point, partly *fricatives* and *liquids*, formed by a partial process of compressing or narrowing the air-passage; and secondly, they are distinguished in regard to the exact spot, where the process of articulation takes place. The lowest articulation takes place in the *faucal region*, close to the larynx (here, for example, h is formed); next comes the guttural region, at the throat, near the soft palate and uvula (here k is formed); it is marked, when necessary, with a dot above the consonant; then the *palatal region*, the hard palate, (here the German ch is formed in 'ich'); the mark is a stroke like the acute accent in Greek over the consonant; then the *dental region*, at the teeth and gums (d, t, s, sh), and finally the *labial region*, at the lips (b, p, m). There exists a further class of consonants in the Indian languages, and also in modern Tibetan, which are styled *cerebrals;* they are most of them modified dentals, formed by bending or curling the tongue upwards, and bringing the tip of it into contact with the hard palate in the centre or toward the hinder part of its roof; mark, a dot under the consonant.

Many of these letters, in order to become audible, require in pronouncing them a certain *vocalic effort*; others, to say the least, allow or suggest such an effort; the mark of these vocalized consonants is a small *ring* under the letter. When this vocalic effort is made by the medium of the nasal channel alone, the oral passage being simultaneously closed at some one of the points indicated above, we get the nasal consonants as a result. When the stoppage is made at the guttural point, ng is obtained (to be marked *ṅ*); at the dental point, n; at the labial point, m. In order to conform with the two final rules, cited above from Lepsius, the Greek letter *χ* is used to represent the German ch, when it is guttural and hard, as in the word 'doch'; use is made of the Greek *γ*, when it is soft or accompanied by a vocalic tone (the Dutch g); *χ́* gives the force of a palatal ch (German 'ich' = *iχ́*, 'milch' = mil*χ́*); *ϑ* is used to represent the strong English th (as in 'through'); *δ* renders the softer or vocalized tone (as in 'that'); a hard, sharp and hissing s or ss (as in 'yes', 'press') is marked as s; the soft vocalic s (as in 'his', 'rise') is represented by z; the hard rushing sound sh, German sch, is rendered by *š*; the sound of the French j by *ž*. If one attempts to give at the palatal point, where the English y (in 'year'), or the German j (in 'Jahr') is formed, the sound sh, German sch, one obtains the palatal *ś*, or the softened and vocalized *ź*. In the Dictionary *ŝ* and *ẑ* have been substituted for these marks.

Further, in many languages, what are properly combinations of two consonants come to be regarded as simple forms, this happening, either because they are gradual growths upon an original simpler form, or because they have a natural affinity to each other. Thus properly dental sibilants should be distinguished thus: *tš*, *dž*; but for the sake of simplicity Lepsius, in his second edition, marks them č and ǰ, or, with their palatal force, ċ and ȷ̇ (instead of ć and ȷ́).

A further example of the combination of consonants is presented in what is known as *aspiration*, when the letter *h* is brought into more or less intimate connexion with another consonant. This introduces us to a very important distinction, belonging to the Tibetan language, which it is necessary to explain at some length, in accordance with which explosive consonants, as they have the force of tenues, mediae, or aspiratae, are treated. The tenues are produced by a sudden opening of the air-passage at one of the points above mentioned: throat, teeth, lips, such opening being unaccompanied by any sensible operation of the breath whatsoever. Thus, when quite exactly sounded, k, t, p are produced. The mediae, g, d, b, are produced by the same process, carried out in a milder and less abrupt way. (the peculiar English pronunciation will come under consideration later). The aspiratae require a decided pressure by the breath (they will be found marked by the spiritus asper above the letter: *k̔*, *t̔*, *p̔*). In northern Germany, in England, and in Scandinavia, modern educated speech recognizes only mediae and aspiratae, for we give an aspirated sound to every k, t and p. The French and the Magyars distinguish consciously the pure tenues from the mediae; on the other hand they ignore the aspiratae. Tibetan pronunciation makes room and requires a mark for all three gradations. Nay more, it augments the class of explosive consonants or mutae by the addition of the dental sibilants in all three ranks or grades of aspiration: ཅ, ཆ, ཇ and ཙ, ཚ, ཛ, or according to the Standard Alphabet: ċ, č̔, ȷ̇ and *ts*, *t̔s*, *dz*. At a later stage of the language some further modifications were introduced, which we shall subsequently allude to.

Let us now, passing from these general observations, draw attention to a few details of the Phonetic Table, which has been drawn up in deference to a wish that reached me from several quarters.

The first column of the Table, now under review, gives the ancient literal pronunciation, as it was in vogue in the seventh century of our era, and was settled at the time of the invention of the alphabet. Such a pronunciation relies, after all, for its justification on the hypothesis, that the inventors of the alphabet had for their first object to reproduce, as exactly as possible, an artistic reflection of the natural value of sounds as spoken by their contemporaries: that, therefore, a later pronunciation is most in conformity with the original genius of the language, if it gives with the greatest distinctness a special power to each written character. A reference to the Table will amply illustrate the fact, that a pronunciation, adopted on these principles, has actually maintained itself in one or the other provincial dialect, and it is very interesting to notice, that the purest and most striking forms of this survival have their homes in those districts, which are most remote from and least subject to the disintegrating and dissolving influences of the actual centre of Tibetan civilisation, the capital Lhasa. Thus the prefixes and the superscribed consonants, for the most part, are still sounded at each extremity of the whole territory, within which the language is spoken, both on the Western and the Eastern frontier, alike in Khams, which borders on China, and in Balti, which merges into Kashmere. Moreover, in both localities the same minor irregularities occur, transgressions against an exact rendering of the pronunciation according to the letters, the same frequent transformations of the tenues into the aspiratae, g and d (compare lower down) becoming *γ* or *χ*, b becoming w. Now, about twenty degrees of longitude separate Balti from Khams, and the former, embracing Islam, long since cut itself adrift from spiritual and religious cohesion with Tibet, and there, too, the dialect in other respects has greatly deteriorated, has admitted many foreign elements and has fallen altogether from the position of a literary language. The resemblances and correspondences noted can, therefore, scarcely be accounted for in any other way, than by assuming that an old and strong instinct of speech lived on in oral tradition for more than ten centuries on the outskirts of the Tibetan domain, which in the intermediate provinces has gradually surrendered and submitted to the spirit of change.

Columns 2—6 contain, on most pages, the provincial dialects in their geographical sequence from West to East. The dialects of Ladak, Lahoul and Spiti correspond to what in my smaller Tibetan dictionary I called the dialect of Western Tibet. The last named, Spiti, represents in some respects the transition to the dialects of Eastern Tibet, under which heading Tsang and Ü are to be classed. At the date of the publication of my former dictionary I was unacquainted with the dialect of Khams. Where a space is left vacant in the columns, the provincial pronunciation agrees with the model provided under column 1. Towards the end of the Table, where the anomalies become much more frequent, I have for the sake of clearness repeated the word.

The sign ྭ (which does not occur in this Table) was pronounced = ཝ, or བ in the substantive terminations *ba* and *bo* (v. Dict. p. 362), viz. = the English w, so that རྭ sounded exactly like the French word *roi*.

The *Accent* has seldom been marked, because, as in our Teutonic dialects, it generally rests on the root of the word. In the case of compounds, it more frequently falls on the last than on the first of the component parts. But accentuation, altogether, is not of great significance in this language.

With regard to *Quantity*, vowels are pronounced shorter, even in open syllables, than is the case for instance in England and Germany. This applies particularly to the Central Provinces. Absolutely long vowels occur only as a peculiarity of dialect. They indicate that a consonant has been dropped, in most provinces, s, in Ü, gs, in Tsang, l. A long vowel may also indicate the blending of vowels. But when in Ü and Tsang the d, (as in *čě'-pa*) and when in Lahoul the g (as in *to', pu'-rón*) is partially dropped, the vowel likewise maintains a short abrupt pronunciation. Moreover, the region, to which I have just referred, is that in which the spoken language has been greatly affected by a foreign linguistic principle. A system of Tones has been introduced under manifestly Chinese auspices. I am told by European students of reputation, who have made the Tonic languages of Eastern Asia their special department, that only the first principles of what are known as the *high and low Tones*, have made their way into Tibetan. Here, as in the languages of Farther India, generally, which possess an alphabetic system of writing, the Tone is determined by the initial consonant of the word. This I have generally indicated in column 7, which column applies only to the Spiti, Tsang and Ü dialects. The system of Tones, as in Siam and elsewhere, has become of paramount importance in determining distinctions between words. An inhabitant of Lhasa, for example, finds the distinction between ཤ and ཞ, or between ས and ཟ, not in the consonant, but in the Tone, pronouncing ཤ and ས with a high note (as my Tibetan authorities were wont to describe it 'with a woman's voice', shrill and rapidly), ཞ and ཟ, on the contrary with a low note, and, as it appeared to me, more breathed and floating. This latter distinction is still more apparent with regard to those low-toned aspirates, that in the course of time were introduced in Central Tibet instead of the mediae, in contraposition to which now the original aspirates are used as high-toned; so more particularly in the dialect of Spiti. The low-toned aspirate I have indicated by h, the high-toned by the mark of the spiritus asper ʻ

Those letters of the alphabet, which as simple initial consonants have a deep tone, become with a superscribed letter or with a prefix high-toned, so also ལ, when subscribed. The tenues remain, it would appear, unaffected by the Tone. With reference to the modifying effect of a final *n*, *d*, and *ṅ*, in different provinces, the Table may be consulted. The characterisation of the rushing sounds as 'palatals' is no doubt correct and agrees with the generally prevailing pronunciation; but the learner need not consider it as being of much importance.

The two letters, འ and ཨ, introduce us to a very interesting linguistic phenomenon. We meet here with the idea of the *vowel absolute,* the pure vocalic note, freed altogether from any presence of a consonant. This vowel-tone is rendered by the letter of the alphabet འ, in contradistinction to ཨ, which represents the Semitic א, the spiritus lenis of the Greeks, the audible re-opening of the air passage of the larynx. The difference may be observed, for example, in the manner of uttering the words, 'the lily, an endogen' and in the pronunciation of 'Lilian' (a name), in Tibetan ལི་ལི་ཨན་ and ལི་ལི་འན. Thus, whenever in the middle of a word one vowel succeeds another (hence also in all diphthongs), འ is used. Again, in Tibetan, as in every form of human speech, it cannot but be the commonest of occurrences for a vowel to follow a consonant, and the strict rule might seem to require the vocalic tone to be always indicated, which, according to Csoma, was originally done. However, as the Tibetan language, adopting the principle from Sanskrit, deems the sound of *a* to be naturally inherent in every consonant, while the other four vowels, as mere subspecies of the vowel absolute, are indicated by little hooks above or below the letter, and as the end of a syllable is always marked by a dot (called *tseg*), the function of འ in this capacity was soon seen to be quite superfluous. Its use is necessary only to obviate ambiguities, when for instance one of the five letters, used as prefixes, precedes a consonant with *a*; e.g. the word མད་, would be read '*mad*'; whereas མདའ་, written thus, implies that the vowel does not precede but follow the consonant d, and consequently the m is prefix, and the word to be read '*mda*'. If the vowel is not *a*, the sign of such vowel suffices, e.g. མདོ་ *mdo;* མདའོ་ *mdao*, standing now for མདའའོ. Some practical difficulty attends the pronunciation of the pure vowel as an initial letter. In order that the effect of the consonant ཨ may not be produced, it is necessary, after opening the larynx, to allow the tone gently to set in and then to let it gradually gain fulness and force. I shall indicate this process by the mark ˓. The sound would be still more accurately represented than it is in the Table, thus: ˓*ár-po*, ˓*úṅ-pa* etc. Improper are the expedients of some of the dialects, the sound being hardened to *γ* in Khams, to ཨ in Western Tibet; also Csoma's device of indicating it by an h is inadequate. This is a case in which the true pronunciation has been preserved in the Central Provinces, perhaps, because it almost necessarily implies the effort connected with the low Tone, above referred to, so that, when the invading system of Tones had here established its authority, it acted as a conservative element.

Finally, this vocalic tone can be used in connexion with certain consonants. It is unnecessary to indicate it in Tibetan, when it accompanies liquidae (*m, n, ṅ, r, l*) and sibilants; but with the mutae it must be marked, where the effect is that, with which we are familiar in the case of the English mediae, b, d, g, j, for instance in 'be, do, go, jew'. In Tibetan the vocalic effect accompanies aspirates too, and is marked by འ, placed as a prefix, which I transcribe thus ₒ, e.g. འཐུ་ *ₒdu* = the English do. The pause on the tone is of course in the case of mutae a very short one. Here again, though only in the case of the mediae, we find this peculiarity preserved in its purity in Central Tibet. It is not difficult to understand, how, if one is careless about closing the nasal passage, a nasal articulation of this prefix can easily grow common. This has happened throughout Khams, and in the rest of Tibet at least in compound words; at Lhasa it is considered inelegant, as is also the sounding of any prefix. On the other hand, the dialect of Central Tibet neglects the distinction between མ and འ and pronounces the former only as a vocalic initial. In words from the Sanscrit the འ is used in some respect as a 'mora', to denote a long syllable, e.g. ཤྲཱི for श्री; hence the opinion of Lamas of Lhasa, that it expresses prosodical length, when used as above in མདའ.

མྱ་ *mya*, is not found in use in any of the dialects. The sole confirmation of its literal pronunciation depends upon the word *myaṅ-ba* which, perhaps a thousand years ago, found its way into the Bu-nan language (Tibar-skad, Cunningh.) and which the people of Lahoul, when speaking Tibetan, pronounce *nyaṅ-wa*. The process of transition to the cerebral ṭ-sounds in the words *krad-pa* etc. is in many places not yet completed, so that the sound of r is still more or less clearly distinguishable. The *Prefixes* have always constituted the most perplexing phenomena in the Tibetan language, At the time of the invention of the alphabet they must have represented a sort of anticipatory sound in close connexion with the initial consonant of the word. Certain seeming impossibilities of pronunciation, when one has, for instance, to deal with a prefix together with a threefold initial consonant (བསྒྲ་, བསྐྱ་) become less formidable, and not more embarrassing than those which meet us, for example, in the Polish language, when we ascertain that in Balti and Khams the three explosive prefixes are pronounced as fricatives, in which case *v* must be written for *w*. Thus གཅི་བ་ *γči-wa*, བཀྲ་ *wkra*, བསྒྲགས་ *wsgrags* call for no greater exertions, than do the Polish *chciwy*, *wkrótce*, *wskroś*. Our strongest ground for assuming this fricative pronunciation to be that of antiquity is, I think, that, had it been explosive, words like གཡུ་, གཡོན་ would have coincided with གྱུ་, གྱོན་. Yet it must be acknowledged that a pronunciation *bču*, *bka* etc. exists, side by side with *wču*, *wka* etc. — མ, as a liquid, offers no difficulty. — འ, as a prefix, is no consonant.

A doubt must still cling to ད, and I do not venture to determine its ancient pronunciation. It is by a strange anomaly that, in most dialects, when prefixed to བ, both it and the initial consonant die away into a spiritus lenis; and almost still more singular it is, that where it still asserts an independent force, in Khams and in Balti, it is sounded like ག with the power of *γ*. The investigations of Lepsius go indeed to prove, that ད and ག are complements to each other; but how came, at the beginning, two letters to be chosen as signs for one and the same sound? Most probably the original sound was *δ*, which then very soon passed into *γ*. The variations between r and s in Ladak afford no sure hold for drawing inferences.

The purpose, for which the Phonetic Table was drawn up, will have been attained, if I succeed in convincing my readers, 1. that for scientific objects the pronunciation, as it is given in Column 1, is the most suitable, and that with a good conscience it can be recommended in the place of that introduced by Csoma; 2. that its system is regular enough to render it unnecessary to give the pronunciation of every individual word throughout the work; 3. that I present in this Table, in regard to the various dialects, as much in the way of results as, down to the present, it has been possible for European students to acquire and to put into shape for the service of a European public.

III. PHONETIC TABLE
FOR COMPARING THE DIFFERENT DIALECTS.

The columns 2—6 are arranged according to the geographical site of the provinces from West to East.

I. Words containing only simple consonants and vowels.

1	2	3	4	5	6	7
	West. Tibet		Central Prov.			
	Ladak	Lahoul	Spiti	Tsang, Ü	Khams	
ka-ra						
kug = cook		*ku'*				
kun				*kün*	*kün*	
ḱań-pa						in C. high-toned
gań			*ghań*	*ghań*		
ńal				*ńā* Ts.		in C. deep-toned
ńan-pa				*ńem-pa* Ü.		
ċi					*ċe*	
čad-pa				*čẹ'-pa*		
čan-pa				*čem-pa*		high-toned
čen-po				*čem-po*		
ja			*jha*	*jha*		deep-toned
nyin					*nyen*	
tib-ril				*tib-rī* Ts.	*teb-rel*	
ťań					*ťeń*	
ťab = *ťäp*						
ťog		*ťŏ'*				high-toned
ťod-pa				*ťọ̈'-pa*		
da			*dha*	*dha*		
dud-pa			*dhud-pa*	*dhü'-pa*		deep-toned
nad = *năt*				*nẹ'*		
ṕan-pa				*ṕẹm-pa*		high-toned
ṕug-ron		*ṕu'-ron*		*ṕug-rọn*		
ba			*bha*	*bha*	*wa*	
bal			*bhal*	*bhā* Ts. *bhal* Ü.	*wal*	
bu			*bhu*	*bhu*	*wọ*	
bu-mo			*bhu-mo*	*bhu-mo*	*wọ-mo*	deep-toned
bod			*bhod*	*bhọ̈'*	*wod*	
mig		*mi'*				
me						
ṫsil				*ṫsī*	*tsel*	high-toned
dza-ti						
wa-tse						
ža			*ša*	*ša*	*ža*	
žag		*ža'*	*šag*	*šag*	*žag*	
za			*sa*	*sa*		
zan			*san*	*sen*		
ˌar-po	*'ar-po*	*'ar-po*			*γar-po*	in C. deep-toned
ˌug-pa	*'ug-pa*	*'ug-pa*			*γug-pa*	
ˌo-ma	*'a-ma*	*'o-ma*			*γo-ma*	
ˌod	*'od*	*'od*		*ö͡ö'*	*γod*	
ˌol-mo	*'ol-mo*	*'ol-mo*		*ö͡é-mo* Ts.	*γol-mo*	
yań					*yeń*	
yan-pa				*yā-ga*		
yal-ga				*yem-pa*		
yin					*yen*	
yul				*yū*, *yü* Ts		

1	2 West. Tibet: Ladak	3 West. Tibet: Lahoul	4 Central Prov.: Spiti	5 Central Prov.: Tsang, Ü	6 Khams	7
yod				*yọ'*		
ral				*rā*		deep-toned
rol-mo				*rŏ-mo* Ts.		
ιo-ma						
ša						
šel						high-toned
sa						
'a-ma						

II. Words terminating in བ་ or བོ་.

1	2, 3 Ladak, Lahoul	4 Spiti	5 Tsang, Ü	6 Khams	7
za-ba	*za-wa*	*sa-wa*	*sa-wa*		deep-toned
ži-ba	*ži-wa*	*ši-wa*	*ši-wa*	*ži-wa*	
ši-ba	*ši-wa*	*ši-wa*	*ši-wa*	*ši-wa*	high-toned
žu-ba	*žu-wa*	*šu-wa*	*šu-wa*	*žu-wa*	
jo-bo	*jo-wo*	*jho-wo*	*jho-wo*		deep-toned
dar-ba	*dar-wa*	*dhar-wa*	*dhar-wa*		
sol-ba	*sol-wa*		*sŏ-wa* Ts.		high-toned

III. Words terminating in ས.

1	2 Ladak	3 Lahoul	4 Spiti	4 Kun.	5 Tsang, Ü	6 Khams	7
K̔ăs	*K̔as, k̔ẹ̄*	*K̔ai, k̔ẹ̄*	*k̔ẹ̄*	*k̔ā*	*k̔ẹ̄*	*k̔ē*	high-toned
ris	*ris, rī*	*rī*	*rī*	*rī*	*rī*	*rī*	
gus	*gus, gụ̈̄*	*gui, gụ̈̄*	*ghụ̈i*	*gū*	*ghụ̈̄*	*gụ̈̄*	
dus	*dus, dụ̈̄*	*dui, dụ̈̄*	*dhụ̈i*	*dū*	*dhụ̈̄*	*dụ̈̄*	deep-toned
des	*des, dē*	*dē*	*dhē*	*dē*	*dhē*	*dī*	
K̔os	*K̔os, k̔ọ̈̄*	*K̔oi, k̔ọ̈̄*	*k̔ọ̈*	*k̔ọ*	*k̔ọ̈̄*	*kọ̈̄*	high-toned
gos	*gos, gọ̈̄*	*goi, gọ̈̄*	*ghọ̈̄*	*gō*	*ghọ̈̄*	*gọ̈̄*	deep-toned
'os	*'os, 'ọ̈̄*	*'oi, 'ọ̈̄*	*'ọ̈̄*	*ō*	*'ọ̈̄*	*γọ̈̄*	
čos	*čos, čọ̈̄*	*čoi, čọ̈̄*	*čọ̈̄*	*čō*	*čọ̈̄*	*čọ̈̄*	high-toned
nags	*nag(s)*	*nag*		?	*nag, nā*	*nāg*	deep-toned
rigs	*rig(s)*	*rig*		?	*rig, rī*	and	
tugs	*tug(s)*	*tug*		?	*tug, tụ̄*	so forth	high-toned
legs	*leg(s)*	*leg*		?	*leg, lē*		deep-toned
p̔ogs	*p̔og(s)*	*p̔og*		?	*p̔og, p̔ö*		
t̔abs	*t̔ab(s)*	*t̔ab*	*t̔au*		*t̔ab*	*t̔ab*	
čibs	*čib(s)*	*čib*	*čiu͡*		*čib*	*čib*	high-toned
šubs	*šub(s)*	*šub*	*šū*		*šub*	*šub*	
p̔ebs	*p̔eb(s)*	*p̔eb*	*p̔ĕ͡ü*		*p̔eb*	*p̔eb*	
'obs	*'ob(s)*	*'ob*	*'ŏ͡ü*		*'o͡ŏb*	*γob*	deep-toned
t̔ams-čad	*t̔am(s)-čád*	*t̔am-čád*	*t̔am-čád*		*t̔am-čẹ̄'*	*t̔am-čad*	high-toned
goms-po	*gom(s)-pa*	*gom-pa*	*ghom-pa*		*ghom-pa*	*gom-pa*	deep-toned

IV. Words with diphthongs.

1	2 Ladak	3 Lahoul	4 Spiti	5 Tsang, Ü	6 Khams	7
K̔ai	*k̔ẹ̄*	*K̔ai, k̔ệ*		*k̔ẹ̄*	*k̔ē*	high-toned
čii, čī	*čī*	*čī*		*čĭ*	*čī*	
bui	*bui, bụ̈̄*	*bui, bụ̈̄*	*bhui*	*bhụ̈̄*	*bụ̈̄*	deep-toned
dĕ͡ī	*dei*		*dhĕ͡ī*	*dhĕ͡ī*	*dī*	
soi					*sọ̈̄*	high-toned
gă͡ü			*ghă͡ü*	*ghau*	*ga-γọ̈*	
lĕ͡ü					and so forth	
mĭ͡ü						deep-toned
ră͡ŏ					(*rȧ-γo*)	
reo						

1	2	3	4	5	6	7
	West. Tibet		Central Prov.			
	Ladak	Lahoul	Spiti	Tsang, Ü	Khams	
rio						deep-toned
roo, rŏ						deep-toned
ruo						deep-toned

V. Words with subscribed letters.

1	2	3	4	5	6	7
kyaṅ					*kyeṅ*	
kyir-kyir					*kyer-kyér*	
kyu					*kyo̱*	
k̔yi					*k̔ye*	high-toned
k̔yu					*k̔yo̱*	high-toned
k̔yed				*k̔yĕ'*		high-toned
k̔yod				*k̔yŏ'*		high-toned
gyi			*ghyi*	*ghyi*		deep-toned
gyon-pa	Pur. Bal.; Ld.		*ghyon-pa*	*ghyo̱m-pa*		deep-toned
p̔yag	*p̔yag čag*	*čag*	*čag*	*čag*	*čag*	high-toned
p̔yi	*p̔i*	*p̔i*	*či*	*či*	*či*	high-toned
p̔yug-po	*p̔yug-po čug-po*	*čug-po*	*čug-po*	*čug-po*	*čug-p*	high-toned
p̔ye	*p̔e*	*p̔e*	*če*	*če*	*če?*	high-toned
p̔yogs	*čog(s)*	*čog*	*čog*	*čog* Ts. *čŏ* Ü.	*čog*	high-toned
bya-mo	*bya-mo ǰa-mo*	*ǰa-mo*	?	*ǰha-mo*	?	deep-toned
byi-ba, byi-wa	*bí-wa*	*bi-wa*	?	*ǰhi-wa*	?	deep-toned
bye-ma	?	*be-ma*	?	*ǰhe-ma*	?	deep-toned
b̥yos	?	*ǰos, ǰoi, ǰö̱*	?	*ǰho̱*	?	deep-toned
mya-ṅán	?	*ṅya-ṅán*	*nya-ṅán*	*nya-ṅé̱n*	?	high-toned
krad-pa	?	*ṭad-pa*	*ṭad-pa*	*ṭe̱'-pa* Ts. vlg. *ke̱'-pa* Ü	?	
k̔rag	*k̔rag*	*ṭ̔ag*	*ṭ̔ag*	*ṭ̔ag*	*ṭ̔ag*	high-toned
k̔rims		*ṭ̔im(s)*	*ṭ̔im*	*ṭ̔im*	*ṭ̔em*	high-toned
k̔rus	?	*ṭ̔us; ṭ̔ü̱*	*ṭ̔ui*	*ṭ̔ü̱*	*ṭ̔ü̱*	high-toned
k̔ron-po	?	*ṭ̔on-pa*	*ṭon-pa*	*ṭo̱m-pa*	*ṭon-pa*	high-toned
gri	*gri*	*ḍri, ḍi*	*ḍhi*	*ḍhi*	*ḍi*	deep-toned
dron-mo		*ḍon-mo*	*ḍhon-mo*	*ḍhon-mo*	*ḍon-mo*	deep-toned
p̔ru-gu	*p̔ru-gu*	*ṭ̔u-gu*	*ṭ̔u-ghu*	*ṭ̔u-ghu*	*ṭ̔o̱-go̱*	high-toned
bra-bo, bra-wo		*bra-wo, ḍa-wo*	*ḍha-wo*	*ḍha-wo*	*ḍa-wo*	deep-toned
braṅ-sa	(B. *blaṅ-sa*)	*ḍaṅ-sa*	*ḍhaṅ-sa*	*ḍhaṅ-sa*	*ḍaṅ-sa*	deep-toned
sran-ma	*stran-ma?*	*ṡran-ma*	*ṡran-ma*	*ṡrém-ma* vulg. *sem-ma*	*stran-ma*	high-toned
sriṅ-mo	*striṅ-mo* B.	*ṡriṅ-mo*	*ṡriṅ-mo*	*ṡriṅ-mo* vulg. *siṅ-mo*	*striṅ-mo*	high-toned
hrul-po	*ṡrul-po*	*ṡrul-po*	*ṡrul-po*	*ṡrul-po*	*ṡrul-po*	deep-toned
klog-pa	?	*log-pa*	*log-pa*	*log-pa*	?	high-toned
glog	*γlog* B.	*log*	*log*	*log*	*γlog*	high-toned
bla-ma	?	*la-ma*	*la-ma*	*la-ma*	*wla-ma*	high-toned
zla-ba, zla-wa	*lza* B.	*(l)da-wa*	*da-wa*	*da-wa*	*lda-wa*	?
rlaṅs-pa		*(r)laṅ(s)-pa*	*lã-pa*	*laṅ-pa*	*rleṅ-pa*	high-toned
sla-mo	?	*la-mo*	*la-mo*	*la-mo*	*sla-mo*	high-toned

VI. Words with superscribed letters.

1	2	3	4	5	6	7
rkaṅ-pa	?	*(r)kaṅ-pa*	*kaṅ-pa*	*kaṅ-pa*	*rkeṅ-pa*	these and all the rest are high-toned
rgad-po	?	*(r)gad-p̔o*	*gad-po*	*ge̱'-po*	*rgad-po*	these and all the rest are high-toned
rṅa	?	*(r)ṅa*	*ṅa*	*ṅa*	*rṅa*	these and all the rest are high-toned
rǰes	?	*žes, žē*	*ǰē?*	*ǰē*	*rǰī*	these and all the rest are high-toned

1	2	3	4	5	6	7
	West. Tibet		Central Prov.			
	Ladak	Lahoul	Spiti	Tsang, Ü	Khams	
rnyiṅ-pa	*(r)nyiṅ-pa*	*nyiṅ-pa*	*nyiṅ-pa*	*nyiṅ-pa*	*rnyiṅ-pa*	
rta	*rta, sta, ta*	*ta*	*ta*	*ta*	*rta*	
rdo	*(r)do*	*do*	*do*	*do*	*rdo*	
rnon-po	*(r)non-po*	*non-po*	*non-po*	*nom-po*	*rnon-po*	
rba	*wa*	*ba*	*ba*	*ba*	*rwa?*	
rmig-pa	*mig-pa*	*mig-pa*	*mig-ba*	*mig-pa*	*rmig-pa*	
rtsa	*sa*	*sa*	?	*tsa*	?	Pur. Bal.
rtswa	*sa*	*sa*	?	*tsa*	?	*rtsoá, stsoá*
rdza-ma	*za-ma*	*za-ma*	?	*dza-ma*	?	
lṅa	*ṅa, šṅa*	*ṅa*	*ṅa*	*ṅa*	*lṅa*	
lċaṅ-ma	*lċaṅ-ma*	*ċaṅ-ma*	*ċaṅ-ma*	*ċaṅ-ma*	*lċeṅ-ma*	*lċaṅ-ma*
lǰaṅ-k'u	*(l)ǰaṅ-k'u*	*ǰaṅ-k'u*	*ǰaṅ-k'u*	*ǰaṅ-k'u*	*lǰeṅ-k'u*	
ltad-mo	*(l)tad-mo*	*tad-mo*	*tad-mo*	*tè'-mo*	*ltad-mo*	*ltad-mo*
ldag-pa	*(l)dag-pa*	*dag-pa*	*dag-pa*	*dag-pa*	*ldag-pa*	
lham	*lam*	*lam*	*lam*	*hlam* or *χlam*	*lham*	*lham*
skom	*skom*	*kom*	*kom*	*kom*	*skom*	*skom*
skra	*šra*	*šra, ṭa*	*ṭa*	*ṭa*	*štra*	
sgo	*γo*	*go*	*go*	*go*	*sgo*	*sgo*
sgra	*ḍa, ra*	*ḍa, ra*	*ḍa*	*ḍa*	*zdra*	
sṅon-po	*ṅon-po*	*ṅon-po*	*ṅon-po*	*ṅom-po*	*sṅon-po*	
snyiṅ	*nyiṅ*	*nyiṅ*	*nyin*	*nyiṅ*	*snyeṅ*	
stag	*stag*	*tag*	*tag*	*tag*	*stag*	
sdoṅ-po	*(s)doṅ-po*	*doṅ-po*	*doṅ-po*	*doṅ-po*	*sdoṅ-po*	
sna	*na*	*na*	*na*	*na*	*sna*	
spu	*(s)pu*	*pu*	*pu*	*pu*	*spo*	
spyod-pa	*(s)ċod-pa*	*ċod-pa*	*ċod-pa*	*ċö'-pa*	*šwod-pa*	
spreŭ	also *šrĕŭ*	*ṭĕŭ*	*ṭĕŭ*	*ṭĕŭ*	*štre-γö*	
sbal-ba	*(s)bal-wa*	*bal-wa*	*bal-wa*	*bā-wa* Ts. *bal-wa* Ü.	*zual-wa*	
sbyar-ba	*żar-wa*	*żar-wa*	*żar-wa*	*ǰar-wa*	*zuar-wa*	
sbraṅ-bu	also *ḍaṅ-bu*	*ḍaṅ-bu*	*ḍaṅ-bu*	*ḍaṅ-bu*	*ḍeṅ-wo*	
sman	*(s)man*	*man*	*man*	*men*	*sman*	
smyon-pa	*nyon-pa*	*nyon-pa*	*nyon-pa*	*nyom-pa*	*snyon-pa*	
smra-ba	*mra-wa*	*mra-wa*	?	*m(r)a-wa*	*šna-wa*	
stsal-ba	*(s)tsal-wa*	*tsal-wa*	*tsal-wa*	*tsā-wa* Ts. *tsal-wa* Ü.	*stsal-wa*	

VII. Words with prefixed letters.

γċes-pa	*ċes-pa*	*ċē-pa*	*ċē-pa*	*ċē-pa*	*γċī-pa*	
γtam	*tam*	*tam*	*tam*	*tam*	*γtām*	
γduṅ-ba	*duṅ-wa*	*duṅ-wa*	*duṅ-wa*	*duṅ-wa*	*γduṅ-wa*	
γnaṅ-ba	*naṅ-wa*	*naṅ-wa*	*naṅ-wa*	*naṅ-wa*	*γneṅ-wa*	
γnam	*nam*	*nam*	*nam*	*nam*	*γnam*	Bal. *γnam*
γtsaṅ-po	*tsaṅ-po*	*tsaṅ-po*	*tsaṅ-po*	*tsaṅ-po*	*γtseṅ-po*	
γżu	*żu*	*żu*	*šu*	*šu*	*γżo*	
γzig	*zig*	*zi'*	*sig*	*sig*	*γzig*	
γyog-po	*yog-po*	*yo'-po*	*yog-po*	*yog-po*	*(γ)yog-po*	
γšer-pa	*šer-pa*	*šer-pa*	*šer-pa*	*šer-pa*	*γšer-pa*	or *gšer-pa*
γser	*ser*	*ser*	*ser*	*ser*	*γser*	Bal. *γser*
dkar-po	*kar-po*	*kar-po*	*kar-po*	*kar-po*	*γkar-po*	
dkyil	*kyil*	*kyil*	*kyil*	*kyil*	*γkyil*	
dgu	*gu*	*gu*	*gu*	*gu*	*γgo*	
dgra	*ḍa*	*ḍa*	*ḍa*	*ḍa*	*(γ)ḍa*	Bal. *χṅul*
dṅul	*ṇul* (vulgo	*mul*) *ṇul*	*ṇul*	*ṇū* Ts. *ṇul* Ü.	*γṇul*	or *χmul*
dpe-ča	*pe-ċa*	*pe-ċa*	*pe-ċa*	*pe-ċa*	*γpe-ċa*	*χpe-ċa*

1	2	3	4	5	6	7
	West. Tibet		Central Prov.			
	Ladak	Lahoul	Spiti	Tsaug, Ü	Khams	
ma-dpe	*mas-pe*	*mar-pe*	*ma-pe*	*ma-pe*	*maγ-pe?*	
dpyid	*(s)pid*	*pid*	*ċid*	*ċi'*	*χšid*	
dbaṅ.	*uaṅ*	*uaṅ*	*uaṅ*	*uaṅ* (vlg. *aṅ*)	*γweṅ*	
dbu	*'u**	*'u*	*'u*	*'u*	*wo̤*	* = ཨུ etc.
dbugs	*'ug(s)*	*'u'*	*'ug*	*'ug* Ts. *'ū* Ü.	*wug*	
dbul-po	*'ul-po*	*'ul-po*	*'ul-po*	*'ū-po* Ts. *'ul-po, ṳl-po*	*γwo̤l-po*	
dben-pa	*'en-pa*	*'en-pa*	*en-pa*	*'em-pa* [Ü.	*γwen-pa*	
dbyar	*yar*	*yar*	*yar*	*yar*	*wyer*	
dmar-po	*mar-po*	*mar-po*	*mar-po*	*mar-po*	*(γ)mar-po*	
dmyal-ba	*nyal-wa*	*nyal-wa*	*nyal-wa*	*nyā-wa* Ts. *nyal-wa* Ü.	*mnyal-wa*	
ḃka, vka	*ka*	*ka*	*ka*	*kā*	*vka*	
bkra-šis	*ṭa-ši(s)*	*ṭa-šī*	*ṭa-šī*	*ṭa-šī*	*bṭa-šī*	
ḃgo-ba	*go-wa*	*go-wa*	*go-wa*	*go-wa*	*vgö-wa*	
brgyad	*gyad*	*gyad*	*gyad*	*gyẹ'*	*vrgyad*	Bal. *vrgyad*
bču	*ču*	*ču*	*ču*	*ču*	*vču, bču*	
bčug-sum	*čug-súm*	*čug-um*	*ču-súm?*	*ču-súm* *ču-sum*	*včug-súm*	
bčub-ži	*čub-ži*	*čub-ži*	*ču-ži*	*ču-ží*	*včub-ží?*	
brǰed-pa	*žed-pa*	*žed-pa*	*ǰed-pa*	*ǰĕ'-pa*	*vrǰed-pa*	
btum-pa	*tum-pa*	*tum-pa*	*tum-pa*	*tūm-pa*	*bto̤m-pa*	
bdun	*dun*	*dun*	*dun*	*dṳn*	*vdun*	Bal. *vdun*
brtse-ba	*se-wa*	*se-wa*	*tse-wa*	*tse-wa*	*vrtse-wa*	
brdzun	*zun*	*zun*	*dzun*	*dzun*	*vrdzun*	Pur. *rdzun*
bži	*ži*	*ži*	*ši*	*ši*	*vže*	
bžib-ču	*žib-ču*	*žib-ču*	*ši̋-ču?*	*ši-ču*	*vžeb-ču?*	
bzaṅ-po	*zaṅ-po*	*zaṅ-po*	*saṅ-po*	*saṅ-po*	*vzeṅ-po*	
bšal-ba	*šal-wa*	*šal-wa*	*šal-wa*	*šā-wa*	*všel-wa*	
bsu-ba	*su-wa*	*su-wa*	*su-wa*	*su-wa*	*vso̤-wa*	
bsreg-pa	*šreg-pa*	*šreg-pa*	*šreg-pa*	*šreg-pa* (*seg-pa*)	*vstrag-pa*	
bslab-pa	*lab-pa*	*lab-pa*	*lab-pa*	*lab-pa*	*vslab-pa*	
mṅar	*k̕ar*	*k̕ar*	*k̕ar*	*k̕ar*	*mk̕ar*	
mgo	*go*	*go*	*˳go*	*˳go*	*mgo*	
mgron	*ḍon*	*ḍon*	*ḍon*	*˳ḍo̤n*	*mḍon*	
mṅar-(b)wa	*ṅar-wa*	*ṅar-wa*	*ṅar-wa*	*ṅar-wa*	*mṅar-wa*	
mčin-pa	*čin-pa*	*čin-pa*	*čin-pa*	*čim-ga*	*mčen-pa*	
mǰiṅ-pa	*ǰiṅ-pa*	*ǰiṅ-pa*	*˳ǰiṅ-pa*	*˳ǰiṅ-pa*	*mǰiṅ-pa*	
mt̕iṅ	*t̕iṅ*	*t̕iṅ*	*t̕iṅ*	*t̕iṅ*	*(m)t̕eṅ*	
mda	*da*	*da*	*˳da*	*˳da*	*mda*	
mt̕so	*t̕so*	*t̕so*	*t̕so˚*	*t̕so*	*mt̕so*	
mdzo	*dzo*	*dzo*	*˳dzo*	*˳dzo*	*mdzo*	
˳k̕ol-ba	*k̕ol-wa*	*k̕ol-wa*	*k̕ol-wa*	*k̕ō-wa* Ts.	*ṅk̕ol-wa*	
˳gul-ba	*gul-wa*	*gul-wa*	*˳gul-wa*	*˳gū-wa* Ts *˳gul-wa* Ü.	*ṅgul-wa*	
˳čam-pa	*čam-pa*	*čam-pa*	*čam-pa*	*čam-pa*	*nčam-pa*	
˳ǰam-po	*ǰam-po*	*ǰam-po*	*˳ǰam-po*	*˳ǰam-po*	*nǰam-po*	
˳t̕ag-pa	*t̕ag-pa*	*t̕ag-pa*	*t̕ag-pa*	*t̕ag-pa*	*nt̕ag-pa*	
γge-˳dún	*gen-dun*	*gen-dun*	*ge(n)-dún*	*ge(n)-dṳn* Ts. *ge-˳dṳ̈n* Ü.	*γgen-dún?*	
˳dod-pa	*dod-pa*	*dod-pa*	*˳dod-pa*	*˳dö̤'-pa*	*ndod-pa*	
˳p̕ur-ba	*p̕ur-wa*	*p̕ur-wa*	*p̕ur-wa*	*p̕ur-wa*	*mp̕ur-wa*	
˳p̕yi-ba	*p̕i-wa*	*p̕i-wa*	*p̕i-wa*	*či-wa*	*nči-wa*	
˳prod-pa	*ṭ̕od-pa*	*ṭ̕od-pa*	*ṭ̕od-pa*	*ṭ̕ö̤'-pa*	*nṭ̕od-pa*	

1	2	3	4	5	6	7
	West. Tibet		Central Prov.			
	Ladak	Lahoul	Spiti	Tsang, Ü	Khams	
˳bab-pa	*bab-pa*	*bab-pa*	*˳bab-pa*	*˳bab-pa*	*mbab-pa*	
vka-˳búm	*kam-bum*	*kam-bum*	*kam-búm*	*ka(m)-búm*	*vkam-búm*	
˳tsir-wa	*tsir-wa*	*tsir-wa*	*tsir-wa*	*tsir-wa*	*ntsir-wa*	
˳dzin-pa	*dzin-pa*	*dzin-pa*	*dzin-pa*	*dzim-pa*	*ndzen-pa*	

ABBREVIATIONS.

abbr.	= abbreviated, abbreviation
acc.	according to
acous.	accusative case
act.	active, -ly
adj.	adjective
adv.	adverb, -ially
A.R.	Asiatic Researches
Ar.	Arabic
B.	books, book-language
Bal.	Balti, the most westerly of the districts, in which the Tibetan language is spoken.
Bhar.	Bharata, a dialogue, ed. by Dr. A. Schiefner.
Bhot.	Bhotan, province.
Burn. I.	Burnouf, Introduction au Buddhism Indien.
II.	Burnouf, Lotus de la bonne loi.
C.	Central Tibet, esp. the provinces Ü and Tsang.
c.	cum, with
c.c.	construitur cum, construed with.
c.c.a.	construed with the accusative, etc.
ccapir	construitur cum accusativo personae, instrumentativo rei
ccirdp	construitur cum instrumentativo rei, dativo personae etc.
cf.	confer, compare
Chr. P.	Christian writings by Protestant missionaries.
Chr. R.	Christian writings by Roman Catholic missionaries.
cog.	cognate, related in origin
col.	colloquial, -ly
collect.	collective, -ly
com.	commonly
comp.	compound -s
conj.	conjunction
contr.	contracted
corr.	correct, -ly
correl.	correlative, -ly
Cs.	Csoma de Körös, Tibetan-English Dictionary.
Cunn.	Cunningham, General, Ladak and the surrounding country.
dat.	dative case
deriv.	derivative
Desg.	Desgodins, La Mission du Tibet de 1855—1870.
Do. or Dom.	Do-mang, a collection of incantations.
dub.	dubious
Dzl.	Dzanglun, an ancient collection of Legends of Buddha.
e.g.	= exempli gratia, for instance
eleg.	elegant, -ly
elsewh.	elsewhere
emphat.	emphatical, -ly
erron.	erroneous, -ly
esp.	especially
euphemist.	euphemistical, -ly
expl.	explain, explanation
extr.	extremo, towards the end of a longer article.
fem.	feminine gender
fig.	figurative, -ly
frq.	frequent, -ly
fut.	future tense
gen.	general, -ly
gen.	genitive case
Glr.	Gyalrabs, a history of the kings of Tibet.
Gram.	native grammarians or grammatical works
Gyatch.	Gyatcherrolpa, Biography of Buddha.
Hd.	Hindi language.
Hook.	Dr. Hooker, Himalayan Journals.
ibid.	ibidem, in the same place.
id.	idem, the same
i. e.	id est, that is
imp.	imperative mood
impers.	impersonal, -ly
incorr.	incorrect, -ly
inf.	infinitive mood
init.	initio, at the beginning of a longer article.
inst.	instead
instr.	instrumentative case
interj.	interjection
interr.	interrogative, -ly
intrs.	intransitive
i.o.	instead of
irr.	irregular, -ly
Kh.	Khams, eastern part of Tibet.
Köpp.	Köppen, Die Religion des Buddha.
Kun.	Kunawur, province under English protection.
Lat.	Latin
Ld.	Ladak, province.
Ld.-Glr.	Ladak-Gyalrabs, a history of Tibet, ed. by Dr. E. Schlagintweit.
Lew.	Lewin, Manual of Tibetan.
Lex., Lexx.	Lexicons, native dictionaries.
Lh.	Lahoul, province.
Lis.	Lishigurkhang, glossary.
lit.	literally, also literature
Ma.	Ma-ong-lung-bstan, a kind of Tibetan Apocalypse.

masc.	=	masculine gender
Med.		medical works
med.		medio, about the middle of a longer article
metaph.		metaphorical, -ly
meton.		metonymical, -ly
Mil.		Milaraspa's hundred thousand Songs.
Mil. nt.		Milaraspai nam-tar, Milaraspa's autobiography.
Mng.		Man-ngag-rgyud, a medical work.
n.		name
neut.		neuter gender
nif.		ni fallor, if I am not mistaken
n.p.		noun proper
N.T.		New Testament
num.		numeral
obs.		obsolete
opp.		as opposed to
p.		page
partic.		participle
pass.		passive, -ly
perh.		perhaps
Pers.		Persian
pers.		person, personal
pf.		perfect tense
pl.		plural number
pleon.		pleonastic, -ally
p. n.		proper name
po.		poetically
pop.		popular language
postp.		postposition
prep.		preposition
prob.		probably
pron.		pronoun
prop.		properly
prov.		provincialism, provincial, -ly
Pth.		Padma thangyig, a collection of legends of Padma Sambhava.
Pur.		Purig, province.
q.v.		quod vide, which see
rel.		relative
resp.		respectful, -ly
Sambh. or Sb.		Shambhala, a fabulous country in the north and a book: Guide to Sb.
sbst.		substantive
Sch.		Prof. Is J. Schmidt, Tibetisch-Deutsches Wörterbuch. Tibetische Grammatik.
Schf.		Dr A. Schiefner.
Schl.	=	Dr. E. Schlagintweit, Buddhism in Tibet.
Schr.		Schröter, editor of the first Tibetan Dictionary.
S.g.		Shad-gyud, a medical work.
Sik.		Sikkim, province
sim.		similar in meaning, similarly
sing.		singular number
s.l.c.		si lectio certa, if the reading is to be depended upon
S.O.		Ser-od, a religious work.
Sp.		Spiti, province.
Ssk.		Sanskrit
Stg.		Stan-gyur, a collection of commentaries.
symb. num.		symbolical numeral
syn. or synon.		synonymous
Tar.		Taranatha, history of the propagation of Buddhism in India.
termin.		terminative case
Thgr.		Thos-grol, Direction for the departed soul to find the way to eternal happiness.
Thgy.		Thargyan, scientific treatises.
Trig.		Triglot, a collection of Buddhist terms in Sanskrit, Tibetan and Mongolian.
trop.		tropically, figuratively
trs.		transitive
Ts.		Tsang, province of Central Tibet.
Ü		Ü, " " " "
Urd.		Urdu, a dialect of Hindustani.
v.		vide, see
vb.		verb
vb. a.		verb active
vb. n.		verb neuter
vulg.		vulgar, low expression
vulgo		in common life
W.		Western Tibet.
Was.		Prof. W. Wasiljew, Der Buddhismus.
Wdk.		Waidurya Karpo, a mathematical work.
Wdn.		Waidurya Nonpo, a medical work.
w. e.		without explanation
Will.		Williams, Sanskrit-English Dictionary.
Wls.		Wilson, Sanskrit Dictionary.
Wts.		Wai-tsang-thu-shi, a description of Tibet, originally Chinese, ed. by Klaproth.
Z.		Zangskar, a Kashmere-Tibetan province.
Zam.		Zamatog, a treatise on Tibetan grammar and orthography.

EMENDATION.

Page 122, 1st. column, 4th. line from the top, after dignity, are to be inserted the following words· 2. *Cs.* exaggeration. *sgro-$_{o}$dogs-pa* 1. *Sch.* to bestow the peacock's feather.

Other misprints in the English text will be easily recognized as such, and hardly require a specification.

ཀ

ཀ་ *ka* 1. the letter **k**, tenuis, = French *c* in *car*. — 2. as numerical figure, used in marking the volumes of a work: **one.** — *ka-t'o* **alphabetical register** *Sch.* — *ká-pa* the first volume of a work. — *ka-dpé* **a-b-c-book.** — *ka-p'réṅ*, *ka smad sum-ću*, *kā-li* the Tibetan **alphabet.**

ཀ་ *ka* 1. an additional syllable, so-called article, affixed to some substantives, numerals and pronouns, v. the grammars. — 2. **pillar,** v. *ka-ba.*

ཀྭ *ka (kva)* **oh!**

ཀ་ཀ་ *ka-ká* **excrement,** (nursery word), **ka-ka taṅ-će* W.* = French: *faire caca.*

ཀཱ་ཀ *kā-ka Ssk.* **crow.**

ཀཾ་ཀ *kaṅ-ka, Ssk.* कङ्क, **heron.**

ཀ་ཀ་ནི་ *ka-ka-ni* a small coin of ancient India *Cs.*

ཀ་ཀ་རང་ *ka-ka-ráṅ* **cucumber** *Kun.*

ཀ་ཀོ་ལ་ *ka-ko-la, Ssk.* कक्कोल, a plant bearing a berry the inner part of which is a waxlike and aromatic substance. — *ka-ko* prob. means the same.

ཀ་ཁ་ *ka-k'á* the **a-b-c, alphabet;** *ka-k'ai t'o* **alphabetical register,** *ka-k'ai dpe* **a-b-c-book;** *ka-k'a-pa* **abecedarian.**

ཀ་ཁོལ་མ་ *ka-k'ól-ma* v. *k'ol-ma.*

ཀ་ཅ་ *ká-ća* also *ká-ća*, **goods, things;** *ká-ćai ṅés-su ₒbráṅs-pai rgyálpo* n. of a demon.

ཀ་ཏ་ཡ་ *ká-ta-ya*, also *ka-tya.* n. of a locality *Mil.*

ཀ་ཏུ *ka-tu* v. *ke-tu.*

ཀ་ཏོ་ར་ *ka-tó-ra*, more correctly *ka-ṭo-ra*, *Hd.*, **metal cup, dish, basin.**

ཀ་ཐ་ར་ *ka-t'a-ra Kun.* a sort of **peach.**

ཀ་དག་ *ka-dág*, also *ka-nas dag*, pure from the beginning *Lex.*

ཀ་དར་ *ka-dár* (from خبردار *Urd.?*) only in the phrase: **ka-dar ćo-će** **to be cautious, take care, take heed,** *-la*, of.

ཀ་པཱ་ལ་ *ka-pā-la Ssk.* **skull.**

ཀ་པི་ཏ་ *ka-pi-ta* **gum, resin** *Sch.*

ཀཾ་པོ་རྩེ་ *kam-po-rtse*, absurd spelling instead of *kam-bo-ja Wdk.*

ཀ་བ་ *ká-ba* **ka-wa** 1. **pillar, post;** *k. ₒdzug-pa* to erect a pillar. — 2. a large vein or artery in the abdomen. — **Comp.** *ka-skéd* shaft of a column. — *ká ćan* having columns. — *ka-γćig-sgo-γćig* a small house, poor cottage; also a mode of capital punishment is said to be called so, when the culprit is fastened to a pillar in a dungeon until he dies of hunger. — *ka-γćig-pa* having one pillar, *ka-máṅ-ma* having many pillars. — *ka-čén* the principal p. (cf. στῦλος Gal. 2. 9) *Tar.* 182. 10. — *ka-rtén* base of a p. *Lex.* — *ka-stégs*, *ka-γdán* pedestal, base of a p. — *ka-spúṅs* many pillars. — *ka-méd* without a pillar; helpless, destitute. — *ka-rtsé*, *ka-yáṅ-rtse* capital of a pillar. — *ka wd-*

čan, súl-čan a channeled pillar. — *ka-γžú* capital of a pillar. — *ka-γžu-γdúṅ* beam of the capital (pillars are mostly made of wood).

ཀ་བེད་ *ka-béd* prob. a sort of **gourd** *Wdṅ.*

ཀ་མ་རུ་ *ka-ma-ru* 1. **alabaster** *Sch.* — 2. n. of a country.

ཀ་མ་ལ་ཤི་ལ་ *ka-ma-la-śi-la* n. of a famous ancient pandita or Brahmanical scholar.

ཀ་མུལ་རྡོ་རྒྱད་ *ka-mul-rdo-rgyád* is said to denote a sort of **alabaster** or of **steatite** in *C.*

ཀ་ཙ་ལིནྡི་ *ka-tsa-lindi* n. of a fabulous, very smooth, stuff or cloth, *Gyatch.*

ཀ་རྩམ་ *ka-rtsam, Ld.* **ka-sam**, prob. a sort of **oats**; differing from *yug-po*, accounted superior to buckwheat, but inferior to wheat.

ཀ་ཚིགས་ཆེན་པོ་ *ka-tsigs-čén-po* title of a book cited in *Glr.*

ཀྭ་ཡེ་ *ka-yé (kwa-ye)* **oh! holla! hear!** so e. g. at the beginning of a royal proclamation *Pth.*

ཀ་ར་ *ká-ra C. & B.* **sugar**; *šel-ka-ra* crystallized s., sugar-candy, *rgyál-mo-ka-ra* id. *Sch.*; *byé-ma-ka-ra* ground sugar. — *ka-ra-ǰa* tea with sugar; *Sch.* 'a sweet soup'? — *ka-ra tog-tóg* sugar in lumps. — *kara-šiṅ* sugar-cane. (*W. k̔a-ra*).

ཀ་ར་བཱི་ར་ *ka-ra-bī-ra*, also *ka-ra-wī-ra (Ssk.)* **oleander flower,** *Nerium odorum.*

ཀ་རཉྫ་ *ka-raṅ-dza Ssk.* a medicinal fruit, *Galedupa arborea.*

ཀ་རནྡ་ *ka-ran-dha Pth.* more correctly ཀ་རཎྜ་ *ka-raṇ-ḍa, Ssk.*, a species of **duck.**

ཀ་རུ་ *ká-ru* **wedge.**

ཀ་ལཱ་པ་ *ka-lā-pa* a fabulous place or country in the north of Asia; also n. of a grammar *Cs.*

ཀ་ལ་པིང་ཀ་ *ka-la-piṅ-ka Cs.*: 'Ssk., n. of a bird', *Will.* 'kalāpin peacock; the Indian cuckoo'.

ཀ་ལ་ཤ་ *ka-la-śa Ssk.* **pitcher, jar.**

ཀ་ལག་ *ká-lag W.* **mud,** mixture of earth and water used instead of clay (*C. & B.*: *ǰim-pa*); the word is also used for other similar compounds.

ཀ་ལནྟ་ཀ་ *ka-lan-taka Ssk.* n. of a bird.

ཀ་ལི་ *ka-li* 1. **skull** *Lex.* — 2. = *ka-lé W.*

ཀཱ་ལི་ *kā-li* the **Tib. alphabet,** v. *ka.*

ཀ་ལིང་ག་ *ka-liṅ-ga Ssk.* n. of different tracts in the eastern part of India; *Sch.*: 'Korea', without giving further explanation; perh. Mongol writers call it so?

ཀ་ལིབ་ *ka-lib, Ar.* كالب **bullet-mould** *W.*

ཀ་ལེ་ *ka-lé.* also *ka-léb,* **saddle-cloth.**

ཀཱ་ཤ་ *kā-śa Ssk.* a sort of grass, Saccharum spontaneum; Tibetans often seem to mistake it for *ku-śa* q. v.

ཀ་ཤི་ཀ་ *ka-śi-ka Ssk.*, adj. of Kāsi (Banāras): inhabitant of Banāras; *ka-śi-kai ras*, a sort of fine **cottoncloth.**

ཀ་ས་ *ká-sa*, also **ká-so, kas** (perh. a mutilated form of *bka-stsal)* resp. **yes, Sir! very well, Sir! at your service!** (*W.* also: **ká-sa-ǰu** v. *žu) W.* frq., also *C.* ni f., never in *B.*

ཀག་གིས་ *kág-gis* **suddenly** *Sch.*

ཀག་མ་ *kág-ma* **mischief, harm, injury** *Cs.*

ཀང་ཀ་ *kaṅ-ka Ssk.* **heron.**

ཀང་དང་ཀིང་ *kaṅ-daṅ-kiṅ* n. of a terrifying deity *Glr.*, prob. = *kiṅ-káṅ*, which is said to signify Rāhula (v. *sgra-γčan & drag-γšed.* in *drag-pa).*

ཀཎྜ་ཀཱ་རི་ *kaṇḍa-kā-ri Ssk.* ('thorny') Wilson: *Solanum Jaquini;* in *Lh.* a sort of wild Rubus.

ཀད་ *kad, Ld.* sometimes instead of the affix *ka*, e. g. *γnyis-kád, tsaṅ-kád*; perh. also in *mnyam-kád, Thgy.?*

ཀན་ *kan Med.* = *bad-kan.*

ཀན་མ་ *kán-ma* **middle finger.**

ཀབ་ཟ *káb-za* (قبضه *Ar.*) *W.* **hilt, handle** of a sword.

ཀབ་ཤ *káb-ša* (کفش *Pers.*) **shoe;** in *W.* esp. the leather shoes of Hindu fashion, which are also bought by wealthier Tibetans.

ཀམ་བོ་ཛ *kam-bo-dza Ssk.* n. of a country in the northwest of India, *Wdṅ.*: *kam-po-rtse.*

ཀའུ *kau* **watermelon** *Sch.*

ཀར *kar,* also *kar-kar,* **great pain, suffering** *Lex.*

ཀརྐ་ཏ *karka-ta Ssk.* the constellation of **Cancer.**

ཀར་སྐྱིན *kár-skyin* **loan,** when respectfully requested, cf *skyin.*

ཀར་ཆག *kar-čág* **register, list.**

ཀརྨ *kárma Ssk.* ('deed, action'); *kar-ma-pa* (in Nepal *karmika*) name of a philosophical school of Buddhism.

ཀར་ཡོལ *kar-yól* **porcelain. china-ware, -cup** etc.

ཀར་ལང་བ *kár-lan-ba,* also *kér-lan-ba,* **to stand up, to rise.**

ཀར་ཤ་པ་ཎི or ཎ *kar-ša-pa-ni* or *na, Ssk.* **कार्षापण,** a coin in ancient India, or rather a weight of gold and silver, of different value (not = 'cowries', as *Sch.* seems to think).

ཀལ་ཡ *kál-ya,* also *kal-yór, W.* col. instead of *kar-yól,* the former seems to be a corruption of قلعی.

ཀི *ki* numerical figure: 31, *ki-pa* the 31st (volume).

ཀི་ཀང *ki-káṅ* **wild leek** *Sch.*

ཀི་གུ *ki-gu* n. of the vowel-sign for *i,* ི.

ཀི་མ *ki-ma Dzl.* ༣༡༩ acc. to *Schf.* a corruption of the Chinese *khin,* a lyre with 7 strings. (Pilgrim. of Fa-Hian Calc. 1848 p. 265).

ཀི་ཙི *ki-tsi* **tickling** *W.,* **ki-tsi kúg-če** **to tickle.**

ཀིང་ཀང *kiṅ-káṅ* v. *kaṅ-daṅ-kiṅ.*

ཀིམ་པ *kim-pa* n. of a fruit, *Lex.*

ཀུ *ku* numerical figure: 61; *kú-pa* the 61st (volume).

ཀུ *ku, kú-sgra B.,* **kú-čo** *W* **clamour.**

ཀུ་ན་ལ *ku-na-la, ku-nā-la Ssk.,* n. of a bird in the Himalaya.

ཀུ་བ *kú-ba Wdṅ.* **gourd.**

ཀུ་བེ་ར *ku-be-ra Ssk.* the god of riches, also *Nag-ku-bera, Rnam-tos-kyi-bú, Rnam-tos-sras, Lag-na-rdó-rje* etc.

ཀུ་མུ་ད *ku-mu-da Ssk.* the flower of the red and white **lotus,** *Nymphaea rubra* and *esculenta.*

ཀུ་ཡ *kú-ya* **sediment of urine** *Med.*

ཀུ་རུ་ཀུལ་ལེ *ku-ru-kul-le* n. of a female deity *Mil.*

ཀུ་རུག *ku-rúg Ld.* **colt of an ass.**

ཀུ་རེ *ku-ré,* also *ku-res* **jest, joke,** *ku-re byed-pa* **to jest,** cf. *kyal-ka.*

ཀུ་ལིག *ku-lig* **key,** also **lock;** more accurately: **pé-ku-lig** key, *čúg-ku-lig* lock, padlock; **ku-lig-búr-* (or *bor-*) *tse** in *Ld.* a contrivance used instead of a doorlatch. *W.*

ཀུ་ཤ *ku-ša* a sort of grass, Poa cynosuroides, often used in sacred ceremonies.

ཀུ་ཤུ *ku-šu* **apple** *Dzl.; W.* (Cf. *sli*).

ཀུ་སུ་མ *ku-su-ma Ssk.* **flower.**

ཀུ་ཧུ *ku-hu* **ring-dove** *Cs.* (*Ssk.*: the cry of the cuckoo).

ཀུག *kug,* also *kug-kúg,* **crooked; a hook;** *gri-kug* a curved knife, short sabre; *lčags-kug* an iron hook; *nya-kug* a fishing-hook; **kug-kug jhé-pa** *C.* **taṅ-če** *W.* **to bend, curve; clinch** (a nail); **go kug taṅ-če** *W.* **to nod,** **lag kug taṅ-če** *W* **of beckon.** (Cf. *kum-pa.*)

ཀུག་རྩེ *kug-rtse,* **kug-se** **cuckoo** *W.*

ཀུན་ *kun (C.: *kụn*)* **all, every, each; whole;** *spui ḱúṅ-bu kún-nas* from every pore *Dzl.*; *dé-dag kun* all these; *γžan kun* all the others; also pleon. *kun ťams-čád* all of them, they altogether; *kún-gyis mťóṅ-ba, ťós-pa* seen, heard by every body, generally known; *kún-tu* 1. into all, in all etc. 2. adv. everywhere, in every direction; *kun-tu-bzáṅ-po* Allgood, n. of the first of the celestial Bodhisattwas, *Samanta-bhadra*, sometimes confounded with Adibuddha, *ťóg-mai Saṅs-rgyas*; in later works even a *Kun-tu-bzáṅ-mo Yum* is mentioned *Thgr.*; *kún-tu rgyú-ba* to go everywhere, wander about; *Kun-tu-rgyu* **परिव्राजक** n. of a class of Brahmans, itinerant monks, *Dzl.*; *kún-nas* **from everywhere, round about, wholly, thoroughly** e. g. overpowered by passions, cleansed from sin *Dzl.*; *kún-nas ͺdod-pa* to wish from the bottom of the heart *Thgy.*

Comp. *kun-dkris* **general corruptness, misery, sin** *Lex.* — *Kun-ḱyáb* comprising, pervading all things. — *Kun-mḱyén-(pa)* **omniscient.** — *Kun-dgá-bo*, *Ssk. ānandā*, n. of the favourite disciple of Buddha; *Kun-dga* is to this time frequently used as a name of (female) persons. — *Kun-dga-rá-ba*, also *kun-dga Thgy.*, or *kun-ra*, *Ssk.* **आराम** or **संघाराम** 'garden of all joys' 1. the **grove** in which a monastery is situated. 2. the **monastery.** 3. in Tibet, which is destitute of groves, more particularly the **auditory** or **library** of a monastery — *Kun-brtágs*, in the Mahayana: a personal, erroneous supposition *Was.* — *Kun-ͺdús* **all-gathering, all-uniting.** — *Kun-dbáṅ* **almighty.** — *Kun-rdzób* **altogether vain, delusive;** *kún-rdzób-kyi bdén-pa* subjective truth *Was.* — *Kun-γži* lit.: the primary cause of all things, viz.: 1. the **soul** or **spirit**, *kun-γžii sems* (opp. to *ͺbyúṅ-ba bžii lus* the body consisting of the 4 elements), *kun-γžii séms-la yo mo ma mčis-te* as no difference of sex exists in souls (we, though being women, would beg etc.) *Mil.* 2. With more precise distinction: *kun-γži* **soul** as the seat of the passions, opp. to *sems-nyid*, the very soul, the spirit as the seat of reason *Mil.* 3. To the followers of the Adibuddha doctrine *kun-γži* is = **God, Adibuddha,** *kun-γžii Saṅs-rgyas.* — *Kun-γzigs* **all-seeing.** — *Kun-slóṅ Lex.* v. *sloṅ-ba.*

ཀུན་ད་ *kun-da Ssk.* **jessamine.**

ཀུན་དུ་རུ་ *kun-du-ru Ssk.* **incense,** Boswellia.

ཀུམ་པ་ *kúm-pa*, also *kum-kúm, kúm-po,* **crooked, shriveled, dried up;** **kum táṅ-če* W.* **to bend together, to double.** (Cf. *skúm-pa).*

ཀུམ་བྷ་ *kum-bha Ssk.* earthen **jar.**

ཀུམ་བི་ར་ *kum-bi-ra Ssk.* **crocodile.**

ཀེ་ *ke* numeral: 91, *ke-pa* the 91st (volume).

ཀེ་ཀེ་རུ་ *ke-ke-ru*, also *kerketana & ketaka Ssk.* 'n. of a precious white stone' *Cs.*; our Ssk. dictionaries give but the last of these names, and as its only signification the name of the tree Pandanus odoratissima.

ཀེ་ཏ་ར་ *ke-ta-ra Sambh.*, n. of a mountain, prob. Kedāra, part of the Himalaya. *Will.*

ཀེ་ཏུ་ *ke-tu Ssk.* **a fiery meteor, shooting star; the descending node.**

ཀེ་རྩེ་ *ke-rtsé* v. *keu-rtsé.*

ཀེ་རེ་ *ke-ré* v. *kye-ré.*

ཀེ་ལ་ཤ་, ཀཻ་ལ་ཤ་ *ke-la-ša, kai-la-ša Cs.*, **कैलास** *Will.*, n. of a lofty region of the Himalaya, mythological rather than geographical, seems to be the same as Ti-se q. v., though modern geographers apply the name to different ranges.

ཀེ་ལན་ *ke-lan*; the fraternity or association, which Huc mentions under this name (Voy. II ch. 6), seemed to be totally unknown to our Tashilhunpo Lama, although the expectation of a final war between Buddhist believers and infidels, in which the latter will be destroyed, is widely spread through Tibet.

ཀེ་ཤུ་ཀ་ *ke-śu-ka Wdṅ.* n. of a plant, perhaps *keċuka*, Arum Colocasia, with edible root; or = *keṅ-su-ka?*

ཀེག་མ་ *kég-ma* = ཀག་མ་ *kág-ma Cs.*

ཀེང་རུས་ *keṅ-rús* **skeleton.**

ཀེང་ཤུ་ཀ་ *keṅ-śu-ka Lex., Sambh., Wdṅ.*, n. of a tree.

ཀེའུ་རྩེ་ *keu-rtse*, also *ke-rtse*, **jacket** *Mil*

ཀེའུ་རི་ *keu-ri* n. of a female terrifying deity *Thgr.*

ཀེའུ་ལེ་ *keu-le Dzl.* ཀཱ, 1: *keu-lei rgya*, acc. to the Mongol version: **customary seal,** — dubious.

ཀེར་གྱིས་ *kér-gyis* **suddenly** *Sch.*

ཀེར་བ་ *kér-ba* **to raise, lift up,** e. g. the finger towards heaven *Glr.*; *ker láṅ-ba* **to rise, stand up.**

ཀོ་ *ko* 1. num.: 121; *kó-pa* the 121st (volume). — 2. affix, = *ka col. Ld* — 3. **all, whole** *Schr.*, cf. *kob.*

ཀོ་ཀོ་ *ko-kó* 1. also *ko-sko*, **throat, chin** *Sch.*, *ko-sko degs Lex.?* 2. = *kaka W.*

ཀོ་ཀོ་ཐང་མ་ *ko-ko-tʻáṅ-ma* n. of a country in or near Ceylon *Pth*

ཀོ་ཉོན་ཙེ་ *ko-nyon-tsé*, also *ko-nyol-tsé*, *ko-lon-tsé* the kernel of the pine-apple *Cs.*; more particularly the edible seed of the Neosa-pine in the valley of the Sutledj; also *skan-nyan-tsé Kun.*

ཀོ་ཋ་ *ko-ṭa*, *Ssk.* **कोठ**, a kind of **leprosy** *Wdṅ.*

ཀོ་པང་ཙེ་ *ko-paṅ-tsé* a sort of **tea** *Schr.*

ཀོ་ཕོངས་ *ko-pʻóṅs* **guitar** *Ld.*; it is tuned in 3 fourths.

ཀོ་བ་ *kó-ba* 1. **hide, skin.** — 2. **leather,** **kó-wa nyé-kʻan** **tanner** *C.*; *gláṅ-ko* **neat's leather.** — *ko-krád* **leather-shoe.** — *kó-mkʻan* 1. **tanner.** 2. (acc. to some also:) conductor of a leather-boat, **boatman.** — *ko-btúm* 'leather-wrapping' is said to be a criminal punishment in *C.*, in different degrees of severity, e. g. **lág-pa ko-túm**, when the culprit's hands are cut off, the stumps sewed up in leather, and the wretch thrown as a beggar upon public charity etc. — *ko-tʻág* **strap, thong.** — *ko-ₒtʻágs Cs.*: a small instrument of leather to weave lace with. — *ko-gdán* a piece of leather put under the saddle *Sch.* — *ko-lpágs* **hide, leather.** — *ko-ₒbúgs Sch.*: three-edged needle for leather. — *ko-tsʻúg* **leather-sieve.** — *ko-rúl* a rotten hide.

ཀོ་བོ་ *kó-bo* n. of a country *Wdk.*

ཀོ་མ་ *kó-ma* n. of a bird *Wdṅ.*

ཀོ་ཝག་ *ko-wág* is meant to express the voice of a raven.

ཀོ་ར་ *ko-ra*, *Hindi* **कोरा**, more tibetanized *ko-rás*, unbleached coarse cotton cloth.

ཀོ་རེ་ *ko-ré*, in compounds *kor W.*, **cup** for drinking; *śiṅ-kor* wooden cup, a utensil every Tibetan carries with him in his bosom; *śél-kor* (European) **tumbler.** (Cf. *pʻór-pa*).

ཀོ་ལོང་ *ko-lóṅ*, a dubious word. *Sch.* has *ko-loṅ-ba* to hate, envy, but in a passage in *Mil.*, where the connection admits of no doubt, *ko-loṅ mdzad-pa* must be taken for: to disdain.

ཀོ་ཤམ་བི་ *ko-śam-bi Dzl., Glr., Ssk.* **कौशाम्बी** n. of an ancient city on the Ganges, in the Doab.

ཀོ་ས་ལ་ *ko-sa-la Sambh., Ssk.*: **कोसला**, = *Ayodhya*, Oude.

ཀོག་པ་ *kóg-pa* I. subst., also *skóg-pa*, *skógs-pa* **shell, peel, rind;** *śún-kog* id.; *pʻyi-kog* exterior shell, **bark;** *kóg-pa śu-ba* **to peel, pare.** — II. vb. n. **to splinter off, to chink;** *kog laṅ-ba* 1. id. 2. **to** rise suddenly and run away.

ཀོང་ *koṅ*, also *koṅ-kóṅ*, 1. **concave, excavated.** — 2. **crooked,** **pí-śi tsʻig-pa koṅ-kóṅ ċo** the cat makes a crooked back *W.* — *kóṅ-po* 1. **cup, bowl.** 2. **crucible.** 3. **breach, gap** *Sch.* 4. n. of a province S. E. of Lhasa. — *kóṅ-bu* small cup, bowl. — *mċʻód-kóṅ* offering-bowl; *snág-koṅ* **inkstand** for black ink, *mtsál-koṅ* for red ink, vermilion; **lúg-koṅ* **casting-mould** (

ཀོད་ *kod* ('a gathering'?) 1. *lag-kód Ld.* an armful of corn, a **sheaf.** 2. affix = *kad, ka, ko:* **nyis-kód, ṅa-kód** all the two, all the five *Ld.* ·

ཀོབ་ *kob* all, *Ld.* col.

ཀོར་ *kor*, root denoting anything round or concave, hence: *kor-kór* 1. adj. **round,** circular *C.* (= **kyir-kyir* W.*); roundish, globular *C.*; concave, deep, as a soup-plate (opp. to flat) *W.* 2. sbst. a thick **loaf** of bread, (opp. to a flat, thin cake) *C.*; **a pan,** saucepan *W.*; a hollow in the ground, a pit not very deep *W.*; *stód-kor* a little circle above a letter, *Ssk.* anuswara; *klád-kor* id., a dot, zero, naught; *gdúb-kor* bracelet *Cs.*; *pád-kor* a certain way of folding the fingers, so as to represent the form of a lotus-flower; *ˌód-kor* a radiant circle *Cs.* Cf. *skór-ba, ˳kór-ba, ko-ré.*

ཀོར་དོ་བ་ *kor-do-ba* **boot** *Ld.?*

ཀོལ་ཏོ་ *kol-to* **dumb, mute** *Sp.?*

ཀོས་ཀོ་ *kós-ko* = *ko-ko; kos-snyúṅ* with a pointed chin *Sch.*

ཀྱ་སིར་རླུང་ *kya-sir-rlúṅ* v. *kyiṅ.*

ཀྱག་ *kyag*, also *kyag-kyág*, **thick,** run into clots *Cs.*

ཀྱག་ཀྱོག་ *kyag-kyóg* **curved, crooked;** **go kyag-kyóg čo-če* W.* to shake one's head, viz. slowly, in meditating; **ri-mo kyag-(ga-) kyog-(gé)** **a flourish** (in writing) *W.* Cf. *kyog-kyóg.*

ཀྱང་ *kyaṅ* I. adj., also *kyaṅ-kyaṅ, kyaṅ-po,* **straight, slender,** as a stick; **kyaṅ-kyaṅ riṅ-mo** **tall, slender,** as a man, a tree etc. *W.* — II. adv. = *yaṅ*, **too, also,** always used enclitically, after the letters g, d, b, s.

ཀྱང་ཀྱོང་ *kyaṅ-kyóṅ*, also **kyaṅ-ṅa-kyoṅ-né*,* **indolent, lazy, idle** *W.*; **kyaṅ-kyoṅ čo-če* to lounge, to be idle *W.*

ཀྱར་ཀྱར་ *kyar-kyár*, also *kyar-po* **flat,** not globular *Cs.*

ཀྱར་ཀྱོར་ *kyar-kyór*, also **kyar-ra-kyor-ré*,* **still feeble,** as convalescents after a disease.

ཀྱལ་ཀ་ *kyal-ka* 1. **joke, jest,** in words *(Lis. ku-rei tsig).* — 2. **jocular trick,** *ku-re daṅ kyál-kai ṗyir* by way of jest, for fun. — 3. any **worthless, foolish, indecent talk** *Stg.*

ཀྱལ་ཀྱལ་ *kyal-kyál Lex.* w. e.; *Sch.*: *kyal-kyal-ba* to go round (?).

ཀྱལ་ཀྱོལ་ *kyal-kyól* = *kyar-kyór, ˌdúd-ˌgro kyal-kyól ˌga* some poor ill-conditioned **beast,** speaking of cattle, *Mil. nt.*

ཀྱི་ *kyi*, **affix** I. to sbst.-roots, ending in d, b, s: sign of the genitive case. — II. to verbal roots, after the same final letters, and then without an essential difference from *kyis*, to which we add in this place also examples of the other terminations *gi(s), gyi(s), yi(s), i* (the *s* by itself is not used after verbal roots): **a.** in the sense of a gerund, meaning **by** (doing something), **because,** *dgós-kyis ˌdóṅ-ṅo* we come because it is necessary . . . , or more freq. **though.** *dgai* though she is glad . . . *Dzl.*, in which case it may often be rendered in English by **but**: she is glad, but . . . ; *zas bzáṅ-po mi ˳dód-kyis ta-mál-pa zos* he did not care for dainties, but ate vulgar food *Dzl.*; or it has to be omitted: *bdén-pa yin-gyis rdzún-pa ma yin* it is true, no fiction *Dzl.* — b. as an adjective, forming, like *kyin* (q. v.), with *ˌdug* or *yod* a periphrastical present tense e. g. *ˌgroi ˳dug* he is walking, *ˌoṅ-gi yod* he is coming. — c. at the end of a sentence in the sense of a finite verb and more particularly in the 1. pers. fut.: *ˌgyod mi rmoi* I shall not make you suffer for it *Dzl.*, *ṅas grogs byá-yis* I shall help *Glr.*, *bžag-gi*, and: *bžág-gis* I shall put *Glr.* This use of *kyi(s)* is said to be quite common at the present time in *C.*, whereas in *W.* not only the whole gerundial use, but even the distinction of *kyi, gyi, gi* in the genitive case of a sbst. has disappeared from colloquial language, instead of which the last consonant is repeated and the vowel i added: šiṅ-ṅi of the wood, *yid-di* of the mind, *bál-li* of the wool.

Note 1. kyi(s) when combined with adjective roots, includes the verb to be, e. g. máṅ-gi = máṅ-po yin-gyi. — 2. In colloquial language and later literature the genitive of the verbal root often takes the place of the genit. infinitivi, which seldom occurs in the old classical style, e. g. nam °ts̔oi bár-du lifelong. — 3. ǰi nús kyi(s), ǰi t̔úb-kyi(s) or vulg. *t̔úb-bi*, as much as (I, you etc.) can (could etc.) — 4. kyi(s), when denoting an antithesis, is often followed by a pleonastical °ón-kyaṅ.

ཀྱི་ལྕེ་ kyi-lče a medic. plant, Gentiana decumbens L., k. dkár-po a variety of it with white flowers.

ཀྱི་ལྡིར་ kyi-ldir **iron hoop** Ld.?

ཀྱི་བུན་ kyi-bún **a feeling cold, a chill** Sch.

ཀྱི་ཧུད་ kyi-húd the sound of weeping, lamentation.

ཀྱིག་རྩེ་ kyig-rtse **unburnt brick** Sch.

ཀྱིང་སིར་རླུང་ kyiṅ-sir-rlúṅ Mil. also kya-s. l., C., an onomatopoetic word: a **blowing wind.**

ཀྱིན་ kyin, used alternatively with gyin and gin, after a vowel: yin, denotes a partic. present, e. g. smón-lam °débs-kyin soṅ proceed on your way praying! With yod or °dug it forms a periphrastical present tense: smón-lam °débs-kyin yod he is praying (just now); in Ld. even as a real subst.: *šúg-ra °t̔ón-gyin (žig) daṅ* 'with a whistling sound proceeding from it', *dó-yin-daṅ* 'together with walking' = in walking.

ཀྱིར་ཀྱིར་ kyir-kyir W. (= kor-kór C.) **round, circular**; a round thing, **disk**, e. g. the little silver saucer which the women of Lh. wear as an ornament on the crown of their head; kyir-mo id., esp. **a rupee** Ld.; *da kyir-kyir* the disk of the moon.

ཀྱིས་ kyis, after d, b, s. 1. sign of the instrumentative case, and therefore generally indicating the personal subject of the action. — 2. combined with verbal roots = kyi.

ཀྱེ་ kye **oh! holla!** in calling to somebody; in solemnly addressing a person or an auditory; also merely the sign of the vocative case B. (in W. *wa!*) kye-kyé id. emphatically.

ཀྱཻ་ abbrev. for kye-kyé v. kye.

ཀྱེ་ག kyé-ga n. of a bird. Med.

ཀྱེ་ཕང་(པ་) kye-p̔áṅ-(pa) n. of an idol in Lh., consisting like most of the popular idols in those countries of a wooden stick or log decked with rags, but much dreaded and revered; said to be identical with Pe-dkar in C. Its worship probably dates from a time before Buddhism was introduced.

ཀྱེ་མ་ kyé-ma **oh! alas!** mostly expressive of sorrow, often combined with kyi-hud; also sign of the vocative case. Seldom it expresses joy. — kye-mao id.

ཀྱེ་རེ་ kye-ré **upright, erect**; *kye-re laṅ-wa*, resp. *žeṅ-wa C., kyer-kyér-la dad-če, resp. žaṅ-če* W. to stand; *°go kyer ǰhe'-pa* to raise one's head, to look up C. Cf. kyer-ba.

ཀྱེ་ཧུད་ kye-húd, = kyi-hud.

ཀྱེ་ཧོ་ kye-hó **hollo! heigh! well!** also like the **behold** of the Holy Scriptures.

ཀྱེད་ཀྱེད་ kyed-kyéd, also braṅ-kyéd, with the upper part of the body stretched forward Ld.

ཀྱེར་ kyer, v. kye-re.

ཀྱོ་བ་ kyó-ba, **hook** Sch.

ཀྱོག་ kyog, also kyog-kyóg, kyóg-po, **crooked, bent, winding,** rtse kyog with its point bent, crooked at the top. Med.

ཀྱོང་ kyoṅ, also kyoṅ-kyóṅ, kyoṅ-po 1. **hard,** as e. g. stale bread, ču kyóṅ-po hard water; **obstinate, unmanageable**; kyoṅ-°búr a sort of relievo-work in metal. — 2. **oblong** Cs. — Sch.: kyóṅ-k̔a **quarrel,** kyoṅ-mgó cause of a quarrel (?). Cf. gyoṅ, k̔a-gyoṅ.

ཀྱོང་ *kyoṅ*, also *kyóṅ-bu*, **small shovel, scraper** *Sch.*

ཀྱོམ་ *kyom*, also *kyóm-kyom*, 1. **flexible,** but without elasticity, **flabby, loose, lax.** — 2. also *k'yom-k'yóm*, **of irregular shape,** not rectilinear.

ཀྱོར་ *kyor*, also *kyor-kyór* **weak, feeble, unfortified** *Cs.*

ཀྱོལ་ *kyol*, also *kyol-kyól* = *kyor Cs.*

ཀྲག *krag* v. *bkrag.*

ཀྲང་ངེ་ *kraṅ-ṅé* **standing,** *kraṅ sdod-pa* to **stand** *Zam.* *cf. kroṅ.*

ཀྲད་པ་ *krád-pa* **leather half-boot** or **shoe,** as it is worn by the lower class of people, often with a woolen leg; *krad-rgyún Cs.* a long narrow piece of leather to fasten the sole to the upper-leather; **tad-kyi* W.* **ṭa'-kyi* C.* (or *gyi*, from *gyi-na?*) a worn-out leather sole.

ཀྲབ་ཀྲབ་ *krab-kráb* v. *ₒk'rab-pa.*

ཀྲམ་ *kram W.* **cabbage,** *kram-mṅár* sweet or fresh cabbage; *kram-skyúr* sour or macerated cabbage *Cs.* (?)

ཀྲི་ཀྲི་ *kṛi-kṛí* n. of a fabulous king of India *Glr.*, not mentioned in the Ssk. dictionaries.

ཀྲྀཥྞ་སཱ་ར་ *krišṇa-sā-ra Ssk.* **the spotted antelope** *Pth.*

ཀྲུ་ཀྲུ་ *kru-krú W.* **windpipe.** **ṭu-ṭú dam-te ši-če** to be strangled.

ཀྲེ་ནག་ *kre-nág* **smut** of a kettle *Sch.* (= *sre-nag?*)

ཀྲོང་ཀྲོང་ *kroṅ-króṅ* **standing upright,** e. g. books (opp. to **gyél-k'an** laid down, lying *W.*); when used of persons it means also: standing on one's knees, kneeling in an upright position.

ཀྲོན་ཀྲོན་ *kron-krón* **hanging,** **ton-ton-la dug-če** to hang, to be suspended in the air W.

ཀླ་ཀློ་ *kla-klo* 1. *Ssk.* म्लेच्छ **barbarian.** — 2. in later times: **Moslem, Mahometan; Mahometanism.** *Was.*

ཀླག་ཅོར་ *klag-čor* **clamour, noise** *Cs.*

ཀླད་ *klad*, acc. to *Lis.* = *goṅ* what is above; hence *klád-pa*, also *glad*, 1. **head.** 2. **brain,** and *klad-ma* **beginning, top** *Sch.*; *gur-klád* chimney of a felt-tent. — *klad-kor* v. *kor.* — *klad-rgyá* the skin covering the brain, **pia mater;** *klad-rgyas*, = *lhá-ba*, 'the bloody marrow in the bones' *Sch.*, or simply **'brain'** *Schf.* — *klad-sgo* the **fontanel** in the infant cranium *Sch.* — *klad-čúṅ* the **cerebellum** *Sch.* — *klad-yžúṅ* **spinal marrow.** — *klad-yzér* **headache** *Med.* — *klad-šúbs* = *klad-rgyá Sch.*

ཀླན་ཀ་ *klan-ka* 1. **censure, blame** *Cs.*, *klan byéd-pa*, *ₒdebs-pa* to blame, cf. *skur-klán.* — 2. *klan ₒtsol-ba* to seek **brawls** *Pth.*

ཀླན་པ་ *klán-pa* v. *klon-pa.*

ཀླུ་ *klu*, *Ssk.* नाग, originally: hooded snake, cobra di capello; in this specific sense, however, it is never used in Tibetan, whereas every child knows and believes in the mythological signification: **serpent-demon,** a demigod with a human head and the body of a serpent, living in fountains, rivers etc., commanding over great treasures, causing rain and certain maladies, and becoming dangerous when in anger; *ydúg-pa* is therefore a usual epitheton of such demons. *klui skad* means the Prakrit language, *klui yi-ge* the Nagari character of *Ssk.* letters, viz. that which is called *varttula*, in contrast to the holy *landza*, *lhai yi-ge.* — *klui ynod-pa* or *skyon* diseases of unknown origin. — *klu-mo* a female serpent-demon. —

klu-sgrúb, prop. n., Nagarjuna, a famous Buddhist divine. — *klu-mdúd* Codonopsis ovata. — *klu-nad* = *klui-ynod-pa.* — *klu-p'rúg* a young Lu. — *klu-smán* 'n. of a medicine' *Cs.*, but *sman* and *klu-smán* are also synonyms for *klu*, *Glr.*, *Mil.* etc.

ཀླུང་ *kluṅ* **river,** more com. *ču-klúṅ*, *B.*

ཀླུངས་ *kluṅs* 1. **cultivated land, field,** *klúṅs-su skye* it grows on cultivated ground *Wdṅ.* — 2. **a complex of fields,** *dkar-*

mdaṅs-kyi kluṅ ṫsáṅ-ma all the fields belonging to Kardang (n. of a village).

ཀླུབ་པ *klúb-pa, pf. klubs,* **to cover,** e. g. the body with ornaments *Pth.*

ཀློག *klog* v. *klog-pa.*

ཀློག་པ *klóg-pa* I. *sbst.* **earwax** *Sch.* — II. *vb., pf. (b)klags, ft. (b)klag, imp. klog, lhogs,* **to read,** *B., C., yid-kyis klóg-pa* to read without uttering **a sound**; *klog-pa* or *klog sbst.* **reading,** *klog bzáṅ-po šés-pa Mil.* to be a good reader; *klóg-gi slób-dpon* a reading-teacher. — *klóg-gra* a reading-school. — *klóg-ṫabs, klóg-ṫsul* art, way of reading.

ཀློང *kloṅ* acc. to *Lex.* = *Ssk. urmi,* **wave;** in the living language it is **used for middle;** in ancient literature for **expanse,** esp. *nám-mk̔ai* of the heavens, *rgyá-mṫsoi* of the sea; *raṅ-byúṅ kloṅ yaṅs brjod-méd* the unspeakably vast uncreated **space**; hence: the space of heaven, the heavens, *klóṅ-du ldíṅ-ba* to soar, to hover in the sky. This vagueness of meaning makes the word suited to the idle fancies of mysticism, as in: *klóṅ-du ˛gyúr-ba,* which seems to denote a soaring into mystic perfection. — *dba-klóṅ Sch.:* wave; Tibetans of to-day, and *Schr.:* the midst of the waves. — *klóṅ-brdól Glr.* was explained by Lamas: emerging from amidst the waves. (The significations 'depth, abyss, plenty, body' added by *Sch.* seem to be erroneous). *Cf. dkyel.*

ཀློན་པ *klón-pa,* also *klán-pa,* **to mend, patch** v. also *lhán-pa.*

ཀྵ་ཡ *kša-ya Ssk.* prop. **phthisis pulmonalis;** but acc. to Tib. pathology *kša-ya nág-po* denotes a bilious disease, prob. **icterus niger, black jaundice.**

དཀགས་མོ *dkágs-mo W.* for *dka-bo.*

དཀན *dkan,* also *rkan (Ld. *skan*)* 1. **the palate,** *yá-dkan,* the upper, *má-dkan* the lower part of the palate; **kán-da ˳déb-pa** **to smack** *C.; dkan-ynyér* the wrinkles of the roof of the mouth *Cs.* — 2. *dkan yzár-po Lex.* w. e, *Sch.* steep declivity, precipice.

དཀའ་བ *dka-ba* 1. adj., **also** *-bo,* seld. *-mo,* **difficult,** *slób-pa dká-ba* learning is difficult *Dzl.,* gen. with supine: *slób-tu* or *slób-par dka* it is difficult to learn, or with the root: *go-dká* difficult to understand; *dkár-ba byuṅ* it has become difficult, it is difficult (to me, to him etc.) — 2. sbst. *dká-ba* **pains, exertion, hardship, suffering,** *dká-ba méd-par* without difficulty, easily, *dka-ba spyod-pa* to undergo hardships = to use exercises of penance ([illegible], [illegible]).

dka-˛grél Cs. 'a difficult commentary', acc. to Tib. dictionaries = **पञ्जिका** perpetual commentary, lit.: explanation of difficulties. — *dka-ṫúb, dka-spyód, dka-spyád* 1. **penance.** 2. **penitent;** *dka-ṫúb-pa, dka-spyód-pa, dká-ṫub-čan,* penitent, *˳ṫsó-ba dka-ṫúb-ba rtén-pa* to live as a penitent. — *dka-sdúg* **trouble,** *dka-sdúg máṅ-po byéd-pa* to take great pains *C.* — *dka-ṫségs* = *dká-ba.* — *dka-lás* 1. **a troublesome work.** 2. **trouble, distress.**

དཀར་བ *dkár-ba* I. adj., also *-po,* seld. *-mo* 1. **white, whitish, gray.** — 2. **morally good,** standing on the side of virtue — 3. candid, sincere? *las dkár-po* good action; *k̔a-zàs dkár-po* v. *dkar-zás; dkár-la dmar-mdáṅs-čan* white and red of complexion *Pth.*

II. sbst. **whiteness.** — *dkár-mo* sbst. 1. the goddess Durga. — 2. **white rice** *Cs.*

Comp. *dkar-skya* **light-gray.** — *dkar-k̔úṅ* 1. **window-hole** in a wall *W.* — 2. opening for the smoke in the roof *C.* — *dkar-goṅ C.* a piece of quartz, (acc. to popular belief porcelain is made of quartz,) hence *Cs.:* 'porcelain-clay.' — *dkar-rgyá* **rose-coloured.** — *dkar-čág* **register.** — *dkar-ṫog* = *dkar-zas.* — *dkar-mé* a light (?), *dkar-mé sbor-ba Sch.* 'to light a candle.' — *dkar-dmar* **light-red** *Sch.* — *dkar-rtsi* **white-wash,** consisting of lime or some other earthy colour *C., W.* — *dkar-zás, k̔a-zás dkar-po, dkar-ṫóg* **clean food, lenten**

diet, viz. esp. milk, curd, cheese or butter, as *dkar-γsúm Schf. Tar.* (Germ. translat. p. 335); also honey, fruit. — *dkar-γól,* resp. *C.* **žal-kar, W. sol-kar** **porcelain, china-ware,** cups or plates of porcelain, *dkar-yol sgrig-pa* to place the china-service on the table, for: to lay the cloth. — *dkar-γyá W.* **tin, pewter,** **kar-γá dañ žár-če** **to solder.** — *dkar-sér* **yellowish white.** — *dkar-γsál* 1. **shining white,** *sku-mdog dkar-γsál gáñs-ri ̥dra* of a bright white colour like a glacier *Glr.* 2. **window** *Sch.* (?)

དཀུ་ *dku* 1. the **side** of a person's body *Cs.*, *dkur* or *dkú-la rtén-pa* to carry a thing at one's side *Zam.*; *dku brtólba* to open the side (in child-birth, v. *mñal).* — *2.* v. *dkú-ba. Comp. dku-lči* a heavy feeling in the side, as a symptom of pregnancy. — *dku-mda* (**kúm-da**) *W.* (= *mčan-mda?)* **pocket** in the clothes. — *dku-nád* apparently a disease of the kidneys. — *dku-zlúm, Lex.* कक्षि cavity of the abdomen, womb.

དཀུ་ལྟོ་ *dkú-lto* **craft, cunning, trick, stratagem,** esp. if under specious pretence one person induces another to do a thing that proves hurtful to him.

དཀུ་བ་ *dkú-ba* **'sweet scent'** *Cs.; Zam.:* = पूति **stench.**

དཀོན་མཆོག་ *dkon-mčog (W.: *kon-čóg, kon-čóg, C.: kon-čó')* 1. **the most precious thing.** Buddhism has always sought the highest good not in anything material, but in the moral sphere, looking with indifference, and indeed with contempt, on everything merely relating to matter. It is not, however, moral perfection or the happiness attained thereby, which is understood by the 'most precious thing', but the mediator or mediators who procure that happiness for mankind, viz. Buddha, (the originator of the doctrine), the doctrinal scriptures and the corporate body of priests, त्रिरत्न, *dkon-mčóg γsum.* Now, although this triad cannot by any means be placed on a level with the Christian doctrine of a triune God, yet it will be easily understood, how the innate desire of man to adore and worship something supernatural, together with the hierarchical tendency of the teaching class, have afterwards contributed to convert the acknowledgment of human activity for the benefit of others (for such it was undoubtedly on the part of the founder himself and his earlier followers) into a devout, and by degrees idolatrous adoration of these three agents, especially as Buddha's religious doctrine did not at all satisfy the deeper wants of the human mind, and as its author himself did not know anything of a God standing apart and above this world. For whatever in Buddhism is found of beings to whom divine attributes are assigned, has either been transferred from the Indian and other mythologies, and had accordingly been current among the people before the introduction of Buddhism, or is a product of philosophical speculation, that has remained more or less foreign to the people at large. — 2. As then the original and etymological signification of the word is no longer current, and as to every Tibetan '*dkon-mčog*' suggests the idea of some supernatural power, the existence of which he feels in his heart, and the nature and properties of which he attributes more or less to the three agents mentioned above, we are fully entitled to assign to the word *dkon-mčog* also the signification of **God,** though the sublime conception which the Bible connects with this word, viz. that of a personal, absolute, omnipotent being, will only with the spread of the Christian religion be gradually introduced and established.

Note 1. *rañ-grub-dkon-mčog* with *Schr.* is evidently the appellation of the Christian God adopted by the Rom. Cath. missionaries of those times. — 2. In the older writings *dkon-mčog* occurs (as far as I know) never without *γsum,* and combinations such as *dkon-mčog-la mčod-pa byed-pa* or *ɣsol-ba ˏdebs-pa,* as well as *bla-ma dkon-mčog,* are to be found only in writings of a comparatively recent date. — 3. Instead of the phrase of asseveration: *dkon-mčog šes,* God knows! the mere words *dkon-mčog ɣsum* are frequently used in the same sense.

དཀོན་པ་ *dkón-pa C., B., -mo W.* **rare, scarce,** and therefore **dear, precious, valuable** (in an objective sense, cf. *ɣčes-pa) ˏǰig-rtén-na dkón-no* is exceedingly rare in the world *Dzl., ˏǰig-rtén-na dkón-par bzáṅ-ṅo* it is of a beauty rarely to be met with in the world *Dzl.; ḱyod ˏdra mtóṅ-na dkón-rgyu med* to see a person like you, is nothing particular *Mil.; ǩe bdé-mo-la lhá čos dkon* with a prattler religion is scarce, there is generally not much religion about him *Mil.* — *dkon-nór* riches, valuables *Mil.*

དཀོར་ *dkór* 1. **wealth, riches.** — 2. *mtíl-dkor, yaṅ-dkor, sa-dkor* are expressions current in *C.* which I could not get sufficiently explained. — *dkor-nór* = *nor.* — *dkor-pa Cs., dkor-mi Sch.* **treasurer.** — *dkor-mdzód* frq., **treasury.** — *dkor-rdzogs* (pronounce **kor-zog(s)**) n. of a monastery in southern Ladak, situated 16 000 feet high.

དཀྱར་ *dkyar Z., Ld.,* a sort of **snow-shoes.** (*Sch.:* 'stocking-boots'?)

དཀྱིལ་ *dkyil* **the middle,** *dkyil-du, -na* in the middle, c. genit. in the midst of, amidst; *dkyil nas* from the middle, from amidst; relative to time: **yar-ri kyil-la** *W.,* in the middle of summer *dkyil-ma* the middle one, e. g. room, = dwelling-room *Ld.*

Comp. *dkyil-dkrúṅ* v *skyil-dkrúṅ.* — *dkyil-ˏḱor* 1. **circle, circumference,** frq 2. **figure,** e. g. *dkyil-ˏḱor gru-bži-pa* **quadrangle, square;** a certain mystical figure; **diagram, model.** 3. **a circle of objects,** *ˏḱor-gyi dkyil-ˏḱor* the circle of the attendants. 4. **the area of a circle, disk,** e. g. of the sun; *žál-gyi dkyil-ḱor bstan* = he showed his full countenance *Pth.* 5. **sphere,** *rlúṅ-gi dkyil-ˏḱor* the atmosphere, *meï-dkyil-ˏḱor* the sphere of fire, and similarly of the other elements, *lhai dkyil-ˏḱor* may perh. likewise be translated by: the sphere of the power of a certain god. In mysticism and magic, however, several other more or less arbitrary significations are assigned to the word, e. g. it is said to be used for *lús-kyi dkyil-ˏḱor* the whole extent or bulk of the body, = the body, *dkyil-ˏḱor-gyi ɣnás-su ˏčáṅ-ba* to wear on one's body (e. g. an amulet); or instead of *čós-kyi dky.: dkyil ḱor mtóṅ-ba* to behold the whole extent of religious doctrine (?).

Note. In Lex. *dkyil* is said to be = मण्ड; perh. merely because *dkyil-ˏḱor* is used for मण्डल? But *mán-dal-gyi dkyil-ḱor* is the Buddhistic map of the world, representing mount Sumeru with the surrounding continents etc.

དཀྱུ་བ་ *dkyú-ba* 1 **to run a race** *Cs.* — 2. **to wring out, to filter** *Sch.* — 3. **to caper about** *Ld.* *dkyú-byai rta* race-horse *Cs., dkyu-sa* race-course *Cs.*

དཀྱུག་པ་ *dkyúg-pa* **to lose colour** by washing *Ld.,* perh. more correctly *skyúg-pa.*

དཀྱུས་ *dkyus* 1. **length,** *dkyús-su* in length, *dkyus-riṅ* **long** *C., spyan-dkyús* length from one corner of the eye to the other (e. g. in an image) *C.* (*Sch.:* bold, insolent?) — 2. **untruth, falsehood, lie.** Tar. 108. 7. *dkyus-nyid* seems to be used so, whilst 188, 5 is totally obscure.

དཀྱུས་མ་ *dkyús-ma* **common, every-day,** e. g. *na-bza* every-day clothes, *dbu-ža* work-day hat; hence *mi dkyús-ma* common people (without office or authority) *C.*

དཀྱེལ་ *dkyel* seems to be acc. to *Cs.* a synonym of *kloṅ.* I only met with the word *dkyél-po če* in a medical work; *Sch.* explains it by **universe,** and a native Lex. by *ḱaṅ yáṅs-pa* the wide house, which possibly may signify the same.

དཀྲི་བ་ *dkri-ba pf. dkris, vb. a.* (cf. *ˏḱri-ba)* **to wind, to wind up,** *grú-gu* a clew or ball of thread, *lús-la gos* (or *gós-*

kyis) dkr., **to wrap a** garment round the body; *rtsá-bar ₒKór-lo dkris-pai yčeu Med.* was explained to me: a magic spell in circular writing, wrapped round the lower end of a clyster-pipe, *fig.: sér-snas kún-nas dkris* quite **ensnared** in avarice; *kun-dkris* **'all-ensnaring'** = sin. — *dkri-ma (Glr.* 47. where the text has *drima)* means very likely **necker-chief,** which col. is called **kog-ṭi* or *Ka-ṭi C. 'og-śri, Ka-śri, kya-śri' W.* — In the sense of *ₑkrid-pa* to conduct *(Sch.)* it never came to my notice.

དཀྲིགས་པ་ *dkrigs-pa* 1. **darkened, obscured, dim,** = *krigs-pa.* — also *dkrigs-ṗrág,* term for a very large number, *Cs.:* a 100 000 billion, acc to *Zam.* = *ytúms-pa,* which *Cs.* renders, a 1000 billion. The one may be, after all, as correct as the other, for all these large numbers are, of course, not meant to be used in serious calculations, but are mere imitations of fantastic Indian extravagancies.

དཀྲུག་པ་ *dkrúg-pa pf. dkrugs (W. *śrug-če*)* **to stir, stir up, agitate** (as the storm does the sea); **to trouble, disturb, confound** (as enemies of religion confound the doctrine, or as passions disturb the mind); *dkrugs-śiṅ* 1. **stirring-stick, twirling-stick.** 2. **disturber, enemy** e. g. of the doctrine *Glr.* — *dkrugs Schr.:* turning-lathe (?) — *dkrugs-maSchr.:*quarrel.—*Dzl.* ༢༥༡7. *dkrugs byéd - pa* dubious; a safer reading is *dkú-lto byéd-pa.*

དཀྲུང་ *dkruṅ* v. *skyil.*

དཀྲུམ་པ་ *dkrúm-pa Cs. & Sch.:* **broken.**

དཀྲོག་པ་ *dkróg-pa* (= *skróg-pa)* 1. **to stir, churn** frq. 2. **to rouse, scare up,** *Glr.* — 3. **to wag** e. g. the tail *W.*

དཀྲོལ་བ་ *dkról-ba* v. *ₑkról-ba.*

བཀག་པ་ *bkag-pa* v. *ₑgégs-pa; bkág-ča byéd-pa* **to forbid** *Sch.*

བཀང་བ་ *bkáṅ-ba* v. *géṅs-pa* to fill.

བཀད་ *bkad? Lex.* quote *tágs-kyi bkad,* which was explained to me by: the crossing of threads in weaving; similar: *mgó-spui bkad, mgo-bkád* the crossing or entangling of the hair on the head. — *bkád-pa* seems = *ₒKad-pa.*

བཀད་ས་ *bkád-sa* 1. **a bake-house, kitchen, cook's shop** *Lex.* — 2. **open hall** or **shed,** erected on festive occasions *Tib.-Ssk. Glossary; Tar.* 18, 12.

བཀན་པ་ *bkán-pa* **to put, to press,** *rkáṅ-pa rtsig-pa-la* one's foot against a wall; **to apply,** *yšó-mo* the plane, *lág-pa* the hand *Zam.,* to put the hand on or to something (or: stretch it out? *Sch.)*

བཀབ་པ་ *bkáb-pa* v. *ₑgébs-pa.*

བཀའ་ *bka (resp.* for *ytam, tsig, skad)* **word, speech** of a respected person (wherefore **order, commandment** may often be substituted for it), *rgyál-poi bka* the word of the king, *bká-la ytsógs-pa* to belong to the word, i. e. to be under the commandment or dominion (of somebody) *Glr.; rgyál-bai bka* the word of Buddha (this is named as one of the five 'means of grace', so to speak, Glr. fol. 70; the four others are: *mdo-rgyúd* the sacred writings *(sutra* and *tantra), bstan-bčós* doctrinal and scientific writings *(śāstra), luṅ* oral benedictions and instructions of Lamas, *man-ṅág* admonitions given by them). After quotations *bka* or *bkao* (= *skad & skad-do)* means: thus says (the holy book or teacher). *bka* as first part of a compound is frequently used to give the word adjoined the character of respectfulness, and is therefore not to be translated separately.

Phrases and compounds: *bka bkód-pa* **to publish, proclaim; publication, proclamation** *C.* — *bka-bkyón* (col. **kab-kyon*)* 'verbal blows' **reprimand, rebuke** (given by a superior), *bka-bkyón byéd-pa, mdzád-pa B. C., *tón-če, ṗiṅ-če* W., bka bkyón-pa,* all of them construed with dat., **to rebuke** somebody. — *bka-bKríms* **law, commandment,** *rgyál-pói bka-Kríms ynyán-pas* by the cruel order of the king *Dzl.* — *bka bgró-ba* **to consult, to deliberate,** *naṅ-blón bču* *dan bka-žib-tu bgrós-pa-la* deliberating carefully with the ten ministers of the interior *Pth.* (*Schr.* gives also. *bka-grós ₒdri-ba* to ask, — *byéd-pa* to give advice), — *bka-ₒgyur* (**ká-gyur,** com. **kan-gyur, kan-dyúr,** in Mongolia **kan-jur**) the word of Buddha, as translated from the original Sanskrit, the holy scriptures of the Buddhists (100 volumes). — *bka ₒgrol-ba* **to dismiss** *Pth.*, *bka-bkrol* **leave of absence,** *gsol-ba* to ask for, *gnaṅ-ba* to grant leave *Schr.* — *bka-rgya, bka-šog,* resp. for *rgya-ma* and *šog-bu*, letter or paper from a superior etc., **diploma, missive, communication** etc. *bka-rgyúd* 1. = *bkai rgyud* 'thread of the word', the oral tradition of the word of Buddha, which is supposed to have been delivered through a continual series of teachers and disciples besides the written scriptures; *bka-rgyud bla-ma* a Lama deriving his religious knowledge in this manner from Buddha himself *Mil.* 2. perh. also = *bka dan rgyud* 'word and tantra', oral and written instruction; *bka-rgyúd-pa* n. of a Lama-sect *Schl.* 73.; *bka-bsgos* **commandment, precept.** — *bka-sgyúr* order, *bka-sgyúr gnaṅ-ba* to issue an order *C.* — *bka sgyúr-ba* 1. to translate the words (of Buddha etc.) 2. to issue an order (viz. in the name of a superior). — *bka sgrog-pa* 1. to publish an order. 2. to proclaim, read, preach the word. — *bka gčog-pa* to act against an order, *yab-kyi bka bčag-tu med* the order of the father must be obeyed *Glr.* — *bka-čéms* resp. for *ka-čéms* **testament.** — *bka-mčid* resp. for *mčid*, words or speech of a superior or any person to be honoured. — *bka nyan-pa ccyp.* 1. *vb.* **to obey.** 2. *adj.* **obedient,** *bka mi nyan-pa* 1. to disobey. 2. disobedient. *bka gnyan* 'the cruel commander', acc. to a Lex. = *btsan-pai sa-bdag* 'the mighty lord of the ground', is said to be the first of gods, either Siva or a pre-buddhistic deity. — **ka tan-ce** *W.* **to permit.** — *bka btags-pa* (*Lex.*: = *krims bsgrags-pa*) **a proclaimed order,** cf. *bkar.* — *bka-rtags Cs.*: **mark, seal, precept, maxim** (?) — *bka-stod Sch.*: **'a subaltern, agent'** (?) — *bka-tan* **order, edict.** — *bka-drin* resp. for *drin*, **favour, grace, kindness, benefit,** *bka-drin mdzád-pa* to bestow a favour, *mi-la* upon somebody; *blá-mai bka-drin-gyis* through the kindness of his (your) reverence *Mil.*; *bka-drin-čé* the usual phrase of acknowledgment, as our: you are very kind! many thanks! *B.* and *col.* — *bka-druṅ* **secretary** (of a high person) *C.* — *bka-gdáms,* = *žal-gdáms* **advice, counsel, instruction;** *bka-gdáms-pa* 1. **adviser** *Sch.* 2. n. of a sect of red Lamas, founded by Brom-ston *Schl.* 73. — *bka-ₒdógs-pa* **to proclaim; proclamation.** — *bka-bsdú-ba* collection of the doctrine *Tar.* — **ka-nán** **instruction** *C.* — *bka gnáṅ-ba* 1. *vb.* **to order, command; grant, permit;** 2. *sbst.* **order; permission;** *ṅed bód-kyi rgyál-poi btsún-mo-la bka gnáṅ-bar žu* I beg you will give her as a consort to my (the Tibetan) king *Glr.* — *bka-pébs Sch.* **a supreme order.** — *bka-priṅ* **message.** — *bka ₒbáb-pa* the going forth of an order, *bka-ₒbáb* order, edict *Schr.* — *bka-ₒbúm*, vulg. **kam-búm**, the hundred thousand precepts (title of a book). — *bka stsol-ba, pf. stsal* (*stsál-to, stsál-pa*), resp. for *smrá-ba* **to speak, to say** (acc. to circumstances: to command, ask, beg, relate, answer etc.), esp. in ancient literature, in which it is almost invariably used of Buddha and of kings. — *bka-blo-bdé Lex.*: = सुवचस् speaking well, eloquently; *Sch.*: *bka-blo-bdé-ba* to acknowledge to be wrong (?); *bka-blón,* (*bkai blón-po Glr.* f. 94) **prime minister; any high official.** — *bka-šóg* any writing of a superior, **decree, diploma, passport, official paper, letter.** — *bka gságs* 1. **a high official, counsellor.** *C.* 2. **court of justice, judgment-hall.**

བཀར་ *bkar term.* of *bka* in or to the word etc; *bkar ₒdógs-pa Cs.* **to legalize,** *Dzl.* cap. 4: **to proclaim, publish.** *bkár-btags-pa* **published; publication.**

བཀར་བ་ *bkár-ba* v. *dgár-ba.*

བཀལ་བ་ *bkál-ba* v. *ₒkál-ba* and *ₑgél-ba.*

བཀས་ *bkas* instr. of *bka; bkás-pa* v. *ₑgés-pa.*

བཀུ་བ་ *bkú-ba Lex.:* **to extract,** to make an extract of a drug by drawing out the juice *(kú-ba ₑbyin-pa); bkús-te ₑbór-ba id.; smán-bku* medicinal extract.

བཀུག་ *bkug* v. *kug; bkúg-pa* v. *ₑgúgs-pa.*

བཀུམ་ *bkum* v *kum; bkúm-pa* v. *ₑgúms-pa.*

བཀུར་བ་ *bkúr-ba* I. 1. *vb.* **to honour, esteem** (synon. *mčód-pa), máṅ-pos bkúr-bai rgyál-po,* महासम्मत, the king honoured by many, frq.; *kún-g is bkúr-žiṅ mčód-pai ₑos* worthy of general honour and respect *Mil.; mis bkúr-bar mi ₑgyur* is not esteemed by men *Dzl.* — 2. *sbst.* **honour;** more frq., *bkúr sti,* **honour, respect, homage, mark of honour,** *bkúr-stis mčód-pa* to distinguish (a person) by marks of respect *Zam.; ráṅ-la bkúr-stí ₒbyuṅ dus* when honour is shown to yourself *Mil.; bkúr-sti byéd pa* to do honour frq.; to make a reverence, to salute. — II. *pf.* of *ₒkúr-ba* **to carry;** in the term *máṅ-pos bkúr-bai rgyál-po* the legend combines this signification with the preceding one *Glr.*

བཀོག་པ་ *bkóg-pa* v. *ₑgóg-pa.*

བཀོང་བ་ *bkóṅ-ba* v. *ₑgóṅ-ba.*

བཀོད་པ་ *bkód-pa* v. *ₑgód-pa.*

བཀོན་པ་ *bkón-pa* v *ₒkón-pa.*

བཀོབ་ལྟ་ *bkób-lta* (**kób-ta**) **the plan** of an undertaking *W.* (vulg. pronunciation for *bkod-blta?*)

བཀོར་འདྲེ་ *bkór-ₒdré Mil.* seems to be a kind of goblins.

བཀོལ་བ་ *bkól-ba* v. *kól-ba.*

བཀྱལ་བ་ *bkyál-ba Cs.:* **to talk nonsense,** v. *kyál-ka; bkyál-pai ṅag = kyál-ka Lex.*

བཀྱིག་པ་ *bkyig-pa* v. *ₒkyig-pa.*

བཀྱེ་བ་ *bkyé-ba* v. *ₑgyéd-pa.*

བཀྱེད་པ་ *bkyéd-pa* **to bend back, recline** (vb. nt.), *rgyaṅs byéd-de* bending or turning far aside.

བཀྱོན་པ་ *bkyón-pa* **to beat** (= *rdúṅ-ba) Mil. nt.; bka bkyon-pa resp.* to chastise with words, **to scold,** frq. (v. *bka,* phrases); *Schr.* mentions also *bkyon-bkyál* chiding.

བཀྲ་བ་ *bkra-ba (Lex.:* = चित्र, *cf.* also *krá-bo)* 1. **variegated.** — 2. **beautiful, blooming** (of complexion); **glossy, well-fed** (of animals); *ša-bkrá* n. of a cutaneous disease.

Comp. *bkra-bzáṅ* n. of a mountain in Tibet. — *bkra-lam-mé* v. *kra-lam-mé.* — *bkra-šis Ssk.* मङ्गल 1. **happiness, prosperity, blessing,** *ₒbáṅs-rnams-la bkra-šís šog* happiness to my people! may they prosper! *Glr.; *nád-med tsád-med ṭa-ši p̔un-sum-tsóg žu** I wish you good health and immeasurable and perfect happiness! (new year's wish in *W.); bkra-šís-kyi ču* holy water *Glr.; bkra-šis-kyi mál-kri* nuptial bed *Cs.; bkra šís-kyi tsig* or *smon-lam* blessing, benediction; **ṭa-ši šig!** Good bye! May you be happy! **kyód-la ṭa-ši čo!** I wish you joy! (also ironically) *W.; bkra-šis-šiṅ* being happy, enjoying prosperity *Glr.; bkra-šís srúṅ-bai gó-ča* instruments used for insuring happiness (to a new-born infant) *Lt.* — 2. sacrificial ceremony by which blessings are to be drawn down, *bkra-šis byéd-pa* or *mčód-pa* or **yóg-če** *(W.,* barley being scattered — *γyog-pa* — on that occasion), to perform this ceremony, - *bkra-šis-pa* **propitious, lucky,** perh. also: **happy;** *bkra-šis-pai ltas* lucky signs; *bkra-šis-pai rtags* lucky configurations or semblances (such as e. g. devout imagination seeks to discover in the outlines of mountains etc. *Glr.* fol. 58.) *bkra-šis-ma* n. of a goddess, *Sch.:* goddess of glory *Dzl.* — *bkra-mi-šis* **misfortune, calamity,** *bkra-mi-šis-pa* **un-**

happy; calamity, *bkra-mi-šis-pa ťams-čád* all manner of calamities. (The expression *bkra-mi-šis* c dat. for: 'Woe to . . . ' in our translation of the New Test. does not rest upon classic authority, but has been adopted as analogous to the above mentioned *bkra-šis šog.*) *bkra-šis-čos-rdzoṅ* (**ta-ši-čo-dzóṅ**) 'Tassisudon' in Bhot., *bkra-šis-lhun-po* (**ta-ši-hlum-po**) 'Tashilunpo' in Tsaṅ.

བཀྲག་ *bkrag* 1. **brightness, lustre** = *mdaṅs*, also *bkrag-mdáṅs*, e. g. of jewels. 2. **beautiful appearance, colour**, of the face or skin, also *ša-bkrág; ša bkrag-mdaṅs* pure **gloss** of the skin *Mil.; bkrág-čan* **bright**. *bkrag-čór* without gloss, **dim**.

བཀྲབ་པ་ *bkráb-pa* 1. **to select, choose**; *mčóg-tu bkrab* **exquisite, choice** *Lex.* — 2 = *ₒkráb-pa, skráb-pa W.*

བཀྲམ་པ་ *bkrám-pa* v. *ₒgrém-pa*.

བཀྲལ་བ་ *bkrál-ba* 1. *pf.* of *ₒgrél-ba Cs., Tar.* 124, 14. — 2. **to appoint**, *lás-la* to a business.

བཀྲས་པ་ *bkrás-pá* 1. *Sch.: pf.* of a verb *bkrá-ba*, adorned, decorated (?) 2. *Cs.: bkras* abbreviation for *bkra-šis, bkras-btags* for *bkra-šis ka-btags = ka-btags*.

བཀྲི་བ་ *bkri-ba* 1. for *dkri-ba* to wrap. — 2. for *ₒkrid-pa* to conduct. — 3. to try to acquire, **to search for** *Dzl.* ༢༩ **to lay up**, = **šri-če* W.*

བཀྲིས་ *bkris* abbrev. for *bkra-šis*.

བཀྲིས་པ་ *bkris-pa* for *dkris-pa* v. *dkri-ba*.

བཀྲུ་, བཀྲུས་ *bkru, bkrus*, v. *ₒkrúd-pa*.

བཀྲུག་པ་ 1. *Dzl.* ༧༤༥ 1. prob. an incorrect reading. 2. prov. instead of *dkrúg-pa*, v. *ja bkrúg*.

བཀྲེན་པ་ *bkrén-pa* 1. *Cs.* **poor, indigent, hungry**, *sai p̓yogs bkr.* a poor, barren country *Stg.* — 2. **miserly, stingy** *C.*

བཀྲེས་པ་ *bkrés-pa vb.* **to be hungry**; *adj.* **hungry**; *sbst.* **hunger** *B., C.* where it is now used as the respectful term; *bkres-skóm* hunger and thirst; *bkres-skóm-pa-las čóg-par ₒbyín-te* leading after hunger and thirst to satiety; *bkrés-ṅnab-pa Sch.:* to have a ravenous appetite.

བཀྲོངས་ *bkroṅs* v. *ₒgróṅs-pa*.

བཀྲོལ་བ་ *bkrol-ba* v. *ₒgról-ba*.

བཀླག་པ་ *bklag-pa* v. *klóg-pa*.

རྐ་ *rka* 1. **a small furrow** conveying water from a conduit (*yúr-ba*) to trees or plants; **furrow** between the beds of a garden; hence: 2. **flower-bed.**

རྐང་ *rkaṅ* (*Ld. *skaṅ, γaṅ**) 1. **marrow**, *rkaṅ-már* id.; *rkáṅ-bro-ma* tasting of marrow *Sch.; rkáṅ-gi kóṅ-nas byáms-pa* love from the innermost heart *Thgy.* — 2. the upper part of the arm or thigh, or the large **marrow-bones** of them, *dpúṅ-rkaṅ, rlá-rkaṅ Med.* — 3. **kernel** of a nut etc. *W.* — 4. = *rkaṅ-pa* no. 5, **stalk**; also **quill** of a feather. — 5. in compounds for *rkáṅ-pa*.

རྐང་པ་ *rkaṅ-pa* (resp. *žabs*) 1. **foot**. — 2. **leg**. — 3 (cf. *lag-pa*) **hind-foot**. — 4. **lower part, lower end**, e. g. of a letter, *rkaṅ-pa-čan* 'having a foot', so the nine letters are called that extend below the line (ཀ, ཁ etc.) *Glr.* — 5. **stem, stalk**, esp. leaf-stalk, *lo-rkáṅ*. — 6 **verse**, metrical line; *ťsig-rkáṅ*, prop.: *ťsigs-su-bčad-pai rkáṅ-pa, id., ťsig-rkáṅ mťar nyis-šád ťob* at the close of a verse a double *shad* is placed; hence: **verse** of the Bible *Chr. Prot.* — 7. **base, foundation**, *rdzu-p̓rúl-gyi rkáṅ-pa bži Dzl.* the four 'pillars' of performing miracles (**ऋद्धिपाद**) *Trigl. fol.* 17.

Comp. **kaṅ-kyóg** **bandy-legged** *C.* — *rkaṅ-kri* a piece of cloth to wrap round the legs (*Lat.: tibiale*) *Sch.* — *rkaṅ-ₒkúm Lex.* w. e., prob. having a foot contracted by disease — *rkaṅ-ₒkór* **bandy-legged** *Sch. rkaṅ-mgyógs-pa* **nimble-footed**, *rkaṅ-mgyógs-kyi rdzas lham-la byúgs-te* oiling his boots with swiftfootedness, a miraculous ointment imparting this gift *Glr., Tar.* 67. — *rkaṅ-ₒgró* a vassal or subject paying his duty by serving as a messenger or porter *Cs.* — *rkan-₍gros* or *-brós* 1. **walking on foot.** 2. **domestic cattle; breeding-cattle.** — *rkan-rgyu Cs.*: 'the hollow of the sole'. — *rkan-γčig-pa* **one-footed.** — *rkan-rjén* **bare-footed.** — *rkan-rjés* **footstep, trace.** — *rkan-γnyis-pa* **two-footed, a biped,** po. for **man, mankind.** — *rkan-stégs* **footstool; trestle.** — *rkan-tán* **on foot,** *rkan-tán-pa* **pedestrian. foot-soldier,** *rkan-tán-du grul-ba (Sch.* also: *rkan-tán-ba)* to walk, to go on foot. — *rkan-mtil* **sole** of the foot. — *rkan-₍tún* (erron. also *-tun) Ssk.* पादप 'drinking with the foot' po. for: **tree** *Mil.* — *rkan-dún* trumpet made of a human thigh-bone (*Hook.* I 173). — *rkan-drúg-pa, rkan-drúg-ldan-pa* **six-footed; insect,** *po.* — *rkan-γdúb* **foot-ring** (ornament). — *rkan-ₒdrén* (v. also *žabs-₍drén)* **disgrace,** *rkan ₍drén-pa* c. genit. to get a person into disgrace, to deprive him of his honour and good name, to be a disgrace to another, e. g. a son to his father by criminal actions etc. *rkan-rdúm* **a maimed foot; lame** *Cs.* — *rkán-snam* **trowsers,** *snám-bui rkán-snam γčig* one pair of cloth-trowsers. *rkan pags lhun S. g.* fol. 9? — *rkan-pyin* felt for covering the legs, v. *rkan-dkri.* — *rkan-ból* upper part of the foot. — *rkan bám* a disease in the foot, *Sch.*: gout. *rkan-ₒbrós* or *bros* v. *rkan-₍grós.* — *rkan-tségs* v. *tségs.* — *rkan-mdzub-₍dzér-pa Sch.*: **corn** (on the toe). — *rkan-mdzér* **iron pricks** fastened to the feet for climbing mountains. — *rkan-bži-pa* **four-footed; quadruped.** — *rkan-lág* hands and feet, *rkan-lag bšál-ba Lt., Schr.*: 'numbness or rheumatic pain in hands and feet'; *rkan-lág sér-kar ₍on* hands and feet chap *Sch.* — *rkan-lám* **foot-path.** *rkan-šin* **treadle,** of a loom. — *rkan-šúbs* **stocking, sock.** — *rkan sór* **toe.**

རྐན་ *rkan* v. *dkan.*

རྐམ་པ་ *rkám-pa* I. *vb.* **to desire, to long,** *nór-la* for money. II. *sbst.* 1. **longing** (*cf. kam* extr.) — 2. v. *skam-pa.*

རྐུ་བ་ *rkú-ba, pf. (b)rkus, ft. brku, imp. rkus,* **to steal, to rob,** *brkú-bya* to be stolen, *brkú-byai rdzas* things that may be stolen.

རྐུན་མ་ *rkún-ma* 1. **thief** frq. 2. **theft.** *rk. byéd pa (W.: *čo-če*)* to steal; **kún-ma zos son* W.* it has been carried away by a thief; **ka-kún gyáb-če* W.* 'to steal with the mouth', to promise to pay without ever doing so, or: to deny having known a thing missing, until all inquiry has ceased and it may be safely appropriated (a common practice of servants in India); *dur-rkún* robber of graves. — *rkún-tabs-su blan-ba* to take away thievishly *Stg.* — *rkun-nor* stolen goods. — *rkún-po, fem. -mo* **thief.** — *rkún-dpon* the head of a gang of thieves or robbers *Cs.* — *rkún-zla* a thief's accomplice.

རྐུབ་ *rkub (Lex.* पायु) 1. **the anus** *B.* — 2. **vulva** *W., C.* — 3. **backside, posteriors** *C.* — *rkub-stégs* **sitting-bench** *C.* — *rkub-tsós* **buttocks** *Cs.*

རྐེ་བ་ *rké-ba (cf. skémpa)* **lean, meagre** *Cs.*

རྐེད་པ་ *rkéd-pa,* also *skéd-pa, W.: *skéd-pa** 1. **the waist,** *sén-ges mčóns-sar was mčons rkéd-pa ₍čag* if the fox takes a lion's leap, he breaks his neck *Mil.*; **skyed kug tán-če* W.* **to bow;** **sked-zér** (?) the arms **a-kimbo** *W.*; more particularly that part where the girdle is worn, **loins;** *rked-rgyán* ornament of the girdle; *rkéd-pa-nas gri bton* he took a knife from his girdle *Pth.*; **ke-pa bhab** 'her waist fell', euphem. expression for: she has got her menses *C.* — 2. **the middle** of a building, of a mountain, **kar-skyéd* W.* the middle story of a castle; *rkéd-pa tsam brtsigs tsár nas* when the building was half finished *Glr.*; *Ti-sei rkéd-pa-na yar bslebs son* he is already half-way up the Ti-se *Mil.*

རྐོ་བ་ *rkó-ba, pf. (b)rkos, ft. brko, imp. rkos* 1. **to dig, dig-out, to hoe,** e. g. *sa* earth; *rko-byéd* digger; po. also a spade, mattock; *brkó byai sa* soil to be turned up. — 2. **to engrave** (*cf. ₒbúr-ba*); *brko-spyád* **a gouge** *Sch.*; *brkós ma* **sculpture.**

རྐོ་མ་ *rkó-ma* n. of a bird *Wdn.*, prob. = *ko-ma.*

རྐོག་མ་ *rkóg-ma* v. *lkóg-ma.*

རྐོང་པ་ *rkóṅ-pa Cs.:* **itch**, *za-rkóṅ* id.; *Lt.: rkóṅ-po.* Others describe it as a scabby eruption of the skin, chiefly affecting animals, but occasionally also men *C.*

རྐོད་པ་ *rkód-pa,* = *rkó-ba Ts.*

རྐོན་པ་ *rkón-pa,* also *skón-pa* 1. **basket;** the word is said to be used in Kun.; perh. also the Ladakian word **kun-dúm*,* a large cylindrical or bottle-shaped basket, may be traced to the same form. I never found it in books. — 2. **net**, fowler's net *Lex.*

རྐྱག(པ་) *rkyag(-pa),* also *skyag(-pa),* **dirt, excrement;** **kyág-pa tóṅ-wa* C.,* **kyág táṅ-ċe* W.* to cack, vulg. — *mig-skyág* the impurity in the eyes *Cs.; *na-skyág** ear-wax *W.*

རྐྱང་ *rkyaṅ* **the wild ass** or horse of Central Asia, Chigitai, *ṗo-rkyáṅ* male, *mo-rkyaṅ* female of it; *rkyaṅ dár-ma* a young wild ass, *rkyaṅ-rgan* an old one, *Cs.* — *rkyaṅ-ču* n. of a lake in the south of *Ld.,* in the neighbourhood of which these animals are particularly numerous.

རྐྱང་པ་ *rk'yaṅ-pa* **simple, single;** *ras rkyaṅ* a single sheet of cotton cloth *Dzl., Mil.; *mi kyaṅ** a single i. e. free, unemployed man, one that carries no burden *C.; yi-ge rkyáṅ-pa* a letter that forms by itself a syllable, or one that is not *brtségs-pa* and without any other consonant or a vowel-sign superscribed; *rkyáṅ-pai graṅs* are called 1, 10, 100 and the further powers of 10; *miṅ rkyáṅ-pa* a word that has no affix-denoting case etc. attached. — **kyaṅ, kyaṅ-kyáṅ, kyáṅ-ka, k̔a-(r)kyáṅ*,* col. (in *B. ša-stag)* **only, nothing but,** **pé-ča ṅags k̔ár-kyaṅ dug** the book contains nothing but charms. — **kyaṅ-kyáṅ** also: living by one's self, childless *W.* — **kyaṅ-ltab** single folded.

རྐྱང་བ་ *rkyáṅ-ba* v. *rkyóṅ-ba.*

རྐྱང་མ་ *rkyáṅ-ma* n. of a vein, v. **rtsa.**

རྐྱན་ *rkyan (Ld. *skyan*)* 1. a brass-vessel like a tea-pot, with a spout, *rag-rkyan id.; *'o-kyan* W.* milk-pot. — 2. **pot-belly, paunch** *Sch.*

རྐྱལ་ཀ་ *rkyál-ka,* sometimes for *kyál-ka.*

རྐྱལ་པ་ *rkyál-pa,* दृति, **leather bag** *frq.; ṗúṅ-po mi-gtsaṅ-rdzás-kyi rkyál-pa* a poetical term for the body *Mil.; rkyal-bu (*kyal-lu*)* **small bag, pouch;** *ra-rkyál* bag of goatskin; *ṗye-rkyál (*če-kyal* C., *ṗe-ky.* W.)* bag for flour.

རྐྱལ་བ་ *rkyál-ba* **to swim,** **kyal gyáb-ċe* W. id.; rkyal rtséd-pa* to amuse one's self by swimming.

རྐྱེན་ *rkyen,* प्रत्यय *Will.: 'with Buddhists: a co-operating cause, the concurrent occasion of an event as distinguished from its proximate* (or rather primary, original) *cause', rgyu* हेतु. (The right meaning was given already by *Schr.,* whereas afterwards, by a mistake of *Cs.,* the totally erroneous sense of 'effect, consequence' has become current among philologists.) 1. **cause, occasion,** *rkyén-gis* c. gen. **by, on account of,** *čii rkyén-gis* whereby? *dei rkyén-gyis* thereby, therefore, *dei rgyu dei rkyén-gyis id.* As a medical term, opp. to *rgyu* (the anthropological or primary cause of a disease) it denotes the pathological or secondary cause of it. — 2. **event, occurrence, accident, case, circumstance,** in a general sense, in as far as the Buddhist conceives every thing that happens in the mutual connexion of cause and effect; *rkyen ṅán-pa* unfortunate accident; *rkyen ṅán-pas ₒdas* he has perished by a fatal accident *Glr.; tse ₒdir byúṅ-bai rkyen ṅán-rnams* the adversities of the present life *Mil.; raṅ mi ₒdód-pai rkyen* an event disagreeable to one's own self; *bló-bur rkyen* a sudden accident *Mil.; rkyen dé-la brtén-nas* owing to that circumstance *Tar.* 8. 1. *méd-pai rkyén-la bltás-te* or *brtén-te C.* considering the case of not being . . . , not having . . . , thus *nad-kyi rkyen, ži-bai rkyen* stands also for: a case of disease, of death; *ₒgal-*

rkyén any circumstance or event adverse to the success of an action, **obstacle, hinderance**, any thing opposite or hostile to the existence of another thing, *mtun-rkyén*, **a happy, favorable circumstance, furtherance, assistance, supply**, *mtun-rkyén byéd-pa* c. genit. to assist in, to help to; *mtun-rkyén ꜀dzom-po* altogether successful. — 3. **misfortune, ill luck, calamity**, *rkyen zlóg-pa* to avert a misfortune, *tégs-pa* to endure, *túb-pa* to brave it *Mil.* — *cf. rgyu.*

རྐྱོང་བ་ *rkyóṅ-ba pf. & ft. brkyaṅ*, **to stretch, extend, stretch forth** (one's hand to a person), **put out** (the tongue), **spread, distend** (the wings, a curtain), *žabs ɣnyis brkyaṅ-bskúm* one leg stretched out, the other drawn in *Pth.*; **kyaṅ-šád-če** *W.* to stretch one's limbs. — *brkyaṅ-šiṅ* 1. 'extending-wood', an instrument of torture in Tibet, a wooden frame on which the extended arms and legs of the delinquent are fastened down, whilst burning pitch or sealing-wax is dropped on his naked breast, which procedure is called *brkyaṅ-šiṅ sprád-pa*, *brkyaṅ-šiṅ-la bčúg-pa* or *brkyáṅ-ba* 2. **cross** *Chr. Prot.* This word has been adopted on account of its etymological signification, although it differs in its form and use from the σταυρός of the N. T., which is unknown in Tibet and India. Additional explanation will be at any rate required on the part of missionaries; but much more so in the case of the *kro-če (Ital. croce)* of the Rom. Cath. missionaries of the last century. In favour of the word *ɣsal-šiṅ*, pointed stake for **empaling** a delinquent, speaks the circumstance, that this is also the original and classical signification of σταυρός, and that Buddhists from their own legends are well acquainted with the idea of martyrdom inflicted in this manner. Still *ɣsal-šiṅ* leads to a conception of the death of Christ historically untrue and revolting to our feelings and is therefore better not employed; moreover it is to be assumed that in the times of the Evangelists σταυρός was the term generally used for cross, whilst in the case of *ɣsal-šiṅ* no Tibetan thinks of anything else but empaling.

རྐྱོང་ཙེ་ *rkyóṅ-tse W.*, resp. **zím-kyoṅ, zím-tiṅ**, **lamp, candle**, (spelling uncertain).

ལྐུགས་པ་ *lkúgs-pa* 1. **dumb, mute**; *ka lkúgs-par byed-pa* to put to silence *Do.*; *lkúgs-pa-pa* a dumb man, *-ma* woman *Cs.* — 2. **dull, stupid** *Sch.*

ལྐོག *lkog* **secrecy**, *lkóg-gi čúṅ-ma Cs.*: a wife kept secretly, a private concubine, *lkóg-tu* in secrect, secretly frq.: *lkóg-tu gyúr-pa, lkyog-gyúr,* परोक्ष, secret, hidden, out of sight *Mil., Tar.*; *lkóg-tu gléṅ-ba* to converse secretly; *lk. sdód-pa* to keep in retirement. — *lkog-rṅan* a reward given secretly, a bribe. — *lkog-čós Sch.*: 'a secret doctrine'; but *lkog-čos byéd-pa* is gen. understood: to apply one's self to religious studies or exercises in secret. — *lkog ǰab byéd-pa* to hide one's self in a lurking place: *lkog ǰab byed-nas lta-ba* to watch, to witness from a lurking-place. — *lkog-zán zá-ba Sch.* to take usury-interest in secret. — *lkog-láb* backbiting, slander.

ལྐོག་མ་ *lkóg-ma* (vulg. **og-ma**) 1. **gullet, oesophagus.** — 2. **wind-pipe.** — 3. **throat.** — 4. **neck.** *lkóg-mai lha-góṅ Sch.*, (acc. to others: *lhar-gór*) the larynx, **koi lkóg-ma** or **og-ma šraṅ soṅ** *W.* his throat is swollen, he has the croup. — — *lkog-dkár* a small nocturnal carnivorous quadruped with a white throat, marten? — *lkog-gágs* hoarseness of voice *Cs.* — *lkog-šál* **dew-lap** (of oxen). — *lkog-sóg* **crav., maw** (of birds) *Cs.*

ལྐོབ་ *lkob* **fat, heavy, plump** *Sch.*

ལྐོལ་མདུད་ *lkol-mdúd*, also *'ol-mdúd*, **larynx.**

སྐ་ཅིག *ska-čig* v. *skad čig, skad* **no. 4.**

སྐ་ཅོག *ska-čóg* n. of a grammarian *Zam.*

སྐ་བ་ *ská-ba* **thick** (of fluids, *cf. slá-ba*); *ska-slád (Ld.: *kas-lád*)* **consistence, density.** — *W.: *skán-te**.

སྐ་རགས་ *ska-rágs B. & C.*, also *ske-rágs, W.* **kye-rágs**, *resp. sku-rágs* **girdle,** *ska-rags ₒčiṅ-ba* to put on the girdle, *ska-rágs bǹur-ba Sch.:* a girdle with a clasp (?).

སྐག་ *skag* 1. *Cs.: = kag, keg,* **mischief; unlucky.** — 2. v. *rgyu-skar.*

སྐང་བ་ *skáṅ-ba = skoṅ-ba; skaṅ-γsó* 1. **satisfaction** *Sch.* — 2. a kind of **expiatory sacrifice,** to make amends for a duty not performed.

སྐང་ཤ་ *skaṅ-ša Sch.:* **sods** cut out.

སྐད་ *skad (C.:* **ka̤**) 1. **voice, sound, cry** *(cf. sgra), gláṅ-po-čei skad lta-bui sgra* a sound like the voice of an elephant, **ka̤'-la čig-pa dho̤n mi-čig-pa** *C.* (words) equal as to sound, but of different sense (= homophone), *sdug-bsṅál-bai skad ₒbyiṅ-pa, snyiṅ-žei skad dón-pa* to utter lamentable cries; *skad stér-ba Sch.,* **ke̤' gyág-pa** *C.,* **skad táṅ-če** *W.* **to sound;** **ke̤' taṅ-wa** *C.* **skad gyab-če** *W. ccdp.* **to call** to a person; *skad mťún-par* with one voice, with one accord. — 2. **speech, words, talk, news,** **ka̤' či naṅ ꜀dug** what is your pleasure? what did you say, Sir? *C.; zér-ba de či-skad yiṅ* the (words) spoken what speech are they? = what do they mean? *Pth.; ₒdi-skad-(du)* in these words, thus. (before a literally quoted speech), *dé-skad-(čes)* id. (after it); it is also used in a more general sense instead of *dé-ltar: dé-skad ma byed* don't do that *Mil.; skad smrá-ba* to give account, to relate *Ld.-Glr. fol.* 12. b. *Schl.,* acc. to another reading instead of *sra smrás-te; skad byéd-pa id., rmi-lám-du byúṅ-ba skad byás-te* reporting it as having been revealed to him by a dream *Pth.* — 3. **language,** *bód-skad* the Tibetan language, *rgya-gár-skad* the Sanskrit language, *bód-skad-du, col. -la,* into or in the Tib. language, *yúl-skad-du* into or in the provincial dialect. — 4. a **snap** with the fingers, always with *čig: skád-čig-(ma),* gen. as a measure of time: **a moment;** also adv.: for a moment, *skád-čig-la* in a moment, instantly, in one moment, *skád-čig de-nyid-la* in the very same moment. (Some mathematical books compute the *skád-čig* = ⁴/₄‴, others as long as ¹/₃″).

Comp. and Deriv. *skad-꜀gágs* **hoarseness of the voice,** *Cs.* — *skad-ṅán* 1. **a bad voice.** 2. **cry, screaming.** — *skád-čan* having a voice, **sounding.** — *skád-ča* 1. *C.:* discourse, conversation, **ka̤'-ča láb-pa** or **ǰhé'-pa** to converse, to have a chat. 2. *C.* talk, rumour, **mii ká'-ča re** it is (but) talk of the people. 3. *W.:* news, tidings, intelligence. — *skad-čé, -čén* 1. **a loud voice** *Sch.* 2. n. of an animal *Lt.* — *skad-γnyá Sch.:* **a high voice.** — *skad-snyán sgyúr-ba Mil.* to sing or whistle in a quavering, warbling manner, of birds, flute- players etc., *꜀gyúr-skad* a singing or playing of this kind. — *skad-dód* **an equivalent word,** *čúṅ-mai sk.* another word for wife *Gramm.* — *skád-pa* v. the separate article below. — *skad-ₒdzér Cs. = skad-꜀gágs.* — *skad-bzáṅ* 1. **a good voice.** 2. *W.:* **good news.** — *skad-lúgs* **dialect.** — *skad-lóg* **clamour, screaming.** — *skad-γsáṅs mťo Sch.:* **a loud voice,** *skad-γsáṅ nyams-čúṅ ꜀gyur* the voice is getting weak *Wdṅ.*

སྐད་ *skad* **ladder,** v. *skás-ka.*

སྐད་པ་ *ská̤d-pa* I. vb. 1. **to say, tell, relate,** *žiṅ-ǩáms šig yód-do skád-par ťos* that a land (of bliss) exists I heard say *Mil.;* more frq. at the end of a sentence *skád-do* or *skad* for: it is said (= dicitur), *grags skad id. Mil.* — 2. **to name, call,** *skád-pa* partic. = *byá-ba* **named, called.** — 3. *Ld.:* **skád-če, χád-če** **to measure, take measure.**— II. sbs. **interpreter; language-master, teacher.**

སྐན་ཏེ་ *skán-te, W.* instead of *ská-ba* **thick, turbid.**

སྐབས་ *skabs* 1. **time, opportunity, case, circumstances;** *mťóṅ-(bai) skabs* opportunity of seeing, *skabs rnyéd-pa* to find an opportunity, *skábs-su* or *skabs-skábs-su* now and then, under certain circumstances, *skábs-su* or *skabs* with genit. at the time of, on occasion of, during, while, when; *dé-ka skáb-su* in a moment, instantly, *skabs ₒdir* now, here, in this case, in this place (of a book etc.) frq., *skabs-ɣre* once, for a time, **skabs-tóg* Ld. (col.)* now, *bár-skabs* **interval, interlapse of time** *Tar.*; *dús-skabs, ťsé-skabs, ɣnás-skabs,* **time, state, situation,** *skabs daṅ sbyár-ba, dús-skabs daṅ bstún-pa* fit for, adapted, suited to the occasion. — 2. *Cs.* **'mode, method'**, or perh. rather, **way, manner;** so the word seems to be used in *Wdṅ.: ldúm-bui skabs la-ṗúg daṅ skyé-lugs ₒdrá-bar* the manner (nature) of the plant being similar to that of a radish as to growth. — 3. **section, chapter** *(cf. ɣtam* no. 3), so esp. in *Tar.*; *skabs bču* the ten sections of Buddhistical theology, also: one that has absolved them.

སྐམ་ *skam* v. *skám-pa* and *-po.*

སྐམ་པ་ *skam-pa* I. *vb.* 1. = *rkám-pa* **to long for.** — 2. = *ském-pa (bskam-pa).* — II. *sbst.* 1. = *rkám-pa* **longing,** 2. **a pair of tongs;** *skam-čúṅ* small tongs, **pincers;** also several other instruments of a similar shape. — III. *adj.*, com. *skám-po* **dry,** *skam-rlón* 1. **dry and wet.** — 2. **dryness** in a relative sense, **skam-ši* Ld.* **very lean** (like a mummy), *skám-sa* **the dry land, the shore,** *skam* id., *skám-sar ṗyin-pa, skam-la sléb-pa* to get ashore, *skam-lam* **journey by land** *Wts.*; **skam-saṅ* Ld.* **meat perfectly dried.**

སྐར་ *skar;* this and the compounds *skar-ka* and *skar-ťsad* v. under *ska-ba; skar-kúṅ* etc. under *skar-ma.*

སྐར་བ་ *skar-ba Cs.:* 'a penning of cattle, assortment, separation, to pen, to fold, to separate'. But as these significations seem to belong to the spelling *bkar-ba* and *dgar-ba,* it will be safer to confine the verb *skar-ba, pf. bskar, imp. skor,* to the following, 1. **to hang up,** **skar-taṅ-če, čár-la skár-ce** id. *Ld.* (e. g. clothes). — 2. **to weigh,** and **skar** **weight,** **gau ṅul gui skar** a little box weighing 9 rupees (about 4 ounces); **skár-ka** or *-ǩa** **weight;** **skar-ťsád** **measure, scale.** *W., C.* — 3. **skar-tág ťáṅ-če** **to inquire rigorously; to restrict, to bind down, to flog;** **skar-lčág** a rigorous inquiring, a flogging *W.*, also *C.*

སྐར་མ་ *skár-ma Ssk.* तारा 1. **star,** fixed star, *nyi zla ɣza skar* sun, moon, planets and stars; sometimes it is used generally: **skar-čén** a very large, uncommonly bright star, esp. Venus when appearing as evening- or morning-star; *nyin-moi skár-ma* a star seen in the daytime (a thing of very rare occurrence). — 2. **constellation, asterism;** *btsas-skár* constellation of nativity *Med;* *ɣyaṅ-skár* propitious constellation (such are the nakšatras no. ༡ to ༢༧ v. *rgyu-skár*).

Comp, *skár-ǩuṅ* (the same word as *dkar-ǩuṅ*, but of a different etymology) **window.** — *skar-ǩóṅs Cs.:* 'the angular distance between two stars or planets' (?) — *skar-lṅá* a weight ('5 points' on the steelyard for gold) = 1 *žo* or $^1/_{20}$ ounce; as money = $^1/_3$ rupee. — *skar-čú* 'star-water'; bathing under the constellation *skár-ma rib-či* (prob. *rewati*, the 28th *nakšatra*, is meant) in October is considered beneficial for every kind of complaint, because *Saṅs-rgyás smán-pai rgyál-po* (quasi 'Buddha Aesculapius', to whom the origin of the medical science is ascribed by Tibetan Buddhists), bathed in that season, and therefore Tibetans, though not particularly fond of washing and bathing in general, are said to follow this example pretty frequetnly. — *skar-mdá (Cs.:* 'ignis fatuus'?) **a shooting star,** *ltuṅ* or *sa-la dril* is coming down, *ₒṗaṅs Mil. id.* — *skar-dpyád, -rtsis* **astrology.** — *skar-ṗrán* **a small star.** — *skar-ťsógs* the starry host. — *skar-ₒdzin* 'star-catching', making one's self sure of a propitious constellation, e. g. for an intended journey, by a sham departure, conveying luggage or goods to the next village etc., but then interrupting and postponing it to a more convenient time.

སྐལ་བ་ *skál-ba* *Ssk.* भाग, *resp. sku-skál* 1. **portion, share;** *bgo-skál* allotted portion; *zas-skál* portion of food, **ration;** *raṅ-skál* personal share; *nor-skál* or *ẏal-nór Glr.* hereditary portion, **inheritance;** *skál-ba ma čád-par* without being shortened of his portion *Mil.; ma mṫóṅ-ba skál-ba ma mčis-pa ₒdra* it does not seem to fall to my lot to see my mother. — *skal-čád* dried up, withered *Sch. (?)* — 2. in a special sense: the portion of good or bad fortune that falls to a man's lot, as a consequence of his former actions, **lot, fate, destiny,** a. relatively: *skál-ba bzáṅ-po, ṅán-pa* good, bad fortune; *ṫse ₒdii grogs-s' ál* the matrimonial share of the present life, the connubial fate for which a person is predestinated *Glr.* (The Buddhist priests pretend to be able to calculate the *skál-ba* of any one after his death) b. in a positive and good sense, denoting either prosperity and blessing as a consequence of good actions, or those actions themselves as being pious and meritorious, so that *skal-ldán* means **happy, blessed** as well as **pious, devout,** and *skal-méd* **unhappy, irreligious, impious.** *skal-ldán* are all those who have devoted themselves to virtue and treasured up more or less good works, and who may expect to be promoted in proportion. The term **worthy,** therefore, though not quite correct as to the word itself, is still very appropriate as it regards the subject; even **venerable, holy** may be applied occasionally, cf. भगवत् and भगवान्. Also some single blessing or spiritual gift may be meant by *skál-ba* and so the Ommanipadmehūm is called the *čos-skál*, 'the religious treasure', of Tibet *Glr.*

སྐས་ཀ་ *skás-ka B., C., skás-ḱa, skás-pa C., skrás-ka* (pronounced **tẹ́-ka* ₋ *C., šrás-ka, šrẹ́-ka W.*), even *skas, skad* **ladder,** generally consisting of the notched trunk of a tree; *rkyáṅ-skad C.* 'single ladder', the same, compared with two or three of them joined together, to make a sort of staircase with broader steps; **do-tá C., do-šrás, do-šrẹ́* W.* a flight of stone-steps; **gya-šrás, gya-šrẹ́ W., gya-kẹ́* C. (Schr.)* a regular **staircase** as in European houses; *gru-skás Glr.* prob.: flight of steps at the corner of a building; *gro-skad Glr.* fol. 7 appeared to be unknown to those that were consulted; *skas-kyi rim-pa Cs.* **steps;** **šra-ldaṅ, šral-dáṅ* W.* **spokes** of a ladder; *skas ₜgram Cs.* the two **side-pieces** of a staircase or ladder; *skas ₒdzug-pa* to apply a ladder *Schr., Cs.*

སྐུ *sku, Ssk.* काय, sometimes मूर्त्ति 1. also *sku-lus, sku-ẏzugs, resp.* for *lus:* **body;** by being prefixed to the names of parts of the body and even of everything that has reference to the bodily existence of a person, it imparts to them the character of respectful terms: *sku-stod, -smad* the upper, lower, part of the body; *sku-ša* flesh; *sku-mṫsál (for sku-ḱrag)* blood *Cs.; sku-mdóg* colour of the skin, *sku-ná* age; *sku-ṫse* lifetime, life; *sku-ḱáms* state of health; *sku-skál* portion, share, *sku-čás* goods, stores *Mil., sku-bsód* virtue, happiness *Tar.; sku-skyés* a present (given to or received from a respected personage); *sku-ₒbág* image, statue *Glr.; sku-mdun-pa (C.: *kun-dụm-pa*)* or *-druṅ-pa* attendant of a man of rank; **ku-ǰar-wa** ('adherent', v. *ₒbyar-ba) id. C.; sku-nye Sch.* relation, kinsman; *sku-ẏšegs-pa* dying, death (of a king etc.) *Glr.; sku-bstod* praise *Sch.; sku-šogs* (acc. to *Cs.* instead of *sku ẏšogs* 'the side' = your presence) a title of honour, when we should say: your or his honour, your or his worship, in *W.* only for clerical dignitaries, in *C.* also for other persons of rank. Even buildings (monasteries etc.) are honoured by these respectful expressions· *sku-dkar ẏsol-ba* to 'administer' whitewash — 2. in a special sense: **the person of Buddha,** whom philosophers represent in three forms of existence called *sku-ẏsum* त्रिकाय, viz.: *čós-kyi sku,* धर्मकाय, *loṅs-spyód-kyi sku* संभोगकाय and *sprúl-pai sku* निर्माणकाय. These three 'persons', however, have as little as *dkon-mčog-ẏsum* any thing in common with the Christian Trinity, nor even with the Indian Trimūrtti, for the first state, the 'body of law', the absolute body, is Buddha in the Nirvāna, the so-called first world of abstract existence i. e. non-existence, which is the ultimate aim and end of every existence and the ideal aspired to by every believing Buddhist; the second state, the 'body of happiness or glory' is Buddha in the perfection of a conscious and active life of bliss in the second world (heaven or Elysium), which state however is inferior to the first; the third, the 'body of transformation and incarnation', is Buddha in the third or visible world, as man on earth. Notwithstanding the altogether abstract character of *čós-sku*, as a philosophical conception, Buddhistic fancy is pleased to represent it as a visible image of Buddha, shining in the colours of the rainbow, or at least as a brilliant apparition of light, though impalpable and unapproachable; and this is not only a notion of the vulgar, but is acknowledged also in literature. More recent speculators have even added a *ṅo-bo-nyid-kyi sku* superior to the three, viz. that which is **eternal** in the essence of a Buddha, even *čós-sku*, the absolute body, being described by these philosophers as transient. The unintelligible passage in *Cs.'s* dictionary, p. 305 b. might be corrected thus: adding to the former three as a fourth' etc. — To this signification belong the compounds *sku-rim*, *resp.* for *rim-gro* **reverence, respect,** particularly in the special sense of a solemn **sacrificial ceremony,** performed on public and private occassions, e. g. in cases of disease: *sku-rim byéd-pa* to perform such a ceremony. — *sku-rtén*, *sku-tsáb*, *sku-yzúgs*, *sku-ḍrá* (*W.* **kun-ḍá**) **image of Buddha** etc. — 3. **image, statue,** of Buddha or other holy persons. *ysér-sku* a gold image, *rdó-sku* a stone image, *ǰim-sku* an image of clay, *bris-sku* a painted image, *búr-sku* a basso-relievo, *rkós-sku* an engraved, *blúgs-* or *ldugs-sku* a molten, *tágs-sku* a woven image *Cs.* — *sku-búm* 'mausoleum' or acc. to another etymology 'the 100 000 images', n. of the famous monastery Kumbúm east of the Kokonor (v. Travels of Huc and Gabet). — *sku ysuṅ tugs* 1. (cf *sku* no. 1) resp. f. *lus ṅag yid* the three spheres of a man's doings or sufferings, works, words and thoughts. — 2. the *rten ysum*, the three representations of Buddha: the image of his person, the books containing his doctrine, the pyramid (*mčod-rtén*) as the symbol of his grace. — *sku-lṅa-rgyál-po* five deities of degenerated Buddhism *Schl.* 157.

སྐུ་རུ་ *skú-ru* a **paddle-wheel,** without a rim; such are the water-wheels of all the mills in the Himalaya *skú-ru-ka* **the figure of a cross** + ×. The latter is common in books as an abbreviation like our 'etc.', to save the repeated writing at full length of the same sentence, as refrains etc.

སྐུགས་ *skugs* **the stake** in a game or wager received by the winner. — *skugs-stóṅ Sch. id.?*

སྐུང་བ་ *skuṅ-ba pf. bskuṅs, ft. bskuṅ* 1. **to hide in the ground.** — 2. **to bury, to inter.** — 3. **to tie** in a doubled or twisted position, e. g. a corpse before it is burnt, **to cord** on all sides. — *bskúṅs-sa* **lurking-place, hiding-place** *Mil.*

སྐུད་ *skud sbst.* v. *skúd-pa.*

སྐུད་པ་ *skúd-pa* I. *sbst.* **thread, yarn; wire;** *skúd-pa yčód-pa* to cut off the thread, also *fig. Cs.* to divorce; *ras-skúd* cotton thread, *lčags-skúd* iron wire; *tson-skúd* coloured thread; *skud-ró* the thread-ends of a seam; *skúd-bris-mkan* an embroiderer.

II. *vb. pf. bskus, ft. bsku, imp. skus, col. kú-wa C.* **skú-če** *W.* **to smear** **tá-gir-la mar skú-če** to butter the bread *W.*, **di-la nág-po ma sku** don't make that dirty *W.*; **to besmear, to daub** *snyiṅ-po(-la) snúm-gyis* a wick with grease *Dzl.*; *sgó-la rtsi* **to paint** a door; *spós-kyis skúd-pa* **to anoint;** *skud* **ointment,** **sra-skúd** **pomatum** *W.*

སྐུད་པོ་ *skúd-po* 1. **brother-in-law** *Cs.* — 2. **father-in-law.**

སྐུན་བུ་ *skún-bu* = *kóṅ-bu Lex.*

སྐུམ་པ་ *skúm-pa pf. bskums, ft. bskum, imp. skum(s)* **to contract, to draw in,** e.g. the leg.

སྐུར་པ་ *skúr-pa,* also *skur-klún, skur-žús* **abuse,** occasionally **blasphemy;** *skur-ₒdebs-pa, byed-pa, smra-ba* **to abuse,** viz.: persons to whom respect is due, esp. holy men or things, e.g. *ₒṗágs-pa-la* the venerable *Dzl.; dkon-mčóg γsum mi bdén-par ltá-žiṅ skúr-pa ₒdébspa* to blaspheme by denying the 'Three Most Precious' *Thgy. sgro-skúr* v. *sgro.*

སྐུར་བ་ *skúr-ba* I. *pf. skur,* at the end of a sentence *skúr-ro,* sometimes for *skúr-pa ₒdebs-pa Mil.* —

II. *pf. ft. & imp. bskur, pf.* at the end of a sentence *bskur-to* 1. **to send, to transmit,** e. g. news, objects, also an army, but not a messenger; *mdún-du skúr-ba* to send on in advance, to have carried before, e.g. a banner; *skur γnaṅ mdzád-pa* resp.: to be pleased to send. — 2. **to give, hand over, deliver, consign, give in charge, commit,** e. g. an army to a general; *dbaṅ skúr-ba* to invest with power, **to authorize,** *ji dgá-bar gyid-du dbaṅ skúr čig* give me power, permission, to do what I like *Dzl.; rgyál-por dbaṅ skúrba* to authorize somebody to be a ruler, to appoint, create, designate as king. The ceremony observed in such a case is a kind of anointing or baptism, pouring holy water on the crown of the head, *spyi-bo-nas dbaṅ skúr-ba,* and as supernatural powers are supposed to be active during this process, *dbaṅ skúr-ba* means also: **to bless, consecrate, endow** with miraculous power; esp. four mystical powers of meditation are imparted in this way.

སྐུལ་བ་ *skúl-ba pf. bskul,* at the end of a sentence *bskúl-to, Ssk.* चद, **to exhort, admonish, enjoin,** *mi žig las byéd-par* a person to do a thing; **to appoint,** *mi žig lás-la,* in the same sense; **to impose,** *mi žig-la las,* work on somebody, — perh. a mere provincialism; *dei tsig-gis bskúl-nas* **induced** by his words; *rnám-šes las daṅ nyon-móṅs-kyis bskúl-nas* the (departed) soul **urged on, influenced, driven,** by its former works and sins *S. g.; lha-srin mčod skul kyaṅ* though I tried **to determine, to bring round,** the gods and the evil spirits by sacrifices *Pth.; gliṅ sogs drág-tu skúl-šiṅ* flutes and other (instruments) **calling,** resounding, fortissimo and so animating the actors; **yid skúl-če* W.* **to remind, admonish;** **šaṅ** (for *γčaṅ*) **skúl-če** **to rouse** by shaking. — *bskúl-ba* and more frq. *bskul-ma* **exhortation, admonition;** *bskúl-ma ₒdébs-pa, C.* also *skúl-rgyag-pa, skul-čág byéd-pa Mil. nt.* **to admonish, exhort.** — **skúl-ḱan W.* **overseer.**

སྐེ་ *ske, vulg. skye,* seld. *skya,* **neck, throat,** *frq.;* neck of a bottle *Cs.;* **skye tsir táṅ-če, *kyig-če, sdám-če* W.* **to choke, strangle,** **skyé-la ťág-pa ťág-na sád-če* id.; ske γčód-pa, γtúb-pa, ₒbrég-pa* **to behead, slaughter;** *sker ₒťám-pa* to seize by the throat, to worry *Sch.; sker dógs-pa* to tie round the neck e. g. an amulet; *ske-ₒḱór* necklace *Schr.; ske-čá* ornament for the neck, **necklace** *Mil.; ske-stóṅ Med., Sch.:* cavity of the throat; *ske-rmá Sch.:* a wound of the throat, a jugular gland that has opened.

སྐེ་ཚེ་ *ske-tsé Wdṅ., Ssk.* राजिका Sinapis ramosa, **black mustard; mustard seed,** a grain of m. s.

སྐེག་ཚོས་ *skeg-tsós* **paint, rouge** (for the face) *Sch.*

སྐེད་པ་ *skéd-pa* v. *rkéd-pa.*

སྐེམ་པ་ *ském-pa* I. *vb. pf. bskams, ft. bskam, imp. skom(s)* **to make dry, lean, meagre; to dry up; exsiccate.** — II. *adj.,* also *ském-po,* **dry, dried up; meagre.** — *skem-byéd* a demon that causes drought *Lt.* — *skem-nád Bhar.* consumption.

སྐོ་བ་ *skó-ba, pf. (b)skos, ft. bsko, imp. skos* 1. **to appoint, nominate, commission, charge** a person, *lás-su* with a work *Dzl.,* much more freq.: *rgyál-por,* *dpón-du* to be king, chief; *rgyál-sar skó-ba* to raise to the throne; *ma bskós-šiṅ* without mandate, unbidden *Glr.* — 2. *lás-la bskós-pa* **destined** to the works i. e. destined to a man in consequence of his works; *ṅéd-kyi las-bskós* my **destiny, fate, lot** *Mil.*

Note. The signification: to elect, to choose *(Cs., Sch.)* cannot be proved and was expressly denied by Tibetans.

སྐོ་ཙེ་ *sko-tsé* 1. a kind of wild onion *Cs.* — 2. a mixture of the leaves of several kinds of leek, pounded, formed into balls and dried; when used, a small portion is broken off, fried in butter and then added to the food. This spice forms a lucrative article of commerce and is exported from *Ld.* to Cashmere and from *Lh.* to India.

སྐོག་པ་ *skóg-pa* v. *kóg-pa.*

སྐོང་ *skoṅ* v. under *koṅ.*

སྐོང་བ་ *skóṅ-ba pf. bskaṅs, ft. bskaṅ, imp. skoṅ(s)* 1. **to fulfil**, e. g. a hope, a vow etc., **nyiṅ** the desire *W.*; *ḱa skóṅ-ba* to fill up what is open, to make up a deficiency *Zam.*, also *dgé-bai ḱa-skoṅ* to fulfil perfectly the laws of virtue, *ḱa-skóṅ, ḱa-bskáṅs, ḱas-skoṅ* 1. **appendix, supplement,** *γšám-du ḱa-skóṅ-du bšad* will be said, described, below in the appendix *Wdṅ.* 2. By Tibetan copyists of books a short prayer is called so, consisting of a stanza of 4 verses, which they are accustomed to write down or recite after having finished the copy of a work, in order to make amends for the mistakes they may have committed. — *ṫugs-dám bskaṅ-rdzás* a certain ceremony v. *Schl* 260. — 2. v. *dpa.*

སྐོན་པ་ *skón-pa* I. *sbst.* v. *rkón-pa.* — II. *vb. pf. & ft. bskon* **to dress,** to clothe another person *(resp. γsól-ba).*

སྐོབས་ *skobs* = *skabs Schr., Sch.*

སྐོམ་ *skom* 1. **thirst,** *skóm-gyis γdúṅs-pa* tormented by thirst *Dzl.* — 2. *resp. žal-skóm,* **drink;** *zas (daṅ) skom* food and drink. — 3. *i.o. skam* the **dry land** *Glr., provinc.* — *skóm-pa* 1. **to thirst, to be thirsty.** 2. **the thirst.** 3. **thirsty,** *skóm-pa-dag ni skóm-pa daṅ brál-bar* ˳*gyur* the thirsty will get rid of their thirst *S. O.* — *skom-dád (dad-pa* = ˳*dod-pa)* **thirst** *Med.* — *skom-ṫsád* **burning thirst** *Mil.* — **skóm-ri** **thirst** *W.*

སྐོར་ *skor (cf. kor)* 1. **circle,** *mig-skor* eye-ball *W.*; *sba-skór* hoop of bamboo *Schr.* — 2. **appurtenances,** *yi-ge* ˳*bri-bai skor* writing utensils, *ṫáb-kyi skor* everything that belongs to the fire-place *C.* (perh. provinc.) — 3. **section, division,** e. g. of a book, similar to *leu,* chapter *Mil., Tar.* — 4. **repetition,** *skor ldáb-pa* to repeat *Schr.* — 5. **theme, subject,** *gaṅ skór-la* ˳*bri* ˳*dug* what is the subject of this writing? Answer: *rtai skór-la* a horse *C.*; *de skór-la* on that account, therefore *Ld.* — 6. *skor, skór-zas* **food presented to Lamas;** laymen are deterred from laying their hands on it by the mysteriously menacing verse: *skór-zas zá-la lčag-gi* ˳*grám-pa dgos* he that eats Lama's food, wants iron jaws. — 7. v. *skór-ba* no. II.

སྐོར་བ་ *skór-ba* I. *vb. pf. & ft. bskor* 1. **to surround, encircle, enclose, besiege** *cca & d.*; also of inanimate objects: *dé-la skór-bai ri* the mountains surrounding it *Glr.*; *ri nágs-kyis bskór-ba Sambh.* a mountain surrounded by a forest. — 2. **to go, move, ride round a thing;** esp. the reverential ceremony of प्रदक्षिण transferred from Brahmanism to Buddhism, which consists in going round a holy object with one's right side turned towards it — one of the most meritorious and indispensible religious duties in the eyes of a Buddhist; *č́ós-skor-la byon* they walked round in the religious direction, i. e. according to the precepts of Buddhism, *bón-skor-du soṅ* in the Bon manner, i.e. the opposite direction *Mil.*; *ṗyag daṅ skór-ba byéd-pa,* as a specification of religious duties: to make salutations and circumambulations.

སྐྱག་པ་ skyág-pa

3. **to wander through, traverse,** *rgyál-ḱáms,* the countries, *Mil.* — 4. **to return, go home** *Sch.* — 5. **to turn round, twist,** *mii ltág-pa* a man's neck, i.e. to choke, to strangle him *Glr.* **Phrases:** *mgo skór-ba, mgo skor byéd-pa (W. *ċo-ċe*)* **to befool, delude, deceive** a person, by intoxication or flattery *Glr.*, also by a flood of words. — **ḱa kór-wa C., kór-ċe* W.* to make one alter his sentiments, to divert one from a plan etc. — **lan** or **dugs skór-ċe** to take vengeance *W.* — **si kór-ċe* (v. *rtsis) W.* **to count, calculate.** — *tsóys-kyi ḱórlo skór-ba* to arrange the objects of the *maṇḍal* (q.v.) in a circle n.f. — *skor lóg-pa, skor lógla ₀gró-ba* to go round the wrong way *Mil.*; **pé-ra kor-re-lóg táṅ-ċe** to talk foolishly, to twaddle *W.* — **lag kór-ċe** the putting a seal under a document which is done by several persons one after another *W.*
Comp. *skór-ḱaṅ Glr.*, prob. = *skór-lam.* — *skor-rgyúgs* turning the enemy, getting into his rear *Mil.* — *skór-mḰan, skór-pa* **a turner** *Cs.* — *skor-spyád, skor-ḋin* a turner's **lathe** *Cs.* — *skor-tíg* **a pair of compasses.** — *skor-dbyúg* a sling, for throwing *Sch.* — *skor-lám* 1. the pathway round-about a monastery, used for the holy processions. 2. a veranda surrounding a house. 3. col. also: round-about way. II. 1. **the going, moving round, encircling** etc. — 2. **the way** round a thing, = *skor-lám*, in the compounds: *náṅ-skor* the inner, *bár-skor* the middle, *ṗyi-skor* the outer roundway, *ṗyi-skor ċén-po* the outermost. — *sá-skor* round-about way, by-way.

སྐོལ་བ་ skól-ba pf. & ft. *bskol* **to boil** (vb. act., cf. *Ḱól-ba).*

སྐོས་པ་ skós-pa 1. v. *skó-ba.* — 2. *Sch.:* 'to order', but this is *sgó-ba.*

སྐྱ་ skya 1. **oar** *C., Thgy.*; *skya-léb* id.; *skya-mjúg* **rudder**; *skya rgyáb-pa* **to row** *Schr.* — 2. **spatula** *Schr.* — 3. **pot-ladle,** *C.* — 4. **wall** of stone or clay, *bár-skya,*

partition-wall, **bhár-kya ċa̱'-pa** to make a partition-wall *C.*

སྐྱ་ skyá-ka, skyá-ga *Lt.,* n. of a bird, *Cs.:* **magpie.**

སྐྱ་བ་ skyá-ba I. vb. 1. pf. *bskyas,* ft. *bskya* 1. *Lex.:* = *₀ṗó-ba* **to change place,** cf. *skyas.* — 2. **to carry, convey** to a place (a quantity of stones, wood, water etc.) *W.,* v. *skyéd-pa.* — 3. *Sch.* **to swim** (?) II. sbst. 1. **kettle** *Sch.* — 2. prob. = *skya* 1.

སྐྱ་བོ་ skya-bo, *Ssk.* पाण्डर and पाण्डु, **whitish gray, yellowish-white**; **skya ċág-ċe* to fry or toast a thing so that its whitish colour turns partially into brown *Ld.*; *mi skya* one clothed in light-gray, (not in red or yellow, as monks are), a layman; *sno-skya* **light-blue,** *ljaṅ-skyá* **light-green,** and so of the other colours; therefore *ser-skya* ought to denote **light-yellow,** but it is also used as an equivalent of कपिल, n. of a saint, (Ser-skyai-₀groṅ = Kapilavastu, an ancient city in Oude, and Buddha's birth-place); originally: 'monkey-coloured', **tawny,** *lto-skyá* 'pale' i. e. poor, insipid, miserable food *Mil.nt.*
Comp. **kya-ko-ré, kya-te-ré** **pale, white** *C.* — *skya-skyá* id. *Sch.* — *skya-nár,* पाटलि n. of a flower, Bignonia graveolens; *Skya-nár-gyi-bu* n. of a city of Old-India Pāṭaliputra, now Patna. — *skya-snár* acc. to *Stg.* the colour of the skin of the Indians, brown. — *skya-rbáb Cs.:* a kind of dropsy, *Sch.:* a grayish oedematic swelling; *skya-rbab-skráṅs Lex.* — **skya-már** **fresh** (i. e. not melted) **butter** *W.* — **skya 'ód* W., skya-réṅs* **morning-twilight, dawn.** — *skya-lám* = *skyá-bo Thgy., C.* — *skya-séṅ* 1. n. of a tree. 2. translation of Pāndu, *skya-séṅ-gi bu* a Pandava. — *skya-sér* 1. *Sch.:* **tawny,** cf. *ser-skya.* 2. 'white and yellow' viz.: men, **lay-men and priests** *Mil.nt.*

སྐྱ་རུ་ར་ skyá-ru-ra n. of a drug *Med.*

སྐྱག་པ་ skyág-pa 1. = *rkyág-pa.* — 2. pf. *bskyags,* ft. *bskyag,* imp. *skyog* **to**

spend, lay out, expend; *skyag-sgó* **expenditure,** *skyag-tó* **account of expenses.** — 3. *W.:* **skyag táṅ-če** **to slaughter, to murder.**

སྐྱང་ནུལ་ *skyaṅ-núl* **pavement, clay-floor, mud-floor** *Lex., Cs.; skaṅ-núl byéd-pa* **to pave, to plaster** (*Sch.* also; to rub, polish).

སྐྱབས་ *skyabs* (*cf. skyób-pa*) *Ssk.* **शरण protection, defence, help, assistance;** *me-čú-la skyabs* is a protection against water and fire; *skyabs méd-do* I am (or: he is etc.) lost! *skyabs byéd-pa, skyábs-su ˳gyúr-ba* ccgp. **to protect, help, save** a person, frq. with *srog-gi* added; *skyábs-su ˳gró-ba* eleg. *mčíba, W.:* **skyab čól-la yóṅ-če** to seek help, *mii* or *mi-la* of some body, *skyabs-˳grós* 1. the seeking of help, **शरण गमन** 2. the formula *Saṅs-rgyás-kyi skyabs-su mčio, čós-kyi sky. mčio, dge-˳dún-gyi sky. mčio,* the Buddhistic creed or confession of faith.

Comp. *skyabs-mgón* **helper, protector, deliverer;** this is applied to certain highly esteemed and respected persons, mythological as well as living, ni f.; *Chr. Pr.* use it for **Saviour, Redeemer, Christ.** — *skyabs-˳grós* v. above. — *skyabs-γnás* 1. **place of refuge,** shelter; also of persons, = **helper,** frq; *mi-la skyabs-γnás byéd-pa Mil.* to take refuge to a person, to seek his assistance. 2. seld. for *skyábs-su γnás-pa* **client,** *ṅá-yi skyábs-γnas ṗó-mo-rnams* all my clients, men and women *Glr.* — *skyabs-sbyin* a gesture of the right hand, like that for giving benediction *Glr.* — *skyabs-yúl* = *skyabs-γnás.* 1.

སྐྱར་གོག་ *skyár-gog* **naked** *Pur.*

སྐྱར་པོ་ *skyár-po Sch.:* **snipe, wood-cock;** *skyar-čúṅ Sch.:* **'a large snipe'** (??); *skyár-mo Sch.* **heron;** *skyar-léb Sch.* **spoon-bill;** *ču-skyar Cs.* **duck,** *Sch.:* **bittern,** but the **कारण्डव** of the *Lex.*, 'a kind of goose' speaks in favour of *Cs.*

སྐྱར་བ་ *skyár-ba* v. *skyór-ba.*

སྐྱས་ *skyas* a changing of abode; *skyas ˳débs-pa* to change one's dwelling-place (cf. *skya-ba*), *skyas čén-po ˳débs-pa* to die

སྐྱས་མ་ *skyás-ma* 1. v. *skyes.* — 2. *Sik.:* **fern.**

སྐྱི་ *skyi Cs.:* the outward side of a skin or hide (opp. to *ša*); *skyi γyá-ba* to shiver, tremble with fear *Cs.* **Comp.:** *skyi-dkár Cs.* dressed leather; hide. — *skyi-lpágs Sch.:* chamois, wash-leather. — *skyi-búṅ Mil.?* — *skyi-bún* prob. an itching of the skin *Mil.?* — *skyi-šá* 1. outward and inward side of a hide. 2. *Sch.:* the anus.

སྐྱི་བ་ *skyí-ba* I. sbst. 1. a medicinal plant *Med.* — 2. also **kyi-u, ṗi-liṅ kyi-u,** **potato** *C.*

II. vb. pf. *bskyis*, ft. *bskyi*, imp. *skyis* **to borrow,** esp. money or goods (cf. *γyár-ba* and *skyin-pa).*

སྐྱིག་པ་ *skyíg-pa* **to hickup;** *skyig-bu* **the hickup** *Med.*

སྐྱིང་སེར་ *skyiṅ-sér Mil.,* eagle, vulture.

སྐྱིད་པ་ *skyid-pa* vb., sbst., adj.: **to be happy, happiness** (*Ssk.* **सौख्य**), **happy;** *skyid-do* (I, thou etc.) am, art etc. happy; *bdé-žiṅ skyid-la* being happy and glad; *skyid-pai nyi-ma* sun of felicity, propitious day *Glr.; skyid-po = skyid-pa* adj., frq., *skyid-de-ba* id. *Tar.* 5, 19.

Comp. *skyid-glu* song of joy. — *skyid-mgo* beginning of happiness *Mil.* — *skyid-sdúg* good and ill luck, happiness and misery; *skyid sdug ji byuṅ kyaṅ* whatever may happen *Glr.; skyid sdug bsré-ba* to share pleasure and pain. — *skyid-čú* n. of the tributary of the Ya-ru-tsaṅ-po, on which Lhasa is situated.

སྐྱིན་ *skyin* **wild mountain goat,** Capra ibex.

སྐྱིན་གོར་ *skyin-gór* **lizard** *Lex.,* = *da-byid.*

སྐྱིན་ཐང་ *skyin-táṅ Sch.:* **hail, sleet.**

སྐྱིན་པ་ *skyin-pa, W.* **skyin-po**, resp. *kar-skyin* **a loan,** a thing borrowed; money advanced without interest; *skyin-pa skyi-ba* to ask a loan; *ṅá-la ˳di skyin-du ˳tsal* he asked me to lend him this *Dzl.; skyin-pa lén-pa Cs.* to take on credit; *skyin-pa spród-pa, ˳jal-ba* to pay back or return a loan *Cs.; nór-skyin* a loan of goods or money, *gós-skyin* of clothes. — *skyin-mi Schr.* debtor. — *skyin-tsáb C.:* the pledge for a loan; acc. to others, however, it just means the object lent or its equivalent when being returned.

སྐྱིབས་ *skyibs* everything giving **shelter** from above, an overhanging rock, a roof etc.: **čar skyib** shelter from rain; **ḍag-skyib** under a *ṗa-boṅ* q. v. (*gyam* is much larger, *ṗúg-pa* deeper) *W.; bka-sky.* प्रघाण, a covered terrace or small portico before a house.

སྐྱིལ་བ་ *skyíl-ba*, pf. & ft. *bskyil* 1. **to bend,** esp. the legs when sitting on the ground after Oriental fashion, also another's leg by a kick from behind; to bend the bow. — 2. **to pen up, shut up,** cattle, **to dam up,** a river, also: *ču rdziṅ-du skyíl-ba* **to collect** water into a pond *Glr.*, or *rdziṅ-bu sky.*; to dam up a pond (but not 'to dig it' *Schr.*); **to keep back, retain, detain** a person *W.; *ḱa kyíl-če** to keep a person from doing something, to dissuade from *W.* — *skyil-krúṅ*, also *skyil-mo-krúṅ*, the posture of **sitting cross-legged,** *skyil-krúṅ byéd-pa* (resp. *mdzád-pa*), *skyil-mo-krúṅ-gis* (or *du*) *ˌdúg-pa* (*resp. bžúgs-pa*) to assume such a posture; *séms-dpai skyil-krúṅ* the usual manner of sitting, in which the feet are not seen, *rdo-rjei sky.* the posture in which the soles of the feet are seen turned upwards, *rdzógs-pai sky.* another posture requiring particular practice. (The spelling *dkyil-krúṅ*, though frequent, is expressly rejected by grammarians.) — **skyil-díṅ* W.* a small hole filled with water. — **skil-ldir* W.* **handle, ring** fixed to a thing, for carrying it, hanging it up etc.

སྐྱུ་གང་ *skyu-gáṅ Lex.* w.e., *Sch.:* **a gulp, draught.**

སྐྱུ་རུ་ *skyú-ru* a sour fruit *Med.; skyú-ru-ra Med.* (*Lex.:* आमलक wood-sorrel) the same (?); in later times the word seems to have been used also for the **olive,** and *skyú-ru-šin* **the olive tree,** which in *Sik.* is called *ḱa-skyúr-poi šiṅ*.

སྐྱུ་རུམ་ *skyu-rúm Cs.:* **'condiment, sauce, pickle',** acc. to others, at least in *W.*, only the resp. word for *spags:* 1. **sauce, gravy.** 2. **dish, mess.**

སྐྱུག་པ་ *skyúg-pa* pf. *skyugs.* 1. **to vomit, eject,** e.g. blood, *skyúg-tu ɉúg-pa* to cause to vomit, *skyúg-pa dřěn-pa* to excite vomiting *Tar.; skyúgs-pa* (partic. pf.), *ṅan-skyúgs*, **the vomit** (it is the food of certain demons, and being boiled in it, is one of the punishments of hell). — 2 to lose colour, **to stain.**

Comp. *skyug-ldád* **rumination,** chewing the cud; *Sch.* also: **eructation.** — *skyúg-bro-ba* nausea, *skyúg-bro-bai nad* disease of nausea; *skyúg-bro-bas* from disgust; *skyug-bro C.* also **impure** with regard to religion, = *W. *tsid-du**. — *skyug-smán* **an emetic.** — *skyúg-log-pa Sch.* to feel disgust.

སྐྱུང་ཀ་ *skyúṅ-ka*, also *lčúṅ-ka*, **jack-daw** (black, with a red bill); *skyúṅ-kas zos Lex.* eaten or stolen by a jack-daw.

སྐྱུང་བ་ *skyúṅ-ba* pf. *bskyuṅs*, ft. *bskyuṅ*, imp. *skyuṅ(s) Cs.* **to leave behind, to lay aside,** e.g. a task *Lex.*, pride *S.g.*

སྐྱུད་པ་ *skyúd-pa* 1. *Cs.:* **to forget, leave off.** 2. *Sch.:* **to comminute; to swallow.** (?)

སྐྱུར་བ་ *skyúr-ba* I. adj. **sour,** sbst. **acidity;** more frq.: *skyúr-po C.*, *-mo W.* adj. **sour,** *Ssk.* अम्ल; *skyur ɉúg-pa* 1. to turn sour. 2. to suffer a substance to turn sour, v. *ɉug-pa.* — *ḱa(-ša)-skyúr-po* **olive,** *ḱa(-ša)-skyur-pói šiṅ* olive tree *Sik.* — *skyúr-ḱu Cs.*, *raṅ-skyúr Cs.*, *skyúr-ru* (*Sik.*), *skúr-mo Lh.* a sour liquid, **vinegar.** (Vinegar seems to be little known as yet in Tibet, and the above mentioned expressions may have been framed by different persons on different occasions, but are not in general use. The same may be said of *Cs.'s skyúr-pa* and *skyur-rtsi* for **acid** in a chemical sense.)

II. vb. pf. & ft. *bskyur* 1. **to throw, to cast,** *ṗyir* out, *lhuṅ-zéd nám-mḱa-la bskyur-nas* having flung his mendicant's-bowl up into the air *Dzl.*, *čur skyúr-ba* to throw into the water, *rgyáb-tu* behind one's self = to turn one's back upon a thing; **to throw away, throw down,** a stone, a corpse etc.; **to eject,** *lúd-pa* phlegm; **to throw off,** a rider; **to give up, abandon,** a work; **to forsake,** a friend; **to abort.** — *skyúr-ma* **abortion** *W. (?)* — *ču skyúr, γyańskyúr* capital punishment in *C.*, when the delinquent, with a weight fastened to his neck, is thrown from a rock into a river.

སྐྱུས་ *skyus? Sch.: skyus ťóg-pa* **altogether;** *skyús-su klóg-pa Gramm.:* to pronounce **jointly,** viz two consonants without a vowel between them.

སྐྱེ་ *ske* 1 v. *ske.* — 2. v. *skyed* and *skyé-ba.*

སྐྱེ་བ་ *skyé-ba* I. vb. (**जन**) pf. *skyes* 1. **to be born;** *ńá-la* (seld. *las) bu skyés-pa yin* I have given birth to a son *Glr.; ṗó-skyes* a man, *mó skyes* a woman, female; *skye-rga-na-ₒči-bai sdug-bsńál* the evil of birth, old age, sickness and death (which constitute what in the opinion of the Buddhist is the greatest evil of all, that of existence); *ťóg-ma skyés-nas, má-la skyés-nas B.,* *'á-ma skyé-sa-na* *W.* from one's birth; *sḱye či-* (or *ši-*) *méd pa* subject neither to birth nor to death, eternal; *skye-ₑgag-méd-Thgy., Lex.,* is said to mean the same. In the special sense of the doctrine of metempsychosis *skyé-ba* has often to be rendered by: **to be re-born,** *mí-ru* as man, *bur* as (somebody's) son. — *mi skyé-bai čós-la bzód-pa* v. *bzód-pa.* — *W.:* *skyé-če* 1. as inf. **to be born, reborn.** 2. as sbst. the being born; **birth.** 3. as adj. being with child, **pregnant; big with young,** also *sḱyé-če-ma*. — 2. **to become, to begin to exist, arise,** *nad kun mi skye, skyés-paań ži-bai ṗyir* ut ne morbus ullus nascatur, natus quoque sedetur *Med.; skye-ba dań ₒjig-pa* to arise and pass away; frq. of thoughts, passions etc. (the person as well as the thing in the accus.): *ḱyeu ḱrós-pai sems skyés-te* the youth — thoughts of wrath arising (in him). — 3. **to grow** *(nasci) lúń-pa ₒbru skyé-ba* valleys where corn grows; *ru mgó-la skye* a horn is growing on the head. — 4. **to grow** *(crescere) čer or čen-por skyé-ba* to grow up, to grow tall; *ras kyań lús-ḱyi ťsád-du skyés-so* the garment also grew in proportion to the growth of the body, or: with the body *Dzl.; rtúl-pod-par skyés-so* he grew up a valiant man, became a valiant man; **to bud, germinate, sprout,** *sbúns-te skye čúg-ce* to accelerate the germinating of the seed by maceration *W.*; even = *ₒṗél-ba Dzl.* ? — 5. sometimes = *skyá-ba* 2. unless in that case *kyé-če* should be spelled *bskyás-čes W.*

II. sbst. (**जाति**) 1. the being born, the **birth,** *skyé-ba mťo-ba, skye-mťó or mťón* **high birth;** of high birth, **noble, man,** male; *skyé-ba dmá-ba, skye-dmá, -dmán* **low birth;** of low birth, **ignoble, woman,** *mí-lus ťob kyań skyé-ba dman* born a human being, it is true, but only a female *Mil.; skyes-dmán* col. *kyer mán* in *C.* the usual word for **woman** and **wife,** *ńe ḱyer mén* my wife. — In the special Buddhistic sense: **re-birth** *mir skyé-ba bžén-pa* to take or assume re-birth as a human being; also **period of re-birth = existence, life,** *skyé-ba ₒdi-la* in this, my present, period of life; *skyé-ba bdun* seven periods of life; also **manner of re-birth,** v. *skye-γnás*; in a concrete sense: the **re-born individual,** *yúm-gyi skyé-ba yin* she is the re-birth of the queen dowager, the re-born q. d. — 2. the **arising** etc. — 3. the **growing** etc.

Comp. *skye-dgú* v. *skyé-bo.* — *skye-ₑgró = ₑgroba* being (q.v.) — *skye-sgó* 1. **entrance to re-birth,** viz. to one of the six regions of birth, v. *ₑgró-ba* II., *skye-sgó γčód-pa* to lock it up. 2. **face,** *légs-pa* a handsome, *žan-pa* an ugly face; also *ḱa-sgó skye-ₒbrás légs-pa* is said for: having a handsome exterior *C.* — *skye-mčéd* (**आयतन**) the five (or six) seats, i. e. **organs, of the senses** (the sixth is **मनस्** the inner sense); the **senses** themselves; this conception, however, has been greatly altered and varied by the fanciful theories of medical and philosophical authors, cf. *Burn.* I, 500. *Was.* (240). — *skye-γnás* 1. **birthplace; station or locality** of a plant.

2. **class** or **region of birth** or re-birth, **class of beings** (v. *ₒgró-ba); byol són-gi skye-ba* the being born as an animal 3. **manner of birth** **उपपाद**, *skyé-ba bži*, also **चतुर्योनि**. the four kinds or ways of being born: *mńál-las* (or *nas*) out of a womb (so, acc. to Stg., elephants and some men are born), *sgo-ńá-las* out of an egg (birds, some *klu*, some men), *drod-γšér-las* out of heat and humidity (insects, some men etc.), *rdzús-te* in a supernatural way (so the *lha*, the Buddhas, when they spring from lotus-flowers; also the inhabitants of infernal regions, souls in the bardo and some men). — *skye-γzúgs* prob. = *byad-γzúgs* **stature, figure.** — *skye-rábs* **series of the births** of a man, **history** of them, and esp. so of the births of Buddha, — so in the title of a work. — *skye-šiṅ* = *skyed-šin Wdn.*

སྐྱེ་བོ་ *skyé-bo* 1. **being,** (animans) *mi-la-sogs-pa sḱyé-bo* man and the other living beings *Dzl.* — 2. **human being, man,** gen. as a collective noun: **mankind,** *ₒḱrúl-bčas skyé-bo* infatuated men *Pth.; skyé-bo mḱás-pa γžán-rnams* other sensible people *Tar.; skyé-bo máṅ-poi yid-du ₔóṅ-ba* universally beloved *Dom.; mi nag skyé-bo* **laymen** (on account of the dimness of their religious knowledge); *so-sói skyé-bo* **पृथग्जन** (cf. *Will.)* the lower clergy, common monks *Tar.*, but also simple laymen, if they are not quite without religious knowledge; *skye-bo-čog, (skyeo-čog Cs.* is a less accurate pronunciation), *skyé-dgú*, or (less correctly) *rgu*, **men, mankind;** *skye-dgui-bdág-mo* **प्रजापती** fem. pr. n., the aunt and first governess of Buddha *Glr., Gyatch.*, also a name of *dpal-lhá-mo's* q.v.

སྐྱེ་ཚེ་ *skye-ťsé* = *ske-ťsé Lex.*, **mustard.**

སྐྱེ་རགས་ *skyé-rágs W.* for *ska-rags* **girdle.**

སྐྱེག *skyeg Cs.:* = *kég, kag* **misfortune.** But *rtsis-kyi skyeg Lex.* w.e.?

སྐྱེགས་ *skyegs* 1. n. of a bird: *ču-sky. Lex.* w.e., *Sch.:* **coot, water-hen;** *ri-skyégs Lex.* w.e., *Cs.:* a large singing-bird, *Sch.;* **grouse, heath-cock.** — 2. *rgya-skyégs* **shell-lac.**

སྐྱེང་བ་ *skyeṅ-ba* and *skyeṅs-pa* **to be ashamed,** also *ḱa-skyeṅ-ba*, B. and col. frq.

སྐྱེང་སེར་རླུང་ *skyeṅ-ser-rluṅ* also *skye-* or *skya-ser-luṅ Mil.*, **cold wind.**

སྐྱེད་ *skyed* and *skye*, 1. **growth, increase,** *skyed če-bar ₔgyur-ba* to grow much; *γžan-gyi zla-skyed-pas dei žag-skyed če* his daily growth was greater than the growth of others in a month etc. *Pth.* — 2. **progress, the getting on, improvement** *skyed yoṅ* progress comes, I am making progress *Mil.;* **profit, gain** *nad-la skyed med* (this) is of no **use** for that disease, of no **benefit** *S.g.fol.* 10. — 3. **interest** *C.*, *dńul-skyed* of money, *ₒbru-skyed* of corn *C.*, *skyed-du γtoṅ-ba* to give on interest *Cs.; skyed ṕog pa Cs.:* 'to be the full term of payment', more accurately: *skyed ṕog* I (you, he etc.) am struck or hit by the term of payment; *skyed-čan* yielding interest, profit *Cs.*

སྐྱེད་སྒོ *skyed-sgo Mil.nt.* prob. = *rgyal-sgo* principal door.

སྐྱེད་པ་ *skyed-pa* I. vb pf. *bskyed*, act. to *skye-ba*, in *W.* pronounced alike: **skye-če** 1. **to generate, procreate;** seldom in a physical sense: *bskyed-pai yab ὁ γεννήσας πατήρ Pth.*, (opp. to *bltams-pai yum Pth.*, for which however *skyed-ma Cs.* does not seem to be an appropriate substitute). — 2. **to produce, form, cause** (opp. to *med-par byed-pa* to destroy, annihilate) e. g. diseases, fear, roots of virtue, merit, *bsod-nams-kyi ťsogs, sa-bon* (fig.) *Dzl.*, *ₒbras-bu* retribution; **to reproduce,** *zad-pa* what has been consumed *Med.;* to create certain thoughts or affections either in one's self or in others: *spró-ba bskyed-pas dei ṕa-má yan spró-ba čún-zad skyés-nas* by his own rejoicing also to his parents a little joy arising *Dzl.* 22. 5; *ťams-čad-kyis brtson-ₔgrús bskyed-do* they all created zeal, took great pains *Dzl.; čes bsam-pa bskyéd-nas* thus they thought. — 3. **to cause to germinate** or **grow,** *yúr-bai čú-yis žiṅ skyed* *ᴄdra* just as the water of the ditch makes the fields green *Med.; sá-bon Dzl.* (v. before, but it may as well be referred to this signification); *γsos skyéd-pa* **to bring up, to nurse up** *Dzl.; skyed sriṅ-ba* id. *Glr.* — 4. = *skyá-ba*, **to bring on, carry, convey** to a place *Pth.*

Comp. *skyed-mos-ṫsál* **grove, park.** — *skyed-rdzógs*, instead of *skyed-rím* and *rdzogs-rím*, **उत्पत्तिक्रम** and **सम्पन्नक्रम**, two kinds or degrees of meditation. — *skyed-ŝiṅ Cs.*: a planted tree (?) prob. a fruit-tree, *Dzl.*

II sbst. 1. **the generating, producing** etc. — 2. = *skyed*, e. g. *skyéd-pa lén-pa* **to gain flesh, to thrive** *C.* — 3. = *rkéd-pa*.

སྐྱེན་པ་ *skyén-pa* adj. 1. **quick, swift** *Lex.*, *k̔ró-* or *sdáṅ-skyen-pa* quick to wrath *Stg.; byéd-skyen-pa* rash, hasty, precipitate *Glr.* — 2. **nimble, dexterous** *C. W.; ᴄp̔óṅ-skyen-pa* dexterous in shooting, **a skilful** archer *Dzl.* (Besides: vb. to make haste, to strive; sbst. zeal, ardour; adj. strong *Cs., Sch.* ??)

སྐྱེམ་པ་ *skyém-pa* resp. **to be thirsty.**

སྐྱེམས་ *skyems* resp. 1. **thirst.** — 2. **drink, beverage,** esp. **l r,** also *żal-skyéms* or *-skyoms, skyems ᴄdrén pa* to offer or set before an honoured person something to drink, *bżés-pa* to accept of it, to take it; *skyems-la γsol-rés byéd-pa* to drink beer in company *Glr.; γŝegs-skyéms* a carousal on the departure of an honoured person; *γser-skyéms* beer together with grains of corn, as an offering to the gods for the good success of an enterprise, a journey etc., in religious dancing-festivals, *γser-skyéms-pa* sbst. the priest or dancer who offers it. — *skyems-čáṅ* **beer.** — *skyems-čú* **drinkable water.** — **skyéms-ḍaṅ* W.* (?) **brandy.** — *skyéms-ṫsúgs Sch.*: **cup, dish.** — *skyéms-siṅ* **small-beer.**

སྐྱེར་པ་ *skyér-pa Lex.*: **हरित** curcuma, **turmeric;** in *W.* **barberry.**

སྐྱེད་དམན་ vulgo for *ske-dmán* **woman** *C.* (v. *skye-ba* II).

སྐྱེལ་བ་ *skyél-ba*, pf. & ft. *bskyel*, imp. *skyol* 1. **to conduct, accompany,** resp. *γdan-skyél-ba; skyól-la ŝog* conduct him hither! *Pth.; *skyel-la-la** (for **skyél-wa-la**) *soṅ* he has gone to accompany (him) *W.* — *bsu-bskyál* going to meet, and accompanying on departing *Dzl., γŝegs-skyél byéd-pa* resp. to accompany an honoured person on departing, to see him off *Mil.* — 2. **to convey, bring, take** e. g. a child to a place, food to somebody, *Dzl., C. W.* id.; **to carry off, to take away** *C.*: **ŝiṅ ma kyal čig** do not bring any more wood! more accurately **kyal ŝog** bring! **kyal soṅ** take away! — 3. **to send** *B. & C.* e.g. clothes to somebody *Dzl.* — 4. **to risk, to stake,** *raṅ-srog Mil.* — 5. *C.*: **to use, to employ** **bá-laṅ lẹ ǰhé-pa-la** an ox for work; **to spend,** **lẹ ǰhé-pa-la mi-ṫse** one's whole life in working, **lé-lo̱ náṅ-na** in idleness. — 6. **k̔a kyél-wa** *C.* to kiss; *γnód-pa skyél-ba, B.* **kyal-wa** *C. W.* col., **to do harm, to hurt, inflict an injury, to play** one a **trick;** *mna skyel-ba B., C. W.*, **to swear,** take an oath; **lo kyél-če** *W.* **rel;, depend upon, confide in.** — *skyel-ṫuṅ byéd-pa* = *γŝegs-skyél byéd-pa*, (prop.: to accompany one to a short distance). — *skyel-bdár Lex.*, also col., present of the departing person to those that accompany him. — *skyel-ma* **an escort, convoy;** *skyél-mar yod* he is a guide (to me) *Mil.; skyél-ma żu* we ask for a safe-conduct *Glr.; dmag daṅ bčás-pai skyél-ma* a military escort *Glr.*

སྐྱེས་ *skyes*, also *skyás-ma, skyós-ma, k̔yós-ma*, resp. *γnaṅ-skyés*, **a present,** *skyes skúr-ba* to give or send a present; *ᴄbyon-skyés, p̔ebs-skyes* a present given to or received from somebody on his arrival. — *sk̔yas-čáṅ* a present of beer, *skyes-k̔úr* of cakes, *skyes-nór* of merchandise or money; *skyes-lán* a present made in return *Cs.*

སྐྱེས་སྡོང་ *skyes-sdóṅ Sik.* **banana, plantain.**

སྐྱེས་ནག *skyes-nág*, also *skye-nág C.* **widower.**

སྐྱེས་པ་ *skyés-pa* 1. pt. pf. of *skyé-ba.* — 2. sbst. **man, male person,** *skyés-pa* *dañ bud-méd*, men and women *B. & C.*; emphatically: *rgyál-po γčig-po skyés-pa yin* the king alone is a man *Dzl.*; **husband** *Glr.*; = *skyés-bu* **a holy man?**

སྐྱེས་བུ་ *skyés-bu*, *Ssk.* पुरुष **man, people**; *skyés-bu gañ* **whosoever; man** opp. to the rest of nature *Med.*; **one** (French: *on*), *skyés-bu lág-pa brkyáñ-ba tsám-gyis* as quick as one stretches out his hand *Dzl.* — Though this word may also be applied to culprits and criminals (*Pth.*), it is chiefly used of **holy men**: *skyés-bu dám-pa* the saint; *dad-ldán sky.* the believing, the faithful *Glr.*; *skyés-bu čén-po*, महापुरुष the great saint, in Buddhistic writings nearly identical with Buddha; *skyés-bu mčog* id. (For the 32 chief characteristics and the 80 subordinate marks distinguishing such a person refer to *Köppen.* I. 433. *Burn.* II. 553 ff. *Gyatch.* c. VII.)

སྐྱེས་མ་ *skyés-ma* 1. fem. of *skyés-pa*, she that has been born *Mil.* — 2. **fern**, = *skyás-ma Sik.*

སྐྱོ་ངོགས་ *skyo-ñógs Cs.*: **quarrel**, *Lex.* = *ₒkrug-lóñ.*

སྐྱོ་བ་ *skyóba* 1. vb. **to be weary**, c c. r: *bdag kyim-gyis skyó-ste* I being weary of living in the world *Dzl.*; in a more general sense: **to be ill-humoured, grieved, vexed, to feel an aversion** *Tar.* 12. 13; *skyo mi šés-par* or *skyo mi šés-pa tsám-du* without being tired, **indefatigably**; *nam skyo-na* when he was tired of it *Dzl.* — 2. sbst. **weariness** *ₒtsol-ₒtsól-nas skyó-ba yañ skyé-bar dug* we are quite tired of that constant seeking *Mil.*; *yid yóñs-su mi skyó-ba* **indefatigableness, perseverance** *Thgy.* — *skyó-mo* adj., **sems skyó-mo rag** I feel **discontented, disheartened** *Ld.*

Comp. *skyo-grógs* **comforter, companion** *Glr., Mil.* — *skyo-glú Cs.*: **a mournful song.** — *skyo-ñál, skyo-dúb* **weariness**, *skyo-ñal-méd-pai dád-pa* unwearied faith *Mil.* — *skyo-šás* **disgust, aversion.** — *skyo-sáñs* **recreation**, *skyo-sáns-la ₒgró-ba*, resp. *ₒbyon-pa* to take a walk or a ride, to promenade. — *skyo-bsún-pa* to be grieved *Sch.*

སྐྱོ་མ་ *skyó-ma* 1. **pap** of parched meal and beer; any **pap, paste** or **dough**; *skyó-ma ₒbyúg-pa* to spread paste (upon a wound, as a salve) *Med.*; *ša-skyó Med.*? (it may denote a paste of meat as well as one of mushrooms). — 2. **blame, slander**, *skyó-ma máñ-la* when he slanders a great deal *Mil.*

སྐྱོགས་ *skyogs* 1. **scoop, ladle.** — **me-kyóg** **coal-shovel** *C.*; **žu-kyóg** **melting-spoon, crucible** *C. W.* — 3. **drinking-cup, bowl, goblet.** — *γser-skyógs, dñul-skyógs* gold, silver goblet. *žal-skyógs C. B.*, **don-skyógs* W.* resp.: drinking-cup. *krag-skyógs* bowl for drinking blood, a skull used for that purpose *Pth.*; **kyog-žáb sal** may I ask your honour for the foot of your cup (viz the remnant of your drink)? *W.* — 3. *srab-skyógs Cs.*: **the rein** of a bridle. —

སྐྱོགས་ལྟོ་འབུ་ *skyógs-lto-ₒbu* **snail** *W.* **'ol-skyógs** id.

སྐྱོགས་པ་ *skyógs-pa* **to turn**, *mgrin-pa* the neck, = to look round, back, *Mil.*, also = to turn away, aside *C.*

སྐྱོང་བ་ *skyoñ-ba*, pf. *bskyañs*, ft. *bskyañ*, imp. *(b)skyoñ(s)* Ssk. पा, रक्ष **to guard; to keep, to tend**, cattle; **to defend**, the religion; **to save, preserve**, the life, the body; **support, to take care of**, poor people, e.g. *drin bzáñ-pos* by benefits, favours. *tábs-kyis* by various means; **to attend to; to be given to**, *tugs-dám* meditation, *lag-léñ* exercise; *rgyal-srid skyóñ-ba* to rule, govern a kingdom, *čos bžin-du* in conformity with the law of religion, justly. — *čos-skyóñ* '**protector, defender of religion**', धर्मपाल, is used for a certain individual deity, or = *ₒjig-rten-skyóñ*, or for a class of magicians in the monasteries of *C.*, v. *Schl.* 157. *Kö.* II. 259. — *ₒjig-rten-skyóñ*, लोकपाल '**guardian of the world**'; there are four of them, identical with *rgyal-čen bži* the four great spirit-kings, q.v. — *skyoñ-dál* **assistance** *C.*, **kyoñ-dhál jhé'-pa** to help. — *skyoñ-ma* = *brtán-ma* the goddess of the earth.

སྐྱོད་པ་ *skyód-pa* pf. & ft. *bskyod*, *Ssk.* चल. 1. **to move, to agitate**, *rlúñ-gis yál-ga* *skyod-na* when the wind agitates the branches *Dzl.*; **to shake**; hence *Mi-skyód-pa*, Akshobhya, n. of the second Dhyani-Buddha. — 2. *W.*: resp. **to go, to walk,** (= *ɣšégs-pa, ˛byón-pa B. C.*) **nán-du skyod** step in, if you please! — 3. *W.*: **to go down, to set,** of the sun, moon etc., **to expire, to pass, to elapse,** of time.

སྐྱོན་ *skyon* दोष 1. **fault, defect** (opp. to *yon-tan*), *skyon gaṅ yaṅ med* I have not to complain of anything, I do not want anything *Dzl.*; **damage, harm, disadvantage, misfortune,** *˛k̔rul-pa-la skyon či yod* what harm is there in erring? *Thgy.*; C.: **mi kyon, kyon me'**, no harm, no matter (*W.* more freq.: **mi sto**); *ɣžán-gyi skyon tós-na dgá-ba* rejoicing in the calamities of others, malicious *Glr.*; *skyón-du mťóṅ-bá* to consider it a loss *Glr.* — 2. **bodily defect, fault,** as lameness; **derangement, disorder** in the mixture of the humours *Med.* — 3. **spiritual defect, sin, vicious quality,** *rdzún-du smrá-bai skyon* the sin of lying *Dzl.*; *skyón-gyis ma gos* not defiled by sin; *lar skyon če* but that is very bad (of you) *Glr.*; *skyon byéd-pa Cs.* to commit a fault, *sél-ba Lex.* to remove, amend, correct a fault, *spáṅ-ba* to leave off, to quit it; *mi-là skyon ˛bébs-pa, ˛dógs-pa* (col. **tág-pa, tág-če**) to charge one with a crime, to calumniate *Glr.*; *ɣžán-gyi skyon gléṅ-ba, rǰód-pa*, to name the faults of others, to speak ill of them, to slander *B., C., Schr.* also: to blame, criticise. — *skyón-čan* 1. **faulty, defective, incorrect,** e.g. *dag-yig* the spelling of a word. 2. **sinful,** subject to vice. — 4. symb. num: 18.

སྐྱོན་པ་ *skyón-pa* pf. *(b)skyon* **to put astride** upon a thing, (causative form to *žón-pa*), *mi žig rtá-la* (or *rtá-ru*) to cause a man to mount, to go on horseback: to fix something on a stick; *mi žig ɣsál-šiṅ-la* **to empale** a man.

སྐྱོབ་པ་ *skyób-pa*, pf. *(b)skyabs*, ft. *bskyab*, imp. *skyób(s) Ssk.* त्रा **to protect, defend, preserve, save** frq., *˛ǰigs-pa-las* from fear, *˛ǰig-pa-las* from destruction; *bskyáb-pa* the protecting power, the preserving cause *Mil.* (ni f.).

སྐྱོབས་ *skyobs* **help, assistance,** seldom for *skyabs*; *skyóbs-ma Thgy.* id.; **šrog-kyób** col. preservation of life, escape; also: he that saves another's life, helper.

སྐྱོམ་པ་ *skyóm-pa*, pf. *bskyoms*, ft. *bskyom*, imp. *skyom(s) Cs.*: **to shake, agitate, stir up.** *Lexx.* give: *ču skyóm-pa* and *snód skyom-pa*, to stir the water, to shake a vessel.

སྐྱོར་ *skyor* = *k̔yor*, the hollow of the hand filled with a fluid, e.g. *ču-skyór* a handful of water.

སྐྱོར་བ་ *skyór-ba* I. vb. pf. & ft. *bskyar* 1. **to hold up, to prop,** — 2. **to paste.** — 2. **to repeat,** *bskyár-te btaṅ* it was repeatedly sent *Dzl.*; to repeat word for word what the teacher says, in order to learn it by heart *Mil.*; to say over again; to **recite by heart** (opp. to *sgróg-pa* to read); *glu de rǰes skyór-nas ma bláṅs-na* if one does not sing the hymn afterwards repeatedly *Mil.*; **kyor ǰaṅ ǰhé'-pa* C.* to practise repeatedly.

II. sbst. **enclosure, fence.**

སྐྱོལ་བ་ *skyól-ba* sometimes for *skyél-ba*.

སྐྱོས་མ་ *skyós-ma* v. *skyes*.

སྐྲ་ *skra*, *resp. dbu-skrá* (*C.*: **ṭa*, *W.*: *šra**) **the hair** of the head, **šra-ló* Ld.* id., used caressingly in speaking to children and women; *skra daṅ k̔á-spu* the hair of the head and of the beard; *skra bsgril ba Cs.*: plaited or curled hair; *skra nyag ɣčig* a single hair. — *skrá-čan* having long hair. — *skra-do-kér* the hair plaited together on the crown of the head, as Buddha and Hindu-women wear it. — *skra-mdúd* the bow of ribands at the end of the long plaits of the women in *Ld.* etc. — *skra-ťsáb Cs.*: **false hair, a peruke.** — *skra-šeṅ Sch.* thin hair.

སྐྲག་པ་ *skrág-pa*, with instr., **to be terrified, frightened by, afraid of something** *˛ǰigs-skrag-pa, dṅáṅs-skr.* id. *B., C.*

སྐྲང་བ་ *skráṅ-ba* pf. *skraṅs*, **to swell,** **ṡraṅs-soṅ** it is swollen, a tumour, a bile, a weal has formed itself *W.; skráṅs-po Sch.* a swelling, tumour; *skraṅs-ₒbúr Sch.* an abscess not yet open.

སྐྲན་ *skran* 1. *Ssk.* गुल्म *Cs.:* a fleshy etc excrescence in the abdomen, a concretion under the skin, in the bowels, womb etc., *Sch.* also: a swelling of the glands. Wise (Commentary on Hindoo Medicine) says, that very different diseases are comprised unter the term *gúlma*, tumours of the pylorus, partial enlargements of the liver, diseases of the large intestines, fixed and moveable swellings; — perhaps also herniae, which I did not find mentioned elsewhere. — In *S. g.* I found *skran-nád* described as a consequence of great fatigue and want of breath, and *skran-γzèr* as pain in consequence of suppressed winds. — 2. *rdo-skrán, bad-skrán,* two sorts of **steatite** *C.*

སྐྲབ་པ་ *skráb-pa Cs.:* 'to beat the ground with one's feet,' **to stamp, tread,** cf. *ₒḱráb-pa; Lex.: bró-skrab-pa,* to dance.

སྐྲས་ཀ་ *skrás-ka* v. *skás-ka.*

སྐྲི་བ་ *skrí-ba* 1. *Cs.* **to conduct** (?) 2. *W.* **ṡri-če** f. *dkri-ba.*

སྐྲུ་བ་ *skrú-ba* pf. *bskrus* ft. *bskru, Sch.:* to wait; the latter would suit well in a passage of *Mil.*, perh. also in *zás-la skru* of the *Lexx.;* but *ṡiṅ-skrus-pa Lexx.* remains unexplained.

སྐྲུན་པ་ *skrún-pa* pf. & ft. *bskrun* **to produce,** fruits *Mil.*, a root of virtue (v. *rtsá-ba) Stg.*

སྐྲུམ་ *skrum* **meat,** resp. viz. when spoken of as the food of respected persons.

སྐྲོག་པ་ *skróg-pa* = *dkróg-pa,* perh. also f. *skrág-pa. Lexx. ḍá-ru skróg-po* **to beat** the drum: *W.* **kopóṅ ṡróg-če** **to play** on the guitar.

སྐྲོད་པ་ *skród-pa* pf. & ft. *bskrad* **to expel, drive out, eject,** out of the country *Dzl., Mil.;* to deprive of cast; **ṡrád-de taṅ če** to expel a thief publicly out of the village *W.*

བཀ…, བསྐ…; words beginning with these letters will in most cases be found arranged under rk.. and sk..

བསྐང་རྫས་ *bskaṅ-rdzás* a sacrificial ceremony v. *Schl.* 360.

བསྐ་བ་ *bská-ba, Ssk.* कषाय, **astringent,** as to taste, *Cs.* erron.: bitter.

བསྐལ་པ་ *bskál-pa, Ssk.* कल्प, **a kalpa, a** fabulous period of time; the fantastical reveries of the Buddhists concerning this subject v. *Kō.* I. 266, also *Will.* under *kalpa bskól-pa čén-po* the great kalpa; *bár-(gyi) bskal-pa* the intervening or middle 'kalpa'; *bsk. bzáṅ-po* the happy, blessed period, viz. in which Buddhas appear; *bskál-pa ṅán-pa* the bad 'kalpa'; *bskal-mé* conflagration of the universe.

བསྐུ་བ་ *bskú-ba* v. *skúd-pa* II vb.

ཁ

ཁ *ḱa* 1. the letter **k'**, aspirated, like c in *'call'*. — 2. numerical figure: **two,** *ḱa-pa* the second volume.

ཁ་ *ḱa* I. additional syllable, = *ka,* but less frequent. —

II. in compounds instead of *ḱá-ba* **bitter** and *ḱá-ba* **snow;** for the latter signification it is in *W.* the only form existing.

III. i. o. *ḱag* **part.** *ḱa γnyis-su* into two parts (e. g. to cleave) *Stg.;* **ḱa-ghaṅ** one **part**; in a special sense: the sixth **part** of a rupee *C.*; *k'a-čig* part, **some, several**, frq.

IV. (also *Ssk.* ख) resp. *žal*, cf. *k'á-po* 1. **mouth**, *k'a k'a* bitter mouth, bitter taste *Med.*; *k'a dúl-po* (soft mouth), manageable, tractable, *k'a gyóṅ-po* hard-mouthed, refractory; *k'a sgyúr-ba* (= *k'a-lo sgy.*) to govern, to rein the mouth (of a horse), to lead, guide, influence other persons *Glr.*, to turn off (a river) *Tar.*; *k'a ᶜt'én-pa* (to pull the mouth) to stop a beast of draught *Tar.*; *k'a ₒbyed-pa*, *W*, **p'é-če** to open one's mouth, *γdáṅs-pa* to open it wide, *ₒdzúm-pa*, *W.*, **čug-če** to shut it; *k'a brdáb-pa* (or *kráb-pa?*) **to smack**; **k'a dab** (or **ṭab**) **zér-wa** to produce a smacking, snapping sound, col.; *k'a rég-pa* c. dat. to put one's mouth to a thing, in order to eat or drink it; *k'a ᶜjúg-pa* c. dat. **to interfere, to meddle with**; *k'a t'ál-ba* 1. col. = *k'a ᶜjug-pa*, 2. *Cs.*: **to promise**; *k'a γtúgs-pa*, *k'a ₔo γtúgs-pa*, *k'á-la ₔo byéd-pa*, *k'a sbyór-ba* *B.*, *C.*, **k'a lán-če** *W*, **k'a kyél-wa** *C.* **to kiss**; **k'a kyé-če** *W.*, **to inveigh**, to give ill language; *k'a bsré-ba* to have intercourse, social connexion with one another, viz. in eating, drinking and smoking together, which is a matter of no little social consequence; *k'a ₒdzin byéd-pa* c.genit. to receive friendly, to be kind to, assist *Mil.*; *k'a γtád-pa* *Glr.* 16. 3. was explained: to bring together personally, to confront, = *k'a sprád-pa*; *k'a ₒbúb-tu nyal-ba* to lie in that position; *k'a bsláṅ-ba* the contrary of the preceding; *k'a ₔóg-tu bltás-te ši-ba* to be killed by a precipitous fall. Especially: the speaking mouth, *k'á-nas*, col. also **k'á-na**, **orally**, by word of mouth, e. g. to state, report, **k'á-nẹ zér-na** in the colloquial language *C.*; **k'a dé-mo ṅyiṅ sóg-po** *W.* hypocritical; *k'á-la slá-te dón-la bka* easily spoken after, but difficult to be understood (e. g. a doctrine); **k'a šór soṅ** 'my (his etc.) mouth has run away', **nor soṅ** 'has erred', the former denoting inconsiderate talk, the latter a lapsus linguae; *k'as lén-pa*, *bláṅ-ba* 1. 'to anticipate with the mouth', **to promise** frq., with direct speech or term. inf., sometimes also with the term. of a sbst. e. g. *bráṅ-du k'as blaṅs* he promised or engaged himself as a servant, — also: **to presume, to arrogate** *Mil.* 2. 'to accept, adopt with the mouth', **to acknowledge, admit** *Tar.*; *k'as ₒčé-ba* *B.*, *k'a t'ál-ba* *Cs.*, to promise; *k'a sṅá-ba*, *sṅás-pa* to blurt out, speak out inconsiderately; *k'a ₒčám-pa*, *mt'ún-pa*, *col.* **t'úg-pa** to agree upon; *k'a sdóm-pa*, *mnán-pa* to silence, *W.*; **k'a kág-če*, *kyíl-če** id.; *k'a skyór-ba*, *slú-ba* to speak cunningly, to try to persuade etc.; *k'a róg-pa*, more freq. **k'a róg-(te) dúg-pa*, *dád-pa*, **to be silent**; *k'a ᶜp'áṅ-ba* *Tar.*, prob. = *k'a ₒk'yam dbyúg-pa* *C.* to divulge ill rumours; *k'a lóg-pa* to reply, contradict; *k'a gáṅ dgar smrá-ba* (**gaṅ tad*, *gaṅ dran zér-če** *W.*) to talk at random; *k'a- (la) nyán-pa* **to obey**, *k'a nyán-po* **obedient** (resp. *bka* i.o. *k'a*); *γsál-k'a* clear, intelligible language; *k'a ṅán-du smrá-ba*, *W.*: **k'a sóg-po zér-če** to use ill language; also without **ṅán-pa** or **sóg-po*, *k'a zér-če** or **k'a tóṅ-wa** means the same. — 2. **mouth, opening, orifice**, of a vessel, cavern, pit etc., *k'a γčód-pa*, *ᶜgébs-pa* to cover, shut an opening; *k'a ₒbyéd-pa* to open, is also used of a book, a letter etc. (for holy books *žal* is employed i.o. *k'a*); *k'a ₒbye-ba* to open or unclose itself, to begin to appear, *k'a ₒbú-ba* id., of flowers; *k'a búb-tu* the opening turned downward, *k'a bslán-du* turned upward; *k'a-t'úg skóṅ-ba* to fill to the brim; *k'a skóṅ-ba* to fill up a void, to make up a deficiency, *γžan-nas* or *las* from elsewhere; *k'a naṅ* the inward brim, *k'a p'yi* the outer edge *Glr.* — 3. **the front side, face**, *k'a lhor stón-pa* or *ltá-ba* to be directed southwards *Glr.* — 4. **surface**, *k'a ₒbri-ba*, to be diminished, of a fluid the surface of which is sinking; *k'á ᶜp'ri-ba* to diminish, to make less, by taking away from the surface; **the outside**, *k'a dkar γtiṅ nag* outside white, inside black, fig. *Mil.*; in a special sense: **colour**, v. *k'á-dóg*; therefore *k'á-ru*, *k'á-na*, *k'á-la*, *k'ar* 1. **on, upon, above**, *šiṅ-k'ar* upon the tree (e. g. he sits), up the tree (he climbs) *Dzl.*; *ču kar* on the water; *ṗyogs bži ká-ru* all round *Glr.* 2. **on, at,** *ču kar* on the river side, *mtso kar ṗebs* he came to the lake *Pth.* 3. **above, besides,** = *stén-du Mil.* 4. **towards, in the face of,** *mtson kar sra* proof against thrust or blow *Mil.* 5. **at the time of, when,** *sléb-pai kar, sleb kar, ₒbyon kar* when (he) arrived; *ré-bai kar* in the hope of; — *ká-nas* down from, away from, *rta ká-nas ₒbébs-pa* to alight from the horse *Glr.*; **ká-na, ká-nę, ká-la** col. for *sgó-nas*, **tábs-si ká-na** by way of the opportunity, on occasion, **yun riṅ-gi ká-ne** by little and little, gradually. — 5. **sharpness, edge,** of a knife etc., **ka túg-po soṅ** the edge has become blunt, **log soṅ** has become bad; **ka mi ₒdug** the edge is wanting; *meï, čui, rlúṅ-gi ka nón-pa* to suppress the sharpness of the fire, water, wind, to stop the flames, floods etc. (viz. by means of incantations) *Glr.*; **ka tón-če, ṗiṅ-če** *W.* to grind, to sharpen; *ka lén-pa* to become sharp *Sch.*

V. **yesterday,** also: **the day before yesterday,** *kai nyin* id., cf. *ka-rtsaṅ*.

Compounds. *ka-dkri* (*C.* **-ṭi**, *W.* **-ṣri**) **neck-cloth,** sometimes worn as a protection against cold. — *ká-skóṅ, kas-skóṅ* **appendix,** of a book. — *ka-skyur-po* **olive, olive-tree** *Sik.* — *ka-ka-sán* or *siṅ* about two months ago *C.* — *ka-kébs* **cover, lid** *Sch.* — *ka-kór, ka-kyér* **border** *Sch.* — *ka-kral Cs.*: respect, regard, with respect to. — *ka-ₒkór* the circumference of the mouth *Cs.* — *ka-gáṅ* (cf. *ka* III) **quadrate, square,** *ka-gáṅ-ba* square *adj.*, *ka-gáṅ-ma* id., e.g. pieces of cloth so shaped. — *ka-gáb Sch.* **cover, lid.** — *ka-góṅ* **snow-ball.** — *ka-grú* corner of the mouth. — *ka-mgál* v. *ka-só*. — *ka-rgán Mil.* privilege of old age n. f. — *ka-rgód Sch.*: ill language; a slanderer. *ka-rgyúg Glr.* acc. to the context: idle talk, unfounded assertion. — *ka-rgyúd* or *-gyún*, resp. *žal-rgyun*, oral tradition, esp. certain mystical doctrines not allowed to be written down. — *ka-bsgós* advice, = *ká-ta*; commandment, cf. *bka-bsgós*. — *ka-mṅár* bitter and sweet. — *ka-čig* (v. *ka* III) **some,** — *ka-γčáṅ* clever talking, cf. *ka sbyáṅ-po* **eloquent** (*Cs.*: fair words?) — *ka-γčód* **cover, lid; cork.** — *ka-bčól Sch.* idle talk, prattle. — *ka-čág Mil.*, was explained: **abuse,** ill language. — *ka-čád*, resp. *žal-čád* **agreement, convention, covenant,** **k. zúm-če** *W.* to conclude a convention. — *ka-čár Mil.* snow and rain; *ka-ma-čár* both falling promiscuously, sleet. — *ka-čiṅs* the appeasing of wild beasts etc. by witchcraft *Mil.* — *ka-čú* 1. spittle *Cs.* 2. snow-water. — *ka-če* 1. a large mouth. 2. a person that has to command over much (cf. *ka-drág, ka-žán*). 3. n. of a mask in the religious plays. 4. n. of a country, Cashmere, v. below. — *ka-čéms* **last will,** *ka-čéms ₒjóg-pa* to make a testament. — *ka-čos* **hypocrisy.** — *ka-mču* 1. **lip.** 2. *Sch.*: word, voice (?) 3. **quarrel, dispute.** — *ka-rjé* 1. great lord, mighty personage *Cs.* (?) 2. good luck, good fortune *Cs.*; but in *C.* it is only used for **fortune = goods, wealth.** — *ka-nyúṅ Sch* sparing of words, **laconic.** — *ká-ta*, also *ká-lta* **good advice, lesson,** *byéd-pa* or *ₒjóg-pa* to give, *C. W.* — *ka-tód-la* (or **-na**) *Ld.* = *ka-tóg la*, **on, upon.** — *ka-tón Cs.*: 'a reading or saying with a loud voice' (*Lex.* वचस), better: **the saying by heart,** *klóg-gam ka-tón-du dón-nas* reading or saying by heart, *ka-tón-du šés-pa* to know by heart *Dzl.*; gen. in reference to religious texts. — *ka-γtám Cs.* **tradition.** — *ka-stóṅ* not yet having eaten anything. — *ka-túg C.* to the brim. — *ka-tóg-la* or **-na,** = *ká-la*, **above, upon,** on the top or surface of, *ka-tóg-tu* id.; *ka-tóg-nas* down from. — *ka-tór Sch.* pustules in the mouth. — *ka-dig, ka-ldig-mkan W.* **stammerer.** — *ka-dóg*, also *ka* (v. *ka* IV. 4.) **colour** *skra mton-mtiṅ-gi ka-dóg-tu gyúr-to* the hair became blue *Dzl.*; *ka sgyur-ba* to change colour, *ka ₒgyur* the colour changes, cf. also *mdog*. — *ka-drág* 1. **mighty.** 2 **haughty.** — *ka-draṅ W.* **over-against, just before, opposite, straight on.** — *ka-šdáms*, = *ká-ta, γdáms-ka*, **advice** *W.* — *ka-ₒdúr*

Cs.: 'one who speaks too fast', *Sch.*: 'too loud'. — *ḱa-₀dig* **cork, bung, stopple.** — *ḱa-nan* **yesterday morning** *C.* — *ḱá-nar-čan* **oblong.** — *ḱa-nin* **last year.** — *ḱá-po* sometimes f. *ḱa* 1. **mouth,** e.g. **ḱá-po dúl-mo** *W.*, **ḱá dúl-po C.*, tractable. 2. **speech** *Mil.* 3. **bitter** *C.* — *ḱá-lpágs* **lip,** *gón-ma* upper, *₀óg-ma* lower lip; *W.*: *ḱál-pag (s) pág-če, dáb-če** to smack. — *ḱá-spu* hair of the beard, *skra dan ḱá-spu* hair of the head and beard, frq. — *ḱá-ṕó* **boasting,** *ḱa-ṕo-čé* id. — *ḱa-pór* = *ṕór-pa,* **a cup.** — *ḱa-ṕyis* **napkin.** — *ḱá-ba* v. below. — *ḱa-bád* the humidity of the air or the moisture of the earth caused by snow. — *ḱa-búb* mouth or face being turned downwards. — *ḱa-brág* v. below. — *ḱa-rbád Cs.*: 'a boast, proud speech'; others: idle talk. — *ḱa-sbyán* **eloquence** *Mil.*, *ḱa-sbyán-po* eloquent, cf. *ḱa-yčán?* — *ḱa-ma-čár* **sleet,** rain and snow. — *ḱa-múr* bit (bridle) *Sch* — *ḱa-rtsán, ḱa-sán* 1. *B. C.* **yesterday forenoon,** *ḱa-rtsán-gi ľyis-pa* the boy that was here yesterday forenoon *Mil.* 2. ***W.*** (**kar-sán**) **the day before yesterday;** some days ago; **kar-sán za-nyi-ma** last sunday: **ḱar-sán (s)tón-ka** last autumn. — *ḱa-ťsa* 1. **bitter and acrid** *Med.* 2. **'hot in the mouth'** *a.* a very acrid sort of radish, e.g. horse-radish. *b.* aphthae, thrush, a disease of the mouth, incident to horses, cows, sheep. *c. ḱa-ťsá rin-ne-ba Mil. nt.* daily warm food. — *ḱa-ťsúb* **snow-storm.** — *ḱa-ťsó* **boasting,** *ḱa-ťsó šin-tu čé-ba* a great swaggerer *Glr.* — *ḱa-ťsón* v. below. — *ḱa-mťsúl* **muzzle, mouth** (of a dog etc.); the lower part of the human face col. — *ḱa-₀ťsóg* abuse? **ḱa-ťsóg čém-po** *C.* a great abuser, reviler. — *ḱa-žán* the contrary of *ḱa-drág,* low, unimportant, having no authority, *ḱa-žán-pai sdug-bsnál* the misfortune of being of low birth *Mil.* — *ḱa-žé* 1. 'mouth and mind', *ḱa-žé mi mťsúns-pa* **hypocrisy, hypocrite** *C.* 2. 'mouth-mind', meaning the same as the phrase just mentioned: **hypocrisy** *Mil.*, *ḱa-že-méd-pa* unfeigned, sincere *Mil.* — *ḱa-žén* **breadth, expanse,** e.g. of the heavens *Mil.* — *ḱa-zás* **food, victuals** *B. C.* — *ḱá-ya* lit.: 'being one's partner or match **as** to speaking', also *ḱai ya,* — gen.: **partner; match;** **ḱá-ya ǰhé'-pa** *C.* to assist, **ḱo ḱe ya** (or **ḱa-ya) ne mi ťub** I am not his match, not able to compete with him; with regard to things: I am not equal to the task. — *ḱa-ras* **neck-cloth,** cf. *ḱa-dkri.* — *ḱá-ru-ťsa* **alum** *Med.* — *ḱa-rúd* **snow-slip, avalanche,** — *ḱa-ró* taste in the mouth. — *ḱa rog* v. *ḱa* IV. 1. extr. — *ḱa-lán* 'mouth-requital' 1. **thanks-giving** *Mil.* 2. **reply,** esp. angry reply. — 3. **requital** for food received *C.* — *ḱa-leb* **cover, lid.** — *ḱá-lo* 1. 'mouth leaves', *snoi ḱá-lo Mil.* the young, tender leaves of several wild herbs, used as vegetables. 2. v. below. — *ḱa-šá* 1. v. *ḱa-skyúr-po.* — *ḱá-šá šá-ba S.g.*, 'snow-deer', **elk** *Sch.*; shoe-leather from the skin of this animal is mentioned in *Mil.*, and is known in Tibet. In *Sik.* however **the deer** of the neighbouring Tarai is called *ḱa-ša,* in other parts of the country **the spotted deer,** — *ḱa-šágs* **jest, joke,** **ḱa-šág ťáb-če, tán-če** *W.* to jest. — *ḱa-šúgs-čan, -šéd-čan W.* **eloquent.** — *ḱa-šés Cs.* **some.** — *ḱa-šób* col. **lies, falsehoods; obscene talk; idle talk.** *ḱa-bšád* **talk, gossip** *Mil.* — *ḱa-sán* v. *ḱa-rtsán.* — *ḱa-sin* several weeks ago *Cs.* — *ḱa-só* mouth and teeth; similar: *ḱa-mgál* mouth and jawbone, **ḱá-só** or **ḱa-gál čag yin** I shall break your chops *W.* — *ḱá-sró? Ld.* **ḱa-šró lám-če** to fry (meat) in butter. — *ḱa-slób,* = *ḱa-tón,* learnt by heart, (used by children) *W.* — *ḱa-lhág* remnant of a meal *Mil.*

ཁྭ *ḱa (ḱwa?)* v. *ḱwa-ta.*

ཁ་ག་པོ *ḱá-ga-po Sch.*: difficult (?).

ཁ་ཆུལ *ḱa-čúl W.* col. for *ḱa-če-yul,* **Cashmere.**

ཁ་ཆེ *ḱa-čé* **Cashmere;** amongst other things it produces much saffron, hence *ḱa-če-skyes* **saffron;** in Cashmere Buddhism was once flourishing (v. the legend relative to its being introduced there: Introduction du Buddhisme dans le Kashmir par L. Feer Paris 1866), but afterwards it came under Mahometan rulers, and *ḱa-čé* denotes therefore now in *C.* a mussulman (cf. Huc & Gabet's journey); *ḱa-čéi dpé-ča* the koran *Schr.*; *ḱa-čéi ͦgrón-ḱaṅ* an inn kept by a mussulman *Mil.*

ཁ་ཏ་ *ḱá-ta (ḱva-ta?) Ssk.* 1. **crow.** — 2. **raven,** = *bya-róg, ṕo-róg.* — 3. *ḱa-ta ḱrá-bo* **magpie.**

ཁ་ཏོ་ཤིང་ *ḱá-to-šiṅ* is said to be = *γsál-šiṅ*, a pointed stake used for the execution of criminals.

ཁ་ཏྭཾ་ག་ *ḱa-tváṅ-ga, ḱa-ṭv.*, gen. pronounced *ḱa-tóm-ga Ssk., Will.*: 'a club or staff with a skull at the top', the weapon of Siva, also carried by ascetics; Tibetans refer it also to the trident.

ཁ་བཏགས་ *ḱa-btágs* **handkerchief** or **scarf of salutation,** a piece of veil-like and generally worthless silk-fabric, about as large as a small pocket-handkerchief, which in Tibet is given or sent, with or without other presents, to the person one intends to visit; cf. Huc's journey.

ཁ་འདའ་ *ḱa-ͦdá,* v. *ḱan-da.*

ཁ་བ་ *ḱá-ba* I. col. *C.* **ḱá-po*, W. *ḱán-te*, Bal. *χo** **bitter.** — II. *W.* **ḱa** **snow,** *ḱá-ba duṅ ltar γsal* bright as snow and shells *Pth.*; *ḱá-ba ͦbab,* col. **ḱa yoṅ** it snows; **ḱa páṅ-ċe* W.* to remove the snow (with a shovel); *ḱá-ba-čan* snowy, and as a subst.: the snow-country, Tibet; *ḱá-ba-čan-pai séms-čan-rnams* the Tibetan beings *Glr.* — III. correspondently to the Arabian word قهوة the missionaries in *Lh.* have given to *ḱa-ba* the signification of **coffee,** which is otherwise unknown in Tibet.

ཁ་བད་ *ḱa-bád* 1. the architectural ornament of a Tibetan house formed by the projecting ends of the beams which support the roof (not 'parapet' *Cs.*) — 2. v. *ka.*

ཁ་བྲག་ *ḱa-brág* **fork** (not generally used in eating); any forked object.

ཁ་མོ་ *ḱá-mo Cs.* **enchantment, irresistible influence.**

ཁ་ཚར་ *ḱa-tsár* **fringes, threads,** such as the loose threads at the end of a web.

ཁ་ཚོན་ *ḱa-tsón Sch.* decision; but in the only passage where I met with this word, viz. *Dzl.* ༢༥༧ 13, this meaning is not applicable, but something like surface or width.

ཁ་ཞུར་ *ḱa-žúr Sch.* **water-hen.**

ཁ་ཟུར་ *ḱa-zúr (Ssk.* खर्जूर, *Hindi* खजूर) col. *ḱa-zúr-pa-ni* **date,** *ḱa-zur šiṅ* date-tree.

ཁ་གཟེ་ *ḱa-γzé* 1. *W.*: **rake** (gardening). — 2. *Sp.*: a carrier's **load,** **ḱa-zé-pa** a cooly.

ཁ་ཡོག་ *ḱa-yóg* **a false charge,** *C.*: **ma nyé-pẹ ḱa-yóg ǰhuṅ** he was innocently accused.

ཁ་ར་ *ḱá-ra* 1. *W.* f *ḱá-ra* **sugar.** — 2. *Sch.*: **trough, manger.**

ཁ་རི་ *ḱa-ri,* or *ḱa-rú,* v. *ḱál-ri.*

ཁ་རོག་ *ḱa-rog,* v. *ḱa rog-pa, ḱa* IV. 1. towards the end.

ཁ་ལེ་ *ḱá-le* v. *ḱyá-le.*

ཁ་ལོ་ *ḱá-lo* 1. v. *ḱa* Comp. — 2. *Schr.* **prow** of a ship, others: **helm;** the word is very often used in the phrase: *ḱa-lo sgyur-ba,* esp. *gru-γziṅs-kyi,* to turn a ship, to steer, to lead, govern, rule, *ḱa-lo sgyur-mḱas-pa* skilful in driving, *ḱa-lo-ṕa* a charioteer. — 3. *Cs.*: the glans penis.

ཁ་ཤྱ་ *ḱa-šya* n. of a mountainous country in the N.E. of India *Tar.* 21. 10.

ཁ་སུར་ *ḱa-súr* v. *ḱa-zur.*

ཁག་ *ḱag* 1. **a task; charge, business, duty; responsibility; importance;** *ḱag ͦḱúr-ba* to be charged with, *ḱág ͦgél-ba* to lay upon; **kag ťég-pa** or **kyág-pa* C.* to warrant, become responsible; *dér ͦtsó-ba yóṅ-ba kag ťeg* I warrant you will get something to eat there *Mil.*; **ḱag -ťég, ḱag-ḱyág* C.* a bail; *ḱág-čan* important. — 2. *W.*: **part,** *bču-ḱág* the tenth part, tithe, **ḱag-nyi čo-té čád-če** to cut in two; **division, section** (of a book); **place,** **ḱág nyi-la ṕog soṅ** I have hurt myself in two places; **ḱag čig-la rúb-če** to press towards one point; in a more general sense: **ḱag čig-la 'i* *sás-ka čos** finish this work at once! — *yul-ḱág* **province, district**; *rgyal-ḱág* **kingdom.** — 3. *W.*: **ḱag** or **ḱág-ga tág-če** **to hang** (by the neck)

ཁག་པོ *ḱág po C.* 1. **difficult** (*W.* **ḱág(s)-po**); **hard** (to bear), **ḱág-po ǰhuṅ** it proved hard, **ḱág-po ǰhē-pa** to suffer want. — 2. **bad, spoiled, rotten,** **mar ḱág-po soṅ** the butter has become rancid.

ཁག་ལ (?) *ḱág-la, Md.*: **ḱág-la mar** **fresh** butter, just made.

ཁང་ *ḱaṅ C.*: vulg. f. *ḱoṅ*, sometimes also in books.

ཁང་པ *ḱáṅ-pa* **house,** *ḱáṅ-pa-la W.* home, at home; in compounds also for a part of the house: **room, story, floor** etc., *steṅ-, bár-, ˳óg-ḱaṅ* upper story, middle story, ground-floor *Glr.*; *bár-ma, dkyil-ma* or *ǰzúṅ-ḱaṅ* means also the usual dwelling-room, opp. to *ǰugs* and *sgo* (v. *sgo*): *bzó-ḱáṅ* **workshop;** *báṅ-ḱaṅ* **store-house, store-room;** *sgó-ḱaṅ* **entrance, vestibule;** *skór-ḱaṅ* (*Glr.* 68, 9) seems to be a passage running round a building; **šóg-ḱaṅ** *W.* the scooping-form or **mould** used in the manufacture of paper; **ʦ́sás-ḱaṅ** **bed** (garden).

ḱaṅ-glá **house-rent.** — *ḱaṅ-čúṅ* house or room reserved for decrepit parents; *ḱaṅ-čúṅ-pa* inhabitant of such; *yaṅ-ḱaṅ-čúṅ-pa* such a person of the second degree, (if, during his life, his son enters into the same right). — *ḱaṅ-stóṅ* **an empty house,** which is thought a fit place for sorcery and necromancy. — *ḱáṅ-bu* 1. little house, **cottage.** 2. **room,** *mya-ṅán-gyi ḱ.* room of mourning *Dzl.* — *ḱaṅ-mig* **room.** — *ḱaṅ-rtsá* **foundation of a house** *Sch.* — *ḱaṅ-žábs* **flooring** of a room. — *ḱaṅ-bzáṅs* **residence,** chiefly of gods. — *kaṅ-rúl Sch.* **a house in ruins.**

ཁང་བུ *ḱáṅ-bu Pth.* n. of a (fabulous) country.

ཁད་ *ḱad* 1. **litter, barrow.** — 2. **like, as,** = *ltar Glr.* — 3. = *ḱod, ḱad-snyáms* v. *˳ḱod-snyóms.*

ཁད་པ *ḱad-pa.* 1. the same as *˳ḱód-pa* **to stick fast, to be seized, stopped, impeded,** v. *˳ḱad-pa*; hence also *ma-ḱád* = *ma-ʦ́ág* **as soon as:** *dbugs čad ma-ḱád-du* as soon as the breathing ceases *Thgr.*; **de ma-ḱád** instantly, directly, *bu skyes-ma-ḱád čig Glr.* a child born **just now.** — 2. **to approach, draw near,** with *la*, *núb-la ḱád-pai ʦ́e* when the evening drew near *Pth.*; frq. with the perfect-root of a verb: *dbugs čád-la ḱád-pai dus* when the ceasing of the breath approaches *Thgr.*; *zin-la ḱad yód-pa-la* as we were just about to seize him; *ḱád-du* postpos. c.a.: *rtíṅ-pa ḱád-du* **as far as** the heel *Mil.*; *ḱád-kyis* adv. **by degrees** *Mil.*; *ḱád-la, ḱád-du* id. *Tar.*

ཁན་པ *ḱán-pa*, also *ḱén-pa* 1. sbst. *Schr.*: wormwood, probably a mistake for *ḱám-pa.* — 2. vb. **to add** (arithm.) *Wdk.*

ཁན་ད *ḱán-da*, more correctly *ḱáṇ-ḍa*, also spelled *ḱá-˳dá, Ssk*, treacle or molasses partially dried, **candy;** *dé-la ḱán-da bčos-pa* the candy made of it *Med.*; *skyér-ḱan-da* candied *skyer-pa.*

ཁན་མན *ḱan-maṅ* (corrupted from *ḱa-dmaṅ?*) **modest** *Lh.*

ཁབ་ *ḱab* 1. **court, residence** of a prince, *rgyál-poi ḱáb-kyi mi-rnams* courtiers. — 2. **wife, spouse,** *ḱab čén-ma* the first wife (in rank); *dé-la ḱab ˳ós-pa ma rnyéd-nas* as there was not found a wife worthy of him *Glr.*; *˳di ǰnyis ṅai ḱáb-tu byúṅ-ba rmis-so* I dreamt that these two would become my wives *Glr.*; *ḱáb-tu bžés-pa* to take for a wife, to marry. (*Schr.* has even a verb: *čúṅ-mar ḱáb-pa.*) — 3. **needle,** *ḱab-rtse* point of a needle, *kab-rúl*(?) *Sch.* needle-case, *ḱab-mig* eye of a needle, *ḱáb-mig-tu skúd-pa ˳ǰúg-pa* or *rgyúd-pa* to thread a needle; *ṗra-ḱáb* a small needle, *sbom-ḱáb, mo-ḱáb Dzl.*, *ʦ́a ḱáb W.*, *blo-ḱáb W.*, *ḱab-rúl W.* a large, thick needle, packing-needle; *ḱab-spú* **bristle** *Sik.*; *ḱab-lén (rdo)* **loadstone, magnet.**

ཁབ་ཏ་ཀ *ḱab-tá-ka* col. **knapsack, pouch.**

ཁབ་ལེ *ḱáb-le* (or *las?*) *W.* **difficult.**

ཁབས *ḱabs* n. of a disease *Med.*

ཁམ་ *ḱam* 1. **a bit**, a small piece of anything, *ḱam-čuṅ* a small bit, *ḱam-gáṅ*, *ḱam γčig* a mouthful, *ḱam-tsád-du γčód-pa* to cut 'in the size of bits' *Dzl.* (infernal punishment); *ḱam-zán* a mouthful of food *Mil.*; *zas ḱam γčig* id. — 3. *W.*, *C.* **appetite**, **zá-če-la ḱam yoṅ** *W.* I get an appetite for eating; **ḱam dig soṅ** *W.* I have no appetite; *ḱam-lóg* want of appetite, **nausea**, aversion (*Cs.* also: hatred); **ḱam-lóg-pa** inclined to nausea, easily sickened *C.*; **ḱam-lóg-ḱaṅ** *W.* id.; **ḱam-ḱám čo dug, nyíṅ ḱam-ḱám čo dug** (with *la*) *W.* he has a desire, a longing for, perh. only provincial pronunciation for *rkám-pa*.

ཁམ་ཁུམ་ *ḱam-ḱúm* high and low *Schr.* (?)

ཁམ་དར་ *ḱam-dár* **walnut** *Sch.*

ཁམ་པ་ *ḱám-pa* 1. **fox-coloured, sorrel, brownish.** — **2. porcelain-clay, china-clay.** — 3. **Tanacetum tomentosum**, a very aromatic plant, frequent on high mountains.

ཁམ་ཕོར་ *ḱam-ṕór* a cup made of dough, used as a lamp in sacrificing.

ཁམ་བིར་ *ḱam-bír* (perh the *Ar.-Hd.* خمیر leaven) thick bread-cakes leavened with butter-milk *Ld.*

ཁམ་བུ་ *ḱám-bu* 1. **apricot** *B.*, *C.*, *ḱám-bui tsí-gu* the stone of an apricot; *ḱam-bu-már* the oil pressed out of apricot-stones, smelling and tasting of bitter almonds *Med.*; *mṅa-ris kám-bu* dried apricots, v. *ṕá-tiṅ*. — 2. **peach** *Sik.* — 3. v. *ḱam*.

ཁམ་གཡག་ *ḱam-γyág Sch.* cherries, morels; these not being known in Tibet, the word must be either of Khotan or Chinese origin, or else the signification of 'stones of apricots' is to be adopted, as given in *Wts.*

ཁམས་ *ḱams* (*Ssk.* धातु) 1. physical constitution of the body, **state of health**, *ḱams bdé ba* healthy constitution, good health; *rje-btsún-gyi ḱams bde lágs-sam?* is your Reverence well? asks a layman, and the Lama answers: *ṅa šin-tu bde; ḱyed ḱams bde-am?* I am quite well; are you well? *Mil.*; *W.* more frq.: **ḱam-záṅ-po**, *C.* also *ḱam sáṅ* good **health**; *ḱams-rmyá Med.*, acc. to *Cs.* **nausea**, feeling sick; *ḱams-sós Sch.*: rest, comfort, health, prob. more accurately: recreation, recovery, restoration (of health), so: *ḱams sós-par gyur Mil.*; sometimes it seems to be a synonym of *lus*, body, *ḱams dúb-pa bsóṅ-ba* to recreate the exhausted body *Mil.nt.* fig.: *γnod-sems-méd-pai ḱams šas če* the peaceable disposition predominates *Stg.* — 2. (synon. of *yul*) **empire, realm, territory, domain;** *yul-ḱáms* empire, in a geographical and political sense, e.g. Nepaul *Glr.*; *rgyal-ḱáms* 1. for *rgyál-poi ḱams* kingdom, *ḱa-ba-čan-gyi rgyal-ḱáms* the kingdom of Tibet. 2. for *rgyál-bai ḱams* the empire of Buddha, the world; *rgyal-ḱáms ˳grim-pa* to roam over the kingdoms, the countries *Mil.*; **region, dominion,** *bar-snáṅ-gyi ḱams* the aërial regions, where the *lha* live *Pth.*; in physiology: *mḱris-pai ḱams* the dominion of bile *Med.*; *ḱams γsum* the three worlds acc. to Buddhistic speculation, viz. the earth with the six heavens of the gods, as the 'region of desire', *˳dód-pai ḱams*; above this is the 'region of form', *γzúgs-kyi ḱams*, and ultimately follows the 'region of formlessness', *γzugs-med-pai ḱams*. — 3. **element** (syn. *˳byúṅ-ba*), *ḱams drug* the six elements of some philosophical systems, consisting, besides the four elements familiar to us, also of *nám-mḱa* and *rnam-šés*, the ether and the substance of the mind. In chronology, in naming the single years of the cycle, five elements are assumed, which (according to Chinese theory) are wood, fire, earth, iron, water. — 4. p.n. **Khams**, Great Tibet, the parts between Ü and China; *smad-mdo-ḱams-sgáṅ γsum* the low-land, the three provinces Do, Kham, and Gong, cf. *mṅa-ris*; *ḱáms-pa* a man from Khams.

ཁར་སྟང་ *ḱar-rstáṅ* v. *ḱá-rtsáṅ*.

ཁར་གོང་ *ḱar-góṅ* **steatite, soapstone**, *Sch.* prob. = *dkar-goṅ*.

ཁར་རྐྱང་ *Ḱar-rkyaṅ* v. *Ḱa-rkyaṅ*.

ཁར་རྩང་ *Ḱar-rtsaṅ* v. *Ḱa-rtsaṅ*.

ཁརྶ་པ་ཎི་ or ཁ་སར་པ་ན་ *Ḱarsa-pa-ni* or *Ḱa-sar-pa-na* n. of a deity *Glr.*; *Tar.* p. 110 gives a (rather absurd) legend concerning the origin of the name.

ཁལ་ *Ḱal* 1. (cf. *sgal*) **burden, load,** *Ḱal ḱyér-ba* to carry a burden; *Ḱál-gyi stéṅ-du* on the top of the luggage *Glr.*; *Ḱal gyél-ba* to load a burden, to put a load upon, *Ḱal bógs-pa* to take off the burden, to unload; **load, freight;** as a fixed quantity, *lúg-Ḱal* a sheep-load, *bóṅ-Ḱal* load of an ass; *brui Ḱal* a load of corn. — 2. **bushel,** a dry measure = 20 bre; therefore = a score or 20 things of the same kind; in *W.* **Ḱal-ċig* frq. for *nyi-śu*, also with respect to persons; *gźór-Ḱal* a 'measuring-score', 20 *bre*, actually measured, as is usual with corn; *dégs-Ḱal* a 'weighing-score', the weight of 20 points on the steel-yard *(rgya-ma)*, in weighing wood, hay, butter etc.

ཁལ་ཁ་ *Ḱál-Ḱa* n. of a Mongol tribe, Khal-ka.

ཁལ་ཁོལ་ *Ḱal-Ḱól* **stunned, insensible** *Thgy.*

ཁལ་ཅག་ *Ḱal-ċág* the best sort of wool for manufacturing shawls, coming **from** Jang-thang.

ཁལ་པ་ *Ḱál-pa* 1. **wether,** castrated ram. — 2. **sow-thistle,** Sonchus.

ཁལ་མ་ *Ḱál-ma* **beast of burden, sumpter-mule** *B.*, *C.* *Ḱál-ma-rnams bzán-la skyél-ba* to drive beasts of burden to the pasture, to turn them on grass-land *Glr.*; *Schr.*; **mi Ḱal nyis-kyi la** *C.* payment for carriers and beasts of burden; though in *W.* it might be understood as: payment for twice twenty men.

ཁལ་རི་, ཁལ་རུ་ *Ḱal-ri*, *Ḱal-rú*, also *Ḱa-ri*, *Ḱa-rú* twenty bushels.

ཁས་ *Ḱas* instr. of *Ḱa*; *Ḱas-lén-pa* etc. v. *Ḱa*, 4; *kas-skóṅ* = *Ḱá-skóṅ*, q.v.; *kas-stóṅ* with an empty stomach; *Ḱas-dmán*, *kas-žán*, **weak, poor.**

ཁི་ *Ḱi* numerical figure: 32.

ཁིའུ་ *Ḱiu* *C.*: **Ḱyiu** **a cutting-out knife.**

ཁུ *Ḱu* 1. numerical figure: 62. — 2. for *Ḱú-lu* (?) *Lil.*

ཁུ་གུ་ *Ḱú-gu* *Cs.* '1. uncle. 2. an address'(?)

ཁུ་ཏུ་ *Ḱú-tu* **a hut, cottage,** constructed of branches *Lh.*

ཁུ་ནུ་ *Ḱú-nu* p. n. **Kunawar,** also Bissáhar, country on the upper Sutledj, bordering on Tibet, and inhabited in the northern part by Tibetans. Here are situated Kanám, a monastery with a considerable collection of Tibetan books, and Poo, a missionary station of the Church of the United Brethren, founded 1865.

ཁུ་བ་ *Ḱú-ba* 1. **fluid, liquid,** also (but less frq.) *Ḱu-ċú*; *lhuṅ-bzéd bkrús-pai Ḱú-ba*, the fluid in which a beggar's bowl has been washed *Tar.*; *Ḱrús-Ḱu* dish-wash, swill *Tar.*; *brás-Ḱu* *Cs.*: rice-soup, *Schr.*: rice-water; *śiṅ-Ḱu*, *rtsá-Ḱu* the sap of trees, of plants *Cs.*; *śá-Ḱu* broth, gravy; *már-Ḱu* melted butter. — 2. **semen virile,** *Ḱu-ba byin-pa* emittere semen; *Ḱu-Ḱrág* the mixture of the semen with the uterine blood, by which process, acc. to Indian physiology, the fetus is formed, *Med.*, *Ssk.* संक्लेद.

ཁུ་བོ་ *Ḱú-bo* **uncle,** on the father's side *B.* and *C.*; *ṕa-Ḱú* father and uncle; *Ḱu-dbóṅ* and *Ḱu-tsán* uncle and nephew. But owing to polyandry, the degrees of kindred lose their precision, in as far as all the brothers that have become the husbands of one wife may be called 'father' by the children.

ཁུ་བྱུག་ *Ḱu-byúg* *B.*, also *Ḱu-gyúg* and *yug.* **cuckoo,** called *byá-yi rgyál-po* and described as a sweetly singing bird, whence prob. *Cs.* has conjectured nightingale, which however is scarcely known in Tibet. — *Ḱu-byug-rtsá* n. of a medicinal herb.

ཁུ་མག་ *Ḱu-mág* *Lh.* purse, money-bag, col. for *Ḱug-ma.*

ཁུ་ཚུར་ *Ḱu-tsúr* *Cs.* the clinched hand, **fist,** *Ḱu-tsúr snún-pa* (*Sch.* also *rgyáb-pa*) to strike with the fist. This signification, however, seemed not to be known to the Lamas consulted, who interpreted the word: a religious gesture, the forefinger being raised, and the others drawn back. Some native dictionaries have मुष्टि fist, others खटक half-closed fist.

ཁུ་ཡུ་ *Ḱu-yú*, in *C.* also **'a-yú**, **hornless,** having no horns, used of cattle *Sch.*

ཁུ་ལུ་ *Ḱú-lu* 1. the short woolly hair of the yak. — 2. *Lh.*: venereal disease, **syphilis.**

ཁུ་ལེ་ *Ḱú-le Sch.*: **steel-yard** and its weight; but *Dzl.* ༢༧, 17 the word refers to an ordinary pair of scales and denotes that **scale** of the two which contains the weights.

ཁུག་, ཁུགས་ *Ḱug*, *Ḱugs* **corner,** concave angle, **nook;** of rivers, lakes etc.: **creek, bay, gulf, cove,** also *ču-ḱúg*; *Ḱúg-tu* within a recess, on the farther side of a cavity.

ཁུག་ཏ་ *Ḱúg-ta* (or *rta*), *a-li-ḱúg-ta*, a kind of **swallow** *Cs.*; the lights (lungs) of this bird are used as a remedy against pulmonary diseases, *Med.*

ཁུག་རྣ་ *Ḱug-rná* and *Ḱug-sná* **fog, mist, haze,** during a calm, esp. in spring-time.

ཁུག་པ་ *Ḱúg-pa* I sbst. 1. *Cs.*: "part of a long period of time" (?) — 2. a certain part of the body *Med.* — II. vb. 1. also *Ḱúgs-pa*, **to call** = *gúg-pa Mil.* (cf. also *γyaṅ*). — 2. **to find; get, earn;** *nor Ḱúgs-pa-aṅ srid* there is a possibility that we may yet replenish our cash *Mil. nt.*; *γnyid Ḱúgs-pa* to get sleep; *sraṅ γsum Ḱugs*, it drew i.e. weighed three ounces.

ཁུག་མ་ *Ḱúg-ma* **pouch,** little bag, *me-lčags-kug-ma* tinder-pouch *Mil.*; *dṅúl-Ḱug* money-bag, purse; **rdzóṅ-Ḱug* Pur.* knapsack; *rtsám-Ḱug*, resp. *žíb-Ḱug*, little bag for flour; *nú-Ḱug* sucking-bag, for babies.

ཁུང་ *Ḱuṅ* **hole, pit, hollow, cavity,** originally used only of dark holes and cavities; *sna-Ḱúṅ* nostril, *rna-Ḱúṅ* the ear-hole, *mčan-Ḱúṅ* arm-hole, arm-pit; *brag-Ḱúṅ* cleft in a rock, cavern; *byi-Ḱúṅ* mouse-hole; *čab-Ḱúṅ* a sink; *bso-Ḱúṅ* peep-hole; *mda-Ḱúṅ* loop-hole; in *C.* **'i-Ḱúṅ, mig-Ḱúṅ, te-Ḱúṅ** are used of any hole in walls, clothes etc., caused by decay or daily wear. *γtor-Ḱúṅ* a sink, gutter; *Ḱúṅ-dregs* soot of an oven or chimney *Sch.*; *Ḱúṅ-pa*, *Ḱúṅ-po Cs.* a large hole, *Ḱúṅ-bu* a small hole, e.g. *spui Ḱúṅ-bu* pore, passage of perspiration *Dzl.*

ཁུངས་ *Ḱuṅs* 1. the original meaning perh. is **mine, pit** *Cs.* — 2. **origin, source** (fig.), *γyoi Ḱuṅs snubs*, he stopped the source of the deceit *Ld.-Glr. Schl.* 13, b. *Ḱúṅs-čan*, and prob. of similar meaning *Ḱuṅs-btsún*, of noble descent, or when applied to statements etc.: well founded; *Cs.* also fine, excellent; *Ḱuṅs-méd*, *Ḱuṅs ṅán-pa* having no 'origin', mean, pitiful, ill founded; in the last sense it seems to be used of historical accounts, *Tar.* 43, 5, and more esp. of religious records *Pth.*, *Glr.*; *γtam-Ḱúṅs Tar.* 66, 18, prob.: historical source, record, document; in *Pth.* facetiously: *γtam-Ḱúṅs čaṅ yin* the source of that speech is beer.

ཁུད་ *Ḱud* **coat-lap,** or any cloth serving in an emergency as a vessel; **Ḱu' ze'** hold forth the lap of your coat, words frequently used to beggars, to whom the alms, chiefly consisting in flour, are poured into that receptacle, *C.*

ཁུད་པ་ *Ḱúd-pa* **pocket, pouch** *Sch.*

ཁུད་མ་ *Ḱúd-ma* **side, edge** *Cs.*; *Ḱúd-du* aside, apart, secretly; *Ḱúd-du ǰog-pa* to put, to lay aside.

ཁུན་ཏི་ *Ḱún-ti*, or **Ḱyen-ti**, is stated to be used in *Pur.* for **he, she.**

ཁུན་པ་ *Ḱún-pa* **to grunt** (*Sch.*: to groan).

ཁུན་བུ་ *Ḱún-bu Glr.* 97, 12?

ཁུམ(ས)་ *Ḱum(s)* v. *gum-pa*; *Ḱúms-pa*, **crooked.**

ཁུམས་ *Ḱums Sch.*: so it is said; *Mil.*: *ló-tstsa-bai snyáṅ-pa rgyáṅ-nas kums* might be rendered: the interpreter's renown was proclaimed from afar; the word, however, is of rare occurrence.

ཁུར་ *Ḱur* 1. **burden, load,** for men, more fully: *mi-Ḱur*; *Ḱúr-skyed-pas* *tsó-ba žig* one that lives by carrying loads *Tar.* — 2. rarely **porter**, carrier of a load; *kúr-po* **load, burden**; *kúr-bu*, col. **kúr-ru** prop. a small load; a load in general; *kúr-pá* carrier, cooly; *kur-rtsá, kur-lám* cooly-station, a day's journey, gen. 10 to 12 English miles; *kur-rtsá-pa* a station-cooly.

ཁུར་བ་, འཁུར་བ་ *kúr-ba, ˏkúr-ba* 1. sbst. *Cs.*: **bread, food,** *Sch.* also forage, fodder. It is, however, not the common word for bread, but only for certain sorts, such as *bra-kúr*, bread of buckwheat, *rtsabs-kúr* q v., and more particularly it is applied to cakes and pastry-work baked in fat or oil. — 2. vb. v. *ˏkúr-ba.*

ཁུར་མ་, ཁུར་མང་(ས)་ *kúr-ma, kur-máṅ(s)* **dandelion** *C.*, used as a pot-herb and medicinal plant; as the former it is also called *kur-tsód.*

ཁུར་ཚོས་ *kur-tsós C.* and *B.* **cheek,** the ruddy part of the face below the eyes (cf. *ˏgrám-pa*); **kur-tsóg W.*

ཁུལ་ *kul* 1. *Sch.*: "the soft **down** of furs", abbreviation of *kú-lu; kul-mal* small basket for wool *Ts.* — 2. **ravine** *Kun.* — 3. **district, province, domain;** *lhá-sa kul* all that belongs to Lhasa *Georgi Alph.*; **dei kul-la ˏdug** is subject to him *C.*

ཁུལ་མ་ *kúl-ma* the bottom, or the side of a thing *Cs.*

ཁེ་ *ke* numeral, ninety-two, 92.

ཁེ་, ཁྱེ་ *ke, kye (Sch.: ke-ma)* 1. **profit, gain;** *ke-spógs B.* and *C.*, **ke-béd* W.* id.; *ke-tsóṅ byéd-pa* **to trade,** to traffic *Pth.*; *šés-kyi ke* gain, advantage obtained by knowledge and attainments; *ke-pa* **tradesman,** dealer; *tsóṅ-ˏdus ké-pa* trader in a market *Mil.*; *ke-nyén Sch.*; profit and loss, risk; *ke-sgrúb-pa Cs.*, **kye-béd tób-če* W.*, to make profit, to gain, *ke brgyáb-pa*, to make a good bargain *Sch.*; **ke-ru ˏdo-wa* C.* to abate, to go down in price; **ké-čan, ke-mé**, profitable, unprofitable; **kyé-mo* W.* **cheap.** — 2. **tetter, herpes, ringworm** (eruption of the skin) *Sch.*

ཁེགས་ *kegs* v. *kegs.*

ཁེངས་པ་ *kéṅs-pa* 1. partic. of *ˏkéṅs-pa*, filled, replete with. — 2. adj. puffed up, **proud, haughty,** arrogant; sbst. pride etc.; *keṅs-séms, keṅs-drégs* pride. *keṅs-po Med.* with reference to food: producing flatulence.

ཁེན་པ་ *kén-pa* 1. *Schr.* worm-wood, prob. erron. for *kám-pa.* — 2. *Sch.*: to lean, to repose on, erron. for *bkán-pa.*

ཁེབས་ *kebs*, col., *W.*: **kyebs**, *Cs.*: *kébs-ma* **covering,** coverlet: **keb sáṅ-pa**; to take the covering off *C.*; *čár-kebs* a covering against rain, rain-cloak; *stén-kebs, lčóg-kebs*, table-cloth *Cs.*; *tód-kebs Lt.* **cap, hood;** *ydúṅ-kebs*, a certain beam or board above the capital of a pillar; *ydóṅ-kebs*, **veil,** cloth to cover the head; **dúṅ-kyebs* W.* **apron;** **paṅ-kéb* C.* **napkin, apron.**

ཁེམ་ *kem* v. *kyem.*

ཁེར་རྒྱག་པ་ *kér-rgyag-pa*, **to defraud; to usurp** *Sch.*

ཁེལ་བ་ *kél-ba* prob. for *ˏkél-ba*, **to load** upon; *blo kél-ba* is said to be used in *C.* for *blo skyél-ba W.*, v. *skyél-ba* no. 6.

ཁེས་ཉེན་ *kes-nyén* the day before yesterday *Sch.*

ཁེས་པ་ *kés-pa C.* **to hit,** *ˏtsáms-la* (or *mtsáms-la?*) to hit the right thing, the exact point or line; *ynád-la* to strike the vital parts, to hit mortally, fatally.

ཁོ་ *ko* 1. numeral, 122. — 2. *Bal.* (**χ'o**) for *ka-ba*, bitter.

ཁོ་ *ko* pers. pron. of the third person, **he, she, it,** but almost exclusively in col. language. In ancient writings it occurs but rarely, being either omitted or supplied by *de*, but in later works that come nearer to the present language, it is to be found the more frequently. *koi* his, her; **kó-pa, kó-wa** plur. **they,** *W.* and *C.*, v. *Georgi Alph.*, in an edict; **kó-čag, kó-tso** id. *C.*; **kó-wa nyi* W.*, both of them: *ko-ráṅ* 1. he himself. 2. he, = **ko** col.; with partic.: *ko dá-či snon la soṅ-ba de, Mil.*, he that just went on in advance, proceeded in front.

Note. The word prob. has been originally a sbst., denoting essence, substance (like ṅó-bo); má-ko, γži-Ko, rgyú-Ko are said to be used in C. for: the essential, the most important part of a thing, the main point, and the noun substantive may possibly have changed into a substantive pronoun, in a similar manner, as ṅa, I, is connected with ṅó-bo; cf. also Kó-na, Kó-bo.

ཁོ་ཏི Ko-ti C. (Chinese?) **tea-kettle.**

ཁོ་ཐག་གཅོད་པ Ko-ťág γčód-pa c. termin. **to despair of** Mil.; **to resign, to acquiesce in, to reconcile one's self to;** also sems Ko-ťág γčód pa Pth.

ཁོ་ན Kó-na adj. and adv. 1. **just, exactly, the very,** rgyál-pos ˏdod-pa Kó-na yin that is just what has been wished for by the king Dsl. ༡༧. 17. sṅá-ma Kó-na bžin-du just as before; ˳di Kó-na yin-par ṅes he is evidently the very same (man) Mil.; srin-bu Kó-na ˳drá-ba just like a worm Thgy.; ťsul de Kó-nas by the very same process Tar. 13, 12; de Kó-na nyid-du gyur čig just so may it happen! (at the conclusion of a prayer) Glr.; but de-Ko-na-nyid, as a philosophical term, is also the translation of the Ssk. táttva, essentiality, truth, implying to the Buddhist nothing but **vacuity,** the Nirvāna Trig. 20. — 2. **only, solely, exclusively,** skád-čig Kó-na, only for a moment Dzl. ༢༥་༢, 12. ˳dod Kó-nas brél na, if taken up merely with lust: séms-čan Kó-na bdé-bar ˳dód-tsa-na as he intended only the welfare of beings Thgy.; Tar.

ཁོ་བོ Kó-bo mas., Kó-mo fem. pers. pron. 1st. person, I, pl. Kó-bo-čag we, indiscriminately as to the rank of persons, B. and C.; mi Kó-boi rnam-šés the soul of me the man, i.e. my human soul Mil.; also pleon. Kó-bo ṅa.

ཁོ་བོམ Ko-bóm, the Tibetan name for **Khatmandu,** the capital of Nepaul Glr., Mil.; sometimes also called klui po-bráṅ, prob. on account of the mineral treasures supposed to abound in that country.

ཁོ་མ Kó-ma, perh. misprinted for Kom **knapsack, wallet** Mil., or else a secondary form of that word.

ཁོ་གཡུ Ko-γyú, occurs only in *Ko-yú skór-če (perh. col. for ˏKor-γyúl) W. **to thrash,** which is done by driving a number of oxen fastened together round a pole that stands in the middle of the thrashing-floor.

ཁོར Kó-ra, Cs. also Kór-sa, **circumference;** circumjacent space; also **fence,** surrounding **wall;** Kó-ra Kor-yúg-tu, (Kor-) Kor-yúg-tu, in a circle, in circumference, frq. in measuring; also round about, all round, e.g. to flow, to encompass; Kor-yúg kún-tu in the whole circuit, round about.

ཁོ་ལག Ko-lág 1. Cs.: **bigness,** robustness (Lex. पीवरगात्र), Ko-lág-yáṅs-pa big, prominent limbs; Sch.: Ko-lág čé-ba a large space. — 2. Lh.; **dumpling,** made of rtsám-pa and beer; Ld.: **pap** of rtsám-pa and tea, called spags in C.

ཁོག Kog 1. frq. for Koṅ(-pa), **the interior, inside;** v. also Kóg-pa and Kóg-ma. — 2. for Kogs, ˏkogs q.v. — 3. for ˏgégs-pa.

ཁོག་པ Kóg-pa, sometimes Kóg-ma, Kog, the trunk of the body, ša-Kóg the body of an animal cut up for food; *ša-Kóg ḍál-če, šig-ce*. to cut up a carcass; *Kóg-tu, Kog náṇ-du* within the body.

ཁོག་མ Kóg-ma C. **pot,** earthen vessel = pru; Kog-čén large pot.

ཁོགས Kogs **cough** Med., Kógs-pa to cough.

ཁོང Koṅ, rarely Kóṅ-pa, pers. pron. 3d. person, **he, she;** like Ko it is of far less frequency in the earlier literature than in the later; at present it is in W. used as the respectful word for he, but in C., acc. to Lewin, as plur., = they; Kóṅ-gi his, her; pl. Kóṅ-rnams, Kóṅ-čag, Kóṅ-tso Kóṅ-čag-rnams; Koṅ-ráṅ and Koṅ-nyid he himself; rgyál-po Koṅ-ráṅ yin dgóṅs-nas the king supposing that he himself was meant Glr.

ཁོང་པ Kóṅ-pa 1. prov. for Kóṅ-pa. — 2. **the inside,** inward parts, prov. Kóg-pa (Cs. also: the veins); Kóṅ-du, Kóṅ-na, Kóṅ-nas adv. and postp. **in, within, from**

within, out of; *k'óṅ-du* (also *k'oṅs-su*) *čúd-pa* or *tsúd-pa*, with or without *sems* (resp. *tugs*) being prefixed 1. **impressed on**, fixed in the mind, thoroughly understood, known. 2. very restless, **uneasy, sorry, anxious** in one's mind; — *k'óṅ-du sdú-ba* to impress on the memory, to learn (by heart) *Glr.*; *k'óṅ-nas snyiṅ p'yúṅ-ba ltar* as if their heart was torn out, *Pth.*; *snyiṅ k'oṅ rús-pai dkyil-nas γsól-ba btab* he prayed from his inmost heart *Thgy.*; *k'óṅ-nas šés-pa, smrá-ba* to know by heart, to say, recite by heart *Cs.* **k'óg-la yid-du med** *W.* I have no recollection of it; *k'óṅ-pai dród-la p'an* it helps against internal heat *Med.*; *k'óṅ-par sóṅ-bai dug bžin-no* it is like a poison that has entered into the internal parts (or the veins) *Thgy.*; **k'óg-paṅk'an-pa**, a bad character *W.*, **k'óg-pa čén-mo** *W.* generosity, magnanimity (?) —

Comp. *k'oṅ-k'rág*, the blood contained in the veins *Cs.* — *k'óṅ-k'ro (-ba)* **wrath, anger**; *k'óṅ-k'ro spóṅ-ba Mil.* to put away, subdue anger, **zá-ba** *C.* to 'conceive' anger, take a dislike; *k'óṅ-mi-k'ro-ba* quiet, calm, mild *Pth.* — **k'og-t'úg** col. uneasiness, **sorrow, anxiety**; **k'og-t'úg jhé-pa** *C.*, **čó-če** *W.* to be uneasy, anxious. — *k'oṅ-gáṅ* full, filled up in the inside, **solid**, *k'oṅ-stóṅ* **hollow, tubular.** — **k'og-t'én, k'og-dén**, *W.* grudge, ill-will, **hatred.** — *k'oṅ-tsil* **suet.** — **k'oṅ-lóg** *W.* **cholera.** — **k'og-šiṅ** *W.* 1. **the core** of a tree, heart-wood. 2. **tenon.** — **k'og-šúgs** **a groan, sigh** *W.*, **k'og-šúgs táṅ-če** **to** sigh, to groan. — **k'og-šúbs-la sil-če** *W.* to read low, softly, whisperingly; **k'og-sil táṅ-če** *W.* to read noiselessly, so as not to be heard. — *k'oṅ-(γ)seṅ* inner caverns, not opening to the daylight; (those of the Rirab are the habitations of the Lha-ma-yin or Asura).

ཁོངས་ *K'oṅs* 1. sbst. (*k'óṅs-ma Cs.?*) **the middle, the midst**; *gaṅs-k'óṅs-na* in the midst of alpine snows *Mil.*; respecting time: *žág bdún-gyi k'óṅs-su* **within, during,** seven days *Pth., Tar.*; respecting money: *de nyid-kyi k'óṅs-na γnás-so*, (this) **is contained,** included in that (sum) *Tar.* ༣༢, 15; *k'óṅs-su γtógs-pa Lex., Cs.*: annexed to, united, incorporated with. — 2. adj. **crooked**; *W.*: **k'oṅs ča dug** it is **bent, curved,** e.g. paper by heat, the limbs by the gout; **k'óṅs-kan** *W.*, **k'oṅ-ril** *C.* **crippled.**

ཁོད་ *K'od* I. v. *ᵒk'ód-pa* and *ᵒgód-pa.* — II. inst. of *ᵒk'od.*

ཁོན་པ་ *K'on-pa* **anger, grudge, resentment;** *k'on ᵒdzin-pa, k'ón-du ᵒdzin-pa* to hate, **k'ón-la k'úr-če** *W.* id.; **k'on-gúg-ste dád-če** *W.* ("to sit waiting with hatred") id.; **k'on-bér** *W.*, the sting, the burning of anger or hatred in the soul.

ཁོབ་ *K'ob* 1. fat, heavy, clumsy *Sch.* — 2. sometimes for *ᵒk'ob.* — 3. v. *ᵒpebs-pa.*

ཁོམ་ *K'om* **wallet, leather trunk** *C.*, *Cs.*: felt or skin bag; *γzims-k'óm Cs.* id. (prob. resp.); *k'om-ᵒbóg Cs.* a cloak-bag; more accurately: the cloth in which the trunk is wrapped and carried by the porter.

ཁོམ་པ་ *K'óm-pa Schr.*; to be able, esp. **to be enabled** to do a thing by the absence of external impediments; *k'óm-pa min Cs.*, **k'óm-ce mi rag** *W.* I have no time, I cannot do it now; *sdod mi k'om* I cannot sit and wait now *Pth.*; *mid mi k'óm-par* without your having time to swallow it down *Dzl.* ༧༥༠, 17. *mi-k'óm-pa brgyad*, the eight obstacles to happiness, caused by the re-birth in places or situations unfavourable to conversion *Trig.* no. 66. Acc. to *Schr.* the word is also used in that special sense: to be able to carry on a law-suit, to which there are likewise eight obstacles.

ཁོར་མོ་ཡུག་ *K'or-mo-yúg Sch.*, *k'or-yúg*, *k'ór-sa* v. *k'ó-ra*; *k'or-yúg-tu* **continually, incessantly** *Mil.*

ཁོལ་ *K'ol Cs.* = *k'ól-bu*; *k'ól-du p'yúṅ-ba*, **abridgment,** epitome *Cs.*

ཁོལ་པ་ *K'ól-pa* 1. *Cs.* **boiled.** — 2. *Sch.* **boiling, bubbling,** *zaṅs k'ól-pa* a bubbling kettle *Dzl.*

ཁོལ་པོ་ *K'ól-po*, also *k'ol-brán*, **servant,** man-servant, *k'ól-por rjés-su bzúṅ-ba* to take, to hire for a servant *Pth.;* frq. fig. *séms-kyi ḱól-por γda* (the body) is a servant of the mind *Mil.; ǰig-rtén srid-pai ḱól-po* a servant of the world i.e. of mammon *Mil.*

ཁོལ་བུ་ *ḱól-bu* **a small piece**, *ḱól-bu nyúṅ-°bru tsam źig kyaṅ ma lus Pth.* not so much as a grain of mustard seed is left.

ཁོལ་མ་ *ḱól-ma* 1. *Cs.* 'anything boiled'; perh. more accurately: anything boiling, *ču ḱól-ma* **boiling** water; *dúg-mtso ḱól-ma* a boiling lake of poison. — 2. *Sch.:* an outlet for the smoke in a roof.

ཁོལ་མོ་ *ḱól-mo* 1. **maid-servant** *B.* — 2. a coarse sort of **blanket** usually given to slaves *Schr.* — 3. mowed corn, **a swath** *C.*

ཁོས་ *ḱos* v. *gés-pa.*

ཁོས་པ་ *ḱós-pa* **wished for,** wanted *Sch.*

ཁྱ་ལེ་ *ḱyá-le Cs.,* **ḱá-le** *W.,* as much as fills the hollow of the hand, **a handful,** e.g. of water.

ཁྱག་པ་ *ḱyág-pa* to lift, v. *°kyog-pa.*

ཁྱག(ས)་པ་ *ḱyág(s)-pa* 1. **frozen; ice.** — 2. **the frost, cold,** *ḱyág-ṫog-ḱar* on the ice *Glr.; ḱyág-pa °ḱyág-pai bód-yul* 'Tibet frozen up with frost' *Pth.;* **ḱyág-la ǰar* (v. *byór-ba*) **soṅ** *W.* it has stuck fast by freezing. — **ḱyag-žu-ko-kó** *Ts.* mud caused by a thaw, **snow-water.** — **ḱyág-sran-čan** *W.* hardened against the cold. — *ḱyag-rúm, ḱyag-róm* ice, pieces of ice, floating blocks of ice (also *čab-róm*); cf. *°ḱyag-pa.*

ཁྱད་ *ḱyad* 1. **difference, distinction** *B., C., W.* **gaṅ táṅ-na ḱyad med** *W.* it is no matter which you give me; *ṅá-daṅ-ṕrad-pa dáṅ ḱyad-méd-do* it is quite the same as if they came to myself; *séms-la ḱyad byuṅ* a difference of opinion arose. — *ḱyad-čos* mark of distinction. — 2. **something excellent, superior,** *bzoi ḱyad, bzo-ḱyád* an excellent work of art *Glr.; bsgrúb-pai ḱyad γoṅ* prob.: it shall be instantly performed in the very best manner *Pth.* — *ḱyad-nór* the principal or chief wealth *Cs.* — *ḱyad-dóṅ* the principal sense *Sch.* — 3. syllable employed to form abstract nouns. A transition to such formations appears in the following sentence: *dkar-nag-čós-kyi če-ḱyád blta Mil.* we wish to examine the difference of greatness or worth of the white and the black religion; so also whenever a certain measure is given, and in general, when such abstract nouns are used in a relative sense, as: *mṫo-ḱyád* **height,** *zab-ḱyád* **depth,** *ṕyug-ḱyád* **wealth.** — 4. **part, division,** the same as *ḱyád-par* 2; **sa-ḱyád** *W.* **place,** corresponding exactly to **sa-ču** *C.*

Derivatives. **kyę'-tsar-čęn** = *ṅó-mtsar-čan* wonderful *C.* — *ḱyád-du* adv. especially, particularly, *ḱyád-du °ṕágs-pa* particularly (uncommonly) lofty, sublime *Glr.* *ḱyád-par* adv. = *ḱyád-du Glr.* 50, 7, and more frq. sbst.: 1. **difference, dissimilarity** *B.* and *C., ṅa daṅ ḱyod γnyis ḱyád-par-če* I and you — that is a great difference *Glr.; de daṅ kyád-par-ma-mčis-pai rten* an image not differing from this *Glr.; míṅ-gi ḱyád-par yin* it is (only) a difference of name *Glr.* — 2. **sort, kind,** *°brás-bui ḱyád-par kun* all sorts of fruit; *ri-dvágs-kyi ḱyád-par žig* a particular kind of game; perh. also: **division, part,** *yúl-gyi ḱyád-par* **province** *Tar.* ༢༠. 14. — 3. = *ḱyad* 2. something of superior qualities, an excellent man *Tar.* ༢༠, 7. *ḱyád-par-čan* **superior, excellent, capital,** *blá-ma ḱyád-par-čan čig Mil.* an excellent spiritual teacher; *ḱyád-par-du* adv. **particularly,** chiefly, especially. Rather obscure as to its literal sense, but of frq. use is the phrase *ḱyád-du γsód-pa, γsád-pa,* c. accus. but also dat., **to despise,** e.g. *dmá-la* an inferior, *rgyu-°brás* the doctrine of retribution, *ṅyon-móṅs-pa* trouble etc.

ཁྱབ་ *ḱyab* v. *ḱyáb-pa.*

ཁྱབ་པ་ *ḱyáb-pa* **to fill, penetrate; to embrace, comprise,** c. accus., also dat., *mi-γtsáṅ-bas ḱyáb-pai sa-ṕyógs* a place full of dirt *Thgy.; °brúm-pa máṅ-pos* full of, quite covered with pustules, pocks *Med.; mḱris-*

pas filled, impregnated with bile *Med.*; *lus sems dga-bdės ḱyáb-par gyúr-nas* body and soul (filled with) full of joy *Glr.*; *bar ḱyáb-pa* to fill up an intermediate space; **to make** (a country etc.) **full** of light, religion, happiness, frq.; *ťams-čád-la drín-gyis* to embrace all creatures with benevolence; *kún-la ḱyab-pa* in grammar: capable of being joined to any word, comprising all of them, *Glr.*; *ḱyab-čé-ba* comprehensive; used also in the way of censure: everywhere and nowhere, to be met with everywhere *Mil.*; *ḱyab-γdál* or *rdól* comprehensive, extensive. — *ḱyab* seems also to be a sbst. in *ḱyab-čé-ba*, and still more so in *rgya bod yoṅs ḱyáb-tu grágs-pa-la* according to what is spoken in the whole compass of India and Tibet *Tar.* 87.

ཁྱབ་འཇུག *ḱyab-ḥjúg* **Vishnu**, a Brahmanical divinity, appearing, like Brahma and Shiva, also in Buddhist legends, yet principally known in his quality as *γza-sgra-γčan-ḥdzín* (Rahula), conqueror of the demon that threatens to devour sun and moon; hence *ḱyab-ḥjug-γzér Med.*, **ḱyab-ḥjúg-gi nad* W.*, **ra-hu-lẹ nẹ* C.*, **epilepsy.**

ཁྱམས *ḱyams Cs., Sch.* **yard, court-yard,** *Cs.* also gallery. It is, like *ťsoms*, a space that is to be found in many Tibetan houses, and may be compared to the compluvium of the Romans, being open in the middle, and on the sides generally enclosed by verandas. *Ḱyams* may therefore be called court-yard, when it is on the same level with the ground, (so also perh. *Tar.* 89, 4, reading *ḱyams-su* for *ḥḱyams-su)*; but in the upper stories such a construction is unknown in European architecture. *Ḱyams-stód* the upper court-yard, *ḱyams-smád* the lower one; *ḱyams-ťóṅs Cs.*: 'impluvium'.

ཁྱམས *ḱyams Cs.*: p. n. = *ḱams*, v. *ḱams* 3.

ཁྱམས་པ, ཁྱར་པ, ཁྱལ་པ *ḱyáms-pa, ḱyár-pa, ḱyál-pa* v. *ḥḱyáms-pa*, etc.

ཁྱི *ḱyi* **dog,** *ḱyi rmug B.* and *C.*; the dog bites, *W.*: barks; **so tab* W.*; bites; **ťam* W.* lays hold of; *ḱyi bós-nas ma brduṅ* proverb: if you call the dog, then you must not beat him *Glr.* — *ḱyi rkaṅ-γnyis Sch.* 'a bastard dog, a cur' (?) — *ḱyi-skád* the barking. — *ḱyi-ḱáṅ* **dog-kennel,** — *ḱyi-gu* **a puppy.** — *ḱyi-rgán* an old dog. — *ḱyi-rṅó* the itch of dogs. — *ḱyi-ḍám* 'dog's seal', a mark burnt in; **stigma** *C., W.* — *ḱyi-dúg* poison of hydrophobia *Sch.* — *ḱyi-mdúd-pa* the pairing of dogs *Sch.* — *ḱyi-pul* **dog-kennel, dog-house.** — **ḱyi-pal-ǰór* W.* Blitum virgatum. — *ḱyi-spyáṅ W.* **jackal.** — *ḱyi-ṗo* a male dog. — *ḱyi-brú Sch.* a vicious, biting dog. — *ḱyi-sbráṅ* dog's fly. — *ḱyi-mo* a female dog, **bitch.** — *ḱyi-smyón* canine madnes, **hydrophobia** *C., W.*; also mad dog = *ḱyi smyón-pa*. — *ḱyi-rdzi* dog-keeper. — *ḱyi-γžóṅ* trough for dogs and other animals, **manger.** — *ḱyi-šig* **flea.**

ཁྱི་གུ *ḱyi-gu* 1. v. *ḱyi*. — 2. *W.* **bud** (of leaves and branches, not of blossoms), **eye** (of a plant).

ཁྱི་ར *ḱyi-ra* **chase, hunting,** esp. of single huntsmen, not of a party; stable-stand, cf. *liṅs*; **kyi-ra-la čá-če* W.* to go a hunting, **ḱyi-ra čo-če, gyáb-če, gyúg-če** id.; **ḱyi-ra-la čá-ḱan** hunter, sportsman; *ḱyi-ra-ba B.* and *C.*, **ḱyi-ra-pa* W.* huntsman.

ཁྱི་རོང *ḱyi-róṅ* p.n., v. *skyid-gróṅ*.

ཁྱི་ལ་ཝ་རི *ḱyi-la-wa-ri* a sort of treacle made of *seṅ-ldeṅ Wdṅ.*

ཁྱིག *ḱyig* v. *ḥḱyig-pa*.

ཁྱིད *ḱyid* breadth of the hand with the thumb extended, a span.

ཁྱིམ *ḱyim (Ssk.* गृह) 1. **house,** not as a building, but as a dwelling-place of man, **a home.** Even when in *Sik.* they speak of **šiṅ-ḱyim, nyúg-ḱyim** a house of wood, of bamboo, the idea of habitation, dwelling-place predominates in these expressions. *ḱyim-na* at home, *ḱyim-du* home (to go home); *ḱyim daṅ ḱyim-na* house for house, each in his house *Tar.* 151. 22; *ḱyim spó-ba* to remove to another place; *ḱyim skyóṅ-ba* to have a household, to gain a livelihood; *ḱyim-gyi so-tśis* household, housekeeping, farming; *ḱyim-gyi rig-pa* knowledge, experience in housekeeping and farming; *ḱyim-med-pa* homeless, without a home; therefore esp. as opp. to the life of a homeless and unmarried priest: *ḱyim-gyi byá-ba* or *las*, 1. domestic business, 2. lay-life, worldly life; cf. also many of the compounds. *ḱyim-la ᵒóṅ-ba, ɣtóṅ-ba* to get married, to be given in marriage, respecting the female part *Glr., Mil.* — 2. **the signs** of the Zodiac, which is called *ḱyim-gyi ᵒḱór-lo*, viz. *lug* ram, *ɣlaṅ* bull, *ᵒḱrig-pa* (pairing) twins, *kárkata (Ssk.)* crab, *séṅ-ge* lion, *bú-mo* virgin, *sraṅ* balance, *sdig(-pa)* scorpion, *ɣžu* (bow) archer, *ču-srin* (sea-monster) capricorn, *búm-pa* water-bearer, *nya* fishes. To these 12 signs however the corresponding Tibetan figures are not ༡ to ༡༢, but o to ༡༡, as seems to be the usage in astronomical science. There is moreover a division into 27 'lunar mansions' much in use; v. *rgyu-skár.* — 3. **double-hour,** the time of two hours; or the twelfth part of the time of the apparent daily rotation of the heavens and consequently also of the zodiac, or, as we should say, the time of the passing of a sign of the zodiac through the meridian. — 4 *Cs.:* **halo,** or circle round the sun or moon. — 5. Symbolic numeral: 12.

Comp. and deriv. *ḱyim-ťáb(s)* **husband,** frq.; also wife; *ḱyim-ťáb-la ɣtóṅ-ba* to give in marriage, to give away a woman for a wife; *ḱyim-ťáb-mo* **wife,** housewife, *Cs.* — *ḱyim-bdág* master of the house, **husband;** owner of a house, **citizen;** *ḱyim-bdág-ma* fem. — *ḱyim-pa* 1. **layman,** 2. *Cs.:* surrounded by a halo (*ḱyim* 4); *ḱyim-pai ṕyógs-su sbyin-pa* given away to laymen *Dzl.;* *ḱyim-par ᵒdug* or *ɣnas* he lives as a layman; *ṕyis ḱyim-pai ťsúl-čan-gyi rnál-ᵒbyor-pa* a devout man, who lives outwardly like a layman *Mil.* — *ḱyim-pa-pa* **a houseowner, peasant, farmer, husband;** *ḱyim-pa-ma* **housewife.** — *ḱyim bya* **domestic fowl, cock, hen, poultry** *W., C.* — *ḱyim-mi* family of a house, household *Cs.* — *ḱyim-ťsáṅ* id. — *ḱyim-ťsér Glr.* 51, 10, usually *ḱyim-mťsés, ḱyim-mťsés-pa*, fem. *ḱyim-mťsés-ma* **neighbour.** — *ḱyim-žág, ḱyim-zlá, ḱyim-ló* 'a zodiacal day, month, year' (?) *Cs.* — *ḱyim-sa* earth, **dust,** dirt (in a house), **sweepings** *W.*, **ḱyim-sa dú-če, spúṅ-če* to sweep (a floor), to sweep together.

ཁྱིམ་ཉ་ *ḱyim-nya Sch.:* **whale** (if at all correct, it must be taken as mythological signification, no Tibetan having ever known of the existence of real whales).

ཁྱུ་ *ḱyu, ḱyú-bo Cs., ḱyú-mo Pth.* **flock, herd,** *lúg-ḱyu* a flock of sheep, *mdzó-mo-ḱyu* a herd of bastard cows, *ɣnág-ḱyu* of horned cattle; *ḱyu skóṅ-ba* to keep, tend a flock or herd; **company, band, gang, troop,** *mi-ḱyu Cs.* a company of men, *bú-mo-ḱyu* a bevy of girls, *dmag-ḱyú* a troop of soldiers; *ḱyú-nas ᵒbúd-pa* to exclude from the company *Pth., C.;* *ḱyu-sná ᵒdrén-pa* to go before, to take the lead of a troop, a flock *Mil.;* *ḱyu-mčóg* **bell-wether;** also the most distinguished amongst a number of men, the first, **chief, head** *Pth., ḱyu-mčóg-ma* fem.; *ḱyu ťságs-pa* vb.n., *Sch.* to collect, to gather in flocks.

ཁྱུ་ *ḱyu Sch.* 'ell', prob. incor. for *ḱru.*

ཁྱུ་བྱུག *ḱyu-byúg* acc. to *Lex.* = *ku-hú.*

ཁྱུག *ḱyug* v. *ᵒḱyúg-pa.*

ཁྱུང་ *ḱyuṅ (Sch.* also *ḱyúṅ-mo)* the Garuda bird, a mythical bird, chief of the feathered race. *ḱyúṅ-šog-čan* = *ṕyag-rdór.*

ཁྱུང་དཔྱད་ *ḱyuṅ-dpyad* a small round **basket** of reed *Cs.;* *ḱyuṅ-ril* is said to be in *C.* a large cylindrical basket, the same as *kun-dúm Ld.*, v. *rkón-pa.*

ཁྱུང་སྡེར་ *ḱyuṅ-sdér* ('Garuda claw') *Med., Cs.:* n. of a medicinal root, pseudo-zedoary; *ḱyuṅ-rgód Med.* id (?).

ཁྱུད་ *ḱyud* v. *ᵒḱyúd-pa.*

ཁྱུད་མོ་ *ḱyúd-mo* **rim** of a vessel *Sch.*

ཁྱུར་མིད་པ་ *Kyur-mid-pa* **to swallow** *Med.*; *Kyur-mid-du sóṅ-ste* suffering himself to be swallowed (from the story of an Indian idol) *Pth.*

ཁྱུས་ *Kyus* wall-side *Ts.* (?)

ཁྱེ་ *Kye* 1. for *Kyeu Mil.* — 2. for *Ke* q.v.; *Kyé-mo* v. *Ke.*

ཁྱེ་མ་ *Kyé-ma* n. of a disease *Med.*

ཁྱེའུ་ *Kyeu* (diminutive of *Kyó-bo?*) 1. **male child, infant boy.** 2. **youth, adolescent** *B.*

ཁྱེད་ *Kyed* pers. pron. 2nd. person, **thou,** and particularly in the plur. **you,** in *B.* eleg., in addressing superiors, but also used by superiors in speaking to inferiors, and even contemptuously: *Kyed ltá-bui má-rabs* such vulgar, mean people, as ye are *Dzl.* — *Kyéd-kyi* thy, your. — *Kyed-ráṅ* (*kyed-nyid* seems to be little used) thou thyself, you yourself; plur. particularly expressed: *Kyéd-ċag, Kyéd-rnams, Kyed-ťso; dge-ťsúl Kyéd ɣnyis* you two Getsuls *Glr.*; *Kyed ɣsúm-po* you three (a mother speaking to her sons) *Glr.*; *Kyéd-ċág* you, when speaking to one person *Glr.*, = *nyid-ċag.*

ཁྱེད་ *Kyed* 1. = *Kyid W.* 2. v. *ₒKyéd-pa.*

ཁྱེན་ཏི་ *Kyén-ti Pur.* **he, she,** v. *Kún-ti.*

ཁྱེབས་ *Kyebs* v. *Kebs.*

ཁྱེམ་ *Kyem* (*Sch.* also *Kem*) **a shovel,** *W.*: **kyem daṅ páṅ-ċe** to shovel away, to remove with a shovel; *Kyém-gyi ₒdáb-ma* the blade of a shovel, *yú-ba* the handle of it *Cs.* — *gru-Kyém, ču-kyém W.* **oar,** *lċags-Kyém* **spade;** *me-Kyém* fire-shovel; *wa-Kyém* a scoop, hollow gutter-shaped shovel *Cs.*; *Kyém-bu* spoon *Cs.*

ཁྱེར་ *Kyer* v. *ₒKyé-ba*; *Kyér-so* v. *ₒKyer-so.*

ཁྱོ་ *Kyo B.* frq., also *Kyó-po Pth.* 1. **man** (seldom). 2. **husband,** *Kyo byéd-pa* ('to act a husband' cf. *byed-pa* I. 1) to take a wife; *Kyod ṅai Kyo mi byéd-na* if you do not marry me *Dzl.* — *Kyo-méd* **single, unmarried.** — *kyó-mo* wife *Cs.* — *Kyo-šúg* husband and wife, married couple; *Kyo-šúg ɣnyis grógs-nas soṅ* these two married people went together; *Kyo-šúg mdzá-ba-rnams* a loving couple; *Kyím-bdag Kyo-šúg ɣnyis* the citizen with his wife; *ɣsér-lha Kyo-šúg ɣnyis* about the same as: Mr. and Mrs. Serlha; *Kyo-šúg-tu sdú-ba* to join a couple in marriage *Dzl.*

ཁྱོ་ག་ *Kyó-ga* 1. **man** emphatically, as: *skyés-bu ṅa hór-pa yaṅ Kyó-ga yin* we Turks are men, too; **hero,** *Kyó-ga-po* id. — 3. **heroic deed, exploit.**

ཁྱོག་པོ་ *Kyóg-po* **crooked, curved, bent;** *Cs.* **also cunning.**

ཁྱོག་ཐོང་ *Kyog-ťóṅ* (v. *Kyó-ga* and *ťoṅ*) *W.* **young man, youth.**

ཁྱོགས་ *Kyogs* **litter, bier** *Pth.*, **palanquin** *Cs.* also scaffold (?) *Cs.*

ཁྱོང་ *Kyoṅ* v. *Kyóṅ-ba.*

ཁྱོད་ *Kyod* pers. pron. 2nd. person sing. and plur., **thou, you;** *Kyod-kyi* thy, thine, your; if plurality is to be especially expressed, it is done by adding *ċag*: *Kyód-ċag Mil.*; occasionally also *Kyód-rnams,* cf. *Kyed*; *kyod-ráṅ* 1. thou thyself, you yourself. 2. thou, you (*W.* **Kyo-ráṅ**).

ཁྱོན་ *Kyon* **size, extension, width, circumference, area, height** e.g. of Dzambuling *Dzl.*, of the Sumeru *Glr.*, of the lunar mansions or the zodiac *Glr.*; *Kyon-yáṅs-pa* a wide extent, *Kyoṅ-yáṅs sa-ɣži* all the wide world (earth); *Kyon-sdóm Cs.* 1. narrow-extent. 2. sum, contents. — *Kyón-nas* **thoroughly,** *Kyón-nas mi sdig-ċan* thoroughly a sinner; *Kyón-nas med* not at all *C.*

ཁྱོམ་ཁྱོམ་ *Kyom-Kyóm* 1. **oblique, awry,** irregularly shaped. — 2. v. *ₒKyóm-pa.*

ཁྱོར་ *Kyor* (*Cs. Kyór-pa*) as much as fills the hollow of the hand, **a handful,** cf. *skyor*; *Kyor gaṅ, Kyor re* one handful, *Kyor do* two handfuls.

ཁྱོལ་བ་ *Kyól-ba* v. *ₒKyól-ba*; *Kyós-ma C.* = *skyós-ma, skyás-ma.*

ཁྲ་ *Kra* 1. a small bird of prey, **sparrow-hawk, falcon,** used for hunting, also *bya-Krá*; *Kra-žúr Sch.*: a species of eagles; *Krá-pa* falconer. — 2. v. the following article.

ཁྲ་བོ *ḱrá-bo* perh. also *ḱrá-mo* **piebald,** two-coloured, (not many-coloured, which is *bkrá-ba); rgya-stág-ḱrá-bo* the streaked Indian tiger *Mil.;* **ṫa-ṫá** *C.* id.; **ṫa-wo-pi-wo, ṫa-si-pi-si** *W.* id. (spelling uncertain); *nag-ḱrá* black-spotted, so that black is the predominating colour of the whole; *dmar-ḱrá* red-spotted, red being the predominating colour. — The significations of the various compounds of *ḱra* have all a reference to the peculiar effect produced on the eye by the blending of two or more colours together, especially when seen from a distance; so: *ḱra-čam-mé Glr.* is said of a rainbow-tinted meteor, *ḱra-lam-mé Mil.,* (or *lham-mé,)* of a similar phenomenon, *ḱra-čem-čém Pth.* of a flight of birds; **ṭa-čám-se, ṭa-čem-mé, ṭa-čém-se** *C.,* **čam-ṭá-ṭiṅ-ṅé** *Ld.,* **ṭa-śig-ge‘ ṭa-₀čig-ge, ṭa-róg-ge** *C.,* — all these seem to be of nearly the same import. — These compounds have also assumed the character of an adverb, signifying, **together, altogether,** *ḱra-me-ré Mil.* id.

ཁྲ་མ་ *ḱrá-ma* 1. *Cs.* **register, index.** — 2. *C.* **judicial decree.** — 3. a species of grain, acc. to *Wdṅ.* = *mgyogs-nás* a kind of barley growing and ripening within 60 days; v. *nas.*

ཁྲག་ *ḱrag* (in *Bal.* still pronounced **ḱrag** elsewhere **ṭag**), *Cs.: resp. sku-mṫsal,* **blood;** **ṅal-ṭág, žaṅ-ṭág** *W.* vulg. blood discharged by menstruation, from which, acc. to some authorities, **paṅ-ṭág** blood of the childbed is to be distinguished; *γzuṅ-ḱrág* healthy, nourishing blood *Cs.; nad-ḱrág* bad blood *Cs.: ḱrag ₒdón-pa, W.* **tón-če**, to bleed a person; *γtár-ba* id.; *ḱrag γčód-pa* to stop, to stanch the blood; *ḱrag čád-pa* vb. n. to cease to bleed, cessation of bleeding; **nyiṅ-ṭág ₒḱól-la rag** *W.* I feel my blood boiling, e.g. from ascending a steep hill; *ḱrag ₒdzág-pa* menstruation (the plain undisguised expression): *ḱrag čág-pa* clotted blood, gore *Cs.; ḱrag-śas-čé-ba* plethoric *Med.*

Comp. *ḱrag-ₒḱrúgs Sch.:* agitation, flutter, orgasm of the blood. — *ḱrág-čan* bloody, e.g. *ral-grí.* — *ḱrag-γčód* n. of a medicinal herb *Med., ḱrag-čags-rtá* a ‘blood-bred’ horse, i.e. a real horse, opp. to a metaphysical one *Mil.* — *ḱrag-ₒṫúṅ* a class of terrifying deities *Thgr.* — **ṭág-ṫuṅ-bu** *W.* **leech.** — *ḱrag-γzér W.* rheumatic pain (?) — *ḱrag-ró* clotted blood (?) *Med. ḱrag-líṅ* a clot of blood. — *ḱrag-śór* hemorrhage, bloody flux (?) *Med.*

ཁྲག་ཁྲིག་ *ḱrag-ḱrig* one hundred thousand million, an indefinitely large number *Cs.;* acc. to *Lex.* = **प्रयुत** one million, cf. *dkrigs-pa.*

ཁྲག་ཁྲུག་ *ḱrag-ḱrúg Cs.* **complicate, confused;** *Zam.:* like a troop of fighting men, or like the loose leaves of a book, when out of order.

ཁྲག་ཁྲོག་ *ḱrag-ḱróg Lt.?*

ཁྲང་ *ḱraṅ* v. *mḱraṅ.*

ཁྲད་པ་ *ḱrád-pa Cs.* stretched out; *ḱrád-por sdód-pa* to sit (with the legs) stretched out (?). *ḱrád-por skyé-ba Wdṅ.* a botanical term applied to the leaves of plants.

ཁྲབ་ *ḱrab* shield, buckler; coat of mail, scales *Sch.;* acc. to oral communication the word in the first instance denotes **scale** (scale of a fish), and secondly **coat of mail;** consequently *ḱráb-čan* 1. scaled, scaly. 2. mailed, armed with a coat of mail; *ḱrád-mḱan* armourer *Glr.*

ཁྲབ་ཁྲབ་ *ḱrab-ḱráb* 1. a weeper, one that sheds tears on every occasion *Sch.* — 2. *Mil.* 92, 4?

ཁྲམ་ཁ་ *ḱrám-ḱa* **a cut, a notch** (in wood), lines cut into wood so as to cross one another, as an ornament; *ḱrám-śiṅ* a club-like implement, carved in the manner just mentioned, representing the attribute of a god. *nyag-ḱrám* a notch.

ཁྲམ་པ་ *ḱrám-pa* I. *C.:* **a liar,** *slu-bar byéd-pai ḱrám-pa Pth.; ḱrám-ma* fem. *Cs.; ḱa-ḱrám* a lie *Mil.; ḱrám-sems-čan* **lying, mendacious** *Mil.* — II *W.:* 1. **lively, brisk, quick,** like boys, kids etc. (the contrary of *γlén-pa* slow, indolent, apathetic); **ṭám-pa čo** *W.* a wish of good speed, addressed to one going on a journey, such as: good success! may all go well! — 2. **modest,** attentive to the wishes of others.

ཁྲལ་ *ḱral* (*Lex.* दण्ड punishment) 1. **punishment, chastisement** for sins, **visitation**; in this sense the word is said to be used still, but much more frq. it signifies 2. **tax, tribute, duty,** service to be performed to a higher master; *ḱral sdú-ba* to collect taxes, *ˌjál-ba, skór-ba* to pay taxes, *bkál-ba* to impose taxes; *dṅúl-kral* money-tax, tax to be paid in money, *ˌbrú-ḱral* corn-tax, tribute paid in corn, *til-már-ḱral* tax, tribute to be paid in sesame-oil.

ཁྲི་ *ḱri* (*Cs. ḱri-ma*), *ḱri-ḱrág, ḱri-tsó* **ten thousand**, a myriad, *ḱri ṗyed daṅ ɣnyis* 15 000; *nyi-ḱri* 20 000; *bži-ḱri* 40 000; *brgyad-ḱri bži-stóṅ* 84 000, a number frq. occurring in legends.

ཁྲི་ *ḱri*, also *ḱriu*, seldom *ḱri-bo*, resp. *bžúgs-ḱri*, **seat, chair; throne; couch; frame,** sawing-jack, trestle etc.; *gya-ṭi* an Indian (Anglo-Indian, European) chair; *čós-ḱri* a professorial chair, pulpit *Pth.*, reading-desk, table for books, school-table; *nyé-ṭi* (v. *snyé-ba*) a contrivance to rest the head on when sleeping on the ground *W. nyál-ḱri*, resp. *ɣzim-ḱri*, bed-stead; *sén-ge-ḱri* throne; *ḱri-la bskó-ba* to raise on the throne; *ḱri-la ˌḱód-pa* to preside, to hold the chair. — As the Tibetans generally sit on the bare ground, or on mats, or carpets, chairs are rather articles of luxury.

Comp. and deriv. *ḱri-ɣdúgs po.* **the sun.** — *ḱri-pa Cs.* **a chairman**; one sitting on a throne. — *ḱri-ˌṗáṅ* 1. *Cs.*: the height of a chair, a high chair. — 2. *mčod-rtén-gyi ḱri-ˌṗáṅ* the same as *baṅ-rím.* — *ḱri-mún* or *món Pth., Tar.*, **prison, dungeon.** — *ṭi-šiṅ, ṭiu-šiṅ*, the common, plain word for chair.

ཁྲི་ལེ་བ་ *ḱri-le-ba* **fear** *C.* (?)

ཁྲིག་ཁྲིག་ *ḱrig-ḱrig* 1. *so ḱrig-ḱrig byéd-pa* to gnash, grind the teeth *Mil.*; *ɣzúgs-po* to shiver, shake with cold, terror, rage *Mil.* — 2. col. for *tig-tig.*

ཁྲིགས་ *ḱrigs* **plentiful, abundant** *Sch.*; *za-ˌóg ḱrigs-se* silk-fabrics, silks, in abundance *Mil.*; *ḱrigs-se gaṅ* quite full *Sch.*; *ḱrigs-se byéd-pa* to treat, to entertain plentifully *Sch.*

ཁྲིད་, འཁྲིད་ *ḱrid, ˌḱrid*, **instruction, teaching**; *ḱrid ˌdébs-pa* to give instruction, to instruct, *ḱrid-pas-čog* I am willing to give you instruction, you may have lessons with me *Mil.*; *ḱrid bšád-pa* to give instruction, to make admonitory speeches, to give parenetical lectures; *ḱrid záb-po* thorough instruction; *slu-ḱrid* instruction to an evil purpose, seduction, v. *slú-ba*; *sna-ḱrid Lex.* guide, leader. — *ḱrid-mḱan* col. teacher. — *ḱrid-ṗrúg* scholar, pupil. — *ḱrid-pa* v. *ˌḱrid-pa.*

ཁྲིམས་ *ḱrims* 1. **right,** not in the abstract sense in which the word is generally understood with us, but in more or less concrete applications, such as administration of justice, law, judgment, sometimes also implying **custom, usage, duty.** Accordingly *rgyál-po*, or *btsún-po ḱrims-méd* means an unjust king, an unprincipled priest or ecclesiastic; *ḱrims bžin-du, ḱrims daṅ mṫun-par* conscientiously, justly; in conformity with custom, duty, law; *čos-ḱrims* religious right, coming nearest to our abstract right; when, for instance, in *Glr.* king Sroṅ-btsan-sgam-po says: *rgyál-ḱrims čós-ḱrims-su bsgyur* I have changed the right of a king into that of religion, he means to say: I have subjected my own absolute will to the higher principle of universal right. A somewhat different sense conveys *Glr.* 97, 4: *čós-ḱrims ˌǰig-pai gros byas* they conspired to extirpate the religious principle of administration. — 2. **law,** *dgé-ba bču daṅ ldán-pai ḱrims* a general law, founded upon the ten virtues *Glr.*; *des čós-ḱrims daṅ rgyál-ḱrims ɣnyis ɣtán-la ṗab*, he regulated the spiritual and secular law *Glr.* 97, 1.; *bka-ḱrims* resp. law, as a collection of precepts, **decree, commandment;** *ḱrims čá-ba* to enact a law, to publish a decree, frq.; *ḱrims sgróg-pa* to proclaim an edict; *mtó-ba ḱrims-kyis ynon* he limited the power of the nobility by laws *Glr.*, *ḱrims-yig* code of law *C.*; *ḱrims* also a single **precept, rule, commandment** *Dzl.*; *Burn.* I, 630. — 3. **administration of justice,** *čós-kyi ḱrims* the ecclesiastical, *dpón-gyi ḱrims* the secular civil, exercised by the *ḱrims-dpon*; *lugs ynyis-kyi ḱrims* a twofold jurisdiction, a combination of the ecclesiastical and secular administration of justice (as it existed among the Jews); *ḱrims srúṅ-ba* to observe, to act according to right, custom, duty; also to exercise jurisdiction, to govern, to reign; to bridle, to keep in check *Glr.* 95. 9.; *ḱrims byéd-pa* id. ni f. — *tsúl-ḱrims* a spiritual precept or duty; also a frequent man's name. — 4. **action, lawsuit,** *W.* also **ṭim-šágs** or only **šags; gaṅ žig ṭim-si ṗi-la* W.* for the sake of some law-suit, **ṭim táṅ-če** to sit in judgment, to try, to hear causes; **ṭim čǒ-pa* C.* = **ṭim táṅ-če* W.*, means also to pass sentence, to punish, **ṭim ḍág-po tóṅ-wa** to inflict a heavy punishment; *mi-la ḱrims-bčad ṗog* he incurs, suffers punishment *Pth.*; **ṭim žú-če* W.* to go to law, to commence an action; **ṭim žú-ḱan* W.* plaintiff; **ṭim táṅ-ḱan* W.* magistrate, judge; *ḱrims-dpon B., C., W.*, superior judge, chief-justice; **ṭim-kyi ḍág-po* C. id.*; *ḱrims-yyóg* apparitor, beadle *Cs.*; *ḱrims-pa* lawyer, advocate *Cs.* (seems to be little used); *ḱrims-ḱaṅ* court, court of justice, tribunal; *ḱrims-ra* id.; place of execution. — 5. **use, custom, usage** — that power to which people in general show the readiest obedience, and which in every sphere of life forms the greatest obstacle to reforms and improvements.

ཁྲིལ་ *ḱril* v *ḱril.*

ཁྲིས་ *ḱris?* *ḱris-ǰágs* **peace,** v. *ǰags.*

ཁྲུ་ *ḱru* (*ḱrú-ma Cs.*) **cubit,** a measure of eighteen inches, from the elbow to the extremity of the middle finger. The average height of a man is assumed to be four cubits, that of a short man three. — *ḱru ǰál-ba* to measure with a cubit measure *Cs.*

ཁྲུ་བ་ *ḱrú-ba* sometimes for *ḱru-ba.*

ཁྲུ་གཟར་ *ḱru-yzár* a kind of **stew-pan** *Sch.*

ཁྲུ་སློག་ *ḱru-slóg* a pit filled with corn (?) *Sch.*; in *Mil.* *ḱru-slóg-pa* stands for digging, breaking up the soil, gardening.

ཁྲུང་ཁྲུང་ *ḱruṅ-ḱruṅ* (*Ssk.* क्रौञ्च) **crane,** Grus cinerea.

ཁྲུན་ *ḱrun* **height, length, extension** *Lex.*, *Cs.*

ཁྲུལ་ *ḱrul* 1. *ḱrul ytoṅ-ba* to let fall, **to drop** (several things at intervals), *mči-ma* tears *Mil.* — 2. **da-ṭúl* W.* **intercalary month.**

ཁྲུལ་པོ་ *ḱrúl-po C.* 1. **cheerful, merry.** — 2. **fornicator.**

ཁྲུལ་མ་ *ḱrúl-ma* 1. *W.* **ḱú-wa ṭúl-ma** crooked handle, **crank** (spelling uncertain). — 2. *C.* **a whore.**

ཁྲུམ་ཁྲུམ་ *ḱrum-ḱrúm*, *Sch.*: *ḱrum-ḱrúm byéd-pa*, *Lt.*: *ḱrum-ḱrúm brdúṅ-ba* **to pound** in a mortar.

ཁྲུམས་སྟོད་ *ḱrums-stód*, and *-smád*, two Nakshatras, v. *rgyu-skár* ༢༥.

ཁྲུས་ *ḱrus* 1. pf. of *ḱru-ba.* — 2. sbst. **bath, washing, ablution;** *ḱrús-ḱu*, water for bathing, washing or rinsing; dish-water; *ḱrus byéd-pa* to bathe, to use baths *Dzl.*; *ḱrús-la ǵró-ba* to go to bathe *Dzl.*; *ḱrus ysól-ba* resp. to take a bath *Glr.*, also to administer a bath to another (cf. *ysól-ba*) *Glr.*, *Pth.*; esp. as a religious ceremony, consisting in the sprinkling with water, and performed, when a new-born infant receives a name, when a person enters into a religious order, or in diseases and on various other occasions (cf. *Schl. Buddh.* p. 239, where the word is spelled *bkrus*). Therefore 3. **baptism,** and *ḱrus ysol-ba* **to baptize** *Chr. R.* and *P.*— *ḱrús-kyi rdziṅ*, pond, pool for bathing; *ḱrus-ḱáṅ* bathing-room or house; *ḱrus-sdér* basin, washing-bowl *Sch.*; *ḱrus-búm* sacred watering-pot; *ḱrus-yžóṅ* bathing-tub *Sch.*; *ḱrus-ysér* bathing-water *Sch.*, but in *Lt.* this word relates to a certain medical procedure or method of curing.

ཁྲེ་ *ḱre* (*Ssk.* **प्रियङ्गु**) **millet,** *ḱre-čáṅ* Murwa-beer *Sik.*, v. *Hook. Himal. Journ.*

ཁྲེ་ཙེ་ *ḱre-tsé* Chinese **vermicelli** *C.* (**ṭ́e-tse**).

ཁྲེགས་པ་ *ḱrégs-pa* v. *mḱrégs-pa.*

ཁྲེལ་ *ḱrel,* resp. *tugs-ḱrél* 1. **shame, shamefacedness, bashfulness, modesty;** **ṭ́el ḱáb-će* W.* v. *gébs-pa.* — 2. **piety,** esp. *W.* — 3. *C.* **disgust, aversion.**

Comp. and deriv. — *ḱrel-gád* a scornful laughter. — *ḱrél-čan Cs.* bashful, timid; *W.* **pious, faithful, conscientious.** — *ḱrel-ltás, ḱrel-ltos,* dread of wicked actions; *ḱrel-ydoṅ* (lit. a face capable of shame) id. — **ṭ́él-dad-čan, ṭ́él-₀dod-čan* W.* fond of making others ashamed. — *ḱrel-ldán* = *ḱrél-čan.* — *ḱrél-ba* vb. to make or to be ashamed, **ṭ́ el ṣoṅ** he was ashamed, **ṭ́él-će mi yoṅ* W.* he is not put to shame; *C.* also: to get into a passion; sbst. shame, *ḱrél-ba daṅ ṅó-tsa-ba med* he has no shame nor dread *Dzl.*, **ṭ́él-wa yod* W.* it is a shame. — *ḱrel-méd (-pa), W. *ḱrel-méd- (ḱan)* shameless, insolent. — **ṭ́él-₀o** object of disgust, *C.* — *ḱrél-yod* **chastity, modesty, decency,** *ḱrél-yod-pa* chaste etc., *ḱrél-yod-par byéd-pa* to behave chastely etc. — *ḱrel-šór* = *ḱrel-méd.*

ཁྲེས་པོ་ *ḱrés-po Thgy.* **load, burden,** = *ḱur.*

ཁྲོ་ *ḱro* 1. a kind of **bronze,** of about the same quality and worth as *₀ḱár-ba,* but inferior to *li,* q.v.; *ḱró-ču* liquid, melted bronze; *ḱró-čus sdóm-pa* to fill up joints, grooves etc. with melted bronze, to solder *Glr.* — 2. **kettle** *Schr.*

ཁྲོ་པ་ *ḱró-pa W.* for *ḱrod.*

ཁྲོ་བ་ *ḱró-ba* 1. **anger, wrath,** (cf. *₀ḱró-ba* vb.) frq.; *ḱóṅ-ḱró-ba* inward anger *Thgy.* — 2. **angry, wrathful** *Cs.*; *ḱró-bar byéd-pa, ₀gyúr-ba* to be, to grow angry *Cs.*; *ḱró-bo,* fem. *ḱró-mo* angry, fierce, ferocious, e.g. *yčan-yzán* a ferocious beast; esp. applied to the 54 (or 60) deities of anger and terror (**भैरव**), e.g *ḱró-ba-čén-po* = *yšin-rje* the ruler of hades; **ṭ́o-túm-po** furious with rage, raging with anger *C.*: *ḱro-ynyér* distortion of the face by anger: *ḱró-ba-ma, ḱró-ba-čan* she whose face is wrinkled with anger, n. of a goddess *Glr.* 17, 12. — **ṭ́o-ṭ́á* W.* **dissatisfaction, grumbling.** — *ḱro-món Sch.* prison (perh. *ḱri-món*). — *ḱro-žál* an angry, frowning countenance *Glr.*

ཁྲོག་ *ḱrog?* — *ḱrog brgyáb-pa* to drink hastily, to gulp down *Glr.*; *ḱrog-ḱrog* plump! the sound caused by something falling heavily on the ground *W.* — *ḱrog-smán* the raw, unprepared substance of a medicine *Sch.*

ཁྲོག་པོ་ *ḱróg-po* botanical term, used of leaves standing round the stem scattered or alternately.

ཁྲོང་ངེ་ *ḱroṅ-ṅé* **upright, straight, erect,** (cf. *kroṅ,*) *Glr., Mil.*

ཁྲོང་པོ་ *ḱróṅ-po, *ṭ́óṅ-po* Ts.* **close-fisted, stingy.**

ཁྲོད་(པ་) *ḱród (-pa), W. *ṭ́ó (-pa)** **crowd, assemblage, mass, multitude;** *mi-ḱród* a troop, crowd of men, *ri-ḱród* an assemblage (mass) of mountains: *rtsva-ḱród* a heap, stack, rick of hay; *nags-ḱród* a dense forest, *mun-ḱród* thick darkness; *dur-ḱród* cemetery where the corpses are cut into pieces for the birds of prey; *dei ḱród-du lha-yčig ₀jóg-pas* placing the princess among their (the girls') company *Glr.*; in *W. *ṭ́ó-pai náṅ-na** and **náṅ-du** c. genit. is the usual expression for **among.**

ཁྲོན་ *ḱron* **claw, fang;** *ḱrón-kyis rkó-bai sde* the class of the gallinaceous birds *S.g.*

ཁྲོན་པ་ *ḱrón-pa* 1. **well, spring.** — 2. *Lh.*: a wooden **water kennel;** *ḱrón-bu* a little well; also n. of a medicinal herb, a purgative against bilious complaints *Med.* *ḱron-rágs* enclosure of a well *Sch.*

ཁྲོམ་ *ḱrom* 1. **market-place, market-street, bazar;** *ḱrom skór-ba* to wander, to ride round the market *Glr.*, to ramble through; *ysaṅ-sṅágs króm-du klog* secret spells (magic formulas) are read in the market (a crime and sacrilege in the eyes a Buddhist). — 2. **crowd of people,** multitude of persons; *ḱrom-čén* a great crowd; *tsógs-pai ḱróm-rnams* the assembled crowd *Pth.*; *ṗo-ḱróm* a multitude of men; *rgyal-ḱróm* prob. an assembly, a gathering of kings *Mil.*; *ḱrom dmar-nág ˛ḱyil-ba* a motley crowd, throng of people *Pth.*

Comp. — *ḱróm-čén (po) Thgr.* chief market-place, principal street *Cs.* — *ḱróm-dpoṅ* overseer, police-officer who is charged with the supervision of the market. — *ḱróm-skor-ma* harlot, strumpet *Cs.*

ཁྲོམ་པོ་ *ḱróm-po Glr.*, n. of a province (?). *ḱróm-po-pa* an inhabitant of it.

ཁྲོམ་མེ་ *ḱrom-mé* sparkling, glittering, *zil-pa ḱrom-mé* a sparkling dew-drop *Pth.*

ཁྲོམས་ *ḱroms* v. *˛grém-pa*.

ཁྲོལ་ *ḱrol* 1. v. *˛ḱról-ba* and *˛gról-ba*. — 2. **a sound;** *ḱról-gyis soṅ Glr.* (the ring) slid sounding (across the azure-floor); *ḱrol-dóṅ* is said to denote a large hand-bell, and *ḱrol-lóg* the same as *ḱrog-ḱróg W.* — Cf. *˛ḱról-ba*. — 3. kettle (?) v. *lčags*.

ཁྲོལ་ཁྲོལ་ *ḱrol-ḱról* adj 1. **bright, shining,** = *ḱról-po*. — 2. *ḱrol-ḱról byéd-pa Glr.*, *mig ṭol-lé ṭol-lé tá-wa* *C.* to stare, *la*, at.

ཁྲོལ་ཆ་ *ḱról-ča* the act of forgiving, pardon *Sch.*

ཁྲོལ་པོ་ *ḱról-po* 1. **sparkling, glistening, dazzling,** e. g. water when the sun shines upon it; *'od ṭól-po* *W.* brightness, splendour. — 2. **distinct, intelligible,** *(s)pé-ra ṭól-po zer mi śe(s)* *W.* he cannot speak distinctly.

ཁྲོལ་མོ་ *ḱról-mo W.* **brittle, fragile,** opp. to *mnyén-po*.

ཁྲོལ་ཚགས་ *ḱrol-tságs Lex., Cs.* **a sieve.**

ཁྲོས་པ་ *ḱrós-pa* v. *˳ḱró-ba*.

མཁན་ *mḱan*, an affix to substantives and verbal roots, denoting 1. one who knows a thing thoroughly, making a trade or profession of it, *sá-mḱan* one who knows the country, the road, a guide, a pilot (*Dzl.* ༢༧༥, 7); *lám-mḱan* id. *Mil.*; *śiṅ-mḱan*, worker in wood, carpenter, joiner etc. — 2. affixed to a verbal root, it is often (at least in later literature) equivalent to the periphrastic participle, signifying: he who in any special case performs an action; so *˛dógs-mḱan Glr.*, one who is binding, fastening; also with an objective case: *ṅai bú-mo ˛dód-mḱan Glr.* such as are courting my daughter; *bsád-mḱan* the man having killed, the murderer. — 3. In colloquial language, esp. in *W.*, it has on account of its more significant form entirely displaced the proper participle termination in *pa*: *dúṅ-ma ḱyer-ḱan-ni mi* *W.* the men carrying the beam; contrary to its original signification, it is even used in a passive sense: *sád-ḱan-ni lug* *W.* the slaughtered sheep.

མཁན་པོ་ *mḱán-po (Ssk.* **उपाध्याय, पण्डित**) a clerical teacher, **professor,** doctor of divinity, principal of a great monastery, **abbot,** who, as such, is endowed with the *mḱan-rgyúd*, or spiritual gifts, handed down from Buddha himself by transmission, viz. *dbaṅ, luṅ, ḱrid*; next to him comes the *slób-dpon*, or professor in ordinary. *mḱán-po ṫón-mi sámbho-ṭa* Dr. Thon-mi Sambhota; *mḱán-mo* **mistress, instructress** *Cs.*: *mḱán-bu* **pupil, scholar** *Tar.*; *mḱan-čén* a great Doctor, a head-master; *mḱan-slób* for *mḱán-po daṅ slób-dpon*, e.g. *blá-ma mḱan-slób-kyi bka* the words of the Lamas, abbots and masters; also for *mḱán-po daṅ slób-ma Glr.* 100, 4. — *mḱan-rábs* the series or succession of the abbots in the great monasteries *Cs.* — *mḱan-rim* the respective prospects of being elected abbot, as depending on the different ranks of the expectant individuals.

མཁའ་ *mḱa (Ssk.* **ख**) 1. **heaven, heavens,** gen. *nam-mḱa*; *mḱa-la* in the heavens, *mḱá-la ṗúr-ba, rgyú-ba, ldiṅ-ba* to fly, wander, soar, in the air. — 2. **ether,** as the fifth element. — 3. symb. num.: **cipher, naught.**

Comp. — *mḱa-klóṅ, mḱa-kyáb, mḱa-dbyiṅs* the whole compass or extent of the heavens *Cs.* — *mk'a-₍gró-ma*, in *Mil.* gen. *mk'a-p'ro-ma, Ssk.* डाकिनी, fabulous beings of more modern legends, 'wise' women of supernatural powers, sometimes represented like angels, at other times like fairies or witches. — *mk'a-mnyám Lex.* like the heavens, infinite. — *mk'a-ldiṅ* the sky-soarer, the bird Garuda, v. *k'yuṅ*. — *mk'a-spyód* wanderings through heaven *Tar.* 112, 4, also: enjoyment of heaven, enjoying or inhabiting heaven; *mk'a-spyód-du γšégs-pa* to go to heaven, to die *Mil.*

མཁར་ *mk'ar* 1. resp. *sku-mk'ár. Glr.*, **castle**, nobleman's seat or mansion, manor-house, frq.; **citadel, fort** *Pth.;* **house** in general *Mil.* — 2. termin. case of *mk'a*.

Comp. — *mk'ar-dpón* governor of a castle, commander of a fortress. — *mk'ar-lás C.* and *B.*, the work of constructing a castle, of raising an edifice; **k'ar-lén** *W.* id. — *mk'ar-srúṅ* the guard or garrison of a castle, fortress *Cs.* —

མཁར་བ་ *mk'ár-ba* 1. (also *ₒk'ár-ba) B.* and *C.*, **staff, stick;** *mk'ar-γsil* staff of the mendicant friars, the upper part of which is hung with jingling rings; *p'yag-mk'ár* resp. for *mk'ár-ba*. — 2. **bronze, bell-metal,** v. *₍k'ár-ba*.

མཁལ་མ་ *mk'ál-ma* **kidney, reins,** *mk'ál mdog* 'kidney-colour, dark red' *Cs.*

མཁས་པ་ *mk'ás-pa Ssk.* पटु, (originally like σοφός) **skilled; skilful,** in mechanical work, and so it is frq. used in col. language; further in a more general sense: *smán-pa mk'ás-pa* a skilful, clever physician; **experienced, learned, prudent, shrewd, wise;** c. accus. or dat., in a thing; *so-tšís-la* in farming, *č'os* in religion; *slób-ma skyóṅ-ba-la mk'ás-pa* an able tutor, pedagogue *Mil.; mk'as-btsun-bzáṅ* prop. denotes the qualities of a right priest: learned, conscientious, good, but sometimes it indicates only the position in society, the clerical rank, so esp. *mk'as-btsún* learned clerics, reverends *Glr.*, *mk'ás-po* or *-pa* a learned man, **a scholar,** *sṅón-gyi mk'ás-po-rnams* learned men of former times; *mk'as-γrúb* id., *rgya-gár-gyi mk'as-grúb-rnams* Indian scholars; it is also used like our 'most wise', 'very learned', and similar expressions in a pompous address *Glr.; mk'as-mč'óg* profound scholar *Zam.* I never found the word applied to inanimate things in the sense of 'wisely contrived', and the correctness of *Cs.: t'abs mk'ás-pos* 'by wise means' may be questioned.

མཁུན་པ་ *mk'ún-pa Sch.* v. *k'ún-pa*.

མཁུར་ཚོས་ *mk'ur-tšós* v. *k'ur-tšós*.

མཁོ་བ་ *mk'ó-ba* **desirable,** to be wished for, *mk'ó-bai yo-ₒbyád*, in *C.* also **k'o-ǰhę**, desirable things, requisits, wants, desiderata; **hindu-tęn-gyi mi-la k'ó-wę tsoṅ-zóg** articles of commerce, goods, commodities, such as they are called for in Hindostan; *nyé-bar mk'ó-ba* indispensable, most necessary. Cf. *ₒk'o*.

མཁོས་ཕབ་ *mk'os-p'áb Lex.* v. *₍k'os*.

མཁྱུད་པ་ *mk'yúd-pa Cs.:* to keep, to hold, to embrace, = *₍k'yúd-pa; dpe-mk'yúd Lex.* w.e.; *Cs.*: unwillingness to lend books, *dpe-mk'yúd-čan* unwilling to lend books, *dpe-mk'yúd byed-pa* to be unwilling to lend books; *mk'yud-spyád* a sort of bag or vessel for carrying something (?); sorcery, witchcraft *Sch.*

མཁྱེན་པ་ *mk'yen-pa*, resp. for *šés-pa, rig-pa, gó-ba*, **to know,** *yab-yúm-gyis mk'yén-par mdzód-čig* my esteemed parents may know *Dzl.;* to know, one man from another, *rgyál-po mk'yén-tam* does the king, does your majesty know the . . . ? (the king himself will answer: *ṅas šés-so) Dzl.* It is frq. used of the supernatural perception of Buddha and the saints, *bsám-p'a dág-par mk'yén-pas* as he (the Bodhisattwa) perceived the sentiments (of his scholar) to be sincere *Dzl.; mk'yén-par gyúr-to* perceived, found out, discovered; **to understand,** *mk'yen sóṅ-ṅam* did you understand it? *mk'yen-rgyá-čan* possessed of much understanding, very learned *Mil.; mk'yén-ldan-yáṅs-pa* profoundly learned; *mk'yen-brtsé Glr.* prob.: omniscient-merciful; *t'ams-čad-mk'yén* all-knowing, a later epithet of Buddha; *ye-mḱyén*, *mṅon-mḱyén* = *ye-śés*, *mṅon-śés*. — *tugs-mkyén* is known to me only as a sbst. abstr.: the knowing, **knowledge, prophetic sight,** *rje-btsún-gyis tugs-mḱyén-gyis yzigs-pa lágs-sam* has your reverence seen by your prophetic sight? *Mil.*; acc. to *Cs.*, however, *sku-mḱyén*, *ysuṅ-mḱyén* and *tugs-mḱyén* are identical in meaning with *mḱyen-mḱyén*, a form of entreaty which, as a Lama told me, properly has the sense: you know yourself best what is good for me! In accordance to this explanation we find in *Mil.* after an entreaty: *blá-ma ḱyed mḱyen-mḱyen.* It is gen. added without any connecting word, like our **pray,** or **please,** but sometimes it is construed with the inf.: *mdzád-pa(r) mḱyen-mḱyén*, please to do.

མཁྲང་(བ་) *mḱraṅ (-ba)*, also *ḱraṅ* **hard, solid, compact;** *srá-mḱráṅ-čan ˳gyur-méd Thgy.* **firm, hearty, sound,** of a strong and robust constitution. — *mḱráṅ-pa* denotes the fourth stage of the development of the foetus *Thgy.*

མཁྲིག་མ་ *mḱrig-ma* **the wrist** of the hand.

མཁྲིགས་པ་ **ṭigs-pa** col. *W.* (also *Bunan*) for:

མཁྲིས་པ་ *mḱris-pa B.* and *C.* (*Ssk.* पित्त) **bile, gall.** — 1. the vesicle of the gall, the gall-bladder, as part of the intestines. — 2. generally: the substance of the bile, the bilious fluid, which acc. to Indo-Tibetan philosophy is connected with the element of fire, and which, conformably to its functions, is divided into five species, of which physiology gives the oddest details. — *mḱris-nád* bilious disease; *mḱris-tsád* prob. bilious fever; *gráṅ-mḱris* a feverish shivering, a chill.

མཁྲིས་མ་ *mḱris-ma Lex.* w.e., perh. = ˳*ḱris.*

མཁྲེགས་པ་ *mḱrégs-pa*, *W.* **ṭág-mo** (*Ssk.* सार) **hard, firm,** e.g. snow; **yo-ṭág-čan** *W.* **obstinate, stiffnecked, stubborn.**

འཁང་བ་ ˳*ḱáṅ-ba* (not: to put a fault or crime on another *Cs.*, but:) **to hurt** or **offend, to annoy, to vex,** *tsúr-la ˳ḱaṅ* we cause vexation to ourselves (by minding too much the affairs of others): ˳*ḱaṅ* **animosity**, ˳*ḱaṅ maṅ* there occur many collisions, quarrels *Mil.*, *dpon-slób re ˳ḱaṅ ˳byuṅ* there arise mutual differences, animosities, between masters and scholars *Mil.*

འཁད་པ་ ˳*ḱád-pa* esp. *W.* 1. **to sit, to sit firm,** *rtai ḱá-ru* on the back of a horse. — 2. to remain sitting, **to stick fast,** to be stopped, kept back, e.g of a bird, *rnyius*, in a snare: *rkáṅ-pa ˳ḱád-de ˳gyél-ba* to get entangled with the foot so as to fall; *sgo ˳ḱad ˳dug* the door sticks. Cf. also *ḱad-pa* and *bkad-pa.*

འཁམ་པ་ ˳*ḱám-pa* 1. **to faint away, to swoon.** — 2. *Sch.* also: to take into one's mouth.

འཁར་བ་ ˳*ḱár-ba* I. sbst. 1. **staff** v. *mḱár-ba.* — 2. **bronze, bell-metal,** ˳*ḱár-(bai) čú* molten, liquid bronze, ˳*ḱár-bai mé-loṅ* a metallic mirror; ˳*ḱar-ṙṅá* **gong,** used in India and China instead of bells: *Cs.*: a drum of bronze; yet it is rather a large bronze disk, producing, when struck, a very loud sound like that of a bell. — ˳*ḱar-yžóṅ* a dish or basin of metal: ˳*ḱar-záṅs* a metallic kettle. — II. vb., in *C.* the same as ˳*ḱád-pa.* — 2. in *W.* intrs. to *dgar-ba.*

འཁར་འཁུ་བ་ ˳*ḱár-˳ḱu-ba* to resist *Sch.*

འཁལ་བ་ ˳*ḱál-ba*, pf. and fut. (imp. *ḱol?*), *W.* **kál-če** 1. *B.*, *C.*, *W.*: **to spin,** *bal*, wool, *skúd-pa* a thread, *srád-bu* yarn. — 2. *W.* **to send, to forward,** things.

འཁུ་བ་ ˳*ḱú-ba* **to offend, insult,** *Bhar.* (*Lex.* = द्रोह injury); ˳*ḱu-˳ḱrig*, acc. to the context, denotes certain passions that disturb the tranquillity of the mind, such as malignity and covetousness: ˳*ḱáṅ-ba* is synon. — *Cs.*'s 'to emulate, contemn, hate, long for', and *Sch.*'s 'pride' I am not able to verify.

འཁུན་པ་ ˳*ḱún-pa* **to groan,** to fetch a deep sigh, not so much as a sign of pain or sorrow, but rather as a mere physical deep and hollow sound *Med.*; ˳*ḱún-sgras ḱáṅ-pa ḱeṅs* he filled the house with groanings *Pth.; sdáṅ-bai dgrá-la γyag ltar ₒk'un* he groans (grunts, bellows) like a yak against a fierce enemy *Mil.*

འཁུམ་པ་ *ₒk'úm-pa* pf. *k'ums* (cf. *skúm-pa*) **to shrink,** to be contracted, e.g. of the limbs, by gout; **yúr-ra raṅ-žin ₒk'úm-ĉe yin** W.* the ditch will get narrower of itself; *k'úms-pa* shrunk, shrivelled, contracted; fig. reduced, restricted, deprived of power.

འཁུམས་པ་ *ₒk'úms-pa Lex.* and *Cs.* to comprehend, understand; *Sch.* also: to practise, to impress on the mind.

འཁུར་བ་ *ₒk'úr-ba* I. sbst. = *k'úr-ba*, **pastry.** II. vb., pf. and fut. *k'ur*, rarely *bkur* (v. *bkúr-ba*) 1. **to carry, convey,** *k'ur(-ru) ₒk'úr-ba* to carry a load; *mi t'ég-par ₒk'úr-ba Med.* to carry too heavy loads, prop to carry what one cannot carry; **k'ur šog** C., **k'ur kyoṅ** W. bring! fetch! **k'ur soṅ** C., **k'ur k'yer** W. take away! carry off! *ₒk'úr-du t'ógs-te* taking up in order to carry, taking on one's back *Dzl.*; **lág-par k'úr-ĉe** W. to hold in one's hand. — 2. **to carry away or off,** *ro ₒk'úr-ba Pth.*, to carry away a corpse; **to take along with,** in W. even: **to pocket,** **sém-la k'úr-ĉe** W. to take to heart; **'á-ne ₒk'úr-ĉe** to take a wife, to marry. — *ₒk'úr-t'ag* carrying-girth, rope or strap *Thgy.* Cf. *k'ur, k'úr-ba* etc.

འཁུར་ཚོས *ₒk'ur-tsós* v. *k'ur-tsós.*

འཁུལ་བ་ *ₒk'úl-ba* **to subdue, to subject** *Cs.*; *Sch.* also: to be uneasy about. *Lex.*: *γyóg-tu ₒk'úl-ba*; v. also *k'ul* 3. *Zam.*; *k'ral ₒk'úl-ba* perh. to force a tax, a rate, on a person.

འཁེགས་པ་ *ₒk'egs-pa* pf. *k'egs* **to hinder, stop, shut off, debar,** *lam* the way *Mil.*; *ji-ltar bkag ruṅ ma k'égs-pas Mil.*, although they prohibited, tried to proh. him), he was not prohibited; *rgyál-bai p'yág-gis kyaṅ mi k'égs-pa Mil.* not being hindered even by Buddha's power.

འཁེངས་པ་ *ₒk'éṅs-pa*, pf. *k'eṅs*, **to be full,** *ĉus keṅs yod-pa Glr.*; *blo-grós ma k'éṅs-te* his mind not being satiated *Tar.* 135, 13.

འཁེབ་པ་ *ₒk'éb-pa* pf. *k'ebs*, **to cover, to spread over,** *yoṅs-su k'ébs-te* being covered all over *Stg.*; *k'a t'ams-ĉad k'ebs-te* over the whole face *Stg.*; **to overshadow** *Dzl.* ༥༢, 17.

འཁེལ་བ་ *ₒk'él-ba* pf. *k'él* 1. **to put on, to load, to pack on,** = *ₒgél-ba*; *bĉu-t'óg k'él-na* when the ten stories or lofts shall have been put on *Mil.nt.* 2. **to spin,** = *ₒk'ál-ba C., Glr.*

འཁོ་བ་ *ₒk'ó-ba* (vb. to *mk'ó-ba*), **to wish, to want,** to think useful, serviceable, necessary, to have occasion for *Mil.*; *ₒk'ó-ste ₒoṅ* he will be able to make use of it *Mil.*; **ₒk'óa mi ₒk'o** or **ₒk'ó-ĉe med** W. I do not want it, I do not like it; *ₒk'o-bjéd* fit for use, **useful.**

འཁོགས་པ་ *ₒk'ógs-pa* weak from old age, **decrepit, decayed;** *rgan* or *rgas-ₒk'ógs* id.; *sṅo-kóg, skya-k'óg* (sic) *Thgy.* with a complexion blue or pale from old age.

འཁོང་བ་ *ₒk'óṅ-ba* (cf. *sgóṅ-ba*) to contract one's limbs, to sit in a cowering position, **to squat; to hide one's self;** *dpa ₒk'óṅ-ba* to become discouraged, disheartened *Thgy.*

འཁོད, ཁོད་ *ₒk'od, k'od* 1. **surface, superficies;** *sai ₒk'od snyóms-pa* to remove inequalities of the surface, to level, to plane, *ₒk'ód-snyoms-pa* levelled, made even, plain; also fig.: *bár-gyi k'od snyoms* gaps were filled up, i.e. distinctions of rank, wealth etc. were done away with, not in consequence of a revolution, but as an act of kindness, forced upon the people by a despotic government. — 2. **a mill-stone,** **yá-k'o'** the upper stone, **má-k'o'** the nether stone *C.*

འཁོད་པ་ *ₒk'ód-pa* **to sit down, to sit;** *bar-snáṅ-la*, suspended in the air, floating, soaring, frq. of gods and saints in legends; *rgyal-srid-la* to have been raised to the throne *Tar.*; **to live, to dwell** *Dzl.*; gen. used like a passive to *ₒgód-pa* **to be put, placed, established** (in virtue, in a doctrine, = to be converted to); *glegs-bám-du* to be put down in writing, to be recorded *Tar.* Cf. *ₒk'ád-pa.*

འཁོན་པ་ ˳*ḱón-pa* (*Lexx.* have a pf. *bkon*) 1. c.c. *daṅ*, **to bear a grudge** or ill-will against a person, **to be dissatisfied** with a thing; ˳*ḱón-nas* when they (the states) were at war with one another (opp. to *mtʼún-nas* in peaceful relations) *Glr.*; ˳*ḱón-med-par* honestly, without insidious intentions, e.g. in negotiations *Glr.*; *čʼos daṅ* ˳*ḱón-pa* to wish to keep aloof from religion, or to have done with religion; in a special sense: to be tired of the clerical profession *Glr.*; ˳*ḱón-žugs-pa*, ˳*ḱón-du* ˳*dzin-pa* = ˳*ḱón-pa*; ˳*ḱon res byéd-pa Sch.* to quarrel, prob. more accurately, to have a spite against each other. — ˳*ḱón-po* **dissension, discord** *Sch.* Cf. *ḱón-pa*. — 2. *C.* = ˳*ḱar-ba* II.

འཁོབ་ ˳*ḱób Sch.* **barbarous, rough, rude,** gen. combined with *mtʼa*, *mtʼa-*˳*ḱób*, with or without *yul*, **barbarous border-country.** So the Tibetans always designate their own country, in comparison with India, the holy land of Buddhism, as being *mtʼa-*˳*ḱób ḱá-ba-čan*. The rarely occurring *yaṅ-ḱób* seems to indicate a still more distant and barbarous country.

འཁོབས་པ་ ˳*ḱóbs-pa* to be startled, agitated, alarmed. in one Lex. however, it is explained by *ḱyáb-pa*.

འཁོར་ ˳*ḱor* 1. **circle, circumference**; the persons or objects encircling, surrounding (a certain point or place); *lté-ba daṅ dei* ˳*ḱór-rnams* the navel and the circumjacent parts *Med.*; **de-ḱór-la** *W.* thereabout; *nye-*˳*ḱór* v. *nye*; more esp. **retinue, attendants.** ˳*ḱor daṅ bčas-pa* (**सपरिवार**) with attendants, suite: ˳*ḱor rnám-pa bži Tar.* frq., the attendants of Buddha's hearers, divided into four classes (viz. in the earliest times: *dge-slóṅ*, *dge-slóṅ-ma*, *dge-snyén*, and *dge-snyén-ma*; at a later period: *nyan-tʼós*, *raṅ-sans-rgyás*, *byaṅ-čʼub-séms-dpa*, and *so-sói skyé-bo-rnams* q.v.) ˳*ḱor dgra-bčóm-pas bskór-te* surrounded by the retinue of the Arhants (v. *dgra-bčóm-pa*); ˳*ḱór-du bsdús-so* he gathered them round himself as his retinue *Dzl.*; also **fig.**: the train of thoughts, reminiscences etc., which the soul, when passing into a new body, cannot take along with it *Thgy.*; it is also used for a single servant or attendant (*Cs.* has ˳*ḱór-po* or ˳*ḱór-pa* male attendant, and ˳*ḱór-ma* female attendant), ˳*ḱor yčig Mil.*; ˳*ḱor ynyis* two attendants *Glr.*, hence ˳*ḱor-rnams* sometimes for domestics, household servants; but if ˳*ḱor* with a numeral is preceded by *ytsó-bo*, or a similar noun, this preceding word is acc. to the Tibetan mode of speaking included in the number given, so that *ytsó-bo* ˳*ḱor lṅa* should be translated: the master and four attendants (not five). — 2. instead of ˳*ḱór-ba*, or *ḱór-lo*, esp. in compound words; *lo-*˳*ḱór* = *lo-skór* a cycle, comprising a space of twelve years.

Comp. ˳*ḱór-mḱan* **attendants** *Glr.* — ˳*ḱór-*˳*báṅs* **subjects** *Cs.* — ˳*ḱor-yyóg* = ˳*ḱór* **retinue, servants** etc. — **dhuṅ-ḱór** *C.* **waiting man,** valet de chamber, = *sku-mdún-pa* which is the respectful word for it. — *naṅ-*˳*ḱór* household servants, domestics. — **ḱor-gyág** *W.* **latch.** — ˳*ḱor-*˳*dás* v. sub ˳*ḱór-ba* II.

འཁོར་བ་ ˳*ḱór-ba* I. vb. (cf. *skór-ba*), **to turn round, to turn about, to go round** in a circle: ˳*ḱór-gin yod* he is walking (running, flying etc.) round the . . . *Glr.*; esp. of the successive transmigrations of metempsychosis, v. II: *mgo* ˳*ḱor* my head turns, I am getting dizzy, confused; also **I am duped,** cheated, imposed on, *ḱyéd-kyi ḱa-sbyáṅ-gyis ṅed mgo mi* ˳*ḱor* we are not to be taken in by the volubility of your tongue *Mil.*; **to pass away, to grow full, to be completed,** *lo-dús* ˳*ḱór-ba-na* when one year was past *Glr.*; *srás-kyis lo* ˳*ḱór-te* when the prince had completed one year, was one year old; **da bú-lon ḱor** *W.* now the debt is entirely paid off, cleared: **ḱor mi tʼub** it cannot be paid off; **mi ḱor**, the sum is not full, not sufficient to cover the debt: **to walk about, roam, ramble** *W.*; **to return** from a journey, to come home: **ráṅ-la ḱór-ba** to come or fall back (on the head of the author, originator); to come together, **to contract, to gather,** e.g.

clouds, frq. water, *koi ká-ču kor* W. it makes his mouth water; *dgrá-bo ₒkor Mil.* enemies are collecting (we create ourselves enemies); also impersonally: *kor soṅ* it has become cloudy; *ɣnam kor* the sky is getting overcast, clouded; therefore even **to arise, to be produced, formed,** *zil-pa ₒkor* dew is produced, *ɣyá*, rust, even: *lus-la sras ₒkor* a child has been formed, produced, in the womb *Pth.* —

II. sbst. 1. the turning round or about etc.; more particularly 2. **the orb** or **round** of transmigration within the six classes of physical beings. Though the Buddhist has not a more ardent wish, than to be finally released from the repeated wanderings of the soul, yet he believes so firmly in these migrations, that he will rather follow the doctrines of his philosophers, and doubt the reality of the perception of his senses, than think it possible, that the whole theory of the *ₒkór-ba* with all its consequences should be nothing but a product of human imagination. — *ₒkór-bar ₒkór-ba* to turn round, to wander about in the orb of transmigration; *ₒkór-bai btsón-ra, ₒdam, mtso* the dungeon, the swamp, the sea of the *ₒkór-ba; ₒkór-ba-las ₒdás-pa* to escape from the *ₒkór-ba,* = to enter into the Nirwana *ₒkór - ₒdas* 1. abbreviation of the foregoing. 2. for *ₒkór-ba daṅ ₒdas-pa* the stay in the *ₒkór-ba* and the escape from it; *ₒkor ₒdas ɣnyis-su ṅas ma mtoṅ* I have not seen that there is a difference between these two *Mil.*

འཁོར་ཡུག་ *ₒkor-yúg* **a wall, rampart** *Cs.*, v. *kó-ra.*

འཁོར་གཡའ་ *kór-ɣyá C.* **latch.**

འཁོར་ལོ་ *ₒkór-lo (Ssk.* **चक्र, मण्डल**) 1. **circle,** *tsógs-kyi ₒkór-lo* offerings arranged in a circle, v. *tsogs: ₒkór-lo ₒbri-ba* to describe a circle *Tar.* More frq.: 2. a circular body, **a disk, roll, wheel,** any modification of the cylinder, *bču-ɣsum-ₒkór-lo* the column on the *mčod-rtén* consisting apparently of thirteen circular disks; *ₒkór-lo brtsib-brgyád* the wheel with eight spokes, a frq. attribute of deities; *rdza-mkán-gyi ₒkór-lo* potter's wheel; *čós-kyi ₒkór-lo* praying-cylinder, cf. below; also a complication of wheels, wheel-work, engine, *ₒprúl-(gyi) ₒkór(-lo)* 'magic wheel', a phantastic attribute of gods, but also any real machine of a more ingenious construction, e.g. sugar-press *Stg.*, electrical machine etc.; *čú-tsod-ₒkór-lo* a clock; *šiṅ-rta-ₒkór-lo* waggon, carriage, also cart-wheel. — Figuratively: *bdé-ba daṅ sdug-bsṅál-gyi ₒkór-lo,* vicissitude of fortune; *dús-kyi ₒkór-lo* (**कालचक्र**) acc. to *Cs.'s* Chronological Table (*Cs.'s Gram.* p. 181) a later philosophical system, contained esp. in the *rtsa-rgyúd, Mūlatantra,* in which the Adibuddha doctrine, prophecies, chronology etc. are propounded. It was introduced into Tibet about 1000 p. Chr.; cf. also *Schl.* 45. — *ₒkór-lo sgyúr-ba,* or *skór-ba,* with *čós-kyi,* to turn the wheel of doctrine, = to preach, to teach religion, (vulgo understood only of the turning of the praying-cylinder); **čö-kyi kór-lo léṅ-mor bé'-pa* C.* to devote one's self to the preaching of religion. On the other hand: *ₒkór-los sgyúr-bai rgyál-po* (**चक्रवर्तिन्**) *Will.*: 'a ruler, the wheels of whose chariot roll everywhere without obstruction, emperor, sovereign of the world, the ruler of a *čakra*, or country extending from sea to sea'. In this Indian explanation two different etymologies are given, the former of which is undoubtedly the original one. Buddhism and the Tibetan language have added a third signification, 'praying-wheel'; modern scholars a fourth, that of the 'orb' or round of transmigration or metempsychosis: hence the confusion attaching to the import of this word.

འཁོར་ལོག་ **kor-lóg** is said to be used in col. language instead of *ka-ló* 3. *W.*

འཁོར་ས་ *ₒkór-sa* =. *skór-lam* v. *skór-ba* I. extr.; *ₒkór-sa bár-pa, čén-po Glr.*

འཁོར་གསུམ་ *ₒkor-ɣsum,* lit. three circles, *Ssk. trimaṇḍala*; *Sch.*: 'every thing that belongs to archery'; more correctly: arrow, knife, and spear.

འཁོལ་བ་ ˳ḱól-ba I. pf. ḱol, cf. *skól-ba*, **to boil, to be boiling,** *ču ḱol* the water is boiling; *˳ḱol ˳ǰúg-pa* to make boil, to set to the fire for boiling, = *skól-ba*; **to ferment** (dough), **to effervesce, to sparkle** (beer) *W.* — II. pf. *bkol*, imp. *ḱol* 1. to oblige a person to be a servant or bondman, **to use as a servant;** in full: *bran-du*, also *γyóg-tu*, *˳ḱól-ba*; therefore *bran-ḱól*, *ḱól-po* **servant, man-servant:** *bkol-spyód-kyi sdug-bsṅál* the calamity of servitude, current expression for designating the lot of animals; *γžán-dag-gis dbáṅ-med-par bkól-ba* to be enslaved by others, to be compelled to do slave-work *Thgy.*; *dgé-bai lás-la bkól-ba* to make a person minister to works of virtue. — 2. **to save, to spare,** to enjoy with moderation *Cs.*, *zúr-du . . . bkól-ba Lex.*; *Sch.:* saved, laid up, put by. — 3. *Sch.:* **to become insensible, to be asleep, to get benumbed,** in reference to the limbs; seems to be used in *Med.*

འཁོས་ ˳ḱos 1. *C.* also *˳ḱós-ka* (cognate to *˳ḱó-ba*), **worth, value, importance** *Cs.*; *˳ḱós-čan* important, mighty, of great influence, *˳ḱos-méd* the opposite of it. — 2. *˳ḱós-su-ṗab-pa* **clyster** *Sch.*; one Lex. has *mḱos-ṗáb*, w.e.

འཁྱག(ས)་པ་ ˳ḱyág(s)-pa 1. **to freeze** (of water, earth, provisions); **to coagulate, congeal** (melted fat etc.). — 2. **to feel cold,** *˳ḱyágs-na gós gyon* if you feel cold, put on clothes *Glr.*, *ḱyag ǰhuṅ* *C.*, *ḱyágs-sa rag* *W.* I feel cold; *˳ḱyágs-gri* a feeling cold, a shivering (cf. *ltógs-gri*) *Mil.*; *ḱyágs-ša* *W.* id., the cold fit of the ague. — *˳ḱyags-rúm*, *˳ḱyags-róm* **ice** *Glr.*; *˳ḱyags-lhám* snow-shoe *Sch.*

འཁྱམ་པ་ ˳kyám-pa **to run about, to wander,** e.g. *čá-med yúl-du* in an unknown country *Glr.*; *˳ḱór-bar* in the orb or round of transmigration, v. *˳ḱór-ba*; *˳ḱyám-ste nor mi bdóg-pa žig* one who lives as a vagabond *Dzl.*; *dé-dag-ni rnám-par ˳ḱyám-pao* they are mistaken, on the wrong track *Wdṅ.*; *˳ḱyám-dù ˳ǰúg-pa* to cause to ramble or rove about, to scatter; *˳ḱyáms-pa* strayed, lost, wandering, vagrant; erroneous, erring *Tar.* 153, 15. — *˳kyám-ḱyi* a vagrant dog. — *˳ḱyáms-po* 1. a vagabond. — 2. n. of a disease *Med.* — 3. erroneous *Tar.* — *ču ˳ḱyám-pa* inundation, flood *Ma.*

འཁྱར་བ་ ˳ḱyár-ba **to err, to go astray, to deviate from,** *yan ḱyár-la ma ča* *Ld.* do not step out of your rank! do not absent yourself! *˳ḱyar dogs yod* one should be afraid of going astray *Thgy.*; *dpe ˳ḱyár-po* a defective simile; *tsig ˳kyár-po* an inadequate designation. — In *Tar.* 48, 4 *dpe ˳ḱyár-po* is translated 'epitome' by *Schf.*, but the whole passage is somewhat obscure.

འཁྱལ་བ་ ˳ḱyál-ba = *kyal-ka* q.v.

འཁྱི་བ་ ˳ḱyi-ba *Sch.*, prob. an incorrect reading for *˳ḱyil-ba*.

འཁྱིག་པ་ ˳ḱyig-pa, pf. *bkyigs*, fut. *bkyig*, **to bind** (a prisoner, a bundle of straw etc.); *kye* (v. *ske*) *ḱyig-pa* *C.* to strangle, suffocate.

འཁྱིགས་པ་ °ḱyigs-pa **to comprise, encompass** *Pth.*, v. *páṅ-pa*.

འཁྱིད་པ་ ˳ḱyid-pa, *Sch.:* *mig ˳ḱyid-pa* **to turn** or **roll** one's eyes.

འཁྱིམས་པ་ ˳ḱyims-pa 1. **to be encircled** with a halo, as the sun and moon sometimes are *Cs.*; *˳og-˳ḱyims Lex.* = परिधि halo; also *˳ja-ód ˳ḱyims* a rainbow-coloured halo appears *Pth.* — 2.: *na-búṅ* or *múg-pa ḱyims, dúd-pa ḱyims*, fog, smoke, **comes floating on.**

འཁྱིར་བ་ °ḱyir-ba **to turn round** in a circular course *Cs.*, *Lex.: γdugs ˳ḱyir-ba* to turn a parasol round (?).

འཁྱིལ་བ་ ˳ḱyil-ba vb. n. 1. **to wind, to twist;** *duṅ γyás-su ˳ḱyil-ba* a triton or trumpet-shell, wound to the right, and then considered particularly valuable, these shells generally being wound to the left; of the hair: *gyén-la ˳ḱyil-ba* wound or twisted (on the crown of the head) *Glr.*; *ro-smád °brúl-du ˳ḱyil-ba* the lower part of the body being wound into a serpent (the usual manner of representing the '*klu*'); *˳ód-du ˳ḱyil-žiṅ*, the body enveloping itself in light *Mil.*; to roll: *nya γser-mig ˳ḱyil-*

ba yod the fish rolls its golden eye *Mil.*; to whirl, to eddy, to move round rapidly, of the water, so prob. *Dzl.* ༡༢, 13; ༢༨༡, 2; *k̓rom dmar-nág ₒk̓yil-ba* the motley crowd in a whirling motion *Pth.*; to hang or flow down in folds, of a tent or a curtain *Glr.* 33, 12. — 2. **to flow** (whirling) **together**, used of rivulets and brooks overflowing so as to form small lakes *Mil.*; of persons: to meet, to flock or crowd together, *mi mán-po dé-ru ₒk̓yil-bar gyúr-te Pth.*; **k̓yil-ču,** and **ču-k̓yil** col. puddle.

འཁྱུ་བ་ ₒk̓yú-ba, pf. ₒk̓yus **to run** *Lex.*

འཁྱུག་པ་ ₒk̓yúg-pa, pf. k̓yug 1. *Cs.*: **to run**; ₒk̓yug-po a runner; ₒk̓yúg-yig running hand, current hand-writing, as is used in the writing of letters etc.; ₒk̓yúg-po ₒk̓yú-ba *Lex.* is explained by *Sch.*: to run away hastily. The signification of running, however, seems to be obsolete, whilst the usual meaning is: 2. **to dart** or **sweep rapidly along**, frq. used of a flash of lightning, also of the rapid motion of a fish in the water *Mil.*; of spectral apparitions *Mil.*; of acute rheumatic pains; of the light: to flash, to shoot rays of light, *k̓ra-k̓yug-k̓yúg-pa* to gleam, to sparkle with light, to shine in various colours *Pth.*; *ser-ₒk̓yúg-ge-ba* glittering in yellow lustre *Mil.*; to glitter, to shine, of the rainbow; to shine through, of the veins through the cuticle etc. — **k̓yúg-šar-čán** *W.* hasty, hurrying, careless.

འཁྱུད་པ་ ₒk̓yúd-pa 1. **to embrace** frq., *mgúl-nas ₒk̓yúd-pa* to clasp round the neck, **to hug**; to encompass by spanning *Pth.* and elsewhere, cf. ₒk̓yigs-pa. — 2. **to glide** in or into (as serpents), *mnál-du ₒk̓yúg-pa* of the soul in the new conception, like the synonym ₒkríl-ba, for ₒǰúg-pa. — 3. **to be able,** **núd-pa mál-sa-na lán-ña** (instead of *lan-bar*) **mi k̓yud** the sick man is not able to rise from his bed. — *blos mi ₒk̓yúd-pa byéd-pa Thgy.* (not clear).

འཁྱུར་བ་ ₒk̓yúr-ba *Cs.*: to be separated, divorced; *Lex.*: *bskúr-bas ₒk̓yúr-ba,* therefore prob. the vb. n. to *skyúr-ba,* to be deserted, cast off.

འཁྱེང་བ་ ₒk̓yéṅ-ba seems to be = ₒgéṅs-pa *C.* col.

འཁྱེད་པ་ k̓yéd-pa (1. cf. ₒgyed-pa) *Cs.* **to be distributed**, e.g. food, *Dzl.* — 2. *C.* and *W.* **to be sufficient, to suffice, to be enough, to hold out,** **mi k̓yed** there is not enough. — 3. *C.* to gain (a law-suit), **to be acquitted.** — 4. *p̓yir k̓yéd-pa* **to bow** without uncovering one's head, as a less humble way of saluting *Mil.nt.*

འཁྱེར་བ་ ₒk̓yér-ba pf. ₒk̓yer (Northern *Ld.* **k̓yers**), at the end of a sentence *k̓yér-ro Tar.* and others, (*Cs. k̓yer-to?*), nearly the same as ₒk̓ur-ba; (the **नय** of the Lexx.: to lead, to guide, does not fully agree with the sense in which it is generally used) — 1. **to carry away, to take away**; *čus* to be carried or swept away by water; fig.: *lé-los* to be overcome, carried away by idleness *Mil.*; *ldé-mig k̓yer* take the key with you! — 2. **to carry, to bring,** in a more general sense, *C.* and *B.*: *k̓yer šog* bring! *k̓yer soṅ* carry off! take away! (in a like manner as ₒk̓úr-ba); *des ču bláṅ-nas k̓yer ₒóṅ-bai lám-k̓a-na* he having fetched water, being on his way to bring it *Pth.*; *k̓yer-la šog* bring me (word), let me know (the result of your investigation) *Mil.* — ₒk̓yér-so 1. **appearance,** esp. a neat, handsome appearance of persons or things. 2. **advantage, superiority, pleasantness,** *Mil.*, *C.*

འཁྱེལ་བ་ ₒk̓yel-ba *Ld.* **to hit, to strike.**

འཁྱོག་པ་ ₒk̓yóg-pa, pf. k̓yag, imp. k̓yog, **to lift, lift up,** = ₒt̓ógs-pa, t̓égs-pa *Glr.*; **to carry, bring,** **sól-ǰha k̓yog** bring in the tea *C.*, cf. sub *k̓ag*.

(འ)ཁྱོག་པོ་ ₒk̓yóg-po or k̓yóg-po **crooked, bent;** *k̓yóg-poi ri-mo* a crooked figure, a curve, flourish, crescent etc.; *nyas p̓ar ₒk̓yog t̓sur ₒk̓yog byás-šiṅ* the fish winding its body, writhing *Pth.*; ₒk̓yog-čan, ₒk̓yog-ₒk̓yóg tortuous; ₒk̓yog-bšád a crooked, out of the way construction or explanation. — ₒk̓yog stón-pa to fly into a passion (?) *Sch.*

(འ)ཁྱོགས་ °*ḱyogs* or *ḱyogs* **palanquin, sedan-chair, litter** *Pth.*; °*ḱyogs-dpyáṅ* id.; a lath or pole for carrying burdens *Sch.*

འཁྱོང་བ་ °*ḱyóṅ-ba* pf. and imp. *ḱyoṅ* **to bring** *W.*

འཁྱོམ་པ་ °*ḱyóm-pa* pf. °*ḱyoms* 1. **to rock, to wave,** of a ship *Schr.*, of the water *Sch.* (not quite clear); **ḱyom-ḱyom do-ba** *C.* **to reel, stagger,** **čáṅ-ghi ḱyom-pa dug** he is staggering under the influence of beer; to be dizzy *Med.*; *mtso-°ḱyóm* dizziness, vertigo, ni. f.; *lug-glád mgo-°ḱór °ḱyóm-pa ɣso* the brain of a sheep cures the swimming of the head (vertigo) *Med.*

འཁྱོར་བ་ °*ḱyór-ba* 1. **to miss, fail,** not to hit *Cs.* — 2. **to reel, stagger,** from intoxication. — 3. **to warp,** of wood.

འཁྱོལ་བ་ °*ḱyól-ba*, pf. °*ḱyol*, cf. *skyél-ba*, **to be carried, to be brought** (somewhere) *Pth.*; with *ɣnód-pa* to be done, inflicted *Mil.*; **to arrive at, come to, reach,** *sku-tsé mṫá-ru* the end of life.

འཁྱོས་པ་, (འཕྱོས་པ་) °*ḱyós-pa* (°*pyós-pa*) *Sch.*, °*ḱyós-ma Mil.*, **a present, gift,** = *ḱyós ma, skyás-ma.*

འཁྲ་བ་ °*ḱrá-ba* I. vb., pf. prob. °*ḱras* **to lean to, to incline towards** *Cs.*; °*ḱrá-sa* a support to lean against, a prop, back (of a chair) *Lex.* — II. adj. **hard,** = °*ḱráṅ-ba, mkráṅ-ba Sch.*

འཁྲབ་པ་ °*ḱráb-pa*, pf. *bkrab* (?), cf. also *skráb-pa*, 1. **to strike, to beat,** in repeated strokes, as in swimming and rowing; **to thrust, stamp, thump,** tread heavily, *bro °ḱrab-pa* to dance in that manner *Mil.*, *Pth.* — 2. **to winnow, to fan** *Stg.*, col. **ṭáb-pa**. — 3. **miy ṭab ṭab** (or **ṭab-ṭab**) **ȷhé-pa** *C.*, **čó-če** *W.*, **to blink, twinkle, wink** with the eyes. — 4. **ḱa-šág ṭab-če** *W.* **to jest, to joke,** to crack jokes. — 5. *Sch.*: **to leap, jump,** *Schr.* for joy. — 6. **to scoop out, to bail out** *Sch.* — 7. **to fight, to combat** *C.*, *W.*

འཁྲལ་འཁྲུལ་ °*ḱral-°ḱrúl* **confusion, disorder.**

འཁྲི་བ་ °*ḱri-ba*, pf. °*ḱris*, cf. *dkri-ba*, cognate to °*ḱril-ba*, 1. **to wind, roll; twist** one's self, **to coil** (of snakes) *Dzl.*; *ḱyim-ṫáb-kyi °ḱri-ba* conjugal embrace *Pth.*; **'óg-ma ṭi-se** (for °*ḱri-ste*) **rag** *W.* I have a sore throat, prop. I feel my throat tied up, I am choking; fig.: *kún-la °ḱris-pa*, either as an adj. 'ensnaring', or as a sbst. 'ensnarer' = sin, cf. *kun-dkris* in *dkri-ba*; °*ḱri-šiṅ* = °*ḱril-šiṅ.* — 2. mostly as a sbst.: **the being attached to,** given to, c.c. genit. (synonym of *čágs-pa*): *raṅ-dón-gyi*, to one's own advantage, *bu-smád-kyi* to wife and children *Mil.*; **fondness, attachment;** *žen-°ḱris* id. — 3. *ḱral °ḱri-ba* **to impose** a tax *C.*, *Lex.*

འཁྲིག་པ་ °*ḱrig-pa* I. sbst. 1. (*Ssk.* **मिथुन**) **coitus** (of the two sexes), **copulation, pairing,** the usual, not exactly obscene, yet not euphemistic term for it; °*ḱrig-pa spyód-pa*, also °*ḱrig-čágs spyód-pa B.* and *C.*, **ṭig-pa čó-če** *W.*, to lie with etc.; °*ḱrig-pai čós-la rtén-pa* to indulge in lust, to be given to voluptuousness; °*ḱrig-skád Sch.*, °*ḱrig-tsig Lexx.*, obscene words, unchaste language; °*ḱrig-pa °byin-pa* to talk smut. — 2. a sign of the zodiac, **the twins.** — 3. symb. num.: 2.

II. vb. 1. **to cohere, to stick together** *Cs.* — 2. **to be clouded** (of the sky), *ɣnam °ḱrig* the sky is getting overcast; also **ṭigs soṅ** *W.* without a sbst., it has become cloudy, dull; *'ód-zér daṅ ȷa-'ód °ḱrig-pa* wrapt in rays of light and the splendours of the rainbow *Pth.*; *ṫaṅ ṫams-čád mes °ḱrig-pa* the whole plain was enveloped in a flame of fire *Mil.* Cf. *dkrigs-pa.*

འཁྲིད་ °*ḱrid* v. *ḱrid.*

འཁྲིད་པ་ °*ḱrid-pa*, pf. *ḱrid*, fut. *bkri?*, **to lead, to conduct** men or beasts to a place; **to command, to head** (an army); **to bring** along with, °*ḱrid-de ma 'óṅs-so* he has not brought (his wife) with him *Dzl.*; therefore °*ḱrid* equivalent to 'with': *bú-tsa °ḱrid byuṅ-nas* coming out with their children

Glr. — *blo ˳k̔rid-pa* perh. a mistake for *brid-pa*.

འཁྲིམས་ ˳*k̔rims*, *bréd(-nas)-˳k̔rims Lexx.* w.e.

འཁྲིལ་བ་ ˳*k̔ril-ba* 1. **to wind** or **coil round** (of serpents), **to embrace** closely, **to clasp round**, e.g. in the act of coition; *ma byams bú-la ˳k̔ril* a loving mother clasping her child *Pth.*; *˳k̔ril-mk̔an* a plant furnished with tendrils or claspers *W.*; *˳k̔ril-šin Wdṅ.* a climbing plant, creeper. — 2. **to glide, slip into,** of the soul when entering another body, = *˳k̔yúd-pa*. — 3. *k̔a ˳k̔ril-ba W.* to speak imperfectly (like children), **to stammer,** — 4. **to heap up,** = *˳dril-ba, sgril-ba*.

འཁྲིས་ ˳*k̔ris* 1. syn. with *˳gram*, **bank, shore, coast,** *rmá-čui ˳k̔ris-na yód-pai mk̔ar*, a castle on the banks of the Hoangho *Glr.*; **k̔yo'-rán-gi ṭ̔i-na yo'* C.* it lies just before you, under your nose; *blá-mai sku-k̔ris-su* = *blá-mai p̔yógs-la Mil.nt.* — 2. v. *˳k̔rí-ba*.

འཁྲུ་བ་ ˳*k̔rú-ba* 1. *Cs.* **to wash, to bathe,** = *˳k̔rud-pa*, cf. *k̔rus*. — 2. **diarrhoea, looseness**; dysentery (?); *˳k̔ru-nád, ˳k̔ru-sbyóṅs* (**अतिसार**) id.

འཁྲུག་པ་ ˳*k̔rúg-pa* 1. vb., pf. *˳k̔rugs*, cf. *dkrug-pa, bkrug-pa*, to be in disorder, agitation, commotion, **to be disturbed;** *˳k̔rúg-par ˳gyúr-ba* to get disordered; of the blood: *rtsa t̔ams-čád ˳k̔rúg-tu bčug*, it made all his blood boil *Glr.*; of the sea frq.; esp. of the mind, disturbed by wrath, fear, anxiety, or some other passion, cf. *k̔og-˳k̔rúgs*: **to quarrel, fight, contend,** *de gnyis ˳k̔rúgs-nas*, the two quarrelling; *bod če naṅ ˳k̔rúg-go*, the nobles of Tibet are contending among one another, have internal feuds; *mči-ma ˳k̔rúg-pa* tears appearing, coming forth, (lit. tears being stirred up, excited *Thgy.*, *Mil.*, *Tar.* — 2. sbst. **disorder, tumult, war,** also **single combat, duel,** *˳k̔rúg-pa šor* disorder arises; *˳k̔rug-dús byas* he appointed the time of the duel *Glr.*; *˳k̔rúg-dpon* = *dmág-dpon*: *˳k̔rúg-pa byed-pa* to take up arms, to begin war; respecting subjects: to rebel; *˳k̔rúg-pa byéd-pai dús-su* in times of war *Glr.*; *dmag-˳k̔rúg, ˳t̔ab-˳k̔rúg* war. — *mi-˳k̔rúgs-pa* n. of a Buddha (not = *mi-skyód-pa*). — *˳k̔rug-lóṅ* is the explanation given by *Lexx.* for *skyo-ṅógs*, hence prob.: contest, strife. — **ṭ̔ úgs-mk̔an* W.* having small cracks, flaws, of potter's ware.

འཁྲུང་བ་ ˳*k̔rúṅ-ba* or *˳k̔rúṅs-pa* 1. resp. for *skyé-ba* **to be born,** *bčom-ldan-˳dás ˳k̔rúṅs-pa daṅ dus-mnyám-du* at the same time when Buddha was born *Glr.*; *gnyis-la sras ma ˳k̔rúṅs-par* as by neither of the two (queens) a son was born *Glr.*; *˳k̔ruṅs-dkái skyés-bu* (holy) men, such as are but rarely born (lit. with difficulty) *Mil.*; **to arise, to originate,** *˳k̔ruṅs-rábs* legend of the origin . . .; *k̔yed-ráṅ-gi t̔úgs-la ˳k̔rúṅs-pai tsig* words as they may just arise in your honour's mind *Mil.*; *snyiṅ-rje t̔úgs-la ˳k̔rúṅs-pas* compassion arose in the soul of his reverence *Mil.*; *tiṅ-ṅe-˳dzin ˳k̔rúṅs-pas* meditation arising. — 2. **to come up, shoot, sprout, grow,** of seeds and plants frq.

འཁྲུད་པ་ ˳*k̔rúd-pa*, pf. *bkrus*, fut. *bkru* **to wash, to bathe,** *gos* clothes, *k̔a-lág* face and hands *Dzl.*; **to wash off,** *dri-ma* dirt; fig. *sa nán-gyis ˳k̔rud Ma.* is stated to mean: the country is fleeced, thoroughly drained of its resources.

འཁྲུམས་ ˳*k̔rums* **carcass, carrion,** game torn by beasts of prey, *Sch.*, (the word seems to be very little known).

འཁྲུལ་བ་ ˳*k̔rúl-ba* (*Lex.*: *Ssk.* **भ्रम** to turn out of the way, to wander, to stray, hence perh. originally:) 1. **to be dislocated, sprained, distorted,** **tsig ṭul* W.* the limb is dislocated; usually: 2. **to be out, to be mistaken,** almost always used in the pf tense, *˳k̔rúl-pa* mistaken, deceived, *ṅa mig ˳k̔rúl-pa yin-nam* does my eye deceive me? *Mil.*; *rná-ba ˳k̔rul dogs túr-re gyis* take care not to hear wrong *Mil.*; *gnyis gčig-tu ˳k̔rúl-bar byéd-pa* to make by mistake two to be one, to confound one thing with another *Tar.*; *˳di dge-slóṅ-mar ˳dód-pa ˳k̔rúl-pa yin-la* she being frustrated in her wish to become a nun *Tar.* 85, 1; *˳gró-ba ˳k̔rúl-pa* the deceived creature *Glr.*;

frq. with *snaṅ: raṅ-snáṅ ₒk̓rúl-par ₒdug* I have been mistaken, it was a deception of the senses *Mil.*; *snaṅ-ₒk̓rúl* and *ₒk̓rul-snáṅ* **illusion, delusion**; *ₒk̓rul-snáṅ-ċan* **delusive** *Glr.*; to err, as a syn. of *nór-ba: k̓yód-ċag ₒk̓rúl-pai ₒǰig-rten-pa* ye deluded children of the world! *Mil.*; *žes ₒdón-par-nams ₒk̓rul* they who pronounce (read) in this manner, are mistaken; *ₐa ₒdogs ₒk̓rul* the adding of *ₐa* is a mistake; *nor-ₒk̓rúl* mistake, *nor-ₒk̓rúl sél-ba Schr.*, **tón-ċe, sál-po ġyáb-ċe**, *W.* to remove mistakes, to correct. — 3. **to be insane, deranged,** syn. of *smyós-pa Dzl.* and others. — *ₒk̓rúl-pa* 1. adj. **mistaken, deceived.** — 2. sbst. **mistake; frenzy, madness**; *ₒk̓rul-ġži* **mistake, error**; *ₒk̓rúl-so (errandi locus)* occasion for committing mistakes, a wrong way, **peril; mistake, error,** cf. *gól-sa*; *ₒk̓rul-ₒk̓ór* artifice *Sch.*, (*Cs.*: machine, contrivance; but this is spelled more correctly *ₒp̓rul-ₒk̓ór*).

འཁྲེན་པ་ *ₒk̓rén-pa* 1. **to wish, to long for,** *zas-skóm Med.*, *k̓yím-la Lex.* — 2. *W.* **to look upon with envy, jealousy.**

འཁྲོ་བ་ *ₒk̓ró-ba*, pf. *k̓ros*, **to be angry,** *la* at.

འཁྲོག་པ་ *ₒk̓róg-pa* **to roar, rush, buzz, hum,** *rná-ba k̓úr-la ₒk̓rog Med.*, a tingling noise is caused in the ear; *rgyu-lóṅ ₒk̓róg-ċiṅ* a rumbling in the bowels *Med.*; *sbo-ₒk̓róg* in the belly; *ₒk̓rog-k̓róg* roaring, rushing, buzzing.

འཁྲོལ་བ་ *ₒk̓ról-ba* pf. and fut. *dk̓rol*, imp. *k̓rol* 1. **to cause to sound, to make a noise, to play,** *ról-mo* on an instrument, **to ring** (a bell), **to beat** (a gong, cymbal); *ma dk̓ról-bar* without being played on. — 2. **to sound, resound,** **ḍód-pa ṭ ól-la rag** *W.* my bowels croak; *ₒk̓ról-po* a player, performer, bell-ringer etc., cf. *k̓ról-po*: **ṭrol-lo-lo-tsé** *W.* a tinkling of bells.

ག

ག *ga* 1. the letter **g**, originally, and in the border countries still at the present time, as initial letter = the English hard g, as final letter = ck; in *C.* as initial deep-toned and aspirated (gh), as final letter more or less indistinct; as a prefix (in *Khams* and *Balti*) fricative = γ or χ: v. Preface. — 2. as numerical figure: 3, cf. *ka* 2.

ག *ga* affix (article) to some substantives, like *ka*.

ག *ga* (*C.* **gha**) 1. = *ₒga* (*C.* **gā**). — 2. = *gaṅ*.

ག་ཁྲལ་ *ga-k̓rál C.* (pron. **gha-ṭal**) **tax, duty** (on cattle and butter).

ག་ག *ga-gá W.* a title of honour: **the old gentleman, the old squire** e.g. **ga-gá ta-ra-ċán** the old Squire Tara Chand, opp. to *no-nó* the young Squire; instead of it in *C.*: *'*a-ǰho-lág**.

ག་ག་ཚིལ་ *ga-ga ts̓il*, **tickling** *Cs.*; *ga-ga-ts̓il byéd-pa* **to tickle.**

ག་གེ་མོ་ *ga-gé-mo* **such a one, such a thing** *Cs.*; **such and such**; v. *če-ge-mo*.

ག་གོན་ *ga-gón* **a melon** *Cs.* (some Lexx. have: cucumber, others: barley).

ག་ཅེན, ག་ཆེན་ *ga-ċén, ga-čén* **some** (people), **a good many; a good deal** *W.*, *C.*

ག་ཆད་ *ga-čád* **without cause, involuntarily,** e.g. to weep *Med.*

ག་ཏ་ *gá-ta Ssk.*, *ga-tai sde-ts̓an* a particular kind of Indian hand-writing, besides Nagari and Lantsa *Glr.*

གད་ *gá-da* (गदा), **club, mace.**

གདུར་ *ga-dúr* medicinal herb of an astringent taste.

གདོར་ *ga-dór* *Lex.* w.e.: *ša-bai ga-dor*: *Sch.* explains: the growth of a new branch on a stag's horn.

ག་འདྲས་ *ga-ₒdrás* *C.* (pronounced **ghandę**) **how?**

ག་ན་ *gá-na* = *gaṅ-na*, **where**, used interr. and correl., frq.; *gá-na-ba* and *gáṅ-na-ba* the same as a sbst., **the whereabouts** of a person, his place of residence: *rgyál-po gá-na-bar*, (or *gá-na-ba der*, *gá-na ₒdúg-par*, *gá-na bžúgs-par*) *soṅ* he went where the king was *Dzl.*, frq. — **ga-na-méd** *W.* **absolutely, at all events,** **ga-na-méd kal gos** it must be sent by all means; **ga-na-méd lóg-te taṅ yin** I shall give it back at all events (*B. c̀is-kyaṅ*).

ག་པུར་ *ga-pur* **camphor** *Med.*

ག་བྲ་ *ga-bra* n. of a medicine *Med.*

ག་ཚམ་ *ga-tsám* **how, how much, how many how long,** interr. and correl.; **as much as,** e.g. as much as you like (you may take) col.

ག་བཙོན་ *ga-btsón* an eruption of the skin *W.*

ག་ཚོད་ *ga-tsód* *C.* **how much,** **rin gha-tsö̤** what is the price?

ག་ཞ་, ག་གཞའ་, ག་ཤ་ *gá-ža*, *gá-γža*, *gá-ša* **a jest, joke, laughter,** *gá-ža daṅ rtséd-mo rtse Pth.* they jest and play; also adj.: inclined to jesting, **di-riṅ gá-ša mi dug** he is not in a good humour, in good spirits, to-day *W.*

ག་ཟུག་ *gá-zug* *W.* **how,** interr. and correl.

ག་གཟི་ *ga-γzi* *W.* **squinting.**

ག་རི་, དགའ་རིས་ *ga-ri*, *dga-ris* = *gá ža W.*; **ga-ri mi rag** I am in low spirits, **dejected.**

ག་རུ་ *gá-ru* = *gan-du* 1. **whither,** which way, to which place, whereto. — 2. **where,** interr. and correl.

ག་རུ་ཌ་ *ga-ru-ḍa* the Garuda-bird. v. *k̔yuṅ.*

ག་རེ་ *ga-ré* 1. **where is?** *B.* and col. — 2. *Ld.* a species of Lathyrus.

ག་ལ་ *gá-la* for *gáṅ-la*, *c̀i-la C.*: **ghá-la tén-ne ne ǰhun** owing to what, or from what cause did the disease arise? **ghá-la ṗen** to what does this serve, of what use is this? *Sch.*: **whither,** to what place? **ghá-la ₒdö-ghi yim-pa** *Ü.* where are you going to? — *gá-la-ba* = *gá-na-ba.*

ག་ལེ་ *gá-le* *C.* **slowly, softly, gently,** gen. in a good sense, opp. to every thing turbulent; therefore in exchanging compliments on meeting or parting: **₊o-ná ghá-le ku žu naṅ** (perh. to be spelled *sku bžugs snaṅ*) says the person that has paid a visit, **₊o-ná ghá-le ṗeb** he that received the visit, when taking leave of each other, both phrases implying about the same as our **farewell! good-bye!** Cf. *snaṅ-ba.*

ག་ལོག་ *ga-lóg* *W.* **squinting.**

ག་ཤ་ *gá-ša* 1. v. *ga-ža.* — 2. **girth** or **rope** slung across breast and shoulder in order to draw or carry anything; also **dog-harness;** also the **bandoleer** or **shoulder-belt,** worn as a badge of dignity by constables and the like officers; sobriquet for the rope of meditation, v. *sgom-t̔ág.*

ག་ཤས་ *ga-šás*, *C.* **gha-šę**, **some, part;** **bhú-mo yaṅ gha-šę čo̤ ǰhé-pa yin** even girls, in part, take to religion (become nuns).

ག་ཤེད་ *ga-šéd* v. *šed.*

ག་ཤེལ་ *ga-šél* **glass-beads, glass-pearls** *Sch.*

ག་སིར་ *ga-sír*, instead of تعزير **punishment** *Ld.*

གག་ *gag* 1. **silver** in bars, ingots, small pieces etc., **uncoined** *W.* — 2 **wad, wadding** (for loading muskets) *W.* — 3. *Cs:* = *bya-gág*, *gag-ts̔é* a water-fowl.

གག་པ་ *gág-pa* *Med.*, a swelling in the throat *Cs.*; *gag-lhóg* id. (?)

གང་ *gaṅ* I. interr. pron. 1. **who? which?** *B.*, *C.*, *W.*; when used adjectively, it generally follows its sbst. (so at least in good language), and if preceding it, it stands in the genit. case: *ṗyogs gaṅ* which region or part of the world? *gáṅ-gi dus* which time? in the latter case it may also mean **whose**: *gáṅ-gi lam* whose way? *p̔yi naṅ γnyis čós lugs gaṅ bzaṅ* which of the two doctrines, the Brahmanic or the Buddhist, is the right one? *p̔yogs gáṅ-nas oṅ, ṅo mi šés-pas* not knowing from what part of the country she comes *Glr.; ma ni gaṅ yin bu ni gaṅ yin bye-brág p̔yes* decide which is the mother and which the child *Dzl.; gaṅ žé-na* lit. 'if one asks which?' corresponds sometimes to the English 'namely, to wit, viz.'; *gáṅ-na* where? *gaṅ-la* whither? *gáṅ-nas, gáṅ-las* whence? *gáṅ-du* where? whither? *gáṅ-na-ba = ga-na-ba* v. above; *gáṅ-pa, yul gáṅ-pa*, col. **gaṅ-yúl-pa**, from what country? — 2. *C.* for *či* **what?** **ghaṅ zér-ra(m)** what shall I say? **k̔yö'-kyi míṅ-la ghaṅ zér-ghyi yö'-dham** what is your name? **gháṅ-la yoṅ** what are you coming for? what do you want? — 2. rel., or rather correl. pron., **who, which, he who, she who, whoever, whichever, whatever,** ὅςτις: *gaṅ p̔yir ṭ̔óṅ-ba de ni* she who follows *Dzl.*; *gaṅ gos ͦdód-pa-la gos byuṅ* whoever wanted clothes, to him they were given *Dzl.*; *rig-pa gaṅ rnó-ba čig-la stér-ro* I give it to him who is the sharpest as to sagacity *Glr.*: *k̔yód-kyi dpá-ba gaṅ yin-pa-la k̔ó-bo mgu* the bravery which you have shown pleases me *Tar.* 21, 13: *rgyál-bu gáṅ-du ṫse ͦp̔ós-pai γnás-su sóṅ-ṅo* they went to the place where the prince had changed life *Dzl.*; *gáṅ-gi lam sṅón-du grub-pa des . . .* he whose way (of sanctification) will be completed first, shall . . . *Stg.* Often *ṫams-čád* or a plural-sign accompanies the partic.: *gaṅ mi šés-pa-dag* they who do not understand *Dzl.* Rarely in *B.*, but frq. in the col. language of *W.*, the *pa* after the verb is supplied by a gerundial particle, such as *na, nas*: **gaṅ ṫáṅ-na k̔yad med** which you intend to give is all the same. Sometimes, however, particularly in more modern literature, no *pa* is added to the verb at all, esp. when *gaṅ* is joined with *yin, yod*, or *dug*, so that such sentences in their form are very similar to the relative sentences of occidental languages; but that this omission of *pa*, although sanctioned by long continued use, is after all an incorrect breviloquence, and that *pa* must always be understood, appears from the frq. occurrence of the plural sign immediately after *yod* etc.: *de γnyis-kyi srid gaṅ yód-rnams* the claims to government which both of these maintained *Glr.*; *gáṅ-ṫse — déi-ṫse* **when — then**; *gaṅ žig* **whoever, if any body** etc. frq.; vulgo in *W.* often pleon. = any or some, **gaṅ žig ṫims-si p̔i-la** on account of some law-suit, instead of *ṫims žig-gi p̔yir*; *gaṅ la-lá žig* is of a similar meaning, but less frq. The import of the word is still more generalized by *yaṅ* being added to *gaṅ* or to the verb: *dṅós-po gaṅ mṫoṅ yaṅ Mil.* whatever he sets his eyes upon; *gaṅ ltár-na yaṅ, gaṅ yin kyaṅ* whatsoever it may be, however that may be, be that as it may, at all events, esp. *C.*: *gaṅ-yaṅ-rúṅ-ba, gaṅ-rúṅ, gaṅ-či-yaṅ-rúṅ* whosoever he may be, whatsoever it may be, *quicunque*; *γnas gaṅ-yaṅ-rúṅ-ba-na* wherecever; *gáṅ-nas gáṅ-du skyes kyaṅ* out of which class of beings and into whichsoever I shall be re-born *Dzl.* — 3. indefinite pron., used absolutely, **each, every, any, all,** when followed by a negation = **not any, none, no**: *žo dar ču sogs gaṅ yaṅ k̔a*, curdled milk, buttermilk, water, every thing tastes bitter *Med.*; *saṅs-rgyás gáṅ-gis kyaṅ ma bčágs-pa* not yet trodden by any Buddha *Glr.*; *p̔an gaṅ ṫogs gyis* be as useful as ever possible *Mil.*; *gáṅ-dag* all *Glr.* and elsewhere; *dé-dag mi ͦbyuṅ gaṅ yaṅ med* these are to be found everywhere; *gáṅ-la gaṅ-ͦdul* converting each in the manner best suited to him; *gáṅ-gis kyaṅ ≐ čis-kyaṅ* by all means; *gáṅ-gis kyaṅ dgós-pa méd-pa* altogether useless *Mil.*; *gaṅ daṅ gaṅ Cs., Sch.* (more frq. *gaṅ daṅ či*) every thing whatsoever *Glr.*

གང་ག་ཆུང་ *gaṅ-ga-čuṅ* an officinal plant *Med.*

གང་གཱ *gaṅ-gā Ssk.* the river **Ganges.**

གང་བ་ *gáṅ-ba*, sometimes *gáṅ-po*, also *gaṅ* 1. **full**, *rin-po-čés baṅ-mdzód gáṅ-ba žig* a treasury full of jewels *Dzl.*; *ťál-ču ḱól-mas gáṅ-ba-ste* being filled with boiling lye *Thgy.*; *γser-ṗyé bre gáṅ-po, γser γžóṅ-pa gaṅ* a measure filled with gold-dust, a basin full of gold; *˴óbs-kyi náṅ-na sbrul γdúg-pas gáṅ-ṅo* lit.: in the ditch it was full of poisonous snakes *Dzl.*; *brgyud gáṅ-bar gyúr-to* the progeny increased *Glr.*; *mčód-rten ḱru gáṅ-pa Glr.* a pyramid, a full cubit in height. — 2. *W.* also **heaped** (measure), opp. to **gaṅ-ċád** (lit. *bċad*) **smoothed** (measure).

གང་བུ་ *gáṅ-bu* **pod, shell, husk** (*Sch.* also also flower-bud?) *˴od-zér-gyi gáṅ-bur ˳dril-nas* enveloping himself in a veil of rays, wrapping himself in a garment of light (another reading: *góṅ-por* in a lump, in one mass) *Glr.*; *gaṅ-ló* an empty pod, freed from the kernels *W.*

གང་ཟག་ *gaṅ-zág* 1. **man**, as an intellectual being, **a person**; *gaṅ-zág γžán-gyis brda sprád-pas* another person describing it to you (opp. to what we know by our own perception and observation) *Mil.*; hence philosophical term for the **I** or **self**, **पुद्गल** *Was.*; *bstan-bċós-la mḱás-pai gaṅ-žág-rnams* learned or lettered men, men of science *Glr.*; esp. man in relation to religion: *čos ṗyi-bšól byéd-pai gaṅ-zág Mil.*, men who postpone religion, not troubling themselves about it: *˳ṗágs-pai gaṅ-žág-rnams-kyi rgyál-po* the king of reverend persons, i.e. Buddha; *lóg-lta-ċaṅ-gyi gaṅ-zág* heretical people; *gaṅ-zág ṗál-pa, ťa-mál-pá* common people *Mil.* and others; also explicitly: people favourably disposed towards religion, religious people *Gyatch.* c. 26 & 27. (at present the word is generally understood in the latter sense); *dus ṗyís-kyi gaṅ-zág Glr.*, *ma-˴óṅs-pai gaṅ-zág skál-ba daṅ ldán-pa Mil.* a pious posterity. The word, however, so little implies the clerical state, that it is used directly for 2. **layman**, one that has not taken orders *Dzl.* ༢༦༠, 5 and elsewhere. — 3. (resp. *žal-zág*) **tobacco-pipe**, not the hukka, but a small sort, similar to ours, gen. made of metal; *gaṅ-mgó* **bowl** of a tobacco-pipe; *gaṅ-mǰúg* mouth-piece or **tip** of it *C.*

གངས་ *gaṅs* 1. **glacier-ice, glacier;** *gáṅs-ċan* adj. abounding in snow, in glaciers, also as a sbst. a glacier; *gáṅs-ċan-las ˳byúṅ-bai ču* the water issuing from a glacier *Med.*, and even as a p.n.: Tibet; *gáṅs-ċan-gyi skad* the Tibetan language; *gáṅs-bšóg-pa* to cleave the snow, i.e. to have it trodden down by yaks sent in advance, in order thus to form a path for the travellers (v. Huc Voyage II. 421). — *gaṅs-rgyúd* a chain of snow-mountains. — *gaṅs-čen-mzod-lṅá* 'the five receptacles of the vast glacier-ice', or *gaṅs-čen-rǰé-lṅá* 'the five kings of the same', pronounced **ghaṅ-čen-˳dzö'-ṅá**, or **ǰe-ṅá**, n. of a high mountain in Sikkim, commonly spelled Kinjinjunga; *gaṅs-čen-mtsó-rgyál* name of a deity (?) *Glr.* — *gaṅs-ťigs Med.* perh. stalactite. — *gaṅs-ri* a snow- or ice-mountain, as p.n. = Ti-se. — Seldom 2. col. **ice** in general; **gaṅs-soṅ** it has frozen *W.* — 3. **snow** in general, **ghaṅ ˳bab** it snows *Ts.*; **ghaṅ-ma-ċár** sleet. — 4. **the sclerotic** of the eye *Sch.*

གད་པ་ *gád-pa* 1. **a bluff;** precipitous river-banks, such as frequently inclose the mountain rivers of Tibet. — 2. In *W.* the word seems to refer more to the species of rock, which is favourable to the formation of such banks: **conglomerate;** *gad-ṗúg* a cavern in such a bank; *gad-rgyál* the gigantic walls of conglomerate rock, through which mountain rivers have cut their way.

གད་མོ་ *gád-mo* **laughing, laughter,** *ǰig-rtén-pai gád-mo* a laughter, a laughing-stock, to wordly-minded people; *ṅai gád-moi γnas* this is to me an object of laughing, it is ridiculous to me *Mil.*; *gád-mos ˳débs-pa* to laugh at a person *Tar.* 25, 15.

གན་ *gan B.* and *W.*, *gám C.*, **nearness,** proximity, used only in such connections as *gan-du* **to, towards, up to,** *ṅai gán-du šog* come to me; *rgyál-poi gán-du* he went to the king; *ḱáṅ-pai gán-du soṅ* he went towards the house; *rgyál-poi gán-nas ṗyin* he came from the king; in col. language also c. accus.: **ḍóg-po gáṅ-du** *W.* close by the brook, and c. termin. case, **čur gán-te** *W.* hard by the water: *rir-gán-pa* one living close to a mountain or hill.

གན་རྐྱལ་ *gan-kyál*, and *rkyal*, **supine,** lying on the back, with the face upward, *gan-kyál (du) nyál-ba* to lie in that position; *˳gyel-ba* to fall backward; *sgyél-ba* to make one fall on his back; **ghan-kyál lóg-pa** to perform a somerset, to tumble over head and heels *C.*

གན་རྒྱ་ *gan-rgyá C.*, **gam-rgya** *W.*, **a written contract, an agreement.**

གན་དར་ *gan-dár Sch.:* a silk handkerchief offered as a present in exchanging compliments on meeting, = *ḱa-btags*

གན་མཛོད་ *gan-mdzód* **store-room, storehouse** *Sch.*

གནྡྷོ་ལ་ *gándho-la* n. of a famous temple in *rdo-rje-γdán* (Vajrāsana near Gaya in Bengal) *Tar.* 16, 4 and elsewhere frq.; yet the words in *Glr.* 8, 10: *ṗyi gándho-la náṅ-du lhá-ḱaṅ byás-pas* 'making outwardly a gandhola, inside an idolshrine', seem not to admit of a noun proper; a Lama explained it by *γtsug-lag-ḱaṅ;* more correctly perh. = *dri-γtsaṅ-ḱaṅ*, i.e. = **गन्धकूट**. Cf. also ghánḍhola.

གཉྫི་ར་ *gáñji-ra Glr.* 65, 8 obviously a *Ssk.* word, though not in our dictionaries; Lamas described it as an architectural ornament, consisting in small turrets or spires along the edge of a flat roof.

གབ་སྒྲ་ *gáb-sgra W.* **a belch** (vulgar).

གབ་པ་ *gáb-pa* **to hide,** to conceal one's self *Dzl.* and elsewhere frq.; *gáb-yig*, writing in secret characters, cryptography *W., C.; gáb-sa* a place of concealment, hiding-place.

གབ་སྤངས་ *gab-spáṅs Glr.*, panels or little boards beneath the cornice of a roof, often filled out with paintings.

གབ་ཙེ་, གབ་ཚེ་ *gáb-tse, gáb-ťse* a tableau containing numerous mythological and astrological figures, and used for fortune-telling.

གབ་ཚད་, གབ་པའི་ཚ་བ་ *gab-ťsád, gáb-pai ťsá-ba* a disease *Med.;* acc. to *Schr.* a hectic, consumptive fever.

གམ་ *gam* v. *gan.*

གམ་བུ་ར་ *gám-bu-ra W.* **citron, lemon.**

གའུ་ *gau* 1. **a chest, box** *Pth.;* a little box or case; when containing amulets, it is worn suspended by a string round the neck (v. *Schl.* 174). — 2. a squeaking sound *W.*, **gau zér-če** **to squeak.**

གར་ *gar* I. (*Cs. gár-ma*) **a dance,** *gar byed-pa, W.* **gár se-če**, to dance; *glu gar rtsed-mo byéd-pa Glr.* to sing, to dance and play; *gár-mḱan* 1. one dancing, a dancer, a performer, e.g. even Buddha or any saint, when displaying miracles. — 2. n. of a god *Tar.* 11, 17, acc. to *Schr., Siwa; gar-stábs* a dancing gesture or motion. — II. = *gá-ru, gáṅ-du*, **whither, whereto, where;** *gar yaṅ* anywhere, *gár yaṅ skyé-ba* growing everywhere *Wdṅ.; gar yaṅ mi ˳gró-ba* to go nowhere, to remain where one is *Mil.; Pth.* — **gar-méd** *W.* at all events, by all means, = **ga-na-med** — *gar-báb* at random, hit or miss, at hap-hazard *Sch.*

གར་ནག་ *gar-nág* n. of a medicine *Lt.*

གར་བ་ *gár-ba* **strong,** *gar-čaṅ strong beer.*

གར་བུ་ *gár-bu* **solid,** not hollow *Sch.*

གར་མོ་ *gár-mo* **thick,** e.g. soup, = *ská-ba; gar-slá Sch.:* thick and thin; thickness.

གར་ཞ་ *gár-ža*, native name of the district called by the Hindoos Lāhul or Lāhōl (acc to Cunningham 'Lahul' is a corruption of *lho-yul*, southern country, which latter appellation, however, is not in use in that district itself). Here, in the village of Kyelang, a missionary station was established in 1857, by the Church of the United Brethren (Moravians), together with a school and a lithographic press, for diffusing Christian knowledge by means of books and tracts.

གར་ལོག་ *gar-lóg*, *Tar.* 91, 7. 10. Transl. p. 317: 'acc. to *Was.* a rapacious mountain tribe, north-east of Tibet; in the Tibetan-Sanskrit dictionary mentioned as 'Turushka". They are doubtless the same robbers, that are called 'Kolo' by Huc (II. p. 187), who were known to our Lama from Tashilhunpo as *mgo-lóg*, or *lčan-mo-mgo-lóg*, they having received this name ('queer-heads') in consequence of having their hair closely cropped. Possibly *gar-lóg* is the older and more correct form; cf. *dar-rgyas-glin.*

གར་ཤ་ *gar-šá* the muscles of the thumb (?) *Med.*

གལ་ *gál* 1. **importance,** *gál-du ˳dzín-pa* to consider of importance, to esteem highly *Mil.*; *gál-čan Cs.*, more frq. *gal-čé-ba* important, *de mi šin-tu gál-čé-bar yód-do Glr.*, *bsláb-bya gal-čé-ba Glr.* important precepts; *gal-čún* unimportant, insignificant; undervalued, slighted *Mil.*; *gál-po* prob. = *gal*, *Schr.*; *gal-po-čé-yi bzá-dpon* the important, indispensable master of the house *Mil.* — 2. **constraint, compulsion,** **na-la ghal jhun** *C.* I have been compelled. — 3. **trap, snare** *C.*, *W.*, also *Mil.*; **gal-tém** *W.* id.; *gal ˳dzúg-pa* to set a trap or snare.

གལ་འགག་ *gál-˳gág Med.* ?

གལ་ཏུ་ *gál-tu W.* **crow-bar, handspike.**

གལ་ཏེ་ *gál-te* I. sbst., *gál-te mčán-kun bčug Pth.* ? — II. conj. **if, in case,** serves to introduce a conditional sentence, ending with *na* (which is the essential word, whereas *gal-te* may be left out as well): *gál-te . . ˳ón-na* if . . comes (ἐάν . . . ἔλθῃ); also followed by *yan* (*kyan*), although black snow fell *Dzl.* (*nas* instead of *na*, frq. to be met with, is either merely a slip of the pen, or an impropriety of speech). — *gál-te-na* as one word, and with the signification of **perhaps,** or the Greek ἄν (not 'if', *Cs.*) I found only in a few passages of the Kyelang manuscript of *Dzl.*, where the edition of *Sch.* has *gál-te*, which makes no sense. *gal-srid W.* = *gal-te.* In Lewin's Manual it often occurs in the sense of **but, however.**

གལ་མདོ་ *gál-mdo* n. of a disease *Med.*

གལ་བ་ *gál-ba* **to force, to press** something on a person (cf. *gal* 2), *mi-la btson gal* in-door confinement is forced on men *Mil.*

གལ་རོ་ *gal-ró W.* **refuse, rubbish.**

གས་ *gas* v. *˳gás-pa.*

གི་ *gi* 1. num. for 33. — 2. affix instead of *kyi*, after *g* and *n*; for the signification v. *kyi.*

གི་གུ *gi-gu* the vowel-sign ི, **i.**

གི་གུ་ཤེལ་, གི་གུ་ཤ་ *gi-gu-šél*, *gi-gu-šá Sch.*; 'having a white speck in the eye, wall-eyed (of horses)'.

གི་ཝང་ *gi-wán*, *Glr.*, *gi-bám Lt.*, also *giu*, or *giu-wán*, *Cs.*: 'n. of a concretion in the entrails of some animals, used for medicine'. But *Glr.* 35, 9 an elephant has it on its neck, and acc. to oral assertions it is to be found also in the human head; a man for instance, is said to have *gi-wán* in his brains, if in his sleep he is heard to utter long-drawn humming sounds.

གི་ལིང་ *gi-lin* a strong-bodied, durable horse *Sch.*

གི་ལིན་ *gi-lin Wts.* a fabulous animal.

གིང་ *gin Pth.* prob. a little drum, or the beating of it, as an accompaniment to dancing.

གིན་ *gin* affix, v. *kyin.*

གིར་མོ་ *gir-mo Ld.* the Indian **rupee,** = 5 *jau.*

གིས་ *gis* instead of *kyis* after *g* and *n*, v. *kyis.*

གུ་ *gu* 1. num. for 63. — 2. sign of diminutives, e.g. *kyi-gu* puppy, little dog. — 3. **extension, extent, room, space** *gnás-sa gu-dóg*, *lún-pa gu-dóg*, *lam gu-dóg* a narrow place, valley, road; *gu-yáṅs* (*-pa*) spacious, roomy, wide, *gu yáṅs-pa ˳dug* there is much room here.

གུ་གུ་ཤ་ *gú-gu-ša Ts.* **plate, flat dish.**

གུ་གུལ་ *gú-gul* (गुग्गुलु) Amyris Agallocha, a costly incense, one kind is white, another black.

གུ་གེ་ *gú-ge* n. of a province in the south-western part of Tibet.

གུ་ཏི་ *gú-ti W.* **deaf** (?).

གུ་རུ་ *gú-ru Ssk.*, spiritual teacher, father-confessor.

གུ་རུག་ *gu-rug Ld.* **colt** or **foal** of an ass.

གུ་ལང་ *gu-láṅ* n. of a deity, resorted to by mothers for being blessed with 'children; acc. to *Sch.: Siva.*

གུ་ལེ་ *gú-le W.* for *gá-le* q.v.; *gú-le-la* id., **slowly, softly, gently,** without noise, **yo gú-le-la čug** shut the door gently! *gu-yár Sch.* apparently the same.

གུ་སུ་ *gú-su Wdk.* **garment, dress** (?).

གུག་གེ་བ་ *gúg-ge-ba* **bent,** bent downwards (?), of leaves *Wdṅ.*; *gúg pa* id.

གུག་པ་ *gúg-pa W.* to rub or scratch gently, **to tickle.**

གུང་ *guṅ* I. *Sch.:* 'the broad-headed tiger of Central Asia, Charachula' (*Mongol.*); it is said to differ from *stag*, and is not found in Tibet. — II. also *dguṅ* (*Cs. gúṅ-ma*) 1. **the middle,** *gúṅ-la* in the middle, e.g. the king in the middle (between his two wives); *stód-kyi gúṅ* (*-nas*) *ton* taken out of the middle of the upper part *Mil.*; *gúṅ-du byéd-pa Thgy.* prob. to divide through the middle, to dissect (anatomically); *gúṅ sgrig-pa Sch.* 'to unite'; with respect to time: *dbyár-gyi gúṅ-la W.* in the middle of summer; *nyin-gúṅ*, and *mtsán-gúṅ* mid-day, mid-night *Cs.*; *guṅ-gnyis*, the two middle times, mid-day and mid-night; *nám-gyi guṅ-tún-la* at the hour of mid-night. — 2. **mid-day,** *guṅ ˳báb-pa* to take a noon-rest on a journey; *guṅ-tsigs* dinner *Schr.*; *guṅ sáṅs-la ˳gró-ba* (*W.* **čá-če**) to take a walk about the middle of the day, at noon; perh. also generally: to take a walk; *guṅ-lón Sch.:* 'at noon', more prob.: afternoon. — 3. **mid-night,** *gúṅ-la* at mid-night *Glr.*; *dguṅ-gčig* one night (?) *Sch.* — 4. (Chinese?) title of a magistrate in Lhasa, something like Privy Counsellor; v. *dguṅ.*

གུང་སྟག་ *guṅ-stág* prob. = *stag Ld.-Glr. Schl.* fol. 13, 6.

གུང་ཐང་ *guṅ-táṅ* n. of a monastery in *Máṅ-yul Mil.*

གུང་མོ་ *gúṅ-mo* **the middle finger;** **guṅ-dzúg** *C.* id.

གུང་དམར་ལ་ཕུག་ *guṅ-dmár-la-p̔ug C.* **carrot.**

གུང་ལ་ཕུག་ *guṅ-la-p̔ug C.* **radish.**

གུད་ *gud* 1. **slope, declivity** *Cs.* — 2. **separation, solitude, seclusion** *Sch.*; *gúd-du ˳bór-ba* to place obliquely *Cs.*; *gúd-du ɟségs-pa Dzl.* ༢༢V, 18 to separate, to disperse (?) *Sch.* — 3. *C.:* **loss, damage** = *gun, god.* — 4. *Ld.:* **heavy** or **thick of hearing,** **gud-nág** quite deaf, deaf as a post. — 5. *gúd-du ɟúg pa* v. *˳gúd-pa.*

གུད་པ་ *gúd-pa* v. *˳gúd-pa.*

གུན་ *gun* (*Cs. gún-pa*) **loss, damage,** **ṅá-la gun p̔og** *W.* I have suffered a loss (prop. damage has come over me).

གུན་པོ་ *gún-po Lh.* **expensive, dear.**

གུན་དུམ་ *guṅ-dúm* a bottle-shaped or cylindrical **basket** to put fruit in, *Ld.* (perh. akin to *rkón-pa*).

གུམ་པ་ *gúm-pa* v. *˳gúm-pa.*

གུར་ *gur*, resp. *bžugs-gúr, gzim-gúr Cs.*, also *dbu-gúr C.*, **tent,** *gos-gúr Cs.* a tent of silk, *p̔yiṅ-gúr* of felt, *sbra* and *re-gúr* of coarse yak's hair felt, *ras-gúr* of cotton cloth; *rgyal-gúr Cs.* 'a king's pavilion', *dmag-gúr* a military tent. — *gur-mčóg* a magnificent tent, or *gur-rgyál*, is used by Chr. Prot. for the tabernacle. — *gur-tág* the tent-ropes, **gur-bér** *W.*, or *gur-šiṅ Cs.* the tent-poles. — *gur-tóg Cs.:* 'the upper covering or outer fly of a tent'. — *gur-gžól Cs.:* 'the walls of a tent'. — *gur-klád* passage for the smoke out of a tent, *gur-*

ₒgram lattice in the side of it, and gur-lcám stakes supporting the roof Sch., — peculiar expressions relating to the felt-tents of the Mongol nomads.

གུར་ཀུམ་, གུར་གུམ་ gur-kúm, gur-gúm 1. **saffron,** Crocus Glr., Lt. — 2. **marigold,** Calendula, and similar yellow flowers C.

གུར་གུར་ gur-gúr Ld. a small **churn** used for preparing tea.

གུར་ལྤགས་ gur-lpágs a perforated skin, a hide full of holes Sch.

གུལ་གུལ་ gul-gúl Bal. **slowly,** for gú-le.

གུལ་ནག་ gul-nág Lt. n. of a medicine.

གུས་པ་ gús-pa sbst. **respect, reverence, devotion;** also adj **respectful, devout;** dge-ₒdún-la gús-pas p̓yag ₒtsál-lo the priesthood I respect with devotion; ma-gús-pa unbelieving, undevout Thgy.; *gus-žáb cʻó-ce* W. to show a respectful willingness to serve; **humble,** gús-par ₒgyúr-ba Cs.: 'to humble one's self'; in modern letters = p̓ran. your most humble servant.

གུས་པོ་ gús-po C., W., **expensive, costly, dear.**

གེ་ ge num. for 93.

གེ་ཤ་ ge-šá a kerchief for the head hanging down behind.

གེ་སར་ ge-sár 1. Cs. n. of a flower, Lt. and elsewhere, prob. = केसर; it is said to grow in Nepal, and to be called also pád-ma ge-sár. — 2. Sch.: **pistil,** but, like ze-ₒbrú, it signifies undoubtedly the organs of fructification in general, as the natural science of Tibet is certainly not acquainted with the sexual difference in the parts of flowers; ge-sár-can the lotos flower Sch. — 3. n. of a fabulous king in the north of Tibet, with the epithet dmág-gi-rgyál-po Glr. and elsewh.; ge-sár-gyi sgrun the fabulous history of the same.

གེགས་ gegs **hindrance, impediment, obstacle,** gégs-med-par without hindrance, unimpeded, tʻe-tsʻóm dan gegs sél-ba to remove doubts and hindrances Mil.; gegs-byéd bgegs a malignant spirit, causing impediments or mischief Zam.; čʻos-mdzád yóns-la gegs byéd-pa to throw obstacles in the way of all pious people Pth.; sans-rgyás mi tʻób-pai gegs bži four obstacles to attaining the Buddhaship Thgy.; also without a negation: tʻób-pai grogs ₒgró-am gégs-su ₒgro will you help me or hinder me in obtaining . . . ? Mil.; ₒgrúb-pai gegs impediment to perfection.

གེལ་པ་ gél-pa **branch** of a tree, šin-gel-pa.

གོ་ go 1. numerical sign for 123. — 2. num. inst. of dgú-bcu, in the abbreviated numbers go-gčig etc., 91—99 — 3 for gó-ča. — 4. for gó-bo.

གོ་ gó 1. **place, room, space** (prob. = gu); in this sense it is used in go-mtsʻams-méd-par without intermediate spaces, continuous; ₒbru sna tsʻogs go-mtsʻams-med-par skyes grain of every kind grew densely, luxuriantly; go-mtsʻams-méd-par gán-ba closely filled Tar. 13; prob. also in go-čʻód: 'the space is cut off, or filled i. e. the matter is done with, settled, satisfaction has been made; col. also: I have got enough, I am full, (the thing lost or missed) has been found, restored'; *gho čʻo' son* or *ǰhun* C., *go čʻód-kʻan yod* W. he has managed the business well, he has executed his commission satisfactorily; des rgyál-bai gó mi čʻod by this the victory has not yet been fully decided Mil.; tʻos bsam sgom gsúm-gyi go čʻod (by only once looking at the Ommanipadmehūm) every other hearing, thinking, or looking at is done away with, any thing further is rendered unnecessary Glr.; kʻyéd-la go mi čʻód-pai čʻos a doctrine not satisfactory to you Mil.; bu tsʻab na spyugs či p̓yir go mi čʻod why should it not be sufficient that I be condemned to exile instead of my son? Pth. — 2. **the proper place** of a person or thing among other persons or things, **position, rank,** condition of life, so in many of the following compounds, the word being seldom used alone: p̓ai gór in the place, office, dignity of his father Dzl.; gó-nas according to, in proportion to Glr.; go rgás-na when rank and dignity are grown old and gone, when the position in life has been lost *Glr.*; hence *go-rgás* may be applied to an old maid (*Schr.*); *ráṅ-gi go ₒdug* that is my place, my business, like *ča;* also **place, space, spot** in a still more general sense: *'á-mai gó-na* at the place of my mother, with my mother *Glr.*; *raṅ-ₒťág-gi gó-na* near the mill *Glr.; go ldóg-pa (zlog-pa, lóg-pa)* to change place, esp. to turn to the contrary *S.g.*; *nád-go* the seat of a disease *Sch.*; *go-byéd* is mentioned as a quality of the air *S.g.*; *sprin-gyi go-bar ṗyé-nas ₒoṅs,* we came parting the space between the clouds *Mil.; sprin dkar ldiṅ-gi go-čóg Mil.?* — 3. **armour**, gen. *gó-čá.* —

Comp. *go-skábs* lit. a chance of taking place, of existing, *bdé-bai go-skábs gá-la yod Pth.*, where is there a possibility of being happy? — *go-skál C.* the share or portion due to a person in accordance to his rank. — *go-ḱáṅ* **arsenal** *Schr.* — *go-ḱráb* coat of mail with helmet, **armour.** — *go-grál* **rank, dignity** *Cs.* — *go-grás* id. *Cs.* — *go-rgás* v. *go* 2. — *gó-ča* 1. **armour;** often fig.: *bzód-pai gó-ča bgó-ba*, or *gón-pa*, to put on the armour of patience; *mi-ɉigs-go-ča* the harness of intrepidity. 2. **gear, implements, tools** in general, *bkra-šis srúṅ-bai gó-ča* (charmed) instruments used for securing future happiness (in behalf of a new-born infant) *Med.* — *go-mnyám C.* of equal rank. — *go-ťém* degree of dignity or rank *Cs.* — *go-ₒdún = sna-ₒdún*, of different sorts, **various** *Lex.* — *go-ldóg* (cf. *go-ldóg-pa*) **the contrary, reverse, opposite; wrong, perverse,** *dé-las go-ldóg* the contrary of it *Med.*: **go ɉug go-lóg-la** *W.* head fore-most; **go-lóg čó-če** *W.* to go to work in the wrong way, **go-lóg ḍí-če** to write wrong. — *go-ṗáṅ(s)* 1. **degree, rank, dignity,** *blón-poi go-ṗáṅ-la bkód-par ₒgyúr-ba Pth.* to be installed into the dignity of a minister; *go-ṗáṅ spár-ba Lex.* to raise the dignity. **2. model, pattern,** standard of perfection (?) *Cs.* — *go-mtsáms* v. *go* no. 1. — **go-mtsón* harness and weapons. — *go-rím* 1. **order** of rank *Glr.* — 2. **succession,** successive order, turn.

གོ་ཁ་ *gó-ḱa* the place (near the hearth) for firewood *Mil.*

གོ་བ་ *gó-ba* I. vb. 1. **to understand, comprehend,** *W.* **há-go-će**; *go-dká-ba* difficult, hard to be understood, *go-slá-ba* easy to be understood, intelligible; **gho-dé-wa yoṅ** *C.* now it becomes intelligible, thus it will be understood; *go-byed-brdá Lex.* an explaining, illustrating symbol; *gó-žiṅ rtóg-pa* to take in and comprehend; *brdá-ru go* this I understand to be a symbol *Pth.; gó-bai yul, gó-byai yul* a subject intelligible to all *Schr.* — 2. **to mean, to imagine,** *par* that. *Glr.; go-nór-ba* to misunderstand, to mistake, to be mistaken. —

II. sbst. **perception, comprehension,** *gó-ba bláṅ-ba Mil.* to come to a right comprehension, a clear perception (of some philosophical or religious truth); *gó-bai mɉál-ba Lex.*: '*mɉál-ba* in the sense of perceiving'.

གོ་བོ་ *gó-bo* a large **eagle** or **vulture,** *C., W.* and *B.*; *go-sér* the common black-bearded vulture of the Himalaya, with a yellow neck; *go-brún* excrements of it *Med.*

གོ་བྱི་ལ་ *go-byi-la Med.* n. of a poisonous medicinal fruit *Cs.*; *go-bye Med.* id.?

གོ་ཡུ་ *go-yú Med.*, n. of a flower *Cs.*

གོ་ར་ *go-rá Cs.*; 'prison, jail'; prop. a court surrounded by a wall.

གོ་རེ་ལོང་ *gó-re-lóṅ* a waiting-servant, **page** *Cs.*

གོ་ལ་ *gó-la Ssk.* **ball, bullet**

གོ་ལོག་ *go-lóg* v. *go-ldóg* sub *go* Comp.

གོ་ཤེན་ *go-šén* v. *go-čén.*

གོ་ས་ *go-sá* **rank, dignity,** **go-sá čén-po, ťón po** *W.* high in rank.

གོ་ཏ་མ་, གཽ་ཏ་མ་, གོའུ་ཏ་མ་ *Gó-ta-ma, Gau-ta-ma, Gou-ta-ma*, **the Gotamide,** the descendant of Gotama, which, among others, was the name of the founder of the Nyaya philosophy in India (Banerjea Dialogues on Hindoo Philosophy p. 56f); but in the Buddhist legends it is mentioned as the name of one of the ancestors of the Sakya-race, on which account Buddha is often called Gautama. The different forms of this name are used promiscuously by Tibetan writers.

གོག *gog* W. for *góṅ-po* **a lump.**

གོག་ཐལ་ *gog-tál* **ashes,** **gog-tál yúm-ċe, yóg-ċe, tiṅ-ċe** W. to spread ashes (viz. on the snow, in order to increase the effects of the sun, and to accelerate the thawing of the snow).

གོག་པ་ *góg-pa* 1. **to crawl** (of little children). — 2. **to crumble off, to scale off** (of the plaster of a wall, of scurf etc.).

གོག་པོ་ *góg-po* **dilapidated, ruinous,** *ḱáṅ(-pa) góg(-po)* a house in ruins; *mḱar-góg* a dilapidated castle; of clothes: out of repair, ragged; *žiṅ-góg* a field lying waste; *dpe-góg* an antiquated, worthless book; *gog-góg Cs.:* 'the sound of a somewhat broken vessel'.

གོང་ *goṅ* 1. **price, value,** also *goṅ-ṫáṅ Glr.*, frq.; *goṅ dpyád-pa* (often also *bċád-pa*, inconsistent with etymology) to apprize, to fix a price; *goṅ brgyáb-pa C.* (*goṅ ˳grig-pa Schr., Sch.*) id. — 2. **the above,** in space as well as in time, (in *Khams* e. g. it is used as a sbst., signifying: elevated, alpine pasture-grounds): **the above said, the former,** referring to a preceding part or passage of a book, *goṅ daṅ mṫun, goṅ daṅ ˳drá-bar, goṅ-bžin, goṅ-mṫsúṅs* as above (mentioned); *ṗrin goṅ ˳og ˳dzól-ba* to confuse a message, to make a medley of it *Glr.*; *góṅ-du, góṅ-na, góṅ-nas, góṅ-la* 1. adv. over it, on it, thereon, above, from above. 2. postp. c. genit. or accus.: on, above, over, before, *sgo góṅ-du* over the door; *yáb-kyi góṅ-du ˳das*, he died before his father *Glr.*; *déi góṅ-du* before this time *Glr.*; *ma ṫsogs góṅ-du* before they are assembled; *góṅ-gi* the former, the above mentioned; *góṅ-gi dé-rnams* those preceding; *góṅ-du bšád-pa ltar* as has been said, explained above; *góṅ-du smós-pa* the above mentioned; *góṅ-gi ... žes smós-pa* the above statement that ...; *sṅa goṅ bód-kyi rgyál-po* the former (ancient) Tibetan kings; *goṅ* and *˳og* like our subdivisions of *a* and *b*, the first and second part, division or section of a book, *ba-góṅ* and *ba-˳óg* Volume XV Section 1 and 2; the face and the back of a leaf: *bži-góṅ* folio 4, a. — *goṅ-sku-ɣžógs*, a title, like our: his highness, excellence, eminence *Sch.* v. *sku*.

གོང་པོ་, གོང་བུ་ *góṅ-po, góṅ-bu, W. *gog**, **lump, mass, heap, clot,** *šá-goṅ-po* a lump of flesh *Dzl.*; *ḱrag-góṅ* a clot of blood *Glr.*; **bol-góṅ* C.*, **sa-góg* W.*, clod, glebe; **ḱa-góg* W* snow-ball.

གོང་བ་ *góṅ-ba, W. *góṅ-ṅa*, gós-kyi góṅ-ba,* **collar,** *goṅ-ba-nas ˳dzin-pa* to seize by the collar.

གོང་མ་ *góṅ-ma* a higher one, **a superior; the former,** the first named, *góṅ-ma bžín-du* like the former; *rgyál-ba góṅ-ma* the most high, the divine Buddha *Mil.*; *góṅ-ma ċe, góṅ-ma ċén-po* the most high, applied to worldly sovereigns, as: *rgya-nág. góṅ-ma* the emperor of China *C.*; *góṅ-ma-rnams Mil.* the gods (the 'superi' of the ancients), among whom according to the doctrines of Buddhism the Lamas are included.

གོང་མོ་ *góṅ-mo* **ptarmigan, white grouse,** *lhá-bya góṅ-mo B.* and *C.*, **ri-bya góṅ-mo* W.*, *goṅ-sróg* id. (?); *goṅ-yag Sch.:* wood-grouse, cock of the wood, Tetrao urogallus.

གོང་ཞུ་ *goṅ-žú C.* **paper lantern.**

གོད་ *god, W. *gód-ḱa* Dzl. gód-pa, Cs. gód-ma* 1. **loss, damage,** *god ˳gyúr-ba Thgy.*, **gho̱'-la ˳dó-wa* C.*, **god-la ċá-ċe* W.*, to suffer loss, e.g. *nór-la* or *nor*, a loss of money and property; *gód-pa* vb. id., **nor gód-da* W.* have you had a loss? 2. *C.* **punishment.**

གོན་ *gon* the common **gourd, pumpkin** *W.*

གྱོན་པ་ *gón-pa* I. vb. **to put on** (clothes, shoes), *mgó-la ža gón-pa* to put on a cap.

— II. sbst. **coat, clothing** *Sch.*; **gón-če** *Lh., Ld.*, **gón-ma** *Bal.* id.

གོབ་ནོན་ *gob-nón* (spelling uncertain), **gob-nón čó-če, tán-če, gyáb-če** *W.* **to tease, vex, irritate.**

གོམ་པ་ *góm-pa* 1. **a pace, step,** *góm-pa ₒbór-ba* to make a step, to pace; *góm-pa bdun ₒbór-ba Glr.* 5, 2 and elsewh.: to make seven steps, as a ceremony, which may also be counted equivalent to a religious pilgrimage, the actual performance of which is not possible: *góm-pa ₒdór-ba* prob. = *ₒbór-ba; góm-pa ₒdébs-pa* and *skyél-ba Lt.* ? ? — *góm-pai stabs* the (peculiar) manner of stepping *Zam.*; **prú-gu-la gom-tán láb-če** *W.* to teach a little child to walk; **gom čág-če** to stride solemnly along; **gom-jór** col a veranda (?). — 2. **the 'pas'** in dancing.

གོམས་པ་ *góms-pa* **accustomed, wonted, wont** c. dat.; *klóg-pa-la góms-šin* practising (the art of) reading *Dzl.*; *góms-par byéd-pa*, and *ₒgyúr-ba* c. dat. and accus., to accustom one's self to a thing, to practise; *mi góm-pa* unaccustomed; **mi dan góm-te** *W.* accustomed to man, tame, domesticated: **ghom-kyé?** *C.* a habit, custom.

གོར་མ་ *gór-ma Cs.*: a general name for stone; *Sch.*: stones, rubble, bowlder-stones.

གོར་མ་ཆག་ *gor-ma-čág*, eleg. *gor-ma-bkúm*, **certain, sure, indubitable,** *de ₒbyin-ba gor-ma-čág-go* his coming is quite sure *Wdn.*; *dé yin gor-ma-čág-go* that it is this, is quite certain *Stg.* frq ; *gor-ma-čág-par* adv. certainly.

གོར་མོ་ *gór-mo* 1. **round, circular** *Sch.*; *gor-gór Med.* id. — 2. *W.* **a rupee.**

གོར་ཤི་ཤ་ *gór-ši-ša* v. *tsán-da-na.*

གོལ་བ་ *gól-ba* v. *ₒgól-ba.*

གོས་ *gos* 1. resp. *ná-bza*, **garment, dress.** — 2. in some compounds **silk.** — *rgyán-gós* fine clothes *Glr.*; *rgyún-gos C., W.*, an every day coat; *čos-gos* clerical garb or garments *Schl.* 170, *Burn.* I. 306, *Köpp.* I. 339, II. 266; *mtán-gos* a sort of petticoat worn by the monks, having many plaits and folds, like the kilt of the Highlanders, but longer and of one colour; *pó-gos* man's dress, *blá-gos* an upper garment, a kind of toga; *mó-gos* a woman's gown; *ₒzáb-gos* holiday clothes, opp. to *rgyun-gos C., W.* — *gos gón-pa, gyón-pa* to put on, *ₒbúd-pa* to take off, *brje-ba* to change clothes; *brtségs-pa Sch.*: to put one garment over the other; *gos btég-pa* to tuck up, by drawing the front skirts under the girdle; *gos ldáb-pa* to lay or fold a coat together; *gos spú-ma* a coat of napped cloth.

Comp. *gos-skúd* **silk-thread.** — *gos-sgáb* **skirt** or **flap** of a coat. — *gos-sgám* box, chest, or press for clothes, **wardrobe.** — *gos-čén*, col. *go-šén*, silk fabrics, **silks.** — *gos-rnyín* an old coat or dress. — *gos-túṅ* **trowsers** *Glr., C.* — *gos-mtá* = *gos-sgab.* — *gos-nág* a black garment, a female dress. — *gos-bzáṅ* a beautiful dress, fine clothes (as an object of show), festival raiment. *gos-lúg* (in *W.* also pronounced **goi-lág, go-lág** in *C.* **gho-lág**) **dress, clothes,** body-linen; **gos-lág ṭú-če** *W.* to wash linen.

གོས་པ་ *gós-pa*, pf. of *bgó-ba.*

གྱ་ *gya* num. instead of *brgyád-ču*, in the abbreviated numbers *gya-gčig* etc. 81—89.

གྱ་ *gya*, a root, the meaning of which is not quite settled yet; it occurs in the following combinations: *gya-gyú* (*Cs.*: crookedness?) **intrigues,** secret machinations *C., W.*; *gnód-séms dan bslú-bai gya-gyú sogs* malice, deceitful tricks and the like; *gya-gyu-čan* crafty, deceitful, fraudulent, e.g. *sems*; *gya-gyú byéd-pa* to intrigue, to plot. — *gya-ma-gyú* 1. of rivers etc.: **quiet, calm,** gently flowing along *Mil.* 2. of a man: **cautious, close, reserved,** so that one does not know what to think of him, ni f. — *gya-nyés Mil.* was explained: **marvelous, inexplicable,** of men, occurrences etc. — *gya-nóm-pa Cs.*: 'contentment, joy'; yet the context in several passages of *Mil.* suggests the signification: abundance, sufficiency. — *gya-rtsóm, gya-tsóm* haste, hurry, rashness *Cs.*

གྱབ་ *gyá-ba* **deformed, disfigured, having lost his or her former beauty** *Cs.*

གྱག་པ་ *gyág-pa* diminished *Cs.*; v. *˳gyág-pa*.

གྱང་, གྱེང་ *gyaṅ, gyéṅ* **pisé**, earth or clay stamped into moulds, and frequently used as building-material in *Sp.*, *Ld.*, and other parts of Tibet; *gyaṅ-sgróm* pisé-mould; *gyaṅ-skór* pisé-wall round an estate or village *Glr.*; *gyaṅ-ra* cattle-yard constructed of pisé; *gyaṅ-tse* terrace wall of pisé *Ld.*; *gyaṅ-rim* one layer of pisé, i.e. as much as is stamped in at a time, about one ell in height; this frequently serves for a measure of the depth of the snow *Mil.*; *gyaṅ-ris* fresco or wall-painting.

གྱད་ *gyad*, also *gyád-pa*, *Ssk.* मल्ल 1. **a champion**, a man of great physical strength, **an athlete**, frq.; *da-dúṅ gyád-gyi tsal ˳gran* let us try once more our strength in fighting *Mil.*; *gyád-rdo* giant-stone, i.e. a stone which only a giant is able to lift *Mil.* — 2. n. of a people *Tar.* 11, 10.

གྱན་རྒྱུ་ *gyan-rgyu Med.*, *gyan-rgyui bu-ga*, *gyan-rgyui mtu?*

གྱམ་ *gyam* **a shelter, a grotto** large and wide, but not deep (cf. *skyibs*), *brág-gyam* a shelter under a rock; *gád-gyam* a grotto beneath a conglomerate rock; *p̔oṅ-gyám* (for *p̔a-boṅ-gyam*) a shelter under a beetling rock: *gyám-bu* a little cover or shelter *Cs.*

གྱར་གྱོད་ *gyar-gyód* prob. = *gyod-k̔a, god-pa* loss, damage.

གྱི་ *gyí* for *gyi*, after *n, m, r, l*; v. *kyi*.

གྱི་ན(བ) *gyi-na*(*-ba*) 1. **bad, coarse, mean, poor, miserable**, of food, clothes etc.; *gyi-na ˳ts̔ó-ba* a miserable, starving life *Pth.* — 2. **unsteady, fickle** *Schr.*

གྱི་ལིང་ *gyi-liṅ Glr.* n. of an excellent breed of horses.

གྱིག་ *gyig* **caoutchouc, India rubber**, *gyig-šiṅ*, *gyig-sdóṅ* caoutchouc-tree *Sik.*

གྱིང་ *gyiṅ* n. of a deity *Pth.*, perh. = *kiṅ-káṅ*.

གྱིང་མོ་ *gyiṅ-mo W.* gently **sloping**, gradually descending or subsiding.

གྱིན་ *gyin* v. *kyin*

གྱིམ་བག་ *gyim-bág* **amalgam**; *gyim-bág-gis ˳byúg-pa* to gild in the fire *Schr.*

གྱིས་ *gyis* 1. inst. of *kyis*, after liquid letters. — 2. v. *bgyid-pa*.

གྱུ་ *gyu Cs.* = *gya-gyú*; cf. also *sgyu*. — *gyú-ba* v *˳gyú-ba*.

གྱུང་རོ་ *gyúṅ-ro* v. *gyóṅ-ro*; *gyur* v. *˳gyúr-ba*.

གྱེ་གུ་ *gyé-gu* **crookedness, curve; hunch, hump**, crookback, crooked; *gyé-gu-čan* of a camel, *gyé-gur ˳dúg-pa* being crooked, of trees, opp. to *draṅ-po*, *Stg.*

གྱེ་གོང་ *gye-góṅ* n. of a Bonpo idol (?) *Mil.*

གྱེང་ *gyéṅ* v. *gyaṅ*.

གྱེད་པ་ *gyéd-pa* v. *˳gyéd-pa*.

གྱེན་ *gyen* (opp. to *t̔ur*) **up, upward, up-hill**, mostly followed by *du* or *la*, *gyén-du ˳dzég-pa* to mount up, to ascend; *gyén-du rdzé-ba* to turn up, to cock (a hat or cap); above, on the surface, *gyén-du lús-pa* to keep above (water) *Glr.* *gyen-la ḍáṅ-po* *W.* **perpendicular, vertical**; *gyen-čád* (opp. to *man-čád*) the upper part of a country, *pú-rig gyen-čád* Upper Puríg, *Ld.-Glr. Schl.* 26, b. also sbst.: *gyen ɣzár-po* a steep ascent *C.*

གྱེར་ *gyer* v. *dgyér-ba*.

གྱེས་ *gyes* v. *˳gyé-ba*.

གྱོ་མོ་ *gyó-mo* 1. **gravel, grit** *Dzl.*, *Stg.* — 2. **potsherd** *Cs.*; *gyo-dúm* id. — 3. **tile, brick** *Sch.*; *gyo-mgó* id.; clay-vessel. In an allegorical comparison of the body with a house, the hair of the head is said to be like a *p̔ó-gyo mo-gyói rdza Med.?* *gyo-rtsi Wdṅ.?*

གྱོག་པ་ *gyóg-pa* **curved, crooked** *Cs.*; *gyóg-po* **left-handed, awkward** *Sch.*

གྱོགས་ *gyogs C.* pronounced *ghyog, ghyo*, for *sgyogs* **cannon**, large gun.

གྱོང་ *gyóṅ* **want, need, indigence**, *lto-gós-kyi gyóṅ tég-pa* to be able to endure **want** of food and clothes *Mil.*; *˳k̔ur-ba* to be reduced to want. — *gyóṅ-po* (cf. *kyoṅ-po*) **hard, harsh, rough, rude, impolite,** (*srab-*) *k'a-gyóṅ-po* hard-mouthed; *gyoṅ-ró* a dried up body, a mummy *Sch.*; metaph. *dgra-gyóṅ* a hard, cruel, dangerous enemy; *k'a-gyoṅ-čé* very rude, impudent *Mil.*

རྒྱོད་ *gyod* v. *ˌgyód-pa.*

རྒྱོད་ཁ་ *gyód-k'a* **loss; quarrel, law-suit** *Sch.*

རྒྱོན་པ་ *gyón-pa* **to put on, to wear** = *gón-pa*; *lús-la gyón-pai gos* the garment that one wears *Dzl.*; *gyóṅ-rgyu* materials for clothing. *Mil.*

རྒྱོས་པོ་ *gyos-po* **father-in-law,** *gyós-mo* mother-in-law, *gyos-sgyúg* parents-in-law *Dzl., Stg.* (In *Ld.* this word is rather avoided, sounding, as it is pronounced there, much like the obscene *rgyó-ba.*)

གྲ་ *grva* 1. **angle, corner** *Dzl.* ༡༢༥, 13; **lap, lappet, extremity,** *gós-kyi grva* coat-tail *Tar.* 98, 10 (seldom used). — 2. **school,** *klóg-grva* a reading-school *Cs.*; *sgóm-grva Glr.* and elsewhere: a meditating-school; *sṅágs-grva* a school for mystical theology *Cs.*; *ˌdúl-grva Glr.* a training-school, seminary; *smán-grvá* a medical school; *rtsis-grva* a school where mathematics are taught; *yig-grva* a writing-school *Cs.* — 3. **a cell** *Cs.* (?) — 4. sometimes for *grvá-pa.*

Comp. *grvá-k'aṅ* **school-house, school-room;** **láb-ḍa-k'aṅ* W.* id. — *grvá-pa* **scholar, disciple,** generally; **monk,** the lowest ecclesiastical grade; *grvá-pa byéd-pa* to become or to be a monk. — *grvá-dpon* **school-master** *Cs.* — *grva-p'rúg* **school-boy.** — *grvá-tsáṅ* the apartments in great monasteries, where the monks belonging to the same theological confession live together. — *grva-tsógs* convention of monks. — **ḍa-šág** **cell** *C., W.* — *grva-sa* **monastery,** *grva-sa čén-po* a great monastery; a school attached to such a one; *mtsan-nyid-kyi grvá-sa žig* a school of the Tsannyidpa sect; *dei stón-pa-rnams* the teachers of such a school *Mil.*

གྲ་ཏི་ *grá-ti* **plate, dish** *Ld.*

གྲ་བ་ *grá-ba* 1. sbst., also *gra-p'ád* **'a muzzle'** *Sch.*; a net before the window, to prevent passers-by from looking into the room *Schr.* — 2. vb. to carve in wood.

གྲ་མ་ *grá-ma* 1. **a beard** of corn, **awn,** *ˌbru grá-ma-čan* bearded, awned plants, such as corn etc. (opp. to *ˌbru gáṅ-bu-čan* leguminous plants) *S.g.*; **the bones** of fish v. *nya.* — *Zam.:* a tree or shrub, prob. the Tibetan **furze,** Caragana versicolor. — 3. a disease of the genitals, perh. venereal boils (condyloma) *Med*

གྲག་པ་ *grág-pa* I. sbst. 1. **noise, rumour, talk,** *Cs.* — 2. the principal or most distinguished amongst several persons *Mil.* — II. vb. = *ˌgrág-pa, miṅ yaṅ mi grág-par* so that not even the name is mentioned any more *Pth.*

གྲགས་པ་ *grágs-pa* I. vb. 1. **to bind** *Thgy., C., W.*, e.g. *grés-po* a load, a burden, also *grás-pa Thgy.*; perh. also *ˌgrágs-pa, ˌgrógs-pa* q.v. — 2. pf. of *ˌgrág-pa.* — II. sbst. 1. **fame, reputation,** character by report, *grágs-pa ṅán-pa* ill name, bad repute *Pth.*; **rumour, report,** *deï grágs-pa čén-po byuṅ* the report of it spread, was circulated; in most cases it signifies **good name, renown,** *snyán-pa daṅ grágs-pas sai steṅ t'ams-čád k'yáb-pa Glr.* the whole earth was filled with (his) fame and renown; *snyan-grágs* id. (*Cs.:* good tidings); *grágs-pa-čan, snyán-grags-čan* illustrious, renowned; *rgyáṅ-nas grágs-pa če-ba* of great renown, of celebrity at a distance, (of less significance when more closely examined); **fame, glory,** *rnyéd-pa daṅ grágs-pa-la čágs-pas Dzl.*, greedy of gain and fame; *grágs-pa-čén-po* is also the name of a goddess = *dpal-lhá-mo.* — *grags* = *grágs-pa: grágs-ˌdod-čan* desirous of glory *Mil.*; *grágs-čan W.* (pronounced **rág-čán**) **famous, renowned; beautiful, splendid, glorious; proud, haughty** (in this case perh. for *drégs-pa-čan*). — *grágs-ˌdzin-ma, Ssk.* यशोधरा, यशोवति, the second wife of Buddha, acc. to others the second name of his first wife. — 2. **cry, outcry, clamour** (perh. better written *grág-pa*), *dga-grágs* *‚úr-ba* to raise shouts of joy.

གྲང་བ་ *gráṅ-ba*, *W.* **ḍáṅ-mo**, I. adj. **cold, cool**, *gráṅ-bai γnas* a cool place; **dáṅ-mo rag* W.*, **ḍháṅ-ghi ₒdúg* C.* I am cold.

II. sbst. **coldness, cold**, *gráṅ-ba ni dró-bar gyur* the cold changed into warmth *Dzl.*: **mén-tog ḍáṅ-mo ṗog* W.* the cold has struck, killed, the flowers. — *graṅ-ṅád* the cold fit of the ague, **ḍhaṅ-ṭi** (lit. *mḱris*) *C.* id. — **daṅ-ṅád* W.* synon. with *grúm-bu*, **gout, rheumatism, arthritic pain**; *graṅ-dro* **cold and warmth**, *graṅ-dro-méd-pai rás-kyáṅ ₒdi* this thin cloth which constitutes my clothing, in warm and in cold weather *Mil.*, v. *méd-pa*; also warmth in a relative sense, **temperature.** — *graṅ-śúm Lt.*, *graṅ-śúm byéd-pa* to shiver with cold *Schr.*

III. vb., also *graṅs-pa* 1. **to get** or **grow cold**, *gráṅs-su bćúg-pa Lex.* to let grow cold; *graṅs ₒgró-bar ₒdug* it will grow cold *Mil.*; *graṅ mi bya* one must not suffer (the child) to catch cold *Lt.* — 2. **to count, judge, consider**, v. *bgráṅ-ba*; also *Zam.*: *ćes gráṅ-naaṅ* though such may be supposed; *Cs.* and *Schr.* have also *graṅ* **perhaps**, *yin graṅ* perhaps it may be so.

གྲངས་ *graṅs*, col. also **ḍaṅ-ka**, *Ssk.* संख्या **number**, frq., *lan graṅs-dú-mar* a number of times *Mil.*; *graṅs-méd-pa*, eleg. *graṅs-ma-mćis-pa* innumerable; *gráṅs-ćan* numerous (?) *Cs.*; *gráṅs-ćan-pa* the atheistic Sankhya sect of the Brahmans (Ban. p. 66); **dá-ḍáṅ žág-ḍaṅ gyáb-će* W.* to date (lit. to write down the number of month and day); *graṅs ₒdébs-pa* or *rtsí-ba* to count *Cs.* — *graṅs-brdá* (*Cs.* Gram. § 235) symbolical numerals, certain nouns, which in some books are used instead of the usual numerals, e.g. *mig*, eye, for 'two'.

གྲངས་པ་ *gráṅs-pa* to grow cold, v. *gráṅ-ba* III.

གྲབ་རྒྱག་ *gráb-rgyág* pride, boasting *Sch.*

གྲབས་ *grabs* 1. **preparation, arrangements, measures; a contrivance**, *grabs byéd-pa* to make preparations for, to be on the point of, frq., *ₒgró-bai grabs byéd-pa*, to make preparations for departing, *γsód-grábs yód-pai tsé-na* just as preparations were made for slaughtering them *Mil.*; **ḱo kyug ḍhab ǰhe'* C.* he is getting sick, is going to vomit; *ḱáb-grabs*, *ₒdzíṅ-grabs* the making one's self ready for combat. — 2. col. also for *gros*, **deliberation**, **nẹ čir dhab ǰhe' dug* C.* they are deliberating about me; **naṅ-náṅ-ṅi ḍabs tún-nẹ* W.* on mutual agreement.

གྲམ་པ་ *grám-pa* 1. **swamp, marsh, fen** *Lex.* — 2. *ₒgrém-pa Mṅg.*

གྲལ་ *gral*, *Ssk.* पङ्क्ति 1. **row, series, class**, esp. a row of persons, *gral(-du) sgrig-pa* to order, to dispose in rows, in rank and file; *grál-gyi tóg-ma*, *ltag*, *goṅ*, more frq. *gral-mgó* the upper end of a row, the uppermost place, the seat at the head of the table; *tá-ma*, *‚og* or *gral-mǰúg(-γžug)* the lower end; *gral mgó-ma* the first, the head person *Mil.*; *γyas-grál* the right-hand end, *γyon-grál* the left-hand end; *gral-rím C.* **claim, title**, *rgan-γžon-gral-rím* the right of seniority; *grál-pa* a beer-house customer; *gral-γtám* tap-house talk *Mil.*; *dbaṅ-grál* the row of supplicants for a benediction; *mčed-gróǵs daṅ dbaṅ-grál mtun dús-su Mil.* if you sit with your fellow-believers in one row, on one mat; **če-ḍál-la čud soṅ* W.* he has entered into the row, the class, of adults. — 2. **bench.** — 3. **proportionality** (?), **žeṅ-ríṅ ḍal-méd daṅ* W.* with his disproportioned length and breadth, his unwieldiness. — 4. **mi žig-la ḍal žig ḍig-će* W.* (lit. *sgrig-pa*) *W.* to play **a trick** to a person.

གྲལ་མ་ *grál-ma* a small beam, **rafter**, *Cs.*; *grál-bu*, *gral-ṗyám S.g.* roof-laths, sticks which are laid close together and covered with earth.

གྲས་ *gras* **class, order, series; rank, dignity; tribe** *Cs.*

གྲས་པ་ *grás-pa* 1. for *drás-pa.* — 2. **to bind**, v. *grágs-pa.*

གྲི་ *gri* (so pronounced in *Pur.*) 1. **knife**, *gris γćód-pa*, **ḍi daṅ ćád-će* W.*, to cut with a knife, but also *grir ṅám-pa*, *γsód-pa*, *ₒgúm-pa Ma*: to kill with a knife;

gri-só, gri-dňó, gri-ḱá the edge of a knife; *gri-lám* lit. 'the path of the knife', the cut, incision; *gri-gúg Pth.* a short, crooked sabre or sword, **falchion, cimeter;** *gri-šá* flesh of a man that has been killed with a sword, (used in sorcery). — 2. *Lt.: dar-mai gri?*

གྲི་མག་ *gri-mág* v. *grib-ma.*

གྲིན་པ་ *grin-pa Mil.*, prob. = *sgrin-po* **skilful, clever.**

གྲིབ་ *grib* 1. **shade,** *grib-kyi ṕu Glr.* the shady part of a valley on the north side of a mountain-range, cf. *sribs*; *grib-pyogs* the side not exposed to the sun, north side, col., *grib-lhágs* the coolness of the shade, the cool shade *Sch.*; *grib-ma* **ḍi-mág** *W.* **shadow** (cast by an object); *dei grib-ma gáň-la ṕóg-pa* on whom his shadow falls; *grib-tsód* a dial *Cs.* — 2. **spot, filth, defilement, contamination,** mostly in a religious sense: *grib yoň* pollution arises; *ro-grib* defilement by a corpse; *grib-sél* name of a Buddha; *grib-(kyis) nón-gyi ydon* a demon that defiles and poisons the food, a harpy; **ḱó-la ḍib ṕog soň** *W. C.* he is crack-brained, not in his right mind; **ḍib-čan** stubborn, refractory, whether from stupidity, or from ill-will.

གྲིམ་པ་ *grim-pa* **to hasten, to hurry** *Sch.*

གྲིམ་ཙེ་ *grim-tse Sik.* a pair of **scissors.**

གྲིམས་ *grims Med.?* (*Lex.* **चतुरस्र** quadrangular, regular, harmonious) Schr.: intelligent, clever.

གྲིལ་ *gril* (cf. *ˌgril-ba*) **a roll,** *šog-gril* rolled paper, a paper-roll; *gos-gril* a garment folded up *Cs.*; *gril-ḱa byéd-pa* to make up a parcel *Sch.*

གྲུ་ *gru* 1. **boat, ferry, ship, vessel,** also a hide blown up with air, used for crossing rivers = **ko-ḍhú** *C.*; *gru-šán* id.; *gru-šán-pa* ferry-man; *grú-la žón-pa* to go on a ferry. **Comp,** *grú-ḱa, gru-šán-ḱa, grú-btaň-sa C.* starting- or landing-place of a ferry. — *gru-glá, gru-btsás* fare, passage-money, a boat-man's fee. — *grú-pa* ferry-man. — *gru-dpón* ship-master, master of a vessel. — *grú-bo,* gen. *gru-yzins,* ship. — *gru-ˌdzin* (**पोतल**) ancient name of Tatta, at the mouth of the Indus, ancestral seat of the Shakya race, whence the name is transferred to the residence of the Dalai Lama in Lhasa, v. Köpp. II. 342. — 2. (*Cs. grú-ma*) **angle, corner,** convex or concave, also **edge, border, brim;** *gru-ysum, gru-bži* etc. triangle, quadrangle; *gru-ysúm-pa* triangular; *dkyil-ˌḱor gru-bži-pa žig ˌbri-ba* to draw a quadrangular figure, a square; *ˌdom-gáň gru-bži,* a surface six feet square; *dbyibs gru-bžir yod S.g.*; **ḍu-nar-čan** *W.* rhomboidal; *gru-yon, Cs. gru-gyél,* oblique angled; *gru-dráň* right-angled *Cs.*; *gru-ḱún* v. *mto-gon.* — *yúl-gru* **place, village, town, country.** — 3. **lustre,** of precious stones, *gru-dmár* a reddish lustre *Mil.nt.*

གྲུ་གུ་ *grú-gu* 1. **clew, hank.** — 2. **n. of a** country.

གྲུ་ཆར་ *gru-čár* 'a fine, fertile rain' *Sch.*

གྲུ་མོ་, གྲེ་མོ་ *grú-mo, gré-mo* **elbow,** *grú-mor ḱa-trám-ka bzúň-ba* holding a trident in his arm *Pth.*; *dé-la grú-moi ṕul-rdég čig byás-nas* pushing him with his elbow *Mil.*; *gru-súg byéd-pa* id.; *grú-moi ḱug,* the hollow of the elbow-joint *Glr.*

གྲུ་ཤ་ *gru-šá,* or *gru-šé,* n. of a country *Pth.*

གྲུག་པ་ *grúg-pa* to break into small pieces, **to crumble, to bruise** *Dzl.*; *grúg-pai ˌbras* bruised rice *Schr.*; *rús-pa čag-grúgs* fracture of a bone *Med.*; *grúgs-bu* something broken.

གྲུང་བ་, གྲུང་པོ་ *grúň-ba, grúň-po,* fem. *grúň-mo* 1. **wise, prudent** *Mil.*; also: *grúňs-pa lags* very learned Sir! *Thgr.* — 2. **meek, mild, gentle** *Cs.*

གྲུབ་ *grub Ld.* **all,** **ḍub ši soň** all are dead; **ḍub zas soň** it has all been eaten up, (v. the next word).

གྲུབ་པ་ *grúb-pa,* pf. of *ˌgrúb-pa* 1. **made ready, complete; perfect;** (*ma grúb-pa* also: not existing); *grúb-pai raň-byón spyan-ras-yzigs Glr.* the perfect, by himself originated, Awalokiteswara = *lhún-gyis grúb-pa; don tams-čád grub-pa, don-grub,* **सर्वार्थसिद्ध, सिद्धार्थ** 'the fulfilment of every wish' n. of Buddha, also of a spell or magic formula. — *grúb-pa lus Med.* either: the frame, the structure of the body, or more prob. an abbreviation of *pʼúṅ-po lṅá-las grúb-pai lus Med.*, v. *pʼúṅ-po*. — 2. **the state of perfection,** *grub-pa tʼob-pa* to attain to this state, *grub-tʼób* **सिद्ध** one that has attained to it, **a saint;** *grub-brnyés, grub-mčʼóg* id.; *grub mtʼá* (*C.*col. **dhum-tʼá**) *Ssk.* **सिद्धान्त opinion, theory** *Zam.*; *pʼyi-náṅ-gi grub-mtʼa ma ˳čʼáms-par Glr.* there being no conformity of opinion between Brahmanists and Buddhists; also n. of a philosophical work, *Was.* 262. — *ma-grúb-pa, grub-pa-méd-pa?*

གྲུམ་པ་ *grúm-pa* 1. *S.g.* n. of a burrowing animal, *Sch.*: **badger.** — 2. pf. of *˳grúm-pa* **lamed, crippled,** *grúm-po* a maimed person, a cripple; *grúm-bu, grum-nád* **gout, rheumatism,** = *tsig-nád; drag-grúm* gout, podagra; **ṡa-dúm** *W.*, a feeling of lameness in the limbs.

གྲུམ་ཙེ་ *grúm-tse* a thick woolen **blanket** *Mil.nt.*

གྲུལ་བུམ་ *grul-búm* a class of demons, *grul-búm-mo* female demons; there are also horned demons of this kind.

གྲུས་པོ་ *grús-po C.* a yak two or three years old.

གྲེ་ *gre* a Naksatra, v. *rgyu-skár.*

གྲེ་ག་ *gré-ga C.* **a sheet of paper** (*W.* **ṡog-gáṅ**)

གྲེ་བ་ *gré-ba* the fore-part of the neck, the **throat,** both the wind-pipe and the gullet; **dé-wa dé-mo**, or **nyán-pa dug** *W.* he has a good voice, sings well; *gre (-ba) gágs(-pa) Med.* hoarseness; **dé-wa tán-će** *Ld.* to join in singing or shouting; *gré-ba dár-ba* a snoring or rattling in the throat; **de-bsál táṅ-će** *W.* to hawk, to hem, to clear the throat.

གྲེ་བོ་ *gré-bo* a species of demons; *gré-mo* 1. female demons of this kind. — 2. v. *grú-mo.*

གྲེ་མག་ *de-mág*, vulg. for *grá-ma* **awn.**

གྲེ་མོག་འབུ་ *gré-mog-˳bu W.* **ant, emmet.**

གྲེའུ་ *greu* **pea, pease,** *món-sran-greu* acc. to *Wdṅ.* = **माष.**

གྲེས་མ་ *grés-ma* **the flashing, lightening, shining** *Schr.*

གྲོ་ *gro* 1. **wheat,** *gro-yós* parched grains of wheat, parched corn; *gro-sóg* stalk of wheat, wheat-straw. — 2. **breakfast,** taken late in the forenoon or about noon, *gro ˳dégs-pa Glr.*, also **dho ˳bóg-pa** *C.* to take breakfast, = *tsʼál-ma zá-ba.* — **do žig** *W.* a morning's march, short day's march, reaching quarters already at 10 or 11 o'cl. a.m.

གྲོ་ག་ *gró-ga, W.* also **dó-wa**, the thin **bark of the birch-tree,** frq. used to write on (esp letters), or for ornamenting bows etc. *Mil.*

གྲོ་བོ་, གྲོ་མོ་ *gró-bo, gró-mo* **reddish gray.**

གྲོ་མ་ *gró-ma* 1. = *gro* 2. — 2. n. of a medicinal herb *Wdṅ.* — 3. **dhó-ma, gya-dhó** *C.* **potato.**

གྲོག་པོ་ *gróg-po* (*Lex.* **श्वभ्र**) 1. a deep **dell, ravine,** lateral valley *C.*; *gróg-ču* brook, rivulet; *grog-yzár* a torrent pouring down in a ravine. — 2. *W.* = *gróg-ča.*

གྲོག་མ་, གྲོག་མོ་ *gróg-ma, gróg-mo* **ant, emmet;** *grog-tsʼáṅ, grog-mkʼár* ant-hill; *grog-spúr* acc. to some = *gróg-ma*, acc. to others some other insect.

གྲོག་ཞིང་ *grog-žiṅ* n. of a medicine *Wdṅ.*

གྲོགས་ *grogs*, col. **rog** 1. **friend;** the more definite form is *grógs-po*, fem. *grógs-mo; kʼa-grógs* a seeming friend, a false friend; *ytiṅ-grogs* a true friend; *sdig-pai grógs-po-la rten-na* if he attaches himself to bad friends *Dzl.*; *snyiṅ-gi grógs-po* intimate friend, bosom-friend *Pth.*; *grógs-po(r) byéd-pa* to make friendship, to enter into connexion with, to make a league, *ma-mtʼoṅ-ma-pʼrád-pai grógs-po byas,* they joined in friendship without knowing each other *Glr.* — *kye grógs-po* ho, friend! *Pth.* — 2. **associate, companion, comrade,** *grógs-po-dag* company, society *Dzl.* also used as address: comrades! friends! or more respectfully: honoured friends! honoured gentlemen! *Stg.*; **fellow**, *grógs-k̔yeu* play-fellow, play-mate *Dzl.*; *dpúṅ-grógs* fellow-combatant, brother in arms; *ₒdúg-grogs*, resp. *bžúgs-grogs* inmate, fellow-lodger *Mil.*, **ḍáṅ-rog** *W.*, (v. *braṅ-sa*) id.; also neighbour *W.*, *C.*; *dgá-grogs*, *γtán-grogs*, *grogs*, companion in life, **spouse, husband, wife,** *grogs mi rnyed* she cannot get a husband *Mil.*; *tse ₒdii grogs-skál* a man's destination **as to marriage**, the matrimonial lot assigned by fate *Glr.*; *ₒdód-grogs*, *mdzá-grogs*, *bzáṅ-grogs C.* one beloved, **lover, sweet-heart,** *mál-grogs* resp. *γzim-grogs* bed-fellow (not only 'concubine' *Cs.*); *dmág-grogs* ally, confederate (in war), hence also: — 3. **assistant, fellow-labourer,** *lás-grogs* journeyman, under-workman; *grogs byéd-pa* to help; *rgán-mo mč̔ód-rten skúd-pai grogs byas* they helped the old woman in anointing the pyramid *Dzl.*; *rtsig-grogs byéd-pa* to help in building a house; at present in *C* a word of courteousness in making requests: **tẹn rog naṅ (γnaṅ)* be so kind as to show me; **naṅ rog dzẹ'** would you kindly give me; **dha ṅa t̔oṅ rog dzọ'** now please let me go! cf. *rogs*.

གྲོང་ *groṅ* an inhabited place, a human habitation, **house, village, town,** *brgyá-groṅ*, *stóṅ-groṅ* a place of a hundred, of a thousand houses or house-holds (*mi-k̔yim*). —

Comp. *groṅ-k̔yér* 1. a large town, **city,** *B.* and *C.*, *groṅ-k̔yer (gyi) mč̔og* chief city, capital *Tar.* 2. fig. **place, scene, sphere,** (e.g. this world is a scene of illusions *Mil.*) — *groṅ-graṅs* the number of houses in a village or town. — *groṅ-mč̔óg Mil.*, *groṅ-mč̔óg ₒdrím-pa*, *ₒgró-ba*, *rgyúg-pa* one that wanders about among the peasantry as a fortune-teller; clerical charlatan, hedge-priest. — *groṅ-γtám* prob. = *groṅ-tsig* — *groṅ-rdál* (*Lex.* जनपद 'an extension of houses') a large town, also a suburb. — *groṅ-pa* 1. *W.* **a villager, peasant.** 2. *C.* = *groṅ*. — *gróṅ-po* = *groṅ Mil.* — *gróṅ-dpon* **village-chief,** *Sch.* — *gróṅ-mi* **peasant.** — *groṅ-tsig Lex.* **provincialism.** — *gróṅ-tso* **village, borough.** — *groṅ-bžis* **farm** *Sch.* — *gróṅ-yul* **village** *Mil.*

གྲོང་བ་ *groṅ-ba C.* col. for *graṅ-ba* **cold,** in *Glr.* occasionally.

གྲོད་པ་ *gród-pa* 1. **belly,** *grod-tsil* **suet.** — 2. col. **stomach;** of ruminating animals the first stomach or paunch. — 3. a dried paunch, or bullock's stomach, for keeping oil etc. *Glr.*

གྲོན་ཅན་ *grón-čan* disadvantageous, injurious, *gron-č̔é* very noxious, *gron-méd* harmless, innoxious *Lex.*

གྲོལ་བ་ *gról-ba* pf. of *ₒgról-ba*, as sbst. = मुक्ति the having been delivered, **deliverance** (from the pain of existence).

གྲོས་ *gros* 1. **advice, counsel,** *gros ₒdebs-pa B.* to give advice; *gros byéd-pa B.*, **dós gyáb-če** *W.*, to consider, to deliberate; to resolve, decide; *gros ₒdri-ba* to ask (a person's) advice, to consult (with one); *grós-ₒdri-sa* the place where advice may be asked, **an oracle** *Glr.*; *grós-pa* adviser, counsellor, senator; *grós-mi* id., head-man of a village; *gros mt̔ún-par* by unanimous decree, unanimously *Dzl.* — 2. **speech, talk,** = *γtam Mil. nt.* — 3. **council** (?). — 4. *Cs.*: **care, heed, caution,** *grós-čan* careful, cautious, *grós-med* careless, heedless.

གླ་ *gla* **pay, wages, fee,** *gla zá-ba* to live on wages, to work for daily wages *Dzl.*; *gla-ltó* food and wages; *glá-pa*, *glá-bo* (col.), *gla-mi* a day-labourer, hired workman, *glá-mo* (*Cs. glá-pa-mo*) fem.

གླ་བ་ *glá-ba* 1. **the musk-deer,** Moschus moschiferus, *glá-mo* the female of it, *gla-p̔rúg* the young of it; *glá-bai lté-ba* musk-bag (lit. navel); *glá-rtsi* (*W. *lar-si**), *Ssk.* कस्तूरी **musk,** *glá-rtsi-me-tog* Pedicularis megalantha, **gla-dá-ra** *W.* Delphinium moschatum, two alpine plants smelling strongly of musk; *gla-sgáṅ* n. of a medicinal root *Cs.*; *gla-glád* v. *glaṅ-glad*. — 2. n. of a pretty large tree, similar to, or the same as *stár-bu Glr.*

གླག, བྱ་གླག་ *glag, bya-glág* **eagle, vulture;** *glag k̔rá-mo Sch.*, **lag-k̔yi** *W.* (an eagle which is said to bark like a dog), *rgyab-glág* perh. different species of eagles.

གླག་པ་ *glág-pa* often used erroneously instead of *rlag-pa*.

གླགས་ *glags* **opportunity, occasion, possibility,** *glags ˳tsól-bá* to seek an occasion, to look for an opportunity; *da glags rnyéd-par dug* now the favourable point of time seems to have come *Glr.*; esp. opportunity of doing harm to another, of getting a hold on him; *glags rnyéd-par mi gyur*, he will not be able to get at you, to do you harm; *ysó-jlags med* there is no possibility of helping him, he is incurable *Med.*; *bzód-glags med* intolerable, insupportable, frq.

གླང་ *glaṅ* (*Bal.* *χlaṅ*) 1. **ox, bullock.** — 2. **elephant.** — 3 **Taurus,** the Bull, in the zodiac.

Comp. *glaṅ-glád* 'bullock- or elephant-brains'; soap being made of such, acc. to popular belief: *C.* **soap** (*Schr. gla-glad*). — *gláṅ-to* the Indian **bison,** Bos taurus indicus, *Lh.* — *glaṅ-túg*, *glaṅ ˳óg-can* **a bull.** — *glaṅ-dár-ma* n. of a king of Tibet, living about 1000 after Christ, notorious for his hostility against the hierarchy of the Lamas. — *glaṅ-dór* **a team** of bullocks. — *glaṅ-sná* **the trunk** or proboscis of an elephant; a plant so called on account of the long spiral spur of its corolla, Pedicularis Hookeriana. — *glaṅ-po* = *glaṅ*. — *glaṅ-po-čé*, *glaṅ-čén*, **elephant,** *gláṅ-mo* a female elephant, *glaṅ-ṕrúg* the young of an elephant. — *glaṅ-bu* a young bullock, *glaṅ-rú* a bullock's horn; also a large fork used by the Tibetan soldiers to rest the musket on, when firing (Hook. II., 235). — *ṕa-gláṅ* = *glaṅ-túg*.

གླང་, གླང་ཐབས་ *glaṅ*, *glaṅ-tábs Med.*, *yzer-gláṅ W.*, **colic, gripes, spasms** in the stomach, and similar affections; *glaṅ-šú Med.?*

གླང་མ་ *gláṅ-ma* a large kind of alpine **willow.**

གླད་ *glad* 1. **the head,** *glád-la* round the head, e.g. to brandish a sword, *Glr.*; as postposition used in a general sense: **close over,** *čui glád-la* close over the water. — 2. **brain** *Med.*, cf. *klád-pa*.

གླད་པ་ *glád-pa* **to thin** *Sch.* Cf. *lhad*, *slád-pa*.

གླན་པ་ *glán-pa* 1. = *glón-pa*, **to patch, botch, mend;** *glan brgyáb-pa Sch.*, *glán-par byéd-pa Lt.* id.; *lhán-pa glán-pa* to sew on a patch *Lex.* — 2. **to return,** *lan* an answer, to reply, rejoin *Lex.* — 3. *C.* col for *glén-pa*; so also occasionally in books.

གླལ་བ་ *glál-ba* **to yawn.**

གླིང་ *gliṅ*, द्वीप, prop. **island,** but usually: **continent,** part of the globe, viz. one of the four imaginary parts of the earth, as taught by the geographers of Tibet, or rather of ancient India: *lus-ṕágs* the part east of the Sumeru, of a semicircular shape; *˳dzam-bu-gliṅ* in the south, triangular; *ba-glaṅ-spyód* in the west, circular; *sgra-mi-snyán* in the north, square. The general character of the first of these parts is described as being *ži-ba* tranquil; that of the second as being *rgyás-pa* rich; that of the third as being *dbaṅ-ldán* strong, and that of the fourth as being *drág-po* wild. In a more general sense: **region, country,** so Nepal is frq. denominated *rin-po-čei gliṅ* the country of jewels and treasures, Urgyan *mk'a-groi gliṅ* the country of the Dakini, as is also Lahoul, in local chronicles; *byai gliṅ* region or country of birds *Glr.*; the word is also not unfrequently a component part of the names of towns and villages. — *gliṅ-ṕrán* prop. a little island, generally one of the small continents, of which there are eight, acc. to the above mentioned geographical system; also island in general. — *gliṅ-ka* a small uncultivated river-island, or low-land *C.*

གླིང་བུ་ *gliṅ-bu* (*Ssk.* वंश) **fife, flageolet,** made of one piece of wood and much like those used in Europe as play-things for children; it is the common musical instrument of herdsmen, and often consists of two pipes; *ṕred-gliṅ* **flute, piccolo-flute,** mostly of metal; *dge-gliṅ* a larger musical instrument like **a hautboy**, used in sacred ceremonies; *rkaṅ-gliṅ* lit. a fife made of the human femural bone, but sometimes also of metal.

གླུ *glu* (*Ssk.* गीति) **song, tune**, mostly, though not always, of a profane nature, opp. to religious hymns; *glu-dbyáṅs*, *glu-sgrá*, id.; the word is also used of the singing of birds; *glu-čúṅ* a little song, ditty, hummed by a person *Glr.*; *glu-rés* **alternate song**; *glu-gar-rtséd-po* rejoicings of every kind *Glr.*; *glu lén-pa B.*, **lu gyáb-pa* C.*, **táṅ-čé* W.*, to sing.

གླུད, བླུད, གླུད་ཚབ་ *glud*, *blud*, *glud-tsab* **a ransom**, a thing given as **a ransom**, *srog-gi glud* a ransom for one's life *Lex.*; *k'oi glúd-du lug brgya gsód-pa*, to slaughter a hundred sheep as a ransom *Mil.*; **lü'-la taṅ* C.* he is made an expiator, a scape-goat; **mi-lü* C.* in a special sense: a man's image which in his stead is cast away in the *gtór-ma*: therefore **k'o mi-lü' yin* C.* he is a curse, an anathema, one deserving to be cursed (ni.f.).

གླུམ་ *glum* **boiled barley, wheat, or rice, used** instead of malt in brewing beer (not for food).

གླེ་ *gle* 1. *Glr.* 60. a small uncultivated island, = *gliṅ-ka* (*Ld.* **zal**). — 2. n. of the capital of Ladak, usually *sle*.

གླེ་འདམས་ *gle-ˌdams* n. of a distemper *Cs.*; involuntary discharge from the bowels, or of urine *Sch.*

གླེགས་ *glegs* (*Cs.* *glégs-ma*) **table, board, plate**; *záṅs-kyi glégs-bu* copper-plate *Tár.* 26, 10; *glegs-bám* (पुस्तक) **book**, also *dpé-ča glegs-bám Glr.*; *glegs-bám máṅ-po bžéṅs-so* he made a present of, dedicated, many books (for the use of a temple); *glegs-šiṅ* the wooden boards which in a Tibetan book supply the binding; *glegs-tág* a thong etc. fastened round a book; *glegs-čáb* a buckle, clasp, or ring attached to this thong. — *sgó-glegs* the pannel of a door; **núm-lag** writing-tablet, a small board, blackened, greased, and strewed over with scraped chalk, on which the school-children write with wood-pencils.

གླེང་བ་ *gléṅ-ba*, pf. *gleṅs* **to say, talk, converse**, *gtam* (*-du*) *gléṅ-ba* id., resp. *gsuṅ gléṅ-ba*; *'lám-la ma tar' žes gléṅs-nas* as word was sent: 'the road is not passable!' *Glr.*; *gtam gléṅ-ba ni bdág-gis byas* I have made this speech *S.O.*; *gčig gléṅ gnyis gleṅ rím-pas mčéd-de btsún-moi bár-du gléṅ-žiṅ* the rumour spreading from one to the other, until it came before the queen *Pth.*; *čós-kyi sgrog-gléṅ byéd-pa*, (resp. *mdzád-pa*), **to preach** *Glr.*; *gros-gléṅ* **council, consultation**, perh. also disputation.

Comp. and deriv. *gléṅ-brjód*, *gléṅ-mo* sbst. **conversation, discourse, lecture**, *gléṅ-brjód ma maṅ dar-gčig gson* listen a little to a short discourse *Mil.*; *čós-gtam gléṅ-mo byed* let us converse on religious subjects *Mil.*; *gléṅ-mo* the act of **speaking**, opp. to *yi-ge*, the act of writing, the **written letter** etc. *Lex.* — *gleṅ-gži* 1. **the subject of a** discourse *Cs.* 2. table of **contents, index** *S.O.* and elsewh. 3. **place, scene,** of a conversation or discourse *Stg.* frq. — *gléṅ-ba-po*, *gléṅ-mo-mk'an* a **story-teller** *Cs.*; *glen-ˌbúm* 'a hundred thousand stories', title of a book, *Sch.*

གླེན་པ་ *glén-pa* 1. *B.* and *C.* **stupid, foolish,** *glen lkugs bkol-spyód-kyi sdug-bsṅál* the misery of stupidity, of dumbness and of servitude (the state of animals) *Thgr.*; *byol-sóṅ-las kyaṅ glén-po* more stupid than a brute *Mil.*; **fool**, *k'yód-rnams re glen* fools that you are all of you *Dzl.*; often in the sense of 'fool' in the Bible, = the **wicked**, the ungodly: *glén-pa gti-mug-čan* **infatuated** fools *Dzl.* ༢༩, 9 = profaners of holy things; **len-nág* W.* id.; **len-nág-gi pé-ra** **foolish talk**. — 2. *W.*: **idle, lazy, dull, imbecile**, e.g. a sickly child, an animal affected with a disease (opp. to **tám-pa, šáṅ-po** being in good health, active, lively).

གླེབ་པ་ *gléb-pa*, pf. *glebs*, **to make flat, plain** *Cs.*, *léb-mor gleb Lex.*

གླེམ་པ་ *glém-pa* **to press, squeeze; to crush, squash** *Stg.*, *C.*

གློ *glo* (*Ld.* ལྷོ **lho**), resp. *gžogs*, 1. **the side**, esp. of the body, *glos p'áb-pa* to lie down on one's side (lit. by means of the side); *gló-ča* (*Ld.* **ldó-ča**) ornaments, suspended on the side of the body, strings of pearls, shells etc., worn by women in the girdle; also in a general sense: *sráṅ-gi glo γyas γyón-na* on both sides of the street *Stg.*; perh. also side of a house, wall, in the expression: **kún-mo lo tol** the thieves broke through the wall *W.*; *glo-skár* window *Pth.* — 2. **saddle-girth** *W.* — 3. **cough**, **lo gyág-pa** *C.* to cough; (*Sch.* has: to err, to act foolishly, to lose, to neglect); **lo láṅ-wa** *C.* to cough; *glo-ḱa sra* a bad cough *Sch.*; **lo-ḱóg** *C.*, *W.*, cough; *glo-rgyál Lt.* a chronic cough; *glo-bstúd Lt.* a permanent short cough. — 4. Not quite clear is the etymology in *glo rdég-pa Sch.*: to be frightened, timid, and *glo rdég* (*-tu*) suddenly, = *gló-bur* q.v.

གློ་བ་ *gló-ba* **the lungs**, *gló-ba ma lṅa* prob. the five posterior lobes of the lungs, *gló-ba bu lṅa* the five anterior ones *Med.*; *gló-ḱa* of a colour like the blood of the lungs, **pale-red** *Sch.*; *glo-dóṅ* **windpipe** *Cs.* — *glo-rdól* a disease of the lungs; *glo-rkó* perh. the same. — *glo-sbúbs* (*Sch. spub*) wind-pipe. — **gló-ro** *W.* prob. pulmonary consumption. — *glo ḱú-ba Lt.* 'convulsion of the lungs' *Cs.*, or simply: cough, v. *ḱú-ba*.

གློ་བུར་ *gló-bur* 1. **suddenly, instantaneously,** also *gló-bur-du*, *glo-bur-bar*; *glo-bur-du mi máṅ-po ˳čí-bai sdug-bsṅál* the calamity of many men dying suddenly; *glo-bur-nád* diseases that arise on a sudden (opp. to *ṙhan-skyés* inherited diseases) *Med.* — *gló-bur-ba* adj., *gló-bur-bai don* the signification of suddenness *Lex.* — 2. *Cs.*: 'recently, *gló-bur-du óṅs-pa* a new comer'.

གློ་འབུར་ *glo-˳bur* **a rise**, an elevation above a surface *Sch.*

གློག་ *glog* (*Bal.* and *Kh.* **χlog**), col. also *glóg ka*, **lightning**, flash of lightning; *glog ˳bar* it lightens; *glog ḱyug* id.; *glog ḱyúg-pai yun tsám-las ma lón-par* with the rapidity of lightning *Mil.*; *glog rgyú-ba* the flashing of light, *Dzl.*; *glog-sprin* thunder-cloud, also as a symbol of the transitoriness of things.

གློག་པ་ *glóg-pa* a disease, = *lhóg-pa*.

གློད་པ་ *glod-pa* 1. **to loosen, relax, slacken** vb.a. *Cs.* — 2. **to comfort, console; to cheer up** *Sch.*; *glód-la rgyún-du bžugs* your honour may be easy about staying here always *Mil.*, cf. *lhód-pa*. — 3. *Ü:* **to give,** *ma bzuṅ ma glód*(*-par*) without any regard to taking or giving *Glr.*

གློན་པ་, གླན་པ་ *glón-pa*, *glán-pa* 1. **to return an answer, to reply.** — 2. **to patch, to mend,** cf. *klón-pa* etc.

གྷན་ཌྷོ་ལ་ *ghán-dho-la* n. of a mountain in *Lh.*, perh. incor. instead of *gan-dho-la* q.v.; it may also be derived from घण्टा bell, and thus the word would signify the same as *dril-bu-ri*, which is the name of another holy mountain, at the foot of which the nobleman's seat **Gondla** is situated.

དགག་པ་ *dgág-pa* v. *˳gégs-pa*.

དགང་བ་ *dgáṅ-ba* v. *˳géṅs-pa*.

དགང་གཟར་ *dgaṅ-γzár* v. *γzar*.

དགད་མོ་ *dgád-mo* v. *gád-mo*.

དགབ་པ་ *dgáb-pa* v. *˳gébs-pa*.

དགའ་བ་ *dgá-ba* (*Ld.* col. **γá-če**) I. vb. **to rejoice,** to be rejoiced or glad, *la* at, in, or of; *dé-la dgá-ste*, rejoiced at it, glad of it, — *mi dgá-ste* grieved, vexed, indignant at it; *ḱrims yód-pa-la dgá-nas* if you wish to have the law introduced *Glr.*; *γsód-pa-la dgá-žiṅ* sanguinary, delighting in blood-shed *Dzl.*; *bu-mo de-nyid-la dgá-bas*, as I wish to have none other but this girl *Dzl.*; *bód-la dgá-ba γčig kyaṅ ma byuṅ* nobody took an interest in Tibet *Glr.*; *ḱyed čii ṗyir mi dga* why are you so dejected, low-spirited? *dga bžin-du* with pleasure (e.g. I shall accept it); rarely with the gerund: *bram-ze da-ruṅ ˳dug-ste rab-tu dga-nas* much rejoicing, very glad, when (that) the Brahmin was still there *Dzl.*; with the termin. of the inf.: to do a thing readily, willingly, *nyán-par dgá-ba* **to like** to hear, to listen eagerly; **to be willing,** *su žig ₒdúg-par dgá-na* if anybody will stay here voluntarily *Dzl.;* **to have a mind, to intend, to wish,** *ḱyod ráb-tu byúṅ-bar dgá-am* do you intend to take orders? *Dzl.; bdág-gis ras ₒdi . . . sbyin-par dgao* I should like to present this cloth to . . . *Dzl.: méd-par byá-bar dgá-na* as I wish to annihilate . . . *Dzl.; gar dgá-bar* (or *gar dgá-ba der*) *soṅ* go whereever you like *Dzl.;* seldom with the accus.: *ₒdzóm-pa de dga-sté* as you now enjoy an abundance *Mil.;* with the instr. case: *des dgá-bar šóg-čig,* may you be cheered, comforted by it *Dzl.*; frq. absolutely: *dgá-bar byéd-pa* to make glad, to rejoice, *C.* also: to caress, to fondle.

II. sbst. **joy,** *dgá-bai ɤtam byéd-pa* to express one's joy *Dzl.*; *dgá-bai sems* id.; *dé-la ráb-ťu dgá-bai sems skyés-so* he found great delight in it *Dzl.*; compounds v. below.

III. adj. 1. **glad, pleased, enjoying,** *ṅa dgá-ba ma yin-pas* as I was not pleased with it *Dzl.; de-la mi dgá-ba, W. *mi gá-ḱan**, not favourably disposed towards, unfriendly, inimical to; *dgá-bar byéd-pa* to make glad, to delight, *bu čuṅ dgá-ba byéd-pai yo-byád* things which delight little children, play-things *Glr.* — Less frq. 2. **charming, sweet, pleasing, agreeable, beautiful,** *lhág-par dgá-ru ₒgro* she is getting more and more beautiful; *C.* in a general sense: **good,** cf. below: *dga-bdé.* — 3. as a proper name = नन्द *Tar.*

Comp. and deriv. *dga-grágs ..úr-ba* to give cheers, to raise shouts of joy *Mil.* — *dga-grógs* a participator of joy, gen. with reference to husband or wife (col. **ga-róg**). — *dga-mgú* great joy, *dga-mgú-ba, dga-mgu-ráṅ-ba* to have great pleasure, to be very glad, to be delighted, frq., *dgá-žiṅ mgú-la yi-ráṅs-pár ₒgyúr-ba* id. *Glr.* frq.; yet *dga-mgúr spyód-pa* to indulge in sensual pleasure *Pth., Stg., bú-mo daṅ* with a girl. — *dga-stón* **feast,** public festivity; *dga-stón-gyi ɤdán-sa* the place of a feast *Glr.*; *bsú-ba dgá-ba* festivities of welcome *Glr.*; *dga-stón byéd-pa* to celebrate a festival; *ₒgyéd-pa* to spread a feast, to distribute festival dishes; fig. *rná-bai dga-stón* a feast or treat to the ears *Glr.* — *dga-bdé* 1. **joy,** *lus sems dga-bdés ḱyáb-par ₒgyur Glr.* 2. (*Ts.* col. **gan-dé**) **good,** = *yág-po,* (of servants, dogs etc.) *C.*; **mí-la ga-dé ǰhé-pa** to treat a person kindly, with affection *C.* — *dga-ₒdún* wedding, nuptial festivities *Sch.* (seems to be a word not generally known). — *dga-ₒdód* n. of the plain of Lhasa, or at least of the northern part of it. — *dga-ldán* joyful 1. n. of a residence of gods, or of one of the heavens, *Ssk.* तुषित v. *Köpp.* I. 265. 2. n. of one of the great monasteries near Lhasa, founded by Tsongkhapa, about the year 1407, v. *Köpp.* II, 345. 3. *ɤžúṅ-sa dga-ldan* n. of the royal castle of residence at Lhasa; *dga-ldán-pa* n. of a sect = *dge-lúgs-pa.* — *dgá-bo* = *dga-bdé* 2. **good** *C.* — *dga-sdug-drag-žan* good and bad, strong and weak, of articles of merchandise and the like *C.* — *dga-spró* **joy,** *dga-spró dpag-tu-méd-pa ťób-pa yin* he entered into a state of indescribable joy *Mil.* — *dgá-ma* n. of the goddess of joy *Cs.* — *dga-ma-ₒdár C., W.* (col. **gá-man-dár**) the trembling with joy, the state of being enraptured, in ecstasy. — *dgá-mo* 1. **delightful, pleasing, charming,** of news, of a speech *W.*, of a landscape *Mil.* 2. **delighted, joyous, cheerful** *W.*, **sem gá-mó rag** I am cheerful; **gá-mo-čan* W.* id.; **gá-mo ǰhé-pa* C.* to caress, to fondle. 3. **pure, holy** *Sch., Dzl.*, prob. also *Mil.*; *čós-pa dgá-mo* a godly priest. — *dga-ťsór* **joy,** **ḱo ga-ťsór máṅ-po ǰhé* C.* he is very joyful; *dga-ťsór čé-ba* gratifying, delightful *Mil.* — *dga-ráṅs* being glad, **rejoicing,** **dhé-la ga-ráṅ dhág-te* C.* being greatly delighted with it, — *dga-rís* v. *ga-ri,* = *gá-ža.*

དགར་ *dgar* = *dgá-bar, raṅ-dgár* **at pleasure,** ad libitum, frq.: *či dgar Pth.* seems to mean: **why.**

དགར་བ་ *dgár-ba* I. **to separate, confine, fold up** (men, cattle, goods), *dgar-byá pyugs* cattle to be penned in a fold *Cs. ɤnás-nas dgár-ba* to banish, to exile; *dgár-bai dón-du* in a special sense, in particular *Sch.* — *gár-te bór-ċe* W. to set apart, exclude, shut out; to lock up, shut up, to lay up or by, to preserve; *gár-gya ċó-ċe* W. to store up; *tób-ċi gár-ċe* to button up. — 2. **to hang up, to fasten, to attach,** *dhar-ċóg ťág-pa-la* C. a flag to a rope. Cf. *skár-ba.*

དགལ་བ་ *dgál-ba* v. *ₒgél-ba.*

དགས་པ་ *dgás-pa* v. *ₒgás-pa.*

དགུ *dgu* 1. **nine,** *dgú-bċu (ťám-pa)* ninety; *dgú-bċu rtsa γċig*, or *go-ċig*, W. *gu-bċu-go-ċig* ninety one etc.; *dgú-pa* 1. the ninth. 2. having, comprising, measuring, nine, e.g. *ǩru-dgú-pa* measuring nine cubits (in length, height etc.); *dgú-po* the nine, those nine; *lan-dgú* nine times; *dgu-niń* three years ago *col.* — 2. **many,** *dgú-ċig* id. *Mil.*; *ťabs dgus bsags*, gathered by many efforts, with great difficulty; used as sign of the plural: *skyé-dgu* men, *skye-dgui bdág-po* (*Ssk.* प्रजापति) the lord of creatures, the lord of men; *skye-dgui-bdág-mo* n. of the aunt and wet-nurse of Buddha; *yód-dgu Lex.* those that are, the existing beings; *nor yód-dgu-ċog Mil.* the goods that one has, property; *bzáń-dgu Lex.* the good and the brave (among men); *lus ₒdod dgur sgyúr-ba* to be changed, transformed, ad libitum *Mil.*; *ńan-dgu ťúb-pa Lt.* to overcome every evil; *mi šes dgu šés-po Thgy.* he that knows every thing; *mi jhe' gu jhe' mi yoń gu yoń* C. if you do many things which ought not to be done, many things will take place which ought not to take place; *ċi-ba yid-kyi dgú-la mi bgéd-de Thgy.* not counting death among things to be thought of. — 3. inst. of *dgun*, *dgu-zlá* winter-month *Mil.* frq — *zer-dgu, smra-dgu??*

དགུ་ཁྲི་ *dgu-ǩri* **litter, bier** C.

དགུ་གཏོར་ *dgu-γtór*, for *ťses nyer-dgúi γtor-ma*, a sacrifice on the 29th day of the month W.

དགུ་ཐུབ *dgu-ťúb* 'all-conquering', n. of a plant.

དགུ་ཕྲུགས *dgu-ṗrúgs Mil., Thg.*, a particular kind of meditation.

དགུ་བ *dgú-ba* 1. vb. **to bend,** to make crooked; *go gú-ċe* Ld. to bend, bow, stop; to submit. — 2. sbst. the act of bending, bowing, **inflection.** — 3. adj. **bent, stooping;** *dgú-po, dgú-mo Cs.* id.

དགུ་རྩེགས་ *dgu-rtségs* n. of a yellow flower *Cs.*

དགུ་ཚིགས, དགུ་ཚིགས་སྐྱ་མོ *dgu-ťsigs, dgu-ťsigs skya-mo* **the galaxy, the milky way** *Mil.*

དགུ་མཚན *dgu-mtsán* **prize** (of combat) C.

དགུག་པ་ *dgúg-pa* v. *ₒgúg-pa.*

དགུང *dguń*, another form for *guń* (the former of the two appears to be prevalent) 1. **the middle.** — 2. **noon, mid-day.** — 3. **mid-night.** — 4. **heaven.** *dgúń-la reg* it reached up to heaven *Mil.*; *dguń snón-po* the blue heaven, *yá-gi dguń-snón* the blue heaven above *Mil.*; *dgúń-du* (or *-la*) *γšégs-pa* (lit. to repair, to withdraw, to heaven) to die *Mil.* and elsewh. — 5. before dates, esp. before the word *lo*, it serves as a respectful word, and is e.g. frq. used in stating the age of a Buddha or a king; yet it occurs also in compounds, where no such bearing is discernible: *dguń-žág, dguń-zla Cs.*; *dguń-do-núb Mil.* this evening, to-night; *dguń-snyiń* a year, a year of one's life; *dguń-ǩág* division of time (?); *dguń-bdún* a week. (*Cs.* has also *dguń-ťig*, and *dguń-ťig-gi dkyil-ₒǩor*, which terms were prob. framed by him, and meant to denote the meridian line and meridian circle.)

དགུང་མོ་ *dgúń-mo* **evening** *Sch*, perh. a corruption of *dgóń-mo.*

དགུན, དགུན་ཀ *dgún, dgún-ka*, W. *gún-ǩa* **winter;** *dgún* is also used adverbially: in winter(-time), during winter; *dgún-dus* winter-time; *dgun-ťóg, dgun-ťog-ťág*, W. *gun-ťag-ťóg*, all the winter through; *gun ťse re* W. every winter; *dgun gráń-bai dús-na* during the cold of winter *Dzl.*; *dgun-nyi-ldog* the winter solstice; *dgun-nyi-ldog-gi ťig*, or *kor-ťig* the tropic of Capricorn *Cs.* (cf. the remark at the end of *dguṅ*); *dgun-stód*, *dgun-smád* the first and the last half of winter, (v. *dus*).

དགུམ་པ་ *dgúm-pa* v. *ₒgúm-pa*.

དགུར་, རྒུར་, སྒུར་ *dgur*, *rgur*, *sgur*, three different spellings of the same root, all of them pronounced **gur**, **crooked,** *dbyibs-dgur* of crooked stature *S.g.*; *rgur žig* stoop down! bend your back! *Dzl.*; *sgúr-te* writhing (with pain) *Dzl.*; *sgúr-po* crooked, humpbacked, by birth *Lt.*; with age *Thgy.*; *C.* col. **gur-gúr** id.; *mgo dgúr-ba* to duck, to bend vb.n.; to submit, to humble one's self (cf. *dgú-ba*). *Cs.*: *dgúr-po*, *dgúr-mo* a crooked man, a crooked woman; *ťsigs-dgúr* a crooked back, crook-backed; *lag-dgúr* having crooked hands etc.; *dgur-ₒgro* of a stooping gait.

དགུས་ *dgus* 1. instr. of *dgu*. — 2. *C.*, *W.*, **this day five days** (the present day included).

དགེ་བ་ *dgé-ba* (*Ssk.* शुभ, कुशल, श्रेयस; also स्वस्ति, कल्याणं, seldom पुण्य) 1. **happiness, welfare; happy, propitious,** *dgé-žiṅ šis-pa Wdṅ.* More frq.: 2. **virtue** (opp. to *mi-dgé-ba*, and *sdig-pa*), also adj. **virtuous,** *sems dgé-ba* a virtuous mind *Glr.*, *las dgé-ba*, *mi-dgé-ba* good and bad actions *Stg.*; *dgé-bai rtsá-ba* roots of virtue, meritorious actions, from which afterwards the fruits of reward come forth; *dgé-rtsa skyéd-pa* frq., *spyód-pa Thgy.*, *byéd-pa Mil.* to produce such a root, to achieve a meritorious action; *dgé-ba séms-par ₒgyúr-ba* to become inclined to virtue, i.e. converted *Dzl.*; *dge-ťsógs* (v. *ťsogs*) a virtuous work, a good deed; *dgé-ba bču* the ten virtues, viz. 1. *srog mi γčód-pa*, not to kill anything living (by which Buddhism has replaced our scriptural interdiction of murder); 2. *ma byin-par mi lén-pa* not to take what has not been given (those who closely stick to the word go even so far, that they will not touch or accept an alms, unless it be put into their hands); 3. *lóg-par mi γyém-pa* not to fornicate; 4. *rdzun mi smrá-ba* not to tell a lie; 5. *ťsig-rtsúb mi smrá-ba* not to abuse or revile; 6. *ṅag-kyál* (or *ₒkyal*) *mi smrá-ba* not to talk foolishness (cf. *kyál-ka*); 7. *prá-ma mi byéd-pa* not to calumniate; 8. *brnáb-sems mi byéd pa* not to be avaricious or covetous; 9. *γnód-sems mi byéd-pa* not to think upon doing harm or mischief; 10. *lóg-lta mi byéd-pa* not to entertain heretic notions, or positively, *yáṅ-dag-par ltá-ba Stg.* to be orthodox. — 3. **fasting, abstinence,** in the phrase: *dgé-ba sñúṅ-ba* to fast, to abstain from food, frq. — 4. **alms, charity; banquet, treat,** as a religious work, *ši-dge γsón-dge* largesses, treats, taking place at funerals, or given in one's life time *Mil.* (*W.* **yá-tra**, and **ku-rím**).

Comp. and deriv. *dge-bskos* **censor,** and at the same time **provost** and **beadle** in a monastery, who has to watch over strict order, and to punish the transgressors Köpp. II. 259, 276; in *Ld.* he is also called *čos-ₖrims-pa* (vulg. **čosrimpa**). — *dge-rgáṅ* **surety, moral bail,** a monk that is made answerable for the moral conduct of an other, who is placed under his care and called *dge-γžón*; also in a gen. sense: **teacher, schoolmaster.** — *dge-bsnyén*, fem. *dge-bsnyén-ma* (*Ssk.* उपासक and उपासिका) 1. the pious of the laymen who retaining their secular occupations have renounced the five cardinal sins (murder, theft, fornication, lying, and drunkenness) and provide for the maintenance of the priests (so in *Dzl.* and gen. in the earlier writings). 2. in in later times as much as **a novice, probationer, catechumen,** i.e. either a kind of clerical apprentice (the Shabi of the Mongols, *šrāmanera Ssk.*, v. *Köpp.* II., 252), or one of a next higher degree, a candidate (v. *Schl.* 162). — *dge-ltás S.g.* **a propitious omen,** a favourable prognostic. — *dge-ₒdún* (col. **gen-dún**), prop. *dge-slóṅ-gi ₒdun* (*Burn.* II., 435) *Ssk.* संघ, the whole body of the clergy, **priesthood;** *dge-ₒdun-dkon-mčóg* the priesthood as one of the three great jewels, or as part of the godhead (in which latter sense the word now is usually understood) cf. *dkon-mčóg*; *dge-ₒdun-dpal-čén Mahāsāṅghika*, n. of a Hinayāna school *Tar.*, *Was.*; *dge-ₒdun-grúb-pa* n.p., the first Dalai Lama about the year 1400; *dge-ₒdun-rgyá-mtsó* n. of the second Dalai Lama, v. *Köpp.* II., 131. — *dge-ldán* **virtuous**; *dge-ldan-pa* n. of the most numerous sect of Lamas, founded by Tsonk'apa; it is also called *dge-lúgs-pa*, or *dga-ldán-pa* from Galdan, a monastery near Lhasa which, as well as Sera and Ḍa-puṅ, belongs to his sect. The Lamas of this community wear for the most part yellow garments; they are said to approach nearer to perfection in mysticism (the highest aim of Buddhist priests) than any other sect, since they apply themselves more systematically to the preparatory studies of morality etc. — *dge-sdig* for *dge-ba daṅ sdig-pa*. — *dge-sbyóṅ Ssk.* श्रमण a Buddhist ascetic, or mendicant friar, *Burn.* I. 275. *Köpp.* I., 330. — *dge-sbyór* seems to have corresponded in its original acceptation to our conception of piety, sanctification and practical religion, but in later times the sense of expertness in the art of meditation was attached also to this word, as: *dge-sbyór p̓el* (this man's) expertness increases, is making progress *Mil.* — *dgé-rtsa* instead of *dgé-bai rtsá-ba* v. above. — *dge-rtsis* the amount of virtue, the sum of merit, *dge-rtsis rgyás-pa* a considerable amount of merit. — *dge-tsúl* 1. a young monk; in the older writings it may be understood as novice; 2. in later literature it denotes the degree next to the *dge-bsnyén*, being that of a subordinate or under-priest, *Köpp.* II. 252, 335. *Schl.* 162.; *dge-tsul-ma* a young nun, a novice. — *dge-mtsán* a lucky omen *Glr.* — *dge-γzón* v. *dge-rgán*. — *dge-γyóg* (seems to be pronounced *ger-yóg* in col. language) **constable, beadle,** a servant of the *tsógs-čén zal-ṅó*, or chief-justice of Sera and other monasteries. — *dgé-las* a good deed or action, but by later writers also applied to magic ceremonies and the like. — *dge-lúgs-pa* v. *dge-ldán-pa*. — *dge-légs* good fortune, prosperity *Glr.* — *dge-slóṅ* Gelong, 1. originally 'beggar of virtue', mendicant friar, भिक्षु one that has entirely renounced the world and become a Buddhist priest, 2. in later writings the highest clerical degree, a priest that has received the highest ordination, v. *Köpp.* I., 335. The Gelong is bound to observe all the 233 commandments of the *so-sór tar-pai mdo*. — *dge-slób-ma* a young nun *Cs.* — *dge-bšés* 1. v. *bšes-γnyén*. 2. n. of priests or monks. — *dge-sloṅ-šiṅ* is said to be a provincial name of the cedar, Cedrus Deodara.

དགེང་ལ་ *dgéṅ-la*, also *dgáṅ-la*, **on, upon, in, at** *Ts.*

དགེར་བ་ *dger-ba* = *γyo-ba*, **to prepare,** (food), *ₒk̓úr-ba dgér-ba* to bake pastry; **tú-ma gér-wa** *C.* = *ₒtúd-pa*.

དགེས་པ་ *dgés-pa* = *dgyés-pa* frq.

དགོ་ *dgo*, in *Lexx.* explained by *dúm-bur*, to divide (?).

དགོ་བ་ *dgo-ba*, a species of **antelope,** living on high mountains, Procapra picticaudata *Hodgson*, v. *Hook.* II. 157 and 139; *dgó-ba-mo* the female of this antelope *Cs.*

དགོག་ *dgog Lexx.* w.e.; *dgog-tiṅ* **pestle** *C.*

དགོང(ས)་ *dgoṅ(s)*, also *dgóṅ(s)-mo*, *Sch.* *dgóṅ(s)-ka* 1. **evening,** *dgoṅs-γčig* one evening, once on an evening *Glr.*; *naṅ re dgoṅs re* every morning and evening; **goṅs-zán** *W.*, **góṅs-ze̥** *C.*, resp. *dgoṅs-γsál* evening-meal, supper; *dgoṅs-ǰám* resp. evening-soup; *dgóṅs-su Dzl.*, *dgóṅs-mo* and *dgoṅs Glr.* in the evening; *dgoṅs daṅ to-ráṅs* in the evening and in the morning *Med.* frq.; *dgoṅs ₒbáb-pa* to hold an evening's rest, to take up night-quarters. — 2. **supper** *C.* — 3. **a day's journey,** *dgoṅs-žúg* col. id.; *rta-dgóṅs* a day's journey for one travelling on horseback, *lug-dgóṅs* a day's journey for a drove of sheep.

དགོངས་པ་ *dgóṅs-pa*, resp. for *sém-pa*, *snyám-pa* etc., and *sems*, *blo* etc. I. vb.

1. **to think, to meditate,** *dgoṅs-pa-la ȷug-pa* to enter into meditation *Glr.*; *ₒdi snyám-du dgóṅs-par ġyur-to* he thought so in his mind *Dzl.*; *rġyál-po k'oṅ-ráṅ yin dġóṅs-nas* the king thinking that he himself was meant, referring the allusion to himself *Glr.*; **to regard as,** *bu daṅ ₒdrá-bar dgóṅs-pa* to treat one like a son *Dzl.*; **to remember, to think of, to devise,** *mṅa-ris-kyi ɣdúl-bya-la* remembering those of Nari that were to be converted, thinking of the conversion of Nari *Glr.*; also with *p̔yir Pth.*; *ṅá-la t̔ugs-brtsé-bar dgoṅs-šig* remember me graciously, frq.; so in a similar manner: to hear graciously, to take a kind interest, share, or concern in, to interest one's self for, to try to promote; so our Lama explained the passage *Glr.* 101, 9: *saṅs-rgyás-kyi bstáṅ-pa-la dgóṅs-nas* = *bstán-pa ₒp̔él-bai p̔yir bsám-blo btáṅ-nas*; **to intend, to purpose,** with the termin. of the inf., frq., *t̔ugs-kyis ma dgoṅs-so* he did not intend, he had no mind *Pth.* — 2. **to die,** *més-kyi dgóṅs-dus-kyi mč̔ód-pa btsug Glr.* is stated to mean: he instituted sacrifices for the remembrance of his grandfather's death; and so similarly in other passages.

II. sbst., also *t̔ugs-dgóṅs*, 1. the act of **thinking, meditating, pondering,** *t̔ugs-dgóṅs ɣtóṅ-ba Mil.* to meditate; **thought,** *rgyál-poi t̔úgs-kyi dgóṅs-pa-la 'gáṅ-du p̔yin' snyám-pa* lit. in the king's 'mind-thoughts' was thought: where shall I go? *Glr.*; **meaning, sense,** esp. the sense of sacred words or writings, therefore *dgóṅs-pa ₒgrél-ba* to explain that sense, *dgoṅs-ₒgrél, dgoṅs-bgról* commentary; **a will, a wish,** *rgyál-poi* (or *-pos*) *dgoṅs-pa bžin-du bsgrub nús-so* I am able to fulfil your majesty's wish *Dzl.*; *skyóṅ-bai dgons-pa-čan Glr.* 104, poetically, one having the desire of protecting, one wishing to protect. — 2. **soul,** *dgóṅs-pa mya-ṅán-las ₒdás-so* his soul quitted (the abode of) misery. — 3. **permission** *C., W.,* **góṅ-pa žú-wa** to beg leave, to ask permission, **góṅ-pa táṅ-wa**, resp. **náṅ-wa** to give permission, in *Sik.* also: to grant admission; but gen. it is used for **leave of absence,** and **k'ó-la góṅ-p̔og ȷhuṅ soṅ** *C.* signifies: he has been dismissed, turned out.

དགོད་པ་ *dgód-pa* 1. **to laugh,** *Glr.*; gen. in such expressions as the following **gọ'-dhó* (lit. *bro*) *yim-pa** *C.* to make one's self ridiculous, a laughing-stock, also *Glr.*; **hab-gód čó-če** *W.* to set up a loud laugh, to burst out into laughter: *dgod-bág* a jest, joke *Sch.*; cf. *bgad-pa.* — 2. v. *ₒgód-pa.*

དགོན་པ་ *dgón-pa* 1. **a solitary place; desert, wilderness,** *dgón-pai ɣnas* a desolate place or region *Stg.*; *dgon-dúṅ* a sandy desert, sands *Sch.* (*Zam.* अङ्गल and *dgón-pa:* अरण्य forest). — 2. **hermitage.** — 3. **monastery,** frq.; *dgón-pa-pa* 1. a man dwelling in a desert, a hermit. 2. a man dwelling in a monastery, a monk; *dgon-pa-ma* fem.

དགོས་པ་ *dgós-pa* I. vb. implying necessity, as well as want: **to be necessary, to be obliged** or **compelled; to want,** to stand in need of; also where we use 'ought': it is gen. used with the verbal root or with the termin. of the inf. present, *byed dgos,* but sometimes also of the inf. future or perfect, e.g. *rin-po-č̔es brtsigs dgós-na rin-po-č̔e méd-pas sa-las bya dgos* though it ought to have been built of precious stones, yet for want of such, it will have to be constructed of earth *Dzl.* — *la* gen. denotes the person standing in need of a thing, e.g. *ṅá-la dgos* I want, I stand in need of, but it also refers to the object for which a thing is wanted: *rgya-gár-du ₒgró-ba-la ɣser dgos-pa yin* for a journey to India gold is wanted (required); in such a case the termin. may also be used: *či žig-tu dgos,* for what purpose is it wanted? *zas za ma dgos* I did not want to eat *Mil.*; *dgós-pai dús-su blaṅs* they took them when they wanted them *Glr.*; *bžéṅs ma dgos* he was not obliged to erect . . . *Glr.* — In commanding, the word is used to paraphrase the imperative of a verb: *ₒóṅ-bar dgos* come! in entreating, the respectful term is chosen: *ₒbyon dgos Mil.*, or in *W.*: **skyod dgos žu** 'you must come, pray!' =

please, do come! *ₒkrid dgós-pai γsól-ba*, or *žú-ba*, a request to be taken along with (by another person) *Mil. C.*: **to wish**, *kyo' še-pa ₒdi ňa go-pa yin* I wish you to know this *Lew.*

II. sbst. **necessity, want, use, purpose** (*W. dgós-če*, pronounced **gó-še(s)**), *máň-po ₒtsol dgós-pa byuň* we have been under the necessity of looking for you a long time *Mil.*; *ňá-la γyui dgós-pa med* I have no use for that turkois, I do not want it *Mil.*; **tiň-la gó-še ṕi-la* W.* for future use; *dgós-pai čún-bas* as it is rather useless; *dgós-pa čii ṕyir* for what purpose? frq.

III. adj. (*C.* also **gó-gyu**, and **go**, *W. *gó-še**, as in II.), **necessary, due, needful, useful**, *med kyaň dgos-pai kral-bsdud* a tax necessarily to be paid, unrelentingly exacted *Mil.*; *ráň-la dgós-pai skál-ba* the portion due to you *Mil.*; *dgós-pai bsláb-bya* useful doctrines *Glr.*; *dgós-pa yin* or *yod B.* and *C.*, **gó-šes yod* W.* it is requisite; *dgas(-pa) med B.*, **gó-gyu men* C.*, **gó-še man** or **med* W.*, it is unnecessary, unfit, not wanted; *mi-dgós-pa* **useless, noxious**, *mi-dgós-pai ṕra-mén* pernicious witchcraft *Pth.*; *dgos-byéd* **useful**, *don dgos-byéd či ₒdug* what there is in it of useful contents *Mil.*; *dgos-ₒdód* **wishes and wants**, *dgos-ₒdód ₒbyúň-bai dpal* a treasure out of which all wishes and wants come, i. e. are satisfied *Glr.*; *dgos-ₒdód nags-tsál* a forest for wishes, i.e. a forest which grants every wish; *dgos-ₒdód* **necessary** expenses *Cs.*

དགྱེ་བ *dgyé-ba* **to bend, to be curving** or **crooked**; *dbyibs dgyé-ba* stooping, cringing, ducking *S.g.*

དགྱེར་བ *dgyér-ba*, *glu dgyér-ba* for *glu lén-pa* **to sing, chant**, expression of the Bonpas; the word is also pronounced **ghyér-wa**.

དགྱེལ་བ *dgyél-ba Sch.* = *sgyél-ba.*

དགྱེས་པ *dgyés-pa*, resp. for *dgá-ba*, **to rejoice, to be glad**; often with *tugs*: *rgyál-poi* (or *-po*) *tugs dgyes* the king rejoiced; with *la* (to rejoice) at or in, (to be glad) of; **to please, to be pleased, to choose,** *ió-bo ₒbyón-pa-la tugs-dgyés-par ₒdug* it seems the lord is pleased to walk *Glr.*; *mi dgyés-te* sorrowful, sad, discouraged, dejected; angry, indignant; cf. *dgá-ba.*

དགྱེས་སུ་འཇུག་པ *dgyés-su ₒjúg-pa* **to bend,** to double down *Sch.*, v. *dgyé-ba.*

དགྲ *dgra*, also *dgrá-bo*, *Ssk.* शत्रु 1. **enemy, foe.** *sdáň-bai dgra* the hating enemy, (opp. to *byáms-pai γnyén*), frq. used of imaginary hostile powers, that are to be attacked and withstood only by witchcraft; *dgra γnyen med* there is no difference between friend and enemy = no such thing exists (viz in the golden age); *dgrar ₒgyúr-ba* to become an enemy (to one) *Tar.*; *dgra byéd-pa*, *dgrá-ru ldáň-ba*, *láň-ba* to act in a hostile manner, *la*, against; *dgra slóň-ba*, causative form, to make a person one's enemy *S.g.*; *dgrar sém-pa*, *ₒdzín-pa* to look upon one as an enemy, to take him for an enemy; *dgrar šés-pa* id.; *dgrá-bčóm-pa* Arhant, Arhat, the most perfect Buddhist saint (*Ssk.* अर्हत् venerable; the Buddhists, however, explain it as a compound of *ari* enemy and *han* to extirpate, he who has extirpated the enemies i.e. the passions *Burn.* I. 295, II. 287. *Köpp.* I. 400). Also *dgra bgegs ₒdúl-ba Glr.* is interpreted as referring to the subduing of spiritual enemies. — *sňá-dgrá* a former foe, *dá-dgra* a present foe, *ṕyi-dgra* a future foe *Cs.*; *ṕyi-dgra* prob. also a foreign enemy. — *ₒči-dgra* a mortal, deadly enemy *Cs.* — *dgrá-ča* weapon, arms *Wdň.*, *dgrá-sta* battle-axe; *dgrá-lha* v. *lha.* — 2. In *W.* also **punishment**, **kó-la da ṕog soň** he was punished; also for any self-incurred misfortune: **kyód-la da ṕog yin** you will draw upon yourself trouble, fatal consequences.

དགྲམ་པ *dgrám-pa* v. *ₒgrém-pa.*

དགྲོང་བ *dgróň-ba* v. *ₒgróň-ba.*

དགྲོལ་བ *dgról-ba* v. *ₒgról-ba.*

བགག་པ *bgág-pa Cs.* another form for *ₒgégs-pa.*

བགད་པ *bgád-pa* to laugh *Dzl.*, cf. *dgód-pa.*

བགམ་པ་ *bgám-pa* v. *ₒgám-pa.*

བགེགས་ *bgegs* 1. = *yegs*, **hindrance, obstruction**, seldom. — 2. an evil spirit, **demon, devil,** like *ydon*; *bgégs-kyi rgyál-po bi-na-ya-ka Mil.* frq. (*Ssk.* विनायक a remover, of obstacles; the god Ganesha etc.).

བགོ་བ་ *bgó-ba* I. vb. 1. **to put on clothes** etc., pf., imp. *bgos; lham rtág-tu bgos* always wear shoes *S.g.*; esp. to put on armour. — 2. v. under *bgod-pa.*

II. sbst. **clothes, clothing,** *bgó-ba dan bzá-ba* food and clothes *Dzl.*

བགོད་པ་ *bgód-pa* (*bgog-pá Sch.* is perh. a provincialism) pf., imp. *bgos*, fut *bgo*; *W.* inf. **gó-ĉe**; imp. **gos ťóṅ** **to divide,** *nor* an inheritance; **to divide** in ciphering, *grańs* a number; **to distribute,** *śas-śás-su* into shares, *mi-rnams-la* to or amongst people *Dzl.*

Comp. *bgod-byéd* **divisor** *Wdk.*, and accordingly also *bgo-byá* **dividend.** — *bgo-skál* 1. **share, lot,** *B.* and *col.* 2. **the doctrine of strict retribution** *Thgr.* frq. — **gó-kan* W.* **sharer, partaker, heir, joint-heir,** — *bgo-bśá* = *bgo-skál, bgo-bśá byéd-pa* to distribute, allot, apportion, *nor* the property *Thgy.*, *la* among *Stg.*

བགོམ་པ་ *bgóm-pa*, pf. *bgams Sch.*, **to walk. to step, to stride,** *góm-pa bgóm-pa Lex.* to make steps; *ₒdém pa-la bgóm-pa* to step over the threshold; *bgom ₒgró-ba* to pace, to walk slowly; *bgoms ťúb-pa* to begin to walk (?) *Sch.*

བགོར་ *bgor*, supine of *bgó-ba.*

བགོར་བ་ *bgór-ba*, *Cs.* = *ₒgór-ba.*

བགྱང་བ་ *bgyáṅ-ba*, acc. to *Zam.* = *brgyáṅ-ba*, v. *rgyóṅ-ba.*

བགྱི་བ་ *bgyi-ba*; eleg. for *byá-ba*, 1. fut. of *bgyid-pa.* — 2. sbst. **action, deed.**

བགྱིད་པ་ *bgyid-pa*, pf. *bgyis*, fut. *bgyi*, imp. *gyis*, eleg. for *byéd-pa* 1. **to make, to manufacture;** *gyis zér-bai yzugs* the images regarding to which there had been said: 'make them!' i.e. the bespoken, ordered images *Glr.*; **to do, to act, to perform,** *las bgyid-pa* to do a work, *bká bžin-du bgyio* according to the word will be acted *Dzl.*; *nye-ynás bgyid-pa* to act the disciple = to be a disciple *Dzl.*; *mi-la ynód-pa bgyis* I have hurt the man, I have done him harm *Dzl.*; *bu yód-par gyis šig* make, bring it about, that a child be (born)! *Dzl.*; *rgyál-bu ma šór-ba gyis šig* see that yo do not let the prince escape *Pth.* (*bu* for *bar* in the more careless popular style). — 2. **to say,** *žes bgyis* so he said *Dzl.*; *žes bgyi-ba* the so called *Dzl.*

བགྲང་བ་ *bgráṅ-ba*, pf. *bgrańs*, **to number, count, calculate** *bsód-nams-kyi ťsad* the amount of merits *Glr.*; *bgráṅ-bya* what may be numbered, numerable; *bgráṅ-bar mi byá-ba, bgráṅ-du méd-pa, bgraṅ-yás* innumerable; *bgraṅ-ṗréṅ* rosary, **beads** *Glr.*, also the garland of human skulls, often seen as an attribute of terrible deities.

བགྲད་པ་ *bgrád-pa* 1. **to open wide,** *mig bgrád-pa* to stare, goggle, *ka bgrád-pa* to gape *Glr.*, *Cs.*; *rkáṅ-pa* to part the legs wide, to straddle, cf. *bsgrád-pa.* — 2. **to scratch** *Sch.* (spelled more corr. *ₒbrád-pa*).

བགྲུང་བ་ *bgrúṅ-ba*, pf. *bgruṅs* to cause to deposit, **to strain, to depurate** *Cs.*, e.g. *rnyóg-ma* impure water *Lex.*.

བགྲུད་པ་ *bgrúd-pa*, pf. *bgrus*, fut. *bgru*, to clear from the husks, **to husk, to shell,** *bgrús-pai ₒbras Lex.* husked rice.

བགྲེ་བ་ *bgré-ba*, pf. *bgrés*, resp. **to grow old,** often with an additional *sku-nas* in years (v. *na*) *Dzl.*; *bgres-rgyúd* weakness of old age, infirmity *Pth.*: *bgrés-po*, in *W.* pronounced **ré(s)-po**, an old man, a man gray with age, hoary; **ré(s)-mo** fem.

བགྲེང་བ་ *bgréṅ-ba*, occasionally for 1. *sgréṅ-ba.* 2. *bgráṅ-ba.*

བགྲེན་པ་ *bgrén-pa*, *Sch.* = *bkrén-pa.*

བགྲོ་བ་ *bgró-ba*, pf. *bgros* (resp. *bka-bgrós mdzád-pa Pth.*) **to argue, discuss, deliberate, consider;** the subject discussed is gen. a direct quotation: *ĉii ṗyir ₒdi-ltar gyur ĉel bgrós-nas* to converse on the cause of the present state of things *Dzl.*; *žes ṗan-*

tsún-du bgrós-nas thus declaring their opinions to one another *Tar.*; **to ask advice,** *ci-ltar bya žes bgrós-nas* asking what they should do *Dzl.*; **to resolve, decide,** *byá-bar* to do *Dzl.*; *bgro-gléṅ byéd-pa* to dispute, to debate *Lex.*

བགྲོང་བ་ *bgróṅ-ba Tar.* = *bgráṅ-ba* **to count.**

བགྲོད་ *bgrod* 1. **the walk, gait,** mode of walking. — 2. symbol. num.: 2.

བགྲོད་པ་ *bgród-pa* **to walk,** *bgród-la p̓an* this assists in learning to walk *Lt.*; **to go, wander,** *lam bgród-pa* to travel over *Glr.*; **to get through,** *k̓yód-kyis bgród-pai skabs med ruṅ* although until now you have not been able to get to this place *Mil.*; *ču bgród-par dká-ba* a river difficult to cross; *nyi-ma-lho-bgród* the sun's going to the south, in the winter half-year, the sun's south **declination,** *byaṅ-bgrod,* north declination, *bgród-dus γnyis S.g.* both declinations; *bud-méd-la bgród-pa* to lie with a woman *Schr., Cs.*

བགྲོས་པ་ *bgrós-pa* v. *bgró-ba.*

མགར་ *mgar* n. of a noted crafty vizier of the king Srontsangampo *Glr.*

མགར་བ་ *mgár-ba* (col. **gár-ra**) **smith,** *mgár-bai bzo* smith's work; **gár-zo có-ce* W.* to forge; *mgár-k̓aṅ, mgár-sa* smithy; *γser-mgár* gold-smith *Cs.*

མགལ་ *mgal* **jaw, jaw-bone,** *ya-mgál* the upper, *ma-mgál* the lower jaw-bone; *mgal-čág* a broken jaw-bone, *mgal-búd* a dislocated jaw-bone *Cs.*

མགལ་པ་ *mgál-pa,* also *ˏgál-pa* **a billet of wood;** *mgal-dúm* 1. a large piece of wood split or cut, 2. a piece of wood half-burnt *W., C.*; **gal-dó, gal tsig* W.*, **gal-rö* C.* id.; **gal-me** a burning piece of wood, **a fire-brand; torch,** consisting of long chips or thin billets of wood; *mgal-méi ˏk̓ór-lo* a circle of light produced by whirling round a fire-brand.

མགུ་བ་ *mgú-ba* **to rejoice, to be glad, joyful, content;** *mgú-nas* delighted *Mil., Tar.*; *mgú-bai lan ma byuṅ* he did not receive a gratifying, satisfactory answer *Tar.* 17, 27; *tams-čád byin yaṅ mgú-dus med* he is never content though every thing be given him *Mil.*; *mgú-bar byéd-pa, W.*: **gu cúg-ce**, to exhilarate, to gladden, to make content; *dga-mgú-ba, dga-mgu-ráṅ-ba* are intensive verbs; *mgur* = *mgú-bar.*

མགུར་ *mgur* (*Ssk.* कण्ठ) resp. 1. **throat, neck,** *gyu mgur-du p̓ul-nas* presenting (the great teacher) with a turkois for his neck *Ma.* — 2. **voice,** *mgur snyán-pa* a sweet, harmonious, voice *Cs.* — 3. (col. **gúr-ma**) **song, air, melody,** hence a religious song is always designated by the respectful word *mgur* (not by *glu*), although the term in itself has no immediate reference to it. *mgur (-du) γsúṅ-ba, bžés-pa* resp. for *glu lén-pa* to sing a song; *Sch.*: *mgur ten-pa* id. — *mgur-ˏbúm* a hundred thousand Songs, title of the Legends of Milaraspa, which are richly interwoven with songs. — *Sch.*: *mgur bsál-ba* to clear the throat, to hawk, to hem; *čú-boi mgur* 'by-water', a tributary, a subsidiary stream (?).

མགུར་ལྷ་ *mgúr-lha* the god of hunting with the Shamans *Sch.*

མགུལ་(པ་) *mgúl (-pa) Ssk.* कन्धर 1. **neck, throat,** *mgul-du ˏdógs-pa* to tie, fasten to one's neck e.g. magic objects; *ráṅ-gi mgúl-pa γcód-pa* to cut one's own throat *Dzl.*; *mgúl-pa sub* his throat is stopped, choked *Mṅg.*; *mgúl(-pa)-nas ˏdzín-pa, ˏjú-ba,* to seize by the throat, sometimes also used for *mgúl-pa-nas ˏk̓yúd-pa* to fall on a person's neck, to embrace. — *mgúl-nad* disease of the throat, **sore throat.** — *mgul-cíṅs dkár-po* a white **neck-cloth** *Pth.* — *mgul-dár* or *dpa-dár* a silk cloth tied round the neck as a badge of honour. — 2. **the shoulder** of a mountain *Mil.*, *γyón-mgul-na* on the left slope.

མགེའུ་ *mgeu* = མགོའུ་ *mgou Cs.* v. *mgo.*

མགོ་ *mgo* (*Ssk.* शिर) resp. *dbu* 1. **head,** **gó-la zug rag** I have a headache, a pain in my head *W.*; **mgo ˏk̓or** my head turns, **I feel dizzy,** I am getting confused, perplexed; *mgo skór-ba* to cheat, swindle, deceive; *mi-mgo ma skor* do not cheat people! *Mil.*; *mgo dgú-ba, dgúr-ba* v. *dgú-ba, mgo ₒtóm-pa* v. *ₒtóm-pa; mgor ǰóg-pa* to carry on the head *Sch.*; **go yúg-če** *W.* to shake one's head, **kug tán-ce** *W.* to nod with the head, either as a sign of affirmation, or of beckoning to a person; **kyog-kyóg čó-če** to wave the head from one side to the other, expressive of reflection. — 2. **summit, height, top,** *ri-mgo ḱá-bas γyogs Mil.* the hill-tops were covered with snow. — 3. **first place, principal part,** *mgo byéd-pa* to lead, to command, to be at the head *Glr.*; to educate cf. *dbu mdzád-pa*; to inspect, look after, superintend, control, *bú-mo žig-gis mgo byéd-pai mi mán-po* a number of (labouring) people looked after by a girl (the farmer's daughter) *Mil.*; **dos gó čó-če** *W.* to preside in a consultation. — 4. **beginning,** *W.*, **go-ma**; *grós-mgo* the beginning of a consultation: *mgo ₒdzúg-pa* to begin; *bod sdúg-pai mgo ₒdzugs* that was the beginning of the misfortunes of Tibet *Ma*; *brtán-gyi skyid-mgo dé-nas tsugs* with this my constant good-fortune commenced *Mil.*; *ló-mgo-la* at the beginning of the year *Mil.*; *mgó-nas* from the beginning *Dzl.* — 5. *Gram.*: a superscribed *r, l, s* e.g. *rá-mgoi ka*, རྐ, *k* with *r* superscribed; *dé-rnams bas ṗul sá-mgoi kao* these are the words beginning with *bsk*.

Comp. and deriv. *mgo-klád* **brain** *Cs.* — *mgo-dkyil* col. crown of the head, **vertex.** — **go-kár**, or **gar** *Ld.* a tight under-garment, drawn over the head when put on, (*Ssk.* परिधान, *Hd.* प्रहिरवन) something like a shirt, but not in general use. — *mgo-skór* **imposture, deceit,** *bdud-kyi mgo-skór de ṅa mi ₒdod* I detest these diabolical tricks *Mil.* — *mgo-skyá* a gray head, *mgo-skyá-čan* a gray-headed person *Cs.* — **go-kyóṅ** *C.*, *W.*, **protector, patron,** = *mgo-ₒdren.* — *mgo-ḱra* scald, scald-head *Sch.* — *mgo-mḱrégs-čan* **obstinate, pertinacious, stubborn,** esp. in buying and bartering, selfish, bargaining, haggling: **go ṭ ag čó-če** *W.* to have these qualities. — *mgo-rgyán* head-ornament. — *mgo-čan* having a head, **mi-go-čan** having a man's head, such as English rupees and other coins (bearing the image of a head) *W.* — **go-čiṅ** *C.*, *W.* = *go-ₒdrén.* — **go-(l)cág** a blow or knock on the head *Ld.* — *mgo-lčógs* little **shoots, sprouts, branches** *Sch.* — *mgo-čá* = *mgo-rgyán.* — *mgo-mǰug* beginning and end (head and tail), *šiṅ ₒdii mgo mǰug gaṅ yín-pa bye-brág ṗyes šig* find out which is the upper and which the lower end of this piece of wood *Dzl.* — *mgo-ǰóṅ Cs.*: 'an oblong head.' — *mgo-rǰén* bare headed. — *mgo-nyág Cs.*: 'a compressed, contracted head'. **go-nyī-pa** *C.* two-headed, double-tongued; a double-dealer, backbiter. — *mgo-snyóms* indifferent, unconcerned. — **gor-tiṅ tsáṅ-ma** from head to heel, the whole from top to toe, = **go-lus-ča-tsaṅ**. — *mgo-ₒdón* = *mgo-ₒdrén*, with *byed-pa* = *mgo ₒdon-pa* to bring or draw forth, to raise, to lift up a person's head, gen. with *raṅ*, one's own head, used in the sense of: **to be self-dependent,** one's own master, to come off well, **to be uppermost** *Mil.*; *mgo ₒton-pa* id. — *mgo-ₒdrén* **protector, patron,** used frq. in letters as a complimentary title. — *mgo-nág* po. for **man** *Glr.* — *mgo-nád* **headache.** — **gó-bu** *W.* **first-born.** — *mgó-ma* 1. adj. **first,** *gral-mgo-ma* first in order, the first in a row or line of persons *Mil.* 2. sbst. **the beginning** *W.*, **go-ma tsug-če** to begin. 3. adv. **in the beginning, at first** *W.* — *mgo-tsém* 'stitched at the head' denoting a book which is so stitched, that the lines run parallel to the back, whilst one stitched in our way is called *rta-mgó-ma.* — *mgo-γžún*, col. **gog-žún** **crown** of the head. — *mgou, mgeu* a small head *Cs.* — *mgo-yór* = *tsá-bai nad Ts.* — *mgo-γyógs* **a covering for the head** (hat, cap etc.). — *mgo-ríl* 1. **a round head.** 2. **cattle without horns** *W.* — *mgo-rég* for *mgo brégs-pa* one that has his head shaved, **a monk;** *mgo-rég btsún-ma Lt.* monks and nuns, or: nuns that have their heads shaved — **go-lus-ča-tsáṅ** a complete **suit of clothes,** **gor-tiṅ-tsáṅ-ma** id.; **go lus sum kón-če** *W.* to furnish a person with new clothes; **go lus spó-če** *W.* to give one's own clothes to a person (e.g. when a king honours any body by arraying him in splendid garments). — *mgo-léb* a flat head *Cs.* — *go-šóg*, resp. *u-šog* **cover,** of a copy-book etc. *Cs.* — *mgo-srin* 1. of a disease *Lt.*

མགོན་པོ *mgón-po*, *Ssk.* नाथ **protector, patron; principal, master, lord; tutelar god;** *ₒgro-mgón* protector of beings; *skyabs-mgón* v. *skyabs*; *ći pyir nai mgon mi byed* why do you not assist me? *Dzl.*; *lhai, bdúd-kyi, γšin-rǰei mgón-po* the principal of the gods, of the devils, the lord of death *Cs.*; *mgón-po mčód-pa, stód-pa, rbád-pa* to honour, to praise, the tutelar god, to stir up or urge him to aid one's cause The special tutelar god of Tibet, called *mgón-po* by preference, is Awalokiteśwara, Spyan-ras-γzigs; *ₒǰig-rten-mgón-po*, or *mi-mǰed-žiṅ-gi mgón-po* lord of the world, *ₒǰig-rten γsúm-gyi mgón-po* (Hindi: *triloknāth*), lord or ruler of the three worlds, an epithet 1. of Buddha, 2. of Awalokiteśwara, 3. of the Dharma-Rājā of Bhotān.

Comp. *mgon máṅs* many patrons or defenders of religion; many small pyramidical sacred buildings *Cs.* — *mgon-méd* unprotected, *mgon-med-zas-sbyin*, अनाथपिण्डद, n. of a certain house-owner in Buddha's time, often mentioned in legends.

མགྱོགས་པ *mgyógs-pa*, *C.* **gyóg-po** **quick, speedy, swift;** *mgyógs-par* (seldom *mgyógs-la Mil.*) adv. **quickly, speedily, soon;** **gyog-riṅ** *W.* speedy, hasty, rash, **gyog-lám** *W.*, *C.*, a straight, short way, a short cut; *rkaṅ-mgyógs* v. *rkaṅ*. — *su-mgyógs*, pronounced **sun-gyóg(s)** *W.*, (lit. 'who is quick?') a race, a racing or running-match.

མགྲིན་པ *mgrín-pa*, (*Ssk.* ग्रीवा) 1. **neck**, *mgrin riṅ-ba*, a long neck, *mgrin túṅ-ba* a short neck *Lt.*; *mgrin-snón* blue-necked, an epithet of gods. — 2. **throat,** as passage or organ of the voice, *mgrin γčig-tu* (to call as) with one voice, frq.; *mgrin-bzáṅ* a loud voice *Cs.*

མགྲོན *mgron* **feast, treat, banquet, entertainment,** *mgron γtóṅ-ba*, resp. *sku-mgrón ₒbúl-ba* to entertain; **dón-taṅ-kan** *W.* host, entertainer; *mgrón-la ₒbod-pa*, resp. *mgrón-du spyan-ₒdrén-pa*, to invite to an entertainment; *mgrón-du γnyér-ba* to treat, to regale *Dzl.*; *mgrón-du ₒgró-ba* to go to an entertainment, a party *Dzl.* (cf. *ₒgrón-du ₒgró-ba* to go abroad); *zas-mgrón* an entertainment consisting in eating; *ǰa-mgrón* a tea-party; *čaṅ-mgrón* a treatment with beer or wine *Cs.*

འགག *ₒgag* 1. **obstruction, stoppage,** esp. in comp.: *yi-ga-ₒgág* want of appetite; *γčin-ₒgág*, also *-dgag*, strangury. — 2. a place or spot that has to be passed by all that proceed to a certain point, **zám-pe gág-tu gúg-na kúm-ma ₒdzin tub** *C.* the thief may be stopped, if you are on the watch in the thoroughfare of the bridge; *ri-bo dpal-ₒbár-gyi ₒgag* the place on the Palbár mountain, where there is the only passage *Mil.*; *sgo-ₒgág* the door of the house, because through it all that enter or leave have to pass; *ka-ₒgág* the mouth, through which every thing must pass that is eaten; fig.: *tar-lám-gyi γnad-ₒgág*, the main point for obtaining salvation; *ₒgag γčig-tu dril-ba* to unite, to be concentrated in one point *Mil.*

འགག་པ *ₒgág-pa* 1. vb, (cf. *ₒgegs-pa*) **to stop, to cease,** to be at a stand-still; mostly in the perfect form *ₒgags*; *dáṅ-ka ₒgags* the appetite is gone *Mil.*; it is also used of the passions having been suppressed, having ceased *Mil.* — 2. sbst. **door-keeper,** v. *sgo-ₒgág* sub *ₒgag*.

འགང *ₒgaṅ* v. *rgaṅ*.

འགངས་པ *ₒgáṅspa* **difficult, troublesome** *Sch.*

འགན་(པོ) *ₒgáṅ(-po)* the **burden** of an office, business, commission, *ₒgan ₒkúr-ba* to bear such a burden, *bskúr-ba* to impose it on a person.

འགབ *ₒgáb* = *mtá-ma, mǰúg-ma*, **the end,** of a bench, a garment etc. *Mil.nt.*; as postpos. c.genit. **after, behind** *C.*

འགབ་པ *ₒgáb-pa* 1. *Sch.*: **to take care, to be cautious; orderly, decent.** — 2.

W. **to suffice,** **mi gáb-če med** the workmen will not suffice.

འགམས་པ་ ₒ*gám-pa*, pf. *gams Sch.*, *bgams Cs.*, fut. *bgam*, imp. *goms* 1. **to put,** or rather **throw, into the mouth,** e.g. grains of wheat, a mouthful of meal, as Tibetans use to do; *ŋye ťúr-mgo re tsam ₒgams* I took a small spoonful of meal *Mil.* — 2. **to try,** *bgám-mo* I will try him, I shall put him to the proof *Dzl.*; *ťsód ₒgám-pa* id. *Lex.* — 3. *W.* **to threaten, to menace.**

འགའ་ ₒ*gá* (ₒ*ga-bo Cs.?*) **some, a few, several,** *ḱyi-ra-ba* ₒ*ga* some huntsmen *Mil.*; *γžón-pa* ₒ*ga žig* some young men *Mil.*; *ḱo-rán* ₒ*ga* some of them *Mil.*; ₒ*ga-ré* = ₒ*ga žig Pth.*: *gál-te nán-gyis* ₒ*ga žig bžág-na* if I appoint some by a peremptory decree *Dzl.*; *skabs* ₒ*gar* in some cases; *lan* ₒ*ga* (*žig*) sometimes, now and then (opp. to frequently, as well as to once, one time); *res*ₒ*ga* 1. sometimes. 2. col. for some, several; *bar* ₒ*ga* sometimes; *lan* ₒ*ga* — *lan* ₒ*ga*, *res* ₒ*ga* — *res* ₒ*ga*, *bar* ₒ*ga* — *bar*-ₒ*ga* at one time — at another time, some — others; ₒ*ga tsam* a few, few *Thgy.*: ₒ*ga šás* some, part (of them) *Mil.*; ₒ*ga yan* followed by a negation: no, no one, not any, none.

འགའ་ ₒ*ga Glr.*, also ₒ*ga-ti* n. of a place in the east of Tibet.

འགར་ ₒ*gar*, termin. of ₒ*ga*.

འགར་བ་ ₒ*gár-ba* 1. sbst. (*W.* also **gár-ru**, *Ts.* *ₒ*gar*, ₒ*gir**) masc. ₒ*gár-po*, fem. ₒ*gár-mo*, a mixed breed of cattle, of a *mdzo* (q.v.) and a common cow, or a bull and a *mdzó-mo*. — 2. vb. v. sub *dgár-ba*.

འགལ་དུམ་ ₒ*gál-dúm* v. *mgal*.

འགལ་བ་ ₒ*gál-ba*, c. *las* or *dan*, **to be in opposition** or **contradiction to,** as: *rtág-pa dan dṅós-po γnyis* ₒ*gál-ba yin* the ideas of 'perpetuity' and of 'thing' are contradictory; commonly of persons: **to counteract,** to act in opposition to, **to transgress, violate, infringe, break,** a promise, law, duty; *yid dan mi* ₒ*gál-bar Dzl.*, resp. *ťugs dan mi* ₒ*gal-bar*, (he gives them) to their wish, to their heart's content; *bka bžin-du mi* ₒ*gal-bar bgyio* I shall act faithfully according to the order *Dzl.*; **gal mi dug** *W.* he has not committed anything, he is innocent; *lha* or *klu dan* ₒ*gal-ba* not to honour a Lha or Lu according to duty.

Comp. ₒ*gal-rkyén* **mishap, untoward accident, impediment** (opp. to *mťun-rkyen*); ₒ*gal-rkyen sél-ba*, or *méd-par byéd-pa*, or *zlóg-pa* to avert, to remove such accidents or impediments. — ₒ*gal-*ₒ*ḱrúl* **transgression,** ₒ*gal-*ₒ*ḱrúl spans-te*, conscientiously; **gal-ťúl só-wa** to make amends, to atone for a transgression. — ₒ*gal-mťún-šes-pa Chr. Prot.*, the knowledge of what is conformable or contrary to the divine law, meant to express our **'conscience'**; the term was formed after the Tibetan phrase: *dge mi-dgé šés-pa*, or *rig-pa*, knowledge of what is virtue and what is vice; cf. however *šés-bžin*, *γnón-ba*, and *byas-čós*. — ₒ*gál-ba-po Cs.*, ₒ*gál-po Sch.*, a transgressor. — ₒ*gal-ťsábs Cs.* a great fault, a crime: ₒ*gal-ťsábs-čan* faulty, criminal, a criminal (?).

འགས་པ་ ₒ*gás-pa*, pf. *gas* (cf ₒ*ges-pa*) **to be cleft** or **split,** of rocks etc.; **to chap,** of the skin, the lips; to break open, **to burst,** of a bag etc., *ḱa lṅá-ru* into five rents, in five places; **to crack, to break** or **burst asunder,** of a vessel, the heart, a fruit, *bdún-du* into seven pieces; *šín-gi rigs-la byás-na ni* ₒ*gas* if it be made of wood, it will split, crack *Glr.*

འགིའུ་ ₒ*giu* v. *gi-wán*.

འགུ་མདའ་ ₒ*gu-mdá* **gun-stock,** (spelling not certain) v. *sgum-mdá*.

འགུ་བ་ ₒ*gú-ba*, incorr. for *mgú-ba*.

འགུག(ས)་ ₒ*gug(s)* **a mesh** *W.*

འགུག(ས)་པ་ ₒ*gúg(s)-pa*, pf. *bgug*, fut. *dgug*, imp. *ḱug* 1. (cf. *kug*) **to bend,** to make crooked, *γnya* ₒ*gugs-pa C.* to bend, bow, stoop; *mgo* ₒ*gugs-*ₒ*gúgs-par sóṅ-ṅo* he went off bowed down, crestfallen. — 2. **to gather,** to cause a gathering, *rnág-tu* of matter, pus, to suppurate. — 3. **to call, to summon, to send for,** e.g. the gardener *Dzl.*, one's daughters *Dzl.*; **to conjure up,** ghosts, *des bdag ˳gúg-par ˳gyúr-ro* by this (charm) I may be conjured up; *blo náṅ-du ḱúg-la* calling the spirit back into its inner domain, abstracting the mind from the external world. — 4. **to draw back, to cause to return, to convey back** *Mil., C.*

འགུད་པ་ *˳gúd-pa,* pf. *gud,* = *rgud-pa? gúd-du bćúg-pa* **to ruin,** to reduce to an extremity *Schr.*; *rtsa byiṅ-gúd dal Med.* a pulse slow and sinking.

འགུམ་པ་ *˳gúm-pa* 1. pf. *gum, ˳gums* eleg. — **to die.** — 2. pf. *bkum, fut. dkum,* imp. *ḱum(s),* **to kill,** to put to death *Dzl.* frq.; **to slaughter** (butcher), *γsár-du bkúm-pai ša,* meat of an animal just killed, fresh meat *Dzl.* — 3. **to bend, curve,** make crooked, to contract, v. *ḱum* and *skúm-pa.*

འགུལ་ *˳gul* **neck,** v. *mgul.*

འགུལ་བ་ *˳gúl-ba* (cf. *sgul-ba*) to change place or posture, **to move, shake, to be agitated,** **ri-gu ḍód-pa-la gul dug**the kid moves in the womb (of the goat); *˳gul-dká* (the limb) moves with difficulty *Med.* frq.; *˳gul yaṅ ma nús-so* (they) would not even stir (from terror) *Dzl.*; **to waver, tremble, shiver,** *˳dár-žiṅ ˳gúl-ba; sa-˳gúl* (pronounced **saṅ-gúl**) earthquake *W.*

འགེག(ས)་པ་ *˳gégs-pa* pf. *bkag,* fut. *dgag,* imp. *ḱog* **to hinder, prohibit, stop,** *bdág-gis bkág-na yaṅ ma ṫúb-kyis* though I was preventing it, I could not (carry my point) *Dzl.*; *ma bkág-ste náṅ-du btaṅ* he admitted him without impediment *Dzl.*; **kág-će med zér-ḱan-gyi ka-šóg** a warrant, a permit to traffic without hinderance, a pass-bill, and the like *W.*; **to shut, to lock** (up), **to close,** *sgo* the door *Glr., lam* the road frq., to close one's nose with the hand *Pth.*; **to retain, keep back** excretions *Med., bšaṅ-dgág* obstruction (cf. *˳gag*); **zá-će kág-te ši** *W.* his food sticking fast he died; **to lock up, shut up** (things for keeping), **to pen up** (sheep, cattle), **kág-te bór-će** *W.* id; *dgag-dbyé* the ending of the seclusion, viz. of the monks who have to stay in their houses during the rainy season *Schf., Tar.* 10, 10, cf. *Köpp.* I, 369; **to forbid,** *dgag-sgrúb Sch.*: 'to forbid and to allow'(?); *gág-pai sgra, ˳gag-ṫsig* a prohibitive particle *Gram.*; *bkág-ća byéd-pa* to forbid, prohibit *Sch.*; **ḱa kág-će** *W.* to silence, to hush; *dgág-pa* a negative, a negation; *bkág-ća* the negative side *Was.* (282).

འགེངས་པ་ *˳géṅs-pa,* pf. *bkaṅ,* fut. *dgaṅ,* imp. *ḱoṅ* 1. **to fill,** *tib-ril ćus* or (seld.) *ćú-las,* or *ṫib-ril-du ćus,* or *ću,* (to fill) a tea-pot with water; **to soil, smear, stain,** the bed with blood *Glr.*; *dgáṅ-dka* difficult to be filled, not to be satisfied, insatiable *Stg.* — 2. **to fulfil** (more frq. *skóṅ-ba*) *ṫugs-dám Lex.* — 3. *gžu ˳géṅs-pa, mda ˳géṅs-pa* to prepare bow and arrows for shooting, frq.; **tú-pag káṅ-će** *W.* to load a gun.

འགེད་པ་ *˳géd-pa, Cs.* = *˳gyéd-pa.*

འགེབས་པ་ *˳gébs-pa,* pf. *bkab,* fut. *dgab,* imp. *ḱob* (*W.* **bkob**), **to cover,** e.g. one's breast with the hand; to cover up, *ḱa* an opening, aperture; **to spread** over or on, **to set up, to put on,** a cover, lid, cork, plug etc.; **to protect,** *btsún-mo mi-ma-yin-gyis ˳gébs-su ˳ǰúg-pa* to have the queen protected by ghosts; **to disguise,** metaph: **bkáb-ste** in disguised language, euphemistically *W.*, **káb-će ṗi-la** in order to express it euphemistically.

འགེམས་པ་ *˳gém-pa,* acc. to *Cs.* another form for *˳gúm-pa,* **to kill, to destroy;** *Schr.*: *klád-pa ˳géms-pa* to surprise; to overthrow an argument by reason; cf. *mgo-˳géms Lex.* w.e.; as a partic.: stupid *Schr.*; the few passages, where I met with the word, leave its meaning doubtful.

འགེལ་བ་ *˳gél-ba,* pf. *bkal,* fut. *dgal,* imp. *ḱol,* 1. **to load, to lay on** a burden, *brui ḱal čig bkál-te* loaded with a load of grain *Dzl.*; fig. to put a yoke upon a person's neck, *byur* to bring down misery on a person; *W.* to bring accusations against a person, **mi 'ós-pe lás-ka žig mi žig-la kal táṅ-na** *Ld.* if one is accused of an unlawful action; *ḱral ˳gél-ba* to impose tribute *Lex.*; **to commission, to charge with, to make, appoint, constitute,** **mi žig gád-po-la kál če** *Ld.* to appoint some one to be an elder or senior, cf ˳*čól-ba.*— 2. **to put, to place** on or over, *ydúṅ-ma bkál-ba* a beam placed over it *S.g.*; **to set** or **put on,** e.g. a pot on a trevet; **to hang up,** *gos-˳gel-ydúṅ* a stand to hang clothes on; fig. ˳*či-bar nús-pai tog ˳gel dgos* one must set on it the roof of being able to die, i.e. one must crown the whole edifice by being free from fear of death *Mil.*

འགེས་པ ˳*gés-pa*, pf. *bkas*, fut. *dgas*, imp. *k'os*, trs. to ˳*gás-pa*, **to split, cleave, divide.** *bkas-šiṅ Lex.* cleft or chopped wood; *dúm-bur* (to divide) into pieces *Lex.*, **to cut up** or **open,** e.g. a fish, gourd, pumpkin, *Dzl.*

འགོ ˳*go*, = *mgo* in some figurative applications of the word: *dmág-˳go* **commander** of an army *Cs.*; *mk'ár-˳go, rdzóṅ-˳go* commander of a fort *Cs.*; ˳*go snám* a sort of fine cloth made of shawl-wool, or also: Europe-cloth, i.e. broad cloth = *sag-lád*; ˳*gó-pa* **officer, captain, head-man** of a village or district, esp. in *W.*; in a general sense: **kon-čóg ǰig-ten-gyi gó-pa yin** God is the ruler of the world; **koṅ-čóg-gi saṅ gó-pa med** God is the only and highest ruler; **˳go-pǫ́n* C.* **rector, director, head-master, principal** e.g. of a school; ˳*gó-ma Zam.* **beginning, origin, source;** ˳*gó-mi Lex.* = ˳*gó-pa*; **go-yód** = ˳*gó-pa Ld*; ˳*gor* in the beginning, at first, originally *Sch.*, *sér-bai ˳gor* when it began to hail *Mil.nt.*

འགོ་བ ˳*gó-ba*, pf *gos* (or ˳*gos*), cf. *bsgo-ba*, 1. **to stain,** to lose colour; **to dirty, sully** one's self, *dé-la* with it, *naṅ-skyúgs lús-la* to soil one's self with vomit. — 2. **to infect,** with a disease, ˳*gó-bai nad*, ˳*go-nád*, ˳*gó-bai rims*, a contagious or epidemic disease, **a plague,** frq.

འགོག་པ ˳*góg-pa*, pf. *bkog*, fut. *dgog?* imp. *k'og* 1. **to take away** forcibly, **to snatch, tear away, pull out,** *rtsá-ba* a root *Lex.*, so a tooth *Schr.*; **to tear up,** e.g. a floor *W.*; **to peel** *Sch.*; **kóg-te k'yér če* W.* **to rob, plunder** frq.: **kóg-te k'yers* Ld.* it has been robbed. — 2. **to take off,** a cover, a lid, a pot from the fire *W.*

འགོགས་པ ˳*gógs-pa* another form for ˳*gégs-pa*, **to prevent, to avert** unfortunate events, fatal consequences; **to suppress,** the symptoms of a disease by medicine; **to drive back** or **away, to expel** e.g. spirits, ghosts; **to repel** people that are trying to land.

འགོང་བ ˳*góṅ-ba* 1 *Cs.*: to bewitch, enchant (?), *góṅ-ba-po*, ˳*góṅ-po* **an enchanter, sorcerer,** *góṅ-ba-mo* enchantress, sorceress *Cs.*; more frq. ˳*góṅ-po* **an evil spirit, demon,** also fig. demon of concupiscence, of fear, of terror *Mil.*; ˳*góṅ-mo* fem. — 2. pf. *bkoṅ*, perh. more corr. *sgóṅ-ba*, *spú-sgoṅ-ba Lex.* **to despond.**

འགོད་པ ˳*gód-pa*, pf. *bgod*, fut. *dgod*, imp. *k'od* (cf. *k'ód-pa*), the Latin *condere*, 1. **to design, to project, to plan** *Schr.* — 2. **to found, to etablish, to lay out** (a town), **to build** (a house); hence *bkód-pai rig-byéd* books on architecture *Glr.*; **to manufacture, to form, to frame.** — 3. **to put, to fix, to transfer,** into a certain state or condition, *bdé(-ba)-la Dzl.*, *bder Lex.*, into a happy state, *dge-ba-la Dzl.* into virtue, *čós-la Pth.* into the true doctrine, *rnám-par ˳gról-ba-la Dzl.* into salvation, *mya-ṅán-las ˳dás-pa-la* into delivery from existence *Dzl.*; *žag-gráns* **to fix** a certain time or term *Schr.*; *tsad* (to determine) the measure or size of a thing *Schr.* — 4. **to set, put,** or **place in order,** *gral-p̔yám bgód-pa ˳dra* as the rafters of a roof are placed side by side *S.g.*; *mt'ar dgód-pa* **to add** or **affix** e.g. ciphers to a certain number *Wdk.*; *bkód-par mdzés-pá* beautiful as to arrangement, nicely ordered, *(b)rgyan dgód-pa Lex.* to arrange ornaments (tastefully), **to decorate, adorn, to construct** or **adjust** grammatical forms, sentences *Zam.* — 5. to put down in writing, **to record,** *miṅ ká-ba-la* to write names on a column *Pth.*; **to compose, draw up, write,** a narrative etc., frq.; **to mention, to insert,** in a writing; **ka kǫ́-pa* C.* **to publish,** to make known. — 6. **to rule, to govern** *Schr.*; *byol-sóṅ bkód-pai rgyál-*

po yin he is king over all subjugated animals *Mil.*

The partic. pf. *bkód-pa* is also sbst.: 1. **plan, ground-plan, draught** of a building *Schr.* — 2. **delineation, sketch,** *žiṅ-bkód* **map.** — 3. **form, shape, figure** *Schr.* — 4. **sample, copy,** even of one's own body, e.g. when a person multiplies himself by magic virtue, = *sprúl-ba.* — 5. **building, edifice, structure,** *bkód-pa mdzes* the structure (is) beautiful *Glr.* — 6. **frame, body,** *bkód-pa lus* id. *Mil.; ṅai bkód-pa nám-mk'ai raṅ-žin* my body of an ethereal nature *Pth.*

Note. The Lexx. have for *bkód-pa* always **ञास** putting down, depositing; but often it has the signification of **व्यूह** orderly arrangement; as vb. it comes nearest to **वपरच्**. As the meaning of the word is almost quite the same as that of *κτίζειν* and *condere*, it recommends itself as the most suitable term for **'to create',** to call into existence, *ₒgód-pa-po* for **creator,** and *bkód-pa* for **creature,** notions which are otherwise foreign to Buddhism.

འགོམ་པ་ *ₒgóm-pa, Cs.* = *góms-pa, Sch.* also = *ₒgém-pa, ₒgúm-pa.*

འགོར་ *ₒgor* 1. v. the following article. — 2. termin. of *ₒgo,* in the beginning, at first *Sch.* — 3. supine of *ₒgó-ba.*

འགོར་བ་ *ₒgór-ba* **to tarry, linger, loiter,** *W.* frq. **máṅ-po gor soṅ** you stayed away very long; **lúm-la gor** he lingers on the way; **máṅ-po ma gór-te** without long delay, = *riṅ-por ma lón-par,* and *riṅ-por mi t'ogs-par B.*; *de ₒgor-γži yin* that impedes, delays; *zlá-ba γnyis ₒkor* (the work) lasted two months *Glr.*

འགོལ་བ་ *ₒgól-ba,* pf. *gol* 1. **to part, to separate** vb.n.; *ₒgól-bai γnas* a hermitage *Pth., ₒgól-po* hermit, recluse. — 2. **to deviate, err,** go wrong or astray; *ₒgól-sa* 1. the place where two roads separate. 2. **error, mistake.**

འགོས་ *ₒgos* n. of a monastery *Tar.*

འགོས་པ་ *ₒgós-pa* v. *ₒgó-ba.*

འཀྱག་པ་ *ₒkyág-pa* cf. *skyág-pa,* **to be sold, spent, expended** *Cs.*

འགྱང་བ་ *ₒkyáṅ-ba,* pf. *ₒgyaṅs,* **to be delayed, deferred, postponed,** *p'yir ₒgyaṅ-na* if one defers it; **nyin ₒgyaṅ žag ₒgyaṅ ǰhé-pa** *C.* to delay again and again; *lo maṅ-po mi ₒgyaṅ-bar* before many years shall have passed; *dus ₒgyaṅs Lex.* w.e.

འགྱིང་བ་ *ₒgyiṅ-ba* 1. to look about haughtily, **to look down upon, to slight,** *mi-la* a person; also of things: **to despise, contemn, neglect** them *B.* and col.: **ₒgyiṅ-bhág ǰhé-pa** *C.*, **gyiṅ čó-čé** *W.* id.; **gyiṅ-čan** supercilious, contemptuous. — 2. = *sgyiṅ-ba Glr.*; *Mil.* — *šél-kyi ₒgyiṅ-ₒk'ar* a sceptre of crystal, an attribute of gods, in pictures represented as a plain, unadorned staff.

འགྱུ་བ་ *ₒgyú-ba,* pf. *ₒgyus,* **to move quickly** to and fro, e.g. as lightning, the quivering air in a mirage, the motion and versatility of the mind etc.

འགྱུར་བ་ *ₒgyúr-ba* I. vb., pf. *gyur(-to, -pa)* imp. *gyur (-čig),* cf. *sgyúr-ba,* 1. **to change,** to be altered *B.* and col.; *mi-rnams-kyi spyód-pa ₒgyur* the behaviour of men changes *Ma.*; *ₒgyúr-bai čos* a changeable (and therefore perishable) thing *Cs.*; and *ₒgyúr-du yód-pa* changeable, variable, *ₒgyúr-du méd-pa, ₒgyur-med* unchangeable, invariable; sometimes **to decrease, abate, vanish, die away,** *mt'u-stóbs, ṅád-med-pa, γzi-rǰid yóṅs-su ₒgyur-ba* the total decay of strength, health, and esteem (in old age) *Thgy.*; *bdág-gi sems ma gyur, ma nyáms-so* my mind has not been altered, nor my resolution weakened *Dzl.*; also with *las: dád-pa ₒdi-las ma gyur čig* do not **depart** from that belief *Mil.* (I have therefore availed myself of this word, combined with the active (transitive) form *sems sgyúr-ba* 'to change the mind' for expressing the *μετανοεῖν* and *μετάνοια* of the N. T., though the Buddhist is wont to regard the *mi-gyúr-ba* as the thing most to be praised and desired.) With the termin. it signifies **to be changed, transformed into,** *B.* and col.; hence — 2. **to become, to grow,** *dge-slóṅ-du ₒgyúr-ba, rgyál-por ₒgyúr-ba* to become a monk, a king *Dzl.; skra mťon-mťiṅ-gi k'a-dóg-tu gyúr-to* his hair turned azure (sky-blue) *Dsl.*; *sbrúm-par ˌgyúr-ba* to get with child; *bdún-du ˌgyur-ba* to reach the number of seven *Dzl.* (In all these cases the more recent writings and the col. language in *C.* usually have **ˌdó-wa*, in W. *ǩá-ce*.*) *ˌgyúr-ba* is also frq. used in conjunction with verbs: *yód-par ˌgyúr-ba* 'to become being', i.e. to begin to exist, 'to become having,' i.e. to gain possession; *sróg-la mi ltá-bar ˌgyúr-pai dṅós-po ˌdi-day* these acts of having become indifferent to life, i.e. acts of contempt of death *Dzl.*; *ná-bar gyúr-na ˌdi mťóṅ-ba tsám-gyis nad sós-par ˌgyúr-ro* when taken ill, they get well again, as soon as they obtain a sight of this *Glr.; ċaṅ mi smrá-bar gyúr-to* he became speechless *Dzl.*; *ˌgyúr-ba* denoting both the pass. voice, and the fut. tense, the context must decide in every instance, how it is to be understood: *su żig rgyal-srid byéd-par ˌgyur* who shall have the government, who shall rule? *Tar.* 21.; *de rgyál-por ˌgyúr-bar śés-so* they knew that this man is made king (for: would be made king); *k'ó-mos k'yód-kyi bu bsád-par gyúr-na* if your son has been killed by me *Dzl.*; *k'yod mi-śa zá-bar gyúr-ċig* may you be obliged to eat human flesh! *Dzl.; ċii p'yir k'yod ˌdi-ltar gyur* by what means have you come into this state? *Dzl.*; *ya-mťsán-du* (or *-par*) *ˌgyúr-ba* to be surprised, astonished; with *ynás-su:* **to come** to a place, **to arrive** at *Mil.*; *ˌdód-pai dṅos-grúb-tu ˌgyúr-ba* to be endowed with the perfect gift of wishing, viz. of having every wish fulfilled; **to happen, to take place, to occur,** *ya-mťsán-du ˌgyúr-ba ċi yod* lit. what is there that has wonderfully happened, what wonderful things have happened? *ɣyós-par ˌgyúr-ba* to become moving, to begin to move. — 3. **to be translated,** *bod-du* into Tibetan *Tar.*;- *bka-ˌgyúr* the **translated** word, v. *bka*; cf. *sgyúr-ba.* — 4. joined to numbers it signifies **time** or **times,** *ɣżán-pas brgya-ˌgyur stoṅ-ˌgyúr-du ˌp'ágs-pa* a hundred times, nay a thousand times more sublime than others *Dzl.*; *k'yód-pas brgya-ˌgyúr-bas lhág-par bzáṅ-ba yod* there are (girls) a hundred times prettier than you *Dzl.*; *ɣsum-ˌgyúr ltá-bur* three times as much *Dzl.*; *de ɣnyis-ˌgyúr tsam żig* one twice as large as that *Mil.*

II. sbst. **change, alteration, vicissitude,** *dus bżii ˌgyúr-bas* through the change of seasons *Thgy.* — *ˌgyur-skád,* or also *ˌgyur-k'ugs* singing or humming a tune in a trilling manner *Mil.; ˌgyur-lċam nya Mil.* perh. a fish swiftly moving to and fro; *ˌgyur-rtén bżág-pa* to pay money in hand, as an earnest that the bargain is not to be retracted. — Instead of the imp. *gyur, śóg* is frq. used.

འགྱེ་བ *ˌgyé-ba,* pf. (and imp.?) *gyes,* **to be divided,** e.g. a river that is divided into several branches; *rnám-pa ɣnyis-su* (a ray of light divided) into two parts *Dzl.;* **to separate, to part,** *bem rig ˌgyes dus* when body and soul part from each other *Mil.;* **to disperse,** of a crowd, with or without *so-sór Dzl.* and elsewh.; of a single person: **to part, withdraw, go away,** **mi-tsóg daṅ ghyē-nẹ* C.* withdrawing from the crowd; **to issue, proceed, spread,** *dé-dag-las gyés-so* they have proceeded from those (their ancestors); of a disease: *gyén-du gyes* (opp. to *t'úr-du zug*) *Med.?*

འགྱེད་པ་ *ˌgyéd-pa* (*W. *kyé-ce**) pf. *bgyes,* fut. *bkye,* 1. **to divide** (trs.), **to scatter, disperse, diffuse,** e.g. rays of light; it is also used when the neutral form *ˌgyé-ba* would seem to be more correct; **to let proceed,** *sprúl-pa,* an emanation; hence **to send,** a messenger *Lex.* and *Schr.;* **to dismiss,** *tsogs,* an assembly *Sch.* — 2. *ˌt'áb-mo ˌgyéd-pa, ɣyul ˌgyéd-pa,* also *ˌgyéd-pa* alone, to fight a battle, **to fight, to combat,** *ˌgyéd-pai tse* in the dispute; similarly *ˌdziṅ-ga bkyé-ba* **to quarrel** *Med.;* hence prob. *W.: *k'a kyé-ce** to abuse, to menace. — 3. *stón-mo ˌgyéd-pa* frq. **to give** an entertainment, banquet, prop. to dispense a feast; *nor ˌgyéd-pa* **to distribute** a property *Lex.*

འགྱེར་བ་ *ˌgyér-ba* **to drop** or let fall, to throw down *Schr.;* **to quit, abandon,** throw away *Sch.*

འགྱེལ་བ་ *˳gyél-ba*, pf. *gyel (-to)*, imp *gyel*, **to fall, to tumble,** **gyel ma gyel** *W.* don't tumble, take care not to fall; **gyél-kan** *W.* lying, (not standing), e.g. a bottle.

འགྱེས་པ་ *˳gyés-pa*, another form for *˳gyé-ba*, *p̓yi-gros-su ˳gyés-par ˳gyur* back foremost they retreat *Glr.*

འགྱོད་པ་ *˳gyód-pa* (*Ssk.* **कौकृत्यं**) vb. (*W. *gyód-ċe**) **to repent, to grieve for,** and sbst. **repentance,** sorrow for, not only for bad, but also for good actions, when the latter are attended with disadvantage or loss; *p̓yis ˳gyón-par ˳gyur* you will have to repent it hereafter *Dzl.*; with *la*, to repent of a thing; *˳gyód-pa skye* repentance arises, I feel repentance, I repent frq.; *sems ˳gyód-par ˳gyur* id.; **da gyód-pa yoṅ dug** *W.* id.; *˳gyód-pa med* I do not regret it; *˳gyód-pa-ċan* repenting *Pth.*; *˳gyód-pai sems méd-par k̓yód-la sbyin-no* I give it you readily and with all my heart *Pth.*; *˳gyód-med* without repentance, without grudging, also: in good earnest; *˳gyod-tsáṅs byéd-pa*, *˳tól-źiṅ ˳gyód-pa*, *˳gyód-ċiṅ bšág-pa Dzl.* to acknowledge repentingly, to confess with compunction; *˳gyod-tsáṅs byéd-par ɣnáṅ-ba* to accept a repentant confession = to forgive, to pardon *Dzl.* (p. ༥༧, ༤༧, ༦༠, ༢༢༨); *˳gyód-rmo-ba*, c. *la*, to make repent, to make one suffer, feel, or pay (for a thing) *Dzl.*; *ɣnoṅ-˳gyód* repentance proceeding from consciousness of guilt *Pth.*

འགྲག(ས)་པ་ *˳grág(s)-pa*, pf. *grags*, **to sound,** to utter a sound, of men, animals, thunder etc. *Dzl.*; **to cry, to shout,** *dei rná-lam-du ˳grágs-par ˳gyúr-na* if it is shouted into his ear; *ċes grags* so it is called, so he was called, by this name he goes, under that name he is known, celebrated; *bód-la yi-ge med ċes grags* Tibet, so it is said, was without letters, without a written language; *Zam.*

འགྲགས་པ་ *˳grágs-pa* **to bind,** v. *grágs-pa.*

འགྲང་བ་ *˳gráṅ-ba* 1. *Cs.* **to number, to count,** v. *bgráṅ-ba.* — 2. **to satisfy** with food, **to satiate,** **ḍáṅ-ċe med** *W.* he is insatiable; gen. only the pf. is in use: *˳graṅs rjes* after having eaten one's fill *Med.*; *šá-ba bsád-pas mi ˳gráṅ-te* not yet having enough of deer-killing *Mil.*

འགྲད་པ་ *˳grád-pa Cs.* = *bgrád-pa*, **to spread, to extend** (vb. a).

འགྲན་པ་ *˳grán-pa* (*Ssk.* **स्पर्धं**) 1. **to vie** with, **contend** with, **to strive** (for victory), *wa séṅ-ge-la* a fox (contending) with the lion *Dzl.*; *ċo-˳p̓rúl* in magic tricks *Dzl.*; *rig-pa* in shrewdness, cunning *Glr.*; *p̓yug-k̓yád rnam-tós-kyi bu daṅ ˳grán-te* to cope even with Plutus as to riches *Dzl.*; *bstód-par ˳gran* let us vie with one another in songs of praise *Glr.*; *˳grán-pas ċog* let us now draw a parallel between (these two) *Glr.*; *˳grán-du ˳júg-pa* to cause (two persons) to strive (for the victory) *Dzl.* — 2. in a general sense, **to fight,** to defend one's self, to make resistance.

Comp. *˳gran-tsig* words of contention, **a quarrelling speech** *Glr.* — *˳gran-sems* 1. **contention, emulation.** 2. **jealousy.** 3. **quarrelsome temper, spirit of controversy;** *˳gran-sems ɣċóg-pa* to stop, put an end to contention. — *˳grán-zla* (pronounced **ḍál-za** in the north of *Ld.*), **rival, competitor,** equal match; *˳grán-zla-med-pa*, *˳gran-zla daṅ brál-ba*, also *˳grán-gyi do-méd*, *˳grán-ya-med*, without a rival, **matchless, unequalled,** applied also to things.

འགྲམ་ *˳gram* 1. **shore, bank,** *ċu-˳grám* id.; *ċu ċén-poi ˳grám-du soṅ* they went to the bank of a large river *Dzl.* — 2. **side,** *sgo-˳grám ɣyás-na* on the right side of the door *Glr.*; *sgoi p̓yi-˳gram-na* before the door, outside, out of doors *Pth.* — 3. **wall,** *k̓áṅ-pai ˳óg-˳gram* the lower wall of a house (opp. to the roof) *Mil.*; *˳gram-ɣźi C., S.g.* **foundation, basis,** *˳gram-ɣźi ˳díṅ-ba* to lay a foundation. — In a more general sense: *˳grám-du* **near, close to, just by,** *rgyáṅ-nas sgra ċé-la ˳grám-du don ċuṅ* he has a great voice, is making much noise, at a distance, but looking nearer, you do not find much in him *Mil.*; *šiṅ-gi ˳grám-du* close to the tree.

འགྲམ་པ་ ༄grám-pa **cheek** (cf. *k̔ur-tsós*), **ḍám-pa hom soṅ** *W.* his cheeks are fallen; *lág-pa ༄grám-pa-la rtén-pa* to lay one's hand on the cheek (in a pensive or sorrowful mood) *Dzl.*

Comp. *༄gram-lčág* a slap on the face, box on the ear; **ḍam-čág gyáb-če** *W.* to box a person's ears. — *༄gram-ču ldaṅ* that makes one's mouth water *Sch.* — *༄gram-p̔ug Lt.?* — **ḍam-dzóg** *C.* a blow or cuff with the fist upon the cheek, **gyág-pa** to deal such blows. — *༄gram-rús* **cheek-bone, jaw-bone.** — *༄grám-ša* the flesh of the cheek. — *༄gram-γšóg* the hinder part of the jaw-bone *Sch.* — *༄grám-so* **cheek-tooth**, molar-tooth, grinder.

འགྲམ་ཡིག་ *༄gram-yig* **edict, proclamation, publication** *Sch.*

འགྲམས་པ་ *༄gráms-pa* **to hurt** *Lt.*; of wounds: to get inflamed, ni f. *Mil. nt.*

འགྲམས་ཚད་ *༄grams-tsád*, a disease, fever in consequence of great exertions *Med.*

འགྲས་པ་ *༄grás-pa* **to hate,** to bear ill-will, to have a spite against, **ṅa k̔ó-la že ḍé ༄dug** *C.* I hate him in my heart.

འགྲིག་འགྲིག་ *༄grig-༄grig* 1. **gelatine, jelly** of meat *C.* 2. v. the following article.

འགྲིག་པ་ *༄grig-pa* (cf. *sgrig-pa*) **to suit, agree, correspond, to be right, adequate, sufficient,** in *B.* seldom, col. very frq., **ḍig-pa yin** *C.* that will do, I am satisfied; **da ḍig** *W.* now that will do! just enough now! **ḍig-ḍig** *W.* to be sure! quite so! of course! **༄o ḍig gog** *W.* yes, to be sure! **tsó-če mi ḍig** *W.* it is not yet time for cooking; **t̔ó-re tság-na ḍig-ga** *W.* will it be early enough, if I sift it to-morrow? **de yaṅ mi ḍig-pa dug** *W.* also that is not practicable; *ṅa ǰo̱'-yaṅ di ma ḍig-na* if my pronunciation is not correct *C.* (Lewin).

འགྲིབ་པ་ *༄grib-pa*, pf. *grib*, 1. **to grow less, to decrease, to be diminished,** syn to *༄bri-ba; mi ༄grib mi lúd-pa* neither to grow less nor to flow over *Dzl.*; but gen. *༄p̔él-ba* is opposed to *༄grib-pa*, and both words refer not only to bulk, size, and quantity, but also to strength, well-being etc., so that *༄grib-pa* also means to sink, decay, be reduced; *bskál-pa mar ༄grib*, acc. to *Schr.* = Treta yuga v. *dus* 6; *mar ༄grib-pa* also opp. to *yar skyé-ba* to be re-born in lower regions. — 2. **to grow dim, to get dark,** cf. *sgrib-pa Cs.*

འགྲིམ་ *༄grim*, in *lag-༄grim Glr.* 45: *lag-༄grim-gyis brgyus-pas* passing from hand to hand, v. *༄grim-pa* II, 1.

འགྲིམ་པ་ *༄grim-pa* I. sometimes for *༄brim-pa Pth.* II. pf. *༄grims* 1. **to go, walk, march about, perambulate, to rove** or **stroll** idling about, *rgyal-k̔ams* over the countries *Mil.*; *γčig-pur ri-k̔ród-la Mil.*; *bár-dor* in the bardo (q.v.) *Thgr.*; *mi-sér ǰág-pai ༄grim-sa yin* it is a resort of robbers *Mil.*; it is also used of the course of the veins in the body *Med.* — 2. *W.* **to go off, to sell,** to meet with a ready sale. — 3. *rig-pa ༄grim-pa* v. *rig-pa.*

འགྲིལ་བ་ *༄gril-ba*, pf. *gril* (cf. *sgril-ba*) 1. **to be twisted** or **wrapped round,** *Dzl.* ༢༥, 17. acc. to one manuscript, for *༄k̔ri-ba Sch.*; to be collected, concentrated, to flock or crowd together, *kun ༄gril-nas* all in a heap, all together *Mil.* — 2. **to be turned, rounded, made circular** or **cylindric,** e.g. a stick *Mil.* — 3. **to fall,** e.g. leaves from a tree; in *B.* seldom, in *W.* frq. (*༄dril-ba* is the same word).

འགྲིས་ *༄gris* v. *༄dris.*

འགྲུ་བ་ *༄grú-ba*, pf. *grus*, **to bestow pains** upon a thing, *slob-pa-la* upon study *Dzl.*

འགྲུབ་པ་ *༄grúb-pa*, pf. *grub* 1. **to be made ready, to be finished, accomplished;** *༄grúb-pa mi srid* it is not possible that this be accomplished *Glr.*; *ma ༄grúb-par* before its having been finished *Glr.*; *ma-༄grúb-pa-rnams ༄grúb-par ༄gyur-ro* (frq. of charms, regarding their desired effect) prob. means: all that has not yet been effected, will be accomplished by it; *grúb-pa-rnams* is applied in a special sense to the ordained Gelongs (v. *dge-slóṅ*); *šúgs-la ༄grub* the thing is brought about quite of itself *Mil.*; so esp. in the phrase: *lhún-gyis grúb-pa* being produced spontaneously (opp. to making, procuring) e. g. clothes, food etc. were always at his disposal, viz. in a supernatural way *Dzl.*; *dpál-las grub* it devolved on me in consequence of my perfection, my superior qualities *Mil.*; *dón-la grúb-pa med kyaṅ* though it did not actually happen so (still, being meant to frighten by appearances etc.) *Glr.*; *byéd-na don čen ₒgrub* if you do so, you will have many advantages (lit. great welfare) by it *Mil.*; *gru ₒgrúb-pa Tar.* 25,6; 34,20 *Schf.*: to take in a full cargo, though from the wide meaning of the word, it may also signify: to accomplish a journey happily, so esp. in the passage *Tar.* 35,3 — 2. **to be made, fabricated**, *rdó-las* out of stone. — 3. **to be fulfilled, granted,** of wishes etc., also with *bžin-du*. — 4. **to be performed according to rule,** of charms; cf. *sgrúb-pa* and *grúb-pa*. — *ₒgrúb-sbyór* is an expression occurring in almanacs, relative to the proving true of certain astrological prognostics of good luck, similar to, but not identic with *rten-ₒbrél*.

འགྲུམ་པ་ *ₒgrúm-pa*, pf. *grum*(?), **to pinch** or **nip off** (the point of a thing), **to cut off, to prune, lop, clip,** the wings, *W.*, cf. *grúm-pa*.

འགྲུལ་བ་ *ₒgrúl-ba* I. 1. **to walk, to pass, to travel,** *ₒgrúl-bar byéd-pa* to cause to go, to send off, despatch, a messenger *Dzl.*; **ṅáṅ-la dul** *W.* walk first! take the lead! *ₒgrúl-ba-po*, *ₒgrúl-po Sch.*, **dúl-k̔an, dúl-mi** *W.* a walker, foot-traveller, pedestrian; *ₒgrúl-pa Sch.* id.; *ₒgrúl* sbst. passage, the possibility of passing, *γnya-náṅ-gi ₒgrúl čád-pas* the passing from Nyanaṅ being made impracticable (viz. by snow) *Mil.* — 2. fig. **to walk, to live, act,** or **behave,** **ṫim-si** (or **tim-mi*) *naṅ-tar** *W.* (to live) in conformity with one's duty, in accordance to the law. — 3. **to pass, to be good, current,** of coins.

II. i. o. *brúl-ba Mil.*

འགྲུས་པ་ *ₒgrús-pa* 1. pf. of *ₒgrú-ba*. — 2. sbst. **zeal, diligence, endeavour;** more frq. *brtson-ₒgrús*.

འགྲེ་བ་ *ₒgré-ba* 1. **to roll** one's self, *sá-la* on the ground; *ₒgre-ldóg Glr.* (or *ₒgre lóg Pth.*) *byéd-pa* id., e.g. from pain, despair etc.; also of horses etc. — 2. **to repeat** *Cs.*

འགྲེང་བ་ *ₒgréṅ-ba* (cf. *sgreṅ-ba*) **to stand** (not in use in *W.*) *dóṅ-gi k̔ar ₒgréṅ-nas* standing at the top of the pit *Dzl.*; *dṅáṅs-pa ltar ₒgréṅ-bar ₒgyur* they start up as if frightened *Dzl.*; of the *ṗo-mtsán*: to be erected *Med.*; *mi ₒgreṅ γsum* three lengths of a man *Tar.* — *ₒgréṅ-bu*, also *ₒgréṅ-po* (*Glr.*) the sign of the vowel e.

འགྲེམ(ས)་པ་ *ₒgrém(s)-pa*, pf. *bkram*, fut. *dgram*, imp. *k̔roms* (*W.* **ṭam-če**, imp. **ṭom**) 1. **to put** or **lay down** in order, e.g. beams, spars etc. *B.* and col.; **to spread out, to display,** goods, books, on the table or ground; **to scatter,** blossoms by the wind *Stg.*; **to draw,** a curtain. — 2. **to sprinkle,** water, *B.* and col. — 3. **to distribute,** for *ₒbrim-pa C.*

འགྲེལ་བ་ *ₒgrél-ba*, pf. *bkral*, another form for *ₒgrol-ba*, **to explain, comment, illustrate,** *dgóṅs-pa* the import (of the words or writings of the saints); *ₒgrél-ba Cs.*, *ₒgrel-pa Zam.*, *Tar.* explanation, explication, commentary; *don-ₒgrél*, resp. *dgoṅs-ₒgrél* explanation of the meaning; *tsig-ₒgrél* explanation of a word, of the words; *γžuṅ-grél* 1. explication of the text 2. text and commentary; *raṅ-ₒgrél* prob. self-explanation, an explanation contained in the book itself *Wdṅ.*; *ₒgrél-ba-po Cs.*, *ₒgrél-po Sch.*, *ₒgrel-byéd Cs.* an explainer, commentator. (*ṗan-tsún ₒgrél-ba*, and *k̔ral ₒgrél-ba Lexx.?*)

འགྲོ་སྒོ་ *ₒgró-sgo C.* **expense, expenditure,** of money, **ḍo-gor táṅ-ba** to lay out (money), to spend.

འགྲོ་ལྡིང་ *ₒgro-ldiṅ* Dramila, country in the south of India *Schf.*; another reading gives Draviḍa (coast of Coromandel).

འགྲོ་བ་ *ₒgró-ba* I. vb., pf. and imp. *soṅ*, the imp. *ₒgro(s)* seldom used, 1. **to**

walk, *ḱyeu ˳gro mi nús-pa góg-pa tsam* an infant, a child, that creeps only, and is not yet able to walk *Dzl.*; *˳gró-ba daṅ nyál-ba daṅ ˳dúg-pa* the walking, lying and sitting *Dzl.*; com. in a more gen. sense: **to go, to move,** *˳gró-am mi ˳gro* will you go or not? *rgyál-poi mdún-la ˳gró-bai lág-ča* the things going, i.e. carried, before the king *Glr.*; **to go away,** *da ṅa ˳gró-bar žu* now I beg to be permitted to go *Pth.*; *γnás-nas ˳gró-ba* to go away from a place, to leave, *ḱyim-nas ˳gro mi ṗód-na* if one cannot leave his house, part from home *Pth.*; **to go out,** *ḱyod nyin-par rtág-tu ˳gró-na* if during the day you always go out, are from home *Dzl.*; **to travel,** *ṗan-tsún-du ˳gró-ba Dzl.*, *ṗar ˳gro ṫsur ˳gró-ba Pth.* travelling there and back; *yar ˳gro mar ˳gró-ba* to travel up and down, up hill and down hill *Glr.*; *˳gró-čos-su* as a spiritual vademecum *Mil.*; *˳gró-ṫse* on the way, on the road; opp. to *˳óṅ-ba* (more fully: *ṗar ˳gro ṫsur ˳oṅ-ba*, col. *yoṅ-ba)* to go and to come back; hence *˳gro-ṫse* may also mean: on the way thither; *˳gro-˳oṅ-méd-pa* a thing that is neither going nor coming, but always remaining in its place *Mil.*; **to go, move on,** to continue one's way, esp. in the phrase *soṅ(-soṅ)-ba-las.* Connected with adverbs and postpositions: *ṗyir ˳gró-ba* to return, go home, to come back, also: to go out, *mdún-du, sṅón-du, sṅún-la ˳gró-ba* to go before, pass before, precede (*mdún-du* referring to space only, *sṅón-du* and *sṅún-du* both to space and time); *rǰés-su ˳gró-ba* to follow, come after or later, to succeed, also to give one's self over to, to addict one's self to (e.g. ill courses) *Ld.-Glr. Schl.* p. 7, b; *˳gro čug, C.* let it be, let it take its course! — *rkyál-˳gro* a swimming fish *Cs.* — *dgúr* (or *rgur*)-*˳gro* = *dud-˳gro.* — *˳grúl-˳gro* pacing, walking *Cs.* — *rgyúg-˳gro* running, galloping *Cs.* — *ṅán-˳gro* going to damnation, *ṅán-soṅ* having gone to damnation, *ṅán-soṅ γsum* the three damned, or not saved, classes of beings (v. sub II); *ṅán-soṅ γsum* is opposed to *bdé-˳gro*, and often used in a general sense = 'hell'. — *sṅón-˳gro* 1. **preceding, foregoing, previous, former.** 2. **preface, introduction,** opp. to *dṅos-γži*, the thing itself, the text etc. *Thgr.* and elsewh. — *čos ṫams-čád-kyi sṅón-˳groi sláb-bya* Petersb. Verzeichniss no. 409) does not mean: 'advice given by the former (teachers)' *Sch.*, but: introductory and preparatory doctrines. — *mčóṅ-˳gro* (going in leaps) **a frog** *Cs.* — *nyál-˳gro* (creeping, crawling) **a worm.** — *ltó-˳gro* (crawling, sliding on the belly) **worm, snake,** frq. — *dúd-˳gro* (*Ssk.*, तिर्यच्) walking in an inclined posture, **an animal,** v. sub. II. — *bdé-˳gro* going to happiness: **the happy, the blessed,** also *bdér-˳gro Was.*, opp. to *ṅán-˳gro*, v. above; usually in a gen. sense, like our 'heaven'; *bdé-˳gro mṫo-ris-kyi lus ṫób-pa* to receive a heavenly, glorified body, v. *lus.* — *˳dúr-˳gro* **trotting** *Cs.* — *ǰur-gro* **a bird** *Cs.* — *˳ṗyé-˳gro* = *ltó-˳gro.* — *láṅs-˳gro* walking erect, **man.** — 2. **to get, to get into, to enter** *či-bdag-gi dbáṅ-du sóṅ-ba* having got into the power of death *S.g.*; *grál-gyi ṫá-mar soṅ* they got (in a miraculous manner) to the end *Dzl.* ༧༥, 4. b.; *de nyid mig-tu sóṅ-na* if the same (a little hair) gets into the eye *Thgy.* — 3. **to find room in, to be contained in,** like *šóṅ-ba*: *til-rǰáṅ ḱal brgyád-ču ˳gró-ba žig* a sesame store-room that will hold 80 bushels; *ḱal γčig ˳gró-bai žiṅ* as much land as can be sown with a bushel of corn (prop. a field holding a bushel) *Pth.* — 4. **to turn to, to be transformed into,** syn. to *˳gyúr-ba* and often used instead of it, but only in more recent writings, and in the col. language of *C.* (in *W.* **čá-če** is much more in use): *dúg-tu ˳gro* it turns to poison, it is changed into poison *Mil.*; *ḱyi-mo žig-tu soṅ* she was changed into a bitch *Mil.*; *mṫar gyúr-nas sdug-bsṅál-du ˳gró-bas-na* because they finally change and are turned into misery *Thgy.*; *lóg-par ˳gró-ba* to take an unfavourable turn, to have a fatal issue (of a cure) *Lt.*; *da sgrúb-γnas-su soṅ yod* it has now become a place of meditation, it has been transformed into sacred ground

Mil.; *stobs čúṅ-du ˳gró-ba* the state of declining, the decay of strength *Med.*; *čól-bar ˳gro* they get intermixed, confused *Ma.*; similarly *Tar.* 210,10; *las zin ˳gró-na* when there is no more work, when work ceases. In a somewhat different sense: *mé-tog smạn-la ˳gro* the blossom is used for medicines. — 5. In *W.* *˳gró-ba* is gen. joined to a supine in *te*, and used to express uncertainty or probability: **dí-riṅ der léb-te ḍo** he has probably arrived there to-day; **zér-te yod ḍo** very likely he has said so; **šro ži-te ḍo** his anger will have abated, I think. The origin of this particular use of the word may perh. be traced to such sentences as the one following: *ṗúṅ-ste ˳gro* we are going to be ruined, we are likely to be ruined. — 6. **to be spent, expended,** v. *˳gró-sgo*; **sóṅ-to** col., account of expenses.

II. sbst **a being, a living creature,** *˳gró-ba mi* the being 'man', *Mil.*; *˳gró-ba rin-čén Cs.*, *˳gro-mčóg*, the highest being, or creature, man; *˳gró-bai rigs drúg*, *˳gro-drúg* the six classes of beings, viz. *lha, lha-ma-yin, mi, dúd-˳gro, yi-dvags, dmyál-ba-pa*. The *lha-ma-yin* are sometimes omitted, or placed after man. — *˳gro(-bai) don byéd-pa*, or *mdzúd-pa* to care for the welfare of beings, which expression is frq. applied to the benevolent activity of the Bodhisatvas etc., at present as much as: to perform divine service, to officiate, = *sku-rim byéd-pa*. — *˳gro-ṗán* = *˳gro-dón* *Tar.* 13,16. — *˳gró-sa* 1. **way, road** *W.*, **ḍó-sa med** one cannot go there. 2. **aim, scope,** *˳gró-sar ṗyin* he reaches his aim, attains his end *Glr.* 3. **access, approach,** *˳gró-sa mi ˳dug* one cannot gain access, admission.

འགྲོགས་པ *˳grógs-pa* 1. (cf. *grogs*) **to be associated,** *ḱyo-šúg γnyis ˳grógs-pa* husband and wife together *Dzl.*; *de daṅ ˳grógs-te ˳oṅs* he came with him, had joined him *Dzl.*; *˳grógs-te dóṅ-ṅo* let us go together *Dzl.*; *ṅa daṅ ḱyéd-rnams ˳bral-méd rtág-tu ˳grogs* I and you, we shall always remain inseparably united *Glr.*; *˳grógs-dgos-rnams* those with whom we are to keep close fellowship, our nearest relations and associates *S.g.* — 2. cf. *˳grágs-pa, sgróg-pa*) **to cry, to shout** *Dzl.*, esp. joined with *˳bod*. — 3. (cf. *grás-pa, grágs-pa* I.) **to bind, to tie,** *ṫág-pa-la dar-lčóg*, a flag to a rope; **to hang, fix, fasten,** *nyi-mai zér-la* hanging on a sun-beam *Glr.*

འགྲོང(ས)་པོ *˳gróṅ(s)-po*, or *˳gróṅs-po*, **straight,** = *bsráṅs-pa*, *Ts.*

འགྲོང་བ *˳groṅ-ba* 1. pf. *groṅs* 1. resp. **to die**; *˳gróṅs-ka* the very time of one's death *Cs.*, cf. *˳čí-ka*; sometimes it stands 2. for *˳drén-pa*, *Mil.* and *C.* — 2. pf. *bkroṅs*, fut. *dgroṅs*, resp. **to be killed, murdered, put to death,** of Lamas and kings.

འགྲོད་པ *˳gród-pa*, = *bgród-pa*, **to go, to travel** *Glr.*

འགྲོན *˳gron* **alienism,** the state of being a foreigner; *˳grón-du ˳gró-ba* to go on travels, to go abroad *Dzl.*; *˳grón-po*, fem. *˳grón-mo*, guest, foreigner, stranger, traveller frq.; *˳grón-po ˳bód-mḱan* one inviting guests, an inviter col.; *γžis-˳gron* a native guest, *byés-˳gron* a foreign guest *Cs.*; *˳gron-ḱáṅ* inn, public house *Mil.*; *˳gron-γnyér* 1. that servant in a household who has to announce visitors, to receive and hand over requests etc.; in *W.* an official in the monasteries attending on strangers and travellers. 2. a mediator, one supporting a petition, one taking care of sacrifices etc. — *˳gron-lám* road *Cs.*

འགྲོན་པ *˳grón-pa*, *Cs.* = *˳gród-pa*.

འགྲོན་བུ *˳grón-bu* (. col. **rúm-bu**) **a small shell, cowry,** at present chiefly used as ornament, or as a medicine, after having been burnt and pulverized; *˳grón-bui ṫal* the ashes of this shell *Med.*; *˳gron-ṫód* an ornament for the head, consisting of cowries *Mil.*

འགྲོར *˳gror*, supine of *˳gró-ba*.

འགྲོལ་བ *˳gról-ba* I. vb. neut., pf. *grol*, **to become free, to be liberated, released from,** *bčíṅs-pa gaṅ yin-pa dé-dag ni gról-bar gyúr-to* **all that were bound** were released; *lus dé-las* from this body *Glr.*; *nád-las* from disease, *ṅas* by me *Mil.* In a specific Buddhistic sense: *yid*, or *sems rnám-par grol* the soul or spirit is released, made free, viz. from every impediment arising from imperfect knowledge or perception, the latter being no longer subject to dimness and uncertainty, but perfectly clear; *raṅ(-sar) gról-ba* what has become clear of itself (without any study or exertion) *Glr.*; yet *raṅ gról-ba* seems also to denote: to be set free, to get released (from the *˳kor-ba*) through one's self; *čos-nyid-kyi gliṅ-du ˳gról-ba* to be released and elevated into the region of the highest perception *Glr.*; *˳gról-ba*, used absolutely, always signifies, like *tár-ba*, to be released from the evil of existence.

II. vb. act., pf. *bkrol*, fut. *dgrol*, imp. *krol* (*W. bkrol*, pronounced **ṭol**) 1. **to loose, untie, unbutton, unfasten**, a knot, a bag, a garment; **to put down, take off**, arms, ornaments etc. — 2. **to release, redeem, liberate**, *bčiṅs-pa-las* from fetters *Tar.* — 3. **to remove**, do away with, put an end to, *sdug-bsṅál* misery, *te-tsóm* doubts. — 4. **to remove obscurities**, to free from uncertainties, **to explain, interpret, comment**, = *˳grél-ba*, e.g. *dgóṅs-pa* the sense, import *Lex.*; *˳grol-byéd*, *˳gról(-ba)-po* commentator *Cs.*

འགྲོས *˳gros* the act of **going, walking**, *pyi ˳grós-su* v. sub *˳gyés-pa*; *skyabs-˳grós* v. *skyabs*; *spyod-˳grós* manner of walking, gait, carriage; *séṅ-gei spyod-grós Mil.* the manner of a lion; also manner or mode of living, of transacting business, *dé-tso ṅá-yi spyod-˳grós yin* these are my occupations *Mil.*; *mig-gi spyod-˳grós* the language of the eyes, of looks; *rkaṅ-grós* 1. a going or travelling on foot, a march. 2. breeding cattle, *rkaṅ-˳grós spél-ba* to breed cattle, to be a grazier. — *ču-˳grós* a current of water; **šiṅ ču-˳grós-la kyál-če** to float timber *W.* — *˳gros-čén* amble (of a horse) *Sch.*

རྒ་བ *rga-ba*, pf. *rgas* 1. **to be old, aged**, *rga-šis γzir-ba* to suffer under (the infirmities of) old age *Zam.* (cf. *skyé-ba* init.); *rgas-pai stéṅ-du* beside my being already old *Dzl.*; *rgas-kógs* v. *˳kógs-pa.* — 2. fig. **to go down, to set**, of the sun etc.; *go-rgás* v. *go* 2.

རྒ་ཝང་ཀྲད་ཀྱི *rga-wan-krád-kyi*(?) **bat, flitter-mouse** *Ts.*

རྒག་ཅིག *rgag-čig* a large gray species of **lizard** *Ld.*

རྒང *rgaṅ*, also *˳gaṅ-γzér-ma* **hedgehog** *Sch.*, or perh. rather **porcupine.**

རྒད་པ *rgád-pa*, or *rgán-pa*, **old, aged**; more frq. *rgád-po* 1. an **old man**, a man gray with old age. 2. an **elder, senior, headman** of a village; *rgád-mo* an old woman; *rgan-bgrés* old people *Sch.*; *rgan-rgón γnyis Sch.*: 'both the old man and the old woman' (?); *rgan-rgón-rnams-kyi skyo-grógs* the comforter of old people (so *Mil.* calls himself) — *rgan-byis* old people and children, old and young *Mil.* — *rgan-mi-máṅ* = *rgan-γsum.* — *gan-tsir-žón-tsir W.*, *gen-žon-dhal-rim C.* the privileges of seniority. — *rgan-žúgs* those that are grown old *Cs.*, 'an old monk' (?) *Sch.* — *rgan-rábs* the aged, *rgan-rábs-la rim-gro byéd-pa Stg.*, *rgan-rigs pu-dúd-du kúr-ba S.g.* to respect old age. — *rgan-γsúm*, *rgan-mi-máṅ* the elders of a village.

རྒལ *rgal W.* **a ford.**

རྒལ་ཅིག་པ *rgal-čig-pa* = *rgag-čig Ld.*

རྒལ་བ *rgál-ba*, pf. and fut. *brgal*, imp. *rgol*, c. *las*, or accus., or *la*, **to step** over (a threshold) *Glr.*; **to pass** or **climb** over (a mountain); *la brgál-bai byáṅ-ṅos* the north-side of a pass crossed *Glr.*; **to leap** over (a wall) *Dzl.*; **to ford** (a river); **to travel** through, **to sail** over, **to pass** (a river or lake), *rgyá-mtso-la gru-γziṅs-kyi lám-nas brgál-te* after having crossed the sea in a ship.

རྒལ་ཚིགས *rgal-tsigs Sch.* = *sgal-tsigs.*

རྒས *rgas*, v. *rgá-ba.*

རྒས་ཀ *rgás-ka* **old age**; *rgás-ka sra* a vigorous old age.

རྒུ *rgu* sometimes for *dgu*; *rgu-tub* = *dgu-tub Med.*; *-gu-drús?*

རྒུད་པ་ *rgúd-pa* **to decline, to sink, to get weak, frail,** esp. with old age *Mil., Pth.*; in *W.* used in a more general sense: **gud soṅ** 1. he has grown thin. 2. he is impoverished, much reduced, in declining circumstances; *dar-rgúd* the rise and fall in the world.

རྒུན་ *rgun* **the vine; grape;** *rgun-dkár* white grapes, *rgun-nág* black, or purple grapes *W.*; *rgun-rgód W.* **raisins;** *rgun-˳brúm* grapes; raisins; *rgun (-˳brum)-šiṅ* vine; *rgun(-˳brum)-ṫsás* **vineyard;** *rgun-čáṅ Mil.* **wine,** resp. *rgun-skyéms Cs.*

རྒུར་ *rgur* v. *dgur.*

རྒོ་ *rgo,* sometimes for *sgo.*

རྒོ་བ་ *rgó-ba* = *dgó-ba.*

རྒོངས་ *rgoṅs S.g.?*

རྒོངས་མོ་ *rgóṅs-mo Mil.* for *dgóṅs-mo* (?).

རྒོད་ *rgod* 1. **laughing, laughter** *S.g.* — 2. **bird of prey.** — 3. **wild.** — 4. **prudent** (v. the following word).

རྒོད་པ་ *rgód-pa* I vb. 1. **to laugh,** aloud *Mil.*; (*Bal. *rgód-ċa**) cf. *gád-mo, dgód-pa, bgád-pa.* — 2. **to grow weak, languid,** or **indolent,** syn. to *γyéṅ-ba,* often joined with *byiṅ,* for emphasis; *rgód-bag-čan* weak, languid, indolent *Stg.*

II. adj. 1. **wild,** *ra-rgód* wild goat, *ṕag-rgód* wild boar, *γyag-rgód* wild yak or ox; *rgod-γyag-rwá* horn of the wild yak *S.g.*; *bya-rgód* vulture, bird of prey = *bya-rgyál*; *rgód-po,* and *rgod* id.; *rgód-kyi rtse-rgyál* an eagle's feather, stuck as ornament on the hat *Pth.*; *mi-rgód* a wild or savage man; a robber, ruffian; *mi-rgód byéd-pa* to rob (usually named together with murdering and lying) *Dzl.*, but as the Tibetan always attaches to this word *mi-rgód* the notion of some gigantic hairy fiend, it cannot in every instance be applied to beings really existing. — Fig. furious, angry (seldom); *dbugs-rgód Med.?* — 2. **prudent, able** *C., Zam.*

རྒོད་མ་ *rgód-ma, rta rgód-ma* (*Bal. *gún-ma**) **a mare;** *rgod-skám-ma* a barren mare *Sch.*; *rgod-brúṅ* dung of a mare *Med.*

རྒོལ་ *rgol* 1. v. *rgál-ba.* 2. v. *rgól-ba.*

རྒོལ་བ་ *rgól-ba,* pf. and fut. *brgol,* **to dispute, combat, fight,** *mi-la* with or against a man; *ṕá-rol-poi dmág-la rgól-du ˳gró-ba* they are about to fight against the hostile army *Dzl.*; *γžán-gyis rgol ma nús-so* nobody could fight them, could make head against them *Glr.*; **to offer resistance,** to make opposition, *sus ḱyaṅ rgól-ba ˳dzúgs-pai mi ma byuṅ* nobody arose to offer resistance *Pth.* (evidently incorrect; it should be either; *sus kyaṅ rgól-ba ˳dzúgs-pa* [inf.] *ma byuṅ,* or: *rgól-ba ˳dzúgs-pai* [partic.] *mi su yaṅ ma byuṅ*); sometimes as much as **to accuse, to charge,** *ḱyód-kyis ṅai bu bsád-do žes brgál-te* 'you have killed my son', thus accusing me *Dzl.*; *ṫsur γnyis rgol* he quarrels at a double rate *Mil.*; *mi-la rgól-ba zú-ba* to find fault with another (higher in rank), to pick a quarrel with him *Mil.*; *rgól-bai žu-dón* a speech provoking a quarrel with a superior *Mil.*; *ṕas-rgól* a quarrel or contest begun by the counter-party *Sch.*; *ṕas-rgol-mi, ṕas rgól-pa mi* adversary, opponent *Dzl.* ༢༥༠, 2. — *sṅá-rgol,* and *ṕyi-rgol* (*Ssk.* पूर्ववादिन् & परवादिन्) 1. acc. to *Cs.* **plaintiff** and **defendant,** but these terms are not quite adequate, as *sṅá-rgol* prop. denotes him who begins a quarrel, **the aggressor, assailant,** both in war and in common life, e.g. in court, and *ṕyi-rgol* designates him, who is intent on defending himself against the attacks and accusations of the opponent. by surpassing him in abusive language and esp. by having recourse to witchcraft. Hence *ṕyir-rgól-bai γnód-pa* is a kind of danger against which every one tries to protect himself, and chiefly again by charms and witchcraft. — 2. *sṅa-rgol* and *ṕyi-rgol* are also said to signify those students that are contending with one another in academical disputations.

རྒྱ་ *rgya* 1. resp. *ṕyag-rgyá,* **seal, stamp, mark, sign, token;** (*ṕyag-*) *rgyás ˳débs-*

pa, Cs. rgya brgyáb-pa, to seal, to stamp; to seal up, *búm-pa-la* a bottle *Glr.*; *nám-mkʼai dbyáṅs-su* (to seal up) into the heavenly regions, i.e. to cause to disappear, to hide for ever *Glr.*; to confirm or pledge solemnly by a sealed document; *ri-rgya lúṅ-rgya ₒdzúg-pa* 'to seal up hills and valleys', i.e. to protect the living beings inhabiting them from being harmed by huntsmen or fishermen, an annual performance of the Dalai Lama, consisting in a variety of spells and incantations; *rgya gcóg-pa* to break open a seal *Cs.* — Further expressions v. compounds. — 2. (*Cs. rgyá-bo?*) **extent, width, size,** *rgyar dpag-tu-méd-pa* immeasurable in extent *Glr.*; *séms-čan-gyi rgyai tsad ni či tsam* how vast must be the extent (of love) with respect to beings! *Thgy.*; *rgyá-čan* having extent, *mkʼyén-rgya-čan* of extensive learning *Mil.*; *rgya-čʼén(-po)* of very large size, very extensive, of a building, a pond etc.; grand, enormous, prodigious, of banquets feasts, sacrifices, assemblies; c. accus. very rich in, *Schr.*; in a general sense: great, *stón-pa rgya-čʼé-ba* a great master or teacher *Thgy.*; *rgya-čʼén spyód-pai blá-ma* may be rendered: a very virtuous Lama, po.; *rgya-čʼúṅ* denotes the contrary of all this; *rgya-čʼe-čʼúṅ* v. *rgya-kʼyón* in Compounds; *rgya-čʼér* adv. = *rgyás-par* in detail, at large, at full length, e.g. to explain; *rgya-čʼér byéd-pa* to extend *Feer Introd.* etc. p. 72; *rgya-čʼer-ról-pa Lalitavistara* or *Lalitavistāra*, title of a biography of Buddha, translated and edited by *Foucaux* (a conjecture concerning the signification of the Sanskrit word v. *Fouc. Rgyatcherr.* II. p. XXII.; some statements relative to the Chinese translations of this work, v. ibid. p. XVI., and *Was.* 176; on the historical value of it v. *Was.* 3, 4); *rgya bskyéd-pa Zam.*, *Cs.* to widen, augment, enlarge, extend, *rgya bskúm-pa* to contract, to diminish the extent. Lastly, it also denotes, like *dkyil-ₒkʼor*, a plain surface, a disk: *nyi zlai rgya dkar šar Mil.* the bright disks of the sun and moon appear, cf. *rgyas* in *zla-rgyás*; v. also the compounds. — 3. (*Cs. rgyá-mo*, perh. also *rgyá-ma*) **net**; *byá-rgya* fowling-net, *nyá-rgya* fishing-net, *ri-dags-rgya* hunting-net, — 4. for *rgyá-ma*, v. compounds. — 5. for *rgyá-mo* **beard,** *rgyá-čan* having a beard, bearded *C.* — 6. for *rgya-gár, rgya-gár-pa*, and *rgya-gár-skad.* — 7. for *rgya-nág, rgya-nág-pa*, and *rgya-nág-skad.* — 8. for *rgya-ru.* — 9. for *rgya-skyégs.* — 10. erron. for *brgya.*

Comp. and deriv. *rgya-dkár* 1. *nyi-zlái rgya-dkár* v. above no. 2. extr. 2. *Cs.* = *rgya-gár* India, 3. *Cs.* a dog with white spots on the nose. — *rgya-skád* 1. Sanskrit language, 2. Chinese language. — *rgya-skás* (*W.* **gya-šre̥**) **a** (European) **staircase,** cf. *skás-ka.* — *rgya-skégs, rgya-skyégs, Ssk.* लाक्षा, Williams: 'a kind of red dye, lac, obtained from an insect as well as from the resin of a particular tree'; in medical works it is mentioned as an astringent medicine; the adjectives *dkar-rgyá* light-red, and *rgya-smúg* violaceous *C.* are derived from this word. — *rgya-kʼúr Med.?* — *rgya-kʼyi* a Chinese dog. — *rgya-kʼyón* **width, extent, area** *Pth.*, col. **gya-čʼe-čʼúṅ**. — *rgya-kʼri C.* **chair.** — *rgya-gár* (the 'white extent or plain') **India,** *rgya-gár-pa* an Indian, *rgya-gar-skad* Sanskrit language. — *rgya-grám* a figure like a cross; *rdo-rje-rgya-grám* shaped like a quadrifid flower; *rluṅ rgya-grám žés-pa Glr.* seems to be = *rlúṅ-gi dkyil-ₒkʼor* atmosphere (connected with some phantastic association); *lám-po rgya-grám* a cross-road *Sch.* — *rgya-čáṅ* a kind of girdle *Lex.* — *rgya-čan* v. *rgya* 2 and 5. — *rgya-čʼu-kʼúg-pa* n. of a river in China near the Tibetan frontier (also *rgya-čʼu-rabs-med*) *Glr.* — *rgya-čʼe* etc. v. *rgya* 2. — *rgya-ṭám Bhot.* = *ṭám-ka*, the third part of a rupee. — *rgya-rtags* **mark, signature, stamp** *Sch.* — *rgya-tʼél* a kind of seal or stamp *Cs.* — *rgya-mtʼóṅs* 1. a platform, an open pavilion on the house-top, 2. a vent-hole for smoke. — *rgya-ₒdré* **a quarrel** *Mil.nt.* — *rgya-nág* (the 'black extent') **China,** *rgya-nág-pa*, and *-ma* a China-man and woman; *rgyá-rnams* the Chinese *Glr.*

— *rgya-nón W.* the great royal seal, of a square form; surpassing (*nón-pa*) all others in influence and power. — *rgya-dpé* a Sanskrit book *Tar.* 33, 2. — *rgya-ṗi-liṅ* n. of the country, *rgya-ṗi-liṅ-pa*, n. of the people, through which the Tibetans heard first (prob. at the beginning of the eighteenth century) of the civilized nations of the occident, hence n. for **British India**, for Englishman, or European resident of British India, and also (sometimes without *rgya*) for Europe and European in general. The word is of course not to be found in literature. Some derive it from 'Feringhi', which term, in the slightly altered form of *ṗa-ráṅ, ṗe-ráṅ*, is current in *C.*, along with the above mentioned *rgya-ṗi-liṅ*; it is therefore not improbable, that *ṗi-liṅ* represents only the more vulgar pronunciation of the genuine Tibetan word *ṗyi-gliṅ*, an out-country, a distant foreign country and esp. **Europe**, *Chr. Prot.* — *rgya-ṗib(s)*, *rgya-ṗúb(s)* a Chinese roof *Glr.* — *rgyá-ba* 1. vb. to be wide, extensive, pf. *rgyas* (q.v.), 2. sbst. width, extent, 3. adj. wide; *rgyá-bar ˳gyúr-ba* to extend, to increase, to become copious *Cs.*, perh. no longer in use. — *rgyá-bo* 1. *Cs.* and *Lex.* **beard.** 2. **a Chinese** *Glr.*, but not without an allusion to the former signification. — *rgya-dbáṅ rin-po-čé* title of the Dalai Lama, v. *Huc* II., 275, where '*kian ngan*' stands erroneously. — *rgyá-ma* 1. **a large steel-yard** *C.*, *rgyá-ma-la ˳dégs-pa* to weigh *Glr.*, **gyá-ma-la tég-ne** *C.* being weighed out by retail, e.g. meat; **gyá-ma-la ma tég-ne** *C.* wholesale. 2. a sealed paper, document. — *rgya-mí* **a Chinese.** — *rgyá-mo* 1. **net** *Cs.* 2. **a Chinese woman** *Glr.*; *rgyá-mo-bza* id. — *rgya-rmá* **the venereal disease** *Sch.* — *rgya-smúg* **violet colour** *C.* — *rgya-ṫsá* **sal ammoniac** *Med.* — *rgya-ṫsós Med.*, perh. = *rgya-skyégs.* — *rgyá-mṫso* 1. **sea, ocean;** *rgyá-mṫsor ˳ǰúg-pa* to go to sea *Dzl.*, *γtóṅ-ba* to let one go to sea *Dzl.*; *ṗyii rgyá-mṫso* the outer sea, ocean; *náṅ-gi rgyá-mṫso* an inner sea, inland sea, lake. 2. *Bal.* (**rgyám-ṫso**) **river.** 3. **dropsy** *Mṅg.* 4. symb. num.: *four.* — *rgya-γži W.* is stated to be a kind of *γtór-ma.* — *rgya-zór Mil.* = *zor* **reaping-hook, sickle.** — *rgya-γzéb Sch.* 'a large net', *C.* a large **rake**, used in reaping. — *rgya-γyúl* 1. a large country 2. China *Glr.* — *rgyá-ra, rgyá-ru*, occasionally *rgya* alone, **the Saiga-antelope** *Sch.* — *rgya-ri* **a portion of meat,** (= *sder-gáṅ* a plateful) small or large, *Pth.*, *W. C.*; it also denotes a measure = ½ *dum*, or ¼ *lhu.* — *rgya-róg* **beard** *C.* — *rgya-láb* **talk, gossip.** — *rgya-lám*, **high-road, high-way.** — *rgya-šóg* **Chinese paper.** — *rgya-sér* 1. **gap, cleft, fissure, chasm,** in rocks, glaciers etc., 2. a dog with yellow spots about the nose *Cs.* 3. **Russia,** *rgya-sér-pa* a Russian; cf. *rgya-gár.* — *rgya-sóg* 1. *W.* **a saw** 2. *Sch.*: 'a Chuichui, or Chuichur, an infidel, a Mahometan; also Turkestan'. — *rgya-sráṅ* the open **street** (opp. to house) *Glr.*

རྒྱག་པ་ *rgyág-pa* another form for *rgyáb-pa*, used esp. in *C.*, **to throw, cast, fling,** *mda rgyág-pa* to shoot arrows *Glr.*; *brág-la ču rgyág-pai ˳ṗraṅ* a path along a precipice, where the water rushes against the rock, i.e. where there is a cataract *Glr.*; *dgón-pa žig rgyág-pa* **to found** a monastery (= *˳débs-pa*) *Georgi Alph. Tib.*; **gó-la zug gyag** *C.* = *mgó-nad ˳debs.*

རྒྱགས་ *rgyags*, or *brgyags*, **provisions, victuals, food,** in full: *˳ṫsó-bai rgyags*, *˳ṫso-rgyágs*; *lam-rgyágs* provisions for a journey; *dgun-rgyágs* prov. for the winter; *rgyágs-ṗye*, provisions of meal or flour; *rgyags-zóṅ* merchandize to buy or barter victuals with.

རྒྱགས་པ་ *rgyágs-pa* **fat, stout,** *Schr.* also **mighty, powerful, proud;** *rgyags-ṗrúg Pth., Schr.*: bastard-child.

རྒྱང་ *rgyaṅ* (so pronounced in *Bal.*) instead of *gyaṅ*, **wall.**

རྒྱང་བ་ *rgyáṅ-ba*, for *(b)rkyáṅ-ba*, *Pth.*: *rgyáṅ-nas bžag* they laid him down with his hands and feet stretched out.

རྒྱང་མ་ *rgyáṅ-ma* **distance** 1. absolutely: *rgyáṅ(-ma)-nas* at a distance, from afar, e.g. to see, to call to; *rgyáṅ (-ma)*

-nas grágs-pa čé-ba famous, celebrated, from afar *Mil.*; *rgyáṅ-du lús-pa* lingering far behind *Sch.*; *rgyaṅ mig mi mťóṅ-mkʻan W.* short-sighted; *rgyaṅ mčoṅ btáṅ-gin* moving forward by long leaps; *rgyáṅ-so ₒdzúgs-pa* to look over *Sch.*, (ought perhaps to be spelled *rgyaṅ-zo* one looking, spying into a distance); *rgyaṅ-šél* spy-glass, *rgyaṅ-bsríṅs-pa* lengthened to a great distance *Lex.*; *rgyaṅ-pʻán, rgyaṅ-pʻén* n. of a philosophical (atheistical! *Cs.*) sect in ancient India, *Tar.* 22, 8: *ₒjig-rten-rgyaṅ-pʻán*. — 2. used relatively: *rgyaṅ-riṅ-po* **far**, *rgyaṅ-riṅ-por soṅ* he went far away *Mil.*; *rgyaṅ-ťúṅ-ba* **near**; *rgyaṅ-grágs* the reach of hearing, **ear-shot**, (gen. the distance at which the sound of a trumpet may be heard, i.e. about 500 fathoms; however, as this number is much in favour with the Tibetans, such estimates are not to be depended upon). — *mig-rgyáṅ Glr.* distance of sight, i.e. the distance at which a man may be well distinguished from a woman, or a horse from an ass; — *rgyáṅs* adv. far, *rgyaṅs bkyéd-de Mil.nt.* moving far away, e.g. in order to increase one's distance from an unpleasant neighbour at table).

རྒྱང་རྩེ་ *rgyáṅ-tse* n. of a village and monastery in Tibet, not far from the frontier of Bhotan, *Köpp.* II., 358.

རྒྱན་ *rgyan* I. 1. **ornament, decoration**, *rgyán-gyis brgyán-pa* decked with ornaments *Dzl.*; *rgyan-ₒdógs-pa* to adorn one's self *Mil.*; *kʻa-rgyán* an ornament at the mouth, edge, or brim of a vessel, e.g. peacock's feathers about the mouth of a *bum-pa* (sacred bottle), flowers in a glass etc.; *kʻa-rgyán-čan* decorated in the front-part, e.g. a coat trimmed with fur of different colours, an arrow gaily painted at its notched end; *rgyán-rnams Dzl.* ornaments, *rgyán-ča* id.; *rgyan-gós Glr.* festival garment, beautiful vesture; *dbu-rgyán* an ornament of the head, a diadem. — 2. in relation to spiritual things: *séms-kyi rgyan* something good, **a blessing**, for the heart *Mil.*; *rgyán-du ₒčar* it proves a blessing, a moral advantage or benefit *Mil.*

II. 1. **a stake** or **pledge** at play, = *skugs*, **gyan tsúg-če* W.* to bet, to wager, e.g. a rupee: (also *rgyal? Schr.*). — 2. **lot**, *rgyan rgyáb-pa* to cast lots, without religious ceremonies, whereas *rtags-ríl* and *mo* are connected with such.

རྒྱབ་ *rgyab*, resp. *sku-rgyáb*, *Ssk.* पृष्ठ 1. **the back** of the body, the back part of any thing; *rgyáb-kyis pʻyógs-pa*, in later literature also *rgyab-pʻyógs-pa Thgy.* to turn one's back to a person or thing, c. *la*, also fig. *Dzl.*; *rgyáb-kyis pʻyógs-par byéd-pa* to put to flight; *rgyab stón-pa* to turn one's back, to turn round *Glr.*; *rgyáb-tu skyúr-ba* to throw to the back, to leave behind, to give up, to quit, frq.; *rgyáb-tu ₒbór-ba* id.; *rgyab brtén-pa* to lean one's back against or upon, to lean or rest on, to rely upon, confide in *Mil.*; *rgyab byéd-pa* to protect *Sch.*; *rgyáb-tu, rgyáb-na, rgyáb-la* **behind**, behind hand; **after, back**; *rgyab-nas* from behind; *rgyab mdún gnyis-la Glr.*, **gyab daṅ dún-la** col. behind and before; *ti-seï byaṅ-rgyáb-tu sleb tse* as we came behind to the north-side of the Tise *Mil.*; *rgyáb-kyi skyed-mos-tsal-du gšégs-so* let us go into the garden behind us *Dzl.*; *rgyab-rdzi* one standing behind working people, in order to watch and superintend them. — 2. as much as one is able to carry on his back, **a load**, *drel-rgyáb gsum* three mules' loads *Glr.*

Comp. *bal-rgyáb*, or **rgyab-bál* W.* a **fleece** of wool. — *rgyab-kʻál* 'a back's load', a burden carried on the back *Sch.*, *Schr.* — *rgyab-snás* a cushion or pad for the back *C.* — *rgyab-rtén* something to lean against, a safe retreat, **prop, support** *Mil.*, *rgyáb-rtén byéd-pa* to be a support *Mil.* — *rgyab-ríṅ* **serpent, snake** *Sch.* — **gyab-lóg jhe'-pa* C.* 1. **to turn one's back** 2. **to rebel, revolt**; **gyab-lóg dád-če* W.* to sit backward, with the back in advance. — *rgyab-lógs* **the back, back-part, reverse** of a thing

རྒྱབ་པ་ *rgyáb-pa*, pf. and fut. *brgyab*, imp. *rgyob*, **to throw, to fling**, aiming at a certain point, hence **to hit**, also **to beat** with a stick, = *rdúṅ-ba*; **to strike**, *mó-la mčus brgyáb-nas bsad* he (the male bird)

killed his mate by a stroke of his bill *Bhar.*; **tsá-ge-la gyob* W.* throw into the centre! hit the mark! *sdóṅ-po-la brgyab ṗog* (the ray of light) fell upon the stem *Glr.*; *dé-la ču rgyob* sprinkle this with water! *Pth.*; *ṗyugs nágs-seb-tu rgyáb-pa* to let the cattle run into the wood; **žag-ḍáṅ gyab-če* W.* to put down the date, to date; **la gyab-če** to cross a mountain pass. — *rgyáb-pa* is particularly used in *W.* in many phrases, whilst in *C. rgyág-pa*, and in *B. ₒdébs-pa* are more in use, as may be seen by referring to the several substantives, e.g. **lud gyáb-če* W.* to throw dung upon the fields, to manure; **par gyáb-pa* C.*, and **gyáb-če* W.*, to print; *gyáb-pa* stands also alone, elliptically: **ka gyab dug** here (is printed) the letter *ka*.

རྒྱམ་ཚྭ་ *rgyam-tsva Med.*, *Cs.*: 'a kind of salt, like crystal'.

རྒྱར་ *rgyar* v. *rgya* 2.

རྒྱལ་ *rgyal* 1. **victory**, in certain phrases: **gyal tób-če* W.* to gain the victory, to conquer, overcome; to win a law-suit, opp. to **ṗam ṗóg-če**. — 2. *Schr.* and *Sch.*: *rgyal-rgyán* **a pledge, a stake,** *rgyal btsúg-pa* to bet, wager, gamble *Sch.*; *rgyal bžag-pa* to contend with an other person about the first place, to try to get the precedence(?) *Sch.*; perh. also ornament, v. sub *rgód-pa* 2. — 3. **fine, penalty**, for theft *C.* — 4. n. of two lunar mansions, v. sub *rgyu-skár*; *rgyál-gyi zlá-ba, skár-ma rgyál-la báb-pai nyin-par, skár-ma rgyal daṅ ₒdzom-par, dpyid-zla rá-bai skár-ma rgyál-gyi nyin-par*, are dates relating to them. — 5. for *rgyál-po* and *rgyál-ba*.

རྒྱལ་བ་ *rgyál-ba* I. vb. neut. **to be victorious,** to obtain the victory, always with the sbst. in the nom. (not instr.) case, and gen. with *las*, **over** or **against**, *nág-poi ṗyógs-las* over the powers of darkness, *ₒjigs-pa-las* over fright, fear; also *γyúl-lás* in battle; prob. also *tsod ltá-ba-las* to pass an examination successfully; but also without *las*, *rtsód-pa* (to win) in a contest *Glr.*: very frq. *rgyál-bar ₒgyúr-ba* id.; *ṅa ṗám soṅ ḱyod gyal soṅ* I have lost, thou hast won (also in business): **to be acquitted,** to gain a law-suit; *dmag-ₒḱrúgs-kyi rgyal-ṗám-gyi γnas-tsúl ḱol* send (us) news concerning the progress of the war; in a similar sense: *rgyal ṗam ₒi-ltar byuṅ B.*; *rgyál-bar gyúr-čig, rgyál-ba daṅ tse-riṅ-bar šog čig* victory and long life! *Dzl.*

II. sbst. 1. (*Ssk.* जय) the act of conquering, **the victory**, **ḍi gyál-wa tob* C.* this bears away the palm or prize, this is the most excellent of all. — 2. the conquering party or person, he that prevails, **the conqueror** (opp to *ṗám-pa* the conquered, vanquished). Much more frq.: 3. **the most high, Buddha** (*Ssk.* जिन), *rgyál-bai sku* his person, *rgyál-bai bka*, his word; *rgyal daṅ de sras* (po. instead of *rgyál-ba daṅ dei sras*) Buddha and his children, his disciples *Pth.* 1, 1; *rgyál-ba góṅ-ma* the highest Buddha, **God,** *Mil.* — 4. *rgyál-ba rin-po-čé* His Highness, His supreme Majesty, title of the Dalai Lama.

III. adj. 1. **conquering, superior, eminent, excellent,** *rnám-par rgyál-bai ḱaṅ-bzáṅs* the most magnificent palace (of Indra) *Glr.* — 2. *W.* (gen. pronounced **gyálla**, in *Pur.* **rgyál-wa**) **good,** instead of *bzáṅ-po*; **gyál-la dád-če** or **lús-če** to continue in good condition, entire, uninjured; *mā gyalla* excellent! capital!

Comp. and deriv., belonging partly to *rgyál-ba*, partly to *rgyál-po*: **gyal-kár** **window** *C.* — **gyál-ḱa, ḱa-gyál** **victory, gain, advantage** *W.* — *rgyal-ḱág* **country, empire.** — *rgyal-ḱáms* 1. **kingdom.** 2. **realm, dominion of Buddha, the world.** — *rgyal-ḱrid Ld.* for *rgyal-srid*. — *rgyal-ḱrims* v. *ḱrims*. — *rgyal-ₒgóṅ* n. of a demon *Mil.* — *rgyal-brgyúd*, and *rgyal-rábs* 1. succession of kings of the same line or family, **dynasty** *Glr.* 2. a single **generation** of a dynasty, *rgyal-brgyúd lṅá-bču-na* in the fiftieth degree (in the line of descent). — *rgyál-sgo* **principal door,** entrance-door, **gate** *C.* — *rgyal-sgrúṅs*, legend of the kings, esp. that of Gesar. — *rgyal-čén bži* the four kings of the spirits or guardians of the universe

(˳jig-rten-skyóṅ v. *skyoṅ-ba*), residing just below the summit of Meru, the protectors of the gods against the Asuras, v. *Köpp.* I, 250; II, 261. — *rgyal-stód* lunar mansion v. *rgyu-skár.* — *rgyál-po* 1. **king**, *rgyál-po čén-po* **great king, emperor**; *rgyál-por ˳júg-pa, bskó-ba*, to inaugurate a king, to raise to the royal throne; *mi-la rgyál-po ˳čól-ba* id. *Pth.*; *rgyál-po byéd-pa* to act the king, to be(a) king; *ṅa rgyál-po mi ˳dod* I do not wish to be king *Dzl.*; *rgyál-po mi tób-na* if I do not obtain royalty *Dzl.*; *ṅas ni rgyál-po mi nús-so* I cannot be king *Dzl.* The word is also used for: government-authorities, police etc.; *rgyál-poi čád-pa* public punishment, *rgyál-pos ysód-pa* to be publicly executed. (As a characteristic sign of Asiatic views it seems worth mentioning, that the *rgyal-po* is usually spoken of much in the same manner, as robbers, conflagrations etc. are, i.e. as a kind of calamity against which protection is to be sought, esp. by charms and spells, cf. *˳jigs-pa*). 2. a local god, *˳gro-táṅ rgyál-po* the Dewa of Dotaṅ *Mil.* 3. fig. something excellent, superior in its kind; not only as with us the word is applied to the lion, as the king of animals, but also to distinguished flowers: the Udumbara (Ficus glomerata), to mountains, Meru and others; and col. *gaṅs-rgyál* a large glacier, *brag-rgyál* a huge rock, *smón-lam-gyi rgyál-po* a very comprehensive prayer, the *bzaṅ-spyód Glr.* 4. symb. num.: 16. — *rgyal-ṗrán* vassal or feudatory prince. — *rgyál-bu* prince. — *rgyal-blón* king and ministers, council of state. — *rgyál-mo* 1. queen. 2. pupil of the eye, together with the iris; *rgyál-moi mdaṅs nyams* the brightness of the eye-ball disappears *Med.* 3. like *rgyál-po* 3, e.g. a charm of particular power. — *rgyal-smád* lunar mansion, v. *rgyu-skár.* — *rgyal-tsáb* (for *rgyal-poi tsab*) 1. vice-roy, regent. Such a vice-roy under Chinese supremacy is now the king of Tibet, who about a century ago was still an independent ruler. 2. **successor** of a king. 3. (for *rgyál-bai tsab*) **Maitreya**, the future Buddha. — *rgyal-mtsán* sign of victory, **trophy**, a kind of decoration of cloth, of a cylindrical shape, erected upon a flag-staff, or carried on a pole. — *rgyal-rábs* 1. = *rgyal-brgyúd.* 2. **history, annals**, of the kings, title of several books. — *rgyal-rigs* 1. **the royal family, house, lineage**, 2. **warrior-caste** ཀྵ. — *rgyál-sa* 1. **a king's** or prince's **residence**, city where a court is held, and hence often **capital, metropolis.** 2. col., esp. in *W.*: **town.** 3. **throne** fig.; *rgyál-sar ységs-pa* to ascend the throne, *rgyal-sa bzúṅ-ba* to occupy the throne, *rgyál-sar bskó-ba* to raise to the throne, *rgyal-sa ˳ṗrog-pa* to usurp the throne; *˳di-nas rgyál-sa rgyai miṅ rgyál-po-la šor* from him the dominion passed over to the Chinese Ming-dynasty *Glr.* — *rgyal-srás* 1. **prince.** 2. **son of Buddha, a saint**; *sṅón-gyi rgyal-srás* saints of the olden time, of past ages. — *rgyal-srid* 1. **government, reign**, *rgyal-srid bzúṅ-ba* to enter upon the reign, to take possession of the throne. 2. *rgyal-srid sna-bdún* the seven jewels of royal government, v. *rin-čén.*

རྒྱས་པ *rgyás-pa* (prop. pf. to *rgyá-ba*) 1. vb. **to increase** in bulk or quantity, **to augment, to spread**, *bá-yi nu ltar rgyas* (the swollen uvula) gets as big as a cow's dug (these are in Tibet particularly small) *Lt.*; *˳ja-tsón rgyás-pa ˳dra* like an expanded rainbow *Glr.*; *bstán-pa rgyás-šin* the doctrine gaining ground, spreading *Glr.*; **to grow, develop** itself, of blossoms frq., of the body etc. — 2. adj. **extensive, large, ample, wide; copious, plentiful, manifold, numerous; rich in, abounding in; great in, strong in** cca.; **detailed, complete, full**; esp. adv. *rgyás-par* (col. **gyás-pa, gyẹ-pa**), *rgyás-par šes ˳dód-na*, often also *rgyás-par ˳dód-na* if you wish to know it fully, to hear it in detail; **tsáṅ-ma gyás-pa zér-na** *W.* if all the particulars are to be told; *rgyás-par byéd-pa* 1. to make bigger, to augment, to increase, to bestow or confer plentifully, *mi-la* on a person *Glr.* 2. to describe, narrate, state at large, in detail frq.; *don rgyás-par byed-pa* to be very **useful**, to exert a beneficial influence, *la* on, *Glr.* — *zla-ba rgyás-pa* full moon *Pth.*; *nya-rgyás zla-ba* id. — *rgyás-pai ťsá-ba, rgyas-ťsád* n. of a disease *Med.* — *ži-rgyás* etc. v. *glin̄*, and *ži-ba*.

རྒྱུ *rgyu Ssk.* हेतु I. 1. **matter, substance, material**, *rgyu šél-las* crystal being the material; *čán-rgyu* ingredients for making beer, i.e. barley, barm etc.; *rgyu dgé-ba bságs-pas ťób-pa yin* (the human body) is a substance obtained by accumulating virtue *Thgy.*; *ná-la dgós-rgyu čun̄* I have few wants *Mil.*; also for substance in an emphatical sense, = nervus rerum, money *Mil.*; *bzó-rgyu* matter or substance of which any thing is made or manufactured, material *Glr.*; *zá-rgyu med* we have nothing to eat *Glr.*; hence **opportunity, chance, possibility**, *dá-ltar rgyu žig snán-no* an opportunity offers now *Dzl.*; **arrangements, preparation**, *°dó-gyu ǰhé-pa* C. to make preparations for a journey. In a special sense: material, stuff for weaving, **warp, chain.** — 2. **cause, reason, motive**, main condition, *mya-n̄án-las °dás-pai rgyur °gyur* it becomes the cause of Nirwana, i.e. it leads to Nirwana *Dzl.*; in elliptical speech: *lha dan̄ mii rgyur gyúr-pai dgé-ba* the virtue that leads to (the re-birth amongst) gods or men *Dzl.* ༣༧, 17 (*Sch.* incorr.); in the same manner *n̄án-son̄ rgyú-ru °gro*; *rgyus* c. genit. by reason of, on account of, in consequence of *Tar.*; *čii rgyus* why *Stg.*; *rgyu méd-du, méd-par* without the impulse of a foreign cause, spontaneously; without sufficient reason, without good cause, the Latin *temere*; *rgyu dan̄ rkyen Cs.* and *Sch.* 'cause and effect', more correctly (cf. *rkyen*): primary and secondary cause, which, certainly, sometimes coincides with 'origin and further development', and so, too, with 'cause and effect'; *rgyu dan̄ rkyen deï pyir, deï rgyu deï rkyén-gyis, deï rgyu-rkyén*, therefore, on that account; in *Med.*: *nyé-bai rgyu* the three anthropological causes or conditions of diseases, the three 'humours', air, bile, and phlegm; *rín-bai rgyu* the ultimate cause of diseases, and of every evil, viz. ignorance (*ma-rig-pa*, v. *rig-pa*); *skyéd-byed rgyu* the creative cause *Zam.*; *°pél-bai rgyu ni lté-ba* the main condition, the efficient cause, of growth is the navel-string *Med.*; *rgyu byéd-pa* to be the principal cause of, to lie at the bottom of a matter *Mil.*; *rgyu skyéd-pa* to lay the foundation of *Dzl.* — 3. after verbal roots *rgyu* implies necessity, like our **I am to, I have to, I am obliged to, I ought to**; in later literature, as well as in the present col. language of *C.*, it indicates the fut. tense: *čós-skor γyás-nas byéd-rgyu-la* whereas the holy circumambulation (v. *skor-ba* I, 2) ought to be performed from the right (to the left) *Mil.*; *sdán-dgra yál-rgyu-la* as the enemy must vanish, or: is sure to come to an end *Mil.*; **sol-čóg ṭal-ḍig ǰhá-gyu yin-nam** *C.* am I to lay the cloth? **dhá-ta tó-ča zá-la °dó-gyu yin** *C.* now I will go and dine; *nai drún-du °ón-rgyu yin-pa* those that intended to come to me (the Latin 'venturi') *Glr.*; *dé-la rgyal-srid γtád-rgyu-la* when the government was to be conferred upon him, when he was to enter upon his reign *Glr.*; *rta žón-rgyu med* (riding-) horses were not to be had *Glr.* — When appended to adjectives, it is a mere pleonastical addition: *dkón-rgyu med* that is not a very precious thing, there is nothing particular in that *Mil.*; *čún-rgyui lha-ḱán* a very small temple *Mil.*; *γžán-pas légs-rgyu med* he is not more beautiful than others *Glr.*; *ya-mťsán-rgyu-med* that is not to be wondered at; **gó-gyu man** *C.* that is useless.

Comp. *rgyu-rkyén* (v above sub no. 2) **connection**, meaning, signification, *rgyu-rkyen bšad-du γsol* please explain to me the connection, which is often used in a general sense = what does that mean? what is that? *Glr.*, but also in a special sense relative to law-suits: **kyö́-kyi gyu-kyén žú-la °do** *C.* I am going to tell what it is with you, i.e. I shall inform against you, bring an action against you. — *rgyu-čá* col. that which belongs to a thing, **an appurtenance**, necessary implement etc. —

rgyu-°brás cause and effect or consequence, gen. in a moral sense: actions and their fruits (*lás-kyi rgyu-°brás*); also the doctrine treating on this subject, the doctrine of retribution, the principal dogma of Buddhism, prop.: *las-rgyu-°brás-kyi čos*; *las-rgyu-°brás-la yid-čes-pa* to believe in the doctrine of retribution *Glr.* — *rgyu-mtsán* (*Ssk.* निमित्त) 1. **cause,** *rgyu-mtsán °dri-ba* to ask after the cause *Glr.*; *rgyu-mtsán lo-rgyús °dri-ba* to question closely, to examine rigorously *Mil.*; **the connection of events,** the manner in which a thing has come to pass, *ṅai náṅ-nas ṕye ḱyér-bai rgyu-mtsán šod* tell me how it was that you could fetch the flour from my house, how you were able to accomplish it *Mil. nt.* 2. **token, sign, characteristic, proof, evidence,** *°dúg-pai rgyu-mtsán* as an evidence of being... *Glr.*

II. instead of *rgyú-ma.*

རྒྱུ་བ་ *rgyú-ba* **to go, walk, move, wander, range,** of men, animals, and fig. of lifeless things, *čú-la rgyú-bai °dab-čágs* birds frequenting the water; *kún-tu rgyú-ba* to wander from one place to another, hence: *kun-tu-rgyú* itinerant monk, n. of a sect of the Brahmans *Dzl.*; *rluṅ rgyú-bai rtsa* those veins in which air is circulating, cf. *rtsa* and *rluṅ*; also c. accus.: *yul,* or *groṅ rgyú-ba* to rove through countries, through villages; *rgyu-sráṅ, btsáṅ-gyi rgyu-sráṅ* the road that is frequented by the *btsan* (a kind of demons). — *rgyu-skár* v. below.

རྒྱུ་མ་ *rgyú-ma* 1. **entrails, intestines, bowels,** esp. the small intestines, opp. to *loṅ-ka* the large intestines; *rgyu °ḱril-ba convolvulus intestinorum Sch.*(?); *rgyu °ḱróg-pa* the croaking of the bowels *Sch.*; *rgyu-sgróg* the **caul,** covering the lower intestines; *rgyu-stód* the upper bowels, *rgyu-smád* the lower bowels *Cs.*; *rgyu-nád* disease of the bowels; *rgyu-γžér* **colic.** — 2. **sausage,** **gyú-ma gyáṅ-wa** *C.* (v. *sgyóṅ-ba*), **káṅ-če** *W.* to stuff sausages; **gyú-ma kar-gyáṅ** meat-sausage, meat-pudding, **gyú-ma naq-gyáṅ** black-pudding *C.*

རྒྱུ་སྐར་ *rgyu-skár* **the lunar mansions,** *Ssk.* नक्षत्र, or those 'constellations' through which the moon 'passes' in her revolution round the heavens; acc. to *Wdk.* and others they are the following: ༠ *ta-skar* (also *dbyug-gu*) three stars in the Ram's head; ༡ *bra-nye* (conceived by the Brahmans to be the image of the *yoni*); ༢ *smin-drug,* the Pleiades; ༣ *be-rdzi, snar-ma;* ༤ *mgo, smal-po;* ༥ *lag;* ༦ *nabs-so, rgyal-stod, nam-so;* ༧ *rgyal-smad;* ༨ *skag, wa;* ༩ *mču, rta-pa, rta-čen* (with Regulus its brightest star); ༡༠ *gre, rtau, rta-čuṅ;* ༡༡ *dbo, ḱra;* ༡༢ *me-bži, bya-ma;* ༡༣ *nag-pa, byau* (with Spica); ༡༤ *sa-ri;* ༡༥ *sa-ga;* ༡༦ *lha-mtsams, lag-sor;* ༡༧ *snron, ldeu* (with Antares); ༡༨ *snrubs, sog-pa:* ༡༩ *ču-stod;* ༢༠ *ču-smad, ṕul;* ༢༡ *gro-bžin* and *byi-bžin* (considered as one constellation); ༢༢ *mon-gre, mon-dre;* ༢༣ *mon-gru, sgrog;* ༢༤ *ḱrums-stod;* ༢༥ *ḱrums-smad;* ༢༦ *nam-gru, še-sa.*

རྒྱུག་པ་ *rgyúg-pa,* pf. *brgyugs,* fut. *brgyug* 1. **to run,** frq.; **to make haste, to hurry, to rush,** *sgor* to the door (out of the room) *Dzl.* ... *kyi tóg-tu* upon ... *Dzl.*; **há-la gyug** be off! get you gone! *C.* 1. **to start** (of a rail-way train) *W.*; *rta-rgyúg-pa* to ride full speed, **to gallop;** also sbst. **race** *Glr.* — 2. **to go, to pass, to circulate, to be current; to be valid, to have force.**

རྒྱུགས་ *rgyugs Lex.*; *Sch.*: **limit, term, aim, end;** *W.*: **task, lesson.**

རྒྱུགས་པ་ *rgyúgs-pa* **pride, ambition** *Sch.*; **grief, sorrow** *Schr.*(?).

རྒྱུང་བ་ *rgyúṅ-ba* **the nerves, sinews** *Sch.*; cf. *brgyúṅs-pa.*

རྒྱུད་ *rgyud* 1. *Ssk.* तन्तु, तन्त्री **string, cord,** but only in certain relations: the string of a bow; *rgya-rgyúd* Chinese string *Mil.*; string, chord, of a musical instrument, *rgyud-máṅs* harp; chain, v. *lu-gu*; mostly fig.: *ri-rgyúd, gaṅs-rgyúd* chain of mountains, ridge of snowy hills; also thread of tradition, i.e. continuous, uninterrupted tradition, so in: *ḱa-rgyúd, dgoṅs-rgyúd, čos-rgyúd, bka-rgyúd* (v. *bka,* compounds); *sňyan-rgyúd* = *bka-rgyúd,* frq. in *Mil.*; *γtam-rgyúd Zam.* legendary tradition. — If used for expressing a succession of generations or families, the word is gen. written *brgyud*, rarely *rgyud*, e.g. *rje-btsún slob-rgyúd daṅ bčas-te* his reverence (the venerable divine) with his race of scholars, in as much as the disciples of a saint are frequently called his spiritual children *Mil.* — 2. **treatise, dissertation,** *Ssk.* **तन्त्र,** also *rgyud-sdé*, esp. the necromantic books of the mysticism of later times *Was.* (184), in four classes, the so-called four classes of Tantras (*rgyud-sdé bži*): *byá-bai rgyud, spyód-pai rgyud, rnal-ₒbyór rgyud, rnal-ₒbyór bla-na-méd-pai rgyud;* yet *rgyud bži* is also the short title of a medical work consisting of four parts: *rtsá-bai rgyud, bšád-pai rgyud, man-ṅág rgyud, p̔yi-mai rgyud.* — 3. **connection, relation, reference,** e.g. of a word.(?) — 4. **character, disposition** of mind, natural quality; **heart, soul;** *rgyud bzáṅ-po* a good disposition, *rgyud ṅán-pa* a bad disposition; *rgyud ži-ba* a mild disposition, good nature, *rgyud ₒjám-pa* a soft temperament *Cs.*; *rgyud ma-rúṅs-pa* a wicked character *Thgy.*; *sem-gyú' C.*, *šē-gyü' C.*, *Mil.*, prob. also *rig-rgyúd Mil.*, character; *raṅ-rgyúd ṅán-pai ₒgón-po t̔ul* restrain the demon of your own wicked heart *Mil.*; of thoughts, feelings, passions, also of a *tiṅ-ṅe-ₒdzin* is said: *rgyúd-la skye* they arise in the soul; *rgyud smin* the mind ripens *Mil.*; in some phrases and passages it designates a man's whole personality: *ráṅ-gi rgyud t̔óg-tu lén-pa* to take (other people's) sufferings altogether upon one's own person (not merely to heart) *Glr.*; *raṅ-rgyúd-la brtág-pa, gžan-rgyúd-la sbyár-ba* to think a matter through in one's own mind, to draw conclusions from an attentive observation of others, *Thgy.* — Concerning *raṅ-rgyúd*, and *gžan-rgyúd* (**स्वतन्त्र & परतन्त्र**) in the more recent philosophical writings, and in medical works, v. *Was.* — *rgyud-čágs Tar.* 15, 14, acc. to *Schf.* sentence, thesis, point. — *don-rgyúd, sgrub-rgyúd Mil.?*

བརྒྱུད་པ་ *rgyúd-pa* I. vb., pf. *brgyus* and *brgyud*, fut. *brgyu*, imp. *rgyud*. 1. **to fasten or file** on a string, to string, *t̔á-gu-la brgyús-pa* strung, filed on a string *Stg.*; *gsér-nyag-t̔ag gyu brgyús-pa* a gold chain with turquoises inserted *Mil.* — 2. **to pass** through or over, **to traverse** (later literature and col.) *mú-ge rgyúd-nas ₒoṅ* famine passes over, prevails in the country *Ma.*; **náṅ-na naṅ gyúd-de dul* W.* he passes from one room to the other, he visits room after room; **nyúṅ-ti-ne gyúd-na gár-la t̔on* W.* he is passing through Kullu to Gar; *lag-ₒgrim-gyis brgyús-pas* v. *ₒgrim; yig-ṅór brgyúd-pa* an error in writing has crept in *Tar.*; *stón-pa gsum ras-čúṅ-pa brgyúd-nas zer* the three teachers, using *Ras-čuṅ-pa* as a go-between, said ..., = they sent word by *Ras-čuṅ-pa* to this effect *Mil.*

II. sbst. and adj. 1. prop. a participle used a. actively; *rgyúd-pa* (or *brgyud-pa*) one that is transmitting knowledge, **a teacher;** *rgyúd-pa bzáṅ-poi byin-rlabs-čan* one that enjoys the blessing of having an excellent spiritual teacher *Mil.*; *ṅai rgyúd-pa rdo-rje-ₒčaṅ-čén yin Mil.* (in this instance it would be justifiable to write *brgyúd-pa*, and, regarding this as a derivative of *brgyúd*, to translate it with 'ancestor'). — b. used passively: *rdo-rje-ₒčáṅ-nas nyams-rtógs rgyúd-pa de ná-ro lags* he to whom knowledge was communicated by *Dor-je-čáṅ* is *Nāro Mil.*; *nā-ro čen-poi rgyud-pa* **a scholar** of great *Nāro Mil.* — 2. a derivative of *rgyud* 2., a Tantrika, **a mystic.**

རྒྱུད་རིས་ *rgyud-ris* a term used in architecture, **wall, panel** (?).

རྒྱུད་ལོང་ *rgyud-lóṅ* **bolt, door-bar** *Sch.*

རྒྱུན་ *rgyun*, *Ssk.* **स्रोतस्** a continual flowing, **the flow, current** or **stream** (seldom river; perh. *smig-rgyui rgyun Lex.* a river seen by a mirage or fata morgana(?); *gáṅ-gai rgyun* the river Ganges); *ču-rgyún-gyis ₒkyér-ba* to be carried away by the current; *rgyún-du žúgs-pa* v. *ₒbrás-bu bži*; frq. fig. *t̔úgs-rjei rgyun* stream of grace *Glr.*, and sim. in some compounds; often in reference to time, hence *rgyún-du* **continually, perpetually, always,** *dus-rgyún-du* id.; **dhū-gyün ta-bhu jhē šig* C.* make it as usual!

sṅár-gyi rgyun all the time before, opp. to *du-ltar* now; also for **ordinarily, predominantly,** e.g. ordinarily it is white, only by way of exception it is of another colour; *k̔a-rgyún* = *ka-rgyúd* tradition; *rgyún-gos* an every day coat, opp. to *γzáb-gos*; *rgyun-ₒgág*, and more frq. *rgyun-č̔ád* an interruption of flowing, of progress, hence *rgyun-č̔ad-méd-par*, or *rgyun-mi-č̔ád-par* uninterruptedly; *rgyun-zás* daily food; *rgyun-riṅ-ba* lasting, of long continuance; *rgyun-lám* an endless, interminable way, to be pursued again and again, e.g. *ₒk̔ór-bai* of transmigration, *byaṅ-č̔úb-kyi* of virtue, holiness *Mil.*

རྒྱུས་ *rgyus* 1. v. *rgyu*. — 2. (*Cs. rgyús-ma*) **notice, intelligence, knowledge,** *ṅá-la dé-ī gyus yod* I am acquainted with it, I know the thing, I am up to it, frq.; *W.*: **gyus yód-k̔an** one that knows about it; **gyus yód-pai lam** a well-known road; *č̔a-méd yúl-du rgyus-méd ₒk̔yam* as a stranger I am rambling through a foreign country *Glr.*; *lo-rgyús* 1. **annals, chronicle,** 2. in a general sense **history, story, tale, narrative,** *lo-rgyús bśád-pa* to relate a story *Glr.*, **ṅá-la lo-gyús śád-č̔e máṅ-po yod** *W.* I have much to relate, to tell; *lo-rgyús žib-tu ₒdri-ba* to ask closely, to inquire minutely into a story *Mil.*; *góṅ-gi lo-rgyús bśád-do* he reported what was related above *Pth.*; also used of any short notice or intelligence, without reference to things past: *der ₒbyón-pai lo-rgyús γsuṅs* he mentioned that he was going there *Mil.*

རྒྱུས་པ་ *rgyus-pa* the fine threads or **fibres** of which animal muscle, plants etc. are composed; *rgyús-pa-č̔an* fibrous; *rgyus-skúd* **catgut.**

རྒྱོ་བ་ *rgyo-ba*, pf. *brgyos*, fut. *brgyo*, imp. *rgyos*, to unite in sexual embrace. This word is an undisguised, and therefore somewhat obscene expression, which in books and in col. language is avoided, though referring to an act not criminal in itself, as *Cs.* seems to have understood it, when he translates *rgyo-ba* by: to abuse, constuprate, ravish: hence it is allowable, yet vulgar, to say: **'á-pa daṅ 'á-ma gyó-wa ǰhe**: *C.*

རྒྱོང་བ་ *rgyóṅ-ba*, pf. *brgyaṅs*, fut. *brgyaṅ*, seems to be a secondary form of *rkyóṅ-ba*, **to extend, stretch, spread** (vb. a.); the word is to be found in *Lexx.*, but seems to be little used; *brgyáṅs-pai má-tsa Pth.* a disease consisting in some parts of the body being morbidly distended (?).

རྒྱོབ་པ་ *rgyób-pa Cs.*, a secondary form of *rgyáb-pa*, prob. but a provincialism.

ལྒ་ *lga*, also *sga*, शृङ्गवेर **ginger** (fresh or dried); *lga-rlon* fresh ginger.

ལྒང་ངེ་ *lgaṅ-ṅé Pth.*: *skya-lgaṅ-ṅé*, is stated to mean: **perfectly white.**

ལྒང་པ་ *lgáṅ-pa*, *lgaṅ-p̔úg* **urinary bladder** *Med.*

ལྒང་བུ་ *lgáṅ-bu*, = *gáṅ-bu*, **husk, pod, shell.**

ལྒའུ་གསེར་ *lgau-γsér Cs.* = *lga-rlon*.

ལྒོ་ *lgo Cs.* = *p̔a-ba-dgo-dgó* **puff-ball.**

ལྒྱམ་ཚྭ་ *lgyám-tswa* = *rgyám-tsa Zam.*, a kind of **rock-salt.**

སྒ་ *sga* 1. gen. *lč̔á-sga*, *bč̔a-sga*, **ginger,** = *lga*; *sga-skyá Lt.* id. (?); *sgá-pi-p̔o Lt.* prob. for *sga daṅ pi-pi-liṅ daṅ p̔ó-ba-ri* ginger and two kinds of black pepper; *sga-spyód Sch.* = *sga-skyá*. — 2. **saddle,** *rta-sga* (*Ld.* **stásga**) horse-saddle; *sga bstád-pa*, resp. *č̔ibs-sga bstád-pa Glr.*, to lay the saddle on, to saddle; *sga-k̔ébs* saddle-cloth, *Sch.*: the leather cover or coating of a saddle; *sga-gló* saddle-girth *W.*, *C.*; *sga-lág Cs.*: frame of the saddle; saddle-bow, saddle-tree; *sga-śá* straps for fastening the travelling-baggage to the saddle, cf. *śa-stág* 2.

སྒ་ཕོང་ *sga-p̔óṅ* **bat, flitter-mouse** *Sch.*

སྒང་ *sgaṅ* 1. a projecting **hill** or **spur,** or the side of a larger mountain; *sgaṅ-γšóṅ* elevations and depressions on a hill-side, in *Kun. sgaṅ-k̔úl*: *sgáṅ-k̔a-la yod* (the village) is situated on a mountain-spur; **sgaṅ gyáb-na** *W.* when you have passed round the extremity of the hill. — 2. *č̔u-*

sgáń **a blister,** caused by vesicatories, by long marches etc., *C., W.*; cf. *bsgań*.

སྒང་བ་ *sgań-ba*, pf. *bsgańs*, fut. *bsgań*, **to grow** or **become full** *Cs.; bud-méd ná-so sgań* a marrigeable girl.

སྒབ་པ་ *sgab-pa*, secondary form of *ˏgébs-pa, byá-mas bú-la sgab-pa* the covering of a young bird by its mother *Glr.*; *gos-sgáb Lex.*, skirt or lap of a coat, *sgab-túń* a short skirt.

སྒམ་ *sgam* **chest, box, trunk**; *sgam-čúń* a little chest or box; *sgam-bu* id.; *sgam-sgo-máńs* a chest of drawers, cabinet *C.*; *šiń-sgam* a wooden chest, *lčágs-sgam* an iron chest; *kó-sgam* a leather trunk; *ró-sgam*, resp. *spúr-sgam* coffin *Cs.* — syn. *sgrom*.

སྒམ་པ་ *sgám-pa*, or *sgám-po Cs.* **deep, profound,** *Sch.* also **prudent, quiet**; *Lex. blo-sgam* w.e. Only the following phrase came under my notice: *tugs šin-tu sgám-mo* he (the prince) is very clever (as a legendary explanation and confirmation of the name *sroń-btsan-sgám-po*). Prob. obsolete.

སྒར་ *sgar* **camp, encampment,** *dmag-sgár* a military camp, *sgar ˏdébs-pa* to pitch a camp; *sgar-míń C.* watch-word, parole, = *bso-sgrá*.

སྒལ་ *sgal* **load** of a beast of burden, *rta-sgal* a horse-load, *šiń-rtai sgal* a cart-load, waggon-load *Cs.*; *sgal ˏgél-ba* to put on a load, *ˏpán-ba* to throw it off, *ˏbógs-pa* to take it off, *sgal bsráń-ba* to adjust or balance it; *sgál-rta* pack-horse, *sgál-pyugs* beast of burden.

སྒལ་པ་ *sgál-pa* 1. **the small of the back,** *sgál-ˏdabs* the lumbar region *Med.* — 2 **the croup, crupper,** back of a horse *Glr.*; **gál-pa ton dug* W.* the back comes out, i.e. has become sore or galled; *sgal-tsigs-Med., sgal-rus* col. backbone, spine; *sgal-rmá* a sore on a animal's back caused by the load.

སྒུ་སྟེགས་ *sgu-stégs Lex.* w.e.; *Sch.* **elbow, angle.**

སྒུ་རྡོ་ *sgu-rdó* **a sling** *Sch.*

སྒུག་པ་ *sgúg-pa*, pf. *bsgugs*, fut. *bsgug*, imp. *sgug(s)*, **to wait,** *zlá-ba γčig sgúg-pa* to wait for a month *Glr.*; **to await, to expect,** *ˏči-ba* death *Mil.*; *lám-na sgúg-pa* to wait on the road *Mil.*; *sgúg-čiń sdód-pa, W.: *gúg-te dád-če** to sit waiting; **'i-ru gúg-te dód* W.* wait here! *sgug-tu ˏjug-pa* to keep one waiting *Glr.*; **to lie in wait** (for a person), **to waylay;** *jág-pas sgúg-pai sa* a place where robbers are lying in ambush *Mil.*; **kon gúg-te dád-če* W.* to bear a grudge, to have a spite against a person.

སྒུང་ *sguń Ld.* **clap, crack, crash, report** (of a gun).

སྒུད་པོ་ *sgud-po* **father-in-law,** *sgud-mo* mother-in-law *Sch.* prov.

སྒུམ་མདའ་ *sgum-mda Schr.* butt-end of a gun, **gun-stock** *C., W.*; spelling dubious.

སྒུར་ *sgur* v. *dgur*.

སྒུལ་བ་ *sgúl-ba* vb. a. (cf. *ˏgul-ba*), pf. and fut. *bsgul*, **to move; agitate,** put in motion, *rgyud kyań ma sgúl-to* he could not even move the bow-string *Dzl.*; to pull (e.g. the bell-string).

སྒེའུ་ *sgeu* 1. diminutive of *sga*, **ginger,** *sgeu-γsér Med., Ssk.* आर्द्रक (*Hind. adrak*), fresh ginger. — 2. **a small door.**

སྒེག་པ་ *sgég-pa Cs.:* **to boast, brag;** yet not so much with respect to words as to looks and demeanour, so that it may be applied to the airs of coquettish girls (*sgég-čiń mdzés-pa* coquettish *Mil., Stg.*) as well as to the bearing of insolent youngsters and bullies. *sgég-ma* n. of a goddess; *sgég-mo Lex.* लास्या, a dancing girl.

སྒེང་ལ་ *sgéń-la*, or *dgeń-la* (?) **on, upon** *Ts.*

སྒེར་ *sger Sch.:* 'different, dissimilar, foreign'. This word I repeatedly met with in books of physical science, without finding the signification given above applicable.

སྒོ་ *sgo* 1. **door,** the aperture itself, as well as the wood-work of the door: *sgo ˏbyéd-pa, W. *pé-če**, to open the door; **júg-pa** 1. *C.* to put in a door, to hang a door on hinges 2. *W.* to close, to shut the door;

γčód-pa 1. to shut, 2. to lock (a door); **gyág-pa, gyáb-pa** *C.*, to shut (the door); *γtán-pa Sch.:* 'to lock up', prop. to bolt, to bar, v. *sgo-γtán; bkúm-pa, bskúm-pa Cs.:* resp. to shut (a door); *sgo bdúṅ-ba* to knock, to rap at the door; **go šrúg-ga rag** *W.* I hear a rattling or rapping at the door. The ground floor of a house into which the door leads, is generally occupied by the cattle, hence: *sgoi p̀yugs* the cattle near the door, opp. to: *p̀úgs kyi nor* the money in the inner chamber farthest from the door, cattle and money being thus the two poles or terminating points of household property. — *rgyál-sgo* the principal door or entrance of a house or chamber (in *Ld.* also: **gyáz-go**). — *sgrig-sgo* folding-door *Cs.* — *čáb-sgo* resp. for *sgo Cs.*, cf. *γsáṅ-sgo.* — *rtá-sgo* a door which may be passed through on horseback, viz. the door or gate of a court-yard or garden, open at the top, or a high castle-gate; in the latter case syn. to *rgyál-sgo.* — *náṅ-sgo* the innermost door, *bár-sgo* the middle door, *p̀yi-sgo* the outer door *Pth.* — *ťsé-sgo* v. 2, *lás-sgo* v. 3. — *šél-sgo* glass-door; wing of a window, casement; *γsáṅ-sgo* secret door; *Cs.* resp, for *sgo* (?). — 2. **the boards** that form the pane or square of a door, hence **board, plank,** v. *sgo-rnám*; *ťsé-sgo* a Chinese punishment, consisting of a thick board with an opening for the neck of the culprit, and resting on his shoulders; *sgo γyóg-pa* to put on the board of punishment. — *bsé-sgo daṅ lčágs-sgo bdun sbrags* a door constructed of sevenfold layers of leather and iron, used as a butt for shooting at. — 3. the aperture of a door, and hence **aperture** in general: *sgo kún-nas* from all the apertures (of the body); *žál-gyi sgo* resp. mouth *Dzl.*; *mṅál-sgo* the opening of the womb (v. *mṅal*) frq.; *skyé-bai sgo* id. less frq. *Thgy.*; *dkyil-ˬkor sgo-bži-pa* a square figure with four openings, about thus: ⌜⌝⌞⌟; the opening of a semicircle; **entrance, passage, outlet,** connecting passage, communication; also fig.: way of mediation, of bringing an agreement about, *ṅan-sóṅ-gi sgo* the entrance, the road, to misery viz.: to hell; *dbáṅ-p̀oi sgo* the organs of sense, also *sgo lṅa* alone; *sgo-γsúm* the three media or spheres of moral activity, *lus, ṅag, yid*, action, word and thought frq.; *bzá-ba daṅ btúṅ-bai sgo ˬp̀rog-pa* to cut off the supply (of provisions) *Pth.*; *bdag čos sgor ˬjug-pa žu* I beg to allow us to enter religion, to receive us as students or disciples *Mil.*; *ˬgró-sgo Schr.* 1. also *búd-go, kyág-go W.*, expense, expenditure 2. *dó-go-tar šé'-pa C.* to relate accurately how a thing came to pass; *lás-sgo* 'door of intercourse, of trade', a commercial place or town, emporium *Glr.* Hence *sgó-nas* with the genit. **by means of, by,** in the way of, according to, but never as connected with a person or joined to an infinitive: *ťabs dú-mai sgó-nas* in different ways, variously (often coinciding with: by various means); *lus ṅag yid-kyi sgó-nas* in or by actions, words, and thoughts (e.g. to strive for virtue, cf. above *sgo-γsúm*) *Dzl.*; *rnám-pa sna-ťsógs-kyi sgó-nas* in every possible way *Dzl.*; *dpei sgó-nas* (to explain) by way of comparison *Thgy.*; *mťsan-nyid-kyi sgó-nas* (to describe a thing) according to its characteristics *Thgy.*; *rigs-kyi sgó-nas* (to divide) according to the species *Lt.*; *ˬdrá-bai sgó-nas btags-miṅ ste* it being a name given to it from its resemblance to ... *Wdṅ.*; ... *la p̀rag-dóg-gi sgó-nas* from envy of ... *Mil.*; *mi-snáṅ-bai sgó-nas* by way of invisibility, by being invisible *Wdṅ.*

Comp. and deriv. *sgo-k̀áṅ* the entrance into a house, **vestibule, porch, portal** — *sgo-k̀úṅ* opening of the door *Mil.* — *sgo-k̀yi* a door-guarding dog, **watch-dog.** — *sgo-ˬk̀ór* **hinge** of a door or gate. — *sgo-glágs Zam.* = *sgo-γtán* (?). — *sgo-glégs* **the board** or **plank** of a door *Cs.* — *sgo-ˬgrám* the space near the door. — *sgo-ˬdrig* (*Ld.* **sgon-dig**) **door-frame,** window-frame. — *sgo-rgyáb* the space behind the door, within the door *Glr.* — **go-čág** (*lčags*) *C.* **lock** of a door. — **go(g)-tán** a bar or bolt (a small beam) to secure the door with. —

sgo-ṫém **threshold,** also **the head-piece** of a door. — *sgo-bdág* = *sgo-dpón*. — *sgo-rnám* a single **board,** e. g. of the floor. — *sgó-pa*, resp. *čábs-sgo-pa* **door-keeper, porter;** *sgo-dpón* the first, principal door-keeper. — **go-ṗiṅ** *W.* **door-hinge.** — *sgo-ₒpár* **board** or **plank** of a door *Cs.* — *sgo-bár Ld.* **chinks** between the separate laths of a door (for of such the doors in Tibet frequently consist, owing to the scarcity of wood). — *sgó-ma* 1. **pane** or **square** of a door, **fold** of a folding-door; 2. a masked dancer in religious dramatic entertainments, representing one of the four guardians of the world (v. *rgyal-čén*). — *sgó-mo* 1. **a large door, a gate, castle-gate, town-gate;** 2. **beginning,** *rtsis-kyi sgó-mo Pth.* = *rtsis-ₒgo Cs.* (Chronol. Table) beginning of a new epoch. — *sgo-mtsáms* the small opening left between door-post and door, when the latter does not perfectly fit. — *sgo-yig Cs.* 1. **inscription,** 2. **lampoon, libel,** 3. a magisterial **advertisement** fastened to a door. — *sgo-lá* n. of a high and difficult mountain-pass between Lhasa and Paṅ, v. Huc. I. p. 244. — *sgo-sruṅ* **door-keeper, porter** *Dzl.*

སྒོ *sgo*, in *skyé-sgo* v. sub *sgó-po*.

སྒོ་ང་ *sgo-ṅá* or *sgoṅ-ṅá* and *sgoṅ*, **egg, eggs, spawn,** also **egg** as a measure *Lt.*; *sgoṅ-dkrís* the pellicle, membrane of an egg *Sch.*; *sgóṅ-čú* the white of an egg *Sch.*; *sgoṅ-šún*, or *kog*, the shell of an egg; *sgoṅ-sér* yolk of an egg *Sch.* — *sgo-ṅa ṗyed* a scholastic term, v. *Was.* (274).

སྒོ་པུར་ *sgo-púr* **foreskin, prepuce** *C.* vulg.

སྒོ་པོ་ *sgó-po* also *sgó-bo*, (*Ld.* **gó-po**) *W.* 1. **the body,** with respect to its physical nature and appearance, **gó-po čén-mo, riṅ-mo, go-riṅ, go-záṅ** tall, **gó-po čúṅ-se** of small stature, short; **róm-po** stout, lusty; **ṭ̔á-mo** slender, thin; **dé-mo** healthy, well; **go-yál** a man that has lost his own body by gaming and become the slave of another. — 2. = *skyé-sgo* **face, countenance,** *skye-sgo legs* a beautiful face, *žáṅ-sgo* an ugly face *Mil.* — *sgó-lo* 1. **body,** 2. **face,** as a flattering word; also directly for a nice or pretty face, **gó-lo min dug bag ṫsogs yod** she has not a pretty face, but looks like a fright *W.*

སྒོ་བ་ *sgó-ba*, pf. *bsgo* (*bsgos* in *Lexx.*, prob. obsolete) **to say,** when used of superiors, hence mostly **to bid, to order** (cf. the article *bka* init.), frq. in early literature, in later times more and more disappearing, being unknown to the common people.

སྒོ་ཙམ་ *sgo-tsám* **a little** *Sch.*

སྒོ་ལོ་ *sgó-lo* 1. v. *sgó-po*. — 2. *Ld.* also = *sgo-ṅá*.

སྒོག་པ་ *sgóg-pa*, (*Ssk.* लशुन) **garlic, leek,** (Allium); *ri-sgóg Med.* Allium sphaeroceph. *L.*, or a species allied to it; *sgog-skyá Med.* Allium nivale Jacqm. (?); *sgog-sṅón Med.* perh. A. rubellum, a blue species, very common in the Himalaya. — *sgog-tiṅ* mortar, *sgog-ytún* pestle, for bruising leek.

སྒོག་པ་ *sgóg-pa* 1. *Cs.*: 'pf. *bsgags*, fut. *bsgag*, to make one swear, *sgóg-po* one that makes a person swear.' I only met with *mna-sgóg Lex.* w. e. — 2. *yya sgóg-pa* v. *yya*.

སྒོང་ *sgoṅ* 1. v. *sgo-ṅá*. — 2. n. of a country, prob. = *koṅ Glr.* — 3. *sgoṅ-ṫóg-pa* n. of a plant *Med.*

སྒོང་བ་ *sgóṅ-ba*, pf. *bsgoṅs*, fut. *bsgoṅ*, imp. *sgoṅ* (*s*), 1. **to make round, globular** *Cs.*; so it is prob. to be understood in: *bu-rám bsgár-žiṅ bsgráṅs-nas bsgoṅs Lex.*, he having boiled down the sugar and allowed it to grow cold, formed it into balls (in this form the sugar is usually kept in Tibet). — 2. **to hide** or **conceal** a thing *Sch.*, thus in **góṅ-te bór-če** *W.*; cf also *dpá-sgoṅ-ba*.

སྒོབ་སྒོབ་ *sgob-sgób* **unable, deficient,** wanting in strength *Sch.*; **lág-pa gob-soṅ** *Kun.* the hands are unable (to move), stiff (from cold).

སྒོམ་ *sgom* **reflection, meditation, contemplation,** *sgom šór-gyi dógs-pa* the fear lest contemplation should be prejudiced or rendered impossible *Mil.*; *sgom srúṅ-ba* to sustain, to preserve meditation (undisturbed) *Mil.*; *sgom-méd* without meditation *Thgr.*

སྒོམ་པ *sgóm-pa* I. vb., pf. *bsgoms*, fut. *bsgom*, imp. *sgom(s)*, resp. *tugs sgóm-pa* (*Ssk.* भू, *causative* भावय) 1. originally: **to fancy, imagine; meditate, contemplate, consider,** c. accus. and dat.; **to have, to entertain, to produce** in one's mind, = *skyéd-pa*, e. g. *bzód-pa*, *snyíṅ-rje*, *byáms-pa* etc.; *rgyún-du nam ₒči čá-med sgom* always consider that it is uncertain at what time you shall die *Mil.*; with the accus. and termin., or with a double accus.; **to look upon,** to represent to one's self as . . ., *ₒgró-drug-séms-čan p̔á-mar sgom* look upon the beings of the six classes as being your parents *Mil.*, viz. with the same respect and affection, or even so, that you imagine your father's or your mother's soul inhabiting just now the animal body of one of those beings; *rmí-lam sgyú-ma sgom* look upon it as being the illusion of a dream *Mil.* — 2. In later times *sgóm-pa* became the usual term for the systematic **meditation** of the Buddhist saint, so that this word, and the expressions *tiṅ-ṅe-ₒdzín-du ₒjúg-pa*, and *bsam-γtán sgrúb-pa*, which in classical writings denote the concentration of the mind upon one point or subject, e. g. upon a certain deity, *lha*, prob. imply one and the same thing. Three degrees of this systematic meditation are to be distinguished, viz. *ltá-ba* contemplation, *sgóm-pa* meditation, properly so called, (which requires *γsal daṅ mi-rtog má-γyeṅs γsum*, i.e. that it be performed in a clear and decided manner, without suffering one's self to be disturbed or distracted by any thing), and the third degree *spyód-pa*, exercise and practice, which three distinctions will be somewhat elucidated by the following: *bzá(-bai)-γtad(-so) yód-na bltá-ba min, byíṅ-rgod yód-na sgóm-pa min, bláṅ-dor yód-na spyód-pa min*, if one lives plenteously, there is no contemplation (possible); where there is inattention and a distracted mind, meditation cannot take place; where there is desire or disgust, exercise and practice are not (to be thought of) *Mil.* 14, 11. Hence contemplation would seem to be more immediately opposed to the rule of sense, meditation to the rule of imagination, practice to the rule of passion; v. also *Was.* (137), *Köpp.* I, 585. Sometimes contemplation and meditation are also opposed to *tós-pa*, and *bsám-pa*, hearing and knowing, as to mere acts of memory and intellect. — *sgóm(-pa)-po Cs.*, *sgom-byéd*, *sgóm-mk̔an Mil.* one that meditates, **an ascetic;** *sgóm-ma* fem. *Mil.* — *sgom-čén* 1. **a great meditator** (so *Mil.* often calls himself). 2. a kind of **field-mouse,** Lagomys badius *Hook.* II, 156. — *sgom-tág* 'meditating-cord', a cord or rope slung by the laxer sects round their bodies, in order to facilitate the effort of maintaining an erect and immoveable posture during meditation, which expedient of course is scorned by the more rigid devotees.

II. sbst. 1. **meditation.** — 2. *Cs.*: 'the state of being accustomed to' (prob. erron. for *goms-pa*).

སྒོམ་འབྲོག *sgom-ₒbróg* (?) **holly,** Ilex. *Sik.*

སྒོར་ *sgor* a spindle in turning-lathes? v. the next word.

སྒོར་བ་ *sgór-ba* 1. pf. and fut. *bsgar*, **to boil down,** to condense by boiling, e. g. *bu-rám* sugar. — 2. **to turn** on a lathe, *W.* **gór-la tén-če**.

སྒོར་མོ *sgór-mo* (perh. also *skór-mo*) 1. **round,** e. g. of leaves, *Wdṅ.* and elsewh. — 2. **a circle.** — 3. **a disk, a globe;** hence **a** rupee *W.*; a semi-globular bowl or **vessel** *W.*, *sgor-tig* circular line, circumference, circle; *sgor-tig p̔yé-ba Cs.*, *p̔yéd-ka Schr.* semicircle.

སྒོས་ *sgos*, in compounds and as adverb: **private, separate, distinct; privately** etc., opp. to *spyi*, e. g. *spyi-γdugs* a parasol for several persons, awning, shelter, *sgos-γdugs* a parasol for one person *Glr.*; *sgós-skal* share of a single person, individual lot

Mil.; *sgós-su*, or *sgos* adv., (opp. to *spyir*) particularly, especially; *sgos-(kyi), dpon* a subaltern officer *Cs.*; *sgós-pa Sch.*: 'to choose, to find the right thing'.

སྒྱིའུ་, སྒྱིག་གུ *sgyiu, sgyig-gu* **bag, purse;** *sgyig-gu čád-poi dbáṅ-du sóṅ-nas* our purse being at low ebb; *dṅul-sgyig* money-bag, purse.

སྒྱིང་བ་ *sgyiṅ-ba*, pf. *bsgyiṅs*, fut *bsgyiṅ*, 1. acc. to *Lexx.* = *Ssk.* जभ syn. to *glál-ba*, **to yawn, gape,** and perh. to stretch one's self after having slept; it is almost exclusively used in describing the attitude of a dying lion, and so also the dying attitude of Buddha. — 2. perh. also = *ˌgyiṅ-ba*.

སྒྱིད་(པ་) *sgyid(-pa)* 1. the hollow of the knee, bend of the knee; **knee-joint;** *sgyid-pa γčód-pa* to lame the knee-joint, to hamstring (a horse) *Glr.* — 2. **the calf** (of the leg) *Mil.*; *sgyid skyúr-ba* acute pain in the knee and leg e.g. of a woman with child *Med.; Cs.*: 'to despair'? — *sgyid-ḱúṅ* the hollow of the knee *Med.* — *sgyid-ḱyól* one lame in his legs *Cs.* — *sgyid-lug-pa Lex.* w. e., *Cs.*: slothful, idle, lazy; *sgyid-lhód Sch.* id.

སྒྱིད་བུ་ *sgyid-bu*, also *sgyéd-bu*, **a hearth, fire-place,** consisting of (three) stones on which the kettle is placed; *lčags-sgyid* iron trevet, tripod, cf. *sgyéd-po*.

སྒྱུ *sgyu* **artifice, imposture** *Dzl.* and elsewh., *γyo-sgyú* id.; *γyo-sgyu-med-na* if he is without guile *Dzl.*; *sgyu-čan* artful, crafty, cunning, *Cs.* — *sgyu-ˌṗrúl-ma*, माया, the name of Buddha's mother. — *sgyú-ma*, माया, **illusion,** false show, deception of sight, opp. to *dṅos* reality; *sgyu-ma sprul-ba* to exhibit a false show *Cs.*; *ṅas snáṅ-ba tams-čád sgyú-mar śes* I know that every thing visible, the whole external world, is only an illusion *Mil.*; *sgyú-mai nor* apparent riches, hence riches in general *Mil.* (cf. *sgyu-lús*); *sgyú-ma-mḱan* **a juggler** *Mil.*; *sgyú-ma-mḱan-gyi mčán-bu, sgyu-mai mčán-bu* a juggler's apprentice *Lexx.* — *sgyu-rtsál* **art, skill, dexterity,** frq., the Indians, and so also the Tibetans counting 64 arts (or 60 in a round number) *Tar.* 21, 2. — *sgyu-zóg* **deception, hypocrisy** *Pth.* — *sgyu-lús* 1. the immaterial, subtile and pure body of the soul in the Bardo, hell etc., hence = *yid-kyi lus Thgr.* 2. the animal and human body in general, in as much as it is only an apparent body, a phantom, when considered from a higher philosophical point of view *Mil.*

སྒྱུག་མོ་ *sgyúg-mo* **mother-in-law** *Stg.*; *mna-sgyúg* both daughter-in-law and mother-in-law.

སྒྱུར་བ་ *sgyúr-ba*, pf. and fut. *bsgyur*, (vb. a. to *ˌgyúr-ba*) 1. **to transform,** *lus ˌdod-dgúr* to transform one's body (i. e. one's self) at pleasure, (*Dzl.* ༢ཿ *lus* is to be supplied, or *gyúr-te* to be read); to transform the royal prerogative into a religious one, v. *ḱrims*. — 2. **to change** (colour, one's mind), **to alter** (something written), hence **to correct, to revise.** — 3. **to give up, leave off** (customs, scruples, doubts, timidity) *Glr.*, *ṗyi-rol-pai čós-lugs* the non-Buddhist religion. — 4. **to turn** off or aside (the course of a river); **to dissuade, divert,** *las.* from *Dzl.* — 5. **to turn,** **ǰiṅ pa gyúr-če* W.* to turn round on one's heel; **ǰiṅ-pa gyúr-te ltá-če* W.* to look back; *ḱór-lo sgyúr-ba* to turn a wheel = *skór-ba*; *skad sgyúr-ba* to vary, to modulate the voice, also to hum a tune, to sing or whistle, as birds do. — 6. **to govern,** *rtai ḱa sráb-kyis*, a horse's mouth by the bridle; also fig. **gyál-po ḱa lón-gyi gyur, ḱyo̱ ḱa čúṅ-mẹ gyur* C.* the king is governed by his minister, the husband by his wife; *ˌdod-čágs ṅán-pas ḱa-sgyur* he is governed by evil passions *Mil.*; *ḱá-lo sgyúr-ba* to govern, prop. and fig., v. *ḱá-lo*; *śiṅ-rta sgyúr-ba* to drive a carriage; in a similar sense *dbaṅ sgyúr-ba* c. *la*, to have command or control of, to command, dominate, frq.; prob. also to possess *Mil.* — 7. **to translate,** *sgra sgyúr-ba* id. — 8. **to multiply** *Wdk.* (cf. *ˌgyúr-ba* 4, and *lóg-pa*); *bsgyúr-bya* the multiplicand *Wdk.* — 9. *Lad.*, *Pur.* **to kill, to slaughter.** — 10. **to publish, proclaim, announce** **ka-sál gyúr-če* W.* to publish an order; **lon gyur** *W.* announce me! send in my name!

སྒྱེ་སྒུར *sgye-sgúr* **crooked** *Sch.*, better *dgye.*

སྒྱེ་བོ *sgyé-bo* is said to denote in *C.* one of the lower classes of officials or noblemen.

སྒྱེ་མོ *sgyé-mo* 1. sbst. **a bag** (not of leather); *ras-sgyé* a bag of cotton stuff *Pth.*; *sgyeu* diminutive. — 2. adj. **quiet, gentle** (of horses) *Sp.*

སྒྱེད་པོ *sgyéd-po* a stone for a fire-place, **hearth-stone, three of** which are so placed together, that a fire may be kindled between them and a kettle put on; *sgyid-bu* a fire-place constructed in this manner.

སྒྱེལ་བ *sgyél-ba*, pf. and fut. *bsgyel*, vb. a. to *ˏgyél-ba*, **to throw down, to overthrow, overturn,** *gan-kyáb* on the back *Lex.*; **to lay** or **put down** (a bottle, a book); **to thwart** (the charm of an enemy); **to kill** (horses); **mi sẹ', ta gyel** manslaughter and the killing of horses, *Ç.*

སྒྱོགས *sgyogs* 1. a warlike engine to shoot darts or fling stones with, **catapult, ballista,** *sgyógs-kyi ˏp̔rul-ˏk̔ór Thgr.* id; *sgyogs-rdo* a stone flung from such a machine *Sch.*; in later times: 2. **mortar, cannon, gun,** in Tibet even at the present day without wheels, col. **ghyog**. — 3. a surgeon's instrument for setting broken limbs *Cs.*

སྒྱོང་བ *sgyóṅ-ba*, pf. *bsygaṅs*, fut. *bsgyaṅ*, perh. originally = *sgóṅ-ba* to hide, but actually used 1. in *C.*: **gyú-ma gyáṅ-wa** **to fill, to stuff** (a sausage) 2. col. in *W.*: **gyáṅ-če** **to put** into (the pocket, a box, a coffin); **gyáṅ-du bór-če** **to keep, lock,** or **shut up** (things); **úgs gyáṅ-če** to hold one's breath; *gla p̔yir sgyóṅ-ba* **to retain** the wages due to another person *Sch.* The form *rgyaṅs* often occurs in *Mil.*, in passages where 'to retain, lock up, put into' or a similar term would suit very well. Other passages cannot yet be sufficiently accounted for, and upon the whole the roots *gyaṅ* and *kyaṅ* (*rgyaṅ* etc.) require to be more closely investigated.

སྒྲ *sgra*, *W.* also **ra**, 1. **a sound, noise; voice;** *há-sgra* the sound *h Glr.*; *sgrá-bčas ˏk̔ru* noisy evacuations **take place** *Lt.*; *ˏón-pa-dag sgrá-rnams ťos* the deaf hear sounds; *sgra sgróg-pa* to produce sounds, noises *Mil.*; *sgra dag γsal γsum* (read) loud, correctly, and distinctly, those three (a precept for reading or reciting); **nyid-ra ťúṅ-če** *W.* to snore; **šóg-ra** the noise made by a flight of birds passing; *miṅ-sgra* a mere word, name, or sound *Was.*, as a philosophical term. — 2. **word, syllable,** *bdág-sgra Cs.*, *bdág-poi sgra Gram.*, the name given in grammar to the so-called article *pa*, e.g. in *rtá-pa* horseman, rider; *dgág-sgra* prohibitive or negative particle. — 3. **language,** science of languages, **philology.**

Comp. *sgra-skád* (= *sgra* 1.) **sound, voice,** *sgra-skád snyán-pa* frq. — *sgrá-čan* **sounding, sonorous.** — *sgra-čé* **far-famed, renowned** *Mil.*. *sgra čer graγspa Stg.* id. — *sgra-snyán* 1. **a well-sounding, agreeable voice,** 2. *C.* **a guitar.** — *sgra-brnyán* **echo** *Mil.* — *sgrá-ldar* **sounding, sonorous.** — *sgra lbyáṅs* 1. **pleasing tone, harmony, euphony,** e.g. *glu daṅ ról-moi Tar.* 2. n. of a goddess *Cs.* — *sgra-sbyór Zam.*, *Tar.*, *Schf.*, a coalition or connection of letters. — *sgra-mi-snyán* (a disagreeable voice) n. of a larger and two smaller northern continents of the fabulous geography of ancient India. — *sgra-ťsád* (*sgra daṅ ťsad-ma*) *Tar.*, *Schf.*: grammar and logic; yet *yi-gei sgra-ťsád*, *sgra-ťsad-yi-ge Glr.* seem to denote philology.

སྒྲ་གཅན *sgra-γčán*, *Ssk.* राहु *Rāhu*, 1. a demon or monster of Indian mythology, esp. known by his being at enmity with the Sun and Moon, on whom he is continually wreaking his vengeance, occasionally swallowing them for a time and thereby causing their eclipses. The Buddhist representation of the Rāhu-legend is given by *Schl.* p. 114 — 2. *Cs.*: **the ascending node** of the moon, determining the time of the obscurations. — *sgra-γčán-*

dzin, राहुल *Rāhula* 1. 'seized by Rāhu' (*Fouc. Gyatch.* II, LVII), obscured, eclipse of the sun or moon, 2. 'catcher of Rāhu,' acc. to the Tibetan legend an epithet given to the deity *ṗyag-rdór*, acc. to Indian mythology, to Vishnu, who in Tibetan is called *ḱyab-ǰúg* (also *ḱyab-ǰug-γsód Cs.*); sometimes, however, he is identified with Rāhu himself, for the names *γza-sgra-γčan*, *γza-sgra-γčan-dzin*, *γza-ḱyab-ǰúg*, *γza-rā-hu-la*, and even *γza-du-ba-ǰug-riṅ* (comet!) are used promiscuously. — 3. a son and disciple of Shakyamuni, who received this name on account of an eclipse of the moon taking place at his birth, v. *Fouc. Gyatch.* II, 389.

སྒྲང་བ་ *sgráṅ-ba*, *Cs.*: pf. *bsgraṅs*, fut. *bsgraṅ*, imp. *sgroṅ*, 1. **to enumerate**, to reckon up separately. — 2. **to upbraid, to reproach.**

སྒྲལ་བ་ *sgrál-ba* **to cut** into small pieces, viz. the picture of an enemy whom one wishes to destroy.

སྒྲིག་པ་ *sgrig-pa*, pf. *bsgrigs*, fut. *bsgrig*, imp. *sgrig(s)*, *W.* **rig-če**, **to lay** or **put in order, to arrange, adjust,** *paṅ-léb* boards or planks, *so-ṗág* bricks or tiles *Glr.*, *kar-yól* plates and dishes, = to lay the cloth; *γdan* stuffed seats or chairs *Dzl.*; **to put** or **fit together, to join** the separate parts of an animal body *Glr.*; to put close together, side by side, hence *W.*: **žiṅ de nyis rig-te yod** these two fields are adjacent, **ťa daṅ rig-te yin** it is situated close to the border; **to compile, to write** books *Glr* — **rig-mo** *W.* **tight, close,** e.g a joint, commissure, seam.

སྒྲིན་པོ་ *sgrin-po*, *Zam.*: = *mḱás-pa*, **prudent, skilful, clever,** *blo sgrin-pa* a penetrating mind *Sch.*

སྒྲིབ་པ་ *sgrib-pa* 1. vb. pf. *bsgribs*, fut. *bsgrib*, imp. *sgrib(s)*, *W.* **rib-če**, to deprive of light, **to darken, to obscure,** *W.* **rib ma rib** get out of my light! *nyi-mai ʼod-zér bsgribs-nas* the light of the sun being obscured, by clouds *Glr*, by a curtain *Zam.* — 2. sbst. the state of being darkened, **obscuration,** gen. fig., mental darkness, **sin,** also *sgrib*; *séms-čan ťams-čád-kyi sgrib-pa sél-ba* frq., hence *sgrib-pa-rnam-sél* n. of a Boddhisatva; *sgrib-pa lňa Dzl.*, the five obscurations caused by sin, prob. = पञ्चकषाय *Burn.* II, 360. — 3. adj **darkened, obscured, dark; sinner,** *bdag-ráṅ sgrib-pa čé-am* am I so great a sinner? *Pth.* — **dib-ma** *C.*, **rib-ma** *W.* **shelter, fence,** e.g. at the side of a field against the wind.

སྒྲིམ་པ་ *sgrim-pa*, pf. *bsgrims*, fut. *bsgrim*, imp. *sgrim(s)*, *Cs.*: **'to hold fast, to force** or **twist together; to endeavour'**; *Sch.* also: **'to squeeze in, cram in; to be overhasty, confused'.** Only the following phrases came to my notice: **ḱúʼ-pa ḍim-pa** *C.* to twist or twine a thread; **rig-pa ḍim** *C.* take care! (collect your thoughts!); **ḍim-tog-čan** *Sp.* inquisitive, curious. Some passages in *B.*, e.g. *blo-bsgrims* (explained by *blo-ʼdás Zam.*) are as yet dubious as to their sense.

སྒྲིལ་བ་ *sgril-ba*, pf. and fut. *bsgril*, *W.* *(*s*)*ril-če**, (cf. *ʼgril-ba* 1. and *ʼḱril-ba*), 1. **to wind** or **wrap round** e.g. a bit of cloth round one's finger; **to roll, wrap,** or **wind up;** *ril-bur* to roll or form into a pill *Med.*; **to make fast** or **tight,** *lhód-pa* what is loose; *ṗyogs γčig-tu sgril-ba* to gather into a heap, **to heap** or **pile up, to sweep together;** hence *sgril-bas* (also *dril-bas Glr.*) **to sum up all,** taking all together, in short *Lt.*; *mǰúg-ma sgril-ba* **to wag** the tail, *mi-la* at a person (of dogs) *Mil.*; **to roll,** e.g. a large stone to some place. — 2. **to multiply** *Wdk.*, frq.; *bsgril-ma* a doubled and twisted thread or cord *Sch.*; *sgril-šiṅ* a wooden roll, round which paper etc. is wound; the rolling-pin of bakers. — *sgril-šóg*, *W.* **šog-ril**, rolled paper *Cs.*

སྒྲུག་པ་ *sgrug-pa*, pf. *bsgrugs*, fut. *bsgrug*, imp. *sgrug(s)*, *W.* **rúg-če(s)**, **to collect, gather, pluck, pick up** e.g. wood, flowers, vermin etc.

སྒྲུང(ས)་ *sgruṅ(s)*, *Ld.* **šruṅs**, *C.* **ḍum**, **fable, legend, tale** (to the uncultivated mind of the Tibetan, destitute of any physical and historical knowledge of the countries and people beyond the boundaries of his native soil, the difference between truth and fable is but vague and unsettled); *sgruṅ ˳čád-pa* to relate fables, stories etc.; *sṅon-rábs sgrúṅ Zam.*, *sṅón-gyi sgruṅ-rgyúd Glr.*, *sgruṅ-ɣtám* tales of ancient times, of the days of yore; *sgrúṅ-mk'an Cs.*, *sgrúṅ-pa Sch.* the inventor or writer of fables and tales, also a narrator of tales.

སྒྲུང་བ་ *sgrúṅ-ba*, pf. *bsgruṅs*, fut. *bsgruṅ*, 1. **to mix.** 2. **to invent, to feign** *Cs.*

སྒྲུན་པ་ *sgrún-pa*, pf. and fut. *bsgrun* 1. **to compare** c. *la* and *daṅ Dzl.* — 2. **to emulate, vie, contend with** *Cs.*

སྒྲུབ་པ་ *sgrúb-pa* I. vb. pf. *bsgrubs*, fut. *bsgrub*, imp. *sgrub(s)* (cf. *˳grúb-pa Ssk.* साध) 1. **to complete, finish, perform, carry out,** an order, a wish, hence usually with *bžin-du Dzl.*; **to make, achieve, manufacture, obtain, attain,** *dṅúl-rdo-la dṅul bsgrúb-tu btúb-pa ltar sems-čan-la Saṅs-rgyás bsgrúl-tu btúb-pa yin-no* in like manner as silver is obtained from silver-ore, Buddha may proceed from beings *Thgy.*; *don sgrúb-pa* to attain to one's aim, to obtain a blessing, a boon; *tse ˳dii don sgrúb-pa* to care for the wants of this life; **to procure,** *rgyágs-p̀ye* flour, as provision for a journey *Mil.*; *nor sgrúb-pa* **to gain** riches; **to furnish with, to supply,** one's self or others *Mil.* — 2. *lha-sgrúb-pa* implies, in accordance to Brahmanic-Buddhistic theology, not so much the making a deity propitious to man (*Cs.*), as rendering a god subject to human power, forcing him to perform the will of man. This coercion of a god seems to be effected in a twofold manner. The practise of the common people is to perform a vast amount of prayers and conjurations, specially intended for the god that is to be made subject. Another method is adopted by saints, who are advanced in every kind of religious knowledge. They continue their *sgóm-pa*, or profound meditation, for months and years, until the deity, finally overcome, stands before them visible and tangible, nay, until they have been personally united with and, as it were, incorporated into the invoked and subjected god. Whilst the conatus, the labouring in his arduous undertaking, is often called *sgrúb-pa*, the arriving at the proposed end is designated by *grúb-pa*, e.g. *rgyál-pos rta-mgrin sgrúb-pa mdzád-pas ˳grúb-nas rta-skád btón-pas* etc., the king began to coerce *Taḍin* (*Hayagrîwa*), and when the latter was made obsequious, so as to appear, a neighing was heard etc. *Glr.*; *sgom-sgrúb byéd-pa* for *sgóm-pa daṅ sgrúb-pa byéd-pa Mil.* — *bsgrub-k'áṅ*, *sgrub-ɣnás*, *sgrub-p̀úg* the house, the place, the cavern, where a saint applies himself to *sgrúb-pa*; *sgrúb-pa-po* one effectuating the coercion described above, *Sambh.* frq. — *sgrub-rtágs* tokens, proofs of perfection, of an accomplished saint. — *sgrub-ťábs* the method of effecting the coercion, of obliging a god to make his appearance; *sgrub-byéd* 1. he that accomplishes the coercion (cf. *Schl.* p. 247). 2. a kind of bile *Med.* — *sgrub-ɣšén* the Bon-doctrine *Mil.*

II. sbst. 1. one that contemplates and meditates, like *sgom-čén Mil.* 2. n of a sect of Lamas, with whom marriage is permitted.

སྒྲེ་བ་ *sgré-ba* I. *Cs.* adj. **naked,** gen. *sgren-mo.*

II. vb. pf. *bsgres*, fut. *bsgre* (cf. *˳gre-ba*) 1. **to roll** *Glr.*, *Pth.* — 2. **to multiply** *Wdk.* — 3. **to repeat** *Cs.* — 4. **to put** or **place in order, to put together, to compare,** e.g. records *Tar.* 174, 14 *Schf.*

སྒྲེ་ཟློག *sgre-zlóg* a sea-washed beach *Sch.*

སྒྲེག་པ་ *sgrég-pa* 1. vb. pf. *sgregs*, **to belch.** — 2. sbst. **belch, eructation,** *sgrég-pa ˳dón-pa, ˳byin-pa Med.* **rul-ḍág** *C.* a belch of a fetid smell.

སྒྲེང་བ་ *sgréṅ-ba*, pf. *bsgreṅs*, fut. *bsgreṅ*, imp. *sgreṅ(s)*, cf. *˳gréṅ-ba*, 1. **to raise, erect,** lift up, hold up, plant up, e.g. a finger, a beam etc. — 2. **to stretch out** a limb and hold it stiff *C.*

སྒྲེན་མོ་ *sgrén-mo* **naked,** *sgrén-mor ˳byúṅ-ba* to appear in a naked state, to show one's self naked *Dzl.*; *Bhar.* 59. *Schf.* 'orbus', orphaned (cog. to *bkren?*).

སྒྲོ་ *sgro* 1. a large **feather**, esp. quill-feather, used for an ornament of arrows, as a charm etc.; *sgro-mdóṅs* peacock's feather, as a badge of dignity. 2. **to elevate, exalt, increase;** *Cs.:* **to exaggerate.** *Was.* however has p. (305): 'Vorurtheil (Anerkennung des Nichtwahren), Gegensatz: *skur-₀débs* Lästerung (Leugnung des Wahren)', and p. (297): '*sgro-skúr* Verneinen und Lästerung'. *Cs.* renders *sgro-skúr* by 'exaggerated praise and blame'; *sgro-skúr ₀débs-ba* occurs also in *Mil.* The phrase *sgro-₀dógs γčód-pa* might therefore be rendered: to put an end to overrating and to prejudice; this meaning, however, does not suit in every instance, and acc. to expressions heard from people in *C.*, *sgro-₀dógs γčód-pa* would signify: to turn to account, to work one's way up, to contest for a prize. Finally ought to be mentioned that acc. to *Schr. sgro-₀dógs spyód-pa* (sic) denotes 'logic'. A connection between these heterogeneous significations is not discernible, but a clew may perhaps be found hereafter. — 3. **sack, bag** (?), *tál-sgro Glr.* was explained by: a sack full of ashes.

སྒྲོ་ག་ *sgro-ga C.* the little bubbles in sparkling beverages, **čáṅ-la ḍó-ga ḍug** the beer sparkles.

སྒྲོ་གུ *sgró-gu*, v. *sgróg-gu* sub *sgrog.*

སྒྲོ་བ་ *sgró-ba* I. sbst. 1. *Wdṅ.*, acc. to *Sch.* **the bark** of a species of willow, but prob. the same as *gró-ga.* — 2. *C.* **the penis.**

II. vb., pf. *bsgros*, fut. *bsgro*, imp. *sgro-Lexx.* w.e., *Cs.:* **to debate, discuss,** so that it would be only another form of *bgro-ba*; but in *C.* **do-šẹ' ʒhé'-pa** is said to mean: **to talk at random,** to chatter away thoughtlessly.

སྒྲོག(ས)་ *sgrog(s)* **cord, rope,** for tying, fettering: **fetters** *Mil.* and *C.*; *lčags-sgróg* iron fetters, chain; *lčags-sgróg lág-pa sbrél-nas* the hands tied or chained together; *lčags-sgróg-pa* a convict put in irons; *šiṅ-sgróg* fetters made of twisted twigs *Cs.*; *lham-sgróg* **shoe-strap,** lace, latchet. — *sgróg-gu, sgró-gu, W. *róg-bu**, **string, strap,** for binding, fastening, strapping; *Sch.* also button; *sgrog-ril Sch.* **button,** *sgrog-ril sgróg-pa* to button up.

སྒྲོག་པ་ *sgróg-pa*, pf. *bsgrags*, fut. *bsgrag*, imp. *sgrags(s)*, **to call, call out,** call to *Dzl.* and elsewh.; **to publish, proclaim, promulgate,** *γtam-snyán* good news *Mil.*; *ši-bai γtam bsgrágs-na* if his death becomes known, *Tar.*; *čos sgróg-pa*, resp. *čós-kyi sgrog-gléṅ mdzád-pa Glr.* **to preach;** *dril-sgrog-pa* to publish by ringing a bell, to publish, proclaim; *sgróg-pa-po* a proclaimer, a preacher *Cs.* — 2. **to shout, to scream,** *ṅú-skad drág-por sgrog* (the infant) weeps and screams *Lt.* — 3. *C.* (in *W.* only resp.) **to read,** *γsuṅ sgróg-pa* to read words of Buddha *Ma.*; even: *séms-kyis sgróg-pa* to read silently. — 4. **to bind,** like *₀grógs-pa*; v. also *sgrog* extr.

སྒྲོད་པ་ *sgród-pa*, another form of *₀gród-pa* to go; not much used.

སྒྲོན་མ་ *sgrón-ma* **a lamp, lantern, torch,** *sgron-mé* a burning lamp, (prop. a lamp-fire); often fig. — *sgroṅ-pa* vb. **to light, to kindle,** *dpé-ča-la me sgrón-nas* lighting (burning) the book *Pth.* — *sgron-bskál* the enlightened age *Cs.*, opp. to *mun-bskál* the dark age. — *sgron-drégs* **lamp-black.** — *sgron-(me-) šiṅ Sch.* the yew-leaved fir, Pinus picea, which tree, however, is scarcely known in Tibet; in *Sik.* it denotes Pinus longifolia, and prob. also in every other province, the most resinous species of coniferous trees prevailing there.

སྒྲོན་པ་ *sgrón-pa*, pf. and fut. *bsgron* 1. **to cover, to lay over, adorn, decorate** *Glr.* — 2. **to light, to kindle,** v. *sgrón-ma.*

སྒྲོབ་ *sgrob* **haughtiness, arrogance, pride,** *Lexx.*

སྒྲོམ་ *sgrom* **box, chest, trunk, coffer** = *sgam*; *sgróm-bu* a small box or chest: *smyug-sgróm Cs.* = *γzéb-ma* a chest or trunk made of bamboo; *ro-sgróm, rús-pai sgrom Zam.* **coffin.**

སྒྲོལ་བ་ *sgról-ba*, pf. and fut. *bsgral* 1. **to rescue, deliver, save,** *las* from, out of, *sgról-bai ded-dpón-du ₀gyur* he becomes a guide to salvation *Glr.* — 2. **to lead,**

transport, carry, to cross (a river) by boat or ferry, *ču-bsgrál Lex.*: तीर्ण passed over; *čú-boi p̔á-rol-tu bsgrál-bar mdzód-čig* have the goodness to take me over to the other bank *Sambh.*; *ₒk̔ór-ba bsgrál-bai gru-γziṅs yin Glr.* it is a boat that carries over the river of transmigration. — 3. **to remove,** do away with, drive away, *ₒdré-rnams p̔yii rgyá-mts̔o č̔én-po-la bsgrál Glr.* the demons were driven to the uttermost parts of the sea; *bdud sgról-ba* to expel the devil; *sdig-č̔an rgyál-po sgról-bar ₒgyur* the guilty king will be removed out of the way! *Glr.*; *dgra-bgegs bsgral-bai ša k̔rag rus-pa daṅ naṅ-rol glo snyiṅ bčás-pa mč̔od-par ₒbul* the flesh, blood, bones, heart, lungs and entrails of slaughtered enemies of the faith are offered by us as a sacrifice. This saying, the tendency of which is often justified by the sophism, that it is an act of mercy to kill an enemy of the faith and thus prevent him from accumulating more sin, shows that even 'mild Buddhism' is not incapable of bloody fanaticism, and instances like that of king Laṅ-dar-ma of old, and of the recent martyrdom of Roman Catholic christians at Bonga confirm this fact from experience.

སྒྲོལ་མ་ *sgról-ma*, sometimes also *sgrol-yúm Cs.*, *W.* **ról-ma**, 1. n. of two goddesses, *Ssk.* तारा, known in the history of Tibet as the white and green Tara, incarnated in the two wives of Srongtsangámpo, *Schl.* 66 and 84; *Köpp.* II., 65. — 2. a name of females, of frequent occurrence.

སྒྲོས་ *sgros* 1. *Cs.* **manner, method, way,** *bšád-sgros* way of explaining, instructing, informing: *sgroγs bšád-sgros Sch.*: 'the method of instruction which is to be proclaimed' (?); *γtám-sgros Cs.*: 'way or manner of speaking' (?). — 2. *Cs.* **edge, brim, lip;** *Sch.* also mark from a wound, **scar;** *žál-gyi mč̔u-sgrós* seems to signify only 'lip'.

བརྒད་པ་ *brgád-pa* = *bgád-pa* to smile, to smile on *Stg.*

བརྒལ་ *brgal* 1. v. *rgál-ba*, 2. v. *rgól-ba*.

བརྒོལ་བ་ *brgól-ba Sch.* 'das Gegenseitige', mutual relation, contrast, contrary?

བརྒྱ་(ཐམ་པ་) *brgya* (*t̔ám-pa*) **a hundred,** one hundred; *brgya-p̔rág* the hundred, a century; *brgya-p̔rág bču* 1000; *brgyá-pa* the hundredth; *brgyá-po* consisting of one hundred (cf. under *dgu*); *brgya daṅ bču-bži* 114; *brgya-nyi-šu* 120; *bži-brgya* (*daṅ*) *go-brgyád* 498; *brgyá-rtsa* v. *rtsa*; *brgyá-la* (*Cs.*: *brgya-ma-lan-γčig*, or *brgyá-lam-na?*) once among a hundred (cases or times) i.e. very rarely, e.g. (*dus*) *brgyá-la brnyed kyaṅ* though it be found for once at last *Mil.* frq., cf. *Schf.* Erläut. zu *Dzangl.* p. 45; also = finally, in short, the Latin *denique, Mil. nt.*; *brgyá-č̔an* erron. for *rgyá-č̔an*. — *brgya-mč̔ód* a hecatomb of 100 lamps, offered on certain festival occasions *Sik.* — *brgyá-ₒdaṅs* about or nearly a hundred *Sch.* — *brgyá-dpon* a captain of a hundred men, the Latin centurio. — *brgya-byin* (शतक्रतु) '(honoured by) a hundred sacrifices', epithet of Indra, cf. ἑκατόμβαιος) 1. Indra. 2. n. of a medicine *Wdṅ.*

བརྒྱ་ *brgya?* 1. in *smrá-bai brgya Sch.*: noisy conversation; *Lexx.* simply आलाप speech, conversation (with the remark that the word is obs. and prov.). — 2. often erron for *rgya*.

བརྒྱང་བ་ *brgyáṅ-ba* 1. v. *rgyoṅ-ba* 2. **to call** to a person from a distance, *C.*

བརྒྱད་ *brgyad* **eight**; *brgyád-pa* the eighth, *brgyad-po* consisting of eight, *brgyád-ču* eighty, *brgyad-ču-rtsa-γčig* (*W.* **gyad-ču-gya-čig**), *gya-γčig* 81; *brgyad-brgyá* 800; *brgyad-stóṅ* 8000; *brgyad-k̔ri* 80 000.

བརྒྱད་(བ)ཀག་ *brgyad-(b)kág* **a reproach, rebuke,** *brgyad-kág byéd-pa* to rebuke, to chide *Dzl.*

བརྒྱན་པ་ *brgyán-pa*, vb. **to adorn, decorate; to provide with** (c. instrum.), cf. *rgyan* sbst.; *nya mgo sá-yis brgyán-pa* the letter *nya* (ཉ) being provided with an *s* above it, = *sny..*, *Zam.*

བརྒྱལ་བ་ *brgyal-ba* 1. **to sink down** senseless, **to faint**; **brgyál-te dád-če**

W. to lie in winter-sleep; *o-brgyál-te* very much exhausted, v. *o.* — 2. **to howl**, of the fox. *Sch.*

བརྒྱུངསཔ *brgyúṅs-pa Lex.*; *Cs.*: **'the marrow in the back-bone'.**

བརྒྱུད *brgyud*, cf. *rgyud*, *Ssk.* परम्पर **family** (*gens*), **lineage; relations, ancestors, descendants, offspring**, *mi-brgyúd* 1. = *brgyud*, *dei mi-brgyúd yin-pa* being of his family *Glr.* 2. people, nation, *bód-kyi mi-brgyúd* the Tibetan nation. 3. the human race, mankind *Cs.*; *rigs-brgyúd*, resp. *ydun-brgyúd* family; issue, progeny, *rigs-brgyúd pél-bar gyur* there will be a numerous offspring; *bla-rgyúd* succession or descent of Lamas *Cs.* — **mig ná-če gyúd-la yod* W.* diseases of the eye frequently occur in that family; **dé-nę gyud mi čad yin* W.* then the race will not die out; **spél-gyud-la bór-če* W.* to set apart cattle for breeding; *brgyúd-nas brgyúd-du* from generation to generation *Cs.*; *bu tsa brgyúd-du bdeo* he is blessed even to his children and children's children *Dzl.*

Comp. *brgyud-brgyúgs* a continuous succession *Sch.* — *brgyúd-čan* like his progenitors *Cs.* — *brgyúd-pa* 1. belonging to a race or family. 2. v. *rgyud* and *rgyúd-pa.* — *brgyud-méd* degenerate *Cs.*, cf. *brgyúd-čan.* — *brgyúd-ma* 1. *Cs.* = *brgyúd-čan.* 2. *W.* fruitful, fertile. 3. *brgyud-ma-brgyab Lex.* w.e. — *brgyud-dzin* **a first-born male, heir and successor.**

བགྲད *brgrad* is acknowledged by *Lexx.*, but evidently an incorrect form for *bgrad.*

བསྒ... *bsg*... words beginning thus will for the greater part be found under *sg*...

བསྒགཔ *bsgág-pa* v. *gégs-pa* and *sgój-pa.*

བསྒང *bsgaṅ* (*Lexx.* = *dṅos-yži*, मुख?) **point of time, moment, instant, conjuncture,** *lo-ysar-bsgáṅ-gi lhágs-ma* a chilling gale on newyear s day *Mil.*; esp. **the proper time** or season for doing a thing, *byá-bai bsgaṅ*; *bri-bai, zá-bai bsgaṅ* the time for writing, eating. (A different word from *sgaṅ*).

བསྒོབ *bsgó-ba* 1. v. *sgó-ba.* — 2. pf. *bsgos*, vb. a. to *gó-ba*, **to soil, stain, defile,** lit. and fig., **kyon-ghyi ma gö* C.* he was not tainted with any spot or blemish, nothing could be laid to his charge; **to infect** with disease; rarely in a good sense: *dri sna-tsogs-kyis legs-par bsgos-pa Stg.* well **anointed** with salves and perfumes.

བསྒྲངབ *bsgráṅ-ba* 1. **to enumerate, count up** (?) *Cs.* — 2. **to cause to grow cold** *Lexx.*

བསྒྲདཔ *bsgrád-pa Lexx.* = *bgrád-pa.*

ང

ང *ṅa* 1. the letter *ṅ*, sounded as a nasal guttural, the English ng in singing, in the Tibetan language often the initial letter of a word. — 2. as numerical figure: 4. — 3. as numeral adjective = *lṅá-bču*, in the numbers 51—59.

ང *ṅa*, pers. pron., first person sing. and pl. **I, we,** the usual word in familiar speech; *ṅai* my, our; mine, ours; *ṅa mi rgan* old man that I am *Mil.*; *ṅa rgyál-po sroṅ-btsan-sgám-po daṅ* with me, king Srongtsangampo *Glr.*; *blá-ma ṅa* I, the Lama *Mil.*; *de mi rgan ṅai ká-la nyon* listen to my word as that of an old man *Mil.*; *ṅai di* this my (doing) *Glr.*; *ṅai rje-btsún* my honoured masters! *Mil.*; *ṅai* *yid-*₍*ón* my dearest! *Pth.*; *ṅa-ráṅ* I my self, esp. col. very frq.; **ṅa ráṅ-ka** *Ts.*, **ṅa tsog** *Ü*, *ṅa nyid*, *ṅa k̇ó-na*, *ṅa bdag* (?), *ṅa-bo* (??) *Cs.* id.; *ṅa ráṅ-gi yaṅ* moreover, what concerns my own affairs *Mil.* Distinct expressions for the pl. **we** are: *ṅá-ċag B.* and *C.*; **ṅá-ża** *W.*, **ṅá-ya** *Bal.*; in *W.* **ṅá-ża** seems to be used in an exclusive sense: I and my people, i.e. excluding you or the person or persons addressed, so that when Europeans use it in *Ld.* or *Lh.*, in addressing their hearers, meaning to include themselves (all of us, we and you), they are generally misunderstood; **ṅa daṅ** 'he or those with me', is said to be used in a similar manner; **ṅa daṅ nyis** both of us; *ṅa-rnams* we *Cs.* Synonyms are: *ṅed, ṅos, bdag*, **k̇o-bo**; and *ṅaṅ, ṅo, dṅo, dṅos, ṅogs* may prob. bederived from the same root.

ང་རྒྱལ་ *ṅa-rgyál* ('I the first') **pride, arrogance,** frq.; *ṅa-rgyál skyéd-pa* to be proud *Dzl.*; *γċog-pa* to break (another's pride), to humble, humiliate *Mil.*; *ṅa-rgyál-ċan* proud; *W.* also naughty, of children.

ང་ངུར་ *ṅa-ṅúr* a species of **duck,** v. *ṅúr-ba*; perh. Anas casarca.

ང་བ་ *ṅá-ba*, rarely for *ṅán-pa*; *dri ṅá-ba* stench *Stg.*; cf. *nyám-ṅa-ba, yá-ṅa-ba.*

ང་ར་ *ṅá-ra* (cf. *ṅad*) **air,** *ṅa gáṅs-kyi ṅá-ras mi ȷigs* I am not afraid of the air of glaciers *Mil.*; **ṅá-ra ḍáṅ-mo rag, ȷám-po rag** *W.* I perceive the air to be cold, to be mild; esp. cold air, *ṅá-ra-ċan* fresh, cold.

ང་རོ་ *ṅá-ro* **a loud voice, a cry,** *kye-hud-kyi ṅá-ro* ₒ*bód-pa* to raise woeful cries *Pth.*; *skád-kyi ṅá-ro ċ̌én-pos bsgrágs-so* they proclaimed, shouting at the top of their voices *Pth.*; *séṅ-gei ṅá-ro* the loud voice, the roaring, of a lion *Mil.*; *γdúg-pai ṅá-ro* prob. voices foreboding mischief *Mil.*; **the roar, roaring, rushing,** of waves etc.; *ṅá-ro sgróg-pa* to roar, to rage; in a relative sense: *skád-kyi ṅá-ro drag-żán* a loud and a low sound, the different force or effort required in producing it *Gram.*; *ṅá-ro-ċan* loud, noisy, roaring; a crier, bawler, noisy fellow.

ངག་ *ṅag*, sometimes *dṅags*, resp. *γsuṅ*, **speech, talk, word,** *ṅág-gi nyés-pa* sins committed with the tongue, in words, (*rdzun, ṗrá-ma, ṫsig-rtsúb*, prob. also *kyál-ka*); *ṅag-gi lhá-mo* the goddess of speech, of eloquence, Sarasvati; *ṅág-gi dbaṅ-ṗyúg* = ₒ*jam-dbyáṅs* Manjusri; *ṅag* ₒ*jám-po* kind, polite speech or words; *ṅag-*ₒ*jám smra-mk̇ás* of a soft tone in speaking and prudent in words *Glr.*; *smán-pai ṅag bżin-du byed-pa* to obey the words of the physician; *ṅag sdóm-pa, ṅag bċád-pa* silence, as a monastic duty or religious exercise, resp. *γsuṅ-bċád Mil.*; *γżan-gyi ṅag γċóg-pas* not doing according to another's word, not obeying him *Tar.*, frq.; *ṅag mnyán-pa* to be obedient *Dzl.*

Comp. *ṅag-kyál*, or -ₒ*k̇yal* = *kyál-ka.* — *ṅag-*ₒ*gròs, smrá-bai ṅag-gròs* 'a manner of speaking or uttering words' *Cs.* — *ṅag-rgyún* tradition, not recorded history, *Cs.* — *ṅag-snyán, snyan-ṅág, snyan-dṅágs* 1. **poetical expression, figure, metaphor.** 2. **poem,** piece of poetry *Glr.* — *ṅag-dbáṅ* 1. **eloquent.** 2. p. n., e. g. *ṅag-dbáṅ blo-bzáṅ rgyá-mtso* Dalai Lama, born 1615. — *ṅag-sbyór* arrangement of speech *Cs.* — *ṅag-ṫsig* = *ṅag.* — *ṅag-lám żú-ba* to apply to a person by word of mouth, resp.

ངང་ *ṅaṅ* (not in the earlier literature) 1. **the nature, essentiality, idiocrasy** of a person, the peculiarity of a thing, *saṅs-rgyás-kyi ṅaṅ yin* he is (partaking) of the nature of Buddha, Buddha-like (corresponding to our 'divine', which consequently might be expressed by *dkon-mċ̌óg-gi ṅaṅ*) *Mil.*; *stóṅ-pai ṅaṅ-nyid* the essentiality of the vacuum itself *Glr.*; frq. used only paraphrastically or pleonastically: *tiṅ-ṅe-dzin-gyi ṅáṅ-la żúgs-pa* to enter into meditation *Mil.*; *ṫugs-mnyés bżin-pai ṅáṅ-la* in a cheerful mood *Mil.*; *ċ̌ágs-med-kyi ṅáṅ-la γnás-par gyis* continue in that passionless state of mind *Thgr.*; ₒ*jigs-skrág-gi ṅáṅ-nas* ₒ*ċ̌i-ba* to die of fear or anxiety; *ṅáṅ-nas* in general is used nearly like *sgó-nas Mil.* frq.; **character, disposition,** *ṅáṅ-bzáṅ, ṅaṅ-ṅán Sch.*; *ṅaṅ-ṫsúl*, and esp.

ṅaṅ-rgyúd id., *ṅaṅ-rgyúd bzáṅ-po Wdṅ., dgé-ba Glr.*, a naturally good, virtuous character; very frq.: *ṅaṅ-rgyúd riṅ-ba* forbearing, longsuffering, not easily put into a passion *Glr.*; not easily excited to action, **phlegmatic**, cool, also **ṅaṅ riṅ-wa* C.*; even *ṅaṅ* alone may have this meaning: *ṅaṅ ma tuṅ* don't lose your patience *Mil. nt.*; *ṅáṅ-gis adv.* not only signifies spontaneously, of one's own accord, but also **slowly, gradually, gently** *Mil.* (so already *Schr.*) — 2. **dominion, sphere, province,** parallel to *kloṅ* and *dbyiṅs Mil.*; **ṅa ma-ši-kai ṅáṅ-la dug** I belong to the kingdom of Christ, said one of our Christians, in order to show the meaning of **ṅaṅ**. Hence it might be used for expressing the ἐν of the N. T. (I John 5, 6 and many other passages) denoting a pertaining to, belonging to, being connected with. *ṅáṅ-la ₒjóg-pa* (*bžág-pa*) *Mil.* and *C.* is an expression not explained as yet.

ངང་པ་ *ṅáṅ-pa* 1. **goose,** more accurately *ṅáṅ-pa* a gander, *ṅáṅ-ma* a goose *Cs.* The domestic goose and the breeding of it is not yet known in Tibet, at least not in *W.* — 2. **a light-bay horse,** an isabel-coloured horse *Ld.-Glr.*

ངད་ *ṅad* 1. cog. to *ṅá-ra*, **air,** **ṅád-la skám-če* W.* to dry in the air; in a general sense the air in its chemical qualities, in its influence on the senses: **scent, fragrance,** *spós-kyi ṅad ldáṅ-ba* the rising of an aromatic breeze; *ṅad yal* the fragrancy, the aroma evaporates; **vapour,** *ká-ṅad, čú-ṅad* snowy vapour, aqueous vapour; **aromati csubstance,** *sṅó-ṅad* aromatic vegetables, such as onions *Med.*; **cold air, the cold, coldness,** v. *ṅad-čan.* — 2. *W.* (cf. *ṅár-ba, ṅár-ma*) **severity, roughness,** **ṅę ṅad jigs dug** he fears I might address him harshly; *ṅád-čan* 1. fragrant, fresh, cool, *W.* cold. 2. *W.* rough, impetuous.

ངན་ *ṅan* 1. **evil, mischief, misfortune,** *ṅan čén-po byas* it has done great mischief *Glr.*; esp. harm done by sorcery and witchcraft *Mil.*; *ṅan-dgú* every possible evil *Lt.* — 2. **curse, imprecation,** *ṅan ₒdébs-pa, W. *táb-če**, to curse, to execrate; *mtu ṅan ₒdébs-pa* to curse by means of witchcraft. Cf. *mṅan.*

ངན་པ་ *ṅán-pa*, col. also **ṅán-po**, **bad,** of food etc.; **mean, miserable** *Dzl.*; **poor, humble, low,** (prop. *rigs-ṅán*), *ṅan-lóṅ* poor and blind (people) *Glr.*; *lo ṅán-pa* a year yielding no crops, an unfruitful or bad year; of men, actions etc.: **wicked,** *ṅán-pa kyod gnyis* ye two villains! *Glr.*; **noisome, pernicious,** *gsol-ṅán* pernicious food, i.e. poison, resp., *Glr.*; . . . *la ṅán-du rjód-pa* to revile, blaspheme; *mi-la mig ṅán ltá-ba* to look with an evil or envious eye upon a person *Glr.*; *ráṅ-rnams spyod ṅan byás-nas dus ṅan zer* acting badly themselves they speak of bad times *Ma.* — *ṅan-ₒgro, ṅan-soṅ* v. *ₒgro-ba* I. extr. — *ṅan-ṅón Cs.* mean, pitiful, very bad. — *ṅan-ṅón tsám-gyis čog šés-pa* prob.: to be satisfied with any thing, and be it ever so poor. — *ṅan-ne-ba* bad. — **ṅan-pe* W.* meal of parched barley, roasted meal. — *ṅán-so* 'bad place', hell; cf. *ṅán-ₒgro* under *ₒgró-ba* I. extr.

ངན་བུ་ *ṅán-bu C.*, **we,** eleg., = *bdag*, when speaking humbly of one's self.

ངམ་གྲོག་ *ṅam-gróg*, *Cs.* 'torrent', *Sch.* 'ditch filled with water, water-ditch; the bank of a river grown high and steep by having been gradually washed out by the current'; (only this latter sense of the word was authenticated to me). In *Glr.* Tibet is poetically called '*ṅam-grog-čé*', which is a very appropriate name when rendered: having large and deep erosions.

ངམ་དུར་ཅན་ *ṅám dur-čan* given to gluttony and drinking *Stg.*

ངམ་རུ་ *ṅam-ru* n. of a disease *Med.*

ངམ་ཤུགས་ *ṅam-šúgs* **reluctantly.**

ངར་ *ṅar* 1. **fore- or front-side, forepart,** *ṅar-gdóṅ* id.; esp. of the leg, the shin-bone, also knuckle ni f.; *lag-ṅár, rkaṅ-ṅár* fore-arm, lower part of the leg; *rje-ṅar* seems to be an appellation for both, (in *W.* **nyar** instead of it). — 2 v. *ṅár-ba* 1. —

3. termin. of *ṅa*, 'to one's self', *ṅar-˳dzin* = *bdag-˳dzin*, selfishness, self-interest. *Mil.* — 4. *ṅar ˳dón-pa* to set on or against, **to instigate,** *nyams-kyi ṅar ˳dón-pa* irritations of the mind, excitements *Mil.*; *nyam-ṅár Lex.* id. (?) — 5. v. *ṅar-ṅár-po.*

ངར་སྐད་ *ṅar-skád* **the roaring,** of lions etc., *˳dón-pa, sgróg-pa Mil.*; *W.* **táṅ-če** also to call to, to shout at.

ངར་ངར་པོ་ *ṅar-ṅár-po* **hoarse, husky, wheezing,** e.g. in old age *Thgy.*; *ṅar-ṅár ˳kún-sgra* a hoarse groaning *Pth.*; *ṅar-glúd* hoarseness and phlegm *Med.*; *gré-ba ṅar-ba* a hoarse throat *Med.*

ངར་ཅན་ *ṅár-čan* v. *ṅár-ba.*

ངར་སྣབས་ *ṅar-snábs* **mucus, snivel,** (affords food to certain demons).

ངར་པ་ *ṅár-pa* **stalk** of plants *Med.*

ངར་པོ་ *ṅár-po W.* **strong, ferocious,** of the tiger etc.

ངར་བ་ *ṅár-ba* 1. **strength, force; hardness,** of steel; cold, frost, cold wind *Mil.* (cf. *ṅá-ra, ṅad*); *ṅar γtoṅ-ba, W.* **táṅ-če, čúg-če**, *Sch.* also *ldúd-pa*, to steel, to temper. — *ṅár-čan* 1. strong, vigorous 2. tempered; *ṅár-ldan* id.; *sems ṅár-ldan* a strong mind *Mil.*; *ṅar-méd* weak, soft. — 2. (v. *ṅar* 1.) a sort of flap (of breeches).

ངར་མ་ *ṅárma* 1. **irritable, passionate, impetuous** *Sch.* — 2. **strong, powerful,** e.g. a powerful protection, *Mil.*

ངལ་བ་ *ṅál-ba* **to be fatigued, tired, wearied; fatigue, weariness,** resp. *sku ṅál-ba*, or *tugs ṅál-ba*, also *mnyél-ba*; *ṅal soṅ* I am tired; *spóbs-pa ṅal* the strength decreases *Med.*; *ṅál-čad-pa, ṅál-dub-pa* intensive forms of *ṅal*; *ṅal ˳júg-pa* vb. a. **to tire, fatigue, weary;** *ṅal γsó-ba* 'to cure weariness', **to rest,** frq.; *ṅal-stégs* a rest, a sort of crutch or fork, which coolies sometimes carry with them, to support their load, whilst taking a momentary rest in standing; also any bench or seat inviting to repose. To provide such conveniences for wayfaring men is considered a meritorious act.

ངས་ *ṅas* 1. instr. of *ṅa.* — 2. *mi-ṅas Tar.* 37, 16. is undoubtedly a typographical error, instead of *mi-nad. Schf.* has left it without an annotation.

ངི་ *ṅi* num. fig.: 34.

ངུ་ *ṅu* num. fig.: 64

ངུ་བ་ *ṅu-ba*, pf. *ṅus*, resp. *šúm-pa*, 1. **to weep,** 2. *W.* also **to roar,** used of swelling rivers, not of the wind; *Schr.*: 'to groan like a turtle-dove'; **ṅu ma ṅu** *W.* do not weep! *ṅús-pai mči-ma* tears that have been shed *Dzl.*; *ga-čád ṅús-pa* weeping without a cause, hysterical weeping *Med.*; *ṅú-ru ˳júg-pa* to cause to weep *Lt.*; **ṅú-ma-god** *W.* weeping and laughing at the same time; *šes ṅús-so* thus he said weeping *Glr.*; **ṇu ḍhó-wa** (lit. *gro-ba*) *C.* to be sorrowful, sad. — *ṅú(-ba)-po Cs.*, *ṅú-mk'an* col. one weeping, a weeper. — *ṅú-šur-čan Sch.*, *ṅú-mk'an* col. a child that is continually crying. — *ṅu-˳bód, ṅu-rdzi, W.* **ṅu-zi**, sbst. a crying, howling, lamenting.

ངུ་རུ་ *ṅú-ru W.* for *ṅúr-ba* 1.

ངུག་པ་ *ṅúg-pa Ts.* = *ṅúr-ba* 2, **to grunt; to snore; to pur** (of cats).

ངུད་མོ་ *ṅúd-mo* **a sob** *Cs., Schr.*

ངུར་བ་ *ṅúr-ba* 1. sbst. **duck,** esp. the red wild duck, **चक्रवाक** Anas casarca; *ṅúr-ka* as red as fire, fiery red; *ṅur-smrig* yellowish red, **saffron colour,** the original colour of the monks' habit, though not the common high-red of the Brug-pa monks in *Sik.* and in *W.* — 2. vb. **to grunt,** of pigs and yaks.

ངུས་ *ṅus* v. *ṅu-ba.*

ངེ་ *ṅe* num. fig.: 94.

ངེད་ *ṅed* pers. person. first person, eleg. for *ṅa*, **I, we;** *ṅéd-kyi* my, our; *ṅed γnyis(-ka)* we two; *ṅed γsum(-po)* we three; *ṅed spun γsum* we three brothers *Glr.*; *ṅéd-kyi bu-dód mdzod* have the goodness to become our foster-son *Mil.*; sometimes *ṅa* and *ṅed* are used promiscuously in the same sentence, so: *ṅas* I, and directly after: *ṅéd-kyi* our *Mil.* The plural number is specially indicated in: *ṅéd-cag, ṅéd-tso, ṅéd-rnams, ṅéd-dag Mil.; ṅéd-čag-rnams Cs.* — *ṅed-rán* 1. I myself, we ourselves. 2. I, we *Glr.*; *ṅed-nyid, ṅed-ḱó-na Cs.* id. (*Ld.* **ṅad**).

ངེའུ་ཅག *ṅeu-čag Dzl.* ཟཱ༢, 11.15. is prob. an incor. reading in *Sch.'s* edition, instead of *ₒu-bu-čag.*

ངེས་པ *ṅés-pa* 1. adj. **certain, true, sure, firm,** *bdag-la ṅés-pa žig stsál-du ɣsol* I ask you to communicate to me something certain, i.e. authentic news; *ṅés-par byéd-pa* to fix, settle, establish, ascertain, e.g. facts of chronology, v. *Wdk.* chronological table in *Cs.'s* Grammar; to ratify *Schr.*; *ₒči-bar ṅés-pa yin* or *ṅés-so* death is certain; *de bdén-par ṅés-sam* is it certain that this is true? *Glr.*; *mi btúb-tu ṅés-na* as it is certain that I am not able (to do it) *Dzl.*; *nam ₒḱyer ṅés-pa med* it is not certain at what time they will be carried off *Glr.*; *bdag ḱyód-kyi bu yin ṅés-na* if I am actually, for certain, your son *Pth.*; *p̓an ṅés-pai čos* that religion which is sure to lead to salvation *Mil.*; *ṅés-pai dón-las gol* he is missing the true sense *Pth.*; *ma-ṅés-pa* untrue *Tar.* 109, 17; *ɣnás-la ṅés-pa méd-pa yin* as to abode I am changeable, I have no fixed abode *Mil.*; also *ṅes-méd* alone: **homeless** *Mil.*; **undefined,** *ṅes-méd-kyi ri-la* somewhere on the mountains *Mil.*; sometimes it is but a rhetorical turn, like the English **evidently, obviously,** *bú-la bkra-mi-šis ṅés-kyis*, as our son has evidently met with an accident *Dzl.*; *bud-méd yin-du ṅés-so* they are evidently women, they do not deserve to be called men *Dzl.*; also sbst. **certainty, surety, truth;** *tsé-la, ṅág-la, lús-la ṅés-pa med* (man's) life-time, word, body have no certainty, are transient *Glr.* Hence *ṅés-pa-čan* **real, actual,** *ṅés-pa-čan-du* really, truly, in fact, in reality, opp. to deceitful appearances, false opinions, wrong calculations etc. *Glr.*; *ṅes-pa-nyid-du* adv. 1. in reality *Glr.* 2. truly, in truth, verily *Glr.*; *ṅés-par* adv. 1. really, certainly, to be sure, frq.; *sdig-pa byás-na rnam-par-smin-pa ṅés-par myóṅ-ste* as retribution for a sin committed is sure to take place, will certainly follow *Dzl.*; *dé-ḍra-ba žig ṅés-par yód-na* if such a one is really present *Dzl.*; *ṅés-par či-ba* the certain dying, the certainty of death *Thgy.*; *bdag ṅés-par byao* I will surely do it *Dzl.* 2. **by all means,** to add force to the imperative mood *Tar.* 16, 11. — 2. often it is used subjectively, esp. in *C.*, when *séms-la* is to be supplied, so that it may be rendered by **to know:** *bdén-par ṅes, rdzún-par ṅes* I know (I am certain) that it is true, untrue; *ṅés-pa čer med* I am not quite sure, I do not know for certain, I do not fully understand, I do not clearly see through it *Mil.*; *séms-čan ₒdi bdág-gi p̓a-má yin ṅés-na*, if we take it for granted, if we try to realize the fact, that this being is our father or mother *Thgy.*; to remember, to bear in mind **sém-la ṅe túb-bam** *C.* shall you be able to remember that? *ṅés-dón*, also *yáṅ-dag-doṅ*, is said to mean immediate knowledge of the truth, which may be obtained mystically by continued contemplation, and is opp. to *dráṅ-don*, knowledge obtainable through the medium of the sacred writings *Mil.*, also *Lexx.*; *ṅes (-par) ₒbyuṅ-(ba) Mil.* frq., *Schr.*: 'deliverance from the round of transmigration', *Sch.*: 'to appear, to prove true'; another explanation still: 'knowledge of one's self' is not borne out by etymology. — *ṅes-bzúṅ* acc. to *Lexx.* a synonym of *brnán-pa*, q. v. — *ṅes-(par) légs(-pa) Thgy.*, 'that which evidently is the best', is said to denote deliverance from the round of transmigration.

ངོ *ṅo* num. fig : 124.

ངོ *ṅo* 1. resp. *žal-ṅó* (cf. *ṅó-bo, ṅor, ṅos*) **face, countenance, air, look,** as the expression of a man's personality and mind (*ṅo mdzés-pa Cs.*, and *ṅán-pa Schr.* are dubious), *bdág-gi ṅo-la ɣzigs-nas* when she (my mother) shall see my face, *ṅod kár-po* a cheerful face; *ṅo nág-par ₒdug-pa* to sit with a sad and gloomy face *Glr.*; *ṅo nág-par ˏgyúr-ba* to grow sorrowful, to turn pale with fright, pain etc.; *ṅo bab* courage fails(me); *ṅo srúṅ-ba* frq. 'to watch the countenance', to pay much or even too much regard to other people's opinions; *ṅo ḍzin-pa Mil.* seems to signify the same, and *ṅo čógs-pa* the contrary: not to comply with a person's wishes *Mil.*; *ṅo spród-pa* to lay open the features, to show the nature of a thing, to explain; *ṅo ˳ṗród-pa* to understand, to learn, in later literature frq.; *ṅo šés-pa* to know *ccap: ṅa ṅo kyód-kyis ma šés-na* if thou dost not know me *Mil.*; with termin. inf.: to know (that something happens); to find out, e.g. by calculation; to perceive; *ṅo mi šés-pa* 1. not to know 2. unacquaintance, ignorance 3. unknown: *ṅó-mi-šes-pa-la ldáṅ-ba* to rise before a stranger; *ṅó-mi-šes-pai yul* an unknown country *Thgy.*; *ṅo ltá-ba Glr.* is said to signify: to submit (vb. n.); **ṅo lén-če** *W.* to beg pardon, cf. *ṅos bláṅ-ba*; *ṅo ldóg-pa* or *lóg-pa* to turn away, always fig. = to desert, *˳k̔ór-bai yul ṅo lóg-na* if you will desert, get rid of, the land of transmigration; more frq.: *ṅo-lóg byéd-pa* to revolt, rebel, *rtsóm-pa* to bring about a revolt, *ṅo-lóg-mk̔an* mutineer, agitator, *ṅo-lóg-čan* seditious, faithless, *ṅo zlóg-pa ccg.* to oppose, resist, not comply with a person's wish *Dzl.* — 2. **side**, like *ṅos*, esp. *W.*: **a ṅó-la soṅ** he has gone to that side, in that direction; **sám-pa 'a ṅo 'i ṅó-a soṅ** he is absent, inattentive. — 3. **self, the thing itself**, cf. *ṅó-bo* and *ṅos*; v. *ḏál-ba*; also sbst. **the self, the I,** *ṅo-tsáb* the representative of the I; cf. also *ṅo-čén*. — 4. **likelihood, prospect of,** c. genit. inf. or root, *˳kyér-bai ṅo* a probability of its being taken away; *bu čig ˳byuṅ ṅo če* a great chance of (getting) a son. — 5. (also *ṅos*) a. **the waxing and waning moon,** with regard to shape; one half of the lunar month with regard to time, *yar-ṅo* the former, *mar-ṅo* the latter half; *yár-ṅo zla ltar* like the crescent moon. b. in a special sense the **increasing moon,** or the first half of the month; thus vulgo; so also in *B.*: *zlá-ba dgu ṅo bču lón-pa-na Glr.*, *ṅo bčú-nas, zlá-ba ṅo bčú-na Pth.* in the first half of the tenth month (to denote the duration of pregnancy).

Comp. and deriv. *ṅo dkar* v. above 1. — *ṅo-lkog* prop. adj.: **public** and **private, open** and **secret,** but it is generally used as a synonym of *zol* or *rdzun*, **fraud, imposture, deceit, eye-service.** It may be explained by its contrary: *ṅó-med lkóg-med* acting in the same manner in public as in private life, the open and the secret conduct being alike *Mil.* (cf. *ṅos*). — *ṅó-čan* natural (?) *Cs.* — *ṅo-čén* ('the greater self'), a man of influence interceding for another person, **an intercessor;** *ṅo-čén byéd-pa* to intercede *Glr.*; *mi-la ṅo-čén ˳čól-ba* to use a person as negotiator, to make inquiries through him *Glr.* (*Sch.* incorr.) — *ṅo-rtóg W.* 1. (like *ṅés-pa* of *B.*) **certain,** e.g. **ṅo-tóg šé-če** to know for certain. 2. (like *dṅos, yaṅ-dag-pa*) **real, actual; true, genuine,** **˳ṫul yin-na ṅo-tóg yin** is it counterfeit or genuine? illusion or reality? **ṅo-tóg sád-k̔an** the actual murderer, he who really occasioned the death. — **ṅó-stod-k̔an W.* he who praises another to his face, **a flatterer.** — *ṅo-nág* v. above 1. — *ṅó-bo-nyid*, **entity,** *ṅo-bo-nyid-méd-pa* non-entity *Tar.* 90,2.; **essence, nature, substance,** e.g. *séms-kyi Mil.*; **character** *Was.* (278, 294); **marrow, main substance, quintessence** (= *snyiṅ-po*) *Glr.* and elsewh.; *ráṅ-gi ṅó-bos* in itself, according to its intrinsic nature *Mil.*; also col. **ṅó-bo k̔o-ráṅ** *C.* the thing itself, opp. to a surrogate; *ṅó-bo γčig rtógs-pa γnyis Was.*: 'one quality, two (different) ideas' (*Schl.* has *ldóg-pa* instead of *rtóg-pa*). — *ṅo-˳báb-pa* adj. **discouraged, timorous, bashful** *W.* — *ṅó-ma* acc. to *Cs.* = *ṅo*. — *ṅó-ma-γyog C.*: master and servant. — *ṅó-mig W.* **boldness;** **ṅó-mig-čan**, or **čén-po** bold, daring, courageous; **ṅó-mig čuṅ-se** shy, timid, fainthearted *W.* — *ṅó-tsa* ('heat of the face') 1. the act of **blushing, shame,** *ṅó-tsai γnas* shameful things *Sch., Schr.*; *ṅó-tsa-čan,* *ṅó-tsa-šes-pa* shamefaced, chaste, ashamed; *ṅó-tsa-med-pa, mi-šes-pa* shameless, barefaced, impudent; **ṅa ṅó-tsa rag** I am ashamed, **ko ṅó-tsa dug, ṅó-tsa-čan dug** *W.* he is ashamed; *ṅó-tsa byéd-pa* to be ashamed. 2. a shameful thing, *kyod ṅó-mi-tsa-la ṅó-tsar byed* you are ashamed where there is no occasion for it *Mil.*; *ṅó-tsa-ba* to be indecent, indecorous, unbecoming, *yúl-du lóg-na ṅó-tsa-la* as it would be a shame if we returned *Glr.*; *ycér-bur ˳gró-ba ṅó-tsa žiṅ* as it would be indecorous to go naked *Pth.* — *ṅo-mtsár-ba* v. *mtsár-ba.* — *ṅó-ru, ṅor* 1. into the face *Sch.*, e.g. *skúd-pa* to smear; *rtsúb-pa* to say rude things to another's face *Thgy.*; *ṅo-ráṅ-du* id. 2. in the face of, before the eyes, *yžán-gyi* of others. 3. by reason of, in consequence of, *des bskúl-bai ṅor* in consequence of a summons, of a request of him *Glr.* and elsewh. — *ṅo-šés* **an acquaintance, a friend** (the usual word in *W.*). — *ṅo-só* **joy,** *ṅo-só čé-bar ˳oṅ* you will have great joy, you will be delighted, highly satisfied; *sbyin-pa ṅo-só byéd-pa* to make presents to another to his full satisfaction *Mil.*, also *Tar.* 211, 2. — *ṅo-srúṅs* regard to the opinion of others, an aiming at applause *Mil.*

ངོགས་ *ṅogs* 1. **mountain-side, slope** (cf. *ṅos*); river-side, **bank, shore,** *rgyá-mtsoi Dzl.* — 2 **ford,** *ču-ṅógs* id. *C.*

ངོམ་པ་ *ṅóm-pa*, pf. *ṅoms*, 1. **to satisfy one's desire** by drinking, *krág-gis*, also *krág-las Dzl.*; *ma ṅoms* I am still thirsty: *ṅóm-par*, also *ṅoms-tsád, ˳túṅ-ba* to drink one's fill; also of sleeping, *nyid ma ṅom* I have not yet had my full share of sleep; fig.: *čós-kyi bdud-rtsis*, to fill one's self with the nectar of doctrine *Dzl.*; *bltá-bas mi ṅoms mdzés-pa* so beautiful, that one cannot gaze at it long enough, frq.; also *bltá-bas mi ṅoms bžin-du* not being able to look at it sufficiently *Pth.*; *ṅoms(-pa)-méd(-pa)* insatiable. — 2. **to show** with design (boastingly, or indecently, e.g. one's nakedness) *Glr.*, *Pth.* — 3. col. for *snóm-pa* **to snuffle,** to pry into, to spy.

ངོར་ *ṅor* 1. v. under *ṅo*, *Comp.* — 2. n. of a monastery of the Saskya, *Wdk.* chronological table in *Cs.'s* Gram.

ངོས་ *ṅos* 1. **side,** *mdún-ṅos* front-side, front of the body *Lt.*; of a pyramid, a mountain, *lhó-ṅos* southern side or slope of a mountain, **side, margin, edge,** of a pond etc.; *rgyáb ṅos yyás-na* on the right hand behind, *yyás ṅos mdún-na* on the right hand before *Glr.*; **surface, plain,** of the table; *sai ṅos* surface of the earth *Cs.*; hence *ṅós-su* (opp. to *lkog-tu*) *Mil.*, **ṅó-la** (opp. to *sbás-te* (**bé-te**) *W.* manifestly, notoriously, publicly, openly (cf. *ṅo*); **side, direction,** like *pyogs*, *W.* — 2. a thing itself (cf. *ṅo* 3), examples v. under *˳jál-ba.* — 3. pers. pron. first person **I, we;** esp. in *Ld.* in epistolary correspondence, eleg. — 4. instrum. of *ṅo*, = *ṅó-yis*; *ṅos ˳dzin-pa Mil.* (*dṅos ˳dzin-pa Thgy.*) vb. 1. to be selfish, self-interested, also adj. selfish, cf. *ṅos* 3. 2. more frq. to perceive, to know, to discern, also *ṅó-yis ˳dzin-pa; ṅos zin-par gyis šig*, know it! be sensible of it! *Thgr.*; with the termin.: to acknowledge as, to take for, to look upon as *Tar.* 189, 1. In a special sense: diagnosis, discriminating a disease *Med.* **nóṅ-ṅo láṅ-wa** *C.* (lit. *ynoṅ ṅos blaṅ-ba*) = **ṅo lén-če** v. **ṅo** 1.

དངགས་སྙན་ *dṅags-snyán* v. *ṅag* (*Lex.* = काव्य).

དངང་བ་ *dṅáṅ-ba*, pf. *dṅaṅs* 1. **to be out of breath, to pant,** to feel oppressed e.g. when plunging into cold water *C.*, but esp. when frightened and terrified, hence 2 to be frightened, **to fear, to be afraid,** *sbrúl-gyis* of a snake; *čes dṅáṅs-nas* thus he spoke in dismay *Dzl.*; *dṅáṅ-par ˳gyúr-ro* you will (or would) be terrified *Dzl.*; *dṅaṅ-skrág, skrag-dṅáṅ* great fear, fright, terror; *dṅaṅ-skrág-pa* intensive form of *dṅáṅ-ba*, frq.

དངན་འཐེན་པ་ *dṅan-˳tén-pa Lex.* not to return things taken away from another.

དངར་ *dṅar* 1. for *mṅar*, **sweet** *Mil.* and elsewh. — 2. also *zil-dṅár Lex.* w.e.;

Sch.: order, succession(?); *ṫsár-du dṅar Lex.*, *Sch.* put in order, placed in array.

དངུད་མོ་ *dṅúd-mo* = *ṅúd-mo Sch.*

དངུལ་ *dṅul* (col. often **mul**) 1. **silver.** — 2. **money.** — 3. **a rupee.** — 4. **a tola** or Indian half ounce; *dṅúl-gyi ṫóg-nas dṅul ɣsúm-ču ṫob* he gets 30 rupees out of the ready money; *dṅúl-ḱa* a silver mine, a vein of silver; *dṅul-kúg, dṅul-sgyig* money-bag, purse; *dṅúl-ču* quicksilver, mercury; *dṅul-dúl-ma* refined silver *Sch.*; *dṅul-rnig*, lump, bar, ingot, of silver *Sch.*; **ṅul-záṅ(s)* W.*, *C.*, silvered or plated copper.

དངོ་ *dṅo* 1. **shore, bank** *Lex.* — 2. **edge** of a knife *Cs.*; fig. *rta-lčág-gi dṅo* whip-cord, lash of a whip *C.* — 3. handle of a knife(??) *Cs.*

དངོམ་པ་ *dṅóm-pa*, *dṅom-brjid*, **brightness, splendour**; *dṅóm-po*, *dṅóm-čaṅ* shining, bright *Cs.*; *Lex. dṅom-čé* very bright. Cf. *rṅám-pa.*

དངོས་ *dṅos* 1. **reality, real,** *dṅos daṅ sgyú-ma* reality and illusion; *rgyál-bu dṅos* the real prince (opp. to a spurious one); **proper, true, genuine; positive** (opp. to negative) *Gram.*; **personal,** *dṅós-la yód-pa* to be personally present; *dṅós-su*, resp. *žal-dṅós-su* **bodily** e.g. to appear bodily; *ạ-yig dṅós-su med kyaṅ*, even though the *ạ* is not actually written there, *Gram.*; *dṅós-su grúb-pa méd-pa* to have no real existence *Thgy.* — 2. *Cs.*: pers. pron. **I**, cf. *ṅos*; *dṅos-ḍzin-pa* to be selfish *Thgy.*; *dṅos-ḍzin* **selfishness, selfinterest,** *dṅos-ḍzin ɣdón-gyis zin-pa* to be possessed by the demon of selfishness *Thgy.*; *dṅos-ḍzin-čan* selfish, self-interested. Thus it was explained by Lamas, though it cannot be denied that sometimes the version: belief in existence, a clinging to reality, a signification equally justifiable by etymology (v. below), would be more adequate to the context. — 3. *Tar.* 150, 14: thou, you; except in this passage I did not meet with the word in this sense, yet it may be used so, in the same manner as *nyid* q.v.

Comp. and deriv. *dṅos-grúb*, *Ssk. siddhi*, 1. **perfection, excellence,** any thing of superior value, e.g. honour, riches, talents, and esp. wisdom, higher knowledge, and spiritual power, as far as they are not acquired by ordinary study and exercise, but have sprung from within spontaneously, or in consequence of long continued contemplation. This *dṅos-grúb* is, as it were, the Buddhist caricature of the χαρίσματα of the N.T. (v. I. Cor. 12,4). — 2. name of male persons, col. **ṅo-rúb* W.* — *dṅos-ṅán* having little flesh, **ill-fed**, emaciated *Mil.* — *dṅós-čan* **material, real** *Cs.* — *dṅós-dad* true faith, opp. to *blún-dad* 'a fool's faith', superstition *Mil.* — *dṅos-sdig* prob.: real, or still effective sin, unatoned, unexpiated sin *Dzl.* ༣༧, 14; or less emphatically: sinful actions in general ༣༠, 15. — *dṅós-po*, *Ssk.* भव, वस्तु, **thing, natural body,** *ser dṅúl-la sógs-pai dṅós-po Glr.*; **matter, subject,** *dgá-bai dṅós-po* matter of rejoicing *Wdṅ.*; **goods, utensils,** *dge-slóṅ-gi* wearing-apparel of a Gelong; **occurrence, event, action,** *dṅós-po sgrúb-pa* to bring a thing about, to set it on foot or a going *Dzl.*; as a philosophical term: **substance, matter,** *Was.* (270. 294); *dṅós-por ḍzin-pa* the belief in the reality of existence *Mil.* — *dṅós-ma Cs.* **natural** (opp. to artificial), natural productions. — *dṅós-miṅ* 1. **the proper** or **real name** for a thing; so *Zam.* uses the paraphrase: *po-mṫsán-gyi dṅós-miṅ*, in order to avoid the plain expression *mje*, which is considered obscene. 2. **noun substantive,** *Chr. Prot.* a newly coined grammatical term. — *dṅos-méd Lex.* = *Ssk. abhava*, *Cs.* **immaterial,** not existing, *Was.* (281): **not real.** — *dṅos-slób* a real, **a personal pupil** *Tar.* often. — *dṅos-ɣži* (*Lex.* = *Ssk. mūla*) the main part of a thing, **the thing itself,** e.g. the subject-matter of a treatise, the ceremony itself, opp. to *snóṅ-ạgro* introduction, *sbyór-ba* preparation, and eventually also *rjes* that which follows.

མངག་པ་ *mṅág-pa*, pf. *mṅags*, **to commission, charge, delegate, send** (a messenger, commissary etc.) *Dzl.*; also used of Buddha's sending a Bodhisatva on the earth to convert all mortals. — *mṅag-γžúg* **a servant, slave,** but esp. a messenger of the gods.

མངན་པ་ *mṅán-pa* **to curse, to execrate;** *mṅan bsgraṅ-ba Cs.* 'enumeration of curses'; but *mṅan mi bgraṅ? Lex.* w.e.

མངའ་ *mṅa*, resp. for *dbaṅ*, **might, dominion, sway,** *mṅa mdzád-pa* to govern, to rule, *la* over; *mṅa brnyés-pa* to have obtained power *Glr.; mṅa sgyúr-ba Tar.* id.; to possess (books, knowledge etc); to have mastered, to understand thoroughly; *mṅa γsól-ba* 1. to name, nominate, appoint, *rgyál-por* a king *Pth.; btsún-mor* to declare a woman one's wife *Glr.* 2. to praise *C.*: *bkra-šis mṅa γsól-ba C.* to congratulate. — *mṅa-ťáṅ* **power, might.** — *mṅa-bdág* **ruler, master, owner,** frq. — *mṅá-ba* 1. vb. resp. for *yod-pa*, **to be** (to have), *rgyál-po-la sras γsum mṅá-ste* the king having three sons *Dzl.; btsún-poi skú-la bsnyuṅ mi mṅa lágs-sam* (I trust) your majesty is not unwell? *Glr.* 2. adj. (partic.) being owned by, **belonging to,** *Dzl.* ༧༥, 3; **having, owning,** = *daṅ ldán-pa*, frq. — *mṅa-mdzád* = *mṅa-bdág.* — *mṅa-žábs Glr., mṅa-ˎǒg Glr., mṅa-ris Lex.* **subject to; a subject.**

མངའ་རིས་ *mṅa-ris* p.n., in a wider sense the whole country round the sources and the upper course of the Indus and Sutledge, together with some more western parts; the Cashmere, English, and most western Chinese provinces, where Tibetans live; in a more limited sense *mṅa-ris skor γsum* denotes Rutok, Guge, and Purang. — *mṅa-ris-k̇ám-bu C.* (*pú-tiṅ* W.), **dried apricots** from Balti: *mṅa-ris ču, mṅa-ris γtsáṅ-po*, also *γyas-ru-γtsáṅ-po*, and *rta-mčóg-k̇a-bub*, the principal river of Tibet.

མངར་བ་ *mṅár-ba*, W. *ṅár-mo*, C. *ṅár-po*, **sweet,** frq.; *mṅar γsum* the three sweets, sugar, molasses, and honey; cf. *dkar γsum.*

མངལ་ *mṅal*, resp. *lhums* (ལྷུམས) **womb;** *mṅál-gyi dri-mas ma gós-par* not contaminated by the impurity of the womb (so all the Buddhas are not born like other mortals, but come forth out of the side of the breast); *mṅal daṅ ldán-par ˎgyúr-ba* to be with child; *mṅal mi bdé-bar ˎgyúr-ba* to be taken by the labours of child-birth; *mai mṅál-nas byúṅ-nas rtág-par* constantly from one's birth; *mṅál-du čágs-pa* 1. the originating in the womb, conception, 2. the foetus or embryo *Med.; mṅál-du ťógs-pa* a disease; *mṅál(-du) γnás (-pa)* foetus, embryo *Thgy.; mṅál-du ˎjúg-pa* to enter the womb, relative to a Buddha: his incarnating himself, his assuming flesh; *mṅál-du ˎdzin-pa Wdṅ.* to conceive, to be with child. — *mṅál-k̇a* mouth of the womb, orifice of the uterus *Med.* — *mṅal-grib* contamination of the womb; *Cs.* adds: original sin, yet prob. it signifies nothing more than *mṅál-gyi dri-ma* v. above; (the said contamination is considered to extend to the least contact with a woman in child-bed). — *mṅál-sgo* the canal of the uterus, vagina; also in a more special sense the extreme orifice of the vagina *Med.;* frq. without any immediate physiological reference, the same as *mṅal*, e.g, when the subject of re-birth is spoken of. — *mṅal-ťúr* a spoon used in midwifery for extracting a dead fruit (in the artificial delivering of a live child the obstetric art in Tibet is rather helpless). — *mṅal rlúgs-pa* **abortion,** *mṅal rlúgs-par byéd-pa* to cause abortion *Cs.*

མངོན་པ་ *mṅón-pa* **conspicuous, visible,** e.g. continents, because they stand out of the water; more frq. fig.: **evident, manifest, clear,** *mṅón-par ˎgyúr-ba* to become manifest; to be verified, proved, e.g. gold by refining *Dzl.* — Tibetan writers regularly translate the *Ssk. abhi* by *mṅón-pa*, hence *čos mṅón-pa Dzl.*, and *mṅón-pai bka Pth.*, the *Abhidharma* (v. *Köpp.* I., 595; *Was.*), *mṅon-pai sde-snod Abhidharma-piṭaka, mṅon-pa-mdzod Abhidharma kośa* (v. *Burn.* I. and *Was.*); as a vb.: to be evident, to appear clearly, *bdén-par čis mṅon*, from what is it evident that it is true? *Dzl.; γnód-par bgyid-du mṅóṅ-no* they are evidently bent on doing mischief *Dzl.; mṅón-du byéd-pa* to manifest, to make public; to show something to others; *Tar.* 24, 1 should be understood: to make clear or manifest to one's self, to perceive, know, understand; *mṅón-du ˳byin-pa* to disclose, reveal (secrets, the future) *Glr.*; to make known (one's wishes) *Glr.*; *mṅón-du ˳gyúr-ba* to be revealed or disclosed, to make one's appearance, *raṅ-byúṅ ye-šés mṅón-du gyúr-pas* as the self-originated wisdom has revealed itself to us *Mil.* — *mṅón-par* adv. manifestly, openly, evidently; often = entirely, highly, greatly, very, *mṅón-par rdzogs Was.* (246) complete fulfilment; in the sense of 'very' it may also be taken in *mṅón-par dgao*, in the legends of Buddha, 'they rejoiced very much', though also one of the other significations of *abhinanda* might help to explain these words.

Comp. *mṅón-(par) brjód(-pa)* = *abhidāna*, a collection of synonyms, of which some are mentioned in *Burn.* I. and II. — *mṅon-rtágs* **proof, argument**; sign or token of the truth of a thing *Dzl.* ༢༢, 2. — *mṅon-(par) rtógs(-pa)* 1. a clear comprehension *Was.* (287). 2. a hymnlike description of a Lha from top to toe, v. also *Schl.* 260. — *mṅon-mtó* re-birth as Lha or as man *Thgy.* (*Schr.*); also n. of a region in Paradise. — *mṅón-pa-pa* an Abhidharma scholar. — *mṅon-spyód Sch.* cruelty, severity; *Schf.* more corr.: **witchcraft**, *Ssk. abhičāra*, *Pth.*, *drág-po mṅon-spyód-kyi las Tar.* frq. — *mṅon-mtsán Lex.* w.e., *Sch.*; an evident sign. — *mṅón-(par) šés(-pa)*, resp. *mkyén(-pa)*, *Ssk. abhijñā*, a kind of **clairvoyance**, gift of supernatural perception, of which five species are enumerated, viz. assuming any form at will, seeing and hearing to any distance, knowing a man's thoughts, knowing a man's condition and antecedents; originally used as a vb.: to be clear-seeing *Pth.* — *mṅon-súm-du* 1. **openly, publicly** *Dzl.*; more frq. 2. **bodily, personally**; like *dṅós-su*, e.g. to appear, to instruct, in person (*Tar.*); to know by one's own personal experience (*W.*).

རྔ་ *rṅa* I. **kettle-drum, drum**, *˳kár-rṅa* v. *˳kar*; *rdzá-rṅa Glr.*, *Cs.*: 'a drum of earthen ware'; *rgyál-rṅa* the beating of drums after a victory, *bág-rṅa* at nuptial festivities, **lhá-ṅa* Ld.* for the king; **žéṅ-ṅa**, and **zim-ṅa* Ld.* a morning and evening serenade with an accompaniment of drums; *krims-kyi rṅá-bo če brdúṅs-te* the beat or sound of the large proclamation drum (prop. law-drum) *Glr.* —

Comp. *rṅa-sgrá* 1. sound of the drum or kettle-drum 2. n. of a Buddha, = *dón-yod-grub-pa* or Amoghasiddha. — **ṅa-lčág* W.*, *rṅa-rdég Sch.*, *rṅa-dbyúg Cs.*, *rṅa-yáb Sch.* **drum-stick**. — *rṅá-pa* **a drummer** *Cs.*, *rṅa-dpón* a chief drummer. — *rṅa-lpágs* **drum-skin**. — *rṅa-yu* handle of a kettle-drum (the larger kettle-drums being held up during the play by means of a handle or stick). — *rṅa-šiṅ* the wooden body of a drum *Cs.* — *rṅa-šón* kettle-drum music *Sch.* — *rṅa-ysáṅs* (also *rṅa-bsaṅs*) a loud beat or roll of the kettle-drum *Sch.*

II. for *rṅa-bóṅ*, and *rṅá-ma*.

རྔ་བ་ *rṅá-ba*, pf. *brṅas*, fut. *brṅa*, imp. *rṅos*, **to mow, to cut, to reap**, *˳bru*, or *lo-tóg zór-bas* to cut the harvest with a sickle; *brtsás-ma brṅás-pa* the reaped corn; *rṅá-mkan* the mower, reaper.

རྔ་བོང་ *rṅa-bóṅ W.*, **ṅa-móṅ* C.*, **camel**, *rṅa-yséb* male camel, *rṅá-mo* female camel; a camel in general; *rṅa-prúg* the young of a camel; *rṅa-rgód* a wild camel; *rṅa-búl* camel's hair.

རྔ་མ་ *rṅá-ma* 1. **tail**. 2. in a special sense: **yak's tail** *Mil.* — *rṅá-ma yyúg-pa Sch.*, **ṅá-ma ṫóg-če** (lit. *skrog-pa*) *W.*, to wag the tail. — *rṅa-yáb* 1. a yak's tail, used for fanning and dusting. 2. *rṅa-yáb*, and *rṅa-yab-yžán*, n. of two fabulous islands in the south of Asia *Cs.*

རྔན་ཆེན་ *rṅan-čén Lex.*, *C.* and *W.*, **contempt, disdain**; **ṅan-čén jhé-pa* C.*, **čó-če* W.* to despise, contemn.

རྔན་པ་ *rṅán-pa* I. sbst. 1. **reward, fee, hire, wages**; *rṅán-pa máṅ-po* the wages are high; *rṅán-pa sbyín-pa* or *ytóṅ-ba* to pay wages; to bribe, to corrupt. — 2. in *C.* at present a kind of **sacrifice.**

II. vb. **to reward, to recompense,** perh. better *brṅán-pa.*

རྔབ་པ *rṅáb-pa* 1. (cf. *rṅam-pa*) **to desire** earnestly, **to crave,** *bkrés-rṅab-pa* to be greedy, to have a craving appetite *Lex.* — 2. *W.* col. for *rṅá-ba* **to mow;** **ṅáb-sa** (lit. *ṅáb-rtsva*) *W.* grass or corn that is to be mown or cut.

རྔབས་རྭ *rṅábs-rva Med.*, a hollow horn, used for sucking *Sch.*

རྔམ་པ *rṅám-pa* 1. sbst. (cf. *dṅom*), also *rṅam-brǰid, rṅom-brǰid,* **splendour, magnificence, majesty,** an appearance, commanding awe or inspiring terror (but not = awe *Cs.*); *rṅám-pai ṅá-ro* a voice of that kind; *rṅám-po, rṅám-čan* adj. bright, shining, grand, majestic. — 2. vb., also *rṅáms-pa*, pf. *brṅams*, **to breathe,** *rṅám-pa bde* the breathing is regular *Mṅg.*, frq ; *rṅám-pa tuṅ* short breath *Sch.*; esp. to breathe heavily, **to pant,** *rṅám-pa rgod* wild puffing *Med.*; c. dat. **to pant for, to desire ardently,** *srog γčód-pa-la* to be blood-thirsty *Ma.*; *rṅám-pai tsúl-gyis* greedily (devouring) *Thgr.*; *rṅám-čan* adj. greedy, avaricious, covetous; **za-ṅam-pa** voracious, gluttonous, ravenous *W.*; to rush upon, fly at, throw one's self on, *γžán-la* on others *Mil.*; **to rage,** to be in a fury; **to destroy** or murder in a state of fury; *mi pal-čér grir rṅom* (like *grir γsod*) the people are in numbers murdered by the sword *Ma.*; to call out in a rage, *čes kros-rṅam-nas* thus she called furious with rage *Dzl.*; *rṅáms-pai (kro)-žal* an angry face, wrathful look *Glr.*

རྔམས *rṅams* **height;** in height *Glr.*, *rṅáms-su* id.

རྔས *rṅas*, v. *sṅas.*

རྔུ *rṅu* **pain,** v. *zug-rṅu.*

རྔུབ་པ *rṅúb-pa*, pf. *(b)rṅubs*, fut. *brṅub*, imp. *rṅubs*, **to draw in,** *dbugs* air, *sna* into the nose *Med.*; to breathe *Med.*; *dbugs rṅub mi ₒton* (?) is mentioned as a sign of great sadness and affliction *Pth.*

རྔུལ *rṅul* **perspiration, sweat,** *rṅúl-ču* id., esp. col.; *rṅul ₒdu Med., ₒbyuṅ Dzl., rṅúl-ču ₒton, *yoṅ**, col. perspiration is breaking forth; *rṅul ₒdóṅ-pa* to cause to sweat or perspire *Cs.*; *rṅúl-ba*, pf. *brṅul*, to sweat, to perspire *Cs.*

རྔེའུ *rṅeu* 1. also *rṅeu-čúṅ, rṅa-čúṅ*, a little **drum,** diminutive of *rṅa.* — 2. the young of a camel, v. *rṅa-móṅ.*

རྔོ *rṅo*, is stated to be a kind of **leprosy,** covering the whole body, of a whitish colour, itching very much, and contagious; **ṅo pog, gyab** he is affected with leprosy; *rṅó-čan* leprous (cf. *mdze*).

རྔོ་བ *rṅó-ba* **to be able** *Cs.*, *rṅo-tóg-pa* id., so *Fouc. Gyatch.* ༢༣༠, 9, **ṅób-če* Ld.*; *Sch.* has: *rṅo mi tóg-pa* to look at one with uncertainty, not being able to recognize; the passage of *Mil.*: *rṅo ma togs kyaṅ* is not to be explained by either of these significations; *Lex.*: *rṅo mi togs* w.e.

རྔོ་བག་ཅན *rṅó-bag-čan Cs.* v. *rṅom-bag-čan.*

རྔོ་ལེན་པ *rṅó-len-pa* **to roast, fry,** (?) *Sch.* v. *rṅód-pa.*

རྔོག *rṅog* 1. also *ze-rṅóg*, **the hunch** or **hump** of an animal *Lex.*, more esp. a hump consisting of fat (like that of the camel); *tsil-rṅóg* the fat around the kidneys, suet *Mil.*; *rús-kyi rṅog Lex.* w.e. — 2. *rṅog(-ma)* **the mane** of horses etc. (not of the lion, v. *ral-pa*), *rta-rṅóg* a horse's mane, *dre-rṅóg* a mule's mane; *dreu-rṅóg* a kind of stuffed seat or mattress *Cs.*, a thick-haired carpet *Sch.*; *rṅóg-čan, rṅóg-ldan* having a mane; *rṅogs-čágs* a beast that has a mane *Cs.*

རྔོད་པ *rṅód-pa* I. pf. *brṅos*, fut. *brṅod Cs.* (perh. erron. for *brṅo*) imp. *rṅod, rṅos*, *W.* **ṅo-če** 1. **to parch** (barley), *ser tsam* (to parch a thing) so that it turns yellowish *Glr.* — 2. **to roast, to fry** e.g. meat in a pan.

II. **to deceive** (acc. to *Cs.* = *rṅón-pa* to deceive wild beasts, to hunt); **to seduce,** esp. to sensual indulgence, *bud-méd Lex.*; similarly *Tar.* 39, 2.

རྔོན་པ་ *rṅón-pa* 1. vb., pf. and fut. *brṅon*, **to hunt, pursue**, wild animals *Cs.*, *Sch.*; **to fish** *C.* — 2. sbst. a hunter, huntsman *Dzl.* and *Ler.*; *rṅón-pa-mo* a hunting woman, a huntress *Cs.*

རྔོབ་པ་ *rṅób-pa Ld.* **to be able**, v. *rṅó-ba*.

རྔོམ་བརྗིད་ *rṅom-brjid* (cf. *rṅám-pa* 1) **splendour, stateliness, majesty**; *rṅóm-bag-čan*, also col. **ṅóm-jig-čan**, grand, majestic; terrible, of a judge, of terrifying deities. (A sbst. *rṅóm-bag* = *rṅom-brjid Cs.* prob. does not exist.)

ལྔ་ *lṅa* (*Bal.* **γa**), **five**, *lṅá-bču*(*-tam-pa*) fifty; *lṅa-brgya* five hundred; *lṅa-bču-rtsa-γčig* (*W.* **ṅa-bču-ṅa-čig**) or *ṅa-γčig*, fifty one etc.; *lṅá-pa* the fifth, *lṅa-po* consisting of five, cf. *dgu*; *lṅá-ga Cs.*, *lṅá-ka Pth.* all the five, each of the five. The number five very often occurs in legends, as well as in sacred science, v. the Index to *Burn.* II., and to *Fouc. Gyatch.* II. under *'Cinq'*. *lṅa-lén*, *Ssk.* **पञ्चाल**, n. of a country in the north of ancient India.

སྔ་ *sṅa* (**पूर्व**) a root signifying **before, soon, early**, rarely referring to space, and seldom used alone as adj. or adv., e.g. *Dzl.* ༢༣༥, 8: *ₒdá-ba ni há-čaṅ yaṅ sṅa čés-so* deliverance (sc. from existence) takes place much too soon; *ṅa ni tém-pa sṅa brgal yin* I was the foremost, the first, to cross the threshold *Glr.*; *bstán-pa sṅa dar bar dar p̔yi dar γsum* the first, intermediate, and last propagation of the doctrine *Glr.*; gen. it is used with an adjective termination, with postpositions, or in compounds.

Deriv. *sṅá-ba* 1. adj. **ancient**, belonging or referring to former ages, *rgya-nág-gi rgyál-po sṅá-ba* an ancient king of China *Glr.*; of an early date, long ago, . . . *las dá-lta sṅá-ba ₒdúg-gam* is it already a long time, since . . . ? *Mil.*; 2. sbst. **antiquity**, the olden time; **the morning**; = *sṅá-dro*, *Mil.*; 3. vb. pf. *sṅas*, **to be the first, to come first, to be beforehand**, (φθάνειν): *rjé-yi sku mtoṅ ṅa sṅá-bas* as I was the first to see the king's face *Glr.*; *ₒgran-tsig sṅás-pa yin* you were beforehand with me in disputing *Glr.*; **k̔a ṅe son** *Sp.* you promised it. — *sṅá-bar* in former times, **formerly, in the morning**; *saṅ sṅá-bar* to-morrow morning *Glr.* — *sṅá-ma* adj. 1. **earlier, former, preceding, afore-said**, frq.; *sṅá-ma sṅá-ma* always the anterior in time and place; *sṅá-ma ltar*, or *bžin-du*, as before, frq. 2. **the first**, the foremost in a series or succession *Dzl.*; *ldáṅ-bai sṅá-ma* **she** who takes the first turn in getting up ***Mil.*** — *sṅá-mo* 1. **earlier, by-gone**; *sṅá-mo-nas* **long ago** *Mil.*; 2. *W.*: **the morning, in the** morning, **nā ṅá-mo** early in the morning, **t̔ó-re ṅá-mo** to-morrow morning; also: **early enough**, in due time (opp. to **p̔i-mo**). — *sṅá-ru* v. *sṅar*, as a separate article. — *sṅá-na* **before, previously**, (gen. *sṅar* is used inst. of it). — *sṅá-nas* id., prop. of former times.

Comp. *sṅá-góṅ*(*-nas*) adv. **before, previously, at first**, a little while ago, **just now** *Mil.*; **formerly**, = late, deceased, *sṅa-góṅ yab* your late father *Glr.*; *sṅa góṅ bód-kyi rgyál-po* the earlier Tibetan kings *Glr.* — *sṅa-dgóṅs* morning and evening *Sch.* — *sṅa-sṅá* very early *Sch.* — *sṅa-čád* **formerly, hitherto**, till now, up to this time ***Dzl.***, = *sṅan-čád*, *sṅon-čád*. — *sṅa-rtiṅ-du* **earlier** or **later**, not at the same time, e.g. *brós-so* they escaped *Glr.* — *sṅa-ltás* **omen, presage, prognostic**; also the fate or destiny portended. — *sṅa-t̔óg* 1. **forenoon.** 2. **the first-fruits** of harvest *Cs.* — *sṅa-dús* **antiquity, time of old.** — *sṅa-dro* **the morning**, the earlier part of the forenoon, 'the time before the heat of the sun'; *sṅá-dro γčig-la* in half a forenoon *Glr.*; *sṅá-dro dgóṅs-mo* morning and evening *Sch.* v. **above**; *saṅ sṅá-dro* to-morrow morning *Mil.* — *sṅa-p̔yi*(*r*) **sooner** or **later**, like *sṅa-rtiṅ-du* v. above *Dzl.* frq. — *sṅá-rol* **time of old, past ages** *Cs.*; *sṅá-rol-tu* before *Tar.* (cf. *sṅón-rol*). — **ṅá-lo** *W.* **last year.** — *sṅa sgrags ₒdrén-pa Cs.*: 'the accenting of the first syllable'. — *sṅa-sár* **early**, *sṅa-sar-sár* **very** early *Cs.* — *sṅa-sór* 1. in the **first place**, first of all, **at first** (cf. *rtiṅ-sor*) *Glr.* 2. **anciently**, in old times *Cs.*

སྔ་སྔོ **sṅa-sṅó vegetables, greens** Thgy. (v. sṅo).

སྔགཔ **sṅág-pa,** also **sṅágs-pa,** pf. bsṅags, fut. bsṅay, imp. sṅog, **to praise, commend, extol; to recommend;** ₀gró-bar sṅags it is recommended to go Wdn.; bstod-sṅág-pa to praise, to sing praises, frq.; sṅág-(pa-)po a praiser, commender, Cs.; sṅag-(par) ₀os(-pa), sṅág-ldan praiseworthy; praised; also n. of the horse of Buddha Cs. — sṅag-ysól **praise, thanks.**

སྔགས **sṅags (मन्त्र,** also **धारणी & तन्त्र)**
1. **incantation,** magical formula, a set of words, consisting mostly of a number of unmeaning Sanskrit syllables, in the recital of which however perfect accuracy is requisite; hence detailed rules and instructions for a correct pronunciation of the Sanskrit sounds have been drawn up for Tibetan devotees. (On magical formulas v. Burn. II., 21, and note; on Buddhist magic in general v. Was. 142.177, Köpp. II., 29.) — rzuṅs-sṅágs, rig-sṅágs, and ysaṅ-sṅágs prob. = sṅags. — sṅags sgrúb-pa, spél-ba, zlá-ba, C. also *gyág-pa*, to recite, to pronounce charms, incantations; ₀ćán-ba, ₀dzín-pa, to carry (charms) about one's self. — sṅágs-kyi tég-pa Tantrayāna, Mantrayāna, v. tég-pa. — sṅágs-pa, sṅágs-mk'an, one versed in charms and their use, i.e. in orthodox and legitimate magic, as contained in the sacred books of religion. Opposed to this are ṅan-sṅágs, ṅan-sṅágs-mk'an, diabolical sorcerers and necromancers, and also common swindlers, jugglers, conjurers, fortune-tellers etc. — 2. **praise, encomium** Cs.

སྔངས **sṅaṅs** = dṅaṅs, v. dṅáṅ-ba Glr., Pth.

སྔན **sṅan,** for sṅa, sṅon, e.g. sṅan-ćád, **formerly, before, previously, beforehand,** opp. to npw Mil.; sṅan-ćád tó-₀tsams-pa bzód-par ysol pardon our former scoffing Mil.; esp. W.: *ṅán-la* for sṅón-la, sṅar, before, previously; *ṅán-ma* for sṅá-ma, *ṅán-me gyál-po* the former or last king, *ṅán-ma naṅ-tar* just as before.

སྔནབུ **sṅán-bu** a medicinal herb, Wdn.

སྔར **sṅar,** prop. sṅá-ru, **before, beforehand, previously, formerly, at first;** sṅar de byás-pai ₀óg-tu not until that has been previously done Dzl.; sṅar méd-pa, sṅar ma byás-pa, sṅar ma skyés-pa what has not existed, or has not been done before, where we only say **new,** frq.; sṅar loṅs get up first! Dzl.; sṅár-bas kyaṅ(lhag-pár) still more so than formerly, frq.; sṅár-gyi what has been hitherto in use, frq.; sṅár-gyi yi-ge rnyiṅ-pa-rnams the old writings of antiquity Glr.; sṅar yin-na adv. = sṅar Mil.; sṅar ltar, sṅar bẑin as before; sṅár-nas from before, from former times Mil.; also with reference to space: foremost, ahead, in advance, on, onward, joined to verbs of motion Dzl.; sṅár-ba the former, first-mentioned (?). In the sense of a postposition (c. accus.) sṅar is used but seldom, as far as I know only in spyan-sṅár.

སྔརམ **sṅár-ma intelligent,** quick of apprehension Sch.

སྔས **sṅas a bolster, pillow, cushion;** yo-byád sṅás-su júg-pa Glr., C. col. *yo-jhḗ-la ṅe ćúg-pa*,using the luggage as a pillow; sṅas-stán, sṅas-₀ból, resp. dbu-sṅás pillow; rgyab-sṅás a cushion for the back; sṅas-mál a couch constructed of pillows or cushions; sṅas-₀páns (?) pillow, cushion Cs.; W. *nyę* for *sṅas*.

སྔསཔ **sṅás-pa** v. sṅa-ba.

སྔུན **sṅun,** col. for sṅon; sṅún-la c. genit. **before, ago,** like gón-du; *dá-wa ṅyi-śi ṅún-la* two months ago; *ṅún-la soṅ* he walked in advance, or ahead; *ṅún-ma* former, last; *ṅún-ma-ẑag* W. two days before yesterday, *yan ṅún-ẑag* three days before yesterday.

སྔུརབ **sṅúr-ba to snore** Lex. (cf. ṅur-ba).

སྔེུ **sṅeu** Lex., Cs.: **a kind of pulse** or **pease;** Sch. = món-sran, v. greu.

སྔོ **sṅo, a root signifying blue or green;** as sbst. **plant, herb, vegetable, greens** Mil.; sṅo skyé-na when it is getting green or verdant.

Comp. sṅo-skyá **blue bice, pale blue,** e.g.

the skin of emaciated persons *Med.*; **ṅo gyaṅ-gyáṅ** *W.* greenish-yellow (spelling dubious). — *sṅo-sgá* officinal herb, *Wdṅ.* (green ginger?) — *sṅo-ṅád* v. *ṅad.* — *sṅo-ljáṅ* **bluish green.** — *sṅo-ṭóg Schr.* 'unripe, sour, of fruits'(?); more corr.: green, unripe fruits. — *sṅo-drégs* green mud or mire *Sch.* — *sṅo-nág* **deep blue.** — *sṅó-ba* 1. vb. **to get green, verdant;** 2. adj., also *sṅó-bo*, more frq. *sṅón-po, sṅón-mo* **blue, green,** also used of the livid colour of diseased or famished people *Glr.* — *sṅo-smán* a medicinal herb. — *sṅo-tsód* **vegetables; herbs.** — *sṅo-ló* the leaf of a plant; *Cs.*: '*sṅo-ló ᵒčár-ba* to become notorious'. — *sṅo-sáṅs* **pale blue** e.g. of the sky; *sṅo-sáṅs-ma* night *Sch.*

སྔོ་བ *sṅó-ba*, *Cs.* also *sṅód-pa*, pf. *bsṅos*, fut. *bsṅo*, imp. *sṅos*, 1. **to become green** *Cs.* — 2. (*Lex.* परिणाम?) **to bless,** **ṅó-wa gyáb-če* W.*, though in most cases as a requital for a present given; *Dzl.* ༢༥༣, 16: to bless, to pronounce a benediction, hence also in litanies the words of the priest seem to be indiscriminately called *sṅó-ba*, whereas the responses of the congregation of monks are termed *mťun-ᵒgyúr*; generally: **to dedicate, devote,** e.g. one's property to the *dkon-mčóg ysum*, i.e. in reality to the priesthood; *dgé-ba ᵒgro-drug dón-du sṅos*, to devote alms, charitable gifts, to the (temporal and eternal) welfare of beings. *Mil.*; also **to design, to intend,** *ṅá-la bsṅós-pai γyu* the turkois intended for me (by you) *Mil.*; *Dzl.* ༧༥, 3: *sá-la káṅ-bu daṅ rin-po-čér bsṅós-nas rtse-ba*, fancying the earth to consist of cottages and jewels, and thus playing with it.

སྔོག་པ *sṅóg-pa Lex.*, prob. pf. *bsṅogs*, fut. *bsṅog*, imp. *sṅogs*, **to vex, to annoy;** cf. *skyo-ṅógs, skyo-sṅógs.*

སྔོན *sṅon* = *sṅa* and *sṅan*, **formerly, before, previously;** *sṅon ťós-na* having formerly heard *Dzl.*; *sṅon máṅ-du ḱyer yaṅ* although you have taken a good deal with you before; *sṅon ᵒdás-pai* or *byúṅ-bai dús-na* in by-gone times, frq.; *sṅon bčom-ldan-ᵒdás* a former Buddha *Glr.*; *sṅon mi dbúl-po ḍe* this man formerly poor *Dzl.*; *bdág-las sṅon bdág-gi pʼa* my father before me (has ...); *sṅón-gyi* adj. former, last; *sṅón-ma* the former (when two persons or things are spoken of), *sṅón-ma-rnams* the former (persons or things) *Glr.*; **beginning,** *lha-ḱáṅ ǰig-pai sṅón-ma lhá-sa-la byás-te* making a beginning with the destruction of the temples in Lhasa *Glr.*; *sṅon-du* adv. and postp., **before,** at the head, in advance, in the front of, *sṅón-du ᵒgró-ba* to go before or in advance, to precede, also of words and letters; *sṅón-du ᵒǰúg-pa* to put or place before, *Gram.*; *sṅón-la* = *sṅón-du*: *sṅón-la soṅ* walk first! *Mil.*; *stón-pai sṅón-du* (he died) before the Teacher (Buddha) *Tar.*; sooner, earlier, before the time supposed, *sṅón-la tsár-ro* they were first in finishing (their task) *Glr.*; *ᵒo-ná sṅón-la ᵒdi pʼul čig* oh yes, but first give me that *Mil.*; *sṅón-nas* from a former time, from the beginning *Mil.*; *sṅón-bžin* as formerly *Mil.*

Comp. *sṅon-skyés* **the first-born,** eldest son. — *sṅon-gró* v. *ᵒgró-ba* compounds. — *sṅon-čád*, *sṅon-čád Dzl.*, v. *sṅan-čád.* — *sṅon-ᵒǰúg* **a prefixed letter** *Gram.* — *sṅon-dús, sṅon-tsé* **antiquity;** adv. **anciently,** in times of old. — *sṅon-byúṅ Cs.* = *sṅon-rábs.* — *sṅón-rábs* ancient race, ancient history, **antiquity,** पुराण. — *sṅón-rol* (cf. *sṅá-rol*) **former time** or **period,** *ma γtád-pai sṅón-rol žig-tu* formerly, in former times, when (the chair) was not yet transferred (to ...) *Tar.* — *dus ná-niṅ sṅón-bai sṅón-rol-na* a year ago (an expression with an unnecessary redundancy of words!) *Mil.* — *sṅon-lás* **former actions.**

སྔོན *sṅon* = *sṅo*, *sṅón-po*, v. *sṅo.*

སྔོན་བུ *sṅón-bu* n. of a medicinal plant, acc. to *Cs.* poisonous; in *Lh.* Delphinium Cashmirianum, officinal. — *sṅon-bum* n. of a botanical work: 'the hundred thousand vegetables' *Cs.*

བངའ་བ *bṅá-ba*, v. *rṅá-ba.*

བངད་པ *bṅád-pa Sch.*: 'ausziehen, ausreissen'.

བརྙན་པ་ *brñán-pa*, = *rñán-pa* sbst. *Glr.*, vb. *Lex.*

བརྙབ་པ་ *brñáb-pa* 1. *Sch.* = *brñád-pa.* — 2. *Lex.* = *rñáb-pa, rñams-pa.*

བསྙལ་བ་ *bsñál-ba* **to be faint** or exhausted *Cs.*; v. *sdug-bsñál.*

བསྙས་པ་ *bsñas-pa* to place upon a cushion *Sch.*

བསྙོ་བ་ *bsñó-ba* 1. v. *sñó-ba.* — 2. **a blessing,** cf. *sñó-ba.* — 3. *Cs.* also: **mouldy, rotten** (prob. only livid, discolonred. v. *sño).*

ཙ

ཙ *ča* 1. the letter *č*, tenuis, palatal, like the Italian ci in *ciascuno*, or c in *cicerone.* — 2. as numerical figure: 5. — 3. = *lča* **excrement,** alvine discharges, *ča ,dór-ba* to discharge excrements *Mil.*

ཙ་ཅིར་ *ča-čír* lark *Ld.*

ཙ་ཙུས་ *ča-čús* **warped, distorted, awry** *Sch.*

ཙ་ཅོ *ča-čó* **clamour, cries,** *snyiṅ tsim-gyi ča-čo* shout, exclamation of joy *Pth.*; **noise,** of many people *Thgy.*; *da čá-čó ma zer* now do not make such a noise! (so *Mil.* rebukes the aërial spirits); **chirping, twitter** *Glr.*; *čá-čo-čan* **shouting, bawling; talkative, loquacious** *Stg.*

ཙ་དར་ *čá-dar*, also *ťsá-dar, tsá-sar,* **a sheet, blanket, toga.**

ཙ་ར་ར་ *ča-ra-rá*, or *či-ri-rí*, *W.* **čár-pa ča-ra-rá yoṅ dug**, it rains heavily, it is pouring.

ཙ་རི་ *ča-rí W.* **bug.**

ཙ་རེ་ *ča-ré* **continually, always** = *čar.*

ཙག *čag* termination of the plur. of pers. pronouns.

ཙག་ཀྲུམ་ *čag-krúm* **cartilage, gristle;** *snai čag-krúm* bridge of the nose.

ཙག་དཀར་ *čag-dkár W.* **quartz.**

ཙག་ག *čág-ga*, *C.* **čág-ga ǰhé-pa**, = *nyára byéd-pa*, c. *la*, **to take care of;** **čág-ga dág-po ǰhe'-pa** to look after, to keep, preserve carefully; **čág-ga dág-po** careful, orderly, regular, tidy, of persons.

ཙག་ཙག, ཙག་པ *čag-čág, čág-pa* **smacking** in eating *Cs.*

ཙག་ཙེར་རེ་ *čag-čer-ré* closely pressed or crowded, in standing or sitting *Ld.*

ཙག་རྡོ་ *čag-rdó* = *čag-dkár W.*

ཙང་ *čaṅ*, (v. *čiaṅ, či-yaṅ*), **every thing, any thing whatever,** *čaṅ-šés* knowing every thing, epithet of deities or saints; more frq. followed by a negative particle and then signifying: **nothing;** **čaṅ mi sto** it does not matter, it is indifferent (to me), frq.; **čaṅ med** there is nothing here, or at hand; also = **čaṅ mi sto; čaṅ mi šés-ḱan** ignorant, stupid; blockhead, simpleton.

ཙང་ཏེའུ་ *čaṅ-téu Glr.*, also *čaṅ-čaṅ-téu* (**डमरु**) a sort of **small drum** *Pth.*

ཙན *čan*, affix, adjective termination, prop. signifying: **having, being provided with,** = *daṅ ldáṅ-pa*, corresponding to the English adj. terminations -ous, -y, -ly, -ful, e.g. *ťsér-ma-čan* thorny; sometimes also = -like or -ish: *bón-čan* Bon-like, heretical *Mil.*, *hin-du-čan* Hindoo-like, Hindooish; seldom affixed to verbs: *byéd-pa-čan* a doer, maker; in *C.* also for the possessive pron.: *ṅá-čan, kó-čan*, my, his (her), **nag-góṅ sá-hib-čen** the Sahib's inkstand. It may also be affixed to a set of words that form one expression: *ťsér-ma nón-po-čan* having sharp thorns, *séṅ-gei mgó-čan* having a lion's head.

ཅན་ *čan*, po., prop. *čán-du*, postp. c. accus., **to, with**, *koṅ čán-du mi ༠gro* I do not go to him *Mil., Pth.*; *ṅa čán-du* with me, in my presence *Mil.* The word seems to be rather obsolete; more recent editions having *gán-du* and *drún-du* instead of it.

ཅན་ཅིལ་ *čan-čil* (?) *W.* the green shell of a walnut.

ཅན་ཅེ་, ཅན་ཅེར་, ཅན་ནེ་ *čan-čé, čan-čér, čan-né, Sch.*; a small bowl or dish; *Cs.*: continually.

ཅན་དྭན་ *čan-dván* green, unripe *W.* (?).

ཅན་ས་ *čán-sa* (?) kitchen, fire-place *W.*

ཅབ་ཅོབ་ *čab-čob Cs.* **nonsense** e.g. *smrá-ba*.

ཅམ་ *čam* 1. *Cs.* **slow**; *Lex. čám-gyis ༠jog*, and several other passages, the sense of which is not quite clear; cf. *čam-mé*. — 2. **glistening, glittering** (?) cf. *lčam-mé*. — 3. *W.* **whole, unimpaired**, *sa* (*lit. rtsva*) *čam-mé yod* the whole store of hay is still left (entire).

ཅམ་པ་ཏ་ལོ་ *čám-pa-tá-lo Ts.* **mallow**.

ཅམ་པོད་ *čam-pód Ld.* **a bunch** of flowers, sprigs etc., a handful of ears of corn.

ཅར་ *čar* 1. *Lex. čar-ré, Cs. ča-ré, Sch.* also *čar-már*, **always, continually** *Cs.* — 2. also *čar, čór-du*, with numerals, esp. *yčig-čar* **at the same time, simultaneously**, opp. to one after the other, successively (viz. doing or suffering a thing, sleeping, dying etc.) *Dzl.*; **at once, on a sudden**, opp. to gradually *Mil.*; *lṅá-car* all the five together *Thgy., ɤnyis-čar, drúg-čar* etc.

ཅར་རས་ *čar-ras* v. ༠*doms-ras*.

ཅལ་ *čal Cs.*: 'noise, *čal-čal* id.; *čal-rgyug* rumour, (false) report'; *čal-čól* idle talk, nonsense, *čal-čól ɤtam* id. *Mil.*

ཅས་ *čas Pur.*, v. *čes* 2.

ཅས་ཅུས་ *čas-čús Sch.* = *ča-čús*.

ཅི་ *či*. num. figure: 35

ཅི་ *či* I. interr. pron. in direct questions: 1. **what?** (*C.* gen. *gaṅ* instead of *či*) *či šes* (like the *Hind.* क्या जाने) who knows? col. *W.*; also pleon. at the end of a question after the... *am: ṅa ṅó-šes-sam či?* do you know me? do you? *Dzl.*; *cii* of whom? whose? followed by *pyir, don, čed, slad* (*-du*): why? wherefore? inst. of *čii pyir* also *či-pyir* etc.; *de čii pyir žé-na* 'this wherefore? (= why this?) if so it is asked'. (This phrase, besides the gerundial particles — esp. *pas* — is the only way in which in *B.* the causal conjunction 'for' (*Lat. nam, enim*) can be expressed, and in translating into Tibetan, the English conjunction must therefore often be altogether omitted.) *čii ༠brás-bu* what sort of fruit? *čii ri* what kind of a mountain? i.e. of what consisting? *Pth.*; *či* also, like an adj., is placed after the word to which it belongs: *rgyu či-las* for what reason? on what account? *Thgy.* — 2. **why? wherefore?** but only in negative questions: *bdág-la des či ma čog* why should not that suffice me? *Thgy.*; *či mi sgrúb* why do you not procure...? inst. of the imp. procure! *Mil.*; *bsám-na či ma legs* if you considered..., why would not that be a good thing? = you had better consider, you ought to consider *Mil.*; frq.: *de ༠byúṅ-na či ma ruṅ* if that happened, why should it not be desirable? = would that it happened! oh, may it happen! — 3. **how?** in conjunction with other words, v. below. — 4. inst. of a note of interrogation, e.g. in: *či ɤnaṅ*, for *ɤnáṅ-ṅam, ɤségs-par či ɤnaṅ* do you allow(me) to come? *Dzl.* ཟེར་, 13; ཟས་, 5.

II. correlatively: **which, what; whatsoever; every thing**, much like *gaṅ*, q. v., esp. the syntactical explanations given there. *či*, as a correlative, ought prop. always to be written *ji*, yet not even in decidedly correlative sentences is this strictly observed: *či byed(-na- aṅ)* whatever I may do *Glr.*; *či ཏྱྀ bka nyan(-te) ṅéd-kyis bsgrub* whatever we may be bidden to do, we shall obediently perform *Pth.*; *či myur*, also *či myur žíg-la Pth.* as quick as possible;

also *či* alone: by all means, at all events, *spyan či draṅs* he must be conducted here at all events *Glr.*

Comp. and deriv. *či-ga* **what?** col. — *či-dgar*, *či dgá-bar* whatever one may wish, **at pleasure, ad libitum.** — *či snyed* v. *snyed.* — **či toṅ** (lit. *γtoṅ*) **žig** **some, something** col. — *či lta-bu* **of what sort,** manner, fashion, quality or nature? *Lat. qualis.* — *či ltar* **how?** in what manner? **what?** *da či ltar bya*, *W.* **da či čó-če**, what is now to be done? — *či ltar gyúr-pai γtam byás-so* he related what had happened, frq. — *či-ste*, followed by *na* or (rarely) *te*, in most cases = the *Lat. sin*, **but if,** if however; even supposed that; sometimes for *gál-te*, **if,** in case. — *či sto* what does it matter? *ši yaṅ či sto* if he dies, what does it matter? *Thgy.* (cf. *čaṅ*). — *či-*₀*dra-ba* similar to what? of what kind? also: of whatever description it may be *Glr.* — *či-nas* from which or what? out of which or what? by which? etc. (*Bal.*: **či-ne** how?), *či-nas kyaṅ* = *čis kyaṅ* q.v. — *či tsam* **how much?** *B.*, *W.*; *či tsam yod kyaṅ* though he have ever so much *Mil.*; *či tsám-du* how far? to what distance? — *či-tsug* *Cs.*, col. **či-zug, gá-zug** how? in what manner? — *či žig* 1. **what? what a?** 2. **some one, any one, something, anything;** *či žig-tu dgos* for what (purpose) is it wanted? *Dzl.*; *či žig-na* once, one time, at any time *Pth.*; *či žig-nas* after that, afterwards *Pth.* — *či yaṅ*, *či-aṅ*, *čaṅ* **whatever,** any thing, all kinds of things, **ṅul yǫ̀-na tsóṅ-gyu či yaṅ yǫ̀** *C.* if there is money, you may sell any thing; followed by a negative: **nothing.** — *či rigs-pa* adj., *či rigs-par* adv. 1. **in some measure,** to a certain degree; in part, partly *Tar.*; 2. **of every sort** *Dzl.* and elsewh. — *či-la* **why? wherefore?** *Glr.*, *W.* col.; also for the *de čii p̔yir žé-na* of *B.*; further it is used inst. of an affirmative; e.g. question: shall we get rice there? answer: **tob yin; či-la mi tob** of course, why not? **či-la žu** **why! well!**

ཅི་ལིམ་ *či-lim* (*Hind.* چلم) 1. the **bowl** of a **hukka (water-pipe).** — 2. **a hukka.**

ཅི་ཙེ་ *či-tse Kun.*, also *tsé-tse*, **millet.**

ཅིག་ *čig*, enclitic, a modification of *γčig*, after *s* usually changed into *šig*, after vowels, and the liquids *ṅ, n, m, r, l* into *žig* (exceptions, however, in provincialisms and in literature are not unfrequent) 1. after nouns, the indefinite article **a,** or **a few,** when following after a plural; sometimes also untranslatable: *bud-méd-dag čig* some women; *máṅ-po žig* many (sometimes expressly opp. to *máṅ-po*, *the* many, *Tar.* 7, 15); *gaṅ žig* v. *gaṅ;* **a little, some,** *šiṅ žig* ₀*tú-ru* ₀*gro dgos* I must go and pick up some fire-wood *Mil.*; after infinitives: *k̔rims daṅ* ₀*gál-ba žig byéd-pa* to commit a trespass, to make one's self guilty of a transgression *Dzl.*; *tse* ₀*p̔ós-pa gráṅs-med-pa žig myaṅ* he suffered innumerable deaths *Dzl.*; it is even added to numerals, and not only when 'nearly', 'about' or similar words leave a given number undefined (*mi lṅa tsam žig* some five people), but also in sentences like the following: *čú-mig bži žig yod* there are four springs or fountains. In all these cases, however, it may also be omitted. The numeral for 'one' ought always to be written *γčig* and never *čig*, but prefixing the *γ* is so often neglected (e g. in *t̔abs čig-tu, lhan čig* etc.) that even grammarians let it pass. — 2. when affixed to verbs (to the root of the imp. mood, or, in negative sentences, to the root of the present tense) it is a sign of the imperative. In ancient literature it is used without reference to rank, whether it be in making prayers to Buddha, or in giving orders to a servant; at present in *C.* only in the latter way; in *W.* it is of rare occurrence.

ཅིང་, ཤིང་, ཞིང་ *čiṅ, šiṅ, žiṅ*, a gerundial particle, the initial letter of which is changed acc. to the rules obtaining for *čig*; it corresponds to the English participle in **ing,** is used in sentences beginning with **when, after, as,** and is affixed to verbal roots and adjectives, in the latter case including the auxiliary verb to be: *γžón-por dúr-du bčúg-čiṅ bui ša zá-bar* *gyúr-ċig* (= *bċúg-nas*, or *bċúg-ste*) may I, after having been buried alive, be obliged to eat my own son's flesh! *Dzl.*; usually however employed in the minor clauses of accessory sentences: *brós-śiṅ ·gáb-pas* having hid themselves after running away *Dzl.*; frq. also where coordinate ideas are in English connected by **and** or **but:** *šá-la zá-žiṅ ḱrág-la ₒṫúṅ-ba* eating flesh and drinking blood; *čé-žiṅ légs-pa* tall and well-shaped; *drod ɣnód-ċiṅ bsíl-ba p̔an* heat is hurtful (but), cold is beneficial *Lt.* It is also used like the ablative of the gerund in Latin: *nya bśór-žiṅ ₒtsó-o* we live by fishing (piscando) *Dzl.*; and = *kyin* (q.v.): *ri-la draṅ-sroṅ byéd-ċiṅ ₒdúg-go* he sits on the mountain acting the part of an anchorite *Dzl.*; *smre-sṅágs ₒdón-ċiṅ ₒdug* he sits wailing *Dzl.*; *raṅ-dgár ₒgró-žiṅ ɣda* he is wandering at pleasure *Mil.*; *ċes smrá-žiṅ yód-pa-la* as they were thus speaking *Glr.*; *čos stón-ċiṅ yód-pai tse* as he was just giving religious instruction *Tar.* 11, 12.

ཅིའུ་རི་ *ċiu-ri* n. of a female demon *Thgr.*

ཅིར་, ཅི་རུ་ *ċir*, *ċi-ru*, termin. of *ċi*, 1. **whereto** etc., little used. — 2. with *yaṅ*: **everywhere**, in every direction, for any purpose, by all means, with a negative: **nowhere** (so at least it is to be explained in several passages of *Pth.* and *Thgy.*).

ཅིས་ *ċis*, instr. of *ċi*, *ċis yid-čes-par ₒgyur* **by what** am I to believe it? what shall make me believe it? **whereby** can I know it to be true? *Dzl.*; *ċis kyaṅ mi skrág-pa yin* he is not to be frightened by any thing *Dzl.*; *ċis kyaṅ*, and *ċi-nas kyaṅ* frq. used as adv.; **by all means**, at all events, at any rate, *ċis kyaṅ ₒgró-na* if you wish to go by all means, at all hazards; *da ċis kyaṅ gegs byao* now I will at any rate play him a trick *Dzl.*; *ċis kyaṅ bžes-pa žu* I beg of you most earnestly to accept it *Mil.*; *ċis kyaṅ slobs* **never mind!** teach it me at any rate! *Pth.*

ཅུ་ *ċu* 1. num. figure: 65. — 2. inst. of *bċu*, used in compound numerals for the tens, when the preceding numeral ends with a consonant: *sum-ċu*, *drug-ċu*, *bdun-ċu*, *brgyad-ċu*.

ཅུ་གང་ *ċu-gaṅ Med.*, *Cs.*: 'a sort of lime used for medicine'.

ཅུ་ཏི་ *ċu-ti* (*?ɣċu-ti*) **pig-tail, cue,** worn by boys and men in Tibet proper, *Ld.* and *Sp.* Cf. *ċo-to*.

ཅུ་ལི་, ཅོ་ལི་ *ċu-li*, *ċo-li* 1. *W.* **a fresh apricot.** — 2. *C.* **dried apricots** without stones. — 3. a sort of wild-growing vegetable *Sik.*, *C.* — *ċu-li ta-gir* the pulp of apricots boiled down to a conserve and formed into cakes *W.* — *bun-ċu-li* a kind **of peach** *Kun.*

ཅུག་ཅུག་ *ċug-ċug* = *ċag-ċág Sch.*

ཅུང་ *ċuṅ* 1. *C.* **gourd, pumpkin.** — 2. n. of a place. — 3. for *ċuṅ žig*: *da ḱyod ċuṅ p̔yis-pa yin* you are **a little** too late now *Pth.*; *ċuṅ yó-ba* a little slanting *Glr.*

ཅུང་ཞིག་, ཅུང་ཟད་, ཆུང་ཟད་ *ċúṅ-žig*, *ċúṅ-zad*, *čúṅ-zad*, **a little,** *B.* and *C.*, *mú-ge ċúṅ-zad ċig* a partial famine *Mil.*; *ċúṅ-zad-kyi p̔yir* for the sake of a trifle, through an insignificant circumstance *Dzl.* ༢༢༤, 15; **some,** *Lat. nonnulla*, of rare occurrence, *Was.* (242); *ċuṅ žig skyéṅ-bar gyúr-nas* rather ashamed, somewhat confounded *Glr.*; *ċúṅ-žig p̔án-nam blta* I shall see, whether it will help, or has helped, a little *Mil.*; a little while, a short space of time, *ċúṅ-zad ċig sdod ċig* wait a little (while) *Dzl.* When followed by a negative, it may either be translated as in: *ċúṅ-zad ma bdé-ba* a little unwell, uneasy etc. *Mil.*, or as in: *dbaṅ ċúṅ-zad med*, there is not even a slight possibility = there is no possibility at all *Pth.* and elsewh.

ཅུང་ཞོ་ *ċúṅ-žo*, also *ċúṅ-žu*, *ċuṅ-ži*, *ɣċoṅ-ži*, a kind of white stone.

ཅུབ་ *ċub W.*, from the *Hind.* चुप्, **ċub ċád-de dug** he keeps silence, holds his peace.

ཅུར་ *ċur*, in *ċur mid-pa* **to devour** food **entire** *Sch.*

ཅུར་ནི་ *ċúr-ni* **meal, flour,** only in medical writings.

ཅེ་ *ċe* numer. figure: 95.

ཅེ་ན་, ཤེ་ན་, ཞེ་ན་ *ċé-na, śé-na, žé-na* (cf. *ċig*), inst. of *ċes smrá-na*, **'if one says so, asks so'** etc., after words literally quoted, frq. (*W.* **zér-na**).

ཅེ་སྤྱང་ *ċe-spyáṅ* **jackal.**

ཅེ་རེ་, ཅེར་རེ་ *ċe-ré, ċer-ré* **envious, jealous,** *mig ċe-ré* (*ċér-gyis Thgr., ċér-te Glr.*) *ltá-ba* to look with an evil or envious eye upon; *ċe-ré lóṅ-ba* dim-sighted, purblind *Cs.*

ཅེམ་མེ་བ་ *ċém-me-ba* **bright, shining,** of polished metal *Glr.*, cf. *k̔rá-bo*.

ཅེམ་ཙེ་ *ċém-tse* **scissors** *C.*

ཅེའུ་ *ċeu* 1. a small **sucking-pipe** for drinking the Murva-beer, in which millet grains are swimming *Sik.* (v. *Hook.* I., 175). — 2. **a clyster-pipe.**

ཅེར་ *ċer*, v. *ċe-ré*.

ཅེས་ *ċes* 1. (*Lex.* इति), also *śes* and *žes* (cf. *ċig*) **so, thus,** in ancient literature regularly placed after words or thoughts that are literally quoted, and so continuing the sentence; the quotation itself is gen. preceded by *˳di skád-du*, or *˳di snyám-du*. In later literature *ċes* and the introductory words are often omitted, in col. language always. Inst. of *ċes smrás-so, ċes γsúṅs-so*, so he said, thus he spoke, so has been said or spoken, so it is said, often only *ċés-so* is used, and in like manner *ċés-pa* for *ċes smrás-pa*, this word, this speech; *ċés-pa-la sogs-pa* these and similar words; *ċés-pa ˳di yaṅ* also the preceding poem (is written by him); *snyun žés-pa nád-kyi miṅ yin* the word *snyun* is a term for 'disease' *Zam.*; *žés(-pa) daṅ* 'such, and', if a quotation is followed by another, where we say 'further', 'moreover'; *ċés-pa-la* after words have been quoted, which form the subject of further discussion; *ċes byá-ba*, or *ċés-pa* the so called, frq. after names; *ċés-su* rarely for *ċes*. — 2. acc. to the usual spelling and pronunciation (*ċes, ċe*) of the Lamas of *Ld.* it is the ordinary termination of the infinitive in *W.* (in *Pur.* and *Bal.* *ċas*, in *Kun.* *ċä*), though etymologically as yet not accounted for; sometimes used also as a sbst. or adj. i.e. partic.: *bsád-ċes* killing, *bsád-ċes yin* it is to be killed; *skyé-ċes* pregnant, v. *skyé-ba*.

ཅོ་ *ċo* 1. num. fig.: 125. — 2. *ċo-˳dri-ba* *Lex., C.*, **to blame, reproach, slight; to vie with.**

ཅོ་ག་, ལྕོ་ག་ *ċó-ga, lċó-ga Mil.* **lark** (not common in Tibet).

ཅོ་གེར་ *ċó-ger*(?), *ċó-ger bžugs Glr., W.* vulgo: **ċó-gan dug** he sits **motionless.**

ཅོ་ཏོ་ *ċó-to*, also *ċó-ti, Cs.*: **a tuft of hair** on the head, thus *Lex.*: *ċó-toi tor-ċóg* (= *ċú-ti?*); cf. *lċaṅ-lo*.

ཅོ་རི་ *ċó-ri* = *ċor*, *čáṅ ċo-ri Lex.* (?).

ཅོ་ལི་ *ċó-li* = *ċu-li*.

ཅོ་ལོ་ *ċó-lo* **the prattling** or **chattering** of little children *Mil.*; cf. *ċá-ċo*.

ཅོག་ *ċog Cs.*: a plural-sign; *Schr.* all (people). This, or a similar original meaning of the word is also to be traced in an expression usual in *Ld.*: *ċóg-mdo* a place where three roads meet, v. *mdo*; cf. also *ċag*. When affixed to a word, it must be preceded by the vowel *o*, the final consonant of the root being at the same time repeated. Affixed to verbs, it seems to convert them into participles: *˳óṅs-so-ċog-la Dzl.* ༢༧, 6, to those arrived, to the (persons) arrived, *yin-no-ċog, yód-do-ċog* those being, existing (things or persons); *Cs.*: *γċés-so-ċog* things that are valuable, precious, to a man.

ཅོག་ཅོག་པ་ *ċóg-ċog-pa W.* **grasshopper, cricket.**

ཅོག་པ་ *ċóg-pa C.* **to have leisure** *ċóg-na yoṅ go* if you have leisure, come! **ċóg-ka** **leisure,** **dhe-riṅ ċóg-ka me** to-day I have no leisure; **ċóg-ka ǰhé** is an affirmative answer, when having been asked for some little service, something like: well, I'll do it.

ཅོག་བུ čóg-bu a sort of **small tent** *Cs.*

ཅོག་ཙེ *čóg-tse*, v. *lčog-tse.*

ཅོག་ལ་མ *čóg-la-ma* a mineral (?) *Med.*

ཅོང་ *čoṅ* 1. *Lex.* a musical instrument, *Schr.*: a bell. — 2. *Mil: čoṅ-la skyur-ba* to push one down a precipice in order to kill him (the only meaning the context here will admit); cf. *tson-dóṅ.* — 3. v. *γčoṅ.*

ཅོང་ཅི *čóṅ-či* a small **bowl** or **dish** *Sch.*; v. *čan-če.*

ཅོང་ཅོང་ *čoṅ-čóṅ* **jagged, indented, serrated.**

ཅོང་མོ *čóṅ-mo*, col. for *lčúṅ-mo.*

ཅོང་བ *čóṅ-ba*, *Pth.: ṅu-₀bód čóṅ-ba* acc. to the context: to raise loud lamentations, wailings (at funerals); perh. etymologically connected with *čo-ṅés.* Cf. *γčóṅ-skad.*

ཅོང་ཞི *čóṅ-ži* = *čúṅ-žo.*

ཅོང་རོང་ *čoṅ-róṅ*, perh. = *čoṅ-čóṅ*, *Mil. čoṅ-róṅ tsér-ma.*

ཅོད་པན་ *čod-pán*, མུ་ཀུ་ཊ, ornament for the head, worn by kings, **tiara, diadem, crown**; **the crest** of gallinaceous birds.

ཅོབ་དར་ *čób-dár Ld.-Glr.*, *Schl.* p. 29, a (?).

ཅོར་གང་, ཅོར་ཅིག *čor-gáṅ*, *čór-čig* **a mouthful, a gulp, a little** *Sch.*; cf. *čo-ré.*

ཅོལ་ཆུང་ *čol-čúṅ Thgy.* childish **prattle** or **babbling.**

གཅགས་པ *γčágs-pa* 1. **to apprehend, to grasp** (with the understanding), **to impress**, gen. with *yid-la*, on the mind, e.g. the doctrine *Dzl.*; also *bka nan-γčágs čén-po γnáṅ-ba* to give a thoroughly solid, impressive instruction; *γčágs-po byéd-pa* = *γčágs-pa;* with additional force: **do čág-po ǰhé-pa* C.* to impress (to one's mind) as firm as a rock. — 2. relative to persons it is synon. to *čágs-pa* **to love.**

གཅང་པོ *γčáṅ-po*, *W.* **šáṅ-po** **clever; lively, sprightly;** *W.* also **attentive to, regardful of;** *γčáṅ-po drúṅ-po* clever and sagacious *Mil.*, *γčaṅ-drúṅ ldán-pa* id. *Pth.*; hence also *γčaṅ* sbst. sagacity, cleverness; *ḱa-γčáṅ* clever words, clever speech *Cs.*; cf. also *ḱa-sbyáṅ*; *W.*: **šaṅ čó-če** to watch for; to keep guard, to watch; **šaṅ-rig čó-če** to be very attentive, to listen with fixed attention, **šáṅ-rig-čan**, *C.* **čáṅ-rig-čen** very attentive; *W.*: **šaṅ skúl-če** 1. to exhort, admonish 2. to wake, to rouse from sleep; **čós-si šaṅ-skúl táṅ-če** to give religious exhortations, to hold parenetic lectures.

གཅད་པ *γčád-pa*, v. *γčód-pa.*

གཅན་(ཁ་)ཟན *γčan-(γ)zán* frq. beast of prey, *Lat. fera*, but more in a systematic sense, so that the cat, and even the dog may be included; *Glr.* po. *γčan-(γ)zán ťá-ma* 'the last of the beasts of prey', the cat.

གཅམ་བུ *γčám-bu Cs.* **humbleness, servility, flattery,** *Sch.* also **untruth, lie;** *γčám-bui ṅag*, or *tsig* a servile speech; *γčám-bu smrá-ba* to speak submissively *Stg.* (not much used).

གཅར་བ *γčár-ba* 1. *Sch.*: **cut out, put out, knocked out**, e.g. *mig* an eye (cf. *bčar-ba.* — 2. *Mil.?*

གཅལ་བ *γčál-ba*, *γčál-du bkrám-pa* **to spread, display, lay out** e.g. precious stones, jewels, on a table, on the ground, *Glr.*, also *Lex.*

གཅི་བ *γči-ba* 1. vb. v. *γčid-pa.* — 2. sbst. = *γčin; bšaṅ γči* both kinds of alvine discharges. *Dzl.*

གཅིག *γčig*, num. **one;** *γčig kyaṅ* even but one; **one and the same,** *dus γčig-tu* at the same time (whereas *dus čig-na* once, one day, which however is also written *dus γčig-na*); *γčig byéd-pa* to unite (vb. n.), to join (in an act), to act in concert; sole, alone; **dear,** beloved, *yab γčig* dear father! *Glr.: šin-tu γdúṅ-bai ma γčig* my own (only) beloved mother! somebody, some one *Dzl.*, *γčig ... γčig* the one — the other, somebody or other, very frq.; *γčig-gis γčig*, *γčig-la γčig* etc. one another, each other frq.; *mi-γčig C.* **differing, different.**

Comp. and deriv. *γćig-ka* **single, only,** opp. to several, *Mil.* — *γćig-ćar, γćig-čar* v. *ćar.* — *γćig-ćig*, pronounced **ćig-ćig**, **a certain, some one,** εἷς τις, *slób-ma-las γćig-ćig Dzl.; bud-méd γćig-ćig Dzl.* ༢༥༧, 5 (where *Sch.* has *ćig-γćig* erron.); *γćig-γćig*, pronounced **ćig-ćig**, 1. **one at a time; separately, alone,** esp. *W.*; 2. **of the same kind, not different** *W.* (v. *Fouc. Gram.* p. 21. 42), 3. adv. **by one's self, only, solely** *W.* — *γćig-ćóg* **all-sufficient** *Glr.* — *γćig-nyid Cs.* 'unity'(?) — *γćig-tu* 1. **into one,** into one body, **together,** *γćig-tu sdú-ba* to unite e.g. six countries, *Dzl.*; to contract, to simplify *C.* 2. at once, wholly, altogether *Dzl.* ༢༢, 3; 3. firstly, in the first place, *γćig-tu-ni*; then follows *γnyis-su-ni* etc. *Dzl.* 4. only, solely *Thgy.* — *γćig-dú* unity and plurality, *γćig-du-brál* not having these two qualities *Was.* (308). *γćig-pa* 1. **the first** *Wdn.* (little used). 2. **having** etc. **one,** cf. *dgu.* 3. **of one kind,** not different or manifold, *mi γćig-pa* different *B.* and *C.* — *γćig-pu* (also *γćig-bu?*) **alone, single,** *γćig-pus mi stoṅ túb-pa* to be able to cope alone with a thousand men *Dzl.; γćig-pur lus-pa* to remain alone behind *Glr.*; **only, sole,** *bu γćig-pu* the only son, frq. — *γćig-po* 1. **alone,** *rgyál-po γćig-po skyés-pa yin* the king alone is a man, *Dzl.* 2. **being one,** or the one, *ma γnyis-la skyés-pai bu γćig-po* thou (being the) one son of two mothers, viz. claimed by two, *Glr.* 3. *Pur.* **the one — the other.** — *γćig-šós* **the other,** when speaking of two.

གཅིད་པ་ *γćid-pa*, also *γći-ba*, pf. *γćis*, fut. *γći*, imp. *γćis*, **to make water, to piss.**

གཅིན་ *γćin* **urine**, *γćin γćid-pa*, or *γći-ba*, *W. tán-će*, **to make water;** *γćin šor* urine is discharged involuntarily; *γćin-rkyág*, both discharges, vulg.; *γćin-ʼgág* the retention of urine *Med.; γćin-snyí* gonorrhoea, clap(?) *Med.*

གཅིའུ་ *γćiu* 1. clyster-pipe = *ćeu*; *γći-ui sman* clyster *Lex.* — 2. *clyster*(?) *Cs.*

གཅིལ་བ་ *γćil-ba* **to spoil, to destroy** *Sch.*

གཅུ་བ, ལྕུ་བ་ *γćú-ba, lćú-ba*, v. *γćúd-pa; γću* or *lću-ʼkór Cs., γću-skór W., γćús-bu Ts.,* **screw.** — *γćú-ti* v. *ću-ti.* — *γću-dóṅ* screw-box *Cs.*

གཅུ་གལ་ *γću-gál* **importance,** *Cs.*

གཅུགས་པ་ *γćúgs-pa*, prob. not different from *γćágs-pa.* The word occurs in: *yid(-la) γćugs(-pa)* beloved, a friend *Dzl.; mdza-γćúgs byéd-pa* to treat amicably *Wdn.; ḱon-γćúgs* having conceived a hatred *Lex.*

གཅུང་པོ་ *γćúṅ-po*, resp. **a younger brother.**

གཅུད་ *γćud? γćud-(la) ʼbór(-ba) Lexx.* w.e.; *Sch.*: **to forsake, to cast out, to reject;** (cog. to *ćud-zán?*)

གཅུད, ལྕུད་པ་ *γćúd-pa, lćúd-pa*, pf. *γćus lćus*, fut. *γću, lću*, imp. *γćus*(?) **to turn,** turn round, **twist, twine, plait, braid;** **ćud log táṅ-će* W.* to untwist, untwine a rope; **ćus zum táṅ-te nol dug* W.* they wrestle and scuffle (prop. they fight scuffling); **sen ćus gyáb-će* W.* to press and bore with the knuckle; **ćús-spu** a low expression for the hair; *lág-pa γćus Zam.?*

གཅུན་པ་ *γćún-pa*, secondary form of *ʼjún-pa, Lexx.*: *rtsád-nas γćún-pa*, prob. **to subdue** completely; *γćúr-žiṅ γćún-pa* prob. to beat or press a thing until it is soft.

གཅུར་བ་ *γćúr-ba*, secondary form of *ʼjur-ba; γćúr-pe Ld.* a coarse sort of **vermicelli.**

གཅེ་བ་ *γćé-ba* **to esteem, to hold dear, to love** *Sch.*

གཅེན་ *γćen* (*Cs. γćén-po*) resp. *Cs.*: one's **elder brother** *Dzl.* ༡༡༦, 11; acc. to *Zam.*: first-born son.

གཅེར་བ་ *γćér-ba* v. *bćér-ba.*

གཅེར་བུ་ *γćér-bu* **naked,** col., also *Mil.; γćer-nyál* id.; *Kun.*: **ćer-góg**; resp. *sku γćér-bu; γćér-bu-rnams ʼgábs-par byéd-pa yin-pa* being one that covers the naked *Stg.; γćér-bur ʼbyin-pa* **to make naked, to strip** *Pth.; γćér-bu byúṅ-ba, W. *ćer-nyál tón-će** to show one's self naked; *γćér-*

bu-pa, *γčér-nyal-mk'an Mil.* (*Ssk. nirgrantha* a naked man, gymnosophist; *čós-sku γčer mtóṅ-du gról-bas* having been delivered so far as to see the *čós-sku* (v. *sku*) unveiled *Glr.*

གཅེས་པ་ *γčés-pa* (*Lh.* *šé-pa-*) **dear, beloved,** ... *ltar γčés-na yaṅ* although he is to me as dear as ... *Glr.*; *ṅéd-kyi mi γčés-pa* a man dear to us, our beloved, our darling *Mil.*; *γčés-ma* a favourite, sweetheart *Cs.*; *γčes-p'rúg* dear child *Mil.*; **excellent, precious, valuable,** *šín-tu γčes-pai lṅa* the five important letters (viz. the prefixed letters) *Glr.*; *šés-pa γčes* it is of importance to know *Med.*; often as superlative: *ʾjig rtén ʾdi-na γčés-pa raṅ-srog yin* the dearest thing in the world is one's own life *Pth.*; *γčés-par byéd-pa Stg.*, *ʾdzín-pa Glr.* c. accus, *W.*: *šé-pa čó-če* gen. with the dat., to hold dear, to love, to esteem, persons or things, but not applicable to the deeper affections of the heart. — *γčes-bsdús Lex.* w.e.; *γčes-btús Cs.* choice pieces (out of books).

གཅོག་པ་ *γčóg-pa*, pf. *bčag*, imp. *čog(s)*, *W.* *čág-če*, imp. *čog* trs. to *ʾčág-pa*, **to break,** *dúm-bur* to pieces; **to break off,** or **asunder; to smash,** a glass; **to crack,** nuts; **to burst; split, blast,** a gun, a rock; fig.: **to break, to violate,** a promise, a vow, a law etc. frq., *yáb-kyi bka bčág-tu med* the word of my father may not be violated (by me) *Glr.*

གཅོང་, གཅོང་ནད་ *γčoṅ*, *γčoṅ-nád*, **consumption, phthisis,** *γčoṅ-čén dmú-ču* prob. dropsy in the chest or in the pericardium *Med.*; gen. any **chronic disease** *čoṅ-la tsu' ma soṅ-ṅam* *C.* it has not taken a chronic turn, has it? also fig.: *sem čóṅ-po dug* *C.* the heart is sick, afflicted.

གཅོང་སྐད་ *γčóṅ-skad Lex., Sch.*: **lamentations, wailings, plaintive voices,** cf. *γčóṅ-ba.*

གཅོང་བ་ *γčóṅ-ba* 1. pf. *bčoṅs*, **to excavate, wash out, undermine** through the action of water, *túr-du γčoṅ-bar mi gyúr-ro* they are not undermined (by the water) *Stg.*; *γčoṅ-roṅ* a narrow passage, a defilé *Cs.* — 2. from *γčoṅ*, **to get faint, languid, wearied** in mind, *C.*

གཅོང་ཞི་ *γčoṅ-ži*, v. *čoṅ-ži.*

གཅོད་པ་ *γčód-pa*, pf. *bčad*, fut. *γčad*, imp. *čod*, *W.* *čád-če*, imp. *čod* 1. **to cut,** *čád-bya γčód-pa secanda secare Gram.*; **to cut asunder,** *k'am-tsal-du* into small bits; **to cut off, chop off,** the hands; **to cut down, to fell,** trees; **to cut out,** the tongue *Dzl.*; **to rend asunder, to break,** a thread, a rope, chains, fetters. — 2. **to cut off** fig.: *ču*, the water, by damming it out, frq.; **to reduce,** the wages; **to cure,** a disease; **to suppress,** a passion; **to discontinue, to give up,** *zan*, *zas*, eating i.e. to abstain from food, to fast; *srog*, to kill, to murder, frq.; **to stop** a thing in its origin, **to obviate, prevent, avert; to avoid; to lock,** the door, frq.; ... *kyi*, or *la*, *bár-du γčód-pa* to throw obstacles in a person's way, to hinder, impede, frq.; *srόg-la bár-du γčód-pa dé-dag* all these life-endangering beings *Glr.*; (for more examples refer to *bar*); **to stop,** to make a pause, in reading, *šad yoṅ-na drág-por bčád-pa* making a marked stop, when there is a *shad*, *Gram.*; *rnam(-par) γčód(-pa)*, or *bčad(-pa)*, section, paragraph; stop, pause; *yoṅs-γčód* id. *Gram.*; **to decide,** *čes bčád-do* thus he decided *Dzl.*; *krims*; or (*Dzl.*) *žal-čé*, to pass sentence or judgment; to judge, condemn, cf. also *tág-γčod-pa.* — 3. **to cross** (little used), *čú-bo grú-yis* a river in a boat *Glr.* — 4. *rjes γčód-pa* **to follow** the track, used both of men and dogs; *már-dzi* (to follow) the smell of butter (viz. of roast-meat), *kyúr-dzi čǫ'-pa* *C.* to follow the sourish smell (viz. the smell of beer); (*γ*)*sár-* (also *tsar Pth.*) *γčod-pa* to search into, to investigate, to examine or study thoroughly *Ld.-Glr. Schl.* p. 20, b. — *čád-pas γčód-pa* and other phrases v. under the respective noun. — *čǫ'-tán* *C.* **the Tibetan rupee,** having lines (*radii*) of division marked, by which they may be cut into smaller pieces. — Note: In some phrases the spelling of *γčód-pa* and the assonant verbs *spyód-pa* and *dpyód-pa* is variable.

གཙོམ་, བཅོམ་ *γčom*, *bčom*, **pride, haughtiness, arrogance**, *bskyúṅ-ba* to put it off, give it up *Lexx.*; *bčom čuṅ-ṅus Tar.* 20, 6 despondingly, low-spirited; *gros-γčóm Lex.* obs. or prov. for *gros-bčám*, v. *ₒčám-pa*.

གཙོར་བ་ *γčór-ba* **to spread, scatter, disperse** *Cs.*

བཅག་པ་ *bčág-pa* v. *γčóg-pa* and *ₒčág-pa*.

བཅང་ *bčaṅ? Sch.*: '*bčaṅ-rgya-čén-po* comprising much, comprehensive, very extensive; *bčaṅ-rgyár mdzad-pa* resp. to apply one's self, to bestow pains upon'.

བཅད་ཀ་ *bčád-ka W.* a whole that has been cut into, or a piece cut off.

བཅད་པོ་ *bčád-po W.* something **old, torn, worn out.**

བཅབ་པ་ *bčáb-pa* v. *ₒčab-pa*.

བཅམ་བཅོམ་ *bčam-bčóm Sch.*: trivial things, medley, hodge-podge.

བཅའ་སྒ་ *bčá-sga* v. *sga*.

བཅའ་བ་ *bčá-ba* 1. v. *čá-ba*. — 2. sbst. drinking; gen. used connected with *bza-ba*; *bčá-ba daṅ bzá-ba*, or *bza-bča* food and drink.

བཅའ་འཕྲང་ *bča-ₒpráṅ Mil.*, declivity, precipice *Sch.*

བཅའ་མག་ *bča-mág*, the usual pronunciation of *lčags-mag*.

བཅར་བ་ *bčár-ba* 1. = *bčir-ba* **to squeeze, to press** in a press *Thgy.*; **to crowd, to throng**, **yár-la bčar* C.*, stand (or sit) more closely together! — 2. **to pull** or **force from, to wrest** *Cs.* — 3. *Lexx.*: *mig bčár-ba* the same as in *γčar-mig* (?). — 4. *Sch.*: *logs bčár-ba* to prop sideways. — 5. *Sch.*: *bčar bžúgs-pa* to have a permanent residence (this would however be more correctly expressed by *čar*). — 6. *bčár-bai rta-bčibs*, and *lan-bčár? Lexx.* w.e.

བཅལ་བ་ *bčál-ba* v. *ₒǰál-ba*.

བཅས་པ་ *bčás-pa* 1. originally pf. of *ₒčá-ba*, little used. — 2. adj. **together with, connected with, having, possessing, containing** a thing, with *daṅ* or termin. (the latter in prose only when a second *daṅ*, signifying 'and', occurs in the sentence); gerundially: *bčás-te*, sometimes also *bčás-pas* or *bčás-šiṅ*; adverbially: *bčás-su* frq.; *ₒkor daṅ bčás-pa* (*-te*, *-su*) with attendance, with a retinue or suite, frq.; *bu-mo bču bod-blón daṅ bčás-pas skór-te* surrounded by ten virgins together with the Tibetan ambassadors *Glr.*; *btsún-mo daṅ sráṣ-su bčás-te* with (his) wife and son *Glr.*; *gos daṅ bčás-su* (to go into the water) having one's clothes on *Dzl.*; *žal ₒdzúm-pa daṅ bčás-te* with a smiling face *Glr.*; *šér-sna daṅ bčás-pa* infected with, subject to, avarice; without *daṅ* or termin. (esp. po.); *ₒkrúl-bčas* infatuated, fascinated *Pth.*; *ₒbru-ťáṅ ťun bčas* together with a small parcel of Dutan tea; it is also, like *rnams*, a collective sign, used in enumerations, referring to several nouns, *Wdṅ.*, or like *la-sógs-pa* and other (things), and more (such things), and the like: *rgyags daṅ bčas bskyál-lo* provisions and other necessaries we shall supply *Mil.*

བཅིང་བ་ *bčiṅ-ba*, fut. of *ₒčiṅ-ba* **to bind.**

བཅིངས་པ་ *bčiṅs-pa*, pf. of *ₒčiṅ-ba* **to bind.** Both verbs (*bčiṅ-ba* and *bčiṅs-pa*) are also used as substantives: **bonds, fetters,** whether of a material, spiritual, or magical nature.

བཅིབ(ས)་པ་ *bčib(s)-pa* v. *ₒčib-pa*; *Sch.* also: **carriage, conveyance.**

བཅིར་བ་ *bčir-ba* v. *ₒčir-ba*.

བཅིལ་བ་ *bčil-ba* v. *ₒǰil-ba*.

བཅུ་ *bču* (*Bal.* **wču**) **ten**, *bču ťam-pa* id.; *bču-pray* a decade; *bču-γčig*, *bču-γnyis* (*Bal.* **wču-ṅas**) eleven, twelve etc., (v. also *bčo*); *bčú-pa*, *bčú-po* as in *dgú-pa*, *dgú-po*. — *bču-skór ₒťon*, *bču-gyúr ₒťon* (the field) yields a tenfold crop. — **čú-ka, čú-kai ṭal* C.*, **ču-kág* W.*, tithe, tithes; *bču-kág-pa* a collector of tithes, *bču-kag ₒdón-pa* to tithe, to decimate *Cs.* — *bču-dpón* corporal, Lat. *decurio*. *bču-ₒóg* (**ču-*

wáy Ts.*) a band of ten soldiers. — *bċu-γċig-žál* the eleven-faced (Awalokiteswara) *Glr.*

བཅུ་བ་ *bċú-ba* v. *₀ču-ba.*

བཅུག་པ་ *bċúg-pa* v. *₀jug-pa.*

བཅུགས་ *bċugs*, from the phrases: *sems k'ón-med-pa dan bċúgs med-pa dan γnód-pa med-pa Stg.*, and *Pratihārya Avadāna* (v. *Feer*) p. 3: *lha-byin-gyis bċugs byás-te* = **देवदत्तविगृहोतेन**, it appears, that *bċugs* signifies hatred, hostility, damage, loss, which when compared with *γċugs* seems rather strange, yet is in accordance with **कौक्रत्य** (for this must probably be read inst. of **कौकृत**).

བཅུད་ *bċud* (**रस**) **moisture, juice, sap,** but gen. combined with the notion of a certain inherent virtue or power; *zlá-bai bċud* a fructifying moisture, to be compared in its effects to the warmth of the sun, and prob. means night-dew (if after all it is any thing real); hence **essence, nutriment,** *rkán-gis bċud ₀gyur* nourishment comes from the marrow *Med.*; *bċúd-la son, Mil.* also *bċúd-la bor*, (this food) has proved a nutritious fluid, it agrees with him; *bċúd-ċan* nutritious, succulent, of grass, food etc.; *bċud-méd* not nutritious, *Med.*; invigorating **cordial, quintessence,** *bċud-lén* an elixir of life; frq. fig.: *čos t'ams-ċád bsdús-pai bċud Glr.*

བཅུམ་པ་ *bċúm-pa* 1. v. *₀júm-pa.* — 2. **to use artifices, to chicane** *Sch.*

བཅུར་བ་ *bċúr-ba* 1. **to be flattened down** *Sch.* — 2. *Kun.* **lún-po ċúr-te yon** there is a draught (here). — 3. *C.* like *bkág-pa* **to bar, obstruct, block up,** e.g. of snow obstructing a road. Cf. *₀júr-ba.*

བཅེ, བཅེས་ *bċe, bċes* v. *₀čé-ba.*

བཅེར་བ་ *bċér-ba* 1. **to heap** or **pile up** *Cs.*; *Lex.*: *šin p'ún-por bċér-ba* to pile up wood. -- 2. = *bċir-ba* 1. **to squeeze, to press** *C., W.*; **to squeeze in,** *ri-brág γnyis-kyi bár du* something between two rocks *Pth.*; **ċer tán-ċe** *W.* to squeeze, press, screw in; **ċer-ċér tán-ċe** *W.* to throng, to crowd.

བཅོ་ *bċo*, for *bċu* in *bċo-lná* 15, and *bċo-brgyád* 18; *lo lna γsum bċo-lná* 3 times 5, 15 years (*lna γsum* standing pleon.) *Mil.*

བཅོ་བ་ *bċó-ba*, pf. and imp. *bċos*, prop. root of the fut. tense of *₀čós-pa*, but in *W.* the usual word for *byéd-pa* **to make, perform; to prepare, manufacture, construct;** employed in all kinds of phrases; **k'ó-la zún-ċan ċó** *W.* (he) makes him a liar.

བཅོག་ *bċog? Glr.* 99.

བཅོམ་ *bċom* for *γċom*, **pride.**

བཅོམ་པ་ *bċóm-pa*, pf. of *₀jóms-pa*, **conquered, subdued; having conquered** or **subdued,** e.g. *dgrá-bċoms-pa*, v. *dgra*; **victory** *Cs.*; *₀p'rog-bċóm*, and **ċom-ṭóg** *W.* **robbery** and **acts of violence.** — *bċom-brlág* p.n., Mathura, town of ancient India, in the neighbourhood of Agra, *Zam., Tar.* — *bċom-ldán* victorious *Cs.*; *bċom-ldan-₀dás* (*Kh.* **wċom-ldan-dé**, *Ld.* **ċom-dan-dás**, *C.* **ċom-dän-dé**) **भगवन्त** *Cs.*: victorious, *Sch.*: 'the victoriously consummated', *Burn.* le bien-heureux, the usual epithet of Buddha, *Burn.* I., 71.

བཅོལ་བ་ *bċól-ba*, v. *₀čól-ba*; *bċól-ma* a thing committed to a person's charge, **a trust.**

བཅོས་པ་ *bċós-pa*, a verb of its own, though as to form resembling a participle, 1. **to treat medically,** hence **to cure, to heal,** *mk'as kyan bċós-su med* he cannot be cured even by the best physicians *Med.*; *bċós-(pai) t'abs* the way of treating, the method of curing *Med.*; *sman-bċós* medical treatment *Med.* — 2. to do (a thing) for the sake of appearance, for form's sake, **to affect,** *bċós-su byéd-pa* **to perform a sham work,** e.g. blowing into a blazing fire *C.*; hence as sbst.: **a false conception,** wrong idea, *bċós pa dan ₀k'rúl-bar gyúr-ba* to give way to odd fancies, to have crotchets in the brain, e.g. in consequence of old age *Thgy.* — 3. partic.: made or contrived by art,

artificial, feigned, fictitious, *ma-bčós* artless, unaffected, genuine; it also seems to denote an absence of mental activity, or a forbearance of exercising such activity, in short that indifference to the world, which is so highly valued by the Buddhist, *Mil.* — *bčós-pai ras*, or *ras bčós-bu*, washed or prepared cotton-cloth *Cs.*; calico, chintz *Cs.*; in *S. O.* it seems to denote a costly, valuable fabric; *bčos-ma* sbst. and adj., a production of art, any thing made or contrived by art, esp. every thing imitated, counterfeit, mock, sham, not genuine, frq.; *bčós-ma ma yin-pa* natural, unfeigned, genuine, e.g. respect, reverence *Glr.* — *ṫsúl-bčos-mḱan*, one that is shamming, a hypocrite. Cf. *ₒčós-pa*.

ལྕ་ *lča*, *Ld.* for *lči-ba*, **excrement, dung, manure.**

ལྕ་སྒ་ *lčá-sga* = *bča-sga*, **white ginger,** v. *sgá*.

ལྕ་བ་ *lčá-ba* 1. *Cs.*: a sort of **carrot,** *Med.* frq., but not known to the common people, at least not in *W.* — 2. कम्बल acc. to *Was.* a garment made of wool or felt *Tar.*

ལྕག་ *lčag* 1. **rod, switch, stick, whip;** *glaṅ-lčág* ox-whip; *ṙṅa-lčág* kettle-drum stick; *lčaṅ-lčóg Lex.* willow-twig, osier-switch; *rta-lčág* horse-whip, whip in general, also a scourge, consisting of several straps with sharp knots; *spa-lčág* a cane, bamboo *Mil.*; *ber(-ma)-lčág* stick *Mil.* — 2. (*lčág-ma*) **stroke, blow, cut, hit,** *lčag rgyáb-pa* to give a blow or cut, *rtá-la* to the horse *Glr.*; *mgo-lčág* (*Ld.* **go-lčág**) a blow or stroke upon the head; *ₒgram-lčág* a smack on the cheek, slap on the face, box on the ear *Cs.*; *ṫal-lčág* id. — 3. forepart of a coat of mail *Sch.* — 4. a kind of Daphne, v. *re-lčag-pa*.

Comp. *lčág-rdo W.* **flint,** flint-stone. — *lčag-ₒbrás Mil.* **whip-cord,** lash of a whip; *lčag-ₒbréṅ*, and *lčag-dṅó* id. — *lčag-ṫsán* = *rta-lčág C.* — *lčag-yú* **whip-stick,** handle of a whip.

ལྕག་ལྕིག་ *lčag-lčig Lex.* w. e.

ལྕག་པོད་ *lčag-pód* **a girdle,** made of plaited and interlaced strips and resembling a chain; one *Lex.* adds: *dáṅ-mai ₒdríl-du lhás-pa* (?).

ལྕགས་ *lčags* 1. **iron,** *lčágs-kyi* of iron; *lčágs-bton-mḱan* a miner digging for iron; *rgya-lčágs* Chinese iron; *ṗo-lčágs* an inferior sort of iron, *mo-lčágs* a finer and better sort of it, *Cs.* steel (?) — 2. an iron instrument, tool, esp. **lock** (of doors), **fetter, shackle,** *sgo ṫams-čad lčags btab-čiṅ* locking every door *Pth.*; **ḱáṅ-čag lág-čag** *C.* fettered on hands and feet; *γnam-lčágs* 1. thunderbolt, 2. a flash of lightning just striking an object; *me-lčágs* a steel to strike fire with, fire-steel.

Comp. and deriv. *lčags-kyú B.* an iron hook, esp. fishing-hook, angle; often fig.: *ṫúgs-rjei*, or *čós-kyi lčags-kyús ₒdzín-pa* to seize with the hook of grace or of religion *Dzl.*, *Glr.* and elsewh. — *lčags-dkár* tin-plate, white iron plate. — *lčags-sḱúd* **thin wire.** — *lčags-ḱém* or *ḱyém* **a spade.** — *lčags-ḱról Sch.* a big iron kettle (= *W.* **čag-dol** **stew-pan,** large iron pan or pot?) — *lčags-mgár* iron smith, **black-smith.** — *lčags-sgór* iron pan. — *lčags-sgyid* **trevet, tripod.** — *lčags-sgróg* **fetter, shackle.** — *lčags-čás* **implements of iron, hardware.** — *lčags-tig* a kind of **gentian,** cf. *tig-ta*. — *lčags-ṫág* **chain** or **chains.** — *lčags-ṫál Cs.* an iron **dish** or **plate,** prob. from *ṫá-li*. — *lčags-drégs* (*W.* **čag-rág**) 1. **iron dross,** scoria or slag of iron; 2. **dirt** of the intestines. — *lčags-rdó* 1. perh. more correctly *lčag-rdó* **flint-stone.** 2. iron-stone, **iron ore** (?). — *lčags-ṗrá Ü*, a kind of musket, imported from Rum (Turkey). — **čag-bér** *W.* an iron bar, **crowbar, hand-spike.** — *lčágs-mag*, *bčá-mag*, the Turkish چقمق **flint-stone, tinder-box** *W.* — *lčags-ṫságs* an iron **cribble** or **sieve, colander.** — *lčags-zám* iron bridge. — *lčags-záṅs* iron kettle. — **čag-záṅ** *C.* good iron, **steel.** — *lčags-γyá* **rust** *Med.* — *lčags-ri* a wall encircling an estate, a town etc. — *lčags-sláṅ* a large iron pan for roasting or kiln-drying corn. — *lčags-šán* iron hoop, hasp, cramp-iron. — *lčags-sá* iron ore *Cs.* — *lčags-bsró* **smoothing-iron** *Sch.*

ལྕང་མ་ *lčáṅ-ma* **willow,** Salix viminalis, almost the only leaved tree in Tibet, frq. planted in the vicinity of villages: *rgyál-lčaṅ* the specific name of this tree in *Kun.*; *róṅ-lčaṅ, sér-lčaṅ* different species of it; *lčaṅ-dkár Kun.* a white kind with birch-like bark, cf. *šo*; *lčaṅ-ló* willow-leaves, 2. (**जटा**) **matted hair,** *lčáṅ-lo-čan,* or *-pa,* one with matted hair, a penitent; also n. of a place in ancient India, of another in Lhasa, and of a third on the top of the fabulous Rirab. 3. **queue, pig-tail** *C.* — *lčaṅ-rlóm* a flat willow basket *Ts.* — *lčaṅ-šiṅ* willow-tree, willow-wood. — *lčaṅ-šól Sch.*: 'the red willow'. — **čaṅ-sil* W.* coolness, shade under a willow-tree.

ལྕང་ལྕོང་ *lčaṅ-lčóṅ Cs.* = *saṅ-šóṅ* **a craggy place, a broken country.**

ལྕམ་ *lčam,* also *p̔yam,* 1. **lath, pole, rafter, spar** of a roof. In Tibet the rafters are placed horizontally, and support a layer of earth; in Mongol tents they are slanting, supporting the felt-covering. — 2. also *brag-lčám,* n. of an officinal herb used for healing wounds *Med.* — 3. *ḥgyur-lčám* prob. denotes a glittering fish, or a fish rapidly darting along — 4. v. *lčám-mo.*

ལྕམ་མེ་བ་ *lčám-me-ba,* perh. **variegated, shining, dazzling** *Glr.*

ལྕམ་མོ་ *lčám-mo,* resp. for *spun,* and esp. for *sriṅ-mo,* acc. to *Cs.* also for *čúṅ-ma,* **a royal consort,** a great man's **sister** or **wife**; *lha-lčám* a princess *Pth.*; *lčam-čúṅ* a young princess or lady, a young unmarried lady of noble rank; *lčam-drál, mčéd-lčam-drai, lčam-sriṅ* brother and sister.

ལྕམ་པ་ *lčam-pa* 1. n. of a flower *Wdṅ.*; 2. n. of a kind of vegetables *S.g.*

ལྕི་བ་ *lči-ba* 1. sbst. (*Ld.* **lča**, *Lh.* **či-a, čé-a**), **dung,** esp. of cattle; *bai lči-ba, bá-lči* cow-dung; *lči-skám* dry dung (used as fuel), *lči-rlóṅ* fresh dung. — 2. adj. **heavy,** *W.* **čin-te**, *yaṅ lči* 1. light and heavy; 2. weight, **yaṅ-či ḍáṅ-ḍa čó-če** *W.* to balance equally, to counterpoise; with regard to food, perh. heavy, oppressing the stomach; but also in a favourable sense: **substantial, nutritious;** fig.: **weighty, important,** *k̔yéd-kyi skyes daṅ bka-stsal lči-ba des* in consequence of your weighty presents and requests *Glr.*; **nám-čog čin-te** *W.* hard of hearing; *k̔a-na-ma-t̔ó-ba lči ba* a heavy, deadly sin, frq.

ལྕིད་ *lčid* v. *ljid.*

ལྕིན་ཏེ་ *lčin-te* v. *lči-ba.*

ལྕིབས་ *lčibs* denotes a. things, which serve to protect the hands, when having to deal with hot or otherwise disagreeable objects; so gloves may be called *lčibs Sch.*, but esp. *ťsa-lčibs* (*W.* **ťsalčib**) **pot-cloth** (to take pots from the fire), **re-čib** *C.*, also **lag-čib** id.; hence prob. *mig-lčibs,* resp. *spyan-lčibs* **eyelid;** *mig-gi lčibs-t̔ór* sty, wisp in the eye, and perh. from some remote similarity *sgo-lčibs, sgoi ya-lčibs* the lintel or head-piece of a door; *nya-lčibs* fishgills, *Lex.* and *Cs.*; b. contrivances to facilitate the handling of different objects, as: **the handles** of pots and vessels, the handles, **hilts, bows, ears, loops** etc. of knives, scissors, pincers and other working-tools.

ལྕུ་བ་ *lčú-ba* v. *γčú-ba.*

ལྕུག་པ་ *lčúg-pa Cs., mnyen-lčug Lex.,* **flexible, pliant; a supple branch;** *lčug-lčúg byéd-pa* to bend repeatedly *Cs.*; *lčúg-ma* **a root-shoot** of a willow or a poplar-tree, **a rod, switch;** **čúg-gu** *C.* the bud of a twig; *lčug-p̔rán* a thin branch or twig.

ལྕུགས་ *lčugs, gri-yi lčugs Lex.* w.e.

ལྕུང་ཀ་ *lčúṅ-ka* = *skyúṅ-ka,* **jack-daw.**

ལྕུང་མོ་ *lčúṅ-mo* **thimble** *Glr.*

ལྕུད་པ་ *lčud-pa* v. *γčud-pa.*

ལྕུམ་ *lčum Med., lčum-ťsa Cs.*: **'a plant,** the stalks of which are used as a purgative'; *lċum-dkár* prob. another species of that plant *Med.*

ལྕེ་ *lċe* 1. resp. *ljags* (**जिह्व**) **tongue,** *lċe rkyań-ba* to put forth, to show the tongue *Mil.*; *lċe brgyá-yis yon-tan ċúń-zad brjód-par nus ma mċis* even with a hundred tongues we should not be able sufficiently to praise the merit . . . *Pth.* — 2. **blade,** *Cs. gri-lċe.* — 3. (**अशनि**) **thunderbolt,** *lċe ₒbébs-pai glog* a flash of lightning accompanying a thunderbolt. — 4. **flame,** *mé-lċe.*

Comp. *lċe-kyigs* **the frenum** of the tongue *Cs.* — *lċe-čúń* **uvula,** *lċe-čuń ₒbabs* inflammation of the uvula *Med.* — *lċe-γnyis-pa* **double-tongued, deceitful,** *lċe-γnyis byéd-pa* to be double-tongued. — *lċe-ťéb, lċe-ₒdrá* a fleshy excrescence below the tongue *Cs.* — *lċe-bdé* a nimble tongue a babbler *Mil.* — *lċe-spyáń* = *ċe-spyáń Thgy., Stg.* - *lċe-ₒbúr* a swelling on the tongue *Cs.* — *lċe-myań-ťsá* **alum** *Med.* — *lċe-rtsá* the root of the tongue, *lċe-rtsá-ċan* a letter pronounced from the root of the tongue, a guttural. — *lċe-rtsé* the tip of the tongue *Cs.*, *lċe-rtsé-ċan* a letter sounded with the tip of the tongue, a lingual. — *lċe-ťsá-(-ba)* a sharp-tasted, pungent medicinal herb *Med.* — *lċe-γžór* a tongue-scraper *Cs.*

ལྕེག *lċeg* a coat of mail for a horse *Sch.*

ལྕེབ་པ་ *lċéb-pa* to go to kill one's self, **to seek death**, esp. by a leap into the water or down a precipice, but not every kind of suicide; also used of insects that fly into a flame etc.

ལྕོ་ག་ *lċó-ga*, also *lċóg-ma* or *mo* **lark.**

ལྕོག *lċog* 1. *B.*, *C.* **a turret** on a house-top, pinnacle (*W.* **speu**). — 2. v. *lċóg-tse.*

ལྕོག་པོ་ *lċóg-po* prob. **low,** *lċóg-por skye* (a certain plant) is low-growing, it does not grow high.

ལྕོག་ཙེ, ལྕོག་རྩེ་ *lċóg-tse, lċóg-rtse*, resp. *γsol-lċóg*, **table**, in Tibet, esp. in *W.*, a very rare piece of furniture, and always small and low; *lċog-ḱébs* table-cloth, *lċog-ḱébs btiń-ba* to lay the cloth; *rgya-lċóg* a large table, a European table; *mdun-lċóg* 'fore-table', a sort of table before an idol, for spreading offerings on it, v. e.g. *Hook.* I, 172; but it is not the same as altar.

ལྕོགས་ *lċogs, zer-lċógs* **pronunciation** *C.*(?)

ལྕོག(ས)་པ་ *lċóg(s)-pa* I. **to be agitated, to shake, to tremble,** *mé-tog mgo-lċóg Zam.* a flower shaking, waving its head (little used).

II 1. vb. **to be able,** *de ma lċóg-na* if (he) is not able (to do that); *ji lċóg-kyi Mil.* as much as possible, to the utmost; **ńa-ráń-ghi gań ċóg-pa** *C.* as far as I am able. More used: 2. adj. **able,** *šéd-kyis mi lċóg-pa* unable, feeble, weak, *rig-pas mi lċóg-pa* ignorant; **ńę ťsar ċig-la ċóg-pa me'** I am not able to carry the whole at once *C.*; **ċóg-ċan** clever, skilful, handy, **ċog-méd** awkward *W.*; **ḱę ċog mi dug** he does not get on with his mouth, he lisps; also **ḱa ċóg-pa** irreverent, disrespectful in speaking *W.*(?)

ལྕོང་ *lċoń, sbol-lċóń* a frog in its first stage of development, **tadpole** *Pth.*

ཆ

ཆ་ *ča* 1. the letter *č*, the aspirated *ċ*, pronounced hard and forcibly, like **ch** in *chap* or *church.* — 2. numerical figure: 6, *ča-pa* the sixth volume.

ཆ་ *ča* I. **part, portion, share** 1. opp. to the whole, *ča γsúm-du bgos* divide it in three parts! *brgyai ča* 1/100 *Glr.*; *stóń-gi ča* 1/1000; *bań-mdzód γsúm-ča γċig* one third of the provisions *Dzl.*; *dbui ča tsam cig ɣsér-gyis ma lóṅ-bar* there being still wanting about as much gold as (the weight of) his head *Glr.*; *náṅ-par sṅá-bai ča* the following day's first part, i.e. the following morning *Mil.*; *sá-ča* a piece of land *Glr.*, *C.*, also land, territory, country in general, *ghai sa-ča* the country of Gha *Glr.*; *zúr-ča* frontier parts, frontier province; *ča-snyoms* at equal parts, equally, e.g. *ču sbyar* mixed with the same quantity of water *Lt.*; *ča-mnyám* id., *ča-mnyám žib bteg* accurately weighed in equal parts *Lt.*; *ča tsam*, *ča ₒdra tsam* in part, in some measure; *ča ma ₒdra* or *ma mťún-pa* partly not equal, differing a little; *ča tsam šes kyaṅ* even if one knows but a little *Mil.*; *yid smon ₒos ča tsam mi ɣdá-bas* it being not in the least desirable; *ča-rdzógs* being complete in every part, entire, integral *Sch.* — Esp. 2. **the half,** *nám-gyi ča stod,* the first half of the night, *nám-gyi ča smad* the second, the last half of it. Hence 3. **the one part** of a pair, similar to *ya*, *lham ča ɣcig* the one boot; *ča sgríg-pa* to pair, to match, to couple *Sch.*; an equal, a match, *ča-mťún-pa*, *ča-ₒdrá-ba*, *C.* also **ča-lóṅ-wa**, similar, resembling *Wdṅ.* and elsewh.; *la-lá ťár-pa ča-mťún dgé-ba med* some have no virtue befitting (i.e. leading to) final salvation *Thgy.*; *ča-méd* without an equal, matchless; *čá-ma-yin-pa* unfit, improper, unbecoming *Sch.*, *ṅag ɣcóg-pa ni ča ma yin* not obeying will not do, is out of place *Tar.* 110, 11. — 4. **a pair,** = *zuṅ Sch.*; *Zam.*: युग. — 5. **share, portion, lot,** *mtsar-sdúg bltá-bai čá-nas mnyam* being equal as to their (respective) share of beauty *Glr.*; *dmán-ča ₒdzín-pa* to choose the humbler (inferior) share, i.e. to be humble, = *dmán-sa ₒdzín-pa Mil.*; in general: *ča ₒdzín-pa* c. genit. to adhere, to be attached to a person or thing *Pth.*; *žiṅ rmó-ba ṅai ča yin* ploughing is my business, my lot, my department *Dzl.*; *čá-la* equally, in equal parts, equally divided, *ká-ba nyin dgu mtsan dgu babs, čá-la nyin mtsan bco-brgyád babs Mil.* there was a fall of snow during nine days and nine nights; it fell equally portioned out to days and nights, (together) eighteen (the peculiar mode of reckoning is here to be noticed)

II. **news, intelligence, notice,** construed like *rgyus* and *ɣtam*; *ɣtám-ča ₒdri-ba* = *ɣtam ₒdri-ba*; *ča yod*, *ča med* like *rgyus yod* and *rgyus med*; *nam ₒči ča méd-kyi čos* the doctrine of the uncertainty of the day of death *Mil.*; ... *par ča mčis-te* there coming news or intelligence that...; *skád-ča* v. *skad*; physically: **voice, sound,** *brág-ča* echo; intellectually: **prospect, auspices,** *Mil.*: *sróg-ča* prospects of life (as to its length and preservation), *kyim-ča* prospects regarding the household, *dgra-ča* prospects, expectations as to one's enemies; **lám-ča* C.* prospects of a safe journey (cf. *ṅo* 4).

III. **thing, things,** relating to clothes, ornaments, materials etc., cf. *čas*; **yo-lus-ča-tsáṅ* W.* a complete suit of clothes; but mostly used in compounds: *ské-ča* neck-ornaments, *glo-ča* ornaments suspended to the belt or girdle, e.g. strings of shells; *dgós-ča* necessary things *Cs.*; *mčód-ča* things necessary for sacrifices, requisites for offerings *Glr.*; *mtsón-ča* weapons; *yig-ča* prob. writings, deeds, documents *Glr.*; **rẹ-ča** cottons, cotton fabrics *C.*; *lag-ča* implements, utensils, goods, baggage etc. *Glr.* — There is still to be noticed the expression: *ča-bžág-pa*, lit. to add one's own share to a thing, 1. to adhere, stick, or cling to, to follow, obey (laws); *saṅs-rgyás-kyi bká-la ča bžag* they adhere to the words of Buddha; *rgyál-poi bká-la* to obey the king's commandment. 2. to refer to (?) *C.*

ཆ་རྐྱེན *ča-rkyén Lex.*, *Sch.*: 'share of destiny, of fate; consequence of one's actions' (?).

ཆ་མཁན *čá-mkan* **soothsayer, fortune-teller** *Sch.*

ཆ་ག *čá-ga Mil.*, **hem, edge, border;** *čá-ga ₒdebs-pa* to hem, to turn in (the edge of cloth).

ཆ་ག་འབུ་ *čá-ga-ₒbu C.*, *Lex.* also *čá-ga-pa*, **grasshopper.**

ཆ་ཆོ་ *čá-čo Lex., Sch.*: 'things homogeneous, matched'.

ཆ་བ་ *čá-ba*, pf. and imp. *soṅ* (the regular form *čas* being nearly obs. at present), in *W.* the usual word for *ₒgro-ba* to go, in *B.* little used and only in later writings, 1. **to go,** **śór-te čá-če** to retire, to retreat slowly; **da ča yin**, or **da čen** adieu, good bye, farewell! **da čen žu** resp., your servant! (in taking leave); **'á-ru-soṅ** go thither, or that way! **'á-ru ma ča** do not go to this place, do not step this way! **to travel,** **gyál-la** (or *dé-mo, yág-po*) *ča žig** I wish you a safe journey, a pleasant trip to you! **lóg-te čá-če** to return, to go or come back; **tiṅ-la čá-če** to follow, to come after or later; **ča čug** let (him) go! give (it) up! let (it) alone! **to be gone, consumed, spent, used, wasted,** **śiṅ máṅ-po ča yin** a great deal of wood will go, will be consumed. — 2. **to become, grow, get, turn,** **tsan ča dug** it grows night, it is getting dark; **gas čá če** to grow old; **nág-po soṅ** that has turned black; **śés-k'an čá-če** to get information; also with *la*: **bág-ma-la čá-ba** (= *bág-mar ₒgró-ba, ₒgyúr-ba*) to become a bride *Ma.*; **mán-la mi ča** this is not used for medicine. — 3. with a supine (*B.*) or a verbal root (col.): **to be about, to be on the point, to be going,** *sléb-tu čá-bai tse* when they were on the point of arriving *Mil.*; *nyi-ma ₒčár-du čá-ba daṅ* when the sun was just going to rise *Mil.*; **me ši ča dug** the fire is on the point of going out; **nad ži ča dug**, the disease is decreasing. — 4. with the gerund it expresses a continuous progress, a gradual operation, an effect by little and little, **ču p'él-te ča dug** the water increases from day to day. — 5. with the inf. it is used in the sense of the future tense, or like the Greek μέλλειν: **to intend, to purpose,** **či śríd-de dir śriṅ-če ča dug** how long does he (do you etc.) intend to stay? **nam lug sád-če ča dug** when are you going to kill the sheep?

ཆ་བུ་ *čá-bu*, a kind of little ornament worn in the ears *Ld.*

ཆ་བྱད་ *ča byád* 1. **thing, implement, instrument,** e.g. a musical instrument *Dzl.*, a surgical instr. *Med.* — 2. **clothing, dress,** *mi-sdúg-pai ča-byad-ṅan* poorly clothed, ragged *Mil.*; **external appearance,** also of animals.

ཆ་ཚམ་ *ča-tsám* v. *ča* I, 1.

ཆ་ཚད་ *ča-tsád* = *čag-tsad.*

ཆ་ཚན་ *ča-tsán* **species, division, class** *Sch.*

ཆ་འཛིན་ *ča-ₒdzin* v. *ča* I., 5.

ཆ་རྫོགས་ *ča-rdzógs* v. *ča* I, 1.

ཆ་ར་ *čá-ra* 1. **oak,** also *mon-čá-ra* (on account of its growing only on the southern ranges of the Himalaya mountains, inhabited mostly by Non-Tibetans) in several species, with pointed, evergreen leaves, a tree much inferior in beauty to the English oak. *čá-ra p'reu Sch.*: 'the stunted or dwarf-oak'. — 2. also *ča-ri, ča-li, ča-lú*, a coarse sort of **blanket** made of yak's hair.

ཆ་ལ་ *čá-la* v. *ča* I., 5.

ཆ་ལག་ *čá-lag* 1. *C.* **implements, instruments,** required for the carrying on of a business. — 2. *W.* **things, effects,** luggage. — 3. *Tar.* 43, 18: *čá-lag daṅ bčás-pa rdzógs-par śés-pa Schf.*: 'the systematic and complete understanding'.

ཆ་ལང་ *ča-láṅ* joined with *rdéb-pa Lex.* and *Mil.*, meaning not known; *Wts.* gives: petite lance des bonzes.

ཆ་ལམ་ *čá-lam* = *há-lam*, **some; for the most part, rather** *C.*

ཆ་ལི་, ཆ་ལུ་ *ča-li, ča-lú* v. sub *čá-ra.*

ཆ་ལུགས་ *ča-lúgs* **clothing, costume, appearance.**

ཆ་ཤས་ *ča-šás* **part, portion, share,** *lús-kyi ča-šás* a part of the body, a limb etc.

ཆ་ཧར་ *ča-hár* Chakhar, a Mongol tribe *Sch.*

ཆག *čag* 1. **dry fodder** for horses and other animals, as hay, barley etc.; *čag-yžoṅ* trough, manger, crib. — 2. **the fourth finger** *Med.* — 3. resp. for **shoe** *Glr.*, also *p̔yag(-lhám)*. — 4. *čag-p̔éb-pa Glr.* = *p̔yag p̔éb-pa.* — 5. **the breadth of a fist,** *čag gaṅ* id., *Mṅg.* frq. — 6. v. *čág-pa.*

ཆག་(ད)ཀྲུམ(ས)་ *čag-(d)krúm(s)* **piece, fragment** *Lex.*, *Thgy.*; **čag-túm-la soṅ* C.* it has gone to pieces.

ཆག་སྐྱ་བ་ *čag-skya-ba Sch.*: 'having only one purpose, pursuing but one aim; unremitting, indefatigable'.

ཆག་ག་ཆོག་གེ་ *čag-ga-čog-gé* (or *p̔yag-ga-p̔yog-gé?*) various things mixed up or thrown together, medley.

ཆག་གྲུམ་ *čag-grúm Lex.* = *čag-dkrúm(?)*.

ཆག་རྒྱག་པ་ *čag-rgyág-pa* **to doubt** *Sch.*

ཆག་ཆག་ *čag-čág* I. 1. with *byed-pa*, *ₒdebs-pa*, **to sprinkle, besprinkle,** *čus* with water, *k̔áṅ-pa*, *lám-rnams* the house, the streets *B.*, *C.* (*W.* **čab-čáb**). — 2. *Sch.*: *čag-čág ydab-pa* **to starch, to stiffen.**

II. *W.* *čag-čág čó-če** **to tread, to trample,** e.g. the narrow paths or furrows between garden-beds; **to clap the hands.**

ཆག་ཆད་ *čag-čád* **rent, break, rupture** *Sch.*

ཆག་དུམ་ *čag-dúm* **fragment, piece, crumb, scrap, bit.**

ཆག་འདིང་ *čag-ₒdiṅ* **doubtful, incredible** *Sch.*

ཆག་པ་ *čág-pa* 1. a large **tuft** or **bunch** of flowers, ears of corn etc. — 2. pf. of *ₒčág-pa*, **broken;** *ma-čág(s)-pa*, and esp. adv. *ma-čág(s)-par* also *čág-med-par* uninterrupted, unintermitting; uninterruptedly; *gas-čag-méd* without a crack, flaw, or chink. — 3. *lam čág-pa* v. *ₒčag-pa.*

ཆག་པོ་ *čág-po* **broken; a broken vessel, pot** etc., **a pot-sherd;** *tsel-(po) čág (-po)* a broken dosser or pannier.

ཆག་བུ་ *čág-bu*, diminutive of *čag-pa*, **a little bunch.**

ཆག་མོ་ *čág-mo* **bunch,** *ₒbrás-bu čág-mo* a fruit growing in the form of bunches or clusters, like the grapes of the vine, the berries of the elder etc. *W.*

ཆག་ཙེ་ *čág-tse* a small **grain,** e.g. of ground grits, **čág-tse-čan** **granulous;** **bág-p̔e čág-tse-čan** ground grits, *W.*; *Hind. soojee.*

ཆག་ཚད་ *čag-ṫsád Sch.*: **the right measure,** *dug ster čag-ṫsád* if a sufficient quantity of poison has been administered to a person, *Med.*

ཆག་ཤིང་ *čag-šiṅ* a wooden **splint** for a broken limb, **čug-če** to put it on *W.*

ཆགས་པ་ *čágs-pa* I. frq. for *čág-pa* 2.

II. vb. **to be begotten, produced;** *ma-čágs-pa* not begotten or produced in the usual way of propagation, but = *rdzús-te skyés-pa*, or *lhún-gyis grúb-pa Pth.* frq.; *mṅál-du čágs-pa* to be produced in the womb, as the foetus is; hence *čags* in compounds: animal, *ₒdab-čágs*, *yšog-čágs* winged animal, bird; *srog-čágs* in general: a living being, an animal, = *séms-čan;* *ₒp̔rúl-gyi ṫsul-čágs Glr.* prob. as much as a wonderful child, a prodigy; *šiṅ-la čágs-pa* to grow on a tree, of fruits; and in general: **to rise, arise, spring up, originate,** of the world, of new works, buildings, empires, customs, of eruptions on the skin; **zil-pa čags soṅ* W.* dew has fallen; **to come forth, to appear,** = *ₒbyúṅ-ba*, e.g. *ₒód-du čágs-pa* to come to light, to appear *Mil.*; **ṅul čags* W.* sweat comes forth, breaks out, I perspire; even: *ráb-tu čágs-pa* = *ráb-tu ₒbyúṅ-ba* to become a cleric (little used); *čags-rábs* genesis, history of the beginning, esp. of the world; *čags-ṫsúl* 1. manner of beginning, origin, procreation *Med.* 2. *W.* form, figure, demeanour, **čags-ṫsúl sóg-po** coarse, rude, rough.

III. 1. vb. **to love,** (ἐρᾶν), *bú-mo-la* a girl; *skyés-pa daṅ na-čúṅ ycig čágs-pa* the mutual affection between a man and a maiden; tender attachment in general, connubial, parental and filial love, *yid-la čágs-pai bú-mo-rnams* my dearly beloved daughters *Pth.;* ardent desire or longing for something, *grágs-pa-la* for glory; **to be attached to, to cling to,** e.g. *lus daṅ sróg-la čágs-pa* to life, *yúl-la* to one's home, to one's native country; often: to suffer one's self to be enticed by a thing, **to indulge in;** *čágs-par mi bya ˏjigs-par mi byá-ste* allowing neither desire nor fear to have any influence upon himself *Samb.* — 2. sbst. **love** (ἔρως), **lust, passion** for, **affection, attachment,** *čágs-pa skyés-so* he fell in love *Dzl.*; *čágs-pa spyód-pa* = *ˏkrig-pa spyód-pa.* According to Buddhistic theory all *čágs-pa* is a great evil, as it betrays a troubled state of mind, and a reprehensible attachment to external things; yet even a saint, so far advanced in dispassion and apathy as Milaraspa, may sometimes be caught in very tender affections and sensations of *čágs-pa,* very like those of other human creatures.

Comp. *čags-sdáṅ* 1. *Schr.* **love and hatred,** 2. *Glr.*, *Pth.* **jealousy** (love showing itself in hatred), also *čags-sdáṅ-gi ṗrag-dog.* — *čags-spyód* **coition, copulation,** cf. *čágs-pa* III., 2. — *čags-žén,* also *žen-čágs* = *čágs-pa* sbst. *Mil.*; **čags-žén čó-če** *W.*, to love, c. *la*; *čags-žén méd-pa* dispassionate, indifferent to all terrestrial things. — *čags-séms* = *čags-žén.* — *čágs-sred-čan Pth.* **lustful, libidinous, wanton.**

ཆང་ *čaṅ* (मद्य) resp. *skyems*, *ysól-čaṅ*, *mčód-čaṅ C.*, a fermented liquor, **beer, wine,** (not 'brandy' *Sch.*); *bu skyés-pa-la miṅ, čaṅ dráṅs-pa-la ytam* proverb: to the new-born child a name (is due), to the beer to be drunk a talk; *nás-čaṅ* beer made of barley (the usual kind); *brás-čaṅ* of rice *Glr.*; *gró-čaṅ* of wheat *Cs.*; *bú-ram-čaṅ,* or *búr-čaṅ* of sugar *Med.*; *rgún-čaṅ* wine; *sbráṅ-čaṅ Med.* honey-wine, mulse, mead? *rús-čaṅ Med.?* — *zás-čaṅ, zán-čaṅ* eating and drinking, meat and drink. — *sloṅ-*, *tig-*, and *bsu-čaṅ* v. sub *bág-ma.* — Fig.: *btúṅ-ba dran-šes bdúd-rtsii čaṅ* my drink is the wine of wisdom's nectar *Mil.* —

Here the process of brewing may be mentioned. When the boiled barley (*Ld.* **sbo-bód**, *Ts.* **ṫab**) has grown cold, some **ṗabs** (q. v.) is added, after which it is left standing for two or three days, until fermentation commences, when it is called *glum.* Having sufficiently fermented, some water is poured to it, and the beer is considered to be ready for use. If proper care is taken (and the people of Ü and Ladak generally do so), the pale beer, thus obtained, is not amiss, and sparkles a good deal, but not being hopped it does not keep long. The people of Lahoul are accustomed to press out the *glum* with their hands, instead of filtering it, and mismanage the business also in other respects, so that their *čaṅ* is a gray muddy liquor, that has hardly any resemblance to beer. The residue of malt, called *sbáṅ-ma,* may be mixed with water or milk, pressed through a strainer, and used instead of barm in baking bread, cakes etc.

Comp. *čáṅ-ḱaṅ* **beer-house, pot-house, tavern.** — *čáṅ-čan* **drinking-cup** or **bowl** *Sch*, *Wts.* — *čáṅ-čem-čan* **an intoxicated person.** — *čáṅ-čem-sa Lex.* prob. = *čáṅ-sa.* — *čáṅ-ˏtuṅ-mḱan* **a beer-drinker;** **čáṅ-ˏtun-ḱan máṅ-po dzom** a great beer-drinking bout takes place *W.* — **čáṅ-dad-čan** **a drunkard, tippler** *W.* — *čáṅ-tsúgs* = *čaṅ-čan Sch.* — *čáṅ-ˏtsoṅ-gi ḱyim* **beer-house** *Dzl.* — *čáṅ-sa* 1. **beer-house** 2. **beer-carousal,** *čáṅ-sa čén-po byéd-pa* to give or arrange a great beer-drinking bout *Mil.*

ཆང་ཅུང་ *čaṅ-čúṅ* **a little** *Sch.*

ཆད་ *čad* 1. also *čad-dón, čad-mdó, W.* **čád-ka**, **promise, engagement, agreement** *ḱa-čád* oral, verbal engagement, *lag-čád* pledge of faith by hand; *čad-dón byéd-pa,* **čád-ka čó-če, zúm-če** *W.*, to give a promise, make a contract; *ytóṅ-(bai) čad(-don) byéd-pa* to agree about giving; *čad-dón ltar byéd-pa* to keep, fulfil a promise; *čad-rdó* 1. the stone which is broken in the ceremony of *rdo ycóg-pa* q. v. 2. monument, memorial of a covenant. — 2. in compounds also for *čád-pa* punishment, *lus-čád* corporeal punishment.

ཆད་པ་ *čád-pa* I. sbst., resp. *bka-čád*, **punishment**; the preceding genit., contrary to our usage, is the genit. of the punishing person, thus: *rgyál-poi čád-pa* a punishment of the magistrates, i. e. a punishment decreed or inflicted by the magistrates, frq.; seldom, if ever, genit. of the punished action, and never that of the punished person. In classical language the usual construction of the words is the following: *čád-pas yčód-pa* to punish, *mi žig-la* somebody, ...*pas* or ... *pai p̓yir* for having ...; in more recent literature: *čád-pa yčód-pa Thgr.*, *Glr.*; *čád-pa tób-pa* 1. to receive the fine incurred by another 2. to suffer punishment, to pay a fine; *ṅá-la čád-pa p̓og* punishment is inflicted on me, I am punished.

II. 1. **to promise**, e.g. *bká-las mi ₒgál-bar* to obey. — 2. v. sub *ₒčád-pa*.

III. adj. **begotten, born, descended** from; the Tibetans are *sbreu daṅ srin-mo-nas* (or *las*) *čád-pa* the offspring of a monkey and a Rakshasi *Glr.*; *šá-nas čád-pai bu* a full child *Glr.*

ཆད་པོ་ *čád-po* 1. **rent, torn, worn-out, ragged, tattered,** *sgyi-gu čád-po* a leaky purse. — 2. a limited time, **a term** *Sch.*

ཆད་ཡིག་ *čad-yig* **a written contract**; *čad-mál-gyi yi-ge Glr.* id.

ཆད་ལུས་པ་ *čád-lus-pa* not to obtain the things hoped for, to be disappointed *Sch.*

ཆད་སོ་ *čád-so* 1. a limited time, **a term.** — 2. **a time-purchase** *Sch.* — 3. **an agreement** *Tar.*

ཆན་ *čan*, also *čan-túg Sch.*, **boiled corn** or **barley** etc.; *ₒbras-čán* rice-pap, *nas-čán* barley-pap.

ཆན་པ་ *čán-pa* a pair of **scissors**, but the common people know only **shears**, which are for various purposes; the scissors mentioned in surgical books are prob. of a nicer construction.

ཆབ་ *čab*, resp. and eleg. for *ču* 1. **water,** *dri-čáb* scented water; *sṅa-čáb*, *p̓yi-čáb*, water which at the beginning and close of the meetings in the large monasteries is handed round, and of which every one present takes a few drops on his tongue, as a symbol of purification, in place of the original ablutions. — 2. for other fluids, as *spyan-čáb* **tears,** *žal-čáb* **spittle,** *ysaṅ-čáb*, or *čab-ysáṅ* **urine,** *ba-čab* cow's urine (so with the Hindoos in *Lh.*, the cow being to them a sacred animal). — 3. in some compounds: **power, dominion, authority.** — *čab-rkyán* **brass can, brass-(tea) pot** with a long spout for pouring out tea, *W.*; also n. for Tibet, perh. on account of the large consumption of tea there. — *čab-k̓úṅ* **privy** *Cs.* — *čab-sgó* **door,** *čab-sgo-pa* **door-keeper, porter.** — **čab-ḍá** (spelling dubious) a wooden **pail,** of a similar shape as *čab-rkyán W.* — *čab-bróm*, *čab-róm* **ice.** — *čab-blúg C.* a vessel for rinsing one's mouth with water. *čab-mig* eleg. for *ču-mig* **fountain, spring.** — *čab-ṫsód* eleg. **a watch, a clock.** — *čab-ₔóg* what is subjected to a person's sway, territory, dominion etc., *čab-ₔóg-tu sdú-ba* to subject; *čab-ₔóg-gi rgyál-po* a vassal, feudal tenant *Trig.*; *čab-ₔóg-pa*, also *čab-ₒbáṅs* one owing allegiance to a sovereign, a subject. — *čab-šóg Cs.* eleg. for **letter, diploma** etc. — *čab-sér* eleg. for *ču-sér* **matter, pus.**

ཆབ་མ་ *čáb-ma W.*, *C.*, also *Mil.*, **lid, valve; buckle, clasp,** *čáb-tse*, or *čáb-rtse C.* id.

ཆབས་ *čabs Lex. čabs-yčig Sch.* = *tabs-yčig* **together.**

ཆམ་ *čam*, in *čám-la ₒbébs-pa Lex.* w.e.; *Sch.*: to throw down, to cause to lie down; to subdue, subject; to spend, consume, **to have done with**; by this last signification it would be a syn. to *zin-pa*, and the circumstance that *čams* is used in Balti as an auxiliary vb. of the pf. tense agrees with that supposition, e.g. **zan zós-se čams** I have done eating, = *zos zin B.*

ཆམ་པ་ *čám-pa* 1. **cold** (in the head), **catarrh;** *sne-čám* id.; *gre-čam* catarrh in the throat, bronchial catarrh; *glo-čám* catarrh in the lungs; *rims-čám* an infecting or epidemic catarrh. — 2. *Cs.* = *ₒčám-pa* **accord, accordance.**

ཆམ་མེ་ *čam-mé* **slowly, by degrees, gradually** *Schr.* (cf. *čem-mé*).

ཆར་ *čar*, termin. of *ča*, 1. **into parts**, e.g. *bgó-ba* to divide into parts. — 2. **as an equal, as a match,** . . . *la čar mi ṗod* he is not an equal to, cannot come up to . . . *Thgy.*; . . . *daṅ stóṅ-ṗrag-čar mi nye* prob.: he does not come up to . . . at all (lit. not for the thousandth part) *Pth.*; so in a similar manner: *brgyai čar yaṅ mi sleb Tar.* — 3. affixed to numerals, and sometimes, though less correctly, written *čar*, q.v. The terminations of the cases mag be affixed to it: *lṅa čár-gyis* every fifth day *Thgy.*

ཆར་ *čar*, also *čár-pa*, 1. **rain**, *čar čén-po* a plentiful rain, *čar drág-po*, or *drag-čár* a heavy rain; *čar čén-pas* or *čé-bas* as it rained heavily *Pth.*; *čar ₒbébs-pa* to cause to rain; *čar ₒbab* it rains, *W.* **čár-pa yoṅ**; *čár-gyi rgyun* a sudden or violent shower of rain *Tar.* — 2. at Kyelang for **watering-pot;** this utensil having never been seen there before, the word was at first applied to it jestingly, but is now generally adopted; *ču-ṫság* 'water-sieve' would be more correct.

Comp. *čar-skyibs* **a shelter, pent-roof,** protecting from rain. — *čar-ḱébs* dress against rain, **rain-cloak.** — *čár-čan*, *čár-ldan* rainy *Cs.* — *čár-ču* **rain-water.** — *čár-dus* **rainy season.** — *čar-ₒdód* (*-byeu*) n. of a bird, water-ousel. — *čar-sprin* a rain-threatening cloud. — **čar-bhi** (?) *C.* rain-cloak. — *čar-rlúṅ* rain and wind *Cs.* — **čar-šiṅ** = *čar-skyibs W.* — *čar-lén* the coping or water-tile of a wall *Cs.*

ཆལ་ *čal*, *sku-čál* resp. **belly, abdomen,** *Cs.*

ཆལ་ཆིལ་ *čal-čil Lex.*, wavering, fluctuating *Sch.*

ཆལ་ཆོལ་ *čal-čól Tar.* 184, 20 = *ₒčal-la-ₒčol-le.*

ཆལ་མར་བརྡལ་བ་ *čál-mar brdál-ba* to spread equally, uniformly (vb. a.)

ཆས་ *čás* (*Sch. čás-ka*) cf. *ča* III., 1. **thing, tool, requisite** etc., *sé-mo-do-la sógs-pai čás-kyis brgyán-te* adorned with ornaments of pearls and other things *Mil.*; *dga-stón-gyi čas rgya čén-po* grand festival arrangements; *čas dé-rnams bšig* overturn the whole affair! *Glr.*; *bág-mar rdzóṅ-bai čas* things to be given to her as a dowry *Tar.* 121, 5; *lčágs-čas* iron tools or utensils; *ltó-čas* food; *dmag-čas* military stores, requisites for war *Pth.*; *ₒṫsó-čas* provisions *Mil.*; *lág-čas* tool, instrument *Cs.* — 2. **dress, garment,** *ṗó-čas* man's dress; *čas-gós*, *W.* **gon-čé**, coat, dress; in a more general sense: **appearance, form, shape,** *búd-med-kyi čás-su byáste* appearing in the shape of a woman *Glr.*; *hór-čas byed* he puts on a Mongol dress *Ma.*; *bú-moi čás-su žugs* he puts on a girl's dress, disguises himself as a girl *Glr.*, *Pth.*; *čas sgyúr-ba* to put on, to assume another dress.

ཆས་པ་ *čás-pa*, originally the pf. of *čá-ba*, but always used as a separate vb. 1. **to set out, set forth, depart,** *čas dgós-par* as I must depart from here *Thgy.*; *bód-du čás-so* they set out for Tibet *Glr.*; *dus-ɣčig-tu čás-so* they departed at the same time *Dzl.*; *čás-su ₒǰúg-pa* to send away, dispatch; *mgyógs-čas ɣtóṅ-ba* to rush, run towards. — 2. **to set about, to begin,** *ɣsód-par* to kill; *ₒgró-bar čás-pa-las* when he made arrangements to depart *Dzl.*; also in the following manner; *da ṗyir ₒdóṅ-ṅo žes čás-pa* 'now we will return' they said, making preparations, or: saying thus, they made preparations *Dzl.*; *ṫugs čás-so* he had set his mind on departing *Mil.*

ཆི་ *či* num. fig.: 36.

ཆི་ཀ་ *či-ka* **wallet, knapsack** *W.*

ཆི་ཏྲ་ *či-tra W* **variegated, figured,** of fabrics.

ཆི་ལི་ལི་ *či-li-li* onomatopoetic word for snuffing up scents by the nose; **žim-žim ḍi-ma či-li-li ḱyer** *C.* sweet odours of cakes are meeting us; *mé-tog dri-ma či-li-li* the perfumes of flowers are perceptible *Mil.*

ཅིག *čig* = *γčig* **one**, as the first part of compound numbers: *čig-bču* 10, *čig-brgya* 100, *čig-ston* 1000, *čig-k̔ri* a myriad etc.; also: *čig-rkyáṅ Lex., Schr.*: 'separate, single, one alone'; *čig-skyés Med., čig-táṅ Med.?* — *čig-túb* n. of a plant *Med.*; *Sch.* also: *čig-túb-pa* to be able to do a thing alone; *čig-dril Sch.*: rolled, wrapped, packed up (in one parcel or bundle); *čig-láb byéd-pa* to talk to one's self, to hold a soliloquy *Schr.*

ཅིང(ས) *čiṅ(s)* v. *ₒčiṅ-ba.*

ཅིད་པ *čid-pa* v. *p̔yid-ba.*

ཅིབ་པ *čib-pa* equal, uniform, suitable *Sch.*

ཅིབས(་པ) *čibs(-pa)* resp. **horse**, riding-horse, saddle-horse, *čibs-la ₒčib-pa* (for *rtá-la žón-pa*) to get on horseback, to mount; to go on horseback, to ride; *čibs-las γžól-ba* to dismount, **čibs žól-la naṅ* C.* may your honour please to dismount; *k̔yéd-kyi čibs-su ₒbul* I give it you for a riding-horse *Mil.*

Comp. *čibs-ka ₒk̔rid-pa* to lead a horse by the bridle *Schr.*; *čibs-k̔a túb-pa* to have the command of the bridle, fig.: to be expert in ruling *Ld.-Glr.* p. 14, a, *Schl.* where *p̔yibs* is incorr.). — *čibs-čás* a horse's furniture, **harness** *Cs.* — *čibs-tur* **the head-piece** of a bridle. — *čibs-dpón* a master groom, **equerry.** — *čibs-rá* **a stable** for horses.

ཆུ *ču* I. num. fig.: 66.

II. sbst. (resp. *čab*) 1. **water;** *ču daṅ sai bu* is said to be a poetical name for wood; *ₒbáb-ču* lit. descending water, viz. brook, river, also rain. — 2. **brook, river,** *ču ₒk̔yám-po* overflowing rivers, floods *Ma.*; *táṅ-ču* a river or rivulet of the plain; *ri-γzár-ču* cataract, mountain torrent *Glr.* — 3. **water in the body:** *snyiṅ-ču* dropsy in the pericardium, *págs-ču* anasarca *Med.*; *págs-ču-zugs* one suffering from anasarca; v. also *ču-sér*; esp. euphem for **urine;** *mi-ču* urine of men, *bá-ču* of cows *Med.*: *ču ni ču ₒdra* the urine is like water *Med.* — 4. v. *ču-žéṅ.*

Comp. *ču-klúṅ* **river,** e.g. *ču-kluṅ gaṅ-gā* the river Ganges *Dzl.* — *ču-klóṅ Cs.*: 'the body of a river', yet v. *kloṅ.* — *ču-dkyil* the middle of a river. — *ču-rkyál* a leather bag for water *Cs.* — *ču-skád* the voice of the waters, the sound of rushing water. — *ču-skór, raṅ-túg-ču-skór* **water-mill** *Glr.* — *ču-skyúr* n. of a bird *Thgy., Sch.*: **'bittern, snipe'**; also n. of a plant. — *ču-skyúr* 1. *Lt.*: acidulous mineral waters 2. *C.*: **vinegar.** — *ču-skyés* 'water-born', the lotus *Glr.* — *ču-skyór* a handful of water. *ču-k̔a* the bank or brink of a river. — *ču-k̔úg* **bay, gulf.** — *ču-ₒk̔úr* containing water, po. for **cloud;** a native proposed to use this word also for **sponge,** which is a commodity hitherto unknown in Tibet. — *ču-ₒk̔yil* **puddle, pool.** — *ču-gáṅ* 1. full of water. 2. = *ču-sgáṅ* (v. *sgaṅ*) which latter is prob. the more correct spelling. 3. *Dzl.* ༡༡༦, 2; ༢༦༡, 18 = सत्त्व virtue, honesty, v. *Schf.* on this passage. — *ču-gri* a sort of knife; *Tar.* 43, 1 *Schf.* razor; also the attribute of a god, a weapon with a curved blade *Stg.* — *ču-gróg Sch.*: rivulet, brook; dish-water, rinsings; boiled water (?). — *ču-mgó C.* **source** or **head** of a river. — *ču-gágs* stoppage or retention of urine, **ischury,** *ču-gágs ₒbigs* the ischury is removed (lit. bored through) *Med.* — *ču-ₒgrám* **bank** of a river; *ču-grám-gyi šiṅ* a tree on the edge of a river, a metaphor for frail and perishable things. — *ču-rgyún* the streaming, continual flowing, **current,** often fig. — *ču-sgóṅ* the water-egg, po. for moon *Sch.* — *ču-ṅógs* v. *ṅógs.* — **čú-ta-gir* W.* flour-dumplings, boiled in water. — **ču-stán* W.* **swaddling-cloth.** — **ču-tág* W.* calamus, sweet-scented flag, or some similar plant. — *ču-túms Sch.*: 'a swelling in the flesh, or a tumour filled with water'. — *ču-mtá* the side or **bank** of a river, **ču-tá tsúg-pa** (the avalanche came down) even to the river side. — *ču-dár Wdk.* a small prayer-flag stuck up close to the river, in order to avert inundations. — *ču-dúg Sch.*: 'a poisonous plant, hemlock', but Tibetans usually understand by it the stupefying power ascribed to certain rivers. — *ču-doṅ* a deep **well.** —

— *ču-mdá* **a jet,** a spouting forth of water *Med.* — *ču-mdó* 'mouth (of a river), spout (of a tea-pot)' *Sch.;* but v. *mču.* — *ču-mdóg* the colour of urine *Med.* — *ču-rdó C.* small rounded pebbles, as in brooks. — *ču-nág* inundation, flood (?) *Ma.* — *ču-rnág* matter, pus *Sch.* — *ču-snód* **1. pitcher, jug.** 2. *Schr.:* **chamber-pot** (yet in *W.* at least this article of luxury is not known). — *čú-pa* **water-carrier.** — *ču-pyág-pa* is enumerated among other synonyms to *grú-pa,* signifying **a ferry-man,** water-man. — *ču-prán* a little river, **brook.** — *ču-bár* 1. ('between the waters') **isthmus,** neck of land. 2. p. n. of a place in Tibet. — *ču-bál* n. of an aquatic plant *Wdn.* — *ču-bún* white paint for the face *Sch.* — *ču-bór* 1. **bubble,** also *čui ču-búr* 2. **blister, bladder, vesicle,** e.g. occasioned by a burn or a vesicatory *Lt.* 3. **boil, ulcer, abscess** *Thgy.,* 4. *šai ču-búr* a word describing the foetus five days after conception *Thgy.* — *čú-bur-čan* 1. n. of a hell *Thgy.* 2. the eye *Schr.* — *čú-bo* **river,** frq., *čú-bo-ri* n. of a mountain with a monastery two days' journey from Lhasa *Glr.* — *ču-byá* **a water-bird;** *Sch.: ču-byá dkár-po* swan, *ču-byá mgo-dmár* stork (not known in *W.*). — *ču-byi* **water-rat** *Sch.* — *ču-lbág* v. *lbag.* — *ču-sbúr* 1. *Sch.:* 'driftwood and the like', prob. more correctly: thin pieces of wood, chips, chaff etc. floating on the water. 2. **water-beetle** *Med.* — *ču-sbrúl* **water-snake,** not a mythological conception, like *klu,* but a really existing animal, though for Tibetans a somewhat faboulous one, as they have never seen the creature itself. The eel (*Sch.*) can hardly be meant by it. — *ču-mig* 1. **spring, fountain** frq. 2. n. of a vein *Med.* — *ču-rtsá* v. *ču-ču,* as a separate article. — *ču-tságs* 1. **a strainer, sieve,** 2. **watering-pot.** — *ču-tsán* 1. hot water, 2. warm water, not too hot for drinking *Med.* 3. a hot spring *Sch.* — *ču-tsód* 1. the clepsydra or **water-clock** of ancient India. 2. **clock** in general, *ču-tsod-ₒkór-lo* a wheel-clock. 3. **the Indian hour** = ½ *Kyim* or 24 minutes. 4. **the European hour;** *W.:* **ču-tsód nyis ma leb** it is not yet two o'clock. — *ču-ₒdzin* po. **cloud** *Mil.* — *ču-rdzá* earthen vessel for water, **water-jar.** — *ču-žén* (*Lex.* **परिणाह**) **long and broad, area, superficial extent,** *ču-žén kru-brgyád-pa* eight cubits long and broad *Dzl.;* also *ču-žen-gáb-pa,* e.g. *ču-žen-gáb-pa-la dpag-tsád brgyád-ču Glr.;* *ču-žen-srab-túg* in length, breadth and height; also separately: *čur dpag-tsád* ༢༥༠༠, *žén-du yaṅ* ༢༥༠༠, *mta-skór-du dpag-tsád* ༡༠༠༠༠ *yód-pa* 2500 miles in length, 2500 miles in breadth, 10000 in circumference; yet except in this connexion *ču* alone is never used for length. As another signification of *ču-žen-gáb-pa Schr.* mentions moreover: proportioned, symmetrical; others have: beautiful, great, considerable, which e.g. is its proper meaning in: *ču-žen-gáb-pa nya-grodha Stg.* the stately fig-tree. — *ču-zém* **water-tub.** — *ču-zlá* 1. the image, the reflexion of the moon in the water; a sort of deception of the senses by witchcraft. 2. the water-month, the first month. — *ču-γzár* a large **ladle** *Cs.* — *ču-bzóm* **a covered bucket** for carrying water. — *ču-ₒóbs* **water-ditch** *Sch.* — *ču-yar* col. water-rat (?) — *ču-rágs* **dam, dike.** — *ču-rí* 'hill of water', **billow.** — *ču-rúd* water rushing in, **inundation, deluge.** — *ču-rlábs* **wave, billow** *Dzl.* — *ču-lág* the arm of a river *Glr.* — *ču-lúd Sch.* dung, manure (?) — *ču-ló* n. of an edible plant *S.g.* — *ču-lóg* **floods.** — *ču-lón,* **dam, dike** *Tar.* 56, 15. *Lis.* — *ču-šíṅ* wood drifted away by the water = *ču-ₒgrám-gyi šiṅ* v. above; or the translation of **कदली** plantain or banana-tree with its spongy wood, in the place of which the Tibetan thinks of the *ₒom-bu,* a shrub of similar qualities, at any rate a symbol of perishableness, of the frailty of life. — *ču-šúṅ Sch.* surface of the water (?) — *ču-šél* v. *šel.* — *ču-γšóṅ Dzl.* ༢༧༠, 17. a ravine containing water. — *ču-sá* **river-mud,** as manure. — *ču-sér* 1. animal water, **serum,** whether normal, or of a morbid character *Med.* — 2. **matter, pus.** — *ču-sráṅ,* = $\frac{1}{60}$ *ču-tsod,* i.e. **a minute;** the Indian or Tibetan minute is equal to 24 of our seconds, = 6 *dbugs Wdk.*, cf. *ču-tsód.* — *ču-srín* a water- or **sea-monster,** also Capricorn in the Zodiac. — *ču-lhá* **water-god** (*Varuṇa*); also = *klui rgyál-po.*

ཆུ་ཆུ་ *ču-čú*, = *la-čú*, **rhubarb,** *ču-rtsá* its root, used as dye and as a laxative *C.*

ཆུ་ཉིང་ *ču-niṅ* **four years ago** *C., W.*

ཆུ་པ་ *čú-pa* 1. *C.* a man's dress, **coat,** — 2. **water-carrier.**

ཆུ་བ་ *čú-ba* a large **sinew,** of which there are 16 acc. to Tibetan anatomy; *čú-ba ldóg-pa* a contraction of the sinews *Cs.*, *žá-ba* lameness, paralysis of the sinews *Sch.* — *ču-rgyús* (स्नायु) sinews, ligaments and nerves (there are 900 *rgyús-pa*); with respect to these, as well as to the veins, Tibetan science seems to be rather in the dark. — *ču-rtsá* 'sinew-veins', a term coming nearest to what we call the nerves. — *ču-ba-lṅa-ldán*, and *lṅa-lén Cs.* names of countries in India.

ཆུ་མ་རྩི་ *ču-ma-rtsí* a medicinal herb *Med.*

ཆུ་མ་ལོང་ *ču-ma-lóṅ*, **ṭu-gu ču-ma-loṅ* Ld.* **an infant, baby.**

ཆུ་སོ་ *ču-só* the external and internal **urinary organs.**

ཆུག *čug* v. *°jùg-pa.*

ཆུང་བ་ *čúṅ-ba* 1. adj. col. *čúṅ-nu*, *W.* also **čúṅ-se**, **little, small,** *čuṅ-čés-pas Dzl.* when he was very little; **young,** *bu čúṅ-ba* or *-ṅu* the younger or the youngest son; *lo-čúṅ* young in years; *ma-čúṅ* the younger sister of the mother; **'á-pa čúṅ-ṅu** the younger brother of the father; the younger or the youngest of the fathers (in polyandry); *čúṅ-ṅu-nas* up from infancy; *čuṅ-gróǵs* an early friend, friend of one's youth; *čuṅ-zád* a little, cf. *čuṅ-zad*; *čuṅ-(gyi) sri* a devil devouring infants, infants-devil; **nyiṅ-ḱám-, ṅo-mig-, ṗod-**, or **nyom-čúṅ-se* W.* shy, timid. — 2. vb. **to be little, small** etc., *snyiṅ ma čuṅ čig Glr.*, be not timorous, do not fear! *°dún-ma rgya ma čuṅ čig* let the consultation not be trifling, let at once something of moment be consulted; *°dún-ma rgya mi čúṅ-bar byed-do* let us now decide on important things *Glr.*; *čúṅs-pa* pf., *čúṅs-pa yin-nam* is it too unimportant? *Mil.* (*čuṅ-°jùg* v. *°ja*).

ཆུང་མ་ *čúṅ-ma*, *C.* also **čuṅ-gróǵs, čuṅ-°dris**, resp. *btsún-mo*, **wife, consort, partner** *B., C.*; *lén-pa* to marry; *mi žig-gi čúṅ-mar byéd-pa* to be made a man's wife, to be married.

ཆུད་ *čud* occurs only in *čúd-γzon-pa, -γson-pa, -γsan-pa, -za-ba*, seldom *-°dza-ba* (*Lex.*) **to consume, spend, waste;** *čud mi zá-ba* inexhaustible.

ཆུད་པ་ *čúd-pa* = *°tsúd-pa, °jùg-pa*, **to go, get in** or **into, to enter, to put in** or **into** etc., to go into a town *Dzl.*; of food entering the body *Dzl.*; *gaṅ yaṅ rúṅ-ba mi čúd-pa med* all without distinction may enter (my religion), says Buddha, in opposition to the aristocratic exclusiveness of Brahmanism *Dzl.*; *ṫúgs-su čúd-pa*, resp., to impress on one's mind; *ḱoṅ-du* v. *ḱoṅ-pa*; *°óg-tu* to subject *Tar.*; *grúbs-su* c. accus. to procure, to provide or furnish one's self with a thing *Mil.*

ཆུན་ *čun*, occurs in *žiṅ-čun* one that is watering or taking care of fields, *ṫsás-čun* gardens *°ól-čun* meadows *Ld.*

ཆུན་པོ་ *čún-po* (दामा) 1. **bunch, bundle.** 2. **tuft, tassel, ornament,** of silk, pearls etc.

ཆུན་མ་ *čún-ma* **the second wife** in rank.

ཆུན་ཙེ་ *čún-tse Bal.* **little, small.**

ཆུབ་པ་ *čúb-pa*, a corruption of *čúd-pa*, *kun čúb-par byao* all this is to be well impressed on the mind; *dbaṅ-po ṫams-čád-du čúb-pa* to pass through, to penetrate, every organ *Stg.*

ཆུམ་པ་ *čúm-pa*, *°jigs-čum-pa Mil.*, **to shrink, to crouch** with fear.

ཆུར་ *čur*, termin. of *ču*; *čur °čí-ba* to be drowned.

ཆུར་བ་ *čúr-ba* a kind of vermicelli, prepared from butter-milk boiled *Med.*, *Ld.* **čúrṗe**.

ཆུས་ *čus* 1. instrum. of *ču; Sch.* also *čús-γtoṅ-ba* 'to melt'; more correctly: **to gild, to plate** (in the warm or in the cold way), to overspread with a gold or silver liquid. — **after five days** *C., W.*, or, the present day included, on the sixth day, cog. to *bču.*

ཆེ་ *če* 1. num. fig.: 96. — 2. v. *če-ba.*

ཆེ་གེ་མོ་ *čé-ge-mo* **such a one,** *lo čé-ge-mo žig-la* in such and such a year *Dzl.*; *čé-ge-mo k̔yod* you so and so *Thgr.*

ཆེ་འགྲན་ *če-ₒgrán W.* being jealous of one's own honour, ni f.

ཆེ་ཐབས་ *če-t̔ábs* **arrogance, haughtiness,** *sde-pai če-t̔abs* the arrogance of the great *Ma.*; **če-t̔ábs-med-k̔an** *W.* affable, condescending, kind; *če-t̔ábs-čan* proud, arrogant, haughty; *če-t̔ábs byéd-pa B.*, **čo-če** *W.*, **zuṅ-wa** *C.*, to be arrogant, haughty.

ཆེ་དོན་ *če-dón* **a missive** to an inferior, **an edict.**

ཆེ་བ་ *čé-ba* 1. adj. **great,** (for *čén-po*); *bu čé-ba* the eldest son, the elder; *čé-bar ₒgyúr-ba* to become great or greater, to grow, increase e.g. of passions; *čé-bar ₒgró-ba, čer ₒgró-ba* id., cf. *čer, čé-bar byéd-pa* to make great; frq. in conjunction with nouns: *že-sdáṅ čé-ba* great with respect to anger, i.e. very prone to anger; *rigs čé-žiṅ* being of high extraction; also in compounds, v. below. — 2. sbst. **greatness, high degree** *Mil.*; **superiority, excellence,** ... *kyi čé-ba stón-pa* to show the superiority of a thing *Mil.*; **čé-wa šrúṅ-wa** *Ld.* to behave decently, respectably. — 3. vb., pf. *čes* **to be great,** not only in *čé-žiṅ, če-o,* but also in: *ṅa-rgyál ma čé-žig* do not be great in pride, i.e. do not allow pride to become great *Mil.*, and so in similar cases; cf. *čes.*

Comp. *čé-ka Sch.*: 'chiefly; the plurality. — *če-kyád* **greatness, size** *Dzl.* — **če-dál** *W.*, **če-dál-la čud soṅ** he has entered the class of adults, he has come to full age. — *čé-rgyu* = *čé-ba,* cf. *rgyu* 3. — *če-brgyúd* perh. lineage by the eldest sons *Glr.* — *če-čúṅ* **great and small; size;** *če-čúṅ ni* in size. — *če-ₒdón* the coming to full age *Mil.nt.* — **če-mi** *W.* **an adult.** — **če-lóṅs** *C.* grown up, **adult** (*Sch.* 'chiefly'?)

ཆེ་ཞེ་ *če-žé* one's **elder sister** *Cs.*, **the elder wife** *Sch.*

ཆེ་བཞི་ *če-bži Lis.* = *bden-dpáṅ*, **witness, eye-witness; witness, testimony;** *če-bžir dris-te* being questioned as a witness, or asked for a testimony *Stg.*

ཆེད་ *čed,* as sbst. of rare occurrence, *Schr.*: reason, signification = *don; Sch.*: *čed čén-po* a great thing, an important business or affair. Mostly *čéd-du* postp. c. genit. **on account of, because of, for;** *ltá-bai čéd-du yin* it is in order to see *Pth.*; *rin-gyi čéd-du* as an equivalent *Pth.*; *lhai čéd-du ₒdzin-pa* or *γnyér-ba*, also *rǰés-su ₒdzin-pa* or *γnyér-ba* to admit to the discipleship or communion of a god *Mil.* — As an adv. *čed-du* seems to signify 1. for a certain purpose, **designedly, purposely, expressly,** e.g. with *byéd-pa* to do, to make a thing; *mṅágs-pa* to send off, dispatch. — 2. **again, once more, once again,** = *p̔yir Mil.* — *dgos-čéd* the construction of any noun with *p̔yir-du, čéd-du* etc., regarded by Tib. grammarians as a case of declension.

ཆེད་དོན་ *čed-dón* v. *če-dón.*

ཆེན་པོ་ *čén-po B.* and *C.*, **čén-mo** *W.*, **great** (*čén-mo* in *B.* only as fem. *Dzl.* ༢༥, b), *čén-por ₒgyúr-ba, W.* **čen čá-če**, to become great, to increase, col. also for to grow up; *skyes-bu čén-po* a great man, a man of great worth (by his talents and actions), a saint; **mi čén-mo** *W.* a man of quality, of rank, a nobleman, a rich man; *čén-ma* the first wife in rank; *čen čun γnyis* the first and second wife *Glr.*; **čén-mo** *W.* also: **old,** **ṭ̔ú-gu lo ču čen-mo** a child ten years old.

ཆེམ་མེ་བ་ *čém-me-ba Lex., Cs.* **stillness, silence,** *čém-mer ₒdúg-pa Schr.*, *čém-mer ₒk̔ód-pa C.*, to sit still without speaking.

ཆེམ(ས)་ *čem(s)* in compounds: 1. *čaṅ-čém(s)* v. *čaṅ.* — 2. *k̔a-čém(s)*, resp. *žal-čéms(s)*, *bka-čém(s)* **farewell exhortation; last will, testament,** *srás-la k̔a-*

čém(s) °jóg-pa to deposit a testamentary disposal or devise for a son *Glr.*

ཆེམ(ས)་ཆེམ(ས)་ *čem(s)-čém(s)* 1. **the noise** made by thunder, by the shock of an earthquake etc., *°brúg-sgra čem-čém sgrógs-pa* the rolling, roaring, clapping of thunder; *bżad-gád °ur čém-pa* a roaring laughter. — 2. *ḱra čem-čém* v. *ḱrá-bo.*

ཆེར་ *čer* termin. of *če*, *čer °gró-ba* to grow, increase; *čer skyé-ba* to become great; to grow up, *čer skyés-pa* partic. grown up, adult; *da-dúń čer toń* go on! go on! *Mil.*; *rgyal-srid byá-ba čer ma byuń Glr.* his government was not (yet) of much consequence (as he was too young); *ńés-pa čer med* this is not quite evident to me *Mil.*; perh. *Tar.* 36, 16; 101, 22; 120, 21; 169, 14 will allow a similar interpretation of *čer.* — *čér-na S.O.* yea; still more (?).

ཆེས་ *čes* 1. instrum. of *če.* — 2. pf. of *čé-ba*, as adv. **very,** *ḱa-zás ńan čés-kyi* as the food is very bad *Dzl.*; *čes sgrin-pa* very prudent or clever *Sch.*; *čes dár-bar gyúr-to* it spread very much *Tar.*

ཆེས་པ་ *čes-pa* 1. pf. of *čé-ba* to be great, *ha-čań yań čes-so* he is much too great *Dzl.*; *dmag-dguń čes-pa* a great army; *dbań čes-pas* being very mighty *Glr.*; *čar čes-pas* as it rained heavily *Pth.*; *dga čes-nas* greatly rejoicing *Mil.* — 2. **to believe,** but only when preceded by *yid* (resp. *ṫugs*), or *bden* (col.), c. *la*, also c. accus., or *par*, that, *Dzl.* ༡༥, 18.

ཆོ་ *čo* 1. num. fig.: 126. — 2. as a word for itself seldom to be met with, e.g. *Ld.-Glr. Schl.* fol. 13, 6; *Tar.* 129, 20; signification not clearly to be made out. **čó-med-pa** *C.* = *dón-med-pa* to no purpose, vain; fickle.

ཆོ་ག་ *čó-ga* (**विधि**) the way or **method** of doing a thing, e.g. of solving an arithmetical problem *Wdk.*, of curing maladies *S.g.*, esp. used of magic performances, *čó-ga-pa Cs.*, *čó-ga-mḱan Mil.*, a performer of such ceremonies. Whether it may safely be used for religious rites or ceremonies in general, is doubtful.

ཆོ་གོ་ *čo-gó Bal.* **great.**

ཆོ་ངེ་, ཆོ་ངེས་ *čo-ńé, čo-ńés,* **lamentation, wailing,** esp. lamentations for the dead, dirge, *°débs-pa Dzl.*, *°bód-pa*, *°dón-pa* in more recent literature, *byéd-pa Sch.*, to lament, wail, cry, clamour; with *la* to cry to a person; the crying of a new-born child *Thgy.*

ཆོ་འཕྲུལ་ *čo-°p'rúl* **magical trick, jugglery,** often put to *rdzu-°p'rúl*, also used of the apparitions and doings of goblins *Mil.* Cf. *rdzu-°p'rúl.*

ཆོ་བ་ *čó-ba* **to set on** (a dog), *čó-čo-ba* to set on repeatedly *Cs.*

ཆོ་འབྲང(ས)་ *čo-°bráń(s) Mil.; Cs.*: the mother's family or lineage; *čo-rigs Dzl.* frq. *Cs.*: 1. the father's lineage, descent by the father's side; 2. an honourable extraction. — *čo-ris Mil.*, frq. = *čo-rigs*, also applied to things, e.g. a cane: *čo-ris yé-nas btsún-pa* a cane of an excellent kind, not coming from any mean or noxious plant.

ཆོ་ལོ་ *čó-lo* 1. **die, dice,** game at dice. — 2. **seal** (?) — *čó-lo-mḱan* a dice-player *Cs.*, *čó-lo rtsé-ba* to play at dice *Cs.*; *čó-lo-ris Glr.* the figure of a die, a square figure, in *Glr.* 47, 9 the Mongol translation substitutes a wheel, v. *°ḱór-lo*; a checkered colouring or pattern, e.g. of cotton cloth *C.*

ཆོག་ *čog* 1. for *čó-ga*; *bón-čog Mil.* the ceremony of the Bonpos. — 2. v. *ycóg-pa.* — 3. v. *čóg-pa.*

ཆོག་པ་ *čóg-pa* vb., sbst., adj. 1. **to be sufficient, sufficiency, sufficient,** ccdpir: *ńéd-la dé-kas čog* it is sufficient for us, we are satisfied *Mil.*; *dris-pas* (instr. of *pai*) *čog-go Dzl.* ༢༠༡, 10 (there has been) enough of asking, = don't ask any more! *gáń-du bżugs kyań čóg-par °dug* it is sufficient (for him) wherever he may live, i.e. he is satisfied with any place of living *Mil.*; *ńéd-la nor lońs-spyód-kyis čóg-pa yod* we have money and goods enough *Mil.*; *°di ysúm-gyis čóg-na* if these three are sufficient for you *Mil.*; *rin-po-čes čóg-par* *gyúr-nas* when they had precious stones enough *Dzl.*; *ₒdi-tsam-gyis čóg-pa ma yin-no* that is not enough, that will not do *Dzl.*; *sgál-pa mi brgya žon čóg-pa* his back (is) large enough for a hundred men to ride on it *Glr.*; adv.: *čóg-par* sufficiently, e.g. *sbyin-pa* to give *Dzl.*; **ma čóg-pá** or **-ga* W.* (col. for *čóg-par*). **dúṅ-če ma čóg-ga sad soṅ** he not only struck but killed him; *p̔yin-pas čóg-gi* it being sufficient (for the present) that I have come *Mil.*; *t̔ams-čád-la čóg-par gyúr-te* as all were satisfied *Dzl.*; *čóg-par ₒdzin-pa* to deem a thing sufficient, to be contented or satisfied with it; *čog šés-pa* vb., sbst., adj. to be contented, contentment, content; *ltá-bas čog mi šés-pai rdzas* a thing at which one cannot look enough *Glr.*, *Pth.*; *yo-byád-kyi* (better *kyis*) *čog šés-pa* easily satisfied as to the necessaries of life. — 2. **to be allowed, permitted, at liberty,** construed in the same manner: *k̔rid-pas čog* you may have lessons with me, I will instruct you *Mil.*; *ₒgrán-pas čog* I am quite at liberty to compete with you, we may safely compete with each other *Glr.*; *ₒtsó-ba dráṅs-pas čog* you can have meat set before you *Mil.*; with a root: *bu byin čog* then you may render up your son; hence it is in *W.* the usual word for *rúṅ-ba*, **náṅ-du ča čóg-če yin-na man** is it allowed to enter or not? **šrád-ma za čog** eating pease is allowed, also: pease are edible; **lé-na k̔yoṅ čog ka taṅ** he issued an edict, that it should be permitted to fetch wool, i.e. he (the Maharajah of Kashmir) permitted the export of wool; **léb-na p̔ul čog* when it arrives, I shall take the liberty of sending it to you.

ཚོགས་པ *čógs-pa* seldom for *ₒčág-pa* **to be broken** *Mil.*

ཚོང, མཚོང *čoṅ, mčoṅ* a transparent, variegated, half-precious stone brought from India to *Ld.* and considered less valuable than *γzi*; perh. cornelian sardonyx?

ཚོད *čod* 1. *C.* **the cutting off; deciding;** **ṭ al-čọ̈ gya čém-po ǰhé-pa** to bring about a great remission of taxes, **bhu-lọn-čọ̈** remission of debts; **sa-čọ̈ gya čem-po ǰhé-pa** to make a great way; cf. however *p̔yod.* — 2. **partition-wall** *Sch.*, *čod rgyág-pa* prob. to construct a partition-wall. — 3. v. *γčód-pa.*

ཚོད་པ *čód-pa* 1. **to be cut off,** *lám-sgo γnyis k̔á-bas čód-de* both approaches being cut off or obstructed by snow *Mil.*; *bčad kyaṅ mi čód-do* impossible to be severed, *caedendo non caeduntur*, *Glr.*; *mi-čód-rdó-rǰe* a diamond that cannot be cut to pieces, an epithet of a firm unbending king *Pth.* — 2. **to be decided, settled, fixed,** *goṅ-t̔áṅ dpyád-kyis* (or *pas*) *mi čod Glr.* the value (of the stone) cannot be fixed, though one should attempt to apprize it i.e. it is invaluable, priceless; *gŏ čód-pa* v. *go.*

ཚོད་པོ *čód-po W.* 1. **split, cut through;** 2. **distinct,** of words or writings.

ཚོན *čon* 1. *W.* (cog. to *čud?*) **useless,** to no purpose, *rin čon soṅ* the payment has been useless, thrown away; gen. adv. **čón-la** gratuitously, in vain, for nothing, **čón-la k̔ón-če** to hate without cause or reason; **čón-la dád-če** to sit idle, to spend one's time unprofitably. — 2. **tent** (?), *čon-t̔ág* tent-rope *Mil.*, *čon-p̔úr* tent-pin.

ཚོམ(ས) *čom(s)* 1. **robbery,** *čóms-kyis zas ₒtsól-ba* to live on robbery *Ma.*; *čóm-po* robber *Dzl.*, *čóm-po rkún-ma* robber and thief, gen. *čom-rkún*, *čom-rkún-gyi ₒǰigs-pa* fear of robbers and thieves; *čom-rkún-pa* id. *Stg.* — 2. imp. of *ₒǰóms-pa.*

ཚོམ་པ *čóm-pa* **to be finished, accomplished,** *W.*, **tó-re čom yin** to-morrow it will be finished, **da čom soṅ** now it is done, completed; cf. *čam.*

ཚོལ *čol* 1. **inconstant** *Cs.*; *dpyid-čol* fickle spring-weather. — 2. *Cs.*: for *čó-lo* in compounds, *rus-čol* **a die** made of bone; *šiṅ-čól* a wooden die; *duṅ-čól* shells used inst. of dice(?).

ཚོལ་ཁ *čol-k̔a Sch.*: 'a hole made by a blow; a nest'.

ཚོལ་ཟངས *čol-zaṅs* a shallow shore *Sch.*

ཆོས་ čos (धर्म) 1. **doctrine**, a particular doctrine, **tenet**, or **precept**; *γsáṅ-bai čos šig* an esoteric doctrine, a mystery *Dzl.*; *k̔yád-čos* for *k̔yad-par-čan-gyi čos* a peculiar, distinguished, sublime, and therefore difficult doctrine; *ʼjig-rtén-gyi čos brgyad* the eight doctrines or principles of the world (though frq. mentioned, I found them nowhere specified) cf. Foucaux Gyatcherr., Translation p. 264; *čos-brgyád-mk̔an*, a man of the world, worldling *Mil.* — More esp. 2. **moral doctrine**, whether any separate dogma, or the sum of various doctrines, **religion** in general, both theoretically (system of morality, ethics) and practically (faith, exercise of religion); *lha-čós* the religion of the gods or (Buddhist) deities, i. e. the Buddhist religion, as the only true one, in opposition to all other heresies and false religions (*log-čós*), as well as to irreligiousness (*čos ma yín-pa*); *k̔a-čós* profession with the lips, hypocrisy *Glr.*; *ʼk̔rig-pai čós-la brtén-pa* those practising the religion of voluptuousness (an expression designedly forcible, like St. Paul's: 'whose god is their belly'); *mi-čos* v. below; *čos ʼčád-pa*, or *bšád-pa*, *stón-pa*, *smrá-ba*, *sgróg-pa*, resp. *čós-kyi sgrog-gléṅ mdzád-pa Glr.* to expound, to teach, to preach religion; *čos smrá-bai žál-la ltá-ba* to watch the mouth of the preacher *Pth.*; **čo ḍóg-pa* C.* to read a religious book; **čos šád-k̔an* W.* a preacher; *čos ʼčád-pai ʼdun-k̔áṅ* place where sermons are delivered, church *Dzl.*; *čos nyán-pa* to hear religious discourses *Dzl.*; *čos žú-ba* to ask for religious discourses; partic.: one eagerly desiring or asking for religious instruction, an inquirer *Pth.*, *Mil.*; *čos byéd-pa* to act or live religiously, righteously, = *čos bžín-du byéd-pa*; also merely to wish to become pious, to strive after piety; *k̔yed snyíṅ-nas čos byéd-na* if you are in good earnest about religion, if piety is the aim of your heart *Mil.*; lastly in a special sense: to become or to be a monk *Pth.*; *čós-la sems sgyúr-ba Mil.* to show an inclination for religion, to turn religious; *čós-su*, or *čós-la ʼjúg-pa* 1. vb. nt. to enter into religion, to be converted, also: to go over to a religion, to turn (Buddhist), 2. vb. act. to convert, to turn a person from a bad life to a good one, to make him a believer, to make another a convert, a proselyte; *čós-la ʼgód-pa* = *ʼjúg-pa* 1; *čos spyód-pa* to practise religion; the exercise of religion, worship *S.g.*; *bka-čós* the word of Buddha, the doctrine as taught by Buddha himself; *rtógs-pai čós Thgy.* the knowledge acquired by meditation, independently of books, scarcely different from *ṅes-dón*, or *ṅon-šés*; *bstán-pai čos Thgy.* any knowledge derived from other sources. — 3. in a special sense the **religion of Buddha**, Buddhism, *dám-pai čos*, and frq. *dám-pa čos* id. (cf. ἡ πίστις Acts 6, 7); *čos daṅ bon* Buddhism and Bon-religion *Mil.*; *čós-la lóṅ-spyod-par ʼgyúr-ba* to live in the enjoyment of true faith. — 4. **religious writings**, and **writings, books, literature** in general, in as much as the Tibetans derivate every science from religion; *bón-gyi čos t̔ams-čád* all the Bon-writings *Mil.* — 5. **custom, manner, common usage, fashion**, *mi-čos* manners of the world *Mil.*; *mi-čos-kyi dús-su* as long as he lived according to the ways of the world *Mil.*; *yúl-čos-kyis* according to the custom of the country *Dzl.*; *kyád-čos* the way of distinguishing, of pointing out the characteristics *Glr.* (cf. under 1); **nature, quality**, *Dzl.* ༡༤༣, 18 cf. *čos-nyid.* — 6. **substance, being, thing**, *čos t̔ams-čád mi-rtág-pa yín-gyi* as every thing existing is perishable *Dzl.* — Other philosophical expressions containing the word *čos* v. *Was.* (296).

Comp. **ós-skad* W.* **book-language**, as opp. to *p̔ál-skad*. — *čós-sku* v. *sku*. — *čos-skyóṅ* v. *skyoṅ-ba*. — *čos-k̔ri* **reading-desk, lecturer's chair, pulpit** *Pth.*; **reading-table, school-desk**. — *čos-k̔rims* v. *k̔rims*. — *čos-k̔rims-pa* v. *dge-bskós*. — *čos-ʼk̔ór* vulgo **prayer-mill**; the column of disks on the *mčod-rtén Pth.* v. *ʼk̔ór-lo* 2, also *ʼk̔ór-lo* extr. — *čos-grá* **school**. — *čos-(kyi) rgyál(-po)* 1. honorary title of kings deserving well of religion. 2. = γšin-rǰe *Schl. Buddh.* 93, 3. also as a p. n. — *čos-rgyúd* **religious tradition,** also = **confession, creed,** *rǰe-btsún-gyi čos-rgyúd ₒdzin-pa-rnams* those embracing the religious tradition of his reverence, his fellow-believers *Mil.*; *čos-rgyúd γčig-pa* one confessing the same faith or religion *Thgr.* — *čós-čan* 1. **pious, devout.** 2. v. *čos* 5, *ₒǰig-pai čós-čan yin* **having the properties** of perishableness, being subject to the law of mutability *Thgy.* — *čos-rǰé* 'lord of the faith', viz. 1. Buddha *Lex.*, 2. devout or righteous lord, title of honour given to distinguished scholars *Tar. transl.* 331, and elsewh.; perh. also = *čos-rgyál.* — *čos-nyid* 1. = *čos* 5, **quality, nature,** *rgyá-mtsoi čos-nyid-kyis* in a manner peculiar to the sea, *Dzl.* ༤༥, 9 (112, 9?). 2. philosophical term: **existence, entity,** = *de-bžin-nyid* (acc. to *Thgy.*) by which the Buddhist however means a negation of being, non-existence, non-entity. — *čos-stégs W.* — *čos-kri.* — *čos-stón* religious festive entertainment given to saints *Glr.* — *čos-dráṅ-po* **righteous** with regard to the laws of religion (adopted by Prot. Miss. for the scriptural term 'righteous' or 'just'), *čos-dráṅ-ba* justice, righteousness. — *čos-ldán* = *čós-čan.* — *čos-sdé* **convent, monastery,** *Wdk., Glr.* — *čós-pa* a religious man, **a divine, a monk.** — *čos-spún* **a religious brother;** such brotherhoods e.g. are formed by two devotees, before going on a pilgrimage. After having been consecrated by a priest, who consults the lot on such an occasion, they owe hospitality and mutual assistance to each other for life. — *čos-spyód* **exercise of religion;** *čos-spyód-bču* = *dgé-ba-bču.* — *čos-sbyín* is said to be frq used in book-titles: *bkra-šis-lhún-po-nas čos-sbyin ₒdzad-méd spel pyir bris* written from Tashilhunpo as a religious gift for infinite increase and blessing. — *čos-blón* **a pious functionary** or official (*bdud-blon* an impious or wicked one) *Glr.* *čós-ma* a religious woman, **a nun** *Cs.* — *čos-méd* without religion, **irreligous, wicked.** — *čos-myón* **religious frenzy,** *W.*: **čos-nyón žugs** he has become deranged, his brains are turned (in consequence of meditating). — *čos-zóg* **priestcraft** *Mil.* = *čos-lúgs* religious party, **denomination, sect.** **čós-sem-čan** *W.* inclined to religion, **pious.**

མཆད་པ་ *čád-pa Lex.*: = 'tomb, sepulchre; = *pramārita Ssk.* killed, slain; *mčád-pa-med-pa* entire, perfect; *mčád-par byá-ba* = *mahimān Ssk.* greatness; also the magical power of increasing size at will'.

མཆན་ *mčan* 1. **the side of the breast,** *mčán-gyi bu* bosom-child, darling, *mčán-gyi mčis-bráṅ* bosom-wife (cf. our 'bosom-friend'); *mčán-du ₒǰúg-pa* to put into one's bosom *Glr.*; *mčán-kuṅ* **arm-hole, arm-pit,** often = *mčan*; *mčán-kuṅ γyás-pai rtsib-mai bár nas* (the Buddhas are born) from between the ribs of the right side (cf. *mṅal*); **čán-da** *W.* **pocket,** in clothes, cf. *dkú-mda.* — 2. v. the following article.

མཆན་བུ་ *mčán-bu* 1. **apprentice,** *bzoi* in a handicraft, trade or art, *rig-pai* in a science, disciple *Cs.*, *sgyú-ma-mkan-gyi* appr. of a juggler, conjurer *Zam.* — 2. *yi-geī mčán-bu* words or lines, printed or written in a smaller character than the rest, and inserted in the text (called *má-yig Cs.*) like our parenthesis, but without brackets; hence 3. **note, annotation** (*Sch.* also: testimony?).

མཆི་བ་ *mči-ba,* eleg. for 1. **to come, to go,** *slád-bžin-par mčio* I shall come later *Dzl.*; **to appear,** used of a god; *skyábs-su* (to put one's self) under the protection of another person, ccd.; *ₒbáṅs-su mčio* I will obey *Mil.* — 2. **to say,** *žes mčio* thus he said.

མཆི་མ་ *mči-ma,* resp. *spyan-čáb* **a tear,** *ₒbyin-pa*; *ₒdón-pa Glr.*, *blág-pa Dzl.*, *γtóṅ-ba Mil.* to shed (tears); *ském-pa* to dry up tears *Cs.*; *ₒpyi-ba* to wipe off tears *Cs.*; *mči-mas brnáṅ-ba* to be choked with tears, to sob violently *Sch.*

མཆིག་ *mčig* 1. *Cs.* a stone for grinding spice etc., **a mortar;** *mčig-gu* a small mortar *Sch.*, **a pestle** *Cs.* — 2. **the nether mill-stone,** *mčig-ma* the runner or upper mill-stone, *Sch.*, *mčig skór-ba* to grind *Sch.*

མཆིང་ *mčiṅ Cs.* = *kloṅ*; one *Lex.* = *dkyil*; v. *kloṅ*.

མཆིང་བུ་ *mčiṅ-bu Cs.* = *₀čiṅ-bu*.

མཆིད་ *mčid, bka-mčid, γsuṅ-mčid, W.* **mol-čid** resp the talk, discourse, speech (of an honoured person) *Cs.*; *mčid.-lán* answer to such speech *Mil.*

མཆིན་པ་ *mčin-pa*, resp. *sku-mčin* **the liver;** *mčin-dri, mčin-ri* **the midriff** or **diaphragm;** *mčin-k'a* liver-coloured; *mčin-nán* 'liver-pressing', first breakfast, because according to popular belief water rises from the human liver in the morning, which is depressed and appeased by taking some food; *mčin-nán byed-pa* to breakfast.

མཆིལ་པ་ *mčil-pa* 1. **fishing-hook** *Dzl.*, *mčil-pas nya ₀čór-ba* to fish with a hook, to angle *Cs.* — 2. **a little bird,** *W.* **či-pa**, *Ts.* **čil-pig; či-pa skyú-wo** *W.* sparrow; *mčil-k'ra* sparrow-hawk; *mčil-mgó* a fabulous stone, like a bird's head, supposed to possess a variety of marvelous qualities.

མཆིལ་མ་ *mčil-ma* 1. *W.* **mčil-mág**, resp. *ljags-mčil, ljags-čáb* **spittle,** prob. also other similar fluids *Lt.*; *₀dór-ba* (*W.* **p̀áu-če*) to spit; *mčil-lúd* (*W.* **mčil-ldúd**) morbid saliva, e.g. of people affected with a cough or with hectic fevers; *mčil-snábs* prob. id.; *mčil-snód*, resp. *žal-bzéd*, spitting-box; *mčil-zúm, mčil-bkáb W.* slavering-bib or cloth. — 2. = *mčil-lhám Tar.* 72, ୨?

མཆིལ་ལྷམ་ *mčil-lhám* **shoe, boot,** *mčil-lhám γnyis ₀dor-ba* to lose both shoes *Wdṅ.*; *mčil-lhám-mk'an* shoemaker, cobbler, seller of boots; *mčil-lhám-gyi yú-ba* the leg of a boot *Cs.*

མཆིས་པ་ *mčis-pa* 1. also *mčis-lágs-pa*, eleg. for *yod-pa*, **to be, to be there, to exist,** *du mčis* how much is there, how many are there? *Cs.*; *sú-la dám-pai čos mčis-pa* whoever has the holy doctrine *Dzl.*; *yul dbús-nas mčis-so* (he) is (comes) from the country Ü *Dzl.* — 2. pf. of *mčí-ba* 1. *lam riṅ-po-nas mčis-te* having come from afar. 2. *žes mčis-pa* so-called.

མཆིས་བྲང་ *mčis-bráṅ* 1. eleg. **dwelling, abode, domicile;** also when speaking modestly of one's own dwelling: *bdág-gi mčis-bráṅ* my humble roof *Dzl.* — 2. *Lex.* **wife, partner.**

མཆིས་མལ་ *mčis-mál* **bed, bed-stead** *Cs.*

མཆུ་ *mču* 1. **lip,** *ya-mču* upper lip, *ma-mču* lower lip; *mču btud mk'as Wil.* prob.: one must be wise in lowering the lips, i.e. one must yield, giving up pouting; *k'a-mčú*, resp. *žal-mčú* 1. **lip** 2. word, voice (?) *Sch.* 3. quarrel, strife, *k'a-mčú rgyal-p̀ám ǰi-ltar byuṅ žé-na* if one asks, which are the details of the quarrel; **k'am-čú ǰhé-pa** *C.* **gyág-pa** *Cs.* to quarrel. — 2. **beak** or **bill** of birds, *mčú-la t́ógs-te ₀gró-ba* to fly, carrying something in the bill *S. O.*; *mču-lto* (or *ču-mdo?*) *W.* id. — 3. n. of. one of the lunar mansions, v. *rgyu-skar*.

Comp. *mču-skyé* muzzle *Sch.* — *mču-sgrós* v. *sgros.* — *mču-t́ár Sch.* (prob. a. mis-print for *mču-t́ór*) pustules, tubercular elevations on the lips. — *mču-riṅs* long-beaked, n. of a bird, and also of an insect (a large musquito).

མཆེ་བ་ *mčé-ba, Cs.* also *mče-só*, **corner-tooth, canine tooth, eye-tooth, fang, tusk** of an animal, *mčé-la γtsigs-pa, W.* **žé-če**, to show one's teeth, to grin; *mče-ba-čan-gyi sde* the class of the tusked animals, viz. the carnivora (lion, tiger, leopard), and the tusked pachydermata (elephant, boar etc.).

མཆེད་ *mčed, sku-mčéd, mčed-lčám*, resp. for spun, **brother, sister;** *mčed γnyis* my two brothers *Dzl.*; *srás-mo lha-lčám mčed bži* four princesses, sisters; *deĭ mčed* his illustrious brother, in reference to a king, prince etc. *Glr.*; esp. of gods: *mčed bži* four divine brothers *Glr.*; *mčed-grógs, grogs-mčéd* clerical brother, *mčed-grógs máṅ-po t́sógs-par* where many clerical brothers assemble; *mčed-grógs dam-t́sig γčig-pa Thgr.* betrothed brothers, religious brothers, = *čos-spún;* also *mčed-lčám* has this signification.

མཆེད་པ་ *mčéd-pa* 1. **to spread,** to gain ground, esp. of a fire. frq.; also fig.: *bdág-gi ₒdod-čágs-kyi me mčéd-pas* as the fire of voluptuousness spread or increased within me *Dzl.*; also in the following sense: *már-me γčig-la γčig mčed ltar* as one kindles one light by another *Mil.*; *γčig gleṅ γnyis gleṅ rím-pas mčéd-de* as (the news) spread more and more by gossiping people *Pth.* — *skye-mčéd* v. *skye.* — 2. = *γyó-ba, mi-mčed-pai dád-pa* = *dád-pa brtạn-po.*

མཆེར་པ་ *mčér-pa* **the milt, spleen.**

མཆོག་ *mčog* **the best**, the most excellent in its kind, *skyés-bu mčog, mii mčog, rkaṅ-γnyis-rnams-kyi mčog* Buddha; *nyes-ltúṅ-gis ma p̓óg-pa* (or *na*) *mčog yin-te p̓og-rtiṅ bšágs-pa byéd-pa rab yin Mil.* the best thing is, not to have been surprised by sin, but after having been surprised, it is the best to confess it (and thus to atone for it); *γsuṅ-mčóg* chief or fundamental doctrine, main dogma, principal commandment etc. *Glr.*; *ṅa ni ₒjig-rtén ₒdi-na mčog* I am the highest in the world (says Buddha immediately after his birth) *Glr.*; *γnas-mčóg* the most glorious or splendid country *Glr.*; *ro-mčóg* excellent taste or flavour *Mil.*; *mk̓as-mčóg-rnams* most learned gentlemen *Zam.*; also as a complimentary word; *mi mčog k̓yod* most honoured Sir! *Pth.*; *mčog-dmán, mčog daṅ tun-móṅ, mčog daṅ p̓ál-pa*, good and bad, first-rate and common, fine and ordinary, of goods etc.; eminent and ordinary, of mental gifts, talents etc.; *mčóg-tu gyúr-pa* = *mčog*, e.g. *mi-rnams-kyi náṅ-na mčóg-tu gyúr-pa γčig* one that has risen among men, so as to become their chief *Glr.*; *yúl-rnams-kyi mčóg-tu gyúr-pa* the most splendid of countries. — Adv.: *mčóg-tu* very, most, with verbs: *bón-po-la mčóg-tu mós-pa žig* a great admirer of the Bonpos *Mil.*; gen. with adjectives: *ro mčóg-tu mṅár-ba* extremely sweet; with the comparative: much, far, by far, greatly, *dé-bas mčóg-tu čeo* ... is far or much greater than that *Dzl.*

Comp. *mčog-sbyin p̓yag-rgyá* a gesture made in practising magic, in conjuring up or exorcising ghosts. — *mčog-zúṅ* the model pair, the two most excellent amongst Buddha's disciples, Shariibú and Maudgalgyibú, v. *Köpp.* — *mčog-ríṅ* longest *Thgy.*

མཆོང་ *mčoṅ* v. *čoṅ.*

མཆོང་བ, མཆོངས་པ་ *mčóṅ-ba, mčóṅs-pa* to leap, to jump, frq., e.g. *čur* into the water; *mi-seb-la* among the people, e.g. of a mad dog).

མཆོད་པ་ *mčód-pa* (पूज) I. vb. 1. **to honour,** revere, respect, receive with honour, *kún-gyis bkúr žiṅ mčód-pai ₒos* worthy of being honoured and praised by all; usually ccapir. (rarely dp.) in the special sense: to honour saints or deities by offering articles of food, flowers, music, the sound, odour and flavour of which they are supposed to relish, hence to treat, entertain, regale (the gods), and in a more general sense applied also to lifeless objects, e.g. to honour a sepulchre in such a manner; *Glr. mčód-pa* may therefore in English be sometimes translated by: to offer, to sacrifice, but it should always be borne in mind, that no idea of self-denial or yielding up a precious good (as is implied by the English word), or of slaughtering, as in the Greek θύειν, can be connected with the Tibetan word itself, though in practice bloody sacrifices, abhorred as they are by pure Buddhism in theory, are not quite unheard of, not only animals being immolated to certain deities, but also men notoriously noxious to religion slaughtered as *dmar-mčod*, red offering, to the *dgrá-lha* q.v. — 2. *C.* resp. **to eat, drink, take, taste,** (in *W.* expressed by **dón-če**).

II. sbst. **offering, oblation, libation,** *mčód-pa ₒbúl-ba, W. *p̓úl-če** frq., also *byéd-pa*; *ról-mo mčód-par ₒbúl-ba* to bring an offering of music *Mil.: mčód-pa sna-tsógs tógs-te* carrying along with them all sorts of offerings *Glr.; mčód-pai kyád-par bču* the ten kinds of offerings *Tar.*; *lha-mčód* offering or libation brought to a *lha*; *˳bru-mčód* an offering consisting of grain; *dus-mčód* offerings presented at certain times *Pth.; rgyun-mčód* daily offering; fig. *dád-pai mčód-pa Mil.; ytaṅ-rág-tu sgrúb-pai mčód-pa p̔ul* as a thanksgiving bring the offering of meditation! *Mil.* —

Comp. *mčód-k̔aṅ* **house** or **place of offerings,** of worship, *Pth.*; adopted as an appellation for the temple of the Jews, as *lhá-k̔aṅ* could not be used *Chr. Prot.* — *mčód-k̔ri* **offering-table,** Jewish **altar,** *Chr. Prot.* — *mčod-lčóg* prob. the same, *C.* — *mčod-čá Glr.* = *mčod-rdzás.* — *mčod-brjód* words of adoration, doxology. — *mčod-rtén Ssk.* चैत्य (religious building) and स्तूप (elevated place, elevation, tumulus) 1. etymologically; receptacle of offerings; 2. usually: a sacred pyramidal building, of a form varying in different countries and centuries, esp. near temples and convents, where often great numbers of these structures are to be seen. They were originally sepulchres, containing the relics of departed saints, and therefore called *ydun-rtén*; afterwards they were erected as cenotaphs, i. e. in honour of deceased saints buried elsewhere, but in more recent times they are looked upon as holy symbols of the Buddhist doctrine, v. *Köpp.* I, 533. — *mčod-stégs* offering-table, **altar.** — *mčod-stód Sch.*: an offering with a hymn of praise. — *mčod-stón* **an entertainment,** as sort of libation, given to the priests *Dzl.;* perh. also **a sacrificial feast.** — *mčod-sdóṅ* 1. *Sch.* = *mčod-rten* (?), 2. **offering-lamp** *Sch.*, 3. **the wick** of such a lamp (in this sense it is used in a little botanical book). — *mčod-ynás* 1. prop. place where there is offered, **place of sacrifice.** 2. the object to which veneration is shown, image of a god *Glr.*, **sanctuary.** 3. the offering priest, **the sacrificator.** — *mčód-pa-po* a sacrificer *Cs.* — *mčod-˳búl* the offering of a sacrifice *Cs.* — *mčod-sbyin* id. (though elsewhere *mčod-pa* sbst., as a gift to deities, is distinct from *sbyin-pa* a gift to men), also: sacrificer; *mčod-sbyin-gyi ˳dun-k̔áṅ* house where people assemble in order to perform sacrifices; *sróg-gi mčod-sbyin* bloody offerings or sacrifices *Tar.* — *mčod-mé* **offering-lamp,** lighted in honour of a deity, and very common in the houses of Buddhists; **čod-mé p̔úl-če* W.* to light such a lamp, (prop. to offer it). — *mčod-rdzás*, *mčod-čá*, *mčód-pai yo-byád* instruments, utensils, requisite for festival processions in honour of a deity. — *mčod-šóms* or *-bšáms* the upper shelves in the holy repositories, containing the little statues of Buddha etc.

མཆོར་པོ་ *mčór-po,* sometimes *˳p̔yór-po* 1. **pretty, handsome,** neat, elegant, *p̔o mčór-po* a handsome man, *bud-méd mčór-mo* a pretty woman, esp. a smart gaily dressed female. — 2. *W.* also **vain, conceited.**

འཆག་ཅན་ *˳čág-čan* col. **trodden, stamped; solid, firm, compact,** like the Hindustani *pakka.*

འཆག་པ་ *˳čag-pa* I. pf. *čag* (s) 1. **to break** vb. n., *snod čag-pa* a broken vessel *Dzl.*; fig. *ṅa-rgyál čag* my pride is broken, frq.; *der-˳byón-stabs čag* the opportunity of going there has been cut off *Mil.; *lam čág-pa* (also *šog-pa)* C.* a. a beaten, practicable road (a road broken through, v. *˳čég-pa*) b. *W.* an impracticable, broken-up road. — 2. **to be broken off,** abated, beaten down from the price, *žu-čág-med-par* there being no room for either asking or abating *Mil. nt.* —

II. also *čágs-pa*, pf. *bčags*, **fut.** *bcag* (imp. *˳čog?*) 1. **to tread, to walk, to move,** esp. when speaking respectfully or formally, *yab més-kyi žábs-kyis bčágs-pai sá-ča* the place where my ancestors did walk *Glr.; žabs čágs-pai p̔yag p̔yir ˳gro* follow me on my walk *Mil. nt.* — *˳čág-tu* or *˳čágs-su ˳gró-ba* to take a walk *Dzl.*; **góm-čag-če* W.* to step along solemnly; *čág-p̔eb-pa* v. *p̔yág-p̔eb-pa.* — 2.

like ˳*gró-ba* in a more general sense: *bžón-pa-la, čibs-la* to ride in a carriage, on horseback *Cs.*

འཆགས་པ་ ˳*čágs-pa* 1 v. ˳*čág-pa.* — 2. sometimes for ˳*čég-pa.*

འཆག(ས)་ས་ ˳*čág(s)-sa* a place for walking, *Lexx.*, *Cs.*

འཆང་བ་ ˳*čáṅ-ba*, pf. *bčaṅs*, fut. *bčaṅ*, imp. *čoṅ(s)*, 1. **to hold, to keep,** to take hold of, *skrá-la* by the hair *Mil.* — ˳*čaṅ-zúṅs* handle, crook of a stick, *Mil.* — 2. **to carry, to wear,** to carry about one, e.g. amulets etc. — 3. (*yid-la*) **to keep** in memory, in one's mind. — **4. to have, to assume,** e.g. the body of a goddess, of a Rakshasi *Pth.*

འཆངས་པ་ ˳*čáṅs-pa W.* a (closed) handful e.g. of dough; **čáṅs-bu** a clod (of clay), a snow-ball etc. formed in the hand.

འཆད་པ་ ˳*čád-pa* I. pf. *čad*, vb. n. to *γčód-pa*, like *čód-pa*, **to be cut** into pieces, **to be cut off, to decay,** *dúm-bur* (to fall) to pieces *Med.*; **to cease, end, stop,** of diseases *Glr.*, of life *Lex.*; **to cease to flow** or **to blow,** of water or wind; **to die away, to become extinct,** of a family, a generation; **to be consumed,** of provisions *Pth.* of bodily strength *Thgy.*; **to be decided,** *kyód-kyis bsád-par* ˳*čád-na* you being determined to kill me *Dzl.* —

II. pf. and fut. *bšad*, imp. *šod* 1. **to explain,** ˳*óg-tu* ˳*čad* it will be explained below *Lt.*; *yid-la byos šig daṅ bšád-do* give heed, and I will explain it to you *Stg.*; ˳*čad nyán-pa* to listen to an explanation *Sch.*; ˳*jig čos γtam* ˳*čád-pa* to teach the transitoriness of existence *Sch.* (?) — 2. **to tell, to relate.**

འཆབ་པ་ ˳*čáb-pa*, pf. *bčabs*, fut. *bčab*, imp. *čob* **to conceal,** to keep secret, ˳*čáb-pa-med-pai sems* a candid mind, openheartedness *Stg.* (cog. to ˳*jáb-pa*).

འཆམ་པ་ ˳*čám-pa* I. vb. (pf. *bčam Lex.*), also adj. and sbst. **to accord, to agree, agreeing, agreement,** *srid-la mi* ˳*čám-pas* as they did not agree about the government *Glr.*; ˳*čam byéd-pa* to make agree, to reconcile *Mil.*, **čam mi čam** col. they do not agree; *ka* ˳*čám-pa* to agree upon, to concert, e.g. an escape; *ka* ˳*čám-par* by concert, unanimously.

II. 1. **to dance,** ˳*čám-par byéd-pa Sch.* 2. a dancer, *kro* ˳*čám-pa* a dancer with a frightful mask; *gar-*˳*čám(s)* a dance; ˳*čám-po* a dancer *Glr.*; ˳*čam-dpón* leader of a dance; ˳*čám-yig* book or programme of a dance.

འཆའ་ ˳*ča Ld.*, *Sp.* **cupboard.**

འཆའ་བ་ ˳*čá-ba* I. pf. *bčas*, rarely ˳*čas*, fut. *bča*, imp *čos*, **to make, prepare, construct,** but used only in reference to certain things; 1. *γnas*, vulg. *tsaṅ*, ˳*čá-ba Pth.* to prepare a place, house or abode, to settle; *mal* ˳*čá-ba* to make a bed or couch *Cs.*; *dmag-sgár* ˳*čá-ba* to pitch a camp; *krims-ra* ˳*čá-ba* to establish a court of justice *Glr.* — 2. *rgyal-krims* ˳*čá-ba* to draw up a law, to give laws, frq. — 3. *dam* ˳*čá-ba* to make a vow, **to promise, assert, protest,** frq; *yi-dam* ˳*čá-ba* id.; also to utter a prayer; *dám-bča* v. sub *dam.* — 4. *skyil-krúṅ čá-ba* = *skyil-krúṅ byéd-pa*, v. *skyil-ba.* — 5. *blo-γtád* ˳*čá-ba*, c. c. *la*, **to place confidence in.**

II. **to bite,** *γčig-la γčig* ˳*čá-žiṅ zá-la* to bite and devour one another *Dzl.*; *so* ˳*čá-ba* to bite with the teeth (?) *Mṅg.*, or to gnash or grind the teeth (?); *šiṅ* ˳*čá-ba* **to gnaw** at a piece of wood *Stg.*

འཆར་རྒྱན་ ˳*čar-rgyán*, or ˳*čar-čán* a present given reluctantly *Sch.* (?)

འཆར་བ་ ˳*čár-ba*, pf. *šar*, **to rise, appear,** become visible, of the sun etc., also of the sun's appearing above a mountain, from behind a cloud etc., frq.; **to shine,** *gaṅs-ri-la nyi-ma šar-ba* the shining of the sun upon a mountain covered with snow, a snowy mountain lit up by the rays of the sun *Glr.*; *γzugs-brnyán mi* ˳*čar-ba* the not appearing of the image which is formed by the reflection of a mirror (as something strange and surprising) *Wdṅ*; *γzugs* ˳*čár-ba byéd-pa* to cause an image to be reflected (in the water);

dpyid-ka šar spring has appeared; frq. of thoughts: *nyáms-su*, or *yid-la ˳čár-ba* (thoughts) rising in one's mind; *yid-la šar kyaṅ Mil.* though I can figure it in my mind; *grógs-su ˳čar* (they) appear as friends *Mil.*; *rgyán-du ˳čar Mil.* it turned into a blessing. — *˳čár-sgo* **thought, idea, conception,** *˳čár-sgo ˳byuṅ* an idea comes, a (happy) thought, a (new) light, bursts upon me *Mil.*; *˳čar-ga Mil.* **the rising, the rise.**

འཆལ་བ་ *˳čál-ba*, secondary form to *˳čól-ba* II., 1. *Cs.:* **to fluctuate** mentally; in this sense prob. *Zam. ytad-méd ˳čál-ba* to fluctuate, to waver, without aim or object. — 2. **to be confused,** in disorder, *smra-˳čál*, also *˳čal-ytám smra Lt.*, as a morbid symptom, prob. he raves, he talks nonsense. — 3. morally: *tsul-ḱrims ˳čál-ba S.g.* **to break** one's vow, *bsláb-pa* to act contrary to the doctrine, **to violate** it *Tar.*; in a more restricted sense: — 4. **to fornicate,** to commit adultery, *bud-méd smad-˳čál byéd-pa* a whore, harlot *Mil.*; *˳čál-pa, -po* lecher, fornicator *Stg.*; *˳čál-pa-rnams-kyi tsig* obscene language, mentioned as sub-species of *kyál-ka*; *˳čál-mo* whore. — **čal-la-čol-lé* W.*, *čal-čól Tar.* 184, 20 confusedly, pellmell.

འཆི་བ་ *˳či-ba*, pf. *ši*, 1. vb. **to die,** of a flame: to go out; *raṅ ˳čio* I will seek death *Dzl.*; *˳či-ba yin* he dies, will die *S.g.*; *˳či* or *ši-ba-las sós-par ˳gyúr-ba Dzl.* to be saved from imminent danger of death (but not: to rise from the dead); *˳či-bar byéd-pai ču* water causing death *Sambh.*; *ši-bar gyúr-to* they perished *Pth.* — 2. sbst., the state of dying, **death,** *˳či-ba tsám-du ˳gyúr-ba* to die almost (of grief etc.) *Mil.*; *dus-min ˳či-ba nyúṅ-ba yin* premature death rarely occurs *Sambh.*; *˳či-ba nam yoṅ ča med Mil.* when death will come one does not know, (*W. *ši-če** to die; death; **ši soṅ** he has died, **ši yin** he will die).

Comp. *˳či-ḱa Cs.:* 'the very act of dying,' but I doubt whether such a sbst. exists; I only know the adv. *˳či-kar* at his very dying, at the point of death *Mil.*, when being exstinguished *Glr.* (v. *ḱar* sub *ḱa* IV. 4, 5), and *˳či-ka-ma* 1. adj. dying, *dúd-˳gro ˳či-ḱa-ma* a dying animal *Glr.*; 2. sbst. the dying, *˳či-ka-ma-ru* = *či-ḱar* (doubtful); *˳či-kar* and *˳či-gar* may be incorrect spellings. — *˳či-ltas*, more rarely *˳či (-bai) rtágs* **forebodings, foretokens of death** *Med.* — *˳či-bdág* the lord of death, perh. = *ysín-rje*, but it seems to be more a poetical expression than a mythological personage; *˳či-bdág bdud* id. — *˳či-nád* a disease causing death, **a fatal disease** *Tar.* — *˳či-ba-po Cs.*; a person dying(?) — *˳či-(ba)-méd(-pa)* immortal; cf. *ši-ba.* — Note. *˳či ˳pó-ba* is prob. only a rather incorrect, yet common expression for *tse ˳pó-ba* to change one's place of existence, to transmigrate.

འཆིག(ས)་པ་ *˳čig(s)-pa* **to bind** *Sch.*, prob. an incorr. spelling for *˳kyig-pa.*

འཆིང་བ་, འཆིངས་པ་ *˳čiṅ-ba, ˳čiṅs-pa* I. vb., pf. *bčiṅs*, fut. *bčiṅ*, imp. *˳čiṅ(s)*, *W. *čin-če**, **to bind** (in general); **to fetter** (a prisoner) *Dzl.*; **to bind** or **tie up, to cord,** a bundle or package; **to tie round,** to put on, a girdle *Glr.*; **to bind up, to dress,** wounds; fig. **to render harmless, to neutralize, paralyze,** esp. by witchcraft, **to exorcise,** frq.; *bčiṅs ˳gról-ba* to untie, to loosen, to take off the dressings *Lt.* —

II. sbst. any binding-material 1. **ribbon,** *mgul-čiṅs* necklace, neckcloth; neckerchief. — 2. **fetter, shackle,** also fig. for magic curse, anathema. — 3. **string, tie.** — 4. **cramp, spasm** *C.*

འཆིང་བུ་ *˳čiṅ-bu* a spurious, glass jewel (*Schf. Tar.* 142, 9); *bsam-yas-˳čiṅ-bu* p. n. *Ma.*

འཆིབ(ས)་པ་ *˳čib(s)-pa*, pf. *bčibs*, fut. *bčib*, imp. *čibs* resp. **to ascend, to mount,** a horse or carriage, *rtá-la*, or more correctly *čibs-la*, **to ride,** to proceed on horseback.

འཆིམས་པ་ *˳čims-pa* **to be full, to get full** *Sch.*

འཚིར་བ་ ˳*čir-ba*, evidently a present-form of the pf. *ċir-ba*, **to press, to squeeze.**

འཚུ་བ་ ˳*čú-ba* I. acc. to grammatical analogy 1. vb. n. to *γċúd-pa*, **to be twisted, distorted,** pf. ˳*čus.* — 2. sbst. **curvature, crookedness, distortion.** — 3. adj., more frq. ˳*čús-pa* **crooked, wry,** *ḱa-˳čús Wdṅ.* the mouth being wry, distorted *Lt.;* also obstinately perverse; fig. *yig-˳čús Med.* frq., prob. = *ḱam-lóg.*

II. pf. *bċus*, fut. *bċu*, imp. *čus*, *W.* **ċu-ċe**, 1. **to lade** or **scoop** (water), *ču-mig-la ču* to draw water from a well *Dzl.; ču-ṫóm* water-conduit *Sch.* — 2. **to irrigate, to water,** *ẑiṅ* a field *Cs.* (?)

III. *nán-gyis ˳čú-ba-la Tar.* 127, 6, when he was pressed hard, was urged with importunity; (this signification, however, seems to rest only on this passage).

འཚུག་པ་ ˳*čúg-pa* **to be mistaken** *Pth.*, v. ˳*ṗyúg-pa.*

འཚུན་པ་ ˳*čún-pa*, evidently vb. n. to ˳*ǰúṅ-pa*, hence 1. **to be tamed, subdued, made to yield,** *stóbs-kyis* by force, *lás-kyis* by hard work. — 2. **to confess** *Cs.* — 3. **to wrap** or **twist** *Sch.* — 4. **to fix** *Sch.* — 5. **to fix one's self** *Sch.*; ˳*čál-sar ˳čun* entangled in vicious indulgences *Sch.*

འཚུམ(ས)་པ་ ˳*čúm(s)-pa* 1. **to wish, to long for** *Lex.* — 2. **to shrink** *Cs.*

འཚེ་བ་ ˳*če-ba*, pf. *bċes*, ˳*čes* (*Sch.*), fut. *bċe*, imp. *čes*, 1. **to assure, to promise,** *ḱas ˳čé-ba Lex.*, resp. *ẑál-gyis ˳čé-ba* id. — 2. resp. for *smrá-ba*, like *γsún-ba* (?)

འཚེག་པ་ ˳*čég-pa*, also ˳*čág(s)-pa*, pf. *bšags*, fut. *bšag*, imp. *šog*, *W.* **šág-ċe**, 1. **to cleave, to split,** *šiṅ* wood; *sóg-les ˳čég-pa* to saw *Sch.; ˳čeg-byéd* (a thing) that cleaves, a hatchet *Cs.* — 2. **to confess, to acknowledge;** v. also *bšág-pa* and *šóg-pa.*

འཚེད་པ་ ˳*čéd-pa* an incorr. form of *čád-pa* or *mčéd-pa.*

འཚེམས་པ་ ˳*čéms-pa*, pf. *bċems*, fut. *bċem*, **to chew** *Med.*

འཚེལ་བ་ ˳*čél-ba Cs.* 1. **to believe, give credit to;** *blo-˳čél-ba* (?) col. id. — 2. *Lexx.* = *ẑén-pa* **to wish** (?).

འཚོག ˳*čog* **wall** *Sch.*

འཚོང་བ་, འཚོངས་པ་ ˳*čóṅ-ba*, ˳*čóṅs-pa Sch.* = ˳*čáṅ-ba.*

འཚོམས་པ་ ˳*čóms-pa* 1. = ˳*čám-pa Glr.* and *Lexx.* — 2. vb. n. to ˳*ǰóms-pa* 4 *W.*, **da čoms soṅ** now it is done.

འཚོར་པོ་ ˳*čór-po* = *mčor-po.*

འཚོར་བ་ ˳*čór-ba* I. vb. n., pf. *šor*, 1. **to escape, slip, steal away; to drop from,** *stón-mo šór-gyis* as the meal escaped him, as he was deprived of the meal *Dzl.; rtsa-ḱrág ˳čór-ba* **hemorrhage, bloody flux** *Med.; bkrag-˳čór* without splendour, lustreless; *nor ˳čor* the money is gone, spent, lost *Thgy.; sdóm-pa ˳čor* the duty is violated *Glr.; mé-la, čú-la ˳čór-ba* to be consumed by fire, carried off by water; **čaṅ mi ṫuṅ dé-ne ḱa mi šor* W.* I will not drink any beer, then the mouth cannot run away, i. e. then no indiscreet words will escape my mouth; **to flow out, to run,** of a leaking vessel, **to run over,** of a full one. — 2. **to come out, to break out,** frq. of fire; ˳*ḱrúg-pa šor* a quarrel, a war broke out, also of water breaking through an embankment etc. — 3. **to go over, to pass,** from one person or thing to another, *rgyál-sa Bód-nas Me-nyág-la šor* the supreme power passed from Tibet to Tanggút *Glr.; γẑán-gyi dbáṅ-du šor* then I shall get into the power of another *Mil.; rkún-ma-la šor* it became the prey of a thief. — 4. *W.* **to run away, flee, escape, elope,** inst. of ˳*brós-pa*, **šór-te ča-dug** he retires, falls back.

II. vb. a., pf. (*b*)*šor*, fut. *γšor* (?) 1. **to pursue, chase, hunt** after, *ri-boṅ rgyas* hares by means of nets; *nya ˳čór-ba* to fish *Dzl.*; *Cs.* also to strain (?); ˳*čor-sgég* a seducer; a swaggerer *Sch.* (cf. *sgég-pa*). — 2. **to light, kindle, set on fire** (?)

འཚོལ་པ་ ˳*čól-pa* 1. **disorderly, dissolute, immoral.** — 2. disorderly action or conduct, **dissoluteness,** ˳*čól-pa sna-ṫsógs spyád-pa* committing several acts of immorality *Wdṅ.* — *ḱro-bo-˳ól-pa* n. of a demon. (Cf. ˳*čól-ba* II).

འཆོལ་བ་ $_{o}$čʻól-ba I. pf. bčol, fut. γčol (?) 1. **to entrust** a person with a thing, to commit a thing to another's charge; **to make, appoint,** *dé-la rgyál-po $_{o}$čʻól-lo* they made him king *Pth.*; *btsún-mo-la rtá-rdzi bčól-lo* they made the queen tend the horses *Glr.*; *tʻab-γyóg $_{o}$čʻól žig* he may be employed as a kitchenboy, scullion *Pth.*; *dbaṅ-méd-du $_{o}$čʻól-ba* to make one powerless, to compel by authority *Glr.*; *bčól-bai γnyer Lex.* manager; *$_{o}$čʻól-bai ṅo Ler.* intercessor; *pi-wáṅ-la ram-$_{o}$dégs bčól-nas glu blaṅs* she sang with accompaniment of the guitar (lit. committing the accompaniment to the guitar) *Glr.*; **kyab čʻól-la** (for *$_{o}$čʻol-du*) **yoṅ-če** *W.* to place one's self under another man's protection. — 2. **to commit, commend, recommend,** *lás $_{o}$čʻól-ba* to commission one with an affair or transaction; resp. *pʻrin (-las) $_{o}$čʻól-ba*, though *pʻrin (-las)* seems to be sometimes a mere pleonasm: *bán-so yul deĩ lha-sruṅ-rnams-la pʻrin-bčól mdzád-do* (the king) recommended the sepulchre to the tutelar gods of the country *Glr.*; **čʻól-te bór-če** *W.* to deposit a thing for temporary keeping.

II. = *$_{o}$čʻál-ba* 1. *Cs.* **to change, to turn aside** (?) — 2. **to be thrown together** confusedly, e.g. of the loose leaves of a (Tibetan) book; *$_{o}$čʻól-bar byéd-pa* to put in disorder, to confuse, to confound *Ma.*; *dge-sdíg $_{o}$čʻól-bar $_{o}$gro* virtue and vice are confounded *Ma.*; **'i lé-ka čʻól dug** *W.* this affair goes wrong, turns out badly; in a special sense: **to rave, to be delirious** *C.*; **čʻol-láb gyáb-pa** *C.* id.; **nyid-čʻol láb-pa, gyag-pa** *C.*, to talk confusedly whilst being heavy with sleep; **čʻól-kʻa** *C.* senseless talk; **čʻól-kʻan-ni ṭʻú-gu, čʻol-ṭúg** *W.* being of a mixed race; illegitimate or bastard child, bastard. — 3. morally: **to break a vow;** **a-ne čʻol son** he has broken his vow on account of a woman, i.e. by having married.

འཆོལ་མ་ $_{o}$čʻól-ma *Cs.*: 1. a thing committed to another's care. — 2. **a sly, crafty woman,** *Sch.* **a dissolute woman.**

འཆོས་པ་ $_{o}$čʻós-pa I. pf. bčos or $_{o}$čʻos, fut. bčo, imp. čʻos, supine *bčós-su Dzl.* ༢, 4, *W.* **čó-če**, pf. and imp. **čos**, **to make, make ready, prepare, to construct, build,** a bow, a road etc. *Glr.*; *$_{o}$čʻós-sam* am I to build? *Glr.*; *drés-ma tʻág-par $_{o}$čʻós-pa* to make ropes out of *drésma* (a kind of grass) prop. to work *drésma* into ropes, *Glr.*; *γzab $_{o}$čʻós-pa* to adjust one's ornaments *Sch.*; *lus $_{o}$čʻós-pa* to dress, to trim one's self up *Sch.*; *γsár-du $_{o}$čʻós-pa* to renew, renovate, repair *Sch.*; *ltúṅ-ba pʻyir $_{o}$čʻós-pa Tar.* 95, 20 perh. to retouch, amend, correct, improve. — *tsʻúl-$_{o}$čʻos* hypocrisy, a mere outward performance of religious rites and observances *Mil.*, *tsʻul-$_{o}$čʻos ma byas spyód-pa* to live without hypocrisy *Mil.*; *tsʻúl-$_{o}$čʻos-mkʻan* hypocrite. — *tsʻúl-$_{o}$čʻos-pa* or *bčós-pa* acc. to *Cs.* also an established rule or canon.

II. *Sch.*: **to gnaw off** (secondary form to *$_{o}$čʻá-ba*).

ཇ

ཇ་ ǰa 1. the letter ǰ, media, palatal, like the Italian *gi* in Giovanni, *g* in giro; in *C.* as initial deep-sounding and aspirated, ǰh. — 2. numerical figure: 7. — 3. **tea,** resp. *γsol-ǰa.* For the trade in Central Asia it is pressed into brick-shaped lumps, a portion of which, when to be used, is pulverized and boiled, having been well compounded with butter and salt or soda (*bul*) by means of a kind of churn of bamboo (*gur-gúr*), after which it is drunk as hot as possible. Of late years tea grown on the southern slopes of the Himalaya Mountains finds its way into

Central Asia. The tea called ˳bru-ṭáṅ is considered the best, and of other teas *Cs.* mentions *rtsé-ǰa, zi-liṅ-spú-ǰa* hairy (?) tea from Siling, (a province in the neighbourhood of the Kokonor); *Schr.: γnám-ǰa, míṅ-ǰa, ˳bó-ǰa, ǰa-γzúṅs, zau, hu-čág, ˳u-si; bzaṅ-ǰa,* or *ko-tse* is, acc. to *Cs.*, good ordinary tea, *čuṅ-˳ǰug*, or *čuṅ-čuṅ* are sorts of inferior quality. The shepherds in *W.* make use of a surrogate, viz. the Potentilla Inglisii (*spáṅ-ǰa*), growing on the mountains at a height of 15 000 feet; poor people in *Sik.* use the leaves of the maple (*γya-li*).

Other **comp.** *ǰa-bkrúg* (pronounced **ǰhab-ṭúg**), prob. for *ǰa-dkrúg*, **twirling-stick** *Ts.* — *ǰa-mčód*, libation of tea. — *ǰa-˳ṭág*, or *btág* **grinding-stone,** in India and Tibet used for kitchen purposes inst. of our little mortars. — *ǰa-dám Sch.* **tea-pot** (?) — *ǰa-blúg W.* a little pitcher-shaped **brass vessel.** — *ǰa-˳biṅ* (pronounced **ǰham-biṅ**) *C.* **tea-kettle, tea-pot.** — *ǰá-ma* the man that prepares the tea in a monastery, **tea-cook;** *ǰai dpon* head-tea-cook. — *ǰa-ril* 1. *W.* **grinding-stone**; 2. *Lex.* **skull.** — *ǰa-sun-čan* 'a cup of tea, or: as much as a cup of tea' *Sch.* — *ǰa-seg* tea-dust *Sch.*

ཇ་ཧོད་ *ǰa-hód Lex.* **yellowish red.**

ཇག་ *ǰag* **robbing, robbery,** *ǰag rgyág-pa* to rob, to be a robber; *rku-ǰag-gyu-zól byéd-pa Glr.*; *ǰág-pa* frq. robber (not robbery *Sch.*); *ǰag-dpón* captain of a gang of robbers *Mil.*

ཇི་ *ǰi* 1. num. fig.: 37. — 2. the correlative form of the pron. *či*, **what.** For the construction of a sentence containing *či* or *ǰi*, v. *gaṅ* II. The explanation there given shows, that in correct language *ǰi* is always followed by a participle: *ǰi yód-pa de ṕul žig* offer what you have, make a libation of what you have. Owing, however, to the slight difference in the pronunciation of *či* and *ǰi*, the former is frq. written in the place of the latter; *ǰi*, of course, is used in conjunction with the same words as *či*; a few more instances may follow here: *ǰi-skad* whatever, relative to words spoken: *ṅas ǰi-skad smras kyaṅ* whatever I may say *Glr.* — *ǰi-snyéd* 1. as much as, as great as; 2. *C.* very much, every thing possible. — *ǰi-lta-ba* 1. adj. of what kind, of what nature, ... *ǰi-lta-ba bžin-du* ... *la yaṅ de-bžin-no* as it is with ... so it is with ... *Stg.* 2. sbst. quality, nature, condition *Cs.* — *ǰi-lta-bu* such as, like as, Lat. qualis. — *ǰi-ltar* adv. as, in what manner; *'á-mas ǰi-ltar zér-pa bžin-du* according to what the mother has said *Glr.* — *ǰi-ste* = *či-ste.* — *ǰi nús-kyis* to the utmost, to the best of one's ability *Dzl.* — *ǰi ma ǰi-bžin-du* (?) according to custom or common usage *Sch.* — *ǰi-mi-snyám-pai bzód-pa* a patience prepared for every event *Sch.* (?) — *ǰi-tsam* = *ǰi-snyéd*; *lo lṅa lón-pa ǰi-tsam-pa de-bžin-no* they are (as tall) as (children) five years old *Stg.*; *ǰi tsam byas kyaṅ* whatever they had done *Tar.*; *ǰi-tsam-na* or *nas* as soon as, when. — *ǰi-bžin* as, like, how, *ǰi-bžin ˳tso mi ruṅ* (he) can in no wise, by no means, continue to live *Lt.*; *ǰi-bžin-du γsuṅs* elliptically: he said how (it was), he answered according to the state of the case (*Schf.*) *Tar.* 89, 9. — *ǰi-srid* as long as.

ཇུ་ *ǰu* num. fig.: 67.

ཇུ་ཏིག་ *ǰu-ṭig* denotes a way of drawing lots by threads of different colours, whence a class of Bonpos is called *ṕya-bon ǰu-ṭig-čan Glr.*

ཇུ་པོ་ *ǰú-po Lis.*, **ǰu-lúm* W.*, a globular stone used for grinding spices, = *ǰa-ril.*

ཇུས་ *ǰus C.* **strategy.**

ཇུས་མ་ *ǰús-ma* a sort of silk stuff *Cs.*

ཇུས་ལེགས་ *ǰus-légs* 1. *Sch.*: 'possessed of good manners, of propriety of conduct, **decent, agreeable;** *ǰus-bdé* sincere' (?) — 2. *Cs.* **clever, skilled, able, experienced.** **žiṅ-gi lẹ** in agriculture, **mag** in military matters *C.*

ཇེ་ *ǰe* 1. num. fig.: 97. — 2. a particle, used for expressing the comparative degree of an adj. or adv., and esp. a gradual growing or increase, often with termin. or *la*: *ǰe man̄ ˳gro* (they) go on increasing or multiplying in number *Mil.*; *ǰe γsál-du son̄* it has become more and more clear or evident *Thgr.*; gen. repeated: *ǰe nye ǰe nye són̄-ste* going nearer and nearer *Mil.*; *ǰe č̔un̄ ǰe č̔ún̄-la son̄*, also *ǰe č̔ún̄ ǰe nyún̄ Mil.* less and less; sometimes also for the superlative degree, *Cs.*: *ǰe dán̄-po* the very first, also *Lex.* — 3. *ǰé-žig* a little while, = *ré-žig Lex.* — 4. *Bhar.* 14, *Schf.*: 'an adhortative particle, often connected with a vocative'; *Sch.* has: *ǰe k̔yod* 'now you, you first!' — 5. = *dbyan̄s Lex.*

ཇོ་ *ǰo* 1. num. fig.: 127. — 2. v. the following word.

ཇོ་བོ་ *ǰó-bo* (आर्य) 1. *C.* **the elder brother**, also **ǰo-ǰó** and **á-ǰo** (the latter also in *W.*), resp. *ǰo-légs*. — 2. **lord, master**, esp. **nobleman, grandee**, *W.* **ǰo**, *yar-lún̄ ǰó-bo Glr.* the lord of the manor of Yarlung; **ti-nán ǰo* W.* the nobleman of Tinan; *ǰo-ǰo min̄-po* my noble brothers (says a princess) *Glr.*; in *C.* used as honorary title for noblemen and priests, in *W.* also for noble Mussulmans; in ancient times for certain divine persons, and idols, particularly for two, famous in history: *ǰó-bo mi-skyod-rdó-rǰe*, and *tsan-dán-gyi ǰó-bo*, also *ǰó-bo šá-kya, ǰó-bo rin-po-č̔é* v. *Glr.*

ཇོ་མོ་ *ǰó-mo* 1. **mistress**, the female head of a household, a woman that governs as mistress of her servants *Dzl.* — 2. **lady**, esp. **a cloistress, nun** *Mil.*; in *W.* frq. — 3. **goddess** (cf. sub *ǰo-bo* 2), *ǰo-mo sgrol-ma* the goddess *Dolma Glr.* — 4. p. n. *ǰo-mo-lha-ri* one of the highest mountain summits in West-Bhotan, usually called 'Chumulhari'; *ǰo-mo-k̔a-nag* another summit in southern Tibet.

མཇལ་བ་ *mǰál-ba*, imp. *mǰol*, 1. **to meet** c. *dan̄*, = *˳p̔rad-pa*, without any respect to rank, *Mil.* often. More frq. 2. resp.: **to obtain access** to an honoured person; *žal-dn̄ós-su mǰál-bar yod* he (the incarnated Buddha) may personally be seen and spoken to *Glr.*; **to wait on, to pay one's respects** to a person, *yab dan̄ mǰal ˳tsál-lo* I will pay a visit to my father *Dzl.*; *p̔yis myúr-du mǰál-du yon̄* I shall take the liberty of soon coming back *Mil.*; *rgyál-bai sku dan̄ t̔a-mal mǰal* to thee, Buddha, my own humble self approaches (says a prince to his father who appears to be an incarnated Buddha) *Glr.*; *mǰál-bar žú-ba* to ask for an audience *Glr.*; *mǰál-du mi btub* (they) cannot get in, cannot obtain admittance *Pth.*; **ǰal-č̔ág čó-če** (or **č̔ag-ǰál* Cs.*) *W.* to salute, to exchange compliments on meeting; *mǰal-p̔rád-byéd-pa* = *˳p̔rad-pa*; used also of a king and his ministers: *mǰal-p̔rád dan̄ dgá-bai γtam mán̄-po mdzad* (they) exchanged many compliments and expressions of joy *Pth.*; to visit or pay one's respects to holy places, as pilgrims do, **to go on a pilgrimage**, also *žal mǰál-ba Mil.*; *γnas mǰál-ba* id., *γnas-mǰál-pa* partic., a pilgrim, palmer; *˳di mǰól žig* do make your pilgrimage to this place. — 3. **to understand, comprehend**, *Zam.*: '*gó-bai mǰál-ba* ज्ञा'; *don mǰál-ba* to understand the sense *Mil.*, yet cf. *˳ǰál-ba* 3. — 4 often erron. for *ǰál-ba*.

Comp. *mǰál-k̔a* **audience, access, admittance**, *mǰál-k̔a γtón̄-ba*, or *γnán̄-ba* to give audience, *˳gégs-pa* to refuse it *Mil.* — *mǰal-dár* = *k̔a-btágs*. — *mǰál-sna-pa* **an usher**, master of ceremonies *Cs.* — *mǰal-p̔yág* **salutation.** — *mǰal-mán̄s* a visit paid by many together, a grand reception *Cs.*

མཇིང་པ་ *mǰin̄-pa* 1. = *˳ǰin̄-pa*. — 2. *rtswa-mǰin̄* **meadow** *Bhar.* 82, *Schf.*

མཇུག་ *mǰúg* what is behind, **hind part**, e.g. of the body, resp. *sku-mǰúg*, **posteriors, back-side, tail**, often also *mǰúg-ma*; *mǰug skór-ba* col. to turn one's back (on another); *mǰúg-ma sgríl-ba* to wag the tail; fig.: the further progress and final issue of an affair, **the consequences** = *rǰes*, opp. to *dn̄os-γži* the thing itself, and to *sn̄ón-˳gro* the preparations *Thgy.*; **the lower end** or extremity, e.g. of a bench, a stick, a river (= mouth), of a procession, train etc.; with regard to time: **the end**, *zlá-ba brgyád-pai mǰúg-la*, at the end of the eighth month;

in general *mjúg-la, mjúg-tu* adv. and postp., = *mťar*, at the end of, at last, behind, after, with the genit. inf., or the verbal root, gen. opp. to *mgo*. — *mjúg-sgro* (*W.* **júg-ro**) lower or inferior part, underpart, buttocks (cf. *γžug*); *mjúg-to* id. — *mjug-btág* (for *btég*), and *mjug-ldéb W.* wagtail. — *mgo-mjúg* above and below *Dzl.*

མཇེ *mje*, resp. *γsáṅ-mje*, **शिश्न, शेफ the penis;** *Zam.* avoids the term by making use of circumlocutions, others employ it, esp. *Med.*; also in vulgar use; *mje láṅ-ba* erection of the penis; *mje sbúbs-su nub* the penis recedes; *mje-mgo* glans penis. — *mje-rlig* the penis and testicles. — *mje-šúbs* the membraneous covering or sheath of the penis.

མཇེད་པ *mjéd-pa*, *Zam.* **सह** suffering, enduring, bearing patiently; *Cs.*: obnoxious; *mi-mjéd* prop.: free; gen. **the world, the universe,** acc. to Buddhistic ideas; except in the last mentioned sense the word seems to be little used.

འཇག་པ *jág-pa*, pf. *jags*, *Cs.*; *Sch.*: to establish, settle, fix, found; hence prob. *bde-jágs* and *kris-jágs*, *jags-kris* (*Lexx.* and elsewh., but not frq.) **time of prosperity,** of peace, of rest, a time without disturbances, war, epidemies etc. (*kris* by itself is not known).

འཇག་པོ *jág-po* 1. *Lex.* = *klu*, or n. of a Lu, also *jóg-po*. — 2. vulgo = *yág-po*.

འཇག་མ *jág-ma* 1. *Sch.*: a sort of **coarse** and **thick grass** of inferior quality; so *Pth.* of a hut: *jág-mas p'úb-pa* covered with such grass. -- 2. *Lex.* **वीरण a fragrant grass**, Andropogon muricatus. — 3. *Glr.*: **a blade** (of grass), **stalk** (of corn), *jág-ma reï stén-na* on every blade, *kú-šai jág-ma p'on čig* a bundle of blades of Kusha grass; *jag-rgód Sch.* horse-tail, pewter-grass, Equisetum. — 4. *Sik.* **squirrel**, perh. = *bya-ma-byi Sch.* (?).

འཇགས *jags*, v. sub *jág-pa*.

འཇགས་པ *jágs-pa C.* **to give,** to make a present *Georgi Alph. Tib.*

འཇང་བ *jáṅ-ba* **to devour, swallow,** *Sch.*

འཇན་པོ, འཇན་མོ *ján-po, ján-mo* **consort, husband, wife** *Cs.*

འཇན་ས *ján-sa*, v. *čán-sa*.

འཇབ་པ *jáb-pa*, pf. prob. *bžabs*, fut. *bžab*, **to sneak, slink,** creep privily; **to lie in wait,** in ambush, *tsé-la jáb-pa* to attempt a person's life *Pth.*; **p'ág-nẹ jáb-te sad táṅ-če** *W.* to assassinate; *lkog jab byéd-pa* v. *lkog*; *jáb-bus ma byin-par lén-pa Thgy.* to steal clandestinely. Cog. to *čáb-pa*.

འཇབ་ཙེ *jáb-tse* nippers, tweezers.

འཇམ་མགོན *jam-mgón* = *jam-dpál*.

འཇམ་པ *jám-pa B.*, **jám-po** *W.*, **jam-jám** *C.* col. (opp. to *rtsúb-pa, rtsiṅ-ge*) **soft, smooth, tender, mild,** e.g. of cloth, hair, a meadow, a plain without stones or rocks, of fruit, the air, the character of a person, a person's way of speaking (*ṅag C.*, **pé-ra** *W.*, **pé-ra jám-po daṅ** with mild expressions, fair words, in a friendly manner), of a law; of beverages: **weak** *W.*; of a (hay-)rake: **close** *W.*; **jám-po ṅáb-če** *W.* to mow off close; *jam-búd* blowing or playing (the flute) softly, piano; *jam-rtsi Med.*, seems to be a kind of medicine; **jam-sáṅ** *W.*, *C.*, plain, without ornaments.

འཇམ་དཔལ *jam-dpál* (**मञ्जुश्री**) *jam-mgón* (•**नाथ**), *jam(-pai)-dbyáṅs* (•**घोष**) one of the two great Bodhisattvas of the northern Buddhists, the Apollo of the Tibetans, the god of wisdom, demiurge, and more particularly the tutelar god and civilizer of Nepal (v. Kŏpp. II, 21), incarnated in *Thonmi Sambhota,* and afterwards in king *Kri-sroṅ-sde-btsán* and others. Cf. *spyan-ras-γzigs*.

འཇམ་མ, རྗེ་འཇམ *jám-ma, rje-jám*, resp. for *tug-pa*, **soup.**

འཇམ་མོ *jam-mo* **post-stage** *Sch.*

འཇའ, འཇའ་ཚོན *ja, ja-tson* **rainbow** frq., *ja-od* light, splendour of the rainbow *Pth.*; *ʒa-tson yal-ba* the vanishing of the rainbow frq.; *ʒa-lus* v. *lus.*

འཛའ་བ *ʒa-ba* 1. also *ʒa-mo Sch.* **lame,** gen. *ža-ba; ʒa-bar byed-pa* to make lame, to lame *S.g.* — 2. **to bespeak, to concert, to confederate** *Sch.*

འཛའ་ས *ʒa-sa, ʒa-mo,* **edict, diploma,** a permit *Cs.*, who declares this word to be Chinese.

འཛར་བ *ʒar-ba Lex.* w.e., acc. to *Cs.* = *byar-ba* **to stick together, to cohere.**

འཛལ་བ *ʒal-ba*, pf. *bčal*, fut. *γžal*, imp. *ʒol, W.* **čal-če**, 1. **to weigh,** *ʒal-byed sraṅ* (a pair of) scales for weighing *Lex.*, *sráṅ-la γžal-ba Glr.* — 2 **to measure,** *riṅ-tuṅ-tsád ʒál-ba C.* to measure the length. — 3. **to appraise, to tax;** to weigh in one's mind, **to ponder;** more fully expressed by *blos-ʒal-ba* to understand *Sch.*, although native grammarians refer this signification with less probability to *mʒal-ba.* — 4. **to pay, pay back, repay,** *bú-lon* a debt, *skyin-pa* a loan, *k̔ral* a tax; **to retaliate, return, repay,** esp. with *lan: p̔an-lán γnód-pas* or *légs-pai lan nyés-pas* to return evil for good. The following is a Buddhist principle of law, but prob. existing only in theory: *dkon-mčóg-gi rdzás-la k̔ri ʒal, dge-dún-gyi rdzás-la brgyád-ču ʒal, p̔ál-pai rdzás-la bdún-gyur ṅo brgyad ʒal* divine or sacred objects are to be repaid or made good tenthousandfold, things or property of the clergy eightyfold, of ordinary men sevenfold, and besides the object itself, hence eightfold *C.*; in *Glr.* there is the following passage: *brkús-pa la brgyad ʒal ṅos daṅ dgu.* — 5. often erron. for *mʒál-ba*; thus prob. also in: *ʒal búl-ba* to bring a present *Sch.* (more correctly: a present of salutation). — *ʒál-k̔a* the act, or business of measuring *C.*

འཛི་བ *ʒi-ba* 1. *Cs.*, also *lʒi-ba,* **a flea.** — 2. *Lex.* and *Cs.*: = *ʒim-pa.* — 3. *Cs.* = *ʒám-pa* **soft, smooth.** — 4. *Sch.*: **disgusting, nasty,** e.g. of a fishy smell.

འཇིག་རྟེན *ʒig-rtén* (receptacle of all that is perishable) 1. **the external world:** a. acc. to the common (popular) notion: the whole earth, the universe, *ʒig-rtén-na dkón-pa*, what is rare, the only thing of its kind in the world *Dzl.*; *ʒig-rtén-gyi lha* the god of the world, a deity of the Bonpos *Mil.*; *ʒig-rtén-las ʼdás-pa* one that has escaped from this world, one emancipated, blessed *Cs.* — b. the external world acc. to Brahmanic and Buddhist theories, as set forth: *Köpp.* I, 231; *ʒig-rtén-gyi k̔ams* id. *Glr.*; *ʒig-rtén čágs-pa* origin, bēginning, *γnás-pa* duration, *ʒig-pa* destruction, *bžág-pa* arrangement of the world, cosmography (title of a volume of *Stg.*) *ʒig-rtén γsum* the three worlds, earth, heaven, and hades; *ʒig-rtén (γsúm-gyi) mgón-po (Triloknāth Hind.)* lord or patron of the three worlds, which is also the title of the third of the three highest Lamas, viz. of the Dharma Raja, residing in Bhotan, v. *Cunningh. Ladak* 371; Buddha *Sakya-t̔úb-pa* seems to have the same title, *Pth.* — c. fig.: *bdé-ba-čan-gyi ʒig-rtén*, or *bdé-ʼgro mt̔o-ris-kyi ʒig-rtén* the world of the blessed, like our 'heaven', but of rare occurrence. — 2. **world,** in a spiritual sense, *ʒig-rtén-gyi byá-ba* worldly things or affairs; *ʒig-rtén-la dgós-pa* (or *p̔án-pai*) *bsláb-bya* useful maxims of life, moral rules *Glr.*; *ʒig-rtén-gyi čos brgyad*, v. *čos*; *ʒig-rtén byéd-pa* short expression for *ʒig-rtén-gyi las byéd-pa Mil.* — 3. symb. num.: **three.** — *ʒig-rtén-pa* 1. an inhabitant of the world, or the inhabitants of the world, the world as the totality of men, and more particularly of the worldly-minded; *ʒig-rtén-pa ni ma-dúl-ba yin-pas* as the world is unconverted, in which sense also *ʒig-rtén* (by itself) seems to be used. 2. a layman.

འཇིག་པ *ʒig-pa* I. vb. 1. act. pf. *bžig*, fut. *γžig*, imp. *(b)šig*, *W.* **šig-če, šig táṅ-če**, **to destroy,** buildings etc., frq.: **to cut to pieces, to divide,** e.g. a killed animal *W.*; **to ruin, to annihilate,** existing institutions or things, also other people; **to abolish, annul,** a law *W.*: **to dissolve,** an enchantment; **to lay aside** an assumed appearance or manner (= to unmask one's self) *Mil.*; **to break, violate,** one's duty, a vow, *Dzl.*;

rma - ǰig Med. was explained: **healing** wounds. *ǰig-par byed-pa = ǰig-pa*, frq. — 2. vb. n. pf. *bžig*, and more frq. *žig*, *W.* **žig-če, žig čá-če**, **to be ruined, undone,** e.g. by mischief-making people *Dzl.*; **to fall to pieces, to decay, to rot,** of the human body etc.; **to be lost, to perish,** *ǰig - par šin-tu sla* (earthly goods) may be easily lost again *Thgy.*; **to vanish, disappear,** *ǰig* (or *žig*)-*par gyur-ba* id.; *sem žig soṅ W.* he was quite dejected or cast down; *žig ysós byed-pa B., C.,* **žig-só* (or *-sób*) *čó-če* or *táṅ-če** *W.* to 'restore from destruction', to rebuild c. dat. frq., also c. genit. *Pth.*; prob. also c. accus. — 3. **to suck,** draw out moisture *Sch.*, v. *ǰib-pa*.

II. sbst. **decay, destruction, ruin,** entire overthrow, *skyé-ba daṅ ǰig-pa kún-la srid-na* as it is the lot of all men to rise and to decay *Dzl.*; *lús-kyi mtar ǰig-pai ltas* symptoms of the final decay of the body *Wdṅ.*; **čáṅ-la koi žig-pa yod** beer proves his ruin, beer is his destruction *W.*; **ǰig-pe čó-čen** *C.*, *ǰig-pa-čan Cs.* frail, perishable.

III. adj., but only in conjunction with a negative: *mi-ǰig-pa* **imperishable;** *mi-ǰig rtág-pa* as explanation of a synonym *Lex.*

འཇིགས་པ་ *ǰigs-pa* I. vb. (भी) resp. *tsábs-pa*, to be afraid of a thing, is gen. connected with the instr. (lit. 'by'), in later literature and col. with *la*, *srin-pos ǰigs-šiṅ* from fear of the Rakshasa *Dzl.*; *dé-la ṅa mi ǰigs* I am not afraid of that *Mil.*; in *W.* frq. in conjunction with **rag**: **kó-la ǰig rag** I am afraid of him; also relative to the future, like *dógs-pa: yi-ge máṅs - pas ǰigs - nas = máṅ - gi dógs - nas*, fearing lest there should be too much writing, i. e. from want of room *Pth.*; *ǰigs-su-ruṅ-ba* dreadful, frightful, frq.; **ǰig-te dár-ri spé-ra zér-če** *W.* to speak trembling and shaking with fear; **máṅ-po ǰig soṅ** *W.* I am very much afraid; *ǰigs-par gyur-ba* to be frightened, *ǰigs-par byéd-pa* to put in fear, to frighten.

II. sbst. (भीत) **fear, dread,** *srin - poi ǰigs-pas* from fear of the Rakshasa *Dzl.* ཞཝ༧, 14 (unless *srin-pos* ought to be read, as above); *ǰigs-pa brgyad* the eight fears of life (so among the rest: *rgyál-poi ǰigs-pa* the standing in fear of the king, who in the East is always supposed to be an arbitrary despot); *mi-ǰigs-pa* 1. fearlessness, intrepidity; *mi-ǰigs-pa sbyin-pa* to impart intrepidity; *mi-ǰigs-pai lág-pa* a fearless hand, heroic vigour. 2. pardon, quarter, safety *Cs.* — *ǰigs* (*-pa*)*-čan Cs.* 1. fearful, timorous. 2. dreadful, frightful (I never found it used in this sense).

III. adj. 1. (fearing) **fearful, timorous,** *ǰigs-pai gró-ba-rnams* timorous beings *Pth.* — 2. (feared) **dreadful, frightful,** *ǰigs-pai mtsón-ča* dreadful weapons; *kyod-pas lhag-par ǰigs-pa yod* there is something even more formidable than you are *Dzl.*

Comp. *bár-do-la ǰigs skyób-mai smón-lam* a prayer efficacious in the Bardo-horrors *Thgr.* — *ǰigs-skrág* **fear;** also a terrible object, *ǰigs-skrág-tu soṅ* he has been changed into **a fright, a monster** *Mil.*; **ǰig - tág tom - pa** *C.* (lit. *btón - pa*) to frighten, deter; intimidate, **threaten;** *ǰigs-skrág-pa* to fear, to be **afraid** *Dzl.* — *ǰigs-mkan* col. **timid, timorous.** — *ǰigs-čan* v. *ǰigs-pa-čan* above. — *ǰigs-čúm-pa* v. *čum-pa*. — *ǰigs*(*-pa*)*-po* one **afraid** *Cs.* (?) — *ǰigs-byéd* one that is **terrifying** *Sch.*, appellation of Yamāntaka, who is invoked, e.g. in drawing lots. — *ǰigs-brál*, *ǰigs-méd* **fearless, intrepid, bold;** also noun pers. — **ǰigs-ri** *W.* **fear, terror,** **ǰig-ri tsór-če** to be afraid, **ǰig-ri kúl-če** to **frighten,** to menace, to intimidate. — *ǰigs-sa Mil.*, *ǰigs-sa čé* it is **a** very dangerous **quarter** or region, in that place there is much occasion for being afraid.

འཇིང་ *ǰiṅ* 1. acc. to *Cs.* = *mčiṅ, kloṅ*, e.g. *rgyá - mtsoi*; *Sch.*: *mtso - ǰúṅ* the whole circumference of a lake; prob. more corr.: **the middle,** *Lex.*: *lus-ǰám ǰág-po mtsó-ǰiṅ ǰug* the smooth-bodied Lu alights in the middle of the lake. — 2. *srod-ǰiṅ Lex.*; or *srod-byiṅ* **twilight.**

འཇིང་པ་ *ǰiṅ-pa*, also *mǰiṅ-pa*, **neck,** resp. *sku-ǰiṅ*; **ǰiṅ-pa gyúr-če** *W.* to turn or move round (as vb. n.), **ǰin-pa gyúr-te ltá-če** *W.* to look round, or back; **ǰin-pa čág-če** *W.* to break one's neck; **ǰin-pa zúm-če** *W.* to hug, to embrace; *ǰin-kyóg* a wry neck *Cs.*; *ǰin-kin* the nape of the neck *Glr.*; *ǰin-ltág* the back part of the neck *Cs.*

འཇིབ(ས)་པ་ *ǰib(s)-pa* (*Sch.* also *ǰigs-pa*) pf. *bžibs* (*γžibs*), fut. *bzib* (*γžib*), **to suck**, e.g. of a suckling baby; *mčus* with the lips *Lex.*; *krag ǰibs-pa* to suck blood *Lex.*; **to suck out, in,** or **up, to imbibe, absorb**, also **to blister**, *ǰib-mán W.* vesicatory.

འཇིབ་རྩི་ *ǰib-rtsi* 1. *Cs.* a kind of sirup. — 2. *Wdn.* a medicinal herb.

འཇིམ་པ་ *ǰim-pa B., C.,* a compound of earth and water, **mud, clay, loam** etc. (*W.* **ká-lag**); *ǰim-skon* a small cup of clay, a crucible *Cs.*; *ǰim-γzugs* a figure formed of clay *Glr.*; *rdó-rǰei ǰim-pa* v. *rdó-rǰe.*

འཇིལ་བ་ *ǰil-ba*, pf. *bčil*, fut. *γžil*, **to expel, eject, remove, turn off,** *pyir ǰil-ba Lex.* id., e.g. noxious animals, vices etc.

འཇུ་བ་ *ǰú-ba* I. vb. 1. pf. *ǰus*, **to seize, grasp, take hold of,** c. dat., *dpрál-bai mdá-la ǰú-ba* grasping the arrow sticking in his forehead *Glr.*; *γčig-la γčig ǰú-ba* taking firmly hold of each other (in a storm at sea) *Glr.*; to seize a person (in taking him prisoner) *Pth.*; *lág-pa-nas* to grasp by the hand, to shake hands (in greeting) *Dzl.* — 2. pf. *bžus*, fut. *bžu*, *W.* **žú-če** (or *ǰu-če?*)* **to melt, to digest,** *zas ǰú-ba* to digest the food; *ǰu slá-ba* digestible, *ǰu dká-ba* difficult of digestion; **ra ǰú-če** *W.* to digest intoxication, to sleep the fumes of wine away; *ǰu-byéd* a sort of bile, the bile as the promoter of digestion *Med.* Cf. *žú-ba* II.

II. sbst. 1. **digestion,** *ǰú-ba slao* the digestion is in order, is easy *Med.*; *ǰu-stóbs čun* the digestive power is weak *Med.* — 2. **a flea** *Sch.* = *ǰi-ba.*

འཇུག་ *ǰug*, sometimes for *mǰug.*

འཇུག་ངོགས་ *ǰug-ńógs Cs.* **entrance,** way of access, to a tank or river, Ghāt (*Hind.*).

འཇུག་པ་ *ǰúg-pa*, I. pf. and imp. *žugs*, *W.* **žúg-če**, vb. n., 1. **to go** or **walk in, to enter,** *kán-pai*, or *čui nán-du ǰúg-pa* to go into the house, or into the water; *rgyá-mtsor ǰúg-pa* to put to sea, to set sail *Dzl.*; *lám-du ǰúg-pa* to set out, to start, to prosecute a journey; **mál-sa-la žúg-če** *W.* to go to bed. In a special sense: a. of a demon, entering into a man to take possession of him, hence **dé-žug-kan** *W.* possessed (by a demon); *ǰúg-sgo Med.* the place where the demon entered the body. b. *dgé-ba-la ǰúg-pa* to walk in the path of virtue; acc. to *Schr.* *ǰúg-pa* by itself, without *dgé-ba-la,* implies the same, and in conformity with this a Lama gave the following explanation of the expression *ǰúg-pai las* in *Thgy.*: works that are a consequence of having really entered upon the practice of virtue, positive good works, opp. to the negative good works of the ten virtues. *čós-la ǰúg-pa* to turn to religion, to be converted; *čos* or *bstán-pa žig-la ǰúg-pa* to adopt a certain religion, a certain doctrine. c. *bud-méd-la ǰúg-pa* to lie with, sleep with a woman *Med.*; **bár-la žúg-če** *W.* euph. expression for: to commit adultery. d. **dún-du žúg-če** *W.* to appear, in reference to gods. e. *rǰés-su ǰúg-pa* v. *rǰés-su.* — 2. **to set** or **fall to, to begin,** *rig-pa sbyán-bas rtsóm-pa kún-la ǰug* a skilled, an experienced man is prepared for anything, knows how to set about it, how to manage it *Med.*; gen. with the inf.: to begin to do, to commence doing a thing, *rtóg-pa-la*, resp. *dgóns-pa-la ǰúg-pa* to begin to think upon *Dzl.*, *Glr.*; *stón-pa-la ǰúg-pa* to begin to show *Dzl.*; *γčig-la γčig rnám-par brlág-pa-la žúgs-pas* being in the best way of entirely exterminating one another *Stg.* — 3. pass. of *ǰúg-pa* II, 3, of letters: **to be combined, to be preceded, to be followed,** *zla yig snón-du ba žúgs-čan* (words) having *zl* preceded by *b*, i.e. beginning with *bzl Zam.* — **4.**

to take place, to exist, *če-čuṅ-k̔ydd žúgs-par mṅón-pas* as evidently a difference in size is existing (?) *Dzl.* ༧༠, 3.

II. pf. *bčug* (perh. also *ǰugs Lex.*), fut. *γžug*, imp. *čug*, *W.* **čúg-če**, vb. a., with *naṅ-du* or termin.: 1. **to put into**, e.g. meat into a pan, a key into the key-hole, a culprit into prison; **to infuse, inject**, *γžúg-par bya* this must be infused *Med.*; also fig. **nyiṅ-rus čúg-če* W.* to inspire with courage. In a special sense: a. *dé-la blo ǰúg-pa* to set one's mind on, to apply one's self to *Glr.* b. *mi žig čós-la ǰúg-pa* to convert a man, to induce him to adopt a certain religion; *ǰúg-pa* also without an object, to missionate successfully *Feer Introd. du B. au Cachem.* 68. — 2. **to make, render, appoint, constitute,** with the accus. and termin., or col. with two accus.: *mi zig rgyal-por ǰug-pa* to make one king *Dzl.*; *mṅon-du ǰug-pa* to make public or manifest, to disclose, to show *Samb.*; **siṅ čug-če* W.* to clear, clarify; frq. with the supine or root of a verb: a. **to cause, compel, prevail on,** *zar ǰug-pa* to prevail on another to eat something *Dzl.*; *skrod-du γžug-go* I shall induce (them) to expel (you) *Dzl.*; *bžugs ǰug rgyu yin* he will induce (the god) to take his abode *Glr.*; *groṅs-su ǰug-pa* to be the cause of somebody's death *Mil.*; *yid-la ǰug-tu ǰug-pa* to cause a thing to enter a person's mind, to put in mind, to remonstrate; *p̔el-bar ǰug-pa* (resp. *mdzad-pa*) = *spel-ba* to increase, as vb. a.; **ǰuṅ čug-če* W.* to cause to exist, create, procure; **k̔ol ǰug-če* W.* = **skol-če** to cause to boil; *dar-du čug čig* cause it to spread *Glr.* b. **to command, order, bid,** *dmag dzin-du bčug* he ordered the soldiers to take (the man) prisoner (but he escaped) *Dzl.* ༢༢༢, 3; *byed-du ǰug-pa* to bid one do a thing, frq.; *btsun-mo blon-pos gebs-su bčug* he gave orders for the queen being protected by the minister. c. **to let, suffer, permit,** *smon-lam debs-su čug* allow me to say a prayer; *rtsig-tu mi ǰug* I shall not give permission to build *Glr.* d. **to give an opportunity** *Thgy.* e. in a general sense: *dal-du ǰug-pa* to do things slowly, to be slow *Mil.* — 3. **to put grammatically**: *sṅon-du ǰug-pa* to put or place before, *sṅon-ǰug* a prefixed letter, a prefix; *rjes-ǰug* final letter, *yaṅ-ǰug* the last but one; also to put, to use a word in a certain signification, *rgyu-mtsan-la ǰug* is used with reference to cause *Gram.* — 4. **to banish, to exile** (prob. erron. for *sp̔úg-pa*), *byáṅ-la* to northern regions *Glr.* — 5. *sgo ǰúg-pa* v. *sgo.* — 6. inst. of *byúg-pa.*

འཇུག་པ *ǰúg-pa* sbst. 1. **the going into, the entering;** in a special sense 2. the beginning, **the first stage** of a disease *Mṅg.* — 3. (**अवतार**) the incarnation of a deity.

འཇུངས་པ *ǰúṅs-pa* **avarice,** *Dzl., Lex.*; *ǰúṅs-pa-čan* avaricious; *ǰuṅs-ǰúr* a miser, niggard.

འཇུད་མཐུན་མ *ǰud-mt̔ún-ma*, or *ǰud-t̔ún-ma Lex.* ('accessible to all') **a prostitute;** *ǰud-mt̔ún byéd-pa* to be a harlot.

འཇུད་པ *ǰúd-pa*, and more frq. *dzúd-pa*, secondary forms of *ǰúg-pa.* Cf. *čúd-pa*, *tsúd-pa.*

འཇུན་པ *ǰún-pa*, pf. *bčun*, fut. *γžun* (cf. *bžun, žun*) *W.* **čún-če**, *Cs.*: **to subdue,** make tame; to make confess; *W.*; **to make soft, to soften,** e.g. iron; **to punish,** by words or blows; **to convert.**

འཇུམ་པ *ǰúm-pa*, pf. *bčum*, fut. *γžum*, imp. *čum*, **to shudder, to shrink.** (Acc. to grammatical analogy *ǰum-pa* ought to be vb. a., to cause to shudder, and *čúm-pa* vb. n.) *ša ǰúms-pa Lex.*, contraction of the muscles, shrinking, shuddering *Sch.*

འཇུར་ *ǰur*, supine of *ǰú-ba*; *ǰur mi dod* indigestible *Sch.* (?).

འཇུར་བ *ǰúr-ba* 1. (pf. *bčur*, q. v.) *Cs.*: complication; *Sch.* also: to struggle against, to resist. *Pth.*: *ǰúr-bar gyúr-ba* **to be entangled;** *ǰúr-bu Sch.*, **ǰúr-pa* C.* tangled yarn; *srád-bui ǰúr (-pa) Lexx.* w. e., *Sch.*: 'the tightness of the yarn'; *ǰur-mt̔úg* wrinkled, as the skin is in old age *Thgy.*; *ǰur-míg* a wire-drawing plate, *ǰur-míg-nas drén-pa* to draw through this plate *Thgy.* — 2. = *dzúr-ba*

to evade, to shun, to go out of the way, *ǰur-méd* unavoidable *Mil.*

འཛུས་ *ǰus*, v. *ǰu-ba* I, 1.

འཛེབས་པ་ *ǰébs-pa*, *ǰébs-po*, **well-sounding** *Stg.*; *snyan-ǰébs* harmony, euphony.

འཛེམ(ས)་པ་ *ǰém(s)-pa* 1. **dexterity, cleverness** *Lex.* 2. **skilled, clever**; *Sch.* **decent**; *ǰéms-po* id.

འཛོ་སྒེག *ǰo-sgég* a coquettish, alluring, seducing attitude or posture; *Lex.*: *ǰud-mlún ǰo-sgég ǰog* the harlot assumes such an attitude.

འཛོ་བ་ *ǰó-ba*, pf. *bžos*, ft. *bžo*, imp. *ǰos*, **to milk**, *rá-ma ǰó-ba* to milk a goat, *o-ma ǰo-ba* 'to milk the milk'; *kyód-kyis ó-ma bžos dug, ṅas ni bžós-pa med*, it is you, not I, that have 'milked out the milk' *Glr.*; *ǰó(-ba)-po*, *ǰó-mk̔an*, milker, milk-man, *ǰó(-ba)-mo* milkmaid; *dód-ǰoi ba* a cow that is able to fulfil every wish.

འཛོག་པ་ *ǰóg-pa* I. pf. *bžag*, ft. *γžag*, imp *žog*, *C.* col. **žág-pa**, 1. **to put, to place**, e.g. the foot on the ground; also to place persons, to assign them a place *Dzl.*, *Glr.*; fig. = *gód-pa* (e.g. *dgé-ba-la, byaṅ-čúb-la, byaṅ-čúb-kyi lám-la*) v. *gód-pa* 3; **to put in order, to arrange**, *ǰig-rtén-bžag-pa* the arrangement (system) of the world; *lus dráṅ-por bžág-ste* sitting straight, bolt-upright *Dzl.*, *Mil.*; *bžág-na mi sdod* if one places her any where, she will not remain there *Mil.*; *stéṅ-du yar bžag* (the anchors) were placed above, were weighed *Pth.*; *lás-su ǰóg-pa* to set one a task, to employ one in a certain service *Dzl.*, *rgyal-srid-la ǰóg-pa* to appoint one to the government i.e. to make one king; *séms* (resp. *t̔ugs*)-*la ǰóg-pa* to take to heart *Glr.*, *Mil.*; *lús-la grui du-šés bžág-la* if we fancy the human body to be a ship *Thgy.*; *nám-mk̔a ráṅ-gi ṅáṅ-du žog* transfer it to the nature of the ethereal space, i.e. figure it to yourself as ether *Mil.*; *p̔yir ǰóg-pa* 1. to leave behind, at home *Dzl.*; 2. to put by, to lay aside *Dzl.*; (another reading omits *p̔yir*). — 2. **to lay** or **put down**, a burden etc., **žóg-la šog** put (it) down and come! *C.*; *nor (γ)sog ǰog med* heaping up treasures and depositing them was not, i.e. was never heard of; *γsóg-ǰog-mk̔an* a hoarder up, a miser *Cs.*; **to leave, to leave behind**, *lag-rǰés* a trace or mark of activity, monumentum *Glr.*; **to leave, quit, abandon**, *ráṅ-gi yul* one's own country *Glr.*; *p̔óṅs-par ma bžág-par* so that it is not abandoned, given up, to poverty *Thgy.*; **yúg-le žog* C.* (= **p̔áṅ-te bor* W.*) throw it away! **to depose**, *yi-ger bris ǰóg-pa* to depose in writing, *literis mandare Glr.*; *sá-bon, γduṅ-brgyúd ǰóg-pa* to leave an offspring behind, to propagate the species; **to lay up, to keep**, as holy relics; **to lay aside**, *ré-žig žóg-la* setting aside, apart, for a while *Dzl.*; *mnyám-par žóg-pa* v. *mnyám-pa*; *sgról-lam ǰog* shall we turn them out or leave them? *Mil. nt.*

II. pf. *(b)žogs*, fut. *γžog*, imp. *žog*, *W.* **žog-ce,** **to cut, to hew, to square**, a pen, timber etc.; **to carve, to chip**, a thin piece of wood etc.

འཛོག་པོ་ *ǰog-po* n. of a Lu *Mil.*, = *ǰag-po.*

འཛོང་ *ǰoṅ* = *lčoṅ*, **tadpole.**

འཛོང་འཛོང་ *ǰoṅ-ǰóṅ* col., *Sch.* *ǰóṅ-po*, **oblong, longish, oval, elliptical, cylindric, bottle-shaped** etc.; col. also applied to stature: **tall**; *ǰoṅ-nyáms-čan Wdṅ.* oblong shaped, in relation to leaves, cones of fir etc.; *ló-ma ǰoṅ-stábs nyág-ga-čan* split into narrow slips, wing-cleft (leaves of caraway) *Wdṅ.*; *dbyibs-ǰóṅ* an oval form.

འཛོང་ཚེ་ *ǰóṅ-tse Cs.* = *lčóg-tse.*

འཛོམས་པ་ *ǰóms-pa*, pf. *bčom*, also *žom*, fut. *γžom*, imp. *čom*, *W.* **čóm-če** 1. **to conquer, subdue, oppress, suppress**, an enemy; *dód-čágs-kyis kún-nas ǰóms-pa* to be quite overpowered by lust; *nad ǰóms-pai sman* a medicine for a disease (to overcome it); *ráb-tu γžóm-pa di* the following overpowering (charm);

bčóm-mo an exclamation like: I am done for! *perii!* — 2. **to destroy**, towns etc. *Glr.*; *bčóm-la γžág-go* id. *Glr.* — 3. **to plunder, spoil, rob,** *˳ǰóms-pai grabs byás-pa-la* as they were about to rob him *Mil.* — 4. **to finish, accomplish** *W.*, cf. *čóm-pa.*

འཇོར་ *˳ǰor* 1. *C.*, also *γžor*, **hoe, grubbing-hoe, mattock, pick-axe** (*W.* **tóg-tse**), *˳ǰór-gyis rkó-ba* to turn up with the hoe; *˳ǰór-po* a large mattock, pick-axe, spade, *˳ǰór-bu* a small one, a hoe; *˳ǰor-yú* the handle of a hoe, *˳ǰor-lčágs* the iron of a mattock *Cs.* — 2. supine of *˳ǰó-ba.*

འཇོལ་བ་ *˳ǰól-ba* I. vb. 1. **to hang down,** of a cow's udder, of the long hair on a yak's belly, of tails etc.; *˳ǰol-˳ǰól* hanging-belly, paunch. — 2. gen. *˳byól-ba* **to turn aside, to make way.**

II. sbst., also (*Cs.*) *˳ǰol-˳ǰól* and *γžól-a*, **train, trail; retinue** *Cs.*; *˳ǰól-gos Cs.*, *˳ǰól-ber Wdk.*, *Pth.*, a robe or garment with a train; *˳ǰól-čan* having a train; *˳ǰol-méd* without a train *Cs.*

འཇོལ་ལེ་ *˳ǰol-lé* **hanging,** cf. *ṗyaṅ-ṅé, gród-pa ˳ǰol-lé* hanging-belly, paunch, cf. *ṗyal Lex.*

འཇོལ་མོ་ *˳ǰól-mo*, acc. to the descriptions given by natives, a bird of the size of a blackbird, of lively motions and an agreeable whistling, in the neighbourhood of Lhasa, building in willow-trees and thorn-bushes; *Cs.* has: a turkey-hen.

རྗང་མ་ *rǰáṅ-ma*, or *rdzaṅ-ma*, **store-room** *Thgy.*

རྗིད་པ་ *rǰíd-pa* **lean** *Cs.*, gen. *ríd-pa.*

རྗིབ་ལས་ **žib-las**(?) *W.*, **service** done in socage, compulsory service, in the fields, on roads etc.

རྗུད་པ་ *rǰúd-pa*, *rdzúd-pa*, = *rgúd-pa Lex.*

རྗུན་ *rǰun*, *nad-rǰún Mil.* a disease.

རྗེ་(བོ་) *rǰé(-bo)*, also *rǰe-u*, **lord, master,** 1. **ruler, king**, *yúl-gyi rǰe mdzád-nas* ruling over a country, acting the part of a sovereign *Glr.*; *bod-ḱáms-kyi rǰé-bor gyur* he became sovereign of Tibet *Wdk.*; *sá-yi bdág-po mi-yi rǰe Mil.* lord of the ground, ruler of the people; *rǰé-bo daṅ bran*, *rǰe-ḱól Stg.*, master and servant; *rǰe-blón* king and minister; *rǰe či lags* sir, what does that mean? *Glr.*; also a title before names, esp. names of kings, *ǰó-bo rǰe Dipangkāra Glr.*; *rǰe-bdúd rǰe-btsán* the gentlemen devils and the gentlemen goblins (messieurs les diables et messieurs les farfadets); *rǰe dkon-mčóg-la γsól-ba ˳débs-pa Mil.* is in fact an empty phrase in the mouth of a Buddhist philosopher, but may nevertheless be used in Christian language for addressing God as 'our Lord'. — 2. **a nobleman**, a person of rank, *rǰeu(i) rigs*, *rǰe-rigs* = *rgyal-rigs* the caste of nobility. — *rǰe-dpón* (*Lex.* आर्य) = *rǰe*, master, lord, prince *Cs.*; *rǰé-ma*, also *γcés-ma Cs.*, col. **šé-ma**, a lady of rank, *rǰe-čúṅ* a young lady, a miss; *rǰé-srás* a young gentleman; also a term of address *Cs.* — *rǰe-btsún* **reverend sir**, a title of the higher priesthood, *rǰe-btsún-ma* fem. — *rǰé-sa* (or *žé-sa*) *byéd-pa* to show deference, to pay one's respects; *žé-sai γtam*, or *žé-sai skad* courteous words, esp. ceremonial and complimentary terms, e.g. *dbu* for *mgo* etc. *W.*: **yá-ša čó-če, yá-še pé-ra**.

རྗེ་ངར་ *rǰe-ṅár* the lower part of the leg, **the shank** (*W.* **sug**); *rkaṅ-lág rǰe-ṅár* the lower part of the arms and the legs *Med.*

རྗེ་བ་ *rǰé-ba*, pf. *brǰes*, fut. *brǰe*, imp. *brǰes*, *W.* **žé-če**, **to barter,** to give or take in exchange; *˳di-dag-gis brǰeo* it may be exchanged for these *Dzl.*; **zan daṅ srog žé-če** *W.* to risk one's life for the necessary food (as thieves do); *brǰé-byai nor* articles of barter; in a more general sense: **to change, to shift,** *miṅ* the name, *gos* the clothes *Dzl.*, *γnas* the place, *tse* the life; i.e. to die *Cs.* — *brǰé(-ba)-po* a barterer *Cs.*

རྗེད་པ་ *rǰéd-pa*, pf. and fut. *brǰed* 1. **to honour, reverence** c. dat., *mčód-čiṅ brǰéd-pa* id. *Dzl.*; *brǰéd-pai ˳os* venerable *Lex.* — 2. **to forget,** frq. (cf. *lus-pa*); *brǰéd-du ˳ǰúg-pa* to make forget, to cause to forget.

Comp. *rjéd-ṅas-čan Lex.* (**मुषितस्मृति**) **forgetful, oblivious;** *Cs.* gives inst. of it: *rjéd-ṅes-čan,* but also thus no clear etymological explanation is obtained. — *rjéd-ču* draught of oblivion, of Lethe *Cs.* — *rjed-bsnyén* (etymology?) *sgúg-pa* technical term for the common practice of Indian servants to hide an object belonging to their master in some obscure corner, and after waiting (*sgúg-pa*) for some months, until it may be assumed that the thing is altogether forgotten (*brjéd-pa*), to appropriate it to themselves. — *rjéd-to* list of notes, memorandum-book, journal, diary, cash-book etc. *Glr., C., W.* — *rjed-rdó* prob. monumental or **memorial stone.** — *rjed-byáṅ* specifications or **lists of goods,** pieces of luggage etc. which the Tibetans number and mark with the letters of the alphabet. — *rjed-byéd* 1. a demon that takes away the power of memory, also *rjed-byéd-kyi γdon.* 2. epilepsy (**अपस्मार**) *Med.* — *rjed-zás Cs.:* 'the meat of forgetfulness'.

ཇེན་ནེ་བ་ *rjén-ne-ba* v. the following word.

ཇེན་པ་ *rjén-pa* 1. not covered, **bare, naked,** *B., C.* (*W.:* *čer-nyál*), *rkaṅ-rjén* (*-pa*) barefooted, unshod; *žabs-rjén-par γdá-ba* or *γšégs-pa*, resp., to be barefooted, to go barefoot; *γdoṅ rjén-du sdód-pa* to sit with unveiled face, *mgo-rjén-pa* with uncovered head, *rgyab-rjén* with a naked back *Cs.*; *rjén-par ₒdón-pa C.* to strip perfectly; *dmar-rjén* stark naked *Sch.*; *rál-gri rjén-pa* a naked sword; *žén-pa toṅ* *W.* give it (me) not wrapped up! *sa-rjen* the bare ground, not covered with a carpet *Cs.*; *rjén-ne-ba* undisguised, obvious to the understanding, manifest *Mil.* — 2. **raw,** not roasted or cooked, *ša-rjen* raw meat, *dmar-rjén* red raw meat; *mar-rjén* not melted butter; *nas-rjén* raw barley, not prepared or roasted; also the meal of it: *W.* *nar-jén* barley-flour, cf. *Sch.: bra-rjén* bu kwheat-meal. — *rjen-zás Med.* (*Cs.* also *rjen-rigs*) victuals that may be eaten raw. — 3. not ripe, **unripe** *W.*

ཇེས་ *rjes* 1. **trace, track, mark left,** impression made (on the ground), *p̓yi-rjés Med.* prob. id.; *mi-rjés* a man's track, *rta-rjés* a horse's track *Glr.; šiṅ-rtai rjes* the track of a waggon or cart, a rut; *rkaṅ-rjés*, resp. *žabs-rjés,* the trace of one's foot, footprint, *rkaṅ-rjés byuṅ* a footprint is made; *rkaṅ-rjes ₒjóg-pa* to leave a footprint behind *Mil.; byas-rjés* proof of an accomplished deed, whether it be the work itself or some indubitable result of it; *lag-rjés*, resp. *p̓yag-rjés* impression or mark left of one's hand, hence fig.: action, deed, charitable institution, pious legacy, whereby a person wishes to immortalize his name. — 2. **the hind part** of a thing *Sch.* (?) — 3. in relation to time: that which follows, **the consequence, the course** or **progress** of a thing, **the last,** = *mjug.* — 4. adv. and postp. inst. of *rjés-su*, v. below. — *rjes γčód-pa* 1. *Sch.* to destroy, blot out, efface a track or trace, in *Med.* to eradicate the trace of a disease, to cure it thoroughly, 2. *Sch.*: to separate, disjoin the hind part(?) 3. *W.* *žes čád-če* to follow a trace or track, to find out or to come upon the track. — *rjes dzin-pa* to 'seize' the track, to overtake *Glr.*, also to be able to follow the track, *rá-ma k̓yui rjes mi zin-pa* a goat that cannot follow the flock *Mil.* — *rjés-la, rjés-su, rjes,* adv. and postp., afterwards, hereafter, for the future, later; after, behind, *deï rjés-la, de-rjés* after that, afterwards, later *Mil.; dé-dag ₒdás-pai rjés-su* after these were gone *Glr.*; *bžag-rjés po.* = *bžág-pai ₒóg-tu Lt.; ṅai rjés-su* after my death. *rjés-su* in conjunction with verbs corresponds to the *Ssk.* **अनु** and is often not to be translated, or serves only to give additional force to some other word or expression: *rjés-su ₒgró-ba, ₒbráṅ-ba* to go after, to follow, to come after; also fig.: *spyód-pa tams-čád ya-rábs-kyi rjés-su ₒbróṅ-ba* to imitate the nobility, the free-born, in their whole demeanour *Glr.; lé-lo daṅ spyód-pa ṅán-pai rjés-su ₒgró-ba* to imitate idleness and wickedness, or idle and wicked people *Ld.-Glr.*; *slób-dpon-gyi rǰés-su brǰód-de* saying after the teacher *Thgy.* — *rǰés-su ʼdzín-pa* **to receive** *Pth.*: *kól-por rǰés-su bzúṅ-nas lto-gós-kyis bskyáṅ-du ɣsol* pray take me (the orphan) into your service, and provide me with food and clothes; to receive as a disciple or follower = *čéd-du ʼdzín-pa* frq.; **to draw after** (after death) *Mil.*; **to assist,** *ʼdi rǰés-su zuṅ žig* do take care of, or provide for this man (as a future co-disciple) *Mil.*; finally with respect to charms and spells: to commit to memory or keep in memory ni f. — *rǰés-su ʼǰúg-pa* 1. vb. a. **to add, affix,** 2. vb. n. **to follow,** *bdag daṅ bdág-gi rǰés-su ʼǰúg-pai slób-ma-rnams* I and the disciples that follow me *Mil.*; in a similar sense: *mi-la rǰés-su slób-pa* to follow another as a disciple *Dzl.* ༢༨༠, 3 (༡༨༣, 7 seems to be a corrupt reading). Also in the following phrases *rǰés-su* may be understood in the sense of: afterwards, subsequently: *rǰés-su dráṅ-pa* **to remember, recollect,** keep in mind, *rǰés-su dráṅ-par byéd-pa* to bring to one's remembrance, to remind *Pth.*; *rǰés-su ʼgyód-pa* **to repent** *Cs.*; pleon. or without any obvious meaning in: *rǰés-su mťún-pa Thgy.* **to agree,** to accord, *rǰés-su rnyéd-pa Stg.* **to find,** *rǰés-su dpág-pa* **to weigh, to ponder** *Cs.*, *rǰés-su snyiṅ-brtsé-ba Thgy* **to pity,** *rǰés-su bstán-pa Tar.* **to instruct,** and thus in similar expressions, esp. in one of frq. occurrence in legends: *rǰés-su yi-ráṅ-ba*, resp. *rǰés-su ťugs-ráṅ-ba* (*Sch.* erron. *ťúgs-pa!*) **to rejoice, to enjoy,** for which sometimes also *rǰés-su ṕyógs-pa* is used, e.g. *dbyé-ba-rnams-la rǰés-su yi-ráṅ-ba* to rejoice at people disagreeing, to enjoy dissensions and jarrings *Stg.*

Comp. *rǰes-skyés* (**अनुज**) born later; younger brother. — *rǰes-grúb-kyi miṅ* **by-name, surname** *Cs.* — *rǰes-ʼǰúg* 1. **following,** coming after, *ṕyi-rábs rǰes-ʼǰúg ťams-čád* all the following generations *Pth.* 2. **final consonant.** — *rǰes-ťóg* prob. the same as *rǰés-la Wdṅ.* — *rǰes-ťób Mil.* is said to denote short interruptions of meditation by taking food, but no more than is absolutely necessary for the preservation of life. — *rǰes-dpág* 1. consideration, deliberation. 2. *Was.* (297) a syllogism consisting of three propositions. — *rǰés-ma* = *rǰes* 2 hinder part *Cs.* — *rǰes-méd* without leaving any traces, **trackless,** *ʼǰig-pa* to destroy thoroughly *Glr.*

རྗེས་པ *rǰés-pa* v. *rǰé-ba.*

རྗོད་པ *rǰód-pa* pf. and fut. *brǰod*, **to say, pronounce, utter,** e.g. a charm or magic formula; *ṅe miṅ žód-da rag* W.* I hear my name mentioned; *saṅs-rgyás-kyi mtsán-nas* to pronounce or invoke the name of Buddha *Dzl.*; **to propound, promulgate,** *čos* a religious doctrine; **to enumerate, set forth,** *légs-pa* or *nyés-pa* the good or bad qualities, actions etc., *yón-tan* the excellence or superiority of a person *Dzl.* and elsewh.; **to treat** of a subject in writing: *lhág-pa-rnams ni ʼdir brǰód-bya* we have now to treat of the rest *Zam.*; an author even says *žes bržód-de* with regard to his own words (after a bombastic poetical exordium, like the 'dixi', of Roman orators) *Glr.*; *rǰód-du méd-pa* unspeakable, inexpressible, ineffable, *rǰód-du méd-čiṅ dpág-tu méd-pa* id. *Dzl.*; *brǰod(-kyis) mi láṅ-ba* (or *lóṅ-ba*) id.; also vb.: to be inexpressible or inexhaustible, frq.; *re-réṅ míṅ-nas rǰod mi laṅ* one cannot mention or enumerate them all *Mil.*; *don mdzád-pa rǰod mi láṅ-ṅo* his utility is beyond description *Dzl.*; *rǰód-kyis mi láṅ-bai ṕyir mi bkod* I do not write it down, because it is impossible to relate every thing *Pth.* (v. *brǰod*).

ལྗགས *lǰags*, resp. for *lče*, **tongue,** *lǰágs-kyis čab ʼdór-ba* to spit, to spit out; *lǰags-čáb* spittle, saliva; *lǰags-dbúgs* breath.

ལྗང་མོ *lǰáṅ-mo* p. n. of a district 1. in Ü, 2. in Kams.

ལྗང་ཁུ *lǰáṅ-ku*, or *lǰáṅ-gu Lt.*, *W.*, **green** (gen. expressed by *ṅón-po*, notwithstanding the ambiguity), *lǰaṅ-skyá* greenish white, *lǰaṅ-nág* greenish black, dark green. — *lǰáṅ-pa* green corn, in the first stage of its growth (in the second stage it is called *sóg-ma*, in the third *snyé-ma*). — *lo-ljáṅ-ba* having a green blade. — *ljáṅ-bu* greenness, verdure (grass, foliage, shrubs), *Lex.*: शाद्वल — *ljaṅ-dmár* greenish red; *ljaṅ-sér* greenish yellow.

ལྗང་དུང་ *ljaṅ-dúṅ* (spelling?), **solid,** not hollow, *W.*

ལྗན་ལྗིན་ *ljan-ljín* **filth, dirt, dust, sweepings;** *lúd-pa ljan-ljín maṅ* a great deal of foul mucous expectoration *Lt.*

ལྗབ་ *ljab W.* **flat, plain, even;** **ljab-ljáb-ba bor** lay or put it down flat; **ljab čó-te dug** sit down flat (on the ground)!

ལྗི་བ་ *ljí-ba*, 1. **a flea** (*ₒ ji-ba*). — 2. **heavy, weighty.**

ལྗིད་པ་ *ljíd-pa*, **heaviness, weight,** *yser daṅ ljíd-pa mnyám-pa dgos* it must be weighed up with gold *Glr.*; *de daṅ ljid mnyám-pa* of equal weight, equal in weight *Med.*; *ljíd-čan*, *ljid-ldán* heavy; *ljid-čé-ba* very heavy; *ljid-med* light, not heavy; *lus tams-čád-kyi ljid pab* he sat down with the whole weight of his body *Cs.*; *ljíd-kyis nón-pa* pressing down by his(its) weight.

ལྗེན་པ་ *ljén-pa Cs.* **to enter, to penetrate,** *bló-la* one's mind, = to be perceived, understood; *tson-ljén* a die or colour penetrating and remaining fixed in cloth etc. Cf. *žén-pa.*

ལྗོངས་ *ljoṅs* **a large valley, principal** or **main valley; region, district, province** *Dzl.*; *ljoṅs daṅ yul-ₒkór* countries and provinces; *ljoṅs čén-po* a large country; *kʼá-ba-čan-gyi ljoṅs ₒdi*, *gáṅs-čan(-gyi) ljoṅs* Tibet, frq.; *nágs-ljoṅs* woody country; *smán-ljoṅs* a country of medicinal herbs *Zam.*; *mú-gei ljoṅs* a very poor country, starving country *Mil.*; *ljóṅs-la* in the valley, in the plain; *ljóṅs-mi-rnams* country-people *Cs.* — *ljoṅs(-su) rgyú-ba* to rove about, *ljoṅs sgyúr-ba* the end of the estival fast of the monks (about the end of August), when they are permitted to rove about the whole district of their monastery.

ལྗོན་པ་ *ljón-pa* a country of gods, **paradise;** *ljon-šiṅ* a tree from paradise, or any large and beautiful tree; *ljón-pai nágs* a beautiful forest.

བརྗིད་ *brjid*, *Tar.* 11, 14, but more frq. *yzi-brjid*, **brightness, splendour, lustre,** gen. of gods and saints, v. *yzi*; also *dpal-brjid Lex.*; *brjid-pa* to shine, glisten, glitter *Cs.*, *brjid-kyis brjid* shining with brightness *Lex.*

བརྗེ་བོ་ *brjé-bo* a making up, a compensation by **barter,** *brjé-bo byéd-pa Glr.*, **brjé-bo gyáb-če** *W.*, to give an equal measure in bartering, e.g. of salt for barley.

བརྗོད་ *brjod* (cf. *rjód-pa*) **sound; talking; speech,** *brjod bdé-ba* euphony; also well-sounding, agreeable speech; *brjod mi bdé-ba* the contrary; also: **dha jo' mi de** *C.* it is not meet now to speak about it; *brjód-pa* speech, utterance; *mṅon-brjód* synonymy, explanation of words; *Cs.* also: 'a poetical term'; *mčod-brjód* praise, eulogy, *Sch.*: invocation of a deity; *če-brjód Schr.*(?), and *čéd-du brjód-pa*, *Tar.* 140, 2 acc. to *Schf.*: preface, introduction, in *C.*: to approve, sanction, commend, *Was.* (270) in the title of a book: = उदान वर्ग w.e.

Comp. *brjód-bya* sbst., *Zam.* also *brjód-pa*, = साध्य an attribute, predicate *Lex.* — *brjod-méd* 1. a speech not earnestly meant, empty words, mere talk. 2. *Mil.*: the unspeakable, the transcendental, identified by some with the Nirvana, by others not. — *brjod-ₒdód Tar.* 210, 7: *brjod-ₒdód-tsam* acc. to *Schf.*: 'a mere supposition'; but in a passage in *Mil.* it seems to denote the (conceited) habit of constantly proposing one's own opinion, and so it might also be understood in *Tar.*

ཉ

ཉ་ *nya*, I. the letter *ny*, double-consonant, distinctly pronounced like *n + y* (*Ssk.* ञ), and used only as initial letter; therefore differing in its nature and sound from the *Ssk.* ञ, though representing it in Sanskrit words.

II. symb. num. for eight.

III. **fish** (मत्स्य), *nya* ˳*dzin-pa*, *W.* **nya zúm-če**, *nya* ˳*čór-ba* (or *bšor-ba*) *Dzl.*, *nya lén-pa* (*bláṅ-ba*) *Pth.* to catch fish; ˳*dám-nya Ld.*, an eel *Cs*; *rgyál-poï γsól-nya* the king's table fish *Pth.*

IV. also *nyá-ču* (cf. *čú-ba*). 1. **tendon, sinew**; *W.*: **ḱáṅ-pe nya did soṅ** my foot is asleep. — 2. col. **mark**, left by a blow, **a weal**, **nya laṅs** the blow has left a weal *W.*

V. 1. the fifteenth day of a lunar month, the day of the full moon. — 2. = *tses* ni f.: *zlá-bai nya drúg-la* on the sixth day of the month *Mil.*

VI. *nya Sch.* 1. lock (?) — 2. **muscle** *Med.*, *nya-bži* the four principal muscles, viz. those of the arms and the calves of the leg, v. also the compounds.

VII. **nya čád-če** *W.* to arrive sooner by a short cut; cf. also **ťad-nya**.

Comp. *nya-rkyál* **the bladder** of a fish *Cs.* — *nya-skyogs* **gills.** — *nya-ḱrá* **sea-eagle,** white-tailed eagle *Sch.* — *nya-ḱráb-čan* **carp** *Sch.* — *nya-ḱrab-čén* **sturgeon** *Sch.* — *nya-ḱróm* **fish-market.** — *nya-gáṅ* 1. full of fish *Sch.* 2. full moon *Cs.* — *nya-grá*, *nyai grá-ma* small **fish-bones.** — *nya-*˳*gyúr* = *nya-lóg* 2 *S.g.*, *C.* — *nya-rgyá* **fishing-net.** — *nya-rgyáb C.*, earth heaped up (like the back of a fish) on the top of outer walls to prevent the entering of the wet. — *nya-rgyás* (*zlá-ba*) full moon *Pth.* — *nya-sgóṅ* **fish-spawn, roe** of fish. — *nya-lčibs* **fish-gills** *Cs.*; mother of pearl *Schr.* — *nya-čú* **tendon, sinew**; perh. also a large nerve in the nape of the neck. — *nya-dól* fishing-net; **nya-dól-pa** fisherman *W.* — *nyá-dós* a load of fish *Sch.* — *nya-ldir* 'a muscle' *Sch.* — *nyá-pa* **fisherman** *Cs.* — *nya-p̓yis* (*Cs.*: fish-gills) **mother of pearl** *S.g.* and col — *nya-mid Sch.*: a sea-monster (this word seems not to be generally known). — *nyá-mo* a (female?) **fish** *Mil.* — **nya-tsél** bow-net, kiddle *W.* **nya-tság C.* id. — *nya-tsil* the fat of a fish. — *nya-tser* **fish-bones** *Sch.* — *nya-tsóṅ-pa* **fish-monger.** — *nya-*˳*dzin Cs.*, **nya-kúg** *W.*, angle, fishing-hook. — *nya-zán* a fish-eater, one feeding on fish *Cs.* — *nya-rús* fish-bone *Cs.* — *nya-lóg* 1. *Cs.*: 'a contraction or sinking of the sinews'. 2. *Sik.*: **cholera** (*Urd.* هيضه) — 3. *Med.*, also *nya-lhóg*, a name for a disease. — *nyá-ša* 1. flesh of fish 2. *W.*: meat cut into long narrow strips and dried in the sun, in *C.* **ša-bčug**. — *nya-γšóg* the fin of a fish *Cs.* — *nya-ság* fish-scale. — *nya-sóg* prob. the back-bone with the bones attached to it, resembling a saw.

ཉ་ག, ཉག *nyá-ga*, *nyag*, a steel-yard.

ཉ་བོ *nyá-bo* body, figure *Sch.*

ཉ་མ *nyá-ma* (*Sch.*: 'mistress of the house, housewife'?) **hearer** of a **Lama**, without being a regular disciple *Mil.* frq.; *nyá ma p̓ó-mo-rnams Mil.* (cog. to *nyán-pa*?)

ཉ་ར *nyá-ra* **care**, *nyá-ra byéd-pa Sch.*, **nyá-ra čó-če** *W.*, to take care of, to provide for a person, to keep a thing well; **nyar go** *C.* for *nyá-ra byed dgos*; cf. *γnyér-ḱa.*

ཉ་ར་ཉོ་རེ *nya-ra-nyo-ré* **weak, feeble, frail,** e.g. of a worm *Thgy.*

ཉག *nyag* 1. v. *nyá-ga.* — 2. v. *nyág-ma.* — 3. also *nyág-ga*, *nyag-ḱrám*, **notch, indenture,** *ló-ma p̓rá-la nyág-ga-čan* having multifid leaves, like those of caraway *Wań.*; *nyág-ga méd-pa* not cleft, not indented. — 4. of wool, *nyág-tu ₒdrén-pa* to draw out into threads, to spin *Mil.*

ཉག་ཉིག *nyag-nyig Cs., Sch.* also *nyag-nyóg* **filth, dirt.**

ཉག་ཉུག *nyag-nyúg Mil.* = *sna-tsogs* (?), of rare occurrence.

ཉག་ཐག *nyag-tág* **thread; chain,** of gold *Mil.*, of iron *Mil.*; cord for stringing turkoises *Mil.*; a cable *Schr.*

ཉག་མཐིལ་ *nyag-mtil* **scale of a steel-yard,** *nyag-rdó* weight of a steel-yard.

ཉག་ཕྲན་ *nyag-prán* a small beam, **a pole** *Cs.*; **an arrow**; *nyag-pran-mdá* arrow *Mil.*

ཉག་མ་ *nyág-ma*, also *nyag-ré*, **single;** *nyag γčig* 1. id., *skra*, or *spu nyag(-ma) γčig* a single hair, frq.; *skrá-yi nyág-ma* id. (a man has 21 000 of them *Med.*) — 2. **a minimum** *Mil.* — 3. *Sch.* also: **bachelor,** old voluntary bachelor. — *saṅs-rgyas-nyag-γčig Thgy., Pth.*, only Buddha, or nothing less than Buddha.

ཉག་མོ་ *nyág-mo Lex.* w.e.; **woman** *Sch.*

ཉག་ཤིང་ *nyág-śiṅ* **beam of a steel-yard.**

ཉང་ཀ, ཉང་གེ *nyáṅ-ka, nyáṅ-ge Sp.* **currant,** Ribes.

ཉན་ཏི *nyán-ti Pur.* **thy, your** (?).

ཉན་པ་ *nyán-pa* (*nyán-to, nyán-tam*), imp. *nyon* 1. (also, though seldom, *mnyán-pa*) c. dat. or accus. **to hear,** to give ear to, **to listen** (cf. *tos-pa*); *slób-dpon-gyi tád-du čos nyán-pa* to attend to the religious instruction of the teacher; *ṅag* or *tsig nyán-pa Dzl.*, *ḱá-la*, or resp. *žál-la*, or *bka-nyán-pa* to obey, to yield; *ṅas ǰi-ltar zér-pai ḱá-la nyán-na Glr.*, *ṅa zer nyán-na Mil.* if you listen to my word; *Tar.* 14, 14; 17, 16 c.c. *las.* — 2. **to listen secretly,** to be an eaves-dropper, **pag-nyęn ǰhe-pa** *C.*, **pag-nyán čó-če, táṅ-če** *W.*, id.; *nyán-mḱan* col. *nyán(-pa)-po*, fem. *nyan(-pa)-mo, B.*, a hearer, auditor; *nyan-tós* id.; but esp of the personal disciples of Buddha, the Sravakas. *Köpp.* I., 419; *Burn.* I., 296; *nyan-tós bču-drúg* the sixteen *γnas-brtán* q.v.; *nyan-tós-ma* a female hearer; *ḱa-la nyán-po, nyán-mḱan* obedient, *ḱá-la mi nyán-po* disobedient. — 3. **to be able,** later *B.*, and col., gen. with a negative: *ₒgró ma nyán-pas* not being able to walk (on account of illness) *Mil.*; also like *ma btúb-pa* not being willing; without a negative: **nyán yin** *W.* yes, I shall be able; inst. of *rúṅ-ba*: **za-nyán yód-na ḱyoṅ** *W.*, bring it me, if it is still eatable.

ཉམ་ *nyam*, also *nyam-tig, nyam-yós* **cricket, locust** *Sik.*

ཉམ(ས)་ *nyam(s)*, resp. *tugs, tugs-nyám(s)* 1. **soul, mind,** *nyáms-kyi grogs* companions of the soul, viz. the murmuring springs and rivulets in the solitude of alpine regions *Mil.*; *nyáms-kyi čaṅ* the soul's wine, i.e. religious knowledge *Mil.*; *nyams dgá-ba* 1. well being, comfort, cheerfulness, *nyams mi-dgá-ba* an unhappy state, discomfort, *nyams-dgá glú-ru bloṅs* sing a song of joy! *Mil.* 2. gen. adj.: agreeable, delightful, charming, *nyáms-dga-bai sa-γnás* a charming country *Glr.*. — 2. **thought,** *nyams skye* or *śar* a thought rises. — 3. **strength, magnitude, height, state, manner,** *nyams-(kyi) tsád byéd-pa Pth.* (also with *bčád-pa* or *lén-pa C.*) to try, to put to the test, e.g. one's strength; *tugs-dám-gyi nyams sád-pa* to try the degree of a person's devotion or spiritual progress *Mil.*; *smra-nyáms, byed-nyáms* manner, — and particularly a pleasing, agreeable manner, — of speaking or dealing.

Other phrases are: *nyáms-su lén-pa* to take to heart, to interest one's self in or for a thing *Dzl.*, to commit to memory, to learn (v. below); *nyáms-su myóṅ-ba* to suffer, undergo, experience *Dzl.*; *nyams ṅá-ba* v. the compounds; *nyams bčád-pa C.* to try, to examine; *nyams ₒbrú-ba C.* to irritate, provoke, vex; *nyams myóṅ-ba* = *nyáms-su myóṅ-ba*; *nyams bžág-pa* is said to be = *drán-pa ṇyé-bar bžág-pa*, v. *nyé-ba*; *nyams lén-pa* 1. = *nyáms-su lén-pa*, v above, 2. col. to measure out, to take the measure, the dimensions of, to survey, *sa* land, *nor* the property, to take an inventory, to ascertain or compute the state of one's property, 3. *C.* = the following; *nyams sád-pa* ccg. 1. to try, to test, *byéd-dam mi byed* whether he will do it or not *Mil.*, to tempt, *tugs-dám-gyi nyams sád-pa* v. above. 2. to mock, scoff, trouble maliciously, provoke, irritate *C.*

Comp. *nyams-dgú* v. *nyams-tábs.* — *nyams-rgyúd Mil.* = *nyams, nyams-rgyúd-la sbyáṅs-pa*, intellectually skilled, well versed. — *nyams-ṅá* **anxiety, fear, dread,** of a thing, with the dat. or instr. *Mil.*; *nyams-ṅá-las tár-ba* to be delivered from anxiety *S.g.*; *nyams-ṅá-ba* vb. to be alarmed, to be in great anxiety *Sch.*; adj. dreadful, horrible, *nags-tsál nyams-ṅa-ba* a horrible forest *Dzl.* — *nyams-bčág* is said to be used resp. or euphem. for *skyon*, e.g. for damage done to an image of a god by water *C.*; *nyams-čágs* sin *Schr.*; in *Thgr.* it seems to be used in this sense. — *nyáms-čún* 1. **faint, weak, languid, exhausted,** by hunger, illness etc. *Dzl.*; **poor** in learning, destitute of knowledge, ignorant *W.*; destitute of money, destitute of virtue *C.* 2. *W.* col. for *snyems-čún.* — *nyams-rtógs* resp. **knowledge, cognition, perception,** *nyams-rtógs šig yod, nyams-rtógs bzáṅ-po skye* or *ˏkruṅs*, a perception, a good thought arises (in my mind); in a general sense: *nyams-rtógs-kyi mtar pyín-pa* to obtain perfect knowledge *Mil.*, frq. — *nyams-stóbs* **strength,** *zin* is gone *Med.* — *nyams-stoṅ-ysál* v. *ysál-po.* — *nyams-brtás byed-pa* **strengthening, restorative, nourishing** *Med.*, (but *nyams-brtas* he recovered, grew well, got up again *Dzl.*) — *nyams-tág-pa* **suffering, tormented, exhausted** *Dzl.*; *nyams-tág-pai skad* or *sgra* lamentation, doleful cries. — *nyams-tábs, nyams-dgú Sch.*: 'appearance, colour, figure, state' (?). — *nyams-myóṅ Tar.* **enjoyment, delight,** *nyams-myóṅ ma skyes ruṅ*, although I had no real enjoyment of it *Mil.nt.*; *tsór-bai nyams-myóṅ* prob. perception by the senses, knowledge acquired through the medium of the senses *Mil.* — *nyams-rtsál* *Dzl.* ༧༠, 7 **skill.** — *nyams-mtsár-ba C.* **wonderful,** most beautiful. — *nyams-lén* a memorial verse, a rhyme or verse serving to retain things in memory *Mil.*

ཉམས་པ་ *nyáms-pa* **injured, hurt,** e.g., by a fall *Dzl.*; of lifeless things: **spoiled, damaged** *C.*; **impaired, imperfect,** *stobs-nyams, dbáṅ-po nyáms-pa, yán-lag nyams Lex.* (as explanation of *žá-bo*); *smra-nyáms* (the sick person) speaks little *Med.*; **sem-nyám sóṅ-kan* W.* discouraged, disheartened; esp. relative to a violation of duty, failing in, *tsúl-krims* (or *tsúl-las*) *nyáms-pas* because he has failed in, acted against the moral law *Dzl.*; *bzód-pa nyáms-par ˏgyúr-bas* because their patience failed *Dzl.*; also **stained** *Glr.*, e.g. *krág-gis* with blood; *nyáms-par byéd-pa Wdṅ.*; *nyáms-su ˏjúg-pa Glr.* to spoil, deteriorate, destroy; *ma nyáms-pa* entire, complete, untouched, uncorrupted.

ཉར་ *nyar* 1. v. *nya-ra.* — 2. *Cs.*, also *nyar-nyár*, **oblong.**

ཉར་གདོང་ *nyár-ydóṅ W.* inst. of *ṅar-ydóṅ*, **shin, shin-bone.**

ཉལ་ཉིལ་ *nyal-nyil*, or *nyal-nyól* **filth, dirt,** foul matter, loose and dry dirt that may be removed by sweeping *Pth.*, *Dzl.*

ཉལ་བ་ *nyál-ba*, imp. *nyol*, 1. **to lie down,** e.g. before a tigress *Dzl.*; to lie down, **to sleep,** *nyal(-du) soṅ* (he) went to bed *Glr.*; *rgya-sráṅ-la nyal ˏdúg-go* (he) slept in the street *Glr.*; *mi nyal tsám-la* when people go to bed, at curfew *Mil.*; *rta nyal byéd-pa* to make a horse lie down *Glr.*; rarely of things: *rtsva nyal* the grass is laid-down (by the wind or rain) *Dzl.*; *ra ˏog nyál-bai nya* so *Zam.* calls the letter *rnya*; fig. to rest, *bdé-bar nyál-du méd-do* (he) had no rest, viz. from envy *Dzl.* ༧༢, 12. — 2. with *daṅ* or *la*, **to lie with** (a woman) *Dzl.* and elsewh. — 3. fig. **to dwell, to live** *Mil.*

Comp. *ṅyal-kri* **couch, bed, sofa** *C.* — *nyal-gós* **counterpane, quilt, blanket** *Sch.* — *nyál-po* **coition,** *nyál-po byéd-pa* to practise cohabitation, *máṅ-du* immoderately *Med.* —

nyál-bu bastard, whoreson *Ma.* — *nyál-sa* sleeping-place.

ཉི *nyi* 1. num. fig.: 38. — 2. num. inst. of *ɣnyis* in compounds, *nyi-brgyá*, *-stóṅ*, *-k̔ri* etc., *nyi-k̔ri* also title of a book, the Prajna Paramitā, containing 28 000 Sloka. — 3. for *nyi-ma*.

ཉི་ཁུད *nyi-k̔ud* a lake in Nepal *Pth.*

ཉི་མ *nyi-ma* (*Bal.* **nyó-ma**, 1. **the sun,** *˳čar* becomes visible, rises; *šar* id., also: has risen, shines; *nub*, *rgas*, *W.* also **skyod, bud**, sets, is setting; *nyi-ma nub ts̔e bar* (for *ts̔eí bár-du*) until sun-set *Sch.*; *nyi-mai ɣnyen.* akin to the sun, the Sākya race *Cs.*; **da nyi-ma riṅ-mo* W.* now the sun stands already high in the heavens; **nyi-mia-gaṅ-šár** sun-flower, Helianthus. — 2. **day,** = *nyin-mo*, opp. to night, frq.; **nyi-ma-ts̔e* W.* the whole day, all day long; **nyi-ma-p̔ed* W.* noon, mid-day; *nyi-ma ɣčig* one day, once *Dzl.*: *nyi-ma-re-rér* daily.

Comp. *nyi-dkyil* **disk of the sun** *Sch.* — *nyi-gúṅ*, *nyi-mai guṅ* **noon, mid-day;** meridian(?) *Cs.* — *nyi-dgá* seems to be the n. of a medicinal herb *Med.* — *nyi-rgás* **sun-set.** — *nyi-ldóg* **the solstice,** *dgún-nyi-ldog* winter solstice, *dbyár-nyi-ldog* summer solstice *Wdk.* — *nyi-núb* = *nyi-rgás.* — *nyi-ts̔é* 1. *Sch.*: the time or duration of one day. 2. *Lex.*: = प्रदेश direction, place, country(?); *nyi-ts̔é spyód-pa Lex.*: a kind of ascetic; *nyi-ts̔é-ba Sch.*: ephemeral; single, simple; *Thgy.*: n. of a class of infernal beings. — *nyi-ts̔ód* **sun-dial,** *nyi-ts̔ód-kyi k̔ór-lo* the circle of a sun-dial *Cs.* — *nyi-˳dzín* **eclipse** of the sun (cf. *sgra-ɣčán*). — *nyi-zér* **sun-beam,** *nyi-zér rtá-la žón-nas* riding on a sun-beam *Mil.* and elsewh.; *nyi-zér-gyi rdul* a mote floating in a sun-beam. — *nyi-zlá* sun and moon; also the figures of sun and moon connected, crowning the top of the *mč̔od-rtén*; *nyi-zlá bsdad mi oṅ* sun and moon will not stand still *Mil.* — *nyi-˳óg* below the sun; the earth *Was.* (49); *nyi-˳óg-gi rgyal-k̔ams Glr.* id.; it seems, however, to denote a certain country, acc. to Mahāvyutpatti the same as Aparāntaka, *Williams*: the western country; cf. *Schf.* on *Tar.* ༧༣. — *nyi-˳od* **sun-shine.** — *nyi-yól* any **screen** or **shelter** from the sun's rays: awning, curtain, parasol, pent-house *Sch.*; **nyi-rib** (prop. *sgrib*) *W.* id., umbrella. — *nyi-šár* **sun-rise** *Cs.* — *nyi-lhag Sch.* a cold day (?) — Cf. *nyin-mo.*

ཉི་ཤུ *nyi-šu* (inst. of *nyis-ču*), often in conjunction with *t̔ám-pa*, **twenty,** *nyi-šu-rtsa-ɣčig B.*, *C.*, **nyi-šu-nyer-ɣčig* W.*, *nyer-ɣčig*, twentyone.

ཉིག་ཉིག *nyig-nyig W.* **loose, slack, lax,** not tight or tense.

ཉིང་ཁུ *nyiṅ-k̔u*, *Ssk.* मज्ज *Cs.*: 'heart, spirit, essence', cf. *snyiṅ-po.*

ཉིང་ཏོ *nyiṅ-to Sch.*: **sure, trustworthy,** *Lex.*: *nyiṅ-tor* = *ṅes-par.*

ཉིང་ལག *nyiṅ-lag*, a category not familiar to us; gen. mentioned together with *yán-lag*; it might be translated by: members of a second order, parts of the *yán-lag*; the exact meaning must however remain undetermined, as the Tibetans themselves are not able to give a clear definition of it. In *C.*: inner parts of the body, opp. to outer. In books, phrases like the following are to be found: *yán-lag daṅ nyiṅ-lag t̔ams-čád daṅ ldán-pa*; *yán-lag daṅ nyiṅ-lag ná-ba*; *yán-lag daṅ nyiṅ-lag ɣčód-pa*; evidently the *nyiṅ-lag* are smaller, but more numerous than the *yán-lag*. In *Pth.* also *nyiṅ-sprúl* is found besides *yaṅ-sprúl*, emanation of the third order; v. *sprúl-pa.*

ཉིང་མཚམས་སྦྱོར་བ *nyiṅ-mtsáms sbyór-ba* **to be re-born** *Stg.*

ཉིད *nyid* 1. **self, same,** opp. to other persons, *ma nyid* the mother herself *Dzl.*; *mi de ni rgyál-po nyid yin-no* this man are you yourself, o king! *Dzl.*; the very, just he, just it etc., *las byéd-pai ɣnas nyid-la* just where I am working *Dzl.*; *deí druṅ-nyid-na* (or *du*) close by, to, or before, hard by, *Thgy.*; *dus de-nyid-du* at the very moment, frq.; *mč̔ód-bya nyid* that which is venerable par excellence *Tar.* 15, 13; *yón-*

tan nyid Tar. 15, 14 id.; dé-nas mi riṅ-ba-nyid-na a very short time after Tar.; when added to adjectives it denotes abstract nouns, as in English the terminations: -ness, -ship, -ty, -cy, -y etc., but it is chiefly limited to the language of philosophical writings, from which a few expressions only (such as *stoṅ-pa-nyid* the emptiness, the Buddhist vacuum) have found their way into col. language. — 2. In the more recent literature it is used resp. for *k̓yod*, **thou, you**; *nyid-kyi* **thy, your** *Pth.*, *Ma.*; *nyid-ráṅ* **you** (col. **nyi-ráṅ, nyo-ráṅ**) *W.*, *C.*, resp., like the German '*Sie*'; *nyid-čag(-raṅ)* **you**, addressed to one person or to several, *C.* (in *Glr. k̓yed-čag* seems to be used in the same way). — 3. **only**, *grańs-kyi lṅa nyid Zam.* only the numeral *lṅa*; *za nyid-do* the letter *za* alone (without a prefix).

ཉིན(མོ) *nyin(-mo)* 1. **day**, = *nyí-ma* 2; *nyin-gyi riṅ-la* during the day-time *Pth.*; *nyin-mor ˌgyur* it dawns *Cs.*; *nyin-mor byed* 'making day', an epithet of the sun *Cs.*; *nyin* adv. in the day-time *Glr.*; *nyin-čig* one day, once *Dzl.*; *nyin čig bžin-du* daily *Dzl.*; *nyin-par* during the day-time *Dzl.*; by day-light *Dzl.*; *deĩ nyin-par* on that day, frq. *Dzl.*; *p̓yir nyin, p̓yi de nyin, deĩ p̓yi nyin* the following day, on the f.d. *Dzl.*; *tses bčo-lṅái nyin* the 15th., on the 15th. *Glr.*; fig.: *bstán-pa nyín-par mdzád-pai skyés-bu* a saint that restores the doctrine, a reformer of faith; hence *Schr.*: *dád-pai nyin-byed* evangelist, apostle. — 2. **propitious day**; **ṅa ča nyin-mo mi ˌdug** *W.* this day is not propitious for me to go.

Comp. *nyin-dkár* a white, a **lucky day** *Sch.* — *nyin-gáṅ, nyin-t̓og-t̓ág* (*W.* **t̓ag-t̓og**) all the day long. — *nyin-gúṅ* **noon.** — *nyin-gla* daily pay, a day's hire *Cs.* — **nyin-tse-ré** *W.* all the day long, the live-long day. — *nyin-mtsán* 1. **a day and a night**, *nyin-mtsán bčo-brgyád Mil.* for nine days and nine nights. 2. **day and night** *Dzl.*, *nyin-mtsan-méd-par* id., frq.; *nyin-med-tsán-med W.* id.; *nyin-mtsán-du* id. *Mil.*; *nyin-mtsán mnyám-pa* equinox. — *nyin-žág(-γčig)* 1. a day with the night, 24 hours, divided into 12 portions of time, called *k̓yim* (q. v.): *nam-p̓yéd* midnight, *nam-p̓yed-yól* 2 o'clock a. m., *t̓o-ráṅs* 4 o'cl. a. m. (in popular language also: **ˌjá-po dáṅ-po** about 2 o'cl., **nyís-pa** 3 o'cl., **súm-pa** 4 o'cl., *nam-laṅs* 6 o'cl a. m. (i. e. the time when the sun first illumines the mountain tops; it is from this moment, and not from midnight, that in daily life the date is counted); *nyi-šár* 8 o'cl. a. m. (when the sun rises upon the valley); *dros-ˌjám* (col. **nyi-ḍúl**) 10 o'cl. a. m.; *nyin-gúṅ, nyi-p̓yéd* 12 o'cl., noon; *p̓yed-čól* (*W.* **zá-ra p̓i-mo**) 2 o'cl. p. m., *myur-smád* 4 o'cl. p. m., *nyi-rgás* 6 o'cl. p. m., *srod-ˌk̓ór* 8 o'cl. p. m. (col. **sa-rúb, srod-rúb**), *srod-čól* 10 o'cl. p. m. (col. **tiṅ-nyi**) — thus acc. to *Wdk.* By adding the names of the 12 years' cycle (*nam-p̓yéd byi-ba, p̓yed-čól glaṅ* etc., v. the word *lo*), these terms have been rendered still more convenient for astrological calculations. Of course, all the terms given are strictly correct only at the time of the equinoxes, and deviate at the summer and winter solstices for more than an hour from the time indicated by our clocks. 2. *nyin-žág* as symb. num.: 15. — *nyin-bžin-gyis Pth.*, *nyin-ré bžin Glr.*, daily adv., with *-gyi* adj. — *nyin-lám* a day's journey *Glr.*, *rkaṅ-t̓áṅ-gi, rtá-pai, lúg-pai nyin-lam* a pedestrian's, a horseman's, a sheep-driver's daily march. — *nyin-ráṅs Tar.* (= *t̓o-ráṅs*) day-break, morning twilight *Schf.*

ཉིབ་ཕྱོགས *nyib-p̓yógs*, *W.* **nyib-čóg(s)** the sunny side of mountains.

ཉིལ་བ *nyil-ba* **to decay**, to crumble to pieces, of rocks, mountains etc.; rarely to run down, of tears, to flow down, of locks of hair.

ཉིས *nyis* 1. instrum. of *nyi*. — 2. in compounds for *γnis*.

ཉུ *nyu* num. fig.: 68.

ཉུ་ཏི *nyú-ti* **pear** *Ld.*

ཉུག་པ་ *nyúg-pa* 1. **to besmear,** *spos* to perfume; **to rub gently, to stroke, to caress** *Sch.*, in this sense perh. *Gyatch* ༢༧, 14. — 2. **to touch,** = *rég-pa* ccd. *W.*; *C.*? — 3. **to search after** (feeling, groping) *Cs.* — 4. **to put out, stretch out,** *ču-nas mgo* one's head out of the water, to look or **peep out,** resp. *dbu nyug mdzád-pa Glr.*; *nyug-nyúg-pa Tar.* 80, 21 **to stand out, to project** (*Sch.*: to run to and fro?).

ཉུག་རྩ་མེ་ཏོག་ *nyúg-rtsa mé-tog* **Carthusian pink** *C.*

ཉུག་རུམ་, ཉུང་རུམ་ *nyug-rúm, nyuṅ-rúm* **a eunuch** *Dzl.*

ཉུང་བ་ *nyúṅ-ba* 1. adj. col. **nyúṅ-ṅu**, **little;** **nyuṅ-ṅu žig**, *Ld.* col. **nyúṅ-ṅa-rig**, *nyúṅ-zad čig* id. *Dzl.*; *nyuṅ-šás Wdṅ.*, **a little, a few, some;** *nyúṅ-bar byéd-pa* to make less *Cs.* — 2. vb. **to be little.**

ཉུང་མ་ *nyúṅ-ma* **turnip,** *la(-pug daṅ) nyuṅ (-ma)* radishes and turnips *Glr.* — *nyúṅ-ku, nyúṅ-loi ǰa* turnip-soup, turnip-tea, an infusion of dried turnip leaves, much used, e.g. in Bhotan, and considered very nourishing(?). **nyuṅ-dó** *C.*, mentioned by *Wts.* p. 137. as 'navets ronds', large sweet, red turnips (perh. turnip-rooted cabbage?). — *nyuṅ-γži* seed-turnips (*Cs.* turnip-seed). — *nyúṅ-lo* a turnip leaf.

Note. In writing and speaking this word is often confounded with *yuṅ(s)* mustard, so that e.g. *yúṅ-ma* is said for turnip inst. of *nyúṅ-ma*, *nyuṅs-dkár* for white mustard, inst. of *yuṅs-dkár.*

ཉུང་རུམ་ *nyuṅ-rúm* v *nyug-rúm.*

ཉུལ་བ་ *nyúl-ba* **to wander** or **rove about, to pass privily** or **steal** through, e.g. towns, countries, mountains *Mil.*, burying-places, tombs (as jackals) *Mil.*; (*lta*) *nyúl-pa, nyúl-mi Pth.*, *sa-nyúl* a spy *Cs.* (Also *γnyúl-ba, myúl-ba.*)

ཉེ *nye* num. fig.: 98.

ཉེ་ཏི *nyé-ṭi* a pear *Schr.* (cf. *nyú-ti, nyó-ti*).

ཉེ་བ་ *nyé-ba* I. vb., **to be near, to approach,** always with the supine of a verb, *dus byéd-du nyé-bas* when he was near dying *Dzl.*; *zlá-ba ṫsáṅ-du nyé-bas* (when she was) near the completion of the months, i e. the time of giving birth to a child *Dzl.*, frq.; *slób-dpon p̓yir ˏóṅ-du nyé-bas* when the time of the teacher's return drew near *Dzl.*; *zín-du mi nyé-ste* being not near having done *Dzl.*; even used as follows: *γnas der sléb-tu nyé-bai ṫse* when he came near the place *Mil.*

II. adj., col. **nyé-mo** **near,** both as to space and time, *lam-riṅ-gi γnyén-pas k̓yim-mṫses nye* the neighbour is nearer than a kinsman living far off; *ká-ba daṅ nyé-bai sar* at a place near the pillar *Glr.*; *ṫag-nyé-ba* id.: *ri ṫag-nyé-ba žig* a near or neighbouring hill *Ma.*; standing near, fig. being closely connected with by consanguinity: *nyé-ba-rnams C.* relations, kindred (*Dzl.* ༢༠, 13 *γnyén-pas* prob. is preferable to *mo nyé-bas*); allied by similarity: *mṫsáms-med-pa lṅa daṅ de daṅ nyé-bai sdig-pa* the five worst sins, and those coming nearest to them; near by friendship and affection: **nyé-mo yin** *W.* he is closely connected with us, he is desirous to enter into an intimate connection with us; *blo*, or *snyiṅ*, or *sems nyé-ba* (or **nyé-mo**), friendly, kind, amicable, *blo nyé-ba ltar byéd-pa* to affect a friendly manner *Glr.*; **nyé-mo ǰhé-pa** *C.* to love, e.g. parents loving their children or vice versâ; *nyé-bai sras brgyad Glr.* the eight intimate disciples (of Buddha, not historical, but mythical persons, Mandshusri etc.).

III. adv. *nyé-bar* or *nyer* 1. **near,** *daṅ* to, *dé-dag daṅ nyé-bar lhá-k̓aṅ bžens* near to them he built a temple *Tar.*; *nyé-bar ˏóṅ-ba, sléb-pa,* to come near, to approach; *nyé-bar ˏgyúr-ba* id., *stóṅs-su nyé-bar ˏgyúr-ba daṅ* when it was nearly empty *Pth.*; *dár-la nyé-bar gyúr-to* it began to spread, to extend itself *Pth.*; *nyé-bar γnás-pa* to be near, to stand near, e.g. of a star *Wdṅ.* — 2. *nyé-bar byéd-pa,* with la, **to adhere to, to keep** (one's promise) *Pth.* — 3. *nyé-bar bžág-pa* **to make use of, to employ,** *drán-pa nyé-bar bžág-pa* (स्मृत्युपस्थान, *Burn.* I.,

626. उप near, though Tibetan dictionaries write उप) to make use of one's intellectual powers. To do this rightly forms part of Buddhist wisdom (v. *Köpp*. I, 436) and instruction (*Dzl.* ༡༢༣, 7, where *Sch.*'s version is incorr.), being divided into four divisions or degrees (*Burn.*); *sańs-rgyás-la dkón-pai ₒdu-šés nyé-bar bžág-pa* to apply to Buddha the notion of rareness *Tar.* 5, 13. — 4. **intensely, urgently, speedily,** *ₒjigs-pa nyé-bar ži* fear is speedily allayed *Glr.*; *nad nyé-bar ₒtso* the disease is speedily cured *Thgy.*; *nyé-bar lén-pa Mil.*, *Thgy.* to seize eagerly, to strive for earnestly, to aspire to, esp. to the re-birth as a human being; cf. also *nyer-lén*; *nyé-bar mk'ó-ba* of urgent necessity, frq. *Tar. nyer ₒpel* it increases rapidly *Med.*

IV. sbst. v. *nyé-šiń.*

Comp. *nye-skór Sch. nye-ₒk'ór* **those about us,** the company around us, *k'yed-rán-gi nye-k'ór-gyi ldóm-bu-ba* a beggar belonging to the people around you *Mil.*; esp. relations, kindred, *des nye-k'ór yań šúgs-kyis yoń* in this way family-connections are formed of themselves *Mil.* — *nye-mk'ón = nye-rin Cs.* (?) — *nye-grógs* **neighbour, fellow-creature** *Cs.* — *nye-č'ár* **now** *Sch.* — *nyé-dag Cs., nyé-du,* and most frq. *nye-ₒbrél* (*ŷnyen-ₒbrél*) **kindred, relations** (these being considered a main obstacle to moral perfection, they are to be shunned accordingly). — *nye-ŷnás* **disciple,** *kyéd-kyi nye-ŷnás bgyio, nye-ŷnás-su mčio* I wish to become your disciple *Dzl.* — *nye-tsán, nye-rigs* **relative, kinsman.** — *nye-rín* 1. **near and far,** near and distant relations. 2. **distance,** *sgor nye-rín či-tsam yod* how far is it from here to the gate? 3. **partial,** *rgyál-po nye-rín č'es* the king is very partial *Glr.*, *nye-rin-méd-pa* impartial *Glr.* — *nye-lám* **near; now** *Sch.*

ཉེ་ཞོ *nye-žo* **damage, mishap, accident** (syn. to *bar-č'ad*), *nye-žo-méd-par* without an accident, safely *Dzl.*

ཉེ་རེག་པ *nye-rég-pa Lexx.* **to wash.**

ཉེ་ཤིང་ *nyé-šiń*, or *nyé-bai šiń Med.*, a tree the fruits of which are used as a sweet medicine.

ཉེག་མ, ཉེག་ཕྲག *nyég-ma, nyeg-t'ág*, v. *nyág-ma.*

ཉེད་པ *nyéd-pa* = *mnyéd-pa.*

ཉེན་ *nyen* 1. = *nye, ngen-k'ór*, or *nyen-skór* = *nye-ₒk'or* **a relative,** *Pth.*: *nyen-k'ór žig yin* he is a kinsman; also alone, like *ŷnyen.* — 2. with a vb.: **danger, risk,** *myúr-du ₒjig-nyen yod* there is a danger of its being soon destroyed *Glr.*; *dmyál-bar ₒgro-nyén ŷda* there is a danger of going to hell; *sróg-gi bar-č'ád-du ₒgró-bai nyen yod Mil.* of risking one's life; *°dúń-nyen° C.* he has the chance of receiving a good beating; occasionally also: to be near, to impend, in reference to happy events; in col. language it is simply used for danger, *nyén-čan* dangerous, e.g. *lam, las, sbrul* etc.

ཉེན་པ *nyén-pa*, pf. *nyén-to*, **to be pained, pinched, pressed** hard, e.g. by hunger, cold, enemies; **to toil and moil, to labour hard, to drudge;** v. *bań.*

ཉེར་ *nyer* 1. = *nyé-bar.* — 2. v. *nyi-šu.*

ཉེར་སྣོགས *nyer-snógs Thgy.*, **theme, task** *Sch.*

ཉེར་ཉེར་ *nyer-nyér, nyer-že*; *W.* **dregs, sediment.**

ཉེར་བ *nyér-ba* 1. *Sch.* **to tan, curry, dress,** make soft. — 2. *W.*, also *°nyer-kád tán-če°*, **to snarl, growl.** — 3. *W.* **to tarry, stay, linger** (*snyér-ba* for *bsnár-ba?*).

ཉེར་མ *nyér-ma W.* for *ŷyér-ma*, **red pepper.**

ཉེར་ལེན *nyer-lén*, or *nyé-bar lén-pa*, is said to be = *rgyui rgyu*, original cause.

ཉེལ་བ *nyél-ba* taken **ill, sick** *Sch.*

ཉེས་པ *nyés-pa* I. sbst. any thing **wrong** or **noxious,** or liable to become so, and the consequences of it; hence 1. **evil, calamity, damage,** *nyés-pa t'ams-čád deï lús-la ₒduo* all sorts of plagues are collecting upon his body *Dzl.*; *lo-nyés* a bad harvest, failure of crops, *lo-nyés byúń-bai tse* when the harvest had been bad; in a special sense in medicine: the three **humours** of the body, air (v. *rlun*), bile, and phlegm, gen. called त्रिदोष *γnod-byéd nyés-pa γsum* the three noxious matters (most diseases being ascribed to a derangement of one of them). — 2. **moral fault, offence, sin, crime,** *nyés-pai skyon*, being contaminated by a crime *Dzl.*; *lus dan nág-gi* (or *kai*) *nyés-pa* sin in word and deed *Dzl.*; *nyés-pa byéd-pa* to commit a fault, a crime; to sin, frq.; also: *mi žig-la nyés-pa byun* a slip has occurred to a person *Dzl.*; *bdág-la nyés-pa či žig yód-de ma γnan* what crime have I committed, that you will not give me permission? *Dzl.* — 3. **punishment** *C.* **nyē-miy** id., resp. **ka-nyē*; *nye-pa pog-kan** he that has got a punishment.

II. vb. **to commit an offence,** *ₒdis či nyés-te bzun* what offence has he committed that he is taken prisoner? *Dzl.* (cf. above); *snón-čad bdág-gis nyés-pa bden* it is true that formerly I committed a fault *Dzl.*; *snár ma sbrán-pa nyés-so* the not reporting sooner was a fault *Dzl.*; *γyógs-pa nyés-so* you have committed a fault by covering... *Dzl.*; *bdag nyés-na* if harm is done to me; hence *či nyés* in a general sense: *kyod či nyés-pa smros šig* tell me what has happened to you *Dzl.*; *btsón-na či nyés* quid mali, si vendideris? *Dzl.*; *mi drán-nam či nyes* is she out of her senses, or, what is the matter with her? *Dzl.*; *či nyés-na* why, *či nyés-na kán-pai nán-na rdzin-bu bkyil* why is there a pond within the house? *Dzl.*; *ma nyés-pai ₒgró-ba* innocent beings *Mil.*; *ma nyés-pa pyir byun* he came out again unhurt *Dzl.*; *nyés-byas* a wicked action, a sin *Cs.*; *nyés-ltun* sin, sinful deed, trespass, *nyés-ltun-gis pog* he has been overtaken by a sin *Mil.*

ཉོ *nyo* 1. num. fig.: 128. — 2. **carrot** *Cs.*

ཉོ་ཏི *nyo-ti* **a pear** *Ld.*

ཉོ་བ *nyó-ba*, pf. and imp. *nyos*, 1. **to buy,** *dnul brgyas* for a hundred rupees; *nyó-(ba-)po* a buyer, purchaser, *nyo-(ba-)mo* fem.; *nyó-mkan* a buyer, customer; *nyó-to* account, bill; *nyo-ₒtsón* commerce, traffic; *nyo-ₒtsón byéd-pa* to trade. — 2. **to take at rent, to take the lease** (of a field, by buying the crop).

ཉོག་པ *nyóg-pa* **soiled, dirtied,** made unclean, e.g. of victuals *Mil.*; *nyóg-ma Sch.*, *ču-nyóg Lex.* muddy, foul water; *nyog-nyóg-po* confused (story) *Tar.*

ཉོགས་བྱིང *nyogs-byin Sch.*: **too soft;** *nyog-nyón Sch.* **soft, tender, weak,** inclined to weep; **šés-nyog-čan** (for *γšés-nyog-čan*) dandling, fondling *W.*

ཉོད་པ *nyód-pa* **food** *Lex.*

ཉོན་མོངས་པ *nyon-móns-pa* (seldom without *-pa*), *Ssk.* क्लेश 1. **misery, trouble, pain,** frq.; also used as a verb: *nyon-móns-šin*; *tsá-bas nyon-móns-te* molested by the heat *Dzl.*; *nyon-móns-par ₒgyúr-ba* to get into trouble *Dzl.*; *nyon ma móns-sam* had you to experience any hardship? *Dzl.* — 2. in a restricted sense: **the misery of sin,** *nyon-móns-pa-las pan-pai don med* this does not avail for being delivered from such misery *Dzl.*; **sin,** *nyon-móns-pai nad, dri-ma Dzl.*; *sér-sna-la sógs-pai nyon-móns-pa* avarice and other sins *S.O.*; *nyon-móns-pa-méd-pa* free from sin, sinless *S.O.*; *nyon-móns-čan-gyis nyá-ša nyos Zam.* the offender buys the flesh of a fish.

ཉོབ་ཉོབ *nyob-nyób* weak, feeble-minded *Sch.*

ཉོར *nyor* 1. v. *nyó-ba*. 2. **a rectangle** *Cs.*

ཉོལ *nyol*, imp. of *nyál-ba*; *nyól-ba* prov. for *nyál-ba*.

ཉོས *nyos*, imp. of *nyó-ba*; *nyos-mi* a slave *Cs.*

གཉང་བ *γnyán-ba Sch.*, prob. = *rnyán-ba*.

གཉན *γnyan* 1. a pestilential disease, epidemic, or contagious disorder, **plague,** *mdze dan ₒbrum-bu γnyan Ma.*; *γnyan-nád* id.; *γnyan-dúg* a poison against, or a remedy for the plague *Med.*; *dka-γnyán* a destructive plague *Sch.* — 2. a species of wild sheep, **argali** (Ovis ammon).

གཉན་པ་ γnyán-pa **cruel, fierce, severe,** *lha γnyán-rnams Glr.* gods of vengeance, deities of terror; *klu-γnyán* id.; *k̔rims γnyán-pa* a cruel commandment, frq.; *dam-tsig γnyán-pa* prob. a rigid vow, a solemn oath *Mil.*; of mountains: **wild, rugged, precipitous;** *γnyán-sa* a rugged country *Mil.*; in *γnyán-pai γnad* (v. *γnad*) prob.: dangerous. — *γnyán-po* sbst. *Mil.?*

གཉའ་(བ) *γnya(-ba)* 1. **neck, nape,** *γnyá-ba brtuṅs* the neck is contracted or shortened *Med.* — *γnyá-ko* hide, or leather of a beast's neck *Cs.* — *γnya-k̔óbs* screen of the neck (attached to a helmet) *Sch.* — *γnya-rgyáb* (?) *C.* breast-work, parapet. — *γnya-rtsé* vertebra prominens, the cervical vertebra with its projecting process *Mil.* — *γnya-tsígs* cervical joint. — *γnya-réṅs* stiff neck, *γnya-réṅs-čan* 1. having a stiff neck; 2. stiffnecked, obstinate. — *γnya-šíṅ* a yoke (for oxen) *Glr.*, *Lex.* — 2. *skad-γnyá* v. *skad.*

གཉའ་ནང་ *γnya-náṅ*, or *snya-náṅ*, a village on the frontier of Nepal

གཉའ་བོ་ *γnyá-bo* **a witness,** one that gives evidence *Cs.*, *Lex.* = *dpáṅ-po*; *γnyá-bo byéd-pa* to pledge for, to be surety for; *Dzl.* ༢༣༠: *bskyi-γnyá byas*, *Sch.*: 'he made an attested loan'.

གཉི་ག *γnyi-ga* for *γnyis-ka Stg.*; *γnyi-zér* for *nyi-zér Lex.*

གཉིག་ཏུ *γnyig-tu Lex.* = *γčig-tu.*

གཉིད་ *γnyid*, resp. *mnal*, **sleep,** *γnyid-du ₒgró-ba* to fall asleep *Glr.*, *Mil.*; *W.* *nyid ma yoṅ* sleep has not come, I am sleepless; *nyid ma k̔ug, nyid k̔ug ma nyan*, also *nyid saṅ soṅ* id.; *γnyid mi t̔ub* he cannot find sleep *Med.*; *γnyid-t̔úm-pa* one uninterrupted portion of sleep *Glr.*; *γnyid mt̔úg-pa* a sound sleep, *γnyid-sráb* a light sleep, a slumber *Med.* — *γnyid-log-pa* (prop. *γnyid-kyis lóg-pa*) *Dzl.* to fall asleep, *Dzl.* ༢༠༢, 16; ༢༩༨, 9 (thus correctly translated already by *Schr.*), prob. also to sleep; *γnyid-la ₒgro-ba*, *W.* *ča-čé*, to fall asleep; *γnyid t̔úg-por soṅ* he fell into a deep sleep *Mil.*; *da-rúṅ γnyid ma lŏg-mk̔an-ₒdug* *W.* I am still awake; *γnyid sád-pa* to awaken, to awake vb. n.; *γnyid-yúr-ba* to be overcome by sleep *Sch.*, *Tar.* 31, 22, *Pth.*, — *γnyid-rdól C.* somnambulism; *nyid-ma-mún-la ḍúl-čé* id., *Ld.*; *nyí'-čŏl gyáb-pa* id. *C.* — *γnyid-čan* sleepy *Cs.*; *γnyid-méd* having no sleep, sleepless; *γnyid-yér* morbid sleeplessness; *γnyid-yár Med.*, *Pth.*, id ? *γnyid-lam C.* = *rmi-lam* dream.

གཉིས་ *γnyis* 1. also *γnyis šig* (v. *čig*), **two,** *de γnyis*, *γnyis-po*, *γnyis-ka* the two, both; *γnyis(-su)-méd(-pa)*; *mi-γnyis-pa Tar.*, not being two, i.e. not differing, identical, the same, *ṅa daṅ rgyál-ba γnyis-su med* I and Buddha, we are one, i.e. I am an incarnation of Buddha *Glr.*; *Cs.* also: indubitable, thus perh. used by *Mil.*; *γnyis-su ₒbyúṅ-ba* to be divided into two, to become two *Glr.* — 2. a (married) **couple,** *brám-ze γnyis* Brahmin man and wife. — 3. **both** (v. above), in Tibetan often added, where two nouns have the same predicate, either disjunctively, and then usually followed by *re*: *j̔ó-bo daṅ byams-mgón γnyis mdzó-mo reï stéṅ-du bžugs* both the lord and the Maitreya were mounted on bastard-cows *Glr.*; *ṅa-ráṅ re γnyis* either of us *Mil.*; *p̔yi naṅ γnyis čós-lugs gaṅ bzaṅ* which is the better of the two religions, the esoteric, or the exoteric? *Glr.*; — or copulatively: *k̔yo-šúg γnyis-la rás-čug γčig-las mi bdóg-ste* as they both, husband and wife, had only one cloth together *Dzl.*; — and reciprocally: *čos daṅ bon γnyis rtsód-pa* the contest between the religion of Buddha, and the religion of the Bons *Glr.*; *k̔yod daṅ ṅa γnyis bza-mi byao* we two shall marry each other *Glr.* In most cases mentioned sub 3, *γnyis-po* (the two), *γnyis-ka*, *(γ)nyi-ga*, *W.* col. also *nyi-ko, nyi-kad, nyi-kod*, *Sp.* *nyi-mo*, may be used inst. of *γnyis*; *γnyis* may also refer to several nouns on one or on both sides: *k̔yed daṅ ṅa γnyis* both you (referring to several persons) and I; but it may also be quite omitted, as in other languages: *ga daṅ bai ₒjug-tsúl* the way of employing the (two) letters g and b *Gram.*

Comp. and deriv. *γnyis-skyes* one that is **born twice** i.e. a bird *Cs.*; also one that has entered into a religious order *Cs.* — *γnyis-čár* v. *čar.* — *γnyis-γnyis* **two a piece.** — *γnyis-lláb* **twofold, double,** v. *ldab.* — *γnyis-₀ťúṅ* (**द्विप**) 'drinking twice', the elephant. — *γnyis-pa* 1. **the second.** 2. **having two,** possessed of two, e.g. *mgo-γnyis-pa* having two heads. two-headed; also double-tongued, deceitful *W.* 3. **having doubts, doubting**(?) *Wdn.* — *γnyis-po* the two, both (v. above). — *γnyis-méd* v. beginning of this article. — *γnyis-₀dzin* prob. the state of being affected or influenced by contrary things: doubt, unsteadiness, wavering *Glr.*; *γnyis-₀dzin ltá-ba* prob. to look upon two things as differing, to think them different *Mil.*

གཉུག་མ་ *γnyúg-ma Cs.* **natural,** opp. to *bčós-ma* artificial, hence (*Sch.*) = *dṅos-ma*; *Lexx.* = **निज** innate, peculiar. It occurs in the expressions: *sems γnyúg-ma*, and *γnyúg-mai sems Mil*; *γnyúg-mai ye-šés Mil.*; *γnyúg-mai don Mil.* and *Lex.*; *ma-bčós γnyúg-mai ṅáṅ-du ₀dres*, perh.: is dissolved into the uncreated primordial existence *Mil.* Our Lama explained it differently in different passages, and was not certain of the true meaning of the word.

གཉུང་དཀར་ *γnyuṅ-dkár* **rape-seed** for pressing oil; but cf. *nyúṅ-ma.*

གཉུལ་བ་ *γnyúl-ba* = *nyúl-ba.*

གཉེ་བ་ *γnyé-ba*, *Glr.* also *γnyeo*, *smyé-bo*, **a wooer, courter.**

གཉེ་མ་ *γnyé-ma* the twisted part of the **colon** or **great gut,** *Med.* and col. (*Sch.* erron.: rectum).

གཉེན་ *γnyen*, resp. *sku-γnyén* 1. **kinsman, relative,** *byáms-pai γnyen* loving relations, frq.; *γnyén-la byáms-pa byéd-pa* to love one's relatives; *γnyén-gyi sgyúg-mo*, *sgyúg-mo* as a degree of relationship *Lex.*; *γnyen byéd-pa* to become related, or allied, by marriage *Dzl.* — 2. gen. *γnyén-po* **helper, friend, assistant,** esp. spiritually: *rgyud γnyén-po bzáṅ-bar byin-gyis rlobs* bless my soul, that it may become a good spiritual helper (to these people) *Mil.*; *γnyén-po-la ma ltós-par* without looking up to a spiritual adviser *Mil.*; frq. used of supernatural helpers: *bod ₀dúl-bai γnyén-po* the promoter of the conversion of Tibet (the special Saviour of Tibet, as it were), Awalokiteswara, frq.; applied to things: **remedy, means, expedient, antidote,** *nád-la γsó-bar byéd-pai γnyén-po* assistants in curing maladies (e.g. medicine, diet etc.) *Med.*; *dei γnyén-por* as a remedy for *Thgy.*, frq.; *sgrúb-pai ťabs mi šés-pai γnyén-por* as a remedy for helplessness in acquiring a certain object, i.e. direction or instruction how to obtain it *Thgy.*; *γnyén-po γsáṅ-ba* mysterious helpers, or sources of good (relative to fetish-like objects frq.) — 3. *Cs.*: '*γnyén-po* adversary, antagonist, enemy; contrary, opposite, adverse'; *Sch.*: '*γnyén-por rtén-pa* to adhere to the counter party'; *Lexx.* have '*spáṅ-byai γnyén-po*' a *γnyén-po* to be shunned, explaining *γnyén-po* by **प्रतिभव** (prob. to be corrected into **पक्ष**) opponent, adversary. Sure proofs of this signification of *γnyén-po* I seldom met with in literature, but Lewin mentions some instances scarcely to be doubted. — 4. i.o. *mnyen* and *bsnyen.*

Comp. *dpuṅ-γnyén* **helper, assistant,** frq. — *ṕá-γnyén*, *má-γnyen* a relation on the father's side, on the mother's side *Cs.* — *bšes-γnyén* friend, esp. spiritual friend, v. *bšes.* — *γnyen-grás* (*Sch.?*), *γnyen-₀brél*, *nyen-dúṅ-po* *W.* relations, esp. of the same blood; *γnyen-sdé*, *γnyen-ṫsán*, *γnyen-srid Mil.* id., col. — *γnyen-₀dún* 1. *Sch.*: '**concord, harmony,** amongst kinsmen', in which sense it seems to be used in *Stg.*: *γnyen-₀dún zád-pa yin* this harmony ceases. 2. **relations,** *ṕa yaṅ ma yin, γnyen-₀dún min* neither father nor relations *Thgy.* — *γnyen-zlá* prob.: qualified, fit for matrimonial alliance (as to birth etc.). *kyéd-rnams kyaṅ ṅed rgya-nág-pai γnyen-zlá yin-pas* as ye Tibetans may enter into connubial connexion with us Chinese *Glr.*; in a concrete sense: a good match, *γnyen-zlá ma rnyéd-*

kyis Dzl. ༢༧, 14; *ḱyod daṅ γnyen-zlá min* I am not allied with you by marriage, with you I am not on terms of affinity. — *γnyen-šál* (?) reconciliation *C.* — *γnyen-bšés* relatives and friends, also separately: *ḱyód-la γnyen med bšes kyaṅ med Mil.*

གཉེར་བ་ *γnyér-ba* c. accus. **to take pains with, to take care of, to provide for,** to try to get; **to procure, to acquire,** *γnyer byéd-pa* id.; as a sbst. *Tar.* 165, 22: the procurer, provider *Schf.*; gen. in conjunction with *don* in various ways, as: *bdag don žig γnyér-te* as I have to look after a business *Dzl.* ༢༠, 7; *don γnyér-ba* to earn money; *dón-du γnyér-ba* c. accus., rarely c. dat.: to provide for, to strive to procure, *nor dón-du γnyér-ba* to endeavour to make money, frq.; *yo-byád dón-du γnyér-ba-rnams* people who desired to have goods *Tar.* 169, hence *don-γnyér* **exertion, effort, zeal,** *don-γnyér čén-po dgos* great exertions are necessary *Mil.*; in this sense prob. also *Tar.* 4, 8: earnest exertion (in investigating); *don-γnyér byéd-pa* c. *la* to study, investigate (a thing) *Glr.*; *don-γnyér-čan* 1. zealous, painstaking. 2. *Sch.* also: liked, welcome, *mgron* a welcome guest. — *dkon-γnyér Tar.* 183, 21, *Schf.*: administrator of valuable property; acc. to others: the first secular functionary of a *γtsúg-lag-ḱaṅ*, about the same as **bailiff** (steward) of a convent, = *lha-γnyér* Georgi Alph. Tib. (in an edict); also the manager of the daily sacrifices (*dgon-γnyér?*); *slob-γnyér* **a student,** *čos-slob-γnyér* a religious scholar (a student of theology) *Mil*, *slob-γnyér gáṅ-du bgyis* where did you study? *Mil.* — *γtad-γnyér byéd-pa* to trust (a person with), to intrust (a thing to) *Glr.*; *čéd-du γnyér-ba*, and *rjés-su γnyér-ba* v. *čed.* — *γnyér-ḱa* **attention, care,** *γnyér-ḱa byéd-pa ccg.* to pay attention to, attend to, take care of *Pth.*; *γnyér-ḱa γtád-pa* to commit (a thing) to a person's charge, to put a person in trust of *Glr.* — *γnyér-pa* **farm-steward,** in convents etc. — *γnyér-byáṅ* prob. = *γnyér-ḱa.* — *γnyer-tsáṅ* **store-room, store-house,** (if under the charge of a special *γnyér-pa*).

གཉེར་མ་ *γnyér-ma* a fold of the skin, **wrinkle** *Med.*; *γnyer-ma réṅs-pa ɔgyur* the wrinkles are made straight, are smoothed *Stg.*; *γnyér-ma-čan* wrinkled; *ḱro-γnyér* (भृकुटि) a frown, a severe or angry look v. *ḱró-ba*; *γnyér-ba* to wrinkle, *sna-góṅ γnyér-ba* to knit the brows, to frown *Pth.*

གཉེལ་བ་ *γnyél-ba* = *mnyél-ba Sch.*

གཉོག་པ་ *γnyóg-pa* **to desire,** to wish earnestly *Cs.* v. *snyóg-pa.*

གཉོད་ *γnyód* **strength, durability, stoutness** of cloth etc., *C.* and *W.*, *γnyód-čan* strong; *γnyod-čúṅ*, *γnyod-méd* weak; *Lex.* *lus γnyod-čúṅ* a weakly body or constitution.

གཉོད་པ་ *γnyód-pa* **to draw, stretch, strain** *C.*, *W.*

མཉན་ *mnyan C.* **boat, skiff, wherry;** *mnyán-pa* boat-man, ferry-man.

མཉན་པ་ *mnyán-pa* 1. = *nyán-pa Dzl.* etc. — 2. v. *mnyan.*

མཉན་ཡོད་ *mnyan-yód*, श्रावस्ती, a town in the northern part of Oudh.

མཉམ་ *mnyam* v. the following word.

མཉམ་པ་ *mnyám-pa* (सम) col. **nyám-po**, 1. **like, alike, equal, same,** *mnyám-po yód* they are alike, equal, not differing, col.; with *daṅ*, seldom with the termin., *lha daṅ mnyám-pa yod* they are like unto the gods *Pth.*, *Glr.*; *zlúm-por mnyám-pa* roundish *Sambh.*; *rigs mnyám-pa* of equal birth, rank *Dzl.*; *dus mnyám-pa* contemporary, simultaneous. frq. *mnyám-par gyúr-ba* to become equal, to be equal *Dzl.* — 2. **even, level, flat,** *lag-mtʼil ltar mnyám-pa* flat like the palm of the hand *Glr.* and elsewh.; *mnyám-pa* (or *-par*) *byéd-pa* to make even or level, to even, to equalize *Dzl.*; to divide equally; *sems mnyám-pa* imperturbation, evenness of mind, not to be affected by kindness or the reverse; *sems mnyám-par ɔjóg-pa* to compose the

མཉེད་པ་ mnyéd-pa mind to perfect rest, for meditation, frq.; mnyám-pa sbyór-ba id. (?) — mnyám-du adv. (col. *nyám-po*) c. daṅ: together with, in company of, blá-ma daṅ nyám-du ₀grogs dús-su Mil.; ma daṅ mnyám-du₀či-ba Thgy.; col. *ṅa daṅ nyám-po šog* or merely *nyámpo šog* come along with me! *nyam šoṅte* going along with; nyí-ma šár-ba daṅ mnyám-du with the rising sun Mil.; col. *ḍul daṅ nyám-po* in walking, ambulando; *len daṅ nyám-po* in taking it away (it was broken); *k̔úr-pa nyám* (to send something) by (with) a cooly. — mnyam-méd, mnyam-brál unequalled, matchless; mi mnyám-pa 1. unequal, 2. uneven. — p̔yag (or lag) y̔nyis mnyám-bžag-tu yód-pa both hands laid together on the stomach, mnyámbžag p̔yág-rgya-čan id. — mnyam-pa-nyid, समता, equality, parity; impartiality, justice.

མཉེད་པ་ mnyéd-pa, pf. and imp. mnyes, fut. mnye, W. col. *mnyo-če*, 1. to rub, between the hands or feet, e.g. ears of corn; one's body Tar.; esp. hides, hence to tan, curry, dress; kó - ba mnyés - pa a tanned hide, dressed leather; *šed daṅ nyé - če* W. to rub in or into with force. — 2. Cs. also: to coax.

མཉེན་པ་ mnyén-pa, W. *nyén-mo*, flexible, pliable, supple; soft, smooth, of the voice frq.; of the mind Dzl.; mnyén-par byéd-pa to make soft, smooth, flexible, ₀gyúr-ba to become soft, of the skin etc. Med.; mnyen - mnyél - ba to make soft by tanning Sch. — mnyen-mnyés y̔šin-pa to caress, to fondle Sch.

མཉེལ་བ་ mnyél-ba 1. also y̔nyél-ba, to tan, to dress (hides) Sch. — 2. resp. for ṅál-ba to get tired Pth.

མཉེས་པ་ mnyés-pa, resp. for dgá-ba, in more recent writings and col. for the dgyés-pa of ancient literature, to be glad, to take delight in, ccd.; to be willing, to wish, often with t̔ugs; mnyés-par byéd-pa to make glad, to give pleasure; e.g. to the king by presents Glr., to Buddha by worshipping him Glr. — mnyes-bšin-pa Lex., Sch.: to love much; to be rejoiced at.

མཉོ་མཉོ་ཅན་ mnyó-mnyo-čan W. fondling, petting, p̔rú-gu-la a child.

རྙ་ལོ་, སྙ་ལོ་ rnyá-lo, snyá-lo, several wildgrowing species of Polygonum Med.

རྙང་བ་ rnyáṅ-ba Cs. = bšál-ba, to rinse; W. to suffer diarrhoea, rnyaṅ-nád diarrhoea; rnyáṅ-pa diarrhetic stool; rnyáṅma, y̔nyáṅ-ma id., ni f.

རྙང་རྙིང་ rnyaṅ-rnyiṅ, worn-out clothes, rags Cs.

རྙན་ rnyan = y̔nyan wild sheep, argali.

རྙབ་རྙབ་པ་ rnyab-rnyáb-pa to seize or snatch together Sch.

རྙས་ rnyas, sometimes used for brnyas.

རྙི་, སྙི་ rnyi, snyi, W. ʼnyiu, nyiṅ-ṅu* (cf. rnyoṅ) 1. snare, for catching wild animals, rnyi ₀dzúg-pa to lay snares, also fig. — 2. trap, p̔úr-rnyi mouse-trap (consisting of a flat stone supported by a little stick (p̔úr-pa). — 3. net Sch. (?).

རྙིང་པ་ rnyiṅ-pa old, ancient, of things, e.g. clothes, y̔sar - rnyiṅ new and old snár-gyi y̔i-ge rnyiṅ-pa-rnams ancient records Glr.; brda-rnyiṅ the ancient orthography Zam.; lo-rnyiṅ = na-niṅ last year Wts.; draṅ-sróṅ rnyiṅ-pa the old rishi, i.e. the well-known, of long standing, opp. to a new - comer Dzl. — rnyiṅ - ba vb., pf. brnyiṅs, to grow old, g̔os brnyiṅs old clothes, lham brnyiṅs old shoes Lex.; rnyiṅ - bar ₀gyúr-ba id.; rnyiṅ-bar b̔yéd-pa to wear out or away in a short time Dzl.

རྙིང་མ་ rnyiṅ-ma, n. of the most ancient sect of Lamas, clothed in red, v. Köpp.; Schl. 72; rnyiṅ-ma-pa one belonging to this sect.

རྙིད་པ་ rnyid-pa, pf. brnyid, (b)rnyis, fut. y̔nyid, 1. to wither, to fade, also fig. — 2. to grieve, (vb. n.) Sch.

རྙིལ་, སྙིལ་ rnyil, snyil, so-rnyil, the gums.

རྙིལ་བ་ rnyil-ba v. snyil-ba.

རྙེད་པ་ rnyéd-pa 1. vb., pf. brnyed, brnyes, fut. brnyed, (नम) to get, obtain, acquire; to meet with, find, B. C. frq.; gáṅ-

nas rnyed where did you get that? *Dzl.*, also: whence shall I get it? *Dzl.*; *mi rnyéd-du mi rún-ṅo* it must be got or procured by all means *Dzl.*; *ṅas rnyed* I obtain; *rnyéd-par dká-ba* दुर्लभ difficult to be obtained, found, or met with, frq.; *sdug-bsṅal daṅ bsdós-te čos rnyéd-pa* to purchase the acquisition of religion by suffering tortures *Dzl.*; *zas daṅ skom ma rnyéd-de* having nothing to eat or to drink, frq.; *don rnyéd-pa* v. *don*: *da ni ré-ba rnyéd-do* now my hopes are realized *Dzl.*; *gri rnyéd-pas* as he found a knife *Dzl.*; *skabs rnyéd-pa* to find an opportunity *Dzl.*; *btsál-na yaṅ ma rnyéd-de* not finding it in spite of every search *Dzl.*, (*W.* **tob-če**).

II. sbst. लाभ **profit, gain, acquisition, property, goods.** *rnyéd-pa máṅ-po rnyed-pa* (or **tób-če**) to gain much profit; *bdag rnyéd-pa daṅ ldán-na mi dga* if I have got some earnings, he envies me for them; often in conjunction with *grágs-pa* and similar expressions: riches and honour. — *rnyed sdú-ba, rnyéd-pa p̔róg-pa Sch.*: to make booty, to plunder. — *rnyed-bkúr Lex.*, prob. riches and honour. — *rnyed-nor* v. *tob-nór*.

རྙོག་པ་ *rnyóg-pa* (cf. *nyóg-pa*) vb., pf. *brnyogs*, fut. *brnyog*, 1. **to trouble, to stir up** *Cs.*; also adj.: **thick, turbid.** **ču nyóg-pa* W.* — 2. **to rub** one's self, *ká-ba-la* against a pillar *Dzl.* (*snyóg-pa*). — **nyóg(-pa)-čan, nyóg-po* C.*, troubled, turbid, dirty; *rnyóg-pa méd-pa* clear, limpid, *mtso Wdṅ.* — *rnyóg-ma* dirty, muddy water; mud, mire. *rnyóg-ma-čan* muddy, miry.

རྙོགས་ *rnyogs Lt.?* *rnyogs-tsád* a disease *Med.*

རྙོང་ *rnyoṅ* seems to be the same as *rnyi Lex.*; *rnyóṅ-ba*, pf. *brnyoṅs*, fut. *brnyoṅ* 1. *Cs.*: 'to ensnare, entrap'. 2. *Sch.*: 'to stretch out'. I met with *rnyoṅ* in the following expressions, not satisfactorily to be explained either by *Cs.* or by *Sch.*: *rkáṅ-pa rnyoṅ Lex.*; *dku ma rnyoṅs Lex.*; *lus rnyóṅ-ba S.g.*: frq.; *γyal-rnyóṅs S.g.*; *mgul-rgyab zug daṅ rnyoṅ S.g.*; *rnyoṅs-tsád Mng.*

སྙ་ནང་ *snya-náṅ* v. *γnya-náṅ*.

སྙ་ལོ་ *snyá-lo* v. *rnyá-lo*.

སྙག་པ་ *snyág-pa*, col. for *snyég-pa*; also in *Mil.*

སྙགས་ *snyags Lex.* w.e.; *C.* = *dbyaṅs* music, harmony.

སྙད་ *snyad* **malicious** or **false accusation** or **imputation,** *snyad ₒdzúg-pa* (*W.* **tsug-če**) to bring in an action against, to prosecute; **nyad ḍú-če* W.*, **nyẹ' k[illegible]a* C.* id., esp. to irritate, to provoke another, by accusations; *snyad ₒdágs-pa* id. *Glr.*; *snyad ₒdág-pa, W.* **dág-če** to clear one's self of an accusation, to refute it; *snyad byéd-pa* c.dat. to use as a pretence or pretext *Glr.*; **nyẹ' čọ' (or čẹ') táṅ-wa* C.*, **nyad-sé tág-če* Ld.* to weary another by too great punctiliousness, ni f.; **nor-nyád čó-če* W.* to extort money by false accusations, *la* from; *snyad méd-par* without cause, pretence, or provocation *Thgy.*; **nyád-zer-čan* W.* one that makes false accusations.

སྙད་པ་ *snyád-pa*, pf. and fut. *bsnyad*, imp. *snyod*, **to relate, to report,** e.g. *lo-rgyús* a story *Pth.*, *rmí-lam* a dream *Dzl.*; *γtam snyád-pa* 1. to speak, state, inform, give notice (*W.* **hun táṅ-če**). 2. *Cs.*: 'to rehearse' (?).

སྙན་ *snyan* 1. resp. **the ear,** *rgyál-poi snyán-du tos* it came to the king's hearing *Glr.*; *snyán-du žus* or *brǰod* they told or informed him *Pth.*; *snyán-du zuṅ* listen, pay attention, give ear to! *Pth.*; *snyán-du p̔ul* they sang to him or before him (lit. they made him hear) *Mil.* (cf. sub *snyán-pa*); *snyán-(gyis) γsán-pa* to hear *Mil.*; *snyan-γsán bébs-pa* to give ear to one, to hear one *Cs.*; **nyẹ̄n-žu ₒbul-wa* C.* to address a superior, to apply to him; *snyan-kúṅ* the ear-hole; *snyan-dbáṅ* the organ of hearing *Cs.*; *snyan-šál* the lap or tip of the ear *Cs.*; *snyan-p̔rá žú-ba* to slander, *mi mi-la* to calumniate one person to another. — 2. = *γnyan* **argali.**

སྙན་པ་ *snyán-pa* (यशस्) 1. sbst. **renown, glory, fame, praise, rumour,** *k̔yód-kyi* *snyán-pa ṗyogs bcur grags* every part of the world rings with thy praise; *deï snyán-pa rgyáṅ-nas ṫos Mil.* his praises are heard far and wide; *ċes deï snyán-pa brǰód-ċiṅ* thus speaking praisingly of him *Mil.*; *čés-pai snyán-pa-la rtén-nas* owing to a rumour of this purport *Mil.*; *ċes snyán-pa daṅ grágs-pa čén-po byuṅ* so was said far and near *Mil.*; *deï snyán-du* to his praise *Mil.* (cf. *snyan*). — 2. adj., *W.* **nyán-po**, **well-sounding,** sweet to hear, of voice, words etc.; **ṫsor-náṅ-la nyán-po** *W.* pleasant to the ear; also: *dge-slóṅ dbyaṅs ráb-tu snyán-pa* a monk having a well-sounding voice *Dzl.*; *ṫsig snyán-par* with pleasant words *Dzl.*; *snyán-pai ṫsíg-gis* id.; **low,** not loud; *snyan-skád* also *C.*: elegant, well-sounding, poetical language; *mi snyán-pa* 1. unharmonious; 2. offensive, insulting, *gaṅ žig bdág-la rtsód-ċiṅ mi-snyán-brǰod* he who in a dispute says to me insulting words; *mi-snyán-par zér-ba dáṅ-du lén-pa* to put up with, to pocket offensive remarks. 3. lamentable, *skad mi snyán-pa zér-ba* to utter lamentable cries, plaintive tones, also of animals, *Dzl.*; *γtam-snyán(-pa)* 1. good, joyful news, glad tidings, *byéd-pa* to bring them *Dzl.*, *Mil.* 2. a pleasing talk, conversation *Cs.* (?) — *snyan-grágs* v. *grágs-pa*. — *snyan-rgyúd* oral instruction of the Lamas, = *bka-rgyúd*. — *snyan-(d)ṅág(s)* v. *ṅag*. — 3. vb. **to praise, extol, glorify,** *stód-ċiṅ snyán-par grágs-te* he extolled him in songs of praise *Dzl.* (?)

སྙབ་པ་ *snyáb-pa* **to smack** with the lips *Sch.*

སྙམ་པ་ *snyám-pa* 1. vb. **to think, suppose, fancy, imagine,** *ḃdág-ċag riṅ-po-čc btaṅ* (better: *γtaṅ*) *snyám-mo* we think we shall give jewels *Dzl.* ༣༤༧, 16.; *ṅa lčeb dgos snyám-nas* thinking, I must seek death (v. *lčéb-pa*) *Pth.*; *yón-tan daṅ ldán-par snyám-ste* fancying to be possessed of excellent qualities *Dzl.* — 2. sbst. **thought, sense, mind, feeling,** *čos byás-na snyám-pa yóṅ-gin γda* (cf. *na* III., 2) we have a mind to renounce the world *Mil.*; similarly: *ǰigs-so snyám-pa yod re-skán* I am far from any thought of fear *Mil.*; most frq. *snyám-du bsams* he thought in his mind; *snyam-byéd*: *ṗan snyam-byéd kyaṅ* though one may imagine that it will help *Med.*; *skyúg-pa, brduṅs, dkris snyam-byéd* there arises a feeling like that of nausea, like that of being beaten, of being (tightly) wrapt up, *Med.*

སྙི་ *snyi* v. *rnyi*.

སྙི་བ་ *snyi-ba* 1. adj., also *snyi-bo, snyi-mo, snyin-po Cs.*, **nyin-te** *W.*, **soft, smooth,** to the touch; **tender, delicate,** of the skin; **easily broken** or **injured; loose, crazy,** not durable, not strong or stout, of cloth, ropes etc.; not hard or tough, **tender,** of meat, rendered so by beating or boiling. — 2. sbst. **softness.** — 3. n. of a plant.

སྙི་ཕུལ་ *snyi-ṗúl* corn of luxuriant growth *Sch.* (?)

སྙི་མ་ *snyi-ma* prov. for *snyé-ma*; also *Glr.*

སྙི་ཤང་ཀ་ཏྱ་ *snyi-śaṅ-ka-tya*, and *snyi-śaṅ-gur-rta*, names of mountains in Nepal.

སྙིགས་པ་ *snyigs-pa* **degenerated, grown worse** *Cs.* *snyigs-ma* (**कषाय**) 1. **impure sediment,** *már-gyi* in butter; *daṅs snyigs ḃyéd-pa* to separate the clear (fluid) from the sediment *Med.* — 2. the degenerated age (iron age), prop. *snyigs-(mai) dus*.

སྙིང་ *snyiṅ* (**हृद**) **the heart** 1. physically, also *snyiṅ-ka, snyiṅ-ga*, resp. *ṫugs (-ka)*; also **the breast;** **nyiṅ-ka ṗár-ra rag** *W.* I feel my heart palpitate; *snyiṅ ḃdár-žiṅ ḃgul* the heart trembles (with fear) *Domaṅ*; *bdág-gi lús-kyi snyiṅ ltar γċes* as dear to me as my own heart *Glr.* — 2. intellectually: **the mind,** *snyiṅ dgá-ba, snyiṅ bdé-ba* gladness, cheerfulness; *snyiṅ daṅ mig ḃṗróg-pa* to transport, to ravish *Sch.*; courage, *snyiṅ ma čuṅ ċig* be not afraid! sentiment, feeling, will, **nyiṅ sóg-po ċó-te ma ċag** *W.* I have not broken it wilfully; **k̔a daṅ nyiṅ ma dé-te** *W.* hypocritical; **nyiṅ-sém dáṅ-po** *W.* sincere, candid; in a more g ıeral sense: *snyiṅ γdón-gyis bslus* the heart is infatuated by a demon *Glr.*; even madness may be attributed to the heart *Do.* — *snyiṅ-nas* 1. heartily, zealously, earnestly, e.g. looking for or to a thing *Dzl.*; *snyiṅ tág-pa-nas* with all one's heart, most earnestly, devoutly, e.g. to say one's prayers *Thgy.* 2. actually, really, *koṅ snyiṅ-nas mi ₒbyiṅ-ba yin* really he does not sink! (the water actually bears him) *Mil.* 3. v. *snyiṅ-po*.

Comp. and deriv. *snyiṅ-ku* v. *nyiṅ-ku*. — *snyiṅ-kàms* **courage** *Sch.* — **nyiṅ-ṭág kol** *W.* my heart's blood is boiling (with anger etc.) — *snyiṅ-dgá* v. above. — *snyiṅ-čan* **courageous, spirited** *Ld.* — **nyiṅ-ču žug** *W.* **afflicted with dropsy in the pericardium,** hydrocardia. — *snyiṅ-rje*, resp. *túgs-rje* (करुणा) **kindness, mercy, compassion,** *mi-la snyiṅ-rje sgóm-pa* to commiserate, to pity a person *Mil.*; *snyiṅ-rjes kyáb-pa* id. with respect to a great number of beings, to embrace with affection *Dzl.*; *snyiṅ-rjes nón-te* overpowered by compassion; **nyiṅ-že tsór-če** *W.* to have compassion; *snyiṅ-rje-čan, snyiṅ-rje daṅ ldán-pa* compassionate, merciful *Dzl.*: *snyiṅ-rje-skad* lamentation, a cry of compassion *Dzl.*; *snyiṅ-rje-mo:* 1. *kyod snyiṅ-rje-mo raṅ žig ₒdug* you are much to be pitied *Mil.* 2. col.: **dearest, most beloved, amiable, charming;** also *snyiṅ-rje* for *snyiṅ-rje-mo, snyiṅ-rje mdzá-bo* my poor little friend. — *snyiṅ-nyé-ba*, col. **nyiṅ nyé-mo**, **friendly, amicable, loving, affectionate; friend; friendship,** *snyiṅ-nye bú-mo* a woman connected by friendship with, a woman, the friend of (a sick person mentioned) *Lt.* — *snyiṅ-ɣtam* **a confidential speaking,** for exhortation, consolation, or encouragement; *brtsé-bai snyiṅ-ɣtam* affectionate exhortation *Glr.*; *pán-pai snyiṅ-ɣtam* useful admonition etc. *Mil.* — *snyiṅ-stobs* **courage.** — *snyiṅ-ₒdód-pa* **to wish, to desire, to long for,** *za-snyiṅ-ₒdód-pa* to wish to eat, to be craving for food *Thgy.*; *ₒgro-snyiṅ-ₒdód-pa* to wish to go. — *snyiṅ-rdúṅ-ba* palpitation of heart *Sch.* — **nyiṅ daṅ* (etymol. dubious) *čó-če** *W.* ccd. to interest one's self for, to take an interest in. — *snyiṅ-sdúg W.* **liked, beloved; darling, favourite,** e.g. a child; *nyiṅ-dúg šig dug** *W.* he is a general favourite; **ṅa di nyiṅ-dúg čo dug** *W.* I am very fond of this, it is my favourite (pursuit etc.); but *snyiṅ-ma-sdúg* bad people *Mil.* — *snyiṅ ná-ba* 1. = *snyiṅ-nád.* 2. **'heart-sickness', grief,** on account of injury suffered from others, curable only by indemnity paid or revenge taken. — *snyiṅ-nád* **disease of the heart.** — *sniṅ-po* (सार, गर्भ) **the chief part, main substance, quintessence,** e.g. the cream of the milk *Med.*; the soft part of a loaf, the wick of a lamp *Dzl.*; frq. fig.: the main substance of a doctrine, a book etc., *don-snyiṅ ₒbyin-pa* to give a summary, the sum and substance (of a writing); *séms-čan tams-čád saṅs-rgyás-kyi snyiṅ-po-čan yin-na* if all beings have the pith and essence of the nature of Buddha in themselves *Thgy.* 5, 8; the Ommanipadmehūm is called the *snyiṅ-po* of religion *Glr.*; *snyiṅ-po-méd-pa* worthless, null, void, *snyiṅ-pos dbén-pa* id. *Tar.* 185, 2; *de-bžiṅ-ɣšégs-pai snyiṅ-po* the spirit of Tathāgata *Was.*; *snyiṅ-po-byaṅ-čúb-* (or *byaṅ-čub-snyiṅ-po*) *-la mčis-pa* to become Buddha *Thgy.*; *srog(-gi) snyiṅ(-po) ₒbúl-ba Mil.* frq. to offer one's heart's blood, to pledge one's own life. — *snyiṅ-rtsa* (col.) the great veins connected with the heart, perh. = *snyiṅ-luṅ.* — *snyiṅ-rtse* the tip or apex of the heart, mentioned by *Mil.* as a particular dainty (perh. only by way of a jest). — *snyiṅ-brtse-ba*, resp. *túgs-brtsé-ba*, vb., also sbst. and adj., not much differing from *snyiṅ-rje*: **love, pity** etc. frq.; *Dzl.: bú-la snyiṅ-brtse-nas*; *tams-čád-la snyiṅ-brtse-ba yin-na*; *de-dag-la snyiṅ-brtse-bai pyir*; *snyiṅ-brtse-bai sems skyés-te* etc. — *snyiṅ-tsim* **contentment, satisfaction,** sometimes also pleasure felt at the misfortune of others *Pth.*, *snyiṅ-tsim ₒdébs-pa* to manifest such an enjoyment. — *snyiṅ-tsil* the fat about the heart *Cs.* — *snyiṅ-žo-ša* v. *žó-ša.* — *snyiṅ-rús*, resp. *tugs-rús* (acc. to *Mil.*: *snyiṅ-gi rús-pa tón-par gyis* let energy and diligence arise in you); **firmness of mind** (heart) i.e. 1. **diligence, zeal, perseverance**

Mil. and *C.* 2. **courage** *W.* — *snyiṅ-re-rǰé* (*snyiṅ-rǰe*, with *re* placed between, v. *re*) **o the poor man!** the poor people! either standing absolute or as predicate to a preceding noun: *˳dí-rnams snyiṅ-re-rǰé* these (people) are indeed much to be pitied *Mil.*; *kyod-raṅ . . . ˳dzín-pa snyiṅ-re-rǰé* you (would) comprehend that? poor wretches that you are! *Mil.*; even as an adjective: *séms-čan snyiṅ-re-rǰé* the poor creatures! frq.; *snyiṅ-re-rǰé-bai sdig-čan* the lamentable sinner! — *snyiṅ-rluṅ Sch.*: 'low spirits, melancholy, mental derangement'; I met with it only in *Mil.*, as signifying **heart-grief, deep sorrow,** e.g. *snyiṅ-rlúṅ drág-po ldaṅ* great affliction is caused. — *snyiṅ-lam-na Sch.*: 'in one's mind'. — **snyiṅ-lúṅ** *W.* the heart, liver, and lights of a slaughtered animal, the **pluck.** — *snyiṅ-šubs* **pericardium.**

སྙིང་བ་ *snyiṅ-ba W.* **to swell** (in water), **lum nyiṅ soṅ** the soaked barley has swollen.

སྙིད་པ་ *snyid-pa* prob. = *rnyid-pa Pth.*

སྙིད་མོ་ *snyid-mo Lex.* the sister of a woman's husband.

སྙིན་པ་ *snyin-pa*, *snyin-po*, *snyin-te*, v. *snyi-ba.*

སྙིམ་པ་(གང་) *snyim-pa(-gaṅ)* a measure for liquids, as well as for flour, grain and the like, as much as may be taken up by both hands placed together.

སྙིལ་ *snyil* = *rnyil.*

སྙིལ་བ་ *snyil-ba*, or *rnyil-ba*, pf. and fut. *bsnyil* (cf. *nyil-ba*) 1. **to pull** or **throw down, to break down, to destroy,** houses, rocks etc.; *ṕyé-mar snyil-ba* to reduce to powder *Lex.*, *Sch.* — 2. *ṕyir* (*bskrad*) *snyil-ba Lex.*; *Sch.*: **to expel, banish, exile.**

སྙུག་པ་ *snyúg-pa*, also *smyúg-pa*, pf. *bsnyugs*, fut. *bsnyug*, **to dip in, to immerge.**

སྙུག་མ་ *snyúg-ma*, more frq. *smyúg-ma*, **reed, rush, bulrush**; *snyúg-gu* reed-pen; *snyúg-bzo* basket-work of reeds *Pth.*; *snyúg-šiṅ* bamboo.

སྙུགས་ *snyugs C.* **duration, continuity, time** *Cs.*; **nyúg-čẹn* C.* continual; *snyugs-sríṅs Lex.* protracted, lengthened out.

སྙུགས་སྦྲུལ་ *snyugs-sbrúl* **lizard** *Sch.*

སྙུང་ *snyuṅ*, resp. for *nad*, *W.* **nyuṅ-zúg**, **disease, illness, sickness,** *btsún-pai skú-la snyuṅ mi mṅá-am* is your Majesty well? *Glr.*; *snyúṅ-du mdze byuṅ Glr.* leprosy arose to him as a disease, he was attacked with the disease of leprosy; *snyuṅ mdzes btab* id. *Tar.*; *snyúṅ-γži* = *nád-γži.*

སྙུང་བ་ *snyúṅ-ba* I. vb., pf. *bsnyuṅs*, fut. *bsnyuṅ*, 1. **to make less, to reduce, to diminish**; *Sch.*: **to disparage.** — 2. resp. **to be ill, sick, indisposed;** *ťugs snyúṅ-bai mi* people that are disagreeable, annoying to others *Mil.*

II. sbst. 1. the state of being ill, **illness, indisposition.** — 2. *W.* **awl, pricker, punch;** also *snyúṅ-bu.*

སྙུན་ *snyun* = *snyuṅ*, *skú-la snyún-gyis bzuṅ* he was taken ill *Dzl.*; *snyun ˳dri-ba Mil.*, *rmé-ba Sch.*, *γsól-ba Dzl.*, *snyún-dri žú-ba Mil.*, to inquire after a person's health; to wait on, to pay one's respects *Dzl.* ༣༨༧, 16.

སྙུན་པ་ *snyún-pa*, pf. and fut. *bsnyun*, **to be ill,** to labour under a disease.

སྙེ་ཐང་ *snye-ťaṅ* a village and convent near Lhasa.

སྙེ་བ་ *snyé-ba*, pf. *bsnyes*, fut. *bsnye*, imp. *snye* **to lean against, to rest on,** *rtsig-pa-la* against a wall; **to lie down, recline, repose on,** *mál-stan-la* on a bed, *sṅás-la* on a cushion or pillow; **gyáb-nye** col. a support or cushion for leaning against with one's back. — *snye-ḱri* v. *ḱri.* — *snye-stán*, *snye-˳ból* **pillow** or **cushion** to rest on.

སྙེ་མ་ *snyé-ma*, also *snyí-ma*, 1. **ear** of corn. 2. **corn forming ears** (v. *ljáṅ-pa*), *snyé-ma mig-čan* fruitbearing ears, **nye-lóṅ** *W.* empty ears; **nye-ma ťon** *W.* the corn blows, is in flower; **nye čág-pa** *C.* to thrash, **nye-čág-gi dhụ'-ḍo** an animal used for treading out the grain. — *snye-dkár* diseased ears. — *snye-mgó* = *snyé-ma* 1.

སྙེག(ས)་པ་ *snyeg(s)-pa*, pf. *bsnyegs*, fut. *bsnyeg*, imp. *snyog(s)*, *W.* **nyág-ċe**, 1. c. accus. **to hasten** or **run** after, **to pursue,** frq.; also with *rjés-nas*, *rjés-su*, *rjés-bžin-du*, *pyi-bžin-du*; *raṅ-ₒgró-sa snyogs* hasten towards your aim! *Mil*; *snyég-sar snyogs Lex.* id.; *bsnyég-tu*, or *snyégs-su ₒdoṅ-ba* to walk hastily, to make haste or speed *Dzl.* — 2. **to overtake,** *snyégs ma nús-pas* not being able to reach *Dzl.* — 3. c. dat. **to hasten** to some place, *ltád-mo-la* to the play *Mil.*; **to rise,** *γnám-la* rising up to heaven, as a flame, *Glr.*, a cedar *Wdṅ.*, frq.; **to strive** or **struggle for, to aspire to,** *nór-la* riches, *sde-čén-la* increase of territory, *žiṅ-kams-bzáṅ-la* the region of eternal bliss. — *snyég-ma* pursuer *Dzl.*

སྙེགས་ *snyegs* **straight, stretched out** *Sch.*

སྙེང་བ་ *snyéṅ-ba* 1. inst. of *rmyéṅ-ba*, to stretch *Mil.* — 2. also *snyéṅs-pa*, resp. for *ₒjigs-pa*, vb. (pf. *bsnyeṅs*, fut. *bsnyeṅ*) and sbst., *rgyál-pos ma snyeṅs šig* do not be afraid of the king! *Dzl.*

སྙེད་ *snyed* I. the **crupper** attached to a saddle *Sch.* II. = *tsam*: 1. *ₒdi-snyéd* (*-ċig*), *de-snyéd*(*-ċig*) **so much, so many,** frq.; also for: **how many!** e.g. . . . *yón-tan ₒdi-snyéd mṅao* how many excellent qualities has . . .! *Dzl.*; *ċi-snyéd*, *ji-snyéd* how much? how many? also *snyed* alone (examples v. sub *byé-ma*). — 2. after round sums: **about, near,** *stoṅ snyed*, also *stoṅ ji-snyéd Mil.* about a thousand.

སྙེན་པ་ *snyén-pa Cs.*: 1. **to come** or **go near, to approach,** gen. *bsnyén-pa*. — 2. **to gain, to procure,** inst. of *rnyéd-pa*(?).

སྙེམ(ས)་པ་ *snyém(s)-pa* 1. vb., pf. *bsnyems*, **to be proud** or **arrogant, to boast,** *ṅa-rgyál snyéms-pas* to be swollen with pride *Dzl.*; *mtu-rtsál* (to be proud) of one's strength *Dzl.* — 2. sbst. **pride, haughtiness,** *snyém-pa-ċan* prideful, proud, *snyems-čúṅ* 1. prideless, humble, affable, kind, col. **nyom-čúṅ**, and **nyam-šúṅ**. 2. poor, indigent *C.*

སྙེས་ *snyes* v. *snyé-ba.*

སྙོ་བ་ *snyó-ba* sometimes for *smyó-ba.*

སྙོག་པ་ *snyóg-pa*, or *bsnyóg-pa*, secondary form of *snyég-pa*, esp. when signifying **to wish earnestly, to crave** for or **lust** after, also *ka-snyóg-pa Cs.*

སྙོད་ *snyod*, = *go-snyód*, **caraway.**

སྙོད་པ་ *snyód-pa* I. pf. *bsnyad*, 1. **to draw out** and **twist,** as in spinning *Stg.*, *C.* — 2. *Cs.*: **to tell, to relate,** = *snyád-pa*.

II. pf. *bsnyod*, *bsnyos*, fut. *bsnyod*, **to feed,** to give to eat and to drink, *ccapir.*

སྙོན་པ་ *snyón-pa* I. 1. pf. and fut. *bsnyon*, **to deny, to disavow dishonestly,** *Dzl.* ༢༢, 2; ༢༠, 8 **to assert falsely,** *snyon byéd-pa Glr.* — 2. **nyon ḍú-ċe* W.* is said to signify the same as **nyad ḍu-ċe** v. *snyad.*

II. inst. of *smyón-pa*

སྙོབ་པ་ *snyób-pa*, pf. *bsnyabs*, fut. *bsnyab* 1. **to stretch out,** e.g. the hand, *Lex.* — 2. *W.* **to reach,** by stretching one's self out, **to arrive at,** **nyob mi tub**.

སྙོབས་ *snyobs* = *snyoms Lex.*

སྙོམ(ས)་ *snyom(s)*, *Lex.* = तन्द्रि I. 1. **weariness, lassitude; laziness, idleness,** *lus snyoms-lċi-ba yin* one is exhausted and dull *Med.*; *snyóms-la ṅúl-ba* to be tired and exhausted. — *snyóms-las* 1. **indolence, unconcern,** esp. religious indifference, *Glr.*; *snyóms-las byéd-pa*, or *drán-pa Glr.* to be lazy, indolent, indifferent; *snyóms-las-ċan* adj. lazy etc. *Glr.* — 2. *Sch.*: an idle person(?).

II. col., also *Mil.*, inst. of *snyems.*

སྙོམ(ས)་པ་ *snyóm(s)-pa* I. vb., pf. *bsnyoms*, fut. *bsnyom*, to make even 1. **to level,** *γnas* a place, *Dzl.*; *sá-la snyóms-pa* to level with the ground, **to demolish** *Dzl.* — 2. *pan-tsun* **to equalize** different things, **to arrange uniformly,** *zas* one's meals, i.e. not cold and warm promiscuously *Thgy.*; **to level, to reduce** to an equality of condition, *ltogs-pyug* rich and poor (according to the principles of the communists) *Glr.*; similarly *bú-lon Tar.* 74; *tams-ċád-la snyóms-na bdag kyaṅ snyóms-par mdzad*

˳ťsal I wish to be treated fairly like any other people *Dzl.* ༢༧; *ká-lo snyóms-pa* to regulate (a matter), **to manage** or **direct** (a business) **justly,** uniformly *Glr.* — *snyóm-du med*, he has not his like *Dzl.*; **tag nyóm-la* C.* always uniformly, without variation.

II. sbst., also *btaṅ-snyóms*, evenness, or **calmness of mind, equanimity,** *snyóms-par ˳júg-pa* to assume it, = *sems mnyám-par bžág-pa*, v. *mnyám-pa*. — *snyoms-˳júg byéd-pa* 1. id., 2. euphem. for *˳ḱríg-pa spyód-pa*. — *mgo-snyóms* impartial *Mil.* — *snyóms-po* equal, even, uniform, e.g. in every part equally thick.

སྙོལ་བ་ *snyól-ba*, pf. and fut. *bsnyal* (cf. *nyál-ba*) 1. **to lay down; to bed** a person, to assign him his couch or bed *Pth.*; **ṭú-gu mál-du* C.* (to lay) a child on its bed, to put to bed; **nyál-te žág-pa* C.*, *bór-če W.*, to lay or put down, opp. to *laṅ-te* etc., to set or place upright, to set on end, e.g. a book. — 2. fig.: **me nyál-wa* C.* to put the fire to bed, i.e. to scrape it together and cover it with ashes; *spú snyól-ba* to smooth down the bristling hair, i.e, to abate one's anger; *čaṅ, žo, snyól-ba* to allow the beer to ferment, the milk to curdle, in a state of rest (undisturbed).

བརྙ་བ་ *brnyá-ba*, pf. *brnyas,* 1. **to borrow** *Dzl.* ༢༧༠, 12. 14; ༢༧༣, 6. 2. **to seize** by force, **to usurp** *Sch.*

བརྙང་ *brnyaṅ Lex.* prob. = *rnyáṅ-pa*.

བརྙད་པ་ *brnyád-pa* for *bsnyád-pa*.

བརྙན་པ་ *brnyán-pa Cs.* **to borrow**; *brnyán-po* borrowed; also fig.: borrowed, reflected, *γzugs-brnyán* (*Lex. snaṅ-brnyán*) a reflected image प्रतिबिम्ब frq.; also image, picture in general; even a little statue *Pth.*; *rmi-lam-gyi γzugs-brnyán* vision, visionary image; *sgra-brnyán*, प्रतिश्रुत reflected sound, echo; *mgo-brnyán* a mask, a fearful apparition *Thgr.*, *mgo-brnyán sér-po Schl.* 234. — *p̀yag-brnyán* servant *Cs.* — *brnyán-poi gos Cs.*: 'a garment marked with the figures (sic) of the rainbow' — *brnyán-poi brnyas Lex.* interest for a loan, rent for things borrowed *Sch.*

བརྙབས་པ་ *brnyábs-pa* **diligence, painstaking; to take pains** *Sch.*

བརྙས་པ་ *brnyás-pa* I. borrowed, v. *brnyá-ba*.

II. 1. **to despise, contemn** c. dat., frq.; *ma brnyás šig* do not despise! *Dzl.*; *brnyas smád-pa* id. *Dzl.* — **contempt,** *brnyás-pa byéd-pa*, *W.* **nya-šé tág-če**, ccd. to despise, to treat contemptuously, frq.; *brnyas-bčos* (*Thgy. brnyas-čos*) contempt, scorn.

བརྙོངས་ *brnyoṅs* **convenient, suitable** *Sch.*

བསྙིགས་པ་ *bsnyígs-pa* 1. **to return, restore, deliver up** *Cs.* 2. **sediment.**

བསྙུག *bsnyug* full *Sch.*; *skyu-gaṅ bsnyug Lex.* a full draught (?).

བསྙུལ་བ་ *bsnyúl-ba* to wash *Lex.*

བསྙེན་པ་ *bsnyén-pa* 1. **to approach, to come near,** c. dat., also *drúṅ-du*, *ḱó-boi drúṅ-du bsnyen čig* come to me *Dzl.*; *góm-pa re-ré bór-žiṅ ˳či-ba-la bsnyén-pa ltar* as with every step we come nearer to our death *Thgy.*; **to join, to stick to** a person *Dzl.* — 2. **to propitiate, soothe, satisfy,** a deity *Cs.* — 3. **to accept, receive, admit** *W.*; *bsnyén-par rdzógs-pa* to be ordained, consecrated, frq.; c. *las* by *Tar.* — *dge-bsnyen* v. *dgé-ba*. — *bsnyen-bkúr* **reverence, veneration, respect,** *byéd-pa* to pay one's duty or respect, esp. to the priesthood by various services, *ṅá-la bsnyén-pa byás-te Dzl.* and elsewh., frq., also *bsnyén-žiṅ bkúr-ba Glr.*, and **nyen kúr-če* W.*; *bsnyén-bkur žú-ba* to ask permission for performing such services *Mil.* — *bsnyen-bsgrúb* priestly function, religious office, esp. *sṅags* q. v. — *bsnyen-γnás* fasting, abstinence; *bsnyen-γnás srúṅ-ba*, *W.* **zúm-če**, to abstain from food, to fast.

བསྙེར་བ་ *bsnyér-ba* to make grimaces or gesticulations *Cs.*

བསྙེལ་བ་ *bsnyél-ba*, *Lexx.*: resp., **to forget**; *bsnyel-méd* not forgetting or forgetful, mindful; *bsnyel-ysó-ba* to remind, to put one in mind of a thing *Mil. nt.*

བསྙོན་ *bsnyon* v. *snyon*.

བསྙོར་བ་ *bsnyór-ba*, *Lex.* nas *bsnyór-ba*, acc. to *Sch.*: to sift barley.

ཊ

ཊ་ *ṭa*, the letter *ṭ*, cerebral *t*, *Ssk.* ट.

ཊ་ཀཱ་ *ṭá-kā*, *Hind.* टका in *W.* imaginary coin, money of account, = 2 paisa or 1 d. — Different from it is ཊཾ་ཀ་, ཊང་ཀ་, ཊང་ཁ་, ཏང་ཀ་ *ṭáṅ-ka*, *ṭaṅ-ka*, *ṭaṅ-k̔a*, *taṅ-ka*, *Hind.* तङ्का 1. in *C.* $\frac{2}{5}$ rupee = 9 d., v. also *γc̔od-taṅ* (v. *γc̔od-pa* comp.). — 2. a gold and silver coin *Tar.* 112, 6. — 3. *W.* **money** in general.

ཊི་ཀེད་, ཊྲི་ཀེད་ *ṭi-ked*, *tri-ked* **card, ticket; postage-stamp.**

ཌ

ཌ་ *ḍa*, the letter *ḍ*, cerebral *d*, *Ssk.* ड.

ཌཱ་ཀི་ *ḍá-ki* (डाकी *Hind.*: 'husband of a Dākinī, *Shaksp.*) in *Mil.* prob. = *Dākinī*, *mk̔á-ₒgro-ma*.

ཌ་མ་རུ་, ཌ་རུ་ *ḍá-ma-ru*, *ḍá-ru*, (डमरु) a small **tympan** or **drum**, with a handle and two balls fastened to it by a strap.

ཌཱཀ་ *ḍák*, gen. **drag**, *Hind.*: डाक, **the post, letter-post.**

ཌཎ་ཌི་ *ḍaṇ-ḍi*, *Hind.* डण्डी, **the beam** of a pair of scales; a kind of litter.

ད

ད་ *ta*, 1. the letter t, tenuis, French t. — 2. num. fig.: 9. — 3. inst. of *btags*, v. *ya-btags*.

ད་ཀ་རི་ *tá-ka-ri* (*Hind.* तराकड़ी) common **scales**, *Ld.*

ད་ཀུ་ *tá-ku W.* stick with a hook, hooked cane, **crutch**; **ta-ku-rú-ku** *Ld.* **crooked, contracted, crippled.**

ད་གིར་ *tá-gir W.* **bread**, esp. the flat bread-cakes of India, commonly called '*chapátee*'; **č̔ú-ta-gir** *Ld.* boiled flour-dumplings; **túl-ta-gir** pancakes.

ད་བ་ *tá-ba* (Pers. تابا) gen. **tao** *W.* a flat **iron pan** without a handle.

ད་བག་ *tá-bag W.*, *t̔ár-ₒbag C.*, **a plate**, **tá-bag dal-dál** *W.*, **ter-t̔ér** *C.*, a flat plate, *kor-kór* a deep plate, soup-plate.

ད་བེར་ *ta-bér* (spelling?) *W.* **fence** of boards or laths.

ད་ཟིག་ *ta-zig*, or *ta-zig-yúl*, **Persia**, *ta-zig (-pa)* a Persian.

ད་ར་ཙེ་ *ta-ra-tsé* (*Pers.* ترازو) *W.* a small pair of scales, **goldweights.**

ད་རེ་ *ta-ré* v. *re.*

ད་ལ་ *tá-la* 1. ताल **the palmyra tree,** *Borassus flabelliformis* (not the date-tree *Cs.*) *B.* — 2. In more recent times, and already in *Mil.*, *tá-la* seems to denote **the plantain** or banana tree, *Musa paradisiaca.*

ད་ལ་ལ་ *ta-la-la Lex.* **lamp, lantern.**

ད་ལའི་བླ་མ་ *ta-lai-blá-ma* (*ta-lai Mong.* ocean, sea), the Dalai Lama, v. *Huc.* II., 155. *Köpp.* II., 120.

དག་དག་ *tag-tág W.* the imitative sound of knocking, **tag-tág zer** there is a knock, **tag-tág čó-če** to knock at the door.

དང་ *taṅ* **through,** v. *toṅ* and *lteṅ.*

དང་ཀུན་ *taṅ-kun* n. of a medicinal herb *Med.*

དང་ག་ *taṅ-ga* v. ཏཾ་ཀ་ *ṭaṅ-ka.*

དཏྐཱ་ལ་ *tatkā-la Ssk.* **the present moment** *Wdk.*

དན་དུར་ *tan-dúr Ld.* a sort of hard **cake** or bread, resembling biscuit or rusk.

དབ་དབ་ *tab-táb* v. *tob-tób.*

དར་དར་ *tar-tár*, **tar-tár-čó-če** *Ld.* to smooth (wrinkles or folds in cloth, paper etc.)

དལ་བ་ *tál-pa*, or *tál-ma*, *Cs.*: 'a moment', *Sch.*: 'quick, decisive, penetrating'; *tál-par*, *Cs.* also *tál-mar*, 1. **instantly, immediately, quickly** *C.*, e.g. *soṅ* go without delay! *Lex.* — 2. *Sch.*: **completely, quite through**, *ɣčód-pa* to hew, to cut (quite through), *ₒbigs-pa* to bore through, to perforate; also *tal ₒbigs-pa.*

དལ་བ་ *tál-ba* a tool with holes in it, used by nailers *Sch.*

དི་ *ti* 1. num. fig.: 39. — 2. Not originally Tibetan, designating 'water'; this word has found its way into *Ld.*, where it however occurs only in **ḱá-ti** saliva (water of the mouth), and in **ná-ti** mucus (running from the nose). — 3. v. *spyi.*

དི་ཀ་ *ti-ka* (टीका) **explanation, commentary.**

དི་ཐུག་ *ti-ťúg*, (*Sch.* *ɣti-ťug*) **bad, mean, silly** *Cs.*; **obstinate, stubborn** *Schr.*

དི་ནག་ *ti-nág* **heath-cock** *Sch.*

དི་ཕི་ *ti-ṗi*(?) *W.* **cap, hat** (from the *Hind.* टोपी?).

དི་ཕུ་ *ti-ṗu*, *Sch.*: *ti-ṗu mjug-riṅ* **pheasant.**

དི་ཙ་ *ti-tsa Sty.*, *tú-ťsa Sch.*, **anvil.**

དི་ཚ་ *ti-ťsa* 1. *tig-ťsa* **zinc** *Med.*; *ti-ťsa sér-po* cadmia, calamine (?) *Med.* — 2. a musical instrument, constructed of metal *Sch.*

དི་སེ་, དེ་སེ་ *ti-se*, *té-se*, the snow-peaks around the lake Manasarowar in *Mṅaris*, which are considered to be the highest and holiest of mountains.

དིག་ *tig* 1. also *tig-tig*, *Lex.* w.e.; *Sch.*: 'certainty, surety; certain'. In col. language **tig, dig, ťig, ṭig**, is frq. used for: **to be sure! well, well! very right!** also as an adj.: *nór-dag tig-tig* the right, the lawful heir. Cf. **ₒgrig; tig ltá-če, tig tsam**, *tig-ťsád* v. sub *ťig.* — 2. *Sik.* the great **hornet.**

དིག་ད་ *tig-ta* (from तिक्तक the n. of several bitter herbs, e.g. of Gentiana Chirayta) several species of **gentian.**

དིག་མེན་ *tig-mén Cs.*, *tig-tsé Ld.*, the ribands which are wound round the felt-gaiters that cover the lower part of the legs.

དིག་ཚ་ *tig-ťsa* = *ti-tsa.*

དིག་རིག་ *tig-rig Sp.* inst. of *ta-gir.*

དིང་ *tiṅ* 1. a small **cup** of brass used esp. in sacrificing. — 2. the sound of metal, **tiṅ zér-ra rag** *W.* I hear a tinkling.

ཏིང་ངེ་འཛིན་ *tiṅ-ṅe-˳dzin* (**समाधि** *Trigl.*, *Was.* also **समापत्ति**) **contemplation,** profound meditation, perfect absorption of mind, cf. *bsam-ytán,* and *sgóm-pa*; *tiṅ-ṅe-˳dzin byéd-pa Sch.*, gen. *tiṅ-ṅe-˳dziṅ-du ˳júg-pa* to be absorbed in deep meditation; *tiṅ-ṅe-˳dzin ˳k'ruṅ* devout meditation takes place; also meton.: the faculty, the power of meditating e.g. *ṗel Mil.*

ཏིང་རྗིང་ *tiṅ-rjiṅ Sik.* **shrew**(-mouse).

ཏིང་ཏིང་ *tiṅ-tiṅ* **clean, well-swept** *Ld., Ts.*

ཏིང་ཏི་ལིང་ *tiṅ-ti-liṅ* **snipe** *Ld.*

ཏང་(ཏིང་)-ཤགས་ *tiṅ* (*-tiṅ*) *- ṡags* little bells moved by the wind *Sch.*

ཏིབ་རིལ་ *tib-ril,* resp. *ysol-tib,* **tea-pot,** *zaṅs-tib* a copper tea-pot,* *rdza-tib* an earthen tea-pot.

ཏིམ་པི་ *tim-pi Mil.* goat's leather, kid-leather, from India, dyed green or blue.

ཏིམ་བུ་ *tim-bu Ts.* **funnel.**

ཏིལ་ *til* (**तिल**) **sesame,** *til-már* sesame-oil, seed-oil.

ཏུ *tu* 1. num. fig.: 69. — 2. an affix, denoting the terminative case, or the direction to a place, joined to the final consonants g and b; cf. *du, ru, su.*

ཏུ་པག་ *tú-pag* (*Turk.* توپک) *W.* **gun, musket, fire-lock, fowling-piece,** **gyáb-če** to discharge, fire off; **tú-pag-man** gunpowder.

ཏུ་རུ་ཀ་ *tu-ru-ka Ma.* **the Turks, Turkomans,** **तुरुष्क**, ترک.

ཏུ་ཙ་ *tú-tsa* v. *ti-tsa.*

ཏུ་ལཱ་ *tú-lā* (*Ssk., Hind.*) **a balance, pair of scales,** *C.* **tú-la tég-pa** to weigh.

ཏུག་གིན་འདུག་ *túg-gin ˳dug* 'cannot' *Sch.* (?)

ཏུག་རིང་ *tug-riṅ,* or *tug-čúm,* prob. also *tug-čém, Cs.:* a wooden rattle's sound or noise; *Sch.* also: the trotting of horses heard in the distance; *tug-riṅ-čan Stg.* noisy (?).

ཏུབ་ *tub, tub yčig-tu rgyúd-do?*

ཏུབ་ཏུག་ *tub-túg Lex.* w.e.; *Sch.:* 'either — or, whether I be able (to do it) or not' (?).

ཏུར་བ་ *túr-ba* (?) *W.* **to darn** (stockings).

ཏུར་རེ་ *túr-re* **clear, distinct,** syn. to *wál-le*; *yid túr-re ˳dug* it is clear to my mind; *túr-re bzuṅ Mil.* prob. watch it! have a sharp eye upon it! *že-sdáṅ láṅs dogs túr-re gyis Mil.* take care lest an emotion of anger arise in your mind! *túr-gyis sad Mil* prob.: he awakes, stirs, is evidently roused; *túr-re-ba Glr.*: adj. (or abstract noun), *rjed-yeṅ-méd-par túr-re-ba* clear, firm with regard to perceptions, opinions etc., without omission or digression.

ཏེ *te* 1. num. fig.: 99. — 2. an affix denoting the gerund, and used after the final letters *n, r, l, s* (v. Grammar), to be translated by the participle in ing, or sentences beginning with when, after, as etc.; also used as a finite tense (though seldom in *B.*), and in that case followed by *˳dug* or *yod,* or also without these words: **dád-de ˳dug** I sit *W.*; *˳gró-ba yin-te Mil.* I go.

ཏེ་པོར་ *té-por Lex.* = *légs-par*; *Sch.:* very, really, actually.

ཏེ་བོར་ *té-bor Sch.* constantly, continually.

ཏེ་སེ་ *té-se* v. *ti-se.*

ཏེག་པ་ *tég-pa,* imp. *tog, C., W.,* = *˳tégs-pa,* **to pack up, put up; to put in** or **into,** **'am-bág-la** into one's bosom; **tag-ṭul** or **ṭug** preparations for a journey, **taṅ-če** *W.* to make.

ཏེའུ་ *teu? Ld.-Gir.* (*Schl.* f. 25, b); *teu sér-po; Mil.* 59, 4 of my edition; *Lex.: teu ṡiṅ-k'ri,* where *Sch.* translates: a square table.

ཏེལ་པ་ *tél-pa Cs.:* an instrument for burning *Med.*; *lčágs-tel* such an instrument of iron *Cs.*; *sprá-tel Lt.?*

ཏོ *to* 1. num for 129 — 2. affix added to certain verbs, when they terminate a sentence.

ཏོ་ཏོ་ལིང་ལིང་ *to-to-liṅ-liṅ W.*, an adv. denoting a swinging motion;

hence *to-to-liṅ-liṅ sed sé-ċe* to play at swinging, to swing.

ཏོལ་ *tó-la* for *tú-lä C.*

ཏོག་ *tog* 1. (केतु *Cs.*: **'the top** of any thing, **a top ornament'**; esp. the button on the cap of Chinese dignitaries, as a mark of distinction; *tog-dkár*, श्वेतकेतु n. of Buddha in paradise (*dga-ldán*) before his incarnation *Ld.-Glr.* 8, a.; *mdúṅ-tog* point, thorn, nail. — 2. for *tog.* and thus prob. also used in *skabs-tog* now, at present *Ld.*

ཏོག་སྒྲ་ *tóg-sgra, tóg-tog-sgra Lex.*, a rolling sound *Sch.*, acc. to *Wdṅ.* also a cracking sound.

ཏོག་ཏིལ་ *tog-til* **a bump, a swelling**, by a knock against the head.

ཏོག་ཙེ་ *tóg-tse W., tóg-rtse Lex.*, **hoe, mattock, pickaxe** *W.* (in *C.* ˳*jor*); *tog-lċags* the iron of the hoe, *tog-yu* the handle of it; *tog-leb* a spade (?) *Cs.*

ཏོང་ཏོང་བྱེད་པ་ *toṅ-tóṅ byéd-pa Lex., Sch.*: to perforate; to produce a whirling noise.

ཏོབ་ཅི་ *tob-ċi W.* **button,** **tób-ċi brgyáb-ċe** to button up; cf. *tób-ču*; (buttons are not in general use in Tibet).

ཏོབ་ཏོབ་སྨྲ་བ་ *tob-tób smrá-ba* to talk confusedly *Sch.*; *W.*: **tab-táb**, or **tab-tób ma ċo** keep your temper! do not talk with such agitation!

ཏོའུ་ལོ་ *tou-lo* **polecat** *Sch.*

ཏོལ་ *tol? Mṅg. bem-tól? Sch. tol-ẏċód-pa* = *tal-ẏċód-pa* q.v.

ཏྲམ་པ་ *trám-pa* hard (of rare occurrence); *ša-trám, rus-tram, rtsa-tram, tram-dkár, tram-nág*, are different species of gout *Med.*

ཏྲི་ཀེད་ *tri-ked* v. *ṭi-ked.*

ཏྲི་ཤུ་(ལ་) *tri-šu(-la)*, from त्रिशूल trident *Wdk.*

ཏྲེ་ཏྲེ་ཧོ་ *tre-tre-ho* (by the context) a dangerous disease of the stomach or a serious symptom of it *Pth.*

ཏྲེ་བ་ཅན་ *tré-ba-ċan* coloured *Sch.*

ཏྲེ་སམ་ *tré-sam* a medicine in the shape of a powder *Med.*

ཏྲོན་ *tron* **diligence, industry** *Cs.*; *tron byéd-pa* to be diligent, to exert one s self.

གཏག་གཏོང་ *ɣtag-ɣtoṅ Lex.* w.e.; *ɣtag-ɣtoṅ-ba* to disperse *Sch.*

གཏང་རག་ *ɣtaṅ-rág* **thanks, thanksgiving,** and prob. also thank-offering, esp. rendering thanks to a deity; *ɣtaṅ-rág byéd-pa*, ˳*búl-ba Mil., Lt., W.* **ċó-ċe, ṗúl-ċe** to render thanks.

གཏད་ *ɣtad* (v. *ɣtód-pa*), in the direction of, **towards,** *ɣyón-gral-du ɣtad ṗyin-nas* going towards the left end of the row *Glr.*; **doṅ-tád* W.* directly opposite, just over against.

གཏད་པ་ *ɣtád-pa* 1. vb, v. *ɣtód-pa*, also *brtád-pa*. — 2. sbst. **hold, steadiness, firmness,** *ɣtád-pa-med* it has no hold, no firmness *Mil.*; *ɣtad-méd* ˳*čúl-ba Zam.* prob to vacillate, to waver, to be unsteady.

གཏད་སོ་ *ɣtád-so* a refuge, resource, esp. store of provisions; **tẹ̄-so žág-pa** *C.* to procure such a store.

གཏན་(པ་) *ɣtán(-pa) Cs.*: 'series, order, system; a bar for a door'; *Sch.* also 'anvil', and 'to lock up'. People from *C.* knew only one signification of *ɣtán-pa*, viz. **mortar,** = *ɣtun*; **bar, door-bar** occurs in *sgo-ɣtán C.* and *W.* But a different word seems to be *ɣtan*: 1. **order, system,** in the current phrase *ɣtán-la* ˳*bébs-pa* to put in order, to arrange, to reduce to a system, *bre-sráṅ* measure and weight *Glr.*, the Tibetan alphabet *Glr.*, the civil law and the canon law *Glr.*, laws, books, = to compose, draw up, write *Glr.*; *raṅ-séms ɣtán-pa* in a mystic sense: to regulate, compose, and purify the mind *Glr.*; also to fashion, to train *C.*, to set right *Mil.* (Cf. *bsam-ɣtán.*) — 2. **duration,** perh. also entireness, completeness, hence *ɣtán-gyi* constant, continual, *ɣtan-grogs* consort, partner for life *Mil.*; *ɣtan-méd Sch.*: 'perishable, without duration or continuity'; *ɣtán-du* 1. **always, continually, for ever,** *ɣtán-du bžúgs-pa* living there continually *Tar.* 2. **entirely, completely** (which is the usual signification of ẏtan-du) e.g. to cut off, to deliver completely; ẏtán-nas id.; ẏtan-ḱrigs agreement, stipulation, convention, ẏtan-krigs byéd-pa *Mil.*

Note. Owing to its second signification ẏtan is often confounded with *brtan(-po)*, or even with *bstan(-pa)*. Not only illiterate people, but well-educated Lamas from *C.* were occasionally doubtful as to the correct spelling of this word.

གཏན་ཚིགས་ *ẏtán-ṫsigs* (*Ssk.* हेतु, *Stg.*, *Do*, ཟྲེ f. 344 *ẏtan-ṫsigs-kyi de-ḱo-na-nyid bstán-pa* = हेतुतत्त्वउपदेश) 1. **argument,** syllogism *Cs.*; evidence before a court of justice *Dzl.* ༢༢༥, 6. — 2. *Sch.*: **a standing proposition,** indisputable point *Thgy.* (where in my *Ms. brtan-ṫsigs* is erron. written; v. the note to the preceding word). — 3. **logic, dialectics** *Cs.*; *ẏtan-ṫsigs-méd-par smrá-ba* is in *Stg.* the term applied to a kind of *kyál-ka*, evidently: illogical, irrational talk; *ẏtan-ṫsigs-su bżéd-nas Glr.* 96. wishing to clear up, to render evident (?); *ẏtan-ṫsigs-mḱan* dialectician, logician.

གཏམ་ *ẏtam* (कथा) **talk, discourse, speech.** 1. in a general sense: **tam ċig-pa** *C.*, **tam ċig-ċig** *W.*, that is one and the same talk, that means the same; *ẏtam bsdúr-ba* to compare depositions, to examine, to try judicially, **tam-dúr** *W.* trial, judicial examination. — 2. **news, tidings, intelligence,** *ẏtám bzáṅ-po* good news; *ṗyis ẏtam mi ˳dug* after which there are no further accounts *Mil.*; **tam śád-ċe** to tell a tale, a story *W.*; **report, rumour, fame,** *de ṗul zér-bai ẏtam rgyál-pos ṫós-nas* when the king heard the report that ... had been delivered up *Pth.*; *ṫag-riṅ-gi ẏtam* fame of remote matters or events; *bdág-gis ẏtám-du ṫós-na* as I have learned, have been told *Dzl.* — 3. **section, chapter** *Tar.*, frq.

Phrases. *ẏtam gléṅ-ba S.O.*, *Dzl.*, *ẏtám-du gléṅ-ba Dzl.* to speak, to converse, to discourse; *ẏtam byéd-pa*, *smrá-ba*, *zér-ba* id.; *ẏtam byar ˳groo* I shall go and speak to him *Dzl.*; the genit. preceding *ẏtam* always denotes the person or thing spoken of, not the person speaking; *ċi-ltar gyúr-pai ẏtam byas* he gave an account of the manner how it had happened *Dzl.*; *mṫún-pai ẏtam byéd-pa* to negotiate about peace *Glr.*; *ċos(-kyi) ẏtam byéd-pa* to begin a religious conversation *Mil.*; *na dé-ltar byéd-pai ẏtam mi-la ma lab* do not tell any body that I am doing this *Mil.*; in a similar manner: *mi rúṅ-bai ẏtam bsgrág-go* he shall declare it to be unbecoming *Thgr.*; *ṗa-mái ẏtam dris* he inquired about his parents *Dzl.*; *bú-moi ẏtam ṫos* he heard of the girl *Dzl.*

Comp. *ẏtam-rgyúd* **tradition, oral account;** *deï ẏtam-rgyúd* the legend of him. — *ẏtam-ṅán* **ill report,** slander. — *ẏtam-snyán* **joyful news, glad tidings,** *sgróg-pa* to announce *Mil.* — *ẏtam-bsdúr* v. above. — *ẏtám-dpe* a proverb, a saying *Cs.* — *ẏtam-rtsúb* rough speech, **abusive language.** Note. In *W.* **(s)pé-ra** is more in use than **tam**

གཏམ(ས)་པ་ *ẏtám(s)-pa* 1. adj **full,** *spú-gri ẏtám(s)-pa* quite full of razors *Thgy.*; also *Lexx.*; more frq. it is spelled *(b)ltám(s)-pa*. — 2. vb. to appoint, to commission, of rare occurrence. — 3. sbst. *Cs.*: a term for a thousand billion, yet v. the remark to *dkrigs-pa*.

གཏའ་(མ་) *ẏtá(-ma) Lexx.* (cf. *ẏté-pa*) **pawn, pledge,** *ẏtá-mar ˳jóg-pa* to pawn, to give as a pledge, *ẏtá-ma blú-ba* to redeem a pledge *Cs.*; **nór-ta** *W.* jewels, precious stones, given as a pledge (*Cs.*: 'pecuniary security, bail'); *mi-ẏta* a hostage *Cs.*

གཏར་བ་ *ẏtár-ba*, with *ḱrag*, **to bleed,** to let blood *Med.*; *ẏtár(-bar) byéd-pa*, *rtsá-ba-la* from a vein, or also *ẏtár-ga ˳débs-pa* id.

གཏི་ཁེ *ẏti-ḱé* a kind of louse *Sch.*

གཏི་ཐུག *ẏti-ṫug* insane, mad *Sch.*, = *ti-ṫug.*

གཏི་མུག་ *ẏti-mug* (तमस्) **gloom, mental darkness, ignorance, stupidity.** *gléṅ-pa ẏti-mug-ċan* infatuated fools *Dzl.*; *mṫsán-mo ẏti-mug-ẏnyid-du soṅ* at night I fell into a profound sleep *Mil.*; in a special sense: the lowest of the three *guṅa* or psychological qualities of animated beings, सत्त्व, रज, तमस्, virtue, passion, stupidity, acc. to the Brahminical theory, for which however Buddhism has substituted the three moral categories: *₀dod-čágs*, *že-sdáṅ*, *γti-mug*, voluptuousness, anger, inconsiderateness (*Köpp.* I, 33); *γti-mug*, as for example, is the source of falsehoods told with a pretended good intention, *Stg.*; the symbol for it is the pig *Wdṅ.* Note. The philosophical term *ma-rig-pa* is altogether different from *γti-mug*.

གཏིག(ས)་པ་ *γtig(s)-pa Lex.* **to fall in drops, to drop, to drip.**

གཏིང་ *γtiṅ*, *Ld.* **ltiṅ**, **bottom,** *rgyá-mtsoï γtiṅ-dkrugs* he turned up the bottom of the sea; *γtiṅ-du núb-pa* to sink to the bottom *Cs.*; **depth,** hence *γtiṅ záb-po Dzl.*, *γtiṅ riṅ-ba* deep, *γtiṅ nyé-ba* not deep, shallow; *rgyá-mtso-bas γtiṅ-záb-bo* it is deeper than the sea *Dzl.*; *γyáṅ-sa γtiṅ-ríṅ-ba* a deep abyss *Thgr.*; *čú-bo γtiṅ-záb-po žig* a deep river *Dzl.* ༢༧༢, 1. (in the third line however *záb-bo* would be the correct reading for *zab-po*); *γtiṅ-zab-ḱyád ḱru-brgyád-pa* eight cubits deep (lit. with regard to depth holding eight cubits) *Dzl.* ༡༢༦, 5; fig. *γtiṅ-nas* from the bottom of the heart, *ṅá-la dád-pa γtiṅ-nas gyis* believe in me with all your heart *Mil.*; *ḱa-grógs* and *γtiṅ-grógs* v. *grogs*; *ḱa-dkar-γtiṅ-nág* white without, and black within (fig.) *Mil.*; the following passage of *Mil.*: *rgyá-mtso čé-la dpe lóṅ-la ḱa-γtiṅ-méd-pai sgom čig gyis*, is not perfectly clear, yet the real sense seems to be: resembling the ocean, be so lost in contemplation, that you do not know any longer a difference between surface and bottom; *γtiṅ-rdó* a stone or piece of lead (*žá-nyei γtiṅ-rdó Pth.*) fastened to a rope, and used as plummet, as anchor, as a clock-weight, as a means for drowning delinquents etc.; **ču nyóg-po-če-la tiṅ med** *W.* a very muddy water has no depth; *γtiṅ-čan* deep, *γtiṅ-méd* shallow *Cs.*; also fig. deep, reserved, covert, difficult to fathom, to form an opinion of, and the contrary: shallow, superficial; *γtiṅ-mi-lón C.* of unknown depth; *γtiṅ-dróṅs-pa* fathomed, penetrated, ascertained *C.*

གཏིབ(ས)་པ་ *γtib(s)-pa* 1. **to be gathering,** of clouds, *sprin-ṗuṅ γtib-pa* thick clouds gathering *Wdṅ.*; *bdug-spós sprin-bžin γtib* incense wafts along like clouds *Glr.*; *mún-pa γtib Lex.*, col. also **nam-ḱa tib-tib yod** cf. *₀tib-pa*. — 2. sometimes for *rdib-pa*.

གཏིམ་པ་ *γtim-pa* v. *tim-pa*.

གཏུག་པ་ *γtúg-pa*, pf. *γtugs*, also *btúg-pa*, cognate to *ṫúg-pa*, 1. **to reach, to touch,** *yi-dam-gyi ṫúgs-kar γtúgs-nas* putting or pressing (his forehead) against the breast of the image *Glr.*; *mi žig-gi žábs-la mgó-bos γtúg-pa*, or only *žábs-γtug-pa* to touch as a supplicant a person's feet (or skirt) with the brow, to cast one's self at another's feet, frq.; *btug ṫúg-pa daṅ* was explained: when it (the danger) draws quite near *Ma.*; **to overtake, to reach,** ni f., e.g. *mṫa* the end *Lex.*; **to meet with, to join** *Tar.* 172, 14. — 2. to bring an action against a person, **to sue** *Sch.*, thus prob. *Dzl.* ༡༡༠, 3, and *Pth.* — 3. = *zád-pa* to be exhausted, to be consumed(?) *Zam. zád-pai γtúgs-pa*.—

Note. Not only *γtúg-pa*, but also many of the following words have b as well as g for their initial letter, and moreover a corresponding form beginning with *ṫ*, of the same or nearly the same signification.

གཏུན་ *γtun*, *Sch.* also *rtun*, col. **gog-tún** (spelling dubious) 1. **pestle;** there are small ones, like ours and large ones, in shape of poles, as thick as a man's arm, and about 6 feet long, by means of which the pounding is effected in an excavation made in a rock, called *γtun-ḱúṅ*; *γtun(-gyis) rdúṅ-ba* to pound with a pestle *Dzl.*; *γtún-po* mortar *Cs.*; *γtun-bu*, *γtun-šiṅ* pestle *Cs.* — 2. **mallet, knocker** *Dzl.*

གཏུབ་པ་ *γtúb-pa*, more frq. *btúb-pa*, = *ṫúb-pa*, **to be able,** *ṗyir ₀óṅ-du btúb-pa-am* shall you really be able to come back? *Dzl.*; *mi btúb-pa* very frq. not to be able to prevail upon one's self, **to be unable**, also: **to be unwilling, to have no mind** (to do a thing).

གཏུབ(ས)་པ་ *ytúb(s)-pa, btúb(s)-pa, Ld.* **stúb-če**, = *˳túb-pa*, **to cut to pieces, to cut up**, meat, wood etc.; in *W.* also **to mince;** (in *C. btsáb-pa*); *ytubs-spyád* chopper *Sch.*

གཏུམ་པ་ *ytúm-pa* 1. **ferocity, rage;** also adj. **furious;** *k̔ró-žiṅ ytúm-la snyiṅ-rje-med* in furious wrath, merciless *Dzl.*; *ydúg-čiṅ ytúm-pai klu* a Lu in a deadly rage *Sambh.*; *ytúm-pai sgra sgróg-pa* to roar furiously *Pth.*; *k̔ró-ytum-pa* furious with rage *Glr.*; *ytúm-žiṅ rgód-pa* obstinate and unmanageable, of a boy; *ytúm-po Mil., ytúm-čan, ytum-ldán* cruel, fierce, furious *Cs.*; *blá-ma t̔ugs-ytúm-po ˳oṅ* the Lama grows angry *Mil. nt.*; *ytúm-mo* fem. a fury of a woman *Dzl.* ༢༠༠, 10; *Sch.* also: hangman (?); *rluṅ ytúm-mo Cs.* a furious wind, a hurricane — 2. = *btúm-pa, ˳túm-pa*, **to veil, to cover; to wrap up**, e.g. the head; with the instr. to wrap up or cover with a thing.

གཏུམ་པོ་ *ytúm-po* 1. v. *ytúm-pa* 1. — 2. चण्ड (hot) in the more developed mysticism the power which meditating saints by dint of long continued practice may acquire of holding back their breath for a great length of time, by which means the air is supposed to be drawn from the *ró-ma* and *rkyáṅ-ma* (two veins, v. *rtsá-ba*) into the *dbú-ma* (*sróg-rtsa, dhú-ti*, aorta?) thus causing a feeling of uncommon warmth, comfort, and lightness inside, and finally even emancipating the body from the laws of gravity, so as to lift it up and hold it freely suspended in the air, *Mil.* frq.; v. also *Tar.* 186, 20; *ytúm-poi bde-dród* the feeling of warmth just mentioned *Mil.*; *ytúm-po ˳bar* the warmth of meditation commences *Mil.* The three above-named veins are symbolically represented by *a-shád*, i.e. the second half of an ཨ, viz. ད, hence *a-šad-ytúm-po* the three veins'-meditation-warmth, *Mil.* — 3. n. of the goddess Durga or Uma.

གཏུར་བུ་ *ytúr-bu Lex.* w.e.; *Cs.* **bag, sack, wallet.**

གཏུལ་བ་ *ytúl-ba* **to grind, to pulverize,** colours, medicinal substances etc.; cf. *˳t̔ág-pa*.

གཏེ་པ་ *yté-pa W.* (*Ld.* **sté-pa**) *yté-ba, yté-ma C., ytéṅ-pa Lexx.*, **pawn, pledge, bail** (*Sch.* also: a present); cf. *ytá-ma*; *yteu* id.? hostage? *Tar.*

གཏེར་ *yter* (निधि, कोश) 1. **treasure,** frq. — 2. symb. num. for 9. — *yter-mdzód* **a treasury.** — *ytér-k̔a* **a mineral vein, mine,** *nór-gyi ytér-k̔a rnyéd-pa* to find a mine of precious metals.

གཏོ་ *yto Lt., Thgy.* a magic ceremony for the purpose of averting misfortune; *yto-bčós* id.

གཏོག་པ་ *ytóg-pa* 1. also *btóg-pa, ˳tóg-pa*, **to pluck off, gather, crop, tear out** (one's hair) *Lex.* — 2. v. *se-gol.*

གཏོགས་པ་ *ytógs-pa* **to belong, appertain to; belonging,** *rgyál-poï ydúṅ-la ytógs-pa yin* you belong to the royal blood or family *Dzl.*; *deï náṅ-du mi ytógs-sam* am I not included in them? *Dzl.*; *˳dzam-bui-gliṅ-la ytógs-pa* belonging to Dzambuling *Glr.*; **di lé-ka daṅ ma tog** *W.* do not meddle with that! *ma-ytógs-pa*, gen. adv. *ma ytógs-par* **except, besides.** — *ytogs-˳dód Sch.*: 'to love, to like, to wish; a good-for-nothing fellow' (?).

གཏོང་བ་ *ytóṅ-ba*, pf. *btaṅ*, fut. *ytaṅ*, imp. *toṅ* (*W.* **taṅ-če**, imp. **toṅ**) त्यज 1. **to let** a. **to let go**, to permit to go, **to dismiss**, *čii p̔yir bdág-čag-rnams-kyis ytoṅ* why should we let you go, suffer you (our teacher) to go? **to let escape** (a prisoner) *Dzl.*; **to let loose** (a dog against a person) *Mil.*; **to let go,** to quit one's hold *ma ytoṅ*, col. **ma taṅ** don't let him go, stop him! **to leave, abandon, renounce,** *č̔os* one's religion; more definitely: *blos ytóṅ-ba*, v. *blo*; *yóṅs-su ytóṅ-ba* to abandon altogether *Dzl.*; to leave off, to abstain from, *ysód-par byá-ba ytóṅ-ba* to leave off killing *Dzl.* b. **to let in, to admit,** *sgó-nas* through the door *Dzl.*, *náṅ-du ytóṅ-ba* to permit to enter. — 2. **to let go,** i.e. to make go, **to send,** *mi* a man, a messenger, very frq.; *ₒdzam-bui-gliṅ kún-tu btáṅ-nas* he made him go all over the country of Dzambuling *Dzl.*; *skyél-du ytóṅ-ba* to dispatch for conveying (a message); *lĕn-du ytóṅ-ba* to send (a person) for (a thing); *ₒtsól-ba btáṅ-ba-las* he sent out searchers (people in search) *Dzl.* ༢༠, 18., unless this passage should be read *ₒtsól-bar*. — 3. **to let have, to give,** so in *W.* almost exclusively; *sman ytóṅ-ba* to give medicine, *ytóṅ-tsul* the way of giving medicine, for 'a dose' *Med.*; *ytóṅ-pod-čan* liberal, bounteous *Mil.*; *ytóṅ-sems-ldan* id. *S.g.*; *ytóṅ-sems* liberality, bounty; **tóṅ zer** he says, give me! he wants to have, he tries to get *W.*; *čós-la ytóṅ-ba* to give a person up to religion, i.e. to destine him for the priesthood, to make him take orders. — 4. **to make, to cause,** e.g. a smoke by lighting a fire *Glr.*; with the termin. **to turn into,** *byé-taṅ néu-taṅ-du* sandy plains into meadows *Glr.*; *rims(-nad) ytóṅ-ba* to cause, **to send down,** epidemies, plagues (of gods); **to construct, fix, place,** chains before a building *Glr.*; in *W.* **(s)kad táṅ-če** to utter sounds, **kú-čo, bó-ra táṅ-če** to raise, to set up a cry; **kug** or **kum táṅ-če** to make crooked, to bend; in forming intensive verbs: **go čád táṅ-če** to decapitate; **tón toṅ, piṅs toṅ** take out! throw out! **tsa toṅ** put salt into it! **ču táṅ-če** to water (the garden); **lud táṅ-če** to manure (the fields). The participle **táṅs-pa** is used adverbially in *Ld.*; **i-ne táṅs-pa á tsúg-pa** from here to there, from this place to that place (= *bzuṅs-te*).

གཏོད་ *ytod?* *ytód-la mnán-pa*, of the sun *Pth.*, of the galaxy *Mil.*, evidently denotes the disappearing of these celestial bodies by enchantment or only as a poetical figure; perh. = *ydos*, or to be explained by *ytód-pa* II.

གཏོད་པ་ *ytód-pa* I. also *ytád-pa*, pf. *btad*, *ytad*, fut. *ytad*, imp. *btod* (*Mil.*; *Cs. tod?*) 1. **to deliver up,** *lág-tu* into the hand, to hand over *Glr.*, to hand to a person the subject for a theme or problem *Glr.*, to commit the management of the household to another *Dzl.*, to commit a child to a teacher *Dzl.*, *dge-ₒdún-la dbaṅ* to confer important offices on the priesthood *Glr.*, *rig-pa* to teach; *ycig snyiṅ ycig-la ytád-pa* to communicate one's feelings to one another *Glr.* — 2. **to lean against** or **upon** c. dat., e.g. to rest one's head on one's arm; to lay or put against, to, or on, one's mouth to a person's ear *Thgr.*, the tip of the tongue against the palate *Gram.* — 3. **to direct, to turn,** *mi-la mgó-bo*, one's face towards a person *Lt.*, *mi-la mdzúb-mo*, or *sdig-mdzúb* to point at a person (with the finger) *Glr.*; *sgo nub-pyógs bál-poi yúl-du ytod Glr.*, the door points south, towards Nepal; *ₒbém-la* to take aim, to aim at *Lex.*; *rná-bai dbáṅ-po ytód-pa* to listen to, to give a person a hearing *Mil.*; *sems*, resp. *tugs*, *ytód-pa Mil.* id.; *ₒod-zér-la ytád-nas yzigs-pas* turning after a ray of light, following it with the eye (= *brtén-nas*) *Glr.*; **also used** absolutely: *dkar-kúṅ ytód-pa* the projecting windows *S.g.* (?) — *ka ytód-pa Glr.?*

II. inst. of *rtód-pa*, **to fasten** (cows etc.) to a stake (driven into the ground), **to tedder.**

གཏོམ་པ་ *ytóm-pa* **to talk, to speak** *Sch.*, cf. *ytam* (?).

གཏོམས་པ་ *ytóms-pa* **filled up, full,** for *bltáms-pa*, *ytáms-pa*, *Sch.*

གཏོར་བ་ *ytór-ba* (*Lex.* **ལྷགས**) cf. *ₒtór-ba*, 1. **to strew, to scatter** ccirdp., *mé-tog-gis ytór-ro Dzl.* they strewed flowers, also *ytór-to Dzl.*; *sá-la sas ytór-ba* they that threw earth upon me *Dzl.*; *sá-la ytór-ba* to scatter over the ground *Glr.* — 2. **to cast, to throw,** ccar., books into the water *Glr.*, a ring into the air *Glr.*; **to throw** out, e.g. spittle into a person's ear, for healing purposes (= *ₒdór-ba*); **to cause to circulate** the chyle through every part of the body *Med.*; **to waste, to dissipate** *Dzl.*, occasionally with the accus. of the vessel containing the substance thrown out: *nú-*

ma γtór-ba *Glr.* (a cow) emptying its udder by discharging the milk. — 3. *Sch.*: '*srub γtór-ba* **to rend,** to tear to pieces'.

གཏོར་མ་ *γtór-ma* **strewing-oblation,** an offering brought to malignant demons, either as a kind of exorcism or as an appeasing gift, in order to prevent their evil influences upon man; *mčód-pa dan γtór-ma sbyin-pa* to offer such an oblation, *γtór-mar snó-ba* to devote something for it. The ceremonies are similar to those used in *sbyin-srég Schl. Buddh.* 249; the offerings consisting of things eatable and not eatable, of blood, and even of animal and vegetable feces, scattered into the air (the benefit being shared by the *dri-za* q.v.). There are various sorts of Torma-offerings, according to the nature of the substances offered (*ču-* or *čab-γtor*, *pye-γtor*; *lhag-γtor*, an oblation of the fragments of a meal *Mil.*), or according to the time at which (*dgu-γtór* v. *dgu*), and the purpose for which they are offered (*mtsún-γtor* v. *mtsun*). Other names of Torma-offerings are: *blud-rgyá*, *mar-me-rgyá*, *tin-lo*(?)*-rgyá*, *ča-γsúm* etc. Tormas in general belong to the ceremonies most frequently performed; *γtor-čá* are the vessels and other implements used for that purpose; *γtor-sdéb Sch.*: 'a bowl for these offerings'(?). — *γtor-zán Lex.* **बलि** oblation of the remnants of the daily meal to creatures of every description.

གཏོལ་ *γtol*, only in *γtol-méd*, = *ča-méd*, **not known, dubious,** *pó-am mó-am γtol-méd-do* one does not know yet, whether it will be a boy or a girl *Dzl.*; *či byá-bai γtol méd* not knowing what to do *Dzl.*; *gar tál-bai γtol med* not knowing where she had gone to; *bdág-la γtol méd* I do not know any thing about it *Dzl.* — (*Sch.* has a verb *γtól-ba* to perforate, pierce; to discover, disclose; v. *rtól-ba*).

གཏོས་ *γtos* **size, width, quantity,** *rí-boi γtos tsam* as high as a mountain *Lex.*; *rim-gro γtos-čé-ba*, like *rgya-čé-ba*, great marks of honour, extraordinary homage.

བཏག་པ་ *btág-pa* v. ˳*tág-pa*.

བཏགས་པ་ *btágs-pa* v. ˳*dógs-pa*, and *ka-btágs*.

བཏང་བ་ *btán-ba* v. *γtón-ba*.

བཏད་པ་ *btád-pa* v. *γtód-pa*.

བཏབ་པ་ *btáb-pa* v. ˳*débs-pa*.

བཏང་སྙོམས་ *btan-snyóms* (cf. *snyoms*) **उपेक्ष** complete **indifference,** perfect **apathy** (acc. to *Schr.* prop. 'a liberality perfectly impartial'?).

བཏང་བཟུང་ *btan-bzún Lex.* **मुचिलिन्द** n. of a hill where Buddha was teaching.

བཏིག་པ་ *btig-pa*, pf. *btigs*, *Cs.* **to drop,** to let fall in drops, *rná-bar sman*, medicine into the ear, v. ˳*tig-pa*.

བཏིང་བ་ *btin-ba* v. ˳*din-ba*.

བཏུ་བ་ *btú-ba* v. ˳*tú-ba*.

བཏུང་བ་ *btún-ba* v. ˳*tún-ba*.

བཏུག་པ་ *btúg-pa* v. *γtúg-pa*.

བཏུད་པ་ *btúd-pa* v. ˳*dúd-pa*.

བཏུད་མར་ *btúd-mar Glr.* in rapid or close succession, **tụ-tụ-pa-la** *C.* id.

བཏུབ་ *btub*, *Lex.* = *run*, **fit, convenient, practicable, becoming,** *btúb-bo* it is convenient etc.; *btúb-pa* v. *γtúb-pa*.

བཏུམ་པ་ *btúm-pa*, *γtúm-pa*, 1. **to wrap round, to envelop;** hence 2. in *W.* **to shut,** a book, valuable books being wrapped up in a cloth before being laid by; *btum-póg* **bunch** or **knot**, produced by money and the like being tied up in the girdle.

བཏུལ་བ་ *btúl-ba* v. ˳*dúl-ba*, *γtúl-ba*.

བཏེག་པ་ *btég-pa* v. ˳*dégs-pa*.

བཏོད་པ་ *btód-pa* 1. = *rtód-pa*, **to fasten** (grazing horses or cattle) by a rope to a stake, **to tedder;** *Mil.* declares relations to be the *btod-tág* (the tedder) in the hands of the devil. — 2. **to erect, raise up, produce, cause, occasion;** *srol-btód-*

pa (*Lex.* w.e.) may accordingly imply: to introduce a custom.

བརྟོན་པ *btón-pa* v. *ₒdón-pa.*

བརྟོལ་བ *btól-ba Sch.* = *γtól-ba.*

རྟ *rta* (*rtá-po C., Mil.*), resp. *čibs*, 1. **horse**, *p̓o-rta* a gelding, *mó-rta*, or *rta-rgód-ma*, a mare; *rta ₒdúl-ba* to break in, train, a horse; *rta rgyúg-pa* to gallop; to run horses for a wager, to race *Glr.*; **sta śrul-če* Ld.* id.? — 2. the lower front part of a pair of breeches, *dór-rta, ăṅ-rta.*

Comp. *rta-rkyá(-pa)*, or *-skyá(-pa)* one skilled in horsemanship. — *rta-bskrágs* (**stab-rágs* Ld.*) a clattering train of horsemen. — *rta-gál Ts.* pouch or bag of a horseman, saddle-bag. — *rta-grás* = *rta-rá.* — *rta-bgád* a horse-laugh, *rta-bgád-kyis ₒdébs-pa* to set up a horse-laugh *Sch.* — *rta-mgó* a horse's head; *rta-mgó-ma* v. *go-tsém.* — *rta-mgrin* (हयग्रीव) n. of a demon (*Schl.* 110), a terrifying deity. — *rtá-sga*, *W.* **tá-ga**, **saddle.** — *rta-sgám* a large box or chest. — *rtá-sgo* v. *sgo.* — *rta-sgyél*, gen. connected with *mi-bsád*, the slaughtering of men and killing of horses. — *rta-ṅán* Tibetan horses, small, strong, unshod, v. *Hook.* II, 131, and so already in *Marco Polo*'s travels. — *rta-rṇa* **horse-tail,** **te ṅá-ma yod* W.* it is (made) of horse-hair. — *rta-lčág* horse-whip; whip in general — *rta-čág* dry fodder or provender given to horses, corn, oats. — *rta-mčóg* the best horse, a splendid horse, state-horse; gen. a fabulous horse, a sort of Pegasus, thus e.g. *Glr.* chp. 6, where it partakes of divine properties (*rtai rgyál-po čan-šés bá-la-ha*; acc. to *Schl.* p. 253 *rlúṅ-rta* is the same). — *rta-mčóg-k̓a-ₒbab* = *γyas-ru-γtsáṅ-po* = *mná-ris-ču* n. of the principal river of Tibet. — *rta-ljáṅ* he with the green horses, the sun, po. *Glr.* — *rta-rná* horse-ear, n. of one of the seven gold-mountains, surrounding the Rirab. — *rtá-pa* horseman, rider, **tá-pa ta-žón* Ld.* a balancing-board, **see-saw;** *rtá-pai dpúṅ* horse, **cavalry** *Cs.* — *rta-lpágs* a horse's skin; n. of a medicinal herb *Med.* — *rta-bábs* 1. a large stone or raised place for alighting from a horse(?) *Cs.* 2. the superstructure of a large door or gate, the arch of a gate-way, *Lex. twa-ra-ṇa*, द्वारण? — *rta-dbyáṅs* अश्वघोष n. of a great scholar *Thgy.* — *rta-bél* a horse's front-hair *Cs.* — *rta-sbáṅs* **horse-dung.** — *rta-rmíg* a horse's hoof; n. of a plant *Med.* — *rta-rmíg-ma* a lump of silver bullion like a horse's hoof *Cs.* — *rta-rdzí* one that tends horses; **a groom** *Glr.* — *rta-žúṅ* a good horse. — *rta-zám* 1. **post-station,** *rta-zám-gyi tsúgs-pa* a post-house; *rta-zám gyi spyi-dpon* postmaster-general *Cs.* 2. in *Ld.* also for *rta-zám-pa.* — *rta-zám-pa* **postillion, courier, express, estafet.** An estafet rides day and night, mounting fresh horses at certain stations, and making the way from Lé to Lhasa (for ordinary travellers a journey of 4 months) in 18 days. — *rta(i)-ₒú-lag* a compulsory service consisting in the supply of horses. — *rta-rá*, *rta-grás* **inclosure, stable,** for horses. — *rta-šá* 1. horse-flesh. 2. the oblique abdominal muscles of the hips. — *rta-šád* **curry-comb** *Sch.* — *rta-γsár* a horse not yet broken in or dressed *Schr.* — *rta-bséb* **stallion.** — With regard to the colour of horses (*spú-k̓a*), the following distinctions are made: *rta-dkár* a gray or white horse; *rta-rkyaṅ-nág*, or *k̓am-nág Sch.* a dark-brown horse; *rta k̓ám-pa Ld.* a yellowish-brown horse (*Sch.* a dark-brown horse); *rta-k̓am-dmár Sch.* a light-bay horse, a sorrel horse; *rta k̓rá-bo* a piebald or a dappled horse *Ld.-Glr.*, *Schl.* fol. 26, a; *rta-gró Sch.* a gray horse, *rta gro-dkár* a light-gray horse, *rta gro-sṅón Sch.* a dapple-gray horse, *rta gro-dmár* a roan horse, a roan; *rta rgya-bo Sch.* a chestnut-bay horse (a bayard, a brown horse) with white breast and muzzle; *rta ṅáṅ-pa* an isabel *Ld.-Glr.*; *rta rṅog-dkár* a bright bay horse; *rta-sṅo-k̓ra*, *rta-sṅo-tig-čan Sch.* a dapple-gray horse; *rtá-sṅo-nag Sch.* a dark-gray horse; *rta-tig-k̓ra Sch.* a spotted horse; *rta nag* a black horse; *rta-brau* = *rgya* *bo Sch.*; *rta-mog-ro Glr.* a yellowish-brown horse; *rta zag-pa Sch.* a horse having gray and white spots; *rta ˳ól-ba Mil., Ld.-Glr.*, a black horse; *rta ra-rá Sch.* a yellow-dun horse; *rta rág-pa Ld.* a tawny horse (*Sch.*: 'a white and red spotted horse'); *rta rag-rág* an ash-gray horse; *rta rag-sér*, or *rta ser-sér Sch.* a yellowish-red horse; *rta sram-srám Sch.* a gray horse with a black mane and tail.

རྟག་པ *rtág-pa* (नित्य) 1. **perpetual, constant, lasting, eternal.** 2. **perpetuity, duration** to all futurity, a quality which, acc. to Buddhist views, can be ascribed only to the vacuum, to absolute emptiness, the *stoṅ-pa-nyid*; *mi rtág-pa* not durable, perishable; *de yaṅ mi-rtag ṫsul-du ydа* this, too, is subject to the law of perishableness *Mil.*; *mi rtág-pai čos* the principle of transitoriness; *rtág-par ˳dzin-pa* to look upon (transitory things, i.e. the world) as lasting, and hence: to be worldly-minded *Glr.*; as partic. one that is earthly-minded, a worldling; *nyál-ba-la rtág-pa* steady in lying, i.e. disposed to lie down, to be continually at rest, *Stg.*; *rtag-čad* lasting and transitory, frq.; *rtag-par*, or more frq. *rtag-tu*, **always**, i.e. 1. continually, 2. at each time (*Dzl.* ༢༥, 5); *rtág-tu-ba* perpetuity, eternity *Cs.* — *rtág-po, Ld.* **stágs-po**, **lasting**, durable, reliable, *rtag-brtan* id. *C.*; *rtag-snyóm-la C.* adv. uniformly, equally. — *rtag-rés ˳kór-ba Sch.*: a constant change(?).

རྟགས *rtags* (cf. *rtógs-pa*) 1. resp. *ṗyag-rtágs*, **sign, token, mark, characteristic**, **tag-ẓi** *W.*, **tags-pa** *Ld.*, id.; *rtags byéd-pa*, vulg. **tag rgyáb-pa** to make a mark; *ráb-tu byúṅ-bai rtags yód-pa* (partic.) one having the outward marks of an ecclesiastic *Glr.*; *bkra-šis rtags* v. *bkra-šis*; **omen, prognostic,** = *ltas*, *bú-mo skyé-bai rtags* a prognostic of a girl being born *Med.*; **proof** of a thing, c. genit., frq.; *mṅon-rtágs Dzl.* id.; **proof, argument, evidence,** **či tágs-pa-ne zum** *Ld.* upon what evidence have they seized him? **tágs-pa ẓig gos** you must prove it, **tágs-pa-aṅ mi dug** there is no trace, no evidence, left. — 2. **inference, deduction** *Was.* (320). — 3. **the black, the centre** of a target, *W.* **tág-la čúg-če** to take for a mark. — 4. **sexual organ,** organ of generation, *rtágs-sam bhá-ga* as two synonyms for the same thing *Wdṅ.*, *ṗó-rtags, mó-rtags* frq. — 5. **gift, present,** resp. *ṗyag-rtágs.* — 6. any mark for denoting grammatical distinctions, such as terminations etc., ni f.; *rtags ˳júg-pa* using such marks, making grammatical distinctions, seems to imply about the same thing as our etymology, the etymological part of grammar. — *rtags-yig* 1. **stamp, type**(?) *Cs.* 2. letter of recommendation, **credentials** *W.* — **tag-ril** *W.*, **lot,** **tag-ril túṅ-če** to cast or draw lots (a half-religious proceeding) cf. *rgyan.*

རྟབ་པ *rtáb-pa*, also *rtab-rtáb-pa*, and *stáb-pa*, **to be in a hurry, to be confused, frightened,** in a state of alarm, e.g. of fowl frightened by some cause (*Zam.* = *bréd-pa*); *rtáb-po* adj.; *stab-stáb-por sóṅ-nas* having become quite startled and confounded *Pth.*; *rtab-rtób* sbst., *rtab-rtób-tu náṅ-du ṗyin-te* she ran into the house in haste (full of joy) *Mil.*; *rtab-rtáb-la ra mi ˳dren* I cannot help you with such speed *Mil. nt.* It is also spelled *brtabs-pa.*

རྟས་པ *rtás-pa* v. *brtá-ba.*

རྟིག་གི *rtig-gi Ts.* for *rtéu*, **foal, colt.**

རྟིང་ *rtiṅ* (in more recent literature and col.) what is **behind** or **after**, with regard to space, and more particularly to time, *rtiṅ-du, rtiṅ-la, rtiṅ-na* adv. **afterwards,** *rtiṅ-du bčós-so* they were made afterwards, were added later *Glr.*; postp. c. genit., or less corr. c. accus., after; *byon rtiṅ-la* after their appearance *Pth.*, *byuṅ-rtiṅ* after he has come *Mil.*; *de-rtiṅ-la* after that *Glr.*; **tiṅ-ne ḍáṅ-če** *W.* to follow, to come after or later; *rtiṅ-ma* adj. and sbst. the last *Tar.*; *γtám-gyi rtiṅ-ma yin* this is my last, my farewell-speech *Glr.*; without *ma*: **dus tiṅ ẓig-na** *W.* some day **hereafter,** some future day; **tiṅ-ma ẓag, tiṅ-ma nyi-*

*ma** *W.* the following day; **tiṅ-ǰúg** remaining part, the last remainder, **di-riṅ ǰa tiṅ-ǰúg len soṅ** *W.* to-day I have used the last of my tea. — *rtiṅ-pa* 1. the end, extremity, lowest part, e.g. of a stick *Glr.*; gen.: 2. the heel of the foot, *rtiṅ-lčags* a spur, *rtiṅ-lčags rgyáb-pa* to prick with the spurs, to spur; *rtiṅ-ču* the Achilles-tendon.

རྟིབ་པ *rtib-pa*, pf. *brtibs*, fut. *brtib*, imp. *rtib(s)* **to break** or **pull down** (cf. *rdib-pa*).

རྟིའུ་ *rtiu*, sometimes for *rteu*, **a foal.**

རྟུག་པ *rtúg-pa* 1. **excrement, dirt** *rtug-skám* or *-ském* dry excrements *Med.*; *rgyal-srid rtúg-pa bžin-du dór-ba* to throw off royalty like dirt *Pth.*; *rtúg-pa p̓yis-pai rdo* a stone for wiping one's self *Mil.* — 2. *C.* **wind, flatulence.** — 3. *(b)rtug* v. sub *ťógs-pa.*

རྟུང་བ *rtúṅ-ba*, pf. *brtuṅs*, fut. *brtuṅ*, also *stúṅ-ba*, **to make shorter, to shorten, to contract**, e.g. a rope, a **dress**; *ynyá-ba brtuṅs* his neck is contracted *Mṅg.*

རྟུན *rtun* v. *ytun*; *rtun-ril* **a trituration-bowl** *Sch.*

རྟུན་པ *rtún-pa*, *brtún-pa*, **diligence,** *rtún-pa skyed-pa* to be diligent *Zam.* Cf. *dún-pa.*

རྟུལ་པོ *rtúl-po*, or *rtúl-ba*, **blunt, dull,** *mtson-rtúl* a blunt weapon *Cs.*; gen. fig.: *dbáṅ-po rtúl-po* (opp. to *rnón-po* or *rnó-ba* sharp, and *ₒbriṅ-po* middling) dullness, stupidity, imbecility of mind; dull, stupid; *blo-rtúl* weak intellect. — *(b)rtul-p̓ód-pa* (**वीर**) boldness, courage; bold, brave *Dzl.*

རྟེའུ་ *rteu* **foal, colt,** *rteu ₒbraṅ-ba* to bring forth a colt, to foal *Cs.*

རྟེན *rten* (cf. the next article) that which contains, keeps, or supports a thing, 1. **a hold, support,** esp. in compounds: *ka-rtén* the plinth or base of a pillar *Cs.*; *rkaṅ-rtén* (resp. *žabs-rten*) a foot-stool *Cs.*; *žu-rtén* **a** present given to support a supplication, and never omitted by Orientals when making a petition; **sem-tén** *W.* token, keep-sake; — esp. **a visible representation, a statue** or **figure** of Buddha or of other divine beings, which the pious may take hold of, and to which their devotions are more immediately directed (v. the explanation in *Glr.* chp. II, init.) — 2. **receptacle,** resp. *ydun-rtén*, for the bones or relics of a saint, *mčód-rten* for oblations, v. *mčód-pa*, compounds; *rig-pai rten* receptacle of the soul, i.e. the body *Schr.*; *rig-pa rtén-med-pa*, *rten daṅ brál-ba* the houseless, bodiless soul *Thgr.*; *ₒjig-rtén* v. *ₒjig*; *snyiṅ ni tse srog séms-kyi rten* the heart is the seat of life and of the soul *Mṅg.*; **seat, abode, residence,** of a deity, **sanctuary, temple** (*Dzl.*), **shrine,** *rtén-gyi ytsó-bo* the deity residing in a shrine *Glr.*; **visible representation, symbol,** of divine objects or beings, esp. the *rten ysum*: *sku-rten* an image of Buddha, *ysuṅ-rten* symbol of the doctrine, gen. consisting in a volume of the holy writings, *túgs-rten* symbol of grace, a pyramid, *Köpp.* II, 294. Hence *rten* might very suitably be used for denoting the material element in the Christian sacraments, viz. the water, and the bread and wine. — 3. **present, gift,** prop. for *žu-rten* (v. sub no. 1), and then in a more **general** sense, resp. *p̓yag-rtén*, *W.*, for *p̓yag-rtágs*; also **offering, oblation.** — 4. **sex,** specified as male, female, or hermaphrodite, independently of age *S.g.*; sometimes comprising age *S.g.*; or denoting age alone, as child, man, old man *Lt.*; **calling, situation** in life *Tar.* 163, 15 (where *gyi* ought to be changed into *ni*) 176, 15; 178, 18; some compounds follow still at the end of the next article.

རྟེན་པ *rtén-pa* 1. vb., pf. and fut. *brten*, imp. *rton* (*brten?*), **to keep, to hold, to adhere to, to lean on,** *ₒkár-ba-la* on a staff *Pth.*; *ká-ba-la* against a pillar; *lág-pa ₒgrám-pa-la* to lean one's head on one's hand, in meditating *Dzl.*; fig. **to depend** or **rely on,** *brtén-pai blá-ma* the priest to whom one holds; *snúm-la rtén-pa* to keep to the fat, i.e. to eat much fat *Med.*; *ₒkrig-pai ťós-la* **to be given, addicted,** to sensuality; **ču táṅ-wa máṅ-po-la tén-ne** *C.* if one is intent on watering; *ₒtsó-ba dka-ṫúb-la* v. *dká-ba* compounds; *k'yéd-kyis ɣsúṅ-ba-la brtén-nas* following, obeying (your) orders *Glr.*; *ṅai nús-pa-la rtén-nas* relying on my strength, i.e. by the help of my strength (you will be able to get to that place) *Mil.*; hence *(b)rtén-nas* is frq. used for: in consequence of, with respect to, concerning etc.: *rkyen dé-la rtén-nas* in consequence of this event (the doctrine spread) *Tar.* 8, 1; **ɣha-la tén-nas** why? wherefore? *C.*; *yul k'yád-par-čan-la rtén-nas* (to sin) with regard to a noble object *Thgy.*; **to hang on, to depend on, to arise** or **issue from**; *rtén-par ₒbrél-ba* v. *rten-ₒbrél*; **to be near, to border on,** **tén-te yod* W.* (the two villages) are contiguous to each other; = *ɣtád-pa, stón-pa* to be directed, to be situated, to lie towards, *lhó-p'yogs-la* to be situated towards the south *Sambh.*; *ₒod-zér-la rtén-nas ɣzigs-pa* to look after or pursue with one's eye a ray of light, like *ɣtód-pa* I. 3. Cf. *stén-pa.* — 2. sbst. **that which holds, keeps up,** *rgyál-poi rtén-pao* (these) are **the supports** of **kings** *Dzl.*; *brtén-pa rús-pai ɣnás-lugs bstán-pa* 'the doctrine of the hold-giving bones', osteology *Mṅg.* 3. adj. attached to, faithful *C.*

Comp. *rtén-grogs, ṫse hril-por ₒgrógs-pai rtén-grogs* perh. erron. for *ɣtán-grogs.* — *rtén-ɣnas Gram.*: the case which denotes **the place of a thing or person, the locative.** — *rten-ₒbrél,* or in full: *rtén-par ₒbrél-bar ₒgyúr-ba* or *ₒbyúṅ-ba* 'the coming to pass in continuous connection' (the explanation of *Burn.* I, 623 is grammatically not quite correct) i.e.: 1. in a general sense: **the connection between cause and effect**; in a special sense, the Buddhist doctrine of the *rten-ₒbrel bču-ɣnyis,* निदान, the twelve **causes** of existence *Wdk.* 551 (with illustrations); *Schl.* 23, *Burn.* I. 485, *Köpp.* I., 609. 2. **the auspices** of an undertaking, in as much as the complete knowledge of the causal connection of things implies also a certain prescience of future events; *rten-ₒbrél rtóg-pa* to investigate the auspices, *šés-pa* to know them, (a physician e.g., when treating a patient, must try to find out the auspices) *Med.*; *rten-ₒbrél bzaṅ* or *legs* good auspices, *ṅan* bad auspices, frq.; so also frq. col. — *rtén-ma* **prop, support, pillar** *S.g.*, **tén-šiṅ* W.* a pole used as a prop; *rtén-sa Mil.*?

རྟོག་གེ་བ་ *rtóg-ge-ba* (तर्क) the act of **arguing, reasoning; dialectics** *Cs.*; *Sch.* distrust, suspicion (?); *k'a-bšád rtóg-geï slób-dpon* seems to describe a teacher who talks in a hypocritical manner with a mere appearance of wisdom. — *rtóg-ge-pa* an arguer, disputer, reasoner, dialectician *Cs.*

རྟོག་པ་ *rtóg-pa* I. vb., pf. *brtags* (*rtogs* q.v.), *brtag*, imp. *rtog(s)*, 1. **to consider, examine, search into, look through,** cca (also dat.), *brtágs-na mi šes* though one meditates (upon the soul), one cannot understand or fathom it *Mil.*; frq. with a single or double indirect question: to examine whether (or whether not); *brtag-dpyód* (or *rtóg-ɣžig*) *ɣtóṅ-ba Pth.*, *Mil.* id.; *brtags-dpyód* examination, trial *Zam.*; c. termin. **to discern, to recognize** as, e.g. *mk'ris-par brtag* it is ascertained to be bile, to be caused by bile *Med.*; *so-sór rtóg-pa Stg.* prob. to recognize as being different. — 2. **to muse, to ruminate,** to trouble one's head about a thing, which is considered a fault much to be guarded against, and the more so, as religious faith as well as meditation require the mind to be strictly directed and entirely devoted to the one subject in question; hence *ma-rtóg tíṅ-ₒdzin Mil.* contemplation without any disturbing reflections and by-thoughts; cf. no. II. — 3. v. *dog-pa.*

II. sbst. 1. **consideration, deliberation, reflection,** cf. I., 2; *rtóg-pa skyé-ba, rtóg-pa-la ₒjúg-pa* to reflect on a thing, to indulge in musings *Dzl.* — 2. **scruple, hesitation,** *rtóg-pa skyés-te* to grow doubtful, hesitating *Mil.*; *rtog(-pa)-med(-pa)* simple, unsophisticated; simplicity; singleness of heart. — *dé-la rtog-ₒjúg mi byed Glr.* he does not meddle with that.

རྟོགས་པ་ *rtógs-pa* (prop. the pf. of *rtóg-pa*, like *novi* of *nosco*) 1. vb. **to per-**

ceive, to know, to understand, *dpyád-na ma rtógs-so* they did not understand, though they inquired into it *Dzl.*; *rtógs-par ₒgyúr-ba* to obtain information, to convince one's self of a thing *Dzl.*; *rtógs-par byéd-pa* to teach, to demonstrate, to convince a person of *Dzl.*; *má-rtógs-pa* stupid, ignorant; ignorance *Mil.* — 2. sbst. (but in Tibetan always construed as an infinitive with the accus. inst. of the genit., and with an adv. inst. of an adj.) **knowledge, perception, cognition,** frq.; *sems rtógs-pa* the knowledge of (one's own) soul *Mil.*; *mṅón-par rtógs-pa* (**अभिसमय**) clear understanding or perception, in modern Buddhism the same as *stoṅ-pa-nyid Trig.* 21. — *rtógs-pa-čan*, *rtogs-ldán* rich in knowledge *Mil.* — *rtógs-(pa) brjód(-pa)*, for **अवदान** cf. *Burn.* I. 64, a moral legend. — *rtogs-spyód* theory and practise, *rtogs-spyód byéd-pa* to know and to do, *rtogs-spyód la mk̔ás-pa* theoretically and practically religious. — *rtógs-ₒdod-čan* desirous of knowing or learning, inquisitive *Mil.* — Sometimes for *togs-pa*.

རྟོད་པ་, གཏོད་པ་, བཏོད་པ་ *rtód-pa, ɣtód-pa, btód-pa* 1. sbst., also *rtod-p̔úr*, **a stake**, in the ground, for teddering a horse, for securing a boat etc.; **a peg**, in a wall, for hanging up things; *rtod-t̔ág* a tedder (v. *btod-pa*); *rtód-pa brgyáb-pa* to drive in a stake or peg. 2. vb. **to tedder, fasten, secure** *Dzl.*

རྟོན་པ་, བརྟོན་པ་, བརྟན་པ་ *rtón-pa, brtón-pa, brtán-pa*, with or without *yid*, ccd., **to place confidence in** a person, **to rely on.**

རྟོལ་ *rtol? čos-rtól Tar.* 164, 20, *Schf.* the pith or marrow of a doctrine; *rtól-skyes-kyi šés-pa Mil.?* — *brtól-šes-pa Tar.* 197, 8, *Schf.* to know thoroughly.

རྟོལ་ *rtol Cs.*, *rtol-góg Lex.* w.e.; *Sch.*: **a bastard**, an animal of a mixed breed, *rtól-po* a male, *rtól-mo* a female bastard *Cs.*; acc. to Desgodins the cross-breed of a yak-bull and a *ₒgar-mo*. Cf. *ltor.*

རྟོལ་བ་ *rtól-ba*, pf. *brtol* (*Ld.* **stól-če**) 1 **to bore, to pierce,** to bore into, cci. & t., *Stg.*; to bore through, **to perforate** cca., a board etc., *sgo-ṅa* the shell of an egg (of chickens creeping out) *Sch.*, **to open** (**an** abscess) by a puncture; **to make an incision;** **bi-gaṅ* W.* to bore a hole. — 2. **to come to, to get to, to arrive at,** *ɣnás-su* to (at) a place *Lex.* (cog. to *t̔ál-ba, t̔él-ba*); *yoṅs-ₒdus-brtol Lex.* w.e.; *Tar.* 30, 22, *Schf.*: **पारिजातक**, the coral-tree, Erythrina indica; also a tree of paradise. (In *Dzl.* ༢༠༣, 13 the manuscript of Kyelang has: *dé-dag-las rtól-ba* it outpassed them).

ལྟ་ *lta* 1. more correctly *blta*, v. sub *ltá-ba*, I. 1., **we will see,** *Mil.*, frq. — 2. in various phrases and expressions, in which its special signification is no longer clearly discernible: a. *lta či smos Dzl.* and elsewh., the most frq. form, *lta smos či dgos Thgy.*, *lta smos či ₒtsal* (eleg.) *Stg.*, *W.* more distinctly: **lta dgos či yod**, also **zer dgos či yod**, **far from, not to mention, to say nothing of, how much less, how much more;** with a preceding infinitive or noun: *ₒdi-dag ₒdul-ba lta či smos* to say nothing of the conversion of these! how much easier is it to convert these! *Dzl.*; *ₒó-skol lta či smos* how much more we! *Thgy.*; *lta žog* is much the same: *lo zlá-ba lta žog* to say nothing of years and months; **tar žog, tá-la žog* C.* id. — b. the word is frq. used after participles or adjectives ending with *pa*, when, judging in each case from the connection in which it happens to stand, it may be deemed equivalent to: **evidently, indeed, thus then etc.,** spoken either with emphasis, or ironically, or in a sorrowful tone. As it is next to impossible to learn from the Tibetans the exact import of those little words, which slightly modify the grammatical and logical relations of a sentence, European translators have generally passed them over. Cf. *Dzl.* ༢༠༠, 18, ༢༥༦, 2 (where a **shad** ought to be added), ༤༢, 7 (where *ste* means though), ༣༥༩, 18; *Tar.* 7, 17, 19. In *Dzl.* ༢༠༢, 7 *lta*, in accordance with the manuscript of Kyelang, is to be omitted. — c. **like, as,** (*ltá-ba* sbst. abstr., *ltá-bu* adj., *ltá-bur* or *ltar* adv.), *dú-ba ltá-bur yód-*

pa žig one having the nature or the colour of smoke *Glr.; rta bčus rgyúg-pa ltábui sgra* a noise as if ten horses were galloping *Glr.;... ltá-bu mḱás-pa žig* a man as wise as ... *Dzl.; p̔a-má ltá-bur gyúr-to* he was (to him) like a father *Dzl.; bai dzí-ma ltá-bu daṅ ldán-te* having eyelashes like those of a cow *Stg.; ráṅ-la mi-mḱó-ba bú-la byíṅ-pa ltá-bu ma yin* not as if she (the mother) would give her child only what she does not want herself *Thgy.*; *žés-pa ltá-buo* is the usual expression for quoting a passage from an author, and always follows the quotation; *ḱyod ṅá-lta-bu min* you are not my equal, and also: you are not in my situation *Mil.; ₒdi-lta-bu, dé-lta-bu*, one like him, such a one as he; *či-lta-bu* what sort of? *saṅs-rgyas šes byá-ba či-lta-bu yin* the so-called Buddha, what sort of being is he? what is meant by 'Buddha'? *Dzl. či-lta-bu-la bskal-pa žes bgyi* what sort of a thing is called 'Kalpa'? *ji-lta-ba* v. *ji*; *ji-lta-bu* of what kind, as a rel. pron. Sometimes *lta* alone is used for *lta-bu: ḱyód-lta* your equal! *Mil.*; so prob. also in the passage *Dzl.* ༡༠༤, 8, where *yód-pa lta či mťoṅ* would be = *yód-pa ltá-bu gaṅ mťoṅ* (better than taking *lta či mťoṅ* for *lta či smos Schf.*). In *Dzl.* ༢༤༠, 13, and ༢༤༤, 3 *ltá-žig* is prob. to be altered into *ltá-žog*, v. sub a, 2, above. — d. *lta* is sometimes a mere expletive, e.g. in *dá-lta* (v. *da*), and after the conditional *na* (*Dzl.* ༡༠༦, 1; ༤༦, b; ༤༢, 16, ༢༤༨, b.).

ལྟ་བ་ *ltá-ba* I. vb., pf. *bltas*, fut. *blta*, imp. *ltos, blta*, resp. *gzigs-pa* (cf. *ltos-pa*) **1. to look** (as an act of the will, cf. *mťóṅ-ba*), **to view**, often with *mig*, or *mig-gis* (v. below); *bltás-na mi mťoṅ* though you look (for it) you do not see it *Mil.*; **nán-tan žib-ča ltos* Ld.* look at it accurately! **to̤ šig* C.* look (before you)! have your eyes open! **to̤ šig nyo̤n čig* C.* attention! mind! be careful! *ltá-bas čog mi šés* I never can look enough at it; with *nas:* to look from or through, *sgo-šéṅ-nas* (to peep) through the narrow opening of a door *Tar.*; *bltá-na sdúg-pa* pleasing when looked upon, charming to look at; also n. of the city of gods on the Riráb *Stg.*, and of one of the seven golden mountains around the Riráb *Glr.; ltá-ru soṅ* go there and look (at it)! **lta-la toṅ* W.* let me look (at it)! show it me! *p̔an-tsun-du ltá-ba* to look around *Dzl.; *čog-čóg-la**, or **ye-yón-la** col. id.; *p̔yi mig*, or *p̔yir* (to look) back *Dzl.; *p̔i mig log lta-če**, or **jiṅ-pa gyúr-te ltá-če* W.* id.; **to inspect**, ccd., rarely c.a., frq. *Glr., Dzl.; ḱyed mi-nús-pa-la bltás-na* if one views, considers, your inability *Dzl.; ṅas ma bltas-na* if I do not inspect it *Glr.; *ghán-la te̤ ruṅ* C.* whatever one may fix his eyes upon = whatever it may be; **to look after or into, to revise, to examine, to try**, *rtsa ltá-ba* to feel a person's pulse *Med.*; *p̔án-nam blta* I will see, if I can help *Mil.*; also: I will see, whether it has done good; *su če blta* let us see who is taller *Mil.*; *é tsud ltos šig* see, if you can put it through *Glr.; rtiṅ-sor blta* we shall see that afterwards *Mil.; yáṅ-dag-par ltá-ba* to examine or search into minutely *Mil.; *tsod ltá-ba** in col. language is the expression most in use for **to examine**, to put to the proof, **to test, to try, to sound** etc. Lastly, as a mere act of the mind: **to meditate, reflect, muse, ponder, investigate**, *du ₒdug blta* let us see how many there are *Mil.*; *lta rtog byéd-pa*, or *gtóṅ-ba Mil.* to investigate closely. Also in a mystic sense, v. *sgóm-pa* I, 2. — 2. ccd. (or accus.) and termin., to look upon a thing as, *šés-pa-la zóg-tu* to look upon knowledge as deceitful; *dkon-mčóg gsum mi bdén-par ltá-ba* to think the three treasures to be untrue, not real, = not to believe in them. — 3. c. dat. (rarely termin.): **to have regard to, to pay attention to, to take notice of**, and with a negative: **to be indifferent to, not to care about**, *sróg-la mi ltá-ba* not to care about one's life (from heroism or desperation). — **4. to be situated or directed towards**, *mdo ni núb-tu lta* the lower part of the valley is situated towards the west. — 5. *ṅas bltás-pa* in my opinion:

ṅá-la bltás-na(s), or *rtén-nas*, with regard to me, as for me, for my sake *Glr.*; *γžán-ma-rnams-la bltás-pas* as far as the others are concerned, with regard to the others *Glr.* —

II. sbst. 1. the act of **looking, beholding,** v. I, 1. 2.; *ltá-ba yáṅs-šiṅ* circumspect *Glr.* — 2. **contemplation** (mystical) v. *sgóm-pa* I, 2. — 3. (दर्शन) **opinion, doctrine, theory, philosophical system, school** (in Tibetan a verb, cf. *rtógs-pa* II), *rtág-par ltá-ba* the theory of perpetual duration (of earthly things); *ṅán-par ltá-ba* a false opinion, = *lta-lóg*.

Comp. *lta-nyúl-pa* **a spy, scout,** *lta-nyúl byéd-pa* to spy, to explore, v. *nyúl-ba*. — *lta-stáṅs*, resp. *γzig-stáṅs Pth.* **the look,** or manner of looking, air, mien, *ži-bai lta-stáṅs* a mild look, or countenance, *Cs.*; *ḱró-bai lta-stáṅs* an angry or fierce look *Cs.*; esp. the magical and powerful look of a saint, *lta-stáṅs šig mdzád-pa* to cast such a magical look *Mil.*; *lta-stáṅs-la bžúgs-pa*, *lta-stáṅs-kyi ṅáṅ-nas čá-ba Mil.* to sit, or stride along, with such a look, i.e. with great solemnity of deportment, as of one in a trance; *lta-stáṅs-bži* the four magical looks, viz.: *ₒgúgs-pai lta-stáṅs* the attracting look, *skród-pai lta-stáṅs* the repulsive look, *lhúṅ-bai lta-staṅs* the precipitating look, *réṅs-pai lta-stáṅs* the paralyzing look *Cs.*; also *séṅ-geï*, *gláṅ-po-čeï lta-stáṅs-kyis γzígs-pa* to look at a person with a lion's look, with an elephant's look. — *lta-lóg*, in later lit. and col. *lóg-lta*, **false sentiment,** not only false doctrine, heresy, but any irreligious impulses of the mind, perverse and sinful thoughts, e.g. *lóg-lta skyés-te* is used for conspiring against a person's life *Glr.*, giving way to doubt or weakness of faith *Glr.*, falling in love with a woman *Pth.*; *mi-la lóg-lta byéd-pa* to slander, to abuse a person *Glr.*

ལྟག་ལྕིར་ *ltag-lčin* **puff-ball** *Sch.*

ལྟག་པ་ *ltág-pa* 1. the back part of the neck, **nape** *Med.* and elsewh., frq. — 2. **the upper part** or **place,** *grál-gyi* of the divan, the seat of honour *Dzl.* — 3. **the back,** *gri-ltag* the back of a knife. — 4. *ltag ₒog sgyúr-ba* to turn upside down *Dzl.*; *ltóg-na(s)*, *ltag*, **above,** *sgó-ltag* above the door, *gróṅ-ltag dgón-pa Mil.* the convent above and behind the village, the front-side of the houses being gen. turned towards the valley and the river; thus 'behind' is equivalent to 'higher up'; *ltág-na-med-pa* (of rare occurrence) for *blá-na-med-pa* the highest, अनुत्तम; *ltag skór-ba* to strangle, to suffocate *Glr.*; *ltag γčód-pa* 1. *Cs.* to cut off a man's neck, to behead. 2. *W* to make a person change his mind, to alter his sentiments; **ṅe ḱó-la gyóg-pa tag čad yin** I hope I shall talk him out of it, shall dissuade him from doing it; *ltag nyal-ba* to lie backward *Sch.*

Comp. *ltág-sgo* the back-door of a house, v. above. — *ltag-γčód* or *-čód* 1. **decapitation,** 2. *Sch.*: **changeable, fickle, inconstant.** *ltag-čú Med.*; *Sch.*: 'sinew of the neck, the covering of the neck'. — *ltag-mdúd Sch.*, *ltag-sdúd Lt.*, the hole in the occiput, the connexion of the brain with the spinal marrow. — *ltág-spu* neck-hair, **mane,** of the horse, of the lion *Ld.-Glr.* — *ltág-ma* what is uppermost, e.g. words written over other words.

ལྟང་ *ltaṅ* 1. **a bale** of goods, carried on one side of a beast of burden, half a load, *ltaṅ γnyis* two bales, or a whole load. — 2. also *lteṅ*, *W.*: **through, quite through,** **pí-sta-ne náṅ-la ltaṅ toṅ dug** one sees from the outside into the interior; **ltaṅ bug toṅ** bore through! **ltaṅ tón-te ča dug** he is passing through, he does not make a stay here. — Cf. *toṅ*.

ལྟད་མོ་ *ltád-mo*, col. also **ltán-mo**, resp. *γzigs-mo*, the looking on, **a sight, scene, spectacle,** *ltád-mo-la ₒtsogs* they came together in order to look on *Glr.*; *ltád-mo ltá-ba* to look at a scene, to be an eye-witness; *ltád-mo ltá-bai sa* a place where there is something to be seen; a theatre. — *ltád-mo-ḱaṅ* a playhouse, exhibition, puppet-show etc. — *ltád-mo-pa Pth.*, **ltád-mo-lta-mi**, **ltád-mo-la yóṅ-ḱan**

W., a spectator, a visitor; *ltád-mo-mḱan, ltád-mo stón-pa* a showman, actor, mimic etc. — *gróṅ-yul-gyi ltád-mo ma dran žig Mil.* forget the scenes of village life!

ལྟབ་པ་ *ltáb-pa*, pf. *bltabs*, fut. *bltab*, imp. *ltob* (*W.* **ltabs toṅ**), **to fold** or **gather up, to lay** or **put together,** **kyaṅ-tab, nyi-tab tab-če** *W.* to fold single, to fold double; *ysúm-ltab byéd-pa* to fold or bend together threefold, e.g. a corpse previous to cremation; *ltáb-ma Cs.* **a fold, crease plait;** *ltab-gri* a clasp knife

ལྟམ(ས)་པ་ *ltám(s)-pa*, pf. *bltams*, fut. *bltam*, 1. **to be full,** also *ytáms-pa.* — 2. resp. **to be born,** *skyéd-pai yab daṅ bltáms-pai yum* the father by whom one is begotten, and the mother by whom one is born *Pth.*

ལྟར་ *ltar* 1. also *bltar*, supine of *ltá-ba*, **in order to see;** *bltár-ruṅ-ba* visible; *Sch.*: 'pleasing to the eye'; *gaṅ ltár-na yaṅ, či ltár-na yaṅ*, be that as it may *Glr.* — 2. postp. c. a., **like, as,** after the manner of, *ri-ltar* like a mountain; *p̔yag byéd-pa ltar byéd-pa* to make a saluting gesture *Glr.*; *ṅo-šes ruṅ mi šés-pa ltar byas* although they knew . . ., they affected not to know . . . *Mil.*; *ₒbral mi p̔ód-pa ltar yód-na yaṅ* being like one that cannot part with, = being scarcely able to part with, *Glr.*; *ltar snáṅ-ba* to appear like, hence prob. *ltar-snáṅ* appearance, similarity *Sch.*, (*Lex.* w.e.); *lúṅ-bstan-pa ltar* (to do a thing) in conformity with a prediction *Tar.*; also *ltár-na*, and *ltár-du*, *mi-lo ltár-na . . . yod* computed by human or terrestrial years it amounts to . . . *Thgy.*; *bód-rnams ltár-na* according to Tibetan (sources) *Tar.*; *či-ltar(-na)* how? in what manner or way? *či-ltar* also serves to paraphrase the English 'so that' e.g. 'he played so that all were enraptured' is thus expressed: he played — how did he play? — all were enraptured; *ji-ltar(-na)* as *ji-lta ji-ltar . . . dé-lta dé-ltar Sambh.* even as . . . so; *ₒdi-ltar, dé-ltar(-na)* so, thus, in that manner; *ₒdi-ltar mi rgan k̔yod* such an old fellow as you are; frq. also in referring to the words of others, where we use 'that': *dé-ltar bdén-na* if that is true.

ལྟར་ལྟར་པོ་ *ltár-ltar-po Lex., Cs.*: of a liquid nature, as an embryo first in the womb.

ལྟས་ *ltas* **prognostic, omen,** more distinctive *sṅá-ltas;* **miraculous sign, miracle, prodigy,** more accurately: *ṅo-mtsár-bai ltas; bkra-šis-pai ltas* a propitious omen; *rmi-ltas bzáṅ-po* a good sign in a dream *Pth.*; *dgé-ltas* a favourable sign; *ṅán-ltás*, or *ltas-ṅán* a bad sign *Dzl.*; *ltás-mḱan* a soothsayer, fortune-teller; *ltas stón-pa* to soothsay *Cs.*

ལྟི་རི་ *lti-ri* **pitcher** *Sch.*

ལྟིག་ཐུང་ *ltig-túṅ C.* a person of small stature, perh. a corruption of *lte-túṅ.*

ལྟིབ་པ་ *ltib-pa* to fall through *Sch.*

ལྟིར་བ་ *ltir-ba* v. *ldir-ba.*

ལྟུང་བ་ *ltúṅ-ba* 1. vb., pf. *lhuṅ,* **to fall, to fall off, down, into;** fig.: *mtó-ba de yaṅ mtar lhúṅ-ṅo* what is high will finally fall down *Dzl.*; more esp. to fall into sin, to commit sin, hence *nyes-ltuṅ* an actual sin, a sinful deed, *ltúṅ-byed* a transgression, crime; also *ṅán-soṅ-du* (v. *ₒgró-ba* I, 5), or *dmyál-bar* to fall into damnation. — 2. sbst. **the fall,** esp. the moral fall, *ltúṅ-bas gós-pa* polluted by sin; *ltúṅ-ba bšágs-pa* confession of sin.

ལྟེ་བ་ *lté-ba* 1. **navel-string, umbilical cord,** *yčód-pa* to cut it *Med.* — 2. **navel,** *lté-bai k̔úṅ(bu) Lt.* id.; *glá-bai lté-ba* musk-bag. — 3. the middle of a thing, **centre,** *dkyil-ₒk̔or-gyi* of a circle; *mu-k̔yúd ysúm-gyi lté-bar* in the middle of three (concentric) circles *Lt.*; *raṅ-ťág-gi lté-ba* the axle-tree of a water-wheel *Glr.*; *sai lté-ba* the centre of the earth, in the opinion of the natives: *Tibet*; also cognomen of several fabulous kings of Tibet *Köpp.* II., 52. — *lté-ba yžuṅ-ráṅ* Lhasa, or, in a more special sense, the palace of the Dalai Lama — *lte-túg W.* = **tig-túṅ** *C.*

ལྟེང་ *lteṅ* 1. v. *ltaṅ.* — 2. *lteṅ-rgyás* n. of a Buddha.

ལྟེང་ཀ་ *lteṅ-ka* **pool, pond** *Dzl.*

ལྟེབ་པ་ *ltéb-pa* (cog. to *ltáb-pa*), **to double down, to turn in,** *mṫa*, or *sné-mo* to hem, by turning in the edge, cf. *sné-mo.*

ལྟེམ་རྒྱང་ *ltem-rgyáṅ* **humour, whim, caprice,** *ltem-rgyáṅ byéd-pa* to be whimsical or capricious *Cs.*

ལྟེམ་པ་ *ltém-pa* the state of being full, e.g. a vessel full of water; **full, overflowing,** *ltém-po* full; *ltem-ltém* so full that it runs over.

ལྟོ་ *lto*, seldom *ltó-ba* (*C., Mil.*) 1. **food, victuals,** *lto(b)za-ba* 1. to eat, *lto yaṅ ma zos* he did not eat anything *Glr.*; 2. to gain or get one's living *C.*; *ltó-la byin* give him to eat! *Lt.*; *lúg-la lto ster* feed the sheep; *lto γyó-ba* to prepare food *Mil.*; **to nyo śrog ṫsoṅ** *C.* he risks his life in order to procure food; *gla-ltó* wages and food; *lto-gós, lto-rgyáb*, food and clothes *Mil.*; *lto-rgyab-skyid Lex.* prob. food, clothes, and good health (comfort); **dha tó-če za gyu yin** *C.* now I will go and eat (something). — *lto-čuṅ, lto-ráṅ Sch.:* a person temperate in eating. — *ltó-°dun-čan* **an epicure, parasite, sponger.** — *lto-žiṅ* provision ground which a person receives for his subsistence. — *žim-lto-čan* dainty-mouthed, lickerish. — 2. **goat's beard,** Tragopogon., used as a kitchen-vegetable.

ལྟོ་བ་ *ltó-ba* **belly, stomach;** also the belly of a bottle; *ltó-ba sá-la °bébs-pa* to prostrate one's self.

Comp. *lto-gáṅ* a full belly, also: with a full belly or stomach. — *ltó-°gro, ltós-°gró* 1. moving or creeping on the belly, **a worm, a snake.** 2. symb. num.: 8. — *lto(-ba)-°gróg(-pa) Cs.*: 'belly-fretting, a nervous excitement of the belly'. — *lto-stóṅ* with an empty stomach, **jejune, empty.** — *lto-ldir* belly of a vessel, *ltó-ldir-čan* swelling out, bellied, like vessels. — *ltó-na-ba, ltó-zug* stomach-ache. — *lto-°ṗyé* crawling or creeping on the belly, a snake; *lto-°ṗye čén-po*, **महोरग**, a fabulous monster of the serpent kind, similar to the klu.

ལྟོག་འདྲེ་ *ltog-°dré* a demon *Sch.*; *°dre-ltúgs* prob. the same

ལྟོགས་པ་ *ltógs-pa* I. vb. 1. **to be hungry,** *ltógs-so* I am hungry *Cs.*, *ltógs-su °bór-ba* to suffer a person to hunger, to starve *Dzl.* — 2. *Sch.:* **to regret,** *ltogs nyal ma byeb* do not always lie in grief and regret! *Sch.(?)*; *ltógs-par bžúgs-pa* resp. to be full of regret.

II. sbst. **hunger.**

III. adj. **hungry,** *séms-čan ltógs-pa-rnams Dzl.*; *ltógs-par °gyúr-ba* to grow hungry; *ltógs-gri Mil.*, col. **ltóg-ri** *W.* hunger. **ṅa(-la) ltóg-ri rag** I am hungry, **ǩyod (-la) ltóg-ri rag** you are hungry, **ǩo ltóg-pa yod** he is hungry. — *ltogs-ṗyúg* hunger (i.e. poverty) and wealth *Glr.* — *ltog-ṫsór* the feeling of hunger, *ltogs-ṫsor če* I am very hungry *Mil.*

ལྟོང་ག་ *ltóṅ-ga* **notch, incision, indentation,** *mdá-ltoṅ* the notch in an arrow; **a depression,** *ri-tóṅ* in a ridge of mountains, *la-tóṅ* the indentation of a mountain-pass.

ལྟོངས་ *ltoṅs* **summit** *Mil.*, frq

ལྟོབ་ *ltob* v. *ltáb-pa.*

ལྟོར་ *ltor*, *śras-ltór* a bastard prince *Glr.*

ལྟོས་ *ltos* 1. v. *lta-ba.* 2. *Sch.* = *γtos.*

ལྟོས་པ་ *ltós-pa* 1. vb., = *ltá-ba*, **to look at,** on, or to, ccd., *γnyén-po-la ma ltós-par* without looking to a spiritual guide *Thgy.*; *ǩyod dé-la ltos mi dgos-pa žig yin* you need not care for that *Mil.*; *ré-žiṅ ltós-pa Glr.* to look at (a thing) hopefully; *dé-la ltós-na* if I look at, consider, this *Mil.*, if one compares this with... *Thgy.*; **(s)ṅá-ltos či-čug (?) tsáṅ-ma čó-ǩan** *W.* a person acting with great circumspection — 2. sbst. **the looking at** or on, *ltós-pa méd-par* without looking at it (e.g. in playing at dice); **relation, respect, regard** *Cs.*

སྟ་གོན་ *sta-gón* **preparation, arrangement,** *sta-gón byéd-pa* to make preparations, to prepare, arrange, fit out; *°ṫsó-*

bai sta-gón-la bžeṅs he rose to make preparations for dinner *Mil.*

སྟ་ཟུར་ *sta-zúr* **hip, hip-bone,** e.g. as the seat of strength *Mil.*; *stá-zúr yan-čád* from the hip upward *Dzl.*

སྟ་རི་ *sta-rí W.*, originally *sta-grí Mil.* and *C.*, *sta-ré B.*, **axe, hatchet;** *dgrá-sta* battle-axe *Lex.*; *star-ltág Cs.* the back of an axe or hatchet, *star-míg* the hole for putting the handle in, *star-yú* the handle, *star-só* the edge of an axe.

སྟག་ *stag* 1. **tiger,** *rgya-stág* the Bengal tiger *Mil.*; *stag-prúg* a young tiger, *stág-mo* a tigress; *stag-ṫsáṅ* a tiger's den; *stag-ris* the stripes of a tiger's skin. — 2. *Tar.* 166, 2?

སྟག་ཆས་ *stag-čás Mil.* utensils carried by men about them, such as a knife, smoking-implements, weapons etc.

སྟག་པ་ *stág-pa* **birch-tree;** *stág-ma* n. of another tree.

སྟག་གཟིག་ *stag-gzig* a not unfrequent form (which prob. has been adapted to Tibetan etymology) for *ta-zig*, **Persia, Persian.**

སྟག་ཤ་ *stag-ša* a medicinal herb, *Glr.*, *Med.*; *stag-ša-dé-ba Glr.*

སྟག་ཤར་ *stag-šár* **a youth, young man** *C.*, *Mil.*

སྟང་ཟིལ་ *staṅ-zil Cs.*: n. of a black stone, acc. to *Zam.* a silver-ore.

སྟངས་ *staṅs*, *Sch.* also *stáṅ-ka*, **manner, style, posture,** *gom-pai staṅs* manner of walking, gait; *brdég-staṅs byéd-pa* to assume a fighting posture *Mil.*; *ltá-staṅs* v. *ltá-ba* comp.; *stón-pai bžúgs-staṅs* the sitting posture of Buddha; *C.*: **ko ghó-ghon-taṅ dé-mo** his style of dressing is fine, he is well dressed; **tám-zer-taṅ ké-pa** eloquent; even like a mere termination for forming verbal substantives: **zá-taṅ**, or **túṅ-taṅ lég-mo** good eating, drinking.

སྟད་པ་ *stád-pa*, pf. and fut. *bstad*, imp. *stod*, **to put on, to lay on,** *rtá-la sga* to put the saddle on a horse, to saddle; *rtá-la ˳gró-čas* to load the baggage on a horse.

སྟན་ *stan* **mat, carpet,** esp. a carpet for sitting on, also **a cushion,** resp. *bžúgs-gdan*; **saddle-cloth;** *stan ˳diṅ-ba* to spread a mat (on the ground), *˳gébs-pa* to lay (a mat) on; **ču-stán** swaddling-cloth *W.*; **bol-tén** mattress, **ṫul-tén** (lit. *prul-stán*) a light travelling-mattress *C.*; sometimes substratum of any kind, also of hard materials, e.g. *gtsub-stán*, *btsab-stán*.

སྟབ་ *stab* 1. v. *rtab.* — 2. *Sch.*: *stab stáṅs-pa* to suffer, to tolerate, to yield.

སྟབས་ *stabs* (cog. to *tabs*, also syn. of *staṅs*), **mode, manner, way, measure,** *séṅ-gei stábs-kyis* (or *su*) *˳gró-ba* to walk in the manner of a lion; *gar-stábs* v. *gar*; **opportunity,** *˳byón-stabs* an opportunity for going; **tábs-si ká-na** (also **ká-ne**, or *ká-la**) *W* when an opportunity offers; *riṅs-stabs-su* hastily, speedily *Mil.*; **kón-stabs** dearth, famine, want *Ld.*; **riṅ-stabs** a describing at full length, copiousness (*stabs*, in this instance, corresponds to the English termination 'ness', changing the adj. into an abstract noun).

སྟར་ *star*, for *sta-ri* q.v.

སྟར་ཀ་ *stár-ka Sch.*, *stár-ga Lex.*, *stár-ka Glr.*, **walnut,** *star-(gai) šiṅ*, *ljón-šiṅ stár-ka* walnut-tree *Glr.*; *star-skógs* nutshell; *star-sdóṅ* trunk of a walnut-tree. *stár-ka byéd-pa Ld.-Glr. Schl.* f 15, b (?).

སྟར་བ་ *stár-ba*, pf. and fut. *bstar*, imp. *stor*, 1. **to file** on a string, e.g. pearls; **to tie fast, to fasten to,** e.g. sheep to a rope, in a bivouac, *stár-la rgyúd-pa* id. — 2. **to clean, to polish** *Lex.* — 3. *Sch.*: **to ornament, decorate** (?).

སྟར་བུ་ *stár-bu*, or *star-žún Med.*, frq., the berries of Hippophaë rhamnoides, a shrub or tree very frequent in Tibet; acc. to a *Lex.* also a kind of Rumex in India.

སྟི་བ་ *sti-ba*, pf. *bstis*, fut. *bsti*, imp. *stis*, 1. **to rest, to repose, to refresh** one's self, *sti-(bai) gnas* resting-place. — 2. **to honour** (?); *(b)sti-stáṅ* **honour, respect, reverence,** *byéd-pa* ccd., to show a person honour, frq.; **kó-la ti-táṅ čaṅ med** *W.* he is not esteemed at all, he enjoys no credit whatever; *bkúr-sti* id., v. *bkúr-ba.*

སྟིང་བ་ *stiṅ-ba*, pf. *bstiṅs*, fut. *bstiṅ*, imp. *stiṅs*, **to rebuke, scold, abuse** *Lexx.*

སྟིབ(ས)་པ་ *stib(s)-pa* to offer (sacrifice), rarely used.

སྟིམ་པ་ *stim-pa*, pf. *bstims*, fut. *bstim*, imp. *stims*, prop. vb. causative to *ₒtim-pa*, gen. = *ₒtim-pa*, **to enter, penetrate, pervade, to be absorbed in**, *tugs čos-nyid-kyi klóṅ-du stim Pth.* the soul is absorbed in the expanse of the *čos-nyid*.

སྟུ་ *stu* **cunnus**, orifice of the vagina, the vulg. and obscene expression for the pudendum muliebre.

སྟུག(ས)་པ་ *stúg(s)-pa* 1. abstract noun and adj., **thickness, density, thick;** *stugs-po* adj., = *ₒtúg-pa*, *ₒtúg-po*, **thick, dense**, e.g. a forest, *Dzl.*; **sound, heavy** (sleep, clouds etc.); *dpal-stúgs* right noble, most noble *Cs.*; *stugs-po-bkód-pa Pth.* one of the heavens of Buddha. — 2. **a wind,** flatulence *C.*

སྟུང་བ་ *stúṅ-ba*, pf. *bstuṅs*, fut. *bstuṅ*, imp. *stuṅs* = *rtúṅ-ba*.

སྟུད་པ་ *stúd-pa*, pf. and fut. *bstud*, **to repeat, to reiterate,** to give or offer repeatedly (medicine, food, beer etc.), *bstúd-na* if it is repeated *Mṅg.*; *sbrid-pa máṅ-po stúd-čiṅ ₒoṅ* repeated sneezing ensues *Lt.*; *bstúd-nas ná-ba* to be always ill *Sch.*; cf. *btúd-mar*.

སྟུན་པ་ *stún-pa*, pf. and fut. *bstun*, prop. causative to *ₒtún-pa*, gen. = *ₒtún-pa*, **to agree,** *dgé-ba bčú-la bstún-pai rgyal-ḱrims* a law agreeing with the ten virtues *Glr.*; *ₒdod-yón lṅa daṅ stún-pai loṅs-spyód* a life of pleasure in accordance with the five enjoyments *Glr.*; *dus-skábs daṅ stún-te* agreeably to the (proper) time, in due time *Glr.*; *ṅai žiṅ rmó-ba ₒdi daṅ stún-pai mgúr-ma* a song having reference to this my labour in the fields *Mil.*; *γžuṅ daṅ stún-pa Lex.*, *Cs.*: 'to confer, to make agree with the original text'.

སྟུབ་པ་ *stúb-pa*, or *sté-pa*, *Ld.*, for *btúb-pa*, *γté-pa*.

སྟེ་ *ste* an affix for the gerund, inst. of *te*, after *g*, *ṅ*, **and** vowels, v. *te*. — As *ste* contains the copula, it may be added also to other words than verbs, e.g. *kyod rigs čé-žiṅ mtó-ba-ste* as you are of high and noble extraction *Dzl.*; like *ₒdi-lta-ste* it is also used for **namely, to wit, videlicet** (viz.), that is to say, esp. before translations of foreign words and names: *ši-ra-ste mgó-bo žes-byá-ba Tar.* 11, 11; 4, 11; 189, 2 and elsewh. In the latter case it may also be rendered by **or** (Lat. *sive*). After an enumeration of several things, it serves to point back, or to comprise: *ža, za, a, ya, ša, sá-ste drug-ni* the six letters *ž*, *z* etc.; *γsum ná-ro kyi-gu grén-bu-ste* three signs, o, i, and e *Glr.*, *Tar.* 188, 16; *dá-ste žag bdún-na* as to the being now, in seven days, i.e. in seven days from to-day *Dzl.*; sometimes *ste* seems to stand in the place of a preceding verb, *Feer Introd.* 73, s.l.c.; at other times it is used, where its exact meaning is not obvious.

སྟེའུ་ *sté-po*, or *steu*, carpenter's **axe, adz,** an axe with its blade athwart the handle (*Cs.*: 'paring axe'), used by Indian and Tibetan carpenters, *Hind. basūla*, *ste-ltág* its back, *ste-yú* its handle, *ste-ḱa Cs.* its edge, though in *S.g.* 32 *sté-ḱa so-γnyis-pa* it must be the name of the tool itself. — *ste bžog γtóṅ-ba* to pare, to smooth, to hew with the axe. — **ṗág-ste* W.* a plane.

སྟེགས་ *stegs*, also *stégs-bu*, any contrivance for putting things on, **a stand, board, table, stool** etc.; *ká-stegs* the pedestal or base of a pillar *Cs.*; *rkáṅ-stegs* foot-stool, jack, horse (wooden frame with legs); **kyóṅ-stag* W.* candlestick; **čós-stag; čó-tag* W.*, book-stand; *ₒdug-stegs* a board, stool, bench, to sit on *Cs.*; **do-tég* C.* a stone-seat, whether artificial or natural; *snód-stegs Cs.* 'a board to put vessels on'; *ṗór-stegs* a cupboard *Cs.*; **ṗó-stag* W.* a bench; *žábs-stegs* resp. for *rkaṅ-stegs*; **žún-teg* C.* candlestick; *γžag-stegs* a board to place things on *Cs.*; *zá-stegs* dining-table *Schr.*; *γsól-stegs* id resp., and table in general, col. **sol-tág**; *lám-stegs* seat, resting-place by the road-side *Glr.*; **ŏṅ-teg* C* candlestick.

སྟེང་ *steṅ* **that which is above, the upper part, top, surface,** *sai steṅ tams-càd* the whole face of the earth *Glr.*; *sén-moi stéṅ-gi sa* the earth here upon my finger nail *Dzl*; *stéṅ-gi nám-mk'a* the heavens above *Dzl.*; *stéṅ-gi p'yogs* the zenith; *steṅ-ʻóg* above and below, *steṅ-ʻóg-gi ydon* demons of the upper and lower regions; *stéṅ-na* adv. and postp.: above, overhead, on high, up-stairs, on the surface, answering to the question where or in what place; *stéṅ-du* adv. and postp. 1. id , answering to the question whither, to what place, but also where or in what place, e.g. to sit on a lotos, to throw down to the ground, to send a thing or a messenger to a person *Dzl.*, frq. 2. above, over, moreover, besides, in addition to, *rgás-pai stéṅ-du* in addition to my old age *Dzl.*; *byás-pai stéṅ-du* he made it and besides... *Dzl.*; *bdag čós-la mi mós-pa méd-pai stéṅ-du bón ráṅ-la mos* I am not only no despiser of religion, but a regular Bon-worshipper *Mil.*; *stéṅ-nas* down from. — *stéṅ-ka* (*W.* **táṅ-ka**), also *stéṅ-tse* a terrace. — *stéṅ-k'aṅ* upper story of a house, garret. — **steṅ-dúṅ**(?) *W.* pestle, pounder.

སྟེན་པ་ *stén-pa*, pf. and fut *bsten*, imp. *sten*, **to keep, to hold; to adhere to, to stick to, to rely** or **depend on,** almost like *rtén-pa*, but c. accus., *blá-ma mk'ás-pa stén-pa* to adhere to a learned Lama; to stick or keep to certain victuals, medicines etc., using them regularly, frq.; even *saug-bsṅál* to have to taste misfortunes *Thgy.*; **to addict one's self** (to virtues or vices), *sér-sna* to avarice *Stg.*; *mi stén-pa* = *spáṅ-ba* to avoid, shun, abstain from *Glr.*; *Cs.* also: *γyog stén-pa* to keep a servant in pay.

སྟེམ་པ་ *stém-pa*, pf. and fut. *stems* (= *stén-pa*?), **to hold, to support** *Mil. nt.*; **to shut** or **fasten** a door, **to secure** it by a beam or bar. *C.*

སྟེམས་ *stems* **curse** (?) *Tar.* 181, 20. Cf. *byad.*

སྟེའུ་ *steu* v. *sté-po.*

སྟེར་བ་ *stér-ba*, pf. and fut. *bster*, ccdp. 1. **to give** *B.*, *C.*, frq.; **to bestow, present, grant, concede, allow;** with the supine or root of a verb: **to let, permit,** *náṅ-du ʻgro(r)*, *náṅ-du ʻóṅ-du* to let enter to grant admission *Dzl.* — 2. *W.* in a special sense: to give to eat or to drink, **to feed** (infants, animals). — 3. **to add** (in arithmetic) *Wdk.* — **tér-go** **aid, contribution** *C.*

སྟེས་དབང་ *stes-dbaṅ Lex.*, where *staṅs-legs* is added for explanation; in *Tar.* 134, 7 *stes-dbaṅ-gis* is translated by *Schf.*: power of fate.

སྟོ་ཐག *sto-tag* **rope** *Sch.*

སྟོ་བ་ *stó-ba*, most frq. in the col. phrase *čaṅ mi sto* it does not matter, it makes no difference, it is all the same (also *čaṅ mi rtog*); *Mil.*: *ši ruṅ mi stó-ba ʻdug* it does not matter if they die; *ši yaṅ či stó-ste* what does it matter if they die?

སྟོ་ར་ (?) *stó-ra W.*, a circle of dancers.

སྟོང་ *stoṅ* 1. **thousand,** *stoṅ-p'rág* id., *stoṅ-p'rag-brgyá-pa* (the work) containing ten thousand (viz. Sloka) *Köpp.* II, 272; *Burn.* I, 462. — *stóṅ-dpon* a commander over a thousand; *stoṅ-ʻk'ór-lo* a wheel with a thousand spokes; *las stoṅ byed Med.* that is a remedy producing a thousand good effects. – 2. **a fine for manslaughter,** to be paid in money or goods to the relatives of the person killed; *če-čúṅ-gi stoṅ byéd-pa Glr.*, to proportion this fine to the rank of the man killed. — 3. v. *stóṅ-pa.*

སྟོང་གྲོགས་ *stoṅ-grógs* v. *stóṅs-pa.*

སྟོང་པ་ *stóṅ-pa* (शून्य) **empty, clear,** *k'áb-kyi rtsé-mo tsam yzúgs-pai sa stóṅ-pa* about so much clear space, as to allow the point of a needle to be stuck in *Dzl.*; **hollow,** not charged or loaded (of a gun); not written upon, **blank; indifferent,** having no distinct or definite quality, e.g. as to taste or smell; *rlúṅ-gi raṅ-bžin ni stoṅ mód-kyi* though wind (or air) in itself is without smell *Dzl.*; **waste, deserted,** *brag-stóṅ* a rocky desert, *luṅ-stóṅ* **a desolate** valley *Mil.*; **žaṅ - stóṅ* Ld.*, **dom - stóṅ* Pur.*, bare-bottomed, having the bottom bare, vulg.; **mi tóṅ-pa* W.*, = **mi kyaṅ**, v. *rkyaṅ-pa; kaṅ-stoṅi* a desolate house, as a place suitable for enchantments; fig. **sem tóṅ-pa rag* W.* I feel lonely. — *stoṅ-pa-nyid.* शून्यता, **emptiness, vacuity, the void,** the chief product of the philosophical speculations of the Buddhists, and the aim and end of all their aspirations, v. *Köpp.* I, 214; *Burn.* I, 442; 462. (Five synonyms v. *Trig.* f. 20). *stóṅ-zád-la skyél-ba* to squander, to waste, *tse* one's life *Mil.*; *stoṅ-saṅ-ṅé* absolute vacuity, *stóṅ-saṅ-ṅé byás-nas* making tabula rasa, keeping, retaining nothing whatever *Thgy.* — *stoṅ-ysál* v. *ysal-po.* — Adv. *stóṅ-par* in vain(?) *Mil.*

སྟོང་ཟིལ་ *stoṅ-zil*(?) *W.* Corydalis meifolia.

སྟོངས་པ་ *stóṅs-pa* 1. pf. *bstaṅs* (*Dzl.*), fut. *bstaṅ*(?), **to accompany,** **tóṅ - te ḍó-wa* C.* to go along with a person; *čis kyaṅ mi stóṅs-par ₒči* I die without any thing following me *Thgy.*; more frq. *stoṅ-grógs byéd-pa* ccgp. (also dat.?) **to help, to assist** a person *Mil.* — 2. **to make empty; to be empty, to become waste** or **desolate,** *ráṅ-gi ynas stóṅs-šiṅ S.g.*, *raṅ-šúl stóṅs-nas Mil.*, your own place becoming desolate; *stóṅs-su nyé-bar gyur* it had become nearly empty, was almost spent or exhausted *Pth.*; *mis stóṅs-pai káṅ-ro* ruins forsaken by men; *saṅs-rgyás-kyis stóṅs-pa Thgy.* the period during which no Buddha appears, a *mi-kóm-pa* v. *kóm-pa*; *sa-yžir stóṅs-pa* to level with the ground, to raze, to demolish entirely.

སྟོད་ *stod, Ssk.* उत्तर, **I. the upper, higher, former part** of a thing, **the upper half** opp. to *smad;* 1. esp. the upper part **of the body,** resp. *sku-stód Pth.*; *stod-kóg* the upper part of a carcase *Sch.*, also *stód-po Mil.*; *stod-kyébs* a sort of frill or ruffle of the Lamas; *stod-ₒgág* doublet of the Lamas, without sleeves; *stod-túṅ* a short coat, jacket. — 2. the upper or higher part **of a country,** *stód-pa* an inhabitant of it, highlander. — 3. with respect to time: **the first part,** of the night *Dzl.*, of life *Glr.*, of winter and the like; *stód-la* at the upper part of, above.

II. v. *stád-pa,* and *stód-pa.*

སྟོད་པ་ *stód-pa* 1. vb., pf. and fut. *bstod* ('to raise, to exalt', opp. to *smád-pa*) **to praise, commend, laud,** *bdág-stod-pa, W. *ráṅ-tod-če**, to praise one's self, **raṅ-tod-čan** a self-admirer, self-flatterer; **to extol, to glorify,** men, gods etc., frq.; *stod-(čiṅ) bsṅags-pa* id.; *stod-tsig* an epithet of praise, a commendable quality. — 2. sbst. **praise, eulogy,** also **tód-ra* W.*; **compliments,** complimentary phrases e.g. in letters; hymn of praise, also *stod-bsṅágs, stod-dbyáṅs, stod-glú; stód-pa(r) byéd-pa, W. *pul-če**, ccd. (the former also c. accus.) to praise, to extol; *stod-ₒós* laudable, commendable, worthy of praise.

སྟོན་ *ston* 1. **autumn** (more about it v. *dus*, *ston brgya mtóṅ-bar gyúr čig* may he live to see a hundred autumns! *Lt.* — 2. **in autumn,** during autumn *B.*, frq. — 3. = *ston-tóg.*

Comp. *stón-ka, stón-ka,* **autumn,** **stón-ka-na, stón-ka-la** in autumn, during autumn. — *ston-tóg* autumnal fruit, **harvest,** *ston-tóg sdú-ba* (*W.* also **dóg-če**) to gather in the produce of the fields, to harvest. — *ston-dús* **harvest-time, autumn,** — *ston-zlá* autumnal month.

སྟོན་པ་ *stón-pa* I. vb., pf. and fut. *bstan,* at the end of a sentence *bstan-no* (so prob. also in *Dzl.* ༧༠, 10 the correct reading), *W. *(s)tán-če**, 1. **to show,** *lam stón-čig B.*, **(s)tán toṅ* W.*, **ṭeṅ rog ǰhe šig* C.* show me the way! *stón-mkan žig yod* somebody has shown *Glr.*; *bú-mo sgo stón-mkan* the girl that has shown the door *Mil.*, *mtsán-mkan-la bu stón-pa* to show the soothsayer a child *Dzl.*; *lus stón-pa*, applied to deities etc.: to show one's self, to appear *Dzl.*; *rdzu-ₒprúl stón-pa* to show, to exhibit magic tricks, v. *rdzu*; *dmág-pa yin-no žes bstán-te* 'this is the bridegroom!' with these words showing, i. e. introducing him as the bridegroom

Dzl. ཝཛ, 3. — 2. = *ytód-pa*, **to face, to front, to look towards**, *sgo lhó-pyogs-su ston* the door faces the south *Glr.* — 3. **to point out, to indicate, describe, explain**, *čé-ba* the greatness or superiority of a thing *Mil.*; *bú-mo skyé bar ͦgyúr-bar stón-pa yin* it indicates that a girl will be born *Wdṅ.*; *či-ͦdra žig (yod) ston dgos* give me a description of her person *Glr.*; *bstán-par byao* now I will explain that, frq.; *ji-ltar byón-pa bstán-pai leu* the chapter describing the arrival; hence **to teach**, *čos* religion; *luṅ* v. *luṅ*. — 4. *W.* **to make** one **undergo** or **suffer, to inflict** (just as **tóṅ-če** to suffer), **mi-la nag stón-pa** to torture a person, **dug-ṅálstón-pa** to plague, torment, grieve. — 5. *W.* as a vb. nt., **to show one's self, to appear**, *'*i-ru tan-te yod** this appears here, this turns up or occurs here.

II. sbst. **a teacher**, frq., *lúṅ-ston-pa* **a prophet**, v. *luṅ*; the *stón-pa* par excellence is Buddha, frq.; — *ston-min*, and *tse-min* two false doctrines *Glr.* 92, 3. (the translation given by *Sch.* is but an arbitrary one).

སྟོན་མོ་ *stón-mo* **feast, banquet** (v. also *yá-tra*), *stón-mo bzáṅ-po, čén-po*, a grand, splendid feast *Dzl.*; *šóm-pa* to prepare, arrange (a feast), *byéd-pa* to give, hold, celebrate it, also c. dat. in honour of; *stón-mo ͦdrén-pa* to serve it up *Mil.*, *ͦgyéd-pa* to distribute the dishes, *dmáṅs-kyi stón-mo ͦgyéd-pa* to distribute of the viands of the table to the common people *Mil.*, *zá-ba* to eat, or partake, of such a festive entertainment *Dzl.*; *stón-mo-ynaṅ-sbyin* a present of meat, of provisions *Glr.*; *dgá-ston* festive entertainment, frq.; *rná-bai dgá-ston* a feast or treat to one's ears *Glr.*; *čós-ston* a religious feast *Glr.* (might be used for agapē, love-feast, feast of charity); *dús-ston* a periodical festival, one connected with certain times or periods *Tar.*; *bag-ston* wedding-feast, frq.; *miṅ-ston* feast given at the solemnity, when a name is given to a child; *ráb-ston* a feast after settling some important business *Cs.*; *btsás-ston* a feast given after the birth of a child; *tsógs-ston* sacrificatory feast; *yšid-ston* funeral feast.

སྟོབ་པ་ *stób-pa*, pf. *bstab* (*Cs.* *bstob*), fut. *bstob Cs.*, imp. *stob*, (causative to *tob-pa?*), to put into another's mouth esp. food, **to feed**; also applied to a mare that shoves the grass to her foal *Dzl.*; *nán-tan-gyis stób-pa* to press a person to accept of a dish etc. *Dzl.*; in a more general sense: *láṅ-ste stan stób-par byéd-pa* rising to offer one's own seat *Stg.*; to make a donation *Dzl.*; also capir.: *yo-byád tams-čád-kyis stób-pa* to provide a person with every thing within one's power *Tar.*

སྟོབས་(པོ) *stóbs(-po)* **strength, vigour, force**, frq.; *lús-stobs* bodily, *snyiṅ-stobs* mental strength; *ͦjú-stobs* digestive power *Med.*; *stóbs-po če* of great physical strength *Dzl.*; *stóbs-kyis* by virtue, by means of; *stobs-ͦpel-nyams-brtás byéd-pa* strengthening, nourishing, of food *Med.*; *stóbs-čan, stobs-ldán*, strong, robust; *stobs-čúṅ, stobs-'méd*, powerless, weak; the five powers of a Buddha v. *Burn.* II, 430; *Köpp.* I, 436; the ten powers v. *dbaṅ bču*. — *stobs-čén* 1. n. of a Lu-king, *S.O.* — 2. **rammer, pile-driver**, (or *rdob-čén?*) *C.*

སྟོར་བ་ *stór-ba* **to be lost, to perish, to go astray**, *bu stór-ro* a child has been lost *Dzl.*; *lus daṅ srog* (to lose) one's life *Dzl.*, *sems* one's senses, *lam* one's way (also fig. to err from true religion *Pth.*); **tor ma čug** *W.* do not lose it, do not drop it, carry it carefully; *stór-sa med* it cannot be lost or antiquated *Mil.* — *stór-kuṅ* for *ytór-kuṅ* drain, gutter *Lex.*

བརྟ་ *brt...* v. chiefly sub *rt*.

བརྟ་བ་ *brtá-ba*, pf. *brtas*, *Lex.*: *lus sems brtas*, explained by *rgyás-pa*, **to grow wide, to extend**; gen. **to grow stout**, esp. with *nyams Dzl.*; cf. also the expression for strengthening sub *stóbs(-po)*; also *rtas byéd-pa Med.*; fig. strong or great: *ͦgyód-pa rtas* the greatest, the sincerest repentance *Pth.*; *bág-čags rtás-pa* high passion *Thgy.*

བརྟག(ས)་པ་ *brtág(s)-pa*, v. *rtóg-pa;* as sbst., preceded by a genit., **inquiry, examination,** *Stg.*, frq.; gen. c. accus. *rmi-lam brtág(s)-pa* examination of dreams *Stg.; rin-po-če brtág(s)-pa-la mḱás-pa* connoisseur of precious stones *Dzl.*; *brtágs-pa brgyad Tar.* 21, 2.?

བརྟད་ *brtad* a kind of imprecation, which consists in hiding the image and name of an enemy in the ground underneath an idol, and imploring the deity to kill him; *brtad ˳ǰúg-pa* to perform that ceremony *Mil.*

བརྟད་པ་ *brtád-pa* 1. *Lex.* = *bló-bur* **new, recent.** — 2. *Sch.* **haste, speed,** for *rtáb-pa* (?) (*Tar.* 180, 2 it should prob. be *ɣtád-na.*)

བརྟན་པ་ *brtán-pa* adj. and abstract noun; *brtán-po* adj., **firm, steadfast, safe; firmness** etc.; *brtán-par ɣnás-pa*, **tán-po dád-čc* W.*, to last, hold out, abide, continue, frq.; *brtán-pa ťób-pa* to become firm or durable (lit. to acquire firmness or durability) *Mil.; brtán-par ˳gyúr-ba*, **tán-po cá-če* W.* id.; *brtán-gyi skyid* a continued or abiding happiness *Mil.; dbaṅ brtan* their strength is holding out *Med.*; *brtán-du ˳ǰúg-pa Glr.*, **tán-po čó-če* W.*, to watch, keep, preserve carefully; **tán-po kur* W.* carry it carefully or safely! *dám-bčas-pa brtán-par šes* he knew his word to be inviolable *Dzl.*; *yi-dam-la brtán-pas* because he firmly kept his word *Dzl.*; *dus brtán-gyi bdé-ba* eternal welfare, everlasting happiness *Mil.* (perh. this ought to be *ɣtan*).

བརྟན་མ་ *brtán-ma*, or *bstán-ma*, and *bstán-pa-mo*, n. of the goddess of the earth, (also *skóṅ-ma*, *yá-ma*), used in practising magic.

བརྟུལ་བ་ *brtúl-ba* 1. **deportment, behaviour** *Cs.* — 2. *Sch.* also diligence, painstaking (?). — *brtul-žúgs*, व्रत 1. *Cs.* manner, way of acting. 2. *Sch.* and gen.: exercise of penance, *brtul-žugs byéd-pa* or *spyód-pa*, to perform such exercises, to do penance. 3. penitent. — *brtul-žugs-čan* **penitent** (adj. and sbst.) — *brtul-ṕód-pa* v. *rtul-ṕód-pa.*

བསྟང་བ་ *bstáṅ-ba* v. *stóṅs-pa.*

བསྟན་པ་ *bstán-pa* 1. v. *stón-pa.* — 2. sbst. **doctrine,** a single doctrine, or a whole system of doctrines; *saṅs-rgyás-kyi bstán-pa* the doctrine or religion of Buddha, *ťub-bstán*, for *ťúb-pai bstán-pa*, id.; *ɣnás-lugs bstán-pa* the doctrine of the position of... *Med.*; *bstán-pa ɣnyis* with Urgyan Padma etc., the same as *mdoi* and *sṅágs-kyi lam*, v. *mdo* extr. — *bstán-˳gyur* the second great literary production of Buddhism, containing comments on *Kan-˳gyur*, and scientific treatises (v. *bka-gyur* in *bka*) *Köpp.* II, 280. — *bstan-bčos* (शास्त्र) a scientific work. — *bstan-rtsis* a chronological work relative to the year of Buddha's death. — *bstan-˳dzín* follower, adherent of a doctrine, *saṅs-rgyás-kyi bstan-˳dzin Mil.*, Buddhist; also frq. used as a noun personal. — *bstan-(b)šig* col. a destroyer of the doctrine, in general a good-for-nothing fellow, a mischief-maker, an obnoxious person or thing. — *bstan-srúṅ* 1. **a keeper, guardian of the doctrine;** perh. also = *bstan-˳dzín.* 2. **keeper, warden, guardian** in general, *lha-ḱáṅ-gi bstan-srúṅ; lhá-sai bstan-srúṅ* the tutelar goddess of Lhasa, acc. to *Glr.* = *dpal-lhá-mo.* 3. in general the contrary to *bstan-bšig.*

བསྟིར་ *bstir* supine of *sti-ba; bstir-méd* 'restlessness', one of the infernal regions.

བསྟུགས་པ་ *bstúgs-pa* **to make lower, to lower** *Sch.* (?).

བསྟེན་པ་ *bstén-pa* 1. vb. v. *stén-pa.* 2. sbst. **confidence,** = *brtón-pa Bhar.*

བསྟོད་པ་ *bstód-pa* v. *stód-pa.*

ཐ

ཐ *ta*, the letter **t** aspirated, like the English t in 'tea'.

ཐ *ta* 1. num. fig.: ten. — 2. **every thing, all, total** *Sch.* (?).

ཐ་སྐར་ *ta-skár* a certain star, *ta-skár-zla-ba* a month, prob. = वैशाख (April-May); *ta-skár-gyi bu* अश्विनी twin half-gods.

ཐ་ཁབ་ *ta-káb Lh.* a large **needle.**

ཐ་ག་པ་ *tá-ga-pa* **a weaver** *Dzl.*

ཐ་གུ་ *tá-gu*, vulg. *ti-gu*, 1. a short **cord** or **rope.** — 2. **string, twine,** for making garlands *Stg.*; a bell-rope *Dzl.*

ཐ་གྲུ་ *ta-grú*, originally *tag-grú Pth.*, **extension, width, breadth,** *ₒdzam-bu-glin-gi ta-grú kún-la Glr.* in the whole extent of Dzambuling; *ta-grú čé-ba Pth.* extensive.

ཐ་རྒོད་ *ta-rgód* 1. **obtuse, rounded off** *Sch.* — 2. *Mil.!*

ཐ་ཆད་ *ta-čád* **very bad, mean** *Cs.*

ཐ་ཆུང་ *ta-čún* **the last month** of a season (v. *dus*), e.g. *dpyid-zla ta-čún* the last month of spring, opp. to *rá-ba*, (and *ₒbrin-po*); **the youngest** of three or more sons, opp. to *rab* (and *ₒbrin-po* the middle one).

ཐ་སྙད་ *ta-snyád* 1. **appellation,** *žes ta-snyád-du grags* so it is called *Wdṅ.*; *Tar.* 96, 13; 178, 3; *Was.* (296): **supposition; condition,** *ta-snyád-pai bdén-pa* conditional truth. — 3. *Schr.*: **etymology,** *Cs.* only: part of grammar; so frq. used by grammarians, e.g. *tsig dan ta-snyád slób-pa* to learn spelling and etymology. 4. In col. language I heard it used only for talking or disputing in a conceited, foolish manner, so also in *Mil.* — *Lex.* in conformity with each of these significations = व्यवहार, from व्यवह्व to distinguish, to name; to dispute. — *ta-snyad-yčig-pa* n. of a school, of a system or doctrine *Tar.*; *ta-snyad-grúb-pa* n. of a literary work.

ཐ་དད་པ་ *ta-dád-pa* **different, various, sundry,** gen. opp to *yčig* or *yčig-pa*; *dgós-pa ta-dád-pa* the various wants of a man *Dzl.*; *ta-mi-dád-pa* alike, equal.

ཐ་ན་ *tá-na* **even, so much as, up to,** *tá-na-srog-čágs gróg-sbur yan-čád* even the smallest insect *Stg.*; *tá-na yig-ₒbru re-ré yan-čád* even every single letter *Thgy.*; at the close of an enumeration: **finally also** *Ld.-Glr. Schl.* 20, 6.

ཐ་པི་ཐུ་པི་ *ta-pi-tú-pi* **confusion, disorder** *Sch.*

ཐ་དཔག *tá-pag* v. *tár-dpag.*

ཐ་བ་ *tá-ba* (= *tú-ba*) **bad** *Mil.*

ཐ་མ་ *tá-ma* **the last** of several things, with respect to number, time, rank, the lowest, meanest, most inferior, often opp. to *rab* and *ₒbrin*, and also to *kyád-par-čan*; it appears somewhat singular, that *yčan-zán-gyi tá-ma* signifies a cat, and *ₒdab-čágs-kyi tá-ma* a hen *Glr.*; *dús-kyi tá-ma-la* in the last times *Glr.*, prob. also alluding to the general decline taking place towards the end of the Kalpa; sometimes it is to be translated: **in the last place, finally, at last** *Glr.*, like *tá-mar Dzl.* ༢༧, 11; last = parting (parting-cup, parting-kiss); for the last time: *ynyén-gyi tá-mas bskor* he sees his relations for the last time around him, *zás-kyi tá-ma za* he eats for the last time *Thgy.*; *tá-ma-la* c. genit. at the end of, after. — *ₒprád-pai tá-ma ni ₒbral, ysón-pai tá-ma ni ši-ba yin* the end of every meeting is parting, the end of every living is dying.

ཐ་མ་ཁ་ *ta-ma-ka Cs.*, vulg. *W.* **tá-mag**, **tobacco,** *ₒtun-ba*, *W.* resp. **dón-če** to smoke (tobacco).

ཐ་མལ་པ་ *ťa-mál-pa* (*ťa-mál* abbreviated from *ťá-ma-la*) 1. **mean, vulgar, plebeian**, *ťa-mál-par* *ˌdúg-pa* to live like the vulgar *Dzl.* — 2. **ordinary, usual**, *ťa-mál-pa ma yin* that is no usual thing *Dzl.*; *ťa-mál* adv. = *ṗal-čér*.

ཐ་ཚིག་ *ťa-tsig Sch.* 'oath'; but in two passages of *Dzl.* *čii ťa-tsig* can only mean: **'what signifies?'**

ཐ་ར་ཐོ་རེ་ *ťa-ra-ťo-ré W.* **wide asunder, wide**, **ťa-ra-ťo-ré žág-pa* C.* to scatter, to throw loosely about.

ཐ་རམ་ *ťa-rám* 1. *Sch.*: 'the breadth of a plain'. — 2. a medicinal herb *Med.*, in *Lh.* Plantago major.

ཐ་རུ་ *ťa-rú Tar.* 20, 17, *Schf.*: 'the utmost limits', or it may be a p. n.

ཐ་ལི་ *ťa-li W.*, **ťe-li* C.*, *Hind.* **थलिया**, **a tin plate**.

ཐ་ལོང་ *ťa-lóṅ W.* a sort of red cloth.

ཐ་ཤལ་ *ťa-šál Sch.*: 'the end, the consequence; bad'; *Bhar.*: *skyés-bu ťa-šál nyid Schf.*: homo nequam, a good-for-naught.

ཐག་ *ťag* 1. sometimes for *ˌťag*, *Glr.* — 2. **distance** a. relatively (prob. from *ťág-pa* measuring-cord, surveyor's chain) only in: *ťag-riṅ-ba* adj. and abstract noun, *ťag-riṅ* (*-po*) adj., *W.* **ťag-riṅ-(mo)** **distant, a great distance,** *sa ťag-riṅ(s)* a far country *Glr.*; with *daṅ* or *las* far from; *ťag-mi-riṅ-ba* not far *Pth.*; *ťag-riṅ(-po)-nas* from **afar**, from a distance *Thgy.*; *ťag-nyé-ba* **near; proximity**; *W.* adj. **ťag-nyé-mo**; *ťag či-tsam* how far? *Cs.*; *ťag-gru* v. *ťa-gru*. b. absolutely, only with respect to time, in: *ma-ťág* **but just, just now**, gen. with a verbal root, *sleb ma-ťág yin-pa* he that has arrived just now *Glr.*; *sṅar bšad ma-ťág-pa* (the passages) that have been explained just now *Gram.*; as an adv. gen. *ma-ťág-tu*, or only *ma-ťág*, frq., e.g. *ťos ma-ťág-tu* as soon as he had heard; *de ma-ťág-tu* directly, immediately, in *W.* **ma-ťóg-tse**. — 3. *ťag-ťóg* v. *ťog-ťág*. — 4. *ťag-γčód-pa* v. *ťág-pa* I.

ཐག་ཐག་ *ťag-ťág*, with **ǰhé'-pa* C.*, **čó-če** **to knock,** *sgo* at the door.

ཐག་པ་ *ťág-pa* I. **rope, cord** (in *Lh.* hempen ropes, as a foreign manufacture, are often distinguished from other ropes, by being called **रस्सी**, *bal-ťág* rope made of wool, *ral-ťág* rope of goat's hair, *rtsid-ťág* rope of the long hair of the yak, *rtsa-ťág*, or *ṗon-ťág Glr.* rope of grass; *lčágs-(kyi) ťág-pa* chain, wire-rope, used as fetters or otherwise; **ras-ťág* W.* **bandage;** *ťag-mig* **mesh** of a net *Sch.*; *ťag-zó* **rope-maker's work** *Pth.* — *ťág γčód-pa* vb. a. (*ťag čód-pa*, or *čád-pa* vb. n. or pass.) 1. to cut a cord, *bdag nyé-du daṅ ˌbrél-ťag bčád-pas bde* I am glad of having cut the cord (tie) which united me with my family *Mil.*; gen. with *re*, the cord of hope, e.g. *ˌgró-bai ré-ťag čad* the cord of the hope of going on a journey is cut off, i.e. the journey has been given up *Glr.; Schr.*: *ˌó-ťag γčód-pa* to wean (a child); *bló-ťag čod* deliberation is cut off, the matter is decided or resolved upon; hence frq. without *blo*: 2. **to decide, resolve, determine,** *rgyal-po bkróṅ-bar ťag-bčád* it was determined to murder the king *Glr.*; *ḱyod γnyis ṅá-la čúṅ-ma mi len ťág-čód-pa-na* if you positively refuse to give me a wife *Pth.*; **ťag-čád mi ḱyul* W.* I have no right to decide on that point; *ťag-čód-pa byéd-pa* to decide, pass sentence, give judgment *Mil.*; **to be sure, decided, certain,** . . . *gróṅs-par ˈťag-bčád-de* (cf. above) as it is quite certain that he has died *Mil.*; . . . *yod ťag-čód* there are certainly . . . *Glr.*; *čos dar ˌóṅ ťag-čód* it is quite certain that religion will spread *Mil.*; *ltá-bas ťag-bčád-nas* being immovable in contemplation; with termin.: to know for a certainty, to understand or see clearly, *ráṅ-sems čós-skur ťag-čód-čiṅ* knowing one's own mind to be vain and frail (v. *čós-sku* sub *sku* 2) *Mil.*: *snáṅ-ba séms-su* the visible world as a thought, as imaginary, i.e. as nothing *Mil.*; *ťag-čód* **certainty, surety, evidence,** *ˌóṅ-kyaṅ ťag-čód byed dgos* but one should know it for certain, one must be sure of it *Mil.*; *ltá-ba ťag-čód-kyi rnál-ˌbyor-pa* you, the ascetic, firm in meditation! *Mil.* — **ťag-čọ'-rbẹ'-čọ'* C.* resolute.

II. prob. = *dág-pa*, in *snyiṅ* (or *že*, or *bsám-pa*) *ťág-pa-nas* with a faithful heart, with all my heart, **heartily**, *že ťág-pai žú-ba Mil.* a sincere prayer or entreaty.

Note. In *ťag-pa* and other words beginning with *ť*, (e.g. *ťaṅ*, *ťo*), *d* sometimes takes the place of *ť*, and this uncertainty in the use of the initial letter dates perh. from a time, when the aspirated pronunciation of the media first began to be adopted in *C.*, and was not yet generally introduced.

ཐགས *ťags* **texture, web,** *ťags ˳ťág-pa* to weave *Dzl.*, *ťágs-˳ťag-mkan* col. for *ťá-ga-pa*, also *ťágs-mkan Pth.* a weaver; **ťser-ťág** *W.* thorn-hedge, fence consisting of thorn; *ťags-kri* (weaver's) loom *Ld.-Glr.*; *ťágs-gra-˳bu Cs.*, **ťágs-kan-bu** *W.*, **spider**; *ťágs-ča* weaver's implements; *ťágs-γnas*, *ťágs-ra*, a weaver's place or shop *Cs.*; *ťags-brán byéd-pa Mil.*, **ťag rán-če** *W.*, to begin the warp.

ཐགས་ཐོགས *ťags-ťógs* **impediment** *Cs.*

ཐང *ťaṅ* 1. also *ťáṅ-ma Mil.*, *ťáṅ-bu Dzl. Ms.*, **ťáṅ-ka** *W.*, flat country, **a plain, steppe**; also fig. like *žiṅ*, *bde-čén-gyi ťaṅ* land of bliss *Mil.*; *ťáṅ-la* (from the house) into the plain or steppe, = into the open air *Dzl.*; *ťáṅ-la ltúṅ-ba* to fall to the ground; **ma-ťáṅ** *W.* the unfloored bottom of a room; *gram-ťáṅ* a fenny or swampy plain *Cs.*; *spaṅ-ťáṅ* a green grassy plain or steppe, meadow, prairie; *byaṅ-ťáṅ* the northern steppes or plains of Tibet (used as a noun proper); *bye-ťáṅ* a sandy desert or plain; *˳ol-ťáṅ* ground covered with (snail-) clover, **pasture ground,** grassy plain; *šag-ťáṅ* a gravelly plain; *ťáṅ-du byéd-pa Cs.* to lay waste, to make a desert of, *ťáṅ-du ˳gyúr-ba* to become a desert. — 2. *Cs.* **price, value,** perh. also amount; *rin-ťáṅ* id. *Dzl.*; *rin-ťaṅ-čan* **dear, precious,** *Mil.*; *yoṅ-ťáṅ* 1. *W.* **income, profit,** 2. *C.* = *yón-tan* **talent**, natural gift, faculty; *lo-ťáṅ* yearly tribute, *γčód-pa* to fix, to order it *Tar.*; *za-ťáṅ* (a person's) capability of eating *Thgy.* — 3. *W.* for *dwaṅs* **clear, serene,** **nam ťaṅ** a cloudless sky, fine weather; **daṅ ṗi-ro ťáṅ-te yod** (the sky) was cloudless last night. — 4. **potion** *Med.* — 5. = *bka-ťáṅ*, **order, command,** (*bka*) *ťaṅ-yig* **decree;** *pad-ma-ťaṅ-yig* is the abridged title of a collection of legends about Padma Sambhava. — 6. (**resin?**) *ťaṅ-čú* **resin, gum,** e.g. of fruit-trees. — 7. a very short space of time (the statements as to its length vary from five seconds to one minute and a half), **a moment, a little while,** gen. *ťaṅ γčig*, not seldom joined with *skad čig* and *yud tsam*; *ťaṅ tsam* id. *Pth.*; *čig-ťaṅ*, *bži-ťaṅ* one moment, four moments; *Lt.*, *ťaṅ-ré S.g.*, one after the other *Sch.* — 8. v. *ťaṅ-ka.* — In a few instances the meaning of *ťaṅ* is not quite evident.

Comp. *ťaṅ-krúṅ* bastard *Sch.* — *ťaṅ-čú* v. *ťaṅ* C. — *ťaṅ-stóṅ* uninhabited, desolate; wilderness. — *ťaṅ-˳brú Sch.* 'cedar-nuts', perh. = *ko-nyon-tsé* q.v. — *ťaṅ-már* tar *Cs.* — **ťaṅ-ma-la-la-tsé** a small lizard *Ld.* — *ťaṅ-γži* market-price, **ťaṅ-ži čag** *C.* the market-price abates. — **ťaṅ-zi** *W.* fata morgana — *ťaṅ-rág* cedar (?) *Sch.* — *ťaṅ-šiṅ* fir, pine.

ཐང་ཀ, ཐང་ག *ťáṅ-ka*, *ťáṅ-ga*, resp. *žal-ťáṅ*, *W.* **sku-ťáṅ**, *Tar.* *ťáṅ-sku*, **image,** prop. of human beings, at present = picture, **painting,** in a gen. sense, also of landscapes etc.

ཐང་དཀར *ťaṅ-dkár* the white-tailed eagle *Sch.*

ཐང་ཐང *ťaṅ-ťáṅ* v. the following word.

ཐང་པོ *ťáṅ-po*, **tense, tight, firm** (= *˳ťáṅ-po?*); *ťaṅ-lhód* tight and loose; also tenseness fig. *Mil.*; *ťáṅ-ša γčód-pa* to strain, to stretch, *čód-pa* vb. n. or pass. *Stg.*, *Mil.*, *C.*; **zúg-po ťaṅ-ṅam** *C.* are you well? — *rkaṅ-ťáṅ-du* or *la* **on foot,** v. *rkáṅ-pa* comp.; *ťaṅ γčod-pa* **to tire, to fatigue** *Mil.*, *ťaṅ čod-pa* or *čad-pa* to be tired, wearied *Pth.*; **gom-ťáṅ láb-če* (*ṭú-gu-la*)* *W.* to lead a child in walking, to teach a child to walk; *ša-ťáṅ-ťáṅ* to the utmost of one's power *Sch.*

ཐང་ཕྲོམ *ťaṅ-ṗróm* a medicinal herb *Med.*, *Wdṅ.* = *dha-tu-ra* thorn-apple (?).

ཐང་ཤ *táṅ-ša* v. sub *taṅ-po; taṅ-šiṅ* v. *taṅ* comp.

ཐད(ཀ) *tád(-ka)* 1. **the direction straight forward,** *steṅ daṅ ˏog daṅ tád-ka tams-čád-du* upward and downward, and in every other direction *Stg.*; *steṅ-ˏog-tád-kar* straight upward and downward *S.g.*; *ṗo-bráṅ-gi tád-kar ṗyin* they came straight towards the castle; *tád-ka-na* directly before *Thgy.*; *deï nub-tád-kyi* that which is situated to the west of it *Tar.*; most frq. *tád-du* c. genit. **towards,** in straight direction; **over against; in presence of** e.g. to assemble, to propound, to lay before one, to study under a professor *Dzl.*; **exactly in the place** of a thing *Tar.* 17, 1; *šai tád-nas čod Tar.* 159, 4 prob.: cut off only from the flesh; **tẹ̈-kya, tẹ̈-kaṅ-la* Ts.* **straight on;** *tad-draṅ-na* **directly before** *Wdṅ.*; **tad-nyá* W.* **over against, opposite, facing;** *tád-so-na* = *tád-ka-na Mil.* — 2. *tád-kar* **each for himself** *Glr.* — 3. **entire, whole, untouched, safe** (integer) *C.* and perh. *Thgy.*

ཐད frq. abbreviation for ཐམས་ཅད *tams-čád,* **whole, all.**

ཐན *tan, Hind.* थान, = *yug,* **a piece of cloth.**

ཐན་སྐོར *tan-kór, tan-skór Lex.*, surrounding country *Sch.*

ཐན་ཐུན *tan-tún* (*Schr. tad-tún*) **a little** *Sch.*

ཐན་པ *tán-pa* **dry weather, heat, drought** *Glr.*

ཐབ *tab* 1. resp. *ysol-táb,* **fire-place, hearth,** *me-táb,* id.; also for **stove,** *lčags-táb* iron stove; *tab šor* 'the hearth is running over', i.e. the food placed on it runs over in boiling, a mis-hap the more serious, as the household god is offended by the evil smell caused thereby. — 2. v. sub *čaṅ.*

Comp.: **táb-ka* W.* fire-place, **táb-ka tsam yod** how many fire-places, i.e. households, are there? — *tab-kúṅ* opening or mouth of a stove, furnace, or fire-place; v. also *Schl.* 249. — *tab-ynás* fire-place, furnace, oven *Cs.* — **tab-tsáṅ* W.* kitchen. — *tab-ṗyis, W. *tab-ṗis** clout, dish-clout, wiper. — *tab-yžób* burnt smell. — **tab-lás čó-kan* W.* cook. — *tab-yyóg* kitchen-boy, scullion *Pth.* — *tab-šiṅ* fire-wood, fuel. — *tab-lhá* deity of the hearth.

ཐབ་ཐོབ *tab-tób W.* = *tom-tóm.*

ཐབས *tabs* (cog. to *stabs*), **opportunity, chance, possibility,** **tóṅ-*or *dúl-táb ma ǰuṅ* W.* I had no opportunity of seeing or going; **tab šig nyi-ráṅ-ne mi ǰúṅ-na* W.* if you offer no chance, if on your part it is not made possible; *tabs mi tub Dzl.* and col. I am not able, I cannot; *ydan-dráṅs-pai tabs med* I then shall lose the opportunity of meeting (the princess) *Glr.*; *ˏbrós-pai tabs med* there is not any chance of escape *Glr.*; *lám-la yžól-tabs med* there is no occasion for stopping or tarrying on the road *Mil.*; **way, manner, mode,** *klog-tabs* way of reading, e.g. Sanskrit; *rkún-tabs-su* in a thievish manner, by theft *Stg.*; *rgyál-poi tabs ytóṅ-ba* to give up the way (of life) of a king, to resign the crown *Dzl.*, *tabs ycig-tu* together, in company, jointly, e.g. to sit down with one another, to go together to a place, frq.; **means, measures,** *tabs byéd-pa, W. *čó-če, kyóṅ-če** to use means, to take measures; *blo tabs ˏtsól-ba* to contrive means *Ma.*; *tabs stón-pa* to show means or ways, to give directions, to instruct *Glr.*; *ˏtsó-tabs* **livelihood, subsistence;** *tabs zad* there is nothing else to be done *Glr.*; *ži-bai tábs-kyis* in a fair way, amicably, not by constraint or compulsion *Glr.*; *tábs-kyis* by various means, by artifice, cunningly, craftily: *tábs(-la)-mkás-pa, tábs-šes-pa, W.* also **táb-čan*,* **skilful, dexterous, clever, full of devices;** *da bód-du ˏgró-tabs gyis šig* now take steps, make preparations, for a journey to Tibet *Glr.*; *de ysón-poi tabs yód-dam* is there a means of recalling those men to life? *tabs-čág Mil.*, **tab-šág** or **teb-šág** vulgo, a shift, make-shift, surrogate; *tabs (daṅ) šes (-rab)* the mystical union of art and science, or (*Sch.* less correctly) of matter and spirit, cf. *Was.* (144).

ཐམ་ག, ཐམ་ཀ *tám-ga, tám-ka* **a seal, sign** *Cs.*, v. *dám-ka.*

ཐམ་ཐམ་ *tam-tám Sch.* 1. also *tám-me-ba*, **unconnected, scattered, dispersed.** — 2. *tam-tám* (*byed*) *-pa* = *ₒtúm-pa*.

ཐམ་པ་ *tám-pa* (sometimes *tém-pa*) **complete, full,** almost exclusively used as a pleon. addition to the tens up to hundred.

ཐམས་ཅད་ *tams-čád* **whole, all**; added to the singular number: *rgyal-kʻáms tams-čád* the whole empire *Glr.*; *lus tams-čád na* the whole body aches (opp. to one part of it); *bód-kyi zaṅs tams-čád* all the copper of Tibet *Glr.*; more frq. added to a plural (though usually in the form of the singular number): all (the persons or things), *de tams-čád*, rarely *dé-dag tams-čád*, all those; *tams-čád-kyis so-só-nas* all of them one by one, each.

ཐམས་པ་ *táms-pa* (= *ₒtám-pa?*), *sa*, or *bye-táms-su ₒjug-pa* to suffer (a person or beast) to stick fast in the mud, in the sand (?) *Glr.* 84.

ཐའུ་ *tau Wdṅ.* **capsule** (?), *Wts.* **peach** (?).

ཐར་ *tar* v. *tar-tór*.

ཐར་ཐོར་(ལ་) *tar-tór(-la)* = *ta-ra-to-ré* (cf. *ₒtór-ba*); **tar čós-se dug* Ld.* sit wide asunder, not too close together! *tar byed-pa Mil.* **to break to pieces, to smash, to crush.**

ཐར་ནུ་ *túr-nu* a purgative *Med.*

ཐར་དཔག་ *tar-dpág, C.* **tar-ₒbág*, W.* **tú-bag** a large **plate, dish, platter.**

ཐར་བ་ *túr-ba* **to become free, to be saved,** **tar gos*, or *goi* W.* he must become free, *las* from; to be not hindered or prevented, **to get through, to get on, to be able to pass,** *čú-la* through the water *Mil.*; *zas mi tar* the food cannot pass through *Med.*; to be released, acquitted, discharged, **ṭim-na* C.* by a court of justice; *tár-du ₒjúg-pa* to set at liberty, to acquit, with *tse* (col. **tse-tár-la táṅ-wa**) to pardon (a malefactor), to grant him his life, frq., to let live (animals) *Mil.*; often in a religious sense (with or without *rnám-par*) **to be saved, freed, released,** viz. from the transmigration of souls; more frq. the pf. *tár-pa* 1. to be free etc., *lam tar* the road is free, passable 2 sbst. **freedom, liberty, happiness, eternal bliss,** मोक्ष, *tár-pai rgyur ₒgyur* it will be serviceable for (my) liberty; *tár-* (*pai*) *lam* the road to happiness (a common expression); *tar-méd-kyi dmyál-ba* hell without release. 3. adj. **free,** *tár-par ₒgyúr-ba* to become free, *byéd-pa* to make free, to liberate, to save; *tár-sa* place of refuge, asylum *Thgy.*

ཐལ་ *tal*, sometimes for *ta-li*; *tál-gyis* v. *tál-ba* II. 3.

ཐལ་བ་ *tál-ba* I. sbst. 1. **dust** (cf. *rdul*), **ashes, and similar substances;** *gog-tál* ashes; **tug-tál** ('soup-dust') roasted barley-flour *C.* — *tal-kár* a kind of elephant, *Cs.*, perh. the ash-coloured. — *tál-ču* lye. — *tal-čén* ashes of the dead; also a sort of light gray earth, representing the former, and used for bedaubing the face in masquerades *Mil.* — *tal-tág Ld.* unleavened bread. — *tal-mdóg* ash-coloured, cinereous. — *tal-pyágs* broom *Sch.* — *tal-byi* the gray or cat-squirrel. — *tal-tsá* a sort of salt *Med.* — 2. *bya-tal* **dung of birds** *Glr.*

II. vb. (*Cs.* also *ₒtál-ba*) 1. **to pass, to pass by,** **tal ča dug* W.* he goes past, he does not come in; **zúm-pa tal ča dug**, he goes past the bridge, does not pass over it; to **miss** the **mark,** of an **arrow** or ball; *rba tal-tál ₒoṅ* the waves flow past *Mil.* — 2. **to go, step, pass beyond,** *lo lṅá-bču tál-nas* when the age of fifty has been passed *Wdṅ.*; **ču-tsód γčig tsá-big tal* W.* a little past one o'clock; *sṅo-ba-las tal-nas dmar-žiṅ* Thgy., prob. inclining from blue to red; **to be in the advance** *C.*; **to project, to be prominent,** hence *tal-túṅ* different lengths, one object projecting beyond another; **to play a prominent part, to take the lead** *W.*; *tál-čes-pa* **to exceed the due measure** *Sch.*; **ka tal-wa** to be forward in speaking, bold. — 3. **to go or pass through,** *brág-la yar tal mar tal*, and *par tal tsur tál-du ₒgró-ba* to soar up and down befor rock, and to pass actually through it (the saints not being subject to the physical laws of matter) *Mil.*, *Thgr.*; **to shine, to light through;** *tal-°byúṅ-du ₒgró-ba* to go straightforward, to act without ceremony or disguise *Dzl.* ༢༥༢, 3; *tál-ma Sch.*, *tál-le C.*, **through and through;** *tál-gyis* **directly, straightway, unhesitatingly** *Mil.* — 4. **to come or get to, to arrive at** (*W.* **tél-če**), *tál-nas lo ɣsum lon* three years have elapsed since they arrived; *p̓a-má gar tál-bai ɣtol-méd*; *bzaṅ-tál* safe arrival *Thgr.*; *yár-gyi bzáṅ-tal čén-por ₒgró-ba* to arrive at, attain to (a blessed state) in a pleasant and speedy manner *Thgr.* — 5. **to be over, past, finished, done,** *tál-lo* of a song: it is over, finished *Mil.*; *drúg-ču tál-lo* the number of sixty is full; *yál-nas tál-ba Mil.* having disappeared, vanished; *stór-te* (or *stór-nas*) *tal* he is undone, it is all over with him *Mil.* frq.; *rim-gyis ǰe nyúṅ ǰe nyúṅ tal* by degrees it vanishes, dies away *Mil.*; *sṅar čad-tsig tal* the former agreement is no longer valid; *tal soṅ* col. = *tsar soṅ.* — *Tar.* 46, 5. 12? 172, 5: *tál-gyur-pa Schf.* **follower, adherent,** or the name of a certain sect.

ཐལ་མོ་ *tál-mo* **the palm of the hand,** *tál-mo sbyár-ba* to hold together the palms of the hands, as a gesture of devotion; *tál-mo snún-pa Dzl.*, more frq. *tal-lčág rgyáb-pa* to give a slap on the face, a box on the ear; *tal-brdáb-pa* to clap with the hands *Sch.*

ཐི་ *ti* num. fig.: 40.

ཐི་གུ *ti-gu* v. *tá-gu*; *ti-gu-k̓ró-bo* (?) *C.* = **ar-gón** *W.*

ཐི་བ་ *ti-ba* 1. **wood-pigeon, stock-dove** *Sch.*; *ti-bo* **plover, peewit, lapwing** *Sch.* — 2. *C.* = *té-ba*.

ཐིག་ *tig*, prob. from *ti-gu*, 1. **carpenter's cord** or string to mark lines with, **marking-string,** *tig(-gis) ₒdebs-pa* to use such a string, to draw lines. — 2. any instrument used in drawing lines; *skor-tig* a pair of compasses, *ɣya-tig* slate-pencil, lead-pencil; also a line drawn with a lead-pencil; **tig-ta taṅ-če** *W.* c. genit. to examine, try, test. — 3. **a line,** *tig-ₒdebs-pa*, *rgyag-pa*, *rgyab-pa*, to draw lines; *guṅ-tig* the meridian line *Cs.*; *nag-tig* or *snag-tig* a black line, *tsal-tig* a red line; *tsaṅs-tig* diameter; equator *Cs.* — 4. symb. numeral for **zero.** — 5. v. *tig*.

Comp. *tig-skód* string to mark lines with. — **tig-nyá** *W.* **over against.** — *tig-nág Stg.*, *Sch.*: that part of hell, where the damned are sawn to pieces, lines being drawn upon them. — *tig-tsám* **a little.** — *tig-tsád Cs.* **proportion, symmetry,** *Ld.-Glr.* f. 27, 6, *tig-tsad byéd-pa* to proportion; **tig-tsád zúm-če** *W.*, to determine the relation or proportion of things. — *tig-šiṅ* **a ruler,** to rule lines with.

ཐིག་ལེ་ *tig-le* 1. **a spot** like that of a leopard's skin, *tig-le-čan* **spotted, speckled;** **tig-ma** *W.* id., of variegated woolen fabrics; *čos tig-le nyag čig Mil.*, the centre of all religion, in which finally all the different sects must unite. — 2. **zero, naught** *Wdk.* — 3. **semen virile.** — 4. **contemplation.** The two latter significations are mystically connected with each other, as will be seen from a passage of *Mil.*, which is also a fair specimen of the physiological and mystical reveries of the more recent Buddhism: *yoṅs lús-la ɣtúm-mo ₒbár-bas bde; rluṅ ro rkyaṅ dhú-tir čúd-pas bde; stod byaṅ-čub-séms-kyi rgyún-ₒbab bde; smad dáṅs-mai tig-le k̓yáb-pas bde; bar dkar dmar tug p̓rad brtsé-bas bde; lus zag-med-bdé-bas tsim-pas bde; de rnál-ₒbyor nyáms-kyi bde drug lags*, he (the Yogi) feels well in general, when the warmth of meditation is kindled (cf. *ɣtúm-mo*) in his body; he feels well, when the air enters through *ró-ma* and *kyáṅ-ma* into the *dhúti*; he feels well in the upper part of his body by the flowing down of the *bódhi*; he feels well in the lower parts by the spreading of the chyle (chylous fluid, semen); he feels well in the middle, by being affected with tender compassion, when the red (the blood in the *kyáṅ-ma*) and the white (the semen in the *ró-ma*) unite; the whole body is well, being pervaded by the grateful feeling of sinlessness; this is the sixfold mental happiness of the Yogi.

ཐིགས་པ་ *tigs-pa* **a drop,** *tigs-pa re-ré-nas* in drops, by drops *Glr.*; *čar-tigs* a drop of rain; *γsér-tig-po* (sic) *Mil.* seems to denote a drop or globule of molten gold, which in this form is offered for sale by gold-washers.

ཐིང་ *tin* v. *ₒdin-ba.*

ཐིབ་པ་ *tib-pa* v. *ₒtib-pa* and *γtib-pa; tib-tib* **very dark** *Sch.*; *byin-rlábs tibs-tibs Pth.* seems to imply the descending of a blessing upon a person; *tib(s)-po, mo* **dense,** *Cs.* or perh. nothing but **obscure, dark,** *nágs Stg.*

ཐིམ་པ་ *tim-pa*, also *ₒtim-pa, γtim-pa* and *stim-pa*, gen. with *la* or *nán-du*, **to disappear** by being **imbibed, absorbed; to evaporate,** of fluids; of a snake: **to creep away,** to disappear in a hole; frq. of the vanishing of rays of lights, of gods etc.; **to be melted, dissolved** (salt or sugar in water); **to sink,** *dran-méd-du* into unconsciousness *Mil.*

ཐུ *tu* 1. num. fig.: 70. — 2. **tu gyáb-če* W.* **to spit,** with *la*, to spit at or on. — 3. often erron. for *mtu.*

ཐུ་བ *tu-ba* 1. also *tú-pa*, **skirt, coat-flap** *Glr.* — 2. rarely *ₒtú-ba*, **bad,** e.g. wood *Mil.*; **gyal-tú* W.* good and bad promiscuously; *sdug-bsṅál tú-ba* a bad accident *Thgy.*; **malicious, wicked, vicious** *Glr.* — 3. vb., v. *ₒtú-ba.*

ཐུ་བོ *tú-bo* **ཇོ་བོ** **a chief; an elder brother,** *Dzl.*, *Tar.*; *tú-mo Cs.*: mistress, lady (?).

ཐུ་མི *tu-mi* p. n., v. *ton-mi.*

ཐུ་རེ *tu-ré* **uninterrupted** *Sch.*

ཐུ་ལུམ་ *tu-lúm* **a lump of metal** *B.*; *W.* **cannon-ball:**

ཐུག *tug*, *C.* also **túg-pa**, c. accus. **until, to,** in reference to time and space; **žag zib-ču tug** for forty days; only col.

ཐུག་ཅོམ་ *tug-čóm Sch.*: **'dreadful noise'**; *Thgr. tug-tsóm; Mil. tug-sgrá* id.

ཐུག་པ *túg-pa* I. sbst. **soup, broth,** *ₒbras-túg* rice-soup, *bag-túg* meal-soup, gruel, *rgya-túg* Chinese soup, a sort of vermicelli-soup *C.*; *tug-tál* v. *tál-ba.*

II. vb. 1. **to reach, arrive at, come to,** c. dat. or termin., *tseī mtar túg-pa* to reach the natural term of life *Dzl.*; to come or go as far as *Dzl.*; *rús-pa-la túg-pa* to pierce to the quick *Dzl.*; *ši-la tug tse Mil.*, *ₒči-bar túg-pa-la Lt.* when one is near death; ... *la túg-gi bár-du* till, until *Dzl.*, *Tar.*, *Pth.*; *bzúṅ-la tug* he was just on the point of seizing her *Dzl.*; **sád-da tug* W.* going to kill; *ši-la* (or *bsád-pa-la*) *túg-pa* often means deserving death (of culprits) *Dzl.*; *tse ₒpó-ba-la tug kyaṅ* though life is at stake *Dzl.*; in like manner *W.*: **lus šrog daṅ túg-te ča dug** he goes at the peril of his life; *tug-yas* not to be reached, endless *Cs.* — 2. **to meet, to light upon,** c. *la* or *dan*, = *ₒprád-pa*, esp. col. **nyi-rán-la túg-ga-la yoṅs* W.* he has come to see you; **tug yin* W.* we shall meet again, = till we meet again! à revoir! *ȷ̀ág-pa daṅ túg-pa Mil.* to fall in with robbers; *γdoṅ túg-pa* = *túg-pa*; *či-la tug ruṅ Mil.*, **ghá-la tug kyaṅ* C.* whatever may happen to me; *tug-čád* agreement to meet *Sch.* — 3. col. **to touch, to hit or strike against,** *W.*: **ī-ru túg-kan** here it touches, or strikes against; here is the rub; **lag-pa mi tug yin** I shall not touch it, I shall not come near with my hand; **dé-la tug kyaṅ ma tug* W.* do not even touch it!

ཐུགས *tugs*, resp. for *snyiṅ, yid, sems, bsám-pa, blo* etc., and whenever mental qualities or actions are spoken of in respectful language, v. below. 1. **heart, breast,** in a physical sense, gen. *túgs-ka*; *túgs-kyi sprúl-pa* the incarnation of a deity, originating in a ray of light which proceeds from the breast of that deity *Glr.* — 2. **heart,** in a spiritual sense, **mind, soul, spirit, will,** v. below; **design, purpose, intention,** *sbyin-pai tug zlóg-tu γsol* we beg to desist from the intention of giving *Dzl.*; **understanding, intellect** *Glr.* (v. *sgám-pa*); *túgs-*

su čúd-pa = *ḱóṅ-du čúd-pa*; *túgs-su ̥byón-pa* to be kept in mind, in memory *Mil.*; also = *yid-du ̧óṅ-ba* ni f.; cf. ̥*gró-ba*. — 3. *túgs-la btágs-so* v. ̥*dógs-pa*. — 4. for *túgs-rje* or *bka-drin*, *tugs mdzád-pa* **to grant or show a favour** *Dzl.* — 5 in the phrase *tugs mi túb-pa*, with the genit. of the inf., it is used without ceremonial distinctions for **to venture, to risk, to dare** *Dzl.*

Comp. *túgs-ka* v. above — *tugs-mḱyén* resp. for *mṅon-šés Mil.* — *tugs-̥ḱrúgs* resp. for *ḱoṅ-̥ḱrúgs Ma.* — *tugs-dgóṅs* = *dgóṅs-pa* II.; *tugs-dgóṅs γtóṅ-ba* = *bsam-bló γtóṅ-ba* **to muse, meditate, reflect** *Mil.* — *túgs(-su)* ̥*gró-ba* resp. for *yid-du ̧óṅ-ba* **to be agreeable; agreeable, pleasant, delightful; pleasure, delight**, ... *la* in (a thing) *Mil.* — *tugs-rgyál* resp. **anger, wrath, indignation** *Mil.*, *tugs-rgyál bžeṅs* anger arises, is roused. — *tugs-ṅán* **grief, sorrow, affliction** *Dzl.* — *túgs-čes-pa* resp. for *yid-čes-pa* to believe. — *túgs-rje* prop. respectful word for *snyiṅ-rje* **pity, commiseration, compassion**; gen. **grace, mercy, generosity**, *ṅa-la túgs-rje(s) γzigs* pray, look graciously upon me! *Mil.*; even thus: *sá-bon žig túgs-rje γzigs dgos*, pray, be so kind as to send me some seeds! *W.* — *túgs-rjes ̥dzin-pa*, *túgs-rje mdzád-pa* id. — *túgs-rje-čan* **gracious, merciful, generous.** — (*lha*) *túgs-rje čén-po* the All-merciful, Awalokiteswara. — *tugs-dám*, prop. resp. for *yi-dam*, 1. **oath, vow, solemn promise,** e.g. *bčá-ba* to take (an oath), to make (a vow). 2. **a prayer,** a wish in the form of a prayer, = *smón-lam*. 3. **contemplation,** the act of contemplating a deity (cf. *sgóm-pa* and *sgrúb-pa*); **meditation** in general, *Mil.* frq., *tugs-dám ̥pel* meditation increases, proceeds successfully; **devotion.** 4. **a deity, a tutelar god** or **saint, a patron** *Glr.* — *tugs-nyid* v. *sems-nyid*, sub *sems*. — *tugs-múg* resp. for *yi(d)-múg* despair. — *tugs bdé-ba*, *mi bdé-ba*, v. *bdé-ba*. — *tugs-γtsigs-pa* to be cautious *Sch.*; v. however *γtsigs-pa*. — *tugs-brtsé-ba* **love, affection of the heart, compassion,** resp. for *snyiṅ-brtsé-ba*, frq., *tugs-brtse-bar dgóns-pa*, *γzigs-pa*, with *la*, to look upon compassionately, to remember in mercy. — *tugs-ráb Sch.* = *šes-ráb*. — *tugs-rús Mil.* = *snyiṅ-rús*. — *tugs-(kyi) sras Mil.*, *Tar.*, **spiritual son,** an appellation given to the most distinguished scholars of saints.

ཐུང་ང་ *tuṅ-ṅa* **three years old,** of animals *Sch.*

ཐུང་བ་ *túṅ-ba*, col. *túṅ-ṅu*, *Ld.* **túṅ-se**, **short,** relative to space, time, quantity of vowels etc.; *tuṅ-ṅu ̥gro-ba* to become shorter; but the word is not so much used as 'short' is in English; *yid túṅ-ba Dzl.*, *spro túṅ-ba Wdṅ.* **passionate, hot-tempered, hasty.**

ཐུད་ *túd* **cheese** made of buttermilk, or of *čúr-ṕe*, butter and milk *Ld.*, *Glr.*, *Pth.*; *̧o-túd* milk-cheese, made of curd, or of milk coagulated with runnet.

ཐུན་ *tun* I. a regular amount, a fixed quantity 1. of time, a certain length of time, as long as a man is able to work without resting, **a shift,** six, four, or three hours; *Schf.* translates *Tar.* 67, 17 even by one hour; **a night-watch,** *mel-tse tun ̥ḱor* the night-watch is over *Dzl.*; *tun bžii rnal-̥byor* the meditation of a whole day *Mil.*; **tun čád-če** *W.* (the cock) announces the watch (by crowing); *tun bzuṅ-ba Pth.* prob. to have the watch; *nam-gyi guṅ-tun-la* at or about midnight; *sród-kyi gúṅ-tun-la Mil.* prob. id. — 2. **a dose of medicine** *Med.* frq. — *tun-log?*

II. **in sorcery:** bodies or substances which are supposed to be possessed of magic virtues, such as sand, barley, certain seeds etc., *tun-dóṅ* a hole in which such substances are concealed; *tun-rá* a horn to carry them; *tun γsó-ba* to revive a charm *Mil. nt.*

III. one who collects, **a gatherer** (from ̥*tú-ba*), *šiṅ-tún* one who picks up or gathers sticks *Mil.*; *rtsa-tun* a gatherer of grass, *snye-tún* a gatherer of ears of corn *Cs.*; *tun-zór* reaping-hook, sickle *Sch.*

IV. *tun*, or more frq. *tun-móṅ(s)*, **usual,**

daily, what is done or is happening every day; **common, general**, *dṅos-grub tun-moṅs* earthly goods, as well as intellectual endowments, considered as common property, but not spiritual gifts; *tun-min, tun-moṅs ma yin-pa* **unusual, uncommon**, not for every body; **čig-la čig tun-móṅ čo** take good care to live together in harmony *W.*; *tun-móṅ-du* or *su* **in common, in company, jointly**; *tun-moṅ* by itself is also used as adv., = *tun-spyir*, **in general.**

ཐུབ་པ *túb-pa* (जय) I. vb., c. accus., sometimes c. dat., 1. **to get the better of, to be able to cope with, to be a match for** (an enemy), **to be able to stand or bear** (the cold etc.), **to be able to do one harm, to get at one**, *dug-gis ma tub-čiṅ* as the poison could not do him any harm *Dzl.*; **to be able to quench, extinguish, keep off** e.g. fire, hail *Glr.*; *γžán-gyis mi túb-pa* **invincible**, not to be overcome; *ṅan dgu túb-pa* to be able to subdue every thing that is bad *Lt.*; **to have under one's command** or **control, to keep under**, e.g. one's own body; **to be able to bear**, e.g. *mis túb-par dka* (water from a glacier) is not easily borne by man, i.e. does not agree with him *Med.*; *ras rkyaṅ tub-pa* to be able to bear a simple cotton dress *Mil.*; *lo brgya túb-pa* to live to (the age of) a hundred years, frq. — 2. with a supine or verbal root, **to be able**, col. the usual word, in B. gen. *nús-pa*; cf. *γtúb-pa*.

II. sbst. 1. मायक **a mighty one, one having power and authority**, *šā-kya-tub-pa* Buddha; a wise man, a sage, a saint in general, मुनि. — 2. symb. num. for 7.

ཐུམ(ས)་ *tum(s)*, also *túm-pa Cs.*, *túm-po Sch.*, 1. **cover, covering, wrapper**, of a book or a parcel; *rgyáb-pa Sch.* to put (a cover round a thing), to wrap up; **šig-pa* C., W.*, **sáṅ-pa* C.* to take off (a covering); *túm-čan* having a cover. — 2. **a parcel wrapped up** (in paper etc.); *ₒbru-taṅ-túm bčas* together with a small parcel of tea.

ཐུམ་པ *túm-pa* 1. v. *tum*. 2. v. *γnyid*.

ཐུམ་བུ, ཐོམ་བུ *túm-bu, tóm-bu* **a large spoon, a ladle**; *rag-túm* a brass ladle, *zaṅs-túm* a copper ladle.

ཐུར་ *tur* 1. *Cs.* **a declivity** (?), prob. only adverbially: **down**; *tur-lám* a downhill road; *túr-la, túr-du* down, downward, *ₒgró-ba* to go down, *núb-pa* to sink down; *mgo túr-du bstán-te* head down, head over heels *Stg.*; **ti-pi túr-la súb-če* W.* to uncock one's cap. — 2. v. *túr-mgo*, and *túr-ma*.

ཐུར་མགོ *túr-mgo* 1. **the tip of a spoon**, *túr-mgo tsam* as a measure *Mil.* — 2. also *tór-mgo* halter, **túr-go čúg-če* W.* to bridle, to bit (a horse); **túr-la tén-če* W.* to strive, to struggle against; to rear. — *tur-tág* the rein, *tur-mta* the end of the rein.

ཐུར་བུ, ཐུར་རུ *túr-bu, túr-ru* **foal, colt, filly.**

ཐུར་མ *túr-ma, W. *tur-maṅ**, 1. **spoon.** — 2. Chinese **chopsticks.** — 3. **a pole** *Dzl.* ༢༥༧, 4. — 4. a whole class of surgical instruments *S.g.*

ཐུལ་ *tul* 1. **egg** (acc. to Cunningham a Cashmiri word), *túl-ta-gir* pancake. — 2. v. *ₒdúl-ba*, also substantively: *tul de min* besides this **way of converting** (people) *Pth.*; *tul ₒóg-tu ₒjúg-pa Tar.* 25, 16 to keep a tight hand over a person, to discipline one; *žiṅ-gi tul ₒdébs-pa Ld.-Glr.* to clear land for tillage, ni f.

ཐུལ་པ་ *túl-pa, Cs.* also *túl-po*, dress made of the skins of animals, **a furred coat** or **cloak** *Mil.*; *lúg-tul* dress of sheep-skin, *rá-tul* dress of goat-skin, *túl-lu* the common sheep-skin dress; **túl-čan* W.* wide, not fitting close or tight.

ཐུལ་བ་ *túl-ba* 1. pf. to *ₒdúl-ba*, **to tame, curb, check, restrain**, *Mil.*: *ṅás ₒdré-rnams túl-nas* the goblins having been subdued by me; *las nyon-moṅs túl-ba dka* it is difficult to check a sinful deed *Mil.*; participle: tamed, civilized; converted. — 2. **to roll** or **wind up** *Lh.*

ཐུལ་ལེ་ *túl-le Ld.* **impressive**, nearly the same as *túr-re*.

ཐུས་པ *tús-pa* 1. **bad** = *tú-ba*, prov.; 2. v. *ₒtú-ba*.

ཐེ་ *te* 1. for *té-mo*; 2. num.: 100.

ཐེ་རྟོག་ *te-rtóg* **scruple, doubt, uncertainty, hesitation**, occasionally used for *te-tsóm*.

ཐེ་བ་ *té-ba*, *C.* also **ti-ba**, pf. *tes Sch.*, the col. syn. of *γtógs-pa*, seldom in *B.*, 1. **to belong, appertain to**, c. *la*. — 2. **to occupy one's self** with a thing, **to meddle with, to interfere**, c. *dan* (= *ₒdri-ba*); *té-mk'an* belonging together, c. *la*, belonging to a thing; **ma-té-a* W.* for *ma-té-bar*, = *ma-γtógs-par*; *te-rég* the connexion or relation of ownership, *dí-la yáb-kyi te-rég med* to this my father has no claims *Mil. nt.*

ཐེ་བོ་, ཐེ་བོང་ *té-bo*, *te-bón W.* **thumb**, v. *téb-mo*.

ཐེ་མོ་ *té-mo*, col. *té-tse*, diminutive *teu*, resp. *p'yag-té* **seal, signet, stamp**, **té-tse gyáb-če*, or *nán-če** to seal, to stamp; *sa-té Tar.* 79, 12(?); **té-tse lag-kór tán-wa** to engage, to bind one's self by a seal in some common concern.

ཐེ་ཚོམ་ *te-tsóm* **doubt, scruple, uncertainty, perplexity**, *te-tsóm skyes*, *byed* (*W* **čo**), *za*, *te-tsóm-du gyur* I am doubtful; *te-tsom za-ba-rnams* scrupulous, irresolute persons *Pth.*; **te-tsom man-po rag* W.* I am in great perplexity, I am quite at a loss; *te-tsom žig ₒdri-ba* to utter a doubt *Dzl.*

ཐེ་རང་ *te-ran* v. *teu-ran*.

ཐེ་རེ་ *te-ré* col. **straight, upright, firm; smooth,** without folds or wrinkles; *te-ré tin C.* draw (the carpet) smooth.

ཐེ་རེལ་ *te-rél W.* **incomplete, defective, unfinished**, *te-rél-la lus son* (the loaf) is not whole, there has already been cut from it.

ཐེ་ལི་ *te-li* v. *ta-li*.

ཐེག་པ་ *tég-pa* I. sbst. **यान**, 1. **vehicle, carriage, riding-beast**, *rtai tég-pa-la žon* he mounted on horseback *Dzl.*; *tég-pa lna-brgyá bsams* he procured five hundred conveyances (horses, elephants, carriages) *Dzl.* 2. for attaining to salvation, *tég-pa γsum* **three conveyances** are generally mentioned, but in most cases only two are specified, viz. *tég-(pa) dman(-pa)*, **हीनयान**, and *teg(-pa) čen-po*, **महायान**, gen. called 'the little and the great conveyance or vehicle', by means of which the distant shore of salvation may be reached. Yet mention is also made of a *snágs-kyi tég-pa*, **मन्त्रयान** *mantrayāna*, e.g. *Tar.* 180, 13. For more particulars about these vehicles, and other more or less confused and contradictory notions, the works of *Köppen* and esp. *Wasiljew* may be consulted.

II. vb. 1. **to lift, raise, hold up, support** *Mil.*, *Glr.*; hence *k'ri-tégs* leg of a table *Sch.*; *teg-k'úg C.* knapsack, travelling-bag. — 2. **to raise, set up** fig. *bśad-gád* to raise a loud laugh *Mil.* — 3. most. frq. **to be able to carry**, *ji tég-pa* as much as you are able to carry *Dzl.*; *mis teg-tsád γčig* as much as one man is able to carry *Tar.*; esp. with a negative: *ma teg* he was not able to hold him up *Dzl.*; *mi-teg k'ur* to carry what is too heavy to be carried (by ordinary muscular strength), to strain one's self by lifting, *Med.*; to endure, tolerate, stand, *k'ón-rnams-kyi nan ma teg-par* not being able to stand their urgent demands *Mil.*; **to bear, to undergo without detriment,** *skyid teg sdug teg* to be able to bear good fortune and ill fortune. Cf. *ₒtégs-pa*, *ₒdégs-pa*. —

ཐེང་ *ten* 1 *ten-ró Mil.*, **ša-tén* Ld.*, the dead body of an animal killed by beasts of prey. — 2. **tén-la* C.* **down, downward**, e.g. **kyúr-wa, yúg-pa, bór-wa**, to fling down.

ཐེང་པོ་ *tén-po Pth.*, *tén-bu Sch.*, **tén-k'an* W.*, **lame, hobbling, limping.**

ཐེངས་ *tens* **time, times**, *tens lna* five times *Pth.*; *dbugs-tens čig-la* in one breathing, at a stretch; without intermission *Pth.*

ཐེན་ *ten* 1. **a little while, a moment.** — 2. v. *ₒten-pa*.

ཐེན་པ་ *tén-pa* **tax, duty, impost** *Sch.*

ཐེབ *teb* 1. for *tem*, **full** *Glr.* — 2. for *tabs* *Glr.*, *C.* — 3. *téb-mo*, *teb-čén* the thumb, *teb-čún* the little finger; v. *mte-boṅ.*

ཐེབས *tebs* **series, order, succession** *Sch.*, *tebs-re byed-pa* to do successively; *tébs-pa* v. *ₒtebs-pa.*

ཐེམ་པ *tém-pa* I. 1. **threshold**, *rgál-ba* to cross it *Glr.*; *sgo-tém* door-sill, threshold; *yá-tém* head-piece of a door-frame, lintel, *ma-tém* sill, threshold *Glr.* — 2. **staircaise, stairs, flight of steps,** *tem-skás* id.; **tem-sǒ** *W.* **step, stair;** *tem-rim* *Cs.* 1. the several steps of a staircase. 2. **rank, dignity.** — *rdo-tém* stone staircase; *ḱor-tém* winding stairs *Cs.* — II. 1. **to be full, complete,** *zla-dus tem-pa daṅ* when the time of the months was fulfilled *Glr.* frq.; *žag γčig ma tém-pa-la* one day being still wanting *Glr.*; *brgya tém-pa* v. *tam-pa Glr.* — 2. *W.*: **to be sufficient, enough.** — 3. **to receive** (?) *Sch.*

III. *Sch.* = *tén-pa*, **tax, impost, tribute.**

ཐེམ་བུ *tém-bu*, *tem-tsaṅs* **stopping, closing, shutting up; a stoppage** *Sch.*

ཐེམས་ཡིག *tems-yig Sch.* **memorial.**

ཐེའུ་རང *teu-rán Glr.*, *te-brán Lt.*, *te-rán Ma.*, a sort of **demons.**

ཐེར *ter* 1. **bald, bare,** *spyi-tér Thgy.* a bald head; a bald-headed person; *ter-tér C.* flat. — 2. = *te-ré* (?) *ṗyi ter naṅ gog* strong and hale outside, decayed within *Mil.*; *ter-zúg-pa* = *rtág-pa Thgr.*

ཐེར་འབུམ *ter-ₒbúm Sch.* 1000000000; *ter-ₒbum-čén-po* 10000000000.

ཐེར་མ *tér-ma* a kind of thin woollen cloth, a flannel-like fabric, *le-ter* made of shawl-wool, *bal-ter* of common wool.

ཐེལ *tel* for *te-li*, *rag-tél C.* a plate made of latten brass.

ཐེལ་བ *tél-ba W.* frq. = *sléb-pa* **to arrive,** cf. *tál-ba* II., 4.

ཐེལ་སེ *tél-se Sch.* and *Wts.* **a seal, stamp,** = *te-tse.*

ཐེས་པ *tés-pa Sch.* pf. to *té-ba*; = *tes-bsún Lt.*?

ཐོ *to* 1. num. for 130. — 2. **register, list, catalogue, index;** *to ₒbri-ba* to register, to make out a list or catalogue *Schr.*; *sléb-to*, *ₒbyúṅ-to* account of receipts, *sóṅ-to*, *búd-to*, *skyág-to* account of expenditures; *btáṅ-to* account of money or goods lent out; *nyó-to* account of goods bought, bill; *lo-to* **calendar, almanac;** *dei lág-tu ṗrin-bor-to* list of orders or directions given to him (lit. laid down in his hands); *dei rgyúd-la tób-to* a list of things which his relations shall receive.

ཐོ་གར *to-gár Pth.*; acc. to *Sch.* **the Turkomans;** *Tar.* 18, *Schf.*: **Tukhara,** name of a people in the northwest of India; prob. the **Togarmah** of the Bible.

ཐོ་ཅོ *to-čo Mil.*, **a foolish joke,** unbefitting a sensible man.

ཐོ་ཕྱི *to-ṗyi Schr.* **love** (?), in *Pth.* it seems to signify the **sky.**

ཐོ་བ, མཐོ་བ *tó-ba*, *mtó-ba*, **a large hammer,** *tó-bas rdúṅ-ba* to hammer, to forge; *rdó-to* a stone hammer, *šiṅ-to* a wooden hammer, mallet; **to-čúṅ** 1. an ordinary hammer. — 2. **the cock of a gun.** — 3. **a soldering-stick.** *Lh.*

ཐོ་འཚམ་པ *to-ₒtsám-pa* **to scorn, scoff, jeer, sneer at, vex, insult, mock,** c. *la*, by words *Dzl.*, also by actions *Dzl.*; *snan-čud to-ₒtsám-pa bzód-par γsol* pardon our having sneered at you before! *Mil.*; also *mto-mtsám-pa*, *-btsám-pa*, *-brtsám-pa.*

ཐོ་ཡོར *to-yór* **stone pyramid, heap of stones** (cairn).

ཐོ་རངས *to-ráṅs* 1. **dawn, break of day, early morning,** *to-ráṅs(-kyi) dús-su* early in the morning; 2. **the following, the next morning,** c. genit.; both also adverbially: *de daṅ mǰal-bai to-ráṅs* on the morning after having met him.

ཐོ་རེ *tó-re W.* **to-morrow** (*B.*, *C. saṅ*).

ཐོ་རེ་བ *tó-re-ba*, *tor-tsál Cs.*: **a few;** *Mil.*, *tog-re-tsal* **a little while.**

ཐོ་ལུམ *to-lúm* v. *tu-lúm.*

ཐོ་ལེ *to-lé* 1. *to-lé ₒdébs-pa* **to spit,** c. *la*, at or on *Pth.* (cf. *tu*). — 2. **button** *C.* — 3. *to-lé dkár-po C.* **chalk.** — 4. *to-le-rgyal Mil.*?

ཐོ་ལོག་ *to-lóg C.* **mule, hinny.**

ཐོག་ *tog* I. **what is uppermost** 1. **roof,** *tog ₒbúbs-pa* to cover with a roof, to roof (a house) frq.; *tog ₒgél-ba* id.; also fig. **to complete, to crown a thing** *Mil.*; **tóg-sa nán-če* W.* **to roof, to finish a roof** by beating and stamping down the earth or sods, of which the covering consists; *tog-rdzís γtóṅ-ba Mil.* id.; also fig. **to impress,** c. genit., *Mil.* — **tog-kár* W.*, the opening for the smoke in a roof. — *tog-čan* having a roof, **tóg-yog* W.* under cover. — 2. **ceiling**; *yá-tog* ceiling, *má-tog* floor of a room. — 3. **story,** *dgu-tóg* having nine stories or floors, frq. — 4. in a general sense: *tog ₒdrén-pa Mil.* **to be at the head, to lead, direct, govern**; *tog-k̔ar, W. *k̔a-tóg-la**, **on, upon,** *k̔yág-tog-k̔ar* on the ice *Glr.*; *tóg-tu*, and *tog-tóg* adv. **up, up to; above**; *ydáṅ-tog-tu* in the uppermost place, quite at the top, *Glr.*; postp. c. genit. (or accus.) 1. **on, upon,** e.g. to lay on, to place upon *Pth.*; *sems tóg-tu lji-bar byúṅ-nas* lying heavy, weighing heavily, upon one's mind *Glr.*; *ṅai tóg-tu byuṅ* my heart was smitten (by that); that has touched, has grieved my heart *Mil.*; *tog-tu k̔el-ba Mil.*, vb. act. to it. 2. **above** *Glr.* 3. **towards,** in the direction of, e.g. running towards, *mai tog-tu Dzl.*; *yá-tog, má-tog* ad. **above, below,** or **up to, up stairs,** and **down, down stairs** *Mil.* 4. **to,** e.g. to send to *Dzl.* 5. *dmag-tog* **at the head of** the army, or only **with** the army. 6. **during, as long as, throughout; whilst** (*tog* gen. without *-tu*), *dgun-tog* throughout the whole winter; **dir á-k̔u sem tser tog** whilst her husband is here in great anxiety *Ld.*; *bgros-tog* during the walk. Cf. also *ṅa-og, p̔i-tog* as sbst.: **morning, evening, forenoon, afternoon** *W.* 7. **directly after,** *bžos-tog ₒó-ma* fresh milk, *S.g.* (s.l.c.). — *tog-nas* 1. **above, more than,** **lo ṅab-ču tog-ne ma lus* Ld.* they remained, i.e. lived not more than fifty years. 2. **on the part of,** *Thgy.*, analogous to *p̔yógs-nas.*

II. **thunderbolt, lightning;** *tog daṅ sér-ba* lightning and hail, *tog-sér-gyi γnód-pa* damage done by the elements; *tog ₒbáb-pa* lightning descending, *rgyab-pa* striking, *tog-bábs-su ₒbyón-pa* to arrive, to approach quick or suddenly like lightning *Tar.*, resp.; *tóg-gis γsód-pa S.g.*, *tog báb-ste ₒči-ba Do.* to be killed by lightning.

III. 1. **fruit, produce,** *dkár-tog* v. *dkár-po*; *žiṅ-tog* produce of the fields *Dzl.*; *lo-tóg* a year's produce; *šiṅ-tóg* produce of a tree or other plant, fruit; *γsar-tóg* this year's crop *S.g.*; *tog-p̔úd* first-fruits, **as an** offering; *tog-šás* id. (?). — 2. *W.* **fortune, wealth, property,** **ṇúl-li tog** property in money, cash in hand; *(s)pi-tog* common property, property belonging to a community.

IV. in *ma-tog(-tse)* for *ma tag*, col. and *Thgy.*, s.l.c., v. *tag*. Cf. also *tog-tág, tóg-ma, tógs-pa.*

ཐོག་ཐག་ *tog-tág*, prob. augmentative of *tog*, v. *tóg-tu* 6, also *tag-tóg*, **during, as long as, throughout; quite,** *mtsan tog-tág-tu* all night long; *nyi-ma-γčig-gi bár-du tog-tág* during a whole day; *lam tog-tág gáṅ-ṅo* the roads were quite full (of snow) *Dzl.*

ཐོག་མ་ *tóg-ma* **what is uppermost,** 1. **the upper end, the uppermost place,** *grál-gyi tóg-ma-la ₒdúg-go* they sat down in the first, or uppermost, place *Dzl.*; gen. 2. **origin, beginning;** *tóg-mai saṅs-rgyás kun-tu-bzáṅ-po* Adibuddha Samantabhadra, so a deity is called, by which a prayer has been appointed that is supposed to be particularly efficacious; *tóg-ma čo-rigs mtó-ba* of noble birth, as regards his origin *Dzl.*; *tóg-ma btsás-pai tsé-na, tóg-ma btsás-nas, tóg-ma skyés-nas* already at his birth, from his very birth *Dzl.*; *tog-ma méd-pa-nas, dus tog-méd-nas* time out of mind, from eternity; *tóg-ma-nas* from the very beginning; of itself; as a matter of course *Dzl.*; *bsúbs-pai tog-tág-la* as soon as they began to fill up *Glr.*; *tog-mta-bar-du* at first, later, in conclusion (lit. in the beginning, end, and middle) *Lt.*; most frq. *tóg-mar* 1. **at first, first,** the Lat. primum, primo, and primus. — 2. postp. c. genit. **before**, with respect to time *Mil.* — *ťog-draṅs-pa Pth., Glr., Sch.*: 'at first, begun'; our Lama explained it by **'to lead, to guide'**, v. *ťog* I, 4.

ཐོག་ཚད་ *ťog-tsád W.* **story** (of a house); *ťóg-so Mil. nt.* id.

ཐོགས་ *ťogs* v. *˳dógs-pa*, and *˳ťógs-pa*.

ཐོགས་པ་ *ťógs-pa*, c. *la*, **to strike, stumble, run against** (like *ťúg-pa* v. 3); **to be hindered, impeded, delayed**, frq.; *mi ǩyi gáṅ-laaṅ ťógs-pa méd-du* without being hindered by men, dogs, or anything else *Mil.*; *ťogs-pa-méd-pa, ťogs-méd, ťogs-brdúgs-*(or(b)*rtug-*)*méd-pa*, असङ्ग **not hindered, unimpeded, unchecked; all-searching, all-penetrating.**

ཐོང་ *ťoṅ, ťoṅ-šól* **a plough.**

ཐོང་ཁ་ *ťóṅ-ǩa Mil., ťoṅ-ga Mṅg.?*

ཐོང་པ་ *ťóṅ-pa* 1. *Cs.* **a ploughman.** — 2. *Cs.*: '**a ram** that is castrated, **wether**; *ra-ťoṅ* a castrated he-goat'; according to my authorities, however, *ťóṅ-pa*, and *ra-ťóṅ* signify a ram and he-goat **one year old**, *ťoṅ-tsér* and *ra-tsér* being the feminine forms (?) — 3. *ťóṅ-pai lo Mil.* the years between childhood and manhood, **juvenile years**, *Sch.* *ťóṅ-po*, cf. *ǩyóg-ťoṅ*.

ཐོང་སྤུ་ *ťóṅ-spu* **mane of the camel** *Sch.*

ཐོངས་པ་ *ťóṅs-pa Mil.?*

ཐོད་ *ťod* 1. *Cs.* **a head-ornament, crown**; gen. the usual covering for the head in the East, **turban**, *la-ťód Glr.* id.; *dbu-ťód* resp.; *sá-yig ťód-du bčiṅs-pai ka* the letter k having for a crown the letter s: སྐ *Zam.* — 2. = *ťog* I.: *go-ťö* *C.* **over** or **above** the door; *ǩa-ťód-la, ǩa-ťóg-la, ǩa-ťód-la*, **up, upon** *Ld.* — 3. **threshold**, *yá-ťod, má-ťod* = *yá-re, má-re.* — 4. v. *ťód-pa.* — 5. *ťod-rgál čé-ba* (*ťoṅ?*) *Mil.*, acc. to the context: **angry, wrathful.** — 6. *ťod-ťód* v. *su.*

ཐོད་པ་ *ťód-pa* 1. **skull, cranium**; skull of a dead person, **death's head**; *ťod-skám* a dry skull, *ťod-rlón* a fresh skull *Thgr.*; *ťod-ǩrág* a skull filled with blood *Thgr.*; *ťod-p̔ór* a drinking-cup made of a skull. — 2. col. **forehead, brow**; *ťod-rtsá* vena frontalis *Lt.*; *ťod-čiṅs, ťod-ǩebs, ťod-brgyán*, turban.

ཐོད་ལེ་ཀོར་ *ťod-le-kór Lex.* **alabaster**; *Tar.* 67, 18 *Schf.* — खटिका, chalk.

ཐོན་ *ťon* v. *˳ťón-pa* and *˳dón-pa*; *ťón-pa C.* also: **good, fair, beautiful**; *smrá-bar ťón-pa* eloquent.

ཐོན་མི་ *ťón-mi*, or *ťú-mi sam-bhó-ṭa* n. of the minister that was sent to India by king Sroṅbtsansgampo, in order to procure an alphabet for writing.

ཐོབ་ *ťob* 1. v. *ťób-pa.* — 2. v. *˳debs-pa.*

ཐོབ་ཆུ་ *ťob-ču Schr.*, *ťob-če, ťob-či, ťeb-ču* *C.*, **button** (v. *ťob-či*).

ཐོབ་པ་ *ťob-pa* I. vb. (synon. to *rnyed-pa*, and exclusively in use in *W.*) 1. **to find**, frq. — 2. **to get, obtain**, *ṅas ťob B.*, *ṅá-la ťob* col., I find, I get; *ťob-par ˳gyúr-ba* id.; **to partake of, to come to**, *dád-pa* faith (to come to the faith) *Mil.*; **to obtain, to get possession of, to subject to one's power** *Dzl.*; *da-drág ťob-mťár Gram.*: after (words) that have got a *da-drág*; *saṅs-rgyás, rgyál-po, bdág-po, ťób-pa* (lit. to get the Buddha etc.) **to become** a Buddha, a king, a lord; *ťag-dzód ťob-če* *W.* to become frq. (cf. *rgyál-po*). —

II. sbst. that which has been got or obtained: **the sum, result**, of a calculation etc. *Wdṅ.*

III. *ťób-če(s)* *W.* adj. that which is **to be got** or **received**, e.g. *búlon ťób-čes-si bún-yig* a list of demands to be called in, of money owing.

Comp. *ťob-rgyál byéd-pa* **to rob, pillage, plunder** (?) *Sch.*; *ťob-čá* the share which one gets *C.* — *ťob-ťáṅ Cs.* 'income, revenue'; more accurately: that which falls to one's share, as a reward or pay, for work, services etc., e.g. bits of cloth or silk, which a tailor may keep for himself. — *ťob-nór* 1. **share, quota.** 2. **quotient.** — *ťob-bló C.* **desire**, *bkúr-sti ťób-pa* **ambition** *Schr.* — *ťob-tsir* (lit. the turn of getting, receiving) **claim, right; duty, due,** *tob-tsir ná-la yod* I have a claim, a right to it *W.*; **tob-tsir tán-ce* W.* to give each his share in his turn (prop. acc. to the due turn). — *tob-rim Glr.* id. — *tob-yig* **repertory, index.** — *tob-sról* prob. = *tob-tsir*, **right of succession** *C.* — *tob-šá C.* **contest, quarrel, strife; scramble,** e. g. for money thrown among the people.

ཐོམ་བུ་ *tóm-bu* = *túm-bu.*

ཐོམས་པ་ *tóms-pa* v. *ₒtóms-pa.*

ཐོར་ཁོད་ *tor-kód*, or *tor-gód*, **a Mongol tribe.**

ཐོར་མགོ་ *tor-mgó* v. *tur-mgó.*

ཐོར་ཅོག, ཐོར་ཙུགས་ *tor-cóg, tor-tsúgs*, (also *do-kér*) **a plaited tuft of hair, toupet,** *Lex.*: *có-tai tor-cóg*; *tor-cóg dar sna lṅa bcins Pth.* he bound his tuft of hair with a silk string of five colours; prob. = *γtsug-tór* q.v ; *tór-to(r) Lex.* id.

ཐོར་པ་ *tór-pa*, also *ₒtór-pa Med.*, **the small-pox** *Sch.*; in *Sik. tór-ba* signifies **pimple, pustule,** but the usual word for this is *srin-tór*, and in *W.* **pul-tór** has a similar meaning, whereas *tór-bu Med.* denotes a whole class of diseases, comprising dyspepsy and cutaneous disorders. — *dmar-tór* **measles** *Sch.*

ཐོར་བ་ *tór-ba* 1. v. *ₒtór-ba.* — 2. v. *tór-pa.*

ཐོར་བུ་ *tór-bu* **single, separate;** *Tar.* 120, 19: *prá-mo tór-bu-pa* separate little works, books *Schf.*

ཐོར་མོ་ *tór-mo* the growing fat of cows, goats etc. in consequence of sterility *Sch.*

ཐོལ་བ་ *tól-ba* 1. v. *ₒtól-ba*, pf. to *rtól-ba*, what has come forth, what has been raised, elevated (?) *Sch.* cf. *tol-tól Mng.*; *tol-byún* to arise, to begin, suddenly *Sch.*

ཐོས་པ་ *tos-pa* 1. vb. **to hear** *B., C.* (*W.* **tsór-ce**), *rgyál-po žig-gi γtam tós-sam*, or only *rgyál-po žig tós-sam Dzl.* have you heard of a king? *ₒbrós-so zér-bai γtam rgyál-poi snyán-du tós-so* it came to the king's hearing that he had escaped. *Glr.* — 2. adj. *mán-du tós-pa* **far-famed, renowned,** frq.; *ma tós-pa* **unheard of;** *tos-gról* the title of a book which is read to the soul of a deceased person (**to-dhól* C.*, **to-dól* W.*), and the full title of which is: *tós-pa tsám-gyis gról-ba tób-pai čos* a doctrine by the hearing of which a man is instantly saved *Thgr.*; *tos-čún Mil.* **hearing little.**

ཐྲིག་ཐྲིག་ *trig-trig* **the creaking of shoes.**

ཐྭག་ *twag Ld.* the sharp sound, **the cracking,** which is heard, when a branch of a tree is breaking off; cf. *tsa-rág* and *ldim.*

མཐང་ *mtan Cs.*: **the lower part of the body,** *mtan-gós* a vestment for it, a sort of petticoat (acc. to others: toga) worn by Lamas.

མཐའ་ *mta* (cf. *tá-ma*) 1. **end, ending,** 1. relative to space: **edge, margin, brink, brim,** of a well *Glr.*, skirt of a forest, gen. *mtá-ma*; **limit, bound, border, confines, frontiers,** *mta skór-ba* to go round the confines (of a place); *mtá-las ₒdás-pa* exceeding all bounds, very great, e.g. *sdug-bsṅál Thgr.*; used even thus: *rgyál-po bžúgs-pai mtá-ru bskor* to walk round him that sits on a throne *Glr.*, po.; adverbially: *dé-mta* round this (mountain) *Mil.*; *mta dbus kún-tu* in the whole country (in the frontier districts and in the central parts); *mtai rgyal-kams* neighbouring or border-country; *mta* id., e.g. *mta bži* the four border-countries, i.e. all the surrounding territory, frq.; *mtai nor* the treasures of the border-country *Glr.*; *mtai dmag* border-war.; in the Tibetan part of the Himalaya mountains *mta* denotes in a special sense **Hindoostan;** — in grammar: **termination,** *na ma ra la žés-rnams mtá-can* words ending in n, m, r, l; *ga-mtá* a final g. 2. relative to time: *bskál-pai mta Dzl.* the **termination** of a Kalpa; *dus-mtái me* the conflagration at the end of the world, the ecpyrosis; in a more general sense: *mta ńán-pas* as this will end badly; *mta γcig-tu Wdṅ.* and *Tar.* 4, 7 *Sch.*: **on the one hand, in part, in a certain degree, in some respect;** *Schf.*: 'schlechthin' (?) —

mta-γčód-pa final or definitive sentence or judgment *Sch.; dei mta γčod-pai ṗyir* in order to settle it definitely, viz. by counter-proof, *Gram.*; *yáṅ-dag-mta* the true end, i.e. objective truth *Was.* (297); **the rest, remainder,** *re-dógs-kyi mta spaṅ* having given up also the last remnant of fear and hope *Glr.*, cf. *mtá-dag; mtá-ru, mtar* 1. **towards the end,** towards the boundary or the neighbouring country; **at the end** etc.; *mtar túg-pa* to reach, to attain to the end, frq.; *tsei mtar túg-pai graṅs* the number of those that reach the (natural) end of life *Dzl.; mtar-tug-pa-méd-pa* inexhaustible *Dzl.*; *mtár-ṗyin-pa* (rarely *mtar-ₒkyil-ba*) id.; also absolutely as sbst. *mtár-ṗyin-pa* **a perfect, a holy person, a saint;** *mtár-ton-pa* id. (?) *Mil.; mtár-byed-pa* to give a work its finish *C.*, (*Sch.*: 'to destroy, demolish'?) 2. adv. **lastly, finally, in conclusion** *Dzl.*, *Thgy.*; perh. also **to the very last, wholly, altogether.** 3. postp. with genit. **after, behind,** *rgyal-rábs sum-brgyái mtar* after 300 royal generations *Glr.*; *sá-mtar šiṅ, šiṅ* is to be written after a final s, *Gram.* — 2. **aim, purpose** *Cs.* — 3. **system,** opinion *Tar.* 107, 4 *Schf.*, perh. for *grub-mta.*

Comp. and deriv. *mtá-klas-pa Cs.* = *mtá-med-pa*, yet v. *mtas.* — *mta-skór* **circumference, perimeter,** v. *dpag-tsád.* — *mta-ₒkób* v. *ₒkob.* — *mta-grú Glr.* 42? — *mta-rgyás* **very wide** *Schr.* — *mta-lčags* frame, of a mirror etc. *Schr.* — *mta-čag Med.?* — *mta-rtén* final consonant *Gram.; mta-rten-med-pa* ending with a vowel *Gram.* — *mta-tig* boundary line *Sch.* — *mta-tog-tág* **unceasing** (?) *Sch.* — *mtá-dag* **several, sundry; all,** frq.; *maṅ-tsig mtá-dag* the plural sign *mta-dag Gram.* — *mta-draṅs Gram.?* — *mtá ma* **the end,** *grál-gyi mtá-mai bú-mo* the girl at the end of the row (opp. to the middle or the other end, not necessarily to the beginning, like *mγúg-ma*); **border, hem, seam,** of dresses *Dzl.; deṅ mtoṅ-ba mta-ma* to-day we see (him) for the last time *Glr.* (*tá-ma* would be more correct, like *Dzl.* ༢༧, 16). — *mta-mal-pa* sometimes for *ta-mal-pa.* — *mtá-mi* **borderer; neighbouring people.** — *mtá-med-pa, mtá-yas-pa* **infinite, endless.** — *mta-γséb Wdṅ.?*

མཐར་ *mtar* 1. v. *mta.* 2. for *tar.*

མཐར་སྐྱོལ་ *mtar-skyól* the bringing to an end, **carrying through, persistence, perseverance** *Mil.*

མཐར་གྱིས་ *mtár-gyis* **by turns, successively,** *Dzl.*; **by degrees, gradually.**

མཐས་ཀླས་ *mtas-klas*, *Zam.* = པར྄ཡནྟ, **border, limit?** cf. *mta* compounds.

མཐིང་ *mtiṅ* acc. to *Cs.*: 'indigo', and '*mtiṅ-šiṅ* indigo-plant'; acc. to a Lama from Lhasa however: 1. **mountain-blue** (which is found, together with malachite, in the hills near Lhasa). — 2. from the resemblance: **indigo-colour** (whereas indigo as a substance is *rams*), and esp. a light **sky-blue, azure;** cf. *mton-mtiṅ.*

མཐིང་རིལ་ *mtiṅ-ril*, *Lex.* a certain bird; *Sch.*: a sort of wild duck; acc. to *Pth.* a smaller bird.

མཐིའུ་ *mtiu* v. *mteu.*

མཐིལ་ *mtil* 1. **bottom,** of a vessel, of the sea; **floor,** of a room *Glr.*; **foundation,** of a house. — 2. the lower side of a thing; **inner or lower part of a thing,** *lág-mtil* (resp. *ṗyág-mtil*) **the palm of the hand;** *lag-mtil-na* in the closed hand; *lag-mtil gaṅ* a closed handful; *rkaṅ-mtil* (resp. *žabs-mtil*) the sole of the foot; *lham-mtil* the sole of a shoe; *mtil bži* the palms of the hands, and the soles of the feet. — 3. **the background, the far end,** of a cave, a tunnel etc. — 4. *C.*: **the centre, the principal or chief part,** of a town; **the principal place, chief city, capital,** of a country.

མཐུ *mtu* 1. **power, force, strength,** of the body, of the mind, of Buddha, of a prayer, of witchcraft etc.; **ability, power** or **authority** to do a thing; *mtu daṅ ldán-pa* **strong, powerful, efficacious, able** etc., *mtu-méd* **powerless, feeble, unable;** **mi za tu mè** *C.* I must eat it; *bsgrub-mi-nus-mtu-méd-la soṅ* we must be able to fulfil it *Mil.*; *mtu-*

žig-gis by an extraordinary manifestation of power or strength *Dzl.*; *klui mťu yin* that is an effect of the Lus, is produced, comes from the Lus *Stg.*; *mťus* **by virtue of**, frq.; *mťu-stóbs = mťu.* — 2. **magic, witchcraft,** *mťu ɣtóṅ-ba Mil.*, *mťu ˳débs-pa*, **táb-ċe* W.*, to practise witchcraft, to injure a person by magic spells, to bewitch *Mil.* and col. frq.; *mťu ser brtad ɣsúm-po rdzógs-par bslabs* conjuring, raising tempests, exorcising ghosts, all these things I have learned thoroughly *Mil.*; *mťu-bo-čé* **high-potent, high and mighty** *Tar.*

མཐུག་ *mťug* v. *˳ťug*.

མཐུད་པ་ *mťud-pa* v. *˳ťud-pa*.

མཐུན་པ་ *mťún-pa*, also *˳ťún-pa*, **to agree, to harmonize; agreement, harmony; agreeing** etc., 1. in a general sense, c. c. *daṅ*, .. *yin-par don mťún-no* they agree in the opinion of her being ... *Glr.*; *mťún-par byéd-pa* to make agree, to bring to an agreement, to make consistent, *mťún-par ˳gyúr-ba* to be made agreeing or consistent *Glr.*; *dgóṅs-pa ɣċig-tu mťún-pa* unanimous; *lhai lugs daṅ mťun* god-like (in deeds) *Glr.*; *rigs mťún-pa* of equal birth; *lo mťún-pa* of the same age, contemporary; *blo mťún-te* being of the same mind, similarly disposed, *čos byá-bar* with respect to religion *Glr.*; *ḱa mťún-par* with one mouth, *gros mťún-par* with one accord, unanimously, as one man; *grabs mťún-pa* to live in harmony; — **to be adequate, corresponding to,** e.g. *yid (daṅ) mťún-par*, resp. *ťúgs daṅ mťún-par*, to one's wish, as one could desire = *yid bžin-du*; *nad daṅ mťún-par* corresponding to the disease, fit or proper for the disease. — 2. in a special sense 1. viz. *yid daṅ*, **to be wished for, desirable,** particularly in *mťun-rkyén*, v. *rkyén*; also: **to wish, to like, to delight in,** *ḱyed rnams-kyis mťún-pai rdzas* things wished for by you, desirable to you *Mil.*; 2. with or without *ɣċig-la ɣċig*: *mťún-nas* whenever they (the two nations) lived in peace with each other (opp. to *˳ḱón-nas*) *Glr.*; *mťún-pai ɣtam byéd-pa* to converse amicably *Glr.*, to enter into negotiations of peace *Glr.*; *mťún-par byéd-pa* 1. v. above, 2. **to caress, to fondle, to dandle** *Glr.*; *šin-tu mťún-par yod* they are on the best terms with each other, are making love to each other *Glr.*; *mťún-po bsdad ˳dug* col. id.; *mťún-po byéd-pa* to be kind, affable, condescending *Mil.* (opp. to being proud, cold, reserved); *rgya bod ɣnyis mťun ˳oṅ* there will be a good understanding between China and Tibet *Glr.*; *mi mťún-pai ṗyogs ťams-ċád-las rgyál-ba* to gain the victory over all the hostile parties; *mťún-˳gyur-gyi yi-ge C.* **letter of recommendation**; *mťún-ċan W.* **gentle, peaceful.**

མཐུར་ *mťur*, also *mťúr-mgo*, v. *ťúr-mgo*, **halter,** *rta-mťur Lex.* id.; *mťur-ťág* **rein, reins** *Sch.*; *mťur-mťá* the end of the reins, e.g. to place them into the hands of another.

མཐུས་ *mťus* v. *mťu* 1.

མཐེ་བོ་ *mťé-bo*, col. *mťé-bóṅ*, *mťe-čén*, *mťéb-mo* (v. also *ťe bo*), **thumb,** *rkáṅ-pai mťé-bo* **the big toe**; *mťeb-čúṅ* the little finger, the little toe *Glr.*

མཐེའུ་ *mťeu* 1. **a little hammer**; 2. *mťeu-čúṅ* **the little toe.**

མཐོ་ *mťo* 1. **a span,** from the end of the thumb to the end of the middle finger when extended; *mťo ˳jál-ba* or *ɣžál-ba*, *W. *táb-ċe**, to span, to measure by the hand with the fingers extended; *mťo gáṅ*, *mťo ré tsam* a span (in length), *mťo do* two spans. — 2. v. *mťó-ba.*

མཐོ་གོང་ *mťo-góṅ* a little triangular receptacle into which the likeness of an enemy is placed, to whom one wishes to do harm by witchcraft *W.*

མཐོ་རྒྱབ་ *mťo-rgyáb* **earnest-money** *W.*

མཐོ་བ་ *mťó-ba* 1. **to be high; highness, height; high, lofty, elevated,** *B.* (cf. *mťón-po*), frq. fig; *rigs če-žiṅ mťó-ba-ste* being of high and noble birth *Dzl.*; *dé-las mťó-ba* more elevated than that, surpassing, surmounting that; c. accus. or instrum., high as to (stature, rank etc.) *mtó-na* when I am high, when I rise; *mtó-ba γnón-pa* to lower what is high, to bring down, to humble, frq.; *ṅas mto-mtó byás-pas dma-dmá byuṅ* the more I was aspiring, the more I was brought low *Pth.*; *sbyin-pa mtó-ba Stg.* was explained: gifts or alms bestowed from a sincere heart. — 2. **hammer,** v. *to-ba*; *mto-po-tog* a stone used as a hammer *Cs.*

Comp.: *mto-kyad* **height, highness** *Dzl* — *mto-dógs Pth.* (together with *γyo-sgyú*, and *prag-dóg*) perh. mistrust, suspicion; **tón-dod-čan* W.* **ambitious,** aspiring, aiming at things too high. — *mto-spyód W.* a haughty manner. — *mto-dmán* 1. *Cs.* high and low, uneven; also *Schr.* 2. **height,** *mto-dmán mnyám-pa* of equal height *Glr.* — *mto-ₒtsám(s)-pa* v. *to-ₒtsám-pa.* — *mto-ris* **heaven,** abode of the gods, **paradise,** Elysium.

མཐོང་ག་ *mtóṅ-ga Sch.*, *mtoṅs-ka Pth.*, **chest, breast,** *mtóṅ-ga-nas ₒdzin-pa* to seize by the breast *Pth.*

མཐོང་བ་ *mtóṅ-ba* **to see,** 1. vb. n. to have the power of vision, often with *mig(-gis)*; *mtóṅ-bar ₒgyúr-ba* to obtain the faculty of seeing, to recover one's sight; *mtóṅ-bar byéd-pa* to make (the blind) see *Dzl.*; *mig-gis nye mtoṅ riṅ mi mtoṅ* he sees only when the object is near, not when it is far, he is short-sighted *Med.*; *nye-mtóṅ* short-sighted *Sch.* — 2. vb. a. 1. **to perceive,** by the eye, **to see, to behold,** *bód-kyi ri mtóṅ-bai ri* an eminence from whence one can see the mountains of Tibet *Glr.*; *mi γžán-gyis mtóṅ-sar* (a place) where one can be seen by others; *de bú-mos mtóṅ-bar mdzád-do* he made it visible to the girl, he made her see it *Dzl.*; *mtóṅ-ba žig yód-na* if there is one that has seen it, if there exists a witness *Dzl.*; *de mtóṅ-ste šes* seeing this, I came to know, i.e. from this I saw, I perceived; *mtoṅ tos dran reg*, frq., the seeing, hearing, touching, thinking of (e.g. a form of prayer, or magic formula); *ma ₒóṅ-bar*, (or *ₒóṅ-ba*) *mtóṅ-nas* as he saw his mother coming. 2. **with accus. and termin.: to regard, consider, take for,** *Thgy.*; *rdzas dkar sér-por mtoṅ Lt.* taking white things for yellow ones. 3. **to meet, find, catch.** 4. **to know, understand, perceive** (mentally) *Mil.* 5. col. **to undergo, suffer, endure,** misfortunes, pain etc. (cf. *stonpa* 4), *mi mtoṅ mtóṅ-ba* to suffer what is not to be suffered, not bearable nif., cf. *ltá-ba.*

Comp. *mtóṅ-kuṅ Cs.* **'a window',** prob. for *mtoṅs-kuṅ.* — *mtóṅ-sgom-čan Thgy.* was explained: one who instantly knows and understands every thing he sees(?) — *mtóṅ-ₒkor*, *mtóṅ-mta*, **the reach of sight, range of vision** *Cs.*, **tóṅ-ₒkor-la bor* W.* do not take them (the horses) farther than you can see them; **the horizon** *Cs.*; *mtoṅ-dúg* ('eye-poison') **evil-eye** *Sch.*; **envy, grudge, jealousy.** — *mtoṅ-snáṅ* v. *snaṅ-ba.* — *mtoṅ-byéd* that which sees, the eye *Cs.*; the substance which is the source of vision, a species of gall, **आलोचक.** *Med.* — *mtoṅ-lám* the path of obtaining the power of sight, a mystical state *Was.* (139) — *mtóṅ-lugs* the way of beholding, of viewing a thing; **notion, idea, opinion** = *snáṅ-ba*, *mtóṅ-lugs γsúm-du byuṅ* three different opinions were forming *Glr.*

མཐོངས་, རྒྱ་མཐོངས་ *mtoṅs*, *rgya-mtoṅs* 1. **an opening for the smoke** in a ceiling or roof, also *mtóṅs-kuṅ.* — 2. also *mtóṅs-ka*, **pavilion, platform, open gallery,** on a flat roof *Glr.* (*Cs.*: 'impluvium, or the opening in the middle of a square building', for which, however, the Tibetan word seems to be *kyams* or *kyams-mtóṅs*).

མཐོངས་ཀ་ *mtóṅs-ka* **silk ornaments** on the borders of a painting *Cs.*

མཐོངས་པ་ *mtóṅs-pa Cs.*: **to lose one's senses;** perh. *ₒtóms-pa.*

མཐོན་ཀ་ *mtón-ka*, or *mtón-ga Lex.*; *Cs.* 1. **azure, sky-blue** (?). — 2. n. of a flower. — 3. *Glr.* one of the five celestial gems; *mtón-ka čén-po* another of these gems. —

མཐོན་པོ་ *mtón-po* **high, elevated,** *B.* and col. (cf. *mtó-ba*), of water **deep,** of the voice **loud,** of weight and measure **full,** of rank **high;** **čós-skad tón-po* W.* high-sounding words, pompous style; **lág-len tón-po** *W.* highly skilled, well practised. — *mton-mtiṅ* 'the high blue (thing)' viz. the hair of the head of Buddha, always represented as of a light sky-blue.

མཐོལ་བ་, འཐོལ་བ་ *mtól-ba, ₒtól-ba*, **to confess, to avow,** *nyés-pa Dzl.*; *mtol tsáṅs* (cf. *ₒgyod-tsáṅs*) **confession, acknowledgment,** *mtol-tsáṅs byéd-pa Dzl.*, *mtol bšags-pa* to make confession, to confess, which acc. to Buddhist doctrine involves atonement and remission of sins.

མཐོས་ *mtos* 1. *Ld.* **high, elevated,** **ṭím-si saṅ tos ma len** do not take more than is right! — 2. *Mil.?*

འཐག་པ་ *ₒtag-pa*, pf. *btags*, fut. *btag*, imp. *tog*, 1. **to grind,** *raṅ-tág-gis* in a mill *Dzl.*, *gro* wheat, *p̓yé-mar* to flour: to reduce to powder, **to pulverize,** by means of two stones (cf. *ytun*); **to mash.** — 2. **to weave,** *snám-bu* cloth; *ₒtág(-pa)-po, ₒtág-mk̓an* **a weaver;** *dar-tag-bú-mo* the daughter of a silk-weaver *Glr.* — *tag-stán* loom *Sch.* — *ₒtag-rdó* **mill-stone, grinding-stone**(?) *Sch.*

འཐང་པོ་ *ₒtáṅ-po Wdṅ.* a bodily defect or deformity, prob. *téṅ-po.*

འཐད་ *ₒtad* **liking, pleasure; will; joy,** v. the following article.

འཐད་པ་ *ₒtád-pa* I. 1. **to be pleasant, agreeable, well-pleasing** ccdp., *ysuṅ de kun šin-tu séms-la ₒtád-pa žig byuṅ* all these sayings have pleased me very much *Mil.* — 2. (not governing a case) **to please, to be acceptable, to be considered as good,** to be (generally) **admitted,** *mi ₒtád-par mtoṅ* I see that (this reading) is not generally accepted *Zam.; žes-paaṅ ₒtád-do* it occurs also in this form *Zam.; mi-ₒtád-de* **wrong!** *Was.* (294); **to be fit, proper, suitable** (syn. to *ₒos-pa*), *sems zér-ba mi ₒtád-la* as it is not proper to call it soul, as it cannot fitly be called soul *Mil.* — 3. a familiar word, very frq. used, in *W.* almost the only word for *dgá-ba* and *ₒdód-pa*, **sem tád-de** cheerfully, joyfully *W.*, *ₒtád-rgyu méd-pa tsam žig-la* prob.: as he became angry *Mil.*; **sém-mi náṅ-ne tad soṅ**, also **tiṅ* (q. v.) **tág-pa-ne tad-soṅ** *W.* I have been heartily glad; *ₒtad-ₒtád-ₒdra yaṅ Mil.* though apparently rejoicing; **mā tad-tád** *W.* I am very glad of that; **sem tád čúg-če** *W.* to make glad, to exhilarate; **sá-heb-bi žó-la mi tád-da** *W.* does your honour not like curdled milk? **tád-k̓an** *W.* willing, ready; **gá-ru tád-na soṅ** *W.* go wherever you like; *lóg-pa-ₒtad* let us turn back *Glr.*; *ráṅ-ñi ₒtád-la* voluntarily, spontaneously.

II *Sch.* = *ₒtán-pa, ₒtad-ldán* = *ₒtán-po.*

འཐན་ *ₒtan* **bad,** *ₒtan-ₒdré* a demon *Sch.*

འཐན་པ་ *ₒtán-pa* (cog. to *brtán-po* and *táṅ-po?*) *Cs.* also *ₒtád-pa*, **firmness, constancy,** in *Lex.* explained by *nán-tan*: *mi ₒtán-po* a steady, resolute man *Cs.*

འཐབ་པ་ *ₒtáb-pa* **to combat, to fight,** in a battle; **to quarrel, to dispute, to brawl;** *k̓a-tsúb daṅ ₒtáb-pa* to struggle with a snow-storm *Mil.*; *ₒtáb-pa méd-čiṅ ši-ba* to die peaceably, without a struggle; *ₒtáb-pa ₒdúm-na* when quarreling (persons) are reconciled; *k̓a-ₒtáb Cs.* a fighting with the mouth, altercation; *lag-ₒtáb Cs.* a fighting with one's hands, a close fighting, a scuffle (*Sch.* gesticulation?); *ₒtab-król Lex.* dispute, contest; *ₒtab-ₒkrúg* prob. id.; (*Lex.* **आयुध** weapon?); **tab-dháb* C.* weapons, arms; *ₒtab-čás* ammunition, requisites for war *Schr.*; *ₒtab-brdúṅs, á-k̓ui ₒtab-brdúṅs* the quarreling and thrashing of my uncle *Mil.*; *ₒtáb-mo* quarrel, fight, row, fray, battle, *B.* and col. frq., *ₒtáb-mo byéd-pa B.*, **čó-če* W.*, to quarrel, fight etc.; *ₒtáb-mó spród-pa* to fight a battle, to join battle *Glr.*; *ₒtab-žób* a dry cough *Sch.* — *ₒtáb-rtsód* altercation, quarrel, brawl, frq. — *ₒtab-ya* antagonist, *k̓yód-kyis ṅai ₒtáb-ya byed dgos* thou must contend with me *Glr.* — *bdúd-moi ₒtáb-ya* a termagant, a she-devil to struggle with *Mil.*; *ynás-skabs-kyi ₒtáb-ya* the antagonists of life, i. e. the family and relations a secular man has to struggle with *Mil.* — *ₒtab-rágs* intrenchment, breast-work, fortification *C.*

འཐབ་འབུ ₒ*táb-ₒbu* a cricket *Sch.*

འཐམ་པ ₒ*tám-pa*, pf. ₒ*tams*, 1. **to seize,** to lay hold of, **to grasp,** to take a firm hold of, esp. with the teeth (dogs), or the jaws (serpents *W.*); to sting (of bees *W.*); **to embrace,** **rkaṅ-pa ₒtám-če* W.* to put one's arms around a person's feet, as a supplicant; to grasp intellectually, to comprehend (?) *Glr.* — 2. **to gnash,** so one's teeth; **to shut closely,** *k̔a* one's mouth, frq. — 3. **to join, unite** (vb. n.), *grógs-su, grógs-por Stg.*, in friendship, *byá-bar* in an act, an undertaking *Dzl.*

འཐལ་བ ₒ*tál-ba* v. *tal-ba.*

འཐས་པ ₒ*tás-pa*, *Lex.* = *mk̔régs-pa*, **hard, solid;** *bag-čágs rgyúd-la ₒtas* prob.: inordinate desire has taken a firm hold of your minds; *sra-ₒtás Sch.* **strong, robust, sinewy;** *ȧ-ₒtas-te*, and *ȧ-ₒtas-kyi bag-čags Pth.?*

འཐིག་པ ₒ*tig-pa* 1. vb. n., pf. ₒ*tigs* **to drop, to fall in drops, to drop from,** *k̔rag ma ₒtigs-par Lt.* without any blood dropping out. — 2. vb. a., pf. *btigs*, fut. *btig* **to cause to fall in drops, to instil** etc.

འཐིང་སླད ₒ*tiṅ-slad Cs.* a term of blame or abuse; *Lexx.*

འཐིབས ₒ*tibs* **a cover, covering;** ₒ*tibs-ₐog tsud? S.g.*

འཐིབས་པ ₒ*tibs-pa*, pf. *tibs* and *ytibs* (cf. *ytibs-pa*), **to gather,** of clouds, storms; *ná-bun bžiṅ-du ₒtibs-par gyúr-to* (all the Buddhas) came drawing nearer like clouds of mist *Glr.*; **to condensate,** vb. n. *ljón-šiṅ tams-cád dgá-bai tsál-du ₒtibs* all the trees afford a delightful shade *Glr.*; *byiṅ ₒtibs* drowsiness overcomes me; po. and fig. **to grow dark or dim,** *šés-pa* consciousness *Med.* — ₒ*tibs-po* **dark, close, dense.**

འཐིམ་པ ₒ*tim-pa* v. *tim-pa.*

འཐུ་བ ₒ*tú-ba* 1. adj. v. *tu-ba.* — 2. vb., also ₒ*tún-pa*, pf. ₒ*tus*, *btus*, fut. *btu*, imp. *tus*, *btu* (*Cs.*), **to gather, collect, pick up,** *šiṅ, me-tog*, frq.; *tus-mi* an assemblage of men, council, *Cs.*

འཐུང་བ ₒ*túṅ-ba*, pf. ₒ*tuṅs* (*Cs.* also *btuṅs* I have drunk out), (fut. *btuṅ Cs.*), imp. ₒ*tuṅ*, (*Cs.* also *btuṅ* drink out!), *W.* **túṅ-če**, **to drink,** frq.; **to suck, to smoke** (tobacco), **to eat** (soup); **to be soaked, drenched** (cloth) *Dzl.*; *ṅóms-pa ₒtúṅ-ba* to drink one's fill *Dzl.*; *žo-ₒtuṅs*, *ₐo-ₒtuṅs* suckling baby; *žo-ₒtuṅ dus-na* during the time of giving suck *Med.*; ₒ*túṅs-pa tsám-gyis* immediately after drinking *Thgy.*; ₒ*túṅs-so* they were engaged in drinking *Glr.*; ₒ*túṅ-du ruṅ-ba, W.* **tuṅ-čóg**, **drinkable;** *btúṅ-ba* sbst. **drink, beverage,** *bzá-ba daṅ btúṅ-ba, bza-btúṅ* (*W.* **zabtúṅ**) meat and drink, frq.; *btúṅ-ču* water for drinking *Mil.* —

འཐུག་པ, མཐུག་པ ₒ*túg-pa*, *mtúg-pa*, adj. and abstr. sbst., ₒ*túg-po* adj, **thick,** *mta-ₒtúg* thicker toward the margin or edge *Mṅg.*; gen. of woven stuffs, opp. to *sráb-pa*; *srab-ₒtúg* 1. **thin and thick,** 2. **thickness** relatively; also **consistency,** of liquids, opp to *slá-ba Med.*; **dense,** *nags*, frq.; **sound, heavy,** *ɣnyid ₒtúg-po* a sound sleep; **strong,** *bag-čágs ₒtúg-po* a strong inclination *Mil.*

འཐུད་པ, མཐུད་པ ₒ*túd-pa*, *mtúd-pa* **to make longer** by adding a piece, to piece out, to prolong, *p̔u-dúṅ W.* a sleeve; *skyé-ba ₒtud mi dgos* he has no need of adding a re-birth, a new period of life *Pth.*; ₒ*tud-ma* 1. **addition, prolongation,** **sróg-gi túd-ma táṅ-če* W.* prolonging life (by medicine, careful nursing). — 2. **aid, assistance, subsidy,** e.g. to a needy betrothed couple; also **a gift of honour, a** present, offered to a departing benefactor or respected Lama *W.*; *dmag-ₒtúd* **subsidies; auxiliary troops.** — 3. **help, assistance** in general.

འཐུན ₒ*tun* **gatherer,** *šiṅ-ₒtún* a gatherer of wood, *rtsa-ₒtún* of grass.

འཐུབ་པ ₒ*túb-pa*, pf. ₒ*tubs*, fut. *ytub*, imp. ₒ*tub*, *btub*, *W.* **túb-če**, **to cut into pieces,** v. *ytúb-pa.*

འཐུམ་པ ₒ*túm-pa*, pf. ₒ*tums*, *btums*, fut. *btum*, imp. ₒ*tum*, *btum*, *W.* **túm-če**, **to cover** or **lay over, to put over, to**

coat, *záṅs-kyis Glr.*; **to wrap up, to envelop,** v. *γtúm-pa.*

འཐུམས་ ₒ*tums* **barren, sterile; addled** (eggs); *blo-*ₒ*túms* **stupid** *Lexx.*

འཐུར་ ₒ*tur* supine of ₒ*tu-ba.*

འཐུལ་བ་ ₒ*túl-ba* **to rise, to spread,** of smoke, vapours, perfumes, *ga-pur* ₒ*tul* it smells of camphor *Lex.*; *rdul mi* ₒ*túl-bar byás-pai* ₒ*óg-tu* after having laid the dust *Dzl.*; *la-lás bdug-spós* ₒ*tul* some persons were spreading perfumes *Pth.*

འཐེགས་པ་ ₒ*tégs-pa Cs.* **to set out on a journey.** (To me only **tág-če* W.* is known.) 1. **to pack up.** 2. **to depart.** It prob. signifies the same as *tég-pa*, ₒ*dégs-pa* **to lift, raise, take up,** cf. *γži btág-čes*, or ₒ*degs-pa* **to shift, to change,** lodgings, to remove; *teg-k̔úg* carpet-bag, knapsack.

འཐེང་ ₒ*teṅ*, perh. only another spelling for *teṅ*; *Sch.* has ₒ*téṅ-la* ₒ*bór-ba* **to throw away as unfit,** and if that be correct, it may serve to explain both significations mentioned under *teṅ.*

འཐེང་བ་ ₒ*téṅ-ba Cs.* **to be lame, to go lame,** cf. *téṅ-po*; also adj.: *bsu-mk̔an byiu* ₒ*teṅ-ma čig kyaṅ med* not even a lame chicken came to meet me *Mil. nt.*

འཐེན་པ་ ₒ*tén-pa* 1. **to draw, to pull,** *gyén-la* up, upward, *mdún-du* forth, out; *p̔ar* ₒ*ten tsur* ₒ*ten* they pulled to and fro, this way and that way *Pth.*; *nur-gyis* by jerks, by little and little *Glr.*; *yól-ba* ₒ*tén-pa* a curtain drawn before *Glr.*; **u' tén-če* W.* to draw breath, to breathe; in *W* esp. used for **to draw out** (a cork) **to take off** (a pot-lid), **to draw** or **take away** (a pot from the fire). — 2. **to stop, to stop short, to wait,** ₒ*tén-pa bzaṅ* it will be advisable to stop, to wait. — In *W.* also = *rtén-pa* to lean, recline, repose on. — **gór-la tén-če* W.* to form on a lathe, to turn. — *Sch.*: ₒ*ten-*ₒ*k̔yér* forgetting and remembering (?).

འཐེབ་ ₒ*teb* **overplus, extra, supernumerary,** *gos-*ₒ*téb* a supernumerary dress *Lex.*; *mal-gos* ₒ*teb-kyis* ₒ*túm-pa* to wrap up in an extra blanket *Lex.*; *žag γčig* ₒ*teb* one day over, or too much; ₒ*téb-pa* to have too much (?) *Sch.*

འཐེབས་པ་ ₒ*tébs-pá*, pf. *tebs*, (prop. the passive or neuter vb. to ₒ*débs-pa*, but often not differing from it, v. ₒ*débs-pa*) 1. **to be thrown, strewed, scattered,** *sá-bon Mil.*; **to be afflicted with, befallen by,** *nád-kyis* a disease, frq., also with *lús-la Glr.*; *lan* ₒ*tébs-pa* to answer; *γsal* ₒ*tébs-pa* to be explained minutely; to be understood perfectly *Thgr.* — 2. *W.* **to be hit** or **struck** (= *k̔és-pa*; **'i-ru teb soṅ** I have been hit here (stung, bitten etc.); **teb čúg-te toṅ** put it down, hitting (the right place), i.e. put it just in its proper place; **mi téb-če** not to hit the mark, to miss the aim; **ma teb** the blow did not strike home; even of a prayer is said: **teb**, it has hit, it has been heard. — 3. *Cs.* in a general sense: **to take, seize, hold fast;** ₒ*tebs-lčib Cs.*: 'a tailor's instrument for holding fast cloth etc. in sewing; a thimble'; but the latter is undoubtedly to be spelled *mteb* (or *teb*)-*lčibs*; v. *lčibs.*

འཐེམས་པ་ ₒ*téms-pa Cs.*: '**to shut, comprise, cover, include**; v. ₒ*tams-pa*'; the *Lexx.* have only: *nan-čags-*ₒ*téms*, and ₒ*tems-nán* w.e. In *W.* it is 1. vb.n. to ₒ*tams-pa*: **lág-pa tem** my hand has been squeezed in, **tém-čei čá-lag** a thing (e.g. a machine) giving chances of being squeezed. — 2. **to suffice,** = ₒ*k̔yéd-pa, ldáṅ-ba.*

འཐོ་འཚམས་པ་ ₒ*to-*ₒ*tsáms-pa* v. *to* etc.

འཐོག་པ་ ₒ*tóg-pa Cs.* = *γtóg-pa*, *Sch.* also = ₒ*tág-pa.*

འཐོགས་པ་ ₒ*tógs-pa* pf. and imp. ₒ*togs*, 1. **to take, to seize, to take up,** a knife, a sword *Dzl.*, provisions in order to distribute them *Dzl.*, esp. **to carry** *Dzl.* and elsewh.; *ról-mo* ₒ*tógs-pa Glr., Tar.* 21, 16, prob. to carry musical instruments (or to make music?); = *tób-pa* to receive, **mii lus togs re-ré*, or *togs tsád** all that have received human bodies by the metempsychosis *C., W.* — 2. = ₒ*dógs-pa* with *p̔an*, frq., v. ₒ*dógs-pa*; *Tar.* 159,16 = **to name, to call.**

འཐོན་པ་ *₀tón-pa*, pf. and imp. *ton*, vb.n. to *₀dón-pa*, in *W.* very frq., in *B.* less so, = *byúṅ-ba*, 1. **to come out, to go out.** **dág-sa kʼáṅ-pa-ne ton** he is just coming out of the house; *kun pʼyir ₀tón-te* all coming out *Mil.*; **to remove** (from a house or place), **to leave,** **ton-čág* W.* the last farewell; **to depart, to emigrate;** *ču pʼá-gar tón-nas* when I shall be beyond the river *Mil.*; more carelessly: **yul tón-na, lúṅ-pa tón-na* W.* when one has passed through, the village, the valley; **dún-du tón-če** to step or come forth (from the crowd etc.); **to rise, arise, originate,** v. *snyiṅ-rús.* — 2. for *₀óṅ-ba*, **to come,** esp. *Bal.* — 3. **to come from, to proceed from, to have origin,** *bod kʼo-ráṅ-nas ₀tón-pa yin* these are products of Tibet itself; hence: **to occur,** like *₀oṅ-ba, tsóṅ-pas kʼúr-nas ₀ton ₀dug* (these goods) occur as imported, are imported; *rig-pa-čan miṅ ₀ton yin-te* known as being acute, sagacious.

འཐོབ་པ་ *₀tób-pa*, v. *tób-pa.*

འཐོམ(ས)་པ་, ཐོམས་པ་ *₀tom(s)-pa, tóm(s)-pa*, **to be dim, dull, clouded,** of the senses and the understanding, **nyid tóm-če* W.* **to slumber, to doze,** **nyid yúr-če** id.; *mgo-(bo) ₀tom* consciousness is clouded or darkened, by intoxication, disease *Med.*; also of religious darkness *Pth.*; **mig tom-tóm ča dug* W.* he is dazzled (by the brightness of the sun); *ldoṅs-šiṅ ₀tóms-par gyur* having become blind *Dzl.*

འཐོར་ *₀tor* **fragment,** of a book *Tar.*, cf. *tór-bu.*

འཐོར་བ་ *₀tór-ba*, pf. *btor*, fut. *γtor*, imp. *₀tor*, 1. prop. vb.n. **to be scattered,** of leaves by the wind *Dzl.*, **to fly asunder, to be dispersed; to fall to pieces, to decay,** of the body after death *Mil.*; **to burst,** of a gun; but also vb.a.: *mé-tog ₀tór-ba* to strew flowers *Glr.*, *Dzl.*; *₀tor-₀tuṅ* **libation** *Cs.*, *ču-₀tór* libation of water *Sch.*; cf. *γtór-ba.* — 2. *W.*: **to have notches, flaws,** of edge-tools.

འཐོལ་བ་ *₀tól-ba* v. *mtól-ba.*

ད

ད་ *da* 1. the letter **d**, originally, and in the frontier districts also at present, pronounced like the German d, i.e. not quite so soft as the English d; in *C.* as initial aspirated and low-toned, **dh**; as final letter half dropped, and changing a preceding a, o, u into *ä, ö, ü*; as prefix in *Kh.* and *Bal.* = *γ*, not differing from the prefixed **g.** — *da-drág* is a term used by grammarians, for the now obsolete *d* as second final, after n, r, l, e.g. in *kund*, changing the termination *du* into *tu*; *no, ro, lo* into *to*; *nam, ram, lam* into *tam.* — 2. num. figure for 11.

ད་ *da* 1. gen. at the head of a sentence: **now, at present, just,** esp. before the imp. mood: *da kar-dáṅ-la soṅ* just go to Kardang! **directly, immediately, forthwith, instantly;** in narration sometimes (though rarely) for **then, at that time.** — 2. in col. language after the emphatical word of the sentence: **it is true, to be sure, indeed,** **loṅ da yod ṅul med** time I have, it is true, but no money.

Comp. *da-ko Sch.* = *da.* — *dá-či* **a little while ago, lately.** *Mil.* and col. — *dá-ča* **in future, henceforward.** — *da-nyid* **the present time; but just now.** — *dá-lta(r)*

1. **now, at present,** *dá-ċi-nas dá-lta p̔án-la* from lately till now *Thgy.*; *dá-ltai* (or *dá-ltar-gyi*) *bár-du* until now; *dá-ltai spyód-lam* our course of acting during this life *Glr.*; *dá-ltar-gyi byá-ba*, or *dṅós-po* a person's experience or actions during the present period of his life. *Dzl.*; *da-lta-nyid-du Glr.*, *da-lta-ráṅ Mil*, *Pth.*, instantly; *dá-lta-ba Cs.*, *dá-ltar-ba Gram.*, *dus dá-lta-ba* the present time, presence; the present tense 2. *W.* **hereafter, afterwards,** **dág-sa mi gos, dál-ta toṅ** I do not want it now; give it me afterwards. — *dá-ste* **henceforth, from this time forward** *Dzl.* — *da-dúṅ* (frq. pronounced and spelled *da-rúṅ*) v. below. — *da-dé Glr.* and *C.* **now.** — *da náṅ* **this morning.** — *dá-ni* 1. **now,** 2. **henceforth** *Glr.* *da-p̔yi(n)-ċad Dzl.*, *da-p̔yis Glr.* **henceforth.** — *dá-byuṅ* a man of yesterday, **an upstart.** — *dá-tsam* about this time. — *da-t̔súṅ* henceforth *Pth.* — *da-γzód* **but now, but just, not until now.** — **da-ráṅs** *C.* = *da-naṅ.* — *da-rúṅ*, *da-dúṅ* **still, still more,** *da-rúṅ toṅ* give still more! *da-rúṅ légs-par γsúṅ-bar žu* please, explain it more in detail *Ma.*; **still longer, once more,** *da-rúṅ yaṅ* again and again, over and over again; **da-rúṅ t̔sá-big ma t̔sar** *W.* it is not quite finished yet. — *da-rés* (*Sch.* also *da-ré-ba?*) 1. **now, now at least, but for this time** (opp. to *sṅán-ċad, sṅar, p̔yis*) *Mil.* 2. *W.* **formerly, heretofore** (opp. to *da* **now**). — *dá-lo* **this year, in this year.**

ད་ཁ་ *dá-k̔a* **horse-shoe,** **dhá-k̔a gyáb-pa** to shoe a horse *C.*

ད་ཅི་ *dá-ċi* (*stá-ċi?*) **sickle hook,** for cutting off briers *Lh.*

ད་ཆུ་ *dá-ċ̔u* **mercury** *Med.*

ད་ཏྲིག *da-trig* a medicine *Med.*

ད་དྲག *da-drág* v. the letter d.

ད་ཕྲུག, དྭ་ཕྲུག, ད་ཚེ་ *da-p̔rúg*, *dwa-p̔rúg*, *da-tsé*, **orphan.**

དྭ་བ་ *dwá-ba* a plant *Med.*, yielding an acrid drug; *da-tsód* id.(?); *da-rgód*, and *da-γyúṅ* are two species of this plant, the former of which is considered to be of greater virtue *Wdṅ.*

ད་བག *dá-bag* v. *tá-bag*, *t̔ar-ₒbág.*

ད་བེར་ *da-bér* v. *ta-bér*, *mda-bér.*

ད་བྱིད་ *da-byid* **lizard,** *Med.*; *Lex.* = *skyin-gór.*

ད་ར་ *dá-ra* col. and sometimes *B.* = *dár-ba* **buttermilk.**

• ད་ལི་ *da-lí* several low-growing kinds of Rhododendron.

དག *dag* 1. sign of the plural, eleg. for *rnams*; often added to the pronouns *de* and *ₒdi*, and sometimes to numerals; also in the combination *dag-rnams.* In translations of Sanskrit works it denotes the dual number. — 2. *ṅá-dag*, *k̔yéd-dag*, seems in *Mil.* often to be used for *ṅá-lta-bu-dag* **my equal,** or **equals** (another reading is *ṅá-lta*, v. *lta* 2). — 3. *W.* col. = *da*, esp. in the compounds **dág-sam, dág-sa** now; also **certainly, it is true** (v. *da* 2) *Mil.* — 4. v. *dág-pa.*

དག་ཁ་ *dág-k̔a* is said to be used in *Ts.* for *dé-k̔a.*

དག་ཅི་ *dág-ċi Lh.* **mint,** aromatic plant, Mentha Royliana.

དག་ག་དོག་གེ་ *dag-ga-dog-gé Ld.* for *dog-dóg.*

དག་པ་ *dág-pa* (prop. pt. of *ₒdág-pa*), **clean, pure; cleanness, purity;** as adj. also *dág-po*, *W.* **dág-mo**; *dág-par ₒgyúr-ba* to become clean, *dág-par byéd-pa* to make clean, to cleanse, to purify, *dág-par ₒk̔rú-ba* (*W.* **dág-mo t̔ú-ċe**) to wash clean; more frq. fig.: **k̔a ma dhag** *C.* impure, incorrect, vulgar pronunciation, cf. *sgra* 1; *rigs ma dag* impure blood or kindred; com. **pure** with regard to religion and morals, (also = **holy, sacred,** relative to lifeless objects), *lus daṅ ṅag daṅ yid-kyi las yóṅs-su dág-pa* quite pure in word and action *Dzl.*; *lus dag sems dag dbáṅ-po dag*, also *lus-γtsaṅ* etc. id.; *dág-par ₒtsó-ba* to lead a pure, a virtuous life; *smón-lam dág-pa* is stated to mean a **sincere** prayer *Glr.*; *rnám-(par) dag(-pa)* quite pure, most holy, frq.;

hence *rnam-(par) dag(-par) rtsi-ba*, or *mdzád-pa* is used for: to justify, in a scriptural sense, by *Chr. Prot.*; *mi* or *ma-dág-pa* **impure; impurity,** *bkrús-na mi-dág-pa méd-do* when they have bathed they are quite clean *Dzl.* — Adv. *dág-par*, e.g. *ḱrú-ba* v. above; *dág-tu* **assuredly, certainly** *Lt.*(?); *dág-gis* purely = quite, entirely *S.g.*(?); **dág-mo** *W.* id., **dág-mo šrág-če** to burn completely, **dág-mo za-če** to eat all, to consume entirely. — *yáṅ-dag-pa Skr.* सम्यक् *Trigl.*, **actual, real,** *yáṅ-dag-par ču yin* in reality it is water *Dzl.*; more frq. construed thus: *de yin yáṅ-dag-na* if it is really that, *btsoṅ yáṅ-dag-na* if you are really willing to sell it, *dod yáṅ-dag-na* if you really wish it, *ḱyód-la yod yáṅ-dag-na* if you really have *Dzl.*; *yáṅ-dag-pa daṅ bdén-pai ťsul bžiṅ-du* in truth and in reality *S.O.*; *yaṅ-dag-pa ni bden-pa-ste* since that which is real is true *S.O.*; *yaṅ-dag-pa-nyid* reality *S.O.*; *dgé-bai čós-rnams yáṅ-dag-par bláṅ-ba* to assume, to adopt, virtuous habits earnestly *Stg.*; *yáṅ-dag-par rdzógs-pa* really accomplished *S.O.*; *yaṅ-dag-par ltá-ba* to be orthodox, v. *dgé-ba bču*; *yaṅ-dag lam* the right way, = *ťár-lam Mil.*; *yaṅ-dag-dón* seems to be = *ṅes-don Mil.*, but *yáṅ-dag dón-du γnyér-ba* to aim at, to aspire to, truth *Mil.*; *yáṅ-dag-pai dón-la ǰúg-pa* to be pious *Thgy.* —

Comp. *dag-brǰód* orthoepy *Cs.* — *dag-ťér-ba*, *dag-ťér byéd-pa Sch.* to clean, to cleanse; *Tar.* 189,22; *dag-ster(-čer)mdzád-pa.* — *dag-(pai) snaṅ(-ba) Schr.* 'good opinion'(?), prob.: **a pure, sound view** or **knowledge** *Glr.*; in *Mil.* it has a similar meaning; **dhag-náṅ ǰón-wa** *C.* to lead a holy life. — *dag-žiṅ* holy country *Sch.* — *dag-yig* orthography; *sṅón-gyi-dag-yig* the older orthography; *brda-dág* = *dag-yig*.

དག་པ་ *dág-pa*, *W.* **dag-če**, v. *tég-pa.*

དང་ *daṅ*, postp. c. accus, **with** (Lat. cum), *ṅa daṅ* with me (often with the addition of *bčás-pa*, *lhan-γčig*, *mnyám*, q. v.), e.g. to go, speak, play, quarrel with; *bud-méd daṅ nyál-ba* to lie with a woman; in some cases it must be omitted in English, or rendered by other words, as: *groṅ-kyér daṅ nyé-ba*, *riṅ-ba* near the town, far from the town; *de daṅ drá-ba* equal to that. Some particular ways of using *daṅ* are the following: 1. for **and,** *γser daṅ dṅúl daṅ lčags-la-sógs-pa* gold, and silver, and iron, and the other (metals). The shad is here always put after *daṅ*, which shows that in the mind of the Tibetan *daṅ* never ceases to be a postposition; it can therefore be used only for connecting nouns and pronouns. In enumerations it is employed in different ways, and often quite arbitrarily, e.g. after every single noun or pronoun except the last one, or also after the last; it is used or omitted just as the metre may require it; or when a sum is mentioned, in the following manner: *byúṅ-ba bži ni: sa (daṅ) ču (daṅ) me (daṅ) rluṅ daṅ bžio* the four elements: earth, and water, and fire, and air, four they are; or, esp. in col. language, thus: *sa daṅ γčig, ču daṅ γnyis* etc. — 2. **distributively:** *žag daṅ žag, lo daṅ lo*, day by day, every year; *ḱyim daṅ ḱyim-na Tar.* every one in his house. — 3. after a personal pronoun col. almost like a sign of the plural: *ṅa daṅ γnyis-ka* we two, both of us. *ṅa daṅ ťsán-ma* all of us. — 4. after the inf., and in *W.* after the gerund in *gin*, *nyi-ma šár-ba daṅ* at sun-rise, as soon as the sun rises, when the sun rose; *lo brgya lón-pa daṅ* when a hundred years had (or shall have) passed away, after a hundred years; *smrás-pa daṅ ḱyim-du soṅ* with saying so, he went home, is gen. translated: he said so and went home, and so frq. in narration; *W.: *šúg-ḍa ťon daṅ** with a whistling, **ťóṅ-gin žig daṅ** at beholding. — 5. after an imperative for **and,** *sgo rduṅs šig daṅ de-dag oṅ-ṅo* knock at the door, and they will come *Dzl.*; *yid-la byos šig daṅ bšád-do* give heed, and I will explain it to you *Stg.*; or it is used in the following manner: *légs-par sems šig daṅ ma nór-ram* consider it well; have you not made a mistake there? *nyon čig daṅ sṅón-dus-na* listen to me!

Now, there was in olden times etc. *Dzl.* and elsewh., frq.; *loṅ žig daṅ ṅá-la dbáṅ yod* do take it! I have the power, you know, i.e. I shall answer for it *Dzl.*; in more recent times it is used (also when not followed by any other words) as an imperative particle = *čig*: '*da zo daṅ*' *byas-pas* saying 'eat!' *Glr.*; '*da ltos daṅ*' *ysuṅs* 'now just see', he said *Mil.*; even after *žu*, which in its application is like a verb in the imperative: '*ysúṅ-ba žu daṅ*' *žes zér-bas* saying 'pray, teach (us)!' *Mil.* — 6. In *W. daṅ* is used improperly for the instrum.: **bér-ka daṅ duṅ** strike with the stick! and for by or through with respect to persons: **yóg-po daṅ šab-šób zer** he cheats me, tells me a lie, through his servant.

དང་ *daṅ* 1. **meadow** *Lh.* — 2. *daṅ*, or perh. better *taṅ*, (cf. *tiṅ*), **taṅ táṅ-če*, or *taṅ čó-če, taṅ šan čó-če**, **to read in a singing or drawling manner** *Ld.* — 3. *dáṅ-du lén-pa*, c. *la*, **to submit, yield to, comply with,** *Glr.*, *Tar.*; ç. accus **submissively to put up with** (*Sch.* and *Wts.* are hardly right).

དང་ག་, དང་ཁ་ *dáṅ-ga, dáṅ-ka*, 1. **appetite,** *daṅ-ga ˳gag* my appetite is gone, *mi bde* is bad, *Med.* and *Mil.* (*Sch.* 'the **will**'?). — 2. *C.* for *dám-ka*.

དང་པོ་ *dáṅ-po* 1. **the first,** with respect to number, time, rank, *dáṅ-poï ytam de sus zer Pth.* who spoke (raised) the first rumour? who was it that first got up the rumour? *dáṅ-poi nyin-par* on the very first day; *na-tsód dáṅ-po-la ynás-pa* being still in the prime of life *Wdṅ.*; the former, he that is mentioned before another, *dáṅ-po ynyis* the two first named *Thgy.*; **the former, the earlier,** he that precedes another in point of time, = *sṅá-ma*, opp. to *pyi-ma*, *˳óg-ma*, **the latter.** — 2. **the first thing, part** etc., *nyin-moï dáṅ-po-la* at the beginning of day, at day-break *Tar.*; *daṅ-po-nyid-du* **in the first place, before the rest, above all, before every other thing** *Thgy.*; *dáṅ-po-nas* from the very beginning *Thgy.*, *Tar.*; *dáṅ-por*, and very frq. *dáṅ-po* adv., **firstly, in the first place; at first, in the beginning.** — *las-dáṅ-po-pa* **a beginner,** *las-dáṅ-po-pai dús-su* as long as he is only a beginner *Thgy.*; *las-dáṅ-po-pai byis-pa* like νήπιος (child) in the N.T., *Mil.*

དང་བ་ *dáṅ-ba* 1. **to be pure,** *nám-mka dáṅ-nas Mil.*; gen. adj. **pure, clear,** *˳bras dáṅ-ba* picked rice *Lt.*; of inclinations, dispositions, feelings: *séms-čan kún-la rab dáṅ-ba* full of love towards all creatures; *dge-séms dáṅ-ba* a pure, sincere disposition to virtue *S.O.*; most frq. **devout, pious; devotion, faith;** *dáṅ-bai sems* id. (in *W.* often confounded with *ydeṅ-ba*). — 2. *lag dáṅ-ba* = *dár-ba*, v. *darba* II. 2.

དང་ཙེ་ *dáṅ-tse W.* **a field-terrace.**

དང་ར་ *dáṅ-ra* (spelling dubious) **stable,** for cattle, *C.*, *W.*

དང་ལ་ *dáṅ-la* 1. *Sch.* **'a tract of land abounding in springs'.** — 2. n. of a high mountain pass, north of Lhasa, called *Tantla* by Huc II., 231.

དྭངས་པ་ *dwáṅs-pa*, *C.* also **dháṅ-po**, **pure, clean, clear,** = *daṅ-ba* I., of air, water; *ynam-dwáṅs* a clear sky, fine weather (*W.* **taṅ**); *daṅs-smug* reddish gray *Sch.* — *dwaṅs-ma* 1. **the chyle,** *Ssk.* रस, concerning which Brahmanical and Buddhist physiology has led to a great many phantastical ideas, *Med.* frq.; also fig., mostly in an obscure and unintelligible manner. — 2. *Sch.*: **'the spirit, the soul',** a signification not found hitherto in any book, but acc. to a Lama's statement the word denotes the soul, when purified from every sin, and to be compared to a clear and limpid fluid, in which every heterogeneous matter has been precipitated. — *daṅs* is also not seldom met with erron. used for *dṅaṅs* and *mdaṅs*.

དད་པ་ *dád-pa* 1. secondary form of *˳dód-pa* **to wish** *Dzl.* and elsewh.; hence in compounds: *skom-dád* **thirst,** **tágs-dad-čan** fond of dress or finery (cf. *˳dogs-pa*) *W.*, and in similar expressions. — 2. **to believe** (cf. श्रद्) in a religious sense, more significant than *yid-čes-pas* and including a devotedness full of confidence, like πιστεύειν in the N.T.; also sbst. **faith,** more fully *dád-*

pai sems, and adj. **faithful, believing**, *yón-bdag. dád-pa* the faithful giver of alms *Mil.*: more fully *dád(-pa)-čan, dad-ldán*: *ma-dád-pa*, and *dad-méd* **unbelieving**; often with *mos* or *gus*: *kun dad-dad-mos-mós-su ₒdúg-pa-la Mil.*; *dad-čiṅ-gus-par ₒgyur-ba Glr.*; *dad-par ₒgyúr-ba, dád-pa byéd-pa* **to become faithful or believing, to believe**, frq.: *dád-bžin-du* full of faith; *dad-brtsón* for *dád-pa daṅ brtson-ₒgrús Tar.* — Note. **mi žig-la dád-pa tob* W.* col. a man becomes a believer, v. *tób-pa*; but *Tar.* 35, 1 *págs-pa Dhi-ti-ka-la dád-pa tob* means: he was brought to believe by hearing the Reverend Dhitika.

དན་ད་ *dán-da*, and *dan-róg*, medicinal herbs *Med.*

དན་ད་ལི་ *dán-da-li*, or *dan-dál*, *Ld.* **a sieve**, gen. consisting of perforated leather and a wooden frame; *rás-dan-dal* a sieve made of cloth (inst. of leather).

དན་མོ་ *dán-mo* (spelling?) the female of the ibex, and of the musk-deer.

དམ་ *dam* (a root signifying bound, fast, fixed, from which the following compounds, as well as *sdóm-pa*, are to be derived), sbst., also *dam-tsig* and *yi(d)-dam*, resp. *tugs-dam*, **a solemn promise; vow, oath, confirmation by oath**, like *bden-tsig*; *dam bčá-ba* 1. **to promise**, 2. **the act of promising, the promise**; also *dám-bča Mil.* and col.; *dám-bča ₒbúl-ba* resp. to make a promise, e.g. *mi ₒbáb-pai* not to descend *Mil.*; to promise solemnly *Mil.*; hence *yi-dam*, and (more popularly) *dám-bča* **the sacrament** *Chr. Prot.*; *dam bčás-pa* a promise made; *dam sruṅ-ba, dám-la γnás-pa*, or *nyé-bar byéd-pa, dám-bčas-pa spyód-pa, dám-bčas-pa bžin-du byéd-pa, dám-bčas-pa daṅ mi ₒgál-ba*, to keep one's promise; *nyáms-pa* to break (a promise, a vow); *dam-nyáms-kyi lás-rnams* **violations of duty**; *dám-la ₒdógs-pa* **to exorcise** demons etc. *Glr., Pth.*, but only by gentle persuasion, which induces them to promise to do no harm anymore, not by magic power (so it was expressly stated by a Lama); *dám-la ₒjóg-pa Tar.* 125 id. (ni f.); *dám-čan, dam-tsig-čan Mil.* bound by an oath etc.; *dám-ču* prob. water which is drunk in taking an oath *Pth.*

དམ་ཁ་ *dám-ka Glr.*, *dám-ga Wts.*, *tám-ga Cs.*, **a seal, stamp**, resp. *pyag-dám*, esp. for the seals of Lamas; *dám-ka rgyáb-pa* **to seal, to stamp**; *kyi-dam* v. *kyi*; *dam-rgyá* = *dám-ka Tar.*; **dam-čúg* W.* seal of a Lama, used as an amulet.

དམ་པ་ *dám-pa*, acc. to the explanation of a Lama: **bound by an oath** or **vow, consecrated**; but *Lexx.* render it by **परम, चय** i.e. = *mčog*, thus *Dzl.* ༢༣༥, 4; ༣༡, 9, and *Cs.*: **noble, brave, excellent**, which is prob. also the sense of the word when compounded with *čos, skyés-bu*, and other words. Its usual rendering, however, is 2. **holy, sacred**, *blá-ma dám-pa, skyés-bu dám-pa*, a holy Lama, a holy man, and most frq. *dám-pai čos, dám-pa čos, dám-čos*, the holy doctrine, the holy religion of Buddha. Yet, in the interpretation of passages the original meaning (noble, excellent) ought to be resorted to much oftener. So also *γyóg-mo dám-pa čig Glr.* signifies an excellent, a favourite female slave, but not exactly a holy or a faithful one.

དམ་པོ་ *dám-po* 1. **strong, firm; tight, narrow**, of fetters etc.; gen. adverbially *dam-du*, e.g. to bind, to lock up, to seize firmly, securely. — 2. of laws, commandments, **severe, strict, exact.**

དམ་དུམ་ *dam-dúm* **various** *Sch.*; yet cf. *dum*.

དར་ *dar* I. 1. **silk**, *dár-gyi* **of silk, silken**; *mjal-dár* resp. for *ka-btágs C.*; *rgyaṅ naṅ dar* fine Chinese silks *Thgy.* — *dar-dkár* white silk *Glr.* — *dar-skúd* silk-thread; *gos-méd dar-skúd ₒdra* stark naked *Ma.* — *dar-gós* silk dress, *Cs.* also silk-stuff. — *dar-čún* a bunch or fringe of silk *Cs.* — *dar-čén Ld.-Glr.*, acc. to *Schl.* = *ka-btágs*, yet cf. the significations given sub I. 2. — *dar-ₒtág-mkan* a silk-weaver; *dar-ₒtag-bu-mo Glr.* the daughter of a silk-weaver. — *dar-pón* = *dar-čún*. — *dár-bu* a coarse kind of silk *Cs.* — *dar-búbs* a whole piece of silk-stuff rolled together. — **dhar-ma-rę* C.* 'neither silk nor cotton', half silk half cotton; acc. to others velvet. — *dar-dmán-pa* raw silk *Schr.* — *dar-ts'óṅ-pa* a dealer in silks, a silk-mercer. — *dar-záb* the finest silk, frq.; a piece of such silk. — *dar-yáb* a silk fan. — *dar-yúg* a narrow ribbon-like piece of silk-stuff *Glr*, *Mil.* — *dar-liṅ* = *dhar-ma-rẹ*. — *dar-šám* the lower border of a silk dress *Glr.* — *dar-(gyi) srín(-bu)* silk-worm. — 2. **a cloth**, made of whatever material; **flag** *Wts.*, **sail** (v. *γyór-mo*); *ˌp'yar-dár* a hoisted flag; *mduṅ-dar* a little flag fixed to a lance; *ru-dhár* *C.* military banner. — *dar-lčóg* little flags fixed on houses, piles of stones, and the like (v. *Schl. Buddh.* 198). — *dar-po-čé* 1. **a large flag** fastened to a flag-staff; 2. **flag-staff, mast.** — *dar-ts'ó* a military division, squadron *Sch.* — *dar-šiṅ, dar-bér*, prob. flag-staff.

II. **ice, icy plain;** *dar čágs* ice is forming; also substantively = *dar*, *mts'ó-la dar-čágs btab Mil.* — *dar-zám* ice-bridge. — *dar-ǰár* ('clinging to the ice'?) *W.* a dark-gray aquatic bird.

III. v. *dar-γčig, dár-ba, dár-ma.*

དར་རྒྱས་གླིང་ *dar-rgyas-gliṅ* v. *rdo-rje-gliṅ.*

དར་སྒ་ *dár-sga* **walnut.**

དར་གཅིག་ *dar-γčig* (col. also *dal-γčig*), **a little while, a moment;** *dar-γčig lón-pa-na* after a little while *Glr.*; adverbially: **for a little while, for a moment** *Mil.*: **directly, instantly, in a moment** *Mil.*; *dár-tsam Sch.* id.

དར་དིར་ *dar-dír* **humming, buzzing** *Mil.*; **wailing, lamenting** *Pth.*

དར་རྡོ་ *dar-rdó* **grinding-stone** for Indian ink *Sch.*; *bdár-rdo* would perhaps be more correct.

དར་པོ་, དར་མོ་ *dár-po, dár-mo*, col. for *dál-po, dál-mo*, v. *dál-ba.*

དར་བ་ *dár-ba* I. sbst., also *dá-ra, dar*, **buttermilk,** *dar-γsár* fresh buttermilk.

II. vb. 1. **to be diffused, to spread**, of influence, power, opinions, diseases, *čes dár-ba* to gain much ground, to increase exceedingly *Lt.*; *dár-du ˌǰúg-pa* (act.) to extend, enlarge, e.g. academies *Glr.*; *dar-gúd* spreading and decaying, increase and decrease; *dhár-po* *C.* **grand, magnificent,** of a feast, drinking-bout. — 2. with *lag*, **to take in hand, to put hand to a work.** c. *la Dzl.*; also *dáṅ-ba.*

དར་མ་ *dár-ma* 1 **the age of manhood, manly age, prime of life,** gen. reckoned from 30 to 50, but acc. to *S.g.* from 16—70; *dár-la báb-pa*, or *dar-báb*, a person in the prime of life, frq.; *dar-γáṅ* col. id.; *dar-yól* a person beyond that age. — 2. **a man,** and *dár-mo* **a woman in the prime of life.**

དར་མོ་ *dár-mo* v. *dár-po, dár-ma.*

དར་སྨན་ *dar-smán* v. *dar-ts'ur.*

དར་ཙམ་ *dár-tsam* v. *dar-γčig.*

དར་ཚིལ་ *dar-ts'il Sch.* 'groin' (?).

དར་(མ)ཚུར་ *dar-(m)ts'ur Wdṅ.* = *dar-sman*, **alum** *Sch.*

དར་ཡ་ཀན་ *dar-ya-kan* a medicinal herb *Med.*

དལ་ཡམས་ *dal-yáms Mil.*, *rims-dál Mil.*, **epidemic disease, plague,** or perh. n. of a particular disease.

དལ་ཅིག་ *dál-čig*, col. for *dar-γčig.*

དལ་ཐོག་འཇུག་པ་ *dal-t'óg ˌǰug-pa* **to attack and disperse an enemy** *Sch.*

དལ་བ་ *dál-ba, dál-bu*, **slowness, ease, quietness, leisure** (opp. to haste, hurry, vehemence), *dhál-wa* (or *dhál-bu*) *yö'-dham* *C.*, have you time? *dál-ba žig-gi skábs-su* when he happened to have nothing to do *Dzl.*; *dál-bar ˌdúg-pa* to be disengaged, unemployed; *dál-ba brgyad* **the eight conditions of rest,** the state of being free from the eight *mi-k'óm-pa*; to these belong the *ˌbyor-pa bču*, i.e. ten goods or blessings which, in part, are but more particular definitions of the eight rests, yet include also other blessings; hence both together are called *dal-ˌbyór bčo-brgyád* (another instance of this peculiar way of reckoning v. sub *nyin-mts'án*) As these various conditions are partly characteristics of 'humanity', and attainable only by human beings, they might be denominated 'the (eighteen) specific blessings of humanity'. Often they are also used directly for 'condition of humanity, or of human nature', this kind of existence being, from a religious point of view, the best and most desirable. *rnyed-dkái dál-ba mi lus*, and similar expressions frq. occur (*Cs.* has calmness, tranquillity of mind, evidently mistaking it for *rnal-₀byor*). *dál-ba, dál-bu, dál-po, dál-mo, W.* also **dál-čan**, **quiet, calm,** of the mind, the water; **gentle,** of the wind; **slow, lazy;** **šē-gyü' dhál-wa*, or *šé-pa dhál-wa* C.* phlegmatic disposition. — Adv. *dál-bar* (v. above), *dál-gyis, dál-bus*, **slowly, softly, gradually,** e.g. to draw, opp to *drág-tu*; *dál-₀groi rgyun bžin* like a stream flowing gently and softly; *mi-dál-bar Dzl.* incessantly.

དལ་མོ་ *dál-mo* **chine, loin.**

དལ་བཙོང་ *dal-btsóṅ* (spelling dubious), **dal-tsóṅ táṅ-če* W.* **to carry on compulsory trade.** This is frequently done by Eastern rulers, who in time of personal need make a sale of goods, compelling people to buy at fixed prices.

དི་ *di*, num. fig.: 41.

དི་གར་ཅི་ *di-gar-či* is said to be a provincialism, and secondary form of *γži-ka-rtsé*, n. of a town near Tashilunpo.

དི་མར་ *di-mar Sch.*: 'a certain worm or insect'.

དི་རི་རི་ *di-ri-rí* **buzz, murmur, hum, low confused noise,** as of crowds, of a number of praying people, of wailing prisoners, of birds on the wing *Glr.*

དིག་ *dig*, the Persian دیگ, **a large kettle, washing-copper, brewer's copper.**

དིག་པ་ *dig-pa* 1. *Cs.* **a stammerer,** also *ka-dig*, cf. *₀dig-pa*. — 2. *C.* **reeling, staggering, intoxicated.**

དིང་དིང་ *diṅ-diṅ, gád-mo diṅ-diṅ Tar.* 158, 4 prob. an onomatopoetic word, *Schf.* **'laughing aloud'.**

དིང་སང་ *diṅ-sáṅ* = *deṅ-saṅ*.

དུ་ *du* 1. num. fig.: 71. — 2. for *tu* (q.v.) after final *ṅ, d, n, m, r, l.* — 3. **how many?** *bslébs-nas zlá-ba du lon* how many months is it ago that he came? — *du-dú* **how much, how many each time?** *dú-žig* how much about? *dú-ma* many, *žag dú-ma* many days; *dú-mar p̓ye* it is divided into **several** (parts) *Wdṅ.*; *lan dú-mar* **many a time, often** *Cs.*; **dú-ma rákša* C.* col. a great many, very much (perh. 'devilishly much', from *rākšas*).

དུ་བ་ *dú-ba* (cf. *dúd-pa*) **smoke,** *₀tul*, or *gyén-du ₀p̓yur* smoke rises *Zam.*; *dú-ba-pa Sp.* very poor people that pay but a trifling tax, **proletarians** (prop. 'smoke-people' that have nothing but the smoke of their fire). — *du-ba-mǰug-riṅ* **a comet.** — *du-žág C.* the smoke or vapour hanging over towns and large villages in the morning.

དུག་ *dug* **poison,** *dug blúd-pa* to administer a poisoned potion to a person, to give him poison to drink; *dug-mi-γnód-par ₀gyur* he becomes proof against poison *Dom.*; *čú-la dug ₀débs-pa* to poison the water *Pth.*; *dug γsum* in a moral sense, *₀dod-čágs, γti-mug, že-sdáṅ*; sometimes *dug lṅa*, five moral poisons, are mentioned.

Comp. *dúg-čan* poisonous. — *dug-γnyén* an antidote *Cs.* — *dug-mdá* a poisoned arrow. — *dug-sbrúl* venomous serpent. — *dug-méd* not poisonous. — *dug-šóg* poisonous paper *Mil., Pth., Glr.* — *dug-sél* that which neutralizes a poison *Cs.* — *dug-srúṅ* a preservative against poison *Cs.*

དུག་ཏི་ *dúg-ti* (or *dúg-ste?*) *Ts.*, **so, thus, in this manner,** also *núg-ti*.

དུག་པོ་ *dug-po*, esp. *Ü* (= **ču-pa* Ts.*, **gon-če* W.* **coat, garment, dress** *Mil.*

དུགས་ *dugs*, esp. in medical writings; it seems to denote 1. **heat:** *Tar.* 31, 21 *tsád-pai dugs-kyis* by the glowing heat of the day *Schf.*; *S.g.*: *čui dri dugs rláṅs-pa če* the water (i. e. urine) has a strong smell and emits much heat(?) and vapour; *Lt.* ༢༢, 4. 5; ༢༣, 4; ༤༥, 5; ༥༤, 4; ༢༤༧, 10. *čui rigs šin-tu dúgs-pa Mṅg.* adj.? — 2. **revenge, grudge, rancour,** **dug kór-če, dugs-*

*lán ldón-če** to take vengeance, to revenge one's self.

དུགས་པ་ *dúgs-pa W.* 1. **to make warm, to warm,** *mé-la* at the fire, e.g. one's hands, a plate. — 2. **to light, to kindle,** **me dúg-če** to light a fire; **kán-pa mes dug soṅ** the house has begun to burn, has caught fire; **zá-če dug ťsár-ḱan** burnt food, a burnt meal; **dúg-ḍi** a burnt smell.

དུང་ *duṅ* 1. **a tortoise shell,** *duṅ-rdó* a petrified tortoise shell *Cs.* — 2. **a shell,** both small shells, worn as an ornament (*skye-duṅ-p̓réṅ* necklace of shells), and more particularly **the great trumpet-shell,** which is sounded on certain occasions; it is usually of a pure white, hence *duṅ-dkár* 1. **trumpet-shell,** 2. **white rose** *C.*, *dúṅ-so* snow-white teeth *Pth.*, *dúṅ-ru* snow-white horns *Mil.*; a trumpet-shell wound to the right (*γyás-su ₒḱyíl-ba*) is regarded as valuable as it is rare *Glr.* — 3. **trumpet, tuba,** *duṅ ₒbúd-pa* to sound, to blow a trumpet; *ḱrims-duṅ* judgment-trumpet, trumpet used in courts of justice, *čos-duṅ* church-trumpet, trumpet used in religious ceremonies, *dmag-duṅ* war-trumpet, *liṅs-duṅ* hunting-bugle; *rkaṅ-duṅ* a trumpet or cornet made of a hollow thigh-bone; *zaṅs-duṅ* a copper trumpet, a bass tuba eight feet long; *dbaṅ-duṅ* a similar instrument, but of less dimensions; *rwa-duṅ* a trumpet of horn, *rag-duṅ* a brass trumpet. — 4. **skull** (?) *Sch.* has: *duṅ-čen* 1. skull, 2. = *rkaṅ-duṅ*; in *Glr.* Brahma is called *duṅ-gi ťor-ťsogs-čan.*

དུང་ངེ་ *duṅ-ṅe* **constant, continual** *Dom.*; *duṅ-ṅe-ba Thgr.* id.

དུང་དུང་ *duṅ-dúṅ* **staggering, reeling, tottering, wavering** *Sch*

དུང་པན་ *duṅ-pán, C.* **dhuṅ-pẹ́n**, **basin.**

དུང་འཕྱར་ *duṅ-ₒp̓yár Pth.*, **100 million** *Sch.*

དུངས་པ་ *dúṅs-pa*, secondary form of *γdúṅs-pa*, **love,** *dád-pa daṅ dúṅs-pa žig skyés-te Mil.*, frq.; *yid-dúṅs* = *snyiṅ-brtse-ba*, frq.; **dhúṅ-bhu** *C.* love, **ṭ́u-gu-la dhúṅ-bu ǰhé-pa** cf. *γčés-pa.*

དུད་པ་ *dúd-pa* I. sbst. (cf. *dú-ba*, and the Pers. دود) **smoke,** *W.*: **ḱáṅ-mig dúd-pa mā méd-ḱan dug** there comes very little smoke into the room. — *dúd-ḱa Sch.* 1. having the colour of smoke, **dark-gray.** 2. **family, household.** 3. **chimney** (?). — *dúd-ḱu Sch.* 'liquid soot'; prob. soot mixed with water, smut; *Lt.* compares morbid evacuations or matter ejected from the stomach with *dud-ḱu.* — *dud-bál* soot *Sch.*, prob. **flocky soot.** — *dud-bún* a cloud of smoke *Cs.* — *dud-rtsí* soot, smut *Cs.* — *dud-lám* chimney.

II. vb. 1. **to tie, to knit, to knot,** v. *mdúd-pa.* — 2. pf. of *ₒdúd-pa*, **stooping, bent,** hence *dúd-ₒgro* **quadruped, beast, animal,** opp. to man that walks erect *Stg.*

དུན་པ་ *dún-pa* **great diligence, assiduity,** *dún-pa drág-po*; **dún-čan** very diligent *W.* (cf. *ₒdún-pa*, and *rtun*).

དུབ་པ་ *dub-pa*, vb. **to be** or **get tired;** adj. **tired;** sbst. **fatigue;** *mi dúb-bo* they do not get tired *Dzl.*; *ṅál-žiṅ dúb-nas Glr.*; *lus daṅ ṅag yid dub Pth.* he is tired in body, mouth, and soul, i.e. he has no strength for doing, saying, or thinking anything good. — *dúb-čan* **tiresome** *Cs.* — *dúb-rgyu* **anxious, sorrowful** *Sch.*

དུབས་ *dubs, Stg.* frq.: *nyé-žiṅ dubs nyé-bar* acc. to the context it might mean: **very probably;** but the word seems to be little known.

དུམ་ *dum* **a piece,** frq.; as a measure or certain quantity of meat, v. *γzugs*; *dúm-po* **a large piece** *Cs.*; *dúm-bu* **a small piece,** frq.; *dúm-bur γčóg-pa, γčód-pa, byéd-pa* to break, to cut to pieces. — *dam-dúm* several small pieces or things *Cs.*; perh. = *dum-dúm Ld.*, e.g. *yul dum-dúm*, or *groṅ dum dúm* several scattered farms, hamlets or villages, which have together one common name.

དུར་ *dur* **tomb, grave,** *dúr-du ₒǰúg-pa, ₒdzúd-pa* (*Cs. ₒdébs-pa*) **(s)kúṅ-če** *W.*, **to bury**; *dur rkó-ba* to dig a grave. — *dúr-rkun* grave-robber, plunderer of tombs. — *dúr-kuṅ* **grave, tomb.** — *dúr-ḱrod* acc. to etymology denotes **a cemetery, burial-**

ground, but in Tibet it signifies a place to which corpses are brought to be cut into pieces for hungry dogs and vultures, this being considered a very honourable mode of burying (or rather disposing of) dead bodies, *Köpp.* II, 322. These places of course are haunted by demons and foul spirits; *dúr-k'rod-pa* an ascetic living at such a place, *Burn* I, 309. — *dúr-rgyas* the last food which a dying man eats. — *dúr-sgam, dúr-sgrom* **coffin.** — *dúr-rdo* **tomb-stone** *Cs.* — *dúr-spyaṅ* **jackal.** — *dúr-p'uṅ* **barrow, tumulus, mound, cairn.** — *dúr-byaṅ* **epitaph** *Cs.* — *dúr-tsun, dúr-tsod,* food offered to the dead *Cs.* — *dur-mtséd* a place for burning dead bodies *Sch.* — *dúr-sri* a grave-devil, a sort of sepulchral vampire.

དར་བ་ *dúr-ba* 1. sbst. **weed, weeds,** *Sch.* — 2. vb. **to run** *Mil., dúr-te rgyúg-pa* to run towards a place or object, to hasten to, *zás-la dúr-ba* to hasten to dinner, *lás-la* to work *C.*; cf. *ṅám-dur-čan.*

དར་བིན་ *dur-bin W.*, the Persian دوربین **spy-glass.**

དར་བྱ་ *dúr-bya* a **paring-axe; a hoe** *Sch.*

དར་བྱིད་ *dur-byid* **a purgative root,** prob. = *tár-nu S.g.*, acc. to *Wdṅ.* = *tri-byi-ta* (sic), prop. **त्रिवृता,** Ipomoea Turpethum.

དལ་བ་ *dúl-ba*, prop. pf. of *˳dúl-ba*, **soft,** of the skin etc.; **tame; gentle** (temper), **easy** (disposition), **mild;** also sbst. **softness** etc.; *dul-po, W.* **dúl-mo** id., but only adj.; *ma dul-ba* **untamed, rude,** *Dzl.*; **sráb-k'a* (or *k'á-po*) *dúl-mo** *W.* **soft-** or **tender-mouthed; tame, manageable, tractable.** *Tar.* 11, 14 a better reading prob. would be: *dbaṅ-po ˳dul-bai brjid* a splendour that dazzles the senses.

དལ་མ་ *dúl-ma* a kind of **water-colour** made of pulverized gold and silver, for painting and writing.

དུས་ *dus* 1. **time,** in general, *dús-kyi k'ór-lo* v. *k'ór-lo*; *dús-kyi* means also: **happening sometimes** *Mil.*; *dus* adv., for a while, for some time *Lt.*; *deï dús-su, dus de tsa-na, dé-dus, dus der*, at the time, at this time; *dus de-nyid-du* then immediately, directly afterwards; *dáṅ-poi dus nyid-du* in the very first time; *dús-su*, or *dus-dús-su, dus ˳ga-ré*, sometimes, now and then; *de daṅ dus mnyám-du* simultaneously with that *Glr.*; *dus γčig-tu* or *la* at one and the same time, together; *dús-čig-na* (erron. *γčig*), also *dus re* (or *nam*)-*žig-gi tse, dus-re* (-*žig*), once, one day, some day; *dus lan-čig* id. *Glr.*; *dus p'yi žig-na* some future day; *dus γžan žig-na* another time; *dus či tsam-na* at what time? when? *Glr.*; *dus*(-*na*) after a genit., inf., or verbal root = when, after, *žag γnyis soṅ dus* when two days had, or will have passed *Mil.*; *ṅa bú-moi dús-na yin-te* when I was still a girl *Glr.*; *mgú-dus med* the time of being satisfied never arrives *Mil.*; *btsá-dus-te* as the time of giving birth has come *Lt.*; frq. with *˳báb-pa: bdag ˳dúl-bai dús-la bab* the time of my conversion has come; sometimes *dús-la sleb Lt.*; col.: *dus sleb* the time is come; *˳gro-bai dus ˳débs-pa Dzl., byéd-pa* frq., to fix a time for going, also thus: *nam ˳gró-bai dus byéd-pa Dzl.*; *dus kún-tu, dus rgyún-du* always; almost pleon. in: *dus dá-nas* henceforth, from this time forward *Mil.*; *de daṅ dus ˳dzom* as to time it coincides with that *Glr.* — 2. **the right time, proper season; for** is expressed by the genit. of the inf. (cf. above: the time of my conversion); *dús-su* at the right or proper time, e.g. for paying off *Glr.*; *dus ma yin-pa* the wrong time; *dus ma yin-par, dus-min* unseasonably, not in due time; esp. too soon, prematurely, e.g. to die; *dus-ma-yin-pa spóṅ-ba* to abstain from doing unseasonable things. — 3 *dus γsum* **the three times,** viz. *dá-ltai*, or *dá-ltar-gyi, ˳dás-pai*, and *ma-˳óṅs-pai*, frq., thus in *dus γsúm-gyi saṅs-rgyás* the Buddhas of the three times; often also with special reference to metempsychosis, **the present, the former,** and **the future period of life;** with respect to the times of the day: **morning, noon, evening;** besides *nyin-dus γsum*, also *mtsán-dus γsum* occurs. —

4. **season.** Here Tibetans, of course, distinguish the four seasons of the temperate zone, *dpyid* spring, *dbyar* summer, *ston* autumn, *dgun* winter; but in books, originally written in India, either three are counted, *tsá - dus* hot season, *grán - dus* cold season, *čár-dus* rainy season, or more accurately six: *dpyid* (वसन्त) spring, i.e. March and April, *sos-ka* (ग्रीष्म) hot season, May, June, *dbyar* (वर्ष) rainy season, July, August, *ston* (शरत्) damp season, September, October, *dgun - stód* (हेमन्त) first part of winter, November, December, *dgun-smád* (शिशिर) last part of winter, January, February. — 5. **conjunctures, times, circumstances,** **dus dé - mo** *W.*, **dhy - dé (sa - ̥ǰám)** *C.*, *dús-kyi ̥krúg-pa méd-pa Ld.-Glr.*, *dus bzáṅ-po Dom.*, peace. — 6. a particular period of time, as distinguished from others, **an age,** युग (= ı̥ʊ̍ʊ̥ʊ कल्प), *yar-ldán*, or *rdzogs-ldán* (कृत or सत्य) *yar-rábs*, or *γsum-ldán* (त्रेता) *rtsod-ldán*, or *γnyis-ldán* (द्वापर) *snyigs-ma* (कलि), to be compared to the four ages of Greek mythology. — 7. **year** *Lt.* — 8. symb. num.: 6. — Note. *dus byéd-pa* also signifies (cf. 1 above) **to fulfil the time,** *tsei dus byéd-pa* to die, to perish, also to commit suicide *Dzl.* frq.; *̥či-bai dus byed-pa* id. *Wdṅ.* — *dus dzin-pa* to take the day-service upon one's self (?) *Dzl.* ༢༥༤, 3.

Comp. *dus-skabs* v. *skabs.* — *dus-čén*, *-bzáṅ*, *-stón*, **festival,** *byéd-pa* to keep one. — *dus-mčód* v. *mčod-pa.* — *dus-sbyor Cs.*: **'judicial astrology',** *dus-sbyor-pa* an astrologer. — *dus-me* **comet** *Cs.* — *dus-rtsi-ba Cs.* **'the counting of time'.** — *dus-tsig Sch.*: '*dus-tsig γsár-ba* new, fresh provisions, **'produce of the year'** (?). — *dus-tsigs*, *dus-mtsams* 1. **period, epoch;** 2. **season** *Cs.* — *dus-tsód* 1. **space** or **measure of time.** 2. often for *dus*, *de dus-tsód-kyi mi-rnams* the men of that time or period, *deï dus-tsod-la* at that time; also for hour. — *dus-ziṅ Sch.*: 'time of depravity'. — *dus-bzáṅ* v. above *dus-čén.* — *dus-rlábs* **'wave of time'** i. e. **ebb and flood, the tides,** *Stg.* — *dus-lóg* a year yielding no crops, **a sterile, bad year** *Pth.*

དེ་ *de* 1. num. figure: 101. — 2. affix of the gerund, for *te*, after a final *d.*

དེ་ *de* demonstrative pron. (in *B.* gen. placed after the word to which it belongs, in col. language before it, even without the termination of the genitive) **that, that one,** opp. to *̥di* this, this one, yet with occasional exceptions. 1. when words or passages are literally quoted, the Tibetan begins with *̥di-skad* or some similar expression, and places a *čes* or *dé-skad* after it. *̥di*, in such a case, corresponds about to **'the following',** *de* to **'such',** or **'thus',** (cf. τοῦτο and τόδε). But elsewhere *̥di* may also refer to what has been said before, e.g. in a reply: *tsig ̥di ni bdén-pa yin-nam* is this word (that has just been said) true? *Dzl.* In the context of a narrative, however, *de* is usually employed. — 2. It frq. stands in the place of the definite article **the:** *pa de lóg-ste sóṅ-ṅo* the father went back *Mil*; esp. after adjectives and participles, where it adds to perspicuity: *γžón-nu de na-ré* 'the younger one said *Mil.*; *sṅón-la sóṅ-ba de* he that has gone on before *Mil.*; *deï dón-du, deï pyir(-du), čéd-du, slád-du*, **therefore, on this account, for this reason;** *deï ̥óg-tu* **under that, after that, afterwards;** *deï dús-su, tse(-na)* **there, then, at that time.** — 3. **he, she, it,** for *ko*, which in classical style is not in use. — 4. for *deï*, in *de-pyir*, *de-dus*, (abbreviations of *deï pyir-du*, *deï dús-su*, v. above). Plural: *dé-dag*, *dé-rnams*, *dé-tso.*

Comp. and deriv. *dé-ka*, *dé-ka*, **the very same,** *γsa dé-ka ṅa yin* the very same snow-leopard (you saw) was I myself *Mil.*; *dé-ka ltar* **just so** *Thgy.*; *dé-ka yod* (in answer to a question) **indeed! yes, yes! to be sure!** *Mil.*, *C.*, frq.; *dé-ka lags Mil.*, id.; *de kyed lags Pth.*, oh, this ... is you?! — *de-kó-na*, *de-nyid*, col. *de-ráṅ*, **the very same,** cf. *kó-na*; *de-nyid*, and *de-ko-na-nyid* are also sbst.: **essence, nature** *Thgy.*: *séms-kyi de-nyid* the essence of the soul

Mil. — *de-snyéd* **so many.** — *dé-lta, dé-ltar* (*-du*, or *-na*) **so,** *p̓a ni dé-lta ma yin-te* as it is not so with the father *Stg.*; *dé-lta-bu* of that kind, quality, or manner, **such,** esp. in *B.* — *de-dé* = *de*, but more emphatic, **exactly that;** *de-de-bžin-no* **yes, so it is!** **dhén-da, de** *C.* = *dé-lta* etc. — *dé-na* **therein, in that place, there, here.** — *dé-nas* **from, thence, from that place; afterwards, then, at that time,** very frq. — *dé-pa, dé-ma Cs.* one of that place, sect, religion etc. — *dé-bas* 1. after a comparative, **than that;** 2. also *dé-bas-na, dés-na, des,* **therefore, consequently, now then** (δή) *B.* frq. — *dé-bo* = *de Cs.* — *dé-tsam* **so much;** *dé-tsam-na, dé-tsa-na,* **then, at that time.** — *dé-tsug, W.* gen. **dé-zug**, **so, thus.** — *dé-bžin(-du)* **according to that, thus, so;** frq. for **it,** *dé-bžin-du ɣnáṅ-ṅo* he allowed it *Dzl.*; *dé-bžin ṅó-šes-nas* perceiving it *Glr.* — *de-bžin-nyid* (तत्त्व) **essence,** *Was.* (272), **identity** (297), like *čos-nyid* and some other similar expressions, = *stoṅ-pa-nyid,*' *Trigl.* fol. 20. — *dé-zug* = *dé-tsug.* — *dé-yaṅ, dé-aṅ,* 1. **this,** or **that, too; he also.** 2. **namely, to wit, viz.,** preceding specifications and detailed statements, sometimes also after a gerund, in which case it cannot be rendered in English. — *de-rag* **directly, immediately** *Sch.* — *de-ráṅ* = *de-k̓ó-na, de-ráṅ yin* that is just the thing! exactly! to be sure! col. — *de-riṅ B.* and *C.* **to-day,** *de-riṅ-gi* **of this day.** — *dé-ru, der,* 1. **into that, thereinto, into that place, thither, that way.** 2. **in that, therein, in that place, there,** frq. — *dé-la* **to this, to that; in, on,** or **at this; thereat, therewith, thereto, thereon; about that, concerning that; thereof, therefore.** — *dé-las* **from, out of, from that;** after a comparative and *ɣžan,* **than that.** — *de-srid* to such a length of time.

དེ་བ་ *dé-ba* a medicinal herb, *Med.*

དེང་ *deṅ,* also *diṅ,* **to-day,** *déṅ-nas* from this day forward *Mil.*; *deṅ p̓yin-čád* or *čad Dzl.* id.; *déṅ-gi dus* the present time or age; *deṅ-sáṅ* to-day and to-morrow, **now-a-days;** *deṅ-sáṅ lhá-rje* the physicians of the present day *Wdṅ.*; *déṅ-dus smáṅ-pa Lt.* id.

དེང་བ་ *déṅ-ba,* pf. and imp. of *ₒdéṅ-ba,* **to go, to go away;** *déṅs-pa* seems to be the same form: *so-sói ɣnás-su deṅs Mil., ráṅ-sar déṅs-so Pth.* they went each to his own place; *nám-mk̓ar deṅ Mil.* prob. it melted away, dissolved into air; *sór-mo-rnams deṅs mdzád-pa* to turn the fingers upwards (?). *Schr. déṅs-pa* to ascend.

དེད་པ་ *déd-pa,* pf. of *ₒdéd-pa.*

དེབ་(པ་) *déb(-ma)* **poultice, cataplasm,** applied to sores and inflamed parts of the body *Sch.*

དེབ་ཐེར་, བཏེར་, སྟེར་ *deb-t̓ér, -ɣtér, -stér,* tibetanized form of the Persian دفتر **documents, records, catalogues, registers, lists, books;** *deb-t̓ér-pa, deb-t̓er-mk̓an Cs.* keeper of the archives or records, **recorder, archivist, librarian;** *déb-k̓aṅ* **chancery, government office** *Schr.*; *déb-yig* **cover, envelope, stitched book** *Sch.*

དེམ་ཙི་ *dém-tsi* (perh. *Bu-nan*), **a small, narrow bridge, foot-bridge** *Lh.*

དེའང་ *déaṅ,* v. sub *de.*

དེའུ་(རེ་) *déu(-re)* **one day, some future time,** *Dzl.* frq.; *deu ... deu ...* now ... now, at one time ... at another time *Mil.* (*Tar.* 165, 18 is prob. an incorr. reading).

དེར་ *der,* for *dé-ru,* esp. as adv., **then, at that time;** *der zad, der bas Cs.* that is all, there is nothing more, finis.

དེས་ *des* 1. instrum. of *de; des čog* with that it is enough, **that will do** *Sch.* — 2. for *dé-bas,* v. *de* comp.

དེས་པ་ *dés-pa Cs.*: **'fine, brave, noble, chaste;** a title'; occurs frq. in *Dzl.* as a commendable quality of women.

དོ་ *do* 1. num. figure: 131. — 2. **two, a pair, a couple,** used only in counting, measuring etc.: *žo do re* two drams of each *Med.*; **tá-bag do* W.* two platefuls. — 3. **this,** *Schr.*: *dó-ɣi dón-du*; gen. only in *do-núb* this evening, to-night *Mil.*; *bdag do-núb sáṅ-gi mi* I, a man only for to-day and to-morrow *Mil.*; *Cs.* also *do-žág, do-*

mód to-day. — 4. **an equal, a match; a companion, associate,** *W.* **yá-do** **fellow, yoke-fellow, mate, comrade, consort;** *do-zla* 1. id. *Mil.*; 2. **party** in a lawsuit(?); **dó-da ṕan-tsún žib čé'-pa** *Cs.* seems to mean: carefully to investigate (the right of) both parties; *do-med* unequalled, matchless; **dho-med zaṅ-po**, *C.*, *W.*

དོ་ཀེ(ར)་ *do-ké(r)* = *ťor-tsúgs Lex.*

དོ་གར་ཁ་ *do-gar-ḱá W.* **light-blue.**

དོ་གལ་ *do-gál* **importance, weight; important, weighty** *C.*, *W.*; **dho-ghál mi ǰhé'-pa** *C.*, **do-gál mi čó-če** *W.*, to treat lightly, to make light of, to slight; **ₒdi tsig-po dho-ghál mi ₒdug** *C.*, this word is unimportant, of no consequence; *do-gál-čan* important, of consequence *Cs.*

དོ་དམ་ *do-dám* **commission, charge, superintendence;** **dho-dhám ǰhé'-pa** *C.*, **do-dám ḱúr-če** *W.*, to have the superintendence, direction, or charge of a business, to have the keeping of a thing; *do-dám-pa* 1. a commissioned, authorized person, **overseer** etc.; 2. **bishop** *Chr. Prot.*

དོ་པོ་ *dó-po* **a load,** for a beast of burden, cf. *dos*; **do-góm** *W.* saddle-cloth, housing; *do-ḷógs* the load on one side of a sumpter-horse, half a load, *do ya-ɣčig*; *do-nón-pa* the equalizing of the load, by increasing or lessening it on one of the sides.

དོ་བ་ *dó-ba* 1. Jerusalem artichoke *Sik.* — 2. secondary form of *sdó-ba* c. accus., to be a match for, to be equal in strength etc., to cope with *Mil.*; **šrog dhaṅ dhón-da re** *C.* his life is at stake (*da?*).

དོ་བོ་ *dó-bo Med.*, prob. = *dó-ba* I.

དོ་མོད་ *do-mód* **to-day,** this day, v. *do.*

དོ་ར་ *do-rá Mil.?*

དོ་རེ་ *do-ré* v. *do* 2.

དོ་ཤཱ་ལཱ་ *do-šā-lā Hind.* a thick **shawl** or **wrapper** *W.*

དོ་ཤལ་ *do-šál Cs.* n. of an ornament hanging down from the shoulders; *Schr. mu-tig-gi do-šál* pearl-necklace; *Mil.* id.

དོ་སེ་ *do-sé* (from *tse?*) **now, at present** *Bal.*

དོག་ *dog* col. an auxiliary vb., acc. to Lamas of *W.* and *C.* = *rtóg-pa,* but of different pronunciation (*W.* **dog**, *C.* **dhog**). It seems to correspond to the expressions: as far as I know, as much as you know, to your knowledge etc. So a person may be asked: **yóg-mo me bar dóg-ga(m)** has your maid-servant, for what you know, lighted a fire? whilst, if the servant herself were asked, the question could only be: **me bar-ra(m)*, or *bar ťsar-ra(m)**.

དོག་ *dog* sbst., in *B.* mostly *dóg-pa,* 1. **bundle, clew, skein,** e.g. of wool, weighing about two pounds, as much as one can hold conveniently with the hand or twist round it (*lag-dóg*). — 2. **capsule,** *ár-dza-kai* of the cotton plant. — 3. **ear of corn** *Lex.*; *Col.* more in use: *dog-dóg* a larger piece, *ḱá-ra dog-dóg,* lump-sugar (opp. to ground sugar); **clod, clump, lump, loaf,** **dog-dóg čó-če** *W.* to form loaves; or in general: to press, to press together, to crush, to crumple; **a piece of wood, a log** *W.* (differing from *rdog*); **dúg-ga-dog-ge** *Ld.* broken in pieces, e.g. *ḱa-ra.*

དོག་པ་ *dóg-pa* 1. v. *dog* sbst. — 2. adj. and sbst., **narrow, narrowness;** *dóg-po, dóg-mo* adj.; *dóg-pai ɣnas-las ťar-ba Wdṅ.*; fig. *šin-tu dóg-par gyúr-to* they were kept within narrow bounds *Glr.*; **ṭim dhóg-po** *C.* strict administration of justice.

དོག་ལེ་ *dóg-le* an iron pan with a handle *C.*, *W.*

དོགས་པ་ *dógs-pa* 1. vb., **to fear, to be afraid of, to apprehend,** gen. with the root of the pf tense, which in earlier writings is placed in the instrum. case: *nyés-pa byúṅ-gis mi dogs Dzl.*; whereas *Glr.*: *ser byuṅ dógs-pai dús-su* (fearing) when a hail-storm is threatening; *Tar.* 188, 9: *rgyal-srid ma zin-gyi(s) dógs-te* being afraid (the prince) might not be able to govern; *ma zin dógs-pas Glr.* fearing lest he should not finish the matter; γsó-mk'an ma byuṅ dógs-nas Glr. fearing that no deliverer would make his appearance; hence for **that not, lest** and similar expressions, bu mis mt'óṅ-gis dógs nas that his son might not be seen by the people Pth.; že-sdáṅ laṅs dogs túr-re gyis be on your guard lest anger should arise, take care not to grow angry! Mil.; ₒgos dógs-pai lčibs dusters to prevent (things) from getting dirty Lex.; γžán-gyis γsál-bar šés-kyis dogs(-na) using distant allusions, so that the drift of a speech is not at once clear and intelligible Gram.; rarely with the supine: dé-dag bág-tu. or ₒbrós-su dogs fearing lest they should become faint-hearted or take to flight Dzl. — 2. sbst. **apprehension, fear, scruple,** dógs-pa skyes-te Dzl.; also dogs skyés-te Glr.; dogs bsál-ba, dogs γčód-pa to remove doubts or apprehensions Tar.; dogs dpyod ni dogs γčód-do examining a scruple is as much as removing it Sch.; re-dógs hope and fear (things which a saint ought to be no longer subject to) frq.

དོང་ doṅ 1. **a deep hole, pit, ditch,** an excavation deep in proportion to its breadth, e.g. a trench in fortifications, Glr.; sa-dóṅ id.; ču-dóṅ **a well, a deep cistern;** me-dóṅ a fiery abyss, pool of fire Dzl.; Sch. proposes to use it also for **crater.** — 2. **depth, deepness, profundity;** dóṅ-čan Cs., *dóṅ-po* W., **deep;** doṅ-méd not deep, shallow Cs. — 3. v. ₒdóṅ-ba.

དོང་ག་ dóṅ-ga n. of a tropical climbing plant, and of a sweet-tasted lenient purgative Med.

དོང་པ་ dóṅ-pa **padlock,** dóṅ-pa ₒjúg-pa to put a padlock on.

དོང་པོ་, ལྡོང་པོ་ dóṅ-po, ldóṅ-po 1. **tube,** any hollow cylindrical vessel, = pu-ri; dóṅ-bu a small ditto; spa-dóṅ a tube etc. of bamboo, šiṅ-doṅ a tube etc. of wood; lčags-doṅ of iron; mda-doṅ **a quiver,** dóṅ-ba Glr. id; dóṅ-mo, ldóṅ-mo **a small churn,** = gur-gúr. — 2 **a shuttle,** made of a piece of bamboo.

དོང་ཙེ་ dóṅ-tse, Sch. also dóṅ-ťse, dóṅ-rtse, piece of money, **coin,** γsér-gyi gold coin Dzl.; esp. a small coin, used (like penny) proverbially for a small sum, Dzl. ༣༠༧, 9; ༧༧, 6.

དོང་ཟིལ་ doṅ-zil(?) W. Corydalis meĭfolia.

དོང་ཟེ་ dóṅ-ze **wasp** Cs.

དོད་ dod **an equivalent,** *ṅul méd-na dod čig tob gos* W. if you have no money, I must receive an equivalent; dei dod či-ₒdra yod what is the equivalent, what shall we get for it? Mil.; bu-dód adoptive son, ṅéd-kyi bu-dód mdzod pray, suffer yourself to be adopted by us Mil.; skad-dód verbal equivalent, **synonym, translation** Lex.; dód-du **as an equivalent, as payment, for, instead of, at,** e.g. at a moderate price; k'yód-kyis ṅai stóbs-kyi dod mi p'er Glr., gen. *mi nyn* C., you cannot cope with me in strength, you are no match for me.

དོད་པ་ dód-pa **to project, to be prominent,** gen. with ₒbur-du; also **elongated** (Botany) Wdṅ.

དོན don (Ssk. अर्थ), resp. (at least in some of its applications) žabs-don Pth. 1. **sense, meaning, signification,** gó-ba to understand, ₒgrél-ba to explain; don rnyéd-par dká-bai yig-ₒbrú letters the meaning of which is not easily understood Glr; don mi ₒdug that makes no sense; ₒdii don či yin what does that mean? žal ni k'ai don yin: 'žal' signifies the same as k'a; dpe bži don daṅ lṅai mgur a psalm, containing four parables, together with their explanation, as being the fifth (part) Mil.; ráṅ-gi-séms-la don gyis refer the signification, make the application, to your own soul Mil.;.. kyi dón-du bšad, it is explained in the sense of..., as having the same meaning as... Gram.; don mt'ún-no they agree in this sense, on that point, they say so unanimously Glr.; don dé-la soms think over this sense, i.e. over the meaning of this significant example Mil.; žu-dón application, petition, request; contents, Tar. 45, 19.; also opp. to ťsig (word, form); čos-byuṅ-na spri-ti-ma zer-ba ₒdug-ste don mtun in the čos-byuṅ, it is true, he is called Spritima, but the contents (i.e.

the things related about him) agree, are the same *Glr.*; *ńés-don*, and *dráṅ-don* v. *ńés-pa*, extr.; **idea, notion, conception** *Was.* (283); as the heading of a chapter or paragraph, e.g. *sdíg-pa dág-pai don* of the expiation of sin. Rarely in a subjective sense: *don-méd byis-pa* thoughtless children *Mil.* — 2. **the true sense, the real state of the case, the truth,** (cf. *don-dám*), esp *dón-la*, sometimes also *dón-gyis Tar.* 102, 12, in truth, in fact, really *Glr.* and elsewh.; to speak the truth *Thgy.*; *dón-la bltá-na* col. id.; also for: true! surely! indeed, forsooth. — 3. **intent, purpose, design; profit, advantage,** *ₒdii don ċi yin* what is your meaning and intent (of doing that)? *soṅ-sóṅ-bai don med Dzl.* going on is to no purpose; *don med bžin-du* without seeing the use of it, without understanding the purpose *Wdṅ.*; with the genit. of the noun: **the profit, advantage, the good,** of a person, *mii don byéd-pa* to promote a person's welfare; esp. with reference to holy men, *ₒgro(-bai) don byéd-pa* to work for the welfare of (all) beings, very frq.; of priests col.: to act officially, to sacrifice; **gain, profit,** v. *ynyér-ba*; in a concrete sense: **some particular advantage, prerogative, good** or **blessing** obtained, frq.; *p̔án-pai don* a useful thing, *bdé-bai don* a gift of fortune, *rnyéd-pa* to obtain it; *dṅos-grúb mčóg-gi don* the excellency of the highest perfection; hence *dón-du* postp. c. genit. 1. **for,** for the good or the benefit of; 2. **for the sake of, on account of;** c. genit. of inf. **in order to, that;** 3. rarely: **in the place of, instead of, against, for,** *zas nór-gyi dón-du ₒtsóṅ-ba* to sell food for money *Mil.* — 4. in a general sense: **affair, concern, business,** *raṅ-(gi) don* one's own affairs, one's own interest (cf. n. 3); *yžan-(gyi) don* the interest of others; also meton. for **disinterestedness** *Mil.* (*Ssk.* परार्थ); *don máṅ-bas* on account of much business (syn. *brel-bas*) *Dzl.*; **chief or main point** (ni f.), *ysó-ba-rig-pai dón-rnams mdor sdú-ba* to sum up the principal points of medical science; *čos don ysúm-la ₒdús-te* religion being reduced to three main points (*lus, ṅag, yid*) *Glr.*; *don sgrúb-pa*, or *ₒgrúb-pa* to settle an affair, to obtain one's end, to attain to happiness. — 5. in anatomy *don lṅa* are: **the heart, lungs, liver, spleen,** and **kidneys** *Med.*; cf. *snod.* — 6. **document,** *čád-don* a written contract, agreement; *ċe(d)-don* a letter (to an inferior person).

Comp. *don-ċan*, *don daṅ ldán-pa* 1. **useful, profitable, expedient,** e.g. *tsig Thgy.* 2. **enjoying an advantage.** 3. having a certain sense. — *don-mt̔un* **a merchant** *Cs.*; *dpal daṅ ldán-pai don-mt̔un-dag* most honourable merchants! — *don-dág* 1. *Sch.* business, affairs (?). 2. col. = *don* 1. *don-dám* (परमार्थ), **the true sense,** subjectively: **good earnest,** col *W. yáṅs-pa man don-dám yin* it is not (said in) jest, but in good earnest; objectively: *don-dám-par dbyer-méd* in truth, (after all, upon the whole, in the end), it is all the same *Gram.*; *don-dám rnám-par ńés-pai čos Glr.* prob. = *don-dám-pai bdén-pa* absolute truth *Was.* (293); in later times = *stoṅ-pa-nyid Trigl.* 20; *Mil.* — **don-ḍás** *W* (lit.-*ₒbras*) = *ċe-dón?*

དོན་ *don* num. for *bdún-ċu*, *don-yċig* etc. 71, 72 etc. to 79.

དོན་པ་ *dón-pa* for *ₒtón-pa Glr.*, in one passage, prov. in *C.*

དོབ་དོབ་ *dob-dób*, *dob-dób smrá-ba* **to talk stuff, nonsense** *Sch.*

དོམ་ *dom* **the brown bear;** *dóm-bu* 1. *Sch.* the cub of a bear, 2. *Cs.*: a species of black dogs, resembling a bear.

དོམ་དོམ་ *dom-dóm Cs.*: ornamental fringes hanging down from the neck of a horse; *Wdṅ : mé-tog rtá-yi dom-dóm ₒdra.*

དོམ་ར་ *dóm-ra* **screen, shade** for the eyes and the like *Sch.*

དོར་ *dor* **a pair** of draught cattle; *glaṅ-dór* a yoke of oxen

དོར་བ་ *dór-ba* v. *ₒdór-ba.*

དོར་མ་ *dór-ma* **breeches, trowsers,** *dor-t̔úṅ* short breeches, *dor-riṅ* long drawers, trowsers *Cs.*; *snam-dor* from *snam-bu*; *dór-rta* 1. that part of the breeches which covers the privy parts, v. *rta*; *yúgs-sa-moi dór-rta des yza sruṅ, rmá-la p̔an Wdṅ.*, the middle part of a widow's drawers prevents epilepsy and heals wounds. — 2. *W.* = *dór-ma?*

དོལ་ *dol* 1. **net,** esp. fishing-net, **tám-pa** to spread, to fix it *C., W.*; (*nya-*)*dól-pa* **a fisherman,** cf. *ydól-pa.* — 2. *W.* **stew-pan.** — 3. *dol ycód-pa* **to split, to cleave** *Sch.*

དོས་ *dos* **a load** (of a beast of burden) that has to be carried by compulsory service, without being paid for; *k'al-dós* id.; *ja-dós* a load of tea carried in this manner; *dos* *ₒgél-ba* to load (on), to pack, *dos ₒbógs-pa* (not *ₒp'óg-pa Cs.*) to unload; *dós-pa* a conductor of such loads *Cs.*, *dos-dpon* the leader of a caravan of such loads; *dos drág-pa* 1. *Mil.* prob.: **hard compulsory service;** 2. perh. also: **severe in exacting it,** e.g. a feudal lord.

དྲ་ཅི་, དྲང་ཅི་ *drá-ci, drán-ci Pur.* a flat basket.

དྲ་པ་ *drá-pa* a small copper coin, used in the western part of the Himalaya, **a thick paisa,** of the value of half a penny.

དྲ་བ་ *drá-ba* I. sbst. **जाल,** 1. **grate, lattice; net, net-work,** *lús-la drá-bar ₒbrel* (the veins) are spread throughout the body like net-work *S.g.*; *rús-pai drá-ba* the frame-work of bones, the skeleton *Thgy.*; *ₒod-zér-gyi drá-la* a pencil or aggregate of rays of light (lit. lattice-work of rays) *Glr.*; *dra mig* id., esp. col.; *lcágs-*(*kyi*) *dra*(*-mig*) **iron railings; grate; gridiron;** *rgyá-dra* **wooden rails, fence** *C., W.*; *dra-*(*ba*) *p'yed*(*-pa*) *Lex., Glr.* 'half-lattice', technical term for a kind of silk ornament; *drá-ba-can* latticed, grated; *dra-lag-drá-lag-can* having many forked ends or branches, of the horns of a stag. — 2. a bag made of net-work *Cs.*, *dra-p'ád, dra-čún* id. — 3. the web of water-fowls.

II. vb., pf. *dras, W. *dé-če**, **to cut, clip, lop, dress, prune, pare** (leather, cloth, paper, wings etc. with knife or scissors); also fig.: *p'ai miṅ-nas drás-te* borrowing (a syllable) from the father's name *Glr.* (twice); cf. also *Tar.* 107, 13; **t'éb-dhe-pa* C.* one that cuts the strings (of a purse) on his thumb, i.e. **a cut-purse, pick-pocket;** *gos-drás* cloth cut out for a garment *Cs.*; *dras-spyád* **scissors** *Sch.*; *dra-gri Cs.*: 'a tailor's knife used for shears'; *drai* (sic) *ro Sch.*, **de-rúg, ta-dé* W.* **clippings, cuttings, remnants.**

དྲ་མ་ *drá-ma* **experienced, practised, learned** *Sch.*; so perh. *Pth.*, where however *bra-ma* and *tra-ma* is the usual form.

དྲ་ཟུ་ *dra-zu*, or **dra-su* W.* a small pan with a handle; **a ladle.**

དྲག *drag* 1. *W.* **the post; any parcels** or **goods conveyed by post,** the *Hind.* **डाक.** — 2. **expedient, profitable, of use,** *p'ul-ba drág-gam* will it be of any use, well-applied, if I give? *Mil.*; *ji byas kyaṅ ma drag* whatever I did, it was of no use *Pth.*; *na či-ltar byás-na drag* what course will it be expedient to take? what shall I do best? *Pth.*; **či dhag, ghaṅ dhag* C.* what is right? what is expedient? *nád-pa drág-pas čog* it is sufficient, if the patient is getting better *Mil.*

དྲག་པ་ *drág-pa* 1. **noble, of noble birth** *C.*, **drág-po* W.*; *mi drág-pa*, or merely *drág-pa*, **a nobleman;** *drag-rigs* **nobility, gentry;** *drág-par byéd-pa* to raise to nobility, *drág-par ₒgyúr-ba* to become a nobleman *Cs.*; *drag-šos* an inferior officer or magistrate *Cs.* — 2. gen. *drágs-po, W.* also *drag-čan,* (*Ssk.* **तीव्र, उग्र**) **strong, vehement, violent** *ču drag-pa* a rapid river, violent current; *brtson-ₒgrus drag-pa ₒbád-pa* or *ₒdún-pa drag-pa* unbending, unwearied application; *skad drag-pa* a powerful voice; *k'rims drag-pa* a severe punishment; *snyiṅ-rje drag* yearning compassion; **strong, forcible,** of expressions or language; moreover an epithet of terrifying deities, particularly of Siwa (*Ssk.* **रुद्र**), *drag-mo* fem.; *ži rgyas dbaṅ drag* v. sub *ži-ba.* — Adv. *drag-tu* **vehemently, violently,** e.g. to pull, to lament, to implore; **hastily, speedily,** e.g. to come *Wdṅ.*; *drág-por*, e.g. *drág-por bčad-de bklág-par byao* in reading a marked stop should be made *Gram.*; *ha-čaṅ mi-drág-par* very gently, softly; *drág-gis, dád-pa* to believe firmly *Mil.* — 3. *drág-pa* possessing a quality in a high degree, *dug-drag-pa Stg.* very poisonous. — 4. symb num. 11.

Comp. *drag-nád*, v. *dreg-nád*, **gout.** — *drág-rtsal-čan* = *drág-po*, of deities. — *drag-žán* **strong and weak,** e.g. the relative force of sound *Gram.*; also **high and low,** with respect to rank. — *drag-šúl* **frightfulness,** *drag-šul-čan* **frightful, terrible, powerful; cruel,** frq., yet chiefly with respect to the power manifested by gods and sorcerers. — *drag-γšed* lit. 'cruel hangman', a terrifying deity v. *Schl.* 111, 214.

དྲགས་ *drags* adv. **very, much, greatly,** *mañ-drags Mil.* **very much;** adj. **much, strong, intense,** *bza-btuñ-drags* eating and drinking a great deal *S.g.*; *dran-drágs* an intense, most vivid, remembrance of a person *Mil.*, an ardent longing or desire; *dga-drágs-nas* being very happy, highly rejoiced *Pth., C.*; *ₒgyod-drágs-nas* feeling deep repentance *Mil.*; *bsteñ drágs-na* if one continues it too long *S.g.*

དྲང་ *drañ* a kind of bear *Sch.*

དྲང་པོ་ *dráñ-po* (ऋजु) **straight** 1. not deviating from the direct course, not crooked or oblique, *ťig*, *lam* etc. frq.; *lus dráñ-po ₒǰóg-pa* to sit straight; **ka búb-ne dáñ-po čó-če** *W.* to place a thing straight or upright again; **ťéd-la dáñ-po** *W.*, horizontal. — 2. **right,** e.g. *lam*, opp. to *lóg-pa*. — 3. **sincere, honest, upright, truthful,** *dráñ-poi rañ-bžin-čan-gyi pyir* because they have an upright character *Dzl.*; *las dráñ-po* good actions, righteous deeds, opp. to *rtsúb-po* violent, unjust *Stg.*; *ḱrims dráñ-po* 1. **a just sentence, righteous judgment,** opp. to *log-pa*. — 2. applied to men, with regard to their acting according to justice and the law (v. *ḱrims*); *čós-drañ-po* **honest, upright,** with respect to religion and the divine law; also *dráñ-po* alone, whenever it is not to be misunderstood, may be used for our **just.** — *drañ-por*, *tsig dráñ-por smrá-ba* **to be candid, to speak the truth,** frq. *drañ-don* v. *ñés-pa* extr.

དྲང་བ་ *dráñ-ba* 1. abstract noun to *dráñ-po*. 2. pf. to *ₒdrén-pa*.

དྲང་སྲོང་ *drañ-sróñ*, ऋषि, 1. **a holy hermit,** an order of men, introduced from Brahmanism into Buddhism. These saints are looked upon partly as human beings, partly as Dewas, and at any rate as being endowed with miraculous powers *Dzl.* frq. — 2. At present the Lama that offers *sbyin-sreg* is stated to bear that name, and whilst he is attending to the sacred rites, he is not allowed to eat anything but *dkar-zas* (v. *dkar-po*). — 3. symb. num.: 7.

དྲན་དྲི་ *drán-dri Lh.* **the beam of a pair of scales,** *Hind.* डण्डी.

དྲན་པ་ *drán-pa* I. vb. स्मृ, 1. **to think of,** c. accus., with or without *yid-la*, gen. to think of past events, **to remember, recollect, call to mind,** *drin* benefits, v. *drin*; *byúñ-ba-rnams* that which has happened *Glr.*; more emphatically: *rjés-su drán-pa* frq.; but also *dkon-mčóg drán-pa* to think of, to remember, God; *sdúg-po yóñ-ba de ma drán-pa yin* do not think of, do not trouble yourself about, future evils *Mil.*; *bskyis-par mi drán-no* I do not recollect having taken anything on credit *Dzl.*; *drán-pa tsám-gyis* as soon as one thinks of it, quick as thought *Thgr.*; *so-só-nas... drán-par gyis šig* every body should think of... *Dzl.* (the simple imp. seems not to be used); (*rjés-su*) *drán-par byéd-pa* also: **to remind of, to put in mind of, to revive the memory of,** = *drán-du ₒǰúg-pa*, *dran-skúl byéd-pa Lex.* — 2. **to become conscious of, to recollect,** *rmi-lam* a dream *Pth.*; *drán-par ₒgyúr-ba* to recover one's senses, to be one's self again *Dzl.*; *čiañ mi drán-pa* insensible *Dzl.*; *mi drán-pai ₒóg-tu* after they had become insensible *Dzl.* — 3. **to think of with love** or **affection, to be attached to, to long for,** *ǎ-ma* for the mother col.; **dran-sém** *W.* **love, affection, attachment;** *dran-mčog-rje* dearest Sir! *Mil.*

II. sbst. स्मृति, स्मर, 1. **remembrance, recollection, reminiscence; memory** frq.; *drán-pa γsál-po* a retentive memory. — 2. **consciousness,** *stor* is lost; *ťugs dran-méd-du ťím-pa* to lose one's senses, resp. *Mil.*; *dran-méd-du brgyál-pa* id.; *drán-pa rnyéd-*

pa to recover one's senses *Pth.*; *γsó-ba* id.; *dran-ₒdzin-méd-pa* being out of one's senses (with joy) *Glr.*; **self-possession, consideration,** *dran-méd* without consideration, inconsiderate; *séms-ċan smyón-pa-dag drán-pa so-sór rnyed* insane persons regained the respective faculties of their minds *S.O.*, *drán-pa γžúṅs-pa* prob. quickness of apprehension, good capacity; *drán-pa nyáms-pa* weak-minded; *dran-yód, dran-ldán,* remembering, being in one's senses *Cs.*; *dran-šés* for *drán-pa daṅ šes-ráb Mil.*; **ḍhem-pa maṅ-po k̔o-la šar** *C.* he is uneasy, troubled, full of scruples and apprehensions.

དྲལ་ *dral* 1. v. *lċam-mo.* 2. v. *ₒdral-ba.* 3. for *gral.*

དྲལ་ཙེ་ *dral-tse* a kind of courier or messenger *Cs.*

དྲས་ *dras* v. *dra-ba* II.

དྲི་ *dri,* col. also *dri-ma,* **odour, smell, scent,** *dri-žim(-po), dri-bsúṅ Dzl.* an agreeable smell, sweet scent; *dri-bzáṅ(-po)* 1. id., 2. *Cs.* also **saffron;** *dri-ṅán,* prob. also *dri-lóg, W.* **dri sóg-po**, *Cs. dri-mi-žim* an unpleasant smell, a stench; *dri bró-ba* to exhale an odour *Glr.*; **ḍi núm-pa** or **nóm-pa** to inhale an odour; *W.*: **k̔yúr-ḍi, nyiṅ-ḍi, dúg-ḍi, mé-ḍi, rúl-ḍi, hám-ḍi rag** I perceive a sour, stale, burnt, smoky, putrid, mouldy smell; **ťsig-ḍi, žob-ḍi** a smell of burnt food, burnt wool; *dri lṅa* five odours or perfumes used in offering; *dri-k̔a Sch.*: urinous smell (?); *dri-ṅád* vapour, exhalation, fragrance; *dri-ċan lté-ba* bag of the musk-deer; musk *Wdṅ.*; *dri-ču* scented water, perfume *Cs.* (yet cf. *dri-ma*), *dri-čén* a medicinal herb *Lt.* — *dri-γtsaṅ-k̔áṅ,* **गन्धकूट, a sacred place, a chapel,** conjectures about the etymology of the word v. *Burn.* I, 262. — *dri-ₒdzin po.,* the nose. — *dri-za,* also *dri-za-mo* fem., **गन्धर्व an eater of fragrance,** in Brahmanism **the heavenly musicians,** and so also in Buddhism painted as playing on guitars, but usually (in accordance with the etymology) thought to be **aërial spirits,** that feed on odours of every description. They are supposed not only to be fond of flowers and other fragrant objects, but also to visit dunghills, flaying-places, shambles etc., the various substances of which are accordingly dedicated to them (cf. *γtór-ma*). The insects, swarming about such places, the Tibetan believes to be incarnated *dri-za.* — *dri-zai groṅ(-k̔yer)* **mirage, fata morgana.**

དྲི་བ་ *dri-ba* **question,** *dri-ba ₒdri-ba* to ask a question, *mi-la* a person; *dri-bai lan, dris-lán,* answer; *dri-rtóg ma maṅ Mil., C.,* **ḍhi gya ma ǰhé** or **čé** *Cs.*, don't ask long! do not ask many questions!

དྲི་བོ་ *dri-bo* **an enchanter, sorcerer, magician.** *dri-mo* **enchantress, witch** *Mil.*

དྲི་མ་ *dri-ma,* **मल, 1. dirt, filth, impurity; excrement, ordure;** *lag-(pai) dri(-ma)* marks left by dirty fingers on books etc.; *sná-dri* mucus, snot, snivel *S.g.*; *dri-ma γzum* the three impurities, excrement, urine, sweat; but sometimes more are enumerated; frq. fig.: *nyés-pai, nyon-móṅs-pai, k̔a-na-ma-ťó-bai dri-ma*; *dri-ma kun zád-nas* after all impurities have been put off *Dzl.*; *dri-ču* 1. **urine,** *ₒdór-ba* to urinate *Glr.*; *rés-ₒga raṅ-byuṅ-gi dri-ču sten* sometimes (in my extremity) I had recourse to my own water *Mil.* — 2. v. sub *dri.* — *dri-čén* feces of the intestinal canal. — *dri-ma-ċan* **dirty, sluttish,** as to dress; *dri-ma-méd-pa* clean, cleanly. — 2. for *dkri-ma,* v. *dkri-ba.*

དྲིང་ *driṅ Cs.* = '*drin* **kindness, favour;**' yet, *γžan driṅ mi ǰog Lex., γžán-gyis driṅ-la mi ǰog-ċiṅ raṅ-gi čos žugs-so Dom.?* One dictionary renders it by **प्रत्यय,** knowledge; certainty, faith, confidence

དྲིན་ *drin,* resp. *bka-drin,* rarely *sku-drin Glr.*, **kindness, favour, grace,** *blá-mai drin-gyis* by the grace of my Lama, of my spiritual father, of my patron saint *Mil.*; in addressing a person, *k̔yed* (or *k̔yod*)-*kyi bka-drin-gyis* is gen. used; *mai drin* benefits conferred by a mother *Thgy.*; *drin-ċan, drin-čé* **kind, gracious, benevolent; benefactor,** *drin-ċan p̔a-má* the parents, these benefactors; *drin-ċan már-pa,* Marpa full of grace (Milaraspa's Lama); *tse* ₒ*di-la drin če-šós rán-gi ma yin* the greatest benefactress for this life is one's own mother; *bód-la bka-drin čé-ba lags-so* this turned out the greatest benefit for Tibet *Glr.*; *ǎ-ma drin-čén* kindest mother! (says a king to a wonder-working female saint) *Pth.*; *drin drán-pa* as a vb., **to acknowledge a kindness, to feel obliged**; as a sbst. **thankfulness, gratitude** *Thgy.*; *k̔yód-kyi drin rtág-tu drán-pas* as I shall always feel greatly obliged to you *Dzl.*; *dei bka-drin drán-čiṅ* full of thankfulness towards him *Dzl.*; *drin rjéd-pa* unmindful of obligations; *drin γzó-ba, drín-du γzo-ba, drín-lán glán-pa, drin-lán bsáb-pa, W.* **ḍin-zó taṅ-če** to return benefits, to show one's self grateful; *drin γzó-žiṅ lan byao* you shall not have done it for nothing *Dzl.*; *drin-lán-du* as a gift made in return, a return-present.

དྲིབ་ཤིལ་ (*drib-šil*) **ḍib-šil**, a corrupt form for *dril-bu γsil, Ld.*, = *γyér-k̔a.*

དྲིམ་ *drim* (spelling?) **stump, trunk,** of a tree or plant, deprived of top and branches *Ld.* —

དྲིའུ་ *driu* v. *dre.*

དྲིལ་ *dril*, gen. *dril-bu,* **bell;** *dril sróg-pa* to ring the bell; to publish by ringing a bell; *dril-lče* the tongue of a bell, the clapper; *dril-γzúgs* the body of a bell *Cs.*, *Glr.*; *dril-sgrá* the voice or sound of a bell, peal of bells; *dril-k̔aṅ* bell-tower, belfry; *dril-stégs* the frame of timber, on which bells are suspended.

དྲིལ་བ་ *dril-ba* v. ₒ*dril-ba.*

དྲིས་པ་ *dris-pa* v. ₒ*dri-ba.*

དྲུ་བུ་ *drú-bu* = *grú-bu, grú-gu,* **a clue** or **ball,** of wool etc.

དྲུག་ *drug* num. **six,** *drúg-pa, drúg-po* cf. *dgu*; *yi-ge drúg-pa* or *-ma* the prayer of the six letters, the Ommanipadmehūm, *Glr.*; *drúg-ču* sixty; *drúg-ču-rtsa-γčig* (*W.* **ḍug-ču-re-čig**), or *re-γčig*, sixty one; *drug-brgyá* six hundred; *drug-stóṅ* six thousand; *drug-ču-skór* a cycle of sixty years. — *drúg-sgra* the so-called article, presenting itself in the following six forms: *pa, ba, ma, po, bo, mo.*

དྲུག་དཀར་, དྲུག་དམར་ *drug-dkár, drug-dmár,* **two sorts of turkoise** *Cs.*

དྲུང་ *druṅ* the space **near,** and esp. **before** a person or thing, *p̔o-bráṅ-gi druṅ gáṅ-na-ba der* ₒ*dúg-nas* alighting on the place before the palace *Dzl.* ୨ᴠ, 3; gen. with *na, du, nas.* 1. adv. **near to, near by, to or at the side of, before, to, off from;** *drúṅ-du rtóg-pa* to examine personally, face to face, orally *Dzl.*; *drúṅ-du* ₒ*gró-ba* to go near or up to. 2. postp. c. genit. (less corr. c. accus.), *šiṅ-gi drúṅ-na* near, or under the tree, *drúṅ-du* id.; to or towards the tree; *drúṅ-nas* away from (the tree); *rgyál-poi drúṅ-du* to the king, before, in presence of (coram) the king; *drúṅ-pa,* resp. *sku-drúṅ-pa,* one standing near, **a waiting man, a page in ordinary** *Cs.* — *drúṅ-*ₒ*k̔or* **train, retinue.** — *drúṅ-γnas-pa* **companion, associate.** — *drúṅ-yig(-pa)* **secretary.** — *drúṅ-*ₒ*tso-ba* **private physician,** physician in ordinary *Cs.* When preceded by *žabs* it becomes a respectful term, e.g. in the direction of a letter, where it stands for our **'to'** (lit. 'to the feet of *N.N.*').

དྲུང་པོ་ *drúṅ-po* 1. **prudent, sensible, judicious, wise** *Mil.*, in conjunction with *γčáṅ-po*; so also *Pth. γčaṅ-drúṅ-ldaṅ-pa.* — 2. **sincere, candid** *C.* — 3. **diligent?**

དྲུངས་ *druṅs* **root,** of rare occurrence; *druṅs (-nas) p̔yuṅ* exterminated, destroyed root and branch, *Lex.*

དྲུངས་པ་ *drúṅs-pa* **clarified, clear** *Cs.*; *bžes-druṅs* resp. for *čaṅ,* **beer,** *Ts.*

དྲུད་ *drud* 1. v. ₒ*drud-pa.* — 2. *drud-drúd* **pelican** *Sch.*

དྲུབ་པ་ *drúb-pa* v. ₒ*drúb-pa.*

དྲུམ་པ་ *drúm-pa* **to have a strong desire, to long, languish, pine,** for, *Sch.*

དྲུས་མ་ *drús-ma* **millet** *Sch.*

དྲེ་ *dre Ts., dreu Lex., ḍiu Lh., drel Glr.,* **mule,** *dré-p̔o, p̔ó-dre* he-mule, *dré-mo, mó-dre* she-mule.

དྲེ་བོ་ *dré-bo Lt., dre-mo Mṅg., *de-móṅ* W.,* **elbow.**

དྲེག་པ་ *drég-pa, drégs-pa* 1. any **dirt** that is removed by scraping, whereas *dri-ma* is washed off; more particularly: — 2. **soot,** which is also used as a medicine *Wdṅ.*; *k̔uṅ-drég* id.; *sgrón-dreg* lamp-black; *sláṅ-dreg* soot on a kettle; *lčágs-dreg* v. *lčags*; *t̔ál-dreg, rdó-dreg Med.?* — *só-dreg* **tartar** incrusting the teeth *Med.* — *dreg-bál* flakes of soot. — *dreg-nád* **gout;** *dreg-grúm* id.

དྲེགས་པ་ *drégs-pa* 1. **pride, haughtiness, arrogance,** *k̔eṅ-dégs* id.; *drégs-pa nyams* pride is put down, humbled; *drégs-pa skyáṅ-ba* to lay aside, to put off pride; *nór-gyis dregs* purse-proud *Lex.* — 2. **proud, haughty, arrogant,** = *drégs-pa-čan*; *drégs-pa (-čan t̔ams-čád* the great, the proud, the people of high rank, the great ones of this world *Pth.*; in the world of spirits, with or without *bgegs*: the powerful demons. — 3. as a vb.: *ró-tsas dregs t̔se* when the sexual impulse **is strong** *Med.*

དྲེད་ *dred* (*Zam.* तरक्षु) **hyena,** which name has prob. been transferred by the inhabitants of the mountainous districts to the *dred*, an animal better known to them) **the yellow bear;** *mi-dred* a bear that devours men *Mil.*; *p̔yúgs-dred* a bear destructive to cattle; *dréd-p̔o* he-bear, *dréd-mo* she-bear. — *dred-t̔sáṅ* a bear's den. — *dred-siu-šiṅ* hazel-nut tree *Sch.*

དྲེད་པོ་ *dréd-po* 1. *Sch.*: **'evasive, lazy',** yet *č̔os-méd dréd-po zol-zóg γyo-rgyú-čan?* — 2. **load, burden,** esp. a heavy load *C.*, *dréd-po dréd-pa* = *k̔rés-po grág-pa*, to cord a load.

དྲེད་མ་ *dréd-ma, rtsa-dréd-ma Glr.* = *drés-ma; dám-dréd-ma Mil.?*

དྲེའུ་, དྲེལ་ *dreu, drel*, v. *dre*; *dreu-rṅóg* 1. **the mane of a mule.** — 2. **a couch,** or **stuffed-seat** *Cs.* — 3. a kind of **long-haired cloth.**

དྲེས་མ་ *drés-ma* 1. *C.* a kind of grass, of which ropes and shoes (of great durability) are made; *Glr. dréd-ma; drés-mai ge-sár S.g.* the filaments of *drés-ma*; *dres-*ₒ*bru Cs., dres-*ₒ*brum S.g.* the seeds of *drés-ma.* — 2. *W.* Iris kamaonensis.

དྲོ་ *dro* (cf. *dró-ba*), 1. **the hot time of the day,** from about 9 o'cl. a. m. till 3 o'cl. p. m.; *dró-la báb-nas* when this time arrived *Dzl.*; *sṅá-dro* the morning, *p̔yi-dro* 1. the later part of the afternoon, 2. *W.* *p̔i-ro* evening, night. — 2. a meal taken about noon, **lunch;** *dro btáb-pa* to lunch; *dro-lúg* a sheep intended to be eaten for a luncheon; *dro-šá* meat intended for such a purpose.

དྲོ་བ་ *dró-ba* 1. **to be warm,** v. *drós-pa*; gen. adj. **warm,** *dró-bai γnas* a warm place; *dró-bar* ₒ*gyúr-ba* to grow warm. — 2. **warmth** (*bág-dro* v. sub *ur*).

དྲོགས་ *drogs Sch.*: 'packed up, made up into pack or parcel'.

དྲོང(ས)་ *droṅ(s)* v. ₒ*dren-pa.*

དྲོང་མ་ *dróṅ-ma* **a large basket** or **dosser,** provided with a lid, and carried on the back, *Hind.* पतारा.

དྲོད་ *drod* 1. **warmth, heat,** e.g. of the sun; *drod-γšér* warmth and moisture; *dród-kyi šiṅ* a tropical tree *Wdṅ.*; *me-drod* 1. **the heat of the fire** *Lt.* 2. prob. **animal heat,** perh. because it is supposed to arise from a union of the fiery element with a germ originated by conception. — 2. *k̔a-dród zuṅ γčig* a small piece of food, = *k̔a-zás*, and prob. incorrect for *k̔a-bród* enjoyment of the mouth. — *lám-la drod t̔ób-pa Mil.* was explained: to have a cheerful mind, free from doubts and apprehensions on the way (to heaven), *drod*, therefore, seems to stand here for *brod.* — *drod-rtags, Mil.*, was explained as being new knowledge, new perceptions, as a fruit of long meditation; one *Lex.* has *dród-rig-pa* = मात्रज्ञ experienced or well-versed in measure.

དྲོན་མོ་ *drón-mo* col. **warm,** *zan-drón* warm food.

དྲོལ་ *drol* v. ₒ*drol-ba.*

དྲོས་ *dros, Sch.* = *dro*; *dros-č̔én* **noon, mid-day,** *dros-č̔úṅ* forenoon(?).

དྲོས་པ་ *drós-pa*, pf. of *dró-ba,* **heated, grown warm,** esp. of the ground by the heat of the sun, of men, by warm clothing; *dros soṅ* the ground has grown warm, the snow is beginning to melt; *drós-na* when it is getting warm; *di gón-na dros lags* if you put that on, you will be warm *Mil.*; *tse γčig drós-pai gos* warm clothing for one period of existence *Mil.* — *ma-drós-pa* n. of the Manasarowara or lake of Mapam in Nari. The Hindoos describe it as something like a northern ocean, inhabited by Nagas (v. *klu*), and the Tibetans in good faith repeat such fables, at least in their literature, although they know better.

དྷ་མན་ *dha-mán Ld.-Glr. Schl.* fol. 17, b., v. *lda-mán.*

དྷུ་ཏི *dhú-ti*, (धुति a shaker, agitator?) a word of more recent mystical physiology, 'the middle vein', = *dbú-ma* (cf. *γtúm-po* and *tíg-le*) *Thgr.*, *Mil.*, *Wdṅ.* The Lamas consulted by me asserted, not quite in accordance with books, *dhu-ti* to denote a kind of *rluṅ* in the body (which would agree with ཕུ to blow, and with πνεῦμα), a vital power closely connected with the soul, supporting it during lifetime, and leaving it only when separated by death. This would be a new or second signification of *dhu-ti*, although I cannot vouch for the correctness of the above statement, nor am I able to decide, whether *dhu-ti* and *à-ba-dhuti* are quite the same. — *à-ba-dhuti-pa Tar.* 187, 8 is a proper name, *Schf.*

དྷེ་ལ་ *dhe-lâ, Hind.* धेला, **half a paisa,** the smallest coin, equal to the tenth part of a penny, *W.*

གདག(ས)་ *γdag(s)* 1. fut. of *˳dogs-pa.* — 2. *γdags* **the light, day** *Cs.*, opp. to *sribs.* — 3. in *Stg. γdágs-pa* occurs frq. as a translation of प्रज्ञा **wisdom.**

གདང, རྡང་ *γdaṅ, rdaṅ* (*ldaṅ?*) 1. **clothes-stand, rack** or **rail** for hanging up clothes, *γdáṅ-la gos ˳dzár-ba, ˳gél-ba*; *γdáṅ-bu* 1. **peg** or **nail,** for the same purpose. 2. *skás-kyi γdaṅ(-bu) Lex.*, **šral-dáṅ** *W.*, **step of a ladder.** — 2. col. for *γdeṅ.*

གདང་བ་ *γdáṅ-ba, γdáṅs-pa,* to open wide, mouth and nostrils, **to gape** *B.* and col.; *γdáṅ-pai k̔ro-žál* an angry face with the mouth wide opened *Glr.*

གདངས་ *γdaṅs* 1. **music, harmony, melody,** = *dbyaṅs, snyags,* also *γdaṅs-snyan*; *γdaṅs byéd-pa* to make music *C.* — 2. resp. for *dprál-ba* **forehead** *Cs.*

གདངས་པ་ *γdáṅs-pa* 1. v. *γdáṅ-ba.* 2. resp. one recovering from illness, **convalescent,** with *snyun, bsnyuṅ-ba Lex.*; **ra daṅ** *W.* he has recovered from his drunken fit, has become sober again.

གདན་ *γdan,* आसन, resp. *bžugs-γdan W.*, **a bolster,** or seat composed of several quilts or cushions, put one upon the other (five for common people, nine for people of quality), cf. *˳bol; γdan-k̔ri* **a throne** *Glr.*; *γdan-rábs* **a succession of teachers** *Tar.* 199, 4. The word is much used in polite expressions: *γdan ˳dégs-pa* **to take leave, to withdraw, to depart;** *γdán-sa* 1. **place of residence,** *bla-mai Mil.*; *dga - ston - gyi* place of a festival *Glr.* 2. **situation, position, rank,** ni f., *Mil.*; *γdán-˳dren-pa* **to invite,** = *spyán-˳dren-pa,* **to appoint, to nominate,** *dpon-du* a chief, a leader *Glr.*; **to go to meet** *Glr.*; **dan-su-če** *W.* id.; **dan-kyal-če** *W.* **to accompany,** as a mark of attention; *dan-p̔eb-pa* **to arrive** *Sch.*

གདབ་པ་ *γdáb-pa,* fut. of *˳debs-pa.*

གདམ་ཀ་ *γdám-ka W.*, *γdam-ṅa Lex.*, **choice, election,** **dám - ka čó - če** *W.* **to choose, to elect;** *γdám-ṅa byéd-pa Lex.* id.

གདམ་པ་ *γdám-pa,* fut. of *˳dóms-pa, γdáms-pa,* pf. of *˳dóms - pa,* **to advise,** *rgyál-po-la γdám-pai mdo* adviser of kings, a mirror for sovereigns *Thgy.*; *γdáms-pa* sbst. **advice, counsel, doctrine, precept,** *γdáms-ṅág, W.* **γdáms-ka, γdáms-k̔a** (cf. *k̔á-ta, k̔á-lta*), resp. *žal-γdáms, bka-γdáms* id.; *γdáms-pa čig žu* we ask for some advice *Glr.*; *p̔án-pa γdáms-pa* a good advice; *γdams-ṅág stón-pa Lex.*, **dám-ka,* or *k̔á-ta táṅ-če** *W.* to give an advice, to advise; *γdams-ṅág ˳dóms-pai tsig* **the imperative mood,** expressing command or exhortation *Gram.*

གདའ་བ་ *γdá-ba,* eleg. for *˳dúg-pa B.* and *Khams,* 1. **to be, to be there,** *du* *γda* how many are there here? *Zam.*; *sgyúr-gin γda Glr.*; *rtóg-tu γdao* he or it may be discerned, distinguished *Dzl.*; *p̔yin-nas γda* he had arrived *Mil.*; no other negative than *mi* can precede it: *žábs-mtil-la ču rég-pa tsám-las mi γda* the water did not reach above the soles of the shoes *Mil.* — 2. with *par* it expresses uncertainty, vagueness, *γšégs-par γda* he may possibly go, *Pth.*; *ₒdi yin-pa* (col. for *par*) *γda* he seems to be this (man) *Pth.*; cf. *ₒdug-pa.* — 3. to say, cf. *mči-ba.*

གདལ་བ *γdál-ba* another form for *rdal-ba.*

གདིང་བ་ *γdiṅ-ba* another form for *ₒdiṅ-ba*; also sbst.: *γdiṅ-ba daṅ bgo-ba* **carpets** and **clothes,** i.e. all sorts of textures, *Stg.*

གདུ་བ་ *γdú-ba* 1. another form for *sdú-ba* **to gather, to collect.** 2. another form for *γdúṅ-ba*(?) *Sch.*: **to love**; cf. *rnyed-la γdu Zam.*

གདུ་བུ *γdú-bu Glr.*, *γdú-gu Glr.*, *γdúb-bu* the usual form, **ring for the wrist, bracelet,** or for the ankle, an ornament of Hindoo women; *lag* (resp. *p̔yag*) - *γdub* bracelet; *rkaṅ* (resp. *žabs*)-*γdub* foot-ring; *sór* (col. *ser*)-*γdub* finger-ring *Glr.*; *γser-γdub* gold-ring, *dṅul-γdub* silver-ring; *γsér-ser-γdub* a golden finger-ring; **tág-če** *W.* to put on (a ring).

གདུག་པ་ *γdúg-pa* 1. **poison** = *dug*, *γdúg-pa γsum Dzl.* = *dug γsum*; *zás-su γdúg-pa zá-ba Dom.* — 2. in general: any thing hurtful, or any injury, mischief, harm done; as adj. **noxious, mischievous, dangerous,** *γdúg-pa-čan*, of animals, demons, wicked men; *dug-sbrúl γdúg-pa-čan* dangerous venemous serpents *Glr.*; *dre-srin γdúg-pa maṅ* many mischievous demons *Glr.*; *γdúg-pai bsám-pa* propensity to destroy, destructiveness, ferocity, of beasts of prey *Glr.*; *γdúg-pai ṅá-ro* wild screams *Mil.*; *γdug-rtsúb* **ferocity, malice, spite** *Mil.*; *stár-bu γdúg-pa ts̒ér-ma-čan* **buckthorn** with horrible spines *Wdṅ.*; also for **mischief done by evil spirits** *Mil.*

གདུགས་ *γdugs* I. resp. *dbu-γdúgs* 1. **parasol, umbrella,** *B., C.* — 2. **canopy, baldachin**; *spyi-γdugs* a covering, shelter, awning, for several persons *Glr.*; *γdugs ₒbúbs-pa* to raise a canopy, to put up a shade or screen; of peacocks: to spread the tail.

II. eleg. **mid-day, noon,** *sáṅ-gi γdúgs-la* for to-morrow noon *Dzl.*; noon-tide heat (cf. *dugs*), *γdugs-méd γdóṅ-pa γdúgs-kyis γdúṅs* an unprotected face is molested by the heat *Lex.*; *γdugs-ts̒ód* 1. **noon-tide, dinner-time,** 2. **dinner.**

གདུང་ *γduṅ*, resp. for *rus* (-*pa*), 1. **bone, bones, remains,** esp. as *riṅ-srél*, also *γduṅ-rús*, *sku-γdúṅ*; *γser-γdúṅ*, *dṅul-γdúṅ* the gold and silver palls covering the remains of the highest Lamas. — 2. **family, lineage, progeny, descendants,** *rigs ni rgyal-rigs-so, γduṅ-ni gau-ta mao* as to caste, he belongs to that of the ruler, as to family, he is a descendant of Gotama; also fig.: *saṅs-rgyás-kyi γduṅ Dzl.* the spiritual children of Buddha, the saints; *γduṅ-brgyúd yod* the house, the family, is still existing *Glr.*; *γduṅ*(*brgyud*) *ₒdzin-pai sras* a first-born male, by whom the lineage may be continued, frq.; also for any single descendant *Glr.* — *γduṅ-sgróm Sch.* **coffin,** *Schr.* **funeral urn.** — *γduṅ-rtén* funeral pyramid containing relics, cf. *mčod-rten.* — *γduṅ-rabs* **generation,** *ṅá-nas γduṅ-rábs lṅá-pa-la* in the fifth degree after me *Glr.*

གདུང་བ་ *γdúṅ-ba*, *γdúṅs-pa* I. vb. 1. **to desire, to long for,** *zás-la*, *ltó-la*, *Glr.* and elsewh.; **duṅ duṅ čó-če** *W.* id. — 2. **to love,** *šin-tu γdúṅ-bai ma γčig* my own dearly beloved mother! cf. *brtse-γdúṅ.* — 3. **to feel pain, to be pained, tormented, afflicted,** by heat or cold, thirst, lust, distress; **nyiṅ dúṅ-te** *W.* sad, sorrowful; *γdúṅ-bar byéd-pa* to make sad, to distress, *γžán-gyi séms-la*, the mind of others. — 4. **to be dried,** *nyi-mas* by the sun, of a dead body *Dzl.*

II. sbst. 1. **desire, longing, lust,** *γdúṅ-ba ži* (sensual) desire ceases *Stg.* — 2. love, *mos-gus-γdúṅ-ba dpag-méd skye* immense veneration and love arises *Glr.* — 3. **affliction, misery, distress, torment, pang,** *γdúṅ-bai skad* a plaintive voice, doleful cry *Glr.*

III. adj. 1. **longed for, earnestly desired.** — 2. **beloved,** v. above. — 3. **grieved, tormented** frq.; *yduṅ-dbyáṅs* a song expressive of longing or of grief, an elegy *Mil.*;. *yduṅ-séms* love-longing *B.*, and col.; **ǎ-ma-la dúṅ-sem-čan ₒdug* W.* he tenderly loves his mother.

གདུང་མ་ *ydúṅ-ma* **beam, piece of timber,** *má-yduṅ* principal beam, *bú-yduṅ* cross-beam; *yduṅ-ḱébs* beams projecting over the capital of a column *Glr.* — *yduṅ-sgrig* a raft *Ld.* — *yduṅ-ₒdébs S.g.* pedestal, base(?) — *yduṅ-zám* a bridge of timber or of poles. — *ydúṅ-šiṅ Sik.* fir-tree (Pinus abies).

གདུད་པ་ *ydúd-pa* **love, longing** *Sch.*, cf. *ydú-ba.*

གདུབ་བུ་ *ydúb-bu* v. *ydú-bu.*

གདུབ་པ་ *ydúb-pa Stg.*: *zás-la,* adj., **frugal, temperate?**

གདུམ་(པོ་) *ydúm(-po)* **a piece** *Sch.*, = *dum.*

གདུལ་ *ydul* v. *ₒdul-ba.*

གདུས་ *ydus* v. *ydú-ba.*

གདེག་ *ydeg* v. *ₒdégs-pa.*

གདེང་ *ydeṅ* **confidence, assurance, cheerfulness** *Mil.* very frq.; *ydeṅ ťób-pa* to become confident, to take courage, to be reassured; *ₒči-tse ydeṅ čiaṅ med* when dying, he has no confident hope *Mil.*; *mi-ₒǰigs-pai ydeṅ* a strong confidence *Mil.*, *Thgr.*; *ydeṅ-tsád* id., *de-riṅ tsam yaṅ sdód-pai ydeṅ-tsád ma mčis-pas* not being sure whether his life will be spared for one day more; *ₒči-bród ydeṅ-tsád med* without confidence, without any readiness to die *Mil.*; *blo-ydeṅ Mil.* and col. = *ydeṅ.*

གདེང་བ་ *ydeṅ-ba*, pf. *ydeṅs*, *Cs.* **to threaten, to menace;** *Sch.* **to brandish** in a menacing way, *mtson-ydeṅ* brandishing a weapon *Lex.*; I also met with: *lag ydeṅ-ba Glr.* to raise and move one's hand (in a suppliant manner), cf. *dáṅ-ba* II., and: *bya yšog ydéṅ-pa* a bird with its wings raised and spread *Ma.*

གདེངས་ཀ་ *ydéṅs-ka* **head and neck of a serpent,** *sbrúl-gyi Glr.*

གདེངས་པ་ *ydéṅs-pa* 1. v. *ydéṅ-ba*, 2. = *ydeṅ*(?) **dáṅ-pa-čan* W.*, **ló-deṅ-pa* C.*, **deserving** or **enjoying confidence; faithful, trusty,** of servants, husbands, wives etc.

གདོང་(པ་) *ydoṅ(-pa)*, resp. *žal-ydoṅ*, 1. **face, countenance,** *ydoṅ skya* a pale face *Lt.*; *ydoṅ-dmar bod-yul* the country of the red-faced (more accurately: brown-faced) Tibetans *Pth.*; *ydoṅ-nág(-po)* 1. a black face; 2. **a frowning countenance;** *ydoṅ-čúṅ* dejected, disheartened, *ḱrel-méd ydoṅ-čúṅ mi byed-par* impudent and saucy *Glr.*; **doṅ-šrán táṅ-če* W.*, **doṅ-šran-te čá-wa* Kun.*, to be forward, bold, brazen-faced; *ṕág-gi ydóṅ-pa* pig's face, pig's head *Sambh.*; *ydoṅ-bži-pa* Brahma ('the four-faced'). — 2. **surface, superficies,** *sa-yžii;* **fore-part, front-part,** *dóṅ-la* adv. **in front, in advance** e.g. to go *C.*; *ydoṅ-ytád*, *Ld.*: *doṅ-stád* **just opposite;** *ydoṅ(-la)-ₒdéd-pa* **to push** or **press forward, to urge on** (a donkey, a coward to the fight), **to haul** (a culprit before the judge); *snáṅ-ba ydóṅ-ded-pa* to pursue one's course regardless of others (both in a good and in a bad sense) *Mil.*; *ydoṅ-ṕyis* handkerchief *Sch.*; **doṅ-si* W.* complexion, *gyur soṅ* he has changed colour; to *ťúg-pa*, and *bsú-ba* it is joined pleon.; *ydoṅ-lhógs* is stated to imply the same as *grúm-bu Lt.*

གདོད་མ་ *ydód-ma* = *yzód-ma,* **the beginning,** *ydód-mai dus*; *ydód-mar* **in the beginning, at first** *Mil.*; *ydód-kyi(s)* **first, at first, previously, before** *Mil.*; *ydód(-ma)-nas* from the beginning; *ydód-nas dág-pa* of primitive purity *Mil.* and elsewh.; *da-ydód Lex.* prob. = *da-yzód.*

གདོན་ *ydon* (ग्रह) **evil spirit, demon,** causing diseases etc , *steṅ ₒog-gi* superior and inferior (spirits), Rahu e.g. is *stéṅ-gi ydon,* an evil spirit of the aërial or heavenly regions; *stéṅ-ydon-gyis ₒči-ba Glr.* = *yzas ṕóg-pa* to die of epilepsy (*W.?*), or of apoplexy (*Sch.*); *ydon-čén bčo-lṅá*, or *bčo-brgyád*, frq.; *ydón-gyis brláms-pa Lt.*, *brlábs-pa Sch.*, infatuated or possessed by some evil spirit; *ɣdon ₒǰúg-pa* the entering of a demon into a person; *ɣdón-mi-za-ba* **certainty, surety;** *de byuṅ-ba-la* or *de byuṅ-bar ɣdon mi za* there is no doubt of such a thing having happened; gen. adv.: *ɣdón-mi-za-bar* undoubtedly, indubitably, *ɣdon-mi-ₒtsal-bar Dzl.* id.

གདོན་པ་ *ɣdon-pa Cs.* fut. of *ₒdon-pa.*

གདོལ་པ་ *ɣdól-pa, Lexx.* = *rigs-ṅán*, चण्डाल, **an outcast**, a man of the lowest and most despised caste, still below the *dmáṅ-rigs.* The Tibetan word for this caste was perh. originally *dól-pa* fisherman, and has afterwards been transferred to all persons that gain their livelihood by the killing of animals, and consequently are despised as professional sinners.

གདོས་ *ɣdos* 1. **fetter, chain;** *ɣdos-ťág* fetter in a fig. sense, bondage, *Thgy.* — 2. **material existence** (?), **matter** (?). *ɣdos-bčás*, *(b)rdos-bčás*, **material, corporeal,** *ɣdos-bčás-kyi lus Thgr.*, frq.; *ɣdos-bčas-su grúb-pa med* (these things) are nothing material, they have no substance *Thgr.*; *ɣdos-med* **immaterial, unsubstantial;** *ɣdós-su čé-ba* seems to be the same as *ɣdos-bčas*, and perh. also *ɣdós-pa ₒdzin Lex.* — 3. *ɣdos brgyáb-pa C.* for *W.* **ǩa kun gyáb-če**, v. *rkún-ma.*

གདོས་པ་ *ɣdós-pa* 1. = *ɣdos* (?) — 2. *Cs.* **mast, sail-yard;** acc. to Lexx. something pertaining to a ship; *ɣdós-bu* oar *Sch.*

བདག་ *bdag* 1. **self,** *ṅa bdag* for *ṅa nyid Dzl.* ༢༩, 14; gen. in the objective case: **myself, thyself, one's self;** *bdag ston ɣžan smad* to praise one's self, to blame others; *bdag sruṅ-ba* to devote one's self to solitary contemplation; or as a genit.: *bdág-gi* one's own, my, mine; *bdág-gi séms-la smad* he reproved himself *Dzl.; bdág-tu ₒdzín-pa; bdag-ₒdzin* the clinging to the I, the attachment to one's own self, **egotism,** frq.; *bdag daṅ bdág-gir ₒdzin-pa* attachment to the I and mine *S.O.*; *bdág-tu ltá-ba* prob. id., *Tar.* 35,18, *Schf.*: Atmaka-theory, *bdag-méd-pai čos Tar.* 36, 1 the Anātmaka, the contrary; *bdag-méd rnám-pa ɣnyis* are mentioned in *Thgy.*, prob. = *gáṅ-zág-gi bdag-méd*, and *čós-kyi bdag-méd Mil.* c. XII.; *bdág-gir med S.O.*; *bdag-méd* ultimately coincides with *stoṅ-pa-nyid*, *Burn.* I., 462 med. In common life, *bdag-med* is also used for **another**, **dag-méd-kyi mi** id.; **dag-méd-la ma taṅ** do not give it to another; *bdag-ɣžan* I and others, one's self and others; *bdag-nyid* 1. = *bdag* **I myself, thou thyself, he himself,** *bdag-nyid-la ɣsón-čig* listen to me! *Pth.*; *rgyál-po bdag-nyid* the king himself *Dzl.*; *ǩa-čig ni bdag-nyid ráb-tu ₒbyúṅ-bar ɣsol* some ask for the permission of becoming priests themselves *Dzl.*; *bdag-nyid ₒba-žig* only for their own persons *Thgy.* 2. sbst. **the thing itself, the substance, the essence,** *byaṅ-čub-séms-kyi bdag-nyid yin* I am the essence of bōdhi, the personified bōdhi, says *Mil.*; *ťúgs-rǰei bdag-nyid dkon-mčog-ɣsum* o grace personified, Triratna! *Glr.*; the Ommanipadmehūm is *saṅs-rgyás ťams-čád-kyi dgóṅs-pa ťams-čád ɣčig-tu bsdús-pai bdag-nyid Glr.*, i.e. the sum and substance of all the sentences of all the Buddhas concentrated in one word; *bdag-nyid-čén-po*, *čé-bai bdag-nyid* = *rdzógs-pai saṅs-rgyás* chief Buddha, Sākyathubpa, *S.O.* — 2. sbst. pronoun, first person, **I,** eleg., expressing modesty and respect to the hearer or reader, without amounting to our 'my own humble self', v. *ṗrán-bu;* plur. *bdág-čag, bdág-rnams, bdág-čag-rnams*, also in a general sense: we mortals *Thgy.*; *bdág-čag ťsóṅ-pa-rnams* we, these merchants here *Dzl.* — 3. **the I,** the ego = *gáṅ-zag Was.* (269). — 4. **master, lord,** for *bdág-po*, v. below. — 5. in natural philosophy **the element of solid matter;** also for **air** *Stg.* — *bdág-po* 1. **proprietor, master, lord;** *bdág-poi sgra* the syllable *pa*, as denoting the active agent, i.e. him that has to do with a thing, e.g. *rtá-pa* (not to be taken as 'definite article' *Cs.*); thus in many compound words: *ǩáṅ-bdag, kyim-bdag* etc.; *ťúgs-rǰei bdág-po* lord of grace, Awalokiteswara, *Glr.* init.; supreme lord, liege-lord, *klui bdág-po* = *dbáṅ-po, rgyál-po*; patron. 2. **husband, lord, spouse;** hence **á-ma dág-po*, or *sriṅ-mo dág-po**, a vulgar and obscene word of abuse. — *bdag(-po) byéd-pa* to reign over, to possess, prop. with *la*, but also with accus. *gha - sá - ča bód-kyis bdag byas* Tibet reigned over the province of Gha; *W.* also: to treat rudely, to handle roughly; *bdág - tu byás - pai bud - méd* a married woman *Thgy.*; *bdag-po-med-pa* (col. *mk̓an*) **unowned,** e.g. of a dog, *Pth.*; **forlorn, friendless,** without a patron, **a vagabond;** also for an unmarried woman; also as an abusive word.

Comp. *bdag-rkyén* (as yet not found in books) seems to denote **kindness, attention, help,** received from a superior, (yet, it would seem, not without some obligation or other existing on the part of the latter, and thus the word differs from *bka-drín*). — *bdag-nyid*, *bdag-méd* v. above. — *bdag-bzúṅ Glr.* prob. = *bdag-po*. — *bdag-bsrúṅ* **hermit.**

བདའ་བ་ *bdá - ba* I. adj. resp. **savoury, well-tasted,** for *žim-pa*; *C.* col. **dán-te**.

II. vb., pf. *bdas* = *ₒdéd-pa*, 1. **to drive, to drive out,** *p̓yugs* cattle; **to chase, to put to flight** *Dzl.*; *lás-kyis*, *lás-kyi rlúṅ-gis bdás-nas* in consequence of works, of certain actions, frq. — 2. **to carry away, along,** or **off, to hurry off,** *čú-bos bdás-pai gliṅ* land carried away by water *Cs.* — 3. **to call in, collect, recover,** *bú-lon* debts *Dzl.* — 4. **to reprove, rebuke, accuse** *Sch.*; *bda-ₒdéd byéd-pa Lex.*, *Cs.*: 1. **to drive, to carry.** 2. **to examine, to investigate.**

བདར་ *bdar* for *bda-bar*.

བདར་བ་, རྡར་བ་ *bdár-ba*, *rdár-ba*, **to rub,** i.e. 1. **to file, to polish** *Glr.*, **to grind, to whet;** *bdár-rdo* whet stone, hone. 2. **to rasp,** e.g. sandal-wood *Glr.*; **to grind, to pulverize,** *p̓yé-mar bdár-ba* to grind to powder, *Lexx.*; *lčágs-bdar* **a file,** *sá-bdar* **a rasp.** — 3. *so bdár - ba C.* **to gnash** or **grind the teeth;** *p̓yag bdár-ba* to sweep *B.*; *byi* and *p̓yi bdár-ba* **to clean, to polish** *Dzl.* — *Ma.* in two passages: **to pray earnestly,** which is the meaning required by the context, confirmed also by several Lamas. — *mdún-du bdár-ba Lex.*: पुरस्कृ, to place in front: to lead; to appoint; show; inspect; prefer; honour. — *skyel-bdár* fee or reward given to an escort *Sch.* — *brdár-ša Sch.*: '*séms-kyi brdár-ša* the nerves, sinews' (?); *bdár-ša γčód-pa*, and *rtsa-brdár γčód-pa* to examine closely *Mil.*; *raṅ-gi séms brdar-ša čod C.* take it seriously to heart.

བདལ་བ་ *bdál-ba* v. *rdál-ba*.

བདུག་པ་ *bdúg-pa* 1. vb. pf. *bdugs*, **to fumigate, to burn incense, to swing the censer** *Dzl.* — 2. sbst. **the burning of incense; perfume, frankincense,** more frq. *bdug-spós*, *bdug-spós-kyis bdúg-pa*, *Dzl.*; *bdug-spós ₒful* odours of incense arise *Pth.*

བདུང་བ་ *bdúṅ-ba* v. *rdúṅ-ba*.

བདུད་ *bdud*, *Ssk.* मार, Mong. *šimnus*, the personified evil principle, **the Evil One, the Devil,** the adversary of Buddha, and he that tempts men to sin, but not like Satan of the Bible, a fallen spirit, nor like Ahriman of the Persians, an antagonist of Buddha of equal power and influence, but merely an evil genius of the highest rank, by whose defeat Buddha will finally be the more glorified. He is also identified with the god of love (Cupid), काम; v. *Köpp.* I. 88. 111. 253. In later times he has been split into four, and subsequently into numerous devils; also female devils, *bdúd-mo*, are mentioned. — *bdúd-rtsi* (अमृत. सुधा) 1. **the drink of gods, nectar,** frq.; fig.: *čos-kyi bdúd-rtsi* the nectar of the doctrine, and similar expressions; even common beer, when drunk by a Lama, may resp. be called so. — 2. a praising epithet of medicines; *bdud-rtsi-lṅa-lúm* a bath prepared of a decoction of five holy plants, viz. *šúg-pa*, *bá-lu*, *ṫse-pád*, *k̓ám-pa*, and *ₒóm - bu*. — 3. **myrobalan,** Terminalia citrina, *Wdṅ.* — 4. a kind of brandy (?) — 5. *bdud-rtsi-dmár-po* a demon.

བདུན་ *bdun* 1. **seven,** *bdún-pa*, *bdún-po*, cf. *dgu*; *bdún-ču* seventy; *bdun-ču-rtsa-γčig*, (*W.* **bdun - ču - don - γčig**), *don-γčig*, seventy one etc.; *bdun-brgyá* seven hundred, *bdun-stóṅ* seven thousand etc. — *lús - kyi bdún-po* the seven (principal) parts of the body, viz. hands, feet, shoulders, and neck, (those of holy men are of a goodly size, long and stately) *Stg.* — *bdun-ṗrág* (ἑβδομάς) seven days, a week, *S.g.* — **dún-na-tsẹ** *W.* a child born before the natural time, a seven months' child.

བདུར་བ་ *bdur-ba Sch.* **to belong to a class** (?).

བདེ་བ་ *bde-ba* (शुभ, सुख) vb., adj., sbst., *bdé-po* adj. *Mil., C.* (of rare occurrence), *bdé-mo* adj., col., esp. *W.*, 1. **to be happy** or **well; happy; happiness**; *mi bdé-ba* the contrary of *bdé-ba*; *ṅa bdé-ste* as I am quite happy *Dzl.*; *bdeo* he is happy, prospers, flourishes; *bdé-bar byéd-pa* to make happy; *bdé-bar ṗyin-pa* to come to a state of happiness, of rest, to a place of safety; *bdé-bar ɣnás-pa* to be happy, to live in prosperity; *bdé-bar ɣtóṅ-ba* to let alone, to let another be happy; *ḱyod bdé-bar btaṅ mi yoṅ* we shall not allow you to be quiet *Mil.*; in *C.* col.: **žọ' dé-mo-la mi žag** id.; *bdé-bar gyur-čig*, resp. *bžúgs-šig*, **be happy! farewell!** *W.* **dé-mo ča žig**; *bdé-bar btsá-ba B.*, **dé-mo-la kyé-če** *W.*, to be safely delivered of a child; *bde-bar ɣšégs-pa* he that has entered into eternal bliss, the blessed, *Sch.* (*Köpp.* I, 91?) an epithet of former Buddhas, *Ssk.* सुगत; *lus daṅ sems mi-bdé-bar ˳gyúr-ba* to be bodily and spiritually afflicted *Dzl.*; *mi-bdé-bai bág-med-na* fearless of adversity *Dzl.*; *mi-bdé-bar ˳gyúr-ba* **to ache,** of parts of the body; *mṅal mi-bdé-bar ˳gyúr-ba* to be in travail, to suffer the pangs of childbirth; *sems-bdé, blo-bdé, snyiṅ-bdé* **cheerful, merry, glad;** *šin-tu ṫugs-ma-bdé-bar dám-bčas-te* promising with a heavy heart, very reluctantly *Glr.*; *dga-bdé* v. *dgá-ba* comp.; *dus-bdé* (*-*mo** *W.*) **peace, a state of peace,** in *C.* frq. in conjunction with *žod-˳ǰágs* or *sa-˳ǰám*; *ži(-bai)-bdé(-ba)* **the happiness of rest, a happy tranquillity** *Glr.*; **peace** *Thgy.*; esp. the happiness of Nirwana *Thgy., Mil.*; *˳ǰig-rtén-gyi bdé-ba-la čágs-te* fond of a worldly life of pleasure *Dzl.*; *bdé-ba daṅ ldán-pa* happy, *bdé-ba-čan* v. below; ; *nas-skábs-kyi bde-ba* a happy situation *Glr.*; *mya-ṅán-las ˳dás-pai bdé-ba ṫób-pa* to attain to the happiness of Nirwana *Dzl.*; *dus-brtán-gyi bdé-ba-la bkod dgos* I must help him to attain to eternal bliss *Mil.*; *ṗan-bde* v. *ṗan.* — 2. **good, favourable, suited to its purpose** ... *na bdeo* (*W.* **dé-mo-yin**) the best thing will be, if I ... *Dzl.*; **gho dé-wa yoṅ** *C.* so it becomes intelligible; **good, well-qualified, well-adapted,** *ḱa lče bdé-ba* with good organs of speech *Pth.*; *smra-bdé-žiṅ* knowing to speak well, well-spoken *Pth.*; *nyáms-rtogs-kyi smra lče bde* a tongue skilled in speaking wisdom *Pth.*; in *W.* it is opp. to *rtsóg-po*: **lam de-mo** the road is good, may be passed without risk. — 3. in *W.* *bde* is also the usual word for **beautiful,** more accurately: *(*l*)*tá-na de-mo*; *mā de-mo** splendid indeed! **dé-mo man-na-méd** it is only for show

Comp. *bde-skyid* **happiness, felicity,** frq.; *bdé-˳gro* going to happiness, joining the happy (spirits in heaven), also *bdér-˳gro*, opp. to *ṅán-˳gro*; usually in a general sense, like our 'heaven'; *bdé-˳gro mto-ris-kyi lus ṫób-pa* to receive a heavenly (glorified) body. — *bde-čén* felicity, consummate bliss, frq. — *bde-mčóg*, शम्बर. सम्बर, a deity of more recent Buddhism, *Schl.* 108; *Tar.* — *bde-˳ǰágs* **prosperity, welfare.** — *bde-stóṅ* (acc. to a Lama's statement for *ṫabs bdé-ba, šes-ráb stoṅ-pa-nyid*), an expression for contemplation, v. *Was.* (144 and 141). — *bde-spyód W.*, **de-čód** *C.* **de-čӧ**, col. euphemism for **privy.** — *bdé-ba-čan* सुखवति, *bdé-ba-čan-gyi žiṅ-ḱams* **the land of bliss,** a sort of heaven or paradise, in the far west, the abode of Dhyani Buddha Amitabha, v. *Glr.* chapt. IV., *Köpp.* II., 27. — *bde-byéd* he who or that which makes happy *Cs.*, शंकर. — *bde-byúṅ* शम्भु, शम्भव, source of happiness, n. of *Siva*; as symb. num.: 11. — *bde-blág* **ease, content** *Cs.*, acc. to our Lama: **quickness, speed,** *nád-pa bde-blág-tu ɣsós-par ˳gyúr-bai mtsan-nyid Wdṅ.* a sign that the patient will soon recover. — *bde-légs* **well-being;** ... *las bde-légs-su gyúr-čig* they shall recover from ..., they shall prosper again after ... *Dom.*

བདེན་པ་ *bdén-pa*, सत्य, I. vb. 1. **to be true,** and adj. **true,** *ḱyod zér-ba bdén-no* what you say is true, you are right *Dzl.*; *bdág-gis nyés-pa bdén-gyis* it being true that I committed a fault *Dzl.*; *dé-bžin-du bden srid* it might be true after all *Glr.*; *šin-tu yaṅ bden* to be sure, that is true! *Glr.*; *de bdén-par ṅés-sam* is it quite certain that this is true? *Glr.*; *č'bden ltós-la bdén-par ˳dúg-na* ... see whether it is true, and if it is, then ... *Pth.*; *bdén-par ˳dzín-pa* to believe to be true, to take for granted *bdén-˳dzin žig-na* the illusion being destroyed *Thgr.*; **dén-če-če** *W.* (for *yid-čes-pa*) to believe, to be persuaded of the truth, frq.; *bden bden* very true indeed! certainly; *bden-bdén-ma* prob. something in which there is much truth *Tar.* — 2. to be in the right, to be right, *kyed bod-blon-rnams bden* ye Tibetan ambassadors are in your full right *Glr.*; **ṅa á-sál-la dén-pa soṅ** *W.* I have evidently been right.

II. sbst. 1. **truth**, in the abstract; but usually: **something true**, true words etc., *bdén-pa smra-ba* to tell or speak the truth; as adj.: **true, veracious** *Stg.*, (*W.* **dén-pa zér-k'an**); *mi-bden-rdzún* this is not truth but falsehood *Glr.*; *bden-pa mtóṅ-ba* to discern, to know, the truth, a degree of Buddhist perfection *Tar.*; *bdén-pa bži* the four truths, the four realities, viz. pain, the origin of pain, the annihilation of pain, and the way of annihilating it, v. *Köpp.* I., 220. Whether, when *bdén-pa gnyis* are mentioned, they refer to two of the just named realities, or whether they always denote absolute (objective) truth (*don-dám-pai bdén-pa*) and subjective truth (*kun-rdzób-kyi bdén-pa*) as mentioned by *Was.* (293), I am not prepared to decide, nor am I able to explain the meaning of *lám-gyi bdén-pa* and *˳góg-pai bdén-pa* (*Thgy.* frq.). *bden-pa-nyid* seems to be a technical term for truth, though the Buddhist understands by it nothing but *stoṅ-pa-nyid*. Nevertheless, the possibility of its being misapprehended from this reason ought to be no obstacle to the word being used in its original sense, and re-established in its proper right, the more so, as Buddhist philosophy makes but a mockery of truth by identifying it with a negation of reality. — 2. = *bden-tsig*, v. below; *Mil.*

Comp. **dén-daṅ, dén-da** *W.* **in truth, certainly.** — *bden-po* **a true, a just man** *Cs.* — *bden-brál Cs.*: 1. **'void of truth, unjust.** 2. **southwest part** or **direction'.** — *bden-tsig* 1. a true word *Mil.*, but usually 2. a solemn asseveration, often combined with a prayer, to which the power of securing infallible fulfilment is ascribed *Dzl.* and elsewh., frq. — *bden-˳dzin* v. above.

བདེར་ *bder* = *bdé-bar*; *gaṅ-bdér* **whichever you like, at your pleasure**; *či-bdér* has a similar meaning, v. *Tar.* 69, 14, and prob. also 192, 4; *bder-bkod* v. *˳gód-pa bdér-˳gro* v. *bdé-ba*.

བདོ་བ་ *bdó-ba* 1. *Cs.* **'abundance, exuberance'**; more corr., acc. to *Zam.*, where it is explained by *dár-ba* and तीव्र (unbounded), **to extend** (intr.) **without bounds.** — 2. with *la*, **to hurt, to injure** a person *Dom.* and elsewh.; *dgra bdó-ba* v. *sdáṅ-ba*.

བདོག་པ་ *bdóg-pa* I. vb. 1. *W.* **to get** or **take possession of, to stow away, to house,** **ston-tóg** the harvest; **to put into,** **gám-mi náṅ-du** something into a box; **to lay up or by, to keep,** esp. **dóg-te bór-če** in store, on hand; **ug náṅ-du dóg-če** to hold one's breath — 2. *B.* **to be in possession, to be possessed of,** gen. with *la*, like *yód-pa*, *dé-la rás-yúg gčig bdog* he is in possession of only one piece of cloth *Dzl.*; *k'yód-la ˳dí-˳dra-bai slób-ma bdóg-gam* have you such scholars? *Dzl.*; *nor mi bdóg-pa Dzl.* poor; *dgón-pa ni gáṅ-na bdog Mil.* where have you (where is) your monastery? *bdág-la p'úg-pa bdog* I have a cavern *Mil.*; in an absolute sense: *t'abs bdóg-gam mi bdog* are there any means or not? *Ma.*; *W.* **yin-dog-čan** is stated to mean **proud, arrogant**; **yóg-dog-čan** one that saves money, a scraper.

II. sbst. **wealth, riches,** *B.*; cog to *bdág-po*.

བདྲལ་བ་ *bdrál-ba*, pf. of *˳drál ba*, *Dzl.* frq. (s. l. c.)

མདག་པ་ *mdág-pa* a sort of large **unburnt bricks** of mud or clay *Cs.*

མདག་མ, མེ་མདག mdág-ma, me-mdág, **glowing embers, live** or **burning coals,** mdág-mai doṅ a pit for keeping them, e.g. for the purpose of melting metals *Stg.*

མདང་ *mdaṅ*, also *mdaṅs*, 1. *C., B.* **yesterday evening, last night,** frq.; *mdáṅ-gi rmi-lam*, also *mdaṅ-súm-gyi rmi-lam Glr., Pth.*, last night's dream. — 2. *W.* **yesterday** (cf *ḱa-rtsáṅ*); *mdaṅ-sáṅ Lex., Cs.*: 'yesterday and to-morrow, now-a-days'; perh. erron. for *deṅ-sáṅ.*

མདང་བ་ *mdáṅ-ba Sch.*: *mdáṅ-bai ɣnas* **place of cremation,** the spot where the burning of the dead takes place.

མདངས་ *mdaṅs* I. *Ssk.* ओजस्. तेजस्, 1. resp. *sku mdaṅs* **brightness of face, fresh and healthy complexion,** also with *bžin-gyi Cs.*; *mig-gi mdaṅs* bright eyes *Lt.*; *ɣzi-mdáṅs* = *mdaṅs*; *dmár-bai mdaṅs* fresh, ruddy complexion *Glr.*; *dmár-bai mdáṅs-kyis* with a face beaming with joy *Dzl.* and elsewh.; the brightness is destroyed by disease, *ₒṗrog*, frq., or is fading away, *ₒčor Lt.*; in a relative sense: **appearance, exterior, look,** *mdaṅs-ṅán* bad, ugly appearance *S.g.* — 2. *Med.*: a hypothetical fluid, the most subtile part of the semen, a substance that pervades the whole body, esp. the skin, and is the primary source of vitality; cf. *Wise*, Hindu Syst. of Med., Calcutta 1845, p. 42. 54. 201. — *mdaṅs-bsgyúr* n. of a species of bile. — 3. **brightness, lustre, splendour,** in general, *nyi-mai, ₒjai B.* and col.; fig.: *dbáṅ-poi mdáṅs-ma mig ni ṅá-la med Pth.* I am destitute of the eye, that brightest of the senses, as much as: the most excellent of possessions is denied to me.

II. resp. *dprál-ba* **forehead.**

མདའ་ *mda* 1. **arrow,** *rgyáb-pa, ₒṗén-pa* to shoot (an arrow); *smyúg-mda* an arrow of reed, *lčágs-mda* an iron arrow; *dúg-mda* a poisoned arrow *Mil.*; *dprál-bai mda* an arrow lodged in the forehead *Glr.*; *mé-mda* 1. **a fiery dart.** 2. **gun, firelock** *C.* — 2. any straight and thin pole or piece of wood, e.g. the stem or tube of a tobacco-pipe; *šiṅ-rtai mda* pole or beam of a carriage; *lčágs-mda* an iron bar or rod, a ramrod etc.; *čú-mda* a jet or shoot of water, frq.; *(s)kár-da* *W.* a shooting star. — 3. = *mdo* 1. — 4. symb. num.: 5.

Comp. *mda-ḱúṅ* **loop-hole, embrasure.** — *mdá-mḱan* 1. **an archer.** 2. **an arrow-maker** *Glr.* — *mda-rgyáṅ* the range of an arrow-shot *Glr.* — *mda-sgró* the feathers of an arrow *Cs.* — *mdá-ču* the waters discharged from the lower parts of a valley, opp. to *ṗú-ču*, those of the upper part *Glr.* — *mda-ltóṅ* the notch at that end of an arrow which is placed on the bow-string *Pth.* — *mda-dár* a little flag fastened to an arrow; esp. an arrow with silk ribbons of five different colours. By hooking such an arrow into the collar of a bride, the match-maker draws her forth from among her maiden companions *Glr.* *mda-dóṅ* **quiver.** — *mdá-pa* **an archer;** *mda-dpón* **the commander of the archers,** a high military rank *C.* — *mda-sprád* v. *spród-pa.* — *mda-bér* perh. the more correct form of *ta-bér.* — *mdá-bo* a large arrow. — *mda-mó* **arrow-lot,** a kind of fortune-telling by means of arrows. — *mda-rtséd byéd-pa* to amuse one's self with the shooting of arrows *Cs.* — *mda-ts̀o* a troop of archers *Cs.* — *mda-ɣyu* bow and arrows *Dzl.* — *mdá-bzo-pa* arrow-maker. — *mdá-yáb Glr.* 1. *Lex.* = *pú-šu,* **fence;** hence **parapet, railing;** yet a Lama from Tashi-lhunpo declared it to be the projecting part of the (flat) roofs of large temples, on which the parapet is erected. — 2. **a covered gallery** on the top of a house *C.*

མདུང་ *mduṅ* 1. **lance, spear, pike,** *mduṅ-skór-ba* to brandish, to whirl a spear *Cs.*; *mduṅ-ḱyim Dzl.* 96, 9 a frame for leaning spears against; *mdúṅ-mḱan* a maker of spears; *mduṅ-túṅ*, or *ₒtáb-mduṅ* a short lance or pike, a javelin. — *mdúṅ-ṫogs Mil.*, *mdúṅ-pa* a spearsman, a lancer. — *mduṅ-dár* a lance with a little flag at the top. — *mdúṅ-rtse* top of a spear, spear-head; *mdúṅ-šiṅ* shaft of a lance. — *mdúṅ-bzo-pa* =

mdúṅ-mḱan. — *mduṅ rtse-ɣsúm-pa* trident. — 2. **sting,** of insects *C.*, *W.*, *mduṅ brgyáb-pa* to sting. — 3. *ɣser-mdúṅ*, *dṅul-mdúṅ* prob. the **two frontal muscles** *Med.*

མདུད་ *mdud Lt.* a medicine (?).

མདུད་པ་ *mdúd-pa* **a knot,** *mdúd-pa bór-ba* frq., *dúd-pa Lt.*, *byéd-pa Cs.*, **gyáb-ĉe** *W.*, to tie or make a knot, *sgrol-ba*, *ₒgrol-ba*, to untie (a knot); **ḍól-dud** *W.* sliding-knot, slip-knot, **šin-dud** *W.* a regular knot; *skra-mdúd* knot or bow of ribbons holding together the long plaits of the women; frq. fig. *sér-snai mdúd-pa* bonds of avarice *Mil.*; **nyiṅ-dud ḍól-ĉe** *W.* (to untie) to open one's heart to a person; *mdúd-pa-ĉan.* 1. **full of knots, knotty.** 2. **cloddy** (?) *S.g.* — *mdúd-ₒdra* a disease of the membrum virile, prob. paraphimosis *Mṅg.*

མདུན་ *mdun* **the fore-part, the front-side of a thing; the vis-à-vis,** *mdún-gyi nám-mka-la* in the heavens before him, over against him, *Glr.* and elsewh.; *mdún-gyis* adv. coram, **face to face,** *mdún-gyis ltá-ba* to behold face to face; gen. c. *la*, *na*, *du*, *nas:* 1. adv. **before it, at it, to it, from it;** 2. postp. **before, at, to** etc.; *mdún-la ₒóṅ-ba*, or *sleb-pa* to come up or near, *ráṅ-gi mdún-la sleb ma bĉug* he did not allow (the pursuer) to come near; *mdún-du skúr-ba* to send in advance; *mdun-du ṗyin-pa* to come near, to approach; to hasten to *Pth.*; *mi máṅ-po ťsógs-pai mdún-du* in the presence of a great number of people *Dzl.* — *sku-mdún-pa* **a waiting-man, valet de chambre,** v. *sku.* — *mdun-lĉóg* v. *lĉóg-tse.* — *mdun-na-ₒdon* (*C.* **dụn-nán-dọn**) 1. *Lex.* पुरोहित, **court-chaplain, domestic chaplain** or **priest;** so prob. also *Tar.* 58, 17. — 2. at present: **a high civil officer** or **functionary,** = *bka-blón*, vizier, *Stg.* and elsewh.

མདུན་མ་ *mdún-ma*, frq. in later lit.; one Lama explained it by *mós-pa*, another by: 1. **wife,** 2. **things, concerns;** *ₒjig-rtén-gyi mdún-ma* = *ₒjig-rtén-gyi bya-ba.*

མདེའུ་ *mdeu*, *Sch.* also *mde-ḱa*, **arrow-head** *B.*; *mde-súl Cs.*: 'the furrows or grooves of an arrow-head'.

མདོ་ *mdo* 1. **the lower part of a valley,** where it merges into the plain (opp. to *ṗu*), = *mda;* more frq. the place where one valley opens into another, hence in general: the point where two valleys, roads (*lám-mdo*), rivers (*ĉú-mdo*) meet; *lám-sraṅ-mdor* at the street-corners *Dzl.*; *ɣsúm-mdo*, *bži-mdo*, *ĉóg-mdo* the point where three, four, several (roads etc.) meet, esp. *bži-mdo* **a crossing, cross-road,** as a place of incantations; *mdo* prop. n. (in full: *dar-rtse-mdo*) province of the eastern part of Tibet, v. *ḱams*; **ₒdó-ru** in *C.* used as postp. = near, with, by, **ṅe ₒdo-ru** with me, **yul-gyi ₒdo-ru** near the village. — 2. *Ssk.* सूत्र, **aphorism, short sentence** or **rule, axiom;** hence *mdó-ru*, *mdor*, *mdó-tsam sdu-ba* to contract, abridge, epitomize, to give only the main points, frq.; *mdor(-sdu)-na* **in short, in general, altogether, on an average,** denique, frq. — 3. **Sūtra,** in the more recent Buddhist sense, religious treatise or dissertation, a sacred writing, *mdo-sdé* a collection of Sūtras, a part of the Kangyur; *mdo-sdé-pa*, *mdo-sde-ₒdzin* Sautrāntika, a school of philosophers, v. *Tar.*; *mdo-mdṅ* title of several collections of Sūtras; in quoting passages: *mdó-la*, *mdó-las*, in the *mdo*, according to the *mdo* (viz. is said, is written etc.) *Stg.*; *mdo-sṅob* giving a benediction to the host for his entertainment *Mil.*, cf. *Köpp.* I, 143. At present a distinction is to be made between *mdoi* or *dbú-mai lam*, and *sṅágs-kyi lam*, i. e. between the doctrine of the sacred writings and a faithful and systematic study of them, — and of the more modern mysticism, which is mixed up with Siwaism, and seeks to obtain spiritual gifts by means of witchcraft, thus saving trouble and time; v. *Was.* (142. 177), *Köpp.* II, 29. — 4. *Cs.* *mdó-ĉan* **prudent,** *mdo-med* **imprudent,** cf. *ₒdo.* —

མདོ་ལེ་ *mdo-lé*, the tibetanized डोली *Hind.* **sedan-chair** *Pth.*

མདོག་ *mdog*, resp. *sku-mdóg*, **colour** (cf. *k'a-dóg*) *B.*, *C.*; *mdog-légs* of a beautiful colour; *mdog-mdzés* 1. id., 2. **a rose.** *Cs.*; *mdog-dkar-k'á* perh. the more corr. spelling for **do-gar-k'á** *W.*, light-blue; *mdog-γsál* a species of gall, lit. '**purifier of the skin**', *Med.*

མདོངས་ *mdoṅs* 1. the white spot, **blaze, star** on the forehead of a horse *Glr.* and elsewh.; 2. **the eye in a peacock's feather;** *rmá-byai mdoṅs*, *sgro-mdóṅs*, *mdóṅs-sgro* **peacock's feather;** *mdóṅs-mt'a-čan* **turkey-hen** *Cs.*

མདོངས་པ་ *mdóṅs pa* = *ldóṅ-ba*, **blind,** physically and morally, *B.*, *mig-mdoṅs-pa*, *mdóṅs-par ˳gyúr-ba*, to get blind, to be made blind *Dzl.*

མདོངས་གསོལ་བ་ *mdóṅs-γsol-ba Mil.*, *mdoṅs-sól žú-ba* or *byéd-pa Cs.*, **to congratulate, to wish joy** to another *Cs.*; *Zam.* explains it by *˳dún-pa* to wish, another *Lex.* by *ṅó-dga* joy; in the passage of *Mil.* it seems to signify thank-offering.

མདོམས་ *mdoms*, sometimes written for *˳doms.*

མདོས་ *mdos* a cross formed of two small sticks, the ends of which are connected by coloured strings ⊕, and used in various magic ceremonies.

འདག་པ་ *˳dág-pa* 1. *Sch.*: '**clay; cleaving, adhesive, sticky.**' In *C.* = *˳jim-pa* (*W.* **ká-lag**) a mixture of clay and water; *˳dag-žál S.g.* prob. id.; *˳dág-pa sbyáṅ-ba* to make such a mixture, *Cs.*; *˳dag-sbyár* covering, or stopping up with clay, e.g. the chinks of a wall or door, **˳dag-jár ˳búl-ba** to render such service to a meditating Lama as an act of piety. In *Pth.* *˳dág-pa* is mentioned as a kind of plastic art, and evidently signifies to mould, to model, to shape. — 2. = *ldág-pa Cs.*; *˳dág-gu Lex.* = *skyó-ma*, pap, pulp, prob. = *ldé-gu*. — 3. pf. *dag*, 1. **to clear, to wash away, to wipe off,** *dri-ma*, frq.: *rtá-la sol-byúg* (to clean) a horse marked or blackened with charcoal *Glr.*; *sdig-sgrib* (to wash off) the filth of sin *Glr.* 2. **to disappear,** of sinful thoughts *Glr.*, sometimes *γnás-su* to their own place, is added pleon. *Mil.* — Participle *dág-pa* clean, v. *dág-pa.*

འདང་ *˳daṅ* v. *˳dad.*

འདང་བ་ *˳dáṅ-ba Sch.* **to come to, to arrive at;** cf. also *brgya-˳daṅs*, sub *brgya.*

འདད་, འདང་ *˳dad*, *˳daṅ*, resp. *sku-˳dad* or *daṅ Lex.* **funeral-repast.**

འདབ་ *˳dab* **a train** of persons, *˳k'or-˳dab* **retinue** *Cs.*

འདབ་མ་ *˳dáb-ma* 1. **wing,** *sprúg-pa* to shake (the wings) *Cs.*, *γyób-pa* to clap them *Cs.* — 2. **ladle, float-board** of a water-wheel. — 3. **petal,** flower-leaf, frq.; *˳dab-brgyad* eight-petaled *Glr.*; v. *Schl. Buddh.* 248. — 4. **any leaf, a broad leaf,** also *lo-˳dab.* — 5. **fan** *Cs.* — 6. **flag** *Cs.* — *˳dab-čags* a winged animal, **bird,** frq. — *˳dab-ráṅs-pa* **full of leaves;** with leaves fully developed *Sch.* — *˳dab-γšóg* **flag-feather, quill-feather.**

འདབས་ *˳dabs*, rarely *˳dab*, **the side, lateral surface,** of a hill, of the body etc.; **surface,** *mčin-˳dabs* of the liver *Med.*; in a more general sense: *sgál-˳dabs* **the lumbar region** *Med.*; pleon.: *nágs-˳dabs-na* = *nágs-na* in the woods *Mil.*

འདམ་ *˳dam* **mud, mire, swamp,** earth and water, = *˳dág-pa*, but as a product of nature; *˳dam rdzáb B.*, **dam-tsóg* W.* id.; *˳dám-du*, *˳dam-rdzáb-la ˳byiṅ-ba* to sink into a swamp; **dam-pág(s)* W.* muddy plash, slough. — *˳dám-bu* **reed** for thatching, writing etc.; *Cs.* also **sugar-cane;** *˳dam-bu ka-ra?* prob. a species of reed in wells or ponds *Wdṅ.*; **dam-búr* W.* sugar-cane.

འདམ་ཀ་ *˳dám-ka Zam.*, *˳dám-ga*, *˳dám-ṅa*, *˳dám-pa Cs.* **choice, option,** *deṅ saṅ ˳dám-ka byéd-pa* to choose whether to-day or to-morrow *Zam.*; cf. *γdám-ka.*

འདམ་པ་ *˳dám-pa* (or *˳dóm(s)-pa Glr.* prov.) pf. *˳dams*, imp. *˳dom(s)*, **to choose, to select,** a bride *Glr.*; *mi-γtsáṅ-ba ˳dám-pa* such as choose impure things, cynical, lascivious characters *Stg.*; *˳dam-riṅ* choosing, turning over in one's mind a long while; *dgrá-bo γán-pa mi γtaṅ ˳dam-riṅ t'ábs-kyis γdul* prob.: not losing sight of your enemy, constantly watching, put him down, as soon as an opportunity offers, *S.g.*, and hence *že-sdáṅ ₒdam-ríṅ* a long lingering, lurking grudge *S.g.*

འདའ་བ་ *ₒdá-ba*, pf. *ₒdas* (prob. vb. n. to *bdá-ba*, *ₒdéd-pa*) **to pass over, 1. to travel over, to clear a certain space,** *taṅ de* this plain *Sambh.*; *žag dú-mai lam* (to perform) many day's journeys *Dzl.* — 2. c. *las*: **to go beyond, to surpass** *Dzl.*; *lhá-las dás-pai spos* incense surpassing that of the gods, i.e. that which is burnt to them *S.O.*; **to exceed,** *tsád-las* the measure *Lt.*; *gráṅs-las ₒdás-pa Tar.* surpassing number, innumerable; *bsám-byai yúl-las* (surpassing) the understanding or imagination, inconceivable *Glr.*; **to transgress, to trespass against,** *bká-las*, *krims-las*, a commandment, a law = *ₒgál-ba*; **to get over a thing, to get the better of, to overcome,** = *rgyál-ba*; **to go away from,** *mya-ṅán-las* q.v.; **to let go, leave off, abandon,** *čós-las* one's religion *Thgy.*; *bló-las ₒdás-pa?* — 3. with or without *dús-las*, *tse*, resp. *sku*, **to depart this life, to die;** *das-po* **the deceased, defunct, late,** *Lex.*; **de-lóg* W.* the soul of a deceased person, **ghost, apparition;** the re-appearing is possible only for about forty days after death, as long as the Bardo lasts, v. *bar-do*. — 4. **to pass by,** = to disappear, *nyi-zlá ₒdás-nas* when the sun and the moon have disappeared (for a time); very frq. relative to time: **to pass away, to elapse,** *ₒdás-pai dus* the time that has passed, is gone, past time, v. *dus* 5.; *zla dgu ₒdás-nas* after nine months *Lt.*; *ₒdus-ló* the year past, *ₒdas-zlá* the month past, *ₒdas-žág* the day past; **de-zág-la* W.* **the other day, lately;** *nyin-mtsán čós-kyis ₒdá-bar bya* day and night are spent in religious exercises; *dgé-bai byá-ba kó-nas dus ₒda Tar.* (time) spent in none but works of virtue. — *ₒdá-ga (-ma) Cs.* **hour of death,** *ₒda-ga-ye-šés* मृति ज्ञान, knowledge of the hour of death (title of a book).

འདར་བ་ *ₒdár-ba* **to tremble, shudder, shiver, quake,** *gráṅ-bas ₒdar-ba* to shiver with cold; *ₒjigs-pas* (to tremble) with fear; *ₒdár-žiṅ ₒgúl-ba* id.; *ₒdár-bar ₒgyúr-ba* to begin to tremble; *ₒdar-yám Sch.* doubting, wavering, undetermined, *ₒdar-yám byéd-pa* to doubt, to waver.

འདལ་ *ₒdal* (?) *ru-ₒdál*, *ru-ₒdrél* **a single horn** *Sch.* — *bad-ₒdál* prov., being left exhausted on the road, sinking under fatigue.

འདལ་འདལ་ *ₒdal-ₒdál* v. *tá-bag*.

འདལ་བ་ *ₒdál-ba* = *dál-ba*, *ču-ₒdál* **still water** *Lex.*

འདི་ *ₒdi* demonstr. pron. **this,** *ṅai bu ₒdi* this my son; *ṅai ₒdi* this of me, i.e. that which I am doing just now *Glr.*, what I am experiencing just now *Mil.*: **the present, the respective,** *ₒgrúb-pa-po ₒdi* the respective performer (of an incantation) *Dom.*; such a one, *bdag miṅ ₒdi žes-byá-ba* I, such and such a one *Thgr.*, also *ₒdi daṅ ₒdi (-lta-bu)* and similar expressions, *ṅas kyód-la ₒdi daṅ ₒdi-lta-bu žig sbyin-no* I give you such and such a thing. On the difference between *ₒdi* and *de* v. *de*; the plural forms and derivatives of both of them are in conformity; only the following may be particularly mentioned: *ₒdi-ka-ráṅ* is used also for **just here, just now** *Mil.*; *ₒdi-lta-ste* **for instance, to wit, such as, viz.;** also pleon. with *žé-na: gnyis gaṅ že-na ₒdi-lta-ste Wdṅ.*; *či pyir žé-na ₒdi-lta-ste Pth.*; *ₒdi-ltar* **so, in this manner,** *čii pyir kyod ₒdi-ltar gyur* in what manner have you become so, how did you get into this condition? *Dzl.* frq.; *ₒdi-ltar-ro* it ran thus, it was to this effect, of this purport *Glr.* frq.; *ṅa ₒdi-ltar yin* such I am, I am, live, go, just as you see me here *Mil.*; in the verse: *ₒdus-byas čos-rnams ₒdi-ltar blta* 'compounded things must be regarded thus' — the word *ₒdi-ltar* is meant to be accompanied by a snap of the fingers (*se-gól*, or *skád-čig-ma*); *ₒdi-nas* **from this place, from this time present, as yet, still.** *ₒdi (daṅ) pyi (-ma)* the present and the future life, frq.; *ₒdi pyid sdéb-pa*, *rjé-ba* to exchange this life for the future one, i.e. *tse pyi-ma blós-btaṅ-ste ₒdii don sgrúb-pa* to be earthly minded *C.*; **di-zug*, *ï-zug* W.*, so, thus; **di-riṅ* W.* to-day; *ₒdi-ru* (come) **in here, into this place; here, at this place,** frq.; **now,** seldom.

འདིག ˳*dig* **stopper, stopple,** also *ƙa-˳dig;* **dig-če** *Ld.* to put in a stopper; **to stop up,** to close with a stopper; **dig-ril** *C.* **musket-ball.** Cf. *dig.*

འདིང་བ ˳*diṅ-ba,* pf. *btiṅ, fut. ydiṅ, imp. tiṅ(s),* **to spread on the ground,** a mat, carpet etc.; **to scatter, sprinkle, strew,** grass or hay to lie upon, ashes on the snow etc.; **btin-ba** sbst. *W.* **a small carpet,** on which the Lamas use to sit: **mal-btin** *C.* **bedding, pillow,** or **blanket.** — ˳*diṅ rgyáb-pa Sch.* **to weigh in one's mind,** to consider; to suspect, to entertain a suspicion.

འདུ(ན)་ཁང་ ˳*dú(n)-ƙaṅ* **meeting-house, house of assembly;** *čos˳čád-pai* (quasi) **church, chapel** *Dzl.*

འདུ་འཁྲུག ˳*du-˳ƙrug* **tumult, riot, uproar** *Cs.*

འདུ་བ ˳*dú-ba,* pf. ˳*dus,* (vb. n. to *sdúd-pa*) 1. **to come together, to assemble,** of men and animals; ˳*dun-ƙáṅ-du Dzl.;* ˳*dús-sam ma* ˳*dus* are they already assembled? *daṅ* with (a person) *Tar.*; in order to fight *Stg.*; of things: *nyés-pa ťams-čád dei lús-la* ˳*duo,* v. *nyes-pa;* ˳*du-ba* and ˳*dus-pa* sbst. **a coming together, an assembling, a gathering,** esp. in *Med.* a (somewhat indefinite) **disease, or cause of disease;** ˳*dus-sa* **meeting-place** *Glr.*; *las-mi maṅ-po* ˳*dus-sa* an establishment comprizing many workmen, **manufactory, workshop, workhouse,** **dzóm-˳du yóṅ-gin* ˳*dug** *C.* they flock or crowd together; *ťsoṅ-˳dus* the assembled traders or dealers, **the market** frq.; *skyabs-kun-˳dus* 'a collection of all the refuges' is a name given to Milaraspa. — 2. **to unite, to join one another,** *ƙyo-šúg-tu* as husband and wife, **to get married;** in a special sense in philosophical language: 1. **to unite** (opp. to ˳*brál-ba*), e.g. the soul uniting with an organ of sense, like *sdéb-pa, Mil.* 2. ˳*dus-byás* composed of two or more ingredients, ˳*dus-ma-byas* consisting of one thing, simple, elementary; only this is eternal, every thing compounded is perishable, frq. — 3. **to be pressed** or **crowded together,** **šril dús-te dug** *Ld.* they stand crowded, in serried files or ranks; intellectually: *dam-čos* ˳*dus-pa* a compressed system of religion. — 4. ˳*dús-pa* **to consist of** or **in,** *γnyis-su* ˳*dus-so* (religion) consists of two things *Thgy.; snaṅ-srid séms-su* ˳*dús-te γda* the external world consists of spirit, is spirit, i.e. is nothing *Mil.* — 5. col.: **to be drawn together, to contract, to shrink,** **dus ča dug** *Ld.* it shrinks, e.g. wood or paper from heat; **tsa-˳du** *C.* prob. **cramp, spasm, convulsion;** **dús-ƙan** *Ld.* **elastic, springy.**

འདུ་བྱེད ˳*du-byéd, Ssk.* **संस्कार,** (the Tibetan word is nothing but a literal translation of the *Ssk. saṅskāra;* cf. also ˳*du-šés* and *p̔úṅ-po*) 'one of the obscurest and most difficult terms of Buddhist philosophy' *Köpp.* I, 603, where the various translations are enumerated that have been attempted, such as: idea, notion, imagination (cf. *Burn.* I, 503), action (*Was.*) etc. It should, however, at once be acknowledged, that the word cannot be translated into a European language, as the meaning given to it is not the result of honest research and observation, but a product of arbitrary and wild speculation.

འདུ་འཛི ˳*du-˳dzi* **noise, bustle, din, clamour,** ˳*du-˳dzi méd-pai dbén-pa* ˳*di* this solitude without any noise *Mil.;* ˳*du-˳dzi-la γnás-pa* to live in the midst of the bustle of worldly affairs; ˳*du-žiṅ,* ˳*du-lóṅ Cs.* id.

འདུ་ཤེས ˳*du-šes, Ssk.* **संज्ञा** ('con-scientia') corresponds in most cases to our **idea, notion, conception, image,** although sometimes **perception, feeling, sense, thought, consciousness** may be employed for it: *nór-la rtág-tu yód-pai* ˳*du-šés skyéd-pa* to combine with earthly goods the idea of constant possession *S.O.* and thus frq.; *lús-la γrui* ˳*du-šés* ˳*júg-pa* to unite with the human body the idea of a ship, to represent the body as a ship, *Thgy.*; *skyó-bai* ˳*du-šes byuṅ* the perception, the feeling of discomfort arises *S.g.*; *ƙró-bai* ˳*du-šés-spán-ba* to detest the idea, the thought of anger *Dzl.; dgé-bai p̔yógs-la* ˳*du-šés čúṅ-zad kyaṅ ma γyos* no thoughts, no inclinations, tending to virtue, arose (in him), virtuous emotions never stirred in his mind; *ťágs-pai* ₒdu-šés-čan entertaining thoughts of sensual pleasure *Glr.*; ₒdu-šés slar rnyéd-pa to recover from a state of insensibility; as vb.: ₒdu-šés-pa, mya-ṅan-ₒdás ťob du-šés-te imagining that I shall obtain Nirwāna *Thgy.* As one of the five p̀uṅ-po it is translated by **idea** (*Burn.* I, 511), by **perception** (*Köpp.* I, 603). The three terms ₒdu-šes-čan, ₒdu-šes-méd-pa, ₒdu-šes-med-min may be rendered: having the faculty of thinking, having no faculty of thinking, neither thinking nor not thinking (*Dzl.* ༢༣༦, 7), ₒdu-šes-čan refers to human beings, the two other terms relate to celestial beings (v. *Köpp.* I, 261, 17 and 26), that are evidently so much the more excellent and exalted, as they are far above all reasoning and thinking. According to another, and (it would seem) more natural interpretation, the first of these three terms implies **rational** beings (man), the second **irrational** beings (higher animals), and the third **quite irrational** creatures (lower animals, worms, reptiles, that are not even possessed of the sensitive powers of the higher animals), whilst the 'long-lived Lhas' of the 17th. heaven are classed together with the common Lhas (who however taken strictly, belong to the 'first world') and on account of their stupidity are believed to be incapable of ever being converted, *Thgy.*

འདུག་པ་ ₒdúg-pa (eleg. ydá-ba, resp. bžúgs-pa) 1. **to sit**, syn. with sdód-pa; with *na*, *la* etc.; **to sit down** with termin. or *la*; **to sit up** (in bed); ₒdúg-par ₒgyúr **to get seated** *Dzl.* ༥༦, 6; **to remain sitting**, to keep one's seat, *Dzl.* ༥༦, 7; **to remain, to stay**, ₒdir ma ₒdúg-par soṅ žig *Dzl.*; **to remain behind, to stay at home**, with or without p̀yir, k̀yim-na etc. *Dzl.* — 2 **to be, to exist, to live** *Glr.*: ... skabs-med ₒ'dug-go!' there is no chance of ... Yes, there is! ... ₒdug šés-nas knowing that ... is still alive *Dzl.*; dráṅ-sroṅ byéd-čiṅ ₒdug he lives as a hermit *Dzl.*; **to be, to live at a certain place**, ynás-na ₒdúg-pa the being somewhere *Gram.*; p̀a-má gáṅ-na ₒdug where are my parents now? **to be at home** *Dzl.* and elsewh.; **to be extant, to be found**, čaṅ mi ₒdug nothing is, or was to be found, nothing was there *Mil.*; as partic. joined with, or put inst. of the possess. pron.: k̀o-ráṅ daṅ (k̀oi) bu brgyad ₒdúg-pa he and his eight children being with him *Mil.* (yód-pa is construed in the same manner); in quotations: to be found, to be written, to be met with, ... yod zér-ba ... na ₒdug the account of being ... is to be found in ..., *Glr.* — 3. **to be**, as copula, in *B.* often with termin.: k̀yim-par ₒdúg-pa to be a layman *Stg.*; rkáṅ-pa k̀ra-bor ₒdug the foot was variously coloured *Dzl.*; ₒdi-rnams mi-ma-yin-du ₒdúg-pas as these are spirits *Mil.* Generally speaking, this termin case is not to be pressed, nor always to be explained by: **to have become**, or to be translated by: **in**, as in the following: rgya-gár-gyi yi-ger ₒdúg-pas to be (written) in the Indian language *Glr.* — 4. **to be**, as auxiliar vb., 1. with the termin. of the inf., often merely paraphrastically, e.g. yód-par ₒdúg-pa = yód-pa *Glr.*; frq., however, indicating doubtfulness and uncertainty: ṅa ni šaṅ či-bar ₒdug may be I shall die to-morrow *Glr.*; k̀yed ... yin-par-ₒdug you seem to be, you are, I dare say *Mil.*; ₒgro dgós-par ₒdug I suppose you must go *Glr.*; stér-bar ₒdug it will probably be given *Glr.*; ma mťóṅ-na mi rtógs-par ₒdug if we had not seen it, we should probably not have known it *Mil.*; in the same manner it is used with yód-pa, q.v. — 2. with a verbal root, in ancient lit. hardly ever occurring, in more recent writings used paraphrastically like ₒdúg-pa, with the termin. of the inf. (v. above 1), but not indicating a certain tense, e.g. rdol ₒdug it makes its appearance, comes to light, *Glr.*, bšig ₒdug they were destroyed *Glr.*; in col. language (in *W.* at least) it is gen. a sign of the pres. tense: zer ₒdug I say, thou sayest etc.; only in *Bal.* it indicates the fut. tense. — 3. with the gerund in *te* or *nas* vulgo for the pres. or preterite tense, frq.; in *B.* of so rare occurrence, that it is prob. to be regarded as a vulgarism to be charged on the copyists, and to be corrected accordingly. — **4.** with *gin* (*B.* and col.) and *čiṅ* (*B.*), denoting **a continued action, state,** or **condition,** as in English: I am looking. — ˳*dúg-ynas*, ˳*dúg-sa*, **place of residence, abode.**

འདུད་པ ˳*dúd-pa*, pf. *btud*, fut. *ydud* (*Cs.*), imp. *dud*, *tud* (*Cs.*), **to bend** or **bow down, to incline,** *rná - ba*, to incline one's ears to hear, (also used of animals), cf. our 'to prick the ears', *Dzl.*; **to bow, to make a bow,** *la*, to a person; *žábs-la* at a person's feet, to kneel down before a person.

འདུན ˳*dun*, *go-*˳*dún*, = *sna-tsogs* **of several kinds, divers, sundry, various,** *Lex.*

འདུན་པ ˳*dún - pa* 1. vb. **to desire, to wish earnestly,** with *la*, *nyán-pa-la mi* ˳*dún - par* they not having any desire to hear *Pth.*; *dgé-ba-la* to strive after virtue, frq.; also ˳*dún-pa* alone (without *dgé-ba-la*) id. *Thg.*; **lo čö-la* ˳*dụm - pa** *C.* religious interest, concern for religion; to be zealous, to take a warm interest *Mil.* — 2. sbst. **a desire** *Thgy.*; **a supplication** *Dzl.*, *Glr.* Cf. *dún-pa.*

འདུན་མ ˳*dún-ma* 1. **advice, counsel,** *ṅán-pa* a bad advice *Ma.*; ˳*débs-pa* to give advice; *byéd-pa* to take a resolution *Mil.* — 2 **consultation** (v. examples sub *čúṅ-ba*), ˳*dun-grós* id.; *da lán-gyi* ˳*dun-grós* ˳*di-la* at this present consultation *Glr.*; *˳*dụm-ma jhé'-pa** *C.* to consult, to confer with (a person about a matter). — **3. council,** ˳*dún-mar bsdus* they called a council together *Mil.*; esp. in compounds: ˳*dún-k'aṅ* = ˳*dú-k'aṅ* q.v.; ˳*dún-sa* **meeting-place, assembly, union, association, society,** *dge-*˳*dun* an association of clerical persons. — 4. v. ˳*dum?* *ynyen-*˳*dun* harmony amongst relations, *Stg.* — **5. the state of being a bride; bride,** *C.*, and perh. *Glr.*; cf. also *dga-*˳*dún* sub *dgá-ba.* — 6. = *mdún-ma?*

འདུབ་སྙོམས ˳*dub - snyóms* *Sch.* **a state of comfort, ease;** ˳*dub-*˳*k'rúgs*, an interruption of that state, discomfort.

འདུམ་པ ˳*dúm-pa* 1. vb. **to reconcile one's self to, to be reconciled with,** *t'áb-pa* ˳*dúm-na* if contending parties are reconciled with one another; *rtág-tu mi* ˳*dúm-mo* they are constantly at variance *Dzl.*; *˳*dụm-ṭ'a** (lit. *k'ra*) *C.* contract, agreement, = *čad - don.* — 2. sbst. **concord, unison, peace** *Cs.*

འདུར ˳*dur* **thick and clammy** *Sch.*

འདུར་བ ˳*dúr-ba* **to trot;** ˳*dur-grós* **the trot.**

འདུལ་བ ˳*dúl - ba* I. vb., pf. *btul*, *t'ul*, fut. *ydul*, imp. *t'ul*, *W.* **túl-če** 1. **to tame, to break in,** *rta*; **to subdue, conquer, vanquish,** *dgra*; sometimes even **to kill, to annihilate** *Pth.* — 2. **to till, cultivate,** waste land; **to civilize,** a nation, which with the Buddhist is the same as **to convert**, frq.; **to educate, to discipline, to punish;** *ydúl-bai rigs-pa* those fit for and predestinated to conversion *Dzl.*; *ydúl - bya* id. frq.; also used substantively: ˳*gró - ba ṅá - yi ydúl-bya yin* the beings are to be converted by me *Glr.*; *bdag k'yéd-kyi ydúl-byar šog čig* may we become your converts!

II. sbst. **विनय 1. the taming** etc. — 2. also ˳*dúl-bai sde*, the disciplinary part of the Kangyur, ˳*dul-ba-las* from, or according to the Dulwa; ˳*dúl - bai brda* an expression (taken) from the Dulwa.

འདུས་པ ˳*dús-pa*, v. ˳*dú-ba.*

འདེ་གུ ˳*dé-gu*, v. *ldé-gu.*

འདེ་བ ˳*dé-ba*, v. *ldé-ba.*

འདེག(ས)་པ ˳*dég(s) - pa*, pf. *bteg(s)*, fut. *ydeg*, imp. *t'eg*, *W.* **tág - če**. imp. **tog**, **to lift, to raise, to elevate**, the head, the tail, also fig.; *sgrón - me Glr.*, *'*od-ṭ'o** *W.*, to hold up a lamp, a light; also fig.: to let one's light shine to others; *grágs-pai gó - sar* ˳*dégs - pa* to raise to a high rank; **to support, sustain, maintain, keep up,** *Pth.*; *rám-bu* ˳*dégs-pa* to join in singing, to fall in with, *Dzl.* and elsewh. (*Sch.* erron. 'to bawl, to blare'); *rá-mda* ˳*dégs-pa* to help; for **ži tág - če** and similar phrases cf. the secondary forms *tég - pa*, *tégs-pa*, ˳*t'égs-pa*; with or without *srán-la*, *rgyá-ma-la* etc.: to put on the balance, **to weigh,** *B.*; *žib-btégs* weighed accurately

Lt.; ₒ*dégs-k̔al* 'a bushel by weight' *Cs.*, or rather: twenty points on the large steelyard. — **ǰug-tág** *W.* **water-wagtail.** — **dég-k̔a** *C.*, *W.*, **weight.** — ₒ*dégs-dpon* is said to denote a military dignity, but is not generally known; as 'servant waiting at table', it ought to be spelled *stégs-dpon.* — ₒ*dégs-šiṅ* *Sch.* **yoke,** fitted to a person's shoulders, for carrying water-buckets etc.

འདེང་བ་ ₒ*déṅ-ba*, pf. *deṅ*, imp. *deṅ(s)*, **to go,** esp. *p̔yir ₒdéṅ-ba* **to go back, to return,** *Dzl.*, *Lex.* Cf. ₒ*doṅ-ba.*

འདེད་པ་ ₒ*déd-pa*, pf. and imp. *ded*, sometimes preceded by *rǰés-su*, **to go** or **walk behind,** hence 1. **to drive,** cattle, the herdsman walking behind the animals, whereas of the shepherd ₒ*k̔rid-pa* is used; *rlúṅ-gis gru* ₒ*ded* the wind drives the ship, frq.; also to drive through (a tube) by blowing, to blow through *Glr.*; to drive (animals, birds) from a place of rest, **to rouse, start.** — 2. **to pursue, chase, run after,** *rgód-ma* ₒ*déd-pa* to be in the rut (of a stallion); **ded táṅ-ċe** *W.* to chase, to hunt; **déd-de bó-ċe** *W.* to call after a person. — 3. vb. n. **to follow in succession, to succeed,** *rím-pa bžin* successively, of generations, *Glr.* — 4. **to call in, to recover,** money, debts; *bú-lon-*ₒ*ded drág-po* a severe dun *Mil.*; ₒ*déd-mi* a driver, e.g. the person walking behind the horse of a rider, driving it on *Lt.*; **the pursuer** of a fugitive *Glr.* — Cf. *bdá-ba.*

འདེབས་ ₒ*debs* 1. **puncheon** (tool). — 2. **time, times,** = **lan** *W.*(?).

འདེབས་པ་ ₒ*débs-pa*, pf. *btab*, fut. *γtab*, imp. *t̔ob*, *supine* ₒ*débs-su*, and *γdáb-tu*, *W.* **táb-ċe**, imp. **tob**; **to cast, throw, strike, hit,** variously applied, cf. *rgyáb-pa*, in *B.* gen. with instr., even if there is a dative in the same sentence, v. the examples; **ċog-tse-la táb-ċe** *W.* to strike upon the table; *rlúṅ-gis, γdón-gyis, nád-kyis* ₒ*débs-pa*, to be beaten by the wind, to be possessed by a demon, to be seized with an illness, frq.; *sṅágs-kyis* ₒ*débs-pa* *B.*, *mtu btáb-pa* col., **to pronounce a charm** against a person or thing, with *la*; *lan, ṅo-spród, gros* ₒ*débs-pa*, **to answer, to explain, to advise;** *γsól-ba* ₒ*débs-pa* **to make a request,** *smón-lam* ₒ*débs-pa* to offer up a prayer; *γsal-*ₒ*débs byéd-pa* **to remember well** *Mil.*; *γsal* ₒ*débs-su šes-pa* prob **to have a distinct recollection of a thing** *Glr.*; *rtsis* ₒ*débs-pa* prob. **to cast up an account, to reckon, to compute,** *dei rtsis-γdáb bdág-la med* I do not take that into account *Mil.*; *lús-la γzér(-gyis)* ₒ*débs-pa* *Dzl.*, **zér tab-ċe*, or *gyab-ċe** *W.*, knocking nails into the body; *rgyas* ₒ*débs-pa* **to seal;** **lúd tab-ċe*, or *gyáb-ċe** *W.* to spread dung (on the ground), to manure; *č̔us* ₒ*debs-pa* to sprinkle with water *Dzl.*; *ts̔a, ša t̔úg-pa-la* ₒ*débs-pa* to put salt, meat, into the soup; *sá-bon* ₒ*débs-pa* to sow; *gur* ₒ*débs-pa, sga-*ₒ*débs-pa*, to pitch a tent, a camp (driving in the tent-pins); also without a sbst.: *sṅar btab-pai č̔u-γšoṅ-du* (pitching) in the same dell where they had encamped before *Dzl.* ༢༧༡, 1. (*Sch.* incorr.): hence in general: **to found, to establish,** e.g. a monastery, frq.; *dus* ₒ*débs-pa* to fix a time.

འདེམ་པ་ ₒ*dém-pa* **to prove, to examine** *Sch.*

འདེར་ ₒ*der* *Glr.* prob. for *lder.*

འདོ་ ₒ*do*, for *mdo* 3., *Cs.* ₒ*do-yód* **prudent, clever,** ₒ*do-méd* *Lex.*, *Cs.* **imprudent, silly.**

འདོ་བ་ ₒ*dó-ba* 1. sbst. *Sch.*: **'a breed of fine horses'**; one *Lex.* has ₒ*do-rta* w. e. — 2. vb. *Cs.*: = *zló-ba*, **to say, to repeat;** *ma-*ₒ*dos-par* **unspeakable** (?) *Dzl.* ༢༥༡, 4 (the reading of *Sch.* dubious, v. *Schf.*'s remarks on this passage).

འདོག་པ་ ₒ*dóg-pa*, prob. an incorr. reading for *dógs-pa.*

འདོགས་པ་ ₒ*dógs-pa*, pf. *btags* (also *γdags!*), fut. *γdag(s)*, imp. *t̔ogs*, *W.* **tag-ċe**; imp **tog* or *tag toṅ**, 1. **to bind, fasten, tie to,** (opp. to ₒ*gról-ba*), *W.* **k̔yi tág-te bor**, tie up, fasten, the dog well; (v. ₒ*bór-ba*); *la* to a thing, frq.; also in a more general sense: **to fix, to attach,** e.g. a balcony to a house *S.g.*; **to tie round, to buckle on,** *go-mts̔ón lús-la* the armour *Pth.*; **to** put on, *rgyan* gay clothes, finery, *rgyan bzáṅ-po btágs-pa* beautifully attired *Mil.*; col. also without *rgyan*, e.g. **túg-dad-čan** *W.* fond of dress and finery. — 2. in particular phrases: *bkar-ₒdógs-pa* v. *bkar*; *mi-la skyon ₒdógs-pa* **to charge a person with a fault, to upbraid;** *sgro ₒdógs-pa* v. *sgro*; *túgs-la ₒdógs-pa* **to interest one's self in** or **for, to take care of;** *k̔yod túgs-la mi ₒdógs-pa ₒdi či yin mi šes* why he does not interest himself in your behalf, I know not *Mil.nt.* 37, 6.; with reference to things: **to have near at heart;** *túgs-la btágs-so* you have taken great care of me, a phrase frq. used, where we should say: I am much obliged to you! though Tibetans deny its implying acknowledgment and expression of thanks. — *dám-la ₒdógs-pa* v. *dam*; *p̔an ₒdógs-pa* v. *p̔án-pa*; *miṅ ₒdógs-pa* **to give a name;** *drá-bai sgó-nas* according to likeness or analogy *Mṅg.*; *k̔yeui miṅ či-skad ydags* how is the boy to be called? *Dzl.* *miṅ mi-ydúṅ-ba žes* (or *mi-ydúṅ-bar*) *btágs-so* they named him... *Mil.*, *Dzl.*; *miṅ* may also be wanting. — 3. *Gram.* **to join, subjoin, affix,** *rar btags ga* a *g* joined with *r*, i.e. *rg*; *ra-la ǰa* a *ǰ* joined with *r*, i.e. *rǰ*; *sa-la btags-pai ta-yig*, *st*; *ya-btags*, or shorter, *yá-ta*, the *ya* which is written underneath, the subscribed *ya*, = ◌ྱ; *yá-ta btágs-pa yi-ge bdun*, seven letters are joined with *yá-ta(gs)* *Glr.*; *smád-ₒdogs ysum* the three subscribed letters, *ya*, *ra*, and *la* *Zam.*; *ₒdogs-čan* 1. having a letter subscribed; 2. an open syllable with a vowel-sign, as *go* གོ, *de* དེ, *mdo* མདོ, etc. (not *da* ད or *mda* མདའ) *Zam.*; *a-ₒdogs* consonants with *a* (འ) subscribed, syllables with a long vowel. — 4. in philosophical writings: *btágs-pa* **conditional,** not absolute, *Was.* (228. 270), *btags-med* **nominal** *Was.* (281).

འདོང་བ་ *ₒdóṅ-ba*, pf. and imp. *doṅ* or *ₒdoṅ*, **to go, to proceed,** *so-sór* *Dzl.* **to separate, to disperse;** *rgyál-poi tád-du* (to go) to the king; *p̔yi-rol-tu ₒčág-čiṅ* to take a walk *Dzl.*; *dóṅ-ṅo* let us go *Dzl.*; *lóg-la ₒdoṅ-ṅo* let us turn back *Glr.*

འདོད་པ་ *ₒdód-pa* I. vb. (*W.* more frq. *tád-pa*), **to have a mind, to like, to be willing,** *zas bzáṅ-po mi ₒdod* *Dzl.*; *mi za ₒdod tsul byed* he pretends not to like this food *Lt.*; *sbyin (-par) ₒdód-pa ₒgyur* he gets inclined to give; *mi ₒdód-par ₒgyúr-ba* to feel no longer inclined; **to wish,** *nyán (-par)* to listen; *či daṅ či ₒdód-pa* whatever you may wish *Dzl.*; *rgyál-po ₒdód-pa* to wish to be a king *Dzl.*; as adj.: **wished for, desirable**, esp. with negatives, v. below; *ₒdód-par byá-ba* adj. **agreeable, pleasing, obliging, flattering,** *Stg.*, *Cs.*; **to desire to long for,** *k̔yim ₒdod* I wish I were at home *Dzl.*; *me daṅ nyi-ma* (I am longing) for fire and for sunshine *Med.*; *bú-mo ṅa mi ₒdod* I do not wish for a girl; *raṅ-ₒdód-žen-pa* **self-love** *Glr.*; (*raṅ-*) *bzáṅ-ₒdod* **self-complacency, vanity,** *Glr.*; **to ask for, to demand,** *koṅ-ǰo ₒdód-pa-la slebs* they came in order to ask for *Koṅǰo* (in marriage) *Glr.*; **to strive for, to aspire after,** *saṅs-rgya-bar* for holiness, for being like Buddha, for Buddhaship, *Dzl.*; **to be willing, to intend;** also ironically: *ná-ₒdod-pa* one that wants to grow ill, that does not take any care of himself; **to be ready, willing,** *bsnyen-bkúr byéd-par* to take charge of the waiting on (Buddha); *ₒdód-par byéd-pa* to make willing, disposed, to persuade to it *Dzl.*; **to maintain, to assert; to suppose; to pronounce to be** (cf. *ₒtád-pa?*) *Mṅg.*, *Tar.* and elsewh. frq. — *mi ₒdód-pa* to be not willing, not liking; **to detest,** *btsógs-pas kún-gyis mi ₒdód-na* as she was detested by all on account of her sluttishness *Dzl.*; **to be angry, indignant,** *žes mi ₒdód nas* thus exclaiming indignantly *Dzl.*; *mi-ₒdód-pa*, and *ma-ₒdód-pa* adj. **not wished for, disagreeable, adverse,** *mi-ₒdód-pai las* hard drudgery; *mi-ₒdod(-lóg)-pai rluṅ* adverse wind, frq.; **tsig mi-dód-pa zer-k̔an** *W.* one that slanders.

II. sbst. *Ssk.* काम 1. **lust, desire** in general; *ₒdód-pa kun zád-de* after all desires have ceased *Dzl.*; *ₒdód-pa-rnams-la čágs-pa* to indulge one's desires or passions; in a special sense, **carnal desire, lust, vo-**

luptuousness, = ₒdod - čágs, frq.; meton., coitus, ₒdód-pa spyód-pa to practise it; ₒdód-pai dus ₒdébs-pa to agree upon the time for cohabiting *Tar.* — 2: *Ssk.* इच्छा, **a wish,** ₒdód - pa γsum γnáṅ - na if three wishes are granted *Dzl.*; meton. the object of desire, ₒdód - pa tób - pa; ₒdód - pa daṅ ₒbrál - ba to be separated from the object of one's desire. — 3. **supposition** *Tar.* 45, 21. — 4. *W.* semen virile. — 5. **Kama, Cupid,** the god of love and of lust. — 6. symb. num.: 13.

Comp. ₒdod-k̔áms the world of sensual pleasure, the world of Brahma; ₒDod-k̔ams-bdág-ma, prop. n. = Skye-dgui-bdág-mo, = Dpal-lhá-mo. — ₒdód-mk̔an he that wishes, seeks, sues, **a lover, suitor,** cca., nai bú-mo ₒdód-mk̔an máṅ-po ₒdug there are here many suitors of my daughter *Glr.* — ₒdod-dgu all wishes, lus ₒdod-dgúr sgyúr-ba to transform one's self at pleasure *Mil.*, *Stg.* — ₒdód-čan, ₒdod-ldán, ₒdód-pa-čan eager, desirous *Cs.* — ₒdod - čágs (राग) **passion, carnal desire, lust,** frq., ₒdod-čágs skyés - te, ₒdod-čágs-kyis γdúṅs - te; as the highest of the three **guna** (cf. γti-mug) it corresponds to सत्त्व, **virtue,** and is symbolized as cock or hen, though Tibetan readers probably never understand anything else by it than sensual indulgence. — ₒdod-ₒjó v. ₒjó-ba. — ₒdod-dún strong desire *Cs.* — ₒdod-dpál prop. n. **Dodpál, a** large hardware-manufactory and mint at the foot of the Potala in Lhasa. — ₒdod-brál, ₒdod-méd, free from passions. — ₒdod-(pai) yón-(tan) 'wished for goods', earthly goods and pleasures, whatever is grateful to the senses, such as ₒdód-pa lṅa, a delight to the ears, the eyes, the palate etc. — ₒdod-lóg **unchastity, lewdness, prostitution,** spyód-pa to have illicit, esp. incestuous intercourse, daṅ with. — ₒdód - sred - čan **avaricious, greedy** *Pth.*, yet cf. čags - sred - čan; both words prob. signify the same. — ₒdod-lha = ₒdod-pa 5.

འདོན་ ₒdon *Lt.*, n. of a medicine (?) dkar, dmar, skyur-ₒdon.

འདོན་པ་ ₒdón-pa, pf. bton, fut. (*Cs.*) γdon, imp. ton, *W.* *tón - če*, the vulg. word for ₒbyin-pa, vb.a. to tón-pa, ₒbyúṅ-ba, **to cause to go out** or **to come forth,** i.e. 1. **to expel, throw out, eject,** from the house, village etc.; to take out, from a box; **to draw forth; to dig out,** metals; *záṅ-ton-sa* *W.* a copper-mine; *tón-te bór-če* *W.* **to put, set, lay, place out; to let out,** of prison *Pth.*; **to drive** or **turn away, to dismiss,** a servant, a wife etc., frq.; *ṅa k̔oi k̔a - ne čaṅ ma ton* *W.* I could not get or force any thing out of him; mči-ma ₒdón-pa to shed tears *Glr.*; with skad and similar words: **to utter, to set up** (a cry), **to make one's self heard;** hence 2. **to pronounce,** yi-ge γnyis-γnyis-su ₒdón-pa to pronounce two consonants as two distinct sounds *Gram.*; to pronounce a magic formula; klóg-pa daṅ ₒdón-pa-la góms-šiṅ practising reading and pronouncing *Dzl.*; **to say, to repeat; to recite** (sacred texts) with a singing, drawling tone, like that of mendicant friars; hence in general, to perform one's devotions; žal-ₒdón - du mdzád - pa, *Tar.* 95, 11, prob. resp. = k̔a-tón byéd-pa to repeat by heart; túgs-la ₒdón-pa prob. to read silently. — 3 fig. **to elevate, to raise,** k̔ri tóg-tu *Pth.*, or rgyál-sar *Glr.*, to raise to the throne; mgo v. mgo - ₒdon, sub mgo compounds; γžán - gyi srog to prolong a person's life, by affording him a (scanty) subsistence *Thgy.*; *sróg - ton - k̔an (-po)* *W.* the giver of life, ζωοποιός. — 4. *k̔a tón - če* *W.* **to sharpen** a scythe **by means of a hammer.** — 5. **to edit, to publish,** books, *Tar.* 47, 17. — 6. čos mtá - ru ₒdón - pa to arrive at the end and scope of religious knowledge *Mil.* — 7. *W.* resp. **to take, to taste,** to eat or to drink, don yin-na would you like a taste of that? dón-k̔aṅ dining-room; dón-gir resp. for ta-gir; dón-rag for ä-rag.

འདོམ་པ་ ₒdóm-pa 1. **to come together** *Lex.*, *Lt.* — 2. for ₒdám-pa **to choose, to make a choice** *Glr.* — 3. also ₒdóms-pa, pf. γdams, ft. γdam, imp. ₒdoms, 1. **to advise,** cf. γdám-pa. 2. **to exhort,** bág-med-pa-rnams-la wicked persons, brtsón-par to give diligence *Tar.* 3. **to recommend** *Glr.*, **to bid, to command,** v. γdám-pa. — 4. *Cs.*: **importance; business, occupation** (?).

འདོམ(ས)་(པ) ˳*dóm(s)* (*-pa Cs.*). 1. a long-measure, **a fathom,** = 6 feet, ˳*dom-gáṅ* one fathom, *S.g.*, as the usual length of a man, = *ḱru bži; šiṅ* ˳*dom dó* a piece of wood two fathoms long *Dzl.;* ˳*dom bčui doṅ* a well ten fathoms deep; ˳*dóm-gyis*, or ˳*dóms-su* ˳*ǰál-ba* to measure by fathoms *Cs.*; ˳*dom-gaṅ-gru-bži* 1. adj. measuring a square fathom; also a cubic fathom; 2. sbst. **a strong jail** or **dungeon.** — 2. imp. of ˳*dam-pa* **to choose.**

འདོམས་ ˳*doms* the pudenda, **privities,** regio pubis, ˳*doms(-kyi)-spu* the hair of that region, ˳*doms-spu* ˳*tóg-pa* to pluck out such hair *Cs.*; *rṅa-ma* ˳*doms óg-tu* ˳*ǰúg-pa* col. to take to one's heels; ˳*doms-stóṅ* vulg. without breeches; *sdoms-lpágs* foreskin, prepuce (?); ˳*doms-γtsáṅ(-ma) C.* a pure virgin; a nun; ˳*doms-γtsáṅ-pa* a chaste monk (if not rather *sdom* is meant); ˳*doms-rás* (also *čar-rás Cs.*) a small apron to cover the privy parts *Cs.*

འདོར་བ་ ˳*dór-ba*, pf. and imp. *dor* (cog. to *γtór-ba*, *stór-ba*, *byi-dór*, *ṕyag-dár*). 1. **to throw** or **cast away,** like *γtór-ba* and ˳*bór-ba Stg.;* esp. **to throw out, to eject,** spittle, frq.; *dri-ču* ˳*dór-ba* to make water *Glr.*; fig. *srog* ˳*dór-ba* to fling away one's life *Dzl.;* **to sweep out** or **away** *Dzl., Stg.* — 2. (opp. to *lén-pa*, *bžéd-pa*) **to decline, refuse, reject, despise,** things offered *Dzl.*; to reject, a reading, a passage *Gram.*; **to disapprove,** of an action as immoral; *blaṅ-dór*, ˳*dor-lén*, accepting and rejecting, deciding for or against, e.g. *dge-sdig-gi Glr.* — 3. **to subtract,** *dór-bai lhág-ma Wdk.* the remainder left after subtracting; perh. also **to divide.** — 4. *srog* ˳*dór-ba* also signifies: **to endanger life,** or **to deprive of life,** used e.g. of diseases *S.g.*; *góm-pa* ˳*dór-ba* (= ˳*bór-ba*), to pace, to step, to stride, frq.; *dmód-pa* ˳*dor-ba* v. *dmód-pa.*

འདོལ་ས་ ˳*dól-sa Lex.*, **fertile ground** or **soil** *Sch.*

འདྲ་བ་ ˳*drá-ba* 1. adj., *C.:* **dá-te**, **similar, equal** (which two notions gen. are not strictly distinguished from each other); ˳*drá-ba* ˳*di-dag* these equal things, for: these comparisons, *Pth.*; *kyed γnyis* ˳*drá-bar* ˳*dug*, ˳*dra-ba yin*, ˳*drao*, you two resemble each other very much; with a pleon. *mnyam: riṅ-ťúṅ mnyám-la* ˳*drá-ba* equally long *Dzl.*; gen. with *daṅ* or accus., seldom with termin., in various applications: *ḱyed(daṅ)* ˳*drá-ba ni* your equals *Dzl.; bud-méd-du* ˳*drá-bai náṅ-na* amongst woman-like, effeminate (men), *Dzl.;* ˳*dii byin ťsáṅs-pa daṅ* ˳*drao* his brightness is equal to (that of) Brahma *Dzl.*; *γžán-gyi dón-laaṅ ráṅ-gi* ˳*drar séms-pa* esteeming our neighbour's advantage as high as our own *S.g.;* *ťams-čád-la bu γčig-pa daṅ drao* he behaved to all as (to) an only son *Dzl.;* with a negative: *γžan yaṅ de daṅ* ˳*drá-ste γnáṅ-ba med* others shall allow it just as little as he himself *Dzl.; Saṅs-rgyás daṅ* ˳*drá-bar byá-bai ṕyir* in order to be equal to Buddha, to come up with Buddha *Dzl.*; *brtsigs-pa mi* ˳*dra skyés-pa* ˳*dra* not as if (it had been) built, but as if it had grown up spontaneously *Glr.*; *bdag* ˳*dra bud-méd blo-dmán kyaṅ* even a stupid woman like myself; *skra* ˳*drá-ba yód-dam* whether any thing like hair is still left? *Mil.; ťéṅ-ro* ˳*dra rnyed* he found the remnants of a carcass or something like it *Mil.*; *ro daṅ* ˳*drá-ba* as much as dead *Wdṅ.*; *mnyán-pa daṅ* ˳*drá-bai bšes-γnyén* a teacher like as a ferryman (conveying to the shores of happiness) *Thgy.*; *rtag-rtág* ˳*dra yaṅ* seemingly eternal *Mil.*; *skyid-skyid* ˳*dra yaṅ* even if it appears a blessing *Mil.; rúṅ-ba daṅ* ˳*drá-na* if it appears feasible *Dzl.;* *ster dgós-pa* ˳*dra* it seems I shall be obliged to give it *Glr.; da-lán ḱyod nús-pa če-čé* ˳*dra bžin byúṅ-ste* as your strength this time at least seems to be rather great *Mil.;* *ḱyed slu-slú* ˳*dra* you might easily be ensnared *Mil.; mi-*˳*drá-ba* **unequal, unlike, different,** *sṅon-čád daṅ mi* ˳*drá-bar* quite otherwise than formerly *Dzl.*; *čós-pa mi* ˳*drá-bar* not like, not befitting, a priest *Mil.*; **various, several,** **ḱa-zé mi-dá-wa* C.* several dishes; ˳*di-*˳*dra-ba*, *dé-*˳*dra-ba* **such;** *dé-dras*, (**dhén-de* C.* vulg.) **so, thus;** *či-*˳*dra-ba*, *ǰi-*˳*dra-ba* **of what kind** (qualis), *či-*˳*dra čig légs-*

par ston dgos you must tell me minutely how she looks, what kind of appearance she has *Glr.*; *p̓ug ci ₒdra cig ₒoṅ* what will be the upshot? where is this to end? *Glr.*; *ṅa ǰi-ₒdra-bar de bžin ₒgyur* he becomes just what I am *Stg.*; **ghán-dẹ** *C.* col. **how?** *ₒdra-ₒdra* (*W.* **ḍán-ḍa**) very frq. for *ₒdrá-ba*, e.g. *ša-dkár-gyi rgyu ₒdrá-ₒdra-la tíg-rtse-zer* something similar to the substance of tin is called zinc; *ₒdra mi ₒdra* like and unlike; **equality, likeness, similarity,** *ₒdra mi ₒdra ltá-ba* to examine the likeness *Glr.* — 2. sbst. 1. **resemblance, likeness,** v. *ₒdógs-pa* 2. — 2. **form, shape, appearance, phase.** *Thg.*

འདྲངས་ *ₒdraṅs* v. *ₒgraṅs.*

འདྲད་ *ₒdrad* v. *ₒbrad.*

འདྲན་ *ₒdran* v. *ₒgran.*

འདྲལ་བ་ *ₒdrál-ba*, pf. *dral* (cf. *rál-ba* and *hrál-ba*), **to tear to pieces, to rend asunder;** also **to pull down,** a house; **to rip up, to cut open,** an animal.

འདྲི་བ་ *ₒdrí-ba*, pf. and imp. *ₒdris*, 1. **to ask,** ... *la*, *W. nas*, a person; with accus. **to enquire after** or **about** a thing; *grós-ₒdri-sa* a place for asking advice, **oracle** *Glr.*; *blá-ma ₒdrí-ba* to inquire after one's Lama *Mil.*; *p̓a-mái ytam* after one's parents *Dzl.*; *ₒdrí-bai tsig* **interrogative pronoun,** e.g. *ci Gram.*; v. also *dri-ba.* — 2. inst. of *ₒbri-ba.*

འདྲིང་བ་ *ₒdriṅ-ba Glr.* fol. 57, 12? another reading: *ldiṅ-ba.*

འདྲིད་པ་ *ₒdrid-pa* for *ₒbrid-pa.*

འདྲིམ་པ་ *ₒdrim-pa* for *ₒbrim-pa.*

འདྲིལ་བ་ *ₒdril-ba*, pf. *dril*, I. vb. n., cf. *ₒgril-ba* and *hril-ba*, 1. **to be turned, rolled round** or **twisted into** a thing, *od-zér-gyi gáṅ-bur* to be wrapped into a covering of light *Glr.*; **to gather, to flow together,** as *p̓ó-bai bád-kan*, the gastric phlegm *Med.*; fig.: *blo-sems yċig-tu ₒdril-te* whilst our minds were flowing together *Glr.*; *yúl-pa-rnams k̓á-ₒdril-te ṅó-log-pa* **a conspiracy** *Schr.* — 2. **to roll down,** *ri-bo ṅos-la* the slope of a hill *Thgy.* — 3. **to fall, to fall down** *W.*

II. vb. a., cf. *sgril-ba*, **to wrap up,** *rás-kyis* in a handkerchief *Glr.*, *dar sna lṅas* in five sorts of silk *Glr.*; *zaṅs-kyis* (covered or sheathed) with copper *Mil.*; **to heap together, to pile up,** *mé-tog p̓úṅ-por dril* the blossoms are aggregated, heaped together in a panicle *Wdṅ.*; *dril-bas* **in short, to sum up all, in summa** *Glr.* — *ljags ₒdril-ba Sch.*: to play with the tongue, moving it to and fro.

འདྲིས་པ་ *ₒdris-pa* **to be accustomed to, to be acquainted with,** gen. with *daṅ*, *Glr.* and col.; rarely with accus.: *ynyen ǰi tsam ₒdris bžin* the more friends you get familiar with; *mig ₒdris čés-na* if persons constantly see one another, get perfectly used to one another, *Mil.*; mostly adj. (= *góms-pa*) **accustomed, used,** *mi* or *k̓áṅ-pa daṅ*, to men, to one's house; also *dris-pa* used absol. = **tame** *W.*; *dris-pa mi* an acquaintance, a sympathizing friend, an assistant *Thgy.*; *sṅar-dris-kyi mi* an old acquaintance, an old crony *Thgr.* A derivation of *dris-pa* from *ₒdrid-pa*, *ₒbrid-pa*, to deceive, to bait, to decoy, and hence to tame, was suggested by some Tibetans, but is after all scarcely to be authenticated.

འདྲུ་བ་ *ₒdrú-ba* v. *ₒbrú-ba.*

འདྲུགས་པ་ *ₒdrúgs-pa* **to fall into small pieces, to crumble** (away) *Sch.*

འདྲུད་པ་ *ₒdrúd-pa*, pf. and imp. *drud* (*ₒdrus?*), rarely *ₒbrúd-pa*, 1. **to rub,** *lus* the body; **to file, to rasp,** *šiṅ* wood, *Lex.*; **to rub off, to scour,** **bé-ma daṅ W.*; **to polish, to smooth, to plane,** *p̓ag-ste* with a plane *W.*; **to grind, to powder, to pulverize** (?). — 2. **to drag, to draw** or **pull along** on the ground, by a rope, *ro sá-la* a dead body on the ground (*ma-ₒdrús-par* without slipping (?) *Med.*) — 3. **dúd-de gyur toṅ** *W.* move, or push it a little aside; *dud cád-ce W.* to cut off obliquely (?).

འདྲུབ་པ་ *ₒdrúb-pa*, pf. and imp. *drub* (s) 1. **to sew** *Sch.*, so perh. *Dzl.* ༢༣༠, 11.

— 2. **to embroider** *C.* — 3. **to heal,** *rma* wounds *S.g.* — *tsem-drúb* needle-work *Sch.*

འདྲུལ་བ་ *ₒdrúl-ba*, pf. *drul*, gen. *rul* (q.v), **to become putrid, to rot, to putrefy,** *drúl-bar gyúr-ba* id.; *ₒdrúl-bar byéd-pa* to cause to be decomposed *Med.*; *rten-ₒdrúl* prob.: putrefied substances, *bšan-yčis ₒbyin-par-byed* are removed with the faeces *Med.*

འདྲེ་ *ₒdre*, also *lhá-ₒdre*, *W.* **lán-de**, **goblin, gnome, imp, demon, evil spirit, devil,** col. the most frq. word for such beings; quite in a general sense: *klu-ynyán-la sógs-pai lha-ₒdre-rnams; byá-ₒdre, ₒdre-rgód Lt.* prob. two particular species of demons; *zá-ₒdre* is said to be a word for 'owl'; *ₒdres ₒkyér-ba* to be carried off by goblins *Ma.*; *ₒdres-ynód, ₒdrei ynód-pa* mischief done by evil spirits; *ₒdre ₒjúg-pa* the entering of evil spirits, the state of possession; *ₒdré-žugs-pa* (*W.* **-kan**) one possessed by a devil, a demoniac; *skród-pa* to cast out, *ₒdúl-ba* to subdue (devils).

Comp. *ₒdre-ₒjigs-šiṅ* = *gu-gul-šiṅ*, 'devil's fear', a resinous wood, by the burning of which goblins are smoked out. *ₒdre-paṅ-ka* n. of the fruit of *sgóṅ-tog Wdṅ.* — **de-pu* (or *bu?*)*-tsúb** *W.* **whirlwind, water-spout.** — *ₒdré-po* a male devil, *ₒdré-mo* a female d., *ₒdré-bu* a young d., an imp *Cs.* — *ₒdre-me-bud* ignis fatuus, will-o'the wisp, Jack with the lantern *Schr.* — *ₒdre-dmág* a goblin host. — *ₒdre-lág* the left hand, the left side of the body being supposed to belong to the evil spirits *C.* — *ₒdré-šig* **'devil's louse', bed-bug** *C.* — *ₒdre-srin* goblins and Rakshasas, demons in general, frq.

འདྲེ་བ་ *ₒdré-ba* I. pf. and imp. *ₒdres*, prop. vb. n. to *bsré-ba*, 1. **to be mixed with,** *de ynyis ₒdrés-(-na) Lt.* if the two are mixed with each other; *pyogs-yčig-tu ₒdres* mixed together, miscellaneous *Lex.*; *ₒdres-mtsáms* (*ₒtsams Tar.*) the 'limit of mixing', *rgyá-mtso daṅ gáṅ-gā ₒdrés-mtsáms* the influx of the Ganga into the sea *Tar.* 178, 9; *tsig yžan ma ₒdrés-par* without mingling other talk with (the conversation); *ka daṅ snyiṅ ma ₒdres* a man with whom word and sentiment differ, **a hypocrite;** *čos daṅ čos ma yin-pa ₒdres* right and wrong were mixed together; in an absol. sense: *spyód-pa ₒdrés-te mú-stegs-par gyúr-to* his course of life degenerated, and he became a Brahmanist *Pth.*; *dúd-ₒgro ₒdrés-pa* an animal of a mixed race, **half-breed, mongrel;** *ma ₒdrés-par* without any confounding or mixing together, sharply discriminating *Mil.*; *ma-ₒdrés-pa* prob. **pure, unadulterated.** — 2. **to interfere, to meddle with,** **de le-ka daṅ ma de** *W.* do not meddle with that; **to have intercourse with, to engage in,** *B.* and col.; *ráṅ-sems blá-ma ₒdrés-pas bde* through your, the Lama's, intercourse with my soul, in your society, I am happy *Mil*; *ytam ₒdré-ba* id.

II. erron. for *ₒgré-ba Pth.*

འདྲེག་པ་ *ₒdrég-pa* v. *ₒbrég-pa.*

འདྲེགས་ *ₒdreys* v. *drég-pa.*

འདྲེད་པ་ *ₒdréd-pa* **to slide, glide, slip,** **déd-de gyel** *W.*, **ₒdéd-tag(?) šór-ne gyel** *C.* he slipped and fell.

འདྲེན་པ་ *ₒdrén-pa*, pf. *draṅ(s)*, fut. *draṅ*, imp. *droṅ(s)*, 1. **to draw, drag, pull,** a carriage *Glr.*; a person by his arm *Dzl.*; *drág-tu* violently *Dzl.*; **to draw tight,** a rope *Dzl.*; **to draw from, to pull out,** an arrow out of a wound *Glr.*; **to press** or **squeeze out,** matter, pus, *Med.*; **to tear out,** *ysóṅ-poi rgyú-ma* the intestines of a living person; fig. *ka-čig tser-snón-gyi rigs-suaṅ ₒdren* some reckon it (lit. **draw** it) to the species of Meconopsis *Wdṅ.*; **to cause, to effect,** *bde-čén* felicity *Thgy.*, *skyúg-pa* vomiting *Tar.* — 2. **to conduct,** water (*W.* **rán-če**); **to lead, to guide;** with or without *sna*, *lam ₒdrén-pa* to direct a person in his way; also sbst. **guide,** *ₒdren-méd* without a guide, without a king *Dzl.*; esp. to lead to happiness, felicity, frq.; opp. to *lóg-ₒdren-pa* q.v.; *yúl-du-dmag* to lead an army into a country, to wage war against it, frq. — 3. **to cite, to quote,** *luṅ* a religious authority *Cs.* — 4. **to invite,** a guest; **to call, to go to meet; to cause to appear, to conjure up,** a ghost, a deity; resp. *spyán-ₒdren-pa, ydán-ₒdren-*

pa; also for **to fetch, to go for,** if the object is of a sacred character, e.g. relics; *spyan ma dráṅs-par ₒgró-ba* to go uninvited *Cs.* — 5. **to place before one, to serve up,** dishes, meals; **to pour out,** beer, wine etc., ccdpar., frq.; resp. with *žál-du Pth.*; **to taste,** to eat or drink what has been offered, resp. *W.* (cf. *mčód-pa, ysól-ba*). — 6. **to count, to number,** esp. with *re,* or *re-ré-nas,* separately, one by one, *Glr.*, *Mil.*; **to enumerate,** *ma draṅs* ... are here not enumerated *Wdṅ.*; c. termin. **to count for, to consider, to look upon as,** *dpé-ru* as a parable, as not existing *Mil.* — 7. *W.* in a general sense: **to convey, to remove,** **zá-če ťúr-maṅ uaṅ den** food is conveyed by a spoon, **ka kyem daṅ den** snow is removed by a shovel. — 8. further: *rkaṅ* (resp. *žabs*) *ₒdrén-pa* **to insult, to scoff, to deride** *Thgy.*, *C.* — *me ₒdrén-pa* the blazing, flaring of a flame *Sch.* — *mgo-ₒdren* v. *mgo,* comp.

འདྲེན་མ་, འདྲེས་མ་ *ₒdrén-ma*, *ₒdrés-ma*, **mixture, medley,** e.g. in border-districts a mixed dialect, a mixed religion; a mixed colour, e.g. gray.

འདྲོངས་པ་ *ₒdróṅs-pa* = *ₒdrén-pa*, esp. in conjunction with *spyan: spyán-ₒdroṅs-sam ltos šig; mi ₒdroṅs-na* try whether you can invite him (whether he will come); if not, then ... *Mil.*, also *Mil. nt.*

འདྲོག་པ་ *ₒdróg-pa* 1. **to wince, shrink, quiver, start,** from fear: **to shy,** of horses; *ₒdróg-čan* **shy, skittish, easily frightened** *W.* 2. — *ₒdrog-slóṅ-ba Sch.*: **to take by surprise, to deceive by cunning, to outwit;** *blo-ₒdróg Lex.* w.e.

འདྲོབ་སྐྱོང་ *ₒdrob-skyóṅ Sch.*: 'the keeper of light' (?).

རྡང་ *rdaṅ* v. *ydaṅ.*

རྡབ་པ་ *rdáb-pa* v. *rdéb-pa.*

རྡར་བ་ *rdár-ba* v. *bdár-ba.*

རྡལ་བ་ *rdál-ba*, pf. and fut. *brdal,* imp. *rdol,* also *ydál-ba, bdál-ba,* 1. **to spread,** sand, stones, manure, esp. as done by means of a stick, rake, shovel etc.; **to extend,** a canopy *Pth.*; **to cover,** *rdziṅ-gi žabs byé-mas,* the bottom of a pond with sand *Dzl.*; fig. *dam-čos ťaṅ-mar bdál-ba-la* now when holy religion lies before you as if it were spread out in a plain, i.e. when it is accessible to all, *Mil.*; *kyab-ydál* or *rdál* spreading far and wide, all-embracing, *sems nám-mka ltá-bu, čós-kyi kloṅ, čos-dbyiṅs,* and the like; *groṅ-rdál* v. sub *groṅ.* — 2. *sos-ydál Lex.* w.e.; *Sch.*: **slowly, not in a hurry.**

རྡིག་ *rdig* = *yo-byád? náṅ-gi rdig kun Mil.* seems to mean: all the utensils and furniture of a house.

རྡིགས་པ་ *rdigs-pa* **to beat** *Sch.*, prob. = *rdég-pa.*

རྡིབ་པ་ *rdib-pa*, pf. *rdibs*, vb. n. to *rtib-pa,* **to fall to pieces, to give way, to break down,** of a roof, rock, tree, the heavens. — 2. **to get dinted,** battered, like tin-vessels by a blow or knock, *C.*, *W.*

རྡུ་བ་ *rdú-ba Cs* **thistle,** not generally known, but perh. the same as *ma-rdu.*

རྡུག་པ་ *rdúg-pa*, pf. *brdugs*, fut. *brdug,* 1. **to conquer, to vanquish** (?), *klú-rnams-kyis lha-ma-yin ťúb-čiṅ rdúg-par byás-te* the Nagas having overcome and vanquished the Asuras *Stg.*; hence prob. **to annihilate, destroy, undo,** *der ťabs brdugs-pas* as all resources were destroyed *Pth.* — 2. **to strike against, to stumble at,** *C.* (cf. *ťúg-pa* II, 3); *ťogs-rdug* (or *brtug*)-*méd-pa,* v. *ťógs-pa,* without impediment.

རྡུང་ *rduṅ*, **a small mound, hillock,** *Ld.*

རྡུང་བ་ *rdúṅ-ba*, pf. *brduṅs*, fut. *brduṅ*, imp. (*b*)*rduṅ*(*s*), also *bdúṅ-ba,* **to beat, to strike,** a person, a drum etc.; **to cudgel, to drub,** also *rdúṅ-ₒtsog-pa* (*Sch.* -*ₒtsob-pa?*); **to beat with a hammer, to hammer,** *lčags*; *rdúṅ-du rúṅ-ba* malleable, ductile; **to knock,** *sgo* at a door; **to break to pieces, to smash,** *rdo-yis* with a stone (the sacrificial vessels) *Glr.*; **to beat out,** *brá-bo* buckwheat, with a stick; hence to beat out with a flail, **to thrash; to pound, to bray;** *stéṅ-rduṅ* a pestle *Ld.* — *bro rdúṅ-ba* **to dance.** — *yžu rdúṅ-ba* **to bend the bow,** v. *Schf.* on *Dzl.* ༢༥༢, 11. — *rdúṅ-mkan* **a fighter, bully;** of horses:

a kicker; of oxen, **butting**. — *rduṅ-ytág Lex.* w.e., prob. a drubbing, a sound thrashing; *rdun-ytag byuṅ* I have got a drubbing.

རྡུམ་པོ་ *rdúm-po Cs.* **maimed, mutilated,** *rdúm-po byéd-pa* **to mutilate**, *lag-rdum* a maimed hand, *rkaṅ-rdúm* a maimed foot, *rwa-rdúm* a mutilated horn; having a maimed hand, foot etc. *Mil.*

རྡུལ་ *rdul* **dust**, not so much as a deposited mass, but rather as particles floating in the air, **motes, atoms**; thus esp. *rdul-p̔rán*, *rdul-p̔rá-mo*, *rdul-p̔ra-ráb*, *nyi-zér-gyi rdul*, yet less to express minuteness than infinite number; **atom**, in a philosophical sense, *k̔u-k̔rág-gi rdul t̔ams-čád* all the atoms of the procreative fluid *Wdṅ.*; **monad**, *rdul-p̔ra-rab-ča-med*, acc. to *Was.* (279); *rdul ˳tul*, *ldaṅ*, dust arises *Dzl.*; *rdul mi t̔úl-bar* (or *ma ldáṅ-bar*) *byéd-pa* to lay the dust *Dzl.*; *sprúg-pa*, *W.* **šrúg-če**, to shake off, to beat out; *rdúl-du rlóg-pa* (in this case also *t̔ál-bar rlóg-pa*) to crush or pound a thing, until it is reduced to powder *Lex.*; *glaṅ-rdúl Cs.*: 'a mote in the dung of an ox' (?), *Sch.*: 'a small particle of cow-dung.' — *rdo-rjei rdul* diamond-powder (?) *Lex.*; *sól-bai rdul* coal-dust.

Comp. *rdúl-čan* **dusty**. — *rdul-p̔yágs* **dusting-whisk, dusting-brush** *Sch.* — *rdul-ts̔ub* a whirling cloud of dust. — *rdul-ts̔ón* coloured stone-dust, employed in certain ceremonies, for making figures drawn in the sand more visible *Mil. nt.* — *rdul-γzán* a blouse (?), travelling-cloak against the dust, *Wdk. fol.* 144 a Lha wears such a garment.

རྡུལ་པོ་ *rdúl-po*, prob. erron. for *rtúl-po Dzl.* ༢༢༥, 2.

རྡེ་ *rde* in compounds for *rdeu*.

རྡེ་བ་ད་རུ་ *rde-ba-da-ru Wdṅ.*, tibetanized from देवदारु, **cedar**.

རྡེག(ས)་པ་ *rdég(s)-pa*, pf. *(b)rdegs*, fut. *brdeg*, imp. *(b)rdeg(s)*, **to beat, strike, smite**, c. accus., or (less corr.) c. dat., chiefly in *B.*, *rdég-čiṅ spyód-pa*, verberando concumbere, to compel a wife by blows to fulfil the conjugal duty *Thgy.*; *mé-loṅ-la brdég-čiṅ* beating the looking-glass in anger *Glr.*; *rdeg-˳ts̔óg-gi sdug-bsṅál* the ill-fortune of getting a beating *Thgy.*; **to push, thrust, knock, kick,** *p̔ul-rdég* a blow with the fist, *byéd-pa* to give one *Mil.*; *rdeg-čós Lex.* w.e., *Sch.* a dance; *rdeg-čós-pa* to dance, so perh. *Thgy.*, if *brdog-čós-pa* is not a better reading, *glo-rdég(-tu)* = *glo-búr-du*, **suddenly**.

རྡེབ་པ་ *rdéb-pa*, sometimes for *sdéb-pa*.

རྡེབ(ས)་པ་ *rdéb(s)-pa*, prob. the original form, but of rare occurrence, for *rdáb-pa*, pf. *brdabs*, fut. *brdab*, 1. **to throw down with a clap,** to clap the coat-tail on the ground *Glr.*; with a clashing sound, a potsherd *Tar.*; **to fling or knock down,** a person *Mil.*; *lus sá-la* **to prostrate one's self,** very frq.; *rtas* (to be thrown) by the horse *Sch.*; **k̔a dáb-pa** 1. *C.* **to fall upon one's face.** 2. *W.* **to smack with the tongue,** also of the snapping of a spring, of the clapping down of a lid or the cover of a book; **ká-lpags déb-pa* W.* to smack with the lips (in eating). — 2. **to throw to and fro, to toss about,** *mgó-bo rdébs-šiṅ ˳dré-ldog-pa* to turn one's head this way and that way *Pth.* — 3. **to stumble** *Sch.*, so perh. *Lt.* fol. 196, 6; *čal rdáb-pa Lex.*, *rdáb-čal-ba Sch.* to slip and stumble. — 4. **to kill, to slaughter** *Bal.* — 5. **deb-šóg šé'-pa, táṅ-wa* C.*, **ur deb táṅ-če* W.*, **to talk big, to exaggerate.**

རྡེའུ་, རྡེ་, རྡེལ་པོ་ *rdeu, rde, rdél-po,* dimin. of *rdo*, 1. **a little stone, pebble,** *rdeu bskúr-ba bžin* like a little stone thrown on the ground *Glr.* — 2. **the stone,** calculus, in the bladder or the kidneys, *p̔o-rdé* calculus in males, *mo-rdé* in females; *rdeu čúgs-pa* the concrescence of a calculus, *rdeu ˳dón-pa* the removing it *Cs.* — *rdel-dkár* a white pebble, *rdel-k̔rá* a coloured pebble *Cs.* — *rde-˳grám* ('the spreading of little-stones') the counting with pebbles *Cs.* — *rde-γžál* a pavement of pebbles. — 3. **a musket-ball** *C.*, *rdeu-pár* a bullet-mould; a bullet-founder *C.*

རྡོ་ *rdo B., C., rdó-ba* in *W.* the usual form, in more recent lit. frq., 1. **stone.** — 2. **weight,** for weighing things by a balance, col.; *rdoi* of stone, *rdoi ťúb-pa* a stone Buddha *Glr.*; *rdo skyéd-pa, skyá-ba*, to carry or drag stones to a place; **do-čág čóg-pa** *C.* a ceremony observed in making a contract, by breaking a stone and using the fractured side as a seal, cf. *mdzúg-gu* *ₒtúd-pa*; *rdo-bčál btín-ba Sch.*: 'stones arranged according to their species'; **do-rúb-la táṅ-če, do-rúb táṅ-te sád-če** *W.* to pelt, beat, or kill with stones, **to stone;** *rdo rus tug* to the last extremity *Sch.*; *dṅúl-rdo* a stone containing silver, silver-ore *Lex.*; *sprín-rdo* a sort of marble *Cs.*; *sbrá-rdo Sch.*, (perh. *spra-rdo?*) asbestus; *mé-rdo* fire-stone, flint; *rmaṅ-rdo* foundation-stone; *zúr-rdo* corner-stone; *γsér-rdo* a stone containing gold, gold-ore *Cs.*

Comp. *rdo-klád* a stone resembling a sheep's brain, and used as a remedy for diseases of the brain *S.g.* — *rdo dkár Cs.* a white stone; *Sch.* **alabaster.** — *rdo-skrán* a kind of steatite or soap-stone. — *rdo-ḱá* a vein in a stone. — *rdo-ḱóg* a stone pot. — *rdo-mḱris* gall-stone(?) *S.g.* — *rdo-rgyúd* various kinds of soft stone, as serpentine, soap-stone, chalk. — *rdo-rgyús S.g.?* **do-čág** *C.* oath taken in the above mentioned ceremony. — *rdo-čál Sik.* = *rdo-γžál.* — *rdo-čár* a shower of stones; **hail** *Schr.* — *rdo-ₒčáṅ, W.* **dom-čáṅ**, a stone of such a size as may be grasped by the hand. — *rdo-mnyen Cs.* = *ka-ma-ru* a soft kind of stone, alabaster. — *rdo-snyiṅ* jasper *Sch.* — *rdo-ťál Cs.* stone-ashes, **calcined stone;** *Sch.* **quicklime,** *Schf. Tar.* 103, 14: **chalk;** *rdo-ťál byúgs-pa* to rough-cast, to plaster. — *rdo-drég S.g.? Sch.* dirt on stones. — *rdo-snúm* **rock-oil, petroleum** *Schr.* — **do-pé** *W.* stone-dust, small particles or grains of stone. — *rdo búṅ-ba* a shining black stone *Cs.* — *rdó-bos* (perh. *do-bos*) **a large hammer, mallet** *Ld.* — *do-dbyúg* **a sling-stone** *S.g.* — *rdo-ₒbum* a sacred heap of stones, **a mani.** — *rdo-sbóm* large, heavy stones *Sch.* — *rdo-rtsig* stone-wall — *rdo-tsád* (= *yám-bu, rta-rmig-ma Cs.*) **a bar of silver-bullion,** of about 156½ tolas (4 pounds) in weight, the common medium of barter in Central Asia. — *rdo-žun Lt.* = *brag-žun* **bitumen, mineral pitch** (?) — *rdo-žó* **lime,** both quick lime and slaked lime *C.* — *rdo-γžál* **a stone-pavement.** — *rdo-γžógs* a cut or wrought stone *Cs.* — *rdo-zám* a stone-bridge; a rock-bridge, natural bridge formed by overhanging rocks. — *rdo-riṅ(s)* a stone pillar, obelisk, as a land-mark, monument, or an ornament of buildings *Glr.* — *rdo-ríl* a globular stone *Pth.* — *rdo-léb* a stone slab to sit upon; or to write on etc. — *rdo-sraṅ* a stone weight *Cs.* — *rdo-srín Glr.* 50, 10, evidently a corruption of *dar-srín.*

རྡོ་རྗེ་ *rdó-rje*, gen. **dór-je** *W.* **dór-že**, वज्र, (*Zam.* also उपल) 1. **precious, stone, jewel,** esp. **diamond,** more precisely: *rdó-rje pa-lám*; *rdo-rjei γtun* a knocker made of precious stones *Dzl.*; *rdó-rjei sku* an adamantine body *Pth.*; *rdó-rjei ťse* an adamantine life *Glr.*; *zag-med-rdó-rje-lta-bui ťsé-la mña brnyéd-pas Pth.* as much as immortality; *rdó-rjei ₒjim-pa*, or *rin-po-čei ₒjim-pa Glr.* mortar composed of pulverized precious stones and water, and considered a cement of marvelous properties. — 2. **thunderbolt,** originally the weapon of Indra, with the northern Buddhists the ritual sceptre of the priests (v. *Köpp.* II, 271; *Was.* 193), held by them during their prayers in their hands and moved about in various directions; symbol of hardness and durability, also of power; source of many phantastic ideas and practices; frq. forming part of names. — 3. euphem. for *po-rtágs C.*

Comp. *rdo-rje-gliṅ* seems to be the popular spelling of the Sanitarium in British Sikkim, which by the English generally is written Darjeeling. (Here Csoma died, and Dr Hooker staid here for some time.) Acc. to several titles of books in the Petersb. list of manuscripts, it ought properly to be spelled *dar-rgyas-gliṅ.* — *rdo-rje-rgya-grám* v. *rgya* comp. — *rdo-rje-γčód-pa*, वज्रच्छेदिका, title of a religious book most extensively used among Buddhists; *Was.* (145), *Burn.* I, 465. — *rdo-rje-ₒčáṅ*, वज्रपाणि, less frq. *ₒdzin*,

°धर, also *lág-na,* or *ṕyág-na-rdo-rje,* and abbreviated *lag-*, or *ṕyag-rdór*, **holder of the sceptre**, originally the Indra of the Brahmans; in Buddhism, in the first place, the Dhyani Bodhisatva of the Dhyani Buddha Aksobhya, and secondly a terrifying deity, the guardian of the mystical doctrine (*Was.* frq.), hence confounded with the *čos-skyoṅ-bži,* as well as with *ku-be-ra,* prince of the *γnod-sbyin,* and special deity of Milaraspa; v. *Köpp.* and *Schl.* — *rdo-rje-γdán,* वज्रासन. prop. the diamond seat or throne of Buddha at Gaya, *Köpp.* I, 93, and hence also proper name applied to that town, frq. — *rdo-rje-ṕa-lám* diamond v. above. — *rdo-rje-ṕág-mo,* वज्रवाराहि or भद्रोाहि (*Wts.* 136) 'diamond-sow', a goddess of later Buddhism, frq. worshipped (also in *Lh.*, where she has a sanctuary at Markula near Triloknath), and incarnated as abbess in a nunnery, situated on an island of the lake Pal-te, v. Georgi *Alph. Tib.*, *Wts.* 135. — *rdo-rje-ṕúr-pa Glr.* an instrument the upper part of which is a dorje and the lower a purpa. — *rdo-rje-légs-pa,* abbrev. **dor-lág**, a local deity in *Lh.*, originally an honest village black-smith. — *rdo-rje-sems-dpa,* वज्रसत्त्व. gen. = *rdo-rje-˳čáṅ* (*Was.* 188), sometimes differing from it, v. *Schl.* p. 50; also = *mi-skyód-pa,* Aksobhya; also *mi-skyoṅ-rdó-rje Glr.* Respecting the word *rdo-rje* cf. *Burn.* I, 526.

རྡོ་ར་ *rdo-ra,* or *rto-ra* **circle of dancers** *W.*

རྡོག *rdog C.* **root,** **dog dhaṅ ló-ma** root and leaves; **lab-dog** radish-root; yet cf. *rdóg-po.*

རྡོག་པ་ *rdóg-pa* **step, footstep; kick,** *rdóg-pa ˳bór-ba* **to step, to pace, to walk** *Cs.*; *rdóg-sgra* the sound of steps, the clattering of hoofs; *rdog-stán* a straw-mat for cleaning one's shoes *C.*; *rdóg-pai ˳óg-tu ˳júg-pa Dzl.* ༢༦༧, 13 (*Ms.*; *Sch.*: *rdóg-pai žábs-su?*) to prostrate, to throw under one's feet; *rdóg-pas rdúṅ-ba Sch.*, *˳ṕúl-ba Sch.*, *snón-pa, mnán-pa Sch.*, *rdog-ṕúl rgyáb-pa Pth.*, **dog-tó ṕúl-wa** *C.*, **dog-čóṅ gyab-če** *W.* to strike with the foot, to apply a good kick, to stamp the ground; *rdog-bstád byéd-pa* prob. id.; prop. to load, to pack on (?).

རྡོག་པོ་ *rdóg-po* (*Cs.* also *rdóg-ma*), **a grain of corn, sand, sugar; a drop of rain** *Glr.*; *sran rdog bdun* seven peas; *˳ṕreṅ-rdog* the bead of a rosary, which often consists of grains of seed; **a piece,** *rdog-γčig* (how many turnips do you want?) one *C.*

རྡོངས་པ་ *rdóṅs-pa* v. *sdóṅs-pa.*

རྡོམ་ཆན་ *rdom-čáṅ* v. *rdo-mčáṅ.*

རྡོར་ *rdor* 1. in compound words for *rdó-rje.* — 2. n. of a monastery in Tibet *Cs.* Chronolog. Table 1223 p. C. — 3. = *sdor Cs.*

རྡོལ་པ་ *rdól-pa* **a cobbler** *Cs.*, prob. = *γdól-pa.*

རྡོལ་བ་ *rdól-ba,* pf. and fut. *brdol,* vb. n. to *rtól-ba,* 1. **to come out, to break forth from, to gush forth, to issue from,** of a well of water (issuing from) *Pth*; **to come up, to sprout, to shoot,** of seed; **so ma dol** *W.* the teeth are not yet cutting; *kóṅ-nas rdól-bai glu* a song streaming forth from within *Mil.*; *mi-nad rdól-žiṅ* diseases breaking out among men *Mil.*; **to flow** or **run off,** of the water of a lake; *kloṅ rdól-ba* to come forth, to proceed from the middle or the midst of *Glr.* (the meaning of this passage is not quite clear); *rdol-γzér* an instrument for boring metals *Sch.* — 2. of vessels: **to leak, to be not tight, to have holes,** *snod žabs-brdól* a vessel with a leaky bottom *Thgy.*; also of shoes, covers, tent-cloth etc. not being watertight; **to break, to burst,** of ulcers, wounds; *glo-rdol Med.* v. *gló-ba*; *rdol-γnyán Sch.*: 'fistula; gonorrhea'. — 3. **to rave, to delirate; to be sleep-walking, lunatic,** also *bla rdól(smrá)-ba Lex.*, where it is explained by *bab-čól*; *γnyid-rdól, mig-rdól C.* id.

རྡོས་པ་ *rdós-pa* 1. sbst., *Cs.* = *γdos*; *lus rdos-čé Lex.* w.e. — 2. vb. n. *Sch.*: '**to break, burst, flow out,** *dbú-ba,* or *lbú-ba* the bursting of a bubble'.

རླ་ *lda... Ld.* frq. for *kla..., gla..., zla...*

ལྡ་གུ· *ldá-gu* **discourse, speech, conversation;** *W.*: **ldá-gu táṅ-če** **to speak;** **ldá-gu śé-če med** one cannot understand what is spoken or said; *ldá-gu-čan* **talkative** *Cs.*

ལྡ་མན· *lda-mán*, *Ld.-Glr. dha-mán*, **a couple of small kettle-drums,** one hanging in front, the other behind, the latter being beaten by a second person that follows the bearer.

ལྡ་ལྡི· *lda-ldi* a kind of ornament of silk or cotton, **a fringe** or **tassel,** *dár-gyi, rin-po-čéi*, esp. worn in sacrificing, *Lex.*

ལྡག་པ· *ldág-pa*, pf. *bldags*, fut. *bldag*, imp. *ldog*, **to lick,** *ḱrag* blood; *klad ldág-pa* the brain being licked up, a punishment of hell *Thgy.*; *ná-bza-la*, or *-nas* to lick a person's coat *Mil.*; **ldag-ldog** *W.* = *ṕe-srul*, lit. **'a lick'**, i.e. a pap prepared of *rtsám-pa* and *čaṅ*, licked from the fingers, or eaten with a spoon.

ལྡང· *ldaṅ* 1. v. *ldáṅ-ba*. — 2. for *ydaṅ* **stand, frame, trestle.** — 3. *W.* **ldaṅ-ldáṅ-la kur** carry it lengthways! opp. to *ṕred*; **ldaṅ-ldáṅ-la dád-če** to rock with one's chair.

ལྡང་མགོ· *ldáṅ-mgo* **the yarn-beam** of a loom *Sch.*

ལྡང་སྒོ་སྐ· *ldáṅ-sgo-ska. Ssk.* **शरभ,** *Fouc. Gyatch.* 256; if the text is correct, it would seem preferable to connect *ri-dags* with *ldáṅ-sgo-ska*, and to render it: 'the animal Sarabha', a fabulous eight-footed creature of the snowy mountains.

ལྡང་བ· *ldáṅ-ba*, pf. *ldaṅs* or *laṅs*, imp. *ldoṅ*, 1. vb. n. to *sláṅ-ba*, **to rise, to get up** (cf. the more frq. secondary form *láṅ-ba*), *₀gyél-ba-las* from a fall *Wdṅ.*; *nyál-las* from a lying position *Lex.*; *stán-las* from a seat; *ťo-ráṅs* in the morning *Lt.*; *ṅó-mi-śes-pa-la* before, or in presence of a stranger; also used of the bristling of the hair, *Lt.*, of the rising of vapours, perfumes, dust, of a wind springing up; **to extend, to spread,** *dri ṅán-pa ṕyogs bčur ldaṅ* an offensive smell is spreading in every quarter *Tar.*; *₀ḱrúgs-pa dbús-nas* the rebellion (spread) from the province of Ü, *Ma.*; **to break out,** *mé-ro ldaṅ* the smothered flame breaks out again; in a special sense of morbid matter that has accumulated (*ysóg-pa*) *Med.* frq., e.g. *ḱa-zás žú-nas ldaṅ* during digestion the symptoms break out anew; *dgrá-ru ldáṅ-ba* to show one's self an enemy, to break out into hostilities frq.; **to arise, originate, break out,** of disease, despair, *Mil.*; also for: **to have risen, to stand,** but only in certain combinations, *ldaṅ dub byéd-pa* tired from having been standing (so long) *Lt.* — 2. *W.* **to suffice, to be sufficient, enough** (cf. *loṅ-ba*) = *₀ḱyéd-pa*, of food, clothes, money; hence *ldaṅ*: **complete, perfect, entire, whole,** **ras náṅ-śa rág-ma gos ldaṅ čig** cotton cloth with lining (sufficient) for a whole dress; **ḍú-gu gos ldaṅ nyis** woolen yarn for two complete dresses. — *ldaṅ* prob. signifies also quite through, cf. *ltaṅ* II.; *ldaṅ-ťsád* occurs in medical works, and in many cases seems to imply **quantity;** *neu-ldáṅ Lex.* = *na-mnyám* of the same age (*Sch.* not corr.).

ལྡད་པ· *ldád-pa* 1. vb. pf. and fut. *bldad*, imp. *ldod*, **to chew** *Zam.*, *W.*; *skyug-ldád Cs.*, v. *skyug bldeg-čiṅ ldad-pa* (?) *Sch.* to chew the cud, to ruminate; *log Cs.* 1. id., 2. rumination, deliberate reflection; *Pur.*: **spá ldad-čas** to taste, to try; *Ld.*: **ḍi ldad-če** to smell at. — 2. *Ld.* for *glád-pa*

ལྡན་པ· *ldán-pa* I. sbst., also *mdán-pa Lex.*, **cheek,** *ldán(-pai) so* cheek-tooth, molar tooth; *ldan-lčág Cs.* **a** blow on the cheek, a box on the ear; **dẹn-tsóg** *C.* id.; **mi dhé-la dẹ́n-tsog gyag* (or *gyab*) *soṅ, mi dhe dẹ́n-tsog-ghī máṅ-po duṅ soṅ** his ears have been soundly boxed; metaph. *grog-ldán* the cheek or side of a ravine *Mil. nt.*

II. vb. and adj. 1. originally: **to be near to, hard by,** a thing, (juxta), hence *W.* **ldán-la, ldán-du**, adv. and postp., **near to, by,** **ṅẹ ldán-la dug** sit down by my side; **śiṅ-gi ldán-du** close by the tree; **ṅai ldán-du śog** come near to me! **gám-mi ldán-du** near the box; **tser-máṅ-ṅi ldán-la ḍúl-če** to go along the side of a hedge. — 2, in *B.* and *C.* only used with reference to possession (penes), mostly as partic. or adj., and construed like *bčás-pa*, **having, being possessed of, provided with**, = *čan* (which in *W.* is almost exclusively used in this sense). The objects may be things of any description, also physical and mental properties, so that *ldán-pa* differs in this respect from *bčás-pa* (*Tar.* 136, 14. 15); *nor dan ldán-pa* rich, wealthy; *sems-čan dan ldán-pa* with child; *bu dan bu-mor-ldán-pa* having children; *rig-pa dan ldán-pa* wise; with a negative: *nor dan mi ldán-pa*; *dan ldan-par ˳gyúr-ba* **to get, to obtain**, frq.; *ldán-du lén-pa Glr.* 101, 1 is stated to mean the same. Poetically, and forming part of certain expressions and names, without *dan* and *pa*, like *čan*: *nor-ldán, dga-ldán, ˳byor-ldán*. — 3. *ldán-pa* and *ldan dan ˳dús-pa* seem to imply: **mixed, compound** (opp. to *rkyan-pa*) with regard to temper and disposition of mind *S. g.* — 4. **to add up, sum up**, *Wdk.* — 5. *W.* **gún-ka tsúg-pa ldan yin** it will be **enough**, it will hold out, till winter-time, prob. only a corruption of *ldán-ba*. — 6. *Pur.* = *˳grig*, **regularly, properly, duly, rightly**.

ལྡན(པ་)པོ་ *ldán(-pa)-po* one that has, that is able, a man of ability *Cs.*

ལྡན་མ་ *ldán-ma* n. of a country *Ma.*

ལྡན་ཚད་ *ldan-tsád* equivalent to *˳dus-tsád Mng.* 35 (?).

ལྡབ་ལྡིབ་ *ldab-ldib* (*skad*) *Lex.* **silly talk, tittle-tattle.**

ལྡབ་ལྡོབ་ *ldab-ldób Lex.* w.e., *Cs.* **indolence, dullness, drowsiness**; acc. to others, **a hasty, volatile manner.**

ལྡབ་པ་ *ldáb-pa*, pf. *bldabs*, fut *bldab*, imp. *ldob*, 1. *Cs.* **to do again, to repeat**; *skyár-ldáb Lex., Sch.*: **repeatedly, anew, afresh, again**; *nyis-ldáb Lex., Sch.*: for the second time, doubly, twice; **čú-(l)dab de san čén-mo yod* W.* it is ten times as large as that, yet cf. *ltáb-pa*; **ldáb-ste zér-na* W.* saying it once more, again, in short. — 2. ? *Ld.*: **ldab zúm-te k'yer** take a firm hold of him (or it) with your hand, and carry him (or it) away!

ལྡམ་ལྡམ་ *ldam-ldám Cs.*, *ldam-pa*, **very idle, slothful.**

ལྡམ་ལྡུམ་ *ldam-ldúm Cs.*: **'mean, pitiful, sorry, idle'.**

ལྡམ་ལྡེམ་ *ldam-ldém Ld.* **dubious, uncertain,** used of things.

ལྡར་བ་ *ldár-ba Cs.* **to be weary, tired, faint, languid**, *ldar-ldár-du ˳gyúr-ba*.

ལྡི་རི་རི་ *ldi-ri-ri* (v. *ldir-ba*) **the rolling of thunder** *Thgr.*

ལྡིག་པ་ *ldig-pa* **to fall** or **sink through** *Sch.*

ལྡིང་བ་ *ldin-ba* **to be swimming, floating,** cf. *rkyál-ba*, *W.*: **čán-ni k'a-tóg-la pabs ldin dug**, opp. to **til-la ner* or *nub*;* **to be suspended, floating, soaring** (in the air), *ynám-la, nám-mk'a-la*; *mk'á-ldin* v. *mk'a*.

ལྡིང་ཁ་ *ldin-k'a* v. *ltin-k'a*.

ལྡིང་ཁང་ *ldin-k'an* **a bower** formed by the branches of a tree, **the leafy canopy** of a dense wood *Mil.*; *šin yyú-lo rgyás-pai ldin-k'an* the wide shady porches of turkois-leaved trees.

ལྡིང་དཔོན་ *ldin-dpon* an officer over fifty, acc. to others, over a hundred men, = *brgya-dpon*, a sergeant, captain, distinguished by a copper button on his cap, *Hook.* II, 160. 200.; *ldin-˳og Sch.*, *ldin-tso*, the troop under this officer's command.

ལྡིང་སེ་ *ldin-se*, or *ldin-si Ld.*, adv. **quite, very, very much**, **na ldin-se k'ams zán-po yod** I am quite well; **na ldin-se ma ˳tád son** I was very much displeased, very vexed; perh. also **ldins tág-pa-nas** for *ytin*, cf. *lins-pa*, or perh. in *Ld. ldin* is the form for *ytin*.

ལྡིབ་པ་ *ldib-pa* 1. vb., pf. *bldib*, *Sch.* = *ldig-pa*. — 2. adj. *Cs.*: **not clear, not intelligible**, **k'a-dib* W.* **stammering, stuttering**; *ldib-ldib* = *ldab-ldib*.

ལྡིམ་ *ldim W.* **the crash** of a falling tree, **the report** of a gun, **ldim zér-ra rag** I hear a crack.

ལྡིར་ལྡིར་ *ldir-ldir* is said to be = **di-ri-ri* C.*

ལྡིར་བ་ *ldír-ba* 1. also *ltír-ba*, **to be distended, inflated, to belly;** *lto-ldír* a big belly; *ltó-ldir-čan* big-bellied. — 2. **to rush, to roar,** of the wind *W.;* **to roll,** of the thunder, *ₒbrag ldir* it thunders; *ldir bžin* like thunder; *ldir-sgra* a thundering, roaring noise; *ldir-čé-ba* thundering *Thgr.*

ལྡུ་གུ་ *ldú-gu* = *γdú-ba*, *γdú-gu*.

ལྡུག(ས)་པ་ *ldúg(s)-pa*, pf. *ldugs* (*Lex.*), *blugs* (usual form), fut. *blug*, imp. *blug(s)*, col. *blug-pa*, **to pour,** *snód-du*; *lág-ču blugs* pour some water on my hands, give me water for washing; **to sprinkle,** to strew, sand *Glr.*; **to cast, to found,** metals. Cf. *blugs* and *lugs*.

ལྡུད་པ་ *ldúd-pa*, pf., fut. and imp. *blud*, col. *blúd-pa*, **to give to drink, to water,** cattle etc., with accus of the drink given, *dug blúd-čiṅ mi ₒči* he does not die by a poisoned draught, *btúṅ-ba blud* he gives (him) to drink *Thgr.*; *ṫúg-pa légs-par blúd-čiṅ* making (another) eat plenty of soup *Lt.*, as one also says: *ṫúg-pa ₒṫúṅ-ba* to eat soup.

ལྡུམ་ *ldum* 1. **vegetables, greens,** in general. — 2. *W.* **lettuce, salad;** *ldum-nág*, a kind of lettuce *Cs.*; *ldúm-bu* 1. *Cs.* **plant, stalked plant.** 2. prob. for *ldóm-bu Mil.*; 3. *C.* vulgar pronunciation for *sdóṅ-po*. — — *ldúm-ra* 1. *W.* **kitchen-garden;** 2. **fruit-garden, orchard,** and 3. esp. **flower-garden** (better *sdúm-ra*); *ldúm-ra-pa* **gardener** *Pth.*

ལྡུམ་པོ, ལྡུམ་ལྡུམ་ *ldúm-po*, *ldum-ldúm*, 1. for *dúm-po Glr.*; 2. *Ld.* for *zlúm-po*, **round;** *Mil.* also *ldúm-la ₒgríl-ba* made round, rounded off.

ལྡུར་ལྡུར་ *ldur-ldúr Lex.*; *Sch.*: **roaring, rushing.**

ལྡེ *lde?* *Lexx.* *miṅ(-gi)-lde* w. e.; *lde-ka Sch.*: '**belonging together, of the same species**'.

ལྡེ་གུ, ལྡེའུ་ *lde-gu*, *ldeu Med.* 1. *Cs.* **mixture, syrup** (?); 2. **ointment** *Wdṅ.*

ལྡེ་བ་ *ldé-ba* (*Sch.* also *ₒdé-ba*), pf. *(b)ldes*, fut. *blde*, imp. *ldes*, **to warm one's self,** c. accus., *me*, at the fire; *nyi-ma*, in the sun (not *me-la*).

ལྡེ་མིག *lde-mig B.* and *C.* (*Ts.* col. **de-mág** *Bal.* **le-mig*, otherwise not in use in *W.*) 1. **key,** *lde-čáb Glr.* prob. id. — 2. **introduction, preface** *Cs.*

ལྡེའུ་ *ldeu* 1. *Cs.* also *sdeu*, a kind of **pease,** *Hind.* मुङ्गा — 2. v. *lde-gu*.

ལྡེག་པ་ *ldég-pa* (pf. *bldeg?*) **to quake, shake, tremble,** e. g. of the palace of the gods *Dzl.*

ལྡེང་ཀ་ *ldéṅ-ka*, *ldiṅ-ka*, v. *ltéṅ-ka*, **a pond.**

ལྡེབ་ *ldeb* 1. *Sch.* **leaf, sheet,** of paper; 2. = *ldebs* 1.

ལྡེབ་པ་ *ldéb-pa* 1. *Cs.* = *ldég-pa*; 2. *Sch.* **to bend round** or **back, to turn round, to double down.**

ལྡེབས་ *ldebs* 1. **side,** *Lex.* = *ₒdabs*, e.g. of a mountain *Sch.*, the flat side of a sword or knife *Cs.*; *rús-pai ₒbúr-poi ldebs* by the side of, near, the protuberance of a bone. — 2. **compass, enclosure, fence** *Sch.* — 3. *C.*, *W.* **a large cloth,** in which a person is carried by several others, either by means of a pole, or by taking hold of the four corners. This mode of conveyance is called **Dandi** (डण्डी *Hindi*). — 4. in the *Wdṅ.* it seems to have still another signification.

ལྡེམ་ *ldem* 1. v. *ldém-pa* I. — 2. **statue, idolatrous image, idol,** standing upright, cf. *ldém-pa* II., *C.* — 3. **suspension-bridge** (?) *Ld.-Glr. Schl.* 17, a; v. *ldém-pa* III.

ལྡེམ་པ་ *ldém-pa* I. sbst. 1. *Cs.*: '**contrariety, opposition, irony**', which seems not to be quite inconsistent with the explanation given by *Zam.*, *draṅ-min*, as being an intentional concealing of the true sentiment. — *ldém(-po)* **riddle, enigma** (cf. *ṫsód-bya*); *mi-ldem*, *byá-ldem*, *bém-ldem* an enigma or allegory applied to men, to birds, to inanimate beings; *ldém-poi ṅag*, *ldém-γtam* **parable, allegory;** *ldem-dgóṅs Lex.* = *Ssk.* अभिसंधि, prob.: a concealed deceitful intention, *Sch.*: 'a mysterious opinion'; *ldém-rjód-pa Cs.* to say a riddle or parable, **ldem ṭad-če** *W.* to propose a riddle, *ldem ṫsód-pa Cs.*, *čód-pa Sch.*, to solve a riddle. — 2. *W.* **a trap** (*C.* **pur-nyi**), **bi-ldém** mouse-trap, *wa-ldém* fox-trap, *tsúg-ce* to put a trap.

II. adj. 1. (*Schr. ldém-po*) **straight, upright; tall, well-made**, *Mil.*, prob. also *Wdn.* — 2 partic. of III., **inconstant; unstable, variable, perishable** *Cs.*

III. vb., also *ldem-ldém-pa Sch.* **to move up and down**, striking, trembling, vibrating; *γšog-sgró ldém-pa* the clapping of wings *Mil.; ldem-ldém* **flexible, supple, elastic, pliant.**

ལྡེར་ *lder, Ts.* = *ldebs* I., *skyai ldér-la* **on the side** of a wall, **on** a wall, e.g. to paint, to scrawl; *rii lder.*

ལྡེར་བ་ *ldér-ba Cs.:* '1. **toughness, clamminess,** 2. **potter's clay**'. *lder-tso Cs.* 1. **clay,** 2. **an idol made of clay** *Mng.* — *ldér-sku Glr.* prob. = *ldér-tso* 2.; acc. to others: a picture on a wall. — *ldér-bzo* figures modelled of clay, **plastic work**, *ldér-bzoi lha Zam.* = *ldér-tso* 2.; *lder-bzoi-ldebs Lex.* a clay-enclosure (?) — *ldér-so Glr.* 88, 1. 2., by the context also **figure, image.**

ལྡོ་ *ldo* side, *Ld.* for *glo.*

ལྡོག་པ་ *ldóg-pa*, pf. and imp. *log*, vb. n. to *zlog-pa*, 1. **to come back, to return, to go home, to depart.** — 2. **to come again**, often with *pyir*, of diseases, = **to relapse**; in a specific religious sense v. *ₒbrás-bu bži*, frq.; *dgrar* to come forward again as an enemy, to renew the war (ni f.) *Mil.* — 3. **to change, to undergo a change**, as to colour, smell etc. *Med.*; *ₒgyúr-ldog*, and *ldog-ₒgyúr Mng.* **changeableness, inconstancy, fickleness.** — 4. **to turn away** (vb. n.) *las* from; *blo ldóg-pa* id. *Thgy.*; *no ldóg-pa* v. *lóg-pa*. The partic. as adj.: *dé-las ldóg-pai* (the thing) **opposed** to that, **contrary** to it, *Wdn*; *go-ldóg* id. *Lt.*; *mgo-ldóg Lex.*? — *Sch.* has also *ldog-pyé-ba* **distinguished, different**, from each other, and *ldóg-pa* **reciprocal, mutual, each separately.** Cf. *lóg-pa*.

ལྡོང་བ་ *ldóṅ-ba* 1. vb, pf. *ldoṅs, loṅ*, **to become blind, to be blind; to be infatuated.** — 2. adj., also *ldóṅs-pa, mdóṅs-pa*, **blind; infatuated.** Cf. *lóṅ-ba*.

ལྡོང་མོ་ *ldóṅ-mo*, resp. *γsol-ldóṅ*, **a small churn**, used for preparing tea, = *gur-gúr*, v. sub *ja*. Cf *doṅ-dús* *Ld.* **a stave;** *ldoṅ-rus?*

ལྡོང་རོས་ *ldoṅ-ros Cs.:* n. of a yellow earth, **bole, ochre**, used for staining the walls of houses; *ldoṅ-ros-sa Lt.*

ལྡོན་པ་ *ldón-pa* **to give** or **pay back, to return,** = *klón-pa, glón-pa*, esp. with *lan*, **to answer** *Dzl.*

ལྡོབ་པ་ *ldób-pa* **to apprehend quickly; to be witty, to be quick in repartee** *Cs.*; *ldobs-skyén Lex.*, explained by *šés-sla-ba* understanding readily?

ལྡོམ་པ་ *ldóm-pa? rag-ldóm-pa* is stated to be = *rag-lús-pa Ld.*

ལྡོམ་བུ་ *ldóm-bu*, less frq. *ldúm-bu*, often preceded by *ro-snyóms* **alms**, consisting of food; *ldóm-bu byéd-pa* to ask such alms; *ldóm-sa* alms-house, house where beggars receive food; *ldóm-bu-ba* a person living on alms, a beggar, *Mil.*, *Pth.*

སྡང་བ་ *zdáṅ-ba*, pf. *sdaṅs*, I. **to be angry, wrathful**, *mi dgá-žiṅ sdáṅ-ste* growing angry, flying into a passion *Dzl.*; gen. c. *la*: **to hate, to be inimically disposed**, frq.; *sdáṅ-bai dgra* opp. to *byáms-pai γnyen*; *sdáṅ-bar séms-pai dgrá-bo* id. *Wdn.*; *kyim-mtses-kyi dgrá-sdaṅ-ba*, or *dgrá-bdo-ba* the neighbour's grudge; *sdáṅ(-bai) sems, sdáṅ-blo*, most frq. *že-sdáṅ*, **hatred, enmity, hostility, ill-will;** (cf. dug) *sdáṅ-ba tams-cád ₒjig-pa* to subdue all hostile powers; *sṅar sdáṅ-ba* the former, the old hatred *Mil.*; *sdaṅ-mig Lex.* an angry look, a scowl.

II. for *γdáṅ-ba*.

སྡང་བུ་ *sdáṅ-bu* v. *γdáṅ-bu*.

སྡད་པ་ *sdád-pa* v. *sdód-pa*.

སྡམ་པ་ *sdám-pa* v. *sdóm-pa*.

སྡར་མ་ *sdár-ma* **trembling, timorous, timid** *Dzl.*, *Zam.*

སྡི་བ་ *sdi-ba*, pf. *bsdis*, v. *sdig-pa*.

སྡིག་ *sdig* 1. **thick** (?) *γsús-pa sdig Mng.* — 2. **foundation** *C.*, *rgyág-pa* to lay a foundation.

སྡིག་པ་ *sdig-pa* I. also *sdig-pa rwá-čan*, col. **rá-tse**, **scorpion,** also as sign of the zodiac; *sdig-pa dkár-po, nág-po*; *sdig-rwá*, the sting of a scorpion; *sdig-dúg* the poison of a scorpion; *sdig-tsáṅ* a scorpion's nest; *sdig-srin* **crab, crawfish,** used both as food and medicine *Med.*, but not as designation for the respective sign of the zodiac, v. sub *k'yim*; *sdig-srin-*ₒ*bu Lt.* id.?

II. (पाप) **sin,** moral evil as a power, *sdig-pa-la yid-čes-pa Dzl.* ༢༥༢, 11 to believe in sin as such; ₒ*jóms-pa* to conquer sin, as something hostile to man *Dom.*, and so meton. = sinners, adversaries; sometimes perh. for **sinfulness,** sinful state, but gen. in a concrete sense: **offence, trespass,** in thought, word, or deed, *k'a-na-ma-tó-bai sdig-pa*, or *nyés-pa* prob. a grievous sin *Dzl.*; also with a genit., *rgyál-poi sdig-pa sbyóṅ-ba* to wash away, to expiate, the king's sin; also ₒ*dág-pa, sél-ba, W.* **čád-če**; ₒ*byáṅ-ba* id., but more in an intransitive or passive sense; so also ₒ*čégs-pa* (*yšág-pa, bšags-pa*) to confess, as acc. to Buddhist views, confession is almost tantamount to expiation of sin, cf. also ₒ*gyód-pa* and *bzód-pa;* there seems to be, however, no word strictly corresponding to our 'forgiving' of sin; *sdig-(pai)-las* a sinful deed; *sdig-pa-la dgá-ba* **to love sin, to be wicked;** *sdig-(pai) grogs* a companion in vice, **an associate in crime** *Dzl.*; *sdig-pa byéd-pa, spyód-pa*, **to commit sin, to sin;** *sdig-pa mi byéd-pai yul* a country where no sins are committed, a pious country; *sdig-byéd, sdig-spyód* **impious, wicked; a wicked person,** *sdig-pa-rnams byás-pa* id. (more accurately: *πολλὰ ἡμαρτηκώς*) *Stg.*; *sdig-čan* id. (*sdig-pa-čan* seems not to be in use); *sdig-sgrib* the filth, the contamination of sin, *sdig-sgrib tams-čád sél-ba* to cleanse from every defilement of sin *Glr.* (which the Ommanipadmehūm is sufficient to do); *sdig-po* **a sinner, a bad character,** *sdig-po če* a vile sinner *Glr., Mil.*; *rdig-to-čan*, पापीय, = *sdig-čan*, but only as epithet of Dud; *sdig-blón* a wicked officer *Glr.*

སྡིག(ས)་པ་ *sdig(s)-pa*, pf. *bsdigs*, fut. *bsdig*, imp. *sdigs*, and *sdi-ba*, pf. *bsdis*, ft. *bsdi*, 1. **to show, to point out,** *sdigs-mdzúb* a pointing finger, . . . *la sdigs-mdzúb ytád-pa* to point at . . . (with scorn or derision); *sdigs-mdzúb nám-mk'a-la ytad* pointing with the fingers toward heaven, yet not in a 'menacing' (*Cs.*) way. — 2. **to aim** *C.*, *bsdi(g)s-sa* the place that is aimed at, **aim, butt; goal** *Thgy.*; *bsdis-pai p'yógs-su* in the direction of the aim *Thgy.* — 3. **to menace, to threaten,** *čád-pas* with punishment *Mil.* (ni f.); **dig-če p'i-la** *Ld.* as an alarm-shot; ₒ*di-la bdág-gis* ₒ*jigs-pa žig-gis ma bsdigs-na* if I do not threaten him with something frightful, if I do not strike him with fear, *Dzl.*; *sdigs-mo byéd-pa* to assume a menacing attitude *Mil.*, to threaten tauntingly *Thgy.*

སྡིངས་ *sdiṅs* **a cavity** or **depression,** *spáṅ-sdiṅs* a depression on a grassy plain, *ri-sdiṅs* on a mountain-ridge; the significations given by *Cs.*, 'middle part, heart, core', were not known to our men of Tashilunpo.

སྡིབ་པ་ *sdib-pa* 1. *Sch.* = *ldib-pa.* — 2. *Tar.* 8,18 = *rtib-pa.*

སྡུག་པ་ *sdúg-pa* I. adj. **pretty, nice,** *ltá-na* to look at *Dzl.*; **tsa-ḍhi-dúg-pa** *C.* **mint,** Mentha, *ἡδύοσμον*; gen. with reference to a person: what is **agreeable, pleasing, dear,** to a person *Ssk.*: प्रिय, *bdág-gi bu náṅ-gi sdúg-pa-la* the most beloved of my sons *Dzl.*; *ṅai bu sdug* my dear son *Pth.*, *sdúg-par* ₒ*dzin-pa Dzl.*, *sém-pa Dzl.* frq., *rtsi-ba Mil.*, to love, c. dat., gen. with regard to parental love; *sdúg-par* ₒ*gyúr-ba* to become dear to a person, to be endeared to, *Dzl.*; *mi-sdúg-pa* **not fair, ugly, disagreeable,** of the body, of a country etc.; *mi-sdúg-pai tiṅ-ṅe-*ₒ*dzin Tar.* 10, 11 contemplating one's self and the world as a foul, putrid carcass (v. *Tar.* Transl. 285, foot of the page); *mi-sdúg-par byéd-pa* to disfigure, pollute, profane, a temple *Dzl.*; *sdúg-gu* beautiful, pretty, handsome, *bud-méd sdúg-gu tams-čad* all pretty women *Dzl.*; there is also a form for the fem. gender: *sdúg-*

gu-ma Dzl.; sdú-ge-ba Cs.: 'the state of being somewhat pleasing'(?); in a prayer occurs: *bod-báṅs sdúg-ge snyiṅ-re-rjé* the good, poor Tibetans, just as in W. **sdug-pa-tsé** is used; often (but not necessarily) rather pityingly: *k'o sdug-pa-tsé* the good man (will do his utmost); **ri-pa sdug-pa-tsé** the good fieldmouse (speedily made off); but also: **sab dug-pa-tsé ă-lu žig toṅ** W. good sir, give me a few potatoes!

II. vb. **to be oppressed, afflicted, grieved,** like *γdúṅ-ba, sems lás-kyis sdúg-nas* by sorrow *Mil.; *sem máṅ-po máṅ-po dug soṅ** C. I was very, very sorry for it; . . . *pas sdúg-go* we are miserable, because . . . *Dzl.*; *sdúg-par ₒgyúr-ba* to become unhappy, to get into distress *Dzl.*

III. sbst., *Ssk.* དུཿཁ, **affliction, misery, distress,** *bod sdúg-pai mgo ₒdzugs* that is the beginning of the misfortunes of Tibet *Ma.; ṅéd-la sdúg-pai ré-mos bab* (then) came our turn of being visited by affliction *Mil.*; more frq. *sdug*, and *sdug-bsṅál* (v. below) *sdúg-tu mi yoṅ ₒdug-gam* are you not in distress? *Mil.*; *sdug k'ur byéd-pa* to undergo hardships (voluntarily), to bear affliction (patiently), to suffer, in an emphatical sense, *Mil.; sdug mi t'eg* you cannot endure the hardships *Mil.; *ka-dúg máṅ-po ǰhé'-pa** C. to work hard, to drudge; *skyid-sdúg* good and adverse fortune, good luck and ill luck, very frq.; *bde-sdúg* id.; *sdug-sógs byéd-pa* (the contrary to *ts'ogs-sógs byéd-pa*) to accumulate misery upon one's self *Mil.*; **dug máṅ-po táṅ-wa** C. to plague or vex a good deal, to inflict injury, c. *la*; *γžan-sdúg-gi sdig-pa* the sin of having done evil to others *Mil.*; **dug zö'-la táṅ-wa** C. **to torture, to put to the rack;** *sdug ₒbáb-pa* **to be in mourning** *Cs.; sdug srúṅ-ba* **to mourn** *Cs.*; *sdúg-čan* col. **fatiguing, worrying.** — *sdug* as adj., **unhappy, miserable,** *Pth.*, is of rare occurrence.

Comp. and deriv. *sdug-k'áṅ* **a chamber of mourning,** a darkened room *Cs.* — *sdug-gós* **a mourning dress** *Cs.* — *sdug-bsṅál* the most frq. word for **misfortune, misery, suffering;** also **pain,** *sdug-bsṅál-gyis γdúṅs-pa Dzl., sdug-bsṅál myóṅ-ba* (W. **ťóṅ-če**) to be in calamity, to suffer pain; **dug-ṅál ťóṅ-wa, tér-wa** C. (**táṅ-če** W.), to inflict pain, to grieve, to torment; *sdug-bsṅal daṅ ldán-pa, sdug-bsṅál-čan* **unhappy, miserable; misery, distress, affliction;** **dug-ṅál ǰhé'-pa** C. to lament, wail, moan; *sdug-bsṅál-du ₒgyúr-ba* to become sorrowful or melancholy; **ṅá-la ná-ga-ri ma šés-pe dug-ṅál yod** Ld. I regret my not knowing Sanskrit; *sdug-bsṅál-ba* (vb.) **to be unhappy,** (sbst.) **the state of unhappiness,** *Thgy.*; *sdug-bsṅál-bai skad* lamentable, doleful cries. — *sdug-mťúg* C. accumulating calamity. — *sdug-ₒdré* a demon *Sch.* — **dúg-po** C. **wretched** (road), **savage** (dog), **ill-bred, naughty, unamiable; evil** (sbst.), *dúg-po byéd-pa* to do evil *Mil.*; **mi-la dúg-po táṅ-wa** C. to do evil to a person, **to molest, trouble, annoy, injure,** a person. — *sdug-p'óṅs-pa Stg., C.,* **poor.** — *sdug-žwa* a mourning-hood *Cs.* — *sdug-srán* inured to hardships; the being hardened *Mil.*

སྡུད་ *sdud* 1. *Sch.*: the **folds** of a garment; *sdúd-k'a* string for drawing together the opening of a bag, **drawing-hem.** — 2. *Cs.* **synthesis,** *ₒbyed-sdúd* analysis and synthesis.

སྡུད་པ་ *sdúd-pa*, pf. *bsdus*, fut. and likewise for the pres. tense) *bsdu*, imp. *sdus, bsdu*, vb.a. to *ₒdú-ba*, 1. **to collect, gather, lay up, amass, assemble,** riches, flowers, broken victuals, taxes, crops, earnings, men, cattle etc., frq.; **to put together, to compile,** *miṅ-rnams . . . nas bsdus* the names have been put together out of . . . *Glr.*; **to brush** or **sweep together,** *W.*: **k'yim-sa ŏl-mo-ne* (or *daṅ*)* the dust with a broom; *dbáṅ-du* **to subject, subdue,** frq. — 2. to **unite, join, combine,** *šiṅ γsum mgo* three pieces of wood at their upper ends *Dzl.*; six kingdoms into one *Dzl.* (to join) actions, words, and thoughts in the path of virtue *Dzl.*; *dmág-rnams k'ór-du* (joining) the troops with his retinue *Dzl.*; *k'yo-šúg-tu* to unite in matrimony, to give in marriage. — 3. **to condense, to comprise,** all moral precepts in three main points, the letters of the alphabet in five classes *Gram.*; esp. with *nyúṅ-ṅu*, *zúr-tsam*, **to contract, compress, abridge,** frq., *de yaṅ bsdú-na* if one shortens it still more, if it is abridged a second time *Gram.*; **dús-k̔an** *W.* **brief. concise, compendious;** **dú-yig** *C.* **abbreviation, abridgment;** *bsdus-ˌgrel* an abridged commentary *Tar.* 177,7; **to close, conclude, finish, terminate,** *mǰug sdúd-pa* to close a train, opp. to *sna ˌdrén-pa Mng.*; *slár-bsdu-ba* concluding a sentence or period with the finite verb in *o*, *Gram.* — 4. *bsdús-pa* **to consist of** or **in**, c. instrum., e.g. *yi-ge drug-gis* of six letters *Thgy.* — 5. **to boil down, to inspissate** *Lt.*, *bsdús-k̔u*, *ydús-k̔u*, a preparation thus obtained *Med.*; *bsdus-t̔áṅ* prob. id. *Med.* — 6. scil. *bsód-nams: bsdú-ba rnam bži* the four ways of collecting merit *Glr.* — 7. *dbugs sdúd-pa Med.?* *bsdú-ba* sbst. **collection, gathering** *Tar.* 33, 16. — *bsdus-yžom* or *ˌǰom Schr.*: a machine for executing criminals constructed in such a manner, that the head is crushed by two stones striking together; *Stg.*: n. of one of the hells

སྡུམ་པ་ *sdúm-pa* 1. vb., pf. *bsdums*, fut. *bsdum*, imp. *sdum(s)*, vb.a. to *ˌdúm-pa*, **to make agree, to bring to an agreement,** *mi-mt̔ún-pa-rnams* things not agreeing *Sch.*, **to reconcile, to conciliate,** *mi-mdzá-ba-rnams* enemies *Thgy.*; *sdúm-par byéd-pa* id.; *sdum-byéd* (resp. *mdzad*), *sdúm(-pa)-po*, *sdúm-mk̔an*, **conciliator, pacifier, peace-maker;** *res ˌk̔rúgs-pa res bsdúm-pa máṅ-du byúṅ-ṅo* at one time they were at odds, at another they were at peace with one another *Tar.* — 2. sbst. **house, mansion** *C.*; *yzim-sdum* (resp.) **bed-room;** *sdúm-ra* garden near the house, cf. *ldúm-ra*.

སྡུར་བ་ *sdúr-ba*, pf. and fut. *bsdur*, **to compare,** *go-sdúr byéd-pa* id., v. *go* 2; *nyams sdur byéd-pa C.* to compare different texts: **taṅ-dúr** *W* **judicial examination, trial.**

སྡུར་ལེན་, སྡུར་བླང་ *sdur-lén*, *sdur-blaṅ*, **amber** *Ts.*, for *sbur-lén*.

སྡེ་ *sde* (*Ssk.* in compound words सेना) **part, portion,** of a whole, e.g. of a country, also *yúl-sde*, **province, district, territory,** even **village** *C.*, *bón-sde* the places or villages of the Bonpas *Glr.*; *sde-čeṅ-la snyég-pa* to aim at an extension of territory *Dom.*; part of the human race: **nation, people, tribe, clan, community,** *p̔á-rol-gyi sde ˌǰóms-pa* to conquer hostile nations; **class,** e.g. of letters: phonetical class; *sde sder bgó-ba* to divide into classes *Cs.*; classes of books: *mdó-sde* the Sūtras, v. sub *mdo; rgyúd-sde* the Tantras, v. sub *rgyud; sbyór-sde bži* the four volumes treating of pharmacy *Glr.*; of monks: community of monks, body of conventuals (consisting of not less than four persons); hence **convent, monastery,** *sde btsugs* he founded convents *Glr.*; *čos-sde* id.; class of religious followers, philosophical school, *sde bži* the four (principal) schools *Tar.*; *lha srín-gyi sde brgyad, lha k̔lú-la sógs-pai sde brgyad* the eight classes of spirits, frq.; it is also used for a great quantity, great many, lots of; and by improper use, or by way of abbreviation for *sdé-pa*, *sde-dpon*, commander, ruler.

Comp. and deriv. *sde-skór Glr.* **district.** — *sde-k̔rugs* **insurrection,** general revolt of a people, *byéd-pa* to excite one *Ma.* — *sde-snód ysum*, त्रिपिटक, **'the three baskets',** viz. the three classes of the sacred Buddhist writings, *ˌdúl-bai* (discipline), *mdó-sdéi* (Sūtras), *sṅágs-kyi sde-snód* (Mantras, i.e. metaphysics and mysticism), hence *sde-snód-la sbyáṅ-ba* to study the sacred writings *Mil.* — *sdé-pa* 1. **the chief** or **governor** of a district *C.*, = *ˌgó-pa W.*, **majordomo** of the Dalai Lama, *Köpp.* II., 134; in a general sense: **a man of quality, a nobleman** *Ma.* 2. **a letter** of a certain phonetic class, or the phonetic class itself, *sdé-pa bži-pa* the fourth phonetic class, the labials *Gram.* So the word is also used for denoting a certain class or **school** of Buddhist philosophers, *Tar.*, frq. — *sde-dpón* = *sdé-pa* 1, signifies also a class of **demons** *Dom.* — *sde-tsán* **class,** e.g. phonetic class, = *sde*; a particular kind of writing, *nā-ga-ri sde-tsán Glr.*; — *sde-yzár Sch.* **lawlessness, anarchy,** *sde-yzár čén-po* general anarchy (?) — *sde-yaṅs* (spelling?) **court, court-yard,** = *k̔yams*. — *sde-rigs* **dominion, territory,**

Glr. — *sde-srid* 1. **province, kingdom** *Cs.* 2. **regent, administrator,** in more recent times title of the *sdé-pa* of the Dalai Lama, and the rulers of Bhotan. *Köpp.* II., 154.

སྡེ་བ་ *sde-ba*(?) *W.* **ĭ-ru dé-če med** there is here no room any more.

སྡེབ་ *sdeb* (? *ₒdebs*) **time, times,** = *lan W.*, e.g. four times.

སྡེབ་པ་ *sdéb-pa*, pf. *bsdebs*, fut. *bsdeb*, imp. *sdebs*, 1. **to mingle, mix, blend** (*ṗyogs*) *γčig-tu* together, *Lex.*, cf. *sbyir-ba*. — 2. **to join, unite, combine,** *drás-su sdéb-pa Mil.*, by the context: sewed well together, — but *drás-su*? — Gen. vb.n.: **to join, to unite,** *daṅ* with, also *la*, *sems mig daṅ bsdébs-nas lta, rná-ba daṅ bsdébs-nas nyan Mil.* the soul sees by joining the eye, it hears by joining the ear; **to join company, to associate, to hold intercourse with,** *Mil.*; also to have sexual intercourse *Pth.*, cf. *ₒdré-ba, ₒgrógs-pa, dzóm-pa*. — 3. **to prepare, dress, get ready** (victuals) *Sch.*, cf. *sbyór-ba*. — 4. **to exchange, barter, truck for,** **bág-ṗe ḍás-la** *W.* flour for rice; in this sense prob. also used by *Mil.*; **to change,** money, **nul deb sal** please change me a rupee (not so in *C.*). — 5. **to make poetry, to compose verses,** at the end of poems: *žés-pa . . . kyis sdéb-pao* the above verses have been composed by . . .; = *sbyór-ba*.

སྡེབ་སྦྱོར་ *sdeb-sbyór* 1. **composition,** esp. poetical, **poetry,** — 2. *yi-gei sdeb-sbyór* **orthography** *Schr.*, *Cs.*, *Sch.*

སྡེར་མ་ *sdér-ma*, resp. *γsol-sdér*, **dish, platter, plate, saucer**; *sder-gáṅ* a plateful, a dish (of meat etc.), esp. *C.*

སྡེར་(མོ) *sdér(-mo)* **claw, talon,** *sdér-kyu Sch.* id.; *sdér-mo rno* a sharp claw; *sdér-čan* furnished with claws, *sder-méd* without claws; *sder-ₒdzin byéd-pa* to seize with the claws *Cs.*; *stag(-gi)-sdér* a tiger's claw *Lt.*; *sder-čágs* animals provided with claws *Mil.*

སྡོ་ཁམ་ *sdo-ḱám Sch.* **belonging together, a pair**(?).

སྡོ་བ་ *sdó-ba*, pf. (*b*)*sdos*, fut. *bsdo*, imp. *sdos* (also *dó-ba* q. v.) 1. **to risk, hazard, venture,** gen. c. *daṅ*, also c. dat. or accus., *bdág-gi lus* one's own body *Dom.*; *lus srog daṅ* frq., *lus daṅ sróg-la Dzl.* — 2. **to bear up against,** *sdug-bsṅal, nyon-móṅs-pa daṅ*, against heavy trials, against toil and drudgery *Dzl.*; **to bid defiance,** to an enemy *Dzl.*, also **to behave with insolence, contemptuously** *Dzl.* — 3. *lág-pas Dzl.* ༢༢ཁ, 6(?).

སྡོང་པོ་ *sdóṅ-po* (*C.* vulg. **dúm-po**) 1. **trunk, stem, body** of a tree *Glr.* — 2. **stalk,** of a plant, *pádmai* of a lotus; *sdóṅ-po ḱoṅ-stoṅ* a hollow stalk *Wdṅ.*; *sdóṅ-poi sde* the class of stalked plants *Cs.* — 3. **tree,** also *śiṅ-sdóṅ(-po)* frq.; *śiṅ-sdóṅ rkaṅ-γčig* a tree of a single stem *Glr.*; *śiṅ-sdóṅ ḱoṅ-rúl* a tree rotten at the core; col. fig. barren, of females, prob. jestingly. — 4. **block, log.**

Comp. *Cs.*: *sdar-sdóṅ* trunk of a walnut-tree, *śug-sdóṅ* stem of a juniper-tree; *ṫsil-sdóṅ* **a tallow-candle**; *ḱyags-sdóṅ* **an icicle.** — *mčod-sdóṅ* (*Sch.* = *mčod-rtén*), in a botanical work it was explained by 'wick', = *sdoṅ-rás*, which seems to be more to the purpose, as a blossom is compared with it. — *sdoṅ-rkáṅ* v. *sdoṅ-rás*. — *sdoṅ-dúm* **stump of a tree,** *sdóṅ-dúm ṫsig-pa* the burnt stump of a tree *Cs.* — *sdóṅ-bu Cs.* 1. **a small trunk.** 2. **stalk.** 3. **wick.** — *sdoṅ-rás, sdoṅ-śiṅ, sdoṅ-rkáṅ C.* a wick of cotton, of wood, of pith; cotton wicks are used esp. for sacred lamps.

སྡོང་བ་, སྡོངས་པ་ *sdóṅ-ba, sdóṅs-pa* (*Sch.* also *rdóṅs-pa*) pf. *bsdoṅs*, fut. *bsdoṅ*, **to unite, to join** (in undertakings), **to enter into a confederacy, to associate one's self with,** c. *daṅ* (also accus.?); *ḱyod daṅ ṅa sdóṅ-ste ₒgro* you and I, we will go together; *sdóṅs-zla* prob. = *zla-grógs*.

སྡོད་པ་ *sdód-pa*, pf. and fut. *bsdad*, resp. *bžés-pa, W.* **dád-če**, 1. **to sit,** frq., **sil-la dod** *W.* sit down in the shade! *dál-bar sdọ́d-pa* to sit still *Lt.* — 2. **to stay, to tarry, to abide,** *ṫóg-mar der bsdad* for the present I will stay here yet a little longer *Mil.*; *nyál-nas bsdad-ₒdug-pa* to lie down and to continue lying *Mil.*; **dọ́-du ǰúg-pa** to receive hospitably, **mi ǰúg-pa** to deny reception, to send away *C.*; **to stop, to halt,** in running, walking *Dzl.*;

to wait, *re žig ma bsád-par sdód-čig* wait a little yet before beginning to kill *Dzl.*; *skád-čig kyaṅ sdód-pai loṅ méd-par* without waiting even for a moment *Glr.*; *Ld.*: **ltós-te dád-če** to wait and see whether etc.; **sám-te dád-če** to wait for, hope for, to look forward to, **gúg-te dád-če** id.; *mdó-sde ˳di ˳tsó-žiṅ sdód-na* as long as the authority of this book is acknowledged *Dom.*; **zag daṅ kyir-kyír dad dug** *W.* (this thing) always remains round (crooked), it will not get straight. — 3. **to be at home,** **dẹ' yọ'** he is at home, **dẹ' me'** he is not at home *C.*; **to live, reside, settle at** *B.* and col.; *bka-sdód Lex.*, *C.*: 1. **attendant, waiting servant,** 2. **aid-de camp.**

སྡོམ་ *sdom* 1. *Lex.* and *C.* **spider.** — 2. **summary, contents,** *spii sdom* 1. **table of contents, index** *S.g.* 2. **general introductory remarks, introduction,** also *sdom-ṫsig; sdóm-la* **summarily, to be brief, in short.**

སྡོམ་པ་ *sdóm-pa* I. vb., pf. *bsdams, bsdoms,* fut. *bsdam, bsdom,* imp. *sdom(s), W.* **dám-če** 1. **to bind,** *lčags-sgróg-gis* **to fetter** *Cs.*; **to bind** or **tie fast, to pinion; to bind up, to dress,** wounds. — 2. **to fasten, to fix firmly,** e.g. by a screw-vice; *k'ro-čús* by melted metal, i.e. to solder; *so,* to press, grind, or strike the teeth together, **to gnash,** as in anger *Pth.*; **to fasten securely,** the door *Dzl.*, *Pth.*; *rtsá-k'a* **to close** an opened vein *Med.*; hence in general, 3. **to stanch, stop, to cause to cease,** *rtsa-k'rág šór-ba* the bloody flux *Med.*; **to bind, constrain, render harmless, to neutralize,** *nyés-pa* an evil *Lex.*, *Sch.* — 4 *W.* **k'áb-ša dam dug** the shoe **pinches.** — 5. to make morally firm, **to confirm,** *spyód-pa*, one's conduct, to conform it strictly to the moral law. — 6. with or without *bdag-nyid,* **to bind one's self, to engage** *Cs.* — 7. **to add together, to cast** or **sum up,** *rgyud bži bsdóms-pas leu* ༡༥༤ all the four Gyud together have 154 chapters; *yóṅs-su bsdús-pa-la* taking all together *Tar.*

II. sbst. **सम्वर obligation, engagement, duty,** *sdóm-pa len-pa Glr.*, *˳dzin-pa Cs.*, to enter into an engagement, to bind one's self to perform a certain duty, *mi-la ˳bógs-pa* **to bind a person by duty,** by oath, **to swear in** *Glr* (e.g. in convents, in the relations of priests and laymen); *srúṅ-ba* to be true to one's duty, to keep one's engagements; *˳čor* a duty is violated *Glr.*; *ṅá-la sdóm-pa med* I have renounced my vow *Glr.* — *sdóm-pa ɣsum,* acc. to *Glr.* and other more recent authors, are: *so-ṫár* (v. *so-só*), *byaṅ-séms,* and *ɣsaṅ-sṅágs-kyi sdom-pa.*

Comp. *sdom-ltóṅ(?)* **neck-bell,** bell attached to the neck of cattle. — *sdom-byéd* 1. **one that binds,** by duty etc. 2. **an astringent medicine** *Cs.* — *sdom-ɣzér* **rivet** of a pair of scissors or tongs *Sch.*

སྡོམ་བུ *sdóm-bu Sch.*: **a ball; a round tassel.**

སྡོར་, རྡོར་ *sdor, rdor* 1. (like ὄψον) that which gives relish to food, **seasoning, condiment,** esp. *ṫúg-sdor* that which gives substance to soup, viz. **meat;** *ṫsa-sdór* salt and meat. — 2. **spice,** *sdór-gyi rkyál-pa* spice-bag *S.g.*; *sdor-ṫál* spice-powder *Sch.* —

བརྡ་ *brda* (संकेत) **sign,** i.e. 1. **gesture,** *čágs-pa ˳dód-pai brda máṅ-du bstán-nas* making many wanton gestures (or giving hints, intimations v. 2), *lág-brda* signs with the hand, *saṅs-rgyás la ɣsól-čig čes lág-brda byas* they beckoned to him to ask Buddha *Dzl.*; **míg-da táṅ-če** *W.* to give a hint with the eye, to wink. — 2. **indication, intimation, symptom, token,** *mi-rtág ˳gyúr-bai brdao* it is an indication of their frail condition *Thgy.*; **symbol** *Pth.*, *brdar* as a symbol, symbolically; *de gaṅ yin ˳dri-bai brda stón-pa* to ask for a thing by symbolic signs, in symbolic language *Glr.*; *brda spród-pa, ˳pród-pa, sbyór-ba, ˳grol-ba* **to explain, describe, represent,** with accus., and prob. also with genit.: *yin-lugs-kyi brda ˳gról-ba Mil.* to explain the essence or nature of things (ni f.); meton. *dei brda či lags* what may be the symbolical meaning of it *Mil.* — 3. **word,** *˳bód-pai brda* interjection *Liš.*; *˳dúl-bai brda* word out of the Dulwa *Zam.* *dris-pai brda-rnyiṅ* an obsolete word for being asked', *Lex.*; *brdá-sgyur-pa Sch.* **interpreter, dragoman** *Sch.*; *brdai blá-ma* is stated to be a Lama who instructs by word of mouth *Mil.*; esp with regard to the spelling of words: *brda yaṅ mi ₒdra sna-tsogs gyur* there came also into use various spellings *Zam.*; *brda - rnyiṅ* old orthography, *brda-ɣsár* new orthography *Zam.*; *bód-kyi brdai bstan-bčós* title of the Zamatog; *tsig-brda* = *tsig*, *tsig-brda-yis ₒgrol-ba* to explain by words *Mil.*

Comp. *brdá-skad* **language by symbolical signs** *Mil.*; prob. also nothing but the usual language by words *Glr.* — *brda-čád* (prob. for *ₒčad*, from *ₒčád-pa* II.), *me-loṅ-gi brda-čád* the language or evidence of the mirror; so prob. also *Tar.* 210, 22. — *brda-spród*, *brda-sbyór* 1. **explanation**, *miṅ - dón brda-spród* explanation of the import of names, title of a small Materia Medica by a certain Wairocana. 2. **orthography** *Gram.*, *Pth.* — *brda - lon Mil.* is said to be = *tsig-lan*, verbal answer. — *brda-lags* 'insignis', acc. to *Cs.* in *Journ. As. Soc. Beng.* V, 384.

བརྡུལ་བ་ *brdúl-ba* 1. *Lex.* w.e.; *Sch.* **to deceive, to cheat** 2. *Sch.* **to swing, brandish, flourish**, *ɣyáb-mo* a fly-flap.

བརྡོག་འཛོས་པ་ *brdog-ₒčos-pa* **to slip, to slide, to lose one's footing.**

བསྡར་བ་ *bsdár-ba*, *Sch.*: *mdún-du bsdár-ba* **to hope, to expect** or **wait for a** favour. In *Dzl.* ༢༣༨, 18 the better reading (accordant with the manuscript of Kyelang) is *sdur* (= *sdú-bar*).

བསྡོགས་པ་ *bsdógs-pa*; the *Lexx.* add: *grabs*, *Cs.* **to compose, prepare, make ready**, *nyer bsdógs-pa* id.; *sna-tág bsdógs-pa* to wind the rope, which is fastened in the nose of an ox or a camel, round the horns or the neck of the animal.

ན

ན *na* 1. the letter **n.** — 2. num. figure: 12.

ན་ *na* **meadow**, *C.* also *ná-ma*; *nar skye* it grows on meadows, *Wdṅ.* and elsewh. (cf. *neu*).

ན་ *na* I. sbst. 1. **year** (?) v. *na-niṅ*. — 2. **stage of life, age**, also *na-tsód*, and *ná-so*, resp. *sku-ná* (also *sku-nás?*); *na-tsód rgás - pas Wdṅ.* old, of an advanced age; *ná-so ɣžón-te Glr.* young; *sku-nás pʼrá - mo Mil.* of a tender age; *na-tsód-kyi dbyé - ba* the different ages or stages of life; (*sku-*) *nár-son-pa* (*Sch.* grown old?) *Glr.*: of full age, adult, grown up; **ná-so-tsír-la** *W.* according to age; *na - čúṅ girl*, maiden, virgin, *na - čúṅ bzáṅ - mo bču* ten beautiful girls *Dzl.*; *na-mnyám*, -*ₒdrá*, -*zlá*, *neu-ldáṅ Lex.* of the same age, coetaneous; **ná-da-tom-mo** *C.* a festivity given by wealthy parents on their son's birthday to him and his playmates, also **ló-da-tom-mo**; *na-pʼrá young*, tender; *na-ɣžón* = *ɣžón - nu*. II. postp. c. accus., signifying the place where a thing is, 1. added to substantives, **in**, (more accurately *náṅ-na* c. genit.), sometimes also to be rendered by **on, at, with, to** etc. *mdó-na* in scripture, *lo-rgyús-na* in a book of history *Glr.*; *dé - na* there, in that place; of time: *dus-ɣčig-na* at the same time, *dei tsé-na* at that time, then etc. — 2. added to verbs, either to the inf., or more frq. (col. always) to the verbal root: **in, at, during** (the doing or happening of a thing), hence a. **when, at the time of**, *bós-na* when I called *Dzl.*, *zér-ba-na* when he said *Tar.*; *bdág-gi pʼa tse pʼós-na* when my father shall have died *Dzl.*; with *nam*: *nam dús-la báb-na* (*W.* **dus léb-na**) when the time comes, frq.; *nam ₒgró-na* when I (you etc.) go, was going, shall go. — b. **if, in case, supposing that** (ἐάν), the different degrees of possibility, however, cannot be so precisely expressed by the mood in Tibetan, as in other languages; with or without a preceding *gál-te*, *či-ste* etc. (cf. the remarks sub *gaṅ* II.); . . . *ma mtóṅ na* . . . *mi rtógs-par dug* if we had not seen . . ., we should not have known . . . *Mil.*; but in most cases also the vb., to which it is subordinate, is put in the gerund: *ₒdi byás-na brám-ze ma yin-pas* as I should be no longer a Brahmin, if I were to do that *Dzl.*; further: **if even** . . ., how much the more . . .! in asseverations: **if** . . ., then indeed may . . .! then I would that . . .! it is well, that . . ., it will be well, if . . ., *na légs-so* frq.; if *légs-so* is elliptically omitted, *na* answers to: **o that! would that!** also: **I will;** in an interrogative sentence, viz. '*légs-sam*' being omitted, to: **must I? shall I?** *Mil.*: *čos byás-na snyam* (when we are with you) we think, we will be pious! *ₒjig-rtén byás-na snyam* (when we have come home) we think, let us take care of temporal things! *či drág-na* (better *či byás-na drag*) what shall we consider the most advantageous? — c. of a more general signification: **as, since, whilst, by** (with the partic. pres.), = *te* or *pas* *Dzl.* frq., *dug zós-na yaṅ* even by eating poisonous things (he was not hurt) ༢༥, 3; *na* is used thus, however, only in conjunction with *yaṅ*, and *dug zós-na yaṅ* is the more popular phrase for *dug zos kyaṅ* In careless speaking or writing *na* is also used for *čé-na* *Thgy.* frq. — 3. pleon. added to the termination of the instr. of substantives and verbs: *rgyu dés-na* **for that reason, therefore,** *čii rgyús-na* **for what reason, why, wherefore** *Stg.*; *dé-bas-na* **hence, thus, so then, accordingly,** very frq.; *kúr-bas-na* because they carried *Glr.*; also added to the termination of the termin.: *ji-ltar-na* frq.; *ɣčig-tu-na*, *ɣnyís-su-na*, **in the first place, firstly** etc. *Dzl.*; *skád-du-na* *Dzl.*; *rgya-gár skád-du-na* *Thgy.* — 4. incorr. for *nas*, col. frq.; its being used for the termin. is very questionable, and the rare instances of this use in books may be regarded as errors in writing (e.g. *Dzl.* ༢༥༠, 17 *náṅ-na soṅ* inst. of *naṅ-du*), whereas the contrary, *du* for *na*, occurs frq., and is to be considered as sanctioned.

III. conj. **and,** *Bal* (?) — IV. v. *ná-k'a*, *ná-ba*.

ན་ཁ་ *ná-k'a*, = *spaṅ*, **greensward, turf.**

ནཱ་ག་ *nā-ga*, *Ssk.* for *klu*.

ནཱ་ག་རི་ *nā-ga-ri* **Sanskrit, Sanskrit-letters.**

ནཱ་གི་ *na-gi* *Sch.* 1. **being ill** (?). 2. **the claws of a sea-monster** (?).

ནཱ་གེ་སར་ *nā-ge-sar* *Lt.* = Hindi, for नागकेसर, Mesua ferrea.

ན་འཇའ་ *na-ₒja* *W.* **mock-suns** and similar phenomena, v. *na-bún*.

ན་ཉིང་ *ná-niṅ* (*Cs.*: 'for *na-rnyiṅ*') **the last year;** gen. adv. **last year;** *ná-niṅ-gi* adj. **of last year** or **last year's** (crop).

ན་བ་ *ná-ba* 1. **to be ill, sick;** inf. also the state of being ill, **illness, sickness,** *ná-ba ɣsó-ba* to cure it *Lt.*, though *nad* is more in use; partic.: a sick person, **patient,** *ná-ba daṅ ₒči-ba* disease and death; *skye rga na ₒči* v. *skyé-ba* I., *rgás-pa daṅ ná-ba* old and sick people; *mi-ná-ba ɣnás-pa* to remain in health *S.g.*; *ná-ba-pa*, *ná-ba-ma* *Cs.* a sick person, an invalid (male and female); *ná-mo* a female patient *Mil.*; *ná-ba-mk'an* a sickly person, an invalid *Cs.*; *ná-ba-čan* sickly, *na-ba-méd* healthy *Cs.*; *na-t'óg* after falling ill *Sch.* — 2. of the separate parts of the body: **to ache,** *rná-ba* (not *-bai*) *ná-ba* pain in the ear, earache; *lus t'ams-čád na* (my) whole body aches *Dom.*; *so ná-na* having the toothache; *nán-na na* it aches, when pressed (with the fingers) *S.g.*; *klád-pa ná-ba-la* (good) for the headache, for diseases of the brain; *na-ₒp'réṅ* complication of diseases or fits *Sch.*; *na-(ba daṅ)zúg(-rṅu)*, *na-tsá* disease and pain.

ན་བུན་ *na-bún* **fog, thick mist,** *t'ibs*, *ₒk'yims* comes on; *byin-rlabs-kyi* prob. a cloud, a flood, of blessing *Mil.*

ནམ་ *ná-ma* 1. v. *na* I. 2. also *ná-mo* (नमस्), **praise, glory, adoration**, *na-mo gu-ru* praise to the teacher!

ནཱ་མ་ *ná-ma Ssk.* = *žes byá-ba* **so called**, frq. in titles of books.

ན་བཟའ་ *ná-bza* (**ná-za**, vulg. **náb-za, nám-za**) resp. for *gos*, **garment, dress**, frq.; *ɣsól-ba* to put it on.

ནའུན་ *na-ún* obs. or vulg. for *na-bún*, old edition of *Mil.*

ན་རག་ *na-rag*, *Ssk.* नरक, **hell.**

ན་རམ་ *na-rám* medicinal herb, *Med.*; in *Lh.* Polygon. viviparum.

ནཱ་རི་ཀེ་ལ་ *na-ri-ke-la Ssk.* **cocoa-nut.**

ན་རེ་ *ná-re*, by form and position an adv., like *ₒdí-skad-du*; before words or sentences that are quoted literally, mostly followed by *smrás-nas*, *zér-ba-la*, but not always, in which latter case it stands for **'he says, he said'** etc., the noun being always put in the nom. case, never in the instr.: *ₒpags-pa na-re* the Reverend said; rarely in accessory sentences: *gál-te ɣžán-dag ná-re* (not *ná-re-na*) si forte alii dixerint *Wdṅ.*; even without *gál-te* in the same sense *Thgy.* It hardly occurs in old classical literature, nor in the col. language of *W.*, but pretty frq. in later literature. In *Kun.*, however, there exists a vb. *ná-čas* (**ná-čā**), pf. *nas* (**nā**), *imp. nos* (**nō**) which is used for *zér-ba* (not in use there), and is construed with the instr.: *ă-pa-su nā soṅ* the father has said.

ན་རོ་ *ná-ro* the sign for the vowel **o**, ◌ོ.

ནཱ་རོ་ *ná-ro* n. of a holy Lama *Mil.*; *nā-ro-pa Tar.* 181, 10 id.? *ná-roi sems-ₒdzin-gyi lčags-ťág* a sort of puzzle.

ན་ལནྡ་ *na-landa Pth. nā-len-dra Wdk.*, n. of a monastery in Magadha.

ན་ལི་ *ná-li* **bowl, basin**, an iron or china dish *W.*

ན་ལེ་ཤག་ *na-le-šag Lt.*, *šal S.g.*, = *ši-kru Wdṅ.* (शिग्रु?) n. of an acrid medicine.

ནག་ *nag* (blackness?) **crime, offence, transgression**, v. *nág-pa* comp.; *nag-ku-be-ra* v. *ku-be-ra.*

ནག་པ་, ནག་པོ་ *nág-pa*, gen. *nág-po*, **black**, *ber p̔yi nág-pa naṅ dkár-ba* a garment outside black, inside white *Glr.*; **nág-po ma ku** do not blacken it, do not soil it! of the countenance **dark, frowning, gloomy, mournful** *Glr.*; *mi nag* (*-po* or *-pa*) a black one, a layman, (on account of his not being clad in a red or yellow clerical garb); *nág-po* n. p. **Krishna** *Tar.*, *nág-po čén-po* = महाकाल **Siwa**; *nág-mo* 1. **a black woman,** 2. **Kali, Uma;** *nág-moi-ₒbaṅs* or *kol* Kālidāsa. — 3. **woman,** in general *Sch.* — *nag-ₒgrós*, *nág-po ₒgro-šés* 'easy to be understood' *Sch.*; acc. to our Lama from Tashilunpo *nág-po ₒgro-bšér* implies: illustrating a sentence by comparing it with similar passages; *nág-čan* 1. **a person guilty of a crime** *Sch.*; *mi nág-čan dóṅ-nas ťár-pa* a criminal released from prison *Mil.* 2. **a married man** *Sch.* — *nag-čágs* **black-cattle, horned cattle** *Sch.*; v. also *ɣnág-pa.* — *nág-ču* n. of a river north of Lhasa, *Huc* II, 238; *nág-ču-ka-pa* people living on its banks, notorious for their thievish propensities. — *nag-čén*, *nag-nyés C.* **a heinous crime.** — *nag-ťúm*, *nag-ťóm*, *Sch.*, *nag-siṅ-ba Thgy.*, *nag-hur-ré Sch.*, **coal-black, jet-black.** — *nag-nóg* (*-čan*) **dirty, dingy; not clear,** as bad print; fig. **stained, polluted,** with sin, guilt, *sems.* — *nag-p̔yógs* v. *p̔yogs.* — *nag*(*-ma*)*-ťsúr* **a black mineral colour,** *Sch*: **green vitriol**(?). — *nag-tsíg* **a point, dot,** *W.* — *nag-zúg* (?) **darkness,** *nag-zúg-la snóm-bžin soṅ* he groped about in the dark.

ནག་ཤ་ *nág-ša Sch.*: **linden-tree, lime-tree** (hardly to be found in Tibet; the word perhaps introduced from Mongol dictionaries).

ནགས་(མ་) *nágs* (*-ma Glr.*) *B.*, *C.*, *W.*, **forest,** *rtsi-šiṅ-nags-kyis mdzes* beautified by forests, richly wooded *Glr.*; *ₒtúg-po* dense forest; *nags-kród* a thicket *Glr.*; *nágs-čan* woody, covered with forests; *nags-ljóṅs* woodland country, a well-wooded province; *nags-sbál Lt.* tree-frog (?); *nags-ťsál* = *nags*, *nyám-ṅa-ba* a dreadful forest *Dzl.*; *yid-du-ₒoṅ-ba* a lovely wood *Sambh.*; *nags-*(*ɣ*)*séb* an intersected forest, v. (*ɣ*)*seb.*

ནང་ *naṅ* I. the space within a thing, 1. **the interior, the inside,** *p̔úg-pai naṅ k̔un* the whole interior of the cavern *Mil.*; *γžóṅ-pai, dóṅ-gi naṅ* the interior of a basin, of a pit (e.g. being filled up) *Dzl.*; *k̔áṅ-pai naṅ pyag-dár byéd-pa* to sweep the inside of a house *Dzl.* — 2. **space, room, apartment, chamber** col. — 3. **dwelling, domicile, house,** esp. *C.* — 4. meton **inmates, family, household,** **naṅ ťsaṅ** *W.* the whole family. — 5. **the interior** (spiritually), **heart, mind, soul,** *ye-šés náṅ-na šar* wisdom begins to shine in the mind; *žen-ₒdzin naṅ-nas ₒgrol* affection, interest, disappears from the heart *Glr.* — 6. sometimes adv. for *náṅ-na.*

II. *náṅ-gi*, genit., used 1. as an adj.: **inner, inward, esoteric** (opp. *to p̔yii*), *náṅ-gi k̔rims, náṅ-k̔rims,* a private law, an esoteric precept or doctrine not intended for the public; **ge-dün-gyi naṅ-ťim dhaṅ ₒgal ťsé** *C.* if priests violate their special moral duties, (very different from *náṅ-pai k̔rims* the Buddhist law, merely opp. to Brahmanism); *náṅ-gi sbyin-pa* inward offerings, i.e. spiritual sacrifices, opp. to outward and material offerings; but *Dzl.* ༢༣༧, 4 it denotes personal sacrifices, the surrendering of parts of our own self, e.g. a member of the body, opp. to outward property; the meaning also reminds of Rom. 12, 1, and I Pet 2, 5. — *náṅ-gi byá-ba* internal affairs *Glr.*; v. also the compounds. — 2. for *náṅ-na* **among, amidst,** frq. c. accus.: *bu náṅ-gi ťa čuṅ, p̔úg-ron náṅ-gi čúṅ-ṅu Dzl.* the smallest among etc.: for *dé-dag-gi náṅ-na* **of it, of them, among them** etc.: *náṅ-gi čúṅ-ṅu* the least of them *Dzl.*; *náṅ-gi lhá-mo sṅá-ma* the foremost among the goddesses; sometimes more pleon., without distinct reference to a preceding noun, *Dzl.* ༢༥, 18; ༢༣༧, 16 (where *Sch.* prob. translates incorr.).

III. with *la, na, du, nas;* 1. as sbst., acc. to the significations given above, e.g. *nád-pai náṅ-du ₒǰúg-pa* to go **into** the room of a sick person *Wdṅ.*; *dei náṅ-du γdan-dráṅs-te* inviting **into** their house *Mil.* — 2. as adv. *náṅ-na* **in it, therein, within, among it** or **them;** *náṅ-du* and *náṅ-la* **thereinto, into it;** *náṅ-nas* out, thereout, from among; among it or them = *náṅ-na.* — 3. postp: **in, into, among** etc., e.g. *rdziṅ-gi náṅ-na k̔rus byéd-pa Dzl.* to bathe in a pond, *čui náṅ-du žúgs-pa* to go into the water; *groṅ-k̔yér dei naṅ daṅ p̔yi-rol-na* in the town and out of it *Dzl.*; **sém-mi náṅ-na zér-pa** *W.* he said to himself; *snai náṅ-nas byuṅ* it came out of his nose (again) *Dzl.*; *mii náṅ-na(s) bzáṅ-po žig* one very beautiful among men *Dzl.*; *gliṅ dé-rnams-kyi náṅ-na(s) mčóg-tu gyúr-pa* the most important among or of these countries *Glr.* (here at least the sing. is as frq. als the plur.); in col. language the word is much used, though often inaccurately; so it is frq. employed, where the later literature has *ṅáṅ-la, ṅáṅ-nas;* **wáṅ-gi náṅ-na** by force; **só-me náṅ-na zer gos** *W.* that should have been mentioned, when it was fresh (in remembrance); **lo tóṅ-ni náṅ-na ťsá-pig ma ťsar** not yet quite in a thousand years, i.e. it is not full a thousand years *W.* — There is still to be noticed: ***naṅ*** = *naṅ-mo.* — ***naṅ-méd-la*** col. frq. suddenly; in *B.* of rare occurrence; ***naṅ-méd nor rnyéd-pa*** to become rich unexpectedly *S.g.*

Comp. and deriv. *naṅ-kyóg Sch.*: having legs bending inward, **bandy-legged.** — *naṅ-skór* v. *skór-ba* extr. — ***naṅ-k̔rims*** v. above. — *naṅ-k̔ról*, vulgo *-rol*, **bowels, entrails, intestines;** also any separate part of them; *naṅ-k̔ról dróṅ-ba* spasmodic contractions of the bowels *Sch.*; *naṅ-k̔rol-bžág* seems in *Lexx.* to be taken synon. with *mnyam-bžag.* — *naṅ-góg* v. *ťer.* — **naṅ-gyóg** *W.* **a large bolt, door-bar.** — *náṅ-ča* = *naṅ-k̔rol.* — *naṅ-čags-su* in one's self, in one's own mind *Sch.* — *náṅ-rǰe* **minister of the interior, home-minister** *Sch.* — *náṅ-lta Glr* 89, 11? — *naṅ-ťáb byéd-pa* to be involved in intestine war *Pth.*, = *naṅ-ₒk̔rúgs.* — *naṅ-dág* 1. *Sch.* 'the interior being cleansed'. 2. col. (or *naṅ-brtags?*) v. *snaṅ.* — *náṅ-don* **the intrinsic meaning, the true sense,** *náṅ-don rtóg-pa* to investigate, to study, the real meaning; **náṅ-don tóg-k̔en,* or *ghó-ḱęn** C., *náṅ-don-ċan (or -yod-ḱan)* W. most learned, very erudite; acc. to Cs. more particularly the mystical sense of religious writings, a higher degree of theology, as it were; *ndṅ-don-gyi rab.byáms-pa* a Doctor of Divinity Cs. — *naṅ-náṅ-gi, naṅ-náṅ-nas = naṅ-gi, naṅ-nas* among. — *náṅ-pa* **Buddhist**, opp. to *pyi-pa*, Non-Buddhist, Brahmanist; *náṅ-pai lta-ba, bstán-pa, čos, stón-pa, čá-lugs,* the theory etc. of the Buddhists. — *náṅ-po* an intimate, a bosom-friend *Sch.* — *náṅ-mt́* members of a household, inmates (ni f) *Dom.* — *náṅ-miġ* room, apartment, C., W. — **naṅ-yáṅs** W. wide, spacious, roomy. — *naṅ-ról = naṅ-ḱrol* — *náṅ-śa* lining, *náṅ-śa tán-wa* to cover on the inside, to line, *náṅ-śa-ċen* C. lined. — *naṅ-sél* **dissension, discrepancy.** — *naṅ-ysés* **reciprocal, mutual** *Wdṅ.* frq.

ནང་མཆོད་ *naṅ-mčód* **a sort of potion** (thin pap?) consisting of the 'ten impurities', viz. five kinds of flesh (also human flesh), excrements, urine, blood, marrow, and '*byaṅ-sḿs dkár-po*' (?), all mixed together, transsubstantiated by charms, and changed into *bdúd-rtsi* or **nectar**, a small quantity of which is tasted by the devotees, with the Lama at their head. This delicious drink is considered of great importance by the mystics, who seek to obtain spiritual gifts by witchcraft (cf. *mdo* extr.); hence every offering is sprinkled with this potion.

ནང་ལྟར་ (*náṅ-ltar*) *náṅ-tar* W., C., *náṅ-żin* C. col. for *bżin-du, ltar,* **according to, in conformity with, like, as,** c. genit. or accus., *bka náṅ-tar, bḱai naṅ-tar.*

ནང་མེ་ *náṅ-me,* resp. for *me* **fire** W. (*snáṅ-me?*).

ནང་མོ་ *náṅ-mo (ma Pth.?)* **the morning;** in the morning; *náṅ-mo ẏċig bżin-du* every morning *Pth.; naṅ re* id.; *naṅ re dgoṅs re* every morning and evening; *da-náṅ* this morning; *da-náṅ ni ġáṅ-nas byon* where do you come from to-day? *Mil.; da-nan-ġi tsó-ba* this. day's breakfast *Mil.; naṅ-nub in the* morning and in the even-

ing; *naṅ-nub nyi-pyéd ysúm-la* in the morning, in the evening, and at noon. — *naṅ-par* 1. in the morning, *naṅ-par śna* early in the morning *Dzl.* 2. **the morning** esp **the following morning,** *náṅ-par-ky' skál-ba*—the allowance, the ration for the following morning *Glr.*

ནང་ས་ *naṅs W.* (?) *naṅ-ċuṅ yod* that is a mere **trifle,** not worth while, cf. *mnog.*

ནང་པར་ *náṅs-par Cs.,* *náṅ-la* *W.,* **the day after to-morrow,** *B. ynaṅ.*

ནད་ *nad* **disease, distemper, malady, sickness,** cf. *ná-ba;* (the Tibetan science of medicine distinguishes 404 kinds of diseases); *mi-nad pyúgs-nad* diseases among men and animals *Glr.; nad yso-ba* to cure a disease, *nad ₒtsó-ba, nad sós-par,* or *żí-bar,* or *daṅ brál-bar ₒgyúr-ba* to be cured of a disease, to get well, to recover; *nád-kyis ₒdébs-pa, ₒtébs-pa,* to be attacked by a disease, to be taken ill *B.; C.* more frq.: **nę́'-kyi gyáb-pa, zir-wa*, W.:* **ná-la nad yoṅ(s)**; *nád-kyi rgyu,* and *rkyen,* v. *rkyen* 1 and 2.

Comp. *nad-rkyál Wdk.* emblem of a deity (meaning not clear). — *nád-ḱaṅ* **hospital** *Cs.* — *nád-go* **seat of a disease** *Sch.* — *nád-ċan* **ill, sick** (little used). — *nád-pa* 1. **a sick person,** male or female. 2. adj. **ill, sick,** *sḿs-ċan nád-pa-dag S.O. = nád-po* and *nád-bu = nad Cs.,* *nád-bu-ċan* *W.,* weak in health, **sickly, poorly.** — *nad-méd* **healthy, hale, in health,** (the usual word); *nad-méd-par gyúr-ċig* may you recover your health, may you remain in good health, all hail to you! *Cs.* — *nád-med-pa* **health,** *nád-med-pa tób-pa, rnyéd-pa* to get well, to recover one's health; *nád-med-pa ₒgyúr-ba* declining health *Thgy.* — *nad tsúl* **the character of a disease** *S.g.* —*nad-yżí* **seat, primary cause** of a disease(?) *Lt.* — *nad-ẏyóg* one attending to sick persons, **a nurse;** *nad-ẏyóg byéd-pa W.* *ċó-ċe*, **to nurse.**

ནན་ *nan* **the act of pressing, urging; pressure, urgency, importunity,** *ḱóṅ-rnams-kyi nan ma tégs-par* not being able to resist their importunity *Mil.; náṅ-gyis* with urgency, pressingly, e.g. *žú-ba* to request, to solicit *Glr.*; *nán-gyis zar ȷúg-pa* to urge, to compel (a person) to eat *Dzl.*; *nán-gyis skór-ba* to press, to crowd, round *Dzl.*; *nán-gyis gúg-pa* to make a person come near by calling to him *Mil.*; *nan-čágs* 1. sbst. **certainty, surety,** **da nan-čág tob soṅ* W.* now I have certainty, now I know for sure; *nan-čags temś? Zam.* 2. adv. **certainly, surely** *W., C.*; adj. **lon nan-čág* W.* certain news. — *nán-tan* 1. sbst. **earnest desire, application, exertion** *Cs.*; *byaṅ-čúb-la nán-tan byéd-pa* to strive earnestly for perfection *Dzl.*; *nán-tan-du byéd-pa Thgy.*; in *čós-kyi nán-tan ysuṅs Pth.* '*kyi*' is perh. to be cancelled. 2. adv. *C.*: **certainly, positively,** **ṅe nén-ten láb-pa, nen-čág zér-pa**, I have told him so definitively, as my unalterable decision; *W.*: **earnestly, ardently, accurately,** **nán-tan žib-ča ltos** look at it, examine it, accurately! **nán-tan čos** do it well, most carefully! **nán-tan šrág-če** to burn entirely. — *nán-tar* very, *nán-tar bzaṅ Lex.*; **very much, all the more, altogether** *Mil.*; *nan-túr*, of rare occurrence, = *nán-tan.* — *nón-pa, ynán-pa* are cog. to *nan.*

ནན་ཏེ་ *nán-te* 1. *Ts.* for *ná-ba* **sick, ill.** — 2. *W.* **ču nán-te kyoṅ**, for *ran-te, dren-te*, conduct the water this way!

ནན་ཞག་ *nán-žag W.* **late, recent,** what has happened a few weeks or months ago.

ནབས་ *nabs* **put on** (your clothes)! *Sch.*, v. *mnáb-pa.*

ནབས་སོ་ *nábs-so* **one of the lunar mansions,** v. *rgyu-skár* ༦.

ནམ་ *nam* I. sbst. 1. **night,** *nam láṅs-te*, or *-nas*, when night departs, **at day-break,** frq.; *nam-gáṅ Sch.*: the last day of the lunar month on which there is no moonshine at all; *nam-gúṅ* **midnight,** *nám-gyi gúṅ-tun-la* in the hour of midnight *Dom.*; *nam-stód* the first half of the night, *nam-smád* the second half of the night; *nám-gyi ča stod, smad*, id. — *nam-pyéd* **midnight** *Dzl., Glr.*; *nam-žóṅ* (?) *Sch.* in the morning; *nam-riṅ Sch.* a long day (??) — *nam-láṅs* **day-break,** *nam-laṅs-kyi-bar-du Dzl.* — *nam-sród* **darkness of night,** *nam-sród byiṅ soṅ-bai tse* as it was almost quite dark *Mil.*, **nam-šród yol sóṅ-nas* C.*, *nam-srós-nas Sch.* id. — 2. for *nam-mka* q. v.

II. adv. of time, also *dus-nám-žig*, 1. **when?** frq., **how long a time?** seldom; *rgyún-du nam či ča med sgom* always keep in mind that you do not know when you will die *Mil.*; *dus-nám-žig-gi tsé-nas* **since when? since what time? how long ago?** *Mil.*; relatively: *nam gró-bai dus byéd-pa* to appoint the time, when one is going to start *Dzl.*; *nam žig sgyú-lus ȷóg-pai tse*, when he shall lay aside his phantom-body *Mil.*; **nam tsúg-pa ko ma léb-na, de tuy*...,* as long as he has not come, so long . . . *W.* — 2. *nám(-du) yaṅ* (col. **nám-aṅ, náms-aṅ**) with a negative, **never,** in sentences relating to the past, or the future, or containing a prohibition, cf. *mi* and *ma*, *nam-yaṅ mi ziṅ-to* it will never be finished *Dzl.* ༢༤༦, 9; *sṅon nam yaṅ ma tos* (that) has never been heard of formerly; without a negative in *B.* rarely, col. frq.: **always;** *nam žag brtan Mil.*; **nám-žag gyúṅ-du* C.* id.

ནམ་མཁའ་ *nám-mka* (cf. *mka* and *ynam*) the space or region above us, **heaven, sky,** where the birds are flying, and the saints are soaring, where it lightens and thunders etc.; **the ether,** as the fifth element *S. g.*; **the principle of expansion and enlargement** *Wdṅ.*; *nám-mka daṅ mnyám-pa* like unto the heavens, as to wide expanse, frq.; inaccurately also for an **innumerable multitude,** *nám-mka daṅ mnyám-pai séms-čan-rnams Mil.*; *nám-mkai dbyiṅs, nám-mka-ldiṅ(-mo)* v. sub *mka*; *nám-mkai mtoṅs* **celestial vault, firmament** *Glr., S. O.*; *nám-mka-mdog* the blue colour of the sky, **azure;** it is supposed to be produced by the southern side of mount Rirab, which consists entirely of azur-stone, *Mil.*; *kyim-gyi nám-mka-la* in the air above the house, like *bar-snáṅ-la, Tar.* ༢༦, 2; *nam-páṅs ycód-pa*, also *nam-*

dpáṅs spyód-pa Mil., to cross the height of the heavens, to fly across the sky. — nam-gru v. rgyu-skar.

ནམ་ཟླ་ (nám-zla) pronounced *nám-da, and nám-la*, Mil., Pth., col., **season,** nám-zla dus bźí the four seasons; da nam-da st·n šar now autumn has set in; *da nam-da ̥dan-mo soṅ*; fig. nám-da ̥das the (favourable) season has passed Mil.

ནམ་སོ་ nám-so = nábs-so.

ནར་ nar v. na I. and II., 2; also ná-k'a.

ནར་མ་ nár-ma adj., and nár-mar adv., continuous, without interruption Sch.; *či-ma nár-te ṭon or šor* C. torrents of tears gushed from his eyes, cf. k'rul; nár-re Mil., more vulg. *nár-ra-ra* in a long row or file, ̥grúl-ba to walk

ནར་མོ་, ནར་ནར་པོ་ nár-mo, nár-nar-po **oblong** Mil., Med.; k'a-nar-čan having the shape of a rectangle; gru-nar-čan **rhombic, lozenge-shaped.** Cf. (b)snár-ba.

ནལ་ nal n. of a precious stone Sch.

ནལ་(མ་) nál(-ma) Cs. **incest, fornication;** nal-grib pollution by it. nal-p'rúg frq., *nal-lé* Ts., bastard-child; nál-bu Sch. a libidinous woman (??).

ནལ་བྱི་ nál-byi Pth. n. of a poison-tree.

ནས་ nas I. sbst. 1. **barley,** in three varieties: mgyógs-nas (Ld. yáṅ-ma, or drug-ču-nas, Wdṅ. k'rá-ma) early barley, ripening in about 60 days; sér-mo late barley, the best sort; če-nas a middling sort. — 2. **barley-corn,** nas-tsam as much as a barley-corn Glr. — nás-čaṅ beer brewed of barley. nas-rjén v. rjén-pa. — nas-p'yé barley-flour. — *nas-zir* (spelling not certain) aim or sight on a gun W.

II. postp., sign of the ablative case (almost like las) 1. added to sbst.: **from,** byáṅ-p'yogs-nas from the north, often joined with bzúṅ-ste (Ld. *táṅs-te*), commencing **from,** extending **from,** with a following **to, as far as; till, until,** with respect so space and time; **by,** lág-pa-nas ̥dzin-pa or ̥ǰú-ba to take a person by the hand, míṅ-nas rjód-pa, smó-ba to call by name, t'igs-pa re-ré-nas (to count) by single drops, so-só-nas **one by one, each by himself; through,** dúṅ-nas bšád-pas speaking through a trumpet Glr., sgo-sáṅ-nas ltá-ba looking through the chink of a door Tar.; sgó-nas ytóṅ-ba to admit through the door Dzl.; *bi-yaṅ-nẹ p'aṅ* W. he flung it through the hole (cf. also rgyúd-pa I., 2); made, manufactured, built etc. **of,** pá-gu-nas of bricks; (made, worked, struck etc.) **with,** *lág-pa-nẹ dun* W. struck with the hand; denoting **distance:** rgyaṅ-grágs yčig-nas pó-ta-la yod C., Potala lies within reach of the ear; ̥di-nas gáṅs-ri-la far from here on the snowy mountain Glr.; with respect **to time: after,** žag bdún-nas after seven days: dé-nas **after that, afterwards, then.** — 2. added to verbs, as gerundial particle, rarely to the inf., gen. (col. always) to the verbal root, prop. **after, since;** also equivalent to te, when added to a pres. or pf. root (instances of which are to be met with almost on every page of Tibetan books); together with ̥dug or yod added to a pres. or pf. tense, col. frq., in B. rarely: ṅa lčeb dgos snyám-nas yod I think I must seek death Pth.; tsós-nas yod it is boiled Pth.; só-nam-gyi byá-ba-la žúgs-nas yód-pa-la as they began to till the ground Glr. — Col. also for na.

ནི་ ni I. 1. particle, col. also *niṅ*; Cs. justly remarks: 'an emphatical particle', serving to give force to that word or part of a sentence, which rhetorically is most important, esp. also (though not exclusively, Sch.) to separate the subject of a sentence from its predicate, thus adding to perspicuity: k'yod ̥dir ̥óṅs-pa ni ṅai mt'us ̥oṅs-so thy coming hither has been effected by my (magic) power Dzl.; bdag ni brám-ze yin myself am a Brahmin Dzl.; de ni ṅa yin that one am I; ̥di ni mi p'ód-do this I am not able to do Dzl.; t'a-mál-pa ni ma yin a vulgar person she is not Dzl.; des ni it is by this (that . . .); stobs ni as to strength (I . . .); gál-te nús-na ni if he can (— well!); *da ni, sṅar ni, ˳di-las ni, sṅon-ćad ni* etc.; *ṡiṅ-mk'an ni* now, as to the carpenter, he... *Dzl.; dár-ba ni* now, with respect to the propagation (of the doctrine). In a similar manner it is frq. used, where we begin a new paragraph, heading it with its principal contents. In col. language the word before *ni* is rendered still more emphatic by repeating it once more after *ni*: **zer ni zer dug* W.* (it is true) they say so; **ḍi ni ḍi-te yod** it has been written, (to be sure); **ǰhe ni ǰhe* C.*, **ćo ni ćo dug* W.* (certainly) they are working at it, (but...). In metrical compositions, esp. in mnemonic verses, it is often added as a mere metrical expletive, without any meaning, esp. after *daṅ*. — 2. *Ts.*: demonstrative pron., **ri ni-lẹ ni ťo-wa dug** this mountain is higher than that.

II. num. figure: 42.

ནི་ལ་ *ni-la* (*Hindi* **नील** blue) 1. *Cs.* **indigo.** — 2. *W.* **the blue pheasant** of the South Himalaya, manāl.

ནི་ལམ་, ལི་ལམ་ *ni-lam, li-lam* (*Hindi;* Shaksp.: 'from the Portuguese *leilam*') **auction, public sale.**

ནིང་ *niṅ* 1. col. for *ni*. 2. for *rnyiṅ?* v. *na-niṅ, že-niṅ.*

ནིམ་བ་ *nim-ba*, **निम्ब**, n. of a plant, Melia Azedarachta.

ནིའི་ལི་ *nii-li Sch.*: **the great buzzard** or **mouse-hawk** (?).

ནུ་ *nu* num. fig.: 72.

ནུ་བ་ *nú-ba* pf. and imp. *nus*, **to suck** *Cs.*, *nu(-ba)-po, mo*, **a suckling** *Cs.*, *nu-kúg* sucking-bag.

ནུ་བོ་ *nú-bo*, resp. *γćuṅ-po, W.* **no**, **a man's younger brother** *B.* and *C.*

ནུ་མ་ *nú-ma*, *Cs.* also *ćáb-nu* (resp.?), **breast,** as two correspondent parts of the body, 1. **mammary gland, female breast, bosom** *S.g.* — 2. **nipple, teat,** also of males. — 3. **dug, nipple** of a cow's udder; *nu-k'yim, -γdan, -˳bur, -˳bor, Cs.* id. — *nú-ša* **the thoracic muscle.** — *nu-rtsé, nu-sór Cs.* the tip of the breasts, nipple. — *nú-žo* mother's milk, *mai nú-žo Dzl.*; *nú-žo snún-par byéd-pa* to suckle, to give suck, *Lt.*; *nú-žo skám-na* if she has no milk *Lt.*

ནུ་མོ་ *nú-mo* 1. *W.* **nó-mo**, **the younger sister of a female,** *B.* and col. — 2. v. *nú-ba.*

ནུག་སྟེ་ *núg-ste* (pronounced **núg-te**) *Ts.*, **so, thus.**

ནུད་པ་ *núd-pa* **to suckle,** *W.*: **pi-pi nud toṅ** give to suck! (= *snún-pa*).

ནུབ་ *nub* 1. **the west,** *nub-(kyi) p'yogs(-rol)* id.; *núb-p'yogs-su* towards the west; *nub-byáṅ* north-west; *núb-kyi* of the west, western; v. also *bdé-ba-ćan*. — 2. **evening,** *do-núb* this evening, to-night.

ནུབ་པ་ *núb-pa* 1. vb., **to fall gradually, to sink,** *mťil-la* to the bottom; **to sink in,** *pús-mo núb-pa tsam* knee-deep *Dzl.* frq.; **to go down, to set,** of the sun, moon, frq.; fig. **to decay, decline,** of religion; *núb-par ˳gyúr-ba* id.; *núb-par byéd-pa Sch.* = vb. a. *snúb-pa.* — 2. sbst. **an inhabitant of the West.**

ནུབ་མོ་ *núb-mo* **evening; in the evening,** frq.; *nub gráṅ-gi* happening every evening *Sch.*

ནུམ་ *num*, *W.* col. for *mun.*

ནུར་ནུར་པོ་ *núr-nur-po* denotes the form of the embryo in the second week: **oval, oblong;** *mér-mer-po* id.

ནུར་བ་ *núr-ba* (cf *brnúr-ba, snúr-ba*), 1. **to change place** or **posture, to move a little,** **rig-te nur** (v. *sgrig-pa*) *W.* move a little nearer together, stand or sit a little closer! *núr-gyis ˳ťén-pa* to pull gradually, to give short pulls *Glr.*; *p'a-bóṅ ˳dam rdzis-pa bžiṅ-du nur* the rock yielded, i.e. received impressions, like foot-prints on soft clay, *Mil.*; **to step aside, to draw** or **fall back; to get out of its place, to be dislocated;** **pi núr-la ḍúl-ćé, pi-log-la núr-će** *W.* to move slowly back. — 2. **to crumble to pieces,** *Mil.* of mountains during an unearthly storm, according to some Lamas, cf. *snúr-ba.* — 3. *Cs.*: **to approach, to come near to**(?), yet cf. *snúr-ba.*

ནུས་པ་ *nús pa* I. 1. vb. **to be able,** to have sufficient moral or physical power, also = *ṗód-pa*; *ǰi* (or frq. *či*) *nús-kyis* **to one's best ability; to be able to do** or **to perform,** *dká-las gaṅ yaṅ mi nus* he cannot perform any difficult task *Thgy.*; *rgyál-po mi nus* he cannot be a king; **to venture, to dare.** *ʼgro nús-pa* one that dared to go. (In *W.* **ṫúb-pa** is used almost exclusively instead of it.) — 2. adj. **able,** *nús-pa su čé-ba lta* let us see who is more able, more efficient, who can do more, *Mil.*; *C.* also **active, diligent, assiduous.** — 3. sbst. **power, ability, faculty, capability,** c. genit.: *ṅai nús-pa-la brtén-nas* by my power, through my agency (you shall obtain it) *Mil.*; *rtsig-pai nús-pa yód-dam med* whether there will be a capability of building . . . *Glr.*; **de čós-la nús-pa med* W.* this religion has no power; *nús-pa bšig-pa ṫams-čád* all the destructive powers; *byéd-nus-pa, stón-nus-pa* the capability of doing, of showing *Thgy.*; *rnam-smin-nus-pa* the power of retributive justice (Nemesis, as it were) *Mil.*; **efficiency, efficacy, virtue** (of a remedy), *smán-nus ʼjoms* they hinder the efficacy of the medicines *Med.*; *nús-pa smin* the efficacy becomes complete *Mil.*; in a more particular sense: **the effect of a medicine** in the stomach (opp. to its taste etc.); there are eight different effects: *lči, snum, bsil, rtul, yaṅ, rtsub, ṫsa, rno S.g.*; *nús-pa γnyis daṅ ldan* they have both qualities *S.g.*; *nus-stóbs* = *nús-pa Sch.*

II. pf. of *nú-ba.*

ནེ་ *ne* num. figure: 102.

ནེ་ཐང་, ནེའུ་ཐང་ *ne-ṫáṅ, neu-ṫáṅ,* **meadow, grass-plot, green-sward,** *B., C., W.*

ནེ་ནེ་མོ་ *né-ne-mo* **aunt,** the father's sister, or wife of the mother's brother.

ནེ་མ་ *né-ma* **meadow, green-sward,** *C., W.*

ནེ་ཙོ་ *né-tso* **parrot.**

ནེ་རེ་, ནེར་ནེར་ *ne-ré, ner nér* (v. *ner-ba*), *W.* **sediment, settlings, dregs.**

ནེ་ལེ་ *ne-lé Sch.*: **'mouse-hawk',** a species of large hawk or vulture, differing from *gó-bo,* frequently to be met with in Kullu, but not in Ladak.

ནེ་བྲེ་ *ne-we Sch.* mason's **trowel,** *ne-we rgyag-pa* to plaster, to roughcast.

ནེ་གསིང་, ནེ་བསིང་ *ne-γsiṅ, ne-bsiṅ* = *neu-(γ)siṅ.*

ནེན་པ་ *nén-pa W.* col. for *lén-pa,* **to take, lay hold of, seize; to take out, off, away; to hold.**

ནེམ་ནེམ་ *nem-ném* denotes **a nodding, waving,** or **rocking motion,** *Mil.*; cf. *nems* and *snem.*

ནེམ་བུ་ *ném-bu* **doubt, error** *Sch.*

ནེམས་ *nems*; *Stg.* describes an elastic floor in the following manner: *rkáṅ-pa bžag-na ni nems šes byéd-de, rkáṅ-pa btégs-na ni spar žes byed*: hence *nems,* **it sinks a little, gives way.**

ནེའུ་ལྡང་ *neu-ldáṅ Lex.* = *na-mnyám* one of the same age, **coetaneous, contemporary;** *Sch.*: *neu-ldáṅ* **friend,** and *neu-ldáṅs* **protector, defender.**

ནེའུ་ལེ་ *neu-lé, Hindi* **नेवला**, *Ssk.* **नकुल**, **ichneumon,** Herpestes Pharaonis, *Liš.*; represented in *B.* as a fabulous animal, cat-like and vomiting jewels.

ནེའུ་(ག)སིང་ *neu-(γ)siṅ* 1. *C.* = *ne-ṫaṅ.* — 2. **grass-plots** on high mountains, **alpine pastures** (*C. spaṅ*).

ནེར་བ་ *nér-ba* **to sink, to fall gradually,** *mtíl-la* to the bottom, = *núb-pa.*

ནེར་ནེར་ *ner-nér* = **ne-ré* W.*

ནོ་ *no* 1. *W.* for *nú-bo.* — 2. num. fig.: 132.

ནོ་ནོ་ *no-nó Ld.* title of young noblemen, *no-nó čén-mo* the eldest of a nobleman's sons, *bár-pa* the second, *čúṅ-se* the youngest; *Sp.* title of the highest magistrate of the country.

ནོ་མོ་ *nó-mo* (*Bal. nó-ño*) *W.* for *nu-mo.*

ནོག་ *nog Sch.*: **cervical vertebra; hump of a camel.**

ནོག་པ་, ནོག་པོ་ *nóg-pa, nóg-po,* prob. prov. for *nág-po*; *nog-nóg* **very dark, deep-black.**

ནོང་བ་ *nóṅ-ba*, pf. *noṅs*, **to commit a fault, to make a mistake, to commit one's self,** *ċi noṅs* what have I done amiss? *bdág ma nóṅs-par ₒdí-ltar ɣnód-pa bgyis* I have thus been injured without my fault *Dzl.*; *nóṅs-pa* **fault, crime,** *nóṅs(-pa) mi byéd-pa* not to commit a fault or crime *Dzl.; bzód-pa* to pardon, to forgive, v. *bzód-pa*; *nóṅs-pa bzód-par ɣsól-ba* to ask pardon for a fault committed (in *C.* even: **nóṅ-pa sol-wa**); *nóṅs-pa-ċan* **culpable, liable to punishment;** **noṅ-ċan-ni (s)pe-ra* W.* a reprehensible speech.

ནོངས་པ་ *nóṅs-pa* resp. **no more alive, dead** *Dzl.*, *rje-btsún sku ma nóṅs-par ṗébs-pa* that your Reverence has arrived safe and sound *Mil.*

ནོད་པ་, མནོད་པ་ *nód-pa, mnód-pa*, pf. and imp. *mnos*, **to receive** instruction, directions, favours, from a superior, esp. priest, *Dzl., Glr.*; but also to receive punishment.

ནོན་པ་ *nón-pa* I. also *ɣnón-pa*, pf. *ɣnan, mnan*, 1. **to press,** **mán-po ma non** do not press too hard! **nán-te ṗé-ċe* W.* to open a thing by pressing; with or without *rkáṅ-pas* to tread under foot, to crush; **to pour over, to cover with,** *sas, byé-mas*, with earth, with sand; **to be drenched,** *ċár-pas* by a shower of rain *Dzl.*; to lay over, to overlay with *Tar.* 9, 11, 21; more frq. fig. **to oppress, suppress, overcome, conquer, humble, keep under,** *mtó-ba ḱrims-kyis* the great people by laws *Glr.;* enemies frq.; evil spirits by magic, e.g. *sri ɣnán-pa* by burying heads of animals in the ground, in order that the evil spirits may remain shut up there; *bgegs nón-pa* to keep the spirits away from the fields during harvest by hatchets etc. stuck in the ground; po. *ḱá-bai ɣdoṅ sri mnan* I have crushed, subdued, the face of the snow (i. e. its surface) that was adverse to me *Mil.; sa ɣnón-du* the sitting posture of a saint, when his left hand rests in his lap, and his right hand hangs down, keeping down, as it were, the earth and her powers; cf *mnyam-bžág*. — Frq. also: *mya-ṅán-gyis, snyiṅ-rjes* etc. to be overcome by misery, by compassion. — 2. **to overtake, to catch, to reach,** *bdás-pas* in the pursuit *Mil.* and *W.* — 3. *sgo-ṅa* **to brood, to hatch, eggs,** *Sch.*

II. *W. lo tsam-non*, for *ḍon*, how old is he?

ནོམ་པ་ *nóm-pa*, pf. *noms*, 1. *Cs.* **to be satisfied, contented** (*ṅom-pa?*) — 2. **to seize, to lay hold of** (*snóm-pa*); *Sch.*: *noms-nyúg byéd-pa*.

ནོར་ *nor* I. (*Ssk.* धन, also वसु) 1. **wealth, property, possessions,** *nor(-la) gód-pa Mil.* to suffer a loss of property; **nor gód-da** or **ṗóg-ga* W.* have you suffered damage or loss? **nor nyams ċó-pa* C.*, **lén-ċe* W.*, to examine the inventory, the amount of property; *ṗágs-pai nor bdun Mil.* the seven (spiritual) possessions of a saint, v. *Trig.* 17; proverb: **ráṅ-nor-ḱa man mi-nor-la dhug* (sc. *tar to*)* *C.* look upon your own property as a medicine, upon that of others as a poison; **thing, substance,** much the same as *rdzas*, *Zam.* (nif.). — 2. more or less exclusively: **money,** *nór-la ltá-ba* to care for money, to be avaricious, easily bribed etc.; *nor skyi-ba* to borrow money, *nor bsri-ba* to save money, to scrape together; *nor sog-ₒjóg-pa* to accumulate riches. — 3. *Sch.:* **cattle,** even in such phrases as: *nor ₒḱrig-pa* the pairing of cattle. *Sch.*, *nor-dpon Desg.* chief neatherd (provincialism of *C.?*). — 4. **heritage, inheritance,** *bḱó-ba* to divide (it among the heirs); *ṗá-nor* heritage from the father, *má-nor* heritage from the mother. — 5 symb. num.: 8 (cf. *nór-lha*).

Comp. *nór-skal* **inheritance, hereditary portion;** *nór-skal-rnams* **funds, capital** *Mil.* — *nor-rgyún* imperishable riches *Cs.*; *nor-rgyún-ma* a goddess, *nor-ċan* **wealthy, opulent, rich** *Cs.* — *nór-bdag* 1. **a man of wealth.** 2. **an heir.** 3. **a money-changer, usurer,** *Hind.* महाजन्, *nór-bdag-mo* fem. of it; also n. of a goddess; *nór-bdag-bu* heir. — *nór-ₒdus Pur.* **the gathering of taxes.** — *nór-brnab-ċan* covetous, greedy of money. — *nor-ṗyúgs* amount, or stock of cattle, *nor-ₒbrú* store of corn. — *nór-bu* v. that article.

— *nor-₀dzin* po. **the earth.** — *nor-rdzás* = *nor* I., 1. *B.* and col. — *nór-lha* = *ku-be-ra*, god of riches; there are eight such gods.

II. v. sub *nór-ba*.

ནོར་བ་ *nór-ba* **to err, to make a mistake, to commit a fault,** *gas ₀ǰul nór-ro* it is wrong (to write it) with the prefix *γ* *Gram.*; *nor soṅ* it is a mistake, I (thou, he etc.) am wrong; *ka, lúg-pa, lam nor soṅ*, it was a slip of the tongue, I got hold of the wrong thing, I lost my way; to stray, *dé-las ₀di-ru* from one thing to another *Thgy.*; *mi-nór-ba, ma-nór-ba, nor-ba-méd-pa* **infallible,** not liable to fail, e.g. of a charm; where one cannot miss or go wrong, *lam*; *mi-nór-bar*, strictly according to prescription or direction. — *nór-ba, nór-pa Cs.* 1. **a wanderer,** from the right way. 2. **an error, a mistake.** — *nor-₀krúl* id., frq.; *nór-ra-re Sch.*: he might possibly be mistaken.

ནོར་བུ་ *nór-bu* (**मणि**) 1. **jewel, gem, precious stone,** *nór-bu-čan* adorned with jewels, set with precious stones; *nór-bu-pa, nór-bu-mkan Cs.* **a jeweler,** a connoisseur of gems; *nór-bu-₀preṅ-ba* a rosary or chaplet composed of precious stones; also as title of a book; *nór-bu rin-po-čé*, **चिन्तामणि**, a very costly jewel; also jewel, par excellence, a fabulous precious stone, the possession of which procures inexhaustible riches; acc. to *Wdk.* 488, it has the shape of an oval fruit of the size of a large lemon. — 2. **a noun personal,** or family name, much in use. — 3. gen. pronounced **nór-ru, nór-ro**, **good, excellent, noble,** e.g. *mi, Bal., Pur.*

ནོར་སོ་ *nór-so, nór-so-čan*, *Wdṅ.* 173, 11; 182, 4?

ནོལ་བ་ *nól-ba* to agree, to come to terms *Cs.*

ནོས་པ་ *nós-pa* v. *nód-pa.*

ནྱ་གྲོ་དྷ་ *nya-gro-dha Ssk.*, Ficus indica, = *byaṅ-čub-šiṅ.*

གནག་པ་ *γnág-pa*, a secondary form of *nág-pa*, of rare occurrence, 1. **black;** *γnag-sbágs* **sooty** *Sch.*; *γnag-p̔yúgs* **black cattle,** esp. the yak; *γnag rta lug γsum* cattle, horses, and sheep, these three; *γnag-kyú* a herd of cattle; *γnag-rdzí* a keeper of cattle, cow-herd; *γnag-lhás* an enclosure for cattle. — 2. fig. black-hearted, **wicked, impious.** — 3. (looking black upon) **frowning;** *Glr.* fol. 96: *sems šin-tu γnág-par byuṅ* (notwithstanding their friendly appearance) they had a spite against each other in their hearts. — 4. sbst. **misfortune, grief, affliction, pain,** *γnág-pa daṅ ldán-pa* unfortunate, unhappy *Stg.*; **nag-čan* W.* **cruel, tormenting;** **nag stán-pa* Ld.* to torture, to torment. — 5. *Sch.*: (well) **considered,** (carefully) **weighed** in the mind; v. however *bnág-pa.*

གནང་བ་ *γnáṅ-ba* I. vb., pf. *γnaṅ(s)*, imp. *γnoṅ*, *B.*, *C.* (in *W. stsál-ba* is gen. used for *γnáṅ-ba*) 1. **to give,** resp., i.e. only used when a person of higher rank gives or is asked to give; cf. *₀búl-ba*; **dág-la dá-wa čig-gi ǰog kyáb-rog náṅ-wa žu* C.* please, have the kindness to give me my month's pay; sometimes it is preceded by a pleon. *rǰés-su, Cs.*, **to bestow, to confer, upon,** frq.; **to commit to,** to place under a person's care, e.g. a pupil (resp. for *γtód-pa*) *Mil.*; **to grant, to concede,** what has been asked, *γnáṅ-du γsol* (ancient lit.), *γnáṅ-ba žu* (later lit.) I request you to grant; *skur-γnáṅ mdzád-pa mk̔yen-mk̔yén* I beg you for the favour of sending me ... (in modern letters); **to allow, permit, approve of, assent to,** *γšégs-par γnáṅ-no* he accepted the invitation, he promised to come *Dzl.*; *bdag ráb-tu ₀byúṅ-ba(r) γnoṅ žig* allow me to take (holy) orders, to become a priest *Dzl.*; *bdag ni sbyin-pa žig byéd-kyis γnoṅ žig* allow of my making a donation *Dzl.*; *de bžin-du γnáṅ-ṅo* yes, I permit it *Dzl.*; *yid bžin-du γnáṅ-ṅo* we allow it; do according to your pleasure! — *či γnaṅ* v. *či* I., 4. — In a looser sense: *blón-por γnáṅ-ṅo* he appointed him his minister; *mi γnáṅ-ba* **to forbid, prohibit,** *čos byar mi γnáṅ-bai krims bčas* he published a prohibitory law concerning the exercise of religion *Glr.*; (*bkas*) *ma γnaṅ Pth.* he refused it, declined to grant it, *byon-du ma γnaṅ* he refused to come *Glr.* — 2. sometimes **to command, to order,** complete form: *bka γnáṅ-ba; γnáṅ-tsig skúl-ba* to order a person to do a thing *Pth.* — 3. in complimentary phrases used in *C.* the precise meaning of *γnáṅ-ba* is not always quite obvious: *γnaṅ-rógs mdzad-pa* (v. above) to give, to help to, to assist in(?); **góṅ-pa tsóm-pa ma naṅ**, do not be put out, do not give way to any misgivings (towards me)! sometimes *snaṅ* (q.v.) would make a better sense.

II. sbst. **concession, permission, grant,** *ₒgró-bai γnáṅ-ba žú-ba Mil.; mi-las γnáṅ-ba tób-pa* to obtain permission from a person; *bka-γnáṅ-ba* (magisterial) permission, order (of government); *γnaṅ-sbyin* very frq., **gift, donation, present,** *stón-mo γnaṅ-sbyin* a present of provisions *Glr.*; **gift of honour, reward, favour, privilege, price of victory** held out etc.

གནང(ས)་ *γnaṅs* adv. 1. **on the third day,** e.g. he came *Glr.*; gen. of the future: **the day after to-morrow,** *saṅ γnaṅs Glr.*; **tó-re náṅ-la** *W.* to-morrow and the day after to-morrow; *saṅ ₒgro γnaṅs ₒgro γód-pa yin* to-morrow or the day after to-morrow I must be off *Pth.*; *γnaṅs-γžés* on the third and fourth day *Lex.* — 2. *γnaṅs-čé* **rather** (too) **large,** *γnaṅs-čún* **rather** (too) **small** *Mil. nt.*

གནད་ *γnad*, *Ssk.* मर्मन्. 1. **the main point, object** or **substance, the pith, essence,** *γnad ₒgról-ba* to explain the main point *Mil.; γnad-dón* the proper meaning, the pith of the matter *Tar., Schf.*; **γnád-šes-mkan** *W.* one that knows a thing thoroughly, that is up to it, knows how to do it; **nė'-šė'-pa, nė'-kyi žú-wa búl-wa** *C.* to excuse one's self, to defend or justify one's self (prop. to account for the circumstances that led to an action); **pog da pog; nad-du** (or **nad-čan**) **ma teb** *W.* I have hit (him), but not mortally; so *B.*: *γnád-du snún-pa* to pierce mortally. — 2. in anatomy: by *γnad bdun*, or 'the seven important parts of the body', acc. to *S. g.* are meant: flesh, fat, bones and veins, and *ču-rgyus, don,* and *snod* (*Wise*, Hindoo Medicine p. 69, gives a somewhat different explanation). — 3. in mysticism: the seven physical conditions requisite for successful meditation, *lág-pa mnyam-bžág-tu bžág-pa* (the hands joined over the stomach in such a manner, that the fore-joints of the fingers cover each other, whilst the thumbs are stretched out without touching), *lus rdo-rje-skyil-krúṅ sdód-pa, gal-tsig mdu ltar srúṅ-ba, dpúṅ-pa rgód-šog-pa ltar srúṅ-ba, mig sna-rtsér ₒbébs-pa, mču raṅ-ₒbab-tu bžág-pa, lčé-rtse ya-dkán-la sbyár-ba;* there are also *séms-kyi γnad Mil.* certain conditions of the mind required, such as abstaining from *rtóg-pa*, speculative thinking.

གནན་པ་ *γnán-pa* v. *nón-pa*

གནབ་པ་ *γnáb-pa* v. *mnáb-pa*

གནམ་ *γnam* 1. **heaven, sky,** = *nám-mka; γnám-ga* id. *Cs.*; *γnám-gyi gó-la* **the sphere** or **globe of heaven** *Cs.* (?); *γnam ₒgyúr-ba Mil.*, mentioned in connexion with an earthquake, and prob. corr. translated by *Schr.* with thunderstorm, tempest; **nam kar-kór** *W.* now the sky is cloudless, now overcast (inst. of **dkar-ₒkor**?); *γnám-sgo* 1. *Sch.* **the gate of heaven** (?). 2. *C.* **trap-door.** — *γnam-lčags, γnam-lče Cs.* **thunderbolt, lightning** that has struck; *γnam-stóṅ* the thirtieth day of the lunar month, the day of new moon *Pth.*; **nam-táṅ** *W.* serene sky, fine weather. — *γnam-tel-dkár-po Glr.* 99 is said to be a deity of the Horpa or Mongols, as likewise *sa-tel-nág-po*, and *bar-tel-kra-bo.* — *γnám-mda Pth.* shooting an arrow straight up into the air. — *γnám-rdo Cs.* = *γnam-lčágs*, *Schr.* **hail.** — *γnam-zlúm* vault of heaven *Sch.* — *γnam-yás Glr.* 95 is said to be a n. p., the name of a building — *γnam-rú*, resp. for *γžu*, **bow** (for shooting), *Cs.* **rainbow.** — *γnám-sa* heaven and earth, *γnám-sa brdéb-pa tsam* so that heaven and earth were mixed *Glr.* — 2. v. *nam*, **faulty, incorrect.**

གནའ་བ་ *γná-ba Glr., Lt., rnab Sg., Ld.* **ná-po**, fem. **ná-mo**, an **antelope,** found in *Ld., Sp., Kun., Nepal* and other countries;

its flesh is well-tasted, and its hair is supposed to cure cases of poisoning(!) *Med. Hook.*, (Him. Journ. II, 132) seems to mean this animal by his 'gnow', prob. confounding γna with γnyan (q.v.) which latter, acc. to Cunningham's Ladak p. 198, and by the statements of the natives, is the argali.

གནའ་བོ་ γná-bo **ancient** *Cs.*, γna-snón **formerly, in old times** *Cs.*; γná-dus *Lex.* **former times, time of yore**; γná-nas ma mtoṅ never seen or heard of before *Dzl.*; γná-rabs *Cs.* men who lived in old times, the ancients.

གནའ་མི་ γná-mi *Lex.* w.e.; *Sch.* **witness.**

གནས་ γnas 1. **place, spot,** *B.*, *C.* (in *W.* sa(-k̔yád), sa-ćá) dbén-pai γnas šig a lonely place; mtó-bai γnas a raised place, an elevation *Dzl.*; γnás-na ˳dúg-pa, γnás-su sdód-pa the being somewhere, γnás-su ˳gró-ba the going somewhere, γnás-nas skrod-pa the expelling from a place *Gram.* — 2 **place of residence, abode, dwelling-place,** (in *W.* not in use) γnas ˳bébspa *Sch.*, ˳ćá-ba *Ma.*, ˳débs-pa, to establish one's self at a place, **to settle,** γnas γtóṅ-ba, šóm-pa, **to quarter, lodge, take in,** a person *Stg.*, γnas méd-par ˳gyúr-ba to become homeless; a house, family, or race no longer existing, extinct, *Dzl.*; γnás-su sóṅ-ṅo they returned to their place, their home *Dzl.*; γnas daṅ skyabs méd-par ˳gyúr-ba to be at one's wit's end, not knowing what to do *Schr.* — 3. **a holy place, place of pilgrimage; hermitage, monastery;** **nás ǰal-pa, nás-kor-pa** *W.* **a pilgrim;** **dor-ǰe-liṅ-gi ne** the hermitage, or Buddhist parsonage in Darjeeling; acc. to *Sch.* also Lama, cf. mćód-γnas. — 4. **a clerical dignity** or **degree,** γnas sbyin-pa to confer such *Sch.* — 5. (cf. the Latin *locus*) **object,** like yul, but not so frq., gád-moi γnas an object of laughter; ṅó-ts̔ai γnas words, actions, which ought to be an object of shame *Schr.*; **point, head, item** *Was.* (225); **sphere, province,** fig. *S.g.*; rig-pai γnas lṅa the five classes of science. — γnas ˳gyúr-ba *Sch.*: to appear embodied (?); γnás-su ˳gyúr-ba and byéd-pa *S.O.* and elsewh.?

གནས་པ་ γnás-pa, (imp. prob. only in the periphrastical form γnás-par byos) 1. **to be, live, lodge, dwell, stay,** of persons, animals and things, mṅál-na γnás-pai k̔yeu the babes in their mother's womb *Dom.* — 2. **to remain, hold to** or **on, adhere to,** e.g. a doctrine, opinion, way of acting etc., dgé-ba bcú-la γnás-pa to persevere in the ten virtues; byáms-pai séms-la γnás-pa to remain, to continue in love; in a general sense: ćós-la γnás-pa 'one abiding in religion', a clerical person *Dzl.* ༣༩, 13; **to exist permanently,** opp. to the moment of first taking existence *Was.* (278). — 3. **to hesitate** (?). — ráb-tu γnás-pa v. ráb-tu.

Comp. and deriv. (also of γnas): γnás-skabs 1. **state, condition,** or perh. more accurately **period,** mṅál-gyi γnás-skabs ltár-ltar-po *Lex.* 2. **temporal life,** γnas-skabs-kyi bdé-ba temporal happiness (opp. to mt̔ár-tug-gi snyiṅ-po, or don, ˳brás-bu, *Schr.*, the essence or result of perfection, here, therefore, = eternal felicity); γnás-skabs-ts̔e-yi bar-γćód mi ˳byúṅ-žiṅ if my temporal life be not endangered. — γnás-k̔aṅ **dwelling, dwelling-house** or **room** *Dzl.*; γnás-k̔aṅ-la sógs-pa a furnished house or room *Dzl.* — γnas-ćén a great resort of pilgrimage, a great sanctuary *Tar.* — γnas brtán (loco firmus, stabilis, lit. translation of स्थविर 1. firm, 2. old) **an elder, senior,** n. of the (16) highest disciples of Buddha; afterwards, when various schools had been formed, n. of the orthodox Buddhists, *Burn.* I, 288; *Köpp.* I, 383; *Was.* (38). (*Cs.* seems to have confounded brtan with brten, when he translates: subaltern, vicar). — γnás-po **host, landlord, master of a house, head of a family** *C.*, γnás-mo fem. *Glr.* — γnas-mál *Lex.*, शयासन, sleeping-place, night-quarters, couch *Schr.*; *Cs.* dwelling-place (?) — γnas-med v. γnas 2. — γnas γtsáṅ-mai ris n. p., name of an abode of the gods. — γnas-ts̔áṅ **dwelling, quarters, lodgings,** mi-la γnas-ts̔áṅ γyár-ba to ask for a lodging; to be lodged, to be received into another's house *Tar.*; **nẹ-tsaṅ ˳ǰuṅ** *C.* you will be lodged here, you may stay here (over night), *W.* **ḍáṅ-sa.** — *γnas-ṫsúl* 1. **the state** in which one is, good or bad, **condition of life,** *séms-kyi* the state of one's soul or heart. 2. **an account**, of one's state of mind. 3. **story, tale, narration; event,** col. 4. in philosophy: **the reality of being** (opp. to non-existence) *Was.* (297). — *γnas-γži* 1. = *γnas* 3, *Tar.* frq. 2. **the locative,** that case which relates to being **in** or **at** a place *Gram.* — *γnás-lugs* 1. **position, disposition, arrangement,** *lús-kyi* arrangement of the parts of the body, the science of anatomy *Med.* 2. in mystical works: *γnás-lugs rtógs-pa* **the knowledge of the essence of things,** the knowledge of all things, or in a Buddhist sense, of the non-existence of all things, *Tar.* and elsewh. — *γnas-bšád* 1. **topography and geography** col. 2. narration of legendary tales connected with some holy place. — *γnás-sa* (v. *γnás-pa*) the permanent residence of a person, or the constant place of a thing, opp. to **bór-sa** *W.* temporary place or residence; **place, room,** in general, **nẹ́-sa γáṅ-pa duγ** *W.* there is much room here. — *γnas-bsrúṅ* 1. *W.* ('locum tenens') **earnest, earnest-money, pledge, security**; it might also be used for **ticket**, ticket of admission etc. 2. *Sch.*: **guardian**, or **warden** of a monastery.

གནོང་ *γnoṅ* 1. v. *γnaṅ-ba.* — 2. **consciousness of guilt,** *γnoṅ laṅ* (his) conscience smites (him) *Mil.*; *˳gyod-čiṅ γnoṅ bkúr-bai sems* repentance and a sense of guilt *Dzl.*

གནོང་བ་ *γnóṅ-ba* 1. **to be conscious of one's guilt, to feel remorse,** to be stung in one's conscience, *γnóṅ-žiṅ ˳gyód-pai sgó-nas* from a consciousness of guilt *Pth.*, *γnoṅ-˳gyód drág-pos* id. *Pth.*; **nóṅ-ṅo láṅ-na ṭim-čọ de** *C.* where there is repentance, it is easy to pass judgment. — 2. **to be seized with anguish,** as the effect of poisoning. —

གནོད་པ་ *γnód-pa* 1. vb. (cf. *snád-pa*) **to hurt, harm, injure, damage,** *rkáṅ-pa-la γnód-par ˳gyúr-gyi dógs-pas* in order not to hurt one's foot *Dzl.*; *γnód-par ˳gyúr-bai dgra* a dangerous enemy *Dzl.*; **ná-la nod yin** *W.* (he or it) will hurt me. — More frq.: 2. sbst. **damage, harm, injury,** *byéd-pa, skyél-ba, Glr., Mil.*, **kyál-čẹ** *W.* **to do harm, to inflict injury, to hurt,** with *la*; *γnód-pa med-par, ma ˳gyur-nas* without any harm, without injury *Sch.*; *γnod-byed-nyés-pa* v. *nyés-pa* I. — *klui γnód-pa* damage done by Nagas. — *γnod-sbyin,* यक्ष, a class of demons.

གནོན་པ་ *γnón-pa* v. *nón-pa.*

གནོབ་ *γnob* v. *mnáb-pa.*

མནག་པ་ *mnág-pa Sch.* = *γnág-pa* 5.

མནད་མནད་ *mnad-mnád Sch.*: **falsehood, calumny;** *W.* **nad-nád čó-ḱan** one doing damage maliciously.

མནན་པ་ *mnán-pa* v. *nón-pa.*

མནབ་པ་, (ག)ནབ་པ་ *mnáb-pa, (γ)náb-pa,* resp. for *gyón-pa,* **to put on,** *ná-bza Lex.* the garment; v. also *nabs.*

མནབ་རྩལ་ *mnab-rtsál Cs.* **mean, worthless;** *Lex.* and *Sch.*: **nourishment, food,** *mnab-rtsál-gyi bu(-tsa) Cs.*: the child of an indigent person, *Sch.*: **foster-child;** the word is not much known.

མནམ་པ་ *mnám-pa* **to smell of,** cca., *dri-ma glá-bai ril-ma mnam* as to its smell, it smells of the dung of a musk-deer; **to smell agreeably, to exhale fragrance,** e.g. the scent of lotus *Glr.*; more frq. **to smell badly,** to spread an offensive smell, to stink, *rṅul maṅ dri mnam* profuse and badly smelling perspiration *Lt.*; *lus btsóg-pa mnám-pa* (or *-po*) *˳di Dzl.* this foul stinking body. Note: The transitive signification (to smell = to perceive by the nose) belongs only to the form *snám-pa*, and *Dzl.* ༢༥, 14 should be translated: the medicine stank.

མནའ་ *mna* **oath,** *mna ˳bór-ba, ˳dór-ba, byéd-pa, skyél-ba B.*, **kyál-čẹ** *W.*, **to take an oath, to swear;** *lha dpáṅ-du btsúgs-nas mna byéd-pa* to swear by the Lha *Glr.*; *˳di-skad čes mna bór-ro Dzl.*; *bar daṅ mná-*

dpaṅ byéd-pa to act as a mediator and witness of the confirmation of the peace by oath *Glr.*; **mna zá-ba** *C.* **to swear falsely, to commit perjury.**

མནའ་མ་ *mná-ma Dzl.* and elsewh., *Cs.*: a son's or grand-son's wife, **a daughter-in-law;** but the word is also used for the daughter-in-law 'in spe', i.e. for the bride of the son, who is usually selected by the parents and lives with these for one or two years before being married; so also bridegroom and son-in-law are nearly synonymous; v. *bág-ma* and *mág-pa*; cf. also the Hebrew חָתָן and כַּלָּה.

མནར་བ་ *mnár-ba* **to suffer, to be tormented,** *B.*, *C.*, *sdug-bsṅál ṗúṅ-pos* under a mountain of misery *Glr.*; *nyes-méd γtsó-bo rgyál-poi ˳ǰigs-pas mnar* the innocent lords had to suffer in consequence of the king's fears *Pth.*; *lás-kyis mnár-ba* to suffer in consequence of former actions, to be damned; *lás-kyis mnár-bai brág-srin-mo žig* a Srinmo in the state of damnation; *raṅ-nyid mnar-sdaṅ* (?) *byed* you make yourselves suffer the torments of damnation *Mil.*

མནལ་ *mnal*, resp. for *γnyid*, **sleep,** *mnál-du ṗéb-pa* or *˳gró-ba* to fall asleep, *mnál-ba* to sleep, *mnál-γzim-pa* id.; *mnal sád-pa* to awake *Mil.*; *mnal-láb* the talking in one's sleep; *mnál-lam* **dream** *Glr.*

མནོ་བ་ *mnó-ba* 1. **to think, fancy, imagine,** *de ṅá-la zér-ba yin mnós-nas* thinking it had been said **to him.** — 2. **to think upon, to consider,** *sṅa bsam ṗyi mno méd-par* neither considering before hand, nor thinking of the consequences; *bsam-mnó γtóṅ-ba* id., *Mil.* (cf. *bsam-bló*).

མནོག་པ་ *mnóg-pa* **contentment** *Cs.*; *zas-mnóg Lex.* w.e.; *Sch.*: moderate fare, frugal diet; *mnog-čúṅ* insignificant, trifling, v. *naṅs.*

མནོང་བ་ *mnóṅ-ba* v. *γnóṅ-ba.*

མནོད་པ་ *mnód-pa* v. *ṅód-pa.*

མནོལ་གྲིབ་ *mnol-grib Cs.* = *mnal-grib*; *mnol-rig* **weak intellect,** want of quick perception *Sch.*

མནོས་ *mnos* 1. v. *ṅód-pa.* — 2. v. *mnó-ba.*

རྣ་བ་ *rná-ba* 1. resp. *snyan*, col. **nám-čog*, or *ăm-čog**, (*Pur.*, *Bal.* **rna, sna**), **the ear,** *séms-čan ˴ón-pa-dag rná-bas sgrá-rnams ťos* the deaf hear; *rná-bai mé-loṅ* the drum or tympanum of the ear *Cs.*; *rná-bai dgá-ston* a treat for the ears *Glr.*; *rná-bai dbáṅ-po γtod* lend me your ear, listen to me *Mil*; *ṅed rná-ba mi sun* I am not tired of hearing *Mil.*; *rnar snyán-pa* pleasant to the ear, tickling the ear *Stg.*; *rná-ba ˳dúd-pa* v. *˳dúd-pa*; *rná-ba byá-ba, byó-ba, blág-pa Sch.*, **to listen,** *rná-ba ná-ba* disease of the ear, **ear-ache;** *rná-ba ˴úr-ba Med.* a tingling, humming, or buzzing in the ears; *rná-ba sra* hard or dull of hearing *Sch.* — 2. v. *γná-ba.*

Comp. *rna-kór* ear-ring *Sch.*—**na-kyág** *W.* ear-wax, cerumen. — *rna-ḱúṅ* ear-hole, *˳či-bai rná-ḱuṅ-du* (or *rná-bar*, or *rnar*) *brǰód-pa* to cry into a dying man's ear. — *rna-ḱébs* that part of a helmet which protects the ear *Sch.* — *rna-gyán* ornament worn in the ears, e.g. *mé-tog-gi Stg.*; *rna-čá* id., *γsér-gyi Mil.* — *rná-mčog* col. 1. = *rná-ba.* 2. the pan of a fire-lock. — *rna-ltág* the back-part of the ear *Cs.* — *rná-ťeg-čan, bzód-pa sgóm-pai rná-ťeg-čan* one that is able to listen to all that (stuff) with patience *Mil.* — *rna-γdúb* ear-ring *Cs.* — *rna-mdá γzér-ba C.* the piercing of the ear with an arrow, a chinese punishment. — *rna-spág* (sic), or *-spábs* ear-wax *Sch.* — *rna-rál* an ear torn by pendants. — *rna-lúṅ Cs.* **the ear or handle of a vessel.** — *rna-šál Med.* ear-lap, tip of the ear. — *rna(-pa)-γšóg Lex.* and *Lt.*, perh. = *sna-γšog.* — *rna-slán* (**nas-lán**) a fur-cover for the ears, worn by Tibetan ladies.

རྣག *rnag* **matter, pus, suppuration,** *rnag smin-pa* pus grown ripe *Cs.*; *˳drén-pa Sch.*: 'to draw out the pus'; (I only met with *rnag sná-˳dren-pa S.g.*, which can hardly have this signification); *rnag-rdól-ba* discharge of matter; *rnag-rtól-ba* prob. causing such a discharge by a puncture; *rnag ˳dzág-pa* the dropping or running of pus

Cs.; *rnág-par rnág-pa* to form pus, to ulcerate *Cs.* — *skráṅs-pa rnág-tu k̔ug* v. *gug-pa.* — *rnag-k̔rág* matter and blood. — *rnág-čan* containing pus, purulent. — *rnag-ₒbrúm* abscess *Sch.* — *rnag-šubs* prob. the core of an ulcer.

རྣགས་ *rnags W.*, *C.*, **ready money, cash,** **nag kyaṅ** id.; **nag-zog** money and goods; **gir-mo gyad nag* Ld.* eight rupees in cash.

རྣང་བ་ *rnáṅ-ba* pf. *brnaṅs* **to be checked, stopped, shut off;** with or without *gré-bar*, to stick fast in one's throat; **to be choked** (complete form *brnáṅs-te ₒči-ba*); *dbúgs-kyis rnáṅ-šiṅ* (his) breath stopping short (from fright) *Pth.*; *skád-kyis rnáṅ-te* not being able to utter a word *Dzl.* ༢༧, 1; *zás-kyis rnáṅ-te* the food sticking fast in his throat, *mya-ṅán-gyis* from sorrow *Dzl.*

རྣམ་ *rnam*, in compounds for *rnám-par*, v. *rnám-par* extr.

རྣམ་པ་ *rnam-pa* 1. **piece, part,** e. g. the parts of a panel of a door, **riṅ-gi nám-pa** a longitudinal piece, **žéṅ-gi nám-pa** a cross piece *W.*; *rnám-pa γnyis-su gyes* (a ray of light) is divided into two parts or rays; **section, distinct part of a treatise; part, ingredient,** *lús-kyi rnám-pa p̔rá-rags-rnams* the subtile and the coarse ingredients of the body *Wdṅ.*; *rnám-pa kún-tu, t̔ams-čád-du* in every respect, to all intents and purposes, through and through, entirely, perfectly; this phrase is used, whenever people of rank are addressed: *rnam-kún t̔úgs-rǰe mgo-ₒdrén bka-drin mt̔suṅs-brál* most honoured patron, altogether incomparable as to grace and goodness! or, *rnam-kún t̔úgs-rǰe daṅ bka-drin mt̔suns-brál*; European gentlemen are thus addressed in letters: *rnam-kún t̔úgs-rǰe ₒgyur-méd sá-heb* most honoured Sahib, invariably kind in every respect! — 2. things or persons taken **individually,** often pleon., *ₒod-zér rnám-pa bži* four (separate) rays of light; *ǰó-bo rnam(-pa) γnyis* the two lords (sc. gods) *Glr.*; *bdag ₒdir t̔sogs bú-mo rnám-pa lṅa* we five girls here assembled *Mil.*; **sá-heb nám-pa nyi* W.* the two European gentlemen; *čo-ₒp̔rúl rnám-pa bčo-brgyád* the eighteen wonderful feats; *ₒbyúṅ-ba rnám-pa lṅa Wdṅ.* the five elements; *žal-zás rnám-pa Dzl.* ༧༦, 17 the separate dishes of a meal (another reading: *žal-zás-rnams*); when used in quite a general sense, the exact meaning is to be understood only by the context: *lhá-sa rnam-pa γnyis t̔sár-nas* after finishing the two Lhasa affairs, viz. the erecting of two buildings previously mentioned; *rnám-pa t̔ams-čád mkyén-pai ye-šés S. O.*, or *spyan Dzl.*, as much as omniscience; *γzugs ni k̔a-dóg daṅ dbyibs-kyi rnám-pao* '*γzugs*' is that in which both colour and form are included *Wdṅ.* — 3. **division, class, species,** *dpuṅ rnam bži* the four species of troops (cavalry, elephants, chariots, infantry); *rnám-pa bži* of four different kinds. — 4. **manner, way,** *rnám-pa sna-t̔sógs-kyis*, *rnám-pa sna-t̔sógs-kyi sgó-nas* in manifold manner, variously, frq.; *rnám-pa drúg-tu* (the earth shakes) in six ways, i.e. directions (whenever extraordinary works of charity are performed by holy men) v. *Burn.* I., 262 (not 'six times' *Sch.*); *rnám-pas = sgó-nas*, or *p̔yir*, *bslú-bai rnám-pas* by arts of seduction *Dzl.*; *dé-la mi dgá-bai rnám-pas* from vexation at it *Mil.*; *bsér-mai rnám-pas* in consequence of the cold wind *Mil.* — 5. **outward appearance, exterior,** **आकार**, as to form, figure, shape: *lčágs-kyui rnám-pa* in the shape of a hook, hooked *Wdṅ.*; *stón-pai rnám-par sprul* he assumed the appearance of the Teacher *Tar.*; *čós-skui rnám-par ₒgyúr-ba* to appear in a misty form *Glr.*; *lus ₒdi ni roi rnám-par ₒgyur* this body turns into a corpse *Thgy.*, and so in most cases with regard to the whole appearance; of colour alone it is used only, when *dbyibs* (the shape) has already been stated, as in a passage from *Pth.*: as to its *rnám-pa* (colour), it is spotted like a leopard; **deportment, demeanour, gesture,** *yid-du ₒóṅ-bai rnám-pas* of graceful manners *Mil.*; further: **state, manner of existence,** of certain inhabitants of hell *Thgy.*; in philosophical writings: 'Form der Erkenntniss' *Was.* (274); mentally: **disposition, temper, state of mind** *Thgy.*; **k̔o nám-pa-la* = sám-pa-la C.* in his mind.

རྣམ་པར་ *rnám-par* 1. termin. of *rnám-pa:* **into the form** etc., v. above. — 2. as postp. **like,** = the Lat. instar, *Wdṅ.* — 3. adv. (possibly an abbreviation of *rnám-pa kún-tu*), **entirely, perfectly, thoroughly;** in negative sentences: **by no means, on no account;** often only adding force to another word, *Ssk.* वि; frq. in the shorter form *rnam.*

The following expressions most in use, containing the adv. *rnám-par* or *rnam,* are alphabetically arranged with reference to the second word: *rnám-par klúb-pa* **to adorn, embellish** *Cs.* — *rnam-gráṅs* 1. **enumeration,** *rgyál-poi* of kings *Glr.* 2. **the whole amount, sum total,** *S.g.*; **full number** or **quantity,** where nothing is wanting *Glr.*90, 3.; *mts̔án-gyi rnam-gráṅs* the component parts of his name according to their etymological value *Tar.*69, 3. 3. **treatise, dissertation, a paper,** *č̔ós-kyi* frq. 4. by grammarians the signification of *de* is thus defined: *rnam-graṅs-γžan-brǰód-pa* demonstrative pronoun(?). — *rnam-ₒgyúr* (cf. above *rnám-pa* 5) 1. **form, figure, shape,** *yi-gei rnam-ₒgyúr* the form of the letters (written or printed) *Glr.*, or in this passage also = the graceful form of letters, caligraphy, penmanship, v. below. 2. **behaviour, demeanour,** *lus-ṅág-gi Wdṅ.*; of a sick person *S.g.*; **gesture,** e.g. devout gestures *Mil.*; *rnam-ₒgyúr rdzés-pa Pth.* mimic gestures, mimical performance, ballet. More esp.: 3. **beautiful form, graceful carriage** of the body, **graceful attitudes** (of dancers etc.) *Pth.*; *bzoi rnam-ₒgyúr* the beauty of a work *Glr.* 4. **pride** *C., W., Mil.*; *rnám-ₒgyur-čan* **fine, smart, gayly dressed; proud, vain, foppish** col. — *rnám-par rgyál-ba* conquering completely, gaining a full victory *Pth.*; *rnam-rgyál* a surname much in use; *rnam-rgyal-púṅ-pa,* acc. to *Schl.* 247 *búm-pa,* water-bottle for sacred uses. — *rnam(-par)-bčád(-pa)* section, paragraph, *rnám-par bčad-pa daṅ-po-o* first paragraph; also mark of punctuation at the end of a paragraph, i.e. double-shad. — *rnam-bču-dbaṅ-ldan* a certain way of writing the Ommanipadmehūm, v. *Schl.* p. 121; but I should rather explain it in accordance to *rnám-pà* 2, as the 'ten powerful things', scil. letters or written characters, else the words would have been: *rnám-par dbaṅ-ldán bču.* — *rnám-par ǰóg-pa* v. *rnam-bžág.* — *rnám-par rtóg-pa* (cf. *rtóg-pa* I. 2, and II., 2), gen. sbst. *rnam-rtóg* (विकल्प distinction; doubt, error) 1. **discrimination, perception;** so perh. *S.g.*: *rnam-rtóg ṅan bčom* the perception of what is disagreeable is weakened; **reasoning, mental investigation,** opp. to *ye-šes,* the sublime wisdom of the saint. 2. **scruple, hesitation,** *rnam-rtóg ma mdzád-par č̔aṅ ₒdi γsol* please drink this beer without any scruple! *Pth.*; so also in col. language. 3. in philosophy: **obscuration,** viz. of the clear and direct (nihilistic) knowledge of truth by reasonings in the mind of the individual, **error,** *Was.* (305). 4. in pop. language **disgust, distaste,** *rnám-rtog skyéd-pa* to feel disgust *Glr.*, *zá-ba Pth.* prob. id. — *rnám-(par) t̔ár(-ba).* 1. **to be entirely released** or **delivered,** and sbst. **complete deliverance,** *rnam-t̔ár γsum Trigl.* fol. 12, three ascetic notions (in themselves of little consequence), *stoṅ-pa-nyíd, mtsán-pa-med-pa,* and *smón-pa-med-pa.* 2. sbst. *rnam-t̔ár* **biography, legendary tales** about a saint; **tale, story, description,** in general. — *rnam-t̔ós-(kyi) bu, sras, rnam-sras* = Kuvera, *Ssk.* वैश्रवण. — *rnam-(par) dág (-pa)* thoroughly cleansed, frq.; by *rnam-(par) dág(-par) rtsi-ba,* or *mdzád-pa* I have attempted to express the Scriptural doctrine of δικαιοῦν or **justification.** — *rnam-ₒdúd* n. of one of the seven golden hills round Mount Meru *Glr.* — *rnam-ₒdrén* (cf. *ₒdrén-pa* 2) the saviour, Buddha; *rnam-log-ₒdrén* the reverse. — *rnam-par-snaṅ-mdzád,* वैरोचन, n. of the first of the Dhyani Buddhas. — *rnam-(par) ₒp̔rul(-ba)* **sorcery, magic tricks,** *byéd-pa Dom.* — *rnam-p̔yé, rnam-p̔yéd,* prob. = *rnam-(par) dbye(-ba)* 1. **distinction, division, section.** 2. *rnam-dbyé* **case** or **cases,** of which the Tibetan grammarians, from an excessive regard of the Ssk. language and in fond imitation of its peculiarities, have also adopted seven in number. — *rnam-(par) smin(-pa)* **retaliation, requital,** of good or evil deeds, committed in former lives, of good actions by prosperity (*las-ₒpró*), of bad ones by misery and sufferings (*lan-čágs*), very frq.; *sdig-pai rnam-par smin-pa myóṅ-ba Dzl.* — *rnam-(par) bžág(-pa)* 1. **to distinguish, to put in order, arrange, classify** *Wdṅ., Thgy.,* . . . . . *sgó - nas* according to . . . .(certain points or facts). 2. to consider a person or thing as fully equal or equivalent to another, to substitute one for the other, *C.*; *rnam-bžag* sbst., *Lex.* **व्यवस्था** 1. **placing apart, separating; distinction.** 2. **arrangement, position,** = *γnás - lugs* 1. — *rnam - (par) rig(-pa)* and *šés(-pa)*, as a vb., 1. **to know fully, to understand thoroughly.** 2. *rnám-par šés-pai lús-čan-rnams Dom.* **rational,** or at least **animated,** beings, opp. to inanimate nature; as a sbst., gen. *rnam-šes,* **विज्ञान**: 1. etymologically: **perfect knowledge, consciousness,** *Köpp.* I, 604. 2. in philosophy: one of the five *p̔úṅ - po,* **perceptions, cognitions,** *Was.* (of which there are six, if the knowledge acquired by the inner sense is included) also in *Mil.* frq., e. g. *sgo lṅai rnam - šes* (cf. *sgo γsúm*). 3. in pop. language: **soul,** e.g. of the departed, (later literature and col.) (The significations 2 and 3, I presume, should be distinguished, as is done here, according to the different spheres in which they are used and not be explained one out of the other, as is attempted *Burn.* I, 503. *Schr.* gives here, as in most cases, the signification used in col. language.) 4. *rnam - rig Was.* (307) **idea, notion;** *Tar.* often = **न्याय**, also **चित्त**, *rnam-rig-tu bkrál-pa* 'explained in the sense of the idealists', *Schf.*; *rnam-rig daṅ rtóg-gei bstan-bčos* logical and dialectical Shastras. — *rnam-bšád* **explanation** *Tar.*

རྣམས་ *rnams,* in *B.* the usual sign of the plural, in col. language little used, esp. in *W.*, meaning, acc. to its etymology, **piece by piece;** hence its use is not a strict grammatical rule, but more or less arbitrary; it is mostly omitted, when the plural is otherwise indicated, e. g. after definite and indefinite numerals; it may be used, however, not only in these instances (*ₒk̔or máṅ-po-rnams* many servants), but also after collective nouns (*dge-ₒdún-rnams*), at the end of enumerations (= *de ťams-čád*), after general expressions, such as: *gaṅ yód(-pa)-rnams* whatever they were, after other plural-signs (. . . *dag - rnams* etc.). Cf. *rnám-pa* 2.

རྣར་ *rnar,* for *rná-bar,* q. v.

རྣལ་(མ་) *rnál(-ma)* I. 1. **rest** *Cs., lús rnál-du γnás - par gyúr - to* his body obtained rest *Tar.*; esp. **tranquillity of mind, composedness, absence of passion,** *sems rnál-du mi γnás - par* his soul having no rest *Tar.*; *rnál-du ₒdúg-pa,* or *ₒk̔ód-pa, Mil.*: *rnál-mar sdód-pa* id.; *rig-pa rnál-du ₒbébs-pa* to give one's mind up to perfect rest *Thgr.*; *rnal-ₒbyór* 1. **योग, meditation,** nearly the same as *tiṅ-ṅe-ₒdzín* and *bsam - γtán Mil.*, but chiefly when it is considered as the business of life; *rnal - ₒbyor - rgyúd,* **योगतन्त्र**, *Tar.* frq. 2. often for *rnal-ₒbyór-pa.* — *rnal - ₒbyór - pa* **योगिन्, योगाचार्य, devotee, saint, sage, miracle-worker** frq. — 2. *Sch.* also: **personal, visible, essential** (?) — *Tar.* 201, 6. 22: *bstán-pa rnál-ma?* — II. often for *mnal.*

རྣུར་བ་ *rnúr-ba* v. *snúr-ba.*

རྣོ་བ་ *rnó-ba B.*, རྣོན་པོ་ *rnón-po* usual form, 1. **sharp, acute, edged, pointed;** *rno-méd C.* **dull, blunt;** *rno p̔yúṅ-ba* to sharpen, grind, whet *Sch.* (like *k̔a ₒdón-pa*); *rno lén-pa* to get sharp, to be sharpened; *rno-p̔yuṅ* name of males. — 2. this word is applied by the Tibetans to the chemical qualities of things, though not quite in the same way as we do, as they ascribe a 'sharp' taste to the flesh of beasts of prey, to the bile etc. *Med.* — 3. *rig-pa rnó-ba* **sharp, clever, shrewd,** *Glr.*, *blo rnó - ba* **talented, gifted,** *dbáṅ-po rnó-ba* **acute, sagacious.**

རྣོང་ *rnoṅ Mil.*? *rnóṅ-la ˳ṕog.*

སྣ *sna* 1. (resp. *šaṅs*) **the nose,** *B.*; in col. language *sna-mṫsúl*, v. below; *snai rús-pa* bridge of the nose, *snai ċag-krúm* cartilage of the nose; *skad sná-nas ˳dón-pa* to utter (nasal) whining tones *Mil.*; *sná-nas ˳ḱrid-pa* to lead or turn by the nose; *sna ˳ṕyi-ba* to blow one's nose. — 2. **trunk, proboscis,** *ṕág-pai Glr.*; *gláṅ-sna* v. *glaṅ*. — 3. a mountain projecting from some other mountain in a lateral direction, **a spur** *Glr.*; it might also be used for **cape, promontory.** — 4. **end,** *ṫig-sna* the end of a string *Glr.*, *rál-pai sna* the end of a lock of hair *Glr.*; **hem, edge, border,** *gós-kyi sna* the border of a garment *Cs.*; esp. **the nearer end, fore-part,** *˳od ċén-po żig-gi sná-la* foremost of a bright ray of light (that was approaching) *Mil.*; *sna ˳drén-pa* **to lead, to head** (a body of men) cf. *mγug-ma*; *dmág-sna ˳drén-pa* to take the command of an army *Pth.*; more indefinitely, like *˳drén-pa*: **to draw along, to lead, to guide,** esp. with *lam*, to direct the way or course of a person, (having the person always in the genit. case); *˳gro drúg-gi lam-sna ˳dren* as a guide he leads all beings *Mil.*; **ċú-na ḍem-pa* C.* **to conduct water** (by a water-course); **to bring upon, to cause,** v. below, compounds; *rnág-sna ˳drén-pa* to cause suppuration *Med.*; *lám-sna ˳dzín-pa* to have taken a certain road *Mil.* — In some cases it is difficult to account for the signification, so: *sna-ċén-po Cs.* **a deputy; commissioner;** *sna-lén byéd-pa* c. genit. **to shelter, harbour, lodge, take in,** *Pth., C.*; *sna (b)stád-pa Lex.*, *bdág-gi sna-stád ḱyód-la re Cs.* I place my full confidence in you; **ná-do ṫóg-ne* C.*, (**nár-do gyáb-te* W.*) **˳gyél-ba** either: to fall by striking with the fore-part of one's foot against a stone, or by striking one's foot against a stone lying before one. — 5. **sort, kind, species,** mostly with *ṫsógs(-pa)*, *W.* with **so-só**, **diverse, various, all sorts of,** *spos sna-ṫsógs-kyis ˳débs-pa Dzl.* to strew all sorts of spices over . . . .; *rnám-pa sna-ṫsógs* frq.; less frq. *sna-maṅ Lex.*, *sna dpag-tu-méd-pa Glr.*, *sna-ṫsád Glr.* **of every sort;** *rin-po-ċe sna-bdun* seven kinds of jewels; *dár-sna lṅa* five sorts of silk; also *sna* alone is added to substantives, inst. of *sna-ṫsógs*, or = *rnams*: *šiṅ-snai dúd-pa* smoke from different sorts of wood *Glr.*; *˳brú-sna smín-pa* the ripening of corn *Glr.*; *sna-γċig* a single one *Mil.*; *ċós-sna Tar.* 166, 4 prob. is not so much a kind, as a part of doctrine, *Schf.* — 6. *mi-sna*. *bló-sna* v. *mi* and *blo*.

Comp. *sná-skad*, **ná-kad ton* W.*, he speaks through his nose. — *sna-ḱúṅ* nostril. — *sna-ḱrág*, *sna-ḱrág ˳dzág-pa* a bleeding from the nose, *sna-ḱrág γċód-pa* to stop it, *ċad*, it ceases, it is stanched. — *sna-ḱrid* guide, leader; the leader of a choir. — *sná-ga* col. = *sna* 3. — *sna-góṅ* trunk, proboscis *Sch.* — *sna-sgáṅ* bridge of the nose *Cs.* — *sna-sgrá* the noise made through the nostrils *Cs.*, snuffling. — *sna-ċú* a running nose, *sna-ċú ˳dzag* mucus is dropping from the nose *Lt.* — *sna-ċén Thgr.* a demon(?). — *sna-mċú* an elephant's trunk *Pth.* — *sna-ṫág* 1. a rope passed through the nose of a beast to lead it by. 2. proboscis, *sna-ṫág* or *sna-mċú sríṅ-ba* to stretch it forward *Pth.* — *sna-drí* prob. = *snabs Med.* — *sna-γdóṅ* bridge of the nose *Sch.* — *sna-˳dág* (spelling?) *W.* **snuff.** — *sna-˳drén* **leader, commander;** *sdug-bsṅál-gyi sna-˳drén* **one that causes misfortune, author of it.** — *sna-nád* disease of the nose. — **na-ċi* C.*, **na-ṕi* W.*, pocket-handkerchief. — *sna-bábs* the glanders *Sch.* — *sná-bo* 1. **leader, commander, chief.** 2. **a guide,** *gom γsum ṫsam-laaṅ sná-bo dgos* about every third step one wants a guide *Mil.* — *sna-búg S.g.*, *sna-sbúgs Cs.*, nostril. — *sna-sbyóṅ*, *sna-smán* snuff *Med.* — *sná-ma Lex.* w.e., *Cs.* = *sna* 4. — *sna-rtsá* root of the nose *Cs.* — *sna-rtsé* tip of the nose. — *sna-ṫsógs* v. *sna* 5. — **nam-ṫsúl* W.*, **nam-súl* Bal.* = *sna* 1 and 2. — *sna-˳dzúr* an aquiline or crooked nose *Cs.* — *sna-léb* a flat nose *Cs.* — *sna-šá* the flesh of the nose; the nose *Cs.*; *sna-šá sbyin-pa* to suffer one's self to be led by the nose *Cs.* — *sna-ɣsóg* 'the hair in the nostrils'; *sna-ɣsógs* 'the wings of the nose (alae nasi), together with the nostrils' *Sch.*; *sna-ɣsór* id. *Sch.* — *sna-bšál Lt.*, prob. an injection into the nose.

སྣ་ནམ་ *sna-nám* **Samarkand** *Glr*

སྣ་སྙེམ་ *sna-sném, sna-sném ma ₒdúg-čig* do not sit here so idly, without any particular object! *Sch.*

སྣ་སྦྲང་ *sna-sbráṅ* **arrow-head** *Sch*

སྣ་མ་ *sná-ma* 1. *Cs.*: 'the blossom of the nutmeg-tree'(?). — 2. v. *sna*, compounds.

སྣ་རུ, རྣ་རོ *sná-ru, rná-ro*, = *ná-ro Sch.*

སྣག་ *snag* 1. = *rnag Cs.* — 2. also *snág-ṫsa* **ink, Indian ink,** *rgya-snág* China ink, *bod-snag* Tibetan ink, *ċe-snág* Cashmere ink; **nág(-ṫsa) lug soṅ** *W.* the ink has run, i. e. a blot has been made. — **nag-koṅ** *W.*, **nag-bhum** *C.*, inkstand. — *snag-ṫig* an ink-spot, a dash, a stroke, made with the pen. — *snag-ṗyé* ink-powder. — *snag-rís rgyág-pa* to paint over with ink. — 3. *míg-gi snág-lpags Pth.?*

སྣག(ས)་ *snag(s)* = *ma-ɣnyén*, **relationship by the mother's side;** *snág-gi ɣnyen-mtsáms* id. *Pth.*; *snag-dbón Lex.* w.e.

སྣང་བ་ *snáṅ-ba* I. vb. 1. **to emit light, to shine, to be bright;** *snáṅ-bar byéd-pa* **to fill with light, to enlighten, to illuminate,** *ₒgyúr-ba* **to be filled with light, to be enlightened,** e. g. by the light of wisdom *Dzl.*; *šin-tu mi-snáṅ-bai mún-pa* darkness entirely devoid of light *Dzl.* — 2. **to be seen** or **perceived,** to show one's self, to appear, e. g. blood appears on the floor *Dzl.*; (*ṗyi*) *snáṅ-ba ṫams-čád Mil.*, *ṗyi snáṅ-ba gaṅ ₒbyuṅ Mil.*, *ṗyi snáṅ-bai yul Mil.*, *snaṅ-ṫsád Glr.*, every thing visible, all that is an object of sense, the external world; *dá-lta rgyu žig snáṅ-ṅo* now an opportunity shows itself *Dzl.*; *lus mi snaṅ yaṅ ɣsuṅ snáṅ-ba ma-čád-pa byuṅ* although the body had become invisible, yet the voice continued to appear, to be heard *Tar.* 127, 11; it seems even to be capable of being extended to mental perceptions, the partic. being equivalent to imaginable; **to have a certain appearance, to look** (like), *čád-pa ltar* as if it had been suddenly cut off *Wdṅ.*; *snúm-bčas* (to look) greasy *S.g.*; *ₒṗrúl-du snáṅ-ṅo* it looks like sorcery *Glr.* (cf. *ₒṗrul*); *mi-snáṅ-ba* **invisible,** *mi-snaṅ-bar ₒgyúr-ba* to disappear frq.; *btsún-mo-rnams mi snáṅ-ba daṅ* as their wives were not to be seen, were not present *Dzl.* ༢༠, 17; *mi-snáṅ bar byéd-pa* to make invisible, to efface the traces of a thing. — 3. = *yód-pa Lex.*, sometimes in *B.*, and in the col. language of certain districts; *žes ṗrál-skad-la snaṅ* so it occurs in vulgar language *Gram.*; *zér-ba snaṅ* it is said, *dicitur*, *Tar.* 34, 4, and in a similar manner 33, 22; 34, 14; prob. also: **to be in a certain state** (of health), **in a certain condition, situation** etc., *C.*: **dhá-ta ghaṅ náṅ-ghin yö-dham** how are you now? **čag peb žu naṅ** is the usual salutation in *C.*, like our: good morning! or: how do you do? however, the literal sense of it seems to have been forgotten, as even educated Lamas seldom know how to write it correctly. The proper way of spelling it seems to be: *ṗyag ṗeb bžud snaṅ*, and the words hardly imply much more than those addressed to inferior people, viz. *da leb soṅ* well, so you are come! well, there you are! Cf. *gá-le*.

II. sbst. (**दर्शन, आलोक** etc.) 1. **brightness, light,** *snáṅ-ba yód-pai dús-su* when there is light, broad day-light *Thgy.*; fig. *čós-kyi snáṅ-ba* the light of doctrine *Dzl.* — 2. **an apparation, phantom,** *mi máṅ-pos déd-pai snáṅ-ba ₒbyúṅ-ṅo* there is an appearance as of being pursued by many people, i.e. a phantom of many pursuing people *Thgr.*; *rmi-lam-gyi snáṅ-ba-rnams Mṅg.* — 3. physically: **seeing, sight,** *bdag-ráṅ-gi snáṅ-ba ma dág-pa yin* my faculty of vision, my sight, is dimmed *Tar.*; more frq. intellectually: **view, opinion,** *saṅs-rgyás-kyi snáṅ-ba-la . . . ɣzigs-so, mi-nág-gi snáṅ-ba-la . . . mtóṅ-ṅo* by the Buddhas he was looked upon as . . ., by laymen as . . . *Glr.*; **thought,** idea, notion, conception, c. genit., ₒdi ťams-čád ráṅ-gi séms-kyi snáṅ-ba yin all these things are only conceptions of your mind, your fancies Thgr.; skyid-sdúg-gi snaṅ-ba šar Thgr.; ₒkyágs-pai snáṅ-ba ₒbyuṅ Mil.; bkres-snáṅ ye-méd-par gyúr-to he was even without a thought of hunger Mil.; absolutely: *kyód-di náṅ-wa gá-ru taṅ soṅ* W. where are your thoughts wandering? čós-la snáṅ-ba sgyur turn your mind to religion! Mil.; snáṅ-ba ₒgyúr-ba (τὸ μετανοεῖν) change of heart, conversion (not to be confounded with snáṅ-bar ₒgyúr-ba v. above). snáṅ-ba bdé-ba pleased, cheerful, happy Pth.; in some expressions it is equivalent to soul. Most of the significations mentioned sub 3 seem not to have been in use in the older language. — ₒkrul-snáṅ, ₒprul snáṅ illusion, deception of the senses, deceit, error Mil., Glr., col. — ynyis-snáṅ the arising of two ideas in the mind, ynyis-snáṅ-gi rtóg-pa hesitation, irresolution, wavering Mil. — mtoṅ-snáṅ 1. the act of seeing, the sight, mtoṅ-snáṅ-gi sprúl-pa phantom, apparition, *toṅ-náṅ dé-mo* W. a sight beautiful to look at, *toṅ-náṅ sóg-po* of ugly appearance. 2. Cs.: manner or mode of viewing, point of view; yzigs-snáṅ id. resp.; Pth.: yzigs-snáṅ-la according to his (supernatural) intuition (with reference to a holy person). — tsor-snáṅ the hearing, *tsor-náṅ-la nyán-po* W. delightful to hear, pleasing to the ear. — bar-snáṅ v. bar. — raṅ-snáṅ one's own thoughts, ideas Mil.; the own mind Glr.; raṅ-snáṅ ₒkrúl-pa an illusion of fancy Thgr.; snaṅ-grágs things seen and heard Mil. — snaṅ-stoṅ Mil. frq., prob. not 'empty show, delusive appearance' Sch., but: things (really) appearing and (yet) void, one of those frq. instances, where two words of opposite meaning are placed together, dbyer-méd often being added, as a tertium quid (cf. Köpp. I, 598). — snaṅ-dág (naṅ-rtágs, brtág?? Ld. naṅ-stag) col. the inward man, the heart, the soul, *naṅ-dág-la sám-pa šar soṅ* W. a thought has risen in my soul; *naṅ-dág čad soṅ* now he has felt it in his inmost soul, this will have struck home to his heart W.; *ṅá-la naṅ-dhág ma ǰhuṅ* C. I have not heard it, perceived it, minded it; *naṅ-dhág ma ǰhē* C., *ma čọ* W., I was not heedful, I made a mistake! — snáṅ-ba-mta-yás = ₒod-dpag-méd Amitābha, the fourth Dhyāni Buddha. — snáṅ-me v. naṅ-mē. — snaṅ-tsád v. above I., 2. — snaṅ-tsúl 1. the outward appearance, of a landscape = scenery Mil.; 2. appearance opp. to essence, ynas-tsul Was. (297). — snaṅ-mdzád v. rnám-par. — snaṅ-šás thoughts, fancies (?) — snaṅ-srid (Ssk. संसार) the visible, external world frq. — snaṅ-ysál shining brightlo, brilliant; čós-kyi snaṅ-ysál sgrón-me the bright light of doctrine Pth. — snaṅ-ṅor ral ₒdrum Tar. 16 (?).

སྣད་པ་ snád-pa, pf. bsnad, imp. snod, to hurt, to harm, to injure, c. accus., lus snád-nas being hurt in the body Dzl.; ṅai rta snad ₒgro or ₒoṅ my horse might be hurt Mil.; snád-kyis dógs-te afraid of hurting him Dzl.; of horned cattle: to butt Sch.

སྣབས་ snabs, resp. šaṅs, mucus, snivel, snot, snabs pyi-ba to blow one's nose, snabs-pyis pocket-handkerchief; snabs-lúg snotty nose, snotty fellow Sch.; snabs-lúd, prob. also dar-snábs Dom. = snabs; bé-snabs thick phlegm Cs.; snám-pa v. snom.

སྣམ་བུ་ snám-bu woolen cloth; the common sort is not dyed, very coarse, and loosely woven; snám-bu spú-čan hairy cloth, napped cloth; snam-prúg, dbus-snám Mil., fine cloth; ₒgo-snám C. id.; snam-sbyár Lex. a sort of loose mantle for priests Cs. — *nám-ya* W. trowsers. — snam-yúg, yúg-snam a whole piece or roll of woolen cloth. snam rás woolen cloth and cotton cloth Mil.

སྣམ་བྲག་ snam-brág (Ü: *ṅám-bág*) bosom, snam-lógs, snam-yžógs resp. side.

སྣར་ snar, termin. of sna; snar-bkáb Wdk. fol. 464 nose-band (?) pocket-handkerchief (?); snár-kyu guide-rope for camels, passing through their nose.

སྣར་ཐང་ nar-táṅ n. of a monastery, Köpp. II. 256; n. of a philologist Gram.

སྣར་པོ་, སྣར་མོ་ snár-po, snár-mo Cs. 1. of a white or light red colour (cf. skya-nár). — 2. long, oblong; cf. nár-mo.

སྣར་བ *snár-ba* prob. the original form of *bsnár-ba.*

སྣར་མ *snár-ma* n. of one of the **lunar mansions**, v. *rgyu-skar* 3.

སྣལ་བ *snál-ba* v. *bsnál-ba.*

སྣལ་མ *snál-ma* **thread, silk-thread, woolen thread** etc.: **knitting-yarn,** or yarn used for other purposes; also for **warp, abb-yarn.**

སྣུན་པ *snún-pa*, pf. and fut. *bsnun*, 1. **to prick** *Lt.*; **to stick** or **prick into,** e.g. a stick into the ground *Mil., mtson* a weapon *Lex.* — 2. **to suckle** (cf. *nú-ba, núd-pa*), *nú-ma* ~~or~~ *nú-žo snún-pa Pth., Lt.*, id. — 3. **to multiply** *Wdk.* — *ɣnad snún-pa Lex.* w.e, *Sch.:* 'to excavate the interior, to get or penetrate into the inside'(?).

སྣུབ་པ *snúb-pa*, pf. *bsnubs*, fut. *bsnub*, imp. *snub(s)* vb.a to *núb-pa*, **to cause to perish;** gen. fig. **to suppress, abolish, abrogate, annul, destroy, annihilate,** a religion, a custom etc.

སྣུམ་པ *snúm(-pa S.g., -po Cs.)*, 1. **fat, grease, any greasy substance,** *snúm-gyis skúd-pa* **to grease, to smear;** in *C.* esp. **oil** (*W.* **már-nag**), *snum-zád-kyi már-me* a lamp, the oil of which is consumed; also fig., *snum* being added pleon., e. g. *Mṅg.: lus-zúṅs snum-zád*, and parallel to it: *lus-zúṅs zad Lt.*; *rlan-snúm* raw fat, *žun-snúm* melted fat *Cs.; sol-snúm* cart-grease, composed of pulverized charcoal and fat *Glr.* — 2. fig. of luxuriant grass or pasture, *ri snúm-pa* a hill clothed with luxuriant pastures *C.* (cf. *rug-gé*); *snúm-la ǰám-pa* luxurious and soft *Mil.* — *snum-kóṅ* a little bowl for oil etc. — *snum-ₒkúr* a kind of pastry baked in suet. — *snum-glégs*, *W.* **num-lág**, a wooden tablet, blackened, greased, and strewed with ashes, used for writing upon with a wood-pencil, thus serving for a slate. — *snúm-čan, snúm-bčas, snum-ldán* **fat, oily, greasy.** — *snúm-dri* a smell of fat. — *snúm-nag* **oil** *Kun.* — *snúm-rtsi* a greasy liquid, **oil** etc.; **greasy, oily** *C. snúm-pa* vb. = *snóm-pa* I.

སྣུར་བ *snúr-ba*, pf. and fut. *bsnur*, vb. a. to *núr-ba*, 1. **to put** or **move out of its place, to remove, to shift** *W.*: **to move** or **draw towards one's self** *Cs.*, so *mdún-du snúr-ba Zam.* is explained by *ₒtén-pa.* — 2. *Sch.:* **to cut into pieces, to fracture, to crush,** *žib-mor* into small pieces (to reduce), to powder; so it seems to be frq. used in *Lt.*, though one *Lex.* explains it by *ₒdás-pa* (scarcely corr.). — 3. *Cs.* **to bring near** = **to shorten,** *dus* a term, a space of time. Cf. *brnú(r)-ba Lexx.*

སྣེ་(སྣོ) *sné(-mo)* 1. **extremity, end,** *snál-mai Lex.*, of a thread, *ťág-sne* the end of a rope *Sch.;* **hem, seam,** *né-mo* **ltáb-če** *W.* to fold down and sew the edge of a piece of cloth, **to hem**; **né-mo gyáb-če** *W.* to trim with cord or lace. *sne-ₒkór* **to warp, to get twisted** *Sch.* — 2. *sne-rgód, sne-dmár, sne-ťsód, món-sne, sneu,* names of plants.

སྣེམ་པ *sném-pa* **to shake, to cause to move slightly,** *bsném-byai sa-ɣži* a quagmire, shaking or yielding under one's feet *Sch.*; *nem-ném bsném-pa Lex.*, pf. *bsnems.*

སྣོ་བ *snó-ba Cs.* = *snúr-ba*, **to reduce to small pieces, to crumble.**

སྣོད *snod* I. sbst. (भाजन) 1. **vessel,** *snod-spyád.* id., *Lex.* and col. frq.; *ɣser-snód* a gold vessel; *p̀ye-snód* a vessel for meal or flour; *ču-snód* water-pot, pitcher; *bu-snód* **uterus, womb,** *Lt.* and col.; *snód-kyi ka* mouth of a vessel, *snód-kyi žabs* bottom or foot of a vessel, stem of a glass. — 2. in anatomy: *snod drug* (the six vessels) are: gall-bladder, stomach, the small and the large intestine, urinary bladder and spermatic vessels (in the female: uterus); *don-snód*, the six vessels and the five *don* together, v. *don* 5. — 3. with reference to religion v. *sde*, compounds. — 4. fig. 1. in ascetic language denoting **man,** as far as he is susceptible of higher and divine things; so already in *Dzl.* a man is called *snod yóṅs-su dág-pa* a very pure and holy vessel; *snod-ldán slób-ma* a disciple eager to be instructed *Mil.; snód-du rúṅ-ba* one fit for, worthy of (instruction); *snód-du méd-pa* unfit, insusceptible, rude, vulgar.; *ṅés-par légs-pai snod mčog, ṅes-legs bsgrúb-pai snod* *mčog* a most perfect vessel of religion (most susceptible of etc.) *Thgy.*; *snod ma yin* insusceptible of religion *Thgy.*, *Tar.* — 2. in metaphysics: *p̔yi-snód* **the external world,** or rather **inanimate nature,** *p̔yi-snód-kyi ˳jig-rtén Glr.* and elsewh. frq., opp. to *nan-bčúd*, viz. the sentient beings composing it; so *Mil.*; *Sch.*: matter and spirit. — II. v. *snád-pa*.

སྣོན་ *snon* **rest, remainder**(?) *Dzl.* ༢༥༢, 4 *Sch.*

སྣོན་པ་ *snón-pa*, pf. and fut. *bsnan*, 1. **to add, superadd, increase, augment,** **la nán-če** *W.* to add to the wages, to raise the wages; **ǰa ťsá-big nan sal** *W.* please give me some more tea! *γnyis bsnán-te* two being added to them, (their number) increasing by two *Mil.*; *mán-du snón-pa* to augment by a great number frq. — *nón-ka*, or *nón-k̔a W.*, **increase, growth, augmentation,** and in a special sense: **agio, premium**; *snón-ma*, *bsnán-ma*, id.; **puṅ-nón** *W.*, **gyab-nón** *C.*, *dmag-ťsógs snón-ma* **reinforcements, auxiliary troops.** — 2. **to add up, sum up** *Wdk.*

སྣོབ་ཟོག་ཅན་ *snób-zog-čan* (spelling?) **curious, inquisitive,** **nob-zóg čó-če** *W.* to pry into, to ferret.

སྣོམ་པ་ *snóm-pa* I. also *snúm-pa*, pf. *bsnums*, fut. *bsnum*, imp *snum(s)*; and *snám-pa*, pf. *bsnams*, fut. *bsnam*, imp. *snom(s)*, 1. **to smell,** to perceive by the nose (cf. *mnám-pa*), *snas dri-rnams bsnáms-pa* to perceive scents by the nose *Stg.*; **da num** *W.* there, smell at that! **zi núm-te dúl-če** *W.* to go about smelling and prying; **ṅa čiaṅ mi num** *W.* I do not smell any thing. — 2. **to grope,** **mun-nag-la nom-ne čin* = *nag-zúg-la nóm-žin soṅ** *C.*, v. *nag-zúg*.

II. pf. *bsnams*, fut. *bsnam*, *W.* **nam-če**, resp. for *lén-pa*, *˳dzín-pa*, *ťógs-pa*, *˳čáṅ-ba*, **to take,** relics from a sepulchre *Glr.*; **to seize, to take up,** the alms-bowl *Dzl.*; **to hold,** a stick *Mil.*; **to put on,** a sacred garment; **nam yin-na** *W.* would you please (to take), would you like (to have a cup of tea etc.)?

སྣོར་བ་ *snór-ba*, pf. and fut. *bsnor*, **to confound, mingle, mix, disturb** *Cs.*

སྣོལ་བ་ *snól-ba*, pf. and fut. *bsnol*, 1. **to unite, join, put together, fit together,** e.g. bricks or stones in building *W.*; *Cs.* **to adjust**; *Sch.*: to mend holes in stockings, **to darn**; **to cross** one's hands, *bráṅ-k̔ar*, resp. *ťúgs-kar*, on the breast *Thgr.* and elsewh. frq.; *˳ťam snól-ba* **to put together, to embrace** *Cs.*; *ltá-snol-ba* to look at each other, *˳ó-snol-ba* to kiss each other, 'and thus frq. denoting reciprocity' *Cs.* (though not to my knowledge). — 2. **to wrestle, scuffle, fight,** of boys, dogs frq., also *Mil.*; *stag snól-ba* a fighting tiger that rushes upon the enemy *Ma.*; **to contend with, fight against, subdue,** *me*, a fire *Tar.*

སྣྲུབས་, སྣྲོན་ *snrubs*, *snron*, the names of two of the lunar mansions, v. *rgyu-skár*.

སྣྲེལ་(ག)ཞི་ *snrel-(γ)ži Lexx.* = *p̔red*; *Cs.* **sloping, oblique**; *Sch.*: **confusedly, pellmell**; *Cs.* also **mediocrity.**

བརྣག་པ་ *brnág-pa* 1. **to devise, contrive, to take care, to be concerned about, to strive for** or **after,** ... *žes γčig-tu brnágs-pas* striving only after (that one thing) *Tar.*; as sbst. *brnág-pa čoṅs* keep (it) well in your mind, pay all attention (to it)! c. genit., cf. *brnán-pa*. — 2. *Lex.* = *bzód-pa*, **to suffer, to endure**; *brnag-dka* **intolerable, insupportable** *Lex.* — 3. *Cs.*: **to be full of corrupt matter.**

བརྣང་བ་ *brnáṅ-ba* v. *rnáṅ-ba*.

བརྣན་པ་ *brnán-pa* 1. *Cs.* **to attend, to look on attentively,** *˳bri-klóg brnán-pa* to attend while a person is reading or writing. — 2. *Sch.*: **'to be desirous of, to long for,** *čós-la* for religious instruction, *ltó-la* for food'. With the first signification agrees a quotation in *Zam.*: *nán-tan-brnan*, with the second the word **zá-nan-čan** *W.*, = *zá-brnab-čan*.

བརྣབ་སེམས་ *brnáb-sems Cs.*: **covetousness, selfishness**; *Thgy.*: *bdág-gi-la brnáb-sems* predilection for one's own things, *γžán-gyi-la brnáb-sems* desire for things belonging to others; *W.*: **zá-nab-čan** **greedy, ravenous;** **nór-nab-čan** **greedy of gain** or **money, covetous.**

བརྣུ་བ་, བརྣུར་བ་ *brnú-ba, brnúr-ba Lex.*; *Cs.* **to draw to, to attract,** (*Sch.* also: 'to remove a thing from its place?'), prob. another form for *snúr-ba.*

བརྣོགས་པ་ *brnógs-pa* **to hide, conceal,** *Lex.*

བསྣང་བ་ *bsnáṅ-ba* v. *rnáṅ-ba.*

བསྣད་པ་ *bsnád-pa* v. *snád-pa.*

བསྣན་པ་ *bsnán-pa* v. *snón-pa.*

བསྣམ་པ་ *bsnám-pa* v. *snóm-pa.*

བསྣར་བ་ *bsnár-ba* 1. **to extend in length, to lengthen, to pull out,** e.g. a piece of India rubber *W.* — 2. **to draw** or **drag after, to trail,** *mjúg-ma Lex.* the train of a robe, the tail etc.; fig. **to have in its train, to be attended with,** *nyon-moṅs-bsnár* the consequences of sin *Sch.*

བསྣལ་བ་ *bsnál-ba* **to spin out, to protract** *Cs.*

བསྣུན་པ་ *bsnún-pa* v. *snun-pa.*

པ

པ *pa* 1. the letter *p*, (tenuis), the French p. — 2. num. figure: 13.

པ་ *pa*, an affix, or so-called article, the same as *ba* (q. v.) which, when attached to the roots of verbs, gives them the signification of nouns, or, in other words is the sign of the infinitive and the participle; in the language of common life, however, it is frq. used for the finite tense, and for *par;* affixed to the names of things, it denotes the person that deals with the thing (*rtá-pa* horseman, *čú-pa* water-carrier); combined with names of places, it designates the inhabitant (*bód-pa* inhabitant of Tibet); with numerals, it either forms the ordinal number (*γnyis-pa* the second), or it implies a counting, measuring, containing (*bú-mo lo-γnyis-pa* a girl counting two years, i. e. a girl of two years; *k̔ru-gáṅ-pa* measuring one cubit; *súm-ču-pa* containing thirty viz. letters, like the Tibetan alphabet); frq. it has no particular signification (*rkéd-pa* etc. etc.), or it serves to distinguish different meanings (*rkaṅ* marrow, *rkáṅ-pa* foot) or dialects (*k̔á-ba B.*, **k̔a** *W.* snow); *pa daṅ* with a verb, v. *daṅ* 4; in certain expressions it stands, it would seem, incorr. inst. of *pai*: *γsó-ba rig-pa* science of medicine, *grúb-p̔a lus* structure of the body, *dám-pa čos* holy doctrine (of Buddha).

པ་ཏ་ *pá-ta W.* **cross,** St. Andrew's cross (thus ×).

པ་ཏིལ་ *pa-til* v. *p̔a-til.*

པ་ཏོ་ *pá-to* a medicinal herb *Wdṅ.*

པ་ཏྲ་, more corr. པཏྲ་, *pā-tra* (also *pa-ṭa Pth.*) *Ssk.*, **cup, basin, bowl** (esp. for sacrifices); beggar's bowl = *lhuṅ-bzed.*

པ་ཎ་ *pa-ṇa Ssk.* = *ṭaṅ-ka Tar.* 112, 6: in Bhotan 1 rupee *Schr.*; in *W.* (also **pé-ṇa**) a copper-coin = Paisa, esp. of foreign coinage.

པ་ཎི་ *pa-ṇi Hind.* पाणी, **water** *Lt.*

པ་བེན་ *pa-ben* **a strip of wood, ledge, border (?)** *W.*

པ་(ཝ་)སངས་ *pa(-wa)-saṅs* 1. **the planet Venus.** — 2. **Friday.**

པ་ཡག་པ་ *pa-yag-pa* a medicinal herb = *smug-čuṅ Med.*

པ་ཡུ་ *pa-yu* salt *Bal.*

པ་ཡོ་ཏོ་ཡོ་ *pa-yo-tó-yo*, **srog daṅ pa-yo-tó-yo taṅ-te soṅ* Ld.* for *srog daṅ bsdos*, v. *sdo-ba*.

པ་རུ་ཁ་ *pá-ru-k'a W.* **cross** (a straight one +).

པ་རང་ *pa-ráṅ* (spelling doubtful, at any rate not *ṕa-raṅ*) n. of a mountain pass, 19 000 feet high, between Ladak and Spiti.

པ་རི་ *pá-ri W., pá-ru C., B.* 1. **box**, cylindrical or oval, high or flat, of wood or metal. — 2. *pá-ru*, also *pá-tra Sch.* — 3. v. *bá-ru*.

པ་ཤི་ *pa-ši Sch.* '**a teacher**'; *Lex.*: n. of a Tibetan priest that went to China.

པ་སངས་ *pa-saṅs* v. *pa-wa-saṅs*.

པག་, པག་བུ་ *pag, pág-bu Bal., pág-gu Dzl., pau W., ṕag Glr., ṕau Wdṅ.*: **brick**; *pág-gu byéd-pa Dzl.*; *ṕibs-pag* roof-tile *Cs.*; *wá-pag* gutter-tile *Cs.*; *rdzá-pag*, *so-pag Glr.* burnt-brick *Cs.*; *sá-pag Glr.* unburnt-brick *Cs.*; *pag(-bu)-mk'an* mason *Cs.*; *pag-rtsig* brick-wall *Cs.*; **pag-tsir W.* a row or layer of bricks; frq. used as a measure = a small span, **k'a pag-tsir nyis yod** the snow is as deep as two layers of bricks. — Not quite plain is the etymology of *og-pag*, *Lex.*: *ska-rágs-kyi rgyan*, *Sch.*: 'a girdle ornamented with glass-beads'; and of *pag-ṕór Sch.* cup or vessel with a lid.

པགས་པ་ *págs-pa*, *Mil.* also *-po* (cf. *lpags*) 1. **skin, hide**; *šu-ba* to skin, acc. to *Schr.* also merely to fret the skin; *págs-pai gos* skin or fur-clothing *S.g.* — 2. **foreskin**, when the connection of words does not admit of a misconception, *Mng.* — 3. **skin** or **peel** of fruit, **the bark** of trees, also *pags-šún*, and *šún-pags*; **pag-tág* C.* bark-cord, match-cord; *págs-ču* anasarca, skin-dropsy; *págs-ču-žugs* affected with this disease.

པང་ *paṅ*, ཕང་ *ṕaṅ*, resp. *sku-páṅ*, 1. the bend or hollow formed by the belly and the thighs in sitting, **lap**, *B., C., W.*; *paṅ-du soṅ* he sat down on the lap of . . . *Glr.*; *paṅ-k'ebs* apron; *paṅ-k'rag* the blood flowing off during child-birth; **paṅ-big* W.* urinary bladder; **paṅ-ri* (for *dri?*) *suṅ* C.* she has the bloody flux; *ṕáṅ-yyog-ma Cs.* midwife (a kinswoman generally has to officiate as such; a hired one receives a new dress for her services). — 2. the bend or hollow formed by the arm and the chest in carrying something; **bosom**, usually *ṕáṅ-pa*; *šiṅ-paṅ-pu gaṅ* an armful of wood; *ṕáṅ-par ˳k'yér-ba* to carry (a child) on the arm *Dzl.* and elsewh.; *sdóṅ-po ṕáṅ-pas ma ˳k'yigs-pa tsam žig* a tree not to be encompassed by a man's arms *Pth.*; **paṅ-gód, paṅ-k'ód* W.* an armful.

ཕང་ཀ་ *ṕáṅ-ka, ṕáṅ-k'a* 1. *W.* an implement for stirring the fire; for scraping = *rbad*. — 2. *Ts.* = *paṅ*.

པཉྩ་, པན་ཙ་ *pañtsa, pan-tsa*, seems to be the n. of a tree *B., C.*; *Ssk.* only: five.

པད་པ་ *pád-pa C.* = *srin-bu pád-ma*, v. *pád-ma*.

པདྨ་, པད་མ་ *padma, pad-ma Ssk.* in *C.* pronounced **pé-ma** 1. **water-lily, lotos**, Nymphaea, if not nearer defined, the blue species, whilst the less frq. form *pád-mo* (acc. to *Glr.* fol. 62) seems to denote the white kind of this flower. — 2. (not in *Ssk.*, at least acc. to *Wls.* and *Williams*, though *Köpp.* II, 61 seems to dissent): **genitals**, of either sex, *Med.* — 3. *srin-bu pád-ma* **leech**. — *pad-kór, pad-skór* 1. a particular way of folding the fingers during prayer *Cs.* and *Sch.*; a certain gesture with the hand. 2. a kind of **toupet** of the women, also *pad-ló C., W.* — *pád (-ma) dkár(-do)* 1. white lotos. 2. **title** of a celebrated **Sutra**, translated by Burnouf, *Was.* (151). — *pad-dkár žal-laṅ* an astronomical work by Púgpapa, v. *Cs.* timetable. — *pad-ma-čan* full of lotos; more particularly lotos-lake, with and without *mtso Glr.* — *pad-(ma daṅ nyi-ma daṅ) zlái ydan Glr.* and elsewh., carpet with representations of lotos, sun and moon. — *pad-ma-pa-ni* lotos-bearer, name of Awalokiteswara, *Köpp.* II, 23. — *Pad-ma-ₒbyuṅ ɣnás, Sskr.* P. Sambhava, also: *U-rgyan-pád-ma*, one of the most famous divines and holy magicians, in the 8th century, from Urgyén (*Ssk.* Udayana) i.e. Kabul, who acc. to his own declaration (v. the fantastic legend concerning him, entitled: *pad-ma taṅ-yig*) was greater than Buddha himself, v. *Köpp.* II, 68. — *pad-ma-ra-ga Ssk.* ruby. — *pád-rtsa* a medicinal herb *Wdṅ* (= *pe-tsé?*).

པཎྜི་ཏ་ *paṇḍi-ta Ssk.*, **Pandit,** Indian scholar or linguist; *paṇ-čén* great Pandit; *paṇ-čén rin-po-čé, boy-do* (Mongolian) *rin-čen*, title of the second Buddhist pope, residing at Tashilunpo, *Köpp.* II, 121. — *pan-ža* Pandit-cap.

པན་པོན་ *pan-pón* (also *pan-pün?*) not considered perfect in dignity, as for instance the Lamas in *Lh.*, that are married; yet cf. *ban-bón.*

པར་ *par* I. **form, mould,** *blugs-par* casting-mould; *rdéu-par* bullet-mould; *blúgs-par*, as well as *śiṅ-par*, printing form, a stereotype plate cut in wood; *par rkó-ba* to cut types; *rgyáb-pa, par-du ₒdébs-pa*, to print, to stamp; *par (-yig) ₒbri-ba* to write the exemplar or manuscript for printing. — *pár-rko-pa, pár-rko-mk'an*, cutter of types. — *pár-k'aṅ* printing-office. — *par-rgyáb* print, **par-rgyáb ts'ógs-ṡo** *W.* like a print or impression. — *par-snág* printing-ink. — *pár-pa* printer *Cs.* — *pár-dpon* fore-man of a printing-office. — *pár-ma* a printed work, book; **di pár-ma yaṅ yod** this is also to be had printed. — *par-ɣyóg* a printer's man, assistant. — *par-śóg* printing-paper. — *par-ɣži* = *par.*

II. v. *pár-ma.* — III. termin. of *pa*, also sign of the adverb; combined with verbs, it represents the supine, or adverbial sentences, commencing with **whilst, so that;** *mi byéd-par* without doing.

པར་ཏང་ *par-taṅ Lex.*, **a hairy carpet** *Sch.*

པར་པ་ཏ་ *par-pa-ta* n. of an officinal plant *Med.*

པར་བུ་ *par-bu Lexx., Sch.* = *pa-tra.*

པར་ཙ་སོ་ཏི་ *par-tsa-só-ti W.* **a kind of cotton cloth.**

པལ་ལ་ཏུ་ལ་ *pal-la-tú-la Hind.* **scales of a balance** *Sik.*

པས་ *pas* 1. the instr. of *pa;* combined with verbs, it signifies **by, in consequence of, because;** also **as, since, when.** — 2. = *las*, as sign of the comparative; after vowels, however and the final consonants d, r, l, *bas* stands in its place; *rtá-bas k'yi čúṅ-ba yin* the dog is smaller than the horse; *k'yód-pas, stág-pas, rtá-pa-bas, sṅár-bas*, or *sṅá-ma-bas ce*, bigger than you, than a tiger, than a rider, than formerly; it rarely stands for the partitive: *bu ḻia-brgyá-bas ɣčig*, or for *las* with the signification: except, *Mil.*

པི་ *pi* num. fig.: 43.

པི་ཆག་ *pi-čág* (*Turk.* چاكر) **large butcher's knife.**

པི་པི་ *pi-pi* 1. *Schr., Sch.* **fife, flute.** — 2. *W.* **nipple, teat;** **pi-pi nud táṅ-če** to suckle. — 3. **icicle** *W.*

པི་(པི་)ལིང་ *pi(-pi)-liṅ, Ssk.* पिप्पली. Piper longum, a spice, similar to black pepper, yet more oblong.

པི་ཕོ་ *pi-p'o* v. *pi-śi.*

པི་ཚེ་ *pi-tse* **skin,** or **leather bag** for water etc. *Lh.*

པི་ཙི་ *pi-tsi*, and *ma-tsi*, interjections of anger, *Foucaux Gyatch.* २६८, *transl.* 292.

པི་ཝང་ *pi-wáṅ* or *pi-báṅ*, *Zam.* = वीणा, **guitar,** also *da-nyén-pi-waṅ C., pi-waṅ ról-mo Glr.* = *k'ó-poṅ W.; pi-waṅ rgyud ɣsum* a three-stringed guitar *Stg.*; *rgyud-máṅ* a guitar with many strings *Cs.*; *sgróg-pa* to play (the guitar); *pi-waṅ-mk'an*, or *pi-waṅ-pa* a player on the guitar.

པི་ཤི་ *pi-śi* (perh. from the Persian) **cat,** *W.*; *pi-p'o* male cat, *pi-mo* female cat.

པིག་མོ་ *pig-mo* v. *pás-mo.*

པིར་ *pir* **brush, pencil;** *byúg-pir* large brush, for house-painting; *bčád-pir* small brush or pencil for artistic painting, Chinese writing; *pir-togs(-pa)* painter *Cs.* — *pir-don* receptacle or case for brushes. — *pir-spu* pencil-hair. — **pir-nyúg** *W.* = *bcad-pir*; also for lead-pencil. — *pír-šiṅ* pencil-stick.

ཕིར་བ་ *pír-ba* (spelling?) **to crush, to grind** (to powder) = *mnyéd-pa Ld.*

ཕིལ་ཙེ *pil-tse Ld.* **sieve.**

ཕིས་མོ *pis-mo* v. *pús-mo.*

ཕིསྤལ་ *pispal,* acc. to *Cs. Ssk.*, yet not to be found in *Lexx.*, **the wild fig-tree,** *Hindi: pipal.*

ཕུ་ *pu* num. figure for 73.

ཕུ་ཏི་ *pu-ti* **milfoil,** (millefolium), yarrow; *Lh.*

ཕུ་ཏྲི་ *pú-tri* (*Ssk.* पुत्री, daughter), a common female name (perh. *bu-krid.*)

ཕུ་སྟི་ *pú-sti, Glr.* = *pó-ti,* **book** (perh. formed out of *pústak*).

ཕུ་ན་ཁ་ *Pu-na-ka* town in Bhotan.

ཕུ་བྱི་ *pú-byi* v. *spú-byi.*

ཕུ་ཙེ་ *pú-tse, pú-se,* **a** little rat-like animal, v. *bra* and *zlum; pu-tse-šel* prob. = *pu-šel-tse.*

ཕུ་ཚེ་ *pu-tsé* **husks of barley** *W.*; *Cs.* **bran.**

ཕུ་རངས་ *Pu-ráṅs Mil.*, a district in *Ṅá-ris.*

ཕུ་རི་ *pu-ri* **tube,** any thing tubular and hollow, box of tin or wood, pen-case etc.; also = *dóṅ-po* the Tibetan shuttle; **pu-ri méd-kan** *W.* full, solid, not hollow, cf. *pá-ri.*

ཕུ་རུ་ཥ་ *pu-ru-ṣa Ssk.* **man; soul;** = *skyés-bu.*

ཕུ་ལིང་ག *pu-liṅ-ga Cs.: Ssk.* **masculine gender.**

ཕུ་ལུ་ *pú-lu* **hut,** built of stones, like those of the alpine herdsmen *W.*, (*Ts. rdzi-skyor*); *kyi-pul* dog-kennel.

ཕུ་ཤུ་ *pú-šu* **fence,** *Lex.* = *mda-yáb* and *lín-kan.*

ཕུ་ཤེལ་ཙེ་ *pu-šel-tse* a medicinal herb *Med.*

ཕུག་ཏ་ *púg-ta* (?) **shelf, partition** in a box.

ཕུག་མ་ *púg-ma Pur.* **collar-bone.**

ཕུང་བ་ *púṅ-pa, púṅ-pa C., W.* **an urn-shaped vessel** of clay or wood, for water, beer etc. (seems not to be the same with *búm-pa*).

ཕུན་པ་ *pún-pa W.*, **pún-ce** = *lúd-ce* to run over.

ཕུཎྜ་རཱི་ཀ *puṇḍarika Ssk*, **white lotos.**

ཕུར་ *pur Cs.* 1. **steel-yard.** — 2. *púr-gyis* v. *ₒpur-ba.* — 3. v. *spur.*

ཕུལ་ *pul* v. *pú-lu.*

ཕུཥྐ་ར *puṣkara Ssk* **blue lotos.**

ཕུསྟ་ཀ *pustaka Ssk.* **book.**

ཕུས་མོ་ *pús-mo, W.* **pis-mo, pig-mo**, **knee;** *pis-mo sa-la ₒdzug-pa* to kneel; **pig-mo tsúg-ce, pi-tsúg gyáb-ce** *W.* id.; **pig-mo tsúg-te dad-ce** to sit in kneeling (which is considered indecorous); cf. *tsog.*

ཕེ་ *pe* num. figure: 103.

ཕེ་(ད)ཀར་ *pe-(d)kár,* also *be-kár, pe-hai-ra. bi-hár Lt., Glr., Mil.*, a much worshipped deity, v. *kye-páṅ*, and *Schl.* 157.

ཕེ་ཏེ་ཧོར་ *pe-te-hor* n. of a people *Sch.*

ཕེ་ནེ་ *pe-ne, pé-na* v. *pa-ṇa.*

ཕེ་བན་ *pe-bán* (*Pers.* پیوند), **graft, scion;** **pe-bán tsúg-ce** *W.* to graft.

ཕེ་ཙམ་ *pe-tsám* **little, small, a little** *Sch.*

ཕེ་ཙེ་ *pe-tsé, pi-tsi, Chin. pai-tsái,* **Chinese white cabbage** in *C.*; of late also known in Europe.

ཕེ་ར་ *pé-ra* **a flat basket.**

ཕེ་ས་ *pé-sa, paisa, Hind.*, copper coin, not quite a half-penny.

ཕེན་ཙེ་ *pén-tse* a kind of wood of which vessels are made *Cs.* (= *pán-tsa?*)

ཕོ་ *po* 1. sign of nouns, in like manner as *-pa*; it particularly designates concrete nouns and the masculine gender, frq., in contradistinction to abstract nouns with *-pa* or *-ba*, and to feminines with *-mo*; connected with a numeral, it supplies the definite article: *lṅá-po* the five (just mentioned); *γnyís-po* the two, both, = *γnyís-ka*. — 2. num. figure: 133.

པོ་ཏ་ལ་ *pó-ta-la* (*Ssk.* पोत ship, ल to receive, hence: harbour, port; *Tib.* *gru-dzin*) 1. ancient n. of Tatta, a town not far from the mouth of the Indus. — 2. n. of a three-peaked hill near Lhasa, with the palace of the old kings of Tibet, now the seat of the Dalai Lama. (The spelling '*Buddha-la*' arises from an erroneous etymological hypothesis, and the fact of its being found even in Huc's writings may be attributed merely to a thoughtless adherence to what had become a custom; v. *Köpp.* II, 340.)

པོ་ཏི་ *pó-ti* (acc. to one *Lex.* a corruption of *pu-sta-ka*, for which also the form *pu-sti* seems to speak) = *glegs-bam*, **book** (of loose leaves).

པོ་ཏུམ་ *po-túm Sik.* **large wasp.**

པོ་ཏོ་ *po-tó C.* **bullock.**

པོ་ཏོག་ *po-tóg* v. *mto-po-tog.*

པོ་ལ་ *po-lá* the well-known Turkish mess of **pilaw**, *Hind.* **pulao**, rice boiled with fowl; in *Ld.* however sweet rice, prepared with butter, sugar, and 'pating'; fig. *bsám-bloi pó-la byéd-po* to concoct and deal in plans and plots.

པོ་ལོ(ན)་ཤན་ *po-lo(n)-šán* n. of the mountains bordering on China *Ld.-Glr. Schl.* 21, a (where in the translation the word has not been recognized as being a proper name).

པོག་ཕོར་ *pog-ṕór* **censer, perfuming-pan.**

པོགས་ཏ་ *pógs-ta* v. *ṕúgs-ta.*

པོད་ *pod, pon, pón-to* v. *ṕod, ṕon, ṕón-to.*

པོབ་ *pob C.* **castrated ram.**

པོལ་ *pol Ts.* = *tsá-bai nad.*

པྲ་ *pra* small **turkoises**, 1 or 2''' in size, strung together for finger-rings, v. *tsom.*

པྲ་(མོ་) *pra(-mo) Cs.* 1. **lot;** *pra ˳débs-pa* to cast lot. — 2. **sign, token, prognostic;** *Sch.*: *pra ˳bebs-pa* 'ein Zeichen geben, ein Bild darstellen'.

པྲ་ཅལ་ *pra-čál, spra-čál Lex.* w.e. *Sch.* **jest, joke, fun,** nonsensical talk; *byéd-pa* to make sport, to play the buffoon; *slóṅ-ba* to cause merriment; *pra-čál-pa*, or *-mḱan* wag, buffoon.

པྲ་ལི་ *pra-lí Sch.*: hill-mouse (marmot?), hare (?); cf. *brá-ba.*

པྲང་འགོས་ *praṅ-˳gós* an alpine herb, said to be very wholesome to sheep (so for instance in Purig); acc. to recent investigations, of little value. Acc. to *Cs.* = *ȧ-króṅ*, but this is denied by the people of Lahoul.

པྲི་ཡང་གུ་ *pri-yaṅ-gu Ssk.*, n. of several kinds of Indian aromatic plants *Med.*

པྲོག་, ཟེ་པྲོག་ *prog, ze-próg Lex.*, **the crest of a cock** *Cs.*; *próg-žu, bróg-žu, spróg-zu* = *čod-pán.*

དཔའ་(བ་) *dpá(-ba)* (शूर, वीर), also *spá-ba* 1. **bravery, strength, courage; brave, strong, courageous;** *dpa bsgóṅ-ba Lex., ḱóṅ-ba Thgy.*; *góṅ-ba, bkóṅ-ba Lex.*, to despond; to dishearten (?); *šin-tu dpá-žiṅ* he becoming very brave *Dzl.*; *dpá-la stobs kyaṅ gyad daṅ bnyám-ste* being brave, and in strength equal to an athlete *Dzl.* — 2. **beauty; beautiful.** — 3. *W.* **taste, agreeable taste, flavour.**

Comp. *dpá-čan* 1. brave. 2. beautiful. 3. *W.* savoury. — *dpa-méd-ḱan W.* tasteless, v. also *ldád-pa.* — *dpa-čén* very brave; a great hero. — *dpa-dár* = *mgul-dár*, a piece of silk, tied round the neck, as an honourable distinction for some brave deed. — *dpa-ldán* = *dpá-čan* 1 and 2. — *dpá-bo*, वीर, 1. strong man, hero. 2. demigod. — *dpa-bo-dkár* a medicinal herb *Med.* — *dpá-mo* 1. heroine (more frq. than the masc. *dpá-bo*). 2. = *mka-gro-ma*, Dākini *Mil., Thgr., Glr.* — *dpa-tsúl Mil.* = *dpá-ba* 1. sbst., ni f.

དཔག་ཚད་ *dpag-tsád* **mile**, acc. to *Cs.* = 4000 fathoms, hence a geographical mile; yet there are mentioned *dpag-čén* and *dpág-čúṅ*, the latter = 500 fathoms. The word seems altogether to belong more to the phantastic mythical literature, than to common life; so at least in *W.*

དཔག་པ་ *dpág-pa* v. *dpóg-pa.*

དཔག་གཡེངས་ *dpag-γyéṅs* the bustle or tumult of a festival *Ld.*

དཔག་བསམ་ཤིང་ *dpag-bsam-šiṅ* n. of a fabulous tree, that grants every wish; acc. to *Pth.* = *tsán-dan-sbrúl-gyi snyiṅ-po.*

དཔང་(པོ་) *dpáṅ(-po)* **witness,** both the deponent, and the evidence deposed. Fully authenticated are as yet only: *lha dpáṅ-du ₒdzúg-pa* to call a deity for a witness in taking an oath, to appeal to *Glr.*; also: *dpaṅ byéd-pa* to bear witness, to attest, v. *mna.* More conjectural are the meanings of: *blo-séms dpáṅ-du ɉóg-pa Glr.*, or *raṅ-séms dpáṅ-du ₒdzúg-pa Mil.*, to be sincere, to be conscious of speaking the truth; *dpáṅ-du ₒgyúr-ba* to be witness of, to see, to know (cf. *spyán-du ₒgyúr-ba*); *bden-dpáṅ Liš.* as explanation of *če-bži*, witness or proof for the truth of a thing; **páṅ-po lóg-pa zér-če** *W.* to give false evidence (*Schr. rdzun-dpáṅ*). — *mi-dpáṅ* (*Ld.* **mir-paṅ**) *W.*, *C.*, is used as syn. to *dpáṅ-po* (also *Schr*), 1. witness. 2. defender, advocate; *mi-dpaṅ* (or *dpaṅ-po*) *byéd-pa* c. genit. or dat., to defend in a court of justice; (*dpáṅ-pos dpóṅ-ba Sch.* seems to be unknown and doubtful).

དཔངས་ *dpaṅs* **height;** *dpáṅs-su* in height *Samb.*; *dpaṅs-mtó Lex.* high, cf. *ₒpaṅs.* — *dpaṅs-tsád* great heat *Schr.* (?).

དཔར་བ་ *dpár-ba* v. *dpór-ba.*

དཔལ་ *dpal Ssk.* श्री 1. **glory, splendour, magnificence, abundance;** *dpal reg-pa-méd-pa* unattainable glory *Glr.*; *yón-tan dú-mai dpal* splendour of numerous accomplishments; *skyéd-pai dpál-la loṅs-spyód-pa* enjoying the utmost happiness *Glr.*; frq. as an epithet, or part of the names of deities, e.g. *dpal-čén hé-ru-ka*, and esp. *dpal(-ldan)lhá-mo*, *dpal-čén-mo*, Durga Uma, Kāli, the much adored spouse of Siva; *ₒdod-dgúi dpal* the fulness of all that can be desired *Glr.*; *dpál-gyi dúm-bu*, श्रीखण्ड, 1. sandal-wood. 2. *Cs.* a kind of syrup, prepared of *bsé-šiṅ*, used as a purgative. — 2. **wealth, abundance,** *Glr.* and elsewh. — 3. **welfare, happiness, blessing,** *ₒgró-bai* of creatures *Mil.* and elsewh.; *kún-gyi dpál-du ₒgyúr-ba* or *šár-ba* to be (become) the salvation, the saviour of all beings *Glr.* and elsewh.; *dpal skyéd-pa*, *γžán-gyi*, *ráṅ-gi dpal* to work for the elevation of others or for one's own. — 4. nobility, *dpál-gyi γnáṅ-ba* privilege of nobility; *dpál-gyi γnaṅ-šóg* diploma of nobility, *dpál-gyi γnaṅ-šóg-pa* one having a diploma of nobility *Cs.* — *dpal-k̄yád Dzl.* = *dpal* 1. — *dpal-rtúg* majesty, full glory *Sch.* — *dpal-ldán* a man's name (very common). — *dpal-ɉó* an illustrious man, *dpál-mo* an illustrious woman *Cs.* — *dpal(-gyi)-béu* is said to denote the figure ࿌ *Glr.* — *dpal-byéu* glow-worm *Sch.* — *dpal-byór* 1. glory, wealth, magnificence, as a man's possession. 2. *W.* strawberry; 3. a man's name (very common).

དཔུང་ *dpuṅ* 1 **host, great number,** *ₒbaṅs t̄ams-čád-kyi Dzl.*; esp. of soldiers. — 2. **troops, army,** *dpuṅ bži* the four species of troops: *rtai*, *gláṅ-po-čei*, *šiṅ-rtai*, and *rkaṅ-t̄áṅ-gi dpuṅ* (or *dpuṅ(-bu)-čuṅ*); *dpuṅ-(gi) tsógs*, *dmag-dpúṅ*, army frq.; *dgra-dpúṅ* hostilearmy. — 3. (auxiliaries?), **help, assistance,** **púṅ-la táṅ-če** *W.* to send assistance. — *dpuṅ-grógs*, *-rogs*, helper. — *dpuṅ-(gi) γnyen* friend, protector, defender, assistant, frq. — **puṅ-nón** *W.* reinforcement.

དཔུང་པ་ *dpúṅ-pa* 1. **shoulder,** *dpúṅ-pa k̄ar* on the shoulder *Glr.*; *dpuṅ-pa daṅ dpyi γnyis* both the shoulders and hips *S.g.*; upper arm, *dpuṅ-pa-rkáṅ* upper arm-bone; *dpuṅ ɉúm-pa Sch.* to contract the arm (?); *dpuṅ-pa-lág* upper and lower arm *Cs.*; *dpuṅ-pa-rgyán* an ornament for the arm *Cs.* — 2. **sleeve,** *gos dpúṅ-pa-čan* a garment with sleeves *Cs.*; *dpuṅ-pa-bčád* the part of a woman's dress covering the chest *Zam.*; *Sch.*: *dpuṅ-bčad-rás*.

དཔེ་ *dpe*, *Ld.* **spe**, 1. **pattern, model,** *dé-la dpe Glr.*, or *de dper byás-nas Zam.*, taking this for a pattern: *rgyá-yul-nas rtsis-kyi dpe blaṅs* it was from China that mathematics were learned *Glr.*; . . . *pai dpe mi ̥dug* there are no patterns for . . . *Glr.*; *dpe či ltar* with what to be compared? according to what analogy? *Thgy.*; similitude, parable, example, *mťún-pai dpe* an example that may be followed, a good example; *bzlóg-pai dpe* an example to the contrary, a warning example *Thgy.*; **pe záṅ-po*, and *ṅém-pẹ pe*,* as well as **yár-la* and *már-la žág-pẹ-pe*, or *mar-pe** *C.* id.; *dpe stón-pa* to teach or to prove by examples; hence the participle, used substantively, serves as an epithet of the Sautrantikas, *Was.* (112); *dpe bšád-pa*, *dpe bžág-pa* = *dpe stón-pa*; *dper rǰód-pa* to set up for a parable or comparison; *dpér-na*, in later times also *dpé-ni*, *dpe byéd-na Mil.*, **pe gyáb-na** *W.*, 1. (in order) to quote an example, by way of a comparison, just as if, followed by *bžin-du* or *ltar*, very frq.; 2. like our 'for instance', e.g., before enumerations, where in the older writings gen. *̥di-lta-ste* is used: *dper ̥ós-pa Cs.* what may be compared, *dper mi ̥ós-pa* not to be compared; occasionally also: worthy or not worthy of imitation; *ḱá-dpe*, *ytám-dpe* proverb, adage *Cs.*; *̥drá-dpe* allegory, parable *S.g.*; *má-dpe W.*, *Ld.* **má-spe**, *Lh.* **már-pe**, pattern, (writing-) copy (cf. also *má-dpe* and *bú-dpe* below). — 2. **symmetry, harmony,** beauty, (in certain phrases). — 3. **book,** *ḱrims brgyad-kyi dpe* the book of the eight commandments *Dzl.*; *ká-dpe*, *ka-ḱái dpe* abc-book, primer; *ṗyág-dpe* resp. for *dpe*, if used by a Lama (cf. *ṗyag-mḱár*); *má-dpe*, *bú-dpe* original and copy of a book *Cs.*; *yig-nág dpe* a real book, not of a fig. meaning, as the book of nature, *Mil.*; *dpe rtsóm-pa* to write, to compose, *bšú-ba* to copy a book; *̥dógs-pa*, *̥tsém-pa* to bind, to stitch a book.

Comp. *dpé-ka* little book, vulgo. — *dpe-ḱáṅ* library; bookseller's shop. — *dpe-ḱri* a table to put books on, book-stand. — *dpe-mkyúd*, *̥ḱyud Cs.* v. *mḱyud-pa*. — *dpe-mgó*, *dpe-mǰúg* beginning, end, of a book. — *dpe-sgám* chest for books, book-case. — *dpé-ča* not frq. in *B.*, but vulgo the common word for book. — **dpé-ča ṗé-če*, *túm-če** *W.* to open, to close a book; v. *btúm-pa*. — *dpe-rǰód* v. *dper*. — *dpe-ťó* list of books. — *dpe-byád* proportion, symmetry, beauty. *dpe-byád bzáṅ-po brgyád-ču* the eighty physical perfections of Buddha. — *dpe-byád-čan* well-proportioned. — *dpé-tsoṅ-pa* bookseller — *dpe-šúbs* case or covering for a book. — *dpe-bšús* copy of a book. — *dper* v. 1. — *dpe-brǰód* 1. example, comparison, *dpe-brǰód byéd-pa* to compare, to cite an example *Cs.*; *dpe-brǰód rtógs-pa Gram.* id. (?). 2. paradigm, example *Gram.* —

དཔེ་སྒྲ་ *dpé-sgra* (?), *(*s*)*pé-ra** *W.*, **speech,** for *ytam*; *(*s*)*pé-ra zér-če*(*s*), *táṅ-če*(*s*)*, to speak, to talk; *ĭ-zug* (*s*)*pé-ra ma taṅ* do not say so! *(*s*)*pé-ra zér-če*(*s*) *med-ḱan soṅ** he became speechless (with terror etc.).

དཔེར་ན་ *dpér-na* v. sub *dpe*.

དཔོག་པ་ *dpóg-pa*, pf. *dpags*, fut. *dpag*, 1. **to measure, to proportion, to fix,** *ytóṅ-tsul ťe-ťúṅ-la* (to proportion) the dose to the size *Lt.*; . . . *kyi ťsód-las* after the measure of . . ., *Lt.*: *nad-stóbs-la* according to the violence of the disease *Lt.*; *dpag* (*tu*) *med* (-*pa*), less frq. *dpag-brál*, *dpag-yás*, immensely large, very much; *ťugs dpag-med* infinite grace, *mdzád-pa* to show *Dzl.* — 2. **to outweigh, to counterbalance,** *loṅs-spyód tams-čád-kyis mi dpóg-pa* not to be counterbalanced by all the wealth . . . *Tar.* — 3. **to weigh, to judge, to prove,** *rǰés-su dpóg-pa* to examine *Tar.*; *rǰes-dpág Zam.* अनुमान, inference, conclusion.

དཔོན་པོ་ *dpón-po* **master, lord,** over men (generally); (cf. *bdág-po* owner) master, over working-men, overseer, foreman, leader, *grá-pai dpon-po*, director, =

ₒgo-dpon: **dpón-po-la čag ṕul dug žu zer, tug-šró ma kyod, ṅa yóṅ-loṅ med* W.* make your master my compliment, and he should not take it amiss that I had no time to come; *ḱrims-dpon* 1. prop.: superior judge, lord chief-justice. 2. now: high officer of state, prefect, = *mi-dpón*; *mḱar-dpón* commander of a fortress; *ₒḱrúg-dpon* general *Ma.*; *ₒgó-dpon* v. *go*; *brgyá-dpon* centurion, captain; *bčú-dpon* corporal; *čibs-dpon* master of the horse, equerry; *rjé-dpon = rje*; *rtá-pa-dpon* (sic) (cf. *pa* extr.) general of cavalry *Glr.*; *stégs-dpon* (?) v. *stegs*; *stoṅ-dpon* leader of a thousand (seems to be no longer in use); *déd-dpon* sea-captain; *mdá-dpon* is said to be in *C.* the modern word for general, and *ₒdégs-dpon* the same as *stóṅ-dpon*; however v. *stegs*; *ldiṅ-dpon* v. *ldiṅ*; *spyi-dpon* governor general *Cs.*; *mi-dpon* prefect; *rtsig-dpon* master-mason; *rdzóṅ-dpon* = *mḱár-dpon*; *yúl-dpon* prefect of a district *Wts.*; *rú-dpon* something like colonel; *šiṅ-dpon* master-carpenter; *slób-dpon* teacher, frq., also title of the higher and more learned Lamas, corresponding, as it were, to *M.A.*, master of arts; *γsól-dpon* head-cook, butler. — *dpón-mo* fem., *ṅai dpón-mo yin* she is my mistress *Glr.* — *dpón-yod* standing under a master or mistress. — *dpon-med* free *Cs.* — *dpon-γyóg* master and servants, frq. — *ḱóṅ-jo dpon-γyóg* (princess) *koṅ-jo* and her suite *Glr.* — *dpon-tsáṅ* physician *Schr.* and *Sch.* — *dpon-yig* secretary *Schr.* — *dpon-slób* 1. inst. of *dpón-po daṅ slób-ma Ma.* and elsewh. 2. title of the four independent rulers in Bhotan, the 'Penlow' of English news-papers, acc. to the pronunciation of **pŏn-lob, pŏn-lo**.

དཔོར་བ་ *dpór-ba*, pf. and fut. *dpar*, **to dictate**, *Cs.*; **por-tsóm (jhe')-pa* C.* id.

དཔྱ་ *dpya* **tax, duty, tribute**, *ₒbúl-ba* to pay, *Dzl.*, *ₒbébs-pa* to impose *Tar.* 21, 11; *dpya-ḱrál* id., *rgyál-poi dpya-ḱrál Lex.*; likewise *dpya-ṫáṅ Cs.*

དཔྱང་བ་ *dpyáṅ-ba*, *spyáṅ-ba*, **to suspend, to make hang down**, prop. vb. a. to *ṗyáṅ-ba*, with pf. *dpyaṅs* and *spyaṅs*, imp. *dpyaṅs*, *Sch. dpyoṅs*, but also vb. n., **to rock, to pitch** (of a ship) *Pth.*; *dpyáṅ-la γtóṅ-ba* trs. *Thgy.*; **gyóg-čaṅ**, perh. more corr. **ḱyog-čáṅ**, also **ṗeb-čáṅ* C.* sedan-chair, palanquin; *dpyaṅ-ṫág*, *ₒṗyaṅ-ṫág*, cord or rope, by which a thing is suspended, e.g. a plummet, a bucket a miner; hence fig. *tugs-rjei dpyaṅ-ṫág γčód-pa Thgr.*: *ču-snod daṅ dpyaṅ-ṫag sbá-ba* to hide the bucket together with the rope *Schr.*; a rope-swing, *dpyaṅ-ṫág rtséd-pa* to swing (one's self); *dpyaṅs*, *spyáṅs-pai ṗan*, hanging ornaments, *dar-dpyáṅs* silk ornaments *S.g.*

དཔྱད་ *dpyad* 1. v. *dpyód-pa*. — 2. *Stg.*: an instrument to open the mouth by force; perh. also in a more general sense: crow-bar(?); *dpyád-pa* v. *dpyód-pa*.

དཔྱས་པོ་ *dpyás-po* **offence, fault, blame** *Cs.*; *dpyás-čan* faulty, blamable; *dpyas-méd* faultless, blameless *Cs.*; *dpyas ₒdógs-pa* to blame *Tar.*; cf. *ₒpyá-ba*.

དཔྱི་ *dpyi* (*Cs.* also *spyi*) *W. *(s)pi**, **hip** *Lt.*; *dpyi-mgó Cs.*, *dpyi-zúr*, *dpyi-rús*, hip-bone; *dpyi-mig* socket of the hip-bone, perh. also vulg. = hip.

དཔྱིད་ *dpyid* (cf. Phonetic Table), **spring,** also adv. in spring *Dzl.*; cf. also *dus* 4; *dpyid-ka*, **pid-ḱa* W.*, id., also *Glr.*; *dpyid-zla* month of spring.

དཔྱིས་ *dpyis*, *dpyis ṗyin-pa Sch.*: to come to the last, to arrive at the end; *dei rig-pa ₒdi dpyis ṗyin-pa sus kyaṅ mi šes dgóṅs-nas Schf.*: as he reflected, that no body would thoroughly understand his arguments.

དཔྱོང་བ་ *dpyóṅ-ba*, perh. primitive form of *dpyáṅ-ba*.

དཔྱོ་བ་ *dpyó-ba* **to change** *Sch.*

དཔྱོད་པ་ *dpyód-pa*, pf. and fut. *dpyad*, **to try, to examine**, *nyés-pa daṅ ma-nyés-pa* innocence and guilt, right and wrong *Dzl.*; *dpyád-na ... ma rtógs-so* after ever so much investigating ... they found out nothing *Dzl.*; *bye-brág-tu dpyád-pa ste* having now been separately examined *Zam.*; *sa-dpyád*, or *ri-dpyád γzigs-pa* to examine the country, or the mountains, i.e. their general features, with regard to omens and auspices *Glr.*; *sai dpyad bzáṅ-bar šés-pa* to know that this examination will turn out favourably *Glr.*; **rin čád-če** (gen. written **bčad-če**, cf. *bčód-pa* extr.) *W.* to tax, to estimate; *goṅ-táṅ dpyád-kyis* (or *-pas*) *mi čod Glr.* v. *čod-pa* 2; esp. in medicine: *smáṅ-pas . . . dpyad byás-te . . . žes dpyad byás-so* the physician having tried, tried thus, (pronounced the following as the result of his examination) *Dzl.* ༢༧༡, 12; *sman-dpyád byéd-pa* to treat medically, *dpyad má-la bya* then the mother (not the child) must be placed under medical treatment *Lt.*; *ₒbrás-kyis btsún-moi sman-dpyád byed-pa* to cure (the illness of) the queen with rice *Dzl.*; *sman-dpyád-la mḱás-pa* to be skilled in medical science *Dzl.*; *ču-byád dpyád-kyi γnas* instrumental therapeutics i.e. surgery *S.g.*; *rtog-dpyód, brtag-dpyád*, examination; *rtog-dpyód ráb-tu γtóṅ-ba* to examine very closely *Pth.*; *rtog-dpyód ṫoṅ* examine! *Mil.*; *bzaṅ-dpyód* examining the worth of a thing. — *dpyód-pa-pa*, and *spyód-pa-pa*, *Ssk.* **मीमांसक**, an Indian sect of philosophers (the former of the two spellings seems to be more correct).

དཔྲལ་བ་ *dprál-ba* (resp. *γdaṅs Cs.*), **ṭál-wa**, *Ld.* **šrál-wa**, **forehead,** *dprál-bai mda* an arrow sticking in the forehead *Glr.*; *dprál-bai mig bžin-du* 'like the eye of the countenance', to designate something highly valued (as the scriptural 'apple of the eye'); *dprál-bai ṗyógs-kyi ṫad dráṅ-na* just before one in front *Wdṅ.*; fig. **ṭal-wa ṅán-pa** *W.* unlucky; a luckless person.

དཔྲུལ་དཔྲུལ་ *dprul-dprúl* (or *ṗrul-ṗrúl?*), **ṭul-ṭúl-la tóṅ wa** *C.* to hang one's self.

ལྤགས་ *lpags*, as second part of compounds inst. of *págs-pa*, e.g. *wá-lpags* fox-skin, *stág-lpags* tiger-skin; *šún-lpags* skin, bark, peel, shell.

སྤ་ *spa* 1. v. *dpa*. — 2. also *sba*, **cane** (seems to be distinguished from *smyúg-ma* more in a popular and practical way, than scientifically); *spa-skór* hoop of a cask *Schr.*; *spa-ḱár Mil.*, *spa-lčág Mil.*, *spa-bér Pth.*, *spa-dbyúg Lex.*, walking-cane; *spa-glíṅ* cane-flute *Sch.*; *spa-til* lunt, match, v. *ṗa-til*; *spa-dóṅ* or *-ldoṅ* little cask, made of bamboo prob. = *gur-gúr dóṅ-mo*; **pa-ₒbár** *C.*, *W.* torch; *spa-dmyúg* or *-smyug*, cane *Cs.*; *pa-šiṅ Sik.* strong bamboo sticks.

སྤ་མ་ *spá-ma* 1. **juniper,** Juniperus squamosa, and some other small species; cf. *šúg-pa*. — 2. **cypress** *Sik.*

སྤག་པ་ *spág-pa* 1. v. *spóg-pa*. — 2. **ḱál-pag pág-če** *W.* **to smack** (in eating). — 3. *C.*, *W.* **to dip**, e.g. meat into the gravy; cf. the following.

སྤགས་ *spags*, resp. *skyu-rum*, 1. *C.* = *zan* (= **ḱó-lag, pág-ḱu** *Ld.*), **pap,** esp. made of tea and 'tsampa'. — 2. *W.* = **ša-rúg** *C.*), **sauce, gravy,** for dipping in (sops); **dam-pág** *W.* mire, sludge. — 3. **food, dish, mess:** *W.*, *C.* **pag na so-só**.

སྤང་ *spaṅ*, I. also *spáṅ-po*, 1. **turf, green-sward, meadow,** *mdún-na spaṅ-po mé-tog bkra* in front a flowery meadow-ground *Mil.* — 2. **moss,** also *ču-spaṅ Cs.* — 3. **bog,** *spaṅ-skóṅ* 1. p.n. ('turf-ditch'), a large valley, with a lake in it, on the frontier of Ladak and Rudog. 2. *spaṅ-skóṅ ṗyag-rgyá-pa* n. of an ancient work on religion *Glr.*; *spaṅ rgyan* a medicinal herb *Med.*; *spáṅ-čan* covered with turf; *spáṅ-ču* green mud *Sch.*; *spaṅ-ljóṅs* grassy country; *spaṅ-ṫáṅ* a plain covered with verdure; *spaṅ-spós* Waldheimia tridactylites, a pretty, very aromatic composite, growing on the higher alps; *spaṅ-bóg* piece of turf, sod; *spaṅ-ma Med.*, **तुत्थ**, blue vitriol; *spaṅ-rtsi S.g.* (?); *spaṅ-žún* verdigris *Sch.*; *spaṅ-ri* a grassy hill *Mil.*; *spaṅ-γšóṅ* a mountain-meadow *Mil.*

II. **board, plank,** gen. *spaṅ-léb Glr.* and vulg.; also **a slab, slate, flag** *Lh.*; *spaṅ-sgó* board or panel of a door *Cs.*; *spaṅ-ḱri Schr.*, **ṭi-páṅ** *Ld.*, **paṅ-dáṅ** *Ld.*, book-stand.

སྤང་བ་ *spaṅ-ba* v. *spoṅ-ba*.

སྤངས་ *spaṅs*, sometimes inst. of *dpaṅs*.

སྤད་ *spad*, only in *ṗa-spád* **father and children;** cf. the more frq. *ma-smád*, *Lex.*

སྤན་སྤུན་ *span-spún* **brothers, relatives** *Cs.*

སྤབས· *spabs, rna-spábs C.* **ear-wax**; *Lex.* also *riul-* (or *rdul-?*) *gyi spabs* w.e.

སྤར· *spar* for *par* 1. *Sch.*

སྤར་ཁ· *spar-ka, spar-ka brgyad* the **pah kwah**, or eight diagrams of Chinese science, ☰☷ etc.

སྤར་བ· *spar-ba* I. sbst., also *spar-mo* (*Ld.* **wár-mo**, acc. to the spelling *sbar-mo*) 1. **the grasping hand, paw, claw,** *spráṅ-poi spár-mor spa-dbyúg sprad* he puts the staff into the beggar's grasp (hand) *Lex.*; **wár-mo gyáb-ce** *W.*, *spár-mos ˳brád-pa* to clutch, to scratch; *spár-mos ˳débs-pa Cs.*, *spar byéd-pa Sch.*, to seize with the hand, the paw, or the claws; *ydoṅ tams-cád spar-šád rgyáb-pa Pth.* to scratch the whole face ('combing it with the claws'); **sbar-ˏju** *C.* rail, for taking hold of; *spár-mo ˳byéd-pa, bsdám-pa* to open, to close the hand *Cs.* — 2. as a measure: as much as may be grasped with the hand, **a handful** (of wood, grass, earth etc.), *(*s*)*pár-ra yaṅ** one handful, (*s*)*pár-ra yaṅ do* two handfuls etc.; *spar-tsád lṅa-brgyá* 500 handfuls *S.g.*; *sa spar-gáṅ Mil.* a handful of earth.

II. vb. v. *spór-ba.*

སྤར་མ· *spár-ma* a low-growing shrub of very hard wood *Mil.nt.*

སྤི་ཏི· (*s*)*pi-ti* **Spiti,** the valley, situated to the west of Lahul, watered by the Spiti river, belonging to the British Punjáb, and inhabited by a race of pure Tibetans.

སྤིའུ· *spiu* col. for *spéu.*

སྤུ· *spu, Ssk.* रोमन्, 1. **hair** ('*pilus*', cf. *skra*), *lús-kyi* of the body in general, *Lex.*; *mgó-spu, ká-* or *ydóṅ-spu, mčán-spu, ˳doms-spu* (or *spu-ṅán Cs.*), *bráṅ-spu*, hair of the head, the beard, arm-pits, lower-parts, chest; *bá-spu* the little hairs of the skin, frq.; *rtá-spu* horse-hair; *spu ˏfyi* or *ytog* the hair is plucked out *Lex.*, *byi* falls off *Dzl.*, *yžob byed* is singed off *Sch.*, *ldaṅ, laṅ Dzl.*, *lóṅ-yyo Mil.*, the hair bristles, stands on end; *spu ziṅ byed B.*, *brtse Sch.*, **se-ziṅ** *W.*, a shuddering of fear comes over (me, him etc.); *tams-cád spu-ziṅ byéd-caṅ Pth.*; *byad spus keṅs-pa* with a face all hairy *Glr.*; *spui kúṅ-bu* passage of perspiration, pore *Dzl.*; *spu nyág-ma tsám-gyi ˳gyód-pai sems* repentance as much as one single little hair *Dzl.* — 2. **feather**, *byá-spu rluṅ-giš kyer-ba* a down (feather) blown off; **feathers, plumage.**

Comp. *spú-ka* **colour** of horses and other hairy animals. — *spú-gri* 1. **razor**; also allegorically, as a title of books. 2. knife *C.* — *spú-čan* hairy. — *spu-čim*(?) false hair *Sch.* — *spú-ja* v. *ja.* — *spú-byi nág-po, spu-nág* also *pú-byi*, **sable** (furred animal) *Sch.* — *spú-ma* hairy, carded (cloth). — *spu-méd* hairless. — *spu-ytsaṅ-ma* v. *spus.* — *spu-hrúg* short-haired *Sch.*

སྤུ་རངས· *spu-ráṅs Glr.* v. *pu-ráṅs.*

སྤུག *spug Lex.* n. of a precious stone *Cs.*

སྤུང· *spuṅ* **heap**, col. also for *púṅ-po*; *spúṅ-ba* pf. and imp. *-spuṅs,* to heap, accumulate, pile up (coals etc.); *rin-čén spúṅs-pa* a heap of precious stones *Glr.*

སྤུད་པ· *spúd-pa* **to decorate**; *rgyáṅ-gyis Lex.* (cf. *spus*).

སྤུན· *spun* 1. children of the same parents, **brothers, sisters,** *kó-mo-cag spun ynyis* we (his) two sisters *Dzl.* ༢༤༠, 17; *ṅed spun ysum* we three brothers *Glr.*; *kyed bú-mo spun lṅa-po* you five sisters *Mil.*; pleon. *bu spun ysum Tar.*; *spun yžán-rnams* his other (six elder) brothers *Tar.*; *spun-ycés* dear brother! *Chr. P.* — *pá-spun,* brothers and sisters of the same father; *má-spun* of the same mother; *spún-zla,* (*s*)*pun-da,* or *-la* 1. = *spun*; 2. in *C.* it is said to be used also for attorney, advocate; *spún-ma* sister, as a more particular designation of the sex. — 2. in a wider sense: **cousins, brothers-** or **sisters-in-law**; *grógs-spun* mate, comrade; *čós-spun* a brother of a religious order; *pá-spun, pás-spun,* several neighbours or inhabitants of a village, that have a common Lha, and thus have become *'*rus-pa čig-čig*'*, members of the same family; this common tie entails on them the duty, whenever a death takes place, of caring for the cremation of the dead body (cf. *čos-spún*) *Mil.* and elsewh.; *mdza-spún* friend *Cs.* — 3. **weft, woof** in weaving.

སྤུན་པ་ *spún-pa* 1. sbst., also *sbún-pa B.*, *C.*, *sbur(-ma) Dzl.*, *Ld.*, **chaff, husks** etc. — 2. adj. a botanical term, description of the stalk of a plant *Wdṅ.*

སྤུབ་པ་ *spúb-pa*, pf. *spubs*, vb. a. to *ḥbúb-pa* **to turn upside down.**

སྤུར་ *spur, pur*, also *sku-spúr*, resp. for *ro*, **dead body, corpse,** *spur sbyáṅs-pa C.* to burn a dead body; *spur-k̔aṅ* house for keeping dead bodies, or rather, in most cases, the place of cremation; *spur-sgam* or *sgrom* coffin; *spur-t̔al* ashes of a dead body; *spur-ts̔a* the salt for preparing a dead body; *spur-śiṅ* wood for burning a corpse.

སྤུར་བ་ *spúr-ba*, vb. a. to *ḥpúr-ba*, **to make fly, to scare up, to let fly;** *dus spúr-ba* to pass time quickly *Cs.*; *stoṅ-spúr* exaggeration, bombast *Cs.*

སྤུས་ *spus* 1. **goods, merchandize, ware,** *spus ltá-ba* to examine goods before purchase *Cs.*; **spus gyúr-če* W.*, **pu ḥgyúr-wa* Cs.* = **dal tsoṅ táṅ-če**. — 2. **goodness, beauty,** *spús-čan, spus-ytsáṅ, spus-bzáṅ*, of fine appearance; *spus-méd* ill-looking, unsightly. — 3. *Sch.*: for *spos.*

སྤེའུ་, སྤིའུ་ *speu, spiu*, **turret,** on a castle or gate *W.*, (*C. lčog*). High towers or steeples are seldom met with in Tibetan architecture; **peu gyú-čan riṅ-mo**, *mk̔ar* or *k̔áṅ-pa dgu-t̔óg* are the terms denoting such.

སྤེག་ཤིང་ *speg-śiṅ Cs.*: n. of part of a cart.

སྤེན་ཏོག་ *spen-tog*, **ornament, finery.**

སྤེན་པ་ *spén-pa, yza-spén-pa* 1. the planet **Saturn;** the proper meaning is said to be a broom, hence the sign for it is somewhat resembling that implement *Wdk.* — 2. **Saturday.**

སྤེན་མ་ *spén-ma, spén-śiṅ*, n. of a tree, prob. tamarisk; *spen-bád* a parapet, formed of the stems of tamarisk and raised on the roofs of monasteries.

སྤེལ་བ་ *spél-ba*, vb. a. to *ḥpel-ba*, 1. **to augment, to increase,** *nor* the wealth *Lex.*, *bkra-śis* the welfare; *rkaṅ-ḥgrós spél-ba* to breed cattle *Dzl.* and elsewh.; **spel-gyúd-la bor-če* W.* to keep cattle for breeding. — 2. **to multiply** (arithm.) *Wdk.* — 3. **to spread, to propagate** (news, secrets) *Dzl.* and elsewh.; more emphatically: *spel rgyás-par*, or *sgróg-par byéd-pa* to blaze about *Sch.* — 4. **to join, to put together,** e.g. letters (almost = to spell); to mingle, to mix; *spél-ma* mixture, e.g. of prose and verse *Cs.*; acc. to *Was.* however, couplets, similar both as to metre and contents; composition, combination, *yser yyu spél-mai k̔ri* a chair of gold and turkoises *Pth.*; *spél-mai nor* mixed goods *Cs.*; *spél-gos* clothes of various colours *Cs.*; *spel-ts̔ig Sch.*: a combination of verses, poetry(?); *spél-mar byéd-pa* to mix *Lex.*

སྤེས་ *spes* **edge, brim, border,** *Sch.*

སྤོ་ *spo* **summit of a mountain,** *brag-dmar spo-mt̔ó-nas* from the height of Bragmar *Mil.*; *rdo-rje-ydan-gyi spó-la* on the top of Gayā *Pth.*; *spó-bo* 1. (top, point =) bud *Ts.* 2: district to the east of Lhasa *Glr.*

སྤོ་ཏོ་ *spo-to* 1. **bullock** *C.* — 2. n. of a village in Panyul.

སྤོ་རེ་ *spo-re* v. *spor.*

སྤོ་བ་ *spo-ba*, pf. and imp. *spos*, vb. a. to *ḥpó-ba*, **to alter, to change;** with and without *ynas* (*W. *sa**): to change the place (of residence), to remove, to shift; also to transpose, transplant; *miṅ spó-ba* to change the name *Mil.*; *gos spó-ba* to change one's dress; *mgo-lús* v. *mgo* extr.; to remove (an officer) to another station; to dismiss (a servant), *W.*, also *B.* frq.; *yžan mk̔ás-pa yód-na spós-pa bzaṅ* if another skilful (physician) is to be had, it will be better to dismiss (the present one); to alter, to mend, to correct *W.*; *spó-sa* a place newly occupied by nomads *Sch.*

སྤོག་པ་ *spóg-pa*, pf. *spags*, fut. *śpag*, **to remove and to bring near by turns** *Cs.*; *Lexx.* w.e. —

སྤོགས་ *spogs* **gain, profit,** *k'e-spógs* id.; *spogs byed-pa* to make profit, to gain money; *tsoṅ-spógs byéd-pa* to gain money by traffic *Dzl.*; *tsoṅ-spógs-la ˳gró-ba Dzl.*; *skyed-spogs* interest (of money); *spógs-su ǵtóṅ-ba* to give money on interest *Cs.*; **mi-póg lém-pa** *C.* to demand a tax from emigrants or travellers.

སྤོང་བ་ *spóṅ-ba, spáṅ-ba,* pf. *spaṅs,* fut. *spaṅ,* imp *spoṅ(s)*, (*Ssk.* वृच्) 1. **to give up, to declare off,** *bdag daṅ bdag-gir Sambh.* to give one's self up and all that one has; *sman-dpyád mi byéd-par spóṅ-na* if he gives (the patient) over without even attempting a cure *Dzl.* ༥༠, 1; **to renounce** (all pleasures) frq.; **kód-gu-ru spaṅ mi p'od** he cannot give up Kotgur (his former residence) or forget it; without an object: *yóṅs-su spóṅ-ba* (partic.) they (the Bodhisattvas) who entirely renounce *Thgy.*; **to shun, avoid, abstain from** (faults, sins, certain food) frq.; **to reject** = *˳dór-ba*: *bde-sdúg-la spaṅ-blaṅ med* between happiness and unhappiness there was no need to choose (sc. because only bliss prevailed) *Glr.*; *spoṅ-bláṅ ˳dzin-pa żig-pa* the cessation of every inclination and disinclination, or also, of every interest in choosing or rejecting. — 2. **to throw off, to drop,** a letter, *p'yi-tség* (to omit) the dot after a syllable *Gram.*

སྤོང་བྱེད་ *spoṅ-byéd* **Vaisali,** ancient town near Allahabad, *Tar.* 7, 5 and elsewh.; also Vriji, acc. to *Schf.*

སྤོད་ *spod* **spice** *Med.*; *spod ˳débs-pa* to season; *spód-can* seasoned.

སྤོད་པ་ *spód-pa* 1. **hermit,** *spód-k'aṅ* hermitage *Sch.* — 2. **vow,** *spód-pa nyáms-pa* one that has broken his vow *Sch.*

སྤོབས་པ་ *spóbs-pa* (*W.* also **spós-pa**), 1.vb. **to dare, to venture,** *˳jú-bar mi spóbs-pas* not daring to take hold of *Pth.*, also *Dzl.* ༡༦༠, 4; ༢༠༢, 16; *spóbs-par byéd-pa* 1. id. 2. to enable, empower, authorize *Cs.* — 2. sbst. **courage, confidence.**

སྤོམ་ཡོར་ *spom-yór* diffuse (in words), **prolix, long-winded,** *byéd-pa, smrá-ba, čád-pa Cs.* 'to say circumstantially'.

སྤོར་ *spor, spo-ré,* **steel-yard;** *W.* particularly a little one.

སྤོར་བ་ *spór-ba, spár-ba,* pf. and fut. *spar,* 1. **to lift up,** *rdó-rje* the praying-sceptre *Dom.*; (a hatchet) to fetch a blow; *W.* **šed spár-la** (or *spár-te*) *rgyob** swing (the hatchet) well and strike! **spár-la čoṅ** run and leap! cf. also *nems;* to raise, promote, advance, *go-p'án* in rank *Lex.* — 2. v. *dpór-ba.*

སྤོལ་ *spol Ts.* for **me-mé** *W.* (v. *mes-po*).

སྤོས་ *spos* 1. sbst. **incense;** *bdug-spós* id.; less frq. **perfume** in general; *byug-spós* sweet-scented water or ointment; *spos sbyór-ba, sgrúb-pa,* also *rgyáb-pa* and *rgyág-pa Cs.*, to prepare incense, perfumes, *bdúg-pa* to burn (incense); *˳byúg-pa* to cover (with perfume); *rgya-spós, brag-spós, spaṅ-spós,* different kinds of perfume; *spos-(kyi) réṅ (-bu)* pastil, long and thin straws being covered with an odoriferous substance, which generally consists of pulverized *šugpa,* and sandal-wood, combined with some *gugul,* musk and the like; they are made by the Lamas, and frequently presented to travellers as an offering of welcome. *spos-dkár* frankincense, = *gugúl dkár-po.* — *spós-mk'an* perfumer. — *spos-čág* incense in pieces or cakes. — *spos-čú,* resp. *čab,* sweet-scented water, diluted ointment, *lús-la ˳byúg-pa Pth.*; *spós-čus čag-čág ˳débs-pa Pth.* to sprinkle with such water. — *spos-snod Cs.*, *spos-p'ór* (also *pog-p'ór*), censer, perfuming-pan. — *spós-tsoṅ-pa* = *spós-mk'an.* — *spos-ǵżóṅ* basin for incense *Cs.* — *spos-šél* (col. **po-šél**) amber. — 2. vb. v. *spó-ba* and *spóbs-pa.*

སྤྱ་དངོས་ *spya-dṅos Cs.* = *yo-byád; Lexx. spyad-dṅós* and *dṅos-spyád,* as explanations to *ka-ča.*

སྤྱང་ཀི་ *spyáṅ-ki Mil., Sg., -gi Dzl., -ku, -gu, k'u Cs., Lh.* **šáṅ-ku**, **wolf.** (Wolves, where more frequent, as e. g. in Spiti, commit ravages among the sheep; but are other wise not much dreaded by man). *spyáṅ-mo* female wolf; *spyaṅ-p'rúg* young wolf; *spyaṅ-tsáṅ* wolf's den; *spyaṅ-dóṅ* wolf's trap (used in *Sp.*); *spyáṅ-ku ṅú-ba* the howling of a wolf *Cs.*; *če-spyáṅ Lex.*, lče-spyáṅ Stg., dur-spyáṅ Cs., *kyi-čáṅ* W., jackal. — spyaṅ-dug-pa Cs., spyaṅ-tsér Med., thistle, or kind of thistle, mentioned as an emetic.

སྤྱང་བ་ spyáṅ-ba 1. sbst. and adj.; spyáṅ-po adj., **skill; skilful, clever,** Lex., Glr. and elsewh.; prob. = γčán(-po), q. v.; sometimes confounded with sbyáṅ-ba, sbyáṅs-pa, practiced, expert; ríg-pa spyáṅ-bas rtsóm-pa kún-la ˳jug Lt. the clever man finds his way in every thing; spyaṅ-γlén Cs. the clever man and the dunce: Glr.: spyaṅ γlen ma nór-ba čig byed dgos, prob. to be read ˳byed, and to be translated: then it must evidently appear, who is clever and who is stupid — 2. vb. = dpyáṅ-ba.

སྤྱད་ spyad v. spya.

སྤྱད་པ་ spyád-pa v. spyód-pa.

སྤྱན་ spyan, resp. for mig, **eye**; spyan bgrád-pa, γdáṅ-ba, to stare Cs.; spyan ˳gyúr-ba v. spyán-pa; spyan ˳drén-pa, rarely dróns-pa, resp. for ˳drén-pa, to invite, v. ˳drén-pa; spyan ˳ṗyi-ba to wipe the eyes; spyan btsúm-pa to shut the eyes Cs.

Comp. and deriv. spyan-kyúg or kyug eye-brow Cs. — spyan-dkyús v. dkyus. — spyan-bskyúṅs mdzád-pa to protect, to preserve the eyes Sch. — spyán-sṅa before, with, in presence of a dignitary, spyán-sṅai grá-pa-rnams the scholars standing in presence of his Reverence Cs.; mostly in the termin. case: spyán-sṅar, as adv. and postp., rgyál-poi spyán-sṅar kríd-pa to lead (another) before the king, frq.; rarely in reference to the first pers.: ṅai spyán-sṅar ˳oṅ they came to me, before my face (sc. Buddha's) Dzl.; less corr. spyán-sṅar mdzés-pai skúd-ris Mil. in front (on the fore-part of the shoes) beautifully embroidered figures. — spyán-čan having eyes. — spyan-lčibs eye-lid. — spyan-čáb tears, ˳byin-pa to shed; čór-ba to flow from; also to shed, rgyál-bu spyan-čáb šór-ro Pth. the prince shed tears. — spyan-˳drén one who invites, one that calls to dinner. — spyán-pa Cs. 1. eye-witness; 2. commissary; 3. Sch. overseer; spyán-du ˳gyúr-ba = dpáṅ-du ˳gyúr-ba, to see, to know; spyán-pa byéd-pa to watch, guard, keep, protect, inspect Sch.; bá-glaṅ-gi spyán-pa cow-herd(?) Sch. — spyan-˳brás apple of the eye. — spyan-˳nig-bzáṅ the western 'king of ghosts', v. rgyal-čén sub rgyál-ba. — spyan-dmigs Sch.: 'the object of vision; the inclination of the mind'. — spyan-sman medicine for the eyes. — spyan-rtség the wrinkles of the eye-lids Cs. — spyan-zúr Sch., corner of the eye. — spyan-γzigs, costly offerings dedicated to the gods, Mil.; also applied to presents of food, offered to men, Mil.; ˳búl-ba to offer such; also ˳drén-pa. — spyan-yás, Sch., without eyes, blind. — spyan-rás, Sch. the brightness of the eye, a glance of the eye. — spyan-ras-γzigs W.; *čan-re-zig* Cs.: *čen-re-sig* or -sī*, Ssk. अवलोकितेश्वर, the other (cf. ˳jam-dpal) of the two great half-divine Bodhisattvas of the northern Buddhists, who more particularly is revered as begetter (not creator), redeemer, and ruler of men, and in the first place of the Tibetans, incarnate as king Sroṅ-tsan-gám-po, Köpp. II, 22. — spyán-lam-du seems to be = drúṅ-du, spyán-sṅar, Mil. and elsewh.

སྤྱི་ spyi, I. adj. (synon. tun, also dbyiṅs, opp. to sgos) 1. **general, relating to all, standing higher than all:** *ṭim-pon či*, chief prefect, governor general C.; adv. spyi, spyir(-du), less frq. spyi-la, spyi-na, spyir-gyis, **generally, in general,** frq. followed by sgos(-kyis), kyád-par, **in particular, singly;** also like cum tum in Latin; spyi daṅ ˳dir, generally, and here, in this work, Wdṅ.; spyii sdom, v. sdom; — spyii kog ji daṅ ji bžin-du (?) Sch.: 'according to general custom'. — 2. **all,** C.; lhá-kaṅ spyii bstan-sruṅ Glr. — 3. for spyi-bo, v. below. — spyi-sgra Cs., **general meaning,** more corr. sgra-spyi, Was. (294), **general expression.** — spyi-γčér, spyi-ter Cs., bald-headed. — spyi-tór = gtsug-tór Lex. spyi-tóg, property of the community, common property; W.: *pi-tog-ne toṅ* bestow it out of the common funds! — spyi-gdugs, v. sgos. — spyi-pa, **head, chief, leader, superintendent,** Sch.;

spyi-dpon, much the same, v. *sgos*; *spyi-bo*, 1. (rarely *spyi*), **crown of the head**, top, *spyi-bor ₒkúr-ba* to carry on the head; — *spyi-bos p̔yág-ₒtsal-ba* to bow down bending the head; *žabs spyi-bor lén-pa*, frq., to place the foot of a superior on one's own head; *dei spyi-bo-nas byúg-nas*, pouring over his head, anointing him, *Domaṅ*; more frq: *spyi-bo-nas dbaṅ skúr-ba*, v. *skur-ba*: *spyi-bo-nas dbaṅ bskúr-bai rgyál-po*, the anointed king; *spyi-glugs*, the vessel used for anointing (resembling a tea-pot). — 2. the end of a piece of cloth, *dar-yúg-gi*, *Glr.* — 3. name of a king of China *Glr.*; *spyi-miṅ* common appellation: *dkor ni nór-gyi spyi-miṅ*, '*dkor*' is a general word for property, *Lex.* — II. often incorr. for *ċi*, also *dpyi*.

སྤྱི་ཏི *spyi-ti*, a fantastic, mystical doctrine of **Urgyen-Padma**, *t̔ég-pa č̔én-po spyi-ti*, *spyi-ti yóg-brdai dkyil-k̔or Pth.*; *yáṅ-ti*, another of his doctrines.

སྤྱི་བརྟོལ *spyi-brtól*, *Cs.*: **impudence, impertinence**, *Sch.*: **lewd**; *spyi-brtól-čan*, impudent; *spyi-brtól byéd-pa*, to be impudent *Cs.*

སྤྱིང་བ *spyiṅ-ba*, pf. *spyiṅs*, imp. *spyiṅ(s)*, the vb. a. to *ₒbyiṅ-ba*, **to sink, to lower, let down, dip under**; *č̔ur*, *Lexx.*

སྤྱིན *spyin* (*W.* *(*s*)*pin**), **glue, paste**: *spyin skól-ba*, to manufacture glue: *skúd-pa* (*Sch.* also *bdár-ba?*) to spread glue on; **pin daṅ ǰár-če** *W.* to glue; *ko-spyin*, glue made of skins, *nya-spyin*, fish-glue, isinglass; *bág-spyin* paste or rather a kind of putty, compounded of flour and glue; *rá-spyin* glue made of horn; *ša-spyin*, meat-jelly; *spyin-ǰor* glue-pot.

སྤྱིམས *spyims* (? *čims*), *Ld.* = *spyi*; **čimsi miṅ** = *spyi-miṅ*.

སྤྱིར *spyir* v. *spyi*.

སྤྱིལ་པོ *spyil-po*, 1. **hut** *Mil.*, *Pth.*; *rtsai*, **thatched hut** *Lex.*; *spyil-bu*, id.; *lo-mai spyil-bu*, hut constructed of twigs, fastened together on the top, **arbour**; **a cot**, a mean house. — 2. **inmate of such a one**, *Cs.*; also *spyil-pa*, fem. *-ma*.

སྤྱུག་པ *spyúg-pa*, pf. *spyugs*, imp. *spyug(s)*; **to expel, to turn out, to banish**; *yúl-nas* out of the country; *yul gžán-du Glr.*; *mt̔á-la*, *mt̔ar* into the neighbouring country, over the frontier (v. *mt̔a*); when the place of banishment is named, the otherwise faulty spelling *bčúg-pa* is allowable; v. *ₒǰúg-pa*.

སྤྱོ་བ *spyó-ba*, pf. and imp. *spyos*, **to blame, to scold** *Dzl.*; *č̔úṅ-ma rtág-tu spyó-žiṅ*, as my wife is always scolding; *čes spyós-so* thus they spoke in a blaming way, *Dzl.*; *Cs.* also: **to mock, to ridicule** (?). synon. *ǵšé-ba*.

སྤྱོང་བ *spyóṅ-ba* = *dpyáṅ-ba*.

སྤྱོད་པ *spyód-pa*, I. vb., also *spyád-pa*, pf. *spyad*, *Ssk.* चर 1. = *byéd-pa*, **to do, to act**, v. *tsáṅs-par*, yet gen. with an object in the accus. **to accomplish, perform, commit**; *sdig-pa*, *sdig-pai las*, *dgé-ba*, *dká-ba* (v. *dká-ba*), *č̔os spyod-pa*; *mi-dge-ba dé-dag spyód-na* if one commits these sins *Thgy.*; *bdag či spyád-pas ₒdir skyes*, what having done, or because of which doing of mine am I re-born here? *Dzl.*; even like *byéd-pa* = to be, *mṅa-ₒóg spyód-pai ₒbáṅs Glr.*, simply = subjects; rarely c. dat.: *sdig-pa ₒbá-žig-la spyód-pa*, *Thgy.*, *dgé-ba bčú-la*, *Dzl.*, denoting a habitual doing; cf. *žá-ba*. — 2. **to treat, to deal with**, *zas-skóm légs-par spyód-pa*, (to deal with) food and drink in the right manner *S.g.*; gen. with the dat.: *žiṅ-la lhú-ru spyad*, the fields were disposed of in lots, divided *Glr.*; hence gen. **to use**, to make use of, to employ, to enjoy: *bá-glaṅ nyin-par* to use an ox during the day (for ploughing) *Dzl.*; *yun-riṅ-dus-su bdé-bar spyad kyaṅ*, even if one has long and in tranquillity used, enjoyed (this world's goods), *Thgy.*; so frq. with *loṅs*: *lóṅs-spyod-pa*; to have for a sphere of activity, v. *mk̔á-spyod*, *sá-spyod*, *sa-ₒóg-spyod*; also a euphemism for sensual indulgence: *bud-méd-la spyód-pa* to use, to cohabit with, a woman, *Dzl.*; *mi-rigs-par* or *lóg-par*, to violate (a woman) *Thgy.* & others; *dga mgúr spyód-pa*, of a like meaning; the other synonymous phrases: *ₒdod-lóg spyód-pa, mi ₒós-pai spyód-pa byéd-pa*, *Glr.*, *nyál-po, čágs-pa, ₒkrig-pa spyód-pa*, belong by their construction properly to 1; so also: *bud-méd brgya spyod nus* he can get done with a hundred wives, *Lt.*

II. sbst. 1. **action, practice, execution**, opp. to *ltá-ba*, theory, esp. in mysticism, v. *sgóm-pa*. — 2. **activity:** *spyód-pa šin-tu dóg-par gyúr-to* they were much restrained, narrowly watched *Glr.*; *séms-kyi spyód-pa* seems to be: faculty of mind, *Wdṅ.* — 3. **way of acting, conduct, course of life,** = *spyód-lam*; *byaṅ-čub-séms-dpai* frq.; *ṅán-* or *nyés-spyod* bad actions, *bzáṅ-* or *légs-spyod* good actions *Cs.*; *spyód-pa žib-pa*, 'the strict', a monastic order *Pth.*; **behaviour, deportment,** frq.: *spyód-pa rtsiṅ-ba*, rude, rough, in manners *Glr.*; *spyód-pas skád-čig kyaṅ mi ťsugs*, of an extremely variable conduct (lit. not for one moment the same) *Glr.*

Comp. *spyod-ₒgrós* **gait and deportment** *Mil.* — *spyod-ṅán* = *ṅán-spyod*, *spyod-ṅán byéd pa*. — *spyód-ťsul*, *Sch.* = *spyód-pa* II. *spyód-yul*, **sphere of activity;** *kún-gyi spyód-yul ₒdi ma lags*, that is not a thing to be attempted by every body *Mil.*; *mťóṅ-bai spyód-pa* range of vision *Tar.*; cf. गोचर. — *spyód-lam*, 1. **demeanour, deportment, mode of life** frq.; 2. **good behaviour,** graceful demeanour, noble deportment; otherwise *spyód-pa mdzés-pa*; hence *spyód-pa daṅ ldán-pa*, *spyod-ldán* of genteel manners *Dzl.*; *spyód-pa daṅ mi ldán-pa Dzl.*, **čod-ṅán-čan** *W.*, **čọ̈-lóg ǰhé-ken**, *C.* **rude, unmannerly, ill-bred, disobedient.** 3. *Med.*: **diet,** and more particularly **bodily exercise;** *zas-spyód*, food and exercise. 4. **attitude:** *spyód-lam rnam-bži* the four attitudes of sitting, lying, standing and walking.

སྤྱོད་པ་པ་ *spyód-pa-pa* v. *dpyód-pa*, extr.

སྤྱོད་པད་ *spyod-pad* or *dpyod-pád* (spelling not quite certain), pronunc.: **čọ̈-pẹ̈**, **lemon, citron** *C.*

སྤྱོན་པ་ *spyón-pa*, rarely for *ₒbyon-pa*.

སྤྱོམ་པ་ *spyóm-pa*, pf. *spyoms*, **to boast, to exhibit with ostentation,** e.g. virtues, (the Greek καυχᾶσθαι). Notwithstanding the detailed explanations of the *Lex.*, the word is after all so little known, that I never met with it in books, nor heard it used by the people. — *spyoms*, sbst., **self-praise, boasting** *Zam.*

སྤྲ་ *spra*, monkey. *Mil.*, prob. the large dark-gray, long-tailed **monkey** of the southern Himalaya; *sprá-mo*; *spra-ṗrúg*.

སྤྲ་(འ)ཚལ་ *spra-čál* v. *pra-čál*; *spra-tél* v. *tél-pa*.

སྤྲ་བ་ *sprá-ba*, I. sbst. *W.* **šrá-wa**, **spunk, German tinder,** prepared of the fibres of a thistle (Cousinia); *spra-mé*, glowing tinder, *Pth.*; *ṗyi ni sprá-ba dkár-por γyogs*, white-nappy, as a botanical term, *Wdṅ.*, the colour of the tinder, referred to, being a light gray; *sprá-bai ťóg-gu* a medicinal herb *Wdṅ.*

II. vb. pf. *spras*, imp. *spros*, 1. **to adorn, to decorate:** *rgyán-gyis* frq., *mťsán-dpes Mil.* and elsewh. — 2. *γčes spras*, *Lex.?* *sprá-ba byéd-pa* **to love, to caress.** — 3. perh. identical with **šrá-če(s)**, **to empty** (a dish). — 4. *spra ₒkrid-pa* **to lead, to direct right.** — Cf. also *γtsaṅ sprá-wa*.

སྤྲ་ཚིལ་ *spra-ťsil*, *Med.*, *C.* **wax** (*W.* **mum**).

སྤྲག་པ་ *sprág-pa* v. *sbrúg-pa*.

སྤྲང་བ་ *spráṅ-ba*, *Cs.*, **to beg;** (the verb I never met with, and *Zam.* explains the sbst. only by *nor-méd*): *spráṅ-po*, **beggar,** *Dzl.*, *Glr.*, frq. (*Wts.* 'filou', rather bold, though not far from the truth); **ṭaṅ-lóṅ** *C.*, id.; *spraṅ-rgán Mil.*, an old beggar; *rdzús-mai spráṅ-po* a sham-beggar *Glr.*; *spraṅ-ṗrúg* beggar boy; *spraṅ-bán* mendicant friar *Glr.*; *spraṅ-zás* beggar's livelihood *Mil.*; *dkar-spraṅ* begging for lenten food, also such food obtained by begging, v. *dkar-zás*; *skyur-spráṅ* begging for beer *Mil.*

སྤྲད་པ་ *sprád-pa* v. *spród-pa*.

སྤྲི་སྟི་མ་རྫ་ཡ་, སི་ཆེན་ *spri-sti-ma-rdza-ya*, *si-čẹn*, n. of the emperor of China, during whose reign Buddhism was introduced into that country,

Glr.; acc. to Chinese accounts: *Miṅg-ti*, 58—76 after Christ.

སྤྲི་མ་ *spri-ma, spris-ma, sris-ma*, *W.* **šri**, **cream,** and other fatty substances, gathering on the surfaces of fluids; *ₒó-mai spris, Lt., žo(i)-spris, Wdṅ.*; gen. *ₒo-sri*, cream (of milk); *túg-spri*, the greasy surface of soup; ditto of urine *Med.*

སྤྲིང་བ་ *spriṅ-ba*, pf. *spriṅs*, **to send a message, to give information, to send word;** *ṕrin*, tidings *Dzl.*; *žes spriṅ-no* so I send him word *Dzl.*

སྤྲིན་ *sprin*, **ṭin**, *Ld.* **šrin**, *Bal.* **spin**, **cloud,** also as an emblem of transitoriness frq.; **šrin ṭigs, kor**, *W.*, clouds are spreading; *sprin-gyi ɣséo-nas* from between the clouds *Glr.*; *glóg-sprin* thunder-cloud *Glr.*; *čár-sprin* rain-cloud; *ₒjá-sprin* cloud tinged with rainbow colours *Pth.*; *mig-sprin* v. this; *lhó-sprin* a southern cloud, picturesque expression, the clouds in Tibet generally coming from the south *Mil.*; *sprin-skyés* lightning; *sprin-dmár* clouds reddened by the sun, morning or evening red; *sprin-ṕuṅ, sprin-tsógs*, an accumulation of clouds; *sprin-gyi ṕó-nya* the messenger of the clouds, Meghadūta, a poëm by Kalidāsa *Tar.*

སྤྲིབས་པ་ *sprıbs-pa* **to be hungry** *Sch.*

སྤྲིས་མ་ *spris-ma* v. *spri-ma.*

སྤྲུ་མ་ *sprú-ma*, *Cs.*, **hellebore;** *spru-dkár, -nág Med.*

སྤྲུག་པ་ *sprúg-pa*, pf. and imp. *sprugs*, **ṭúg-pa**, *W.* **šrug-če** **to shake, to shake off, to beat out,** *rdul* dust; **to stir up,** *rdul-tsúb*, **to raise,** whirl up dust; *lus sprúg-sil-ba, lus sprug-sil byéd-pa Glr.*, to shake one's self (used of horses); fig. *nus mṭu rtsal sprúg-pa*, to strain every nerve, to work with might and main *Pth.*; **to shake about, to stir up** (synon. **šrul-če, rum-če** *W.*); *Cs.* also: to rub, to scratch, to brush??

སྤྲུལ་བ་ *sprúl-ba* (cf. *ₒṕrúl-ba*), **to juggle. to make phantoms** (*sprúl-pa*) **appear, to change, to transform** (one's self), which according to the doctrines of Buddhism is the highest acquisition of any man, that by his own holiness has assumed divine nature, viz. as long as he is capable of acting, not having yet been absorbed into the blessed state of nothingness. This power of transformation on the part of the Buddhist is the evidence of what he understands by divine omnipotence; but as this conception is a mere product of fancy, it varies in its import. On the one hand it is opposed to reality, *dṅos*; thus e. g. beings, whom no Buddha could convert through his personal agency, *sku-dṅós-kyi sgó-nas*, are converted (acc. to *Pth.*) *sprúl-pai tábs-kyis.* Frequently Buddha avails himself of jugglery, *rdzu-ṕrúl ston*, converting thousands of beings in a trice. *Dzl.* & elsewh.; further: *drág-poi sprúl-pa byás-pa yin Glr.*, I caused terrifying phantoms to appear, viz. the spectral bodies of executed culprits, in order to scare the rude Tibetans into the way of virtue. From the foregoing it is evident that the term in question by no means conveys the scriptural idea of **a creative and miraculous power;** the Tibetan, however, when he becomes acquainted with christianity, is always apt to substitute his *sprúl-pa* or *rdzu-ₒṕrúl*, and *sprúl-ba* for it. On the other hand, a real and material existence is as often attributed to a *sprul-pa*, when it designates the incarnate and embodied person, the Avatāra of a deity, (Mongol. Chubilgan), who like any human being is capable of acting, and exerting an influence on the material world around him, or of suffering by it, without any docetic admixture. Occasionally it is also to be translated by **emanation:** *yáṅ-sprul*, emanation of the second degree, i.e. one emanation going forth from another; *nyíṅ-sprul* or *ɣsúm-sprul*, an em. of the third degree *Pth.*; *sprúl-pa ₒgyéd-pa*, to let emanations go forth, *Lex.* — Further: *sprul-pa mkyén-pa*, to be an adept in the art of *sprúl-pa*, i. e. witchcraft, *Glr.*; *ri ɣnyis sprúl-te* producing two mountains by magic, *Dzl.*; ... *mṭó-ba* ... *bžúgs-pa sprúl-nas*, changing himself into a high enthroned person, *Dzl.*; *dge-*

slóṅ žig-tu, transforming himself into a friar, *Dzl.* frq.; *dúd-ₒgro ťsím-par sprúl-ba*, to satiate animals by fictitious food *Dzl.*; *ťams-čád sprúl-par ₒdúg-pa*, these were all metamorphoses, mocking phantoms, *Glr.; sku-lús-kyi sprúl-pa brgya-rtsa-brgyád mdzád-de* or *sprúl-te*, to centuple one's self, *Glr.*; *sprul-pai rgyál-po*, the phantom-king, viz. Buddha, Avalokitesvara, or some other divine person, incarnate as a king; *gaṅ-la-gan-ₒdúl-gyi sprúl-pa*, all-converting Avatara, frq.

སྤྲེ་ *spre*, gen. *spreu*, rarely *sprel* (*Ld.* **śreu; spriu**) **monkey**, of a grayish yellow brown, common in the forests of the southern Himalaya, (cf. *spra*); sometimes a distinction is made between *spre* and *spra*, in which case the former is the long-tailed monkey. — *spré-mo*, female monkey, *Cs.*; yet also *spreu žár-ma*, a blind female monkey, *Dzl*; *spre-ṗrúg*, young monkey. — *spre-rtséd*, apish tricks; foolery.

སྤྲོ་བ་ *spró-ba* I. vb. pf. *spros*, prop. the transitive of *ₒṗró-ba* **to make go out, to disperse, to spread**; gen. however intransitive: 1. **to go out, to proceed, to spread,** of rays of light, of the wind, *Wdṅ.* — 2. fig. **to enlarge upon,** by way of explaining, representing, *Zam.*, *Pth.; ycig-las sprós-pa, Was.* (115), enlarging (proceeding) from the number one in an ascending progression of numbers; *rnám-par sprós-pa*, to have come to a full development and restoration from the consequences of sins, *Stg.*

II. 1. vb. (pf. unaltered), **to feel an inclination for, to delight in:** *dgé-ba-la*, in virtue, *Dzl.*; *byá-ba gáṅ-la yaṅ spró-ba čuṅ*, feeling little inclination for doing any thing, *Thgy.; bsád-par spró-ba su yaṅ ma byuṅ*, none was found that had a mind to kill, *Stg.;* so also *Tar.*; **to be willing, to wish,** *Tar.*; in an absolute sense: *sems*, or resp *ťugs*, *spró-bar ₒgyúr-ba*, **to get cheerful, merry,** *Mil.* — 2. sbst. **joy, cheerfulness:** *spró-ba skyéd-pa*, to feel joy, pleasure, *Dzl.* and elsewh.; *spró-ba skyé-bai ṗyir-du*, for an encouragement, for a comfort, *Glr.*; *spro-siṅ-ba Sch.*, great joy (cf. *siṅ*); *spro-siṅ-gé-ba, Sch.*, to one's wish (?); *spro śi-ba, Sch.*, 'not to be joyful', lit. the cessation of joy; *spro ťúṅ-ba*, 'short cheerfulness', i.e. a passionate disposition; or as adj. **passionate, irascible,** *Wdṅ.*; *dga-spró*, **joy,** *dga-spró dpag-tu-méd-pa ťob*, he got into a most cheerful humour, *Mil.* — **ṭo-ḱáṅ**, *C.*, pleasure-house, summer-house, pavilion; *spro-séms* and (*Ld.*) **spro-śés, śro-śés**, joy; *spro-séms, Thgy.* also youthful joy, alacrity, cheerfulness in working, readiness to act.

སྤྲོག་མ་ *spróg-ma*; *Sch. spós-kyi spróg-ma*, **little box for frankincense.**

སྤྲོག་ཞུ་ *spróg-žu* v. *ṗrog.*

སྤྲོད་པ་ *spród-pa*, secondary form *sprad*, the vb. a. of *ṗrod-pa* (by the illiterate it is often used for *ytod-pa*, not very current in common life) 1. **to bring together, to put together, to make to meet:** *ṅai blá-ma-la spród-do*, we will bring you together with our Lama, *Mil.*; so also resp. . . . *ynyis žal spród mdzád-pa*; in another passage *de daṅ žal-spród-du bžúgs-śin* prob. means sitting exactly opposite to one another, (a whimsical idea, relative to two idols many miles distant from each other; possibly it should be read *ytod-du*); *bdág-čag spród-čig*, bring about a meeting between our two parties! *Dzl.; yyul* or *ťáb-mo*, to commit a battle; *rál-ḱa, Ma.*, to put the edges of the swords together, prob. meaning the same; *mťeb spród-pa*, to put the finger to the bow-string, *Glr.*; **lág-ṭo ťéb-ṭo kál-wa**, to suspend by the thumb and big toe, a kind of torture in *C.* (The special meaning: to cohabit, *Cs*, never came to my notice). — 2. **to deliver** (a letter, message) *Pth.*; *spár-mor, lág-tu, Lex.*, to put into one's hand; **to set, to put, to propose,** **gyugs, ldem**, a task, a riddle, *W.*; **to pay** (cf. *ₒṗrod-pa*), *ṗyir sprod-pa*, to repay. — Moreover: *ṅó-sprod-pa*, **to explain,** *don daṅ spród-pa* seems to signify the same in *Mil.*, *Pth.*; *brdá-sprod-pa*, **to explain, to describe** v. *brda*; *brda-spród*, ibid. seems to denote grammar.

སྤྲོས་པ་ *sprós-pa.* 1. pf. v. *spró-ba* I. — 2. **business, employment, activity;** *Cs.:*

'spros-pa-čan, busy, **employed, occupied;** sprós-bčas, id.; čós-kyi and ₒjig-rtén-gyi sprós-pa, spiritual and secular business'; *Sch.*: 'spros kun, all affairs'; I met only with sprós-pa méd-pa or čód-pa, or spros-brál, denoting the state of an absolute inactivity, such as belongs to Buddha in the state of čos-sku, (v. sku 2) *Pth.*, *Mil.*

ཕ

ཕ ṕa 1. the letter ṕ, aspirate, the English p in pass. — 2. num. figure: 14.

ཕ་ ṕa I. vulgo ཨ་ཕ་, ཨ་པ་, ǎ-ṕa, ǎ-pa, (*Cs.* also ཨ་ཏ་ ǎ-ta) 1. **father,** resp. yab (yet also ṕa is used, e.g. when Milaraspa is addressed by his female disciples, as well as in prayers to defunct saints *Mil.*) — 2. a male, not castrated, animal (vulg. likewise á-ṕa). **Comp.** ṕa-gláṅ bull. — ṕa-rjes-bú, *Sch.*, a child born after its father's death. — ṕa-rtá, stallion. — *ṕa-nóṙ*, patrimony *C.*, *W.* — ṕa-spád (*Sch.* also ṕad) v. spad; ṕa-spún v. spun. — ṕa-ṕág, boar. — ṕa-má, parents, ṕa-má-la gús-pa, *Stg.*; *ṕa-ma-méd-k̔an*, *W.*, orphan; also father or mother, parent; ṕa-má-γčig-pa, brothers and sisters born of the same parents. — ṕa-miṅ, relations on the father's side; btsún-moi ṕa-miṅ bós-so, *Glr.*, he invited the relations of his wife's father; ṕa (daṅ) més (-po), ancestors; ṕa-més ši-bai dón-t̔u, for the (defunct) ancestors, *Wdṅ.*; — ṕa-tsáb 1. foster-father, guardian, *Sch.* 2. father to a country(?). — ṕa-tsán, *Mil.* 1. cousin by the father's side (patruelis) *C.* 2. also = ṕa-spún(?). — ṕa-γží = *ṕa-nóṙ*, *C.* — ṕa-yáṅ, *Sch.*, step-father; — ṕa-yúl, fatherland, native country, frq.; ṕa-yúl-la čágs-pa or srég-pa, love of country. — ṕa-γyág, yak-bull. — ṕa-γyár, step-father, foster-father, *Cs.* — ṕa-rá, he-goat, buck.

II. root for the terms: **beyond, onward, farther on**; ṕá-ga, the opposite side; ču ṕá-γar t̔ón-nas, to get to the opposite bank or shore, *Mil.* (not frq.). — ṕá-gi, 1. that which is on the other side, *Sch.* 2. *C.*, also *Pth.*, *Mil.*: **yonder;** ṕá-gii ri de, that mountain yonder, *Pth.* 3. col.: **he.** — ṕá-gir, **there, thither.** — ṕá-ṅos = ṕá-rol, ṕá-rol-tu *Lh.* — ṕá-mt̔a, the other end, the other boundary, *Cs.*; ṕa-mt̔a-méd, without boundary, endless, *Cs.* — ṕa-ṕyogs *C.* = ṕá-ga. — ṕa-tsád, ṕa-zád, **distance;** ṕa-tsád čig-na, at a small distance (from the town), *Pth.*; dé-nas ṕa-zád čig-na, a bit farther on, *Dzl.*; ṕa-tsad čig-tu ₒtón-nas, stepping a little aside, *Pth.*; ṕa-zád ₒgró-ba, to go on, *Dzl.* frq. — ṕa-rí the mountain on the other side. — ṕá-rol, in *B.* very frq. 1. **the other side; opposite side, counterparty.** 2. for ṕá-rol-pa, -na, -tu v. below; ṕá-rol-tu, over to the other side, sk̔yél-ba, to carry, ṕyin-pa, to get to the other side, esp. in reference to the Mahāyāna doctrine of crossing the stream of time to the shore of rest, of Nirwāṇa; gen. as sbst. = पारमिता, means of crossing (*Was.* **perfections,** *Köpp.* **cardinal-virtues**); gen. six of them are reckoned: sbyin-pa, ts̔úl-k̔rims, bzód-pa, brtson-ₒgrús, bsam-γtán, šes-ráb; sometimes only five, at other times even ten, by adding t̔abs, smón-lam, stobs, ye-šés; sbyin-pai, šes-ráb-kyi ṕá-rol-tu ṕyin-pa, to have stepped over or crossed by means of beneficence, wisdom etc. (or more naturally: to have got to the end of beneficence etc., to have fully achieved, accomplished it; sbst. the full accomplishment of etc.). — ṕá-rol-na, adv., **on the other side;** postp. e. gen. **beyond, behind,** with regard to space, *Sambh.*; **extending**

beyond, both as to the future and the past, e.g. *bskál-pa gráṅs-med-pai pá-rol-na*, innumerable Kalpas ago, frq.; *pá-rol-pa*, 1. **one living on the other side.** 2. also *po*, **enemy, adversary,** *pá-rol-pai rgyál-po*, *pá-rol-pai dmag*, *pá-rol-gyi dmag-tsógs*, the hostile king, hostile army; *pá-rol ynón-pa*, to vanquish the enemy; *pá-rol-gyis mi tsúgs-par gyúr-ba*, not to be molested by the enemy. 3. also *po*, **the other; the neighbour;** *pá-rol-gyi lén-pa*, to take away the neighbour's property; *pá-rol-gyi rdzas, yo-byád, nor*, *Stg.*; *pá-rol ynón-pa*, *Tar.* 12,20: excelling others, *Schf.* **exceedingly.** — Cf. also *par* and *pan* II.

ཕ་གུ་ *pá-gu*, *Sch.* **wall; edge, border;** in two passages of *Glr.* the latter meaning does not suit at all, and the former not well; rather: **tile;** v. *pag*.

ཕ་ཏིང་ *pá-tiṅ*, *W.*, **sweet dried apricots,** in *C.* **ṅa-ri-kám-bu**, in Hind. خوباني, in Russia *bokhari*, *bokharki*, also called Persian fruit, much exported from Balti, Kabul, and other countries of western Asia.

ཕ་ཏིལ་ *pa-til*, *pa-til* (*Ar.* فتيلة) *W.*, **lunt, match;** **dug-će**, to light (a match).

ཕ་བ་དགོ་དགོ་ *pa-ba-dgo-dgó*, **puff-ball, bull-fist** (a kind of fungus) *Wdṅ.*

ཕ་བོང་ *pa-bóṅ*, *Glr.* and elsewh., *C.*, *pa-óṅ Pth.*, *Bal.*, *pa-lóṅ Ld.*, **a large rock** or **block,** above ground.

ཕ་ཝང་ *pa-wáṅ*, 1. **bat** (animal) *Lt.*, *Thgr.*, *C.*; **po-loṅ-hel-kyi*, *pa-waṅ-áṅ-kyé*, *-ár-kyi**, *W.*, **pa-waṅ-tár**, *Sik.*, id. (= *bya-waṅ*). 2. *rdo pa-waṅ*, *Ssk.* sâlagrûma, **ammonite.**

ཕ་ར་ *pá-ra*, 1. **breeding-buck.** — 2. v. *pár-ba*.

ཕ་རང་ *pa-ráṅ*, 1. also *pe-ráṅ*, = **pi-liṅ**, *C.*, **Feringhi, European.** — 2. vulg. **venereal disease.**

ཕ་རི་ *pa-ri* 1. *Lh.*, **a coarse covering** or **carpet.** — 2. a mountain on the other side.

ཕ་ལ་ *pá-la Ssk.*, **fruit,** *Lt.*

ཕ་ལམ་ *pa-lám*, *rdo-rje-pa-lám*, **diamond,** *Lt.*

ཕ་ལི་ *pa-lí*, **shield, buckler.**

ཕ་ཤོད་ཤེད་འདུག་ *pa-śod śed dug*, **he changes colour, turns pale,** with consternation, *Ld.*

ཕག་ *pag*, I. v. *pag*. — II. in *B.* gen. *pág-pa*, **swine, hog, pig** (introduced into *C.* from China, and largely consumed; in *W.* somewhat known from India, **ri-pag* and *lúṅ-pag** being distinguished as the wild boar and the tame hog); *pág-pai sna*, *Glr.*; *rús-pa*, *Med.*; *bćud(?) Lt.*; *pág-gi ydoṅ*, a pig's face, *Sambh.*; *pá-pag*, not castrated, *pó-pag*, castrated boar; *mó-pag*, sow. — *pág-kyu*, herd of swine. — *pág-mgo*, 1. **boar's head** (a valued protective against demons, it being hid in the ground under the threshold of the door). 2. *S.g.* fol. 26, it seems to be **a mineral** used in medicine. — *pag-rgód*, wild boar. — *pag-mće*, tusks of a boar. — *pag-túṅ*, *Sch.*: a large boar(?). — *pag-prúg*, young pig. — *pág-ma*, *Sch.*, gelded hog. — *pág-mo*, 1. sow. 2. a goddess v. *rdo-rje*. — *pag-tsáṅ*, pig-sty. — *pag-tsil*, hog's lard; bacon. — *pag-tsógs* = *pag-kyu*. — *pag-rdzi*, swine-herd. — *pag-zé*, hog's bristle, *Wdṅ.* — *pag-yar-ma*, *Sch.*, the fattening of pigs(?) — *pag-ril*, pig's muck(?) *Lt.* — *pag-śa*, pork.

III. (*Cs. pág-ma*), **something hidden; concealment:** *pág-na mi yód-pa*, a man concealed behind, *Dzl.*, *pág-gam gru źig-tu*, in a corner, in obscurity, *Dzl.*; **tsá-big pág-la yod**, it is somewhat hidden, cannot be seen well (from this place), *Ld.*; **pág-la zá-ce**, to eat (dainties) by stealth, *W.*; *nyi-ma rii pág-tu gró*, *Thgy.*, the sun hides himself behind the mountain; *sgo-pág-nas bltás-pas*, to watch, spy, lurk behind the door, *Glr.*, v. also *jáb, pa*; *pag nyan táṅ-će W.*, **to listen.** — **pag-sté**, *W.* ('a hidden paring-axe' v. *sté-po*) plane; **pag-sté gyáb-će, dúd-će, śrúb-će**, to plane. — *pag-tsóṅ*, smuggling, *có-će*, to smuggle, *W.* **táṅ-kan**, smuggler, *W.* — *pág-ra*, parapet. — *pag-rágs*, rampart, intrenchment. — *pag-lám*, secret path (of smugglers). — **pag-súg**, bribery, *C.*, *W.*; **pag-súg táṅ-će**, to bribe; *zá-će*, to accept a bribe, *W.*

*ཕག་ཕག་ *p̔ag-p̔ág*, the name given in *Pur.* to **Codonopsis ovata**, the thick roots of which plant are cooked like turnips or ground and baked; v. *klu-mdúd*.

ཕང་ *p̔aṅ* I. *ₒp̔aṅ* (*p̔áṅ-ma*, *p̔áṅ-bu Cs*) **spindle;** *p̔aṅ-ló*, 1. the **whirl** of the spindle. 2. *šiṅ-rtai p̔aṅ-ló*, **waggon wheel,** *Dzl.*

II. v. *p̔aṅ*.

ཕང་འགྲོ་ *p̔aṅ-ₒgró*, *Sch.*, the belly or body of a stringed instrument.

ཕང་བ་ *p̔áṅ-ba*, *p̔áṅs-pa* (*Glr.* also *p̔óṅs-pa*, prov.) **to save, to spare, to use economy:** *srog* to spare one's life; *mi-p̔áṅs-te* or *-par* e.g. *ₒbúl-ba*, to give largely, not sparingly; *p̔áṅ-sems*, **thriftiness;** *p̔áṅ-sems-čan*, **thrifty, frugal;** **p̔aṅ-sem čo-če**, *W.*, **to be thrifty, frugal.**

ཕང་མ་ *p̔áṅ-ma*, **a medicinal plant,** *Med.*

ཕང་མེད་ *p̔aṅ-méd*, stated to be = *rin-méd*, *Ts.*

ཕང་ལོ་ *p̔aṅ-lo* v. *p̔aṅ* I.

ཕང་ལོང་ *p̔aṅ-lóṅ*, **vertebra**(?) *S.g.*

ཕཊ་ *p̔aṭ Ssk.*, an unmeaning sound, frequently used in magic spells, on which subject Milaraspa speaks rather obstrusely.

ཕད་ *p̔ad*, **a large bag** or **sack,** *rás-p̔ad*, *rál-p̔ad*, *rtsid-p̔ad*, sack of cotton cloth, goat's hair, yak's hair; *p̔ad-k̔á*, *-skéd*, *-mt̔il*, **the mouth, middle,** and **bottom** of a sack; *p̔ad-gáṅ*, a full sack, a sackful; *p̔ad-stóṅ*, an empty sack; *p̔ád-snam*, sack-twine, sack-cloth; *p̔ád-tsa*, very coarse sack-cloth.

ཕན་ *p̔an* I. sbst., **hanging ornaments,** lappets of silk, similar to the decorations of our tent-cloths, awnings etc., *ka-*, *sgo-*, *γduṅ-p̔an*, on pillars, doors, beams; *p̔an-γdugs*, a parasol so decorated, *S.g.*

II. = *p̔a* II., gen. in the combination of *p̔an-čád* (*Glr.* also *p̔an-čód*), also *p̔án-la* or *p̔an*, **towards, until:** *dá-či-nas dá-lta p̔án-la dar čig soṅ*, from 'but just' till 'just now' a moment has passed, *Thgy.*; *ná-niṅ-nas da p̔an-čád lo γčig son*, *Thgy.*; **da p̔an**, **until now,** *C.*; . . . *nas diṅ-saṅ p̔an* (*-la*) *Glr.* from . . . till now; *p̔yi-ma p̔an-čád-du ₒgró-ba yin*, I am proceeding towards the future, *Thgy.*; *p̔an-čád* also **beyond:** **de p̔en-čé' ma do** *C.* do not go any farther than that place; combined with its contrary *tsun*: *p̔an-tsún*(*-du*) *gró-ba*, to walk to and fro, there and back; to walk past, frq.; *p̔an-tsún-du p̔úl-ba*, to push hither and thither, *Glr.*; *p̔an-tsún mt̔ún-pai γtam*, assurances of mutual friendship, *Glr.*; *p̔an-tsun γčig-gis γčig-la yi-ge ǰtóṅ-ba*, *p̔yag byéd-pa*, *γnód-pa byéd-pa*, mutual correspondence, m. greetings, m. encroachment; *p̔an-tsún sdúr-ba sdébs-pa*, to compare with one another, to mix one with the other, *Zam.*; *γnyis-γnyis-dag p̔an-tsun-gyi ₒdra-bai yi-ge*, two equal letters (ă, ā etc.) at a time *Gram.*: *ma-p̔áṅ-gi ₒgram p̔an-tsún-du* on each of the two shores of lake *Ma-p̔aṅ*, *Mil.*; *don p̔an-tsún bsdu-rgyu yód-pa*, **correlative terms,** having reciprocal relation, *Gram.*: *p̔an-tsún t̔or-ba*, **to scatter, to disperse;** *p̔an-tsún-dag*, *Cs.*, both parties.

III. v. the following articles.

ཕན་དིལ་ *p̔án-dil W.* **kettle, pot** (of tinned copper, the common cooking-vessel in Tibet and India, having the shape of a broad urn); in *C.* **zaṅs(-bu)**, *Pers.* and *Hd.* دیگچی (*dēgči*); *p̔an-čuṅ*, a small vessel of that kind.

ཕན་པ་ *p̔án-pa* I. vb. **to be useful:** *de ni bdag-la mi p̔an*, that is no more of use to me; *p̔án-par mi ₒgyur*, it will be of no use; *bu ₒdis ṅá-la p̔án-par dka*, this son will hardly be useful to me, *Glr.*: *p̔án-par dgá-ba-rnams*, such as wish to make themselves useful, they who are ready to serve, *Thgy.*; *bgród-la p̔an*, useful for learning to walk, *Lt.*; *nad kún-la p̔án-pa yin*, that is good for all diseases, *Lt.*; *ṅai nád-la p̔án-pa yin-pas*, because I have recovered, *Glr.*; **p̔an soṅ**, it has helped, it has got better; . . . *na p̔an*, if . . . , then I shall get well, *Glr.*; *p̔án-pa žig srid*, recovery might be possible, *Pth.*; *mi p̔an*, it is useless, = **hurtful;** also: **it is not enough,** *Mil.*; *mi p̔án-par ₒdód-pa t̔ams-čád*, all the malevolent, *Domaṅ*: *k̔á-la p̔an*, lit. 'it is a mere enjoyment of the mouth', i. e. an outward, temporary enjoyment or advantage; hence *p̔án-pa* and *p̔an-pa yin-pa*, adj., **useful:** *p̔án-pai don*, a useful thing, valuable possession, frq.; *bdag nyon-móṅs-pa-las p̔an-pai don med*, after all it is of no use to me in my misery, *Dzl.*; *bslab-bya p̔an-pai tsig*, a wholesome instructive word, *Glr.*; *p̔an-pai grós*, useful advice, *Dzl.*

II. sbst. **use, benefit, profit:** *bstán-pa-la p̔án-pa žig byed-pa*, *Stg.*; *p̔an-γnod-méd-pa*, bringing neither profit nor harm, *Mil.*; *p̔án-pa daṅ bdé-ba*, *p̔an-bdé* **happiness and blessing,** very frq.; *p̔an-ₒdógs-pa*, *p̔an-ₒdógs byéd-pa*, **to be of use,** and adj. **profitable,** frq.; *p̔an-tógs*, **profit;** *p̔an-tógs če*, *Thgy.*, **čén-mo**, *W.*, **very profitable;** ... *la p̔an gaṅ togs gyis*, render services to ... in every way possible! *Mil.*; *p̔an-grogs* a helping (useful) friend, *Pth.*; *p̔an-γnód*, profit and loss, *p̔an-bdé* v. above; *p̔an-žás*, wholesome diet, *Med.*; *p̔an-yón*, **benefit, blessing,** as a reward for a meritorious action, frq.; *p̔an-(pai) sems*, **benevolence, readiness to help.**

ཕབ་པ་ *p̔áb-pa*, I. v. *bébs-pa*. — II. *Sch.*: **to fall down** (?).

ཕབས་ *p̔abs*, 1. **dry barm** (prepared for inst. in Balti, is said to consist of flour, mixed with some ginger and aconite). — 2. **lees, yeast** (of beer).

ཕམ་པ་ *p̔ám-pa* v. *ₒp̔ám-pa*.

ཕའུ་ *p̔au* v. *pag*.

ཕར་ *p̔ar* I. sbst. **interest** (of money), *W.*: **ṅúl-la p̔ar kál-če**, to impose, demand interest, **čál-če**, to pay interest; **exchange, agio.**

II. in later writings and col. for *p̔a* II.; also for *p̔an-čád*, *p̔a-zád*: **fartner;** *p̔ar ₒgró-ba*, to go on; *p̔ar ₒkyám-pa*, to roam farther and farther, *Thgy.*; **p̔ár-tsam**, *C.*, = *p̔ar*; *p̔ar ₒgro tsur ₒgró-ba-rnams*, people going, travelling, hither and thither; **away, off:** *di-nas p̔ar*, away from here; *p̔ar mi mčio*, I do not go away, *Dzl.* ༢༢༠, 6 (*Sch.* erron. 'to the father'); *p̔ar bžud*, go away!; ... *la p̔ar lta-ba*, **to look** (in a certain direction) *Mil.*, **away from one's self,** as opp. to: *raṅ-rig-séms-la tsur ltá-ba*, to look into one's own heart *Mil.*; *glu p̔ár-čig tsúr-čig lén-pa*, **alternative song,** *Mil.*; *p̔ár-slob tsúr-slob yin*, they are mutually scholars one of the other, *Tar.*; *p̔ar γčig láb-na tsur γnyis rgol*, if you say one word 'towards her', she gives you smartly a double charge back, *Mil.*; *p̔ar-tsúr-la*, *W.* also = **so-sór**, **in opposite directions;** **p̔ar-tsúr-la čo-če** to separate vb. a.; **ḍo-če**, to separate vb. n.

Comp. *p̔ár-ka*, *Thgy.* *p̔ár-ka* = *p̔á-rol*, **the opposite side** (of a valley &.) vulgo frq. — *p̔ár-ṅos*, id., *čui p̔ar-tsúr-gyi-lam.* — *p̔ar-p̔yin* abbreviation for *p̔á-rol-tu p̔yin-pa* v. *p̔á-rol*, *p̔a* II. *Mil.* — **p̔ár-tsam**, *C.*, = *p̔a-zád.* — *p̔ar-ₒdzúg* and *tsur-rgól* prob. = *sṅá-rgol* and *p̔yi-rgol.* — *p̔ar-zád* = *p̔a-zád.* — *p̔ár-la*, 1. = *p̔ar*, **away, onward,** *Schr.* 2. = *p̔á-rol-tu*, *na*, esp. with regard to time: vulgo *lo γčig p̔ár-la*, after one year; *W.* esp. after the gerund in *nas:* **zan zós-ne p̔ár-la**, after dinner. — *p̔ár-lam*, **way** or **journey thither,** *Sp.* ni f.

ཕར་བ་ *p̔ár-ba*, I. 1. **wild dog** (barks, and commits its ravages like the wolf, yet being afraid of man) in *Ld.* — 2. wolf *C.*, also *p̔ar-spyáṅ.* II. v. *ₒp̔ár-ba.*

ཕར་རྫས་ *p̔ar-rdzás*, *Sch.*, **an old heir-loom.**

ཕལ་ *p̔al*, I.? *Ld.* 1. **p̔al čós-se** (or *te*) **dug**, **step aside! make way!** — 2. **p̔al-p̔ál čá-če**, **to feel flattered.** II. v. the following.

ཕལ་པ་ *p̔ál-pa*, **usual, common;** *p̔al-pai miṅ*, his usual (common) name, *Thgr.*; *p̔ál-pa-las p̔ags-par bzáṅ-ba*, a more than ordinary beauty *Dzl.*; *mi* or *gaṅ-zág p̔ál-pa*, common people, *Mil.*; *tsoṅ-p̔ál-rnams bór-ro*, they left the common tradespeople behind, *Dzl.*; *p̔ál-pai rdzas* v. *ₒǰál-ba*; *šiṅ p̔ál-rnams*, common trees, *Mil.*; *snod p̔ál-pa*, common vessels, *Mil.*; *p̔al*, the common people; *p̔ál-gyi náṅ-na γnás-pa*, to live among the people *Dzl.*; *p̔ál-gyis rgyáb-nas ded p̔ál-gyis bskór-te*, the people running after and crowding round him, *Pth.*; **p̔ál-(pai) skad**, 1. *W.* the language of common life, opp. to **čós-skad**, book-language (C. *ṭál-ke'*). 2. Sch.: **rough-copy, waste-book**; *pál-po-* (Cs. also *-mo*) *če,* **a host, a troop**; *mi-rgód pál-po-če žig*, a troop or set of monsters (v. *rgód-pa* II.); gen. like οἱ πολλοί, the mass of the people, majority, great part or number; *pál-čé-ba* id. — *pál-čén*, **a philosophers' school**, called Mahasanghika. — *pál-čér*, **manifold, for the most part, ordinarily,** also = **universally**; *pál-čér ṅo-ñés ₒdégs-so*, they raised a general lamentation *Dzl.*

ཕལ་ཅན་ *pál-čan W.*, **broad, wide**, e.g. a broad valley; *pal-méd*, narrow.

ཕས་ *pás*, instrum. of *pá*, I. **by the father**; v. also *pás-spún*, sub *spun*. II. **of the opposite side, of the counter-party**, e.g. *pás rgól-ba.*

ཕི་ *pí*, 1. num. figure 44. — 2. *W.* for *pyi*, *pí-pa* for *pyi-pa.*

ཕི་ཀེར་ *pí-ker* (Urdu فکر, *Ar.* reflexion) *W.* *čan pí-ker med* = *čan mi sto* it is no matter, it makes no difference.

ཕི་ལིང་ *pí-liṅ* v. under *rgya.*

ཕིག་ཕིག་ *pig-pig*, a kind of jelly *C.*

ཕིང་ *piṅ*, *Sch.*: 1. **earthen-ware pitcher.** — 2. **cup, cupping-glass.** — 3. *W*: *sgó-piṅ*, **door-hinge.**

ཕིང་པ་ *piṅ-pa* v. ཕྱིང་པ་; ཕོང་པ་; ཕིང་ཅེས་ v. འཕྱིན་པ་

ཕིར་བ་ *pír-ba*, *pír-če* *W.* **to fall down.**

ཕུ་ *pu* numerical figure: 74.

ཕུ་ *pú*, I. sbst. 1. **the upper part** of an ascending valley or ravine; *pú bar mdo* (or *mda*), the upper, middle, and lower part of such a valley; *pú-ču*, mountain-torrent, frq.; *pur ma ₒgro, pú yá-gir ma ₒgro*, *Glr.*, do not go to the upper part of the valley; *pú-lhágs*, higher situated and colder places or districts, opp. to *rgya-šód*, lower and milder parts. The not unfrequent phrase: *pú-tág γčód-pa* or *čód-pa* was traced by our Lama to its original meaning: the upper part of the valley is shut up (with snow etc.), which is now used in a general sense; *krúl-bai pú-tág čod, Mil.*, prob. shut out all error, prevent every mistake! *pú-tag-čód-lugs-kyi čos šig, Mil.* seems to be an instruction for making a decision; *ṅa rgás-pa daṅ séms kyi pú-tág čód-pas ₒgró-ba mi yóṅ-bar ₒdug*, prob.: I being old and my spiritual affairs settled (not calling for further improvement), shall probably not travel any more (to India; but you may do so) *Mil.* cf. *pugs.* — *pú-pa*, the inhabitant of an elevated valley. Fig.: *pú γyo mda dkrug*, there is agitation above and below, the higher and the lower faculties of the mind are troubled, excited, *Mil.* — 2. prop. n. **Pu**, e. g. **a village in Upper Kunawar**, missionary station of the Church of the United Brethren. — 3. vulgo **the spirit** or **gaseous element of liquors**, causing them to foam, effervesce or explode, cf. *dbugs;* perh. to be referred to no. II.

II. interjection and imitative sound: *pú ₒdébs-pa Glr.*, *pú gyáb-če* *W.*, **to make pooh, to blow, to puff, to inflate**; *pú skoṅ*, puff it up (the skin etc.), lit.: fill it with pooh! *pús*, with the breath; *pús ₒdébs-pa Sch.* **to blow, howl, cry** (?); *sna-rtsa-pú*, **n. of a disease,** *Lt.*

ཕུ་དུང་ *pú-duṅ*, also *pú-tuṅ Glr.*, *pu-rúṅ Cs.*, **sleeve**; *pu-rdzús* *C.* (false sleeves), *pu-dúṅ-* (or *-tuṅ-*) *rtse* (sleeve-edges) **hand-ruffles**; mittens, cuffs (to keep the wrist warm).

ཕུ་དུད་ *pu-dúd*, **honour, respect, esteem**; *pu-dúd-du byéd-pa, Glr., púd-du kúr-ba, S.g.*, to show honour, respect.

ཕུ་བ་ *pú-ba*, pf. of *ₒbúd-pa*, **to blow**, col. used for the latter.

ཕུ་བོ, ཕོ་བོ *pú-bo, pó-bo,* (*Sch.* also *pun*), a man's **elder brother**: *pu-nú*, the elder and the younger, i. e. the two brothers; also the elder and the younger sons (for examples refer to *tsan-dán*); in the passage of *Dzl.* ༢༠༦, 14, *nu* ought to be canceled, and *pu-nú-mo*, ༧༦, 6. 9. should be translated by sister-in-law. *pu-grás, Sch.*, the elder brothers, dub.

ཕུ་རོན་ *p̒u-rón Pth.*, *p̒ug-rón*, (**p̒ur-gón** vulg.) **pigeon**; *p̒u-rón-gyi k̒yu Pth.*; *p̒ug-skyá Sch.* of a light blue colour, like pigeons.

ཕུ་ལ་, ཕོ་ལ་ *p̒ú-la*, *p̒ó-la Ld.* (from the Turkish), **pilaw**, a dish of boiled rice, with butter and dried apricots.

ཕུ་ཤུད་ *p̒u-šúd* **hoopoe.**

ཕུ་སེ་ *p̒ú-se*, **mouse, souslik** and similar rodent quadrupeds (cf. *bra*).

ཕུག *p̒ug*, 1. = *p̒ugs*. — 2. = *sbugs*, *p̒úg-pa*; *lgáṅ-p̒ug-gaṅ*, **the bladder**, in reference to its capaciousness, *S.g.*; *mje p̒úg-tu nub*, the penis recedes into its cavity, *Wdn.*; **the eye of a needle,** *Lt.* — 3. pf. and imp. of °*bug-pa*. — 4. = *p̒ub Schr.* — 5. for *p̒ug-ron*, q.v.

ཕུག་པ་ *p̒úg-pa*, **cavern**; *brag-p̒úg*, rock-cavern, grotto; *gad-p̒úg*, cavern in a steep river-bank, or in conglomerate; *dbén-p̒ug*, the solitary cavern of an anchorite, *Ma.*; *p̒úg-pa-pa*, n. of an astronomer of the 15th. century, v. *pád-ma*; *p̒ug-rtsis*, and likewise *p̒ug-lúgs Wdṅ.*, his calculations.

ཕུག་རོན་ *p̒ug-rón* v. *p̒u-rón*.

ཕུག་ཤུབ་ཤེ་ལེ་ *p̒ug-šub-še-le* (?) *W.*, **hoopoe;** perh. = *p̒u-šúd*, which occasionally is also spelled *p̒u-γšud*

ཕུག(ས)་ *p̒ug*(*s*), (cognate to *p̒u*; also °*búg-pa* and *sbugs*), **end, termination**; *p̒ug-mda-t̒úg-pai lóṅ-ka*, the entrails, the beginning and end of which lie close together, *Mil.* (*mda*, v. under *p̒u*); **innermost part, an innermost apartment,** = *sbúgs*; *p̒úgs-kyi nor* v. *sgo* init.; perh. also *p̒úg-gi spa-rím ltá-bu Glr.* 45, 4 may be referable to this meaning. *séms-kyi p̒ugs-t̒ag čod-pas bde*, happy (am I), because the final aim of my mind is decided and settled, *Mil.*, evidently = *p̒u-t̒ag čod-pa*, the former being perh. etymologically more correct. Similarly: *bu t̒se* °*dii bló-p̒ugs čós-la γtód-čig Mil.*, may the boy direct the aim of his mind for this life unto religion! — **Time to come, futurity,** (opp. to °*p̒ral*, the present moment); *p̒úgs-su*, *p̒ugs-na*, **hereafter, at last, ultimately** (*Sch.* always?); *p̒ugs-či* °*dra čig* °*oṅ*, how will it end? what will be the final issue? *Glr.*

ཕུགས་ཏ་ *p̒ugs-ta*, *p̒ógs-ta*, *pogs-ta*, *W.* (*Pers.* پُخته), **firm, strong, durable**; *p̒úgs-ta btsems*, sew it well (so that it will hold)!

ཕུང་པ་ *p̒úṅ-pa* v. *p̒úṅ-pa*.

ཕུང་པོ་ *p̒úṅ-po*, 1. **heap**; *p̒úṅ-por spúṅ-ba*, *Lex.* also *bčér-ba*, to gather into a heap; *nás-p̒uṅ*, *rtsá-p̒uṅ*, *lúd-p̒uṅ*, *sá-p̒uṅ*, a heap of barley, hay, dung, earth; **mass,** *me-múr-gyi p̒úṅ-po*, a glowing mass, a mass of fire; *sprín-p̒uṅ*, clouds, a gathering of clouds *Glr.*; *γnyér-mai p̒úṅ-po* (the skin becomes) a heap of wrinkles, *Thgy.*; the body is called *mi-γtsáṅ-ba rnám-pa sna-t̒sógs-kyi p̒úṅ-po*, *dug γsúm-gyi p̒úṅ-po*, *jig-pai p̒úṅ-po*, *zín-pai p̒úṅ-po*, *Thgy.*; **accumulation, mass,** *bsod-nams-kyi*, *čós-kyi*, e.g. *čós-kyi p̒úṅ-po* ༨༤༠༠༠, the whole mass of the 84 000 religious lectures of Buddha (!) *Mil.* — 2. In metaphysics: **स्कन्ध, the so-called five aggregates** (*Cs.*) or **elements of being,** viz. *γzugs*, *t̒sór-ba*, °*du-šes*, °*du-byéd*, *rnam-šés*, (v. *Köpp.* I. 602, and esp. *Burn.* I. 475 and 511), which in the physical process of conception unite, so as to form a human individual or **the body** of a man, (*p̒uṅ-po lṅa-las grub-pai lus Wdṅ.*) which by some of the later and more popular writers is itself called *p̒úṅ-po*. So this word, as being synonymous to *lus*, has found its way into the language of the people, and not in a low sense, in as much as one of our Christian converts used the expression: *ye-šúi p̒úṅ-po dur-k̒uṅ-nẹ žens.* — 3. Symb. num. for 5.

ཕུང་བ་ *p̒úṅ-ba* v. **འཕུང་བ་** °*p̒úṅ-ba*.

ཕུད་ *p̒ud*, sbst. I. (v. °*p̒ud-pa*, pf. *p̒ud*), **a thing set apart**, used particularly of the first-fruits of the field, as a meat- or drink-offering, in various applications: *zas-čáṅ-gi p̒ud* meat- and drink-offering *Glr.*; *t̒óg-pud*, *ló-pud*, an offering of the first-fruits of harvest; *srús-p̒ud* id., consisting of ears of corn, wound round a pillar of the house; *bán-ṗud*, first-fruit offering of the barn; *rdó-ṗud, sá-ṗud*, an offering of stones or earth, when a house is built, these materials then being used for manufacturing images of gods, *Glr.*; **initiatory present**, e.g. the first produce of a work, that has been committed to one *Glr.* (so, according to circumstances, it may be as much as **a specimen**); in a general sense, **a thing done for the first time**; *bág-mai ṗud*, prob the first cohabitation. — II. for *ṗu-dúṅ* and *ṗu-dúd*, q.v.

ཕུད་པ་ *ṗúd-pa*, I. pf. of *ₒbúd-pa*.

II. *Cs.* sbst. 1. **spindle covered with yarn.** — 2 **hair-knot, tuft of hair**; *ṗúd-ċan*, being provided with such a one.

ཕུན་(སུམ་)ཚོགས་(པ་) *ṗun(-sum)-ṫsógs(-pa)* 1. adj. **perfect, complete,** possessing every requisite quality, e.g. *dgón-pa*, a hermit's dwelling; **excellent, exquisite, distinguished,** e.g. *ro*, taste, *bsnyén-bkur*, distinctions, marks of honour *Mil.*, *nor daṅ loṅs-spyod Domaṅ*; adv. *dgé-ba bċu ṗun-sum-ṫsógs-par spyód-pa, Dzl.*, to practise the ten virtues to perfection. — 2. sbst. **perfection, excellence, superior good,** frq.; *ṗa-ról-poi ṗun-sum-ṫsógs-pa-la ċágs-pa* to covet the excellent things which another possesses, *Thgy.* — 3. *ṗun-ṫsógs*, frequent **name** for **males** and **females.**

ཕུབ་ *ṗub* 1. **shield, buckler,** *Glr.*, of a convex shape, with the rim bent round; *ko-ṗúb*, a leather buckler; *ṗub-šúbs*, the cover of a buckler, *Cs.*; *ṗúb-kyi mé-loṅ*, the centre of the shield, *Cs.* — 2. v. the following.

ཕུབ་པ་ *ṗúb-pa*, pf. of *ₒbúb-pa*.

ཕུབ་མ་ *ṗúb-ma*, **short straw**; *ṗúb-ma žig*, a small stalk, a bit of chaff; **ṗúb-ma ṭáb-ċe* or *ṭab táṅ-ċe**, to fan, to winnow; *ṗub-ldír Cs.*, chaff; *gró-ṗub*, wheat-straw.

ཕུམ་ཕུམ་ *ṗum-ṗúm*, **posterior, anus** *Pth.*

ཕུར་ *ṗur* 1. v. *ṗu* — 2. v. *ₒṗúr-ba*. — 3. v. *ṗúr-pa*.

ཕུར་པ་ *ṗúr-pa*, **peg, pin, nail**; *rtsig-ṗur Schr.*, **ṗur-ċa* or *ša** (?) *Ld.*, a peg on a wall, to hang up things; *lċágs-ṗur*, **iron nail**; *šiṅ-ṗur*, **wooden peg**; *ṗur-rnyí* v. *rnyi*, *ṗur-bži brkyáṅ-ba* to fasten the hands and feet of a culprit to four pegs driven into the ground, when he is to undergo the punishment of the *rkyaṅ-šiṅ*, v. *rkyoṅ-ba*. 2. **iron instrument** in the form of a short dagger, used for expelling evil spirits, and fancied to possess great power, *Schl.* 257; *sá-ṗur ₒdébs-pa*, to stick such a dagger into the ground, whereby the subterranean demons are kept off; fig. *mig ṗúr-ṫsugs-su ltá-ba Glr.*, to look at one with a piercing glance of the eye; **lha-la sól-wa ṗúr-ṫsug-tu ₒdéb-pa** *C.*, to implore a god very earnestly. *ṗúr-bu* 1. = *ṗúr-pa*; the usual form of incantation is: *ṗúr-bus ydáb-bo, ṫó-bas brdúṅ-ṅo, ṗyág-rgyas mnán-no!* 2. (*yza*) *ṗúr-bu*, **the planet Jupiter**; its day: **Thursday.**

ཕུར་བ་ *ṗúr-ba, Sch.*: **to emboss**; *ṗúr-ma* or *ₒbúr-ma*, **relief work, embossment.** — 2. **to scratch,** v. *ₒṗúr-ba*; *mgo-ṗúr*, n. of a disease *Lt.*

ཕུར་བུ་ *ṗúr-bu*, v. under *ṗúr-pa*.

ཕུར་མ་ *ṗúr-ma*, v. *ṗúr-ba*. — 2. *ṗyé-mai ṗúr-ma*, **a decoration** resembling a flag.

ཕུར་མོ་ *ṗúr-mo*, a medicament *Wdn.*; *ṗur-tál? S.g.*

ཕུལ་ *ṗul* 1. **a handful**, also *ṗul-gáṅ*, e.g. of corn, *Dzl.*, beer *Lt.* (in which case = *skyor*). — 2. **end?** only in the phrase: *ṗúl-tu ṗyin-pa*, **to reach the highest degree, to be victorious**, to have the better of an argument; *yi-gei sgrá-la ṗúl-tu ṗyin*, he has finished his studies in grammar, *Glr.*; *mḱás-pai ṗúl-tu ṗyin-par gyúr-to*, he became a great scholar, *Pth.*; also *ṗul-(tu) byúṅ(-ba)*, **accomplished, perfect, eminent** *S.g.*; p. n. = *á-ti-ša*. — 3. *ṗúl-ċan*, **thick** = **róm-po** *Ld.*

ཕུལ་བ་ *ṗúl-ba* v. *ₒṗúl-ba* and *ₒbúl-ba*.

ཕེ་ *ṗe* 1. *W.* for *ṗye*; *ṗé-ku-lig*, **key.** — 2. num. figure: 104.

ཕེ་རང་, ཕ་རང་ *ṗe-ráṅ, ṗa-ráṅ*, **Feringhi, Europeans,** *C.*

ཕེག་རྡོབ *ṗeg-rdób* v. under *ṗeb-pa*.

ཕེད་, ཕེན་ *ṕed*, *ṕen* *W.* for *ṕyed*, *ṕyen*; *ṕed-ṕed* v. *ṕyad-ṕyad.*

ཕེབ་པ་ *ṕéb-pa*, 1. pf. *ṕebs*, resp. **to go** *C.*; **to come** *C.* and *W.*; also *ča̓g* (or *ṕyág*)-*ṕeb-pa*; scarcely in ancient lit., but *Glr.*, *Pth.*, *Mil.*; **nyi-rán-la ṕéb-loṅ yód-na** W., if you have time to come; **o-ṅá ghá-le ṕeb** *C.*, well, good bye! **dha sá-hib ṕeb**, id. in speaking to a European; *čag ṕeb žu naṅ* v. *snáṅ-ba* I. extr.; *ṕéb-par smrá-ba Schr.*, to salute; *Sch.* also: to speak politely (??); *ṕéb-par ṕág-pa*, *Sch.*, to rise gracefully, to walk decently (?); *ṕéb-sgo ltar Sch.*: 'according to the given order', but cf. *ₒgro-sgo ltar* under *sgo* 3; *ṕéb-rdog-pa* 'to tramp arrival', to go to welcome a high Lama or other honoured person on his arrival with dance and music *C.*, *Lexx.*; *Cs.* however mentions *ṕeg-rdób* as a musical instrument, 'a small brazen plate for music', and in *Stg.* the same word occurs along with *sil-bsnyán.* — 2. for *ₒbab;* so it seems to be used, *Lt.*: *ťúr-du mi ṕebs*; *ṕó-bar mi ṕebs*, it won't go down his throat.

ཕེར་བ་ *ṕér-ba* **to be able** *Mil. nt.*, cf. also *dod*; *Cs.*: 'to become, to be fit' etc.

ཕོ་ *ṕo* I. num. figure: 134.

II. **man,** opp. to woman, **male,** *ṕo lo lṅá-bču-pa*, men of the age of fifty (opp. to *bú-mo lo-gnyís-ma*) *Ma.*; *ṕo mčór-po*, a handsome man (opp. to *bud-méd mčór-mo*) *Pth.*; as a pleonastic apposition to the pers. pron., like *mi*, *Mil.*; common in *C.*: **ṕo-ṅá**, I (masc.) = *ḱó-bo*; esp. in reference to animals: **male, he** (ass), **cock** (bird), *Dzl.* and elsewh.; as apposition to the names of domestic animals when castrated: *ṕo-rtá*, **gelding**; *rá-ṕo*, **a castrated he-goat.** — *ṕo-skyés*, **man, male person,** *Pth.* — *ṕo-gós*, man's dress, man's coat; *ṕo-čás*, *Mil.* id. (?) — *ṕo-čén Wts.*, *Sch.*, gelding. — *ṕo-tó Bal.*, stallion. — *ṕo-rtágs* 1. *Physiol.* = *ṕo-mťsán.* 2. *Gram.*: sign for the masculine gender, *Cs.* — *ṕo-nád*, 1. *W.* andromany, inordinate desire after men. 2. v. *ṕó-ba.* — *ṕo-mó*, man and woman, men and women, male and female; *ṕo-mó med*, no difference of sex exists. **ṕo-ťsé** *Bal.*, male sex. — *ṕo-mťsan*, membrum virile, man's yard, esp. the penis; the rather vague expression *ṕo-mťsán* (or *ṕo-rtágs*) *ḃčád-pa* is asserted to apply not to castration (*Schr.*), but only to circumcision (which, however, is not generally known in Tibet, Mussulmans being found only in some of the larger cities of the country). — *ṕo-yan Sch.* and *ṕo-raṅ Cs.*, *ṕo-hraṅ C.*, an unmarried man. — **ṕo-ri** *W.*, **ṕo-ré** *C.* a male kid. — *ṕo-lhá*, 1. tutelary deity of a man's right side (ni f.) *Glr.* 2. *Cs.*: **Sir,** as polite address. — (Observation: The circumstance of the consonants of the alphabet and the prefix-letters being divided by Tibetan grammarians into masculine, feminine and neuter, is of no practical moment: careful investigations on that head have been made by Schiefner and Lepsius).

III. v. *ṕó-so.*

ཕོ་གྱོག་ *ṕo-gyóg Sch.* (perh. *ṕo-gyó* v. *gyo-mo*), **hollow tile.**

ཕོ་ཉ་ *ṕó-nya*, less frq. *ṕó-nya-ba* (*Ssk.* दूत), 1. **messenger,** e.g. sent for a physician; *ṕó-nya ɣťóṅ-ba*, *ṕó-nya-mṅág-pa*, to send, dispatch a messenger; *brtsí-ba*, *Cs.* to receive one (?) — 2. **ambassador, envoy.** — 3. Passages like *ɣšín-rjei ṕó-nya* messenger of death, angel of death, and *bdé-ba-čan-gyi ṕó-nya*, honourable epithet of a king, that is looked upon as a demi-god (similarly to ἄγγελος τοῦ παραδείσου) sufficiently justify the application of the word to the scriptural notion of **angel,** which may be rendered still more intelligible by adding *nám-mḱai*, *Chr. P.* (P. Georgi retains the Italian *angelo*, spelling it *án-ₒbye-lo*). Buddhist mythology has no available type for it, and *lha* (*Cs.*) could only be made use of, if already whole generations of the Tibetan nation had become Christians.

ཕོ་ནོ་ *ṕo-nó Bal.* for *ṕu-nú.*

ཕོ་བ་ *ṕó-ba* (resp. *sku-ťog Cs.*) 1. **stomach** — 2. the second cavity of the stomach or **reticulum** of ruminating animals (cf. *gród-pa*). *ṕo-ba ljíd-pa*, *Cs.* to overcharge the stomach, to clog; *śól-ba Cs.* to purge, to cleanse; *ṕo-bai ḱa Cs.*, the upper orifice of the stomach, joining the oesophagus; *ṕo-ńan*, a weak st., *bzaṅ*, a good, sound st. *Cs.* — *ṕo-tér*, swag-belly *Sch.*; *ṕo-nád*, disorder of the st. — 2. v. *ṕo*, above.

II. pf. of *ₒbó-ba* for *ṕos Glr.*

ཕོ་བ་རི་ *ṕó-ba-ri*, also *-ris* or *ṕo-ris Lt.*, **black pepper**; the col. form: *ṕo-ba-ril-bu* **'stomachic pills'** prob. is merely a popular etymology (similar to the English 'sparrow grass', corrupted from asparagus).

ཕོ་བྲང་ *ṕo-bráṅ* resp. for *ḱáṅ-pa*, **house, dwelling**; often also implying **hall, castle, palace,** *B.* and col.; *slei ṕo-braṅ*, the castle (palace) of Lé.

ཕོ་ཚོས་ *ṕo-tsós Schr.* **red paint**; *dúṅ-la ṕo-tsós bskús-pa*, red paint put on a shell *Pth.*; *ṕo-tsos-tsal Pth.*

ཕོ་རིས་ *ṕo-ris* v. *ṕo-ba-ri.*

ཕོ་རོག་ *ṕo-róg*, **raven,** perh. also **crow**; cf. *ḱwá-ta*; *ṕo-rog-mig*, **medicinal herb,** *Wdṅ.*

ཕོ་ལ་, ཕུ་ལ་ *ṕó-la*, *ṕú-la W.*, v. *pó-la.*

ཕོ་ལད་ *ṕo-lád W.* **steel,** *Pers.* پوند, فوند.

ཕོ་ལོ་ལིང་ *ṕo-lo-liṅ W.* **peppermint.**

ཕོ་ལོང་མདུད་ *ṕo-loṅ-mdúd Mil.* a kind of knot, complicated, and of magic virtue.

ཕོ་ལོང་ཧེལ་ཀྱི་ *ṕo-loṅ-hél-kyi* etc. v. *ṕa-wáṅ.*

ཕོ་སོ་ *ṕó-so*, *W.* **haughtiness, pride**; **ṕo-so čo-će**, to demean one's self haughtily, *W.*; **ṕó-so-čan**, proud, haughty, puffed up: *ká-ṕo Mil.* bragging about things, which in reality one is not able to do; *ṕo-tsod*, prob. the same as *ṕo-so*, *Mil.*: *ṕo-tsód mṅón-śes ma ₒčad čig*, do not boast of prophetic sight.

ཕོག་ *ṕog*, 1. *Wts.* **beam, rafter**; *Sch.*: 'the principal beam of the roof'. — 2. v. *ₒṕóg-pa* and *ₒbóg-pa.*

ཕོགས་ *ṕogs*, **wages, pay, salary**; *lo-, zla-, nyin-ṕogs* annual, monthly salary, daily wages; *dṅúl-ṕogs, smár-ṕogs, Cs.*, payment in money; *zóṅ-ṕogs Cs.* payment in goods. 2. **providing for another person in natural produce**, even without any service being done in return, e.g. the maintenance of Lamas; *ṕogs-dód*, maintenance by an allowance of money (in exceptional cases).

ཕོང་ *ṕoṅ*, v. *ₒṕáṅ-ba*; *ṕóṅ-ba Glr.* for *paṅ-ba.*

ཕོངས་པ་ *ṕóṅs-pa* (cf. *ₒṕóṅs-pa*) 1. **poor, needy**; *séms-čan nyam-ťág-ṕóṅs-dgu*, the poor and miserable creatures, *Glr.*; *sdúg-ṕoṅs-pa*, id. *Stg.*, *C.* — 2. **poverty.**

ཕོད་ *ṕod*, *skár-ma ṕod*, *Cs.*, *Sch.*, **comet.**

ཕོད་ཁ་ *ṕód-ḱa*, **masquerade garment** with long sleeves.

ཕོད་པ་ *ṕód-pa*, 1. **to be able,** esp. in a moral sense, **to prevail on one's self,** *ₒbral-mi ṕód-pa ltar yód-na yaṅ*, although he was scarcely able to part with . . . *Glr.*; *ₒdi ni mi ṕód-do*, that I cannot do (moral impossibility) *Dzl.*; *lta mi ṕód*, I cannot bear to see that, *Dzl.*; to be able to resist: *zas žim gos bzaṅ su-yis ṕod* who can resist good food and fine clothes? hence *ṕod-pa-čan*, *Cs.*, **bold, daring**; **ṕod-čúṅ-se**, *W.* **timid, cowardly.** — 2. **to come up to, to be nearly equal in worth,** with *tsam(-la)*: *deï bsód-nams tsam-la ṕód* it is nearly of equal merit as . . . *Dzl.*

ཕོན་(ཕོ་?) *ṕón(-po) Glr.* and elsewh., *ṕób-ṕon Cs.*, *ṕón-po(n)*, *ṕón-to*, *ṕod-ṕód*, *W.*, 1. **bundle, truss,** of hay, straw, reeds; **sheaf.** *C.* — 2. **bunch, wisp, cluster, umbel,** *W.*; **tuft, tassel**; *dár-ṕon*, *skúd-ṕon*, *Cs.*

ཕོབ་ *ṕob* v. *ₒbébs-pa.*

ཕོར་པ་ *ṕór-pa C.*, *B.* (*W.* **kó-re**, resp. **don-kyóg**), **bowl, dish, drinking-cup,** generally made of wood and carried in the bosom, to have it always ready for use; cups made of other materials are called *lčágs-ṕor*, *dṅúl-ṕor*, *ysér-ṕor*, and a glass tumbler *śél-ṕor*. The word is also applied to vessels used for other purposes: *spyin-ṕor*, glue-pot, *ṕóg-ṕor*, perfuming-pan. — *ṕör-ṕyis*, cloth for wiping the cup; *ṕor-kúg*, id. (?); *ṕor-śúg* (*śubs*?), the pocket or fold in the coat for receiving the cup, *C.*

ཕོལ་ *p̔ol, W.* 1. **blister** caused by burning, *p̔ol-mig,* **a bad sore, ulcer, abscess,** *Cs., W.* — 2. *Thgy.*, **a kind of fungus** (mould).

ཕོས་ *p̔os,* 1. v. *ₒbó-ba.* — 2. v. *ša.*

ཕྱ་, ཕྱྭ་ *p̔ya,* **lot,** *p̔ya débs-pa* to cast lots *Cs.*; **lot, fortune** *Cs., p̔ya brtág-pa* to judge of lots or fortune *Cs.*; **prognostic** *Sch., p̔ya-bzáṅ, -ṅán* good, bad fortune or prognostics *Cs.*; *nór-p̔ya, k̔yim-p̔ya* prognostics relative to property, family etc., in drawing lots or playing at dice; *p̔ya (daṅ) γyaṅ* lot (good luck) and blessing, *p̔ya daṅ γyaṅ ₒgúg-pa* to call forth good luck and blessing, to secure it by enchantment *Glr., rgya-nág-gi p̔ya-γyáṅ nyáms-pas* as China's fortune and welfare were prejudiced *Glr.*; *p̔yá-mk̔an* fortune-teller *Cs.*, but v. also the next article.

ཕྱ་མཁན་ *p̔yá-mk̔an,* 1. = *rdzá-mk̔an,* **potter.** — 2. v. the foregoing.

ཕྱ་ཅན་ *p̔ya-čan Lt.?*

ཕྱ་ལ་ལེ་བ་ *p̔ya-la-lé-ba, Sch.,* **coarse, rude, negligent, disorderly** (?).

ཕྱ་ར་ *p̔yá-ra,* **curtain before a door,** *Schr. Sch.*

ཕྱག་ *p̔yag,* 1. resp. for *lag,* **hand**; *bčom-ldan-ₒdás-kyis p̔yag sá-la brdebs,* Buddha struck with his hand on the earth, *Dzl.*; *p̔yag brgyáṅ-ba,* to stretch forth one's hand, *Sch.*; with *la* it denotes also the imposition of hands as a holy ceremony, *W.*: **čag gyaṅ sál-če*.* — 2. **bow, compliment, reverence:** *p̔yag dáṅ-po-la,* whilst making the first bow, *Glr.*; also **compliment** in letters: ... *la p̔yag graṅs-med bčaṅs,* with a thousand compliments to ... (a Lama even of a higher order concluded his letter to a nobleman with 10000 compliments to him as the head of the family, and then to the rest according to rank and age in a descending line with 1000, 100 etc.); therefore *p̔yag byéd-pa* (eleg. *gyíd-pa*; resp. *mdzád-pa,* when e.g. a king is addressed by a Lama, *Pth.*), in *Balti *p̔yag byá-ča,* W.* gen. **čag p̔ul-če* or *čo-če,* resp. *ǰal-čag čo-če*,* to salute, to pay one's respects, with *la,* e.g. ministers waiting on the king, *Glr.*; **čág-ga yoṅ*,* he comes to pay his respects, *W.*; *p̔yag daṅ skór-ba byéd-pa,* to make bows and circumitions, *S.g.*; with or without a preceding *p̔yi* (vulg. *ₒton*), **to take leave, to bid adieu,** *B.* and vulgo (cf. *p̔yi* below), **dé-ne čag p̔ul yin*, W.*, so then I shall take my leave now. — *p̔yag ₒtsál-ba,* pf. *btsal,* imp. *tsol,* to make a very low reverence, the head almost touching the ground; more at large: *γžán-gyi žábs-la mgó-bos p̔yag ₒtsál-ba,* esp. in use before Lamas and kings; in the introductions of books, also, the authors generally address both deities and readers with the phrase: *p̔yag ₒtsál-lo.* — 3. **impurity, dirt** (?); v. some of the following compounds and also *ₒp̔yág-pa.* — 4. sometimes for *čag.*

Comp. *p̔yag-mk̔ár* resp. for *mk̔ar-ba* **staff.** — *p̔yag-ₒk̔ur W.* = *p̔yag-rtén.* — *p̔yag-goṅ* the back of the hand *Cs.* — *p̔yag-rgyá* (मुद्रा) 1. resp. for *rgya* (I.) **seal;** *p̔yag-rgyás ₒdébs-pa* to seal, to confirm by a seal, v. *rgya* I. This meaning is at present hardly any longer known, but only: 2. gesture, the manner in which the hand and fingers are held by Buddha, by stage-players, Lamas or saints etc., when performing religious ceremonies or sorceries; *p̔yag-rgyás mnán-pa* to overcome evil spirits by such gesticulations *Dom.*, *ₒgról-ba* to set them free, by dissolving the charm *Pth.* There is a great number of these gesticulations. *p̔yag-rgya-čen-po* is said to be a figurative designation of the Uma-doctrine. (The other meanings given by *Cs.* and *Sch.* are rather uncertain.) — *p̔yag-ṅár* wrist *Cs.*, yet v. *ṅar* I. — *p̔yag-ča Sch.* 'wrought by the hand; an implement', resp. for *lag-ča,* v. *ča* III. extr.; *p̔yag-čás* attributes, carried in the hand, in performing religious dances, cf. *p̔yag-mtsán.* — *p̔yag-čáb* water for washing the hands and the face. — *p̔yag-mčód Mil.* for *p̔yag daṅ mčod-pa byéd-pa.* — *p̔yag-snyigs Lexx.* = *p̔yag-dár.* — *p̔yag-rtágs* 1. resp. for *lag-rtágs* sign of the hand, impression of a blackened finger in the place of a seal. 2. = *p̔yag-rtén* (?). — *p̔yag-*

rtén B. and col. **a present of welcome,** frq., **a present** in general, also **a fee** *Glr.; ṕyag-rtén rgya-čén* immense presents *Glr.* — *ṕyag-mtíl* resp. **palm of the hand.** — *ṕyag-mtéb* resp. **thumb.** — *ṕyag-dár* **sweepings, dust, rubbish;** *ṕyag-dár byed-pa Dzl.* and elsewh., *ṕyág-pa Lex.*, **gyáb-če** *W.* to sweep, to clean; *ṕyag-dar-pa* a sweeper *Dzl.*; *ṕyag-dár-gyi ṕúṅ-po, ṕyag-dar-ḱród* dust-heap; *ṕyag-dar-ḱród-kyi čós-gos* or *ná-bza* vestment or cowl of a mendicant friar, which according to the rules of his order is to be patched up of rags gathered from heaps of rubbish *Burn.* I, 305. (The explanation given by *Sch.* seems to rest on mere hypothesis.) — *ṕyag-na-rdó-rje, ṕyag-rdór* v. *rdo-rje-ₒčaṅ.* — *ṕyag-dpé* resp. for *dpé-ča* v. *dpe* 3. — *ṕyag-dpúṅ* resp. for arm. — *ṕyág-ṕyi* **attendant, man-servant** = *žabs-ṕyi; ṕyág-ṕyi byéd-pa* to be a servant; *ṕyág-ṕyi-la* or *ṕyag-ṕyir ₒbréṅ-ba* to be a follower (of a Lama); collect. train of servants, retinue. — *ṕyag-ṕyis* resp. **towel.** — *ṕyag-bris* resp. 1. **hand-writing, manuscript.** 2. **drawing** *Glr.* 3. **letter** *W.*, *brtsé-bai ṕyag-bris* your kind letter, your friendly correspondence. — *ṕyag-ₒbúl* resp. **gift, present.** — *ṕyag-sbál Cs.* resp. = *ṕyag-goṅ; Sch. ṕyag-sbál-du bčúg-pa* to hold one's hand ready for taking or receiving, v. *sbal.* — *ṕyag-smán* 1. resp. for *sman C.* 2. = *ṕyag-rtén W.* — *ṕyag-ma* **broom, duster, mop** *C., Lexx.* — *ṕyag-tsaṅ Sch.*: 'the all-filling One, the all-universalizing One' (?) — *ṕyag-mtsán* the attributes or emblems of Buddha and of different deities, carried in the hands (it is indeed nothing else than what, when carried in the hands of men, is called *lag-* or *ṕyag-čás Glr.* and elsewh.). — *ṕyag-mdzúb* resp. for **finger.** — *ṕyag-mdzód* **treasurer,** of kings or in large monasteries. — *ṕyag-rdzás* resp. for *nor-rdzás Mil.* — *ṕyag-žábs* resp. for *rkaṅ-lág Schr.* — *ṕyag-ra* (prob. for *ṕyag-gra*) **privy, water-closet.** — *ṕyag-rás* resp. for **towel** *Sch.* — *ṕyag-lán* the return of a salutation, **reciprocal greeting** *Mil.* — *ṕyag-lás W.* resp. for *las* = *ṕrin-las B.* — *ṕyag-lén* resp. for *lag-lén* **practice, exercise,** also **ceremony** (?) **religious rite** (?); . . . *la-ṕyag-lén ₒdebs-pa Pth?* . . . *la-ṕyag-lén-du ₒgro-ba Mil.* (?) — *ṕyag-šiṅ* an attribute of idols, resembling a rod (birch) or besom *Wdk.* — *ṕyág-sa* = *ṕyag-ra; ṕyag-sén* resp. for *sén-mo; ṕyag-sór* resp. for *sór-mo.* — *ṕyag-sról* **law, regulation; practice, use; tradition.**

ཕྱང་ངེ་བ་ *ṕyáṅ-ṅe-ba, Cs.*: = *ǰól-le-ba,* **hanging down** (belly, v. *ṕyal*); *Lexx.* give ཐགམ, slender, slight-made; *Sch.*: **straight, stretched** (?); *ṕyaṅ-ṕrúl* or *-ₒṕrul Lexx.* pendent ornaments.

ཕྱད་ཕྱད་ *ṕyad-ṕyád,* vulg. *ṕed-ṕéd,* **awkward gambols,** clumsy attempts at dancing.

ཕྱད་པ་ *ṕyád-pa,* also *ₒṕyád-pa,* **constant, firm, persevering;** *ṕyád-par,* **always, continually, perpetually;** *Lexx.* = *rgyún-du* (of rare occurrence); *ṕyad ma ṕyod Mil.?*

ཕྱམ་ *ṕyam* = *lčam* (*Sbh.* also *ḱyam*), *ṕyam-rṅas, -rten, -stegs,* **support** (of rafters); *Sch.*: the resting-point of a beam.

ཕྱམ་ཕྱམ་པ་ *ṕyam-ṕyám-pa, Thgr.* **glittering;** cf. *lčám-me-ba.*

ཕྱམ་མེ་བ་ *ṕyám-me-ba, Glr.* **slow, not hasty, not greedy, indifferent to.**

ཕྱར་ཁ་ *ṕyár-ḱa Sch.* **blame, affront, insult** (v. *ₒṕyá-ba?*) *ṕyar-γyáṅ Sch.* id.; *Lexx. ṕyar-γyéṅ?*

ཕྱལ་ *ṕyal,* resp. **belly, stomach,** *Cs.; ṕyal-ṕyaṅ-ṅe, Lexx.* = *gród-pa ǰól-le-ba,* **paunch, swag-belly;** *ṕyál-mo* id.?

ཕྱི་ *ṕyi* (*W.* **ṕi**) I. **behind** adv.: *ṕyi-bkan-du nyál-ba Sch.,* to lie on one's back; *ṕyi-gros-su gyé-ba, Glr.*; **či-do gyáb-pa** *C.,* to retreat, to recede, with the back in advance; *ṕyi lús-pa,* to lag behind; *ṕyi-rtíṅ Sch.,* **heel;** *ṕyi-sdér, Sch.* **the spur of birds;** *ṕyi-na, Cs.;* **behind;** *ṕyi-nas, Cs.,* **from behind;** **ṕi-nur-la** or **ṕi-log-la dúl-če**, to walk backward, *W.*; *ṕyi-γnón yoṅ,* pursuing he comes rapidly near, *Mil.*; *ṕyi mig ltá-ba,* to look round (back), *Glr.*, *ṕyi mig ma ltá-bar,* without looking round; *ṕyi mig čig γzigs-pas,* resp. just looking round (back), *Mil.*; **ṕi (mig) lóg-te ltá-če** *W.* id. — *ṕyi-ṕyir,* behind, following, e.g. *ṕyi*

ˏgró-ba, to walk behind or after another person, *Pth.* — *ṗyi ˏbrán Lex.* (also *mčis-brán*), spouse, wife. — *ṗyi-ma*, the posterior *Schr.*(?) — *ṗyi-bžin* adv. and postp., **after**; *ˏgró-ba, ˏbrán-ba*, frq.; *ri-dags-kyi ṗyi-bžin rgyúg-pa*, to pursue game, deer; *ṗyir-bžin*, id.; *ṗyi-la*, later lit. and *C.*, id.; . . . *kyi ṗyi-bžin ṗyin-pa, ˏón-ba, ˏgró-ba*, to go after; v. also *ṗyir* and *ṗyis*.

II. **after**; adv.: *sna-ṗyi*, sooner and later; also adj.: the former, the latter; the earlier, the later; *ˏdi-ṗyi* sc. *tse*, the present and the future life; frq.; *dus ṗyi žig-na*, at a later period, some time afterwards *Dzl.*; *deï ṗyi nyin* on the following day *Dzl.*; *nyi-ma deï ṗyi de nyin kó-na*, id., *Tar.* — *ṗyi-dgra* v. *dgra.* — *ṗyi-čad* = *ṗyin-čad* q.v. — *ṗyi-tog W.*, the later part of the afternoon. — *ṗyi-dro, ṗyi-ro* (also *Mil.*) *W.*, gen. **ṗi-tog, ṗi-ro** id., also evening. — *ṗyi-nas*, **in future,** in time to come, *Mil.* — *ṗyi-ṗréd Tar.*: *nyi-ma ṗyi-ṗred-kyi bar-du Schf.*, until sunset; *Schr.*: evening. — *ṗyi-ṗyág byéd-pa*, to greet for the last time, to bid farewell, to take leave. — *ṗyi-ma* adj.: **later, subsequent,** following, *sná-ma ma žu ṗyi-ma zá-ba*, not having digested the first (meal), to eat (consecutive) additional quantities *Lt.*; *ṗyi-ma ṗyi-ma*, each following one, every one consecutive in a series, *S.g.* and elsewh.; *nyál-bai ṗyi-ma*, the last going to bed, *Mil.*; *ṗyi-ma-rnams*, the later ones, the moderns, frq. — *ṗyi-mo* adj. **late,** *da (nyi-ma) ṗyi-mór son dúg-pas*, it having grown late (in the day) *Mil.*; **'i go ṗi-mo ṗe dug**, this door is not opened until later (in the day), *W.* **ṗi-mo čó(s)-kan-ni tá-gir**, the last baked, newest bread, *W.* — *ṗyi-rabs*, the later generation, posterity. Cf. *ṗyin, ṗyis.*

III. **outside,** *ṗyiï žin*, the field outside, as a third part of the property, exclusive of cattle and money (cf. *sgo* init.); *ṗyii só-nam*, husbandry, farming *Glr.*; *ṗyii-rgya-mtso*, the outer sea, the ocean, *Glr.*; *ṗyii mi Dzl.* (Ms.), people from abroad, other, strange people, not belonging to the family, *mgrón-nam ṗyi-mi-dag ˎóns-na*, if (when) guests or strangers come, *Dzl.*; *ṗyi-na*, **out of doors, abroad;** *ṗyi-nas*, from without, from abroad; *ṗyi-ru, ṗyir*, **out** (proceeding from the interior of a place to the exterior), less frq., v. *ṗyi-rol*; *ṗyi-la*, id., *B.* and *C.* frq. *ṗyi-kyóg Sch.*: with knees bent outward. — *ṗyi-glin* v. *rgya-ṗi-lin* under *rgya* comp.; *ṗyi-dgrá* v. *dgra.* — **ṗi-(s)ta-la* and *-ru**. *W.* for *ṗyi-ról-na* etc.; **ṗi-stu-la čá-če**, euphemist. for 'going to the water-closet'. — *ṗyi-nán*, **the outside** and **inside** **ṗi nan lóg-če**, *W.*, *bsgyúr-ba*, *Schr.* to turn inside out, e.g. a bag; *lčágs-kyi sgróm la-sógs-pa sgrom ṗyi nan rim-pa bdun tsam* an iron box (coffin) and moreover a series of 7 boxes one within the other *Tar.* 28 *ṗyi nan gnyis-ka smín-pa*, ripe both as to the outside and inside, *Dzl.*; *ṗyi nan gtsan*, pure as to thought and action. With respect to religion, this expression generally denotes the difference between Non-Buddhism — or in a more limited sense Brahmanism — and Buddhism; frequently *gsan* is added as a third item, being explained by: *ṗyi lus nan nag gsán-ba yid*, which explanation however is insufficient, e.g. in the passage: *čos ṗyi nan gsan Pth.*, in which moreover merely a classification within the Buddhist religion seems to be spoken of. Political distinctions are made in *Glr.*: *ṗyi nan bar gsúm-gyi byá-ba byéd-pai blón-po*, yet without sufficiently elucidating the subject. The terms *ṗyi ltu* and *nan lta, Glr.* fol. 89, as well as *ṗyi ltár-du* and *nan ltár-du, Pth.* p. 10 I am at a loss to explain. — *ṗyi-pa* 1. *B.* and col. **a Non-Buddhist,** more particularly **a Brahmanist,** also for *ṗyi-pai čos*, the doctrine of Brahma *ṗyi-pa-la dga Glr.* 2. *Chr. Prot.*: **heathen,** one that is neither a jew nor a Christian. — *ṗyi-yul* 1. *Sch.* **foreign country.** 2. *ṗyi snán-bai yul*, **the external world,** opp. to: *nán-gi sems, Mil.* — *ṗyi-rol*, 1. **the outside,** *mál-gyi ṗyi-rol*, the outside of the bed, *Glr.*; *ṗyi-rol-na, -tu, -nas*, in *B.* gen. for *ṗyi-na, -ru, -nas*; adv. outside, out of doors, out, from without; postp. on the outside before (the door), (he was turned) out of (the house), (he comes) from without (the village), frq.: *ṗi-log* *W.* id.; **čág-ri ṗi-log la**, outside before the (garden) wall. 2. mystic: *ɣdon bgegs ṗyi-rol-tu ˳dzin-pa*, to believe goblins and demons to be really **existing in the outer world** *Mil.* — *ṗyi-sa*, **excrements** *S.g.*; the supposed food of certain demons *Thgy.* — *ṗyi-lha?*

IV. *ṗyi-la*, **on account of**, v. *ṗyir*.

ཕྱི་ལྕག་ *ṗyi-lċág*, *Cs.*; a **blow** with the side of the hand.

ཕྱི་ཐན་ *ṗyi-ṫán*, **threat, menace**, *Mil. nt.*

ཕྱི་བདར་ (or བརྡར་) བྱེད་པ་ *ṗyi-bdár* (or *brdar*) *byéd-pa*, **to clean, to cleanse** *Dzl.* and elsewh.; *byád-kyi ṗyi-bdár bsól-nas kyaṅ* though you do not wash your face *Mil.*

ཕྱི་ཕུར་ *ṗyi-ṗúr*, a kind of **ornament**, similar to *ṗan*.

ཕྱི་བ་ *ṗyi-ba S.g.*, *˳ṗyi-ba Lt.*, 1. the large **marmot** of the highlands of Asia, Arctomys Boibak. — 2. v. *˳byi-ba*.

ཕྱི་མོ་ *ṗyi-mo*, I. col. *ǎ-ṗyi*, *ǎ-pi*, **grandmother**, *Cs.* II. v. *ṗyi* II.

ཕྱིང་པ་ *Pur.* *ṗyiṅ-pa*; *Ld., Lh.* *ṗiṅ-pa*, elsewh. *čiṅ-pa*, **felt**, *˳déd-pa*, to make felt, to mill, to full *Sch.*; *ṗyiṅ-gúr*, felt-tent, a Tartar hut; *ṗyiṅ-stán*, felt-carpet, felt-covering; *ṗyiṅ-déb Sch.*: a wrapper or cover made of felt.

ཕྱིད་ *ṗyid* = *ṗyi*, **after, following**; *ṗyid-nyin*, the day after to-morrow, *Cs.*

ཕྱིད་པ་ *ṗyid-pa* I. (v. *ṗyi* ni f.) **to retard, prolong, maintain**, with *ṫse*: to maintain one's life, to earn a livelihood, *W.* e.g. *gár-ra ċó-te* or *čós-si náṅ-ne ṫse ṗid-ċe*, to maintain one's self as a smith, or by religion, (being a Lama). — II. **to freeze**, *káṅ-pa ṗid-soṅ*, the foot is frozen, suffering from chilblains; *mig ṗid soṅ*, the eyes are inflamed, snow-blind, *W.* (*C.* *či*). — III. v. *˳ṗyid*; *byid*.

ཕྱིན་ *ṗyin* for *ṗyi*, in certain phrases: 1. *ṗyin-čád*, *-ċád*, **later, afterwards**, *ṗyin-čád sdom*, bound over for the time to come, e.g. not to do a thing again; *da ṗyin-čád*, from the present moment, from henceforth, frq.; *˳di ṗyin*, id.; *de ṗyin-čád*, rarely *de ṗyin-nas*, *Tar.* 57, 2 since, since that time, ever since. — 2. **outside**, *ṗyin rtsig-pa méd-de* as there was no wall outside *Glr.*; *ṗyin-dgrá* a foreign enemy *Glr.*; *ṗyin-las* outward business, foreign affairs *Dzl.*

ཕྱིན་ཅི་ལོག་ *ṗyin-ċi-lóg*, anything **wrong, incorrect, deceptive, fallacious; perversity**; *ṗyin-ċi-lóg-gis bslád-de* corrupt, depraved by perversity *Dzl.*; *ṗyin-ċi ma lóg-pao* it is infallible (of a spell), synon. to *bdén-pa*; *ltá-ba ṗyin-ċi ma lóg-pa* correct view, opinion *Pth.*; *ṗyin-ċi-lóg-tu stón-pa* to teach a false doctrine; *blo ṗyin-ċi ma lóg-par*, with a never erring mind *Mil.*

ཕྱིན་པ་ *ṗyin-pa* I. *B., C.* *čin-pa*, *Sp.* *ṗin-pa*, little used in *W.*: 1. **to come, to get to, advance, arrive**; *lam ṗyed tsám-du*, having got about midway, *Dzl.*; *der ṗyin-pa daṅ*, frq.; *ču ṗrág-pa tsám-du ṗyin-to*, the water reached up to his shoulders, *Dzl.*; *ṗin-na* *Sp.*, is he arrived? *sbyin-pai ṗá-rol ṗyin*, that goes farther than alms-giving, surpasses it, *Glr.*: *dpag-ṫsád lṅar ṗyin-pa*, to be five miles in length, *Dzl.* — 2. **to go, to proceed**, *snón-la ṗyin-pa*, *Pth.*; *ma ṗyin-par sleb*, without going, without moving from the place, he arrives at . . . *Mil.*; *bud-méd deï rtsar ma ṗyin*, he did not go to the woman (euphemist.) *Glr.*; *stab-stob-du naṅ-du ṗyin-te*, he went in, ran in, in a great hurry. (Probably the word is cog. to *ṗyi*, and therefore = *˳byúṅ-ba*, *˳ṫón-pa*.) — II. v. *˳byin-pa*.

ཕྱིར་ *ṗyir*; prop. the termin. of *ṗyi*: I. 1. adv. **back, towards the back, behind**; *ṗyir ˓óṅ-ba*, to come back, to return *Dzl.* and elsewh., frq.; also used in a special sense rel. to re-birth *lan-ɣċig ṗyir ˓óṅ-ba*, *ṗyir mi ˓óṅ-ba* v. *˳brás-bu(bźi)*; *ṗyir ˳gró-ba*, *ṗyir ˳dóṅ-ba* etc., id.; *ṗyir ˳dúg-pa*, to remain behind, at home, *Dzl.*; *ṗyir ˳jóg-pa*, to leave behind, at home, to lay aside, to lay up, *Dzl.*; **again** (*rursus*), *ṗyir láṅ-ba*, to get up again, after having fallen; *ṗyir ldóg-pa*, *lóg-pa*, to come back again, to return; *ṗyir ldóg-pai lam*, the way back, the return, *Dzl.*; *ṗyir mi ldóg-pa*, the not taking place of relapses, the prevention of them, *Lt.*; *p̔yir zlóg-pa,* to bring back, to draw off, to divert from; *p̔yir sós-par ₒgyúr-ba,* to return to life; *p̔yir sáṅs-nas,* having come to himself again, having recovered, *Dzl.*; *p̔yir má-la smrás-pa,* he replied to his mother, *Dzl.*; *p̔yir-lóg skyón-pa,* to make one ride backward, with the face to the horse's tail. — 2. postp. e.g. **behind, after,** *ṅai p̔yir e' ₒgro Pth.,* will you follow me? come with me? instead of this more carelessly: *ṅa p̔yir Mil.*; *p̔yir-bžin = p̔yi-bžin* frq. —

II. **afterwards, hereafter,** at a later time *Thgy.*; *p̔yir ₒóṅ-ba,* to come too late *Dzl.*

III. **out,** *p̔yir-la* out (motion from an interior to an exterior place), *p̔yir t́ón-pa, ₒgró-ba, ₒdéṅ-ba, γšégs-pa* to go out, *skyúr-ba,* to cast out, *p̔yir bstán-nas,* turned inside out (the lining of a coat) *Glr.*; *p̔yir ₒbúd-pa Sch.*: 'to put out, to remove; to come to an end, to be completely exhausted'; *sgo p̔yir mi γtóṅ-ba,* not to let out at the door, to keep locked in or shut up *Pth.* In *C.* also *p̔yi-la* is used in this sense. — *p̔yir-žiṅ* acc. to *Lexx.* = भूयंस more (exceeding in number or degree).

IV. postp. c.g., also *p̔yir-du,* more rarely *p̔yir-na* (*W.* **p̔i-la**) **on account of,** 1. (propter) = **by** or **through,** *ċii p̔ir k̔yod di-ltar gyur,* whereby or through what have you got into this plight? *Dzl.*; without *k̔yod*: where does that come from? *Dzl.*; **i nad ċi p̔i-la yoṅs**, by what has this disease been caused? *W.*; *γnód-pai p̔yir-du,* because I have done you harm *Mil.* 2. **for, for the sake of** (*causa*), for the good or benefit of, from love to *Dzl.*; **for the purpose of,** *brtág-pai p̔yir-du,* in order to try or to prove *Glr.* Whether *p̔yir* with the infinitive, esp. of one-rooted verbs, is to be resolved by **because** or **in order that,** can be determined only by the context.

ཕྱིས་ *p̔yis* I. adv. **behind,** *p̔yis ni sgra ₒbyuṅ,* behind, i.e. behind your back, voices are heard; gen. with respect to time: **afterwards, later,** *p̔yis ₒbyúṅ-ba,* to arise, to follow, to come later *Wdṅ.*; also in reference to things past, of a later date than others that had happened before them *Glr.*; *p̔yis-nas kyaṅ,* **also in future, in after times** *Mil.*; *p̔yis-nyin,* on the following day (= *saṅ*) *Dzl.*; at some future time, some (future) day, *Dzl.*; *da p̔yis = da p̔yin-ċád Glr.*; *dus p̔yis = dus p̔yi žig-na,* subsequently, hereafter *Pth.*; *p̔yis skye-ba-méd-pa,* one that in future will not be re-born *Mil.*; on the other hand: *p̔yis skyes bu Sch.,* a son born after the death of his father; *sú-bas kyaṅ p̔yis* last of all *Dzl.*; *p̔yis-pa* v. *ₒp̔yi-ba* (I.); it is also construed like a sbst.: ... *t́ob-pai p̔yis šig-na,* at a time subsequent to his having obtained, = after he had obtained *Tar.* — II. sbst. in compounds: **clout, rag, duster, cloth,** *sná-p̔yis, lág-p̔yis, p̔yág-p̔yis*; *p̔yis-pa,* v. *ₒp̔yi-ba* II.

ཕྱུག་པ་ *p̔yúg-pa* adj. **rich,** also fig.: *yón-tan du-mai dpál-gyis p̔yúg-par šog,* may I grow rich in the splendour of numerous accomplishments! *p̔yúg-po,* adj. **rich,** sbst. **a rich man,** *p̔yúg-po ċén-po žig* a rich nobleman *Mil.*; *p̔yúg-mo* a rich lady; *p̔yug-k̔yád* riches, wealth, opulence *Dzl.*; *p̔yúg-par ₒgyúr-ba* to grow rich, *byéd-pa* to make rich; *p̔yug-dbúl* rich and poor; *p̔yug dbul med* no difference between rich and poor *Dzl.*

ཕྱུགས་ *p̔yugs,* **cattle,** *sgoi p̔yugs* v. *sgo*; *p̔yugs ₒtsó-ba* to tend cattle *Glr.*; *p̔yúgs-kyi šiṅ-rta Cs.,* a bullock cart; *p̔yúgs-nad* disease of cattle, murrain; *nor-p̔yúgs,* chattels, all kinds of property *Dzl.*

ཕྱུར་བུ་ *p̔yúr-bu Sch.* **hay-rick, shock of sheaves, heap of sticks** (*Schr. ₒp̔yúr-ba,* to heap up).

ཕྱེ་ *p̔ye W.* **p̔e**, resp. *γsáṅ-p̔ye, žib,* 1. **flour, meal,** esp. 2. **flour of parched barley,** = *rtsám-pa.* — 3. for *p̔yé-ma,* **dust, powder** etc.; *p̔ye ₒtág-pa, tság-pa,* to grind corn to flour; to sieve; *p̔yer ₒtág-pa,* to reduce to flour. — 4. v. *ₒbyéd-pa.* — *rgyágs-p̔ye* flour as provision for a journey *Glr.*; **ṅán-p̔e** *W.* = *rtsám-pa*; also parched meal. *lċágs-p̔ye* iron filings; *rdó-p̔ye,* stone reduced to powder, small particles of stone; *spós-p̔ye, tsándan-gyi p̔yé-ma,* sandlewood powder, fumigating powder; *búg-ṗyé* wheat flour; *brág-ṗye* small fragments of stone, produced by stone-cutting *Glr.*; *šiṅ-ṗye* saw-dust; *γsér-ṗye* gold-dust; *ṗye-k̔ug* flour-bag; *ṗye-sgye* flour sack; *Cs.*: 'a double pouch for meal'; *ṗye-snód*, flour-tub; *ṗye-ṗór Cs.* a box for meal; *ṗye-ṗád*, flour-bag; *ṗye-baṅ*, flour-store; *ṗyé-ma*, dust, powder; saw-dust, filings etc.; *ṗyé-mar* termin. of *ṗyé-ma*; *ṗye-már* (*Hindi* घीसत्तू) flour roasted with melted butter, sweetened with sugar, considered a dainty.

ཕྱེ་མ་ལེབ་ *ṗye-ma-léb Lex*, **ṗe-ma-leb-tsé** — *W.*, **butterfly.**

ཕྱེད་ *ṗyed* I. **half;** *ṗyed-daṅ-γnyis* ('which with an additional ½ would be = 2') **one and a half** etc.; *brgya-ṗrág ṗyed-daṅ-γsúm*, two hundred and fifty; **yáṅ-čé' C.*, **yáṅ-ṗed, ṗéd-di(saṅ) ṗed, ṗéd-yaṅ-ṗed** *W.* one fourth, a quarter; *yúṅ-ṗyed* one eighth (little used); *mi-ṗyéd* half a man, also used for woman *Pth.* (n.f.); *zla-ṗyéd* v *zlá-ba*; *zla-ba-ṗyéd-pa*, lasting half a month, e.g. a disease. — *ṗyéd-ka, -pa, -ma, Cs., ṗyéd-po Cs.* and vulg. one half; *ṗyéd-ma* also: partner to one half; *ₒdii náṅ-na ṅai ṗyéd-ma žig kyaṅ yód-de*, as I have still a partner in this business; *ṗyed-krúṅ*, half a *skyil-krúṅ* (q. v.), drawing in one leg, and stretching out the other *Glr.*; *ṗyed-gliṅ*, peninsula; *ṗyed-brgyád* = *ṗyed-daṅ-brgyad* hence sbst.: half a rupee, = 7½ points on the gold-steel-yard *C.*

II. v. *ₒbyed-pa.*

ཕྱེན་ *ṗyen* (vulg. *ṗen*), **wind, flatulence** *Med.*; *γtóṅ-ba*, to let go a wind; *ṗyen šor soṅ*, a wind has escaped (me etc.); *ṗyen-dbúgs Cs.*, id.; *ṗyén-dri*, a low, soft wind.

ཕྱོ་ཕྱོ་ *ṗyo-ṗyó*, **čo-čó zér-wa**, **to set on** or **at** (to set a dog at a person) *C.*

ཕྱོགས་ *ṗyogs* 1. **side, direction;** *ṗyogs gaṅ-nas* from whence? *ṗyogs der*, **there, thither,** in that direction; *yul dei ṗyógs-su* or *-la*) *soṅ*, proceed in the direction of yonder village; *ltág-pa* (for *-pai*) *ṗyógs-su Wdṅ.* towards the nape of the neck; *ṗyogs γčig-tu* or *-la* towards one side, in one direction; also for **together,** e.g. to sweep together, to heap together; vulgo also for **at the same time, at once;** *k̔yim-pai ṗyógs-su byin-pas*, bestowing on lay-men *Dzl.*; *čos ṗyógs-su γtóṅ-ba* to spend for pious purposes *Mil.*; in the same manner: *dge-bai ṗyógs-su*, to devote to benevolent designs *Mil.*; **for, in behalf of, for the benefit of:** *γtán-grogs ṗyógs-su ši-lčébs byéd-pa*, to die, to undergo death for the sake of husband or wife *Mil.*; in letters usually: *dé-ṗyogs-su*, there with you, *ₒdi-ṗyogs-su*, here with us. — 2. **quarter** of the heavens, **the cardinal points** of the horizon; *ṗyogs bži*, the four points of the compass; *ṗyogs bžir*, round about, in all directions; c. g. **round** (a person or place); *ṗyogs bži-nas*, from all sides; frequently also *ṗyogs bču*, the ten points of the compass are spoken of, which are the following: *šar, šar-lhó, lho, lho-núb, nub, nub-byáṅ, byaṅ, byaṅ-šár, steṅ-* and *ₒóg-ṗyogs* (Zenith and Nadir); *ṗyogs-skyóṅ, ṗyogs-skyoṅ-rgyál-po, lha čén-po ṗyogs-skyoṅ-ba bču* similar to *ǰig-rtén-skyoṅ* (v. *skyóṅ-ba*), yet ten in number; *rgya-gár-gyi šár-ṗyogs-na*, to the east of India; *rgya-gár šár-ṗyogs-pa-rnams*, the eastern Indians. — 3. *sa-ṗyogs*, **country, region, neighbourhood, part,** *dben-pai sa-ṗyógs*, lonely region, solitary part; *ǰigs pai sa-ṗyógs*, an unsafe country; *yul-ṗyógs* id., *ṅai sa-ṗyógs-na* in my country *Mil., C.* — 4. **part, party,** also *ṗyogs-ris*; *γžán-la ṗyogs ₒgyúr-ba*, to take another man's part, to side with a certain person *Thgy.*; *ṗyogs-(ris) byéd-pa* c. genit. *W.*, **čog-(ri) čó-če**, *ṗyogs ₒdzín-pa Tar.*, *ṗyogs tsam rig-pa Tar.* 119, 4 id.; *ṗyogs-méd* impartial, *sine ira et studio*, gen. in a Buddhist ascetic sense: indifferent to every thing; *ṗyógs-ča Mil.*, *ṗyógs-lhuṅ Lex.*, prob. also *ṗyógs-žen Tar.* 184, 22, partial, interested; *ṗyogs-čai rtóg-pa*, hesitation, scruples, arising from still feeling an interest in a thing *Mil.*; in a general sense it is used in: *ṗyogs-mtsúṅs-pa* **similar** *Wdṅ., Tar.*; *ṗyogs-mt̔un-du Tar.* 190, 16 ought to be rendered: **appropriate, suitable, adequate;** *ráṅ-ṗyogs* one's own party, *γžán-ṗyogs* the other or opposite party; *γnyén-ṗyogs* friends, *dgrá-ṗyogs* enemies; *dkár-ṗyogs* **the good,**

the well-disposed, esp. the good spirits, *nág-p̓yogs, sdíg-čan-gyi p̓yogs* **the bad, malicious,** esp. the evil spirits, devils. — 5. in popular language the word is used also with respect to time: **k̓a-san-stón-čogs** *Ld.*, **last autumn.**

ཕྱོགས་པ་ *p̓yógs-pa* I. vb. **to turn** vb.n., *čós-la* to turn to religion *Schr.*; *p̓yir p̓yógs-pa* to turn one's self back, to turn aside (*Schr. p̓yir p̓yógs-par byéd-pa*, to divert from, to dissuade from) *Tar.* 12, 14 28, 9. *ₒči-k̓ar p̓yógs-pa* turned to dying — near dying? *k̓ór-ba-la rgyáb-kyis p̓yógs-pa*, to turn one's back to the orb of transmigration; *mnón-du p̓yógs-pa*, **1. to be visible, to be evident, to be exposed to view** (?), *lho-nos-su mnón-du p̓yógs-pai brág-las ₒbyún-ba* growing on a surface rock on the south-side *Sambh.*; *don de mnón-du p̓yógs-par byá-bai p̓yir*, in order to bring this meaning to the light, to express it clearly *Gram.* (?). 2. **to be openly** or **evidently attached to, to adhere to** (?) *rgyúd-la* to a Tantra or treatise *Sambh.*

II. adj., sbst., **attached to, following; a partizan, an adherent.**

ཕྱོད་པ་ *p̓yod-pa Cs.* **progress**, *p̓yod čé-ba*, great progress; *Lex.*: *sa-p̓yod-če* v. *čod.*

ཕྱོར་ *p̓yor Mil.*, prob. for *mčor.*

ཕྲ་ *p̓ra*, *ₒp̓ra*, **ornament** (?), **jewel** (?) *p̓ra rgyág-pa, rgyáb-pa, ₒgód-pa, ₒdébs-pa, Sch.* also *p̓ras sprá-ba*, to insert an ornament of jewels, to stud with jewels; *rmog-la pad-ma-rā-gai p̓ra btáb-pa de*, this set of rubies on the helmet, this helmet studded with rubies *Glr.*; *rin-čén sna-ts̓ógs-kyis p̓ra bkód-pa Mil.*; *p̓ra-ts̓óm* border, trimming, *Lex.*

ཕྲ་རྒྱས་ *p̓ra-rgyás Was.* (241) = *bág-la nyál-ba*, **vanities**, i.e. passions, errors, erroneous notions.

ཕྲ་དོག་ *p̓ra-dóg* v. *p̓rag-dóg.*

ཕྲ་བ་ *p̓rá-ba* 1. v. *ₒp̓ra-ba.* — 2. *Lt.* a disease of children. — 3. adj., gen. *p̓rá-mo* (*Cs.* also *bo*) **thin, fine, minute,** opp. to *sbóm-po* q.v., *sbrul p̓rá-mo žig Tar.*; in a general sense, **little, small,** *séms-čan p̓rá-mo-rnáms*; *nú-p̓ra-mo*, little as to age, young, *Mil.*; **trifling, little, slight,** *rnám-rtog p̓rá-mo* slight scruples, *Mil.*; *rdzun p̓rá-mo*, a little lie, a fib, *Thgy.*; **t̓á-mo-ne t̓ón-wa, láb-pa**, to see, to inspect most accurately, to learn the minutest details, *C.*; **thin, high,** rel. to voice *W.*; *p̓ra-žib Lex.*, fine and exact; *šin-tu p̓rá-ba*, in reference to the doctrine of Buddha, implying prob. its subtilties. Cf. *p̓ran.*

ཕྲ་མ་ *p̓rá-ma*, **calumny, slander,** esp. through tell-tales and intermeddling persons *B.* and col.; *p̓rá-ma byéd-pa Dzl.*, *smrá-ba Cs.*, *j̓úg-pa B.* and *C.*, **čó-če** *W.*, resp. (when referring to a person of higher rank) *γsól-ba, žú-ba*, to calumniate, slander, vilify, blacken; *p̓rá-ma-mk̓an Cs.* calumniator, slanderer.

ཕྲ་མེན་ *p̓ra-mén*, **sorcery, witchcraft** *Schr.*; so prob. *Pth.*: *mi-dgos-pai p̓ra-mén-gyi nan-sngágs*, an evil magic spell of pernicious necromancy; *p̓ra-men-po* and *-pa* masc., *-mo* and *-ma* fem., necromancer, wizard, witch; *p̓ra-mén rdzá-ki* (for *dzo-gi*, योगिन्) id.

ཕྲ་མོ་ *p̓rá-mo*, v. *p̓rá-ba*; ཕྲ་ཤགས་ *p̓ra-šags*, v. *ₒp̓rá-ba.*

ཕྲག་ *p̓rag* provinc. also *dbrag*, *srag*, 1. **intermediate space, interstice, interval,** hence *p̓rág-tu* = *bár-du Thgy.*; **a hollow, ravine, defile;** *smin-p̓rág* v. *smín-ma.* — 2. after cardinal numbers it seems to correspond about to the Greek subst. termination *ας*: *bču-p̓rág* a decade, *brgya-p̓rág* a hundred (century), *ston-p̓rág* a thousand (chiliad), *brgya-p̓rág γčig*, *brgya-p̓rag bču*; *ston-p̓rág bži-bču-žig*, a number of forty thousand *Dzl.*; *bdun-p̓rág*, ἑβδομάς, week (recognized as a measure of time, but in common life not much in use).

ཕྲག་པ་ *p̓rág-pa*, 1. sbst., resp. *sku-p̓rág* **shoulder,** *p̓rág-pa-la ₒgél-ba Glr.*, *t̓ógs-pa Sambh.* to load on one's shoulder; *grógs-poi p̓rág-pa-la ₒdzég-pa*, to mount the shoulder of one's companion *Dzl.*; **upper arm,** *p̓rág-pa γnyis-kyi ša Dzl.*, *p̓rag-gón*

Lt. id. — 2. vb., also *ₒṗrág-pa*, **to envy, to grudge,** *Cs.*; *ṗrag-dóg, ṗra-dóg,* the envy, *ṗrag-dog skye* envy is stirring within me, I envy, frq.; *ṗrag-dóg-čan*, envious, grudging, jealous *Pth.*

ཕྲང་ *ṗraṅ*, v. *ₒṗraṅ.*

ཕྲད་ *ṗrad, ṫsig-ṗrád, ṗrád-kyi yi-ge,* **particle,** e.g. *rnám-dbye-ṗrad* the signs of the cases, *kyi, la* etc.

ཕྲད་པ་ *ṗrád-pa* v. *ₒṗrád-pa*; *ṗrád-po* for *k̇rád-po Wdṅ.*

ཕྲན, ཕྲན་བུ *ṗran, ṗrán-bu,* (*Ts.* also *ṗrán-te*) = *ṗrá-mo*, **little, small, trifling,** yet more in particular phrases, and less used in books, than in common life, esp. in *C.*: **rin ṭém-bhu ṭe'-dhe** (lit.: *spraṅ-de*) having paid, spent a trifle; **žú-ba ṭém-bhu žig** a small request; **ṭem-bhu čig** a little bit *C.*; as sbst.: 1. **part of the body** (whether in a general or a more particular sense, I have not been able to ascertain), in medical writings the *ṗran-bui nad* form a class of their own; *yan-lág-gi ṗran yčód-pa Glr.*, to maim, to mutilate parts of the body (not necessarily to castrate *Sch.*). — 2. **knives** and other small instruments used in surgery *Med.* — 3. *ṗran-ráṅ* in the polite epistolary style the person of the writer, 'my own little self', 'your humble servant'; *ṗrán-la ráṅ-gi* = to me my . . ., inst. of: *ṅá-la ṅa-ráṅ-gi.* — *ṗran-ṫségs,* **trifles, minor matters;** *ₒdúl-ba ṗran-ṫségs-kyi yži* the minutiae of religious discipline, Dulva.

ཕྲན་རྩག *ṗran-rtsáq, ṗran-ne-rtsag-tsi* stated to be = *ṗyin-či-lóg Ld.*

ཕྲན་ཚེགས་ *ṗran-ṫségs* v. *ṗrán-bu* extr.

ཕྲལ་ *ṗral* v. *ṗrál-ba*; ཕྲི་བ་ *ṗri-ba* v. *ₒṗri-ba*; ཕྲིད་ *ṗrid* v. *sbríd-pa.*

ཕྲིན་ *ṗrin*, *ₒṗrin*, **news, tidings, intelligence, message,** *ṗrin bzáṅ-po*, good tidings, favourable accounts; *ṗrin-bkur-mk̇an*, messenger, vulgo; *ṗrin skúr-ba, spriṅ-ba* to send word, information, *k̇yér-ba*, to bring tidings, intelligence; *spród-pa, ₒṗród-pa* to deliver; *smrá-ba, rjód-pa, byéd-pa* to report, to deliver messages orally; to superiors: *ysól-ba, žú-ba*; to inferiors: *sgó-ba, ysúṅ-ba; k̇ó-boi ṗrin yaṅ dé-la byós šig* deliver a message to him also from me *Dzl.*; *ṗrin-ytam* message, report *Cs.*; *ṗrin-pa* messenger; newsmonger *Cs.*; *ṗrin-bzáṅ* gospel *Chr. Prot.*; *ṗrin-yig* letter, epistle; *ṗrin-lán* answer to a message. — *ṗrin-lás* (*W.* **čag-lás**) 1. resp. for *las* **labour, business; deed, work,** frq.; *ráb-tu-ynás-pai ṗrin-las mdzad* (the Buddhas) performed the work of consecrating *Glr.*; *ṗrin-lás rnam bži* the same as *ži-rgyas-dbaṅ-drág-gi ṗrin-lás Glr.*, v. explanation under *ži-ba*; *ṗrin-lás čól-ba, ṗrin-bčól byéd-pa* ccdpar. to commit a thing to another person's care or trust, e.g. before going on a journey; in reference to gods: to recommend to their protection or blessing *Glr.* and elsewh. — 2. po. for *ṗrin-lás-pa* **commissary** *Glr.*, where Avalokitesvara is called *ṗrin-lás* of all Buddhas. — 3. **efficiency, power** *Mil.*

ཕྲུ་གུ *ṗrú-gu* v. *ṗrug.*

ཕྲུ་བ་ *ṗrú-ba, ₒṗrú-ba* = *k̇óg-ma* **earthen pot, pan, stew-pan.**

ཕྲུ་མ་ *ṗrú-ma, ₒṗrú-ma* 1. **uterus, matrix of animals,** or acc. to *Cs.* merely the integuments of the eggs; acc. to some, also **the urinary bladder.** — 2. **encampment,** = *dmag-sgár Lex.*

ཕྲུག *ṗrug* 1. in compounds for *ṗrúg-gu, ṗrú-gu* **child, a young one** (of animals); *ṗrúg-gu-mo* a little girl *Cs.*; *ṗrúg-gu skyéd-pa* to beget children, *ysó-ba* to rear, to bring up (children); *ṗrúg-gu skye* a child is born; *šor* a miscarriage, abortion, takes place; *ṗrúg-gui dus* childhood; *dá-ṗrug* orphan; *nal-ṗrug* bastard; *gláṅ-ṗrug* the young one of an elephant; *séṅ-ṗrug* a lion's cub etc.; metaph. of disciples and subalterns: *ṫsoṅ-ṗrúg* the merchants of a caravan in their relationship to their leader *ṫsoṅ-dpón.* — 2. **fine cloth** or **woollen stuffs** *Wts.*, *snam-ṗrúg* id., *dbus-ṗrug* woollen goods from Ü *Mil.*

ཕྲུགས་ *ṗrugs* one day with the night, a period of 24 hours, — but this signification does not hold good in every case.

ཕྲུད་གཞོང་ *ṗrud-γžoṅ* v. *γžoṅ-pa.*

ཕྲུམ་ *ṗrum Lt* and *S.g.? prum-rús* **cartilage, gristle.**

ཕྲུམ་ཕྲུམ་ *ṗrum-ṗrum Sik.* = *ṗum-ṗum*

ཕྲེའུ་ *ṗreu Cs.* = *ṗrá-mo.*

ཕྲེང་བ་ *ṗréṅ-ba* v. *˳ṗréṅ-ba.*

ཕྲེད་ *ṗred, ˳ṗred,* **cross, transverse; across, athwart, obliquely;** *ṗréd-du,* col. **ṭ éd-ṭ éd-la**, crossways, in a cross direction; *ṗréd-lam,* a path (horizontal or inclined) leading along the side of a mountain, (cf. on the other hand *˳ṗraṅ*); *ṗred-γtán* bolt or bar of a gate; **ṭ éd-la ḍáṅ-po**, horizontal *W.*

ཕྲོ་བོ་ *ṗró-bo* something like: **a child's frock** or **chemise** *Ld.* (?)

ཕྲོག་ *ṗrog* etc. v. *˳ṗrog*; ཕྲོབ་, ཕྲོལ་ *ṗrob, ṗrol* v. *˳ṗrob, ˳ṗrol.*

ཕྲོས་ *ṗros* v. *˳ṗró-ba.*

འཕག་པ་ *˳ṗág-pa,* pf. *˳ṗags,* 1. **to rise, to be raised,** e.g. a post or stake raised by the frost; **to soar up,** to fly up to heaven, a miraculous feat often performed by the saints of legends, *Dzl.* and elsewh.; of rays of light, *Dzl.* and elsewh.; fig.: to be higher, more elevated, *deï stéṅ-du* (or *dé-las*) *dpag-tsád brgyad-k̔ri* (or more accurately *k̔ris*) *˳ṗágs-so Glr., Pth.,* (this region) lies by 80000 miles higher than that *Stg.*; **to grow larger, longer,** of the apparent lengthening of the teeth when aching *W.*; of horses: **to rear, to rise up** on the hind-legs; more particularly of the deifying of saints; thus the demi-god-like king Srontsansgampo in his farewell speech says: *k̔yed kun ˳ṗágs-pai byin-rlabs yin* I am the divine instrument of your elevation (your elevation-blessing), he who will effect your ascent to heaven or deification; part. pf. *˳ṗágs-pa* (*Ssk.* आर्य), **sublime, exalted, raised above,** *ṗál-las ˳ṗágs-par bzáṅ-ba* a more than ordinary beauty *Dzl.*; *γžan-pas ˳ṗágs-par gyúr-to* he far excelled others *Dzl.*; *k̔yád-(par) ˳ṗags-(pa),* **distinguished, excellent, glorious,** *yúl-las k̔yad-˳ṗags rgya-gar-yul* India, the most glorious country; *nór-sna k̔yád-par ˳ṗágs-pa brgyai ˳búl-ba* an offering of a hundred of the most costly kinds of jewels *Pth.*; esp. in reference to holy persons, things, places etc.; title of saints, and teachers of religion, with the fem. *˳ṗágs-ma; ˳ṗágs-pa* 'par excellence' is Avalokitesvara, in *W.* esp. the one, that has his throne at Triloknath in Chamba, v. *re-˳ṗágs*; the word is also frq. used as an epithet, placed at the head of the title-pages of religious writings; lastly it is a name of common persons. — *˳ṗágs-pai nor bdun* the seven treasures of the saints: *sbyin-pa, tsúl-k̔rims, dád-pa* and the like *Mil.* — *˳ṗágs(-pai) yul* 1. elevated country, highland. 2. the holy land of the Buddhists, the tracts of the middle Ganges; *˳ṗags-pai skad,* the Sanskrit language *Lex.* — *˳ṗags-rgyal Tar.* and elsewh. = उज्जयिनी *Schf.*, town and district of Ujain. — 2. the word is stated to imply also **to play, to joke, to make sport** *C.*

འཕང་ *˳ṗaṅ* 1. v. *ṗaṅ* I. — 2. also *˳ṗaṅs, dpaṅs, spaṅs,* **height,** *˳ṗáṅ-du, ˳ṗáṅs-su* in height; *k̔ri-˳ṗaṅ* v. *k̔ri, go-˳ṗaṅ* v. *go*; *γnam-˳ṗaṅ,* the height of the heavens *Lex., Mil.*; *dbu-˳ṗaṅ* fig. highness, sublimity, *dkon-mčóg-gi dbu-˳ṗáṅ smád-pa* to lower, to detract from the sublimity of God (v. *dkon-mčog*), to blaspheme God *Domaṅ*; *˳ṗaṅs-mtó* high *Dzl.*; *˳ṗáṅs-mto-ba, ˳ṗaṅs-mton-dmán* relative height *Dzl.*

འཕང་བ་ *˳ṗáṅ-ba* fut., *˳ṗaṅs-pa* pf. of. *˳ṗén-pa.*

འཕངས་པ་ *˳ṗáṅs-pa* 1. frq. for *ṗáṅs-pa* **to spare, to save** *Dzl.*; kindly and carefully to protect from harm, e.g. a drunken Lama *Thgy.*; hence prob. the version प्रेयंस; *˳ṗaṅs-méd γtóṅ-sems-ldan* liberal, bounteous, without restriction *S.g.* — 2. *Glr.* also for *˳ṗóṅs-pa* provinc.

འཕན་ *˳ṗan* I. v. *ṗan* (I). — II. *˳ṗán-yul Glr., ˳ṗán-po Huc* II, 242; name of the nearest alpine valley north of Lhasa, the inhabitants of which are said to speak an indistinct dialect.

འཕམ་པ་ ₒṗám-pa, pf. ṗam, opp. to *rgyál-ba* **to be beaten, conquered, to come off a loser, to get the worst of,** *ygyúl(-las)* in battle *Dzl.*; *lha-ma-yin-las* by the Asuras *Dom.*; in law-suits, in traffic etc.; *ₒṗám-par ₒgyúr-ba B.*, **ṗam dó-wa* C.* id ; also with *ṗam*, as if it were a sbst.: **ṗam kúr-wa* C.* to put up with, to bear a loss, damage, defeat; *ₒṗam bláṅ-ba Glr., Pth.* prob. id.; *ₒṗám-par byéd-pa* to beat, to defeat, to conquer, *rgyá-rnams ₒṗám-par byas* he conquered the Chinese *Glr.*; *rás-pas bón-po čós-kyis ṗám-byas-te* Raspa overcoming the Bonpo by the doctrine of Buddha (v. *čos* 3.) *Mil.*; **ṗam čúg-če* or *kál-če*, W.* id.; *ṗam ṗog soṅ* I have met with a loss, I suffered damage, opp. to *gyal tob soṅ*; *ṗam-rgyál ma bsrés-na* if one is not inclined now for a serious struggle, will not stand the chance of... *Mil.*; *yid-ₒṗám-pa Mil.*, **sems ṗám-po* C.* dejection; *yid-ₒṗám-ma* a low-spirited, dejected woman *Mil.*; *ṗám-pa Glr.*, *ṗám-po* the vanquished etc.; **ṗam-po ṅo-lèn có-če* W.* to give in, to ask pardon; *mi-ₒṗám* 1. **invincible.** 2. **a man's name.** 3. *mi-ₒṗam mgón-po Zam.*, also *mi-ₒṗám čós-kyi rje* is stated to be = *ₒjam-dbyáṅs.*

འཕར་ ₒṗar *Cs.* in compounds: **board,** *sgo-ₒṗar* board or leaf of a door.

འཕར་བ་ ₒṗár-ba I. sbst. v. *ṗár-ba.*

II. vb. (vb. n. to *spór-ba*) 1. **to rebound,** of stones, **bar-náṅ-la* W.* **to splash up,** of water, **to fly up,** of sparks; **to leap, to bound, to throb,** of the veins, *rtsa ₒṗar*, the pulse is beating; **ṗar tá-če* W.*, to feel one's pulse; **nyiṅ-ka ṗar dug** his heart is throbbing, palpitating; **ṗár-ra rag** I have heart-throbbing (v. *rag*); *ₒṗár-ₒṗro čad* v. *ₒṗró-ba* 2; *sá-la ₒṗár-ba*, **to fidget, to be restless, to jump,** from fear *Pth.*; *pár-gyis ₒṗár-ba Lex.* prob. the same as *ₒṗár-ba.* — 2. *Cs.* **to be raised, elevated, promoted, advanced.**

འཕར་མ་ ₒṗár-ma, *Sch.* **'double, manifold'**; *brgya-ₒṗar-ma, Sch.* 'more than hundred'.

འཕལ་ག་ ₒṗál-ga *Cs.*, **incision, indentation, notch.**

འཕིག་པ་ ₒṗig-pa, *ṗig-pa*, pf. *ₒṗigs Sch.* = *ₒbig(s)-pa.*

འཕིར་བ་ ₒṗir-ba *Ts.* = *ₒṗúr-ba*, **to fly.**

འཕུག་པ་ ₒṗúg-pa *Sch.* = *ₒbúg(s)-pa* (?).

འཕུང་བ་ ₒṗúṅ-ba, pf. *ṗuṅ*, **to sink, to begin to decay, to be in declining circumstances, to get into misery,** either by one's own fault, or that of others (opp. to *tséṅ-ba*) *Glr.* and elsewh.; *bód-yul ₒṗúṅ-bai las* a deed to the detriment of Tibet *Glr.*; in a similar manner *bód-yul ₒṗúṅ-bai ṗuṅ-góṅ*, mischievous conjurers in order to inflict an injury on Tibet *Ld.-Glr. Schl.* 21, b; *mgár-gyis rgyá-yul ṗúṅ-bar byás-pa-rnams drán-nas*, remembering the calamities brought on China by Mgar *Glr.*; *ₒṗuṅ-bar ₒgyúr-ba B.*, **ṗúṅ-du dó-wa* C.*, **ṗuṅ čá-če* W.*, to be ruined, to perish, *ₒṗuṅ-bar byed-pa B.*, *ₒṗúṅ-la sbyór-ba Mil.*, prob. also *ytóṅ-ba*, *ₒjúg-pa* to ruin, to undo *Pth.*; *raṅ-ₒṗúṅ* having been reduced by one's own fault; *ₒṗuṅ-dkrol* or *krol* **the decay of fortune, ruin, destruction** *Mil.* and elsewh.; *ₒṗuṅ-yži* cause, occasion of decay *Mil.*

འཕུད་པ་ ₒṗúd-pa **to lay aside, to put away, to separate,** = *ₒbúd-pa Cs.* (?), *súg-pa ₒṗúd-pa*, to clear, to part the flour from the bran, to sieve *Sch.* (?)

འཕུབ་པ་ ₒṗúb-pa = *ₒbúb-pa* **to cover with a roof** *Sch.* (?)

འཕུར་བ་ ₒṗúr-ba, pf. *ṗur*, 1. **to fly;** *púr-gyis ₒṗúr-ba Lex.*, prob. id.; cf. *ṗár-ba.* — 2. **to wrap up, envelop, muffle up;** *Dzl.* ༢༡༦, 10: *rin-po-če gós-kyi mtá-mar* the gem into the skirt of the coat, and likewise *Dzl.* ༢༠༧, 13 read: *gós-mtar ṗúr-te*, inst. of *byúṅ-ste*; *mgo gós-kyis Mil.* (col. not used). — 3. = *mnyéd-pa* **to rub with the hand,** e.g. linen in washing, leather in tanning *Glr.*; to scratch (softly) *C.*

འཕུལ་(ཡིག) ₒṗul(-yig) **prefix,** *de sogs da-yig ǵás-ₒṗul-čan*, these and others have *d* with the prefix *g*: *bás-ₒṗul-kao* words beginning with *k* with the prefix *b*; *bá-ýis ₒṗúl-bai sla*, viz. *bsla ...*; *das-ₒṗul-méd* these receive no *d* as prefix; *sa-*

ra-lá-rnams ₒp̓úl-tsul ni the manner in which prefixes are joined with words beginning with s, r or l; rkyaṅ-ₒp̓ul words beginning with a simple consonant (to which also ya-, ra-, and la-tags are reckoned), preceded by a prefix; brtsegs-ₒp̓ul, words beginning with two consonants and a prefix e.g. bska Gram.

འཕུལ་བ་ ₒp̓úl-ba I. v. the preceding article. — II. vb. 1. = ₒbúl-ba, **to give.** — 2. **to push, to jostle;** *p̓ul-túg gyáb-ċe*, to push with the fist, with the trunk, (of elephants) etc., W.; grú-moi ₒp̓ul-rdeg ċig byéd-pa, to jostle with the elbow Mil.; vulgo *p̓ul-dag or t̓ug* W., *ₒp̓ul-tsúg* C.

འཕེག་ ₒp̓eg v. p̓eg.

འཕེན་པ་ ₒp̓en-pa pf. ₒp̓aṅs, fut. (and frq. for the pres.) ₒp̓aṅ, imp. p̓oṅ, p̓aṅs, 1. **to throw, to cast, to fling;** nám-mk̓a-la into the air Dzl.; k̓ór-bar, to throw into the orb of transmigration Mil.; dmyál-bar, to cast into hell Thgy.; *k̓a pán-ċe*, to shovel snow (out of the road, from the roof); *p̓áṅ-te bór-ra tsig-te bor* am I to throw down the wood, or pile it up? W.; *pu p̓áṅ-ċe* to cast the hair W.; hence ₒp̓aṅ, spindle, and ₒp̓én-siṅ, acc. to Sch., a weaver's shuttle (it being flung). — 2. **to fire off, to discharge, to let fly,** mda, an arrow, γžan-la, at another Dzl.; ₒp̓eṅ-duṅ dart, javelin Stg.; **to shoot,** ₒp̓en-mi šés-pa, W. *p̓aṅ-mi-šes-k̓an*, one that does not know how to shoot. — 3. Sch. ₒp̓en-pa btaṅ-ba '**to intend, to have a mind, to think upon, to consider**', (yet in the only passage, in which I met with the word, in Thgr., the above meaning does not seem applicable).

འཕེལ་བ་ ₒp̓él-ba I. vb. pf. p̓el (ཕེལ) vb. n. to spél-ba, opp. to ₒgríb-pa, 1. **to increase, augment, multiply, enlarge,** frq.; *sum lan nyi-la tsam p̓el* how many are two times three? W.; ₒp̓el-ₒgrib-kyi dbáṅ-gis in consequence of the increase and decrease Gram.; ₒp̓el-ₒgrib-nád, prob. diseases arising from an excess or deficiency of humours Wdṅ. — 2. **to improve, to grow better,** bsam-γtán or tugs-dám ₒp̓él-ba γin meditation has improved, has proceeded better Mil. — II. sbst., Sch. also ₒp̓él-ka, 1. **increase.** 2. **development** S.g.

འཕོ་བ་ ₒp̓ó-ba pf. and imp. ₒp̓os, prop. intrans. to spó-ba, = γnas-spó-ba; 1. **to change place, shift, migrate** frq.; myur-du ₒp̓os-šig, go speedily elsewhere! Dzl.; in a more general sense **to change,** ₒp̓o-méd bdé-ba changeless happiness; in a similar sense ₒp̓o-ₒgyur-méd-pai rnal-ₒbyór Mil.; yet frq. also vb. a.: k̓ú-ba yaṅ ₒp̓o yaṅ ₒp̓o byás šiṅ pouring off the gravy again and again Pth.; very frq. tse ₒp̓ó-ba, ₒċi-ₒp̓ó-ba, ši-ₒp̓ó-ba, to exchange life, **to die,** (in the earlier literature the most common expression for it); the last of the above terms prob. may be explained by ċi-žiṅ ₒp̓ó-ba; ċi-ₒp̓o-ba ₒdébs-pa, Thgr. frq. seems to mean: to help the soul to a happy departure. — 2. C. **to fall out, to shed,** of wheat and corn in general.

འཕོག་པ་ ₒp̓óg-pa, pf. and secondary form p̓og, **to hit, strike, touch, befal, meet,** mṅár-bai dris ₒp̓óg-pa t̓ams-ċád all whom the sweet odour met, to whom it became perceptible Dzl.; gen. with la: ₒod-zér, gríb-ma mi-la ₒp̓og, a ray of light, a shadow falls upon that man Glr. frq.; k̓ó-la nad, tsád-pa, ċád-pa ₒp̓og, disease, heat, punishment etc. has befallen him; γza-ₒp̓og-mkan **an epileptic person** W., C.; the signification: **to hurt,** seems to be less inherent to the word than dependent on contingent circumstances.

འཕོང་ ₒp̓oṅ Cs. **archery,** ₒp̓óṅ-sa archery ground, ₒp̓óṅ-mkan archer, ₒp̓oṅ-skyén good, skilful archer Dzl.

འཕོང་ཚོས་ ₒp̓oṅ-tsos Cs. **buttocks;** ₒp̓oṅs sitting-part, posteriors Lt., Wdṅ.; ₒp̓óṅ-la skyón-pa Sch. 'the riding of two persons on one horse'.

འཕོངས་པ་ ₒp̓óṅs-pa 1. vb., pf. ₒp̓oṅs or p̓oṅs, **to be poor, indigent;** ₒp̓óṅs-par bžúg-pa to let (another) pine in poverty Thgy.; with instrum. **to be deprived of, to lose,** rgyál-po srás-kyis ₒp̓óṅs-nas the king having lost his son Pth. — 2. also p̓óṅs-pa, sbst. **poverty,** and adj. **poor,** v. *ṗóṅs-pa*; perh. also **dejected, disheartened.**

འཕོད་པ་ *ₒṗód-pa* = *ṗód-pa*, *Cs.*; འཕོན་པོ་ *ₒṗón-po* = *ṗón-po*; འཕོབ་པ་ *ₒṗób-pa* = *ₒbébs-pa Sch.*

འཕྱ་བ་ *ₒṗyá-ba*, pf. *ₒṗyas*, acc. to *Lex.* = *smód-pa* **to blame, censure, chide;** the context however, in which the word occurs, seems to suggest the meaning: **to scoff, to deride,** (*Sch.*) e.g. *Dzl.* ༡༢༢, 13. ༡༥༨, 7. ༢༨༠, 15; also *Pth. mis ₒṗyá-ru ₒoṅ*, people will laugh at you.

འཕྱག་པ་ *ₒṗyág-pa*, pf. *ₒṗyags* or *ṗyag?* **to sweep, to clean** *Lex.*, *Pth.*; cf. *ṗyag-dár.*

འཕྱང་བ་ *ₒṗyaṅ-ba*, pf. *ₒṗyaṅs*, vb. n. to *dpyáṅ-ba*, **to hang down,** *dar sṅon-poi ge-ša ₒṗyaṅ-ba* a handkerchief of blue silk hanging down from the head *Sambh.*; *má-mču ťúr-du ₒṗyáṅ-ba* the lower lip hanging down, as a sign of death *S.g.*; **to cling to a person,** from love etc.; *rje-btsún-gyi skú-la Mil.*, to the Reverend's person (or body?); *jú-žiṅ ₒṗyáṅ-ba* to cling to, to take a firm hold of *Thgy.* — *ₒṗyaṅ-ťág* **plumb-line, sounding-line** *C.* also *dpyáṅ-ťag.* — **čáṅ-ǩem-pa** **rope-dancer,** esp. at the festivities of new-year *C.*

འཕྱང་མོ་ཉུག་ or ཡུག་ *ₒṗyaṅ-mo-nyug* or *-yug Sch.*, **singular, strange.**

འཕྱད་ *ₒṗyad Sch.* = *ṗyad.*

འཕྱན་པ་ *ₒṗyán-pa Lexx.* = *yán-pa* **to ramble, to range, roam about, wander, stray from;** *ₒṗyán-te ₒgró-ba Dzl.* ༢༥༩, 4.

འཕྱར་ཁ་ *ₒṗyár-ǩa Sch.*, **blame, affront, disgrace.**

འཕྱར་བ་ *ₒṗyár-ba*, imp. *ₒṗyor* and *ṗyor* 1. **to raise, to lift up;** *ṗrú-gu nám-mǩa-la Glr.* to lift the infant up to heaven; **to hold aloft,** e.g. the *dor-je* in practising magic, pointing it towards heaven; so also *sdig-mdzúb* to raise the finger *Mil.*; *rál-gri*, to lift up the sword to fetch a blow; to lift up the grain in a shovel, hence: **to fan, to sift, to winnow.** — 2. **to hoist,** a flag, frq.; *ₒṗyar-dár* or *dar-ₒṗyár*, a flag; in a general sense: **to hang up,** so esp. *W.* **čár-la** (*Lad.* **čás-la** for *čárs-la*), **bór-če** id.; **čár-la táṅ-če** to hang a man; *čár-šiṅ* gallows; occasionally too: to cling or stick to an object. — 3. *Cs.* **to show, to represent, to excite, to waken;** *ₒṗyar-γyeṅ*, engaging, winning behaviour (= *ₒjog-sgégs*), *ṗyár-ba byéd-pa* to assume an alluring attitude; *ₒṗyár-ka-čan*, tempting, graceful, charming.

འཕྱི་བ་ *ₒṗyi-ba* I. sbst. **marmot,** *ṗyi-ba.* — II. vb. pf. *ṗyis*, *ₒṗyis* 1. **to be late, to be belated, to come too late;** *gál-te ₒṗyis-na*, if I come too late *Dzl.*; *da ǩyod čuṅ ₒṗyis-pa yin* you come just a little too late *Pth.*; *ₒṗyi-mo* v. *ṗyi* II. — 2. also *ₒṗyid-pa* **to wipe, to blot out,** *mig* to wipe the eyes *Pth.*; *mči-ma* the tears *Glr.*; **to pull out,** *spu* the hair *W.*; **to tear out,** *rlig-pa* the testicles *Sch.*; *ₒṗyi-rás Cs.*, **wiper, wiping-clout, duster;** *lág-ₒṗyi Cs.*, **towel,** v. *ṗyis* II.

འཕྱིག་པ་ *ₒṗyig-pa*, *Sch.* **to bind,** better *ₒǩyig-pa.*

འཕྱིད་པ་ *ₒṗyid-pa* v. *ₒṗyi-ba.*

འཕྱིལ་བ་ *ₒṗyil-ba* for *ₒǩyil-ba* **to wind, to twist,** (the hair) *Wdṅ.*

འཕྱུག(ས)་པ་ *ₒṗyúg(s)-pa*, rarely *čúg-pa* **to be mistaken,** also *W.*; **to miss,** *lam*, the road *Lex.*; *ču-ťsód*, to mistake the hour *Pth.*

འཕྱུར་བ་ *ₒṗyúr-ba* 1. **to mount, to rise up,** of smoke; **to overflow; inundate,** of rivers and lakes *Lex.* — 2. *Sch.* **to heap up, to accumulate?** v. *ṗyúr-bu.*

འཕྱེ་བ་ *ₒṗyé-ba*, pf. *ₒṗyes*, **to crawl, to creep,** like snakes; esp. *lto-ₒṗye*, 'belly-creeper', **snake, serpent;** *ₒṗyé-ba čén-po*, **महोरग**, name of a demon; *ₒṗyé-bo*, fem. *mo* **cripple** *Lex.* = *rkaṅ-med.*

འཕྱེན་ *ₒṗyen Mil.* = *pyen*, **wind,** *γtóṅ-ba*, to let go a wind.

འཕྱོ་བ་ *ₒpyó-ba* pf. *ₒṗyos?* 1. **to swim,** of fishes, *Mil.* — 2. **to soar, to float,** in the air *Thgy.* — 3. **to flow, heave, swell,** of fluids *Mṅg.*; *ₒṗyo-dár-ba Sch.*, to undulate. — 4. **to range, roam about, gambol,** *rtse-žiṅ ₒpyó-ba*, of deer *Mil.*; *rí-la ₒṗyo* *dgu*, po. the wild animals of the field *Sch.* — 5. *snyiṅ ˳ṕyo Sch.*, 'the heart is swelling, courage is rising'; however *šés-pa ˳ṕyo Med.*, seems rather to imply: consciousness gives way, is wavering, flitting; *sems ˳ṕyo Lt.?*

འཕྱོང་བ་ *˳ṕyóṅ-ba Lt.* perh. = *˳ṕyáṅ-ba*; occasionally, like *˳ṕyoṅs-pa* used incorr. for *mčóṅs-pa*.

འཕྱོངས་རྒྱས་ *˳ṕyoṅs-rgyás Sch.*, **pride, haughtiness, insolence.**

འཕྱོན་མ་ *˳ṕyón-ma*, **harlot, prostitute,** *byéd-pa*, to whore, to fornicate *Lex.*

འཕྱོར་བ་ *˳ṕyór-ba*, v. *ṕyár-ba*, also for *čór-ba*; *˳ṕyór-po* for *mčór-po*, hence *˳pyŏr-dga Sch.* **dandy, fop.**

འཕྱོས་མ་ *˳ṕyós-ma Sch.*, purchase-price of a bride.

འཕྲ་བ་ *˳ṕrá-ba* I. vb., also *ṕrá-ba*, pf. *˳ṕras*, **to kick, to jerk, to strike with the foot,** *˳ṕra-šágs* a stroke or kick with the foot, *byéd-pa* to kick about with the feet, in a paroxysm of pain or anguish, *Pth.*; *ṭa-šag gyáb-pa*, to give one a kick. — II. = *ṕrá-ba, ṕrá-mo.*

འཕྲག, འཕྲག་པ་ *˳ṕrag, ˳ṕrág-pa*, **to envy, grudge,** v. *ṕrag.*

འཕྲང, ཕྲང་ *˳ṕraṅ, ṕraṅ, lam-˳ṕráṅ*, **a foot-path** along a narrow ledge on the side of a precipitous wall of rock (not 'a defile or narrow pass' *Sch.*), frq.; *bar-doi ˳ṕraṅ* the road of the abyss of the *bar-do*, (as with us: the valley of death) frq. *Thgr.*; *bár-doi ˳ṕraṅ-sgról*, prob. a prayer for deliverance from that abyss *Thgr.*

འཕྲང་འཕྲུལ་ *˳ṕraṅ-˳ṕrul Sch.* **something hanging down.**

འཕྲད་པ་ *˳ṕrád-pa* pf. and fut. *ṕrad* **to meet together;** *daṅ* **to meet with, to fall in with, to find;** *de daṅ ṕrád-do*, you shall see him *Dzl.*; *de ni ṅa daṅ ṕrad mi ṫub*, him I cannot admit *Dzl.*; *bdag daṅ ˳ṕrád-par šog čig*, come to see me *Dzl.*; *sṅar ṅa daṅ ˳ṕrád-pai ˳óg-tu* not until they have met me (sensu obscoeno) *Dzl.*; *byis-pai ro žig daṅ ṕrád-do* he found the dead body of an infant *Dzl.*; *˳ṕrad-ṫsams Sch.*, intersecting line of two plains, **corner, angle.**

འཕྲབ་པ་ *˳ṕráb-pa* = *˳ṕrá-ba* and *˳ḱráb-pa*; *˳ṕráb-byéd-pa* **to flutter,** of a bird wounded by a shot.

འཕྲལ, ཕྲལ་ *˳ṕral, ṕral*, prob. to be regarded as a sbst., like *druṅ, mdun, sṅa* etc., expressing **immediate nearness;** 1. in reference **to space,** but seldom, as for instance *˳ṕrál-du ḱyi ḱríd-de*, having a dog near at hand *Glr.*; gen. 2. with respect **to time:** *ṕral daṅ ṕugs*, what is going to happen immediately and at a later period, presence and futurity; *˳ṕral-ṕúgs-kyi ˳gal-rkyén ṫams-čád sél-bar byed Glr.* to avert immediate and subsequent disasters; *˳ṕral ṕugs gáṅ-la bzaṅ* that is good both for the nearest and the more distant future; *˳ṕral daṅ yún-du* now and for a long time to come; *˳ṕral-sog-ǰog-méd-par* without having gathered or laid up any thing for daily use *Mil.*; *˳ṕrál-gyi ˳dug-ṫsugs ṅán-pa* a poor temporary dwelling, or also: a common, ordinary dwelling, v. no. 3; *˳ṕral-du ša γžan ma rnyed-de* as at the moment he was not able to procure any other meat *Dzl.*; *˳ṕrál-du sleb yoṅ Mil.* I shall come immediately; *˳ṕrál-du dgós-pai yo-byád* the things necessary for daily use *Dzl.*; *˳ṕrál-du ˳byór-ba ma yin* that is not to be had at a moment's bidding *Dzl.*; also postp. e.g.: *deĭ ˳ṕrál-la ṕan* that will help the moment directly after it; more frq. after verbal roots = *ma-ṫág-tu*: *ṕebs-ṕrál* as soon as he had arrived *Mil.*; *smras-ṕrál* as soon as it has been spoken *S.g.*; *skyes-ṕrál* immediately after birth *Lt.*; in compounds: *ṕral-rkyén, ṕral-dgós, ṕral-ṕúgs* cf. above; *ṕral-grig* finished, ready, prepared, in proper case, (vulgo, esp. in *W.*, a word much used) *ṭal-ḍig čó-če* to prepare, to get ready. — 3. fig., **common, ordinary, of daily occurrence, common-place,** *ṕrál-skad B., C.*, (*W.* *ṕál-kad*) common dialect; *žes ṕral-skad-la snaṅ* so you may hear it in the language of the common people, *Gram., Wdṅ.*

འཕྲལ་བ་ *˳ṕrál-ba*, pf. *ṕral*, fut. *dbral*, imp. *ṕrol*, vb.a. to *˳brál-ba*, **to separate, to part,** *ḱa ṭál-wa*, id., *C.*; *daṅ* from;

rtags daṅ ṗral he deprived them of their insignia *Glr.*; *srog daṅ ˳ṗrál-ba* to put to death, to inflict capital punishment *Glr.*; *zúg-tu ˳ṗrál-ba* to cut into quarters (cattle) *Mil.*; *ltó-ba ṗrál-ba* to cut open, to rip up the belly *Tar.*; *dbrúl-bar dka* difficult to part, hard to be kept asunder *Lex.*

འཕྲས་པ་ *˳ṗrás-pa* 1. pf. of *ṗrá-ba;* as sbst. **stroke, blow, kick** with the foot, *Cs.*; *rkaṅ-˳ṗrás*, id.; *rtas-˳ṗras rgyag-pa*, the kicking of a horse; *lag-˳ṗrás*, a blow with the hand, *Cs.*; *˳či-˳ṗrás Lexx.*, *ši-˳ṗrás* vulg. (*W.* **šin - ṭ ás* or *ṭ e**), the kicking, struggling, moving in convulsions, of a dying man or animal, **agony.** (*Sch.* *˳ṗras*, to lie on one's side?). — 2. instrum. of *˳pra*, *Sch.*: *ṗras spras-pa.*

འཕྲི་བ་ *˳ṗri-ba* pf. and imp. *ṗri(s)*, fut. *dbri*, vb.a. to *˳bri-ba*, **to lessen, diminish; to take away from,** **ka ṭi-ce** to take off at the top, e.g. from too full a measure *W.*; more in the special sense of subtracting, with different construction: *de* (or *dé-yis* or *dé-la*) *ṭig-ro ṗri-ba-yis* 60 diminished by this, or: this being subtracted from 60; (*ṭig-ró* = cipher six) *Wdk.*

འཕྲིག་པ་ *˳ṗrig-pa* 1. **to struggle, flutter,** *Cs.*; **to throb, pulsate,** *Lt.* — 2. *Sch.* **to desire, covet, demand.** — 3. *Sch.* **to be suspected.** — 4. **error?** *Sch.*: *˳ṗrig-ldán*, **erroneous, mistaken, faulty, incorrect.**

འཕྲིན་ *˳ṗrin* v. *ṗrin*; *˳ṗrin-pa* **to inform** *Cs.*

འཕྲུ་བ་ *˳ṗrú-ba*, འཕྲུ་མ་ *˳ṗrú-ma* v. *ṗrú-ba* etc.

འཕྲུག་པ་ *˳ṗrúg-pa*, pf. *ṗrugs*, **to scratch one's self,** *ṗrúgs-na Lt.* if one scratches; *za-˳ṗrúg byed* he scratches himself on account of an itching *Med.*

འཕྲུགས་ *˳ṗrugs S.O.*, perh. = *ṗrug* II.

འཕྲུལ་ *˳ṗrul*, **jugglery, magical deception,** the abstract noun to *sprúl-ba*, q.v.; *˳ṗrul-če-ba* great in magic power *Glr.*; *˳ṗrul-gyi rgyal-po* the magic king, enchanted king, phantom-king *Glr.*; *˳ṗrúl-ghi koṅ-jo* the enchantress *Koṅ-jo Glr.*; *˳ṗrul-gyi spyan-gyis* with a magic eye, by means of magical vision *Dzl.*; *ṗá-rol ynón-pai ˳ṗrul daṅ ldán-pa* possessing magic power for subduing an enemy *Sambh.*; *rnám-(par) ˳ṗrúl (-ba)*, *čo-˳ṗrúl*, *rdzu-˳ṗrúl*, frq.; *sgyu-˳ṗrúl* less frq., id.; *mig-˳ṗrul*, optical deception *Cs.* — *˳ṗrul-gyi ˳kor-lo*, *˳ṗrul-˳kor*, **magic wheel,** in ancient literature merely a phantastic attribute of gods etc.; in modern life applicable to every more complicated machine with a rotating motion, e.g. a sugar-mill *Stg.*, an electrifying machine and the like. *˳ṗrul-dgai lha*, *dga-bži-˳ṗrul-gyi lha*, *yžan-dga-˳ṗrul-dbaṅ-byed-kyi lha*, the names of various regions that are residences of gods. *˳ṗrul-snáṅ* 1. **delusion, mockery.** 2. n. of a monastery in Lhasa founded by the Nepal wife of *Sroṅ-btsan-sgam-po's.*

འཕྲུལ་སྒུར་ *˳ṗrul-túr S.g.* seems to be **catheter.**

འཕྲུལ་བ་ *˳ṗrúl-ba*, 1. by its form intrs. to *sprúl-ba*; acc. to *Cs.* both are identical in meaning; I met with it only as an abstract noun = *˳ṗrul* in *rnám-par ˳ṗrúl-ba* (v. under *˳ṗrul*), e.g. *rnám-par ˳ṗrúl-ba dú-ma*, many transformations, magic tricks, for which *rnam-˳ṗrúl* gen. is used. — 2. **to be mistaken, to err, to make blunders** *Mil.*, better *˳krúl-ba.* — 3. **to separate, part, discriminate,** the good from the bad, truth from falsehood *Ld.* (= *ṗrál-ba?* like *drúṅ-po* and *dráṅ-po*).

འཕྲེ་བ་ *˳ṗre-ba* pf. *˳ṗres Cs.*, *˳ṗre byéd-pa Sch.*, **to incline, to lean against; to put down, to lay down**; *Dzl.* ཞ༧, 12, where however the context is not perfectly clear.

འཕྲེང་(བ་), ཕྲེང་(བ་) *˳ṗreṅ(-ba)*, *ṗreṅ(-ba)* sbst. col. *W.* **ṭáṅ-ṅa**, *Ü*: **ṗaṅ**) *Ssk.* माला, **a string, a thread** or **cord,** on which things are filed, strung, or ranged, e.g. *mé-tog-gi ˳ṗréṅ-ba Glr.* a wreath, garland of flowers; *˳ṗreṅ-ba dmar-po* a wreath of red flowers *Wdṅ.*; *gaṅs-rii* a circle of snow-mountains *Schr.*; *nags-kyi*, of woods *Sambh.*; *šiṅ-rtai ˳ṗreṅ-ba rim-pa bdun* 7 circles of chariots *Pth.*; *yig-˳ṗreṅ* a line of letters; *˳ṗréṅ-ba ˳dógs-pa* to bind a wreath; *˳ṗreṅ-skúd*, *˳ṗreṅ-ṭág* the string or cord of the wreath; *˳ṗreṅ-rdóg* bead, hence ₒp̓réṅ-ba esp.: a string of beads, **rosary;** *bgraṅ-ₒp̓reṅ,* rosary for counting the repetitions of prayers and magic spells, being used also in arithmetic, as an aid to memory; *mú-tig-ₒp̓reṅ* string of pearls, rosary composed of pearls; *nor-bu-ₒp̓reṅ-ba* of precious stones; also title of a book; fig. *don ma go tsig-gi ₒp̓réṅ-ba bzuṅ,* they only keep to the string of words, without understanding their import *Mil.*

འཕྲེང་བ་ *ₒp̓réṅ-ba* vb.n. **to love, to be fond of, greatly attached to,** with accus. of the person, *séms-la* and similar supplementary words being generally added; *blá-ma yid-la ₒp̓réṅ-bai rtags, bú-mo séms-la ₒp̓réṅ-bas Glr.; yáb-kyi túgs-la p̓réṅ-bar gyúr-te,* or *ₒp̓réṅ-bžin-du* as she was very dear to her father *Glr.*; *šin-tu ₒp̓róṅ-ba žig byuṅ* an ardent longing for home came over me *Mil.nt.*

(འ)ཕྲེང་ *ₒp̓reṅ,* sometimes incorr. for *p̓raṅ.*

འཕྲེད་ *ₒp̓red,* v. *p̓red.* — འཕྲེས་ *ₒp̓res,* v. *ₒp̓ré-ba.*

འཕྲོ་བ་ *ₒp̓ró-ba,* pf. *ₒp̓ros,* prop. vb.n. to *spró-ba,* 1. gen. with *las,* from, **to proceed, issue, emanate from, to spread,** in most cases rel. to rays of light; *sku ₒod-zér ₒp̓ró-ba* a body from which rays of light proceed, a body sending forth light *Glr.*; *Cs.* also relative to odours, fame etc.; occasionally in reference to descent or parentage *Thgy.* — 2. **to proceed, to go on, continue,** and *ₒp̓ro* **continuation,** opp. to being finished, at an end (*Sch.* incorr.: 'the end'); **láb-ṭo žeṅ-ghyi čẹ̀-pa* C., Schr.*: the interruption of a conversation by another person; *ₒjig-pro bčad* the process of destruction came to an end *Glr.*; *sbyin-pai ₒp̓ro čád kyaṅ slóṅ-mo-pai ₒp̓ro ma čad Pth.* the gifts had come to an end, but not the begging; *ₒp̓ar-ₒp̓ro čad* the pulse no longer beats *Thgr.*; *čos-bsgyúr-ₒp̓ro-rnams bskyur* the continuations of translating were thrown aside *Glr.*; of the soul: *yód-ₒp̓ro-la mi yoṅ* whilst it is still existing, it does not come forth, i.e. it vanishes imperceptibly, as soon as an attempt is made to find out its seat and to demonstrate its essence *Mil.; ₒp̓ro túd-pa* to annex the remainder, to append the continuation; **ṭo žág-pa* C.* to lay the continuation aside; **šól-wa** to put it off, both expressions implying an interruption of work; *ₒp̓ro lus soṅ* or *las soṅ* a remainder is still left of what has not been used or consumed; **ₒdi ghaṅ ṭó-te** after this has been filled up (by pouring in the wanting quantity) *C.*

འཕྲོག་པ་ *ₒp̓róg-pa,* pf. and imp. *p̓rogs,* fut. *dbrog* 1. **to rob, take away; to deprive of,** ccgpar. *nor, gos, rgyál-poi lág-nas rgyál-sa* to deprive the king of his throne *Glr.*; hence *rgyál-sa p̓rógs-pai mi* usurper *Glr.*; *tsád-pas mii mtu-stóbs ₒp̓rog* the heat deprives a man of his strength *Med.*; yet also: *sems-yid ₒp̓róg-pa* to take another man's heart, to run away with his affections, to captivate him *Glr.*; *ₒp̓rog-byéd,* and also *ₒp̓róg-ma = dbaṅ-p̓yúg* 1. ईश्वर i.e. Shiwa, or also Indra. 2. symb. num.: 11. — *rku-ₒp̓róg,* robbery *Ma.*, **čom-* or *čom-ṭóg*,* id., *W.*; **čóm-ṭóg táṅ-kan** robber, **waṅ daṅ čom-ṭóg čó-te** by violence, *W.* → 2. **to make one lose a thing,** *bdág-gi glaṅ p̓rogs* (by his negligence) he has made me lose my ox *Dzl.*; *sdóm-pa ₒp̓róg-tu byuṅ* my vow is lost to me, i.e. the meditation I had vowed has been disturbed, thwarted *Glr.*, to deprive a person of his power or place, **to overthrow,** kings, dignitaries etc. *Stg.*, analogous to *yyo-ba, ₒgul-ba, ₒkrugs-pa.* — 3. **to remove, do away with, expel,** demons *Glr.*

འཕྲོང་ *ₒp̓roṅ Glr.,* provinc. for *ₒp̓raṅ* and *ₒp̓reṅ,* v. *ₒp̓reṅ-ba.*

འཕྲོད་པ་ *ₒp̓rod-pa* 1. vb.: pf. *p̓rod,* vb. n. to *spród-pa,* **to have been delivered, transmitted,** *lág-tu* into the hands of a person, hence *ₒp̓rod-ₒdzín, *ṭod-zín* W.* **receipt, quittance; ṅo** or *ṅos-ₒp̓rod-pa* **to know, perceive, understand;** so prob. also *snyiṅ-la ysál-bar ma p̓rod Schr.* — 2. adj. **fit, proper, suitable, agreeing with, congenial to,** *p̓ó-bar* agreeing with the stomach *Med.; mi-ₒp̓rod zas* unwholesome food *Med.*; *mi-ₒp̓rod-pa* also signifies adverse fortune, adversity *C.*;

ḱaṅ-pa e' ₒṗrod ce-na it the question is, whether the house is likely to prosper.

འཕྲོབ་པ་ ₒṗrób-pa Sch. = ₒṗráb-pa, འཕྲོལ་བ་ ₒṗrol-ba Sch. = ₒṗrál-ba.

འཕྲོས་པ་ ₒṗrós-pa v. ₒṗro-ba; ₒṗros γtóṅ-ba Schr., ₒṗros-par byed-pa Sch. **to spread, to pour forth,** e.g. light, ₒṗros Tar. 48,3, acc. to Schf.: a detailed work; but Tar. 143,13?

བ

བ *ba* 1. the letter **b,** originally, and in the frontier districts still at the present day, corresponding to the English b; the pronunciation of it, however, varies a good deal in the different dialects of the country: in *C.* this letter, as an initial, is at present deep-toned and aspirated = *bh;* in *Sp.* as a final letter, it is softened down to w; and this softening of its sound prevails throughout Tibet in the substantive terminations *ba* and *bo*, when preceded by a vowel or by *ṅ, r, l*; as a prefix it is sounded in *Bal.* and *Kh.* = *b* or *w*. Regarding the irregularities in the pronunciation of initial *db* v. the Phonetic Table. — 2. num. figure: 15.

བ་ *ba* I. (also *bá-mo Cs.?*) **cow,** *ₒdod-ₒjoi ba* v. *-jo-ba*; *ba-kó* cow-leather; *ba-kyú* herd of cows; *ba-gláṅ* v. below; *ba-γcin* urine of a cow; *ba-lči* cow's dung; *ba-ču*, resp. *-čab* = *ba-γcin* (used by hindooizing Tibetans, the cow being sacred to the Hindoos); *ba-nú* 1. a cow's dug. 2. a stone resembling it in appearance *Med.*; *ba-ṗrúg* calf; *ba-rmig* a cow's hoofs; *ba-rmig-gi ču* the water collected in the impression of a cow's foot on the ground, to denote a very small quantity of water *Dzl.*; *ba-o* for *bai* *ₒó-ma*; *ba-rdzí* cow-herd; *ba-rá* pen or stable for cows; *ba-rú* 1. a cow's horn. 2. vulg. cup for scarifying, the hollow tip of a cow's horn being used as such; *ba-šá* cow-beef.

II. affix or so-called **article,** for *pa,* to substantives the roots of which end with a vowel or with *ṅ, r, l,* except when *pa* has its particular signification, as in *ču-pa* etc. (v. *pa*); in adjectives it is either syn. with *po* (as: *dmár-bai mdaṅs,* a ruddy complexion), or it denotes **'having'** (= ... *po-čan,* as: *sna-dmár-ba* or *sna-dmár-po-čan* having a reddish trunk), or it is the sign of the verb formed from it (*dmár-ba,* to be red), or of the abstract substantive (*dmár-ba,* redness).

བ་དཀར་ *ba-dkár* **lime, lime-stone** *Schr.*

བ་གམ་ *ba-gám, S.g.* and elsewh.; *Cs.*: 'low wall, parapet'; acc. to my authorities a certain part of the timber work of a roof, something like pinnacle, battlement; so also *Tar.* 80,21: the king with his retinue beheld the pinnacles of the Naga palace rising above the surface; v. *nyúg-pa* 4.

བ་གླང་ *bá-γlaṅ* **ox, bull;** **ba-laṅ tsogs** *W.*, like an ox, stubborn, stupid; also dirty, filthy, nasty, for which our vulgar expression is swinish; *ba-glaṅ-spyod* appellation for the western part of the globe, v. *γliṅ.* — 2. or *bál-γlaṅ Dzl.*

བ་ཏི *bá-ṭi, Hind.* **बाटी, a large brass dish.**

བ་ཏི་ཀ *bá-ti-ka Stg.*, a small long-measure, ¼ of a barley-corn.

བ་ཏག *bá-tag W.*, also *Sambh.*, 1. **root.** — 2. **stalk of fruit.**

བ་དན་ *ba-dán* 1. **पताका**, of which the word is a corruption acc. to *Lis.*, an **ensign** with pendent silk strips *Dzl.*, *Gyatch.*, *Glr.* — 2. also *šes-rab-ral-gri*, stated to be a kind of **dagger**, set upright, a semblance of which often attends apparitions of the gods; thus the signification of 'sword', given by *Sch.*, seems to be justified, and also *Schr.* refers to it under *spa-dám*; I never met with it in *B.* in that sense.

བ་དམ་ *ba-dám*, *Pers.*, *Urd.* بادام, from the *Ssk.* वाताम्र, 'windmango' *Shksp.*, **almond.**

བ་སྤུ་ *bá-spu* **a little hair,** the little hairs of the body, *bá-spu lań* or *ldań*, the little hairs stand up, I shudder, *B.*, *C.*; similarly: *bá-spu γyo Glr.*, *Mil.*; *ba-spu tsam yań med* (I feel no repentance) even as great as a hair *Dzl.*; *bá-spu-čan* **hairy, covered with hair,** *ba-spu-méd* bald; *bá-spui bú-ga* or *ḱuń* (*-bu*) **pores.**

བ་བུ་ *bá-bu* (*Pers.* پاپوش, *pāpōš*) **a soft shoe,** *skúd-pai* knitted shoe, *p̓iń-pai* felt-shoe, but in general they are made of wool or goat's hair.

བ་བླ་ *ba-bla* (*Ts.* **bhá-bla**) *Med.* **arsenic.**

བ་འབོག་ *ba-˳bog W.* **clod, lump of earth.**

བ་མེན་ *ba-mén Mil.*, *Wdń.*, *Cs.* and *Sch.*: 'a species of wild cattle with large horns'; *Sch.* also: **buffalo-calf;** though in *Sambh.* *gańs-ri-ba-mén* are spoken of.

བ་མོ་ *bá-mo* **hoar-frost,** *B.* and col.; *ba-tsa* (Campbell in Summer's Phenix p. 142, 5: *pen-cha*), inferior, **impure soda,** incrusting the ground near salt-lakes; it is mixed with the food of cattle (from which circumstance the word may be translated 'cow-salt'), occasionally also for the want of something better put into the tea; *bá-tsai skyúr-rtsi Cs.* muriatic (hydro-chloric) acid.

བ་ར་ཎ་སི་ *bā-ra-ṇa-si*, v. *wā-ra-ṇa-si*.

བ་རུ་ར་ *ba-ru-ra* an astringent medicament *Med.*

བ་ལ་ཧ་ *bá-la-ha*, *čań-šés bá-la-ha*, n. of a demon, v. *rta-mčóg*.

བ་ལུ་ *ba-lu = da-li*, various low alpine species of **Rhododendron.**

བ་ལེ་ཀ་ *bá-le-ka* medicinal plant, belonging to the climbers *Med.*

བ་ཤ་ *bá-ša* 1. v. *ba* I. — 2. prob. = *bá-ša-ha* a bitter-tasted officinal plant, acc. to *Wdń.* an Indian tree; in *Lh.* a rather insignificant radiated flower.

བ་ཤུ་ *bá-šu*, *W.* **a virulent boil, ulcer.**

བ་ཤོ་ *bá-šo Ld.*, *ba-šo-ka C.*, **currants, small raisins.**

བ་སོ་ *bá-so* **elephant's tooth, ivory;** *bá-so-mḱan* worker in ivory.

བག་ *bag* I. a primary signification of this word seems to be: **a narrow space;** thus with *Sch.* fig. *bág-dog-pa* to be straitened, in necessitous circumstances, poor; in another application more frq.: *bág-tsam* a little, *nor bág-tsam re* a little money *Mil.*; *bag-ré Thgr.*, perh. the same; *dáń-ga bág-tsam bde* the appetite is growing a little better *Lt.*; *tsér-ma bág-tsam yód-pa* having a few prickles *Wdń.*; *bág-tsam-pa* **slight, insignificant, trifling,** *sdug-bsńál*, a slight misfortune *Thgy.*; *ma-bdé-ba bág-tsam-la bzód-pa mi byéd-pa Mil.* to be fretting on account of a trifling mischance; most frq., however, the word has a moral bearing: **attention, care, caution,** relative to physical and moral evils or contaminations; *bag-méd*, in a gen. sense: *rá-ro dáń-po bág-med-pa* the beginning of intoxication is the disappearing of attention; in a special sense (*Ssk.* प्रमाद): **careless, heedless, fearless;** *mi-bdé-bai* fearless of misfortune *Dzl.*; *˳di-lta-bui bag méd-par ˳gyur* I shall be freed from the fear of such things *Dzl.*; **fearless,** without fear or consideration, without regard to consequences or to the judgment of others etc., *čáń-la bag-méd ˳di-tsam ˳túń-ba Pth.* without shame drinking such great quantities of beer; *mi-dgé-bai las bág-med-par byéd-pa* to sin without fear or restraint *Dzl.*; *˳dod-čágs-la bág-med-pas* to indulge in sensuality without restraint *Dzl.*; **heedlessness** with regard to good and evil *Tar.* 4, 22; **moral carelessness, indifference, want of principle,** *bág-med-la nyál-ba C.*, stated to be = *bág-la nyal-ba*. v. *bag* II; of an opposite meaning: *bag-yód(-pa)* **reverence, fear, shame,** often parallel to *ṅó-tsa*, *ₒdzém-pa*; **conscientiousness,** almost **religious awe;** adj. **conscientious;** *spyód-pa bág-yod-pa* conscientious dealings (pious course of life) *Dom.*; *bág-yod-par mdzód-čig* act conscientiously, take care not to commit sin (here = do not kill) *Tar.* 32, 7; *de bág-yod-pai p̔yir* as he was conscientious (here = chaste) *Tar.* 39, 2; *bag daṅ ldán-pa* id.; *bag daṅ ldán-par mdzod Glr.*; *bág-tsa-ba* **to be afraid;** *bag mi tsa* I am not afraid *Mil.*; sbst. **fear, timidity, anxiousness** *Mil., Stg.*; *bág-tsa méd-pa* fearlessness *Mil.*; *bag byéd-pa* c. *la*, to fear, to dread, a person *Dzl.*, to take care of, one's clothes *Dzl.*; *bag-yaṅs-su* (or *-kyis*) *Sch.* (*'cura relaxata'*) without fear, fearlessly, coolly; *bag ₒk̔úms-pa Sch.* to be afraid; *bag ₒbébs-pa* to drop, abandon, cast away all fear, *γžan-la* the dread of a person *Mil.* frq.; *bág-pa Dzl.* ༦༨, 15 *Ms.* as a vb. to be afraid, to be fearful, *dé-dag bág-tu dógs-nas* afraid lest they should take fright (another reading: *brós-su*) *bágs-kyis* with fear, with awe *Mil.*; *bágs-kyis byéd-pa* to act carefully, with caution *Dzl.* ༢༥༡, 15; *ma bags-kyis* without fear, unrestrained *Dzl.* ༢༨༨, 1 (*Ms.*; with *Sch.* *ma* is wanting, and both passages are rendered incorr.); *bág-po* adj. = *bág-yod-pa Cs.*; *bag-zón* dread, fear, anxiety *Sch.* —

II. **inclination? passion?** *bág-la nyál-ba Was.* (241) '**vanities** (in Chinese: lullings into security'), the usual sinful temptations, lust, anger etc.; the etymological derivation of the term is, however, not perfectly clear; *bag-méd-la nyál-ba*, which acc. to its primary signification ought to be placed sub I, is said to imply the same. More frq. *bag-čágs* denotes **passion, inclination, propensity,** gen. in a bad sense, *las-ṅan bag-čágs*, *ṅán-pai bag-čágs*, also occasionally without any addition, id.; *bag-čágs yid-kyi lus* the 'intellectual' body of passions *Thgr.*, v. *lus*; less frq. in a good sense: *Tar.* 32, 7 = love, affection; *bag-čágs bzaṅ*, *Mil.* —

III. in compounds also for *bag-p̔yé* and *bág-ma*.

བག་པ་ *bág-pa* 1. vb. **to be afraid,** v. *bag* I. — 2. **purity?** *Cs.*

བག་པོ་ *bág-po* 1. = *bag-yód Cs.* — 2. **bridegroom.**

བག་ཕྱེ་ *bag-p̔ye* (*W.* **bág-p̔e**) **wheat-flour;** *bag-skyó* thin pap or porridge of meal; *bag-zán* thick pap, dough; *bag-drón*, warm porridge; *bag-sbyár* paste; *bags-sbyín* **lute, putty,** a compound of meal and glue; *bag-léb*, resp. *bžes-bág C.* a cake of bread (*Hind. chapāti*).

བག་མ་ *bág-ma* **bride,** *lén-pa* to choose, to take frq.; *bág-ma-la* (or *bág-mar*) *lén-pa* to choose for a bride, *γtóṅ-ba* to give for a bride (wife), *ₒgró-ba*, *čá-ba Ma.*, **čá-če* W.*, to become a bride, to get married; **bág-ma ṭi-te* (or *láṅ-te*) *bór-če**, *W.* to leave the chosen bride with her parents, sometimes for years, which frequently is the case, as betrothals, from reasons of expediency, are often brought about by the parents at a very early age. The common custom is that the young man desirous of marrying proceeds to the parents of his chosen one with the 'wooing-beer', *slóṅ-čaṅ*, which step however may remain yet a private affair; after some time he brings *tig-čaṅ*, the 'settling-beer', and finally *bsú-čaṅ*, the 'taking-home-beer', whereupon follows the wedding, *bág-ston*, and the consummation of marriage, *bza-mi byéd-pa*. — *bag-gós* **wedding-garment;** *bag-grógs-mo* **bride's maid** *Cs.*; *bag-zoṅ Cs.* (prob. more correctly: *rdzoṅs*) **dowry.**

བག་ཚམ་ *bág-tsam* v. *bag* I.

བག་ཙེ་ *bág-tse* a little **basket for wool or clews of wool.** *W.*

བག་ཤིས་ *bág-šis* (also *báxis*, *bóxis* etc.) *Ar.* بخشيش 1. **fee,** drink-money. — 2. *Sp.* **a present, alms.**

བགས་ *bags* v. *bag* I.

བང་ *baṅ* 1. **foot-race,** *baṅ ni γžán-las mgyógs-pa* to be quicker in running than another; *de daṅ baṅ mnyám-par rgyúg-pa* to run with equal swiftness as ... *Pth.*; *baṅ rgyúg-pa Cs.*, **bhaṅ táṅ-wa* C.*; **baṅ tán-*

*če** *W.*; *baṅ* *ₒgrán-pa* to run a race; *baṅ-rtsál sbyóṅ-ba Mil.* to exercise one's self in racing; *baṅ daṅ ₒgró-las-dag-gis nyén-pa* or *baṅ-ₒgrós nyén-pa* to overexert one's self in running *Med.*; **bhaṅ-gyóg, bhaṅ-čóṅ** *C.* **running-match, race**; *baṅ-čén(-pa*, also *-po) Pth.*, *Glr.* **swift messenger, courier**; **bhaṅ-mi** *C.*, **baṅ-mi** *W.*, id. — 2. v. *báṅ-ba.*

བང་བ་ *báṅ-ba, báṅ-k̓aṅ, báṅ-mdzod* **store-room, store-house, corn magazine,** also **treasury** *Dzl.*; *šiṅ-baṅ Kun.* a large box for grain, half underground; *báṅ-p̓ud* first-fruit offering from the barn; **bhaṅ-gha** *Ts.* **repository**; (*dbus-baṅ*, pronounced:) **ü-bhaṅ** *Ts.* **cupboard, press, case.**

བང་རིམ་ *baṅ-rim* = *k̓ri-ₒp̓áṅ*, the part of the *mčód-rten* which has the form of a staircase. — 2. *Sch.* 'a separate part of a house connected by a staircase' (?).

བང་སོ་ *báṅ-so* **grave, tomb,** *ysón-por báṅ-sor ₒdzúg-pa* to bury alive *Glr.*; **sepulchre, monument,** *báṅ-so ₒdébs-pa*, or *rtsig-pa* to build a sepulchre *Glr.*; *báṅ-so mčód-pa* to perform funeral sacrifices, to honour a grave *Glr.*

བངས་པ་ *báṅs-pa Sch.* 1. = *sbáṅs-pa.* — 2. = *báṅ-ba.* — 3. = *báṅ-so.*

བཏྟི *bát-ti* (*Hindi*) 1. a weight = 2 *ser*, about 4 pounds. — 2. **balance, pair of scales**; **bát-ti tág-če** to weigh *W.*

བད་ *bad* 1. **moisture, humidity,** **šiṅ bad k̓ór-na** *W.* when wood attracts humidity; **bád-čan** moist, humid, damp, from rain or dew *W.* — 2. **hoar-frost** *bá-mo Sch.*, *Wts.* — 3. in compounds for *bád-kan.* — 4. **edge, border,** *bad ni yser* the edge is of gold *Sch.*; *mk̓ar-bád S.g.* = *k̓a-bad?* *bad-ₒbúr Mil.?*

བད་ཀ་ *bád-ka C.* a plant, similar to mustard, yielding oil.

བད་ཀན་ *bád-kan* mucus **phlegm,** a. as normal substance of the body comprizing 5 kinds: *rten-byéd* mucus in the joints of the neck and shoulders, *myag-byéd* in the stomach, *myoṅ-byéd* in the tongue and palate, *tsim-byéd* in the brain, eyes etc., *ₒbyor-byéd* in the rest of the joints; b. in a morbid state, as a cause of disease: *bád-kan-las gyúr-pai nad* mucous diseases; *bad-kan-lhén* mucus in the cardiac regions, prob. = gastric catarrh; *bad-kan-lčags-dréys* intestinal catarrh; *bad-kan-mgul-ₒgágs* mucous consumption; *bád-kan grúm-bu dkár-po* etc. *Med.*; *bad-kan-rlúṅ* phlegm and air, *bad-kan-mk̓ris* phlegm and bile; *bad-kan-k̓rag* phlegm and blood *Med.*

བན་ *ban* 1. *C.* **beer-jug, pitcher.** — 2. v. the following articles.

བན་ཆུང་, བན་བུན་ *ban-čúṅ, ban-bún* **a little, a bit**; *k̓yod-ráṅ nyams-ban-bún-gyi snáṅ-ba-la* you, with your little bit of spiritual light *Mil.*; *rtsi-šiṅ sna-tsógs ban-ma-bún* forest-trees of every kind not a few (or also variously mixed?) *Mil.*; *ban-če* in moderate quantity, 'tolerably many'.

བནྡྷ་ *bán-dha Sch.* **skull, cranium**; frq. spelled *bhán-dha*, hence perh. = भाण्ड vessel, in which sense it is gen. to be understood in books; accordingly it may be a skull used as a drinking-vessel.

བནྡྷེ་, བནྡེ་ *bán-dhe, bán-de*, acc. to Hodgson's learned Nepalese authority (Illustr. 75) = वन्द्य, *reverendus, salutandus*, for which also in the Tibetan language *btsún-pa* is always used as an equivalent: **a Buddhist priest**; hence originally = Buddhist in general, the term being also applied to women *Mil.*; *ban-rgán* an old priest *Glr.*; *ban-spráṅ* and *spraṅ-bán* a mendicant friar; *ban-čúṅ* ('*pen-kiong*' *Desg.* 370) pupil, disciple in a monastery; *ban-lóg* col., a priest that has turned apostate; *ban-bón*, *Mil.* and elsewh. 1. (acc. to our Lama:) Buddhist and Bonpo. 2. (acc. to *Sch*): **a Bon-priest,** in which case, however, the word prob would be *bon-bán.*

བན་རྫོན་ *bun-zón Sch.*: for *bag-zón* **dread, fear.**

བབ་ *bab* v. *ₒbáb-pa.*

བབ་ཅོལ་ *bab-čól* **hastiness, rashness,** want of consideration in speaking and acting = *yzu-lúm*; *sdig-pa bab-čól-du byéd-pa* to sin recklessly, without heed or regard *Mil.*

བབ་མོ་, བས་མོ་ báb-mo, bás-mo (?) Ld. **soft, mild;** also **chaste, modest** (corrupted from bág-mo?).

བབས་ babs 1. **sunk, settled,** v. ₒbáb-pa; nú-ma-la raṅ-bábs-kyi rdzas byúg-ste rubbing the breasts with a medicine, so that they sank down of themselves, as if they were full Glr.; bábs-sa **settlement, colony** Sch. — 2. **shape, form, appearance** Sch. — 3. rta-babs v. rta, comp.

བམ་(པ) bám(-pa) 1. **rotten, decayed, putrid,** ro bám-pa putrid corpse Tar., bam-rō, id.; prob. also corpse in general, esp. in connection with sorcery; bam-čén, id.? Thgr. — 2. **mould,** white film on liquids; **mouldy, fusty, musty** W.

བམ་པོ་ bám-po 1. **bundle** of wood or grass Schr., Sch. — 2. **division, section,** of books, (of greater length than a chapter); in metrical compositions it is said to comprize a number of 300 verses; glegs-bám v. glegs; bam-śiṅ Sch. **board,** prob = glegs-śiṅ.

བམ་རིལ་ bam-ril 1. Sch. **dull, weak,** from old age or long labour, **worn out,** by much usage. — 2. W. **mould.**

བར་ bar sbst. (Cs. also bár-ma) 1. **intermediate space, interstice, interval,** mḱar γnyis-kyi bar zám-gyis sbrél-ba Glr. overbridging the space between the two castles; sa-bár **straits, narrow sea;** ču-bár **isthmus, neck of land;** *páṅ-gi bar, láṅ-ḱe bar, ₒče bar* **shelf** of a repository, cup-board etc. W.; **intermediate, middle, mean,** stod smad bar γsum upper, lower and middle country Ma.; bar ₒdir here in the middle countries Glr.; bár-gyi, id., as adj. Tar. and elsewh.; bár-gyi sder-čágs, in Wdṅ. a lizard, as an amphibium partaking of two natures; bár-na, bár-du, bár-la adv. and postp. c. genit. (and accus.), lám-gyi bár-na in the middle of the road (there is a well); on the road, in or on the way, on the journey Dzl.; brág-bar btsir-ba to be squeezed between two rocks Thgy.; ló-ma daṅ yál-gai bár-du between leaves and branches Dzl.; rgya bod bár-la ₒgró-bai mi people travelling between China and Tibet Glr.; deï bár-la, de-bár between Glr.; **in the mean time, at the same time,** Glr.; zla-ba γsum-gyi bár-du (to provide for a person) for the space of 3 months Dzl.; żag bdún-gyi bár-du for seven days (he had not eaten any thing) Dzl.; ṫúṅ-čin byá-bai sá-ča bár-du byon he went as far as the country called tuṅ-čin Glr.; dá-ltai bár-du Glr., da-tsam-gyi bár-du Dzl.; da-bár, Mil. **until now, hitherto;** de(i) bár(du) id., when referring to what is past **until then;** ₒbrás-bui bár-du ṫób-pa to obtain all, even to the fruit (inclusive of the fruit) Dzl.; lan γsum-gyi bár-du at three (different) times Dzl.; frq. with verbs: rtsé-mo-la ṫúg-gi bár-du till even touching the top Dzl. and so frq.; rel. to time gen. with a negative, being then equivalent to **as long as,** ma ṫób-pai bár-du as long as it has not been obtained = until its having been obtained Dzl.; ṅa ma śi bár-du till or up to my death Mil.; ma bsleb bár-du as long as we have not reached, attained Glr.; seldom without a negation: mya-ṅán-las ₒdás-pai bár-du Dzl. LV, 4 (s. l. c.); bár-nas **from between,** rtsib-mai bár-nas from between the ribs Glr. — 2. fig. bar byéd-pa to interpose, intercede, mediate Glr., cf. bár-mi. — 3. Termin. of ba, and cf. par III.

Comp. and deriv. *bhár-kya* partition-wall C. — bar-skábs space of time, period Tar. — bar-skór veranda, exterior gallery of the middle story of a house. — bar-ḱaṅ Sch. a building between two other houses; Schr. a room between two others. — bar-gós Schr. waist-coat. — bár-ₒga some, several; several times, now ... now ... Dzl. — bar-čód, -čad, perh. also -γčod, sbst. to bar-du γčod-pa, (v. γčod-pa) **hinderance, impediment; danger; damage, failure, fatal accident;** ṫsé-la bar-čád ₒoṅ, or byuṅ (my) life is in danger; lús-kyi, sróg-gi bar-čád-du ₒgyur id.; also: to meet with an accident, to perish, to be lost Dzl. and elsewh.; *bar-čad-la śi* W., he met with a violent death; bar-čád sél-ba to protect against fatal accidents, of magic spells frq.; ṅá-la bar-čád méd-par without meeting with an accident Mil.; bar-čád rtsóm-pa to meditate evil, to brood mischief *Mil.*; *bar-čád ma tsúgs-par* without having played me a roguish trick *Mil.*; also in a moral sense: temptation; sin, trespass, *bár-du γčód-pa* to commit sin, to trespass *Mil.* — **bár-ta** *W.* cloth round the loins. — *bar-stóṅ Sch.* empty space. — *bár-do* 1. also *bar-ma-do* the intermediate state between death and re-birth, of a shorter or longer duration (yet not of more than 40 days, ni f.); although on the one hand it is firmly believed, that the place of re-birth (whether a man, an animal, or a god etc. go forth from it), unalterably depends on the former course of life, yet in *Thgr.* the soul is urged and instructed to proceed at once into Nirwana to Buddha (inconsistently with the general dogma). *bár-do γčód-pa Mil.* is explained as putting off and preventing the intermediate state after death, as well as re-birth, by penitentiary exercises. 2. *W.*: **hard, difficult; difficulty,** — perh. Bunan. — *bar-snáṅ* (seldom *bar-snáṅ-ba*) **atmospherical space**; *stéṅ-gi bar-snáṅ-la* in the heavens, in the air, frq.; *bar-snáṅ-la ₒpar* (a fragment of a blasted rock) flies up into the air; *bar-snáṅ-du* or *-la* c. genit., the common word for **over,** *goi bar-náṅ-la*, over (his) head. — **bár-pa** *W.* the middle one, e.g. of three brothers. — *bar-bár-du Ma.* **at intervals, from time to time, now and then**; *bar-bár-la* id.; **mà bar-bár-la**, at long intervals, seldom *W.* — *bár-ma* the middle one of three things *Glr.* — *bar-mí* **mediator, intercessor, umpire.** — **bar-tsód** *W.* middling, **lúṅ-po bar-tsód** a moderate wind. — *bar-mtsáms, bar-ₒtsáms* **interval** (*Sch.*: room; leisure, convenience, comfort?). — *bar-lág-pa* = *bar-mi Sch.* — **bar-lhag** gap, vacancy, deficiency *W.*, **bar-lág káṅ-če** to fill up a gap or vacancy, to supply a want, or deficiency.

བར་ལིག་ *bar-lig W.* **a field** or **estate** let to a person for the term of his life, for usufruct.

བལ་ *bal* **wool,** *bál-gyi* woolen, *bal daṅ ldán-pa* woolly *Wdṅ.*; *bal séd-pa* the first coarse plucking of wool, *rmél-ba* the second, of the finer wool, *šiṅ-ba* the third, of the finest *W.*; **bal táb-če** to beat wool *W.*; *lug-, ra-, rṅá-bal* sheep-wool, goat's and camel's hair; *rás-bal, šiṅ-bal* cotton *Cs.*; *šiṅ-bal* prob. also the down on willow-blossoms *Sch.*; *srín-bal Wdṅ.*, *Schr.*: raw silk, yet perh. also cotton; *čú-bal* a kind of moss on stones in brooks *Cs.* — *bal-skúd* a woolen thread or yarn, worsted. *bal-skyé Sch.*: mould on fermented liquors. — *bal-gláṅ*, *Cs.* also *bál-gyi glaṅ-po-čé*, a kind of elephant, for which sometimes incorr. and ambiguously *bá-laṅ* is used, *Dzl.* and elsewh. — *bal-tér* thin woolen cloth *Cs.*; **bal-ₒdáb** *W.* tuft of wool, as is used for spinning. — *bal-prúg* thick woolen cloth. — *bal-yás Sch.* wool-card (?)

བལ་པོ་ *bál-po, bal(-po)-yúl* **Nepal,** frq. designated as *rin-po-čei gliṅ*, and as the favourite country of the *Klu*, or serpent-demons; *bál-po-pa*, fem. *bál-po-ma, bál-mo Glr.*, a Nepal man or woman; *bal-nyiṅ C.*, (*-snyiṅs*) a Nepal rupee; *bal-srán Tar.*, Nepal pease.

བས་ *bas* I. v *bás-pa.* — II. instrum. of *ba*; *bas-bldágs*, 'licked by a cow', n. of a disease combined with the sensation, as if the skin had been licked off by a cow, cow-itch, cow-pox *Cs.* (?) — III. v. *pas*, where there is to be added: **to say nothing of, much less,** e.g. *kron ₒdom dgu-brgyá-bas brgya yaṅ ₒbru mi tub*, a well a hundred fathoms deep cannot be dug, to say nothing of 900 fathoms (much less one of 900 f.) *Glr.*

བས་པ་ *bás-pa* (cf. Pers., Hind. بس) *Cs.*: pf. of *byéd-pa* inst. of, *byás-pa* in the signification of **'done (with), settled'**; *bás-par byéd-pa*, id. *Sch.*; in *Bal.* frq.: **bas, byas, bas-se*, or also *byás-te yód** it is finished, completed, ready, all right; *der bas* that is all of it, nothing more is left *Sch.*; in *bgyis-su bás-kyis* after having been made, caused, occasioned *Mil.*, it stands as a sign of the preterite, similar to *zin*; or like *zad*: *mi γčig-gi smán-du ma bás-kyis* not only for one man it serves as a medicine *Dzl.*; *bas-mta* **border-country** *Sch.*

བས་མོ་ *bás-mo* v. *báb-mo.*

བི་ *bi* 1. num. figure: 45. — 2. in *W.* gen. for *byi.* — 3. *bi* and *biu Pur.* for *bya* **bird, fowl, hen.**

བི་གང་, བི་ཡང་ *bi-gáṅ, bi-yáṅ* in compounds *big*, **hole** *W.* for *bú-ga*, cf. *ₒbig-pa*; *bi-gáṅ-čan* having holes.

བི་ཏང་ *bi-taṅ*, *Lh.* **door,** prop. Bunan.

བི་ནཱ་ཡ་ཀ་ *bi-nā-ya-ka Ssk.*, v. *bgegs.*

བི་ཤྭ་ཀརྨ་ *bi-šwa-kar-ma Ssk.*, *lhai bzó-bo* the smith of the gods, the Brahman-Buddhist Vulcan *Dzl.*, *Glr.*

བི་ཥ་ *bi-ša* (*Ssk.* word for poison) n. of certain medicinal plants, e.g. *bi-ša-dkar* Polygonatum, in *Lh.*

བིག་པན་ *big pan Cs.* **vitriol;** *Sch.* **potash, garlic-ashes;** mentioned in *S.g.* as a caustic.

བིག་བི་ལིག་ *big-bi-lig Kun.* **quail.**

བིད་བིད་ *bid-bid*(?) *Ld.* **mouth-piece of a hautboy, hautboy reed.**

བིམ་པ་ *bim-pa* **बिम्ब, बिम्ब.** Momordica monadelpha, a cucurbitaceous plant with a red fruit *Wdṅ.*, along with *ka-bed*; the fashion of Indian poets to compare red lips with the bimpa fruit, has been adopted also by the Tibetans, *Gyatch.* p. ༦༦; transl. p. 108; so also *Pth.*: *mču-sgrós bim-pa ltá-bur mdzes* (where *Sch.* gives the signification of **peach,** on which the name possibly may have been transferred, although 'lips of the shape of a peach-tree leaf' seem to be rather a strange fancy).

བིར་བིར་ *bir-bir W.* **crumbs, bits, scraps.**

བིལ་བ་ *bil-ba Ssk.* **बिल्व,** *Hind. billb, bél,* Aegle marmelos, tree with a nourishing and wholesome fruit; the word seems to have been transferred also to the cocoa-nut.

བུ་ *bu* I. sbst., resp. *sras*, 1. **son,** common in *B.* and *C.*; **čé-bu* W.*, the eldest son. — 2. child, *bu btsá-ba* the bringing forth of children, children being born *Dzl.*; *bu máṅ-bar ₒgyúr-ba* to get many children; *bu mi ɣsós-pa* not being able to keep a child alive *Dom.*; esp. in reference to the mother: *ma-bu*, mother and children; also transferred on animals: *rta ma brgya bu brgya* a hundred mares with as many foals *Dzl.*; the word is moreover used in many other instances, e.g. with regard to letters which in writing are placed under other letters, in reference to principal beams and smaller cross-beams, to capital and interest; also as a friendly address of a teacher to his hearers *Mil.* — The fem. *bú-mo* v. below.

Comp. *bu-ₒkrid* (or *pu-tri*?) a fem. noun proper. — *bu-grógs Cs.* **step-brother, foster-brother.** — *bu-rgyúd* **offspring, issue, progeny, generation** *Tar.* 168. 11. — *bu-dód* foster-child, adopted son, *ṅéd-kyi bu-dód mdzod* deign to be adopted by us *Mil.* — *bu-ɣdúṅ* a small cross-beam *Mil.* — *bu-nád* child-bed, *bu-nád log* the child-bed terminates unfavourably *Pth.* — *bu-snód* **uterus, womb** *Med.* — *bú-po* male child, son *Dzl.* — *bu-prug* children. — *bú-mo*, vulg. also *bó-mo* 1. **daughter,** frq. 2. **girl,** *ṅa bú-moi dús-na yin-te* when I was still a girl *Glr.* — *kyeu daṅ bú-mo* lads and lasses *Dzl.*; **maiden, virgin;** *bú-mo ɣtsáṅ-ma, ɣsár-ma, ɣsár-pa* a girl that is still in a virgin state. 3. young woman *Dzl.*; *W.* gen. for *bud-méd*, frq. — *bu-smád*, *Cs.* also *bu-mád* family, children, nearest relations *Mil.* and elsewh. — *bu-tsá* (*Dzl.* ed. *Sch.* also *bu-tsa*) 1. **children's children** *Thgy.*; family = *bu-smád* 2. *W.*, **son,** gen. for *bu*; **boy,** **bú-tsa daṅ bó-mo**. — *bu-tsáb Cs.* = *bu-dod.* — *bu-tsás ₒbrél-ba Glr.* (acc. to the context) to cohabit. — *bu-sriṅ* brother and sister. — *bu-slób* scholar, disciple, follower of a clerical teacher, opp. to *nyá-ma* hearer, who still continues in his secular calling. — II. num. figure: 75.

བུ་ག་ *bu-ga* 1. **छिद्र,** in compounds *bug*, **hole, opening, orifice, aperture,** *bá-spui bú-ga* pore, passage of perspiration *Dzl.*; *sna-búg* nostril; *bú-ga dgu*(-*po*) the nine orifices of the body (eyes, ears, nostrils, mouth, urethra, anus); *tsáṅs-pai bú-ga* and perh. also *yid-ₒjug bú-ga Med.*, appears to be = *mtsog-ma* **the fontanel** or vacancy in the infant cranium, with which various fables are connected; **cavity, vessel,** (anatom.), also **veins** *Med.* — 2. symbol. num.: 9.

བུ་གུ་ *bú-gu* **hole**, *sgoi* key-hole *Dzl.*

བུ་སྟོན་ *bu-stón* name of a learned Lama and author of *čos-byúṅ*, about the year 1300 *Glr.*, an adherent of the Adi-buddha doctrine, v. *Cs. Gram.*

བུ་རྡོ་ *bú-rdo Sch.*, **idle talk, tittle-tattle.**

བུ་ཡུག་ *bu-yúg* **snow-storm** *Mil.*

བུ་རམ་ *bu-ram Hindi* गुड़, *gur*, hence *W.* **gu-rám**, **raw sugar, muscovado; treacle**, *Mil., Lt.; bu-rám sgór-ba* to boil down raw sugar *Lex.*; *bu-ram-śiṅ, bur-śiṅ*, vulg. **gur-śiṅ** **sugar-cane**; *bu-ram-śiṅ-pa*, इक्ष्वाकु, name of the first king of the solar dynasty in India, *Glr.; bu-ram-čaṅ, bur-čaṅ* sugar-beer *Lt.*; *bur-dkár? Lt. búr-stáṅ ycig* (more correctly *ltaṅ*) *Sch.*, a bale of raw sugar packed up in leather.

བུ་ལོན་ *bú-lon* (cf. *bun*) **advanced money, debt,** **ṅul gyę bú-lon mi-la táṅ-ce** *W.* to lend a person a hundred florins; (*bú-lon byéd-pa* to contract debts *Schr., Sch.*??) *bú-lon ˳jál-ba* (*W.* **čál-ce**), *spród-pa Sch.* to pay a debt, *sél-ba* to put out, to cancel a debt, *déd-pa, bdá-ba* to call in, to recover a debt, *čágs-pa* prob. the beginning and running up of debts *Dzl.*; *bú-lon-pa* **debtor,** *dṅul brgyai* of a hundred rupees.

བུ་ཧག་ *bu-hág* v. *sbugs-hág.*

བུག་པ་ *búg-pa* 1. sbst. **hole,** *búg-pa ˳búg-pa* to bore holes *Glr.*, cog. to *bú-ga.* — 2. *Sch.*, to get holes (?).

བུག་ཞོལ་ *bug-žól* v. *sbugs.*

བུག་སུག་ *bug-súg Ld.* **birdsfoot-trefoil,** Melilotus.

བུང་བ་ *búṅ-ba* 1. a humming and stinging insect, **bee** etc.; *buṅ-lčág* sting, and also the wound caused by it; **buṅ-ba čág taṅ soṅ** *W.* the bee has stung. 2 *Cs.* a bright black stone.

བུངས་ *buṅs* **mass, heap, bulk,** *buṅs-čén* a large heap *Lt.*; *dri-čui buṅs-če* a great quantity of urine *Mṅg.*; *buṅs byéd-pa* to heap one upon another, pile up. — *buṅ* **many** (?).

བུད་ *bud*, every darkening of the air through dry matter, **a cloud of dust,** more exactly *tal-búd; bud-tsub* dust from threshing; *búd-kyis btab* wrapt in vapour *Mil.*; perh. also **snow-storm** (*Sch.*), yet not exclusively.

བུད་དྷ་ *búd-dha Ssk.*, **Buddha,** n. of the founder of the religion which is called after him, occurring but rarely in Tibetan writings, and among the people (at least in *W.*) almost unknown, v. *saṅs-rgyas*; *bud-dhai ṗreṅ-ba*, **búd-dẹ́ ṭáṅ-na** **rosary** *Ts.*

བུད་པ་ *búd-pa* 1. *Sch.* = *sbúd-pa.* — 2. pf. cf. *˳búd-pa.*

བུད་མེད་ *bud-méd B.* and *C.*, 1. **woman,** *bud-méd sdúg-gu* a fair woman *Dzl.*; *bud-méd daṅ sbágs-pa* to defile, corrupt one's self with women *Dzl.* — 2. **wife, spouse,** not frq. *Dzl.* (*W. bú-mo* and *ǎ-ne*).

བུད་ཤིང་ *búd-śiṅ* **fire-wood, fuel,** also dung used as such; *búd-śiṅ bśág-pa* to cleave or chop wood.

བུན་ *bun* 1. = *bú-lon Mil.*, *bun toṅ* **lend us!** *Mil.*; *bun btáṅ-du ma nyán-pas* not willing to lend any thing *Mil.*; *kyéd-rnams-la bun dgós-na* if you want an advance (of money) *Mil.* — *bún-to, bún-yig* 1. **debtor's account-book.** 2. **bond** or obligation, **bill of debt.** — *bun-bdág* 1. **creditor.** 2. **money-changer, banker.** — *bún-yig* v. *bún-to.* — 2. **interest,** **bhun kyé-pa** to bear interest *C.*; *bun ˳jál-ba* to pay interest *Cs.* — 3. (house) **rent** *Sch.* (?) — 4. *bun-ré Sch.* **a small matter,** cf. *bun-bún*; *bun-bún Sch.* piece-meal, scattered, dispersed. — 5. v. *˳bún-pa.*

བུན་ལོང་ *bun-lóṅ* — *ču bun-loṅ-lóṅ byed* it is whirling up and down, an expression used of boiling water which contains impurities or extraneous matter; hence *bun-lóṅ-gi snaṅ-sás* troubled, impure, sinful thoughts.

བུབ་པ་ *bub-pa* v. *˳bub-pa.*

བུབས་ *bubs* = *yug*, also *tan* (थान *Hind.*) 1. an entire **piece of cloth** rolled up; *gos-bubs* cotton-cloth *Cs.* — 2. in a general sense one whole, something entire *Sch.*; *bubs-ril* prob. whole, entire, *bubs-ril lus S.g.* the whole body, opp. to separate parts.

བུམ་པ་ *búm-pa*, **bottle, flask**; the water-flask of the hukka; bottle-shaped ornaments in architecture, e. g. on the cenotaphs or Chodtén; *rdzá-mai* earthen-bottle, pitcher; *šél-bum* glass-bottle; *čán-bum* beer-bottle; *mčód-bum Cs.* vessel used in sacrificing; *mé-bum* cupping-glass *Lt.* (cf. *puń-pa*).

བུར་ *bur* 1. **bolt, bar,** vertically fastened to a door etc., *tóg-bur* upper, *yóg-bur* lower bolt. — 2. for *bu-rám*. — 3. for *˳bur*.

བུར་རྟིང་ *bur-rtiń* (or perh. *tiń*) *Sch.*, a kind of **bell** or **gong** in temples.

བུར་ཙེ་ *búr-tse* n. of certain plants in *Ld. & Kun.*

བུལ་ *bul W.*, **bhul, bhṳl, bhṳ* and *bhṳ-tog* C., Med.*, (the spellings of Campbell, *peu* — v. *bá-mo* — and of *Schl.*, *phuli*, have prob. resulted from a mistake in hearing), **soda**, not unfrequently found in Tibet as a white powder on the ground, and used as a medicine, as a ferment, as a means for giving additional flavour to tea, and for various technical purposes.

བུལ་པོ་ *búl-po* **slow, heavy, tardy,** *˳gro búl-te* slow in walking, making but tardy progress *Dzl.*; *W.: *ḍúl-če búl-po**.

བུལ་ཧ་རི་ *bul-ha-ri, *bul-gar* W.*, **Russia leather, jufts.**

བུས་པ་ *bús-pa* 1. for *byis-pa Lt.* — 2. v. *˳búd-pa*.

བེ་ *be*, 1. num. figure: 105. — 2. *W.* for *bye*. — 3. for words here not noted refer to *pe*.

བེ་ཁུར་ *be-k̔ur S.g.?*

བེ་གེ་ *be-gé* v. *beg-gé*.

བེ་ཅོན་ *be-čon*, also *-tson, Ssk.* गदा, 1. **club,** with an ornamental knob, prob. merely an attribute of gods. — 2. n. of a goddess *Thgr.*

བེ་ཏ་ *be-ta* a geographical prop. name, prob. = Himalaya, *Pth.*

བེ་ཏོ་, བེ་དོ་ *bé-to, bé-do*, vulg. **calf.**

བེ་དྷ་ *bé-dha* v. *˳bé-dha*.

བེ་སྣབས་ *be-snábs Cs.*, **thick slime** or **mucus,** e.g. the mucus flowing at childbirth from the vagina *Lt.*

བེ་བུམ་ *be-búm*, also *beu-búm*, **writing, scripture, book** *Glr.*, perh. the same word as the following.

བེ་འབུམ་ *be-˳bum*, are stated to be the sacred writings of the Bonpos, which — as our Lama candidly owned — 'are also perused by Buddhists for their edification'.

བེ་མོ་ *bé-mo* **cow-calf,** female calf *C.*

བེ་རྫི་ *be-rdzi* Nakshatra, v. *rgyu-skár* 3.

བེ་ཟ་ *bé-za W.*, from the *Hind.* ब्याज, **interest,** *ṭá-ka bé-za* a double paisa interest, of 1 rupee, = 4—6 pCt. pro month.

བེ་རག་ *be-rag* (spelling?), **fillet** of the women in *Ld.*, ornamented with coloured stones.

བེ་ལེ་ཀ་ *be-le-ka S.g.*, a kind of **surgical instrument.**

བེ་ལོག་ *be-log Sch.* **great-grandfather.**

བེ་ཤིང་ *be-šiń* **oak-tree,** = *ča-ra*; *be-k̔ród* oak-forest *Wdń.*

བེག་གེ་ *beg-gé Lt.*, a disease; *Sch.:* measles.

བེག་ཙེ་ *bég-tse* a hidden **shirt of mail.**

བེང་ *beń Sch.*, **stick, cudgel, club.**

བེད་ *bed*, 1. = *k̔e, k̔e-béd*, **advantage, profit, gain, high price,** *tsá-la drúg-ču bed yód-pai skábs-su* at a time when salt was a sixty times dearer (than barley) *Glr.; *bed tób-če* W.* to gain, to make profit; *bed-čód Mil.* is stated to be the same as *loń-spyód*; *bed-čód tsod bzúd-de* to be temperate, to keep moderation in the indulgence of the appetites. — 2. **interest,** *C., W.*

བེན་ *ben* **a large pitcher; jug, beer-pot,** *Glr.*; **ču-bhén**, water-pot, *C.*

བེམ་པོ་ *bém-po* 1. **dead matter,** mostly applied to the body, as opp. to the soul, *rig-pa*, e.g. *bem rig ˳gye-dus* when body and soul are parting, *Mil., Thgr.*; *lus bem-rig gnyis-kyi so-mtsáms-su* on the boundary between the physical matter of the body and the soul *Mil.*; *Was.* (272) *bem-reg* is perh. a mistake in writing, although it also makes sense. — 2. *Sch.* **a pestilential disease;** in the *Mṅg.* *bem tol rgyáb-pa* seems to denote a surgical operation. — 3. some receptacle, **box, bag** etc., *bém-poi náṅ-nas ɣser bton* she took gold out of the . . .?

བེའུ་ *beu Cs.* **calf.**

བེའུ་བུམ་ *beu-búm* v. *be-búm, Mil.*

བེའུ་རས་ *beu-rás*, in *Stg.* mentioned as a material for clothing; *Schr.*: **'fine linen'**, which however is as yet unknown in Tibet.

བེར་ *ber* 1. **cloak,** *bér-gyi ṭú-ba* tail of the cloak *Glr.*; *ber nág-po* a black cloak *Glr.* and elsewh.; *˳ǰol-bér* dress with a train *Wdk.*, *Pth.*; *tsem-bér* a cloak patched up of many pieces *Pth.*; *ber-čén* gown of a priest, sacerdotal cloak, without sleeves, with *gos-čén* for a collar; *ber-ṭúl* fur-cloak. — 2. **strength, sharpness, keenness, pungency,** of spices, spirits, snuff etc.; *ber-čan* sharp, pungent, piquant; **á-rág-la ber máṅ-po yod** the gin is very strong *W.*; **bér-ra rag, lčeï bér-če máṅ-po rag** it bites, burns my tongue; *za-bér Cs.* the burning sensation caused by the stinging of nettles; cf. *gár-ba.*

བེར་ཀ་ *bér-ka W.*, *bér-ma*, *ber-lcúg Mil.*, **stick, staff** (cf. *dbyúg-pa*); *spai bér-ma* cane, bamboo *Mil.*; *ber-ma lčug ɣčig* a simple staff *Mil.*; *lčags-bér* iron-bar, crow-bar; *smyug-bér* cane, walking-stick.

བེལ་ *bel Cs.* **leather bag.**

བཻ་ཌཱུརྻ་ *wai-dūr-ya*, *Ssk.*, **azure stone, lapis lazuli** *Dzl.* *wai-dūr-ya dkar-po* and *sṅon-po*, v. table of abbreviations.

བཻ་རོ་ཙ་ན་ *wai-ro-tsa-na Ssk.*, *Tib.*: *rnam-par-snaṅ-mdzad*, 1. n. of the first Dhyani-Buddha. — 2. a Lotsawa v. *Köpp.* II., 69.

བོ་ *bo*, 1. num. figure: 135. — 2. **affix,** to designate some words as nouns.

བོ་ཏོག་པ་, བོ་ལོང་བ་ *bo-tóg-pa*, *bo-lóṅ-ba Ts.*, **ankle, ankle-bone.**

བོ་དེ་ *bo-de Cs.*: 'n. of a tree, the fruits of which are used as beads for rosaries'.

བོ་དྷི་ *bo-dhi Ssk.*, **wisdom;** also n. of **the Indian fig-tree,** ficus religiosa, *byaṅ-čub-śiṅ*; n. of the **white narcissus** (*Lh.*).

བོ་བ་ *bó-ba*, prob. pf. of *˳bó-ba.*

བོ་མོ་ *bó-mo W.* for *bú-mo.*

བོ་ལོ་ *bó-lo*, **ball,** for playing *Ld.*

བོག་པ་ *bog-pa* v. *˳bógs-pa.*

བོག་ར་ *bóg-ra Sch.* **roof.**

བོགས་ *bogs*, *Cs.*, **gain, profit, advantage;** *bogs ˳dón-pa Sch.* to yield profit; whereever I met with the word, it was used only in a religious sense: **gain for the mind,** benefit for the heart, furtherance of devotion of meditation, *Mil.*

བོང་ *boṅ* 1. also *boṅs*, **size, dimensions, volume, bulk,** *boṅ-čé*, *-čén* large, *boṅ če don čuṅ*, large of size, and small of significance are e. g. the lungs (in as far as roasted or boiled they yield little substantial food) *Mil.*; *lus-boṅ-čé*, *-čúṅ*, *˳bríṅ* big, little, middling, as to size of body, *S.g.*; *boṅ-ṭúṅ* little in stature; *boṅ-tsád*, *boṅ-tsód* = *rdzógs-pa* full size, a full-grown body *Thgy.* — 2. v. *boṅ-na.* — 3. also *bóṅ-ba*, *Cs.*: 'general name for small stones, pebbles etc.'; in medical works *zíṅ-gi bóṅ-ba* are mentioned as remedies; in *Pth.* the word occurs in an enumeration of temporal goods, precluding the above signification. — 4. v. *boṅ-bu.* — 5. provinc. for *baṅ Glr.*

བོང་ཁྲ་ *boṅ-krá Sch.* a species of **falcon.**

བོང་གུ་ *bóṅ-gu* v. *bóṅ-bu.*

བོང་ང་ *boṅ-ná*, various species of **wolf's bane,** aconite, *boṅ-dkár*, *-nág*, *-dmár*, *-sér*, used as medicines, or even as poisons.

བོང་ནག་ *boṅ-nág* v. the preceeding and the following article.

བོང་བུ་ *bóṅ-bu*, *Sch.* also *bóṅ-bo*, 1. **ass,** *bóṅ-po* or *po-bóṅ* he-ass, *bóṅ-mo* or *mo-bóṅ* she-ass, *boṅ-prúg* colt or foal of an ass; boṅ-sgál an ass's load; boṅ-sbáṅ dung of an ass; boṅ-rdzi keeper or driver of an ass; dre-bóṅ Cs. 'an ass generating a mule'. — 2. n. of insects, rgyás-poi bóṅ-bu sugar-mite, lepisma, Ld.; boṅ-nág (perh. buṅ-nág) dung-beetle Lh. — 3. Cs.: **blockhead, fool.**

བོད་ *bod* 1. Ssk. भोट, **Tibet,** *bód-(kyi) yul* id. 2. for *bód-pa, bod k'a-čig* some **Tibetans** Tar., *k'yed bód-rnams* ye Tibetans. — 3. for *bód-skad* the **Tibetan language,** *bód-du bsgyur ˳jug* I will have it translated into Tibetan Pth.; *bód-skad*, in a more limited sense, also implies the common language of conversation, opp. to book-language W.; *bód-pa, bód-(kyi) mi* Tibetans, *bód-mo* fem; *bód-kyi mi-rigs* or *mi-brgyúd* the people of Tibet, in contradistinction to other nations, *bod-˳báṅs* the Tibetan people, opp. to its ruler.

བོད་པ་ *bód-pa* 1. v. *bod.* — 2. = *˳bód-pa.*

བོན་ *bon* (acc. to Schf. = बीज) 1. n. of the early religion of Tibet, concerning which but very imperfect accounts are existing (v. Report of the Royal Bavarian Acad. of Sc., 13. Jan. 1866); so much is certain, that sorcery was the principal feature of it. When Buddhism became the religion of state, the former was considered heretical and condemnable, and *lha-čos* and *bon-čos*, or shorter *čos* and *bon*, were placed in opposition, as with us christianity and paganism; v. Glr. and Mil.; at the present time, both of them seem to exist peaceably side by side, and the primitive religion has not only numerous adherents and convents in C., but manifold traces of it may be found still in the creed of the Tibetans of to-day. — 2. = *bón-po*, follower of this religion.

བོར་ *bor*, v. *˳bór-ba.*

བོར་ར་ *bór ra*, **a sack of corn,** holding about 30 *k'al* W.

བོལ་ *bol, bol-góṅ* 1. **the upper part of the foot** Stg. — 2. **the leg of a boot** W. — 3. **clod of earth** C. — 4. v. *˳bol.*

བོལ་གར་ *bol-gár* = *búl-ha-ri.*

བོལ་པོ་ *ból-po* v. *˳ból-po.*

བོས་ *bos*, v. *˳bód-pa.*

བྱ་ *bya* 1. sbst. **bird, fowl, hen,** cf. the following articles. (Pur. *biu* [v. *byiu*], *bi*). — 2. vb. fut. root of *byéd-pa*, v. this and the sbst. *byá-ba.* — 3. *ˀja čó-če* W., **to castrate, to geld.**

བྱཱ་ཀ་ར་ཎ་ *byā-ká-ra-ṇa*, व्याकरण, prop.: **explanation,** 1. = *luṅ-du-ston-pa* **prophecy,** cf. Burn. I, 54 sequ. — 2. in later times: **grammar.**

བྱ་ཁྲི་ *bya-k'ri* Mṅg., *bya-tri* Lt., n. of a medicine.

བྱ་རྐང་ *bya-rkáṅ*, 1. **a bird's foot.** — 2. n. of **a vein** Med. — 3. officinal plant, in Lh. a blue kind of orobanche.

བྱ་སྐད་ *bya-skád*, also *bya-sgrúṅs, bya-čós* title of a book of satirical fables, in which birds are introduced speaking.

བྱ་སྐོན་ *bya-skón* **fowler's net** Lex.

བྱ་སྐྱི་ *bya-skyi* Stg.; Sch.: **roof, shelter.**

བྱ་ཁང་ *bya-k'áṅ* Cs. **bird-cage.**

བྱ་ཁྱུང་, ཁྲ, ཁྲུང་ *bya-k'yúṅ, -k'rá, -k'rúṅ* = *k'yuṅ, k'ra* and *k'ruṅ-k'rúṅ.*

བྱ་ག་ག *bya-gág* Dzl. and elsewh., a species of ducks, Sch.: **the gray duck.**

བྱ་དགའ་ *bya-dgá* **gift, present,** esp. as a reward; *sbyin-pa* to bestow a gift, frq.; *bya-dgár* as a present, for a reward, *stér-ba* to give.

བྱ་རྒོད་ and རྒྱལ་ *bya-rgód* and *-rgyál* **bird of prey** B. and col.; *bya-rgod-spos* Med., vulgo *la-da-ra* (v. *gla*) *bya-rgod-p'úṅ-poi ri*, गृध्रकूट, vulture-hill, in Magadha, a preaching-place of Buddha.

བྱ་རྒྱ་ *bya-rgyá* **fowler's net.**

བྱ་སྒབ་ *bya-sgáb* n. of one of the smaller lobes of the lungs.

བྱ་སྙེན་ *bya-snyén* v. *bya-rmyén.*

བྱ་ཏྲི་ *bya-tri* v. *bya-k'ri.*

བྱ་ཐལ་ *bya-tál* Glr. light-gray **bird's dung.**

བྱ་འདབ་ *bya-ₒdáb* 1. lit. **a bird's wing.** — 2. a part of the roof or vertical projection of the same, a kind of façade, admitting of pictorial decoration *Glr.*

བྱ་འདྲེ་ *bya-ₒdré Sch.*, a winged diabolical creature, **harpy.**

བྱ་ན་ *bya-na* (acc. to *Liš.* corrupted from व्यञ्जन) **seasoning, condiment, sauce,** in a legend; prob. also in a gen. sense: **meat, food,** *byá-nai yo-byád Lex.*, *byá-na-ma*, prob. id.; *ts̔á-ba byá-na-ma žig k̔yér-nas* bringing some warm food *Mil.*

བྱ་ནག་ *bya-nág* **raven,** or some similar bird *S.g.*; *bya-nag-rdó-rǰe Mil.* id., because the raven is said to reach an age of a thousand years.

བྱ་ནན་ *bya-nán Sch.* (sub. *byá-ra*) **earnest endeavour.**

བྱ་པ་ *byá-pa Cs.* **fowler, bird-catcher.**

བྱ་པོ་ *byá-po* 1. **cock,** the male of the domestic fowl, more definitely: *byá(-po) mts̔a-lu B.* and col.; *byá-po dáṅ-po, ɣnyis-pa* etc., the first, the second cock-crow *C.* — 2. **byá-po skyá-po** *W.* **sparrow.** — 3. *bya-po-tsi-tsi Med.*, a medicinal plant, stopping the monthly courses; in *Lh.* the great balsamine, Impatiens Roylei.

བྱ་སྤུ་ *byá-spu*, **down** (feather), *byai spu B.* and col.

བྱ་ཕོ་ *bya-p̔o*, **cock,** the male of any bird.

བྱ་ཕྲུག་ *bya-p̔rug* 1. **a young bird.** — 2. **a young fowl, chicken.**

བྱ་བ་ *byá-ba* 1. inf. and part. fut. of *byéd-pa*, q. v. — 2. sbst. **deed, action, work,** without any reference to time, *ₒǰig-rtén-gyi byá-ba* and *čós-kyi byá-ba* secular and religious works, frq.; *mai byá-ba byéd-pa* to act as a mother, to perform a mother's part *Tar.*; *byá-ba zin-pa* an action completely past *Gram.*; *byá-ba maṅ yaṅ ₒbrás-bu čúṅ-ba* much labour and little fruit, much work and little profit *Tar.*; *der rgyál-po daṅ blón-po-rnams-kyi byá-ba byúṅ-ba yin* then the affairs of the kings and their officers, the concerns of the state and its functionaries, gained ground; also in an absolute sense *byá-ba* = **secularity, worldliness,** *byá-ba btáṅ-ba ǰig rgyán-du če* a resigning of worldly things is fraught with great blessing *Mil.*; *bya-byéd* the doing, doings: *bya-byed nyúṅ-ba ǰig rgyán-du če* the doing little brings great blessing, and so in a similar manner: *byá-rgyu byéd-rgyu ma maṅ ǰig* do not give way to a bustling disposition *Mil.*, i.e. do not permit your contemplative state to be interrupted by a distracting activity of your mind; *bstán-pa-la* (or *bstán-pai*) *byá-ba byás-pai lo-rgyús* an account of what has been done for the spread of the doctrine *Tar.*; *byá-ba daṅ ₒbrél-ba* seems to be a grammatical term relating to the verb.

བྱ་བང་ *bya-báṅ* v. *bya-wáṅ.*

བྱ་བལ་ *bya-bál Sch.* **down** (feathers); *Lt.* 121?

བྱ་བྲལ་པ་ *bya-brál-pa* one free from business, one that has renounced all worldly employment, **an ascetic,** *Ld.-Glr.*

བྱ་མ་ *byá-ma* **a female bird, hen, brood-hen.**

བྱ་མ་རྟ་ *byá-ma-rta* **courier, estafet.**

བྱ་མ་བུམ་ *bya-ma-búm* a tea-pot shaped vessel used in sacrificing.

བྱ་མ་བྱར་སྐྱག་ *bya-ma-byar-skyág*(?) **dandelion,** Taraxacum *Ld.*

བྱ་མ་བྱི་ *bya-ma-byi S.g.*; *Sch.* **flying squirrel.**

བྱ་མ་ལེབ་ *bya-ma-léb Sch.* **butterfly,** = *p̔ye-ma-léb.*

བྱ་མོ་ *byá-mo* 1. **the female** of any kind of birds. — 2. **hen, female fowl,** also in conjunction with *mts̔á-lu*, cf. *byá-po*(?).

བྱ་རྨྱང་བ་ *bya-rmyáṅ-ba Sch.*, *bya-rmyéṅ* (another reading *snyeṅ*) *byéd-pa*, **to yawn** *Mil.*

བྱ་དམར་ *bya-dmár* **flamingo** *Sch.*

བྱ་ཚང་ *bya-ts̔áṅ* **bird's nest.**

བྱ་ཚེ་རིང་ *bya-ts̔e-riṅ Sch.* **the white crane.**

བྱ་ཚོགས་ *bya-ts̔ógs* **a flight of birds.**

བྱ་རྫི་ *bya-rdzi* **one attending to poultry.**

བྱ་ཝང་ *bya-wáṅ S.g.; Sch.:* **night-hawk, goat-sucker,** caprimulgus; **bat.**

བྱ་བཞོན་ **bya-bžón* Bal.* **egg.**

བྱ་ཟེ་ *bya-zé* **crest, tuft** (of feathers) of birds *Sch.*

བྱ་འུག *bya-ug* prob. **owl**; *Sch.* quail(?).

བྱ་ར་ *byá-ra Cs.*: 'heed, care, caution'. This word belonging to the language of the people and to later literature, is not so much an abstract, as a concrete noun, signifying **a watchman,** superintendent (chiefly by day, cf. *mél-ṫse* night-watch); it denotes more particularly that individual of a community, who has to see to it, that the compulsory post-office duties be punctually performed, and that messages from the lord or magistrate of the place be duly dispatched and forwarded to their place of destination; in a more gen. sense *byá-ra byéd-pa Glr.*, **ćó-če* W.*, *ɣtoṅ-ba Mil.* c. *la*, **to give heed, to pay attention, to look sharp, not to lose sight of;** also, **to be on one's guard against, to take a thing seriously,** e.g. *nád-la* a disease *Lt.*; **ǰá-ra i-mig** (prop. *yid-mig*) **ćo**, pay strict attention! *W.*

བྱ་རོག *bya-róg* **crow, raven,** mentioned in S.O. as an inveterate enemy of the *ug-pa* (owl).

བྱ་ལས་ *bya-lás,* **labour, work,** *zin-pa-méd-pai bya-lás* endless labours *Mil.*

བྱ་ལོ་པ་ *byá-lo-pa* 1. v. *lo.* — 2. *Sch.* 'keeping poultry'(?).

བྱ་སོ་མ་ *bya-so-ma Ts, Ld.* **bat.**

བྱག(-པ་) *byág(-pa)* 1. *Cs.* **pliancy, nimbleness, agility of body;** *byag-mḱan* rope-dancer *Lex.* — 2. sometimes erron. for *ǰag* and *ǰág-pa.*

བྱང་ *byaṅ* 1. **north;** *byaṅ-ṗyógs* and prob. also *byáṅ-ḱa Mil.* id.; *byáṅ-gi, byaṅ-ṗyógs-kyi* northern; *byaṅ-ṅós* north side, northern brow or slope of a hill; also n. pr., *Glr.*; *byaṅ-ṫáṅ* n. pr. the heaths or steppes in northern Tibet, more esp. those bordering in the west on *Ld.* — 2. **northern country,** coinciding with *byaṅ-ṫáṅ*: *byáṅ-la bčúg-go* he was banished to the north country *Glr.*; *byáṅ-pa* a man from *Jaṅ-ṫáṅ* — 3. the significations of *byaṅ-snyom-pa Sch.* **to tailor, to cut to a proper shape,** and of several other compounds, require a different etymology yet unknown. — 4. for *byáṅ-bu.*

བྱང་རྐྱང་ *byaṅ-rkyáṅ* **trowsers, small-clothes, breeches** *Mil.*

བྱང་ཁོག *byaṅ-ḱóg* 1. **the inside of the body,** *byaṅ-ḱog-stód* the upper part of the body, cavity of the chest, *byaṅ-ḱog-smád* lower part of the belly, abdomen, bowels *S.g.*; **ǰaṅ-ḱóg-la zug rag** I feel a pain in my bowels *W.* — 2. **rump;** opp. to *yan-lág* limbs *Lt.*

བྱང་ག *byáṅ-ga Lt.?*

བྱང་སྒྲ་མི་སྙན་ *byaṅ-sgra-mi-snyán* the northern continent of the ancient geography of India, v. *gliṅ.*

བྱང་ཆུབ་ *byaṅ-čúb,* **बोधि**, prop. wisdom; with the Buddhists **the highest perfection and holiness,** such as every Buddhist desires to obtain, which however to its full extent only the real Buddha himself possesses, v. *Köpp.* I, 425, 435; *byaṅ-čub-mčóg* id., frq.; *byaṅ-čub-mčóg-tu sems* (or resp. *ṫugs*) *skyéd-pa* to create the thought of such holiness, to direct the mind to it *Dzl., Glr.*; *byaṅ-čub ̥dód-pa* to aim at it, to be anxious to obtain it *Dzl.*; *lén-pa* to attain it; *byaṅ-čub-séms* the mind intent on and suited for it, universal charity; *snyiṅ-rǰe-byaṅ-čub-séms-kyis kun blaṅ-nas* submitting to every thing with a loving and charitable mind; *byaṅ-čub-séms-dpa,* **बोधिसत्त्व**, frq. with the addition of *sems-dpa-čen-po* the saint that has attained the highest station next to Buddha, merely for the welfare of men still tarrying in this world, designated Buddha, as it were; *Köp.* I, 422; *byaṅ-čub-séms-ma* fem. of it *Thgr.*; *byaṅ-čub-šiṅ,* **पिप्पल**, the bodhi-tree, holy fig-tree, ficus religiosa (not indica), emblem of mercy; *byaṅ-čub-snyiṅ-po* **बोधिमण्ड**, n. pr. = *rdo-rǰe-ɣdan.*

བྱང་རྡོ་ *byaṅ-rdo Cs.* **monument,** prop. inscription-stone.

བྱང་པ་ *byáṅ-pa* 1. v. *byaṅ*. — 2. *S.g.? byaṅ-pa-srin Sch.*: an insect.

བྱང་བ་ *byáṅ-ba*, pf. of *ₒbyáṅ-ba* q.v.; *byaṅ-sėms* **a pure, holy mind** *Mil.*, prob. = *byaṅ-čub-sėms.*

བྱང་བུ་ *byáṅ-bu*, བྱང་མ་ *byáṅ-ma* 1. **inscription, direction, label.** — 2. the **tablet** on which an inscription is written, *záṅs-kyi byáṅ-bu-la* (to write) on a copper plate or tablet *Glr.*; *yig-byáṅ*, *k̔a-byáṅ*, resp. *žal-byaṅ*, = *byáṅ-bu* 1; *sgo-byáṅ* inscription over a door, *dur-byáṅ* on a sepulchre; *rtags-byáṅ* a mark on a thing *Cs.*; *bṙjed-byáṅ* list of marked luggage; *miṅ-byáṅ*, resp. *mtsan-byáṅ* list of names *Pth.*; *šog-byáṅ* cards *Sch.*; *byaṅ-rdó* a stone monument.

བྱད་ *byad* I. 1. *Cs.* **proportion, symmetry, beauty,** *dpe-byad Dzl.*, id.; *byád-čan* well-proportioned, fair, beautiful; *byad-méd* the contrary *Cs.* — 2. **face, countenance** *Lex.*; *byad spus k̔éṅs-pa* a hairy face *Glr.*; *byád-kyi bkrags Thgy.*, *mdaṅs Lt.*, brightness, radiancy, beautiful complexion; *byad-bžin* face *Dzl.*, मुख *Lex.*; *byad-yzúgs*, *Sch.*: stature, prob. more correctly: countenance and body *Dzl.* and elsewh. —

II. (*Cs.* also *byád-ma*) 1. **enemy.** — 2. **a wicked demon,** *byád-ma rmė-ša-čan Wdṅ.* — 3. also *byad-stem(s)*, *S. O.* and elsewh., **imprecation, malediction,** combined with sorcery, the name of an enemy being written on a slip of paper and hid in the ground, under various conjurations; *yžán-gyi byad*, *p̔á-rol-poi byad-stéms* a malediction practised by another; *byád-du* or *stéms-su ǰúg-pa*, prob. to curse a person with conjurations.

III. in compounds, *yo-byád*, *ča-byád* q.v. — IV. frq. for *byed.*

བྱན་ *byan* 1. *Ld.* frq. for *byá-na*, **ǰan čo-k̔an, ǰán-ma** **cook.** — 2. v. the following.

བྱན་པོ་ *byán-po Cs.* **married man**; *Sch.*: a free man, one divorced from his wife; *byan-mo Cs.* **wife, spouse**; *Sch.*: 1. **a divorced woman.** — 2. **a whore.** Only this latter signification seems to be known among the common people, e.g. **ǎ-pę ǰán-mo**, as a vulgar abusive term; *byan-ťsud-pa Sch.* 'to allure, entice, seduce'; these significations are, however, not sufficient to explain: *byán-moi byi-bor* (or *-por*) *raṅ byan ťsud Lex.*, and: *séms-la raṅ byan ťsud Mil.*

བྱབ་པ་ *byáb-pa* 1. **to clean, cleanse, wash, wipe,** *naṅ ťams-čád-la* to clean the whole house *Domaṅ.* — 2. **to take up, to gather with both hands,** e.g. barley *C.*; *byab-zed Sch.* instrument for cleaning, brush; *byabs-k̔rus Sch.* shower-bath.

བྱམས་པ་ *byáms-pa* 1. **kindness, love, affection,** *byáms-sems* id. — 2. **kind, loving, affectionate,** used of the love of parents to their children, of the beneficent to the needy, but not in the contrary order, nor of love to inanimate objects; *byáms-pai tiṅ-ṅe-ₒdzin* the meditation of love, compassion, frq.; *mi kún-la byáms-šiṅ* being kind towards every body; *byáms-pai ṙnyen* kind, affectionate relations, frq; *byáms-pa máṅ-na* when I have many well-wishers, patrons *Dom.*; *byáms-pa* as a n. pr., also *byáms-pa mgón-po* **Maitreya,** the Buddha of the future period of the world, who at present is enthroned in the Galdan heaven, and who is frequently represented in pictures, v. *Köpp.*; *byams-bžúgs* sitting like Maitreya, i.e. after European fashion on a chair, with his legs hanging down, opp. to *ťub-bžúgs*, like Sākyathubpa; yet he is by no means uniformly represented in that posture.

བྱར་ *byar*, supine of *byéd-pa*; *byar-méd* 1. prop.: *non faciendum*, **not to be done.** — 2. sbst. **inactivity,** inaction in the specifically Buddhist sense, **apathy, indifference,** *byar-méd-kyi ṅáṅ-la ynás-par gyis Thgr.*

བྱས་པ་ *byás-pa*, pf. of *byéd-pa*; *byás-na 'si feceris', 'sin feceris'*, after a preceding prohibitive *ma byed* also to be rendered by **else**; as sbst. 1. '*factor*'. 2. '*factus*': *byéd-pa byás-pa* a doer of deeds, as the first grade of holiness; *byás-pa šés-pa*, *yzó-ba Sch.* to keep in mind a thing done, to requite, to reward; *byas-čos Mil.*, also known in *C.*, seems to be a notion akin to our **conscience,** **ǰhę-čö záṅ-po, ṅém-pa** *C.*, **ǰhę-lę** id.

བྱི་ *byi* 1. *Glr.*, *Pth.*, *byi byéd-pa* **to commit adultery** or **rape of females,** *byi-čád* punishment for it. — 2. v. *byi-ba.* — 3. *Pur.* **bi** **bird,** cf. *byiu.*

བྱི་དང་(ག་) *byi-táṅ(-ga)* **a medicine** *Med.*

བྱི་ཐུར་ *byi-tur* or *dur,* 1. n. of an animal, inhabiting caves *S.g.*; *byi-dur-ma Sik.* **porcupine.** — 2. **spine** of a porcupine or a hedgehog *Sch.*

བྱི་དར་ *byi-dár* a kind of silk stuff? *Wdk.*

བྱི་དུར་ *byi-dúr* v. *byi-túr.*

བྱི་དོར་ *byi-dór* **the wiping, cleaning;** *p̓yag-bdár žés-pa byi-dór-gyi las dei min* the word *p̓yag-bdár* denotes the act of cleaning *Lex.*; commonly *byi-dór byéd-pa* e.g. *γnás-su* to clean, to sweep a place *Dzl.*; spiritually; to cleanse one's thoughts *Mil.*; *byi-bdár byéd-pa Dzl.* **to dress, trim, decorate one's self, to make one's self smart.**

བྱི་པོ་ *byi-po Sch.* **bosom.** — 2. *W.* **male-cat, tom-cat.**

བྱི་བ་ *byi-ba* I. sbst. *B.* and *C.*; col. *C.* **ǯhi-tsi* Ld.*, *Pur.* **bi-tse**, *Ld.*, *Lh.* **sa-bi-li(g)**, **rat, mouse,** and various other animals: *byi-ba-rkaṅ-riṅ Sch.* rabbit (?); *dṅúl-byi Sch.* white rabbit. — *byi-dkár Sch.* white hare. — *byi-k̓úṅ* mouse-hole. — *byi-rdo Sch.* rat's-bane, arsenic. — *byi-ldém* mouse-trap. — *byi-nág Sch.* fitchet, polecat. — *byi-p̓rúg* young mouse. — *byi-brún Dzl.* mouse-dung. — *byi-blá* v. sub *byi-la.* — *byi-tsáṅ* mouse-nest, mouse-hole. — *byi-tsér* medicinal herb *Med.* — *byi-ₒdzin Cs.* mouse-trap; *byi-bzúṅ Lt.*, **bi-zúm* W.*, etymol. id.; but applied to that troublesome plant, **the bur** (burdock), which is stuck into mouse-holes, to fasten in the skin of the mice. — *byi-loṅ* etym. blind-mouse *Sch.* mole. — II. vb.: *byi-ba byéd-pa Cs.*, = *byi byéd-pa* **1. to mouse; to steal, to pilfer.** 2. **to commit adultery.** — III. pf. of *ₒbyi-ba* q. v.; *byi-ba spu*, *Sch.*. hair that has fallen off.

བྱི་བོ་ *byi-bo Lex.*; *Sch.* **little child, infant,** = *byis-pa.*

བྱི་བཞིན་ *byi-bžin* n. of one of the lunar mansions, v. *rgyu-skár.*

བྱི་ཟེ་ *byi-zé Cs.* = *tabs,* **manner, way, method.**

བྱི་རུ་ *byi-ru* **coral,** frq., also *byú-ru; byi-ru mdog* light red *Glr.*

བྱི་རུག་ *byi-rúg* medicinal plant *Med.*

བྱི་ལ་ *byi-la, B., W.* **bi-la, bi-li** (*Hind.* **billā**), **cat;** *byi-lai brun,* cat's dung *Lt.*; *byi-bla Wdk.* id.? In the latter work it is mentioned as the name of a certain monster, whilst *byi-blai rgyal-mtsán* is an attribute of the gods, resembling a flag with a cat's head at the top.

བྱི་ལམ་ *byi-lám Wdk.?*

བྱི་ཤང་ *byi-šáṅ Wdṅ.?*

བྱིང་བ་ *byiṅ-ba* v. *ₒbyiṅ-ba.*

བྱིང་བྱིང་ཐུ་ལུ་ *byiṅ-byiṅ-tú-lu S.g.* n. of an animal (?).

བྱིངས་པ་ *byiṅs-pa* 1. *Cs.* **general, common.** — 2. *Sch.* **hidden, concealed.** — 3. *Cs.* **root.** The word seems to be a secondary form of *spyi* ano *dbyiṅs,* yet in various passages of medical works none of the above meanings is applicable.

བྱིན་ *byin* 1. **pomp, splendour, magnificence,** e.g. of kings; *byin-čé-bar bžúgs-pa* to be enthroned in great splendour *Dzl.*; *γzi-brjid daṅ byin če Dzl. mtu daṅ byin Dzl.*; *byin-čan* magnificent, splendid, brilliant, *byin-méd* the contrary. — 2. **blessing,** a bestowing of blessings, a power working for good, *byin-báb Lex.*, *-p̓áb Sch.*: conferring blessings (?), *bčom-ldan-ₒdás-kyi byin-gyis* by the blessing, the miraculous power of Buddha; yet also applied to devils, v. below; most frq. *byin-gyis rlób-pa,* pf. *brlabs,* ft. *brlab,* imp. *rlobs,* **to bless,** *mi* a person, *sa-γzi* a place *Mil.*, also followed by the termin.: *séms-čan-gyi sdug-bsṅál ži-bar byiṅ-gyis rlobs* grant thy blessing, that the misery of beings may be assuaged *Mil.*; *bu mtun-rkyén ₒdzóm-bar byin-gyis rlobs* bless the son, that all happiness may be accumulated on him *Mil.*; *rgyud γnyén-po bzáṅ-bar* bless my soul, that it may be an efficient help (to these people) *Mil.*; relative to devils: *log-*

˳drén bdúd-kyis byín-gyis brlabs heretical teachers sent and fitted out by the devil; so also *Tar.* 46, 13; **to create, to change into** *Mil.*, *Tar.*; hence *byíṅ-rlabs* blessing, *byin-rlabs byéd-pa*, resp. *mdzád-pa* frq., *γtóṅ-ba*, resp. *stsól-ba Cs.*, = *byíṅ-gyis rlób-pa*; *byin-rlabs-čan, byin-rlabs daṅ ldán-pa* blessed, sanctified, highly favoured, men or things *Pth.*; so also *byin-rlabs žúgs-pa Mil.*; *˳dre-˳dúl byin-rlabs* blessing pronounced against demons, exorcism of devils *Mil.*; meton.: I am the *˳p̔ágs-pai byín-rlabs* of all of you, he who will help you to go to heaven *Glr.*

བྱིན་རྟེན་ *byin-rtén Cs.*, the **relics** of a saint, or the place where they are kept ('depository of blessings'); also in the shape of pills, which liberal donors receive from their Lamas, and which they swallow, particularly in the hour of death.

བྱིན་པ་ *byin-pa* 1. sbst. **calf of the leg,** *byin-pa ná-ba* pain in the calf; *byin-súl Cs.* 'hollow on the inward side of the thigh'(?). — II. pf. of *sbyin-pa*.

བྱིན་པོ་ *byin-po Sch.* **all, the whole; general;** *byin-gyis p̔rá-ba* by degrees, more and more fine etc.?

བྱིན་རླབས་ *byin-rlabs* v. *byin* 2.

བྱིབ་པ་ *byib-pa*, pf. *byibs* 1. **to cover, to wrap up,** *gós-kyis Lt.* — 2. *Cs.* **to hide, conceal, keep secret, hush up.**

བྱིའུ་ *byiu* 1. *Pur.* **biu**, **little bird, bird** *S.g.* — 2. *Sch.* **alpine hare.**

བྱིལ་བ་ *byil-ba* **to stroke,** *mgó-bo-la byil-byil byéd-pa* to stroke a person's head *Pth.*

བྱིལ་མོ་ *byil-mo* **naked** *Sch.*

བྱིས་པ་ *byis-pa* 1. **child,** esp. **little child;** *byis-(pai) nad* disease of children *Med.*; *byis-pa btsá-t̔abs* obstetric science *Med.*; *byis-stón* v. *ná-zla* sub *na* I, 2; *byis-pai blo Cs.* childishness, want of judgment; *byís-pai skyé-bo* **a plain, ignorant person,** a person not initiated *Thgy.*, *S.O.*; *mo-byis* girl, lass *Mil.*; *byis-pa-zúṅ-žig Cs.*, twins. — 2. **boy, lad,** till about the age of 16 years, frq. (*W.* not in use).

བྱུ་རུ་ *byú-ru* = *byí-ru*.

བྱུག་པ་ *byúg-pa* 1. **unguent, ointment, salve,** whether as colouring-matter, medicine or sweet scent *Dzl.*, *Med.*; *byúg-pa ska* thick ointment, thick plaster; *byúg-pa sla* thin unguent *Cs.* — 2. **foot-bath** *W.*, perh. better: *bčúg-pa*.

བྱུག་རིས་ *byug-ris*, *Lex.* = *gral*, **place,** in a certain succession or row; *byug-ris žog* make room, leave a place empty *Sch.*

བྱུགས་ *byugs* v. *˳byúg-pa*; *byugs-spos* **anointing-oil** *Sch.*

བྱུང་ *byuṅ* v. *˳byuṅ-ba*; *byúṅ-t̔sul* **history, story, particulars** of any event, *ṅai byúṅ-t̔sul dé-ltar γda* that is my story *Mil.*; *byuṅ-rábs Sch.* id.

བྱུར་ *byur B.*, esp. of later times and col., *Ld.* also *byus*, **misfortune, mishap, accident,** *byur čé-žiṅ bu mi γsós-na* if one has the great misfortune not to be able to keep a child alive *Dom.*; *mi-la byur ˳gél-ba* to draw down misfortune on a person *Dom.*; **ṅá-la ǰur čug soṅ** *W.*, **ǰhvr** *C.*, I have had misfortune, I have been unfortunate; *byúr-gyi*, also *byúr-čan* unlucky, disastrous, perilous. — **ǰhur-nág** great calamity *C.* — *byur-sél* preservative against misfortune. — *raṅ-byur-rdó* was explained: a sling-stone with which one hits one's self.

བྱུར་པོ་ *byúr-po*, *Cs.* also *-bu*, vulg. *byur-byúr* **heaped,** a heaped measure of corn or meal; *byúr-por bkaṅ Thgy.*

བྱེ་ *bye* 1. = *byeu* **little bird,** *bye-glíṅ* bird's nest *Ma.*; *bye-p̔rúg* a young little bird *Dzl.*, also *bya-p̔rúg*; *bye-brúṅ* bird-dung *Wdṅ.*; *byeu ˏúr-pa Sch.* **partridge.** — 2. v. *byé-ma*.

བྱེ་མགོ་ *bye-mgó* 1. **bird's head.** — 2. **an officinal mineral** *S.g.*

བྱེ་བ་ *bye-ba* **ten million,** *byé-ba-p̔rag γsum daṅ sá-ya-p̔rag drug* thirty-six million; *byé-ba sa-ya*, eleven million; it seems to be among the larger numbers one of the most popular, as the word million is in English.

བྱེ་བྲག་ *bye-brág*, **विशेष**, 1. **difference, diversity,** *k̔ó-bo daṅ saṅs-rgyás bye-brág či yod* what difference is there between me and Buddha? *Dzl.*; *bye-brág ˳byéd-pa* to find, to show a difference, c. genit. in, of, between things; to analyze, to explain; variety, diversity *Was.* (266); *bye-brág bšád-pa* = *vibhāshā Was.* (147), also *bye-brag-bšad-mtsó* or *-ču-γtér*, title of books; *byé-brag-čan Cs.* different, *bye-brag-méd-pa Cs.*, *mi-ṗyéd-pa Dzl.* equal; *bye-brág-tu smrá-ba Thgy.*, *bye-brág-pa*, **वैशेषिक**, name of a school of philosophers, Atomists *Köpp.* I, 69. — 2. **division, section, class, species,** *dúd-°groi, ról-moi bye-brag* a species of animals, a kind of musical instrument etc. *Lex.*; *yúl-gyi bye-brág* a part of the country, province, *Tar.* 33, 6; *bye-brág-tu* (to go through) according to the separate classes *Zam.*

བྱེ་མ་ *byé-ma* (*C.* *ǰhé-ma*, *W.* *bé-ma*) 1. **sand,** frq. — 2. **sandy plain, sands,** *γsér-gyi byé-mai dkyíl-na* in the middle of a plain of gold sand *Glr.* — 3. **gravel** (disease) *Schr.* — *byé-ma °bru γċig* a grain of sand *Cs.*; *gáṅ-pai klúṅ-gi byé-ma tsam* as much sand as there is on the Ganges; *bye-ma-ká-ra* brown sugar, ground sugar, *Hind.* **चीनी**, *C.* — *bye-dkár* white sand, *bye-nág* black sand. — *bye-čáb Lt.* sandy water, water standing on sandy ground. — *bye-ǰóṅs* a sandy tract *Cs.* — *bye-ťáṅ* a plain of sand, a sandy desert *Glr.* — *bye-ṗúṅ* heap of sand. — *bye-tsúb* sand raised by a whirlwind. — *bye-ril* (*Schr. hril*), small sugar-balls, Indian sweet-meat, imported into Tibet, *C.*

བྱེད་པ་ *byéd-pa* I. vb., pf. *byas*, fut. *bya*, imp. *byos*, vulgo *byas* (*Sp.*, *Bal.* *béd-pa*; in *Ld.* and *Lh.* instead of it gen. *ċó-ċe*), resp. *mdzád-pa*, eleg. *bgyid-pa*, 1. **to make, to fabricate,** with the acc., e.g. a house, an armour etc.; with *las* or *la*, to make out of or of: *γsér-las* out of gold, *šiṅ-la Tar.* 160, 11 of wood; with the acc. and termin. to form to, to work into, *págs-pa šog-šog-tu* to work or manufacture skin into parchment *Dzl.*; with the instrum.: to do with, to make of: *°dis ċi žig bya* what are you going to do with it, to make of it? *Dzl.* **to cause, to effect:** *lhúṅ-ba de ṅas byás-pa yin Mil.* it was I that caused this falling; with the supine, **to take care that:** *byéd-par °dod-par byéd-pa* to make him inclined to do it *Dzl.*, *ma šór-bar byos šig Pth.* take care, that he do not escape; *yód-par byéd-pa* **to produce, procure, provide,** *dei γnás-k'aṅ-la sógs-pa byás-nas* he provided for him a dwelling with appurtenances *Dzl.*; to fit out, equip (a ship) *Glr.*; **to act:** *rgyál-po, draṅ-sróṅ* etc. *byéd-pa* to act a king, a saint, as much as: to rule as a king, to live as a saint *Dzl.*, *blá-ma byéd-pa* to be a priest *C.*; in a gen. sense: **to do:** *byá-ba daṅ bya-ba-ma-yin-pa stón-pa* to teach what men ought to do and what they ought not to do *Thgy.*; **to commit, perform, execute:** *nyés-pa byed-byéd-pa* one that has repeatedly committed himself, *las* or *byá-ba byéd-pa* to perform an action, *las ċi žig byed* what are you doing, what is your business? *ťabs yód-de byéd-mk'an med* there is an expedient, but no one that carries it into effect *Ma*; *mi byar mi rúṅ-bas* as it must be performed, lit. as it cannot remain undone *Dzl.*; *bsám-pa ltar myúr-du byás-na* if an intention is speedily executed, performed; *las byéd-pa* **to work, to be efficient** (of a medicine); **to act, proceed, pretend, affect:** *ċi ltar byás-na legs* how proceeding is good? i.e. which is the best way to proceed, how shall I manage best? *Glr.*; *bsám-γtan-la yód-pai lugs byas* he pretended, affected to meditate *Glr.*; *dei lúgs-su byao* I will act as he does, I will do like that man *Glr.*; *gá-le byéd-pa Mil.* to proceed slowly, to be slow; **to take, to assume, to count:** *žag bži-pa dáṅ-por byás-na* if the fourth day be taken for (counted as) the first *Wdn.*; *byéd-pa* with the termin. of the inf. is frequently used periphrastically or to give force to other verbs; such forms are: *γsód-par byed-pa* to kill, *ṗa-más šés-par byos* (or *gyis*) *šig*, resp. *yab-yum-gyis mk'yen-par mdzod ċig* dear parents, you must know! *Dzl.*; on the other hand: *ṗá-la rig-par gyis šig* let your father know about it *Tar.* 37, 7; in such cases the proper sense is merely to be gathered from the context. Besides the simple fut., *°dúg-par byao* I shall remain *Tar.*, *k'ó-mo grogs byá-*

yis as I shall be with you *Glr.*; — the form *byao* frq. serves to express necessity: *btsál-bar bya* I must seek *Dzl.*; esp. with a negation: *brǰód-par mi byao* they are by no means to be pronounced; the participles in the short forms of *γtoṅ-byéd* and *γtoṅ-byá* differ, in as much as the former is used in an active sense, e.g. one giving, a giver, the latter in a passive sense, one to be given; they may be formed of any verb. For specific combinations, in which *byéd-pa* is differently to be translated, as *dpe byéd-pa, yid-la byéd-pa* etc., refer to these words. — 2. **to say, to call,** yet chiefly only in the pf. tense: *žes byás-pa Dzl.* thus said, so called; *sṅar byás-pa bžin* according to what has been said before *Dzl.; byas-kyaṅ* though saying *Pth.* — and in the fut., which in that case, however, frq. stands for the present: *(žes) byá-bai sgra byúṅ-no* a voice thus speaking was heard *Glr.*; *dé-la dbyaṅs šes byao* these are called vowels *Gram.*; *(žes-) byás-pa*, or more frq. *byá-ba,* the so called, being often joined to a name, that is mentioned for the first time, e. g. Anu, the so called, whilst we should say, a man, called Anu, or of the name of A.; *byá-ba* also implies: of the purport, to the effect, just as *čés-pa* is also used: *'tsol-žig' byá-bai luṅ byúṅ-nas* an order being given to make a search *Glr.* — 3. **to go away, to disappear:** *byas soṅ* he disappeared *Glr.* —

II. sbst. 1. *byéd-pa* and *byéd-mk̔an,* the person that does or has done a thing, **the doer, performer** etc.; **author,** *bstan-bčós byéd-mk̔an* the author of the work *Tar.* — 2. *byéd-pa* **the instrumentative case** *Gram.* — 3. *byéd-pa* **the doing, dealings,** with noun in the instrum. case: *dé-˳dra-ba mi-rigs-pa rgyál-pos byéd-pa* such wrong being done by the king, such unjust dealings of the king *Dzl.*; in the genit. case: *bló-yi byéd-pa dbyiṅs-su sbos* hide the working of your understanding in the heavens, i. e. let it disappear in nothingness; **effect,** also with the noun in the genit. case, *Wdṅ.* — 4. *byéd (-pa)-po,* **doer, accomplisher** etc., *mčód-sbyin byéd-pa-por bos* he invited him as sacrificing priest *Tar.*; *˳dúl-bar byéd-pa-po* converter *Tar.*; *bkra-šís spél-bai byéd-po* augmenter of eternal happiness (from a hymn); *byéd-pa-po* **instrumentative case** *Gram.*; as the twelve *byéd-pa-poi skye-mčéd* I here cite the following from *Wdk.*, without being able to offer an explanation: *bdag, séms-čan, srog, ˳gró-ba, γsó-ba, skyés-bu, gaṅ-zág, šéd-ćan, šed-bdág, byéd-pa-po, tsór-ba-po, šés-pa-po, mtóṅ-ba-po,* where, by the by, it is to be observed, that thirteen are here enumerated, *byed-pa-po* being mentioned again with the rest (a want of accuracy, which is not unfrequently to be met with in the scientific works of the Tibetans). — 5. *byá-ba* q. v.

བྱེའུ་ *byeu* (also *byiu* q.v.) **little bird;** *byeu-zúl byéd-pa* v. *zul; byeu-la-p̔ug S.g.*, a medicinal herb *Cs.*

བྱེར་བ་ *byér-ba* v. *˳byér-ba.*

བྱེས་ *byes, Lexx.* and col.; **foreign country; abroad,** *byes tag-riṅ-ba* a far distant country *Cs.*; *byés-su ˳gró-ba* to go abroad, to travel; *byés-su ˳dég-pa* to remove, to emigrate *Lex.*; *byés-nas sléb-pa* to come from abroad *Lex.*; *byés-pa* traveller, foreigner, stranger; **lam-róg bés-pa yód-pa yin-te** *W.* proceeding together as fellow-travellers.

བྱོ་བ་ *byó-ba Cs. rná-ba byó-ba* **to hear, hearken, listen.**

བྱོན་པ་ *byón-pa* v. *˳byón-pa.*

བྱོལ་བ་ *byól-ba* v. *˳byól-ba.*

བྱོལ་སོང་ *byol-sóṅ* **animal,** esp. **quadruped;** *byol-sóṅ-bas glén-pa* more stupid than a brute *Mil.*; *byol-sóṅ rgyál-po* the lion *Mil.*

བྲ་ཀ་ *brá-ka* v. *ṭá-ka.*

བྲ་ཉེ་ *bra-nyé*, n. of a lunar mansion, v. *rgyu-skár 2.*

བྲ་བ་ *brá-ba,* 1. sbst., n. of a small **rodent,** living under ground (not mole *Cs.*, but rather **suslik, earless marmot** *Sch.*); *brá-p̔u-se Ld.* a similar animal (= *pra-li?*); *bra-mk̔ár, bra-tsáṅ Cs.*, burrow of it; *bra-brúṅ*

Lex., *bra-ril Cs.*, dung of it; *bra-lpágs* skin of it. — 2. vb. **to have** or **to be in great plenty, to abound** (?), *rán-gis za ma bra, btuṅ ma bra, gon ma bra* she allowed herself no abundance of food, drink, or clothing; **za-, tuṅ-, čin-, lab-, zér-ḍha-te** eating, drinking plentifully, walking, speaking, talking a great deal *C.*; **ṫsa-, ḍho-, ḍháṅ-ḍha-te** being very hot, warm, cold *C.*

བྲ་བོ *brá-bo* (prov. **brau**, *Pur.* **bro**) **buck-wheat**; *bra-p̓yé Lex.*, *rǰen Sch.* buck-wheat flour; *bra-sóg* buck-wheat straw, serving as a poor sort of fodder during winter.

བྲག *brag* **rock**, *brag rtse-γsúm-pa* a three-pointed rock; *brag-skéd* the middle height of a rock, opp. to *brag-mǰug* and *rtse* its foot and top *Cs.* — *brag-spós* prob. an aromatic herb, used for incense *Lt.* — *brag-skibs* beetling rock. — *brag-rgyál* a prominent, high and precipitous rock, towering rock. — *brág-ča, -ča* echo; also fig. for something unsubstantial, shadowy, not existing *Mil.* — *brag-mǰúg* foot of a rock *Cs.* — *brag-p̓ug* rock-cavern. — *brag-p̓ye* dust produced by hewing stones *Glr.* — **ḍhag-bhóṅ** = *p̓a-bóṅ C.* — *brag-dmár* name of a rock in or near Lhasa, alledged not to be identic with *dmar-po-ri* (*Sch.*).—**ḍag-tsél-wa, ḍag-šig-pa** mite, tick *W.* — *brag-rtsáṅ* rock-lizard. — *brag-rtsé* top of a rock. — *brag-žún* mineral pitch, bitumen, is said to cure fevers and even fractures. — *brag-rí* rocky hill. — *brag-rúd* fall of a rock. — *brag-róṅ* chasm in a rock, ravine. — *brag-šig* v. *brag-rtsél-ba.*

བྲང *brañ* 1. resp. *sku-bráñ* **chest, breast,** (cf. *nú-ma*); *brañ rdúñ-ba* to beat one's breast *Glr.*; **ṫ́ú-gu ḍáñ-la čir-te k̓yér-če** *W.* to **carry** a child pressed against one's breast. — *brañ-kyéd* (?) *Cs.* a high, prominent chest. — *brañ-dkyil* middle of the breast, cardiac region. — *brañ-lkóg Mil.* prob. = *lkóg-ma*. — *brañ-skás Sch.* the dorsal vertebrae opposite to the chest. — **ḍañ-kúd** **string** of the *brañ-k̓úñ* (*-guñ, -k̓oñ, -goñ*), **pellet-bow,** a bow furnished with two strings, to shoot pellets or small stones, *brañ-rdi* or *-rdeu*, with it *W.* — **ḍhan-k̓óg** *C.* cardiac-region, pit of the stomach. — *brañ-sgró* snake, serpent (like *lto-˳gró*). — *brañ-búr* the middle convex part of the *rdó-rǰe Ma.* — *brañ-ṫsig Lh.*, prob. heart-burning. — *brañ-(γ)žól Cs.* dew-lap. — *brañ-ze Mil.* prob. breast-bone, sternum. — *brañ-γyúñ Sch.* tame, gentle. — *brañ-rus Med.* breast-bone. — **ḍañ-lág** *W.* the hands crossed on the breast. — *brañ-so Glr.* breast, brisket of a butchered animal. — 2. also *˳brañ*, gen. *˳bráñ-sa*, eleg. *mčis-bráñ* (q.v.), resp. *γzim-bráñ*, *bžugs-bráñ* **night-quarters, halting-place,** whether under a roof or in the open air; also as much as **stage** (of a journey); *bráñ-sa ˳débs-pa Tar.*, prob. also **bór-če** *W.*, to take up night-quarters; **dwelling,** particularly a temporary one, **lodgings;** but also a permanent **abode,** esp. in *W.*; **ḍáñ-sa táñ-če, yár-ce** to take in, to lodge a person over night *W.* (cf. *γnas* 2). — *bráñ-k̓añ*, dwelling-house, dwelling-room *Pth.* — *brañ-grógs* house-mate, bed-fellow. — *brañ-dpón* master of the house, landlord. — *p̓o-bráñ* v. *p̓o*; *bla-bráñ* v. *bla.*

བྲང་ངེ *b.. ..ñ-ñé Lex.* = *krañ-ñé.*

བྲང་པ *bráñ-pa* v. *˳bráñ-pa.*

བྲན *bran* 1. **slave, servant,** *mi-bráñ* 'vir servus' *S.g.*; *bran byéd-pa* to be a servant, to serve *Cs.*; *brán-du ˳gyúr-ba* to become a servant *Cs.*; *brán-du ˳k̓ól-ba* to make another be a servant, to use him as a servant *B.*; *brán-du skúl-ba* to engage a person as a servant, to get him to work for one's self *Glr.*; *brán-du k̓as-bláñs-so Pth.* they promised to serve him; *lus ñag yid γsum brán-du p̓úl-te* devoting heart, mouth, and body to his service *Pth.*; *nañ nub lto-gós-kyis brán-du k̓ol* morning and night I am a slave to food and clothing *Mil.*; **subject,** one owing allegiance, **la-dágs-si gyál-po-la ḍán-yul-ṫso** a village subject to, belonging to, the king of Ladak *W.*; *brán-p̓o* servant, slave *Tar.*; *brán-mo* maid-servant, female slave; *bran-k̓ól*, *bran-γyóg* = *bran*; also collectively, servants, domestics, household. — 2. **texture,** in the compound *tags-brán byéd-pa* to weave *Mil.*; *nye-brán Mil.* seems to be some decoration of the shoes; *sño-brán Mil.* something similar. — *ču-brán Glr.*, and *mtso-brán*??

བྲན་པ་ *bran-pa* **to pour out** *Tar.*

བྲན་མོ་ *brán-mo* 1. v. *bran* 1. extr. — 2. also = *ḍan-tsós* *W.* **finger, toe.**

བྲབ་པ་ *bráb-pa* v. *˳bráb-pa.*

བྲམ་ཟེ་ *brám-ze*, from ब्राह्मण् 1. **Brahmin,** Hindoo priest; *brám-ze-mo* female Brahmin; *brám-ze rig-byéd ˳dón-pai sgra* the voice of a Brahmin reciting the Vedas, being taken as a sign of good luck; *brám-ze-pa* an adherent of Brahma. — 2. **a priest** in general *S.O.* (Acc. to *Fouc.* transl. of *Gyatch.* 13 and 52 also = *brāhmaṇa*, the theological part of the Vedas; this is however against the tenor of the Tibetan text, which requires the word to be taken in the former sense.)

བྲལ་ *bral* v. *˳brál-ba.*

བྲི་ *bri* v. *˳brí-ba.*

བྲིད་པ་ *brid-pa* 1. *Sch.* '**to continue, to reiterate, to repeat continually**; *brid-la γtón-ba* to give again and again'. — 2. v. *˳brid-pa.*

བྲིད་བྲིད་པ་ *brid-brid-pa Sch.* **to float,** to move confusedly, before one's eyes.

བྲིད་རྩ་ *brid-rtsa Lt.?*

བྲིམ(ས)་ *brim(s)* v. *˳brim-pa.*

བྲིས་ *bris* v. *˳brí-ba*; *bris-sku, sku-bris* **picture of a saint,** drawn or painted *Cs.* — *bris-˳búr* the art of painting and carving images. — *bris-ma* written book. — *nag-bris* a drawing *Cs.*; *tson-bris* a coloured picture.

བྲུ་བ་ *brú-ba* v. *˳brú-ba.*

བྲུ་བ་ཚ་ *bru-ba-tsá Lex.* **hunger.**

བྲུ་ཞ་ or བྲུ་ཤ་ *bru-žá* or *bru-šá Wdk.*, prob. = *gru-žá* and *gru-šá Pth.*, *˳bru-šál* or *˳bru-šál Ld.-Glr. Schl.* 19, b. 21, a. name of a country to the west of Tibet, bordering on Persia.

བྲུག་པ་ *brúg-pa* **to flow, to stream, to gush** *Cs.*; sbst. **current, flow, flux** *Cs.*; *ču brúg-pa* flowing-water *Lex.*

བྲུན་ *brun* **dirt, dung, excrements,** *mi-brúṅ, bya-brún, sbraṅ-brún* etc. feces of men, birds, flies etc. *Med.* and elsewh.

བྲུབ་པ་, བྲུབས་པ་ *brúb-pa, brúbs-pa* v. *˳brub-pa.*

བྲུལ་ *brul* **small particles, fritters, bits, crumbs,** *bag-brul C.* crumbs of bread; *brúl-ba Mil., C.* **to fall,** into an abyss *Thg.*; to fall off, fall out, fall down, of leaves, seeds etc.; *brúl-bu, brul-lu = brul W.*

བྲུས་ *brus* v. *˳brú-ba.*

བྲེ་ *bre,* *ḍe*, *Sskr.* द्रोण, 1. a measure for dry things as well fluids, about 4 pints; acc. to *Cs.* $\frac{1}{20}$ of a *˳bo*; *bré-bo če, breu čúṅ* large and small *bre, Cs.*; *γsér-pʼyẹ bre gaṅ Glr.* one (small) measure of gold-dust; *bre-do* two measures; *bré-la γšoṅ* that will just fill a *bre Zam.*; *bres bšar-ba* to measure with a *bre Lex.*; *lha-kʼaṅ bre-tsad tsam žig* a miniature temple, not larger than a *bre Glr.*; vulgo also that part of the *Chod-rten,* which has the shape of a corn-measure; in a general sense, **measure,** *bre-sráṅ γtán-la ˳bébs-pa Glr.* to regulate measures and weights. — 2. *bre* *Ld. Lh.* *bre-sé* *Kun.* Eremurus spectabilis, a plant of about a man's height, belonging to the asphodels. — 3. v. *bré-ba.*

བྲེ་ཀོ་ *bré-ko* **basin for washing** *C.*

བྲེ་ག་ *bré-ga* **medicinal herb;** *bré-gu,* id.(perh. the same plant) *Med.*

བྲེ་བ་ *bré-ba* v *˳bre-ba; bla-bré, ka-bré Sch.* **capital, chapiter,** upper part of a column or pillar.

བྲེ་མོ་ *bré-mo Sch.* **unfit, useless, worthless;** *bré-moi γtam Thgy.*

བྲེགས་པ་ *brégs-pa* v. *˳brég-pa.*

བྲེང་བ་ *bréṅ-ba* v. *˳bréṅ-ba.*

བྲེད་པ་ *bréd-pa* **to be frightened, afraid, in fear** = *rtáb-pa, B.* and *C.*; *sbrúl-gyis dṅaṅs-šiṅ bréd-pa* to be frightened by a snake *Wdṅ.*, or *bréd-čin dṅáṅs-pa Pth.*;

bdúd-kyis bréd-na if you are afraid of the devil *Glr.*; *bred-ₒtoms Lex.*; **ḍhē-po** fearful, frightful, terrible *C.*

བྲེལ་བ་ *brél-ba* I. vb. (not the same as *ₒbrél-ba*) 1. **to be employed, busy, engaged, to have business** or **work on hand,** *ṅed mḱar-las-kyis brel nas loṅ mi ₒdug* being engaged in building, we have no time to spare *Mil.*; *ₒdod ḱó-nas brél-na* if one is entirely taken up with lust and pleasure; **dhe-riṅ ṅá-la ḍhél-wa yo', saṅ-nyin šog** to-day I have a great deal to do, come to-morrow *C.*; *brél-bas* on account of much business *Dzl.* — 2. synon. with *ṕóṅs-pa* **to be poor, to be without, wanting, destitute of,** c. instrum.: *loṅs-spyod-kyis brél-ba Dzl.* ༡༢༩,7; more frq. with a negative: *čis kyaṅ mi brél-bar byás-so* they did not let him want anything *Dzl.* ༡༢༠,17, *Sch.*; *ₒtsó-bai yo-byád-kyis mi brél-bar* abounding in every necessary of life *Dzl.* ༡༦༦,3 (acc. to a better reading); combined with another word: *ṕóṅs-brel-te*; *brel-ṕoṅ-med-čiṅ Dzl.*, *mi brel-bar* not sparingly, scantily, niggardly, e.g. to bestow *Dzl.* frq. — II. sbst. 1. *C.* and *B.*, a being engaged in **a multiplicity of business** v. I, 1. — 2. *W.*: **business, affair, concern,** **ṅá-la ḍél-wa žig yod** I have some particular business, concern, suit; **ḍél-wa či yod** what do you want, what are you about, what are you doing there?

བྲེས་ *bres* 1., *W.* also *brés-kyu* **manger;** *rta-brés* manger for horses. — 2. v. *bre.* — 3. v. *ₒbré-ba.*

བྲོ་ *bro* 1. **oath,** *bro -ṫsál-ba* to take an oath(?) *Pth.*, *bro ₒbór-ba* id., *dbu-bsnyuṅ daṅ bro bór-ro Glr.* they swore by their heads, nif. — 2. **dance,** *bro skráb-pa Lex.*, *ḱráb-pa Mil.*, *brdúṅ-ba Glr.*, resp. *žabs-bró mdzád-pa Mil.* to dance, leap, gambol, as a manifestation of gladness and mirth, whilst *gar byéd-pa* is a regular kind of dancing, with gentle and waving motions of the body; *rṅa-bró* drums and dancing *Glr.*; *bró-mḱan Cs.* dancer. — 3. *Pur. bro* v. *brá-bo.* — 4. v. *bró-ba.* — 5. *bro-nád Lex.*, *Mil.* and elsewh.; *Sch.* 'an epidemic disease'; *bro-ₒtsál Sch.* '**cold** (in the head), **cough, catarrh**;' *Tar.*: *ṕágs-pa lo maṅ-por sku-bro ₒtsal-te*; *Mil.*: *šin-tu bro-ₒtsál-bar gyúr-nas.*

བྲོ་བ་ *bró-ba*, I. vb. 1. **to taste, to smell,** vb. a. & n.; *gnyid kyaṅ mi bró-bas*, not even enjoying (tasting) sleep *Dzl.*; *ḱá-ro skyá-ba bro* one has an astringent taste in the mouth *Med.*; *spos bro-o* it smells of incense *Dzl.*; *dri-gsúṅ žim-pa bro-o* it has a pleasant smell *Dzl.* — 2. *C.* **to desire, to wish,** = *ₒdód-pa*, *bló-bro-ba* id.; *ṅu bró-ste* being about to weep *Mil.* — II. sbst. **taste, savour, flavour,** col. *bro-blág* (**ḍob-lág**), *lán-ṫsa ḱa-zás kún-gyi bró-ba skyed* salt imparts flavour to any kind of food *S.g.*; *bro ltá-ba* or *myoṅ-ba*, col. **ḍob-lag nyaṅ-če** *W.* to taste, to savour; to try the taste; *bró-ba-čan Cs.*, **ḍób-lag-čan** *W.* savoury, pleasing to the organs of taste, exciting the appetite; *bro-(ba-)med* tasteless, insipid *Cs.*

བྲོ་མ་ *bró-ma* v. *gró-ma.*

བྲོག་ཞུ་ *bróg-žu* v. *próg-žu.*

བྲོད་ *brod*, = *bró-ba*, **taste** (*žim-po*) **ḍhö'-čen** *C.*, **ḍód-čan** *W.*, well-tasted, savoury; **ḍhö' čém-po** *C.* of a strong, powerful taste.

བྲོད་པ་ *bród-pa* **joy, joyfulness,** *bród-pa skyéd-pa Mil.*; *dga-bród* id. *C.*; *či-bród* readiness to die *Mil.* — Here may be quoted also *drod* 2 and 3.

བྲོབ་, བྲོལ་ *brob, brol* v. *ₒbráb-pa, ₒbrál-ba.*

བྲོས་ *bros* 1. v. *bro* 5; *bros-ṫebs Sch.* — 2. v. *ₒbros-pa.*

བླ་ *bla* I. the space **over, above** a thing, chiefly occurring in compounds; *blá-na* above *Lex.*; *bla-na-méd-pa*, अनुत्तर, having nothing higher over it, the upper-most, the very highest, e.g. *byaṅ-čúb*, *šes-ráb* and the like frq; *bla-na-méd-pai lam*, *bla-med-rdo-rjei ṫég-pa*, = *sṅágs-kyi lam*, the mystical method, v. *mdo* 3; *sá-bla*, above the earth, above ground, opp. to *sa-stéṅ*, *sa-ₒóg* upon and under the earth. Generally fig.: **superior, better, preferable,** *baṅ-mdzód stoṅ yaṅ blao* then even an empty treasury is preferable *Dzl.*; commonly with the pf. root of a vb.:

tse *ₒp̓os kyaṅ blao Dzl.* then I will rather die; less frq. with *na*: *ši-na yaṅ blai* since even death is to be preferred *Dzl.*; frq. it may be rendered by 'may', *rgyál-bar gyur kyaṅ blao* then may rather . . . gain the victory (than that I should . . .) *Dzl.*; also pleon.: *kyod mig-gis mi mťoṅ yaṅ blai* be it that you do not see it (it is of no consequence whether you see or not) *Dzl.* ༢༡༣, 7. In the passage *Tar.* 123, 8 *bla* seems to stand as an adv. for 'very', *Schf.* —

Comp. *bla-gáb, bla-gós* (*W.* vulgo **tsá-dar, tsá-sar**) = *γzán-gos*, upper garment, cloth, serving Indians, and occasionally also Tibetans as a covering, = toga, ἱμάτιον; *bla-gáb p̓rág-pa γčig-tu γzár-ba* to throw the toga over one shoulder, frq.; *bla-gab-méd-pa*, 1. without upper garment *Dzl.* 2. having no wish, no desire, free from passion(?) — *bla-bré*, also *bla-re*, canopy, dais *Dzl.* and elsewh. — *blá-ma* उत्तर 1. **the higher, upper, superior;** *blá-mar byéd-pa* to esteem highly, to honour, syn. to *bkúr-sti byéd-pa Domaṅ, Tar.*; the exact grammatical explanation of *mii blá-mai čós-kyi čo-ₒp̓rúl Dzl.* ༤༤, or of the similar passage *mii čos blá-mai rdzu-ₒp̓rúl Burn.* I, 164, offers some difficulties, although it is evident, that *Burn.* has hit the sense better than *Sch.* Of later date is the signification: 2. **the superior,** i.e. spiritual teacher, father confessor, गुरु, with the genit. of the person *Pth.*; in a more gen. sense: **ecclesiastic, priest, 'Lama'** *Thgr.*, *Pth.*; in East. Tib. a title designing a high eccles. degree, something like 'D.D.' v. Desg. 247, 371; *bla-mčód* for *blá-ma daṅ mčod-γnás* ecclesiastic and sacrificing priest, whether it be one and the same person, or two different individuals *Pth.*, *Mil.*; *bla-(ma-) čén (-po)* **chief Lama, Grand-Lama.** — *bla-bráṅ* resp. for dwelling-room or house of a Lama or Lamas, whilst *γzim-ḱáṅ, p̓o-bráṅ* are the resp. expressions for secular dignitaries. — *bla-slób, blá-ma daṅ slób-ma*, the Lama and his disciple *Sch.* — *smán-gyi-bla* v. *sman.* —

II. *Sch.* **'soul, life';** acc. to oral explanations: 1. **strength, power, vitality,** e.g. in food, scents etc., just like *bčud.* — 2. **blessing, power of blessings,** like *γyaṅ*, e.g. **ṭim-me mi-la la čém-po mi dug = yaṅ mi čag** *C.*, no blessing attends a contemner of the law. — 3. an object with which a person's life is ominously connected; thus very commonly *bla-šiṅ* a tree of fate (gen. a juniper or in *W.* a willow-tree, *ral-lčáṅ*), planted at a child's birth; *rgyál-poi bla-gyú* the king's turkois of life *Glr.*; *bla-dár* a little flag on the house-top, on which benedictions are written; *bla γnás* the omen is lasting, propitious, *nyams* it is vanishing, foreboding danger; so prob. also *Dzl.* ༢༠, 17, where it is not at once equivalent to 'soul' (*Sch.*). —

III. frq. incorr. for *sla.* — IV. in some combinations it has a signification not yet accounted for, e.g. *bla rdól-ba Sch.* to find fault with, to blame, abuse, without a reason; *bla-ťse*(?) *Lex.*

བླ་གབ་, གོས་ *bla-gáb, gos* v. *bla* I.

བླ་ཆེན་, མཆོད་ *bla-čén, -mčód* v. *blá-ma* sub *bla* I.

བླ་གཉན་ *bla-γnyán Med.?*

བླ་ཐབས་ *bla-ťábs Lex.*

བླ་དྭགས་ *bla-dágs Gram.*; *Sch.*: 'a primitive word, an abstract noun'.(?)

བླ་ན་ *blá-na* v. *bla* I.

བླ་བོར་ *blá-bor Sch.*: 'well! that may be! so much the better!'

བླ་བྲང་ *bla-bráṅ* v. *blá-ma* sub *bla* I.

བླ་འཚོ་, གླ་འཚོ་ *bla-ťsó, gla-ťso Sch.*: **hereditary portion, inheritance.**

བླ་གཡུ་ *bla-γyú*, བླ་ཤིང་ *bla-šiṅ* v. *bla* II.

བླ་རེ་ *bla-ré* v. *bla-bré* sub *bla* I.

བླག་ *blag* 1. sub *bde-blág* q. v. — 2. sub *btso-blag* q. v.

བླག་པ་ *blág-pa* 1. pf. *blags*, *rná-ba blág-pa = rná-ba γtád-pa Lex.*: **to incline one's ear to, to lend one's ear, to listen to** (*blág-pa* not by itself 'to hear' *Cs.*) —

2. *mčʻi-ma blág-pa* **to shed tears.** — 3. in *blág-pa méd-pa*, the free translation of आभ्यवकाशिक. *Burn.* I, 309 takes it in the signification given by *Sch.* to *bde-blág*, and explains it by 'bare of every convenience or comfort'.

བླང་བ་ *bláṅ-ba* v. *lén-pa.*

བླད་པ་ *blád-pa* **to chew,** secondary form to *ldád-pa. Lex.*

བླན་པ་ *blán-pa* = *glán-pa Cs.*

བླར་ *blar*, frq. incorr. for *slar.*

བླུ་བ་ *blú-ba*, pf. *blus*, **to buy off, to ransom, to redeem,** *mi de blú-ru ɣtóṅ-ba* to pay in order to redeem a man, to pay as a ransom for him *Glr.*; *pʻug-ron-gyi srog blus* he redeemed the life of the dove *Dzl.*; *ₒdi-dag-gis rgyal-poi mgo blu-o* therewith I will redeem the king's head *Dzl.*; to recover, to redeem, *ɣté-ba*, a pawn, pledge, security *C.*; *blu-rin* the money or price paid for the redeeming of persons or goods, ransom.

བླུག་པ་ *blúg-pa* v. *ldúg-pa.*

བླུགས་སྐུ་ *blúgs-sku* **molten image;** *blúgs-pár* casting-mould; *blúgs-ma* **cast metal, statues, relievos** (cf. *ₒbúr-ba*); *blugs-ɣzár*, *dgáṅ-blugs* v. *ɣzar*; *ǰá-blugs* urn-shaped vessel for pouring out tea etc.; *spyi-blugs* v. *spyi-bo* sub *spyi*; *már-blugs* oil-pitcher.

བླུད་པ་ *blúd-pa* 1. vb. *ldud-pa.* — 2. sbst. to *blú-ba*, **release, ransom, redemption** *Sch.* — *blúd-bu* v. *rlúd-bu.*

བླུན་པ་ *blún-pa* **dull, stupid; stupidity, foolishness;** *blún-po* **stupid, foolish; fool, idiot;** *blún-po la-lá . . . ₒdzin* some fools consider it . . .; *blúṅ-poi lugs* foolery, fool's opinion, fool's wisdom, expressions frq. used in scientific works to defeat antagonistic views; *dgé-ba mi byéd-pai mi ni blún-po yin* the man without virtue is a fool; *ₒdod-yón-la čags šin-tu blun* to be given to lust is folly *Pth.*; *byol-soṅ-pʻyúgs-pas blun* more stupid than a beast *Mil.*; *blün-ɣtam*, *blún-tsig* foolish talk, foolery; *blún-dad* superstition *Mil.* (cf. *dṅos-dad*).

བླུས་ *blus* v. *blú-ba*; *blús-ma* **ransom** *Cs.*

བློ་ *blo* I. rarely *bló-ba* **mind** (*Was.* 314 बोधि) 1. the intellectual power in man, **understanding,** *mkʻás-pai blo daṅ ldán-pa Dzl.*, *blo rno-ba Glr.* talented, gifted; *blo čén-po* (*čúṅ-ṅu*) of great (small) mental abilities *C.*; *blo ɣsál-te* of a clear understanding, sharp-witted *Dzl.*; *šes-pai blo* sagacity, intelligence, judgment *Dzl.*; *blo-rgyá Sch.* comprehensive intellectual power; *blo myur-žiṅ* being of quick comprehension, sharp *Dzl.*; *blo-ráb*, *-ₒbriṅ*, *-dmán-pa* of sound, moderate, weak intellects or mental faculties *Mṅg.*, the last expression is frq. used in modestly speaking of one's self *Glr.* and elsewh.; *bló-yi mün-pa* intellectual darkness, a darkened mind *Glr.*; *blo-bág* narrow-minded, weak in intellect *Sch.*; *kʻyod ni blo nór-ro* you are mistaken; *blos-lčógs-pa* 'to be competent in mind or judgment' *Sch.*; *bló-na-ₒbab* 'I understand' *Sch.* (?) — 2. **mind, thought, memory,** *čos daṅ yi-ge-la blo ǰúg-pa* to direct one's thoughts to religion and to learning to read *Glr.*; *bló-la sbyór-ba* to impresss on the mind, to inculcate *Glr.*; *bló-la bžúgs-pa* what is retained by, treasured up in the memory *Tar.*; *bló-la bzúṅ-ba* to learn by heart *Glr.*, *W.*: **loa* or *ló-na zúm-če**; *blo-tʻag-čód* v. sub *tʻág-pa* I. — 3. **mind, sentiment, disposition** (here in part = *yid*), *bló-la ₒdód-pa* to desire; *blo ₒdún-pa* interest, concern, v. *ₒdún-pa*; *mčʻód-pa byéd-pai bló-čan de* he that has a mind, is disposed, to sacrifice *Dzl.*; *raṅ bdé-bar ₒdód-pai blo méd-par* without any regard to his own welfare *Thgy.*; *blo nyé-ba* friendly sentiment; also: kindly disposed *Glr.*; *sdáṅ-bai blo* a hating mind, malevolent disposition *Lt.*; *blo gró-ba Sch.*: 'to get soft, moved, touched, sad', acc. to a native authority: to be agreeably affected by; *blo mtʻún-pa* to be of the same mind, like-minded, with supine also: to agree *Glr.*; perh. also: to be unanimous, peaceable, on friendly terms *Sch.*; *kʻyéd-kyi blo daṅ mtʻún-pa* agreeably to your wish *Mil.*; *blor ma šoṅ Sch.* 'the mind could not take it in' *Tar.* 51, 7, *Schf.*: 'it did not please me, I could not reconcile myself to it'; **blo skyél-ba* W.*, **k̔el-ba* C.*, *čel-ba Cs.* (?), to rely, to depend upon, *blo gél-ba* to hope *Sch.* (the correct spelling as yet doubtful); *blos γtóṅ-ba* to give up, resign entirely, to risk, venture, e.g. *ráṅ-gi srog Glr., Mil., blo spáṅ-ba,* id. *Mil.; *tse-ₒdi lū-táṅ** monk *C.; ₒó-čag blos ma t̔óṅs-par* as she was so much attached to us *Mil.*; *raṅ-blos ma t̔oṅs-pa* a man attached to himself, in love with himself; *blo γtód-pa Schr* to trust, confide (cf. compounds); *dé-las blo zlóg-pa Thgy.*, to subtract, to draw off, divert, dissuade from; *blo bríd-pa* to deceive, impose upon, cheat *Glr.* (*bló-yi bdag* 'conscience' *Sch.*, acc. to *Schr.* not an authenticated expression).

Comp. *blo-k̔og-čé* confident, courageous, intrepid, undaunted. — *blo-grós* **sense, intellect, understanding;** *blo-grós-kyi śés-bya* what is to be discerned by the understanding; *blo-grós daṅ ldán-pa, blo-grós-čan* sensible, judicious (of persons), *blo-grós čén-po C.* of much sense, of an excellent understanding, *čúṅ-nu C., žán-pa Mil.* of little understanding; *blo-gros-méd* unintelligent, injudicious; *blo-gros-rgyal-po* n. of a medicinal plant, = *smug-čúṅ Wdṅ.* — *bló-čan* having mind, sense; *byis-pai blo-čan* having the mind or sense of a child, thinking like a child *Cs.*; having a mind, v. above *mčód-pa byéd-pai bló-čan de.* — *blo-nyés* **ill-meaning, malicious** *Glr.* — *blo-γtád, blo-γdeṅ* **hope, confidence, assurance,** *bdág-gi blo-γdéṅ sú-la ₒča* in whom am I to place my confidence. — *blo-γdeṅ čós-la byéd-pa Glr.*; *W.: *lor-tád* or *lo-dáṅ čó-če, kyél-če (s)**, c. *la.* — *blo-rtóg* prob. = *blo-grós, blo-rtóg t̔a-dád-pa Pth.* people of different mental abilities. — *blo-stóbs* 1. *C., W.* **courage.** 2. *W.*, **generosity, magnanimity,** or perh. also **equanimity, self-command,** e.g. if a person remains kind and forbearing towards disobedient servants. — *blo-t̔ábs* counsel, expedient, *blo-t̔ábs tsól-ba Ma.* — *blo-bde* **cheerful, happy.** — *blo-ₒdód* **covetous, greedy.** — *bló-sna* 1. *bló-sna maṅ-ba Glr.* was explained by our Lama: having manifold thoughts, being restless, flighty, giddy. 2. *W.* disposition, turn of mind, **ló-na riṅ-mo** slowness, irresolution, also longsuffering, **lo-na t̔úṅ-se** resoluteness, determination, promptness, both also adj.: slow, irresolute, and: resolute, determined etc. — *blo-méd* injudicious, foolish *Cs.* (*Dzl.* ?ᒪᒧ, 18 makes no sense, there being prob. an error in the text. The translation of *Sch.* seems to be a mere conjecture). — *blo-bzáṅ* 'sound sense', col. **'lob-zaṅ'**, a very common name of persons. — *blo-śéd Sch.* 'memory, intellectual power'. — *blo-séms* **mind, soul, heart,** *blo-sems-bdé = blo-bdé Mil.* — *blo-bsám* intellect; *W.: *lo-sám méd-k̔an** foolish, one not knowing what he is about.

II. frq. incorr. for *glo.*

བློ་བ་ *bló-ba* I. vb. **to be able** = *p̔ód-pa*; *k̔yod mi ló-na* if you cannot; **di mi lo** that you cannot (dare not) do, prob. only *W.* vulg. — II. sbst. = *blo*, frq. used by *Mil.* for the sake of the rhythm.

བློ་བུར་ *bló-bur* = *gló-bur* **sudden, suddenly;** *k̔yed dá-ltar-gyi dád-pa bló-bur yin* thy present faith is new, but just sprung up in thee *Mil.*; *mi-spyod bló-bur-du ₒgyur* the conduct of men suddenly changes *Ma.*

བློང་མོ་ *blóṅ-mo*, for *lóṅ-mo*, **bones** or **knuckles** used as dice *Mil.*

བློན་ *blon* 1. *Lex.* = *gros, blón ₒdébs-pa* **to give advice, to counsel;** *Cs.*: to make arrangements — 2. v. the following.

བློན་པོ་ *blón-po* **officer** (prop. counsellor), any magisterial officer of higher rank; *blón-po daṅ ₒbaṅs* commanding and obeying, higher officers and subalterns *Glr.*; more particularly **minister** (of state); *blon(-po) čen(-po) Glr., blón-po bká-la γtógs-pa Glr.*, more commonly *bka-blón(-po)*, **high officer of state, minister, governor;** *k̔rims-blón* minister of justice, officer of justice; *rgyal-blón* king and minister, also = council, privy-council, *Glr.*; *čós-blon* 1. (opp. to *bdúd-blon*) an orthodox, faithful minister etc. 2. *čos-blon čén-po* minister of public worship *Glr.*; *rje-blón* the same as *rgyal-blón Glr.* — *spyi-blon* chief officer *Cs.* — *p̔yi naṅ bar γsúm-gyi blón-po Glr.*, lit outer, inner, middle minister, a distinction not quite intelligible. — *dmág-blon* military, *yúl-blon* civil officer *Cs.* — *naṅ-blon* 1. v. above *p̓yi-naṅ* etc. 2. *Lh.* country-judge.

བྷ· *bha,* sometimes written for བ, either from ignorance, or in order to appear learned, as is also དྷ for ད, and so forth.

བྷ་ག· *bhá-ga Ssk.* **the female genitals,** *Pth.*

བྷ་ར་ཏ· *bhá-ra-ta, bhá-ra-tai dúm-bu, bhár-ta, bár-dha, Ssk.* भरतखण्ड country between Lanka and the Sumeru, viz. Hindustan; also North-India, *Mil.* and elsewh.

བྷ་ལད· *bha-lad, Urd.* ولايت, *Beng.* belati, 'a far distant country', = *p̓i-liṅ,* for **Europe.**

བྷང་གེ· *bhaṅ-ge W., Ssk.* भङ्गा, **hemp.**

བྷེ་དྷ· *bhe-da* v. *ₒbe-dha.*

དབའ· *dba* 1. *Lex.* = *že-sa* **reverence, respect,** obs. 2. (or *rba*) = the following.

དབའ་ཀློང· *dba-klóṅ Glr., rba-kloṅ Mil., Dzl., dba-rlábs* **wave, billow**; *rba-skya* whitish waves *Mil.*; *dba-tsúb* surge, roar, turmoil of waves *Cs.*; *dba-byi* water-rat?

དབག་པ· *dbág-pa,* pf. *dbags Sch.,* v. *dbog-pa* and *bag-pa.*

དབང· *dbaṅ* (*wan, vulg.'*aṅ*) 1. **might, power, potency,** *blón-po dbaṅ čés-pas* because the minister was very potent *Glr.*; *dbaṅ dge-ₒdún-la γtad Glr.,* not only: 'he granted great privileges to the priesthood' *Sch.,* but: he invested it with magisterial power and jurisdiction; rarely used of physical power or strength *S.g.*; *bsdad-dbaṅ-med* it is not in my power to stay *Thgy.*; *búm-pa ǰó-moi yin-te dbaṅ ma mčis-so* as the pitcher belongs to my mistress, I have no power over it, I have not to dispose of it *Dzl.*; *sdod-dbaṅ-méd-par* having no strength, not being able to wait (from eagerness, avidity etc.) *Glr.*; *dbaṅ-méd,* prob. *sdod* to be supplied (if the text be correct), this won't do so any longer *Glr.*; *(raṅ-)dbaṅ-méd-du* or *par* involuntarily, not being able to help it, e.g. to weep, rejoice, believe, *Mil.*: *dbaṅ-méd-du mči-ma ₒcor-du ǰúg-pa* to make one weep; *dbaṅ-méd-du ₒčól-ba* to make a person powerless, to force by absolute power *Glr.*; *dbáṅ-du ₒgyúr-ba* to get into another's power, to be overpowered *Tar.*; *ₒdód-pai* to get into the power of the passions, to be led away by them *Dzl.*; *dbáṅ-du gyúr-pa* seems also sometimes to mean: he who has brought every thing into his power (?), along with *nyon-moṅs-pa-méd-pa* and *sems-rnam-par-gról-ba*; *dbáṅ-du sdúd-pa* to reduce under one's power *Pth.*; *snyiṅ-rǰe* to make the principle of mercy one's own, to practise it freely *Glr.*, (where *ₒdú-ba* stands) *ₒgró-ba* to comprise all beings, *Glr.*; *dbáṅ-du byéd-pa* id.; *dbaṅ byéd-pa* c. la, 1. to rule over, to govern, frq. 2. to possess, *bdág-gis dbaṅ byar méd-pa* what one does not possess *Thgy.* — *dbaṅ-sgyúr-ba c. la,* to govern, to rule, frq.; *dbaṅ ₒgrúb-pa* id. seldom. — *dbaṅ skúr-ba* v. *skur-ba* and *dbaṅ,* 2. **waṅ táṅ-če* W.* to make efforts, to exert one's self, also = the next. — *dbaṅ zá-ba* to offer violence *Dzl.* ?LV, 3. — *dbáṅ-gis* like a postposition, by, by means of, in virtue of, in consequence of, e.g. *lás-kyi* of former actions *Glr.*; *ṅa-rgyál-gyi dbáṅ-gis* from or in consequence of pride *Tar.* — 2. more especially in mythology, *dbaṅ bču Dzl.* ?V?, 14, also *stobs-bču Trigl.* 8, 6; *Gyatch.* II, 46, *Burn.* II, 781 seqq. 1. the ten powers of knowledge of Buddha, v. *Köpp.* I, 437 seqq. 2. in later times *γžan rǰés-su ₒdzin-pai dbaṅ bču* ten powers tending to the benefit of others are ascribed to the Bodhisattva, *Thgy.*: *ts̓é-la dbáṅ-ba* (respecting this form v. below) power over the length of one's own life; *séms-la dbáṅ-ba* power according to one's own pleasure to enter into any meditation; *yo-byád-la* to shower down provisions for the support of creatures; *lás-la* to mitigate the punishments for their sins; *skyé-ba-la* to effect one's own re-birth in the external world, without danger of being infected by its sin; *mós-pa-la* at pleasure to change one object into another; *smón-lam-la* to see every prayer for the welfare of others fulfilled; *rdzu-ₒp̓rúl-la* to exhibit wonderful feats for bringing about the conversion of others; *ye-śés-la* to understand all writings on religion (ni f.); *čós-la* to convey the publication of religion to all creatures at the same time and in every language. 3. in practical mysticism: various supernatural powers (v. *skúr-ba*), e.g. *p̔yi naṅ ysáṅ-gi dbaṅ skúr-ba Pth.* is alledged to signify: to convey externally, i.e. into the mouth, the power of *snaṅ-ba-mťa-yás* (this and the two following are names of Buddhas and demons), internally, into the body, the power of *spyan-ras-yzigs* and lastly into the mind perfect purity, i.e. the *rta-mgrin*, and together with it power over the demons. — 3. **regard, consideration**(?). In later writings the composition of *dbáṅ-du byás-na* (*mdzád-na* etc.) c. genit. (instead of which in *C.* also *dbáṅ-du śór-na, śóṅ-na* are said to be in use), is frq. to be met with, signifying as much as: when... is concerned, when... is in question, for the purpose of, or merely: respecting, as regards: *légs-pai, ǰigs-pai, btsán-pai* when beauty, firmness, formidable appearance (of a royal castle) are concerned, are the points in question *Glr.*; *snágs-kyí dbáṅ-du rtsis-pai śló-ka* prob. the Slokas being numbered with a regard to the Mantras, i.e. including the latter *Tar.* 127, 16. — 4. symb. num.: 5 (*dbaṅ* being taken for *dbáṅ-po*).

Comp. and deriv. *dbaṅ-bskúr* consecration, inauguration, initiation *Was.* (189), = *dbaṅ-bskyúr* might, power, e.g. *saṅs-rgyás-kyi Glr.* — *dbaṅ-grál* the row of those that are to be ordained or consecrated. — *dbáṅ-čan* mighty, powerful *Cs.* — *dbaṅ-ťáṅ* 1. **might,** = *mṅa-ťaṅ, dbaṅ-taṅ-méd-pa* low, mean, of inferior rank *Dzl.* 2. **time, chronology** *Lexx.* 3. **destiny, fate, predestined fate,** or rather the destiny of any creature consequent to its former actions, *ťse daṅ dbaṅ-ťáṅ*, frq.; *dbaṅ-ťaṅ-méa-pa* may therefore imply: having no destiny, i.e. no particular destiny. — *dbaṅ-ˌdus-p̔o-bráṅ* 'Angdophorung' of the Indian papers, n. of a fort in Tibet. — *dbaṅ-ldán* mighty, powerful; *dbaṅ-ldán-gyi p̔yogs Dmaṅ, dbáṅ-poi p̔yogs Sbh.*, is said to be north-east. — *dbáṅ-po* v. the next article. — *dbaṅ-p̔yúg* 1. adj. mighty, also sbst.: *dbaṅ-p̔yúg yžán-las čé-ba Glr.* 2. symb. num.: 11. 3. **noun proper** a. Iswara, Siva *Glr.*, hence also the Lingam as his emblem *Glr.* b. Avalokitesvara *Glr.* — *dbáṅ-ba* 1. vb. c. *la* = *dbaṅ byéd-pa*, e.g. *rgyal-srid-la mi dbaṅ* he does not succeed to the throne; gen. with accus. *yčig ˌdi dbáṅ-ba yin* one... belongs to this one *Mil.*; *bdag dbáṅ-bai rgyal-p̔rán* the vassals under my sway *Dzl.* 2. sbst. = *dbaṅ*, e.g. *tsé-la dbáṅ-ba* (v. above). — *dbaṅ-ris* prob. domain, dominion. — *dbaṅ(-po)-lág(-pa)* a medicine, said to be prepared from a viscid, aromatic root, shaped like a hand. — *dbaṅ-śés* perception, by means of the organs of sense *Was.* (278).

དབང་པོ་ *dbáṅ-po* 1. **possessed of power, dominion,** *nór-gyi dbáṅ-por gyur Dzl.* (*Ms.*); **lord, ruler, sovereign,** esp. divine rulers: Indra, also *lhai dbáṅ-po*; further *rgyál-bai dbáṅ-po, ťúb-pai dbáṅ-po* the highest of the Buddhas *Glr.* — 2. **organ of sense,** *dbáṅ-po lṅa(-po)* a. the five organs of sense, eyes etc., also *dbáṅ-poi sgo lṅa Med.* b. *Trigl.* 17, 6, five immaterial, transcendent senses of Buddha, which are in unison with his five powers, *stobs lṅa*, as stated by *Burn.* II, 430, v. *Köpp.* I, 436. In natural philosophy six organs of sense frq. are mentioned, मनस being added as the sixth; medical writings also treat of *dbáṅ-po dgu* or *dbáṅ-poi sgo dgu*, v. *bú-ga.* — 3. **sense, intellectual power,** *dbáṅ-po rnón-po* of acute intellect, *dbáṅ-po rdúl-po* of obtuse intellect, also as common expressions for sagacious or dull *Dzl.*; *dbáṅ-po nyams* the senses are weakened, become dull *Med.*; *lus sems dbáṅ-po* body, soul, and senses (are glad, are pure etc.) *Dom.*; *dbáṅ-po ysó-ba* to gladden, strengthen, revive, the senses *Mil.*; *ráṅ-gi séms-las dbáṅ-poi rnam-śés ˌbyuṅ* out of the spirit (of the personality which during the time between two periods of existence is in a disembodied state) the sense-endowed soul (of the new individual) is generated (in the process of conception)

S.g. — 4. **genitals,** *Wdn.* and elsewh.; *dbán-po lág-pa* v. *dban-lág* sub *dban.*

དབར་མི་ *dbár-mi Sch.* **a faint-hearted, timorous man.**

དབལ་ *dbal Lex.* = *tog* and *rtsé-mo* **top, summit, point** e.g. of a *mčod-rten Glr.*; the point, or acc. to some the grooves of the *p̓ùr-pa* or exorcising dagger; *rtai dbal bzan-nan Lex.?* — *dbál-ba* v. *₀bal-ba.*

དབུ *dbu* resp. for *mgo,* **head,** frq.; **beginning, commencement,** e.g. of holy doctrine *Glr.*; *'u lán-če* W.,* the mode of greeting between Lamas, by touching each other with their fore-heads; to bless (a layman by imposition of hands); *dbu mdzád-pa* to be the head, the principal person, e.g. in an assembly of believers *Mil.*; more definitely: *dbu mdzád-do* he was my instructor *Mil.* — *dbu-skrá* the hair of the head. — *dbu-rgyan* ornament of the head, diadem *Mil.* — *dbu-rnás Sch.* pillow. — *dbu-čan* furnished with a head, i.e. with a thick stroke at the top (of a letter), hence the name of the Tibetan printing characters. — *dbu-čen* 1. **higher officer.** 2. *dbu-čun* **subaltern officer** *Cs.* — *dbu-rje* **Reverence, Reverend,** title of Lamas. — *dbu-snyún bžés-pa Sch.*, *dbu-snyún dan bro ₀bór-ba Glr.* resp. to swear by one's head. — *dbu-tód* royal cap, crown. — *dbu-mtún drún-du* resp. the same as *žabs drún-du* in directing letters: To ... — *dbu-₀p̓án* **elevation, high rank, dignity,** *stód-pa* to praise, *smád-pa* to despise, to revile (dignities). — *dbú-ma* 1. n. of the goddess **Durga,** the wife of Siva. 2. **principal vein,** v. *rtsá-ba.* 3. **the middle** (-doctrine), **middle-road,** **मध्यम,** which endeavours to avoid the two extremes *Was.*, also *dbú-mai lam* or *ltá-ba*; *dbú-ma-pa* an adherent of this doctrine *Sch.*, cf. however *mdo* extr. — *dbu-méd* **the Tibetan current hand-writing,** cf. *dbú-čan.* — *dbu-rmóg Zam.* w.e.; in *W.* **gyál-po u'-móg čo žig** is said to signify: Long live the king! — *dbu-rtsé* the top, pinnacle, of a temple, monastery *Glr.* — *dbu-mdzád* (cf. *dbu mdzád-pa* above) **chairman, principal, warden,** in convents an official that takes the lead in performing the prayers. — *dbu-zwá* cap — *dbu-šóg* title-page *Sch.*

དབུ་བ *dbú-ba* v. *lbú-ba.*

དབུགས *dbugs* 1. **breath, respiration,** *dbugs rnúb-pa dan ₀byín-pa* or *₀byún-ba* to respire, to inhale and exhale air *Med.*, *W.* **tón-če** for *₀byún-ba*; *dbugs ₀byín-pa* to stop for rest, to recover one's breath *Sch.* (and perh. *Pth.*); *dbugs-dbyún t̓ób-pa* to be eased in one's mind, after despondency *Tar.*; *'ug gyan bór-če* W.* to stop, to keep back one's breath; **'ug sub** or *kor tán-če* W.* to choke, suffocate, strangle, throttle; *skyé-₀gro t̓ams-čád-kyi dbugs lén-pa* to take away the breath of beings (which is ascribed to the demon *pe-dkár*) *Glr.*; *p̓yi-dbugs* seems to be the last breath of a dying man, but *nán-dbugs* is some fantastic physiological notion *Thgr.*; *dbugs mdé-ba* and *mi-bdé-ba* an easy and a hard breathing *Med.* frq.; *dbugs-t̓ún* short breath; *dbugs rdzán-ba* or *brdzúns-pa* shortness of breath, asthma, as a complaint of old age *Thgy.*; *dbugs lheb-lhéb byéd-pa* to pant, to be pursy *Med.* — *dbugs-rgód Lt.?* — *dbugs-nán Sch.* flatulence. — *dbugs t̓cbs-grél Sch.* 'in one breath'? — 2. **a breath, one respiration,** as smallest measure of time = $\frac{1}{1800}$ *k̓yim* = 4 seconds.

དབུང་ *dbun Lex.* = *dbus.*

དབུབ་པ *dbúb-pa* v. *₀búbs-pa.*

དབུར་ *dbur* termin. of *dbu, Sch.* **first, at first.**

དབུར་བ་ *dbúr-ba,* also *₄úr-ba, 'úr-ba* **to smooth,** *šóg-bu* paper, *ras* woollen stuff, *γžál* a pavement *Cs.*; **'ur gyág-pa* C.*, **gyáb-če* W.* to iron, to smooth linen etc., **'ur-čag** smoothing-iron.

དབུལ་བ *dbúl-ba* I. vb. v. *₀búl-ba.* — II. adj. **poor, indigent** *Dzl.*; sbst. **poverty, want, penury,** *dbúl-ba sel-ba* to relieve want *Glr.*; *dbul-žin ₀p̓óns-pai rigs* a poor and indigent generation *Dzl.*; hence frq. *dbúl-p̓ons* poor, a poor man, pauper *Mil.*; poverty *Glr.*; usually *dbúl-po,* fem. *dbúl-mo,* poor.

དབུས *dbus* (*Ld.* *'us*, *C.* *'ü*) 1. **middle, midst, centre,** *t̓ág-pai dbus tsám-du* p̔yin-nas having proceeded about to the middle of the rope *Dzl.*; *skyé-boi dbús-su* in the midst of the people *Tar.*; *t̔aṅ γnyis-kyi dbus-rí* the hill (mountain) in the middle between the two plains *Glr.*; *dbús-kyi ri-rgyál* Sumeru standing in the centre (of the world) *Mil.*; seldom relative to time: *bžúgs-pai dbús-su* whilst he was sitting *Glr.*; in metaphysics: *dbus daṅ mt̔a* 'the medium and the extremes' *Cs.* Asiat. Researches XX, 577 — *dbús-ma* the middle one (of three or more persons) *Mil.*, (of inanimate things) *Glr.* — 2. in a specific sense: **the central province** of a country, a. of India, hence = Magadha, the holy land, land of Buddha *Thgy.* b. of Tibet, the province Ü; *dbús-pa* an inhabitant of it; *dbus-γtsán Ü* and *Tsaṅ*.

དབེན་པ་ *dbén-pa* **solitary, lonely,** e.g. a road *Dzl.*; **solitude, loneliness,** *dbén-pa ₒdí-na* in this solitude *Dzl.*; *dbén-par ₒgró-ba* or *γnás-pa* frq.; *dben*, id.: *dbén-la dga Ma.*; *dben-(pai) γnas, sa* solitary place, esp. hermitage; *dbén-γnas čén-po brgyád-kyi sa* earth from the eight great hermitages, sacred places of pilgrimage in India *Glr.*; like *bstoṅs-pa* the word is construed with the instrum. case: *mas dbén-pa*, solitary as to a mother, i.e. motherless; *snyiṅ-pos dbén-pa* = *snyiṅ-po méd-pa Tar.*

དབོ་ *dbo* 1. n. of a lunar mansion, v. *rgyu-skár*, no. ??. — 2. the belly-side of fur.

དབོ་བ་ *dbó-ba* v. *ₒbó-ba*.

དབོན་པོ་ *dbón-po* (*W.* *'ón-po*, *C.* *'om-po*) 1. *B.* resp. for *t̔sá-bo* **grandson; nephew;** *dbon-srás* id. *Glr.*; *dbón-mo* fem.; *mes-dbón* ancestor and grandchild *Glr.*; *dbon-žáṅ Glr.* 95 seems to denote son-in-law and brother-in-law, with which also *Sch.'s* Mongol transl. agrees, Geschichte d. Ost-Mong. p. 359 med. — 2. **Lama-servant** *C.* — 3. a certain sect of Lamas, clad in red, shorn, and married, = **sor-kyim-pa**, *C.*, *W.* — 4. a Lamā skilled in astrology, who for instance, when a person has died, performs those ceremonies, that serve to avert harm from the survivors *W.*

དབོལ་བ་ *dból-ba Cs.* = *rtól-ba*, *Lex. rdziṅ dból-ba*.

དབྱངས་ *dbyaṅs*, **yaṅ(s)** 1. **singing, song, tune, melody,** *glu-dbyáṅs* id.; *luṅ-bstán-gyi dbyaṅs* prophetic song, psalm *Mil.*; *dbyaṅs(-su) lén-pa*, *dbyaṅs byéd-pa* to sing *Dzl.*; *stód (-pai) dbyaṅs* song of praise, hymn of thanksgiving, **ǰhé'-pa** *C.*, **p̔úl-čé** *W.*; *γduṅ-dbyáṅs* a song of aspiration *Mil.* — *dbyáṅs-čan Glr.* a deity, prob. = *ₒǰam-dbyáṅs-čan-ma* Saraswati, goddess of euphony. — *dbyaṅs-snyán* sweet singing. — *dbyáṅs-pa* singer *Cs.* — **yaṅ-žú** bow for a violin, fiddle-stick *W.* — 2. **vowel,** hence *dbyaṅs-yig* 1. the (four) **signs of the vowels,** *Gram.* 2. *Cs.*: **notes** (of music) or any contrivance for marking the modulation of sounds; so perh. also *Glr.*

དབྱར་ *dbyar* **summer,** in India: **rainy season** (cf. *dus*); also *dbyár-ka*, *dbyár-k̔a Mil.*, *W.*, *dbyár-dus*, *Cs. dbyár-mo*; *dbyar-dgun-méd-par* summer and winter *Mil.*; *dbyar B.*, *dbyár-ka-la* col. in summer; *dbyar-γnás* 1. summer-abode, *Sch.* 2. the solitary summer-fasting of the monks; *dbyar-skyés* 'summer-born'; *dbyar-rṅá* summer-drum, po. expression for thunder *Cs.* — *dbyar-čár* summer-rain *Cs.* — *dbyar-žwa* summer-hat.

དབྱར་པ་ *dbyár-pa* (*Pur.* **sbyár-pa**, elsewh. **yár-pa**) **poplar,** various kinds of which tree are found in the vicinity of villages, cultivated or growing wild. (*Wdṅ.* also *sbyár-pa*.)

དབྱི་ *dbyi* (**yi*, com. *'i**) 1. **lynx,** *dbyi-mo* the female of this animal, *dbyi-p̔rúg* a young one; *dbyi-t̔sáṅ* lair of it. — 2. in Ü: **beer,** = *čaṅ*.

དབྱི་གུ་ *dbyi-gu* = *dbyig-gu* **little stick,** cf. *dbyig-pa*.

དབྱི་བ་ *dbyi-ba*, prob. only fut. to *ₒp̔yi-ba*, **to wipe off, to blot out, to efface,** *Lex.*: *ri-mo*, a drawing. *Sch.* however notices also a perf. *dbyis*.

དབྱི་མོ་ *dbyi-mo* **flax** (?).

དབྱི་མོང་ *dbyi-moṅ* medicinal herb, used against delirium *Med.*; *Cs.*: 'a plant of an acrid taste, used as tea'; in *Lh.* Potentilla Salesovii, of which neither the one nor the other fact is known to me.

དབྱིག(ས)་ *dbyig(s)* 1. = *nor* **wealth, riches, treasures**, *nor-dbyig* id. *Dzl.*; *dbyig-čan* rich, *dbyig-med* poor *Cs.*; *dbyig-mán Lex.* — 2. prob. = *dbyig-γnyén*, **precious stone** or a kind of such *Glr.* and elsewh.

དབྱིག་པ་ *dbyig-pa* **stick**, = *dbyúg-pa*.

དབྱིག་པུ་ *dbyig-pu Sch.:* 'implement for cleaning, scouring, polishing'.

དབྱིང་ཞ་ *dbyiṅ-ža Sch.*: **summer-hat** (?).

དབྱིངས་ *dbyiṅs* 1. syn. with *kloṅ*, com. *nám-mk'ai dbyiṅs* or *dbyiṅs* alone: **the heavens, celestial region,** *rgyáb-la brag dmar nám-mk'ai dbyiṅs* red rocks behind and the expanse of heaven *Mil.*; *k'yeu dbyiṅ-su yal* the youth disappearing was carried up to heaven *Pth.*; *dbyiṅs-na bžúgs-pai ḍá-ki-ma Mil.* — 2. **height** *Schr.*; the above passage was also rendered: red rocks behind, as high as heaven. — 3. in metaphysics an undefined idea of **extent, region, space,** **धातु**, (cf. *kloṅ*), *čós-kyi dbyiṅs*, **धर्मधातु**, not 'the wide diffusion of religion' *Sch.*, but a mere fanciful notion, or as it is expressed *Wts.* 143: le monde intellectuel de Bouddha; of highly learned Lamas the words are used: *tugs-dgóṅs čos-dbyiṅs-su tim C.*; and also *dbyiṅs* alone: *bló-yi byéd-pa dbyiṅs-su sbos Glr.* hide your mental activity in the heavens, i.e. let it be reduced to nothing; so prob. also *Tar.* 38, 10, *p'úṅ-po lhág-mo méd-pai dbyiṅs-su*, where nothing of the skandha is left remaining. *Sch.: dbyiṅs-su* in a body, in one mass, whole, entire (?).

དབྱིན་ *dbyin* or *γyin byéd-pa Sch.*, **to incite, instigate, set on.**

དབྱིབས་ *dbyibs* **shape, figure, form,** *byá-dbyibs-čan* having the shape of a bird *Lt.*; *šiṅ-rtai dbyibs daṅ ˳dra* shaped like a waggon or carriage *Glr.*; *skyés-pai dbyibs-la ṅós-bzuṅ-ba* to learn the nature (of plants) from the shape in which they grow; **ă-me yib dug** he quite resembles his mother in shape *W.*; *dbyibs légs-pa B.* a fine figure, **sóg-po** an ugly figure *W.*, or also: of a handsome (or ugly) form; *dbyibs zlúm-por yod* it has a round shape *Glr.*

དབྱུག་གུ་, དབྱུ་གུ་ *dbyug-gu, dbyú-gu* 1. **small staff, wand, rod,** e.g. used as a magic wand, sun-dial etc. *Cs.* — 2. *Lex.*: = *ču-tsod* q.v.; *Sch.: dbyúg-gu re-bži*, '64 equal parts of weight or measure; 64 quarters of an hour, or 16 hours'; but 64 *ču-tsod* would make as much as $25\frac{3}{5}$ hours.

དབྱུག་རྡོ་ *dbyúg-rdo W.* **sling-stone**; *B.: rdo-γyúg.*

དབྱུག་པ་ *dbyúg-pa* I. vb. pf. *dbyugs* 1. **to swing, brandish, flourish,** a stick, a sword; **to wag,** *ṙṅá-ma* the tail *Cs*; **yug yug ǰhe'-pa** *W.*, to swing to and fro, to dangle; **yug toṅ** *W.*, swing! dangle! — 2. **to throw, cast, fling,** **gyál-kar-ne do** *C.*, to fling a stone through a window; to throw away, to throw down, **yúg-le žog** *C.* (= **p'áṅ-te bor** *W.*), throw it away! — II. sbst, **stick,** *C.*; **yúg-pa gyáb-pa** *C.* to strike, to beat with a stick. *dbyúg-to Glr.*, *dbyúg-to*, id. (*Sch.* club?) *Lex.*: = *bér-ka*, **दण्ड**; *dbyug-to-čan* wielding a stick; n.p.

དབྱུང་བ་ *dbyúṅ-ba*, fut., and in *C.* secondary form to the pres. *˳byin-pa.*

དབྱེ་བ་ *dbyé-ba*, (regular pronunciation **yé-wa*, com. *'é-wa**). I. vb. fut., and in *C.* secondary form of *˳byéd-pa.* — II. sbst. 1. **parting, partition, division, distinction, classification** *Thgy.* — 2. **section, part, class, species,** *dbyé-ba nyi-šu γsuṅs* twenty different species are named *Lt.*; *yi-ge ˳di dbyé-ba γnyis* these letters are divided into two classes; hence like *sna-tsogs: sgyu-rtsál dbyé-ba* manifold arts, artifices *Smbh.* — *dbye-brál Lex.:* **discord, dissension.**

དབྱེན་པ་ *dbyén-pa* (**yén-pa*, com. *'én-pa**, = *dbén-pa*), **difference, dissension, discord, schism,** *dge-˳dún-gyi dbyén-pa byéd-pa* to create discord, to cause a schism among the priesthood *Dzl.*; *dbyen ˳byéd pa* to make a difference, to discriminate *Sch.*

དབྱེར་མེད་, དབྱེ་རུ་མེད་པ་, དབྱེར་ཕྱེད་པ་, *dbyer-méd, dbye-ru-méd-pa, dbyer-mi-p'yéd-pa* in-

separable, not to be distinguished, quite the same, identical *Glr.* and elsewh.; *blá-mar dbyér-med* prob.: identical with a Lama; esp. in the higher philosophy in reference to the impossibility of distinguishing between good and evil (!).

དབྱེས་ *dbyes Schr.*: **magnitude, size, dimensions,** so perh. where *dprál-bai dbyes če* is mentioned as a characteristic of beauty.

དབྲག་ *dbrag*, v. *ṕrag*, **intermediate space, interstice;** ravine, glen, defile, *C.*; *Sch.* also: vise, handvise.

དབྲད་པ་ *dbrád-pa* v. *˳brád-pa.*

དབྲབ་པ་ *dbráb-pa* v. *˳bráb-pa.*

དབྲལ་བ་ *dbrál-ba* v. *˳brál-ba.*

དབྲི་བ་ *dbri-ba* v. *˳bri-ba.*

དབྲེ་བཙོང་ *dbre-btsóṅ* (?) *Sch.*; *Lex. dbre-btsog* dirt, filth.

དབྲོག་པ་ *dbróg-pa* v. *˳ṕróg-pa.*

འབའ་ *˳ba Sch.*: 'seizure, distraint'; or rather the liability of paying higher interest, payment not having been made at the appointed time; *˳ba-gan*, *˳ba-gan-yig* warrant for thus proceeding against a debtor *C.*

འབའ་ཆ་ *˳ba-ča Wdṅ.*; *Sch.*: **lees** from distilling brandy.

འབའ་པོ་ *˳bá-po* **magician, sorcerer, conjurer;** *˳bá-mo* sorceress, witch *Cs.*, *W.*

འབའ་བ་ *˳bá-ba* 1. **to bleat,** *W.* **ba tán-če**. — 2. **to bring, to carry,** *˳bá-šog* bring it hither! *Sik.*, *˳ba-soṅ* take it there! — 3. **to commit adultery** *C.*

འབའ་བོ་ *˳bá-bo*, *Cs.* = *ṕug-pa*, **hole, cave, cavern,** *brág-gi* cleft in a rock, grotto; *˳bá-bo-čan* **hollow, excavated.**

འབའ་བྱི་ *˳bá-byi* a kind of cake, baked of parched rice or maize meal, frequently eaten with the tea *C.*

འབའ་ཞིག་ *˳bá-žig B.* **only, solely, alone,** *bdag ˳bá-žig tár-ro* I alone escaped *Dzl.*; *rkáṅ-pa ˳bá-žig* the foot alone (appeared party-coloured) *Dzl.*: *blón-po de ˳bá-žig-gi čúṅ-ma* only this officer's wife *Dzl.*; **mere, nothing but,** *γser daṅ dṅul ˳ba-žig-gis gaṅ Sbh.*

འབག་ *˳bag* 1. **mask, guise, disguise;** cf. also sub *sgo-lo.* — 2. **imitation, effigy, likeness, figure,** *˳dra-˳bág* resp. *sku-˳bag*, *žal-˳bág* id.; *˳dra-˳bag-gyon-mi* masked persons *Pth* — *˳bag-˳čam*, prop. **masquerade,** masked ball; *Cs.*: buffoonery, grimaces.

འབག་པ་ *˳bág-pa* I. vb. pf. *˳bags*, fut. *dbag?* cf. *sbág-pa*, **to defile, to pollute one's self,** *bud-méd daṅ* with women *Dzl.*; *˳dod-čágs-la* through lust *Dzl.*; **to defile, to soil, to dirty,** *snód-la* a vessel *Dzl.* ༢༢༠, 7? — 2. *C.* **to take away, to steal, to rob; to covet, to wish to take,** c. *la Mil.* (acc. to oral information).

འབག་འབོག་ *˳bag-˳bóg* a slight elevation, **hillock** *W.*

འབག་རག་ *˳bag-rág* **spider,** *˳bag-rág-gi tsaṅ* cob-web *Sik.*

འབགས་ལྷག་ *˳bags-lhag* **rest, remainder, remnant** (of food) *Mil.*

འབང་བ་ *˳báṅ-ba* **to be soaked, macerated,** softened by soaking *Cs.*, cf. *sbáṅ-ba.*

འབངས་ *˳baṅs* **subject,** *rgyál-po ˳báṅs-su ˳oṅ* the king turns into a subject *Ma.*; *˳baṅs byéd-pa* to obey, *bkai ˳baṅs bgyid-par* (or *bka-˳baṅs-su*) *ḱas-blaṅs-so* they promised to obey, to perform the commandment *Mil.* frq.; *báṅs-su byéd-pa Cs.* to reduce under one's dominion; gen. collectively: **the people, the subjects,** opp. to *blón-po* officers, magistrates, or *rje*, *rgyál-po* etc. — *lha-báṅs Tar.* 165, 22 *Schf.*: slaves belonging to a temple.

འབད་པ་ *˳bád-pa* I. vb., imp. *˳bod*, **to endeavour, to exert one's self, apply one's self,** c. *la* or the termin.; *dus-rgyún-du čós-la ˳bád-pa de* this (habit of) constantly applying one's self to religion *Mil.*; also c acc.: *dká-ba brgya-ṕrág* to perform a hundred exercises of penance; col. **to cultivate, raise, rear, take care of,** *žiṅ* or *sá-γzi* to cultivate the ground, *rgun-˳brúm* to grow vines, *dúd-˳gro* to breed cattle; *slob-par* to apply one's self to learning, *gléṅ-mo ḱó-nar* to devote one's self exclusively to public speaking, preaching *C.* — II. sbst.

application, study, exertion, ̥*bád-pa drág-pos* with most persevering application; ̥*bád-pa dan rtsól-ba méd-par* without any exertion *Glr.*; hence ̥*bad-rtsól* id.; *skyés-bus srúb-pai* ̥*bad-rtsól* an assiduous rubbing with a human hand *Wdn.*; *dei* ̥*bad-rtsól-gyis* through his endeavours *Thgy.*; prob. also: **volition, energy of will** *S.g.*; the passage in *Thgy.*: *byan-čúb ci tób-la* ̥*bad* ̥*tsál-lo*, is perh. not quite correct.

འབབ་ ̥*bab* 1. **a fall of snow** *Mil.* — 2. **tax, duty** *Sp.*

འབབ་པ་ ̥*báb-pa*, pf. *bab(s)*, imp. ̥*bob Cs.*, *bobs Glr.*, **to move downward** 1. **to descend,** *lá-nas* col., a defile, in *B.* gen. with *las*, e.g. *rtá-las Dzl.*, also *rtá-ka-nas Glr.* to alight from a horse, mostly with *la*, although *ri-la* ̥*báb-pa* may also mean: to alight (flying) on a mountain *Dzl.* ༢༥༣, 2. — 2. **to fall down,** *γnám-la ká-ba* ̥*bab* snow falls from heaven *Dzl.* — **to flow,** the usual word; to flow off; *mi-γtsán* ̥*báb-pai γtór-kun* sink-hole, for dirty water to run through *Lex.* — 4. **to alight on, to enter into,** of demons *Lt.* — 5. in a general sense, like **to get:** *nya skám-la* ̥*báb-pa* a fish that has got on dry ground; *ná-la ré-mos* ̥*bab Pth.*, or *res* ̥*bab Tar.* it is my turn; *srógla* ̥*báb-bo Dzl.* life is at stake; frq. in reference to time: *či-bai dús-la báb-bo* it has come to the time of dying, the hour of death has arrived; without a genit.: it is time; *skábs-la báb-bo* there is now an opportunity *Dzl.* — ̥*bab-ču* **river, rivulet, brook;** also **rain.** — ̥*bab-stégs* access or descent to the water, steps leading to a bathing-place *Hind.* *ghāṭ*. — ̥*báb-mo* W.* **condescending, affable.**

འབམ་ ̥*bam* 1. *rkan-*̥*bám* a disease of the foot *Sch.*: **gout.** — 2. ̥*bám-yig* v. *yi-ge.*

འབམ་པ་ ̥*bám-pa Cs.* **putrefaction, rottenness; to be putrid, rotten,** cf. *bám-pa.*

འབར་བ་ ̥*bár-ba* (vb.n. to *sbár-ba*) 1. **to burn,** *me* ̥*bár-bai kán-pa* a burning house *Thgy.*; **to catch fire, to be ignited; to blaze** *Dzl.*; also in reference to the passions frq.; **to beam, radiate,** *ód-du* in light *Tar.*; ̥*bár-du rún-ba Cs.* combustible. — 2. **to open, to begin to bloom, to blossom,** frq. — 3. **to talk, rattle, to be garrulous, babbling,** *̥*bar* *ó-pa me** it is not worth while to talk about it *C.*; *ko ná-la mán-po* ̥*bar* ̥*dug* he treats me to a long gossip *C*; esp. **to brawl, quarrel, chide,** *ka-*̥*bár* **quarrelsome, brawling** *Mil.*; *mán-du* ̥*bár-du byún-ba-las* as she was going to brawl still longer *Mil.*; **bar-kád tán-ce** to rail at a person *W.* — 4. *dpal* ̥*bar-ba Cs.* **to be celebrated,** famous.

འབར་འབར་ ̥*bar-*̥*bár* 1. sbst. **a high, pointed hill,** cf. ̥*bag-*̥*bóg.* — 2. adj. **uneven, rough; pock-marked.**

འབལ་བ་ ̥*bal-ba*, used only with *skra*, 1. **to part, dress, arrange,** the hair, as it is customary with the monks and nuns of certain sects; in Kham also national costume; *skra γyas* ̥*bal γyon* ̥*bal byéd-pa* (of a nun) *Pth.*; **bál-*̥*go-cen** a person wearing the hair thus dressed *C.*; *skrá-*̥*bal-can*, prob. id.; *C.*: name of an old Indian sect. — 2. as a sign of mourning, **to have the hair disheveled,** hanging down in disorder *Pth.*; so also *Dzl.* ༡༥༥, 17, acc. to correct reading; ̥*bal-*̥*bál* **shaggy** *Sch.*

འབི་འབི་ ̥*bi-*̥*bi* **small lumps of clay** *Cs.*

འབིག(ས)་པ་ ̥*big(s)-pa*, pf. *pigs*, fut. *dbig*, imp. *pig(s)* and ̥*búg(s)-pa*, *pug*, *dbug*, *pug*, also *pig-pa*, *púg-pa*, 1. **to sting,** of insects *Stg.*; **to pierce,** *rdó-rje-yis ni rin-čén pug* the diamond pierces the precious stone *Pth.*; **to bore,** *šin-la búg-pa* ̥*búg-pa* to bore holes into wood *Glr.*; in a gen. sense, **to make a hole,** *rkán-pa kyis pug* the dog bit my foot *Mil.*; *kán-pa* ̥*big-pa Thgy.* and elsewh., **to break into, to break open;** *̥*big gyáb-pa**, id. *C.*; *ču-*̥*gágs* ̥*bigs* it removes strangury *Med.* — 2. *C.* **to deflower, to lie with,** obscene. — **búg-ce** *W.* to make remarks on an absent person, **to criticize.** — *bigs-byéd*, n. p., n. of the Vindhya mountains (v. विन्द्).

འབིང་ ̥*bin*, **jham-bin** *C.*, resp. **sol-*̥*bin** **tea-pot.**

འབིབ(ས)་པ་ ̥*bib(s)-pa* = ̥*búb(s)-pa Sch.*

འབུ་ ₒ*bu* **worm, insect**, any small vermin, esp. euphem. for louse; ₒ*bu-srin, srin-*ₒ*bu*, id.; ₒ*bu-skyógs* **snail** *Med.*; ₒ*bu-tags Cs.*, **cob-web**; **bu-yáṅ** (prob. a mere corruption of *búṅ-ba*) **humble-bee** *W.*; *ₒ*bu-riṅ** **snake** *W.*

འབུ་བ་ ₒ*bú-ba*, pf. ₒ*bus* 1. **to open, to unfold,** of flowers, esp. with *ḱa Pth.* — 2. *Cs.*: **to be lighted, kindled, set on fire.**

འབུ་མ་ ₒ*bú-ma Sch.*: tool used in forging nails.

འབུ་རས་ ₒ*bu-rás* a coarse silky material, stated to be imported into Tibet from Nepal, and to come from some other insect than the silk-worm.

འབུ་ལ་ ₒ*bú-la* 1. *C.*, *W.* shoe of plaited straw. — 2. *C.*: **kó-wa bú-la**, a kind of leather, resembling chagreen.

འབུ་སུ་ཧང་ ₒ*bu-su-háṅ* medicinal herb *Med.*

འབུག་ ₒ*bug Sch.* **awl, puncher; chisel.**

འབུགས་པ་ ₒ*búgs-pa* v. ₒ*bigs-pa.*

འབུངས་པ་ ₒ*búṅs-pa*, prop.: **to fall upon in a body, to rush in upon,** = *rúb-pa*; *čós-la* ₒ*buṅs* apply yourselves with might and main to religion! it is also used of one person: ₒ*bad* ₒ*buṅs* he summons all his strength, strains every nerve *Dzl.*

འབུད་པ་ ₒ*búd-pa* I. pf. *bus, ṕu(s)* (the latter form prob. transit., the former intransit.) fut. *dbu*, imp. *ṕu(s)* 1. vb.n **to blow,** *lás-kyi rluṅ* ₒ*búd-ciṅ* whilst the wind of works is blowing; *čós-kyi duṅ bus* the trumpet of religion blew (was blown). — 2. vb. a. **to blow,** *duṅ* the trumpet; **to blow away,** *rluṅ-gis sbúr-ma bús-pa ltar* like chaff blown off by the wind *Dzl.;* to blow up, to fan, *me* the fire, frq.; **to blow into, to inject,** e.g. to apply a clyster *C.;* **to blow** or **breathe upon,** *bsér-bus* to be encountered by a cold wind *Med.*; **to inflate, to distend** by injecting air, *lus kun bús-pa ltar skraṅs Mṅg.*; ₒ*bud-*ₒ*duṅ Wdk.* = *duṅ* trumpet. Cf. *sbúd-pa* and *ṕu.* — *W.* **ṕú-ce**. — II. pf. imp. *ṕud*, fut. *dbud W.* **ṕud-ce**, trs.: 1. **to put off, pull off, take off** *C.*, *W.*, the turban, hat, coat, ring etc. *Glr.* and elsewh.; **to throw down,** *ṕud bžág-go Glr.*, = *ₒ*paṅ-ste** *bor W.*, v. sub ₒ*ṕén-pa.* — 2. **to drive out, expel, cast out, chase away,** with the accus. of the person and place, *yul* out of the country *Tar.*; *yul-ṕud* an exile *Schr.*; *drag-pos* by force *Mil.;* **to let out** (out of a cage); **to set free, to set at liberty, to allow to pass** *W.;* **to lay out, to spend,** **ṅul tsam ṕud soṅ** how many rupees have been laid out, spent? — 3. **to pull out, tear out, extract, uproot,** so a tooth, *C.*, *W.* — 4. **to take away, to subtract,** **gú-ne* (or *gu tóg-ne*) *ži ṕúd-pa* (or *ṕúd-na*) *ṅa lus** 4 taken from 9 leaves 5 *W.* — III. pf. ₒ*bud*, vb.n. (limited perh. to *W.*) 1. **to fall from, escape from, drop, fall down,** **láy-pa-ne bud soṅ** it escaped, dropped out of my hand; **to fall off,** of leaves; **to fall through,** **sól-wa da-mig-ne bud soṅ** the coals are fallen through the grate. — 2. **to go away, to leave,** e.g. to leave the service. — 3. **to go out of sight, to disappear,** **nyi-ma bud soṅ** the sun is gone down; **búd-ḱan** a departed (deceased) person; **the ancients, those of old,** *pristini*; **to pass away,** **dus-tsód bud** time passes away (make haste!); **pid-ka šar-na gun bud soṅ** when spring begins, winter has passed away; **bud čug-ce** **to cause to be lost,** or **to suffer to be lost, to lose.**

འབུན་པ་, བུན་པ་ ₒ*bún-pa, bún-pa* **to itch;** **bun, zá-bun** **the itch, itching** *W.*; **bun rag** I feel an itching (*B. yyá-ba*).

འབུབ་པ་ ₒ*búb-pa*, pf. *bub*, imp. *bub(s)*, 1. **to be turned over, upside down,** frq. with *ḱa*, *ḱa-*ₒ*búb-tu nyal* he lies with his face undermost; *ḱa-*ₒ*bub-tu bžag* or *bor* it is placed with its top lowermost, inverted, tilted, turned over; *lag-*ₒ*búb* (or *-bubs*) *byéd-pa Sch.*: stumbling to fall on the hands. — 2. fig., **to be overthrown, destroyed, spoiled,** with regard to meditation *Mil.*

འབུབས་པ་ ₒ*búbs-pa*, pf. imp. *ṕub(s)*, fut. *dbub*, *W.* **ṕub-ce**, **to put on a roof,** or something for a roof; *tog* **to make, construct a roof;** *gur* to pitch a tent; *gru-ṕubs* corner-pavilion *S.g.*

འབུམ་ ₒ*bum* **one hundred thousand,** ₒ*búm-tso* id.; *rgyai dmag* ₒ*búm-tso lṅa*

500 000 Chinese *Glr.*; *˳bum-ṗrág γčig* a hundred thousand; *˳búm-ṫso drug* 600 000; *mgur-˳búm* the 100 000 songs, v. *mgúr-ma*.

འབུམ་པ་ *˳búm-pa* **tomb, sepulchre** *Cs.*, *sku-˳búm*, *γduṅ-˳búm Cs.*, id.; *sku-˳búm* (*kum-búm*) n. p., a large monastery on the Chinese frontier, v. Huc, also *Köpp.*, who traces the name back to the preceding word.

འབུར་བ་ *˳búr-ba*, I. vb. 1. **to rise, to be prominent**, *sbáṅ-la brág-ri ˳búr-ba čig* a rocky hill rising from the green-sward *Mil.*; *˳búr-du dód-pa* v. *dód-pa*; *˳búr-du rkó-ba* to emboss, to work out relievos *Glr.*; *˳bur-kó gyáb-pa* *C.*, *búr-la tón-če* *W.* id. — 2. **to spring up, come forth, bud, unfold**, *ṅo bur dug* it is getting green *W.* — 3. **to increase, augment**, *ṅo kyé-na ŏ-ma bur dug* when the fields are getting green, milk becomes more plentiful *W.* — *kyoṅ-˳bur* gold and silver ornaments in relievo on some other metal. — *glo-˳búr*, *blo-˳bur* seems to be a technical term for some part of a building *Glr.* — *bris-˳búr* paintings and sculptures. — *˳búr-rko-mḱan*, *˳búr-bzo-pa* engraver. — *˳búr-sku* relief-picture — *˳bur-rgód* (s.l.c.) *Ld.-Glr.*, *Schl.* 17, b., mentioned among various musical instruments (?). — *˳bur-ǰóms* with *byéd-pa* to reduce elevations, to smooth uneven ground; fig. *Mil.*, to prostrate an opponent in disputation. — *˳búr-po* 1. *Sch.*: **projecting, prominent; a protuberance, tumor**, *rús-pai ˳búr-poi ldebs* near the protuberance of the bone *Med.* 2. **having protuberances, uneven, rough**, opp. to *˳ǰám-po*, of the skin *Med.* — *˳búr-ma* embossment, relievo — II. sbst. **protuberance**, e g. a boil, pustule etc.

འབུལ་བ་ *˳búl-ba* I. vb., pf. imp. *ṗul*, fut. *dbul* (*ul, yl*), *W.* *ṗúl-če* 1. **to give**, when the person receiving is considered to be of higher rank (cf. *γnáṅ-ba*), *či tsam žig dbúl-bar bgyi* how much shall we give you? *Feer Introd.* p. 70, 18; **to bring in**, e.g. to place a criminal before the king *Dzl.*; *gar daṅ rtséd-mo rgyál-po-la ˳búl-ba* to perform dances etc. before the king *Dzl.*; *γtsúg-lag-ḱaṅ rgyál-po-la γzigs-par ˳búl-ba* to show the king the convent-temple *Glr.*; **to lay before, represent, report**, like *γsól-ba*, *ṫsul rgyas ṗúl-bas* as they had given him a minute report of the manner in which ... *Mil.*; *ṗul žig* communicate it to me *Mil.*; *˳bul-bar ṗul-nas Mil.*, prob. proposing to give, offering; *lam* to put a person in the way of, to put in a condition, to enable *Mil.*; specifically in dating letters: *dkar-mdáṅs-nas ṗul* given at Kardang. — 2. **to add** (arith.) *Wdk.* II. sbst. **offering, gift, present**, *˳búl-ba maṅ-po ṗul Mil.*, also *byéd-pa Pth.*

འབུས་པ་ *˳bús-pa* 1. v. *˳bú-ba*. — 2. = *˳búr-bar*, **prominent**.

འབུས་ཤིང་ *˳bus-šiṅ Sch.* **a coppice of young trees.**

འབེ་དྷ་ *˳be-dha* (*bé-da*), a class of **itinerant musicians**, cf. *mon W.* (This seems not to be a Tibetan word, but to belong to one of the mountain dialects; its spelling also — acc. to *Ld.-Glr.*, *Schl.* 25, b. p. 15 — may be wrong).

འབེན་ *˳ben Pth.*, *˳bem* *W.*, *C.*, 1. **aim, goal, target**, *˳ben ˳dzúgs-pa* to set up a target; *˳bén-la γtod-pa* to aim, to take aim; *˳bén-sa* the place where the target is to be set up; specifically: the central part of the target, the mark. — 2. **scope** *Cs.* — 3. **putrefaction** *Sch.*, = *˳bam*.

འབེན་དུག *˳ben-dúg Cs.* **rags, tatters.**

འབེབས་པ་ *˳bébs-pa*, pf *ṗab*, fut. *dbab*, imp. *ṗob W.* *ṗáb-če*, causative to *˳báb-pa* 1. **to cast down, throw down**, *ltó-ba sa-la* to cast one's self on the ground *Dzl.*; *sa-rdúl ˳bebs bčug* he made (the pigeon) throw down dust *Glr.*; **to cause to rain** (e.g. jewels) frq.; *ḱyeu ču ˳bébs-kyi ri-mo* a picture representing two youths who, driven by piety, conveyed by means of an elephant skins filled with water to the fishes in a dried-up pool *Glr.*; *mig sna-rtsér* to keep one's eyes directed towards the tip of the nose. — 2. **to subject** *Dzl.* ༢༥༠, 12. — 3. **to put off, to lay aside**, e.g. *bag* I. — 4. used in a variety of phrases: *γnas ˳bébs-pa W.* *ži ṗáb-če* to take up one's residence in a place; *dpya ˳bébs-pa*, with *la*, to impose taxes *Tar.*, cf ˳*bab*; *skyon* ˳*bébs-pa* to impute a crime to a person, to calumniate *Glr.*; *(s)*kad pab-če** *W.* to translate; *blo*, resp. *tugs*, e.g. *yul-pyogs* ˳*di-ru* ˳*bébs-pa* to direct one's thoughts to a certain place, to have a mind to settle there; *ytán-la* ˳*bébs-pa* v. *ytan*; **nā núl-la páb-ča** to turn the barley into money *Kun.*

འབེམ་ ˳*bem* v. *ben.*

འབེར་ ˳*ber Cs.*: 'a sort of plastic mass used by smiths'.

འབེལ་(མ་) ˳*bel(-ma)* the hair on the forehead of a horse *Cs.*

འབེལ་པོ་ ˳*bél-po Sch.*: '**temperate, saving, economical;** ˳*bél-po* ˳*dug* a good deal has been saved (by economy), ample provision has been made; ˳*bél-du* ˳*júg-pa* to enjoin temperance, frugality' (?).

འབོ་ ˳*bo* **a dry measure,** which seems to be very variable as to quantity, and little used; *kal-bó Cs.* **bushel.**

འབོ་བ་ ˳*bó-ba*, pf. ˳*bos*, *bo*, *po*, fut. *dbo W.* **bo-če, po-če**, **to pour out,** *krag* ˳*bó-ba* to shed blood *Ma.*; *ma bó-ba byún-nas* there being no spilling *Glr.*; *bdúd-rtsi pó-bas* pouring out nectar *Glr.*; **pos toṅ** *Ld.* pour out! — 2. **to swell (up), to rise,** **bós-te rag** I see it has swelled *W.*; ˳*bós-pai nas Sch.* swelled barley; *srán-ma pós-pa tsam* as big as a swelled pea *Lt.*; *srád-ma pos-pós* grain swelled, and afterwards parched. — 3. **to sprout, shoot forth,** of wild-growing plants, *sa* ˳*bo* ˳*dug* the ground is verdant *C.*

འབོག་ ˳*bog*, a kind of **upper-garment,** *po-*˳*bóg*, for men, *mo-*˳*bóg* for females *Cs.* — 2. *W.*: **a square cloth,** for wrapping up and carrying provisions, also **bog-ča**, hence **bog-tes** a burden thus formed. — 3. *W.*, **a small hillock;** **sa-bóg, be-bóg** a sand-hill; **ri-bóg** a projecting hill, also a clod; **paṅ-bóg** a piece of turf.

འབོག་ཆོལ་ ˳*bog-čol* v. *sbug-čol.*

འབོག་ཐོ་ ˳*bog-tó*, *žwá-mo* ˳*bog-to Cs.*, **hat** with a broad crown of yellow cloth, and trimmed with long-haired fur.

འབོག་(ས་)པ་ ˳*bog(s)-pa*, pf. *bog, pog*, fut. *dbog? W.* **bog-če**, **to be rooted out, uprooted, pulled out,** of teeth *W.*; **to be put out of joint,** *tsigs W.* — 2. **to be taken down** (opp. to ˳*gél-ba*), *kál-rnams pog Glr.* the loads were taken off; **zaṅ mé-ne** the kettle from the fire *W.* — 3. **to grow loose, to come off, to drop off,** leaves from a tree *C.* — 4. **to sink down, to fall to the ground,** esp. in a fainting-fit, ˳*bog - čiṅ brgyál - ba Thgy.*, *brgyál(-žiṅ)* ˳*bóg pa Pth*, id.; ˳*bog yun riṅ-na Lt.* prob.: when the fainting-fit has lasted a long time; *smyo-*˳*bóg* **madness, insanity,** ˳*byuṅ* sets in, takes place *Glr.*; ˳*bog-ši* being quickly carried off, by cholera etc. *W.* — 5. **to wade, to dip into, to submerge,** *ču-la Dzl.* also *ču Lex.* to wade through the water.

འབོགས་པ་ ˳*bógs-pa*, pf. *pog*, fut *dbog, dbag*, imp. *pog*, 1. **to give, to impart,** *ydams-ṅág, luṅ* counsel, advice, directions *Tar.*; *krid, bsláb-pa Mil.* instruction; *sdóm-pa* to impose religious duties, i.e. to receive into holy orders *Glr.*; to bequeath, to give (?), *nor Lex.* — 2. *yži-ma* **to fit up a dwelling,** = ˳*bébs-pa Glr.*; *gro* ˳*bógs-pa* to take breakfast. 3. **to blot, stain, pollute,** v. ˳*bág-pa.*

འབོང་བ་ ˳*bóṅ - ba Cs.*, **roundness, rotundity,** ˳*boṅ -* ˳*bóṅ*, **round;** acc. to my informants **boṅ-bóṅ** **loose, slack, incoherent** *W.* —

འབོད་ ˳*bod* 1. v. ˳*bód-pa.* — 2. v. ˳*bád-pa.*

འབོད་པ་ ˳*bód-pa*, *bod-pa*, pf. imp. *bos*, *W.* **bo-če, bos (boi, bo)**, 1. **to call, to exclaim,** *sdod čig ces bós-so* he exclaimed: wait! *Dzl.*; *mi žig B.*, *mi žig-la* col., to call a person; *rtsar Glr.*, *mdún-du Pth.* to call near; *náṅ-du* to call in; ˳*bód-pai brda* or *tsig* **interjection** *Gram*; *čáṅ-la* ˳*bod-pa* to call, to invite, to a cup of beer *Dzl.*; *ma bós-par* ˳*óṅ-ba* to come uninvited *Dzl*; *kú-čos* ˳*bód-pa Wdṅ.*, ˳*bod-grógs-pa Dzl.* to cry repeatedly; **bós-ra** *Ld.*, **boi-ra, bo-ra** *Lh.*, **táṅ-če** or *gyáb-če** id. *W.*; *ṅu-*˳*bód* howling, v. *ṅú-ba.* — 2. **to call, to name, to denominate,** *yúl-skad*... ˳*bód-pa* commonly called, styled ... *Wdṅ.*

འབོབས་ ₒ*bobs*, not exactly 'stocking' (*Sch.*), but a soft, warm stuffing of the stockings; **bob-zọn** a shoe provided with such stuffing *C.*

འབོར་བ་ ₒ*bór-ba*, pf. imp. *bor*, 1. **to throw, cast, fling,** e.g. the mendicant's bowl up in the air, the sword to the ground *Dzl.*; *zám-pai ₒóg-tu* to precipitate a person from a bridge *Dzl.*; *p̔yir* to cast out *Thgy.*; **ma bhor-wa j̀he'** *C.* don't throw it away! **bhor soṅ** I've lost it *C. bor-ɣtór, bor-stór, bor-dór, dór-ₒbor-ba Mil.* and elsewh. id.; to throw away, pour away, *č̔u* water *C.*; to waste, to squander *Dzl.* — 2. **to leave, forsake,** *k̔yim-t̔ab* husband or wife *Dzl.*; to leave behind, *mi žig bód-du* to leave a person behind in Tibet; *yáb-k̔yis bór-bai tse* when I was left by my father, when my father died *Pth.*; *de bór-la t̔oṅ* let that alone, give it up, keep away from it *Mil.*; **ṅa lé-ka bor taṅ yin** *W.* I shall now leave off working, I shall put aside my work. — 3. = ₒ*j̀óg-pa*, **to place, put, lay,** in *W.* the word commonly used, in *C.* and *B.* only in certain phrases: **ʼi-ru bor** put it here! **tán-ni k̔ar bór-če** to seat a person on the carpet, to invite to a seat on the carpet; **mii lág-tu ṭ̔in bór-če** to place a charge into somebody's hands; **nyér-pa só-ma bór-če** to appoint a new manager; frq. with gerund: **k̔yi tág-te bór-če** to fasten a dog (to a chain). — 4. in particular combinations, e.g. *góm-pa*.

འབོལ་ ₒ*bol* (v. *bol*) **cushion, bolster, mattress;** *snye-ₒból* pillow, v. *snye-ba*.

འབོལ་པོ་ ₒ*ból-po B., C.,* *ₒ*ból-mo** *W.* 1. **soft,** of the ground, beds, leather, fruit etc.; **soft, gentle, pliable,** also as to disposition of mind; ₒ*ból-le šig-ge sdód-pa* to sit still, to remain quiet, tranquil *Mil.* — 2. *C.* = *mód-po*.

འབོས་ ₒ*bos* 1. v. ₒ*bo*. — 2. v. ₒ*bo-ba*. — 3. sbst. **boil, bump, tumour** *C.*

འབྱང་བ་ ₒ*byaṅ-ba* **to clean, cleanse, purify** *Cs.*, ₒ*byaṅ-k̔yád* custom *C., W.*

འབྱམས་པ་ ₒ*byám-pa*, pf. *byams Cs.*, **to flow over, to be diffused.** ₒ*byam-klás-pa Lex., Cs.*: unlimited, infinite; *rab-ₒbyáms Lex., Cs.*: widely diffused, far spread; *rab-ₒbyáms-pa Cs.*: a man of profound learning, a doctor of theology or philosophy; also *Schr.*; *Köpp.* II, 253.

འབྱར་བ་ ₒ*byár-ba* v. ₒ*byór-ba*.

འབྱི་བ་ ₒ*byi-ba*, pf. *byi*, also *p̔yi* and *p̔yis*, vb. n. of *p̔yi-ba* **to be wiped off, blotted out, effaced** *Cs.*; **to fall off,** of the hair *Dzl.* and elsewh.

འབྱིང་བ་ ₒ*byiṅ-ba*, pf. *byiṅ* 1. **to sink in, to sink down, to be swallowed up,** *šiṅ-rṭa byé-ma-la ₒbyiṅ Glr.* the carriage sticks fast in the sand; *gru č̔ú-la* the ship sinks in the water *Dzl.* and elsewh. — 2. **to grow faint, languid, remiss,** *rig-pa byiṅ-ba bsér-ba* to lift up again one's fainting soul *Mil.*; *byiṅ-rgod* seems to signify **languor, distraction,** *byiṅ-rmúgs Mil.*, id., *byiṅ-rmugs-méd-pai sgom*; so also *byiṅ-t̔ibs Lt.*; *sems-byiṅ-ba* **drowsiness, indolence, depression of spirits.** — 3. *C.* **j̀hiṅ soṅ, j̀hiṅ log soṅ**, they have dispersed, separated, are all gone home. — 4. v. ₒ*j̀iṅ*, 2.

འབྱིད་པ་ ₒ*byid-pa*, pf. *byid*, *p̔yid* 1. **to glide, to slip** *Lex.* = ₒ*dréd-pa*. — 2. **to disappear, to pass away,** e.g. *mi-t̔se ₒbyid* human life passes away *Lex.*; in *W.* **tse p̔id-če** vb. a., to earn a livelihood, **gár-ra č̔ó-te** by smith's work (*C. lto zá-ba*).

འབྱིན་པ་ ₒ*byin-pa*, pf. imp. *p̔yuṅ*, fut. (in *C.* also pres.) *dbyuṅ Ld.* **p̔iṅ-če**, trs. of ₒ*byuṅ-ba*, **to cause to come forth: 1. to take out, to remove,** a pillar from its place *Dzl.*; **p̔iṅs(toṅ)** take it out (out of your pocket, out of the box etc.) *Ld.*; **to draw out, pull out,** a sword, a thorn etc., frq.; **to tear out, to put out,** one's eyes etc., *mig dbyúṅ-ba dé-dag* the men whose eyes are to be put out *Dzl.* p. ༤༦, 10, acc. to an emended reading; **to draw forth, produce, bring to light,** something that was hid *Dzl.* — 2. in a more gen. sense: **to let proceed from, to send out, to emit,** rays of light, frq.; *lus-la k̔rag* to draw blood by scratching one's self *Dzl.*; *mči-ma Glr.* to shed tears; *skad* to make the voice to be heard, of a bird *Dzl.*; *sdug-bsṅál-gyi skad* to utter complaints, lamentations *Dzl.*; *skad čén-po* to cry aloud *Dzl.*; **to exhibit, to extol,** *bstán-pai čé-ba* the grandeur of the doctrine *Tar.* 48,9, *Schf.*; **to drive out, turn out, expel,** *ɣnas ₒbyin-pa Tar.*, **yúṅ-wa* Ts.*, to banish. so also *Ld.* **piṅ-če**: **to cast out, throw away** *Ts.*; **to save, rescue, liberate, release,** *nas* from, *Dom.*; absol. *Tar.* 121,19. — 3. particular phrases, such as *k'ól-du p'yúṅ-ba, yid ₒbyin-pa* etc. v. in their own places.

འབྱུག་པ་ *ₒbyúg-pa*, pf. and imp. *byugs* 1. **to wet, moisten, smear, spread over, anoint**, with *la: ša skám-la tsá-ču byúgs-pa* salt-meat *Glr.*; *ɣdóṅ-la sol-snúm ₒbyúg-pa* to daub one's face with coal-salve *Glr.*: also with accus. and instrum.: *lha-rtén spos daṅ byúg-pas* covering the little temple with spices and ointments *Dzl.*; *ɣser ₒbyúg-pa* prob. to gild *Pth.* — 2. **to stroke, to pat,** *mgó la* a person's head *Dzl.*

འབྱུང་བ་ *ₒbyúṅ-ba* 1. vb., pf. imp. *byuṅ* (intrs of *ₒbyin-pa*) **to come out, to emerge,** often with a pleon. *p'yir* etc., from the water, from an egg, a vessel etc. *Dzl.*; *ₒk'ór-ba-las* — to be set free, to be liberated *Dom.*; to go out, *k'yim-nas Dzl.*; *p'yi-rol-tu ₒbyúṅ-ba* to go out into the open air *Dzl.*; **to make one's appearance, to become visible** *Dzl.*; **to show one's self, to appear** *rgyál-poi rmí-lam-du byúṅ-bai lha-ɣčig* the princess that appeared to the king in a dream *Glr.*; also: *ṅá-la rmí-lam bzáṅ-po byuṅ* I have had an auspicious dream *Mil.*; *sgrén-mor ₒbyúṅ-ba* to go abroad naked *Dzl.*; **to be heard, to resound,** *skad* frq.; **to be said, to be told** *Tar.*; **to turn out, to prove, to be found,** *ma bzí-ba su byúṅ-ba* he who is found not intoxicated *Glr.*; *ṅán-pa byuṅ* it proved to be ill founded *Mil.*; ...*pa su yaṅ ma byuṅ* none was to be found that... *Pth.*; to step forward, from the crowd; to step forth, to appear *Glr.*; **to step up to,** with *rtsar* to *Glr.*; *brgyúgs-nas byuṅ* they came running up or near *Pth.*; **to go to, to proceed to, to come,** *rii rtsé-mor Dzl.*; **ka-náṅ-wa ma júṅ-na* W.* if no order (permission etc.) comes; *dbugs p'yir byuṅ-nas* when breathing returned, when they recovered from fainting *Dzl.*; *mun-pai bskal-pa lṅa-brgya byuṅ-ṅo* then came, followed, 500 dark Kalpas *Pth.* — 2 **to rise,** as kings, frq.; **to arise, to originate, to become,** with *nas, las,* from, in consequence of, by, *dé-nas byuṅ* it derives its origin from that *Glr.*; *ₒbrás-bu ₒbyúṅ-bai šiṅ* trees on which fruit is growing *Stg.*; *mi ₒbyúṅ-bar ₒgyúr ba* not to come to a fair beginning, to be suppressed in its first beginnings *Glr.*; *k'yeu žig byuṅ ₒdug* by that time a boy had become of it *Glr.*; *ɣnyís-su byuṅ* they became two, they split in two (systems of doctrine); *ráb-tu ₒbyúṅ-ba* to become a priest, v. *rab*; to come in (money); **to happen, to take place,** very frq., *ltas či byuṅ* what signs have taken place? *Dzl.*; *mi žig-la nyés-pa čén-po byuṅ* = a man has committed etc. *Dzl.* frq.; *ro ₒdi-rnams-la či byuṅ-ba yin* what has happened to these corpses, what is their history? *Glr.*; *sṅar byuṅ-ba* and *ma byuṅ-ba* things heard of and unheard of *Tar.*; *k'á-p'ye-nas yód-pa dé-aṅ de dús-su byúṅ-ṅo* 'at that time also the opened position (of the hands of the image) took place' *Glr.*; *blá-ma-la yaṅ byuṅ lágs-sam* did the same thing happen to your Reverence? *Mil.*; *ṅéd-kyis ₒdi-bžin byuṅ* it is I that brought this thing about *Glr.*; *p'yis-byuṅ* or *ₒbyuṅ* the later time, time to come, also adv. afterwards, latterly, *Tar.* — 3. The word more and more assumes the character of an auxiliary in such phrases as the following: *ₒgro-tub-pa byuṅ* they were able to proceed (the possibility of proceeding was brought about) *Glr.*; *da blama der bžúgs-pa byúṅ-na* in case your Reverence should stay there *Mil.*; with the supine: *ₒbúl-du, žér-du, stón-du byúṅ-ba-la(s)* as they gave, said, showed *Mil.*; *tugs-dám ₒp'él-bar byuṅ* meditation increased; lastly, with the root only: *bod daṅ ₒbrel byuṅ* came into communication with Tibet *Glr.*; *sleb byúṅ-ba-la* when he appeared *Mil.*; *rdo dbyug byuṅ* he threw a stone; and so it is commonly used now, esp. in *C.*; it supplies the place of a copula in: *ɣsuṅ de kun séms-la šin-tu ₒtád-pa žig byuṅ* this song was truly heart-affecting *Mil.*

Comp. ₒ*byúṅ-k̔uṅs* 1. = *ču-mig* **a well, spring** *Sambh.* 2. **origin** *Pth.* 3. **ablative case** *Gram.* — ₒ*byúṅ-k̔uṅs-kyi k̔ams Cs.*, 'a mineral, *byuṅ-k̔uṅs-kyi k̔áms-kyi bčud* a mineral elixir'(?) — ₒ*byuṅ-γnás* (सम्भव), **place of origin** (cf. *padma* ₒ*byuṅ-γnás*); **primitive source**, *yón-tan t̔ams-čád-kyi* ₒ*byuṅ-γnás* source of all accomplishments; *byuṅ-bai γži* id.; *p̔an-bdé t̔ams-čád* ₒ*byúṅ-bai γži* primordial source of all happiness. — II. sbst. 1. **a coming forth, an originating, the state of being,** ₒ*byuṅ-ba-nyid Tar.* 4, 4 *Schf.* the true state of a case. — 2. **element,** usually 4: ₒ*byúṅ-ba bžii γnód-pa* damage done by fire, water, wind and sand *Glr.*; ₒ*byuṅ-ba bžii lus* the physical body, very frq.; ₒ*byúṅ ba γyo* the elements are in motion, are raging *Ma.*; higher philosophy numbers 5 elements, adding the ether, *mk̔a*, as the fifth; accordingly physiology teaches, that in the composition of the human body earth constitutes the mucus of the nose, water the saliva, fire produces the pictures formed in the eyes, air the sensations of the skin, ether the sensations of the ear; even 6 elements are spoken of, v. *Köpp.* I, 602. — 3. symb. num. for 5.

འབྱུང་པོ་ ₒ*byúṅ-po* (भूत) 1. **being, creature,** ₒ*byúṅ-po kun* all beings *Cs.*; ₒ*byúṅ-po čén-po* the great being, Buddha *Cs.* — 2. **demon, evil spirit, foul sprite,** frq., ₒ*byuṅ-po-srúṅ* a preservative, talisman, against such; ₒ*byúṅ-mo* fem. *Cs.*

འབྱེ་བ་ ₒ*byé-ba*, pf. and imp. *bye*, *W.* **be-če(s)**, intrs. of ₒ*byéd-pa* 1. **to open,** *padma k̔á-bye-ba* a lotos-flower that has opened *Glr.*; *mṅal k̔á-bye-nas* when the mouth of the womb has opened itself *S.g.* — 2. **to divide, separate, resolve,** *ska sla γnyis-su bye* it resolves into thick and thin matter *Med.*; *dúm-bu stóṅ-du dbyé-bar* ₒ*gyur* it separates into a thousand pieces *Glr.*; *bye-brág ma byé-bai bár-du* as long as the separation has not evidenced itself *Dzl.*

འབྱེད་པ་ ₒ*byéd-pa*, pf. and imp. *p̔ye, p̔yed, p̔yes*, fut. *dbye*, *W.* **p̔é-če(s)**, pf. and imp. **p̔e(s)**, vb. a., 1. **to open,** **k̔a p̔e(s) toṅ** *W.* open your mouth; *sgo p̔yés-nas* ₒ*jóg-pa Pth*, **p̔é-te bór-če** *W.* to open the door without shutting it again; fig. *čós-kyi sgo rnám-par* ₒ*byéd-pa*; *mig* to open one's eyes, opp. to ₒ*dzúm-pa*; *lóṅ-bai mig* ₒ*byéd-pa* to open a blind man's eyes *Dzl.*; to open again what had been shut or stopped, to restore, *dáṅ-ga, yi-ga B.*, *k̔am W.* the appetite; *ba-p̔yéd* the open b, b pronounced like w, *Gram.*; to get out, work out, fetch out, stone-shivers by means of a chisel *Glr* — 2. **to separate, to keep asunder, to disentangle,** threads *W.*; to disunite, to set at variance, *dé-dag dbyé-bai p̔yir* in order to set them at variance, to create enmity between them *Stg.*; to part, separate, *byaṅ-k̔óg-stod-smad mčin-dris dbyé-ba ste* the cavity of the chest and the abdomen being separated by the diaphragm *S.g.*; **to divide, classify,** *rigs-kyi sgó-nas dbyé-na* if they are classified according to the different species *Lt.*; **to pick, to sort,** pease; hence, **to pick out, choose, select,** **p̔é-te kyoṅ** make your choice, and bring it here! *W.*; *séms-čan-rnams lás kyis rnám-par p̔ye* the beings are severed by their deeds *Thgy.*; *k̔á-p̔ye-ba* to open, to separate, e.g. when hands, that were laid in each other, are separated again *Glr.*; *k̔á-p̔ye-ba* also **to open, to begin to bloom;** ₒ*byéd-pa* **to dissect, to anatomize** *Thgy.*; esp. with *rnám-par*, **to analyze,** to explain grammatically and logically, *don*, the sense, import, *Stg.* frq.; as *sdúd-pa* is the opposite of it: ₒ*byed-sdúd* **analysis and synthesis** *Cs.*; ₒ*byed-sdúd-kyi sgra* term for the affix *am*, the disjunctive particle (ni f.) *Glr.*; *mi-p̔yéd-pa* **inseparable, indivisible, imperishable,** *sku Sch.*; **unshaken, immovable,** *dád-pa Mil.* frq.

འབྱེད་དཔྱད་ ₒ*byed-dpyád Sch.* **tongs, pincers.**

འབྱེམ་པ་ ₒ*byém-pa*, with *byéd-pa*, 'to act with promptness, determination and good success' *Sch.*

འབྱེར་བ་ ₒ*byér-ba* pf. and imp. *byer*, **to disperse in flight,** to flee in different directions *Dzl.* *ts̔óṅ-*ₒ*dus byér-nas mi* ₒ*dúg-ste* the market-people having fled, and no body remaining *Pth.*; **to give way, to be**

removed, of diseases *Lt.*, opp. to *rgyas* and *bsags.*

འབྱོ་བ་ *˳byó-ba*, pf. *p̔yo*, *p̔yos*, imp. *p̔yo*, *byo*, *byos*, **to pour out, to pour into another vessel, to transfuse** *Lex.* and *Cs.*

འབྱོག་པ་ *˳byóg-pa*, pf. *byogs* **to lick** *Lex.* and *Cs.*

འབྱོང་བ་ *˳byóṅ-ba* I. pf *byáṅ-ba* 1. **to be cleansed,** purified, v. *byáṅ-ba.* — 2 **to be skilled, well versed,** *rig-byéd-la* in the Vedas *Tar.* — II. pf *˳byoṅs-pa* **to be finished, perfect, complete,** frq. with *snyiṅ-rǰe Mil* and elsewh., to exercise full compassion(?) cf. *sbyóṅ-ba.* (The above arrangement is nothing more than an attempt; in order to arrive at any certainty as to these roots, a far greater number of observations would be required.)

འབྱོན་པ་ *˳byón-pa*, pf. and imp. *byon*, resp. **to go, proceed, travel,** *dé-nas byón-pa-na* then in proceeding on the way *Glr.*; **to arrive, appear, become visible;** also for *˳byúṅ-ba*, e.g. *raṅ-byón*; with root of the verb: *p̔úr-byon-pas* preparing to fly *Mil.*; *ma-byón-pa* = *ma-˳óṅs-pa* future (Buddhas) *S.O.*; to rise, to appear; with dat. inf. = *˳ǰúg-pa* **to begin, to set about** a certain work *Tar.* 125, 16.

འབྱོར་པ་ *˳byór-pa* **wealth, riches, goods, treasures,** *˳byor-pa zád-mi-śes-pa daṅ ldán-pa* one possessing inexhaustible wealth, *bdé-ba daṅ ˳byór-pa* joy and treasures *S.O.*; *˳byór-pa drug Pth.*, prob. six kinds of temporal goods; *ráṅ-gi ˳byór-pa lṅa* and *γžan-gyi ˳byor-pa-lṅa* five subjective and five objective goods, of a similar nature as those mentioned sub *dal-˳byor*, yet without any evident reason for being thus divided *Thgy.*; *˳byor-ldán* rich, mostly used as a noun personal.

འབྱོར་བ་, འབྱར་བ་ *˳byór-ba*, *˳byár-ba* I. intrs. of *sbyór-ba* 1. **to stick to, adhere to** *Med.*; **k̔yág-la ǰar soṅ**, it is frozen fast *W.*; *˳byár-byed spyin* glue *Lex.*; *˳byor-sman* sticking-plaster *W.*; **to infect,** of diseases, *˳byor-nad* an infectious disease *Cs.* also mentally: **lo* or *sém-la ǰar** it sticks fast, is remembered, borne in mind.

2. **to be prepared,** ready, at hand, extant, *śa ma byór-nas* there being no meat prepared *Dzl.*; *˳p̔rál-du ˳byór-ba ma yin* that is not at once in readiness *Dzl.*; *ċi ˳byór-ba des mčód-pa byéd-pa* to offer sacrifice of such things as are at hand *Dzl.*; *ċi-ste ˳byór-bar mi ˳gyúr-na* but if he has not such a thing at his disposal *Sambh.* — 3. **to agree,** *mi-˳byór-ba k̔á-čig* some disagreements, contradictions *Tar.* — II. resp. **to come, arrive,** *W.*, *C.*; **k̔yé-kyi ku dúṅ-du ǰár-gyu yin** I shall appear before your Honour *C.*; **nyúr-du ǰar yoṅ** I shall immediately attend *C.*

འབྱོལ་བ་ *˳byól-ba*, pf. and imp. *byol*, fut. (and pres. in *C.*) *dbyol* **to give** or **make way, to turn out of the way, to step aside,** *γčig-gis γčig-la Dzl.*; *˳byól-te ˳gro* in walking I make way (to people) *Dzl.*; *W.* with accus.: **rul, las, dig-pa ǰól-ċe** to step out of the way of, to shun, a serpent, toil, sin. Sometimes *˳ǰól-ba.*

འབྲ་གོ་ *˳brá-go* n. of a medicine *Med.*

འབྲང་ *˳braṅ* v. *braṅ* II.

འབྲང་རྒྱས་ *˳braṅ-rgyás Mil.* **sacrifice,** offering of eatables.

འབྲང་བ་ *˳bráṅ-ba* 1. pf. *˳braṅs*, imp. *˳broṅ*, **to bear, bring forth, give birth; to litter,** *bráṅ-mo* an animal going with young, bearing *Cs.* — 2. also *˳bréṅ-ba*, pf. *˳braṅs*, imp. *˳breṅs Mil.* (*˳broṅ Sch ?*) **to follow, to walk at another's heels,** with *p̔yir*, *p̔yi-bžin* (*-du*), *rǰés-su*, *W.* **tiṅ-la** with genit., **to follow, pursue, hunt after,** *dbyúg-pas* with a stick *Pth.*; **to pursue,** in one's thoughts.

འབྲད་པ་, འདྲད་པ་ *˳brád-pa*, *˳drád-pa*, pf. *brad*, imp. *brod* **to scratch, to scrape,** with the nails, claws etc.; **to lacerate by scratching,** *γdoṅ Dzl.*; also **to gnaw, nibble at.**

འབྲབ་པ་ *˳bráb-pa*, pf. *brab*, imp. *brob* 1. **to catch suddenly, to snap away, snatch away,** a fly with one's hand, the prey with a bound. — 2. **to beat, to scourge,** *tser-lčág-gis* with thorns *Thgy.* — 3. **to throw out, to scatter,** magical objects, such as grains of barley etc.

འབྲལ་བ་ *ₒbrál-ba*, pf. *bral*, imp. *brol*, intrs. of *ₒṕrál-ba*, **to be separated, parted from, deprived of**, c. *dan*, e.g. from one's retinue, of the light of doctrine *Dzl.*; *ₒbrál-bar mi ṕod bú-mo ḱyod* thou, my daughter, from whom I am not able to part *Glr.*; *čún-ṅu-nas ṕa-má γnyis dan brál-te* from a child bereft of parents, an orphan from infancy *Pth.*; **to lose, to be bereft**, frq. used in reference to the death of near relations; *mdo-sdé dan láγ-pa mi brál-žin* as the sacred writings never came out of his hands; *skóm-pa dan brál-bar gyúr-to* he got rid of his thirst; *nad dan brál-bar gyúr-to* he recovered from his illness, frq. (in such cases often confounded by the illiterate with *nád-las bsgral* etc.); more particularly: *srog dan* etc. **to die, perish**, frq.; *ₒjig-ṫen ₒbrál-bar ₒgyúr-ba* to be dissolved, of the human body *Dzl.*; *ₒdú-ba yód-na ₒbral-bar on* what was solid, is dissolved in dust *Dzl.*; *ₒbral(-bar) med (-pa)* **inseparable, indissoluble**, frq.

འབྲས་ *ₒbras*, *C.* also *ₒbrás-mo*, resp. *bsan-ₒbrás* (*Pur.* **bras**, *Ld.* **ḍas**, *Lh.* **ḍai**, *C.* **ḍe**) 1. **rice;** *ₒbras-dkár(-mo)* white rice, *ₒbras-dmár* red rice (the inferior and cheaper sort); of the former there seem to be distinguished: *ₒbo-tsa-li* (*Hd.* **basmati**), *rgyal-mo-γsán*, *ham-dzém*, *ₒdzin-ₒdzin* the second sort, acc. to *Cs.*; *ₒbrás-kyi srus* peeled rice *Sch.*; *ₒbras-sá-lu* 'wild rice' *Sch.*; *ₒbras-so-ba Sch.* and *Schr.*, rice not husked *ₒbrás-mo spos-šél* or *dkar-ₒdzóm Ts.* maize.

Comp. *ₒbras-čán* rice-wine, rice-beer. — *ₒbras-čán* boiled rice. — *ša-ₒbrás* rice mixed with small pieces of meat. — *ₒbras-ṫúg* rice-soup. — *ₒbras-žin* rice-field. — *ₒbras-zán* dish of rice. — *ₒbras-yós* parched rice *Med.* — *ₒbras-sil C.* boiled rice, got up with butter, sugar, apricots etc., *W.* **ṕu-lá, ṕo lá**, پلاو. — 2. **tumour**, esp. larger swellings in the groin etc.

འབྲས་ལྗོངས་ *ₒbras-ljón* (**ḍe-jón**) n. p., **Sikim.**

འབྲས་སྤུངས་ *ₒbras-spúns* n. p., monastery near Lhasa.

འབྲས་བུ་ *ₒbrás-bu* 1. **fruit**, e.g. *šin-gi Mil.*; *ₒbrás-bu ye-méd-kyi sa* a country producing no fruit *Thgy.*; **corn, grain,** *ₒbrás-bu zór-bus brñá-ba Mil.*; *ₒbras-ṅan* a failure of fruit. — 2. **testicle** *Wdn.* cf. *rlig-pa*; *mig-ₒbrás* apple of the eye. — 3. fig. **effect, consequence,** esp. as opp. to *rgyu*, hence *rgyu-ₒbrás* cause and effect, more esp. in moral philosophy = **retribution, requital, recompense, reward,** three grades being distinguished: 1. *rnám-par smin-pai ₒbrás-bu* full recompense, in the worst case by the punishments of hell; 2. *rgyu bṫún-pai ₒbrás-bu* by adversity during life; 3. *dbán-gi ₒbrás-bu* by unpleasant local circumstances, — so *Thgy.*; *rgyu-ₒbrás* and *ₒbrás-bu* also directly denote **the doctrine of final retribution,** *ₒbrás-bu mi bden* the doctrine of requital is not true *Thgy.*; further: *ₒbrás-bu* reward of ascetic exercises, the various grades of perfection, of which four are distinguished: a. *rgyún-du-žugs-pa* स्रोतापत्ति or as partic. °पन्न, he who enters the stream (that takes from the external world to Nirwana); b. *lan-γčig-ṕyir-ₒon-ba* सकृदागामिन्, he who returns once more (for the period of a human birth); c. *ṕyir-mi-ₒon-ba* अनागामिन् he who returns no more, being a candidate of Nirwana; d. *dgra-bčom-pa* अर्हत्, the Arhat, the finished saint; v. *Köpp.* I, 398.

འབྲི་ཁུང་ or **གུང་** *ₒbri-ḱún* or *-gun* sect of Lamas and monastery in Tibet, *ₒbri-ḱún-pa* member of that sect.

འབྲི་ཏ་ *ₒbri-ta* a form of medicine, prob. a kind of extract *Med.*; *ₒbri-ta-sa-ₒdzin* medicinal herb, an emetic, *Med.*; in *Lh.* Cuscuta, which however does not agree with the descriptions.

འབྲི་བ་ *ₒbri-ba*, I. pf. and imp. *bri*, intrs. of *ₒṕri-ba* **to lessen, decrease, diminish,** of water, frq. in conjunction with *ḱa*, at the surface, used with regard to size, number and intensity (synon. *ₒgrib-pa*) — II. pf. and imp. *bris* (*Glr.* also *bri*) 1. **to draw, design, describe,** *dkyil-ₒḱor žig* to describe a circle or other figure; also to paint *Glr.* 2. **to write,** *yi-ge* letters, a letter (epistle); *yi-ger* '*literis mandare*', to record, to write down, something from hearing *Dzl.*: *ₒbri-smyúg* writing-reed, pen, pencil etc.

འབྲི་མོ་ *°bri-mo*, **चमरी, tame female yak;** *rgod-°bri Pth.*, or *°broṅ-°bri Cs.*, wild female yak; *°bri-zal* young female yak *Ld.-Glr.*, *°bri-o* yak-milk; *°bri-mar* yak-butter; *°bri-mdzo* (*W.* **brim-dzo**) bastard of bull and yak.

འབྲི་མོག་ *°bri-móg* medicinal herb *Med.*

འབྲིང་ *°briṅ* **middle, midst, mean, middling, moderate,** *°briṅ žig* something moderate, of middling quality, = *tsád-ma* or *tig-tsád W.*; *briṅ-po* the middle one, of three sons *Dzl.* and elsewh.; between *stobs-čé* and *čúṅ-ṅu Lt.*; *bzaṅ ṅan °briṅ ysum*; *rnal-°byór °briṅ-po* one that is moderately advanced in contemplation *Thgr.*; *zlá-ba °briṅ-po* v. *zla-ba*; *°bríṅ-gis* **middling, moderately,** adv.

འབྲིང་བ་ *°briṅ-ba*, in *žabs-°briṅ byéd-pa* for *bráṅ-ba Mil.*

འབྲིད་པ་ *°bríd-pa* 1. also *°dríd-pa*, pf. *brid*, **to deceive, cheat, impose upon,** *blo °bríd-pa* id. *Glr.*; *°bríd-de rṅód-pa-las Tar.*, as she wanted to seduce him deceitfully; *ka-mṅar-bríd* deceitfully, insidiously sweet, being followed by a nauseous, acrid or burning taste *Med.* — 2. *Cs.* = *°prí-ba*.

འབྲིམ་པ་ *°brím-pa*, I. vb., pf. *brim(s)* 1. **to distribute, deal out, hand round,** sweet-meats, flowers, poems *Dzl.*, *Tar.*; ... *la*, to ... → 2. *Ld.* **to throw away,** what is worthless, = **páṅ-čes**. — II. sbst. **distributer, dispenser, waiter at table** *Dzl.*; *°brím(-pa)-po*, id. *Cs.*

འབྲུ་ *°bru* **grain, corn, seed,** frq.; grain of sand, *byé-ma °bru rei stéṅ-na* on every grain of sand *Glr.*; *°bru °tag-pa* to pound grains *Lex.* — 2. a single **grain, piece, letter,** *yi-ge °bru yčig* a single letter; also without *yi-ge*: *°bru drúg* the six letters = *yi-ge-drúg-pa*, v. *drug*. — 3. collectively, **grain, corn,** in gen. *°brui kal* a load of grain *Dzl.*; *°brú-sna mi °kruṅs* no kind of grain is growing *Glr.*; *°bru gáṅ-bu-čan* pulse, legume *S.g.*; *nor dan °bru-rnams °pel* money and corn multiply. — *°bru-rdóg* grain of seed. — *°brú-sna* v. above. — *°bru-báṅ* granary. — *°bru-°bú* corn-worm, weevil *Cs.* *°bru-már* oil extracted from seeds; lamp-oil *Dzl.* — *°brú-tsoṅ-pa* oil-merchant.

འབྲུ་ཐང་ *°bru-táṅ*, n. of a superior sort of tea.

འབྲུ་བ་, བྲུ་བ་ *°brú-ba, bru-ba*, pf. and imp *brus*, *°drú-ba*, *drus* 1. **to dig,** *kúṅ-bu, dur, doṅ* (cf. *rkó-ba*). — 2. **to chisel, carve, cut.** — 3. *Sch.* **to look through,** *yig* a writing; **to examine,** *°bru* grain; hence *mtsaṅ °bru-ba* to spy out, smell out, faults, stirring up brawls and quarrels by it, *Stg.* **to irritate, vex, provoke,** *mtsaṅ °brú-bai tsig* provoking words *Lex.*; *snyad, snyon °brú-ba* **to accuse** *W.*

འབྲུ་མ་ *°brú-ma* **tumour, swelling, weal** *Sch.*

འབྲུ་ཚ་ *°bru-tsa* an angular kind of Tibetan current handwriting, v. *Csoma Gram.*

འབྲུ་ཤལ་, འབྲུ་ཤ་ *°bru-šál*, *°bru-šá* v. *bru-šá*.

འབྲུག་ *°brug* (*Bal.* **blug**) 1. **thunder,** *°brug-skád*, *°brug-sgrá* id.; *skad-čen °brug* loud thunder; *°brug °bód-pa Cs.*, *grág-pa Dzl.*, *ldír-ba Lex.* and elsewh., thundering. — 2. **dragon** (to which thunder is ascribed *Sch.*); *yyu-°brúg snón-po* blue dragon *Glr*

འབྲུག་པ་ *°brúg-pa* I. sbst. 1. **sect of Lamas,** clothed in red, *Schl.* 73., established in the province of Bhotan, acc. to *Sch.* = *ža-dmár*, = *sá-skya*. — 2. **Bhotan.** —

II. vb. for *°brúb-pa Mil.* frq.

འབྲུད་པ་ *°brúd-pa*, = *°brú-ba*, also *°drúd-pa*.

འབྲུབ་པ་ *°brúb-pa* 1. gen. with *ču*, **to cause to overflow, to gush, to spout forth to flow over,** *Mil.*, *Tar.* and elsewh.; *ču-°brub Lex.*, *°brubs Sch.* water that has flown over (?). *°brub-po* **fluid, liquid; fluidity, a fluid,** *Cs.* (?). — 2. *Cs.* **to deal out.** — 3. *Sch.* **to shut up, wrap up.**

འབྲུམ་པ་ *°brúm-pa* 1. *Cs.* **grain, minute particle,** *°brum-rdog*, *°bru-rdóg* a single grain, = *°bru*; **fruit,** *rgun-°brúm* grape; *se-°brúm* hip (fruit of wild brier) *Sik.* — 2. **pustule, pock,** gen. *°brúm-bu*; *°brum-nad* small-pox; *°brum-nág* black or deadly small-pox; *°brum-dkár* white small-pox; *°brum-krá* coloured small-pox *Med.*, *°brum-*

pa and *ₒbrúm-pa nág-po* as name of a disease of the groin, prob. bubo *Med.* — *ₒbrum-rjes* pock-mark. — *ₒbrúm-po* a large grain *Cs.*; *ₒbrúm-bu* a small grain; pock, pustule, v. above.

འབྲུམ་ལྷ་མོ་ *ₒbrum-lha-mo Sch.* a tutelar goddess of little children, worshipped by the Shamans.

འབྲེ་བ་ *ₒbré-ba*, pf. and imp. *bres* **to draw over** or **before, to spread, to stretch,** a net *Glr.*, a curtain *Glr.*, a canopy, awning *Lex.*; **to wrap a thing up in a cloth**, in order to carry it, as books, a corpse *Thgy.*

འབྲེག་པ་ *ₒbrég-pa*, pf. *breg(s)*, imp. *brog(s)*, also *ₒdrég-pa* **to cut off,** *ṡiṅ-ta-lai lo-ma bregs-pa* a plantain branch cut off, as representing a being irremediably cut off from its former state of existence *Mil.*; **to mow** *Sch.*; of parts of the body: *ske* to cut off a person's neck *Thgr.*, *p̓o-mtsán* the membrum virile *Schr.*, *rtai súg-pa* the foot of a horse, prob. only the tendon of it, as much as to lame, to disable *Glr.*; also to sever with a saw; most frq. in reference to the hair, to cut off, **to shave,** with the scissors or a razor, *skra daṅ ḱá-spu* frq.; *ₒbrég-mḱan* **barber, hair-cutter** *Dzl.*; *ₒbreg-spyád* a sharp small knife *Sch.*

འབྲེང་པ་ *ₒbréṅ-pa Cs.*, *bréṅ-ba* **strap, rope,** *ko-ₒbréṅ* leather strap; *ṡa-ₒbreṅ Mil.*; *ₒbreṅ-ťag Cs.* cane-ribbon, made of buck-leather; leading-rope, guide-line. — *ₒbréṅ-bu Cs.* cobbler's strap.

འབྲེང་བ་ *ₒbréṅ-ba* frq. for *ₒbráṅ-ba.*

འབྲེལ་ *ₒbrel* sbst. v. *ₒbrél-ba* II.

འབྲེལ་པ་ *ₒbrél-pa* **connection, conjunction,** yet only in certain applications: 1. **connection between cause and effect,** used also at once for **effect, consequence, efficacy,** *smón-lam-gyi ₒbrél-pa* the efficacy of prayer *Mil.* frq.; *ₒjog-pa* to apply, make use of it *Mil.* — 2. **the vascular and nervous system conjunctively,** the two systems in their totality, ni f., *Med.* — 3. **genitive case**, the sixth case of Tibetan Grammarians, *ₒbrél-pai sgra*, the termination of it, *kyi.* — 4. **a small quantity, a little, a bit,** *zás-kyi ₒbrél-pa żig dgos* I ask for a little bit to eat *Mil.* frq.; *čos(-kyi) ₒbrél(-pa) ťób-pa* to snatch up a little bit of religion *Mil.*

འབྲེལ་བ་ *ₒbrél-ba* I. vb., intrs. of *sbrél-ba*, 1. **to hang together, to cohere, to be connected,** *rtsa daṅ rus-pa tsam ₒbrél-ba* connected only by veins and bones, nothing but skin and bone *Dzl.*; *ₒod-zér-gyi drá-bas ₒbrél-te* covered with a continuous net of rays *Glr.*; gen. with *daṅ*, *bod daṅ rgyai ₒbrél-ťsul* the connection with, or the intercourse between Tibet and China *Glr.*; *de dan ₒbrél-bai las* the functions connected with, and peculiar to (a certain organ) *Lt.*; *ₒbrel-mťsams* 1. **joint**, or **rivet** of pincers etc. *S.g.* 2. **boundary,** *W.* — 2. **to come together, to meet, to join,** *ₒbrél-γtam* gossipings in meeting on the road *Mil.* — 3. **to meet sexually, to cohabit,** *de daṅ lus ₒbrél-ba* to cohabit with (him or her) *Glr.*; (*lhán-du*) *ₒbrél-ba-la(s) bu skyes* they having cohabited, a child was born *Glr.* — II. sbst. *ₒbrél-ba* or *ₒbrel* **union, communication, connection,** *bod daṅ ₒbrel byuṅ* the union with Tibet took place *Glr.*; *rgya bod γnyis ₒbrel čád* the union ceases *Glr.*; **nor-ḍél čó-če, nor-ḍél-la čá-če** *W.*, to form a mercantile connection, to enter into commercial intercourse. — *las-ₒbrel* = *las-ₒp̓ro* q.v. — *γnyis-ₒbrél*, *γsum-ₒbrél* a double, triple consonant, e.g. *sk*, *skr*.

འབྲོག་ *ₒbrog* **solitude, wilderness, uncultivated land,** esp. **summer-pasture** for cattle in the mountains; thus *ₒbrog-skyoṅ-ba Ld.-Glr.*, *Schl.* 15, 6 might imply: to attend to a mountain dairy; *gám-ₒbrog* a near, *rgyáṅ-ₒbrog* a remote summer-pasture; *ₒbrog-ḱyi Cs.* a large shaggy shepherd's dog; *ₒbróg-dgon*, *ₒbróg-stoṅ*, *ₒbróg-sa* = *ₒbrog.* *ₒbróg-γnas* 1. **pasture-land** 2. **people occupying it.** — *ₒbróg-p̓a*, *ₒbróg-mi* id.; more particularly, **inhabitants of the steppe,** nomadic Tibetans *Sch.*, *ₒbróg-mo* wife, *ₒbrog-p̓rúg* child of such a nomad. — *ₒbrog-żád Sch.* **rude,** rough, boorish, *ₒbrog-żad stón-pa* to be rude etc.

འབྲོང་ *ₒbroṅ* 1. (चमर) = *γyag-rgod*, **wild yak** *Glr.*; *byáṅ-ḱai ₒbroṅ*, the yak of

Jang-thang; ˳broṅ-˳brí cow, ˳broṅ-ṕrúg calf, ˳broṅ-ko skin, leather, ˳broṅ-ša flesh, ˳broṅ-ru or -ra *Glr.* horns of the wild yak. — 2. v. ˳bráṅ-ba.

འབྲོམ་ *˳brom* noun personal; *˳brom-stón* a celebrated Lama and scholar in the 11th. century.

འབྲོས་པ་ *˳brós-pa*, pf. and imp. *bros*, **to flee, to run away** (*W.* **šor-če**), *˳brós-šiṅ gáb-pa* to flee and hide one's self *Dzl.*; *ṕyir ˳brós-so* (the army) took to flight *Glr.*; *˳brós-pai γnas Dzl.*, *˳brós-sa Glr.* place of refuge; fig. *mig ḱuṅ-du bros* his eyes are sunk, hollow *S.g.* — *˳bros-ša* a large dorsal muscle *Med.* — *γnyid-˳brós-pa* = *γnyid-lóg-pa* (?) *Dzl.* ༢༧༨, 9.

རྦ་ *rba* v. *dba.*

རྦད་ *rbad* 1. *Sch.* a large species of **eagles.** — 2. *W.* **crutch,** = *paṅ-ka.* — 3. = *rbab.* — 4. **great** (?) v. *ḱa-rbad; rbad-sgra* a strong voice *Sch.*; cf. *rbod-rbód.* — 5. **quite, wholly, entirely** (?) *rbád-γčod-pa*, *rbad-tsér γčód-pa Mil.* to cut off entirely, to extirpate; **ťag-čọ́ bẹ'-čọ̈** **resolute** *C.*

རྦད་སྐྱོགས་ *rbad-skyógs Sch.* **residue, residuum, dregs, husks** etc.

རྦད་པ་ *rbád-pa* 1. vb., imp. *rbod*, **to set on, incite,** *Tar.*, *C.*, e.g. *ḱyi*; **to excite, instigate, animate,** *Cs.*; *rbad-ḱa S.g.* an inciting talk (?). — 2. adj. **undulating, undulatory** *Sch.*

རྦད་རྦོད་ *rbad-rbód*, **thick, dense, close, strong, great** *Cs.*, *skra rbad-rbód Lex.*

རྦབ་ *rbab*, 1. *Med.*, *Sch.*: a kind of **dropsy,** *skya-rbáb Sch.*, also *ša-rbab Lt.* id. (?) — 2. **the rolling down,** also *rbad*, e.g. *rdo-rbáb* loose stones rolling down, a frequent annoyance in high mountains *Pth.*, *rbab ži-bas* after the rolling of detritus had ceased *Mil.*; **bad ṕog soṅ** a piece of rock rolling down hit him *W.*; *rbab sgril-ba Lex.* to roll down, trs.; *rbáb-pa* id. intrs.; *már-la rbáb-tu šor* it rolled down and away *Mil.*

རྦེ་ *rbe Sch.* **'the fur of the stone-fox'.**

རྦོ་ *rbo Sch.* **mitt of fish.**

རྦོད་ *rbod* v. *rbád-pa.*

ལྦ་བ་ *lbá-ba* 1. **wen, goitre.** — 2. **knots, excrescenses** on trees, on account of their speckled appearance often worked into drinking-bowls; *lbá-tsa Med.*, prob. a kind of salt, used as a curative of goitre.

ལྦག་ *lbag* **bubbles** (?), **ču bag gyáb-če** to strike the water, so as to make it splash and foam *W.*

ལྦུ་བ་, དབུ་བ་ *lbú-ba, dbú-ba* **bubble, foam, froth, slaver;** *čú-lbu Lex.*; *lbú-bčas nyuṅ* producing little froth *Lt.*; *lbú-ba bsál-ba* to scum or skim off *Cs.*; *grogs čú-yi lbú-ba daṅ ˳dra* a friend is like water-bubbles.

སྦ་ *sba* v. *spa.*

སྦ་ནག་ *sba-nág Sch.* **a mean house, hovel, hut.**

སྦ་བ་ *sbá-ba* 1. vb. fut. of *sbed-pa* q.v. — 2. sbst. **privy parts, pudenda** *Stg.*

སྦག་པ་ *sbág-pa*, pf. *sbags*, imp. *sbogs* (cf. *˳bág-pa*), **to soil, stain, defile, pollute,** *dri-mas Lex.* — 2. **to mingle, intermix,** *Lex.*

སྦང་བ་ *sbáṅ-ba* v. *sbóṅ-ba.*

སྦང་མ་ *sbáṅ-ma* malt from which beer has been brewed, v. *čaṅ*; *sbaṅ-skóm* id. dried, *sbaṅ-ṕyé* id. reduced to flour (of an inferior quality) *Cs.*; *glum-sbáṅ Ts.* = *sbáṅ-ma*; *sbaṅ-ču* barm prepared from it *W.*

སྦངས་ *sbaṅs* dung of larger animals, *rtai sbaṅs Glr.* (**stal-báṅ(s)* Ld.*), *boṅ-sbaṅs*, *glaṅ-po-čei sbaṅs Cs.*; *sbaṅs-lúd* id., used for manure; *sbaṅs-skám* id. dried for fuel.

སྦབ་ཅ་ *sbáb-ča C.*, **sbáb-ǰa* W.* a certain number or quantity of trading-articles, e.g. of paper, a quire of 10—100 sheets, a bundle of matches etc.

སྦམ་པ་ *sbám-pa*, pf. *sbams*, imp. *sboms*, **to put** or **place together, to collect, to gather,** *ṕyogs γčig-tu Lex.*; *smyúg-ma sbáms-pa ˳dra* like reeds laid together *Wdṅ.*

སྦར་བ་ *sbár-ba*, v. *sbór-ba.*

སྦར་མོ་ *sbár-mo* v. *spár-mo.*

སྦལ་ *sbal* (perh. the same as the following *sbal-pa*), *lág-pai* the soft muscles of the inner hand, cf. also *ṕyag-sbál;* the soft part of the paw of animals.

སྦལ་པ་ and བ *sbál-pa* and *-ba* **frog** (rather scarce in Tibet), one *Lex.* **कर्कट, crab, crawfish** (?); *sbál-pa dkár-po Stg.* stated to be a large species of frog; *nágs-sbal Lt.* prob. tree-frog; *rús-sbal* **tortoise**; *sbal-čúṅ* or *-lčoṅ Pth.* 1. a young frog, **tadpole** *Cs.* 2. vulg. (from ignorance) **lizard**; *sbal-rgyáb S.g.* tortoise-shell.

སྦལ་མིག *sbal-mig* **bud, eye, gem, sprout, shoot,** *ₒton* comes forth, *ₒbye* opens *Stg.*

སྦིད་པ་ *sbid-pa Ts.* for *sbúd-pa* **bellows**, instrument for blowing.

སྦུ་གུ *sbú-gu* **hollow, cavity,** in the stem of a plant or a grass-blade *Mil.*

སྦུ་བ་ *sbú-ba* v. *lbú-ba.*

སྦུ་ལ་ཁ *sbú-la-k̇a Ts.* = *bka-blon-sram* **sable,** *mustela zibellina.*

སྦུ་ལྷན *sbu-lhán Ts.* (**bu-hlṇ**) **plane,** tool used in joinery.

སྦུག་ཅོལ, སྦུབ་ཆལ, *sbug-čól, sbub-čál Cs., *ₒbog-ₒčol** (?) *Ld.-Glr.*; **sbug-žál, sbum-žól* W.* **large brass cymbal;** **dúṅ-će, ṕáb-će* W.* to play the cymbals.

སྦུག་པ་ *sbúg-pa* = *ₒbúgs-pa,* **to perforate, to pierce.**

སྦུག(སྦུག)པོ *sbug-(sbug-)po Cs.* **hollow.**

སྦུག(ས) *sbug(s),* more frq. *sbubs,* **hollow, cavity, excavation, interior space,** *k̇úṅ-bui Lex.* tubular cavity, in bones etc. *S.g.*; **subterraneous passage, conduit, sewer** *C.*; *sbúbs-su ₒǰúg-pa, sbúbs-nas ₒtón-pa* to put into an underground hole or recess, to come forth from it *Glr.*, *Mil.*; *sbúg-tu nor sbá-ba* to hide money in such a place *Lex.*; **hiding-place, hidden recess,** = *saṅ-seṅ*; **hole** for inserting the handle of some instrument *Sch.*; *šáṅs kyi sbubs γnyis* hollow, expanded nostrils *Cs.*; *sbubs-ₒbyár Med.* disease of the penis, prob. stoppage of its orifice by gonorrhoea, cf. *mǰe.*

སྦུགས་དག *sbugs-hág* (**bu-hág**) 1. the **panting of a dog** *Sik.* — 2. **bassoon** with a large and nearly globular bell-mouth *W.* —

སྦུད་པ་ *sbúd-pa* 1. vb. **to light, kindle, set on fire,** seldom, *Lex.*: *mé-čas sbúd-pa* q.v. — sbst. **bellows,** usually consisting of two skin-bags, the orifices of which are opened and shut by the hands, and which are then squeezed together, so that the compressed air passing through a tube is driven into the fire; *sbúd-pa ₒbúd-pa Cs.* or *rgyáṅ-ba Sch.* to blow or work the bellows; *sbud-rgyál* = *sbúd-pa.*

སྦུན་པ་ *sbún-pa* v. *spún-pa.*

སྦུན་གཏེར་ *sbun-γtér Pth.* a small building in the style of a monument, in which sacred writings are deposited.

སྦུར་ *sbur* **ant** *Cs.*, prob. identical with the following (cf. *gróg-sbur*).

སྦུར་པ་ *sbúr-pa* **beetle,** *ču-sbur S.g.; sbur-čén, -čúṅ, -dmár, -mgyógs Cs.*, denoting various kinds of beetles.

སྦུར་མ་ *sbúr-ma,* = *sbún-pa,* **chaff, husks** etc.; *rlúṅ-gis sbúr-ma bús-pa ltar Dzl.*, *sóg-sbur čus γyéṅ-ba ltar Pth.* like chaff scattered by the wind, carried along by the water; *sbu-lén* or *-lóṅ* **amber** *Wts.*

སྦེ་ག *sbé-ga Lex.* w.e.

སྦེ་བ་ *sbé-ba Sch.* **to scuffle, wrestle.**

སྦེག་པ་ *sbég-pa* **lean, lank, thin** *S.g.*

སྦེད་པ་ *sbéd-pa,* pf. *sbas,* fut. and common secondary form *sba,* imp. *sbos, W.* **sbá-će**, pf. *sbas,* **to hide, conceal,** *γter* a treasure, *mdzód-du* in a store-house; *má-mo sbéd-pai ṕug* cavern in which a Mamo is concealed *Mil.*; *dpúṅ-gi ts̆ogs ts̆ál-du* to conceal troops in a wood *Dzl.*; *γtér-du* to deposit as a treasure *Glr.*; *sai ₒóg-tu* in the ground *Dzl.*; also as much as to inter, to bury *Dzl.*; **sbás-te* or *bẹ́-te bor-će* W.* = *sbéd-pa*; **sbás-te** **secretly, clandestinely, by stealth** *W.*; *mi sdig-čan-la lus sba ṕyir* in order to hide our form before sinful men, in order not to be recognized by them *Mil.*;

to hide from, to guard, secure, protect from, *srúṅ-žiṅ sbá-ba* id.; **to keep, preserve,** *sba-sri-med-par* (to bestow) freely, amply, without restriction.

སྦེད་མ་ *sbéd-ma* **a veiled woman;** name of a wife of Buddha *Cs.*

སྦོ་ *sbo Sch.* **the upper part of the belly;** *sbo-tsil* **bacon** *C.; sbo-rkún-pa* **pickpocket** *C.*

སྦོ་བ་ *sbó-ba* pf. *sbos* = *ₒbó-ba* 2, **to swell(up), to distend,** *ltó-ba sbos Lt.* the belly is swollen, turgid; *sbó-ₒḱrog-pa Sch.* 'to wheeze from inflation' (?).

སྦོག(ས)་པ་ *sbóg(s)-pa* v. *sbág-pa; ráṅ-gi bú-tsai tsig-sbóg Mil.,* seems to imply a man that is receiving abusive language from his own sons (?).

སྦོང་བ་ *sbóṅ-ba,* pf. *sbaṅs,* fut. *sbaṅ* **to steep** in water, **to soak, to drench;** **báṅ-te bor* W.* soak it in water!

སྦོད་པ་ *sbód-pa* **tassel, tuft.**

སྦོམ་པ་ *sbóm-pa,* more frq. *sbóm-po* **thick,** *ṕra-ba-las zlog sbóm-po Zam.* the contrary to *ṕrá-ba* is *sbóm-po; sbom-ṕrá daṅ riṅ-túṅ mnyam* of equal length and thickness *Dzl.*; **stout; coarse, clumsy, heavy,** also applied to sins; *sbóm-ma* a stout woman *Cs.*; sbst. **thickness, stoutness, heaviness.**

སྦོར་བ་ *sbór-ba,* pf., fut. and secondary form *sbar,* trs. of *ₒbár-ba,* **to light, kindle, inflame.**

སྦོར་ལོ་ *sbór-lo* Anemone polyantha *Lh.*

སྦྱང་བ་ *sbyáṅ-ba* v. *sbyóṅ-ba.*

སྦྱར་བ་ *sbyár-ba* v. *sbyór-ba.*

སྦྱར་པ་ *sbyár-pa Wdṅ.,* n. of a tree, prob. = *dbyár-pa.*

སྦྱིག་པ་ *sbyig-pa, sbyig-mo Lex.* w. e.

སྦྱིན་པ་ *sbyín-pa,* I. vb., pf. and imp. *byin,* 1. **to give, to bestow** (in *B.* a common word, in *W.* almost unknown; yet v. *smin-pa* II.), without any ceremonial difference between high and low; **to hand, deliver; to give up, deliver over; to give back, give for a present; to offer, proffer, hold out,** *rín-la byin-no* he offered as an equivalent *Pth.*; *ma byin-par mi lén-pa* v. *dgé-ba.* — 2. **to add, to sum up** *Wdk.* —

II. sbst. **gift, present, alms;** the expression *sbyin-pa ɣsum* comprises: *zaṅ-zíṅ-gi* the bestowing of goods, *mi-ₒǰigs-pai* the affording of protection, and *čós-kyi sbyin-pa,* the giving of moral instruction *Cs.*, *sbyin-ɣtóṅ* distribution of gifts, *sbyin-ɣtoṅ čen-po byed-pa Dzl.* — *sbyin-bdag* dispenser of gifts, more especially in the first beginnings of Buddhism a layman manifesting his piety by making presents to the priesthood, v. *Köpp.* I, 487, and in almost all legends; also the reverse, *len-pa* **the receiver of gifts,** Dulva v. Feer Introd. p. 71. — *sbyin-sreg,* **होम, burnt-offering,** v. *Was.* (194), *Schl.* 251 sqq.

སྦྱུ་ *sbyu,* sometimes for *sgyu Sch.*

སྦྱོང་བ་ *sbyóṅ-ba,* pf. *sbyaṅs,* fut. *sbyaṅ* शुध 1. **to clean, remove by cleaning,** clear away, as *ₒdág-pa,* esp. *sdig-pa Tar.*, *sgrib(-pa) Thgy.*; less frq. in a physical sense, e.g. removing phlegm by vomiting *Med.*, *ₒḱru-sbyóṅs* diarrhoea *Lex.*; **to cleanse,** *sbyóṅ-byed* 1. **cleansing, purifying,** *raṅ sbyoṅ-byed-kyi šes-rab Mil.* the knowledge how a man may be purified by his own doings. 2. *Med.*: **purging medicine.** — 2. **to remove, take away,** in a general sense *Cs.*; **to subtract,** *de-rnams tig-mtsams sbyaṅ-ste Wdk.*, 60 being subtracted, cf. *ₒṕri-ba*; **to cease,** of diseases *Med.* — 3. **to exercise, to train,** *blo* one's mind *Cs.*, *ḱa* one's mouth, hence *ḱa-sbyáṅ* eloquence *Mil.* (having reference also to *ḱa-ɣčáṅ* q. v.); *sṅon yón-tan sbyáṅs-pa sóṅ-bai mtus* by dint of formerly cultivated abilities *Glr.*; *tugs yóṅs-su sbyáṅs-pai skyés-bu Mil.* a saint of a thoroughly cultivated (or purified) mind; **to exercise, to practise,** *da-rúṅ sbyaṅ dgos* that must be practised still better; **to study,** *sde-snód-la* the holy scriptures *Mil.*, and with accus. *ɣžúṅ-lugs Tar.* 14, 9 (where *byaṅ* stands); *rtsís-la sbyáṅ-ba* to learn mathematics *Pth.*; **to practise, to perform; to recite, to repeat,** formulas, *bšar-sbyáṅ byéd-pa Mil.*, **kor ǰaṅ čó-če* W.*; **to accustom, familiarize,** **mi daṅ* *ǰaṅ-k̔an** accustomed to man, tame, also without **mi daṅ* W.*; **ǰaṅ-k̔yád** **custom, use, habit** *W.* — 4. **to accumulate** (?) *Cs.* — 5. **to conjure to the spot, to call by magic** (?) *Tar.* 76,15 *Schf.*

སྦྱོར་བ *sbyór-ba* I. vb., pf. and fut. *sbyar*, *W. *žár-ce**, trs. of *ˌbyór-ba*, 1. **to affix, attach, fasten, stick**, a writing, a plaster *W.*: **žar gyab-ce**; **to apply** *lcé-rtse dk̔án-la Gram.*; fig. *bló-la, séms-la* **to impress;** **k̔ár-ya daṅ** **to solder** *W.*; **zer gyáb-la žor** nail it fast! *W.*; **me-sk̔ám žar tsar** the trigger is drawn *W.*; **to put on,** a plaster, v. above, an arrow on the bow-string; **to subjoin, take up, resume,** a subject in a treatise *Thgy.*, *Tar.* 127,14; **to put together, to join, unite,** *rús-pa čág-pa Med.*, *dbáṅ-po γnyis* v. sub II.; **to compile, compose,** a book; *k̔a* 1. **to close, shut,** one's mouth, = *ˌtáms-pa Pth.* 2. **to kiss** *C.*; **to insert, to dispose** in proper classes or divisions *Gram.*, *byá-bai sgra ma sbyar yaṅ* also without the word *bya* being added; *bdé-ba-la, byaṅ-čúb-la Mil.*, like *ˌgód-pa* 3; **to join, connect, combine,** words, letters; *tsig de don daṅ sbyár-tsa-na* if these sentences are joined with their significations, i.e. if their explanation is given *Mil.*; *rtsis-su* **to count together, to sum up** *Dzl.*; *sbyór-la*, gen. written *žor-la*, **joined, connected, combined,** **tsig nyi sum žór-la yoṅ** two or three words are found joined to one another; this word is frq. used to express simultaneousness of action, where in English expressions as 'along with', 'together with', 'at the same time' etc. are used: *žór-la ˌgró-ba* to go along with (another person) *Mil.*; *žór-la k̔ur-k̔yer* take this also along with it! **k̔o čá-te žor daṅ kal soṅ* W.* as he was going, we sent it along with him; *žor-la gyel soṅ* it fell at the same time (by coming in contact with some other falling body); **žór-la k̔yér-wa** to take hold of and take away at the same time; *k̔ó-la žor p̔óg-pa* he was also (simultaneously) affected by (the loss); **žór-la zér-k̔an žig** or even **tsig-gi žor** a mere expletive, without any appreciable meaning *C.*; *bdag sdig-sgrib čés-pai žór-la* (the calamity has befallen the others too), owing to their connection with such a great sinner as I am *Mil.nt.* — 2. **to prepare, procure, to get ready,** *yo-byád* the appurtenances *Dzl.*, *ˌtsó-ba* victuals *Dzl.*; *rta daṅ sbyár-bai šiṅ-rta* a carriage ready to start *Stg.* (or acc. to no. 1, a carriage attached to the horses); **to mix,** *ču daṅ* with water *Dzl.* and elsewh.; *γžán-du* **to prepare, to turn one thing into another, to change, transform** *Thgy.*; frq. **to prepare one's own mind, to compose one's self,** *dád-pa-la sbyór-bar gyis* make up your mind to believe *Mil.* — **to join, fit together, adjust, make agree,** esp. one's course of action; **to conform one's self to,** with *daṅ*, *k̔ó-moi yid daṅ sbyor čig* accommodate yourself to my wishes *Dzl.*; *k̔rims daṅ sbyár-ro Dzl.* then we must conform to the law; most frq.: ... *daṅ sbyár-nas* or *-te* **corresponding, agreeable to, according to,** *k̔rims* according to the law, to usage etc. *Dzl.*; *bú-moi yid* according to the wish of the daughter *Dzl.*; also **to compare** *Tar.* 89, 16, *Thgy.*; *γžan-rgyúd-la sbyór-ba* seems to imply: to gain knowledge by observing others, opp. to *raṅ-rgyúd-la brtág-pa*, to ascertain by one's own immediate judgment.

4. **to compose poetry,** ... *kyis sbyór-bao* = *sdeb-pa* 5 — II. sbst. 1. **adjunction, conjunction, union,** *dbáṅ-po γnyis-kyi sbyór-ba byéd-pa*, '*membrorum amborum conjunctionem efficere*' *Wdṅ.*; hence **coition, cohabitation,** *bud-méd-la sbyór-ba byéd-pa* to effectuate it with a woman *Pth.*; *sgra-sbyor-ba* a joining or combination of sounds (letters), **orthography** (?) *Zam.* — 2. **a mingling, a mixture,** e.g. of medicines, also *sbyar-ťábs Med.*; *sbyor-sde-bži* the four departments of pharmacy *Glr.* (apparently the title of a book); **preparation** = *sṅón-ˌgro Schl.* 240, also mental preparation, esp. the preparation of the mind for prayer, and the arrangement of it, meditation preparatory to it (nif.) cf. *mtsams sbyár-ba.* — 3. **syllogism** *Was.* (278). — 4. **comparison, agreement, harmony,** *γtám-gyi* the harmony of history *Schf.*

སྦྲ *sbra* 1. *W. *(s)bra**, *C. *ḍa** **felt-tent,** *sbra-gúr* id.; *sbra-ťág* ropes, *sbra-šiṅ* frame-work, *sbrá-pa* inmate, of such a tent. 2. v. sub *γtsaṅ*.

སྦྲག་པ་ *sbrág-pa*, pf. *sbrags*, *C.* **ḍág-pa**, *W.* **rág-će** **to lay, to put**, a thing over or by the side of an other, *ṗyogs-γčig-tu Lex.*; gen. used only in the gerund: **ťsa dor rág-ne** together with salt and spices *W.*; **ṅá-ža daṅ rág-te mi dug** he does not belong to us *W.*, or in compounds: *nyi-rág* **double-barreled gun** (one barrel beside the other), *W.*raṅ-bár ḍug-rág** six-barreled pistol, **revolver** *W.*, *bse-sgo bdun-sbrag Pth.*, sevenfold skin-door, used as a target for shooting at.

སྦྲག་མ་ *sbrág-ma* **hay-fork,** *Cs.*

སྦྲང་བུ་ *sbráṅ-bu C.* **ḍáṅ-bu**, *W.* **ráṅ-ṅu, ra-uṅ** **fly,** and similar insects without a sting; *sbráṅ-ma* 1. id. 2. *C.* **bee,** *sbráṅ-mai ťsogs* swarm of bees. — *sbráṅ-rtsi W.* **ráṅ-si** **honey;** **ráṅ-si ráṅ-ṅu** *W.* bee. — *sbráṅ-čaṅ* **mead** or something similar. — *sbraṅ-ťsáṅ* and *sbraṅ-dóṅ Cs.* cells in a honey-comb, the honey-comb itself. — *sbraṅ-búg* bee-hive *Sch.* — *sbraṅ-byí* marten *Sch.* — *sbraṅ-yáb* flap, fly-brush *Cs.*

སྦྲད་པ་ *sbrád-pa* = *ₒbrád-pa* **to scratch** *Sch.*

སྦྲན་པ་ *sbrán-pa* = *sbrón-pa.*

སྦྲམ་བུ་ *sbrám-bu* **unwrought gold** *Cs.*

སྦྲིད་པ་ *sbríd-pa* 1. **to sneeze** *Med.*; *sbríd-pa ₒbyuṅ* I am seized with a sneezing *Med.* — 2. **to become numb, torpid,** **ḱáṅ-pe nya ḍid soṅ** my foot is asleep *W.* — 3. *Dzl.* ༢༥༨, 5 *Sch.* **to flutter** before one's eyes (?).

སྦྲུད་པ་ *sbrúd-pa*, pf. and imp. *sbrus*, fut. and sec. form *sbru, W* **rú-će** **to stir** with one's hand, *zan Lex.*; **to knead** (*Cs.*) is *rdzí-ba* which is not identical with *sbrúd-pa*, at least not in *W.*

སྦྲུམ་པ་ *sbrúm-pa* **pregnant, big with young;** *mi daṅ srog-čags sbrum-ma-rnams Dzl.* women with child and beasts with young; *sbrúm-par ₒgyúr-ba* to conceive, to become pregnant, frq.; *sbrúm-par ťsór-nas* feeling pregnant *Pth.*: *ṗrú-gu sbrum byúṅ-bas* having conceived, being with child *Pth.*

སྦྲུལ་ *sbrul*, *Pur. sbrul*, *Lh.* **rúl**, *C.* **ḍul** 1. **serpent, snake;** *sbrul* and *sbrúl-mo* also mythical demoniac beings; *sbrul γdúg-pa* or *dug-sbrul* venomous serpent; *sbrúl ḱas sdigs-po Sch.* serpent-tamer; *sbrúl-gyi snyiṅ-po* v. *tsán-dan.* — *sbrúl-mgo* 1. a serpent's head. 2. v. *ₒaṅ-ke.* — *sbrul-sgóṅ* a serpent's egg. — **ḍul-nyá** **eel** or some other esculent snake-like fish *C.* — *sbrul-dúg* venom of serpents. — *sbrul-mig* 1. a snake's eye. 2. n. of **a certain vein** *Med.* — *sbrul-ťsil* snake's grease *Med.* — *sbrul-žágs* v. *žags.* — *sbrul-ló* serpent-year, *sbrúl-lo-pa* one born in such a year v. *lo.* — *sbrul-šún* slough, skin of a snake. — 2. symb. num.: 8, = *klu.*

སྦྲེ(ད)་ *sbre(d) Lex.* n. of an animal; *Sch.*: **stone-fox.**

སྦྲེ་བོ་, རེ་བོ་, རེ་བ་ *sbré-bo, ré-bo, ré-ba* a coarse material manufactured of yak's hair for tent-coverings.

སྦྲེང་བ་ *sbréṅ-ba*, pf. *sbreṅs*, *Cs.*: **to play** an instrument; acc. to *Dzl.* ༥༧, 16, **to jerk,** a chord, a bow-string.

སྦྲེབས་པ་ *sbrébs-pa Cs.*: resp. for *ltógs-pa* **hungry.**

སྦྲེལ་བ་ *sbrél-ba*, *W.* **rél-će(s)** **to stitch together,** paper; **to stitch to, to sew on; to fasten on,** a package on a horse; *lčags-sgróg lág-pa sbrél-nas* having one's hands shackled together; *bar zám-gyis sbrel* the chasm is overarched by a bridge *Glr.*; (iron chains) *séṅ-ge daṅ* fastened to (stone) lions; in a gen. sense: **to connect, to join,** *γnyis-sbrél, γsum-sbrél* two or three consonants joined together, cf. *miṅ-γži.*

སྦྲེས་པ་ *sbrés-pa Cs.* **frozen, stiff, hard.**

སྦྲོན་པ་ *sbrón-pa*, pf. and fut. *sbran* 1. **to call to the spot,** *rá-mda, grogs* for assistance *Lex.*; **to send for,** the minister *Glr.* — 2. **to call to** *Thgy.*; **to give information, notice, intelligence,** *rgyál-po-la rmi-lam-du* to warn the king by a dream *Dzl.*; *mi žig sbrán-du btáṅ-nas Dzl.* to dispatch a man in order to convey intelligence. — 3. **to sprinkle, to stain, to pollute,** *ťig-les Sch.*

ཨ

མ **ma** 1. the letter **m**. — 2. numerical figure: 16.

མ་ *ma* I. sbst. 1. **mother**, col. *ă-ma*, resp. *yum; mai rum* womb, matrix; *rán-gi ma yċig-pai sriṅ-mo* full sister by the same mother, whilst *mas dbén-pai sriṅ-mo* denotes half-sister, step-sister, by another mother. — 2. frq. used metonymically, e.g. **capital**, v. below; *ma tsam yod* W., what is the amount of the sum advanced? **original text, copy to write after, pattern** v. below; **a letter written above** another. — Comp.: *ma-ḱál* amount in bushels of grain lent out. — *ma-ḱú* mother and uncle, v. *ḱá-bo.* — *ma-rgyúd Sch.* 1. **original, primary cause.** 2. **line of descent** by the mother's side, when however it should be spelt *brgyud.* — *má-ču* the first infusion of malt or stronger beer, v. *čaṅ.* — *ma-čúṅ Cs.*: 'a mother's younger sister', perh. more correctly: a father's second wife, as to rank; *ma-čen* 1. *Cs.*: 'a mother's elder sister'. or a father's principal wife. 2. v. the respective article. — *ma-ṕár* capital and interest W. — *ma-bu* mother and son; capital and interest; original and copy; *ma-bú mťún-pa ₒbri-ba* to copy accurately *Schr.*; a letter written above and below another letter; principal and cross beam etc. — *má-mo* v. that article. — *ma-tsáb* foster-mother *Sch.* — *ma-yżi* v. sub II. — *ma-yyár* step-mother *Cs.* — *ma-ró* a mother's corpse *Pth.*

II. a root signifying **below**, opp. to *ya: má-gi* the lower one, e.g. *ču-bo Mil.*; *ma-gi-na* below, at the bottom, *má-gi-nas* from below, out of the valley, in *Sik.*: from, out of, the Indian plain (v. *mťa*); *má-mču* lower lip. — *má-tem* sill, threshold. — *má-tog* v. *tog* I, 2. — *má-rdo* = *rmaṅ-rdo.* — *ma-rábs* mean descent, people of low extraction *Dzl.* — *ma-ri Sch.* downward(?) — *ma-ré* = *ma-tém*, v. *re.*

III. **negative adv. not**, however only in some cases: a. in the simplest form of prohibition, where in the Tibetan language inst. of the imperative the root of the present with *ma* is used: *ma ₒgro* do not go, *ma byed* do not do (it). With the form of the future *mi* is placed: *rjód-par mi byao* it shall not, should not be pronounced *Dom.*; *mi de dgrar mi bslaṅ* they should not make the man their enemy *S.g.* — b. with the preterite: *ma soṅ* he did not go, *ma byas* he did not do (it). — c. with the present tense also in conjunction with the words *yin, lags, mčis, red.* — d. without any evident reason, and perh. not always correctly, with many substantives and adjectives that are formed of infinitives or participles, and are conveying a negative sense: *ma-rig-pa* a not knowing, ignorance; *ma-rúṅ-ba* v. *ruṅ-ba* (v. *mi*).

IV. In the col. language of *Lh. ma* is used as an **interrogative**, when a question is returned by a question: *ḱyód-di miṅ či zer* what is your name? *miṅ ma?* my name?

V. Affix, so-called article, frq. denoting the fem. of the masc. in *pa*, if *mo* is not used inst. of it; gen. put to the names of inanimate things, utensils etc., as also to compound adjectives: *zaṅs ru-bżi-ma* a four-handled kettle (cf. *bu lo-ynyís-pa* a boy two years old, sub *pa*).

VI. *mai nyin* **two days before yesterday** *C.*, = *snón-ma żag* W.

མ་ *mā* W. always with a marked accent and long vowel, prob. abbrev. of *maṅs* **very**, before adjectives and adverbs, *mā máṅ-po* very much, *mā gyál-la* very good.

མ་ཀར་ *ma-kár* (Hind. مَکَّار impostor) W. **deceit, imposition, intrigue**, *ma-kár čó-te zer* he speaks hypocritically, with some secret design; *ma-kar-čan*, **hypocritical, fawning**.

མ་ཀ་ར་ *ma-ka-ra Ssk.* **sea-monster.**

མ་ཁ་ *ma-ḱá* 1. *Lt.* = *mts̀an-dbye.* — 2. **Mecca** *Stg.*

མ་ཁལ་ *ma-ḱál* v. *ma* I.

མ་མཁན་ *ma-mḱán* v. *ma-rgán.*

མ་གལ་ *ma-gál Wdṅ., W.* **poplar-tree.**

མ་གི་ *má-gi* v. *ma* II.

མ་རྒད་ *ma-rgád,* **mar-gád** *Glr.*, from **मरकत**, **emerald.**

མ་རྒན་ *ma-rgán W.* **mar-gán** 1. **matron, grandam.** 2. *C.* also **ma-kḗn** **cook; quarter-master.**

མ་ཆེན་ *ma-čén* 1. v. *ma* I. — 2. **head-cook.**

མ་ཏྲི་མུ་ཏྲི་ས་ལ་འཛུ་ *ma-tri-mu-tri-sa-la-ₒdzu* is said to be a form of prayer of the Bonpos, as the Ommanipadmehūm is of the Buddhists; *Desg.* p. 242 has: *ma tchri mou me sa le gou.*

མ་དང་ (?) *ma-dáṅ Ld.* a place on the roof of a house cleared for spreading grain there.

མ་གདན་ *ma-γdán, W.* **mag-dán**, *C.* **ma-dḗn** **ground, basis, foundation;** also for *ma-γdán-gyi ri-mo* **ground-plan.**

མ་རྡུ་, མ་དུ་ (?) *ma-rdú,* **ma-dú W.* **thorn, prickle,** *má-rdu-čan* **thorny, prickly.**

མ་རྡོ་ *má-rdo,* **mar-do** *W.* prob. a careless pronunciation of *rmáṅ-rdo.*

མ་ནིང་ *ma-niṅ* 1. **without sexual distinction** *Med.* and *Gram.* — 2. **impotent, unable to beget** *S.g.* — 3. **barren, childless** *Wdṅ.* (explained by *bu-ts̀a-méd-pa*). — 4. *Cs.*: also **hermaphrodite,** *Wdṅ.* however denotes this explicitly by *mts̀an-γnyis-pa*

མ་ནུ་ *ma-nu Med.? Cs* : = **मनु, मनस्**, *yid*; as symb. num.: 14.

མ་ནུ་པ་ཏྲ་ *ma-nu-pa-tra* a medicine *Wdṅ.*; in *Lh.* Bryonia dioeca.

མ་ཎི་ *má-ṇi* (*Ssk.* precious stone) 1. abbrev. of Ommanipadmehūm; **má-ni táṅ-če** *W.* 1. **to mutter prayers.** 2. **to purr like a cat.** Hence 2. **praying-cylinder,** prop. *ma-ni-čos-ₒḱór Schl.* 230. — 3. **consecrated stone-heaps** or **stone-walls** (Mongul *Obo*) *Schl.* 196; *ma-ni bka-ₒbúm* title of a book; as to its contents v. *Schl.* 84.

མ་ཕང་ *ma-ṕáṅ Mil., ma-ṕám Cs.* = *ma-drós-pa,* v. *drós-pa.*

མ་མ་ *má-ma* **children's nurse** *Dzl., Glr., Cs.*: *nú-ma snún-pai* wet-nurse, *drí-ma ₒṕyi-bai* nurse for cleaning, *páṅ-du ₒḱúr-bai* for carrying, *rtsèd-grogs-kyi* for playing.

མ་སྨུན་ *ma-mún Ld.* col. for *na-bún,* **fog.**

མ་མོ་ *má-mo* 1. *Sch.* **grandmother.** — 2. *Sch.* **ewe,** sheep that has lambed. — 3. *Mil.* and elsewh. frq., a kind of wicked demons.

མ་ཞི་ *ma-ži Lt.* medicinal plant (?).

མ་ཞུ་ *má-žú* v. *žú-ba.*

མ་གཞི་ *má-γži, W.* **máb-ži** 1. **ground-work, basis, elementary principle, component part; prime colour; principal thing, main point.** — 2. *Sch.* **originally** (?).

མཱ་ཡཱ་ *mā-yā Ssk.* = *Tib. sgyu-ₒṗrul-ma* **'delusion',** n. of the mother of Buddha Śākyamuni.

མ་གཡོག་ *ma-γyóg* = *tab-γyóg* **kitchen-boy, scullion** *W.*

མ་རི་, མ་རེ་ *ma-ri, ma-ré* v. *ma* II.

མ་རུ་ *má-ru* n. of a castle, perh. = *rmé-ru.*

མ་རུ་རྩེ་ *ma-ru-rtsé* 1. n. of a medicine *Med.* — 2. n. of a country *Pth.*

མ་ལ་ *ma-la Sch.* **excellent! capital!** — In *Feer Introd.* p. 69 it was explained by our Lama as = *'é-ma* **ah, well!** Also Feer has: *Eh bien!*

མ་ལ་ཁན་ *má-la-ḱan Ld.* **snake-charmer, conjurer.**

མ་ལ་ཡ་ *má-la-ya* **the western Ghauts** famous for sandal-wood; the tracts along their foot, **Malayalim, Malabar.**

མ་ལ་ལ་ཙེ་ *ma-la-la-tsé Ld.* **small lizard.**

མ་ལག་ *má-lag Ld.* **somerset;** **má-lag lóg-če** to perform a somerset, to play the tricks of a mountebank; to roll on the ground with legs turned up, of horses etc.

མ་ལམ་ *má-lam* **high-road, broad passage** *W.*

མ་ཤ་ *ma-ša* 1. *Ssk.* **माष**, **pea**, Phaseolus radiatus, = *mon-srán* or *greu Wdn.* — 2. *W.* the contrary of *ya-ša*, **contempt, scorn, disregard.** — 3. *W.* **trigger of a musket.**

མ་ཤ་ཀ་ *ma-ša-ka Ssk.* **माषक**, *Cs.*: a small gold weight and coin in ancient India.

མ་ཤི་ཀ་ *ma-ši-ka* name formed from the Hebrew מָשִׁיחַ, for **Christ,** the Greek word not being adapted to the Tib. language *Chr. Prot.*

མ་ཧཱ་ *ma-hā Ssk.* **great,** used in names and titles: *ma-hā-kā-la* and *de-ba* = Siva *Glr.*; *ma-hā-tsī-na, ma-hā-tsin* the modern name of China, formerly *rgya-nág*; *ma-hā-tsi-nai skad* the Chinese language *Wdk.*; *ma-hā-rā-dzā* the great king, title of some princes, particularly that of Kashmere.

མ་ཧེ་ *ma-he, Ssk.* **महिष**, **buffalo** *Glr.*, *ma-he-mo* female of it.

མག་པ་ *mag-pa* 1. **son-in-law** *Dzl.*, *mag-skud* son-in-law and father-in-law *Dom.* 2. **bridegroom** col.

མག་མལ་ *mag-mal, Ar.* مخمل, **velvet** *W.*

མང་ *maṅ* 1. *C.* col. for *mi oṅ, mi ₒdug* (?); so also in some passages of the *Ma.* — 2. v. *máṅ-po.*

མང་ག་ལཾ་ *maṅ-ga-lam Ssk.* = *bkra-šis.*

མང་པོ་ *máṅ-po* 1. **much, many,** *mi maṅ-po* (*rnams*) **many people,** also (like οἱ πολλοί) **most people, the gross** or **bulk of the people,** for which *W.* **máṅ-če**, e.g **máṅ-če zer dug** most people say, or, mostly it is said etc.; *ₒkor máṅ-po* (*rnams*) the numerous retinue *Dzl.*; *máṅ-por* adverb **mostly** (not frq.) *Zam.*; *ču maṅ-nyúṅ ltos* look after the height of the water, whether there is much or little of it; *γčig bsgyúr-ba-la maṅ-nyuṅ med* if you multiply by 1, you will get neither more nor less *Wdk.* — 2. **very, very much,** with verbs, chiefly col., *maṅ-po ₒjigs* I am very much afraid.

Comp. and deriv. *maṅ-bkúr* = *máṅ-pos bkúr-ba* v. *bkúr-ba* I. and II. — *maṅ-gé-mo* long ago, long since (?) *Cs.* — **maṅ-ṅa** *W.* col. for *máṅ-por, máṅ-ba(r)*; **žag daṅ žag máṅ-ṅa máṅ-ṅa táṅ-če** to give a little more every day. — *máṅ-če* v. above. — *máṅ-ja* a liberal distribution of tea *Ld.-Glr. Schl.* fol. 27, a, and p. 72. *máṅ-du* is not only the termin. case, but also a compound of *maṅ* and the synon. *du*, being used exactly like *máṅ-po*, both in the nomin. and accus case, *γdams-ṅág máṅ-du bstán-pas ₒbrás-bu bži tób-pa máṅ-du byuṅ* as he gave manifold instructions, many became obtainers of the four fruits *Tar.* 14, 3.

མང་བ་ *máṅ-ba* I. vb. pf. *maṅs*, **to be much,** *ₒdi máṅ-ṅam de maṅ* is this much or that? i.e. which is more, this or that? *Dzl.*; *dgra máṅs-pas* as the enemies had become very numerous *Dzl.*; *sman-dpyád máṅs-pas pán-rgyu med* by making much of medical treatment he will not grow well *Mil*; *ma máṅ čig* be it not much, let it not grow too much *Mil.* and elsewh.; *máṅs-kyis dógs-pa* fearing lest it should grow too much *Wdn.* — II. adj. 1. *máṅ-po.* — 2. **having much,** *bu maṅ-bar ₒgyúr-ba* to get many children, *bu-máṅs* rich in children *Pth.* — *máṅs-tsig* a sign of the plural number, e.g. *dag Gram.* — III. also sbst. **plenty.**

མང་ཡུལ་ *máṅ-yul*, a province of Tibet bordering on Nepal, in which *skyid-gróṅ* is situated, v. *skyid.*

མན་ཛི་ར་ *man-dzi-ra S.g.* a mineral medicine; perh. *man-dza-ri Ssk.* **pearl.**

མཎྜལ་ *maṇḍal Ssk*, prop. *Tib. dkyil-ₒkor* jewels, viands etc. presented as offerings, and arranged in **a cirle** *Glr.* and elsewhere, cf. *tsogs.*

མད་ *mad* 1. = *nad* (?) *lus mad-méd-čiṅ Sambh.* — 2. sometimes for *smad.*

མད་པ་ *mád-pa* **true,** *kyed mad γsúṅ-žiṅ* as you speak what is true *Mil.*; *ma nyés-pai bden-tsig mád-po smras kyaṅ* although he solemnly declared not to have committed it *Pth.*

མན་ *man* I. sbst., also *mán-na, má-na Hind.* **a 'man'** or Indian hundredweight, equal to about 80 pounds, anglicized **maund.** — II *W.* for *ma yin* (*B. min*) 1. it is not;

'i man this it is not; *mán-na* is it not so? isn't it? is it? In conjunction with a negative it is col. almost the only word for **only, but** etc.: *de mán-na mi yoṅ, de mán-na med* only this one is to be met with, besides this there are none; *la-dág-gi lug č́ún-se mán-na mi yon* there are only small sheep in Ladak; *dún-la mán-na mi tóṅ-k'an* he who sees only what is close before him, a short-sighted person; *dé-bu lo gyad tiṅ-la máṅ-na mi yoṅ* fruit will appear only after a space of eight years; *di-riṅ mán-na ma toṅ* I have seen (him, it) only to-day, i.e. to-day for the first time cf. *min.* — 2. **no.** — III. = *ma* II., *man-yán* **below** and **above** *Cs.*; *man-čád, -čád, -čód* 1. adv.and postp.c.accus., **below, downward, on the lower side of, as far as,** *lté-ba man-čád ču náṅ-du nub Glr*, he was immerged in the water below his navel, i.e. up to his navel; inst. of *man-čád* also merely *man: pús-mo goṅ man Mil.*, lit below the parts over the knee i.e. higher than the knee; *de man-čód*, below that *Glr.*; in reference to time, **from,** *do-núb man čad* from this evening *Mil.*; *de man-čád* **since, from that time forward** *Mil.*; *rmaṅ btiṅ-ba man rab-ynás mdzád-pa yán-la* from the foundation up to the consecration *Glr.*; **even to** (the last man), (all) **except** or **save** (one), also *mán-pa, mán-pe, mán-k'an, man-ra* *W.* (*B. min-pa*). — 2. sbst. **lower part** of a country, **lowland,** thus in *Lh.* as a proper name.

མན་ངག *man-ṅág*, *Ssk.* उपदेश, **advice, direction, information,** *stón-pa* to give, *man-ṅag (-gi) -rgyúd* v. *rgyud* 2; in later writings and in the mind of the common people, it coincides with *sṅags*, in as much as the esoteric doctrines of mysticism, i.e. magic art, are concerned, which are communicated in no other way than by word of mouth; cf. *k'a-rgyan.*

མན་ཅད, ཆད, ཆོད, པ, ལྷག *man-čad, čad, čod, pa, lhag,* v. *man* II. and III.

མན་དཱ་ར་བ *man-da-ra-ba*, मन्दारव, a tree in paradise *Stg.*

མན(ན)མུན(ནེ) *man(-na)-mún(-ne) Ld.*, **turbid, muddy, dingy, dim, dull, dusky,** as to water, flames of light etc.

མན་ཙི *mán-tsi Sch.* a kind of silk-cloth.

མན་ཛི *man-dzi* 1. *Sch.* 'a small **square table',** acc. to others **a tripod** with long curved feet, for sacrificial purposes. — 2. *W.* **bed** *Hindi* मञ्च.

མན་ཤེལ *man-šel* **crystal, glass** *Pth.*

མར *mar* I. sbst., resp. *ysol-már* 1. **butter** *Thgy*, *C.*, *W.* — 2. col. also **oil.** — **Comp.** *skya-már*, *Ld. k'ág-la mar* fresh, not melted butter; *ba - már* cow-butter; *ˌbri-már* yak-butter; *ˌbru-már* oil from oleaginous seeds, rape-seed oil etc. *Dzl.* and elsewhere; *rtsi-már* oil from the stones of apricots etc.; *mdzo-már* butter from the bastard-cow; *žun-már* melted butter, *ghi* (*Hind.*), the usual form of butter in India and frq. also in Tibet, highly esteemed both as food and as medicine; *žum-már-pa* *C.* **lamp;** *mar-dkár Med.* = *skya-már.* — *már-k'u* melted, liquid butter — *mar-rnyiṅ* old, rancid butter, recommended by physicians for diseases of the mind, fainting-fits, wounds. — *mar-nág* *W.* oil, *nyuṅ-dkar-mar-nág* rape-seed oil. — *mar-blúg* *W.* a small urn-shaped vessel for butter or oil. — *mar-mé* **lamp,** at present only for holy uses, thus: *mar-mé ghyen-tsen* holy, heavenward burning lamp *C.* (formerly any lamp *Dzl.* ༢༥, 11; *Glr.*); *mar me mdzád* Buddha Dipaṅkara, v. *Dzl.* XXXVII.; — *mar-žógs Mil.* a part cut off, one half of a *mar-ril*, i.e. a globular lump of fresh butter, about one pound in weight, not unfrequently offered to travellers as a gift of courtesy. — *mar-ysár* fresh butter *Lt.* — II. termin. of *ma* I.,to or 'into' the mother; *mar-gyur ˌgró-ba* regarded as a mother, a creature loved like a mother, *Mil.*; v. *ma* II. down, downward, *már-la* id., *B.* and *C.*; v. *rbab* and *ˌgrib-pa*; *mar-ṅo* v. *ṅo* 5.

མར་ཀ་ལ་ག *mar-ka-la-ga* (?) a fine ochreous earth, found e. g. on the Baralasa pass between *Lh.* and *Ld.*, used as ground-colour in staining houses with *dkár-rtsi Ld.*

མར་རྒན་ *mar-rgán* v. *ma-rgán.*

མར་ངོ་ *mar-ṅó* v. *ṅo* 5.

མར་དོན་ *mar-dón* perh. *dmar-ₒdón.*

མར་པ་ *már-pa,* n. of a holy Lama, teacher of Milaraspa, by whom he was highly respected.

མར་བ་ *mar-ba* provinc. for *dmár-ba Sch.*

མར་ཡུལ་ *már-yul Ma.,* n.p. = *la-dwags* Ladak.

མལ་ *mal,* the place where a thing is, its **site, situation,** **mál-du žág-pa** *C.* **bór-če** *W.,* to put a thing in its own place; also where a thing has been, its **trace, vestige,** *šiṅ-rtai* rut, wheel-mark, track; *mal γčig-tu mi ₒdúg-pa* prob. to be unstable, changeable, fickle, restless; more esp. place of rest, **couch, bed,** *mál-gyi ₒog-tu* under the bed *Glr.; dgoṅs-mal* resp. for night-quarters *Dzl.* ༢༩, 3 (so acc. to the xylographic copy; *Sch.* having the less appropriate *dgoṅs-lam*); **mal dúg-če** *W.* to live in a strange place, ἐπιδημεῖν; *mal bdé-ba Sch.* a quiet sleep, *ṅai lus sems mál-du bde* I now may safely lie down, fig. for: the danger is now over *Glr.* — *mal-k̔ri* bed-frame, bed-stead. — *mal-gós Cs., mal-čá Lex.,* **mal-čé** *C.,* **-stán** *C., W.. Dzl.* bedding, bed-clothes. — *mal-ldaṅ Sch.* 'cradle', rather improb., perh. hammock. — *mal-yól* bed-curtain. — *mál-sa,* resp. *γzims-mál* couch, bed.

མལ་ལ་མུལ་ལེ་ *mal-la-múl-le Ld.* **lukewarm,** tepid.

མལ་ལི་ཀ་ *mal-li-ka Ssk.,* properly name of a flower, Jasminum Champaca, used as an epithet in pompous titles of books.

མས་ *mas* 1. instrum. case of *ma* mother. — 2. v. *ma* II, **the lower part,** gen. however with terminative meaning, **downward, towards the lower parts,** *mas btáṅ-ba Med.* to move downward, to purge; **backward, last** *Sch.;* used also as a sbst.: *más-k̔yi* the last, e.g. *yi-ge* final letter *Cs.; más-la* downward, below *Sch., más-nas* from below *Sch.;* cf. the contrary *yás.*

མི་ *mi,* I. num. figure: 46. — II. sbst. **man,** *mi γsod-pa* to kill men, to murder, *mi-méd ri-k̔ród* uninhabited, desolate mountains *Mil.; mi-rnams ná-re* people said *Mil.; mi-la ma lab* tell no body else of it *Mil; ráṅ-gis bságs-pa mi-yis spyod* what we gathered ourselves, is enjoyed by others *Mil.; mi-nor raṅ slóṅ-ba* to gather by begging what belongs to others *Mil.; mii bú-mo* 1. daughters of men, opp. to *lhai bú-mo* e.g. witches appear in the shape of daughters of men *Mil.* 2. daughters of others, opp. to *ráṅ-gi bú-mo Mil.,* cf. also *mi-bu* further on; pleon. before a pers. pron. of the first person: *mi-ṅá, mi-bdág* I, *Mil.* (cf. *p̔o*), and with certain sbst.: *γtsó-bo mi drug* (we) six lords *Glr.*; plur. also *mi-tsó Sch.*

Comp. *mi-k̔a,* (idle) talk of the people, common talk, *yúl-sdei náṅ-nas mi-k̔a sdud* in the whole neighbourhood one is an object of gossip, nif.; defaming talk; imprecating speech, with or without *ṅán-pa, mi-k̔á zug* or *p̔og* (damnation) lights on (me, him) *Dom.* — *mi-kyim* 1. **human dwelling, house,** (the Chinese capital contained) *mi-kyim ₒbúm-tso* 100 000 houses *Glr.* 2. *Ld.-Glr. Schl.* 20. b. and *Glr.* 94, 7 it seems to imply **the people of a household, domestics,** the same as *k̔yim-ghi mi.* — *mi-ₒgréṅ* v. *ₒgréṅ-ba.* — *mi-rgód* v. *rgód-pa* II. — *mi-brgyúd* v. *brgyud.* — *mi-rje* sovereign, king, *mi-rje mdzád-pa* to be king, to reign *Glr.* — *mi-nyid Cs.* 'humanity, honesty'; *mi-nyid-čan* 'humane, honest'(?) — *mi-brdág.* 1. = *mi-rje.* 2. symb. num.: 16. — *mi-mda* (vulgo *min-da*) *Mil.* and *C., W.:* men, persons preceded by a numeral, e.g. six men, six women (prop. a line or row of people). — *mi-sdé* v. *sde. Sch.* has also: *lha-sdé mi-sdé* princes and nations. — *mi-sná* 1. **race of men, class of people** (seldom). 2. **messenger, delegate,** not frq met with in books, yet not unknown in *C.* and *W.,* and used esp. of messengers with an errand or charge given them in words; in our translations introduced for **apostle,** *p̉ó-nya* having been adopted for 'angel'. — *mi-dpón* prefect *Glr., C.* — *mi(i)-bu* 1. **a child of man, a mortal,** po., *Mil.*, cf. *mii bú-mo* above. 2. **son of man,** when Christ speaks of himself as such, otherwise *mii sras Chr. Prot.* — *mí-bo Cs.*, rarely for *mi.* — *mi-dbaṅ*, prince, potentate. — *mi-ma-yin(-pa)* अमनुष, one that is not a human being, *mi daṅ mi-ma-yin-pa t̉ams-čád* all human and not human (adversaries) *Dom.*, esp. ghosts, demons, *dur-k̉ród-kyi mi-ma-yin-pa-rnams* the ghosts of a grave-yard (not the souls of the dead); *mk̉á-la rgyú-bai mi-ma-yin* the ghosts that walk in the air *Mil.*; *dkár-p̉yogs-kyi mi-ma yin-rnams* good genii *Mil.*; *mi-ma-yin-gyi čo-ₒp̉rúl* apparitions of ghosts *Mil.* — *mi-mo* **woman,** yet only in contraposition to *lhá-mo* and other not human female beings *Mil.* and elsewh. — *mi(i)-yul* human world, lower world, earth, opp. to regions of the gods or of infernal beings *Glr., Pth.* — *mi-rabs* mankind. — *mi-rigs* v. *rigs.* — *Mi-la-rás-pa*, often only *Mí-la*, name of a Buddhist ascetic, of the 11 century (*Wdk.*), who between the periods of his meditations itinerating in the southern part of Middle Tibet as a mendicant friar, instructed the people by his improvisations delivered in poetry and song, brought the indifferent to his faith, refuted and converted the heretics, wrought manifold miracles (*rdzu-ₒp̉rúl*), and whose legends, written not without wit and poetical merit, are still at the present day the most popular and widely circulated book in Tibet. — *mi-lág* servant, **mi-lág-tu ₒdó-wa** to do servant's work, to perform drudgery *W.* — *mi-lús* 1. the human body. 2. v. *lús-pa.* — *mi-ser* 1. **subject, servant, menial, drudge.** 2. **robber, thief, sharper.** — 3. v. below.

III. negative adv.: **not,** in all such cases where *ma* (q.v.) is not used. With simple verbs the place of the negation is always immediately before them, in compound forms gen. before the last of the component parts, e.g. *ₒbyúṅ bar mi ₒgyúr-ro*, unless logically it belongs to the first, in which case often *ma* inst. of *mi* is employed. This rule, however, is not always strictly observed, so *Glr.* 70: *de daṅ nám-du yaṅ mi ₒbrál-bar gyis šig*, and immediately after: *skad γčig kyaṅ ma brál-bar gyis šig* do never part with it

མི་ཉག, **མེ་ཉག** *mi-nyág, me-nyág*, and **ཏང་གུད་** Tanggud, names of two provinces closely connected with each other, situated in the north-eastern part of Tibet and forming in ancient times a separate kingdom *Glr.*

མི་མ་ *mi-ma Sch.* **tears.**

མི་སེར་ *mi-sér* 1. n.p., formed after مصر, *mi-sér yul* Egypt, *mi-sér-pa* Egyptian, *Chr. Prot.* — 2. v. *mi.*

མིའམ་ཅི་ *miam-či, Ssk.* **किंनर**, fabulous beings of Indian origin, nearly related to the *ₒdri-za*, and belonging to the retinue of Kuvera; fem *miam-či-mo.*

མིའུ་ *miu* 1. **a little man, dwarf,** also *miu-t̉úṅ Wdn.*; *mig-gi miu* v. *mig.* — 2. perh. applicable also **to puppet, doll.**

མིག *mig*, resp. 1. **eye.** — 2. **eye of a needle; hole** in a hatchet or hammer, to insert the handle — 3. symb. num.: 2. — *mig-gi gaṅs Sch.*, the white of the eye; *mig-gi rgyál-mo* or *miu*, 'the queen or the little man in the eye': 1. **pupil.** 2. **iris** *Stg.*; *mig-gi snág-tsa* or *-mtso Cs.*, vulgo *mig-gi nág-po* id.; *mig-gi mé-tog Sch.* the luminous point of the eye: *mig nyáms-pa Cs.* weak eyes; *mig ltá-ba* to see with the eyes, to look up, to look round *Glr.*; *mig ₒdzúm-pa* to shut the eyes, *ₒbyéd-pa* to open the eyes, v. *ₒbyéd-pa* 1; *ₒdón-pa, ₒbyin-pa* to cut or tear out the eyes, to squeeze them out by a particular instrument, as a torture or punishment *C.*; *mig bčár-ba Lex.*, acc. to *Sch.* id.; *mdóṅs-pa, mdóns-par ₒgyúr-ba* to get blind or blinded, to be deprived of sight *Dzl.*; *mig ₒk̉yid-pa Sch.*, to distort or roll the eyes; *mig skú-ba Dom.* (*bskú-ba?*) n. of a certain magic trick; *mig čid-pa* inflammation of the eyes through cold, snowblindness *C.* (perh. *p̉yid-pa*); **mig zug soṅ**

it has struck my eyes, I should like to have it *C.*, *W.*; **mig log ltá-ce** to eye one obliquely, with envy or jealousy *W.* —

Comp. *mig-kyóg* squinting *Sch.* — *mig-rkyén Mil.*, is said to be the same as *mig-ltós.* — **mig-skyór** *W.* eye-ball. — *mig-skyág* the impurities in the eyes *Cs.* — *mig-k'úṅ* eye-hole, socket *Sch.* — *mig-ₒk'rul Mil.* v. *mig-ₒp'rul.* — *mig-grogs* one's sweetheart *Cs.* — *mig-ₒgram* edge of the eye *Sch.* — *mig-rgyaṅ* 1. v. *rgyaṅ-ma.* 2. farsightedness, *mig-rgyáṅ-čan* one that is farsighted, *mig rgyaṅ-t'úṅ* short-sighted *Bhar.* *mig-sgyu* mirage, looming, Fata Morgana, *sós-kai t'áṅ-la mig-sgyu ₒgyú-ba bžin Thgr.* like the mirage on a plain in the hot season. — *mig-sgyur-ma* = *mk'á-ₒgro-ma Mil.* — *mig-čaṅ* 1. having eyes. 2. having seeds or grains, fructified, of ears of corn *W.* — *mig-čér* v. *če-re.* — *mig-lčibs* eye-lid *Med.* — *mig-č'u* 1. tears *W.* 2. hydrophthalmia *Med.* 3. *mig-č'u dzág-pa* blear-eyes *Schr.* — *mig-brnyás ₒk'yér-ba Mil.* c. dat., to slight, to treat contemptuously. — *mig-rtúl* dim, dull eyes *Sch.* — *mig-lta* (resp. *žál-lta*, *žál-ta*) *byéd-pa* to inspect, superintend (**mig-ta-k'an** overseer of workmen); to keep, to guard; to care for, to minister, to serve. — *mig-ltág Sch.* = *mig-skyág* (?) — *mig-ltós* 1. eye-sight, look, mien *Cs.* 2. *C. W.* learning by observation and close ocular attention, **gár-ža-pe hin-dui mig-tós k'ur**, or **k'yon**, or **lob dug** *W.* the people of Lahoul copy the Hindoos; **mig-tós ṅán-pa k'ur**, or **lob soṅ** *W.* he has imitated what is not good. — **mig-tọ-la p'ém-pa**, or **nọ'-pa** *C.* to derive profit or harm from observing and imitating others (?) **mig-tọ-la p'ẹm-pẹ 'tim** deterring punishment. — **mig-t'ág tóṅ-wa** a kind of torture in *C.*, little hooks, connected by strings, being fastened in the lower eye-lids as well as in the chest, by which means the former are constantly drawn down and prevented from closing. — *mig-t'úṅ* short-sightedness *Cs.*, *mig-t'úṅ-čan* short-sighted. — **mig-ḍa** snow-spectacles, shades formed of a texture of horsehair. — **mig-dól** *C.* = *γṅyid-rdól.* — *mig-ldán* = *mig-čan* po. needle. — *mig-nád*, disease of the eye. — *mig-po* = *mig Cs.*, *mig-po-čẹ́* a large eye *Cs.* — **mig-pág** *C.*, *W.* eye-lid. — *mig-sprin* 'a white spot in the eye' *Sch.*; acc. to *Lt.* it seems to be the white of the eye, sclerotica, in *C.* the cataract is called so. — *mig-p'ór Cs.* = *mig-k'úṅ.* — *mig-ₒk'rúl Mil.* optical deception, *mig-ₒk'rul-mk'an* a showman *Cs.* — *mig-bu* 'Augenklappe' *Sch.* (?) — *mig-ₒbúr* goggle-eyes. — *mig-ₒbras* apple of the eye, eyeball, **mig-ḍás lóg-če**, or **mig-kór lóg-če** *W.* to roll the eyes; *bdág-gi mig-gi ₒbras ltar γčés-na yaṅ* although she is as dear to me as the apple of my eye. — *mig-máṅ(s)* chess-board, game at tables, *mig-máṅ rtsé-ba Dzl.* to play at chess, *mig-maṅ-ris-su bris-pa Glr.* chequered, painted or in-laid work after the pattern of a chess-board. — *mig-méd* eyeless, blind. — *mig-dmár* 1. red eye, as a symptom of disease *Lt.* 2. the planet Mars. — *mig-smán* eye-medicine. — *mig-rtsa* 1. prob. Vena facialis externa *Med.* 2. the blood-vessels of the sclerotica, *mig-rtsa ₒk'rúgs-pa* the blood-vessels irritated, reddened *Med.* — **mig-sál** *W.* sharp-sightedness, **mig-sál-k'an** sharp-sighted, **mig-sal-nyám** the contrary. — *mig-rtsẹ́g* the wrinkles of the eye-lid *Cs.* — *mig-tsil*, 1. fat in the eye *Mil.* 2. the white in the eye *Cs.* — **mig-tsig(-če)** *W.* inflammation of the eye, **k'á-mig-tsig** caused by snow, **dúd-mig-tsig** caused by smoke. — *mig-zi* mist before the eyes *Sch.* — *mig-zúr* corner of the eye *Sch.* — *mig-γzúgs S.g.* optical perception, a picture of objects being formed on the retina by reflected rays of light (merely guessed by Tibetan science, not ascertained by observation and research). **mig-yáṅ(s)** *C.*, *W.* liberal, bountiful. — *mig-yór*, 1. *Sch.* = *mig-rtúl.* 2. = *mig-sgyú Thgr.* — *mig-rig-rig Mil.* timidly, anxiously looking to and fro, hither and thither. — *mig-riṅ-čan* = *mig-rgyáṅ-čan Cs.* — *mig-ris* artificial eye-brows *Cs.* — *mig-rús* eye-bone *Cs.* — *mig-slobs* the act of accustoming the eyes to ..., *mig-slóbs ṅán-pa skye Mil.* you habituate yourself to a faulty look, i. e.

downward, to what is earthly. — *mig-ṡóg* W. eye-lash. — *mig-sér* 1. jaundice, also *gya-nág mig-sér* W. 2. envy, jealousy, *mig-sér-čan* envious, jealous. — *mig-hu-ré* v. *hu-re.*

མིང་ *miṅ*, resp. *mtsan*, **name**, *ḱyód-kyi miṅ či yin Mil.* or **či zer** W. what is your name? *dei miṅ yaṅ med Glr.* such a thing is or was not known at all, such a thing does not exist; *miṅ-tsam-gyi dge-slóṅ Dzl.* priest only by name; W.: **miṅ-gi náṅ-na** id.; C. also: **ṭál-gyi miṅ tsám-le me** this tax exists only nominally; **appellation, designation, word,** *ṫén-pai miṅ* a word for drawing (pulling) *Gram.*; *miṅ-gi mdzod* **dictionary**; **ḱyod-su miṅ daṅ** or **su miṅ-ṅi náṅ-na** or **su miṅ nén-te** or **su miṅ-la tén-te ča dug** W. in whose name or business, upon whose order are you going? **čii miṅ daṅ** W. for what cause, in behalf of what affair? *miṅ-nas rǰód-pa*, or *smó-ba Dzl.* and elsewh., to call by name, also to call upon the name of, hence . . . *kyi miṅ-nas brǰód-de* in the name of; *miṅ ˳dógs-pa* to name v. *miṅ* 2; *dṅós-miṅ* v. *dṅos*; *btágs-miṅ* a name given (e.g. a Christian name) *Cs.*, *rǰes-grúb-kyi miṅ* a surname *Cs.*, *rus-miṅ* a family name *Cs.*

Comp. *miṅ-rkyáṅ* a single syllable or name *Cs.*, cf. *miṅ-sbyár.* — *miṅ-grógs* one's name-sake *Cs.* — *miṅ-sgrá* a mere name, word, or sound (philosophical term.) *Was.* — *miṅ-ṅán* a bad name, infamy *Cs.* — *miṅ-čan* having a name, *dpal-˳byór miṅ-čan* one of the name of Paljor. — *miṅ-ṫon* v. *˳ṫón-pa.* — *miṅ-mṫá* final letter *Cs.* — *miṅ-sbyár* compound name. — *miṅ-méd* 1. nameless. 2. the fourth finger. — *miṅ-ṫsig* word, appellation. — *miṅ-γži* the first letter of the root of a word, in contradistinction to the second, the third, and the prefix-letters, *miṅ-γži rkyáṅ-pa* a single initial, e. g. ཀ, including ཀྱ, ཀྲ, ཀླ, *Zam.*; *γnyis-sbrél*, *γsum-sbrél* a double, triple, letter, like ཀྱ, ཀྱྭ; *Cs.*(?) — *miṅ-bzáṅ* good reputation *Cs*

མིང་པོ་ *miṅ-po* **brother** in relation to his sister, *miṅ-sriṅ* brother and sister; *de ṅa daṅ miṅ-sriṅ-du byao Dzl.* her and myself I shall make to be sister and brother, i.e. I shall raise her to be my sister.

མིད་ *mid* **a large fish** *Cs.*; *mid-mid* id.

མིད་པ་ *mid-pa* 1. sbst. **gullet, oesophagus** *Mil.* and elsewh.; *mid-skráṅ* a tumour of it, incident to horses *Sch.* — 2. vb. **to swallow, to gulp down,** frq.

མིན་ *min*, W. **man**, 1. for *ma yin* (he, she, it) **is not,** *ṡa-min-ṫsil-min Mil.* they are neither 'flesh nor fat'. — 2. abbrev. for *min-pa* and *min-par* v. below; *btaṅ-min* for **btaṅ yin-nam ma yin** W. will it be given or not? *min-pa* and *ma yin-pa* **to be not;** often as a participle supplying the place of a prep. or adv. (for *min-par*), **excepted, except, besides,** *de ma yin-pai ṡiṅ Stg.* the other trees except this one; *klu ma yin-pa γžan mi ṫub Dzl.* except he that is a Lu cannot . . .; *saṅs-rgyás min-pa sus kyaṅ mi ṡes Mil.* besides Buddha no one knows of it, no one knows it except Buddha; *ṅas yug γčig min-pa mi bsdad Mil.* I have been sitting down only this moment; *ro zér-ba min-pa skyab-pai miṅ mi yoṅ-ba ˳dug Mil.* one can only say 'corpse', and the appellation '*skyab-pa*' is not admissible; *de min* **besides, otherwise, else, apart from, setting aside** *Mil.*; even: *de-min-rnams Glr.* those that are not doing so. Cf. *man.*

མིནྡ་ *min-da* v. *mi-mda*, sub *mi* compounds.

མིམ་ *mim*, the Hind. *mĕm*, **Madam,** *mim sá-heb* the mistress or lady of the house.

མིར་ *mir* termin., མིས་ *mis* instrum. case of *mi.*

མུ་ *mu* 1. num. fig.: 76. — 2. sbst. **border, boundary, limit, edge, end,** *žiṅ-mu-la γnás-pai lha* deity residing on the landmark; *mú-la skye* (the plant) grows on the edges of fields *Wdṅ.*; *mṫa méd-čiṅ mu med Stg.* there is neither limit nor end; *mu bži = mṫa bži Mil*, *S.g.* seems to be used in a philosophical sense for 'perfect limitedness'; *mu-ḱyúd* **circumference, compass,** the **hoops** of a cask *Sch.*, the **rim** of a wheel *Stg.*; *mu-ḱyud-˳dzin* n.p., the least of the seven mountains surrounding the Sumeru. *mú-stegs-pa*, also *mú-stegs-čan* *Ssk.* **तीर्थिक** (overlooking the word *stegs*) it is gen. explained in an intellectual sense, so by Cunningham: adherents of the doctrine of finite existence (Bhilsa Topes), *Cs.*: the doctrine of perpetual duration or of perpetual annihilation(?); but should not rather *mú-stegs* be the same as *˳báb-stegs* (v. *˳báb-pa*), being a literal translation of **तीर्थ**. and therefore prop. a Brahmanic ascetic (v. *Ssk.* dict.), in Buddhist literature always equivalent to Brahmanist, Non-Buddhist, heretic (infidel)? — 3. *Sch* has besides: *mú-la* in a circle, continuously; *mu-ltar* or *mú-nas* = *bžin-du C.*; in *W* they say: **mu čig-la bor** throw it together on a heap!

མུགེ་ *mú-ge* 1. *W.* **desire, appetite,** **zan za-če** or **čaṅ ťún-čeï mú-ge rag** I have a longing for food, for beer; *mú-ge-čan* fond of dainties, lickerish, of men and animals. — 2. *B.* and col., **famine,** *mú-ge ˳byuṅ Dzl.*, *Mil.* a famine is caused, breaks out.

མུ་ཅོར་ *mu-čór* **nonsense,** *smrá-ba Stg.* to talk nonsense.

མུ་ཏིག་ *mú-tig* **pearl** frq., *mú-tig-rgyan* a pearl ornament *Cs*; *mu-tig-čún-po*, *mu-tig-drá-ba Glr.* garland formed of pearls; *mu-tig-ṗreṅ* string of pearls.

མུ་ཐི་ལ་ *mu-ťi-la* **mother of pearl** *Sch.*(?).

མུ་ནི་ *mu-ni Ssk.* **saint, ascetic, anchorite,** chiefly in names: *Sā-kya-mu-ni* the saint of the Sākyas, Buddha.

མུ་ནི་ཏི་ *mu-ni-ti Sch.* = *mu-tig*(?).

མུ་མེན་ *mu-mén Glr., Mil.* a precious stone, of a dark blue, yet inferior to the azure-stone, occasionally used for rosaries; mention is also made of *mu-mén dmár-po Wdṅ.*

མུ་རྩོད་ *mu-rtsód*(?) **colt's foot,** Tussilago farfara *Lh.*

མུ་ཟི་ *mú-zi* **brimstone, sulphur** *Med.*, *mú-zi-čan* containing sulphur, sulphurous; *mú-zii skyúr-rtsi* (*snum Schr.*) sulphuric acid *Cs.*(?).

མུ་རན་ *mu-rán* **hoop,** of casks etc. *Sch.*

མཱུ་ལ་ *mū-la Ssk.*, **root;** particular roots, such as those of Arum campanulatum, so perh. *Lt.*

མུག་གེ་ *múg-ge* sometimes for *mú-ge.*

མུག་པ་ *múg-pa*, 1. sbst. **moth, worm,** *múg-ma* id. *Glr.*, also *múṅ-ma*; *gós-mug* clothes-moth, *bál-mug* id., *lčágs-mug* a worm that eats iron away (?) *Cs.*; *múg-zan* moth-eaten, destroyed by worms *Cs.* — 2. vb. with *yid-*, *yi-*, resp. *ťugs-*, **to despair** *Pth.*; *blo múg-po* a gloomy, doleful way of thinking *Sch.*

མུན་པ་ *mun-pa* 1. sbst. **obscurity, darkness,** frq. — *mún-pai smàg-rúm* id., frq.; *mún-pa-nas mún-par ˳gro Dzl.* they wander in eternal darkness; *mún-pa sél-ba* to lighten the darkness; frq. fig. with and without *bloi.* — 2. adj. **obscure, dark.** — 3. vb. in *W.*, *mun soṅ* he has become insensible. — **Comp.** *mún-ḱaṅ* dark room, e.g. the sanctuary containing the images of the gods *Glr.*; prison *Cs.* — *mún-ḱuṅ Dzl.* prison, dungeon. — **mun-ṭig* Lh.*, *mun-ḱród Dzl.*, **mun-nág* W.*, *C.*, *mun-brág Sch.* and *Lh.*(?) close darkness. — **mun-ḍúl*, or *mun-nyúg táṅ-če* W.* to grope in the dark. — **mún-ču*, *núm-ču* W.* the dusk of evening, **mún (-ču) rub** sets in. — **mún-(s)pe-ra táṅ-če* W.* to talk confusedly, wildly. — *mun-sprúl Tar.* 56,17, to judge by the context: ignorance, stupidity; so *Schf.* — *mun-sribs Lex.* the darkness of night. — *mun-sró* furious passion, **mún-sro yoṅ dug* W.* he rages in his passion. — **mun-srós* = *mún-ču* W.*

མུམ་ *mum* (*Hind.*) *W.* **wax.**

མུར་ *mur* 1. termin. of *mu*, hence *mur-ťug* **to the extremity, till the end of** *Cs.*; perh. also *mur-dúm* (or *-zlum?*) *Ld.* **dull,** of knives, hatchets; *múr-˳dug* = *mú-stegs-pa Sch.* — 2. **gills** of fish.

མུར་གོང་ *mur-goṅ* **the temples** *Sch.*; *mur-˳grám* id. *Cs.*; **jaw, jaw-bone** *Sch.* — *mur-ťór* ulcers in the mouth *Sch.*

མུར་བ་ *múr-ba* 1. **to gnaw,** to destroy by gnawing, to bite asunder, e.g. bones *Thgr.* — 2. **to masticate, to chew**(?).

སྨུལ་སྟུག་ *mul-túg W.* **fist,** **mul-túg čó-če, gám-če** to threaten with the fist, **gyáb-če** to strike with the fist.

མེ་ *me* I. num. fig.: 106. — II. sbst. 1. resp. *žugs C.*, **nán-me** *W.*, **fire,** *me ₒbar* the fire burns, *šor* breaks out, *mčed* spreads, *ši* is extinguished; **me són-na** *W.* is the fire burning (again)? *kán-pa mes* (vulgo **mé-la**) *bsregs*, *šor*, *kyer* the house is burnt down, **dugs son** *W.* ignited, burnt (partially); *me sbór-ba, ₒbúd-pa, γtón-ba B.*, *(*s*)*bár-če, pú-če, dúg-če** *W.* to light a fire, *γsó-ba*, **són-te čó-če** *W.* to stir, poke, trim the fire, **nyál-če** *W.* to cover the glowing embers with ashes, in order to preserve the heat; *rgyáb-pa* 1. **to set on fire,** *kyim-la* a house *Glr.* 2. **to strike fire** *W.*, *me ldé-ba B.* and col., to warm one's self at the fire. — 2. symb. num.: 3. —

Comp. *me-skám* cock (of a gun), **me-kám jar tsar** *W.* the gun is cocked. — *me-skyógs C.* a shovel for live coals. — *me-sgyógs, gyogs* = *sgyogs* 2. — *me-mgál* **fire-brand,** *me-mgál-gyi kór-lo* the circle made by a firebrand, when quickly swung round *Cs.* — **me-dón** **torch** *C.* — *mé-čan* fiery, containing fire. – *me-lčágs* fire-steel, pocket-fire. — *mé-lče* flame of fire. — *me-čá* fire-steel (?) *Sch.*, **me - čé** *C.* every thing requisite for kindling a fire, as it is got in readiness for the following morning. — *me-mnyam-rlún* v. *rlun*. — **me-tág** *C.* 1. (*rtags*) a mark of burning. 2. (*ltag* or *stag*) **spark, sparklet,** a bit of live coal in the ashes. — *me-táb* fire-place, hearth; stove. — *me-dón Dzl.* fire-pit, pool of fire. — *me-dród* v. *drod.* — **me-dá** *C.*, musket, pistol; **me-da pag-čén** canon *Schr.*; **me-dá gyáb-pa** to discharge a gun; **me-da-šin** resinous wood, the coal of which is particularly used for making gun-powder. —**me-dág** (*mdag*) *C.* coals glowing underneath the ashes. — *me-rdél* bullet, musket-ball *Sch.* — *me-rdó* flint *Cs.* — *me-núr Sch.* = *me-mdág.* — *me-snód*, or *-pór* coal-pan, chafing-dish, perfuming-pan. — *me-pún, me-búm* cupping-glass, cup *Lt.* — *mé-ba Dzl.* = *me.* — *mé-bo* = *me* a large fire, *mé-bo če Dzl.* — *me-dbál* a disease *Med.*; it is said to be a cutaneous eruption, hot and smarting, perh. erysipelas? — *me-múr* = *me-mdág Dzl.*; *me-ma-múr Thgy.* id.? — *me-btsá* v. *btsa.* — **me - tság** spark *W.* — **me-dzé** **gun-powder** *C.* — *me-γži* anvil *Sch.* — *me-γžób* mark of singeing, of having caught fire. — **me-zi** *W.* = *me-ltág.* — *me-ₒóbs* = *me-dón Sch.* — *mé-ri* fire-mountain, introduced by us for **volcano.** — *me - rís* a figure resembling a flame *Sch.* — *me-ró* an extinguished fire, fig. *bstán-pai me-ró lan Glr.* the extinct doctrine revives again. — **me-lín** *W.* flame. — *me-lén* fire-tongs. — *me-šél* burning-glass. — *me-lhá* the god of fire, v. *Schl.* 251 sqq. — III. v. also *mé-tog.*

མེ་ཉག་ *me-nyág* v. *mi-nyág.*

མེ་ཏོག་ *mé-tog, W.* **mén-tog**, 1. **flower,** *mé-tog ₒbar, ka ₒbus* the flower opens, begins to bloom, *mé-tog-gi prén-ba* chaplet, wreath of flowers. — 2. *W.* **tuft** or **crest** on the head of some birds. — 3. *W.* **snow-flake.**

མེ་ལོང་ *mé-lon* 1. **mirror, looking-glass,** frq.; *lás-kyi mé-lon* a magic mirror, revealing the future *Glr.*; also fig., esp. in titles of books, e.g. *rgyal-rábs-kyi γsál-bai mé-lon* A bright Mirror of the History of Kings. 2. **plain surface,** flat body extending in length and breadth, e.g. the flatness of the shoulder-blade, table-top, door-pannels etc., hence *sgo mé-lon-can Glr.* an opening provided with a frame of boards to close it, not merely an 'ostium', of which description most of the inner doors in Tibetan houses are.

མེའུར་ *meaₒo* **the mewing of a cat.**

མེད་པ་ *méd-pa* for *mi yód-pa* **to be not, to exist not** (v. *yód-pa*), *med* he is not here, he is gone etc.; **ka-čúl-du son-te med** *W.* he is off, having gone to Kashmere; **čag-mag ǎ-pe kyér-te med** *W.* the tinder-box is not here, father has taken it with him; **ši-te med** *W.* he is dead and gone; *skabs med Dzl.* there is, or there was, no opportunity; *čos-kyi min tsam yan med Glr.* religious law does not, or did not, exist at all; *med kyan* even if nothing is extant, though the thing does not exist in reality; **ni méd-na yaṅ yoṅ dug** the '*ni*' may be dispensed with, though '*ni*' be omitted, it will be all right; *rgyá-la méd-pai yi-ge drug Glr.* six letters not existing in Sanskrit; *méd-kyaṅ-ruṅ-bai yig-ₒbru γčig* a letter that may also be wanting, a dispensable letter, e.g. ཟྰ *Glr.*; *méd-kyaṅ dgós-pai k̔ral-bsdúd Mil.* a taxation necessary, and even if one possesses nothing, yet as it were inexorable; *méd-pa* (*W.* **méd-k̔an**) not being, not existing, not having; *blá-ma-la bžúgs-grogs méd-pa lágs-sam Mil.* has your Reverence no fellow-resident in your house? fem. *méd-ma Mil.*; *W.* **mu dud-pa-méd-k̔an** very or quite smokeless; *mi brnáṅs-pa skyúg-tu méd-pa míd-du méd-pa Dzl.* a man about to be choked, being neither able to spit out, nor to swallow down; *bdag* (or *bdag-la*) *čaṅ dbul-du med Dzl.* we are not able to give any thing; *med-mi-rúṅ-gi bu-tsá Mil.* the sons and grandsons that are to get something (as a heritage); *k̔yim der méd-du mi γtúb-pa*, or *mi rúṅ-ba* indispensable in the house *Thgy.*; so also *med-t̔abs-méd-pai blón-po Glr.*; *méd-par ₒgyúr-ba* to be annihilated, to disappear, *stág-mo méd-par gyúr-to Pth.* the tigress disappeared; *γnam daṅ sa yaṅ med-gyur-na Dzl.* when heaven and earth shall pass away; **da ṅa čiaṅ méd-k̔an soṅ** *W.* now I am quite undone; *blón-po-rnams ₒgran-sems-méd-par gyur-to Glr.* the ministers lost their litigiousness, gave up quarreling; *zas brim-du méd-par gyúr-to Dzl.* the distribution of the dishes became impossible; **pé-ra zér-če méd-k̔an soṅ** *W.* he became speechless; *med-par byéd-pa* to annihilate, an enemy *Dzl.*, to put an end to, a quarrel *Glr.*; frq. *méd-pa(r)* may be rendered by 'without': *rgyál-po žig méd-na mi ruṅ*, or *t̔abs-méd Pth.* we cannot do without a king; *mt̔a-rten-méd-pai mt̔a* a termination without a final consonant *Gram.*; *rgyu méd-par S. g.* without cause; or by 'instead of': *rgyál-po méd-par Glr.* instead of the king, *sṅár-gyi lus méd-par Glr.* instead of the former shape; *nyin-mtsan-méd-par* making no difference between day and night, *p̔o-mo-méd-par* between male and female, *rgan-byis-méd-par* old and young; vulgo also *nyin-med-mtsán-med* etc. — *méd-po*, *W.* **méd-k̔an**, fem. *méd-mo*, a poor man, pauper.

མེན་ *men Mil.* **an ornament, piece of finery.**

མེནྡི་ *mendi*, *Ssk.* मेन्धी, Lawsonia alba, a plant used for staining the finger-nails red *Mil.*

མེན་ཙི་ *mén-tsi* **a coloured silk handkerchief** *W.*

མེན་ཧྲི་ *mén-hri* a kind of **fur**? *mén-hri dmár-poi slóg-pa* a fur-coat of red *men-hri* is mentioned as the vesture of a Lha.

མེར་ *mer* termin. of *me.*

མེར་བ་ *mér-ba Cs.*: 'a quaking; thinness; *mér-po*, *mer-mér* thin, as liquids'; *Sch.*: '*mér-gyis gaṅ* full to the brim'. I met with 1. *mer* in *žig-mér* q.v. — 2. *mér-ba* as adj. for *mtso* the lake *Mil.* — 3. **mer-mér** *W.* adj. **like a thin pap**, and sbst. **a muddy substance**, e.g. street-mire; **mer-mér čó-če** to make a mire. — 4. *mér-mer-ba* adj in connection with such sbst. as light, ray, beam, brightness *Thgr.*, *Mil.* — 5. *mér-mer-po* used in medical writings in a similar manner as *núr-nur-po*, to define the shape of an embryo, **oblong, oval**; these descriptions, however, though partly founded on observation, are frequently very arbitrary, vague, and even contradictory. In *W.* the word has only the signification 3; a Lama from *C.* rendered it with **'full'**, which would agree with *Sch.* and no. 1, as well as with 'glittering, quivering', having some relation to no. 2 and no. 4.

མེལ་ཚེ་ or ཙེ་ *mél-tse* or *-tse* 1. **watch, watchman, sentinel; watcher, spy**, *mél-tse byéd-pa* to watch, to keep watch *Dzl.*; *ǰá-ra-mel-tse* = **mel-tse** *W.* — 2. **steatite** or **soap-stone**, of a greenish colour.

མེས་པོ་ *més-po*, vulgo **me-mé**, **grandfather**; also **forefather, ancestor, progenitor**, *saṅs-rgyás t̔ams-čád-kyi spyi-mes kun-tu-bzáṅ-po Thgr. Kuntuzaṅpo*, the common progenitor of all the Buddhas; *mes rgyál-po Glr.* merely equivalent to 'the old king';

ṗa-més the grandfather by the father's, *ma-més* by the mother's side *Cs*; *yaṅ-més* great-grandfather *Glr.*; *ẑe-* or *γẑi-més Sch.* great-great-grandfather; *mes-dbón* grandfather and grandchildren, resp., e.g *rgyál-po mes-dbón* the kings from one generation to another, the royal ancestors *Glr.*; *mes-rábs* id. *Sch.*; **me-mé**, reverential name given to men of a more advanced age *W.* also *C.*

མེ་ཏྲི *me-tri*, **मैत्रेय**, v. *byáms-pa Mil.*

མོ *mo*, I num. figure: 136.

II. **woman, female,** opp. to *ṗo*, = *bud-méd*: *mo na-re* the woman said *Glr.*, *Mil.*; of animals: **female.** — **mo-kyáṅ* W.* virgin. — *mo-gós* woman's gown, petticoat. — *mo-brgyúd* female line of descent. — *mo-bí* female calf. — *mo-byis Mil.*, *mo-dbyis* (**mo-yi**) *C.* girl, female child. — *mo-btsún* nun *Glr.* — *mo-mtśán*, *moi dbáṅ-po* female genitals. — *mo-ráṅ-(mo)* 1. **single, unmarried woman,** so perh. in the passage, *γdoṅ ṅán-gyi ḱyó-bas mo-ráṅ skyid* happier is a single woman than one with a husband of a bad face; more frq., the word implies 2. **a poor, destitute female,** one who did not get a husband *W.* 3. **she, herself** *C.*, *Lew.* — *mo-rí*, *mo-ré* a female kid. — *mo-rigs* female sex. *Cs.* — *mo-lús* the female body *Sch.* — *mo-γšám* a barren female, hence *mo-γšám-gyi bu* a nonsense, an incongruity.

III. **lot,** *mo ˛débs-pa* to cast the lot, always a religious ceremony performed by Lamas (cf. *rgyan* and *rtags-ril*), which however does not preclude the possibility of an imposture; *mó-pa* one dealing with these practices, a soothsayer, *mó-pa ˛dre mtóṅ-ba* a soothsayer that pretends to have seen a ghost; *mó-mḱan Cs.*, *mó-rtsis-pa Glr.* id. (the latter expression in the respective passage = court-astrologer); *mo-ma* the feminine of it *Cs.*, which however is at variance with *Mil.*, who in several places has *bla-ma mḱas-pai mo-ma.*

IV. **affix,** so-called article, corresponding to the masc. terminations *po* and *pa*, and denoting the fem. gender of persons, *bú-mo* daughter, *bód-mo* a Tibetan woman.

མོ་ཁབ *mo-ḱáb* v. *ḱab.*

མོག་པ *mióg-pa* **dark** (coloured) *Cs.*; *móg-ro* of horses, yellowish-brown *Glr.*

མོག་མོག *mog-móg* 1. *Cs.* = *móg-pa.* — 2. **meat-pie,** meat-balls in a cover of paste.

མོག་ཤ *móg-ša* **mushroom** *W.*

མོགས་ཙ་ར *mógs-tsa-ra Lt.* n. of a plant; in *Lh.* *mog-ša-ras* is a large species of Ferula or Dorema, of a yellow flower and a fetid smell.

མོང་གོལ *móṅ-gol* **a Mongul** *Tib.* *sóg-po.*

མོང་རྟུལ *moṅ-rtúl Lex.* = *blún-po* **dull, stupid.**

མོང་ལོ *móṅ-lo*, *W.* for *lóṅ-mo* **knuckle, anklebone.**

མོད *mod* **moment,** occurring only in the following combinations: *láṅ-bai mod (de-nyid)-la* at the very moment of rising *Pth.*, *Mil.*, *dei mód-la* the moment after *Glr.*; gen. *mód-la* **instantly, immediately,** *mód-la dráṅs-so Glr.* he immediately pulled it out; *ḱra yaṅ mód-la ṗyin-te Dzl.* immediately after there came also the hawk; *dé-nas mód-la* id. *Dzl.*

མོད་པ *mód-pa* (cognate to *mád-pa?*) an emphatic word for **to be,** 1. as an augmentative of *yin*, sometimes superadded to this word; occasionally untranslatable, sometimes = **indeed, to be sure,** *ẑes smras mód-kyi Dzl.* though indeed you may say so; *dpag-tu-méd mód-kyi* though indeed it is immeasurable *Dzl.*; *γsa dé-ka ṅa yin mod Mil.* the snow-leopard indeed was I myself; *di ma yin mod ˛on-kyaṅ* ... to be sure, it is not this one, yet... *Tar.*; *˛gró-ba yin mod* (although not invited) yet after all you must go. — 2. as augmentative of *yod*, signifying abundance, plenty *B.*, *C.*, *W.*; *de mi byéd-na dgra mod* if you omit to do this, you will have plenty of enemies, *nad mod* plenty of diseases; *sti-bstáṅ-gi ḱrims šiṅ-tu mód-kyi* although they abounded in compliments; *mód-pa* having an abundance, *loṅs-spyód mód-par ˛gyur* he becomes the owner of great wealth *Dzl.*; *šiṅ-tog mód-*

pa Glr. abounding in tree-fruit; *mód-po* adj. plentiful, abounding, *kúl-lu-ru śiṅ mód-po* in Kullu wood is plentiful, or *śiṅ mód-poi yul* (Kullu is) a country abounding in wood, opp. to *dkón-po*, hence 'cheap' may occasionally stand for it.

མོན་ *mon* 1. n. p., general name for the different nations living between Tibet and the Indian plain *Mil : món-yul-gyi bán-dhe* a monk from Nepal; *Glr.: dpal-gro món-la* Paldo in Bhotan; *mon-ta-waṅ* is stated to be a commercial place in Assam, from whence much rice is brought to Tibet; the people of Lahoul are looked upon by the real Tibetans as Mon, though for the most part they speak the Tibetan language, and they in their turn consider the Hindoos in Kullu as Mon; that this appellation is often extended to the Hindoos in general, appears from such names as, *món-gre, món-sran* Indian pea, *Phaseolus radiatus*, **माष**; *món-ča-ra* the ever-green oak and its fruit, of the southern Himalaya ridges *Wdṅ.*; in *Ld.* the musicians (*Ld.-Glr. Schl.* 25, b), carpenters, and wood-cutters coming from the south, are likewise denominated Mon. — The form *mon-pa Cs.* is not known to me; *mon-mo* fem. *Pth.* — 2. sometimes for *mun.*

མོན་ཞ་ *mon-ža* (or perh. *yža*) *W.*, **popularity, respect, reputation**, *món-ža tob* he makes himself generally beloved, is highly respected; *món-ža-čan* **beloved, popular**.

མོར་ *mor* termin. of *mo.*

མོལ་བ་ *mól-ba* the usual resp. term, esp. in *W.*, for **to say, to speak,** as *bsgó-ba* and *bká-rtsal-ba* are used in earlier, and *ysúṅ ba* in later literature and in *C.*, hence it is often to be rendered by 'to order'; **sá-heb-la sa-lám mol žu** have the goodness to present (say) my compliments to that gentleman; **mól-lče táṅ-če** to flatter, to caress; **mól-la táṅ-wa** *C.* to make known(?).

མོས་པ་ *mós-pa* vb. and sbst. **to be pleased** *la* **with, to wish, to have a mind,** *ˌgró-bar mós-so Glr.* I took a fancy to go there; *ču-la sógs-par mós-na Thgy.* if you wish for water or something of the kind; *mós-pa daṅ ˌdód-pa S.O.* desiring and coveting (are the origin of all the misery of sin); **to take pleasure in, to rejoice at,** *mós-pai glu Glr.* song of rejoicing; as sbst.: **pleasure, satisfaction, esteem** — 2. **to respect, to esteem,** with *la*, to respect with devotion, **to revere, to adore** *čós-la* frq.; *k̔yod gúṅ-la mos* to whom do you direct your devotions? *Mil.*; *mós-nas ˌbúl-ba yin* I give it merely from devout veneration, i.e. I shall take nothing for it *Pth.*; frq. joined with *gús-pa*: *yid-mos-gús drág-pos* with fervent veneration; *dad-mós* devotion; *mos spyód-pa* as participle, a pious man, a devotee *Tar.* 109, 7.

མྱ་ངན་ *mya-ṅán*, **trouble, misery, affliction,** *mya-ṅán-gyis ydúṅ-ste Dzl.*; *mya-ṅán či yaṅ med Dzl.* I have no trouble, no uneasiness, whatever; *mya-ṅán bsal Tar.* the time of mourning is at an end; *mya-ṅán byéd-pa* to lament, to wail; *mya-ṅan-méd*, **अशोक**. n. of a famous king of ancient India *Glr.*, *Tar.* ch. VI; *mya-ṅán-las ˌdás-pa*, abbr. *myaṅ-ˌdas* (and so also pronounced, as for instance in a verse of *Mil.*, where it occurs as a trochee) 'having been delivered from pain', the usual, illiteral, Tibetan version of **निर्वाण**, the absolute cessation of all motion and excitement both of body and mind, which is necessarily connected with personal existence; absolute rest, which by orientals is thought to be the highest degree of happiness, imagined by some as a perfect annihilation of existence, by others, more or less, only as a cessation of all that is unpleasant in human existence, — well set forth by *Köpp.* I. 304 sqq.

མྱ་ངམ་ *mya-ṅam* **a fearful desert** *Lex.*, *Thgy.*

མྱག་པ་ *myág-pa Sch.* **'to chew'**; acc. to medical writings, **the chemical decomposition** of the chyme in the stomach; **to cause putrefaction**; pf. *myags*; *myágs-par byéd-pa* = *myag-pa S.g.*; *rul-čiṅ myágs-pa Dzl.* decomposed, putrefied; *ro-myágs* the watery product of putrefaction, *'tabes' Thgy.*

མྱང་བ་ *myáṅ-ba* v. *myoṅ-ba.*

མྱད་པ་ *myád-pa Sch.* = *mid-pa* sbst.

སྨྱིང་ *myiṅ Sch.* = *miṅ.*

སྨྱུ་གུ་ *myú-gu*, **སྨྱུག་** *myug*, 1. *Sch.* **reed, rush, flag,** also = *smyú-gu.* — 2. *Cs.* **sprout,** the first shoot of corn etc., *myú-gu snón-po Thgy* the young green corn.

སྨྱུག་པ་ *myúg-pa, myúg-myug-pa* 1. **to run, roam, stroll idle about** *Sch.* — 2. **to show, exhibit ostentatiously, to boast with** *Cs.* v. *dmyúg-pa.*

སྨྱུར་བ་ *myúr-ba* **quick, swift, speedy,** *myúr-po* id. *Mil.*; mostly as adv., *myúr-du* **quickly, speedily; soon;** *či-myúr* as speedily as possible; *myur-du-btsá-rtags* symptoms of immediate parturition *Med.*

སྨྱུལ་བ་ *myúl-ba* **to examine closely, to search into, to scrutinize,** c. accus. or termin. of place *Stg.*, *Mil.*, prob. but a different spelling for *nyúl-ba.* — *lče-myúl Mṅg.*, *Lt.* a symptom of disease, acc. to *Wise* p. 282: a quivering motion of the tongue.

སྨྱོ་བ་ *myó-ba* v. *smyó-ba.*

སྨྱོང་བ་ *myóṅ-ba*, pf. *myaṅs*, also *myoṅ*, fut. *myaṅ W.* **nyáṅ-če**, 1. **to taste** *Dzl.*; **to try by tasting,** *myaṅ-bas žim-po ťsor-nas* perceiving the relish by tasting; *ro myóṅ-ba* **dob-lág nyáṅ-če** *W.*, id.; **to enjoy,** *mťo-ris-kyi loṅs-spyód* the bliss of paradise *Dzl.*; *myóṅ-bar byéd-pa* to make, or to permit to, enjoy, *ḱyod čós-kyi zas myóṅ-bar byao* I shall make thee enjoy the food of religious doctrine *Sch.*, yet it may be rendered also more simply: thou wilt enjoy ... *Dzl.* ༧༢, b. — 2. in philosophy: **to perceive,** in relation to the perceptions of sense, *Ssk.* वेदन. — 3. **to experience, to suffer,** both good and evil, *sdug-bsṅal*, distress etc. frq.; **to get,** *mi-sdúg-pai lus* an ugly body; seldom with termin., *γnás-skabs γžán-du myóṅ-bar ˳gyúr-bai lás-rnams* works which would bring upon their author another state of existence (after his death) *Thgy.*; *myóṅ-bar mi ˳gyúr-ba* to be preserved from *Dom.*; *raṅ-gi byás-pa ráṅ-gi myóṅ-ba yin Pth.* your own doings are your own sufferings; as you have brewed, so you must drink. — 4. auxil. of the pf. like *byuṅ*, but chiefly in negative sentences: *btsal ma myoṅ Dzl.* I have never yet sought, *mťoṅ ma myoṅ Mil.* I have never yet seen, *ťos ma myoṅ Mil.* I have never yet heard, — a construction, that has originated from the earlier one c. inf.: *rdzun smrá-ba ma myoṅ, dgé-bai sems skyéd-pa ma myoṅ* dealing with falsehood, producing virtuous thoughts, has never happened to me yet *Dzl.*

དམའ་བ་ *dmá-ba* **to be low,** *dbus dma mťa γnyis mťó-na* if (in pregnancy) the middle parts of the body are low, and the sides high *Med.*; sbst. **lowness;** adj., also *dmá-mo*, **low,** low water, low voice, low rank, short measure or weight, frq.; *dmá-la ḱyád-du γsód-pa* to despise the low and humble *Lt.*; *dmá-na* if I live in humble circumstances *Dom.*; *ṅá-yis mťo mťo byás-pa dma dma byuṅ* aspiring higher and higher, I fell deep *Pth.*; of religion: *čúṅ-zad dmá-bai dús-su* as it had somewhat fallen into decay *Pth.*; *dma ˳bébs-pa* (frq. written *sma*) *W.* **ma bab kál-če**, and intrs. *dma ˳báb-pa* to lower, to degrade, by words: **to abuse, to vilify** *Do.* by deeds: **to deface, to deform, to mar** *Pth.*; **to disgrace, dishonour, profane** *Pth.*; **to humiliate** *Tar.*; **to oppress, to ruin** *Schr.*; **ma-bab-čan** *W.* humiliated, brought low. — *dmá-sa* 1. *Sch.* low land (?) 2. = *dmán-sa.* — Cf. *dmán-pa.*

དམག *dmag Lexx.* सेना 1. **army, host,** *dmag-tsógs, dmag-dpúṅ*, less frq. *dmag-γséb* id.; *dmag daṅ bčás-pa* with an army *Tar.*; *mí-la dmag skyúr-ba* to commit the command of an army to a person *Glr.*; *yúl-la dmag ˳dren-pa* to lead an army against, to invade a country, frq.; *dmag rgyág-pa Glr.*, **mag ťáb-pa** *C.* to war, to make or wage war, *dmag-rgyág* (or *dmag-˳drén*) *res máṅ-du byéd-pa* to make war upon each other *Glr.*; *mú-stegs-pai dmág-gis bzuṅ* he was made a prisoner by an army of Brahmanists *Glr.*; *dmag stoṅ* 1000 men *Pth.*; *dmág-gi ťsogs stoṅ-ṕrág súm-ču* an army of 30000 men *Dzl.* — 2. in a gen. sense, **multitude, number, host,** **mag-liṅ(s)** *W.* a beating up of game, a battue; **mag-nor** property of the community, = *(*s*)*pi-nor** *W.* — 3. *Cs.* and *Sch.* **war.** —

Comp. *dmag-k̔rims* 'martial law' *Cs.* — **mag-ṭ̔úg** *W.* **war, contention, contest.** — *dmag-mgó Ma.* vanguard, front or first line of the army. — *dmag-sgár* encampment, *ₒdégs-pa* to pitch a camp. — *dmag-bsgrig* troops drawn up, battle-array *Sch.* — *dmag-čás* requisites for war, military stores, ammunition *Pth.* — **mag-t̔áb* C., W.* war. — *dmag-nór* v. above sub no. 2 *mag-nór.*—*dmag-sná* = *dmag-mgó Ma.* — *dmag-dpúṅ* army. — *dmag-dpón* commander, general. — *dmag-bráṅ* = *dmag-sgár.* — *dmag-mí* warrior, soldier. — *dmág-mo* = *dmag*, *dmág-mo če bskúr-ba Pth.* to send out a great army. — *dmag-ts̔ógs* = *dmag-dpúṅ.* — *dmag-líṅs* v. above.

དམག་པ་ *dmág-pa* v. མག་པ་ *mág-pa.*

དམངས་ *dmaṅs* **the common people, populace, multitude, vulgar;** *dmáṅs-kyi stón-mo* a banquet for all *Mil.*; *dmaṅs p̔ál-pa* the vulgar, the common people; one of the common people; *dmáṅs-rigs* id.; used also as an abusive word: **mean fellow;** when referred to Indian matters = शूद्र the caste of craftsmen, not so low as *γdól-ba.*

དམད་པ་ *dmád-pa Sch.* invective, abuse, (does not suit to *S.g.* 21).

དམན་པ་ *dmán-pa* (cf. *dmá-ba*) 1. **low,** v. *mt̔ó-ba;* gen. fig., in reference to quantity, **little,** *dman lhag log* either too little, or too much, or badly constituted, e.g. gall, and other humours of the human body *Med.*; *bsód-nams dmán-pa* having little merit, *blo dmán-pa* having little sense *Glr.*; with *skye-ba* v. *skye-ba* II.; in reference to quality: **indifferent, inferior** *Ssk.* हीन, *rim-pas dáṅ-po mčog yin p̔yi-ma dman* in the order (of enumeration) the first is always better, the next following inferior *S.g.*; **men-šár** maiden, girl, virgin *C.* (cf. *skye-dmán*); **depressed in spirits** *Wdṅ.*; **poor, pitiable,** *ri-dwágs dmán-ma* the poor deer *Mil.*; *dmán-sa* or *dman-ča*, *ₒdzín-pa* to choose the low, humble part, to be humble, to humble one's self, frq.; *dmán-sa zuṅ daṅ mt̔ó-sar sleb Mil.* choose what is low, and you will obtain what is high. — 2. *dman* for *skye-dmán* **woman,** opp. to *p̔o Mil.* — 3. in *Mil.* sometimes also for *má-mo, srin-mo.*

དམར་ *dmar* **profit, gain, good success,** *dmar čuṅ* a small profit *Mil*; *dmár-po* adj., *t̔ugs-dám dmár-po byúṅ-ṅam* did it go on well with your meditation? *Mil.*, *dmar-k̔rid Cs.* 'practical instruction', e.g. in the healing art; acc. to my authorities it signifies the last 'finishing' instruction, in religion *Mil.*, in medical science *Med.*

དམར་པོ་ *dmár-po*, fem. *dmár-mo* (seldom), *dmár-ba*, adj. 1. **red,** frq., *mdog-dmár-po* one red-coloured (lit. red as to colour) *Dom.*; *dmár-bai spyan* red eyes *Glr.*; *sna dmár-ba* having a red trunk or proboscis *Glr.*; *dmár-ba*, also **redness and to be red.** 2. v. *dmar.* — **Comp.** *dmar-skyá* pale red. — *dmar-k̔rá Lt.*, red-spotted. — *dmar-k̔rid* v. *dmar.* — **mar-žén** raw meat *W.* — *dmar-ljáṅ* greenish red *Mil.* — **már-t̔ag čod* W.* the red of evening has vanished from the mountains. — *dmar-t̔áb?* — *dmar-t̔ór* v. *t̔ór-pa.* — *dmar-mdáṅs Sch.* 1. **bright red**(?) 2. **ruddy complexion.** — *dmar-ₒdon Lt.* medicinal herb; in *Lh.* = *bya-po-tsi-tsi.* — *dmar-nág, skud-pa dmar-nág γnyis* two threads, one black, the other red, used in magic. — *dmar-smyúg* blackish red. — *mar-zaṅ-záṅ* scarlet-red. — *dmar-yól* red china-ware (? opp. to *dkar-yól*) *Med.* — *dmar-bšál Sch.* dysentery, bloody flux. — *dmar-sér* (*-po*) reddish yellow, honey-coloured *Glr.*

དམས་པ་ *dmás-pa Cs.* **wounded.**

དམིག་པ་, དམིག་བུ་ *dmig-pa, dmig-bu Lex.* and *Cs.* **hole.**

དམིགས་ *dmigs* sbst. v. the following.

དམིགས་པ་ *dmigs-pa* 1. vb. (analogous to *sgom-pa*), **to fancy, to imagine** *Tar.* 73, 5. prob.; **to think, to construe in one's mind,** *dmigs-te Glr.* or vulgo *dmigs-la* in imagination, e.g. to do a thing in one's mind, which at the time one is not able to perform in reality; this according to a Buddhist's belief is permitted in various cases (e.g. **sém-mi mig-la p̔ul-če* W.*, to bring an offering in mind, in imagination); it is attended with the same beneficial effects, as if actually done, and in legends, especially, it is generally followed by a happy realisation of what had been desired. — *dmigs-so S.O.* prob.: it is imaginable, it may be done in mind; *don dmigs-pa* to intend a benefit or profit for another person *Mil.* — Generally 2. sbst., **thought, idea, fancy** **आलम्बन**, vulgo**mig(s)**; *dmigs-pai rten* prob.: a thing only supposed, an object imagined *Thgr.*; *dmigs-pa ži̇g ston-pa*, *ₒbógs-pa* to give (to another person) an idea of, to make a suggestion *Mil.*; **mig-la čo go** *W.* means also: do it, execute it, according to your own mind, I cannot supply you an exact pattern of it; *dmigs-čan* **ingenious, skilful** in contriving *W.*; *dmigs-pa-las ₒdás-pa = bsám-byai yúl-las ₒdás-pa?* — *yéṅs-med(-par) dmigs-pa (daṅ) brál-bas-na* indisturbable by fancies of the mind, free from every working of the imagination *Mil.*; *dmigs-pa-méd-pai snyiṅ-rje Mil.* seems to be, acc to *Thgy.* the pity which the accomplished saint, who has found every thing, even religion, to be vain and empty, feels towards all other beings, in as far as they are still subject to error and mistake, opp. to *séms-čan-la dmigs-pai snyin-rje*, and *čós-la dmigs-pai snyiṅ-rje* the tender sympathies called forth by the sight of beings that are really suffering and of those defective in morality — a play upon empty phrases, in as much as in the very narrative, from which the passage above is quoted, the natural softness of Milaraspa is evidently excited by a very positive case, and not by any reflexions of an abstract nature. — **mig-pa-ne zǒ-pa** (v. *bzó-ba*) *C.* done only in thought, supposed, fictitious; *dmigs tams-čád brjéd-nas* forgetful of all the beautiful fancies, schemes, and airy notions; *dmigs-pa gtód-pa* prob.: to direct one's thoughts, fancies, *la* to *Tar.* 189, 2. (where, no doubt, *gtád-na* is to be read); *dmigs-gtád* **mental object,** *dmigs-gtád brál-bai rnál-ₒbyor-pa* a saint that is free from such objects; acc. to our Lama also = *gtád-so* q.v.; *dmigs-gsál Lex.*; (*Sch.*: 'a clear notion'), perh. misspelt for *dmigs-bsál* exception from a rule *Gram.*; a particular mention, marking out, exemption of a person, in magisterial orders or enactments *W.* — *dmigs-bu* a blind man's leader *Dzl.*, *Lex* = *lóṅ-krid-pa.* — *nyes-dmigs Mil.* and elsewh., punishment. In the last three examples the etymological relationship is not quite evident.

དམུ་, རྨུ་ *dmu*, *rmu* a kind of **evil demon,** rarely mentioned *Lex.*; *rmu-rgód* **wild, angry, passionate;** a violent fellow, not safe to deal with *Mil.*; *dmu-bló* a wild, irascible mind *Sch.*; hence *dmus-byúṅ* terrifying, frightful *Sch.*; perh. also *dmus-lóṅ* blind, bodily blind, whilst *loṅ-ba* may be applied also to spiritual blindness *Dzl.*, *Glr.* and elsewh., and *dmu-čú* **dropsy,** esp. in the chest and in the belly *Med.*; *dmu-skrán Sch.* an oedema, tumour filled with water.

དམུན་པ་ *dmún-pa* **darkened, obscured,** *blo*; *mún-pa.*

དམུལ་བ་ *dmúl-ba* v. *ₒdzúm-pa.*

དམུར་བ་ *dmúr-ba* v. *múr-ba.*

དམུས་ལོང་ *dmús-loṅ* v. *dmu.*

དམེ་བ་ *dmé-ba* v *rmé-ba.*

དམོད་པ་ *dmód-pa* I. vb. *Cs.* **to curse, accurse, execrate,** *dmód-pa byéd-pa* id. *Tar.* 14. 17. — II. sbst. *dmod-pa Dzl.*, *dmod*, *Glr.* and elsewh., **imprecation, execration, malediction;** *dmód-mo* id.; joined with *ₒbór-ba*, *ₒdór-ba*, *ₒdzúg-pa*, *smó-ba:* 1. **to curse, to execrate,** *draṅ-sroṅ-gis dmod-pa bor-bai lo bču-gnyis* the twelve years on which a curse had been pronounced by the saint *Dzl.* 2. **to swear,** to confirm a treaty by an oath *Glr.* 3. **to pronounce a prayer** or **conjuration,** *lha-la* to the deity *Glr.* 4. **to affirm,** e.g. to say **kon-čóg še** or the like. The word seems to be nearly related both to *smód-pa*, and to *smón-pa*, but, as expressly stated by the *Lexx.*, is not synon. with these verbs.

དམྱལ་བ་ *dmyál-ba* I. vb. **to cut up,** to cut into little pieces, meat at dinner *Dzl.*, a punishment of hell *Dzl.* — II. sbst. **hell,** also *sems-čan-dmyál-ba*; *dmyál-bar ₒgró-ba* to go to hell, *dmyál-ba bčo-brgyád* the 18 regions of hell; *ťsa-dmyál* the hot hell, *graṅ-dmyál* the cold hell. → *dmyál-ba-pa*, *-po*, occupant of hell. — **nyál-wa-čan** *W.* **poor, miserable, wretched**; also like غريب *Urd.*, = my own little self, for 'I', in humble speech.

དམྱུག་པ་ *dmyúg-pa Cs.* **to show**, *dmyúg-dmyug-pa*, *dmyúg-pa byéd-pa* to show repeatedly, **to boast.** Yet cf. *myúg-pa*.

རྨ་ *rma* **wound** *B*, *C.*; *ṅá-la rma byuṅ* I was wounded; *rma ₒbyin-pa* to wound, *rma ɣsó-ba* to heal a wound; *rmai lhá-ba Sch.* 'a wound growing worse'; yet cf. *lhá-ba.* — *rmá-ǩa* 1. **the orifice** or **edges** of a wound. 2. *W.* inst. of *rma* **wound,** **rúl-li ťám-te má-ǩa ťon** he has been wounded by the bite of a serpent. — *rma-čás Sch.* **plaster, cataplasm, dressing, bandage.** — *rma-rjes Sch.* **scar,** cicatrix. — *rma-rnyiṅ* an old wound. — *rma-smán*, *rma-rtsis* medicine or salve for a wound. — *rma-mťsan* scar *Bhar.* — *rma-ró Sch.* scurf, scab. — *rma-šú* a festering, suppurating wound. — *rma-šúl* scar. — *rma-srol Sch.* the act of wounding, the wound received(?) — *rma-ɣsál* a fresh wound.

རྨ་ཆུ་ *rmá-ču* n.p., the river **Hoangho** *Glr.*

རྨ་ཆེན་ *rma-čén* v. *rmá-bya.*

རྨ་བ་ *rmá-ba*, pf. *rmas* 1. **to ask,** obs., *Lex.* 2. **to wound** *Dzl.*

རྨ་བྱ་ *rma-bya* (vulgo often **máb-ja**), मयूर, **peacock,** living wild in India, an object of superstition with Buddhists and Brahmanists. — *rma-bya-čén-po* n. of a deity *Dom.*; *rma-čén Wdk.*, महामायूरी *Will*: 'one of the 5 tutelar deities of the Buddhists'; *Sch.: rma-čen ₒbom-ra* 'lord of the yellow stream' (?).

རྨང་ *rmaṅ*, provinc. *rmiṅ Glr.* **ground, foundation.** *rmaṅ ₒdiṅ-ba* to lay a foundation *Glr.*; *rtsig-rmáṅ* id.; *rmáṅ-rdo* foundation-stone.

རྨང་འཚེར་ *rmaṅ-ₒťsér*, *smaṅ-ₒťsér* or *-ťsar Sch.* 1. **pincers** to pluck out hairs; *Cs.* instrument for cleaning the nostrils. — 2. *Sch.* **rake** (instrument).

རྨང་ལམ་ *rmáṅ-lam Sch.* = *rmi-lam*, of rare occurrence.

རྨད་པ་ *rmád-pa* or rather usually: *rmád-du byúṅ-ba*, *rmad-byúṅ* **wonderful, marvelous,** and *ṅo-mťsar-rmád-du ₒgyúr-ba* to wonder, to be surprised at, fq.

རྨན་པ་ *rmán-pa Sch.* **wounded;** *rmás-pa* v. *rmá-ba.*

རྨི་བ་ *rmí-ba*, pf. *rmis*, **to dream;** *rmi-lam* resp. *mnál-lam* **a dream,** *rmi-lam za-zi* a troubled dream *Lt.*; *mi-bzaṅ-ba* a portentous, ill-boding dream *S.g.*; *rmi-lam mťóṅ-ba*, *rmi-ba* to dream, *rmi-lam-du rál-bar rmis-so* he dreamt that he had been torn to pieces *Dzl.*; *rmi-lam-du ₒbyúṅ-ba* to appear in a dream *Dzl.*; *rmi-lam brtág-pa Cs.* to judge of dreams, *bšád-pa Cs.* to interpret dreams.

རྨིག་སྒ་ *rmig-sga Sch.* **a saddle** that may be folded together.

རྨིག་པ་ *rmig-pa* 1. **hoof,** *rmig-pa ǩa-brág*, *rmig-brág Cs.* a cloven hoof, *mig-pa-ǩa-brág-čan* cloven-footed; *rmig-zlúm* an undivided hoof; *rta-rmig* a horse's hoof, also name of a plant *Wdṅ.*; *ɣyág-rmig* a yak's hoof; *rmig-lčágs* **horse-shoe** *Cs.*; *rmig-(ɣ)zer* horse-shoe nail, hob-nail *Cs.* — 2. *W.* **horse-shoe,** *ɣyab-če* to put on a horse-shoe, to shoe.

རྨིག(སྨ)་པ་ *rmig(s)-pa* **lizard,** of a small kind *S.g.*

རྨིང་ *rmiṅ* v. *rmaṅ.*

རྨུ་ *rmu* v. *dmu.*

རྨུ་བ་ *rmú-ba Cs.* 1. **dullness, heaviness.** — 2. **fog.** — *rmus-pa* 1. *Cs.* **dull, heavy;** *Lex.* **peevish, loath, listless.** 2. **foggy, gloomy, dark,** *nam rmús-pa* a dark night *Dzl.*, cf. *rmúgs-pa*; covered with fog, *yul*, *Dzl.* — *rmu-ťag* 1. a cord to which little flags are attached, on convents etc. 2. *Glr.* fol. 24, sqq., here the word seems to denote some supernatural means of communication between certain ancient kings and their ancestors dwelling among the gods.

རྨུག་པ་ *rmúg-pa*, pf. *rmugs*, 1. **to bite,** *B.*, *C.*, — 2. **to hurt, to sting,** of bees etc. *W.*;

to gall, the feet by friction of the shoes *W.* — 3 to bark *W.*

རྨུགས་པ་ *rmúgs-pa* 1. a dense fog, *k̔yim* fog is coming on, *̥t̔ib Cs.* id.; *sans* has cleared away *Cs.*; *rmúgs-pa-čan* foggy; *nam rmúgs-pa Dzl.* ༢༣༠, 12, a dark, foggy night (another reading: *rmús-pa*); *Dzl.* ༡༥༠, 15, *nyin-mtsán-du yul rmúgs-pa* (*rmús-pa*), covered with fog, wrapt in darkness. — 2. *Sch.* eyes heavy with sleep. — 3. inertness, languor, laziness *Mil.*; inert, languid, sluggish, *rmúgs-par byéd-pa Dom.*

རྨུན་པོ་ *rmún-po Cs.* dull, heavy, stupid; *žo rmún-po S.g.* sour milk (?).

རྨུར་བ་ *rmúr-ba* to gnarl and bite each other, of dogs *Lex.*

རྨུས་པ་ *rmús-pa* v. *rmú-ba.*

རྨེ་བ་ *rmé-ba* I. to be economizing, parsimonious *Lex.*; *bsris-* (*Sch. srid?*) and *sér-rme-ba Lex.* id. —

II. also *dmé-ba* and *smé-ba* 1. sbst. spot, speck, mark, a natural mark, on a cane *Mil.*; mole, mother-spot; **mé-žól** *W.* mark of burning; a detestable sin, esp. murder; uncleanness of food, *rme-γtsan-méd* or *γtsan-rme-méd* making no difference as to clean or unclean food *Mil.*; *rme-grib* moral defilement; *rme-ša-čan Wdn.*, **me-ša za-kan** *W.*, eating unclean flesh, as an animal that devours its own young. — 2. adj., also *rmé-ba-čan, rmé-čan Wdn.*, *rmé-po Lex.* unclean, defiled, contaminated.

རྨེ་རུ་ *rmé-ru*, n.p. 1. mountain on the Chinese frontier *Glr.* — 2. a castle in Lhasa *Glr.*

རྨེག་པ་ *rmeg-pa* = *γtan* order, series, row *Lex.*, *rmég-med-pa* disordered, not regulated.

རྨེད་ *rmed* crupper, attached to a saddle, *sgá-yi rméd Lexx.*; *gón-rmed Pth.*

རྨེད་པ་ *rméd-pa* I. also *sméd-pa*, pf. *rmes*, to ask, *dri-žin sméd-par mdzád-pa* id. resp. *Mil.*; *snyún-dri sméd-pa Mil.* = *snyún-dri žú-ba.* — II. to plough and sow; *rméd-du ǰúg-pa* to cause to be ploughed and sown, e.g. rice *Dzl.*

རྨེན་པ་ *rmen-pa Lex.* *rmén-bu Lt.*, *ša-rmén Mil.* and vulgo, gland, swelling of the glands, wen.

རྨེལ་བ་, སྨེལ་བ་ *rmél-ba, smél-ba* 1. to pluck out, *C.*, *W.*, *Lex.*, v. *bal.* — 2. to become threadbare *W.* — 3. *Sch.* to appoint, to call, to invite.

རྨོ་སྔགས་ *rmo-snags Sch.* = *smre-snágs.*

རྨོ་མོ་ *rmó-mo* 1. *Cs.* = *ma-čún.* — 2. *Sch.* grandmother.

རྨོ་བ་ *rmó-ba*, pf. and imp. *rmos* 1. to plough (up), *žin* frq.; to sow and plough in *̥bras Dzl.*; *ma rmós-pai lo-t̔óg* 1. a fabulous kind of grain in the mythical age. 2. maize, *C.*, *W.* — *rmó-po, rmó-mk̔an* ploughman. — 2. *̥gyód-rmo-ba* v. *̥gyód-pa.*

རྨོག་ *rmog* helmet *Glr.*; *rmog-tsáns Cs.* 'the padding in a helmet'; *k̔rab-rmog* coat of mail and helmet.

རྨོང་བ་ *rmón-ba* vb. and sbst., pf. *rmons* to be obscured; obscurity, chiefly in a spiritual sense; also adj. obscured, stultified *Stg.*; more frq. *rmons-pa*, e.g. *blo*, the mind darkened, by false doctrine *Thgy.*; by sorrow, despondency, = despairing, despondent, unnerved *Dzl.*, with *la* or termin., as to, with regard to . . .; *blo ma rmóns-pa*, or *rmons-méd Mil.* a mind lively, unimpaired, susceptible, *la* of; *kun-tu-rmón šas-čé-ba* an ample share of irrationality, the principal obstacle to the happiness (*ma-k̔óm-pa*) of those beings which are born as beasts; *rmón-par ̥gyúr-ba* to be obscured, darkened, *byéd-pa* to obscure, to darken *Glr.*, also: to confound, perplex, deceive, = *mgo skór-ba Tar.*; *rmón-bu Lex.* without expl., *Cs.*: 'a kind of distemper'; *rmón-spu* hair of the abdomen and the pudenda, *ra-t̔ug rmon-spus lhog-pa ̥ǰom S.g.* the belly-hair of a he-goat tends to heal cancer.

རྨོད་པ་ *rmód-pa Cs.* to plough, *rmod-glán* a plough-ox; *rmod-lám Sch.* furrow.

རྨོན་པ་ *rmón-pa* 1. the act of ploughing; *rmón-pa rgyáb-pa* to plough *Cs.* — 2. a plough-ox, *rmon-dór* a yoke of plough-oxen.

རྨྱ་བ་ *rmyá-ba S.g.* sickness, nausea, *k̔ams-rmyá Lex.* id.

སྨྱང་བ, སྨྱེང་བ rmyáṅ-ba, rmyéṅ-ba = snyéṅ-ba **to stretch one's self**, to stretch forward the neck; *bya-rmyáṅ byéd-pa* id. *Cs.* also: to yawn.

སྨ *sma* v. *dma.*

སྨ་ར *smá-ra* **beard** *Mil.*, *smá-ra-čan* **bearded.**

སྨག *smag* 1. a sort of **medicine** of an astringent taste *Med.*; *smág-rgyu* **black pepper.** — 2. **dark; darkness;** *mún-pai smag-rúm* id. *Glr.*

སྨང་ཚེར *smaṅ-tsér* v. *rmaṅ-˳tser.*

སྨད *smad*, अधर, 1. **the lower part**, opp. to *stod*; *smád-la* downward *Sch.*; *lús-kyi smad* the lower half of the human body, frq.; *smad ˳pyés-pa Sch.:* 'to move the posterior to and fro' (?). — *lus-smad-lṅa sá-la γtúg-pa* to bring the five lower parts of the body, the belly, the knees, and the points of the feet in close contact with the ground, i. e. to prostrate one's self; hence *čos-gos smad lṅa Dzl.* ༢༠, 16, the five lower pieces of the priestly apparel, perh. breeches, stockings and boots; the meaning, however, of *sems-smád bčo-brgyád Pth.* I am not prepared to settle — 2. **lowland** = *man-čád.* — 3. **low rank**, v. *smad-rigs* below. — 4. with regard to time, **the latter part, the second half,** उत्तर, of the night, *Dzl.*, of winter, of life etc. — 5. **children**, in relation to their mother, gen. preceded by *ma* or *bu*, thus: *ṅed ma-smád* I and my mother *Mil.*; *rgán-mo ma-smád γsum* the old woman with her (two) sons, those three *Dzl.*; also of animals: *rgód-ma ma-smád γnyis* the mare and her foal, the two *Dzl.*; *bu-smád* (*Cs.* also *mad*) wife and children, family; *nád-pa dei bu-smád Mil.* the sick man's family; *bu-smád-rnams* (my) wife and children *Mil.*

Comp. *smad-˳čal* **lewdness, dissoluteness, prostitution,** *byéd-pa* to indulge in, to practise *Mil.* — *smad-˳dógs* a subscribed letter *Gram.* — *smád-tsoṅ-ma* '*meretrix*', prostitute, harlot, frq. — *smad-γyógs* nether integuments, breeches, trowsers *Wdṅ.* — *smad-rigs* common people, lower caste *Dzl.*

སྨད་པ *smád-pa* I. vb. 1. **to bend down; to hand, to reach down,** the alms bowl to a little boy *Dzl.*; (*Sch.* 'to stoop'?); *γdoṅ smád-pa* to cast down one's eyes, to be abashed, dejected *Tar.*; *sems* to humble one's self, *la* before *Dzl.*, *tugs* id. resp.: **to be condescending, lowly, meek** *Dzl.* — 2. **to vilify,** c. *la* or accus.: **to blame, to chide,** *bú-mo* one's own daughter *Dzl.*, *bdág-gi séms-la* to blame one's self *Dzl* ; **to abuse, defame, degrade, traduce,** *tsig ṅár-pas ˳págs-pa-la* (to abuse) the venerable man with base words *Dzl.*, *dkon-mčóg-gi dbu-˳páṅ* (to degrade) the highness of the excellent, = to blaspheme; **to despise,** the doctrine *Glr.*; **to dishonour, violate, ravish,** *bu-moi lus* a girl *Pth.*; *má-ga-dha nyáms-smad-pai tse Tar.* 192 when (the country of) Magadha had been brought low, had decayed in its prosperity; *smád-pai tsig* or *ṅag* **abusive word, invective, libel;** *smád-ra* (prop. *sgra*) id., more in the language of the common people, but also *Mil.*; *smád-ra γtóṅ-ba Mil.*, *taṅ-če* *W.* to abuse, to revile; *smad-rigs* common people.

II. sbst. **blame, reproof, reproach, disgrace, contempt.**

སྨན *sman* 1. **medicine, physic, remedy,** both artificially prepared and crude: **medicinal herb, drug;** *rii sman ˳tú-ba* to gather officinal plants on the mountains *Dzl.*; *mén-la ˳do* C.*, *man-la ča* *W*, (the plant) is used as a medicine; *sman sbyór-ba* to prepare a medicine, *γtóṅ-ba* to administer, *zá-ba* or *˳túṅ-ba* to take (physic); different forms of medicine are: *táṅ-gi sman* liquid medicine, infusion, decocture; *pyé-mai sman* powder; *ril-bu* pill; *ldé-gu* electuary, sirup; *sman-már* oily medicine (*Tar.* 39, 8); *sman-čáṅ* prob. alcoholic tincture; *˳bri-ta* extract(?). — Further: *kóṅ-sman* medicine taken internally, *byúg-sman* used externally, unguent; *˳byár-sman* plaster; *bzi-sman* soporiferous potion; *skyúg-sman* emetic; *bšál-sman* purgative. — *smán-gyi bla*, or *smán-bla Glr.* and *Med.*; *Sch.*: 'physician general', yet to my knowledge it is never used in that sense, but only as a god or Buddha of therapeutics; there are eight such gods, revered by students of medicine, and frequently invoked in medicinal writings, as well as in medical practice, v. *Schl.* p. 266 sqq. (*sman-gyi lha Glr.*, is prob. but a misprint). — Other compounds: *sman-rkyál* medicine-bag, smaller or larger leather-bags being the usual receptacles for the commodities of grocers and the drugs of physicians. — *smán-k'an* apothecary's shop. — *sman-k'úg* medicine-bag. — *sman-sgá* a kind of officinal ginger (?) *S.g.* — *sman-sgám* medicine-box. — *sman-mč'ód* the best, or a very superior medicine *Pth.* — *sman-ljóṅs* a country rich in medicinal plants. — *sman-rtá* the vehicle or substance in which medicine is taken *Med.* — *sman-snod* medicine glass or vessel. — *smán-pa* physician *Dzl.*, *Glr.*, *Med.* — *smán-dpe* medical book. — *sman-dpyád* v. *dpyád-pa.* — *sman-blá* s. above.

II. the same as, or something like *klu* *Glr.*, *Mil.*

III. *Lex.* = *p'an*; *Sch.* also has: *sman-séms* a beneficent mind, a mind intent on working good'.

IV. incorr. for *dman.*

སྨར་བ་ *smár-ba* 1. sbst, **ready money,** gen. *smar-rkyáṅ*; *zoṅ min smar* money, and not goods *Lex.* — 2. vb. careless and incorr. pronunciation of *smrá-ba.*

སྨལ་པོ་ *smál-po* n. of a lunar mansion v. *rgyu-skár.*

སྨས་པ་ *smás-pa Sch.*, v. *rmás-pa.*

སྨིག་རྒྱུ་ *smig-rgyú* **mirage** *Lex.* = **मरिचि**; prob. also a reflection in water, *č'ur-ₒk'rul-smig-rgyú.*

སྨིག་བུ་ *smig-bu* **lizard** *Sch.*, v. *rmíg(s)-pa.*

སྨིག་མ་ *smig-ma*, provinc. for *smyúg-ma* **cane, reed** *Do.*

སྨིན་དྲུག་ *smin-drúg* 1. also *skár-ma-smin-drúg* **कार्त्तिक**, **the Pleiades;** *smin-drug-zlá-ba* the month in which the moon standing near the Pleiades is full, Oct. or Nov., *Glr.*; *smin-drug-bú*, **कार्त्तिकेय**, the son of Siva, god of war *Lex.* — 2. *Pur.* Eremurus spectabilis, v. *bre.*

སྨིན་བདུན་, སྨེ་བདུན་ *smin-bdún, sme-bdún* **the Great Bear,** *Ursa major.*

སྨིན་པ་ *smin-pa*, I. (**विपाक**) **to ripen, ripeness, maturity;** most frq. **ripe,** *ₒbrás-bu smin-no B.*, *smin soṅ* vulgo, the fruit is ripe; *smin-par ₒgyúr-ba Glr.* *smin ₒóṅ-ba* to ripen; the growing on to maturity of an animal germ; also the 'stadium maturationis', or the full development of a disease *Med.;* applied to conversion *Pth.* and elsewh.; *rgyud smin-čiṅ gról-bar byin-gyis rlobs* give them the benediction for being saved (absorbed into Nirvana) after having attained to maturity of mind *Mil.*; *smin-gról-la* or *smin-gról-gyi lám-la ₒgód-pa* to lead to conversion and salvation *Glr.*; *rnám-par smin-pa* v. *rnám-pa.* — *smin-grol-gliṅ* n. of a monastery *Cs.*

II. *Bal.* to give (*sbyin-pa*).

སྨིན་མ་ *smín-ma* **eye-brow,** *smin(-mai) dbrag Med.*, *smin-p'rag Mil.*, *smin-mtsams Glr.* the space between the eye-brows.

སྨུག་ཆུང་ *smug-čuṅ Med.* a plant = *smug-rtsí* (?).

སྨུག་པ་ *smúg-pa Sch.* for *rmugs-pa* **fog.**

སྨུག་པོ་ *smúg-po* 1. sbst. a disease, acc. to *Cs.* = *ₒdus-nád*, v. *ₒdú-ba*, 1. — 2. adj. **dark bay, cherry-brown, purple-brown;** **gya-múg** *C.* violet coloured; *dmar-smug* brownish white *Wdṅ.; smug-smúg Sch.* dark red. — *smug-rtsi* 1. **red colour,** with which sacrificial utensils are painted *Lex.* — 2. Macrotomia, a plant with dark-red root, used for dyeing, *smug-ts'ós* paint or colour yielded by this plant *Cs.*

སྨེ་བདུན་ *sme-bdún* v. *smin-bdún.*

སྨེ་བ་ *smé-ba* 1. v. *rme-ba.* — 2. *rtsis-kyi smé-ba Lex.* a kind of arithmetical figure in geomancy, which is used together with the Chinese diagrams, *spar-k'a Mil.*

སྨོ་བ་ *smó-ba*, pf. and imp. *smos*, not frq., yet in some cases of constant use, for *smrá-ba* **to say,** *miṅ-nas smó-ba* to call by name, to name *Do.*; . . . *žes smós-pa* the assertion that . . . *Wdṅ.*; *goṅ-du smós-pa* above-mentioned *Do.; lta či smos* v. *lta.*

སྨོད་པ་ *smód-pa*, pf. *smad*, *Lex.* निन्द v. *smád-pa*, **to blame,** *bdag stod γžan smod* to praise one's self, disparaging others; *γžogs-smód byéd-pa* to slander, calumniate *Thgy.*; **to depreciate, to make contemptible,** *smód-par* ₒ*gyúr-bas Stg.* because it would be disreputable, would detract from his honour. For *smod-*ₒ*dzúg-pa* it would prob. be better to write *dmod-*ₒ*dzug-pa.*

སྨོན་པ་ *smón-pa* **to wish, to desire,** with *la*, *skyid-pa γžán-la ṅa mi smon* for another happiness I do not wish *Mil.*; more frq. with termin. of the infinitive, and then = to pray for, *rgyál-po skyé-bar* (to pray for) being re-born as a king *Dzl.*; *smón-pa bžin-du byéd-pa* to fulfil a prayer *Dzl.*; *smón-pai γnas* the object of a wish or prayer *Cs.*; *yid-smón* **wish, desire,** *de ťsúr-šog-gi yid-smon ṅá-la med* I do not wish that he should come *Mil.*; *riṅ-po-nas* ₒ*di-lta-bur yid-smon byéd-par gyúr-te* having long ago entertained this wish *Stg.*; *yid-smon* ₒ*os* worth wishing, desirable; *smon-*ₒ*jug* a wish and its accomplishment, *smon-*ₒ*jug γnyis*; *smón-lam*, प्रणिधि, prayer, whether it be in the general way of expressing a good wish or offering a petition to the deity, or in the specific Brahmanic-Buddhistic form, which is always united with some condition or asseveration, as: if such or such a thing be true, then may . . ., **wishing-prayer.** — *smon-(lam) lóg(-par)* ₒ*débs-pa* to curse, to execrate.

སྨོན་མགྲིན་ or འདྲིན་ *smon-mgrin* or ₒ*drin* **comrade, companion, associate,** = *grógs-po Lex.*

སྨྱན་ *smyan*? *Sch.*: *smyan byéd-pa* to travel on business; *smyan-byed blo-žan* a traveling clerk not very shrewd *Bhar.* 108; this would seem preferable to the Ssk. equivalent, mentioned in *Schf.'s* edition.

སྨྱར་བ་ *smyár-ba Sch.* **to stretch one's self,** after sleep.

སྨྱི(ག)་གུ་, སྨྱུ(ག)་གུ་ *smyí(g)-gu*, *smyú(g)-gu* **thin cane, writing-cane, reed-pen;** **ḍoi nyi-gu** *C.* goose-quill, **čág-gi nyi-gu** *C.* steel-pen.

སྨྱིག་མ་, com. སྨྱུག་མ་ *smyig-ma*, *smyúg-ma* 1. **cane, bamboo,** *smyúg-mai sbubs* tube of bamboo *Cs.* — 2. **a pen of reed,** ₒ*jóg-pa*, *W.* **žóg-če** to make a reed-pen; **ḍi-nyúg** id., improp. also lead-pencil.

Comp. *smyug-ǩróg Cs.*, acc. to others, *smyug-sbróg* tube of bamboo; pen-case; small churn, = *gur-gúr Cs.* — **nyug-ǩyim** *C.* house constructed of bamboo. — *smyúg-mǩan* a worker in cane *Cs.* — *smyug-sgám* a chest made of reed *Cs.* — *smyug-gri* penknife. — *smyug-lčág* flag, flag-stick; long bamboo *Cs.* — **nyug-ťál** *C.* a flat basket. — *smyug-ťógs* writer *Cs.* — *smyug-dóṅ Cs.* = *gur-gur.* — *smyug-γdán* mat of reed, cane-mat. — *smyug-γdúgs* an umbrella made of split reeds *Cs.* — *smyug-sdér* plate, dish or flat basket, coustructed of reed *C.* — **nyug-tsá-me-tog** *C.*, Carthusian pink. — *smyug-ťsigs* knot, node, joint, of reeds. — **nyug-lóm** *C.* flat basket. — *smyug-bšád* comb made of bamboo.

སྨྱུང་བ་ *smyúṅ-ba* **to fast, to observe a strict diet** *Med.*; often in a religious sense, *smyúṅ-bar byás-pa* and *ma byas-pa* he who has strictly observed fasting, and he who has not *Do.*; *smyuṅ-γnás* **the fast, the act of fasting;** **nyén-nẹ nyúṅ-nẹ zúm-če** *W.* to fast, to practise abstinence. V. *Schl.* 240.

སྨྱུར་བ་ *smyúr-ba* **to be quick, expeditious, in a hurry, to hasten** *Cs.* Cf. *myúr-ba.*

སྨྱོ་བ་, སྨྱོ་བ་ *smyó-ba*, *myó-ba*, pf. *smyos*, *myos* **to be insane, mad,** *či-*ₒ*aṅ mi drán-par myós-so* they lost their senses and ran mad (with grief) *Dzl.*; *smyos-sam* is she mad? *Dzl.*; *snyiṅ myós-pas Do.*, being deranged; **nyo dug** *W.* he is crazy; **to be mad,** as dogs *Schr.*; **to be intoxicated,** *smyó-bai ǩú-ba* intoxicating liquor *Dzl.*; *rtág-tu myós-pai γnas* pot-hóuses, fuddling-places *Stg.*; fig. ₒ*dod-čágs-kyis myos Dzl.* he is mad with lust; *smyó-bar byéd-pa* to make one mad or drunk. — *smyo-byéd* 1. **narcotic,** *smyo-byéd-kyi rdzas* narcotic medicine, soporiferous potion, maddening drink. 2. *smyo-byed(-kyi) γdon* a demon that causes a state of stupefaction or insanity. 3. **frenzy, madness.** 4. symb. num.: 13.

སྨྱོན་པ་ *smyón-pa* **insane, frantic, mad,** *la-dág-pa nyón-pa* a madman from Ladak; *glàṅ-po-če Dzl.* a mad elephant, *k̔yi* a mad dog; **nyón-pa čo dug* W.* he raves, he is stark mad; **č̔o-nyón žug* W.* he has been seized with religious insanity, is deranged, which is stated to be occasionally the effect of severe and long continued meditation. Cf. *lhoṅ*.

སྨྲ་བ་ *smrá-ba*, sometimes སྨོ་བ *smó-ba*, also

སྨར་བ *smár-ba*, pf. *smras*, imp. *smros* 1. **to speak, to talk,** *smra ma nús-te Dzl.* growing dumb, speechless, not being able to speak (physically); *čaṅ mi smrá-bar gyúr-to* they grew speechless, did not know what to say *Dzl.*; *smra šés-nas mir gyúr-to* they received the faculty of speech and became men *Glr.*; *bslú-bai rnám-pas k̔yeu daṅ smrás-te Dzl.* speaking to the youth in a seductive manner; *ts̔ig snyán-par smrá-ba Dzl.* to speak in a friendly way; *č̔os smrá-ba* **to preach,** *č̔os smrá-bai žál-la ltú-ba* to hang on the preacher's lips, to listen very attentively *Pth.*; *da ma smra žig Dzl.* do not lose another word; *smra-mk̔as(-pa)* speaking shrewdly, well-spoken, eloquent *Dzl., Glr.*; *smra-ˏdód* **talkative, loquacious** *Cs.*; *smra-nyúṅ* sparing of words, **taciturn,** *Lt.*; *smra-bčád* forbearing to speak; not being bound to speak *Mil.*; *smra-mč̔óg, smrá-bai dbaṅ-p̔yúg, smrá-bai rgyál-po* = *ˏjam-dpál*; also **to treat of,** with reference to books *Was.* — 2. **to say,** *mí-la* to a person; when it precedes the words that are quoted as they were spoken, (the so-called 'oratio obliqua' being very seldom made use of, one instance v. further on): (*dí-skad-čes*) *smrás-pa* or *smrás-so;* when placed after the words spoken, (*čes*) *smrás-so, smrás-te* etc.; *smrás-pa* also is equivalent to **he continued** *Dzl.*; sometimes it is used impersonally, **it is said,** e.g. it is said in that letter, where we should say, 'that letter says', *Stg*; *smrá-gyu ma byúṅ-ṅo* there remained nothing more for him to say (v. above); rarely with termin. inf.: *ytúg-par ni ṅa mi smrao* that they will reach it, I do not pretend to say *Thgy.*; *šés-par smrá-ba* to profess to know, to understand, like '*artem profiteri*' *Dzl.*; *dṅós-por smrá-ba* to acknowledge a thing in substance *Was.*, *med-par smrá-ba* to deny it in sum and substance.

Note. The word which forms the subject of this article, though constantly to be met with in books, seems to be hardly ever used in conversational language.

སྨྲང་, སྨྲེང་ *smraṅ, smreṅ Cs.* **word, speech;** *smraṅ ysól-ba* to beg the word, to beg leave to speak

སྨྲེ་བ་ *smré-ba* 1. = *smrá-ba*(?) — 2. **to wail, to lament** *Pth.*; more com *smre-sṅágs ˏdón-pa* to utter lamentations; *smre-sṅágs-kyi sgó-nas* whining (with joy) *Mil.* — *smre-ytsáṅ*?

ཙ

ཙ *tsa*, 1. the letter sounding **ts**; tenuis, as in the words 'it got so cold', cf. however ཚ *tsa*; ཙ, ཚ and ཛ represent in *Ssk.* and Hindi-words the palatals **च, छ** and **ज** (ཛྷ = **झ**). — 2. num fig.: 17.

ཙྭ་ *tswa Ld.* **spunk,** German tinder.

ཙ་ཀོར་ *tsa-kór*, *Ssk.* **चकोर** **partridge,** = *sręg-pa*.

ཙ་ཀྲ་བཱ་ཀ་ *tsa-kra-bā-ka* **red goose,** *Anas casarca.*

ཙ་དར་, ཙ་སར་ *tsa-dar, tsa-sar, Pers., Hind.* چدر **shawl, plaid, cloak, toga** *W.* —

ཙ་ན་, ཙ་ནས་, ཙ་ལ་ *tsá-na, tsá-nas, tsá-la* v. *tsam.*

ཙ་ན་ཀ་ *tsa-na-ka*, more corr. ཙ་ཎ་ཀ་ *Ssk.*, **chick-pea**, *Cicer arietinum.*

ཙ་བིག་ *tsá-big*, v. *tsa-big.*

ཙ་རག་ *tsa-rág*, **tsa-rág zér-če** *Ld.* **to crackle,** of fire, breaking twigs etc.

ཙ་རུ་ *tsá-ru* 1. *W.* **curled, frizzled,** as hair and similar things. — 2. *Lex.*: *Ssk.* **meat-offering** to the manes.

ཙ་ཤ་(ཀ) *tsa-ša(-ka)*, चाष, *Coracias Indica,* **jay, roller.**

ཙག་གེ *tság-ge W.* **the black mark in a target,** *tság-ge-la gyob* hit the mark!

ཙན་དན་, ཙནྡན *tsán-dan, tsándan,* चन्दन, **sandal-tree,** *Sirium myrtifolium,* sandal-wood, used for elegant buildings, images of the gods, perfumes, medicines *Glr., Med.*; in different varieties: *dkár-po, dmár-po* etc., also of fabulous kinds: *tsán-dan sbrúl-gyi snyiṅ-po, gór-ši-ša, gláṅ-mgo Glr., Dzl.*; fig. **something superior in its kind,** *pa tsán-dan pú-nu mi-lag-tu soṅ* the elder and younger sons of a distinguished father perform menial services

ཙན་དོང་ *tsan-dóṅ* v. *btson-dóṅ.*

ཙབ་ཙུབ་, ཙབ་ཙོབ་, རྩབ་རྩུབ་ *tsab-tsúb, tsab-tsób, rtsab-rtsúb* **hurry, haste** *Cs., tsab-tsúb-čan* hasty *Cs.; tsab-tsúb mi bya Lex.* take your time, don't be in a hurry! *rtsab-rtsub-méd-par* not flitting, like a butterfly, from one object to another *Mil.; tsub-liṅ Sch.* hastily, in a hurry(?) — *rtsab-hrál Lex.*; *Sch.* a loose, dissolute course of life(?) — *rtsáb-pa Sch.* to hurry, to hasten(?).

ཙབས་རུ་ *tsabs-rú* 1. a kind of **salt,** *tsabs-ru-tsá S.g.* — 2. **a tube of horn** *Sch.*

ཙམ་ *tsam* mostly affixed as an enclitic, = *snyed* (sometimes carelessly for *tsám-pa* or *tsám-du*) I. in a relative sense, 1. **as much as** *ₒdi-tsam* as much as this, = so much, so many; *mi ₒdi tsam ɣsód-pa* to kill so many men *Glr.*; *dé-tsam* id.; also emphat.: *čos de tsam žig bšád-nas* after having given you so much religious instruction *Mil.*; by way of exclamation: *či-tsam* **how much!** *W.* and *B.*, *či-tsam byas* how much have you not done! *Glr.*; *ji-tsam ... dé-tsam* how much... so much (as much as) *Cs.* — 2. denoting comparison, as to size, degree, intensity, **like, as-as, so-as, so that:** *ri-ráb tsam* like Sumeru (in height) *Cs*; *yúṅs-ₒbru tsam* as big as a grain of mustard-seed; **de ri tón-po tsam dug dé-tsogs di yaṅ yod** *W.* as high as yon mountain is also this one; *pús-mo núb-pa tsam* even to sinking in up to the knees (knee-deep); *nyi-ma ₒgrib-pa tsam* so much that the sun was darkened *Glr.*; *mtai rgyál-po yaṅ dbáṅ-du ₒdús-pa tsam byuṅ* he became so (powerful), that he could also subdue — or could have subdued — the neighbouring kings *Glr.* — 3. denoting contingency and restriction: **perhaps, if need be, almost, only, but, all but:** *tsab ruṅ tsám-mo Wdṅ.* this may perhaps be used instead, this may, if need be, supply its place; *btaṅ-na nam-mkai bya yaṅ zin-(pa) tsam ɣda* if I let him loose, he might almost catch a bird in the air, = *zin-pa daṅ ₒdrao Mil.;* with a partic.: *rtags yód-pa tsám-la* = *rtags daṅ yód-pa-la* to every one that has the mark *Glr.; rtsa daṅ rús-pa tsam Dzl.* nothing but skin and bones; *ₒgro mi nús-pa ₒyóg-pa tsam Dzl.* one only creeping, not being able to walk; *ča tsam šes kyaṅ* if one knows but a particle, but a little bit; *sems tsám-mo* they exist only in our fancy *Was.; tsigs-ma tsam yód-dam Dzl.* is not the sediment at least still left? *lhág-ma tsam žig Dzl.* but a remnant; *brgya tsam* may mean: about one hundred, or: only one hundred; in some cases *tsam* is untranslatable: *lṅa-brgyá tsam tams-čád tsei dus byas-so* the 500 merchants died all *Dzl.* (15, 9 s. l. c.); *bdén-pa tsam yod Mil.* some grain of truth is in the matter; *tsig daṅ rnám-par ₒdrá-ba tsam ₒdúg-na-ₒaṅ Mil.* though it is all but equal to the words, i.e. very much like the real tenor or wording; it may also be combined **with** the signs of the cases: *ṅa miṅ tsám-gyi dgé-sloṅ ma yin Dzl.* I am Bhikshu not only by name, I am not merely called so; *da tsám-gyi bár-du Dzl.* till about the present time (standing here rather pleon., as frq. is the case); *brám-ze γčig tsám-gyi slád-du Dzl.* for the sake of a single Brahmin; *spu nyág-ma tsám-gyi ₒgyód-pai sems Dzl.* but a whit (lit. a little hair) of repentance. — 4. *tsám-na* referring to time: **about a certain time, at the time when, when:** *nam-p̓yéd tsám-na* about midnight; *de tsám-na* then, at that time; esp. with verbs: *k̓yim-du p̓yin tsám-na Dzl.* when he came home; inst. of *tsám-na* it is very common to say *tsá-na; byéd-gin yod tsá-na* as he was just doing it *Glr.*; *γnyid sad tsá-na* when he awoke *Glr.; zlá-ba brgyad soṅ tsá-na* when eight months had passed *Glr.*; esp. col.: **yoṅ tsá-na* W.* as we came, on our journey hither, when incorr. **tsa-nẹ* (or *sá-nẹ*)* is said, which is justifiable only in such cases, as: **ă-ma kyé-sa-nẹ** from one's birth; *ǰi-tsam-na* or *-nas* **when**, yet mostly pleon., in as far as the sentence beginning with *ǰi-tsam-na* after all concludes with *nas, pa daṅ, dus-kyi tse* etc., v. *Feer Introd.* frq., also *Tar.* — 5. *tsám-du* denoting extent, degree, intensity: **as far as, about so far, nearly up to, even to, till, so that,** and *tsam* in various other applications: *lam p̓yed tsám-du* about half way; frq. with verbs: *bá-spu láṅs-pa tsám-du skrags Dzl.* he was so frightened, that his hair stood on end; *dúm-bur bčád-pa tsám-du sdug-bsṅál-gyis γdúṅs-te Dzl.* tormented by a pain, as if he were cut to pieces; *bus ma mtóṅ-ba tsám-du dgá-ste Dzl.* 'being glad even to a mother's being seen by her child, i.e. so glad as a child is, when beholding its mother again; sometimes *tsám-la* for *tsám-na* and *tsám-du Mil.* yet not frq. and more col.: *ḍib tsám-la* in the shade; **šiṅ-ni tsám-la* W.* under, before, near a tree; *tsám-gyis* instrum.: *ṅan-ṅon tsám-gyis čóg-šes-pa* content with every thing, as poor as it may be; com. added to the inf.: *smrás-pa tsám-du* as soon as it had been said *Dzl.* frq., or also: 'in the mere saying so' *Stg.*; inst. of it, col.: **zer tsam žig-la*; W.: *zér-ra tsám-žig-ga*.* — *tsam yaṅ* with a following negative: **not the least,** *mós-pa tsam yaṅ mi byéd-pa Mil.* to pay not the least respect; **not in the least, not at all:** *nyí-ma daṅ zlá-ba tsam yaṅ ltar med Dzl.* neither sun nor moon is to be seen at all. — *tsám-pa* adj., *mi-tsad-tsám-pa* man-sized, having the size of a man *Tar.* — *tsám-po Mil. mi tsám-po yóṅs-kyi sems-la ₒǰug* prob : I shall enter into the soul of the very first man I meet with; also = *gaṅ* (cf. *rtags gaṅ yód-pa-la* above). — *Cs.* has besides: *tsám-po-ba* a comparing, estimating; *tsam-poi tsig* a comparative expression; *tsám-poi don* a comparative sense (?). II. used interrogatively: **how much? how many?** **rin tsam?* W.* how dear?

ཙམ་པ་ *tsám-pa* 1. v. *tsam* towards end of preced. article. — 2. sbst. **flour** from parched barley, v. *rtsám-pa*. — 3. n. of a country *Tar.* 10,14; 20,16; acc. to *S.* *Lexx.* = Bhagalpore, v. *Köpp.* I, 96; in modern geography: the small Hindu mountain-province **Chamba** on the river Ravi, under British protection.

ཙམ་པ་ཀ་ *tsám-pa-ka Ssk.* **magnolia,** *Michelia Çhampaca.*

ཙམ་ཙོམ་ *tsam-tsóm* **tripping to and fro, fidgeting about** *W.* (cf. *tsab-tsób*).

ཙར་མ་ *tsár-ma* n. of a place, freq. resorted to by *Mil.*

ཙི་ *tsi* num. fig.: 47.

ཙི་ཏྲ་ཀ་ *tsi-tra-ka Ssk.* 1. a painted mark on the forehead, being the badge of various sects *Sch.* — 2. name of several plants, esp. *Ricinus communis*, so perh. *Lt.*; in *Lh.*: *Anemone rivularis*, common there.

ཙི་སྟག་ *tsi-stág* n. of a purgative *Med.*

ཙི་ན་ *tsi-na* चीन, *China Cs.*; now com. *ma-ha-tsin.*

ཙི་ཙི་ *tsi-tsi* **mouse** *C.*, *tsi-ghi* id. *Ts.*; *tsi-čuṅ* **shrew** (mouse) *Sch.*; *táṅ-gi tsi-tsi* **field-mouse** *Schr.*; *sai tsi-tsi* **mole** *Schr.*; *tsi-tsis-ₒdzin* n. of a plant *Wdṅ.*

ཙི་ཙི་རྫོ་ལ་ *tsi-tsi-dzó-la Cs.*, *tsi-tsi-dzó-ba Sch.* **cancer** (disease), said to be a Nepalese word.

ཙི་ཙེ་ *tsi-tsé* v. *tse-tsé*.

ཙིག་ཙིག་ *tsig-tsig byéd-pa* **to quarrel, to be at variance** *Sch.*

ཙིཏྟ *tsitta Ssk.* **the heart** as seat of the intellect, v. *Burn.* I, 637.

ཙིད་ *tsid* **anvil** *Sch.*

ཙུ་ *tsu* num. fig.: 77.

ཙུ་ད་ *tsú-da*, *tsú-dai śiṅ* n. of a tree *Sch.*

ཙུག་ *tsug* for *ċi-ltar* adv. interrog. and correlat., **how, as,** rarely occurring in books; *Pth.: de gar ₒgro, tsug byed* where she is going, and what she is doing. In *W.* com. in the form *zug*, in such combinations as: *gá-zug* for *ċi-tsug*, *ċi-ltar*; **ĭ-zug* or *ₒdi-zug*, and *ă-zug** or **dé-zug**: **so**; **daṅ de-zug de-zug** and more of that kind; *de-tsug lags* in *Lexx.*

ཙུག་ཙུག་ *tsug-tsúg* the noise of **smacking** in eating, *tsug-tsúg mi bya* do not smack *Zam.*

ཙེ་ *tse* num. fig.: 107.

ཙེ་གུར་ *tse-gúr Sch.*: 1. a small **tube.** — 2. **a little.**

ཙེ་པོ་, ཙེལ་པོ་ *tsé-po*, *tsél-po* **a basket** carried on the back, dosser, esp. *W.*; **ċáṅ-tse* or *ċág-tse** a wicker basket, **nyúṅ-tse* or *nyúg-tse** a cane basket *Ts.*; **tsel-ċúg** the wands used for such a basket; **tsel-ċág** a broken dosser *W.*; **tsel-rá** the frame-work of a basket *Cs.*; **tsel-lúṅ** string or strap for carrying it.

ཙེ་ཙེ་, ཙི་ཙེ་ *tse-tsé*, *tsi-tsé* **millet** *Cs.*

ཙེ་རེ་ *tse-ré* 1 **song, tune** *Lex.* — 2. = *tse-ré*.

ཙེག་ཙེག་ *tseg-tség*, *tseg-tség zér-ba* **to rustle,** 'to make a noise like dry hay' *Cs.*

ཙེབ་ཙེབ་ *tseb-tséb* **sharp-pointed,** of needles, thorns.

ཙེམ་ཙེ་ *tsém-tse* = *ċém-tse* **small scissors.**

ཙེའུ་རི་ *tseu-rí* a species of female demons *Thgr.*

ཙེར་ཙེར་ *tser-tsér*, *tser-tsér byéd-pa* **to tremble, shake, quake** *Sch.*

ཙེལ་པོ་ *tsél-po* v. *tsé-po*.

ཙོ་ *tso* num. fig.: 137.

ཙོ་ར་ *tsó-ra Wdṅ.*, *Ssk.* n. for the medicinal herb *srúb-ka*; in *Ssk. Lexx.* no botanical explication is given, but only the notice, that it is a perfume; in Kullu a sweet-scented white lily is called so.

ཙོག་པུ་ *tsóg-pu* (acc. to one *Lex.* = उत्कुटुक, which is not to be found; on the other hand *Burn.* I, 310 gives *tsóg-pu-pa* = नैषदिक, one sitting down) **the posture of cowering, squatting, crouching,** *tsog(-tsog)-pur sdód-pa*, *ₒdúg-pa* resp. *bżúgs-pa Pth.*, col. **tsoṅ-tsóṅ, tsom-tsóm**, **to cower, squat, crouch;** *tsóg-pu mi nus* he cannot even cower, of one sick unto death *Thgy.*; *tsog mi γzúg-pa* of a similar sense *Sch.* — (The version 'to sit on one leg drawn in' *Sch.*, which has also been adopted by *Burn.*, may possibly be founded on a mistake of *Sch.*, who in *Cs.*'s explanation: 'sitting in a crouching posture upon one's legs', prob. read 'upon one leg').

ཙོང་ཁ་ *tsóṅ-ka* n. of a place in Eastern Tibet *Ma.*; *tsóṅ-ka-pa* 1. inhabitant of that place. 2. n. of a celebrated teacher of religion and reformer, about the year 1400.

ཙོང་ཙོང་ *tsoṅ-tsóṅ* 1. = *tsog-tsóg* v. *tsóg-pu*. — 2. *tsoṅ-tsóṅ-la kur* carry it straight *W.*

ཙོན་དོང་ *tson-dóṅ* v. *btson-dóṅ*.

ཙོབ་ཙོབ་ *tsob-tsób*, **tsob-tsób-la dúg-ċe** *Ld.* to stand or sit in different groups, not in rows.

ཙོར་མོ་ *tsór-mo* **a five-finger pinch** *Cs.*

གཙག་པ་ *γtság-pa* v. *ₒtság-pa*; *γtság-bu* also *btságs-bu* **lancet** for bleeding.

གཙང་ *γtsaṅ* 1. **clean, pure** v. *γtsáṅ-ba*. — 2. n. of a province in *C.*, where Tasilhunpo is situated; *γtsáṅ-pa* inhabitant of it.

གཙང་བ་ *γtsaṅ-ba* 1. vb. **to be clean, pure** *Dom.* — 2. sbst. **cleanness, purity.** — 3. adj. **clean, pure.** Most frq. as sbst. with negation: *mi-γtsáṅ-ba* impurity, foulness, filth *Dzl.* and elsewh.; excrement *S.g.*; *mi-γtsáṅ-ba rnám-pa sna-ṫsógs-kyi p̔úṅ-po* heap of all kinds of filth, mass of corruption, sometimes applied to the human body *Dzl.*; *γtsáṅ-ma* adj., clean, as to the body, clothes etc.; *de ni rab-bkrús γtsáṅ-ma yin* that man is well washed and clean *S.O.*; *γtsaṅ-btsog-méd(-pa)* one that knows no difference between clean and unclean (cf. *med*); **dirty, slovenly; rude, uncouth** *Glr.*; *γtsáṅ-mar byéd-pa* 1. **to clean.** 2. **to make one's self clean, smart, tidy;** **tsáṅ-ma ǰhé'-pa* C.*, **čó-če* W.* is said to be a euphemism for circumcision. — **śul-tsáṅ-po* C.* one that clears his plate, empties his cup; one that does a thing thoroughly. — *γtsáṅ-k̔aṅ Cs.*, com. *dri-γtsaṅ-k̔aṅ* v. *dri.* — *γtsaṅ-sbrá* religious purity, **शुचि**; *γtsaṅ-sbrá-čan* (or *daṅ ldán-pa*) morally pure, *γtsaṅ-sbra-méd-pa* impure *Do.*—*γtsaṅ-rís Sch.*: the pure country and its inhabitants, the pure, the saints.

གཙང་པོ་ *γtsáṅ-po*, *Ld.* **tsáṅs-po** **river, stream;** esp. the large stream flowing through Tibet from west to east, gen. called **Yarutsaṅpo**; *γtsaṅ-čú*, resp. *γtsaṅ-čáb*, id.

གཙང་བུ་ *γtsaṅ-bu* **screen, parasol** *Sch.*

གཙང་གཙོང་ *γtsaṅ-γtsoṅ* (or **˳dzaṅ-˳dzoṅ*?*) *Ld.*, **steep, rugged, mountainous.**

གཙབ་པ་ *γtsáb-pa* **to detach with a crow-bar.**

གཙི་བ་ *γtsi-ba*, pf. *γtsis*, **to invite, summon, call, appoint** *Sch.*

གཙིགས་ *γtsigs* 1. **importance** *Cs.*, *γtsigs(su)-če* very important *Lex.*; *γtsigs čé-bar byéd-pa* to make much of *Cs.*; *Sch.* also *mi-γtsigs* **insignificant; unapt,** and *ma-γtsígs* **unimportant; without difficulty,** whereas in one *Lex.* *mi-γtsigs spyód-pa* is explained by *mi-rigs-pa.* — 2. *Pth.* 85: (but as a girl was born, the king and his ministers were quite in despair, and) *btsún-mo-la yaṅ ṫugs γtsigs-čuṅ-bar gyur-to* also the queen's mind was much dejected(?). — 3. *Mil.*: *γtsigs-la ˳bébs-pa* frq.; by the context: **to subdue, to force, compel,** also with supine, *˳baṅs bgyíd-par* to compel to obey. — 4. *Sch.*: *γtsigs-pai blo* quick comprehension, retentive memory.

གཙིགས་པ་ *γtsigs-pa*, with or without *mčé-ba*, **to show one's teeth, to grin** *Glr.*; *rnam-par γtsigs-pa* id. *Glr.*

གཙིར་བ་ *γtsír-ba* v. *˳tsir-ba.*

གཙུག་ *γtsug* 1. **crown of the head, vertex** *Lt.*, *spyi-γtsug* id. *Glr.* frq.; *γtsúg-tu ˳čiṅ-ba* to fasten on the head; fig. *sá-yig γtsúg-tu bčiṅs-pai ga*, cf. *ṫod.* — 2. **tuft, crest,** of birds *Sch.* — 3. **whirlpool, eddy, vortex,** in the water *Sch.*; *γtsug-˳k̔yil Wdṅ.*, also *rtsub-˳kyil*, perh. id.(?); *γtsug-rgyán* head-ornament, *γtsug-(gi) nór(-bu)* jewel of the head; frq. fig.: most high, most glorious among ..., c.genit.; also *γtsúg-gi nór-bur gyúr-pa Glr.*, = *mčóg-tu gyúr-pa.* — *γtsug-tor* = *ṫor-čog*, **उष्णीष**, conical or flame-shaped hair-tuft on the crown of a Buddha, in later times represented as an excrescence of the skull itself, v. *Burn.* II., 558. *Schl.* 209.

གཙུག་ལག་ *γtsug-lág* 1. **sciences,** '*literae*'; *γtsug-lág rnám-pa bčo-brgyád* the eighteen sciences; *k̔yod γtsúg-lag čé-ziṅ ˳dzúṅs-pa* thou, who art rich in knowledge and wisdom. — 2. **scientific work** or **works,** frq.; *γtsug-lag-k̔áṅ* **विहार**, academy, convent-temple and school, cf. also *gándhola*; *γtsúg-lag-mk̔an* or *-pa Cs.* a learned man.

གཙུགས་པ་ *γtsúgs-pa* **to bore out, scoop out, excavate** *Sch.*(?).

གཙུབ་པ་ *γtsúb-pa*, pf. *γtsubs*, **to rub**, *γtsub-śiṅ*, a piece of dry wood that is rubbed against another (*γtsub-stán* or *-γtán*) in order to make fire *Cs.*

གཙེ་བ་ *γtsé-ba*, pf. *γtses* v. *˳tsé-ba.*

གཙེགས་པ་ *γtségs-pa* = *˳dzigs-pa Sch.*

གཙེང་བ་ *γtséṅ-ba* = *γtsi-ba Sch.*

གཙེར་བ་ *γtsér-ba* = *˳tsé-ba Lex.*

གཙོ་ *γtso* 1. v. *γtsó-bo.* — 2. v. *γtsod.*

གཙོ་བོ་ γtsó-bo (Ssk. प्रधानं, consequently = mčog) 1. **the highest** in perfection, **the most excellent** in its kind, γtsó-bor or γtsor byéd-pa, lén-pa to place foremost, to consider the first or most excellent; γtso byás-pai bú-mo lṅa the five noblest of the girls *Mil.*; γtso byéd-pa-rnams the most respectable, the leaders, the heads *Mil.*; des γtsó-byas dpon-γyóg-rnams the higher and lower people subject to him *Pth.* (γtsó-byed-pa to be the first, belongs however rather under the head of no. 2); sṅágs-kyi γtsó-bo, smón-lam-gyi γtsó-bo (the same as rgyál-po) chief spell, principal prayer; yi-ge γtsó-bo súm-ču the 30 principal letters, (the letters of the alphabet) *Glr.*; nad-rnams kún-gyi γtsó-bo the principal disease, viz. fever *Lt.* (more correct from an Indian than from a Tibetan point of view); γtso-čé-ba **very important** *Thgr.*; **eminent** *Tar.*; γtsó-bor and γtso-čér, adv., **especially, chiefly, principally.** Hence: 2. **a chief, a principal, master, lord,** rkaṅ-γnyis-kyi (lord) of men, i.e. Buddha *Dzl.*; rten-gyi γtso-bo the 'lord' of the shrine, the deity to whom a shrine is consecrated, which in the lord's absence is guarded by some servant deity, e.g. *Dzl.* chap. VI.; čós-kyi γtsó-bo čén-po grand-master of the doctrine, a title of Sariibu *Dzl.*; **gentleman,** but chiefly as a title = Sir, Mr., blón-po γtsó-bo drúg-po, γtsó-bo mi drug the six (gentlemen) ministers *Glr.*; γtsó-mo the most distinguished lady, the noblest, first in rank, bú-mo γtsó-mo the most excellent among the girls; γtsó-mor ˳ós-pa žig the one most deserving of preference, the one of the noblest appearance *Mil.*; γtsó-mo mdzád-pa to be mistress, resp.

གཙོ་མ་, བཙོ་མ་ γtsó-ma, btsó-ma **hemp** *Sch.*

གཙོད་, བཙོད་, གཙོ་ γtsod, btsod, γtso (*Ld.* vulgo *stsod*), **the so-called Tibetan antelope,** with straight horns standing close together and in the direction of the longitudinal axis of the head *S.g.*, γtsód-mo fem., γtsod-ṗrúg the young one, γtsod-rús the bones, γtsod-ḱul the wool of it (used for shawls).

བཙའ་ btsa (btsa-ba *Sch.*?) 1. **rust,** lčágs-kyi btsa rust of iron; btsas-zas *Sch.*, ḱyer *Lex.* destroyed by rust. — 2. **rust, blight, smut,** of corn *Sch.* — 3. = btsag, *Sch.* — me-btsá **moxa** *Lt.*; mi-rus-btsa?

བཙའ་བ་ btsá-ba 1. pf. btsas, **to bear, to bring forth,** čuṅ-ma-la bu btsas his wife bore, gave birth to, a son *Dzl.*; bu btsá-bai ṫabs mi ṫub they could not bring forth *Dzl.*; btsás-pa what is begotten, new-born children or animals *Do.*; btsá-zug laṅs pains of labour ensued *Sch.* — 2. resp. **to watch, look on, spy,** spyán-gyis *Cs.*

བཙའ་མ་ btsá-ma **fruit** *Sch.* 2. = btsa *Sch.*

བཙག་ btsag, गैरिक, **red ochre** *Med.* and *Lex.*; used also of earths of a different colour; btsag-ṫáṅ, btsag-ri, btsag-lúṅ plain, hill, valley, of red earth; btsag-yug some other officinal mineral *Med.*

བཙག་པ་ btság-pa v ˳tság-pa.

བཙག་མོ་ btság-mo a certain beverage, = rtsáb-mo.

བཙང་བ་ btsáṅ-ba prob. = ˳tsáṅ-ba.

བཙང་པོ་ btsáṅ-po title of sovereigns *Glr.*, alledged to be but Khams-dialect for btsán-po.

བཙན་ btsan 1. a species of demons, residing in the air, on high rocks etc., mischievous, *Glr.*, *Dom.* — 2. v. the following article.

བཙན(པོ་) btsán(-po) **strong, mighty, powerful,** of kings, ministers etc., esp. as title of honour: **high-potent,** *Dzl.*, *Glr.*; hence of family, race, descent: **illustrious, noble,** lhá-mo btsán-rnams the queens of high descent, in opp. to a third of low extraction *Glr.*; btsan-(žiṅ) ṗyug(-po) noble and rich *Dzl.*, *Mil.*; **strong, violent,** btsan-dúg a virulent poison *Dzl.*; **forcible, violent,** btsan-˳ṗrógs byéd-pa to commit a robbery connected with violence *Pth.*; btsan-ṫabs-su by violent means *Pth.*; **coercive, strict, severe** bka, ḱrims *Glr.*, btsán-par mdzád-pa rigorously to enforce (a law); **firm, staunch, immovable, not wavering,** ṅag-btsán steadfastly abiding by one's word *Sch.*; **firm, safe.**

sure, *dben-ɣnás Mil.* a safe, inaccessible retreat; *rdzoṅ btsan* a firm stronghold *Lex.*; = concealed, hidden, hence *btsan-k̔aṅ* the innermost dark room in a temple, in which the gods reside, or an apartment for the same purpose on the top of a house; **definite, decided, without uncertainty,** *saṅs-rgyás-kyi bstán-pa mi núb-čiṅ mt̔a btsán-par byéd-pai p̔yir* in order that the doctrine of Buddha by being accurately defined may be secured against subversion *Pth.*

བཙབ་པ་ *btsáb-pa* imp. *btsob*, **to cut small, to chop,** wood; **to hash, to mince,** meat *C.*; *bstab-stán* chopping-block *C.*

བཙམ(ས)་པ་ *btsám(s)-pa* for *˳tsám-pa*, v. *tso*.

བཙལ་བ་ *btsál-ba* v. *˳tsól-ba.*

བཙས་པ་ *btsás-pa* v. *btsá-ba.*

བཙས་མ་ *btsás-ma* 1. also *rtsás-ma* **harvest,** *btsás-má rṅa-ba* **to reap, to mow** *C.* and *Lex.*, *btsás-ma ran tsa-na* in harvest time *Mil.*— 2. **wages, pay,** *gru-btsás Lex.*, fare, passage-money; *la-btsás Lex.*, *la-čan-gyi btsas?*

བཙིར་བ་ *btsir-ba* v. *˳tsir-ba.*

བཙུག(ས)་པ་ *btsúg(s)-pa* v. *˳dzúgs-pa.*

བཙུད་པ་ *btsúd-pa* v. *˳dzúd-pa, ˳tsúd-pa.*

བཙུན་པ་ *btsún-pa* 1. **respectable, noble,** of race, family, *rigs čé-žiṅ btsún-pa* id. *Dzl.*; *btsún-pai bud-méd Dzl.* a lady of rank. — 2. **reverend,** as title of ecclesiastics, *btsún-pa-rnams* the ecclesiastics, priests *Glr.*, = *ban-dhe* and *Ssk.* भदन्त (*Tar.* Transl. p. 4, note 7); even *btsún-pa k̔rims-méd* wicked Reverends *Ma.* — 3. **creditable, honourable, faithful** in observing religious duties, so frq.: *mk̔as btsun bzaṅ ɣsum* v. *mk̔as-pa*; *tsig-btsún-pa* grave and virtuous discourse *Schr.*, *Sch.*: polite words (?), *tsig mi btsun-pa Thgy.* was explained to me: one whom nobody believes; applied to things: **good;** thus *Mil.* says of his cane: *spa čo-ris yé-nas btsún-pa de* this cane of quite an excellent quality. — *btsún-po* = *btsún-pa* 1., *rgya-rjé btsún-po* the noble emperor of China *Glr.*; as a title v. *snyuṅ*; *btsún-por byéd-pa Cs.* to reverence. — *btsún-ma* priestess *Cs.* — *btsún-mo* 1. woman of rank, **a lady;** also as a term of address: your ladyship, e.g. in a legend, when a merchant speaks to the wife of a judge *Dzl.*; **spouse, consort,** esp. **queen consort,** with and without *rgyál-poi*, frq.; *btsún-mo čé-ba* = *čen-ma* the principal wife; *btsun-mo-čan* having a wife, *btsun-mo-méd* not having a wife *Cs.* — 2. **nun,** *mo-btsún*, id. *Glr.*, *C.*

བཙུམ་པ་ *btsúm-pa* v. *˳dzúm-pa.*

བཙེ་བ་ *btsé-ba* v. *˳tsé-ba.*

བཙེམ་པ་ *btsém-pa* v. *tsem-pa.*

བཙོ་ *btso*, **purification, refining** (?) **ser-la tso taṅ-wa** *C.* to refine gold (which term eventually is the same as 'to boil') v. *˳tsod-pa*; *btsó-ma*, *btsós-ma* a purified substance, *ɣser btsó-ma*, purified gold, very frq. with regard to a bright yellow colour *Glr.*

བཙོ་བ་ *btsó-ba* v. *˳tsód-pa*; *btso-blag-pa* **to dye, to colour,** *btso-blág-mk̔an* **a dyer,** *Lex.*

བཙོ་མ་ *btsó-ma* 1. = *ɣtsó-ma.* — 2. v. *btso.*

བཙོག་པ་ *btsóg-pa* I. vb. v. *˳tsog-pa.*

II. adj., also *(b)rtsóg(s)-pa*, *W.* **sóg-po** 1. **unclean, dirty, nasty, vile,** *˳di-ni šin-tu rtsóg-pai sa yin* this is a very vile place, says the prince of hades to a saint visiting there; so also every Tibetan will say to a stranger entering his house; *ṅa btsog-čiṅ* when I am getting unclean, i.e. when I am confined *Dzl.*; *lus btsog-pa mnyam-pa ˳di* this vile stinking body *Dzl.* — 2. in *W.* the common word for **bad** in every respect, **useless, spoiled, troublesome, perilous** (e.g. of a road); **injurious;** also in a more relative sense, **inferior, poor,** of goods; *btsog-nág* tobacco-juice, oil from the tobacco-pipe.

བཙོང་ *btsoṅ* **onion** *Med.* and vulgo, eschewed by pious Buddhists and ascetics, but a favourite food of the bulk of the people; *btsoṅ sreg-pa* to roast onions.

བཙོང་བ་ *btsóṅ-ba* v. *ₒtsóṅ-ba*.

བཙོད་ *btsod* n. of an animal, = *γtsod*, q v. — 2. n. of a plant, **madder** **मञ्जिष्ठा**, (*Rubia Manjit*); *btsod-ₒbru* seeds of this plant, *btsod-žiṅ* field on which it is grown.

བཙོན་ *btson*, also *btsón-pa*, **a captive, prisoner,** *nyés-pa byás-pai btson žig* an imprisoned criminal *Dzl.*; *btsón-du ₒdzin-pa* to take prisoner *Dzl.*; *ₒjúg-pa* to put to prison; *btsón-nas ₒdón-pa* to set free, *ťár-ba* to be released; *bzáṅ-btson* undeserved imprisonment or detention (ni f.), e.g. of hostages, fig. of people that are snowed up *Mil* — *btsón-ǩaṅ*, *btson-ra* prison. — *btsón-doṅ* 1. **dungeon,** keep; *Mil.*: *γnás-skabs-kyi btsón-doṅ* the dungeon of life. — 2. *W.* **deep abyss, gulf,** **tsón-doṅ ťóṅ-na mi máṅ-poi go ǩor** many are getting dizzy, when looking into a deep abyss. — *btsón-rdzi*, *btsón-sruṅ* jailer, turnkey. — *btsón-rdzas* prison-fare.

བཙོལ་བ་ *btsól-ba* v. *ₒtsól-ba*.

རྩ་ *rtsa* I. sbst., i. re col. *rtsá-ba* (*W.* **sá-wa**) or *rtsá-bo S.g.* 5, 1. **vein,** *rtsa γčód-pa* to open a vein *Dzl.*, **sá-wa gyáb-če** *W.* id. Owing to the imperfect state of Indian and Tibetan anatomy, resulting from inveterate prejudices both of a religious and intellectual nature, great confusion prevails also in the department of angiology, many different vessels of the human body, and even part of the nerves being classed among the veins, so that it is impossible to find adequate terms for the Tibetan nomenclature. This applies e.g. to the division of the *rtsa* in *čágs-pai*, *srid-pai*, *ₒbrél-pai*, and *tséi* or *srόg-gi rtsa*, which last term does not correspond to what we understand by artery (*Cs.*); so it is also with respect to the three principal veins, which by a mystic theory are stated to proceed from the heart, *dbú-ma* the middle one, white, *rkyáṅ-ma* the left one, red, and *ró-ma* the right one, white, concerning which cf. the articles *γtúm-mo* and *ťig-le*; *rtsa-dkár*, also *rlúṅ-rtsa Med.*, are perh. in most cases the same as **artery,** acc. to the well-known supposition of the ancients, that the veins of dead men, appearing empty, contain air; *p̓ar-rtsa* id., as in the living body it pulsates; *rtsa-nág* or *ǩrág-rtsa*, vein, blood-vessel; *rtsa-sbúbs* is mentioned *Lt.* 147, 10, as a surgical instrument. Some names are more or less clear: *mig-rtsa* seems to be the Vena fac. ext., *rtsa-čúṅ* Vena jugul. ext., *rtsa-čén* or *rtsa-bo-čé* V. saphena magna, *p̓o-mťsan-ghi dbus-rtsa* V. dorsalis penis. *rgyú-grog-rtsa*, on the other hand, are the ureters, ni f., which are represented as proceeding from the small intestine. — *rtsa-rgyus Med.* 1. *Sch.*: 'veins and sinews' (?); *rtsa-rgyus-ₒgag* an obstruction of the veins *S g.* 2. title of a book: Directions how to feel the pulse. — *rtsa-čús*, *C. rtsa-ₒdus* cramp. — *rtsa-mdúd* an inturgescence of the veins. — *rtsa-γnás Mil.* seems to be a net of veins, vascular plexus, any connection of things that may be compared to it, as e.g. the causal connection of the 12 Nidanas (v. *rten-ₒbrel* sub *rtén-pa* comp.) — *rtsa-spún* tissue of veins *Sch.* — 2. **pulse,** so in *rtsa ltá-ba*, or *rtog-pa Med.* to feel one's pulse, and *mťson-*, *kan-*, or *čag-rtsa* the feeling one's pulse with the second, third or fourth finger.

II. sbst, for *rtsá-ba*.

III. particle in conjunction with numerals: 1. gen. connecting the tens with the units, equivalent to **and:** *nyi-šu-rtsa-γčig* twenty and one; less frq. after *brgya* and *stoṅ*, where also *daṅ-rtsa* is not unusual, yet examples as the following: *S g.*, fol. 5, where the sum of 62, 33, 95 and 112 is stated to be = *sum-brgya-rtsa-γnyis*, and *Pth.* p. 34, twice *lṅa-brgyá-rtsa γčig* = *stoṅ-daṅ-rtsa-γnyis*, — exclude any doubt as to the proper use of the word. — 2. inst. of *nyi-šu-rtsa-γčig* to *nyi-šu-rtsa-dgu*, *rtsa-γčig* etc. is also used by itself, as an abbreviation, e.g. *S.g.* p. 3, in describing the growth of an embryo from week to week; this use of the word may account for the assumption, quite general in *W.* and *C.*, that *rtsa* in itself is equivalent to 20, for even Lamas of both districts could be convinced only by an arithmetical proof, that the numbers mentioned in the above passages were 302 and 1002, and not 322 and 1022. — 3. In *bčú-rtsa nyí-šu-rtsa, brgyá-rtsa*, without any units following, e.g *Tar.* 120, 10, the word evidently stands but pleonastically, like *tam-pa*.

ཙྭ་ *rtswa* (*Bal.*, *Pur. rtswa, stswa*) *C.* *tsa*, *Lh.*, *Ld.*, *sa*, **तिणं, grass, herb, plant,** *rtsa-kai* (or *rtsa-rtsei*) *zil-pa* the dew on the grass *Glr.*; *rtsa nyag γčig* a single blade of grass *Cs.*; *snó-yi rtsa, rtsa-snón* green grass; *rtsa-skám*, and often *rtsa* alone, **hay,** *rtsa rná-ba* to mow grass, *ₒtú-ba*, to gather (grass); *rtsá-ka C., W.* pasture, pasturage, **sá-ka gyál-la** *W.* good pasturage. — *rtsá-čan* covered with grass, grassy. — *rtsa-mčóg* Kusha-grass *Lex.*, v. *ku-ša*; *rtsa-mčog* (*-groṅ*) town in West Assam, where Buddha died *Glr.*; Kamarūpa. — *rtsa-tág* grass-rope *Dzl.* — *rtsa-tún* grass-gatherer *Sch.* — *rtsa-γdán* grass-mat *Sch.* — *rtsa-γyáb* manger *Sch.* — *rtsa-ras Sch.* 'linen', prop. the same as *la-ta* q. v. — 2. euphemism for *rkyag*; **tsa táṅ-wa** *C.* to go to stool; *rtsa ču bsdams Mil.* he suffers from obstruction and strangury.

ཙ་བ་ *rtsá-ba*, I. cf. *rtsaṅ* and *rtsad*, *Ssk.* **मूल. 1. root** (*W.* com. **bá-tag** for it), **stalk of fruits;** *rtsá-ba lṅa* five (medicinal) roots, viz. *rá-mnye, lčá-ba, nyé-šiṅ, ǎ-šo* (better *ǎ-ša*)*-gandha, γzé-ma*; *rtsá-ba-nas ₒbyin-pa* etc. to pull out with the root, to eradicate, extirpate, mostly fig., v. below. — 2. **the lower end** of a stick, trunk of a tree, pillar; *má-tog rtsá-ba* id. *Mil.*; the **foot** of a hill, mountain-pass, the latter also *lá-rtsa W.* **lár-sa**; *rtsá-bai žal, lag* the lower faces or hands of those images, that represent deities with many faces and hands *Glr.*; *rtsá-bai ṅos* base of a triangle *Tar.* 204, 1; **fundament, foundation-pillar,** and the like; in later literature and vulgo *rtsá-bar* and *rtsar*, rarely (*Glr.*) *rtsá-ru* postp. with genit., **to, at,** e.g. to go to, to come to, to be at, both of persons and things, *bud-méd-kyi rtsar nyál-ba* or more euphem., *p̓yin-pa* to go to a woman *Glr.*, *šiṅ-gi rtsar*, even *čui rtsar Glr.*; **at, near, to,** a tree, river etc.; so also *rtsá-la* **to, at;** *rtsá*(*-ba*)*-na Glr.* and vulgo (incorr.) **tsá-ne** *C.* **at, near;** without a case following: *rtsar byúṅ-nas* coming near, stepping up to *Glr.* — 3. **root** fig. **origin, primary cause,** also *γži-rtsa*, e.g. *ₒkor-bai γži-rtsa γčod-pa Mil.* to cut off the root of transmigration, to deliver a soul from tr.; *rtsá-ba-nas ₒbyin-pa, ₒdón-pa, ₒgóg-pa* etc., also *tsáṅ-nas, tsád-nas γčód-pa* etc., to exterminate (root and branch), to annihilate; on the other hand: *rtsa-brdár-γčod-pa Mil.*, *rtsád-γčod-pa* to examine closely, to investigate thoroughly. — *nyȯn-móṅs-kyi rtsá-ba γsum* are the three primary moral evils, viz. *ₒdod-čágs, že-sdáṅ, γti-mug*; *rtsa-brál* therefore might signify: he who has freed himself from them; but it seems to mean also: without beginning or end, **unlimited,** e.g. *snyiṅ-rje Glr.*, *sems nyid Mil.*; *dgé-bai rtsá-ba, dgé-rtsa* a virtuous deed, as a cause of future reward, *skyéd-pa, spyód-pa, byéd-pa* to perform such a deed; *rtsá-bai* . . . **the original primary, principal** . . . . e.g. *don*, primitive or first meaning *Cs.*; *rtsá-bai nyon-móṅs-pa Cs.*: 'original sin', *Sch.*: 'sin inherited from former births'; at all events not identical with the original sin of Christian dogmatics, although the word grammatically might denote it; *rtsa* (*-bai*) *rgyud* an introductory treatise, giving a summary of the contents of a larger work, e.g. of the *rgyud-bži*, mentioned sub *brgyud*; also title of other works, *Ssk.* **मूलतन्त्र**, v. *Cs. Gram.*, chronol. table; whether *Sch.*'s translation 'cause and effect' is altogether correct, may admit of some doubt, yet v. below; *rtsá-ba daṅ ₒgrél-ba Cs.* 'text and commentary'; in *rtsá-bai ma Thgy.* the genitive case stands prob. for the apposition: the mother that is the root of me, in a similar manner as *rtsá-bai raṅ-bžin* nature *Cs.*; *rtsá-bai blá-ma* seems to denote the teaching priest, the one by whom in any particular case the instruction is given, opp. to *brgyúd-pa*, he to whom it is imparted. A good deal of confusion however prevails here, owing to the ambiguity of the verbal form in *brgyúd-pa* and the variable spelling;

v. *rgyúd-pa* extr. — *rtsa-ťór Sch.*: 'lower end and top' (?) (should perh. be *rtsa-ťog*); *rtsa-mi Tar.* 191, 3 is rendered by *Schf.* with 'Haupt-Mann', principal man. — *rtsa-lág* (*Schr.*: root and branches) *Lex.* बन्धु relations, kindred; *rtsa-lag-čan* having relations, *rtsa-lag-med* without relations *Cs.* — *rtsa-šés Sch.*: primitive wisdom. — 4. symb. num.: 9. — II. v. *rtsa* **vein.**

Note. *rtsa*, vein, is traced by Tibetan scholars back to *rtsá-ba*, the veins being the 'roots of life'; in a dictionary the words are better treated separately.

ཙ་ལ་ *rtsá-la* v. *rtsá-ba* I, 2.

ཙང་ *rtsaṅ* = *rtsá-ba* seldom, v. *rtsá-ba* I, 3.

ཙངས་པ་ *rtsáṅs-pa* lizard, *brag-gi Lt.* (*W.* **gag-čig**).

ཙད་ *rtsad* = *rtsá-ba* **root,** *rtsád-nas γčód-pa Mil.* to root out, to eradicate; *rtsad γčód-pa,* = *rtsa-brdár γčód-pa,* = *ťsar* and *γsar γčód-pa*, to search, investigate *Mil.*; *gar bžugs rtsad bčád-nas* to inquire, search for a person's place of abode *Pth.*

ཙབ་པ་, ཙབ་ཙབ་ *rtsab, rtsab-rtsab* v. *tsab-tsub.*

ཙབས་ *rtsabs* **ferment, barm, yeast,** prepared of barley-flour; *rtsabs-ǩur* a sweetish sort of bread, made up with it *Ld.*; *rtsábs-mo* a beverage brewed from roasted meal (*rtsám-pa*) and water, and made to ferment by adding butter-milk, esp. liked in winter; also called *btság-mo; žó-rtsabs Sch.* milk-brandy, not known to us.

ཙབས་རུ་ཙ་ *rtsabs-ru-tsa Lt.* n. of a medicine.

ཙམ་པ་ *rtsám-pa*, I. sbst. 1. **roast-flour,** flour from roasted grain, *ₒbras-rtsam* of rice, *gro-rtsam* of wheat, *nas-rtsam* of barley, this last the most common; stirred with water, beer, or tea into a pap, it is the usual food in *C.* — *rtsám-ₒbru* roast-flour and grain = victuals in gen. *Kun.* — *rtsám-rin* the price of flour *Sch.* — 2. **urine** *Lt.* *rtsam-mdóg* colour of urine.

II. vb. v. *rtsóm-pa.*

ཙར་ *rtsar* v. *rtsá-ba* I, 2.

ཙལ་ *rtsal* 1. **skill, dexterity, adroitness, accomplishment;** in the first place **physical skill,** *lag-rtsal-čan* of a skilful, practised hand *W.*; *sgyu-rtsál* id., *stobs daṅ sgyu-rtsál* strength and dexterity *Glr.*, skilfulness; *rtsal(daṅ) ldán(-pa)* skilful, expert, adroit, *rtsal-méd* the contrary; *rtsal ₒgran-pa* to vie in skill, *rtsal sbyóṅ-ba* to practise, or improve one's self in skill *Mil.*; *rtsal šor* all skill is gone, *rgud* id. *Sch.*; *stobs-(kyi) rtsal, Lex.* पराक्रम, strength, energy, *mťu-rtsál* and *rtsal-mťu* prob. id. *Dzl.*, *S.g.*; *rtsal-čé-ba* or *rtsal-po-čé* adroit as a gymnastic, wrestler etc.; also sbst. athlete, juggler etc. *Dzl.*; *rtsál-gyi mčoṅs* a gymnastic feat *Lex.*; *rtsal-sbyoṅ* bodily exercise, nimbleness, agility, *báṅ-rtsal-sbyoṅ* nimbleness in running, *γšóg-rtsal-sbyoṅ* agility in flying *Mil.*; *ču-rtsál* feats performed in the water; the art of swimming *Pth.*; vulgo *W.* also for natural, innate abilities: *mig-rtsal-mǩan* keen-sighted, *mig-rtsal nyams* of a weak sight; *rtsal-ťón Sch.* 'skilful, masterly' (?) — 2. in later times used in a special sense of **skill, expertness in contemplation,** cf. *sgóm-pa;* so frq. with *Mil.*; *byaṅ-čub-sėms-kyi rtsal γsum*; *lam-ₒgag-méd-kyi rtsál-ǩa* such accomplishments 'as will clear the road', — ascetical terms familiar only to the initiated.

ཙས་མ་ *rtsás-ma* v. *btsás-ma.*

ཙི་ *rtsi* 1. all fluids of a somewhat greater consistency, such as the **juice** of some fruits, **paints, varnish** etc., *rtsi-čan* **viscid, sticky, clammy;** **tsi gyág-pa* C.*, **si gyáb-če, kú-če, táṅ-če* W.* to colour, to paint, **tsi táṅ-wa* C.* also to solder; *ldab-pa*(?) *Sch.* to lacker, to varnish; *sbráṅ-rtsi* **honey;** *nád-kyi rkyen rtsi* a medical draught, potion *Dzl.* ༥༦, 7, (another reading: *sman*); *bdúd-rtsi* nectar; *tsón-rtsi* painter's colour, *dkár-rtsi* white-wash, *nág-rtsi* black paint, *dmár-rtsi* red paint; **sér-tsi* C.* gilding, **ṅúl-tsi** silvering *C.* — 2. applied to external appearance: **dóṅ-si* W.* **complexion;** even *spa rtsi ₒjam ǩa-dóg légs-pa de* this cane, as to its outside smooth, as to colour beautiful *Mil.* (unless *rtsi* be = shell, bark, rind?)

— *rtsi-tóg* juicy fruit; *rtsi-śiṅ* 1. **fruit-tree** *Pth.* 2. **tree,** in gen. *Glr.* and elsewh., frq. — *rtsi-gu* fruit-kernel, the kernel in a fruit-stone (not the latter itself *Sch.*); *W.* for **tsi-gu**, q.v.; *rtsi-gu-mar-nag* oil extracted from the stones of apricots; *rtsi-már Lt.* id.

རྩི་བ་ *rtsi-ba*, pf. (*b*)*rtsis*, fut. *brtsi*, imp. (*b*)*rtsi*(*s*) 1. **to count,** **si-te bór-če** *W.* to pay down, money; cf. also *rtsis.* — 2. **to count, reckon, calculate,** *mi ré-la p̓ul re-réi t̓ád-du* reckoning a handful to each *Dzl.*; *žag súm-ču-la zlá-ba γčig, zlá-ba bču-γnyis-la lor rtsi-ba* to reckon a month at 30 days, a year at 12 months *Thgy.*; *mi-lo-ltar rtsi-ba* to count by the years of a man *Thgy.*; *gaṅ bzaṅ rtsi-ba* to calculate which (day) be a propitious one *Glr.*; *dus rtsi-ba* to reckon up, to compute the time *Mil.*; **če-miṅ ḍál-la si-če** *W.* to reckon among the adults; *yón-tan-la skyón-du rtsi-ba* to consider good qualities as faults, = *ltá-ba* I, 2; *brduṅ rtsi* he may be reckoned to strike, i.e. he is very likely to strike, threatens to strike *C.*; *brtsís zin* 1. **the account is closed,** the bill is ready. 2. **product, sum total.**

རྩིའུ་ *rtsiu* n. of a plant, = *pri-yáṅ-ku Wdṅ.*

རྩིག་པ་ *rtsig-pa* I. vb., pf. (*b*)*rtsigs*, fut. *brtsig*, imp. (*b*)*rtsig*(*s*), 1. **to build,** whether of stone or of wood, *k̓áṅ-pa.* — 2. **to wall up,** *sgo* a door *Glr.* — II. sbst **wall, masonry.**

Comp. *rtsig-skyábs Stg.* is said to be = *rtsig-rmáṅ.* — *rtsig-ṅós* side of a wall. — *rtsig-rdó* stone for building. — *rtsig-dpón* master-mason, architect. — *rtsig-p̓úr* a peg in a wall, wall-hook, to hang up things. — *rtsig-rmáṅ* fundament of a wall. — *rtsig-zúr* edge or ledge of a wall *Thgy.* — *rtsig-bzó-pa* brick-layer, mason. — *rtsig-γyóg* journeyman mason.

རྩིགས་ *rtsigs*, *Sch.*: '*rtsigs-čé* very gracious and well-affected' (?), prob. should be *rtsis-če* q. v. no. 3.

རྩིགས་མ་ *rtsigs-ma* **turbid matter, sediment, impurity,** = *tsigs-ma S.g.*

རྩིང་བ་ *rtsiṅ-ba* adj. and sbst., **coarse, clumsy, rough, rude; coarseness** etc., *B.*; *rtsiṅ-po B.* and *C.*, *rtsiṅ-ge C.*, *W.* id., but only adj; *p̓ye* coarse meal, grits (opp. to *žib-po*, *ʼjám-po*); *spyód-pa rtsiṅ-ba* of rude manners *Glr.*

རྩིད་པ་ *rtsid-pa* **the long hair of the yak,** *rtsid-t̓ágs* = *re-t̓ágs* coarse cloth manufactured of it; *rtsid-stán* saddle-cloth *Mil.*; *rtsid-gúr* tent-covering made of it.

རྩིབ(ས)་མ་ *rtsib*(*s*)-*ma* 1. **rib,** *rtsib-mai bár-nas* from between the ribs *Glr.*; *rtsib-lógs γyas γyon* all the ribs of the right and left side *Dzl*; *rtsib-logs ná-ba* pain about the ribs *Do.*; *rtsib-riṅ* the upper ribs (?) — 2. **spoke** of a wheel, frq.; *rtsib-kyi mu-k̓yúd* fellies composing the rim of a wheel *Cs.*; in ornamental designs the *rtsib-ma* are often fanciful figures, supplying the radii of the circle; further: **the sticks** or **ribs** of a parasol, canopy etc. *Glr.*; **the spars** of a felt-tent, **the ribs** or **futtocks** of a boat *Schr.* — *rtsib-ri* n. of a mountain, = *śri-ri.*

རྩིས་ *rtsis* 1. **counting, numbering, numeration,** *rtsis-las ˳das-pa* innumerable *Mil.*; **bód si-la, món-si-la** *W.* according to Tibetan, according to Indian counting or computation of time (is to-day the twentieth); **mi-si, ḍóṅ-si** *W.* numbering of the people, of the domiciliated; **mág-si táṅ-če** *W.* to hold a numbering of military forces. — 2. **account,** *rtsis byéd-pa Glr.*, *˳débs-pa Mil.*, *γyáb-pa C.*, *W.* **kor-če*, (*l*)*ta-če** **to calculate, to compute,** *rtsís-su sbyár-ba* to count together, to sum up *Dzl.*; **calculation, computation** (beforehand), **scheme;** **žag nyi-śu-la ˳gro-* (or *ča-rtsis yod*)* *W.* in about 20 days we calculate, i.e. we intend, to go; **śiṅ-ta gyúg-si yód-pe dus-tsód-la** *Ld.* at the hour, when according to their calculation the carriage was to start; *rtsis-kyis* (or *rtsis byás-nas*) *ṅó-śes-pa* to find by computation *Glr.* — *skár-rtsis* **astrology, astronomy;** *dkár-rtsis, nág-rtsis*, acc. to *Cs.*: Indian and Chinese astronomy and chronology. — 3. **estimation, esteem,** *rtsís-po čén-po byéd-pa* to value, to make much of, *lús-kyi rtsis-po-če* one that makes much of his own body, by indulging and adorning it *Thgy.*; *rtsis-rtsis byéd-pa Sch.* id.; *dé-la bla-*

lhág-tu rtsis-su byed he respected her beyond measure *Tar.*, *Schf.* — **si-rúg** vulgo *W.* for *rtsis* in most of its significations.

རྩིས་པ་ *rtsis-pa* 1. also *rtsis-mk'an* **mathematician, astronomer, soothsayer; accountant** *Cs.* — 2. n. pr. *rtsis-pa ḋ-mgrón* secular, *rtsis-pa mgron-ɣnyér* spiritual name of the late Resident of the Sikim government at Darjeeling, called by the English Cheboo Lama, † 1866, v. Hooker Journ. — *rtsis-dpon* a chief mathematician, chief accountant, receiver general *Cs.*

རྩུབ་པ་ *rtsúb-pa* I. vb. **to revile, abuse,** v. *ṅor rtsub-pa* sub *ṅo.*

II. adj., com. *rtsúb-po, rtsúb-mo Ssk.* **परुष, uneven, rough, rugged,** of the skin, cloth etc.; **coarse-grained,** powder; **rough, wild, dreary,** countries, *roṅ-rtsub* with wild ravines *Glr.*; **bristly,** hair; **harsh, tart, astringent,** of taste *Med.*; also applied to any thing of a highly **aromatic, pricking, pungent** or **acerb** taste, such as onions and similar vegetables, liable to cause both dietetic and religious scruples; *rtsub-zás* food of this description; in music: **strong, forte;** of sentiment and behaviour: **rude, unfeeling, regardless, callous** *S.g.*, *Glr.*

རྩེ(མོ)་ *rtse(-mo)* 1. **point, top, peak, summit,** *k'aṅ-, gri-, ri-, śiṅ-rtse*, or *k'aṅ-pai* etc., *rtsé-mo* **gable** of a house, point of a knife, top of a hill, head of a tree; of convents, royal palaces, resp.: *dbú-rtse Glr.*; *lá-rtse*, *W.* **lár-se** (cf. *rtsá-ba* I, 2.) **lá-se** **summit** of a mountain-pass; *rtse daṅ logs-su* terminal and lateral *Wdṅ.*; *rtsé-sgro Glr.* flag-feather, pinion; *ža rtse-riṅ* hat with a high crown *Tar.*; *rtse ɣčil-ba Sch.*: to break off the point, to blunt; *rtse-reg-čé Mil.* very sensitive, touchy, not to be touched with the tip of the finger. — 2. **point, particular spot,** *rtse ɣčig-tu ltá-ba* to look at one point; also adv., to look **steadily, unremittingly,** as: *ráṅ-gi grib-ma-la rtse-ɣčig-tu ltá-ba Wdṅ.*, also *Tar.* frq.; *sems rtse ɣčig-tu byed-pa* to direct the mind to one point, frq.; *sems rtse-ɣčig-tu byás-pai tiṅ-ṅe-ₒdzin-la žúgs-te Dzl.*; aim, *tse ₒdii rtse ɣčig* as this life's only aim *Mil.*

རྩེ་བ་ *rtsé-ba*, pf. *rtses*, imp. *rtse(s)*, **क्रीड्,** (different from *brtsé-ba*) 1. **to play,** *mig-máṅ* at chess *Dzl.*; **to sport, to frolic,** used also of animals *Dzl.*; *rtse bro ɣtóṅ-ba* to run to and fro, playing and skipping, of deer *Mil.*; **to joke, to jest,** *rtsé-žiṅ dgá-ba, rtse-dgá spyád-pa* id.; **ɣáṅ(s)-pa sé-če** *W.* id.; **to enjoy, amuse, divert one's self, to take recreation,** *tsal-gyi naṅ-du rtser soṅ* they went on a pleasure party into the woods *Dzl*; euphem. of cohabitation, *ₒdi daṅ rtsé-bar byao Pth.* I mean to enjoy her.

Comp. *rtsé-mk'an* player, gambler, gamester. — *rtse-gróg*s, *rtsed-gróg*s play-mate. — *rtse-dgá* v. above. — *rtse-rgód* sport and laughter. — *rtsé-sa* play-ground, place of amusement. — *rtse-sems* a mind fond of play; *k'yód-kyis rtsé-sems yin mod k'yaṅ* though you may still relish pleasures *Pth.*

2. **to touch,** *W.* **lág-pa ma se** do not touch it with your hand. — 3. **to shudder** (cf. *spu*).

རྩེ་ཆུང་ *rtse-čúṅ* = *rtsa-čúṅ*, Vena jugularis externa.

རྩེག་པ་ *rtség-pa*, pf. *(b)rtsegs*, fut. *brtseg*, imp. *rtsog*, *W.* **ság-če(s)** 1. **to lay one thing on or over another, to pile up, stack up, build up,** wood, boards; to put slices of meat on bread; fig.: *ná-ro ɣnyis brtseg* two 'naro' one above the other, ཻ, *Gram.*; gen. **double;** *k'aṅ-pa rtsegs-pa* 1. **'a house of two stories'** = a stately building, palace; by this word *Wdṅ.* explains *k'aṅ-bzáṅ*, v. *bzáṅ-po.* 2. acc. to other *Lexx.*, **an apartment built on another,** an upper chamber; balcony on the roof of a house, **कूटागार**; *rgya-grám brtségs-pai mčód-rten* a chod-ten with a cross (v. *rgya-grám*) on the top *Pth.* — 2. **to tuck up,** clothes *Cs.* — 3. *dbugs rtségs-pa*, *gyén-du dbugs(-kyis) rtség-pa Med.*, **short-breathed, asthmatic, panting, gasping,** from fright etc., or as a sign of approaching death. — *dkon(-mčóg) brtségs(-pa)*; **रत्नकूट** title of a book.

རྩེང་བ་ *rtseṅ-ba*, pf. *brtseṅs*, fut. *brtseṅ*, imp. *(b)rtsoṅ(s)* **to tuck up, truss up.**

རྩེད་པ་ *rtséd-pa* I. also *rtsén-pa*, = *rtsé-ba* **to play;** *rtsed rtsé-ba* id.; *rtséd-mo*

play, game, *dgá-bai rtséd-mo byed-pa Dzl.*; *glu gar rtséd-mo byéd-pa* to sing, dance and play *Glr.*; *rtséd-mo* **toy,** *byis-pai* children's toy *Mil.*; *rtséd-mo-čan* **playful, sportive, merry** *Cs.*; *rkyál-*, *gár-*, *grí-*, *čól-*, *mčóṅ-*, *rtá-rtsed* the sport of swimming, dancing, fencing, dicing, leaping, riding *Cs.*; *γyeṅ-rtséd* **play, amusement, diversion;** *rtsed-dgá* id. *Sch.*; *to-to-liṅ-líṅ rtsed* q. v.; *rtséd-ₒjo*, *rtsén-ₒjo*, *W.* **séṅ-jo** **sport, public amusement, popular pleasure;** *γžón-nu rtséd-ₒjoi tsógs-kyis bskór-nas* surrounded by a number of youthful playmates; **séṅ-jo táṅ-če* W.* to arrange a sport.

II. **to varnish** (?).

རྩེད་མ་ *rtséd-ma* the disagreeable feeling in the teeth produced by acids *Sch.*; *rsed-ám* a shivering, cold shudder *Sch.* v. *rtsé-ba* 3.

རྩེད་མོ་, རྩེན་པ་ *rtséd-mo*, *rtsén-pa* v. *rtséd-pa*.

རྩེན་གོག་ *rtsen-góg Mil*, acc. to *Sch.*: **calf of the leg.**

རྩེས་ *rtses* v. *rtsé-ba*.

རྩོག(ས་)པ་ *rtsóg(s)-pa* v. *brtsóg-pa*.

རྩོད་ལྡན་ *rtsod-ldán* n. of a certain era or period of the world v. *dus* 6.

རྩོད་པ་ *rtsód-pa*, I. vb., pf. *brtsad* **to contend, to fight with arms** *Dzl.*; with words: **to dispute, debate, wrangle,** frq., *daṅ* with, *la* about; *rtsód-čiṅ mi-snyán rǰód-pa* to speak evil words, to use bad language, in quarreling.

II. sbst. **dispute, contention, quarrel; disputation** *Glr.*; *rtsód-pa ₒgrán-pa* to compete in disputation *Glr.* — *ťsád-mai rtsód-pa* a learned debate about words; *rtsód-pa-rnams* points of controversy *Tar.* 132,18, *Schf.* — *rtsod-γží* the subject of a disputation.

རྩོན(མ་) *rtsón(-ma) Pur.* **nausea, vomiting,** **rtson ṗog** he grows sick; **rtsón-čas** **to be sick, to vomit.**

རྩོམ་པ་ *rtsóm-pa* I. vb., pf. *(b)rtsams*, *rtsoms*, fut. *brtsam*, imp. *rtsom(s)* 1. **to begin, commence** a work, **to be about, to set about** an undertaking; *ₒbrós-par brtsáms-te* being about to run away *Dzl.*; *čós-las brtsáms-te rtsód-do* it was about religion that our dispute began *Tar.*; *ṅo-lóg brtsáms-pa-las* beginning, stirring up an insurrection *Glr.*; *dé-nas brtsáms-te* beginning at this place, **from here, from that time** (cf. *bzúṅs-te* sub *bzúṅ-ba*). — 2. **to make, to accomplish,** *γsó-bai las mi brtsám-mo* so he will not accomplish the business of healing; com. **to compose, to draw up,** in writing, *bstán-bčos rtsom-mí* author, writer, composer *Pth.*; *brtson-ₒgrús rtsóm-pa Dzl.* frq., to work diligently, carefully; **to take pains, to exert one's self,** *rtsóm-par*, or *rtsóm-pa-la mḱás-pa* a clever writer, an elegant composer, which title in Tibet is applied to any one, that exhibits in his style high-sounding bombast with a flourish of religious phrases; *čad rtsod rtsom γsum-gyi bšad-gra Glr.* prob. a school, in which religion is taught and explained, combined with disputations and written compositions. —

II. sbt. **beginning, commencement** (**आरंभ**), *rtsóm-pa daṅ-po* the first beginning *Ld.-Glr.*; **a doing, proceeding, undertaking, deed** *Tar.*

རྩོལ་བ་ *rtsól-ba* 1. vb. **to endeavour, to take pains, to give diligence;** *rtsól-bar* adv. **diligently, zealously;** *ḱyód-kyis rtsól-bai dús-la bab* now you must use dispatch *Pth.*; *rtsol-méd* **unsought,** *rtsol-méd ₒgró-bai don byéd-pa* to seek the welfare of beings without their caring for it *Glr.*; *srog rtsól-ba Lex.* and *Mil.*, acc. to *Sch.*: **to draw breath, to take fresh courage,** which seems to be implied by *dbugs rtsól-ba Ma.*; *nyal-po rtsol drag(-na)* if cohabitation is immoderately indulged in *Med.* — 2. sbst. **zeal, endeavour, exertion,** *rtsól-ba skyéd-pa* to use diligence *Zam.*

སྩོལ་བ་ *stsól-ba*, pf. and fut. *stsol* (**sól-wa, sál-wa**), 1. **to give, bestow, grant,** when the person that gives is respectfully spoken to, much the same as *γnaṅ-ba* q.v.; *stsál-du γsol* please to give, to grant etc. *Dzl.*; *bdág-gi lám-rgyags stsol čig* pray, give me provisions (provender) for the journey *Dzl.*; **to give back, to return** what had been lent *Dzl.*; **to grant, bestow, afford, give** (as a present); also for γtóṅ-ba **to send, to send out,** so at least in *W.*; further: *W.* *ǰa sal, šu-gu sal, deb-sal* please to give me some tea, to lend me some paper, pray, give me change; or more pressingly: *ǰa sal gos* I earnestly request you for some tea etc., I entreat you to . . .; *sal mi gos* I thank you, I do not want it; *bká-stsal-ba* v. sub *bka; dṅos-grúb stsól-ba* to bestow spiritual gifts (?). — 3. sometimes incorr. for *bsál-ba* (*sél-ba*) **to clean, to clear, to remove** *Dzl.*

བརྩད་པ་, བརྩམ་པ་ *brtsád-pa*, *brtsám-pa* v. *rtsód-pa*, *rtsóm-pa*, sometimes incorr. for *btsád-pa*, *btsám-pa*.

བརྩེ་བ་ *brtsé-ba* vb. **to love,** sbst. **love, affection, kindness,** nearly the same as *byáms-pa*, frq. preceded by *snyiṅ*, resp. *ťugs*, q. v.; *brtsé-bas* out of love, kindness, e. g. *γnáṅ-ba* to give something out of love; **with love, lovingly, kindly,** e. g. *skyóṅ-ba* to protect; *brtsé-bai ťsig* words of love, kind exhortations *Glr.*; *brtsé-bai p̔yag-bris* your very kind letter; *snyiṅ-brtse-ba*, resp. *ťúgs-brtse-ba* = *brtsé-ba; brtsé-ba-čan, brtse-ldán* **loving, affectionate, kind;** *brtse(-ba)-méd(-pa)* **unkind, unmerciful, ungracious;** *brse-γdúṅ* **love, affection,** *p̔a-má brtse-γdúṅ če yaṅ či žig bya* what could even parental love do? *Glr.*; *lha-p̔rúg γžón-nui brtse-γdúṅ de* this proof of love on the part of young goddesses towards me *Mil.*

བརྩོན་པ་ *brtsón-pa* 1. vb. with *la*, **to strive, to aim at, to exert one's self for,** *ťsógs-pa-la* an accumulation of merits, frq.; *brtsón-par byéd-pa*, or *ₒgyúr-ba*, also with *mṅón-par* preceding it; **to apply one's self,** *lás-la* to business, *ťugs-dám-la* to meditation *Dzl.*, *Mil.* — 2. sbst. (*Ssk.* वीर्य, *virtus*) **endeavour, effort, care, exertion,** *byá-ba-la brtsón-pa* alacrity, readiness to act *Wdṅ.*; more frq. *brtson-ₒgrús* v. below. — 3. adj. = *brtsón-pa-čan, brtson-ldán Mil.*, **diligent, assiduos, studious,** *sgrúb(-pa)-la* eager to obtain power over demons *Mil.*; *brtsón-par* **on purpose, with intention, wilfully;** as sbst. mostly *brtson-ₒgrús*, with *skyéd-pa, byéd-pa, rtsóm-pa* to use diligence, to show energy, zeal etc.; *brtson-ₒgrús drág-po* intense application; *brtson-ₒgrus-čan* **assiduous, studious,** *brtson-ₒgrus nyáms-te Stg.* having lost one's energy.

ཚ

ཚ 1. the letter *ťsa*, the aspirate of ཙ (cf. ཅ), sounded *ťs.* — 2. num. fig.: 18.

ཚ་ *ťsa*, 1. **hot,** v. *ťsa-ba.* — 2. **grandchild,** v. *ťsá-bo.* — 3. v. *ťsa-ťsa.* — 4. resp. **illness, complaint** *C.*

ཚྭ་ *ťswa* **salt,** *ťswa ₒdébs-pa* **to salt,** with *la*; *ťsa nyén-če* *W.* to taste, to try, food prepared with salt; *k̔a-ru-ťswa* **alum** *Med.*; *rgya-ťswa* **sal-ammoniac** *Med.*; *lče-myaṅ-ťswa* **alum** *Lt.*; *rdo-ťswa* **rock-salt** *Cs.*; *ba-ťswa* **impure soda,** v. *bá-mo.* — *bód-ťswa Lt.?* — *lán-ťswa* = *ťswa.* — *ťswa-k̔a* salt mine *Cs.* — *ťsa-(k̔u-)čan* *W.* **saline, salinous.** — *ťswa-sgo* place where salt is found. — *ťsa-tsé* **sal-ammoniac** *C.* — *ťsa-ču* **salt-water, brine;** acc. to some, **vinegar** (?).

ཚ་སྐོར་ *ťsa-skór* v. *ťsá-bo.*

ཚ་ཁང་ *ťsa-k̔áṅ* v. *ťsa-ťsá.*

ཚ་འཁྲུ་ *ťsa-ₒk̔rú* v. *ťsa-ba.*

ཚ་ག་འབུ་ *ťsá-ga-ₒbu*, also *čá-ga-ₒbu*, *ťsag-ťság* **grasshopper, locust** *C.*

ཚ་གཅིག་མ་ *ťsa-γčig-ma* **thick blanket, quilt** *C.*

ཚ་ཆུ་ *ťsa-ču* v. *ťsa-ba.*

ཚྭ་ཚུ་ *ťswa-ču* v. *ťswa.*

ཚ་དྲག་ *ťsa-drág* **haste, hurry,** **ťsa-ḍág ǰhe šig** *C.*, **ťsa-rág toṅ** *W.* make haste! — adv. *ťsa-drág-tu Sch.* but also **mā ťsa-rág šog** *W.* come quickly, without delay!

ཚ་སྣ་ *ťsá-sna* **anxiety** about, **tender care** for **a thing,** ni.f.; **ťsa-na-čan** *W.* **solicitous, careful, attached,** **ťsa-na-méd-ḱan** *W.* **indifferent, unfeeling, callous;** *ḱán-pe* **ťsá-na ḱúr-ḱan** *W.* one that has to care for the welfare of a household or community, superintendent etc.

ཚ་སྣག་ *ťsa-snág Sch.* = *snág-ťsa* **ink.**

ཚ་པན་ཚེ་ *ťsa-pan-tsé C.* **dresser, kitchen-table.**

ཚ་བིག་ *ťsá-big Ld.* **a little.**

ཚ་བ་ *ťsá-ba* I. vb. **to be hot,** *só-ga-(la) nyi-mai ˬod-zér ráb-(tu-) ťsá-bas* as at the time of the Soga the rays of the sun are very hot.

II. sbst. 1. **heat,** *ťsá-bas ydúṅ-ba* to be tormented by the heat *S.g.*; *ťsá-bai dus-su* during the heat of the day, at noon, cf. *dro Mil.*; *ťsá-ba ni bsíl-bar gyúr-to* the heat changed into coolness *Dzl.*; *ťsa yzér-ba* the burning of the heat, or of the sun *Sch.*; *ťsá-bai nad Lt.* the fever-stage in diseases; *ťsa sél-ba* to cure an acute disease *Sch.*; *ťsá-bas rmyá-ba* to lose one's appetite in consequence of great heat *Sch.* — 2. **warm food,** *stér-ba, ˳drén-pa Mil*; *ťsa-yčig-ma* one that in twenty-four hours takes but one regular meal. — 3. **spice, condiment,** *ťsá-ba ysum* त्रिकटु, black pepper, long pepper, ginger.

III. adj. (vulgo **ťsẹ́m-mo** *C.*, **ťsán-te** *W.*) 1. **hot, warm.** — 2. **sharp, biting, pungent,** of spices etc. — 3. **stinging, prickly, thorny** *Pth.* —

Comp. *ťsa-˳ḱru* colic, gripes *Lt.* — *ťsa-góṅ* forenoon *Sch.* — *ťsa-grań* 1. hot and cold. 2. (relative) warmth. — **ťsan-gyal** *W.* inflammatory fever. — *ťsa-lčib* v. *lčib.* — **ťsa-čú** 1. a hot spring *C.* 2. a warm bath *C.* — *ťsa-bra* dinner *Sch.*(?) — *ťsa-mig* red pepper *Ld.* — **ťsẹ́m-mo C.* hot, warm. — *ťsa-dmyál* hot hell. — *ťsa-zér* 'glowing ray', po. for sun. — **ťsan-láṅ** *W.* hot, passionate, ardent; in the rut — *ťsa-lam Sch.*: half a day's journey, a march before breakfast, = *ťsal-mai lam.* — *ťsa-bsubs Lt.?*

ཚ་བོ་ *ťsá-bo*, resp. *dbón-po B.*, *sku-ťsa C.* 1. **grandchild, grandson,** *Ld.* **mē-mé-ťsa-wo**. — 2. **nephew, brother's son** *Dzl.*; *Ld.*: **á-žáṅ-ťsa-wo**. — *bú-ťsa* v. *bu*; *yáṅ-ťsa* **great-grandchild,** *yúṅ-ťsa* **great-great-grandchild,** *yži-ťsa* id. *Sch.* — *ťsa-skór* grandchildren *Sch.* — *ťsá-mo* 1. **granddaughter.** 2. **niece.** 3. **wife** *Lh.* — *ťsa-žáṅ* nephew and uncle *Mil.* — *ťsa-yzúg* nephews and nieces *Sch.* — *ťsa-yúg* grandchildren, *ťsa-yúg máṅ-poi čó-lo* the many grandchildren's tattling *Mil.*; offspring, in gen., *bu-ťsa-yúg* id. *W.*, *C.*; **ťsá-wo ťsa-yúg yáṅ-ťsa yúṅ-ťsa** *W.* children and children's children.

ཚ་མིག་ *ťsa-mig* v. *ťsá-ba* comp.

ཚ་མོ་ *ťsá-mo* 1. v. *ťsá-ba.* — 2. v. *ťsá-bo.*

ཚ་ཚ་ *ťsá-ťsa* 1. little images of Buddha, and conical figures, moulded of clay and used at sacrifices *Schl.* 194, 206; *ťsá-ḱaṅ* place for keeping them *Cs.*; fig. *ḱá-nas mé-yi ťsá-ťsa ˬpro* from his mouth proceeded cones of fire *Pth.* — 2. *Bal.* for *ťsa-drág* **hastily, quickly;** *ťsa-ťsa-méd* **slow, slowly.**

ཚ་གཞུག་ *ťsa-yžúg* v. *ťsá-bo.*

ཚ་ཟར་ *ťsá-zar* v. *ťsá-dar.*

ཚ་རག་ *ťsa-rág* v. *ťsa-drág.*

ཚ་རུ་ *ťsa-rú* **lamb-skin,** **ťsar-lág** *W.* coat made of lamb-skins.

ཚ་ལ་ *ťsá-la* a kind of medicine *Med.*, acc. to *Wdṅ.* = *dar-ťsúr.*

ཚ་ལུ་ *ťsa-lú* 1. also *mtsa-lú*(?) **cock,** *bya (-po)-ťsá-lu Wdṅ.*, *C.*; in *W.* applied only to red-breasted cocks, from *mťsal* vermilion (*Sch.* hen?). — 2. v. *ťsál-ba.*

ཚ་ལུམ་པ་ *ťsa-lúm-pa C.* **sweet orange,** frq. in *Sik.*

ཚ་ལེ་ *ťsá-le* 1. *Ssk.* सुभग, *Hd.* सुहागा, *Pers.* تنکار, *Ar.* بورق, **borax,** *ťsá-lei skyúr-*

rtsi boracic acid *Cs.*; *ťsa-le byéd-pa* to solder *Sch.*(?). — 2. *ťsá-le záṅ-po Lh.*, n. of a flower, *Hemerocallis fulva.*

ཚག་ *ťsag*, 1. v. *ťsags.* — 2. *ťság-sgra* **an appalling tone** *Sch.*(?); **ťsag gyab* W.* a stinging pain is felt. — 3. **ťsag-ṭúg, ťsag-yá* W.* **twins**; **ťsag-lúg** twin-sheep.

ཚག་པ་ *ťság-pa* (cf. *ₒťság-pa*), *mar ťság-pa* **oil-miller** *Sch.* — *ťság-ma* **sieve, filter,** also *ťsags*, q. v. — **ťsag-ré** bolting-cloth, bolter *C.*, *W.* — *ťsag-ró* residuum after sifting, as bran etc.

ཚག་ཚིག *ťsag-ťsig* **dark spots** or **speckles,** on wood etc. *Mil.*; **freckles** *C.*

ཚག་ཚེ་ *ťsag-ťse* **bruised barley** or **wheat** *Sch.*

ཚག་ཤ་ *ťság-ša* **flesh of larger animals,** of cattle etc.

ཚགས་ *ťsags* 1. **cap,** *gos-ťságs* coat and cap *Dzl.* — 2. = *ťság-ma, ťsags-kyis, btsags Lex.*; *ko-ťságs* a sieve made of leather, the one most in use; *k̔rol-ťságs* = *ťság-ma Lex.*; *nya-ťságs* **weel,** for catching fish *C.* — 3. **thin-split bamboo,** for making baskets *Sik.* — 4. *Sch.*: **'the right sort, a choice article,** *ťsags-bzáṅ byás-nas* making a good choice'. — 5. **density**(?) **ťság-čan, ťsag-ťúg-mo* W.* standing close together, e. g. trees, books; *ťsags-dám* dense and strong, as stuffs *Sch.*; *so ťsags-dam-žiṅ* the teeth standing close and firm *Glr.*; **ťsàg čó-te dug** sit close together! *Ld.*; *ťsags-lhód* not dense or compact *Sch.*; relative density. — 6. *ťsags byéd-pa* (*W. *čó-če**), *ťságs-su ₒǰúg-pa* and *čúd-pa Mil.* **to save, spare, lay up** as provision for the future, *ťse p̔yi-mai grabs či yaṅ ťságs-su ma čud* I have not made any provision yet for the future life *Mil.*; **to economize, to be sparing,** *mé-la* of the fire; to be niggardly; *ťságs-ₒdod-čan* **stingy, griping, avaricious.**

ཚང་ *ťsaṅ* 1. **nest,** *byá-ťsaṅ S.g.*; *ťsaṅ bzó-ba* to build a nest *Sch.*; **den, hole, lair, kennel, burrow,** *stág-ťsaṅ, wá-ťsaṅ, p̔yi-ťsaṅ* (cf. *p̔yi-ba*); **cell, honey-comb, hive,** *sbráṅ-ťsaṅ Cs.* — 2. variously applied to human places of abode: *ɣnas-ťsaṅ* **habitation, house;** *ťsáṅ ₒčá-ba* to build a nest, to establish a household *Schr.*; *grwa-ťsaṅ* v. *grwa*; **ťab-ťsáṅ** in *W.* the common word for **kitchen,** *ɣsól-k̔aṅ* being the resp. term for it; *ťsáṅ-zla* perh. brothers and sisters, beside *p̔a-má Mil.* — 3. v. *ₒťsáṅ-ba.*

ཚང་ངུ་ *ťsáṅ-ṅu* **cradle** *Sch.*

ཚང་བ་ *ťsáṅ-ba* I. vb., pf. *ťsaṅs*, **to be complete, full, entire,** *zlá-ba dgu ťsáṅ-ba-na, ťsáṅ-ba daṅ, ťsáṅ(s)-nas* when the nine months were full, completed *Dzl.*, *zla-ba ťsáṅ-du nyé-bas* towards the end of the months of pregnancy *Dzl.*; **dá-wa ťsaṅ soṅ = bud soṅ* W.* the month is completed, is expired; *rgyál-po ɣčig* (also *ɣčig-gis*) *ma ťsáṅ-ba-la* as one king was still wanting, the number not being yet complete *Dzl.*; *ťsaṅ-nas yod* they are complete (in number) *Pth.* —

II. sbst. (seldom) **completeness, entireness,** *yin-min-gyi(s) ma-ťsáṅ-ba byuṅ-na* when there is no completeness, no absolute certainty as to right and wrong. —

III. adj. 1. **complete, entire;** more frq.: 2. **having things complete,** *yón-tan dé-ťso ťsáṅ-bai bú-mo* a girl in full possession of all these qualities *Pth.*; *k̔a-dóg lṅa ťsaṅ-ba* having all the five colours complete *Glr.*; *dbáṅ-po ma-ťsáṅ-ba* one not in full possession of his five senses *Glr.* — *ťsáṅ-ma* 1. **whole, entire, perfect** (the usual adjective form), *bya-p̔rúg ťsáṅ-ma žig* a perfect young bird, i. e. perfectly developed *Dzl.* — 2. esp. *W.* **all,** for *tams-čád.* — **ťsáṅ-ka* W.* **all together, in all,** with regard to smaller numbers. — *ťsáṅ-po* forming a whole. — *ťsaṅ-skám* **perfectly** dry, *ťsaṅ-rlón* **perfectly** wet; *ťsaṅ-ₒgrig* **all right,** frq., **ťsaṅ-dig ǰhé-pa* or *čó-če* W.*

ཚང་ཚིང་ *ťsaṅ-ťsiṅ*, *Cs.*: **wood, grove, copse, thicket;** *Sch.*: a wild, dismal place; *ťsaṅ-ťsiṅ ₒk̔rigs-pa Sch.*: 'dense thicket; horrible and awful'; '*ťsaṅ-ťsiṅ srid-pai ɣnas* the horrible existence in the external world *Mil.*

ཚང་ཡ་ *ťsaṅ-yá* **double-barreled gun** *C.* and *W.*

ཚང་ར་ *ťsaṅ-ra* v. *ₒťsaṅ-ra.*

ཚངས་ *tsaṅs*, W. **kú-lig-gi tsaṅs**, key-hole, col. for *mtsams* (?).

ཚངས་པ་ *tsáṅs-pa* (evid. preterite of *ₒtsáṅ-ba*) 1. **purified, clean, pure, holy,** *tsáṅs-par gyur čig* prob. be clean! be forgiven! *Dzl.* ༣༢, 13; *ₒgyod-tsáṅs*, *mtol-tsáṅs*, v. the two; *tsáṅs-par spyód-pa*, *tsáṅs-pai spyód-pa spyód-pa*, *tsáṅs-par mtsúṅs-par spyód-pa* 1. to be clean, chaste, holy, to do what is right, to lead an honest, upright life. 2. to be a priest, to belong to a holy order, and as sbst. priest, cleric; *mi-tsaṅs-par spyód-pa*, not to be clean, chaste etc., esp. with *bud-méd-la* to commit one's self with a woman *Mil.* — *tsaṅs-skúd*, *Sch.*: 'holy cord, the bond of spirits' (?) — *tsaṅs-tig* **equator,** prob. of *Cs.*'s construction, cf. *dguṅ* extr. — 2. ब्रह्म, **Brahma,** an Indian deity transplanted into Buddhism; he is occasionally called *lha čén-po* (*Glr.*) and proverbial for his melodious voice, yet otherwise not of any consequence. — *tsáṅs-pai bú-ga* = *mtsóg-ma Med.*, *Pth.*

ཚད་ *tsad* (cf. *tsod*) 1. **measure,** a. in **a general** sense, **size:** *če-čúṅ-gi tsád-la* according to the size, in size *Glr.*; *mi-tsad* size of a (full-grown) man *Tar.*; *sku-tsád* stature, size of body, resp. *Glr.*; *zlá-bai dkyil-ₒkór-gyi tsad* the size of the moon's disk *Stg.*; *stobs gyad stóbs-po-čei tsád-du pyin-te* his strength was equal to that of a powerful athlete *Dzl.*; **ṭu súm-čui tsad čo gos** *W.* make it thirty cubits in size; *kam-tsád-du γčód-pa* to cut into bits piecemeal *Dzl.*; *ču-rgyún kyab-tsád-du* as far as the waters covered it *Tar.*; *ñóm-tsad(-du) ₒtúṅ-ba* to drink one's fill; *γnás-tsad* seems to express chronology *Wdk.*; *mnan-tsad* direction how the pulse is to be felt (or pressed) *Med.*; *kyéd-rnams-kyi čós-bslab-tsad* according to your view of religious studies *Mil.*; *dró-tsad* thermometer, *graṅ-droi tsad* id.; *yaṅ-ldii tsad* barometer; *mto-dman-gyi tsad* scale for the rising and falling (of the barometer); all these appear to be proposals of *Cs.* for the respective physical terms; *pa-tsád* distance (v. sub *pa* II); *tsad-méd(-pa)* **unmeasured, immeasurable, innumerable,** e.g. *yón-tan Dzl.*; *tsad-med(-pa) bži* the four immeasurables (viz. merits): *byáms-pa*, *snyiṅ-rje*, *dká-ba* and *btaṅ-snyóm Dom.*, *spyod-pa* to practise them, *tob-pa* to attain to them *Dzl.*; *ṅa-bas mi tsad γžan yaṅ* an infinity of others besides me *Mil.*

b. **the full** measure, which is **not short** of the proper quantity, **standard,** *tsád-du pyin-pa*, *skyé-ba* (*Sch.* also *ₒkyól-ba*) to grow, so as to reach the proper measure; *tsád-du skyés-pa* grown up, full-sized, adj. *Dzl.*; **tsẹ' žág-pa** to set up a pattern, or as a pattern *C.* *tsad-ldán* right (as weight), about the same as 'gaged', just, fair, with regard to persons (ni f.) *C.*

c. **the right** measure, which does **not exceed** the proper quantity: *tsád-γčod-pa* to limit, *bed-čód* the enjoyment *Mil.*; *bza-btúṅ-la* to observe the proper measure in eating and drinking, **tsẹ' dzim-pa**, or **žág-pa** *C.* id.; *tsád-las ₒdá-ba*, *tál-ba* to exceed the proper measure frq.; *yid-pám-pa-la tsád-las ₒdás-pa yoṅ* the dejection increases to an excess *Mil.* — To 1, a. may be referred d. those instances in which the word assuming the character of an affix serves to form abstract nouns, such as *γdeṅs-tsád*, or *rtogs-tsád*, *Mil.* in several passages (cf. also *tsod*) further to 1, b may be reckoned e. the signification **all,** *dgé-ba byed tsad* all the pious *Pth.*, to which also *Tar.* 54, 15 may be referred; *sna-tsád* **of every kind, of all sorts** *Glr.*; **žẹ tsẹ' čụ'-du soṅ** *C.* all his eating agreed with him extremely well; *ₒdir ldóm-bu-ba byuṅ tsad* all the beggars that show themselves here *Mil.*; *mi yoṅs tsad* all the people that come; *snaṅ tsad čós-skur šar* all that happens appears as *čós-sku Glr.*; *γsuṅ tsad* all that is ordered, proclaimed *Sch.*; *tsogs tsád* all the people assembled *Sch.*; and f. **enough,** esp with a negation: *ₒdra-ba mi tsad* not having enough of the comparisons, not resting satisfied with them; **ma tsád-de** *W.* = *ma zád-de B.* not only. — 2. a certain **definite measure,** in compounds: *dpag-tsád* a mile, *sor-tsád* an inch: also pleon. *kru-tsad* an ell *Cs.* = *kru.* — 3. **goal, mark,** the point to which racers run *C.*

— 4. *tsad rgyág-pa* **to guess, conjecture, suppose** *Sch.*, cf. *tsod.* — 5. sometimes for *tsád-pa* **heat**; for *tsad-ma* **logic**, *dbu-tsád* Madhyamika logic *Tar.* 179, 17, *Schf.*

ཚད་པ *tsád-pa* I. sbst. 1. **heat**, in gen.; *tsád-pa byuṅ-tse* when it grows hot *Glr.*; *tsád-pas ydúṅ-ba* to be tormented by the heat *Glr.*; *tsád-pas*, or vulg. *tsád-pa-nas*, *ṗóg-pa* to be struck by the heat, to receive a sun-stroke; also to be taken ill with dysentery, to which the Tibetans, used to the dry atmosphere of the northern Himalaya, are very liable, when during summer they venture into the southern subtropical regions; *tsád-čan* hot, e.g. *yul*; *tsad-ldán* prob. id.; *me-búm tsád-čan, Lt.* a hot cupping-glass (?). 2. morbid heat of the body, **fever** (*W.* **tsan-zug**); *tsad-pai nad* id., but also **dysentery**, v. above *Glr.*, *C.*; *tsad-pa žag-ynyis-ma* tertian fever *Schr.; gya-tsẹ' Sik.* Indian or jungle-fever; **roṅ-tsẹ'** *Sik* common intermittent fever. — II. vb. *Cs.*: **to measure**, = *tsád-du byéd-pa, tsad ˳jál-ba.*

ཚད་འབུ *tsád-˳bu* **grasshopper, locust** *Sch.*

ཚད་མ *tsád-ma*, प्रमाण *Cs.*: '**measure, rule, model, proof, argument; logic**'; *tsád-ma-pa*, or *-mḱan*, *Cs.* logician, dialectitian; *tsád-mai bstan-bčós* a dialectical work *Pth.*; *tsad-ma yžuṅ* an original work on dialectics *Cs.*; *tsád-ma ˳grél-ba* commentary to it *Cs.; saṅs-rgyás-kyi bka tsád-mar bžág-pa* the words of Buddha reduced to a dogmatical system (?) *Pth.* — *tsád-ma kun-˳dús, tsád-ma sde bdun* titles of books mentioned by *Was.*

ཚན *tsan*, 1. a root = *tsa* in *tsá-ba* **hot, warm** *C.* and *B.; tsán-mo* (**tsẹ́m-mo**), *in W.* **tsán-te**, e.g. with *ču*, **ču tsẹ́m-mo** *C.*, **ču-tsán** *W.*, hot water *Dzl.*, warm water *Lt.*; *zan-drón tsán-mo* warm food *Lt.*; *ču-skól tsán-mo* boiling water *Mṅg.;* **ša tsọ́-pa tsẹ́m-mo** boiled meat, in Lhasa brought warm to the market; **tsẹn-˳ḍi táṅ-wa** *C.* to proceed capitally against, ni. f.; *tsán-te* **sharp, biting, pungent**, *W.* also sbst.: **spice**, esp. **red pepper.** — *tsan-žug W.* **fever.** — *tsan-ró Sch.*: '**hot**, the sensation of heat'. — 2. = *tsá-bo:* **ṗa-tsẹ́n** cousin by the father's, **ma-tsẹ́n** by the mother's side *C.*; *ṗa-tsán* also = *ṗa-spún*; *ḱu-tsán* v. *ḱú-bo.* — 3. **series, order, class**, *sde-tsán* id.; *bži-tsán* a class or collection of four things, tetrad *Gram.*; *drug-tsán-du sdébs-pa* to put together in classes of six *Mil.; don-tsán Tar.* 96, 14, a certain class of ideas, range of thoughts *Schf.* — 4. as termination of some collective nouns: *ynyen-tsán, nye-tsan* **kindred, relations**, *nye-tsán bdúd-kyi bšol-˳débs yin Mil.*; *blón-po-tsan lṅá-po* the five embassies, ni f. *Glr.* — 5. *náṅ-tsan* **part**, of a country, **district**, *Tar.* 90, 20. — 6. *čos-tsan* any treatise under **a distinct head or title** in a volume *Cs.* — 7. **difference** *Sch.*; *le-tsan* different divisions, sections, chapters. — 8. **much, large, copious, great**, **ḱa tsan čin-te** *W.* much deep snow; *tsan-čé-ba, tsan-čen* **very much, a great deal**, *las ṅán ni tsan-čé* a great many bad actions *Thgr.*; *lo tsan-če-ba* a plentiful harvest, rich crop *Glr.*; hence *tsán-po* **a dignitary, grandee** *Pth.*; *ḱams-tsán*, 1. **prefect of a provincial association**, in large convents, such as Sera and others. 2. **association, club.**

ཚབ *tsab* (cf. *˳tsáb-pa*), **representative**, com. *tsáb-po C.*, *W.*, **ḱó-la tsáb-po yod** he has got a representative, proxy; in reference to a thing: **equivalent, substitute**, *des tsab ruṅ* it may be replaced by this, *tsab ruṅ tsam-mo* this may perhaps be used as a substitute *Wdṅ.*; **ṫáb-ṗii tsab čó-če** *W.* to use as a mop; *ṅas tsab byao* I shall supply his place *Tar.*; *tsáb-tu* **instead of, in the place of**, *már-mei* instead of a lamp, for a lamp *Glr.*; in *W.* **tsáb-la** very common. Chiefly in compounds: *sku-tsáb* resp. = *tsáb-po* **representative of a superior**, hence, as may be the case, **vice-roy, delegate, commissioner, agent.** — *rgyal-tsáb* v. *rgyál-ba.* — *do-tsab Schr.* prob. = *tsáb-po* = *sku-tsáb.* — *rta-tsáb* a thing given as an equivalent for a horse *Cs.* — *nor-tsáb* goods serving as a compensation for something else. — *ṗa-tsáb* **guardian, trustee.** — *bla-tsáb* representative of a Lama, **Vice-Lama.** — *bu-tsáb* **adopted child, foster-child.** — *mi-tsáb Schr.* **negociator, mediator; hostage** (?).

ཚབ་ཚབ་ *tsab-tsáb, mig tsab-tsáb byéd-pa* **to blink** or **twinkle** with the eyes *C.*, also *W.*

ཚབས་ *tsabs* 1. mostly with *če, čén-po*, **very great, very much**, *sdíg-pa tsabs-čé-bar* ₒ*dug* it proves a very great sin, *mgó-bo* ₒ*k'or tsabs-čé-na* when much dizziness intervenes *Lt.*; **ṭim-dhaṅ-gal tsab čém-po** *C.*, great, serious transgression; ₒ*gál-tsabs-čan* sinning heinously. — 2. *tsábs-pa* and *-po Cs.*, who also designates it as resp., **peril, fear, sin** (rather questionable); **difficulty, trouble** (might perh. be more adequate); *búd-med* ₒ*ó-tsabs-la p̓an Wdṅ.* it is of use in milk-diseases of the women.

ཚམ་དམ་ *tsam-dám* **noisy, blustering, alarming** *Sch.*

ཚམ་ཚུམ་, ཚམ་ཚོམ་ *tsam-tsúm, tsam-tsóm* (cf. *tsóm-pa, té-tsom*) **doubt, hesitation, wavering,** *tsam-tsúm byéd-pa* **to doubt, hesitate, waver;** *tsam-tsúm-čan, tsam-me-tsom-mé* **doubtful, wavering, undecided,** *p̓an-tsúṅ p̓yág-la tsam-me-tsom-mér lús-pai tse* whilst both of them were uncertain as to saluting (who should salute first) *Pth.*

ཚའི་ཏའུ་ *tsai-tau* (Chinese) **chopping-knife** *C.*

ཚའི་སྐྱོགས་ *tsai-skyógs* **scoop, basting-ladle** *C.*

ཚར་ *tsar* 1. also *tser* **time** *Pth.* vulgo; *tsar-γčig* one time, once; *tsar γčig-la* also = *srib-γčig-la* in one moment; *tsar γsum* threefold, in three specimens, copies *Tar.*; *tsar bži Dzl.* ༢༤, 8, in four divisions, sorts, qualities (?) — 2. also *tsar-tsar* **ends of threads, fringes,** in webs, *k'a-tsár Ld.* also *ru-tsár* fringes at the beginning, *p̓on-tsar* at the end of a web *Cs.* — 3. **thin strips of cane,** for wicker-work, *tsar-zám* cane-bridge *C.* — 4. *tsar-slág* v. *tsa-ru.* — 5. v. ₒ*tsar-ba.*

ཚར་བོང་ *tsar-boṅ* officinal plant in *Lh.*, *Carduus nutans*, but not agreeing with the description in *Wdṅ.*

ཚར་མ་ *tsár-ma*, fem. *tsár-mo Bal.* **old.**

ཚར་ཚར་ *tsar-tsar* v *tsar* 2.

ཚལ་ *tsal* 1. provinc. also *tsol*, **wood, grove,** as a place for hunting and recreation, *tsal stúg-po Dzl.*; *nags-tsál* id.; **garden,** *mé-tog-gi* flower-garden *Ph.*; *tsal yaṅ-tse* (*Chin.*) *C.* kitchen-garden. — 2. *smyu-gui-tsal* one kind of the fabulous food of man in the primitive world *Glr.*; also the 'unploughed rice' is called ₒ*bras sa-lu-tsal.* — 3. v. *mtsal.*

ཚལ་པ་ *tsál-pa* (*Sch. tsal-ba?*) 1. also *šiṅ-tsal* **chip** (of wood), **splinter,** *nón-po* a sharp, piercing splinter *Dzl.*; **billet** *Glr.*; **thin board, veneer** etc.; **shiver, fragment,** *tsál-pa bdún-du gas Dzl.*; *tsál-bu* dimin., small chip or shiver *W.*: **tsál-bu ton soṅ** a small piece is broken out. — 2. **bunch,** of flowers, of ears of corn etc., a lock of hair cut off *W.*

ཚལ་མ་ *tsál-ma* vulgo for *dro*, **breakfast,** *tsal-ma za-ba* **to breakfast,** *tsál-ma zá-ba-rnams* 'companions at a great man's table' (?) *Cs.*; *tsál-mai lam* = *tsa-lám* v. *tsá-ba* extr.; *tsal bóg-pa* = *dro btáb-pa* to make a morning-halt on a journey; *tsal-rtiṅ* the time from breakfast till dinner, opp. to *sṅá-dro*, q. v.

ཚས་ *tsas* (*tsás-po Cs.*) 1. *W.* for *tsal* **garden,** *tsas-skór, tsás-k'aṅ* garden-bed, *tsás-mk'an* gardener. — 2. of a woman in child-birth: *tsas-kyis γso* (?) *Med.*

ཚི་ *tsi* num. fig.: 48.

ཚི་ཀ་ *tsi-ka* (or *tsi-rka?*) *C.* **furrow** in a ploughed field.

ཚི་གུ་, ཚིག་གུ་ *tsi-gu, tsig-gu* 1. **kernel** or **nut** contained in the stone of a stone-fruit, *k'ám-bui* of an apricot *Lt.*, *C.* (*W.*: **rtsi-gu**). — 2. *Ld.* a large **muller** or **grinding-stone** = *ǰu-lúm*; **musket-ball, bullet.**

ཚི་བ་ *tsi-ba C., W. *tsi** **tough, viscous, sticky matter,** esp. **clammy dirt,** e.g. in the wool of sheep; *tsi dám-po* solid dirt, *bád-kan-gyi tsi-ba Med.* **tenacious slime;** *tsi(-ba)-čan* **sticky, clammy, dirty;** **tsi-du* W.* **dirty, unclean, filthy,** esp. in a religious sense, = **kyug-ḍho* C.*; **ṅe zúg-po tsi-du soṅ** says a girl euphemistically for: I have the menses.

ཚིག་ *tsig* 1. **word,** in its strict sense, '*bdé-bar γšégs-pa ni' bde-ba daṅ γšegs-pai tsig γnyis-las med, bde-bar γšegs-pa* are only two words, viz. *bde-ba* and *γšegs-pa Lex.*; *ₒdri-bai ťsig* interrogative (word), such as *či*; *ťsig sgrig-pa* to connect or arrange words; as a sbst.: **construction,** the order in which words are to be placed; **grammatical form,** *dá-ltar-gyi ťsig* form of the present tense; *ťsig-grógs, ťsig-grógs-kyi dbáṅ-gis Tar.*; *Schf.*: 'by the force of construction' (?) *ťsig-ₒgrél Tar.* **explanation of words;** *ťsig-ₒgrós Sch.*: **'course of speech,** connexion of words'; *ťsig-ṕrad, ťsig-rgyán* **particle,** a small word not inflected; *ťsig-ₒbrú Schr.*: **a separate word** or **syllable,** *ťsig-ₒbrú-γnyer-pa Sch.* 'linguist, philologist, purist'; *ťsig-ₒbru-lčibs Lex.*? — 2. **word, saying, speech,** subject of a discourse, *ťsig-snyán(-pa)* kind word, friendly speech, *ťsig-ǰám* id., *brtse-bai ťsig* an affectionate word *Glr.*; **ťsig-súb* W.* hard, angry, bad words; **ťsig-ṅán, ťsig-zúr* W.* id.; *rtág-par ma mťóṅ-bai ťsig ťos-nas* always receiving the answer, that (she who was sought) had not been seen; *ťsig-med-par ₒgyúr-ba* not being able to utter a word (from pain) *Dzl.*; but *ḱa-ťsig-méd-par γsól-ba ₒdébs-pa Mil.* prob. to pray without hypocrisy; *ťsig nyúṅ-la don čé-ba Mil.* saying much in few words; *ťsig-ḱyál-pa = kyal-ka Dzl.*; *γžán-gyi ťsig γčod-pa* to interrupt one in his speech; *ťsig-γsal* **a clear word, perspicuous style** *Cs.*; *ťsig-ₒból* **easy** or **fluent style** *Cs.*; *ťsig-la mḱas-pa* skilful in selecting words *Cs.*; *bdén-ťsig* v. *bdén-pa* extr.; *brdzún-ťsig* **falsehood, lie** *Cs.*

ཚིག་གུ་ *ťsig-gu* v. *ťsi-gu.*

ཚིག་པ་ *ťsig-pa* 1. v. *ₒťsig-pa.* — 2. sbst., *W.* also *ťsig-po* **anger, indignation, vexation, provocation,** *ťsig-pa zá-ba* **to be angry** *Pth.*, frq.; **ťsig(-po) ḱol* W.* his anger kindles.

ཚིག་པོ་ *ťsig-po* 1. = *ťsig Cs.* — 2. v. *ťsig-pa* 2.

ཚིགས་ *ťsigs*, less frq. *ťsigs-pa, ťsigs-ma* 1. **member** between two joints, hence *ťsigs-mtsáms* joint *S.g.*; **joint,** *sor-ťsigs* the joints of the fingers, **knuckles** *Cs.*; *ťsigs ₒbúd-pa Cs.*, **ṭúl-ťe, bóg-če* W.* to put out of joint, **to dislocate, to sprain;** *ťsigs ǰúg-pa* to reduce a dislocated joint *Cs.*; *ťsigs-nád, ťsigs-zúg* articular disease, pain in the joints, gout; joint of the back-bone, **vertebra; spine,** also *sgal-ťsigs*, vulgo *ťsigs-rús*, hence **ťsig-gúr* W.* hump, hunch; **joint, knee, knot,** *sog-ťsigs* knot of a stalk of corn or straw, *smyug-ťsigs* knot of cane *Cs.*; member of a generation *Glr.*; **metrical division, verse,** *ťsigs-su bčád-de smrá-ba* to speak in verse, *ťsigs (-su) bčad(-pa)* **strophe, stanza,** *ťsigs-bčád byéd-pa* to compose verses, to speak in verse *Dzl.*; *dus-ťsigs* **division of time,** e.g. season *Pth.* — 2. *ťsigs-ma* **sediment, residuum, residue,** *smán-gyi* of a medicine *Dzl.*; *már-gyi Dzl.* olive-husks, oil-cake; *ťsigs-ró = ťsigs-ma.*

ཚིབ(ས)་ *ťsib(s), ťsib-nad* **measles** *Sch.*

ཚིམ་པ་ *ťsim-pa* vb. **to be content;** gen. adj. **content, satisfied, satiated, consoled,** frq.: *yid ťsim-par gyur* he was satisfied, appeased, consoled; *ǰi ₒdód-pai yid ťsim-ste* all her (their) wishes being satisfied *Glr.*; *dga-bdés ťsim-par gyúr-čiṅ* being indeed over-happy *Pth.*; *ťsim-par byéd-pa* to satisfy, with the dat. or accus. of the person.

ཚིམ་ཚིམ་ *ťsim-ťsim, mig ťsim-ťsim ₒdug C.* the eye is **dazzled.**

ཚིར་ *ťsir* **order, course, succession, turn,** prob. only col., **ṅá-la ťsir yoṅ* or *bab** it is my turn; **ná-so ťsir-la** succession by seniority; **gán-ťsir žón-ťsir** id.; **ťsir-la, ťsir-du, ťsir daṅ** by turns, every one in his turn or course, one thing after the other.

ཚིར་བ་ *ťsir-ba* v. *ₒťsir-ba.*

ཚིལ་ *ťsil* **fat,** not melted, *ťsil-bu* id. *S.g.*; *lúg-ťsil* **mutton fat,** *ṕág-ťsil* pork-fat, **bacon;** *ḱál-ťsil, ḱóg-ťsil, gród-ťsil* **suet, lard;** *sbó-ťsil* **bacon;** *lóṅ-ťsil* **intestinal fat.** — *spra-ťsil* **wax** *B.*, *C.* (*W.* **mum**); *ťsil-ku* liquid fat, in the living body, or melted fat *Pth.* — *ťsil-čan, ťsil-ldán* **fat,** *ťsil-méd* **lean.** — *ťsil-ró* remains of lard after melting. — *ťsil-šúbs* 1. **straight-gut, rectum** *Med.* 2. **sausage** *Cs.* —

ཚིལ་དིང་ *ťsil-diṅ Ld.* **mortar and pestle.**

ཚིས་ *ťsis Mil., Thgy.* prob. secondary form of *rtsis.*

ཚུ་ *tsu* 1. num. fig.: 78. — 2. the contrary of *p̓a* II., root of the words signifying **hitherward, on this side;** *tsú-k̓a Cs.* (*tsúr-k̓a* q. v.), more frq. *tsú-rol* **this side** (opp. to *p̓á-rol*), *tsú-rol-na* adv. **on this side,** postp. with genit. adj. **on this side;** *tsú-rol-tu*, this way, to this place; *tsú-rol-nas* from this side; *tsú-rol-pa* one on this side, one belonging to this (our) party *Stg.*; *tsu-bi* one of this side, *p̓a-bi* one of the other side *Cs.*, provinc. (?). Cf. *tsun, tsur.*

ཚུ་འུ་ *tsu-u*(?) *C.*, prob. Chinese, for the Tibetan *skyúr-ru*, acc. to some: **vinegar,** acc. to others: **a pulpy product,** prepared of various kinds of fruit, mixed with vinegar, sugar, and spices, and having been left to ferment, used, like mustard, as a condiment, which in India is called 'chutney'.

ཚུག *tsug* 1. *Sch.*: **'group, object'** (?); *tsúg-so W.* all the households or villages placed under one Gopa. — 2. rarely for *tsug*; thus *j̓i-tsug Glr.* 49, inst. of *ċi-tsug*.

ཚུག་པ་(ལ) *tsúg-pa(-la) W.* **to, up to, till,** *gaṅ tsúg-pa* **how far, how long?** **ṅa Nyúṅ-ti-ru čá-če tsúg-pa-la** until I go to Sultanpur; *gaṅ tsúg-pa* ... *de tsúg-pa* **so far as.**

ཚུགས་པ་ *tsugs-pa* 1. v. *˳tsugs-pa.* — 2. **to do one harm, to hurt, to inflict,** mostly with a negative, *bar-čád ma tsúgs-par* without having hurt me *Mil.*; *ṅá-la mes, nad-kyis* etc. *mi tsugs* fire, disease etc. can do me no harm, *Glr., Mil.*, frq. — 3. sbst., also *tsúgs-k̓aṅ*, *W.* **tsug-sa**, **caravansary,** or merely a level, open place near a village, where traveller's may encamp, or where public business is transacted; also for धर्मशाला, **hall of judgment; hospital.**

ཚུད་པ་ *tsud-pa* v. *˳tsud-pa.*

ཚུན་ *tsun* = *tsu* 2., gen. with *čad* or *ċad* or *la*, signifying **within, by, not later than,** as postp. c. accus., *rabs bdun tsun-čád* within seven generations, (they will be happy) even to the seventh generation, *Dzl.*; *sáṅ-gi nyi-ma-p̓yéd tsún-la* by to-morrow noon (it must be finished) *Glr.*; **dá-wa če' tsun 'é leb** *C.* shall he come in less than half a month? *bu daṅ bú-mo tsun-čád* even to the children, not even the children being excluded *Tar.* 119, 3. —

Note. In the terms *p̓an* and *tsun*, like *yan* and *man(-čad)*, the significations given by *Cs.*: **from, from a certain place or time forward, till, until,** are not properly inherent to the word, but are to be inferred in each separate instance from the figurative application of the original sense of the root.

ཚུབ་མ་ *tsúb-ma, ˳tsúb-ma* **storm,** *tsub-čéb, rluṅ-tsúb* **gale, hurricane,** *k̓a-tsub* snow-storm; *bu-tsub* (*p̓u-tsub?*) gust of wind, (*lha*) *˳drei bu-tsub* whirlwind; fig. *p̓rag-dóg-gi tsúb-ma Mil.* **a violent fit of envy;** *sems-tsúb* **trouble of mind** *Cs.*

ཚུར་ *tsur* **hither, to this place, hitherward** (cf. *p̓ar*), *tsur šog* (resp. *ɣšegs*, in later lit. *byon*) come hither, come here! also in an objective sense: *tsur ˳óṅ-ba* **to return home** *Pth., Tar.*; *˳di-nas tsur bšád-nas* speaking to me through this (tube) *Glr.*; almost pleon. in *tsúr-la nyon* listen to me! *Mil.* frq.; *tsúr-ka* **this side,** the this side river-bank, declivity, party etc., similarly: *tsúr-logs, tsúr-p̓yogs.*

ཚུར་(མོ), མཚུར་(མོ) *tsúr(-mo), mtsúr(-mo)* **colouring matter, pigment,** prob. = *sa-tsúr Stg.*, acc. to *Cs.* **mineral paint,** *nag-* black, *ser-* yellow, *dmar-tsúr* red-paint; for *nag tsúr Sch.* has: green vitriol; in *Zam.* also *rús-kyi tsur* is named.

ཚུལ་ *tsul* शील 1. **manner, way, form, character, nature,** *tsul j̓i-ltar* ... *de bžin-du* **as — so** *Wdṅ.*, *zér-tsul, ˳grúl-tsul, bsám-tsul* the way in which a person speaks, walks, thinks; *ɣnás-tsul* v. *ɣnás-pa*; *ɣnás-tsul* and *snáṅ-tsul* **being** and **appearing,** philosoph. terms for **reality** and **appearance** *Was.* (297); *ɣtóṅ-tsul* the way of giving, i.e. a certain quantity given, dose *Stg.*; *mi sdug-pai sna-tsógs-kyis* (to damage) in various vicious ways *Mil.*; *tsul de k̓ó-nas* by that same way of proceeding *Tar.*; hence *tsúl-gyis* in consequence of, by means of *Pth.* and elsewhere; *snan smrás-pai tsul* the character of his last speech *Dzl.*; *rgya-bód-kyi ˳brél-tsul* the mode or kind of intercourse, the relations between Tibet and China *Glr.*; *ṗyág-gi tsúl-du* in a way as if he were saluting *Mil.*; *gus-gús-kyi tsúl(-du) byéd-pa* to make a semblance of veneration, to make gestures of reverence *Mil.; mi mḱyén-pai tsúl-du byás-te* pretending not to know *Mil.*; (cf. *tsúl-ₒčos-pa* v. *čos-pa*); *dge-slóṅ-gi tsúl-du* in the guise of a monk *Tar.; mai tsul ₒdzin-pa* to assume the mother's form, figure *Tar.; glaṅ-čén-gyi tsúl-du*, (Buddha came down) in the shape of, or as, an elephant *Glr.*; *dád-pai tsúl-gyis* in the way of faith, with a believing mind *Pth.; mi-rtág tsúl-du yda* it exists in the way of transientness, it is of a transitory nature *Mil.; mdzád-pa bču-ynyis-kyi tsúl-gyis* in the manner, in the order, of the twelve deeds *Glr.*; *ṡas čé-bai tsúl-gyis* for the most part, *Tar.* 50, 15; **way of acting, conduct, deportment, course of life,** *sṅá-mai tsul* your former conduct *Mil.*; *dé-lta-bui dgé-bai tsul dc tós-nas* hearing such an example of virtue related. — 2. emphat.: **the right way**, good manners, order, rule: *tsul (daṅ) mtún(-pa)* **orderly, regular, sensible, reasonable,** *brgyá-la tsul-mtún re tsam ₒbyúṅ-na Mil.* if but once in a hundred cases something sensible is uttered; *tsul-ldán, tsúl-čan* regular, methodical *Cs.*; also **just,** conformable to duty, *tsúl-bžin-pa* adv. *tsul-bžin-du* id.; *tsul-méd, tsul-bžin-min* **irregular. unjust** *Cs.*; *srid-žui tsul spyód-čiṅ* fulfilling a child's duty; *tsúl-las nyams* **growing remiss in one's duty,** neglecting, breaking one's duty; esp. *tsúl-ḱrims* **religious or moral duty, moral law; monastic vows,** *tsúl-ḱrims-čan* 1. being bound by such *Sch.*; 2. observing such *Cs.; tsúl-ḱrims srúṅ-ba* to keep them, *ₒǰig-pa, nyáms-pa* to break them; *tsúl-ḱrims,* as a personal name, is much in favour. — 3. **species, kind,** *nád-tsul* species or kind of disease, *zás-tsul* species of food *S.g.* (not frq.). — 4. joined to the root of a verb: *yóṅ tsul,* **when,** or **as,** he came, *W.*

ཚེ་ *tse* I. num. figure: 108.

II. sbst. 1. **time,** in a gen. sense, = *dus B.*; *yód(-pai) tse(-na),* **when** it is, **when** it was; *gáṅ(-gi) tse(-na), de(i) tse(-na)* **at which time, at that time, then,** frq. *tse-ré* all the time(?), *nyin-tse-ré* the whole day, *tsan-tse-ré* the whole night *W.* — 2. **time of life,** **tse-ghaṅ-tsṓn-čug** imprisonment for life *C.*; *tse yčig-gi drós-pai gos* v. *drós-pa;* **life,** *tse ₒdi* this, the present, life, *tse-ṗyi(-ma)* a future period of life (also merely: *ₒdi ṗyi,* without *tse*); *tse sṅá-ma* an earlier period of existence, relative to the transmigration of souls, yet *tse ₒdi* and *ṗyi* may also be used in a Christian sense; *tse riṅ-ba* long life, *tse túṅ-ba* short life; *tse-riṅ* is also a very common name both of men and women; *rgyál-ba daṅ tse-riṅ-bar ṡóg-čig* happiness and long life (to the king)! *Dzl.*; *tse(-daṅ) -ldán(-pa),* आयुष्मान्, title or epithet of Bodhisattwas; *tse-dpag-méd* name of Buddha; **tse ṗíd-če** *W.* to earn a livelihood; *tse ₒḱyér-žiṅ ṡór-ba* to come off with one's life, to have a narrow escape; *tse tár-du ₒǰúg-pa* v. *tár-ba*; *tse(-las) ₒdás(-pa)* having died *Dzl.* — 3. *Bal.* **sex,** **ṗó-tse, mó-tse**, male, female sex.

Comp. *tse-skábs* v. *skabs.* — *tse-čú* water of life *Glr.* — *tse-ynyis-pa* of an amphibious nature *Cs.* — *tse-ltógs* a poor, starving vagrant, beggar *W.* — *tse-mdáṅs Lt.* = *byad-mdaṅs* healthy appearance, a fine, fresh complexion. — *tse-tsád* duration of life. — *tse-mdzad, Wdk.* 457, an attribute of the gods, resembling a small plate with fruit. — *tse-rábs* period of existence, duration of a re-birth, a great many of which acc. to Buddhist doctrine every man has to pass through *Dzl.; tse-rábs-kyi blá-ma Mil.* a man that is always re-born as a Lama.

ཚེ་པད་ *tse-pád Ephedra saxatilis,* a little alpine shrub with red berries, which are said to be roasted and pulverized, to give greater pungency to snuff.

ཚེ་རེ་ *tse-ré* 1. v. *tse.* — 2. v. *tsér-ka.*

ཚེག *tseg W.* **tsag** 1. **point, dot,** also *nag-tség.* — 2. more particularly **the point separating syllables,** *bar-tség,* id.; *ṗyi-tség* likewise, in as far as it follows a letter *Gram.*; *tseg-bar* that which stands between two points or tsegs, **a syllable.**

རྩེགས་ *tsegs* **troublesome, difficult, hard,** *tsegs-če* very troublesome, *rkaṅ tsegs-čé Mil.* much (fruitless) running to and fro; *tsegs-méd* it is not difficult; *tsegs-méd(-par)* easily adv.; *tségs-pa* trouble, toil, difficulty *Sch.; ṗran-tsegs* little troubles or difficulties *Cs.*

ཚེམ་(པོ་) *tsém(-po),* **seam,** cf. *ₒtsém-pa; tsém-bzo-pa, tsém-pa* **tailor** *W.*; *tsém-po ₒgrol* the seam opens, comes loose; *tsem-méd* without a seam; *tsém-bu Lex., Sch.:* what has been stitched, darned, quilted.

ཚེམས་ *tsems,* resp. **tooth,** *tséms-šiṅ* tooth-pick *Dzl.*

ཚེམས་པ་ *tsems-pa* to have the disadvantage, to come off a loser, not receiving a full share *Sch.*

ཚེར་ *tser* 1. = *tsar* **time** vulgo; *tser-tsér, Mil.,* prob. **many times, repeatedly.** — 2. v. the following.

ཚེར་ཀ་ *tsér-ka W.* also *tse-ré, tse-ri* **sorrow, grief, pain, affliction,** **tse-ré čo mi go** do not grieve! **tser čúg-če** to afflict, to grieve (not in *B.*).

ཚེར་མ་ *tsér-ma, W.***tser-máṅ** 1. **thorn, prick, brier,** *Dzl. tser zug soṅ* I have run a thorn into (my hand, foot); *tser-mai mgo* a deer's head po. spoken of *Mil.; tsér-ma ₒdón-pa* to pull out a thorn; *nya-tsér* fish-bone *Sch.*; *tsér-ma-čan* 1. thorny, prickly, briery. 2. like thorns, *Thgy.* — 2. **thorn-bush, bramble, brake** *tser-dkár, tser-stár,* buck-thorn, *Hippophaë rhamnoïdes,* **tser-tar-lú-lu** *Ld.,* the berries of it (extremely sour). — *tser-tágs* thorn-hedge (in Tibet gen. dead hedges). — *tser-lúm* yellow raspberry *Sik. tser-lhág* n. of a disease *Lt.*

ཚེས་ *tses* अहन्, 1. **day of the month,** *tses-gráṅs* **date,** always expressed by the cardinal number, *tses-γčig* etc., *tses-bčú* the tenth, in certain months a festival day, *tses-bču-mčód-pa* sacrifice and beer-drinking on that day; *tses-bčúi ₒčám-yig* programme of the religious dances performed on that occasion; *zlá-ba tsés-pa* and *tses-γsum-zlá-ba.* — 2. symb. num.: 15.

ཚོ་ *tso* 1. num. figure: 138. — 2. sbst. **troop, number, host,** yet hardly ever standing alone, or governing a genit. case, but like a termination affixed: *gróṅ-mi-tso* the peasants (of the village), *ḱyéd rnál-ₒbyor-pa-tso* ye saints! In some instances its substantive character is more apparent, thus in *tsóṅ-pa-tso, mḱás-pa-tso, bá-tso* it may be rendered by: a troop of merchants, a society of learned men (or the learned), a herd of cows (*Cs.*); but most frq. it stands (at least in later lit.) as plural termination of pronouns, so: *ṅéd-tso* **we,** *ḱoṅ-tso* **they,** *ₒdi-tso* **these,** or it is affixed to numerals: *ₒbum-tso* 100 000. — *yul-tso* v. *yul.* — 3. adj. **hot** *Bal.*

ཚོ་བ་ *tsó-ba* **fat, greasy,** *tso-ḱú* fat gravy, *tso-ldír* unwieldy with fatness (*tso ₒdug mi ₒdug,* or *bud ma bud,* is it fat or not? being with young or not? *Sch.?*)

ཚོ་ལོ་ *tsó-lo W.* vulg. = *ₒṗoṅs,* cf. *ₒṗoṅ-tsos.*

ཚོགས་ *tsogs Ssk.* गण, (cf. *ₒtsógs-pa*) 1. **an assemblage** of men (implying, however, compared with *tso,* a larger number of individuals, not at once to be surveyed), *Cs.: tsogs sdú-ba* to call an assembly, *ₒgyéd-pa* to dismiss it; *tsogs ₒdu* an assembly meets, *ₒgye* it dissolves; *W.:***šol soṅ** it is adjourned, **tol soṅ** it is broken up; *dpuṅ(-gi), dmag(-gi)-tsogs* army frq.; *yul-tsogs* village community, country-parish, **yul-tsog nyi láṅ-te yod** *W.* two parishes have set out; **human society,** *tsógs-kyi náṅ-nas ₒbyúṅ-ba Stg.,* **tsog dhaṅ gyé-wa** *C.* to retire from society; *tsógs-naṅ mi ₒgró-ba* not mixing with society *Dó.*; *čós-tsogs* has been introduced by us, with the concurrence of our native Christians, as the word for **'congregation, church,** ἐκκλησία'. — 2. **accumulation, multitude,** of things, **šiṅ-tsog** *W.* wood, thicket, copse, bush, shrub; *mé-tsogs* mass of fire, *Thgy.*; in a more special sense = *dgé-bai tsogs,* or *bsód-nams-kyi tsogs,* accumulation of merit acquired by virtue, *tsogs γsóg-pa* to accumulate such frq.; *tsogs ma bság-pai mi* almost the same as a wicked, godless person; *tsogs(-kyi) ₒḱor(-lo),* गणचक्र, sacrificial offering, a quantity of victuals, trinkets, and other articles being disposed in a circle as an oblation, *Mil.* and elsewh.; *tsogs-ₒkʻór skor-ba* prob., like *šóm-pa* to prepare such an offering; *tsogs γnyis Glr.* was explained by *bsod-nams-kyi tsogs daṅ ye-šes-kyi tsogs*; *sna-tsógs* of all kinds, merely signifies 'many'. — 3. *tsogs drug Mil.* and elsewh., *Was.* 290, **'kinds' of perception** by the senses, which are supposed to be more or less in number, yet the etymology of the word rather suggests the groups of objects perceptible by means of the (6) senses. —

Comp. *tsogs-kʻáṅ* meeting-house *Cs.* — *tsogs-ₒkʻór* v. above. — *tsogs-grál Mil.* 1. row of people in an assembly 2. row of offerings, ni f. — *tsógs-čan-ma Sch.* 'songstress, prostitute'. — *tsogs-mčóg* a most splendid assemblage, *tsogs-mčog-dge-ₒdún Thgy.* — *tsogs-γtám* speech addressed to a meeting *Cs.* — *tsogs-stón* a high sacrificial festival *Pth.* — *tsogs(-kyi)-bdág(-po)* गणेश, son of Siwa, the god of wisdom, furnished with a thick belly and the head of an elephant; appears also in the Buddhism of later times.— *tsogs-dpón* president or chairman of a meeting *Cs.* — *tsogs-záṅs Sch.*: 'the meeting-kettle, the point of union or its symbol'. — *tsogs-sa* place of meeting *Cs.* — *tsogs-γsóg* accumulated merit, tantamount to offerings and gifts bestowed on priests, also any service or work done to or for a priest *Mil.*

ཚོང་ *tsoṅ* (*Cs.* = *zoṅ* merchandize, but more corr.:) **trade, traffic, commerce,** **pʻag-tsóṅ* W.* smuggling-trade, **čó-če, táṅ-če**; *tsóṅ-gi kʻe* profit, gain, *gun* loss in trading; *tsoṅ byéd-pa Glr.*, **gyag-pa* C.*, **gyab-če* W.* (cf. above), to carry on trade; *tsoṅ brgúd-pa* id. *Sch.*

Comp. *tsoṅ-skad* commercial language, business-like style, terms of trade. — *tsóṅ-kʻaṅ* store-house, magazine. — *tsoṅ-gru* trading-vessel, merchantman. — *tsóṅ-grogs* commercial friend, correspondent. — *tsoṅ-čaṅ* pledging in beer, after a bargain has been struck. — *tsóṅ-čad* bill of purchase, deed of sale. — *tsoṅ-mtun* commercial intercourse. — *tsóṅ-ₒdus* market people *Pth.* — *tsóṅ-ₒdus-sa* market-place. — *tsóṅ-rdal* that quarter of a city which is chiefly inhabited by merchants. — *tsoṅ-pa* **merchant, trader, seller**; *ₒbru-tsoṅ-pa* corn-merchant, *čaṅ-tsoṅ-pa* dealer in wine and other liquors. — *γser-daṅ-dnul-(gyi) tsóṅ-pa* exchanger of gold and silver coins. — *tsóṅ-dpon, Hind. čaudhari*, head of a commercial establishment, the principal merchant in a city, under whose control all the rest, and the market in general, are standing; the chief leader of a caravan, to whom all that have joined in it are subordinate *Glr.* — *tsoṅ-spógs* proceeds of trade; *tsoṅ-spógs byéd-pa, tsoṅ-spógs-la ₒgró-ba* to engage in commercial speculations *Dzl.* — *tsoṅ-ₒpʻrúl* commerce, *tsoṅ-ₒpʻrúl-gyi γnas* market. — *tsoṅ-zán* (cf. *tsoṅ-čáṅ*) meal after settling a business. — *tsoṅ-zóṅ* goods, merchandize. — *tsóṅ-sa* commercial place, market.

ཚོང་ཚོང་ *tsoṅ-tsóṅ* 1. a kind of **ornament** *Cs.* 2. = *tsoṅ-tsóṅ*.

ཚོད་ *tsod* (prop. the same as *tsad*) 1. **measure, proportion,** in a general sense = **the right and just measure;** *tsod ₒdzin-pa, (bzúṅ-ba) W. *zúm-če** 1. to take measure, to measure, to measure out, to survey, *yul* land, **yul-tsód-zum-kʻan** land-surveyor *W.* 2. to estimate, to rate, to appraise, to tax, *raṅ-gi tsod mi ₒdzin* he overrates himself (his own powers) *Dzl.* 3. to observe the right measure, to be temperate, *zas-čáṅ-la* in eating and drinking *Glr.*; *zás-tsod ma zin čuṅs gyúr-na* when below the proper measure, i.e. when too little is eaten *S.g.* 4. to try, to tempt, to lead into temptation *W.*; *tsod-ltá-ba, lén-pa B.* and vulg., *Cs.* also *tsod bgám-pa* **to try, prove,** **tsod ma ltos** I have not tried it yet *W.*, **tig-tsód ma ltos** id., *tsod ltá-ba, len-pa* also **to sound, to sift, examine, spy out,** *tsód-len-pa* sbst., **spy;** *séms-kyi* or *nyáms-(kyi) tsod lén-pa* to examine, find out or sift another's thoughts or sentiments, also **kʻog-tsǫ́' lém-pa* C.*; *tsod ǰal-ba* to measure; *tsod-šes-pa* **to keep measure,** and adj.: **observing due measure, temperate,** *tsod-mi-šés-pa* not keeping measure, intemperate. — *tsod-čan, tsod-ldan* 1. **moderate.** 2. **punctilious, strict, grave** *W.* — *tsod-méd* intemperate, immoderate, impudent. — 2. **measure, instrument for measuring,** *ču-tsód* water-clock. — 3. **division, portion, quantity,** *tsod-čig* part, **nor tsod čig** part of the money, of the estate *W.*; esp. of time, **point of time,** certain hour, cf. *ču-tsod* and *dus-tsod;* **duṅ pú-če tsód-la** *W.* at the time when the signal with the trumpet is given; **tsam tsod** *W.*, at which hour? — 4. **estimation, supposition, conjecture, guess;** *ṅai tsod-la* according to my estimation, *tsod ₒdzin-pa* v. above; **dha léb-pe tso' yo'** by this time he will have arrived, I guess *C.*; hence **tsod-če** *W.* to guess; *tsód-šes, tsód-bya* **riddle** *Cs.*, *tsód-šes smrá-ba* to propose a riddle, *mi-tsod* about men, *bem-tsód* about inanimate objects *Cs.*(?); **tsod-tsód** *W.* at random *Sch.* — 5. *tsod* affixed to an adj. serves to form abstract nouns, thus: *rnyéd-par dká-tsód* the difficulty of obtaining, *ₒjig-par slá-tsod* the facility of destroying, *pan-ₒdógs čé-tsod* the greatness of the advantage *Thgy.*

ཚོད་མ་ *tsód-ma* 1. **vegetables, greens,** *tsód-ma rgod-skyés Cs.*: wild-growing greens, frequently gathered by the Tibetans in spring-time, such as dandelion, nettles, Eremurus etc.; *tsód-ma γyuṅ-skyés Cs.* cultivated vegetables. — 2. **boiled greens, vegetable-soup** *Mil.* and vulgo. — *sṅo-tsód* = *tsód-ma*; *nyuṅ-tsód* a dish of roots, turnips etc. *Cs.; ldum-tsód* a variety of roots *Cs.*(?) — *lo-tsód* all sorts of cabbage; *ša-tsód Cs.*, 'meat',(?) or more probably: prepared mushrooms. — *tsod-sdér* **plate, dish** *Sch.*

ཚོན་ *tson*, I. (cf. *tso-ba* and *tsos*) **colour,** 1. colouring matter, **paint,** = *tsón-rtsi*, or *rtsi-tsón*; *tsón-rtsi dkár-pos ₒbri-ba* to mark with white paint; *ₒbyúg-pa* **to paint;** *tson lén-pa* to take, imbibe colour *Cs.*; *tson sbyór-ba* to mix, to prepare colours *Cs.*; *tsón-gyis btso-ba* **to colour, to dye;** *tson-skúd* dyed thread *Do.*; *tson-spél* a coloured strip *W.* — 2. **colour** = *mdog W.* — II. v. *mtson.*

ཚོན་པོ་ *tson-po* 1. **fat, plump, well-fed** *W., C.* 2. **resinous.**

ཚོན་མོ་སྟེང་ *tson-mo-steṅ* a metal (not known) *Stg.*

ཚོབ་ *tsob* for *tsab Sch.*

ཚོམ་པ་ *tsóm-pa* I. also *tsóm-po Cs.* **bundle, bunch,** *tsóm-bu* id., *mé-tog-gi tsóm-bu* bunch of flowers *Pth.*; *rṅá-ma nág-poi tsóm-pa btágs-pa Mil.*, a kind of collar, made of black yak's tail; *pra-tsóm* a border or trimming set with jewels or pearls. Acc. to our authorities, however, the word properly signifies a mixture or variety of colours, something **variegated, gay-coloured,** e.g. **dii náṅ-du tsom máṅ-po** there is much colouring in this, it is manycoloured, **tsom-tsóm** id. — II. vb. **to doubt, hesitate;** to be timid, bashful, shy; to be ashamed *C.*; sbst. **doubt, timidity** etc.; *tsom-tsóm, tsam-tsóm, te-tsóm* id.

ཚོམས་ *tsoms C., W.* 1. = *kyams*, also *tsoms-skór* **court-yard,** *kan-pai tsoms Lex.* — 2. **set, division, part, chapter** *Sch.*, so perh. in the title of a book, *čéd-du brjód-pai tsoms Thgy.*; **kye-ča yu daṅ zii tsóm-čan** *W.* a neck-lace or string of pearls in sets, divided by turkois-drops and *γzi.*

ཚོམས་རྔམས་ *tsoms-rṅams* **noise, din, clatter** *Sch.*

ཚོར་བ་ *tsór-ba* 1. **to perceive,** sbst. **perception;** as one of the five skandhas = वेदना, a sensation, a feeling; **to perceive,** *γžán gyis ma tsór-bar* without any one perceiving it *Dzl.*; also without *γžán-gyis*: *ma tsór-bar rkú-ba* to steal unobserved, the contrary to robbing forcibly *Thgy.*; **žim-po tsor** he found it well-tasted; *sbrúm-pa tsór-nas* feeling herself to be with child *Pth.*; **yáṅ-mo tsor soṅ** *W.* it felt light to the touch. — 2. **to hear,** for *tós-pa*, common in *W.* —

ཚོར་ལོ་ *tsór-lo* a (flying) **report, rumour.**

ཚོལ་བ་ *tsól-ba* v. *ₒtsól-ba.*

ཚོས་ *tsos* 1. **paint, dye, colouring matter;** *tsos rgyág-pa, rgyáb-pa* **to dye, to colour** *Sch.*; *tsos gyur* (or *log*) *soṅ* it has lost colour, it is faded; *tsós(-kyi) ku(-ba)* liquid paint, = *tsón-rtsi Glr.*; *tsós-mkan* dyer, *tsos-lu Sch.*: a cosmetic, wash(?); *rgyá-tsos* a red pigment from India, perh. kermes *Med.* — 2. **a medicament** *Med.* — 3. v. *kur-tsos, ₒpoṅ-tsos.*

མཚའ་ལུ་ *mtsá-lu* 1. also *rtá-mtsa-lu Lex.*, *Sch.*: a horse with white feet. — 2. v. *tsa-lu*.

མཚགས་ *mtsags Sch.* = *tsags* 4, *tsags-bzáṅ byéd-pa*.

མཚང་ *mtsaṅ* v. *ₒtsaṅ-ba*.

མཚན་ *mtsan* 1. resp. for *miṅ*, **name,** esp. the new name which every one receives that takes orders; *mtsan ɣsól-ba* 1. to give a name *Glr.* 2. to take, to assume, a name *Glr.*, title *W.* — 2. **mark, sign,** v. *mtsan-ma*. — 3. **night,** *mtsán-mo*.

མཚན་(མ་) *mtsán(-ma)* **लक्षण.** 1. **sign** (*rtags* and *ltas*), **mark, token, badge, symptom,** *dón-med-pai mtsán-ma yin* it is a sign that it would be fruitless *Wdṅ.*; *mtsán-ma ₒdébs-pa* to make a mark, to mark (e.g. with paint) *Glr.*; *btsún-mo-la ma ₒjigs-šig byás-pai mtsán-ma byin-nas* making a sign to the queen, signifying: do not fear! (that she had nothing to fear); *mtsán-mas mtsón-pa* to represent a thing by a sign or mark *Lex.*; *rgyal-poi mtsán-ma* (or *rtags*) *lṅá-po* (acc. to Indian notions) the five royal insignia, turban, parasol, sword, fly-flap and coloured sandals; **shape** and **peculiar characteristics of separate parts of the body,** *lus-kyi mtsan Dzl.* ༢༣༤, 5, esp. as marks of beauty, *skyés-bu čén-poi mtsan sum-ču-rtsa-ɣnyis* cf. *skyés-bu*; *mtsan daṅ dbyibs* as to limbs and stature *Dzl.*; *mtsan(-ma) bzáṅ(-po)* and *ṅán(-pa)* good and evil signs, tokens, symptoms, prognostics, frq.; *bkra-šis-pai dge-mtsan* propitious signs *Glr.*, emphat., good, favourable sign, some special (good) quality, *mtsan daṅ ldan-pa* possessing such quality, **superior, excellent,** frq.; *mtsán-ma rtóg-pa* to prove, to examine, signs; *mtsán-mar sgóm-pa* to take as an omen *Sch.*, *mtsán-mar ma bzuṅ* do not regard it as an (evil) omen, be not surprised or alarmed *Sch.* — *mtsan(daṅ) bčás(-pa)*, and *mtsan-méd* having characteristics and having none, (v. also *Was.* 297), terms with which Buddhist speculation loves to play, cf. *Köpp.* I, 597. — 2. **genitals** *Med.*, *Pth.*, gen. preceded by *po* or *mo*; *mtsan-dbye* prob. the genitals open themselves *Med.*; hence in Lhasa the word *tsan-zúg* (q.v.) might be misunderstood for painful affection of the genitals. — 3. *šin-tu mtsan čé-bar gyúr-te* is at one time applied to Buddha, at another to men, thus leaving the true meaning doubtful.

Comp. and deriv. *mtsán-mkan* soothsayer, astrologer, frq. — *mtsan-gráṅ* and *dgu-mtsan* prize, crown of victory *C.* — *mtsan-brjód* calling upon the name of a deity, enumerating its characteristics and attributes *Cs.*; *mtsan-dón* something similar(?). — *mtsan-nyid* prop.: **'the sign'**, the essential characteristic, sometimes even implying the true, innermost essence of a thing, whilst, on the other hand, it is also used merely for 'mark' in general; *čós-kyi mtsan-nyid stón-pa, kóṅ-du čúd-pa* prob. to show the true essence of doctrine, to receive it into one's own mind *Dzl.*; *mtsan-nyid-pa Mil.* n. of a philosophical school of the present day, stated to be the same as *bye-brág-pa*; it is much in favour with the Gelugpa-sect, and the principal object of their studies is, to ascertain the literal sense and original spirit of their doctrine; they love disputations on these subjects, and may be considered the representatives of speculative science among the Tibetan clergy. — *ₒdus-byás-kyi mtsan-nyid mi-rtág-pa yin* the essential property of all that is compounded is liability to decay *Glr.*; **property, quality** *Domaṅ*; **symptom, indication,** *nád-pa sós-pai mtsan-nyid* an indication that the patient will recover *S.g.*; *mtsan-nyid ɣsum* the three marks or characteristics in the doctrine of 'perception' of the Mahayanists, *kun-btágs*, *ɣžán-dbáṅ*, *yoṅs-grúb Was.* 291; *mtsan-nyid bšád-pa Schr.*: **definition**; so it seems to be used in *Thgy.* — *mtsan-rtágs* = *mtsán-ma Wdk.* — *mtsán-pa* **marked,** *ₒkór-los* being marked with the figure of a wheel *Glr.* — *mtsán-dpe* for *mtsan daṅ dpe-byad Glr.* — *mtsan-ɣži Lex.*, *Sch.*: 'the cause of a sign or symptom, an object' (?).

མཚན་མོ་ *mtsán-mo W.*, **tsan**, **night** **tsan ča dug**, *W.* night sets in; adv. **at**

night, by night, in the night time *Dzl., W.:* **tsan-la**; *dei mtsán-mo Dzl.* in that night; *tsan gáṅ, tsan tog-tág, W.* also **tsan-tse-ri**, the whole night; also adv., all night; *mtsan-dkyil, mtsan-gúṅ, mtsan-pyéd* **midnight;** *mtsan-stód, mtsan-smád* the first, the second half of the night; *mtsan-stód-kyi rmi-lam* a dream before midnight *Med.* — *mtsan-dús* **night time.** — *mtsan-byi* (*W. *tsan-bi**) **bat.** — *tsan-šiṅ W.* 1. **chip of pine-wood,** 2. **pine-wood.** 3. **pine-tree.** — *mtsan-só byéd-pa* to keep watch during the night *Sch.*

མཚམས་ *mtsams* 1. **intermediate space, interstice, border, boundary-line,** *rgya-gár daṅ bál-poi mtsáms-na, rgya-bál-gyi mtsáms-su* on the border between India and Nepal *Glr.*; *mtsáms-kyi nags-kród* boundary-forest *Glr.*; *sa-mtsáms* (vulgo *san-tsám*) frontier of the country *Glr.*; *dé-nas* *ₒdoms lṅa-brgyái mtsáms-nas* at a distance of 500 fathoms from that place; *bar-mtsams-na yod* it lies in the middle between; *ri taṅ mtsáms-su* where the mountains are contiguous to the plain; *byaṅ šar mtsáms-su* in the north-east (cf. no. 2 below); *ču ₒgram mtsáms-su* (between the water and the river's bank) close to the edge *Wdn.*; *dei mtsáms-su* (with regard to a royal dynasty) **intervening, a usurper,** interrupting the regular succession *Glr.*; *čés-pai tsig mtsáms-nas* when these words were uttered, at these words *Tar.* 127, 11; *sgo(i)-mtsáms* a narrow opening of the door, *sgo-mtsáms-nas sleb* (he or it) enters through the cleft of a door, equivalent to our 'through the key-hole'; **tsám-la čúg-če* W.* to preserve, to put (plants) between (paper), to pack up (glass in straw). — *mtsams sbyor-ba* 1. **to close interstices, to stitch up, to sew together** (the separate parts of a shoe) *Mil.* 2. *Sch.*: **to occupy a certain space, to enter a womb',** to embody one's self in human flesh, so it seems to be used in *Thgr.* and *Mil.* 3. **to take a resolution, to form a plan, to conceive an idea, to settle in one's mind,** like *ₒgód-pa*, cf. *sbyór-ba* I, 2; II, 2 *C., W.* — *mtsams ₒbyé-ba* to split(?), *skra smin ysár-du mtsams-bye rtsub ₒkyil S.g.* the hair of the head and the eye-brows splits, divides again, is growing thin, crisp, and interspersed with bald places, which is alledged to be a symptom of approaching death, yet hardly founded on correct observation, nor by any means clearly defined; *Schr.* has: *skra mtsams ₒbyéd-pa* to part the hair on the top of the head. — *mtsams-med-pa* 1. adj., *Ssk. ānantarya*, without interstices, continuous, = *go-mtsams-med-pa* v. *go* 1, *Dzl.* 2. sbst., *Ssk. ānantarya, Was.* (240), 'where nothing is to be interposed between a deed and its consequences, where the consequences are not to be averted', **a deadly, capital sin** *Dzl.* and elsewh.; *mtsáms-med-pa lṅa*, i e. inexpiable sins, are: parricide and matricide, murder of an Arhat (*dgrá-bčom-pa*), or of a Tathāgata, likewise causing divisions among the priesthood. — *dus-mtsáms* **intermediate time** *Cs.* — *mtsams-sbyór* the Sanskrit diphthongs ē, ō, ai, au; *mtsams-sbyór-pa* and *-ma*, a bawd, *Cs.* — *mtsams(-kyi)-žu(-ba)*, also *ₒtsams-žu*, an expression gen. occurring in modern Tibetan letters, winding up the complimentary phrases of the introduction, and passing over to the proper business of the letter; for the immediate sense of the phrase I found no explanation. — 2. **the points of the compass,** *mtsams bži* the four cardinal points of the horizon; *mtsams brgyad* includes the intermediate points, south-east etc., *mtsams drug* denotes the four cardinal points together with the zenith and nadir. — 3. **demarcation, partition, break, pause, stop,** *mtsams yčod-pa* to make a stop or pause with the voice in reading *Gram.*; esp. to draw a line of demarcation about one's own person, whether it be by a magic circle (*Dom.*), or by retiring to a solitary house, either for the sake of private study (*Zam.*), or which is most frq. the case, for religious meditation, (**tsám-la dád-če* W.*) in the cell of a cloister, or in a hermitage or cave in the mountains, the seclusion lasting sometimes for several months, during which time the scanty food is silently received from without through a small aperture. Such seclusions are undergone by some in the sincere belief, that they will acquire thereby higher gifts and abilities, by others merely to increase their odour of sanctity. *mtsams sdóm-pa Mil.* has a similar signification. — *spyad-mtsáms* **rules, instructions,** defining the extent and limits of a person's duties. — 4. symb. num.: 6, v. *mtsams drug* above.

མཚར་བ་ *mtsár-ba* 1. **fair, fine, beautiful,** = *mdzés-pa Zam., Glr.* frq., *mtsar sdug dan ldán-pa* id., e.g. *bú-mo Glr.*; also of flowers; **bright, shining,** of metals *Stg.*; **nyám-tsar-wa, ló-tsar-wa** admirably fair, wonderfully fine. — 2. **wondrous, wonderful, marvelous,** gen. with *no, nó-mtsar-čan žig* a wonderful, distinguished, eminent man *Mil.*; *rten no-mtsar-čan* a wonderful image (of some deity) *Glr.*, in both instances equivalent to **wonder-working, miraculous;** *no-mtsar-mčód-pa* a marvelous, extremely rich offering *Mil.*; more frq. *no-mtsar-čé-ba* e.g. marvelous things, events, miracles *Dzl.*; *mi srid no-mtsar-če* impossible! most wonderful! *Glr.*; *no-mtsar-čé-ba ma yin* that is not so very wonderful *Dzl.*; **strange, ridiculous,** *γtam šin-tu no-mtsar-čé Glr.* — 3. *no-mtsár* **wonder, surprise, astonishment,** *no-mtsár skyé-ba, no-mtsár-du ₒgyur-ba* or *ₒdzin-pa, no-mtsar-rmád-du ₒgyúr-ba* to wonder, to be surprised. — 4. *no-mtar-čé* an expression of thanks, = *bka-drin-če, dé-ltar yin-na k̔yed γnyis-ka no-mtsar-čé* if that is so, then both of you receive my best thanks! *Mil.*; *yóns-pa no-mtsar-čé* thanks to you for your coming! *Mil.*

མཚལ་ *mtsal Cs.* also *tsal* **vermilion,** used (among the rest) inst. of red ink for writing; *mtsal-pár* a printing with red ink *Cs.*; *mtsal-lčógs-pa(?) Sch.*: 'clear vermilion'(?); *sku-mtsál* resp. for *k̔rag* blood *Cs.*

མཚུངས་པ་ *mtsuns-pa* (*W.* **tsogs**) **similar, like, equal,** *k̔a-dog* as to colour *S.O.*, *sna-ma dan* like the former, *bdud-rtsir* like nectar *S.g.*; *bdud dan mtsuns* you are to me like a satan, you are a satan to me *Pth.*; *lhai sdug-bsnál dan ča-mtsúns-pai stén-du* besides their sharing all the imperfections of the gods *Thgy.*; *dús-mtsuns-pa* **a contemporary** *Mil.*; *mtsuns-méd, mtsuns-brál,* **without an equal, matchless, incomparable;** *sems dan mtsuns ldán-pa* explained by *Was.* (241) as: manifestations of mind, those outward signs by which the mind manifests itself as existing.

མཚུན་ *mtsun* (*Zam.* = *Ssk.* क्रव्य, raw flesh) 1. *Cs.*: **meat for the manes of the dead,** *γtón-ba* to bring an offering to the dead, *skyel-ba* to send one; *mtsun-γtór* explained in *Wdn.* by *ši-bai dón-du γtór-ma γtón-ba*; *mtsun-γtór stér-ba Wdn.* — 2. *Sch.*: **tutelar deities, household-gods,** or rather **the souls of ancestors;** so *Dzl.* ༢༠, 16 (another reading is *btsun*); also in *mtsun-γtor*, if *mtsun* be taken as a dat., it may have this signification; *mes-mtsún* household-gods of the Shamans *Sch.*

མཚུར་ *mtsur* v. *tsúr-mo.*

མཚུལ་པ་ *mtsúl-pa* **the lower part of the face,** nose and mouth, **the muzzle** of animals *Mil.*; **bill, beak** *Sch.*; *W.* **nám-tsul** **nose;** *mtsúl-pa ₒgag* the effect of the gall entering the nose(?) *Mng.*; *k̔a-mtsúl* (*W.* **k̔am-tsúl**) **face,** seldom in *B.*

མཚེ་སྐྱོང་ *mtse-skyón Wdn.?*

མཚེ་ལྡུམ་ *mtse-ldúm* n. of a medicinal herb *S.g.*

མཚེ་མ་ *mtsé-ma* (*W.* **tsag-túg**) **twins,** *bu mtse-ma γnyis dus γčig-na ₒk̔runs-so Pth.* two twin-sons were born simultaneously; *mtsé-ma γsúm-po* three-twin-child, trigemini *Wdn.*

མཚེད་ *mtsed, Sch.*: *dur-mtséd,* **place for burning the dead.**

མཚེའུ་ *mtseu* **a small lake,** *mtso dan mtseu* lakes and lakelets *Pth.*

མཚེར་བ་ *mtser-ba* = *ₒtser-ba.*

མཚོ་ *mtso* 1. **lake,** frq. — 2. for *rgya-mtso* sea, rarely. — 3. symb. num.: 4. — **Comp.** *mtso-dkyil, mtso-dbús* the middle of a lake. — *mtso-ₒk̔ór* an assemblage of many lakes *Cs.* — *mtso-ₒk̔yóms* v. *ₒk̔yoms.* — *mtso-ₒgrám, mtso-mtá* border of a lake. — *mtso-šnón Glr.*, **sóg-po tso-nọn** *C.* the blue lake, Kokonor, in Mongolia. — *mtso-čú* water, *mťso-rláṅs* vapours, *mťso-rlábs* waves of a lake. — **tso-lág** *C.* **inlet, creek, cove.** — **to-lag-ḍél** *C.* **strait, channel.**

མཚོག་པ་ *mťsóg-pa* v. *˳ťsóg-pu.*

མཚོག་མ་ *mťsóg-ma Lt.*, also *mťsog-γsén Cs.*, 'spot or tender part of the head', vacancy in the infant cranium, = *ťsáṅs-pai bú-ga.*

མཚོགས་ *mťsogs* adv., **ťsógs-se** adj., *W.* for *mtsuṅs* or *˳dra*, **similar, like, equal;** **aṅ-ré-zi ťsogs rgyál-la mi dug** they are not so good as the English; **ko daṅ ṅá-la dug-ṅál ťsóg-se yod** with him and with me there is the like disaster, misfortune visits us equally.

མཚོན་ *mťson,* 1. also *mťsón-ča,* any **pointed or cutting instrument,** *mťsón-čas γtúb-pa* to cut to pieces with such an instrument *Dzl.*; **weapon, arms;** *mťson ťogs-pa* to seize a sword, to take up arms *Dzl.; mťsón-gyis ˳jig-pa* to destroy, to conquer, with the sword *Ma.*; *mťsón-ča rnám-pa bži Stg.:* sword, spear, dart, arrow; *go-mťsón* armory and arms; *ru-mtsón* v. *ru*; *mťson-ḱrág* blood drawn by cuts or stabs (used for sorceries) *Lt.* — *mtsoṅ-gyi dru-bu* an attribute of the gods, resembling a coil or ball of thread *Wdṅ.*; *mťson-skúd sgril-ma Thgr.* id. (?). — 2. also *ťson* **fore-finger,** *mťsón-rtsa* the pulse to be felt with the fore-finger; *mťson gaṅ* a finger's breadth; *mťson gaṅ mar* a finger's breadth lower *Med.*; *mťsón-pa* a four-fingers' pinch (?); *šiṅ mťsón-pa žig* a handful of sticks *Mil.*

མཚོན་པ་ *mťson-pa* 1. v. *mťson.* — 2. vb. **to set forth, bring forward, adduce, state, quote, exhibit,** examples of grammatical forms etc. *Gram.*; *˳dis mťsón-nas* illustrating it by this, setting this up as an example *Gram.*; *des kyaṅ sgyú-mạï dpe čig mťson* also in this may be seen an instance of deception *Mil.*; *dpes mťsón-pa* to illustrate by parables *Mil.*; *mťsán-mas* by a sign *Gram.*; so prob. also: *ăm-ban γnyis dei mtsón-pai dmág-mi* the soldiers brought forward by the two Chinese officials; it is also alledged to stand for **to make, to prepare** *C.* — *rnám-mḱa mťsón-pai rnál-˳byor-pa* prob.: the saint that represents the heavens, that resembles the heavenly space *Mil.*

འཚའ་ལུ་ *˳ťsa-lu* v. *mťsa-lu.*

འཚག་པ་ *˳ťsag-pa* 1. vb., pf. *ťsags*, *btsags*, fut. *btsag*, imp. *ťsog* (trans. to *˳dzag-pa*), **to cause to trickle, to strain, filter, sift, squeeze, press out,** *˳bru-már ťság-pa* (partic.) oil-miller *Dzl.*; **to draw off,** *dmú-ču* to tap (a dropsical person) *S.g.* Cf. *ťság-ma, tsags.* — 2. adj. **thick, fat, obese** *Lex.*

འཚང་, མཚང་ *˳ťsaṅ, mťsaṅ* **fault, error, offence, sin,** *de ˳ťsáṅ-du če* that is very wicked, a great offence; *mii* or *mi-la ˳ťsaṅ brú-ba* or *drú-ba* 1. **to spy out another's faults,** to upbraid him with them, to accuse him *Do., C., W.*; **ťsaṅ ˳og ḍhú-wa** *C.* id. — 2. **to irritate, provoke, make angry** *C.*

འཚང་བ་ *˳ťsáṅ-ba*, vb. I. pf. *ťsaṅs*, fut. *btsaṅ*(?) 1. **to press into, to stuff** *Sch.*, *˳ťsáṅ-ḱa byéd-pa* id. *Sch.*; *náṅ-du ˳ťsáṅs-pa Lexx.* prob. pressed into, stuffed inside, so *Sch.*: *ḱri naṅ ťsáṅs-čan* a stuffed seat; *dbugs ḱar ˳ťsáṅs-pa* out of breath, panting (in the heat of pursuit) *Mil.*; *dbugs stod-du ˳ťsaṅs-nas skad mi ťon Mil.* I am pressed for breath, my breath stops, I cannot utter a word (for ardent longing); *stod-˳ťsáṅs, rluṅ-˳ťsáṅs, ˳ťsáṅs-la p̓an,* all these expressions imply a want of breath, not sufficiently to be reconciled to the original meaning of the word. — 2. **sú-la ťsáṅs-se yóṅ-če** *Ld.* to attack a person with open violence, opp. to a stealthy attack. — II. pf. *saṅs*, which verb, however, occurs only in *˳ťsaṅ-rgyá-bar ˳gyúr-ba* to become Buddha *Dzl.* frq., *˳ťsaṅ rgyá-bar ˳dód-pa* to aim at Buddhaship, and *saṅs-rgyás* (having become) Buddha. Besides this form, there exists also a verb *sáṅ-ba*, pf. (*b*)*saṅs*, to clean, as may easily be proved by examples. The whole will perh. become clear, if we presume that the form *˳ťsaṅ-ba* for the present tense is now obsolete, occurring only in reference to Buddha, as quoted above, and that the root *saṅ* is now used as present tense in the following significations: 1. **to remove** (impurities) — like *˳dág-pa* — **to make clean,** *daṅ sáṅ-te med* W. (the soot) having yesterday been removed, there is none just now; *saṅ dug, saṅ čos* W. it is cleansed, swept clean, *ₒbag saṅ, nyé-pa saṅ* the contamination, the sin, has been removed, done away with C.; snyun saṅs the disease is removed Pth.; skyo-sáṅs byéd-pa to remove melancholy, to recreate or amuse one's self; to comfort others; skyo-sáṅs-la ₒgró-ba, skyo-sáṅs byéd-pa to take a walk, to take a ride Pth., C.; mya-ṅáṅ sáṅ-ba **to comfort** Pth., **to console one's self;** esp. 2. **to recover, to come again to one's senses,** ra-ro-ba-las from intoxication Dzl.; γzim-pa-las from a deep sleep Dzl.; also construed as before: bzi Glr., *ra* W. from a drunken fit, and this agrees with a sufficiently authenticated signification of the Ssk. root budh, so that saṅs-rgyás would after all be the literal translation of बुद्ध (contrary to Burn. I, 71 med.), taking the signification of the name, accord. to Tibetan notions, to be: 'the man that has entirely recovered from error and come to the knowledge of absolute truth'. That saṅs-rgyás be the same as **perfect, holy,** seems to be a mere etymological conjecture of Cs. — 3. **to take away, to take off,** *ḱeb sáṅ-wa* C. to uncover. — 4. **to be spoiled, to become unfit, useless,** *wó-ma saṅ soṅ* C. the milk is spoiled, zom saṅ ₒdug = šaṅ ₒdug the casks are leaky, are running out.

འཚང་ར་ ₒtsaṅ-ra Sch.: the neck of the thigh-bone; tsáṅ-rai tsil the fat attached to it C.

འཚབ་པ་ ₒtsáb-pa, pf. tsabs, bsabs, fut. bsab, imp. tsob, **to pay back, repay, refund,** skyin-pa a loan Lex.; cf. tsab.

འཚབ་འཚུབ་ ₒtsab-ₒtsub **hurry, confusion, perplexity, fear** Sch.; also: ₒtsab-ₒtsáb-mor γnás-pa to tarry in fear, to hesitate in apprehensions Tar.

འཚབས་པ་ ₒtsábs-pa, pf. tsabs, imp. tsobs Sch.: resp. **to be afraid;** Lex. blo-ₒtsábs id. (?).

འཚམ(ས)་པ་ ₒtsám(s)-pa 1. = ₒčam-pa(?) **fit, suitable, in accordance to, in conformity with,** de daṅ ₒtsám-par S.g.; so-sói ₒbyór-pa daṅ ₒtsám-par Tar. according to their ability, in proportion to their property. — 2. frq. and mostly erron. for mtsáms-pa.

འཚར་བ་ ₒtsár-ba, pf. tsar 1. **to be finished, completed, terminated,** sṅón-la tsár-ro Glr. it was the first that was finished; **to be at an end, consumed, spent,** *nor tsár-te soṅ* W. the money is all spent; esp. as an auxiliary, to denote an action that is perfectly past or completed (where in the earlier literature zin stands), in later books with the termin. inf., yóṅs-su rdzógs-par tsár-te when ... was completely finished Glr.; vulgo the mere root is used, esp. in W., *tsog tsar-ra ma tsar* are they assembled, has the meeting begun already? *lam-la žug tsar, soṅ tsar, kal tsar* he is on the way, he is gone, it is dispatched; tsár-ba byéd-pa, tsár-du ₒjúg-pa Cs., *tsar čug-če* W. **to bring to a close, to finish, to terminate.** — tsár-γčod-pa 1. **to destroy, annihilate,** e. g. diabolic influences, infernal powers Pth.; **to defeat, overcome,** in disputation Mil.; **to excel, surpass,** sgyu-rtsál-gyis Glr.; **to punish** Tar. 2. for γsár-γčod-pa Pth. — 2. **to grow, grow up, thrive,** of little children W.; ₒtsar-skyéd growth Mil.

འཚལ་ ₒtsal, sgro-bai-ₒtsal-gyi ḱa-brgyan Mil.?

འཚལ་བ་ ₒtsál-ba, imp. ₒtsol eleg. 1. **to want, wish, desire, ask;** when followed by a verb, the latter stands in the termin. inf., or the mere root of it, and more esp. that of the perf. form, yab daṅ mjal ₒtsál-lo I have a mind to go to see my father Dzl.; bltás-par ₒtsál-te wishing to see Dzl.; túgs-la bžag ₒtsal I wish it may be borne in mind Glr.; γsuṅ ₒtsal I beg you to speak Mil., bzuṅ ₒtsal please take Pth.; pleon. ₒḱrid-par žu ₒtsal Glr.; esp. as an intimation of willingness, dé-ltar ₒtsál-lo yes, we will do that Mil., or like our: very well! Further: ṕá-la nor ma ₒtsál-tam has he not asked the money from his father? Dzl.; gum yaṅ či ₒtsál why does (the king) want to kill me? Dzl.; deï don mi ₒtsal the profit of it I do not desire Glr. — 2. **to eat,** btsan-dúg poison *Dzl.*; *byi-bas ₒtsál-te* eaten by mice *Dzl.*; *ɣdon mi ₒtsál-bar* eleg. for *ɣdon mi zá-bar* without doubt *Dzl.* — 3. **to know** *Cs.*; so *ṅo-ₒtsál-ba* appears to be used for *ṅo-šes-pa*, and in a passage of *S.O.* it seems to imply **to understand.** — 4. in certain phrases: *ₒbad ₒtsál-ba* **to use diligence** *Thgy.*; *bro ₒtsál-ba* 1. **to swear** *Pth.*(?), 2. **to have a cold** *Mil.*; *p̓yag ₒtsál-ba* **to greet, salute,** v. *p̓yag.*

འཚལ་མ་ *ₒtsál-ma Cs.* = *tsál-ma.*

འཚིག་པ་ *ₒtsig-pa*, pf. *tsig*, **to burn, to destroy by fire,** *groṅ-k̓yer mi daṅ bčas-pa* (he burned) the town with its inhabitants *Pth.*; *mes*, *mer*, vulgo **mé-la** with fire; *rnám-par* entirely, completely *Dzl.*; more loosely: *tsig soṅ* he burnt himself, scalded himself etc.; also of food, burnt, injured by the heat; *ₒtsig-gam* am I burning? (thinks one suffering of fever) *Med.*; of inflammation, v. *mig-ₒtsig*; of any violent pain *Dom.*; **to be glowing,** of the evening-sky *W.*; **tsig ₒǰug ₒdug** *C.* **to be in the rut,** the copulating of larger animals.

འཚིང་ and འཚིངས་པ་ *ₒtsiṅ* and *ₒtsiṅs-pa Mṅg.*?

འཚིར་བ་ *ₒtsir-ba*, pf. *tsir*, *btsir*, fut. *ɣtsir*, *btsir*, imp. *tsir W.* **btsir-če** **to press,** *mig* with the finger on the eye *Med.*; *nán-gyis* to press hard *Stg.*; **to press out,** an ulcer; **to wring,** a wet cloth; **to crush out,** *til-már* sesame-oil *Lex.*; *ₒo-ma ₒtsir-ba* **to milk;** **tsir tag jhé-pa*, or *táṅ-wa** *C.* **to press hard, to examine closely, to hold a rigorous inquest;** *btsún-mo-la yaṅ tugs ɣtsir čúṅ-bar gyúr-to Pth.* also the queen's mind was much depressed.

འཚུགས་པ་ *ₒtsúgs-pa*, pf. *tsugs* (intrs. of *ₒdzúg-pa*), 1. **to go into** (more frq. *ₒtsúd-pa*), **to enter upon, begin, commence,** *stód-pa ₒbúl-ba-la tsugs* he began to praise, to flatter. — 2. **to penetrate by boring,** v. *p̓ur-pa*; **to take root, to establish one's self, to settle,** *rtsá-ba ma tsugs* it has not struck root; *ₒbrog ₒtsúgs-su ye ma-ₒdod Mil.*, prob.: they had no longer any mind to establish themselves in this alpine solitude; *brtán-gyi skyid-mgo dé-nas tsugs* this was the beginning of my lasting happiness *Mil.*; most frq. *tsúgs-pa* as partic. or adj.: **firm, steady,** *rk̓aṅ-lág-ma tsúgs-te sá-la ₒgyél-to* his limbs not remaining firm (in consequence of a paralytic stroke), he fell to the ground *Dzl.*; **káṅ-pa tsúg-kyin dug** sit quiet with your feet! *Ld.*; *ₒdug mi tsúgs-pa Med.*, *sa ɣčig-tu mi tsugs-pa Pth.*, **dö̓-tsug mé̓-pa** *C.*, **dád-du mi tsúg-k̓an** *W.* not being able to sit still; not stationary, **unsettled, roving, restless, volatile, flighty, inattentive,** *spyód-pas skád-čig kyaṅ mi tsúgs-pa Glr.* id.; **tsúg-la dod** *W.*, be attentive! **to be able** *C.*

འཚུད་པ་ *ₒtsúd-pa*, pf. *tsud* (intrs. to *ₒdzúd-pa*) **to be put into** (a hole), to prison *Glr.*; **to go into, to enter, to get into** (a good and wholesome way), **to go to** (hell); *k̓oṅ-du* v. *k̓oṅ ₒtsud-pa.*

འཚུབ་པ་ *ₒtsub-pa*, pf. *tsubs*, 1. **to whirl,** of whirlwinds, snow-storms, smoke etc. *Mil.* and elsewh. — 2. **to be choked,** esp. **to be drowned,** *nya čab-la ₒp̓yo-ba ₒtsub mi srid* the fish swimming in the water cannot be drowned *Mil.*; *čus ₒtsúb-pa Mil.*; **tsub-te ši** *W.* he has been drowned. — 3. *spyód-pa ₒtsúb-pa* **pugnacity,** of fowl *Glr.*

འཚེ་བ་ *ₒtse-ba* 1. vb. pf. *btses*, fut. *btse*, *ɣtse* (*Dzl.*) **to hurt, damage, injure, persecute, torment,** *mi-la ₒtsé-žiṅ ɣnód-pa byéd-pa*, or *ɣnód-čiṅ ₒtsé-bar byéd-pa* id.; also sbst., **enemy, persecutor** *Mil.*; *ɣčan-zán-la sógs-pai ₒtsé-ba daṅ bčás-pa* (a place) haunted by beasts of prey or any other noxious creatures *Thgy.*; the term is also applied to horses that bite each other. — 2. sbst. (spelling uncertain) **psalterium,** the third stomach of ruminating animals *W.*

འཚེག་པ་ *ₒtség-pa*, pf. *tsegs*, imp. *tseg(s)*, **to repay** *Cs.*

འཚེང་བ་ *ₒtséṅ-ba*, pf. prob. *ₒtseṅs*, 1. **to increase, improve, thrive,** opp. to *ₒp̓úṅ-ba W.* — 2. **to be content, happy** *Mil.*

འཚེད་པ་ *ₒtséd-pa* 1. v. *ₒtsód-pa*. — 2. v. *bséd-pa.*

འཚེམ་པ་ *ₒtsém-pa* pf. *tsems*, *btsems*, fut. *btsem*, imp. *tsems*, *W.* **tsem-če** **to sew,** **gos tsém-čeï ras** materials for a garment; ˳*tsem-skúd* **thread** for sewing; ˳*tsem-kʼáb* **needle.** — ˳*tsem-drúb* **needle-work** *Cs.* — ˳*tsem-srúb W.* **seam.** — ˳*tsem-méd* without a seam; *Sch.* also: without interruption.

འཚེར་བ ˳*tsér-ba*, I. vb. **to neigh** *Pth.* and vulgo. — II. also *mtsér-ba* 1. vb. **to grieve, to sorrow,** and sbst. **grief, sorrow,** resp. *tʼugs-˳tsér*, cf. *tsér-ka*; ˳*tsér-čan* **sorrowful, anxious,** ˳*tser-méd* **free from sorrow, easy.** — 2. **to be afraid, to fear** *C., Mil.* — 3. **to shine, to glitter,** and sbst. **lustre, brightness, splendour, brilliancy,** of light *Lex.*, of jewels *Dzl.*; *dkár-žiṅ* (or *dkár-la*) ˳*tsér-ba* to be of a shining white *Mil.*

འཚེར་ས, མཚེར་ས ˳*tsér-sa*, *mtsér-sa* 1. *Sch.*: **cause of uneasiness, source of care.** — 2. an old deserted settlement or dwelling; ˳*tser-rnyiṅ* id. *Sch.*

འཚོ་བ ˳*tsó-ba*, I. vb. a. intrs, pf. and imp. *sos*, 1. **to live,** *riṅ-du* a long time, *lo brgya* a hundred years *Med.*; *nam* (or *ǰi-srid*) ˳*tsoï bár-du* **for life, life-long,** *čʼós-kyis*, *rig-pas*, *rṅón-pas* to gain a livelihood by religion, science, hunting *Cs.*, or: to lead the life of a cleric, scholar, hunter; *srid* ˳*tsó-ba* to pass life, **to continue** in a state, **to exist,** frq.; ˳*dú-˳dzii náṅ-du* ˳*tso mi pʼód-do* in the throng of the world I cannot exist *Dzl.* (*W.* **són-če* and *tse pʼid-če**). — 2. **to remain alive,** to be maintained in life, ˳*di ma byás-na mi* ˳*tsoo* else we shall not remain alive, we shall not be able to live *Dzl.*; **to revive, to recover,** from sickness etc. *Dzl.*; *sós-par* ˳*gyúr-ba* id, frq.; *ši-ba-las* to be rescued from peril of death *Dzl.* — 3. **to last, to be durable,** of clothes etc., *W.*: **máṅ-po tsó-če** to last long, to be very durable; ˳*tsó-žiṅ sdód-pa* to remain valid, binding, to retain its virtue, efficacy, of laws, doctrine etc. — 4. **to feed, to graze.** — b. trs., pf. (*b*)*sos*, fut. *γso*, 1. **to nourish,** *lus* the body; to sustain, *srog* life; **to pasture, to feed,** *pʼyugs* ˳*tsó-ba-la kyér-ba* to lead the cattle to pasture *Pth.*, *pʼyugs* ˳*tsor pʼyin-pa* id. — 2. **to heal, to cure,** *nad Lt.*; in this sense the fut. form is used as a vb. for itself, q.v.; ˳*tso-byéd*, *tso-mdzád* **'life-giver',** i.e. physician, medicine.

II. sbst., also ˳*tso*, 1. **life,** *mi žig-gi* ˳*tsó-ba bsól-ba* to prolong life *Dzl.*; ˳*ó-čag* ˳*tsoï rje* the lord of our lives, viz. the king *Glr.*; ˳*tso skyóṅ-ba* to spare, preserve, protect another's life; **to rear, bring up, educate.** — 2. **livelihood, sustenance, nourishment, entertainment,** *zlá-ba γsúm-gyi bár-du* ˳*tsó-ba sbyór-ba* to board a person for three months *Dzl.*; ˳*tsó-ba-la ma bltá-ste* not caring for the entertainment *Dzl.*; ˳*tsó-bab záṅ-po* good eating and drinking *Mil.*

འཚོག་ཆས ˳*tsog-čas* **goods, effects, chattels, tools, necessaries,** = *yo-byad Lex.*; also **provisions, provender.**

འཚོག་པ ˳*tsóg-pa*, pf. *btsags*, fut. *btsog*, imp. *tsog*, *W.* **tsóg-če** 1. **to hew, chop, cut, pierce; to inoculate, vaccinate,** *brúm-pa* the small-pox. — 2. **to cudgel,** ˳*tsóg-čiṅ rdúṅ-ba Pth.*, *brdóg-˳tsog-pa* id. *Dzl.* — 3. also *mtsóg-pa* **to find fault with, to blame, censure, carp at, teaze** *Sch.*

འཚོག་མ, འཚོགས་མ ˳*tsóg-ma*, ˳*tsógs-ma* = *mtsóg-ma.*

འཚོགས་པ ˳*tsogs-pa*, pf. and imp. *tsogs*, **to assemble, to gather, to meet,** frq.; *kʼyed* ˳*dir tsogs*, ye, that are here assembled *Mil.*; *mi máṅ-po tsógs-pai mdún-du* before many assembled people *Dzl.*; ˳*byúṅ-ba lṅa tsógs-pa* the five elements meeting *S.g.*; ˳*tsogs rtén-gyi zas-čáṅ* food and drink to entertain the people assembled *Glr.*; **to unite, to join** in doing something, **to associate,** to make common cause; examples v. *lugs.*

འཚོང་བ ˳*tsóṅ-ba*, pf. *btsoṅs*, fut. *btsoṅ*, imp. *tsoṅ*, *W.* **tsóṅ-če**, **to sell,** *dri* ˳*tsóṅ-bai γnas* place where perfumes are sold *Stg.*; **daṅ gón-če tsóṅ-kʼan-ni mi** *W.* the man that yesterday had a coat to sell.

འཚོད་པ, འཚེད་པ ˳*tsód-pa*, ˳*tséd-pa*, (*Cs.* ˳*tsó-ba?*) pf. *btsos*, fut. *btso*, imp. *tsos*, *tsod*, *W.* **tsó-če**, 1. **to cook, to dress,** in boiling water, meat, vegetables; **ču-tsós** *W.* 'water-boiled', dumplings, = **čú-ta-gir**. — 2. **to bake** provinc. — 3. **to dye,** *gos* a garment. — 4. *tsós-pa*, **tsós-mkʼan** *W.** **ripe,** **tsos soṅ** is ripe; **ldád-pa ma tsos** *Ld.*, he is a green-horn.

འཚོབ(ས)་པ་ ₒtsób(s)-pa **to be a deputy, representative, substitute** *Cs.*; *rigs ₒtsób-pa* to be the first-born male in a family, the support of a family *Dzl.*; *ₒtsób-par byéd-pa* **to substitute,** to put in the place of another *Dzl.*; *γduṅ ₒtsób-po* resp. for **first-born** *Dzl.*

འཚོལ་བ་ *ₒtsól-ba*, pf. and fut. *btsol*, imp. *tsol*, *W.* **tsál-če**, 1. **to seek, to search, to make research**; *tabs* **to think upon means.** — 2. **to try to obtain**, *zas*; **to procure, acquire** *Mil.*; **to fetch** *Thg.*

ཛ

ཛ *dza* 1. the letter sounding **dz**; cf. the observations to ཙ *tsa*. — 2. numerical figure: 19.

ཛ་ *dza* 1. v. *dza-ti*. — 2. *dzá-brduṅ-ba* **to break through** *Sch.*

ཛ་ཏི་ *dzá-ti*, prop. ཛཱ་ཏི, *Ssk.* जाती, **nutmeg** *Lt.* and vulgo; sometimes *dza* for it, *po. Lt.*

ཛ་བོ་ཤིང་ *dza-bo-šiṅ Lex.* **a hollow tree** *Sch.*

ཛ་ཡ་ *dza-ya* 1. *Sch.*: **'muddy deposit,** green slime in the water'. — 2. *C.* **the markings of wood,** speckled and variegated, in consequence of a disease of the tree, cf. *lbá-ba*. — 3. n. of an ancient king of China *Glr.*

ཛ་ལནྡྲ་ *dza-lantra*, more accur. ཛ་ལནྡྷ་ར་ *dza-lán-dha-ra*, n. of a province in the Punjâb, now 'Jellundur'.

ཛ་ལུ་ཀ་ *dzá-lu-ka*, *čui dza-lu-ka Sch.* **'water-spider'**; in *Ssk.* however: **leech.**

ཛབ་ར་ *dzáb-ra*, prob. to be spelt *rdza-bra* q.v.

ཛམ་བུ་ *dzám-bu*, gen. *ₒdzám-bu*, जम्बु, **the rose apple-tree,** *Eugenia*, which figures also in mythology; *dzám-bui gliṅ*, *dzam-bu-gliṅ*, *dzam-gliṅ*, जम्बुद्वीप, acc. to the ancient geography of India and Tibet, that part of the world which comprizes these countries, the triangular peninsula of Hindostan, occasionally including the immediate border-lands; but as in Brahman and Buddhist literature all that does not belong to these two religions is considered as not existing, or at least as hardly human, *ₒdzam-bu-gliṅ* is simply used for **earth, world.** and *ₒdzam-bu-gliṅ-pa*, for inhabitant of the world, **man.**

ཛམ་བྷ་ལ་ *dzám-bha-la*, also *dzám-bha*, *Glr.* the Tibetan **Plutos, god of riches,** = *rnam-tos-srás*, also *rmugs-ₒdzin Lex.*, *γnod-ₒdzin*, and acc. to *Schf.*'s conjecture (*Tar.* 6, 1) also *γnód-pa-čan*; *dzam-sér* this god painted yellow, *dzam-nág* painted black *Cs.*

ཛི་ *dzi*, num. figure: 49.

ཛི་ན་མི་ཏྲ *dzi-na-mi-tra Ssk.* n. of a Buddhist scholar.

ཛུ་ *dzu*, num. figure: 79.

ཛུ་ཏ *dzu-ta Hindi*: **shoe** *C.*, *W.*

ཛུབ་ཛུབ་ *dzub-dzúb C.* **dhsub-dhsúb ǰhé-pa** **to wag, to whisk** the tail, of horses and cattle.

ཛེ་ *dze*, num. figure: 109.

ཛེ་ཙེ་ *dze-tse C.* **dhse-tse**, vent-hole for the smoke, **chimney.**

ཛོ་ *dzo* num. figure: 139.

ཛོ་ཀི་, ཛྭོ་ཀི་ *dzó-ki*, *dzwo-ki Mil.*, *Wdṅ.*, vulg. for *yó-gi*, v. *rnál-ₒbyor-pa*.

མཛའ་བ་ *mdzá-ba* (*Lex.* = *mtún-pa*) **to love,** as friends or kinsmen do, *ḱyo-šúg* *mdzá-ba-rnams* a loving married couple *Dzl.*; *mdza-žiṅ sdúg-par ˳gyúr-ba* loving each other, e.g. like brothers or sisters, *Dzl.*; *mi-mdzá-ba tams-ċád* any hostile, malignant (creatures or powers) *Dom.*; *mi-mdzá-ba-rnams sdúm-pa* to reconcile those that are at variance *Thgy.*; *brám-ze mdzá-žiṅ šés-pa žig yód-de* he had a Brahmin for his intimate friend *Dzl.*; *mdza-bšés* **friend,** frq. in conjunction with *nyé-du* or *k'yim-mtses Glr.*; *mdzá-bo* id. *Dzl.* etc. and vulgo, rarely *mdzao Thgy.*; still more vulg. *Ts.*: **dzán-te*, *dzá-mo** fem.; **dzá-wo ǰhé-pa**, *C.*, = *mdzá-ba*; *mdza-grógs* intimate friend *Sch.*; *C.*: husband, wife.

མཛངས་པ་ *mdzaṅs-pa* (*Ssk.* पण्डित) 1. **wise, learned,** frq.; *mk'ás-šiṅ mdzáṅs-pa*, *γtsug-lag-ċe-žiṅ mdzáṅs-pa*; *mdzaṅs-blun* the wise man and the fool, a relig. composition, publ. by Schmidt, together with a German translation, containing an endless variety of examples relative to the Buddhist doctrine of future rewards and punishments; *mdzáṅs-ma* a wise woman *Glr.* — 2. **gentle, noble,** distinguished as to rank, *ya-rábs mdzáṅs-kyi bu Glr.* po. — (The spelling *˳dzáṅs-pa* is not of unfrequent occurrence, but seems to be objectionable.)

མཛད་པ་ *mdzád-pa*, imp. *mdzod* (*W.* also **dzad**), **to do, to act**, resp. for *byéd-pa* in all its significations, whenever the person acting is the object of respect, hence almost without exception with regard to Buddha; but also in common life: **ċi dzad duy** *W.* what is your honour doing? also together with *byed-pa, grogs byéd-par mdzód ċig* pray, help me! further as a sbst.: **the act of doing, the thing done, the deed,** *mdzád-pa bċu-gnyis* the twelve deeds (or prop. incidents) of an incarnated Buddha, viz. the descending from the gods, conception, birth, exhibition of skill (i. e. going through certain chivalrous exercises), conjugal diversion, relinquishing family-ties, engaging in penitential exercises, conquering the devil, becoming Buddha, preaching, dying, being deposited in the shape of relics; sometimes even hundred (or rather 125) such deeds are enumerated *Cs.* —

Comp. and deriv. *mdzád(-pa)-po* a maker, composer etc.; also to be used for creator. — *mdzad-spyód* resp. deed, action *Mil.*; deportment, conduct, like *spyód-lam Mil.*; course of life, way of acting, e.g. of a heretical king *Pth.*

མཛར་ར་མཛེར་རེ་ *mdzár-ra-mdzer-ré Ld.* pitted with the small-pox, **pock-marked; warty, blotchy,** v. *mdzér-pa.*

མཛུབ་མོ་, vulgo མཛུག་གུ་ *mdzúb-mo*, *mdzúg-gu*, 1. **finger,** esp. **fore-finger;** *tams-ċád k'ar mdzúb-mo ċúg-la sdod Glr.* now sit down and put your finger into your mouth (for our: put your finger upon your mouth), i.e. be silent, as becomes the vanquished; **dzúg-gu ṭá'-pa** *C.* a kind of covenanting, the two parties wetting their fingers with saliva and then striking them against one another, which ceremony is considered more stringent than that of **do ċóg-pa**, v. *rdo.* The different fingers are: *(m)té-bo*, *(m)téb-mo* **thumb;** *mdzúb-mo B.*, **dzúg-gu** vulgo, *ston-byéd Cs.*, *mtsod Med.* **fore-finger;** *srin-lúd*, *bar-mdzúb Cs.*, **gúṅ-dzug** *C.*, *kán-ma Med.* **middle-finger;** *srin-mdzub Cs.*, **srin-dzug** vulgo, *miṅ-méd* (*Cs.*, acc. to *Ssk.*) *ċad Med.* **the fourth finger;** *(m)te(-ba)* or *teu-ċúṅ*, **dzug-ċúṅ** *C.* **the little finger.** — 2. **toe.** — 3. **claw.**

Comp. *mdzub-kér*, *-kyér* or *-kyáṅ Cs.* a stiff finger. — *mdzub-brkyáṅs Cs.* an extended finger. — *mdzub-skyis* finger-ring (= *ser-γdub*) *Lex.* — *mdzub-k'rid* a pointing with the finger, hint, intimation, direction, *blo-té-tsom sél-bai mdzub-k'rid byas* he made an intimation that removed every scruple of the mind *Glr.* — **dzug-gáṅ** *W.* a span, measured with thumb and fore-finger. — *mdzub-gúg* a crooked finger *Cs.* — **mdzub-rtén** vulgo, thimble — *mdzub-mtó* 'a span measured with the thumb and middle-finger' *Sch.* prob. = *mdzug-gaṅ.* — *mdzub-rdúb* a mutilated finger *Cs.* — *mdzub-brdá* a hint or sign given with a finger *Cs.* — *mdzub-rtsé* tip of a finger *Cs.* — *mdzub-tsigs* joint of a finger Cs. — mdzub-žú thimble Cs. — *dzug-ri* W. = mdzub-brdá, *dzug-ri-táṅ-če* to beckon. — mdzub-šúbs a fingered glove Sch

མཛེ་ mdze, Ssk. कुष्ठ, **leprosy** (not cancer, yet infectious, the skin growing white and chapped) Glr., Med.; mdzé-čan **leprous.**

མཛེར་པ་, འཛེར་པ་ mdzer-pa, ₒdzér-pa **knot, excrescence** of the skin, **wart** etc. Med.; rus-mdzér S.g. bony excrescence, exostosis (?); **knag, knot,** in wood Dzl.; mdzer-mál knot-hole, in boards.

མཛེས་པ་ mdzés-pa **fair, handsome, beautiful,** mdzés-pai or -mai bú-mo Glr.; bú-mo mdzés-pa as a tender address to a daughter Glr.; ri-bo nags-tsál dú-mas mdzés-pa a mountain beautified by numerous woods; mdzés-par byá-bai pyir for show, serving as finery, ornament Stg.; fig.: spyód-lam mdzés-pa a deportment outwardly unblamable Dzl.; lus-mdzés a well-made body, ydoṅ-mdzés a handsome face, mig-mdzes a beautiful eye Cs.; mdzes-mdzés **pomp, extravagance, profusion, debauchery** Sch. — ynod-mdzés name of the rig-sṅágs-kyi rgyál-po(?) Dom., Lex.

མཛོ་ mdzo mongrel-breed of the yak-bull and common cow Lt., whilst ₒbri-mdzo (W. *brim-dzo*) is the hybrid of a common bull and a yak-cow, mdzó-po a male, mdzó-mo a female animal of the kind, both valued as domestic cattle; mdzó-mo-kyu a herd of such animals; mdzo-rgód wild cattle; mdzo-prúg calf of such cattle; mdzo-kó leather, mdzo-már butter from a bastard cow, mdzo-sgál load for the same Cs.; mdzo-tsá Wdṅ. n. of a medicine (cf. ba-tsá?).

མཛོ་མོ་ mdzó-mo, 1. v. mdzo. — 2. **oats** Sch.

མཛོད་ mdzod, Ssk. कोष, 1. sbst. **store-house, magazine, depository, strong-box,** mdzód-du ₒjúg-pa, sbéd-pa to secure, to hide a thing in a depository, mdzód-nas ₒdón-pa to fetch forth from it; dkor-mdzód, yter-mdzód Glr. treasury; baṅ-mdzód corn-magazine, granary; dbyig-mdzód a safe for valuables, yser-mdzód for gold; pyag-mdzód (Cs. also mdzód-pa) **treasurer,** with kings, in large monasteries; miṅ-gi mdzod a treasury of words, **dictionary.** — mdzod-kaṅ store-room, larder. — mdzod-sruṅ treasurer Dzl. — 2. vb. v. mdzád-pa.

མཛོད་སྤུ་ mdzód-spu, Ssk. ऊर्णा, smin-mtsams-kyi mdzód-spu Glr., acc. to Cs. **a single hair,** acc. to the majority, **a circle of hair,** between the eye-brows, in the middle of the forehead, one of the particular marks of a Buddha, from which, e.g., he is able to send forth magic or divine rays of light.

མཛོལ་བུ་ mdzól-bu Lex.; Sch.: **'grief, dejection; a snare, a trap'**(?).

འཛའ་ ₒdza 1. **exchange, agio** C. — 2. **interest** or **premium** paid for the use of money borrowed Lh.

འཛའ་བ་ ₒdzá-ba, prob. only in the word čúd-ₒdza-ba **to be expended in vain** Cs. (?).

འཛག་པ་ ₒdzág-pa, pf. (y)zags, fut. yzag, (intrs. to ₒtsag-pa), **to drop, drip, trickle,** sna-krág, sna-ču dzag blood, water, dripping from the nose Med.; *ṅal-tag zág-če* the menstrual flow of females (plain expression for it) W.; mči-ma Dzl.; ₒó-ma ₒdzág-pa dé-las ₒbyuṅ milk is trickling from it Wdṅ.; ₒdzag-ₒdzág-pa to trickle constantly Sch.; in a more gen. sense: **to flow out** spouting; krag yzágs-pa the blood that has been shed Dzl.; mtso žábs-nas zágs-te méd-par soṅ flowing off at the bottom, the lake dwindled away Mil.; *ká-ču zag dug* W. he foams (with rage); bžin zags-te the face dripping (with perspiration); *šú-gu zags soṅ* W. the paper runs, blots; sometimes used transitively: kún-la snyiṅ-btse mči-ma yzag he is shedding tears of universal pity Dzl. ??, 16; sor bar-nas ₒdzág-nas letting (the ashes) fall through between his fingers Mil.

འཛག་འཛོག་ ₒdzag-ₒdzóg **mixed, mingled, promiscuously, pell-mell** Lex. = ₒkrúgs-pa.

འཛང་འཛོང་ ₒdzaṅ-ₒdzóṅ = ytsaṅ-ytsóṅ.

འཛངས་པ་ ₒdzaṅs-pa, Lex. = zád-pa **spent, consumed, exhausted,** construed with nor, of rare occurrence.

འཛད་པ་ *ˌdzád-pa*, pf. *zad* 1. **to be on the decline, pf. to be consumed, spent,** frq., *bsags-pai nor ˌdzad* the gathered wealth goes to an end *Pth.*; *snúm-zad-kyi már-me* a lamp the oil of which is exhausted *Glr.*; *k'yód-kyi bsód-nams zád-pai ts'óṅ-p'rug-rnams* ye (poor) partners in trade, whose stored-up merits are now at an end (whilst the speaker by the strength of his virtue is saved from the danger in which the others perish) *Glr.*; *rgyágs-la zad* that has been spent for provisions *Mil.*; *brlai ša zad kyaṅ yaṅ-ṅo* the flesh of the upper part of the thigh, even after it had been used (after all had been laid on the scales); was nevertheless lighter than .... *Dzl.*; *t'abs-zád* helpless *Glr.*; *ts'e-yóṅs-su zád-pa-las* whilst life is consuming itself *Do.*; *ts'e-zád-kar Do.*, prob. the same as *ˌči-k'ar*, at the hour of death; frq. referred to sin: *ˌdod-čágs-kyi sems, dri-ma kun, nyés-pai skyon t'ams-čád, ˌdód-pa kun yóṅs-su zád-de* sensuality and all sin, desire and defilement being done away with, having ceased *Dzl.*; *dug lṅai lás-la zád-pa med* the effects of the five poisons (q.v.) never cease; *ˌdré-la zad-pa med* of devils there is an infinite number *Mil.*; *zad (-pa) méd(-pa), zad-mi-šes-pa* incessant, endless, everlasting — 2. *ˌdis zad* **with this it is done,** i.e. a. this is **the only thing,** besides which no second is existing; *ˌdis don-ɣnyer-žiṅ ˌtsó-bar zád-na* as this is our **only means** of making a living *Dzl.*; *bu ni k'yod ɣčig-pur zád-de* as thou art **our only son** *Dzl.*; *mt'óṅ-ba k'ó-mo k'ó-nar zád-de* as I am **the only person** that has seen .... *Tar.*; *mts'óṅ-bar zád-de* this is limited to seeing, this refers **only** to sight *Dzl.* ༤༥, 12; *ɣnyis ni miṅ ɣčig-pa tsám-du zád-pas* as the two have **only one name** *Tar.*; hence the frequent *ma zád-de* with the termin. case, **not only,** *srog ˌdór-ba ˌdi ˌbá-žig-tu ma zád-de* having lost his life not only this time (but often so before) *Dzl.* ༧༢, 13; *der ma zad(-kyi)* not enough with that, still more, further, yea even *Thgy.* — b. **it is decided, settled, unquestionable,** *nor rgyál-pos bžés-par zád-na* as the fortune unquestionably falls to the king.

འཛབ་ *ˌdzab* **magic sentence,** *bzlá-ba* to pronounce one *Lex.*

འཛབ(ས)་པ་ *ˌdzáb(s)-pa* **to strive, endeavour; to be studious, to give diligence** *Sch.*

འཛམ་བུ་ *ˌdzám-bu* v. *dzám-bu.*

འཛམ་བུར་ *ˌdzam-bur*, **gun, cannon,** **gyáb-pa** *C.* to discharge.

འཛར་ *ˌdzar* **bob, tassel, tuft** *Lex.*

འཛར་བ་ *ˌdzár-ba Cs.*: **'to hang down'**; yet it is evidently the prop. present-form to the pf. *bzar* and the fut. *ɣzar*, which frq. are used without regard to tense: **to hang up,** clothes on a line *Dzl.*; **to hang** or **throw over,** the toga over one's shoulder *Dzl.* and elsewh.

འཛི་བ་ *ˌdzi-ba* **to abstain from, to be abstinent, temperate** *Sch.*

འཛིང་བ་ *ˌdziṅ-ba* **to quarrel, contend, fight,** *mče-, sder-, rwa-ˌdziṅ byéd-pa* to fight with tusks, claws, horns *Cs.*; *ˌdziṅ-mo* **quarrel, contention, dispute.**

འཛིངས་པ, གཟིང་བ་ *ˌdziṅs-pa, ɣziṅ-ba*, gen. with *skra*, rarely with *myo Glr.*, **bristly, rugged, shaggy,** of beggars *Dzl*, infernal monsters *Dzl.* — *sprin-sna ˌdziṅs-mt'iṅ-nág Mil.?*

འཛིན་ *ˌdzin* 1. **the act of seizing, seizure, grasp, gripe,** v. *ˌdzin-pa*, e.g. *nyi-ˌdzin* eclipse of the sun, *zla-ˌdzín* lunar eclipse, (the heavenly bodies being seized by the dragon Ráhula, v. *sgra-ɣčan*), *ril-ˌdzín* total, *ča-ˌdzín* partial eclipse *Wdk.* — 2. **he that seizes, holds fast, a holder, keeper; receptacle;** *rdo-rje-ˌdzin* v. *rdó-rje*; *ču-ˌdzin* po. cloud, *ro-ˌdzin* po. tongue *Lex.*; **adherent,** e.g. in *srol-ˌdzin.* — 3. **bond, obligation, certificate,** e.g. *p'rod-ˌdzin* **receipt, acquittance.** — 4. **contract, agreement, treaty,** **žág-pa** *C.*, **t'áṅ-če** *W.*, to conclude, make, a bargain, a treaty; *yig-ˌdzín* **a written agreement.**

འཛིན་ཅན་ *ˌdzín-čan W.* **sticky, glutinous** (?).

འཛིན་པ་ *ˌdzín-pa* I. vb. pf. (*b*)*zuṅ*, fut. *ɣzuṅ*, imp. *zuṅ(s)*, also *ɣzúṅ-ba, bzúṅ-ba* and *zín-pa* in all tenses, *W.* **zúm-če**, *Bal.* **zún-čas**, 1. **to take hold of, to seize, grasp,** *lág-pa-nas* to grasp a person's hand *Mil.*; *mgó-nas* taking hold of a skull *Dzl.* ༢༧, 6; *gós-kyi mťá-ma* to seize the coat-tail *Dzl.*; *mi* a man, = to catch, frq.; *čuṅ-mar ₒdzin-pa* to take wives *Glr.;* **to hold,** *lág-na rál-gri* to hold a sword in one's hand *Glr.*; **k̔yi zum toṅ** *W.*, **k̔yi dzin* (or *zin*) *roq ǰhẹ̄** *C.*, hold the dog fast! **to catch,** a ball, rain-water etc.; *bzuṅ-bas mi zin capiendo non capitur*, it (the soul) cannot be taken hold of *Mil.; bdág-gi ɣduṅ-brgyúd ₒdzin-pai rgyál-bu* a prince upholding my race *Glr.*; **to hold, support,** a certain doctrine; **to embrace,** another religion *Glr.*, v. below; to take upon one's self, some religious duty. — 2. **to get, receive, obtain.** — 3. **to occupy, to take possession of,** hold in possession, a country *Ma.*, *rgyál-sa* the throne; **to be seized,** *nád-kyis zin-pa* seized with a malady *Mil.*, — 4. intellectually: **to take in, comprehend, grasp, conceive,** by the faculty of perception or imagination: *dbáṅ-po-rnams-kyi nús-pa zad-pas yul mi ₒdzin-pa-am ɣžán-duₒdzin-pa* to perceive things not as they are, or not at all, in consequence of weakened senses *Thgy.*; with reference to mind or memory: *séms-la, yid-la, bló-la B.* and *col.;* **to be taken in, affected, seized, captivated,** *sdig-pas zin-pa* to be affected, taken, by sin *Mil.*; *ťúgs-rǰes zin-pa* to be kindly, graciously, affected towards a person; *ťugs-ma zin-pa* to be not graciously inclined *Mil. nt.*; *bú-mos zin-pa* taken in love with a girl *Pth.*; *ₒdzin-pa ťams-čád* all that captivates me; **to choose, to follow,** *ri-k̔ród* to choose the solitude of mountains *Mil.*, *dmán-sa* to follow humility, to choose lowliness *Mil.* and elsewh.; **to embrace,** another religion, v. above; **to take for, to consider, esteem,** *ṅa-la dgrar* taking me for an enemy *Dzl.*; *mi* or *mi-la ɣčés-par* or *sdúg-par* to value, esteem, love, a person, v. *ɣčés-pa; ṗar, mar* to esteem, respect one, as a father, as a mother *Stg.*; *méd-pa-la yód-par* to consider the not existing as existing *Thgr.*; *ɣnyis-su* to consider as different, to find a difference between two things, which according to Buddhist philosophy are one and the same, cf. *ɣnyis-ₒdzin;* also absolutely, without an object being mentioned: *dṅós-por ₒdzin-pa* to believe in the reality (of a thing) *Mil.* — 5. *rǰés-su ₒdzin-pa* v. *rǰes.*

II. sbst. 1. **he that seizes, holds, occupies,** *rigs-sṅags ₒdzin-pa* the holder of a magic sentence; **adherent, keeper** etc. — 2. **that which affects, captivates,** in an intellectual sense, v. above *ₒdzin-pa ťams-čád;* the being seized or affected with, or as we should say, **taking an interest in,** v. sub *spóṅ-ba*; also cf. *ɣzuṅ-ₒdzin.* — *ₒdzin-skyóṅ, ṗo-bráṅ ₒdii ₒdzin-skyóṅ gyis* occupy this palace and take care of it *Glr.* — *ₒdzin-pa* **the earth,** as a receptacle of beings *Sch.*

འཛིམ་པ་ *ₒdzim-pa Lt.?* acc. to one *Lex.* = *ₒdzin-pa.*

འཛིར་བ་ *ₒdzir-ba,* = འཛག་པ *dzág-pa* **to drop, to drip** *Lex.*

འཛུ་བ་ *ₒdzu-ba,* pf. *ₒdzus,* **to enter** *Sch.*

འཛུགས་པ་ and ཟུག་པ་ *ₒdzugs-pa* and *zug-pa*, pf. *btsugs, zugs,* fut. *ɣzugs,* imp. *zug(s)*, (trs. to *ₒťsugs-pa*) 1. **to prick** or **stick into, to set,** to prick a stick, to set a plant, into the ground, **to plant,** frq.; **to run, thrust, pierce,** to run one's self a splinter into the flesh etc. *W.*; **to erect,** a pillar, **to raise,** a standard. — 2. **to put down, to place,** a kettle *Dzl.*; to place before, *mi-la ṗór-pa* to place a drinking-bowl before a person (more genteel than *bžag-pa*) *Glr.;* **to put or place on, to touch with,** *mdzúb-mo* the finger; esp. *pus-mo(-i lha-ṅá) sá-la* to place the knee on the ground, to kneel down, v. *pus-mo*; *žábs-ₒdzugs-kyi dga-ston* feast given, when a little child begins to walk *Glr.* — 3. **to lay out,** a garden, **to found,** a town, a convent; **to institute,** a sacrificial festival *Glr.;* **to introduce,** *srol* a custom *Lex.*, hence in a general sense, **to begin, commence,** any business, with or without *mgo*; **ku-rim tsúg-sa ma tsugs** *W.* has the ceremony already begun? is it a going? *rgól-ba ₒdzúgs-pa* to offer resistance *Pth.* — 4. **to prick, sting, pierce,** *mdas* with arrows *Dzl.*, fig. *mi-k̔a zúg-pa* hurting by malicious words *Do.*:

tsig kún-tu zúg-pa a sarcastic, offensive speech *Stg.* — 5. intrs., **to bore or force itself into, to penetrate, to take hold, to stick to,** mostly fig., e.g. *sman ma zug* the medicine has not taken hold yet, does not work *Thgy.*; *zlá-la ḱyéd-kyis mi zug* you do not cling or stick to a companion *Mil.*; **dé-la sem zúg-pa** *C.* to be attached to, to be pleased with a thing; **zúg-pa** *C.*, attached. — 6. **to sting,** like nettles, **to prick,** *tser ltar* like a thorn *Mil.*; *ló-ma zúg-par byed* the leaves sting *Wdṅ.*; *zug-rgyu-méd-pa* not smarting *Wdṅ.*

འཛུད་པ་ *ₒdzúd-pa,* pf. *btsud, Sch.* also *zud,* imp. *tsud* (trs. to *ₒtsúd-pa,* synon. to *ₒǰúg-pa*), **to put, to lay,** into a box, into the grave; **to lead, to guide,** into the right way, to virtue, to religion = to convert; to reduce, to despair, *sdig-pa-la* to seduce to sin *Pth.*; **to prompt** one to do a thing *Gyatch.*; *ₒdzúd-ₒdzud-pa* to put into *Sch.*

འཛུབ་མོ་ *ₒdzub-mo,* sometimes erron. for *mdzúb-mo.*

འཛུམ་ *ₒdzum* **smile,** *byáms-pai ₒdzúm-γyis* with a friendly smile; *ₒdzum byéd-pa* **to smile;** *ₒdzum daṅ ldan* **smiling** *Pth.*; *ₒdzum skyóṅ-ba* to preserve a friendly countenance, to be always mild and gentle; *ₒdzum-skyoṅ* in a special sense, the exhortation given to every daughter on her marriage, to treat visitors with a friendly smile; also fig., **an engaging appearance,** *ri-mo ₒdzúm-gyis ma bslús-par* not to be deceived by an enticing appearance of colour *Mil.*; *ṅo-ₒdzúm,* **smile,** in a relative sense, *ǎ-nei ṅo-ₒdzúm dkar nag bltas* I watched whether the smile, the mien, of my aunt was friendly or unfriendly *Mil.*; *ṅo-ₒdzúm nág-ste* looking sad *Dzl.*

འཛུམ་པ་ *ₒdzum-pa,* pf. *btsum, zum,* fut. *γzum,* imp *tsum* 1. **to close, to shut,** yet only in certain applications, more esp. **to close one's eyes, to shut one's mouth,** *mig mi-ₒdzúm-par ltá-žiṅ* to have one's eyes immovably fixed upon *Dzl.*; also *pád-mai ḱa zum bžin S.g.* just as the lotus-flower closes; *má-ḱa mi zúm-žiṅ Wdṅ.* if the wound will not close; *ḱa zum* the orifice (of the urethra) is closed *Mṅg.* — 2. **to wink,** prob. only **dzum-dzúm ǰhé'-pa* and *čó-če**. — 3. **to smile,** *ráb-tu* to look very friendly *Glr.*; sbst. **the smile,** *bčom-ldan-ₒdás-kyi žal ₒdzúm-pa daṅ bčás-pai sgó-nas* from the portals of Buddha's countenance graced with a smile *Glr.*; *žal-ₒdzúm mdzád-pa* resp. to smile *Glr.*; *bžin-gyi ₒdzum* the smile of the countenance; adj. **smiling; sweet, beautiful** *Mil.*

Comp. *ₒdzúm-ḱa* a smiling mouth; *lha-mo ₒdzúm-ḱa-mo* a smiling goddess *Mil.* — *ₒdzúm-bag-čan* (of a child) sweetly smiling *Mil.* — *ₒdzum-ltag-dgyé Cs.*: **'a smile between the teeth, a sardonic smile, a grin';** *ₒdzum-mdáṅs* a smiling air *Cs.* — *ₒdzum-múl* or *-dmúl* a smile; *dzum-múl-gyis šor* a smile escaped him *Glr.*; *ₒdzum-(d)múl-ba* to smile. — *ₒdzum-méd* frowning, austere *Cs.* — *ₒdzum-ₒdzúm* 1. the winking. 2. the smiling; *ₒdzum-waṅ-wáṅ Cs.*: smiling look.

འཛུར་ *ₒdzur,* 1. sup. of *ₒdzu-ba.* 2. v. the following.

འཛུར་བ་ *ₒdzur-ba,* pf. *bzur,* fut. *γzur,* imp. *zur, Cs.* **zúr-wa** **to give** or **make way,** *lam(-nas)* to step aside; **to keep aloof** *Mil.*; *lás-la ₒdzúr-ba* to shun work, to evade labour *Lex.*

འཛུལ་བ་ *ₒdzúl-ba* 1. vb. **to slip in,** *rtsa-γséb-tu* between the grass *Thgy.*, *sgor* through the door *Lex.*; *čú-la, čur* into the water, i.e. to dive. — 2. sbst. *Sch.*: **'a tippler'.**

འཛུས་ *ₒdzus* v. *ₒdzú-ba.*

འཛེག་པ་ *ₒdzég-pa,* pf. *ₒdzegs,* imp. *ₒdzog,* **to ascend,** *ri-la* frq ; *šiṅ-sdoṅ-po-la Glr.*

འཛེང་ *ₒdzeṅ, ₒdzeṅ-rdo* **whsettone, hone** *Lex.*

འཛེང་བ་ *ₒdzéṅ-ba* **to stick** or **jut out, to project, to be prominent** *Sch.*

འཛེད་པ་ *ₒdzéd-pa,* pf. *bzed,* fut. *γzed,* vulgo *bzéd-pa,* **zé'-pa** *C.*, **zéd-če** *W.*, **to hold out** or **forth,** *ḱud* the coat-tail, *snod* a vessel *Dzl.* (The significations given by *Cs.*: **to receive,** and by *Sch.*: **to meet with,** seem not to be sufficiently warranted.)

འཛེམ་པ་ *ₒdzém-pa* **to shrink,** *la,* from, **to shun, avoid,** *mi-dgé-ba-la Glr.*, *sdig-*

_pa-la_ frq.; _ṅó-ťsa-la mi ˳dzém-pa_ Cs. **insensible to shame, shameless;** _nád-rigs-la mi ˳dzém-na_ unless one is on his guard against the several diseases; also **to feel ashamed,** *_ṅe'-nam-la mi ˳dzem-mam_* C. do you not feel abashed in our presence? _˳dzém-pa-ċan ˳dzém-bag-ċan_ **bashful, modest, temperate** Cs.; _˳dzém(-pa)-med(-pa)_ the contrary; _ḱrel-˳dzém_ **modesty** Cs.

འཛེར་པ་ _˳dzér-pa_ v. _mdzér-pa._

འཛེར་བ་ _˳dzér-ba_ 1. **to say,** to speak, _Stg._ ཁུ 57, 6, obs., v. _zér-ba._ — 2. **to be hoarse,** _˳dzér-po_ hoarse, _skad Dzl., Med.; skad ˳dzer-˳dzér-du ṅú-ba_ to weep with a very hoarse voice _Pth._ — 3. **to solder** _Sch._

འཛོ་སྒྲེལ་ _˳dzo-sgrél Mil.?_

འཛོག་པ་ _˳dzóg-pa_, pf. _btsogs_, fut. _btsog_ **to heap together, to jumble, to throw disorderly together** _Cs._

འཛོང་འཛོང་ _˳dzoṅ-˳dzóṅ Ts._ *_˳dzog-˳dzóg_* 1. **jagged, pointed, conical.** — 2. **oblong, cylindrical** _C._

འཛོམ(ས)་པ་ _˳dzóm(s)-pa_ **to come together, to meet,** *_dzom ťsár-ra ma ťsar_* are they already assembled? _dág-pa mṅón-dgai žiṅ-ḱams der ˳ó-skol ˳dzóm-par ɣdon mi za_ that we shall meet again in the realms of pure bliss, that is certain _Mil._; _ťses bċo-lṅá daṅ ˳dzóms-pas_ as it just fell upon the 15th. _Glr._; *_dzom mi dzom_* _W._ they do not agree with each other; _dé-rnams rnyéd-par dká-ste mi ˳dzom_ as it is difficult to obtain these things, we shall not be able to get all of them together _Glr._; *_dzóm-pa me'-pa ċig kyaṅ me'_* _C._ there is nothing that does not find its way there, that is not to be had there; **to be plentiful** _Mil._; as partic. with termin. case: **rich in, abounding** _Mil._ — _dál-˳byor ˳dzóm-pai lus Mil._ v. _dál-ba._ — _ḱun-˳dzóm_ 'where all meet', name of mountain-passes, e g. between _Lh._ and _Sp._, and of females; in a similar manner _gaṅ-˳dzóm_ and _˳byor-˳dzóm_ ('conflux of goods'). — _˳dzóm-po_ rich in _C._, _rtsa-ču ˳dzóm-po_ abounding in grass and water, fertile _C._; _mťun-rkyén ˳dzóm-po_ fortunate, successful, through a favourable concurrence of circumstances; _ťsos-sna-˳dzóm-po_ variegated, many-coloured.

འཛོལ་པ་ _˳dzól-pa_ **fault, error, mistake,** _dé-la ˳dzól-pa ɣsum byuṅ_ he fell into three mistakes, committed three errors _Glr._

འཛོལ་བ་ _˳dzól-ba_ **to shake about, to stir** or **shake up,** e.g. a feather-bed; **to confound, to confuse,** _ṗrin goṅ-˳og ˳dzol-ba_ to deliver a message confusedly, making a mess of it _Glr._; _W._: *_zol-zól ċo-ċe_*. — *_˳dzól-ťso_* _C._, *_zol-zól_* _W._ **difference.**

རྫ་ _rdza_, _W._ *_za_*, 1. **clay,** gen. _rdzá-sa._ — 2. in comp. for _rdzá-ma_, e.g. _čáṅ-rdza_ **beer-jug,** _čú-rdza_ **water-pitcher** _Cs._ —

Comp. and deriv. _rdza-kór_ earthen bowl, little dish. — _rdza-ḱáṅ_ pottery _Schr._ — _rdza-ḱúṅ_ clay-pit. — _rdza-mḱán_ potter, _rdza-mḱán-gyi ˳kór-lo skor-ba_ to turn the potter's wheel _Dom._ — _rdza-rṅá_ kettle-drum of burnt clay. — _rdza-čág_ potsherd. — _rdza-čú_, or more refined _rdza-čáb_, water issuing from clay-slate rocks _Mil._ and elsewh. — _rdza-čén_ a large, _rdza-čúṅ_ a little pot, v. _rdzá-ma._ — _rdza-snód, rdza-spyád_ earthen vessel. — _rdza-ṗág_ tile, (Dutch) tile for stoves. — _rdza-ṗór C._ = _rdza-kór._ — _rdza-búm_ 1. **pitcher, jar, bottle,** formed of clay. 2. **jar,** in gen., _lċágs-kyi rdza-búm_ iron jar _Stg._ — _rdzá-bo_ an earthen vessel _Cs._ — _rdzá-ma_ **pot** (unglazed, urn-shaped, bellied vessels of various size, not for cooking, but only for holding water, butter and the like). — _rdza-ɣžóṅ_ earthen basin. — _rdza-ri_ mountain consisting of clay-slate. _dza-sá_ argillaceous earth, clay. — _dza-brá_, _C._ *_dzab-ra_*, _W._ *_zab-ra_* a mole-like animal.

རྫ་ཀི་ _rdzá-ki Mil._, for _dzó-gi, yó-gi._

རྫང་ _rdzaṅ_ **chest, box,** for various store = _báṅ-ba Thgy._

རྫང་བ་ _rdzáṅ-ba_ v. _rdzóṅ-ba._

རྫབ་ _rdzab_, _˳dam-rdzáb_, **mud, mire** (_Cs._ **clay**); _rdzab-dóṅ_ **sink, slough.**

རྫབ་རྫུབ་ _rdzab-rdzúb_ **sham, emptiness, falsehood,** _rmi-lam rdzab-rdzúb-čan_ an empty dream _Cs._

རྫས་ *rdzas* 1. **thing, matter, object** (= *dṅós-po Lex.*), *rdzas dkar sér-por mťoṅ* white objects appear yellow *Lt.*; *rdzas ǩa-sáṅ yód-pa dé-riṅ med* the thing of yesterday is to-day no more *Mil.*; *mi-γtsáṅ-bai rdzas* something impure *Pth.;* natural bodies, **substances,** from which e.g. medicines are prepared *S.g.*; **materials, requisites,** *dei rdzas* requisites for this purpose; especially for sacrifices, sorceries etc., hence also used as identical with **magic agency** *Wdṅ.*; **remedy,** *smyo-byéd-kyi* narcotic, soporific *Glr.*; **ointment,** v. *rǩáṅ-pa* and *bábs*; *rdzás-las ₒbyúṅ-bai bsód-nams Tar.* 20, 9, not: merits arising 'from works or any material causes', but: the good, the blessing accruing from a right application of *rdzas*, wonder-working medicines, and consisting in long life etc., with which also *Trigl.* fol. 20, b is in unison, if the Sanskrit word is read *dzaiwatrikam*; *srog-rdzás* **provisions, victuals** *Pth.;* in the context *rdzas* is also found standing alone in the same sense, where it perh. would be more correct to read *zas*; *mé-mdai rdzas*, *me-rdzás*, also *rdzas* alone, **gun-powder,** **dze-ǩúg* C.* cartridge-box, **dze-mé'** (a gun) not loaded *C.*; **goods, property,** *rdzas gaṅ yód-pa-rnams* all his property *Mil.*; *nor (daṅ) rdzas* money and money's worth *Mil.* and elsewh.; **treasures, jewels, valuable productions,** *rgya-gár-gyi Glr.* — 2. in philosophy: **matter** *Was.;* **real substance, realities** *Was.*

རྫི་ *rdzi, W.* **zi**, 1. **wind,** *rdzi-rlúṅ* id., also *bsér-bui*, *rlúṅ-gi rdzi Do.*; *p̓u-rdzi*, or *stod-rdzí* a wind blowing down the valley, *luṅ-* or *mdo-rdzí* blowing up the valley; *dri-rdzi ldaṅ* a fragrant breeze, a wind fraught with the odours of flowers is blowing *Stg.*; **šár-zi yóṅ-ṅa rag** *W.* I perceive an east-wind is setting in; *rdzi-čár* heavy rain with wind, *rdzi-čár drág-po* rain-storm *Tar.* and elsewh.; **zi núm-če* or *tsór-če** *W.* **to smell, sniff, snuffle,** of dogs. — 2. in comp. for *rdzi-bo, rdzi-ma.* — 3. v. *zi.*

རྫི་བ་ *rdzí-ba*, pf. *(b)rdzis*, fut. *brdzi*, imp. *(b)rdzi(s)*, *W.*, **zi-če**, *Pur.* **dzi-čas** **to press, to knead,** dough; **to tread, to beat** (clay, *gyaṅ* q. v.); *gál-te tsér-ma brdzís-na* if I should tread into a thorn *Dzl.*; **to crush,** a worm; **to oppress, to distress;** *rdzi-méd Lex., Sch.:* 'powerless', but *stóbs-rnams-la rdzi-ba-med-pa Stg.* evidently signifies: of invincible strength.

རྫི་བོ་ *rdzi-bo* **herdsman, shepherd, keeper,** frq.; also *rdziu Dzl.*; *rdzi-p̓o* a male, *rdzi-mo* a female keeper; *p̓yúgs-rdzi* herdsman, *γnág-rdzi* neat-herd, *gláṅ-rdzi* cow-keeper; *rá-rdzi* (**rár-zi** *W.*) goat-herd; *ǩyi-rdzi* dog-feeder, *byá-rdzi* person attending to the poultry; *mi-rdzi* 'guarder of man, a god' *Cs.* yet a king might also be thus designated; *rdzi-skór* shepherd's hut = *pu-lu. Sch.* has besides: *dpe-rdzi* **index, register.**

རྫི་མ་ *rdzi-ma* (vulgo **zi-ma**) **eye-lashes** (the eye-lashes of Buddha are sometimes compared to those of a cow).

རྫིག་རྫིག་ *rdzig-rdzig*, with **taṅ-wa** *C.*, **to address harshly, to fly at.**

རྫིང་ *rdziṅ* **pond,** gen. *rdziṅ-bu* e. g. for bathing *Dzl.*; v. also *skyil-ba*; *rdziṅ-po* or *-čén* a large pond *Cs.*

རྫིངས་ *rdziṅs*, *gru-rdziṅs Lt.*, gen. *γziṅs* **ship, ferry.**

རྫིའུ་ *rdziu* 1. for *rdzi-bo.* — 2. **fin of a fish** *Sch.*

རྫུ་བ་ *rdzú-ba*, pf. *(b)rdzus*, fut. *brdzu*, imp. *(b)rdzu(s)* **to give a deceptive representation,** to make a thing appear different from what it is (cf. *sprúl-ba*), with termin. case **to change into,** also **to change** (one's self), **to be changed,** *srín-por* to change into a Rakshasa *Zam.*; **to disguise** one's self, *rnál-byor-par* as a mendicant friar; *rdzús-te skyé-ba* v. *skyé-ba*; *yig-rdzu* a letter filled with falsehoods, a lying epistle *Mil. nt.*; *šá-ru rdzú-bai rgyú-ma* entrails feigning to be flesh, looking like flesh *Mil.*; *rdzu-ₒp̓rúl* (*Ssk.* ऋद्धि) **delusion, miraculous appearances, transformations,** *stón-pa* to produce such, *ₒjig-pa* to destroy the illusion, e.g. by seeing through it *Mil.*; *rdzu-ₒp̓rúl-gyi mťu*, or *stobs* **witchcraft, magic;** *rdzu-ₒp̓rul-čan* gifted with magic power *Thgy. rdzu-ₒp̓rul* is the highest manifestation of the acquired moral perfection, that is known to Buddhism; there is, however, an essential difference between it and the miracles of holy writ, the former bearing the stamp of non-reality and mere appearance, as is not only implied by the name, but also universally acknowledged; and it differs again from *čo-ₒṗrul*, in as much as the latter requires the help of natural magic (jugglery), or of demoniacal influences, and never can be produced, like *rdzu-ₒṗrúl*, at the pleasure of the saint by his own immanent power. Yet there is no doubt that the term *čo-ₒṗrul* is also often used in connection with *rdzu-ₒṗrúl*, and as identical with it; v. *Dzl.* ༣༦ and ༧༩.

རྫུན *rdzun*, *C.* **dzun**, *W.* **zun**, *Pur.* **rdzun**, also *brdzun* **untruthful speech, falsehood, lie, fiction, fable**; *rdzun-tsig*, id.; *mi-bden rdzún* that is falsehood and not truth *Glr.*; *rdzun-smrá-ba*, resp. *ɣsúṅ-ba B.*, *byéd-pa B.*, *C.*, **zér-če** *W.* **to lie**, *rgyál-ba-rnams-kyis rdzun ɣsúṅ-ba mi srid* it is impossible that Buddhas should lie; **to tell tales, to make believe, to impose upon**; **zun yin** *W.* you are not in earnest, you only want to quiz me; **zun gyáb-če** *W.* to lie, to act the hypocrite; **mi še zun gyab** *W.* to feign, to pretend ignorance, to disown a person or thing, **mi tsor zun gyab** *W.* he pretends not to hear it. — *rdzun-ₒkráb Sch.*: 'an adroit liar and deceiver'. — *rdzún-ma* 1. = *rdzun Dzl.* 2. **liar** *Mil.* — **zún-yag-čan** *W.* **clown, buffoon, merry Andrew.**

རྫུབ *rdzub* **deceit, imposture** *Lex.*, *byéd-pa* **to make a false assertion** *Tar.*; cf. *rdzab-rdzub.*

རྫུས་མ *rdzús-ma* something **counterfeit, feigned, dissembled,** *rdzús-mai spráṅ-po* a disguised beggar *Glr.*

རྫེ་བ *rdzé-ba* pf. *(b)rdzes*, fut. *brdze*, imp. *(b)rdze(s) W.* **zé ce**, 1. **to tuck up, truss up,** clothes; **to cock,** a hat; **to turn up,** the upper-lip *Wdṅ.*; *skra gyén-du brdzés-pa* the hair bristling *Do.*; **so* or *čé-wa zé-če** *W.* to show one's teeth, to grin. — 2. **to threaten** *Cs.*

རྫེའུ *rdzéu* dimin. of *rdzá-ma*, **a small pot, pipkin.**

རྫོག(ས) *rdzog(s)?* **fist,** also **dzog-ril** *C.*

རྫོགས་པ *rdzogs-pa* 1. vb. **to be finished, to be at an end, to terminate** (*Lex.* = *zin-pa*), *lam rdzógs-pai mtsáms-su* just where the road terminates *Mil.*; **dá-wa zóg-ne** *W.* as the month has expired; **i-ru pi-ti yúl-tso zog soṅ** *W.* here the villages of Spiti have an end; *mdzád-pa yóṅs-su rdzógs-nas* having accomplished all his deeds *Glr.*; *ji-ltar smón-pa bžin-du yoṅs rdzógs-pas* all prayers and wishes being fully realized *Dzl.*; *yóṅs-su rdzógs-par tsár-te* when the whole (of the building) was completed *Glr.* — 2. adj. **perfect, complete, blameless,** **gó-lo zog dug** *W.* the body (of this horse) is without fault; *stón-pa dág-par rdzógs-pai saṅs-rgyás* the most perfect teacher, Buddha *Glr.*; so in a similar manner *rdzogs (-pa)-čén(-po)*; also *yé-šes yóṅs-su rdzógs-pa* is an appellation of Buddha. — *rdzógs-par* adv. **perfectly, completely, fully** (cf. *lhúg-par*), *bsnyád-pa* to report circumstantially *Dzl.*, *ɣdams-ṅág ɣnáṅ-ba* to counsel well *Mil.*; *rdzógs-par šés-pa žig* one thoroughly conversant *Mil.*; *rdzógs-par bsláb-pa* to learn thoroughly *Mil.* — *bsnyén-par rdzógs-pa* or *bsnyen-rdzógs mdzád-pa* to ordain, v. *bsnyén-pa.* —

Comp. *rdzogs-ldán* v. *dus* 6. — *rdzogs-tsig* v. *slár-sdu-ba.* — **dzog-yél** *C.* obeisance to Chinese officers, in a kneeling posture. — *rdzogsrim* v. sub *skyéd-pa.*

རྫོང(ས) *rdzoṅ(s)*, 1. (*C.* vulgo **dzum**) **castle, fortress**; *rdzóṅ-dpon* lord or governor of a castle, commander of a fortress; **dzoṅ-kyél** *C.*, **zoṅ-lén** *W.* letter-post from one nobleman's seat to another. — 2. **the act of accompanying, escorting,** *ₒdebs-pa* **to accompany, to escort** *Dzl.*, **fee for safe-conduct,** travelling-present; **dowry,** *byéd-pa* to bestow.

རྫོང་བ *rdzóṅ-ba* pf. *(b)rdzaṅ(s)*, fut. *(b)rdzaṅ* **to send, to dispatch,** presents, ambassadors; **to expedite, send off, dismiss; to give to take along with.** — *dbugs rdzóṅ-ba* **shortness of breath, asthma** *Thgy.* and elsewh.

རྫོབ་པོ, མོ *rdzób-po*, *-mo*, 1. **vain, empty, spurious, void;** *kun-rdzób* v. *kun.* — 2. **vain, fond of dress** *W.*

ཝ

ཝ *wa* 1. the letter **w**, which occurs but rarely, and only as an initial, yet it is a true Tibetan letter, the *Ssk.* व being gen. represented by བ, and as second constituent of a double consonant denoted by ྭ (called *wa-zúr* angular or small *wa*); the pronunciation in general is the same as that of the English w. — 2. num. fig.: 20.

ཝ *wa* 1. **water-channel, gutter,** gen. of wood (*Cs.* also: trough); *wa-ka Lex.* id., *Cs.; wa-mču* **spout, lip,** or **beak** of vessels. — 2. **fox** (the name corresponding to the sound of barking) *Dzl.*, vulgo *wa-tsé; wa brgyal* the fox yelps *Sch.* The fox is the riding-beast of the goblins; whenever his barking is heard, it is in consequence of his receiving lashes from his rider. — *wa-skyés* fox-born *Cs.* — *wa-gró* a bluish fox, *gro-gró* a gray fox *Sch.* — *wa-rgán* **an old fox, a knave** *Cs.* — *wa-ldéb* fox-trap *W.* — *wa-nág* a blackish fox *Sch.* — *wa-lpágs* fox's skin. — *wa-spyaṅ Mil*, *wá-ma-spyaṅ Cs.* **jackall.** — *wa-prúg* young fox, cub. — *wá-mo* she-fox. — *wa-tsaṅ* fox-hole. — *wa-róg* black fox *Sch.* — *wa-tswá* a kind of salt *S.g.* — 3. n. of **a lunar mansion,** v. *rgyu-skár.* — 4. *wa-lóg-pa* **to perform somersets** *Sch.* — 5. *W.* **ho!** calling for one.

ཝཱ་ར་ཎ་སཱི་, or སེ་, བཱ་ར་ཎ་སཱི་ *wa-ra-ṇa-si* or *sé, ba-ra-na-si* **Banaras,** a city in the valley of the Ganges, frq mentioned in legends, as a residence of Buddha, at the present time a principal seat of Brahmanism.

ཝ་ལེ་, ཝལ་ལེ་, ཝལ་ལེ་བ་ *wa-lé, wal-lé, wal-lé-ba* **clear, distinct, plain,** *wa-lér drán-pa* to recollect distinctly *Cs.; yid-la* floating distinctly before one's mind *Lex.; don wa-lé gyis* try to gain a clear understanding of the sense of it *Mil.*; also *skad-wál* = आपाठ (?).

ཝ་སི་ *wa-si* a kind of apples *Sch.*

ཝི་ *wi* num fig.: 50.

ཝུ་ *wu* num fig.: 80.

ཝུ་རྡོ་ *wu-rdo* **pumice stone** *Sch.*

ཝེ་ *we* num. fig.: 110.

ཝོ་ *wo* num. fig.: 140.

ཞ

ཞ *ža*, 1. a letter of the alphabet, represented by *ž*, originally, and in the frontier-provinces to the present day, the soft sibilant, which is pronounced like *j* in French, or like the English s in leisure, (*zh*), (still more accurately like the Polish *ż* in *zima*); in *C.* it differs now from ཤ only by the following vowel being deep-toned. — 2. numerical figure: 21.

ཞྭ་, ཞྭ་མོ་ *žwa, žwa-mo,* resp. *dbu-žwa,* a covering of the head, **hat, cap;** fig. *ṅa yig sá-yi žwá-čan* the letter ང having ས for a cap: སྔ *Zam.*; *žwa gón-pa, gyón-pa* to put the cap on, *˳búd-pa* to take it off (in *Ts.* by way of salutation); *rgya-*, *bod-*, *sog-żwa* Chinese, Tibetan, Mongolian cap; *dgun-żwa* winter-cap, *dbyar-żwa* summer-hat (light felt-hats adapted to the warmer season); *p̓yiṅ-żwa* hat or cap made of felt; *wa-żwa* cap made of the fur of a fox. — *żwa-dkár*, *-nág*, *-dmár*, *-sér* white, black, red, yellow cap, denoting occasionally also **the wearers** of such caps, esp. **red-caps** and **yellow-caps**, as belonging to different Lama-sects — *żwa-k̓ébs* the covering of a hat *Cs.* — *żwa-tog* top ornament of a hat *Cs.*, prob. a button, v. *tog.* — *żwa-γżól* brim, *żwa-ri* crown of a hat *Cs.*, in *Ld.* however *ri* denotes the brim or flap. — *Schl.* p. 171 calls a low conical cap of the Chief Lama *ná-ťon-ża.*

ཞ་ཉེ་ or ཞ་ནེ་ *żá-nye* or *żá-ne*, also *rá-nye Cs.*, **lead,** *żá-nyei γtiṅ-rdo* **sounding-lead, plummet** *Pth.*; *ża-nye-rdó* **lead-ore** *Cs.*; *żá-nyei čus sbyár-ba* to fill up (a groove or juncture) with molten lead *Glr.*; *żá-nye dkár-po C.*, **tin,** also *ża-dkár*, *γśa-* or *bśa-dkár*; *żá-nye nág-po* lead, (*Cs.*'s 'white lead and black lead' seem to be a mere conjecture); *ża-śóg* (**tin-foil** *Sch.* (?)), thin plates of lead.

ཞ་བ་ *żá-ba* **lame; lameness;** gen. *żá-bo* **lame, halting;** a lame person, **cripple,** *B.* and col.; *żá-mo* fem.; **żá-wo čo dug** *W.* he is lame, he limps; *rkáṅ-* or *lág-ża-čan* having a lame foot or hand.

ཞ་འབྲིང་ *ża-ₒbriṅ* v. *żabs* extr.

ཞ་ལ་ *żá-la Glr.* and vulgo, v. *żál-ba.*

ཞ་ལུ་ *żá-lu* **cup, bowl,** = *p̓or-pa*, *ko-re Cs.*

ཞ་ལུ་པ་ *żá-lu-pa*, *żá-lu lóts-ťsa-ba* or *lo-čén* n. of the author of a little glossary, called **Zamatog.**

ཞག *żag* 1. *żág-pa* (only *Schr.*, *Cs.*), **żág-po** *W*, **żág-ma** *Lt.*, *W.*, resp. *dguṅ-żág* **a day,** the time from one sun-rise to another (cf. on the other hand *nyi-ma* 2); *żag čig* **a day,** and adv : **once day, once;** **żag čig-gi żág-la** *W.* is also used of a future day: **żag čig de dus leb yin** *W.* once the time will come; *żag ₒga-nas* after a few days *Mil.*; *żag dú-ma lón-par* after many days *Dzl.*; *ṅa di-riṅ ná-niṅ léb-żag** *W.* this is the day of our arrival a year ago; **dé-żag** *W.* **lately,** the other day, a short time ago; **dáṅ-żag** *W.* **yesterday; recently,** **dáṅ-zag za-nyi-ma** *W.* last sunday; **nán-żag** *W.* some time ago, **nán-żag stón-ka** *W.* last autumn; **k̓ár-saṅ-żag** *W.* **the day before yesterday;** *żág-nas żág-tu* **from day to day;** **żág-daṅ(-żag)** *W.* **every day, always;** *żag bdun* seven days, *żag-bdun-p̓rág* **a week,** *żag-bdun-p̓rág że-brgyád* forty-eight weeks *Thgy.* — *żag-gráṅs* **the date,** **żag-dáṅ gyáb-če** *W.* **to date.** — *żag-mál* **a station, day's journey, quarters** *Cs.*, *żág-sa* id. *Cs.* — **żag-záṅ** *W.* **holiday.** — 2. **fat, grease,** in a liquid state, = *ťsil-k̓u S.g.*; also melted and congealed again *W.*; fig. **the fat of the country, fertility,** *yúl-la żag med* the country is barren *Ma.*; *żág-čan* greasy, oily, *żag-méd* lean; *żag-p̓ór* a cup, vessel, for grease *Cs.* — 3. **fog, smoke, dry vapour,** filling the atmosphere in autumn.

ཞགས་པ་ *żágs-pa* **leash,** rope with a noose, e.g. for catching wild horses, *żags-ťág Cs*, *żags-dbyúg Sch.* id., *rgyáb-pa Cs.*, *p̓en pa Sch.* to throw the noose; *żags-pas*, *żags-tag-gis ₒdzin-pa* frq. fig., as *Schl.* 213; *sbrul-żágs* noose consisting of a serpent, for catching any hurtful creature *Glr.*; frq. as an attribute of the gods.

ཞང་(པོ) *żáṅ(-po)*, vulgo *á-żaṅ*, **uncle** by the mother's side, **mother's brother;** *żaṅ-brgyúd* his offspring *Cs.*; *żaṅ - nyén* in a gen. sense, relations by the mother's side *Dom.*; *żaṅ-ťsá* sister's son. — *ťsa-żáṅ*, resp. *dbon-żáṅ* 1. nephew and uncle, by the mother's side, also applied to spiritual brotherhood *Mil.* — 2. **son-in-law** and **brother-in-law** *Glr.*

ཞང་བློན་ *żaṅ-blón Glr.* seems to be a kind of **title** given to a minister (or magistrate).

ཞང་ཞུང་ *żaṅ-żúṅ* ancient n. of the province of **Guge** *Glr.*

ཞན་པ་ *żán-pa* **weak, feeble,** frq., the opp. to *drág-po*; *ṅa ǰi-ltar żan yaṅ* as weak, as miserable as I am (says a cripple) *Pth.*;

k̔ams žán-pa Mil. of a weak body, of delicate health; also applied **to sounds, accent** and the like; cf. *ńá-ro*; **ugly** opp. to *légs-pa*, v. *skye-sgo*.

ཞབས་ *žabs* 1. **bottom** of a lake, of a vessel *Dzl., Mil.*; lower end of a staff *Mil.*; for **under** in compounds, as *mña-žábs* q. v. — 2. resp. for *rkáń-pa* **foot**, *mi žig-gi žábs-la ˳dúd-pa Cs., mgó-bos btúg-pa S.b., ˳o byéd-pa Cs.* to bow down at another person's feet, to touch them with one's head, to kiss them; *žabs drúń-du* c. genit **to the feet of ...**, for **to ...**, in directions of letters; *žabs rjén-par* **barefooted**, e. g. *γšégs-pa Mil.*; *žabs ˳degs-pa Sch.* to help, prob. = *žabs-tóg byéd-pa* v. below; *žabs ˳čág-pa* = *˳čág-pa* II. —

Comp. For the most part they are the same as those of *rkáń-pa;* there are to be mentioned more especially: *žábs-kyu* 1. **spur** *Cs.*(?). 2. n. of the vowel-sign ུ for u *Gram.* — *žábs-mgo Tar.* point of the foot *Schf.* — *žabs-sgróg* garter *Cs.* — *žabs-bčágs Sch.*, 1. partic. of *žabs-˳čag-pa*. 2. = *žábs-čágs*. 3. **grounds, territory.** — *žabs-čág(s), -p̔yágs*, resp. shoe, boot. — *žabs-t̔óg* 1. **service** rendered to superiors, esp. to priests, convents etc., by the erection of buildings, or keeping them in repair, or by any aid or work done in their behalf; *˳tsó-bai žabs-tóg* or *žabs-tog* alone: distribution of victuals, *žabs-tóg bzáń-po p̔ul* he placed dainty food before him *Mil.*; *žabs-tóg ˳o mi brgyál-ba ˳bul* we shall provide you with every thing, so that you shall not suffer want *Mil.*; *žabs-tóg byéd-pa* a. **to render such services** b. **to feed, treat, provide,** offer, *Glr.* and elsewh. 2. = *žabs-tóg-pa* 1. **servant,** regularly employed in monasteries, by Lamas etc., **an official,** *rgyál-poi sku-γsuń-túgs-kyi žabs-tóg* royal page, *Glr.* 2. **dispenser, benefactor** *žabs-tóg-ma* fem. — *žabs-rtiń* **heel.** — *žabs-rtén* 1. **footstool** *Cs.* 2. **boot** *Sch.* — *žabs-˳drén* **shame, disgrace,** from *mii žabs ˳drén-pa* to bring shame upon another, to be a disgrace to him, e.g. a child proving a disgrace to his parents, by a dissolute life, disrespectful deportment etc. *Thgy. žabs-rdul* dust on one's feet *Cs.* — *žabs-pád* lit.: 'a padma below the foot', seems to be an attribute of divine persons, but sometimes nothing more than a high-sounding complimental expression for 'foot'; *byin-pa 'e-na-ya ˳dra žabs-pad ˳bur* his leg displays a calf like that of Enaya *Pth.*; *žabs-pad-la, Zam.* init., seems to stand like *žabs druń-du*, so also *žabs-pád k̔ri drúń-du*, in letters; *mii žabs-pad stén-pa Tar.*, fig. for *žabs-tóg byéd-pa* **to serve; to be a scholar, pupil** *Schf.* — *žábs-p̔yi* **servant** (male or female), in the widest sense of the word, servant to an individual, as well as a minister of the state or the church, only that the latter service is always referred by an Asiatic to the 'person' of the king or priest; collectively: **retinue;** occasionally also to be understood as **an attending, a waiting on,** thus: *rjé-yi žábs-p̔yi ˳gran*, we will vie with one another in our attending the lord *Glr.; žábs-p̔yir ˳bráń-ba, žábs-˳brań-ba* or *˳briń-ba* to follow as a servant, *žam-˳briń(-pa) Do., žam-riń Cs., ža-˳briń Sch.* servant. — *žabs-bró, žabs-bró mdzád-pa* **to dance** *Sch.* — *žabs-ma* drawers, under-petticoat. — *žabs-sén* nail of the toe *Sch.* — *žabs-bsil* water for washing an honoured person's feet. — *žabs-lhám* = *žabs-čág.*

ཞམ་ཆུ་ *žám-ču Sch.:* 'the scum left by the evaporation of water'(?); **žám-če** *W.* to take off, *lbu-ba* the froth, scum; yet cf. *γžám-pa*.

ཞམ་མེ་བ་ *žám-me-ba* **being plentiful, abounding in** *Mil.*

ཞར་བ་ *žár-ba*, fem. *ma*, 1. = *yan lag ma tsań* being not in full possession of one's members, *mig-žár* **one-eyed, half or totally blind;** *lag-žár* having only one hand, being lame in one or both hands; so in a similar manner *rkań-žár*. — 2. (= *mig-žár*) *C., W.* **blind,** rarely in *B.* — **žar-tę** (*žar-ltas*) the winking with one eye *C.*

ཞར་ལ་ *žar-la, Schr.* **'following, succeeding',** prob. = *žór-la*, q.v.

ཞལ་ *žal* resp. for *k̔a* 1. **mouth** 2. **face, countenance** *žál-du γsól-ba, W.* **žál-la rág-ce**, to eat, to drink; **tsá-big žól-la rag** or **žal-rág dzod** please to take some . . .!

rgyal-poi žál-nas ysuṅs the king spoke *Glr.* frq.; *žál-gyi sgo* the door of the face, the mouth (cf. also *ₒdzúm-pa*); *žál-la mi nyán-pa Glr.* to be disobedient; *žál-gyis bžés-pa Glr.* or *ₒčé-ba Sch.* to promise, and other significations of *k̔as lén-pa*, e.g. to accept *Tar.* 126, 10; *žal bgrád-pa* and *ydáṅ-ba* **to gape** *Sch.*, *ₒbyéd-pa* to open the mouth, *žal ₒdzúm-pa* to smile; with *ltá-ba* 1. *žál-la ltá-ba*, e.g. *č̔os smrá-bai* to watch the mouth of the preacher, to hang on his lips *Pth.*; in a similar manner: *gús-pai séms-kyis ṅá-yi žál-la lta Pth.* 2. *žal ltá-ba*, *žál-lta byéd-pa* **to serve** (v. *žál-ta*), *žal yaṅ k̔yéd-la lta mč̔ód-pa yaṅ k̔yéd-la ₒbul* they serve you and honour you *Glr.*; *žál-lta-ru byuṅ* he came to serve him *Mil.*; *žal ydáms-pa* **to bid, order, exhort** *Glr.*; *žal dón-pa* **to pronounce, to deliver, state, report**; *žal mjál-ba Mil.* **to visit, to come to see**; *žal mt̔óṅ-ba* to see a person's face *Tar.*; 'in order to attain the highest *dṅos-grúb*, one must *séms-kyi raṅ-žál mt̔óṅ-ba*, and in order to be able to do this, one must penetrate into the Buddhist doctrine' — thus *Mil.* teaches a Bonpa; *p̔yis žal mt̔óṅ-bao* afterwards his face was seen, he made his appearance *Tar.*; *žal-yzigs-pa* v. sbst. *žal-yzig.*

Comp. For the most part expressions of civility: *žal-kár*, resp. for *kar-yól* plates and drinking-vessels. — *žal-dkyíl* face *Cs.* — *žal-bkód* order, ordinance *Sch.*(?). — *žal-skóm*, *žal-skyéms* drink. — *žal-skyín Glr.* countenance. — *žal-skyógs* cup, goblet *Mil.* — *žal-k̔ébs* cover of an image of Buddha *Sch.* — *žal-k̔rid* oral or personal instruction *Mil.* — *žal-ₒk̔aṅ* biting words of a superior (*Sch.* prob. not quite correct). — **žal-gyá* (*rgya? brgya*) **jhé'-pa* or *žē-pa** to promise *C.* — *žal-rgyán* mustaches *C.* — *žal-ṅó* 1. = *ṅo*, *žal-ṅó nág-par bžugs* he was sitting there with a mournful face *Glr.* 2. *ts̔ogs-č̔en-žal-ṅó* title of the chief-justices of the great monasteries of Sera, Gadan and Depung. 3. *Sch.*: '*žal-ṅo* or *ṅor* (?), noble sons, princes' (?) — *žal-dṅós* **bodily**, in one's own body or person, *saṅs-rgyás žal-dṅós-kyi ₒk̔rúṅs-yul Pth.*, the place where Buddha was born bodily; *žal-dṅós-su mjál-bar yod Glr.* he is bodily to be seen. — *žal-sṅa Cs.* = *spyan-sṅa.* — *žal-čol* resp. for *'ar-čól* handkerchief, napkin *C.* — *žal-č̔ád* v. *k̔a-č̔ád.* — *žal-č̔u*, *žal-č̔áb Schr.*, *Cs.* spittle, saliva. — *žal-mč̔ú* lip, v. *k̔a-mč̔ú.* — *žal-č̔é* **judgment, decision**; *des ₒú-bu-čag-yi žal-č̔é yčád-do* he shall pass sentence on us *Dzl.* ২৩২, 15, and elsewh. (the text of *Sch.* is not quite correct); *žal-č̔é bču-drúg-pa* and *bču-ysúm-pa* '(the code) with the 16 and that with the 13 judgments'; these are two distinct bodies of law, both of them in *C.* of standard authority; *žal-č̔é-pa* judge *Dzl.* — *žal-č̔éms* v. *č̔ems* 2. — *žal-nyód* favourite dish *Sch.* — *žál-ta* 1. also *žál-lta* a. **service, turn.** b. **inspection, visitation, revision**; *žál-ta byéd-pa* a. **to serve,** b. **to inspect, review, superintend; to visit,** the poor, the sick and to take care of them; **to guard,** *žíṅ-la* the field. 2. resp. for *k̔á-ta*, *k̔a-ydáms* **direction, instruction, counsel, advice,** *žál-ta žib-rgyás žú-ba* to ask for accurate and detailed instructions *Mil.*; *žál-ta-pa* = *sku-mdún-pa*, *žábs-p̔yi* waiting-man, valet-de-chambre *C.*, *Tar.* 56,2: servant in a convent; more frq. fem., *žál-ta-ma* waiting-woman, lady's maid, chamber-maid. — *žal-ydáms* **instruction, advice,** *jig-rtén-la dgós-pai žal-ydáms ysúṅs-so* he imparted to her useful maxims *Glr.*; **order, command** *Glr.* (v. above); also, *žal-ydáms bris-mk̔an* **author,** in as much as all printed books are considered to be sacred, and the authors generally are Lamas, whose words are looked upon as divine. — *žal-ydóṅ* **countenance.** — *žal-bdág* in large religious meetings a Lama, who walks about with a wand in order to preserve good order, a verger. — *žal-ₒdébs* **a free-will offering** or **present** *Cs.* — *žal-lpágs* **lip.** — *žal-p̔yis* resp. **napkin.** — *žal-bád* (or *pad?*) *C.* **chief overseer, superintendent.** — *žal-byáṅ* **title, superscription, inscription.** — *žal-ts̔óm* (for *óg-ts̔óm*) *Pth.* **beard.** — *žal-ts̔ós Sch.* (*Cs. žal-tsus*) = *žal-zás Dzl.* **food.** — *žal-zág* **tobacco-pipe,** v. *gaṅ-zag.* — *žal-yzigs* 1. **looking with the face,** *lhor*, southward *Glr.* 2. **apparition,** *žal-yzigs t̔ób-pa* to see an apparition, *bžúgs-par žal-yzigs-šiṅ* appearing in a sitting posture *Mil. nt.* (cf. *spyan-rás*). — *žal-bsró Tar.* 76, 12, *Schf.*: **the act of consecrating,** e.g. a temple.

ཞལ་བ་ *žál-ba* I. sbst., also *žal, žá-la, žál-rtsa* or *-rdza Sch.* **clay, lime-floor,** *Lex.*: *žál-ba* = *skyáṅ-núl*; *ñtíl-gyi žá-la Glr.* **clay, cement of a floor,** cf. *ár-ga*; **plastering, rough-cast,** *sgó-la žal bgyis-te* plastering the door with clay *Glr.*, also applied to the anointing of sacrificial objects with butter *Mil.* — II. vb. **to serve up food, to spread a repast** *Sch.*

ཞི་ *ži* num. fig.: 51.

ཞི་གིལ་ *ži-gil* **chaff** and other impurities removed from the grain by washing.

ཞི་བ་ *ži-ba*, *Ssk.* शम, **to become quiet, calm, to abate, to subside; to settle,** of a swelling *W.*; **to be allayed,** of passion, malice etc. *Glr.*; **to be appeased, relieved, to cease,** of pain, quarrels, intoxication, maladies etc. *Glr.* and elsewh.; **to be atoned, blotted out,** of sins *Tar.*; *ži-bar ˛gyúr-ba B.*, **ži čá-če* W.*, id.; **ra, šro ži soṅ* W.* the drunken fit, the paroxysm of passion has passed over; *ži-la soṅ* (the hobgoblins) became quiet, held their peace *Mil.*; *ži-bar byéd-pa* **to still, sooth, appease, mitigate,** **ži čúg-če* W.*; *ži-byed* a composing draught, संशमन *Wise* 130; more particularly with reference to the affections: **to be dispassionate**, not subject to any mental emotion, *ži-ba čén-por ˛gyur* he is getting very free from passion *Do.*, v. below *ži-ynás*; also sbst. **tranquillity, calmness,** and adj. **tranquil, calm,** *ži-ba daṅ bde-légs-su ˛gyúr-bar mdzád-du ysol* permit us to attain to peace and happiness *Dom.*; *ži-bai ťábs-kyis* **amicably, in a fair way** *Glr.*; so also *ži-bai ytam smrá-ba Glr.*; *ži-bas mi ťul drág-pos ˛dul dgos ˛dug Pth.* if he will not submit by fair means, he must be converted or subdued by force; *ži-bai žal Pth.* the expression of calmness about his mouth, his peaceful countenance; *ži-bar yšégs-pa* to go to rest, to die *Cs.*; *ži-bai* or *lóṅs-skui lha-ťsogs že-ynyis Thgr.* the good, the peaceable deities, opp. to those called *ťró-bo*; differently again the word is used in: *ži-ba daṅ ťró-ba daṅ ži-ma-ťro Pth.*, which has been explained by *Sch.* as: the medium between calmness and passion, 'calm indignation'. *Cs.* moreover mentions *ži-ba* or *rtag-ži-ba*, as 'a name or epithet of Iswara and certain Buddhas', so that *ži-ba* would be equal in sound as well as in meaning to शिव, *ži-ba-pa* and *-ma* being his male and female disciples. A good deal of obscurity attaches, further to the frequent mention of the *ži-rgyas-dbaṅ-drag*, as the characteristic properties of the four parts of the world (v. *gliṅ*), and likewise as qualities and functions of the Buddhas, gods and saints, viz. allaying diseases, conferring happiness and wealth, ruling over all creatures and subduing all that is unruly and hostile; to which are to be added four kinds of burnt-offerings, in the same fourfold sense, v. *Schl.* 250. Finally, in mysticism the term *ži-ba* acts a prominent part: *ži(-bar) ynás(-pa)* and *lhag(-par) mťoṅ(-ba)*, शमथ and विपश्यन, shortened *ži-lhág*, implies an absolute inexcitability of mind, and a deadening of it against any impressions from without, combined with an absorption in the idea of Buddha, or which in the end amounts to the same thing, in the idea of emptiness and nothingness. This is the aim to which the contemplating Buddhist aspires, when, placing an image of Buddha, as *rten*, (v. *rten* 1) before him, he looks at it immovably, until every other thought is lost, and no sensual impressions from the outer world any longer reach or affect his mind. By continued practice he acquires the ability of putting himself, also without *rten*, merely by his own effort, into this state of perfect apathy, and of attaining afterwards even to *dṅos-grub*, the supernatural powers of a saint. The stories that are related of such achievements, and with which the work of Taranātha abounds, are, notwithstanding their absurdity, readily believed by every faithful Buddhist. That there are also cases of failures, cf. *smyón-pa*.

ཞི་མ་ *ži-ma* **sieve,** of cane or wood *Ts.*

ཞི་མི་ *ži-mi Schr.* and *Wts.* (where *ši-mi* stands), gen. *žím-bu Glr.*, or *žúm-bu* **cat**, *C.*

ཞིག *žig* 1. = *čig*. — 2. v. *ʼjig-pa* I., 2, *žig-rál-ba* **demolished, ruined** *Mil.*

ཞིག་མེར་ *žig-mér* (sbst. or adj.?) **dense throng,** or **crowded together** in a mass *W.*

ཞིང་ *žiṅ*, I. sbst. ཀྵེཏྲ (*Cs.*: *žiṅ-ma, žiṅ-po, žiṅ-bu*, perh. provincialisms), 1. **field, ground, soil, arable land;** *táṅ-žiṅ* fields in a plain, level land, *ri-žiṅ* fields on a mountain, hill-land; *túl-žiṅ W.* (ui f.) cultivated land; *žiṅ-k'a* = *žiṅ*, *žiṅ-k'ai bú-mo* the girls in the field *Mil.*; *žiṅ rmó-ba* frq., to plough a field; to carry on agriculture; *ʼdébs-pa* to till, to sow a field, *mi ycig-gis btáb-pai* a field that has been sowed by one man *Glr.*; *žiṅ ʼčú-ba* to irrigate a field (?) *Cs.*; *rná-ba* to mow, to reap, a field, *žiṅ-mk'an* **reaper;** **žiṅ bád-če* W.* to pursue husbandry; *žiṅ bgód-pa* to divide or distribute land *Cs.* — 2. fig., cf. *žiṅ-k'ams, bsód-nams-kyi žiṅ daṅ ʼp'rád-pa* to enter the field of merit, to turn into the path of virtue *Dzl.*; *ydúl-byai žiṅ-du yzigs-te Pth.* seeing him in the land of conversion (yet v. also 3, a.): **region,** *žiṅ bču* (*Sch.*: 'the ten regions') is said to signify something like: the reign of Evil.— 3. equivalent to *saṅs-rgyás-kyi žiṅ* the kingdom of Buddha, a. in an earthly sense: **a holy land, a land of salvation,** where Buddha resides, or at least where Buddhism prevails; so also *ʼdúl-bai žiṅ* land of conversion *Glr.*; acc. to *Wts.* it is a name of the earthly seat of Buddha, the residence of the Dalai Lama at Lhasa; b. supernaturally: **heaven, paradise, Elysium** i.e. one of the heavens inhabited by the Buddhist gods, or also the state of non-existence, Nirwāna; *žiṅ-la p'éb-pa* = *bdé-bar yšégs-pa* **to die.** — 4. **body,** v. *žiṅ-čén, žiṅ-lpágs.* —

Comp and deriv. *žiṅ-bkód* map *C., W.*. *žiṅ-gi bkód-pa* v. *Asiat. Res.* XX., 425. — *žiṅ-k'aṅ* 1. summer-house, pleasure-house, pavilion *W.* 2. field and house, the whole estate or property *W.* (= *yul-yžis*) — *žiṅ-k'áms* = *žiṅ* 2 and 3, frq. — *žiṅ-ʼk'rúṅs, žiṅ-gi k'rúṅs-pa* or *-ma* the produce of the field *Cs.* — *žiṅ-k'ród* many fields together *Cs.* — *žiṅ-rgód* rough, uncultivated ground *Sch.* — *žiṅ-čén* and *-čúṅ* a large and a small field; also: a large and a small body or corpse *Thgr.* — *žiṅ-mčóg* paradise, a most delightful country, an Eden, an Eldorado *Pth.* — *žiṅ-bdág* proprietor of a field, land-owner. — *žiṅ-pa* husbandman, farmer *Dzl.* — *žiṅ-lpags* a skin (pulled off), hide. — *žiṅ-mu* boundary of a field, landmark. — *žiṅ-bzáṅ* good land, productive soil *Cs.* — *žiṅ-yšin* dead, arid, burnt soil *Cs.*— *žiṅ-sa* 1. ground, soil, arable land *Cs.* 2. province *Sch.*

II. gerundial termin. = *čiṅ*, q.v.

ཞིབ་ *žib*, resp. **fine flour,** also **flour in general,** *žib-k'úg* bag, *žib-pór* box, for flour *Cs.*

ཞིབ་པ་ *žib-pa, B., žib-po Cs., žib-mo C., W.* 1. **fine,** of powder and similar things, *žib-rtsiṅ* fine and coarse *Zam.*; *žib-par byéd-pa, B.* *žib-mo čó-če* *W.*, to make fine, to pound, to reduce to powder. — 2. **accurate, exact, strict, precise,** *ltá-ba yáṅs-šiṅ spyód-lam žib-par mdzod* be wide in your views, but strict in your actions *Glr.*; so *Sch.* understands also *žib-žib yod, žib-po med, žib-rgyu med*, which ought however to be translated: 'I have accurate information, I have no precise information, I have no particulars to communicate'; *žib-mo šés-pa* to know accurately; more frq adv. *žib-par, žib-tu B.*, **žib-ča* *vulg., **exactly, precisely, thoroughly** *žib-tu ysól-ba, ytam žib-tu byéd-pa* to report accurately *Dzl.* (the former resp.); *žib-par bšád-pa Glr.* id.; *žib-par (šes-) ʼdód-na* if you wish to know it accurately *Glr.*; *bka žib-tu bgros-pa* resp., to consult carefully *Pth*; *bka-mčid ysuṅ-glén žib-tu bgyid* gentlemen, discourse as freely as you please! *Mil.*; *las-rgyu-ʼbras žib-tu mi rtsi-na* if one does not strictly regard the doctrine of retaliation *Mil.*; "*žib-ča ltos* (or *to*) *W.* look at it well, carefully; **žib-ča zer* W.* pronounce it accurately; **žib-ča čo'-pa* C.* to examine closely; **žib-sál* W.* accurately and distinctly.

ཞིམ་ཐོག་ལེ་ *žim-t'og-le* n. of a medicinal herb *Med.*

ཞིམ་པ་ *žim-pa*, gen. *žim-po*, **well-tasted, sweet-scented,** "*žim-po rag*" *W.* I find the taste or smell of it agreeable; *ŝa ₒdi lhág-par ẑim-na* this meat being of a better taste *Dzl.*; *ẑim-rgyui zas* food prepared of savoury things *Zam.*; *dri-ẑim, dri-ɣsúṅ ẑim-po* pleasant odour *Dzl.*; *dri mi ẑim-pa* disagreeable smell *Glr.*; **ẑim-ze̤** also **ẑim-ẑim** *C.*, **ẑim-zag** *W.* sweet-meats, confectionery; **ẑim-zag-tsóṅ-k'aṅ** *W.* confectioner; **ẑim-lto-čan** *W.* dainty-mouthed, a sweet-tooth.

ཞིམ་བུ་ *ẑim-bu* v. *ẑi-mi.*

ཞུ་ *ẑu*, 1. num. figure: 81. — 2. v. *ẑú-ba.*

ཞུ་དག་ *ẑu-dág*, ཞུས་དག་ *ẑus-dág* **amendment, improvement, correction**; the word is also added at the end of written books, e.g. of Taranatha, as an attestation of a careful revision; *ẑu-dág byéd-pa* **to mend, improve, correct**; *raṅ-rgyúd ẑu-dág byéd-pa* to examine and reform one's self *Cs.* *ẑu-dag-mk'an* **reviser, corrector, censor** *Cs.*, *ẑu-čén-gyi lóts-ťsa-ba* a great corrector or commentator (of *Ssk.* writings), seems to have become a current title.

ཞུ་བ་ *ẑú-ba* I. vb., pf. *ẑus* (esp. in later writings and vulgo, in ancient literature gen. *ɣsól-bar* for it) signifies 1. every kind of speaking to a person of higher rank, therefore **to request, to prefer a suit or petition, to make a report, to put a question** etc., *ẑú-ẑiṅ ɣsól-ba-la ₒgró-bai ťse* when I have to bring in a petition *Dzl.*; *'rmnál-lam de ɣẑán-la mi ɣsúṅ-bar ẑu' ẑús-so* 'pray, do not relate the dream to others', he begged *Glr.*; *ɣnáṅ-bar ẑu byás-pas* saying, 'I beg you will permit', *Glr.*; *sṅar mťóṅ-bai dṅós-po dé-dag ẑuo* I will ask him about the things lately seen, I shall request an explanation of him *Dzl.*; *ṅá-la gáṅ-dag ẑú-ba de légs-so* it is very right of you, thus to ask me about every thing *Do.*; *rgyál-poi drúṅ-du rmi-lam ẑús-pa* he related the dream before the king *Pth*; *ston-pa ẑu* (*pa* col. for *par*) I request (you) to explain *Mil.*; *der ₒbyón-pa ẑu* 'thither to come I request' *Mil.*; *dé-la mk'án-po ẑus* they besought him to be their abbot *Glr.*; *ɣnáṅ-ba ẑú-ba* to ask permission *Cs.* — 2. In *W.* this *ẑu* has become a word of civility to the widest extent, as it is not only added to almost every sentence of a speech or a letter, something like our 'with your permission' or 'if you please', e.g. **ẑan či méd-na ṅa do yin ẑu** if you have nothing further (to say), I shall go, with your permission; **k'o leb soṅ ẑu** he is arrived, if you please; but it also supplies every kind of salutation in coming or going, hence **ẑu zér-če**, resp. **ẑu ẑú-če**, to make or give one's compliments, **ǎ-pa-ne̤ ẑu máṅ-po ẑu dug** my father's best respects (cf. *p̔yag*). Inst. of *ẑu*, *ǰu* is also frq. heard (vulgo), e.g. **ǰu sab ǰu!** good day, Sir, good day! which prob. is only an intensation of sound, and not to be referred to the Indian जी. — **či-la ẑu** *W.* **why, well then, mind!** **či-la ẑu, nyi-ráṅ ṅe̤ tsar ma kyód-pa yun-riṅ kyod** well, I have not seen you this age! — The word is also used as a sbst., for **request, wish, question**, **ẑú-wa ₒbúl-ba** *C.*, **p̔úl-če** *W.*, *ɣtóṅ-ba Glr.* to make a request, to put a question; *ɣdan-ₒdrén-pai ẑú-ba nán-čan p̔úl-bas Mil.* assailing him with pressing invitations.

II. (prop. fut. of *ₒǰú-ba*) pf. (*b*)*ẑu*(*s*), fut. (*b*)*ẑu*, (imp.?) 1. **to melt**, trs. and intrs., *bẑu-btúl* v. sub *lugs*; *bẑu-byai ɣser* gold to be melted *Cs.*; *ẑú-bai k'ams* whatever is melting or fusible, **metals** *Sch.*; *ẑuo* it melted (from the heat) *Dzl.*; *ₒód-du ẑu-nas* dissolving in light *Glr.* frq. — 2. **to digest**, *ẑú-byed-kyi sman* digestive medicine *Cs.* (cf. *ₒǰu-byéd*); *ma-ẑú(-ba)* undigested, *zas ma ẑú-ba* undigested food, also **indigestion**, sufferings arising from it; *ma-ẑúi nad* id.; *ma-ẑú ₒǰú-ba* to decompose what is undigested *Med.*; opp. to *ẑu-rǰés* it seems to denote more particularly **the chyme** before it is mixed with bile, and perh. also **the duodenum** where this takes place; so the region of *ẑu daṅ ma-ẑúi bár-na* is stated to be the place, where the bile is principally operating *S.g.* Cf. *ₒǰú-ba.*

Comp. *ẑu-skyogs W.* crucible, melting-spoon. — *ẑú-mk'an* 1. **petitioner.** 2. **digester;** n. of an officinal plant, = *spaṅ-ẑún Wdṅ.*

— žu-gléṅ, žu-gléṅ byéd-pa to address, accost, resp. *C.* — žu-rgyá (v. rgya-ma) 1. petitionary letter, petition, suit. 2. any writing addressed to superiors. — žu-rgyú the subject of a petition or suit. — *žu-ṅó-pa*, *C.*, intercessor, advocate, mediator, *žu-ṅó ǰhé'-pa* to intercede, to advocate. — žu-rǰés 1. **the chyme mixed with bile** (cf. ma-žu above). 2. **the place of it,** žu-rǰés na I feel a pain there *Med.* 3. **eructation, rising,** ḱá-la zu-rǰés skyur *S.g.* caused by beer; ro daṅ žu-rǰés mṅár-mo *Med.* a sweetish taste and rising (from the stomach). — žu-rtén **the present** which, according to oriental notions, has necessarily to attend or introduce a petition. — žu-dón prop. drift, subject of a petition; in a general sense = žú-ba request, suit, address, communication etc. — žu-sná (pronounced *žu-ná*) *W.* = žu-ṅó. — žú-po, žú-ba-po = žú-mḱan 1. — žu-byéd v. above — žu-ₒbúl, pronounced *žum-búl*, petitioning, making a suit in an humble posture with folded hands *Cs.* — žú-yig, žú-šog, žú-bai ṗrin-yig a petition, žú-yig-gi rten = žu-rten. — žu-lán answer to a petition. — žu-lóg a feigned, false, designing suit, *gyáb-pa* to address such a one *C.*

ཞུགས་ žugs, resp. **fire,** e.g. the fire lighted for cremation *Tar.* 7, 4.

ཞུགས་པ་ žúgs-pa v. ₒjúg-pa.

ཞུང་ཞུང་ žuṅ-žúṅ with byéd-pa **to nod or bow repeatedly,** of a pigeon *Mil.*

ཞུད་པ་ žúd-pa 1. **to twine, to twist** *W.* *žúd-če, žú-če*. — 2. **to spin** *Cs.*, žu-ḱór spindle, distaff. — 3. **to rub** *Cs.* — 4. **to hang up, to suspend** *Ts.* — žud-ťág = dpyaṅ-ťág.

ཞུན་པ་ žún-pa **melted** *Cs.*; *žun táṅ-če* *W.* **to melt,** trs; žun-ťár byéd-pa to melt and beat to pieces *Mil.*; žun-ťigs spark flying from red-hot iron *W.*; žún-ma that which is melted, ysei sogs žún-mai ṗúṅ-po heaps of melted gold and other metals *Glr.* — žun-mar v. mar. — žún-mo melted, whatever melts easily *Cs.* (who spells it bžun-mo).

ཞུམ་པ་ žúm-pa 1. sbst. **fear, dismay, despondency, faint-heartedness,** sems žúm-na if I continue undismayed *Dzl.*; dkon-mčóg ysúm-la žúm-pa-med-par bkúr-bsti byéd-pa to honour the three most Precious undauntedly, with a cheerful heart; sems ráb-tu žúm-par gyúr-to they became greatly dejected in mind, their spirits were much cast down *Pth.* — 2. vb. *lbú-wa žúm-če* *W.* **to scum, to skim** (off).

ཞུམ་བུ་ žúm-bu = ži-mi.

ཞུར་ žur, 1. **snout, muzzle, trunk.** — 2. sup. of žú ba.

ཞུལ་ཞུལ་ žul-žúl, *Ts.*: *žū-žū ǰhé'-pa* **to stroke, to caress.**

ཞུས་དག་ žus-dág v. žu-dág, ཞུས་པ་ žús-pa v. zú-ba.

ཞེ་ že (cf. žen) 1. **inclination, affection, heart, mind; volition;** there is a proverb in *C.*: *mi ḱá-ǰo-čé-la že me', ču nyóg-po-čé-la tiṅ me'* a braggart has no mind, as muddy water has no bottom, i.e. as in muddy water you cannot see the bottom, so you cannot rely on the solid principles of a braggart; ḱa-žé v. ḱa, comp.; že bkon-pa or ₒḱon-pa a hating mind, rkám-pa *Sch.* a covetous, ťág pa *Mil.* a sincere, nág-po *C.* a wicked, ytsáṅ-ba *Sch.* a pure heart or mind, or also hating, covetous etc. as to mind (several other combinations of this kind, given by *Sch.*, are too doubtful to be copied); že-ycód-pa *Sch.*: 'to lose courage, to have no longer any inclination for', perh. better, **to resign,** and že-bčád **resignation,** as a Buddhist virtue *Mil.*; on the other hand, že ycod-pai ťsig *Sch.*: 'slanderous words' which, e.g. *Dzl.* ༢༠, 11, well agrees with the context, but is not clear in point of etymology. — že-dúg damage, destruction *Sch.*, byéd-pa to cause, to inflict. — že-lóg v. žen-lóg sub žén-pa. — že-sún angry, cross, ill-humoured, vexed. — 2. numerical word for bži-bču in the abridged numbers že-yčig etc., 41 to 49. — 3. numerical figure: 111.

ཞེ་ན་ žé-na, rarely žés-na. v. čé-na.

ཞེ་ས་ žé-sa **reverence, respect, civility, politeness,** žé-sa daṅ bčás-pa **reverential, respectful** *Pth.*: dei dús-su mis ṗyag daṅ *żé-sa mi śés-pas* because at that time people knew little of compliments and politeness *Pth.*; *żé-sa byéd-pa* to show honour, respect, *rnám-gyur mdzés-pai żé-sa* ₒ*bul-ba* to arrange mimic performances in honour of some persons, (which also at the present time is frequently done in these countries); complimentary word (for *żé-sai ťsig*), *rná-bai żé-sa snyan* the complimentary word for *rna-ba* is *snyan Zam.*

ཞེང་, གཞེང་ *żeṅ*, *γżeṅ Cs.* (*W.* **żaṅ**) 1. **breadth, width,** *żéṅ-čan* **broad** (road, valley), **wide, spacious,** **żéṅ ḱa-čém-po** *C.* id.; *żeṅ-méd*, *żeṅ-ṗrá-mo*, **żeṅ-čúṅ-se** *W.* **narrow**; *żéṅ-du* in breadth *Sambh.*; *żeṅ-śiṅ* writing-tablet = *snum-glegs*. — 2. **plain, surface, side,** *żeṅ-čé-ba γnyis* the two broad sides (of a pillar) *Glr.*

ཞེད་པ་ *żéd-pa* **to fear, to be afraid,** synon. to ₒ*jigs-pa Thgr.* frq.; *żéd-nas* full of apprehensions *Pth.*

ཞེན་པ་ *żén-pa* (cf. *że*), vb. c. *la*, 1. **to desire, to long for, to be attached to, to be partial to, to be taken with,** *ḱyéd-la żén-čiṅ čags* I love you ardently (ἐρῶ) *Glr.*; *bod-ₒbáṅs ṅá-la żen-čé-żiṅ dgá-ba-rnams* the people of Tibet, that are affectionately attached to me *Glr.*; sbst.: **desire, longing,** e.g. to hear more of a thing *Mil.*; also **greediness. covetousness**; *ráṅ-ₒdod-żen-pa* **self-love, selfishness, egotism** *Glr.*; *ṗyógs-żen Tar.* 184, 22, **party-spirit, party-agitation**; *čágs-med żén-med* free from passion or interest *Mil.*; *żén-pa zlog* suppress your passion *Mil.*; *ťse ₒdi-la żen ldóg-pa* to be disgusted with this life *Thgy.*; **żém-pa ma lóg-na dhé-pa mi yoṅ** *C.* before one has renounced every desire, one cannot believe. —

Comp. *żén-ḱa*, *żé-ḱa* = *żén-pa* sbst., *Sch.* — *żen-ḱris Mil.*, *żen-čágs* frq., also vulgo, *żen-ₒdzín Glr.* inclination, desire, passion, attachment, **żen-dzin čó-če** *W.* to love, to be attached. — *żen-dón*, resp. *bżed-dón*, object of desire *Cs.* — *żen-lóg*(-*pa*, cf. above), disinclination, antipathy, disgust; in an ascetic sense: resignation *Mil.*; ₒ*jig-rtén żen-lóg-gi gaṅ-zág* a man tired of this world *Mil.*; *żen-lóg-pa*, or -*mḱan* fastidious, squeamish, easily disgusted; **że-mi-lóg-ḱen** *C.* one that is not easily disgusted, not squeamish. — 2. = *ljén-pa* **to penetrate, to be fixed,** of colours etc., *ras dkar-po ťson żen-pa ltar* as a colour is fixed in white cloth, is **lasting** *Dzl.*

ཞེམ་ཞེམ་ *żem-żém Ld.* an inferior kind of silk, of which the handkerchiefs consist, that are presented to foreign visitors etc. as a welcome or mark of respect, cf *ḱa-btágs.*

ཞེར་ *żer*, *żer ₒdébs-par byéd-pa Cs.*: **to chide, rebuke,** which, however, in the only passage, where I met with the word, does not suit the sense very well.

ཞེར་པོ་ *żer-po* **'mean, pitiful, coarse'** *Cs.*

ཞེས་ *żes* v. *čes.*

ཞོ་ *żo*, 1. **dram,** a small weight = $\frac{1}{16}$ ounce, of *skar-lṅa*, v. *skár-ma*; *γser-żo-gaṅ Pth.* a dram of gold; *γser żo γsum-brgyá* between 1 and 2 pounds of gold; as a coin it is stated to be = $^2/_3$ rupee. — 2. resp. *γsol-żo* **thick milk, curds,** *żo bsnyál-ba* to place milk to curdle; **milk** in gen., esp. *mai nú-żo Dzl.*, *má-żo* col., mother's milk; *żo-ₒťúṅ dús-na* during the time of suckling, *żo-spáṅs zas zai dús-na* after the child has been weaned *Med.*; *żo dkróg-pa*, *skróg-pa*, *bsrúb-pa* **to churn, to butter** *Lex.* — 3. **a small white spot,** *sen-żo* on a finger nail, *so-żo* on a tooth *Glr.* — 4. num. figure: 141.

Comp. *żó-ka* prob. = *żo*, *Thgy* — *żo-skyá Med.?* — *żo-čágs Med.?* *żo-ṗrúm Sch.*: 'a vessel for thick milk' (?), perh. *ṗru.* — *żo-rás Med.*, *Sch.*: spoiled milk. — **żo-ri** *W.*, (like *rú-ma C.*) **sour milk,** used to acidify new milk; in a gen. sense: **ferment, leaven,** **żo-dzi** *Ts.* — *żo-śi Sch.* = *żo-rás.* — *żo-sri*, *żoi spris-ma Wdṅ.* **cream.**

ཞོ་ཤ་ *żo-śá* 1. **force, efficiency** *Cs.* — 2. n. of a medicinal fruit, *żo-śá γsum*, viz. *mḱál-żo-śa* kidney-shaped, healing diseases of the kidneys (in *W.* the chesnut bears this name), *snyiṅ-żo-śa* heart-shaped, healing diseases of the heart; *gla-gor-żo-śa* is said to be given to horses; besides *mčin-pa-*

and *mčér-pa-žo-ša* are mentioned. — 3. **toll** (?), **pay** (?), *žo-šás ₒtsó-ba Tar.*, *Stg.* a publican *Cs.*, a soldier *Schr.*, prob. any officer that receives salary or pay.

ཞོག་ *žog*, imp. of *ₒjóg-pa.*

ཞོགས་ *žogs* v. *mar-žógs.*

ཞོགས་པ་ *žógs-pa Med.*, *žóg-ka Sch.*, = *sṅá-dro* **morning, fore-noon;** *žógs-ja* **tea at breakfast** *Cs.*

ཞོང་ *žoṅ* **lower, nether,** *žóṅ-k̔aṅ-pa* the lower part of the house, *žoṅ-rtsé* the lower and the upper part; *žoṅ-žóṅ* **deepened, excavated, hollow, uneven** *C.*

ཞོད་ *žod* 1. the original meaning of the word is yet uncertain; at present used in *C.*: **žo' dé-wa, žo-jág**, **peace, quietness, tranquillity,** **k̔o žo'-dé-la mi žag** he gives him no rest, causes him much trouble; **sém-kyi zo' dé-mo** peace of mind, evenness of temper; **žo'* or *zo' dé-mo* or *ₒjám-pa* gentleness, meekness. — 2. *Sch.*: **high-water, floods, inundations** *Wts.*, *C.*; *sṅa t̔an p̔yi žod* first drought, then inundation *Wdk.* — 3. **udder** *W.*, *C.*

ཞོན་པ་ *žón-pa*, resp. *ₒčib-pa* **to mount**, c. *la*; *rtá-la žón-pa* to ride, on horseback, *šiṅ-rta-la* to ride, in a carriage, frq.: *rtá-la žón-nas lhó-p̔yogs-su ₒgró-ba* to ride southward, to travel on horseback towards the south *S.g.*; also c. accus.: *bžón-pa žón-pa* to mount a horse or a carriage *Lex.*; *žón-du ₒjúg-pa* (= *skyón-pa*) to let mount.

ཞོམ་པ་ *žóm-pa*, = *ₒjóms-pa?* *rgas žóm-ste* **weighed down by old age** *Sch.*; cf. *γžóm-pa.*

ཞོར་ *žór*, ཞོར་ལ་ *žór-la* etc. v. *sbyór-la.*

ཞོལ་ *žol* 1. *žol-γyág*, **yak-bull,** *Bos grunniens Sch.*; *rá-ma žól-mo* a long-haired goat *Mil. nt.* — 2. **village belonging to a convent** *Mil.*, so Shikatse is the *sde-žól* of Tashi-lhunpo. — 3. postp., **under,** *Sch.* (cf *γžol-ba* II).

གཞའ་བ་ *γža-ba Sch.*: 1. **to sport, joke, play, sing,** (cf. *ga-γža*). — 2. **to believe, trust, confide.**

གཞའ་ཚོན་ *γža-tson* earlier form for *ₒja-tsón* **rain-bow.**

གཞའ་གསང་ *γža-γsaṅ* = *γyuṅ-druṅ Lex.*

གཞག་པ་ *γžag-pa* v. *ₒjóg-pa.*

གཞང་ *γžaṅ* 1. **anus** *Med.*, *γžáṅ-k̔a* id.; *γžaṅ-nád*, *γžaṅ-ₒbrúm* **piles, hemorrhoids** *Med.*; *γžaṅ-srín* a kind of intestinal worms *Lt.* — 2. **privy parts,** **žaṅ-ₒt̔ág* W.* catamenial blood; **žáṅ-tsoṅ-ma* W.* = *smád-tsoṅ-ma; *žaṅ-stoṅ* W.*, without breeches, with a bare posterior.

གཞད་གད་, གཞད་མོ་ *γžad-gád*, *γžád-mo* v. *bžád-pa.*

གཞན་ *γžan*, *γžán-pa*, *γžán-ma* (the last esp. in *W.*), 1. adj. and sbst., **other, the other, another,** *žan mi* the other men *Dzl.*, *γžán-pas lhág-par* more than others *Dzl.*; *slób-ma γžán-dag* the other scholars *Dzl.*; *mtsan γžán-pa* the other signs *Dzl.*; *blón-po γžán-ma-rnams* the other ministers *Glr.*; *bú-mo γžán-pas čé-rgyu med* she is not taller than the other girls (*pas* = *las*, not from *pa*) *Glr.*; *γžan rgol ma nus* others were not able to resist them (= nobody could do them any harm) *Glr.*; *γžán-du* to some other place, *ₒgró-ba* to go (to some other place) = **to go away, to start; elsewhere;. in another way,** v. example *ₒdzín-pa* 1, 4; also: *γžán-du ma sems šig Dzl.*, suppose or believe nothing else, do not think that the matter can be otherwise, frq. used like our 'of course'; *γžán-na* **elsewhere;** *γžán-nas* **from some other place;** *γžán-nas ₒgrúb-tu med* it cannot be accomplished from any other quarter, by any body else *Mil.* — 2. adv. **otherwise, else, on the other hand** *W.*; *γžán-yaṅ* **further, furthermore, or else,** (just) to mention some other circumstance, frq. — *γžan-bsgrúb Lex.* seems to be some logical term *Gram.* — *γžan-ₒp̔rúl* n. of a heaven inhabited by certain gods *Glr.*, *Mil.* — *γžan-dbáṅ* **dependent on others** *Was*, cf. *raṅ-dbáṅ.*

གཞབ་པ་ *γžáb-pa* **to lick** *Sch.*

གཞམས་པ་ *γžáms-pa* v. *bžáms-pa.*

གཞར་ཡང་ *γžár-yaṅ Lex.* = *nám-yaṅ*; *Pth.*: *γžar-yaṅ mi* **never** (*Sch.* and *Schr.* prob. incorr.).

གཞལ་བ་ *γžál-ba*, fut. of *ˌjál-ba*, **to weigh,** *sráṅ-la γžál-bar nús-kyi* if one could weigh with a pair of scales *Glr.*; *γžál-dgos-kyi rdzas Sch.*: 'goods for which duties are to be paid', liable to duty, to custom; *γžal-du-méd-pa* **imponderable** *Stg.*; **immensely much** *Pth.*; **immeasurable, incomparable, infinite, vast;** *γžal méd*, *γžal-yás* id.; *γžal-med-ḱáṅ*, more frq. *γžal-yas-ḱaṅ*, also *γžal-med-kaṅ-bžaṅ* palace, rarely used of human palaces (so *Glr.* in one passage, when speaking of the house of a Brahmin), mostly of the abode of gods *Pth.* and elsewh.; also Tibet, in po. language, is called a *lha-γnás γžal-yas-ḱáṅ*, the heavens with the sun a *ṅo-mtsár lhai γžal-yas-ḱáṅ*. — *γžal-ts̒ád* **measure, scale, standard** *Sch.*

གཞས་ *γžas* **play, sport, jest, joke** *Sch.*, *Lex.*: *glu-γžas.*

གཞི་(མ་) *γži(-ma)* 1. that from which and on which a thing arises, exists, depends; **ground, foundation, original cause, exciting cause** (**मूल** *Was.* 234); *dge-légs ťams-čád ˌbyúṅ-bai γži(-ma)* the primitive source of all happiness (is the doctrine of Buddha) *Glr.*; *γži-skye-méd* without origin and birth *Mil.*; *γžir bžág-pa* prob.: to use as a foundation *Mil.*, *Tar.*; **gór-ži* W.* cause of delay; *má-γži* v. as an article of its own sub *ma*; *rtsig-γži* foundation of a wall *Cs.*; *nyúṅ-γži, lá-γži* turnips, radishes, left for seed (being the foundations, as it were, of new plants); in *γži-sems-nyid, γži-čos-nyid* it prob. stands as an apposition, in the sense of *kun-γži*: the spirit, the primeval cause; in a special sense: the innermost essence, inherent nature; *γži-nas* **actually,** opp. to 'apparently' *Mil.*; **fundamental law, statute,** *γži čén-po* title of a book *Was.* 264: in certain cases it may be translated by **action,** v. *ruṅ-ba* 2, c. — 2. **ground, floor,** *γži-ma gru-bži* a square floor *Glr.*; *stéṅ-gi γži* the upper base, top-surface *Stg.* — 3. **residence, abode, home,** *γži ˌdzin-pa* to take up one's residence in a place *Mil.* and elsewh.; *γži ˌbébs-pa W.* **pab-če** id.; *γži-ma rab čig ṕóg-nas bžág-go* he assigned to him a nice dwelling-place and established him there *Glr.*; **seat, place,** *čos-γži* seat of religion, monastery *Tar.* and elsewh.; school of religion *Tar.* 44, 17; *γži γčig-tu skád-čig kyaṅ mi sdód-de* in no place resting for a moment (the arrow flies towards its goal) *Thgy.*, **ži čig-tu* C.* the same as *rtse γčig-tu.* — 4. in philosophy: **axiom, proposition** *Was.* (58); **contents, tenor** (299); **basis, support** (273). — 5. *Sch.*: **enmity**?? — 6. also *že* (cf. *γžes*) a definition of time or of relationship: *γži-niṅ*, *že-niṅ* two years ago, *γži-més* great-great-grandfather, *γži-més-mo* great-great-grandmother, *γži-ts̒á* great-great-grandchild *Sch.* —

Comp. *γži-dgón* monastery of the place, in or near a village, usually very small and harbouring but a few monks. — *γži-ˌji-bžin-pa* a recluse, 'who stays where he is' *Burn.* I, 310. — *γži-bdág* lord of the manor, lord of the soil, may denote a king or nobleman, but gen. it is **a local deity,** presiding over a certain district, to whom travellers are bound to offer sacrifice, and whom to offend they must carefully avoid.

གཞིག་པ་ *γžig-pa* 1 **to examine, search, try,** *rtog-* (or *brtag-*) *γžig légs-par γtóṅ-ba* to select and arrange carefully, e.g. books *Pth.*; *lo daṅ zlá-bar rtog-γžig žib-tu γtóṅ-ba* to search minutely as to the day and year *Pth.*; *bsam-γžig γtóṅ-ba* = *bsam-bló γtóṅ-ba* to weigh, consider *Pth.* — 2. fut. of *ˌjig-pa.*

གཞིབ་པ་ *γžib-pa* fut. of *ˌjib-pa.*

གཞིབས་པ་ *γžibs-pa* **to put** or **lay in order** *Lex.*, **žib-žib čó-če(s)* W.*, **toṅ-wa* C.* id.

གཞིལ་བ་ *γžil-ba* fut. of *ˌjil-ba*, = *ˌjóms-pa.*

གཞིས་ཀ་ *γžis-ka* **native place, native country** *Lex.*; *yul-γžis* house, estate, property *Mil.* = *žiṅ-ḱáṅ* paternal estate; *pa-γžis* the father's domicile as inheritance; *γžis sgríl-ba* to change one's abode, to remove to another place *Sch.*; *γžis-pa* **a native** *Sch.*; *γžis-mad* **family, household, wife, children** and

domestics; *γži-byés Sch.:* native and foreign, at home and abroad.

གཞུ་ *γžu,* also *γžu-mo Mil.*, resp. *γnam-rú B.* and col., 1. **bow,** for shooting, *γžu bčos* he constructed a bow *Glr.; γžu ₒgéṅ-ba, W.* **káṅ-če**, to bend the bow and have it ready, frq.; *ₒtén-pa Pth.*, and *ₒgúgs-pa Cs.*, id.; *ₒbúd-pa* to unbend (the bow) *Cs.*; *rdúṅ-ba* (*Dzl.* ༦༥, 15, ༡༤༢, 11. *Gyatch.* ༡༣༥, 10), acc. to explanations given by Lamas: to make the bow-string sound by a sudden pull or jerk, = *γžú-rgyúd sbréṅ-ba Dzl.*, which both as to matter and language seems preferable to other explanations that have been given. — 2. **arch,** in architecture *Cs., γžú-lugs-su ₒbúb-pa* 'to arch in the form of a bow' *Cs.*; **capital, chapiter**, v. *ka-ba.* — 3. resp. for **žum-már-pa** **lamp,** **zim-žu** id., **góṅ-žu** lantern *C.* (spelling uncertain).

Comp. *γžú-mk'an* bow-maker. — *γžu-rgyúd* bow-string *Dzl.* — *γžú-čan, γžu-ldán* furnished with a bow. — *γžu-mčog Lex., Sch.:* 'the two ends of a bow'; *γžu-mčóg ₒdzúgs-pa* to rest one end of the bow on some object(?) *Mil.* — *γžu-t'óg* an arched roof *Cs.* — *γžu-t'ógs* holding a bow, archer *Ld.-Glr.* — *γžu-brtán* n. of an ancient Indian king *Gl.* — *γžu-dóms* a cord, fathom, as a standard measure, opp. to any abitrary measure (so explained by a Lama). — *γžú-pa* bow-man, archer. — *γžur-šúbs,* bow-case *Wdṅ.*

གཞུ་བ་ *γžú-ba* **to strike, to lash,** *lčág-gis* with a whip.

གཞུག *γžug* 1. = *mjug,* q. v., **end, extremity;** *γžug-gu, γžug-čuṅ Med.* **coccyx; rump** or **ventlet** of birds *Sch.*; *γžug-rmén* the glands of it *Sch.*; *gral-γžúg* the end of a row *Glr.*; *mgo-γžúg* upper and lower end, e.g. of a stick *Glr.*; *lo-γžúg-la* at the end of the year *Mil.*; *mṅag-γžúg* household-servants, suite *Sch.* — 2. v. *ₒjúg-pa.*

གཞུང་ *γžuṅ* 1. **the middle, midst.** — 2. **spinal marrow** *S.g.*, also *klad-γžuṅ Sch.*, *γžuṅ-riṅs Mil.* — **gyab-žúṅ-la zug rag** *W.* I feel a pain in the middle of my back; *lče-γžuṅ* the middle of the tongue; *γžuṅ-nas* in a direct way, opp. to *zúr-nas.*

Comp. **žúṅ-go** *C.* middle door, principal door or gate. **žuṅ-čág** *W.* partition-wall, **čád-če** to construct one. — *γžúṅ-pa* a man from the middle part of the country, neither *stód-pa* nor *šám-pa W.* — *γžúṅ-ma* 1. **the middle of a thing** *Cs.*; as a proper name: the middle part of Lhasa, containing the royal palace, also *γžuṅ-sa-dga-ldán.* 2. the back-part of fur *Sch.* 3. **kernel, pith, main substance** *Sch.* 4. **the original, the source, text;** *γžuṅ-lúgs* id. *Tar.*

གཞུང་བ་ *γžúṅ-ba* pf. *γžuṅs Cs.*: **'to attend, to be heedful; attention,** *γžúṅs-pa* heedful'; *Sch.* has: 'sincere, orderly', and for the current phrase *yid γžúṅs-pa* he gives: 'a quiet and prudent mind or behaviour'. But the way in which the word is used in books, where it frequently occurs in conjunction with *mk'ás-pa,* as well as in the popular expressions *žúṅ-k'an* and *žuṅ-méd-k'an* = *blo-rnó* and *blo-dmán,* would rather suggest the version: **acuteness of perception,** a good and quick comprehension.

གཞུད་པ་ *γžud-pa Sch.:* **'to go, to walk, to put into'.**

གཞུན་པོ་ *γžún-po* **excellent in its kind,** *γser γžún-po* the purest gold, *ston-tóg γžún-po* a capital crop *C.*

གཞུར་བ་ *γžúr-ba* **to shear, shave, cut off,** **ta** the hair *C.*, leaves, branches *Cs.* (cf. *bžár-ba*?).

གཞེ་ར་ *γžé-ra* **parsley** *C.*

གཞེང་ *γžeṅ* v. *žeṅ.*

གཞེན་ *γžen* the act of **remembering** or **reminding,** **nyíṅ-la žen yóṅ-če ḍi-la ḍi** *W.* in order not to forget it, I have written it down; *γžen skúl-ba Lex.* to remind a person; *γžen btád-pa* or acc. to another reading *btáb-pa,* i.e. *ₒdébs-pa* to admonish, exhort *Dzl.* ༡༥༡, 9.

གཞེན་པ་ *γžén-pa* **to light, kindle, inflame** *Sch.*; *ráṅ-byuṅ-gi mes žúgs-la,* prob. to be set in flames by spontaneous fire (?) *Tar.* 7, 4.

གཞེས་ *γžes* **the second day after to-morrow** *Lex.*; **to-re náṅ-la že-la** *W.*, to-morrow, the day after to-morrow, on the fourth day; *γžes-rnyiṅ Cs.* = *γži-niṅ.*

གཞེས་པ་ *γžés-pa* (= *bžugs-pa* yet less used), resp. for **to sit, stay, wait,** *čuṅ tsam γžes šig* wait a little! *Dzl.* ᠒᠓᠒, 12 (another reading: *bžugs šig*).

གཞོ་བ་ *γžó-ba* for *bžó-ba,* v. *ʼjó-ba.*

གཞོག་པ་ *γžóg-pa* v. *ʼjóg-pa.*

གཞོགས་ *γžogs* **the side of the body,** = *glo*; *γžogs γyas γyon* the right and left side *Sch.*; *γžógs-su* sideways *Sch.*; *γžogs slóṅ-ba Lex., γžogs-sloṅ byéd-pa Cs.* to speak allusively; *γžogs-smód byéd-pa* to prejudice a person against another insidiously, to create enmity *Thgy.*; it is also used like a verb: *γžógs-te rtsáb-pa* to be insolent with a fair appearance, opp. to *ṅor* downright *Thgy.* — *γžogs-ṗyéd ná-ba Do.* prob. an inaccurate expression for pain in one side.

གཞོང་པ་ *γžóṅ-pa* **wooden basin, trough, tub, washing-tub**; *ḱyi-γžóṅ* (col. **ḱyib-žóṅ**) trough for feeding dogs and other animals, also manger *W.*; **ṭud-žoṅ* W.* prob. id.; **čag-žóṅ*.W.* trough for dry horse-meat; **ṭab-žóṅ** winnowing-tray, inst. of a shovel; in books the word is used in a wider sense, in such expressions as *γser-, dṅul-, ʼkar-, rdo-γzoṅ.*

གཞོངས་ *γžoṅs Lex.* = *ljoṅs.*

གཞོན་པ་ *γžón-pa* 1. sbst. v. *bžón-pa.* — 2. adj. **young,** *γžón-pa de na-ré* the younger one said *Mil.*; *rgyál-po sku-ná γžón-pa* the young king; *bdag γžón-pas* as I am still young, I as the younger one, the youngest *Dzl.*; *γžón-pa ʼgá-žig* some young people *Mil.*; *γžón-dus bu-méd* who in their younger years had no children; *γžón-nu* **a youth,** frq., *γžón-nu-ts̒o* plur. *Mil.*; *γžón-nu-ma* or *bú-mo γžón-nu Dzl.* **virgin, maiden, girl**; *sé-ba γžón-nu* a young rose *Wdṅ.*; *γžón-nu daṅ brál-bar byéd-pa* to deprive a girl of her virginity *Cs.*, *γžon-nu-brál* a girl that has lost her virginity *Cs.*; *γžón-nu-nas* from a child, from infancy *Mil.*; *γžon-grógs* youthful companion *Mil.*; *γžón-ša-čan* with youthful flesh, *γžón-ša-čan-du ʼgyúr-ba Glr.* to grow young again.

གཞོབ་ *γžob* 1. *me-γžób* **singeing,** or what has been **singed,** wool, hair, feathers etc.; **a mark** from burning; *γžób-dri Sch.* also *γžob-ró* smell of singeing; *γžób-tu ʼgyúr-ba* to be singed, seared *Pth.*; **žob gyáb-pa* C.* to singe off; fig. *ṅai lus-séms γžób-tu ṫal Glr.* my body and soul were seared, deeply afflicted. — 2. *W.* **a crash,** e.g. of a tree breaking down.

གཞོམ་པ་ *γžóm-pa* 1. v. *ʼjoms-pa.* — 2. **to break in two, to tear** *Sch.*; in *W.* used of metal vessels **bent** or **bruised.**

གཞོར་ *γžor* v. *ʼjor.*

གཞོལ་བ་ *γžól-ba* 1. **to apply one's self diligently** *Cs.*, *čós-la ṫugs γžól-ba Pth.* id. resp. — 2. **to comprehend, to fathom**(?) *Sch.* — 3. resp. for *ʼbáb-pa* **to alight, light from, dismount,** v. *čibs*; cf. also *žol.*

གཞོས་ *γžos* for *bžos,* v. *ʼjó-ba.*

བཞ་ *bža,* in *Lexx.* mentioned as the same with *brlán-pa.*

བཞག་ *bžag* 1. **large intestine,** = *γnyé-ma*; *bžag-sgór-mo* the windings of the intestines *Glr., Mil.* — 2. certain muscles under the arms *Mṅg.* — 3. *Sch.*: 'flesh of animals that died of disease'.

བཞག་པ་ *bžág-pa* 1. v. *ʼjóg-pa.* — 2. **to tear, wear,** intrs., of cloth etc.; **to burst, crack, split** *C., W.*

བཞད་ *bžad,* also *bžád-pa Pth.* **swan**; *bžad-dkár Lex.*; *bžad-ldán Schr.*: 'a pond with swans on it'.

བཞད་པ་, གཞད་པ་ *bžád-pa, γžád-pa* **to laugh, smile** *Glr.*; *bžád-ḱa-ma* a girl with a smiling face *Mil.*; *bžad-gád* **laughter,** *ṫég-pa* to raise (a laughter) *Mil.*, *bžad-gád-mḱan Tar.* buffoon, jester; *bžád-mo* **smile, laughing, laughter,** *bžád-mo bžád-pa* to laugh; *bžád-pa-mo, bžad-ldán-ma* n. of a goddess, *Ssk.* Hasawati *Cs.*

བཞབ་པ་ *bžáb-pa* v. *ʼjáb-pa.*

བཞམས་པ་ *bžáms-pa* 1. also *γžáms-pa Schr.?* **to stroke,** *ṗyág-gis* resp. with the hand, **to coax, caress;** hence *bžáms-te Dzl.*

༢༢,5, might perh. be rendered: **to appease, to pacify.** — 2. *bžams-bsgó byéd-pa Lex.* **to remind of, to call to mind.**

བཞར་བ་ *bžár-ba* **to scrape,** with a knife, **to shave** or **shear,** with a razor *Med.*; *skra bžár-ba* the hair.

བཞི་ *bži* 1. **four;** *bži-pa, bži-po* cf. *dgu*; *bži-bču* (col. **žib-ču**) 40, *bži-bču-rtsa-γčig* (*W.*žib-ču-že-čig*), *že-γčig* etc. the numbers 41—49; *bži-brgyá* 400, *bži-stoṅ* 4000 etc.; *bži-ča* one fourth, a quarter; *bži-tsan-gyi-sdé-pa pyed-daṅ-brgyád* the 7½ tetrads (of letters) *Gram.* — 2. often incorr. for *ži* or *γži.*

བཞིན་ *bžin* 1. sbst. **face, countenance,** *rób-tu mi-sdúg-pa* (of) a very ugly face *Dzl.*, *légs-pa, mdzés-pa Glr.* (of) a handsome, a pretty face; *bžin-mdzés-ma* a woman or girl with a pretty face; *bžin zágs-te* the face dripping (from perspiration); *bžin ₒdzúm-pa daṅ bčas-pa* with a friendly smiling countenance *Mil.*; *bžin-pags sér-po* the skin of the face being yellow (as in bilious complaints) *Mṅg.*; *bžin-rás* the appearance, *ṅán-pa Med.*; *bžin-bzáṅ*, fem. *bzin-bzaṅ-ma*, a polite address: my dear Sir; *kye bžin-bzaṅ-dag* much respected gentlemen! also in other instances as a word of politeness: *bžin-bzáṅ-ma dé-dag laṅs-te* the ladies rose and ...; it seems to be particularly in favour, when apparitions are addressed *Mil.* — 2. particle, the meaning of which corresponds in part to that of the Greek prep. κατά c. acc., gen. used as an adv. *bžin-du* or *bžin*, but also as an adj. with *pa:* a. joined to verbal roots, *bžin* serves to form with them a partic. pres., and *bžin-du* a gerund, *tugs-mnyés-bžin-pai ṅáṅ-la* in a rejoicing frame of mind, in a joyful mood *Mil.*; *kri-la bžúgs-bžin-du* sitting on the chair *Dzl.*; *skrág-bžin-du* from fear *Dzl.* (cf. καθ' ὕπνον); *mdaṅs ₒgyur bžin-du* whilst his colour changes *Dzl.*; *mi šes bžin-du šes-so žes zer* not knowing it he pretends to know it *Stg.*; *dád-bžin-du log soṅ* 'credentes discesserunt', believing they went away *Mil.* b. *bžin(-du)* as postp. c. acc., **agreeably, in conformity, according to,** very frq.; *čos bžin-du* according to the precepts of religion *Dzl.* (cf. κατὰ νόμον), *rgyál-pos bsgó-ba bžin-du sgrúb-pa* to execute a thing according to the king's command, to perform his order frq.; *kyod ǰi-skad smrás-pa bžin-du γžán-dag-la bsnyád-de* relating to the others according to what has been said by you, = relating what you have said *Dzl.*; *yid-bžin-du* to heart's content frq.; **like, as,** *ri ₒgyél-ba* like the breaking down of a mountain *Dzl.*; also with a pleonastic *ltar: mkán-po ǰi-ltar γsúṅ-ba bžin Glr.*, or, which would be the same, *ǰi-bžin γsúṅ-ba ltar*, as the very learned gentleman has said, foretold; *de bžin-du* **so** = *dé-ltar; de-de-bžin-no* yes, that is so; *de-bžin-nyid* (तथता), **truth, reality, substance, essentiality** *Was.* (272), **identity** (297), in mysticism = *čos-nyid Thgy.*, v. *čos*, comp.

c. *pyi-bžin(-du), pyir-bžin(-du)* **afterwards, subsequently** (cf. κατόπισθε). — d. distrib. *nyin-ré-bžin(-du)*, **daily, per day** (καθ' ἡμέραν), *nyin-γčig-bžin-du* id.; *re-re-bžin-gyi mdzad-pa Glr.* his daily doings.

བཞུ་བ་ *bžú-ba*, v. *žú-ba* II. and *ₒǰu-ba*, **to melt.**

བཞུགས་པ་ *bžúgs-pa*, resp. for *sdód-pa* and *ₒdúg-pa*, 1. **to sit,** *bžúgs-su γsol B*, *bžugs (-žu)* col., please sit down! — *bžúgs-kri* chair; throne. — 2. **to dwell, reside,** *bžúgs-pai po-bráṅ* castle of residence *Dzl.*; *bžúgs-pai rten* a small temple in which a deity resides *Dzl.*; *bžugs-grógs* fellow-lodger: — 3. **to remain, stay, exist, live,** *ₒǰig-rtén-du bžúgs-pa* to be in the world, to live on earth, of Buddha and saints; also, still to remain in the world; *stón-pa bžúgs-pai dús-su* during the life-time of the Teacher (Buddha) *Tar.*; *kyed ₒdir bžugs čos-mdzád ye* devout here present = my devout friends! *Mil.*; **žug yo-dham* C.* are you at home? **ku žug naṅ yo-dham* C.* are you coming? = welcome! well-met!; transferred to writings, texts etc., **to be contained,** so in titles of books: *mdzaṅs-blún žes-byá-ba bžúgs-so* the so-styled 'Sage and Fool' is contained (in the present volume); *bló-la bžúgs-pa daṅ glegs-bám-du bžúgs-pa tams-čád yi-ger spel* all that was found in the memories (of individual persons) and in books, was recorded *Tar.*

བཞུད་པ་ *bžúd-pa*, resp. **to go away, to depart,** *B.* frq.; *ṕar bžud* pray, go away! (opp. to *ťsur-byon*).

བཞུན་ *bžun* v. *žun*.

བཞུར་བ་ *bžúr-ba* 1. = *γzúr-ba, bžár-ba Cs.* — 2. **to strain, filter,** *Sch.*

བཞུས་པ་ *bžús-pa* v. *žú-ba*.

བཞེང་བ་ *bžéṅ-ba*, pf. and imp. *bžeṅs Glr.*, resp. for *slóṅ-ba*, **to raise, erect, set up,** an image, temple; **to manufacture, compose,** sacred things, e.g. pictures, books; **to draw up, frame, write, print,** or cause it to be done; **to found, endow, give,** books to monasteries etc.

བཞེངས་པ་ *bžéṅs-pa* 1. pf. of *bžéṅ-ba*. — 2. resp. for *láṅ-ba* **to rise, get up,** intrs. to *bžéṅ-ba*; also with *yár(-la) Glr.*; **nyi-ráṅ žáṅs(-sa*)* *W.* are you risen? **žaṅ(s)** please to get up!

བཞེད་པ་ *bžéd-pa* I. vb., resp. for *ₒdód-pa*, **to wish, desire,** *rgyál-po γzigs bžéd-dam* does your Reverence wish to see the king? *Dzl.*; *rgyál-po náṅ-du ₒbyón-par-bžéd-pa-la* as the king wished to enter *Glr.*; *rta mi bžéd-na* if your Reverence does not wish to have the horse *Mil.*; in science: **to accept,** *mḱán-pa ṕyi-ma-dag mi bžéd—pa legs* it is well that learned men of later times do not accept it, approve of it *Gram.*; **to assert, maintain,** *so-sói bžéd-ťsul máṅ-na yaṅ* although many different propositions are to be met with *Wdk.*; *sṅá-mas bžed* earlier writers are of opinion, insist on *Gram.*; of letters: *ga-ₒṕul bžed* certain letters require ག for a prefix *Zam.* — II. **supposition, view, opinion** *Tar.* 113, 21. — *bžed-don* resp. **wish, desire** *Cs.*, *bžed-don ₒgrub* it happens according to one's wish, as one could wish *Cs.*

བཞེས་པ་ *bžés-pa* I. vb., resp. for *lén-pa* **to take, receive, accept; to seize, confiscate,** *B., C.* (*W.* **nám-če** synon.); *ḱáb-tu bžés-pa* and *žál-gyis bžés-pa* v. *ḱab* and *žal*; esp. at meals, **to take, to eat,** *ǰi bžéd-pa bžes šig Dzl.* please take whatever you like, *bžés-na* if he would take it, if it should be to his liking *Mil.*; instead of *lón-pa* in: *dgúṅ-lo bču-γnyis bžés-pa* he got twelve years old. — II. sbst. **food, meat,** *bžés-pa ₒdrén-pa* to offer, to serve up meat *Mil., Pth.* — **Comp.** **žě-ḍho** *C.* food, sweet-meats (cf. *gro*) *bžes-ťáṅ* food (?) *Sch.* — **žě-ḍhúṅ** (?) *Ts.* beer. —**žě-bhág** *C.* bread —**žě-rág** *W.* brandy. —**žě-hór** *C.*, hookah, oriental tobacco-pipe, the smoke of which passes through water.

བཞོ་བ་, བཞོས་པ་ *bžó-ba, bžós-pa* **to milk.**

བཞོག་པ་ *bžog-pa* v. *ₒǰog-pa*.

བཞོགས་ *bžogs* = *γžogs*.

བཞོང་ *bžoṅ* = *γžon*.

བཞོན་པ་ *bžón-pa* (sometimes incorr. *γžón-pa*) vehiculum, **riding-beast, carriage, vehicle;** *bžón-pa šóm-pa* to order the horses to be put to *Dzl.*; *bžon-pas ₒbrós-pa* to take to flight in a vehicle or on horseback *Dzl.*; *mi-srun bžón-pa* a not gentle riding-beast *S.g.*

བཞོན་མ་ *bžón-ma* **milking cow** *Cs.*, *bžon-ṕyugs* milking cattle *Glr.*

ཟ

ཟ *za* 1. the letter **z**, originally, and in the frontier-provinces to the present-day, sounding like the English z, in *C.* differing from ས, s, only by the following vowel being deep-toned. — 2. numer. figure: 22.

ཟ་, ཟས་ *za, zas, Ld.* any thing **small, neat, elegant, of a miniature size,** **pé-ča za žig** a little book, pocket-edition, **nod-čád za zig** a little pot or can, **čaṅ za žig** a drop of beer.

ཟྭ་ *zwa*, **nettle**, stinging nettle, gen. *zwa-tsód*, being, when young, eaten as greens (v. *tsód-ma*); *zwa(i)-p'yi(mo)*, *'a-ya-zwa-tsód*, *Wdn.*, blind or dead nettle; *zwa-lčág* scourge made of stinging nettles, *zwa-lčág brgyáb-pa* to flog with it *Cs.*; *zwa-ber*, the smart produced by the stinging of nettles *Cs.*; *zwa-ₒbrúm Wdn.* (?).

ཟ་ཁུ་ *za-k'u Med.*, e.g. *bad-kan za-k'ur ₒgyur Mng.* prob. the same word which *Sch.* spells *za-gu*, explaining it by gonorrhoea, morbid discharge of seminal fluid, semen pruriens.

ཟ་བ་ *za-ba*, *bza-ba* I. vb., perf. *zos*, *bzas*, fut. *bza*, imp. *zo*, *zos* (*C.* **zē**) 1. **to eat**, both of men and animals, *zá-bya*, *zá-rgyu* what may or must be eaten, *za-čig-pa Dzl.* (perh. better *bza-γčig-pa*) one that takes only one meal a day, or perh.: one that takes a solitary meal; *zós-pas* having eaten *Dzl.*; *zós-pai ˛óg-tu* after he had eaten *Dzl.*; *zos-ₒgrogs* 'immediately after dinner' (??) *Sch.*; *ma-lús-par zá-ba Dzl.*, **dág-mo za-če** *W.*, to eat up, consume, to clear the plate, the manger; *bzá-ru rún-ba* or *mi-rún-ba* what may or may not be eaten; *Dzl.* ༧༢, 16 has also a supine *zós-su*: *bu zos-su ˛on* she will even be constrained to eat her own young (s. l. c.); *žim-du zo Zam.* may you enjoy your dinner! ni f.; *zá-k'ar* at dinner-time *Sch.*; *za-zá-ba* 'to eat often, to be a glutton' *Cs.* — 2. **to live upon, to live by**, *gla zá-ba* to gain one's subsistence as a day-labourer *Dzl.* — 3. **to itch**, *za ₒp'rúg-pa* v. *ₒp'rug-pa.* — 4. fig. for **to steal**, **kún-ma, gón-mo zos son** *Ld.*, a thief, a witch, has made away with it. — 5. fig. of affections of the mind: **to entertain, to give way to**, *k'ón-k'ro*, *tsig-pa*, *té-tsom zá-ba* to give way to resentment, anger, doubts. — II. sbst. **food, meat, victuals**, *za ču žim* good eating and drinking *Mil.*; **zá-če zá-če, čó-če** *W.* to eat food, to prepare food. — *za-rkón* v. *rkon.* — *za-k'an* dining-room; eating-house, cook's shop *C.* — *za-k'u* v. the preceding article. — *zá-mk'an* one that is eating, an eater. — **za-čóg** *W.* what may be eaten, **za-mi-čóg** what may not be eaten. — **za-t'úr** *C.* chop-sticks. — *zá-ma* **food, victuals**, *zá-ma mi ster run* though you do not give me any food *Mil* — *za-yón* meat-offering to saints etc. *Mil.* — For more refer to *bza.*

ཟ་མ་ *zá-ma* 1. v. above. — 2. also *zá-ma-tog Ssk.* करण्ड, **basket**, in Tibetan only fig., mostly as a title of books, but also used in connection with mysticism.

ཟ་ཟི་ *za-zi* **trouble, noise** *Cs.*, **troublesome chatting** *Sch.*; **troubled, bewildered, perplexed** *Schr.*; in the passage *rmi-lam za-zi man Med.* it seems to signify troubled dreams.

ཟ་ཟོམ་ *za-zóm* a fine cotton fabric *Sch.*

ཟ་ར་ *zá-ra?* **zá-ra p'i-mo** *W.* the later part of the afternoon, v. *rdzá-ra.*

ཟ་རུ་ *zá-ru* v. *γzár-bu.*

ཟ་འོག་ *za-˛óg* **heavy silk cloth**, *za-˛óg-gi gos* a garment made of it *Glr.*; *za-˛óg dgu brtsegs k'ri* a seat formed of nine silk quilts. — *za-báb* id.

ཟ་ཧོར་ *za-hor* n. of a town or district, acc. to *Cs.* in Bengal, acc. to *Pth.* in the north-west of India, by the statements of Lamas the present **Mandi**, a small principality under British protection, in the Punjâb, between the rivers Byās and Ravi, where there is a sacred lake, celebrated as a **place** of pilgrimage, from which the **Brahmins** residing there derive a considerable income.

ཟག་པ་ *zág-pa* 1. sometimes for *γzág-pa*, from *ₒdzágs-pa.* — 2. sbst., *Ssk.* आस्रव **misery, affliction, sorrow**, esp. as a consequence of sin, hence frq. = sin, *zág-pa zad* the woe of this world is over, frq.; *zág-pa-med-pai las* works spotless or without sin *Thgy.*; *zag-méd-kyi bde-ba* untroubled happiness *Glr.*; *zag-bčás* burdened with misery and sin, *zag-bčás-kyi las γsum* the three sinful works *Thgy.*; *zag-bčas-kyi mnon(-par)-šes(-pa) Glr.* and *Thgr.?*

ཟང་ *zan? Sch.*: *zan-t'ál-du* **penetrating.**

ཟང་ཟང་ *zan-zán* 1. v. *dmár-po* extr. — 2. also *zan-zin*, *zin-zin*, *γzin-ba*, v. *ₒdzins-pa*; *W.* also: **muddled, rather tipsy.**

ཟང་ཟིང་ *zan-zin* 1. sbst. **matter, object, goods,** = *rdzas*, *zan-zin čún-zad tsám-gyi* *pyir* even for the most trifling matter *Stg.*; *pyi-rol-gyi zaṅ-ziṅ* external goods, earthly possessions, (opp. to internal, spiritual gifts) *Dzl.*: also *zaṅ-ziṅ* by itself: what is earthly, pertaining to this world *Mil.* — 2. adj., **confused in mind, stupefied** *Sch.*, v. the preceding article.

ཟངས་ *zaṅs* 1. **copper,** *ysér-zaṅs* gilt copper, *záṅs-kyi btsa* prob. verdigris. — 2. **kettle** *B.*, *C.*, v. *pan-dil*; *záṅs-su skól-ba* to boil in a kettle *Dzl.*; *zaṅs ḱól-pa* a boiling kettle *Dzl.*; *˳ḱár-zaṅs* bronze or brass kettle, *lčags-zaṅs* iron kettle. — *zaṅs-rkyán* copper can or jug. — *zaṅs-skyógs* copper ladle. — *zaṅs-čén* a large, *zaṅs-čúṅ* a small kettle. — *zaṅs-tíg* a small species of gentian. — *zaṅs-tib* copper tea-pot. — **záṅ-ton-sa** *W.* copper-mine. — *zaṅs-ťál* copper slacks *Glr.* — *zaṅs-mdóg* copper colour. — *zaṅs-sdér* copper plate or dish *Sch.* — *zaṅs-snód* copper vessel. — **záṅ-bu** *C.*, *W.*, = *zaṅs* 2; **záṅ-bu če čuṅ nyi** two copper kettles, a large one and a little one. — *záṅs-ma* = *záṅs-bu?* *Mṅg.* — *záṅs-γya* *Cs.*: 'copper-green', prob. verdigris. — *záṅs-sa* copper-ore *Cs.*

ཟངས་དཀར་ *záṅs-dkar* south-western province of Ladak, *záṅs-dkar-pa*, *-ma* man or woman of that province.

ཟད་པ་ *zád-pa* v. *˳dzád-pa*.

ཟན་ *zan*, *C.* **zẹn**, I. resp. *bšáṅ-ma*, also *ḱam-zán* *Mil.* 1. **pap, porridge,** of flour and water, thick, boiled or not boiled, warm or cold, also called *bág-zan*, esp. as dough for baking; in *C.* porridge is gen. made of *rtsám-pa*, and if possible of tea; *˳brás-zan* rice-p., *˳ó-zan*, milk-p.; porridge being the daily food, as bread is with us, the word is used also 2. for **food** in gen: *zan zá-ba* to take food, to eat, *bdag daṅ zan mi zá-na* if you will not eat with me *Dzl.*; *zan-dráṅ* cold, *zan-drón* warm food, *zan-čaṅ* meat and drink, *S.g.*; *zan btsos-pa* boiled food; **zan-kón** dearth *W.*; *zan zos* 1. he was eating porridge. 2. as one word: *Bal.* wife, cf. *bza*; fig. *lkog-zán zá-ba* to take unlawful interest *Sch.* — 3. **fodder, provender,** v. *bzan.* —

II. inst. of *za* **eater,** as second part of a compound: *ša-zán* meat-eater; carnivorous animal *Glr.*; *nya-zán* fish-eater, ichthyophagist; *pag-zén* pork-eater.

ཟན་པོ་ *zán-po* v. *γzán-po*.

ཟབ་ *zab* **silk,** fine or heavy silk, v. *dar-záb*; *zab-čén* costly silk cloth *Sch.*; *zab-skúd* *Lt.*, *Mil.* silk-cord; *zab-˳ból* silk covering for a seat, bolster *Pth.*

ཟབ་པ་ *záb-pa*, vb., adj. and sbst, **to be deep, deep, depth,** *záb-po*, gen. *záb-mo*, adj., deep, frq.; often fig., *blo-záb* *Cs.*: a profound mind or understanding; *zab-záb byas kyaṅ záb-mo raṅ mi ˳dug* although people call it deep, it is not deep *Sch.*; *zab-lám*, *záb-moi sgom-ḱrid* a term of Buddhist mysticism, doctrine of witchcraft, = *dbú-mai lam*, or *pyág-rgya čén-po*. — *zab-ḱyád* depth, = *zabs*, *Dzl.*, *Mil.*

ཟབས་ *zabs* **depth,** *zábs-su ˳dom bčui doṅ* a pit ten fathoms in depth.

ཟམ་པ་ *zám-pa* **bridge,** *grú-zam* bridge of boats *Cs.*; *lcágs-zam* iron bridge, wire-bridge; *lčúg-zam* suspension-bridge, by means of cables of twisted birch-tree branches; *˳drén-zam* draw-bridge *Cs.*; *rdó-zam* 1. stone-bridge. 2. natural rock-bridge; *rtswá-zam* common expression for *lčúg-zam* and *ťsár-zam*; the latter: suspension-bridge by cables formed of thin split cane; *šiṅ-zam* wooden bridge; *zám-pa ˳dzúgs-pa* to throw a bridge *Cs.*; *zám-pai ká-ba* or *rkáṅ-pa* the piers or foundations, *spaṅ-léb*, *spaṅ-sgó* the boards or planks, *mda-yáb* or *lag-rtén* parapet, *γžu-tóg* arch, *zam-γdúṅ* beam of a bridge, *Cs.*; *zam-čén* a large bridge, *zam-čúṅ* a little one *Cs.*, *zám-bu* id.

ཟར་ *zar* 1. supine of *zá-ba*; *zar ˳júg-pa* **to give to eat.** — 2. **pitch-fork,** for shaking up the corn, hay-fork, dung-fork; forks at dinner are not yet used in Tibet, spoons and knives, and in Lhasa chop-sticks, answering their end sufficiently.

ཟར་བབས་ *zar-bábs* *Sch.*: **tassel;** acc. to our authorities: **gold-brocade.**

ཟར་བུ་ *zár-bu* *Glr.*, *Mil.* seems to be **tassel.**

ཟར་མ་ *zar-ma Dzl.; Med.* **sesame-seed;** *zar-mai me-tog* flower of sesame, *Sch.*; *zar-ma-ču* is mentioned in *Pth.* as Aphrodisiacum; yet *zar-mai ras* is stated to be a fabric, manufactured from *zwa-ṫsód*, muslin?

ཟལ་ *zal Ld.* a small and uninhabited river-island.

ཟལ་མོ་ *zál-mo* 1. **young cow, heifer,** *₀bri-zál* yak-heifer. — 2. a fabulous bird *Sch.*

ཟས་ *zas* **food, nourishment,** for men and animals, also in a wider fig. sense; *zas-bčád smyúṅ-ɣnas* fasting, abstaining from or withholding food *Lex.*; *zas-bzáṅ(-po)* 1. dainty food *Dzl.* 2. nourishing fare, *Wdṅ.*, *zas-ṅán(-pa)* the contrary; *zas-ni* as to diet . . . *Med.*; *zás-su či za* what does it feed on? *Dzl.*; *zás-sušrag ₀ṫúṅ-ba* to drink blood for nourishment *Do.; zas ₀ṫsól-ba* to seek to obtain a livelihood *Ma.*; *₀ṫsó-ba zas, Mil.* a pleon. expression = *zas*; *k̔a-zás* (resp. *žal-zas B., sól-wa* col.) **food, meat,** for human beings; *dkár-zas* v. *dkár-ba; dmár-zas Sch.:* 'festival dishes', perh. more corr. flesh-meat, animal food? *gró-zas Sch.:* 'dry traveller's fare'; *p̔án-zas*, wholesome nutritive food *Med.* —

Comp. **ze-kón** *C.*, dearth, scarcity. — *zas-skom* meat and drink, solid and liquid food *Med.*; *zas-čáṅ*, id., as travelling-provisions *Glr.* — *zas-spyod* food and exercise, diet, in a wider sense *Med.* — *zas-ṫsód* the due measure of food, *zas-ṫsód ma zin* the portion or share was not full, it was not the full allowance, *S.g.* — *zas-ɣtsáṅ-ma* (clean food), n.p. शुद्धोदन, the father of Buddha; *bdúd-rtsi-zas*, *bré-bo-zas*, *zas-dkár* the names of his three brothers, *zas-ɣtsaṅ-srás* appellation of Buddha himself.

ཟི་ *zi*, I. num. figure: 52. — II. *W.* 1. something of a very **small size** or **quantity,** **zi yaṅ mi dug** not an atom is left, **zi-med-k̔an čo** eat it up to the last crumb! **mé-zi** a spark in the ashes ever so small. — 2. **the black mark** in a target. (cf. *ža*).

ཟི་ངིལ་ *zi-ṅil* v. *zi-líṅ.*

ཟི་བ་ *zi-ba* v. *ɣzi-ba.*

ཟི་མ་ *zi-ma, Sch.*: **green slime** on standing water, *zi-ma-čan* what is covered with such a slime.

ཟི་ར་ *zi-ra, Ssk.* and *Hindi* जीर, **the Asiatic caraway,** *Cuminum Cyminum*, exported from Tibet to India, of a powerful aroma, which to the taste of Europeans is often disagreeable; two kinds are distinguished, *zi-ra dkár-po*, and *nág-po.*

ཟི་རི་རི་ *zi-ri-ri* **the humming of bees,** the singing of a kettle *W.*

ཟི་རུ་ *zi-ru* col. for *ɣzér-bu.*

ཟི་ལིང་ *zi-liṅ* I. also **zi-ṅil, zi-lóṅ** *W.* **noise, bustle, tumult.** —

II. from the Chinese 1. also *zi-lím, zi-láṅ* **a composition metal,** similar to German silver, *zi-liṅ-pan-tse* or *baṅ-tse C.* a basin of that metal. — 2. n. p., province, adjoining the Kokonor, *zi-liṅ-ja* tea from thence.

ཟིང་ཟིང་ *ziṅ-ziṅ* v. *zaṅ-ziṅ.*

ཟིང་རེལ་ *ziṅ-rél W.*, prob. for *₀dziṅ-sbrél*, with **čó-če**, to prepare for battle, or to begin fighting.

ཟིན་པ་ *zin-pa* 1. v. *₀dzin-pa.* — 2. = *₀dzád-pa*, esp. in the pf. tense, **to draw near to an end, to be at an end, to be finished, exhausted, consumed;** *zin-pai p̔úṅ-po* the perishable, mortal body *Thgy.*; **to be finished, terminated,** *nam yaṅ mi zin-to Dzl.* it will never be finished; **to finish, to get done with,** building a wall *Glr.*, **zin čúg-če** *W.* id.; *₀ṫuṅ ma zin dógs-pas* fearing not to be able to drink it all *Glr.*; *rtsé-ba zin-pas* as the playing has ceased, or, as he has done playing *Dzl.*; *zin(-pa) méd(-pai) las* endless working, unceasing labour *Mil.*; hence = *ṫsár-ba*, to denote an action that is **perfectly past,** esp. in *B.*, *p̔rú-gu skyés-su zin kyaṅ* although the child is already born *Do.*; *ɣsón-poi tsé-na ₀ú-čag-gis de spyad zin* we had enjoyed it during our life-time; *zin-bris Cs.*: 1. **abridgment, general view, synopsis.** 2. **lecture,** so *Schf. Tar.* 210, 22. 3. **receipt, quittance; bond** (of obligation), **bill of debt.**

ཟིམ་བུ་ *zim-bu* **fine, thin, slender,** *č̔ar zim-bu mi drág-po žig bab* a fine, drizzling rain was falling *Dzl.*, *Mil.*; *čar zim-zim dál-gyis báb-pa Mil.*, id.; *zim-zim* or *ziṅ-ziṅ* **fine, hair-shaped, capillary,** e.g. the leaves of some plants.

ཟིར་བ་ *zir-ba*, (*γzir-ba?*), gen. **zir táṅ-če** *W.*, **to aim,** *zir-po*, *zir-čan* a good aimer, marksman *W.*; *zir-sa* **aim, dispart,** **nẹ-zir** sight (of a gun) *W.*

ཟིར་མོ་ *zir-mo*, **zir-mo gyún-če* W.* to slide down a snow-hill on the coat spread under, a winter-diversion of children.

ཟིལ་ *zil* 1. (*Cs. zil-ma*), **brightness, splendour, brilliancy, glory,** *rje-btsún-gyi túgs-rjei zil ma bzód-par* not being able to bear the brightness of his Reverence's grace, (the adversary fell down the mountain) *Mil.*; *zil-čan* **brilliant, resplendent;** *zil-gyis nón-pa* to overcome, vanquish, *ḱoi zil-gyis nón-te* overpowered by him *Pth.*; *zil-bar ₒgró-ba* to increase, multiply, spread *Sch.* — 2. in botany: *stoṅ-zil, Corydalis meïfolia*; *γser-zil, dṅul-zil? S.g.*

ཟིལ་དངར་ *zil-dṅár* v. *dṅar.*

ཟིལ་པ་ *zil pa* **dew,** *zil-pa ḱrom-mé* a sparkling dew-drop *Pth.*; *zil-dkár* **hoar-frost** *Sch.*; *zil-mṅar Cs.* = *mdúd-rtsi* **nectar.**

ཟིལ་བུན་པ་ *zil-bún-pa* a slight **shuddering** from fear.

ཟུ་ *zu*, num. figure: 82.

ཟུག་ *zug* 1. also *γzug*, **pain, torment,** physical and mental; **distemper, illness, complaint,** esp. *W.* **zúg rag** I feel a pain, I am ill, **gó-la zug rág-ga** have you the head-ache? **zug čo dug** he is ill, he is suffering from pain; **só-zug** toothache; *zúg-rṅu*, *zug-γzér*, resp. *snyún* or *snyúṅ-zug*, *B.* and col. = *zug*, *mya-ṅán-gyi zúg-rṅus sdúg-bsṅal-žiṅ* weighed down by the grief of misery, *nyon-móṅs-kyi zúg-rṅu Mil.*, of the like import. — 2. also *γzug*, the principal or main pieces in cutting up an animal, **quarters,** *zug-tu ₒṗrál-ba* to cut into such pieces *Mil.*; 1 *zug* = 3 *lhu* = 6 *dum* = 12 *rgya-ri*. — 3. v. *tsug.*

ཟུག་རྔུ་ *zúg-rṅu* v. *zug* 1.

ཟུག་པ་ *zúg-pa* I. vb. 1. v. *ₒdzúgs-pa.* — 2. **to bark** *Dzl.*

II. sbst. **building, erection,** **zúg-pa gyáb-pa* Ts.* to build (cf. *ₒdzúgs-pa* 3).

ཟུང་ *zuṅ* 1. earlier literat. and *W.* **a pair, couple,** *zúṅ-du ma mčis* not occurring in pairs *Wdṅ.*; **čá-bu zuṅ čig**, *Ld.* a pair of pendants (for the ears); *nyi-zlá zuṅ γčig btsón-du bzuṅ* sun and moon are both shut up (covered by clouds) *Mil.*; *zuṅ-mčóg* the model-pair, the two principal disciples of Buddha, Sariibu and Maudgalgyibu, *Köpp.* I, 101; *zuṅ-ldán* **agreeing** in sound, **rhyming** *Cs.*; *zuṅ-ₒbrél* **connection, junction, union,** *zuṅ-ₒbrel ₒdód-na* if one wishes both things to be united *Glr.*; *zuṅ-brél-du* one after the other, or one with the other *Pth.*; *zuṅ sdébs-pa* **to join, connect, unite** *Mil.*; *zuṅ-yá* one half of a pair, a single one, e.g. shoe etc. *Cs.* — 2. **a single, separate piece** *C.* and sometimes in later literat.; *ḱa-dród zuṅ čig* a bit or mouthful of food *Thgy.*; *tsar re zuṅ re bltás-pas* when he had seen a single piece but once, (he knew it immediately) *Tar.* — 3. symb. num.: 2; *zuṅ-ṗyógs* id. — *zuṅ-ₒjúg* a technical term of practical mysticism, the forcing the mind (*sems*) into the principal artery, in order to prevent distraction (of mind) (!) *Mil.* (v. *γtúm-mo*).

ཟུང་མཁར་ *zuṅ-mkár* n. of a royal castle *Glr.*

ཟུང་བ་ *zúṅ-ba* v. *ₒdzin-pa.*

ཟུངས་ *zuṅs* v. *γzuṅs.*

ཟུབ་པ་ *zúb-pa* inst. of *bsúbs-pa*, pf. of *sub-pa Glr.*

ཟུམ་པ་ *zúm-pa* 1. v. *ₒdzúm-pa.* — 2. *W.* for *bzúṅ-ba*, v. *ₒdzin-pa*; hence *zum-ḱáb* **pin, brooch.**

ཟུར་ *zur* 1. **edge,** *gad-zúr* edge of a steep river-bank, or precipice consisting of conglomerate *Cs.*; *ču-zúr* edge of the water, border, brink, bank, *ču-zúr-pa* one that lives on the bank of a river; *zúr-na* at the border (of the place where one happens to be) *Mil.* **žiṅ-zúr-nẹ lam yod* W.* the road leads along the field; **board,** of a ship. — 2. **edge, corner,** *ḱá-ba zur-brgyád-pa* octangular pillar *Stg.*, (v. *zúr-čan* and *zúl-ma* below); *zur bži* the four corners *Sch.* — 3. **side,** **zúr-du* (or *lóg-su*) *žag-pa** *C.* to lay aside; *zúr(-du) bkól-ba Lex.*, *Sch.*: to lay up, put by, spare, save; *zúr-du* ₒ*krid-pa* to take aside, apart, for a private conversation; so also *zur p̓yin-pa Stg.*; *zúr-du*, *zúr-gyis B.*, **zúr-na* W.*, **indirectly, by the way, by the by, incidentally,** *zúr-du smrá-ba* to speak indirectly, by hints *Cs.*; *zúr-gyis mtsón-pa Tar.* to note, point out only by hints or insinuations *Schf.*; hence perh. *tsig zúr* **invective speech,** **tsig-zúr ma zer* W.* no invectives! don't be personal! *zur zá-ba* is prob. the same, where *Sch.* has: to address harshly; **zúr-ne lab-če* W.* to learn or study privately (out of school-time, or, not with the appointed master); *zur bžugs-pa Cs.* (prob. for *zúr-du*) **to lead a private life** (cf. *zúr-pa*); *zur mig ltá-ba* **to look sideways, askance, to leer, squint** *Sch.* — 4. **outline,** *k̓yod dan zur* ₒ*dra tsam yan sa sten med* none on earth is like you, or can be compared to you, even in a general outline *Pth.*; ₒ*di-dag zur tsam bsdú-ba yin-gyis* this is merely a brief outline, extract, sketch *Glr.* and elsewh., frq., also *zur tsam yin-gyis Glr.* —

Comp. *zur-bkód*, *zúr-*ₒ*débs*, *Sch.*: 'founded for a special purpose'. — *zúr-čan* cornered, angular, *yi-ge Glr.* p. 31, a sort of type or printing-letter, = *klui yi-ge*, v. also no. 2 above. — *zur-čág Sch.*: prop., having a broken edge, damaged by being knocked about; gen. fig., of words and grammatical forms: faulty, corrupted, misapplied; *Liš.* and elsewh., *Ssk.* अपभ्रंश. the most vitiated Prakrit-dialect *Was.* (267). — *zur-*ₒ*débs* = *zur-bkód-zur-nór* private goods *Cs.* — *zur-pa* one out of office, a private individual *Cs.*

zúr-ma = *zur* prov. — *zur-γsós* educated by strangers *Sch.*

ཟུར་མོ་ *zúr-mo* **pain,** = *zug*, vulg.

ཟུར་ཕུད་ *zur-p̓úd Glr.* **hair-knot, dressed hair** *Sch.*

ཟུལ་མ་ *zúl-ma W.* **cornered, angular,** = *zúr-čan*; **p̓e'-zúl** lotus-edged, of bowls, dishes, plates, that are of a polygonal or radiated shape.

ཟེ་ *ze* I. num. figure: 112.

II., also *zé-ba B.*, *W.*, *zeu Cs.* 1. **hump** of a camel, zebu etc. *Cs.* — 2. **crest,** of birds, dragons etc. *Glr.*, *S.g.*; also *ze-próg Lex.* — *zé-k̓a Cs.*: 1. 'hump. 2. decorated pad or cushion'. — *ze-rnóg Cs.* = *zé-ba*. — *ze-*ₒ*brú*, *zeu-*ₒ*brú Glr.*, *Mng.* the anthers of a flower.

ཟེ་འབུག་ *ze-búg W.* **the maw** or **fourth stomach** of ruminating animals.

ཟེ་མ་ *zé-ma W.* **elastic spring.**

ཟེ་ཚྭ་ *zé-tswa* **saltpetre** *S.g.*; *zé-tswa-čan* containing saltpetre, nitrous; *zé-tsai skyúr-rtsi* nitric acid *Cs.*

ཟེགས་མ་ *zégs-ma* **impurity, smut, dirt** *Sch.*

ཟེང་ *zen*, *t̓ú-ba γyás-zen γyón-zen byás-pa* the skirts of the coat on the right and left side folded back, tucked up *Mil.*

ཟེད་ *zed* I. sbst. 1. **brush,** *p̓ag-zéd* brush of hog's bristles; *byab-zéd* clothes-brush, dust-brush *Cs.*; *so-zéd* tooth-brush *Cs.* — 2. **edge** *C.* — II. adj *Sch.*: **'broken off, damaged, injured;** *zéd-lans* **chink, crack, rent;** *zéd-*ₒ*dug-pa* to crumble at the top' (?)

ཟེམ་ *zem* 1. **cask, barrel, tun,** often sonsisting merely of an excavated piece of a willow-tree, the Tibetans knowing but little of coopery *C.*, *W.* — 2. **box, chest** *W.* — *zem-šin* the body or wood of a vessel, *zem-mtil* the bottom of a vessel *Cs.*

ཟེར་ *zer* 1. v. *γzer*. — 2. **talk,** cf. *brjod.* — 3. n of a small animal *Med.*

ཟེར་བ་ *zér-ba* 1. (seldom ₒ*dzér-ba*) **to say,** esp. later literat. and vulg; *k̓yod zér-ba bdén-no* you say rightly *Dzl.* (where at other times always *smra-ba* is used inst. of it); *he he zer bgád-pas* they laughed he, he! *Glr.*; *čos dar zer rgyai yig-tsan-na* ₒ*dug* then the doctrine was diffused, say the Chinese records *Glr.*; after words quoted: ... *zér-bar* ₒ*dúg-pas* thus having been spoken, read, heard *Glr.*; *'yin' zer bsnyon byás-so* saying 'it is he', she told a lie *Glr.*, and so frq. *zer*, where in earlier literat. *žes* is used; *zér-na* 1. **if one says,** esp. for the older *že-*

na, frq. 2. **if I may say so, so to speak, as it were;** **di-la či zer** what is this called? frq., also without *la;* to make a noise, e.g. **sag sag zér-wa** *C.* to foam with a hissing noise, to sparkle, of wine, beer; *zér-mkan* 1. he that is saying. 2. *W.*, said, called, mentioned, esp. for the older *žes byá-ba.* — **zér-ke'** *C.* rumour, report. — **zér-ṗog-čan** *W.* speaking in an uncivil or offensive manner. — *zer-ri C.* rumour. — 2 **to drive in,** nails, v. *γzér-ba.*

ཟེལ་མ་ *zél-ma* **small chip,** *šiṅ-zél* **wood-shavings** *W.*

ཟོ་ *zo* I. num. figure: 142.

II. imp. of *zá-ba.*

III. sbst. resp. *sku-zó*, = *lus-kyi ḱams* **physical constitution,** *sku-zo mdog légs-la* as the appearance of your majesty's bodily constitution is so excellent *Glr.*; *zo bzáṅ-ba* a good complexion *Cs.* — 2. **figure, delineation, representation,** perh. better to be spelt *bzo* (?) — 3. **mould,** *zo-čágs* showing mouldy spots *Sch.* (?); *zo-már* old, mouldy butter, so prob. *S.g.*; *zo-ša Lt.* mouldy meat

ཟོ་བ་ *zo-ba* 1. sbst., **pail, bucket,** *šiṅ-zo* wooden pail, *ču-zo* water-pail. — 2. vb. v. *bzó-ba.*

ཟོག་ *zog* 1. **deceit, fraud, falsehood** (*Lex.* = *rdzub*), *zóg-čan* 1. **lying, deceitful; liar** *W.* 2. **adulterate, counterfeit** *W.*; *zog-ldán, zóg-po Cs.* id., *zog-méd* the opp.; *sgyu-zóg* (religious) **hypocrisy** *Pth.*; *čos-zóg* **priestcraft** *Mil.*; **zol-zóg** = *zog W.* — 2. vulg. pronunciation in *C.* and *W.*, inst. of the following.

ཟོང་ *zoṅ* (vulgo *zog*) 1. **ware, merchandise, goods,** *zoṅ-min-smár* not goods but ready money *Lex.*; *rgyágs-zoṅ* goods taken by travellers along with them to be bartered for provisions; *smán-zoṅ* drugs; *ťsóṅ-zoṅ* **merchandise** *Cs.*; *zóṅ-rnams rnám-pa sna-tsógs* goods of all kinds; **zóg-gi dág-po** *Ts.* owner of the goods, master of the estate, heir, = *nór-bdag.* — 2. *Sch.* **worth, price**(?). — 3. *Sch.* **doubt**(?). — 4. *Sch.* **lie**(?).

ཟོན་ *zon* **attention, heed, care,** gen. *zon byéd-pa*, to pay attention, to take heed, to beware, *dgrá-la* of an enemy *Pth.*; also c. accus. *Mil.*; *zon sdig-pa spoṅ mi šes* seems to mean: not knowing the attention needful for renouncing sin *Thgy.*; *zon-méd* **heedless;** *zon-gráb*s **provision, precaution, preventive measure** *Sch.*

ཟོན་པ་ *zón-pa Ts.*, **stuff-** or **woolen shoes;** **bob-zón** id., covered with leather.

ཟོབ་ *zob Ts.*, **zob-zób ǰhé'-pa** **to shake thoroughly,** = *ˏdzól-ba.*

ཟོམ་ *zom* 1. **point, top,** *rdo-rǰei* of the *dor-ǰe Dom*; **summit,** of the Rirab and some other mountains *S.O.* and elsewh.; *zom-ḱóg* **dull, simple, stupid,** *Sch.* — 2. **cave** *Sch.*, *brag-zóm* rock-cavern.

ཟོར་ *zor*, 1. sup. of *zó-ba, bzó-ba Sch.* — 2. sbst. the weapons employed in combating the evil spirits in the *γtór-ma*, such as knife, sword, sling, bow and arrows etc.; *zor-ḱa* the fore- or front-part, the edge, of the weapons directed against the demons, *zór-ḱa ˏṗén-pa Cs.*: to fling those weapons against the spirits.

ཟོར་བ་ *zór-ba* **sickle,** *zór-bas rṅá-ba Mil.*, *γčód-pa Cs.* to cut with a sickle, *zór-lče* sickle-blade; *zor-čúṅ* small, *zor-čén* large sickle, scythe, though in Tibet as yet hardly known; *zor-rtúl* blunt, dull, *zor-rnón* sharp sickle: *zór-bu* = *zor-čúṅ.*

ཟོར་ཡང་ *zor-yáṅ Sch.*: **small, short** (?).

ཟོལ་ཚོ་ *zól-ťso* v. *ˏdzól-ba.*

ཟོལ་ཟོག་ *zol-zóg* **deceit, fraud, imposture, falsehood,** *zol-zóg byéd-pa, W.* **čo-če**, **to deceive, impose on,** e.g in traffic *Thgy.*, *zól-zog-čan* **deceitful, fraudulent,** *zol(-zog)-méd* without deceit, free from guile, artless *Mil.*

ཟོས་ *zos* v. *zá-ba.*

ཟླ་ *zla* 1. for *zlá-ba.* — 2. for *zlá-bo.*

ཟླ་བ་ *zlá-ba* I. sbst. 1. prov. *zla*, **moon,** frq.; *mḱai zlá-ba* **celestial moon** *Lex.*, to distinguish it from 2. *dús-kyi zlá-ba* **temporal moon** or **month,** *zlá-ba γčig, B, W.*, **da čig** *C.*, one month; **zlá-ba ma ˏḱor šog** come before the end of the month *Sch.*; *zlá-ba ťsáṅ-du nyé-bas* towards the expiration of the months (of pregnancy) *Dzl.*; *zla-dús ťém-pa daṅ* at the expiration of those months *Glr*; cf. also *ṅo* 5. — 3. symb. num: 1. — **Combinations and comp.** *zlá-bai dkyil-ˌkor, zla-dkyil,* **da kyir-mo** *W.* disk of the moon; **da gaṅ soṅ** *W.* the moon is full; **da gaṅ-po* or *son-te** *W. zlá-ba rgyás-pa Pth., nya-rgyás zlá-ba Pth.* full moon; *nya* day of full moon; *zla(-ba) kám(-pa), zla-gám, W.* **da-p̔éd** half moon, i.e. the first and last quarter; **semicircle,** *zlá-ba kám-pa ltá-bur bžág-go* they are placed round in a semicircle *Do.*; *dbyibs zla-gám ltá-bur yod* it is semicircular in shape *Glr.*; *zlá-bai ṅo* v. *ṅo*; *zla-ťéb = zla-šól*; *zla-nág* new moon *Sch.* (?); *zla-p̔ógs* monthly wages; *zla-tsés* 1. = *zlá-ba tsés-pa, tses-γsum-zlá-ba Mil.* the moon on the first two or three evenings of her being visible; **crescent,** *zla-tsés ltá-bu* in the shape of a crescent, *S.g.*; it is also used as an image of speedy decay. — 2. **date** *Schr.*(?) — *zla-mtsán* the monthly courses; also the discharges of them, *zla-mtsán ˌdzag* the catamenial discharges flow *Cs.*; *zla-mtsán-čan Stg., zla-mtsán daṅ ldán-pa S.g.* having the monthly courses; *zla(-ba)-šól, -žól, -ťéb, zla-lhág, W.* **da-ṭúl** **intercalary month;** the separate months of the year are usually counted from *zlá-ba dáṅ-po* to *bču-γnyís-pa*, yet there are also particular names for them, viz. acc. to *Cs.*:

1. *ˌbrúg-zla, ťui zlá-ba, rtá-pa zlá-ba,* माघ
2. *sbrúl-zla, krá-zla, dbó-zla,* उत्तरफ-ल्गुनी
3. *rta(i) zla(-ba), nág-zla,* चैत्र
4. *lúg-zla, sá-ga-zla-ba,* वैशाख
5. *spré-zla, snrón-zla,* ज्येष्ठा
6. *byá-zla, ču-snód-zla-ba,* पूर्वाषाढा
7. *kyi-zla, gró-bžin-zla-ba,* उत्तराषाढा
8. *p̔ág-zla, krúm-zla,* भद्रपदा
9. *byi-zla, ťa-skár-zlá-ba,* आश्विनी
10. *glaṅ-zla, smin-drúg-zla-ba,* कार्त्तिका
11. *stág-zla, mgó-zla,* मृगशिर
12. *yós-zla, rgyál-zla,* पौषा

II. vb., also *zló-ba, zlós-pa,* pf. *bzlas, bzlos,* fut. *bzlo,* imp. *zlos,* 1. **to say, tell, express.** *zloam mi zlo* shall you tell it or not? *Pth.*; *γžán-la zló-ba Lex.* to tell others; *yid-ma-raṅs-pa-nyid p̔yir zlós-par byéd-pa* to express one's dissatisfaction *Stg.*(?). — 2. **to murmur** or **mutter over,** to recite softly or quite silently, prayers, spells etc., also *žúb-bus zlá-ba Zam.*; *yi-ge-drúg-pa lan-čig bzlás-pai bsód-nams Glr.* the merit of saying once the six-syllable prayer, and as such saying generally is done repeatedly, it is synon. with **to repeat.** — 3. **to answer, reply** *Cs.*; *Mil.* ni f. — 4. undoubtedly a less correct spelling for *ˌda-ba* (for which reason the secondary forms with o are wanting), **to pass, to get beyond,** *la zlá-ba* to cross a mountain-pass, *nád-kyi la zlá-ba* to be past hope of recovery *Cs.*; also trs., *mya-ṅán-las zlá-ba* to deliver from pain, to help to eternal happiness.

ཟླ་བོ *zlá-bo* 1. = *grogs, W.* **yá-do**, **companion, associate,** *zlá-bo byéd-pa* **to accompany, attend, assist,** *rkún-zla* a thief's accomplice *Dzl.*; *ˌgrán-zla* **rival, competitor** (v. *ˌgrán-pa* extr.); *γnyén-zla,* v. *γnyen*; *bzá-zla* **spouse, consort** (male or female) *Lex.* — *srid-zla Mil.* partner for life; *zla-γzán* a woman whose husband is dead ('who has eaten him'). — 2. **friend, acquaintance** *B.* and col. — 3. **lover, bridegroom; spouse** in *C.* To *zla* standing for *zlá-bo*, may be referred *zlas-dbyé Zam.*, expl. by द्वन्द्व, **pair, couple, combination,** viz. of a thing and its reverse, hence *zlas-p̔yé-ba* **reverse, contrary,** e. g. *yód-pai zlas-p̔yé-ba méd-pa Sch.*

ཟླུག(ས)་པ *zlúg(s)-pa,* pf. *bzlugs,* fut. *bzlug,* **to give notice, send word, inform** *Sch.*, *p̔rin-yig-gis bzlúgs-pa* he informed him by a letter *Stg.*, not frq.; in *Lexx.* explained by *γžán-la snyád-pa,* and *gó-bar byed ˌjúg-pa.* —

ཟླུམ་པ *zlúm-pa* 1 adj., more frq. *zlúm-po,* (= **kor-kór** *C.*, **kyir-kyir** *W.*) **round, circular,** *dbyibs* in shape *Glr.*; **roundish, rounded, obtuse,** *zlúm-por rtsig-pa* to erect a round, cylindrical wall, e.g. for a monument; **clubby, clumsy,** e.g. of a short and thick tobacco-pipe; *rkáṅ-pa zlúm-pa* club-footed *Stg.*; **globular, spherical,** e.g. cavities in the human body *S.g.*; *dku-zlúm Zam.*

(acc. to the *Ssk.*) the interior rounding of the abdomen. — 2. vb. 1. **to mix together** *Sch.*; **to put together, collect,** *ts̓ogs* merit *Lex.* 2. for *btúm-pa Pth.*: *dgé-₀dún dbu-zlúm žabs-rjén* clerics with their heads wrapt up and barefooted. 3. for *₀dúm-pa.* — *zlum-ril* **globular** *Cs.* — **zlúm-bu** *W.* **host, swarm, troop, crowd.**

ཟླུམ་ཕུ་སེ་ *zlúm-p̔u-se* (or *rtse?*) a mole-like animal *Ld.* (whether the same as *rdza-bra?*).

ཟློ་བ་ *zló-ba* v. *zlá-ba,* II.

ཟློག་པ་ *zlóg-pa,* pf *zlogs,* fut. *bzlog,* trs. to *ldóg-pa,* **to cause to return:** 1. **to drive back, repulse,** an army *Dzl.*; **to dispel, expel,** evil spirits *Dom.*; **to send back.** — 2. in a gen. sense: **to send, dispatch,** people to fetch something *Dzl.* frq. — 3. **to turn off, divert,** *bsám-pa-las* from an intention *Dzl.*; with *blo* to divert the mind from, to dismiss a thought, to give up, to banish from one's thoughts *Thgy.*, *γnyén-gyi γduṅ-séms zlog dka* it is hard to give up the love of kindred altogether *Mil.*; *dei t̔ugs slar zlóg-tu γsol* we beg you to dismiss the thought of it *Dzl.*; **to dissuade from** *Tar.* 40, 5; **to avert,** injury, evil consequences, frq.; **to prevent,** *nad-sél* the healing of a disease *S.g.* — *zlog-t̔abs* antidote *Ma.* — 4 **to subvert, overthrow** (?). 5. *mii ṅo* **to resist, to be unyielding, uncompliant** *Dzl.*

ཟློས་གར་, ཟློད་གར་ *zlós-gar, zlód-gar Stg.* **a dance,** *zlós-gar byéd-pa* **to dance,** *slób-pa* to teach or learn dancing; *zlós-gar-mk̔an* a dancer.

ཟློས་པ་ *zlós-pa* v. *zlá-ba.*

གཟའ་ *γza* I. ग्रह 1. **planet,** *γza bdun* the well-known seven heavenly bodies called in ancient times planets, viz. Sun, Moon, Mercury, Venus, Mars, Jupiter and Saturn; sometimes the ascending knot (राहु) is added to the number, sometimes also the descending knot (केतु), and then there are *γza brgyad* or *γza dgu,* eight or nine planets. The former seven denote also the days of the week: *γza-nyi-ma* Sunday, *γza-zlá-ba* Monday, *γza-mig-dmár* Tuesday, *γza-lhág-ma* Wednesday, *γza-p̔úr-bu* Thursday, *γza-pa* (or *-wa*)*-sáṅs* Friday, *γza-spén-pa* Saturday, and the signs for them in the calendar are ?, ?, ?, ?, ?, ?, °; *γzai γnód-pa* hurtful influence of the planets. — 2. *γza-čén-po,* and often *γza* alone, = *rá-hu,* hence *nyi-zla-γzas-₀dzin* or *γzas-bzuṅ* **eclipse** of the sun or moon, v. *sgra-γčan*; acc. to *Pth.* every uncommon or alarming sidereal phenomenon seems to be personified as *γza.* — 3. symb. num.: 9. — 4. vulgo: **rainbow.** — *γza-skár,* 1. **planets and fixed stars,** *nyi-zla-γza-skár* the sun, moon, planets, and stars. — 2. **constellation,** *γza-skar-ṅán* an adverse configuration *S.g.* — *γza-k̔yim Cs.* 'the place', more corr. 'the house' of a planet, the constellation in which the planet stands. — *γza-nád Cs.* and *Schr.*: **apoplexy;** in *W.* it seems to be used only for **epilepsy;** *γza p̔óg-pa* id.; *γzá-p̔og-mkan, γzá-brgyab-pa* epileptic. — *blá-γza, sróg-γza, γšéd-γza, má-γza gróg-γza, bú-γza, dgrá-γza, klúṅ-si-dar-γza Wdk.* and several more, are astrological terms, not to be clearly defined. — II. sometimes for *bza,* q.v. — III. *W.* **rubble-stones, bowlders, detritus,** *γza-róṅ* ravine filled with detritus; a better spelling seems to be *rdza.*

གཟག་པ་ *γzág pa* v. *₀ts̓ág-pa, ₀dzág-pa.*

གཟགས་པ་ *γzágs-pa* 1. v. *γzábs-pa.* — 2. **to magnify, multiply** *Sch.*

གཟན་ *γzan* 1. v. *bzan* and *γzan-pa; γčan-γzan,* q.v. — 2. esp. *W.*, commonly *γzan-gós* **plaid,** = *bla-gós* v. *bla. γzan-stán Zam.* id.? *rṅul-γzán* **napkin,** nif. *Lex.*

གཟན་པ་ *γzán-pa* 1. **to eat, devour** *Cs.* — 2. **to gnaw,** mostly fig.: *ts̓ér-ma žábs-la γzan* the thorn hurts, annoys, the foot *Mil.*; of clothes: **to wear out** *C.*; adj. *γzán-pa* and *γzán-po* **worn-out, threadbare;** *séms-la γzan* it gnaws at the heart *Mil., sróg-la* it preys upon life *Mil.*, **ná-wa-la** *C.* it deafens the ears, = *sún-₀byin-pa; γzán-du skyúr-ba* (lit. to give to devour, e.g. a body to demons), **to scorn, slight, despise** *Mil.*; **to throw away, squander, waste, lavish,** gen. in the forms (*čud*)*-γzón-pa, γsón-pa,* v. *čud.*

གཟབ་པ་ *yzáb-pa* I. *Cs.* **'clean'**, *Sch.* also **'clear, careful'**; *bzáb-pa Cs.* **'fine, elegant'.** In books I met with neither form; in col. language, however, are used: **záb-mo** 1. **dressed up, smart,** = *mčór-po.* 2. **fond of dress, vain.** — **zab-če* W.* to dress one's self up. — **záb-gos* W.* festival raiment, holiday-clothes (opp. to *rgyún-gos*). — **zab-ṭód* W., *zab-ṭö* C.* (lit.: *sprod*) **taṅ soṅ** he is dressed up, very smart. — *Sch.*: *yzáb-yig*, 'elegant writing', the Tibetan printed letters, *dbú-čan.* —

II. v. *yzábs-pa.*

གཟབ་མ་ *yzáb-ma* **bundle, bunch,** of grapes *C.*

གཟབས་པ་ *yzábs-pa*, also *yzáb-pa*, *yzágs-pa Lex.*; imp. *yzobs*, **to use care, diligence,** *lo yčig zas-spyód yzábs-pas* by a careful diet continued for a year *Mṅg.*; **to take care, to beware,** *dé-las yzobs* beware of it, be on your guard against it *Sch.*

གཟར་ *yzar Lex.*, **peg, hook, wooden nail,** for hanging up things; *yzar-sláṅ* a pan that may be hung up.

གཟར་བུ་ *yzár-bu* (col. *zá-ru*) **ladle,** gen. of wood, *yzár-bu ˳p̔yar* she wields the ladle, she swings it for a blow *Mil.*; *dgáṅ-yzar* and *blúgs-yzar* two spoons or ladles, with long handles, used at burnt-offerings *Schl.* 249.

གཟར་བ་ *yzár-ba* 1. adj. *yzár-po*, **steep, rugged, precipitous,** *brag mtó-la yzár-ba-la* near a high, precipitous rock *Mil.*; *ri yzár-po, brag yzár-po* slope, declivity, of a hill or rock; *brag-yyaṅ-yzár Mṅg.* id.; *ri yzár-gyi ṅos* steep declivity, cliff *Thgy.*; *ri-yzar-č̔u* waterfall, cataract *Glr.*; *yzar-k̔yóm-pa* to get dizzy on a steep height *Sch.* — 2. vb. v. *˳dzár-ba.*

གཟས་པ་ *yzás-pa* **to be about, to be on the point, to prepare,** *mčóṅs-par, bsád-par yzás-pa-las* when he was on the point of leaping, of killing *Dzl.*; *rkó-bar yzás-so* he prepared, began, to dig out.

གཟི་ *yzi* 1. **shine, brightness, clearness, splendour;** **táṅ-zi* W.* **looming, mirage.** — 2. n. of a half-precious stone, variously coloured, brown, gray, streaked *Glr.*, *Pth.* — 3. v. sub *yzír-ba.* — 4. v. *bzi.* —

Comp. *yzi-čan* shining, bright, e. g. a star *W.* — *yzi-brǰid* 1. **brightness, beauty,** a fair, healthy complexion, = *mdaṅs*, or joined with it, frq; **majesty,** e. g. of deities etc. *Dzl.* 2. **honour, esteem, celebrity;** *yzi-brǰid-čan* 1. bright, beautiful, majestic. 2. celebrated, famous, distinguished. — *yzi-mdáṅs* 1. **healthy appearance** *S.g.* 2. vulgo also **evening-red, evening-sky,** ni f. — *yzi-byin* = *yzi-brǰid* 1; *yzi-byin nyáms-pa* looking poor, emaciated, worn out, from hunger, sufferings *Stg.*; *yzi-byin-čan* bright, shining; *yzi-˳ód* bright gloss or lustre *Lex.*

གཟི་རུ་ *yzi-ru* col. for *yzér-bu* **a little nail** *W.*

གཟིག་ *yzig* **leopard;** *yzig-ris* its colour.

གཟིག་མོ་ *yzig-mo* **porcupine** *Ssk.*, *yzig-móṅ* id.?

གཟིགས་པ་ *yzigs-pa*, resp. for *mtóṅ-ba* and *ltá-ba* 1. **to see,** *˳óṅs-par* seeing that he had come *Dzl.*; in indirect questions, to see whether? — what sort of? — etc.; **to see through, to get an insight** *Tar.* 94, 6, *Schf.*; **to look,** *šár-la* towards the east *Glr.*; **to look (for),** *yzigs-pas mi ˳dug* when he looked (for it), there was nothing to be seen; **to look at, to regard, mind, esteem,** *sku-tšé-la mi yzigs-pa* not regarding your Honour's life *Dzl.* — 2. equivalent to: **to give, grant,** *sá-bon žig tugs-rǰe yzigs dgos* have the goodness to give me some seed, prob. only breviloquence for *sá-bon žig ynáṅ-bar tugs-brtsé-bar yzigs šig.* — *yzigs-rtén* resp. **present, gift,** *yzigs-rtén-du skúr-ba* to charge a person with the delivery of a present *Pth.* — **zig-dod-čan* W.* vain. — **zig-po* W.* neat, well dressed, resp. for *mčór-po.* — — *yzigs-mo* resp. for *ltád-mo*, *mé-tog dé-la yzigs-mor byón-pa-las* as he came in order to look at the flower *Pth.*

གཟིང་བ་ *yziṅ-ba* for *˳dziṅs-pa Glr.*

གཟིངས་ *yziṅs* **vessel, ship, float, ferry,** also fig.; *gru-yziṅs* id., frq.; *yziṅs čén-po žig byás-te* equipping a large vessel *Glr.*;

γziṅs-čúṅ a small vessel *Cs.*; γziṅs-pa ship-master, captain.

གཟིམ་པ་ *γzim-pa*, also with *mnal*, resp. for *γnyid-log-pa*, 1. **to fall asleep** *Dzl.* — 2. **to sleep,** *rgyál-po γzim-pa-las* whilst the king was sleeping *Glr.* — 3. **to expire, to die** *Tar.* 4, 20. —

Comp. **zim-kyoṅ** W., resp. for *rkyóṅ-rtse*, candle, lamp. — *γzim-k̔aṅ* 1. sleeping-room. 2. dwelling, habitation. — *γzim-k̔ebs* quilt. — *γzim-k̔om* cloak-bag, portmanteau. — *γzim-k̔ri* bedstead. — *γzim-gur* sleeping-tent. — **zim-gág** C. porter, door-keeper. — *γzim-ča* bedding, bed-clothes *Gyatch.* — **zim-tiṅ, zim-ter** W. lamp. — **zim-tiṅ** (lit. *-btiṅ*) *Sik.* bedstead? — *γzim-t̔úl* sheep-skins for night-quarters. — *γzim-dpon* body-servant, valet-de-chambre, = *sku-mdún-pa*; *γzim-p̔rúg* his subordinate servants or pages. — *γzim-mál* bed-linen. — *γzim-yól* bed-curtain.

གཟིམ་གཟིམ་ *γzim-γzim W.*, *C.*, **mig zim-zim ča dug** W. the eyes are dazzled, by a glaring light.

གཟིར་བ་ *γzir-ba* (acc. to *Cs.* fut. of *ₒtsir-ba*, certainly related to it, but chiefly used in an intellectual sense), **to be pressed, harassed, troubled, to suffer,** to be pressed by necessity, to suffer from hunger, disease etc. *B.*, *C.* — *Sch.* also *γzi γzir-ba* a stinging pain in the chest.

གཟིལ་ *γzil, γzil-bun-pa C.* = *spu-ziṅ byed-pa.*

གཟུ་བ་ *γzú-ba* **a lever, bar;** = *γšó-mo Cs.*; *γzu-ṙñás* a prop *Cs.*

གཟུ་བོ་ *γzú-bo Cs.*: 1. **straight, right.** — 2. **upright, honest.** *Lexx.*: *t̔ugs γzú-bo*, from which it appears to be a word of civility, but little known. *Sch.* has besides: *γzu-dpáṅ*, which he renders by 'witness, mediator'.

གཟུ་ལུམ(ས)་ *γzu-lúm(s) Lexx.* = *bab-čol* and सहसा, hence signifying **rashness, impetuosity,** so *Cs.*, and therefore *γzu-lúm-čan* **inconsiderate;** *γzu-lúm byed-pa* **to act rashly;** *Sch.* also: **disobedience, pride, haughtiness.**

གཟུག་ *γzug* 1. v. *zug.* — 2. **top,** *lai* of a mountain-pass *Mil.*

གཟུག་གེ་བ་ *γzúg-ge-ba* **hurting, giving pain,** *žes γzúg-ge-ba žús-nas* as she spoke words that gave so much pain *Mil.nt.*

གཟུག་པ་ *γzúg-pa* **to be able to bear, to sustain,** v. sub *tsoγ.*

གཟུགས་ *γzugs*, *Ssk.* रूप, 1. **figure, form, shape,** *p̔yi-rol-gyi γzúgs-rnams* the forms of the sensible world, the impressions that are made on the eye *Wdṅ.*; *mig-gis γzúgs-rnams mtoṅ* the forms (of things) are seen with the eyes; *ráb-tu-byuṅ-bai γzugs* the (painted) figure of a priest *Glr.*; sim. *klui γzugs γsér-las byás-pa Tar.*; *lus-γzúgs* shape of body, stature, frq.; *srin-moi γzúgs-su byéd-pa* to transform one's self into a Rākshasi *Glr.*; *rnál-ₒbyor-pai γzugs byéd-pa* to assume the outward appearance of a hermit *Mil.*; in metaphysics: form, body, as one of the five Skandhas, v. *p̔úṅ-po.* — 2. resp. *sku-γzúgs*, *W *zúg-po** = *lus*, **body,** **zúg-po ṭú-če** W. to wash the body, to bathe; **zúg-po záṅ-wa mi dug, mi-dé-wa dug** C., **dé-mo mi dug** W. euphem. for: she has just her courses. — *γzugs-ṅán* ill-formed, too short in stature *S.g.*; *γzugs ₒk̔úm-pa* to bend, twist one's body, and *γzúgs-kyis ₒtsó-ba*, *quaestum corpore facere*, are given by *Sch.*; *γzugs riṅ-mo* long-stalked *Glr.* — 3. in physics: **body, matter, substance,** *γzúgs-čan*, *γzúgs-su snáṅ-ba* composed of matter, material, substantial; *γzúgs-čan ma yin-pa*, *γzúgs-su mi snáṅ-ba*, *γzugs-méd* immaterial, unsubstantial; *γzúgs-med-pai* (or *-kyi*) *skad* a ghostlike voice *Mil.*; *γzugs-k̔áms* the range of the material world — *γzugs-brnyán* v. *brnyan.*

གཟུགས་པ་ *γzúgs-pa* v. *ₒdzúg-pa.*

གཟུང་བ་ *γzúṅ-ba* v. *ₒdzin-pa*; *γzuṅ-ₒdzin Mil.* frq., **interest, inclination, bias,** *γzuṅ-ₒdzin-brál* being free from interest, unbiased, apathetic, which always is praised as an indispensable quality and the true happiness of an ascetic, and the literal equivalent to which in *Ssk.* may be regarded to be ग्राह्यग्राह; yet *Was.* p. 304 renders it by 'idea and reason'. — γzuṅ-γzér peg on a wall, = rtsig-ṗúr; a hold, support, rail, balustrade (?) *Stg.*

གཟུངས་ γzuṅs, frq. spelt *zuṅs*, yet properly only in compounds, lit. **a hold,** i.e. 1. **power, strength** *Schr.*; *γzuṅs-žán Sch.*: **loose, weak, without a hold, untenable;** *γzuṅs-zád* **weakened, debilitated,** esp. of women by loss of blood *Cs.*; *γzuṅs-rtén* **prop, support.** — 2. *lus-zúṅs* the seven constituents necessary for **healthy life,** धातु, chyle, blood, fat, muscle, bone, marrow, semen *Med.* — 3. धारणी, also *γzuṅs-sṅágs*, **spells, magic sentences,** first used in the doctrine of Mahāyāna, from which the mysticism of later times originated, v. *Was.* (142, 177); they are for the most part but short, and always end in a string of Sanskrit syllables, that are devoid of any meaning. Whole volumes are filled with them.

གཟུད་པ་ *γzúd-pa*, fut. of *₀dzúd-pa*.

གཟུམ་པ་, གཟུར་བ་, གཟུལ་བ་ *γzúm-pa, γzúr-ba, γzúl-ba* v. *₀dzúm-pa* etc.

གཟེ་བ་ *γzé-ba Sch.* 1. **pannier, dosser** *Dzl.* ༧༥༥, 14. — 2. **home, habitation, nest.** — 3. **swift,** in running *Thgy.*, **quick,** in comprehending *Sch.*

གཟེ་མ་ *γzé-ma Med.*; *Cs.*: 'a horned aquatic plant'; *γzé-mai čaṅ Med.* beer made of it.

གཟེ་རུ་ *γzé-ru*, for *γzér-bu* **a little nail.**

གཟེ་རེ་ *γze-ré* **looking poorly** *Sch.*; *γze-ré byéd-pa* **to be poorly, ailing, ill** *Sch.*

གཟེག(ས) *γzeg(s)*, कण. **a little grain, atom;** *γzeg ča čuṅ* a small particle *Lex.*; *γzég-ma* prob. id. (*Cs.* also: filth?) *γzeg-zán* कणाद. 'atom-eater', n. of the founder of the Vaiseshika-philosophy, also called Kasyapa; *γzeg-zán-pa* its professors *Wdṅ.*

གཟེག་མོ་བྱི་ *γzég-mo-byi* **hedgehog** *Sch.*

གཟེངས་ *γzeṅs* **height, loftiness, sublimity, gloriousness,** esp. in *γzeṅs stód-pa*, also *yar γzeṅs stód-pa Pth.*; to praise, extol, glorify *Mil.* (cf. *seṅ*).

གཟེད་པ་ *γzéd-pa* I. vb. 1. v. *₀dzéd-pa.* — 2. **to hit** *Sch.* — II. sbst. *Sch.*: 'a long spike'.

གཟེད་མ་ *γzéd-ma Cs.*, gen. *γzéb-ma*, also *γzebs Sch.* 1. **pannier,** with lid *Kun.*; a box-shaped **basket** with lid *C.* — 2. **cage, aviary** *Lex.*; **prison** *Sch.* — 3. **net, snare** *Sch.*

གཟེམ་པ་ *γzém-pa*, 1. *Cs.* = *₀dzém-pa.* — 2. **to do a thing gently,** **zém-te dul-wa** *C.* to walk softly, **žág-pa** *C.* to put down softly.

གཟེར་ *γzer*, also *zer*, 1. **nail, tack,** *šiṅ-γzer* wooden nail, *lčágs-γzer* iron nail; *γnám-γzer* 'plug or bolt for fastening a door (at the top)' *Cs.*; **gyáb-če** *W.*, **gyág-pa** *C.*, *γzér-ba Glr.*, *₀dzúg-pa Lex.*, *₀débs-pa* and more frq. *γzér-gyis ₀débs-pa B.* to knock in, drive in, nails; *lag-zér gyág-pa* driving red-hot tacks into the finger-ends, a kind of torture in *C.*; *γzér-bu*, vulgo **zé-ru, zi-ru** a little nail. — 2. **a help to memory,** for retaining a lesson or doctrine, **mnemonic verse** *Mil.* — 3. **ray, beam,** *nyi-γzér* sun-beam, *₀od-γzér* ray of light; *ťsa-γzér* 'a hot beam', *bsil-γzér* 'a cool beam' (?) *Cs.* — 4. **pain, ache, illness,** (*γ*)*zug-γzér* id., *mgo-γzér* head-ache, *rgyu-γzér* gripes, colic, *ṗo-γzér* stomach-ache, *rtsib-γzér* pleurisy, *so-γzér* tooth-ache *Cs.*; **zer-kyáṅ ṅá-la gyáb-ba rag*, or *táṅ-ṅa rág** *W.* I feel the pains of labour; **zer-láṅ** *W.* spasms in the stomach or something similar; *γzer-₀ṗrig-pa* to writhe with pain; *γzer ₀ṗo* the pain passes from one part of the body to another *S.g.*

གཟེར་བ་ *γzer-ba* 1. **to bore into, drive** or **knock into,** *zer C.* nails, **ná-da** *C.* an arrow through the ear, Chinese punishment. — 2. **to feel pain, to be suffering** (= *γzír-ba?*); *čaṅ-₀ťúṅ γzer* beer-tippling produces pain *Med.*

གཟེར་བུ་ *γzér-bu*, v. *γzer* 1, extr.

གཟོ་བ་ *γzó-ba* 1. v. *bzó-ba.* — 2. **to remember, keep in mind, own, acknowledge,** esp. *drin* a favour, also *byás-pa*, as much as **to be grateful;** *dé-dag-gi byas-pa γzó-bai ṗyir* from gratefulness for their kindness *Dzl.*; *byas mi γzo* they are ungrateful; *drin γzó-*

ba, drin γzó-bai sems gratitude, drin mi γzó-ba ingratitude; drin-γzo-čan **grateful.**

གཟོང་, གཟོང་བུ་ γzoṅ, γzóṅ-bu **chisel, graving-tool, puncheon.**

གཟོད་ γsod 1. **now, this moment,** (opp. to dá či, before, a little time ago) *Mil.;* at least just now, *Mil.; da-γzod(-čig),* id.; *da-γzód bu yin-par ča yod* now I know that it is my son; **not until now, then for the first time** (in narratives with preterite tenses) *Pth.;* **then at length** *Pth. — γzód-ťsor-ba, ťos-pa, -rdog-pa Dzl.* **to hear, to receive information, to be informed, to be told,** *γšégs-pa* that he was gone *Dzl. —* 3. *γzód-ma* **beginning, commencement** v. *γdód-ma.*

གཟོན་པ་ γzon-pa, γsón-pa with čud, v. čud and *γzán-pa* extr.; *bsgó-ba rnar γzón-pa* the precept was wastled in the ear, it entered at one ear and left at the other; one *Lex.* gives the explanation: *bsláb-bya-la mi nyán-pai don.*

གཟོབ་པ་ γzób-pa 1. *Sch.* **quick, sharp, clever; caution, circumspection.** — 2. v. *γzáb-pa.*

བཟང་ bzaṅ 1. n. of a medicinal plant in Tibet *Wdṅ.* — 2. whatever is **good,** v. *bzáṅ-ba.* — 3. **agreement, treaty,** v. *sgrig-pa.*

བཟང་བ་ bzáṅ-ba adj. and sbst., *bzáṅ-po* adj 1. **good, (भद्र).** in every respect, answering its purpose, excellent, suited, morally good; *bsam-pa bzaṅ-po* a good resolution *Mil.; bdag bzaṅ-na* if I behave well, keep myself free from blame, *Do.* (cf. *légs-pa*). — 2. **fair, beautiful,** as to the body, frq.; *nags-ťsal bzáṅ-po* a beautiful wood *Mil.; γzugs-bzáṅ* of a fine, tall stature. — sbst.: *bzaṅ* the good, that which is good in the abstract; *bzáṅ-nas byuṅ* 'it came from good' i.e. from a good heart; *dei γzáṅ-lan-du* as an acknowledgment of his goodness *Glr.* —

Comp. *bzáṅ-kyi* a species of large dogs *Cs. — bzaṅ-sgrig* treaty of peace, **ǰhé-pa** *C.*, **čó-če* W.* to make peace, to come to an agreement, to conclude a treaty, frq.; *bzaṅ-sgrig-pa* id. — *bzaṅ-ṅán* good and bad, good and ill, *bzaṅ-ṅan-ₒbriṅ γsum* good, bad, and indifferent; *bzaṅ-ṅán ₒbyéd-pa* to discern between good and evil, to choose one or the other *Schr.; bzaṅ-ṅán rtógs-pai sems* is an attempt to find an adequate expression for the word 'conscience' *Chr. P.* — *bzaṅ-ťál* a good exit out of the *ₒkór-ba* (the cycle of transmigrations), a happy departure *Thgr. — bzaṅ-drúg* 'the six good things' (nutmeg, cloves, saffron, cardamom, camphor, sandal-wood) *C.;* used by *Mil.* also in a fig. sense; in *W.* simply: cloves. — *bzaṅ-ₒdód* self-complacency. — *bzaṅ-spyód* 1. *Cs.* good action. 2. n. of a prayer of particular efficacy *Glr.*, also called *smón-lam-gyi rgyál-po. — bzaṅ-btsón* v. *btson.* — **zaṅ-lúg* W.* good behaviour, good treatment, **mi žig-ne ťób-če** to experience such from a person, **mi-la čó-če** to show it to a person.

བཟངས་ bzaṅs, only in *kaṅ-bzáṅs*, which *Wdṅ.* explains by *káṅ-pa brtségs-pa* a large house of several stories, applied only to the abodes of gods; in *W.* also the cubical part of the Chodten is called so.

བཟད་པ་ bzád-pa rarely for *bzod-pa; mi-bzád-pa* 1. **intolerable** *Dzl., Do.* — 2. **irresistible** *Do.*

བཟན་ bzan, sometimes for *zan,* esp. **food of animals,** *bzan ₒtsól-ba* to seek food *Mil*; **pasture, pasturage,** *bzán-la skyél-ba* to place in pasture, to let feed *Glr.; bzán-pa Ts.* id.

བཟབ་པ་ bzáb-pa v. *γzáb-pa.*

བཟའ་ bza, I. vb., fut. of *zá-ba,* **to eat,** *bza* this is to be eaten, in dietetic prescriptions; v. also *zá-ba.* — II. sbst. 1. (rarely *γza*) seems to denote the members of a family, they being conceived as **eaters** or **fellow-boarders;** *bzá-tso máṅ-poi pa-má* parents that have a large family *Mil.; bza maṅs náṅ-na* among a numerous household *Mil.; bza-drúg* a family, a company at table, of six persons, ni f. *C.;* in certain combinations: **wife, spouse,** *rgyá-mo bza* the Chinese spouse, *bál-mo bza* the Nepalese spouse (of the king), *Glr.* frq. — 2. **meat, food,** *bzá-ba daṅ btúṅ-ba* meat and drink, specially the quality and quantity of food, *zá-*

ma bċud če-la bza če-ba nutritive and substantial food *Mil. nt.*

Comp. *bza-γtád, bzá-bai γtád-so* store of provisions, *bzá-γtad-méd-pa* not having such a store *Mil.* — *bza-mi* 1. = *k̓yo-šug* **husband and wife,** *byéd-pa* to become husband and wife, to marry each other, *k̓yod dan̄ n̄a γnyis bza-mi byao* we will marry each other *Glr.*; *bza-mír byin-gyis rlób-pa* to give the nuptial benediction, to unite in wedlock, to marry *Glr.*; *dbúl-po bza-mi γnyis* a poor married couple *Glr.* 2. in a wider sense: **household,** *bza-mi nyi-šu-rtsa-γnyis* a household of twenty two persons *Mil.* — *bza-med* **ill-fed, lean** *Mil.* — *bzá-ťso* plur. of *bza.* — **za-dá** (lit. *za-zlá*) *W., C.* partner, wife. — *bza-šin̄* **fruit-tree,** *bza-šin̄-rá-ba* orchard, *bza-šin̄-ra-ba-srún̄-pa* watchman or keeper of it *Dzl.* — *bza-šúg* (vulg. *-*šúb**) = *bza-mi C.*

བཟར་ *bzar* sometimes for *zar*; *bzár-ba* v. *ₒdzár-ba.*

བཟས་པ་ *bzás-pa* v. *zá-ba* and *γzás-pa.*

བཟི་ *bzi* (sometimes *γzi, zi*), **drunken fit, intoxication, stupefaction;** *bzi sáns-te* having become sober again after intoxication *Glr.*; **zi-čan** *W.* intoxicated, muddled, *bzí-ba* 1. vb. **to become intoxicated, to get drunk,** *bzi-bar ₒgyúr-ba* id.; *bzi-bar byéd-pa* to intoxicate, to make drunk *Cs.* 2. sbst. **state of intoxication.** 3. adj. **drunk, intoxicated** *C.*

བཟུང་བ་ *bzún̄-ba* v. *ₒdzin-pa*; it is used as an adv. in the form of *bzún̄s-te,* e.g. *dei núb-mo-nas bzún̄s-te* from that evening (prop. beginning with that evening), ever since that evening *Mil.*; *ťses brgyad-nas bzun̄s-te nyai bar-du* during the time from the 8th. to the 15th. (day of the month).

བཟུར་ *bzur* v. *dzúr-ba.*

བཟེ་རེ་ *bze-ré,* also *bze Sch.*: **pain,** *bze-re-čan* suffering pain, *bze-ré byéd-pa* to inflict pain, to torment. (*Cs.*: 'indignation; angry; to be angry with.')

བཟེད་ *bzed* 1. in comp.: *p̓yag-bzéd* **(hand-) basin** *Cs.*; *lhun̄-bzéd* **beggar's bowl, alms-pot,** frq.; *bzed-snód* **salver** *Sch.*; *bzed-žál Lex.,* also *žal-bzéd Cs.*: 'spitting-box; acc. to oral expl. a cup into which the higher class of people skim off the superabundant grease swimming on the tea (v. *ja*); *bzéd-pa* v. *ₒdzéd-pa.* — 2. *bzed-snyóms-pa* **wire-drawing** *Sch.*

བཟོ་ *bzo* 1. **work, labour,** *bzoi rnam-ₒgyur* the beauty of a work or workmanship *Glr.*; *bzo rgya-nág-gi lugs* as to the workmanship it is in Chinese style *Glr.* (by some the word is taken in these passages in the signification 3). — *bzó-la sréd-pa* liking labour, laborious, = *las Stg.*; **zo ťe-rél, mi-la ma (s)tan** *W.* the work is not yet finished, do not let people see it yet! *snai bzo byed-gin ₒdug-pas* being just occupied with working out the noses *Glr.* — 2. **manufacture, art, trade, handicraft,** *rin-po-čei* art of a jeweler, *gos-* trade of a tailor, *dúul-* art of a silversmith, *lčags-* trade of a blacksmith, *tag-* of a rope-maker, *rdo-* of a stone-cutter, *rtsig-* of a mason, *bzan̄-* of a copper-smith, *šin̄-* of a joiner or carpenter, *γser-* art of a goldsmith, *lha-* of an image-maker, *lham-bzo* trade of a shoemaker. — 3. also *zo,* **figure, image, picture, resemblance,** = *dbyibs,* **ă-me zo dug** *W.* he is the exact likeness of his mother; **appearance, physical constitution,** v. *zo.* — 4. sometimes for *bzó-pa, bzó-bo,* so that all the words enumerated sub 2 may also denote the artist or workman. —

Comp. and deriv. *bzó-k̓an̄* **workshop.** — *bzo-k̓yád, bzoi kyad Glr.* **work of art,** masterpiece, elegant piece of workmanship. — *bzo-k̓yúd, bzo-k̓yun Cs.*: 1. potter's wheel. 2. a hydraulic machine(?). — *bzo-grá* **academy** of arts, mechanics' institution *Cs.* — *bzo-rgyú* working-materials *Glr.* — **zó-bsta*(?), *zób-sta, zó-sta** *W.* **form, fashion,** e.g. **style** of a house, its architecture; form, of a bottle, a lamp or candle stick, of any production of art; **zor-dó** anvil-stone *W.* (*bzo-rdo*). — *bzó-pa* **artist,** mechanic, *dúul-bzo-pa,* silversmith, and so forth. — *bzo-dpón* master, over journey-men or the students of an art. — *bzó-ba,* pf. *bzos,* **to make, to manufacture** *C.* (for the *byéd-pa* of *B.,* and **čo-če** of *W.*), **par zó-wa** to print; **sém-kyi zó-wa** *C.* to frame in one's mind, contrive, invent; **zo-*

pe̦ tsa* manufactured salt, *zo̦-pe̦ ser̦* artificial gold *Wdṅ.* — *bzó-bo* = *bzó-pa, bzó-bo mḱás-pa* a skilful artist *Mil.; bzo-byéd* 1. id. 2. **imaginative faculty, imagination,** ni f. — *bzo-lás* work *Sch*

བཟོད་པ་ *bzód-pa* (rarely *bžád-pa*) I. vb., ཀྵམ, 1. **to suffer, bear, endure,** c. acc., *mig ná-ba ma bzód-nas* not being able to bear the pain in his eyes *Dzl.*; *lus ₒdis na mi bzod* with this body pain, disease, cannot be endured *Thgy.*; *saṅs-rgyás-kyi túgs-rǰe čé-bas ma bzód-nas* seems to imply: Buddha in his mercy not suffering this, but checking the mischief; — also c. dat.: *ₒǰám-po-la mi bzod* he cannot bear what is soft or smooth *Dzl.*; *ma-bdé-ba bág-tsam-la bzód-pa mi byéd-de* getting so fretful through a slight indisposition *Mil.*; *ltá-basmi bzód-de* finding it unbearable for his eyes *Pth.*; *drán-pas mi bzód-de* as much as: so that he almost lost his senses over it *Pth.*; *bzód-tabs* (or *bzod-glags*)-*méd-par ₒbyúṅ-ba* or *ₒgyúr-ba* not to be able to bear . . . any longer, frq.; *mi-bzód-pa* or *-bzád-pa* adj., **unbearable, intolerable,** also **irresistible;** *ma bzód-nas* not being able to resist any longer *Dzl.* — 2. **to forgive, pardon,** *sṅan-čad ťo-ₒtsám-pa bzód-par ysol* to pardon our former tricks is what we beg *Mil.*; *rtá-la ma skyón-pa bzód-par bžes ₒtsal* that I did not request you to mount, this I beg you to forgive me *Mil.*; *bzód-par ysól-lo byas kyaṅ* although she begged pardon *Pth.*; *skyón-rnams yé-šes-spyan-ldan-rnams-la bzód-par ysol* with respect to the deficiencies I pray for the indulgence of the very wise (readers); *bzod-ysól byéd-pa* to ask pardon, forbearance *Pth.* —

II. sbst. 1. **patience** (*Ssk.* क्षान्ति), *bzód-pa sgóm-pa* to exercise one's self in patience *Dzl.* ༢, 12; but also, to have patience, to show forbearance; *bzód-pa bžés-pa*, id. resp. (v. also above I, 2); *bzód-pa-čan* **patient;** *bzod-srán* unwearied patience; *bzod-pa-čuṅ* impatient *Mil.*, *bzod-med Cs.* id. — 2. in asceticism: **perseverance, stedfast adherence to the four truths,** constancy in pursuing the path that has been entered upon, *mi skye-bai čos-la bzod-pa* acc. to *Was.* id., being at the same time no longer subject to re-births, p. (140). —

Observ. So far as 'to forgive' implies patience, forbearance, it may be rendered by *bzód-pa*; but as the Scriptural view of 'forgiveness of sin' involves more than that, other expressions, such as *bú-lon sél-ba*, must be resorted to with reference to the latter.

བཟོབ་པ་ *bzób-pa Sch.* = *ysób-pa.*

བཟོམ་ *bzom* **tub,** carried on the back, to convey water, v. *ču-bzóm* sub *ču.*

བཟླ་བ་ *bzlá-ba* v. *zlá-ba.*

བཟླས་བརྗོད་ *bzlas-brǰód* (cf. *zlá-ba* II, 2); *zlá-ba* in a strict sense, is stated to be **the silent,** *brǰód-pa* **the soft, yet audible pronouncing of spells** etc., *bzlas-brǰod* signifying both together; *bzlas-brǰód byéd-pa* to mutter over *Glr.*; *mú-stegs-pai bzlas-brǰód* Brahmanical spell-murmuring *Thgy.*

བཟླུམ་པ་ *bzlúm-pa* v. *zlúm-pa.*

བཟློ་བ་ *bzló-ba* v. *zló-ba.*

བཟློག་ *bzlog* **the contrary, the reverse,** *prá-ba-las bzlog sbóm-po* the contrary of thin is thick *Lex.*

བཟློས་ *bzlos,* v. *zló-ba.*

འ

འ *a*, 1. a letter peculiar to the Tibetan language, which, contrary to ཨ (q.v.) denotes the pure vowel, without any admixture of a consonant sound. The difficulty which attaches to the articulation of this vowel, requiring an opening of the glottis before it is sounded, has occasioned a great variety of pronunciation in the different provincial dialects. Vide Phonetic Table with its explications. — 2. numerical figure: 23.

འ་ཅག་ *ˏá-čag*, Cs. **we,** v. *ˏú-čag*.

འ་ཅི་ *ˏa-či* n. of a country Glr.

འ་ཏི་ཝ་ *ˏa-ti-wa*, with *lóg-pa*, Sch.: **to perform somersets, to tumble over, to roll.**

འ་ན་ཡང་ *ˏa-na-yaṅ* **although,** Sch.; *ˏa-na-ma-na* Sch.; **perfectly alike, having a striking resemblance** (?).

འ་མ་ *ˏá-ma* **but,** e.g. *ˏá-ma ma r̀jed čig* but do not forget! Cs.

འ་འུར་ *ˏa-úr* Sch.: **'shaking or rattling sounds'** cf. *ˏur-ˏúr*.

འང་ *ˏaṅ* 1. like *yaṅ*, attached to conjunctions, and corresponding to the English **ever, soever,** after vowels, col. also after consonants, e.g. *nam-ˏaṅ*. — 2 *ˏáṅ-sgra, bóṅ-bui* Cs. the braying of an ass.

འང་ཀེ་ *ˏáṅ-ke* (not ident. with *áṅ-gi* number), a mystical character, frq. occurring in certain finical ornaments or flourishes called *sbrúl-mgo*, occasionally also in written words.

འབ་པ་ *ˏáb-pa* Ts. **to bark.**

འར་པོ, འར་ཅན *ˏár-po, ˏár-čan* Ts. **angry** = *ɣtúm-po*.

འར་བ་ *ˏár-ba* C. **lot,** *rgyáb-pa* to cast, = *rgyan rgyáb-pa*.

འར་འུར་ *ˏar-ˏúr* v. *ˏur-ˏúr*.

འར་ཡང་ *ˏár-yaṅ* **also, too, likewise** Sch.

འི་ *ˏi* 1. num. figure: 53. — 2. W. demonstr. pron. inst. of *ˏdi*, **this,** also *'i-po*.

འུ་ *ˏu* 1. num. figure: 83. — 2. sbst. **kiss,** v. *ˏo*. — 3. also *ˏo*, Cs.: demonstr. pron., **this,** *ˏú-ni-ru, ˏú-nir, ˏó-nir*, **hither;** Ts. *wú-ahi* **this.**

འུ་སྒྲ་ *ˏú-sgra* Glr. **noise of many foot-steps,** prob. = *ˏúr-sgra*.

འུ་ཅག་ *ˏú-čag* 1. also *ˏó-čag* Glr., *ˏó-čog* Thgy., *ˏú-bu-čag* Dzl. pers. pron. **we.** — 2. **chimney** W. (?).

འུ་ཐུག་ *ˏu-túg* Sch.: 'Lüderlichkeit, auch

ཨུ་ཚུགས་ *'u-tsúgs'*; but in W. *'un-tug čó-če* means **to break out into a violent passion,** and *'ún-tug-k'an* or *-čan* **angry;** in C. *mú-tug-pa* and *dúg-tug-pa* **to be at a loss;** so also in Mil.

འུ་བུ་ *ˏú-bu* v. *ˏú-čag*.

འུ་རུ་རུ་ *ˏu-ru-rú* Sch. = *ur*.

འུ་ལག་ *ˏu-lág* **compulsory post-service,** the gratuitous forwarding of letters, luggage and persons, the supply of the requisite porters and beasts of burden (also more immediately these themselves), — originally a socage-service rendered to lords and proprietors, government officers and priests; in more recent times remunerated and legally regulated in those parts that are visited by European travellers; *mi-la ˏu-lág skúl-ba* to impose such services, by exacting porters etc. Pth., *ˏgél-ba* id.; *skyél-ba* prob. to forward by Ulag; (Cs. limits the signification too much).

འུ་སུ་ *ˏú-su* Lt. **coriander seed.**

འུག་པ་ *ˏúg-pa*, **owl,** Lt.; *ˏug-rgán* Sch. the great horn-owl, *ˏug(-gu)-čúṅ* the little owl; *ˏug-mig* owl's eyes (Cs. 'large languishing eyes', Sch.: 'large protruding eyes'); *ˏúg-mig-čan* having such eyes, *ˏúg mig-pa* or *-ma* a goggle-eyed man or woman Cs. — 2. Ld. also for *yug-po* **oats.**

འུག་སིངས་ *ˏug-siṅs* v. *siṅs-po*.

འུད་ *ˏud* 1. Cs. **swaggering, bragging, bombast, fustian;** *ˏud čer smra-ba* to swagger, brag, gen. *wur sé-pa*, C. — 2. = *yud* Thgy., *ˏud-kyis*, **in a moment, instantly, suddenly.** — 3. **command, order** (?), Sch.: *ˏud-sgrog-pa* to make known an order.

འུབ་པ་ *ˏub-pa* **to sweep** or **rake together** with one's hands, *paṅ-pas ˏub-kyis bsdus-te* Pth. with the arms gathering **all** into one heap.

འུམ་བུ་གླང་མཁར་ *ˏum-bu-glaṅ-mk'ar* n. of the palace of the ancient Tibetan king **Thothori,** Glr.

འུར་ *ˏur* 1. **noise, din, clashing, cracking, roar** of a tempest etc., but also and not less.

a low, humming noise, *rná-bai bú-ga bkág-pai tse ur-úr žés-pai sgra* the humming in the ears produced by stopping them *Wdṅ.*, *ur-úr-po-yi sgra* id. *Wdṅ.*; *rná-ba úr-la krog* there is a buzzing in my ear *S.g.*; *ur ldaṅ* or *byuṅ* a noise is heard; *Cs* more particularly: **talk, babbling, chit-chat,** *ur-ytoṅ-ba* to talk, to chat; **toṅ-ur** *C.* (lit. *stoṅ*) bragging, humbug; *ur-sgra* = *ur* noise caused by many voices, many footsteps, cf. *u-sgra*; of the howling of a tempest, *úr-sgra če* although it (the thunder) makes a great noise *Mil.*; *ur-tiṅ* a brass basin, used to make a noise by striking it *Sch.*; *úr-ba* sbst. **a humming insect, beetle** *Sch.*; vb., **to be noisy, chattering,** *Cs.*; *dga-grágs úr-te* shouting, rejoicing *Mil.*; **ur čó-če** to set a dog on a person *W.*; **ur bšád-pa, ur-brdáb btáṅ-ba** *C. W.* to exaggerate, brag, boast. — 2. *bag-dró ur-úr Pth.* seems to describe the feeling of a genial warmth pervading the body. — 3. **uur gyág-pa** *C*, **'ur gyáb-če, táṅ-če** *W.* to smooth, v. *dbur-ba*. — 4. *úr-rdo* a sling *Sch.*, *úr-rdo pén-pa* to throw with a sling.

འེ་ *e* num. figure: 113.

འོ་ *o* I. num. figure: 143. —

II. sbst. 1. provinc. *u* **kiss** (चुम्ब), *o byéd-pa* **to kiss** *Lt.*, *ká-la* on the mouth *Pth.*; *pyag, žabs* resp. on the hand, the foot *Cs.*; *o ytóṅ-ba Cs.*, **'u lán-če* W*, = *o byed-pa*. — 2. v. *o-ma*. —

III. pron. 1. pers. pron. **we,** v. *u-čag*. — 2. dem. pron. **this** *Cs.* v. *u* III. — IV. interj. (*o ŏ*) 1. like **oh, yes!** as a reply: *o lágs-so* oh very well! *Mil.*; **'o yóṅ-ňog, 'o dig-gog, 'o gyál-log W.*, **o yóṅ-ňe* C.* well! it's all right to me! well, do so! — *o o, ŏ ŏ,* so! well! very well! in *W.* it is a common reply, indicating nothing more, than that attention has been paid to the words spoken, like the English well! indeed! — 2. as a positive affirmative, **yes!** *W.*, cf. *o-ná*.

འོ་སྐོལ་ *ó-skol*, also with *rnams* and *čag*, (*Cs.* also *ú-skol*), *Ld.* *á-yo*, **we,** *Mil.*, *Tar.*, *Thgy.*, e.g. (if all men must die), *o-skol lta či smos* of course also we *Thgy.*; it is very often used as a reciprocal pronoun: *ó-skol ma ši prád-va* the fact, that we have seen each other once more before we die *Mil.*

འོ་བརྒྱལ་ *o-brgyál*, resp. **fatigue, weariness, want,** any kind of hardship, **péb-lam-la ob-gyál ma kyód-da* W.* has not your walk hither fatigued you? *o-brgyál yóṅ-lugs* the getting into difficulties *Mil.*; more frq. as vb.: *o-brgyál-ba*, *kyéd-čag-rnams o ma brgyál-lam* are you perhaps fatigued? *Glr.*; *žabs-tóg o mi brgyal-ba bul* a short expression for: everything shall be at your service, so that you shall not want anything *Mil.*; *o-re-brgyál* = *o-brgyál* 1. **trouble, drudgery, annoyance** *Mil.* 2. **decay, decline, ruin,** of religion, usages etc.

འོ་སྙིག་ *o-snyig* **sour cream** *Sch.*

འོ་སྙིགས་ *o-snyigs* **birch-tree** *Sch.*

འོ་དོད་ *o-dod* **lamentation, wailing, cry for help,** gen. as vb. *o-dód bód-pa* to lament, to call for help *Glr.*, *Pth.*, *Wdṅ.*; *o-dód-pa* one that seeks help, support, redress, a client, a plaintiff, more in pop. language.

འོ་ན་ *o-ná* (cf. *o, on, ón-kyaṅ*), comes nearest to the Greek ἀλλά, used esp. to introduce a new thought or proposition in speech: **now,** what shall you do in that case? *Dzl.*; **well,** what did he say? *Dzl.*; **well,** I hope you have at least . . . *Dzl.*; **why, ay,** *Mil.*; **but now** *Thgy.*; **but,** the Latin *autem*, when a new clause is added *Mil.*, *Thgy.*; **yea,** in a climax, e.g.: I met with a naked man, yea, an insane ascetic *Mil.* — 2. as an answer in the affirmative, **yes** *W.* —

འོ་མ་ *ó-ma* **milk,** *ó-ma jó-ba* **to milk** *Glr.*; *snyól-ba* to let it curdle *Cs.*, *srúb-pa* to churn it *Cs.*; *ó-ma čags* the milk thickens, coagulates *Cs.* —

Comp. *o-táṅ* 'milk-meadow', the plain in which Lhasa now stands; of the former lake, *o-táṅ-gi mtso Glr.*, a sedgy moor is said to be still remaining. — *o-tug* milk-soup *Tar.* — *o-túd* cheese, v. *tud*. — *o-túṅ* suckling-child, baby, = *žo-tuṅ*. — *o-*

snód milk-vessel. — *ˬo-sprí, ˬo-srí,* cream. — *ˬo-már* 1. milk and butter *Sch.* 2. termin. of *ˬó-ma* into the milk. — *ˬo-zó* milk-pail.

འོ་མ་ཟི་ཟི་ *ˬo-ma-zi-zi W.* **pater-noster pea,** the seed of Abrus precatorius, used as beads for rosaries.

འོ་ཡོ་, འོ་ཡོག *ˬo-yó, ˬo-yóg* **terrier** *Sch.*

འོ་རེ་བརྒྱལ་ *ˬo-re-brgyál* v. *ˬo-brgyál.*

འོ་ཤོ་ *ˬó-šo W.*, only in **'ó-šo túṅ-če* or *gyáb-če** **to laugh at,** deride, to feel a pleasure at the misfortune of others.

འོ་སེ་ *ˬo-se* **mulberry,** *ˬó-se-šiṅ* mulberry-tree; *ba-ˬós Med.*, perh. strawberry spinach, Blitum, which in *W.* is called *ba-o-se,* cow-mulberry.

འོག་ *ˬog, W. *yog*, Ts. *wag*,* 1. root signifying **below,** or with reference to time, **after,** opp. to *goṅ; ˬóg-tu, W. *yóg-la** 1. adv. **down, below, underneath; afterwards, later;** in paging books it denotes the second page of a leaf, v. *goṅ;* it is used as an expedient to correct errors in numbering, or to make additions, as with us e.g. 'page 24, b'. 2. postp. **under,** with accus., less frq. with dat., **down from; after** (as to time, rank, succession). — *ˬóg-na, W. *yóg-na*,* 1. adv. **underneath, below.** 2. postp. c. gen. **under, after.** — *ˬóg-nas, W. *yóg-nas** 1. adv. **from under, from below.** 2. postp. c. genit. **forth from below** *ˬóg-tu ˬjúg-pa* to put underneath, to subject, subdue *Glr.*; *k̔a-ˬóg Ts.* = *ˬóg-tu,* e.g. **šiṅ-gi k̔a-wág** under the tree; sometimes (less corr.) with accus. inst. of genit., also *ˬog* alone, inst. of *ˬóg-tu, óg-na: *Ru-tog Gu-lab-siṅ 'og mi dug* W* Rutog does not stand under, is not subordinate to, Gulab Singh; *ldiṅ-ˬog* the division of soldiers under the Dingpon, or a century (division of hundred); *bču-ˬog* a body of ten men under a *bčú-dpon* or corporal. — 2. testicles, of animals, *ˬog-čan* not castrated; **wog čẹ'-pa** (*spyad-pa*) to cover, copulate *C.*

Comp. and deriv. *ˬóg-sgo* the lower orifices of the body for the discharge of the excretions, *ˬóg-sgo γnyis S.g.*; more partic. the anus *Pth.* — *ˬog-rdo* anvil *Sch.* — *ˬog-pag* v. *pag.* — *ˬóg-ma* adj. the lower, later, following one, *dei ˬóg-ma* the one following after that, the second in turn; **lą-mẹ saṅ ge-nyén yóg-ma žig dug* W.* a Genyen is inferior to a Lama. *ˬog-min,* **अकनिष्ठ,** 'the not inferiors' i.e. the highest, the inmates of a certain heaven inhabited by gods, or also that heaven itself. — *ˬóg-rol-tu = ˬóg-tu Tar.* — *ˬog-rlúṅ Lt.* vapour, flatulence. — *ˬog-šál* crop, craw of birds.

འོང་བ་ *ˬóṅ-ba,* pf. *oṅs,* imp. *šog, B.* and *Bal.* (**'óṅ-čas**), for which in common life almost always, and in more recent literature not seldom, *yóṅ-ba, W. *yóṅ-če*,* is used, 1. **to come,** *ma ˬóṅ-ba mťóṅ-nas Dzl.* when he saw his mother coming; *náṅ-du ˬoṅs, Dzl.* he came in; *p̔yir ˬoṅ-ba Glr.* to come back; *mi γnyis ṅai drúṅ-du ˬóṅ-rgyu yin-pa Glr.* two men that were about to come to me; *ˬóṅ-bai lám-du Pth.* when being on their way; *ti-se-la sgóm-du yóṅs-pa yin Mil.* we come to the Tise in order to meditate; *ˬóṅs-pa légs-so* you are welcome *Cs.*; *ṅas ˬo-dód byas kyaṅ ˬóṅ-mk̔an med Pth.* although I was crying for help, nobody came; *k̔yer ˬóṅs-so Glr.* they came to bring, they brought with them; *k̔rid-šog* bring hither! *krid ˬóṅs-so Glr.* they brought thither; with reference to time: *ma-ˬóṅs-pa* not yet come, i.e. future, *dus* etc. very frq.; also poet.: *ma-ˬóṅs dón-du* for the benefit of those that are to come, i.e. of posterity; *čaṅ yóṅ-bai rigs, Wdṅ.*, the kinds (of cerealia) from which beer comes (is made). — 2. **to happen,** *yód-pa yóṅ-gin ˳dúg-pas Mil.* as it sometimes happens that there are . . .; more frq. **to occur, to be met with,** *ˬgréṅ-bu ˬoṅ ˬgyúr-na* whenever an e occurs, wherever an e stands *Gram.*; *mii yul-na mi ˬoṅ* such a thing does not occur on earth *Glr.*; **di-ru mi yóṅ(-če)* W.* that is not to be met with here. — 3. **to fall to the lot of, to be given, to come upon,** c. dat., *sras ˬóṅ-bai γsól-ba btáb-bo Pth.* she prayed that a son might be given to her; **k̔o-la nad yoṅs* W.* a disease came upon him; **sód-nyom yoṅ** I receive alms, **sod-nam yoṅ** I acquire merit *W.*; to come in, *yoṅ-sgo* income, revenue *Schr.*, cf. *yoṅ-*

ťaṅ sub _ťaṅ_ 2. — 4. **to be suitable, practicable, to do**; _bstán-pa γčig-la stón-pa γnyis mi ˛óṅ-pai Glr._ as two preceptors for one doctrine will not do; _yúl-du lóg-pa mi ˛óṅ-bas Glr._ as a journey home is not practicable; _˛o-yóṅ-ṅog_ v. _˛o_; _lús-la óṅ-bai bár-du_ as long as he was fit for work; **to go on well, to do well** _C._, *_da yóṅ-ṅa_* _W._ will it do now? — 5. when connected with verbs, it serves to indicate futurity, like the English auxiliaries **shall** and **will**, as becomes evident from such expressions as the following: _˳či-ba nam yoṅ ča med Mil._ when dying comes, i.e. when we shall die, is uncertain; _mdog ˳gyúr-ba ˛oṅ Glr._ a change of colour is coming, i.e. the colour will, or is going to, change; _˳gró-ba mi yoṅ-bar ˳dug Mil._ I am not likely (_dúg-pa_, 4) to go there any more; *_ṭel-čè mi yoṅ_* _W._ he will not be put to shame, not be disappointed; also with the supine: _srog daṅ brál-bar ˳gyúr-du ˛oṅ Dzl._ it will even come to his dying, it will be his death; _zós-su ˛oṅ Dzl._ he will even get so far as to eat . . .; _ši-bar ˛oṅ_ he will die; still more free and popular are those turns, in which the gerund or the mere root is used: _γnaṅ-ste ˛oṅ Pth._ he will assent to it, allow it; _γčig min kyaṅ γčig yin-te ˛oṅ Glr._ if it is not the one, it will be the other; _sleb yoṅ_ he will come _Mil._ and in _C._ very common; _yid-čés mi ˛oṅ_ they will not believe it; it is also used to express the passive voice, and the English **to become, to grow, to get**: _šés-na ṅa γsod ˛óṅ-bas Glr._ as I should be killed, if she heard of it; *_zer yoṅ_* _C._ so it is said, expressed, i.e. this is the usual way of expressing it; *_p̒él-te yoṅ_* _W._ it is getting larger, increases; or with a noun: _smin ˛oṅ Glr._ it is growing ripe; _rgyál-po ˳baṅs-su ˛oṅ Ma._ the king becomes a subject.

འོང་མོལ _˛oṅ-mól Ld._ for _˛ól-mo._

འོད _˛od_, **light, shine, brightness,** _šar_ flames up, shines, _˳p̒ro_ spreads, proceeds from; _˛od spró-ba_ to emit light, _bkyé-ba_ to spread _Sch._; _˛od lham-mér mdzád-pa_ resp., to shine with a bright light _Sch_; _˛od k̒éṅs-pa_ filled with light _Sch._; _lús-la ˛od yód-pa_ self-luminous, a property of primeval man _Glr._; _nyi-˛ód_ sun-light, _zla-˛ód_ moon-light, _skar-˛ód_ star-light _Cs._; _γnam-˛od_ brightness of the night-heavens, zodiacal-light _Cs._; _me-˛od_ fire-shine _Cs._; lustre, brightness, of polished metal, _˛od byin-pa_ to elicit a gloss or lustre, to give a bright polish _Sch._; metaphor. fair complexion, external beauty, *_k̒áṅ-pe 'od p̒élte yoṅ_* the splendour of the house increases, *_bud ča dug_* declines, decays _W._; _˛od daṅ ldán-pa B._, _˛ód-čan_ 1. **luminous, emitting light**; 2. **bright, polished.** 3. **light,** *_da 'od-čan ča yin_* _W._ now it will grow light. 4. **of a fine colour, of a blooming appearance** _Glr._ 5. **beautiful, splendid, stately**; _˛od-med,_ vulgo _˛od-med-k̒an_, the contrary.

Comp. _˛od-kór_ or _skor_ a luminous circle _Lex._ — _˛od-dkar_ 1. white light. 2. symb. num.: 1. — _˛ód-čan_, v. above. — _˛od-dpag-méd_, अमिताभ, also _snaṅ-ba-mťa-yás_ the fourth Dhyani-Buddha, v. _saṅs-rgyás_. — _˛ód-spro_ (or _˳p̒ro?_) light? — *_ŏd-ṭo_* _W._, *_ód-ṭo tog_* hold up the light! *_ód-ṭo bu_* glow-worm, fire-fly; _˛od-˳p̒ro_ sometimes occurring in the names of gods. — _˛od-γzér_ ray of light _Dzl._ and elsewh. frq.; _˛od-γzér-čan_ n. of a god, _˛od-γzér-čan-ma_ of a goddess _Do._ — _˛od-srúṅ_ n. p. 1. the human Buddha of the preceding period of the world. 2. a king of Tibet, son of Langdarma. — _˛od-γsál_ 1. a bright light or gloss, _˛od-γsál mdaṅs daṅ ldán-pa_ very glossy, of leaves. 2. com. of the supernatural enlightening of the saints, _˛od-γsál-gyi ṅáṅ-nas γzigs-te Mil._ knowing, beholding, by means of prophetic light.

འོད་མ _˛ód-ma_ **cane, bamboo**, _˛ód-ma ťsal_, वेणुवन, cane-grove; such a grove near Rajagriha was a favourite retreat of Buddha.

འོན _˛on W._ **but** (_sed, autem_); (not so often used as in English).

འོན་ཀྱང _˛on-kyaṅ_ **but, yet, notwithstanding** _Dzl._ and elsewh., frq. in _B._; rarely _˛on-yaṅ_ for it _Mil._; it stands at the beginning of sentences, but is also preceded by a gerund with _-kyi_, in which case it is almost pleonastic; _Lexx._ give उताहो as the

Ssk. word for it, which however seems not to agree with its use.

འོན་ཏང་ *˛ón-tañ* = *˛ón-kyañ Lex.*

འོན་ཏེ *˛ón-te B.* and *C.* **or if not, or else, or also,** in double-questions after the termination *am* of the first question.

འོན་པ་ *˛ón-pa* 1. **deaf,** also **to be deaf;** *˛ón-pa-pa, ˛ón-pa-po, ˛ón-po* a deaf man, *˛ón-pa-mo, ˛on-mo* a deaf woman *Cs.*; *˛on-loñ* deaf and blind. — 2. **to give, to bring,** chiefly as imp. *˛ón-čig Dzl.*

འོན་སེང་ *˛on-señ*, with *byéd-pa*, **to pay attention, to watch, to spy** *Sch.*

འོབ་ *˛ob* 1. also *˛obs* **ditch, trench, pit** *Dzl.*; *me-˛ób* fiery pit; also fig.: the fire-pool of passions. — 2. v. *yob.*

འོམ་བུ་ *˛óm-bu* 1. **tamarisk,** Myricaria *Med.* not unfrequent near the rivers of Tibet. — 2. *Sch.*: 'a town, settlement'(?).

འོར་ *˛or* 1. **dropsy,** viz the species **anasarca,** nif., = *págs-ču*; *dbu-˛or* prob. id. *Med.* — 2. **eddy, whirlpool** *Sch.*

འོར་བ་ *˛ór-ba* 1. **to put** or **lay down** *Cs.* — 2. **to feed,** e.g. a little child *W.*

འོལ་ *˛ol* **clover, trefoil,** viz. snail-clover, medic, (Medicago); *˛ol-tán* a plain covered with such clover; *'ol-kyog* *W.* snail.

འོལ་མདུད་ *˛ol-mdúd* v. *'ol-mdúd.*

འོལ་པ་ *˛ól-pa* **vulture** *Sch.*(?)

འོལ་སྤྱི་ *˛ól-spyi* **in a general way, generally speaking, about,** *˛ól-spyir* id. *Sch.*; *˛ól-spyi tsám-du dus mnyám-mo* they are about contemporaries *Tar.*

འོལ་བ་ *˛ól-ba* **black horse** *Mil*, *Ld.-Glr.* (*Ts.* *wál-ba*).

འོལ་མོ་ *˛ól-mo Ld.* *oñ-mol* **besom, broom, brush,** *stag-˛ól* birch-broom, *zed-˛ól* hair-broom *Cs.*

འོལ་མོ་སེ་ *˛ol-mo-sé Wdñ.* an officinal plant; *Cs.*: '*˛ol-ma-sa* 1. a certain small berry. — 2. a small weight'.

འོས་ *˛os* 1. v. the following. — 2. v. *˛o-se.*

འོས་པ་ *˛ós-pa* 1. vb. and adj. **to be worthy, suitable; becoming, appropriate,** with termin. inf., in later times and vulgo, with the root, *sbyin-par ˛os* it is becoming, it is meet to give; *˛di γzigs-par mi ˛os* it is not decent to see this; *ka-lón čá-če 'os* *W.* he is worthy to be a vizier; *ī-sam la tañ mi 'os* *W.* he is not worth such high wages; *la nán-te tañ 'os* *W.* he deserves extra-pay; *yid-smón ˛os* to be wished, desirable; *p̓yag bya-bar ˛os-par ˛gyur* he becomes adorable; *stód-˛os* to be praised, laudable; *bkúr-˛os* deserving honour *Cs.*; *tams-čád-la p̓óg-˛os-pai čád-pa* the punishment condign to all; rarely with genit.: *kún-gyis bkúr-žiñ mčód-pai ˛os Mil.* he is deserving of universal honour and respect, and even: *rjei ˛os min* he was not worth to be a king, for which more frq. the termin. is used: *γtsó-mor ˛ós-pa žig Glr.* the one that is the most deserving of being mistress, i.e. she that has the genteelest appearance, that is most of a gentlewoman; *gróg-su ˛ós-pa* he is worthy to be his colleague, nif. *Mil.* — 2. more particularly in colloquial language: **right,** *W.* *ós-čan, ŏ-šan*; with a negative *mi-ós-pa, os-méd, os-min* *W.*, *mi-ŏ-pa* etc. *C.* wrong (for the *rigs-pa* and *mi-rigs-pa* of earlier lit.); *mi ˛ós-pai spyod-pa byed-pa Glr.* to entertain illicit intercourse; *rdzas ˛ós-pa* a lawful, *mi ˛ós-pa* an unlawful matter *Schr.*; *ŏ-min-ghi ṭim-gál* *C.* a wrong, immoral act, sinful transgression; *'os mi-ós p̓é-če* *W.* to discern between right and wrong; with regard to a man's words, **credible, trustworthy,** or the contrary. — *Sch.* has besides: *˛os či yod*, 'what other means or way is there?' and: *˛os spyi-ba* 'to finish (a thing) for the most part; to be good or tolerably good'(??).

ཡ

ཡ *ya* 1. the consonant **y**, pronounced like the English initial **y**, in yard, yoke etc., in *C.* deep-toned; *yá-btags, yá-ta Glr.* the subscribed y or ◌ྱ. — 2. num. fig.: 24.

ཡ་ *ya* I. often with *γčig*, one of two things that belong together as being of one kind, or forming a pair, also one of two opponents; *mig ya-γčig lóṅ-ba Pth.* blind of one eye; *lham ya-γčig Glr.* one of a pair of boots, an odd boot; *lag-pa ya-γčig-tu γser ťogs, lág-pa ya-γčig-tu bú-mo ǩrid-de Dzl.* in one hand holding the gold, with the other leading his daughter; *stóṅ-pa daṅ γsál-ba γnyis ya ma brál-bar Thgr.* the empty and the clear (emptiness and clearness) being inseparable from each other; *ya-gyál* one of several, e.g. of three things *Gram.*; of six *Lex.*; **yá-do** in *W.* the common word for *grogs* or *zlá-bo* **associate, companion, assistant,** **yá-do čó-če** to assist; **nyi-ka ya yọ'** *C.* they are equal to each other, a match, one as good as the other, **ǩó-la ya me',* or *ǩọ ya ǰhe'-ǩen mi dug** *C.* he finds none that is a match to him, **di lẹ-kẹ ya ṅẹ mi tub** *C.* I am not equal to the task; *ǩai ya* v. *ǩá-ya*; *ya-méd* = *do-méd*; *˳ťáb-ya* adversary, antagonist; *ya-žár* one-eyed; *ya-ma-zúṅ* and *ya-má-brla, ya-ya* v. below. —

II. root signifying **above, up** etc. (opp. to *ma*), cf. *goṅ*; adj. *yá-gi* (also *yá-ki Mil.*), *p̒u yá-gi* the upper or highest part of a valley *Glr.*, *ri-bo yá-gi* the hill up yonder *Mil.*; *yá-gi* upper = heavenly *Mil.*, opp. to *má-gi*; *yar* and *yas* v. the respective articles; the word, otherwise, occurs only in compounds: *yá-rkan* palate; *ya-gád* (for *skad*) ladder *Sch.*; *ya-góṅ* above, over *Sch.*; *ya-mgál, ya-mčú, ya-ťém, ya-ťóg, ya-rábs, ya-ré, ya-só* v. *mgal* etc.; *ya-mťá* the upper end, i. e. the beginning e. g. of a word, opp. to *ma-mťa* the end *Cs.*; *yá-ša* **esteem, honour, love,** shown to a person *W.* (= *žc-sa B., C.*), **yá-šẹ spé-ra** expressions of respect; **yá-šẹ p̒i-la zér-na** if one speaks respectfully; *ya-ša-méd-ǩan* uncivil, regardless, reckless, unfeeling; **yá-ša čó-če** to show love, regard, to treat with tenderness, to fondle, a child, animal etc., opp. to *má-ša*, which however is less in use.

ཡ་ཁ་ *yá-ǩa* **mutual revilings** *Ma.*: *ma smád-la yaṅ yá-ǩa sgrags* mother and children abuse one another. *Cs.*: *yá-ga* bad reputation (?).

ཡ་རྒྱལ་ *ya-gyál* v. *ya* I.

ཡ་ང་(བ) *yá-ṅa(-ba) C.* also **yá-ṅa-bo** (prob. for *γya ṅán-pa*) **shuddering, fright, anguish,** with genit. or accus. of that which is the cause of it *Do.*; *yá-ṅá-bai dmag-ťsógs Mil.* a formidable host; *yá-ṅai gegs* terrible danger *Pth.*

ཡ་ཏ་ *yá-ta* v. letter *ya*.

ཡ་ཏྲ་ prop. ཡཱ་ཏྲཱ *ya-tra* (procession and feast, in honour of some idol) *W.*: **festivity, reveling,** in beer with dumplings and pastry, held in autumn or winter, in memory and for the benefit of the souls of those that died during the last year.

ཡ་དོ་ *yá-do* v. *ya* I.

ཡ་པོ་ *yá-po* **butcher; executioner** *Schr.*

ཡ་བ་ *yá-ba* prob. = *γya-ba.* — *Mil.?*

ཡ་བ་ཀྵཱ་ར་ *ya-ba-kšā-ra Ssk.* **saltpetre** *Med.*

ཡ་མ་ *yá-ma* 1. **the temples.** — 2. **a severe cold, catarrh.** *Med.*; **yá-ma rag** *W.* I have a bad cold. — 3. n. of a goddess, = *brtán-ma*.

ཡ་མ་ཟུང་ *ya-ma-zúṅ* **unsymmetrical, incongruous, not fitting together,** e. g. two unequal shoes; of religions, languages, customs, that have sprung from heterogeneous elements; of behaviour: **inconsistent; unheard of, prodigious,** *čo-ₒpʻrúl* magic feats *Tar.*

ཡ་མ་བརླ་ *ya-ma-brla, *ya-má-la*, Ü: ya-ma-la-po, Ts.: *ya-ma-len-te*, Lis.: = snyiṅ-po-med-pa, mi-bdén-pa* **vain, unstable, fickle, not to be trusted** or **depended upon.**

ཡ་མཚན་ *ya-mtsan* 1. **wonder, miracle, supernatural occurrence.** adopted also as the term for the miracles of Scripture *Chr. Prot.; ltas-sam yá-mtsan či byuṅ Dzl.* what signs and wonders have happened? *yá-mtsan-du ₒgyúr-ba Dzl.* to happen, to come to pass in a marvelous manner; *yá-mtsan-ste Pth.* being a wonderful man; *kyód-la ₒdi-tsam rig-pa-méd-pa ni yá-mtsan-čeo* that you are so ignorant is very strange (wonderful); **yá-tsem-po* C.* marvelous, miraculous; *yá-tsam-can* id. *Schr.* — 2. **wonder, astonishment, amazement,** *rgyál-po yá-mtsan čén-po skyés-te Tar* **the king** greatly wondering; **yám-tsan tsór-če, có-če* W.* to wonder; *yá-mtsan-gyi ɣnás-so Tar.* it is a thing to be wondered at; *dé-tsam yá-mtsan-rgyu med Mil.* that is not so very astonishing.

ཡ་ཡ་ *yá-ya* 1. *Cs.:* **differing, diverse,** *yá-ya-ba* **diversity;** *ya-ya-bor gyúr-ba Sch.:* a subject of dispute, contrariety of opinion. — 2. *ɣyá-ya.*

ཡ་ཡོ་ *ya-yó* **crooked, wry,** col. *Cs.*

ཡ་ལད་ *ya-lád* **corselet and helmet, mail, armour,** *ɣsér-gyi* of gold; also fig. *B.*

ཡ་ཤ་ *yá-ša* v. *ya* II.

ཡ་hu་དཱ་ *ya-hu-dá* **Judah,** *ya-hu-dá-pa* **jew** *Chr. Prot.*

ཡ་ཧོ་ཝཱ་ *ya-ho-wá* **Jehovah** *Chr. Prot.*

ཡག་པ་ *yág-pa* **a small mattock, hoe,** *čág-yag* iron hoe, *šiṅ-yag* wooden hoe *Ts.*

ཡག་པོ་ *yág-po,* prov. also *ₒjág-po,* seldom in B., but otherwise common in *C.* and *W.* **good,** in all its significations, both as to men and things, = *bzáṅ-po; *dei pʻi-la di yág-po* W.* for that purpose this is good, fit, serviceable; **yág-po jhé-pa* C., *čó-če* W.,* c. ç. *la,* **to caress, to flirt,** also in an obscene sense; *yág-po yag-po* well, well!

ཡང་ *yaṅ* 1. (accented), **again, once more: likewise, also, further,** frq., *yaṅ yaṅ Mil., yaṅ daṅ yáṅ-du Tar., yáṅ-nas yáṅ-du Dzl.* **again and again;** joined to adj. and adv. denoting a higher degree, **still:** *yaṅ čuṅ Mil.* still smaller, *ₒdi či-yaṅ-las yaṅ dgá-ba žig byuṅ Mil.* that was still more pleasing than any thing before; *yáṅ sgos Mil.* still more in detail; **yáṅ-ṅon-žag* W.* the third day before yesterday. — 2. (unaccented, throwing the accent back on the preceding word), after the final letters g, d, b, s, gen. *kyaṅ,* after vowels often *ₒaṅ,* **also, too,** the Latin *quoque, ṅa yaṅ, bdag kyaṅ* I too; *bu čé-ba yaṅ Dzl.* my eldest boy too: *bsód-nams daṅ yaṅ ldán-pa Dzl.* having also merit; *yaṅ — yaṅ —,* both — and —; *ₒdi yaṅ — de yaṅ* both this and that, *pʻyi-rol yaṅ naṅ yaṅ* both outside and inside; followed by a negative, **neither — nor;** *yaṅ* singly, with a negative: **not even,** *kar-šá-pa-ni ɣčig kyaṅ mi sbyin-no Dzl.* I shall not even give a cowry for it; *yaṅ* with a comparative (as above) **still,** *sṅár-bas kyaṅ lhág-par* still more than formerly; as effect of a preceding cause, **so then,** *kyeu de yaṅ tse ₒdas-so Dzl.* so then the boy died, *bsád-pa yaṅ graṅs-méd-do Dzl.* so then there were people killed without number; emphat., **even,** *ríṅ-por ma lón-par smra yaṅ šés-so Dzl.* within a short time he was even able to speak; *sṅa-čád kyaṅ Dzl.* even before this; *kar-šá-pa-ni ₒbum yaṅ* even so much as a hundred thousand cowries (I would give); also joined to a verbal root: *tams-čad ₒdus kyaṅ* even if all without exception be gathered; **although,** *btsal kyaṅ ma rnyed* although they were seeking, they did not find, or, they were seeking indeed, **but** did not find; this latter turn is frequently used, where we use **but, yet, nevertheless** etc.

ཡང་སྐྱར་ *yaṅ-skyár* 1. sbst. **postscript.** *Cs.* — 2. adv. **again, afresh, anew** *C.*

ཡང་གེ་ *yáṅ-ge* v. *yáṅ-po.*

ཡང་སྒོས་ *yáṅ-sgos* v. *yaṅ* 1.

ཡང་ཅར་ *yáṅ-čar Bhot.* and *Schr.*

ཡང་ལྕི་ *yaṅ-lči* v. *yáṅ-po.*

ཡང་འཇུག་ *yáṅ-ḥjug* the second of two final letters, viz. *s* after *g, ṅ, b, m.*

ཡང་ཏྲི, ཡང་གི་ཁ *yáṅ-tri, yáṅ-gi-ka* (spelling uncertain), is said to be the n. of a green stone, which is worked into handles of knives etc. *W.*

ཡང་དག་པ་ *yáṅ-dag-pa* v. *dág-pa.*

ཡང་ན *yáṅ-na* **or**, in *B.*, com. pleon. after the affixed *am* (*gam, nam* etc.), which in itself already expresses the **or**; it is also preceded by *daṅ*; **further**, *Thgy.*; **either — or —**, *yaṅ-na (ni) — yaṅ-na (ni) —.*

ཡང་སྤྲུལ་ *yáṅ-sprul* v. *sprúl-pa.*

ཡང་པོ་ *yáṅ-po Cs.*, **yáṅ-mo* C.* and *W.* **yáṅ-ghe* Ts.* adj., *yáṅ-ba* adj. and sbst., **light, lightness,** opp. to *lči-ba*, q. cf.; — fig. *ḥjam-žiṅ yáṅ-ba* what is soft and light, commodious and easy *Dzl.*; of food cf. *lči-ba* II.; **weak,** **de saṅ yáṅ-mo yin* W.* this is a weaker, less emphatic, word than that; **ṅo yáṅ-mo* C., W.* cheerful, happy.

ཡང་མ་ *yáṅ-ma* **early barley,** v. *nas* I.

ཡང་མེས་པོ་ *yáṅ-mes-po* **great-grandfather,** *yáṅ-mes-mo* **great-grandmother** *Sch.*

ཡང་རྩལ་ *yáṅ-rtsal* **very high skill, consummate art** *Mil.*

ཡང་རྩེ་ *yáṅ-rtse* **the highest point, summit,** fig. **the height of perfection.**

ཡང་ཚ་ *yáṅ-tsa* **great-grandson** *Sch.*

ཡང་ར་ *yáṅ-ra W.* **buck, ram, he-goat,** = *pá-ra.*

ཡང་ལ་ *yáṅ-la* prob. = *yáṅ-na S.g.*

ཡང་སོས་ *yáṅ-sos* n. of a hell *Thgy.*

ཡངས་པ་ *yáṅs-pa*. 1. also *-po*, **wide, broad, large,** *taṅ, sa-γži* a large or wide field, plain *Glr.*; *yaṅs-šiṅ rgya-če-ba* large and spacious, of a house *S.O.*; **gnʹ-sa* (or *né-sa*) *yaṅ-pa dug** *W.* here is much room; fig. **mig-yáṅ* C., W.* liberal, generous, bounteous; **yaṅ-méd-la, yaṅ-yáṅ-pa-la* W.* sudden, unexpected, unawares; **yaṅ-lúg čó-če* W.* to hang or throw a coat over, without getting into the sleeves; *yaṅ-šam byéd-pa* id., *Sch.*; **yaṅ-hlúb* C., W.* wide, of clothes. — 2. v. *γyéṅ-ba.*

ཡངས་པ་ཅན་ *yáṅs-pa-čan, Ssk.* **वैशाली**, *Dzl.* and elsewh., city in ancient India, now **Allahabad.**

ཡན་ *yan* (= *ya* II. opp. to *man* III q. v.) **what is uppermost,** *man-yan* **below** and **above** *Cs.*; *yán-na Cs.*: **above, in the beginning, in the first part;** gen. *yan* stands as adv. or postp with accus., = *yán-la, yan-čád(-la), yan-čód(-la),* **above, in the upper part,** *lté-ba yan stéṅ-la yód-do Glr.* lit. above the navel standing out of (the water), i.e. standing in (the water) up to the navel; *sta-zúr yan-čád Dzl.* above the hips; *lo-brgyád yan-čád Pth.* above eight years old; otherwise when referring to time, always **till, to**; often preceded by *nas*, **from ... forth,** *Glr.*

ཡན་གླིང་ *yan-ljiṅ* **dulcimer,** musical instrument in *Ts.*

ཡན་པ་ *yán-pa* adj., **free, vacant, unoccupied, having no owner,** of places and things that are common property, like the air, rocks and stones etc.; *kyi yán-pa* a dog without a master, vagrant dog; *gral yán-la yod* there are yet places unoccupied; of fields: **untilled, fallow-ground;** *yan kyár-la ma ča*, v. *ḥkyár-ba*; *yán-gar-ba* **separate, apart, by itself** *Lis.*, *rgyal-rigs yán-gar-ba žig* a separate dynasty, a dynasty of its own; *yán-gar-du* id., adv. *Was.* (281); *rgya-yán* the external world, *rgya-yán(-gyi) γnyén-pa Glr.* a helper from the external world; *sems rgya-yán-du ma šór-bar byos* take care that the mind be not distracted by outward things; **yan ča-če* W.* to disperse, **lug, nor tsaṅ-ma, sam-pa yan soṅ* W.*, the sheep have dispersed (or a sheep has strayed), the fortune is gone, the thoughts are lost, wandering; *yán-du ḥjúg-pa* to suffer (the sheep) to disperse on the pasture; *nad yán-*

pa wandering (contagious) disease, = *yams Sch.* (*yán-pa* to run about, to wander *Sch.*, is rather doubtful).

ཡན་ལག *yán-lag* 1. **member, limb,** *yán-lag lna* arms, legs, and head *Mng.*; *yán-lag skyón-čan* an injured or defective limb *Lex.*; *yán-lag nyams-pa* weak in the limbs, decrepit, crazy, = *žá-ba Lex.* — 2. fig. **branch of a river, branch of a tree;** *dge-bsnyén-gyi yán-lag γzúṅ-bar bgyio Do.* was explained: I wish to be counted a branch, i.e. a member, of the community of novices; **appendage,** something subordinate to a greater thing, like **branch-establishment** *Tar.* 175, 3; also with reference to books: **appendix, supplement** *Tar.* — 3. **branch, section, separate part** of a doctrine or science, frq., a **particular head, point, thought,** in a treatise.

ཡབ་ *yab*, resp. for *pa*, **father,** *rgyál-po yab yum γsum Glr.* the king and his two consorts; *rgyál-po yab yum* denotes also king and queen as father and mother to the country *Glr.*; *yab rgyál-po-la γsól-to Dzl.* he said to his royal father; *yab-srás* **father and son,** in a spiritual sense: **master and disciple;** *yab-més* 1. **father and grandfather.** 2. **progenitor, ancestors** *Glr.*

ཡབ་པ་, གཡབ་པ་ *yáb-pa, γyáb-pa* 1. **to lock, lock up, secure, cover over** *Sch.*, *yab-ča* things well secured, under safe keeping; *yáb-yob-pa* to hide, conceal *Sch.*; *γyab* or *γyab-sa* **covered place, covert, shelter** *Sch.*; *yab riṅ-po* **portico, veranda,** e.g. of the monastery at Tashilhunpo; *yab-ras* **awning, tent** *Sch.* — 2. *C.* **to skim, to scoop off,** from the surface of a fluid. — 3. *W.* **to move to and fro, hither and thither,** v. *γyób-pa.* —

ཡབ་མོ་, གཡབ་མོ་ *yáb-mo, γyáb-mo* 1. **the act of fanning, waving,** *lág-pa yáb-mo byéd-čiṅ ˳či-ba* dying whilst waving the hand to and fro, considered as a sign of peace *Do.*; *gós-kyi yáb-mo byéd-pa Glr.* to beckon by waving with one's clothes; hence fig. — 2. **the bringing on, provoking,** *dgrá-boi* of an enemy *Mil.*, *˳p̒uṅ-γžii* a calamity *Mil.*; *yáb-mo ǰhé'-pa* or *γyág-pa* to beckon to come, to bring (something adverse) upon one's self. — 3. **fan,** *rṅa-yáb* a. a **yak-tail** fan *Cs.* b. kettle-drum stick *Sch.*; *sbraṅ-yáb* fly-brush *Cs.*; *rluṅ-yáb* ventilating- or cooling-fan *Cs.*; *bsil-yáb* **pankah** (*Hind.*), a large fan suspended from the ceiling and set in motion by means of a string. — 4. **sail** *Cs.?*

ཡམ་བུ་ *yám-bu* = *rdo-tsád* v. *rdo* comp.

ཡམ་མེ་བ་ *yám - me - ba* 1. *Sch.*: **coarsely, roughly, of a coarse make, rough-hewn.** — 2. *Mil.*: *čui k̒á-na p̒ár-la yám-me γšegs* he walked softly gliding across the water to the other bank.

ཡམ་ཡོམ་ *yam-yóm Cs.* also *yam-yám Thgr.* **tottering, not steady** *Cs.* *yam-yóm byéd-pa* **to totter.**

ཡམས་ *yams, yams-nád Cs.*, *nad-yáms Glr.* **epidemic** or **contagious disease, plague,** *má-yams* a plague caused by evil spirits, v. *má-mo.*

ཡར་ *yar*, from *ya*, **up, upward,** also *yár-la*, e.g. *γzigs-pa* to look up *Glr.*, *yár-˳gro már-˳gro byéd-pa Glr.* to travel **up and** down; *yar mar ˳čág-pa B.*, **kyód-če* W.* resp., to walk up and down; *yár-la k̒yer šog* bring or fetch up *Pth.*; *yar ma sgyugs mar ma ˳tón-par Pth.* as it would go off neither upward by vomiting, nor downward; *yár-nas már-la* from top to bottom; *yar ˳tón-pa Thgy.* to come up again, from a depth; **yar mar tsaṅ-ma-ru* W.* in every direction, all over; in such expressions as *yar laṅ-ba* **to rise, get up,** *yar ˳p̒él-ba* **to increase,** it stands pleon.; *yár-la* also denotes a relation to that which is higher, the intercourse with, the deportment towards, superiors (*már-la* the contrary) *Glr.*; esp. with reference to the transmigration of souls and their final deliverance: *yar γčód-pa* to cut off the way to the three upper classes of beings, the so-called 'good natures', *yar skyé-ba* to be re-born in the upper classes, the reverse of which is *mar ˳gríb-pa* to sink down to the lower; *yar ˳drén-pa* to draw or lift up to heaven.

ཡར་ལྟོས *yár-ltos* **imitation** *Sch.*

ཡར་བ་ *yár-ba* **to disperse, ramble, stray** *C.* (= **yan čá-če* W.*); **to spring** or **leap off** *Cs.*; **to be scattered** *Sch.*

ཡར་ལུང་ *yar-luṅ Glr.* a large tributary of the Yangtsekyang coming from the north, in western China, east of the town of Bathang; nevertheless Tibetan historians, from a partiality to old legends, describe it as flowing near the mountain of Yarlhasampo. V. *Köpp.* II, 50.

ཡར་ལྷ་ཤམ་པོ་ *Yarlhaśampo*, a snowy mountain, between Lhasa and the frontier of Bhotan, near which according to tradition the first king of Tibet, *γnya-k̔ri-γtsáṅ-po, Nyaṭitsáṅgpo*, coming from India, first entered the country.

ཡལ་ག་ *yál-ga* **branch, bough,** frq., *yál-gai tsúl-du* ramified *S.g.*, *yál-ga-čan* branchy, full of boughs; *yal-p̔rán Cs.*, *yál-ga p̔reu Sch.* small branch, twig; *yal-₀dáb* a branch full of leaves *Cs.*

ཡལ་བ་ *yál-ba* **to dwindle, fail; disappear, vanish,** *drod yal* animal heat (in a living being) diminishes, (an inanimate object) cools down, grows cold; *ṅad yal* it evaporates *Lt.*; of beer: to get stale, dead (*W.*: **yal čá-če**); *(*s*)*kug*(*s*) *gyál-k̔an-lu yal ča dug** *W.* the stake is lost in going to the winner; *₀ja yál-ba bžin-du Glr.* like the vanishing of the rainbow; *yal-śúl Wdṅ.* in a fruit the remnants of the withered blossom; **to be obliged to yield, to be dislodged** *Glr.* fol. 25, but perh. the signification: **to disappear** is also here admissible; *lus daṅ srog yal Dzl.* body and soul are trifled away, are lost; **go-yál** (v. *sgó-po*) one who has lost himself by gambling and has thus become the slave of another; *yál-bar ₀dór-ba, ₀bór-ba*, 1. *Sch.* **to annihilate, annul.** 2. *Cs.* **to despise,** *γžan* other people. Cf. *yól-ba*.

ཡལ་ཡལ་ *yal-yál Cs.* 100 000 octillions, *yal-yál čén-po* a nonillion; yet cf. *dkriqs-pa*.

ཡལ་ཡོལ་, -ཡུལ་ *yal-yól, -yúl* **inconstancy, inattention, carelessness** *Cs.*, *Sch.*

ཡས་ *yas*, from *ya*, 1. **from above,** *₀báb-pa* to come down from above *Cs.*; **above,** *yás-kyi* the one above, the upper one *Do.*; *yás-nas* from above *C.*, *yas mas*, a. from above and from below *Cs.* b. upward and downward *Cs.*; *yas-byón* coming from above *Mil.* — 2. **off, away,** *yas γtóṅ-ba, ₀p̔aṅ-yás γtóṅ-ba, γtor-yas byéd-pa Glr.* and elsewh., to throw away. — 3. in comp. **without,** *mt̔a-yás* without an end, endless, frq.; *bgraṅ-yás* numberless *Gram.*

ཡི་ *yi*, 1. num. fig.: 54. — 2. in some combinations inst. of *yid*, *so yi γčód-pa yi(d) čád-pa* 1. **to forget,** e.g. a benefactor *Glr.* 2. more frq. **to give up, to despair** *Dzl.*; **despondency, despair** *Mil.*; *yi-p̔ri-ba* a disliking, hatred *Cs.*; *yi(d)-múg-pa*, *yi-múg-par ₀gyúr-ba* to despair, frq.; *yi-ráṅ-ba* to be glad, to rejoice, v. *ráṅ-ba*; *yi-γsád-pa Cs.* = *yi-múg-pa*.

ཡི་ག་ *yi-ga* **appetite,** *yi-ga ₀gag, ldog* the appetite is lost, aversion, disgust is felt, *yi-ga sdaṅ* id. *Sch.*; *₀čus* id. *Med.*; *yi-gar ₀oṅ* it is grateful to the taste, it tastes well *Med.*

ཡི་གེ་ *yi-ge* in comp. *yig*, 1. **letter,** *yi-ge dbú-čan*(*W.* **róm-yig**) the Tibetan printed letters, *dbu-méd*(*W.* **ṭa-yig**) current handwriting, of which there are again different kinds: *dpé-yig* the more distinct and careful, used in copying books, *₀k̔yúg-yig* the cursory and often rather illegible writing in letters, and *₀bam-yig*, the very large and regular style invented for the use of elementary writing-schools (v. specimens of all of them in the lithogr. supplement to *Cs.*'s grammar). — *yi-ge-drúg-pa* the six-syllable (prayer), **the Ommanipadmehum** *Glr.* and elsewh.; *yi-ge-bdún-pa* and *brgyá-pa Mil.?* *yi-ge bsláb-pa* to learn reading and writing, *yig-rtsis* reading, writing, and cyphering; *ká-yig* the letter k. — 2. anything that is written, **note, card, bill, document; inscription, title** (more accurately *k̔á-yig*), esp. **letter, epistle;** *yi-ge bžág-pa* a deposited document, bond *C.*; *dge-sdig-gi yi-ge* register of virtues and iniquities; *yi-gei lan* a written answer *Glr.*; *yi-gei śubs* a. **envelope,** b. **letter-case, pocket-book;** *yi-ge ₀bri-ba* to write a letter, *spriṅ-ba W.* **kál-če** to send off, *tob-*

pa to receive a letter; *yi-ge sleb* a letter arrives; *yi-ger* ˳*bri-ba Dzl.*, ˳*gód-pa* to compose, to pen down; *yi-ger* ˳*brir* ˳*jûg-pa* to get copied; *yi-ger bris* ˳*jóg-pa literis mandatum deponere*; *skú-yig* letter, circular epistle; *k'á-yig* v. above; *čád-yig* contract, bargain; ˳*čáms-yig* dancing-book, rules relating to religious dances; ˳*čól-yig* letter of recommendation *Cs.*; *rtágs-yig* 1. **stamp, signature** *Cs.* 2. **certificate, credentials** *W.*; *ynás-yig* description of a place; *spriṅs-* or ˳*p'rin-yig* = *skúr-yig*; *bú-yig* 1. copy. 2. commentary, opp. to *má-yig* 1. original, first copy; 2. text *Cs.*; ˳*dzin-yig* = *rtágs-yig* 2 *W.*; *žú-yig* memorial, petition; *lán-yig* letter in answer, reply; *lám-yig* 1. **hand-book, road-book, guide,** *šám-bha-lai lam-yig* description of the road to Sambhala (a fantastical book). 2. **itinerary, travelling-journal** (?). 3. **pass-port** *Cs.*

ཡི་དྭགས་ *yi-dwags* (from etymol. subtility written also *yid-tags* or *yid-btags*), प्रेत, the fifth class of beings of Buddhist cosmography, condemned in a fore-hell to suffer perpetual hunger and thirst. a grade of punishment preceding the final and full torments of hell; they are represented as giants with huge bellies, and very narrow throats, inhabiting the air *Köpp.* I, 245.

ཡི་དམ་ *yi-dam*, less frq. *yid-dam* (= *dam-bča*) resp. *túgs-dam* 1. **oath, vow, asseveration, promise,** *yi-dam-la brtén-pas* because he firmly adhered to his word *Dzl.* — 2. a 'wishing prayer' (v. *smon-lam*), *yi-dam bčá-ba* to make a vow *Dzl.*, to pronounce a wishing prayer *Dzl.* — 3. **meditation** (this signification rests only on the analogy with *tugs-dam*, and has yet to be confirmed by quotations from literature). — 4. also *yi-dam-lhá* **tutelar god**, a deity whom a person chooses to be his patron, whether for his whole life, or only for some particular undertaking, and with whom he enters into an intimate union by meditation: frequently also it is a defunct saint or teacher (so e.g. the *yi-dam* of Milaraspa was *rdo-rje-*˳*čaṅ*); sometimes such a connection subsists from infancy through life, or the deity makes advances to the respective person by special revelations, so in the case of king *Sroṅ-btsan-sgam-po Glr.* — 5. acc. to *Cs.*'s proposition: **sacrament**; yet our Christian converts preferred the more popular *dam-bča.*

ཡིག་ *yig* = *yi-ge* as an affix, v. *yi-ge.*

ཡིག་བསྐུར་ *yig-bskúr*, also *yig-mgó*, **epistolary guide**, containing the different addresses and customary phrases used in writing letters *W.* — *yig-k'áṅ* **library** *C.*, **chancery** *Schr.* — *yig-mk'an* **secretary, book-keeper, clerk** *Glr.* and elsewh. — *yig-ča Glr.*, *Tar.* **written accounts, records, books of history.** — *yig-dpon* a 'master-writer' *Cs.* — *yig-p'réṅ* line, written or printed. — *yig-*˳*brú* a single letter. — *yig-tsáṅ* 1. **archives, records, documents** *Glr.* 2. **book-case** *Glr.* — *yig-*˳*dzin* **written contract**, *bžág-pa* to indent (articles of agreement).

ཡིད་ *yid*, resp. *tugs*, I. 1. **soul, mind,** esp. the powers of perception, volition and imagination, cf. *blo*; *yid bžin-du* as one would wish, to heart's content, frq.; *yid-bžin-gyi nór-bu* a jewel or talisman that grants every wish; *yid-du* ˏ*oṅ-ba* adj., rarely *yid-*ˏ*oṅ-po Mil.* **engaging, winning, pleasing,** *skyé-bo máṅ-poi yid-du* ˏ*óṅ-ba Do.* beloved with many; **nice, pretty,** of girls, houses etc., frq.; also *yid-kyi* inst. of it, e.g. *yid-kyi mtso* a pretty lake *Sbh.*; *ṅai-yid* ˏ*oṅ* my dearest! my darling! *Pth.*; *yid-du-mi-*ˏ*oṅ-bai tsig smrá-ba Wdṅ.* to say some unpleasant word; whereas *W.*: **da yid-la yoṅ* or *juṅ** now it comes into my mind; *ṅa yid-du mi rag* I do not recollect; *C.*: **yi'-la ma soṅ** it would not go down with him, he had no mind for it; *ṅai yid-la* **mi* ˳*bab Tar.* it does not please me, I do not like it; *yid-la šar kyaṅ ro mi myoṅ Mil.* though you may fancy it in your mind, yet you do not perceive the taste; *yid-la byéd-pa*, ˳*dzin-pa W.*: **čo-če, bór-če**, **to comprehend, perceive, remember, mind, take to heart,** frq.; *yid-kyis byéd-pa* to do a thing in one's mind, fancy, e.g. sacrificing, like *dmigs-la Thgr.*; *yid-kyis byás-pa* fancied, imaginary. ideal *Cs.*; **yi'-

*kyi lóg-pa** C. to read mentally, softly, inaudibly; before many verbs *yid* stands almost pleon.: **yid k̔ul-če** W. **to exhort**; *yid ˳k̔ul-ba Sch.* 'mental suffering', perh. better: **to be uneasy, troubled, harassed**; *yid ˳k̔rúl-ba* **to be mistaken**; *yid-čad-pa* v. *yi-ycod-pa*; *yid-č̔es-pa* **to believe,** with the accus. or dat. of the thing which one believes, with the dat. of the person whom one believes, ... *par*, that ... (cf. *dád-pa*); *k̔yód-la čun ži̇g yid ma č̔és-pas Mil.* having become a little distrustful towards you; **yid* (or *dén*)*-čö-čeï spé-ra** W. credible words; *yid-brtan-dká-ba Tar.* not to be depended upon, hardly to be believed; *yid-ynyis* **doubt**; *t̔é-tsom dan yid-ynyis ma byed čig Mil.*; *yid ˳p̔ám-pa Mil.* **to be cast down, dejected, depressed**; *yid ˳p̔róg-pa Mil.* **to prepossess, to infatuate**; *yid blon-ba* **to be afraid, full of anxiety** (?) *Sch.*; *yid ˳byun-ba*, resp. *t̔ugs-˳byun-ba Mil.* **to be sad, unhappy, discontented,** *la*, on account of; *na k̔or-bai č̔os-la yid-byun-nas Mil.* I was wearied of the way of (constantly moving in) the orb of transmigration; *yid-˳byin-pa* to make discontented or weary; *yid-múg-pa* v. *yi-mug-pa*; *yid ˳tsim-pa ˳gyúr-ba Dzl.* to become satisfied, contented; **yid tsim co-ce** W. to satisfy; *yid-log-pa* **to be tired** or **weary of** *Sch.*; *yid-t̔ún Dzl.* **forward, rash, overhasty**; *yid-dúns* v. *duns*; *yid-myós* fuddled, tipsy; *yid-smón* v. *smón-pa*; *yid-yžúns* v. *yzúns*; *yid-srúbs Lexx.*, *Sch.*: 'a refractory, stubborn mind', which however does not suit the connection. — 2. symb. num.: 14. — II. = *yud*, *yid-tsam* for *yud-tsam*, *Wdn* frq.

ཡིད་དྭགས་ *yid-tags* v. *yi-dags.*

ཡིན་པ *yin-pa*, resp. and eleg. *lágs-pa* I. **to be,** with neg. *ma yin* or *min*, *W.* **man**; *k̔yod su yin* who are you? *bsa de-ka na yin Mil.* I was the leopard (you saw); with genit., *nai yin* that is mine, belongs to me; **di-rin za-nyi-ma yin** W. to-day is Sunday; *gán-nas yin Mil.* whence are you? *˳di med-pas yin Pth.* it is because this is not here ...; *na bú-moi dús-na yin-te Glr.* when I was still a girl; **yin kyan** C., **yin-na yan** W., C. for *˳on kyan* **yet, nevertheless, notwithstanding**; *yin-gran(-na)* v. *grán-ba* extr.; *yin* for optat or imp.: *de yin* 1. **so it is, yes.** 2. **that may be,** *mi ˳dod run de yin Mil.* if you feel no inclination, never mind, let it be so! *dgrá-bo yin-na-˳an yin Mil.* if he is an enemy, let him be so! *yin-na* stands also pleon. with adverbs etc.: *snar yin-na* = *snar Mil.*; *yin*, so it is! yes! *min*, *W.* **man**, no! *yin-min* truth in a relative sense, *yin-min-gyi t̔é-tsom bsal Glr.* it removes all doubts as to the truth, e.g. the historical truth; *ma yin-pa*, *min-pa* 1. vb. not to be a thing. 2. adj. not being a certain thing, *ma yin-par*, adv.; *č̔os ma yin-par* 'not being law', i.e. contrary to the law of religion, **wrong, unjust,** = *mi rigs-par*; *yul, dus, tsod, rigs-pa ma yin-par spyód-pa Thgy.* to do a thing at a wrong time or place, without observing due measure, in an improper or unnatural manner; hence also *ma-yin-pa* alone: **wrong, unjust**; **ma-yim-pe čö-pa jhe-k̔en-la ten-šig zer** C. whoever commits an improper action is called **ten-šig**; hence also *yin-min* right and wrong. — 3. v. *min.* Cf. moreover *yód-pa* and *˳dúg-pa*, which may be used for *yin-pa*, but not inversely. Sometimes it implies **to mean, to signify**: *rna de či yin Glr.* what does this drumming mean? *rgyál-po k̔on-rán yin dgons* the king thought (the prophecy) meant him, referred to himself; *t̔óg-ma ned-kyi p̔yir ma yin-pas Dzl.* as from the very beginning it was not aimed at me, had no reference to me; also in other instances, where we have to use words of a more precise character: *k̔yód-kyi lo gan yin-pa-la k̔ó-wo dgú-gis Tar.* whilst the sensibility that was with you, i.e. the discretion shown by you, gives me much pleasure. — II. *yin* is joined to a partic. pres., quite analogous to our English construction: *˳gró-ba yin* **I am going** *Mil.*, *C.*; *k̔yód-la lám-mk̔an yód-pa é yin? Mil.* (are you having) have you a guide? *dei nán-na su yód-pa yin? Glr.* who is within? it is also joined to a partic. pf., when referring to the past: *na-rán-la skyés-pa yin Glr.* I have born him; *č̔ád-pa yin-pas Glr.*

because he is descended from . . .; *či byúṅ-ba yiṅ, Glr.* what has become of him? *de-dus či byas-pa yin Mil.* what were you doing just then? so esp. *W.*: **zer-pa yin, zér-pen** he has said it, **kál-pen** it has been sent off; joined to the partic. fut., (or to the partic. pres. or pf., in as far as these are sometimes used also for the fut.) it expresses futurity: *ši-ba yin Pth.* I shall die; *ño su šés-pa-la bskúr-ba yin Glr.* she shall be given to him, that will know her, find her out from amongst the rest; *ₒgró-ba yin mod Glr.* indeed you will have to go now. When joined to a root, it is only in *W.* that it denotes the future: **léb yin, léb-bin** he will come, **táṅ yin** he will give.

Comp. **yin-tog-čan* W.* thinking one's self to be something (great), proud, conceited. — *yin-tsul Mil.* **property, attribute,** ni f. — *yin-lugs* 1. circumstances, **condition** (= *ynás-lugs?*); *kóṅ-rnams-kyi yin-lugs brjod Mil.* she related to him her circumstances. 2. nature or essence of things *Mil.*

ཡིབ་ *yib*, v. *čar-yib* **eaves, shed** *Mil. nt.*, yet cf. the following.

ཡིབ་པ་ *yib-pa* **to hide one's self** *C., W.*; *čar yib byéd-pa Pth.* to take shelter from the rain; **yib-te bór-če* W.* to hide, conceal; *yib-ma* **something hidden** *Sch.*; *yib-sa* **place of concealment, hiding-corner.**

ཡིས་ *yis*, termination of the instrum. case after vowels, po.

ཡུ་ *yu* 1. sbst.? *yu byéd-pa* **to calumniate** *Sch.* (?); *yu-na* if it is true *Sch.* (??) — 2. num. figure: 84.

ཡུ་གུ་, -ཁུ་ *yu-gu, -ku* **oats**, or a similar kind of grain, which, in case of need, may serve for food *C.*

ཡུ་གུ་ཤིང་ *yú-gu-šiṅ* officinal tree, yielding a remedy for wounds and sores *S.g.*; also fig. *Wdṅ.*

ཡུ་གུར་, ཡུ་གེ་ར་ *yu-gúr, yu-gé-ra*, n. of a country and people, *Cs.*, which *Sch.* gratuitously identifies with *Taṅ-gúd*; however *Glr.* p. 32 is stated, that Tibet derived mathematical science and works of art from the east, viz. China and Minyag (i. e. *Taṅ-gúd*), laws and specimens of workmanship from the north, viz. Hor and Yugera (which are frequently mentioned together *Ma.*) — a passage which *Sch.* (History of the Eastern Monguls, 328) translated, but owing to an obscurity in the Mongul text, he failed to recognize Yugera, instead of which he has the word 'Gugi', questionable even to himself. (*Sch.* on the 'Phantom of the Turkish Uigures', v. Preface to *Dzl.* IX.).

ཡུ་བ་ *yú-ba* **handle, hilt, shaft,** *gri-yu* haft of a knife; *stár-yu* helve of an axe; *débs-yu* handle of an awl; *lhám-yu* leg of a boot *Cs.*; *yú(-ba)-čan* provided with a handle, *yu-méd* without a handle *Cs.*; *yu-bčád* 'shoes, slippers' *Sch.* (?).

ཡུ་བུ་ཅག་ *yú-bu-čag Cs.* = *ₓu-bu-čag.*

ཡུ་བོ་, ཡུ་མོ་ *yú-bo, yú-mo* ox, cow, having no horns *Cs.*; for *yú-mo Sch.* has 'hind, female of a stag'; it seems to be little known. *yú-mo srol-góṅ* and *yú-mo mdeu-ₒbyin* names of plants *Wdṅ.*

ཡུག་ *yug* (= *bubs*) 1. **piece of cloth or stuff;** *gós-su ras-yúg yčig-las mi bdóg-ste Dzl.* as they had but one cotton cloth for their clothing. Cotton cloth is generally of very small width, but the silk fabric, designated by *dar-yúg*, seems not to exceed much the breadth of ribbons *Glr.* — 2. for *yud Mil.*

ཡུག་པོ་ *yúg-po, Ld. ₓúg-pa* **oats,** prob. the same as *yú-ku.*

ཡུག(ས)་ས་, ཡུག(ས)་ཟ་ *yúg(s)-sa, yúg(s)-za* **mourning** for a deceased husband or wife, and the state of uncleanness consequent to it, the duration of which varies according to circumstances, whether the first or second spouse has died, and also with respect to the different countries; *yúg(s)-sa-pa*, also *yúg(s)-sa* **widower,** *yúg(s)-sa-mo* **widow**; *yúg(s)-sa p̀óg-pa* being unclean in consequence of mourning; *sáṅs-pa* cleansed, viz. by the expiration of the time of mourning *Cs.*

ཡུང་བ་ *yúṅ-ba Med.*, **yúṅ-pe* W.*, **turmeric.**

ཡུང་མ་ *yúṅ-ma*, for *nyúṅ-ma*, **turnip** *Glr.*

ཡུངས་(ད)ཀར་ *yuṅs-(d)kár* **white mustard,** *yuṅs-nág* **black mustard;** *yuṅs-bṛú* **grain of mustard-seed,** *yuṅs-bru tsam* as small as a grain of mustard-seed *S.g.*; *yuṅs-már* oil of mustard.

ཡུད་ *yud* 1. rarely *yug*, a very small portion of time, **moment,** acc. to *S.g.* = **कला**, stated to be a space of time varying from 8 seconds to 2½ minutes; *yúd tsam (žig)*, *yud ré* but one moment, *yúd-tsam-pa Do.* of a moment's duration; *tse ₒdi yud tsam yin p̔yi-ma-la mta-méd* this life is but like a moment, the future without end; *yúd-kyis*, *yúd-du* in a moment, e.g. *ɣnás-su p̔yin-pa* to get to a place *S.g.*; for a moment, *nám-mk̔a-la ltá-ba* looking up to heaven *Wdṅ.* — 2. acc. to *Stg. k̔u*, fol. 53, *yud* is a space of time of longer duration, 48 minutes; acc. to *Schr.* in *Bhot.* = *ču-tsód* 24 minutes. — 3. **a black** or coloured stripe on woven fabrics, *yud-čan* striped, black or white *W.*

ཡུད་བུ་ *yúd-bu* = *yú-bu*, *ₒú-bu Cs.* (?).

ཡུད་ཡུད་ *yud-yúd Sch.*: *yul-yúd bríd-pa* **a dim and indistinct glimmering** before one's eyes.

ཡུན་ *yun* **time,** when denoting a certain space or length of time, *klog ₒkyúg-pai yun tsam ma lón-par der p̔yin-nas Mil.* in no longer time than a flash of lightning takes he arrived there; *yun riṅ-po, W.* **-mo**, a long time, *yun riṅ-por*, *yun riṅ-du* during a long time, *yun riṅ-po-nas* a long time since or past; **yun máṅ-po bul ča dug* W.* a long time passes; **yun riṅ-ṅi k̔á-na* W.* by degrees, gradually; *yún-du Glr.* for a long time to come; *yun či srid-du* how long? *yun t̔úṅ-ba* a short time.

ཡུམ་ *yum*, resp. for *ma*, 1. **mother,** *btsún-mo yum*, *yum btsún-mo* the queen mother. — 2. *Ssk.* **मातृका**. title of the third and latest part of the sacred writings, which contains the **Abhidharma**, or metaphysical portion (*Köpp.* I, 595. *Burn.* I, 48): *Sch.* mentions also an extract of it, *yum-čúṅ*.

ཡུམ་པ་ *yúm-pa*, only *W.* **to strew,** salt on food, ashes on the snow.

ཡུར་བ་ *yúr-ba* I. vb. 1. **to slumber,** *W.* also **tom yur-če**. — 2. v. *yúr-ma*.

II. sbst. **aqueduct, conduit, water-course, ditch** *Glr.*; *yúr-po če* a large trench, channel, canal, *yur-p̔rán* a small one; *sbubs-yur* a covered, subterraneous canal *Cs.*; *yur(-bai) ču* water conveyed by a canal.

ཡུར་མ་ *yúr-ma* **the act of weeding** *C., W.*; **yur-ma yur-wa**, *C., W.* also **čo-če** to pull out weeds; metaph. to purify the mind, cleanse the heart, e.g. by disburdening one's conscience.

ཡུལ་ *yul* 1. **place,** a. **an inhabited place,** as opp. to desolation, *t̔aṅ stoṅ-pa mi daṅ yul med-čiṅ Pth.* a desert in which there are neither men nor dwelling-places; b. **place,** with reference to a sacred community (college, monastery etc.) near it, e.g. some of the students live in the college, others in the place: so *yul-dgón* village and monastery, *yul-dgón-rnams Mil.* for *yúl-mi daṅ dgón-pa-pa-rnams* laymen and clerics. c. **place, province, country,** in a gen. sense, *yúl-(gyi) skad* provincial dialect, provincialism; *yul-(gyi) mtil*, *mčog* chief place, capital; *yul čen-po brgyad* chief places; as such are enumerated in *Pth.*, without any regard to geography, Singhala, Thogar, Li, Balpo, Kashmir, Zahor, Urgyan, Magata; *rgya-gar(-gyi) yul* India; *rgyá-yul*, *bód-yul*, *sóg-yul* India (or China), Tibet, Mongolia; whenever *yul* precedes a word, as in **yul wa-ra-ṇa-sér**, it is to be understood in this way: as to the place (situation), in Banāras; *skyid-yul* a lucky place, *sdug-yul* an unlucky one; *p̔á-yul* fatherland, native country, home; *raṅ-yul* one's own country, *ɣžán-yul* a foreign country; *ₒbróg-yul* country consisting of steppes, *róṅ-yul* country full of ravines; *lha(i)-yul* **land of gods,** abode of the *lha* also fig., a particularly pleasant country or scenery; *mi(i)-yul* **abode of men,** (ἡ οἰκουμένη) **the inhabited world, earth,** yet in the Tibetan sense always as opp. to the abodes of good or evil deities; *mii yúl-na mi ₒoṅ Glr.* in the world such a thing is not to be found; *rnám-šes dbáṅ-poi yúl-las ₒdás-pa Wdṅ.* the soul that has left the external world, (yet cf. no. 2); *spyód-yul*, q.v. — 2. **the object or objects of perception by means of the senses**; *ýyii yul drug* the provinces of the six senses, viz. forms (the external appearances of bodies), sounds etc. *Mil.*; so prob. also: *yúl-rnams-la lóṅs-spyod-par rmóṅs-te Wdṅ.* dead to sensual pleasures; *yul mi ₒdzin-pa*, or *yžán-du ₒdzin-pa Thgy.* to perceive things either not at all, or not correctly; *brǰód-pai yúl-las ₒdás-pa* is stated to imply: exceeding the limits of speech, unspeakable, unutterable; *bsám-byai yúl-las ₒdás-pa = bsám-gyis mi k̒yáb-pa* frq. unimaginable, inconceivable, which term, however, does not seem to be fully adequate; also *Was.* (311) translates *yul* with **object**; cf. *ynas*, 5. — 3. **weather**, or rather in a more gen. sense, **climatic state** of a country, and condition of the beings in it, v. below *yul-ṅán*, *yul-bzáṅ*.

Comp. and deriv. *yul-k̒áms* kingdom, e.g. of Nepal, China, *Glr.* — *yul-ₒk̒ór* country, province *Glr.* — *yul-gru* id. *Glr.* — *yul-dgón* v. above. — *yul-ṅán C.* tempest, *yul-ṅán-gyi ts̒úb-ma* the turmoil of the tempest *Glr.*; also public calamities, such as famine, murrain etc, *Glr.* — *yúl-čan* 1. **suited, proper, being in its place, fulfilling its purpose,** *Cs.* (?) 2. **that which is treated 'objectively'** *Was* 311, cf. no. 2 above. — *yúl-čos* characteristic properties, manners etc. of a country. — *yul-ljóṅs* district, tract of country. — **yul tum-túm* Ld.* the separate villages of a whole cluster bearing one common name. — *yul-sdé* 1. **district** *C.*, *W.* 2. **village magistrate.** — *yúl-pa* **inhabitant, native,** *gaṅ yúl-pa yin* whence are you? what is your country? — **citizen, burgher** *Mil.*; *yúl-pa-rnams* the people, the public *Mil.* — *yúl-po* gen. with *če*, a large country, *Mil.* — *yúl-dpon* village magistrate, district judge. — *yul-ṕyógs* region, neighbourhood *Mil.* — *yúl-ma* a native woman. — *yúl-mi* 1. = *yúl-pa*. 2. **countryman, compatriot** *Do.* — *yul-méd* 1. **improper, not in its place** *Cs.* 2. *ráṅ-snaṅ yul-méd bstán-du ysol Glr.* was explained: what has no place in my mind, what I do not know or understand, I beg you to teach me. — *yúl-ts̒o* **village, borough,** = *gróṅ-ts̒o.* — **yul-ts̒ód-zum-k̒an* W.* land-surveyor, engineer. — *yul-yzis* v. *yžis.* — *yul-bzáṅ* fair weather *Cs.*, yet cf. *yul-ṅán.* — *yúl-yod-pa = yúl-čan Cs.* — *yúl-len* the mode of forwarding letters from village to village, instead of expediting them in longer and regular stages. — *yul-bšád* geography or topography. — *yul-sá* dwelling-place, habitation *W.* — *yul-srid* government of a country *Schr.* — *yul-sréd = yul-la ₒdód-pa* attachment to one's native place, the love of country and of home, *Mil.*

ཡུལ་བ་ *yúl-ba*, less corr. spelling for *nyúl-ba Tar.*

ཡུས་ *yus* 1. **boasting, bragging, puff,** *yus če don čuṅ Mil.* much bragging, and nothing in it, *yus če šes čuṅ Mil.* one that boasts much, and knows very little; *yus brǰod-pa, byed-pa* to boast *Cs.* — 2. **pride,** *k̒oṅ yus ma če žig* do not take too much pride in your heart *Mil.*; *lás-la byas yus čé-na ṅó-so čuṅ* the more a man is pleased with himself after his deed, the less (real) happiness. — 3. **blame, charge, accusation** *Schr.* (?), false accusation *Sch.* (?), *yus byéd-pa* to charge, accuse *Schr.* — 4. **ardour, fervour, transport,** *dád-pai yús-kyis* in the fervour of devotion, e.g. to shed tears, to fall down on the ground *Pth.* — 5. *yus ₒtúd-pa* to fasten one cord to another, **to knit or join things together** *Sch.*

ཡེ་ *ye*, 1. *Cs.*: *'yé-ma* **beginning and eternity,** *ye-ldán* **eternal'.** This word is known to me only as an adv., **completely, perfectly, highly, quite**; *yé-nas* id.; *ye-dág* quite clean, *ye-rdzógs* quite perfect, *yé-nas bzáṅ-po* altogether good; with a negative following, **not at all,** *ye ma ₒdod* I felt no inclination at all, *ye ma žig-par ₒdug Mil.* he was not hurt at all, *yé-nas mi byed dgos* that is not to be done by any means; *ye-šés* (vulgo *Ld.* **'i-šes**) ज्ञान, the perfect, absolute, heavenly, divine **wisdom**; less frq. resp. *ye-mkyén*; *ye-šés lṅa* the five kinds of divine wisdom, of which, acc. to some, every Buddha is possessed, acc. to others, only Adibuddha; *ye-šés*, in a great measure at least, is inherent to all great saints and divine beings; it will suddenly break forth from the bodies of the terrifying gods in the shape of fire, which puts the demons to flight *Glr.*; *raṅ-byúṅ ye-šés* the self-originated wisdom occasionally is personified in a similar manner, as Wisdom is in the Proverbs of Solomon; in later times this conception coincides in the popular mind also with *stoṅ-pa-nyid*. — 2. provinc. for *yin Glr.* 75. — 3. provinc. for ... *am, ḱyed blá-ma-čan ₒgró-ye Mil.* are you going to the Lama? — 4. in comp. for *ye-šés*, v. *ye-ťig*. — 5. num. figure: 114.

ཡེ་ཏིག *ye-ťig Sch.*: **'the trace, line, or manifestation of divine wisdom'.**

ཡེ་དངས་ *ye-dáṅs Bal.* for *nyid-ráṅ*, **you**, the pronoun of polite address.

ཡེ་འབྲོག་ *ye-ₒbróg* a contagious disease *Cs.*; acc. to oral explanation: **injury inflicted on the soul, harm done to the mind,** which may take place in 360 different ways *Mil.* —

ཡེ་རང་ *ye-ráṅ* n. of a city, next to Khobom (Katmandu), the first in Nepal *Mil.*

ཡེ་རེ་ *ye-ré* v. *yér-re-ba*.

ཡེ་ཤུ་ *yé-šu* **Jesus** *Chr. Prot.*

ཡེགས་པ་ *yégs-pa* **rough, shaggy, hairy** *Cs.*

ཡེང་བ་ *yéṅ-ba* v. *γyéṅ-ba*.

ཡེད་པོ་ *yéd-po* provinc. for *yág-po*.

ཡེན་ *yen*, prob. only in *yén-la* joined to *γtóṅ-ba* and synonyms, **to bestow liberally, amply, plentifully;** *zas daṅ spyód-lam yen-la γtad-par bya* food and exercise should be amply provided for *Lt.*

ཡེར་ *yer Lt.* = *γnyid-yer* q.v.

ཡེར་པ་ *yér-pa?* *ṕyág-tu yér-pa žig mdzád-nas* to raise one's hand with the palm turned upward, as a gesture of (willingly or respectfully) **offering,** *Mil.nt.* (This term might perh. be applied to the 'waving' of the wave-offerings, ordained by the Mosaic law.)

ཡེར་བ་ *yér-ba* **sprinkled, sputtered, spouted**(?) *Sch.*

ཡེར་རེ་བ་ *yér-re-ba* **pure, clear, genuine, unadulterated** *Mil.*; *sṅo ye-ré* a pure blue, *dkar ye-ré* a pure white *C.*

ཡེལ་ཡེལ་ *yel-yél*, *Pth.* frq., e.g. *mdaṅs yel-yél, sems-dgá yel-yél* **clear, light, bright** or something like it(?).

ཡེས་མེས་ *yes-mės* **ancestor** *Sch.*

ཡོ་ *yo* numerical figure: 144.

ཡོ་ག་ *yó-ga Ssk.* = *rnal-ₒbyór, yó-gi* = *yo-ga-pa, yó-gi-ni* = *yó-ga-ma*; more about this word v. *Williams Ssk. Dict.*

ཡོ་བ་ *yó-ba* 1. adj. and sbst., **oblique, sloping, slanting, awry, crooked; obliquity, slope, slant;** *čuṅ-yo-ba* a little slanting, crooked *Glr.*; *ḱa yo* the mouth awry *S.g.*; *yón-po*, col. **yón-te**, adj., id.; *yo sróṅ-ba, yón-po bsraṅ-ba, Lexx.*, to make the crooked straight; **zám-pa yon-yón čo dug* W.* the bridge is unsteady, swings to and fro; fig. **twisted, distorted, perverted, erroneous;** *yon-dpyad* wrong interpretation, false judgment; going crooked ways, **deceitful, crafty,** and sbst. **crookedness**, deceitful dealings *Cs.*; more frq. *γyo*. — 2. **everything, altogether, whole** (?) *Sch.*

ཡོ་བྱད་ *yo-byád*, **tools, implements, chattels, household furniture, necessaries,** *ₒtsó-bai* necessaries of life; *mčod-pai* requisites for sacrificing; *yo-byád sbyór-ba* to procure the needful, to make preparations *Dzl.*; *yo-byád ťams-čád-kyis* (or *bzáṅ-pos*) *stób-pa Tar.* to provide a person with everything necessary, to fit out well; *yo-byád srél-ba* id. (?) *Sch.*; *yo-byád-kyis ₒbrál-ba* to be in want of the needful; *nor ṕyugs yo-byád* money, cattle, and furniture, as a specification of property.

ཡོ་འབོག་ *yo-ₒbóg Wdṅ.* n. of a tree, which by the Lamas of Sikim is stated to grow in Tibet; *Sch.*: **elm,** and in another place: *rii yo-ₒbóg* **linden-tree,** less prob.

ཡོག་ *yog* 1. col. but also sometimes in *B.*, for *ₒog* **below, down stairs**, *yog-ḱáṅ* **ground-floor; cellar.** — 2. v. *γyóg-pa*.

ཡོག་པོ་ *yóg-po* 1. *Sch. yóg-mo, W. yóg-śiṅ*, **pole** or **stick for stirring the fire, poker** *Mil. nt.* — 2. v. *γyóg-po*.

ཡོག་གཅིན་ *yóg-γčin* one that is wetting his bed *Sch.*

ཡོང་བ་ *yóṅ-ba*, pf. *yoṅs*, used throughout Tibet (except in Balti, where they say *'óṅ-čas*); not unfrq. also in later literature, for *₍óṅ-ba* **to come;** *Sch.* has also *yoṅ-čad* (*-ṫsad?*) time and place of coming, and *yoṅ-yé* ever before, at all times (?).

ཡོངས་ *yóṅs*, **all, whole,** *mgo-nág yóṅs-kyi rje Glr.* lord of all the black-haired (i.e. of all men); *yoṅs-ₒdu-ₒṫsal-gyi p̓o-bráṅ Mil.* the palace in which all wish to meet, ni f.; *yóṅs-su* adv. **wholly, completely, altogether,** *yóṅs-su dág-pa* quite clean, *yóṅs-su ṡpáṅ-ba* to give up entirely; *yóṅs-su bslád-de* quite lost in perverseness; **generally, universally,** *žes yóṅs-su grágs-so Glr.* so he was universally called; *yóṅs-grágs-kyi bu čen bži Mil. nt.*, four disciples, followers, of universal fame; *sdug-bsṅál-las yóṅs-su ma gról-la Stg.*, seems to mean: he is not yet quite delivered; cf. however *yé-nas* with a negative. — *yoṅs-grúb* **the absolute,** what is independent and complete in itself *Was.* (202). —

ཡོད་པ་ *yód-pa*, resp. and eleg. *mčís-pa* 1. **to be,** = *yin-pa*, *sgyu yod Dzl.* it is deceit, humbug; often with the termin., like *ₒdúg-pa, dúd-pa ltá-bur yod Glr.* it is smoke-coloured; *śin-tu mṫún-par yod ₒdúg-pas Glr.* as they are very intimate with each other; with a participle joined to it (or a gerund, vulgo, esp. in *W.*), *gró-ba yod* **it is becoming, growing, getting** *Pth.; śár-p̓yogs-su bstán-pa yod* it is pointing towards the east, *stsál-nas yod* he gives, has given; *brtsig-nas yod* he is building, he was building; *léb(s)-te yod* *W.* he is (has) come; with a root often pleon.: *ṅas bśags yod k̓yod-kyis k̓ol čig Mil.* I have been splitting (the tree), do you carry it away now; *ṅan čén-po byas yod Glr.* he has been committing a great evil; *soṅ yód-pas Pth.* as he was gone. — 2. **to be in a certain place,** *der rdziṅ-bu žig yód-pai náṅ-na Dzl.* inn pond which is in that place; *ṅai yul-mi-las bú-mo yód-pa-rnam Dzl.* the girls that are among my subjects; *de náṅ-na yód-k̓an ṫsáṅ-ma* *W.* all that is in it; *yód-sa*, pop. for *gáṅ-na-ba*, place of abode. — 3. **to exist, to be on hand,** *bdé-ba yod ma yin Pth.* no happiness exists; *čúṅ-zad yod kyaṅ srid-kyis Dzl.* as possibly a little might still be on hand; *'é yod* is, or are there (even now)? *Glr.; snáṅ-ba yód-pai dus-su Thgy.* whilst there is day-light. — 4. with genit. or dat. for **to have** (like the Latin *est mihi* I have): *sú-la-₍aṅ yod ma yin Pth.* nobody has . . .; *rgyál-po-la ₒdód-pa čén-po yód-par ₒdug* the king seems to have yet a great wish; *rgyál-moi γyóg-mo žig yód-pa de Pth.* a maid-servant whom the queen had; so in a like manner without a case: *gri žig yód-pa de Mil.* the knife which he had about (him); *yód-pa Thgy.* the things which one has, τὰ ὑπάρχοντα; *k̓rón-pa ₒdom bču-dgu yód-pa Glr.* a well having a depth of 19 fathoms. — 5. *yód-par ₒgyur* a. fut. of *yód-pa* **shall or will be.** b. **to originate, appear,** *bsáṅs-pai śúl-du da-rúṅ yaṅ yód-par gyúr-nas Dzl.* as in the place of (the gold-pieces) that were taken away, always new ones appeared. c. **to get, receive,** *k̓ri γdugs kyaṅ yód-par gyur čig Dzl.* the throne should also receive a canopy! *yód-par byéd-pa* **to beget, produce, effect,** frq., *bu yód-par gyis śig Dzl.* get her a child!

Comp. *Cs.: yod-pa-nyid* existence, *yod-min-nyid* non-existence; *Sch.: yod-ṫáṅ* 'thoroughly clear'; *yod-ṫsód yin* 'it has the semblance of being' (?); *yod-med* a. being and not being, *yod-méd go-bzlóg snaṅ* optical illusions, when one imagines to see what is not existing, or the reverse. b. in *W. yod* is also used merely to give force to *med*, as *yod med* there is not at all . . .

ཡོན་ *yon* 1. **gift, offering,** of free will, to priests and mendicant friars, frq., *zás-yon* a gift consisting in food, *yon ₒbúl-ba* to bestow a gift, to bring an offering; *yón-du ₒbúl-ba* to present as a gift; **fee,** *smán-yon* physician's fee *Cs.; yon snó-ba* to bless the gift received, to return a blessing for it. — 2. = *yon-tan*.

Comp. *yon-mčód* 1. = *yón-bdag Glr.* 2 for *yón-bdag daṅ mčód-γnas Mil.* dispenser (of gifts) and priest. — *yón-bdag* vulgo and in more recent literature for the *sbyin-bdag* of earlier writings, **dispenser of gifts, entertainer, host**, in point of fact identic with **house-owner, citizen, farmer,** and also at the present time used in that sense without any religious bearing; it is also the title generally used by mendicant friars in their addresses, something like 'your honour'. — *yón-γnas* the receiver of a gift *Cs.*

ཡོན་ཏན་ *yón-tan* गुण (opp. to *skyon*) 1. **good quality, excellence, valuable properties,** e.g. the medicinal virtues of plants; also **acquirements, accomplishments, attainments,** *yón-tan slób-pa* to learn something useful *Pth.* and vulgo; *ₒdi bui yón-tan yin Dzl.* for that you are indebted to the boy, this is the boy's merit; **property, quality,** in gen., e.g. the different tastes and effects of medicines *Med.*; also mystic or fantastic properties *Glr.* — *bdag blus kyaṅ yón-tan med Glr.*, even if one would ransom me, it would be to no purpose, not worth while; *ₒdód(-pai) yón(-tan)* v. *ₒdód-pa*; *p̔an-yon* v. *p̔án-pa.* — 2. num.: 3.

ཡོན་པོ་ *yón-po* v. *yó-ba.*

ཡོབ་, འོབ་ *yob*, *ₒob*, **stirrup** *Cs.*; *yob-gón* instep of the foot *Cs.*; *yob-lčágs* 'the iron of the stirrup' *Cs.*; *yob-čén* = *yob Cs.*; *yob-t̔ág* stirrup-leather *Cs.*, *yob-mt̔il* the footing, *yob-lúṅ* (*Sch. yob-lóṅ*) the hoop of the stirrup.

ཡོབ་པ་ *yób-pa* v. *γyób-pa.*

ཡོམ་པ་ *yóm-pa Cs.* vb., adj. sbst., **to swing, totter, tremble, to be unsteady; swinging etc., the swinging etc.**; *yóm-po*, adj., *yom-yóm Pth.*, *yóm-me-ba Mil.* id.

ཡོར་པོ་ *yór-po* 1. **dull, heavy, blunt** *Cs.*; *Tar.*: *yór-yor-ba*; but the expressions *t̔om-yór* shaking, tottering, trembling, like an old man *Mil.*, and *mig-yór* mirage, seem to indicate that the proper signification is **trembling.** — 2. **oblique, slanting,** *C.*

ཡོལ་གོ་, ཡོལ་མ་ *yól-go*, *yól-ma* **earthenware, crockery** *Schr.*, *Cs.*, *dkar-yól* **china-ware, porcelain,** frq.; *yol-gór* **cup, bowl,** *Sch.*

ཡོལ་བ་ *yól-ba* I. sbst. **curtain,** *yól-bas ₒbré-ba Glr.* to stretch a curtain over; *yól-ba ten-pa Glr.* to draw a curtain; *yól-ba γčod-pa* to close the curtain (of a door), *yól-ba ₒbyéd-pa* to open it *Cs.*; *dar-yól* silk-curtain, *ras-yól* calico-curtain; *sgo-yól* curtain before a door. — II. vb. 1. **to be past,** *nyi-ma-p̔yed yol* mid-day is past, it is afternoon (about 2 o'cl.) *Wdk.* (v. *nyin-žág*); *srod yol soṅ* the evening-twilight is gone, it is complete night (about 11 o'cl.) *C.*; *nyi-ma yól-la k̔ad* day is almost over, evening is drawing on, *Dzl.* ༢༠༨, 6; *dús-las yól-ba* **to be past,** both impers., it is past, it is over, and pers., he is past his prime, old, decrepit *Dzl.*; *rluṅ daṅ čar dús-las mi yól-bas* wind and rain setting in and ceasing at the proper time *Dzl.* — 2. also *γyól-ba C.*, *dbyól-ba*, *ₒbyól-ba* **to evade, shun, to go not to a place,** *mig yól-ba* to look away; **lé-yol čém-po yin** he is very shy of work, averse to labour *C.*

ཡོས་ *yos*, 1. **slightly roasted corn,** mostly barley or wheat, which on account of its transportability is generally taken by travellers along with them, as their fare on the road; fresh prepared it is much relished by the people; *ₒbrás-yos* rice, thus prepared *S.g.* — 2. **hare,** but only as an astronomical term, *yós-lo* the hare-year.

གཡག་ *γyag*, चमर, **the yak,** Bos grunniens (reckoned by the Hindu among the antilopes), fem. v. *ₒbri-mo*; *p̔o-γyág* male yak; *p̔a-γyág* uncastrated yak-bull; *γyag-rú* horn of a yak, also n. of a plant, Morina *Ld.*; *γyag-rog-žol-čén* a very long-haired, shaggy yak *Sch.*

གཡང་ *γyaṅ* 1. *Ssk.* श्री, synon. *dpal*, **happiness, blessing, prosperity,** *γyaṅ čágs* blessing comes (from), grows (out of), nif. *Mil.*; *šor* it departs, it is gone; *γyaṅ-skyób*, *γyaṅ-ₒgúgs Schl.* 263, **yáṅ-k̔úg** *W.* **a calling forth of blessing, sacrifices and other ceremonies performed, in order to secure happiness and prosperity.** — *γyaṅ-skár* **propitious stars** or **aspects**; the lunar mansions no. ༦

to 卐 v. *rgyu-skár.* — *γyaṅ-kúg* **beggar's bag** of the Lamas. — *γyáṅ-čan* **happy, blessed, prosperous,** *γyaṅ-méd* the contrary. — *γyaṅ-yíg* a written benediction *Glr.* — *γyaṅ-lhá* a deity of the Shamans, dispensing happiness *Sch.* — 2. **gulf, abyss,** gen. *γyáṅ-sa* also *γyaṅ-γzán; ǰi-tsam mto bžin γyáṅ-sa če* so high as you stand, so deep is the gulf; *lus γyáṅ-du γtóṅ-ba* to plunge, to precipitate one's self *Dzl.*; *γyáṅ-du* or *γyáṅ-la ltúṅ-ba* to fall down *Dzl.*; *mčóṅ-ba* to leap *Glr.*; *ṅán-soṅ-gi γyáṅ-la ₒkor Pth.* he totters on the brink of the abyss of hell; *γyáṅ-sa-las ₒdzin-pa* to snatch from the abyss, to save *Thgy.*; *brag-γyaṅ-γzár* rocky precipice *Mṅg.*

གཡང་ཊི་ *γyaṅ-ṭi Sch.*: 'the precious stone chas'.

གཡང་ཚེ་ *γyaṅ-tsé Mil.* nt., *C.* a bowl or cup of clay or wood.

གཡང་ལུགས་ *γyaṅ-lúgs C.* also *yaṅ-lús,* = *γzán-gos* **skin** of an animal, used for clothing; *Mil.* also fig.: *bzód-pai γyaṅ-lúgs gyon* he wrapped himself in the mantle of patience; *γyaṅ-γži Lex.* अजिन, skin of an antilope, the customary couch of the members of religious orders; also **skin, couch, covering,** in general *Pth.*

གཡན་པ་ *γyán-pa Lexx.* w.e. *Sch.*: a cutaneous eruption, akin to the itch, which is said to invade any part of the body, and to be combined with a copious discharge of matter; hereditary, and not contagious.

གཡབ་ *γyab, γyáb-pa, γyáb-mo* v. *yab* etc.

གཡམ་ *γyam Sch.*: 'the following a good or bad example, with the respective consequences(?)'.

གཡམ་པ་ *γyám-pa Sch.*: 'a certain stone'; **yam-pʻáṅ* W.* **a slab of slate, roof-slate,** for *γya-spáṅ.*

གཡའ་ *γya* 1. **rust,** incorr. verdigris; *lčags-gyá* id.; *lčags gya čags Lt.* iron rusts; **ya kʻor,* or *ǰuṅ,* or *yoṅ* W.* id.; **ya čád-če* W.* to scrape the rust off (from metals), to clean, polish; *γya-dág-pa* freed from rust, clear, polished, e.g. a mirror; *γyá-pa* **rusty** *Sch.*; fig. for **infection, contamination** *Mil.*; *γya ₒdrúl-ba* to be mouldy *Sch.* more corr. **to get rusty,** to get covered with foul extraneous matter; *lčé-la γya-ₒdrúl byed Lt.* the tongue gets furred. — 2. also *γyá-ma,* vulgo **yá-mán**, **slate, slab of slate;** *γya-spáṅ* 1. id. 2. *Cs.* also **oil of vitriol, sulphuric-acid**(?) 3. in *C.* **verdigris;** *γya-tig* 1. **a line drawn with a slate- or lead-pencil.** 2. **slate-pencil, lead-pencil,** also *γya-smyúg.* 3. **bolt, bar,** *γya rgáb-pa* to bolt, to bar, *γya pʻyé-ba* to unbolt, to unbar; *γyá-šir* = *γya; *ₒdzin-ya* C.* pin. — 4. v. *γyá-ba.*

གཡའ་ཀྱི་མ་ *γyá-kyi-ma Lt.* n. of a plant, in *Lh.* a small high-alpine Saussurea.

གཡའ་བ་ *γyá-ba* 1. **to shrink, to start up,** in consequence of a sudden irritation, tickling etc., **to shudder,** *skyi-γya-ba* id. *Mil.*; *W.*: **ya čúg-če** to cause to shrink or start, **to tickle,** *Cs.* also: *γyá-ba* **to feel a horror.** — 2. **to itch,** *dei lus γyá-bas Dzl.* because he felt an itching.

གཡའ་ཡ་ *γyá-ya C.* **yá-ya** **yes!** in speaking to inferiors.

གཡའ་ལི་ *γyá-li* **maple** *Sik.*; the dried leaves of it are said to be boiled by the poor instead of tea.

གཡར་དམ་ *γar-dám Lex.,* **oath**(?) *Sch.*

གཡར་བ་ *γyár-ba* **to borrow, to lend; to hire;** with reference to money, only provinc. (*Lh., Ts.*); *pʻo-braṅ-nas már-me γyár-te Glr.* having borrowed a lamp in the castle; *γnas-tsáṅ γyár-ba Tar., C., *ďáṅ-sa yár-če* W.* with *la,* **to ask for reception,** night-quarters; *kʻáṅ-pa γyár-mkʻan* **lessee, tenant, lodger;** *γyar byed-pa* = *γyár-ba Sch.*; **pʻan-yár čo-če* W.* to succour a person by an advance of money; *pʻa-γyár* **step-father,** *ma-γyár* **step-mother,** *bu-γyár* **adopted child;** *γyár-po* **credit** for what has been lent, advanced; **yár-po táṅ-če* W.* to lend, a thing, *Schr.* to let, lodgings.

གཡར་ཚུས་ *γyar-tsus* **food, nourishment, victuals** *Sch.*

གཡས་པ་ *γyás-pa* **right,** *γyás-ma* the right hand, *γyás-na* on the right (hand), *γyás-su* to the right, *γyás-nas* from the right;

mig-γyás the right eye, *lag-γyás* the right hand, *rkan-γyás* the right foot; *γyas-ños*, *-pyógs*, *-lógs* the right (hand) side: *γyas-γyón* right and left; *γyas-γyón-la`ltá-ba* to look all round; *γyas-rú* 1. the right wing. 2. p.n., district in *Ts.*; **Yĕ-ru tsáñ-po** n. of the principal river in Tibet v. *tsáñ-po.*

གཡི་, དབྱི *γyi, dbyi* **lynx** (*Cs.* erron. ermine).

གཡིག(ས)་པ *γyig(s)-pa* **to be hindered** *Cs.*; *Lex.*: *γyér-mas γyigs-pa?*

གཡུ་ *γyu* **turkois,** *mdún-γyu* the front-turkois in the head-dress of females; *prá-γyu* little turkois-stones; *γyui* frq. for turkois-blue; **yu-dán** *W.* the rib n on which the turkois-stones of the head-dress are fastened; *γyu-mtsó* a blue-glittering lake, po. *Mil.*; **yu-žún-men-tog** forget-me-not *Sp*; *γyu-rál* a mane of turkois-colour *Glr.* — *γyu-rúñ* for *γyuñ-druñ Glr.*

གཡུག་པ་ *γyúg-pa*, incorr. spelling for *dbyúg-pa.* —

གཡུང་དྲུང་ *γyuñ-drúñ*, **स्वस्तिका** (also *γża-γsañ*), **the cross cramponee** ✠, the principal symbol of the Bonpos, but also much in favour in Buddhist mysticism and popular superstition: *γyuñ-drúñ-pa* = *bón-po*; *γyuñ-drúñ dgón-pa* the Buddhist monastery Lama Yurru in Ladak, v. Cunningham.

གཡུང་བ་ *γyúñ-ba* **tame,** opp. to *rgod.*

གཡུང་མོ་ *γyúñ-mo* (*Lex.* **डिम्बिका, a libidinous woman**), *Cs.*: 'a woman having always the menses'.

གཡུར་ *γyur* 1. **sleep** *Sch.* — 2. v. *γyul-ka.*

གཡུར་བ་ *γyúr-ba Lex.*, *C.* also **yór-ba** **to droop, to hang or sink down,** of fading flowers etc.; *γyur zá-ba Lex.* w.e.; *Sch.*: what has become ripe and eatable.

གཡུལ་ *γyul Schr.*: **army;** *Cs.*: **battle;** neither of the two meanings appears to be quite exact (cf. *dmag*); prob. both *γyul* and *γyul-ñó* denote an army facing the enemy and ready for battle; *γyúl-las rgyál-ba* and *pám-pa* to conquer and to be conquered frq.; *γyul ˳gyéd-pa Do.*, *spród-pa Do.*, *Pth.*, *ťáb pa* to fight, strive, struggle, *dañ* with; *γyúl-du* or *γyul-ñor žúgs-pa* to go to battle *Do.*; *γyul šóm-pa* to prepare for battle *Lex.*; *dug lñai γyúl-ño zlóg-pa* to repulse the warlike host of the five poisons *Mil.*

གཡུལ་ཁ་, གཡུལ་འཐག་ *γyul-ka, γyul-˳tag* **thrashing-floor;** both these words appear to be not everywhere current, but provinc., cf. *ko-γyu*; *γyul-ka γcóg-pa Sch.*, **yur ǰhé-pa** *C.* **to thrash.**

གཡེང་བ་ *γyéñ-ba*, less frq. *yéñ-ba*, pf. *(γ)yeñs*, **to move a thing softly to and fro,** e.g. an infant on one's arms, to lull it to sleep *Thgy.*; esp. with reference to the water: *čus γyeñs-te* moved by the waves to and fro *Dzl.*; fig. to run to and fro, like a hunted hare *Ma.*; **to stream into, to overflow,** *yul-káms-su* a country, to inundate it, of floods, hostile armies etc *Ma.*; **to rummage, turn over,** *dpé-rnams* books *Mil* — 2. **to turn off the attention, to disturb the mind,** *rgyál-po spyan γyéñs-pa dañ Glr.* the king looking away, directing his attention to something else: *sems bdud-kyis γyeñs Mil.* the soul is disturbed by the devil; *čos ˳dód-pa-rnams γyéñs-par byéd-pa Thgy.* to put out or confound those that are seeking religion; *ma-γyéñs-par nyón čig* now be all attention! *γyéñ-ba*, *γyéñs-pa* sbst., **inattention, wandering, absence of mind,** *γyéñs su ˳jug-pa Thgr.* to give one's self to inattention; adj. *rnám-par γyéñs-pa* very absent, wandering; *rnám-par mi-γyéñ-ba* or *-γyéñs-pa* quite attentive, not to be disturbed by anything, inexcitable, a character in which Buddha excels, and which every one of his followers must strive to attain. — 3. sbst. *γyéñs-pa* **diversion, pleasure, recreation,** **yáñ(s)-pa-la čá-če**, resp. **ťug-yáñ(s)-la (s)kyód-če** *W.* to take a walk, **yáñ(s)-pa sé-če** *W.* to be playful, like children, kittens etc.; **jest, joke,** **yáñ-pa man, don-dám yin** *W.* I am not joking, I am serious; **yáñ(s)-pa-čan** *W.* jester, buffoon; *yéñs-˳dod-kyi ka-krám ma yin Mil.*, these are no falsehoods spoken in jest. — *γyéñs-ma*, a wanton female, prostitute *Sch.*

གཡེན་ *γyen? γyen-sbyór-ba S.g.* **to calumniate** ni f.

གཡེམ་པ་ *γyém-pa, Lex.* **मिथ्याचर्या, being untrue** in one's dealings, acting **wrongfully,** which also my referees confirmed to be the general import of the word; in books, however, it is usually joined to *ₒdód-pas,* or *ₒdód-pa-la,* adding *lóg-par,* as: *ₒdód-pa-la lóg-par γyém-pa,* or it stands alone as in *γyém byéd-pa,* signifying **'to commit adultery, fornication'** *Dzl.* and elsewh.; *log-γyém* sbst. —

གཡེར་ཁ་ *γyér-ka* (vulg. *'er-ka*), **bell, set of bells,** or **peal** *Glr.*

གཡེར་པོ་ *γyér-po* **wise, prudent, circumspect, thorough-going** *Sch.*

གཡེར་བག་ *γyer-bág Lex., Sch.:* **a light, luminous place.**

གཡེར་མ་ *γyér-ma Med.* frq., **Guinea pepper,** *Capsicum W.* *nyér-ma*; *γyer-šiṅ-pa* medicinal herb *S.g.*

གཡེལ་བ་ *γyél-ba* 1. **to be idle, lazy, slothful; idleness, laziness;** *γyel-ba-méd-par* incessantly, continually, e.g. to pray, to guard *Mil., S.O.* — 2. *ṭugs γyél-ba* resp. to forget *W.*

གཡོ་ *γyo* (rarely *yo*) **craft, cunning, deceit,** more frq. *γyo-sgyú, γyo-zól; γyó-čan* crafty, deceitful, *γyo-méd* honest, *γyo byéd-pa* to deceive.

གཡོ་བ་ *γyó-ba* I. vb., pf. and imp. *γyos,* 1. **to move,** to cause to change place; **to be moved,** agitated, shaken, *γnam sa γyós-so* heaven and earth were shaken *Dzl.; des ni sa ₒdi γyo-bar ₒgyur* thereby the earth may be shaken *Do.;* **to bend, incline, tilt,** e.g. a vessel; **zúg-po yos toṅ* W.* make a bow! *sku γyós-par ₒgyúr-to* the image began to move *Glr.; sa-γyós* earthquake; **to begin to move** or to march *Ma.; tugs-rje γtiṅ-nas γyós-pai rtags* it is a sign that his heart is moved by grace *Mil. nt.*; *dgé-bai p̔yógs-la ₒdu-šés čuṅ-zad kyaṅ ma γyos* he did not allow the least virtuous impulses to rise (in his heart), he kept down every sense of virtue; *γyó-ba* partic., continually moving, restless, uneasy, of the mind *Mil., mi-γyó-ba* **unmoved,** immovable, n. of Siva and of other terrifying deities *Glr.* (cf. **चपल** *Will*) — 2. **to prepare,** victuals for the table *γyós-subyéd-pa* id.; *γyós-kaṅ* kitchen, bake-house, *γyós-mkan* baker, cook.

II. sbst. **moveableness, mobility,** *yáṅ-žiṅ γyo-ba-nyid* an easy mobility *Wdṅ.*

གཡོག་ *γyog* (v. *yog, ₒog*) *Tar.* and elsewh., usually occurring in the more definite form *γyóg-po,* **servant, man-servant,** *γyóg-mo* **maid-servant, female servant,** waiting-maid; when distinguished from *kól-po, kól-mo* and *bran,* it denotes a higher degree, e.g. *γyog-mo γnyis* two waiting-maids and besides 500 *kól-mo* maid-servants *Pth.; γyóg-po daṅ yáṅ-γyog daṅ nyíṅ-γyog* servant, servant's servant, and the servant again of these *Pth.; mii γyog byéd-pa* to be in a person's service, to obey a person; *dpon-γyóg* master (mistress) and domestics, master and attendants, frq.; *nad-γyóg,* a nurse, one that tends sick persons *Dzl.; γyog-ₒkór* attendants, e.g. *γyog-ₒkór bču-drúg* attendants and retinue of 16 persons, *ₒkor daṅ γyog* id.

གཡོག་ནང་ཟན་ *γyog-naṅ-zán* a house-servant *C.* —

གཡོག་པ་ *γyóg-pa,* pf. and imp. *γyogs,* rarely *yóg-pa* 1. **to cover,** *bu gós-kyis γyóg-pa* to cover a child with a garment *Dzl., mgó-la rdzá-ma γyóg-pa* to cover one's head with a pot *Glr.;* also: *rdzá-mai mgó-la drá-bas γyóg-pa* to cover the opening of a pot with a wire grate *Glr.; p̔yii págs-pa γyogs* the external cutaneous covering appears (in the embryo) *S.g.; ri-mgo ka-bas γyogs* the hill-tops were covered with snow *Mil.;* **to pour over** or **upon,** to cover in pouring, *krág-gis* with blood *Dzl.;* **to overlay,** with gold *Dzl.;* **to sprinkle over, besprinkle,** **sig-pa-la ṭág* W.* the wall with blood; **to strew over,** **ká-la gog-ṭál* W.* ashes over the snow. — 2. **to pour away,** to throw away; so *W.;* the people in *W.* understand the words *Dzl.* ༢༦, 6: **ma yógs-pai lhág-ma** the rest which has not been thrown away, whereas others, e.g. the people of Sikkim explain it: the rest that has not been taken possession or care of.

གཡོགས་ *γyogs* 1. **cover, covering,** *mgo-γyógs Lex.* covering for the head, cap; also fig. and po. for self-delusion, self-deception (prop.: a veiling of the head) *Mil.*; *steṅ-γyógs*, *stod-γyógs* upper-garment, mantle, toga, *smad-γyógs* trowsers, breeches *Tar.* — 2. **cover, envelope,** *γyógs-ċan* having a cover.

གཡོད་ *ẏyod C.* the large intestine, colon.

གཡོན་ཅན་ *γyón-ċan Pth.*; *Cs.* = *γyó-ċan* crafty; perh. also **fornicator,** as *γyón-ma*, acc. to *Lex.* and *Sch.*: harlot.

གཡོན་པ་ *γyón-pa* **left,** *γyón-ma* the left hand, *γyón-na* on the left, to the left, *γyón-du* towards the left, *γyón-nas* from the left; *γyón-lógs* the left side or hand, *γyon-lág-byed-pa Pth.* left-handed, *γyon-rú Sch.* the left wing, of an army.

གཡོབ་པ་ *γyób-pa*, pf. *γyobs* **to move about, to swing, brandish,** *γṡóg-pa* the wings; *rkaṅ-lág γyób-pa* to kick, to strike, with the arms and legs.

གཡོར་མོ་ *γyór-mo* 1. **sail,** *γyor-yól* id *Cs.*, *γyor-ṡiṅ* sail-yard *Cs.*, also mast, in a rather obscure description of a ship in *Zam.*, where the sail is called *dar*, cloth. — 2. **wave, billow,** *rgyá-mtsoi Glr.*

Note. Tibetan writers knowing of ships and navigation about as much as a blind man of colours, the obscurity of passages relating to such matters may easily be accounted for.

གཡོར་བ་ *γyór-ba* 1. v. *γyúr-ba.* — 2. v. *γyár-ba.* — 3. v. *yor.*

གཡོལ་བ་ *γyól-ba* v. *yól-ba.*

གཡོས་ *γyos* 1. prov. for *γyas*, in *γyos-skór* circumambulation from left to right (so that the right side is towards the person or object that is reverentially to be saluted) *Wdṅ.* — 2. v. *γyo-ba.*

ར

ར *ra* 1. the consonant **r**, always pronounced with the tongue. — 2. num. fig.: 25.

ར་ *ra* stands for: 1 *rá-ba*, 2. *rá-ma*, 3. *rá-mda*, 4. *rá-ro.*

རྭ་ *rwa* (cf. *ru*) 1. **horn** *W.* **rá-ċó** id. — 2. **sting** e.g. of the scorpion. — 3. *Sch.*: 'the inward side, the horn-side, of a bow'. — *rwa-ċan* horned. — *rwa-snyiṅ* the pith of a horn *Cs.* — *rwa-myúg* 'the first germ of seed that appears after sowing' *Cs.*; *rwá-rtsa* 'the root or bottom of a horn' *Cs.*, *rwá-rtse* 'the top or point of a horn' *Cs.*, *rwá-tsa S.g.* (?).

ར་གན་ *rá-gan*, in comp. *rag*, **brass,** *rá-gan-gyi búm-pa*, *rag-búm* brass cup, can, vessel, *rag-dúṅ* a brass trumpet; *rag-skyá Sch.*: white-copper, packfong, German silver.

ར་སྒོ་ *rá-sgo* hoof, claw *C.*, *W.*

ར་ཉེ་ *rá-nye*, provinc. for *żá-nye* **lead.**

ར་མཉེ་ *rá-mnye* an officinal root *Med.*, *Sch.*: **carrot.**

ར་ཏི་ *rá-ti Cs.*: 'a small weight, a drachm (60 grains)'; but रत्ती (not to be found in *Will.*) is prob. the Hindi word for रत्तिका, the seed or grain of *Abrus precatorius*, as a weight about = 2 grains.

ར་མདའ་ *rá-mda* **help, assistance** (*Cs.* also: companion, **assistant**), *rá-mda ˳bód-pa* to cry out for help *Glr.*, *rá-mdar sbrón-pa Cs.* to call (upon a person) for assistance, *ra ˳dégs-pa W.* **ram tág-ċe** (cf. *żabs ˳dégs-pa*) **to help,** to assist *Sch.*, *ra ˳drén-pa* id. *Mil. nt.*; *rá-mda-pa* **helper, assistant** *Glr.*; *rá-mdai dpuṅ-tsóg* **auxiliary forces** or army *Cs.*

ར་སྡོང་ *ra-sdóṅ Sch.* **weeping willow.**

ར་སྣ་ *ra-sná* n. of a medicinal herb *Wdṅ.* 166, = *sgrón-šiṅ* fir-tree.

ར་བ་ *rá-ba* 1. **enclosure, fence, wall,** frq., esp. in *W.*, also the space inclosed by a fence, wall etc., **yard, court-yard, pen, fold** etc.; *rá-bas skór-ba* to inclose with a fence *Stg.*, *rá-čan*(?), *ra-ldán* having an enclosure, fence, wall etc. *Cs.*; *smyúg-mai rá-ba* bamboo-hedge, bamboo-fence, *ṫsér-mai rá-ba* thorn-hedge, thorn-fence, *šiṅ-gi rá-ba* wooden fence, fence of boards, pickets or rails *C.*; *rá-mo* id., *ra-mo-čé* a large pen or fold *Mil.* and *C.*; *kun-dga-rá-ba*, *kún-ra*, v. *kun*; *ḱrims-ra* place of execution; *lčáṅ-ra* garden with willow-trees; *nyág-ra*(?) wall of stones put loosely together *Ld.*; *rtá-ra* stable or pen for horses; *rdó-ra* 1. stone-wall. 2. circle of dancers; *ṗág-ra* v. *rags*. — *bá-ra* cow-house, pen for cows; *rtsig-ra* *Sch.*: wall round a court-yard; *brtsón-ra* v. *brtson*; *lúg-ra* sheepcot, sheepfold; *šiṅ-ra* v. above. — *ra-šúl* the remnants or traces of an old pen. — 2. the first of the three (or two) months of a season, *zla ra-ba*.

ར་མ་ *rá-ma* (rarely *ra Glr.*) **goat, she-goat,** frq. — *ra-kyál* bag made of a goat's skin. — *ra-skyés Tar.*; *Sch.*: a gelded he-goat. — *rá-gu*, col. *ri-gu*, young goat, **kid.** — *ra-rgód* wild goat, = *ra-po-čé Cuningh. Ld.* p. 199. — *ra-ṫúg S.g.* and *ṗá-ra* he-goat. — *ra-ṫóṅ* 1. a he-goat of two years *C.* 2. a gelded he-goat *W.* — *ra-dó*(?) thread made of goat's hair *W.* — *ra-lpágs* goat's skin. — *ra-ṗó* a gelded he-goat. — *ra-lúg* goats and sheep; *ra-ma-lúg* id., when a particular stress is laid on the impropriety of both species of animals being mixed together; also fig. of improper intermixtures. — *ra-šá* goat's flesh. — *ra-slóg* a coat made of goat's skins.

ར་མེད་ *ra-méd* **infallible,** certain, sure *Sch.*

ར་མོ་ཆེ་ *ra-mo-čé* n. of a plain near Lhasa where the Chinese wife of *Sroṅbtsansgampo* ordered a large Buddhist temple to be built *Glr.*; as a com noun v. sub *rá-ba*.

ར་རི་ *ra-ri Sch.*: *ra-ri-méd-pa* neither high nor low.

ར་རིལ་ *ra-ril* **treddles, dung** of goats.

ར་རེས་ *ra-rés* = *rés-mos*, **skyid dug ra-res yoṅ dug** *Ld.* good fortune and misfortune come by turns.

ར་རོ་ *rá-ro* 1. **intoxication, drunkenness.** — 2. **intoxicated** *B* and col.; *Sch.*: *rá-ro dáṅ-po bag-méd-pa*, v. sub *bag* I. *rá-ro γnyis-pa glaṅ-po-če smyon-pa daṅ ͺdra* drunkenness while continued resembles a furious elephant, *rá-ro γsúm-pa ši-ro ͺdra* the end (of it) resembles a corpse; *ra ži* or *saṅs*, also *γdaṅs* (?) *W.* the drunken fit is over; *rá-ro-ba B.*, *C.*, *rá-ro*(*-čan*) *W.* intoxicated, drunk, *rá-ro-bar byéd-pa* to make drunk *Dzl.*, *rá-ro-ba-las sáṅs-te* having come to one's self again after a drunken fit, being sober again *Dzl.*

ར་ས་འཕྲུལ་སྣང་ *ra-sa-ͺprul-snáṅ* n. of a Buddhist temple erected in Lhasa by the Nepalese wife of *Sroṅbtsansgampo Glr.*

ར་སི་ *rá-si Hind.* **rope,** in *Lh.* **hempen rope,** and as such distinguished from *ṫág-pa*, rope made of goat's hair, which is the one most in use in Tibet.

ར་ཤིད་ *ra-šid* (Pers. رسيد), **receipt,** **ra-šid ṭi-ked** money-stamp.

རཱ་ཧུ་ and རཱ་ཧུ་ལ་ *rā-hu* and *rā-hu-la* v. *sgra-γčán*.

རཀྟ་ *rakta Ssk.* **blood, saffron, minium, cinnabar** *Mil.*

རག་ *rag* 1. sbst. v. *ra-gán*. — 2. adj. (*Ssk.*: *adhina*) subject, subservient, dependent, *rag lás-pa* or *lús-pa B.*, *C.*, *W.*, **rag-ldom-pa** *W.*, with *la*, **to depend on,** *de ḱyód-kyi nús-pa-la rag-lús* that depends on your strength *Mil.*; *dbugs rṅúb-pa sems-la rag-lás-pa yin* breathing depends on the soul *Stg.*; *ͺtsó-ba γžán-la rag-lás-šiṅ* as they depend on others for their lives *Tar.*; *Bhar.* 22 *ḱyod rgyal-srid byed-la rag-go Schf.*: 'regno operam nava!' — 3. *W.* for *reg*, *grags*, *dregs*, *sbrag*, v. *rag-pa*; *rag-čan W.* for *drégs-pa-čan* **proud,** haughty; for *grágs-čan* **famous; glorious, splendid; angry** (?).

རག་པ་ *rág-pa* 1. vb. *W.* for *rég-pa* **to touch, feel,** and in a more generalized sense

= ₒ*tsór-ba* **to perceive,** to scent, taste, hear, see, e.g. **dáñ-mo rag** I feel cold, **dáñ-mo rag-ga** do you feel cold? (but **dáñ-mo dug** it is cold); **gó-la zug rag** (*C.* **rig**) my head aches; **tóg-ri rag** I feel hungry, **tóg-ri rág-ga** are you hungry? **ñai miñ žód-da rag** I hear my name called; **go ḱád-da rag** I perceive the door sticks; **'i lúñ-po ḱyér-ra rag** I see, the wind will carry that away; **go ṕé-te mi rag** the door seems to be locked. — 2. adj. **dark-russet, brownish,** of rocks, horses *W.*

རག་མ་ *rág-ma* 1. *W.* adj. to the gerund **rág-te** (*sbrág-ste*): **be-rág yu-dán** (lit. *γdan*) **rág-te** a fillet together with a strip set with turkoises. — 2. prop. n. of a village *Mil.*

རག་ཙེ་ *rág-tse* **stone** in fruits *W.*

རག་ཤ་ *rág-ša* **a bead of a rosary,** acc. to *Lis.* from रुद्राक्ष Elaeocarpus Janitrus, the berries of which are used for such beads.

རག་ཤི་ *rag-ší* n. of a country.

རགས་ *rags* 1. **dam, mole, dike, embankment,** also *ču-rágs, ču-lón* — 2. any construction of a similar shape: *ṕág-rags* (also *ṕág-ra*) **intrenchment, breast-work;** *ṕúb-rags* stack, rick; *šiñ-rags* stack of wood.

རགས་པ་ *rágs-pa* **coarse, thick, gross,** *lús-kyi rnám-pa ṕra-rágs-rnams Wdñ.* the more delicate and the coarser component parts of the body; *rags-pai dbáñ-du byás-na Wdñ.*, reckoning one with another, on an average; **rough,** as in: *rágs-rtsis-su* by a rough estimate *Tar.*; *rágs-pai mi-rtág-pa dañ ṕrá-bai mi-rtág-pa* the perishableness of the whole mass and of the single parts *Thgy.*; *yán-lag rágs-pa* prob.: strong, firm limbs *Pth.*; of Buddhas is said that they appear *rágs-pai ťsúl-gyis* i.e. **bodily,** or **substantially;** *rags-rís byed-pa Sch.:* to work, mould, form, sketch etc. roughly.

རང་ *rañ* 1. **self** *B.* and col. (*nyid*, with few exceptions, is, in *W.* at least, colloquially not in use) *ña-rán ḱyod-rán* **I myself, thou thyself** etc., in col. language also = **I, thou** etc.; sometimes the person is only indicated by the context, the pronoun I etc. being omitted; *rañ-čag, rán-rnams* plur.; *rán-gi* my, thy etc.; *čúñ-ma de rán-gi lús-la čágs-pas* this wife fond of herself, in love with herself *Dzl.* (yet cf. *de-rán*, below); *des rán-gi ma yin-par rig-nas* he perceiving that it was his own mother *Pth.*; *rán-la rán-gis skra bčád-de* shaving one's own head *Dzl.*; also in a gen. sense: *rán-bas ñán-pa* an inferior person than one's self *Thgy.*, in like manner: *rán-las čé-ba Thgr.*; *rán-la bu méd-na* if a man has no son of his own *Mil.*; *rán-gi srúñ-ba* to keep, to guard one's own property *Thgy.*; **rañ mi-ₒdód-pe kyen ťsán-ma** *C.* all the disagreeable things that fall to one's lot; in compounds: *rañ-séms* one's own soul (opp. to *γžan-lús*) *Mil.*; v. also ₒ*dré-ba* extr.; *rañ-rig rañ-γsal rañ-bde γsum* self-created knowledge, clearness, and happiness (the three fruits of the spirit) *Mil.*; *rañ-sróg rán-gis γčod* you will take your own life *Glr.* — 2. **spontaneously, of one's own accord,** *žal-zás rañ-ₒóñ-ño Dzl.*; *rán-byon-pa, rán-byuñ-ba* originated of itself, v. below; *rañ ₒgról-ba* 1. to get loose, come loose of itself. 2. to become clear or intelligible spontaneously, by intuition. 3. to save one's self; *rán-šar-ba* = *rán-ₒgrol-ba* 2. — 3. **just, exactly, precisely, the very,** *de rán* the very same; *de rañ yin* so it is! exactly so! just so! **dhá-ta rañ** *C.*, **dá-či rañ, dág-sa rañ** *W.* just-now, **di-riñ rañ** just to-day *W.*; **already,** *sñá-mo rañ* already early in the morning *Mil.*; **barely, merely, the mere, the very,** *ña dañ ṕrád-pa rán-gis* by the mere meeting with me *Mil.*; *mi rañ* a person travelling all alone, i.e. without baggage, horse or companion *Kun.*; *mo-rán* v. *mo.* — **really, indeed, actually, truly** (the verb being repeated): *mi-la-rás-pa de yin rañ yin-nam?* art thou really that same Milaraspa? **yoñ rañ yoñ-gyu yin** *C.* he will truly or certainly come; **even,** *sdáñ-po rañ byas* now they even hated him *Mil.*

Comp. *rañ-skal* a person's own share. — *rañ skyu* (?) *ťúb-pa Sch.:* to act after one's own mind. — *rañ-skyur* vinegar *Cs.*(?)

— *raṅ-k'a Sch.* = *ráṅ-bu?* — *raṅ-k'óṅs* = *raṅ-k'úl* territory, district *C.* (?) — *raṅ-*ₒ*k'ós* one's own worth, affairs, necessities *Sch.* — *raṅ-grub* not made or produced by men, **self-produced.** — *ráṅ-dga-ba* **free, independent,** *rán-dga-pa* an unmarried man *Sch.* — *raṅ-rgyál* 1. *Stg.*: = *raṅ-saṅs-rgyás.* 2. *raṅ-rgyál-gyis* ₒ*gró-ba Sch.*: to live after one's own option or pleasure (?) — *raṅ-rgyú Sch.*: 'die eigene Ursache, Selbstfolge' (?!) — *raṅ-ṅó* one's own nature, *šes-pa* to know *Mil.* — *raṅ-nyid* himself, herself etc., one's self *Mil.*, *raṅ-nyid* ₒ*gról-ba* to deliver one's self *Thgy.*, *bdud raṅ-nyid* the devil himself in his own person *Tar.* — *raṅ-*ₒ*t'ág* **mill, water-mill.** — *raṅ-mt'óṅ* **pride,** self-complacency, self-sufficiency *Mil.*, *Glr.* — *raṅ-dón* one's own affairs, one's own profit, *raṅ-dón byéd-pa* to look to one's own advantage *Do.*, *raṅ-*ₒ*dód* **selfishness,** v. *raṅ-rtsis.* — *raṅ-snáṅ* v. sub *snáṅ-ba*; *Sch.* also: self-born. — *raṅ-po Cs.* = *po-raṅ* an unmarried man. — *raṅ-bábs* v. *babs.* — *ráṅ-bu* 1. *Cs.* single, alone, *ráṅ-bur* adv. singly, alone, without a consort. 2. *Cs.*: a single life (?). 3. *Schr.*: one's own child. — *raṅ-byúṅ*, *raṅ-byón* self-born, having originated of itself, = *raṅ-grúb* frq. *raṅ-dbaṅ* **independence, liberty,** *raṅ-dbáṅ t'ób-pa* to become free *Glr.*; *γnás-la raṅ-dbaṅ-méd* they are not master of the place i.e. they are not free to choose the place *Thgy.*, in the same sense, *gar skye raṅ-dbaṅ-med Mil.*; **raṅ-wáṅ* ₒ*ǰúg-pa** to set free *C.*; *raṅ-dbáṅ-čan* **free** *W.* — *raṅ-*ₒ*bar Cs.*: **'musket',** in *W.* it is only used for **pistol;** **raṅ-bár ḍug-rág** *W.* **a revolver.** — *ráṅ-mo Cs.* = *mo-ráṅ* an unmarried woman. — *raṅ-rtsís* the opinion which one has of one's self, *raṅ-rtsis daṅ raṅ-*ₒ*dód ma če žig* think little of your own self! *Mil.* — *raṅ-bžin,* स्वभाव, natural **disposition,** state or **constitution, nature, temper,** *raṅ-bžin-las γžán-du* ₒ*gyúr-ba* to change one's natural constitution *Wdṅ.*, ₒ*bab dé-ltar čé-bai raṅ-bžin-gyis* as a natural consequence of so heavy a snow-fall *Mil.*; *raṅ-bžín-gyis* **of itself, by itself,** from its very nature, **naturally, spontaneously** *Dzl.*, in col. language, *raṅ-bžin-nas* id., also for **self** in the sense: I, he etc. without the aid and independently of others; ₒ*byúṅ-ba lṅai raṅ-bžin-čan-gyi lus* ₒ*di* this body participating of the nature of the five elements *Wdṅ.*; *draṅ-poi raṅ-bžin-čan-gyi p'yir* for *raṅ-bžin-čan yin-pai p'yir Sbh.* — **raṅ-žin ǰö-pa** *C.* needless words, where it is a matter of course; also: talk without any serious intent; **de da raṅ-žin-la zér-če žig yod** *W.* that is nothing but talk. — *raṅ-bzó.* 1. *Lex.*: the right, proper form (of a word)? 2. self-determination, opp. to a punctilious adhering to tradition *Mil.* — *raṅ-raṅ* **each ... himself, each ... his,** her, its etc. (not reciprocally, as *Sch.* has it), *raṅ-ráṅ-gi k'rii* ₒ*óg-tu sbas* he buried each (idol) under its own seat *Glr.*, *raṅ-ráṅ-gi leur γsal* each (subject) will be explained in its own chapter *Lt.* — *raṅ-raṅ-lao* each (final consonant) has itself (joined), i.e. is doubled *Gram.* — *raṅ-ré* 1. = *raṅ-ráṅ*: *raṅ-réi sna-t'ág raṅ-rés zuṅ* each may lead himself, may be his own guide. 2. **we,** *raṅ-réi sgo drúṅ-na* at our own door *Mil.*, *raṅ-ré-rnams* we (the Lamas, opp. to the laymen) *Mil.* 3. polite way of addressing, for our **you** or the German 'Sie' *Thgr.?* -- *raṅ-šúgs-la* **of itself,** spontaneously *W.* — *ráṅ-sa*, *ráṅ-so* one's own place, *ráṅ-sa* ₒ*dzíṇ-pa* to maintain one's place, one's station *Mil.*, prob. like *ráṅ-mgo* ₒ*t'ón-pa*; *ráṅ-sar*, *ráṅ-sor* 1. *bžág-pa* to put (a thing) in its place, fig. for: to leave undecided, to let the matter alone, ni f. *Mil.* 2. of itself, e.g. *ráṅ-sor ži* (a storm) abates of itself. — *raṅ-saṅs-rgyas* Pratyekabuddha, i.e. a Buddha who has obtained his Buddhaship alone by his own exercises of penance, but who does not promote the welfare of other beings.

རང་ག་བ་ *ráṅ-ga-ba Cs.* **coarseness, meanness.**

རང་བ་ *ráṅ-ba*, pf. *raṅs*, **to rejoice,** *sems mi-ráṅs-par* **discontented,** *yid-ráṅ-ba* or *yi-ráṅ-ba* id., frq.; **dhé-la ga-ráṅ-ḍhág-te** highly pleased with it *C.*; *yid ma ráṅs-šiṅ mi mgú-bar gyúr-te* being very much dissatisfied *Stg.*; *ma-ráṅ-bžin-du* unwillingly, reluctantly.

རང་རོང་ཅན *rań-roń-čan Cs.* **rough, craggy,** uneven.

རངས་པ *rańs-pa* 1. v. *rań-ba.* — 2. *nyin-ráńs-par* for *ťo-ráńs-kyi dús-su* early in the morning *Tar.* 111, 17. — 3. in *W.* for *réńs-pa.*

རངས་པོ *ráńs-po Sch.* **rough, rude, unpolished.**

རད་པ *rád-pa W.* for *bgrád-pa.*

རད་རོད *rad-ród* v. *ród-po.*

རན་ད *rán-da* (*Pers.* رندا, رنده) **a plane** *Ld.*

རན་པ *rán-pa* 1. vb. and adj. to keep, or keeping, the proper mean, **to be proportionate, just right,** adv. *rán-par* **moderately,** *rán-par sro* warm yourself moderately (tolerably) *Lt., zas-ťsód rán-par zá-ba* to eat moderately *S.g.; ₒdi-tsam ni rán-no* this is about the proper measure *Dzl.*; with the root of the vb.: *žiń rńá-ran-nas* as it was (the proper) time for harvest *Dzl., ₒgro-ran* it is time to go *Pth., ši ma rán-par ší-ba* to die an untimely death; *bág-mar γtań-rán-pa dań* when it was time to give her in marriage *Dzl.;* not so often with a sbst.: *rtsás-ma rán-tsa-na* when harvest-time had come *Mil.* — 2. *rtsa rán-pa C.* **shave-grass,** *Equisetum arvense.* — 3. col. for *ₒdrén-pa* **to lead** (water); for *bran-pa* v. *ťags.*

རབ *rab* I. **superior, excellent;** the eldest, of three sons, opp. to *bríń-po* and *ťa-čúń,* frq.; *gań-zág dbań-po-ráb-rnams* very able or clever persons (opp. to *ₒbríń-po* or *ťá-ma* having moderate or very little capacity) *Mil., Thgr.,* inst. of which *rab ₒbriń γsum* is often used *Thgy.; ťébs-na rab* if rightly understood, that will be the best *Thgr.,* frq. for: so it is right, that will do; **much, plentiful,** *rab-skrăĭ ₒóg-nas* also with a full head of hair (you may be a holy man) *Mil.; ráb-tu* adv. **very,** with adjectives and verbs, *ráb-tu sdoms* lock (the door) well *Dzl.; ráb-tu ƙrós-par gyúr-te Tar.;* it occurs also in the following phrases: *ráb-tu ₒbyín-pa* to receive or admit into a religious order, *ráb-tu ₒbyúń-ba* to enter into a religious community, to take orders, *slób-dpon čos- bańs-las* being with, or being ordained by the teacher Chosbangs; *rgyál-poi rígs-las* (to take orders) as a descendant of the royal family, of the caste of noblemen *Tar.; ráb-(tu) byúń(-ba)* he that has taken orders, a novice, or in gen.: **a clerical person;** *rab-byúń* is also the name of the first year of the cycle of sixty years; *rab-(tu) γnás(-par) byéd-pa, mdzád-pa* c. acc. or *la,* prop. 'to make firm or permanent', **to consecrate, to hallow,** a new house, esp. a temple, an idol; by this act a house is secured against accidents, and an idol is supposed to acquire life and to become the abode of the respective deity, which occasionally manifests itself by sundry miracles *Glr.; ráb-tu ₒbyéd-pa* (also erron. *byéd-pa*) *Cs.* to analyze, but *Tar.* 96 it is equivalent to प्रकरण treatise, dissertation. *rab-ₒbyáms-pa* v. *ₒbyáms-pa; rab-ₒóg* the second in rank, next in value, excellence etc., thus *Dzl.* ༡༢༤, 5 (as a better reading for *ₒbriń-mo*); *rab-yáńs* very wide, very extensive *Sch.; rab-γsál* 1. very clear, quite evident. 2. sbst. a small **balcony** or **gallery,** frequently seen in Tibetan houses. 3. *Sch.* history (?).

II. also *rabs,* **ford,** *rab-méd* without a ford, *rab-só = rabs Sch.*

རབ་རིབ *rab-rib,* col. also *hrab-hrib,* **mist, dimness,** e. g. before the eyes, in consequence of impaired vision; **ƙo šrab-šrib mán-na mi ťoń** he sees only a mist before his eyes, *W.; skár-ma rab-rib* the faint glimmering of a star.

རབས *rabs* 1. **lineage, succession of families, race, family,** *rgyal-rábs* royal family or lineage, nobility; succession of kings; *mi-rábs* human race; *rabs-čád* a person whose lineage is broken off, i.e. **childless,** issueless, *rabs-čád bza-mí γnyis* a married couple without children *Mil.; yá-rabs* the higher class of people, noblemen; *má-rabs* the lower class, also: one belonging to the higher or lower class; collectively: *rgán-rabs* old men, aged people, *γžón-rabs* youth, young persons; *sńón-rabs* **the ancients** (*veteres*), *p̓yi-rabs* men of modern times, descendants, posterity *Glr., sńon-rabs-sgrúń* an old legend, ancient history *Zam.*, *snón-yyi rabs bčo-brgyad* the 18 Puranas *Tar.* 4, 11. — 2. **generation** *Dzl.*, resp. *ydun-rábs Glr.*, *ná-nas ydun-rábs lná-pa-na* in the fifth generation after me; with respect to individuals, period of life, viz. one of the many periods, which every person is supposed to pass through, or sometimes pleon. denoting a person as being the representative of his generation: *sans-rgyás rabs bdun* the seven Buddhas. — 3. in gen.; **succession, series, development**, e. g. the propagation of the Buddhist doctrine *Tar.* 205, 21; *bskal-rábs* successions of Kalpas, *bskal-rábs-nas bskal-rábs-su.*

རམ་པ་ *rám-pa* 1. *W.* **quick-**(quitch-)grass. — 2. = *rán-pa?* *Lt.*, *Glr.*

རམ་བུ་ *rám-bu* 1. prob. only in: *rám-bu* *degs-pa* to join in singing, to take part in a song, to fall in with, *Dzl.* ༢V, 13 (not: to set up a dismal cry *Sch.*), v. also *čol-ba.* 2. = *na-rám Polygonum viviparum.*

རམས་ *rams* 1. **indigo** *B.*, col. — 2. *Cs.*: 'degree of doctorship, *snags-* or *go-* or *drun-ráms-pa* one having such a degree'.

རལ་ *ral* 1. **goat's hair.** — 2. **rent, cleft,** *pu ral ynyis* a sloping valley dividing into two parts at its upper end; *ral-ysum* n. of Lahoul on account of its consisting of three valleys; cf. *rál-ba.* — 3. v. *rál-pa.*

རལ་ཀ་ *rál-ka* v. *rál-gu.*

རལ་ཁ་ *rál-ka* v. *rál-gri.*

རལ་ག་ *rál-ga Sch.* = *yál-ga.*

རལ་གུ་ *rál-gu* 1. *Sch.*: **cleft, chink, fissure.** — 2. *dar-dkár-gyi rál-gu* and *rál-ka Pth.?*

རལ་གྲི་ *ral-gri*, col. **ral-gyi, ra-gyi** **sword,** also for rapier and other thrust-blades *Dzl.*; *ral-grii dáb-ma* or *lče* **blade,** *so* edge, *šubs* scabbard of a sword *Cs.*; *rál-gri-pa Cs.* a sword-man; a fighting man; *rál-ka* = *rál so*; *rál-ka spród-pa* 'to bring the blades together', to fight hand to hand, (*ral-ka sbrad-pa Sch.* is prob. a misprint).

རལ་པ་ *rál-pa* **long hair, lock, curl; mane** (of the lion, not of the horse etc.); *rál-pa-čan* having or wearing long hair, n. of a Tibetan king that distinguished himself by his bigotry and by his servility to the priests; *ral-lčan* a willow planted at the birth of a child, under which a lock of the child's hair is buried, when it is seven years old *Ld.*

རལ་བ་ *rál-ba* = *drál-ba* and *hrál-ba*, pf. of *drál-ba*, **torn,** of clothes etc., *mtsón-gyis* lacerated, slashed, cut to pieces by the sword *Dzl.*; *žig-rál-ba* id.; *žig-rál* breach, **destruction,** *kán-pa-la žig-rál byún-na* when the house gives way *Glr.*; *ka-rál, rna-rál, sna-rál* a lip, ear or nose, that has been lacerated by wearing rings etc.

རས་ *ras* 1. sbst. **cotton cloth,** cottons, also a piece of cotton cloth, handkerchief etc., *ras sbóm-pa* thick, strong cotton cloth; *lág-ras, pyis-ras Cs.* handkerchief, napkin; *tód-ras* **turban** *Cs.*; *prá-ras* a fine sort of cotton stuff, = *ká-ši-kai ras.*

Comp. *ras-rkyán* cotton cloth. — *ras-skúd Cs.* cotton thread. — *ras-kúg* a small bag made of cotton. — *ras-kra* **calico, chintz** *Cs.* *ras-gós* **cotton dress, gown.** — *re-gá* a strong cotton fabric brought from *Sik.*, *C.* as *bčós-bu Cs.* calico, chintz. — *ras-tág* **fillet, bandage.** — *rás-pa* a person wearing cotton clothes *Mil.*, frq. — *ras-bál* raw cotton. — *ras-búbs* a whole piece of cotton cloth. — *rás-ma* a small piece, a rag *Lex.* **re-zén** *C.* a long, loose cotton garment, shawl. — *ras-yúg* = *ras-búbs.* — *ras-rú* v. *re-rú.* — *ras-slág* a furred garment covered with cotton cloth *W.* — 2. adj. *ka-rás* (**rē**, for *rens?*) hard snow that will bear a man.

རས་པ་ *rás-pa* 1. vb., *Ld.* **ras-če** **to get or grow hoarse,** **skad ras son** the voice has grown hoarse, **skad ras-sa rag** I feel a hoarseness in my throat. — 2. sbst. v. sub *ras.*

རི་ *ri*, also *ri-bo B.*, **ri-ga** *W.* 1. **mountain, hill,** *ri pó-ta-la* the mountain (called) Potala *Liš.*; *ri-bo dpal-bár Mil.*, *rgyal-gyi-sri ri Mil.* the mountain *Pal-bár, Gyal-gyisri*; *rir* on the mountain *Mil.*, *ri-la* id.

frq.; *ri-ťaṅ-mťsams-su* at the foot of the mountains or hills *Med.*; *rir-gán-pa* one living in close vicinity to a mountain, *W.*; *gáṅs-ri* an ice-mountain, snowy mountain, glacier, *nágs-ri* or *šiṅ-ri* a hill covered with wood, *brág-ri* a rocky mountain, *γyá-ri* a mountain or hill consisting of slate-stone or schist; *spaṅ-ri* a hill covered with grass. — 2. **brim** of a hat or cap; **side-leather,** side-piece of a shoe. — 3. symb. num.: 7. — 4. num. figure: 55. — 5. v. *ri-mo.*

Comp. and deriv. *ri-skéd* v. *rkéd-pa.* — *ri-skyégs Stg.*, v. *skyegs.* — *ri-ḱród* chain of mountains, assemblage of hills or mountains, esp. as abode of hermits who, on that account, are called *ri-ḱród-pa*; also directly = *dgón-pa* hermitage. — *ri-mgó* mountain top. — *ri-rgyál, rii rgyál-po* a very high mountain, e.g. Tise *Mil.*, Gandharā *Sbh.*, esp. = *ri-ráb*, q.v. — *ri-rgyúd* chain of mountains, ridge of hills. — *ri-ċan* mountainous, hilly. — *ri-čén, ri-bo-čé* a great mountain. — *ri-nyin* the sunny side, the southern slope of a mountain. — *ri-rnyíl* fall of a mountain, land-slip *Sch.* — *ri-stóṅ* v. *stóṅ-pa.* — *ri-deu* (or *rdeu*) *čúṅ Sch.*, **ri-bóg, ri-de-bóg* W.*, a mountain spur abounding in stones. — **ri-dód* W.* (perh. to be spelled *ri-ḱród*) a hermit (living) in the mountains. — *ri-sná* mountain spur. — *ri-pa* an inhabitant of the mountains, mountaineer, from a Tibetan point of view equivalent to the Latin *paganus* and *agrestis* as opp. to *urbanus*, therefore = peasant, poor uncivilized person. — *ri-ṗrán* a little hill or mountain. — *ri-bo* = *ri*, v. above. — *ri-bór-pa Tar., Cs.: ri-ˏór-pa;* = *ri-ḱród-pa, ri-bór-gyi groṅ* mountain village *Tar.* — *ri-brág, brág-ri* rocky mountain. — *ri-ₒbóg* spur. — *ri-sbúg* mountain cavern. — *ri-rtsá* foot, *ri-rtsé* top of a mountain, *nyi-ma ri-rtsé-la ṗóg-na* when the rising sun illumines the mountain tops. — *ri-rtsé-kan Cs.* n. of a mischievous spirit. — *ri-rdzóṅ* mountain fortress, fort. — *ri-ráb* the centre of the world and king of the mountains, the fabulous Sumeru or Meru, also *ri-rab-lhún-po, ri-rgyál, ri-bo-mčog-ráb Mil.* — *ri-lúṅ* mountain and valley. — *ri-γzéb Sch.* = *ri-ḱród.* — *ri-sribs* the side not exposed to the sun, shady side, north-side of the mountains.

རི་གུ *ri-gu* young goat, **kid** *W.*

རི་རྒྱ *ri-rgyá Sch.*: foxes or fox-skins (?).

རི་དྭགས *ri-dwags* animals of chase, **game.**

རི་བ *ri-ba W.* **ri-če** to be worth, gen. as adj. **worth,** **lug di ṅul čig ri-če yin** this sheep is worth one rupee *W.*; *dṅul brgya ri-bai rta* a horse worth one hundred rupees *Cs.*. cf. *rin* and *rib; ri-bai rin-ťáṅ* the full price *Sch.*

རི་བོང *ri-bóṅ* **hare,** *ri-bóṅ-mo Cs.* female hare; it lives in *Ld.*, but not in the smaller valleys, e.g. not in Lahoul; *ri-bóṅ-gi rwa* the horn of a hare, a nonentity, a thing not existing, cf. *mo-šám-gyi bu.*

རི་མོ *ri-mo* 1. **figure, picture, painting, drawing,** *lha-ḱáṅ-gi Glr.*; *ri-mo-mḱan* **painter**; *ri-mo-ċan, ri-mo-ldan* marked with figures; *ri-mor byéd-pa* to represent by means of figures and colours, to paint *Do.*; **markings** (streaks, speckles etc.) *šai* markings of a (tiger's) skin *Tar.*; *ri-ḱrá* having stripes of various colours, spotted, speckled; *ri-mo* also draught, plan, design, and fig. **pattern,** rule of conduct, law written into the heart. — 2. = *rim-gro* reverence, **veneration,** *ri-mor byéd-pa* to honour, to venerate *Stg.*

རི་ལུ *ri-lu* col., but also *Tar.* 63, for *ril-bu.*

རི་ཤི *ri-ši*, **ऋषि**, = *draṅ-sróṅ* q.v.

རི་ཤོ *ri-šó* n. of a medicinal herb *Med.*

རིག *rig* in *Ld.* col. and provinc. for *žig: *maṅ-na rig** or **nyuṅ-ṅu rig toṅ** give much! give little!

རིག་པ *rig-pa* I. vb., 1 **to know, to understand,** = *šés-pa* with the termin. of a sbst: to know (a person etc.) as, with the termin. of the inf.: to know that, **to perceive,** observe, *ḱrós-par rig-nas* perceiving that he became angry *Dzl.*; *ṗá-la rig-par gyis* let your father know it, inform your father of it *Tar.*; *zlóg-tu rig-par byed* (it or he) teaches how to avert, prevent etc. — 2. v. *sgrig-pa*.

II. sbst. 1. **knowing, knowledge; prudence, talents, natural gifts** *Glr.*; *rig-pa dan ldán-pa* **talented, rich in knowledge, learned** *Dzl.*; *rig-pa ɣsar-ba* new informations, disclosures, knowledge; **news,** *lóg-gi rig-pa bsgrés-na* if one compares the absurd news *Tar.* 174, *Schf.*; *ma-rig-pa* 1. sbst. **अविद्या ignorance,** mostly used in the specific Buddhist sense, viz. for the innate principal and **fundamental error** of considering perishable things as permanent and of looking upon the external world as one really existing, with Buddhists in a certain manner the original sin, from which every evil is proceeding, v. *Köpp.* I, 163 (but cf. *ɣti-mug*). 2. adj. void of reason, **unreasonable,** irrational, *dúd-ˌgro ma-rig-pa Mil.* — 2. **science, learning, literature,** *nán-gi rig-pa* the orthodox or sacred literature, *p̓yi rig-pa* the heterodox or profane literature *Cs.*, *tun-mon-gi rig-pa* literature or science common to both religions (Buddhists and Brahmans) *Cs.*; *rig-pai ɣnas* and *rig-pa* any single science (philosophy, medicine etc.) v. *rig-ɣnás*; *rig-pai ról-tso* or *rig-pai ɣnas tams-čád Cs.* circle of science, **encyclopedia.** — 3. **soul** (prob. only in later literature), *rig-pa lus dan brál-ba* the soul separated from the body, *rten dan brál-ba* the soul separated from her hold or from her abode *Thgr.*; often opp. to *bem Mil.*

Comp. *rig-mk̓an*, *rig(-pa)-po Cs.*, *Sch.* a knowing person, a learned man. — *rig-rgyud* **character** *Mil.* — *rig-snágs* **a spell, charm, magic formula,** *rig-snags-mk̓an* a person skilled in charms. — *rig-ɣnás* a science, one of the sciences; *rig-ɣnás čé-ba lna* the five great sciences or classes of science, frq.; these are: *sgrá-rig-pa* science of language, *ɣtan-tsigs-rig-pa* dialectics, *ɣsó-ba-rig-pa* medicine, *bzó-rig-pa* science of mechanical arts, *nan-dón-rig-pa* religious philosophy; of less consequence are: *rig-ɣnás čún-ba lna* the five minor sciences; and the *rig-ɣnás* or *rig-pa bčo-brgyad* (also *tsug-lag* ?L), which need not be particularly enumerated, though they are often mentioned in the *Dzl.*; they are named by *Cs.* and *Sch.* — *rig(-pa)-po* v. *rig-mk̓an.* — *rig-byéd* 1. conveying knowledge, **instructive,** prob. also learned, *na rig-byéd glú-mk̓an ma yin-te* I am no schooled, accomplished, singer *Mil.* 2. **instruction,** a book conveying knowledge, a scientific work, *bzoi rig-byéd* a technological work *Glr.* 3. **वेद** Veda, the (four) sacred writings of ancient Brahmanism, hence 4. as symb. num.: 4. — *rig-ma*, **वेदमातृ**, Veda-mother, *Gāyatrī*, a certain metre, verse and hymn of the Rigveda, personified as a deity *Mil.* — *rig-ˌdzin*, from *rig-pa ˌdzin-pa* to comprehend a science with ease, to be of quick parts *Dzl.*, as partic.: **a man of parts, a clever fellow;** but usually *rig-ˌdzin* (like *rig-ˌčan*, of rarer occurrence), *Ssk.* **विद्याधर**, denotes a kind of spirits to whom a high degree of wisdom is attributed, like the Dākinis. — *rig-šés* the faculty of **reason** *Tar.* 90, 2, *Schf.*

རིག་རིག་ *rig-rig*, *mig rig-rig byéd-pa* or *dúg-pa* to look about, esp. in an anxious manner, shyly *Tar.*, *Mil.*

རིགས་ *rigs* 1. **family, lineage, extraction, birth, descent,** *rigs-rús* lineage and family *Glr.*, *mai rigs-su nyé-ba* or *ɣtógs-pa* a relation by the mother's side *Dzl.*; emph.: **noble birth** or extraction: *rigs-kyi bu* or *bú-mo* noble or honoured sir! honoured madam! a respectful address, which is also more generally applied; thus in *Thgr.* it is the regular way of addressing the soul of a deceased person; *mi-rigs* 1. the human race, mankind *Cs.* 2. **nation, tribe** *Glr.*; *sdé-rigs* **tribe** *Cs.* 3. rarely = sex, *mó-rigs* female sex *Wdn.* — 2. in a special sense: **caste, class** in society, **rank.** In Tibet five ranks are usually distinguished. viz.: *rgyál-rigs* royal state, royalty, *brám-ze-rigs* caste of priests (Brahman caste), *rjé-rigs* nobility, aristocracy, *dmáns-rigs* the citizens, *ɣdól-pai rigs* the common people. When speaking of India, the appellations of these classes are applied to the castes of Brahmanism, although they do not correspond to each other in every respect. — 3. **kind, sort, species,** *groi rigs ɣsum yod* there are three sorts of wheat, *skád-*

rigs gós-rigs mi-ₒdrá-ba different languages and costumes; ċi-rigs of every sort, ċi-rigs-su in every possible manner, e g. čos stón-pa to teach religion; nyin-moi rigs-kyis or rigs-la by the day, **by days, daily** Glr.; rigs is also used for **some, certain,** nád-rigs-la mi ₒdzém-na if one is not on his guard against certain diseases; sometimes pleon.: yán-lag rigs bži the four limbs, viz. hands and feet Glr.; rgyal-čén rigs bži the four great spirit-kings Thgy., rigs ɣsum mgón-po the three tutelar saints (spyan-ras-ɣzigs, p̔yag-rdór, ₒjam-dbyáṅs) Glr.; saṅs-rgyás rigs lṅai žiṅ-k̔ams Thgr. — rigs-pa vb. **to have the way, manner, custom, quality of,** mgo p̔yir ₒbyúṅ-bai rigs-so the upper end (of a stick, part of which is in the water) has the way of sticking out, i.e. sticks out; often to be translated: **must** necessarily (according to the laws of nature or to circumstances); as partic. or adj.: **necessary,** also **proper, suitable, right, suited to its purpose,** in the earlier literature gen. with the genit. of the infin., sometimes with the termin. of the infin., in later times with the root of the verb; thus: t̔ós-nas ldáṅ-bai rigs-so you must get up as soon as you hear ... Dzl.; da ri žig snáṅ-bai rigs now a mountain must appear Dzl.; bžág-pai rigs-sam would it not be expedient to appoint...? Dzl.; rigs-kyi dús-la báb-bo it is just the right time Dzl.; mi smrá-bai mi rigs-so it is not right to be silent Dzl.; smád-par mi rigs-so it is not right to abuse Glr.; ₒóṅ-rigs ₒdúg-pas because (he) might possibly come Mil. nt.; drán-pa mi zin rigs-la if he should perhaps not retain the recollection of, if there should be any danger of his not remembering Thgr.; ṅan-sóṅ-du ₒgró-bai rigs-la as there is a possibility of going to hell Thgr.; ɣdúl-bai rigs-pa those fit for conversion Dzl.; lhar skyé-ba ni rigs-pa ma lags his being re-born as a deity is not befitting, or also: not possible, not probable Dzl.; mi-rigs-pa wrong, not right, unbecoming, improper etc., mostly as adv.: mi-rigs-par byéd-pa to act wrong, to do badly, frq. — rigs-kyi rjes-ₒbráṅ Was. (274) v. sub luṅ.

Comp. rigs-brgyúd race, **lineage,** extraction, **family** Cs., rigs-brgyud-ₒdzin **male issue,** rigs-brgyúd ₒp̔él-bar ₒgyúr-ba the rising of a numerous progeny Dom. — rigs-ṅán 1. low birth or extraction, *k̔yod mi rig-ṅán-pa daṅ nyám-po ḍé-ċe man* you must not mingle with people of low extraction, with common people W.; rigs-ṅán dpón-du skó-ba to raise a child of low extraction to the royal dignity Glr. 2. **hangman** Dzl. (cf. ɣdól-pa). — rigs-ċan, rigs-ldán of noble birth. — rigs-mnyám-pa, mtún-pa, ₒdrá-ba of the same rank etc., of the same species. — rigs-nyáms **degenerated,** rigs-nyáms dge-slóṅ a monk disgracing his profession Pth. — rigs-méd = rigs-ṅán no. 1.

རིགས་པ་ rigs-pa 1. v. rigs. — 2. often erron. for rig-pa. — 3. adj. of rigs: rgyál-rigs-pa belonging to the reigning family or caste; ċi-rigs-pai sgó-nas in every possible manner Mil.; ċi-rigs-par snyán-pai ťsig-gis with ever so many kind words Dzl.; also: in any way, any how, to a certain degree or extent, in part, partly Tar. 4, 3 etc. — 4. sbst., translation of न्याय **logic, dialectics** Trigl. 15; an infallible, not deceptive idea Was. (297).

རིང་ངེ་བ་ riṅ-ṅe-ba **continual**(?), **daily**(?) k̔a-tsá riṅ-ṅe-ba Mil. nt. every day warm meals.

རིང་བ་ riṅ-ba I. adj , also riṅ-po C., B., *riṅ-mo* W. 1. **long, high, tall,** relating to space; riṅ-mo *k̔ur* W. carry it lengthwise; it also implies distance, in which case ťag-riṅ (q. v.) is the more precise form; da-dúṅ yúl-las riṅ-ste as he is still at a great distance from the place Dzl.; more frq. with daṅ: ɣnas ₒdi groṅ-k̔yér daṅ riṅ-bas because this place is far from the town Dzl.; mi riṅ-ba-na at no great distance. — 2. **long,** with respect to **time,** ťse riṅ-ba sbst. a long life, adj. long-lived, rgyál-ba daṅ ťse riṅ-bar šog ċig may he be victorious and live long! Dzl.; yun riṅ-po (or mo) a long time; yun riṅ-po-nas from a long time, a long time since, riṅ-por ma lón-par, less accurately: riṅ-po ma lón-par soon afterwards, relating to things past, riṅ-por mi ťogs-par id. with respect to the future, = after a little while, in a short time, frq.; *mi-riṅ-bar* id. *Tar.*; *dé-nas mi riṅ-bar* not long after that *Tar.*; *riṅ žig* a long time, *riṅ žig lón-pa daṅ* after a long time *Dzl.*; *riṅ žig-tu* adv. **long, a long while, for a long time,** *riṅ žig-tu ma ₒoṅs-pas* as he did not come for a long time *Dzl.*; *riṅ žig-na* after or during a long time *Glr.*; *riṅ-la*, resp. *sku-riṅ-la* c. genit. **during, at,** *nyín-gyi riṅ-la* in the day-time, during the day *Pth.*, *ₒdir bžugs rin* (provinc. for *riṅ*?) *ₒtso-ča̧s* or *rgyags* provisions for the time of his stay *Mil.*; esp. of kings etc.: **under** a king; during the reign or life of a king, frq.; *dé-riṅ B.*, *C.*, **di-riṅ** (more correct form, but only in *W.*) **to-day.** — 3. **old,** *riṅ žig-na Sch.* long ago, long since, v. also *riṅ-lugs.* —

II. **length, distance** etc., more definite form, but of rare occurrence: *riṅ-ba-nyíd*, *dé-nas mi-riṅ-ba-nyid-na* a very short time afterwards *Tar.*

Comp. *riṅ-ǩyád* **length.** — **riṅ-tab* W.* length, copiousness (of account). — *riṅ-túṅ* 1. long and short. 2. length, relatively. — *riṅ-gág*, also *stod-gág* jacket or waistcoat of a Lama, without sleeves.

རིང་ལུགས་ *riṅ-lúgs Cs.*: 'the sect or followers of a person', *Sch.*: 'old customs'; *Glr.* 92, 2 (?).

རིང་བསྲེལ་ *riṅ-bsrél* ('things which are to be preserved for a long time'), **धातु**, relics of a Buddha or a saint, viz. small, hard particles, acc. to Burnouf the remnants of burnt bones.

རིངས་ *riṅs* sometimes for *riṅ.*

རིངས་པ་ *riṅs-pa* **swift, speedy,** *ríṅs-par rgyúg-pa* to run fast, to hasten, hurry; *riṅs-par yod* I am in a hurry *Mil.*; **riṅ-pa toṅ* W.* be quick! make haste! *riṅs ruṅ* though you be in a hurry *Mil.*; *riṅs-pai bsód-snyoms* alms, gifts of charity (requiring haste), urgently requested, and out of the common course, *Burn.* I, 269. 628 **za-riṅs, ₒtuṅ-riṅs**, waiting impatiently for one's meal, **ₒgrul-riṅs** for setting out *W.*; *riṅs-stábs-su* most speedily *Mil.*

རིད་པ་ *rid-pa* 1. **meager, emaciated** *Dzl.* and elsewh. — 2. *Sch.* also: **rare.**

རིད་པང་ *rid-páṅ* the Neosa pine-tree *Kun.*

རིན་ *rin* 1. **price, value,** *rin γčód-pa* to fix, to determine the price *Cs.* (cf. *taṅ*), *rin rtóg-pa* to ascertain the price, to estimate the value *Cs.*; *rin ₒbébs-pa* to abate, to lessen the price *Cs.*; *rin ₒbáb-pa, rin ₒbri-ba* to go down, to sink or fall in value *Cs.*; **rin tsam* W.*, **rin gha-tsọ* C.* how dear (is it)? what does it cost? *rin-la mi čog Sch.* to sell under cost-price; *rin-čan* dear, costly; *rin-méd* worthless, also: for nothing, gratis; *rin-góṅ*, *rin-táṅ*, *rin-tsád Tar.* ༢༠༢, 17 = *rin*; *rin-čén-po, rin-po-čé* v. the next article. — 2. for *riṅ*, v. *riṅ-ba* I, 2.

རིན་ཆེན་(པོ) *rin-čen(-po)*, also *rin-po-če*, 1. **very dear, precious, valuable;** usually: 2. sbst, **रत्न**, **a precious thing, treasure, jewel, precious stone, precious metal; metal** in general; *Glr.* 7, five jewels of the gods are enumerated, sapphire, indragopa and other three, prob. fabulous, stones, and five jewels as the property of man: gold, silver, pearls, corals, lapis lazuli; in other books other jewels are specified as such. In the Buddha-legends frq. mention is made of the *rin-po-če sna bdun*, i.e. the extraordinary treasures of a Tshakravartin king, viz. the precious wheel (v. *ₒǩor-lo*), the precious elephant, the precious horse, the precious jewel, the precious wife, the precious minister and the precious general (or inst. of him, the precious citizen) v. Gyatch. chap. III. Sometimes *rin-po-čei* may be understood literally: consisting of jewels, of precious stones, at other times it is merely equivalent to: valuable, precious; *rin-po-čei gliṅ Glr.* seems frq. to signify a holy, happy land inhabited by gods. — 3. **a title,** used not only in *rgya-mtso rin-po-če* and *pan-čen rin-po-če* (the honorary titles of the high-priests of Lhasa and of Tashilunpo), but also a title of every Lama of a higher class.

རིན་དི་ *rin-di W.* (*riṅ-dri Bun.*) 1. **lead.** — 2. **musket-ball.**

རིབ་ *rib* = *ri-ba Sch.* (*Dzl.* ༢༧༠, 8. 15, and in *Sch.*'s dictionary): **worth,** costing, standing at; to the Tibetans asked by us the word seemed to be unknown, and the MS. of Kyelang has *ri-ba* in the above cited passage.

རིབ་མ་ **rib-ma** W., **dib-ma** C., **fence, hedge, enclosure** to protect the fields from cold winds, intruders etc.

རིམ་གྲི་ *rim-gri* resp. for **ltógs-ri** **hunger** W.

རིམ་(འ)གྲོ་ *rim-gro* or *rim-ₒgro*, resp. *sku-rim* **honour, homage,** shown more esp. to gods, saints, and priests, **offerings** and other ceremonies (v. sub *sku*), *rim-gros tar-bar ₒgyur* he will yet be cured by religious ceremonies (if medical advise should prove insufficient) *S.g.*; *dei rim-gro-la* as a ceremony for him (the sick person) *Mil.*; *zan-zin-gi rim-gros* by offerings in goods, cattle etc.) *Mil.*; *rim-ₒgro čén-po byas* he arranged a great sacrificial festival *Pth.*; *rim-gro-pa* servant, waiting-man, valet de chambre.

རིམ་པ་ *rim-pa*, *Ssk.* क्रम, 1. **series, succession,** *rim-(pa) bžin(-du) Dzl.*, *rim-par Glr.*, in a row or line, in rows, by turns, successively, one after another, also = by degrees, gradually; *rim-gyis*, *rim-pas Dzl.* id.; *rim-pas dán-po mčog yin pyi-ma dman* v. sub *dmán-pa*; *byá-ba tob-rim bžin byéd-pa* to do a business by turns, each taking a certain share of the work *Glr.* — 2. **the place** in a row or file, constituent part or member of a series, *dei mi-brgyúd rim-pa lnas rgyál-sa bzun* five members of his lineage occupied the throne *Glr.*, and in a still more general sense: *sgo rim-pa bdun* a sevenfold door *Dzl.*; *rim-ldábs Sch.* and *nyis-rim S.g.* double; *rim-gčig* = *lan-gčig* one time, once. — 3. **order, method,** *ₒcád-par ₒgyúr-bai rim-pa ₒdis* by this method which will be explained immediately, *Sbh.*; *rim-bral* disorderly, irregular *Cs.* — *rim gnyis* v. *skyed-rim*.

རིམས་(ནད་) *rims(-nad)* contagious disease, **epidemy, plague,** *nan-rims* id. *Glr.*; *rims gton-ba* to send, to cause a plague, as demons do *Dzl.*; *dus gdon gnyis-kyis ma skyed rims mi ₒbyun* plagues, epidemics, are caused by nothing but the season or by demons; **ṭu-rim** W. **dysentery, diarrhoea,** bloody flux; *rims-só* the 'tooth' of an epidemy, i.e. its contagium, virulency.

རིལ་ཏིང་ *ril-tin Ld.* = *ša-rág*.

རིལ་བ་ *ril-ba* I. more frq. *ril-po*, *ril-mo B.*, *C.*; **ril-ril** W. 1. **round, globular,** in C. also **cylindrical;** *srán-ma ril-mo* peas are round *Wdn.*; **ril-ril** W. also sbst.: a round, globular object, such as a cabbage-head, a round lump of butter etc.; *ril-bai spyi-blugs Glr., Sch.*: 'a bottle, narrow in the middle, a gourd-bottle'. — 2. **whole, entire; wholly, quite** **kon-ril** quite crippled, lamed C.; **nag-ril-ril** W. very black, quite black; *rtág-pa dan ril-por ₒdzin-pa* to consider a thing lasting and entire (not compounded) *Thgy.*; *ril-por na dbán-na* if it belongs to me entirely *Mil.*; *ril-po* the whole, the entire thing (opp. to a part), also in arithmetic *Wdk.*; *ril-poi lhág-ma* the remainder of the whole *Wdk.*; *bubs-ril lus* the whole body *S.g.*; *ril-gyis gyógs-pa* entirely, completely, enveloped, or wrapped up *Sch.*; *ril-mid-pa Sch.*: 'to swallow a thing entire'; *dé-dag dan ril-gyis mči-am pyed dan mči-ba bka-stsól čig* tell me whether I am to come with all, or only with one half (of them) *Dzl.* ༧༥༢, 5 (acc. to the manuscript of Kyelang); *ril-bu*, col. **ril-lu**, **small ball, globule, pill,** *ril-bur bsgril-ba srán-ma tsam* formed into a pill of the size of a pea *Lt.*; *ril-ma* globular dung of some animals, *byi-bai ril* mouse-dung *Mng.* (where Piper longum is compared with it), *glá-bai ril* dung of the musk-deer; *lug-ril* tirdles, sheep-pellets, *ša-ril* 1. dung of the argali *Ld.* 2. small meat-balls C. — II. 1. W.: **ril-če** (for *gril-ba*) **to fall.** — 2. *Bal.* **ril-čas** (for *sgril-ba*) **to wrap up.**

རིས་ *ris* 1. cognate to *ri-mo* and perh. to *ₒbri-ba*: **figure, form, design,** *pádma-ris* the figure of a lotus-flower *Glr.*, *mig-man-ris-su bris-pa Glr.* painted like a chess-board; *skya-ris* the blank parts of a picture, *tson-ris* the painted parts of a picture *Cs.* — 2. *Cs.*: **part, region, quarter,** hence *mto-ris* **heaven,** v. *mto*; *dban-ris* share of power or of territory; *mna-ris* id. and n. of a part of

Tibet; *ṗyogs-ris* **party**; *Cs.* has also: *raṅ-ris* one's own party, *γžán-ris* another's party, *ris-čan* **partial, prejudiced,** *ris-méd* **impartial, indifferent,** hence also **hermit,** because he ought to feel indifferent to every thing. — 3. *Sch.*: '*ris-su* difference, *ris-su čád-pa* equality'(??). — 4. *ris-γza* symb. num.: 7, derived from the number of the great planets together with sun and moon.

རུ་ *ru* 1. **horn,** = *rwa*; *rá-ru* goat's horn, *lúg-ru* ram's horn. — 2. parts of vessels etc. resembling a horn, e.g. the handle of a stew-pan *Mil. nt.*; **gó-ru* C.* door-post. — 3. **part, division,** *dmág-gi* of an army *Stg.*, wing *Cs.*; of a country, *dbu-γtsáṅ-ru-bži Mil.*; *γyás-ru* the right side or wing, *γyón-ru* the left side or wing, *γžuṅ-ru* the middle part or centre *Cs.* — 4. as num. figure: 85.

Comp. *ru-dár Wdk*, *Mil.*, *ru-mtsón Sch.* military ensign, **banner, colours,** *ₒṗyár-ba* to display, to hoist (a flag). — *ru-sná* division of an army *Sch.* — *rú-pa* 'troops, advanced posts of the enemy' *Sch.* — *ru-dpón* commander of a regiment, colonel.

རུ་ང་ *ru-ṅá* **hatred, grudge, malice,** (of rare occurrence); *ru-ṅa-čan* spiteful, malicious.

རུ་རྟ་ *ru-rtá Cs.*: 'a kind of spicy root'; in *Lh. Inula Helenium.*

རུ་ཐོག་ or རྡོག་ *ru-tóg* or *ru-rdóg Cs.* n. of a district in Tibet contiguous to Ladak; an extensive plain, east of lake *Paṅkoṅ.*

རུ་པ་ *rú-pa* v. *ru.*

རུ་པོ་ *rú-po* **ram** *W.*

རུ་བ་ or རེ་གུར་ *rú-ba* or *re-γur* a tent-covering made of yak's hair; *rú-ba-pa* a person living in such a tent; *rú-bai tsogs* a number of such tents, a tent-village.

རུ་མ་ *rú-ma* **curdled milk,** used as a ferment *C.*, *ₒó-mar rú-ma blug-ₒdra* as when sweet and curdled milk are put together *S.g.*; as to its effect, it may also stand for **leaven.**

རུ་ཚར་ *ru-tsár* **fringes** *Ld.* = *ḱa-tsár.*

རུ་རཀྵ་ *ru-rakṡa Med.*; *Cs.*: a sort of berry

རུ་རུ་ *ru-ru Stg.*; *Sch.*: a kind of deer; a species of fruit-trees.

རུ་ལེབ་ *ru-léb* 'flat-horn', acc. to *Sch.* the reindeer (*šá-ba ru-léb* the domesticated, and *ₒbróg-gi ru-léb* the wild r.), more prob. **the elk,** v. *ḱa-ša.*

རུག་གེ་ *rug-gé* appearing (?), *žiṅ snum ruγ-gé* the field had a luxuriant appearance *Mil. nt.*

རུག་པ་ *rúg-pa* 1. *Cs.* a kind of potato. 2. *W.* **to collect, gather, pluck,** v. *sgrúg-pa.*

རུང་ཁང་ *rúṅ-ḱaṅ Cs.*: **bake-house, kitchen.**

རུང་བ་ *rúṅ-ba* 1. vb. **to be fit, calculated, suitable, right,** and adj.: **fit** etc., gen. with termin., rarely with the root of the verb, *tsig ₒdi ₒǰigs-su ruṅ* this word is calculated to terrify, is terrible *Dzl.*; *btsoṅ-du ruṅ* it is salable, vendible *Dzl.*; *slob-dpón-du mi ruṅ* he is not fit to be a teacher *Dzl.*; *γžán-du mi ruṅ* he is good for nothing else, but also in the sense: he is too good for anything else, nothing inferior can be offered to him *Glr.*; *grub rúṅ-du yód-pa* one that is able to perform it *Tar.*; *mi rnyed mi ruṅ* it must be procured by all means *Dzl.*, *mi byar mi ruṅ* it must be done *Dzl.*; *nyál-du mi ruṅ* it would not do to sleep *Dzl.*; *med kyaṅ ruṅ* I (you etc.) can also do without (him) *Glr.*; *dei tse γtáṅ-du rúṅ-ṅam mi ruṅ* would it not be as well to let him go once more? *Dzl.*; *či-ltar yid-čes-su ruṅ* how can one believe you? *Dzl.*; **kon-čóg zun zer mi ruṅ* W.* God cannot tell a lie; *ₒdi yaṅ ruṅ* this, too, is correct, will do *Gram.*; *ṫsab ruṅ tsam* it may perhaps be used instead *Wdṅ.*; *ṅá-la mós-pa ma byas kyaṅ rúṅ-ste* that they do not show me any honour is not so great a loss; but . . . *Mil.*; *ₒdis ruṅ-ṅam* is that the right thing? will that do? *de-ltar ruṅ* (*W.* **čog**) well, let it be so! for aught I care! — 2. several other phrases with *ruṅ*: a. *lus ₒdi či ruṅ* why should we care so much for this our body? *Dzl.*; esp. *či ma ruṅ*, preceded by *na* or (rarely) by *yaṅ*: **why should**

not...? i.e. **o that! would that!** *˳di bdág-gi yin-na či ma ruṅ* would that this were mine! *Thgy.*; *ṅai bú-mo min-na či ma ruṅ* I only wish, she were not my daughter! would it were not my daughter! *Pth.* b. *ruṅ* = *yaṅ* after a verbal root: *de tsam žig bsdad ruṅ* though I have been sitting so long *Mil.*; *mi dgos ruṅ* though it is not necessary *Mil.*; *šes ruṅ mi šes-pa ltar byéd-pa* to plead ignorance although one knows the thing *Mil.*; *či-la tug ruṅ* whatever may happen to me, = **at all events, at any rate**; *či yin ruṅ* whatever it may be *Mil.*; *log yin ruṅ min ruṅ* whether it be an erroneous (opinion) or not *Mil.*; *ši ruṅ γson ruṅ* whether I live or die, living or dead *Pth.*; *gaṅ yaṅ ruṅ, či yan ruṅ* whosoever he may be, whatsoever it may be, frq.; *sa ču gaṅ yaṅ rúṅ-ba-la* on earth, water or whatever it be *Do.* c. *mi-rúṅ-ba* **illicit, improper, unfit,** v. above; *mi-rúṅ-bai γži bču* ten illicit actions, differently specified *Tar.* 33, 9, *Köpp.* I, 147, partly moral offences, partly only infractions of discipline; but *ma-rúṅ-ba, ma-rúṅs-pa* 1. **pernicious, dangerous, atrocious,** as enemies, beasts of prey, malignant gods and spirits, reckless destroyers etc. 2. **spoiled, destroyed, ruined,** *ma-rúṅ-bar byéd-pa* to destroy etc., *ma-rúṅ-bar ˳gyúr-ba* to be destroyed etc. *Dzl.*

རུད་ *rud* **a falling** or **fallen mass,** as: *k̔a-rúd* snow-slip, avalanche, *ču-rúd* deluge, inundation, flood (by the rupture of an embankment and the like), *sa-rúd* land-slide, descent of a great mass of earth; *rúd-zam* a snow-bridge, formed by avalanches.

རུབ་ཆུ་ *rub-čú* prop. n., a district in the south of *Ld.*

རུབ་པ་ *rúb-pa* **to rush in upon, to attack, assault,** *p̔yag žabs kún-nas rub-rúb ˳jús-te* rushing in upon him from every side in order to touch his hands and feet *Mil.*; *bzán-la rúb-pa* **to pounce on** the prey, to fall upon the food *Glr.*; **do-rub tán-te sád-če** *W.* to kill with stones, to stone; **čog-čig-la rúb-pa** *W.* to press or crowd together towards one side; *k̔a-rúb byéd-pa* to outcry, to bear down by a louder crying *Mil.*; **˳go-rub-rúb ˳dug** *C.*, **go-rúb taṅ dug** *W.* they put their heads together; **šrod rub soṅ*, or *mún-ču rub soṅ** *W.* darkness draws on, night is setting in, for which in *C.* **sa rub soṅ** is said to be used, so that it might also be translated by **to darken, to obscure.**

རུབ་སོ་ *rub-šó* **currant** *W.*

རུམ་ *rum* 1. **womb, uterus,** = *mṅal*, but less frq.: *rum mi bde-ba* sensations of pain during pregnancy *Dzl.*, *rúm-du ˳júg-pa* to enter into the womb. — 2. **darkness, obscurity,** *mún-pai rum Glr.*, gen. *smag-rúm.* — 3. prop. n., **Turkey, the Ottoman empire,** the site of which is but vaguely known to the Tibetans, though some commodities from thence find their way to Lhasa; *rúm-pa* a man from Turkey, a Turk; *rum-šam* (شام) Syria *Cs.*

རུལ་བ་ *rúl-ba* **to rot, to get rotten, to become putrid, to turn rancid** etc., *rúl-bar ˳gyúr-ba B.*, **rul čá-če** *W.* id.; *˳o-ma rul soṅ* the milk is spoiled, *k̔a rul* the snow does no longer bear, **be rul** *W.* **drift-sand, quicksand;** *rul-skyúr* 'sour by putrefaction' *Sch*; *rúl-dri* a putrid smell; *rúl-po* for *hrúl-po Cs.* — Cf. *˳drul-ba.*

རུས་ *rus* 1., *W. rus-pa*, **lineage, family,** *miṅ daṅ rus ni ˳di-ltar-ro* their name and lineage are such and such *Glr.*; **ṅa-raṅ-ghi* (or *ṅa-raṅ dhaṅ*) *ru-čig-pa* or *-ḍá-wa** *C. B.*, **rús-pa čig-čig** *W.* we are of the same family; *rus-γčig-pa γsód-pa* a murderer of persons related to him by blood *Lex.*; *t̔u-mi rus Lex.*: *Thu-mi*, a family-name; *rus mt̔ó-ba* high extraction, *rus dmá-ba* low extraction *Cs.* — 2. v. the next article.

རུས་པ་ *rús-pa* (resp. *γduṅ*) 1. **bone,** *rus-čág* fracture of a bone *Med.*; *rús-pai dúm-bu* prob. small bones of which the Tibetan anatomy enumerates 360. — *mi-rus* human bone; *rkáṅ-rus* bone of the foot; *mgó-rus* bone of the skull; *rús-pai rgyan Mil.* a decoration of terrifying deities and magicians, consisting of human bones suspended from the girdle; *rús-pai rgyan drug Pth.*, the like ornament, but fastened to six different parts of the body, the top of the head, the ears, the neck, the upper arm, the wrists, and the feet; *rus ₒbol-ba* mentioned as a morbid symptom *Lt.?* — 2. **the stone** of apricots and other stone-fruits *C.*, *W.*; grape-stone *Wdṅ.* — 3. **energy,** *snyiṅ-gi Mil.*, gen. *snyiṅ-rus* q.v. — 4. v. *rus*.

Comp, *rus-kráṅ* skeleton, **rus-ṭáṅ ťsóg-se** *W.* he is nothing but skin and bones. — *rús-ḱu Lt.* bone-broth(?). — *rus-gróg Sch.:* a dry bone (?). — *rus-bčúd Lt.?* — *rus-nád W.* caries. — *rús-bu* 1. small bone. 2. bones in general *Dzl.* — *rus-ťsád*, *rus-ťsód Med.?* — *rus-šiṅ* 1. *Sch.* firmness, perseverance, repentance. 2. n. of a part of the body (?) *Lt.*

རེ་ *re* 1. indefinite num. or pron., **single, a single one, some** (persons), **something; one to each, one at a time,** *re-ré* or *re* **every, every one, every body, each,** *ráṅ-la bu re méd-na yid-ₒṗam-pa re yóṅ-gi ₒdug, dés-na ḱyéd-la-aṅ bu re dgos* despair comes from having no son, therefore you, too, should have a son *Mil.*; *yud re* for a moment, = *yud tsam Thgr.*; *lan re lan ɣnyis* once or twice *Mil.*; *mi brgya re tsam žon čóg-pa* (a horse) sufficiently (large) for being mounted by about a hundred men *Glr.*; *lo re tsam ma-ɣtógs* with the exception of one year about *Glr.*; *ras-g̊os-rkyáṅ re* a single cotton garment *Mil.*; *čos-ₒbrél re* a small amount of spiritual instruction *Mil.*; *W.:* **bal re** some wool, **šú-gu re** some paper (= *žig*), **kú-šu re** some apples; *bčú-la ṗúr-pa re ɣtád-nas* handing to each of the ten a *ṗur-pa Pth.*; *lág-na dóṅ-tse re-ré yod* in each of his hands there was a gold-coin *Dzl.*; *nyin ré-la séms-čan ḱri re bsad Glr.* he slaughtered every day 10 000 living beings, *ra lṅa lṅa bsad* five goats (every day); *mi res lug re bsad* each man killed one sheep *Glr.*; in a somewhat different sense: **lo ré-ne lo re čúṅ-se yod** *W.* they grow smaller from year to year; *nyuṅ re* little at a time *Glr.*; *re-re ɣnyis-ɣnyis* one and all, one with another, indiscriminately *Mil.*, *re-re-bžin-gyi mgo* every single person's head *Tar.*; *re žig* **somebody, something; some** (persons), **a little;** (with or without *dus*) **a little while,** *re žig sdod* wait a little! *Dzl.*; *re žig čig-na* **after** a little while, *Bhar.* 37; **once, one day, one time, at a future time,** also *dus re žig-gi ťse Pth* — 2. **mutual, reciprocal** (in this sense it is perh. to be spelled *res*, though it is certainly cognate to *re*), *dpon slob re ₒḱaṅ ₒbyuṅ Mil.* there arises mutual discord between teachers and disciples *Mil.*; **different, differing?** *ré-lta-bu* 'of a different kind or nature' *Sch.* — 3. sbst. a. the wooden parts of a door, *re bži* the four parts of a door-frame, *yá-re* the head-piece, the lintel, *má-re* the sill or threshold (= *yá-ťem* and *má-ťem*), **yá-re má-re ḍal toṅ** *W.* pull it down entirely! *logs-ré* the side posts (*C.* *sgo-ru*). b. v. *re-mos* and *reu*. — 4. In such forms as *mór-ra-re*, *mčis-sa-re*, *gyúr-ta-re* (*Dzl.* ༡༦, 1. ༢༥, 9. ༢༩, 2) it may be rendered by an adverb, as: certainly, undoubtedly. — 5. vb., v. *réd-pa* and *ré-ba*. — 6. particle, mostly put between two closely connected words: *nyams-re-dgá*, *blo-re-bdé Glr.*, *ₒo-re brgyál*, *skyug-re-lóg*, *že-re-ₒjigs*, *yi-re-múg*, *don-re-čúṅ*, *snyiṅ-re-rjé* (this **last** very frq.), without essentially modifying the signification, yet only used in emphatic speech. — 7. num. for *drug-ču* in the abbreviated forms of the numbers 61 to 69. — 8. num. figure: 115.

རེ་སྐན་ *re-skán* (etymology?), acc. to the passages which came to my knowledge a strong negative (like οὐ μή), **by no means, never,** *yoṅ re-skan Mil.* frq., that can never happen, that is absolutely impossible (parallel to *yoṅ mi srid*); *ťsim-par ₒgyur re-skán* they never can be satisfied with it *Tar.*

རེ་སྐོན་ *re-skón* n. of a bitter medicinal herb.

རེ་ཁ་ *re-ḱá Sch.* **a picture, painting.**

རེ་འཁན་ *re-ₒkán* v. *re-ba*.

རེ་འཁང་ *re-ₒḱáṅ Sch.: re-ₒḱáṅ ₒbyúṅ-ba* to be not too much (?).

རེ་གུར་ *re-gur* v. *ré-ba* sbst.

རེ་གྲོན་ *re-grón* **addition, increase.**

རེ་ལྕགས་པ་ or **རེའུ་ལྕགས་པ** *re-lčágs-pa* or *reu-lčágs-pa*, *Med.*, a mezereon with white blossoms in the South-Himalaya, of which paper is made.

རེ་ཏོ *ré-to* pumpkin *Kun.*

རེ་དོགས *re-dógs* v. *ré-ba.* vb.

རེ་ལྡེ *re-ldé* v. *ré-ba* sbst

རེ་སྣམ *ré-snám* v. *ré-ba* sbst.

རེ་འཕགས *re-ₒp̓ágs* prop. n., **Triloknath,** a much frequented place of pilgrimage in Chamba, with a famous image and sanctuary of *Avalokitešvara.*

རེ་བ *ré-ba Cs.* sbst., also *ré-bo,* acc. to some *sbré-bo, W.* **re-snam**, *Cs.* sack-cloth, a kind of cloth of yak's-hair, a tent-cloth (also *re-ldé* and *re-yól Cs.*); *re-gúr* a tent of such cloth.

རེ་བ *ré-ba* I. vb., 1. **to hope,** *t̓ams-čád mt̓óṅ-du reo* all hoped to see *Dzl.*; *dé-la p̓án-du ré-nas* hoping it might be good for it *Mil.*; *sú-la re* in whom should they place their hope, in whom should they trust? *loṅ yód-du ré-la* whilst you are hoping still to have time (enough) *Mil.*; *ré-žiṅ ltós-pa* to look up full of hope *Glr.* — 2. **to wish,** v. II. — 3. to beg, to ask alms, **to go a begging,** for victuals, **k̓o ré-a-la yoṅ** *W.* he comes to beg.

II. आशा sbst. **hope; wish,** frq., *ré-ba skóṅ-ba, ré-ba sgrúb-pa* to fulfil a hope; *rnyéd-pa, t̓ób-pa* to get it fulfilled, to obtain what one has hoped for, *ré-ba ltar ₒgyur* it goes to one's wish, as well as one could wish; *ré-ba daṅ ldán-pa* hoping, full of hope, *ré-ba méd-pa* hopeless, despairing.

Comp. *re-t̓ág* v. *t̓ág-pa.* — *re-dógs* hope and fear, *re-dógs med* being without hope and without fear (the principal aim and prerogative of ascetics) *Mil.* — *ré-(bai) ynas Cs.*: room for hope; prob. also = *ré-sa* the person or thing whereon one's hopes are placed *C., W.*

རེ་མོས, རེས་མོས *ré-mos, rés-mos* **turn, series,** or more accurately: the order or change of the series, *ñéd-la sdúg-pai ré-mos bab* then misfortune came to be our turn *Mil.*; *re-mos-su Pth.*, **ré-mos ċ̓ós-la** *Ld.* by turns, alternately, e.g. to strike one's breast with the hands; **ré-mos ré-mos** *W.* by degrees, gradually; *re-móṅs* id. *Ma.*

རེ་ཞིག *ré-žig* v. *re* 1.

རེ་རལ *re-rál* n. of a medicine *Med.*

རེ་རུ་ (རས་རུ?) *re-rú (ras-ru?) W.* the spread- or warp-beam of a loom.

རེ་ས *ré-sa* v. *ré-ba.*

རེག *reg* 1. *Sch.*: *reg-yzig-pa* 'notes taken down, and extracts made, during a course of study'.— 2. v. the following article.

རེག་པ་ *rég-pa* I. vb., 1. (*W.* **rág-če = nyúg-če**, the latter being more in use) **to touch,** to come in contact with, *lág-pa sá-la gar rég-par* where his hands touched the ground *Dzl.*; *rluṅ yál-ga-la rég-na* when the wind touches the branches *Dzl.*; *k̓á-reg-pa* c.dat.: to eat, to taste, to take, *dúg-la-k̓á-reg ré-ba yod* in taking poison there is hope, (viz. so bad are the times) *Ma.*; **tsá-big žal rag dzod* or *žál-la rag** *W.* please, taste a little of it! *sá-la k̓ru gaṅ tsam-gyis ma rég-par ₒbyón-pa* to walk not touching the ground by an ell, i.e. to move in the air, about a cubit distant from the ground *Pth.*; *rég-pa-med-pa* intangible, unapproachable, out of reach, *Glr.* — 2. to feel, to perceive *Cs.?* — II. sbst. *reg* (prob. only abbreviation of *reg-bya*) feeling, touch, sense of feeling *S.g.* 10, 5?

Comp. *reg-dúg* ('poison that has entered the body by contact') *S.g.* 29, is said to signify now in *C.* venereal disease, syphilis. — *rég-bya* 1. what is felt or may be felt, anything palpable or tangible, *reg-bya mi ts̓or* what may be felt is felt no longer *Wdṅ.* 2. **feeling, sense of feeling,** *p̓ágs-pa-reg-bya* the feeling of the skin, *lús-po p̓yii rég-bya grán-la* whilst the outside of the body appears cold to the touch, *rég-bya-rtsúb* rough to the touch *Med.* — *rég-ma Cs.* n. of a goddess.

རེང་བ་ *reṅ-ba*, pf. *reṅs* **to be stiff, hard, rigid,** *rmai reṅ sbyaṅs* to remove the hard parts, of a wound (to clear, to cleanse) *Wdṅ.*; **raṅs soṅ* W.* (the blood) has coagulated, congealed, also of a dead body: it has grown stiff; **ráṅs-te dad dug* W.* he makes himself stiff, he struggles against; *réṅs-pa* **solid** (opp. to liquid), **coagulated, stiff, hard;** *reṅs-par byed-pa* to make hard or stiff; fig.: **stiffnecked, obstinate, unwilling,** *Do.*

རེང་བུ་ *réṅ-bu* 1. **pastil** for **fumigating** *Lt.*, v. *spos.* — 2. *Sch.*: separate, not belonging to anything else.

རེངས་ *reṅs* sometimes for *raṅs*, v. *nyin-reṅs*, *ťo-reṅs.*

རེངས་པོ་ *reṅs-po Sch.* **alone, single.**

རེད་པ་ *réd-pa* 1. **to be,** = *yin-pa*, in *Sp.* and *C.*, rarely in *B.*; also *ré-pa* (*ré-ba*) is met with; *k'yed p'yugs-rdzi ma red rdo-rje-sems-dpar snaṅ* you are not a herdsman, no, you are *Vajrasattva* (viz. a deity)! *Pth.*; **čaṅ yö-pa re' mé-pa re'*?* is there any beer here or not? *C.* — 2. *Cs.*: **to be ready,** *red mda* a ready arrow *Cs.*; *red daṅ ma red rma* a healed wound and one not yet healed (?) *Sch.* — 3. **to be withered** *Ts.*

རེབ་རེབ་པ་ *reb-réb-pa Sch.*: **to be in a great haste** or **hurry, to be very zealous,** *W.*: **reb log čó-če** to do something wicked again and again.

རེམ་པ་ *rém-pa* vb. and adj. (to be) strong, vigorous, durable, sound, hearty, of men and animals, **rem-pa soṅ* W.* now I feel strong again; **gyóg-pa dúl-če-la rém-pa čo!* W.* exert yourself to walk fast! *čos spyod rem* show your ability, in performing ceremonies or incantations *Mil.*; *rém-čig rém-čig ₒdré-ťsogs-rnams* be strong, ye hobgoblins, show your power; do your best! (ironically) *Mil.*

རེའུ་ *reu Mil.* prob. **panel** or **square,** of a wainscoted wall, of a chessboard etc.; *re(u)-mig* id.

རེར་ *rer* termin. of *re*, to each individually; . . . a piece.

རེས་ *res* 1. inst. of *re.* — 2. **change, turn, time, times,** *da ṅed byéd-pai rés-la báb-ste* it being now our turn of acting *Dzl.*; **dí-riṅ ču-ré k'on yod* W.* to-day it is his turn to irrigate (the field); *res byéd-pa* with verbal root, to do a thing by turns with another person, *čáṅ-la ₒťuṅ-rés byéd-pa*, resp.: *skéms-la ysol-rés mdzád-pa* to vie with one another in drinking beer *Glr.*; *skyes ₒbul-rés byéd-pa* to send mutual presents to one another *Glr.*; *res ₒjóg-pa* to change *Sch.*; *rés-kyis* relieving one another (in service), doing (a thing) alternately or by turns, e g *nyál-la mél-ťse byéd-pa* to sleep and to keep watch *Dzl.*; *res* is also used as an adv.: 1. *res če res čuṅ* now great, now small, or partly great, partly small; *res yod res med* at one time it is there, at another not *Cs.* 2. **at** a time, every time, distributively: *res p'ye ťúr-mgo re tsam ₒgams* I always take the tip of a spoon full of meal at a time *Mil.*; *res ycig* once, once upon a time *Tar.*, *res ₒga* sometimes, *res . . . res* now — now, **at** one time — at another, frq.; **lu-ré* W.* **a** change of singing, an alternative song; *rés-mos* v. *re-mos*; *res-yzá* a changing (wandering) star, **a planet** *Cs.*; *res-ₒgrogs-zla-skár* the stars with which the moon is successively in conjunction *Sch.*

རེས་པོ་ *rés-po* **old,** v *bgre-ba.*

རོ་ *ro* I. sbst. **taste, flavour, savour,** *k'a-ro* id.; *ro-myóṅ-ba* to taste; six different kinds of taste are distinguished: *mṅár-ba* sweet, *skyúr-ba* sour, *lán-ťswa-ba* salt, *k'á-ba* bitter, *ťsá-ba* acrid, *bská-ba* astringent, and the medicines accordingly are also divided into six classes; *ro brgya daṅ ldan-pa* of a hundredfold taste, i.e. of the most exquisite **and** manifold flavour, frq. — II. sbst. 1. also *ró-ma?* resp.: *spur*, **dead body, corpse, carcass,** *mi-ro* a dead man, *rtá-ro* dead horse, *srin-bui ro* dead insects *Dzl*; *ro sré́g-pa* to burn a corpse. — 2. **body,** v. comp. — 3. **residue, remains, sediment,** *ťság-ro* (or *ₒťság-ro*) that which remains in a sieve or filter, impurities, husks etc., *já-ro* tea-leaves in **a** teapot, *ťsil-ro* the remains of bacon after **having** been fried, greaves; *gál-ro*, *rdó-ro*, *sá-ro* rubbish; *skúd-ro* the ends of threads in a seam; v. also *ro-tó*.

Comp. *ro-kán*, col. **rom-kan** place for burning or burying the dead, a favourite spot for conjurations and sorceries. — *ro-grib* defilement by contact with dead bodies. — *ro-rgyáb* **back, back part** *Lt.* — *ro-sgám* **coffin.** — *ro-tó Ld.* (= *ro* II, 3) **residue**; **rañ-sii ro-to** **wax**; **sig-pe ro-tó** ruins of walls. — *ro-stód* the upper part of the human body, chest and back *Stg.*; esp. back *Mil.* — *ro-dóm* fees given to the Lamas for performing the burial or cremation ceremonies *Mil.* — *ro-búg Sch.* grave, tomb. — *ro-myágs* v. *myags* — *ro-smád* the lower part of the body *Med.*, *ro-smád sbrúl-du* ˳*kyil-ba* the lower part of the body like a winding serpent *Wdk.* — *ro-rás* cloth of cotton for wrapping up a dead body before cremation; upon it incantations are frequently written against demons and malignant spirits *Pth.* — *ro-lans* = **वेताल** (evil) spirit, or goblin that occupies a dead body (*Will.*) *Tar.* 158. — *ro-šiñ* wood for burning a dead body.

རོ་ཉེ *ro-nyé Stg.* = *ra-nyé*, *ža-nyé* **lead.**

རོ་མ *ró-ma* 1. sometimes for *ro Cs.*, *Schr.* — 2. v. *rtsa* I.

རོ་ཙ, རོ་གཙའ *ró-tsa*, *ró-ytsa* **sexual instinct, carnal desire,** lust *Med.*, *ró-tsa skyéd-pa* to excite, to increase the carnal appetite by medicine *Cs.*; also: to feel it; *ró-tsa-ba* 1. voluptuous, sensual, lustful *Mil.* 2. exciting or animating the sexual instinct *Wdn.*

རོག་པོ *róg-po* 1. *C.* **black**, cf. *bya-* and *pó-róg*. — 2. *W.*= *rág-pa* **reddish, yellowish-brown,** of rocks. — *róg-ge-ba* shining dimly; *žal* ˳*dzum-nág róg-ge-ba* with a face glowing gloomily as it were *Mil.nt.* — *rog-róg* 1. *C.* jet-black. 2. 'dark-grey' *Sch.*, prob. = *róg-po* 2. — 3. **rogue, villain** *Cs.* (a man of dark deeds?).

རོགས *rogs*, vulgar pronunciation of *grogs*, **friend, companion, associate, assistant** v. *grogs*; *rogs-méd ycig-pa* quite alone *Pth.*; **roy-rám có-ce** *W.* = *ra-mda byéd-pa*; **rógs-po** *Ld.* adulterer, **róg-po cò-ce** (of a husband) and **róg-mo có-ce** (of a wife) to commit adultery.

རོང *roñ* **narrow passage, defile, cleft** in a hill, also **valley**; *brag-róñ* dell or chasm between rocks, **ravine**, *roñ-rtsúb* a rough country full of ravines, so Tibet is called *Glr.*; *róñ-yul* id.; *róñ-mi*, *róñ-rta*, *róñ-lcañ* a man coming from, a horse bred in, a willow growing in such a country.

རོད *rod* **pride, haughtiness** *Ts.*

རོད་པ, རོད་པོ *ród-pa*, *ród-po* **stiff,** unable to help one's self, *ród-lci-ba Sch.* id; *Ld.*: **rod-da-rod-de** of decrepit or sick people.

རོམ་཈ང *róm-kañ W.* for *ro-kañ*.

རོམ་པོ *róm-po W* (for *sbóm-po C.*, *B.*) **thick, big, stout,** of men, trees, sticks; **massive, massy, plump; deep,** of sounds, opp. to *prá-mo*. — *róm-yig* type, types, letters used in printing, opp. to *pra-yig*, v. *yi-ge*.

རོལ *rol* 1. **side,** only in the comp.: *náñ-rol* inside, *pyi-rol* outside, *pá-rol*, *tsú-rol* etc.; *mál-gyi pyi-rol* the outside of the bed (e.g. has been soiled) *Glr.*; mostly as postposition: *yáñs-pa-can-gyi náñ-rol-na* within the town of *Yañ-pa-can*; *náñ-rol-nas* ˳*búl-ba* to reach, to hand from within *Dzl.*; *čui pá-rol-na*, *tsú-rol-na* (or *tsú-rol-tu*) on the other side or on this side of the water; *yyás-rol*, *yyón-rol* the right side, the left side; also in a looser sense: *pyi-rol-tu bzuñ-ba* to look upon a thing as externally or really existing *Mil.*; often pleon.: *sñón-rol-nas* **before, previously** *Thgy.*; ˳*óg-rol-tu* for ˳*óg-tu* **after** *Pth.*, *Tar.*; ˳*di-nas nyi-ma-núb-kyi pyógs-rol-na* to the west from here. — 2. *Sch.*: *rol(-tu) bsád-pa* to destroy completely, to kill on the spot(?). — 3. (*Cs.* also *rol-mo*) **furrow**; *rol rmód-pa* to make furrows, to plough.

རོལ་རྟ *ról-rta Sch.*: **the near horse** in a team, the right-hand horse.

རོལ་པ *ról-pa* = *sprúl-pa*, v. *ról-ba* 3.

རོལ་བ *ról-ba* 1. **to amuse** or **divert one's self** (synon. with *rtsé-ba*), thus one of the twelve actions of a Buddha is *btsun-moi* ˳*kor-*

du ról-ba diverting himself with his wives; *bdag-yód daṅ ról-ba* to divert one's self with a married woman (sensu obsc.) *Schr.*; in *rgya-čer-ról-pa* (v. sub *rgya*), and in *ról-pa bkód-pa* (the n. of a certain kind of contemplation *Gyatch.*), it is used for ललित, playing. — 2. **to take, taste, eat, drink,** *srín-mo l ág-la ról-ba* witches or ogresses reveling in blood *Mil.*; *ról-pai stábs-su bžugs* there he sits with greedy mien. — 3. = *sprúl-ba* **to practice sorcery, to cause to appear** by magic power, *rnám-par ról-pa* = *rnám-par sprúl-pa*; *yé-šes ról-pai ḱyeu lha Pth.* for: *yé-šes-kyi sprúl-pa* incarnations of the divine Wisdom; *rol-pai mtso* prob. **enchanted lake,** occurs in the description of the Sumeru, but no Lama seemed to know its exact meaning. — 4. vulg.: **to thrash,** to cudgel.

རོལ་མ་ *ról-ma* 1. v. *rol* 3. — 2. col. for *sgról-ma.*

རོལ་མོ་ *ról-mo* (cf. *ról-ba* 1). 1. **music,** *ról-mo byéd-pa*, *W.* **čó-če**, to make music, *ról-mo spyád pa Sch.* id. — 2. **musical instrument,** = *ról-moi ča-byád Dzl.*, *ról-ča Cs.*, in *W.* esp. cymbal.

རླ་ and རླག་ *rla* and *rlag* sometimes for *bla* and *glags.*

རླག་པ་ *rlág-pa* v. *rlóg-pa.*

རླངས་པ་ *rláṅs-pa* **vapour, steam,** *ḱa-rláṅs* **breath, exhalation,** **ḱa-láṅ táṅ-če** to breathe, to exhale *W.*; **gaṅ-láṅ** cloud-like snow-drifts on high hills, *ču-rláṅs* steam, watery vapour; *rláṅs-ču* ₒ*dón-pa Schr.* **to distil.**

རླན་ *rlan* 1. **moisture, humidity,** *rlan spáṅ-ba* to avoid the wet *Med.*, *rlan steṅ nyál-ba* to sleep in the wet *Lt.* — 2. **a liquid,** *rlan-rlón* id., *rlan-rlón čaṅ* the liquid (called) beer *Lex.*; *rlán-čan* moist, wet, humid, e.g. a country, *rlan-méd* dry. Cf. *rlón-pa, brlan.*

རླབ(ས)་པ་ *rláb(s)-pa Sch.*: 'to remove, to clear away'.

རླབས་ *rlabs* **wave, billow, flood,** *rgyá mtsoi rlabs Med.*; *ču-rlábs* and *dba-rlábs* or *rba-rlábs* = *rlabs*; *dus-rlabs* ebb and flood, **tides** *Stg.*; *rlabs ɣyó-ba* or ₒ*ḱrúg-pa* the tumult of the waves *Cs.*; *rlabs-po-čé* or *rlabs-čén*, *Lex.*: महोर्मि, a large wave or billow, a rolling swell of the sea, surf, surge; also fig.: a high degree, e.g. of diligence *Thgy.*

རླམ་པ་ *rlám-pa* v. *rlóm-pa*; *rlam-ḱyér Sch.* pride (?).

རླིག་པ་ *rlíg-pa*, resp. *ɣsaṅ-rlig*, **testicle, stone,** ₒ*byín-pa*, ₒ*ṗyíd-pa*, *W.* **tón-če** **to castrate,** emasculate (a man), to cut or geld (an animal), *rlig-ṗyúṅ*, *rlig-méd* castrated, emasculated, *rlig-čan* having testicles, *rlig-ɣčig-pa* having only one testicle; *rlig-bu*, *rlig-šúbs* scrotum; *rlig-skráṅs* swollen testicles; *rlig-rlúgs Lt.*, *rlig-blúgs S.g.*, id. (acc. to *Cs.*).

རླིངས་ *rliṅs Sch.* **good, quick,** cf. *brliṅ-ba.*

རླིད་ *rlid Sch.* a closed leather-bag.

རླིད་བུ་ *rlid-bu Sch.*: 'a whole, a lump or mass'; but this seems not applicable in the phrase *dúd-ₒgroi rlid-bu Lex.*, and otherwise it is not known to me.

རླུག(ས)་པ་ *rlúg(s)-pa* 1. *Cs.*: **'to purge,** *mṅal rlúgs-par byéd-pa* to cause an abortion, *rlugs-byéd* purging, procuring abortion; *rlúgs-ma Sch.*: 'the casting out, effusion'; acc. to one *Lex.* excretion of indigested food. — 2. *Ts.*: to overthrow, to pull down, v. *lug-pa.*

རླུང་ *rluṅ* वायु 1. *W.* *rluṅ-po* **breeze, wind,** *rluṅ ló-ma-la reg* the wind touches the leaves *Dzl.*, *rluṅ-gis skyod* (a thing) is moved by the wind *Dzl.*, blown away by the wind *Glr.*; **luṅ laṅ* C.*, **lúṅ-po ṗu dug* W.*, the wind blows, also for: there is a draught (here); **lúṅ-rag máṅ-po yoṅ dug* W.* one feels the wind (here) very much; *rluṅ čén-po Mil.*, *drág-po* a high wind, a gale; *šár-rluṅ* east-wind etc., *čar-rlúṅ* rain and wind; *skám-rluṅ* a dry wind *Cs.*; **lúṅ-po yób-če* W.* to fan; ₒ*og-luṅ* wind (from the stomach), **flatulence** *Lt.*; fig.: *lós-kyi rlúṅ-gis déd-de* impelled or pushed on by the wind of actions, i.e. involved in the consequences of one's actions; and in a similar manner in other instances, frq. — 2. **air,** atmospheric air, *rlúṅ-gyi dkyil-ₒḱor* **atmosphere;** *rlúṅ-gi ₒṗrúl-ḱor* air-pump *Cs.*, *rlúṅ-gi gru* air-balloon *Cs.* — 3. in physiology: one of the three humours of the body (v. *nyés-pa*) supposed to exist in nearly all the parts and organs of the body, circulating in veins of its own, producing the arbitrary and the involuntary motions, and causing various other physiological phenomena. When deranged, it is the cause of many diseases, esp. of such complaints the origin and seat of which is not known, as rheumatism, nervous affections etc. This *rluṅ* or humour is divided into five species, viz.: *srog-ₒdzin* cause of breathing, *gyén-rgyu* faculty of speaking, *k̔yab-byéd* cause of muscular motion, *me-mnyám* of digestion and assimilation, *t̔ur-sél* of excretion; *rlúṅ-las gyúr-pa yin* (the disease) arises from *rluṅ Glr.*; *rlúṅ-gis bzúṅ-ste = rluṅ-ndd-kyis btáb-ste.* — These notions concerning *rluṅ* are one of the weakest points of Tibetan physiology and pathology. — 4. **in mysticism** *rluṅ ₒdzín-pa* seems to be = *dbugs bsgyáṅ-ba*, and to denote the drawing in and holding one's breath during the procedure called *ytum-mo* (q. v.), which is as much as to prepare one's self for contemplation, or enter into a state of ecstasy *Mil.*; *rluṅ sems-la dbaṅ t̔ób-pa Mil.*, frq., is said to imply that high degree of mystical ecstasy, when *rluṅ* and *sems* have been joined into one; he who has attained to the *mgyogs-rlúṅ* is able to perform extraordinary things, e.g. with a heavy burden on his back he is able to run with the greatest speed, and the like. —

Comp. *rlúṅ-rta* **the airy horse,** n. of little flags, frequently to be seen waving in the wind on Tibetan houses, on heaps of stones, bridges etc. The figure of a horse which together with various prayers is printed on these flags signifies (acc. to *Schl.* 253) the deity *rta-mčog.* Huc also mentions superstitious practices that may be called *rluṅ-rta.* — *rluṅ-mdá Sch.* air-gun. — *rluṅ-nád* disease caused by *rluṅ*, v. above. — *rluṅ-dmár*, *rluṅ nág-po* prop. dust-storm, a storm whirling up clouds of dust; further: **storm, tempest** in general, also a gale at sea *Glr.* and elsewh. — *rluṅ-ts̔úb* whirlwind, **snow-storm** *Mil.* — *rluṅ-séms* v. above, *rluṅ* 4. — *rluṅ-sér*, *rluṅ-bsér-bu*, *rluṅ bsir-ba*, a violent wind *Cs.*

རླུབས་ *rlubs* 1. in *C.*: **corner, hole, place for hiding** a thing; *Lex.*: *k̔uṅ-bui rlubs.* — 2. *Sch.*: **ditch, pit, pool, abyss,** *mei rlubs* fire-pool.

རློག་པ་ *rlóg-pa*, pf. *brlags*, fut. *brlag*, imp. *rlog(s)*, *brlag*, vb. a. to *ldóg-pa*, 1. **to overthrow, to destroy**; *t̔ál-bar* or *rdál-du rlóg-pa* to reduce to powder, to destroy entirely *Thgy.* and elsewh.; *rtsa-ba-nas*, or *rnám-par*, to annihilate, e.g. all the infidels *Pth.*, **to break, to smash** e. g. a vessel *C.*; **to lose** *C.*, *'á-ma lag-soṅ* I have lost my mother *C.*, *'lug čig lag soṅ* one sheep has perished *C.* — 2. fig. **to pervert, to infatuate,** *nyés-pai dri-mas yóṅs-su brlágs-te* quite corrupted by the filth of sin *Dzl.*; *čúṅ-mar ₒdzín-pai bsám-rlags-ts̔o* those infatuated by thoughts of marriage *Glr.*; *brlág-po* **foolish, stupid,** of a little child *Thgy.*

རློང་ *rloṅ* sometimes erron. for *kloṅ* or *loṅ*.

རློན་པ་ *rlón-pa* I. 1. adj. (*Cs.* 'moist') *W.* **wet,** *ts̔aṅ-rlón* quite wet, wet through; hence of meat, vegetables and the like, **fresh, green, raw** *B.* and col. — 2. vb., pf. and fut. *brlan*, **to make wet, to moisten,** *čus*, *čar-pas Dzl.*

II. *Sch.*: **to answer,** with *lan*, also *glón-pa*, *ldón-pa*, *blán-pa*, *zlón-pa*.

རློབ་པ་ *rlób-pa*, pf. *brlabs*, fut. *brlab*, imp. *rlobs*, v. *byin*.

རློམ་པ་ *rlóm-pa* I. vb., pf. *brlams*, fut. *brlam* 1. **to be proud of, to glory in, to boast of,** with termin., *bder rlóm-pa* to boast of one's good fortune, *ycig-par* or *ycig-tu rlóm-pa* to be proud of the identity with . . . *Tar.* — 2. **to love, to adhere to, to be attached to** *W.*, **to strive after,** *yžán-gyi nór-la.* — 3. **to be possessed,** of demons, *ydón-gyis brláms-pa Lt.* — II. sbst. **pride,** *bsags kyaṅ rlóm-pas ₒk̔yer* if perhaps (any merit) has been gathered, it is taken away again by pride *Mil.* — Deriv. *rlóm-po* **a boaster,** an arrogant person *Cs.*; *rlóm-sems* **pride, arrogance.**

བརླ་(རླ་? *Cs.*) *brla* (*-bo?*) **the thigh,** *brla ná-ba* a pain in the thigh *Do.*, *brla ygas* the right thigh *Glr.*, *brla-rkáṅ* femoral bone (*Sch.*: hip-bone?). **brla-k̔uṅ** groin *W.*; *brla-bar Sch.*: junction of the legs, genitals; *brla-rús* femoral bone; *brla-šá* muscular part of the thigh; *brla-súl Cs.*: 'side of the thigh'.

བརླག་པ་ *brlág-pa* v. *rlóg-pa.*

བརླང་པོ་ *brláṅ-po Lex.* and *Sch.* **abusive word, invective, abusive language** (*Sch.* also: 'rude fellow, brute'?), *rtsub-brláṅ-ba ma yin-pa* refraining from abusive language *Thgy.*; *brláṅ-po-rnams byéd-pa* to make use of such language *Stg.*; *brlaṅ-spyód byéd-pa* to be coarse, churlish *Sch.*

བརླན་པ་ *brlán-pa* v. *rlón-pa.*

བརླབ་པ་ *brláb-pa* v. *rlób-pa.*

བརླམ་པ་ *brlám-pa* v. *rlóm-pa.*

བརླིང་བ་ *brlíṅ-ba C.* **firm, secure, safe** (*Sch.*: quick?), *brlíṅ-po* id., both of men and things, **liṅ-ghyi' jhe-la k̔ur* C.* carry it safely, carefully! *brliṅ-lóg Sch.*: confused, disorderly, not to be trusted.

བརླུག་པ་ *brlúg-pa Sch.*: = *mdzá-bo* friend, assistant, helper; one *Lex.* explains *bló-brlug* by *grogs.*

བརླུབས་ *brlubs* v. *rlubs.*

ལ

ལ *la* 1. the letter l. — 2. numeral: 26.

ལ་ *la* I. sbst. **mountain pass**, road or passage over a mountain, *lai gyen* the up-hill road or ascent of a mountain, *lai t̔ur* the down-hill road or descent *Cs.*; *la rgál-ba B., C.* (*W.*: **gyáb-ce**) to cross a mountain pass; *lá-la ˳gró-ba Cs.* id.

Comp. *la-rkéd* or *skéd* the declivity or slope of a mountain pass. — *la-k̔á* the highest point of the pass, *la-mgó* the head, or top, of a mountain pass. — *la-sgó*, *Sch.*: 'turnpike of a pass'. — *la-ycán-pa* a collector of duties on a ghat or pass *Cs.* — *la-čúṅ* a small pass *Glr.* — *la-mjúg* = *la-rtsa.* *la-stóṅ* v. *stóṅ-pa.* — *la-t̔óg* = *la-rtsé.* — *la-rtsá* (*W.* **lar-sa**) foot of a mountain pass *la-rtsé* (*W.* **lar-sé**) top of it. — *la-šán Sch.*: = *la-rkéd.*

II. sbst., also *lá-ba*, **wax-light, wax-candle, taper**, from the Chinese *láh* **wax**, *C.*

III. In compounds for *la-p̔ug* and *la-č̔a.*

IV. postpos. c. acc. 1. denoting local relations in quite a general sense, in answer to the questions **where** and **whither:** *sá-la ˳gré-ba* to roll (one's body) on the ground, *sá-la ˳gril-ba* to fall down on the ground, *nám-mka-la ˳p̔ág-pa* to rise to heaven, *nám-mka-la ˳p̔úr-ba* to fly in the air, *mé-la* at, on, in, to, the fire, *ri-la* on, to, the mountain, *čú-la* in, into, to, on, the water, *šár-la* to, towards the east, eastward (e.g. to look), *bód-la* in, to, Tibet; also where we should say: from, as: *ynám-la k̔á-ba ˳bab* snow falls from heaven, *rtá-la ˳bab* he alights from his horse, *brág-la mčoṅs* he leaps down from the rock *Dzl.*, *lús-la k̔rag ˳byin-pa* to draw blood from the body by scratching. This latter use of *la* occurs so frequently, that it cannot always be looked upon as a misspelling for *las*, though this would be the more exact word. — 2. with reference to time: *žag ysúm-pa-la* on the third day, *lo nyi-šú-pa-la* in the twentieth or during the twentieth year, *zlá-ba ysúm-la* (finish it) within three months *Glr.*, *p̔yag dáṅ-po-la* at, during, the first obeisance *Glr.* — 3. in other bearings: *dé-la rtén-nas* (prop. relying on, keeping to) relative to, with respect to, in consequence of: also *dé-la*, without *rtén-nas* id.; with verbs expressing feelings of the mind: **at, off, concerning** etc., *dé-la dgá-ste* glad of, rejoicing at it; *sdig-pa-la ˳dzém-pa* to be afraid of sin; *ma byúṅ-ba ˳di-la ydams-ṅág ysól-to* he asked advice with respect to this not having been done *Mil.*; in introducing a new subject: *rgyál-sa me-nyág-la šór-bai lo-rgyús-la* now, as to the fact of the supremacy having been transferred to *Taṅ-yul*, it . . . *Glr.*; in headings of chapters etc., e.g. *gliṅ bži mìṅ-la* names of the four parts of the globe *Trig.*; *če-čuṅ-gi t'sad-la* with respect to size *Glr.*; *bre-sráṅ-la γyo mi byéd-pa* not to cheat by measure and weight *Glr.*; for the Latin *erga* and *contra*, as: *dgra-la rgol-ba* to struggle against or with an enemy; *bu-la snyiṅ-brtse-nas* from love to her son; *nad-stóbs-kyi če-čúṅ-la dpág-pa* to proportion (the medicines) to the degree of the illness *Lt.*; *sṅár-gyi rgyún-la* in comparison with the former time *Tar.*; *rgyál-poi t'úgs-rje-la* by, or according to the king's favour; *ṅai lúgs-la* by my way of proceeding, according to my system *Mil.*; *žábs-p'yi-la* (to go with a person) as a companion. — 4. most frq. *la* is used as sign of the dat. case, col. also of the accus. following a vb. a. — 5. in all the relations mentioned above, *la* is added to the inf., partic. and root of a vb., wherever the verb will at all admit of it, and besides it is used as gerundial particle in a similar sense as *te:* **a.** after the inf. (only in *B.*): *lha-rtén žig yód-pa-la* as there was in that place an idol-shrine *Dzl.*; often also to be translated by **although.** **b.** added to the root (*B.* and col.): *mt'óṅ-la ma btags* (though) having seen it, yet he did not fasten it *Dzl.*; col. esp. when the root is doubled, for **while, whilst:** **ṅe ša tub-túb-la kyod šiṅ k'ur** fetch thou wood, whilst I am cutting the meat into pieces *W.*; in *C.* and *B.* = *čiṅ*, also added to adjectives, *lus mi-sdúg-čiṅ t'úṅ-la dbyaṅs snyán-pa* ugly as to his body (and) of small stature, (but) having a fine voice *Dzl.*; in sentences containing an imp. it is added to the root of it: *šóg-la ltos šig* come and look!

ལ་ཁྱི་མོ་ *la-kyi-mo W.* **the mountain-weasel;** = *sre-moṅ?*

ལ་རྒྱ་ *la-rgyá Sch.*: government, administration (?).

ལ་ཆ་ *la-čá* **sealing-wax,** *Wdṅ.*, **la-kyir** *W.* balls of sealing-wax, with a hole for stringing them, used like our sticks of sealing-wax; *la-t'ig* drops of sealing-wax; *la-t'ig rgyág-pa* to drop melted sealing-wax upon (a person), as a torture.

ལ་ཉུང་ *la-nyúṅ Glr.*, either a sort of turnip, or (more prob.) for *lá-p'ug daṅ nyúṅ-ma* radish and turnip.

ལ་ཉེ་ *la-nyé Sch.*: 'a mark' (?).

ལ་ཏ་ *la-tá Hind.* لتّه? an imported material like **flax** or a sort of linen-cloth, not in general use; hence in many parts of the country unknown.

ལ་ཏུ, ལ་ཐུ, ལ་དུ་ *la-tu, la-t'u, la-du*, prop. लडू. a sort of pastry of India, composed of suet, coarse meal, sugar and spices; the word may also be used for our gingerbread.

ལ་ཐིག་ *la-t'ig* v. *la-ča.*

ལ་ཐོད་ *la-t'ód* **turban** *Glr.*

ལ་དྭགས་ *la-dwágs*, also *már-yul*, **Ladág, Ladák,** province in the valley of the Indus between *mṅa-rís* and Bálti, inhabited by Tibetans and formerly belonging to Tibet, afterwards an independent kingdom, but recently conquered by Gulab Singh of Kashmere and hindooized as much as possible by his son and successor; capital **Le.**

ལ་པ་ཤ, ལ་པ་ཤག་ *lá-pa-ša* or *lá-pa-šag Cs.* a kind of upper garment without a girdle.

ལ་ཕོ་ *lá-p'o* **buttermilk,** boiled, but not yet dried into vermicelli (*čúr-ba*).

ལ་ཕུག་ *lá-p'ug* **radish,** *bod lá-p'ug* the common black radish, ni f.; *rgya lá-p'ug* a red species, of an acidulous taste. The carrot (*Daucus carota*) is in *C.* also col. called *la-p'ug sér-po.* — *la-bdár*, gen. **lab-*

*dár**, a contrivance for grating radishes, either made of wood, or consisting of a quartz-stone with a crystallized, rough surface.

ལ་བ་ *lá-ba* v. *la* II.

ལྭ་བ, ལྭ་ཝ་ *lwá-ba, lwá-wa, Ssk.* कम्बल, *Will.*: 'a woolen blanket or cloth; a sort of deer'; *skrai lwá-ba Stg.* frq. a kind of woolen cloth. The seat of Buddha is often a slab resembling a *lwá-ba Do.*

ལ་མ་ *la-ma Sch.*: a certain herb.

ལ་མ་སྲོ་ *la-ma-sró* **raspberry** *Kun.*

ལ་འུར་ *la-ᵤúr Cs.*, also *la-gór Sch.*, **quick, swift, speedy,** *ḱyod ma ₒdug ma ₒdug a-ᵤúr ₒdeṅ Mil.* make haste, go without stopping (on the road).

ལ་ཡོགས་ *la-yógs* **retribution**, punishments overtaking a sinner during this life (cf. *lan-čags*) *C., W.*; **la-yóg ťob yin** that will come home to you! *Sch.* has *la-yogs-pa* to return, to come back (?).

ལ་རེ་ *la-ré W.* a sort of long-legged and swift-moving centiped, frequent in houses.

ལ་ལ་ *la-la C., B.* (is said to be pronounced *la-lá* in *Sp.*, but *Thgy.* sometimes accentuates *lá-la*, according to the metre) **some, a few**; when put twice: **partly — partly, what — what;** *la-la žig* also as a singular: some body, some one *Dzl.* ᏙᏙ, 1.

ལ་ལ་ཕུད་ *lá-la-p̓ud* a medicinal herb; in *Lh.* a Bupleurum.

ལ་སོ་ *la-so Sch.* **list** (of cloth), **selvage.**

ལ་སོགས་ *la-sógs* v. *sogs.*

ལག *lag*, also *dbón-lag, dgón-lag, Sch.*: little, not much.

ལག་(པ་) *lág(-pa)* 1. resp. *p̓yag*, **hand, arm,** **lág-pa táṅ-če* W.* to shake hands, also to offer one's hand, as a pledge of faith (for *C.* v. *mdzúg-gu*); *lág pa-nas ₒǰú-ba* to take, to seize by the hand *Dzl.*; *lag-pai rgyab* or *bol* the back of the hand; *lág-pai mdun* the palm of the hand *Cs.*; *lág-tu lén-pa* **to take in hand, to exercise, to practise,** *sgóm-pa* meditation *Mil.*, *tsig-dón* to study and practise the import of a word, to live accordingly *Mil.*, metaph.: *mtso-lág* **arm of the sea,** gulf, **bay,** *mtso-lag-ₒbrél* narrow sea, **straits;** *gliṅ-lág, yul-lág* tongue of land, *gliṅ-lag-ₒbrél* isthmus, neck of land *C.*; fig. for **power,** authority, *mii lág-tu ₒgró-ba* to get into a person's power, to be at his mercy *Thgy.*, *lág-nas ₒp̓róg-pa* to snatch out of a person's hand, to deliver from another's power *Glr.* — 2. **fore-paw;** also **paw** or **foot** in gen., e.g. foot of a cock *Glr.* — 3. symb. num.: 2.

Comp. *lag-kod* **bundle, bunch, armful,** sheaf of corn *Ld.*(?). — *lag-skór Ld.*: **hand-mill.** — *lag-ḱúg* **pouch, hand-bag** *Schr.* — *lag-mgó* 1. *lag-mgo tsam* like a fist *Glr.*, or acc. to others: both hands put together in the shape of a globe or ball. 2. a glove with only a thumb, a mitten *C.* — *lag-grám* leaning one's head on the hand *W.* — *lag-rgyúgs* **railing.** — *lag-rgyún* accustomed manner, **use, habit** *Cs* — *lag-ṅár* **the fore-arm** *Wdṅ.* — *lág-ča* **utensils, tools, implements;** object carried in the hands, e.g. royal insignia at a festival procession *Glr.*; also in a more gen. sense, like *čá-lag*, *ₒḱor-γyóg lág-ča daṅ bčás-pa ťoṅ žig* supply servants and things (wanted for the journey)! *Glr.* — *lag-čág* a broken hand, a lame hand *Cs., Schr.* — **lag-čad* W.* solemn promise by shaking or joining hands. — *lag-rǰés* 1. impression, mark, of the hand, of the fingers. 2. **a work** which immortalizes a person's name, *lag-rǰes ₒǰóg-pa* to leave such a work behind *Glr.* — *lag-nyá*, one *Lex.* has: *lag-nyás = stér-mḱan-med-par lén-pa* to take what is not given, hence *lag-nya* prob. a sbst.: a grasp, a snatch. — **lag-nyár* W.* for *lag-ṅar.* — *lag-tig* (or *dig?*) travelling-bag, pouch *Ld.* — *lag-rtags* 1. resp. *p̓yag-rtágs* q.v., **sign or mark made with the hand, as** a seal of verification, impressed on a legal document, but often only with the finger dipped in ink. 2. any small object, e.g. a needle, which the deliverer of a letter has to hand over together with the letter; present in general? — *lag-stábs Sch. = lag-*

len. — *lag-mtíl* **the palm** of the hand. — *lag-dám Mil.*, *lag-dám-po C.* **close-fisted,** stingy, niggardly. — *lag-dar Lex.*, prob. the same as *láb-dár* (*W.* col.) **grater.** — *lag-ydúb* **bracelet.** — *lag-bdé Mil., C.*, the person that pours out the tea at a tea-carousal. — *lag-ₒdón Cs.* a vassal or subject paying his landlord in money or kind, opp. to *rkaṅ-ₒgró* who performs his services as an errand-goer or a porter. — *lag-rdúm Mil.* having a mutilated or crippled hand. — *lag-ldán* having a hand or a trunk, hence = **elephant,** *Cs.* — *lag-brdá* **sign** or signal made by the hand, **beckoning.** — *lag-na-rdó-rje*, *lag-rdór* v. *rdó-rje.* — *lag-na-yžoṅ-ťogs Cs.* 'holding a basin in his hand', n. of a deity. — *lag-snód* = *lag-tig.* — *lag-dpón* work-master, overseer, esp. builder *Dzl., Glr.* — *lag-p̄yis* a piece of cloth for wiping the hands, **towel, napkin.** — *lag-búbs* v. *ₒbúb-pa.* *lag-bér* **walking-staff.** — *lag-mí* **bail,** surety. — *lag-dmár C.* **hangman.** — *lag-btsúg* **shoot, scion.** — *lag-ťsigs* joint of the hand, **wrist; elbow-joint.** — *lag-yzúṅs*, *W.* **lag-zúm**, **balustrade,** banister, railing. — *lág-yyog-pa* **companion, assistant, associate.** — *lag-rís* the lines in the palm of the hand *Sch.* — *lag-lén*, resp. *p̄yag-lén*, *Sch.* also *lag-stabs*, **practice, practical knowledge, dexterity,** *Cs.*: *čós-kyi lag-lén* the practice of religion, *k̄ríms-kyi* of the law, *rtsis-kyi* of mathematics. — *lag-šúbs* **glove.**

ལགས་པ་ *lágs-pa*, resp. and eleg. for *yin-pa* and *ₒgyúr-ba*, **to be;** *lágs-so* like *yin*, as answer to a question: so it is! yes to be sure! very well! at your service! When a Lama asks a shepherd: *k̄yéd-kyi miṅ či yin* what is your name? the latter answers: *N. N. byá-ba lags* my name, if you please, is N.N., and asks on his part: *blá-ma k̄yed či skad byá-ba lags* what may be the name of your Reverence? *Mil.* — *de k̄yed lágs-sam* is it you, Sir? *Pth.*; *dge-sloṅ de su lags* who is this reverend gentleman? *Dzl.*; *či ltar lags-pa* (for *gyur-pa*) *ysol-pa* he reported (to Buddha) what had happened, *Dzl.*; *blá-ma-la bžugs-grogs med-pa lags-sam Mil.* has your Reverence no attendant? *ltá-ba ma lágs-kyi* that does not mean: to behold, but ... *Dzl.*; *ₒoṅ-ba či lags* 'what is it that this comes here?' i.e. how does this happen to come here? *Glr.*; *rje či lags* what is that, Sir? (when one is surprised at any thing strange or unaccountable, at an unreasonable demand etc., also when we should say: God forbid!) *Glr.*; *yin lags*, *yda lags*, *yod lags* there is, it is *Glr.*; *žal-zás ysol lágs-nas* when we shall have done dining *Dzl.*; a Lama asks: *btsal-le* (= *btsal-lam*) have you looked for it? and the disciple answers: *btsal lags* yes, I have! *Mil.*; in addressing a person: *blá-ma lags* (prop: you that are a Lama) for the mere vocative case, ὦ ἱερεῦ, *Mil.*, frq. — In *W. lags* is not in use now (cf. however *le* 3), but in *C.* it is of frq. occurrence, e.g. in Lhasa: **lā*, *lā-so*, *lā yo'*, *lā yin** for: yes, Sir! very well, Sir! **lā? lā-am? lā-sam?** please? what did you say?

ལགས་མོ་ *lágs-mo* W. **clean,** for *légs-pa.*

ལང་ཀ་ *laṅ-ka* **Ceylon,** *laṅ-ka-pu-ri* city of the Rakshasa in Ceylon, which island is the abode of these beings, according to the belief of many people in Tibet and northern India even at the present day; *laṅ-kar yšegs-pai mdo* the *Sutra Laṅkāvatāra* in the *Kangyur.*

ལང་(ང་)ལོང་(ངེ་) *laṅ(-ṅa)-loṅ(-ṅe)* **weak,** e.g. from hunger, disease *Ld.*

ལང་ཐང་ *laṅ-ťaṅ Scopolia praealta Don.*, a common weed with pale yellowish flowers *Med.*; in *Lh.* a species of Hyoscyamus, of frq. occurrence, seems to be understood by the same name.

ལང་བ་ *láṅ-ba* (provinc. *lóṅ-ba*), pf. *laṅs*, imp. *loṅ(s)*, = *ldaṅ-ba*, I. **to rise, to get up,** *da loṅs* get up now! also with *yar* (pleon.); *laṅs-te sdod-pa* **to stand,** *Lt.* and col; **to arise,** e.g. of a contest *W., C.;* to go away, to depart, esp. fig., of the night: *nam láṅs-te* at daybreak; **to come forward, to step forth,** from among the crowd *Do.*; *p̄yir láṅ-ba* **to recover,** to be restored, to grow well, **to come to one's self,** after a fainting fit *Dzl.*; *bstán-pai mé-ro láńs-pa yin* the dying embers of religion were blown into a flame again *Glr.*; **to appear, to break out,** of a disease, *nad-lańs-dus* when a disease is in its first beginnings *Lt.* — II. *lań-ba* and *loń-ba*, pf. *lońs* to come up to, to arrive at, **to be equal, to reach,** *ˏdi lon soń* with this it is made up, that will do *C.*; *ˏdrén-gyis ma lań* lit.: the serving up (of many dishes) would not do, i.e. there would be no end of serving up *Mil.*; *gráńs-kyis láń-ba* to be numerable *Mil.*, cf. also *ča* (init.) and *rjód-pa* (extr.).

ལང་ཚོ *láń-tso* **youth,** youthful age, *dei láń-tso-la ma čágs-pas* not falling in love with, not being enticed or led away by their youthful appearance *Glr.*, *láń-tso rgyás-pas* grown up to adolescence; *lań-tsoi dpal* the charms of youth *Pth.*; *láń-tso srin-moi ydoń* the face of the youthful Srinmo *Glr.*; *lań-tso-čan Cs.* adolescent, young; *lań-tso-ma* **girl,** maiden *Sb.*

ལང་ལིང་བ *láń-liń-ba Sch.* to be in a confused whirling motion (v. *loń-loń*); *lań-ma-liń Mil.* seems to be a word descriptive of the rising of a cloud, of the soaring of a bird of prey, *sprin-dkár lań-ma-liń.*

ལང་ལོང *lań-lóń* v. *lań-na-loń-ńe.*

ལང་ཤོར *lań-šór Cs.* **stubbornness, obstinacy,** adj. *lań-šór-čan*; sometimes *lań-šór* (without *čan*) seems to be also used adjectively, e.g.: *ˏdre k̔yéd-pas láń-šor bág-ťags yin Mil.* evil passion is more obstinate (i.e. more difficult to be got rid of) than ye hobgoblins.

ལད་པ *lád-pa Cs.* **weak, faint, exhausted,** of men and animals; **blunt, dull,** of knives; *Sch.* also **rotten, decayed.**

ལད་མོ *lád-mo* **imitation,** *lád-mo byéd-pa B., C.*, **čo-če**, *gyab-če* W.*, **to imitate, to mimic, to say after,** *smón-lam ˏdi-skad bdág-gi lád-mo gyis* say after me the following prayer *Thgr.*; *ńéd-kyi lád-mo k̔yéd-kyis mi-ˏoń Mil.* you cannot imitate me.

ལན *lan* (orig. perh.: 'turn', hence): 1. **time, times,** *lan-yčig* 1. once, one time. 2. also *dus-lan-yčig Glr.* once, one day, both as to the past and the future. 3. once for all, decidedly *Glr.* 4. for this time, first, first of all, before all, **lan čig lé-ka ˏdi čo** this work must be done first of all; *da-lán* id.; *lan ynyis* **twice,** *lan-bču* ten times etc.; *lan bdun (nam) ysum* seven times or three times, frq. in rules about ceremonies; *bsgór-ba lan máń-du byás-te* circumambulating round it many times *Mil.*; *lan grańs dpag-tu-méd-pa* innumerable times *Thgy.*; *W.*: **ži lan nyi la tsam ƒiel** how many are 2 times 4? *bži lan ynyis-la brgyad soń* 2 times 4 are 8. — 2. **return, retribution, retaliation,** *lan byéd-pa* (*W.* **čó-če**), *lan ˏǰál-ba* **to return, retaliate, repay**; *p̔án-lan ynód-p̔as* or *légs-pai lan nyés-pas ˏǰál-ba B.*, **p̔ém-pe lén-la nö-pa ǰhé-pa* C.*, **p̔án-pe lán-la nód-pa čo-če* W.* to return evil for good; **lan-zó čó-če W.* to show gratefulness, to be **grateful; punishment,** ... *bčúg-pas lan dug* that is the punishment for having allowed... *Glr.*; *lan lén-pa*, *W.*: **lan k̔ór-če, táń-če, dug-lan ldón-če**, to take vengeance, to revenge one's self; *mig-la mig-lan só-la só-lan sróg-la sróg-lan* eye for eye, tooth for tooth, life for life; *dei lán-la* in return for that; *lan-gráńs* a number of retributions *Thgy.*; *drin-lan* recompense for benefits received, requital of a good action, *bzań-lán* id., *dei bzáń-lan-du* as an acknowledgment for it *Glr.*; hence *ńan-lan* signifies: taking revenge for an injury received, returning evil for evil, not as *Cs.* gives: *bzań-lan* gratefulness, *ńan-lan* ungratefulness(?) — 3. **answer, reply,** *k̔yód-kyi ysúń-ba dei lán-du* as answer to your majesty's question *Glr.*; *lan ˏdébs-pa* frq., also *ˏtébs-pa, klón-pa, ldón-pa Dzl.*, *W.* **zér-če** **to answer;** *lan ysól-ba, žú-ba* id. in answering to the questions of a person superior by rank, age or office,— *lan mdzád-pa* if he, the superior, answers; *ytám-lan glú-yis ˏǰal* I answer to the speech by a song *Mil.*; *dris-lan* an answer to a question, *p̔rin-lan* a reply to a dispatch received, *rtsód-lan Cs.* a defendant's reply (in law), *yig-lan* answer to a letter.

ལན་ཀན, ལན་གན *lán-kan, lán-gan* **railing, fence, enclosure** *Stg.*; *Lex.*: = *pu-šu.*

ལན་སྐྱར་ *lan-skyár W.* prob. = *lan*, **retribution, return,** **de lan-kyár yin** that is all he has gained by it!

ལན་གྱོག་ *lan-gyóg Thgy.*, prob. = *lan-čags;* or perh. the original form of *la-yógs?*

ལན་ཆགས་ *lan-čágs* **misfortune, adversity, calamity,** as a supposed punishment for what has been done in a former life; every unlucky accident, that happens to a person without his own fault, being looked upon as a retribution for former crimes. Thus *lan-čags* denotes about **what** Non-Buddhists would call **destiny, fate, disaster.**

ལན་བུ་ *lán-bu* **braid, plait, tress of hair** (*Cs.* curl, lock of hair? *Sch.* **pigtail**?) *lán-bu slé-ba* or *lhé-ba* to make **plaits, to** plait the hair; *lan-tsár* ornaments, **worn** in the hair *Mil.*

ལན་ཚ་ *lán-tsa*, more accurately *lańtsa* (acc. to Hodgson corrupted **from** रञ्जा) n. of a style of writing in use **among** Nepalese Buddhists. It is a kind of **ornamental** writing, used by caligraphists for inscriptions and titles of books.

ལན་ཚྭ་ *lán-tswa* **salt,** prob. = *tswa*, *lán-tswa ču-la tim-pa* salt which dissolves in water *Thgy.*; *lán-tswa ka-zás kún-gyi bró-ba skyed* salt gives a relish to every dish *S.g.*; *lán-tswai ču* salt-water *Lex.*; *lán-tswa-ba* saline, briny *Med.*

ལབ་བདར་ *lab-bdár* v. *la-bdár* in *lá-púg.*

ལབ་པ་ *láb-pa* **to speak, talk, tell,** *mi-la ma lab* do not tell anybody *Mil.*; *rdzún-ytam láb-pa Bhot.* **to lie,** to utter a falsehood; *lab tsól-ba Sch.:* 'to speak unseemly, to brawl(?)'. — *lab tsám-pa Sch.:* to speak while dreaming, to be delirious. *lab ytóṅ-ba Cs.*, **lab gyáb-če* W.* **to talk, to chat;** **ká-lab-čen** **eloquent,** fluent of words *C.*, *W.*; *rgya-láb* a great deal of talk, *rgya-láb-čan* **talkative** *C.*, *W.*

Comp. *láb-ga Cs.*, **láb-ča* C.*, *W.* **talk.** — *lab-grógs Mil.* companion, intimate friend *Mil.* — *lab-rdól* talking unbecomingly *Sch.* — **láb-ra** (prop. *láb-sgra*) 'noise of tattling', **tattle, talk,** **láb-ra táṅ-če* W* **to chat, babble.** — **lab-lób* or *lab-lo**, with **gyáb-če** to speak indistinctly, to mumble; to speak in one's sleep; **lab-lób-te dul** he walks speaking in his sleep, he is a somnambulist *W.*

ལབ་ཙེ་ *láb-tse* a heap of stones in which a pole with little flags is fastened, esp. on mountain passes *Schl.* 198.

ལམ་ *lam* 1. **way, road** *lam-čén*, *rgyá-lam*, *stóṅ-lam Cs.*, **má-lam* W.* **highway, main road, high-road;** *gyén-lam* an up-hill road, an ascent, *túr-lam* a down-hill road, *préd-lam*, *rtsibs-lam* a horizontal or a sloping road, that leads alongside a hill, *lam-prán* a narrow footpath, *lam dóg-mo* a strait path, *lam yáṅspa* a broad one; **lam dé-mo** a good, **easy** road, **lam sóg-po** a difficult, dangerous, road *W.*; *lam tár* the road is open, may be passed, is not obstructed by snow etc. *Glr.*; *lam byéd-pa Sch.*, **lam čó-če, sál-če* W.* to clear a path, to construct a road; *rgya-gár-gyi lam* or *rgya-gar-du ᵒgró-bai lam* the way to India *Pth.*; *gri-lam* the way of the knife, i.e. **a cut, slit, slash;** **'i-ne dúd-pe lam** here is the way for the smoke, here the smoke escapes *W.* — 2. way, space or distance travelled over, **journey,** *lám-du* on the road, on the journey; *bal-bód-kyi lam* the journey from Nepal to Tibet *Glr.*, *lám-du ᵒjúg-pa* to set out, to travel, also: to continue one's journey, *lam-pyéd tsám-du pyin-pa daṅ* as we had done about half the way *Dzl.*, *lám-nas ldóg-pa* to return home from a journey, *krús-la ᵒgró-bai lám-du* when he went to bathe *Dzl.* — 3. गति, fig. **way** or **manner** of acting, in order to obtain a certain end; *tár(-pai) lam* the way of deliverance, viz. for Buddhists: from the cycle of transmigrations, for Christians: from sin and its consequences; hence the way to happiness, to eternal bliss. The six (sometimes only five) classes of beings (v. *ᵒgró-ba*) are sometimes called the six ways of re-birth within the orb of transmigration. In mystical writings *lam lṅa* are spoken of as the ways leading to the *sa bču* (q. v.) *Thgy.*; *lam(-gyi) rim(-pa) Cs.:* 'a degree of advance; the several steps towards perfection'; also the title of sundry mystical writings; *záb-lam* the profound method or way, *tábs-lam* method of the (proper) means (ni f.) *Mil.*; *bla-med-rdó-rjei lam*, col. *snágs-kyi lam* denotes the Uma-doctrine or mysticism, v. *dbú-ma; skyés-bu čúń-bai, ₒbriń-poi*, and *čén-poi lam* three ways: that of a natural (sinful) man, that of the more advanced believer (but not: 'the happy mean' *Cs.*) and that of the saint, or the walk and conversation of the righteous, so also in *drań-sroń-gi lam* the saint's or hermit's course of life; *dgé-ba bčui lás-kyi lam spyód-pa* to walk the way of practising the ten virtues *Dzl.*

Comp. and deriv. *lám-ka* prob. = *lam*, *lám-ka-na* (another reading *lám-k'ar*), by the road-side *Dzl.* — *lam-mk'an* one well acquainted with the road, **a guide** *Pth.*, also fig. — *lam-gól* by-way, secret path *Sch.* — — *lam-grógs* **fellow-traveller,** travelling companion. — *lam-rgyúd* = *lam* 3? *lam-rgyúd lńa Dzl.* ༢༥༢, 18, the five classes of beings, cf. *ₒgró-ba* II. — *lam-rgyús-pa* = *lám-mk'an.* — *lam-čén Schr.* = *rgya-lám.* — *lam-rtágs* the signs of the way being nearly accomplished i.e. the acquirements and perfections of a saint *Mil.* — *lam-ltar-snań* something looking like a road, but a spurious, wrong way *Sch.* — *lam-stégs* seat, resting-place by the way-side; also fig. *Glr.* — *lam-mdó* v. *mdo.* — *lam-ₒdrén-pa, lam-sná-pa* **guide.** — *lám-pa* 1. **police-officer** stationed on highroads for seizing thieves or fugitives; **toll-gatherer.** 2. **traveller,** wayfarer *Cs.* 3. **bell-wether** *W.* — *lám-po* = *lam, lam-po-čé.* 1. **highway** *Sb.*; also as a place for practising magic, ni f. 2. **way to heaven,** = **t'ar-lam** *W.*(?) — *lám-yig* v. *yi-ge* extr. — *lam-lóg* erroneous *Mil.* — *lam-srań* **lane, street.**

ལར་ *lar* 1. **but, yet, still, however** *Mil.*, *Thgy.*, *Glr.*; *lár-ni* and *lár-na* id.; occurs scarcely any more in col. language. — 2. **lar** (or **la-re**) *me'* *C.* none at all(?).

ལས་ *las* I. sbst., col. *lás-ka*, resp. *p'yag-lás* *W.* **t'in-le**. 1. **action, act, deed, work,** *byi-dór-gyi las* the act of sweeping *Lex.*; *las-bzáń, las-dkár* a good work, virtuous action, *las-ńán, las-nág* a bad, a wicked action, frq.; *lus dań ńag dań yid-kyi las* actions, words, thoughts *Dzl.*; *lás-kyi rnam-smin* retribution, reward or punishment for human actions, frq. (cf. *las-rgyu-ₒbras* below); *lás-kyi mé-loń* mirror of fate, mirror foreshadowing future events *Glr.*; *lás-kyi búm-pa* a certain vessel used in religious ceremonies *Schl.* 248; *las ma zád pas* because the measure of his deeds was not yet full, his destiny was not yet fulfilled *Dzl.*; also **destination** in a general sense *Was.* (282); *lás-kyi lhág-ma lús-pa des* in consequence of the yet remaining rest of (unrequited) works *Stg.*; *snón-las* former action; *las dbań-bčós-su-méd-pa Pth.* an accident which cannot be prevented; **performance, transaction, business,** *las t'ams-čad nus-pa* one who can do or perform every thing *Do.*; also the **functions** of some organ of the body *Lt.*; **work; labour, manual labour,** **lé-ka t'ób-pa** to get work; *las byéd-pa B., C.*, **lé-ka čó-če, tán-če** *W.* to do or perform a work, **to work,** also of things: **to operate, to produce effects** *Wdń*; *mk'ar-las-byed-mi* workmen employed in building *Mil.*; *dúr-las byéd-pa* to attend to the graves, i.e. to perform the sepulchral rites and ceremonies; *zań-zin-las byéd-pa* to carry on business, to trade, to traffic *Mil.*; *lás-su* as a task, according to one's occupation, trade, or business, by virtue of one's office, **ex officio** (ni f.) *Mil.*; *lás-su rúń-bar* duly, rightly, perfectly, *comme il faut Mil.*; *lás-su byá-ba* v. below (extr.). — 2. sometimes: **secular business,** **lé-ka nán-na** in business-affairs, in practical life. — 3. **effect** of actions, and in a special sense: **merit,** *las zád-pa* the merits being over, having an end *Thgy.* (cf. 1, above). — 4. the doctrine of works and their consequences, of retribution, *las mi bden* that doctrine is not true *Thgy.*

Comp. and deriv. *lás-ka* 1. col. work, labour, v. above. 2. *Sch.* and *Wts.*: **dignity, rank, title.** — *las-skál* retributive fate, = *las-p'ró.* — *lás-mk'an* **workman** *Cs.* — *las-rgyu-ₒbrás* either for: *las dań rgyu-ₒbras* works and their fruits (which in *Thgy.* are divided into *bsód-nams-ma-yin-pai las-rgyu-ₒbrás* sinful deeds, *bsód-nams-kyi las-rgyu-ₒbras* virtuous actions, *mi-γyo-bai las-rgyu-°brás* ascetic or mystical works *W.*), or for *lás-kyi rgyu-°brás*: **fruits** of works, retribution and the doctrine of it. — *lás-sgo* **trading-place, emporium** *Glr.* — *lás-čan* 1. laborious, industrious *Cs.* 2. (v. above *las* 3) having acquired merit, **worthy** *Mil.* — *las-čé* in *C.* used for expressing probability, as in *W.* *°gro* with the gerund is used, v. *°gro-ba* I, 5; *mtoṅ las-čé* he will probably have seen it *Mil. nt.*; *ṅas °di °bor las-čé* as possibly I may put this yet aside; *k'yod mi-la-ni min las-čé* you are not Mila, are you? *Mil.* — *las tog-pa Sch.*: **a person employed, an official, a functionary.** — *las-rtágs Sch.* **dignity, rank, title** incident to the office held. — *las-dáṅ-po-pa* v. *daṅ-po.* — *las-dár Sch.*: 'parade, ceremonial'(?) — *lás-pa* 1. **workman, labourer** *Cs.* 2. *Sp.*: vice-magistrate of a village. — *lás-dpon* overseer of workmen. — *las-spyód* works, actions, way of life, *byaṅ-čúb-kyi las-spyód skyéd-pa* to lead a holy life *Pth.* — *las-°p'ró* 'continuation, prosecution of works', blessings following meritorious deeds, *k'yed daṅ ṅa yaṅ sṅón-gyi las-°p'ró-yód-pa yin* a bond of connection is formed between you and me by the merits we acquired in former periods of life *Pth.*; — **happiness,** prosperity in consequence of good works, good luck fortunate event, opp. to *lan-čags.* — *las-°brél Glr.* prob. id. — *lás-mi* **workman.** — *las méd* **idle, lazy, inactive.** — *las-tsán* 1. **office, post, service,** *las-tsán-du °júg-pa* to put into office, to appoint, *las-tsán-nas °dón-pa* to put out of office, to dismiss *Cs.* 2. **official, functionary** **yúl-gyi le-tsen** elders of a village-community *C.*, *las-tsán-pa* id. — **le-lam-k'an** **diligent, industrious,** **le-mi lám-k'an** **idle, lazy** *W.* — *las-su byá-ba* the second case of Tibetan grammar, the **dative** case.

II. only in *B.* and *C.*: postp. c. accus. mostly corresponding in its application to the English prepos. **from,** used also for expressing the ablative case (having nearly the same sense as *nas*): 1. **from,** e.g. delivering from, coming from, often = **through,** e.g. shining into a room through the window *Dzl.*; to hear, get, borrow a thing from a person etc.; to call, to denominate a thing **from** or **after,** according to; *tsád-las dpág-pa* to define **by** or **according to** measure *S.g.* in quotations: *°dúl-ba-las* **out of** the, **from** the Dulva, sometimes also for: **in** the Dulva; for denoting the material **of** which a thing is made: of earth, of clay etc.; partitively: *°bras dé-las šas γčig* a part of this rice, *slób-ma-las γčig* one of the disciples *Dzl.*; *ṅai yúl-mi-las bú-mo yód-pa-rnams* the girls that are found **among** my subjects *Dzl.*, *kún-las °p'ágs-pa* distinguished **amongst** all, more excellent than all the others *Dzl.*; hence 2. **than** after the comparative degree: *ná-niṅ-las bzaṅ* more beautiful than last year *Mil.*; with a negative: *lo bču-drúg-las ma lón-te* not older than sixteen years *Dzl.*; *zlá-ba lṅá-las mi sdod* I shall not stay **longer than** five months *Glr.*; *ras-yúg γčig-las mi bdóg-ste* possessing **nothing but** one sheet of cotton cloth *Dzl.*; *ṅá-las med* there is none besides myself *Glr.*; *brnyas °k'yér-ba-las mi yoṅ* in the end you will probably do nothing else but despise me *Mil.*; in a brief mode of speaking: *γsa-γčig-las rje-btsun ma mtoṅ* we saw nothing but the leopard, your Reverence we did not see *Mil.*; *mi p'án-žiṅ γnód-pa-las med* it is good for nothing, it only does harm *Mil.* — 3. added to the inf. of verbs it signifies not so much **from** as **after,** from doing, i.e. after doing, *nyál-ba-las láṅ-ba* to rise from lying, to rise after having been lying down; **during,** frq., the verbal root being repeated, *soṅ-sóṅ-ba-las* during my going or travelling on *Dzl.*; *náṅ-du °gró-bar bsám-pa-las* when (I) intended to walk in, when (I) was on the point of walking in *Dzl.*

ལས་པ་ *lás-pa Cs.* for *lús-pa*; in *rág-las-pa* and a few other expressions occurring also in *B.*

ལི་ *li* I. **bell-metal,** *li-sku, li-tál, li-túr, li-snód* an idol, a plate, spoon, vessel made of that metal; *li-ma* in gen.: utensil, instrument that is cast of *li Glr.*

II. **apple,** = *sli C.*

III. *li-yul Glr.*, acc. to *Was.* (74) Buddhist countries in northern Tibet, esp. Khoten; acc. to others in northern India or Nepal.

ལི་ཀ་ར་ *li-ka-ra* or *li-ḱa-ra Cs.* a sort of **sugar.**

ལི་ཁྲི་ *li-ḱri Glr.* and elsewh., an orange-coloured powder, acc. to *Lis.* सिन्दूर red lead, **minium.**

ལི་ཐང་ *li-ťaṅ Cs.*: 'n. of a province of Tibet near the Chinese frontier', *li-ťaṅ-pa* inhabitant of that province.

ལི་བ་ *li-ba* **squinting, squint-eyed** *Sch., li-ba mig* squinting eyes *Sch.*

ལི་ཙ་བྱི་ *li-tsa-byi* n. of a noble family of ancient India, often mentioned in the history of Buddha *Dzl., Gyatch.*

ལི་ཡུལ་ *li-yul* v. *li* III.

ལི་ལམ་ *li-lam, Hind.* नीलाम, acc. to Shakspeare from the Portuguese *leilam,* **auction, public sale.**

ལི་ཤི་ *li-ši* 1. *Ssk.* लवङ्ग **cloves** *Med., C.* — 2. *Hind.* इलाएची cardamom *W.*

ལིག་བུ་མིག་ *lig-bu-mig S g., Sch.*: 'malachite'.

ལིང་ག་ *liṅ-ga Ssk.* 1. **sign, mark.** — 2. the image of an enemy which is burnt in the *sbyin-sreg* in order thus to kill him by witchcraft *Lt.* — 3. membrum virile *Pth.*

ལིང་གོལ་མ་ *liṅ-gol-ma* **a large hornet** *Sik.*

ལིང་ངེ་ *liṅ-ṅé* **dangling, waving, floating,** in the wind *Mil.; sprin žig liṅ byuṅ-bas* a floating cloud? *Mil.;* **liṅ-liṅ čó-če** *W.* **to dangle,** to hang dangling, e.g. on the gallows, **liṅ-liṅ sé-če** *W.* **to swing, to see-saw;** *rkaṅ-lág ṕra liṅ-ṅé* ˳*dug-pa* an infant struggling with hands and feet *Pth.*

ལིང་ཏོག་ *liṅ-tóg* or *liṅ-ťóg* **a film** or **pellicle** on the eye *Med.*

ལིང་བ་ *liṅ-ba C.*, also *liṅ-po* or *liṅ* alone, **a whole piece,** *liṅ γčig* of one piece, *liṅ bži* four pieces or parts, = *rnám-pa; γsér-gyi liṅ-ba Cs.*: a piece of unwrought gold; *dar-liṅ Cs.* a piece of silk; *liṅ-gis* ˳*dril-ba* to pack up into a parcel, to roll up into one packet *Sch.*

ལིང་ཚེ་ *liṅ-ṫse* gratings, **lattice** *Cs.*

ལིང་ལིང་ *liṅ-liṅ* v. *liṅ-ṅé.*

ལིངས་ *liṅs* **a hunting** or **chase** in which a number of people are engaged; *dmág-liṅs* id. (cf. *ḱyi-ra*); *byá-liṅs Cs.* falconry, hawking; *liṅs-la* ˳*gró-ba* to go a shooting, a hunting; *liṅs* ˳*débs-pa Sch.* to hunt, to arrange a hunting party; *liṅs γtóṅ-ba* to get by hunting, to hunt down, *liṅs btáṅ-ba* what has been got by hunting, game shot or caught; *liṅs-pa* hunter, huntsman, *liṅs-pa-mo* huntress *Cs.; liṅs-ḱyi* hound, *liṅs-ḱra* hunting falcon or hawk.

ལིངས་སྐོར་ *liṅs-skór* hand-mill *W.* (?)

ལིངས་པ་ *liṅs-pa Sch.*: quite round or globular; *dkár-por liṅs-te Pth.*: prob.: being quite white, cf. **lhiṅs-se** *Ld.* quite.

ལིབ་ *lib,* **all,** *Ld.*: **lib du-če** to sweep all together with the hands; *C.*: **ḱá-we lib kab soṅ** all being covered with snow.

ལུ་ *lu* 1. **knag, knot, snag,** = ˳*dzér-pa;* **lu-big** knot-hole *Ts.* — 2 num. for 86.

ལུ་ཀང་ *lu-kaṅ* (perh. a misspelling for *lugs-koṅ?*) **crucible** for gold and silver *Sch.*

ལུ་གུ་, ལུག་གུ་ *lú-gu, lúg-gu,* diminutive of *lug,* **lamb,** frq.; *lu-gu-rgyúd* 1. rope to which the lambs are fastened, or strung; hence 2. small chain, e.g. watch-chain, chain or row of stitches on knitting-needles; lace-trimming and the like.

ལུ་བ་ *lú-ba* 1. vb. **to cough,** to throw up phlegm, to clear the throat. — 2. sbst. **the cough** *Cs.*

ལུ་མ་ *lú-ma Sb.* pool containing a spring, ground full of springs, *lú-ma-čan* rich in springs.

ལུ་ལུ་ *lú-lu* the fruit of some thorny shrubs, *šib-ši-lu-lu* hip, fruit of the wild rose-tree, *ṫser-stár-lu-lu* berry of *Hippophaë.*

ལུག་ *lug* **sheep,** **ḍó-lug, ši-lug, bsád-lug** *W.* sheep for slaughter. — *lúg-ḱyu* flock of sheep. — *lúg-gu* v. *lú-gu.* — *lug-sgal* sheep's load — *lug-ṅál-ba* and *lug-čúṅ-ba* names of medicinal herbs *Cs., Wdṅ.* — *lug-snyid Sch.* **wether.** — *lug-ťúg* **ram** *B., C.; lug-ťúg-gi rwa dbyibs* like a ram's horn *Wdṅ.; rgya-ru-lug-ťúg* a Saiga ram *S.g.* —

lug-tóṅ Sch. wether. — lúg-pa 1. sbst. shepherd, keeper of sheep Ma. 2. to stick the heads together like timid sheep, to be sheepish in behaviour Ma. — lug-míg n. of a flower Med. — lug-múr and lug-rtsí medicinal herbs. — lug-tságs a sheep-skin with little wool on it Ld. — lug-rá sheep-fold, pen, sheep-cot. — lug-rú ram's horn; n. of several species of Pedicularis. — *lug-lóg* sheep-skin Ld.

ལུག་པ་ lúg-pa I. sbst. and vb., v. sub lug. — II. vb., **to give way, to fall down,** cf. rlúg-pa Ts.

ལུགས་ lugs 1. **the casting, founding,** of metal, lúgs-su blúg-pa Glr., *lúg-la lúg-pa* col. C., to found, to cast; lúgs-ma **a cast,** rgya-gár lúgs-ma an image (statue, idol) cast in India Glr. — 2. **way, manner, fashion, mode, method,** bód-kyi lúgs su gyis šig Glr. make it according to the fashion of Tibet; ṅai lúgs-kyis bon byed dgos you must live according to our, i.e. the Bon-fashion Mil.; bsam-gtán-la yód-pai lúgs-su byas he feigned meditation Glr.; di yin-pai lúgs-su byed they speak, act, make it appear, as if it really were so Tar. 184, 21; ṅa-ráṅ-gi lúgs-kyi mk'ár-las my way of building, what I call my style of building Mil.; **opinion, view, judgment, way of proceeding,** k'yed-ráṅ-gi lúgs-la according to you, if we followed your advice Mil.; čós-lugs **religion,** i.e. a certain system of faith and worship, p'yi naṅ gnyis čós-lugs gaṅ bzaṅ which of the two religions, the Brahman or the Buddhist be the better one Glr.; **established manner, custom, usage, rite,** čá-lugs mode of dress, fashion, čós-lugs religious rites, rgyá-lugs Chinese (or Indian) manners, bód-lugs Tibetan manners etc.; ráṅ-lugs one's own way, gžán-lugs other people's way or manners; ráṅ-lugs-la gnás-pa (= raṅ-sa ˳dzin-pa) Glr.; seems to be only another expression for that Buddhist virtue of absolute indifference to all objects of the outer world: lugs is also used concretely, meaning the adherents of a custom or religion, hence = **sect, school, religious party, denomination,** mdo-lugs follower of the Sutras, the Sutra sect, sṅags-lugs a follower of the Tantras, the Tantra sect; in a special sense: lugs gnyis the two principal classes with regard to religious life, ˳jig-rtén-gyi lugs the laical or profane class, laymen, čós-kyi lugs the clerical or sacred class, priests Cs.; lúgs-kyi that which relates to manners or morals, **ethical** Cs. (v. As. Res. XX, 583). — 3. in conjunction with a verbal root or with the genit. of the inf. it often corresponds to the English termination **ing** as: ldáṅ-lugs the rising, getting up, ˳gró-lugs the going, sdód-lugs the sitting Mil., ˳o-rgyál yóṅ-lugs sogs šól-˳debs-kyi žú-ba the (possibility of) getting into difficulties and other reasons for inducing him to postpone (his setting out) Mil.; bsam-yás bžéṅs-lugs bris he described the building of Sam-yé Glr.; méd-lugs the (circumstance of) not having Mil.; yin-lugs **the condition, state** Mil.; dá-lta ná-lugs či-ltar na as to your present illness, in what does it consist? Mil.; tsógs-nas skyóṅ-bai lúgs-su yód-pa they joined in educating them, they educated them together Mil.; it is also added to adjectives: čé-lugs **greatness** Mil.

ལུགས་མ་ lúgs-ma v. lugs 1.

ལུང་ luṅ I. 1. **a strap,** slung over the shoulder or round the waist, for carrying things; **handle, ear** (curved), of vessels, baskets etc., different from yú-ba a straight handle, hilt. — 2. 'foot-stalk of fruits' Cs.; lúṅ-t'ag Cs.: a rosary, string of beads, suspended by the girdle.

II. Ssk. आगम, = bka, used of words spoken by secular persons commanding respect: p'as gnáṅ-bai luṅ t'ób-nas obtaining (his) father's word of permission Dzl, luṅ ˳byuṅ an **order** is issued (by the king) Glr., tú-ru-ška-la luṅ len dgós-pa being obliged to accept orders from the Turuskas Tar.; more frq.: **spiritual exhortation,** admonition, **instruction,** luṅ gnáṅ-ba to give it (sometimes only: to pronounce forms of prayer etc. before devotees); luṅ gtóṅ-ba id., *luṅ taṅ-k'en* instructor, teacher, admonisher C.; luṅ stón-pa, also lúṅ-du stón-pa to instruct, to give spiritual precepts, also with regard to supernatural voices etc. *Mil.*; esp. **to prophesy,** predict, **to reveal secrets,** with termin.: *dā-na-ši-la yin-par luṅ bstan* it is prophesied that it is Dānasīla, the prediction relates to D., *saṅs-rgyás-su lúṅ-bstan-to* he has received a prediction concerning (his obtaining) the Buddhaship *Dzl.*; *mdaṅ mkhá-ₒgros lúṅ-bstan-pai skyés-bu de* the man foreshown yesterday by the Dākini *Mil.*, hence *lúṅ-ma-bstan-pa* unheard of, unprecedented *Mil. nt.* (*Cs.* also: to demonstrate, *lúṅ-du brtán-du yód-pa* demonstrable?); *luṅ ₒgód-pa Cs.* to make, to establish, precepts; *luṅ ₒdrén-pa Cs.* to cite, to quote, an authority *Tar.* 210, 2; *lúṅ-gi rjes-ₒbráṅ Was.* (274) those who stick to the letter (opp. to *rigs-kyi rjes-bráṅ* to the real quality, viz. the spirit); *luṅ-bstán* exhortation, precept, commandment, *lhai luṅ-bstán bšád-pa* to communicate the precept of the god *Tar.*, ... *žes byá-bai luṅ-bstán byuṅ* there came a divine order or prophecy of this purport, to this effect; hence *luṅ-ston-pa* **prophet** *Chr. Prot.*

ལུང་ཐག *luṅ-ťág* v. above *luṅ* I.

ལུང་པ *lúṅ-pa* 1. **valley,** *ri-lúṅ* mountain and valley; *luṅ-čén* a large valley, *luṅ-čúṅ* or *luṅ-ṗrán* a little valley; *luṅ-kóg Sch.*: 'the cavity of the valley'; *luṅ-stóṅ* a desolate, a solitary valley, as a fit abode for hermits, frq. — 2. **furrow, hollow, groove,** e.g on the surface of a stick *Mil.*, of the liver *Med.*

ལུད *lud* **manure, dung,** *lug-lúd* sheep's dung; *lud ₒgrém-pa* to spread manure (on fields) *Cs.*, *lud ₒdrén-pa* to carry manure (to the fields) *Cs.*, **gyáb-če, táb-če, táṅ-če* W.* to manure the ground; *lud-ku* dung-water; *lud-dóṅ* dung-hole; *lud-ṗúṅ* dung-hill; *lúd-ₒbu* grubs etc. in a dung-hill.

ལུད་པ *lud-pa* 1. sbst. **phlegm, mucus,** *rnag-krág-gi lúd-pas bkaṅ-ste* full of phlegm, matter and blood *Glr.*; esp. in the organs of respiration: *lúd-pa čig bskyúr-bas* throwing up some phlegm *Glr.*; *lúd-pa lú-ba* to throw up by coughing *Dzl.*, *sbrid-pa* by sneezing *S.g.*; *lúd-ṗor* spittoon, spitting-box *C.* — 2. vb., **to boil over** *ču lúd-pas* the water boiling over *Dzl.*; *mtso lúd-pa* the running over of lakes, **inundation** *Ma.*; *ču lúd-nas lúd-nas bkáṅ-ba yin* it filled, by the water rising higher and higher.

ལུམས *lums* **a bath** used as a medical cure; **fomentation.**

ལུམ་བི, ལུམ་བི་ནི *lúm-bi, lúm-bi-ni,* n. of a queen, and of a grove called after her, situated in the north of India, where Buddha is said to have been born.

ལུས *lus,* also *lús-po,* **body,** *lus sá-la brdáb-pa* to prostrate one's self, frq., *lus stón-pa* to show one's self, to appear, to make one's self visible, as gods *Dzl.*, and in a similar manner *lus* is often used for expressing our reflective verbs, when relating to physical processes, cf. *sems*; *lús-kyi dbáṅ-po* the sense of feeling, in as far as it resides in the skin and the whole body of man *Med.*; *rgyál-poi ydúṅ-brgyúd* (or *rgyal-bu*) *lús-la yod* I bear a prince under my bosom *Glr.*; *lus smád-pa* **to violate, to ravish** *Pth.*; *lus ₒgrúb-pai tóg-ma* the beginning of the development of a body as embryo *Wdṅ.*; *grúb-pa lus* v. *grúb-pa*; *lús-la čágs-šiṅ* from love of life *Dzl.*; *lus daṅ sróg-la sdó-ba* to risk or stake one's life *Dzl.*; *mi-lus tób-pa* or *bláṅ-ba* to be born as a human being, *lus-ṅán* (to be born) as an animal, or also as a woman *Mil.*; — often for the whole person of a man: *bráṅ-gyi lus kyaṅ dpón-du ₒgyur* even a servant may become a master *S.g.*; *lús-kyis mi bzód-par nya-ṅán-gyis ydúṅs-te* is used (*Dzl.* ༡༥༡, ༢) of an exclusively mental suffering or infirmity. — In mysticism and speculative science several expressions are employed which, however, do not differ much in their import: *sgyú-lus, ₒjá-lus, bde-ₒgro mto-ris-kyi lus*; *rig-pa ₒdzin-pai lus* (*Tar.* 56, 20), *yid-kyi lus* (frq.), **लिङ्गशरीर,** the immaterial body which is enclosed in the grosser material frame, accompanying the soul in all its transmigrations and not destroyed by death (*Köpp.* I., 66), *yid-kyi lus* might be rendered by 'spiritual body'; another explanation given by Lamas is: the body which exists only in our imagination (*yid*); in that case it would be identical with *sgyu-lús*.

Comp. *lus-rgyágs* a fat body *Cs.*, *lus-rid* a mean, thin, lean body, *lus-sbóm* a thick stout figure, *lus-riṅ* a long tall body, *lus-ťuṅ* a short body *Cs.* — *lús-čan* having a body, hence as sbst. = *séms-čan* creature, being, *lús-čan kún-gyi yid-du ̥oṅ* a favourite of every creature *Stg.* — *lus-stód* upper part of the body, *lus-smád* lower part of the body. — *lus-bóṅs* the bulk of a body. — *lus-byád* form of the body. — *lus-med* having no body, incorporeal, ghostlike, ghostly, *lus-méd-pai skad* a ghostly voice *Mil.* — *lus-smád* v. *lus-stód.* — *lus-zúṅs* v. sub *yzuṅs.*

ལུས་པ་ *lús-pa*, *C.* also *lás-pa*, to remain behind or at home, *bód-du zlá-ba ynyis* to remain in Tibet for two months *Glr.*; **to be remaining or left** *Dzl.*; **to be forgotten,** omitted, left behind; *yyén-du lús-pa* to remain uppermost, floating to remain standing, sitting, lying, e.g. **ka lús-sa mi dug* W.* the snow does not remain, will soon melt away; *lús-par byéd-pa Pth.*, *lús-su ̥júg-pa*, **lus čúg-če* Ld.* to leave behind, to leave a remainder; *ma-lús-par* entirely, wholly, without remainder, without exception, *̥gró-ba ma-lús* or *mi-lús Mṅg.*, all creatures without exception; *má-lus-par* prob. also: surely, undoubtedly, at any rate, in any case, ni f. — *lús-ma*, *rjés-lus*, *pyir-lus*, *lhág-lus Cs.* **remainder, balance, residue.**

ལེ་ *le* 1. a small not cultivated **river-island** *C.*, = *gliṅ-ka* and *zal.* — 2. v. *leu.* — 3. *W.* a word expressive of civility and respect, and added to other words or sentences, like Sir! and Madam! in English, **zu-lé** good day, Sir! it is also added to the word *sa-heb* gentleman, and then *sa-heb-le* is about equivalent to: honoured Sir, dear Sir. — 4. num.: 16.

ལེ་བརྒན་, ལེབ་རྒན་ *le-brgan*, *leb-rgán* 1. *Med.* frq., *Lex.* = वरं saffron, whereas *Cs.* has: 'poppy, *le-brgan-rtsi* the juice of poppies, opium, *le-brgán-ghi mé-tog* the poppy flower, *le-brgán-ghi ̥brás-bu* poppy-seed', and *Sch.* adds: *le-brgan-mdóg* poppy-coloured, light-red, and he translates also *le-brgán Dzl.* ༥༤, 1, by 'poppy-coloured', although it is mentioned there amongst various species of Lotus. But in *W.* poppy and opium are usually called by the Hindi name پيم, *pim*; neither in *W.* nor in *Sik.* did I meet with any body, who knew the significations given by *Cs.* and *Sch.*, but only: 2. **diapered design** of woven fabrics; thus also *Mil.*: *le-brgán dmár-poi ydan* a flowered carpet, *le-brgán ̥jol-bér Pth.* a flowered dress with a train.

ལེ་ན་ *lé-na* the soft downy wool of goats (esp. those of Jangtháng) below the long hair, **the shawl wool;** fine woolen-cloth.

ལེ་མ་ *lé-ma* v. *leu.*

ལེ་ལག་ *le-lág* **appendix, supplement, addition** *Cs.*

ལེ་ལན་ *le-lán Cs.*: consequence; *Sch.*: rebuke, reprimand, reproof, and *le-lán-pa*, *le-lán bdá-ba* to blame, rebuke, reprove; *le-lán-čan Cs.* consequential, important (?).

ལེ་ལམ་མཁན་ *le-lám-mkan* v. *las-lám-mkan.*

ལེ་ལོ་ *lé-lo*, *lé-lo-nyid* **indolence, laziness, tardiness,** *lé-lo ma byed čig* don't be lazy! *Glr.*; *yčig lé-lo byás-nas* as one (of them) had been lazy *Dzl.*; *lé-los ̥kyer* he is overcome by laziness *Mil.*; *lé-loi rjés-su ̥gró-ba* to be given to laziness *Ld.-Glr.*; *lé-lo-čaṅ* **lazy, indolent, slothful.** — **le-šól* W.* = *le-lo.*

ལེགས་པ་ *légs-pa B.*, *légs-po* and *-mo C.* (cf. also no. 3) 1. **good,** serving the purpose, with regard to things; adv. *légs-par* well, duly, properly, *légs-par ̥tsól-ba* to search, to investigate accurately *Glr.*; *bsú-ba légs-po gyis* do care for a proper reception! *Glr.*; *légs-par gyur čig* (*Schr.* adds *kyéd-la*) may you prosper! *Sch.*, *légs-par ̥óṅs-so* you are welcome *Sch.*; **happy, comfortable,** *bdag légs-na* when I am well off (opp. to *nyés-na*) *Do.*; *legs nyes stón-pai mé-loṅ* mirror of fate, of the future *Glr.*; *lo(-tog) légs(-pa) B.*, **lo lag-mo* W.*, a rich, healthy, happy year; *či ltar byás-na legs* which is the best way of doing it? *Glr.*,

Tar.; *sems-čan mis byás-na légs-pa gaṅ yin* which of the actions of human beings are good (in this connection it is nearly the same as *bzáṅ-po*, morally good); *legs* is also used in politely hinting or requesting, like the English 'you had better': *k'yod p'yin-pa légs(-so) Glr.*, and still more polite: *γšégs-par legs* your Highness had perhaps better go etc. *Pth*; *nús-na šin-tu légs-so* if you can do it, very well! *Dzl.*; also *légs-so* alone, very well! well done! *légs-so légs-so* excellent! capital! — 2. **neat, elegant, graceful, beautiful** *C.* — 3. **lág-mo* W.* **good, due,** and adv. **well, duly, properly,** like *légs-par* (v. above), e.g. **me lág-mo ₒbar ₒdug** the fire burns well, **lẹ́-ka lág-mo čos** you have worked well; but most frq.: **clean, pure, clear,** **ču lag-mo** pure or clear water (opp. to *rtsóg-pa*); **fine,** of powder, = *žib-mo*; **lág-mo čó-če** to clean, clear, wash, wipe, sweep etc.; to reduce to fine powder, to pulverize.

Comp. *légs-čan Sch.*, *legs-ldán Cs.* virtuous (?). — *legs-byás*, resp. *legs-mdzád* good deed, good work *Cs.* — *legs-sbyár*, संस्कृत, well constructed, skilfully arranged, high-wrought, hence: the Sanskrit language. — *legs-smón* **patron, protector, well-wisher,** congratulator *Cs.* — *legs-bšad* a remarkable saying, a sententious remark *Mil.*, two works, called after their authors *goṅ-dkár* and *sa-skya-legs-bšád*, are recommended to students of the language. — *legs-γsol* resp. **thanks,** acknowledgment, gratitude *C.*

ལེན་པ་ *lén-pa* (rarely *lóṅ-ba, lóṅ-pa*), pf. *bloṅs* (rarely *loṅs*), fut. *blaṅ*, imp. *lon Cs.*, *loṅ(s) Dzl.*, *Mil.*, *blaṅs Cs.*, *W.*: **lén-če, nén-če, bláṅ-če** to take, i.e. 1. **to receive, get, obtain,** *γnas-ṅán* an inferior place viz. for being re-born *Thgy.* — 2. **to accept,** what is offered or given, opp. to *ₒdór-ba*; also **to bear, to suffer patiently, to put up with.** — 3. **to seize, catch,** lay hold of, **grasp,** e.g. one that is about to leap into the water *Dzl.*; **to catch up; to catch, to take prisoner,** a culprit *Dzl.*; **to carry off,** e.g. the arms of killed enemies; *ma byin-par* to take what is not given, **to steal, to rob**; *lén-pa-ₒdra* it is as if it had been stolen from me *Glr.*; *čúṅ-ma lén-pa* to get or take a wife, frq., also to procure one for another person; *srog lén-pa* = *ₒp'róg-pa* to deprive of life, **to kill** *Mṅg.*; **to fetch,** *lén-du* (*W.* **lén-na-la**) *soṅ* go and fetch it! to take possession of, **to occupy** (by force of arms) *Glr.*

ལེབ་མོ་ *léb-mo* (*Cs.* also *léb-po*) **flat,** *mon-srán léb-mo* Indian pease are flat, lenticular; *léb-čan*, *leb-léb* id. col., **leb-léb-la bor** lay it down flat! *léb-ma*, *leb-ťágs* **lace, bandage, ribbon** *Cs.*, *dar-skúd-kyi leb-ťágs* lace of silk thread; *bhag-leb* a flat loaf of bread *C.*; *šiṅ-léb*, *leb-šiṅ* board, plank, *rdo-léb* a slab, cf. *gléb-pa*.

ལེའུ་ *leu* **division, section** of a speech, of a treatise, of a book, **chapter,** of very different length; *léu-čan Cs.*, *leur byás-pa Zam.* having sections or chapters, being divided into chapters; abbreviated *le*, *bšags-le daṅ šer-le čad-pa yin* the chapters (treating) of the confession of sins and of wisdom are wanting *Tar.*; *lé-ma Cs.*, *le-ťsán Sch.* id.

ལོ་ *lo* 1. **year** (resp. *dgúṅ-lo*, v. *dguṅ*), *lo lṅa-bču-pa Ma.* usually *lo lṅa-bču lon-pa* (*W.* **lon-k'an**) fifty years old, of fifty years; *bú-mo lo-γnyis-ma* a girl two years old *Ma.*; *lo daṅs lo*, *lo-ré (-re)-bžin*, *ló-ltar* (*Sch.* also *bstár!*) **annually, yearly**; *ló-nas ló-ru* from year to year; *sṅá-lo*, *ₒdás-lo* last year; *ₒdi-lo*, usually **dá-lo**, this year; *p'yi-lo*, *C.* *sáṅ-lo* next year; *lo ₒk'ór-te* after one year had passed, *srás-kyis lo k'or-te* when the prince was one year old *Glr.*; the names of the twelve years of the small cycle (v. below) are those of the following twelve animals: *byi* mouse, *glaṅ* ox, *stag* tiger, *yos* hare, *ₒbrug* dragon, *sbrul* serpent, *rta* horse, *lug* sheep, *spre* ape, *bya* hen, *kyi* dog, *p'ag* hog; thus the first year is called *byi-lo* the mouse-year, and *byi-lo-pa* is a person born in that year etc. — 2. for *lo-tóg*, v. the compounds; for *ló-ma* leaf, for *ló-tsa-ba*. — 3. prob.: **talk, report, rumour, saying,** added (like *skad*) to the word or sentence to which it belongs, *če-gé-mo ši lo zér-ba ťos tsá-na* when a rumour is heard, that N.N. has died

Thgy.; *W.*: **da lam ťar lo** they say the road is open now; also with a definitive subject: **'a-čé'kú-lig toṅ' lo** the mistress asks for the key; **ko kóm-se rag lo** he says he is thirsty (yet also in these cases a speaking on hearsay may be meant: somebody tells me that Mrs. N.N. asks for etc.); **ťsór-lo** **report, rumour** *W.*, also **ťoṅ-lo** and **lób* (?)-*lo** are said to have a similar signification; **šé-lo** and **rig-lo** *W.* are expressions of which I cannot give a satisfactory explanation; *bšád-lo byas kyaṅ krám-pa yin Mil.*, prob.: though he may get a name (in the world) by his learned discussions, he is after all a liar. — *lo* 3 prob. occurs only in col. language and more recent pop. literature; *Dzl.* ༢༥ *V*, 17 *lo* is a corrupt reading for *ysol*. — 4. num.: 146.

Comp. *lo-skor* (*Cs.* also *lo-kor*) **cycle of years**, a period of twelve years; it is the usual manner of determining the exact time of an event, which also tolerably well suffices for the short space of a man's life. If for instance a person in a dog-year (e. g. 1874) says that he is a *byi-lo-pa*, it may be guessed by his appearance, whether he is 10 or 22, 34, 46 etc. years old, and thus also in other cases accidental circumstances must help to determine the precise date of an event. Occasionally, however, the cycles are counted, e. g. *lo-skór brgyad* 96 years *Glr.* Besides this cycle of 12 years there exists another of 60 years which is formed (in imitation of Chinese chronology) by combining those 12 names of animals with the names of the (so called) five elements, *šiṅ* wood, *me* fire, *sa* earth, *lčags* iron, *ču* water. Each of these elements is named twice, followed, the first time by *po*, and the second by *mo*; when signs of gender may also be omitted without altering any thing in the matter. Thus *šiṅ(-po)-kyi-lo*, *šiṅ(-mo)-pag-lo*, *me(-po)-byi-lo*, *me(-mo)-glaṅ-lo* are our years 1834, 35, 36, 37, and 1894, 95, 96, 97 etc. — *lo-krims* (v. *lo-tóg-gi krims*) ceremonies, at the beginning of harvest. — *lo-gráṅs* prop. date (of the year), *Sch.* also: *lo-gráṅs ťsáṅ-ma* **being of** (full) **age.** — *lo-mgó Cs.* the beginning of a year, new-year's day. — *lo-rgyús* v. *rgyus*. — *lo-ṅán* a bad year, a poor harvest. — *lo-čág Cs.* 'every second year'. — *lo-čúṅ* or *nyúṅ C.* young, *lo-nyuṅ-nyúṅ* very young. — *lo-nyés* = *lo-ṅán*. — *lo-snyiṅ Sch.* 'year, period or stage of life' (?). — *lo-tóg* or *-ťóg* the produce of the year, **harvest, crop,** *lo-tóg rṅá-ba* to reap it, to gather it in. — *lo-ťó* **almanac.** — *lo-ₒdod Mil.* earthly-minded, sinner? — *lo-dpyá* annual tribute. — **lo-pǘ** = *srus-púd*, *C.* — *lo-pyág* (*Ld.* **lob-čag**) embassy sent every year to the king to renew the oath of allegiance. — *lo-pyéd* half a year. — *lo-ťsán* annual produce, harvest, *lo-ťsan čé-ba* a rich, abundant harvest *Glr.* — *lo-légs* v. *légs-pa*. — *lo-bšád* = *lo-ťó Cs.* — *lo-yséb Sch.* a stack, a heap of corn (?).

ལོ་ཀ་ *ló-ka Ssk.* **world,** *lo-ke-šva-ra* = **अवलोकितेश्वर.**

ལོ་ཏོག་ *lo-tóg*, or *lo-tóg*, v. *lo*, compounds.

ལོ་འདབ་ *lo-ₒdáb* v. *ló-ma*.

ལོ་མ་ *ló-ma*, *W.* **lób-ma**, **leaf,** *ló-ma lhuṅ*, *brul B.*, *C.*, **lób-ma ḍil* or *ḍul soṅ** *W.* the leaves have fallen; **lób-ma ť á-mo** an acerose or pine-leaf; *lo-ₒdáb* = *ló-ma*.

ལོ་ཙ་, ལོ་ཙཱ་ *lo-tsa*, *lo-tsā* (v. *Ssk.* **लोच्** to speak?) the (art of) **translating,** *sgra daṅ ló-tsa slób-pa* to learn the language and the (art of) translating *Glr.*; also *ló-tsa sgyúr-ba* to translate *Pth.*; *ló-tsa-ba* translator (of Buddhist works) *lo-čén* great translator, seems to be a certain title; *lo-páṇ* for *ló-tsa-ba daṅ páṇḍi-ta*.

ལོ་ལི་མ་ *ló-li-ma Ld.* (*Urd.* لولی) **prostitute, harlot.**

ལོག་གེ་བ་ *lóg-ge-ba* seems to be nearly the same as *lóg-pa* adj , *ťe-ťsom lóg-ge-bai ṅáṅ-la* prob.: entertaining irrational doubts or scruples; *baṅ-rim lóg-ge-ba* an inverted *baṅ-rim* q. v.; *lóg-ge-ba-la kyer* he took it back again *Mil.*

ལོག་པ་ *lóg-pa* I. vb., pf. and secondary form of *ldóg-pa*, q. v., **1. to return, to go back,** *yúl-du Glr.*; **nam lóg-te ča dug** *W.*, **nam lóg-ne ḍó-gyu yin** *C.* when will you return? *lóg-pa ₒtad Glr.*, *lóg-la ₒdód-do Glr.* let us turn back, *ṗyir lóg-pai lam* **the way back.** — 2. **to come back, to come again.** — 3. **to turn round, to be turned upside down, to tumble down** *W.*, e.g. of a pile of wood etc.; *ṅo lóg-pa* or *ldóg-pa* to turn away one's face, always used fig. for to turn one's back on, to apostatize *ₒk'ór-ḃai yul ṅó-ldóg-na* if you mean to turn your back to the land of the cycle of existences, more frq.: *lóg-pa byéd-pa* **to revolt, to rebel,** *lóg-pa rtsóm-pa* to plot, to stir up, an insurrection *Glr.*, *lóg-pa-mk'an* a rebel *Glr.*; **lóg-pa-čan** rebellious, seditious *W.*

II. adj. **reversed, inverted; irrational, wrong,** *lóg-pai lam, lam lóg-pa Mil.* a wrong way; *lóg-pa-la žúgs-pa* ('to rush into error, to turn to what is wrong?'), also euphemism for **to fornicate** *Stg.*; *lta-(ba)- log(-pa)* v. *ltá-ba*; *čos-lóg* a wrong faith, false doctrine, **heresy;** *grwa-lóg, ǰo-lóg* col an apostate monk or nun; *lóg-par* and (col.) *log* adv. wrong, amiss, erroneously, *lóg-par sém-pa* to think evil, to have suspicions (about a thing), often = *lta-lóg skyéd-pa* **to sin;** frq.: **log ₒdrén-pa** to mislead, seduce *B.*; **log yóṅ-če** *W.* to come back, to return, **ši-lóg yóṅ-če** to recover life, to revive (after having been nearly lifeless), to rise from the dead, prob. also: to appear as a ghost *W.*; **nad log-gyáb taṅ** *W.* the disease has become worse again, there has been a relapse; **la-lóg (bla-lóg) pó-če** *W.* to turn, e.g. the roast; **čud log taṅ-če** v. *ẏčud*.

Comp. *log-čos Ma.* = *čos-lóg.* — *log-rtógs* wrong judgment, false knowledge. — *lóg-lta* = *lta-lóg*, v. *ltá-ba* — *log-spyod*, *Lt.*: *lóg-spyod ṅán-pa* perverse conduct, a sinful life. — *lóg-ₒtso* with *sgrúb-pa* to live in a sinful manner, as much as: to live by crime, by vice *Mil.*

ལོགས་ *logs* 1. **side,** *rtsig-logs* the side of a wall, *mdún-logs* fore-side, front-side, *rgyáb-logs* back, back part of a thing; *lógs-re* 1. **side-post of a door** (opp. to *yá-* and *má-re*). 2. each side (v. *re* 3); *logs-bzáṅ* the right or upper side, *logs-ṅán* the left or lower side (of a cloth) *Cs.*; **surface,** *sai* of the earth; **side, direction, region,** *rkáṅ-pai-lógs-nas* from the part of the feet, up from the feet (e.g. a pain in the body proceeding up from the feet) *Sch.*; *ẏyas-logs* the right side, *ẏyón-logs* the left side, frq.; *ťsú(r)-logs* this side, on this side, *ṗá(r)-logs* the other side, on the other side; *lógs-su, lógs-la* **aside,** apart, **žág-pa** *C.* to lay by, to put aside, to put out of the way, to clear away, *lógs-su dgár-ba, bkár-ba* means about the same; *lógs-su bkál-ba* to hang aside, to hang up in another place; *lógs-na yód-pa* to be distinct, separate, to live by one's self, solitarily *Schf.*, *Tar.* 45, 18; *lógs-pa* other, additional, by-, co-, spare-, *rgyags logs-pa* spare-provision, so also *logs ẏčig*: *ťág-pai sné-mo logs ẏčig* the other end of a rope. — 2. **wall,** **log-žál** *W.* id.; *logs-bris* mural or fresco painting *Tar.*

ལོང་ *loṅ* 1. **leisure,** spare-time, vacant time, **time,** *loṅ yód-du ré-la nám-zla ₒdas* whilst you are always hoping to have (still) time (enough), you allow the favourable moment to pass away *Mil.*; similarly: *loṅ yod snyam-la mi-ťse zad Mil.*; *sdód-pai loṅ méd-par* without delay, immediately, directly *Glr.*; **ṅa yóṅ-loṅ med** *C.*, *W.* I have not time to come; **ṗéb-loṅ yód-na** if your honour have time to come *C*, *W.*; *rdég-loṅ yóṅ-bas* as there will be yet plenty of time to beat (me, you had better hear me now) *Mil.*; *loṅ-ẏtam Sch*: 'cheerful talk, animated conversation'. — 2. imp. of *laṅ-ba* and *len-pa.*

ལོང་ཀ་, ལོང་ཁ་, ལོང་ག་ *loṅ-ka, loṅ-k'a, loṅ-ga Med.* **intestines, entrails, guts;** strictly taken it is said to denote only the blind gut (?); *yár-'oṅ, már-loṅ Cs.*: the upper gut, the lower gut or thin guts, thick guts; *loṅ-nád* a disease of the guts.

ལོང་བ་ *lóṅ-ba* 1. pf and secondary form of *ldoṅ-ba*, as vb.: **to be blind,** and fig.: **to be infatuated;** as adj.: blind, blinded etc., as sbst.: blind man *Dzl.* — *loṅ-k'rid* (or *ₒk'rid-pa*) the guide of a blind man *Lex.*; *lóṅ-po, lóṅ-ba-po* a blind man *Cs.*; **nye-lóṅ** *W.* an empty ear of corn, a tare. — 2. also *loṅs-pa*, = *lén-pa Glr.* or *laṅ-ba* 1, 2 *Glr.*

ལོང་བུ་ *lóṅ-bu Stg*, *lóṅ-mo Mil.* **ankle-bone. astragal.**

ལོང་ལོང་ *loṅ-loṅ* being in pieces, in fragments *C.*, cf. *bun-loṅ.*

ལོངས་ *loṅs*, 1. pf. and imp. of *lóṅ-ba.* — 2. in conjunction with *spyód-pa:* **to use,** to make use of, to have the use or benefit of, **to enjoy,** e.g. *bdé-ba daṅ skyid-pa-la* happiness and prosperity; *lóṅ-spyod-par byá-bai rgyu* the object of enjoyment, the thing enjoyed *Stg.*; *loṅs-spyód* (*Ssk.* **भोग**) 1. **enjoyment, fruition,** use, esp. with regard to eating and drinking, *loṅs-spyód šá-la byed* they fed on meat, *loṅs-spyód šiṅ dé-las byed* they lived on (the fruits of) this tree *Pth.* 2. **plenty, abundance,** *bza-btúṅ-gi lóṅs-spyod dpag-tu-méd-pa bsag Glr.* they produced or procured an enormous quantity of food and drink; esp.: **riches,** *loṅs-spyod čé-ba* great riches; **wealth, property,** *lóṅs-spyod-kyi bdág-por gyur* he became owner of the property *Dzl.*; *mčód-pa byá-bai lóṅs-spyod med* he was not rich enough to bring an offering (to Buddha) *Dzl.*

ལོད་པ་, ལོད་པོ་ *lód-pa, lód-po*, v. *lhód-pa.*

ལོད་པོ་ *lód-po Sch.*: 'half through, through the middle, one half (?)'.

ལོན་ *lon* **notice, tidings, message,** *lon-bzáṅ* good news, *spríṅ-ba* to give notice, send word, send a message; *lon kyur* or *lon zer* has also the special sense: send in my name! *C.*; *lon žig k'yér-la šog* let me know, send me word *Pth*

ལོན་པ་ *lón-pa* = *lén-pa* 1. **to take, to receive** etc. *Glr., Pth., ču lón-nam* have you fetched the water? i. e. are you bringing the water? *Pth.*; *nór-bu mi lon* I shall not receive the jewel! *Pth.* — 2. more frq. the word is used with reference to time: **to elapse, to pass,** a. in a general sense, *lo máṅ-po žig lón-pa daṅ* after many years had elapsed *Dzl.*, *riṅ-žig lón-te* after a long time, *riṅ-por ma lón-par* after a short time. b. with regard to the age of a person: *lo či tsam lon* how old are you? *bču-drúg-lon* I am sixteen *Mil.*

ལོབ་ *lob W.* sometimes for *lo* year, and *lób-ma* for *ló-ma* leaf.

ལོབ་པ་ *lób-pa*, pf., imp. *lobs*, **to learn,** rarely for *slób-pa*; *lóbs-pa* the act of learning *Dzl.*

ལོས་ *los*, **in truth, indeed,** *mgón-skyabs raṅ los yin* he is indeed the helper (from a hymn in praise of Buddha).

ཤ

ཤ 1. the letter *ša*, the English **sh**, but palatal; in *C.* it is distinguished from ཞ (*ža*) only by the following vowel being sounded in the high tone. — 2. num.: 27.

ཤ་ *ša* I. 1. **flesh, meat,** *γyág-ša* yak's flesh, *lúg-ša* mutton; *ša ₒtsód-pa* (*W.* **tsó-če**) **to** boil meat; *ša rṅod-pa* (*W.* **ṅó-če, šrúg-če** or **lám-če**) to roast meat; *'p'yi-ša* outward flesh, *náṅ-ša* or *náṅ-ča* inward flesh, or the entrails *Cs.*(?); *šá-nas čád-pai bu Glr.* the child of my own flesh and blood; *ša ₒk'rig-pa* sexual instinct; **'á-pe ša, 'á-me ša** in *W.* a vulgar form of attestation; **surface of the body,** *šai ri-mo* spots, stripes etc. on the skin (of an animal) *Tar.* — 2. **muscle,** *nú-ša* thoracic muscle *Mṅg.* — 2. for *ša-k'óg* v. compounds.

II. v. *šá-ba* and *ša-mo.*

Comp. *ša-bkra* n. of a cutaneous disease *Med.* — *ša-skám* meat dried in the sun. — *ša-k'áṅ* **larder**; butcher's stall. — *ša-k'ú* broth. — *ša-k'óg* the body of a slaughtered animal, without the skin, head, and entrails, če-ša of a large — čuṅ-ša of a small animal. — ša-ḱrág flesh and blood, meton. 1. for body, ša-ḱrág γsál-ba a sound body *Mil.* 2. for: children born of the same parents *Cs.* — ša-rgyágs fat meat. — *ša-čúg* (ša bčug) meat cut into strips and hung up to dry in the sun *W.*, *C.* (*Hook.* II, 183). — ša-rǰén raw meat. — ša-ñyóg *Sch.*: 'soup with greens in it'. — ša-rñyiṅ old meat. — ša-mdóg colour of the skin, complexion *Dzl.* and elsewh. — ša-mdog-lóg-pa *Cs.*: *erysipelas*, St. Anthony's fire? — ša-núg the lean of meat *Cs.* — ša-nád a certain disease *Lt.* — *šá-na* (lit.-sna) *W.* ardour, zeal? — šá-spu feathers, downs. — *ša-spin* meat boiled down to jelly *W.* — ša-°ṕróg *Mil.?* — *šá-bhag-leb* a sort of pie baked in oil *C.* — ša-bo sheep, cattle or other animals destined for slaughter *Mil. nt.* — šá-°bu **a maggot.** — *ša-búr* *W.* **boil, abscess, ulcer;** *Sch.*: mark left by a lash, weal. — *ša-dé* rice boiled with small pieces of meat *C.* — ša-sbráṅ **flesh-fly,** blue-bottle-fly. — ša-rmén fleshy excrescence, a little lump in the muscular flesh. — ša-btsós boiled meat. — ša-ťsá 1. hot meat. 2. friend *Pth.*, *S.g.*, ša-ťsa-čan amicable, attached *W.* — ša-ťsán dmár-po *Sch.*: 'a tumour resembling a weal or a wart'. — ša-ťsíl the fat of flesh. — šá-ťsoṅ-pa butcher, dealer in meat. — ša-°dzin 1. a hook for taking meat out of a kettle *C.*, *W.* 2. the **fork** of Europeans. — ša-°dzér wart. — ša-zá, ša-zán 1. prop.: flesh-eater, carnivorous animal. 2. gen.: a class of demons, described as fierce and malignant, *Ssk.* पिशाच. — ša-zúg, ša-γzúg = zug 2. — ša-rág dried apricots, with little pulp, and almost as hard as stone. — ša-ríd lean flesh. — ša-ríl 1. little meat-pies. 2. v. ša-ba. — ša-rúg sauce, gravy *C.* — ša-rúl putrid meat. — ša-ró a disease *Wdṅ.*, is said to be an induration of the skin, callus, or perh. scirrhus. — ša-rlón fresh meat, raw meat, ša-γsár flesh of an animal that has just been killed.

ཤྭ šwa 1. *Dzl.* ཉ༠ོ, 1. *Sch.*: high water, flood, inundation. — 2. *Lt.*: a certain hereditary disease or infirmity?

ཤ་ཀ་ ša-ka some kind of game (?) *Wdṅ.*

ཤ་ཀ་མ་ ša-ka-ma, ḱa-če ša-ka-ma **saffron** *C.*

ཤ་ཀར་ ša-kar *Cs.* a kind of sugar.

ཤ་ཀོན་ ša-kón, or ša-°ḱón, *Wdṅ.*; *Sch.*: grudge, resentment, **hatred.**

ཤཱ་ཀྱ་ šá-kya *Ssk.*, ṕód-pa *Tib.*, **the mighty, the powerful, the bold,** n. of the family of Buddha, the founder of the Buddhist religion, and hence often n. of Buddha himself, also šā-kya-ťúb-pa (*Mil.* rather boldly abbreviates it into šāk-ťub), šā-kya-mú-ni, šā-kya-seṅ-ge.

ཤ་དཀར་ ša-dkár v. γša-dkar.

ཤ་སྐད་ ša-skád the cawing or croaking of ravens *W.*

ཤ་སྐྱོ་ ša-skyó *Mṅg.?* perh. dough mixed with meat.

ཤ་ཁ་མ་, ཤ་ཁ་ར་ šá-ḱa-ma, šá-ḱa-ra = ša-ka-ma and ša-ka-ra.

ཤ་ཁུག་ ša-ḱúg *Sch.* a small bag or purse.

ཤ་ཁྱི་ ša-ḱyi *Sch.* a shaggy dog, a poodle.

ཤ་འཁོན་ ša-°ḱón v. ša-kón.

ཤ་གོས་ ša-gós, col. for šam-gós.

ཤ་ཅེན་ ša-čén *Lt.?*

ཤ་ཉམ(ས)་ ša-nyám(s) *Lex.*, as explanation of *dbal?*

ཤ་སྟ་ ša-sta, = klu *Wdṅ.*

ཤ་སྟག་ šá-stag 1. also ša-dag **mere, merely, only,** ḱyeu šá-dag btsás-te only sons being born *Dzl.*; mi dbúl-°ṕoṅs-pa šá-stag-ste as they are all of them poor people *Dzl.*; bdén-pa-mťoṅ-ba šá-stag-tu gyúr-to they all come to the knowledge of the truth *Tar.* — 2. *Ld.* for (rtai) šám(-la)-btags(-pa) a pack, a bundle, fastened to the saddle behind the rider, *šá-stag-la ḱol or rel toṅ* tie it up, fasten it behind!

ཤ་དི་ šá-di *Ld.*, *Pur.* **ape, monkey.**

ཤ་ན་ ša-na 1. *Ssk.* शण **hemp,** *Cs.*: **flax,** šá-nai ras *Stg.*, *Sch.*: **'fine linen',** šá-nai *gos* a garment made of fine linen. — 2. v. *šá-sna*, sub *ša*.

ཤ་པོས་ *šá-pos* a thick blanket *Ld.*

ཤ་བ་, ཤྭ་བ་ *šá-ba, šwa-ba Cs. W., C., B.* **a hart, a stag,** col. usually **ša-wa-ra-čú* or *ru-ču**; *šá-p'o* the male animal, *šá-mo* the hind, roe, *ša-p'rúg* a young deer, fawn; cf. *k'a-šwa.*

ཤ་མ་ *ša-ma* 1. **after-birth,** placenta. — 2. an ordinary coat made of cloth which has not been napped *W.*

ཤ་མི་ལིག་ *ša-mi-lig* **parsley** *Ld.*

ཤ་མོ་ *šá-mo C., B.* (*W.* **móg-ša**) **mushroom;** the various species of fungus receive their appellations from their colour (*dkar-šá, nag-ša, smug-ša, ser-ša*) or from the place where they grow (*kluṅs-ša, ču-ša, lud-ša, šiṅ-ša*); the damp climate of Sikkim produces moreover **šó-ke, k'á-wa* and *dé-mo* (*sgre-mo*) *-ša-mo**, etc. *Cs.* has also *ša-maṅ*, a thick kind of mushroom.

ཤ་ར་ཤོ་རེ་ *ša-ra šo-ré* (cf. *γšér-pa*) *W.* **moist.**

ཤཱ་རི་ཀ་ *šā-ri-ka Ssk.* n. of a bird, *Gracula religiosa;* a species of jay.

ཤཱ་རིའི་བུ་ *šā-rii-bu*, **शारिपुत्र**, n. of one of the two principal disciples of Buddha.

ཤ་རུ་ *šá-ru* 1. **hartshorn** *Med.* — 2. n. of a vein *Med.*

ཤ་ལོག་ *ša-lóg* **warped, oblique, aslant** *W.*

ཤཀ་ཏི་ *šák-ti Ssk.*: spear, lance, pike, sword, *Cs.* also trident; *Dzl.*

ཤག་ *šag*, in *šag-ter-gás* it broke, it burst asunder *Sch.*

ཤག་མ་ *šág-ma* 1. *C.* small stones or pebbles, **gravel,** *šág-ma-čan* gravelly, *šag-t'áṅ* a plain abounding with gravel. — 2. *W.* **pebble,** *šag-rád* rocky ground, covered with a thin layer of mould which only by dint of much irrigation will yield a scanty produce; *šag-rúg* gravel, *šág-sa* earth mixed up with pebbles, stony, sterile ground.

ཤགས་ *šags* 1. **joke, jest, fun,** *šags čé-ba byéd-pa* to rally maliciously, to turn into ridicule with sarcasms *Glr.; ṅan-šágs Mil.* a bad joke; *k'a-šágs* v. *k'a.* — 2. cause of a contention, object of a dispute or a quarrel, **matter in dispute** *Mil.;* quarrel, dispute, contention, in gen., **šag gyág-pa** *C.* to fight, to quarrel, to dispute.

ཤང་ *šaṅ* v. *γšaṅ.*

ཤང་པོ་, ཤང་སྐྱུལ་ཅེས་, ཤང་རིག་ *šáṅ-po,* **šaṅ kúl-če**, *šaṅ-rig* v. *γčaṅ-po;* **šaṅ-lág** a kind of fur, perh. for *sbyaṅ-slág* fur-coat of wolf's skin *Lh.*

ཤང་ལང་ *šaṅ-láṅ* **sabre, sword** *Pth.*

ཤང་ཤང་ *šaṅ-šáṅ* a fabulous creature with wings and bird's feet, but otherwise like a human being; *šaṅ-šaṅ-téu Cs*: pheasant or partridge (**जीवजीव**).

ཤངས་ *šaṅs*, resp. for *sna*, **the nose,** *šaṅs-rgyúd Pth.*, *šaṅs-sna* id.; *šaṅs-k'úṅ* nostril, *šaṅs-rtsé* tip of the nose.

ཤད་ *šad* 1. the mark of punctuation: །, also *rkyaṅ-šád* or *čig-šád;* it is a diacritical sign of about the value of our comma or semicolon; *nyis-šád* the double shad, །།, dividing sentences, or, in metrical compositions, verses; *bži-šád* the fourfold shad, །།།།, at the end of sections and chapters; *tseg-šád* the dotted shad (༎), an ornamental form of the ordinary shad, always made use of, when a shad is to be put after the first syllable of a line; *šad byéd-pa Lex.*, *ₒtén-pa Sch.*, to make a shad. — 2. v. the following article.

ཤད་པ་, གཤད་པ་, གཤོད་པ་ *šád-pa, γšád-pa, γšód-pa Cs.* 1. **to comb, to curry,** (a horse), also *šad rgyág-pa.* — 2. **to brush, to stroke,** to rub gently with the hand *W.*; *šád-ma Sch.* **curry-comb,** horse-comb; **šiṅ-še'** a wooden rake, **čág-še'** an iron rake *C.*

ཤན་ *šan* 1. **iron hoop** of a barrel *Cs.* — 2. **small boat,** **šém-pa** ferry-man *C.* — 3. snow-leopard *W.* (cf. *γsa*). — 4. **difference, distinction,** *šan ₒbyéd-pa* to distinguish, decide, determine *Mil.* and elsewh., *γžan-gyis šan mi byéd-pas* as nobody else is able to decide it *Glr.*; *skad-γnyis-šan-sbyór* is said to be the title of a certain dictionary.

ཤན་ཁ་ *šán-k'a* 1. **oblique** *W.*, **šán-k'a-la dé-če** to cut off obliquely; *šan-t'ér* id.,

lam śan-ṫér-la č̌a dug the road has an oblique direction. — 2. *C.*: place of passing over a river.

ཤན་པ་ *śán-pa* 1. also *bśan-pa*, slaughterer, **butcher** *Glr.*, sometimes also **hangman**; *śán-ḱaṅ* slaughter-house, butcher's shop, *śán-gri* butcher's knife, *śan-grib* pollution by the sin of slaughtering an animal. — 2. master or rower of a boat, **boatman.**

ཤབ་ཤུབ་ *śab-śúb* 1. *W.* **whispering,** **śab-śúb táṅ-ċe, zér-ċe** to whisper. — 2. also *śab-śób* **lie, falsehood,** *śab-śób byéd-pa* to lie, to cheat; *śab-śúb-ċan* deceitful, fraudulent, crafty.

ཤམ་, གཤམ་ *śam*, * γśam* the lower part of a thing, e.g. of a country, *śám-pa* a lowlander (opp. to *γžúṅ-pa* and *stód-pa*); *γśám-du* adv. and postp. **below,** at foot, *ráṅ-leui śám-du ̥čad* they will be treated of in their respective chapters *Lt.*; *dei śám-du* under it, underneath (e g. to write); *śam-gós*, *śam-ṫábs*, resp. *sku-śám* a garment like **a petticoat,** worn by Tibetan priests and monks.

ཤམ་བུ་ *śám-bu* **flounces, fringes, trimmings.**

ཤམ་བྷ་ལ་ *śám-bha-la Ssk.* in pure Tibetan *bde-̥byúṅ*, n. of a fabulous country in the north west of Tibet, fancied to be a kind of paradise; *śám-bha-lai lám-yig* (not passport, but:) 'guide for the journey to Shambhala'.

ཤར་ *śar* (from *śár-ba*) 1. **east,** *śar-p̒yógs* id.; *śar-pa* inhabitant of an eastern country; *śar-lhó* south-east. — 2. termin. of *śa*, into the flesh.

ཤར་པ་ *śár-pa* 1. young men, grown-up youth (collective noun) *W.*; perh. also: a young man. — 2. v. the preceding article.

ཤར་པོ་ *śár-po* 1. *W.* **adulterer,** **śár-po ċó-ċe* or *ḱúr-ċe** to commit adultery, (on the part of the husband.) — 2. = *śar-pa* 1.

ཤར་ཕོ་ *śár-p̒o* a young man, *śár-p̒o γžón-nu γsum* three young men *Mil.*

ཤར་བ་ *śár-ba* pf. and secondary form of ̥*čár-ba.*

ཤར་མ་ *śár-ma* 1. *Sch.*: **a strip** *Schr.* *śar rgyáb-pa* to sew in long stitches, to baste (*Sch.*: *zuṅs γdáb-pa*). — 2. *W.*, *C.* **grown-up girls** (collective noun); **a female** (?)

ཤར་མོ་ *śár-mo* **adulteress,** cf. *śár-po.*

ཤར་ཤར་ *śar-śár* **straightway, directly,** *śar-śár ̥gró-ba Cs.*

ཤར་ཤུར་ *śar-śur Ld.* furrowed, having small elevations and hollows.

ཤལ་ *śal*, in *rna-śál* **ear-lap,** tip of the ear.

ཤལ་བ་ *śál-ba* 1. *Sch.* **stone-pavement.** — 2. **a harrow,** *śál-śal-ba Sch.*, **śál-la dúd-ċe** *Ld.* to harrow.

ཤལ་མ་ *śál-ma Cs.*: **a flint, sharp-edged stone;** *W.*: stony ground; mountain side consisting of detritus; *śál-ma-ċan* full of sharp stones *Cs.*

ཤལ་མ་ལི་ *śál-ma-li Ssk.* the seven-leaved silk-cotton tree, *Bombax heptaphyllum Stg.*

ཤས་ *śas* 1. **part,** *ċa-śas* id.; ̥*bras de-las śas γċig* part of this rice *Dzl.*; *śas-śás-su bgó-ba* to distribute, . . . *la* among *Dzl.*; *śas-čé-ba* a good deal, much, the greater part of, *zla-mtśán śas-čé-bai ḱu-ḱrág* generative fluid in which uterine blood predominates (cf. *ḱu-ḱrág* in *ḱú-ba*) *Wdṅ.*; *γti-mug śas-čé-bar ̥gyúr-ba* excess of dullness or stupidity *Thgr.*; *śas-čér*, *śas-čés*, *śas-čén* in an eminent degree, in an exceeding measure. — 2. **some, a few,** *žag-śás* some days *Mil.*; ̥*ga-śas* some, a few *Mil.* — 3. instr. of *śa.*

ཤི་ *śi* num.: 57.

ཤི་བ་ *śi-ba* pf. and secondary form of ̥*či-ba.* 1. vb. **to die, to expire, to go out** (as light, fire); *śi-bar gyur-pa-las* when she was in a dying state *Pth.*, *śi-zin-pai ̥óg-tu* after her death; **śi-te lóg(-yoṅ)-ċe** *W.* to rise again from the dead, **láṅ-ċe** (lit. *slaṅ-ċes*) to raise from the dead. — 2. sbst. the state of dying, expiring, *śi-ba-las sos* awakened from a dying state frq.; cf. also comp — 3. partic. and adj. *śi-ba sós-par byéd-par gyur* one already dying still recovers *Do*; *śi-bai lus* the body of the deceased *Do.*

Comp. *śi-ki-ma*, *˳či-K̔a-ma* 1. sbst. **dying, death,** *śi-ki-ma-ru* in dying. — 2. adj. **dying,** *śi-ki-ma yod* (or *˳či-K̔a-ma yod*) he is at the point of death, he is at death's door. — **śi-K̔an** col. the deceased, the dead. — *śi-sṅo* *Sch.*: 'blessing for one deceased'. — *śi-čos* religious ceremonies for the dead *Sch.* — *śi-ša* flesh of animals that have died of themselves, the only flesh which a strict Buddhist is allowed to eat, and which accordingly in Buddhist countries is frequently consumed.

ཤི་རིག་ *śi-rig* *W.* clinking, jingling.

ཤི་རོག་ *śi-róg* *W.* a sort of early barley.

ཤཱི་ལ་ *śi-la* *Ssk.* for *k̔rims*, *tsúl-k̔rims* custom, manner, moral law.

ཤིག་ *śig* 1. for *cig* (q. v.) after a final s. — 2. **louse,** *mi-śig* common louse, *lúg-śig* sheep-louse, tick, *k̔yi-śig* flea, (*lha*)-*˳dre-śig* bug; **dag* (lit. *brag*)-*śig-pa** *W.* mite, wood-louse, tick; *śig ˳tú-ba B.*, **ltá-ce*, *rúg-ce** *W.* to look for lice, to louse, *śig bsál-ba* to clean from lice; *śig-čan Sch.* also *śig-po* or *śig-śig-po* infested with lice, lousy; *śig-nád* pedicular disease; *śig-sró* lice and nits *S.g.*

ཤིག་གེ་བ་, ཤིག་ཤིག་ *śig-ge-ba*, *śig-śig* 1. standing or lying close together, **close-banded** *Mil. nt.*, *C.* cf. *γśig-pa*, *γśib-pa*. — 2. **trembling, tottering, wavering;** with *mig:* looking this way and that, looking about, perh. also: rolling (the eyes).

ཤིགས་(སེ་)ཤིགས་ *śigs*(-*se*)-*śigs* **rocking,** as trees moved by the wind *Mil.; śigs-śigs yom-yóm* waving, moving to and fro, shaken etc., also fig. *Pth.*

ཤིང་ *śiṅ* I. gerundial particle for *ciṅ* after a final s.

II. sbst. 1. **tree,** *bzá-śiṅ* fruit-tree, *rtsi-śiṅ* v. *rtsi*; *ljón-śiṅ* a beautiful green leafy tree, *skám-śiṅ* a dry withered tree. — 2. **wood,** *śiṅ žig* some wood; *k̔áṅ-śiṅ* timber, timber-wood, *búd-śiṅ* firewood, fuel, *skám-śiṅ* dry wood; *yám-śiṅ Cs.*: 'a small quantity of wood thrown into the fire for sacrifice'. — 3. **a piece of wood, log, billet,** **śiṅ ŋyi sum tob** *W.* put two or three pieces (to the fire); **stump, stub** of a tree *Glr.*; **tú-pag-gi śiṅ** *W.* gun-stock; *sróg-śiṅ* axle, axle-tree.

Comp. *śiṅ-kir-ti* **a carrying-frame** *Lh.* — *śiṅ-kyu* a wooden hook. — *śiṅ-rkaṅ Schr.* **a wooden leg, a crutch.** — *śiṅ-rkéd* the upper part of the trunk of a tree. — *śiṅ-k̔aṅ* 1. a wooden house, log-house. 2. shed or out-house for wood. — *śiṅ-k̔u* sap, juice of trees. — *śiṅ-k̔ur* a load of wood. — *śiṅ-k̔ri* wooden chair. — *śiṅ-mk̔an* worker in wood, **carpenter, joiner.** — *śiṅ-rgón Sch.* **wood pecker,** *śiṅ-rgon k̔rá-bo* the spotted woodpecker, *śiṅ-rgon mgo-nág* black woodpecker. — *śiṅ-rgyál* a tree of extraordinary height or circumference, **a giant-tree.** — *śiṅ-mṅár* **licorice** *Sch.*, *Wts.*; a sort of cinnamon *W.* — *śiṅ-čás* 1. wooden utensils, implements. 2. tools for working wood *Sch.* — *śiṅ-tog*, *śiṅ-tog* fruits of trees, **fruit.** — *śiṅ-rta* v. that article. — *śiṅ-stan* **chopping-block** *Ld.* — *śiṅ-t̔ags* wooden enclosure. — *śiṅ-t̔ún* wood-picker, gatherer of wind-fallen wood. — *śiṅ-dúm* log, billet, block. — *śiṅ-dra* wooden lattice-work; wooden paling *C.*, *W.* — *śiṅ-druṅ-pa* one sitting under a tree, i.e. an ascetic, *Burn.* I, 309. — *śiṅ-γdúgs* the leafy crown of a tree *Sch.* — *śiṅ-sdóṅ* trunk, **stem of a tree; a tree; block.** — *śiṅ-p̔rán* **a small tree, a shrub, bush** *Sch.* — *śiṅ-bál* cotton from the cotton-tree *Cs.*, cf. *śal-ma-li-śiṅ.* — *śiṅ-bu* a small piece of wood, *śiṅ-bu sor-bži-pa* a piece of wood four inches broad or long *Tar.* — *śiṅ-˳brás* fruit. — *śiṅ-smán* medicine prepared from wood *Sch.* — *śiṅ-rtsá* root of a tree. — *śiṅ-rtsi* **resin** *Cs.* — *śiṅ-rtsé* **top of a tree.** — *śiṅ-tsa* **cinnamon** (having a 'saltish taste, as is expressly stated *S.g.*); **śiṅ-tse lób-ma** *W.* **bay-leaf, laurel-leaf.** — *śiṅ-tsál* **chip, shaving, splinter.** **śiṅ-tsógs** *W.* **forest.** — *śiṅ-γžoṅ* a wooden basin, trough, tub. — **śiṅ-žóg** (lit. *bžogs*) **chip, splint** *W.*; shavings brought off by the plane *C.* — *śiṅ-zán* **wood-rasp** *Sch.* — **śiṅ-zél** **a small chip,** a very small and thin piece of wood, a splinter, **śiṅ-žél zug soṅ** *W.* I have run a splinter into (my hand or foot).

— *śiṅ-zóg W.* **a rasp.** — *śiṅ-γzér* **a peg.** — *śiṅ-léb* board, plank. — *śiṅ-śún* the bark of trees. — *śiṅ-séd* a rasp.

ཤིང་ཀུན་ *śiṅ - kun* **asa foetida,** used as medicine, and (like garlic) as a spice; also n. of a mountain pass between Lahoul and Zankar.

ཤིང་རྟ་ *śiṅ-rta* ('wooden horse') **waggon, cart,** carriage, also fig. = *tég-pa*, e.g. *śiṅ-rta čén-po* frq. in the writings of *Tsoṅḱapa; śiṅ-rta-ₒḱór-lo* id.; *śiṅ - rtai ḱaṅ - bzáṅ* the body of a carriage, *śiṅ-rtai mda* the pole, beam, shaft of a cart, *ₒṕáṅ-lo* the wheel, *rjes, lam, śul, srol* the track, rut (of a cart) *Cs.*; *śiṅ - rta rkaṅ - γčig Sch.* wheelbarrow; *śiṅ-rta-mḱan Cs.* maker of carts, cartwright; *śiṅ-rta-pa* 1. carter, driver, coachman. 2. charioteer.

ཤིད་ *śid* 1. *Sch.* **hazel-nut.** — 2. also *γśid-γśid-ma, γśid-stón, γśid-zán* **funeral repast,** of which every body may partake; *śid-čós* religious funeral ceremony; *śid-sa Sch.* 1. burying ground, cemetery. 2. a fruitful field = *γśin-sa.* Cf. *γśin.*

ཤིན་ཏུ་ *śin-tu* **very, greatly,** esp. before adj. and adv., in *B.* frq.

ཤིབ་ *śib* v. *śib.*

ཤིབ་པ་ *śib-pa* v. *śúb-pa* **to whisper.**

ཤིབ་ཤི་ལུ་ལུ་ *śib-śi-lú-lu* or *rú-ru Ld.* **hip,** the fruit of the dog-rose.

ཤིམ་ཤ་པ་ *śim-śa-pa Cs.* a kind of tree or wood.

ཤིར་, ཤིར་ཤིར་ *śir, śir-śir*, with *ₒtón-pa Cs.* to gush out, to stream forth with a noise.

ཤིལ་བ་ *śil-ba W.* to drip through.

ཤིལ་ལི་ *śil-li* a gauze-like texture *W.*; *śil-śil* 1. id. 2. *Cs.*: 'a cant word denoting the noise of any thing'.

ཤིས་ *śis* **good luck, fortune, bliss;** *de ₒbyúṅ-na śis* if that happens, it will be an auspicious sign, *śis-pai miṅ* a name foreboding good *Lt.*, *mi śis-pai ltas* an omen foreboding ill *Wdṅ.*; *bstán - pai śis* acc. to *Schl.* 232 denotes the religious plays performed in the convents. *Cs.*: *śis(-pa)-po* one blessed, *śis-pa yin-pa* to be blessed, *śis-par ₒgyúr-ba* to become blessed, *śis-par byéd-pa* to make blessed, to bless; *bkra-śis* v. *bkrá-ba.*

ཤུ་ *śu* 1. acc. to Cunningham and other English authorities the Tibetan word for **stag;** yet as none of the many Tibetans, from different parts of the country, that were consulted by us, seemed to know this word, it is not unlikely, that in consequence of indistinct hearing it is but a corruption of *śa - ba* (q. v.). — 2. **śu-śú ǰhé'-pa** *C.* **to whistle.** — 3. num.: 87.

ཤུ་དག་ *śu-dág* n. of a plant *Med.*; *Sch.*: **the rush.**

ཤུ་བ་ *śú-ba* I. sbst. 1. **an abscess, ulcer, sore** *Cs.*: *śú-ba ₒton* an abscess rises, *na* gives pain, *ṕan* heals; **śu-ₒbúr** *W.*, and prob. also *śu-tór Med.*, id.; **śu-nág* and *bá-śu** *W.* a sore that has become inflamed and rankling. — 2. **scab, scurf, scald** *W.*

II. vb., pf. *(b)śus*, fut. *bśu*, imp. *(b)śu(s)*, 1. **to take off,** pull off, draw off, *γźán-gyi gos* to take off a person's clothes, *gó - ča* armour, *mtśón - ča* arms, weapons *Pth.*; **to strip, strip off,** e.g. leaves, twigs, *págs-pa* the skin, the peel, hence (also without *págs-pa*) **to skin, to pare, to peel** *W.*, e.g. *'*á-lu śú-če** to peel potatoes; *gyab - śús* coat of wool shorn from a sheep, fleece *Ld.* — 2. **to copy,** *dpe* a book, resp. *źal-śús byéd-pa Cs.*; *dpe-bśús* a copied book *C.*

ཤུ་བྷཾ་ *śu-bham Ssk.*, sometimes at the end of books, hail! all hail!

ཤུ་ར་སེ་(ན) *śu-ra-se(-na)* n. of a tract of land in the neighbourhood of Mathura, not far from Agra *Wdk.*

ཤུ་ལི་ཀ *śú-'i-ka Tar.* 63, 8, prob. also *śu-lig Sch.*, n. of a fabulous country in the north-west.

ཤུག་ *śug* 1. **a thrust, push, knock,** **śug čém-po ǰhé'-pa** **to push off,** to give a knock, to elbow, differing from *ₒṕúl-ba* to shove (by a more gentle motion) *C.* — 2. in comp.: *ḱyo-śúg*, v. *ḱyo*: *śúg-bza* **wife,** consort, spouse *Schr.* — 3. *W.*: **old,** but still fit for use. — 4. *śug-śúg-la* col. for *śúb-bur* **softly, gently,** e.g. *ₒgró-ba* to walk, to tread etc.

ཤུག་གུ་ *śúg-gu W.* for *śóg-bu.*

ཤུག་པ་ *śúg-pa* 1. the high, cypress-like **juniper-tree** of the Himalaya mountains, **the pencil cedar** (*Juniperus excelsa*). It covers large mountain tracts, is considered sacred, and much used in religious cer monies; its berries (*śug-₀brás*) are burnt as incense. — *śug-dúd* the smoke or perfume of juniper.— *śug-tsér Med.* the young pointed sprouts of this tree. — *sug-tsód* a sort of mistletoe, *Viscum Oxycedri*, growing on it and gradually killing it. The leaves have a slightly sour taste and are used for culinary purposes *W.* — *rgya-śug* acc. to *Cs.* = *spá-ma Juniperus squamosa*, a low shrub and similar to our *Juniperus communis.* But a passage of the *Stg.* shows that its fruits are eaten like pease or rice, which cannot be imagined of juniper-berries or cypress cones; cf. *spá-ma.* — 2. in *śúg-pa ₀púd-pa Sch.*, v. *sub ₀púd-pa.*

ཤུགས་ *śugs* 1. **inherent strength, power, energy,** c. genit.: *dád-pai*, *byáms-pai*, *dgá-bai śúgs-kyis* by the power or ardour of faith, love, joy, e.g. to shed tears, = to weep with joy etc. *Glr.* and elsewh.; *ċ́in-gyi śugs dgag mi bya* the impulse to make water must not be suppressed *Med.*; *₀dí-dag sṅón-gyi sbyin-śugs yin* this is the power of former alms or presents *Glr.*; *túgs-rjei śúgs-kyis* by the power of grace *Do.*; *der sléb-pai śugs* the power or ability of attaining to that place *Thgr.*; without a genit.: *śúgs-kyis* = *ráṅ-śugs-kyis* spontaneously, of one's own accord, *śúgs-kyis yoṅ* they will, no doubt, come of their own accord *Mil.*; *śugs byéd-pa* to exert one's self(?); *śugs-stóbs* = *śugs*; *sṅá-śugs ₀drén-pa Cs.*: 'the accenting the first syllable'. — 2. col. also *śubs* and *śud*, mostly in compounds: *śúgs-skad Mil.*, *śúgs-sgra*, col. **śúg-ra** **a whistling,** a whistle or whiff; *śúgs-glu* 1. a whistling. 2. a whistled tune, **śúg-da ǰhé-pa** to whistle a tune *C.*; *śúgs-pa* a small whistle which, in sounding it, is put quite into the mouth.

ཤུགས་ནར་ *śugs-nár* (*W.* **k̓óg-śúg**), *śugs-riṅ* **sigh, groan,** *śugs nar byéd-pa* or *₀byin-pa* to sigh, to groan, *śugs-riṅ nar nár ₀dug* **he heaves a deep sigh** *Mil. nt.*

ཤུང་བ་ *śúṅ-ba*, pf. *śuṅs*, 1. **to snore.** — 2. **to hum, to buzz,** e.g. of a large beetle.

ཤུད་ *śud* v. *śugs* 2.

ཤུད་པ་ *śúd-pa* pf. fut. *bśud*, 1. **to rub,** e.g. one thing against another *C.* — 2. **to get scratched, excoriated, galled** (cf. *śún-pa*). — 3. *śud byéd-pa* (*W.* **ċó-ċe**) **to steal silently away, to sneak off** unperceived.

ཤུན་པ་ *śún-pa* **bark, rind, peel, skin,** *śun-kóg*, *śun-págs* id., the last expression is also used of the skin of animals *Lex.* — *p̓yi-śun* the outer rind or skin, *náṅ-śun* the inner rind; *bár-śun* the middle rind, the bast, esp. of willows *Sch.*: *śun-kóg láṅs-pa* the spontaneous chapping or peeling off of the skin; *śun-máṅ* **box-wood.**

ཤུབ་པ་ *śúb-pa*, also *śib-pa*, pf. imp. *śubs*, to speak in a low voice, **to whisper,** *śub byéd-pa* id.; **k̓og-śúb-la sil-ċe** *W.* to read in a low voice, to read whispering; *śúb-bu* a whispering, *śúb-bus zlá-ba* to recite in a low voice *Lex.*, *śúb-bur smrá-ba B.*, **śúb-la zér-ċe** *W.* to speak softly; *śúb-bus smód-pa* to reprehend in a whisper *B.*

ཤུབས་ *śubs* **case, covering, sheath, paper bag** etc. frq.; *rkaṅ-śúbs*, resp. *žabs-śúbs* stocking, sock, *gri-śúbs* knife-case or sheath, *mje-śúbs* v. *mje*; *lag-śúbs*, resp. *p̓yag-śúbs* **glove.**

ཤུམ་པ་ *śúm-pa*, pf. (*b*)*śums*, ft. *bśum*, imp. (*b*)*śum*(*s*), 1. **to weep,** *ma śum mdzod* do not weep! *ṅu-śúm Mil.* **weeping, lamentation.** — 2. to tremble(?) *graṅ-śúm Lt.*, *Schr. graṅ-śúm byéd-pa* to tremble or shiver with cold, to shudder.

ཤུར་བ་ *śúr-ba*, pf. fut. *bśur*, imp. (*b*)*śur*, 1. to burn slightly, **to singe.** — 2. **to cut off.**

ཤུར་བུ་ *śúr-bu* 1. **girdle, belt** *Lex.*; *śur-bu-p̓réu Zam.* id. (acc. to *Sch.*). — 2. *Cs.*: **sore, ulcer.** — 3. *Ts.*: **dumpling of flour,** = *k̓o-lag.*

ཤུལ་ *śul* 1. **an empty place,** a place that has been left, that is no longer occupied, *ráṅ-śul stóṅs-nas* your own place becoming empty, by your quitting it *Mil.* *šúl-du lús-pai nor* all the things left behind in the camp *Glr.*; *dóṅ-tse láṅs-pai šúl-du* instead of the coin which had been taken away (there appeared . . .) *Dzl.*; *k'yód-kyi šúl-du* in the place which you occupied during your life *Thgr.*; hence in a looser sense: *btsún-mo méd-pai šúl-du* on the occasion of the queen's absence *Glr.*; in the same manner *Tar.* 103, 16, 19, and also thus: *dei šúl-du Glr.* 51 during her absence. — 2. **track, rut,** of a carriage, **furrow,** of a plough *Dzl.*, **way, road;** also in a gen. sense: *šul t'ag-riṅ* a long way *Glr.*; *šul-lám* = *šul*; acc. to *Cs.* also **manner, method.** — 3. any thing left behind by a person departed, or by a thing removed, as *ču-šul, mar-šul, p'ye-šul* that little water, butter or flour which adheres to the vessel emptied, but not washed; *me-šul* the extinguished cinders left by a fire; **property left** by a deceased person *šul tsáṅ-ma yóg-po-la t'ob* his servant gets all the property left (by his master) *W.*, *C.*, *p'a-šul* paternal inheritance, patrimony; *p'a-šul-ₒdzin-pa* the heir *C.*; *šul yaṅ mi ₒdug* nothing at all is left; **šúl-med-k'an čo** *W.* finish it at once! eat it all up! *šū-tsaṅ-po* one that eats all up, clears his trencher (a good trencher-man) *Ts.*

ཤུལ་བ་ *šúl-pa, bšúl-pa Cs.*: **backbone, back, posteriors;** *šul-šá* the flesh, the muscles of the back, *šul-rgyús* the fibres, the nerves of the back; *Sch.*: *bšul-dri* smell of excrements, *šul-byi* **polecat, fitchet.**

ཤུས་ *šus* 1. v. *šú-ba.* — 2. *šus ₒdébs-pa* to whistle *S.g.*

ཤུས་མ་ *šús-ma* any thing copied, **a copy** *Cs.*

ཤེ་ *še* 1. *Cs. še-stag, še-dag* = *ša-stág* **mere, only,** nothing but. — 2. num.: 117.

ཤེ་ན་ *šé-na* v. *čé-na.*

ཤེ་པ་ *šé-pa* v. *šés-pa.*

ཤེ་བམ་ *še-bám Cs.*: = *t'o-yig* a kind of contract or bargain.

ཤེ་མ་ *šé-ma* (for *rjé-ma* or *yčés-ma?*) *W.* **noblewoman,** lady of rank or quality, **lady,** **šé-ma čuṅ-ṅu*, *šem-čúṅ** nobleman's daughter, **young lady, Miss.**

ཤེ་མོང་ *še-móṅ Sch.*: 'divine predestination, divine protection; nature, fate, destiny; power; origin of power or authority; strength', force, the latter signification also in *Wts.* (?).

ཤེ་རུལ་ *še-rul Sch.*: **fetid, putrid.**

ཤེག་ *šeg* 1. imp. of *yšégs-pa*, resp. for *šog.* — 2. the Arabian شيخ, chieftain, elder, senior. — 3. *C.* col. for *šed* I.

ཤེད་ *šed* I. **strength, force,** = *stóbs, mt'u, C.* also *šeg*; *dpá-žiṅ šed-čé* a mighty hero *Thgy.*; *šéd-čan* **strong, vigorous, powerful;** *šéd-mo* 1. sbst. = *šed?* 2. adj. = *šed-čan Ts.*, **šé'-mo gyág-pa yin** he is strong and stout, *šed-méd* **powerless, weak,** *šed-méd-kyi rtá-bas rkaṅ-t'áṅ mgyogs* one travels quicker on foot than on a weak horse; *šed-čúṅ* **weak, feeble, frail,** e.g. *lus Lt.*; *šed ₒbri* strength decreases, begins to fail, *ysos* is restored, *nyams* is impaired; *šed skyéd-pa* to **grow** fat *Sch.*: 'to protect; to make haste'; **mi žig-la šed čúg-če** *W.* **to strengthen** a person; **šed daṅ nyé-če** *W.* to rub well, forcibly; **šed žár-te* (*sbyar-te*) *čoṅ** run and jump! **šed žár-te gyob** swing your arm and throw! *W.*; **šed-kyer-nág-po** by force, with violence, e.g. **taṅ** he forced it on (me) *W.* (cf. *nan*): *šed-po-čé* a strong, powerful man *Thgy.*; *šéd-bu Lex.* id.; *šed-bdág Sch.* one having power or authority, a lord, ruler. — **šed - wáṅ** *W.* **force, violence,** **šed-wáṅ daṅ** by force, e.g. to take, **šed-wáṅ táṅ-če** *W.* to violate, to force (a girl).

II. the approximate **direction, region, quarter,** *nyi-mai ₒog šéd-na* below the sun, i.e. between the sun and the horizon *Mil.*; *W.*: **gaṅ šéd-la** in what direction? whereto? **de šed-la** about in that direction; **gaṅ šed ne* (lit. *ynas*) *šig-tu** to some place or other.

ཤེན་ *šen* (?) **floor** of a house or room *W.*

ཤེར་ཕྱིན་ *šer-p'yin* abbreviation for *šes-ráb-kyi p'á-rol-tu p'yin-pa*, the title of a division of the *Kan-gyur.*

ཤེར་བ śér-ba, pf. bśer, **to compare, to confront** *Cs.*

ཤེལ śel **crystal, glass** *Dzl.* and elsewh.; acc. to *Stg.* the moon also consists of such crystal *Cs.*: *rán-śel* native crystal, *bzú-śel* artificial crystal, glass; *mán-śel Pth.* prob. = *śel; spos-śél* amber; *me-śél* burning-glass, *ču-śél* चन्द्रकान्त a fabulous magic stone supposed to have the power of producing water or even rain.

Comp. *śel-kór* or *-ṗor* a tumbler. — *śel-dkár* = *śel Glr.* — *śel-k̔án* glass-works, glass-manufactory *Schr.* — *śel-sgóṅ* globe of glass *Mil.* — *śel-sgó* glass-door. — *śel-rdó* crystal. — *śel-snód, śel-spyád* a crystal or glass vessel. — *śel-ṗréṅ* a string of glass-beads. — *śel-búm* glass-bottle. — *śel-mig* spectacles, spy-glass, telescope.

ཤེས śes v. *čes.*

ཤེས་པ śés-pa (synon. *rig-pa*, resp. *mk̔yén-pa*) I. vb., 1. **to know, perceive, apprehend,** *bzáṅ-bar śés-pa* to find, to know a thing to be good *Glr.*; *brtágs-na mi śes* when (the soul) is searched for, it is not to be perceived or apprehended *Mil.*; *śés-pai blo ingenium sapiens Dzl.*; *mi-śes-pa-dag* those who do not care for knowing (a thing) *Dzl.*; *su śés B., C.,* **či śē* W.* (like the Hindi क्या जाने) who can tell? may be; *čiaṅ mi śē-k̔an* a know-nothing, ignoramus, dunce; **k̔o-ráṅ mā śé-k̔an čén-mo žig tsor dug* W.* he is said to be an extremely clever (learned etc.) man; *mi-śés dgu śés-pa* knowing (even) the unknown things, knowing every thing *Thgy.*; *čaṅ-śés* id.; **ṅa-ráṅ t̔oṅ śē* W.* I know it from having seen it; *śés-par gyur* 1. he will know. 2. he comes to know, he learns; *śes-par gyis śig* 1. know! 2. let it be known! *śes-bžin-du* **knowing, knowingly,** with (my) knowledge; *ṅó-śes-pa = śés-pa*, yet cf. sub *ṅo.* — 2. **to understand,** = *gó-ba, don* the sense *Glr.*; *ṅas rtsis śes* I understand mathematics; **to be able,** in a general sense, also physically: **ghaṅ śē-pa* C.* to one's best ability, to the utmost of one's power (= *ji nus-kyis B.,* **či t̔úb-k̔an* W.*); *k̔rág-gi goṅ ₒgul śés-pa* a clot of blood that could only quiver (though, in fact, a human being) *Glr.*; esp. with a negative: *smra mi śés-pa* not being able to speak, *dgye dgu mi śes* they cannot be bent or curved *Med.* — 3. **to be convinced, to be of opinion, to think,** *sú-la yaṅ mdzá-bor ma śes* do not think anybody to be your friend!

II. sbst. (= *rig-pa*) 1. **the knowing** (about a thing), **knowledge.** — 2. **science, learning,** *śés-pa-la zóg-tu ltá-ba* to look upon science as a (sort of) cheating. — 3. **intellectual power, intelligence,** *śés-pa t̔ibs* the intellect (of infants) is still very weak *Lt.*, *ɣsal* is clear *Pth.* — 4. **the soul** or spirit, separate from the body *Thgy.*, *Mil.*

Comp. **śē-gyá** talent(?) *C., W.* — **śē-gyü** **character** *C., W.*, **śē-gyü ṅém-pa** a bad character. — *śes-ₒdód* **desire of knowledge, curiosity** of mind *Mil.* *śes-ldan*, *śes-blo-ldán-pa* 1. knowing, rich in wisdom. 2. very learned Sir! — *śés-po, śés-pa-po* one that knows or understands, a knower *Cs.* — *śés-bya* 1. what may be known or ought to be known, *śés-bya kun* every thing worth knowing, all the sciences. 2. knowing, conscious, wilful? *śés-byai sgrib-pa* contamination by wilful sins *Do.?* — *śes-byed* that which knows, the understanding. — *śés-bžin* **consciousness** (v. above *śes-bžin-du*), *dran-pa daṅ śes-bžin-čan yin-te Gyatch.* ༡༡༤, 14 (cf. *Burn.* II, 806, 5); *śés-bžin* may, accordingly, be used for **'conscience'** in a christian sense. — *śés-yoṅ Ts.* = *śes-rgya.* — *śes-ráb* (प्रज्ञा) 1. 'great knowledge', **wisdom, intelligence, understanding, talent,** *śes-rab če-ba* very talented, gifted (e.g. a boy) *Mil.*; *śes-ráb daṅ ldán-pa* id.; *śes-rab-spyan* the (mystic) eye of wisdom *Schl.* p. 210. — *śes-rab-rtswa Taraxacum*, dandelion, also used as food. — *śes-ráb-kyi ṗá-rol-tu ṗyín-pa*, प्रज्ञापारमिता, the having arrived at the other side of wisdom, n. of that section of the *Kangyur* which treats of philosophical matters.

ཤོ śo (*Cs.*: *śó-mo*) I. **die, dice,** *śo rgyáb-pa* **to dice,** *śo rtsé-ba* to play at dice, *śo-ₒgyéd-pa* (*Sch.* *k̔yé-žig* as imp.) id.? — *śo rgyál-ba* or *ṗám-pa* to win or lose at playing;

šo-rgyán *Cs.* the money or stake deposited at dice-playing; *rtsis-šoi rdeu Mil.*, *šo-rdél Wdk.*, an attribute of certain deities; *šo-mig* the points of dice, *šo-mig γsúm-par* (or *-pa-la*) *ₒbáb-na* when three points are thrown. Tibetans play with three dice marked with 6 and 1, 5 and 4, 3 and 2 on opposite sides, hence from 3 to 18 points may be thrown.

II. 1. the white willow of *Spiti*, *Ld.* and other Himalayan districts. — 2. other plants *rgya-šo*, *lug-šo? Wdṅ.*

III. = *btsa-ma* blast, blight, smut, mildew *Cs.*

IV. for *šo-gam*, q. v.

V. num.: 147.

ཤོ་གམ་ *šo-gám* **custom, duty, tax,** *šo-gám lči-ba W.* **lčin-te** high duty, *šo-gam len-pa* to take toll, to levy a duty; *šo-gám bzlá-ba Sch.*: 'to smuggle, to circumvent or defraud the customs' (?); *šo-gám-gyi γnas* custom-house; *šo-gám-pa* receiver of the customs, toll-gatherer; **šo-ṭ ál, šo-dú** *Ts.* **tax,** duty.

ཤོ་ཆ་ *šó-ča* a kind of steel-yard *C.*

ཤོ་མ་ *šó-ma*, v. *šá-mo*, **mushroom** *Mil.*

ཤོ་མང་ *šo-máṅ* a medicinal herb *Med.*

ཤོ་ར་ *šó-ra* **saltpetre,** nitre, *šó-ra-čan* nitrous.

ཤོ་རེ་ *šo-ré*, adj., **damaged, spoiled,** by being partially broken, torn etc., sbst.: **a defect, flaw, notch, gap,** also **hare-lip;** **šo-ré soṅ** it is damaged, **šo-ré ťon soṅ** a notch, chink, crack has been caused; **ḱa-šór, na-šór**, with a slit lip, a slit nose.

ཤོ་ལོ་ཀ་ *šó-lo-ka* v. *šlo-ka.*

ཤོག་ *šog* I. *šóg-čig*, prop. from *γšégs-pa*, imp. of *ₒóṅ-ba*, 1. come! let him come! *ₒbrás-bu ťsúr-šog-gi yid-smón ṅá-la med* I do not wish that fruit should come to me from without *Mil.*; *ḱur šog, ḱyer šog bskyal šog* bring hither, (with *soṅ* inst. of *šog*: take away!) *šog zér-ba* **to invite.** *ṅed-la šog kyaṅ mi zer Glr.* we are not so much as invited, you know. — 2. with the imp. = *gyur-čig*, *bsad-par-šog* may (he, I etc.) be killed! *Dzl.* — II. v. *šos.*

ཤོག་པ་ *šóg-pa* I. sbst., also frq. *γšóg-pa*, 1. **wing,** *γšog-rkyaṅ-ba* to spread the wings, also to spread like wings; **šóg-pa dé-če, čád-če, dúm-če** *W.* to clip the wings; *γšóg-pa-čan*, *γšog-ldán* provided with wings, winged, a bird. — 2. **wing-feather, pinion,** *ₒdab-γšóg*, *γšóg-sgro* id.; *mjug-γšog* tail-feather. — 3. **fin,** of fishes. — 4. other things resembling a wing or a feather, *mig-γšog*, resp. *spyán-γšog* eye-lash; *raṅ-tág-gi γšóg-pa* prob.: wing or float-board of a water-mill; of course it might also be used for: wing, sail, of a windmill, though these are not yet known in Tibet.

II. vb., v. sub *γšog-pa.*

ཤོག་བུ་ *šóg-bu*, *W.* **šúg-gu**, 1. **sheet of paper,** and **paper** collectively, *rgya-šóg* China paper, *bod-šóg* Tibet paper, *dar-šóg* silk-paper, *ras-šóg* cotton-paper (also paper of linen-rags), *šiṅ-šóg* bast-paper, *pags-šóg* leather-paper, skin-paper, parchment; *mtiṅ-šóg*, *nag-šóg* dark-blue or black paper, for writing on in gold or silver; *mgo-šóg*, resp. *dbu-šóg*, upper leaf, i. e. cover, covering, wrapper. — 2. *Bal.*: **book.**

Comp. *šog-ḱáṅ* **paper-maker's form.** — *šog-gáṅ* a sheet of paper. — *šog-gráṅs* number of leaves in a book. — *šog-sgril*, *šog-dril*, *W.* **šog-ril** **paper-roll, codex.** — *šog-ldéb Sch.*: 'leaf, sheet'? — *šog-tsár* scrap of paper. — *šog-šiṅ Sch.* palm-tree? — *šog-hril γčig* = *šog-gáṅ*, *Sch.*

ཤོང་(མ)་, གཤོང་(མ)་ *šoṅ(s)*, *γšoṅ(s)* (*Lex.*: སཱནུ 'elevated plain, ridge of a mountain') 1. **mountain-ridge** *Wts.* Usual meaning: 2. **pit, hole, cavity, excavation, valley,** *ču-šóṅs* cavity filled with water *Dzl.*; *spaṅ-šoṅs* valley with meadows, low ground overgrown with grass; *snai bya-γšóg-gi γšoṅs* the cavities near the wings of the nose *Mil. nt.*; *šóṅ-du* valley-ward, down hill *Dzl.*; *šóṅs-čan*, (*γ*)*šoṅ-*(*γ*)*šóṅ* full of cavities, **uneven,** *Sch.* also: **rough, rugged, steep;** *šóṅs-bu* **furrow,** *šóṅs-bu ₒtén-pa* to make furrows, to furrow.

ཤོང་བ་ *šóṅ-ba* I. to go in, **to have room** in or on, with term., *mi šoṅ*, *W.* also: **šóṅ-če mi dug** that is not to be got in, there is no room for it; *bre lṅa šóṅ-bai búm-pa* a can holding five quarts *Dzl.*

II. pf. *bšaṅs*, fut. *bšaṅ*, imp. *šoṅ(s)*, **to empty, remove, carry or take away,** *W.* stones, earth etc., but gen. (with or without *rkyág-pa*) to go to stool, to ease nature, *B.* and col.

ཤོད་ *šod* 1. the lower, the inferior part of a thing, *rtse-šod* upper and lower part, top and bottom *C.*; *rgya-šod Wdṅ.* a low tract of land, with a milder climate, where e.g. apricots are thriving, opp. to *p̔u-lhágs* elevated cold region, scarcely fit for the cultivation of corn and barley; *šód-du* to or towards the bottom, **down, downwards,** *C.*, **šọ̈'-du báb-pa** to descend, come down, **šọ̈'-nẹ ˳dzég-pa** to ascend *C.* — 2. imp. of *˳č̔ád-pa*, *bšád-pa*; yet cf. also:

ཤོད་པ་ *šod-pa*, pf. *bšád-pa*, 1. **to say, to declare** *C.* — 2. **to comb** *Cs.*

ཤོབ་, གཤོབ་ *šob*, *γšob* **a fib, falsehood, lie,** *smrá-ba*, *W.* **gyáb-če**, to tell a lie.

ཤོབ་ཤོབ་ *šob-šób* **loose, soft,** as leaves etc. *W.*

ཤོམ་པ་ *šom-pa*, pf. *(b)šoms*, *bšams*, fut. *bšam*, imp. *(b)šom(s)*, **to prepare, make ready, arrange, put in order, fit out,** *γnas* lodgings, *γdan* a seat, *stón-mo* a festive entertainment, *bžón-pa* a carriage, i.e. to have the horses put to *Dzl.*; *dpúṅ-gi ts̔ogs* an army *Dzl.* — *šóm-ra* 1. **preparation, arrangement, fitting out,** *šóm-ra byéd-pa* = *šóm-pa C.*, so also *Cs.*; but *Sch.*: 2. *šóm-ra* **state, pomp, splendour,** with *byéd-pa* to show off, to dress smartly, *šóm-čan* stately, grand (?).

ཤོར་ *šor* v. *šo-ré.*

ཤོར་བ་ *šór-ba* 1. v. *˳č̔ór-ba.* — 2. to measure *Mil.*, v. *γšór-ba.*

ཤོལ་བ་ *šól-ba* 1. **intercalation, insertion** *Cs.*, *zla-šól* intercalary month. — 2. *Cs*: pres. tense of *bšól-ba* q.v.

ཤོལ་པོ་ *šól-po Sch.*: 'a species of willow', v. *γšól-po.*

ཤོས་ *šos* 1. almost always in conjunction with *γčig*, **the other,** of two, e.g. *bud-méd γčig-šós* the other woman *Dzl.* — 2. *Zam.* तर, col. *šog*, a termination indicating the comparative or superlative degree: *čuṅ-šós*, *γžon-šós* the younger, the youngest, of two or of several, *btsún-mo lṅa-brgyái čuṅ-šós Pth.*; **riṅ-šóg** *W.* the tallest; *yun-riṅ-šós Thgy.* the most long-lived; *drin-čé-šós* the principal benefactress, cf. *drin*; *nad čé-šós rgyás-nad ˳ts̔ébs-pas* because one is suffering under the chief disease, viz. old age, *Thgy.*

ཤྲཱི་ *śrī Ssk.*, = *dpal* **glory, magnificence; magnificent, splendid, grand;** *śrī-ri Mil.*, pr. n., a naked mountain in a sandy plain, about a ten day's journey to the west of Tashi-lhunpo, covered with monasteries, and perh. on that account considered as *nyams-mts̔ár-ba*. *śrī-k̔aṇḍa* v. *dpál-gyi dum-bu.*

ཤློ་ཀ་ *śló-ka Ssk.*, also *šo-lo-ka*, **strophe, stanza,** esp. one consisting of four catalectic trochaical dimeters.

གཤའ་ *γša* I. 1. also *γšá-ma*, *bšá-ma*, **worthy, becoming, fitting, suitable,** *˳tsé-ba mi γšai* as it is unworthy, unbecoming, improper, to persecute (others) *Dzl.*; **de k̔yód-la ša yod** or **šá-če yod** *Ld.* that serves you right. — 2. **righteous, upright, honest, good,** = *skyón-med-pa*, *C.*; *blo γšá-ma* an upright, true heart, *Thgy.*; **lẹ šá-ma ǰhé'-pa** *C.* to perform a work faithfully, in good earnest.

II. **only, merely; mere, nothing but,** (= *šá-stag*) *C.*

གཤའ་དཀར་, བཤའ་དཀར་ *γša-dkár*, *bša-dkár S.g.*, *Wdṅ.*, *C.* **tin,** *W. kar-ya*; yet cf. *ža-nye.*

གཤའ་རིང་ *γša-riṅ* a long skirt or coat-tail *Sch.*

གཤག་པ་ *γšág-pa* v. *γšóg-pa.*

གཤགས་ *γšags* **right, justice,** *Lex.* and esp. *W.*; *γšags ˳byed-pa Lex.* to investigate the rightfulness (of an action), = **ye dig p̔é-če** *W.*; **ṭim-šág táṅ-če** to administer justice, to sit in judgment **ṭim-šág-taṅ-k̔an** judge, **šag (go-) lóg táṅ-če** to warp justice, to judge contrary to justice and right; **ṭim-šág žú-če** to go to law, to bring an action, **šág-pon** superior judge, chief-justice, *W* — *bka-γšágs* v. *bka* extr.

གཤང་ γšaṅ a musical instrument, esp. used by the Bonpo, *Glr.*, *γšaṅ ˳ḱról-ba* to play on that instrument *Mil.*

གཤང་བ་ *γšáṅ-pa Sch.* = *bšáṅ-ba.*

གཤང་གཤོང་ *γšaṅ-γšóṅ* rough, rugged places or tracts *Cs:*

གཤད་པ་ *γšád-pa* 1. = *šód-pa* **to comb.** — 2. = *˳ĉád-pa* II., **to explain, to relate.**

གཤམ་ *γšam* 1. **the lower part** of a thing, *γšám-du* a. adv. **down.** b. postp. **under, below, beneath**; also adv. **farther down,** more towards the end, in the course of; **examples** v. sub *leu*; postp. *dei γšám-du* under it. — 2. **barren,** *B.* and col., *mo-γšám, rgod-γšám, ba-γšám* a barren woman, mare, cow.

གཤར་ *γšar Sch.*: a certain style of writing.

གཤས་མ་ *γšás-ma Sch.* = *γšá-ma.*

གཤིགས་ *γšig-pa* v. *γšib-pa.*

གཤིན་པ་ *γšín-pa* 1. also *γšín-po* **good, fine,** *žiṅ šin-pa B., C.* a fertile field, *sa-ṗyógs γšín-pa* a rich country *Stg.*; *γšín-par rmó-ba* to plough well; *γšín-sa* 1. fertile field or land. 2. v. *γšín-po.* — 2. = *γším-pa.*

གཤིན་པོ་ *γšín-po* **one deceased, a dead man,** *γšín-mo* a dead woman, e.g. **šin-mó ǰor-zóm** the deceased, the late Jorzóm; it may have reference to the body, as well as to the soul, or to both together. — *γšin-rje* the god of the dead, of the lower regions, of hades, also regarded as the judge of the dead, *Ssk.* **यम**; *γšin-rjei γšed* a. id., Yama the destroyer. b. the destroyer of Yama, Siwa; *Ssk.* **यमान्तक**. cf. also *Schl.* 93. **ĉin-dúd** **knot,** opp. to **ṭol-dúd** **a bow,** a slip-knot *W.* — *γšin-˳dré* the soul as a ghost or spectre *Sch.* — *γšin-˳prás* the convulsive motions, the writhings of a dying creature. — *γšin-zas* food presented to the Lamas when a person has died (*Cs.*: food prepared, or exposed for the dead?). *šin-sa* 1. **burying ground, cemetery,** 2. fertile field.

གཤིབ(ས)་པ་, བཤིབ(ས)་པ་ *γšib(s)-pa, bšib(s)-pa,* also *γšig-pa,* 1. *Sch.*: to range, **to compare**; *Ld.* to be ranged, to draw up in files; **gral γšig rgyáb-pa* C.* to induce assembled people by means of a stick to stand or sit closer; cf. *žal-bdág.* — 2. *ral-gri γšib-pa Wdṅ.?*

གཤིམ་པ་, གཤིན་པ་ *γšim-pa, γšin-pa Sch.*: 'ground, crushed'

གཤིམས་བཟང་བ་ *γšims-bzáṅ-ba Sch.* to be irresolute, unsettled in opinion; to be distrustful, suspicious.

གཤིས་ *γšis*, often also *bšis*, 1. **nature, temper, natural disposition,** *γšis-ka* col. id., *raṅ-γšis yin* it is their nature, their natural disposition *Mil.* — *γšis-kyis* by the very nature of the case, without secondary causes, naturally, quite of itself *Mil.*; *γšis-ñán Mil., Do.* was also explained by *rgyú-med-par,* prob. implying merely: not having been one's self the efficient cause. — 2. **person, body,** *γšis ṫams-ĉád-du ˳byúg-go* they anointed the whole body *Do.*

གཤུང་བ་ *γšuṅ-ba Cs.* to rebuke, reproach; the *Lexx.* explain it by: *šúb-bur smád-pa* to blame in a whisper, i.e. behind a person's back.

གཤུམ་པ་ *γšúm-pa* v. *šúm-pa.*

གཤེ་བ་ *γšé-ba,* pf. *γšes,* **to abuse, revile,** with *la, Dzl.* and elsewh.; *γše yaṅ slar mi γšé-ba* even when reviled, (one should) not revile again (rule for monks) *Cs.*

གཤེག་པ་ *γšég pa* v. *γšóg-pa.*

གཤེགས་པ་ *γšégs-pa* (imp. *γšegs, Dulva* in *Feer Introd.* etc. p. 68; but *šog* is prob. the original and older form), *Bal.* **šags-ĉas*,* resp. **to go, to go away,** opp. to *˳byón-pa* to come *Glr.*; in other passages **to come** *Dzl.*; *γšegs-grábs mdzad* he made preparations for setting out *Mil.*; *nám-mḱa-la ˳ṗúr-žiṅ γšegs* he ascended to heaven *Tar.*; *slar γšégs-pa* **to return, to come back.** *γšégs-pa* is col. seldom used, but often in books, and mostly of Buddha and great saints; *bdé-bar γšégs-pa* **to die,** of saints and kings; *sku γšegs-pa Glr.*; *dgúṅ-du* or *dgúṅ-la γšégs-pa Mil*, *mḱar γšégs-pa Glr.,* id.; *bdé(-bar)-γšegs(-pa)* as partic. = **सुगत Buddha;** *de-bžin-γšegs-pa* **तथागत** acc. to the explanation now generally accepted: he that walks in the same ways (as his predecessors), a very frq. epithet of the Buddhas. — *γšégs-bskyés* parting-(beer-) cup, parting-feast or treat *Mil.* — *γšegs-zón Cs.* a banquet or dinner after the death of a great person.

གཤེད་མ་ *γšed-ma*, rarely *γšed*, 1. **executioner, hangman** *Stg.*; *γšéd-ma skó-ba* to engage a hangman, i.e. to pay a murderer *Glr*; fig.: *p̓an ťsun γčig-gi γšed γčig-gis byá-ste Wdṅ.* prob. means: one destroying the other. — 2. in a special sense: **gods of vengeance**, tormenting the condemned in hell, or fighting against evil spirits, *drag-γšéd Schl.*

གཤེན་རབ(ས)་ *γšen-ráb(s) Glr.*, the founder of the Bon-religion, his full name being *bon γšen-rabs-γyuṅ-drúṅ C.* prob. identic with the Chinese philosopher *Lao-tse* — *ye-γšen Mil.* id. — *sgrub-γšén* the Bon-doctrine (opp. to *dam-čós Mil.*)

གཤེར(བ་) *γšér(-ba) B., C.*: **wet, wetness;** *γšér-ba, γšér-pa, γšér-po* adj., *γšér-bar ₒgyúr-ba* to get thoroughly wet, to be drenched *Dzl.*, to get moist, to be moistened; *γšér-bar byéd-pa C., B.*, **šér-pa čó-če** *W.* to wet, to moisten. In *C.* and in *B.* *γšer-ba* seems to be mainly used for **wet**, in *W.* for **moist.**

གཤེར་བ་ *γšér-ba* I. sbst. and adj. v. the preceding article.

II. vb.. 1. **to ask for, beg for,** *šér-te ťob soṅ* I got it by asking for it (I did not buy it) *W.* — 2. **to ask** **šér-len-pa** (lit. *γšér-len-pa*) **to interrogate, to question, to try** (judicially); as partic. and sbst.; the examining or criminal judge *C.* — 3. = *γšór-ba* **to measure** *C.*

གཤོ་བ་ *γšó-ba*, pf. *γšos*, 1. **to pour out, to pour away** *C.*, prob. the same as *bšo-ba.* — 2 (?) **k̓a šós-te k̓yer** he has **alienated** him, enticed him to join his own party *Ld.*

གཤོ་མོ་ *γšó-mo* **lever** **šó-mo gyáb-pa** *C., W*, **taṅ-če** *W.*, **šó-mo kán-pa** *W.*, **kémpa** *C.* to put a lever to (a thing).

གཤོག་པ་ *γšóg-pa* I. sbst. v. *šóg-pa.*

II. vb., also *bšóg-pa, γšág-pa, γšég-pa, ₒčégs-pa*, pf. *γšags, bšags*, fut. *γšag, bšag*, imp. *γšog, Pth.*, 1. **to cleave, to split,** *šiṅ* wood, *rnám-par* entirely, *ťsál-pa bžir* into four pieces *Glr*, *dúm-bur* into pieces; *sgo γšág-pa* **to break open** a door (with a hatchet) *Pth.*; **to break or pierce through,** *dkyil* through the middle *Mil.*, *gaṅs bšóg-pa Mil.* to break through the snow, by means of yaks sent in advance to beat a path (v. *Huc.*), *lam bšog-pa* in a gen. sense: to beat a path; *lam mi šog* or *ma šog-par ₒdug Glr.* the road is not practicable; *sóg-les γšég-pa Thg.* to saw lengthwise; — *γšeg-pa* is also used for: **to rend, to tear,** to make a rent or slit into a dress etc. *C., W.* — 2. **to confess,** *sdig-pa, nyés-pa, ltúṅ-ba* to confess a sin, and thus **to expiate it,** which two, according to the views of a Buddhist, are always united, at least as it regards lighter transgressions. Hence *sdig-pa bšags* frq. means: the sin is atoned for, is blotted out, and *γšeg-pa* is the usual word for **'to forgive'.** *sdig-bšágs* **atonement, expiation,** *sbrul bsád-pai-sdig-bšágs-su* as an atonement for having killed a serpent *Glr*; *mťol-bšágs* = *sdig-bšágs, mťol-bšágs-la ša-k̓óg ₒbúl-ba* to offer a killed animal (a sheep) as an atonement *Mil.*; *sdig-bšags-smón-lam Glr.* **penitential prayer.**

གཤོང(ས)་ *γšoṅ(s)* v. *šoṅ.*

གཤོད་པ་ *γšód-pa* to comb *Cs.*

གཤོན་པ་ *γšón-pa Cs.*: = *skyón-pa* to put on (?).

གཤོབ་ *γšob* = *šob.*

གཤོམ་པ་ *γšóm-pa Thgy.* = *šóm-pa.*

གཤོར་ *γšor Sch.* a basin or **reservoir** of water, seems to be not much known; but in *Zam. yúr-bai γšor* is to be found.

གཤོར་བ་ *γšór-ba* I. vb., *C.* also *γšér-ba*, pf. fut. *bšar, bšor*, 1. **to count,** e.g. sheep, by letting them pass one by one through one's hands, the beads of a rosary (through one's fingers), hence *čos-brjod-bšar-sbyaṅ maṅ-po byed* to read prayers etc. (cf. *sbyaṅ-ba*, 3). — 2. **to measure,** *bres* by the peck *Lex.*; **to weigh;** *γšér-la rá-gan γšár-ba* to weigh out (to exchange) brass for gold. — 3. **to hunt, to chase,** = *ₒčór-ba, ri-dwags* game *Lex.*; *nya-yšór-ba* **to fish** *Dzl.* — 4. *Sch.* to cut through (?).

II. adj., also *yšér-ba,* **rough, bristly, shaggy,** *skra*, *spu Stg.*, opp. to *ₒǰam-po* (*Sch.* rough, gruff, rude?)

གཤོལ་ *yšol* **plough** *Glr.*, *ṫoṅ*, *ṫóṅ - yšol* id. The plough in India and Tibet consists only of a crooked beam, *yšol - mda,* (without wheels) with the share (*yšol-lčágs, toṅ-lčágs*) at the lower end; *yšol-mdá ₒdzin-pa* **to plough,** lit. to take hold of the plough-beam.

གཤོལ་པོ་ *yšól-po* **poplar-tree** *C.*

གཤོས་པ་ *yšos-pa* 1. *yšo-ba* and *bšo-ba.*

བཤའ་ *bša* 1. in *bgo-bša* **portion, share, allowance, ration** *Lex.*, evidently a secondary form of *šas.* — 2. *Dzl.* ༢༧༠, 1 **inundation,** flood; *šwa*, the reading of the manuscript of Kyelang, seems to be preferable.

བཤའ་བ་ *bšá-ba,* pf. *bšas,* **to slaughter, to kill** (animals for food); in a story of *Glr.* it follows the slaughtering and must be understood to denote the cutting to pieces of the killed animal; but our Lama preferred to read *bšús-pa* to skin.

བཤའ་མ་ *bšá-ma* v. *yšá-ma.*

བཤག་པ་ *bšág-pa* v. *yšóg-pa.*

བཤང་བ་ *bšáṅ-ba, Sch.* also *yšaṅ-ba,* alvine discharges, *bšáṅ-ba ₒbyín-pa* to make open bowels, of food, medicines *Med.*; *bšaṅ-dgág* **constipation** *Med.*; *bšaṅ-yči* excrements and urine, *bšaṅ - yčis skú-ba* to dirty therewith *Dzl.*; *bšaṅ -yči bsri-ba* to retain stool and urine *Sch.*; *bšaṅ-lám* the anus *Med.*

བཤངས་པ་ *bšáṅs - pa* **leaky, leaking, full of crevices,** **ču-zóm nyi-ma-la bór-na šaṅ dug** *W.* the water-pail will become leaky, if it is left standing in the sun.

བཤད་པ་ *bšád-pa* (prob. pf. of *ₒčád-pa* q.v.) 1. **to explain,** expound; **to declare,** pronounce, *čos-bšád-pa* to explain religion, to lecture on religious subjects, **to preach;** *ₒči-ba daṅ ₒdrar bšad* he must be set down for dead *Wdṅ.*; *bú-mo skyé-bar bšad* this **indicates** that a girl will be born *Lt.*; *bšád-kyis mi láṅ-ṅo* it is **ineffable, unspeakable; to say,** *ₒbáb-par bšad* they say it flows down *Wdṅ.*, *ṫá-mar bšad* he is said to be on the lowest stage *Thgy.*, *ṅán-par bšad* it is said or declared to be bad, *smán-du bšad* it is **mentioned** as a medicine *Wdṅ.*; **to tell, to relate,** col. the usual word. — 2. **to comb,** v. *šód-pa.* — *bšad-grwa* **school-room, lecture-room.** — **šad-dón** *W.* the subject of a talk. *bšad-yám* a public lecture *Sch.* (?). *bšad-ló byéd-pa* to make many words *Mil.*

བཤན་པ་ *bšán-pa* v *šán-pa.*

བཤར་ *bšar,* supine of *bšá-ba.*

བཤར་བ་ *bšár-ba* v *yšór-ba.*

བཤལ་བ་ *bšál-ba* 1. **to wash, to wash out or off, to clean by washing, to rinse,** plates, dishes, etc. — 2. *ltó-ba bšál-ba* **to purge** the body, hence in gen. *bšál-ba* to suffer from diarrhoea, and *W.* col. **šal** **diarrhoea, looseness, flux,** **šal rag** I have d., **šal dug** he suffers from d., **šal yoṅ** d. begins; *bšal-ₒǰám* a mild d., *bšal-ₒṗyés*(?) a violent flux *Sch.*; *bšal - nád* indisposition from d.; *bšal-byéd B.*, *bšal-smán B.* and col. **laxative,** aperient medicine.

བཤས་པ་ *bšás-pa* v. *bšá-ba.*

བཤིག་པ་ *bšig-pa* v. *ₒdzig-pa* I.

བཤིབ་པ་ *bšib-pa* v. *yšib-pa.*

བཤུ་བ་ *bšú-ba* v. *šú-ba.*

བཤུག་པ་ *bšúg-pa* to sell *Cs.*

བཤུད་པ་ *bšúd-pa* 1. v. *šud-pa.* — 2. *Sch.*: to purify by fire, *bšúd-me* purifying fire (?).

བཤུབ་པ་ *bšúb-pa* to put into the scabbard, **to sheathe** *Sch.*

བཤུམ་པ་ *bšúm-pa* — བཤེར་བ་ *bšér - ba* v. ཤུམ་པ་ *šúm-pa* etc.

བཤེའུ་ *bšeu* (cf. *bša, šwa*) **inundation, flood** *Mil.*

བཤེས་པ་ *bšés-pa*, prop. pf. of *šés-pa*, **to know** (a person or thing), **to be acquainted,** *dan* with *Dzl.*; *ɣnyen-bšés* **a relation, relative.** *ɣnyen-bšes-la ṗán-ɣtogs-par sems-so* they are intent on being of use to their relatives *Dzl.*; *ɣnyen* and *bšes* **may** also be separated: *k̔yód-la ɣnyen med bšes kyan med, Mil.*; *bšes-ɣnyén* on the other hand means: **friend,** *dgé-bai bšes-ɣnyén* (*Ssk.* **कल्याणमित्र**) friend to virtue, **spiritual adviser,** opp. to *mi-dgéi bšes-ɣnyén* **seducer,** *Glr.* (cf. *sdig-pai grógs-po*); *dge-bšés* 1. = *dgé-bai bšes-ɣnyén.* 2. = *dge-bsnyén* **lay-brother.** — *no bšés* v. *ńo-šés.* — *mdza-bšés* **friend.**

བཤོ་བ་ *bšó-ba*, pf. *bšos*, 1. also *ɣšó-ba*, **to pour out** *Lex.* — 2. **to lie with,** to have sexual intercourse with, = *ₒk̔rig-pa byéd-pa*, e.g.: *de dan bšós-pas bu skyes* after having slept with him, she bore him a son *Pth.*; **to engender, to generate, to beget** (v.a.), *ṗág-rdzis bšós-pai bu* the son begotten by the swine-herd *Pth.*, (*bšo-ba* seems not to be considered obscene).

བཤོག་པ་ *bšóg-pa* v. *ɣšóg-pa.*

བཤོད་པ་ *bšód-pa* = *bšád-pa*, **šo'-ri** *C.* **rumour, report.** **šo-ri-la dhé-ḍa zer dúg-te yi' mi če** though it is rumoured I cannot believe it *C.*

བཤོར་བ་ *bšór-ba* v. *ɣšór-ba.*

བཤོར་པོ་ *bšór-po C.*, *W.* **liberal, munificent.** *Schr.*: squanderer, spendthrift(?).

བཤོལ་བ་ *bšól-ba* 1. **to put off, postpone, defer, delay,** *bód-la ₒgró-ba* the going to Tibet *Glr.*; absolutely: *bšól-ba bzan* it is good to wait; — **to prolong,** e.g. *mi žig-gi ₒtsó-ba* the life of a person (by a reprieve) *Dzl.*, also **to grant, to allow** viz. a respite, a reprieve, *bdág-la žag bdun žig bšól-te* granting me a respite of seven days *Dzl.*; **to stop, detain,** e.g. the sun in his course *Thgy.*, a traveller wishing to set out *Pth.*; **to omit,** to neglect doing *Mil.* (ni f.); *ṗyi bšól-ba* **to put off, postpone,** *ṗyi-bšól byéd-pai gán-zag* a person that is always postponing his religious duties *Mil.*; *čós-la ṗyi-bšól byar mi run Mil.* there should be no putting off, whenever religion is concerned; *bšol ₒdebs-pa* and *ₒtebs-pa* = *bšol-ba* frq.; *bšol ma ṫebs* he could not be detained, kept back, diverted from his purpose *Pth.*; relatives are called *bdúd-kyi bšol-ₒdébs* a hinderance on the way of the believer, caused by the devil.

བཤོས་ *bšos* resp. for *zan* or *spags*, **food, victuals, provisions of the table;** *bšos-la ɣšegs-pa* to go to dine, to go to dinner *Dzl.*; *dge-ₒdún-la bšos ɣsol-ba* to treat the priests to a meal *Dzl.*; now almost exclusively applied to food **offered to the gods,** = *lha-bšos*; *bšos-bu Mil.* offering-morsels, e.g. small pieces of butter offered to the gods or the ghosts.

བཤོས་པ་ *bšos-pa* **begotten, generated,** v. *bšo-ba.*

ས

ས *sa* 1. the letter **s**, the sharp English *s*, in *C.* distinguished from **z**, (which is sounded there also as sharp s) only by the following vowel being high-toned. — 2. num.: 28.

ས་ *sa* 1. **earth,** as elementary substance, *sa čʼu me rlun* earth, water, fire, air, the four elements, *sa nyúń-zad čig* a small quantity of earth, opp. to: *sa čén-poi sa* the mass of the whole earth *Dzl.*; *rdzá-sa* clay, argillaceous earth, **bé-sa** *W.* sand and earth, *šág-sa* flint and earth; also for **ore, metal** (like *rdo*), *ɣsér-sa* gold-ore, *dńúl-sa* silver-ore *Cs.*; *k̔yim-sa* sweepings, offscourings;

the ground, *sá-la* (*W.* also **sę ḱá-na**) *ₒdúg-pa* to sit on the ground, *sá-la ltúṅ-ba, gyél-ba* to fall to the ground; *sa-₄óg, sa-stéṅ, sa-blá,* under, on, above the ground; *sa-₄og-spyód* the Nagas (*klu*); **the earth,** the globe which we inhabit, usually more accurately *sa čén-po* v. above. — 2. **place, spot, space,** = *ynas,* and col. more in use than this, *rwai sa ₒbúr-ba Stg.* 'swollen in the places of the horns', i.e. men that had been oxen in a former life, and in consequence of it are distinguished by little knobs corresponding to their former horns; **póg-sa ghá-la dug* C.* where have you been hit or hurt? *ₒdá-sa* and *ₒbém-sa* sharp-shooters' stand and place of the target *C.*; *yod-sa* the place where a person lives, (in the old classical style usually expressed by *gaṅ-na-ba*); **čin-taṅ-sa** vulg. 1. orifice of the urethra. 2. privy, water-closet; *ṅá-la grós-ₒdri-sa čig yod* I have a place where to ask advice, I have an oracle *Glr.*; in a wider sense: **occasion, opportunity, possibility,** *lús-la rég-sa med* one cannot get near him *Glr.*, *rje ḱyód-kyi ységs-sa dé-na med* you cannot go to that place, Sir! *Mil.*; *nor-gyis blú-sa med* you cannot ransom yourself by money *Mil.*; also with respect to men: *ṅa yžán-la zér-sa* (*žú-sa, ré-sa*) *med* I cannot address myself to any body else with my words (requests, hopes); **place, step, degree, grade,** *čun-ma čé-sar bzuṅ* he took and treated his second wife in the place of the first, i.e. he showed the second the honour due to the first; *sa-bču* v. compounds. — 3. it is also said to be the name of a quadruped of the size and appearance of a badger, but not identic with *ysa Sik.*

Comp. *sa-dkár* = *dkar-rtsi Cs.* – *sa-skám Sch.* arid soil, dry ground, **steppe.** — *sa-skyóṅ, sa-skyór Lex.* protector of the earth i.e. king. — *sa-ḱu* made dirty by earth, dust etc., **soiled, turbid.** — **sa-ḱyád* W.* (for *ynas B., sá-ča C.*) **place,** **sa-ḱyád kám-po** a dry place, also: the dry land; **a piece of ground,** **sa-ḱyád čig taṅ** he gave him landed property, **sa-ḱyád-di dág-po** landlord; **dwelling-place, place of residence,** **ḱyód-di sa-ḱyád gá-ru yod** where is your home? — *sa-ḱyáb Cs.* = *sa-bdag.* — *sa-ḱyon Cs.*: 'the earth's extension or compass'. — **sa-ṭa** (*sa-ḱra*) **map** *C.* — *sá-mḱan* one who is well acquainted with a particular place or country, a guide *Dzl.* — *sa-mḱar Glr.* a castle the walls of which consist for the most part of earth. — *sa-gyóṅ Sch.* hard ground. — *sa-dgá* and *sa-dgyés Lex.* = *ku-mu-da.* — *sa-dgra Glr.* the enemy of a country, i.e. in many cases nothing but a demon. — **saṅ-gúl* W.* earthquake. — *sa-ṅós* surface of the earth. — *sa-sṅón Cs.* blue earth. — *sa-bčú*, दशभूमि, acc. to one explanation the ten steps or degrees of perfection which must be attained by those striving after the prize of Buddhaship; *sa ṫób-pa* to reach one step (viz. the first) *Do.*; *sa čén-po* a high degree, e.g. the eighth *Thgy.*; *Foucaux* enumerates them all *Gyatch. Transl.* p. 3. According to another supposition *sa-bču* signifies the ten worlds or dominions of the Bodhisattvas *Was.* (124). — *sa-čá Glr., Mil., C.* **place, country** (*W.* **sa-ḱyád**). — *sa-čen* 1. v. above *sa* 1.; 2. v. *sa-bču*; 3. v. *sa-skya.* — *sa-stéṅ* v. above *sa* 1. — *sa-dúg* evaporation, damp, injurious to those sleeping on the bare ground. — *sa-dó* (v. *do-po*) half a load of earth, a sackful of earth, being half the load of a donkey *Mil.* — **sa-dóṅ* W.* **pit,** hole. — *sa-bdág* 1. **landlord,** master or lord of the ground, sovereign *Stg.*, *sá-yi bdág-po sá-yi rje* are words used in addressing a king *Mil.* 2. more frq.: **god of the ground** of the country, supposed to be a jealous and angry being, of terrific appearance, to whom on many occasions sacrifices are brought, and who prob. was worshipped already before the spread of Buddhism cf. *Schl.* 271. — *sa-mda* 1. mouse-trap, also a large trap for catching leopards and other animals. 2. a fabulous plant (?). — *sa-rdó* a stone of earthy fracture; earth and stones; **sa-dó da tsi-wa** to slight, to disregard, to neglect *C.* — *sa-ynás* (= *ynás-sa*) **place, region, country, landscape,** *nyams-dgá-bai sa-ynás* a lovely landscape *Glr.* — *sa-sna-lṅá* soil of five different places. — *sá-*

pa inhabitant of the earth, of our globe *Sch.* — *sa-spyód* possessing the earth, man *Cs.* — *sa-p̓ág Glr.*, prob. = *so-p̓ág* brick, dried in the sun. — *sa-p̓úg* cavern, cave. — *sa-p̓yógs* **place, region, tract,** *˳jigs-pai sa-p̓yogs* an unsafe place or region *Thgy.* — **sá-bi-lig** *W.* 1. **mouse, rat** 2. *Ld.* also **bar, bolt,** door-bar? — *sa-blá* v. above *sa* 1. — *sa-dbáṅ Cs.* = *sa-bdág*, v. above *sa* no. 1. — *sa-˳bol Cs.* soft earth. — *sa-ma-rdó* or *sa-min-rdó-min Sch.*: 'neither earth nor stone', i.e. a kind of conglomerate. — *sa-mín Sch.*: 'white sand' (??). — *sa-mós Sch.* = *kú-mu-da* or *úd-pa-la.* — *sa-dmár* red earth; *sa-dmar-˳bóṅ* n. of a monastery in the neighbourhood of Darjeeling, situated on a mountain-slope, which consists of a red-coloured soil (*Hook.* I, 171 calls it Simonbong). — **sa-tse** *W.* sand or gravel found in roasted barley etc. — *sa-rtsig, sa-rtsis, sa-tsig* **stage, post-station.** — *sa-mtsams*, *W.* **san-tsam**, **border, frontier, boundary** *Glr.*; *sa-mtsáms ˳gégs-pa* to fix the borders or limits, to mark out the boundaries. — *sa-žag* dust floating on water *Pth.* — *sa-γži* **ground, soil, footing, floor; estate** *Tar.* 99. — *sa-˂óg* v. above *sa* 1, *sa-˂og-spyód* the Nagas (*klu*). — *sa-yáṅs* a wide place or space, an extensive tract of land. — *sa-yúl* = *sa-čá Glr.* — *sa-γyos, sa γyó-ba* earthquake. — *sa-rigs* species of earth. — *sa-ris Pth.*? — *sa-rúl Cs.* rotten or decayed earth (?) — **sa-ró** *W.* **rubbish,** (*Sch.* fallow-ground, fallow-field?) — *sa-lám Mil.*, perh. for *sa-bčui lam.* — *sa-šún Sch.* crust of the earth (?) — *sa-bšin* fertile land, rich soil. — *sa-srán* hard ground. — *sa-srúṅ Cs.* = *sa-bdag* v. above *sa* no. 1. — *sa-srós* evening twilight, dusk *Cs.*

ས་སྐྱ *sa-skyá* a large monastery, S.W. of Lhasa, also the Lamas belonging to it, clothed in red, *Wts.* 132. *Schl.* 73. *sa (-skya)-čén(-po)* honorary title of the Lama *Kun-dga-snyiṅ-po*, born in the year 1090 after Christ; *sa-skyá páṇḍi-ta* a famous Lama of this monastery, born 1180.

ས་ག *sá-ga* n. of one of the lunar mansions, v. *rgyu-skár* no. ༡༦, and hence also n. of a month, part of March and April, ni f.

སཱ་ག་ར *sā-ga-ra Skr.* **the sea.**

ས་གུ་ཙེ *sa-gu-tsé* **worm** *C.*

ས་ཏྲ *sa-tra Tar.* 184 and 187, *Schf.*: **diploma, patent,** not to be found in *Ssk.* dictionaries.

ས་ཐེལ་ནག་པོ *sa-tel-nág-po* deity of the *Hór-pa.*

ས་བོན *sá-bon* 1. **seed,** *sá-bon ˳débs-pa* to sow, *sá-bon btáb-mk̓an* sower, *sá-bon-du byéd-pa* to use as seed-corn *Dzl.*; **seed-corn, corn, grain,** also green corn, *sá-bon tsám-la rṅá-ba* to mow off as if it were green corn *Ma.* — 2. = *k̓u-k̓rág*, v. *k̓ú-ba Med.*; also = *k̓ú-ba*, e.g. *sá-bon ˳dzin-pa* **conception** *S.g.*, *sa-bon zág-pa emissio seminis Glr.*; fig.: **propagation, progeny, issue,** *sá-bon byed mi nus* then no propagation can take place; *sa-bon čig žog* 'propagate thyself!' — 3. fig.: *dgé-bai sá-bon* the seeds or germs of virtue, *sdig-pai sá-bon* the germs of vice, *da sá-bon ma bskyéd-na* if I do not now produce seeds viz. of virtue (else more frq.: 'a root of virtue') *Dzl.*; *byaṅ-čúb-kyi sá-bon Tar.* — 4. *W.* **soap,** acc. to the Hind. سابن, more accurately صابن.

ས་འཚོ་མ *sa-˳tsó-ma* Gopa, the wife of Buddha.

ས་ཡ *sá-ya* **a million;** this number, however, is not much in use with Indians and Tibetans, whereas the lāk, *˳bum*, 100,000, frq. serves to represent a very large sum.

ས་ཡབ *sa-yáb* (sovereign, 'father to a country') a not unfrequent perversion of the title *sa-heb W.*

ས་ར་སོ་རེ *sa-ra-so-ré* also *sar-sór*, coarse-grained and fine-grained (corn, seeds etc.) mixed together *W.*

ས་རི *sa-rí* n. of a lunar mansion, v. *rgyu-skár* ༡༥.

སཱ་ལ *sā-la Ssk.* n. of an Indian tree, *Shorea robusta*, with which also some superstitious fables are connected.

ས་ལང་གི *sa-láṅ-gi*, *Hind.* **सारङ्गी**, a kind of violin,

ས་ལུ *sa-lu Ssk.* **शाली**, *Oryza sativa*, **rice,** as a plant; acc. to *Sch.* also Indian corn (?).

སལེ་སྦྲམ་ *sa-le-sbrám* (cf. *sbram-bu*) *Wdn.* **fine gold.**

སཧེབ་ *sá-heb*, col. *sāb*, *sab*, *Arab.* صَاحِب, formerly in India title of Moslems of high rank, now title of every European, = **gentleman, sir.**

སག་ *sag*, also *nya-sag Cs.*, 1. brawn, callosity; *Sch.* also: hair-side (of a skin); *sag-čan* brawny, *sag-₀túg* a thick brawn. — 2. *W.* **scale,** (of a fish) *nya-sag-čan* scaly.

སག་གདར་ *sag-γdár C.*, **sab-dár** *W.*, *γsag-brdár Sch.* **a rasp,** *sag-γdár rgyag-pa* **to rasp.**

སག་པ་ *ság-pa C.* a little bubble, **sag sag zér-wa** to sparkle, to effervesce.

སག་རམ་རྩི་ *sag-ram-rtsí* **sulphuric acid** *Cs.*

སག(ས)་རི་ *sag(s)-rí* **shagreen.**

སག་ལད་ *sag-lád*, *Pers.* سقلات, 1. fine **cloth,** made of *lé-na*, *C.* **go-nam** (v. *snam-bu*). European broadcloth *W.* — 2. round or twisted lace, round tape, strips of cloth set with spangles? *W.*

སང་ *sań* 1. *B.*, *C.* **to-morrow,** *sań-nyin* id. *Glr.*; *sáń-gi γdúgs-la* for to-morrow noon *Dzl.*; *sań nán-par Cs.*, *sań sńá-bar Glr.* to-morrow morning; also absolutely: on the following day *Pth.*, *dei-sań* id.; *sań-p̀ód*, more frq. *sań-lo* next year; *sań-p̀ód da tsám-du* a year hence, this time a year. — 2. *W.* particle denoting the comparative degree, inst. of *las* or *pas* of *B.*, **de sań i' gyál-la** this is better than that. — 3. *Ld.*, *Balt.* sometimes for *yań.*

སཾ་སྐྲི་ཏའི་སྐད་ *sań-kritai skad* **the Sanskrit language** *Glr.*

སང་གི་ཀ་ *sáń-gi-ka*(?) a greenish stone of which knife-handles and similar articles are said to be made *W.*

སང་ང་ *sań-ńá*, *sań-ńé*, *sań-sún Ld.* **secretly, privately, whisperingly, by report,** = *sám-sum.*

སང་སེང་ *sań-séń* **hiding-place, chink, crevice,** *k̀yim-gyi* of the house *Stg.*, for hiding money and treasures, = *sbugs*; *gós-kyi* folds of the dress, that are a haunt of vermin.

སང་བ་ *sáń-ba*, pf. *(b)sańs*, fut. *(b)sań*, 1. **to do away with,** to remove (dirt etc.), **to cleanse,** cf. *₀tsáń-ba*, where also examples are given. — 2. in a more gen. sense: **to take away** or **off,** *k̀ebs sáń-ba* to uncover; **k̀o-la nyi' sań soń** *C.* his sleep is gone, he cannot sleep. — 3. **to spoil,** to render unfit or useless, **wó-ma sań soń** *C.* the milk is spoiled, **zem sań soń** the cask or tub leaks *C.* Cf. *seń.*

སངས་རྒྱས་ *sańs-rgyás* the Tibetan equivalent for बुद्ध; as to the etymology of the word v. sub *₀tsáń-ba.* The first historical Buddha is *Sańs-rgyas šā-kya t̀úb-pa*, whose family name is *Gaú-ta-ma* and his personal name *Don-grúb*, सिद्धार्थ, which, however, is not much used. In course of time several imaginary predecessors were given to him: *₀Od-srúń*, *Gser-t̀úb* and *₀Kor-ba-₀ǰig*, as having existed and reigned in former periods of the world. A successor also, *Byáms-pa*, was assigned to him, of whom it is supposed that he will reign at the period following this present one. According to others, however, *Sākyat̀ubpa* was already the seventh Buddha that appeared on earth, the four above-named having been preceded by *Tams-čad-skyób*, *Gtsug-tor-čan* and *Rnam-par-γzigs*, this last one being the first of them all. These seven Buddhas then are comprised under the name of *Sańs-rgyas-rabs-bdún.* — But the fertile imagination of devote Buddhists has further increased the number of future Buddhas to not less than one thousand (?), appropriate names for each of them have been invented, and Prof. Schmidt has thought it worth his while, to have these thousand names reprinted in a special pamphlet. Mysticism, however, generally knows only of the five first-named Buddhas (*Gautama*, his three predecessors and his first successor) and to each of these five 'human' Buddhas a celestial Buddha corresponds, called 'Dhyani Buddha' or the Buddha of contemplation, whilst to every Dhyani Buddha again his Dhyani Bodhisattwa is associated. In later times there is even mentioned a supreme or highest god, Adi-Buddha, *tóg-mai Saṅs-rgyás*, which doctrine, however, seems not to have been generally accepted. — Cf. *Köpp.* II, 15—29.

སད་ *sad* **frost, cold air, cold, coldness,** *sád-kyis ˳kyér-ba* to be destroyed by frost *Glr.*; often in conjunction with *sér-ba*, hail.

སད་པ་ *sád-pa* I. **to examine, see, try, test,** *kyod bzód-dam mi bzod sád-par byao* I shall see, whether you are patient *Dzl.*; *ɣser ltar sád-nas mṅón-par ˳gyur* like gold, it is approved by testing *Dzl.*; *nyáms-sad-pa* v. *nyams*; *sád-mi mi bdun* 'the seven men of trial', i.e. the seven most distinguished and talented among the young Tibetans sent by king *Kri-sroṅ-lde-btsan* to 'Kanpo Bodhisattwa, for being thoroughly instructed in religion and sciences *Glr.* 86, also *Tar.* 162, 22; *las sád-pai ɡáṅ-zag Mil.* a tried, a tested man?

II. frq. in conjunction with *ɣnyid*, resp. *mnal* 1. to cease to sleep, **to awake,** *rmis ma-tág-tu* directly from that dream *Dzl.*, *ɣzim-pa-las* from sleep *Dzl.* — 2. **to rouse,** from sleep, **to waken,** more precisely *sád-par byéd-pa*; also fig.: *dgé-bai rtsá-ba* good, virtuous, emotions *Tar.*

སན་གིན་ *san-gin, Pers.* سنگین, **bayonet** *W.*

སབ་ *sab*, col. for *sa-heb.*

སམ་ཏ་ *sam-ta Schr.*, *brtsam-grwa Cs.*, others: *bsám-kra, sáb-dra*, pocket-book, note-book, memorandum-book, tablets *C.*, *W.* (*Cs.* a small writing-desk?).

སམ་དལ་ *sam-dál Ld.*, *yar-sam Lh.* **mustaches.**

སམ་(མ་)སུམ་(མེ་) *sam(-ma)-sum(-me)* with a low voice, **lowly, softly,** e.g. **zér-če**, from politeness etc.; **sam-súm zer** speak in a low voice! *W.*

སར་ *sar* 1. termin. of *sa*, *čé-sar ˳dón-pa Cs.* to promote to high rank or dignity, *sar-ɣnas-dpá-bo* (in a hymn) was explained by: *sa bčú-la ɣnás-pai dpá-bo* i.e. Buddha. — 2. *sár-ɣčod-pa* v. *ɣsar.* — 3. sbst. **wick** *W.*

ས་རྫི་ཀ་ *sa-rdzi-ka Ssk.* **soda,** in *Wdṅ.* it is mentioned as a plant, yielding soda.

སར་སོར་ *sar-sor* v. *sa-ra-so-re.*

སལ་བབ་ *sal-báb W.*, and prob. also *sal-sil Mil.*, gold ornament, **gold lace,** and the like, ni. f.

སལ་ལེ་བ་ *sál-le-ba* **clear, bright, brilliant** *Mil.*, *sal-lér snáṅ-ba* lighted up brilliantly, well lighted *Pth.*, *mdaṅs sal-sál* id. *Pth.*

སས་ *sas* instr. of *sa.*

སི་ *si* 1. in some parts of *Ld.* the termination of the instrum. after vowels, like *su* in *Kun.* — 2. also *si-si*, the sound of whistling through the teeth, *si-skad, si-sgra* whistling, whistle; *si-brda* whistling, whistle, as a call or sign; *si-glu* a whistled tune. — 3. num.: 58.

སཱི་ཏཱ་ *sī-tā* n. of one of the four fabulous streams of the world.

སི་རི་ *si-ri* 1. **pack-thread, twine** *C.*, *W.* — 2. **bar, bolt, door-bar,** **si-ri čúg-če* or *gyáb-če** to bolt, to bolt up, **si-ri tón-če** to unbolt, unbar *W.*

སི་རི་འབུ་ *si-ri-˳bu* **centiped** *W.*

སི་རིལ་ *si-ríl* a kind of inkhorn, case for carrying an inkstand in one's pocket *Ld.*

སི་ལ་ *si-la Ssk.* **सिल्हकी** a sort of incense.

སི་ལི་མ་ *si-li-ma* the breaking up of the ice *Sch.*

སིག་པ་ *sig-pa* **to hitch up,** to give a hitch, as porters do with a load on their back *Cs.*

སིག་བུ་ *sig-bu Sch.*, *sig-ra Schr.*, a sort of basket.

སིང་ *siṅ* v. *siṅ-siṅ.*

སིང་སྐྱུར་ *siṅ-skyúr Sch.* curdled milk, sour milk.

སིང་ག་གླིང་ *siṅ-ga-gliṅ Cs.*, *siṅ-ga-lai gliṅ Glr.*, **सिंहल, Ceylon.**

སིང་གེ་ *siṅ-ge* 1. frq. for *seṅ-ge.* — 2. v. *rtsiṅ-ge.*

སིང་བ་ *siṅ-ba* 1. vb., **bal siṅ-če** **to pick out, sort out,** wool for the third time, by which the finest is obtained. — 2. adj. in compounds: *nág-siṅ-ba* jet-black, very black *Thgy.*; *spró-siṅ-ba* v. *spro.*

སིང་བུ་ *siṅ-bu* liquor made of mare's milk, Tartar arrack *Sch.*

སིང་ཚལ་ *siṅ-tsál Ts.* **tea-pot, tea-kettle.**

སིང་ཡོལ་ *siṅ-yól* v. *seṅ-rás* in *seṅ-po.*

སིང་རི་ *siṅ-ri* 1. n. of a mountain *Glr.* — 2. = *siṅs-po.*

སིང་སིང་ *siṅ-siṅ* **thin, limpid,** of fluids *W.* (yet cf. *séṅ-po*), **siṅ čug-če** to clarify, to purify.

སིངས་པོ་ *siṅs-po* 1. adj. **thin, clear** *W.* — 2. sbst. *Cs.*, also *čaṅ(-ba)-siṅs Pth.*, *Lt.*, **ug-siṅ* Ld.* **small-beer,** the fourth infusion of 'chang', a weak beverage, without any intoxicating qualities, yet not disrelished on that account.

སིད་པ་ *sid-pa* **to whistle** *Sch.*, *sid-sgra* = *si-sgra.*

སིནྡྷུ་ར་ *sindhu-ra,* for सिन्दूर **minium,** red lead, = *li-k̔ri Glr.*

སིབ་པ་ *sib-pa* **to evaporate, to soak in, to be imbibed,** of fluids, *sib-sib* or *sib-kyis,* also *sib-kyis tím-pa* to evaporate quickly.

སིབ་བུ་ *sib-bu Lt.; Cs.:* a sort of **small-pox;** *Schr.:* **the measles.**

སིམ་པ་ *sim-pa Lex.* = *bdé-ba,* सुख, sbst. **good health, prosperity,** vb. **to be well, to be well off.**

སིམ་བིད་(ལ་) *sim-bid(-la)* adv. **sliding, gliding, slipping,** with **čá-če** to move along in this way *Ld.*

སིལ་བུ, གསིལ་བུ་ *sil-bu, ysil-bu* a little piece, **a fragment,** *ro sil-bur ˳tor* the corpse falls to pieces *Mil; sil-sil* col. id.; **sil čó-če** to reduce to small pieces, by breaking, crumbling, plucking etc. *W.*

སིལ་སྙན་ *sil-snyán* (also *sil* and *sil-sil Lex.*) **cymbal,** *lčágs-kyi sil ˳k̔ról-ba Lex., sil snyán ról-mo ˳k̔ról-ba Glr., Dzl.* to strike the cymbals; *sil-snyán-ma* a female cymbal-player *Tar.*

སིལ་མ་ *sil-ma* 1. the tinkling sound of a cymbal, *rdza-čáb sil-mas snyán-pa brjod* tunefully flows the brook over its clay-slate bed *Mil.*; *sil-čáb* gurgling water, rippling brook *Mil.*—2. also *sil-dṅúl* the rupee of Ladak, = 4 *jau,* = ¼ of an Indian rupee, **sil-ṅul gyad-di nas** a patch of barley worth 8 Silma *Ld.*

སུ་ *su* I. pron., also *su žig,* 1. interrog. pron. **who?** *˳di-na su yod* who is here? *k̔yod su yin* who are you? *su či-skad bya-ba yod* who is it and what is his name? *Mil.*; **which?** = *gaṅ, rgyál-poi bu su žig* which son of the king? *Tar., sú-rnams, sú-dag,* col. **sú-su** plural form; in certain popular phrases: **su-gyóg** race, running-match *W.*, **su tob gyáb-pa** to pounce upon, to snatch away, to plunder *C., W.*—2. correlative and indefinite pron.: *su mi di ysód-pa dé-la ... sbyín-no* to him that kills this man, I shall give ... *Stg.*; *k̔yod sṅar sú-la yaṅ ysól-ba ma btáb-bam* have not you already asked somebody before? *Dzl.* ༢༩, 14 (acc. to a better reading); *su de čáṅ-bai gán-du mčio* I shall go to him who has it *Do.*; *su t̔od-t̔ód* whom it concerns *Sch.*(?); *su yaṅ(ruṅ)* **whosoever,** whoever, any body who, also absolutely: **every, every one, all,** *sú-bas kyaṅ p̔yis* later than all (the others) *Dzl.*, when followed by a negative: **nobody,** frq.; *su byuṅ Mil.* = *su yaṅ*; *su med kyaṅ* though nobody be present *Pth.*; *su, su žig, su gaṅ* is also used for **somebody, some one, a certain** (but not frq. and more in col. or vulg. language): *su gaṅ mdzá-bo žig* a certain friend; *su sér-sna-čan žig* a (certain) miser; also in the following manner: **su čad dug su tsem dug** one cuts out, the other sews *W.*; **bóṅ-bu su lo-ču-nyi-pa, su lo-čú-pa yin** some of the donkeys are twelve, others ten years old. — II. termination: 1. of the term. after a final s, cf. *tu, du, ru.* — 2. of the instr. in *Kun.*: **'á-pa-su** from or by the father, inst. of the *p̔as* of *B.* (cf. सु in the Brāj-dialect of the Hindi). — 3. expletive after *nas Mil.* and elsewh. — III. num.: 88.

སུ་གི་ *sú-gi* vulgar corruption of *dzo-ki* q.v.

སུ་མི་ *su-mi* a medicinal root serving as an antidote *Cs.*

སུ་རུ་པན་ཙ་, སུར་པན་ *su-ru-ṗan-tsá, sur-ṗán* Guinea pepper, *Capsicum annuum C., W.*

སུ་ལུ་ *sú-lu? sú-lui ṫsúl-du bżúgs-pa* denotes perh. the usual sitting posture of Milaraspa who, while reciting his songs, used to stretch out his left leg, drawing up the other, and supporting his right arm on it on which his head was leaning.

སུ་སུ་ *su-su* 1. v. *su.* — 2. *su-sú zer-wa* denotes **the drawing in the breath** in blowing up a fire, the lips being nearly closed, to prevent ashes or smoke from entering the mouth.

སུག་ *sug* **reward, recompense,** *sug-rṅán* id., *sug-rǰéd* mark of honour as a reward *Cs.*; *ṗag-súg* a bribe, frq.

སུག་པ་ *súg-pa* I. sbst. 1. **the hand** *Med.*; *sug-bris* handwriting *Sch.* — 2. the lower part of the leg of animals, *rtai súg-bżi*; **súg-gu** *W.* id. — 3. a medicinal herb *Wdṅ.*

II. vb. **to push, jog, nudge a person,** in order to waken him, or to make him attentive; **to push open,** a door with a stick *Mil.*; *súg-pa żig byéd-pa Mil.*, **sug gyáb-pa** *C.* **to push, to shove, to displace,** **sug ča yin** it will get out of its place *W.*

སུག་སྨེལ་ *sug-smél Cs.*: 'a kind of spice, betel, betel-nut' (?); ***sug-smél Lt.*** and *C.* **cardamom.**

སུད་པ་ *súd-pa* **to cough, to breathe with difficulty** *Cs.*, *súd-de ši-ba* to be choked or suffocated *Sch.*

སུན་པ་ *sun-pa* vb. and adj. 1. **to be tired of, weary of, sick of; tired, weary, out of humour** *rná-ba mi sún-te* not tired of hearing *Mil*; *yid sún-par ₒgyúr-ba* to become tired, to get weary of; the more precise form of the adj. is *sún-po*: **żág-daṅ ḍe zá-na sún-po rag** or *sún-na rag* *W.* if one eats rice every day, one gets tired of it; **sems sun-po** id.; **'dm-čog sun soṅ** *C.* one gets tired of hearing *C.*; **sá-heb nyen sun ruṅ** though it may be disagreeable to you, Sir, to hear it *C.*; *ṫugs-sún dgóṅs-pa yin-pa ₒdug* I suppose your Reverence will be tired of it *Mil.*; **sun** (*C.* **sun**) **čug-če** **to make** (a person) **tired of** (a thing), **to vex, annoy, to stun** or **drown with noise,** to deafen. — 2. *sún-par byéd-pa Dzl.*, and more frq. *sún-par byin-pa* 1. to drown with, to overpower by noise, to silence (thus prob. *Mil.* ch. 34 init.); hence 2. **to refute, confute, disprove** *Tar.* 3. c. acc. **to insult, defame, disgrace, dishonour** *Schr.*, *Dzl.* ༣༣༣, 1, 3, ༢༠༥, 2; *Bhar.* 67, *Schf.*; so perh. also *sun-pa* in the following passage of *Mil.*: *ṫúgs-rǰe drág-po sun ma byin* we will not put to shame the great favour (of the Lama). 4. **to renounce,** to resign, *sun ₒbyin-pai stobs* strength to renounce (the world).

སུབ་པ་ *súb-pa,* pf. *(b)subs,* fut. *bsub,* 1. **to stop up, plug up, close, cork; to keep shut,** closed, locked up, **to stop,** *ka sna lág-pas* to stop one's mouth and nose with one's hand *Lt.*; *dbugs súb-pa* to strangle, suffocate, choke (a person); **to fill up,** choke up (with earth, rubbish etc.) a lake *Glr.*; *sna-sub* a disease of the nose? *Lt.* — 2. **to cover, close, shut up** *Sch.*, more frq., fig. *rkaṅ-rǰés súb-pa* to cover the trace or track, to efface every vestige; **ti-pi ṫúr-la súb-če** to turn down the brim of the hat; **to blot out, erase,** *ri-mo* a drawing, *bú-lon-pai miṅ* the name of a debtor; **to hush up, conceal, cover,** e.g. other people's offences; **to suppress, to avoid,** e.g. obscene words; to allow to settle, the mash, in brewing; in all these instances in *W.* also **súb-te bór-če** is used.

སུམ་ *sum,* for *γsum,* **three,** in compounds before consonants: *súm-ču* 30, *sum-brgya* 300, *sum-stóṅ* 3000; *súm-ča, Sch.* also *sum-yar,* **a third,** the third part, *ₒdzam-bu-gliṅ súm-ča γnyis* (or only *sum-γnyis*) two thirds of Dzambuling (i.e. of the world) *Dz.*, *bod sum γnyis* two thirds of (all) the Tibetans *Ma.*; *sum-skyá Sch.* a cord of three twisted threads; *sum-ču-rtsa-γsum* the 33 ancient gods (of the Vedas); *súm-ču-pa* the thirty, i.e. 30 letters, the Tibetan alphabet, *súm-ču-pa daṅ rtags-ₒǰúg Zam.* the alphabet and the punctuation, abbreviated: *sum-rtágs Lexx.*

སུམ་(ཅུ་)ཏིག་ *sum(-ču)-tig* a medicinal herb *Med.*

སུམ་པ་, སུམས་པ་ súm-pa, súms-pa I. adj. **putrid, rancid, rotten.**

II. vb., pf. *bsums*? fut. *bsum*, *Sch.* **to bind** or **tie together**, to draw together; **to condense.**

སུར་ན་ *súr-na*, *Pers.* سُرنا, **hautboy**, larger than the *glíṅ-bu* and sounding sharper; for profane use.

སུར་པན་ *súr-pán* v. *su-ru-pan-tsá.*

སུར་ཡ་ or སུར་ *sur-ya* or *surya Med.*, སཱུརྱ, **colocynth.**

སུར་སུར་ *sur-sur* **coarse-grained**, e.g. grits *W.*

སུལ་ *sul* an artificial **plait** or **gather** made in a dress *W.*; **furrow, channel, groove, trench, ditch** (*Cs.*); *ri-súl* lateral valley, ravine, hollow, *ri-súl-gyi groṅ-k̔yér* ravine as a haunt of evil spirits; *brag-sul* narrow ravine between rocks; *ka-súl* the fluting in a column; *súl-čan* furrowed, having plaits or folds; *súl-ma* an angular, not round, vessel; *sul-mál* the third stomach of ruminating animals, the psalterium or book-tripe *Sch.*, *sul-máṅs Lt.*

སུས་ *sus* 1. instr. of *su.* — 2. *k̔yeu-sús Gyatch.* ༧༥, 13, also *Stg.?*

སེ་ *se* 1. *Ld.* inst. of *te* after *s*, e.g. **zós-se** — 2. num.: 118.

སེ་གོལ་ *se-gól* 1. **snapping** one's fingers. — 2. the time it takes to do this, i.e. **a very short time, a moment, a twinkling** *Cs.*, *se-gól-gyi sgra* the sound produced by snapping the fingers, *se-gól-gyi brda* a signal given by it *Cs.*; *se-gól γtóg-pa Mil.*, *byéd-pa Mil.*, *brdáb-pa Glr.* to snap one's fingers as a sign of contempt or indignation.

སེ་ཏྲང་ *se-tráṅ* yellow beads of a rosary, coming from the central part of Tibet, accounted more valuable than **rág-ša** *W.*

སེ་དུག་ *se-dúg* v. *se-šiṅ.*

སེ་དྲི་, བསེ་དྲི་ *se-dri*, *bse-drí* the disagreeable smell of the sweat of the arm-pits *Lt.*, *se-dri bsnám-pa* having that smell *Pth.*

སེ་ནམ་ *se-nam* vulgar for *bsód-snyoms*, **alms.**

སེ་སྤུར་ *se-spur Sch.* **dung-beetle.**

སེ་བ་, གསེ་བ་, བསེ་བ་ *sé-ba*, *γsé-ba*, *bsé-ba* 1. **rose-bush, rose-tree; rose;** *γser-mdog-sé-ba-me* (for *mé-tog*) *Lt.*, prob. the yellow rose; wild roses with beautiful and rich blossoms frequently adorn the slopes of the lower hills in the Himalaya mountains; whether the *se-rgód Med.* and the 'wild rose' of *Cs.* are identical, seems to be questionable; **se-ḍúm** *C.* **hip, haw.** — *šiṅ-sé-ba* is mentioned as the food of the silk-worm *Glr.*, hence = *ó-se-šin.* — 3. thorn?

སེ་བོ་ *se-bo* **gray**, *skra se-bo* gray hair; *mgo se-bo* (resp. *dbu se-bo*) a gray-headed person. — In col. language many things which we call gray, are styled white.

སེ་འབྲུ་, སེའུ་ *se-ₒbru*, *seu* (*C.* **sen-ḍú**, *W.* **sem-rú**) **pomegranate.**

སེ་མོ་དོ་ *sé-mo-do* or *sé-mo-to Mil.* a kind of **ornament**, e.g. made of pearls.

སེ་མོག་ *se-móg C.* **the venereal disease**; *se-rmá* syphilitic ulcers *Sch.*

སེ་ཡབ་, བསེ་ཡབ་ *se-yáb*, *bse-yáb* **fig** *Med.*

སེ་ར་ *sé-ra*, n. of a large monastery near Lhasa.

སེ་རག་དུར་སྨན་ *se-rag-dur-smán* **carrot** *W.*

སེ་རེལ་ *se-rél* half open, **se-rél čúg-če** to open half (doors, lids, covers etc.) *W.*

སེ་ཤིང་, བསེ་ཤིང་ *sé-šiṅ*, *bsé-šiṅ Cs.*: 'a tree or shrub, good for hedges, *se-dúg* 1. poison contained in that shrub. 2. = *se-móg Cs.*

སེག་, སེག་སེག་ *seg*, *seg-ség* **obliquely, awry, sideways**, *ség-γčod-pa Cs.*, **ség-ḍhe-la ḍhá-wa** *C.*, **ség-ḍe-la ḍé-če** *W.* to cut off obliquely (opp. to **ṭę-kaṅ-la** straight *C.*).

སེག་མ་ *seg-ma* **small stones, gravel** *W.*

སེང་ *seṅ* v. *γseṅ.*

སེང་གེ་ *séṅ-ge*, *W.* **siṅ-ge**, **lion**, *séṅ-ge-mo* lioness, *séṅ-gei rál-pa* the mane of a lion; *seṅ-gei k'ri* सिंहासन **a throne** ('said to be so called from its being supported by golden lions' *Will.*); *seṅ-mgó* lion's head *Glr.*; *seṅ-ydoṅ-ma Sch.*, = *sī-ha-mu-ka* lion's face, **a goddess**, *Glr.; seṅ-prúg* a lion's whelp, *seṅ-tsáṅ* a lion's den.

སེང་ལྡང་ *seṅ-ldáṅ S.g*, *seṅ-tsér Wdṅ.*, a tree growing on the southern, lower ranges of the Himalayas, having red wood, and a bark which by poor people is used for tea (*sdoṅ-ja*); its sap serves as an officinal drug, *Lt.*; acc. to *Schf.* खदिर *Acacia Catechu.*

སེང་པོ་, བསེང་པོ་ *séṅ-po, bséṅ-po* 1. **clean, white**, cf. *skya-séṅ.* — 2. *Sch.:* **thin, airy, transparent, not dense or tight**, *seṅ-séṅ* id. (*Sch.:* **open, free, roomy, spacious**); *skyé-bo seṅ-séṅ-por gyur* they became very thin, lean, pale people, **siṅ-siṅ-po, sings-po* W.* id.; *seṅ-rás Sch.*, **siṅ-yol* W.* a thin curtain, thin cotton cloth.

སེང་བ་ *séṅ-ba*, pf. *bsaṅs*, fut. *bsaṅ, bseṅ*, **to lift up, to raise** what was hanging down or drooping *W.* **saṅ ċo-ċe* or *taṅ-ċe** to lift up (the eyes, the hands, the dress etc.); *sku-k'áms bséṅ-ba-la ˳byon* (his Reverence) goes to take some recreation *Mil.; k'ams dúb-pa séṅ-ba* to refresh the wearied body *Mil.*; *k'ams rmúgs-pa bséṅ-bai rluṅ-ṅád* bracing air; *skyo-bsáṅ-ba* to unbend the mind, to divert one's self; *skyo-séṅ-la ˳gró-ba* (resp. *˳byón-pa*) to take a walk, *séṅ-la mdzád-pa* to drive out, to take the air in a carriage *Pth.; mya-ṅán bsáṅs-te* consolatory, giving comfort *Pth.*

སེང་ཤིང་, སེང་ཤང་ *seṅ-šiṅ, seṅ-šáṅ* v. *yseg-šáṅ.*

སེད་ *sed* **a file**, **ċag-sé'** id., **šiṅ-sé'** **a rasp.**

སེན་ཐབས་ *sen-t'ábs Mil.?*

སེན་མོ་ *sén-mo*, resp. *p'yag-sen* or *žabs-sén*, **nail** of a finger or toe; *sen-t'óg* **a gripe, pinch, nip, twitch**; a pinch (of snuff) *sén-mo ˳débs-pa, W. *túb-ċe* or *gyáb-ċe** **to pinch, squeeze,** **sen-ċus gyáb-ċe** to bore with the knuckles *W.; sen-tsám Sch.* as much as may be put on a finger-nail, a small quantity; *sen-žó* a white spot, such as will sometimes appear on the nails of the fingers.

སེབ་ *seb* v. *yséb.*

སེམ་,སེམས་ *sem*, usually *sems*, *Ssk.* सत्त्व, resp. ཐུགས་, **soul**; esp. as power of perception and volition, **mind**, cf. *yid* and *blo; sems na* the mind is disturbed, disordered *Mṅg.; sem ˳k'rúgs-pa* a mind agitated and troubled by sorrow, affliction, vexation etc., *sem k'óṅ-du* (or *k'óṅs-su*) *ċúd-pa* one very much grieved, deeply concerned; *sem ċúṅ-ba* a timid mind, **sem tsér-ċan* W.* a compassionate disposition, **sem nyé-mo* W.* a friendly disposition; *sem ysó-ba B.*, **sem so táṅ-ċe* or *ċúg-ċe* W.* **to console**, comfort, appease; the mind as imaginative faculty, intellectual power, *sem stór-ba* to lose one's senses *Do.;* **spirit**, *kun-yžii sem* the (eternal) spirit (opp. to *˳byúṅ-ba bžii lus* the material, perishable body) *Mil.*; *sém-kyi spyód-pa* intellectual power, mental faculties *Wdṅ.*; *dṅós-po t'ams-ċád ráṅ-gi sems yin-te* 'as things with me are only mind', i.e. as they exist only in my mind, in my imagination *Thgr.*, cf. *Was.* (136); *sém-la ma soṅ* 'it did not enter his mind', he had no mind, did not like *W.*; *sems ˳gyur* (his) mind is changed, *sems sgyur-ba* to change one's mind, *μετανοεῖν*; *bzód-pai sems* patient indurance, fortitude, **constancy**; *ynod-sems* **malice**; *šes-ráb daṅ ldán-pai sems* **wisdom,** knowledge; *sems skyéd-pa*, c. genit., to suffer thoughts or inclinations to rise in one's mind, as e.g. *˳dod-ċágs-kyi* libidinous (thoughts), frq.; also: to nourish, indulge (desires, passions), to give way to them; often used for our reflective verbs: *sems smád-pa* to humble one's self (*mi žig-la* before a person); also: *bdág-gi séms-la smad* he blamed, scolded, himself *Dzl.* ༧༥, 3, cf. *lus.*

Comp. *séms-mk'an* **intelligent, sensible,** *séms-mk'an mi yċig kyaṅ ma byuṅ* not one sensible person was present *Glr.* — *sems-˳k'rál* a mind afflicted, painfully agitated *Sch.* — *sems-ċan* animated being, **man, animal,** very frq.; *séms-ċan daṅ ldán-pa* being with child, pregnant; *sems-ċan-dmyál-ba* = *dmyál-ba*·

— *sems-nyid Glr., Thgy.*, 'the very soul', but this is often nearly the same as 'spirit', and in the language of the N. T. it may fitly be used for *πνεῦμα*, and *ťugs-nyid* for *πνεῦμα ἅγιον*, Holy Spirit. — *sems-rtén* **keepsake, token** *Pth.* and col. — *sems-dón* an intellectual or spiritual good, gift, or possession *Mil.* — *sems-bdé* **cheerful, merry** *Mil.* — *sems-nád* **heart-grief, affliction,** *séms-kyi nád-du če* he has much heart-grief *Glr.* — *sems-dpá* a brave mind; *byań-čub-sems-dpá* v. *byań-čúb*; *sems-dpa-čén-po*, **महासत्त्व**, a frq. apposition to it. — *séms-tsam* a mere thought, idea *Was.* (134), *séms-tsam-pa* (*Cs.*: **योगाचार्य**) a mystic *Köpp.* II, 25. — *sems-ťsér* **fatigue, weariness, disgust** *Sch.*

སེམ(ས)་པ་ *sém(s)-pa*, pf. *sems, bsams*, fut. *bsam*, imp. *som*, *W.* **sám-če**, **to think,** *ₒdi snyám-du séms-so* or *bsáms-so* he thought as follows, he had the following thoughts; *lóg-par sém-pa* to think ill (of a person) *Dzl.*; **to meditate, muse, ponder,** *sém-bžin-du* absorbed in meditation, lost in thought *Dzl.*, *mi-dgá-bar sém-šiń* immersed in melancholy thoughts *Dzl.*; in *C.* **sém-žin-du** signifies at the present time: knowingly, wilfully, purposely, = *šes bžin-du*; *šin-tu soms šig* think over it seriously! *Dzl.*; **to think of,** c. accus., *grań-bai ɣnas* (to think) of a cool place, i. e. to long for coolness *Dzl.*, and c. dat.: *rań-gi yúl-la ma bsám-par* forgetful of home, forgetting one's native soil *Glr.*, *yi-ge ₒdi-la ma bsám-par* disregarding this contract *Glr.*; also with termin.: *ɣžán-du ma sems šig* do not think of anybody else; **to intend, purpose, have in view,** e.g. *ɣnód-par byá-bar* to do harm *Dzl.*; construed in the same manner, it also signifies: **to fancy, imagine** *Do.*; with *dań ₒdrá-bar* and similar expressions: **to hold, think, consider, to take for, to look upon as;** *da ₒkór-bai nyes-dmigs bsám-šes-na* (for *bsám-žiń*) now that you know with full consciousness the punishment of (going through) the cycle (of animal existences) *Mil.* (yet cf. *bsám-šes* in *bsám-pa*). Sometimes it denotes only an act of memory, a remembering: *lhá-čos ťos-bsam-byéd-pa-rnams* those who have heard and kept in their memory the religion of Buddha, (who remember the words even without understanding them) *Mil.* Cf. *bsám-pa*.

སེའུ་ *seu* 1. **a little tooth** *Lt.* — 2. **pomegranate.**

སེར་, སེར་རུ་ *ser, sér-ru* corruption, putrefaction? **már-la sér-ru gyab** *C.* the butter turns yellow and rancid, *sér-čan* **rancid** *S.g.*

སེར་ཀ་ *sér-ka, sér-ka, sér-ga* 1. **a cleft, slit, fissure, crevice, gap,** *brag-sér* chasm or cleft in a rock; *rgya-sér* a large gap, cleft, chasm; *sér-ka súb-pa* to close, stop up a hole *Pth.* — 2. v. *sér-po.*

སེར་སྐྱ་ *ser-skyá* **Lamas and laymen,** **ser-kyá kun ₒdúm-ma ǰhé-pa** a promiscuous convention, parish council *C.* — 2. v. *skyá-bo.*

སེར་ཁྱིམ་པ་ *sér-kyim-pa* a sect of Lamas = *dbón-po.*

སེར་ག་མ་ *sér-ga-ma Sch.* turmeric, *Curcuma.*

སེར་ཆེ་ *ser-čé Lt.* a yellow aquatic flower; **ser-čen** *W. Saxifraga flagellaris.*

སེར་སྣ་ *sér-sna* **avarice,** frq.; *sér-sna byéd-pa* to be avaricious *Dzl.*

སེར་པོ་ *sér-po* **yellow;** *ser-ₒpréń* clerical procession, parade *Mil. nt.*

སེར་བ་ *sér-ba* **hail;** *ser-král* a kind of insurance against damage done by hail, i.e. money paid to the Lama for his preventive ceremonies.

སེར་བུ་ *sér-bu* v. *bsér-bu.*

སེར་མོ་ *sér-mo* 1. *C.* col. **finger.** — 2. *W.* six-rowed barley, **late barley.** — *sér-mo-ba* the Lamas *Sch.*

སེལ་ *sel* 1. **discord, dissension,** *nań-sél* domestic dispute. — 2. a kind of **incantation,** like *brtad*, *sel ₒǰúg-pa* to exorcise, to make use of conjurations or incantations *Mil.*

སེལ་བ་ *sel-ba*, pf., fut. *bsal*, imp. *sol*, **to remove,** esp. impurities, hence **to cleanse; to pick, pick off; to blot out, cross out,** *bú-lon* a debt; **to clear,** **lam sál-če** *W.* to make a path or road; very frq. fig.: **to remove,** to remedy (an evil), to cure (a disease), to repair (a damage), to redress grievances), to dispel (darkness) etc.

སོ་ so, I. sbst. 1. resp. ťsems, **tooth**, stéṅ-so, yá-so upper tooth; ˳óg-so, má-so lower tooth; mdún-so Sch. γčád-so, Stg. so-drúṅ fore-tooth, front-tooth; sbúbs-so, grám-so, ráṅ-ťag-so Sch. ldán-so cheek-tooth, molar-tooth, grinder, mčé-so Cs, *čód-ten-so* W. eye-tooth, corner-tooth, canine-tooth. — 2. **tooth** of a saw, wheel, comb. — 3. **edge** of a knife.

II. sbst. for sa, in conjunction with certain words, e.g. ṅan-sor skye-ba to be born in an inferior place Mil.; v. also ráṅ-so, sór-bžag-pa, ˳krúl-so.

III. sbst. **joy** (?), so bsod-pa id. Cs. and Lex.; cf. ṅó-so.

IV. sbst., also bso, **look-out, guard, spying,** so byéd-pa to spy, to look out; só-ḱuṅ peep-hole; só-pa keeper, guard, watchman, spy, emissary, zas nor bdúd-kyi só-pa yin money and dainties are the devil's emissaries Mil.; mé-bso a guard or watch kept by several persons round a fire; só-sgra 1. watchword, = sgar-míṅ. 2. v. comp.

V. grammatical termination: *tén-so* provinc. for rtén-no C., also Glr.

VI. num. for súm-ču in the abbreviated numbers 31—39.

VII. num.: 148.

Comp. so-gri a saw. — só-sgra the whistling through the teeth, in the magic performances of the Bonpo, só-sgra ˳débs-pa Glr. — so-čág a broken tooth. — so-drég tartar? Med. — so-búd a tooth that has come out. — so-máṅ comb. — so-žó a small white spot on a tooth, cf. sén-žo. — so-zéd **tooth-brush.** — so-šiṅ **toothpick.** — so-srúb gap in the teeth Sch.

སོ་ག་ só-ga = sós-ka.

སོ་ཆ་ só-ča n. of an emetic Med.

སོ་ནམ(ས་) so-nam(s) **agriculture, husbandry,** so-námsbyéd-pa to till the ground, to practise agriculture, **farming,** sgrúb-pa, ˳bád-pa id., so-nám-pa Cs. husbandman, farmer.

སོ་པ་ só-pa v. so IV.

སོ་པ་རི་ só-pa-ri Cs. a kind of berry, beneficial to the teeth.

སོ་ཕག་ so-ṗág **brick, tile;** also collective noun, brickwork, tiling.

སོ་བ་ só-ba coarse, thick-shelled **barley,** used for fodder.

སོ་བྱ་ só-bya an aquatic bird S.g.

སོ་མ་ só-ma 1. sbst. Ssk. (prop. a climbing plant the juice of which was offered in libations to the gods and was also worshipped itself, on account of its intoxicating qualities, hence): **hemp,** also γtsó-ma, btsó-ma; so-ma-rá-dza id., so-ma-rá-dzai ras **hemp-linen** Schr., so-ma-rá-dzai ťag-pa **hempen rope** Pth. — 2. adj. **new, fresh,** esp. W. *só-me náṅ-na zer gos* this ought to have been mentioned directly (when it was still fresh in every body's memory).

སོ་ཚིས་, སོ་ཚིགས་ so-ťsis, so-ťsigs **house-keeping,** management of domestic concerns, **husbandry,** cf. so-nam agriculture.

སོ་ལུག་ so-lug **lees** of liquors, yeast of beer Sch.

སོ་ལོག་ so-log **high-road, causeway** W.

སོ་སོ་ so-só distinct, separate, singly, individually, zas so-sói lág-tu ˳óṅs-so the victuals came into the hands of the individual persons Dzl.; so-só-nas adv. frq.: so-só-nas snod bzéd-de 'singulatim', each for himself, holding forth his vessel Dzl.; **various** e.g. *na so-só* W. for sna-ťsogs of B.; **diverse, different** sám-pa so-só different opinions, a dissension; **separate, distinct,** so-só byéd-pa, W. *so-só čó-če* to separate, disjoin, divide, so-sór bžág-pa, W. *so-só bór-če* to set, put, lay apart. — so-soi skye-bo, **पृथग्जन,** prop. one separated (from the saints), one outside the pale, a man of the lower classes, of low caste; with Buddhists: **a layman,** and as to his spiritual condition: a man in his natural state, one not yet enlightened (like ψυχικός I Cor. 2, 14, though on account of its derivation, the above term cannot well be used for the Greek word); also the lower classes of clerical persons, monks. — so-só(s)-ťar-pa, so-ťár, **प्रतिमोक्ष,**

liberation, **deliverance,** *so-só-tar-pai mdo* the book of deliverance, code of the moral law, containing about 250 precepts for the priesthood, the monastic rules of the Buddhists.

སོ་སོ་ཚ་ *so-so-čá* a medicinal herb, an emetic *Wdṅ.*

སོག་ *sog* 1. v. *sob.* — 2. for **srog** *Ü.*

སོག་པ་ *sóg-pa* 1. sbst., also *sógs-pa,* **shoulder-blade,** scapula, *sóg-pai mé-loṅ* the flat part of it, *sog-yu* the narrow extremity of it; *sog-mó ͦdébs-pa* (v. *mo* III.) to divine from the shoulder-blade; *sog-lhú* shoulder as a piece of meat for boiling (I Sam. 9, 24). — 2. vb. (also: *γsóg-pa, bsóg-pa, sógs-pa*) pf. *(b)ags,* fut. *bsag,* imp. *sogs, bsag, W.* **ság-če**, **to gather, heap up, hoard up,** *ṗral sog-ͦjog-méd-pa* without having collected and deposited the daily requisites, the things wanted every day *Mil., bsód-nams sóg-pa Mil., ťsogs sóg-pa* frq. to collect, to hoard up merits of virtue, *las-ṅán sóg-pa* to heap up sins; *γsog-ldáṅ* morbid matter consisting in too great an accumulation of humours, ni f., *Med.; dmág-gi dpuṅ sóg-pa* to collect an army *Dzl.;* **to assemble,** children *Glr.;* hence **sag(s)** *W.* **all** (of them), **lug sag tsam** how many sheep are there in all?

སོག་པོ་ *sóg-po* **a Mongol** *Glr., sóg-mo* a Mongol woman, *sog-ṗrúg* Mongol child, Mongol boy, *sog-čás* Mongol dress or fashion of dress, *sog-rta* Mongol horse.

སོག་མ་ *sóg-ma* **blade, stalk; straw;** *sog-ͦbru Sch.* green corn that begins to sprout; *sog-ťsigs* a knot on a stalk *Cs.; sog-sbúr* a small blade of straw, chaff *Pth.; sóg-mai ͦbú-la* a shoe of straw; *sog-rú, sog-rúm, sog-ldúm* stubbles.

སོག་ལེ་ *sóg-le B., C.,* **čad-sóg, gya-sóg** *W.* **a saw,** *sóg-les γčód-pa B.* to saw to pieces, **gya-sóg śrúl-ce** *W.* to saw; *sog-le-ka* the toothed edge of a saw, also botanical term.: serrate, serrated (of leaves) *Wdṅ.*

སོགས་ *sogs* **and so forth, and the like,** mostly preceded by *la: mí-la sógs-pai srog-čágs homo et cetera animantia,* prop. the beings in addition to man; *ba-dán-la sógs-pas brgyán-te* decorated with little flags and the like; less frq.: *la sógs-te,* inst. of which always *la-sógs-pa* or *pai* may be used; often *sogs* alone, also in prose; after *(la) sógs(-pa)* usually a comma is to be supplied, and the words following are to be considered as an apposition: *yi-ge rtsís-la sógs-pa rig-pai γnas lṅa* writing, arithmetic and so on, the five sciences; hence often applicable, when a comprehensive noun appellative does not exist: *γser sogs* gold and the other, viz. metals, *Glr.; tsa sogs γsum* the three *tsa*-sounds, *tsa, ťsa* and *dza Gram.*

Note. In course of time the original grammatical sense seems to have been forgotten, in as much as *la* is now read together with *sógs-pa,* and often also the dot separating the syllables is omitted.

སོང་ *soṅ* perf. and imp. of *ͦgró-ba* to go, 1. **I went, I have** (thou hast etc.) **gone,** v. *ͦgro-ba* 1 and 2, e.g. *der soṅ yód-pas* when he had gone thither *Pth., soṅ-sóṅ-ba-las* going on continually, *Dzl.,* continuing to do a thing *Dzl.; sóṅ-ba yin* it is gone, it is no longer extant *Mil.; dbáṅ-du soṅ* (he or it) came into the power of... *S.g.; da sdig-pa-la sóṅ-na Thgy.* if we now go on to (the topic of sins) *W.:* **da-rúṅ ṅa ma soṅ** it is not yet past five o'clock; **'i-nẹ sóṅ-pa 'a tsúg-pa** from here (adverbially, like *bzúṅs-te*) to that place *Ld.;* imp.: **dí-ru ma dug! soṅ!** do not stand here! walk on! — 2. **became, turned** etc. *kyi-mo žig-tu soṅ* she became a bitch, was changed into a bitch *Mil., dkár-por soṅ* it turned white *Glr.,* **doṅ nág-po soṅ** *W.* his face grew dark; **bi-gúṅ soṅ** *W.* a hole has been made, it got a hole; **gyál-sẹ ka-čúd sóṅ-nẹ** as she got a taste for the town *W.;* **nod ču gaṅ soṅ** the vessel was already full of water (when I came) *W.* — **soṅ-tó** *W.* account of expenses.

སོད་པ་ *sód-pa* 1. *C.* **to wake, rouse.** — 2. sometimes for *γsód-pa.*

སོན་ *son* rarely for *soṅ*; frq. only in *nár-son-pa,* v. *na.*

སོན་པ་ *són-pa* 1. v. *son.* — 2. v. *γsón-pa, γsón-po.*

སོབ་ *sob* 1. also *sog, ɣsob, ɣsog,* **null, void, vain, empty, bad in its quality, not durable.** — 2. also *ɣsob* something **stuffed** (as a chair), *nán-sob, ḱón-sob, ḱóg-sob Wdń.* prob. id.: *sob-stán* **cushion, bolster, mattress,** *pags-sób* the stuffed skin of an animal, *seń(-gei) sób* the stuffed skin of a lion *Pth.*

སོམ་ *som* 1. also *ɣsom, sóm-śiń* **fir-tree, pine-tree.** — 2. also *soms,* imp. of *sém-pa.*

སོར་ *sor* 1. also *ɣsor,* **gimlet,** *rús-pa ₒbúgs-pai sor S.g.* prob. a sort of **trephine.** — 2. v. *sór-mo.* — 3. v. *sar, sor bźag-pa* to put in its place (*Sch.* also: 'quite the same'?); *rán-sor* v. *rań* compounds. — 4. (cognate to *só-ma?*) *sor čúd-pa* (*Sch. ₒjud-pa*) **to restore, renew,** e.g. exhausted strength *Dzl.*, the doctrine of Buddha *Pth.* — 5. term. of *so.*

སོར་མོ་ *sór-mo,* resp. *p̔yag-sór Mil., žabs-sór,* 1. **finger, toe;** *sor-ɣdúb* finger-ring, *sor-ťsigs* the joint of a finger. — 2. **inch,** *sor-bži-pa* four-inched.

སོལ་བ་ *sól-ba* **coal,** esp. charcoal, = *sol-nág; sól-bai me* coal-fire *Lt.*; **sol-mé* W.* live coal, burning coal.

སོལ་པོ་ *sól-po* resp. **friendly, kind, affable** *C., W.*

སོས་ *sos* 1. inst. of *so, sos btáb-pa* **to bite,** *Sch.* also **to backbite,** to calumniate. — 2. v. *ɣsó-ba* and *ₒťsó-ba.*

སོས་ཀ་, སོ་ག་ *sós-ka, só-ga,* 1. in Tibet: **spring,** = *dpyid, Mil.* — 2. in India: **the hot season,** from about the middle of April till the middle of June.

སོས་དལ་ *sos-dál or sos-bsdal Sch.*: **slow.**

སོས་ཟིན་ *sos-zin* disease of the membrum virile, in five forms (prob. different stages of gonorrhea) *Mng.*

སྲ་བ་ *srá-ba* 1. adj., also *srá-bo* and *srá-mo Cs.*, col. **srán-te** (cf. *srán-pa*), **hard, solid, compact, firm,** and abstract noun: **solidity, hardness, compactness,** of wood, meat etc., and often fig.: *ɣžu-srán* a bow difficult to be bent *S.g.*, *rgas-srá* hearty vigorous old age *S.g.*; *mťson ḱar sra* proof against cut and thrust, also: proof against malicious words *Mil.* — *sra-brkyań,* कठिनाक्षर, the coarse blanket of a monk. — *sa-rtsí* **varnish.** — 2. vb. *W.*, **to empty.**

སྲང་ *srań* I. (cf. *srón-ba*) 1. **pair of scales, balance** *B.*, *srán-la ₒdégs-pa Cs.*, *ɣžál-ba, ťsád-pa Sch.*, *srán-ba Sp.* to weigh, to balance. — 2. **steel-yard,** **sran tág-če** to hold the steel-yard, in weighing. — 3. **weight,** in a general sense, *bre-srán* weight and measure, *rgya-srán* Chinese weights *Cs.* — 4. **an ounce,** *srań gáń* one ounce, *srań do* two ounces, *sman srán* ༢༢, two pounds of medicine, the daily quantity taken by Buddha when he had caught cold *Dzl.* ༤༢, 3. — *srán-ča Sch.* balance and what belongs to it. — *srań-mdá* scale-beam or lever of a pair of scales *Sch.* — *srań-p̔ór* scale. — *srań-ťsád Cs.* weight. — *srán-ba* vb. v. above.

II. **street,** *lam-srán* id.; *srań-yár Sch.*: tortuous path, labyrinth (?). — *rgya-srán* street, lane *Glr.*; *rgyu-srán* the road which a person habitually walks.

སྲན་བུ་ *srán-bu* **thread, yarn,** *ₒḱál-ba, sgríl-ba.*

སྲད་མ་ *srád-ma* v. *srán-ma.*

སྲན་པ་ *srán-pa* (cf. *srá-ba*) *Cs.*: pf. fut. *bsran,* imp. *sron,* W. **śrán-če** **to suffer, bear** (with patience), **endure, to be hardened** *W.* frq., **śrán-ťub-ḱan* or *śrán-ťeg-ḱan** one that can endure much; **ḱyod śran gos* Ld.* you must hold out, you must stand it; in *B.* *sran ₒdzugs-pa* is used in the same sense; **ḱyág-śran-čan** hardened, accustomed to frost, **dúg-śran-čan** inured to hardships *W.* — **śrán-te** col. frq. adj.: 1. = *srá-ba* (opp. to *lhód-po* and *ₒból-mo*) **hard, firm, durable, rigid, strict.** 2. fig. **hard, severe, bitter.** — *sdug-srán* hardiness *Mil.*; *sran-čé-ba* = *srán-ťub-mḱan. Cs.*: *srán-pa* sbst. hardship, severe distress or toil, *srán-par* toilsomely, rigorously, *srán-pa-po* one that hardens himself (?).

སྲན་མ་, སྲད་མ་ *srán-ma, srád-ma* 1. **pease, beans, lentils,** *Cs.* mentions also *srad-dkár, srad-nág* and *srad-snón,* also *mḱal-srán,* in *W.*, however, we only met with the common field pea and some dry imported Indian sorts of it (*mon-srán*); *rgya-srán* (*Cs. mon-srán*) was the name the natives were inclined to give to our European bean. — *sran-ṗuṅ* a heap of pease, *sran-ṗub* pease-straw, *sran-ṗyé* flour of pease, *sran-mé* blossom of pease. — 2. **grain,** like *rdóg-po*, e.g. of Indian corn; even *lčágs-kyi sran-čuṅ Wdṅ.* grains of shot(?).

སྲབ་ *srab* **bridle,** *rtai*; *srab sga stan ṫsáṅ-po* a complete riding-gear; **s̀rab čúg-ce* W.* **to bridle, to bit** (a horse), **s̀rab gyúr-ce** **to govern, to rein** (a horse) *srab-skyógs Cs.* **the reins,** — *srab-lčags Cs.* **the bit.** — *srab-mṫúr Sch.* **the halter.** — *srab-mdá Stg., Ld.:* **s̀ram-dá** **reins.**

སྲབ་པ་ *sráb-pa B.*, **sráb-mo* W.* **thin, tender, fine,** e.g. skin *Dzl.*, cloth, leather, paper, clouds; **shallow, loose,** not close; *srab-mṫil Sch.* inner sole, welt; *srab-mṫúg* thickness, dimension.

སྲབ་སྲིབ་ *srab-srib Cs.* **dark, obscure.**

སྲམ་ *sram,* उद्र 1. **otter,** the flesh of which is considered very nourishing, the liver is used as a remedy for strangury *S.g.*, but encountering this animal is regarded as an evil omen *S.g.*; *čʻu-sram* id.? (*Cs.* beaver?) *nyá-sram Mil.*, either the same, or: fishes and otters; *brag-srám* rock-otter? sable? **ka-lon-s̀ram* W.* prob. **sable;** it is nearly black and stated to live near Yarkand, in the mountains as well as in the flat country. The ear-coverings worn by the ladies of Ladak are made of the fur of this animal. — 2. **otter-skin, sable-skin.**

སྲར་ *srar* adv. *Sch.:* **severely, rigorously.**

སྲས་(པོ་) *sras(-po)* resp. for *bu*, **son, child,** *dpon-srás, rgyal-srás* son of the sovereign, a prince; *rgyal-srás* also: son of Buddha, a Buddha; *lha(i) sras(-po)* 1. son of a god *Dzl.* 2. a prince; *ṫugs-srás* spiritual son or daughter *Mil.*; in this sense *sras* may be applied to females: *saṅs-rgyás-kyi sras dág-pao* she has become a spotless child of Buddha *Dzl.* — *srás-bu* = *sras.* — *srás-mo* **daughter, young lady, princess.** — *sras-ṫsáb Cs.* adopted child.

སྲི་ *sri* 1. a species of **devil** or **demon,** devouring esp. children, **a vampire,** also *sri-ṅán Schl.*, *čúṅ-sri Glr.*, *ṗúṅ-sri Mil.* a devil bringing misfortune; they are supposed to live in underground places, and are therefore also called *más-kyi sri*; *sri laṅ* a devil rises from below; *sri nón-pa B.*, **nán-ce* W.* to lay, suppress a devil.

སྲི་བ་ *sri-ba* I. pf. *bsris*, fut. *bsri*, 1. **to retain,** e.g. *bs̀áṅ-ba, γčin* constipation, strangury. — 2. **to be parsimonious, niggardly,** esp. with *nor; sba-sri-méd-par γnáṅ-ba Mil.* to give unsparingly, to bestow very liberally; **s̀ri-s̀es-kʻan* W.* parsimonious.

II. *W.* **to wind, to wrap round,** for *dkri-ba.*

སྲི་ཞུ་ *sri-žu*, less frq. *srid-žu*, **respect, reverence, deference,** *sri-žu-pa, sri-žu-mkʻan* one paying his regards, his respects, showing deference.

སྲིང་བ་ *sriṅ-ba* pf. *bsriṅs*, fus. *bsriṅ* 1. (cognate to *riṅ-ba*) **to extend, stretch, stretch out,** the arm, **to hand, reach,** **de dul soṅ, ṅá-la s̀riṅ toṅ** it has fallen down, hand it to me *W.*; **to fling far away** *C.* — 2. **to postpone, put off,** *˳či-bai ṫse Glr.* the term of death; **to prolong,** *ṫse* life *S.g.*; **to wait, to tarry,** **'á-ṫsig s̀riṅ* Lh.* wait a little, **dag-sa yoṅ-ṅa ṫsa-big s̀riṅ-te yoṅ?** shall (I, you, he etc.) come directly or after a while? *Ld.*; **nam dir s̀riṅ-ce ča dug?** how long shall you stay here? *W.* — 3. **to send** (*skúr-ba Lex.*) *ṗrin, yo-byád Sch.* — 4. *skyéd-sriṅ-ba* **to bring up, train up, to rear** *Glr.*

སྲིང་མོ་ *sriṅ-mo* **sister** (of a male person, cf. *miṅ-po*) *bu-sriṅ, miṅ-sríṅ*, resp. *lčam-sriṅ* brother and sister, cousins.

སྲིད་ *srid* 1. **length, extension,** *ṗug srid-du kʻru-bčo-brgyád-pa* a cavern 18 cubits long *Tar.*; more frq. with regard to time: *˳di* or *de-srid(-kyi bar)-du* (for) so long (a time), *či-srid-du*, also *či-srid-de*, how long (a time)? also: as long as; when followed by *yaṅ*: be it ever so long (in this case *ǰi* would be more correct); also *srid-par*, or *srid* alone, for *srid-du.* — 2. **dominion, government,** *srid-la ma ˳čám-pas* falling out with one another about the government *Glr.*, esp. *rgyal-srid, dbaṅ-srid* id.; *srid byéd-pa* to reign, to govern, *srid ˳ṫsó-ba* id. *Dzl.*; *˳di γnyis-kyi srid gaṅ yód-rnams ṗrog* he seized upon their territorial shares *Glr.; bla-srid Cs.* a Lama's dominion. — *sde-srid* **province**; *čos-srid* clerical goverument, ecclesiastical dominion. — 3. **ruler, commander, regent, reigning prince**; so also in the compounds just mentioned.

སྲིད་པ་ *srid-pa* I. vb., 1. to be, to exist (?). — 2. **to be possible,** often preceded by *yaṅ; skyé-ba daṅ ˳jig-pa kún-la srid-na* since springing up and passing away is the lot of all men *Dzl.; ṗán-pa ži̇g srid* healing is possible *Pth.; ˳di-las sla yaṅ srid* it might be easier (for me) then than now *Dzl.; de-bžin-du bden srid snyám-nas* thinking this might possibly be true; the verb is usually put in the infinitive mood terminating in *pa: de yin-pa-aṅ srid* after all it might be this man, it might be he *Mil.; ˳dir ˳óṅ-ba mi srid-do, bód-du brós-pa srid* he will scarcely come back, he will have escaped to Tibet *Glr.;* sometimes with the root of the verb: *yoṅ mi srid Mil.; bdag ťar kyaṅ srid-kyis* as it is a possible case, that we might be released *Dzl.; ma srid čig* about the same as: God forbid! by no means! In *W.* nearly = **to be obliged:** **ḱyer-wa-la ṡrid** now it will be my lot, now I shall be obliged, to carry (twice as much), **sád-če-la ṡrid** (*B.: bab* or *ťug*) he deserves death, he must die.

II. sbst. भुवन 1. **existence,** state of being, **life,** *srid-pa γžan nyáms-su myóṅ-ba* to experience, to pass through, other periods of existence *Wdṅ., srid ṗyi-ma Sch.:* the future period of life, of existence. — 2. things existing, **the world,** *srid(-pa) γsum* the three worlds, *srid-pai ˳ḱór-lo Cs.:* the revolving system (the world's cycle); *srid-pai mťso* the ocean of existence, *srid-pai ču-klúṅ čén-po* the stream of existence *Mil.*; also a single **being,** commonly however *srid-pa-pa; bár-doi srid-pa, bár-srid-pa Thgy., bár-ma-doi srid-pa-pa Stg.* the beings in the Bardo, v. *bár-do.* — The meaning of *srid* in *srid-pai bar-do*, and in some other expressions, have yet to be determined. — 3. symb. num.: 14.

སྲིན་ཁྲད་ *srin-ḱlád Sch.:* a sort of **flint-stone.**

སྲིན་གླང་ *srin-gláṅ Lt.? W.* **srin-gláṅ-čan** having the staggers (of horses); being mad.

སྲིན་པོ་ *srin-po, Ssk.* राक्षस, fem. *srin-mo*, **demons,** figuring in Indian and Tibetan mythology. They are supposed to be, for the most part, of an enormous size, generally hostile to mankind, going about at night, to ensnare and even to devour human beings. Their chief abode was Ceylon, and also Tibet was originally inhabited by them. The Tibetans are even said to be the descendants of an ape (sent by, or emanated from, Avalokitēshvara) and of a Tibetan Srinmo. *brág-srin* rock-Srinpo or Srinmo; *˳dre-srin* goblins and Srinpos; *čú-srin* v. the following article.

སྲིན་བུ་ *srin-bu,* = *˳bu,* **insect, worm, vermin;** *srin-bu pád-ma (srin-pa Sik.)* **leech,** *srin-bu me-˳ḱyér* **glow-worm;** *rgyu-srin, ḱoṅ-srin* **intestinal worm;** *ṗyi-srin* vermin living on the skin *Lt.*; *dár-srin* **silk-worm;** *srin-bál* acc. to *Wdṅ.* = *rás-bál* **cotton,** *Sch., Schr.:* **flock-silk;** raw silk; *srin-byá* nocturnal bird, **owl** etc. *Lt.; srin-ťór* **small ulcer** or tumour; *srin-šiṅ Med., Sch.:* **mulberry-tree;** *ču-srin* a monster living in the water.

སྲིན་ལག་ *srin-lág* **the ring-finger.**

སྲིབ(ས)་ *srib(s)* 1. **darkness, gloom, night.** — 2. **shady side, north side** of a mountain. — *srib-pa* vb., to grow dark or dusky, *C.:* **sa ṡrib soṅ** night has begun.

སྲིའུ་ནག་ *sriu-nág* **mulberry-tree.**

སྲིལ་ *sril Sch.* **silk-worm.**

སྲུ་ *sru Glr., srú-mo Lex.* and *C.* mother's sister, **aunt.**

སྲུག་པ་ *srúg-pa, W.* for *sprúg-pa, srúb-pa* and *dkrúg-pa:* 1. **to shake, to shake out.** — 2. **to stir, stir up, twirl.** — 3. **to shake,** to make to totter.

སྲུང་བ་ *srúṅ-ba* I. vb., pf. *(b)sruṅs,* fut. *bsruṅ,* imp. *(b)sruṅ(s), Ssk.* रक्ष, 1. **to watch, to keep guard** intrs.; but gen. trans., i.e. **to watch, to keep, to guard, to keep in custody,** *ḱyim* the house *Dzl.;* **to save from, to pro-**

tect, to shelter, e.g. *lus*, the body, but also: **to keep** unpolluted, pure, chaste; *bdag srúṅ-ba* to guard one's self, in a special sense: to live as a *bdag-srúṅ*, as a hermit *Dzl.*; **to preserve,** *bdag γnód-pa ťams-ċád-las sruṅs šig* may I be preserved from every harm! *Do.*; with *la: bdág-la srúṅ-du γsol* I pray to preserve, to protect me *Do.* — 2. **to beware of, to guard against,** *lus daṅ ṅág-gi nyés-pa Dzl.*, = *lus daṅ ṅag srúṅ-ba* (v. above no. 1) *Dzl.* — 3. **to keep, to observe faithfully,** a promise, laws; *bká-sruṅ-mk̒an* **obedient, faithful, trustworthy.** — 4. **to hinder,** forbid, prohibit, *rigs-kyis, bdág-pos, č̒ós-kyis sruṅ* it is forbidden, it is prohibited, by the degree of kindred, by the husband, by religion in general *Thgy.*; **to prevent, to be a preservative** or **preventive** *S.g.* — 5. **to wait,** = *sriṅ-ba*, e.g. **žag nyi** for two days *W.*

II. sbst. 1. **the keeping, guarding, the heed, guard.** — 2. the person or the thing keeping, guarding, esp. **amulet, preventive, preservative,** *btágs-pa* to suspend (an amulet, to the neck or other part of the body).

Comp. and deriv. *sruṅ-skúd*, -*ok̒ór* or -*mdúd* an amulet consisting of threads. — *srúṅ-mk̒an* **keeper, guardian, watchman,** **ťsán-la šrúṅ-k̒an** *W.* (night-) watchman; *srúṅ-pa B.* = *srúṅ-mk̒an*, *bzá-šiṅ-ra-ba srúṅ-pa* keeper of a fruit-garden *Dzl.*; *srúṅ-po Cs.* = *srúṅ-mk̒an*; *srúṅ-ma B.* id., *dmyal-bai sruṅ-ma* guardian of the infernal regions frq. *Dzl.*; *č̒ós-skyoṅ-bai srúṅ-ma ťams-ċád* all the tutelar gods of religion *Mil.*; collectively: body of watchmen, *lhá-rnams-kyi srúṅ-ma dáṅ-po* the first corps of watchmen of the gods, the Nāga; *rgyál-poi srúṅ-mai mi* the men of the king's body-guard *Stg.* —*srúṅ-sems* the taking heed, being cautious.

སྲུན་པ་, བསྲུན་པ་ *srún-pa, bsrún-pa*, **calm, soft, mild,** and: **mildness, gentleness, meekness;** *srún-po* adj. = *srún-pa*, esp. of horses: **quiet, tame;** *šin-tu mi-bsrún-žiṅ* very **malicious, malignant,** of demons *Mil.*

སྲུབ་ *srub* v. *srus.*

སྲུབ་པ་ *srúb-pa*, pf. imp. (*b*)*srubs*, fut. *bsrub*, 1. **to stir, stir up, stir about,** *žo srúb-pa* to churn, to make butter. — 2. **to rummage, to rake up, to stir, to turn over.** — 3. **to rub,** two pieces of wood against each other *Wdṅ.* — **šrub-šiṅ** *C.* 1. twirling-stick. 2. mischiefmaker, disturber of the peace.

སྲུབས་ *srubs* 1. **a cleft, slit, gap, fissure,** *brag-srúbs* chasm or cleft in a rock, smaller than *sér-ka Mil.*; **intermediate space,** interval, interstice; **rent** in a dress; **disunion, separation; wound** *Lt.*; *srubs obye Lt.*, *srubs oťor Sch.* a severing, a wound has been made; *srubs γtór-ba* to rend asunder, to tear *Sch.* **ťsem-šrúb ḍól-ċe** *W.* to rip, to cut open a seam. — 2. seam? — 3. *W.* col. for *srus.*

སྲུམ་ *srum* resp. for **meat,** flesh of animals used as food, *srum-k̒óg* an animal slaughtered and cut up, for a person of quality.

སྲུལ་པོ་ *srúl-po* 1. **evil demon, malignant spirit** *Mil.*; *lús-srul-po Lex.* **sorcerer.** — 2. **putrid, rotten** *Cs.*

སྲུལ་བ་ *srúl-ba*, pf. and fut. *bsrul*, I. **to be corrupted, decomposed,** of the humours of the body *Wdṅ.*

II. *W.* **šrúl-ċe*, = *šrúg-ċe** 1. **to stir,** **ťúg-pa** the soup, **to mix** and stir, **č̒ú-la p̒e** flour with water. — 2. **to shove, to move,** to and fro, **p̒ág-te šrúl-ċe** to plane, **ċad-sóg šrul-ċe** to saw. — 3. **ťa šrul-ċe** to put a horse to a gallop?

སྲུས་ *srus*, *W.* also **šrub**, **unripe ears** of wheat etc. **šrub nyé-ċe** *W.* to rub them between the hands; the grains, thus being shelled, are considered a rural dainty; *obrás-kyi srus* a shelled grain of rice.

སྲུས་པ་ *srús-pa Sch.* **to thicken, to become more consistent,** by evaporation, by boiling.

སྲེ་ད་ *sré-da Wdṅ.*, *sred S.g.*, a species of corn (?).

སྲེ་ནག་ *sre-nág Lex.* **soot;** *W.* **šre-móg**.

སྲེ་བ་ *sré-ba* I. sbst. a certain shrub *Cs.*

II. vb., pf. *bsres*, fut. *bsre*, imp. (*b*)*sres*, trans. to *ₒdré-ba* 1. **to mix with, to mingle, to admix,** *már-la sré-ba* to mix with butter *Lt.*, *čaṅ ču sre-ba* to mix beer with water *Med.*; *dreu sré-ba* to breed mules; *bsrés-pa* mixed up, **confused**, of a narration *Tar.*; fig. *k̔a* or *lus sré-ba* to communicate with another, i.e. to live, to eat, drink, smoke with a person *Do.*; *skyid sdug sré-ba* to share pleasure and pain, joy and sorrow *Glr.*; *W.*, like **žé-če**, **to exchange for:** **zan daṅ šrog** to risk one's life for a subsistence. — 2. **to add; to add up,** cast up, sum up *Wdk.*, **nyī daṅ nyī šre ži** 2 and 2 make 4 *W.*

སྲེ་མོག་ *sre-móg* v. *sre-nág.*

སྲེ་མོང་ *sre-móṅ* **weasel,** prob. = **la-k̔yi-mo** *W.*; *sré-mo Lex.*

སྲེ་ལོང་ *sre-lóṅ* 1. *Sch.*: the sinew above the heel. — 2 n. of a medicine?

སྲེག་པ་ *srég-pa* I. sbst. (*W.* **šrag-pa**) **partridge.**

II. vb., pf. (*b*)*sregs*, fut. *bsreg*, imp. (*b*)*sreg*(*s*), *W.* **šrág-če** **to burn,** i.e. 1. **to consume, to destroy by or with fire** (*mes*, *mé-la*) e.g. a corpse, *dág-mo*, or *W.* **nán-tan**, altogether, entirely, *dgra* an enemy (sc. in effigy); *sbyin-sreg* **burnt-offering; to make red-hot,** *lčags-bsrégs* red-hot iron *Thgy.* — 2. **to roast, fry, bake,** on a spit *C.*, or in a pan, **már-la** in butter *W.*; **tá-gir šrág-če** to bake bread *W.*; **to tan,** to make swarthy, *nyi-mas* (to be tanned) by the sun *Dzl.*; *bsrég-k̔aṅ Sch.* shed for storing up fire-wood.

སྲེང་ *sreṅ*, *mi-sréṅ C.* = *mi-rkyáṅ*, v. *rkyaṅ-pa.*

སྲེད་ *sred* v. *sré-da.*

སྲེད་རྒྱལ་མ་ *sréd-rgyal-ma* a deity of the Bonpo *Mil.*

སྲེད་པ་ *sréd-pa* 1. vb., sbst., adj. **to desire, the desire, desirous,** *zás-la* of food *Lt.*, *k̔a-ṫsai ró-la* of acid or hot substances *Med.*, *ról-mo-la* (liking) music *Stg.*; *yúl-sred-pa čúṅ-ba* not much attached to his native country; *ₒjig-rtén*(*-la*) *sréd-pa* **avarice, covetousness** *Mil.*, *ₒdod-sred-čan* covetous, greedy *Pth.*, *čágs-sred-čan* lecherous, libidinous *Pth.*; *sréd-pa-las yóṅs-su gról-ba* quite free of any desire, (so is Buddha); *sréd-po Cs.* lover, *sréd-ma Cs.* sweet-heart. — 2. symb. num.: 8.

སྲེན་ *sren* (?) **floor** *W.*

སྲེལ་བ་ *srél-ba*, pf. and fut. *bsrel Cs.*, *W.* **šrál če** **to bring up, to rear, to nurse up, to train,** infants, young animals, **šrál-k̔an** nourisher, fosterer, nurse etc.

སྲེས་ *sres Ts.* = *ži-gil* q.v.

སྲོ་ *sro*, resp. *ṫugs-sro. W.*, **heat, ardour, passion, wrath, anger,** **šro yoṅ** anger rises (in a person), he (etc.) grows angry, **šro bab, šro bud** the anger abates; **šro-ríṅ-mo** slow to wrath, **šró-čan** furious, raging, **šro-ṫúṅ** hot, ardent, passionate.

སྲོ་བ་ *sró-ba*, pf. (*b*)*sros*, fut. *bsro*, imp. (*b*)*sro*(*s*), **to warm,** to make warm or hot at the fire, or in the sun *Glr.*, *Lt.*; *ₒjám-pai dród-kyis bu bsro* (a mother) foments her child with a gentle warmth *Thgy.*

སྲོ་མ་ *sró-ma* 1. **egg** of a louse, **a nit** *C.*, *W.*, *šig-sro ₒdu* nits are increasing fast *S.g.* — 2. small **bubble** *W.*, **čáṅ-la šró-ma k̔ol** the beer foams, froths in fermentation. — 3. *sró-ma nág-po*, *sró-ma séṅ-ge* n. of a medicinal herb *Med.*

སྲོ་ལོ་ *sró-lo Med.*, Sedum and similar plants.

སྲོག་ *srog* **life,** *srog γčód-pa* to kill, frq.; *srog lén-pa*, *ₒp̔róg-pa* id., esp. when done by demons; *srog daṅ ₒprál-ba* id., esp. to execute, to put to death *Glr.*, *srog daṅ ₒbrál-ba* to die; *srog ₒbúl-ba Dzl.* ༢༤༢, 12 *Sch.*: to sacrifice, to yield up one's life, but the manuscript of Kyelang has: *srog daṅ ₒbrál-lo*, and *šá-bai srog k̔yéd-la ₒbúl-lo* (*Mil.*) means: I make you a present of the stag's life, i.e. I spare its life for your sake; *srog ₒdór-ba* to sacrifice, one's life, prop. to cast it away *Dzl.*; *srog-la mi ltá-ba* to make light of one's life frq.; *srog daṅ bsdó-ba* to risk, to hazard one's life, frq.; *srog skyób-pa* to save life *Dzl.*, *srog ₒbyin-pa*, *ₒdon-pa* id., *Thgy.*: to save, to preserve (a child's) life (by well caring for it); *srog ₒṫsó-ba* id. *Dzl.*, *S.g.* (*Sch.* also: to recover, to grow well again); *sróg-gi ḱá-ba* n. of a vein; *sróg-gi snyíṅ-po Mil.?*

Comp. **sróg-skyób* W.* **deliverer, redeemer, saviour.** — *sróg-ḱuṅ Mil.* the deep cut or stab, by which Tibetan butchers kill animals (*Huc* I, 443), *sróg-ḱuṅ ˳byéd-pa* to stab in this manner. — *sróg-čan, srog-ldán* having life, living, alive. — *srog-čágs* animated being, *mi-la sógs-pai srog-čágs ťams-čád* all men and other living beings *Dzl.*, *srog-ťág = dpyaṅ-ťág.* — *srog-bdág čén-po = pe-dkár Glr.* — *srog-méd* lifeless, inanimate. — *srog-rtsá* 'root of life, vein of life', aorta *S.g.*, chiefly used rhetor. and fig. — *srog-lén* **deadly, fatal** *Lt.* — *srog-šiṅ* **axle, axle-tree;** *mčod-rtén-gyi srog-šiṅ* the pole in a Chodten; fig. **prop,** *séms-kyi srog-šiṅ Mil.*

སྲོང་བ་ *sróṅ-ba*, pf. *bsraṅs*, fut. *bsraṅ*, imp. *sroṅ(s)*, *bsraṅ*, *W.* **šráṅ-če**, **to make straight, to straighten,** *yón-po* what is awry, crooked *Lex.*, *γzer sróṅ-ba* to beat out nails; **to equal** *Sch.*; *sku dráṅ-por bsráṅs-te* (he sat) straight and erect, cf. also *sraṅ* and *bsráṅ-po.* — *W.*: **sráṅ-te ča dúg-ga 'i-ru dad** will he pass straight through or does he stay here?

སྲོང་བཙན་སྒམ་པོ་ *sroṅ-btsan-sgám-po* Srong-tsangampo, n. of the most famous king of Tibet, a contemporary of Mohammed; he introduced the Tibetan letters, and was the chief promoter of Buddhism and its literature.

སྲོད, སྲོད་འཇིང་ *srod, srod-˳jiṅ* **dusk of the evening, twilight,** **šrod rub* W.* the dusk of evening draws near, it is getting dusky, *srod daṅ ťo-raṅs* in the evening and morning *Lt.*; *srod byiṅ soṅ* night has set in; *srod yol soṅ* id., viz. the time about 11 o'clock at night *C.*; *srod-la* in the dusk of evening *Mil.* — *srod-˳ḱor-ṕag Cs.* (?) the *ḱyim* of evening-twilight, v. *nyin-žag.* — *srod-loṅ* dayblind, nyctalops, seeing better in a mild than in a bright light.

སྲོལ་ *srol* **usage, custom, common use, habitual practice, habit,** *der yi-gei srol méd-pas* as the art of writing is not yet in use there *Glr.*; *sṅár-srol bzáṅ-po-la dgoṅs šig* keep in mind the good old customs *Glr.*; *srol čágs-pa, sról-du ˳gyúr-ba Cs., sról-du ˳ťsúd-pa* to grow into a habit, to become the custom (of a person, a country); *srol ˳dzúgs-pa* to introduce a practice *Glr.*; *srol γtód-pa Lex.* prob. the same; *bka-sról = srol,* but at the same time expressive of reverence for the originator of the custom *Zam.*; *ṕyag-sról Mil.* is said to be a respectful expression for *lag-lén-gyi srol* (?); *legs-pai dpe-srol btsug-ste Glr.* having introduced good customs for imitation; *ťob-sról* **claim, title, right,** founded on old custom.

སྲོས་ *sros* 1. v. *sro-ba.* — 2. *Cs.* sbst. = *srod* twilight, dusk of evening, *mún-sros-pa* dusky, dark; *Glr.*: *sa srós-nas* when it grew dark.

སླ(ང)་ང་ *sla(ṅ)-ṅá* a large iron **pan** for parching grain, *slaṅ-dregs* soot adhering to a pan.

སླ་བ་ *slá-ba* I. adj., also *slá-mo* 1. **thin,** of fluids (opp. to *ská-ba, ťúg-po, réṅs-pa*) *W.* **lan-te**. — 2. **easy,** opp. to *dká-bo* difficult, *šés-pa slá-ba ma yin* knowledge is not easily obtained *Dzl.*; usually with the supine: *rig-par slao* it may easily be found out *Dzl.*, or with the root of the verb: *go-slá* easy to be comprehended.

II. vb., v. *slé-ba.*

སླག་པ, སློག་པ་ *slág-pa, slóg-pa* **fur-coat,** *sgo-slóg Mil.*, more corr. *dgo-slog*, hunting-coat, made of the skin of an antelope; *spyaṅ-slág, W.* **šaṅ-lag** fur-coat of a wolf's skin; *ťsar-slág* coat of lamb's skins; *ras-slág* prob.: a fur-coat covered with calico *Glr.*

སླང་ *slaṅ* 1. v. sub *sla-ṅa.* — 2. v. *slóṅ-ba.*

སླང་ཁ་ *sláṅ-ḱa* **shelf, shelves, stand.**

སླང་བ་ *sláṅ-ba* v. *slóṅ-ba.*

སླད་ *slad*, eleg. = *ṕyi* I, II, IV, 1. *slad-ról* **hind part, back part** *Lex.*, *slád-bžin-du* or *slád-bžin-par* behind, e.g. *˳bráṅ-ba* to walk behind one, *slád-sa = ṕyi-sa* (གྲུ) dung *Bhar.* — 2. **after,** *slád-na* c. genit. = *˳óg-tu Dzl.*; *slád-nas* adv. afterwards, hereafter, subsequently *Lex.* and *C.*; *slád-kyi* subsequent, later, posterior; *slád-ma Cs.*:

the hind part, that which comes after, the later or latter part; *slád-mar*, *slád-kyis* afterwards, hereafter, *slád-mar yaṅ* also for the future. — 3. *slád-du* **on account of, for the sake of.**

སླད་པ་ *slád-pa*, pf. *bslad*, (cf. *lhád-pa*) **to mix,** esp. with something of an inferior quality, hence **to adulterate, vitiate, to spoil, to corrupt,** *skyón-gyis* or *lhád-kyis ma slád-pa* not marred by any defects *Lex.*, *p̓yin-či-lóg-gis yoṅs-su slád-de* quite unfitted by perversity *Dzl.*; *gáṅ-gis kyaṅ ma sláḍ-pa* without any thing detrimental operating, not subject to any noxious influence *Wdṅ.*; *de myós-šiṅ sláḍ-par byás-te* making him drunk and thus disabling him *Dzl.*

སླན་ *slan* 1. (?) **na-slán** *W.* the furred ear-coverings of Tibetan ladies. — 2. = *slad*; *slan-čád* = *p̓yin-čád.*

སླན་ཏེ་ *slán-te* v. *slá-ba.*

སླན་པ་ *slán-pa* 1. **to mend, patch** *Sch.* — 2. v. *bslan.*

སླམ་པ་ *slám-pa*, 1. to roast slightly, **to parch,** to make brown by exposing to heat, e.g. meal *C.*, *W.* — 2. **to roast, to fry,** **már-la** *W.*

སླར་ *slar*, eleg. = *p̓yir*, 1. **again, over again, once more.** — 2. **afterwards, hereafter,** *slár-nas* id. *C.* — *slar yaṅ ˬjug-pa* to be affixed or added again (of letters, to the end of a word) *Gram.*; *slar ˬóṅ-ba* to come back, to return *Dzl.*; *slar-γšegs* he went away again *Dzl.*; *slar stobs skyed* he regains strength *S.g.*; *slár-bsdu-ba* the final o of a verb, indicating the end of a sentence *Gram.*

སླས་ *slas* 1. v. *lhas.* — 2. **retinue, train, attendants,** wives and servants, *p̓o-bráṅ-gi slas* a king's or prince's retinue, **the court,** people at court *Dzl.*

སླི་ *sli C.* acc. to some authorities: a yellowish red **apple,** or Indian apple (opp. to *kú-šu* Tibetan apple); acc. to *Cs.* **cherry;** cherries, however, are scarcely known in Tibet. — *sli-tsi* small, wild-growing, cherry-like dwarf-apples, *Pyrus baccata;* **bi-li-tsi** *W.* gooseberry; **wám-p̓u-li-tsi** the white berries of a species of mountain-ash, *Pyrus ursina* (**wamp̓u** in the Bunan language: 'bear').

སླུ་བ་ *slú-ba*, pf. *bslus*, fut. *bslu*, imp. (*b*)*slu*(*s*), **to entice, allure, ensnare, beguile, seduce,** e.g. to be ensnared by wordly sorrows; less frq. in a direct sense: **to impose on, to deceive,** *rdzun byás-te* by a falsehood *Dzl.*; *slu-k̓rid* enticement, seduction, means of seduction, bait; *bzáṅ-poi slu-k̓rid* enticement to a good purpose; *bslú-ba-mk̓an* deceiver, deluder, impostor *Glr.*; *mi-slú*(*-ba*) infallible, sure *Mil.*

སླེ་ *sle* 1. a coarse blanket *Ts.*, = *čá-ra*, *čá-ri.* — 2. n. of the capital of Ladak.

སླེ་ཏྲེས་ *sle-trés Med.* n. of a creeper or climbing plant.

སླེ་པོ་ *slé-po U*, *slé-ba*, *slé-bo Cs.* a flat **basket.**

སླེ་བ་ *slé-ba* I. vb., *bsle-ba*, *lhé-ba.* pf. *lhas B.*, **lá-če** *W.* **to twist, plait, braid,** the hair, (to make) a basket etc.; **to knit.**

II. sbst. 1. v. no. I. — 2. **distortion, dislocation** (of a limb) *Cs.*; *slé-bo* one that has a distorted limb *Cs.*; *sle-mig* a distorted eye *Cs.*

སླེ་ཡོན་ *sle-yón* **craft, deceit, trickery,** *sle-yón byéd-pa* **to cheat, deceive, impose upon** *Cs.*

སླེད་ *sled* knitting-needle(?) *Ld.*

སླེབ་པ་ *sléb-pa*, pf. (*b*)*slebs*, fut. *bsleb*, resp. *ˬbyón-pa*, *p̓éb-pa* (cf. *ˬóṅ-ba*), 1. **to arrive,** with termin.; *bslebs-zin* I have arrived, he has arrived; in *Ld.* however the future **slebs yin** is also pronounced **leb zin**. — 2. **to reach, to extend,** to a certain place or point *Pth.* and col. — 3. **to come in** (of interest, rent, duties), hence *sleb* income, revenue, public revenue, receipt of customs etc.; *sleb-t̓o* account of receipts.

སློ་དྲོན་ *slo-drón* warm fresh **dung** *Sch.*

སློག་པ་ *slog-pa* I. sbst. v. *slág-pa.*

II. vb., pf. *bslogs*, fut. *bslog*, *Cs.* (trs. to *ldog-pa*) **to turn,** to turn round or about, to turn upside down, inside out, *rkyál-pa p̓yi-náṅ slóg-pa* to turn out the inside of a bag; *mig slóg-pa* to roll one's eyes; **boṅ-bu má-lag slog ˬdug** the donkey is rolling on his back; *sa slóg-pa* to plough up, turn up, to dig the soil; in arithmetic: **sum nyi lóg-pa ḍug** *W.* two times three are six.

སློང་བ་, སླང་བ་ *slóṅ-ba, sláṅ-ba*, pf. *(b)slaṅs*, fut. *(b)slaṅ*, imp. *sloṅ(s)*, *W.* **láṅ-če**, I. causat. and transit. form to *ldáṅ-ba*. 1. **to cause to rise, to help to rise**, one lying on the ground; *dgrá-ru slóṅ-ba* to cause a person to rise as an enemy (cf. *dgrar ldáṅ-ba*), i.e. to make a person one's enemy *S.g.*; *bsád-pai mi-ró slóṅ-ba* to resuscitate the slain; **to excite, cause, inspire,** compassion, fear, terror etc.; *ṗrag-dog-gis, skyo-šas-kyis kun-nas bslaṅs-te Glr., Mil.* quite excited by envy and hatred, ni f.; esp. in pathology of the procatarctic or exciting causes of diseases: **to kindle** (a disease) **into action**, hence *sloṅ-rkyén* the exciting cause (of a disease); — **to raise, to erect**, a pile, post, wall *Mil.; sláṅ-šiṅ* a pile, stay, prop, erected or set up. — *kun-slóṅ Lex., Mil.: nyon-móṅs-kyi sloṅ-kun-sloṅ* excitement (??).

II. (perh. originally quite a different word), 1. **to ask, require**, ccdp. *klu žig ṅá-la dpe sloṅ* a Lu asks me for the book *Dzl.; bú-mo čúṅ-mar slóṅ-ba* to ask a man's daughter in marriage *Dzl.*; esp. **to beg**, to try to get by begging: *čúṅ-zad bsláṅ-ṅo* we beg for a little of it! *Dzl., ṗá-la sláṅs-nas ḱyer* he obtained it from his father by begging *Mil.; bsód-snyoms slóṅ-ba* to collect alms by begging (*slóṅ-ba* partic. and sbst. beggar, mendicant *Dzl*, *slóṅ-mḱan, slóṅ-ba-po* id.); hence. — 2. **to collect, to gather**, *nor Cs.* riches. — 3. **to examine, to probe** (a wound), *rma-γsar mdzúb-mos* a fresh wound with the finger *Thgy.*; also: **to search** a man's **house.** — 4. **to give,** *ḱa-lhág čig sdús-la sloṅ čig* gather some of the remnants of the meal, and give them to me! *Mil.*, so in *Sp.* and *C.* frq.

སློང་མོ་ *slóṅ-mo* **alms**, *slóṅ-mo slóṅ-ba Lex.*, *byéd-pa Cs.* to ask alms, to beg; *slóṅ-mos ₒtsó-ba* to live on alms; *slóṅ-mo-pa* beggar *Pth.*

སློན་པ་ *slón-pa* 1. *Sch.* **to patch, to mend.** — 2. *Sch.*: *dpán-po ṗyir slón-par byéd-pa* to dissemble, to feign (?) — 3. *Cs.*: to thrust out.

སློབ་ *slob* the act of learning, study, *slob ma myóṅ-ba* to have had no instruction or education; *slob ₒḱrid-pa* to teach.

སློབ་པ་ *slób-pa*, I. vb., pf. *bslabs*, fut. *bslab*, imp. *slob(s)*, *W.* **láb-če**, **to learn, to teach,** *ṅa* or *ṅá-la slob* I learn, *ṅas slob* I teach, *dé-la mḱan slob γnyis-kyis lo-tsṫsa bslabs* both the abbot and the instructor taught him the art of translating *Pth.*; *ṅa rtsis šig slob ₒdód-pas slobs* as I should like to learn something of mathematics, teach me! *Pth.*; *bslábs-pas šés-te* when he had learned it *Pth.; bsláb-čiṅ lóbs-pa yaṅ dka* as learning is difficult, even if one is taught *Dzl.*; *slób-tu ₒǰúg-pa* to let one take lessons, to have or get one instructed *Dzl.;* **ṫ ú-gu-la gom-ṫáṅ láb-če** to teach a little child to walk *W.; mi-la yi-ge bslabs* schools were established *Glr.; yón-tan slób-pa* to teach (to learn) good, useful, things *Pth.* and frq.

II sbst. 1. the act of **learning** *Dzl.* — 2. **teacher, instructor,** *brám-ze slób-pa* a Brahman as instructor *Dzl.*; *ₒṗágs-pa slób-pa-rnams* the venerable preceptors (more than *dge-slóṅ*, less than *dgrá-bčom-pa*) *Tar.* 5, 1. 31, 9.

Comp. **lob-ḱyád** *W.* **use, practice, exercise.** — *slob-grwá* **school, school-room, school-house;** **lob-ḍa-ḱáṅ** *W.* id. — *slob-gṙógs* school-fellow, co-disciple. — *slob-γnyér* student, scholar, *slob-γnyér gáṅ-du bgyis* where have you studied? at what college have you been a student? *Mil.* — *slób-dpon* **teacher, instructor, master,** frq.; also a college-title like our bachelor etc.; **'the teacher'** by way of eminence, is either Buddha or *Pad-ma-byuṅ-γnás.* — *slob-ₒbáṅs* **scholar, pupil, disciple,** = *bu-slób Mil.* — *slób-ma* id., frq. **lob-ló** **report, rumour, fame** *W.* — Cf. *bslabs.*

སློབས་ *slobs* **exercise, practice, experience;** *mig-slobs ṅan-pa skye Mil.* a bad custom of seeing begins to prevail (viz. that of looking downward, and minding only earthly things).

གསའ་, བསའ་ *γsa, bsa Mil., C.* (*W.* **šan**) **the snow-leopard**, nearly white, with small clusters of black spots; living on the higher mountains.

གསག་པ་ *ysáq-pa Sch.* **to sew together.**

གསང་ what is **secret, hidden,** *ysan šor* the secret comes out, is made known *Dzl.*

གསང་བ་ *ysáṅ-ba* I. vb. **to do a thing secretly, to conceal,** *ṅa-la ysaṅ-du mi ruṅ* it is not right of you to be so close to me *Mil.*; *ysáṅ-ste brkús-nas* stealing secretly, *ysáṅ-ste bskyál-nas* sending underhand, furtively *Dzl.*; **to hide one's self, to be concealed** *dbén-pai γnas šig-tu ysáṅ-ste* betaking one's self secretly to a solitary place *Dzl.*, *yid-mťún-par ysáṅ-ste* keeping it secret with one consent *Dzl.*; **saṅ-nẹ dad-če** *W.* to sit concealed.

II. sbst. 1. **secret things, a secret;** *ysaṅ-bai bdag-po* = *ysan-dbaṅ* v. below. — 2. **secret parts** *Med.*, also *ysaṅ-γnás Med.*, *ysáṅ-bai pád-ma Med.*, sometimes the anus included; *ysáṅ-bai nad* diseases of the sexual organs *Med.*

III. adj. 1. **secret, hidden, concealed,** *ysáṅ-bai čos* esoteric doctrine *Dzl.*; *p̓yi-naṅ-ysáṅ* v. *p̓yi* III. — 2. *ḱyi-mo nyan-gyi rna ysaṅ-ba* a female dog of very sharp hearing (v. *yseṅ-ba*).

Comp. *ysáṅ-kaṅ* a secret room *Cs.* — *ysáṅ-sgo* a secret door *Pth.* — *ysan-sgro S.g.?* — *ysaṅ-sṅágs* secret charms, mysterious incantations, frq.; even in medical works they are praised as the 'best medicine'. — *ysaṅ-mǰe* v. *mǰe.* — *ysaṅ-γnás* 1. a secret **place.** 2. **mystery,** ni f.: *ysáṅ-bai γnas dú-ma ysuṅs* he taught many mysteries, many secret doctrines. 3. **privities, pudenda.** — *ysaṅ-spyód* **privy, necessary,** water-closet. — *ysaṅ-dbáṅ*, *ysaṅ-rdór Mil.*, *ysaṅ-bai-bdág-po Do.* = *rdo-rǰe-ₒčaṅ*, v. *rdo-rǰe*, comp.

གསན་པ་ *ysán-pa* resp. **to hear, to listen** *Dzl.*; *ḱyod ysan daṅ* listen (to me)! *Mil.*; *bdag-gi ťsig-la yson* id. *Glr.*; with *las* or *la*: to hear a person teaching, expounding etc. *Tar.* Cf. *ysón-pa.*

གསབ་པ་ *ysáb-pa* v. *ysób-pa.*

གསར་བ་ *ysár-ba, ysár-pa,* usually *ysár-po* **new, fresh,** *lúg-ša ysár-ba* fresh mutton *Lt.*; *rma ysár-pa* a raw wound *Thgy.*; *bág-ma ysár-pa* the young, (recently married) wife *Dzl.*; **bhú-mo sár-pa** a girl that is still a virgin *C.*; *ysár-du* adv., *ysár-du bsád-pai ša* flesh of animals that have just been slaughtered, lit.: fresh-slaughtered flesh *Dzl.*; *ḱa-ysár* a new edge; *ḱaṅ-ysár* new house, also a name of villages, castles etc.; *gos-ysár, mar-ysár Lt.*; *rta-ysár Schr.* a horse not yet broken in. — *ysar ₒgrógs-pa Sch.*: 'to tell each other news; to make a new acquaintance'. **sar-zúg čó-če** *W.* to plant (a piece of land) for the first time, to cultivate, to people, to stock with inhabitants. — *ysar-riṅ* old and new, stale and fresh; age, duration, existence. — *ysar yčód-pa* frq., also *ťsar yčód-pa Pth.*, **to search, inquire into, investigate thoroughly, to examine, to study,** *skad* a language. — *ysár-bu* **new beginner, tyro, novice** *Mil.*

གསལ་བ་ *ysál-ba* vb., **to be clear, distinct, bright,** *slar šár-žiṅ ysál-na* when (the sun) shines bright again; *már-me ₒčí-ḱar ysál-ba bžin* flaming up once more, like an extinguishing lamp *Glr.*; *lhaṅ-ṅé lham-mér ysál-te* appearing bright, clear and distinct *Dzl.*; *ysál-lo* it is clear, it is evident; it stands written, it may be read, *ₒdúl-ba-na ysál-lo* it may be read in the Dulva *Glr.*, *Tar.*; *ysál-po* (प्रकाश) **visible** to a great distance, **conspicuous, distinct,** obvious, intelligible; *kun-ysál* id.; **mig sál-po ťoṅ mi ťub, ṅag sál-po zer mi še** *W.* his eye, — his speech, is not clear, he is not able to see, to speak distinctly; *ysal-dag-snyan-ysúm B.* = the popular *sgra-dag-ysal-ysúm,* v. *sgra*; *yi-ge ysál-po* a plain, legible handwriting; **clear, bright,** *ysál-bai mé-loṅ* a bright mirror (a frq. title of books); **bright, light, pure,** of colours, *dkar-ysál* pure white *Glr.*; **pure,** free from faults and deficiencies, **sál-po gyáb-če** *W.* **to correct;** *sa-p̓yógs kyaṅ ysál-bar gyúr-ro* also his whole neighbourhood will be freed from defects, will become **happy** *Do.*; *ysál-le-ba* = *ysal-ba*; *ysál-ḱa Tar.* prob. = *ysál-ča, Mil.*: *ysál-ča žig γnáṅ-ba žu* I request (you) to give me a detailed account, inst. of which also only *sal čig* may be said.

གསལ་སིང་ γsál-śiṅ (like σταυρὸς in its original meaning) **a pointed stake,** for empaling malefactors, *γsál-śiṅ-du* or *γsál-śiṅ-gi ťsé-la skyón-pa* to empale. — Cf. *rkyaṅ-śiṅ*.

གསས་མོ་ *γsás-mo Lexx.*; in *Lt.* prob.: **mother's milk.**

གསིག་པ་ *γsig-pa Cs.*, also *bsig-pa*, to throw up in a backward direction; in *Thgr.* is said of a lion: *rál-pa γsig* he shakes his mane; *dpuṅ-bsig Cs.*: 'the shaking of one's shoulder' (prob. for: **shrugging**); **to winnow, to fan, to sift** *Stg.; W.*

གསིང་མ་ *γsiṅ-ma* 1. **pasture-ground, meadow** *Dzl.* — 2. moor, fen *Sch.?*

གསིར་བ་ *γsir-ba Sch.*, *bsir-ba Cs.* 1. **to whirl about** or round, to twirl, *p̀aṅ* a spindle, *mda γsír-ba Cs.*: 'to whirl an arrow'. — 2. *W.* **to move** by a repeated pushing, *p̀ág-ste* a plane; **to smooth, to even,** with a plane, a knife etc.; **to slide, glide, slip,** down a slope.

གསིལ་བ་ *γsil-ba* 1. **to cut to pieces, to divide, split,** *lhú-ru Mil.*, *dúm-bur Lex.*, *γsor-gyis γsil-ba* to saw to pieces, to saw up. — 2. **to toll, sound, ring,** *dril-bu γsil-ba* to ring a bell *Cs.*, hence *mk̀ar-γsil* v. *mk̀ar-ba*. — 3. **sil-ĉe* W.* **to read.** — *γsil-bu* and *γsil-ma* v. *sil-bu*.

གསུང་ *γsuṅ*, resp. for *skad* and *γtam*, 1. **voice,** *γsuṅ byuṅ* a voice sounded, was heard *Glr.*, *γsuṅ dág-pa* a clear voice, like that of Buddha *Dzl.* — 2. **the act of speaking, talking,** *γsuṅ gléṅ-ba* to converse, discourse, *γsuṅ ₒdré-ba*, *γsuṅ-ₒdré mdzád-pa* id.; that which is spoken, the words uttered, **the speech,** *k̀yéd-kyi γsuṅ dei lán-du* in answer to your words *Glr.*; *γsuṅ k̀lóg-pa* to read the sayings, the apothegms (of Buddha) *Ma.*

གསུང་བ་ *γsúṅ-ba* I. vb., pf. *γsuṅs*, resp. for *smrá-ba B.* and *C.* (in *W.* **mól-ĉe** is used inst. of it) **to speak, talk, say,** the latter also with the termin. of the infin., inst. of direct speech, but rarely; *dé-skad ma γsuṅ* your Reverence should not say so! *Mil.*; *γsuṅ ma γnaṅ* it did not please him to speak *Mil.*; *rdzun γsúṅ-ba* to tell a falsehood, to lie; **to explain,** *don Mil.*; **to ask;** *mi ₒdod mi γsuṅ bžés-par žu Mil.* please accept it without ceremonies (without a refusal); *žal-γdáms γsúṅ-ba* to give advice etc. *Glr.*; *ĉos γsúṅ-ba* to preach *Glr.*; *mgúr-ma γsúṅ-ba* to recite or to sing a song (but also: *mgúr-ma smrá-ba, zér-ba* is said).

Comp. *γsuṅ-bgrós* **report, statement, opinion.** — *γsuṅ-mĉog* **principal word, main dogma** e.g. the Ommanipadmehum *Glr.* — *γsuṅ-snyán* a harmonious voice, an agreeable, pleasant speech; *Mil.* uses it also of the singing of birds (and the screaming of peacocks!) — *γsuṅ-sprós*, *γsuṅ-ₒp̀ró* **conversation** between persons of rank, or between such and inferior people. *γsuṅ-ráb* = *γsuṅ-mĉóg*, also sacred writing, **Holy Scripture** *Chr. Pr.* — *γsuṅ-śóg* = *bka-śóg*.

གསུད་པ་, བསུད་པ་ *γsúd-pa*, *bsúd-pa* 1. *Sch.* **to be lost, to be dispersed.** — 2. *W.* to fill with food beyond satiety, **to stuff, to cram.** *Bhar.* 124 *smán-pa γsud* stands for *Ssk.* विसूचिका (*Will.*: spasmodic cholera), which elsewh. is rendered *zas ma žu-ba*; the meaning is prob. to overeat one's self.

གསུམ་ *γsum* three (cf. *sum*), *γsúm-k̀a*, *γsúm-ga* the three, all the three; *γsúm-pa* the third; containing three; *γsúm-po* the three; *γsum* also elliptically for *dkon-mĉog-γsúm*: *γsúm-la skyábs-su ₒdóṅ-ba* to seek the protection of the Three Precious *Do.*; *bskál-pa gráṅs-med(-pa) γsum* three times innumerable Kalpas (appeared) *Dzl.*, *Glr.*; *rgán-mo ma smad γsum-po ₒdi* the old (woman) with her (two) sons, the three *Dzl.*; *rgyál-po yab yum γsum* the king and his (two) queens, the three *Glr.*; *rab ₒbriṅ γsum* the big, the middle (and the little one), the three. — *γsúm-sprul* emanation of the third degree, = *nyiṅ-sprul*.

གསུར་མ་ *γsúr-ma* a thing slightly burnt, **singed** *Cs.*, *γsur-dri* the smell of it.

གསུས་པ་ *γsús-pa* **belly, stomach,** *γsús-pa sbos* the belly is swollen or distended *Lex.*; *γsus-nád* dropsy of the belly; *γsus-rked* the middle part of the body, the waist *Sch.*; *γsus-ₒp̀yaṅ-po* a deity.

གསེ་བ་ *γsé-ba* 1. v. *sé-ba*. — 2. v. *γséd-pa*.

གསེག་བརྡར་ *γseg-brdár Sch.* **a file** (instrument), v. *sag-γdar*.

གསེག་མ་ *γség-ma* **small stones**; *γseg-seb-čan* full of small stones.

གསེག་གཤང་ *γseg-γšáṅ* = *mḱar-γsil Lex.*

གསེང་, སེང་ *γseṅ, seṅ* 1. **cleft, chink, crevice, fissure, leak,** v. *ḱoṅ-séṅ* sub *ḱoṅ* extr.; *sgo-γséṅ* chink of a door *Tar.*; *γseṅ bsrúb-pa Sch.* to stop up, plug up, crevices etc.; *γséṅs-pa* leaky, cracked, full of fissures *Sch.* — 2. **harmonious,** well-sounding. — 3. *rná-ba γseṅ Sch.*: a sharp, acute, quick ear, cf. *γsáṅ-ba* II, 2.

གསེད་ *γsed* several larger species of Lonicera.

གསེད་པ་ *γséd-pa*, also *bséd-pa* (pf. *γses?*) **to pick, sort, assort,** hair, wool; **to pull or pluck in pieces.**

གསེབ་ *γseb* I. **stallion,** a male horse or camel.

II. also *seb*, 1. the narrow **interstices** between persons or things thronged together, hence with *na, tu* and *la*, **between, among,** with *nas* **from between,** *ḱyi mii γséb-la mčoṅ* the dog leaps into the midst of the people, *ló-mai γséb-tu ˳ǰóg-pa* to put between leaves, *sprin-gyi γséb-nas lus p̀yed ˳ťon* half of his body protrudes from between the clouds, = rises above etc.; *groṅ-γséb-tu bžúgs-pa* to sit among the villagers; *ḱyéd-čag-gi γséb-na Meu-dgál byá-bai bud-méd yód-dam?* is there a woman among you named *Meu-dgal?* *γséb-lam* a secret path, by-way, between rocks or underwood. — 2. **multitude, crowd,** *dmág-γseb* army, *nágs-γseb* forest.

གསེར་ *γser* (*Pers.* زر) **gold**; *γsér-gyi* of gold, golden, *γsér-gyi mé-tog* n. of a medicinal herb.

Comp. *γser-skúd S.g.* n. of an officinal herb. — *γser-skyéms* v. *skyems*. — *γsér-ḱa* a gold mine. — *γser-mḱár* an imperial castle *Wts.* — *γser-glíṅ* Malacca *Cs.* — *γser-˳gyur-rtsi* prob. much the same as: 'philosopher's stone' *Pth.* — *γser-ťúb* n. of the second Buddha, Kanakamuni. — *γser-mdóg* gold-colour, *γsér-mdog-čan* n. of a monastery. — *γsér-pa* gold-searcher, gold-washer *Gram.*; *γser-p̀ud* n. of a medicinal herb, an emetic *Med.* — *γser-˳p̀réṅ* a gold chain. — *γser-byé* gold-sand. — *γser-mé* = *γsér-gyi-mé-tog Med.* — *γser-γtsó-ma, γser-btsó-ma* refined gold *Glr.*, *Pth.* — **ser-záṅ* W.* gilt copper. — *γser-bzó-pa, γser-mgár Cs.* goldsmith. — *γser-yig-pa* 'bearer of a gold-letter', ambassador, envoy *Glr.* — *γser-šóg* leaf-gold, gold-foil, foliated gold *Sch.* — *γser-sraṅ* one ounce of gold; a coin = 16 rupees, gold-mohur.

གསེས་ *γses? raṅ-γsés* **reciprocal, mutual** *Wdṅ.*

གསོ་བ་ *γsó-ba* pf. *γsos*, (*b*)*sos* (= *˳tsó-ba*) 1. **to feed, nourish** *Dzl.*; **to bring up, nurse up, rear, train,** *bu* a child, *dúd-˳gro* an animal; also *γsó-skyoṅ-ba, γso-skyóṅ byéd-pa*. — 2. **to cure,** *nad, rma*; **to stop, remove,** to put an end to, *ṅal* fatigue, i.e. to recruit one's self, to rest; **to mend, to repair,** *ḱyim* a house *Cs.*; **to restore, rebuild, re-establish,** what had been destroyed, **to kindle again, stir up again,** a fire; *žig-* or *šig-γso-ba* id.; **to refresh, recreate,** *sems*, resp. *ťugs*, the soul, i.e. to comfort, console.

Comp. *γso-mḱan* **restorer** *Glr.* *γso-ťábs* **way of curing,** manner of healing *Med.* — *γsó-ba-po* **physician** *Med.* — *γsó-bya* the thing to be cured, the disease *Med.*; *γso-byéd* the healing substance, **the remedy**; the healing person, **the physician.** — *γso-sbyóṅ-ba* v. the following article. — *γso-tsúl* = *γso-ťábs.* — *γso-rig* **pharmacology.**

གསོ་སྦྱོང་བ་ *γso-sbyóṅ-ba*, for *ṅyés-pa γsó-ba daṅ sdig-pa sbyoṅ-ba* to get quit of sin, by making confession to a priest and thus restoring the former state of virtuousness, **to confess**; also *γso-sbyoṅ len-pa, γso-sbyoṅ-la γnas-pa*; such confession does not entail any penalties, but only a renewal of obligations, cf. *Fouc. Gyatch.* II, 16.

གསོ་རས་ *γso-rás Lex.*; *Sch.*: **rag, tatter.**

གསོག་པ་ *γsóg-pa* 1. v. *sóg-pa* II. — 2. v. *sob*.

གསོང་པོ་ *γsóṅ-po* **sincere,** *γsóṅ-por smrá-ba* to speak the truth.

གསོང་བ་ *γsóṅ-ba Cs.* and *Lex.*; usually *γsáṅ-ba*.

གསོད་པ་ *γsód-pa*, pf. *bsad*, fut. (*Lex. γsad*, usually:) *bsad*, imp. *sod*, *W.* **sád-će**, 1. **to kill, slay, murder, slaughter.** *γsód-pa-la dgá-ba* to delight in killing *Dzl.*; *bsad ma-ťág-pai ša*, *γsár-du bsád-pai ša* v. *γsár-ba*; *rgyál-pos γsód-pa* to be executed by the authority *Dzl.*; (*ťse*) *bsád-pa-la ťúg-nas* when he was just on the point of being executed *Dzl.*; **p̔ag ǰáb-te sád-tań-će* W.* to assassinate; *bsád-do! bčóm-mo!* I am lost! it is all over with me! *Wdń.* — 2. **to put out, extinguish** frq. — 3. *k̔yád-γsod-pa* to despise, v. *k̔yad* extr.

Comp. *γsod-γčód* **the act of murdering, murder,** slaughter, *γsod-γčód-kyi ǰigs-pa* fear of murder *Mil.*; *γsod-γčód máń-po byed* he is murdering, slaughtering, a great deal. — *γsod-byéd* killer, murderer, *γsod-byéd rńán-pa* the murderous huntsman *Lex.*; *γsod-byéd-kyi γnas* slaughter-house *Stg.* — *γsód-sa* place of execution *Thgy.* — *γsód-lugs* way of killing, *sńar ma byas* a new (way of killing) *Tar.*

གསོན་པ་ *γsón-pa* I. A. vb., 1. intrs. **to live, to be alive,** *γsón-no* he (she etc.) is alive, **de méd-na mi són-će mi ťub** without that a man cannot live *W.*; **to remain alive, to save or preserve one's own life,** *rdzún-du smrás-na γson kyań* though I could save my life by (telling) a falsehood *Dzl.*; *γsón-par mi ˳dod* I do not wish to live (any longer) *Dzl.*; of the fire: **to burn,** **da són-na* W.* does it burn now? — 2. trs. **to wake, to rouse** from sleep **by shaking, to urge on, to hurry on** (lazy people), by force, whereas *skúl-ba* is only done by words. — B. sbst. **life,** *γsón-pai ťsé-na* or *γsón-pai dús-su* **during** (my, your etc.) **life, in lifetime,** frq.; hence: *γson-pa-nyid* for ζωή John 1, 4 etc. *Chr. P.* — C. adj. **living, alive,** frq. *γsón-po*, col. **γsón-te**, *kyé-ma bu γsón-po mťóń-ńo* ah, there I see my son again alive! *Stg.*; *γsón-por byéd-pa* to call into life, to animate, *γsón-por dúr-du ˳ǰúg-pa* to bury alive *Dzl.*, *γsón-pai rgyú-ma ˳drén-pa* to tear out the bowels of a living man; **son-te* W.* also: **healthy, whole, restored to health again,** **kań-pa, mig, me són-te čó-će** to cure a foot, an eye, to blow a fire into flame again; **entire, whole, undivided,** **són-te k̔yóń-ńa** am I to bring it entire (or cut into pieces etc.)? of the moon: **full.** — *γsón-ma* rarely for *γsón-po*, *p̔úg-ron γsón-ma* a live pigeon *Pth.*; *γson-γšin* both the living and the dead *Cs.*; *γson bsrégs* a creature burnt alive, *mi žig(-la) γson-bsrégs byéd-pa* to burn a person alive *Pth.*

II. vb., pf. *bsan*, fut. *γsan*, imp. *γson Cs.*, prob. the original form of *γsán-pa* **to hear.**

III. *čúd-γson-pa* v. *čud.*

གསོབ་ *γsob* v. *sob.*

གསོབ་པ་ *γsób-pa*, pf. *bsab*, fut. *γsab*, 1. **to fill out or up, to supply, complete, make up,** *hór-k̔ońs* a gap (?) *Sch.*, **to cure,** wounds *W.*, **sob-mán** balm, ointment for wounds. — 2. **to pay, repay, return,** *skyin-pa* a loan *Sch.*, *drin γsób-pa* to return a kindness *Glr.*

གསོར་ *γsor* 1. v. *sór* I. — 2. supine of *γsó-ba.*

གསོར་བ་ *γsórba* **to brandish, flourish,** a staff *Cs.*

གསོལ་བ་ *γsól-ba* I. vb., 1. = *žú-ba* 1, q.v.; *rgyál-po-la sróg-gi skyabs γsól-to* he besought the king to save his life *Dzl.*; *stón-pa-la smón-lam btáb-par γsol čig* ask the teacher to say the prayers *Dzl.*; *bstán-du γsol* I beg to explain, frq.; *lha γsól-ba* to worship a god, by offerings, libations etc. *Glr.* and elsewh. Tibetans when arriving on the top of a mountain-pass generally mutter the words: *γsól-lo γsól-lo*, prob. to express their thankfulness for having been preserved from harm so far, and to implore further protection. — 2. resp. for *gón-pa* and *skón-pa* **to put on:** (*skú-la*) *ná-bza*, *čos-gos*, *dbú-la ťod*, *žábs-la čag* (to put on) a garment, clerical robes, cap, shoes *Dzl.*, *Glr.*; *slób-dpon-la ber-čén skú-la γsól-te* putting the cloak on the teacher *Ma.*; for *zá-ba*, *˳ťúń-ba*, also for *˳drén-pa*, **to eat, to drink, to offer a meal** *Dzl.*; *rgyál-po ˳bras-čáń γsól-nas* as the king had drunk rice-wine *Glr.*; **to take, to give, administer** (medicine) *Dzl.*; **to place** (food etc.) **before, to**

serve up for (clerical persons) *Dzl.*, *γsól-lo mčód-čig* I place it before you, help yourself! moreover: *rgyál-pos čáb-la sku-k̔rús γsol* the king took a bath *Glr.*; *srás-la sku-k̔rús γsól-lo* they administered a bath to the prince *Glr.*; *mts̔an γsól-ba* to assume, to receive, a name *Glr.*, to give a name *Glr.*; even thus: *dei t̔úgs-la γdon γsol* a demon enters his (the king's) body (clothes himself with it) *Glr.*

Comp. **sol-kár* W.*, resp. for *ka-yol* earthen ware, crockery. — *γsol-skrúm* meat prepared for the table of a man of rank. *γsol-k̔á* 1. request, prayer *Sch.* 2. meat and drink *Sch.* — **sól-k̔aṅ** resp. for **yọ́-k̔aṅ* C.*, **t̔ab-ts̔áṅ* W.* **kitchen.** — *γsol-ṅán* poisoned food *Glr.* — *γsol-lčóg* **table.** — *γsol-mčód* **prayer** and **offerings.** — *γsol-ǰá* **tea.** — *γsol-nyá* fish destined or dressed for the table of a respected person, *rgyál-poi Pth.* — *γsol-tág*, *γsol-stégs* **table.** — *γsol-tib* **tea-pot.** — *γsol-t̔áb* **fire-place, kitchen.** — *γsol-ldóṅ* = *gur-gúr.* — *γsól-dpon* prop. head-cook, master-cook, gen. **cup-bearer, butler, waiter.** — *γsol-p̔ógs* **salary** *Sch.* — **γsol-₀biṅ* C.* = *γsol-tib.* — *γsol-már* **butter.** — *γsol-ts̔igs* **dinner.** — *γsol-žib* fine parched **barley-flour.** *γsol-γyóg* under-waiter, under-butler. — *γsol-rás* **distribution of victuals,** by a person of rank to common people, hence *Chr. P.* for **Lord's supper,** holy communion; **donation, gift, present** in gen.

II. sbst. 1. **request, demand, entreaty,** *γsol-ba ₒdebs-pa* to make a request, to entreat frq. — 2. **food** **sól-wa žé-pa** to eat, dine, sup *C.*

གསོས་པ་ *γsós-pa* v. *γsó-ba*, *γsos byéd-pa* **to cure** *Sch.*; *bu mi γsos-pa* not keeping, retaining a child alive *Do.*; *γsós-bu* foster-son, **adoptive son;** *γsós-ma* cure? medicine? *γsós-ma ₒdébs-pa Thgy.*

བསའ་ *bsa* v. *γsa.*

བསག་པ་ *bság-pa* v. *γsóg-pa.*

བསང་བུ་ *bsáṅ-bu* resp. for *zan* **food, fare** *Glr.*; **bsáṅ-ma** id. *W.*; *bsaṅ-ₒbrás* resp. a dish of rice.

བསད་པ་ *bsád-pa* v. *γsód-pa.*

བསབ་པ་ *bsáb-pa* v. *γsób-pa.*

བསམ་ *bsam*, **thought, thinking,** *bsám-gyis mi k̔yáb-pa* beyond the reach of human intellect, **incomprehensible** etc. frq.; *čos bzáṅ-las bsam bzaṅ lhág-pa yin* a good way of thinking is worth more than good (external) religion *Mil.*; *W.*: **sam-ṅan-čan** **malicious, wicked.**

བསམ་པ་ *bsám-pa* I. fut. tense and secondary form of *sém-pa.*

II. sbst. संकल्प, 1. **thought,** imagination, fancy, *bsám-pa ṅán-pa sém-pa* to foster bad thoughts *Do.*; *bsám-pa tsám-gyis* quick as thought; *rtág-tu ₒdi snyám-du bsám-pa skyes* he was constantly haunted by these thoughts *Dzl.* — 2. **will,** *mi žig-gi bsám-pa ltar* (or *bžin-du*) *sgrúb-pa* to execute, to carry out a person's will frq.; *bsám-pa ltar ma gyúr-pas* as it did not go according to their **wish;** *bsam-pa ₒdi-las ma zlog čig* do not try to divert me from my **purpose** *Dzl.*; *bsám-pa bzáṅ-po* good **intention** or **design** *Mil.*; **desire, mind, inclination, liking,** *γnód-pai* or *γdúg-pai* thirst for blood, murderous disposition *Glr.* — 3. **soul, heart** (of rare occurrence), *bsám-pai dón mi ₒgrub* then (by doing so) you injure your own soul *Mil.*

Comp. *bsam-γtán*, ध्यान, 1. **state of complete abstraction,** acc. to *Burn.* '*contemplation*' (cf. *tiṅ-ṅe-ₒdzin*, समाधि, समापत्ति, *Burn.* '*méditation*'), *bsam-γtán byéd-pa* to transpose one's self into the state of contemplation or meditation (the difference between the two is not easily defined), v. *Köpp.* I, 586. With this extraordinary state of mind a strange conception is associated, viz. 2. of **certain regions,** where besides gods and other beings also such men have their abode, that are growing more and more perfect and are stripping off every personal quality, whether good or bad, v. *Köpp.* I, 255. — *bsam-mnó* or *-bló*, also *blo-bsám* **thinking,** wishing etc., *bsam-mnó byéd-pa* or *γtóṅ-ba*, resp *t̔ugs-bsám γtóṅ-ba Pth.*, **to think, to meditate, consider, think upon** frq.; *bzáṅ-byed-kyi bsam-*

bló a mind, directed towards what is good, **honesty, probity** *Glr.* — *bsam-sbyór* **design, device, project** *Mil.*, *bzáṅ-po, ṅán-pa; bsam-byór byéd-pa* to plan, to scheme, to project a plan *C.* — *bsam-šés* **consciousness,** **sam-šé ṅém-pa** *C.* bad conscience (?).

བསམ་བསེའུ་ *bsam-bséu* 1. **seminal vesicle.** — 2. ovary?

བསལ་བ་ *bsál-ba* v. *sél-ba.*

བསིག་པ་ *bsig-pa* v. *ysig-pa.*

བསིད་པ་ *bsid-pa* **to mend, repair, put in order** *Sch.*

བསིར་བ་ *bsir-ba* 1. = *ysir-ba.* — 2. *W.* **to sip,** **sir-te ṫuṅ** he drinks sipping.

བསིལ་བ་ *bsil-ba* I. adj. and sbst. **cool, the cool** (of the day), **coolness,** *ḱáṅ-pa bsil-ba žig* a cool house *Dzl.*, *bsil-ba p'an* coolness is wholesome *Lt.*, *ṫsá-ba bsil-bar ₒgyùr* the heat changes to coolness *Dzl.*; *bsil* id., **sil-la dod** sit down in the shade *W.*, *lčaṅ-bsil* 'willow-shade', shady place under willow-trees; *bsil-žiṅ gráṅ-ba* **cold** *Dzl.*, *Glr.*; *bsil-mo* id., **sil-mo p'i-la** *W* for the sake of coolness.

II. vb., **to cool,** resp. for *ₒḱrúd-pa* **to wash,** *žal* mouth and face, *žabs* the feet, *žábs-bsil* water for washing the feet *Cs.*; even: *ču drón-mos sku bsil-bar mdzád-pa* to wash the body with warm water *Cs.*; **to shed,** *spyan-čáb máṅ-po* many tears *Mil.*

Comp. *bsil-ḱaṅ* a cool room, a summer-house, summer-residence *Stg.* — *bsil-grib* cool shade *Cs.* — *bsil-ₒṫúṅ* a cooling drink or beverage *Sch.* — *bsil-ydúgs* parasol *Do.* — *bsil-bu* coolness (?); *bsil-bui rluṅ* a cool breeze *Cs.* — *bsil-smán* a cooling medicine. — *bsil-zás* cooling food. — *bsil-ₒyáb* a fan.

བསུ་བ་ *bsú-ba*, pf. and imp. *bsus,* **to go to meet,** *ma bu bsur ₒoṅ* the mother goes to meet her son *Dzl.* (usually with accus. as in the preceding case, col. also with dat.); *bsus šig* let him come to meet me *Thgr.*; **to join,** of two armies, generals, kings *Dzl.*; **to make advances, to interest one's self for;** most frq.: **to go to meet** (solemnly), **to welcome** a respected person, *p'o-bráṅ-gi náṅ-du* into the castle *Dzl.*; *páṇḍi-ta ₒbyón-pa-la bsú-ba byéd-do* I will go to meet the arriving Pandit *Glr.*; *bsú-ba rgya-čén-po* very great festivities of reception *Pth.*; *bág-mar bsú-ba yin* we will lead her home as your bride *Mil.*; *ydóṅ-bsu ba* = *bsú-ba Mil.*; **dan sú-če** *W.* for *dan-* or *spyan-ₒdren-pa* of *B.* — **su-kyel* or *kyal** *W.* reception and conduct of honour.

བསུ་སྨན་ *bsu-smán Sch* **clyster,** *W. *sur-nyig*.*

བསུང་ *bsuṅ* **smell,** esp. **sweet scent** *Dzl.*; *dri-bsúṅ* id; *dri-bsúṅ žim-pa broo* it is sweet, scented, fragrant *Dzl.*: *bsuṅ-ṅád Sch.* fragrance; *ro bsúṅ-ba* filled with a cadaverous smell *Dzl.*; **mar suṅ soṅ dog** *W.* the butter smells (rancid).

བསུན་བསྐྱུར་ *bsun-bskyúr Sch.:* irregularity of life, **dissoluteness;** *bsún-par byed-pa Sch.*: to be dissolute; to be dirty; *bsún-tsam* disgusting, obscene *Sch.*

བསུམ་པ་ *bsum-pa* 1. = *ₒdzúm-pa.* — 2. = *súm-pa Cs.*

བསུར་སྨྱིག་ *bsur-smyig W.* **clyster,** cf. *bsu-smán.*

བསེ་ *bse* 1. v. *se, se-ba, se-dri, se-šin.* — 2. also: *bse-kó*, **tanned leather,** *bse-ḱráb Lex.* a coat of mail made of leather; *bse-sgám, bsei sgróm-bu Pth.* leather-box, or a box covered with leather; *bse-sgó* leather-door, or a door-like target made of hides *Pth.* — 3. *bse* or *bse-ru* (*Lex.* བསེ་རུ 'a certain animal') **unicorn,** *Hook.* II., 157 'tchiru', **an antelope,** prob. = *ytsod*; **rhinoceros** *Tar.* 185, 20.

བསེགས་པ་ *bségs-pa Sch.* to come from one side, to come across one's way.

བསེད་པ་ *bséd-pa* v. *ysód-pa.*

བསེད་དཔྱད་ *bsed-dpyád Sch.* the bow for setting a drill in motion.

བསེན་མོ་ *bsen-mo Sch*: a female devil.

བསེར་, སེར་, གསེར་བུ་ *bser, ser, ysér-bu* 1. **a fresh, cold breeze,** *bsér-gyis p'og* he is exposed to a cold wind *Sch.* — 2. of persons, resp. **the feeling cold, catching cold,** *bsér-du yoṅ* you will feel cold *Mil*; also *bsér-mo* adj. or sbst.: **ser-mo* *sér-mo máṅ-po ma kyód-da* W. did you not feel very cold on your way? *bser-mai nad* resp. a catarrh, a cold *Dzl.*

བསེལ་(བ་) *bsél(-ba)*, gen. *lam-bsél* **convoy, safe-conduct, escort;** *Lex.: ʼjag-skyób-kyi kyél-ma* (escort) against robbers; *bsél-pa* safeguard, guide, *(lam-) bsél byéd-pa* to accompany and protect on the way, to escort.

བསོག་པ་ *bsóg-pa* v. *ság-pa.*

བསོད་སྙོམས་ *bsod-snyóms*, **पिण्ड, alms, gifts** presented to clerical persons, *bsod-snyóms-gyis ʼtso-ba* to live on alms, on charity. *bsod-snyóms byéd-pa, sóg-pa, ʼjúg-pa Cs., bsod-snyóms-la rgyú-ba*, resp. *šégs-pa* to beg, ask, collect alms; *bsod-snyóms sbyór-ba* to prepare an entertainment for the priesthood.

བསོད་པ་ *bsód-pa* 1. vb., **to be pleased with, to take a delight in, to like,** W.: **de-la kon-čog sod-če man** God is not pleased with that. — 2. adj., **pleasing, agreeable.** **nyiṅ sod tsor dug** W. I feel well, I am quite happy; *bsód-pa daṅ ṅán-pa* good and bad; *bsód-pai zas* is explained by one *Lex.: zas bzáṅ-poi miṅ* good food, good provisions, by another: = **प्रणीत** prepared, dressed, boiled. — *bsód-bde, bsód-nams*, resp. *sku-bsód* 1. **good fortune, happiness, felicity,** *bsód-bde-čan* happy, *bsód-bde-med* unhappy *Cs.* 2. **destiny, fate,** = *dbaṅ-táṅ*, **tam-čád sód-de-ne juṅ** every thing happens according to a decree of fate W.; prob. also *sku-bsód šin-tu če Ld.-Glr.* 11, b. *Schl.*, his destiny is a very high one; *kyód-kyi bsód-bde-la brdúṅ-ba yód-pa yin* it belongs to your destiny that you get a drubbing. — 3. **merit, virtue, good action,** *byéd-pa* to perform (a good action) *Dzl., bsód-bde sóg-pa* to gather merit, *bsód-nams ma yin-pai las* sinful deed *Thgy.*

བསོས་ *bsos* **indemnification, damages** paid for bodily injury.

བསོས་པ་ *bsós-pa* v. *ɣsos-pa*

བསྲང་བ་ *bsráṅ-ba* v. *sróṅ-ba*; *bsráṅ-po* **straight, upright,** *yór-po dug šráṅ-po-la žog* C. it stands aslant, put it straight!

བསྲུད་པ་ *bsrúd-pa* v. *bsród-pa.*

བསྲན་པ་ *bsrán-pa* v. *srán-pa.*

བསྲབ་པ་ *bsráb-pa*, v. *srab*, **to bridle, keep under, restrain, check, curb, refrain,** *bag-čágs* the passions, *mún-pa* or *sgrib-pa bsráb-pa Cs.* to dispel darkness (prob. only in a spiritual sense)

བསྲལ་བ་ *bsrál-ba* v. *srél-ba.*

བསྲི་བ་ *bsri-ba* etc. v. *sri-ba* etc.

བསྲུང་ *bsrun Cs.* **a tutelar genius.**

བསྲུན་པ་, བསྲུབ་པ་, བསྲུལ་བ་, བསྲེ་བ་, བསྲེག་པ་, བསྲེལ་བ་, བསྲོ་བ་ *bsrún-pa, bsrúb-pa, bsrúl-ba, bsré-ba, bsrég-pa, bsrél-ba, bsró-ba* v. *srún-pa, srúb-pa* etc.

བསྲོད་པ་, བསྲད་པ་ *bsród-pa, bsrád-pa,* = *sró-ba*, **to dry,** by exposing to the rays of the sun *Sch.*

བསླ་བ་, བསླང་བ་, བསླད་པ་ etc. *bslá-ba, bsláṅ-ba, bslád-pa* etc. v. *slá-ba, sláṅ-ba* etc.

བསླབ་པ་ *bsláb-pa* 1. vb., v. *slob-pa.* — 2. sbst. **doctrine,** *bsláb-pa ɣsum Glr.*, acc. to an explanation in the Triglot: *lhág-pai tsul-krims, lhág-pai sems, lhág-pai šes-ráb* (expressions which I am not able to interpret satisfactorily); our Lama explained *bsláb-pa ɣsúm-gyi sdóm-pa Mil.* by: *so-tar, byaṅ-séms* and *ɣsaṅ-sṅágs-kyi sdóm-pa*; *bsláb-pai ɣnas* **dogma, tenet** *Tar.* — **lab-kan** W. **teacher.** — **lab-(s)tán táṅ-če** W. to teach, to keep school. — *bslab-bya* what is to be learned, **doctrine, precept, admonition,** *ʼjig-rten mi-čos-la dgos-pai bsláb-bya mdzád-do* he imparted to her some practical doctrines or rules of life and social intercourse *Glr., bsláb-bya stón-pa B*, **táṅ-če** W. to give admonitions, to exhort, reprimand

བསླུ་བ་, བསླེ་བ་, བསླེབ་པ་, བསློག་པ་ *bslú-ba, bslé-ba, bsléb-pa, bslóg-pa* v. *slu-ba, sle-ba* etc.

ཧ

ཧ *ha* 1. the letter *h* — 2. numeral: 29.

ཧ་ *ha* 1. *W.* **a yawn,** **ha yoṅ dug** I cannot help yawning. 2. **breath,** *ha ˳débs-pa* to breathe. — 3. **the sound of laughter,** **hab-gód čó-če* *W.* to laugh out or aloud, cf. *ha-há.*

ཧྭ་ *hwa* 1. *gós-kyi hwa* **collar** of a coat. — 2. **shin, shin-bone** *Sch.* — 3. **hŏ, hō* *W.* very well! — 4. col. nearly = *p̓a* II., **yonder,** farther off, **há-la gyug* C.* get you gone! be off! begone!; **há-čog = p̓á-rol** the other side, yonder side, **há-gi** that (man) there, **há-gi-ru** there, there above, up there, there behind, thither, that way *C., W.*

ཧ་གོ་བ་ *há-go-ba W.* **to understand,** **ha mi go-a** don't you understand it?

ཧ་ཅང་ *há-čaṅ* **very,** sometimes **too much, too,** *mya-ṅán-las ˳da-ba há-čaṅ yaṅ myur-čés-so* his removal (prop. disappearing) from misery happens really too soon! *Dzl.*; *há-čaṅ-nas* id., **ha-čan-ne ké-pa* C.* very learned, possessed of extensive information.

ཧ་ན་ཧོ་ནེ་, ཧན་ཧོན་ *ha-na-ho-né, han-hón* **very angry,** much enraged *Ld.*

ཧ་ནི་ *há-ni* **all** of them, **all together, in a body** *Sch.*

ཧ་བ་ཧ་བ་ *há-ba-há-ba* **to breathe out steam** or vapour.

ཧ་བོ་ *há-bo* n. of a medicinal herb *Lt.*

ཧ་ཡེགས་ *ha-yégs* **woe** (to you etc.)! *W.*

ཧ་ར་ *há-ra,* with **gyáb-če*,* *W.* **to play at dice.**

ཧ་ར་ཧུ་རེ་ *ha-ra-hu-ré W.* **impetuous, violent, rude, impudent.**

ཧ་རམ་ *ha-rám* with **čó-če* W.* **to deny, disown, disavow.**

ཧ་རི་ *há-ri Ssk.* **parrot.**

ཧ་རི་ཏ་ཀ་ *ha-ri-ta-ka Ssk.* **vegetables, greens, pot-herbs** *Wdṅ.*

ཧ་རི་དྲ་ *ha-ri-dra Ssk.* the turmeric plant, **Curcuma** *S.g.*

ཧ་རི་ཙནྡན་ *ha-ri-tsan-dan Ssk.* **sandal-wood.**

ཧ་རི་ཙམ་ *ha-ri-tsam Pur.* **centipede.**

ཧ་རིབ་ *ha-rib Ld.* music (?).

ཧ་རེ་ཎུ་ཀ་ *ha-re-ṇu-ka Ssk.* a medicine *Med.*

ཧ་ལ་, ཧ་ལ་ཧ་ལ་ *ha-la, ha-la-ha-la Wdṅ.,* a certain poison, also **poison** in general, *Ssk.*

ཧ་ལ་ཧ་ལ་ *ha-la-há-la Cs.:* a name of *spyan-ras-gzigs,* v. *spyan.*

ཧ་ལམ་ *há-lam* **about, near, nearly, pretty, tolerably, rather,** *de daṅ há-lam ˳drá-ba* about or nearly like that *Wdṅ.*

ཧ་ལལ་ *ha-lál Ar.,* **ha-lál čó-če*,* *Urd.* حلال کرنا, to kill (an animal) in the manner prescribed by the Mahometan law *W.*

ཧ་ལས་ *ha-lás* col., **astonished, frightened,** **ha-la-ši** or **ha-la-še** id., **ha-lé čá-če* W.,* *ha-lás-pa B.* **to be astonished, frightened** *Mil., Pth.*

ཧ་ལོ་ *ha-ló* **flower,** esp. a large beautifu[l] **garden-flower** *Glr., ha-ló rkyáṅ-pa* a simple flower, *ha-ló stoṅ-˳dáb* a double flower; **ha-ló-ka** mallow *W.* (?)

ཧ་ཤང་ *ha-šáṅ* 1. *Cs.:* (Chinese word) **a Buddhist priest, doctor, scholar** *Glr.* — 2. id., represented by **a mask** in religious plays, *ha-p̓rúg* an old doctor with boys, his pupils.

ཧ་ཤིག་ *ha-šig* a mineral medicine, used as a remedy for the stone; acc. to *Wdṅ.* = *t̓ód-le-kór,* alabaster.

ཧ་ཧ་, ཧཱ་ཧཱ་ *ha-há, hā-hā* the natural sound of laughter *Mil., ha-há rgód-pa* to laugh out, to set up a loud laugh;

to *Sch.* also an interjection expressive of pain (?).

ཧའི་ *hai* a Chinese word, **shoe** *C.*

ཧའུ་སྤ་བ་ *hau-spa-ba* n. of a medicinal herb *Med.*

ཧགས་ *hags Lex.* **sugar, treacle** *Cs.*, *hágs-kyi lá-tu.*

ཧང་ *haṅ? haṅ-ₒdzom-pa* **to squander, to dissipate** *Sch.*, *haṅ-ča-byed* **a squanderer** *Sch.*

ཧང་བ་ *háṅ-ba*, *W.* **háṅ-če** **to pant, to gasp.**

ཧད་ཀྱིས་ *hád-kyis* **suddenly** *Sch.* — *had-po? Mil.*

ཧད་ཧད་ *had-hád* or *hur-húr*, with **čó-če** **to exert one's self,** to strive *W.*

ཧན་ལྡང་ *han-ldáṅ W.* 1. **dumb, mute,** **han-dáṅ-ṅi (s)pé ra** **a stammering,** also: a confused, unmeaning speech. — 2. **imbecile, weak of mind.**

ཧན་ཧོན་ *han-hon* v. *ha-na-ho-né.*

ཧབ་ *hab* 1. **a mouthful,** *háb-za byéd-pa*, *hab-háb zá-ba* to devour greedily, e.g. of dogs, pigs etc., *hab-bčád* a needy wretch, a starveling, famishing person. — 2. **a stitch,** in sewing, also **háb-ka** *C.* **háb-so** *W.*, *hab-ₒtsem-pa* to make here a stitch and there a stitch, as in quilting *Mil. nt.* — 3. *hab-gód* v. *ha* 3. — 4. v. the following article.

ཧབ་ཤ་ *háb-ša* **a dispute, a quarrel,** *háb-ša byéd-pa Mil.*, *Thgr.*, to dispute, to quarrel; *hab-tób byéd pa* to scramble for, to strive or contend for *Pth.*

ཧམ་པ་ *hám-pa* 1. **avarice, covetousness, greediness;** *W.* also vb.: to covet, **žán-ni nór-la** after a person's wealth; **to long for,** to yearn after, **koi 'á-ne hám-te dad dug** his wife sits yearning (after him); *hám-pa byéd-pa Sch.*: to be covetous. — 2. **strength** *Cs.*; **courage, bravery** *W.*, of men and animals. — 3. white film on liquids etc., **mould** *C.*, **hám-di* or *-ri** a musty, fusty smell *C.*, *W.*; **hám-por čág-kan** *W* **mouldy, musty,** **ham-če** *W.* to get mouldy. — 4. **lie,** falsehood, *C.* — *hám-pa-čan* 1. **covetous, avaricious; greedy, voracious.** 2. **courageous;** one *Lex.* explains *rlam-kyér* by *hám-pas kyér-ba* (?); **hám-pa čúṅ-se** *W.* cowardly.

ཧམ་བུར་ *hám-bur W.* rime, hoar-frost?

ཧར་ *har* **suddenly,** *har láṅ-ba* to rise suddenly *Mil.*; **har se' ǰhé'-pa** to rouse suddenly from sleep *C.*; *har-gyis* (*Sch. had-kyis*) more precise form of the adv. *Tar.*

ཧར་རེ་ *hár-re* **empty, open,** *Tar.* 115,16 *Schf.*

ཧལ་པ་ *hál-pa* a porridge, made of milk, butter and honey.

ཧལ་བ་ *hál-ba* **to pant, to wheeze, to snort,** *hal-kyi* a panting dog *Sch.*; **hal-méd** *W.* **weak.**

ཧས་ *has* **exaggeration, hyperbole,** *has-čer smrá-ba Cs.*, **he gyab-če** *W.* **to exaggerate, to talk big, to brag.**

ཧས་པོ་རི་ *has-po-ri* n. of a mountain in *C.*, *Glr.*

ཧི་ *hi* numeral: 59.

ཧི་དིག་ *hi-dig*, or *hig-dig*, *W.* **zér-če** **to blow one's nose.**

ཧི་མཱ་ལ་ཡ་ *hi-mā-la-ya Ssk.*, = *gaṅs-čan* the snowy mountains, **Himalaya.**

ཧི་ར་ *hi-ra Ssk.* **diamond.**

ཧི་རི་ *hi-ri* **corn-stack,** **hi-ri gyáb-če** *W.* to pile up a stack of corn.

ཧི་ལིང་ *hi-liṅ* **noise,** **hi-liṅ táṅ-kan** *W.*, **bully, brawler.**

ཧི་ཧི་ *hi-hi* = *ha-há.*

ཧིའི་ཀ་ *hii ka Sch.* **breast-bone.**

ཧིག་, ཧིག་ཀ་ *hig*, *hig-ka* **the act of sobbing,** **hig táṅ-te dug* or *gyáb-te dug** he is sobbing *W.*; **hig ǰáṅ* (lit. *sbyaṅ*) *dug** is said to be an expression used of a Lama, when he is watching the gradual departing of the soul of a dying man.

ཧིང་ *hiṅ*, ཧིངྒུ, = *šiṅ-kun*, *Asa foetida.*

ཧིན་དུ་སྟཱ་ནི་ *hin-du-stá-ni*, *C.*: **hin-du-tá-ni ké**, Hindoostanee, the language of the Hindoos.

ཧིས་ *his Pur.*: **hiz yoṅ** **he is panting.**

ཧུ་ *hu* 1. *W.* **breath,** **hu gyáb-če** to breathe. — 2. num.: 89.

ཧུ་ཀ **hú-ka**, *Ar.* حقّه **the hookah,** with an inflexible tube.

ཧུ་ཀུམ *hu-kúm W.,* حكم *Urdu,* **order, command.**

ཧུ་ཁྱུ *hu-ḱyú* the sound of sighing *Pth.*

ཧུ་ན *hú-na Cs.: Ssk.* (*hū-na*) n. of an ancient people, the Huns (?).

ཧུ་འང་དྷི *hu-ʼaṅ-dhi* (?) *Sch.:* title of the Chinese emperor.

ཧུ་རེ *hu-ré, míg hu-ré ˳dug* **he stares, he goggles,** with wonder, horror, confusion *Mil., Glr.; mig-húr Mṅg.*

ཧུ་ཤར *hu-šār* (from the *Hind. hošyār?*) (grown) **well again,** being again lively, active; **diligent, sedulous** *W.*

ཧུ་ཧུ *hu-hú* 1. interj. expressive of pain from cold *Cs.* — 2. 'the sound of one's mouth in eating' *Cs.* — 3. **hu-hú tán-ce* W.* **to whistle.**

ཧཱུྃ *hūm,* **हुम्, हूम्,** mystical interjection, e.g. in the prayer of six syllables, v. ཨོྃ

ཧུན *hun W.* (= *ča, lon, ṕrin*) **news,** tidings, intelligence, information, **hun taṅ-ce** to give account or notice, to inform, acquaint, let know, **ṫsar-na hun toṅ** tell me (let me know) as soon as it is finished! **hun ṫsói-ce** to get intelligence, to receive news; **hun ma yoṅ* or *mi dug** we have no news yet; **disclosure, explanation, opinion, idea,** **ci yód-pe hun ḱyód-la juṅ yin** you shall get an idea of what kind of . . . are to be found, **sém-can ṫún-can žig yin-pe hun ṅá-la juṅ** I have got the notion that this is a very quiet animal; **re-rēi hun cil-tar še** whence have you such accurate information of every one of them? **ser-dub dil-te hun ma juṅ** he did not perceive it when the ring fell off; **hun-méd-la** **unexpectedly, unawares.**

ཧུབ *hub* as much as is swallowed at once, **a gulp, a draught,** *tóg-mar húb re ˳ṫuṅ žig* at first take only one mouthful, one draught at a time *Glr.; hub ṗcig* one mouthful, *hub do* two mouthfuls *Cs.; húb-kyis* by draughts *Sch.; hub-húb byéd-pa* to drink in large draughts, to gulp.

ཧུར *hur* 1. v. *hu-ré.* — 2. *hur-húr* v. *had-had.*

ཧུར་བ *húr-ba* **dexterity, cleverness, skilfulness** *C., hur-ṫág* id., also **zeal, diligence** *Sch.; húr-po* 1. **quick, alert, dexterous, clever.** 2. **hot, hasty, passionate** *Ld.; rta húr-po* a fleet, spirited, fine horse *Cs.*

ཧུས *hus Cs.* **moisture, humidity,** *hús-can* wet.

ཧེ *he* 1. num.: 119. — 2. interj.: **o! holla!** *Cs.; he-he* 1. id. *Cs.* 2. = *ha-há, he-hé zer bgád-pas* she laughed: he, he! *Glr.*

ཧེ་ཏུ *hé-tu Ssk.* **cause, reason, argument, logic.**

ཧེ་བག *he-bag* **provocation, taunts, sarcasms.**

ཧེ་བཛྲ *Ssk. he-vajra,* ཀྱེ་རྡོ་རྗེ *Tibet. kye-rdo-rje Cs.:* n. of a god; n. of a series of treatises.

ཧེ་རུ་ཀ *hé-ru-ka* **terrifying deities,** also *ḱrag-˳ṫúṅ, Thgr.* frq., *hé-ru-kai rgyud* legends of wrathful deities.

ཧེག་པོ *hég-po* having become **putrid, rancid.**

ཧེལ་གེ *hél-ge Sch.:* **soft leather, wash-leather.**

ཧེལ་པོ *hél-po, hél-can, *hel-hél* W.* **wide, extended;** of garments: **wide, easy;** *hél-ba* id. and sbst.: **width** *Sch.*

ཧོ *ho* num.: 149.

ཧོ་མ *hó-ma Ssk.* prop.: **burnt-offering** of butter; = *sbyin-sreg* v. *Was.* (194): *Schl.* 251; *hó-ma byéd-pa* **to sacrifice;** *hom-ḱuṅ* a small pit or a triangular box **used** as an altar for such an offering.

ཧོ་ཧོ *ho-hó* interj. of admiration *Cs.*

ཧོང་ལེན *hoṅ-lén* a medicinal herb, *Picrorrhiza,* frequently to be found on the mountains, *Hook.* I., 272.

ཧོན་ཧོན *hon-hón* **stupid, foolish** *Cs.*

ཧོབ་པ *hób-pa, W.: *hób-te dug** it has got **bent in** or **battered,** of tin ware.

ཧོམ *hom* (Mongol word?) a pad, placed under a camel's load.

ཧོམ་པ *hóm-pa W.* **to fall away,** to lose flesh, e.g. of hollow cheeks, **to shrink, to shrivel,** of withered fruit.

ཧོར་ *hor* 1. formerly: **a Mongol** ,*hor Jiṅ-gin-ḱan* the Mongol Djingiskhan; *hor-sér Shara Sharaighol* n. of a Mongol tribe *Glr.*: *hór-yul Mongolia.* — 2. at present: in *C.* the people living near the *Tengri-nor* (*gnam-mtso*): in *W.* the Turks; *hór-zla* a Turkish month.

Note. *Cs.* has only the second of these significations, *Sch.* only the first (the latter using *Cs.*'s examples and changing all the Turks into Mongols!) The suppositions of Latham seem still less consistent with the real state of the case.

ཧོར་ཁོངས་ *hor-ḱoṅs Sch.*: deficiencies, gaps: separation' (?).

ཧོར་འདྲ་ *hór-˳dra Sch.*: 'confiscation, *hór-˳dra bábs-pa* to confiscate' (?).

ཧོར་པ་ *hór-pa* **wood-grouse** or cock of the wood *Sch.*, *hór-pa dkár-po* a species of hawk *Sch.* (?).

ཧོལ་ཧོལ་ *hol-hól W.* **soft, loose, light,** as the soil in spring, **hol táṅ-ce, hól-te bór-ce** to break up, to loosen (the soil).

ཧྲག་པ་ *hrág-pa* 1. vb., **to require more and more,** to covet incessantly *Ma.*, *W.* — 2. sbst., adj. **hardness, hard** *Cs.*

ཧྲང་བ་ *hráṅ-ba* 1. **alone,** cf. *raṅ*, **šraṅ-šráṅ-la yoṅ soṅ** I came alone *C.*, *ṗo-hráṅ, mo-hráṅ* single man and woman, = *ṗo-ráṅ* etc. *C.* — 2. with *dmar* preceding, **naked** *C.*

ཧྲད་པ་ *hrád-pa* 1. **to thrust, to push violently, to stem** firmly, **káṅ-pa sig-pa-la* W.* to stem the foot against the wall — 2. **to scratch,** *sgó-la ṗyag-hrád-pa ˳ga mdzád-pa* (his Reverence) made several scratchings with his hand, scratched several times, at the door *Mil.* — 3. **to exert one's self,** to make every effort *W.*, **šrád-can zúm-ce** or *táṅ-ce** id. *W.*

ཧྲབ་ཧྲིབ་ *hrab-hrib C.* **šrab-ba-šrib-be* Ld.*, v. *rab-rib.*

ཧྲལ་བ་ *hrál-ba* **to rend, tear up. tear to pieces** e.g. of a beast of prey: to tear up a person's body; **šral soṅ** he has torn it to pieces *C.*, *W*, *hral-hrál Lex.*

ཧྲཱི་ *hri Cs.*: '*Ssk.* essence, substance; a mystical word'.

ཧྲིག་ *hrig W.* **šrig-la táṅ-ce, šrig-ga táṅ-ce** **to hang** (a thief), **šrig-la ši-ce** to hang one's self.

ཧྲིག་པ་ *hrig-pa Cs.*, *mig* (or resp. *spyaṅ*) *hrig-hrig byéd-pa* or *˳dúg-pa*, (= *rig-rig*), to look this way and that, hither and thither *Mil. nt.*; *hrig-ge-ba* looking in that manner *Thgr.*

ཧྲིད་ *hrid*; *S.g.*; *rná-ba hrid ˳byar* is explained by *Wdṅ.*: *rná-ba lhág-pa ṗyógs-su byar* the ear leans feebly on the neck, as a sign of death.

ཧྲིལ་པོ་ *hril-po* 1. **round, globular,** *hril-hril byéd-pa* to writhe with pain, *hril-hril kar-kár byéd-pa* to be writhing, and then again stretching one's self or starting up *Pth.* — 2. **whole,** *tse hril-por* for the whole life *Glr.*, *mgo hril-gyis γtúm-nas* wrapping up his whole head *Glr.* — 3. **close, dense,** *hril ˳dús-te ˳dúg-pa* to sit or stand close together in rows *Mil.*, *C.*, *W.* Cf. *ril-ba.*

ཧྲུད་པ་ *hrúd-pa* adj. and abstract noun, **rough, rugged; severe, austere; roughness** etc.; *hrúd-po* adj. id. *Cs.*

ཧྲུམ་པ་ *hrúm-pa* **to break, to smash** *Sch.*

ཧྲུལ་བ་ *hrúl-ba* adj. and abstr. sbst. **ragged, tattered; raggedness,** *hrul-bai dug-po* a ragged coat *Mil.*; *hrúl-po* id., *gos hrúl-po Dzl* and elsewh. frq. — 2. sbst.: **rags, tatters,** *gós-su hrúl-po gyón-pa* to put on rags for a garment *Pth.*; *hrúl-ḱaṅ* a ruin, **ruins** *Sch.*

ཧྲེམ་པ་ *hrém-pa* **swollen** *Sch.*, *hrem-mé* id. *Mṅg.*

ལྷ་ *lha*, *Ssk.* देव. 1. the first class of beings subject to metempsychosis, **the gods,** both those of Brahminical mythology, and the various national and local gods, with whom Buddhism came in contact. These local gods were incorporated into the system of Buddhism, when they were found to be too numerous and too much endeared to the people, to be entirely discarded and given up; so, most of them are worshipped even nowadays and presented with various offerings. They are also supposed to enjoy a blissful existence (hence: *dé-riṅ lhá-yi nyi-ma śar* 'this day was a day of happiness to me' *Glr.*, and similar expressions are of frq. occurrence; v. also *lha-yul*) and to be possessed of qualities and capacities superior to those of ordinary human beings. Nevertheless, when compared with any Buddhist saint, they are considered to be of inferior rank and power; and a local *'lha'* can never attain to Buddhaship, without having previously assumed the nature of man; v. *Köpp.* I, 122. 248. II, 296. *lhai bu* or *sras*, *bú-mo* or *srás-mo* descendant from the gods, son or daughter of the gods *Dzl.* and elsewh.; *lha mi ťób-pa* to obtain the birth as a god or as man *Thgy.*; *lhai yi-ge* the Lantsa-letters, v. *lan-tsa*; *lha ₒbáb-pa* the (mystical) entering of a deity into a human being, **inspiration,** so that the person inspired pronounces the oracles of the god, *lha žúgs-pa* id. pop.; also: the person thus inspired; *lha ni k̓yab-ₒjúg-la mos* as for gods, they worshipped Vishnu *Pth.*, *lha má-mo-la byed* they worshipped the Mamo as a *'lha' Pth.*; *lhai dbáṅ-po, lha-bdág, = brgya-byin* Indra; in another sense: *lhai rgyál-po byéd-pa* to make the gods subject to one's self, (said to be the blessed consequence of a certain charm) *Do.*; the following gods are occasionally mentioned: *nám-mkai lha* the deity of heaven *Tar.*; that of the sea *Dzl.*; the gods of trees, of houses etc.; *dgrá-lha* and *p̓ó-lha* are two personal gods of every human individual, the one being the god of the right side, the other of the left side of his body *Glr.*, *Mil.*; *yi-dam-lha* v. *yi-dam.* — 2. **the image of a god,** in as much as it is really thought to be inhabited by a deity, after having been duly inaugurated (*ráb-tu gnás-pa*) *Glr.*; the local *'lha'* are not always represented by figures resembling human beings, but even by sticks, stones and similar fetishes; gods also of non-Buddhist nations are called *'lha'* and are acknowledged as such. — 3. fig.: *mii lha* **a king** *Mil.*, and hence *'lha'* is often used in addressing a king, like the French *Sire! lha-rgyal-yab-yúm* the royal father and mother *Pth.*; *lhá-yi lha* the lord of lords, the supreme being, **Buddha** *Cs.*

Comp. *lha-k̓áṅ* **an idol-shrine.** — *lha-gčig* 1. dear Sir! dear Lord and King! *Pth.* 2. **princess** *Glr.* — *lha-lčám* **a princess** *Pth.* — *lha-č̓én* a great and mighty deity. — *lhá-č̓os* v. *č̓os* no. 2. — *lhá-rje* **physician** *Wdṅ.*

lha-rtén **image** or temple of a god or of the gods. — *lha-ťó* (prob. for *lhai ťo-yór*) **heaps of stones,** erected on mountain passes or on the tops of mountains. — *lha-ₒdre* gods and goblins, *lha klu ₒdre srin gdúg-pa man Glr.* 2. **goblin, hobgoblin;** **lhá-ₒdre-ber-ka** mullein (Verbascum) *Lh.*; **lán-ₒde non soṅ** *W.* I have had the night-mare. — *lhá-sde, mi-sde* the class of the gods, the class of men. — *lha-nád Sch.*: **hysterics; madness.** — *lha-p̓yág* honours shown to the *'lha'*, worship paid to them, *p̓yogs bžir lha-p̓yág mán-po btsál-te* bowing towards the four points of the compass in token of reverence to the *'lha' Pth.*, often only: **compliments, kind regards,** offered to respected persons, in letters. — *lha-p̓yi* n. of a mountain in the south of Tibet *Mil.* — *lha-p̓rúg* a descendant from the gods, child of the gods; as a mask *Schl.* 235. — *lha-p̓rán* inferior deities. — *lha-bris-mk̓an* or *-pa* a painter of gods. — *lha-ₒbáṅs Tar.*; *Schf.*: **slaves** (doing service) **in temples.** — *lha-ma-yin, lha-min,* असुर, one of the six classes of beings, living on the slopes of the Sumeru below the *'lha'* against whom, like Titans, they are continually fighting; also *lha-ma-yin-mo* are mentioned. — *lha-ma-srin* gods, Asuras and Rakshasas, or perh. also: *lha-ma-srin sde brgyad* the eight classes of the gods, Asuras, Rākshasas etc., i.e. the whole world of spirits. — *lhá-mo* **goddess.** — *lha-ma-rtá Sch.*: a certain insect. — *lhá-bzo* 1. the art of making images of gods *Pth.* 2. also *lha-bzó-bo* a framer of gods *Glr.* — *lhá-yul* 1. the region of the world where the gods reside, the heaven, seat or abode of the gods. 2. fig.: a blessed country, a paradise. — *lhá-sa* (in early times *lha-ldán*) *Sch.*, *Köpp.* II, 332, n. of the capital of Tibet. — *lha-srin* gods and Rākshasas; *steṅ lha-*

srin, ˬog klu-γnyán, bar γži-bdáγ, are often mentioned in connexion. — lha-srúṅ **tutelar god,** bód-kyi Glr.

ལྷ་ང་ lha-ṅá **knee-pan,** pús-mo γyás-pai lha-ṅá sá-la ˳dzúg-pa to kneel down on the right knee frq.; lha-kúṅ the bend of the knee W.

ལྷ་བ་ lhá-ba Med. and Pth., acc. to Wdṅ. also klad-rgyás, Sch.: 'the bloody marrow in the bones; whilst he translates rmai lhá-ba by: 'the growing worse of a wound'.

ལྷ་རུ་ lha-rú Med.; Sch. **cartilage** (cf. lha-gór sub lkóg-ma).

ལྷག་ lhag 1. **more, beyond,** *dá-wa čig lag soṅ* more than a month has passed W., *nyi-ma-pyéd lag soṅ* W. it is already past noon, rgyá-mtso-bas kyaṅ lhág-ste as this alone would be more than the whole sea Dzl.; nyi-šus lhag more by twenty S.g. — 2. = lhág-ma. — lhág-pa 1. adj. **surpassing, excelling, superior,** ˳di-las lhág-pai γžan čos med Dzl.; nyam-tág-pa ṅá-las lhág-pa yód-dam is there any one that is thinner than I? Dzl.; dé-rnams-kyi náṅ-nas lhág-pa the best amongst these Glr.; rgya hor γnyis-las lhág-pa ṅed bod yin we Tibetans surpass the Chinese and Mongols (in sagacity) Glr. 2. rarely = lhág-ma: dé-las lhág-pa the others, the remaining S.g. 6, 1. de-lhag **besides, moreover.** — lhág-par adv. **more** (magis) frq., mostly with adj., but also with verbs, šin-tu lhág-par **far more; very, exceedingly, uncommonly,** lhág-par légs-pa uncommonly beautiful Dzl.; čes lhág-par **extremely,** excessively Stg.; **further,** furthermore, moreover. — lhág-ye-ba = lhag-pa. lhág-ge mdzád-nas making it project.

lhág-ma 1. **remains, scrapings,** sṅar bšad-pai lhág-ma (the letters) which at the last discussion remained, were left. (unexplained) Gram.; lha lhág-ma-rnams the other, the remaining gods Stg.; **the remainder,** in subtracting Wdk. — 2. **razor-stone, razor-strap** Sch. — 3. being above, being at the upper part of, groṅ the place lying higher up (the valley), opp. to ˬóg-ma Dzl.

Comp. lhag-bčas 1. having **more than** so and so much, bha-ra-ta šlo-ka ˳bum lhag-bčas the Bharata of more than 100,000 verses Tar. 2. the gerund in te (ste etc.) Gram. — lhag-mtóṅ 'seeing more' (than other mortals), in certain states of contemplation v. ži-γnas sub ži.

ལྷག་གིས་ lhág-gis = lhaṅ-ṅer, lhag-gis ˳čar Thgr., ˳byuṅ Mil. he shines bright, lhág-ge-ba = lhaṅ-ṅe-ba Mil.

ལྷག་པ་ lhág-pa I. sbst., also γza lhág-pa 1. **Mercury.** 2. **Wednesday.** — II. adj. **more excellent,** v. lhag.

ལྷག(ས)་པ་ lhag(s)-pa I. sbst. **cold wind,** lág-pa pog the cold wind has withered them (the flowers) W.; lo-γsár lhágs-pa the cold new year's wind Mil. — II. vb., **to come together,** to meet, to assemble, with other persons; perh. also: to join, to be adjacent or contiguous, of houses, beams etc.

ལྷང་ངེ་ lhaṅ-ṅe, lhan-ne, lham-me, also lhag-ge, lam-me, lham-pa **clear, distinct,** to the sight as well as to the ear: lhaṅ-ṅe lham-mer γsal-te (Buddha) appearing clearly and distinctly Dzl., in a similar sense: lham-me lhaṅ-ṅe lhan-ner bžúgs-so Pth.; clear, sonorous; kyi-skad lhaṅ-lhaṅ-pa Mil. the clear (loud) barking of dogs; kyod lhaṅ-lhaṅ glú-len-pa Mil. thou clear-voiced songster; lhaṅ-lháṅ brjód-la speaking with a clear, sonorous voice. — Cs. has: **majestic, glorious, sublime, august.**

ལྷད་ lhad a baser substance mixed with a finer one, an **alloy,** lhad ˳júg-pa or sré-ba with la, lhád-kyis slád-pa with accus. Mil., **to alloy, adulterate,** lhád-čan **adulterated,** e.g. milk C., lhad-méd **unadulterated, pure, genuine, real;** *tsig lhe' šor* C. or *žug soṅ* W. spurious words are admixed, falsehoods have been artfully introduced; pyis lhád-du bčug-pai tsig Tar. a later interpolation. — 2. Bal., *γlad*, **fatigued, exhausted.**

ལྷན་ lhan **together,** lhán-gyis (when referring to the subject of the action), lhán-nas (as ablative case), lhán-du (the most frq. form) **with one another, together,** lhan-γčig (-tu), and often lhan-čig(-tu) id.: bdag dan lhan-γčig zan mi zá-na if you will not eat together with me Dzl., rta bčus lhán-du rgyúgs-pa ltá-bui sgrá a noise as if ten horses were trotting together *Glr.*; *rtá-pa brgya dan̄ lhán-du* accompanied by a hundred men on horseback *Glr.*; *lhan(-čig)-skyes(-pa)* **born together with,** e.g. the '*lha*' or '*ₒdre*' born together with every human being *Mil.; lhan-skyes nad, rma* a hereditary disease or defect *Med. lhan-rgyás* 1. 'partner of the seal', i.e. a colleague using the same seal in official business (*lhan-rgyás-kyi ťé-tse*, or *spyi-dám*). 2. = *lhan-γčig*, **hlẹn-gyẹ́-la ťsog* or *žug** they have come together.

ལྷན་པ་ *lhán-pa* I. vb., **to join, to unite,** **k̔a lán-če** *W.* **to kiss,** *'*u lán-če** id. resp.

II. sbst. 1. **a patch,** *lhán-pas klán-pa B.*, **hlẹ́m-pa gyág-pa** *C.*, **gyáb-če** *W.*, *ₒdébs-pa, rdáb-pa Mil.* **to patch, mend.** — 2. **spot, speck, blot,** place differently coloured, *ₒod-zér šár-čin̄ lhán-pa bžin-du* a sunbeam forming by reflection a bright spot *Dzl.; lhan-ťábs* **appendix, supplement,** title of a medical book.

ལྷབ་ལྷབ་པ་ *lhab-lháb-pa, lhabs-se lhabs Sch.*: 'to flutter to and fro, to glimmer, glisten' (?).

ལྷབ་ལྷུབ་ *lhab-lhúb* **wide, flowing,** *dar-bér lhab-lhúb* a wide silk cloak; prob. also sbst.: the moving to and fro, waving, *mé-tog-gi* of flowers *Do.*, **hlab-hlúb-tu sol** *C.* loosen your dress! make yourself comfortable!

ལྷམ་ *lham* **boot,** also **shoe;** *mčil-lham* id.; *rgyá-lham* a Chinese boot, *sóg-lham* a Mongol boot.

Comp. *lham-skúd* twine, used by shoemakers *Schr.* — *lham-k̔an̄-čén* (prob. a Chinese word) strong Chinese boots *C.* — *lhám-mk̔an* shoemaker *Schr.* — *lham-sgróg* shoe-strap, latchet; string for lacing felt-leggings. — *lham-mťil* boot-sole. — *lham-yú* leg of a boot *Cs.*, *lham yu-rín̄* boots with long legs *Sch.* — *Sch.*: *lham-krád* or *-skrád* pieces of leather, used for the patching of soles; *lham-góg* worn-out boots; *lham-ₒgrám* the upper-leather, the vamp; *lham sgró-gu-čan* buskins; *lham yu-čád* a sort of slippers to which cotton leggings are sewed (?); *rtín̄-lham* quarter-piece (of a shoe).

ལྷམས་ཀྱིས་ *lháms-kyis* at once, all, every thing *Sch.* Cf. *lhem.*

ལྷས་(མ་) *lhas(-ma)* 1. **pen, fold,** inclosure for sheep *C.*, *W.*; also **hlẹ́-ra**. 2. also *lhés(-ma)* **braid; wicker-work; texture;** also of pastry, **twisted cake** or **bun, cracknel** (*W.* **žím-zag**), also *lhas-dóg.*

ལྷས་བསྟན་ *lhas-bstán* n. of the birth-place of the mother of Buddha, *Ssk.* **देवदर्शित**.

ལྷས་པ་ *lhás-pa* v. under *slé-ba.*

ལྷས་བྱིན་ *lhas-byin,* **देवदत्त,** n. of a cousin of Buddha who, as the legends have it, was continually annoying Buddha by malicious artifices, whereby, however, the blameless character of the latter showed itself but the more conspicuously; hence proverbially used for any malicious character *Cs.*

ལྷིང་ *lhin̄*, cf. *lin̄s-pa*; *lhin̄-skrán Sch.*: a tumor filled with matter, **an abscess,** *lhin̄-rtsa* a full vein; *lhin̄ čád-pa Lt.*, acc. to *Sch.*: completely separated.

ལྷུ་ *lhu* **part, portion** of the body of an animal, = $\frac{1}{3}$ *zug*, *lhu-ťsigs bču-γnyis Sch.*: the 12 chief parts (of an animal) resulting from this way of dividing it, — but elsewhere 18 such parts are mentioned; *lhú-ru γsil-ba* to divide, to parcel out *Mil.*; **share** in plough-land, v. sub *spyod-pa* I, 2.

ལྷུག་ *lhug* v. *ldúg-pa* to pour *Cs.*

ལྷུག་པ་ *lhúg-pa*, *Cs.*: '*lhug-pa* and *lhug-ma* **prose;** *lhug-po* **wide, diffuse, luxurious,** *gos lhug-lhug-po* a very ample robe; *lhug-par* **amply, copiously, plentifully;** *lhug-par smra-ba* to speak diffusely, copiously, to speak in prose'. *Sch.* adds: '*lhugs* successive, continuous; *lhugs-ťsig* and *lhug-pa* continuous prose'. The principal meaning, however, seems to be: **uninterrupted, having no gaps;** unreserved; *lhúg-par bšád-pa* = *spas-γsán-med-par bšád-pa* to explain completely, without omitting any thing, **lug tán̄-če** *Ld.* to give unreservedly, without limitation; hence also: liberally, plentifully; *mčí-ma* *lhúg-par śor* or *byuṅ Mil.*, tears were flowing abundantly. — In some other passages the meaning of *lhúg-pa* is not quite clear.

ལྷུང་བ་ *lhúṅ-ba*, pf. of *ltúṅ-ba*; *lhuṅ lhuṅ snyán-pai sgra sgróg-ċiṅ ˳búb-bo* sweetly murmuring (the gentle stream) descends *Mil.*

ལྷུང་བཟེད་ *lhuṅ-bzéd*, *Ssk.* **पिण्डपात्र, the alms-bowl** of Buddha and of the mendicant friars.

ལྷུན་ *lhun* **mass, bulk,** *lhún-ċan* **massy, bulky; well-fed,** **lun-ťúg-po* W.*, *lhun-čé-ba* very large; *lhun-(gyis) grub(-pa)* acc. to *Cs.*: 'formed in mass, or all at once', self-created, not contrived by human labour; *bgó-ba daṅ bzá-ba lhún-gyis grúb-pas* clothes and food coming forth of themselves *Dzl.*; also used of palaces, sacred buildings, images, though in such instances often only by way of compliment; *lhun-grúb* is also noun personal. — *lhún-po*, *ri-rab-lhún-po* the mountain of the universe, **Meru, Sumeru,** frq. *lhun-stúg Sch.*, *lhun-ťúg Thgy.* very great, in reference to the mental darkness produced by sin; prob. also: considerable, sublime, grand.

ལྷུབ་པ་ *lhúb-pa* 1. sbst. **width,** *lhúb-pa-ċan Cs.*, *yaṅ(s)-hlúb*, *hlub-hlúb W., C.* **wide,** of clothes. — 2. vb.: **to bind, tie, fasten,** e.g. ornaments to the ear *Ts.*, = *klúb-pa*.

ལྷུམས་ *lhums*, resp. for *mṅal* **the womb** frq., *lhúms-su žúgs-pai dus-mčód* sacrificial festival of the conception (of Buddha) *Sch.*

ལྷུར་ *lhur*, with *lén-pa* or *byéd-pa* c. acc. **to apply one's self to, bestow pains upon,** = *don-gnyér byéd-pa Dzl.* and elsewh.

ལྷེ་བ་ *lhé-ba* v. *slé-ba*.

ལྷེན་ *lhen Cs.* 'filth or dross in the bowels, causing obstruction'; acc. to others: internal excrescences, v. *skran*; *Sch.*: *lhen* or *lhen-sná* pit of the heart.

ལྷེབ་ *lheb*, *dbugs lheb-lheb-tu ˳dug-pa Pth.* **'ug leb leb ǰhed-de* C.* gasping for breath.

ལྷེམ་ *lhem* **now, at present, directly, instantly** *C.*; **all** (of them) cf. *lhams*.

ལྷེས་མ་ *lhés-ma* = *lhás-ma* 2; also: the act of twisting, plaiting, **hlé-ma gyáb-pa* C.* to twist, **to plait.**

ལྷོ་ *lho* **south,** *lho-núb* south-west, *śar-lhó* south-east; *lhor*, *lho-ṗyógs-su* to the south, towards the south; *lhó-k̔a* prob. = *lho*; *lhó-k̔a món-nas ˳oṅs Mil.* they came from the Mon in the south; *lhó-pa*, *lho-˳brúg-pa* an inhabitant of Bhotan; *lhó-yul* acc to *Cunn.* the original form of the name of that province which is now called Lāhul or Lāhōl by the Hindoos, and Lahoul by the English; *lho-búr Sch.* (also *lho-˳ú-ma*), = *k̔ug-rna*.

ལྷོག་པ་ *lhóg-pa*, *glóg-pa Cs.* **a large ulcer** or **sore,** *Sch.*: **carbuncle, anthrax,** *sbyóṅ-ba* to cure it; in *Med.* also *nya-lhóg* and *gag-lhóg* are mentioned. According to the description, however, which Tibetan physicians gave us of the *lhóg-pa*, it seems to denote a cancerous ulcer, against which they employ the *Aconitum ferox* of Nepal, or in default of it some other species of aconite.

ལྷོང་ *lhoṅ Sch.* vexation, anger, wrath(?); but: '*lhoṅ śor* he has lost the *lhoṅ*', is said of one who was not equal to the exertions of incessant meditation, and who in consequence has lost his senses, v. sub *smyón-pa*.

ལྷོད་པ་ *lhód-pa*, *glod-pa*, *lod-pa* or *-po*, *lhod*, *lhód-po* 1. **loose, relaxed, unstrung, slackened,** *yan-lág* of the limbs, e.g. when death approaches *S.g.*, **zúg-po lód-po čá-na* W.* when one gets tired (one cannot help yawning). *lhód-pa sgrím-pa* to tighten what is loose, *lhod lhod gtóṅ-ba* to slacken; fig. **'ó-ma lód-po* W.* the milk begins to fail, milk is scarce. — 2. of the mind: **easy, careless, unconcerned,** *lhód-de nyol ċig* sleep well! sleep soundly! *Glr.*; *blo lhod gyis-la śod* relate the matter calmly, coolly *Mil.*; *śes-pa lhod-ċiṅ* in good spirits, of a cheerful temper *Pth.*; *ťabs śig yod-kyi rgyal-po ťugs lhod mdzod* there is yet a help; therefore, o king, be of good cheer! *Pth.*

ལྷོན་པ་ *lhón-pa*, *glón-pa* **to return, to give** or **pay back** *Cs.*

ཨ

ཨ a, 1. the consonant which is formed in the lowest and hindmost part of the organs of speech, being produced by the opening of the glottis, like the Greek spiritus lenis, the Hebrew Aleph and the Arabian Elif. (In our modern languages the opening of the glottis is not regarded as a consonant, nor expressed by a particular letter or sign.) Combined with the Tibetan vowel-signs, ཨ, ཨི, ཨུ, ཨེ, ཨོ, it is pronounced *'a*, *'i*, *'u*, *'e*, *'o* (cf. འ). It is also called *skye-ba-méd-pai yi-ge*, probably because all speaking depends on and is rendered possible only by a previous opening of the glottis; hence this letter is a symbol of the deity, of the *čós-sku* that was before every thing else. *Spyan-ras-zig*, therefore, addresses a celestial Buddha with *'a*: *'a skye-méd rnam-dág čós-kyi dbyiṅs*. — 2. num.: 30.

ཨ(འ?) *'a* (*ˌa?*) 1. in *Ld.* and *Kh.* the col. demonstr. pron., for *de* that (q.v.); **'á-ne** from thence, there, *'á-ru* there, thither, that way. — 2. *Lh.*, pronounced very short and sharp, **well? what is the matter? yes! here!**

ཨཿ *'a Cs.*: '*Ssk.*: अ. a mystical exclamation'.

ཨ་ཀ(ཨ་ཁ?) *'á-ka* (*'á-k'a?*) acc. to *Huc* II, 160 = *'á-jo Kh.*

ཨ་ཀ་རུ *'á-ka-ru Cs.*, v. *'á-ga-ru*.

ཨ་ཀཱ་ལ *'a-kā-la Lt.*, *Ssk.*: **untimely.**

ཨ་ཀྲོང *'a-kroṅ* an alpine plant, in *Lh. Arenaria Roylea.*

ཨ་ཁ་ཁ, ཨ་ཁག *'á-k'a-k'a*, *a-k'ág* an exclamation expressive of contempt and detestation, opp. to *'á-la-la*; acc. to *Cs.* *'a-k'ag* is also adj. = *mi-sdug-pa*.

ཨ་ཁུ *'a-k'ú*, *W.* also *'a-kú*, col. for *k'ú-bo* 1. **father's brother, uncle** *Mil*, *C.*, *W.* — 2. **husband, consort** *W.*

ཨ་ག་རུ *'á-ga-ru*, **अगरु, aloe-wood,** agallochum, calambac.

ཨ་གྱིས *'a-gyis* caressing word used by mothers soothing their babies, prob. without any particular signification *Thgy.*

ཨ་ཙུག *'a-čúg* **ankle-bone** *Lt.*

ཨ་ཚུ, ཨ་ཚུ་ཚུ *'a-čú*, *'á-ču-čú* interj. expressive of pain from cold, hence *'a-čú-zer-ba* n. of one of the cold hells.

ཨ་ཆེ *'a-čé*, *'a-ċé*, *Bal.* *'a-šé*, col. for *ċe-že* 1. **an elder sister** of a female person. — 2. *W.* **wife, mistress, madam,** used as address and otherwise.

ཨ་ཇོ *'a-jó C.*, *W.*, *jo-jó C.* (v. *jó-bo*) 1. **an elder brother** of a male person. — 2. **Sir, Mr., gentleman, lord,** used in addressing and otherwise; also like our: **friend!** ho there! hollo! I say! *'a-jho lág C.* **the old Squire,** = *ga-gá Ld.*

ཨ་ཏི་ཤ *'a-ti-ša Ssk.*, *púl-du-byuṅ-ba Tib.*, n. of a celebrated Pandit of Bengal, who lived for many years in Tibet, and died there in the eleventh century of our era.

ཨ་ཐོ་བ *'a-t'ó-ba* beautiful, good *Sch* (?).

ཨ་འཐས *'a-ˌt'as Pth.?*

ཨ་དོགས *'a-dogs Sch.* table(?)

ཨ་དོན *'a-dón Sch.*: 'without sexual distinction; sense of the letter *'a*'.

ཨ་དྲུང *'a-drúṅ C.* **horse-boy,** one tending horses.

ཨ་ན(ན) *'á-na(-na)* an interjection expressive of grief *Sch.*

ཨ་ན་མ་ན *'a-na-ma-na Sch.*: having a striking likeness(?).

ཨ་ནུ *'á-nu* Hindi man's name, also used in Tibet *Glr.*

ཨ་ནེ *'á-ne* 1. = *né-ne-mo* **father's sister, aunt; grand-aunt** *Glr.* — 2. *Cs.*: **nun.**

3. *W.* **wife, partner, spouse,** **'á-ne kúr-če** to take a wife, to marry, **(s)kyá-wo 'á-ne kur čog** a layman is at liberty to marry; **'á-ne-la čó-če** to treat, to use as a wife, sensu obsc. = to sleep with. — 4. **a woman, a female.** — 5. *Sch.* an old woman (?).

ཨ་པ་ *'á-pa* = *'á-p̔a.*

ཨ་པོ་ *'a-po Ü:* **building** (= **k̔ar-lén* W.*), **'á-po gyáb-pa** to construct a house, to build.

ཨ་པྲ་ *'á-pra Sch.* **zizel**, earless marmot, souslik (*Spermophilus citillus*).

ཨ་ཕ་ *'á-p̔a, 'á-pa* col. for *p̔a*, in *B.* of rare occurrence; **'á-pa čén-po** the elder, **čúṅ-ṅu** the younger, of the husbands of a person's mother, hence occasionally = **uncle;** **'á-pe ša* W.* a vulgar oath; also (like *p̔a*) uncastrated male animal, cf. *p̔a.*

ཨ་ཕོ་ང་ *'a-p̔o-ṅá C.* col.: **I**, cf. *k̔o-bo-ṅá.*

ཨ་ཕྱི་ *'a-p̔yi Mil*, **'a-p̔i, 'a-pi**, for *p̔yi-mo* **grandmother.**

ཨ་ཕྱིམ་ *'a-p̔yim* **old woman, goody, dame** *Sch.*

ཨ་ཕྲག་ *'a-p̔rág Sch.:* the bosom of a garment, *'a-p̔rág-tu sdú-ba* to put into the bosom, = *'am-bág.*

ཨ་བ་དྷུ་ཏི་ *'a-wa-dhu-ti* v. *dhu-ti.*

ཨ་བང་ *'a-baṅ*, for *baṅ-po*, the husband of the father's or the mother's sister *Cs.*

ཨ་བི་ཥ་ *'a-bi-ṣa Ssk.:* 'antivenomous', n. of a medicinal herb *Wdṅ.*

ཨ་བོ་ *'a-bo* 1. *Sch.* = *'a-p̔o.* — 2. a medicine *S.g.*

ཨ་བོ་ཙེ་ *'a-bo-tse Sch.:* **'good, tolerable, middling'**, cf. *Bun.: eb-bo* good.

ཨ་བྱག་ *'a-byag* and *'a-ₒbras* names of medicines *Med.*

ཨ་མ་ *'á-ma* col. and sometimes in *B.* = *ma* **mother;** **'á-me ša** a vulgar oath; *'á-ma drin-čén* so a king addresses a wonder-working nun *Pth.*

ཨ་མ་གྱིས་ *'a-ma-gyis Cs.* interj., prob. similar to *a-gyis.*

ཨ་མི་དེ་བ་ *'a-mi-de-ba* the usual Tibetan corruption of **अमिताभ,** v. *ₒod-dpag-méd.*

ཨ་མྲ་ *á-mra Ssk.* **the mango tree** and **-fruit** *Dzl.*

ཨ་མྲི་ཏ་ *'a-mri-ta* (*Ssk.* **अमृत ambrosia;** also various fruits etc.), in the *Lt.* perh. the **guava** fruit, which in Hindoostani is now called *amrūt.*

ཨ་ཙ་(མ་) *'a-tsa(-ma)* interj. expressive of pain by touching hot objects *Sch.*; also used in various other instances, when disagreeably surprised, startled etc. *bdag ma gról-ba ₒdi 'á-tsa-ma* alas! I am not yet released! *Thgr.*; *'á-tsa-ma yi-dwags snyiṅ re-rǰé* alas! ye poor Yidags folk! *Mil.*

ཨ་ཙ་ར་ *'a-tsa-ra Mil.* a species of hobgoblins, or spectres; in *C.* a Bengalee, acc. to *Lew.* The observations of *Huc* (II, 271) concerning this word seem to be mixed with some errors.

ཨ་ཙརྱ་ *'a-tsarya, Ssk.* **आचार्य, spiritual guide** or **father, instructor, professor, doctor.**

ཨ་ཚ་(ཚ་) *'a-ts̔a(-ts̔a)* an interj. expressing discomfort occasioned by heat.

ཨ་མཚར་ *'a-mts̔ar Sch.:* oh dear, what a wonder!

ཨ་ཛི་ན་ *'á-dza-na Wdṅ., 'á-dzi-na Stg.,* **अजिन** *Will.:* the hairy skin of a black antelope, which serves the religious student for a couch, seat, covering etc.; Tibetan writers use it for the animal itself: *ri-dwags 'á-dzi-nai págs-pa Stg.*

ཨ་ཞང་ *'a-žáṅ* 1. col. for *žáṅ-po* **mother's brother,** **'a-žaṅ-ts̔á-wo** **nephew.** — 2. *Cs.:* 'an address' (?).

ཨ་ཝ་ *'á-wa* a medicinal herb *S.g.?*

ཨ་བརྟ་ *'ā-warta, 'ā-barta(-na) Ssk.* ('whirl, whirlpool, eddy') a disease of the *rluṅ*, q.v.; perh. **dizziness?** *Med.*

ཨའུ་ཙི་ *'au-tsi* 1. *Sch.:* it is of no consequence, it does not matter. — 2. n. of a plant = *bya-po-tsi-tsi.*

ཨ་ཡ་ཟྭ་ཚོད་ *'a-ya-zwa-ts̔ód* dead-nettle *Med.*

ཨ་ཡུ་ *'a-yu C.* (= *k̔u-yu*) **hornless,** of cattle.

ཨ་ར་ *'á-ra* **beard** *Ts.*

ཨ་ར་ 'ā-rā *Hind.* **a saw.**

ཨ་ར་པ་ཙ་ན 'a-ra-pa-tsa-na a mystical and symbolical word, *Was.* (183)

ཨ་རག 'a-rág, resp. *bšes-rág C.*, *ₒdon-rág W.*, **arrack, brandy,** the usual barley-brandy, which is distilled in the convents and in nearly every manor-house.

ཨ་རུ་ 'á-ru 1. prob. *Ssk.* a medicinal plant, *Med.* — 2. v. 'a.

ཨ་རུ་ར་ 'á-ru-ra **myrobalan,** an astringent medicinal fruit *Med.* frq.

ཨ་རུམ 'a-rum a species of garlic, with a pale-red blossom, *Allium strictum.*

ཨ་རེ་ 'a-re an interj. the meaning of which is stated differently, *Mil.*; *'a-re paṅs* well then! throw it away!

ཨ་རོག 'a-róg *Sch.*: = *rogs-po, grogs,* **companion, mate, fellow, comrade, friend;** *'a-rog-k̔ya* or *gya Sch.*: 'a complimentary phrase or form of salutation'.

ཨ་ལ(ལ) 'á-la(-la) *Mil.*, also *'ál-la* id. interj. expressive of joyful surprise: aye, ah, that is capital! *dés-na 'á-la-la* well, that is excellent or splendid indeed! *Mil.*; also adjectively: **de saṅ di 'á-la-la* W.* this is much better than that!

ཨཱ་ལི་ 'á-li the Tibetan vowels, *'ā-li-ká-li* the series of the vowels together with the consonants; *'a-p̔reṅ* id.

ཨ་ལི་ *'a-li a* little *C.*

ཨ་ལི་ཁུག་ཏ 'a-li-k̔ug-ta **a swallow** *Cs.*

ཨ་ལུང་ 'a-lúṅ *Sch.* **buckle, clasp (?).**

ཨ་ལོང་ 'a-lóṅ **a ring.**

ཨ་ཤད 'a-šád v. sub *γtúm-mo.*

ཨ་ཤུ 'a-šú **apricot.**

ཨ་ཤོ་ཀ 'a-šo-ka n. of a tree and of a king.

ཨ་སམ 'a-sám *Sch.*: a thick sauce or broth, soup; *'a-sbyár* a thin broth.

ཨ་སྲུ 'a-srú for *srú-mo* **aunt** *Sch.*

ཨ་གསལ་ལ 'a-γsál-la adv. **openly, manifestly, publicly,** = *mṅon-súm-du.*

ཨ་ཧ་ཧ 'a-ha-há interj. expressing joy, pleasure, satisfaction.

ཨ་ཧོ་ཡེ 'a-ho-yé yea, nay even (?).

ཨག་པོ 'ág-po **bad** *C.*

ཨག་ཙེ 'ag-tsé *Melia Azedarachta,* **the 'neem'** of Anglo-Indians, an important remedy for cutaneous diseases.

ཨག་ཚོམ 'ag-ts̔óm *Glr.*, *'og-ts̔óm Sch.*, resp *žal-ts̔óm Pth.*, **beard of the chin, chin-tuft.**

ཨང་ 'aṅ 1. sbst. = *ₒdoms? 'áṅ-rta, 'áṅ-ras* loin-cloth *C.*, *W.*; *'aṅ-t̔úṅ* **under-garment,** χιτών, (hence also to be used for shirt and shift); *'aṅ-rág* **trowsers,** breeches *Pth.* — 2. interj.: **well then! now then! well!** in French: *eh bien!* at the beginning of a speech also *'áṅ-ge, 'áṅ-ke, 'áṅ-ki, Mil.*, without any regard to rank.

ཨང་གི 'áṅ-gi or *'áṅ-ki, Ssk.* **ཨངྐ, figure, number, cipher,** also *'aṅ-graṅs, 'aṅ-yig Cs.*; the last word, acc. to others, means **secret characters,** cryptography.

ཨང་གུ་ལི 'aṅ-gu-li *Ssk.* **finger** *Do.*

ཨང་གར་འཇིག 'aṅ-rgar-ₒǰig acc. to *Lew.* **English,** *Hd. angrezi.*

ཨང་མ་ཙི 'aṅ-ma-tsi *Sch.* **flies,** winged insects.

ཨན 'an *W.* **white chalk.**

ཨན་སྟོང་ 'an-stoṅ *Med.*, *Sch.*: cervical vertebra.

ཨན་གདོས 'an-γdos *C.*: **stocks,** **'an-dǒ-la ǰúg-pa** to put (a person) into the stocks.

ཨན་འདར 'an-ₒdár *C.* 1. **board, plank, deal.** — 2. *lčags-kyi 'an-ₒdár Cs.* an iron instrument of torture; acc. to *Thgy.* a kind of press.

ཨནྡྲ་རྙི་ལ 'andra-rnyi-la *Lex.*, corrupted form for *'indra-nī-la.*

ཨམ་ཆོག, ཨམ་བག **'am-čog, 'am-bag** col. *C.* for *rna-mčog, snam-brag* **ear; bosom.**

ཨམ་བན 'am-ban a Chinese resident, Chinese superior civil officer, in the chief cities and provincial towns of the tributary countries of China.

ཨར་ཀ 'ár-ka, 'ár-ga, 'ár-ka, 'ér-ka 1. *Cs.* **marble.** 2. **plaster-floor**, made of pulverized marble and oil, also *'a-žál.*

ཨར་གོན་ *'ar-gon* an offspring of parents not having the same rank, nor the same religion, and not belonging to the same nation *Ld.*

ཨ་རྒྱམ་ *'a-rgyam Sch.:* 'the offering of sacrifices'; *Will.:* **अर्घ** respectful offering to a god or Brāhman.

ཨརྫ་ཀ *'ar-dza-ka Ssk., Sch.:* **cotton**, *'ár-dza-kai dóg-pa Glr.* cotton-capsule. (This signification is not to be found in our *Ssk.*-dictionaries.)

ཨར་ལ་གཏད་པ་ *'ár-la ytád-pa Sch.:* 'to be reduced to extremities, to extreme misery' (?).

ཨལ་གཅིག *'al-ycig Sch.:* 'the one half of a pair, e.g. **one** eye', = *ya-ycig.*

ཨལ་ད་ *'ál-ta* (for *da-lta*) *Bal.* 1. **now, at present.** — 2. **to-day.**

ཨལ་དིང་ *'al-tiṅ*, *al-tiṅ-la kur-če* *W.* to carry something bulky tied up in the girdle.

ཨལ་དོ་, ཨལ་ཙེ་ *'al-tó*, *'al-tsé* earthen kitchen-pot *Ld.*

ཨལ་ལ་ *'al-la* v. *'a-la-la.*

ཨསྨ་གརྦྷ་ *'asma-gar-bha, Tar.: nór-bu asma-gar-bha Schf.:* **emerald.**

ཨི་ *'i* 1. **beer,** = *čaṅ, C.* — 2. vulgar pronunciation of *dbyi*, *yi*, **the lynx.** — 3. num.: 60.

ཨི་ཁུག *'i-kug*, *'ig*, *W.* **hiccough, sob,** *'i-kug yóṅ-ṅa rag* I have got the hiccough, *'i-kug gyab dug* he hiccoughs.

ཨིནྡྲ་གོ་པ་ *'indra-go-pa*, **इन्द्रगोप**, **cochineal;** yet among the substances devoted to a costly Chodten it is mentioned as one of the five divine jewels *Glr.* 7.

ཨིནྡྲ་ནཱི་ལ་ *'indra-nī-la* **sapphire** (*Sch.:* emerald?).

ཨུ་ *'u* num.: 90.

ཨུ་ཅུག *'u-čúg*, with *čó-če* *W.* **to persuade,** e.g. to buy something.

ཨུ་དུམ་བ་ར་ *'u-dum-ba-ra* (*Ssk. Ficus glomerata*) in Tibetan literature a fabulous lotos of immense size.

ཨུ་མ་ *'u-ma Ssk.*, prob. also spelled *dbú-ma*, n. of the wife of Siwa (Durga, Kāli etc.).

ཨུ་ཙུགས་ *'u-tsúgs Sch.* = *'u-túg.*

ཨུ་རྒྱན་ *'u-rgyán* 1. also *'oḍiyana Cs.*, (not mentioned in *Ssk.* dictionaries), often written in the abbreviated form ཨོྒྱན, a fabulous country in the north-west of India (though *Cs.* supposes it to be Ujain), frequently represented as a kind of paradise. — 2. now a noun personal of frq. occurrence; *'u-rgyan-padma* v. *padma-˳byuṅ-ynás.*

ཨུག་ཆོས་ *'ug-čós* n. of a remedy *Med.*

ཨུང་གུ་ *'úṅ-gu* **oil-lamp** *C.*

ཨུཏ་པ་ལ་, ཨུད་པ་ལ་ *'ut-pa-la*, *'ul-pa-la* a blue lotos which is also used for medicinal purposes. In *Lh.* this name seems to be transferred to *Polemonium caeruleum.*

ཨུན་ཐུག *'un-túg* v. *'u-túg.*

ཨུམ་ *'um* **a kiss,** *'um ǰór-wa* or *gyág-pa* **to kiss** *C.*

ཨུར་རྒྱ་ *'ur-rgyá* a warm meal-porridge; fermenting **dough** *C.*

ཨུར་རྡོ་ *'ur-rdó* v. *ur-rdó.*

ཨུར་བ་ *'úr-ba* v. *dbúr-ba.*

ཨུལ་འཐག *'ul-˳tág* col. for *yyul-˳tág.*

ཨེ་ *'e* 1. in *C.* and later literature, an interrogative, pronounced short, accented, and usually put immediately before the vb. or the pron. which stands in the place of the vb.: *dé-mo é yo'*? do you feel well? are you well? are you getting on well? *kyed daṅ 'e ˳prad mi šes* I do not know whether I shall see you again *Mil.*; *'e nus mi nus* whether we shall be able or not *Mil.*; rarely for **even if, though, although,** *'e sus kyaṅ mi túb-na* though nobody is really able to do it. — 2. num.: 120.

ཨེ་ཉ་ཡ་ *'e-nya-ya, 'e-na-ya, Ssk.* **एण**, a fabulous black antelope with short legs and black eyes.

ཨེ་མ་ *'é-ma, 'e-ma˳ó, 'e-ma-hó* interj. expressing joy, surprise, astonishment, **hey! hey day! indeed! you don't say so!** in asking, beseeching, requesting a person's attention: **please, pray, I say;** or expressive of lamentation, compassion: **alas! oh! would to God! O dear!** e.g.: *'é-ma séms-čan snyiṅ-re-rjé* alas, the poor people! *Glr.*

ཨེ་ཝཾ་ *'e-wam, Ssk.* **एवम्**, **yes, certainly, to be sure** *Wdk.* and elsewh.

ཨེ་ར་ཀ་ *'e-ra-ka Cs.*: 'n. of a country, Irak? Chaldaea?' (In *Ssk.* it denotes a sort of grass, or a woollen carpet.)

ཨེ་ལ་ *'e-la, Ssk.* **एला**, *'é-la prá-mo Wdṅ.* small **cardamoms**, seed of *Electeria Cardamomum.*

ཨེན་ཙམ་ *'én-tsam* **a little, some, a small bit,** *Ü* and *B.*

ཨེན་རེ་ *'en-ré* **quick, fast, speedy** *Sch.*

ཨེན་འདར་ *'en-˳dár* v. *'an-˳dar.*

ཨེམ་ཆི་ *'ém-či, 'ám-či* (Turkish word) **physician** *W.*

ཨེར་ཀ་ *'ér-ka C.* v. *'ár-ka.*

ཨོ་ *'o* 1. for འོ་ *˳o* **a kiss,** *Pth.* — 2. num.: 150.

ཨོ་དཀར་ *'o-dkár W.* = *lkog-dkór*, v. *lkóg-ma.*

ཨོ་ཌི་ཡན་ *'o-ḍi-yán* v. *'u-rgyán.*

ཨོཌྲ་ *'óndra,* **ओड्र** *Oḍra,* the northern part of Orissa, *Wdk.*

ཨོ་མོ་སུ་ *'ó-mo-su* (Mongol word) **stocking** *C.*

ཨོ་ལྡོང་ *'o-ldóṅ, 'o-dóṅ,* col. **'ó-šo* Cs.,* **windpipe;** **'o-le* W.* **throat;** **'o-lé dám-te ši soṅ** he is suffocated.

ཨོ་ལོ་ *'ó-lo* (Mongol word?) *Sch.*: the place where two rivers flow together, **the confluence** of two rivers.

ཨོ་རྒྱན་ *'o-rgyán* = *'u-rgyán Pth.*

ཨོཾ་ *ōm, Ssk.* **ओम्**, mystical interjection, in later Hindooism the symbol of the Hindoo triad, in as much as it consists of the three sounds, a (Vishnu), u (Shiva), and m (Brahma). This interjection frequently occurs in the prayers of the northern Buddhists of Tibet, and especially in the famous 'six-syllable prayer', ཨོཾ་མ་ཎི་པདྨེ་ཧཱུྃ, *ōm ma-ṇi pad-me hūm,* the literal version of which is: 'O thou jewel in the lotus, *hūm*!' The person addressed in these words is not Buddha, but *Spyan-ras-yzigs* (v. *spyan*); by some he is thought to be the author of them. Concerning the import of this short apostrophy the best information is to be found *Köpp.* II, 59—61. — The Tibetans themselves are ignorant of the proper sense of these six syllables, if sense at all there be in them, and it is not unlikely that some shrewd priest invented this form of prayer, in order to furnish the common people with a formula or symbol, easily to be retained by the memory, and the frequent recital of which might satisfy their religious wants. And though there may be no obvious meaning in such exclamations or prayers, yet their efficacy is sure to be firmly believed in by a people, whose practical religion chiefly consists in the performance of certain rites and ceremonies, in a devout veneration of their Lamas, combined with frequent oblations to them, in abstaining from gross sins (regarding even the killing of live animals as such), and in the Pradakshina (v. *skor-ba* 2). — The numerous attempts that have been made to explain the Ommanipadmehūm satisfactorily, and to discover a deeper sense or even a hidden wisdom in it, have proved more or less unsuccessful. The most simple and popular, but also the flattest of these explanations is derived from the purely extrinsic circumstance, that the Sanskrit words of the prayer consist of six syllables, and accordingly it is suggested, that each of these syllables, when pronounced by a pious Buddhist, conveys a blessing upon one of the 'six classes of beings'. — The conjecture with which *Köpp.* closes his disquisition, is certainly nothing but a smart thought of that learned author.

ཨོཾ་ཨཱཿཧཱུྃ 'ō-'a-hūm, another mystical formula, used e. g. for transforming the *mi-γtsáṅ-ba bċu* into *bdud-rtsi*, v. the explanation given under *naṅ-mčód.*

ཨོཾ་ཚུགས 'ō-tsugs *Sch.*: propping one's chin on both fists, *'ō-tsúgs mdzad Mil.*

ཨོག་རྒྱ 'og-rgyá **beard**; *'og-tsúm* = *'aq-tsóm.*

ཨོག་མ 'óg-ma **throat, neck,** = *lkog-ma*; *'og-žó* a beautiful white neck, a 'milk-neck' *Glr.*; *'og-skó* prob. = *'os-sko Med.*

ཨོང་གུ 'oṅ-gu **a lamp,** *'oṅ-rás* **the wick** of a lamp *C.*

ཨོང་ལེ 'oṅ-lé *W.* resp. for *'a*, at your service! at your commands!

ཨོང་ལོག 'oṅ-log **ptarmigan** *Sch.*

ཨོམ་མོག 'om-móg **throat and chest** *Sch.*

ཨོལ་མ 'ol-ma *C.* **throat, windpipe,** = *'ol-ldoṅ*; *'ól-ma dám-te sẹ́-pa** to strangle, throttle; *'ol-rko, 'ol-goṅ, 'ol-kroṅ* id., or acc. to others = *'ol-mdud* the fore-part of the larynx.

ཨོས་སྐོ 'os-sko, also *ō-ku* *C.* **the chin,** resp. *žal-ko.*

ཨོས་ཅོས 'os-čos *Ts.* *ọ-čọ* *Pedicularis Hookeriana.*

ENGLISH-TIBETAN VOCABULARY.

English-Tibetan Vocabulary.

The figures, here and there attached to Tibetan words, refer to the page where the respective article is to be found. — The accent is marked only when, exceptionally, it rests on the last syllable of a word.

A

A, An, article *čig* 140.
Abandon *skyur-ba*; *spon-ba*; *°bor-ba*.
Abate *żi-ba*.
Abbot *mḱan-po*.
Abdomen *čal*, esp. *sḱu-čál*.
Ability *nus-pa*; *rtsal*.
Ablative case *°byuṅ-ḱuṅs*.
Able *mḱas-pa*; to be — *°ḱyud-pa*; *lċogs-pa*; *nyan-pa*; *ṫub-pa*; *nus-pà*; *ṗod-pa*; *°ṫsugs-pa*; *šes-pa*.
Ablution *ḱrus*.
Abode *mċis-bráṅ*; *°dug-γnas*; *°dug-sa*; *γnas (-ṫsaṅ)*; *γżi-ma*.
Abolish *°jig-pa*; *snub-pa*.
Abortion *skyur-ma*; *mṅal rlugs-pa*.
Abounding *rgyas-pa* 109, *mod-po*, *°dzom-po*.
About *tsam-na*, *tsa-na*; round — v. *ṗyogs* 352; to be — *ča-ba* 152; *čas-pa*.
Above adv. *steṅ-na*; *bla*; *yan*, *yan-la* 506; prep. *ḱa-na*, *ḱa-ru*, *ḱa-la*, *ḱar* 34; *goṅ-du*; *ltag-nas*, *ltag*; *ṫog-tu*.
Abridge *sdud-pa*.
Abridgment *zin-bris*.
Abroad v. *byes*; to go — *byes-su °gro-ba*.
Abscess *ču-búr*; *ȷ ol*.
Absolutely *čis-kyaṅ*; *ga-na-méd*.
Abstinence *dge-ba*; *ṫsod-šes-pa* 452.
Abundant *ḱrigs*.
Abuse s. (reviling words) *skur-pa* 23; vb. a. (to revile) *skur °debs-pa* (*byed-pa*; *smra-ba*); *dma °bab-pa*; *smad-pa*.
Abyss *btson-doṅ*; *γyaṅ-sa*.
Academy *γtsug-lag-ḱáṅ*.
Accept *bżed-pa*, *bżes-pa*; *len-pa*.
Acceptable, to be — *°ṫad-pa*.
Access *°gro-sa*; v. also *γtoṅ-ba* 208 and *mjal-ba* 173.
Accident *rkyen*; unfortunate *°gal-rkyén*; fatal — *bar-čád*; *byur*, *byus*.
Accompany *skyel-ba*; *zla-bo byed-pa*.
Accomplish v. *grub-pa*; *čom-pa*; *spyod-pa*; *rtsom-pa*.
Accomplished *pul-tu byuṅ-ba* 344.
Accomplishment *rtsal*; *yon-tan* 516.
Accord, Accordance *°čam-pa*.
According to **naṅ-tar** W. C.; *daṅ sbyar-nas*; *bżin-du*.
Account s. *rtsis*, *lo-rgyús* 113; *γnas-ṫsúl*: on — of v. *rkyen*; *čed-du*; *ṗyir*; *slad-du*.
Account vb. a. *rtsis byed-pa* (*°debs-pa*. *gyab-pa*).
Accountant *rtsis-pa*.
Accumulate *spuṅ-ba*.
Accurate *żib-pa*.
Accusation, false — *snyad*.
Accuse *°gel-ba*; *rgol-ba*.
Accustomed *goms-pa*; *°dris-pa*; to be *°dris-pa*.
Ache vb. n. *na-ba*.
Acid, Acidity *skyur-ba*.
Acknowledge *ḱas len-pa*; frq. only *smra-ba*, *zer-ba* etc.
Aconite *boṅ-ṅa*.
Acquaintance (friend) *ṅo-šés*.
Acquainted, to be *ṅšés-pa*.
Acquiesce *ḱo-ṫag γċod-pa*; *mi rgol-ba*; *daṅ-du len-pa*.
Acquitted, to be — *rgyal-ba*.
Across *ṗred*, *°ṗred*.
Act vb. *byed pa*; *spyod-pa*; *bgyid-pa*; to — the part of *byed-pa*.
Action *spyod-pa*; *bya-ba*; *las*; former actions *sṅon-lás*.
Action (law-suit) *ḱrims*, *šags* W. 51.
Activity *spyod-pa*.

Actual *ṅes-pa-čan*; *ṅo-rtóg*; *yáṅ-dag-pa*.
Actually *γži-nas*.
Acute *rno-ba*.
Adage *ka-dpe*.
Add *snon-pa*; *sre-ba*; *rjes-su ͦjug-pa*; v. *ͦgod-pa*.
Addict, to — one's self *sten-pa*.
Adduce v. *mtson-pa* and *dpe*.
Adequate *ͦgrig-pa*; *mtun-pa*.
Adhere *ͦbyor-ba*, *ͦbyar-ba*; *γnas-pa*.
Adherent *pyogs-pa*; *ͦdzin-pa*.
Adieu v. *pyi-pyag* 347.
Adibuddha *kun-γži* 4.
Adjust *sbyor-ba*; *sgrig-pa*; *ͦgod-pa*.
Admit *γtoṅ-ba*; *kas len-pa*.
Admonish *skul-ba*.
Admonition *bskul-ba*, *bskul-ma*; *bslab-bya*.
Adolescent s. *kyeu*.
Adore *mos-pa*.
Adorn v. *ͦgod-pa*; *sgron-pa*; *brgyan-pa*; *spra-ba*.
Adult s. *če-mi*, *nar son-pa* 298.
Adulterate *slad-pa*.
Adulterer *šar-po*, adulteress *šar-mo*.
Adultery, to commit — v. *ͦjug-pa* 177, *byi byed-pa*; *γyem byed-pa*.
Advantage *don*; *bogs*; *ͦkyer-so*; *rgyal-ka*, *ka-rgyál*.
Adversary *pa-rol-po*.
Advice *ka-γdáms*; *ka-bsgos*; *ka-ta*, *ka-γdáms*; *gros*; *γdams-pa*; *ͦdun-ma*; *man-ṅág*; to ask — *bgro-ba*.
Advise *γdam-pa*, *ͦdom-pa*.
Adviser *bka-γdams-pa*.
Affair *don*.
Affect *bčos-pa* 147.
Affection *čags-pa*; *byams-pa*, *byams-sems*; *brtse-ba*.
Affectionate *brtse-ba-čan*.
Affix *sbyor-ba*.
Affliction *sdug-pa*; *mya-ṅán*; *tser-ka W*.
Afore-said *sṅa-ma*.
Afraid, to be — *skrág-pa*, *dṅaṅ-ba*; *ͦjigs-pa*; *bag tsa-ba*; *bred-pa*.
After adv. *rgyab-tu*; *pyi* 349; *ͦog*; *slad-na*.
After prep. *rjes*, *ͦog*; *slad*; *rtiṅ*; *mtar*; *nas*.
After-birth *ša-ma*.
Afterwards *rjes-la*, *rjes-su*; *rtiṅ-du*; *de-nas*; *pyin-čád*; *pyis*; *pyi-bžin*; *slad-nas*; *slar*.
Again *čed-du*; *pyir*; *slar*; *yaṅ*; — and — *yaṅ-nas yaṅ-du*.
Age *na-tsód*, *na-so*; *dus*.
Aged *rgad-pa*; to be — *rga-ba*.
Agent *byed(-pa)-po*, *byed-mkan*; *tsab-po*, resp. *sku-tsab*.
Agressor *sṅa-rgol*.
Agility *byag-pa*.
Agio *non-ka*; *par*; *ͦdza*.
Agitate *dkrug-pa*; *skyod-pa*; *skyom-pa*; *sgul-ba*; to be agitated *ͦgul-ba*; *ͦkrug-pa*.
Agitation *krag-ͦkrúgs*.
Ago *sṅun-la*; long — *sṅa-mo-nas*.
Agony *γšin-ͦpras*; *koṅ-ͦkrúgs*; *sems koṅ-du ͦtsud-pa*.
Agree *ͦgrig-pa*; *ͦčam-pa*; *stun-pa*; *mtun-pa*.
Agreeable *dga-ba*; *yid-du ͦoṅ-ba*.
Agreement *ka-čád*, resp. *zal-čád*; *gan-rgyá*; *čad*, *čad-so*; *ͦčam-pa*; *bzaṅ*.
Agriculture *so-nám(s)*.
Ague *tsad-pai nád*; *tsan-zug W*.
Aim s. *ͦgro-sa* 102; *ͦben*.
Aim vb. *zir-ba*; v. *γtod-pa* no. 3.
Air (atmospheric air) *ṅá-ra*; *ṅad*; *rluṅ*; cold — *ṅad*.
Air (tune) *mgur*, *glu*, *dbyaṅs*.
Air (mien) *ṅo*, *γdoṅ*.
Alabaster *ka-ma-ru*; *tod-le-kór*.
Alas *kye-ma*.
Alienism *ͦgron*.
Alight *ͦbab-pa*, resp. *γšol-ba*.
Alive *γson-po*.
All *kun*; v. *gaṅ*; *tams-čád*; *mtá-dag*, *tsad*; *yoṅs*; — right! *tsaṅ-ͦgrig*; — seeing *kun-γzigs*; — uniting *kun-ͦdus*; not at — *tsam yaṅ mi (ma)*; *ye mi (ma)*.
Allegory *ͦdra-dpe*.
Allow *γnaṅ-ba*; to be —ed *čog-pa*, *ruṅ-ba*.
Almanac *lo-tó*.
Almighty *kun-dbaṅ*.
Almond *ba-dám*.
Alms *ldom-bu*; *sloṅ-mo*; *bsod-snyóms*.
Alone *γčig*, *γcig-γčig*, *γčig-pu*, *γčig-po*.
Along with *žor-la*.
Alphabet *ka-preṅ*, *ka-ká*; *kā-li* 2.
Alpine pastures *neu-γsiṅ*; *ne-taṅ* C.
Also *yaṅ* 505.
Altar *mčod-stégs*, *mčod-kri*.
Alter *sgyur-ba*; *spo-ba*.
Alteration *ͦgyur-ba*.
Although *yaṅ* 505.
Altogether *kun*, *yoṅs-su*.
Alum *ka-ru-tsa*; *lče-myaṅ-tsá*.
Always *rgyun-du*; *rtag-tu*; *nam-yaṅ*.
Amalgam *gyim-bág*.
Ambassador *po-nya*.
Amber *spos-šél*.
Ambitious *grags-pa-la čags-pa*; *mton-dod-čan*.
Ambush v. (*lkog-*)*ͦjab*.
Amendment *žu-dág*, *žus-dág*.
Among *naṅ*, *naṅ-na* 301; *las* 546.
Amusement *γyeṅ-rtsé*
Analogy v. *dpe*.
Anasarca *pags-ču*.
Anatomy *lus-kyi γnas-lugs*.
Ancestor *pa-mes*, *mes-po*; *brgyud*.

Ancient *sṅa-ba*; — ly *sṅa-sor*; *sṅon-dús*.
And *daṅ* 248; v. also *ċiṅ* 140.
Angel *p̔o-nya* 345.
Anger *k̔ro-ba*; *k̔oṅ-k̔ro*; *k̔on-pa*; *sro*, resp. *t̔ugs-sro W.*; *že-sdaṅ*.
Angle *grwa* 75; *gru*.
Angry *k̔ro-ba*, *k̔ro-bo*, *k̔ro-mo*; to be — $_o$*k̔ro-ba*; *sdaṅ-ba*.
Angular *zul-ma*.
Animal s. *dud-*$_o$*gro*; *srog-č̔ágs*.
Animated being *srog-č̔ágs*; *sems-ċan*.
Animosity $_o$*k̔aṅ*.
Annals *lo-rgyús*; — of the kings *rgyal-rábs*.
Annihilate *med-par byed-pa*; to be annihilated *med-par* $_o$*gyur-ba*.
Annotation *mċan-bu*.
Announce *lon sgyur-ba*; *sbrón-pa*; *γ̔rin smra-ba*; *ṡes-par byed-pa*.
Annoy $_o$*k̔aṅ-ba*; *sṅog-pa*; *sun* $_o$*ǰug-pa*.
Annually *lo-ltar*, *lo daṅ lo*.
Anoint *skud-pa*; *bsgo-ba*; $_o$*byug-pa*.
Another *bdag-méd*; *γžan-ma*.
Answer vb. *lan* $_o$*debs-pa*.
Ant *gre-mog-*$_o$*bu*; *grog-ma*.
Antagonist $_o$*t̔ab-ya*; *p̔a-rol-pa* (or *po*).
Antelope *dgo-ba*; the Tibetan — *γtsod*, *btsod*, *γtso*.
Antidote *γnyen-po*.
Antipathy *žen-lóg*.
Antiquity *sṅa-dús*, *sṅa-ba*; *sṅon-ťsé*, *sṅon-dus*, *sṅon-rabs*.
Anus *rkub*; *γžaṅ*, *γžaṅ-k̔a*; *bṡaṅ-lám*.
Anxiety **k̔og-t̔úg**; col. *nyams-ṅa*.
Anxious (*sems*) *k̔oṅ-du č̔ud-pa*; v. also *bag-tsa*.
Any v. *gaṅ* 65; — one *gaṅ žig*; — thing *ċi žig*, *ċi-yaṅ*; — whatever *ċaṅ*.
Apathy *btaṅ-snyoms*; *byar-méd*.
Aperture *sgo*; *bu-ga*.
Apostle *mi-sná*.
Apothecary's shop *sman-k̔aṅ*.
Apparition *snaṅ-ba*; *žal-γzigs*.
Appear $_o$*č̔ar-ba*; *ston-pa*; *snaṅ-ba*; $_o$*byuṅ-ba*; *yod-par* $_o$*gyur-ba*.
Appearance $_o$*k̔yer-so*; *č̔a-byád*, *č̔a-lugs*; *č̔as*; *snaṅ-ťsúl*.
Appease *ži-bar byed-pa*.
Appendix *k̔a-skoṅ*
Appertain *γtogs-pa*.
Appetite *k̔am*; *daṅ-ga*.
Apple *ku-ṡu*; *sli*; — of the eye *spyan-*$_o$*bras*.
Application $_o$*bad-pa*; *brtson-*$_o$*grus*.
Apply *bkan-pa*; to — one's self *brtson-pa*.
Appoint *skul-ba*; *sko-ba*; $_o$*gel-ba*; $_o$*č̔ol-ba*; $_o$*ǰug-pa*.
Apprehend *γċags-pa*; *dogs-pa*.
Apprentice *mč̔an-bu*.
Approach vb. *k̔ad-pa*; *nye-ba*; *bsnyen-pa*.
Approach s. $_o$*gro-sa*.
Approve *bžed-pa*.

Appurtenance *rgyu-č̔á*; —s *skor*.
Apricot *k̔am-bu*; *ċu-li*, *ċo-li*; dried — *ċu-li C.*, *p̔a-tiṅ W.*; *mṅa-ris k̔am-bu C.*
Apron *dun-k̔ebs*, *paṅ-k̔ebs*.
Aqueduct *yur-ba*.
Arch *γžu*, *γžu-mo*.
Archer $_o$*p̔oṅ-mk̔an*; —y $_o$*p̔oṅ*.
Architect *rtsig-dpón*.
Archives *yig-ťsáṅ*.
Area v. *dkyil-*$_o$*k̔or*; *k̔yon*, *rgya-k̔yón*; *č̔u-žéṅ*
Argali *γnyan*.
Argue *bgro-ba*, *rtsod-pa*
Argument *mṅon-rtágs*; *rtags*.
Arise *skye-ba*; $_o$*k̔or-ba*; $_o$*k̔ruṅ-ba*; *č̔ags-pa*; *ldaṅ-ba*.
Arm *lag*(*-pa*), resp. *p̔yag*.
Armful *lag-k̔ód*; v. also *paṅ*.
Armour *go-k̔ráb*; *go-č̔a*.
Armpit *mč̔an-k̔uṅ*.
Arms *mťson*, *mťson-č̔a*, $_o$*t̔ab-grabs*.
Army *dpuṅ*; *dmag*; *dmag-dpúṅ*.
Aroma *ṅad*.
Aromatic *ṅad-ċan*.
Arrange *sgrig-pa*; $_o$*ǰog-pa*; *γtan-la* $_o$*bebs-pa* 205.
Arrangement *grabs*; *rgyu*; *γnas-lugs*.
Arrive *sleb-pa*; $_o$*byon-pa*; $_o$*byor-ba*.
Arrogance *ṅa-rgyal*; *p̔o*
Arrow *mda*.
Arsenal *go-k̔áṅ*.
Arsenic *ba-bla*.
Art *sgyu-rtsál*; *bzo*.
Artery *rtsa-dkár*; *rluṅ-rtsa*.
Artifice *sgyu*.
Artificial *bċos-pa*.
Artist *bzo-pa*.
As (like) *ltar*; *bžin-du*; (when) v. *ċiṅ* 140; *na* 299; *pas* 323; as — as *tsam* 430; — far — *tsam-du*, *bar-du*, *t̔ug*, *ťsug-pa*; — much — *ga-tsám*; — soon — *ma-k̔ád*, *ma-t̔ag-tu*.
Ascend $_o$*dzeg-pa*.
Ascending node *sgra-γċáṅ*.
Ascetic s. *sgom-po*, *sgom-mk̔an*; *sdom-sruṅ*.
Ashamed, to feel — *skyeṅ-ba*; *k̔rel-ba*; $_o$*dzem-pa*.
Ash-coloured *gro-mo*.
Ashes *gog-t̔ál*; *t̔al-ba*.
Aside *zur-du*; *logs-su*, *logs-la*.
Ask $_o$*dri-ba*, *γsol-ba*, *žu-ba*; *γser-ba*; *sloṅ ba*; 'if one asks so' v. *ċe-na* 142.
Asleep, to fall — *γnyid-du* $_o$*gro-ba*.
Aspire *snyeg-pa*.
Ass *boṅ-bu*, *boṅ-bo*; wild — *rkyaṅ*.
Assailant *sna-rgol*.
Assassinate v. $_o$*ǰab-pa* 174.
Assemblage *k̔rod-pa*; *ťsogs*.
Assemble vb. n. $_o$*du-ba*; $_o$*ťsogs-pa*; *lhags-pa*; vb. a. *sdud-pa*; *sog-pa*.
Assert *dam* $_o$*č̔a-ba*; *bžed-pa*.
Assiduous *brtson-pa-ċan*.

Assist *zla-bo* or *grogs byed-pa.*
Assistance *skyabs*; *skyobs*; *ra-mda.*
Assistant *grogs*; *ya-do W.*; *ra-mda-pa.*
Associate s. *grogs*; *zla-bo*; *ya-do W.*; *rogs.*
Associate vb. *ₒtsogs-pa*; to be — *ₒgrogs-pa.*
Assume *ₒċań-ba.*
Assurance *ydeń*; *blo-ytád*, *blo-ydéń.*
Asterism *skar-ma.*
Asthma *dbugs rdzań-ba.*
Astonished, to be — *ha-las-pa.*
Astonishment *ńo-mtsár*; *ya-mtsan.*
Astray, to go — *ₒkyar-ba*; v. also sub *yan-pa* 506.
Astride, to put — *skyon-pa.*
Astringent *bska-ba.*
Astrology *skar-dpyád*, *skar-rtsis.*
Astronomy *skar-rtsis* 439.
Asunder *so-sor* 578; to tear — *ₒdral-ba.*
At *kar*; *mdun-du*; *na* 298; *rtsar* 437.
Athlete *gyad.*
Atmosphere *rluń-gyi dkyil-ₒkor* 11.
Atom *rdul.*
Atonement *sdig-bšágs.*
Attach *ₒdogs-pa*; *sdom-pa*, *rtod-pa.*
Attached *zug-pa C.* 466; to be — *čags-pa*; *žen-pa.*
Attachment *ₒkri-ba*; *čags-pa*; *žen-ₒdzin.*
Attack *rub-pa.*
Attain *sgrub-pa*; *tob-pa*; *rnyed-pa*; v. also *ṗyin-pa.*
Attend vb. n. *skyoń-ba*; vb. a. *zla-bo byed-pa*; *nya-ra byed-pa.*
Attendant *ₒkor*, *ₒkor-mkan*; *ₒkor-yyog*, *yyog-ₒkor.*
Attention *ynyer-ka*; *zon.*
Attentive *yčań-po.*
Attitude *stańs*; *spyod-lam*; *rnam-ₒgyur*, *tsul*, *sdod-tsul.*
Attribute s. *brjod-pa* gramm.; *rtags*; *mtsan*, *mtsan-nyid.*
Auction *ni-lam.*
Auditory (in a monastery) *kun-dga-ra-ba* 4.
Augment vb. n. *rgyas-pa*; *ₒṗel-ba*; vb. a. *spel-ba.*
Aunt *ne-ne-mo*; *'a-ne*; *sru.*
Auspice *ča*; *rten-ₒbrél.*
Authentic *ńes-pa*
Author *byed-mkan*; *žal-ydams bris-mkan* 473.
Authority *čab*; *mtu.*
Authorize *dbań skur-ba.*
Autumn *ston*, *ston-ka.*
Avalanche *ka-rúd.*
Avarice *ser-sna*; *ham-pa.*
Aversion *skyo-šas*; *kréł*; to feel an — *skyo-ba.*
Avert *zlog-pa*; *yčod-pa.*
Avoid *yčod-pa*; *spoń-ba*; *ₒdzem-pa.*
Await *sgug-pa.*
Away *par* 341; *yas* 508.
Awkward *rtsal-méd*; *mi šes-pa.*
Awn *gra-ma.*
Awry *kyom-kyóm*; *ča-čús*; *yo-ba.*
Axe *sta-ré*; *ste-po.*
Axiom *yži-ma.*
Axle-tree *srog-šiń.*
Ay *ₒo-ná.*

B

Babbling s. *čol-čúń.*
Baby *ṗru-gu čuń-ńu.*
Back s. *rgyab*; *ltag-pa*; the small of the — *sgal-pa.*
Back adv. *rgyab-tu*; *ṗyir.*
Background *mtil.*
Bacon *sbo-tsil.*
Bad *ńan-pa*; *tu-ba*; *gyi-na*; *btsog-po W.*
Badger *grum-pa.*
Bag *sgyiu*, *sgyig-gu*; *sgye-mo*; *pad*; leather — *rkyal-pa*; small — *rkyal-bu.*
Bail (person) *dge-rgan*; *lag-mi.*
Bakehouse *bkad-sa.*
Baker *yyos-mkan.*
Balance (pair of scales) *tu-lā*; *bat-ti*; *srań.*
Balcony *rab-ysál.*
Bald *ter.*
Ball *go-la*; *bo-lo*, musket — *rdeu C.*, *rin-di W.*; cannon — *tu-lúm.*
Ballista *sgyogs.*
Balustrade *lag-yžúńs.*
Banana *skyes-sdóń.*
Band (gang) *kyu*, *kyu-bo.*
Bandage *ras-ṫág*; *leb-ma*, *leb-ṫúgs.*
Bandeleer *ga-ša.*
Bandy-legged *rkań-kyóg.*
Banish *spyug-pa.*
Bank (shore) *ₒkris*; *ₒgram*; *ńogs*; *dńo*; of a river *ču-ka*, *ču-ₒgram*, *ču-mta.*
Banker *bun-bdág.*
Banquet s. *mgron.*
Baptism *krus* 51.
Baptize *krus ysol-ba.*
Barbarian *kla-klo.*
Barbarous *ₒkob.*
Barber *ₒbreg-mkan.*
Barberry *skyer-pa W.*
Bare *rjen-pa*; — footed *rkań-rjén.*
Bark s. *pags-pa*; *šun-pa*; — of a species of willow *sgro-ba*; — of the birch-tree *gro-ga.*

Bark vb. n. *zug-pa.*
Barley *nas*; *so-ba*; boiled — *ylum*; — corn *nas.*
Barm *ṗabs*; *sbaṅ-ču.*
Barter vb. *rje-ba*; *sdeb-pa.*
Base s. *yži*; *rmaṅ.*
Bashful *ṅo-bab-pa*; *dzem-bag-čan.*
Bashfulness *k̔rel.*
Basin *ka-to-ra*; *zi-liṅ-pan-tse.*
Basis *₀gram-yži*; *ma-yži.*
Basket *pe-ra*; *tse-po*; *yzed-ma*; a small — of reed *bag-tse.*
Bat (animal) *ṗa-wáṅ.*
Bath *k̔rus.*
Bathe *₀k̔ru-ba*, *₀k̔rud-pa.*
Battle *yyul*, *₀t̔ab-mo.*
Bawling adj. *ča-čo-čan.*
Bay (gulf) *k̔ug*; *ču-k̔úg*; *mtso-lág.*
Bay-coloured *smug-po.*
Bayonet *san-gin* W.
Bazar *k̔rom.*
Be *yin-pa*, resp. *lags-pa*; *yod-pa*; *₀dug-pa*; *mčis-pa*; *mṅa-ba*; *ynas-pa*; there is, there are *₀dug*; *mčis.*
Beadle (in a monastery) *dge-bskós*; *dge-yyóg.*
Beam (timber) *yduṅ-ma*; — of light *yzer*; *₀od-yzér.*
Bear vb. a. (to bring forth) *btsa-ba*; *skyed-pa*; (to carry) *₀k̔ur-ba*, *₀k̔yer-ba*; *t̔eg-pa*, *₀t̔ogs-pa*; (to suffer) *yzod-pa*, *t̔ub-pa.*
Bear s, brown — *dom*; yellow — *dred* 264; the Great Bear *smin-bdún.*
Beard *rgya-bo*; *sma-ra*; *'ag-tsóm*; — of corn *gra-ma.*
Beast *dud-₀gro*; — of burden *k̔al-ma*; — of prey *yčan-záṅ.*
Beat *rgyab-pa*; *rduṅ-ba*; *rdegs-pa*; *₀ṗam-par byed-pa*; to — the drum *skrog-pa*; to the gong, the cymbal v. *₀k̔rol-ba*; to be beaten *₀ṗam-pa.*
Beautiful *mdzes-pa*; *bzaṅ-ba*; *legs-pa*; *sdug-pa*; *dga-ba*; *bde-ba*; — appearance or colour *bkrag*; *mdaṅs*; — form *rnam-₀gyúr.*
Because v. *kyi* 6; *ṗas* 323.
Beckon *lag-brdá byed-pa.*
Become *skye-ba*; *₀gyur-ba*; *ča-ba* W.
Becoming (comely), to be — *₀os-pa.*
Bed *mčis-mál*; *nyal-k̔rí.*
Bed (garden) *t̔sas-k̔aṅ.*
Bedding *mal-yós*, *mal-čá*; *yzim-čá.*
Bedfellow *mal-grogs*, resp. *yzim-grogs.*
Bedstead *mal-k̔ri*; *mčis-mál.*
Bee *buṅ-ba*; *sbraṅ-ma.*
Beer *čaṅ*; — carousal *čaṅ-sa*; — house *čaṅ-k̔aṅ.*
Beetle *sbur-pa.*
Befool *mgo skor-ba.*
Before adv. *sṅa-ma*, *sṅa-góṅ* 135; *sṅan*, *sṅar*, *sṅun* 136; *sṅon*, *sṅon-du* 137; prep. *druṅ-du* 263; *mdun-du* 273.
Beforehand v. *sṅa*; *sṅan*, *sṅar*; to be — *sṅa-ba.*
Beg *žu-ba*; *ysol-ba.*
Beget *bšo-ba*; *skyed-pa.*
Beggar *spraṅ-po*; *ldom-bu-ba*; — boy *spraṅ-ṗrúg.*
Begin vb. n. *čas-pa*; *ǰug-pa*; *mgo ₀dzug-pa*; to — to exist *skye-ba*; vb. a. *rtsom-pa*: *₀dzugs-pa.*
Beginner *las-daṅ-po-pa.*
Beginning s. *mgo*, *mgo-ma*; *₀go-ma*; *sgo-mo*; *sṅon-ma*; *t̔og-ma*; — and end (head and tail) *mgo-mǰug.*
Begotten *čad-pa*; to be — *čags-pa.*
Behalf v. *don* no. 3, 259.
Behave *₀grul-ba.*
Behaviour *rnam-₀gyur*; *spyod-pa.*
Behead *ske yčod-pa.*
Behind adv. *rtiṅ*; *ṗa-rol-na* 338; *ṗyi*, *ṗyis*; prep. *₀gab*; v. *rgyab* 107.
Behold interj. *kye-hó* 7.
Being s. *₀gro-ba*; *lus-čan*, *sems-čan.*
Belch s. *sgreg-pa*; vb. n. *sgreg-pa ₀don-pa.*
Believe vb. n. *dad-pa* 249; vb. a. *yid* (*t̔ugs* or *blen*) *čes-pa.*
Bell *dril*; — metal *mk̔ar-ba*, *₀k̔ar-ba*; wether *k̔yu-mčóg.*
Bellows *sbud-pa.*
Belly *grod-pa*; *lto-ba*, *ysus-pa.*
Belong *ytogs-pa*; *mṅa-ba*; belonging together *t̔e-mk̔an* W.
Beloved *yčes-pa*; *mon-ža-čan.*
Below adv. *ma* 408; *man-čád*, *man-čód*; prep. *₀og* 501.
Bench *gral.*
Bend vb. a. *k̔ug-k̔úg byed-pa*; *skyil-ba*; *dgu-ba*; *gugs-pa*; *gum-pa*; *₀dud-pa*; vb. n. *mgo dgur-ba*; *dgye-ba.*
Benefit v. *skyed* 29; *don* no. 3, 259; *ṗan-pa*, *ṗan-yón*; for the — of *ṗyogs-su*; *don-du*
Benevolence *ṗan-pai sems.*
Bent (crooked) *k̔oṅs*; *₀k̔yog-po*; *gug-ge-ba*; *dgu-ba.*
Benumbed v. *sbrid-pa.*
Bereave *₀ṗral-ba*; to be bereft *₀bral-ba.*
Besides *k̔a-ru*, *k̔ar*; *steṅ-du*; *min*, *min-pa.*
Besiege *skor-ba.*
Besprinkle *čag-čág byed-pa* or *₀debs-pa.*
Best s. *mčog* 166; *don* no. 3, 259.
Bestow *sbyin-pa*: *ster-ba.*
Better, to get the — of *t̔ub-pa*; *rgyal-ba.*
Between *bar-la*, *de-bár*; *yseb-na*, *yseb-la*; from *bar-nas.*
Beverage *skyems*; *btuṅ-ba* 244.
Beyond *ṗa-rol-na*; *ṗan-čád.*
Bhotan *₀brug-pa.*
Bice, blue — *sṅo-skyá.*

Bid *sgo-ba*; *˳jug-pa*; *˳dom-pa.*
Bier *k̓yogs*; *dgu-k̓ri.*
Big *č̓en-po*; — with child *sems-č̓an daṅ lhan-pa*; — with young *sbrum-pa.*
Bigness *k̓o-lág.*
Bile *mk̓ris-pa.*
Billet of wood *mgal-pa*; *śiṅ-dum.*
Billow *č̓u-ri*, *č̓u-rlabs*; *dba-klóṅ.*
Bind *˳č̓iṅ-ba*; *˳dogs-pa*; *sdom-pa*; *˳k̓yig-pa.*
Biped *rkaṅ-gnyis-pa.*
Birch-tree *stag-pa.*
Bird *bya*; *dab-č̓ágs*; little — *mč̓il-pa.*
Birdcage *bya-k̓áṅ.*
Birdsnest *bya-tsáṅ.*
Birth v. *skye-ba* 28; high — *skye-ba mto-ba*; low — *skye-ba dma-ba.*
Birthplace *skye-gnás.*
Bishop *do-dam-pa* 257.
Bison (Indian) *glaṅ-to.*
Bit (small piece) *k̓am*, *k̓am-tsál*; *č̓ag-dúm*; *brul.*
Bit (of a bridle) *srab-lč̓ágs.*
Bitch *k̓yi-mo.*
Bite vb. *rmug-pa*; *˳č̓a-ba.*
Bitter *k̓a*, *k̓a-po*, *k̓a-ba* 36.
Bittern *č̓u-skyar.*
Bitumen *brag-žún.*
Black adj. *nag-po.*
Black s. (centre of a target) *rtags.*
Blacksmith *lč̓ags-mgár.*
Bladder (urinary) *lgaṅ-pa.*
Blade (of grass) *˳jag-ma*; *sog-ma.*
Blade (of a sword) *lč̓e.*
Blame vb. a. *spyó-ba*; *smad-pa*, *smod-pa.*
Blame s. *klan-ka.*
Blank adj. *stoṅ-pa.*
Blanket *grum-tse*; *tsa-dar*; *č̓a-ra* 152; *śa-pos Ld.*
Blasphemy *skur-pa.*
Blast vb. *gč̓og-pa.*
Blaze s. *mdoṅs.*
Bleat *˳ba-ba.*
Bleed *gtar-ba*, *rtsa gč̓od-pa.*
Bless *sṅo-ba.*
Blessed *skal-ldán*; *bde-˳gro*; *gyaṅ-č̓an.*
Blessing s. *byin*, *byin-rlabs*; *bkra-śis*; *bsṅo-ba*; *p̓an-yón*; *gyaṅ*; *rgyan* 107.
Blind *mdoṅs-pa*; *žar-ba*, *mig-žár*; *loṅ-ba.*
Blister s. (pustule) *č̓u-sgaṅ*; *č̓u-bur*; (plaster) *˳jibs-sman.*
Blister vb. *˳jibs-pa*; *˳jibs-sman ˳jug-pa.*
Blood *k̓rag*; y *k̓rag-č̓an.*
Blooming *bkra-ba.*
Blossom vb. *˳bar-ba.*
Blot out *˳p̓yid-pa*; *sel-ba.*
Blow vb. *˳bud-pa.*
Blow s. *lč̓ag.*
Blue *sṅon-po*, *sṅo-bo*; deep — *sṅo-nag*; pale — *sṅo-skyá*; *sṅo-saṅs*; sky — *mtiṅ.*
Bluff s. *gad-pa.*
Blunt *rtul-po*; vb. also *k̓a* IV. no. 5.
Blushing (the act of) *ṅo-tsa.*
Board s. *spaṅ-léb*; *śiṅ-léb*; *glegs*; *sgo-rnám*; — of a door *sgo-glégs*; — of a ship *zur.*
Boast vb. *rlom-pa.*
Boasting s. *k̓a-tso*, *k̓a-p̓o*; *yus.*
Boat *gru.*
Boatman *gru-pa*; *ko-mk̓an*; *mnyan-pa.*
Bodily *dṅos-su*; *mṅon-sum-du*; *žal-dṅós.*
Body *lus*; *gzugs*; *sku*; — linen *gos-lág.*
Boil s. (ulcer) *č̓u-búr*; *śa-búr W.*
Boil vb. a. *skol-ba*; to — down *sgor-ba*; vb. n. *˳k̓ol-ba*; to — over *lud-pa.*
Boiling adj. *k̓ol-pa*, *k̓ol-ma.*
Boldness *ṅo-mig*; *rtul-p̓od-pa.*
Bolster *sṅas*; *gdan.*
Bolt s. *bur*; v. also *gya* and *si-ri.*
Bolt vb. a. *gya rgyab-pa*; *si-ri č̓ug-č̓e W.*
Bond *˳dzin*; *zin-bris.*
Bonds *bč̓iṅ-ba*, *bč̓iṅs-pa*; *˳č̓iṅ-ba.*
Bone *gduṅ*; *rus-pa*; —s of fish *gra-ma.*
Book *dpe*; *glegs-bám*; *po-ti.*
Books (literature) *č̓os*; book-language *č̓os-skad.*
Bookstand *dpe-k̓ri.*
Boot *lham*; leather half-boot *krad-pa* 8.
Border s. *gru*; *mta-ma*; *sna*; *mu*; *mtsams.*
Bore vb. *rtol-ba*; *˳bigs-pa.*
Born *č̓ad-pa*; to be — *skye-ba*; *btsa-ba*; *˳k̓ruṅ-ba*, *kruṅs-pa*; *ltams-pa.*
Borough *groṅ-tso.*
Borrow *skyi-ba*; *brnyan-pa*; *gyar-ba.*
Bosom *snam-brág*; *paṅ-kébs.*
Botch vb. *glan-pa.*
Both *gnyis.*
Bottle *bum-pa.*
Bottom *gtiṅ*; *mtil*; *žabs.*
Bough *yal-ga.*
Bound vb. n. *˳p̓ar-ba.*
Boundary *mtsams*, *sa-mtsams.*
Bow vb. *˳dud-pa*; "*skyed kug taṅ-č̓e*" 16 *W*
Bow s. (compliment) *p̓yag.*
Bow s. (for shooting) *gžu.*
Bowels *rgyu-ma*; *naṅ-k̓ról.*
Bowl s. *ko-re W.*; *koṅ-po*; *pa-tra*; *p̓or-pa*; *gžoṅ-pa*; beggar's — *lhuṅ-bzéd*; — of a tobacco-pipe *gaṅ-mgó.*
Box s. (chest) *sgam*; *sgrom*; *gau*; *pa-ri*; — on the ear *˳gram-lč̓ag.*
Boy *byis-pa*; infant — *k̓yeu.*
Bracelet *gdu-bu*; *lag-gdúb*
Brag *sgeg-pa.*
Brahma *tsaṅs-pa.*
Brahmin *bram-ze.*
Braid vb. *gč̓ud-pa.*
Brain *klad-pa*; *glad*; *mgo-klád.*
Bramble *tser-ma.*
Bran *tsag-ro.*
Branch (bough) *yal-ga*; *gel-pa*; v. also *lč̓ug-pa* 149.

Brandish *dbyug-pa.*
Brandy *'a-rág.*
Brass *ra-gan*; — can *čab-rkyan.*
Brave adj. *des-pa*; *dpa(-ba)*; *spa-ba.*
Brawls v. *klan-ka* 8.
Bread *bag-leb C.*; *ta-gir W.*
Breadth *k̔a-žeṅ*; *žeṅ*, *γžeṅ.*
Break vb. a. *γčog-pa*; to — one's promise *ₒgal-ba*; v. *ₒčal-ba*; v. *ₒǰig-pa*; vb.n. *ₒgas-pa*; *ₒčag-pa*; to — forth *rdol-ba*; to — out *ₒčor-ba*; *laṅ-ba.*
Breakfast s. *gro*; *dro C.*; *ťsal-ma W.*
Breakfast vb. *ťsal-ma za-ba.*
Breast *nu-ma*; *braṅ*, resp. *sku-bráṅ.*
Breath *ṙṅam-pa*; *dbugs*; *rlaṅs-pa*; to be out of — *dṅaṅ-ba.*
Breathe *ṙṅam-pa.*
Breeze *rluṅ.*
Bribe s. *p̔ag-súg.*
Brick *pag*, *pag-bu*; *so-pag.*
Bricklayer *rtsig-bzo-pa*
Bride *bag-ma*; —'s maid *bag-grogs-mo.*
Bridegroom *bag-po*, *mag-pa* col.
Bridge *zam-pa.*
Bridle s. *srab.*
Brier *ťser-ma.*
Bright *bkrag-čan*; *k̔rol-k̔ról*; *γži-brǰid-čan*; *ₒod-čan*; *γsal-ba.*
Brightness *bkrag*; *dṅom-pa*; *mdaṅs*; *ₒťser-ba*; *zil*; *γzi*; *γzi-brǰid*; *ₒod.*
Brilliant *zil-čan.*
Brim *gru.*
Bring *skyel-ba*; *ₒk̔yer-ba*; *ₒk̔yog-pa*; *ₒk̔yoṅ-ba*; *ₒk̔yol-ba*; to — along with *ₒk̔rid-pa*; to — on *skyed-pa*; to — round *skul-ba*; to — together *sprod-pa*; to — up *γsos skyed-pa.*
Brisk *k̔ram-pa.*
Bristle s. *k̔ab-spú.*
Bristly *rtsub-po.*
Brittle *k̔rol-mo.*
Broad *p̔al-čan*; *žeṅ-čan.*
Broken *dkrum-pa*; *čag-pa*, *čag-po*; country *lčaṅ-lčóṅ.*
Bronze v. *k̔ro* 52; *mk̔ar-ba*, *ₒk̔ar-ba.*
Brook s. *grog-ču*; *ču*; *bab-ču*; *ču-p̔ran.*
Broom *p̔yag-ma*; *ₒol-mo.*
Broth *ša-k̔ú.*
Brother *spun*, resp. *mčed*; father's — *k̔u-bo*; mother's — *žaṅ-po*, *'a-žaṅ W.*; a sister's — *miṅ-po*; elder — *ǰo-bo*, col. *'a-ǰó*; resp. *γčen*; younger — *nu-bo*; *γčuṅ-po*; *no W.*; religious — *čos-spun*; brother — in law *skud-po.*

Bruise vb. *grug-pa.*
Brush s. *pir*; *zed.*
Brute *byol-sóṅ.*
Bubble s. *ču-búr*; *lbu-ba*, *dbu-ba.*
Bubbling *k̔ol-pa.*
Bucket *ču-bzóm.*
Buckle s. *čab-ma.*
Buckler *p̔a-li*; *p̔ub.*
Buckwheat *bra-bo.*
Bud s. *sbal-míg*; leaf — *k̔yi-gu.*
Bud vb. *skye-ba.*
Buddha *saṅs-rgyas*; *rgyal-ba*; *rgyal-ba goṅ-ma.*
Buddhist *naṅ-pa.*
Buffalo *ma-he.*
Bug *ča-ré*; (*lha*) *ₒdre-šig.*
Build *rtsig-pa*; *ₒčos-pa*; *ₒgod-pa*
Building s. *bkod-pa.*
Bulk *boṅ*; *lhun.*
Bull *glaṅ-ťúg*; *ba-glaṅ.*
Bullet *go-la*; *ťsi-gu*; — mould *ka-lib.*
Bullock *glaṅ*; *spo-to C.*
Bun *lhas(-ma)*; *lhas-dóg*; *žim-zag W.*
Bunch *čam-pód*; *čag-pa*; *čag-bu*, *čag-mo*; *čun-po*; *ťsom-pa*; *γzab-ma.*
Bundle *čun-po*; *p̔on-po*; *lag-kód.*
Bung *k̔a-ₒdig.*
Burden s. *k̔al*; *k̔ur*, *k̔ur-po*; *k̔res-po*; *ₒgaṅ* (*-po*).
Burn vb. a. *ₒťsig-pa*; *sreg-pa*; vb. n. *ₒbar-ba.*
Burning-glass *me-šél.*
Burst vb. a. *γčog-pa*; vb. n. *ₒgas-pa*; *ₒťor-ba*; *rdol-ba.*
Bury *skuṅ-ba.*
Bushel *k̔al-bó.*
Business *las*; *don*; *k̔ag*; *gaṅ-po*; *spros-pa*; **ḍel-wa** 382 *W.*
Busy, to be — *brel-ba.*
But adv. (only) *ťsam*; v. *man* 411; conj. v. *kyi*; *ₒon-kyaṅ*; *ₒo-ná.*
Butcher *šan-pa*; *ša-ťsoṅ-pa.*
Butler *γsol-dpon.*
Butter *mar*; fresh — *skya-már.*
Butterfly *p̔ye-ma-léb.*
Buttermilk *da-ra*; *dar-ba.*
Buttock *rkub*; *ₒp̔oṅ-ťsos.*
Button s. *sgrog-gu*, *sgrog-ril*; *tob-či*, *ťob-ču.*
Buy *nyo-ba.*
Buzz vb. *ₒk̔rog-pa.*
Buzzing s. *ₒur.*
By *kyi*; v. sub *rkyen*; *sgo-nas*; *pas*; *p̔yir*; close — *druṅ-du.*

C

Cabbage *kram*; Chinese white — *pé-tsé, pi-tsi.*
Cairn *to-yór; dur-ṗuṅ.*
Calamity *bkra-mi-šis; rkyen; ₒgal-rkyen.*
Calamus *ču-tág.*
Calculate *rtsi-ba; rtsis byed-pa; bgraṅ-ba.*
Calculation *rtsis.*
Calendar *lo-to.*
Calf *be-to, be-do; beu;* — of the leg *sgyid-pa; byin-pa.*
Call vb. a. *skad-pa; skul-ba; ḱug-pa;ₒgugs-pa; sgrog-pa; ₒbod-pa;* v. also *byed-pa* I, 2 and *miṅ ₒlogs-pa* 280;so-called *žes byas-pa;* vb. n. to — to a person *ḱe' taṅ-wa C.; skad gyab-če W.; sgrog-pa; brgyaṅ-ba.*
Calm adj. *gya-ma-gyú;* v. *dal-ba.*
Calm vb. a. *ži-bar byed-pa.*
Calumny *ṗra-ma.*
Camel *rṅa-bóṅ;* male — *rṅa-yséb,* female — *rṅa-mo.*
Camp *sgar.*
Camphor *ga-pur.*
Can s. *rkyan, čab-rkyán* 155.
Cancer (disease) *lhog-pa;* (constellation) *kar-ka-ta.*
Candle *rkyoṅ-tse.*
Candy *ḱaṇ-ḍa.*
Cane *spa, sba; smyi-gu, smyug-ma; ₒod-ma.*
Canine tooth *mče-ba, mče-só.*
Cannon *gyogs, sgyogs; ₒdzam-búr;* — ball *tu-lúm.*
Canopy *ydugs.*
Caoutchouc *gyig.*
Cap *tod-ḱebs.*
Caper vb. n. *dkyu-ba.*
Capital adj. *kyad-par-čan.*
Capital s. (stock in trade) v. *ma* 1,: 2; *tog* III.; (chief city) *mtil; rgyal-sa W.*
Captain *ₒgo-pa; brgya-dpon.*
Captivate *ₒdzin-pa.*
Captive s. *btson.*
Caravansary *tsugs-ḱaṅ.*
Caraway 1.Carum*go-snyod.*2.Cumin*zi-ra.*
Carcass *ro, teṅ-ro; yzugs.*
Card *yi-ge.*
Cardamom *sug-rmél; li-ši W.*
Cardinal points *ṗyogs* 352.
Care s. *nya-ra; ynyer-ḱa;* to take — **ka-dar čo-če*;* to take — of *skyoṅ-ba; *čag-pa jhé-pa* C.; ynyer-ba;* to use — *yzabs-pa.*
Careless *bag-méd.*
Caress vb. a. *mtun-par byed-pa; yag-po; ₒjag-po byed-pa.*
Carpenter *šiṅ-mḱan.*
Carpet *stan.*

Carriage (conveyance) *bčibs-ṅa; bžon-pa; teg-pa.*
Carrion *ₒḱrums.*
Carrot *guṅ-dmar-la-ṗug; lča-ba; se-rag-dur-sman W.*
Carry *ₒḱur-ba; ₒḱyer-ba, ₒḱyog-pa; ₒḱyol-ba; skya-ba; skyed-pa;* to — away *skyel-ba; bda-ba;* to be able to — *teg-pa* 235.
Cart *šiṅ-rta.*
Carter *šiṅ-rta-pa.*
Cartilage *čag-krúm.*
Carve *ₒjog-pa; ₒbru-ba, bru-ba.*
Case (incident) *rkyen; skabs;* in — *gal-te* 68; *na* 299; (sheath) *šubs;* (grammar) *rnam-dbyé* 314.
Cash *rnags* 313.
Cashmere *ḱa-čúl, ḱa-čé.*
Cask *zem.*
Cast vb. a. *skyur-ba; rgyag-pa; ₒdebs-pa; ₒṗen-pa;* to — away *ₒdor-ba;* to — down *ₒbebs-pa; ₒbor-ba;* to (metals) *ldugs-pa.*
Casting-mould *lug-koṅ.*
Castle *mḱar; ṗo-braṅ; rdzoṅs.*
Castrate *rlig-pa ₒbyin-pa.*
Cat *byi-la; bi-la, bi-li, pi-ši W. žim-bu, žum-bu C.*
Catapult *sgyogs* 119.
Cataract *ri-yzar-ču.*
Catarrh *čam-pa; bro-ₒtsál.*
Catch *ₒdzin-pa.*
Catgut *rgyus-skúd.*
Cattle *ṗyugs;* breeding — *rkaṅ-ₒgrós;* hornless — *mgo-ril W.*
Caul (anatomy) *rgyu-sgróg.*
Cause s. *rkyen; rgyu; rgyu-mtsan;* original = *ẏži-ma.*
Cause vb. a. v. *gugs-pa; ₒjug-pa; ytoṅ-ba; byed-pa.*
Causeway *so-log.*
Caution s. *ynyer-ḱa.*
Cautious v. *ka-dár; gya-ma-gyú;* to be — **ka-dar čo-če*; ₒgab-pa.*
Cave, Cavern *ṗug-pa.*
Cavity *ḱuṅ; sbugs.*
Cease *ₒgag-pa; ₒčad-pa; ži-ba.*
Ceiling *tog, *ya-tog.*
Celebrated *gzi-brjid-čan.*
Cell *grwa; *da-šág** 75.
Cellar *sa-ḱáṅ.*
Cemetery *dur-ḱrod.*
Censer *pog-ṗór, spos-ṗór.*
Censor (of a monastery) *dge-bskos* 85.
Censure s. *klan-ka.*
Centiped *la-ré W.; si-ri-ₒbu W.*
Centre *lte-ba; mtil; dbus.*
Cerebellum *klad-čuṅ.*
Ceremony *čo-ga; sku-rim.*

Certain *ńes-pa*; *gor-ma-čág*; *ńo-rtóg*; a — one *γčig-čig*.
Certainly *γdon-mi-za-bar*.
Certainty *ńes-pa*; *ťag-čód*.
Ceylon *lań-ka*.
Chaff *spun-pa*, *sbun-pa*; *sbur-ma*.
Chain s. *lčags-ťág*; *nyag-ťág*.
Chair *ḱri*; *rgya-ḱri* C.
Chairman *ḱri-pa*.
Chalk *ťo-lé dkar-po*.
Chamber *nań*; *ḱań-mig*.
Champion *gyad*.
Chance s. *rgyu* 110.
Change s. *ₒgyur-ba*; *res*.
Change vb. a *sgyur-ba*; *rje-ba*; *spo-ba*; *razu-ba*; to — place *ₒṕo-ba*; vb. n. *ₒgyur-ba*; *ₒṕo-ba*.
Chant vb. *dgyer-ba*.
Chap vb. *ₒgas-pa*.
Chapter *leu*
Character (disposition) *rgyud*; *ńań*; *ńo-bo-nyid*; *ťsul*; *rig-rgyud*; **šē-gyú** C. 562.
Characteristic s. *rgyu-mtsán* 111.
Charge vb. *sko-ba*; *rgol-ba*; *mńag-pa*; to — with (to commission) *ₒgel-ba*.
Charge s. (commission) *ḱag*.
Charity *snyiń-rje*.
Charming *dga-ba*; *yid-du oń-ba*.
Chase vb. *ₒčor-ba*.
Chase s. *ḱyi-ra*.
Chasm s. *rgya-sér*.
Chastisement *čad-pa*; *ťul*.
Chastity *ḱrel-yod*; *ťsańs-par spyod-pa*.
Chat vb. *ˏur γtoń-ba*; *lab γtoń-ba*.
Chattering s. *čo-lo*.
Cheap *ḱye-mo* W.; *rin čuń-ba*.
Cheat vb. *blo brid-pa*; *slu-ba*; *γyo-zól byed-pa*; *mgo skor-ba*.
Cheek *ₒgram-pa*; — bone *ₒgram-rús*; tooth *ₒgram-so*.
Cheer vb. *glod-pa*; *spro-ba skyed-pa*; *dga-bar byed-pa*.
Cheerful *ḱrul-po*; *dga-mo*; *sems-bdé*, *blo-bdé*.
Cheese *ťud*; *ˏo-ťúd*.
Chess-board *mig-máń*; to play at chess *mig-mań rtse-ba*.
Chest (box) *gau*; *sgam*; *sgrom*; (thorax) *brań*, resp. *sku-bráń*
Chew *ldad-pa*
Chicken *bya-ṕrug*.
Chief adj. *dpon*; *γtso*; — justice *ḱrims-dpon*
Chief s. *ₒgo-pa*; *dpon-po*; *γtso-bo*; *ḱyu-mčóg*.
Chiefly *γtso-bor*, *γtso-čér*.
Child *ṕru-gu*; *byis-pa*; *bu*; v. *ḱyeu*.
Children *bu-ṕrug*; — of the same parents (brothers, sisters) *spun*.
Chill s. *kyi-bún*.
Chin *ko-kó*; *ma-lé*.
China *rgya-nág*; *rgya-yúl*; modern name: *ma-hā-či-na*, *ma-hā-čin*; — clay *ḱam-pa*; — ware *kar-yól*; *dkar-yól*; resp. *žal-kar* C.; *sol-kar* W.
Chinese s. *rgya-nag-pa*, *rgya-bo*; fem. *rgya-nag-ma*, *rgya-mo*; *rgya-mi*; plur. *rgya-rnams*.
Chinese adj. *rgyai*, *rgya-nag-gi*, — language *rgya-skád*; — paper *rgya-šóg*.
Chink *sgo-bár*.
Chip *ťsal-pa*; *šiń-ťsal*.
Chirping s. *ča-čó*.
Chisel vb. *ₒbru-ba*.
Chit-chat s. *ˏur*.
Choice adj. *mčog-tu bkrab*; *ḱyad-par ṕags-pa*; *ḱyad-par-čan*.
Choke *dbugs sub-pa*; **skye tsir tań-če** W.; *ske bsdam-ste γsod-pa*; to be choked *rnań-ba*; *ske bsdam-ste ₒči-ba*; *ₒtsub-pa*.
Cholera *ḱoń-lóg* W.; *nya-lóg* Sik.
Choose vb. a. *bkrab-pa*; *ₒbyed-pa*; *ₒdzin-pa*; vb. n. (to like) *dgyes-pa*.
Chop vb. *btsab-pa*; to — off *γčod-pa*.
Chopping-block *šiń-stan*.
Chopsticks *ťur-ma*.
Chord *rgyud* 111
Christ *skyabs-mgón* 26; *ma-ši-ka* 410.
Chronic adj. *yun riń-bai*; — disease *γčoń-nád*.
Chronicle *lo-rgyús*.
Churn vb. *dkrog-pa*; *žo dkrog-pa*.
Churn s. v. *gur-gúr* 70.
Chutney (Indian condiment) *ťsu-u* 449.
Chyle *dwańs-ma* 249.
Cimeter *gri-gúg*.
Cinamon *šiń-ťsa*.
Cipher s. *mḱa*; *ťig-le*.
Circle s. *skor*, *ₒḱor*, *ₒḱor-lo*; *dkyil-ₒḱor*; *sgor-mo*, *sgor-ťig*.
Circular adj. *kyir-kyir*; *gor-mo*.
Circumference *dkyil-ₒḱor*; *ₒḱor*; *ḱo-ra*; *ḱyon*; *mu-ḱyúd*.
Circumstance *rkyen*; *skabs*.
Citadel *mḱar*; *rdzoń*.
Citizen *ḱyim-bdág*; *yul-pa*; *yon-bdag*.
Citron *gam-bu-ra* W.; *spuod-pad* C.
City *groń-ḱyér*.
Civilize *ₒdul-ba*.
Claim s. *ťob-ťsir*, *ťob-sról*.
Clairvoyance *mńon-šés* 133.
Clammy *rtsi-čan*.
Clamour s. *ku*, *ku-sgra*, *ku-čo*; *skad-lóg*; *ča-čó*.
Clandestinely *sbas-te* W.; v. also *lkog-tu*, *γsań-ba*.
Clap vb., to — the hands *čag-čág byed-pa*.
Clap s. (crash) *sguń* W.; *ldim* W.; *ldir-sgra*.
Clasp vb. a. *ₒḱyud-pa*; *ₒḱril-ba*.
Clasp s. *čab-ma*; — knife *ltab-gri*.

Class s. *gral*; *ťa-tsán*; *bye-brág*; *dbye-ba*; *ťsan, sde-ťsán.*
Classify *rnam-par bžag-pa*; *ₒbyed-pa.*
Claw *ќron*; *sder(-mo)*; *spar-ba.*
Clay *ₒǰim-pa*; *rdza*; *žal-ba*; – floor *skyaṅ-nul.*
Clean adj. *dag-pa, γtsaṅ-ba*; *lag-mo W.*; – food *dkar-zás.*
Clean, Cleanse vb. a. *p̓yi-bdar byed-pa*; *saṅ-ba*; *sel-ba*; to be cleansed *ₒbyoṅ-ba.*
Clear adj. *mṅon-pa*; *tur-re*; *wa-lé*; *wa-le-ba*; *lag-mo W.*; *siṅs-po W.*; *lhaṅ-ṅe.*
Clear vb. a. *ₒdag-pa*; *sel-ba.*
Cleave *ₒges-pa*; *ₒčeg-pa*; to be cleft *ₒgas-pa.*
Cleft s. *rgya-sér*; *ral*; *srubs.*
Clerk *yig-mќan.*
Clever *γčaṅ-po*; *sgrin-po*; *ťabs-čan*; *spyaṅ-po*; a – writer *rtsom-par mќas-pa.*
Clew s. *gru-gu.*
Climb *ₒdzeg-pa*; *rgal-ba.*
Cling *čags-pa*; *ča-bžag-pa.*
Clip *ₒgrum-pa.*
Cloak s. *ber.*
Clock *ču-ťsod*; *ču-ťsod-ₒќor-lo.*
Close vb. a. *ₒgegs-pa*; v. also *ₒdzum-pa.*
Close adj. *gya-ma-gyu* 73; – fisted *ќroṅ-po*; *lag-dam-po*; adv. *ₒǰam-pa* 174; – over *glad-la.*
Clot s. *goṅ-po*; – of blood *ќrag-góṅ.*
Cloth *sag-lád*; *p̓rug*; *ťer-ma*; *dar*; a piece of – *yug, bubs.*
Clothes *gos, gos-lág*; *bgo-ba*; to change – *gos brǰe-ba*; to put on – *gos gon-pa*; to take off – *gos ₒbud-pa*; suit of – *go-lus-ča-ťsaṅ W.*
Clothes-brush *byab-zéd.*
Clothes-stand *γdaṅ, rdaṅ.*
Clothing s. *bgo-ba*; *ča-byád, ča-lúgs.*
Cloud s. *sprin*; – of dust *bud.*
Clouded, to be – *ₒќrig-pa.*
Cloudy, it has become – *ќor-soṅ.*
Clove *li-ši C.*; *bzaṅ-drúg W.*; *zer-bu W.*
Club (mace) *ga-da.*
Clumsy *sbom-pa*; *zlum-pa.*
Cluster s. *čag-mo.*
Clyster s. *ₒќos*; *bsur-smyig*; – pipe *čeu.*
Coachman *šiṅ-rta-pa.*
Coagulate *ₒќyags-pa.*
Coal *sol-ba.*
Coarse *rtsiṅ-ba*; *rags-pa*; – grained *rtsub-po.*
Coast *ₒќris.*
Coat s. *gos*; *dug-po Ü*; *ču-pa Ts.*; – lap *ќud*; – of mail *ќrab.*
Coat vb. a. *ₒtum-pa.*
Cock s. *bya-p̓o, bya-po*; *ќyim-bya*; of a gun *ťo-čúṅ*; *me-skám.*
Cock vb. a. *rdze-ba.*
Coetaneous *na-mnyám, na-ₒdrá.*
Coffee *ќa-ba* 37, III.
Coffer *sgrom.*
Coffin *dur-sgám, ro-sgám.*
Cohabit *ₒbrel-ba*; *ₒќrig-pa spyod-pa.*
Cohabitation *sbyor-ba.*
Cohere *ₒbrel-ba.*
Coil vb. (of snakes) *ₒќri-ba.*
Coin s. *doṅ-tse.*
Coition, Coitus *ₒќrig-pa*; *čags-spyód*; *nyal-po.*
Colander *ťsag-ma.*
Cold adj. *graṅ-ba*; – air *ṅa-ra*; *ṅad*; – wind *ṅar-ba*; *lhags-pa*; to feel – *ₒќyags-pa*; v. *kyi-bún*; to get, to grow – *graṅ-ba, graṅs-pa.*
Cold s. *ќyags-pa*; *graṅ-ba*; *ṅad*; *ṅar-ba*; to have a – *bro-ₒťsal-ba*; a – in the head *čam-pa*; *bro-ₒťsál*; *ya-ma.*
Colic *glaṅ, glaṅ-tábs*; *rgyu-γzér*; *ťsa-ₒќru.*
Collar s. *goṅ-ba, gos-kyi goṅ-ba*; to seize by the – *goṅ-ba-nas ₒdzin-pa.*
Collect vb. a. *sgrug-pa, sloṅ-pa*; *sdud-pa*; *sog-pa.*
Colonel *ru-dpón.*
Colour s. *ќa*; *ќa-dog*; *mdog*; *ťson*; beautiful – *bkrag*; prime – *ma-γži*; to lose – *dkyug-pa.*
Colt *ťur-bu*; – of an ass *ku-rúg, gu-rúg.*
Comb s. *so-máṅ.*
Comb vb. a. *šad-pa, γšad-pa, γšod-pa.*
Combat s. *ₒťab-mo*; *ₒќrug-pa.*
Combat vb. *ₒťab-mo ₒgyed-pa, ₒťab-pa*; *ₒќrab-pa*; *rgol-ba.*
Come *ₒoṅ-ba*, resp *ₒbyor-ba, ₒbyon-pa*; *p̓eb-pa*; eleg. *mči-ba*; come! *šog*; to – again *ldog-pa, log-pa*; to – back *p̓yir-ₒgro-ba*; to – forth *čags-pa*; to – out *ₒbyuṅ-ba, ₒťon-pa*; to – to *ₒќyol-ba*; *γnas-su ₒgyur-ba*; to – together *ₒdzom-pa*; to – up (of seeds) *ₒќruṅ-ba, rdol-ba.*
Comfort vb. a. *glod-pa*; *mya-ṅan saṅ-ba*; *spro-ba skyed-pa.*
Comforter *skyo-grógs.*
Command vb. a. *bka γnaṅ-ba, γnaṅ-ba*; (an army) *ₒќrid-pa.*
Command s. *žal-γdáms.*
Commander *dmag-ₒgo*; *dmag-dpón.*
Commandment *bka, bka-ќrims, bka-bsgos*; *ќrims.*
Commence *rtsom-pa*; *ₒdzugs-pa.*
Commend *sṅag-pa*; *ₒčol-ba.*
Comment vb. a. *ₒgrel-ba, ₒgrol-ba.*
Commerce *ťsoṅ.*
Commissary *sku-ťsáb.*
Commission vb. a. *sko-ba*; *ₒgel-ba*; *mṅag-pa.*
Commit *skur-ba*; *ₒčol-ba*; (sin etc.) *byed-pa.*
Common *dkyus-ma*; *ťun*; *p̓al-pa*; *p̓ral*; the – people *p̓al* 341.
Communication *bka-rgya*; *ₒbrel, ₒbrel-ba.*

Communion °*brel-ba*; °*grogs-lugs*; holy — *γsol-rás* 592.
Compact adj *mḱraṅ*; °*čag-čan*.
Companion *grogs*; *rogs*; *skyo-grógs*; *zla-bo*; *ya-do W.*
Company *ḱyu*; in — *ťun-moṅ-du*; °*grogs-te*.
Comparative degree v. *je* 172; *las* II, *pas, saṅ*.
Compare *sdur-ba*; *sgrun-pa*; *sgre-ba*.
Comparison *dpe* 327.
Compass (circumference) *mu-ḱyúd*; points of the — *mťsams* 455.
Compasses, pair of, *skor-tig*.
Compassion *snyiṅ-rje*; *snyiṅ-brtse-ba*.
Compel v. *nan-gyis* 302; *šed-kyer-naq-pos W.*; to be compelled *dgos-pa*.
Competitor °*gran-zla*.
Compile *sgrig-pa*.
Complaint *zug*, *γzug* 488, *nad*.
Complete adj. *grub-pa*; *rgyas-pa*; *ťam-pa*; *ṕun-ťsógs*; *rdzogs-pa*; *ťsaṅ-ba*; to be — *ťsaṅ-ba*.
Complete vb. a. *sgrub-pa*; *ťog* °*gel-ba*; to be completed °*ḱor-ba*; °*ťsar-ba*.
Completely *γtan-du*; *ye-nas*.
Complex of fields *kluṅs*.
Complicate adj. *ḱrag-ḱrúg*.
Compliment s. *ṕyag*; compliments v. *stod-pa* 223.
Compose °*god-pa*; *rtsom-pa*; to — verses *sdeb-pa*; *sbyor-ba*.
Comprehend *go-ba*; °*dzin-pa*; *yid-la byed-pa*.
Comprehension *go-ba*.
Comprehensive *ḱyab-če-ba*.
Comprise *ḱyab-pa*; *sdud-pa*.
Compulsion *gal* 68; *nan* 302.
Computation *rtsis*.
Compute *rtsi-ba*.
Comrade *grogs*.
Concave *koṅ*.
Conceal *sbed-pa*; *γsaṅ-ba*; *sgoṅ-ba*; °*čab-pa*
Concealment *ṕag*.
Conceited *mčor-po*.
Conception *dmigs-pa*.
Concerning (as regards) *rten-nas*; *dbaṅ-du byas-na* 387.
Concession *γnaṅ-ba*.
Concord *mťun-pa*.
Condemn *žal-če γčod-pa*; *ḱrims γčod-pa* or *γtoṅ-ba*.
Condescending *če-taos-med-pa*; to be — *mťun-pa byed-pa*.
Condiment *skyu-rúm*; *sdor*.
Condition (state) *γnas-skabs*; *γnas-ťsúl* 311; *yin-lugs* 548.
Conduct vb. a. *skyel-ba*; °*ḱrid-pa*; °*dren-pa*.
Conduct s. *spyod-pa*.
Cone *ťsa-ťsa*.
Confess °*čeg-pa*; *mťol-ba*; *γšog-pa*; *γso-sbyoṅ-ba* 590
Confession (creed) *čos-rgyud* 164.
Confide (*yid*) *rton-pa* 215; v. *blo-γdéṅ* 385.
Confidence *blo-γtád*, *blo-γdéṅ*.
Confidential speaking *snyiṅ-γtam*.
Confine vb. *dgar-ba*.
Conform vb. *sbyor-ba*.
Confound *dkrug-pa*; °*dzol-ba*.
Confused, to be — *rtab-pa*.
Confusion °*ḱral-*°*ḱrúl*.
Congeal °*ḱyags-pa*.
Conglomerate s. *gad-pa*.
Congratulate *bkra-šis mṅa γsol-ba*.
Conjuncture *bsgaṅ*; *dus*.
Conjure (implore) *nan-gyis žu-ba*.
Conjure up °*gugs-pa*.
Conjurer °*ba-po*.
Connect *sbyor-ba*; *sbrel-ba*; *zuṅ sdebs-pa*.
Connected with *bčas-pa*; to be — °*brel-ba*.
Connection °*brel-pa*, *zuṅ-*°*brél*; v. also *rgyu-rkyén* 110.
Conquer *bčom-pa*; °*joms-pa*; *rgyal-ba*; °*ṕam-par byed-pa* 356; to be conquered °*ṕam-pa*.
Conqueror *rgyal-ba*.
Conscience *gal-mťun šes-pa*; *šes-bžin*; v. also *byas-čos* and *γnoṅ-ba*.
Conscientious *ḱrel-čan*.
Consciousness *šes-pa*; *dran-pa*; — of guilt *γnoṅ-ba*.
Consecrate *skur-ba*; *rab(-tu) γnas(-par) byed-pa* 524.
Consequence *mjug*; °*bras-bu*; in — of *dbaṅ-gis*.
Consider vb. a. *graṅ-ba*; °*dzin-pa*; *bsam-mnó byed-pa*; vb. n. *sgom-pa*; *mno-ba*.
Consideration *dran-pa* 262.
Consign *skur-ba*.
Consist °*dus-pa*, *bsdus-pa*.
Consistence *ska-sládí*.
Consistency *srab-*°*ťúg*.
Console *sems γso-ba*; *mya-ṅan-bsaṅ-ba*.
Consort s. *čuṅ-ma*; royal — *lčam-mo*; *btsun-mo*.
Conspicuous *mṅon-pa*; *γsal-po*.
Constable *dge-γyóg* 86.
Constellation *skar-ma*; *γza-skár*.
Constipation *bšaṅ-dgág*.
Constitute *gel-ba*; *sko-ba*; °*jug-pa* II, 2.
Constraint *gal*.
Construct *bčo-ba*; v. °*ča-ba*; °*čos-pa*; *γtoṅ-ba*; °*goa-pa*; *rtsig-pa*
Construction (grammatical) *ťsig sgrig-pa*.
Consult *bka-bgro-ba*.
Consultation *gros-gléṅ*; °*dun-ma*.
Consume *čud γzon-pa*; *zin* °*jug-pa*; to be

consumed *ča-ba*; *čad-pa*; *ₒtsar-ba*; *ₒdzad-pa*; *zin-pa*.
Consumption *γčoṅ*.
Contain v. *šoṅ-ba*; to be contained *ₒgro-ba*; v. *ₒdug-pa* no. 2.
Contamination *grib*.
Contemplate *sgom-pa*.
Contemplation *sgom*; *tiṅ-ṅe-ₒdzin*.
Contempt *ṅan-čen*; *brnyas-pa*; *smad-pa*.
Contend (fight) *ₒkrug-pa*; *rtsod-pa*; (to strive) *ₒgran-pa*.
Content adj. *čog šes-pa*; *tsim-pa*; to be — *mgu-ba*; to heart's — *yid-bžin-du*.
Contention *ₒgran-sems*; *ₒdziṅ-mo*
Contentment *snyiṅ-tsim*.
Contest s. *tob-šá*.
Continent *gliṅ*.
Continually *rgyun-du*; *čar*, *ča-ré*; *γtan-du*.
Continuation *ₒṕro*.
Continue *ₒṕro-ba*.
Contract vb. a. *skum-pa*; vb. n. *ₒkor-ba*.
Contract s. *gan-rgyá*; *čad-yig*; *ₒdzin*, *yig-ₒdzin*.
Contradiction, to be in *ₒgal-ba*.
Contrary s. *bzlog*, *go-bzlóg*; *go-ldóg*, *go-lóg*.
Contrivance *grabs*.
Convent s. *čos-sde*; *sde*; *dgon-pa*.
Convention *ka-čád*.
Conversation *gleṅ-brǰód*.
Converse vb. *gleṅ-ba*; *gleṅ-mo byed-pa*; *gros-byéd bgro-ba*.
Convert vb. *čos-su ₒǰug-pa*.
Convey *skya-ba*; *skyed-pa*; *skyel-ba*; *ₒkur-ba*.
Convoy s. *skyel-ma*.
Cook vb. *ₒtsod-pa*.
Cook s. *gyos-mkan*; head *γsol-dpon*, *ma-čen*.
Cool *graṅ-ba*; *bsil-ba*.
Cooly (carrier) *kur-pa*; (workman) *gla-pa*.
Coot *skyegs*.
Copious *rgyas-pa*.
Copper *zaṅs*.
Copulation *ₒkrig-pa*; *čags-spyod*.
Copy vb. *šu-ba*.
Copy s. (transcript) *bkod-pa*; *bu-dpe*; (pattern) *ma*, *ma-dpe*.
Coral *byi-ru*.
Cord s. *rgyud*; *sgrogs*; *ta-gu*; *ₒṕreṅ-ba*.
Cordial s. *bčud*.
Core *kog-šiṅ*.
Coriander seed *ₐu-su*.
Cork *ka-γčod*, *ka-ₒdig*.
Corn (grain) *ₒbru*; boiled — *čan*; slightly roasted *yos*; stack of — *rags*, *ṕub-rags*; *hi-ri*; corn on a toe *rkaṅ-mdzub-dzer-pa*.
Corner *kug*; *gru*; *grwa*; *zur*.
Corporal *bču-dpon*.
Corpse *ro*, resp. *spur*.
Correct adj. *skyon-méd*; *nor-méd*; to be — *ₒgrig-pa*.
Correct vb. *sgyur-ba*; *žu-dag byed-pa*.
Correction *žu-dág*, *žus-dág*.
Correspond (to be adequate) *ₒgrig-pa*.
Correspondent (in business) *tsoṅ-grogs*.
Corrupt vb. a. *slad-pa*.
Corruptness *kun-dkris*.
Costly *gūs-po*, *rin-čan*.
Cottage *kaṅ-bu*; *ku-tu*.
Cōtton *ras-bal*, *srin-bal*, *šiṅ-bal*; — cloth (*ka-ši-kai*) *ras*.
Couch s. *kri*; *nyal-kri*; *mal*.
Cough s. *glo*; *kogs*; *bro-ₒtsál*; vb. *kogs-pa*.
Council *gros*, *gros-gleṅ*; *ₒdun-ma*.
Counsel s. *gros*; *bka-γdáms*; *ₒdun-ma*.
Counselor *bka-γšags*.
Count vb. *bgraṅ-ba*; *ₒdren-pa*; *rtsi-ba*; *γšor-ba*; *si kor-če W*.
Countenance *γdoṅ*; *bžin*; *ṅo*; *skye-sgo*; *sgo-lo*.
Counteract *ₒgal-ba*.
Counterfeit adj. *rdzus-ma*.
Counterparty *ṕa-rol*
Counting s. *rtsis*.
Country *yul*, *yul-ₒkór*, *yul-grú*; *sa-čá*; *rgyal-kág*; love of — *yul-sréd*; *yul-la ₒdod-pa*.
Couple s. *zuṅ*; married — *bza-mi*.
Courage *snyiṅ-stobs*, *snyiṅ-rús*; *spobs-pa*.
Courageous *ham-pa-čan*; *dpa-ba*, *dpa-čan*.
Courier *rta-zam-pa*.
Course s. *tsir*.
Court s. (residence of a prince) *kab*; — of justice *bka-γšags*; *krims-kaṅ*.
Courtyard *kyams*; *tsoms*, *tsoms-skór*.
Cove *kug*.
Covenant s. *ka-čád*.
Cover vb. *ₒkeb-pa*; *ₒgebs-pa*; *klub-pa*; *ₒtum-pa*.
Cover, Covering s. *ka-kebs*, *ka-gab*, *ka-γčod*, *ka-leb*; *kebs*, *kyebs*, *kebs-ma*; *go-šog*; *tums*; *γyogs*; *šubs*; covering for the head *mgo-γyógs*.
Cowry *ₒgron-bu*.
Crab *sdig-srin*.
Crack vb. a. *γčog-pa*; vb. n. *ₒgas-pa*.
Crack s. *sguṅ*.
Craft (cunning) *dku-lto*.
Crafty *yó-ba*.
Cram *sgrim-pa*.
Crane (bird) *kruṅ-kruṅ*.
Crash s. *sguṅ*.
Crave *ṅab-pa*.
Craw *lkog-sóg*.
Crawfish *sdig-srin*.
Crawl *gog-pa*; *ₒṕye-ba*.
Cream *spri-ma*, *spris-ma*, *sris-ma*; *ₐo-sri*; *žo-sri*.

Create *₀god-pa.*
Creator *₀god-pa-po*; *mdzad-po.*
Creature *bkod-pa*; *₀gro-ba, lus-čan.*
Credible *₀os-pa.*
Creditor *bun-bdág.*
Creed *čos-rgyud, čos-lugs.*
Creek *ḱug, ḱugs.*
Creep *₀p̓ye-ba, gog-pa.*
Crescent s. *zla-ťses lta-bui ri-mo* or *dbyibs.*
Crest (of fowl) *čod-pán.*
Crevice *ysen, sen.*
Cricket (insect) *čog-čog-pa W.*
Crime *nyes-pa*; *nons-pa.*
Cripple *ža-bo.*
Crippled *ḱons-ḱan W.*; *ḱon-ril C.*; *grum-pa.*
Criticise *₀bigs-pa.*
Crocodile *ḱum-bi-ra.*
Crooked *kug*; *kum-pa, kon*; *kyog-po*; *ḱons*; *₀ḱyog-po*; *dgur*; to be — *dgye-ba.*
Crop vb. *ytog-pa.*
Crop s. *lo-tóg.*
Cross s. *brkyan-šin*; *sku-ru-ka.*
Cross vb. *yčod-pa*; *rgal-ba.*
Crouch *čum-pa.*
Croup, he has the — *ḱoi lkog-ma skrans son* (his throat is swollen).
Crow s. *ḱa-ta*; *p̓o-róg.*
Crow-bar *gal-ta*; *lčags-bér.*
Crowd s. *ḱrod-pa*; *ḱrom*; *yseb.*
Crowd vb. a. *bčar-ba C.*, *bčer-ba W.*
Crown s. *čod-pán*; — of the head *spyi-bo*; *ytsug.*
Crown vb. a. *čod-pan-gyis brgyan-pa*; v. also *ťog ₀gel-ba.*
Crucible *kon-po W.*; *žu-skyógs C.*
Cruel *ynyan-pa*; *drag-šul-čan.*
Crumb *čag-dúm*; *brul*; *bir-bir W.*
Crumble vb. a. *grug-pa*; vb. n. *gog-pa.*
Crupper *sgal-pa*; *rmed.*
Crush *glem-pa*; *rdzi-ba.*
Cry vb. n. *₀grags-pa, ₀grogs-pa.*
Cry s. *na-ro*; *skad, skad-nan*; *ča-čó*; — for help *₀o-dód.*

Crystal *man-šel, šel.*
Cubit *ḱru* 51.
Cuckoo *ḱu-byúg*; *kug-se W.*
Cucumber *ka-ka-rán Kun.*
Cultivate *₀bad-pa*; cultivated land *kluns.*
Cunning s. *dku-lto.*
Cup *ko-ré, kor*; *kon-po*; *tin*; *p̓or-pa*; — bearer *ysol-dpon.*
Cupboard *₀ča.*
Cupping-glass *me-búm, me-pún.*
Curd *žo*, resp. *ysol-žó.*
Cure vb. *yčod-pa*; *bčos-pa*; *₀tso-ba*; *yso-ba.*
Curious (inquisitive) *snob-zog-čan.*
Curl s. (of hair) *ral-pa.*
Curled *tsa-ru W.*
Currant *nyan-ka Sp.*; *rub-šo W.*; (raisins) *ba-šo Ld.*, *ba-šo-ka C.*
Current s. *rgyun*; *ču-rgyún.*
Current adj., to be — (of coins) *₀grul-ba, rgyug-pa.*
Curse s. *nan*; *dmod-pa.*
Curse vb.a. *nan ₀debs-pa*; *dmod-pa ₀bor-ba.*
Curtain *yol-ba.*
Curve s. *gye-gu.*
Curve vb. a. *kug-kug byed-pa*; *₀gum-pa*; curved *ḱyog-po*; *kyag-kyóg W.*; to be curving *dgye-ba.*
Cushion *snas*; *stan*; *₀bol, snye-₀ból*; *sob-stán.*
Custom (use) *ḱrims*; *čos*; *srol*; (toll) *šo-gám.*
Cut vb. a. *yčod-pa*; *₀jog-pa*; *dra-ba*; (to mow) *rna-ba*; to — into pieces *sgral-ba*; *₀ťub-pa*; v. *₀čad-pa*; to — off *grum-pa*; *₀breg-pa, ₀dreg-pa*; v. *čod-pa*; v. *čad-pa*; to — open *₀ges-pa*; to — out v. *yčar-ba* 143; to — up *ytubs-pa*; *dmyal-ba.*
Cut s. *ḱram-ka*; (blow) *lčag*; a short — **gyog-lám**.
Cylinder *₀ḱor-lo* 58; praying — *čos-kyi ₀ḱor-lo.*
Cylindrical *ril-ba*; to be — *₀gril-ba.*
Cymbal *sbug-žál*; *sbum-žól W.*; *sil-snyán.*
Cypress *spa-ma Sik.*

D

Daily adv. *nyin-re-bžin(-du)*; *žag-dan žag.*
Dalai Lama *ta-lai bla-ma.*
Dam s. *ču-rags*; *ču-lon.*
Dam up vb. *skyil-ba.*
Damage s. *skyon*; *gud, gun*; *god*; *nyes-pa*; *ynod-pa*; vb. a. *ynod-pa.*
Damp adj. *rlan-čan.*
Dance vb. *₀čam-pa*; *bro-brdun-ba* or *ḱrab-pa*; s. *gar*; *bro.*
Dancer *gar-mḱan.*

Dandelion *ḱur-ma, ḱur-ťsod.*
Dandy *₀p̓yor-dga.*
Danger *nyen.*
Dangerous *ma-run-ba, ma-runs-pa*; *ydug-pa-čan*; *btsog-pa W.*
Daring adj. *rtul-p̓od-pa*; *spobs-pa-čan*; *dpa-čan, dpa-bo.*
Dark adj. *sgrib-pa*; *mun-pa*; *smag*; to grow — *₀tibs-pa*; *₀grib-pa.*
Darken vb. a. *sgrib-pa*; vb. n. *₀grib-pa.*

Darkness *mun-pa*; *smug-rum*.
Darling, my —! *ṅai yid˛oṅ*; cf. also *sdug-pa*.
Darn *tur-ba*; *snol-ba*.
Dart s. *mda*; vb. n. *˳k̔yug-pa* 60.
Date s. (time) *zag-gráṅs*; (fruit) *k̔a-zúr*.
Daub vb. *skud-pa*.
Daughter *bu-mo*, *bo-mo*; *sras-mo*; — in-law *mna-ma*.
Dawn s. *skya-ód*, *skya-réṅs*; *t̔o-ráṅs*; vb. it dawns *skya-reṅs šar*.
Day *nyi-ma*; *nyin-mo*; *žag*; — and night *nyin-mtsán*; — by — *žag daṅ žag*; all the — long *nyin-tse-ré*; every — *žag-daṅ W.*; from — to — *žag-nas žag-tu*; one —, some — *deu-re*; the other — *de-žag* 471 *W.*; this — five days *dgus*.
Day-break *nam-laṅs*; at — *nam-laṅs-te* or *nas*.
Dazzle vb. n. *t̔om-par ˳gyur-ba*.
Dazzling *k̔rol-po*; *lčam-me-ba*.
Dead adj. v. *ši-ba*; a — man *γšin-po*; *ro*.
Deaf *˛on-pa*.
Deal with vb. *spyod-pa*.
Deal s., a good — *ga-čén*.
Dear *γčig*; *γčes-pa*; *dkon-pa*; *gus-po*; *rin-taṅ-čan*, *rin-čan*; to hold — *γče-ba*.
Dearth *zas-dkon C.*
Death *˳či-ba*; forebodings of — *˳či-ltas*; hour of — *˳da-ga*; to seek — *lčeb-pa*.
Debate s. *rtsod-pa*; vb. *bgro gleṅ byed-pa*.
Debt *bu-lon*; the — is cleared *bu-lon k̔or*.
Debtor *bu-lon-pa*.
Decapitate *ske γčod-pa*.
Decay s. *˳jig-pa*.
Decay vb. *nyil-ba*; *˳t̔or-ba*; *nub-pa*.
Decayed *˳k̔ogs-pa*.
Deceased *γšin-po*.
Deceit *mgo-skór*; *ṅo-lkog*; *rdzub*; *zog*, *zol-zóg*.
Deceitful *lče-γnyis-pa*.
Deceive *mgo skor-ba*; *rṅod-pa*; *blo ˳brid-pa*, *˳brid-pa*; *slu-ba*.
Deceived *˳k̔rul-pa*.
Decency *k̔rel-yod*.
Decent *˳gab-pa*.
Deception *sgyu-zóg*.
Decide *γčod-pa*; *t̔ag-γčod-pa*.
Decided *zad*; v. *˳dzad-pa*; to be *čad-pa*.
Declare *bšad-pa*.
Declination (of the sun) v. *bgrod-pa*; north — *byaṅ-bgrod*, south — *lho-bgrod*.
Decline (decay) vb. n. *rgud-pa*.
Declivity *gud*; *ri γzar-po*, *braq γzar-po*.
Decoction *t̔aṅ-gi sman*.
Decorate *sgron-pa*; *brgyan-pa*; *spra-ba*.
Decoration *rgyan*.
Decrease vb. *˳gyur-ba*; *˳grib-pa*; *˳bri-ba*.
Decree s. *bka-šog*, *bka-k̔rims*; *k̔ra-ma*.
Decrepit *˳k̔ogs-pa*.

Dedicate *sṅo-ba*.
Deed *las*; *bya-ba*.
Deep adj. *γtiṅ-riṅ-ba*; *zab-pa*; — (of sounds) *rom-po W.*
Deer *ka-ša Sik.*
Deface *dma ˳bebs-pa*.
Defeat vb. *˳p̔am-par byed-pa*.
Defect s. *skyon*.
Defective *skyon-čan*.
Defence *skyabs*.
Defend *skyoṅ-ba*; *skyob-pa*.
Defender (of religion) *čos-skyóṅ*.
Defer v. *˳gyaṅ-ba*.
Deficient *sgob-sgób*.
Defile s. *roṅ*.
Defile vb. *bsgo-ba*; *˳bag-pa*.
Defilement *grib*.
Deform vb. *mi sdug-par byed-pa*
Degenerate adj. *brgyud-méd*; *rigs-nyáms*.
Degree (rank) *t̔em-pa*, *t̔em-rim*; sa no. 2; *go*, *go-p̔aṅ*; a high — v. *rlabs*; by degrees *k̔ad-kyis*; *mt̔ar-gyis*; *rim-gyis*, *rim-pa bžin du*
Dejected *žum-pa*; *mi dga-ba*, v. *dga-ba* III; *dman-pa*.
Delay s. *bšol-ba*.
Delay vb., to be delayed *˳gyaṅ-ba*.
Delegate vb. a. *mṅag-pa*.
Delegate s. *t̔sab-po*, resp. *sku-t̔sáb*.
Deliberate vb. *bka-bgro-ba*, *bgro-ba*.
Deliberation *grabs*, *˳dun-ma*, *˳dun-gros*
Delight s. *dga-ba*; *dga-spró*, *dga-t̔sór*, *dga-ráṅs*, *dga-mgú*; to take — in *dga-ba*, resp. *dgyes-pa* or *mnyes-pa*; *spro-ba*.
Delighted *dga-mo*, *dga-ba*, *dga-raṅs*; to be *dga-ba*.
Delightful *dga-mo*, *dga-t̔sor če-ba*.
Delineation *bkod-pa*; *ris*, *ri-mo*.
Deliver (rescue) *sgrol-ba*; (transfer) *sprod-pa*; *γtod-pa*; *skur-ba*.
Deliverance (liberation) *grol-ba*.
Deliverer *skyabs-mgón*; *srog-skyób W.*
Dell *grog-po*.
Delude *mgo skor-ba*.
Deluge s. *ču-rúd*.
Delusion *snaṅ-˳k̔rúl*.
Delusive *kun-rdzób*; *˳k̔rul-snaṅ-čan*.
Demand vb. *˳dod-pa*.
Demeanour *spyod-lam*.
Demon *bgegs*; *˳goṅ-po*.
Den *t̔saṅ*.
Denomination *čos-lugs*.
Dense *stugs-po*; *˳t̔ug-po*.
Density *ska-slád*.
Depart *čas-pa*; *bžud-pa*; (deviate) *˳gyur-ba*.
Depend upon *rten-pa*; *blo skyel-ba W.*, *k̔el-ba C.*
Deportment *spyod-pa*.
Depository *mdzod*.

Depression (incision) *ltoṅ-ga.*
Deprive *ₒṗrog-pa; ₒṗral-ba;* to be deprived *ₒbral-ba.*
Depth *zab-ḱyád; ytiṅ; zab-pa; zabs.*
Deranged *ₒḱrul-ba* no. 3.
Derangement *skyon.*
Descend *ₒbab-pa.*
Descendants *brgyud.*
Describe *ston-pa; ₒbri-ba.*
Description *bšad-pa; bstan-pa; ynas-ṫsul, ynas-lugs; rnam-ṫar; byed-ṫsul, yod-ṫsul.*
Desert s. *dgon-pa; ₒbrog(-stoṅ).*
Deserted *stoṅ-pa.*
Deserve v. *ₒos-pa.*
Design vb. a. (delineate) *ₒbri-ba; ₒgod-pa;* (intend for) *sño-ba*
Design s. *ri-mo.*
Desirable *mḱo-ba.*
Desire s. *ṫob-bló; ₒdod-pa.*
Desire vb. *ₒdod-pa; smon-pa; žen-pa; sred-pa; ṙñam-pa; ṙñab-pa; rkam-pa.*
Desolate adj. *ño bab-pa; žum-pa.*
Despair s. *yi(d) yčod-pa; yi(d) mug-pa.*
Despair vb. *ḱo-tag yčod-pa; yi(d)-mug-pa.*
Despise *brnyas-pa; ṙñan-čen byed-pa; ḱyad-du ysod-pa; ₒgyiṅ-ba; smad-pa.*
Despond *spa-sgoṅ-ba.*
Despondency *žum-pa; yi(d) mug.*
Destine *sko-ba; sño-ba.*
Destiny *skal-ba; sko-ba; bsod-bdé; dbaṅ-ṫáṅ.*
Destitute *kun-gyis btaṅ-ba; mgon-méd; rten-méd.*
Destroy *ₒgem-pa; ṙñam-pa; ₒjig-pa; ₒjoms-pa; ṫsar-yčod-pa* 458; *ma-ruṅ-bar byed-pa; med-par byed-pa.*
Destruction *žig-ral,* v. *ral-ba.*
Detail s., in — *rgyas-par* 109.
Detain *skyil-ba; bšol-ba.*
Detect *rnyed-pa; ṫob-pa.*
Determine vb. a. (induce) *skul-ba;* vb. n. (resolve) *ṫag yčod-pa.*
Detest *spoṅ-ba.*
Develop vb. n. *rgyas-pa* 109.
Deviate *ₒḱyar-ba; ₒgol-ba.*
Devil *bdud; bgegs.*
Devise *dmigs-pa-nas* (or *sems-kyis*) *yzo-ba; dgoṅs-pa.*
Devote vb. *sño-ba.*
Devotion *gus-pa, daṅ-ba.*
Devour *čur mid-pa; hab-háb za-ba.*
Devout *skal-dán; gus-pa; čos-čan; daṅ-ba.*
Dew s. *zil-pa.*
Dexterity *sgyu-rtsál.*
Dexterous *skyen-pa; rtsal-čan.*
Diadem *čod-pán.*
Diagram *dkyil-ₒḱor.*
Dialect *skad-lúgs.*
Diamond *rdo-rje, dor-je-ṗa-lám.*
Diaphragm *mčin-ri.*
Diarrhoea *ₒḱru-ba; šal W.* 567.

Dictionary *miṅ-gi mdzod.*
Die, dice s. *čo-lo, čol; šo;* to play at — *šo rtse-ba; šo gyed-pa.*
Die vb. n. *ₒči-ba, ši-ba;* resp. *dgoṅs-pa,* and *ₒgroṅ-ba;* eleg. *ₒgum-pa;* v. *ₒda-ba;* to — out *ₒčad-pa.*
Diet *spyod-lam;* lenten — *dkar-zás.*
Difference *ḱyad, ḱyad-par; bye-brag;* to find a — *ynyis-su ₒdzin-pa.*
Different *mi-yčig; ṫa-dad-pa; so-só: mi-ₒdra-ba;* not — *yčig-pa.*
Difficult *dka-ba, dka-bo; ḱag-po, ḱab-le.*
Diffuse vb. *ₒgyed-pa.*
Dig *rko-ba; bru-ba.*
Digest *ₒju-ba; žu-ba.*
Digestion *ₒju-ba.*
Dignitary *ṫsan-po.*
Dignity *go-grál, go-ṗáṅ; go-sá; gras, dbu-ₒṗáṅ.*
Dike *ču-rags, ču-lon; rags.*
Dilapidated *gog-po.*
Diligence *brtson-ₒgrus; snyiṅ-rús;* to use — *rtsol-ba skyed-pa.*
Diligent *brtson-pa-čan.*
Diligently *rtsol-bar.*
Dim adj. *dkrigs-pa; bkrag-čór; man-mún Ld.;* to grow — *ₒgrib-pa.*
Diminish vb. a. *ₒṗri-ba;* vb. n. *ₒgrib-pa.*
Dimness *rab-rib, hrab-hrib.*
Din *ₒdu-ₒdzi.*
Dip vb. *spag-pa.*
Diploma *bka-rgya, bka-šog;* — of nobility *dpal-gyi ynaṅ-šóg.*
Direct vb. a. *ytod-pa;* to be —ed *ston-pa, lta-ba.*
Direction *ño, ños; ṗyogs; man-ñág; žal-ta; šed.*
Directly *de-ma-ṫag-tu.*
Director **ₒgo-pón* C.*
Dirt *dri-ma; dreg-pa; rkyag-pa; lčags-dregs.*
Dirty adj. *dri-ma-čan; btsog-pa; gos-pa; mi-ytsaṅ-ba; ṫsi-du W.*
Dirty vb. a. *ₒgo-ba.*
Disadvantage *skyon.*
Disagreeable *mi-sdug-pa; yid-du-mi ₒoṅ-ba.*
Disappear *mi-snaṅ-bar ₒgyur-ba; yal-ba; med-par ₒgyur-ba; ₒjig-pa; ₒbud-pa.*
Disapprove *ₒdor-ba; mi ynaṅ-ba.*
Disciple *grwa-pa; nye-ynas; slob-ₒbáṅs.*
Discontented *skyo-mo; mi dga-ba.*
Discontinue *yčod-pa.*
Discord *dbyen-pa; sel.*
Discouraged *ño ₒbab-pa.*
Discourse s. *gleṅ-brjód, gleṅ-mo; lda-gu.*
Discuss *bgro-ba.*
Disdain s. *ṙñan-čén.*
Disease s. *nad; na-ba; snyuṅ;* chronic — *yčoṅ;* fatal — *ₒči-nád.*
Disfigured *gya-ba.*

Disgrace s. *rkaṅ-°drén, žabs-°drén.*
Disgrace vb. a. *dma-°bebs-pa.*
Disguise s. *°bag; rdzu-ba.*
Disguise vb. a. *°gebs-pa;* v. *čas* 156.
Disgust s. *skyo-šás; ḱrel; rnam-rtóg.*
Dish *ka-to-ra; sder-ma; spags; skyu-rúm W.*
Disheartened *skyo-mo.*
Dishonour vb. *smad-pa; dma °bebs-pa.*
Disk *kyir-kyir; dkyil-°ḱór; °ḱor-lo; sgor-mo.*
Dislocated, to be — *°ḱrul-ba.*
Dismay s. *žum-pa.*
Dismiss *bka °grol-ba; °gyed-pa; γtoṅ-ba; °don-pa.*
Disorder s. *°ḱrug-pa; skyon; °ḱral-°ḱrúl.*
Dispatch vb. *rdzoṅ-ba; zlog-pa; γtoṅ-ba, mṅag-pa.*
Dispel *zlog-pa.*
Dispense vb. (deal out) *°brim-pa.*
Disperse vb. a. *°gye-ba, °gyed-pa; γčor-ba;* vb. n. *°byer-ba; yan ča-če W.*
Display vb. *°grems-pa; γčal-ba.*
Disposition s. (character) *rgyud; ṅaṅ; ṅaṅ-rgyúd; raṅ-bžín; γšis.*
Disputation *rtsod-pa.*
Dispute vb. n. *rgol-ba; rtsod-pa.*
Dispute s. *ḱa-mču, rtsod-pa, °dziṅ-mo.*
Dissatisfaction *mi-dga-bai sems.*
Dissatisfied *mi-dga-ba;* also *°ḱon-pa.*
Dissect *°byed-pa.*
Dissension *°ḱon-po; naṅ-sel, sel; dbyen-pa.*
Dissertation *rgyud, mdo*
Dissimilarity *ḱyad-par; mi-°dra-ba.*
Dissolute *°čol-pa;* to be — *mi ṫsaṅs-par spyod-pa.*
Dissolve vb. a. *°žig-pa;* to be dissolved *ṫim-pa.*
Dissuade *sgyur-ba; zlog-pa.*
Distance *rgyaṅ-ma; nye-riṅ; ṫag; ṗa-ṫsad, ṗa-zád*
Distant *ṫag-riṅ(-mo).*
Distend *rkyoṅ-ba.*
Distinct *ḱrol-po; čod-po; wa-lé, wal-le-ba.*
Distinction *ḱyad; dbye-ba.*
Distinguish *rnam(-par) bžag(-pa).*
Distinguished *°ṗags-pa; ḱyad-par-čan.*
Distorted *ča-čús;* to be — *°ḱrul-ba.*
Distress s. *sdug-bsṅal, mya-ṅan, dka-las.*
Distribute *bgod-pa; °brim-pa;* v. *°gyed-pa.*
District *yul-ḱág; yul-ljóṅs; yul-sde; ḱul; sde.*
Disturb *dkrug-pa; γyeṅs-par byed-pa; bar-du γčod-pa;* to be disturbed *°ḱrug-pa.*
Disturber *bstan-šig.*
Ditch *ču-°óbs; °obs.*
Diverse *sna-ṫsogs; sna-so-só.*
Diversity *bye-ba; mi °dra-ba.*
Divert *sgyur-ba; rtse-ba; zlog-pa.*
Divide *bgod-pa; °gyed-pa; °byed-pa; °ges-pa;* to be divided *°gye-ba*
Dividend *bgo-byá.*
Divine s. *čos-pa.*
Division *dbye-ba; bye-brág; ḱyad, ḱyad-par; ču-ṫsán; rnam-pa; ḱag.*
Divisor *bgod-byéd.*
Dizzy, I am — *mgo °ḱor.*
Do *byed-pa; spyod-pa;* eleg. *bgyid-pa;* resp. *mdzad-pa;* that will — **dig-pa yin* C.; des čog.*
Doctrine *čos; bstan-pa.*
Dog *ḱyi,* male — *ḱyi-ṗo,* fem. *ḱyi-mo;* mad — *ḱyi smyon-pa;* — kennel *ḱyi-ḱáṅ, ḱyi-pul.*
Doll *miu.*
Domain *ḱams; ḱul; dbaṅ-ris.*
Domicile *mčis-bráṅ.*
Dominion *ḱams* 39; v. *rgyal-ḱams* 108; *ṅaṅ; mṅa; čab-°óg; dbaṅ-ris; srid.*
Door *sgo; čab-sgo;* large — *sgo-mo;* little — *sgeu;* principal — *rgyal-sgo;* — bar *γtan-pa;* — frame *sgo-°drig;* — hinge *sgo-ḱor, go-ṗíṅ W.;* — keeper *sgo-pa,* resp. *čabs-sgo-pa, sgo-sruṅ.*
Dose s. *ṫun.*
Dosser *ṫse-po, ṫsel-po.*
Dot s. *ṫseg.*
Double adj. *γnyis-ldáb;* — tongued *lče-γnyis-pa;* — barreled gun *nyi-rag W.;* (v. *sbrag-pa*); *ṫsaṅ-yá.*
Double vb. a. *skum-pa.*
Doubt s. *ṫe-ṫsóm; ṫsom-pa; ṫsom-ṫsóm; yid-γnyis.*
Doubtful *γtol-méd.*
Dough *skyo-ma; bag-zan.*
Down adv. *ṫur; ṫeṅ-la C.; γšam-du;* to go — *nub-pa, °bab-pa.*
Downward *mar, mas; °og-tu, šod-du.*
Dowry *rdzoṅs.*
Doze vb. *nyid ṫom-pa.*
Drag vb. *°drud-pa.*
Dragon *°brug.*
Dram s. (weight) *žo* 478.
Draught s. (drawing) *bkod-pa; ri-mo;* (drink) *hub.*
Draw (pull) *°ṫen-pa; °dren-pa;* to — in *rṅub-pa; skum-pa;* to — out *°ṫen-pa; °byin-pa;* to — up (to compose) *°god-pa.*
Dreadful *°žigs-pa.*
Dream s. *rmi-lam,* resp. *mnal-lam;* vb. *rmi-ba.*
Dress s. *gos, čas;* resp. *na-bza.*
Dress vb. a. (to clothe) *skon-pa;* (to cook) *°ṫsod-pa, °ṫsed-pa;* to — wounds *sdom-pa.*
Dressed up *zab-mo.*
Dried *skam-po;* — up *kum-po*
Drink vb. *°ṫuṅ-ba.*
Drink s. *skyems; žal-skóm;* meat and *bza-bṫúṅ.*

Drinkable water *skems-ču.*
Drinking-cup *skyogs*; *čaṅ-čan*, *por-pa*, *ko-re W.*
Drip vb *ₒdzag-pa.*
Drive vb. *ₒded-pa*; to — back *ₒgogs-pa*; *zlog-pa*; to — out *skrod-pa*; *bda-ba.*
Driver *ₒded-mi.*
Drop s. *tigs-pa.*
Drop vb. a. *krul ytoṅ-ba*; vb. n. *ₒdzag-pa*; *ₒčor-ba.*
Dropsy *pags-ču*; *snyiṅ-ču*; *dmu-ču.*
Dross *lčags-drégs.*
Drowned, to be — *ₒtsub-pa*; *čus ₒkyer-ba.*
Drum s. *rṅa*; — skin *rṅa-lpágs*; — stick *rṅa-lčág.*
Drummer *rṅa-pa.*
Drunk *ra-ro-ba*; *bzi-čan W.*; to get — *bzi-ba.*
Drunkard *čaṅ-dad-čan W.*
Drunkenness *ra-ro.*
Dry adj. *skam-pa*, *skam-po*; *skem-pa*; — weather, drought *tan-pa.*
Dry vb. a. *skem-pa.*
Dryness *skam-pa.*
Duck s. (water-fowl) *ṅur-ba.*
Due adj. *dgos-pa.*
Duel s. *ₒkrug-pa.*
Dulcimer *yaṅ-ljin Ts.*
Dull adj. *lkugs-pa*; *glen-pa*; *rtul-po*; *blun-pa.*
Dullness *rmu-ba.*
Dumb *lkugs-pa*; *smra-mi-nus-pa.*
Dumpling *ču-ta-gir W.*
Dung s. *lča Ld.*; *lči-ba W.*; *brun.*
Dungeon *kri-mún*; *btson-doṅ.*
Dupe vb. a. *mgo skor byed-pa* 25.
During prep. *kons-su*; *na* 298; *riṅ-la.*
Dusky *man-mún.*
Dust s. *kyim-sa*; *tal-ba*; *rdul*; *pye-ma*; cloud of — *bud.*
Duty *kag*; *krims*; *sdom-pa*; moral — *tsul-krims*; (tax) *dpya*; *šo-gám.*
Dwarf *miu.*
Dwell *ynas-pa*, *ₒdug-pa*; *sdod-pa*; resp. *bžugs-pa*; *ₒkod-pa.*
Dwelling s. *ynas-kaṅ*, *ynas-tsaṅ*; eleg. *mčis-braṅ*; temporary — *ₒbraṅ-sa.*
Dwindle *yal-ba.*
Dye s. *tsos*; vb. a. *tsos rgyag-pa.*
Dynasty *rgyal-brgyúd*; *rgyal-rábs.*

E

Each *kun*; *re*, *re-ré*
Eager *ₒdod-čan*, *ₒdod-ldan*; to be — *ₒdod-pa*; *sred-pa.*
Eagle *go-bo*; *glag.*
Ear *rna-ba*; resp. *snyan*; — ache *rna-ba na-ba*; — hole *rna-kúṅ*; — shot *rgyaṅ-grágs*; — wax *klog-pa*; *rna-kyág*; — of corn *snye-ma.*
Early adj. and adv. v. *sṅa* 135; earlier *sṅa-ma*, *sṅa-mo*; earlier or later *sṅa-rtiṅ-du.*
Earn *kug-pa.*
Earnest s., in good — *don-dám.*
Earnestly *snyiṅ-nas*; v. also *yaṅ-dag-pa*, sub. *dag-pa* 248.
Earth *sa*; *sa čen-po*; — quake *sa-yyós*; *saṅ-gúl W.*
East *šar.*
Easy *sla-ba*; *lhod-pa.*
Eat *za-ba*, *bza-ba*; resp. *ysol-ba*; *mčod-pa*; v. also *ₒtuṅ-ba*; to — up *ma-lus-par za-ba.*
Echo s. *brag-ča*; *sgra-brnyán.*
Eclipse of the moon *zla-ₒdzin*, of the sun *nyi-ₒdzin.*
Edge *ka*; *ča-ga*; *mta*; *zur*; — of a knife *dṅo.*
Edict *bka-šog*, *ysuṅ-šog*; *bkar-btags-pa.*
Edifice *bkod-pa* 96.
Educate *ₒtso-ba*; *yso-ba*, *yso-skyon byed-pa.*
Effect vb. a. *byed-pa.*
Effect s. *ₒbras-bu*; effects (goods) *ča-lag W.*, *lag-ča*, *yo-byad.*
Effervesce *ₒkol-ba.*
Efficacy *nus-pa.*
Egg *sgo-ṅá*, *tul W.*
Egotism *bdag-ₒdzin* 268.
Egypt *mi-sér yul.*
Eight num. *brgyad*; eighth *brgyad-pa*; eighteen *ču-brgyad*; eighteenth *ču-brgyad-pa*; eighty *brgyad-ču*; eightieth *brgyad-ču-pa.*
Either — or *yaṅ-na — yaṅ-na.*
Eject *skrod-pa*; *ₒdor-ba.*
Elapse *ₒda-ba.*
Elbow *gru-mo*, *gre-mo*; *dre-bo.*
Elder adj. *če-ba*, *čen-po*; — brother *jo-bo*; *tu-bo.*
Elder s. *rgad-po.*
Election *ydam-ka.*
Electuary *lde-gu.*
Element *ₒbyuṅ-ba*; *kams.*
Elephant *glaṅ*, *glaṅ-po-čé*, *glaṅ-čén.*
Elevate *sgro-ₒdogs-pa*; *ₒdegs-pa*; *spar-ba*; *seṅ-ba.*
Eleven *bču-yčig*; eleventh *bču-yčig-pa.*
Elk *ka-šá ša-ba.*
Eloquence *ka-sbyaṅ.*
Eloquent *ṅag-dbáṅ*; *ka-sbyaṅ-po*; *ka-šugs-čan W.*
Elsewhere *yžan-du.*

Emanate *ₒṕro-ba.*
Emanation *sprul-ba* 336.
Emboss *ṕur-ba.*
Embrace vb. *ₒḱyud-pa*; *ₒḱril ba*; *ₒdzin-pa*; *ḱyab-pa.*
Emerald *ma-rgád.*
Emerge *ₒbyuṅ-ba.*
Emetic *skyug-smán.*
Eminent *ḱyad-par-čan*; *ṕun-sum-ťsogs-pa*; *rgyal-ba*; *ṕul-tu byúṅ-ba.*
Emit *ₒbyin-pa.*
Emmet *gre-mog-bu W.*; *grog-ma.*
Empale *γsal-śiṅ-la skyon-pa.*
Emperor *rgyal-po čen-po.*
Empire *ḱams*; *yul-ḱáms*; *rgyal-ḱág.*
Employ *skyel-ba*; *spyod-pa*; to be —ed or busy *brel-ba.*
Empty *stoṅ-pa*: to make — *stoṅs-pa.*
Emulate *ₒgran-pa.*
Emulation *ₒgran-sems.*
Enabled, to be — *ḱom-pa* 44.
Encampment *sgar*; *dmag-sgár.*
Enchanter *ₒgoṅ-po*; enchantress *ₒgoṅ-ba-mo.*
Encircle *skor-ba.*
Enclose *skor-ba.*
Enclosure *skor-ba*; *ra-ba.*
Encompass *ₒḱyigs-pa*; *ₒḱyud-pa*; *skor-ba.*
End s. *mǰug*; *mťa*, *mťa-ma*; *ǰug*; *γžug*; towards or at the — *mťa-ru*, *mťar*; to be at an — *rdzogs-pa*, *zin-pa.*
Endeavour vb. *rtsol-ba*; *lhur len-pa*; *don-du γnyer-ba*; s. *ₒgrus-pa.*
Endless *mťa-yás*; *mťa-méd.*
Enemy *dgra*, *dgra-bo*; *ṕa-rol-po*; *ₒťse-ba.*
Energy *śugs.*
Engagement (promise) *čad*; *sdom-pa*; v. also *las*, *brel-ba.*
Engrave *rko-ba.*
Enjoin *skul-ba.*
Enjoy *loṅs spyod-pa*; — one's self *rtse-ba.*
Enjoyment *loṅs-spyód*; *nyams-myoṅ.*
Enlarge *rgyas-pa*; *ₒṕel-ba*; *dar-ba*; - upon *spro-ba.*
Enough *ťsad*; *čog-pa*; to be — *ₒḱyed-pa*; *ₒgrig-pa.*
Ensnare *dkri-ba.*
Enter vb. a. *ₒǰug-pa*; *ₒťsugs-pa*; *ₒťsud-pa*; vb. n. *čud-pa.*
Entertainment *mgron*; v. also *mčod-stón.*
Entire *tsaṅ-ma*; *ril-ba*; *son-te W.*
Entity *ṅo-bo-nyid* 129; *čos-nyid* 164.
Entrails *rgyu-ma*, *naṅ-ḱrol.*
Entrance (vestibule) *sgo-ḱáṅ.*
Entrust *ₒčol-ba*; *γtod-pa*, *γnyer-ḱa γtad-pa.*
Enumerate *sgraṅ-ba*, *bsgraṅ-ba*: *ₒdren-pa.*
Enumeration *rnam-gráṅs.*
Envelope *yi-gei śubs.*
Envious *ṕrag-dog-čan*; v. also *če-ré.*
Envoy *ṕo-nya.*
Envy s. *ṕrag-dóg*; *mig-sér.*
Envy vb. *ṕrag-pa.*
Epidemy *rims(-nad)*; *ṅan-rims.*
Epilepsy *ḱyab-ₒǰug*; *γza-nád*; *γza-ṕog-pa.*
Epistle *yi-ge.*
Epitaph *dur-byaṅ.*
Equal *mnyam-pa*; *snyoms-po* 201; *ₒdra-ba*; *mťsuṅs-pa.*
Equality *mnyam-pa-nyid*; *ₒdra-mi-ₒdra.*
Equanimity *snyoms-pa*; *btaṅ-snyóms.*
Equivalent s. *dod*; *ťsab.*
Eradicate *rtsad-nas γčod-pa.*
Erect adj. *kye-ré*; *ḱroṅ-ṅe.*
Erect vb. a. *sgreṅ-ba*; *ₒdzugs-pa*; *bžeṅ-ba.*
Err *ₒḱyar-ba*; *ₒḱrul-ba*; *ₒgol-ba*; *nor-ba.*
Error *ₒgal-sa*; *ₒḱrul-so*, *ₒḱrul-γži.*
Eructation *skyug-ldád*; *sgreg-pa.*
Escape vb. *ₒčor-ba*; *ₒbud-pa.*
Escort s. *skyel-ma*; *bsel(-ba)*, *lam-bsél.*
Escort vb. *rdzoṅ ₒdebs-pa.*
Especially *ḱyad-par-du.*
Essence *ṅo-bo-nyid* 129; *bčud* (quintessence) 147.
Establish *ₒgod-pa.*
Estafet *rta-zam-pa.*
Esteem s. *ṕu-dúd*; *rtsis*; *ya-śa.*
Esteem vb. a. *bkur-ba*; *γčes-par byed-pa* or *ₒdzin-pa.*
Estimation *rtsis*; *ťsod* 453.
Eternal *rtag-pa*; *skye-ₒči-med-pa.*
Eternity *rtag-tu-ba* (?).
Ether *mḱa.*
Etymology *ťa-snyád.*
Eunuch *nyug-rúm.*
Euphony *sgra-dbyaṅs.*
Europe *rgya-pi-liṅ*; *ṕyi-gliṅ*, vulgo *ṕi-liṅ.*
European s. *ṕa-ráṅ*, *ṕe-ráṅ*; *ṕi-liṅ-pa.*
Evade *ₒǰur-ba*, *ₒdzur-ba*; *ₒǰol-ba*; *ₒčor-ba.*
Evangelist *ṕrin-bzaṅ sgrog-pa(-po).*
Evaporate *ťim-pa.*
Even adj. *mnyam-pa.*
Even vb. a (to level) *snyom-pa.*
Even adv. *ťa-na*; *yaṅ*; not — v. *yaṅ* 505.
Evening *nub*; *nub-mo*; *dgoṅs.*
Evenness *nyam-pa-nyid.*
Event *rkyen*; *dṅos-po*; at all events *čis kyaṅ*, *gaṅ yin kyaṅ* 65; *ga-na-méd W.*, *gar-méd W.*
Ever *rtag-tu*; *γtan-du*; *dus-rgyun-du.*
Every *kun*; *re*, *re-ré*; v. *gaṅ* 65; — day *dkyus-ma*; *žag daṅ žag* 248; — thing *čaṅ*; *či*; *kun.*
Everywhere *kun-tu*; v. *čir* 141.
Evidence *rgyu-mťsan* 111.
Evident *mṅon-pa.*
Evidently v. *ṅes-pa* 128.
Evil s. *ṅan*; *nyes-pa.*
Evil adj. *ṅan-pa*; *ťu-ba*; — spirit *ₒgoṅ-po.*
Exact adj. *žib-pa.*

Exactly *ko-na*; *rań*; — that *de-dé* 256.
Exaggerate *sgro-*$_{o}$*dogs-pa.*
Exalt *sgro-*$_{o}$*dogs-pa.*
Exalted $_{o}$*pags-pa.*
Examination *brtags-dpyad.*
Examine *rtog-pa*; *dpyod-pa*; *γžig-pa*; *sad-pa.*
Example *dpe*; *dpe-brjód.*
Excavate *γčoń-ba*; *sbug-pa.*
Excavation *sbugs*; *šoń.*
Excellence *dńos-grub*; *če-ba.*
Excellent *rgyal ba*; *kyad-par-čan*; *γčes-pa*; *pun-tsógs*; $_{o}$*pags-pa.*
Except prep. *ma γtogs-par*; *min*, *min-par.*
Exchange s. (agio) *par.*
Excite *sloń-ba*, *dkrog-pa.*
Exclaim $_{o}$*bod-pa.*
Exclusively *ko-na.*
Excrement *rkyag-pa*; *rtug-pa*; *dri-ma.*
Excrescence *lba-ba*; *mdzer-pa*; $_{o}$*dzer-pa.*
Execrate *ńan* $_{o}$*debs-pa*; *mńan-pa*; *dmod-pa* $_{o}$*bor-ba.*
Exercise s. (bodily) *spyod-lam* 335; — of religion *čos-spyod.*
Exercise vb. a. *sbyoń-ba*; *lag-tu len-pa.*
Exert one's self $_{o}$*bad-pa.*
Exertion $_{o}$*bad-pa*; *brtson-pa*; *don-γnyér*; *dka-ba.*
Exhausted *nyams-tag-pa*; to be — (consumed) $_{o}$*dzad-pa*; *zin-pa*; (tired) $_{o}$*čad-pa*; *ńal-*$_{o}$*čad-pa*, *tań-*$_{o}$*čad-pa.*
Exhort *skul-ba*; *skul-čag byed-pa*; *bslab-bya byed-pa*, or *ston-pa*, or *btań-ba.*
Exhortation *bskul-ba*, *bskul-ma*; *snyiń-γtam*; *luń*, *luń-bstán*; *bslab-bya*; farewell — *ka-čéms.*
Exile vb. a. *γnas-nas dgar-ba.*
Exist cf. $_{o}$*dug-pa*; *yod-pa*; *skye-ba.*
Existence *skye-ba*; *srid-pa.*
Exorcise *dam-la* $_{o}$*dogs-pa.*
Expanse *kloń*; *ka-žéń.*
Expect *sgug-pa.*
Expedient adj. *pan-*$_{o}$*dogs-pa*, *pan-togs-čan*; *rigs-pa* 528; *don-byed-nus-pa*
Expel *skrod-pa*; $_{o}$*jil-ba*; $_{o}$*don-pa*; *spyug-pa*; $_{o}$*bud-pa*; *zlog-pa.*
Expend *skyag-pa.*
Expenditure, **Expense** $_{o}$*gro-sgo*; *skyag-pa*, *skyag-sgo.*
Expensive *gus-po.*
Experience vb. a. *myoń-ba*, *nyams-su myoń-ba*; v. also *sbyoń-ba.*
Experience s. *slobs.*
Experienced (skilled) *mkas-pa.*
Expiation *sdig-bšágs.*
Expire $_{o}$*da-ba.*
Explain $_{o}$*grel-ba*, $_{o}$*grol-ba*; *ńo sprod-pa*; $_{o}$*čad-pa*; *bšad-pa.*
Explanation *brda-spród.*
Exploit *kyo ga.*
Expressly *čed-du.*
Exquisite *mčog-tu bkrab*; *kyad-par* $_{o}$*pags-pa.*
Extend *rkyoń-ba*; *bsnar-ba.*
Extension *kyon*; *gu.*
Extensive *rgyas-pa*; *yańs-pa.*
Extent *kyon*; *rgya*, *rgya-kyon*, *rgya-ba*; *ču-žeń* 158.
Exterior s. *rnam-pa*; *ča-byad* 152.
External *pyii*, v. *pyi* III 349; — appearance *ča-byad*, *pyi-rol.*
Extinct, to become — $_{o}$*čad-pa*; *ši-ba.*
Extinguish *γsod-pa.*
Extra $_{o}$*teb.*
Extract vb. a. *bku-ba*; $_{o}$*byin-pa*; $_{o}$*don-pa.*
Extraction (descent) *rigs.*
Extremity (end) *mta-ma*, *zur.*
Eye s. *mig*, resp. *spyan*; — brow *smin-ma*; — lash *rdzi-ma*; *mig-γšog*, resp. *spyan-γšog*; — lid *mig-pág C. W.*

F

Fable s. *sgruńs.*
Fabricate vb. a. $_{o}$*čos-pa*; *bčo-ba*; *byed-pa*; *bzo-ba*; to be fabricated *grub-pa.*
Face s. *γdoń*; *ńo*; *ka*; *skye-sgó*; *sgo-lo*; *bžin*; in the — of *ka-ru*, *kar.*
Face vb. (to be directed towards) *ston-pa.*
Fail vb. (to miss) *mi kes-pa C.*; *mi-*$_{o}$*tebs-pa W.*; (to err) $_{o}$*gol-ba*; (to dwindle) *yal-ba.*
Faint adj. *nyams-čuń*; to get — *γčoń-ba.*
Faint vb. n. *brgyal-ba*; $_{o}$*kam-pa.*
Fair adj. *mdzes-pa*; *mtsar-ba*; *bzań-ba.*
Faith *dad-pa.*
Faithful *dad-pa*; *γdeńs-pa*; *slu-méd*; *gyo-sgyu-méd.*
Falchion *gri-gug.*
Falcon *kra.*
Fall vb. $_{o}$*gril-ba*; $_{o}$*gyel-ba*; *ltuń-ba*; $_{o}$*bab-pa*; to — in drops $_{o}$*tig-pa*; to — off $_{o}$*byi-ba*; to — to pieces $_{o}$*jig-pa*; $_{o}$*gril-ba W* to — upon $_{o}$*buńs-pa.*
Fall s. *ltuń-ba.*
Fallow *yan-pa.*
False *mi bden-pa*; *rdzus-ma*; *γyo-čan*; charge *ka-yog*; *snyad*; conception *bčos-pa*; — sentiment *lta-lóg*, *log-lta.*
Falsehood *dkyus*; *ka-šób*; *rdzun.*
Fame *grags-pa.*
Family *brgyud*; *γduń*; *bu-smád*; *γžis-mad*; *rabs*; *rigs-brgyúd*; *rus.*

Famine *mu-ge.*
Famous *grags-čan.*
Fan s. *ṅa-yáb.*
Fan vb. a. *ₒḱrab-pa*; v. *yab-mo.*
Fancy vb. a. *sgom-pa*; *dmigs-pa*; *sems-pa*; vb. n. *mno-ba.*
Fancy s. *dmigs-pa*; *sems-kyi snaṅ-ba.*
Fang *ḱron*; *mče-ba*, *mče-so.*
Far *rgyaṅ-riṅ-po*, *rgyaṅs* 107; (*ṫag-*)*riṅ-ba*; *mi nye-ba*; as — as *bar-du*, *ḱad-du*; — famed *sgra-čé*; — from *lta či smos* 215.
Farewell v. *ga-le* 64; to say — v. *ṗyi-ṗyag*, sub *ṗyag.*
Farm s *groṅ-bžis*; — steward *ynyer-pa* 194.
Farmer *ḱyim-pa-pa*; *žiṅ-pa* 475.
Farsightedness *mig-rgyáṅ* 414.
Farther *ṗar.*
Fashion s. *čos*; *lugs.*
Fast adj. *mgyogs-pa*; *myur-ba.*
Fast vb. n. *smyuṅ-ba*; *dge-ba sruṅ-ba.*
Fasten *sdom-pa*; *ₒgrogs-pa*; *ₒdogs-pa*; *sgril-ba*; *sbyor-ba*; *sbrel-ba.*
Fasting s. *bsnyen-ynas*, *smyuṅ-ynas.*
Fat adj. *rgyas-pa*; *ṫso-ba*; *ṫson-po.*
Fat s. *ṫsil*; melted — *ṫsil-ḱu*; *žag.*
Fatal *byur-gyi*; *nyen-čan*; *ma-ruṅ-ba*; *šrog-len*, *šrog-ₒṗrog.*
Fate *skal-ba*, *las-bskos* v. *sko-ba* 24; *bsod-pa*; *dbaṅ-ṫáṅ*; cf. also *lan-čags* and *las-ₒṗro.*
Father *ṗa*, resp *yab*; — in law *gyos-po*; *skud-po.*
Fathom s. *ₒdoms-pa.*
Fatigue s. *ṅal*, resp. *ₒo-brgyál.*
Fatigue vb. a. *ṅal ₒjug-pa*; to be fatigued *ṅal-ba*, resp. *sku-ṅal-ba*, *ṫugs ṅal-ba.*
Fault *skyon*; *noṅs-pa*; *ₒṫsaṅ.*
Faulty *skyon-čan.*
Favour s. *bḱa-driṅ*; v. *ynaṅ-ba* II 309.
Favourable *mṫun-pa*; — circumstance *mṫun-rkyén.*
Favourite s. *snyiṅ-sdúg*; *sdug-pa.*
Fear s. *ₒjigs-pa*, *ₒjigs-skrag*, *ₒjigs-ri*; *bag-ṫsa* (*-ba*).
Fear vb. *ₒjigs-pa*; *dṅaṅ-ba*; *dogs pa.*
Fearless *ₒjigs-méd*; *bag-méd.*
Feast s. *dga-ston*; *mgron*; *ston-mo.*
Feather *spu*; quill — *sgro.*
Fee s. *gla*; *ṙṅan-pa*; *bag-šis.*
Feeble *kyar-kyór*; *kyór*; *nya-ra-nyo-ré.*
Feed *stob-pa*; *snyod-pa*; *ₒor-ba* W.; *ₒṫso-ba*, *yso-ba.*
Feel *reg-pa*, *ṫsor-ba*; to — cold *ₒḱyags-pa.*
Feeling s. *reg-bya.*
Feign vb. n. *bčos-pa* 148; v. *lugs byed-pa* (*lugs* no 2, 548); *ṫsul-du byed-pa* (*ṫsul* no. 1, 450).
Fellow *grogs*; *ya-do* W.; — labourer *las-grogs*: — lodger *ₒdug-grogs*, *braṅ-grogs*, resp. *bžugs-grogs*; traveller *lam-grógs.*
Felt s. *ṗyiṅ-pa.*
Female *mo.*
Fen *ₒdam*; *gram-pa.*
Fence s. *ḱo-ra*; *skyor-ba*; *ta-bér* W.; *pu-šu*; *ra-ba.*
Ferment vb. *ₒḱol-ba*; s. *žo-ri* W. 478; *ru-ma.*
Fern *skyes-ma.*
Ferocious *ṅar-po.*
Ferry s. *gru*; *rdziṅs*, *yziṅs.*
Ferry-man *gru-pa*; *ču-ṗyag-pa*; *mnyan-pa.*
Festival *dus-čén.*
Fetter vb. a. *sbrel-ba*; *ₒḱyig-pa*; *ₒčiṅ-ba.*
Fetters s. *sgrogs*; *lčags*, *lčags-sgrog*; *bčiṅs-pa.*
Fever *ṫsad-pai nád* C.; *ṫsan-zug* W.
Few *nyuṅ-ṅu*; a few *ₒga*, *ₒga tsam*; *nyuṅ-ṅu žig*; *čig* 140; *la-lá* C.
Fib s. *šob*, *yšob.*
Fibre *rgyus-pa.*
Fickle *gyi-na*; *ya-ma-brla*; *ₒgyur-ldog*; *skad yčig kyaṅ mi ṫsugs-pa.*
Fickleness *ₒgyur-ldog*, *ldog-ₒgyur.*
Fictitious *bčos-pa*; *dmigs-pa-nas bzos-pa.*
Fidget vb. *ₒṗar-ba.*
Field *žiṅ*; *kluṅs*; — terrace *daṅ-tse* W.
Fife *gliṅ-bu.*
Fifth *lṅa-pa*; fifteen *bčo-lṅa*; fifteenth *bčo-lṅa-pa*; fifty *lṅa-bču*; fiftieth *lṅa-bču-pa.*
Fight s. *ₒṫab-mo.*
Fight vb. a. *gyed-pa*; *rgol-ba*; *ₒṫab-pa*; *ₒṫab-mo byed-pa*; vb. n. *ₒḱrug-pa*; *ₒgran-pa*; *rgol-ba*; *rtsod-pa*; *ₒdziṅ-ba.*
Figure s. *dkyil-ḱor*; *skye-yzúgs*; *bḱod-pa*; *rnam-ₒgyúr*; *dbyibs*; *yzugs*; *bzo*, *zo*; *ri-mo*; *ris.*
Figured (variegated) *či-tra* W.
File s. (tool) *lčags-bdar*; *sed.*
File vb. (to string) *rgyud-pa*; *star-ba.*
Fill vb. *ḱyab-pa*; *ₒgeṅs-pa.*
Filter s. *ṫsag-ma*; vb. a *ₒṫsag-pa.*
Filth *dri-ma*; *mi-yṫsaṅ-ba* 433; *grib.*
Find *ṫob-pa*; *rnyed-pa*; *ḱug-pa.*
Fine adj. (beautiful) *mdzes-pa*; *sdug-pa*; *mṫsar-ba*; (not coarse) *žib-pa*; *lug-mo* W.; (thin) *srab-pa.*
Fine s. (penalty) *rgyal*, *stoṅ.*
Finger *ser-mo*, *sor-mo*, resp. *ṗyag-sór*; *mdzub-mo*, *mdzug-gu*; — ring *ser-ydúb*, *sor-ydúb.*
Finish vb. *sgrub-pa*; to be finished *ₒgrub-pa*; *ṫsar-ba*; *rdzogs-pa*; *ₒdzad-pa*; *zin-pa.*
Fir *ṫaṅ-šiṅ*; *som*, *ysom*, *som-šiṅ.*
Fire s. *me*; — brand *gal-mé*; — fly *ₒod-ṗro-ₒbu* W.; — place *ṫab*, *me-ṫab*; — tongs *me-lén.*
Firm (solid) *mḱraṅ*; *mḱregs-pa*; *sra-ba*; (trodden) *čag-čan* 167; (tight) *ṫaṅ-po*, *dam-po*; (sure) *btsan*; *ṅes-pa*; (steady) v. *ṫsugs-pa.*

Firmness (of mind) *snyiṅ-rús.*
First *daṅ-po*; *sṅa-ma*; *mgo-ma*; born *mgo-bu*; *sṅon-skyes*; — part *stod* 223; adv. (at first) *mgo-ma W.*; *sṅa-sór*, *sṅa-góṅ*; *sṅar*; *γčig-tu*; *ṫog-mar.*
Firstfruits *ṗud.*
Firstly *daṅ-por.*
Fish s. *nya*; — bone *nya-grá.*
Fish vb. *nya rṅon-pa*; *nya γšor ba.*
Fishing-hook *mčil-pa.*
Fishing-net *nya-rgya*, *nya-dól.*
Fissure *rgya-sér*; *ser-ka.*
Fist *ḱu-ṫsúr.*
Fit vb. a. v. *sgrig-pa* 120; to — out *šom-pa*; to be — *°ṫad-pa*; *ruṅ-ba.*
Five *lṅa.*
Fix vb. a. *°god-pa*; *sbyor-ba*; — a time *dus byed-pa.*
Flabby *kyom.*
Flag s. *dar*; — staff *dar-po-čé.*
Flageolet *gliṅ-bu.*
Flame s. *lče*, *me-lče.*
Flannel *ṫer-ma.*
Flap s. *gos sgáb.*
Flash vb. *°ḱyug-pa.*
Flat adj. *leb-mo*; *mnyam-pa.*
Flatten vb. a. *gleb-pa.*
Flatter *stod-pa*; *mol-lče btaṅ-ba W.*
Flatterer *ṅo stod-ḱan.*
Flattery *γčam-bu.*
Flatulence *ṗyen*; *˛og-rluṅ.*
Flavour s. *bro-ba*; *ro.*
Flaw s. *šo-ré W.*
Flea *ḱyi-šig*; *°ji-ba.*
Flee *°bros-pa.*
Fleece s. *ʼbal-rgyáb.*
Flesh *ša*; — fly *ša-sbráṅ.*
Flexible *kyom*; *mnyen-pa.*
Fling vb. *rgyab-pa*; *rgyag-pa C.*; *dbyug-pa C.*; *°ṗen-pa*; *skyur-ba*; *°bor-ba.*
Flint *lčag-rdo*; *lčags-mag.*
Float vb. n. *ldiṅ-ba.*
Flock s. *ḱyu*, *ḱyu-bo.*
Flog *lčag-gis γžu-ba*, v. also *skar-ba.*
Flood s. *ču-log.*
Floor s. *γži-ma*; (bottom) *mṫil* 240; *šen W.*; *ʼan-°dar C.*; ground — *˛og-kaṅ.*
Flour s. *ṗye*; *žib.*
Flourish vb. *bde-ba*; *°ṫseṅ-ba.*
Flourish s. (in writing) *ri-mo kyag-kyog.*
Flow vb. *°bab-pa*; s. *rgyun* 112.
Flower s. *me-tog*; — bed *rka*; — garden *sdum-ra.*
Fluid s. *ḱu-ba.*
Flute *ṗred-gliṅ.*
Flutter s. *ḱrag-ḱrug* 49.
Fly vb. *°ṗur-ba*; to — up *°ṗar-ba* 356.
Fly s. *sbraṅ-ma.*
Foal *rteu*; — of an ass *gu-rug.*
Foam s. *lbu-ba*, *dbu-ba.*
Fodder s. *čag.*
Foe *dgra*, *dgra-bo*; *ṗa-rol-pa* and *ṗo.*
Fog *kug-rna*; *na-bún*; *rmugs-pa.*
Fold s. (plait) *ltab-ma*; (pen) *lhas-ma.*
Fold vb. a. (to plait) *ltab-pa*; (to pen) *dgar-ba.*
Follow *°braṅ-ba*, *rjes-su °gro-ba*; *γčod-pa.*
Follower *bstan-°dzin.*
Following *ṗyi(s)*, *ṗyir* I, 2; *°di.*
Fond, to be — of ... *la čags-pa*, *žen-pa.*
Fondness *ḱri ba*; *žen-ḱris*, *zen-čags-pa.*
Fontanel *klad-sgo*; *mṫsogs-ma*; *°ṫsaṅs-pai bu-ga.*
Food *zas*, resp. *žal-zás*, *bžes-pa*; *bšos*; *ka-zás*; *za-ba*, *za-ma*; *lto*; — of animals *bzan.*
Fool s. *glen-pa*; *blun-pa*, *blun-po.*
Foolish *glen-pa*; *blun-pa*; *blo-méd.*
Foot *rkaṅ pa*, resp. *žabs*; — bridge *dem-tsi Lh.*; — path *rkaṅ-lam*; *°ṗraṅ*, *lam-°ṗraṅ*; — race *baṅ*; — ring *rkaṅ-γdub*; — soldier *rkaṅ-ṫaṅ-pa*; — stool *rkaṅ-stegs*; — of a hill *rtsa-ba*; on foot *rkaṅ-ṫaṅ-du* or *la.*
Footprint, Footstep *rkaṅ-rjés.*
For *don-du*; v. *ṗyogs* 352; — forty days *žag bži-bčui bar-du*, *žag bži-bču ṫug W.*
Forbear vb. a. *°gyod-mi rmo-ba* 98.
Forbid *°gegs-pa*; *mi γnaṅ-ba.*
Force s. *mṫu*; *dbaṅ*; *ṅar-ba*; *šed-dbáṅ W.*
Force vb. *dbaṅ-med-du °čol-ba*; v. also *nan-gyis*; *šed-ḱyer-nag-pos W.*
Ford vb. *rgal-ba.*
Fore, — arm *lag-ṅár*; — finger *mdzub-mo*; — part, — side *ṅar*, *ḱa*, *mdun ṅos.*
Foregoing *sṅon-gro*; *sṅa-ma.*
Forehead *ṫod-pa*; *dpral-ba.*
Foreign *yan-pa*; *γžan-ma*; *ṗyii*; — country *byes.*
Forenoon *sṅa-ṫóg*; *sṅa-dro.*
Foreskin *sgo-pur*; *mdun-lpags*, *°dom-lpags.*
Forest *nags(-ma)*, *nags-γseb*; *nags-ṫsal*, *nags-ḱrod*; *ṫsal.*
Forget *rjed-pa*; *yi-γčod-pa*, resp. *ṫugs γyel-ba W.*
Forgive vb. a. (not resenting) *bzod-pa* 498; (to leave unpunished) *°gyod-mi rmo-ba*; (to efface) *sel-ba*; (to wash away) *dag-pa.*
Fork *ḱa-brág*; *ša-°dzin.*
Form s. (mould) *par*; (figure) *dbyibs*; *γzugs*; *čas*; grammatical — *ṫsig.*
Form vb. a. *skyed-pa.*
Former adj. *goṅ*, *goṅ-ma*; *sṅon-°gro*; *daṅ-po*; — part *stod*; — time *sṅon-rol.*
Formerly *sṅa-čád*, *sṅa-goṅ*, *sṅa-bar*; *sṅan*, *sṅar*; *sṅon.*
Fornicate *°čal-ba*; v. *γyem-pa.*
Fornicator *°čál-pa.*
Forsake *skyur-ba*; *°bor-ba*; *γtoṅ-ba.*
Fort *mḱar.*

Forte (in music) *rtsub-po.*

Forth *sogs*; *p̀ar*; *yas.*

Fortress *rdzoṅ(s).*

Fortune (lot) *p̀ya*; (wealth) *ḱa-rǰé* C.; good - *bkra-śis*; —teller *p̀ya-mḱan*; *ṅan-sṅags-mḱan.*

Forward vb. *˳ḱal-ba.*

Found vb. *˳yod-pa*; *rgyag-pa*; *˳debs-pa*; *˳dzugs-pa.*

Foundation *rmaṅ*; — of a house *mt́il*; *ḱaṅ-rtsá.*

Fountain *ču-mig.*

Four *bži*; fourth *bži-pa*; fourteen *ču-bži*; fourteenth *ču-bži-pa*; forty *bži-bču*; fortieth *bži-bču-pa.*

Fourfooted *rkaṅ-bži-pa.*

Fowl *bya*; domestic *ḱyim-bya.*

Fowler *bya-pa.*

Fox *wa*; — coloured *ḱam-pa.*

Fragile *ḱrol-mo* W.

Fragment *čag-ḱrúm*, *čag-dúm*; (*y*)*sil-bu.*

Fragrance *ṅad.*

Frail, to get — *rgud-pa.*

Frame s. *ḱri*; vb. a. *˳god-pa* 95.

Frankincense *bdug-pa*, *gu-gul.*

Fraud *ṅo-lkog*; *zog*, *zol-zóg.*

Free adj. *yaṅ-pa*; *t́ar-pa*; to become — *˳grol-ba*; *t́ar-ba*; to set — *t́ar-du ˳jug-pa*; *˳bul-pa.*

Freeze *˳ḱyags-pa*; *p̀yid-pa.*

Freight s. *ḱal.*

Frenzy *˳ḱrul-pa.*

Fresh *ysar-ba*, *ysar-po*; *so-ma* W.; — butter *skya-már* W.

Friday *yza-pa(-wa)-saṅs.*

Friend *grogs*, *rog*; *ṅo-śés*, *mdza-bśés*, *bśes-ynyén*; *mdza-bo*; *zla-bo.*

Friendly *sṅyiṅ-nyé*; resp. *sol-po.*

Fright s. *˳jigs-pa.*

Frighten *skrag-pa.*

Frightened *skrag-pa*; to be — *rtab-pa.*

Fringes *ḱa-t́sar.*

Frog *sbal-pa.*

From *nas* 304; *man-čad* 411; *las* 546; — within *ḱoṅ-nas* 43.

Frontier *sa-mt́sáms.*

Front-side *ḱa*; *ṅar.*

Frost *ḱyags-pa*; *sad.*

Froth *lbu-ba*, *dbu-ba.*

Frozen *ḱyags-pa.*

Fruit *śiṅ-tóg*; *˳bras-bu*; — tree *bza-śiṅ*; *rtsi-śiṅ.*

Fry vb. *sreg-pa*, *slam-pa*, *rṅód-pa.*

Fuel *bud-śiṅ.*

Fulfil *skoṅ-ba*; *sgrub-pa*; *˳geṅs-pa.*

Full *gaṅ-ba*; *ltem-pa*; *mt́on-po*; to be *ltams-pa*; *˳ḱeṅs-pa*; to make — *ḱyab-pa*

Fully *rgyas-par.*

Fumigate *bdug-pa.*

Fun *pra-čál*; *śags.*

Functionary *blon-po*

Fundament *rtsa-ba*; *rkub.*

Fur-coat *slag-pa*, *slog-pa*; *t́ul-pa.*

Furious *ytum-pa.*

Furnish (supply) *sgrub-pa.*

Furniture *yo-byád.*

Furrow s. *rka.*

Further *yžan-yaṅ*, *yaṅ.*

Furtherance *mt́un-rkyen.*

Futurity *ma ˳oṅs-pai dus*; *p̀ugs.*

G

Gain vb. a. *rgyal-ba*, *rnyed-pa*, *sgrub-pa.*

Gain s. *skyed*; *ḱe*, *ḱye*; *ḱa-rgyál*, *rgyál-ḱa*; *rnyed-pa*; *spogs*, *bogs.*

Gait *bgrod.*

Galaxy *dgu-t́sigs.*

Gale *rluṅ-dmár*, *rluṅ nug-po.*

Gall s. *mḱris-pa.*

Gallop vb. n. *rta rgyug-pa.*

Gallows *čar-śiṅ.*

Game s. (animals of chase) *ri-dwags*

Gander *ṅaṅ-pa.*

Ganges *gaṅ-gā.*

Gap *rgya-sér*; *ser-ka*, *ser-ga.*

Gape vb. *sgyiṅ-ba*; *ydaṅ-ba.*

Garden *t́sal*; *t́sas* W.; *ldum-ra*; *sdum-ra*; — flower *ha-ló.*

Garlic *sgog-pa.*

Garment *gos*; *čas*, resp. *na-bza*; under — *˳aṅ-t́úṅ*; upper — *bla-gáb*, *bla-gós*, *yzan-gos.*

Garret *steṅ-ḱaṅ.*

Gate *rgyal-sgo*; *sgo-mo.*

Gather vb. a. *sgrug-pa*; *˳t́u-ba*; *sog-pa*; vb. n. *˳ḱor-ba*; *˳gugs-pa*; *˳t́ibs-pa.*

Gatherer *t́un*, *˳t́un.*

Gear s. *go-ča.*

Gelding s. *p̀o-rtá.*

General adj. *spyi* 333; *t́un-moṅ.*

General s. *dmag-dpón.*

Generate *skyed-pa.*

Generation *rgyal-brgyúd*; *ydun-raus*, *rabs.*

Genesis *čags-rábs.*

Genitals *mt́san(-ma).*

Genitive case *˳brel-pa.*

Gentian *tig-ta*; *kyi-lčé.*

Gentle *$_o$ǰam-po, $_o$bol-po; mtun-čan; sgye-mo.*
Gentleman *γtso-bo; sa-heb*; old —, old squire, *ga-gá Ld., 'a-ǰo-lag C.*
Gently *ṅaṅ-gis; ga-le C., gu-le W.*
Gentry *drag-rigs.*
Genuine *dṅos; ṅo-rtóg; lhad-méd.*
Geography *γnas-bšád, yul-bšád.*
Germinate vb. n. *skye-ba*; to cause to — *skyed-pa.*
Gesture s. *brda; rnam-gyúr*; v. also *ťsul.*
Get vb. a. *ǩug-pa; rnyed-pa; ťob-pa; $_o$dzin-pa; γod-par $_o$gyur-ba*; vb. n. *$_o$gro-ba; ča-ba W.*; to — into *čud-pa; $_o$bab-pa*; to — through *ťar-ba, bgrod-pa*; to — up *ldaṅ-ba, laṅ-ba*, resp. *bžeṅs-pa.*
Ghost *mi-ma-yin(-pa); sems-nyid.*
Ghostlike *γzugs-méd* 494; *lus-méd.*
Gift s. *$_o$ǩyos-pa; γnaṅ-ba; bya-dgá; $_o$bul-ba; sbyin-pa; yon.*
Gild *čus γtoṅ-ba, γser-čus $_o$byug-pa.*
Gills *nya-skyogs.*
Gimlet *sor.*
Ginger *sga, sgeu; lča-sga.*
Girdle s. *ska-rágs.*
Girl *bu-mo; γžon-nu-ma; na-čuṅ.*
Give *skur-ba; ster-ba; γnaṅ-ba; $_o$bul-ba* 394; *$_o$bogs-pa; sbyin-pa; stsol-ba*; to — an entertainment *$_o$gyed-pa*; to — up *sgyur-ba; γčod-pa; spoṅ-ba; blos γtoṅ-ba*; to be given to *skyoṅ-ba; rten-pa.*
Glacier *gaṅs, gaṅs-čan.*
Glad adj. *dga-ba*; — tidings *γtam-snyán*; to be — *dga-ba; mgu-ba*; to make — **sem ťad čug-če* W.*
Glass *šel, man-šel*; — beads *ga-šél*; bottle *šel-búm.*
Gleaner *snye-ťun.*
Glide *$_o$dred-pa; $_o$byid-pa.*
Glistening *ǩrom-mé, ǩrol-po; čam.*
Glitter vb. *$_o$ťser-ba.*
Globe *ril W.*
Globular *zlum-pa, ril-ba*; a — stone *rdo-ril.*
Glorious *grags-čan; $_o$ṗags-pa.*
Glory s. *grags-pa; dpal, dpal-byór.*
Glory vb. *rlom-pa, ṗo-ťsod $_o$čad-pa*; v. *ṗo-so.*
Gloss *bkrag; $_o$od-γsál.*
Glossy *bkra-ba.*
Glove *lag-šúbs.*
Glue s. *spyin.*
Gnash *so ǩrig-ǩrig byed-pa, so bdar-ba; so sdom-pa.*
Gnaw *γzan-pa; $_o$ča-ba, mur-ba.*
Go *$_o$gro-ba; $_o$doṅ-ba; ča-ba W.; rgyu-ba; bgrod-pa; ṗyin-pa*, eleg. *mči-ba*, resp. *ṗeb-pa*; to — about *$_o$grim-pa*; to — abroad *$_o$gron-du $_o$gro-ba, byes-su $_o$gro-ba*; to — astray *$_o$ǩyar-ba*; to — away *$_o$gye-ba*, resp. *bžud-pa, γšegs-pa*; to — in or into *čud-pa, $_o$ǰug-pa*; to — out *$_o$ťon-pa; spro-ba*; to — round *$_o$ǩor-ba, skor-ba.*
Goal *ťsad.*
Goat *ra-ma*; wild — *ra-rgód, ra-po-čé; skyin.*
Goat's hair *ral.*
Goblet *skyogs.*
Goblin *$_o$dre, lha-$_o$dre.*
God *dkon-mčog*; a god *lha*, a goddess *lha-mo*; a tutelar god *yi-dam-lhá, lha-sruṅ; mgon-po.*
Going s. (the act of) *gros.*
Goitre *lba-ba.*
Gold *γser.*
Gong *$_o$ǩar-rṅá.*
Good adj. *bzaṅ-ba; legs-pa; dga-bdé C.; rgyal-ba W.*; col. *yag-po*; to be — (of coins) *$_o$grul-ba.*
Good s. (advantage) *don.*
Good-bye *da ča yin W.*152; **ṭa-ši-šig* W.*; v. *ga-le C.* 64.
Goods *dṅos-po; ka-ča; ǩa-rǰé C.; spus; zoṅ.*
Goose *ṅaṅ-pa, ṅaṅ-ma.*
Gorge s. (ravine) *roṅ.*
Gossip s. (idle talk) *ǩa-bšád; rgya-láb.*
Gourd *ka-béd, ku-ba, gon W., čuṅ C.*
Gout *draṅ-nád W.; grum-bu, grum-nád, drag-grum; dreg-nad, ťsigs-nad, ťsigs-zúg.*
Govern *sgyur-ba; rgyal-srid skyoṅ-ba; dbaṅ sgyur-ba.*
Government *rgyal-po, rgyal-srid.*
Governor *sde-pa; bka-blón.*
Grace s. *bka-drin, ťugs-rǰe.*
Gracious *ťugs-rǰe-čan.*
Gradually *ṅaṅ-gis; gu-le gu-le W.*
Graft s. *pe-bán.*
Grain s. *čag-tse, rdog-po, $_o$bru.*
Grammar *byā-ka-ra-ṇa* 372.
Grandchild *ťsa-bo*; — daughter *ťsa-mo*; — father *mes-po*; — mother *ma-mo, ṗyi-mo*; — son *ťsa-bo*, resp. *dbon-po.*
Grant vb. (*bka*) *γnaṅ-ba; $_o$grub-pa; stsol-ba; γzigs-pa.*
Granulous *čag-tse-čan W.*
Grape *rgun, rgun-$_o$brúm; čag-mo.*
Grasp vb. *$_o$ǰu-ba, $_o$dzin-pa*; cf. *γčags-pa.*
Grass *rtswa.*
Grasshopper *čog-čog-pa, ča-ga-$_o$bu.*
Grate s. *dra-pa, lčags-dra.*
Grateful *drin-γzo-čan*; to be — *drin γzo-ba.*
Grater *lag-dár, lab-dár.*
Gratitude *drin dran-pa.*
Grave s. *dur-ǩuṅ.*
Gravel s. *gyo-mo; šag-ma.*
Gravy *spags; ša-rúg*, resp. *skyu-rúm.*
Gray *se-bo*; light — *skya-bo.*
Grease s. *snum-pa*; vb. *snum-gyis skud-pa.*
Greasy *snum-čan; ťso-ba.*
Great *če-ba, čen-po, rgyas-pa.*

Greatness če-ba, če-kyád.
Greedy ₀dod-sred-čan; blo-₀dód; ham-pa-čan.
Green sṅo-ba, sṅon-po; ljaṅ-ḱu.
Greens s. sṅo-tsód, ldum, tsod-ma.
Greensward na-ḱa; ne-táṅ.
Grieve vb. n. skyo-ba, ₀gyod-pa.
Grind ₀tag-pa; bdar-ba; to — the teeth so bdar-ba.
Gripes glaṅ, glaṅ-tabs.
Gristle čag-krúm.
Grit (gravel) gyo-mo.
Groan s. ₀ḱog-súgs W., sugs-nár, sugs-riṅ.
Groan vb. ₀ḱun-pa.
Groom rta-rdzi.
Grope snom-pa.
Grotto gyam, pug-pa.
Ground s. žiṅ; yži(-ma) 480; sa-yži 570.
Grouse ri-skyégs; goṅ-mo.
Grove skyed-mos-tsal.
Grow vb. n. čer skye-ba; ₀kruṅ-ba; ₀gyur-ba; rgyas-pa; ča-ba; to — dark ₀tibs-pa; to — old bgre-ba; to cause to grow skyed-pa.
Growth skyed, skye.
Grudge s. ḱon-pa; to bear a — ₀kon-pa.
Grumbling s. *to-tá* W.
Grunt vb. ṅug-pa, ṅur-ba, ḱun-pa.
Guard vb. skyoṅ-ba, skyob-pa, sruṅ-ba.
Guardian pa - tsáb; — of the world jig-rten=skyoṅ.
Guess s. v. tsod 453.
Guide s. lam-mḱan, lam-₀dren-pa, lam-yig.
Guitar sgra-snyan; ko-poṅs W.
Gulf ḱug, ču-ḱug; (abyss) btson-doṅ.
Gullet lkog-ma.
Gulp s. hub; skyu-gáṅ, čor-gáṅ.
Gum s. taṅ-ču.
Gun sgyogs; tu-pag W.; me-mda C.
Gunpowder tu-pag-man W.; me-rdzás C.
Gunstock ₀gu-mdá; sgum-da.
Gut, great — or colon ynye-ma.
Gutter wa.
Guttural s. lče-rtsa-čan 150.

H

Habitation groṅ; ynas-tsaṅ, ynas-ḱaṅ, yži-ma.
Haft yu-ba.
Hail s. (frozen rain) ser-ba; (salutation) v. rgyal-ba I 108.
Hair skra; spu, a little — ba-spu.
Hairy ba-spu-čan; skra-čan.
Half (one half) s. ča 151.
Half adj. pyed; — boot krad-pa.
Hall bkad-sa; — of judgment tsugs-ḱaṅ.
Halo ḱyim.
Halter tur-mgo; srab-mtúr.
Halting-place sti-bai ynas; (night quarters) ₀braṅ-sa, resp. yzim-bráṅ.
Hammer s. to-čuṅ; large — to-ba.
Hand s. lag(-pa), resp. pyag.
Hand vb. a. sriṅ-ba; to — over skur-ba.
Handicraft bzo.
Handful ḱyá-le; ḱyor; ₀čaṅs-pa; spar-ba; pul.
Handkerchief sna-pyis; — of salutation ḱa-btágs 37.
Handle s. kab-za, lčibs, yu-ba.
Handsome mčor-po, mdzes-pa.
Handspike gal-ta.
Hang vb. a. (a man) *čar-la taṅ-če* W.: to — up skar-ba, dgar-ba, ₀gel-ba; ₀pyar-ba; vb. n. to — down ₀jol-ba, ₀ṗyaṅ-ba.
Hangman ysed-ma.
Hank gru-gu.
Happen ₀gyur-ba, ₀byuṅ-ba, ₀oṅ-ba.
Happiness dge-ba, skyid-pa, yyaṅ: bkra-šis.
Happy bkra-šis-pa; skal-ldán, skyid-po; legs-pa; to be — bde-ba, skyid-pa; may you be — bkra-šis-šig W.
Hard kyoṅ, mḱraṅ, mḱregs-pa; sra-ba; — to bear ḱag-po; — water ču kyoṅ-po.
Hardened sran-čan.
Hardness ṅar-ba.
Hardship dka-ba, nyon-moṅs-pa 191.
Hardware lčags-čas.
Hare ri-bóṅ.
Harm s. skyon; to do — tsugs-pa, ynod-pa byed-pa or skyel-ba; vb. to — snad-pa.
Harmony (musical concord) sgra-dbyaṅs; (agreement) mtun-pa; concord amongst kinsmen ynyen-₀dúṅ.
Harness s. čibs-čas.
Harrow s. sal-ba; vb. to — sal-ba ₀drud-pa.
Harsh gyoṅ-po; rtsub-po.
Hartshorn sa-ru.
Harvest s. btsas-ma; lo-tóg 552.
Haste s. tsa-drag; to make — rgyug-pa; make haste! *tsa-rag toṅ* W.; *riṅ-pa toṅ* W.
Hasten vb. n. snyegs-pa; riṅs-pa.
Hasty spro tuṅ-ba; yid tuṅ-ba.
Hate vb. ₀ḱon-pa, ₀gras-pa, sdaṅ-ba.
Hatred sdaṅ-sems, že-sdáṅ.
Haughtiness če-tábs, po-so.
Haughty ḱa-drág, ḱeṅs-pa; če-tabs-čan, po-so-čan.
Hautboy dge-gliṅ; sur-na.
Have (possess) bdog-pa; having v. čan 138,

v. *bčas-pa* 146; I have *ṅa-la yod* 515; I have to v. *rgyu* no. 3, 110.
Hawk s. *k̔ra.*
Hay *rtsa-skám*; — fork *sbrag-ma.*
Haze *k̔ug-rná.*
He *k̔o*, *k̔oṅ*, *de* 255; — who *gaṅ* no. 2 65.
Head s. *mgo*, resp. *dbu*; (chief) *k̔yu-mčog* 47; *ɣtso-bo* 434; (of an argument) *yan-lag*; — master *ₒgo-dpón.*
Head vb. a. *ₒk̔rid-pa*, *sna ₒdren-pa.*
Headache *mgo-nád*; *klad-ɣzér.*
Headman *ₒgo-pa*, *rgad-po.*
Heal vb. a. *ₒtso-ba* 460, *ɣso-ba*; *bčos-pa.*
Health *k̔ams*; *nad-med-pa.*
Healthy *nad-méd.*
Heap s. *p̔uṅ-po.*
Heap vb. a *sgril-ba*, *bčer-ba*, *spuṅ-ba*; to — up *sog-pa.*
Heaped *byur-po*, *byur-byúr* 377; *gaṅ-ba W.* 66.
Hear vb. a. *t̔os-pa*, *t̔sor-ba W.*, *nyan-pa*; hear! *ka-yé.*
Hearer *nyan-pa* or *-po.*
Heart *snyiṅ*, resp. *t̔ugs*; *naṅ*; *rgyud* 112; *že* 477; to know by — *k̔a-ton-du šes-pa* 35.
Heart-grief *sems-nád.*
Hearth *me-t̔áb*; *sgyid-bu* 118; — stone *sgyed-po.*
Heartily *snyiṅ t̔ag-pa-nas.*
Hearty *že-t̔ag-pa*; a — request *že-t̔ag-pai žu-ba.*
Heat *t̔sa-ba*, *tsad-pa*; *t̔an-pa.*
Heated *dros-pa* 264.
Heaven *mk̔a*, *nam-mk̔a*; *ɣnam*, *mt̔o-ris* 242.
Heavens *mk̔a*, *dbyiṅs* 390.
Heavy *lči-ba.*
Hedgehog *rgaṅ*, *ₒgaṅ-ɣzer-ma.*
Heed s., to give — *bya-ra byed-pa.*
Heedless *zon-méd.*
Heel s. *rtiṅ-pa.*
Heifer *zal-mo.*
Height *mt̔o-k̔yad*; *k̔yon*; *rṅams*; *dpaṅs*; *ₒp̔aṅ* 355.
Heir s. *nor-bdag*; joint - *go-k̔an W.*
Hellebore *spru-ma.*
Helm s. *k̔a-lo.*
Helmet *rmog.*
Help s. *skyabs*, *skyobs*, *ra-mda.*
Help vb. a. *skyabs byed-pa*, *grogs byed-pa.*
Helper *skyabs-mgon*, *skyabs-ɣnas*; *ɣnyen-po*, *dpuṅ-ɣnyén*, *dpuṅ-grogs.*
Hem s. *sne-mo*, *č̔a-ga.*
Hemorrhoids *ɣžaṅ-nád*, *ɣžaṅ-brúm.*
Hemp *so-ma*, *ɣtso-ma*, *btso-ma*; *bhaṅ-ge W.*
Hen *bya-mo*; *kyim-bya.*
Henceforth *da-ste*, *da p̔yis* 247, *da p̔yin-čád* 350.
Herb *sño*, *sño-t̔sód*, *rtswa.*
Herd *k̔yu*, *k̔yu-bo.*
Herdsman *rdzi-bo*, *p̔yugs-rdzi.*
Here *ₒdi-ru* 275.
Hereafter *p̔ugs-na*, *da-ste*, *da-p̔yis*, *da p̔yin-čad.*
Heresy *č̔os-lóg.*
Heritage *nor-skal.*
Hermit *dgon-pa-pa*; *bdag-bsrúṅ.*
Hermitage *dgon-pa*, *ɣnas.*
Hero *k̔yo-ga.*
Heron *kaṅ-ka*; *skyar-mo.*
Hesitation *t̔sam-t̔súm.*
Hew *ₒjog-pa*, *ₒt̔sog-pa*; v. also cleave.
Hiccough s. *skyig-bu*; *'i-k̔ug*, *'ig W.*; vb. to — *skyig-pa.*
Hide s. *ko-ba*, *ko-lpags*, *pags-pa* or *-po.*
Hide vb. a. *skuṅ-ba*, *sbed-pa*; to — one's self *ₒgab-pa*, *yib-pa*, *ɣsaṅ-ba.*
Hiding-place *bskuṅs-sa.*
High *mt̔o-ba*, *mt̔on-po*; — and low *drag-žán* 261; — road, — way *rgya-lám*; *ma-lam W.*
Hill *ri*; v. *sgaṅ.*
Hilt *kab-za*, *lčibs*, *yu-ba.*
Hinder vb. a. *ₒgegs-pa*, *ₒk̔egs-pa*; to be — ed *t̔ogs-pa.*
Hind-foot *rkaṅ-pa.*
Hind-part *mjug.*
Hindrance *gegs*, *bgegs*, *bar-č̔ód.*
Hinge s. *sgo-ₒk̔ór.*
Hip s. (joint) *sta-zúr*, *dpyi*; (fruit) *šib-ši-lu-lu Ld.*
Hire s. *rṅan-pa*, vb. to — *ɣyar-ba.*
History *lo-rgyús*, *byuṅ-t̔sul.*
Hit vb. a. *k̔es-pa*, *rgyab-pa*, *t̔ug-pa*, *ₒp̔og-pa*, *ₒtebs-pa W.*
Hit s. *lčag* 148.
Hither *t̔sur*; — to *sña-čad.*
Hive s. *tsaṅ.*
Hoangho *rma-č̔u.*
Hoarfrost *ba-mo.*
Hoarse *ṅar-ṅar-po*, *ₒdzer-po*; to be — *ₒdzer-ba*; *ras-pa Ld.*
Hoarseness *skad-gágs.*
Hoe vb. a. *rko-ba.*
Hog s. *p̔ag.*
Hoist vb. a. *ₒp̔yar-ba.*
Hold vb. a. *čaṅ-ba*, *snom-pa*, *ₒdzin-pa*; to — forth *ₒdzed-pa*; to — out (suffice) *ₒk̔yed-pa*; vb. n. *rten-pa* 213.
Hold s. *rten*; to take - of *ₒju-ba.* [413.
Hole s. *k̔uṅ*, *bi-gán*, *bi-yán W.*, *bu-ga*; *mig*
Hollo interj. *ka-yé*; *kye*, *kye-hó*; *W. wa!*
Hollow adj. *k̔oṅ-stóṅ.*
Hollow s. *k̔uṅ*, *sbug(s)*; the — of the hand *skyor.*
Holly *sgom-ₒbróg.*
Holy *skal-ldán*, *dam-pa*; a — man, saint, *skyes-bu dam-pa.*
Homage s. *bkur-ba*, *bkur-sti*; *rim-gro*, resp. *sku-rím.*
Home s. *k̔yim*; to be at — *k̔yim-du sdod-pa.*

Homeless *ńes-méd.*
Hone s. *ₒdzeń.*
Honest *drań-po, č̓os drań-po.*
Honey *sbrań-rtsi, rań-si W.*
Honour s. *bkur-ba, bkur-sti; sti-stań; ya-ša; rim-gro,* resp. *sku-rim; grags pa, p̓u-dúd.*
Honour vb. a. *bkur-ba, mčod-pa, rje-ba.*
Honourable *btsun-pa.*
Hood s. *t̓od-k̓ebs.*
Hoof *rmig-pa.*
Hook s. *kug.*
Hookah (Turkish pipe) *ci-lim;* resp. *že-hór C*
Hoop s. *šan.*
Hoopoe *p̓u-šúd.*
Hope s. *re-ba; blo-ydéń, blo-ytád;* vb. to — *re-ba.*
Horizon *mt̓oń-ₒk̓or.*
Horn *rwa, ru.*
Hornet *liń-gol-ma.*
Hornless *k̓u-yú.*
Horse s. *rta,* resp. *č̓ibs;* black — *ₒol-ba;* — dung *rta-sbańs;* — tail *rta-rña;* — whip *rta-lčag.*
Horseman *rta-pa.*
Horseshoe *rmig-lčágs.*
Hospital *nad-k̓ań, tsugs-k̓ań.*
Host (number of men) *dpuń, p̓al-po-če;* (army) *dmag.*
Hot *t̓sa-ba, t̓san;* to be — *t̓sa-ba;* the — time of the day *dro* 264.
Hour *ču-t̓sod* 158; double — *k̓yim* 47.
House s. *k̓ań-pa; k̓yim; groń; mk̓ar; sdum-pa C.; nań;* — owner *k̓yim-bdag, k̓yim-pa-pa;* — rent *k̓ań-glá.*
Household *ɣžis-mad; bza-mi* 497.
Housekeeping *so-tsis, so-tsigs.*
Housewife *k̓yim-t̓ab-mo, k̓yim-bdag-mo.*
How *či* 139, *či-ltar, či-tsug, ga-zug, či-nę Bal.;* — much *ga-t̓sód; (či-)tsam.*
However *ₒon-kyań.*
Howl vb. *ńu-ba;* (of animals) *ńur-ba.*
Howling s. (of a tempest) *ₒur-sgra* 500.
Hug vb. a. *ₒk̓yud-pa.*
Hum s. *di-ri-ri* 252; *ₒur-sgra* 500.
Hum vb. *ₒk̓rog-pa.*
Human *mii;* — being *skye-bo.*
Humble adj. *gus-pa.*
Humbleness *ɣčam-bu.*
Humidity *bad.*
Humours (of the body) v. *nyes-pa* 191.
Humming (noise) *ₒur-ₒur;* — of bees *di-ri-ri, zi-ri-ri.*
Hump, Hunch s. *rńog; gye-gu.*
Hundred *brgya.*
Hunger s. *ltogs-pa; bkres-pa.*
Hungry *ltogs-pa, bkren-pa, bkres-pa.*
Hunt, Hunting s. *kyi-ra.*
Hunt vb. a. *rńon-pa, ₒčor-ba, ɣšor-ba.*
Hunter *rńon-pa, kyi-ra-ba, lińs-pa.*
Hurricane *rluń-t̓súb.*
Hurry vb. *grim-pa; rgyug-pa.*
Hurry s. *tsab-tsúb.*
Hurt vb. a. *ɣnod-pa skyel-ba, ɣnod-pa, ₒk̓ań-ba, t̓sugs-pa, ₒt̓se-ba.*
Husband s. *k̓yo, k̓yim-t̓abs, k̓yim-bdag; skyes-pa; dga-grogs; bdag-po;* — and wife (couple) *k̓yo-šúg.*
Husbandry *so-t̓sis, so-t̓sigs.*
Husk s. *lgań-bu, spun-pa, sbur-ma.*
Hut s. *k̓u-tu, pu-lu, spyil-po.*
Hydrophobia *k̓yi-smyón.*
Hypocrisy *k̓a-č̓os; sgyu-zóg; t̓sul-ₒč̓os.*
Hypocrite *k̓a-že mi mt̓suńs-pa.*

I

I pron. *ńa, ńed, ńed-rań* 128, *ńos* 130, *bdag-nyid* 268; I myself *ńa-rań, ńed-rań.*
Ice *dar, čab-brom, gańs, k̓yags-pa.*
Icicle *k̓yags-sdóń.*
Idea *ₒdu-šes; dmigs-pa.*
Identic *mi-ɣnyis-pa* 192.
Idiocrasy *ńań* 125.
Idle adj. *le-lo-čan; kyań-kyóń W.*
If *na* 299, *gal-te* 68; but if *či-ste* 140.
Ignoble *skye-ba dma-ba.*
Ignorance *ɣti-mug, ma-rig-pa.*
Ill adj. and adv. (sick) *nad-pa;* — fed *dńos-ńán; bza-méd;* — humoured *skyo-ba;* — looking *spus-méd;* — luck *rkyen;* to be — *na-ba.*
Illness *nad, na-ba, zug W.*
Illusion *ₒk̓rul-snáń, sgyu-ma.*
Illustrate *ₒgrel-ba;* to — by parables *dpes mt̓son-pa.*
Image *sku;* molten — *blugs-sku.*
Imagine vb. a. *go-ba, sgom-pa, dmigs-pa, sems-pa;* vb. n. *snyam-pa.*
Imbecile *glen-pa, han-ldáń W.*
Imbibe *ₒjibs-pa;* to be imbibed *t̓im-pa.*
Imitate *lad-mo byed-pa.*
Imitation *lad-mo; ₒbag.*
Immaterial (not existing) *dńos-med, ɣzugs-méd.*
Immeasurable *t̓sad-méd, ɣžal-du-med-pa.*
Immediate *ₒp̓ral, p̓ral.*
Immediately *mod-la, de ma-t̓ag-tu* 227.
Immoderate *t̓sod-méd.*
Immoral *ₒčol-pa, mi tsańs-pa* 445.
Impaired *nyams-pa.*

Impart *°bogs-pa.*
Impartial *p̓yogs-méd.*
Impartiality *mnyam-pa-nyid.*
Impeded, to be — *k̓ad-pa.*
Impediment *yegs, °gal-rkyén, bar-č̓ód.*
Imperative mood *ydams-ṅag °doms-pai ťsig* 265.
Imperishable *mi-°jig-pa, rtag-pa.*
Impetuous *ṅar-ma.*
Impious *skal-méd; sdig-byéd.*
Implements *ča-byad, ča-lag, go-č̓a, yo-byád.*
Impolite *gyoṅ-po*; very — *k̓a-gyoṅ-čé.*
Imponderable *yžal-du-med-pa.*
Importance *k̓ag, °k̓os, yal, do-gál, ytsigs.*
Important *lči-ba, k̓ag-čan, °k̓os-čan.*
Impose vb. a. (lay on) *°gel-ba, skul-ba*; (to deceive) *°brid-pa, mgo skor-ba.*
Imposture *mgo-skór; sgyu, ṅo-lkog; rdzub.*
Imprecation *ṅan; byad, byad-stems.*
Impress vb. (on the mind) *k̓oṅ-du čud-pa; yčags-pa.*
Improper *mi-ruṅ-ba.*
Improve vb. n. *°p̓el-ba, ťseṅ-ba.*
Improvement *skyed.*
Impure *skyug-bro, ma-dag-pa.*
In prep. *na, naṅ-na.*
Inattention *yyeṅ-ba, yyeṅs-pa.*
Inattentive *mi °ťsugs-pa.*
Incantation *sṅags, ysaṅ-sṅags, yzuṅs.*
Incense s. *kun-du-ru, gu-gul, bdug-pa.*
Incessantly *k̓or-yug-tu, rgyun-čad-med-par, rgyun-du.*
Inch *sor-mo.*
Inclination *yzuṅ-ba, bag-čags.*
Incline vb. n. (to lean) *°k̓ra-ba.*
Inclined, to be — (disposed) *°dod-pa.*
Income *sleb.*
Incongruous *ya-ma-zúṅ.*
Inconsiderate *yzu-lum-čan, blo-gros-med.*
Inconstant *čol, mi °ťsugs-pa, °gyur-ldóg.*
Incorporeal *lus-méd.*
Incorrect *skyon-čan.*
Increase vb. a. *sgro-°dogs-pa, snon-pa, spel-ba*; vb. n. *rgyas-pa, °p̓el-ba.*
Increase s. *skyed, non-ka.*
Incredible *mi srid-pa, °os-méd W.; yid-čes-su mi ruṅ-ba.*
Indecorous *ṅo-ťsa.*
Indeed *de-ka yod* 255, *mod-pa.*
Indefatigably *skyo-mi-šes-par.*
Indented *čoṅ-čóṅ.*
Independence *raṅ-dbáṅ.*
Index *dkar-čag, gleṅ-yži; ťo.*
India *rgya-gár*, British — *rgya-p̓i-liṅ.*
Indian s. *rgya-gar-pa.*
India rubber *gyig.*
Indicate *ston-pa.*
Indication *mťsan-nyid.*
Indifferent *stoṅ-pa*; to be — to ... *la mi lta-ba.*
Indigence *gyoṅ, dbul-bä, °ǰoṅs-pa.*
Indigent *dbul-po, dbul-°p̓oṅs.*
Indigestion *zas ma žu-ba.*
Indigo *rams*; — colour *mťiṅ.*
Indirectly *zur-du, zur-na W.*
Indivisible *mi-p̓yed-pa.*
Indolent *kyaṅ-kyóṅ W., rgod-bag-čan.*
Indubitable *gor-ma-čag-pa, ydon-mi-za-ba.*
Induce *skul-ba.*
Indulge in vb. n. *čags-pa*; v. also *bag-med-pa* 363.
Industrious *le-lam-k̓an W.; brtson-pa-čan.*
Inexplicable *yya-nyés*; it is — to me *rgyu-mťsan mi šes* or *bšad mi nus.*
Infallible *mi-nor-ba.*
Infant *ču-ma-lóṅ Ld.; p̓ru-gu čuṅ-ba*; — boy *k̓yeu.*
Infect *°go-ba, bsgo-ba.*
Inflammation *°ťsig-pa*; — of the eyes *mig-ťsig (če) W.*
Inflate *°bud-pa; p̓u °debs-pa.*
Inflection *dgu-ba.*
Inflict *skyel-ba.*
Influence s. *dbaṅ*; vb. a. *skul-ba.*
Inform vb. a. *spriṅ-ba, lon zer-ba C., hun taṅ-če W.*
Information *man-ṅág; hun W.*
Infringe *°gal-ba.*
Infuse *°jug-pa.*
Infusion *ťaṅ-gi sman.*
Ingenious *dmigs-čan.*
Inheritance *skal-nór, nor-skal.*
Inject *°jug-pa.*
Injure *°ťse-ba, ynod-pa.*
Injured *nyams-pa.*
Injury *ynod-pa.*
Ink *snag-ťsa*; — powder *snag-p̓yé.*
Inkstand *snag-koṅ; *nag-bhum* C.*
Inlet *ťso-lág C.*
Inmate *naṅ-gi mi.*
Inn *°gron-k̓áṅ.*
Inner *naṅ-gi* 301.
Innumerable *graṅs-méd-pa; tsad-méd.*
Inquire *°dri-ba*; to — closely *žib-tu °dri-ba*; to — rigorously **skar-tag taṅ-če* W.*
Inquiry *brtags-pa.*
Inquisitive *rtogs-°dod-čan.*
Insane *smyon-pa*; to be — *°k̓rul-ba, smyó-ba.*
Insanity *smyo-°bóg.*
Inscription *byaṅ-bu, byaṅ-ma; žal-byáṅ.*
Insect *rkaṅ-drug-ldan-pa; °bu.*
Insensible *k̓al-k̓ól*; to get — *°k̓ol-ba.*
Inseparable *mi-p̓yed-pa, °bral-méd.*
Insert *°dzud-pa.*
Inside s. *k̓oṅ-pa, naṅ-rol.*
Inspect *lta-ba, mgo byed-pa* 91, *žal-ta byed-pa* 473.
Inspection *žal-ta.*
Instance *dpe*; for — *°di-lta-ste, dper-na.*
Instant s. *dar, skad, yud*

Instantly *mod-la.*
Instantaneous *dar γčig-gi; ₒṗral-gyi; yud-tsam-pa.*
Instantaneously *glo-bur.*
Instead *dod-du; ťsab-tu, šul-du.*
Instigate *ṅar ₒdon-pa.*
Instinct v. *raṅ-bžin*, v. *šugs*; sexual — *ro-tsa.*
Institute vb. a. *ₒdzugs-pa.*
Instruction *bka-γdams, bka-naṅ; k̔rid; žal-ta*; instructions *spyad-mtsáms* 456.
Instructive *k̔rid-ₒdebs-su ruṅ-ba.*
Instructor *mk̔an-po*; instructress *mk̔an-mo.*
Instrument *ča-byád, ča-lag.*
Insult vb. *ₒk̔u-ba; ₒk̔aṅ-ba; ťsig rtsub* (or *ṅan*) *zer-ba.*
Insurrection *sde-k̔rugs, ₒk̔rug-pa.*
Intellect *blo-grós.*
Intelligence (knowledge) *rgyus*; (news) *ča.*
Intelligent *sems-mk̔an, blo-rno-ba.*
Intelligible *k̔rol-po; go-sla-ba.*
Intemperate *ťsod-méd.*
Intend *dgoṅs-pa, dga-ba, ča-ba W., ₒdod-pa; sems-pa; sno-ba* 137.
Intent s. *don, bsam-pa.*
Inter vb. a. *skuṅ-ba.*
Intercalary month *zla(-ba)-šol, *da-ṭul* W.* 491.
Intercessor *ṅo-čen* 129.
Intercourse *ₒbrel-ba* 402; to have — *ₒdre-ba, k̔a-bsre-ba, sdeb-pa.*
Interest s. (money) *skyed, ṗar, bed*; (concern) *γzuṅ-ba.*
Interfere *k̔a ₒjug-pa.*
Interior s. *k̔og, k̔oṅ-pa, naṅ* I 301.
Intermediate *bar* 366.
Interpret *ₒgrol-ba.*
Interpreter *skad-pa.*
Interstice *bar, dbrag.*
Interval *bar-skabs, bar-ₒťsáms.*
Intestines *rgyu-ma, loṅ-k̔a, loṅ-ga.*
Into *naṅ-du.*
Intolerable *mi-bzad-pa.*
Intoxicated *čaṅ-čem-čan* 154, *ra-ro-ba* 521, *zi-čan W.*
Intoxication *bzi, ra-ro.*
Intrenchment *rags, ṗag-rags.*
Intrigue s. *gya-gyú.*
Introduce *ₒdzugs-pa.*
Introduction (preface) *sṅon-ₒgro.*
Inundate *γyeṅ-ba, lud pa.*
Inundation *ču ₒk̔yam-pa, ču-nag, ču-rúd.*
Inured v. *sran-pa* 580.
Invective *smad-pai ťsig.*
Inveigh *γše-ba, k̔a kye-če W.*
Invent *dmigs-pa-nas bzo-ba; bsam-blo* or *-mno byas-te sgrub-pa; blo-ťabs ₒťsol-ba.*
Investigate *lta-ba, lta-rtog byed-pa.*
Invincible *γžan-gyis mi ťub-pa* 234.
Invisible *mi-snaṅ-ba.*
Invite *ₒdren-pa, γdan-ₒdren-pa, spyan-ₒdren-pa; šog zer-ba.*
Involuntarily *ga-čád,* (*raṅ*) *dbaṅ-med-du.*
Inward *naṅ-gi* II 301.
Iron s. *lčags*; — ore *lčags-sa*; — slag *lčags-drégs.*
Iron adj. *lčags-kyi.*
Irreligious *skal-méd, čos-méd.*
Irresistible *rgol mi nus-pa.*
Irritable *rtse-reg-če* 440.
Irritate **gob-non-čo-če* W., ťsaṅ ₒbru-ba.*
Isabel (horse) *ṅaṅ-pa.*
Ischury *ču-gags* 157.
Isinglass *nya-spyin.*
Island *gliṅ-ṗrán.*
Issue vb. n. *ₒgye-ba, ₒṗro-ba.*
Issue s. *bu-rgyúd.*
Isthmus *ču-bar, gliṅ-lag-ₒbrél* 541.
It pron. *k̔o* 42, *de* 255.
Itch s. (disease) *rkoṅ-pa.*
Itching s. *ₒbun-pa.*
Itself pron. v. *ṅo* 129; *dṅos-γži* 131.
Ivory *ba-so.*

J

Jackal *če-spyaṅ, dur-spyaṅ, wa-spyáṅ.*
Jackdaw *skyuṅ-ka, lčuṅ-ka.*
Jacket *k̔eu-rtse, k̔e-rtse.*
Jagged *čoṅ-čóṅ.*
Jar s. *rdza-búm.*
Jaundice *mig-sér*; black — *k̔sa-ya nag-po.*
Jawbone *mgal, ₒgram-rús.*
Jealous *če-ré, mig-ser-čan.*
Jealousy *gran-sems, čags-sdaṅ, mig-sér.*
Jehovah *ya-ho-wá.*
Jejune *lto-stoṅ.*
Jelly (gelatine) *ₒgrig-ₒgrig C.*
Jessamine *kun-da.*
Jesus *ye-šu.*
Jest s. *ku-ré, kyal-ka, k̔a-šágs, ga-ža.*
Jest vb. *ku-re byed-pa; rtse-ba.*
Jet of water *ču-mda.*
Jewel *rdo-rje, nor-bu; ṗra, ₒṗra; rin-po-če.*
Join vb. a. *sgrig-pa, ₒdogs-pa, sdud-pa, sbyor-ba, sbrel-ba, zuṅ sdebs-pa*; vb. n. *sdeb-pa*; to — (in singing) *ram-bu ₒdegs-pa.*
Joined *sbyor-la, žor-la.*
Joint s. *ₒbrel-mtsams* 402; *ťsigs* 448.
Jointly *skyus* 28.

Joke s. *ku-ré, kyal-ka, k'a-šágs, ga-ža.*
Joke vb. *rtse-ba.*
Journey s. *lam* 544; a day's — *dgoṅs, dgoṅs-žág.*
Journeyman *las-grogs.*
Joy s. *dga-ba* II 83, *dga-bdé, dga-ts'ór; ṅo-só, spro-ba* II 337, *brod-pa.*
Joyful, to be — *mgu-ba.*
Joyous *dga-mo.*
Judah *ya-hu-dá.*
Judge s. *k'rims-dpon*; district — *yul-dpon.*
Judgment-hall *bka-γšágs.*
Jug *č'u-snod, ben.*
Juggler *sgyu-ma-mk'an.*
Jugglery *ₒp'rul, č'o-ₒp'rul.*
Juice *bč'ud, rtsi.*
Jump vb. *ₒk'rab-pa.*
Juniper *spa-ma.*
Jupiter (*γza*) *p'ur-bu.*
Just adj. *draṅ-po, ts'ul-č'an* 450.
Just adv. v. *raṅ* no. 3 522; — before *k'a-draṅ* 35; — by *ₒgram-du* 98; — he, the very, *k'o-na* 43; — now *ma-tág* 227; — so *de-k'a-ltar* 255.
Justice v. *k'rims* 50; *γšags* 564; chief — *šag-dpon W.*
Justification *rnam-dag rtsi-ba* 314.

K

Kalpa s. v. *bskal-pa* 33.
Keep vb. a. *ₒč'aṅ-ba, sruṅ-ba, skyoṅ-ba* 31; to — back *ₒgegs-pa, skyil-ba*; to — in mind *ₒč'aṅ-ba*; vb. n. *rten-pa* 213.
Keeper *rdzi-bo* 468; *sruṅ-mk'an* 583.
Kernel *rkaṅ*; *rtsi-gú, ts'i-gu.*
Kettle *zaṅs, zaṅs-bu*; — drum *rṅa.*
Key *lde-mig*; (*je-*) *ku-lig W.*
Khams v. *k'ams* 39.
Khatmandu v. *k'o-bóm* 43.
Kick s. *rdog-pa, ₒp'ra-šags.*
Kick vb. a. *ₒp'ra-ba*, v. also *rdog-pa.*
Kid *ra-gu, ri-gu W.*
Kidney *mk'al-ma.*
Kill *γsod-pa, srog γč'od-pa*, resp. *ₒgum-pa, ₒgem-pa.*
Kind s. *k'yad-par, rigs, sna* 316; *rnam-pa* 313; *bye-brag*; of every — *sna-ts'ad.*
Kind adj. *driṅ-č'an, byams-pa*; to be — *mt'un-po byed-pa.*
Kindle *dugs-pa, sbor-ba.*
Kindness *driṅ, bka-driṅ, bdag-rkyén, brtse-ba.*
King *rgyal-po, rje-bo.*
Kingdom *rgyal-k'áms, rgyal-k'ág.*
Kiss s. *ₒo, ₒu.*
Kiss vb. *ₒo byed-pa, k'a γtugs-pa, *k'a lan-č'e* W.*
Kitchen *bkad-sa, γyos-k'aṅ*; *t'ab-ts'aṅ W., sol-k'aṅ C.*; — garden *ldum-ra W.*
Knag *mdzer-pa.*
Knapsack *k'ab-t'a-ka, k'om*; *č'i-ka W.*
Knead *rdzi-ba.*
Knee *pus-mo*; — joint *sgyid-pa*; — pan *lha-ṅá.*
Knife *gri.*
Knit *slé-ba.*
Knock s. (the sound of knocking) *tag-tág*; there is a — *tag-tág zer W.*
Knocker *γtun.*
Knot s. *mdud-pa* 273; *mdzer-pa* 463.
Know *šes-pa, ṅo-šes-pa, rig-pa*, resp. *mk'yen-pa, ṅes-pa C.*; to — by heart *k'a-ton-du šes-pa.*
Knowledge *rgyus, rig-pa, šes-pa.*
Known adj. *rgyus-yod-pa, č'a-yod-pa*; not *γtol-méd, rgyus-med-pa, č'a-med-pa.*
Knuckle s. *sor-ts'igs*; knuckles used as dice *bloṅ-mo.*
Kunawar v. *k'u-nu* 40.

L

Label s. *byaṅ-bu, byaṅ-ma.*
Labour s. *las*, resp. *p'rin-las, bzo.*
Labour vb. a. *las byed-pa.*
Labourer *las-pa.*
Laconic *k'a-ñyúṅ, ts'ig-ñyúṅ.*
Lad *byis-pa.*
Ladder *skad, skas-ka.*
Lade (water) *ₒč'u-ba.*
Ladle s. *t'um-bu, γzar-bu, č'u-γzar, skyogs.*
Lady *jo-mo, btsun-mo*; — of rank *rje-ma*, col. *še-ma*; young — *šem-č'úṅ W.*
Lahul *gar-ža* 67.
Lair *ts'aṅ.*
Lake *mts'o.*
Lama *bla-ma*; Grand — *bla(-ma) č'en-po.*
Lamb *lu-gu, lug-gu.*
Lame adj. *ža-ba, ža-bo, rkaṅ-rdúm.*
Lamed *grum-pa.*
Lament vb. n. *smre-ba, mya-ṅan byed-pa, č'o-ṅe debs-pa.*
Lamentation *č'o-ṅe, ₒo-dód.*
Lamp *mar-mé, sgron-ma, 'oṅ-gu, *žum-mar-pa* C., rkyoṅ-tse W.*
Lampblack *sgron-dregs.*

Lampoon s. sgo-yig.
Land s. (cultivated) kluṅs; (dry land) skam-sa; — owner žiṅ-bdág.
Landlord (of a house) bran-dpon; — (of the ground) sa-bdag.
Landscape sa-ynás.
Landslip sa-rúd.
Lane lam-sraṅ.
Language skad, sgra; — master skad-pa.
Languid nyams-čuṅ, nyams-tag-pa, yčoṅ-ba C., šed-méd W.; to get — rgod-pa.
Lantern sgron-ma, paper — goṅ-žu.
Lap s. (coat-tail) grwa; (bosom) paṅ, resp. sku-páṅ.
Lard s. grod-tsil.
Large rgyas-pa, čen-po, rgya-čen-po, yaṅs-pa.
Lark čo-ga, lčo-ga; ča-čir Ld.
Larynx ḱol-mdúd, 'ol-mdúd.
Last adj. rjes 181, ta-ma 226, pyi-ma, rtiṅ-ma W.; — night mdaṅ; — will ḱa-čéms, bka-čéms; — year ḱa-niṅ, sṅa-lo, na-niṅ.
Last vb. n. ˳tso-ba.
Lasting adj. rtag-po.
Lastly mtar 240.
Latch s. ˳ḱor-gyág, ˳ḱor-yya.
Late pyi-mo; later (subsequent) pyi-ma; to be late ˳pyi-ba.
Lately da-či, *dę-zag-la* 275.
Lath lčam, pyam.
Lathe sḱor-spyád.
Latter pyi-ma.
Lattice dra-ba.
Laudable stod-˳os.
Laugh vb. n. dgod-pa, rgod-pa, bžad-pa.
Laughter gad-mo, rgod.
Laurel, — leaf *šiṅ-tse lo-ma* W.
Law ḱrims, bka-ḱrims; to go to — *tim žu-če* W.
Lawsuit ḱrims, ḱrim-šágs.
Lawyer ḱrims-pa.
Lax adj. kyom.
Laxative s. bšal-smán.
Lay vb. a. snyol-ba, sgyel-ba, bsnyal-te bžag-pa; ˳grems-pa; to — aside skyuṅ-ba, ˳pud-pa; to — on ˳gel-ba, stad-pa; to — out (to expend) skyag-pa, ˳dzugs-pa; (to plan) ˳god-pa; (to display) yčal-ba; to — over (to spread over) sgron-pa; to — up bkrí-ba, bdoġ-pa.
Layman ḱyim-pa, gaṅ-zág; mi-nag skye-bo 29.
Laziness le-lo, le-lo-nyid.
Lazy le-lo-čan, kyaṅ-ḱyóṅ W.
Lead s. ža-nye, ža-ne, ra-nye; rin-di W.; — pencil yya-tig, ˳bri-smyúg.
Lead vb. a. ˳ḱrid-pa, tog ˳dren-pa, sna ˳dren-pa.
Leaf lo-ma.
Leak vb. n. rdol-ba.
Lean adj. skam-ši, skem-po, žag-méd.
Lean vb. (against) snye-ba.
Leap vb. mčoṅ-ba, ˳par-ba.
Learn slob-pa.
Learned adj. mḱas-pa.
Learning s. rig-pa, šes-pa.
Lease s., to take a — nyo-ba.
Leather s. ko-ba, ko-lpags, bse; — shoe ko-krád; — sieve ko-tsag.
Leave s. ynaṅ-ba; — of absence bka-bkrol, dgoṅs-pa; to take — v. pyag 347.
Leave vb. ˳jog-pa, ytoṅ-ba, ˳bor-ba.
Leaven s. žo-ri W.; v. ru-ma 531.
Lecture s. gleṅ-brjod, gleṅ-mo.
Lecturer sgrog-pa-po; —'s chair čos-ḱri.
Leech s. ḱrag-˳tuṅ-˳bu W.; srin-bu pad-ma.
Leek sgog-pa.
Left adj. yyon-pa; — hand yyon-ma; handed yyon-lag-byed-pa; gyog-po.
Leg rkaṅ-pa.
Legalize bkar-˳dogs-pa.
Legend sgruṅs.
Legendary tales rnam-tár.
Leisure loṅ, čog-ka; to have — čog-pa.
Lemon gam-bu-ra, spyod-pád.
Lend yyar-ba.
Length dkyus, riṅ-ḱyád, srid.
Leopard yzig; snow — ysa.
Leprosy rno, mdze.
Lessen vb. n. ˳grib-pa; je-nyuṅ je-nyuṅ-bar ˳gyur-ba.
Lesson s. ḱa-ta, resp. žal-ta; rgyugs W.
Lest conj. v. dogs-pa 258.
Let vb. (to — in, to — loose etc.) ytoṅ-ba; ˳jug-pa II, no. 2 178.
Letter (of the alphabet) yi-ge; (epistle) yi-ge, resp. bka-šóg; — case yi-gei šubs.
Lettuce ldum.
Level vb. a. snyoms-pa.
Lever yšo-mo.
Liar ḱram-pa, zog-čan.
Libation mčod-pa, mčod-ston 166.
Libel s. sgo-yig.
Liberal mig-yáṅs.
Liberate ˳grol-ba.
Liberty tar-pa, raṅ-dbán; to be at — čog-pa.
Libidinous čags-sred-čan, ˳čol-pa.
Librarian deb-ter-pa.
Library kun-dga-ra-ba; yig-ḱaṅ.
Lick vb. ldag-pa.
Lid ḱa-ḱébs, ḱa-gáb, ḱa-yčód, ḱa-leb; čab-ma.
Lie s. rdzun, šob, šab-šób W.
Lie vb. (to tell a lie) rdzun smra-ba or byed-pa.
Lie vb. (down) nyal-ba; to — with *tig-pa čo-če* W., bšo-ba.
Life srog, ˳tso-ba, yson-pa, tse 450; — long nam ˳tsoi bar-du.

Lift vb. *ker-ba, ₒk̓yog-pa, ₒdegs-pa, spor-ba, ₒp̓yar-ba, seṅ-ba.*
Light s. *ₒod, snaṅ-ba.*
Light adj. (not heavy) *yaṅ-po*; (not dark) *skya-bo*; — blue *sṅo-skya*; — gray *dkar-skya*; — green *ljaṅ-skya*; — red *dkar-dmar*; — yellow *ser-skya.*
Light vb. a. *sgron-pa, sbor-ba.*
Lightning s. *glog, glog-ka, tog.*
Like adj. (similar) *mnyam-pa, mtsuṅs-pa, tsogs-se W.*; adv. (in the same manner) *lta, ltar. naṅ-tar W. C.*
Like vb. a. . . . *la dga-ba.*
Likelihood *ṅo.*
Likeness *bzo, zo.*
Likewise *yaṅ.*
Limb *yan-lag.*
Lime *rdo-żó.*
Limit s. *mta, mu.*
Line s. *tig*; *yig-p̓rén.*
Lineage *brgyud, rigs, rigs-brgyúd, rus, rus-pa.*
Linger *ₒgor-ba.*
Lining s. *naṅ-śa.*
Lion *seṅ-ge*; lioness *seṅ-ge-mo.*
Lip *k̓a-lpágs, mču, k̓a-mču.*
Liquid s. *k̓u-ba, rlan-rlón.*
List s. *to*; — of goods *rjed-byáṅ.*
Listen *nyan-pa.*
Literature *čos, rig-pa.*
Litter s. (palanquin) *k̓ad, k̓yogs, ₒk̓yogs*; (bier) *dgu-k̓ri C.*
Little adj. *čuṅ-ba, nyuṅ-ba, p̓ra-ba, p̓ran, p̓ran-bu, dman-pa.*
Little s. (a little) *čig, čuṅ, čuṅ-żig, tig-tsám, tsa-big, 'a-tsig W., a-li C.*; adj. *čuṅ-ba.*
Live vb. n. (to be alive) *ɣson-pa* 591; (to dwell) *ɣnas-pa* 310, *ₒdug-pa* 277, *ₒk̓od-pa* 56; (to behave) *ₒgrul-ba* 100; to — by or on *za-ba* 485, *ₒtso-ba* 460.
Lively *ɣčaṅ-po, k̓ram-pa.*
Liver *mčin-pa* 165.
Lizard *skyin-gór, da-byid, rgag-čig Ld.* 103, *ma-la-la-tsé Ld.* 409.
Load s. *k̓al, k̓ur, rgyab, rgyab-k̓al* 107, *sgal* 114, *dos* 260.
Load vb. a. *ₒgel-ba, ₒk̓el-ba.*
Loadstone *k̓ab-lén.*
Loaf *kor-kór, dog W.* 257.
Loan s. *skyin-pa*, resp. *kar-skyin.*
Locality *ɣnas, skye-ɣnás* 28.
Lock s. (of hair) *ral-pa.*
Lock s. (of a door) *lčags, *go-čag* C., ku-lig W.*
Lock vb. a. *ɣčod-pa*; to — up *ₒgegs-pa*; *gar-te* or *gyaṅ-du bor-če W.*, v. *sgyoṅ-ba* 119.
Locust *tsa-ga-ₒbu, ča-ga-ₒbu.*
Lodgings *ɣnas-tsaṅ, ₒbraṅ-sa.*
Log *dog W.*
Logic *tsad-ma, rigs-pa.*
Loins *rked-pa.*
Loiter *ₒgor-ba.*
Lonely *dben-pa.*
Long adj. *riṅ-ba, dkyus-riṅ*; as — as v. *bar* 366.
Long vb. n. *rkam-pa, skam-pa, ɣduṅ-ba, żen-pa.*
Look vb. (to view) *lta-ba*, resp. *ɣzigs-pa*; (to appear) *snaṅ-ba*; to — at or on *ltos-pa*; to — down upon *ₒgyiṅ-ba*; to — upon as *sgom-pa.*
Look s. *lta-staṅs, ṅo*; — out *so, bso.*
Loose adj. *kyom, lhod-pa.*
Loose, Loosen vb. a. *glod-pa, grol-ba.*
Looseness *ₒk̓ru-ba.*
Lop vb. a. *ₒgrum-pa.*
Lord s. *mgon-po, jo-bo, rje-bo, dpon-po, dbaṅ-po, ɣtso-bo*; — of the manor *ɣżi-bdág.*
Lose *rlog-pa, ₒbud-pa W.*; to — colour *dkyug-pa*; to be lost *stor-ba.*
Loss *gud, gun, god, god-pa, god-ma.*
Lot s. (fortune) *skal-ba*, resp. *sku-skál*; *las-bskos* (v. *sko-ba*); *p̓ya*; to cast lots *mo ₒdebs-pa, rgyan rgyab-pa* 107, *rtags-ril btaṅ-ba W.* 212.
Lotus *ku-mu-da, pad-ma* 322.
Loud *mton-po, skad čen-po.*
Louse s. *śig.*
Love vb. a. *čags-pa, *čags-żen čo-če* W., ɣduṅ-ba, ₒp̓reṅ-ba, brtse-ba, mdza-ba* 461, **żen-ₒdzin čo-če* W., ɣčes-par byed-pa* or *ₒdzin-pa.*
Love s. *čags-pa, snyiṅ-brtse-ba*, resp. *tugs-brtse-ba, duṅs-pa, dran-séms, byams-pa, byams-sems.*
Lover *ₒdod-grogs, mdza-grogs, bzaṅ-grogs*; *ₒdod-mk̓an.*
Low *dma-mo, dman-pa*; *snyan-pa.*
Lower adj., — part of a thing *smad, śam, ɣśam, śod*; — — of the body *ro-smád.*
Lowland *smad, man-čád.*
Luck s., good — *śis*, bad — *rkyen.*
Lucky *bkra-śis-pa.*
Luggage *ča-lág.*
Lukewarm *mal-la-mul-le.*
Luminous *ₒod-čan.*
Lump *goṅ-po, goṅ-bu, gog, dog.*
Lunar *zla-bai*; — mansions *rgyu-skar* 111.
Lunch, Luncheon s. *dro* 264.
Lungs *glo-ba.*
Lurk *sgug-pa, ₒjab-ste sdod-pa, lkog-ₒjab byas-te lta-ba.*
Lurking-place *bskuṅs-sa.*
Lust s. *ₒdod-pa, ₒdod-čags, čags-pa, ro-tsa.*
Lustful *čags-sred-čan, ₒčol-pa.*
Lustre *bkrag, ₒtser-ba.*
Lynx *dbyi, ɣyi.*

M

Mace (club) *ga-da.*
Machine *°p̔rul-°k̔or.*
Mad *smyoṅ-pa*; to be — *smyo-ba.*
Madam, dear — *bžin-bzaṅ-ma.*
Madder *btsod.*
Madness *°k̔rul pa, smyo-°bóg.*
Magazine *ts̔oṅ-k̔aṅ, mdzod.*
Maggot *ša-°bu.*
Magic s. *°p̔rul*; adj. *°p̔rul-gyi*; — sentence *γzuṅs*; — tricks *čo-°p̔rul*; — wheel *°p̔rul-°k̔or.*
Magician *°ba-po.*
Magistrate *°go-pa, °go-yod Ld.*; village — *yul-dpon.*
Magnificence *rṅam-pa, dpal, dpal-byór, byin.*
Magnolia *tsam-pa-ka.*
Magpie *skya-ga, ka-ta k̔ra-bo.*
Maid, Maiden *bu-mó*; lady's — *žal-ta-ma*; — servant *k̔ol-mo, γyog-mo.*
Mail (armour) *k̔rab, ya-lád.*
Maim vb.a. *p̔ran γčod-pa, sug-pa °dreg-pa.*
Main adj. *mčog*, v. also *γžuṅ*; — dogma *γsuṅ-mčog*; — point *don* 259, *γnad*; — substance *ṅo-bo-nyid.*
Maintain *smra-ba, °dod-pa*, resp. *bžed-pa*; *smras-pa-la brtan-par γnas-pa.* [*ts̔áb* 375.
Maitreya *byams-pa mgon-po* 109; *rgyal-*
Majestic *rṅom-bag-čan, γzi-brǰid-čan.*
Majesty *rṅam-pa, rṅom-brǰid.*
Make vb. a. *byed-pa*, eleg. *bgyid-pa*, resp. *mdzad-pa, sgrub-pa, °č̔a-ba, bzo-ba, °ǰug-pa, bčo-ba*; to be made *°grub-pa.*
Maker *mdzad-po.*
Malabar *ma-la-ya.*
Male adj. *p̔o*; — child *k̔yeu*; *bu*; — person *skyes-pa.*
Malediction *byad, byad-stem(s).*
Malice *γnod-sems.*
Malicious *blo-nyés.*
Mallow *čam-pa ta-lo.*
Man s. (human being) *mi, rkaṅ-γnyis-pa*; *laṅs-gro, skye-bo, skyes-bu, gaṅ-zag*; (male) *p̔o, skyes-pa*; — servant *k̔ol-po, bran-k̔ól*; waiting — *žal-ta-pa.*
Mane *rṅog, ltag-spu.*
Manger *k̔yi-γžóṅ*; *bres.*
Manifest adj. *mṅon-pa.*
Manifestly *ṅos-su.*
Manifold *sna-ts̔ogs, sna-maṅ-ba*; *p̔al čér.*
Mankind *skye-bo, skye-dgú, skye-rgú*; *mi-rabs, mi-rigs.*
Manly *k̔yo-gai*; — age *dar-ma.*
Manner *ts̔ul, lugs, rnam-pa* no. 4,313; *stabs, staṅs, sgros, čos* no. 5, 163.
Mansion, lunar — *rgyu-skar* 111.
Manufacture s. *bzo.*
Manufacture vb.a. *°god-pa, sgrub-pa, bčo-ba, bzo-ba.*
Manure s. *lud*; vb. a. *lud γtoṅ-ba.*
Many *maṅ-po, du-ma, dgu*, a good — *ga-čén*; how —? *du*; so — *de-snyéd.*
Map s. *bkod-pa, žiṅ-bkod W.*; **sa-t̔a* C.*
Maple *γya-li Sik.*
March vb.n. *°grod-pa, °grul-ba*; to — about *°grim-pa.*
March s. *rkaṅ-grós.*
Mare *rgod-ma, mo-rta.*
Margin *ṅos, zur, mt̔a.*
Marigold *gur-kúm.* [*bkur-sti.*
Mark s. *rtags, mts̔an(-ma)*; — of honour
Market *ts̔oṅ-°dus*; — place *k̔rom.*
Marmot *p̔yi-ba, °p̔yi-ba.*
Married adj., a — man or woman *k̔yim-t̔ab*; a — woman *bdag-tu byas-pai bud-med*; to get — (both of man and woman) *k̔yo-šug-tu °du-ba* 276; (of a woman) *mi žig-gi čuṅ-mar byed-pa* 159.
Marrow *rkaṅ*; *ṅo-bo-nyid*; spinal — *klad-γžuṅ.*
Marry vb. a. (to take a wife) *čuṅ-ma len-pa*; (to unite in matrimony) *k̔yo-šug-tu sdud-pa.*
Mars *mig-dmár.*
Marsh *gram-pa*; *°dam.*
Marvelous (*ṅo*) *mts̔ar-ba* 456; v. also *ya-mts̔an-po* 505.
Mask s. *°bag.*
Mason *rtsig-bzo-pa.*
Masquerade *°bag-°č̔am.*
Mass (lump) *goṅ-po*, (heap) *p̔uṅ-po*, (bulk) *lhun*, (multitude) *k̔rod-pa.*
Mast (flag-staff) *dar-po-č̔é.*
Master *mgon-po, mṅa-bdág, bdag-po, dpon-* [*po.*
Mat s. *stan.*
Match s. (equal) *k̔a-ya, do*; v. *čar* 156; v. *ya* 504; (lunt) *p̔a-til, pa-til.*
Matchless *°gran-zla-med-pa, °gran-ya-méd, do-méd, mts̔uṅs-méd.*
Mate s. (companion) *do-zla*; *ya-do W.*
Material s. *rgyu.*
Material adj. *dṅos-čan, γzugs-čan.*
Mathematician *rtsis-pa.*
Matter s (substance) *rgyu, dṅos-po, rdzas, zaṅ-ziṅ*; (in physics) *bem-po, γzugs*; (pus) *ču-ser, ču-rnag, rnag.*
Matter vb. n.; it does not — *čaṅ mi sto*; what does it —? *či sto.*
Mattock *°ǰor, tog-tse.*
Mattress *sob-stán.*
Maw *lkog-sóg, ze-búg.*
Maxim *bka-rtags.*
Meadow *spaṅ, spaṅ-po, ne-t̔án, ne-ma.*
Meagre *skem-pa, rid-pa.*

Meal (flour) *ṗye.*
Mean adj. *gyi-na, ṅan-pa, btsog-pa.*
Mean vb. *go-ba, snyam-pa, ˳du-ṡes-pa; yin-pa* 510.
Meaning s. *bsam-pa*, resp. *dgoṅs-pa; don.*
Means s. *grabs, ṫabs*; by all — *ṅes-par, gaṅ-gis kyaṅ, čis kyaṅ*; by no — *re-skán*; by what —? *čis*; by — of *sgo-nas* 115
Measure s. *skar-ṫsád, bre, ṫsad, ṫsod*; to take — *skad-če, ṫsod ˳dzin-pa*; measures (arrangements) *grabs*; to take — *grabs byed-pa.*
Measure vb. a. *˳ǰal-ba, dpog-pa, ṫsod ˳dzin-pa, nyams-len-pa, yṡor-ba.*
Meat s. *ṡa*, resp. *skrum; za-ba*, resp. *bżes-pa*; dried — *skam-saṅ*; — and drink *bza-btúṅ*; — jelly *ṡa-spyin*; — pie *mog-móg W.*
Mecca *ma-ḱá.*
Mechanic s. *bzo-pa*; mechanics' institution *bzo-grá.*
Meddle *ḱa ˳ǰug-pa, ṫe-ba.*
Mediator *bar-mi.*
Medicine *sman.*
Meditate *sems-pa*, resp. *dgoṅs-pa, lta-ba, sgom-pa, bsam-mno byed-pa*, resp. *ṫugs-bsam yṫoṅ-ba.*
Meditation *sgom, sgom-pa, rnal-˳byór.*
Medley *čag-ga-čog-gé.*
Meet vb. a. *ṫug-pa, ˳prad-pa, mǰal-ba*; vb. n. *˳dzom-pa*; to go to — *ydan-˳dren-pa.*
Meeting s. *˳du-ba, ˳dus-pa*; — house *˳dun-ḱaṅ, ṫsogs-ḱaṅ*; — place *˳dus-sa.*
Melody *mgur, dbyaṅs.*
Melon *ga-gón.*
Melt vb. a. *˳ju-ba, żu-ba*; melted, molten *żun-pa, żun-mo*; melting-spoon *żu-kyóg.*
Member *yaṅ-lag, ṫsigs* 448.
Memorandum-book *rǰed-ṫo.*
Memorial stone *rǰed-rdó.*
Memory *dran-pa.*
Menace vb. *˳gam-pa.*
Mend vb. a. *glan-pa.*
Mendacious *ḱram-sems-čan.*
Mendicant adj. *spraṅ-po*; — friar *spraṅ-bán.*
Menses, Menstruation *ḱrag ˳dzag-pa, zla-mṫsán.*
Mention vb. a. *˳god-pa*; to be mentioned (in a book etc.) *˳byuṅ-ba.*
Merciful *snyiṅ-rǰe-čan*, resp. *ṫugs-rǰe-čan.*
Mercury (planet) *lhag-pa*; (metal) *dṅul-ču.*
Mercy *snyiṅ-rǰe, ṫugs-rǰe.*
Mere *˳ba-żig.*
Merely *ṡa-stag, ṡa-dag.*
Merit s. *bsod-pa.*
Merry *ḱrul-po, sems-spro-ba, spro-sems-čan; dga-ba, dga-mo.*
Mesh *˳gug(s) W.*
Mess (dish) *skyu-rúm, spags.*
Message *ṗrin, ˳ṗrin, lon*, resp. *bka-ṗrin.*
Messenger *ṗo-nya, mi-sná.*
Metal *żu-bai ḱams*; cast — *blugs-ma.*
Metaphor *ṅag-snyán, ˳dra-dpe.*
Meteor *ke-tu.*
Method *čo-ga, ṫabs, ṫsul, lugs.*
Metropolis *rgyal-sa, mṫil.*
Mewing s. (of a cat) *mea˰o.*
Mid-day *nyin-guṅ, dguṅ, ydugs.*
Middle s. *dkyil, rked-pa, koṅs, guṅ, dguṅ dbus, yżuṅ.*
Middle adj. *bar-pa, bar-ma, briṅ*; — finger *kan-ma, guṅ-mo, bar-mdzub.*
Midnight *nam-ṗyéd, mṫsan-dkyil, mṫsan-guṅ, mṫsan-ṗyed, dguṅ*, v. *guṅ* 69.
Midriff *mčin-dri*
Midst s. *koṅs, dbus.*
Might *mṅa, mṅa-ṫáṅ, dbaṅ, dbaṅ-ṫáṅ.*
Mighty *ḱa-drág, rgyas-pa, dbaṅ-čan, btsan-po.*
Migrate *˳ṗo-ba.*
Milch cow *bżon-ma.*
Mild *dul-ba, srun-pa, bsrun-pa.*
Mile *dpag-ṫsád.*
Milk s. *żo, ˰o-ma*; sour — *żo-ri W*, *ru-ma C.*; — pail *˰o-zó.*
Milk vb. a. *˳jo-ba, ˰o-ma ˳jo-ba, ˰o-ma ˳ṫsir-ba.*
Milky-way *dgu-ṫsigs.*
Mill s. *raṅ-˳ṫag.*
Millet *ḱre, či-tse.*
Million *sa-ya*; ten — *bye-ba.*
Millstone *ḱod.*
Milt *mčer-pa.*
Mind s. *sems, blo, yid, nyams, snyiṅ, snyam-pa, że*, resp. *ṫugs*; to have a — *dga-ba, ˳dod-pa*; to keep in — *dran-pa, yzo-ba.*
Mind vb. a. *lta-ba, ynyer-ḱa byed-pa* 194; never —! v. *čis kyaṅ* 141.
Mine s. *ḱuṅs, yter-ḱa.*
Mine pron. *ṅai* 124.
Minister s. *blon-po*; prime — *bka-blón.*
Mint (plant) *dag-či Lh.*
Minute s. *ču-sraṅ.*
Minute adj. *ṗra-ba, żib-pa.*
Miracle *ltas, ya-mṫsan.*
Mirage *dri-zai groṅ, mig-sgyu.*
Mischief *skyug, ṅan*; — maker *bstan-ṡig.*
Miserable *gyi-na, ṅan-pa, ṫu-ba. sdug-bsṅal-čan.*
Miserly *bkren-pa.*
Misery *nyon-moṅs-pa, zag-pa.*
Misfortune *bkra-mi-ṡis, rkyen, skyon, ṅan, byur, byus.*
Mishap *gal-rkyén.*
Miss s. (young lady) *ṡem-čúṅ W.*
Miss vb. *ṫal-ba, mi ḱes-pa.*
Missive s. *bka-rgya, če-dón* 160

Mist na-bún, rmugs-pa.
Mistake s. ˳ḱrul-pa, ˳ḱrul-γži, ˳gol-sa, nor-ba, ˳dzol-pa.
Mistake vb. nor-ba, ˳ḱrul-ba.
Mistaken adj. ˳ḱrul-ba, ˳ḱrul-pa.
Mistress (instructress) mḱan-mo; (head of a household) ǰo-mo, dpon-mo; (lady) btsun-mo 435.
Mix sdeb-pa, spel-ba 331, sre-ba; to be mixed with ˳dre-ba.
Mixture spel-ma, sbyor-ba II no. 2, 406.
Mock vb. t́o-˳t́sam-pa.
Mode (manner) skabs, stabs, lugs.
Model s. dpe 327.
Moderate adj. ˳briṅ, t́sod-ċan.
Moderately ˳briṅ-gis; ran-par.
Modest ḱan-man, ḱram-pa, ˳dzem-bag ċan.
Modesty ḱrel, ḱrel-yod, ḱrel-˳dzóm.
Mohammedan, Mohammedanism kla-klo.
Moisture bċud, bad.
Moment skad, bsgaṅ, yud.
Monastery dgon-pa, čos-sdé, grwa-sa.
Monday γza-zla-ba.
Money dṅul, nor; ready — rnags; smar-ba, šmar-rkyáṅ; — changer nor-bdag.
Mongol sog-po.
Monk grwa-pa, mgo-rég, čos-pa.
Monkey spra 335, spre, spreu 337.
Month zla-ba; intercalary — ḍa-t́úl W. 51.
Moon zla-ba, zla; full — nya-rgyas zla-ba; half — i. e. first und last quarter da-ṕéd W.; new — zla-nág 491; waxing and waning — ṅo, ṅos v. ṅo no. 5, 129.
Moral adj. t́sul-ċan, t́sul daṅ mt́un-pa; mt́sul-ḱrims-kyi; dge-bai; čos-kyi; also sems-kyi, yid-kyi; — doctrine čos no. 2, 163.
More lhag 600.
Moreover deï steṅ-du 222.
Morning sṅa-dro, sṅa-mo W., naṅ-mo; the next — t́o-ráṅs, naṅ-par; this — da-náṅ; yesterday — ḱa-náṅ; — twilight skya-réṅs, skya-'ód W.
Morrow, to — saṅ, t́o-re W.
Mortal s. mi(i)-bu; adj. (perishable) zin-pai; mi rtag-pa; (deadly) srog-len.
Mortar (for pounding) mčig; (short cannon) sgyogs; (cement) ˳ǰim-pa, ka-lag W.
Most kun-las lhag or maṅ-po; v. also ṕul-čér 342.
Moth mug-pa.
Mother ma, resp. yum; 'a-ma; — in law sgyug-mo; gyos-mo.
Motherless mas dben-pa.

Mother-of-pearl nya-ṕyis.
Motion ˳gul-ba, γyo-ba.
Motionless adv. ma γyo-bar, ma ˳gul-bar, ma γyens-par.
Motive rgyu.
Mould s. (form) par 328; (fungus) ham-pa.
Mould vb. a. ˳god-pa, ˳čos-pa, ˳dag-pa 274.
Mouldy ham-por čags-mḱan W.
Mound dur-ṕuṅ 254.
Mount vb. žon-pa, resp. ˳čib-pa.
Mountain ri; — pass la; — pasture ˳brog.
Mourn mya-ṅan byed-pa.
Mournful mya-ṅan-gyi; — song skyo-glu.
Mouse s. byi-ba, tsi-tsi; sa-bi-lig W.
Mouth ḱa, resp. žal.
Mouthful s. ċor-gáṅ, ċor-ċig.
Move vb. a. skyod-pa, sgul-ba, γyo-ba; to — to and fro γyeṅ-ba 518; *šrul-ċe* W. (v. srul-ba 583); vb. n. rgyu-ba, ˳gul-ba, resp. ˳čags-pa 167; to — a little nur-ba 305; to — on ˳gro-ba; to — quickly to and fro ˳gyu-ba 96; to — round skor-ba.
Mow rṅa-ba, rṅab-pa.
Much drags, maṅ-po, rab; as — as ga-tsám W., tsam 430; so — ˳di-snyéd, de-snyéd; very — maṅ-drags, šin-tu maṅ-po.
Mucus snabs, lud-pa.
Mud ka-lag, ˳ǰim-pa, ˳dam, mer-ba, rdzab, ˳dam-rdzáb; — floor skyaṅ-núl.
Muddy man-mún.
Mulberry ẓo-se.
Mule dre, dre-po, dre-mo.
Multiply vb. a. sgyur-ba, sgril-ba, sgre-ba, spel-ba, ˳ṕel-ba.
Multitude ḱrod-pa, ḱrom, dmag, γseb.
Murder vb. a. γsod-pa; s. γsod-γċód.
Murderer γsod-byéd.
Muscle (anatomy) ša, nya.
Muse vb. n. rtog-pa.
Mushroom ša-mo, mog-ša W.
Music rol-mo.
Musk gla-rtsi; — bag gla-bai lte-ba; — deer gla-ba.
Musket me-dá C.; — ball rdeu, rde.
Mustard ske-t́sé, skye-t́sé, yuṅs 512.
Mute adj. lkugs-pa, han-ldáṅ W.
Mutter vb. a. sam(-ma) sum(-me) zer-ba W.; to — prayers ma-ṇi taṅ-ċe W., zla-ba, zlo-ba 491.
Muzzle s. ḱa-mt́súl, mt́súl-pa.
My pron. nai, eleg. bdag-gi, ṅed-kyi.
Myriad (čig-)ḱri.
Mystic s. rgyud-pa.

N

Nail s. *γzer, zer, p̔ur-pa*; a little — *γzi-ru, γzer-bu*; — of a finger or toe *sen-mo*, resp. *p̔yag-sén, žabs-sén.*
Naked *sgren-mo, γc̀er-bu, rj̀en-pa.*
Name s. *miṅ*, resp. *mts̔an.*
Name vb. *miṅ γtogs-pa, skad-pa, °grag-pa, zer-ba.*
Namely *de-yaṅ, de ˏaṅ*; *°di-lta-ste.*
Nape *ltag-pa.*
Napkin *k̔a-p̔yis, lag-p̔yis, paṅ-k̔eb.*
Narcotic adj. *smyo-byéd.*
Narrative s. *lo-rgyús.*
Narrow adj. *p̔al-méd, žeṅ-méd, dog-pa.*
Nasty *btsog-pa, (b)rtsog(s)-pa.*
Nation *mi-brgyúd* 124, *sde* 295, *rigs* 527.
Native s. *yul-pa.*
Native-place *γžis-k̔a.*
Natural *dṅos-ma, ma bc̀os-pa.*
Naturally *raṅ-bžin-gyis, γšis-kyis* 565.
Nature *ṅaṅ, c̆os-nyid, ṅo-bo-nyid* 129.
Naught (cipher) *mk̔a.*
Naughty *ṅa-rgyal-c̀an.*
Nausea *skyug-bro-ba, k̔am-lóg, k̔ams-rmyá.*
Navel *lte-ba.*
Near adj. *nye-ba*; adv *nye-bar, rtsar* 437, *gram-du*; *rgyaṅ t̔uṅ-ba*; *ldan-la, ldan-du* 289; to be — *nye-ba, rten-pa* 214.
Neat adj. *sdug-pa, sdug-gu.*
Necessaries s. *yo-byád.*
Necessary adj. *dgos-pa, rigs-pa* 528; to be — *dgos-pa.*
Necessity *dgos-pa.*
Neck *ske, mgur, mgul, mgrin-pa, °j̀iṅ-pa*; *γnya-ba*; — cloth *k̔a-dkri, k̔a-ras.*
Neckerchief *dkri-ma, mgul-c̆iṅs.*
Necklace *ske-c̆á.*
Need s. *gyoṅ.*
Needful *dgos-pa.*
Needle *k̔ab, °tsem-k̔áb.*
Negative s. *dgag-pa* 94, *°gag-pai sgra.*
Neglect vb. *°gyiṅ-ba, . . . la mi lta-ba.*
Neigh *°ts̔er-ba.*
Neighbour *k̔yim-mts̔és, p̔a-rol-po.*
Neighbourhood *sa-p̔yógs, yul-p̔yógs.*
Nepal *bal-po, bal-yúl.*
Nephew *ts̔a-bo*, resp. *dbon-po, dbon-srás.*
Nerve *c̆u-rtsá.*
Nest *ts̔aṅ.*
Net *rgya, rgya-mo, dol*; — work *dra-ba.*
Nettle *zwa.*
Neutralize *°c̆iṅ-bá.*
Never v. *nam-yaṅ* 303.
Nevertheless *yin-kyaṅ, yin-na yaṅ W.*
New *so-ma, γsar-ba, γsar-po.*
News *c̆a, skad, p̔rin, °p̔rin, lon, hun W.*; good — *lon-bzáṅ.*

Nice *sdug-pa.*
Night *nam, mts̔an-mo*; — quarters *°braṅ-sa*, eleg. *mc̆is-bráṅ*, resp. *γzim-bráṅ*; — watch *t̔un.*
Nimble *skyen-pa*; — footed *rkaṅ-mgyogs-pa.*
Nine num. *dgu*; ninth *dgu-pa*; nineteen *bc̀u-dgu*; nineteenth *bc̀u-dgu-pa*; ninety *dgu-bc̀u*; ninetieth *dgu-bc̀u-pa.*
Nip vb. a. *grum-pa.*
Nipple *nu-ma* 305, *pi-pi.*
Nitre *šo-ra.*
No, none v. *gaṅ* 65.
Nobility *dpal* no. 4, 326.
Noble adj. *drag-pa, btsun-pa, skye-mt̔ó.*
Nobleman *rj̀e-bo, mi-drag-pa, no-nó* 306.
Noblewoman *btsun-mo, še-ma W.*
Nod vb. a. (beckon) *lag-brda byed-pa*; **go kug taṅ-c̀e* W.*
Node, ascending — *sgra-γc̀an*; descending — *ke-tu.*
Noise *klag-c̆ór, grag-pa, sgra, ˏur, ku, ku-sgra*; — made by thunder etc. *c̆ems-c̆éms* 161; to make a — *°k̔rol-ba.*
Noisome *ṅam-pa.*
Nominate *sko-ba, °c̆ol-ba.*
Nonsense *c̀ab-c̀ob, c̀al-c̀ól*; to talk — *c̀al-c̀ól smra-ba.*
Nook *k̔ug, k̔ugs.*
Noon *dguṅ.*
North *byaṅ.*
Nose *sna, *nam-ts̔ul* W.*
Nostril *sna-k̔úṅ.*
Not *ma* 408, *mi* 413, *med* v. *med-pa* 417.
Notch s. *k̔ram-k̔a, nya-ga, ltoṅ-ga.*
Note s. *mc̆an-bu, yi-ge* no. 2, 508.
Nothing *c̀aṅ mi* 138, *c̀i mi* 140; — but *ša-stag*, col. *k̔a-rkyaṅ* (v. *rkyaṅ-pa*); *°ba-žig* 391.
Notice s. *rgyus, c̆a, lon*; to give — *lon spriṅ-ba.*
Notion *du-šes.*
Notwithstanding *ˏon-kyaṅ* 502.
Noun substantive *dṅos-miṅ* 131
Nourish *°ts̔o-ba, γso-ba.*
Nourishing adj. *nyams-brtas byed-pa.*
Nourishment *zas.*
Novice *dge-bsnyén* 85.
Now *da, da-lta, γzod, ˏo-ná* 500; — and then *bar-bar-du* or *la*; just — *ma-t̔ág* 227; not until — *da-γzód* 247.
Nowhere v. *c̀ir* 141.
Noxious *mi-dgos-pa, nyes-pa, γdug-pa.*
Null adj. *sob, sog, γsob, γsog.*
Number s. *graṅs.*
Number vb. a. *bgraṅ-ba, rtsi-ba.*

Numberless *bgran-yás.*
Numerous *rgyas-pa.*
Nun *čos-ma, btsun-mo, mo-btsún* 435; *jo-mo* 173.
Nurse s. (children's) *má-ma.*
Nurse up vb. a. *γsos skyed-pa, skyed srin-ba* 30.
Nutriment *bčud.*
Nutritious *bčud-čan, lči-ba.*

O

Oak *ča-ra, be-šin*; — forest *be-ḱród.*
Oar *skya, gru-ḱyém*
Oath *yi-dám*, resp. *ṫugs-dám, mna, bro.*
Oats *ka-rtsam, yug-po*
Obedient *bka nyan-pa.*
Obey *ḱa-la* (or resp. *žal-la*) *nyan-pa.*
Object s. *γnas, rdzas, zan-zin, dṅos-po* 131; — of perception *yul* 513; mental — *dmigs-γtád.*
Oblation *mčod-pa, sbyin-pa* 405.
Oblige (compel) v. *nan-gyis* 303.
Obliged, to feel — *drin-dran-pa.*
Oblique *ḱyom-ḱyóm, yo-ba, šan-ḱa.*
Oblong *nar-mo, kyoṅ.*
Obscuration *sgrib-pa* 120.
Obscure adj. *mun-pa, go-dka-ba* 71.
Obscure vb. a. *sgrib-pa*; obscured *dkrigs-pa, rmoṅ-ba, rmoṅs-pa.*
Obscurity *mun-pa.*
Observe *sruṅ-ba*, . . . *la lta-ba* I no. 3, 216.
Obstinate *kyoṅ-po, go-ṫag-čan* W. (lit. *mgo-mḱregs-čan*).
Obstruct *ₒgegs-pa, bčur-ba.*
Obstruction *bgegs, ₒgag.*
Obtain *sgrub-pa, rnyed-pa, ṫob-pa, len-pa.*
Obviate *γčod-pa, zlog-pa.*
Occasion s. *rkyen, glags, skabs*; on — of *skabs-su.*
Occupy *ₒdzin-pa* no. 3, 465.
Occur *ₒgyur-ba, ₒṫon-pa, ₒoṅ-ba.*
Occurrence *rkyen, dṅos-po.*
Ocean *rgya-mtso.*
Odour *dri, dri-ma.*
Oesophagus *lkog-ma.*
Of prep. *kyi* 6, *nas* 304, *las* 546.
Off adv. *ṗar* 341, *yas* 508.
Offence *sdig-pa*; to commit an — *nyes-pa, sdig-pa byed-pa.*
Offend *ₒḱaṅ-ba, ₒḱu-ba.*
Offensive *šin-tu ṫu-ba, mi žim-pa*; *yid-du mi ₒoṅ-ba.*
Offer *sbyin-pa.*
Offering s. *mčod-pa, ₒbul-ba, yon*; — lamp *mčod-sdoṅ*; — table *mčod-ḱri, mčod-stégs*; house or place of — *mčod-ḱaṅ.*
Office *ₒgaṅ-po.*
Officer *ₒgo-pa, blon-po.*
Official s. *bka-blon, bka-γšags.*
Official adj. *blon-poi, bka-blon-gyi*; — paper *bka-šog.*
Offspring *brgyud, ba-rgyúd.*
Oh interj. *ka, ka-ye, kye, kye-ma* 7; oh very well! *ₒo lags-so.*
Oil *mar, mar-nág* W.; — cake *mar-gyi ṫsigs-ma*; — lamp *'uṅ-gu.*
Ointment *skud*; *byug-pa.*
Old *rgad-pa, čen-mo* W., *rnyiṅ-pa, bčad-po*; — age *rgas-ka*; — man *rgad-po*, — woman *rgad-mo*; — squire *ga-ga* 63; to be — *rga-ba*; to grow — *bgre-ba.*
Oleander *ka-ra-bi-ra.*
Olive *skyu-ru, ḱa-skyur-po Sik.*; — tree *skyu-ru šiṅ, ḱa-skyur-poi šiṅ Sik.*
Omen *sṅa-ltás, ltas, rtags.*
Omit *bšol-ba.*
Omniscient *kun-mkyén.*
On prep. *ḱa-ru, ḱar* 34, *ḱa-ṫog-la, ka-tod-la* 35, *dgaṅ-la, dgeṅ-la, sgeṅ-la* 114, *ṫog-tu* 237, *na* 298.
Once (one time) *lan-γčig*; — more *čed-du, da-ruṅ, ṗyir, yaṅ, slar*; at — v. *čar* 139; (at the same time) *ṗyogs γčig-la* 352.
One num. *γčig*, — at a time *γčig-čig* 144; — eyed *mig-žár*; — footed *rkaṅ-γčig-pa*; the one — the other *γčig* . . . *γčig, γčig-po.*
One pron. (French 'on') *skyes-bu* 31; — another *γčig-gis γčig* 143; by one's self *γčig-* [*γčig* 144.
Onion *btsoṅ.*
Only adj. *γčig-ka, γčig-pu* 144; *zad* (v. *ₒdzad-pa* 464).
Only adv. *ka-rkyaṅ* (v. *rkyaṅ-pa* 17), *ša-stag* 555; *ḱo-na* 43, *γčig-tu* 144; *ₒba-žig* 391, *man-na mi* 411, *tsam* 430; not — *ma zad-de* 445.
Open adj. *ṗyes-pa, ṗyes-te*, vulgo *ṗe-te*; *bkag-pa ma yin-pa.*
Open vb. a. *ḱa ₒbyed-pa, bgrad-pa*; vb. n. *ₒbye-ba, ḱa ₒbye-ba.*
Opening s. *ḱa, bu-ga.*
Openly *ṅos-su* 130, *mṅon-sum-du* 133; *'a-γsal-la* W. 605.
Opinion *grub-mtá, lta-ba, snaṅ-ba*; in my — *ṅas bltas-pas* 216.
Opportunity *skabs, glags, rgyu, stabs, ṫabs, sa.*
Opposite *ḱa-draṅ, go-ldog*; — side *ṗar-ḱa, ṗa-rol, ṗar-ṅos.*
Opposition, to be or act in — *ₒgal-ba* c. *las* or *daṅ.*
Oppress *nón-pa.*

Optical deception *mig-₀krúl.*
Or *yaṅ-na* 506.
Oracle *gros-₀dri-sa.*
Orally *ḱa-nas*, col. *ḱa-na.*
Orange *tsa-lum-pa.*
Orb *₀ḱor-lo*; — of transmigration *₀ḱor-ba* 58.
Orchard *bza-śiṅ-ra-ba, ldum-ra.*
Ordain *bsnyen-par rdzogs-pa, bsnyen-rdzogs mdzad-pa* 469.
Order s. (succession) *go-rim* 71; to put in — *śom-pa, ytan-la ₀bebs-pa*; (command) *bka, bka btags-pa, bka-ṫaṅ, bka-ynaṅ-ba*; *żal-ydáms*; *hu-kúm W.*; (purpose) in — to *don-du* 259, *ṗyir-du* 351
Order vb. a. (command) *bka ynaṅ-ba* 13, *sgo-ba* 116.
Orderly adj. *tsul-mtún.*
Ordinarily *rgyun, ṗal-čér.*
Organ (of sense) *dbaṅ-po.*
Orifice *ḱa, bu-ga.*
Origin *ḱuṅs, byuṅ-ḱuṅs, ₀go-ma, ṫog-ma, čags-tsúl, rtsa-ba.*
Originate vb. n. *ḱruṅ-ba, čags-pa*
Ornament s. *rgyan, čun-po.*
Orphan *da-ṗrúg.*
Orthography *dag-yig, yi-gei sdeb-sbyór, brda-spród.*
Other *yżan, yżan-pa, yżan-ma, śos, yčig-śós.*
Otter *sram.*
Ought v. *rgyu* 110.
Ounce *sraṅ.*
Our, ours *ṅai* 124, *ṅed-kyi* 127.
Out adv. *ṗyir* 351, *ṗyi-rol-tu* 349; to be — (mistaken) *₀ḱrul-ba*; out of prep. *nas, ḱoṅ-nas.*
Outcast s. *ydol-pa.*
Outcry *grags-pa.*
Outlet *sgo.*
Outside s. *ḱa, ṗyi-rol.*
Outside adv. *ṗyi* III 349.
Outward adj. *ṗyii*; — appearance *ča-byád.*
Over prep. *goṅ-du, bar-snaṅ* or *la*; *bla*; — against *ḱa-draṅ, ṫad(-ka)*; adv. to be — (past) *ṫal-ba* II no. 5, 231.
Overcome vb. a. *ṫub-pa, non-pa*; vb. n. *sran-pa.*
Overflow vb. a. *yyeṅ-ba*; vb. n. *lud-pa.*
Overhasty *ha-čaṅ riṅs-pa, ha-čaṅ myur-čes-pa.*
Overseer *skul-ḱan, do-dam-pa, mgo byed-pai mi.*
Overshadow *₀ḱeb-pa.*
Overtake *snyegs-pa, ytug-pa.*
Overthrow vb. *sgyel-ba, rlog-pa.*
Overturn vb. *sgyel-ba, rtib-pa.*
Owl *ʼug-pa.*
Own adj. *raṅ-gi, nyid-kyi.*
Own vb. (possess) *bdog-pa, dbaṅ-ba*; owning *mṅa-ba.*
Owner *mṅa-bdág.*
Ox *glaṅ, ba-glaṅ.*

P

Pace s. *gom-pa*; *₀čag-pa, gom-₀čag-pa.*
Pace vb. *gom-pa ₀bor-ba*
Pack vb. a., to — on *₀ḱel-ba*; to — up *teg-pa.*
Paddle-wheel *sku-ru.*
Padlock *doṅ-pa.*
Page s. (waiting-boy) *go-re-lóṅ*; *sku-druṅ-pa, sku-mdun-pa*; — of a book *śog-logs.*
Pail *zo-ba.*
Pain s. (bodily) *zug, yzug*; *yzer*; (mental) *mya-ṅán* 420, *sdug-bsṅal* 294; to take pains *₀gru-ba, ₀bad-pa*; *brtson-₀grus byed-pa.*
Pain vb. a. *₀tse-ba*; to be pained *yduṅ-ba.*
Paint s. *tson*; vb. a. *skud-pa.*
Painter *ri-mo-mḱan.*
Painting s. *ri-mo, taṅ-ka.*
Pair s. *zuṅ, dor.*
Pairing s. (copulation) *₀ḱrig-pa.*
Palace *ṗo-braṅ.*
Palanquin *₀ḱyogs*; **ḱyog-čáṅ* W.*, **ṗeb-čáṅ* C.* (v. *dpyaṅ-ba* 328).
Palate *dkan, rkan*
Pale adj. **kya-ko-ré, kya-te-ré** 25.
Palm s. (of the hand) *lag-mṫil, ṫal-mo.*
Pan (large) *sla(ṅ)-ṅa*; (small) *dra-zu*; (flat) *ta-ba.*
Pancake **ṫul-ta-gir* W.* 234.
Pankah (fan) *bsil-yáb.*
Pannier *yzed-ma.*
Pant vb. n. *rṅam-pa, dṅaṅ-ba.*
Pap (porridge) *skyo-ma, ḱo-lág.*
Paper s. *śog-bu* 563; a sheet of — *gre-ga*; official — *bka-śog.*
Parable *dpe* 327, *₀dra-dpe.*
Paradigm *dpe-brjód.*
Paradise *mṫo-ris*
Paragraph *rnam-bčad-pa.*
Paralyze *₀čiṅ-ba*; *nyams-par byed-pa.*
Parasol *ydugs.*
Parcel s. (package) *ṫums* 234.
Parch *rṅod-pa, slam-pa.*
Pardon vb. a. (to use forbearance) *bzod-pa* 498; (to leave unpunished) *₀gyod mi rmo-ba, čad-pas mi yčod-pa*
Pare *kog-pa śu-ba.*
Parenthesis *yi-geï mčan-bu*
Parents *ṗa-má.*
Park *skyed-mos-tsál.*

Parrot *ne-tso.*
Parsimonious *śri-śes-k̀an W.*
Parsley *γżę-ra C., śa-mi-lig W.*
Part s. *ča, ča-śás, śas, rnam-pa, k̀a, k̀ag, ga-śas, lhu*; in — (partly) *ča ₒdra tsam*; at equal parts *ča-snyems.*
Part vb. a. *ₒṕral-ba*; vb. n. *ₒgye-ba, ₒbral-ba.*
Partake *ča t̀ob-pa, t̀ob-ča ₒdzin-pa, bgo-skal t̀ob-pa.*
Partaker **go-k̀an* W.*
Partial (biased) *nye-riṅ.*
Particle (grammatical) *t̀sig-ṕrad.*
Particularly *k̀yad-par-du, mčog-tu.*
Partition *dbye-ba*; — wall *čod, bar-skya.*
Partizan *ṕyogs-pa.*
Partly *ča tsam, ga-śas*; v. also *ʼa-lá* 541; *k̀a-čig* 34.
Partner *k̀a-ya, ya, ya-do W., grogs, zla-bo.*
Partridge *sreg-pa.*
Party (part) *ṕyogs* 352.
Pas (in dancing) *gom-pa.*
Pass vb. n. *skyod-pa, ₒgrul-ba, rgyug-pa, rgyud-pa, ₒčor-ba, t̀al-ba*; to — away *ₒk̀or-ba, ₒda-ba, ₒbud-pa W.*; vb. a. (to cross) *rgal-ba, zla-ba*; to — over a certain space *ₒda-ba.*
Passage (entrance or exit) *sgo, lam.*
Passion *čags-pa, ₒdod-čágs, bag-čágs.*
Passport *bka-śog, lam-yig.*
Past adj. *ₒdas-pa*; — ages *sṅa-rol*; to be — *yol-ba.*
Paste s. *skyo-ma*; vb. a. *sbyor-ba.*
Pastry *ₒk̀ur-ba.*
Pasturage *bzan.*
Pasture s. *neu-γsiṅ*; — land *ₑol-t̀áṅ, ₒbrog-γnas.*
Pat vb. a. *ₒbyug-pa.*
Patch s. *lhan-pa*; vb. a. *lhan-pas ₒdebs-pa, glan-pa.*
Patience *bzod-pa.*
Patient adj. *bzod-pa-čan.*
Patron *mgo-skyóṅ, mgo-ₒdrén, mgon-po.*
Pattern *dpe, ma, ri-mo.*
Pauper *dbul-ṕoṅs*; *med-po, med-mo.*
Pavement *skyaṅ-núl.*
Paw s. *spar-ba.*
Pay vb. a. *sprod-pa, ₒȷal-ba.*
Pay s. *gla, ṕogs.*
Pea, pease *sran-ma, srad-ma.*
Peace *żod, dus-bde, żi-bde.*
Peach *ka-t̀a ra, k̀am-bu, bun-ču li.*
Peacock *rma-bya.*
Peak *rtse(-mo).*
Pear *nyu-ti, nyo-ti.*
Pearl *mu-tig.*
Peasant *groṅ-pa, groṅ-mi*; *kyim-pa-pa, żiṅ-pa.*
Pebble *rdeu, rde*; *ču-rdó*; *śag-ma.*
Pedestrian *rkaṅ-t̀aṅ-pa.*
Peel s. *k̀og-pa, śun-pa.*
Peel vb. a. *k̀og-pa śu-ba, śu-ba.*
Peep-hole *so-k̀uṅ* 578.
Peg *rtod-pa, γdaṅ-bu, ṕur-pa.*
Pen s. *smyug-gu*; — knife *smyug-gri.*
Pen vb. a. (sheep etc.) *skyil-ba, ₒgegs-pa.*
Penalty *rgyal, stoṅ.*
Penance *dka-t̀úb, dka-spyód*; *brtul-żúgs.*
Pencil *γya-t̀ig, ₒbri-smyúg*; *pir.*
Pencil-cedar *śug-pa.*
Penetrate *k̀yab-pa, ₒdzugs-pa.*
Penis *mȷe, sgro-ba C.*
Penitent adj. *dka-t̀úb, brtul-żúgs.*
Pent-roof *čar-skyibs.*
People s. *skyes-bu*; common — *dmaṅs, smad-rigs.*
Pepper s. *ṕo-ba-ri*; Guinea — *γyer-ma C., *nyer-ma** or **t̀san-te** or *su-ru-ṕan-t̀sá W.*
Peppermint *ṕo-lo-liṅ W.*
Perambulate *ₒgrim-pa.*
Perceive *rtogs-pa, t̀sor-ba, yid-la byed-pa, rag-pa W., rig-pa.*
Perception *go-ba, rtogs-pa*; object of *yul* 513.
Perfect adj. *grub-pa, ṕun-t̀sógs, ṕul-byúṅ, tsaṅ-ma, rdzogs-pa.*
Perfection *dṅos-grúb*; state of — *grub-pa.*
Perfectly *t̀saṅ, rdzogs-par.*
Perform *byed-pa, sgrub-pa, bčo-ba W., spyod-pa.*
Perfume s. *spos.*
Perhaps *gal-te-na, graṅ*; *su śes, či śes W.*
Peril s. *nyen, bar-čód, ₒk̀rul-so.*
Perimeter *mt̀a-skór.*
Period *dus-t̀sigs, dus-mt̀sams*; *γnas-skabs*: former — *sṅon-rol.*
Perish *ₒȷig-pa, med-par ₒgyur-ba.*
Permission *dgoṅs-pa, bka γnaṅ-ba*; with your — *żu W.* 476.
Permit *bka γnaṅ-ba*; to be permitted *čog-pa, ruṅ-ba.*
Pernicious *ṅan-pa*; *ma-ruṅ-ba.*
Perpendicular *gyen-la draṅ-po W.*
Perpetual *rtag-pa.*
Perpetually *rgyun-du.*
Persecute *snyeg-pa, ₒded-pa, ₒt̀se-ba.*
Perseverance *yid yoṅs-su mi skyo-ba* or *mi ₒgyur-ba.*
Persia *ta-zig.*
Person *gaṅ-zág.*
Personal *dṅos.*
Personally *mṅon-sum-du, dṅos-su.*
Perspiration *rṅul.*
Pertinacious *mgo-mk̀regs-čan.*
Peruke *skra-t̀sab.*
Perverse *go-ldog.*
Perversity *ṕyin-či-lóg.*
Pervert *rlog-pa.*
Pestle *γtun, dgog-t̀iṅ C.*
Petting adj. *mnyo-mnyo-čan W.*

Petroleum *rdo-snúm.*
Petticoat *mo-gós, šam-gós.*
Pewter *dkar-γyá.*
Philology *sgra-rig-pa.*
Philosophy *nań-don-rig-pa* 527.
Phlegm *bad-kan, lud-pa.*
Phlegmatic *nań-brgyud riń-ba*; — disposition **šē-gyu'-dhal-wa* C.* (lit. *šes-rgyud dal-ba*).
Physician *sman-pa; 'em-či, 'am-či; γso-ba-po* 590.
Piccolo-flute *p̔red-gliń.*
Pick vb. a. *ₒbyed-pa*; to — up *sgrug-pa.*
Pickle s. *skyu-rúm.*
Picture s. *bzo, zo, ri-mo; t̔ań-ka*, resp. *žal-t̔ań*; — of a saint *bris-sku, sku-bris.*
Piebald *k̔ra-bo.*
Piece s. *čag-krum, čag-dum, dum, rnam-pa*; a single — *zuń* 488; a small — *k̔ol-bu*; to fall to pieces *rdib-pa.*
Pierce *ₒbig(s)-pa.*
Piety *k̔rel; čos-la dga-bai sems.*
Pig *p̔ag.*
Pigeon *p̔u-rón, p̔ug-rón.*
Pigtail *ču-ti W., lčań-lo C.*
Pilaw *p̔u-la, p̔o-la.*
Pile vb. a. *sgril-ba, bčer-ba, rtseg-pa.*
Pilfer *byi byed-pa.*
Pilgrimage, to go on a — *mǰal-ba.*
Pill s. *ril-bu.*
Pillar *ka-ba.*
Pillow *sňas, snye-stán, snye-ₒból.*
Pin s. *p̔ur-pa, ₒdzin-γya C., zum-k̔áb W.*
Pincers *skam-čuń.*
Pinch vb., the shoe pinches **k̔ab-ša dam dug* W.* 297.
Pious *skal-ldan; k̔rel-čan, čos-čan, čos-sem-čan W.; čos-la dga-ba.*
Pisé *gyań, gyeń* 74.
Pistol **me-dá* C., *rań-ₒbár* W.*
Pit s. *k̔uń, k̔uńs, doń.*
Pitcher *ču-snód, ču-rdzá, ben, rdza-búm.*
Pitchfork *zar.*
Pith *γnad.*
Pitiable *dman-pa.*
Pity s. *snyiń-brtse-ba.*
Place s. *k̔ag, sa, sa-k̔yad, go, yul-gru, yul, γnas, sa-ča, groń*; to take — *ₒgyur-ba, ₒbyuń-ba.*
Place vb. a. *ₒǰog-pa, ₒbor-ba, ₒdzugs-pa*; to be placed *k̔od-pa.*
Plague s. *γnyan, ₒgo-bai nad, ₒgo-bai rims; ńan-rims, rims-nád.*
Plaid *γzan-gós.*
Plain s. *t̔ań; ńos.*
Plain adj. (without ornament) *ₒǰam-sań, rgyan-méd.*
Plaintiff **t̔im žu-k̔an* W.*
Plait s. *lan-bu*; vb. a. *lan-bu sle-ba; γčud-pa.*
Plan s. *bkob-lta, bkod-pa*; vb. a. *ₒgod-pa.*
Plane s. *p̔ag-ste W.*; vb. a. **p̔ag-sté šrul-če* W.*
Planet *γza* 492.
Plank *spań, spań-léb.*
Plant s. *sňo, rtswa*; vb. a. *ₒdzugs-pa.*
Plantain *skyes-sdóń; ta-la*
Plaster s. (in surgery) *ₒbyor-sman.*
Plaster vb. a. (to pave) *skyań-nul byed-pa.*
Plastering s. *žal-ba* 474.
Plate s. *glegs, gra-ti Ld., ta-bag W.*; tin — *t̔a-li W.*; iron — *lčags-t̔ál.*
Plate vb. a. *čus γtoń-ba* 160.
Play vb. (to sport) *rtse-ba, rtsed-pa*; to — on an instrument *ₒk̔rol-ba, skrog-pa*; to — a trick *γnod-pa skyel-ba.*
Play-fellow *rtse-grógs, grogs-k̔yeu.*
Play-ground *rtse-sa*
Pleasant *sdug-pa, yid-du ₒoń-ba*; to be — *ₒt̔ad-pa.*
Pleasantness *ₒk̔yer-so.*
Please vb. a. *dga-bar byed-pa*; vb. n. v. *mk̔yen-pa* 55; if you please *žu* 476; to be pleased *dgyes-pa, bsod-pa.*
Pleasing adj. *dga-mo, bsod-pa.*
Pleasure *dga-ba, rtsed-mo, γyeń-rtsed, rtsed-ₒǰo; snyiń dga-ba* or *bde-ba*; at — *rań-dgár, yid bžin-du.*
Plebeian *ma-rabs, p̔al-pa.*
Pledge s. *rgyan, γta-ma, γte-pa.*
Pleiades *smin-drúg.*
Plentiful *k̔rigs, rgyas-pa, mod-po*; to be — *ₒdzom-pa.*
Plenty s. *lońs-spyód.*
Pliable, Pliant *mnyen-pa, mnyen-lčug, lčug-pa.*
Plough s. *γšol*; vb. a. *γšol-mda ₒdzin-pa; rmo-ba.*
Pluck s. (of an animal) *snyiń-luń.*
Pluck vb. *sgrug-pa.*
Plummet *ža-nyei γtiń-rdo.*
Plump *lkob; rom-po W.*
Plunder vb. *ₒgog-pa, *kog-te k̔yer-če W.* 95.
Pock s. *ₒbrum-pa*; — marked *mdzar-ra-mdzer-ré Ld.*
Pocket s. *čan-da, dku-mda, k̔ud-pa*; — book *yi-gei šubs; sam-ta, sab-dra*; — fire *me-lčags*; — handkerchief *na-či C., na-p̔i W.*
Pocket vb. a. *ₒk̔ur-ba.*
Pod *gań-bu, lgań-bu.*
Poem *ńag-snyán; snyan-dńags.*
Poetry *sdeb-sbyór.*
Point s. *t̔seg, nag-t̔seg*; main — *don, ma-γži*; to be on the — *ča-ba*; v. also *las* II extr. 546.
Poison *dug.*
Poker *yog-po.*
Polecat *šul-byi.*
Polish vb. *bdar-ba.*

Polished adj. ˏod-čan
Politeness že-sa.
Pollute ˳bag-pa.
Pollution grib.
Pomatum ṡra-skúd.
Pomegranate se-˳bru, seu.
Pond rdziṅ.
Ponder sems-pa, resp. dgoṅs-pa; bsam-blo γtoṅ-ba.
Pool ču-k̔yil, lteṅ-ka.
Poor dbul-ba, p̔oṅs-pa, ṅan-pa, gyi-na, k̔as-dmán, k̔as-žán; the poor people! snyiṅ-re-ṙje.
Poplar dbyar-pa; ma-gál W.; γṡol-po.
Popular mon-ža-čan W.
Popularity mon-ža W.
Porcelain kar-yól, dkar-yól; — clay k̔am-pa.
Porch sgo-k̔áṅ.
Porcupine rgaṅ, byi-t̔ur, γzig-mo.
Pore spui k̔uṅ-bu, ba-spui bu-ga..
Porridge zan 486.
Portal sgo-k̔áṅ.
Portion s. skal-ba, ča 150, ča-ṡás; tsod, lhu 601; — of meat rgya-ri, sder-gáṅ.
Position go 70.
Positive adj. dṅos.
Possess, to be possessed of bdog-pa.
Possessing adj. bčas-pa 146.
Possession, to hold in — ˳dzin-pa 465.
Possibility glags, go-skábs, rgyu, sa.
Possible, to be — srid-pa.
Post s. (pillar) ka-ba.
Posteriors rkub, ṁjug, p̔um-p̔úm, ṡul-pa.
Postillion rta-zam-pa.
Postpone bṡol-ba, sriṅ-ba.
Postscript yaṅ-skyár.
Post-service ˏu-lág 499.
Post-station rta-zám.
Pot s. k̔og-ma, rdza-ma, p̔an-dil W.; — cloth tsa-lčibs; — house čaṅ-k̔aṅ.
Potato skyi-ba, *kyi-u* C., *ḍho-ma, gya-ḍho* C. 78; 'a-lu W.
Potency dbaṅ.
Potsherd gyo-mo, čag-po.
Pouch s. rkyal-bu, k̔ug-ma, k̔ab-ta-ka Ld.
Poultry k̔yim-bya.
Pound vb.a. rduṅ-ba, k̔rum-k̔rum byed-pa.
Pour ldugs-pa, ˳byo-ba, ˳bo-ba.
Poverty p̔oṅs-pa, dbul-ba.
Powder s. p̔ye-ma.
Power mṅa, mṅa-táṅ, mt̔u, nus-pa.
Powerful rgyags-pa, ṅar-ma, btsan-po
Powerless dbaṅ-méd; to render — dbaṅ-med-du ˳čol-ba.
Practice s. lag-lén, resp. p̔yag-lén; lob-k̔yád W.
Practise vb. a. sbyoṅ-ba.
Praise s. sṅag-γsól; vb a. sṅag-pa, stod-pa.
Prattle s. čol-čúṅ.

Pray vb. n. γsol-ba, žu-ba.
Prayer γsol-ba; — mill čos-k̔or, ma-ni-čos-k̔or.
Preach čos sgrog-pa, resp. čos-kyi sgrog-gleṅ mdzad-pa.
Precede sṅon-du ˳gro-ba.
Preceding sṅa-ma, sṅon-˳gro.
Precept bka-bsgos, bka-rtags, k̔rims, čos, γdams-pa, bslab-bya.
Precious dkon-pa, γčes-pa, rin-čẹn, rin-po-če; the most — thing dkon-mčog 10.
Precipitous γzar-ba.
Precisely raṅ, k̔o-na.
Preface s. sṅon-˳gro.
Prefect yul-dpon, mi-dpón.
Preferable bla.
Prefix s. sṅon-ǰúg, ˳p̔ul(-yig).
Pregnant sbrum-pa; ˏsems-čan daṅ ldan-pa 290.
Preparation grabs, rgyu, sta-gón.
Prepare ṡom-pa, sbyor-ba I, no. 2, 406; bčo-ba W., dger-ba C., ˳ča-ba 168; to — victuals for the table γyo-ba, γyos-su byed-pa.
Prepuce mdun-pags, ˳dom-pags.
Prerogative don.
Presage s. sṅa-ltás.
Presence, in — of mdun-du, resp. spyan-sṅar.
Present s. (gift) skyes, rten, žu-rtén, resp. γzigs-rtén, ˳k̔yos-pa, bya-dgá, sbyin-pa.
Preserve vb. skyoṅ-ba, skyob-pa, sruṅ-ba.
Press vb. bkan-pa, bčar-ba, glem-pa C., non-pa, ˳tsir-ba, to — hard (in an inquest) tsir tag ǰhe'-pa C.
Pressingly nan-gyis 303.
Presume (arrogate) k̔as-len-pa 34.
Pretty adj. mčor-po, sdug-pa, dga-mo.
Prevail on ˳ǰug-pa.
Prevent ˳gogs-pa, γčod-pa, zlog-pa.
Preventive s. sruṅ-ba.
Previous adj. sṅon-˳gro.
Previously sṅa-na, sṅa-goṅ, sṅan, sṅar, sṅon.
Price goṅ, t̔aṅ, rin.
Prick vb. a. snun-pa, ˳dzugs-pa 465.
Pricking (pungent) rtsub-po.
Pricks fastened to the feet for climbing mountains rkaṅ-mdzer.
Pride s. ṅa-rgyal, dregs-pa, p̔o-so, rlom-pa, rlom-sems.
Priest bla-ma.
Priestcraft čos-zog.
Priesthood dge-˳dun.
Primary adj. v. rtsa-ba.
Prime minister bka-blón.
Prince rgyal-bu, rgyal-srás.
Principal adj. mčog, γtso-bo; — part mgo.
Principal s. mgon-po, ˳go-dpon.
Principally γtso-bor.
Print vb. par-du ˳debs-pa, par rgyab-pa W.

Printer *par-pa.*
Printing-office *par-k̔an.*
Prison *btson-k̔an, k̔ri-mun.*
Prisoner *btson.*
Private, Privately *sgos.*
Privilege s. *γnan-ba.*
Privities *ₒdoms, sba-ba.*
Privy s. *čab-k̔un, γsan-spyód.*
Prize s. (reward) *dgu-mťsán.*
Probationer *dge-bsnyén.*
Proboscis *glan-sná.*
Proceed *ₒgye-ba, spro-ba*; to let — *ₒgyed-pa* 97.
Proclaim *bka bkod-pa, bka ₒdogs-pa, sgrog-pa, sgyur-ba W.*
Proclamation *bka bkod-pa, bka btags-pa, bka-ₒdogs-pa.*
Procreate *skyed-pa, bšo-ba.*
Procure *sgrub-pa, γnyer-ba, sbyor-ba, ₒťsol-ba.*
Produce s. *ťog.*
Produce vb. *skyed-pa*; to be produced *čags-pa.*
Product s. (sum total) *brtsis-zin.*
Professor *mk̔an-po.*
Profit s. *skyed, k̔e, k̔ye, don, spogs*; *p̔an-pa, p̔an-ťogs, bed.*
Profitable *drug, p̔an-ₒdogs-pa.*
Profound *zab-pa.*
Prognostic s. *sna-ltas.*
Progress s. *skyed.*
Prohibit *ₒk̔egs-pa, ₒgégs-pa.*
Project vb. a. *ₒgod-pa*; vb. n. *ťal-ba.*
Prolong *bšol-ba, srin-ba.*
Prolongation *stud-ma.*
Prominent, to be — *ťal-ba.*
Promise s. *čad*; vb. *čad-pa, ₒče-ba, k̔as-len-pa, dam ₒča-ba.*
Promulgate *sgrog-pa, rjod-pa.*
Pronounce *ₒdon-pa, rjod-pa.*
Pronunciation *lčogs, zer-lčogs, zer-ťsul W., klog-ťsul, rjod-dbyans C.*
Proof s. *mnon-rtágs, rtags, rgyu-mťsan.*
Prop s. *rgyab-rtén*; vb. a. *skyor-ba.*
Propagation *sa-bon*; *dar-ba.*
Propensity *bag-čágs.*
Proper *dnos* 131; — place *go*; — time *bsgan.*
Property *yon-tan, lons-spyód*; — left *šul* 561.
Prophesy vb. *lun ston-pa.*
Prophet *lun-ston-pa.*
Prophetic sight *mnon-šes, ₒod-γsal*, resp. *ťugs-mk̔yén.*
Propitious *bkra-šis-pa, dge-ba.*
Proportion *ťig-ťsád, byad.*
Propound *rjod-pa, ston-pa, ₒčad-pa.*
Proprietor *bdag-po.*
Prospect (likelihood) *no* 129, *ča* 151.
Prosperity *bkra-šis.*
Prosperous *γyan-čan.*
Prostitute s. *ₒp̔yon-ma, smad-ťson-ma.*
Protect *skyob-pa, ₒgebs-pa, srun-ba, skyabs byed-pa.*
Protection *skyabs.*
Protector *skyabs-mgón*; *mgo-skyon, mgo-ₒdren, mgon-po*; — of religion *čos-skyon* 31.
Proud *k̔ens-pa, grags-čan, rgyags-pa, dregs-pa*; to be — *snyems-pa.*
Proverb *k̔a-dpe.*
Provide *sbyor-ba, yod-par byed-pa.*
Provided with (having, possessing) *čan* 138, *ldan-pa* 290.
Province *k̔ag, k̔ul, sde, sde-srid*; *yul-gyi kyad-par.*
Provincialism *gron-ťsig.*
Provisions *rgyags*; *srog-rdzás*, resp. *bšos*; store of — *γtal-so.*
Provoke *nyams ₒbru-ba, ₒťsan ₒbru-ba.*
Provost *dge-bskos.*
Prudent *mk̔as-pa, grun-ba, rgod-pa, sgrin-po.*
Prune vb. *ₒgrum-pa.*
Ptarmigan *gon-mo.*
Public s. *yul-pa-rnams* 513.
Publication *bkar-btags-pa, bka bkod-pa, gram-yig.*
Publicly *mnon-sum-du.*
Publish *bkar-ₒdogs-pa, sgyur-ba, sgrog-pa.*
Puddle s. *ču-ₒk̔yil.*
Puff s. (ostentation) *yus* 513.
Puff-ball *lgo, p̔a-ba-dgo-dgó.*
Pull vb. a. *ₒdren-pa, ₒťen-pa*; to — along *ₒdrud-pa*; to — down *snyil-ba, rtib-pa, ₒdral-ba*; to — off *šu-ba*; to — out *ₒbyin-pa, ₒgog-pa.*
Pulpit *čos-k̔ri.*
Pumpkin *gon, čun.*
Pungency *ber.*
Pungent *ber-čan, rtsub-po, ťsa-ba, ťsan-te.*
Punish *ₒjun-pa, čad-pas γčod-pa* 155.
Punishment *čad-pa, k̔ral, ga-sir Ld., god, dgra, lan* 543.
Pupil (scholar) *mk̔an-bu*; *slob-ma, slob-prug, slob-bans, bu-slob.*
Puppy *k̔yi-gu.*
Purchase vb. *nyo-ba.*
Pure *dan-ba, γťsan-ba, ťsans-pa*; *lag-mo W.*; *γsal-ba, dga-mo, lhad-méd.*
Purgative s. *bšal-sman.*
Purge vb. *bšal-ba.*
Purity *γťsan-ba.*
Purpose s. *dgos-pa, don*; on — *brtson-par*
Purpose vb. *dgons-pa, sems-pa.*
Purposely *čed-du.*
Purr vb. n. *nug-pa*, v. *ma-ṇi.*
Purse s. *sgyiu, sgyig-gu, sgye-mo.*
Pursue *rnon-pa, snyegs-pa, ₒded-pa.*
Pus (matter) *ču-rnag, rnag, ču-ser.*
Push vb. a. *rdegs-pa, ₒp̔ul-ba, sug-pa.*
Pustule *ₒbrum-pa.*

Put vb. a. *bkan-pa, ₒgod-pa, ₒǰug-pa, ₒǰog-pa, ₒbor-ba W.*; to — astride (e.g. in empaling) *skyon-pa*; to — down *grems-pa, ₒgrol-ba, sgyel-ba, ₒǰog-pa*; to — in or into *sgyoṅ-ba, čud-pa, ₒǰug-pa, teg-pa, ₒdzud-pa*; to — in order *sgrig-pa*; to — off *bud-pa, bšol-ba*; to — on *ₒgebs-pa, gon-pa,* resp. *γsol-ba*; to — together *snol-ba.*
Putrid *rul-ba.*
Putty s. *bag-sbyin* 364.

Q

Quadrangle *dkyil-ₒk̔or gru-bži-pa.*
Quadrate s. *k̔a-gáṅ*; adj. *k̔a-γaṅ-ba.*
Quadruped *rkaṅ-bži-pa.*
Quail s. *big-bi-lig W.*
Quality *čos-nyid*; good — *yon-tan* 516.
Quarrel s. *k̔a-mču, ₒdziṅ-mo, hab-ša, rtsod-pa.*
Quarrel vb. *ₒk̔rug-pa, rgol-ba, ₒgran-pa*; quarreling words *ₒgran-tsig.*
Quarrelsome, — temper *ₒgran-sems.*
Quarter of the heavens *p̔yogs* 352.
Quarters *γnas, γnas-t̔saṅ C., braṅ-sa W.*
Quartz *čag-dkár.*
Queen *rgyal-mo*; — consort *btsun-mo* (*rgyal-poi*).
Question s. *dri-ba, žu-ba.*
Queue (pigtail) *lčaṅ-lo C., čֹu-ti Ld.*
Quick adj. *mgyogs-pa, myur-ba, skyen-pa, k̔ram-pa*; be —! **riṅ-pa toṅ** *W.*
Quickly *mgyogs-par*; *myur-du.*
Quicksand **be-rul** *W.*
Quicksilver *dṅul-ču.*
Quiet adj. *dal-ba, gya-ma-gyú, srun-po*; to become — *ži-ba.*
Quill *rkaṅ.*
Quilt s. *t̔sa-γčig-ma C.*
Quintessence *ṅo-bo-nyid, bčud, snyiṅ-po.*
Quit vb. a. *ₒbor-ba* 396, *ₒǰog-pa* 179, *skyur-ba* 28; *ₒgye-ba, γtoṅ-ba.*
Quite *ye, ye-nas, yons-su*; *ldiṅ-se Ld.*
Quittance *ₒp̔rod-ₒdzín.*
Quiver s. *mda-dóṅ.*
Quiver vb. n. *ₒdar-ba.*
Quotient *t̔ob-nór.*

R

Race s. (generation) *mi-sná, rabs.*
Race s. (contest in running) *baṅ* 364; to run a — *dkyu-ba.*
Radish *la-p̔ug, guṅ-la-p̔ug.*
Rafter *lčam, gral-ma.*
Rag *hrul-ba.*
Rage vb. n. *rṅam-pa.*
Ragged adj. *čad-po, hrul-po.*
Rail s. *lag-rgyúgs* 541.
Rain s. *čar, čar-pa*; — cloak *čar-k̔ebs*; — water *čar-ču.*
Rain vb.n. *čar ₒbab-pa*, it rains *čar ₒbab W.*
Rainbow *ₒǰa, ₒǰa-t̔son.*
Rainy *čar-čan*; — season *čar-dus.*
Raise *sgreṅ-ba, ₒdon-pa, ker-ba, ₒp̔yar-ba, ₒdzugs-pa, bžeṅ-ba, seṅ-ba, sloṅ-ba.*
Raisin *rgun-rgód, rgun-ₒbrúm.*
Rake s. (gardening) *k̔a-γzé W., rgya-γzéb C.*
Ram s. *lug-t̔úg.*
Ramble vb. *ₒk̔yam-pa, ₒk̔or-ba W.*
Rampart *ₒk̔or-yúg.*
Range s. (row) *gral, rim-pa*; — of vision *mt̔oṅ-ₒk̔or, mt̔oṅ-mt̔a.*
Range vb. n. *rgyu-ba, ₒgrim-pa.*
Rank s. *go, go-p̔aṅ, go-sá, go-grál, go-grás, rigs.*
Ransom s. *glud, blud, glud-t̔sab*; *blud-pa*; vb. a. *blu-ba.*
Rare *dkon-pa.*
Rash adj. *yid-t̔úṅ* 570.
Rashness *bab-čol, γzu-lúm.*
Rasp s. *sa-bdar, sag-γdár C.*; *šiṅ-zóg W., šiṅ-séd W.*
Rasp vb. a. *bdar-ba, sag-γdar, gyag-pa C.*
Raspberry *t̔ser-lum Sik, la-ma-sró Kun.*
Rat s. *byi-ba, sa-bi-lig W.*
Rather *ča-lam*; v. *bla* 382.
Ration *zas-skál.*
Raven *k̔a-ta, bya-róg, p̔o-róg, bya-nág.*
Ravine *grog-po, roṅ, sul.*
Raw *rǰen-pa.*
Ray s. *γzer, ₒod-γzér.*
Razor *spu-gri.*
Reach vb. a. *γtug-pa, t̔ug-pa, sniṅ-ba*; to — down *smad-pa.*
Reach of hearing *rgyaṅ-grágs.*
Read vb. *klog-pa, sgrog-pa,* **sil-če** *W.*
Reading-desk *čos-k̔ri.*
Ready *p̔ral-grig* 359; to be made — *grub-pa, ₒgrub-pa*; — money *rnags, smar-ba, smar-rkyáṅ.*
Real *ṅes-pa-čan, dṅos, dṅos-čan*; *ṅo-rtóg W.*
Reality *dṅos*; *yaṅ-dag-pa-nyid* 248; *γnas-t̔sul* 449.
Really *ṅes-pa-čan-du*; (bodily) *dṅos-su* 131.
Realm *k̔ams*; *rgyal-k̔ams* 108.

Reap *rña-ba.*
Reaper *žiñ-mk'an.*
Reaping-hook *zor-ba, rgya-zór.*
Rear vb. (bring up) *srel-ba, ɣso-ba.*
Reason s. (intellect) *blo, blo-grós*; (cause) *rgyu.*
Reasonable *ts'ul-mt'un* 450.
Rebel vb. *ño-log byed-pa* 553, **gyab-log ǰhe'-pa** *C.*
Rebel s. *ño-log-mk'an.*
Re-born, to be — *skye-ba* 28.
Rebound vb. n. *₀p'ar-ba.*
Rebuke s. *bka-bkyón, brgyad-kág*; vb. a. *brgyad-kag byed-pa.*
Receipt *₀p'rod-₀dzín, zin-bris.*
Receive *len-pa*, resp. *bžes-pa*; *t'ob-pa*; *rǰes-su ₀dzin-pa.*
Receptacle *rten* no. 2, 213.
Recite *skyor-ba, sgrog-pa.*
Reckon (count) *rtsi-ba.*
Recline *bkyed-pa, snye-ba.*
Recommend *sñag-pa*; *stod-pa.*
Recommendation, letter of — *mt'un-₀gyur-gyi yi-ge.*
Recompense s. *rñan-pa, ɣnañ-sbyin, bya-dga.*
Recompense vb. a. *brñan-pa.*
Reconcile vb. a. *sdum-pa*; to — one's self *k'o-tág ɣčod-pa.*
Record vb. *₀god-pa* no. 5, 95.
Records s. *deb-t'ér, yig-č'a.*
Recover vb n. *ts'o-ba, p'yir lañ-ba.*
Recreation *skyo-sáñs*; *ɣyeñs-pa W.*; to take — *rtse-ba*; *skyo-sañs-la ₀gro-ba*, resp. *byon-pa.*
Rector *₀go-dpón C.*
Red *dmar-po, dmar-ba*; light — *dkar-dmar.*
Redeem *₀grol-ba, blu-ba.*
Redeemer *skyabs-mgón.*
Redemption *blud-pa.*
Reduce (the wages) *ɣčod-pa.*
Reed *₀dam-bu*; — pen *snyug-gu, smyi-gu*, **di-nyúg** *W.*
Reel vb. n. *₀k'yom-pa, ₀k'yor-ba.*
Reflection (consideration) *sgom, rtog-pa.*
Refuge *skyabs-ɣnás.*
Refuse s. *gal-ró.*
Refuse vb. *₀dor-ba, mi ɣnañ-ba.*
Regard vb. a. *ɣzigs-pa*; to — as *dgoñs-pa*; as regards *dbañ-du byas-na, -la* 540.
Regard s., to have — to *lta-ba* I, no. 3, 216.
Regardful *ɣčañ-po.*
Regent *rgyal ts'áb* 109; *sde-srid, srid.*
Region *k'ams, gliñ, ǰoñs, sa-p'yógs, yul-p'yógs.*
Register s. *dkar-č'ág*; *t'o.*
Regular *tsul-čan.*
Reign s. *rgyal-srid.*
Reinforcements *dmag-ts'ógs snon-ma.*
Reins (of a bridle) *srab-skyógs, srab-mdá.*
Reins (kidneys) *mk'al-ma.*
Reject *spoñ-ba.*
Rejoice vb. n *dga-ba*, resp. *dgyes-pa*; *mgu-ba, rǰes-su yi-rañ-ba* 182.
Relate vb. a. *skad-pa, ₀č'ad-pa, snyad-pa.*
Relation (kindred) *brgyud*; *nye-du, nye-brél*; (reference) *rgyud.*
Relative s. (kinsman) *nyen, ɣnyen, ɣnyen-bšés.*
Relax vb. a. *glod-pa.*
Release vb. a. *₀grol-ba*; to be released *₀grol-ba.*
Release s. *blud-pa, t'ar-du ₀ǰug-pa.*
Relic *riñ-bsrél* 529.
Religion *č'os, č'os-lugs.*
Religious *č'os-kyi*; *č'os-la dga-ba*; *k'rel-čan W.*
Religiously, to live — *č'os byed-pa.*
Reluctantly *ñam-šúgs Sch.*
Rely *rten-pa.*
Remain *₀dug-pa, bžugs-pa, lus-pa.*
Remainder *lus-ma, lhag-ma.*
Remains (dead body) *ro.*
Remedy s. *ɣnyen, rdzas, ɣso-byéd.*
Remember *dgoñs-pa, dran-pa, rǰes-su dran-pa*; *yid-la byed-pa*; *ñes-pa* 128.
Remind *yid skul-ba.*
Remove vb. *₀grol-ba, sgrol-ba*; *₀byin-pa, sbyoñ-ba.*
Rend *ɣčod-pa, ₀dral-ba, ɣšeg-pa, hral-ba.*
Renounce *spoñ-ba.*
Renown *grags-pa, snyan-pa.*
Renowned *grags-pa-čan, grags-čan, sgra-č'é.*
Rent adj. *č'ad-po*; to be — *₀gas-pa.*
Rent s. (fissure) *ral*; (house-rent) *k'añ-gla.*
Repair vb. a. *ɣso-ba.*
Repay *₀ǰal-ba, ɣsob-pa.*
Repeat *skyor-ba, sgre-ba, stud-pa, ldab-pa.*
Repent *₀gyod-pa.*
Repentance *₀gyod-pa.*
Repertory *t'ob-yig.*
Reply s. *k'a-lán, lan*; vb. *lan ₀debs-pa, glon-pa.*
Report s. (of a gun) *sguñ*; (rumour) *(*s*)*lob-lo** *W.*
Representative s *ts'ab-po.*
Reprimand s. *bka-bkyón.*
Reproach vb. a. *čo ₀dri-ba, smad-pa, smad-ra ɣtoñ-ba.*
Reproach s. *brgyad-k'ág*; *smad-pa.*
Reproduce *skyed-pa.*
Reproof *smad-pa.*
Repulse vb. *zlog-pa.*
Reputation *grags-pa.*
Request s. *žu-ba, ɣsol-ba*; vb. *žu-ba.*
Require *bžed-pa* 484.
Requisite s. *č'as* 156; requisites *rdzas* 468.

Requital *ka-lán*; *₀bras-bu*.
Rescue vb. a. *sgrol-ba*, *skyob-pa*, *skyabs byed-pa*, *tar-bar byed-pa*.
Resentment *kon-pa*.
Reserved adj. *gya-ma-gyu* 73.
Reside *bžugs-pa*.
Residence *kab*, *rgyal-sa*; *γži-ma*.
Residue *ro*.
Residuum *tsigs-ma*.
Resign *ko-tág γčod-pa*.
Resin *tań-čú*.
Resist *rgol-ba*.
Resolute *lo-na tuń-se W*.
Resolve vb. n. (decide) *bgro-ba*, *tag-γčod-pa*.
Resound *₀krol-ba*.
Respect s. *bkur-ba*, *bkur-sti*; *sku-rim*, *gus-pa*; *pu-dúd*, *srí-žu*; to pay one's respects *rje-sa* or *že-sa byed-pa*; best respects! *žu W*. 476; in every — *rnam-pa kun-tu*; with — to *la* 540.
Respect vb. a. *rtsis byed-pa*.
Respectable *btsun-pa*.
Respectful *gus-pa*.
Respiration *dbugs*.
Respire *dbugs rńub-pa dań ₀byin-pa*.
Responsibility *kag*.
Rest s. (remainder) *mta*, *lus-ma*, *lhag-ma*.
Rest s. (repose) *sti-ba*; vb. *sti-ba*; *ńal γso-ba* 127.
Resting-place *lam-stégs*.
Restless *₀dug mi tsugs-pa* 459.
Restore *γso-ba*.
Restrain *₀dul-ba*; *₀jun-pa*; to be restrained *dog-par ₀gyur-ba*.
Restrict vb. **skar-tág tań-če* W*.
Retain *skyil-ba*, *₀gegs-pa* 94, *sgyoń-ba* 119.
Retaliation *rnam(-par) smin(-pa)*; *lan* 543.
Retinue *₀kor*, *₀kor-γyog*, *₀kor-₀dab*; *žabs-pyi*, *slas*.
Retribution *₀bras-bu* 400, *la-yógs* 541; *lan*; doctrine of — *bgo-skál* 89.
Return vb. a. *lan byed-pa*, *lan ₀jal-ba*; to — an answer *glon-pa*; vb. n. *₀kor-ba*, *log-pa*, *pyir ₀gro-ba*.
Revenge s. *dugs*, *lan*; to take — **dug** or **lan kor-če* W*.
Revere *mos-pa*.
Reverence *sku-rim*, *gus-pa*, *bsnyen-bkúr*, *bag-yod(-pa)*, *že-sa*.
Reverend (title) *rje-btsún*, *btsun-pa*, *dbu-rjé*.
Reverse s (sideopposite) *rgyab-lógs*; (contrary) *zlas-pye-ba*; *bzlog*, *go-ldóg*, *go-lóg*.
Revile vb. a. *smad-pa*, *γše-ba*.
Revise vb. a. *sgyur-ba*, *lta-ba*.
Revision *žal-ta* 473.
Revolt vb. *gyab-lóg byed-pa*, *ńo-lóg byed-pa*.
Revolver **rań-bar dug-rág* W*. 523.
Reward s. *rńan-pa*, *sug*; vb. *rńan-pa*.
Rheumatism *grum-bu*, *grum-nád*; *grum-pa W*., **zer-ne* C*.
Rhododendron *ba-lu*, *da-lí*.
Rhubarb *ču-čú*, *la-čú*.
Rhyming adj. *zuń-ldán*.
Rib *rtsib(s)-ma*.
Ribbon *₀čiń-ba*, *leb-ma*.
Rice *₀bras*; boiled — *₀bras-čán*; parched — *₀bras-yos*.
Rich adj. *pyug-po*; — in *rgyas-pa*, *₀dzom-po*.
Riches s. *dkor*, *nor*, *dbyig(s)*, *₀byor-pa*.
Rick *pub-rags*.
Riddle s. (enigma) *ldem-po*.
Ride vb. (on horseback) *rta-la žon-te ₀gro-ba*; (in a carriage) *šiń-ta-la žon-te ₀gro-ba*.
Riding-beast *bžon-pa*.
Right adj. (right-hand) *γyas-pa*; (not wrong) *drań-po*, *₀os-pa*; all right! *tsań-grig*; — measure *čag-tsad*; to be — *₀grig-pa*, *ran-pa*.
Right s. *krims* 50.
Righteous *čos-drań-po*.
Rim *kyud-mo*.
Rind *kog-pa*.
Ring s. *a-lóń*; — dove *ku-hu*; — worm *ke*.
Ring vb. a. (a bell etc.) *₀krol-ba*.
Rinse *bšal-ba*.
Ripe adj. *smin-pa*.
Rise vb. n. (to get up) *ldań-ba*, *lań-ba*, *kar* or *ker-lań-ba*, resp. *bžeńs-pa*; (as the sun) *₀čar-ba*; (in the air) *₀pag-pa*; (to come forth) *₀bur-ba*, *₀byuń-ba*.
Risk s. *nyen*, *bar-čod*.
Risk vb. a. *skyel-ba*, *sdo-ba*, *blos-γtoń-ba* 385.
Rival s. *₀gran-zla*.
River *ču*, *₀bab-ču*, *ču-kluń*, *ču-bo*, *γtsań-po* 433.
Rivet s. *₀brel-mtsams*.
Rivulet *ču-pran*.
Road *lam*, *šul*, *šul-lám*, *₀gro-sa*; — book *lam-yig*.
Roam *₀kor-ba*, *₀pyo-ba*, *₀grim-pa*, *yar-ba*.
Roar vb. n. *₀krog-pa*, *ńu-ba*, *ldir-ba*, *ńa-ro sgrog-pa*.
Roar, Roaring s. *ńa-ro*, *ńar-skad*, *₀ur* 499.
Roast vb. a. *rńod-pa*, *sreg-pa*.
Roast-flour *rtsam-pa*.
Rob *rku-ba*, *₀prog-pa*, **kog-te kyer-če* W*.
Robber *mi-sér*.
Robbery *čoms*, *bcom-pa*.
Rock s. *brag*; — salt *rdo-tswa*.
Rock vb. n. *₀kyom-pa*, *dpyań-ba*; vb. a. *dpyań-la γtoń-ba* 328.
Rod *lčag*, *lčug-ma*, *dbyug-gu*.
Roll s. *gril*, *₀kor-lo*; paper — *šog-sgril*, *šog-ril W*.

Roll vb. a. *sgril-ba*, *sgre-ba*; to — one's self *ₒkri-ba*, *ₒgre-ba*; vb. n. *ldir-ba*; the rolling of thunder *ldi-ri-ri*.
Roof s. *tog*.
Room s. (apartment) *kaṅ-pa*, *kaṅ-bu*, *kaṅ-mig*, *naṅ-mig* C. W.; (space) *gu*, *go*; to find — v. *ₒgro-ba*, *šoṅ-ba*.
Root s. *ba-tag* W.; *rtsa-ba*, *rtsad*.
Root up vb. a. *rtsad-nas γčod-pa*.
Rope *sgrogs*, *tag pa*.
Rosary *ₒpreṅ-ba*.
Rose *se-ba*, *γse-ba*, *bse-ba*.
Rose-coloured *dkar-rgyá*.
Rot vb. n. *ₒdrul-ba*, *rul-ba*.
Rouge *skeg-tsós*.
Rough *gyoṅ-po*, *rtsub-po*, *rags-pa*, *rtsiṅ-ba*.
Roughness *ṅad* 126.
Round adj. *kor-kór*; *kyir-kyir* W.; *gor-mo*, *sgor-mo*; *zlum-pa*; *ril-ba*; to make — *sgoṅ-ba*; to be made — *ₒgril-ba*.
Round about adv. *kun-nas*, *pyogs bžir*.
Round s., the — of transmigration *ₒkor-ba* 58.
Rouse *dkrog-pa*; **šaṅ skul-če** W. 23.
Rove *ₒgrim-pa*, *rgyu-ba*.
Row vb. *skya rgyab-pa*.
Row s. (series) *gral*, *rim-pa*.
Row s. (fray) *ₒtab-mo*, *ₒdziṅ-mo*.
Royal *rgyal-poi*; — family *rgyal-rigs*; — residence *rgyal-sa*.
Rub vb. *bdar-ba*, *ₒdrud-pa*.
Rubbish *gal-ró*, *rdo-ro*, *sa-ró* W.
Ruby *pad-ma-ra-ga*.
Rudder *skya-mǰug*.
Rude *ₒkob*; *rtsiṅ-ba*; *gyoṅ-po*, very — *ka-gyon-če*.
Rugged *γtsaṅ-γtsoṅ*, *rtsub-po*.
Ruin vb. a. *ₒgud-pa*; to be ruined *ₒǰig-pa*.
Ruinous *gog-po*.
Ruins s., a house in — *kaṅ-rul*, *kaṅ-gog*.
Rule s. (regulation) *krims* 51; (special direction) *spyad-mtsáms* 456.
Rule vb. a. *ₒgod-pa*, *dbaṅ sgyur-ba* or *byed-pa*.
Ruler (governor) *mṅa-bdag*: *dbaṅ-po*; *srid*; (instrument) *tig-šiṅ*.
Rumination (chewing the cud) *skyug-ldád*.
Rumour s. *grag-pa*, *γtam*, *bšod-pa*; **zer-ke** C.; *tsor-lo* W.
Rump *byaṅ-kóg*.
Run vb. *rgyug-pa*, *ₒčor-ba*; to — about *ₒkyam-pa*; to — (flow) off *rdol-ba*; to — a race *dkyu-ba*.
Rupee *dṅul*; *kyir-mo* Ld., *gir-mo* 68, *gor-mo* W.; Tibetan — **čo-táṅ** C. 145.
Rupture *čag-čád*.
Rush s. (reed) *snyug-ma*.
Rush vb. *ₒkrog-pa*, *rgyug-pa*.
Russia *rgya-sér*.
Russian s. *rgya-ser-pa*.
Rust s. *btsa*, *γya*, *lčags-γya*.
Rut (track) *mal*, *šul*.

S

Sable s. *bka-blon sram* W., *brag-sram* W.
Sack s. *pad*.
Sacrament *dam-bča* 250.
Sacred *dag-pa*.
Sacrifice vb. a. *mčod-pa* 166.
Sacrificial, — ceremony *sku-rim* 22; — feast *mčod-ston*.
Saddle s. *sga*, *rta-sga*; — cloth *ka-lé*, *sga-kébs*; — girth *glo* W.
Saddle vb. a. *sga bstad-pa*, resp. *čibs-sga bstad-pa*.
Safe adj. *brtan-pa*, *btsan-po*.
Saffron *gur-kúm*; *ka-če-skyes* 36.
Saiga-antelope *rgya-ra*.
Sail s. *dar*, *γyor-mo*.
Sail vb. *gru-la žon-te lam-du ₒgro-ba*; v. also *rgal-ba* 103.
Saint *grub-tób* 78; *skyes-bu dam-pa* 31; *rnal-ₒbyor-pa* 315.
Sake, for the — of *pyir* 351.
Sal ammoniac *rgya-tsá*; *tsa-tsé* C.
Salary *pogs*.
Salt s. *tswa*, *lan-tswa*; vb. a. *tswa ₒdebs-pa*
Saltpetre *ze-tswa*, *šo-ra*.
Salutation *pyag*.
Salute vb. a. *pyag ₒtsal-ba*, *ₒbul-ba* or *byed-pa*.
Same adj. *nyid*; at the — time *γčig-čar*; of the — kind *γčig-pa*, *γčig-γčig* W.; one and the — *γčig*; the very — *de-ko-na*, *de-ka*; *de raṅ*, *de-ka raṅ*.
Sample *bkod-pa*.
Sanctuary *mčod-γnas*.
Sand *bye-ma*.
Sandal-tree *tsan-dan*.
Sanskrit *nā-ga-ri*.
Sap s. *bčud*, *ku-ba*.
Satiate *ₒgraṅ-ba*.
Satisfaction *skaṅ-γso*.
Satisfied *tsim-pa*.
Satisfy vb. a. v. *graṅ-ba* 98; v. *ṅom-pa* 130.
Saturday, Saturn *γza-spen-pa*.
Sauce *skyu-rum*, *spags*.
Sausage *sgyu-ma*.
Save vb. a. (deliver) *skyabs byed-pa*, *skyoṅ-ba*, *sgrol-ba*, *skyob-pa*, *ₒpaṅs-pa*, *sruṅ-ba*; (lay up) *sri-ba* 581, *paṅ-ba* 340; to be —d *tar-ba* 230.

Saviour *skyabs-mgon* 26; *srog-skyób W.*
Savour s. *bro-ba.*
Saw s. *sog-le C.*, *cad-* or *rgya-sóg W.*; vb. a. **cad-sog šrul-ce* W.*
Say *sgo-ba*, resp. *mol-ba W.*; *smra-ba*, *zer-ba*, *bšad-pa*, resp. *γsuṅ-ba*; *bka-rtsol-ba*; he says, he said *na-re* 300; to — nothing of (let alone) *lta či smos.*
Scale s. (of a fish) *k̔rab*; (of a balance) *k̔u-le*; (for measuring) *skar-ťsád*; pair of scales *sraṅ.*
Scale off vb. n. *gog-pa.*
Scar s. *rmai rjes*, or *šul*, or *mal.*
Scarce adj. *dkon-pa.*
Scarf *ska-rags*; — of salutation *k̔a-btágs* 37.
Scatter vb. a. *ogrems-pa*, *γtor-ba*; to be scattered *otor-ba.*
Scene *groṅ-k̔yér*, *ltad-mo*; v. *gleṅ-γži.*
Scenery *snaṅ-ťsúl.*
Scent s. (odour) *ṅad*, *dri-bsuṅ.*
Scholar (pupil) *grwa-pa*, *slob-ma*, *slob-baṅs*, *slob-p̔rug*, *k̔rid-p̔rúg*, *mk̔an-bu*, *rgyud-pa*; (man of letters) *mk̔as-po.*
School s. *grwa*, *slob-grwá*, *čos-gra*; — boy *grwa-p̔rug*; — house *grwa-kaṅ*; — master *grwa-dpón*; — room *bšad-grwá*; — table *čos-k̔ri.*
Science *rig-pa*; sciences *γtsug-lág.*
Scientific, — work *bstan-bčos.*
Scissors *čan-pa* 155, *cem-tse C.*, *grim-tse Sik.*
Sclerotic of the eye *gaṅs.*
Scold vb. *bka-bkyon-pa*, *spyo-ba.*
Scoop s. *skyogs*; vb. a. *ǒu-ba.*
Scope *ogro-sa*, *spyod-yul.*
Scorn vb. *to-otsam-pa.*
Scrap *čag-dúm.*
Scrape vb. *obrad-pa*, *odrad-pa.*
Scratch vb. *spar-mos obrad-pa.*
Scream vb. *sgrog-pa.*
Screaming s. *skad-ṅán*, *skad-lóg.*
Screw s. *γču-ba.*
Scripture, Holy scripture, *γsuṅ-ráb*, *γsuṅ-mčóg.*
Scrotum *rlig-bu*, *rlig-šúbs.*
Scruple s. *rtog-pa*, *rnam-rtóg*
Scullion *ma-γyóg*, *ťab-γyóg.*
Sculpture *brkos-ma.*
Sea *rgya-mťso*; — captain *ded-dpon*; — monster *ču-srin.*
Seal s. (stamp) *rgya*, resp. *p̔yag-rgyá*; *ťe-mo*, col. *ťe-tse*; *dam-k̔a*, resp. *p̔yag-dám*; vb. a. *dam-k̔a brgyab-pa.*
Sealing-wax *la-ča.*
Seam s. *mťa-ma*, *sne-mo*, *ťsem (-po).*
Search vb. *otsol-ba*, *γžig-pa*; to — into *sar-* or *ťsar-γčod-pa.*
Season *dus* 255, **nam-da, nam-la** 304.
Seat s. *k̔ri*, *rten*, *γži-ma* 480.
Seclusion *dben-pa*, *dben-γnas* 389.
Secrecy *lkog.*
Secret s. and adj. *γsaṅ-ba.*
Secretary *yig-mk̔an*: *bka-druṅ C.*
Sect *čos-lugs*, *lugs.*
Section *k̔ag*, *skabs*, *skor*, *rnam-pa*, *bam-po*, *dbye-ba*; *yan-lag.*
Sedan-chair *ok̔yogs*, *k̔yogs-dpyaṅ*, *p̔eb-dpyaṅ C.*
Sediment *snyigs-pa*, *ťsigs-ma*, *ro.*
Seduce *ṙnod-pa*, *slu-ba.*
Seducer *mi-dgei bšes-nyén.*
See vb. *mťoṅ-ba*, resp. *γzigs-pa*; to be seen *snaṅ-ba.*
Seed s. *sa-bon.*
Seek *otsol-ba.*
Seize *ojug-pa*, *oťam-pa*, *oťogs-pa*, *odzin-pa*, *len-pa*, resp. *bžes-pa.*
Seizure *odzin.*
Select vb. *odam-pa*, *obyed-pa.*
Self *ṅo* 129, *ṅos*, *nyid*, *bdag*, *raṅ*, I myself *ṅed-raṅ* 128, *ṅa-raṅ* 522; — dependant *raṅ-dbaṅ.*
Selfish *dṅos-odzin-can*; to be — *ṅos odzin-pa.*
Selfishness *dṅos-odzin*, *raṅ-odód.*
Sell *oťsoṅ-ba*; to be sold *ogyag-pa*, *ogrim-pa W.*
Send *skur-ba*, *ok̔al-ba*, *mṅag-pa*, *γtoṅ-ba*, *rdzoṅ-ba*, *zlog-pa*; to — for *ogugs-pa*; to — forth *obyin-pa*; to — word *spriṅ-ba.*
Senior (elder) *rgad-po.*
Sense s. (intellectual power) *blo-grós* 385, *dbaṅ-po* 387; (meaning) *dgoṅs-pa* 87, *don* 258.
Sensible *ťsul-mťún.*
Sentence *žal-čé*; to pass — *žal-če γčod-pa*; *ťag-čod-pa byed-pa.*
Sentiment *blo* 384; false — *lta-lóg* 217.
Sentinel *mel-ťse*, *bya-ra.*
Separate vb. a. *dgar-ba*; vb. n. *ogol-ba*, *ogye-ba*, *op̔ral-ba*; *so-só byed-pa*; to be separated *obral-ba.*
Separate adj. *sgos*; *so-so*
Separation *gud* 69.
Sepulchre *baṅ-so.*
Series *gral*, *gras*, *rim-pa.*
Serpent *sbrul*; — demon *klu* 8.
Serrated *coṅ-cóṅ.*
Serum *ču-sér.*
Servant *γyog-po*, *γyog-mo*; *k̔ol-po*, *k̔ol-mo*; *bran-po*, *bran-mo*; *bran-k̔ól*; *mi-lág*; *žabs-p̔yi*, *mṅag-γžug*; your servant! *da čen žu W.* 152.
Serve vb. *žal-ta byed-pa*; to — up *odren-pa.*
Service *žabs-ťóg* 472; at your — *'oṅ-le*, *'a W.*
Sesame *til*; — oil *til-már.*
Set vb. a. to — about *rtsom-pa*, *čas-pa*; to — at *p̔yo-p̔yó*; to — forth *rjod-pa*; to — in order *ogod-pa*, *γtan-la obebs-pa*; vb. n.

to — (of the sun) *nub-pa*, *skyod-pa W.*; to — out (depart) *čas-pa*.
Settle vb. a., to — a business *go čod-pa*; vb. n. *ₒtsugs-pa* 459.
Settled adj. (decided) *zad-pa*; (at an end) *zin-pa*, *rdzogs-pa*.
Settlement (colony) *babs-sa*.
Seven num. *bdun*; seventh *bdun-pa*: seventeen *bču-bdun*; seventeenth *bču-bdun-pa*; seventy *bdun-ču*; seventieth *bdun-ču-pa*.
Several *ka-čig*, *ₒga*, *mi-ₒdra-ba*.
Severe *ynyan-pa*, *drag-pa*.
Severity *ňad W.*
Sew *ₒtsem-pa*.
Sex *rten* no. 4, 213.
Sexual *rten-gyi*.
Shackle s. *lčags*, *lčags-sgrog*.
Shade s. *grib*.
Shadow s. *grib-ma*.
Shake vb. a. *skyod-pa*, *skyom-pa*, *sgul-ba*, *sprug-pa*; vb. n. *ₒgul-ba*, *lčogs-pa*.
Sham, to perform a — work *bčos-su byed-pa*.
Shame s. *krel*, *ňo-tsa*, *bag-yod(-pa)* 364, *žabs-ₒdrén* 472; it is a —! *krel-ba yod W.* (**fel-wa yod**).
Shamefaced *ňo-tsa-čan*.
Shameless *krel-méd*; *ňo-tsa-med-pa*.
Shape s. *dbyibs*, *yzugs*, *čas*, *bkod-pa*.
Share vb. *bgod-pa*; s. *bgo-skal*, *skal-ba*; *ča*, *ča-šás*.
Sharer *go-kan W.*
Sharp adj. (not blunt) *rno-ba*; (to the taste) *tsa-ba*; *ber-čan*.
Sharpness (of an edge) *ka* IV, no. 5, 35.
Sharpsightedness *mig-sál W.*
Shave *ₒbreg-pa*, *bžar-ba*.
Shawl *do-šā-lā*.
She pron. *ko*, *koň* 41, *de* 255.
Sheaf *lag-kód*.
Shears v. *čan-pa* 155.
Sheath s. *šubs*.
Shed s. (slight building) *bkad-sa* 12.
Shed vb.a. *ldug-pa*, *blug-pa*; (tears) *bsil-ba*.
Sheep *lug*; flock of — *lug-kyu*; — fold *lug-rá*.
Sheet of paper *gre-ga C.*, *šog-bu*; *šog-gáň W.*
Shelf *slaň-ka*.
Shell s. (husk) *kog-pa*, *gaň-bu*, *lgaň-bu*; (mollusk) *duň* 253, *ₒgron-bu* 102; vb. a. *bgrud-pa*.
Shell-lac *rgya-skyégs*.
Shelter s. *skyibs*; *skyabs-ynás*; *yyam*; *čar-skyibs*.
Shepherd *lug-pa*.
Shield s. *pa-li*, *pub*.
Shift vb. n. *ₒpo-ba*.
Shine vb. n. *čar-ba*, *ₒtser-ba*, *snaň-ba*; s. *od*.
Shining (bright) *čem-me-ba*, *lčam-me-ba*; *krol-krol W.*
Ship s. *gru*, *gru-bo*, *yziňs*; — master *gru-dpon*.
Shirt s. *mgo-kár Ld.*
Shiver vb. *ₒgul-ba*.
Shoe s. *lham*; soft — *ba-bu*; — of plaited straw *bu-la*; — strap *lham-sgróg*.
Shoot s. *lčug-ma*; vb. n. *ₒkruň-ba*; vb. a. *ₒpen-pa*.
Shooting-star *ke-tu*, *skar-mdá*.
Shore *ₒgram*, *skam-sa*.
Short *tuň-ba*; in — *sgril-bas* 120, *mdor-na* 273; cf. also *zur-tsam* 489.
Shortsighted *mig-rgyaň-tuň*.
Shoulder s. *dpuň-pa*, *prag-pa*; — blade *sog-pa*.
Shout vb. *ₒgrags-pa*, *sgrog-pa*.
Shovel s. *kyem*; coal — *me-skyogs*.
Show vb. a. *ston-pa*, *ňom-pa*, *sdigs-pa*.
Showman *ltad-mo-mkan*.
Shrewd *mkas-pa*.
Shrine *rten*.
Shrink vb. n. (to be contracted) *ₒkum-pa*, (to recoil) *ₒdzem-pa*, *čum-pa*.
Shriveled, Shrunk, *kums-pa*.
Shudder vb *yya-ba*.
Shun *spoň-ba*, *ₒdzem-pa*.
Shut vb. a. (a door) *ₒgegs-pa*; (the eyes) *ₒdzum-pa*; to — off or out *ₒkegs-pa*; to — up *skyil-ba*, *sgyoň-ba*.
Shuttle *doň-po*.
Shy vb. n. (of horses) *ₒdrog-pa*.
Shy adj. *ₒdrog-čan*.
Sick *nad-pa*; v. also *yi-ga čus* 508.
Sickle *zor-ba*, *rgya-zór*.
Sickly *nad-bu-čan*.
Side s. *logs*, *ňo*, *ňos*, *ňogs*, *ₒdabs*, *rol* 536, *kud-ma*; (of the body) *dku*, *yžogs*, *glo*, *ₒgram*, (direction) *pyogs* 352.
Sieve *lčags-tsags*.
Sigh s. *kog-šúgs W.*, *šugs-nár*, *sugs-riň*.
Sight *ltad-mo*, *snaň-ba*, *mtoň-snáň*.
Sign s. *rgya*, resp. *pyag-rgya*; *mtsan-ma*, *mtsan-nyid*, *rgyu-mtsan*; *rtags*; *brda* 297.
Signature *rgya-rtags*.
Signification *don*.
Signify v. *yin-pa* 510.
Sikim *ₒbras-ljóňs*.
Silence *čem-me-ba*.
Silent, to be — *ka-rog-pa*; *čaň mi smra-ba*.
Silk *dar*, *gos*; — cloth *za-ₒóg*; — thread *gos-skúd*; silks *gos-čén*, col. *go-šén*.
Silk-worm *dar-srin*.
Silver s. *dňul*; — in bars *gag*.
Similar *ₒdra-ba*; **tsogs-se* W.*
Similitude *dpe*.
Simple *rkyaň-pa*.
Simultaneously *yčig-čar*.

Sin s. *saig-pa, nyes-pa, nyon-mons-pa skyon, sgrib-pa*; heinous — *rme-ba* 425; deadly — *mtsams-med-pa* 455.
Since adv. (ever since) *bzuṅs-te*; conj. *pas*.
Sincere *draṅ-po*.
Sinew *ču-ba*.
Sinful *sdig-čan, skyon-čan*.
Sing *glu len-pa*.
Singed, Singeing *me-γžob*.
Single adj. (separate) *γčig-ka, γčig-pu* 144; *nyag-ma, rkyaṅ-pa*; (unmarried) *k̔yo-méd*; *čuṅ-ma-méd*; – combat *k̔rug-pa, ₒdziṅ-mo*.
Sink vb. n. *rgud-pa, nub-pa. ₒbyiṅ-ba*.
Sinner *sdig-po, sgrib-pa*.
Sir *γtso-bo* 434; *s̔a-heb*, col. *sāb* 571; *'a-ǰó* 603; dear Sir *bžin-bzáṅ* 483.
Sister *sriṅ-mo, mčed*, resp. *lčam-mo*; elder — *'a-če* 603; younger — *nu-mo* 305.
Sit *sdod-pa*, resp. *bžugs-pa*; *ₒdug-pa, ₒk̔od-pa*; sitting cross-legged *skyil-krúṅ* 27.
Site *mal*.
Situated, to be -- towards *lta-ba*.
Situation *γnas-skabs*.
Six num. *drug*, sixth *drug-pa*; sixteen *bču-drug*, sixteenth *bču-drug-pa*; sixty *drug-ču*, sixtieth *drug-ču-pa*.
Size *če-kyad, če-čuṅ, t̔sad, boṅ, k̔yon, rgya*.
Skeleton *keṅ-rus*.
Sketch s. *bkod-pa*; *zur tsam bsdu-ba* 489.
Skilful *mk̔as-pa, sgrin-po, t̔abs-šes-pa*; *t̔abs-čan W.*; *skyen-pa, spyaṅ-po*.
Skill *sgyu-rtsál*.
Skin s. *pags-pa, ko-ba*.
Skirt s. *gos-sgab, gos-mt̔a, t̔u-ba*.
Skull *t̔od-pa*.
Sky *nam-mk̔a, γnam*.
Slab *spaṅ, γya-ma*.
Slacken vb. a. *glod-pa*.
Slackened adj. *lhod-pa, lhod-po*.
Slander s. *p̔ra-ma, smad-sgra*.
Slander vb. *p̔ra-ma byed-pa*, or *smra-ba*, or *ₒǰug-pa*, resp. *γsol-ba, žu-ba*.
Slanderer *p̔ra-ma-mk̔an*.
Slanting *yo-ba, yon-po*.
Slate *γya-ma*.
Slaughter s. *γsod-γčod*; vb. a. *γsod-pa, ske γčod-pa*, resp. *ₒgom-pa*.
Slave s. *bran, mṅag-γžúg*.
Sleep s. *γnyid*, resp. *mnal*.
Sleep vb. *nyal-ba, γnyid-log-pa*, resp. *γzim-pa*.
Sleeping-room *γzim-k̔aṅ*.
Sleet s. *k̔a-ma-čár*.
Sleeve *p̔u-dúṅ*.
Slender *kyaṅ-po*; *kyaṅ-kyaṅ riṅ-mo W.*
Slide vb. n. *ₒdred-pa*.
Slight adj. *p̔ra-ba*.
Slight vb. a. *ₒgyiṅ-ba, ₒgyiṅ-bag byed-pa*; *čo-ₒdri-ba*.
Sling s. *sgu-rdo*; — stone *rdo-γyúg*.
Slip in vb. n. *ₒk̔ril-ba, ₒk̔yud-pa, ₒdzul-ba*.
Slope s. *gud, ṅogs*.
Sloping *gyiṅ-mo W.*
Slow *bul-po, dal-ba*; (irresolute) **lo-sna maṅ-ba*; *lo-sna riṅ-mo** *W.*
Slowly *ṅaṅ-gis, gul-gúl*; *gu-le W.*, *ga-le C.*
Slowness *dal-ba, dal-bu*.
Smack vb. *k̔a brdab-pa*; *dkan-sgra ₒdebs-pa W.*
Small *čuṅ-ba, čuṅ-tse W.*; *p̔ra-ba*.
Small-pox *ₒbrum-nad*.
Smart adj. (gaily dressed) *rnam-ₒgyur-čan*; *γzab-mo, γzab-sprod*; *mčor-po*.
Smash *γčog-pa, rduṅ-ba*.
Smear *skud-pa, ₒbyug-pa*.
Smell s. *bsuṅ*; vb. a. *snom-pa*; vb. n. *mnam-pa*.
Smile s. *ₒdzum*, vb. n. *ₒdzum-pa*.
Smith *mgar-ba*.
Smoke s. *dud-pa*; vb. a. (tobacco) *ₒt̔uṅ-ba*.
Smooth adj. *ₒǰam-pa*.
Smooth vb. a. *dbur-ba, ₔur-ba, 'ur-ba*.
Smoothing-iron *lčags-bsró*.
Smuggle *p̔ag-t̔soṅ byed-pa*.
Smut s. *sre-nag*; *sre-mog W.*
Snail *skyogs-lto-bu*; — clover *ₔol*.
Snake *sbrul, ₒbu-riṅ, lto-ₒgro*.
Snap s. (with the fingers) *skad-čig* 19.
Snare s. *rnyi, snyi*.
Snatch vb. *ₒgog-pa*.
Sneak vb. *ₒǰab-pa*.
Sneeze vb. *sbrid-pa*.
Snipe *skyar-po, ču-skyar*; *tiṅ-ti-liṅ Ld.*
Snivel s. *snabs*.
Snore vb. *ṅug-pa, sṅur-ba*.
Snow s. *k̔a-ba, gaṅs*; — ball *k̔a-goṅ*; — bridge *rud-zam*; — fall *ₒbab*; — leopard *γsa. bsa*; — shoe *dkyar*; — slip *k̔a-rúd*; storm *k̔a-t̔súb, rluṅ-t̔súb, bu-yug*.
Snuff s. *sna-ₒdág W.*
So *čes* 142, *de-ltar* 256, *ₒdi-ltar* 275, *de-bžin-du* 256, *de-ₒdras* 282; just — *de-ka-ltar* 255; so as *tsam* 430; so that *tsam-du*; so then *yaṅ* 505.
Soak *sboṅ-ba*.
Soap s. *glaṅ-glád C.*, *sa-bon W.*
Soar *ldiṅ-ba, ₒp̔yo-ba*.
Sob s. *ṅud-mo*.
Socage *ₔu-lag* 499.
Society, human — *t̔sogs* 451.
Socket of the eye *mig-k̔úṅ*.
Sod *skaṅ-ša*.
Soda *bul*.
Soft *ₒǰam-pa, mnyen-pa, snyi-ba, ₒbol-po*.
Softly *ga-le C.*, *gu-le W.*
Soil s. *sa-γži*.
Soil vb. *bsgo-ba*.
Solder *k̔ro-čus sdom-pa*; **kar-ya daṅ žar-ce** *W.*
Soldier *dmag-mi*.

Sole of the foot *rkaṅ-mṫil.*
Sole adj. *γčig, γčig-pu* 144.
Solely *K̇o-na, ₒba-žig.*
Solid adj. (not hollow) *K̇oṅ-gaṅ, gar-bu, pu-ri med-K̇an W.*; (not liquid) *reṅs-pa*; (firm) *mK̇raṅ, ₒčag-čan W., sra-ba.*
Solitary adj. *dben-pa*; — place *dgon-pa.*
Solitude *dben-pa, ₒbrog, gud.*
Some *K̇a-čig, ga-čen, ga-šas, gaṅ-žig, ₒga, res-ₒga*; *či γtoṅ W., čig, čuṅ-žig*; *ča-lam*; *re-žig*; *la-lá.*
Somebody, some one, *γčig, γčig-čig.*
Somerset *ma-lág.*
Something *či žig*; *či-γtoṅ W.*
Somnambulism *γnyid-rdól.*
Son *bu, bu-ṗo, bu-tsa W.*, resp. *sras*; — in-law *mag-pa*; — of man *mii bu, mii-sras.*
Song *glu, mgur, dbyaṅs.*
Sonorous *sgra-čan, sgra-ldaṅ.*
Soon *sṅa, mgyogs-pa*; *myur-du*; as — as *ma-K̇ad, ma ṫag-tu* 227, *tsam-gyis* 431; sooner or later *sṅa-ṗyi.*
Soot *dreg-pa, sre-nág.*
Soothe *ži-bar byed-pa.*
Soothsayer *ča-mK̇an, rtsis-pa, mṫsan-mK̇an.*
Sorcerer *ₒgoṅ-po, ₒba-po*; sorceress *ₒba-mo.*
Sorcery *rnam-ṗrul, ṗra-mén*; to practise — *sprul-ba, rol-ba.*
Sorrel adj. *K̇am-pa.*
Sorrow s. *K̇oṅ-ₒK̇rugs*, col. **K̇og-ṫúg**.
Sorrowful *mi dga-ba.*
Sorry *koṅ-du čud-pa, mi dga-ba, blo mi bde-ba, sems skyo-mo.*
Sort s. *K̇yad-par, sna, rigs*; of what — *či lta-bu.*
Soul *nyams*, resp. *ṫugs-nyáms, dgoṅs-pa*; *rgyud*; *rnam-šes, sems.*
Sound s *skad, K̇rol*; *sgra, sgra-skád.*
Sound vb.n. *K̇rol-ba, ₒgrags-pa*; vb.a. *sgra* [*sgrog-pa.*
Sound adj. *rem-pa, bde-ba.*
Soup *ṫug-pa.*
Sour adj. *skyur-ba, skyur-po C., skyur-mo W.*
Source *ču-mig, ču-mgo*; *K̇uṅs, ₒgo-ma.*
South *lho.*
Sovereign s. *dbaṅ-po.*
Sow s. *ṗag-mo*; — thistle *K̇al-pa.*
Sow vb. a. *sa-bon ₒdebs-pa.*
Space *gu, go.*
Spade *lčags-K̇yém.*
Span s. *mṫo.*
Spare vb. *ṗaṅ-ba.*
Spark *me-ltág, me-ṫság.*
Sparkle *ₒK̇ol-ba W., sag-ság zer-ba C.*
Sparrow *bya-po skya-bo W.*; — hawk *K̇ra, mčil-K̇ra.*
Spasm *rtsa-čus* or *-ₒdus*; *ₒčiṅ-ba C.*
Spawn s. *sgo-ṅa, sgoṅ.*
Speak *smra-ba*, resp. *bka-stsol-ba*; *mol-ba W.*; *lab-pa*, resp. *γsuṅ-ba, zer-ba.*
Spear s. *mduṅ.*
Specimen v. *ṗud* 344.
Speck *rme-ba, sme-ba.*
Spectacles *šel-mig*; snow — **mig-ḍa**.
Spectator *ltad-mo-pa.*
Speech *skad, ṅag, γtam, ṫsig, brjod*, resp. *bka*, resp. *γsuṅ*; *dpe-sgra W.*
Speed, good —! **ṫam-pa čo** *W.*
Speedily *myur-du, nye-bar.*
Speedy *mgyogs-pa, mgyogs-riṅs W.*; *myúr-ba, riṅs-pa.*
Spell s. *γzuṅs, γzuṅs-sṅags.*
Spend *skyag-pa, čud γzon-pa*; to be spent *ča-ba, ₒgro-ba, ₒgyag-pa, ₒṫsar-ba, ₒdzad-pa.*
Sphere *dkyil-ₒK̇or* 11; *groṅ* 79, *ṅaṅ* 126; — of activity *spyod-yul.*
Spice *sdor, spod*; *ṫsan-te W.*
Spider *ṫags-gra-ₒbu, ₒbag-rág.*
Spin *ₒK̇al-ba, ₒK̇el-ba.*
Spindle *ṗaṅ.*
Spirit *sems, sems-nyid*; *kun-γži* 4; evil — *γdon* 267. *ₒgoṅ-po* 95.
Spirited *hur-po.*
Spit vb. *ṫu gyab-če W., ṫo-le ₒdebs-pa W.*
Spittle *mčil-ma*, resp. *žal-čab.*
Spleen (milt) *mčer-pa.*
Splendid *ₒod-čan, grags-čan.*
Splendour *rṅam-pa, dṅom-pa, rṅom-brjid, brjid, dpal, byin, zil, γzi, γzi-brjid.*
Splint (for a broken limb) *čag-šiṅ.*
Splinter s. *ṫsal-pa, šiṅ-ṫsal*; *šiṅ-zél W.*
Split vb. a. *ₒges-pa, γčog-pa, γšog-pa, čeg-pa*; vb. n. *ₒgas-pa.*
Spoil vb. a. (plunder) *ₒjoms-pa*; *γčil-ba.*
Spoiled (corrupted) *K̇ag-po*; to be — *saṅ-ba.*
Spoke *rtsib-ma.*
Sponge s. *ču-ₒK̇úr.*
Spontaneously *raṅ, raṅ-bžin-gyis, šugs-kyis, rgyu med-du* 110.
Spoon *ṫur-ma*; tip of a — *ṫur-mgo.*
Spoon-bill *skyar-léb.*
Sport vb. n. (frolic) *rtse-ba.*
Sportsman *K̇yi-ra-ba.*
Spot s. (locality) *go*; (stain) *grib*; (mark) *ṫig-le.*
Spouse (wife) *čuṅ-ma, btsun-mo, K̇ab.*
Spout s. *wa-mčú.*
Sprain vb. a. *ṫsigs ₒbud-pa* or *ₒbog-pa*; to be sprained *ₒK̇rul-ba.*
Spread vb. a. *rkyoṅ-ba, ₒgebs-pa, ₒK̇eb-pa, γčal-ba, rdal-ba, spel-ba, ₒdiṅ-ba, ₒbre-ba, ₒgrems-pa*; vb.n. *mčed-pa, ₒgye-ba, rgyas-pa, dar-ba, ldaṅ-ba.*
Sprightly *γčaṅ-po.*
Spring up vb. n. *čags-pa* 153.

Spring s. (fountain) *ču-mig, ḱron-pa*; (season) *dpyid.*
Sprinkle *ₒgrems-pa, čag-čag byed-pa.*
Sprout s. *sbál-mig, myu-gu, ṁyug.*
Sprout vb. n. *skye-ba, ₒḱruṅ-ba, rdol-ba.*
Spunk *spra-ba*; *tsa Ld.*
Spur s. (of horsemen) *rtiṅ-lčags*; mountain — *sgaṅ.*
Spy s. *lta-nyul-pa, mel-tse*; — glass *dur-bín, šel-mig.*
Spy vb. *so-byed-pa*; to — out (another's faults) *ₒtsaṅ bru-ba.*
Squander *γzan-pa.*
Square s. *ḱa-gáṅ*; adj. *ḱa-gaṅ-ba, ḱa-gaṅ-ma.*
Squash vb. *glem-pa.*
Squat vb. *tsog-pur sdod-pa* 432.
Squeeze vb. *glem-pa, bčer-ba.*
Squire v. *ga-gá.*
Stack s. *ṗub-rags.*
Staff *mḱar-ba, ₒḱar-ba, ber-ka.*
Stag *ša-ba* 556.
Stage (of a journey) *ₒbraṅ-sa.*
Stain vb. (sully) *bsgo-ba*; stained *nyams-pa.*
Staircase *ṫem-pa, rgya-skás*; *gya-šrás W.*
Stairs *ṫem-pa*; up — *ya-ṫog*, down — *ma-ṫog.*
Stake s. (in the ground) *rtod-pa*; (in a wager) *rgyal-rgyan.*
Stalk s. *rkaṅ, sdoṅ-po, ba-ṫag, rtsa-ba, sog-ma.*
Stallion *γseb.*
Stammerer *ḱa-ldig-mḱan W.*
Stamp s. *rgya*, resp. *ṗyag-rgyá.*
Stamp vb. *ₒḱrab-pa* 61.
Stanch vb. (the flowing blood) *sdom-pa.*
Stand vb. a. (bear) *bzod pa* 498; to be able to — *ṫub-pa, ṫeg-pa*; vb. n. *greṅ-ba, laṅs-te sdod-pa.*
Stand s. *stegs* 221.
Star *skar-ma*; shooting *skar-mdá.*
Start vb. (set out) *rgyug-pa*; (from alarm) *ₒdrog-pa.*
State s. (condition) *γnas-skabs, γnas-ṫsúl.*
Stately *ₒod-čan.*
Statue *sku, rdo-sku.*
Stature *sgo-po, sgo-bo.*
Stay vb. n. *ₒdug-pa, sdod-pa, γnas-pa, bžugs-pa.*
Steadfast *brtan-po.*
Steady *ₒṫsugs-pa.*
Steal vb. a *rku-ba, ma-sbyin-par len-pa*; vb. n. (slip) *ₒǰab-pa, nyul-ba, ₒdzul-ba.*
Stealth, by — *sbas-te W.*
Steam *rlaṅs-pa.*
Steel **čag-záṅ**, *ṗo-lád.*
Steelyard *rgya-ma, nya-ga*; *pur, spor, spo-ré, sraṅ.*
Steep adj. *γtsaṅ-γtsoṅ, γzar-ba.*
Steer vb. a. *ḱa-lo sgyur-ba.*
Stench *dri ṅan-pa, dri ṅa-ba, dri mnam.*
Step s. *gom-pa, rdog-pa*; — of a ladder *šral-daṅ* 21; vb. n. *bgom-pa, gom-pa ₒbor-ba, ₒgrul-ba, ₒčag-pa.*
Stepfather *ṗa-γyár*; stepmother *ma-gyár.*
Stick s. *ber-ka, dbyug-pa.*
Stick vb. n. *ḱad-pa, ₒbyor-ba*; vb. a. *sbyor-ba, ₒdzugs-pa.*
Sticky *rtsi-čan.*
Stiff *reṅs-pa*; to be — *reṅ-ba.*
Still adj. (quiet) *dal-ba, mi γyo-bar*; (silent) v. *ḱa rog-pa.*
Still adv. *da-rúṅ, yaṅ.*
Sting s. *mduṅ*; vb. a. *ₒbig(s)-pa, ₒdzug-pa* 466.
Stingy *lag-dam-po, ṫsags-ₒdod-čan.*
Stink vb. *mnam-pa.*
Stir vb. a. *dkrug-pa, srub-pa*; to — up *rnyog-pa, sprug-pa.*
Stirrup *yob, ₒob.*
Stitch vb. *sbrel-ba.*
Stocking *rkaṅ-šúbs*, resp. *žabs-šúbs.*
Stomach *grod-pa, ṗo-ba.*
Stone s. *rdo*; — of fruits *rus-pa*; vb. a. *rdo-rub-la btaṅ-če W.*
Stool *stegs* 221.
Stoop vb. *mgo dgu-ba, mgo dgur-ba* or *ₒgug-pa.*
Stop vb. a. *sub-pa, ₒgegs-pa*; vb. n. *ₒgag-pa, sdod-pa.*
Stopple, stopper *ḱa-ₒdig.*
Store s. *mdzod*; — room *mdzod-ḱaṅ, baṅ-ba, baṅ-ḱaṅ, ṫsoṅ-ḱaṅ.*
Storm s. *ṫsub-ma, rluṅ čen-po, drag-po.*
Story s. (floor) *ṫog*; (tale) *γnas-ṫsúl, lo-rgyus.*
Stout adj. *sbom-pa, rom-po*; (of cloth) *ṫsags-dam*; to grow — *brta-ba.*
Stove *ṫab, me-ṫáb.*
Straight adj. *draṅ-po, groṅs-po, bsraṅs-pa.*
Straighten *sroṅ-ba.*
Strain vb. a. (filter) *ₒṫsag-pa.*
Strainer *ču-ṫsags.*
Straits *sa-bár, mṫso-lag-ₒbrél.*
Stranger *ṗyi-mi, byes-pa.*
Strangle *ske bsdam-ste γsod-pa.*
Strangury *γčin-ₒgág.*
Strap s. *ko-ṫág, sgrog-gu, rog-bu W., luṅ.*
Stratagem *dku-lto.*
Straw *sog-ma, ṗub-ma.*
Strawberry *dpal-byór W.*
Stray v. *yan-pa* 506.
Street *rgya-sráṅ, lam-sráṅ.*
Strength *nyams-stóbs, stobs-po*; *šed*; of spirits etc. *ber.*
Strengthen *šed čug-če W.*
Stretch vb. *rkyoṅ-ba, šriṅ-ba.*
Strew *γtor-ba, ₒdiṅ-ba.*
Strewing-oblation *γtor-ma* 210.

Strict *dam-po.*
Stride vb. *bgom-pa.*
Strike vb. *°p̓og-pa, rgyab-pa, rduṅ-ba, rdeg-pa.*
String s. *rgyud, sgrog, °čiṅ-ba, °p̓reṅ-ba, t̓a-gu.*
Strip vb. *šu-ba, gos °bud-pa.*
Strive for vb. *snyegs-pa, °graṅ-pa, brtson-pa.*
Stroke s. *lčag, °p̓ras-pa.*
Stroke vb. *byil-ba, °byug-pa.*
Strong *gar-ba, drags-po, btsan-po, rem-pa* 535, *šed-čan.*
Structure *bkod-pa.*
Stubborn *mgo-k̓regs-pa.*
Student *slob-γnyér.*
Studious *brtson-°grus-čan.*
Study s. *°bad-pa.*
Stuff s. (cloth) *ras.*
Stuff vb. a *°tsaṅ-ba.*
Stunned *k̓al-k̓ól.*
Stupid *glen-pa, blun-pa, blo-gros-méd.*
Style s. *bzo, zo-sta W.* 497.
Subdue *°joms-pa.*
Subject s. *skor, gleṅ-γži, mṅa-žábs, bran, °baṅs.*
Subject vb. a. *°joms-pa, °og-tu °jug-pa* 501.
Subsequent *p̓yi-ma.*
Subside *ži-ba.*
Subsidy *°t̓ud-ma.*
Subsistence *°t̓so-t̓abs.*
Substance *dṅos-po, rdzas* 468.
Substantive *dṅos-miṅ.*
Substitute s. *t̓sab.*
Subtract *°dor-ba, sbyoṅ-ba, °bud-pa.*
Succession *t̓sir, rabs* 525, *rim-pa* 530.
Such *°di-°dra-ba* 282, *de-lta-bu* 256.
Suck *°jibs-pa, °t̓uṅ-ba.*
Suckling baby *žo-°t̓úṅs.*
Suddenly *glo-bur, glo-bur-du, har(-gyis); yaṅ-med-la W.*
Suet *grod-t̓sil, k̓oṅ-t̓sil.*
Suffer vb. a. *myoṅ-ba, bzod-pa*; vb. n. *mṅar-ba, γzir-ba.*
Suffice *°k̓yed-pa, ldaṅ-ba; čog-pa.*
Sugar *ka-ra, k̓a-ra*; raw — *bu-rám*; — cane *°dam-búr W.*
Suit s., a complete — of clothes *mgo-lus ča tsáṅ.*
Suitable, to be — *°oṅ-ba* 502, *°os-pa, ruṅ-ba.*
Suitor *°dod-mk̓an.*
Sully *bsgo-ba.*
Sulphur *mu-zi.*
Sum s. *brtsis-zin*; vb. to — up *sgril-ba, sdom-pa, sre-ba.*
Summary s. *sdom.*
Summer *dbyar.*
Summit *mgo, spo, rtse(-mo).*
Summon vb. a. *°gugs-pa.*
Sun *nyi-ma*; — beam *nyi-γzér*; — dial *nyi-tsód.*
Sunday *γza-nyi-ma.*
Superficies *ṅos, k̓a, γdoṅ.*
Superintend *žal-ta byed-pa.*
Superintendence *do-dám.*
Superior adj. *k̓yad, goṅ-ma, rgyal-ba, bla, rab*; s. *goṅ-ma, bla-ma.*
Supernumerary adj. *°t̓eb.*
Supine adj. *gan-kyál.*
Supper *dgoṅs-zas*; Lord's — *γsol-ras* 592.
Supple *mnyen-pa.*
Supplement *k̓a-skóṅ, yan-lag, lhan-t̓ábs.*
Supply vb. *sgrub-pa.*
Support vb. *skyoṅ-ba, °degs-pa, °dzin-pa*; s. *rten-pa, rgyab-rtén.*
Supposition resp. *bsam-pa, snaṅ-ba, bžed-pa, bžed-t̓sul.*
Suppress *non-pa, °joms-pa, snub-pa, sub-pa, °gegs-pa*
Sure *gor-ma-čág*, eleg. *gor-ma-bkúm* 73; *btsan-po* 434; to be sure! **tig, tag, de-ka yod** 255.
Surely *ṅes-par, nan-čágs* 303.
Surety *brtan-pa, γdeṅ-t̓sad.*
Surface *k̓a, ṅos, logs, °k̓od, γdoṅ-pa.*
Surpass *°da-ba.*
Surround *skor-ba.*
Suspend *dpyaṅ-ba, spyaṅ-ba* 328.
Swaddling-cloth *ču-stán W.*
Swallow s. *k̓ug-ta.*
Swallow vb. *mid-pa, k̓yur-mid-pa.*
Swamp s. *gram-pa.*
Swan *bžad, bžad-pa*; *ṅaṅ-pai rgyal-po.*
Swear *bro °t̓sal-ba, dmod-mo °bor-ba* 423.
Sweat s. *rṅul.*
Sweep vb. *p̓yag bdar-ba*; to — together *sdud-pa.*
Sweepings *pyag-dár.*
Sweet *dṅar-ba*; — scented *žim-po.*
Sweet-heart *°dod-grogs, mig-grogs, mdza-grogs, bzaṅ-grogs.*
Sweet-meats *žim-zé, žim-žim C., žim-zág W.*
Swell vb. n. *skraṅ-ba, °bo-ba.*
Swift adj. *skyen-pa, myur-ba, riṅs-pa.*
Swim *rkyal-ba, °p̓yo-ba.*
Swine *p̓ag.*
Swing vb. a. *dbyug-pa, γyob-pa.*
Switch s. *lčag.*
Swoon vb. n. *brgyal-ba.*
Sword *ral-gri.*
Syllable *sgra* 119, *t̓seg-bar* 450.
Symbol *rten* 213.
Symmetry *dpe-byad, byad.*
Symptom *mtsan(-ma), rtags.*
Synonym *skad-dód* 258.
Syphilis *p̓a-ráṅ, reg-dug.*
Syria *rum-šam.*
Syringe *γčiu.*

T

Tabernacle *gur-mčóg* 69.
Table *ćog-tse* 150, resp. *ysol-ćóg* 592; *ysol-stegs*; European — *rgya-ćóg*.
Tablet, bearing an inscription *byaṅ-bu*, *byaṅ-ma*.
Taciturn *smra-nyúṅ*.
Tail *ria-ma*, *mjug-ma*.
Tailor *tsem-pa*.
Take vb. a. *len-pa*, *₀togs-pa*, *₀dzin-pa*, resp. *bžes-pa*; **nam-će** W; to — for *₀dzin-pa* 465, *sems-pa*; to — off *₀bud-pa*, *šu-ba*; to — out *goṅ-pa*, *₀don-pa*, *₀byin-pa*; take away! *ḱur soṅ* C., *ḱur ḱyer* W.
Tale *lo-rgyús*, *sgruṅ(s)*.
Talent *blo*, *rig-pa*, *yon-tan*, *šes-rab*.
Talk s. *ytam*, *₋ur*; vb. *smra-ba*, *lab-pa*, *gleṅ-ba*, *₀bar-ba*, *₋ur ytoṅ-ba*.
Talkative *smra-₀dód*, *rgya-lab-čan*.
Tall col. *sgo-po riṅ-mo*, *kyaṅ-kyaṅ riṅ-mo*, *₀joṅ-₀jóṅ*.
Tallow-candle *tsil-sdóṅ*.
Tamarisk *₋om-bu*.
Tame adj. *dul-ba*, *₀dris-pa*, *yyuṅ-ba*; vb. a. *₀dul-ba*, *tul-ba*.
Tan vb a. *mnyed-pa*.
Tanner *ko-ba mnyed-mḱan* C.
Tardy *bul-po*.
Target *₀ben*.
Tarry vb. *₀gor-ba*.
Tartar (incrusting the teeth) *so-dreg*.
Task s. *ḱag*; *rgyugs* W.
Taste s. (savour) *bro-ba*, *ro*; vb a. *myoṅ-ba*; vb. n. *bro-ba*.
Tattered *čad-po*.
Tavern *čaṅ-ḱaṅ*
Tax s. *ḱral*, *dpya*; *₀bab* Sp; vb.a. (appraise) *₀jal-ba*.
Tea *ja*, resp. *ysol-já*; — pot *tib-ril*, resp. *ysol-tib*; — party *ja-mgrón*.
Teach vb *ston-pa*, *slob-pa*.
Teacher *ston-pa*, *slob-pa*, *slob-dpon*; *rgyud-pa*.
Team of bullocks *glaṅ-dór*.
Tear s. *mči-ma*; to shed tears *mči-ma blag-pa*.
Tear vb. a. *yšeg-pa*; to — out *₀pyid-pa*, *₀byin-pa*; to — to pieces *₀dral-ba*, *hral-ba*.
Tease *gob-nón čo-če* W.
Tedder vb. *btod-pa*; s. *btod-ṫág*.
Tell *₀čad-pa*, *snyod-pa*, *smra-ba*, *zer-ba*, *zlo-ba*, *zlos-pa*.
Temperate *tsod šes-pa*.
Temperature *graṅ-dro*.
Tempest *rluṅ čen-po* or *drag-po*, *rluṅ-dmár*, *yul-ṅán*.
Temple *mčod-ḱaṅ*.
Temporal *tse ₀dii*; — life *ynas-skabs*.
Tempt *nyams sad-pa*, *tsod ₀dzin-pa*.
Ten num. *bču*, *čig bču*; — thousand *ḱri*; tenth *bču-pa*.
Tenant *ḱaṅ-pa yyar-mḱan*.
Tend vb. a. *skyoṅ-ba*.
Tender adj. *snyi-ba*, *₀jam-pa*; *byams-pa*.
Tendon *nya-ču*.
Tenet *čos*.
Tent *gur*, resp. *bžugs-gur*.
Term s. (limited time) *čad-so*.
Terminate vb. n. *zin-pa*; vb. a. *₀tsar-bar byed-pa*.
Termination *mṫa* 239.
Terrace *steṅ-ka*, *steṅ-tse*.
Terrify *₀jigs-pa*, *₀jigs-skrag ₀don-pa* C.; **jig-ri skul-če** W.; to be terrified *skrag-pa*.
Test vb. a. *nyams sad-pa*; *tsod lta-ba* 216.
Testament *bka-čéms*, *ḱa-čéms*.
Testicle *rlig-pa*, resp. *ysaṅ-rlig*, euphem. *₀bras-bu*.
Testimony *če-bži*; v. *dpaṅ(-po)* 326.
Texture *ṫags*.
Than *las* 546, *pas*, *saṅ* W. 571.
Thank vb. *ytaṅ-rág byed-pa* or *₀bul-ba*.
Thanks s. *ytaṅ-rág*, *legs-ysól*; many —! *bka-drin-čé*, *ṅo-mtsar-čé* 456; *žu* W.
That pron. *de* 255; *so-či-ltar* 218.
The def. art. v. *de* 255.
Theatre *ltad-mo lta-bai sa*, *ltad-mo-ḱaṅ*.
Theft *rkun-ma*.
Theme *skor*.
Then *de-tsa-na*, *der* 256.
Theory *lta-ba* II, no. 3, 217.
There *de-na*, *de-ru* 256, *pa-gir* 338.
Therefore *de-bas-na*, *des-na*, *des* 256.
Therein *naṅ-na*.
They *ḱo-pa*; *ḱo-wa* W.; *ḱo-tso*, *ḱo-čag* C.; *de-dag*, *de-rnams*.
Thick *₀tug-pa*, *stugs-po*, *sbom-pa*, *rom-po*; (of fluids) *ska-ba*, *rnyog-pa*.
Thicket *tsaṅ-tsiṅ* 444.
Thickness *srab-₀túg* 244
Thief *rkun-ma*.
Thimble *lčuṅ-mo*, *mdzub-rtén*.
Thin adj. *pra-ba*, *zim-bu*, *siṅs-po* W.; *srab-pa*, *sla-ba*, *sla-mo*.
Thing *dṅos-po*, *ča*, *ča-byád*, *čas*, *rdzas*; things (goods) *ča*, *ča-lag*.
Think (suppose) *snyam-pa*; (meditate) *sem(s)-pa*; *bsam-mno byed-pa* or *ytoṅ-ba*, resp. *dgoṅs-pa*; to — of *dran-pa* 261, *dgoṅs-pa*.
Third num. *sum-pa*; thirteen *bču-sum*; thirteenth *bču-sum-pa*; thirty *sum-ču*; thirtieth *sum-ču-pa*; a third, third part *sum-ča*, *sum-yar*.
Thirst s. *skom*, *skom-pa*, *skom-dád*; vb. *skom-pa*.

This *ₒdi* 275.
Thither *de-ru, der* 256; *p̔yogs der* 352.
Thong *ko-t̔ág.*
Thorn *t̔ser-ma.*
Thoroughly *k̔yon-nas.*
Thou *k̔yed, k̔yod,* resp. *nyid.*
Though v. *kyi* 6.
Thought *bsam-pa,* resp. *dgoṅs-pa, snyam-pa, snaṅ-ba, dmigs-pa, ₒčar-sgo, nyams.*
Thousand num. *stoṅ*; ten — *k̔ri, k̔ri-k̔rag, k̔ri-t̔so*; hundred — *ₒbum, ₒbum-t̔so.*
Thrash vb. *γyul-k̔a γčog-pa, γyur byed-pa* C., **k̔o-yu skor-če** W.
Thread s. *skud-pa, ₒt̔sem-skúd*; *snal-ma* 319, *nyag-t̔ág* 185.
Threaten *gam-pa* W.
Three num. *γsum, sum.*
Threshold *t̔em-pa, sgo-t̔ém.*
Thrifty *paṅ-sems-čan.*
Throat *mgul,* resp. *mgur, lkog-ma, ske, gre-ba, mgrin-pa, 'o-lé* W.; sore — *mgul-nad.*
Throb vb. *ₒp̔ar-ba.*
Throne s. *rgyal-sa, k̔ri, sen-ge-k̔ri.*
Through *ltaṅ, lteṅ* 217; *p̔yir* 351.
Throughout *t̔og-t̔ág* 237.
Throw vb. a. *rgyab-pa, rgyag-pa, skyur-ba, γtor-ba, ₒp̔en-pa, dbyug-pa*; *ₒbor-ba* C.; to — down *ₒbud-pa, ₒbebs-pa*; to — off *spoṅ-ba.*
Thumb s. *t̔e-bo, mt̔e-bo.*
Thunder s. *ₒbrug, ₒbrug-skád, ₒbrug-sgr...*
Thunderbolt *t̔og, lče, rdo-rje, γnam-lčags.*
Thursday *γza-p̔ur-bu.*
Thus *de-ltar, ₒdi-ltar, de-bžin-du, de-ₒdi us* C., *de-tsug* W.
Thwart (frustrate) *sgyel-ba.*
Tiara *čod-pán.*
Tibet *bod.*
Tibetan m. *bod-pa,* f. *bod-mo*; — language *bod-skad*; — printing-characters *dbu-čan* 388; — current handwriting *dbu-méd.*
Tick. s. *lug-šig.*
Tickle vb. **ki-tsi kug-če** W.; *gug-pa* W.
Tide s. *dus-rlábs.*
Tidings *p̔rin*; glad — *γtam-snyán*; (gospel) *p̔rin bzaṅ-po.*
Tie s. *ₒčiṅ-ba,* vb. a. *ₒčiṅ-ba, ₒk̔yig-pa.*
Tiger *stag.*
Tight *dam-po, t̔aṅ-po.*
Till, until *bar-du* 366, *t̔ug* C.; *t̔sug-pa* W.
Till vb. a. *ₒdul-ba.*
Time s. *dus, t̔se, skabs*; (while) *yun*; time, times *lan*; one —, once *lan-γčig*; ten — *lan-bču*; point of —, proper — for *bsgaṅ* 124.
Timid *ₒjigs-pa, ₒjigs-mk̔an, ₒjigs-pa-čan*; *sems-čuṅ-ba.*
Tin s. *ža-nye dkar-po, ža-dkár, dkar-ya*; — plate *ta-li* W.
Tinder-box *lčags-mag.*
Tire vb. a. *ṅal ₒjug-pa.*
Tired *dub-pa*; to be — *dub-pa, skyo-ba.*
Tithe s. *ču-k̔ág* W
Title s. *mt̔san*; (claim) *t̔ob-srol.*
To prep. *mdun* 273, *druṅ-du,* resp. *žabs-druṅ-du* 263, *rtsar* 437, *gan-du* 66.
Tobacco *t̔a-ma-k̔a*; — pipe *gaṅ-zág, žal-zág.*
To-day *de-riṅ* C., *ₒdi-riṅ* W.
Toe *rkaṅ-sór, sor-mo*; the big — *rkaṅ-pai mt̔e-bo.*
Together *γčig-tu, lhan-čig-tu*; — with *bčas-pa, mnyam-du.*
Token *mt̔san-ma.*
Tola (Indian half ounce) *dṅul,* col. *mul.*
Toll s. *šo-gam.*
Tomb *dur, baṅ-so.*
Tongs *rkam-pa.*
Tongue *lče,* resp. *ljags.*
Too adv. (too much) *ha-čaṅ*; conj. (also) *yaṅ.*
Tool *čas*; tools *yo-byád, lag-ča.*
Tooth *so,* resp. *t̔sems*; — ache *so-zug*; — brush *so-zéd*; — pick *t̔sems-šiṅ, so-šiṅ.*
Top s. *rtse(-mo).*
Topography *γnas-bšád, yul-bšád.*
Torch *gal-mé, sgron-ma.*
Torment vb.a. *ₒt̔se-ba*; *sdug-bsṅal* or *γnag ston-pa* W.
Torn adj. *ral-ba, čad-po.*
Tortoise *rus-sbal.*
Torture vb. a. *mi-la γnag ston-pa* W.
Totter *yam-yóm byed-pa.*
Touch vb. *nyug-pa, γtug-pa, t̔ug-pa, reg-pa.*
Toupet *t̔or-čóg, t̔or-t̔súgs.*
Towards *t̔og-tu* 237, *t̔ad-du, p̔yogs-su.*
Towel *lag-ₒp̔yis.*
Tower *mk̔ar dgu-t̔og.*
Town *groṅ, groṅ-kyer*; *yul-gru*; *rgyal-sa* W.
Toy s. *rtsed-mo.*
Trace s. *rkaṅ-rjés, mal.*
Track s. *rjes, šul.*
Trackless *rjes-méd.*
Tractable *srab-k̔a dul-mo.*
Trade s. *t̔soṅ, bzo.*
Tradesman *k̔e-pa.*
Trading-place *las-sgo.*
Traffic s. *t̔soṅ.*
Train vb. a. *sbyoṅ-ba*; to — up *skyed-sriṅ-ba.*
Trample vb. a. *rdzi-ba, rdog-pas rduṅ-ba.*
Tranquil *ži-ba.*
Tranquillity *žod.*
Transaction *las.*
Transfer vb. *spo-ba, ₒgod-pa.*
Transform *sgyur-ba*; to — one's self *sprul-ba* 336; to be transformed into *ₒgyur-ba* 96, *ₒgro-ba* 101.

Transformation *rdzu-ₒṗrul.*
Transgress *ₒgal-ba; ₒda-ba.*
Transgression *ₒgal-k̇rül.*
Translate *sgyur-ba.*
Transmigration, the round of — *ₒk̇or-ba* 58.
Transplant *spo-ba.*
Transport vb. *skyel-ba, ₒk̇yer-ba.*
Trap s. *rnyi, snyi; ldem-pa W.;* — door *ɣnam-sgo;* mouse — *bi-ldém W.,* fox *wa-ldém W.*
Travel vb. *ₒgro-ba, ₒgrod-pa, bgrod-pa; č̇a-ba W.*
Tread vb. a. *rdzi-ba; *čag-čag ċo-ċe* W.;* vb. n. *ₒčag-pa, ₒčags-pa.*
Treadle *rkań-šiń.*
Treasure s. *ɣter.*
Treasurer *dkor-pa, ṗyag-mdzód.*
Treasury *dkor-mdzód.*
Treat s (feast) *mgron.*
Treat vb. n. (to use) *spyod-pa* 334: (to regale) *mgron-du ɣnyer-ba;* to — medically *bċos-pa; sman-dpyad byed-pa* 329; vb. n. to — of *ṙjod-pa* 182.
Treatise *rgyud, rgyud-sdé.*
Treatment, good — *bzań-lúgs W.*
Treaty *bzań-sgrig.*
Tree *šiń, sdoń-po, šiń-sdóń.*
Tremble *ₒgul-ba, ₒdar-ba.*
Trespass vb. n. *bar-du ɣċod-pa* 367.
Trevet *lċags-sgyid.*
Trial (before a tribunal) *ɣtam-sdúr W*
Tribe *sde.*
Tribunal *k̇rims-k̇ań.*
Tribute *dpya*
Trick s. *bar-čad;* to play tricks *to-ₒtsam-pa.*
Trickle vb. n. *ₒdzag-pa.*
Trifling adj. *ṗra-ba.*
Tripod *sgyid-bu, lċags-sgyid.*
Troop s. *k̇yu. pal-po-če, tso;* troops *dpuń.*
Trophy *rgyal-mtsán.*
Trot vb. *ₒdur-ba:* s. *ₒdur-ₒgro.*
Trouble s. *nyon-moṅs-pa, dka-sdúg, mya-ńán;* vb. a. *dkrug-pa.*
Troublesome *tsegs.*
Trowsers *rkań-snam, gos-túń, dor-ma, byań-rkyań, smad-ɣyógs.*

True *bden-pa, ńo-rtóg.*
Trumpet *duń.*
Trunk (of a tree) *sdoń-po;* (of an elephant) *glań-sna;* (box) *sgam, sgrom.*
Truss s *ṗon-po;* vb. to — up *rdze-ba.*
Trustee *ṗa-tsáb.*
Trustworthy *ₒos-pa.*
Truth *ńes-pa, bden-pa, yin-min* 510.
Try *nyams sad-pa* 186, *dpyod-pa,* col. *tsod-lta-ba.*
Tub *ɣžoń-pa, bzom.*
Tube *doń-po, pu-ri.*
Tuck up *rdze-ba.*
Tuesday *ɣza-mig-dmár.*
Tuft *ṗon;* — of wool *bal-ₒdab W.*
Tumble vb *ₒgyel-ba.*
Tumbler (drinking-glass) *šel-kór, šel-ṗór.*
Tumult *ₒk̇rug-pa.*
Tun *zem.*
Tune s. *glu.*
Turban *tod, la-tód.*
Turbid *ska-ba, nyog-pa.*
Turf *spań, spań-po*
Turkey *rum.*
Turkois *ɣyu.*
Turmeric *yuń-ba.*
Turn vb. a *sgyur-ba;* to — off *zlog-pa;* to — out *ₒbyin-pa;* to — round *ₒk̇or-ba;* to — up *rdze-ba;* to — upside down *spub-pa, slog-pa;* vb. n. *ṗyogs-pa, ₒgro-ba, č̇a-ba W.;* to — away *ldog-pa.*
Turn s. *tsir* 448, *res* 535; by turns *tsir-la, tsir-du, tsir dań, res-la.*
Turnip *nyuń-ma.*
Turret *speu, spiu.*
Tusk *mče-ba, mče-so*
Tutelar god *yi-dam-lha, t̤ugs-dám.*
Twelve *bċu-ɣnyis;* twelfth *bċu-ɣnyis-pa.*
Twenty *nyi-šu;* twentieth *nyi-šu-pa.*
Twice *lan-ɣnyis.*
Twilight *srod, srod-ₒjiń.*
Twine s. *skud-pa, si-ri W.*
Twins **tsag-túg*, mtse-ma.*
Twirling-stick *ja-bkrúg.*
Twist vb. a. *sgrim-pa, ɣċud-pa, sle-ba.*
Two *ɣnyis;* v. also *do* 256.
Two-legged *rkań-ɣnyis-pa.*
Tyrant *dpon-po drag-po* or *drag-šul-ċan.*

U

Ugly *mi-sdug-pa.*
Ulcer *šu-ba; ba-šu W.; ṗol, lhog-pa.*
Ultimately *ṗugs-na.*
Umbrella *nyi-rib, ɣdugs.*
Unable *mi šes-pa, ċań mi šes-pa.*
Unaccustomed *mi gom-pa.*
Unadulterated *ma-ₒdres-pa, lhad-méd.*

Unaware *yań-med-la W.*
Unbearable *mi-bzod-pa.*
Unbecoming *mi-rigs-pa.*
Unbelieving *ma-dad-pa, dad-méd.*
Unbutton vb. a. *ₒgrol-ba.*
Unchangeable *ₒgyur-méd*
Unchastity *ₒdod-lóg.*

Uncle *k̔u-bo*; *žaṅ(-po)*, *'a-žaṅ*, *'a-k̔ú W.*
Unclean *mi-γtsaṅ-ba*, *dri-ma-ċan*; *t̔si-du W.*, *skyug-bro C.*
Uncommon *t̔un-min*, *t̔un-moṅs ma yin-pa* 234; *srol-méd*, *t̔a-mal-pa ma yin-pa* 227.
Undefined *ṅes-med.*
Under *˳og*, *˳og-na* 501; v. also *šam* 557.
Under-garment *'aṅ-t̔úṅ.*
Undergo *mt̔oṅ-ba*, *bzod-pa*, *snyoṅ-ba.*
Understand *mk̔yen-pa*, *go-ba*, *ṅos-˳p̔rod-pa*, *rig-pa*, *šes-pa*; *ha-go-ba W.*
Understanding s. *blo*, *blo-grós*; good — (agreement) *mt̔un* 241.
Undertaking s. *rtsom-pa* 441.
Undoubtedly *γdon-mi-za-bar.*
Uneasy *koṅ-du č̔ud-pa*, *mi t̔sim-pa*, *mi dga-ba*, *mi dga-ste.*
Unequal *mi-˳dra-ba.*
Unequalled *˳gran-ya-med.*
Uneven *rtsub-po.*
Unexpectedly *hun-med-la W.*, *yaṅ-med-la W.*; *glo-bur-du*, *har(-gyis) C.*
Unfasten *˳grol-ba.*
Unfinished *t̔e-rél W.*
Unfit adj. *mi-ruṅ-ba.*
Unfold *˳bu-ba*, *k̔a ˳bu-ba.*
Ungracious *brtse-méd.*
Unguent *byug-sman.*
Unhappy *bkra-mi-šis-pa*, *sdug-bsṅal-ċan*, *γyaṅ-med-pa.*
Unimpaired *ma-nyams-pa.*
Universally *p̔al-č̔ér.*
Universe *˳ǰig-rtén.*
Unjust *t̔sul-méd*; *č̔os ma yin-pa.*
Unkind *brtse-méd.*
Unmarried (male or female) *k̔yim-t̔abs-méd*; (female) *k̔yo-méd.*
Unobserved adv. *ma-t̔sor-bar.*
Unoccupied *yan-pa.*
Unquestionable *t̔ag-bċad-pa* 227.
Unquestionably *γdon mi za-bar.*
Unreasonable *mi-rig-pa* 528.
Unripe *rǰen-pa.*
Unsought *rtsol-méd.*
Unsteady *˳dug mi t̔sugs-pa* 459.
Unsubstantial *γzugs-méd* 494.
Unsymmetrical *ya-ma-zúṅ.*
Untie *˳grol-ba.*
Until *bar-du*, *t̔ug C.*, *t̔sug-pa W.*; *p̔an-la* 340, *yan-la* 506.
Untoward *mi-˳dod-pa.*
Untruth *šab-šób.*
Up to prep. *gan*, *druṅ-du*, *mdun-du*, *ldan-du W.* 289; *rtsar* 437; adv. *yar*, *gyen.*
Upbraid *bka-bkyon byed-pa.*
Up-hill *gyen-du.*
Upon *k̔a-ru*, *k̔ar* 35, *t̔og-tu* 237, *steṅ-du* 222.
Upper adj. *ya-gi*; — end *t̔og-ma*; — part *stod.*
Upright (erect) *kye-ré*; *kroṅ-króṅ W.*; (honest) *č̔os-draṅ-po.*
Up-stairs *ya-t̔og.*
Urge vb. a. v. *nan* 302.
Urgently *nye-bar.*
Urinary organs *č̔u-só.*
Urine *γċin*, *č̔u*, *dri-č̔u.*
Usage (custom) *srol.*
Use vb. a. *spyod-pa.*
Use s. *krims*; *p̔an-pa*; *lob-k̔yád W.*
Useful *dgos-pa*, *p̔an-t̔ogs-pa*; to be — *p̔an-pa.*
Useless *mi-dgos-pa*, *p̔an-méd*, *don-mi-č̔on W.* 162.
Usual *t̔un*, *t̔un-móṅ*, *p̔al-pa.*
Usurp *˳p̔rog-pa.*
Utensils *lag-č̔a.*
Uterus *bu-snód*, *p̔ru-ma.*
Utmost v. *bla-ma* 382, *ǰi* 172.
Utter *rǰod-pa*, *˳don-pa.*
Uvula *lċe-č̔úṅ.*

V

Vacuity *stoṅ-pa-nyid* 223.
Vagina *mṅal-sgo* 132.
Vagrant adj. *yan-pa.*
Vain (fond of dress) *mč̔or-po*, *rdzob-po*, col. *zab-mo.*
Valid *stobs-ċan.*
Valley *luṅ-pa*; lower part of a — *mdo*, upper part *p̔u.*
Valuable *dkon-pa*, *rin-po-č̔e.*
Value s. (price) *goṅ*, *t̔aṅ*, *rin*; (importance) *˳k̔os.*
Vanish *yal-ba*, *mi-snaṅ-bar ˳gyur-ba* 317.
Vapour s. *ṅad*, *rlaṅs-pa.*
Variegated *bkra-ba.*
Various *sna-t̔sogs*, *sna-so-só*, *so-só*, *rigs mi-γċig-pa.*
Varnish s. *rtsí.*
Vegetables *sṅo-t̔sód*, *t̔sod-ma*, *ldum.*
Vehicle *t̔eg-pa*, *bžon-pa.*
Veil s. *γdoṅ-k̔ebs.*
Vein (of the body) *rtsa*; (of minerals) *γter-k̔a* 208, *rdo-k̔á* 287.
Venerable *btsun-pa.*
Vengeance *dugs W.*; to take — **dug kor-č̔e*, *lan kor-č̔e* W.*
Venture vb. *spobs-pa.*
Venus *pa(-wa)-saṅs.*
Verdant, the ground becomes — *sa ˳bo C.* 395; or *sṅo skyé* 136.

Vermicelli *γċur-p̔e, čur-ba.*
Vermilion s. *mt̔sal, t̔sal.*
Vermin *srin-bu, ₒbu.*
Verse s. *rkaṅ-pa* 15, *t̔sigs* 448.
Vertex *mgo-dkyil, γtsug.*
Vertical *gyen-la draṅ-po W.*
Very *rab-tu, šin-tu*; *ha-caṅ* 595; *mā W.* 408; the very *k̔o-na* 43.
Vessel (receptacle) *snod*; (anatom.) *bu-ga*; (ship) *γziṅs, gru.*
Vestibule *sgo-k̔aṅ.*
Vestige *mal.*
Vice s. *sdig-pa, mi-dge-ba.*
Vice-roy *rgyal-t̔sab.*
Vicissitude *ₒgyur-ba* II 97.
Victorious, to be – *rgyal-ba.*
Victory *rgyal.*
Victuals *k̔a-zás, za-ba, za-ma.*
Vie with *ₒgran-pa.*
View s. *snaṅ-ba* 317; point of – (mode of viewing things) *mt̔oṅ-snáṅ* 318, *γzigs-snáṅ*; vb. a. *lta-ba.*
Vigorous *rem-pa.*
Vile *btsog-pa.*
Vilify *smad-pa, dma-ₒbebs-pa, ma-bab kal-ba W.* 421.
Village *yul-gru, groṅ, groṅ-t̔so, groṅ-yul, yul-t̔so.*
Villager *groṅ-pa.*
Vine *rgun, rgun-šiṅ.*
Vinegar *skyur-k̔u, skyur-ru Sik., skyur-mo Lh.*
Vineyard *rgun-t̔sás.*
Violate (infringe) *γċog-pa, ₒčal-ba*; (deflower) *lus smad-pa.*
Violent *drags-po, btsan.*
Virgin *bu-mo, bu-mo γsar-ma.*
Virtue *dge-ba, bsod-pa*; by – of *stobs-kyis* 224.
Virtuous *dge-ba, dge-ldán.*
Viscid *rtsi-ċan.*
Vishnu *k̔yab-ǰúg* 46.
Visible *mṅon-pa, γsal-po, mt̔oṅ-du ruṅ-ba.*
Vision (act of seeing) *snaṅ-ba, mt̔oṅ-snaṅ*; range of – *mt̔oṅ-ₒk̔or*; (phantom) *žal-γzigs.*
Visit vb. a. *žal-lta byėd-pa*; . . . *daṅ t̔ug-pa-la ₒgro-ba*, . . . *daṅ mǰal-ba* or *p̔rad-pa.*
Visitation (inspection) *žal-ta, žal-lta.*
Voice *skad, sgra, sgra-skad*, resp. *γsuṅ*; loud – *skad-čé.*
Volcano *me-ri.*
Voluptuousness *ₒdod-pa, ₒdod-ċags.*
Vomit vb. *skyug-pa*; s. *skyugs-pa.*
Vortex *γtsug.*
Vow s. *t̔ugs-dám, dam, dam-t̔sig, yi-dam*; to make a – *t̔ugs-dam bċa-ba.*
Vowel *dbyaṅs.*
Vulgar s. *dmaṅs* 422; adj. *t̔a-mal-pa* 227.
Vulture *go-bo, glag, bya-glág.*

W

Wag vb. a. *sgril-ba.*
Wages *gla, p̔ogs.*
Waggon *šiṅ-rta*; – wheel *šiṅ-rtai p̔aṅ-ló.*
Wailings s. *smre-sṅágs.*
Waist *rked-pa.*
Wait vb. n. *sgug-pa, sdod-pa, sriṅ-ba*; to – on *mǰal-ba*; to lie in – *sgug-pa*; to keep one waiting *sgug-tu ₒǰug-pa.*
Waiting-man *sku-mdun-pa, žabs-p̔yi*; *druṅ-k̔ór.*
Wake vb. a. *sod-pa, γnyid sad-pa.*
Walk vb. n. *bgrod-pa, ₒgrul-ba, ₒgro-ba, ₒčag-pa*; resp. *skyod-pa, γšegs-pa, ₒbyon-pa*; to take a – *skyo-saṅs-la ₒgro-ba* 458; v. also *γyeṅs-pa* 518; the act of walking *ₒgros*; manner of – *spyod-ₒgrós.*
Wall s. *rtsig-pa, lċags-ri, skya.*
Walnut *star-ka, dar-sga.*
Wand s. *dbyug-gu, dbyu-gu.*
Wander *ₒk̔yam-pa, rgyu-ba.*
Want vb. a. *dgos-pa, ₒt̔sal-ba, ₒk̔o-ba*; I – *ṅa-la dgos* 87; I do not want it *ₒk̔o-ċe med W.* 56.
War s. *ₒk̔rug-pa*; *mag-t̔áb C., mag-t̔úg W.*
Wardrobe *gos-sgám.*
Warm adj. *dro-ba, dron-mo, t̔sa-ba.*
Warm vb. a. *sro-ba*; *dugs-pa W.*; to – one's self *lde-ba.*
Warmth *t̔sa-graṅ, drod.*
Warp s. *rgyu.*
Warrior *dmag-mí.*
Wart *mdzer-pa.*
Wash vb. a. *ₒk̔rud-pa*, resp. *bsil-ba.*
Washing s. *k̔rus*; water for – *k̔rus-k̔u.*
Waste adj. *gog-po, stoṅ-pa.*
Watch vb. a. *sruṅ-ba.*
Watchman *sruṅ-mk̔an.*
Water *ču*, eleg. *čab*; – carrier *ču-pa*; – channel *wa*; – closet *p̔yag-ra*; *γsaṅ-spyód*; – jar *ču-rdzá*; – snake *ču-sbrul*; – spout *ₒdre-p̔u-t̔sub W.*; – tub *ču-zêm.*
Wave s. *rlabs, dba-klóṅ.*
Wavering s. *t̔sam-t̔súm.*
Wax s. *spra-t̔sil C., mum W.*
Way (road) *ₒgro-sa, lam*, (manner) *rnam-pa, t̔abs, lugs, t̔sul*; by or in the – of *sgo-nas* 115; to have the – of *rigs-pa* 528; to give – *ₒbyer-ba*; to make – *ₒbyol-ba, ₒdzur-ba.* [ₒo, ₒu-ċag.
We pron. *ṅa* 124, *ṅa-*[illegible], *ṅed, ṅed-raṅ, ṅos,*

Weak adj. *žan-pa, šed-med, šed-čúṅ, hal-med W.*; *nyams-čuṅ, ͺǰam-po W.*
Weal (mark) col. *nya.*
Wealth *nor, dkor, p̓yug-k̓yád, dbyig(s), byor-pa, loṅs-spyód* 554.
Weapon *mťson.*
Wear vb. a. *gyon-pa, bgo-ba.*
Weariness *ṅal-ba, ͺo-brgyál.*
Weary adj., to be — *skyo-ba, sun-pa.*
Weary vb. a. *ṅal ͺǰug-pa*; to be wearied *ṅal-ba.*
Weather, clear — *γnam daṅ-ba, γnam dwaṅs, γnam ťaṅ*; dry — *ťan-pa* 229.
Weave vb. a. *ͺťag-pa.*
Weaver *ťa-ga-pa.*
Wedge s. *ka-ru.*
Wednesday *γza-lhag-ma.*
Weed s. *rtsa-ṅan.*
Weeding (the act of) *yur-ma.*
Week *bdun-p̓rág.*
Weep *ṅu-ba, šum-pa.*
Weft *spun.*
Weigh vb. a. *ͺǰal-ba, ͺdegs-pa, γžal-ba, γšor-ba.*
Weight *rdo* 286, *sraṅ* 580.
Welcome, you are — *ͺoṅs-pa legs-so* 501.
Welfare *bde-ba, bde-ͺǰágs.*
Well s. *k̓ron-pa, ču-doṅ, ͺbyuṅ-k̓uṅs, ču-mig.*
Well adj., are you —? *de-mo 'e yo C.*; adv. *ͺo-ná* 500; very — *de-ltar ͺťsal-lo*; well, well! *yag-po yag-po*; — sounding *snyan-pa*; — tasted *žim-po.*
Wen *lba-ba.*
Went, I went *soṅ* 579.
West *nub.*
Wet adj. *rlon-pa, γšer-ba*; s. *rlan.*
Wether *ťoṅ-pa.*
What interr. *či* 139, *gaṅ* 65, *či-ltar* 140, *ǰi* 172.
Whatever *či-yaṅ*; — it may be *či yaṅ ruṅ* 532.
Wheat *gro*; — flour *bag-p̓yé.*
Wheel s. *ͺk̓or-lo*; paddle — *sku-ru.*
When *k̓a-ru, k̓ar*; *čiṅ*; interr. *nam, dus-nam-žig* 303.
Where *ga-na, ga-ru, gar*; — is? *ga-ré.*
Whetstone *ͺdzeṅ.*
Which interr. *gaṅ* 65.
While s. *yun*; a little — *ťen, dar-γčig, re žig (dus)*; a long — *riṅ žig-tu.*
Whilst *la* 540, *las* 546.
Whip s. *lčag, rta-lčag.*
Whirl vb. n. *ͺťsub-pa.*
Whirlpool *γtsug, γtsug-ͺk̓yil.*
Whirlwind *ͺdre-pu-ťsúb W.*
Whisper s. *šab-šúb*; vb. *šub-pa, šib-pa.*
Whistle vb. *šugs-sgra γtoṅ-ba*; v. also *hu-hú* 597.
White adj. *dkar-ba*; — wash *dkar-rtsi.*
Whither *ga-ru, ga-lá* 64, *gar* 67.
Who interr. *gaṅ* 65, *su* 573.
Whole adj. *ťams-čád* 230; *ťsaṅ-ma, ril-ba, hril-po*; s. *ril-po.*
Wholly *yoṅs-su.*
Why interr. *či, či-la* 140, *čii p̓yir* 351; *ga-la rten-nas* 214; interj. *ͺo-ná* 500.
Wick s. *snyiṅ-po, sdoṅ-ras C., sar W.*
Wicked adj. *čos-méd, sdig-pa-la dga-ba.*
Wide *žeṅ-čan, yaṅs-pa, hel-po, hel-čan.*
Widow *yugs(s)-sa-mo.*
Widower *yug(s)-sa-pa, yug-sa*; *skyes-nág C.*
Width *k̓yon, γžeṅ.*
Wife *čuṅ-ma, čuṅ-grogs*; *'a-ne W.*; *k̓ab* 38, *k̓yo-mo* 48; (housewife) *k̓yim-ťab-mo, k̓yim-pa-ma* 47.
Wild adj. *rgod-pa, γnyan-pa.*
Wilderness *dgon-pa, ͺbrog.*
Will s. *bsam-pa, ťugs*, resp. *ťugs-dgoṅs.*
Willing, to be — *ͺdod-pa.*
Willow *lčaṅ-ma.*
Wind s. *rdzi, rluṅ*; cold — *lhag(s)-pa.*
Wind vb. a. *dkri-ba, ͺk̓ri-ba, ͺk̓yil-ba, sgril-ba*; vb. n. *ͺk̓ril-ba.*
Window *rgyal-dkar C.*; — hole *dkar-k̓uṅ.*
Windpipe *k̓ru-krú W., lkog-ma.*
Wine *rgun-čaṅ*, resp. *rgun-skyéms*; *čaṅ.*
Wing s. *šog-pa, ͺdab-ma.*
Wink vb. n. *mig k̓rab-k̓ráb* or *ťsab-ťsáb* or *ͺdzum-ͺdzúm byed-pa.*
Winter s. *dgun, dgun-ka.*
Wipe vb. a. *ͺp̓yi-ba*; to be wiped off *ͺbyi-ba.*
Wire *lčags-skúd.*
Wisdom *ye-šes, šes-ráb.*
Wise adj *mk̓as-pa, gruṅ-ba, mdzaṅs-pa.*
Wish s. *ͺdod-pa, yid-smon*; resp. *dgoṅs-pa, bžed-don*; vb. a. *ͺdod-pa, smon-pa, ͺťsal-ba, bžed-pa.*
Witchcraft *mťu, p̓ra-mén.*
With *daṅ* 248, *mnyam-du* 195, *bčas-su.*
Withdraw vb. a. *γčod-pa, mi ster-ba*; vb. n. *ͺgye-ba.*
Wither vb. n. *rnyid-pa.*
Within *ťsun-čád.*
Without prep. *med-pa(r)* 418.
Witness s. *dpaṅ(-po).*
Wolf *spyaṅ-ki.*
Woman *bud-méd, mo, 'a-ne W.*
Womb *mṅal* 132, *bu-snod* 319, *rum.*
Wonder s. *ya-mťsan.*
Wonderful *nyams-mťsar-ba, ṅo-mťsar-ba*; *ya-mťsan-po C., ya-mťsan-čan W.*
Wont, Wonted adj. *goms-pa.*
Wood (forest) *nags(-ma), ťsal*; (timber) *šiṅ*; — shavings *šiṅ-zél.*
Woodpecker *šiṅ-rgón.*
Woof *spun.*
Wool *bal.*
Word *ťsig, miṅ, sgra, ṅág* 125; resp. *bka.*

Work s. *bya-ba, bzo, las*, resp. *p̔rin-las*; vb. a. *las byed-pa.*
Workman *las-pa, las-mi.*
Workmanship *bzo* 497.
Workmaster *lag-dpón.*
Workshop *bzo-k̔an.*
World *ɔjig-rtén, srid-pa* 582.
Worldliness *ɔjig-rtén ₒdi-la čags-pai sems*; v. *bya-ba.*
Worm *ₒbu, srin-bu, nyal-ɔgro.*
Worn out *čad-po.*
Worst, to get the — of *ₒp̔am-pa.*
Worth s. *ₒk̔os, goṅ, rin, t̔aṅ.*
Worth adj. *ri-ba.*
Worthless *rin-méd.*
Worthy *γša, γša-ma*; to be — *˛os-pa.*
Wound s. *rma, rma-k̔a W.*
Wrap vb. a. *dkri-ba*; to — round *sgril-ba*; to — up *ₒdril-ba.*
Wrath *k̔ro-ba, že-sdaṅ.*
Wrest vb. a. *snol-ba.*
Wrestle vb. n. *snol-ba.*
Wretched *sdug-po*; *nyal-ba-čan W.*
Wring *ₒtsir-ba.*
Wrinkle s. *γnyer-ma.*
Wrist *lag-t̔sigs.*
Write *ₒbri-ba.*
Wrong adj. *mi-rigs-pa, log-pa, mi-˛os-pa*: *˛os-med W.*
Wry adj. *ₒču-ba, ₒčus-pa* 170.

Y

Yak *γyag*; male — *p̔o-γyág*; female — *ₒbri-mo*; wild — *ₒbroṅ.*
Yard (court-yard) *k̔yams.*
Yarn *snal-ma, sran-bu.*
Yawn vb. *glal-ba, sgyiṅ-ba* 118.
Yea *˛o-ná* 500.
Year *lo*; this — *da-lo.*
Yeast *p̔abs, rtsabs.*
Yellow *ser-po*
Yes *˛o, de yin*; *'a W.*; yes, yes! *de-ka yod* 255; —, so it is *de-de-bžin-no.*
Yesterday *k̔a-rtsáṅ, mdaṅ.*
Yet *˛on kyaṅ, yin kyaṅ, yin na yaṅ W.*; *gal-te.*
Yield vb. a. *γtoṅ-ba*; vb. n. *daṅ-du len-pa.*
Yoke of oxen *glaṅ-dór.*
Yonder *p̔a-gi.*
You pron. *k̔yed, k̔yod* 48, *nyid* 188.
Young adj. *γžon-pa, čuṅ-ba*; the youngest (son) *t̔a-čúṅ*; s. *p̔rug.*
Youth s. (youthful age) *laṅ-t̔so*; (boy or young man) *k̔yeu, γžon-nu.*

Z

Zeal *rtsol-ba, brtson-ɔgrus, ₒbad-pa, bag-čags.*
Zealous *brtson-ₒgrus daṅ ldan-pa*; to be — *brtson-ɔgrus skyed-pa, brtson-par byed-pa.*
Zealously *rtsol-bar.*
Zero *t̔ig-le.*
Zinc *ti-t̔sa.*
Zodiac *k̔yim-gyi ₒk̔or-lo.*

Final remark. The Tibetan words, given in the Vocabulary, are not in every instance to be regarded as exact equivalents for whatever word happens to be sought, but rather as hints, how to attain to the wished for expression. It will, therefore, be frequently indispensable to refer to the Tib. Engl. Dictionary for further explanation, and to examine the different bearings and relations of the word in question, so far as they may have been traced there. — Although this Vocabulary is by no means complete in itself, yet it is to be hoped that it will not prove quite unuseful, but answer the purpose for which it was intended.

CORRECTIONS.

A revision of the Dictionary has brought such a number of misprints to light that, on second thoughts, it seems absolutely necessary not to leave them unnoticed, but to register all that are of any consequence. The unfortunate fact, that such corrections should be required, has to be ascribed to two circumstances, in regard to which the reader's indulgence has already been appealed to in the Preface, namely, the author's weak state of health, and the difficulties with which the printing of a book of this character is necessarily attended. —

---

p. page; a b the respective column, left or right; l. line; when the lines are counted from foot of page, the numerals are provided with an asterisk.

p.	col.	l.		
2	a	8	read	*ka-ma-la-ši-la*
2	b	17	„	*ka-sa ǰu*
3	b	3*	„	to beckon
8	a	18	„	*ṭad-kyi*
9	b	21	„	*dka-ťub-la*
15	a	9	„	*ṭa-ši-hlum-po*
16	a	19*	„	*rkaṅ-˳bám*
16	b	7*	„	dig out
17	a	9*	„	affix denoting
17	a	19*	„	*rkyaṅ-pa*
20	b	10*	„	frequently
21	a	6	„	*skal-nór*
21	b	2	„	*ṭé*
26	a	5	„	*skyaṅ*
27	a	11*	„	*skyil-ldir*
27	b	13*	„	*skyur-mo*
28	a	6	„	*γyaṅ-skyúr*
28	a	15*	„	re-born
28	b	19	„	*kyer-mén*
31	b	16*	„	*lag-lén*
32	b	16	dele	2. to paste. —
32	b	5*	read	*skra-séṅ*
33	a	5*	„	*ḱ*
33	b	7	„	*ḍá-ru skróg-pa*
33	b	12	„	caste
34	a	5	„	soft mouth
34	a	15*	„	to lie on the face
35	b	2*	„	*ḱa-γdáms*
38	a	1	„	*lás-ḱa*
38	a	10	„	*Ld.*
39	a	6	„	*zas ḱam γčig* id. — 2.
41	a	20	„	*ḱúg-tu*
41	a	4*	„	*rna-ḱṅṅ*
44	a	18	„	*kóṅ-pa ṅan-pa*
51	a	14*	read	*ḱrims-ḱáṅ*
52	b	24	„	**ṭó-pa**
54	b	13	„	requisites
56	b	5	„	འཁྲིལ་བ་
56	b	15	„	*˳ḱo-byéd*
59	a	20*	„	འཁྱག(ས)་པ་
59	a	10*	„	*˳ḱyam-pa*
59	b	20*	„	*ʻód-˳ḱyims*
63	a	6*	„	= *gaṅ.* — 3. bald, *W. ga-pi* (v. *spyi* 333).
65	a	24*	„	*ʻóṅ-ba de-ni*
66	a	16*	„	*gaṅ-zág-*
66	a	14*	„	*lóg-lta-čan-gyi*
66	b	15	„	*mdzod-ṅiá*
67	a	20	„	གཎྜེ་ལ་
69	b	17*	„	*gun-dúm*
74	a	18	„	*gyád-kyi*
74	a	13*	„	*gyi* for *kyi*
75	a	11	„	*gyón-rgyu*
76	b	6	„	*ťúb-grabs*
77	b	18	„	གུ་གུ་
78	b	22*	„	*gróg-ču*
79	a	18	„	*mčód-rten*
81	a	11	„	*-rtséd-mo*
84	b	5	„	stoop
85	b	18	„	उपासिका
86	b	11	„	*mdo*; *dge-slóṅ-ma* a nun; *dge-slob-ma* etc.
87	a	19	„	*bstán-pa-la*

p.	col.	l.	
89	b	2*	read *čes bgrós-nas*
92	a	4	„ *'u-šóg*
95	a	11*	„ *ṅan-*
95	b	3	„ འགྲོགས་པ་
95	b	21	„ establish
96	a	10*	„ *˳gor*
96	b	1	„ *˳gyág-pa*
96	b	3	„ *˳gyaṅ-ba*
96	b	15	„ *šél-gyi*
98	a	14	„ *˳gyód-par*
111	b	22	„ རྒྱུག་པ
112	a	20*	„ *tiṅ-ṅe-˳dzin*
113	b	7	„ *na-ṫsa*
121	a	20	„ *bsgrub-*
122	a	4	vide emendation p. XXII.
122	a	8*	read སྒྲོག(ས)·
122	b	24*	„ *sgrón-pa*
128	a	4	„ *ṅéd-čag*
128	b	4	„ *dé-˳dra-ba*
128	b	6	„ *˳či-ba*
128	b	2*	„ *ṅo dkár-po*
131	a	16*seqq.	„ *˳dzir*
132	b	5*	„ *čis*
132	b	3*	„ *mṅón-no*
135	a	4	„ *Lex.*
139	b	6	„ *čii* of what?
140	b	1	„ ཅི་ཅེ
141	b	17	„ *čuṅ*
143	a	20*	„ gallinaceous
146	b	10*, 8*	„ **včú**
147	b	23	„ **včom-ldan-˳dẹ́**
158	a	17	„ *ču-búr*
158	b	14*	„ the water; also =
161	b	10*	„ *dris-pas* (instead of
163	b	10*	„ *čós-skad*
164	a	3*	„ irreligious
165	b	18*	„ *mčé-ba*
166	b	15	„ पूज
168	b	20*	„ *zá-ba*
170	a	13	„ *˳ču-ba* to draw etc.
170	a	22	„ vb. n. to *˳ǰún-pa*
170	b	2*	„ *kro-bo-˳čól-pa*
171	a	12	„ *Lex.*
176	b	24	„ *˳ǰig-ṭág*
177	a	5	„ *˳ǰiṅ-kúṅ*
184	b	10*	„ *nyá-ra byéd-pa*
185	a	13*	„ *dpon-gyi*
186	b	4*	„ *nyal-krí*
195	a	21	„ **mnyé-če**
195	b	6	„ སྐྱང་བ
195	b	7*	„ *γnyid*

p.	col.	l.	
200	a	13*	read ཀླེན་པ·
205	a	4	„ *Cs.*
219	b	7	„ *ma byed*
226	a	11*	„ 178. 3. — *Was.* (296): 2.
231	b	7	„ *ṫig-skúd*
232	a	3*	„ *žib-ču*
233	b	18	„ *Ld.-Glr.*,
233	b	23*	„ translates it
233	b	19*	„ **ṫun čad** *W.*
235	b	24	„ *mi-ṫeg kúr-ba*
237	a	9*	„ *ṅá-ṫog*
237	b	15	„ *spyi-ṫóg*
238	a	14*	„ *ṫod*
256	a	9	„ from thence
256	b	12	„ རེབ་(མ)·
259	b	14	„ *don* 1. — *don-dám*
264	b	7*	„ སྒྲོན་མོ
265	a	10	„ like an arctic sea
267	a	14	dele (Pinus abies)
270	b	14	read *bdé-mo*
273	b	2*	„ जोशी
274	a	4*	dele the words: marked or
275	a	9seqq.	read *˳das-pa*
275	b	6*	„ *pyi*
287	b	16	„ precious stone
287	b	22	„ *Pth.* having obtained immortality
291	a	5	„ *˳brug*
292	b	23	„ *sdáṅ-ba*
293	a	3*	„ *sdig-to-čan*
293	b	1	„ སྡི(ག)ས་པ· *sdi(g)s-pa*
301	b	22	„ *lo tóṅ-ṅi*
303	b	23	„ *zíṅ-to*
304	b	22	„ prep.
305	b	21*	„ ནུར་ནུར་པོ·
312	a	3*	„ མཚོལ་གྲིབ
316	b	8	„ *smin-pa*
317	b	12*	„ apparition
318	b	14	„ brightly
322	b	8*	„ *dkár(-po)*
325	a	10	„ *gru-˳dzin*
326	b	4	„ Durga, Uma
327	a	17	„ *žág-pẹ pe*
328	a	18*	„ *koṅ-ǰo*
338	a	14*	„ the defunct ancestors
338	b	2*	„ postp. c. gen.
340	a	21	„ abstrusely
340	b	17	„ *Gram.*;
353	b	15	„ *˳ǰúg-pa*
354	a	9*	„ *˳prál-ba*

p.	col.	l.		
357	b	12*	read	*°ṕóṅ-mḱan*
374	a	12*	„	དྲུག་(པ་)
383	b	10*	„	གླ་འཚོ་ *gla-°ťsó*
389	a	12*	„	*dbón-mo*
407	a	17*	„	སྦྲིད་པ་
410	b	13*	„	circle
412	b	21*, 19*	„	*mi-ḱyim*
415	a	24*	„	to name v. *°dogs-pa* 2;
427	a	12	„	*sman-mčóg*
431	a	1*	„	*tsám-gyis*
433	a	2*	„	*yaṅ*
439	a	19	„	*mii*
439	b	14*	„	*°gro-* (or *ča-*) *rtsis yod*
442	a	7*	„	*nyáṅ-če*
442	b	17	„	assiduous
446	a	3*	„	*ťsan-zug*
449	a	12*	„	travellers
460	b	10	„	*°ťsó-ba*
466	b	11*	read	whetstone
474	a	20*	„	soothe
480	a	13	„	*γžal-med-ḱaṅ-bzaṅ*
493	b	18	„	*Sik.*
496	a	5	„	*γzod*
496	a	18	„	wasted
508	b	12	„	so *yi γčód-pa, yi čád-pa*
522	a	2, 3	„	*ḍáṅ-mo*
530	b	5	„	རིལ་བ་
540	a	4	„	of
567	a	5*	„	prop.
576	a	14*	*skyo-séṅ mdzád-pa*	
578	b	3	„	སོ་ཕག་ *so-pág*
587	a	20, 21	„	*nyon-móṅs-kyi kun-slóṅ*
589	a	1	„	གསལ་ཤིང་
591	b	23*	„	vb. 1. to beg, to pray = *žú-ba*
592	a	9	„	(the king's) soul

In several of the longer articles some confusion in the use of the figures in large and small type has occurred. In order to restrict this catalogue within the smallest possible limits, these and other slight inaccuracies have not been entered.